Waterstone's

Guide to Books 1989/90

Cover illustration:

China, 1988
by **John Latham**
Glass, book, clamp 77cm x 37cm x 37cm
Image supplied by Lisson Gallery, London
©Lisson Gallery

Printed and bound in Great Britain by Richard Clay Ltd, Suffolk.

ISBN 0 9512589 5 8

Waterstone's

Guide to Books 1989/90

WATERSTONE & CO. LIMITED, LONDON

Editors

General Editor: **Tom Birchenough**   Assistant Editors: **Roger Bratchell**, **A M Campbell**, **John Mitchinson**, **Sue Woodhead**.

Contributing Editors

Art Monographs, Theory, Reference: **Lyn French**   Art History, Architecture: **John Zeppetelli**
Biography: **Roger Bratchell**   Business: **Colin Orr**   Children's: **Elizabeth Hammill**
Crafts and Fashion: **Toni Nealie**   Drama: **Nick Stewart**   Fiction: **David Andrews**,
Freddie Baveystock, Tom Birchenough, A M Campbell, Howard Cunnell,
Tim Dowling, Markman Ellis, Chris Newson   Adventure Fiction: **David Blow**
Crime Fiction: **Andrew Stilwell**   Science Fiction: **Amanda Todd, Steve Andrews**
Film and Photography: **Simone Horrocks**   Food and Drink: **Markman Ellis**
Gardening: **Louise Topping**   Health and Fitness: **Caroline Sanderson**
History: **David McRedmond**   Military History: **Nick Marlowe**   Humour: **Bryn Evans**
Literary Criticism: **Paul Baggaley, Markman Ellis, John Mitchinson**
Music: **Peter French, Simon Whiteside**   Nature and Science: **Sue Woodhead**
Philosophy: **Ray Monk**   Poetry: **Mark Fisher**   Psychology: **Nigel Woodhead**
Reference and Language: **K C Lai**   Religion: **Robin Gorna, Steve Gove**
Social Sciences **Simon Bromley**   Sport: **Bryn Evans**   Travel: **A M Campbell**
Women's Studies: **Lynne Segal**.

Design and Production

Design: Pentagram Design Limited   **Cover Picture Research:** Lyn French
In-house Typesetting: Sue Woodhead, Chris Murgatroyd
Picture Research & Additional Production: Linda Wade
Computer Consultants: Stewart Armstrong, Peter Nunn, Patrick Brown,
Passport Computer Consulting;
Jane Psaila, The Last Word.

Special Thanks

Appreciation is due to **Nick Birch**, who participated in the planning of this edition; to the many **Waterstone's employees** whose work in the Second Edition has been incorporated into the Third; to **Freddie Baveystock, Dominique Enright** and **Simone Horrocks**, for additional editorial assistance; and to **Rachel Butler, Paula Carty, Alison Cowham, Marilyn Dale, Sarah Goodwin** and **Joan Normoyle** for invaluable help during production.

Table of Contents

Features

Literary Prizes

CONTENTS

Art

European Art: By Period
European Art: By Country
World Art
Monographs: By Artist & School
Theory & Criticism

Architecture

ART

General Surveys

CLARK, KENNETH
Civilisation
The book from the highly successful television series. Its giant scope across the centuries provides invigorating reading.
[A1] J Murray hbk **£17.95**
[A2] J Murray pbk **£12.95**

GOMBRICH, ERNST
The Story of Art
One of the finest introductions to Western art. The author's intimate style celebrates and stimulates our interest for the value and beauty of great works of art. Very highly illustrated.
[A3] Phaidon hbk **£15.00**
[A4] Phaidon pbk **£9.95**

HARTT, FREDERICK
Art: A History of Painting, Sculpture and Architecture NEW
Copiously illustrated, well-written survey of world art through the ages. Now available in the revised third edition.
[A5] Abrams hbk **£35.00**

HONOUR, HUGH & FLEMING, PETER
A World History of Art
A truly international survey of art with chapters on Africa, the Far East and Latin America as well as Western art and architecture. An excellent introduction with many illustrations.
[A6] Macmillan hbk **£10.95**

JANSON & CAUMAN
History of Art for Young People
Very clearly written and by no means only of interest to children.
[A7] Thames & H hbk **£16.95**

JANSON, H.W.
History of Art
World survey, now in its 3rd edition. Over 1,200 illustrations, many of which are in colour.
[A8] Thames & H hbk **£25.00**

LEVEY, MICHAEL
From Giotto to Cézanne: A Concise History of Painting
A very concise tour of European art from the 13th to the 19th centuries. A good introduction to the subject, copiously illustrated.
[A9] Thames & H pbk **£5.95**

OSBORNE, HAROLD (ED)
Oxford Companion to Art
Excellent reference work, as are all the companion volumes published by Oxford.
[A10] Oxford hbk **£25.00**

PODRO, MICHAEL
The Critical Historians of Art
Overview of the history of art criticism.
[A12] Yale UP pbk **£8.95**

WOODFORD, SUE
Looking at Pictures
A very good introductory book in the excellent 'Cambridge Introduction to the History of Art' series.
[A13] Cambridge hbk **£11.95**
[A14] Cambridge pbk **£6.50**

European Art by Period

Major Series & Introductory Surveys

Many of the titles listed in the section below are released by publishers in uniform series, the aims and quality of coverage of which remain roughly constsnt from title to title. Details of such major series for art history appear below.

CAMBRIDGE INTRODUCTION TO ART HISTORY
Aimed at students and enthusiasts, these handsome paperbacks offer concise, illustrated introductions to various periods in the history of art.
(Cambridge pbk **£6.50**)

HERBERT HISTORY OF ART AND ARCHITECTURE
Compact, richly-illustrated handbooks.
(Herbert Press pbk **£6.95**)

PELICAN HISTORY OF ART AND ARCHITECTURE
Very concentrated, small-format studies with many illustrations, aimed at the serious enthusiast and the student. They include excellent notes, references and bibliographies.
(Viking/Penguin hbk **£30.00**, pbk **£17.95**)

THAMES & HUDSON WORLD OF ART
The numerous titles in this extensive series represent quite remarkable value. They are small laminated paperbacks with varied, colourful fronts and black spines. The authors are distinguished specialists in their fields, and while the style of writing may vary, the quality of information does not - it is well-organised, and includes indexes and bibliographies. The series gives particularly good coverage to ancient and 20th century art and architecture, as well as to a number of individual artists.
(Thames & Hudson hbk **£10.95**, pbk **£5.95**)

Ancient Art

ALDRED, CYRIL
Eygptian Art
[A15] Thames & H pbk **£5.95**

BOARDMAN, JOHN
Athenian Black Figure Vases
[A16] Thames & H pbk **£5.95**
Athenian Red Figure Vases
[A17] Thames & H pbk **£5.95**
Greek Art
[A18] Thames & H pbk **£5.95**
Greek Sculpture
[A19] Thames & H hbk **£10.95**
[A20] Thames & H pbk **£5.95**
Greek Sculpture: The Classical Period
[A21] Thames & H pbk **£5.95**

BOARDMAN, JOHN & FINN, DAVID
The Parthenon and its Sculptures
A richly illustrated study of the great temple and its exquisite sculptural decoration.
[A22] Thames & H hbk **£25.00**

BOWDER, DIANA (ED)
A very useful series on the historical and cultural circumstances of artisitic production.
Who Was Who in the Greek World
[A23] Phaidon hbk **£18.00**
Who Was Who in the Roman World
[A23] Phaidon hbk **£15.00**

BRENDEL
Etruscan Art
Pre-Roman classical art in Italy from the area of Etruria to the north of Rome.
[A24] Penguin pbk **£18.95**

CARPENTER, THOMAS H.
Art and Myth in Ancient Greece NEW
Possibly the first scholarly study and survey of the relationship between Greek art and myth. The author discusses how depictions in vase paintings, sculpture and engravings on gcms, throw light on the way the Greeks understood the stories of Gods and heroes.
[A25] Thames & H pbk **£5.95**

COOK, A.M.
Greek Art
[A26] Penguin pbk **£7.50**

CORBIN, GEORGE A.
Native Arts of North America, Africa and the South Pacific: An Introduction
Emphasis is on the art in the specific cultural context of each tribal area.
[A27] Harper & Row hbk **£29.95**
[A28] Harper & Row pbk **£12.95**

HAMPE, ROLAND & SIMON, ERIK
Birth of Greek Art
[A29] Thames & H hbk **£35.00**

HENIG, MARTIN
A Handbook of Roman Art
[A30] Phaidon hbk **£15.00**
[A31] Phaidon pbk **£9.95**

HIGGINS, REYNOLD
Minoan and Mycenaean Art
[A32] Thames & H pbk **£5.95**

IMMERWAHR, SARA A.
Aegean Painting in the Bronze Age NEW
The author traces the development of Aegean painting from its early manifestations in Crete through its spread to mainland Greece.
[A33] Penn State UP hbk **£40.00**

LEROI-GOURHAN, ANDRE
The Dawn of European Art
[A34] Cambridge hbk **£22.50**

MEGAW, RUTH & VINCENT
Celtic Art: From it's Beginings to the Book of Kells NEW
The fruit of many years of research and travel, this is the first full survey of Celtic arts and crafts from 700 BC to AD 700. The authors discuss the origins of the Celts and the antecedents to their elusive, non-narrative art. A chapter is dedicated soley to Celtic art in Britain and Ireland. With over 450 illustrations.
[A35] Thames & H hbk **£28.00**

MORRIS, DESMOND
The Art of Ancient Cyprus
[A36] Thames & H pbk **£60.00**

3

MOSCATO, SABATINO (ED)
The Phoenicians
Wonderfully designed and illustrated catalogue to the exhibition held at Palazzo Grassi in Venice. All aspects of Phoenician civilization are covered.
[A37] J Murray hbk £60.00

RICHTER, G. & SMITH, R.
Portraits of the Greeks
[A38] Phaidon hbk £14.95

ROBERTSON, M.
A History of Greek Art: Vols 1 & 2
[A39] Cambridge hbk £80.00

ROLLEY, CLAUDE
Greek Bronzes
[A40] Sotheby's hbk £50.00

RUSPOLI, MARIO
The Cave of Lascaux : The Final Photographic Record
The caves were closed to the public in 1981 for major restoration and they were then photographed. The results shown in this book illustrate the wonder and delight of drawings which the pre-historic 'artists' of the caves produced.
[A41] Thames & H hbk £30.00

SPRENGER, MAYA & BARTOLINI, GILDA
The Etruscans: Their History, Art and Architecture
An exhaustive and well-illustrated survey of this ancient Italian civilization documenting and celebrating its achievements in the arts and observing the cultural environment from which it emerged.
[A42] Abrams hbk £70.00

STRONG, DONALD
Roman Art
[A43] Penguin pbk £17.95

TRENDALL, A.D.   **NEW**
Red Figure Vases of South Italy & Sicily
Southern Italian pottery of the fifth century BC evolved from the style introduced by the Greek Colonists into a highly individual and distinctive form. Trendall, a leading scholar in this field, traces the relations between the Greek settlers and the local inhabitants, and the local interpretation of myth and drama by close examination of both style and content of the red figure vases.
[A44] Thames & H hbk £18.00

WHEELER, MORTIMER
Roman Art and Architecture
[A45] Thames & H pbk £5.95

WOLFF, WALTER
Early Civilisations: Egypt, Mesopotamia, the Aegean   **NEW**
This handbook covers art, architecture and sculpture with over 80 illustrations.
[A46] Herbert Press pbk £6.95

WOODFORD, SUSAN
Greece and Rome
[A47] Cambridge pbk £6.50
Introduction to Greek Art
[A48] Duckworth hbk £24.00
[A49] Duckworth pbk £9.95

Byzantine

BECKWITH, JOHN
Early Christian and Byzantine Art
[A50] Penguin pbk £17.95

CORMACK, ROBIN.
Byzantine Eye: Studies in Art and Patronage   **NEW**
Scholarly study which examines the social and cultural background to monumental Byzantine painting and mosaics.
[A51] Varorium Reprints hbk £40.00

DEMUS, OTTO
Byzantine Mosaic Decoration
[A52] Routledge hbk £27.50

HUTTER, IRMGARD
Early Christian and Byzantine Art
[A53] Herbert Press pbk £6.95

MILBURN, ROBERT
Early Christian Art and Architecture
[A54] Scolar P hbk £35.00

RUNCIMAN, STEVEN
Byzantine Style and Civilization
From a respected historian in the field, a brief but concentrated history of the evolution of style and art in social and political context.
[A55] Penguin pbk £6.99

TALBOT-RICE, TAMARA
Art of the Byzantine Era
[A56] Thames & H pbk £5.95

TEMPLE, RICHARD
Icons: A Sacred Art   **NEW**
From the Greek word for image, 'Icons' simply refers to a very limited range of religious picures painted on panels, the forms and shapes of which were prescribed and seemingly remained unchanged for centuries. This richly illustrated study concentrates on the religious significance of these timeless pictures suggesting the fervour and importance of worship in the Orthodox Church.
[A57] Element Books pbk £15.00

WEITZMANN, KURT; ALIBEGASVILI, GAIANE ET AL
The Icon
Early Christian paintings were very simple, yet highly stylized representations of religious subjects (usually Virgin and Child) which were set up as objects of worship.
[A58] Unwin Hyman hbk £47.50

Romanesque

ATROSHENKO, V.I. & COLLINS, JUDITH
The Origins of the Romanesque
[A59] Lund Humphries hbk £25.00

DODWELL, C.R.
Painting in Europe 800 - 1200
[A60] Penguin hbk £30.00

HEARN, M.F.
Romanesque Sculpture
The standard work on the revival of monumental stone sculpture in the 11th and 12th centuries.
[A61] Phaidon hbk £22.00

Illustration from *The Book of Kells* by Francoise Henry (Thames & Hudson hbk £75.00)

LASKO, PETER
Ars Sacra 800 - 1200
[A62] Penguin hbk £30.00

SCHAPIRO, MEYER
The Sculpture of Moissac
Brilliant essay and visual tour around Moissac Abbey in the South of France - one of the most outstanding and complete examples of Romanesque art.
[A63] Thames & H hbk £27.50
[A64] Thames & H pbk £14.00

WILLIAMSON, PAUL
Catalogue of Romanesque Sculpture
[A65] V & A Mus P pbk £11.95

ZARNECKI, GEORGE
Romanesque   **NEW**
With 200 illustrations, a compact and scholarly handbook on the art and architecture of the period.
[A66] Herbert Press pbk £6.95

Medieval

BACKHOUSE, JANET
Books of Hours
[A67] Brit Lib pbk £5.95
The Illuminated Manuscript
All the major schools and illuminators are dealt with in this short, straightforward and accessible introduction to the subject
[A68] Phaidon pbk £7.95
The Lindisfarne Gospels
[A69] Phaidon hbk £9.95
[A70] Phaidon pbk £7.95

BACKHOUSE, JANET & HAMEL, CHRISTOPHER DE
The Becket Leaves
The story of Thomas à Becket from manuscripts.
[A71] Brit Lib pbk £5.95

BECKWITH, JOHN
Early Medieval Art
[A72] Thames & H pbk £5.95

BERENSON, BERNARD
Studies in Medieval Painting
Reprint of a 1930 edition by the legendary critic who was the foremost authority on Italian painting.
[A73] Da Capo pbk £5.75

CALKINS, ROBERT G.
Illuminated Books of the Middle Ages
The most wide-ranging of the general books on the subject. Shows well how text and illumination work together.
[A74] Thames & H £35.00

CAMILLE, MICHAEL
The Gothic Idol   **NEW**
Specialist study investigating the theme of idol worship in medieval art.
[A75] Cambridge hbk £30.00

CHEETHAM, FRANCIS
English Medieval Alabasters
Includes a catalogue of the collection housed in the Victoria and Albert Museum. A thoroughly researched, scholarly study.
[A76] Phaidon hbk £85.00

CHRISTIANSEN, LAURENCE B. & STREHLKE, CARL BRANDON
Painting in Renaissance Siena   **NEW**
This study and exhibition catalogue concentrates on painting and illumination in 15th century Siena. The

works of Giovanni di Paolo, Sassetta, Matteo and Benvenuto di Giovanni are examined in detail and cultural context.
[A76A] Abrams hbk **£40.00**

DEUCHLER, FLORENS
Gothic `NEW`
A thorough investigation and description of the Gothic styles in art, architecture, book illumination, sculpture and stained glass, that flourished throughout Europe from the mid-12th to the late 15th centuries.
[A77] Herbert P pbk **£6.95**

DUBY, GEORGES
History of Medieval Art 980 - 1440 `NEW`
An overview of art and architecture from the Romanesque through to the early Renaissance, with over 300 illustrations, the majority in colour.
[A78] Rizzoli hbk **£35.00**

ECO, UMBERTO
Art and Beauty in the Middle Ages
English translation of one of Eco's earlier academic works.
[A79] Yale UP pbk **£4.95**

HARTHAN, JOHN
Books of Hours and Their Owners
Books of Hours are not only works of art but cultural documents of their time: Harthan's emphasis here is on their personal and religious aspects.
[A80] Thames & H hbk **£15.00**

HENDERSON, GEORGE
From Durrow to Kells: Insular Gospel Books 650 - 800
A scholarly study of the Gospel books produced in the British Isles in the 7th and 8th centuries. The author examines the commission, purpose and intricate decoration of the books, and reinterprets them in the light of Pictish art. With 261 illustrations.
[A81] Thames & H hbk **£35.00**

HENRY, FRANCOISE
Book of Kells
The largest and boldest in ambition of all the illuminated books which have survived from the 8th and 9th centuries. It is widely praised as a masterpiece of Western art. This facsimile reproduction allows us to consider the importance and virtuosity of the work in all its detail.
[A82] Thames & H hbk **£75.00**

LONGON & CAZELLES
Les Tres Riches Heures du Duc de Berry
Complete facsimile of this most elaborate of works with commentary.
[A83] Thames & H pbk **£14.95**

MARTINDALE, ANDREW
Gothic Art
[A84] Thames & H pbk **£5.95**

PACHT, OTTO
Book Illumination in the Middle Ages: An Introduction
[A85] Oxford hbk **£24.00**

SHAVER-CRANDELL, ANNE
The Middle Ages
[A86] Cambridge pbk **£6.50**

SNYDER, JAMES
Medieval Art `NEW`
The author surveys the whole expanse of medieval art in this fully-illustrated book: from the mosaics and frecoes of early Christian basilicas in Ravenna and elsewhere to the austerely poignant art and

architecture of the Romanesque, it culmiantes in the architectural innovations of soaring Gothic cathedrals.
[A86A] Abrams hbk **£40.00**

STONE
Sculpture in Britain: The Middle Ages
[A87] Penguin hbk **£30.00**

SULLIVAN, SIR EDWARD
The Book of Kells
Facsimile edition of 1920.
[A88] Studio Eds hbk **£6.50**

WATSON, ROWAN
The Playfair Hours
[A89] V & A Mus P hbk **£19.95**

WIECK, ROGER
The Book of Hours in Late Medieval Life
[A90] Sothebys hbk **£22.50**

WILSON, DAVID M.
Anglo-Saxon Art
[A91] Thames & H hbk **£28.00**

Renaissance

AVERY, CHARLES
Florentine Renaissance Sculpture
The author examines the innovative and eloquent work of Donatello, Michelangelo and others, situating them in the cultural environment of Florence during the Renaissance.
[A92] J Murray pbk **£5.95**

BAXANDALL, MICHAEL
Painting and Experience in Fifteenth Century Italy
[A93] Oxford hbk **£19.50**
[A94] Oxford pbk **£4.95**

BECK, JAMES
Italian Renaissance Painting
A scholarly and yet highly readable study of the Renaissance, begining with the declaration of a new era in art, in the work of Masaccio, where attempts at naturalism and the creation of a new pictorial space make their first forceful and eloquent appearance. The author then traces the evolution of art in 15th century Italy by grouping together artists of the same generation and examining the work of Piero, Uccello, Mantegna, da Vinci and others, in their respective contexts, culminating in the work of Raphael and Michelangelo and the emergence of mannerism.
[A95] Harper & Row pbk **£13.95**

BLUNT, ANTHONY
Artistic Theory in Italy 1450 - 1600
A classic study by the distinguished art critic.
[A96] Oxford pbk **£5.95**

BROWN, PATRICIA FORTINI
Venetian Narrative Painting in the Age of Carpaccio
A splendidly illustrated and erudite study of narrative painting in Venice in the late 15th and early 16th centuries where religious, diplomatic and civic scenes decorated many important buildings. Special attention is paid to Vittore Carpaccio and Gentile Bellini.
[A97] Yale hbk **£35.00**

BURCKHARDT, JACOB
The Alterpiece in Renaissance Italy
An illustrated reprint of Burckhardt's classic 1898 essay.
[A98] Phaidon pbk **£75.00**

CASTIGLIONE, BALDASSARE
The Courtier
[A99] Penguin pbk **£4.95**

CHASTEL, ANDRE
Art of the Italian Renaissance
Focusing on contemporary sources pertaining to specific works of art and artists, Chaster's study contributes to a fuller understanding of the established masters of the period.
[A100] Alpine Fine Arts hbk **£26.95**

FREEDBERG, CLEMENT
Painting in Italy 1500 - 1600
[A101] Penguin hbk **£30.00**
[A102] Penguin pbk **£18.95**

GOFFEN
Bellini, Titian & the Franciscans
[A103] Yale UP hbk **£35.00**

GOMBRICH, ERNST
Vol 1: Norm and Form
Gombrich's four books on the Renaissance are designed for students of art history. This is a collection of brilliant essays on style, taste and patronage, and their determining influence on the artist and art of the Renaissance.
[A104] Phaidon pbk **£7.95**
Vol 4: New Light on Old Masters
Gombrich is a major interpreter of art in the most wide-ranging sense, and in this volume sheds new and interesting light on the established masters of the period, Giotto, Leonardo, Raphael and Michelangelo.
[A105] Phaidon hbk **£19.95**

HALE, J.R. (ED)
Concise Encyclopaedia of the Italian Renaissance
[A106] Thames & H pbk **£5.95**

HALL, JAMES
History of Ideas & Images in Italian Art
Recommended for specialists and non-specialists.
[A107] J Murray pbk **£17.50**

HANNING & ROSAND
Castiglione: The Ideal and the Real in Renaissance Culture
Not strictly an art book but Castiglione's famous work of manners, *The Courtier*, acts as an excellent introduction to the Humanist ideals of the Renaissance.
[A108] Yale UP hbk **£28.95**

HARTT, FREDERICK
History of Italian Renaissance Art
700 pages and plenty of pictures on painting, sculpture and architecture. Recently revised, it presents an excellent overview of the period.
[A109] Thames & H hbk **£30.00**

HAUSER, ARNOLD
Mannerism
Subtitled 'The Crisis of the Renaissance and the Origin of Modern Art', this is a scholarly study of the movement which challenged Renaissance ideals in 16th century Italy. The exponents of the mannerist style created personal, anti-classical, anti- naturalistic and expressive works.
[A110] Harvard UP pbk **£16.95**

HAY, DENYS (ED)
The Age of the Renaissance
Subtitled 'The Turning Point of Modern History, 1400-1600', this is a very readable introduction to the social life, thought and art of the period. Richly illustrated.
[A111] Thames & H hbk **£20.00**

HILLS, PAUL
The Light of Early Italian Painting
A splendid and lucid work on the pictorial techniques, historical content and evocation of light in the work of painters from the early 13th to early 15th centuries.
[A112] Yale UP hbk **£22.50**

LETTS, ROSA MARIA
The Renaissance
[A113] Cambridge pbk **£6.50**

LEVEY, MICHAEL
Levey's two works on the Renaissance offer lucid reading for all levels of interest, covering the period briefly but with clarity.
Early Renaissance
[A114] Penguin pbk **£6.95**
The High Renaissance
[A115] Penguin pbk **£6.99**

MULLER
Sculpture in the Netherlands, Germany, France and Spain 1400 - 1500
[A116] Penguin hbk **£30.00**

MURRAY, LINDA
The High Renaissance and Mannerism
Very clear study of a difficult period. See Shearman's book on Mannerism for a more detailed discussion.
[A117] Thames & H pbk **£4.95**

MURRAY, PETER & LINDA
Art of the Renaissance
A very useful introduction and general survey.
[A118] Thames & H pbk **£5.95**

PANOFSKY, ERWIN
Studies in Iconology
A study of the representation of Humanist ideals in Renaissance art by one of the leading experts.
[A119] Icon pbk **£8.95**

POPE-HENNESSY, JOHN
This excellent trilogy on Italian sculpture spans approximately five centuries, and is a detailed account of the works, and cultural context, of sculptors from the Gothic period to Ghiberti and Michelangelo in the Renaissance, culminating in the Baroque era with the ecstatic, dynamic sculpture of Gian Lorenzo Bernini.
Italian Gothic Sculpture
[A120] Phaidon pbk **£20.00**
Italian High Renaissance and Baroque Sculpture
[A121] Phaidon pbk **£20.00**
Italian Renaissance Sculpture
[A122] Phaidon pbk **£20.00**

ROSAND, DAVID
Painting in Cinquecento Venice: Titian, Veronese, Tintoretto
A handsome and intelligent book.
[A123] Yale UP pbk **£24.95**

SEYMOUR
Sculpture in Italy 1400 - 1500
[A124] Penguin hbk **£30.00**

SHEARMAN, JOHN
Early Italian Pictures in the Collection of Her Majesty the Queen
[A125] Cambridge hbk **£75.00**
Mannerism
Derived from the word 'maniera', Mannerism means an affectation of style, based on intellectual rather than direct visual observation, in which figures and colour are consciously distorted; it usually describes Italian art and architecture of the Cinquecento.
[A126] Penguin pbk **£5.99**

SNYDER, JAMES
Northern Renaissance Art: 1350 - 1575
All too often studies of the Renaissance focus only on Italy, and fail to appreciate the cultural interchange between North and South: this helps to redress the balance.
[A127] Abrams hbk **£35.00**

STRONG, ROY
Art and Power: Renaissance Festivals 1450 - 1650
Dense authoritative study.
[A128] Boydell P hbk **£25.00**
[A129] Boydell P pbk **£9.95**

TURNER, NICHOLAS
Florentine Drawings of the 16th Century
High Renaissance and Mannerist drawings in the collection of the British Museum, with text by the Assistant Keeper of the Department of Prints and Drawings.
[A130] Brit Mus P hbk **£25.00**
[A131] Brit Mus P pbk **£12.50**

WHITE, JOHN
Art and Architecture in Italy 1250 - 1400
A definitive study, recently updated.
[A132] Penguin pbk **£30.00**
Birth and Rebirth of Pictorial Space
A useful study which explains ways of looking at early Renaissance paintings.
[A133] Faber pbk **£12.50**

WILDE, JOHANNES
Venetian Art from Bellini to Titian
Excellent study for the academic reader.
[A134] Oxford pbk **£16.00**

WIND, EDGAR
The Eloquence of Symbols
A study of Renaissance iconography.
[A135] Oxford hbk **£27.50**

WITTKOWER, RUDOLF
Allegory and the Migration of Symbols
Wittkower is particularly good at expressing difficult artistic concepts. This book and the next are typically well written.
[A136] Thames & H pbk **£9.95**
Idea and Image
Collected essays on the Italian Renaissance.
[A137] Thames & H hbk **£16.00**

Baroque & Rococo

ARGAN, GIULIO CARLO
The Baroque Age **NEW**
A complete overview of art and architecture of the Baroque period of the 17th and 18th centuries, mainly in Italy, its bithplace and stronghold. Includes the work of Caravaggio, Bernini, Pietro da Cortona, Charles le Brun and Rubens.
[A137A] Skira pbk **£14.95**

BAZIN, GERMANE
Baroque and Rococo
[A138] Thames & H pbk **£5.95**

HUBALA, ERICH
Baroque and Rococo
A very reliable and concise introduction to Baroque art and architecture from it's earliest announcements in 16th century Italy to it's lighter and more intimate version of the 18th century, known as Rococo.
[A139] Herbert Press pbk **£6.95**

MAINSTONE, MADELEINE & ROWLAND
The 17th Century
[A140] Cambridge hbk **£11.95**
[A141] Cambridge pbk **£6.50**

WHITFIELD & MARTINEAU (EDS)
From Caravaggio to Giordano: Painting in Naples 1606 - 1705
[A142] Weidenfeld hbk **£15.00**

WOLFFLIN, HEINRICH
Renaissance and Baroque
The 19th century German critic established in this work an indispensable critical vocabulary, still in use today, by his comparison of two distinct periods in the history of art: 'closed/open', 'painterly/linear' and 'unity, multiplicity' are among the many descriptive categories Wolfin introduced.
[A143] Collins pbk **£4.95**

18th Century & Romantic

ANDREWS, MALCOLM
The Search for the Picturesque
[A144] Scolar P hbk **£45.00**

CLARK, KENNETH
The Romantic Rebellion: Romantic versus Classic Art
Clark at his best, on the debate between the styles of Romantics, such as Blake and Turner, and Neoclassicists such as David in France and Adam in England.
[A145] J Murray pbk **£13.95**

DENVIR, BERNARD
The 18th Century: Art, Design and Society 1689 - 1789
A well-documented history of taste in 18th century Britain.
[A146] Longman hbk **£8.95**

HONOUR, HUGH
Neo-Classicism
A thorough guide to this late 18th and early 19th century revival of classical styles, which was inspired by the excavations at Pompeii and Herculaneum in 1748.
[A147] Penguin pbk **£5.95**
Romanticism
New edition with over 400 illustrations. Covers the revolutionary Romantic movement at its height between 1790 and 1840, the protagonists of which favoured sensibility and imagination over reason.
[A148] Penguin pbk **£9.95**

JONES, STEPHEN
The 18th Century
In the 'Cambridge Introduction to the History of Art' series.
[A149] Cambridge hbk **£11.95**
[A150] Cambridge pbk **£6.50**

LIPPINCOTT, LOUISE
Selling Art in Georgian London: The Rise of Arthur Pond
[A151] Yale UP hbk **£30.00**

PALEY, MORTON D.
Apocalyptic Sublime
The Romantic movement was accompanied by a powerful sense of a new beginning and a sense of impending apocalypse. The expression of passions, the exotic evocations, and the recurring sense of absurdity, contribute to an image of terror and

violence which is counteracted, however, by painterly eloquence and transcendence.
[A152] Yale UP hbk **£35.00**

PAULSON, RONALD
Emblem and Expression
The 'meaning' of English Art in the 18th century. It is illuminating on the relationship between art and literature of this period.
[A153] Thames & H hbk **£16.00**
Literary Landscape: Turner and Constable
Convincing and unusual study of these popular painters in the light of Romantic poetry and literature.
[A154] Yale UP hbk **£26.25**
Representations of Revolution: 1789 - 1820
[A155] Yale UP pbk **£12.95**

ROSENBLUM, ROBERT
The Romantic Child: From Runge to Sendak NEW
The changing attitudes towards children in the Romantic era are discussed here with respect to pictorial depictions of them both in the form of portraiture and in allegorical painting. The author then describes the influence that Runge has had on this kind of art, and finds similarities and overlaps with the work of Sendak.
[A156] Thames & H hbk **£5.95**

ROSENFELD, SYBIL
Georgian Scene Painters & Scene Painting
[A157] Cambridge hbk **£45.00**

VAUGHAN, WILLIAM
Romantic Art
A good volume in the series. It includes the world of Blake, Turner and Constable.
[A158] Thames & H hbk **£10.95**
[A159] Thames & H pbk **£5.95**

19th Century

Art and Design in Europe and America 1800 - 1900
[A160] Herbert P hbk **£18.50**
[A161] Herbert P pbk **£11.95**

BENDINER, KENNETH
An Introduction to Victorian Painting
[A162] Yale UP hbk **£33.00**

DENVIR, BERNARD
The Early 19th Century: Art, Design and Society 1789 - 1852
[A163] Longman pbk **£8.95**

EITNER, LORENZ E.A.
Outline of 19th Century European Painting Volume 1
A thorough investigation and assessment of all the styles and schools of painting in the 19th century, which includes neo-classicism, romanticism, realism, salon painters and impressionism.
[A164] Harper & R pbk **£9.95**
Volume 2
[A165] Harper & R pbk **£12.95**

GERRISH, NUNN PAMELA
Victorian Women Artists
[A166] Women's P hbk **£19.95**
[A167] Women's P pbk **£10.95**

HAMILTON
Painting and Sculpture in Europe 1880 - 1940
[A168] Penguin pbk **£18.95**

HAWES, LOUIS
Presences of Nature: British Landscape 1780 - 1830
[A169] Yale UP pbk **£13.95**

HOLT, ELIZABETH GILMORE
From the Classicists to the Impressionists
[A171] Yale UP pbk **£13.95**

HOOK & POLTIMORE
Popular 19th Century Painting
A Dictionary of European genre painters. Excellent for those who are interested in Greuze, Landseer et al.
[A172] Antique Coll Club hbk **£39.50**

JANSON, H.W.
19th Century Sculpture
Famous for his monumental *History of Art*, Janson here looks at the sculpture of Canova, Thorvaldsen and Rodin in the context of social, political and economic forces. Richly illustrated throughout.
[A173] Thames & H hbk **£35.00**

MAAS, JEREMY
Victorian Painters
Reissue of this well-illustrated book.
[A174] Barrie & J pbk **£14.95**

NEWALL, CHRISTOPHER
Victorian Watercolours
The study of Victorian watercolours is neglected in books, but they remain very popular with collectors.
[A175] Phaidon hbk **£25.00**

NOCHLIN, LINDA
Realism
A brief and vigorous investigation of the 19th century movement which concerned itself with mirroring reality in it's most unadorned and sometimes squalid state, in an attempt to enhance experience.
[A176] Penguin pbk **£5.99**

NOCHLIN, LINDA (ED)
Realism and Tradition in Art 1848 - 1900
A stimulating selection of sources and documents.
[A177] Prentice-Hall pbk **£27.80**

NORMAN, GERALDINE
19th Century Painters and Painting
[A178] Thames & H hbk **£25.00**

NOVOTNY
Painting and Sculpture in Europe 1780 - 1880
[A179] Penguin pbk **£17.95**

READ, BENEDICT
Victorian Sculpture
Excellent study of Victorian public sculpture.
[A180] Yale UP hbk **£50.00**
[A181] Yale UP pbk **£17.95**

REYNOLDS, DONALD
The 19th Century
[A182] Cambridge hbk **£11.95**
[A183] Cambridge pbk **£6.50**

REYNOLDS, GRAHAM
Victorian Painting
Newly updated classic from the Keeper of the Department of Prints and Drawings at the V & A.
[A184] Herbert Press hbk **£16.95**

ROSEN & ZERNER
Romanticism and Realism: The Mythology of 19th Century Art
Eight essays on 'high' art versus 'low' genre art from David and Géricault to Bewick and Manet.
[A185] Faber pbk **£7.99**

ROSENBLUM & JANSON
Art of the 19th Century
Excellent general survey.
[A186] Thames & H hbk **£25.00**

VOGT, A.M.
The 19th Century NEW
Lucid and abundantly illustrated introductory survey of art and architecture.
[A187] Herbert Press pbk **£6.95**

20th Century

ARNASON, H.H.
History of Modern Art
Large and comprehensive.
[A188] Thames & H hbk **£25.00**

BOULLION, JEAN-PAUL
Art Deco NEW
A beautifully illustrated and readable history of Art Deco in all it's manifestations throughout Europe, America and Japan. The author traces the origins of this decorative art to the early years of this century and demonstrates how it permeated all aspects of artistic production and craftsmanship.
[A189] Rizzoli hbk **£50.00**

BOWNESS, ALAN
Modern European Art
Broad survey by former director of the Tate Gallery.
[A190] Thames & H pbk **£5.95**

CHIPP, HERSCHEL B.
Theories of Modern Art
Important series of essays on interpretative theories in 20th century art.
[A191] California UP pbk **£7.50**

CORK, RICHARD
Art Beyond the Gallery in Early 20th Century England
A valuable survey of a less obvious artistic tradition which includes the work of mural painters and the Omega Workshops.
[A192] Yale UP hbk **£50.00**

DAVAL, JEAN-LUC
History of Abstract Painting NEW
A well-illustrated survey of abstract art from Kandisky to minimalism, which includes 165 biographies of artists.
[A193] Art Data hbk **£19.50**

LAMBERT, ROSEMARY
The 20th Century
[A194] Cambridge hbk **£9.50**
[A195] Cambridge pbk **£6.50**

LEMOINE, SERGE
Dada
A concise history and appreciation of the artistic movement which flourished simultaneously in many countries between 1915-1922, and which violently challenged tired ethical and artistic conventions in art and society by celebrating the sense of the irrational, questioning the criteria for exhibition and ultimately extending the boundaries of what art can be.
[A197] Art Data pbk **£6.95**

Mondrian and De Stijl
A concise history and evaluation of Piet Mondrian, a founding member of the early 20th century movement which literally translates as 'style', and sought a comprehensive aesthetic idiom which could be applied to painting, decorative arts and architecture.
[A198] Art Data pbk £6.95

LISTA, GIOVANNI
Futurism
[A199] Art Data pbk £6.95

LUCIE-SMITH, EDWARD
Art of the 1930s
[A200] Weidenfeld hbk £20.00
Lives of the Great 20th Century Artists
[A201] Weidenfeld hbk £20.00

LYNTON, NORBERT
The Story of Modern Art
The second edition of this best-selling introduction with a new chapter on the art of the 1980s, and many more colour illustrations.
[A202] Phaidon hbk £19.95
[A203] Phaidon pbk £11.50

MCLEISH, KENNETH
Companion to the Arts in the 20th Century
Comprehensive reference book covering the arts of this century.
[A204] Viking hbk £17.95
[A205] Penguin pbk £5.95

OSBORNE, HAROLD (ED)
Oxford Companion to 20th Century Art
Excellent work of reference covering a wide area.
[A206] Oxford hbk £22.50
[A207] Oxford pbk £12.95

READ, HERBERT
Concise History of Modern Painting
A lucid, philosophical, richly illustrated and highly enjoyable introduction to the history of painting since Cézanne. The author deftly evaluates the implications and evocations of modern painting and its relation to the thought and conditions of 20th century experience.
[A208] Thames & H pbk £5.95
The Philosophy of Modern Art
Outstanding study by the prominent art historian and aesthetician.
[A209] Faber pbk £4.95

ROSENBLUM, ROBERT
Modern Painting and the Northern Romantic Tradition
[A210] Thames & H pbk £6.95

Sketch by Picasso from *Demoiselles D'Avignon Sketchbook* (Thames & Hudson hbk £32.50)

RUSSELL, JOHN
Meanings of Modern Art
[A211] Thames & H pbk £14.95

SCHAPIRO, MEYER
Modern Art: 19th and 20th Centuries
Brilliant and influential US critic.
[A212] Penguin pbk £7.95

SPALDING, FRANCES
British Art Since 1900
[A214] Thames & H pbk £5.95

STANGOS, NIKOS (ED)
Concepts of Modern Art
[A215] Thames & H pbk £5.95

STEINBERG, LEO
'Primitivism' in 20th Century Art
[A216] Thames & H 2 vols pbk £27.50
Other Criteria
A scholarly work which examines the criteria by which modern art is judged. Useful for anyone who finds abstract art inaccessible.
[A217] Oxford pbk £4.95

WHITFIELD, SARAH
Fauvism　**NEW**
The work of the Fauves is characterized by stong colour and brush technique, stripping art of its sophistication in an attempt to give painting a primitive and basic rawness, and creating a shockingly different pictorial effect in the process.
[A218] Thames & H pbk £5.95

Contemporary Art

Forty Years of Modern Art 1945 - 1985
[A219] Tate pbk £7.95

ART AND DESIGN SERIES
Art in the Age of Pluralism　**NEW**
This volume in the series examines ideas of internationalism and the consequent multiplicity of practices in present art production.
[A220] Academy Eds pbk £7.95
The New Romantics　**NEW**
Looks at the re-emergence of exotic subject matter, brilliant color and passion, in the contemporary re-appropriation of the Romantic tradition.
[A221] Academy Eds pbk £7.95

BEAL, GRAHAM; COOKE, LYNNE ETC (EDS)
A Quiet Revolution: British Sculpture since 1965
Illustrated essays on Flanagan, Long, David, Nash et al.
[A222] Thames & H hbk £17.95

BILLETER, WENDY
Art-Expo 88
[A223] Phaidon hbk £35.00

GODFREY, TONY
Drawing Today　**NEW**
With the emergence of the New Image painters, drawing has reclaimed a pre-eminent position in art-making. The author examines drawing as an instrument of both experimental and traditional art, and also traces the legacy of abstraction with the achievements of Twombly, De Kooning and Penck.
[A224] Phaidon hbk £25.00
The New Image: Painting in the 1980s
[A225] Phaidon hbk £19.95

GOODYEAR, FRANK H. JUN.
Contemporary American Realism since 1960
[A226] NY Graph Soc pbk £14.95

HEWISON, ROBERT
Too Much: Art and Society in the Sixties 1960 - 1975
[A227] Methuen hbk £14.95

JENCKS, CHARLES
Post-Modernism: The New Classicim in Art and Architecture
The most enthusiastic evaluation and appreciation of post-modernism, concentrating on the re-emergence of ornament and the classical ideal. Splendidly produced and illustrated.
[A228] Academy Eds hbk £45.00

KRAMER, HILTON
Revenge of the Philistines: Art and Culture 1972 - 1984
[A229] Secker hbk £12.50

LUCIE-SMITH, EDWARD
Art in the Seventies
[A230] Phaidon pbk £6.50
Movements in Art since 1945
[A231] Thames & H pbk £5.95
The New British Painting
[A232] Phaidon pbk £9.95

MCSHINE, KNASTON
International Survey of Recent Painting and Sculpture
[A233] Thames & H pbk £15.95

NAIRNE, SANDY
State of the Art: Ideas and Images in the 1980s
[A234] Chatto hbk £19.95
[A235] Chatto pbk £12.95

WHITFORD, FRANK
Understanding Abstract Art
[A236] Barrie & J pbk £5.95

WOODS, G. ET AL (EDS)
Art without Boundaries
[A237] Thames & H hbk £10.95

Sculpture

BEATTIE, SUSAN
The New Sculpture
A good guide to contemporary (especially British) sculpture with excellent photographs.
[A238] Yale UP hbk £50.00
[A239] Yale UP pbk £16.95

ELSEN, ALBERT
Rodin's Thinker and the Dilemmas of Modern Public Sculpture
[A240] Yale UP hbk £26.25
[A241] Yale UP pbk £9.95

KONSTAM, NIGEL
Sculpture: The Art and the Practice
Really a practical book but a help in understanding the labour behind great sculpture.
[A242] Collins hbk £12.95

LUCIE-SMITH, EDWARD
Sculpture since 1945
A much-needed book on modern and contemporary sculpture, with good photographs.
[A243] Phaidon hbk £19.95

MONTAGU, JENNIFER
**Roman Baroque Sculpture:
The Industry of Art** **NEW**
The scuplutral monuments of 17th century Rome represent among the most important and beautiful of the artistic achievements of Italy. This study examines the complex industrial structure of the baroque sculptor's profession, raising important questions regarding the actual practice of the artist such as where and how the block of marble was obtained, what part did the bronze founder play in the creative process, how was the artist trained. The role of the assistants in the workshop and the extent to which the artist exercised total creative control are also questioned. A highly intriguing study, not only for the specialist.
[A244] Yale hbk **£25.00**

READ, HERBERT
Modern Sculpture: A Concise History
[A245] Thames & H pbk **£5.95**

TUCKER, WILLIAM
Language of Sculpture
A series of essays from this articulate British sculptor. He discusses the sculptural revival from Rodin at the end of the 19th century to the present day.
[A246] Thames & H pbk **£6.95**

European Art by Country

British & Irish

A Paradise Lost: The Neo-Romantic Imagination in Britain 1935 - 1955
[A247] Lund Humph pbk **£14.95**

Bloomsbury: The Artists, Authors and Designers by Themselves **NEW**
Over 200 illustrations of the varied artistic production of the Bloomsbury group supplement the writings of some of its members.
[A248] MacDonald Orbis hbk **£35.00**

Thames & Hudson Encyclopaedia of British Art
An excellent short reference book which includes information on techniques, writers on art and a world gazetteer of museums and galleries.
[A249] Thames & H hbk **£10.50**
[A250] Thames & H pbk **£5.95**

The Dictionary of British Artists 1880 - 1940
[A251] Antique Coll Club hbk **£39.50**

ARCHIBALD, E.H.H.
The Dictionary of Sea Painters **NEW**
This is a revised and expanded edition with over 1,000 illustrations and over 1,000 painter entries.
[A252] Antique Coll Club hbk **£45.00**

ARNOLD, BRUCE
Concise History of Irish Art
[A253] Thames & H pbk **£5.95**
The Art Atlas of Britain and Ireland
Produced in association with the National Trust this is a guide to Fine Art collections in the British Isles.
[A254] Viking hbk **£20.00**

ARTS COUNCIL OF GREAT BRITAIN
English Romanesque Art 1066 - 1200
[A255] Weidenfeld hbk **£19.95**

BARON, WENDY
The Camden Town Group
An acclaimed study of the important early 20th century group of painters, who included Sickert, Robert Bevan, Gore and Gilman.
[A255A] Scolar P hbk **£48.50**

BARRELL, JOHN
The Dark Side of the Landscape
The Rural Poor in English Painting.
[A256] Cambridge pbk **£12.95**

BILLCLIFFE, ROGER
The Glasgow Boys
The Glasgow School of Painting was a group of artists of international reputation at the end of the 19th century including Guthrie, Lavery, Roche, Henry and many others. Their style was, broadly, one of vigorous and painterly realism.
[A257] J Murray hbk **£40.00**

BLUNDELL, JOE WHITLOCK
Westminster Abbey: The Monuments
A photographic guide to the sculptural monuments which adorn the chapels, aisles and transepts of Westminster Abbey.
[A258] John Murray pbk **£9.95**

BREFFNY, B. (ED)
Ireland: A Cultural Encyclopaedia
[A259] Thames & H hbk **£14.95**

BROOKE-HART, DENYS
19th Century British Marine Painting
[A260] Antique Coll Club hbk **£29.95**
20th Century British Marine Painting
[A261] Antique Coll Club hbk **£29.95**

CASTERAS, SUSAN
English Pre-Raphaelitism & It's Reception in America in the 19th Century **NEW**
Examines the influence in America of Millais, Hunt and Rossetti and the Pre-Raphaelite Brotherhood.
[A262] Associated UP hbk **£25.00**
Images of Victorian Womanhood in English Art **NEW**
[A263] Associated UP hbk **£37.50**

CORK, RICHARD
A massive and comprehensive study, in two volumes, of the pre-First World War Vorticist movement, which was centred around Wyndham Lewis.
Vorticism and Abstract Art in the First Machine Age
Vol 1: Origins and Developments
[A263A] G Fraser hbk **£40.00**
Vol 2: Synthesis and Decline
[A263B] G Fraser hbk **£40.00**

DALY, GAY
Pre-Raphaelites in Love **NEW**
In examining the relationship between the exponents of the brotherhood and their models, the author draws on a wealth of biographical information and thereby creates a 'group portrait'.
[A265] Collins hbk **£15.00**

FAIRLEY, JOHN
Great Racehorses in Art
[A266] Phaidon hbk **£38.50**

FARR, DENNIS
English Art 1870 - 1940
[A267] Oxford pbk **£12.50**

FOSKETT, DAPHNE
Miniatures: Dictionary and Guide
[A268] Antique Coll Club hbk **£45.00**

GAUNT, WILLIAM
English Painting: A Concise History
[A269] Thames & H pbk **£5.95**

GODFREY, RICHARD
English Caricature: 1620 to the Present
[A270] V & A Mus P pbk **£6.95**

GORDON, DILLON
British Paintings
A National Gallery publication.
[A271] Phaidon pbk **£7.90**

GRIERSON, MARY
An English Florilegium
Companion volume to the *Irish Florilegium* (see Wendy Walsh below). A large, quality book of exquisite botanical illustrations.
[A272] Thames & H hbk **£75.00**

HARDIE, MARTIN
**Watercolour Painting in Britain
Vol 1 - The 18th Century**
[A273] Batsford hbk **£50.00**
Vol 2 - The Romantic Period
[A274] Batsford hbk **£50.00**
Vol 3 - The Victorian Period
[A275] Batsford hbk **£50.00**
Watercolour Painting in Britain
[A276] Batsford hbk (3 vols) **£125.00**

HEMMING, CHARLES
British Landscape Painters: A History and Gazetteer **NEW**
Hemming sketches a history of landscape painting and painters in Britain from it's emergence as a distinct art form in the 18th century to the present day.
[A277] Gollancz hbk **£16.95**

HICKS, ALISTAIR
The School of London: The Resurgence of Contemporary Painting **NEW**
British painting has gained much prominence over the last 30 years and established masters of the school of London such as Bacon, Freud and Kitaj have exerted great influence. Hicks describes how the passion for imagery and materials still has a hold on many exponents of contemporary British painting. Extensively illustrated in colour.
[A278] Phaidon hbk **£30.00**

HOWARTH, DAVID
Lord Arundel and his Circle
A study of the great Stuart collector and patron of artists and architects such as Inigo Jones. A rare book on the vital aristocratic patronage of this period.
[A279] Yale UP hbk **£35.00**

INGRAMS, RICHARD (ED)
The Ridgeway: Europe's Oldest Road
A book which celebrates the Ridgeway through a number of landscape artists and the words of Richard Ingrams.
[A280] Phaidon hbk **£14.95**

JEFFREY, IAN
British Landscape 1920 - 1950
Extensive book covering the work of Nash, Spencer and Sutherland, among many others.
[A281] Thames & H hbk **£14.95**

JENKINS, ALAN C.
A.R. Quinton's England
[A282] Webb & B hbk **£14.95**

LEVEY, MICHAEL
The Painter Depicted
[A283] Thames & H pbk **£4.50**

LISTER, RAYMOND
British Romantic Painting
A richly-illustrated survey of the Romantic era, examining all areas of painting: from landscape to portraiture, from genre to book illustration. The author discusses the intellectual and historical background which informed the work and describes the reasons for which later generations would refer to this style as 'Romantic'. Biographical and stylistic commentaries accompany full-colour plates of Turner and Constable through to Palmer and Cotman, creating a vibrant history of one of the most interesting and important periods of British art.
[A284] Cambridge hbk **£22.50**

MACMILLAN, DUNCAN
Painting in Scotland: The Golden Age
A catalogue of the Tate exhibition in 1986, covering painters of the Scottish Enlightenment including Ramsay and Wilkie.
[A285] Phaidon hbk **£19.95**

MALLALIEU, H.L.
Dictionary of British Watercolour Artists up to 1920
Vol 1: Text
[A286] Antique Coll Club hbk **£35.00**
Vol 2: Plates
[A287] Antique Coll Club hbk **£29.95**

MAYOUX, JEAN JAQUES
English Painting: From Hogarth to the Pre-Raphaelites `NEW`
A survey of English painting from the 18th century of Hogarth, Gainsborough and Reynolds to the landscapes of Constable and Turner, which culminates with the Pre-Raphaelite return to Quattrocento ideals in the age of Millais, Rossetti and Hunt.
[A287A] Skira pbk **£19.95**

MCCONKEY, KENNETH
British Impressionism `NEW`
In the second half of the 19th century, in response to academic Victorian art and through contacts with the French, many different artists came together to refine and question ideas of art and established a truly British style of impressionism.
[A288] Phaidon hbk **£25.00**
Edwardian Portraits
[A289] Antique Coll Club hbk **£19.95**

MITCHELL, SALLY (ED)
The Dictionary of British Equestrian Artists
[A290] Antique Coll Club hbk **£39.50**

MULLINS, EDWIN
A Love Affair with Nature
A personal view of British art, from a Channel 4 series looking at the peculiar relationship of British artists with the natural world.
[A291] Phaidon hbk **£14.95**

MURDOCH, JOHN
The English Miniature
[A292] Yale UP hbk **£35.00**
[A293] Yale UP pbk **£12.95**

ORMOND, RICHARD L.
Dictionary of British Portraiture
A comprehensive set of four volumes.
[A294] Batsford hbk 4 vols **£175.00**

PEVSNER, SIR NIKOLAUS
The Englishness of English Art
Classic essay on what characterises English art.
[A295] Penguin pbk **£5.95**

POINTON, MARCIA
Pre-Raphaelites Reviewed `NEW`
The author attempts to shed new light on the political, social and philosophical questions raised by the Pre-Raphaelites.
[A296] Manchester UP hbk **£25.00**
[A297] Manchester UP pbk **£7.95**

QUARM, ROGER & WILCOX, SCOTT
Masters of the Sea: British Marine Watercolours 1650 - 1930
Catalogue of exhibition held at the Yale Centre of British Marine Art, New Haven, and the National Maritime Museum at Greenwich
[A298] Phaidon hbk **£17.95**
[A299] Phaidon pbk **£11.95**

REDHEAD, BRIAN
The Inspiration of Landscape: Artists in National Parks `NEW`
Leading British artists have been invited and commissioned to portray and reflect upon the outstanding beauty of landscapes in the National Parks. The texts respond to both the artists and the works produced as well as commenting on archaeology, history, agriculture, wildlife and monuments.
[A300] Phaidon hbk **£14.95**

ROSENTHAL, MICHAEL
British Landscape Painting
A general survey.
[A301] Phaidon hbk **£15.00**

SANDERS, ROSANNE
The English Apple
Stunning book which celebrates 122 varieties of the English apple in exquisite colour botanical drawings by this prize-winning artist.
[A302] Phaidon hbk **£17.95**

SIMON, ROBIN
The Portrait in Britain and America 1680 - 1914
An interesting work of reference, covering in considerable detail the work of portrait painters from both countries.
[A303] Phaidon hbk **£60.00**

SPENCER, MICHAEL
The Glory of Watercolour
A catalogue from the Royal Society of Painters in Watercolours 1987 exhibition.
[A304] David & Ch hbk **£25.00**

STAINTON, LINDSAY & WHITE, CHRISTOPHER
Drawing in England from Hilliard to Hogarth
Major survey of drawing in 17th century Britain. 200 works from the 1987 exhibition are discussed, with excellent illustrations.
[A305] Brit Mus P hbk **£15.00**

STRONG, ROY
Artists of the Tudor Court
[A306] V & A Mus P pbk **£6.95**
English Renaissance Miniature
'Sir Roy Strong is the prime expert in the field ... and a very readable writer.' (*The Times*)
[A307] Thames & H pbk **£12.95**

VINCENT, ADRIAN
19th Century Maritime Watercolors `NEW`
A splendid pictorial tour of maritime painting in Britain in the 19th century, with commentary on style and techniques.
[A308] David & Ch hbk **£25.00**

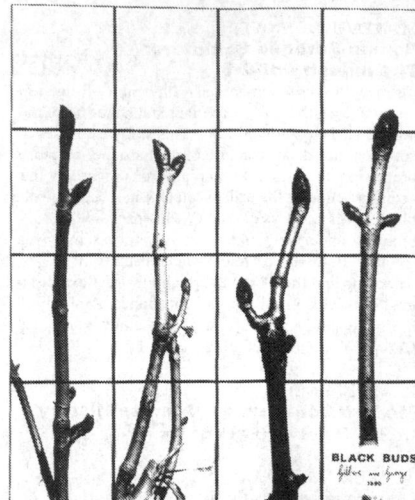

'Black Buds' from *The Art of Gilbert & George* by Wolf Jahn (Thames & Hudson hbk £20.00)

WALKER, STELLA
British Sporting Art in the 20th Century `NEW`
150 illustrations.
[A309] Sportsman Press hbk **£24.95**

WALSH, WENDY
An Irish Florilegium II
Wild and garden plants of Ireland: a superlative horticultural-botanical book with exquisite watercolours by Wendy Walsh and text by the distinguished botanist Charles Nelson.
[A310] Thames & H hbk **£80.00**

WATERHOUSE, ELLIS
Painting in Britain 1530 - 1790
[A311] Penguin pbk **£17.95**
The Dictionary of British 18th Century Painters in Oils & Crayons
[A312] Antique Coll Club hbk **£35.00**

WHINNEY, MARGARET
Sculpture in Britain 1530 - 1830
The only comprehensive survey of sculpture in Britain from the Reformation to the accession of Queen Victoria.
[A313] Viking hbk **£18.95**

WILDER, F.L.
English Sporting Prints
[A314] Thames & H pbk **£9.95**

WOOD, CHRISTOPHER
Olympian Dreamers
Victorian classical painters 1860-1914.
[A316] Constable hbk **£15.00**
The Dictionary of Victorian Painters
[A317] Antique Coll Club hbk **£39.50**

Dutch & Flemish

BROWN & STEVENS (EDS)
Images of the World: Dutch Genre Painting in its Historical Context
[A318] Weidenfeld hbk **£16.95**

BROWN, CHRISTOPHER
Dutch Landscape
Well-designed catalogue of 1986 exhibition.
[A319] Phaidon pbk **£11.95**

Dutch Paintings
[A320] Collins pbk £6.95
Flemish Paintings
[A321] Phaidon pbk £8.95

DAVIES, MARTIN
The Early Netherlandish School
[A322] Phaidon pbk £7.95

DE GROOT, IRENE
Landscape Etchings by the Dutch Masters of the 17th Century
[A323] Gordon Fraser hbk £9.95

FUCHS, GEORG
Dutch Painting
[A324] Thames & H hbk £10.95
[A325] Thames & H pbk £5.95

HAAK, BOB
Golden Age: Dutch Painters of the 17th Century
A splendid volume with over 1,000 illustrations celebrating and assessing the work of the Dutch masters, in what is generally considered to be the greatest period of artistic achievement in Holland.
[A326] Thames & H hbk £45.00

HAND, JOHN OLIVER
Age of Breugel: Netherlandish Drawings in the 16th Century
[A327] Cambridge hbk £42.50

MARIUS
Dutch Painters of the 19th Century
Good basic work of reference by turn-of-the-century historian. Some colour illustrations.
[A328] Antique Coll Club hbk £29.95

MCLAREN, NEIL
The Dutch School
A National Gallery publication.
[A329] Phaidon pbk £20.00

OLIVER, JOHN & WOLFF, MARTHA
Early Netherlandish Painting
[A330] Cambridge pbk £42.50

PANOFSKY, ERWIN
Early Netherlandish Painting Vol 1: Text
[A331] Icon pbk £14.95
Early Netherlandish Painting Vol 2: Plates
[A332] Icon pbk £14.95

ROSENBERG ET AL
Dutch Art and Architecture 1600 - 1800
[A333] Penguin pbk £18.95

SMITH, ALISTAIR
Early Netherlandish and German Paintings
[A334] National Gall pbk £7.95

STECHOW, WOLFGANG
Dutch Landscape Painting of the 17th Century
[A335] Hacker hbk £50.00

SUTTON, PETER C.
Masters of 17th Century Dutch Landscape Painting
Explores the 'Golden Age' of Dutch landscape painting, which had such a wide influence on all other landscape art, including that of England.
[A336] Herbert P hbk £40.00

TROCHE, E.G.
Painting in the Netherlands: 15th and 16th centuries
[A337] Hacker Art Books hbk £42.50

WRIGHT, CHRISTOPHER
The Dutch Painters
100 17th Century masters. The artists are arranged according to which town they come from, which helps put the less well-known into context. A remarkably readable text, and very good value.
[A338] Macdonald pbk £10.00

French

French Paintings from the USSR: Watteau to Matisse
National Gallery catalogue. Covers three centuries of French art; includes masterpieces by major artists which have rarely been seen. Essays describe their acquisition by Russian collectors. 38 colour illustrations, 5 black and white.
[A339] Phaidon hbk £16.95
[A340] Phaidon pbk £9.95

BERNSTEIN, DAVID J.
The Mystery of the Bayeux Tapestry
Shows that the tapestry may have many layers of meaning and is more complex and subtle than its popular image would suggest.
[A341] Weidenfeld hbk £15.00

BJURSTROM, PER
The Art of Drawing in France: 1400 - 1900
[A342] Wilson hbk £29.50

BOIME, ALBERT
The Academy and French Painting in the 19th Century
[A343] Yale UP hbk £15.95

BRYSON, NORMAN
Tradition and Desire from David to Delacroix
An original and stimulating structuralist approach to French Romantic painting.
[A344] Cambridge hbk £37.50
[A345] Cambridge pbk £15.00
Word and Image: French Painting of the Ancien Régime
This discussion of narrative styles won the most distinguished European prize for art history, the Prix de la Confédération des Négotians en Oeuvres d'Art.
[A346] Cambridge pbk £17.50

CLARK, TIMOTHY
Absolute Bourgeois: Artists and Politics in France 1848 - 51
[A347] Thames & H hbk £14.50
[A348] Thames & H pbk £7.95
The Painting of Modern Life
[A349] Thames & H hbk £18.00

CROW, TOM
Paintings and Public Life in 18th Century Paris
Very interesting on the social background to Rococo and Neo-classicsm, this also examines the confrontations with public taste which many groups of painters caused with their salon exhibitions.
[A350] Yale UP hbk £37.50
[A351] Yale UP pbk £10.95

HARDING, JAMES
Artiste Pompiers
These were extreme Neo-classicists who were given the nickname by French Romantic painters. A 'pompier' is a fireman - models at the academy would pose as warriors in firemen's helmets, and from these eccentricities their name was derived.
[A352] Academy Eds pbk £7.95

HARDOUIN-FUGIER; GRAFE & MITCHELL
French Flower Painters of the 19th Century: A Dictionary **NEW**
Destined to become a standard work of reference, both because it is scholarly and unprecedented, and perhaps more importantly, because of the special appeal of the subject matter. The dictionary also contributes to a greater understanding of French painting in the 19th century and provides important background to the 3,500 painters included.
[A353] Philip Wilson hbk £55.00

HARGROVE, JUNE (ED)
The French Academy **NEW**
Examines the historical role of the Academy, and it's relationship to the 'classical ideal'.
[A354] Associated UP hbk £20.00

JOHNSON, D. & M.
The Age of Illusion
Art and Politics in France 1918-1940. Rich documentation of the inter-war years in France which were a time of extraordinary cultural activity.
[A355] Thames & H hbk £14.50

LEVEY, MICHAEL
Rococo to Revolution
Interesting volume from the former director of the National Gallery, London.
[A356] Thames & H pbk £5.95

MILNER, JOHN
The Studios of Paris
The capital of art in the late 19th century. An engaging account of what it was like to be an artist in Paris in its artistic heyday, and an examination of the city itself.
[A357] Yale UP hbk £25.00

WAKEFIELD, DAVID
French 18th Century Painting
Contains a guide to the location of the paintings, many of which are to be found in obscure French galleries.
[A358] Gordon Fraser hbk £30.00

WECHSLER, JUDITH
Human Comedy
A study of caricature and physiognomy in 19th century Paris. A most stimulating and intelligent book for the academic reader.
[A359] Thames & H hbk £20.00

WILSON, DAVID M.
The Bayeux Tapestry
Very popular and handsome book with the best photographs of the tapestry by far.
[A360] Thames & H hbk £55.00

WILSON, MICHAEL
French Paintings after 1800
[A361] Phaidon pbk £6.95
French Paintings before 1800
[A362] Phaidon pbk £7.95

Germany & Austria

EBERLE, MATTHIAS
World War I and the Weimar Artists: Dix, Grosz, Beckmann, Schlemmer
[A363] Yale UP hbk £18.00

KOSCHATSZKY, WALTER
Viennese Watercolors of the 19th Century
[A364] Abrams hbk **£67.50**

NORMAN, GERALDINE
Biedermayer Painting
[A365] Thames & H hbk **£28.00**

REIMANN, G. & ROBINSON, W. (EDS)
The Romantic Spirit NEW
A study of German drawing between 1780 and 1850.
[A366] Oxford hbk **£45.00**

SCHORDKE, CARL
Fin de Siècle Vienna
An authoritative study of politics and culture in Vienna at the end of the century.
[A367] Cambridge pbk **£12.95**

SCHRADER & SCHEBERA
The 'Golden' Twenties
Subtitled 'Art and Literature in the Weimar Republic', the authors chose to retain the epithet 'Golden' in quotations to suggest the conflicting artistic products in the 15 years of cultural activity between 1918 and 1933, where avant-garde experiments rubbed shoulders with mediocre entertainment extravaganzas, and the spectre of Nazi rule hovered ominously.
[A368] Yale hbk **£25.00**

VARNEDOE, KIRK
Vienna 1900: Art, Architecture, Design
[A369] MOMA hbk **£32.00**

VAUGHAN, WILLIAM
German Romantic Painting
Vaughan's books are characterised by good illustration, infectious enthusiasm and elegant writing.
[A370] Yale UP hbk **£45.00**
[A371] Yale UP pbk **£16.95**
German Romanticism and English Art
German Romanticism exerted an enormous influence on the art and literature of Britain, as is outlined here.
[A372] Yale UP hbk **£45.00**

VERGO, PETER
Art in Vienna 1891 - 1918
Superb overview of art, architecture and philosophy which shocked the conservative public of the time. Much contemporary source material.
[A373] Phaidon pbk **£11.95**

VON DER OSTEN, VEY
Painting and Sculpture in Germany and the Netherlands 1500 - 1600
[A374] Penguin hbk **£30.00**

WILLET, JOHN
New Sobriety: 1914 - 1933
Subtitled 'Art and Politics in the Weimar Period', this is a well-researched and illustrated study.
[A375] Thames & H pbk **£8.95**

Italy

Many other titles will be found in the preceding *Renaissance* section of the History of European Art.

BORSOOK, EVE
The Mural Painters of Tuscany
From Cimabue (c. 1240 - 1302) to Andrea del Sarto (1486 - 1531). Third edition of this classic work illustrated with black and white photographs.
[A376] Oxford hbk **£82.00**

BRAHAM, ALAN
Italian Painting of the 16th Century
[A377] Phaidon pbk **£7.95**

DAVIES, MARTIN
The Early Italian Schools before 1400
[A378] Phaidon pbk **£9.95**

HASKELL, FRANCIS
Patrons and Painters
A study in the relations between Italian art and society in the age of the Baroque.
[A379] Yale UP hbk **£37.50**
[A380] Yale UP pbk **£14.95**

NATIONAL GALLERY OF ART WASHINGTON
Age of Correggio and the Carracci: Painting in Emilia in 16/17th Centuries
This excellent book fills a yawning gap on the subject. It was produced for a major exhibition in America and includes high quality plates.
[A381] Cambridge hbk **£45.00**

ROYAL ACADEMY OF ARTS
Painting in Naples from Caravaggio to Giordano
An exhibition catalogue which shows the profound influence of Caravaggio on the Neapolitan school of the 17th century.
[A382] Weidenfeld hbk **£15.00**

SMITH, ALISTAIR
Early Italian Paintings
[A383] Phaidon pbk **£9.95**

WITTKOWER, RUDOLF
Art and Architecture in Italy 1600 - 1750
[A384] Penguin hbk **£30.00**
[A385] Penguin pbk **£18.95**

Russia & Scandinavia

100 Years of Russian Art: 1889 - 1989 From Private Collections in the USSR
Exhibition catalogue.
[A386] Lund Humphries pbk **£17.50**

BIRD, ALAN
A History of Russian Painting
A comprehensive survey of Russian and Soviet painting, including foreign artists working at the court of Peter the Great in the early 18th century.
[A387] Phaidon hbk **£35.00**

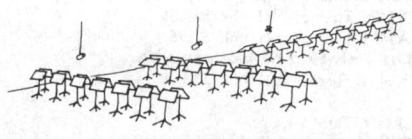

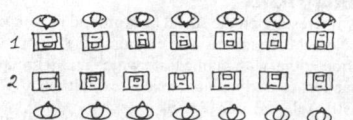

Orchestral plan by Ilya Kabakov from *Ten Characters* (ICA pbk **£10.95**)

BORISOVA, ELENA & STERNIN, GRIGORY
Russian Art Nouveau NEW
Art nouveau in Russia developed specific stylistic traits. This is a very handsome, first-of-its-kind survey, charting the social and cultural context of turn of the century Russia, and delineating the singularly Russian aspects of the movement as it expressed itself in art, architecture, graphics, pottery and other crafts.
[A388] Rizzoli hbk **£65.00**

BOWLT, JOHN E. (ED)
Russian Art of the Avant-Garde: Theory and Criticism 1902 - 1934 NEW
In the first third of this century Russian art produced a very exciting body of avant-garde work which would eventually send shock waves throughout the whole world. This is a collection of writings by artists and critics of the Russian avant-garde and is essential reading for anyone interested in this extraordinary epoch of Soviet artistic and political history.
[A389] Thames & H pbk **£15.95**

BOWN, MATTHEW CULLERNE
Contemporary Russian Art NEW
Very little of the art produced in modern Russia has been seen in the West and now that Soviet artists are experiencing new freedom of expression, the work produced is arousing enormous interest both at home and abroad. This is the first survey of artists working in the Soviet Union today. With the great achievements of Russian art as a backdrop, the author discusses the evolution of contemporary Soviet art and introduces more than fifty artists.
[A390] Phaidon hbk **£25.00**

ELLIOT, DAVID
New Worlds: Russian Art and Society 1900 - 1937
Interesting photographs of artists and designers in the revolutionary period.
[A391] Thames & H hbk **£14.50**

FAUCHEREAU, SERGE
Moscow 1900 - 1930 NEW
Traces the artistic and cultural output of the Russian capital in the exciting first 30 years of this century. Highly illustrated.
[A392] Rizzoli hbk **£39.95**

GRAY, CAMILLA & BURLEIGH-MOTELY, MARIAN
The Russian Experiment in Art: 1866 - 1922
[A393] Thames & H pbk **£5.95**

HAMILTON, G.H.
Art and Architecture of Russia
[A394] Penguin hbk **£30.00**

KENT, NEIL
Triumph of Light and Nature: Nordic Art 1740 - 1940
[A395] Thames & H hbk **£20.00**

NAKOV, ANDREI
Avant-Guarde Russe
[A396] Art Data pbk **£6.95**

PIOTROVSKY, BORIS; GALANINA, LIUDMILLA & GRACH, NONNA
Scythian Art
Art of the tribes which roamed Eastern Europe from 7th-3rd centuries BC. The book shows the many gold objects in the Hermitage and other Russian museum collections.
[A397] Phaidon hbk **£25.00**

SMIRNOVA, E.
Moscow Icons `NEW`
The school of painting of medieval Moscow included significant artists such as Andrei Rublev. With over 500 illustrations this study examines the influence exerted by the 14th century icon painters on later developments in Russian Art.
[A398] Phaidon hbk **£50.00**

VARNEDOE, KIRK
Northern Light: Nordic Art at the Turn of the Century
[A399] Yale UP hbk **£29.95**

Spain

HELSTON, MICHAEL
Painting in Spain during the Later 18th Century `NEW`
The catalogue to this important exhibition introduces little-known painters of the period and contributes to the critical re-appraisal of artists such as Melendez and Paret.
[A400] Phaidon pbk **£10.95**
Spanish and Later Italian Paintings
[A401] Phaidon pbk **£6.95**

JORDAN, WILLIAM B.
Spanish Still Life in the Golden Age 1600 - 1650
Splendidly produced and researched book on still life painting in the age of Zurbaran and Murillo.
[A402] Abrams hbk **£29.95**

MACLAREN, NEIL
The Spanish School
[A403] Phaidon pbk **£8.95**

World Art

Africa

BASSANI, EZIO & FAGG, WILLIAM B.
Africa and the Renaissance: Art in Ivory
Exhibition catalogue of African ivory carvings of extraordinary beauty and complexity, supported by dozens of colour illustrations.
[A404] Prestel-Verlag hbk **£38.00**

GILLON, W.
A Short History of African Art
[A405] Viking hbk **£25.00**
[A406] Penguin pbk **£10.95**

SCHMALENBACH (ED)
African Art: The Barbier-Mueller Collection
Includes aesthetic analyses and studies of the anthroplogical significance of the work.
[A407] Prestel-Verlag hbk **£31.51**

VOGEL, SUSAN
African Masterpieces from the Musee de l'Homme
[A408] Abrams hbk **£37.50**

WILCOX, A.R.
The Rock Art of Africa
[A409] C Helm hbk **£50.00**

WILLET, JOHN
African Art
[A410] Thames & H pbk **£5.95**

YOUNG, GAVIN `NEW`
Art of the South African Townships
With a foreward by Desmond Tutu and 100 colour illustrations, art from a 'hot' political climate - focusing on the township art of the 1980s.
[A411] Thames & H pbk **£6.95**

America

A Graphic Muse: Prints By Contemporary American Women
A survey of graphic work by 24 leading American women artists.
[A412] Phaidon hbk **£25.00**

ADES, DAWN (ED)
Latin American Art `NEW`
This is an exploration of art in Latin America from the years of the independence movements at the begining of the 19th century to the present day. This wide-ranging and richly illustrated book examines all aspects of the artistic production of the various countries, analysing the colonial and post-colonial experiences, the landscape painters of the last two centuries, the popular graphic tradition, the Mexican muralists, the surrealists, the optical experiments of the 50s and 60s and finally commenting on a selection of contemporary art-making.
[A413] Yale UP hbk **£45.00**
[A414] Yale UP pbk **£19.95**

AUPING, MICHAEL (ED)
Abstract Expressionism
Overview of one of the most exciting movements in modern art, which glorified gesture and foregrounded the painting process, and established New York as the artistic capital of the world.
[A415] Thames and H hbk **£36.00**

BADDELEY, ORIANA & FRASER, VALERIE
Drawing the Line: Art and Cultural Identity in Contemporary Latin America `NEW`
An examination of how the artists and muralists of Latin America have helped to shape and determine the cultural identity of this part of the world.
[A416] Verso hbk **£29.95**
[A417] Verso pbk **£9.95**

BROWN, MILTON W; HUNTER, SAM ET AL
American Art
[A418] Abrams hbk **£35.00**

CAMPBELL, MARY
Harlem Renaissance: Art of Black America
A wonderful evocation of the cultural capital of Black America at the dawn of the jazz age in the 1920's, sketching the life and work of poets such as Langston Hughes, musicians Duke Ellington and Louis Armstrong and painters William Johnson and Palmer Hayden.
[A419] Abrams hbk **£25.00**

FEEST, C.F.
Native Arts of North America
[A420] Thames & H pbk **£4.95**

GROCE, GEORGE C.
American Folk Painters of Three Centuries
[A421] Thames & H pbk **£18.00**

A linoleum relief print entitled 'Lets Get Together' from *Art of the South African Townships* by Gavin Young (Thames & Hudson pbk £6.95)

NY Historical Society's Dictionary of Artists in America 1564 - 1860
[A422] Yale UP hbk **£62.95**

LANE, JOHN R. & LARSEN, SUSAN C.
Abstract Painting and Sculpture in America 1927 - 1944
An exhibition catalogue, this provides a thorough survey of American abstraction from 1927 to the emergence of the abstract expressionists.
[A425] Abrams pbk **£22.50**

LEVIN, GAIL
20th Century American Painting: The Thyssen-Bornemisza Collection
A collection specialising in pre-World War II painting, the greatest collection of its kind outside the United States.
[A426] Sotheby hbk **£49.50**

LUBIN, DAVID M.
Act of Portrayal: Eakins, Sargent, James
A study of the art of three society portrait painters, who lifted the genre to a higher artistic status.
[A427] Yale UP hbk **£22.95**

LUCIE-SMITH, EDWARD
American Art Now
[A428] Phaidon hbk **£20.00**

PISANO, RONALD G.
Idle Hours: American Leisure Activities 1865 - 1914 `NEW`
The author charts the rise of the American upper class in the second half of the 19th century and its newly found leisure pursuits such as boating, golfing and reading, and studies the group of impressionist painters who emerged and reflected these interests.
[A430] NY Graph Soc hbk **£35.00**

SCHIMMEL & STEIN
The Figurative Fifties: New York Figurative Expressionism
This beautifully-illustrated book focuses on the lesser-known figurative painters eclipsed by the eruption of the abstract expressionists in post-war NY City.
[A431] Rizzoli pbk **£12.95**

WILMERDING, JOHN
American Marine Painting
Stunning book containing colour reproductions of

Winslow Homer, Edward Hopper, Andrew Wyeth and many others.
[A432] Abrams hbk **£28.50**

India & Islamic

CRAVEN, ROY
Concise History of Indian Art
[A433] Thames & H hbk **£10.95**
[A434] Thames & H pbk **£5.95**

EARLE, J.C.
Art & Architecture of the Indian Subcontinent
[A435] Penguin pbk **£18.95**

ETTINGHAUSEN & GRABER
Art and Architecture of Islam 650 - 1250
A new volume in this invaluable series.
[A436] Penguin pbk **£17.95**

GRAY, BASIL (ED)
The Arts of India
An illustrated survey of all the arts of the Buddhist, Hindu, Jain and modern periods in India.
[A437] Phaidon hbk **£25.00**

KALTER, JOHANNES
Arts and Crafts of Turkestan
[A438] Thames & H hbk **£12.95**

LERNER, MARTIN & FELTEN, WOLFGANG
Thai and Khmer Sculpture from the 6th to the 14th Centuries **NEW**
A survey of bronze and stone sculpture from Kampuchea, Thailand and Vietnam.
[A439] Sotheby hbk **£70.00**

LEVEY, MICHAEL
The World of Ottoman Art
From the founding of the Ottoman Empire to 1909.
[A440] Thames & H pbk **£5.95**

ROGERS, J.M.
The Topkapi Saray Museum
Ottoman albums and illuminated manuscripts.
[A443] Thames & H hbk **£70.00**

SKELTON, ROBERT ET AL
The Indian Heritage
The Victoria and Albert Museum has a good collection both of Indian arts and crafts and of work influenced by them, of which this is a brief survey.
[A444] V & A Mus P pbk **£6.95**

TITLEY, N.M.
Persian Miniature Painting
An absorbing study on this jewel-like art form.
[A446] Brit Lib hbk **£25.00**

WACZIARG, FRANCIS & NATH, AMAN
Arts and Crafts of Rajasthan
Colourful. Includes minatures and woodcarving.
[A447] Thames & H hbk **£27.50**

Oriental

Asian Art: An Illustrated History
[A448] Phaidon pbk **£14.95**

HUTT, JULIA
Understanding Far-Eastern Art
[A449] Phaidon hbk **£19.50**

LEE, SHERMAN E.
A History of Far Eastern Art
A wonderfully illustrated, well-written work tracing the development of all arts in the Far East.
[A450] Thames and H hbk **£38.00**

TANABE, WILLA J.
Paintings of the Lotus Sutra
A survey of the several genres of visual art related to this religious classic, this book is of interest to both the art historian and the student of religion or Asian culture.
[A451] Weatherhill hbk **£37.50**

Chinese

CHENGUYUAN MA
Ancient Chinese Bronzes
[A453] Oxford hbk **£40.00**

CLUMAS, CRAIG
Chinese Export Watercolours
[A454] V & A Mus P hbk **£14.95**

DIEN, ALBERT E; THORPE, ROBERT L. ET AL
The Quest for Eternity
A description of Chinese ceramic tomb sculpture.
[A455] Thames & H pbk **£15.95**

MEDLEY
The Chinese Bronzes of Yunnan
48 tombs in Mount Shizhai contained over 4,000 works of art from the 4th century BC and later. The animals and figures show an agricultural society of some sophistication and are charming in themselves. Excellent photographs.
[A456] Sidgwick hbk **£35.00**

RAWSON, JESSICA
Chinese Bronzes: Art and Ritual
Authoritative and well-illustrated.
[A457] Brit Mus P pbk **£5.95**
Chinese Ornament: The Lotus and the Dragon
A study of the flower and animal symbolism so eagerly copied in the West. It demonstrates that many Chinese flower designs actually have their origins in the mediterranean world of Alexander the Great.
[A458] Brit Mus P pbk **£12.95**

RIDDELL, SHEILA
Dated Chinese Antiquities 600 - 1650
Classic archaeological study.
[A459] Faber hbk **£25.00**

SULLIVAN, MICHAEL
Symbols of Eternity: The Art of Landscape Painting in China
A serious study, containing more text than pictures.
[A460] Oxford hbk **£22.50**

TREGEAR, MARY
Chinese Art
[A461] Thames & H hbk **£10.95**
[A462] Thames & H pbk **£5.95**

WATSON, WILLIAM
Art of Dynastic China
[A463] Thames & H hbk **£65.00**

Japanese

BAKER, STANLEY
Japanese Art
[A464] Thames & H pbk **£5.95**

BLAKEMORE, FRANCES
Who's Who in Modern Japanese Prints
[A465] Weatherhill hbk **£9.95**

ELISSEEFF & ELISSEEFF
Art of Japan
Splendidly illustrated and researched work examining all the arts of Japan through the ages.
[A466] Abrams hbk **£66.00**

HARRIS, VICTOR
Netsuke: The Hull Grundy Collection in the British Museum
'Netsuke' are toggles, fixing a small purse to the belt of Japanese national dress and carved in a wide variety of ways (though predominantly as animals), from jade, ivory or other semi-precious materials. Over 600 examples are included in this study.
[A467] Brit Mus P hbk **£35.00**

HILLIER, J.
Hokusai: Paintings, Drawings and Woodcuts 1860 - 1949
Probably the Japanese printmaker best-known to Europeans (artist of 'The Wave') and widely influential.
[A468] Phaidon hbk **£9.50**
Japanese Colour Prints
[A469] Phaidon pbk **£6.95**
Japanese Prints
From 300 years of albums and books here are 100 selected examples of this exquisite art together with full captions.
[A470] Brit Mus P pbk **£7.95**

MUNSTERBERG, HUGO
The Japanese Print: A Historical Guide
Good introduction to the Japanese art form most influential in the West. This publisher specialises in the art of Japan and all Weatherhill titles are recommended.
[A471] Weatherhill hbk **£14.95**

PAINE & SOPER
Art and Architecture of Japan
[A472] Penguin pbk **£18.95**

PRICE & SINGER
Japanese Painting of the Edo Period 1616 - 1868
The period of exquisite courtly paintings on screens when the art of Netsuke was at its height.
[A473] Thames & H pbk **£15.95**

ROBERTS, LAURENCE O.
A Dictionary of Japanese Artists
Covers painting, sculpture, ceramics, prints and lacquer. Very useful for the collector.
[A474] Weatherhill hbk **£22.50**

SMITH, LAWRENCE
Ukiyoe: Images of Unknown Japan
More prints from the British Museum's excellent collection. Well illustrated.
[A475] Brit Mus P hbk **£12.50**

TERUKAZU
Japanese Painting
[A476] Rizzoli pbk **£14.95**

WICHMANN, SIEGFRIED
Japonisme
The Japanese influence on Western art since 1858. After 200 years of isolation the opening up of Japan to the West had an explosive effect on the arts. This impressive study includes over 1,100 illustrations.
[A477] Thames & H hbk **£35.00**

Monographs on Artists & Schools

Major Series

A number of the titles listed below appear in major series, the aims, format and extent of coverage of which remain constant from title to title. The most important are:

PENGUIN CLASSICS OF WORLD ART

Large-format paperbacks on a selection of famous painters, with a brief introduction followed by a critical history of the artist. The bulk of the books consist of a selection of large colour plates. A good catalogue of works, which also lists questionable attributions at the end.
(Penguin pbk **£7.95**)

PHAIDON COLOUR LIBRARY

Large-format paperbacks on popular artists and schools. The series is being reprinted to upgrade the quality of colour reproduction.
(Phaidon pbk **£10.00**)

THAMES & HUDSON LIBRARY OF GREAT PAINTERS

Originally published by Abrams, these large books have texts by leading art historians and tipped-in colour plates.
(Thames & Hudson hbk **£25.00**)

THAMES & HUDSON WORLD OF ART

The numerous titles in this extensive series represent quite remarkable value. They are small laminated paperbacks with varied, colourful fronts and black spines. The authors are distinguished specialists in their fields, and while the style of writing may vary, the quality of information does not - it is well-organised, and includes indexes and bibliographies. The series gives particularly good coverage to ancient and 20th century art and architecture, as well as to a number of individual artists.
(Thames & Hudson hbk **£10.95**, pbk **£5.95**)

Artists & Schools A-Z

ALBERS, JOSEF (1888 - 1976)
Born in Germany, Albers was one of the first of the Bauhaus lecturers to emigrate to the United States in 1933, becoming, in 1950, Chairman of the Department of Architecture and Design at Yale University. At this point, he began work on a series of paintings and lithographs based on the square - it is this extensive body of work entitled *Homage to the Square* that Albers is best known for.
Interaction of Colour
[480] Yale UP pbk **£7.95**
WEBER, NICHOLAS FOX ET AL
Josef Albers: A Retrospective `NEW`
This volume, published for the first museum retrospective of Albers' work held at the Guggenheim, documents the amazing breadth of Albers' *oeuvre*: early figurative drawings and paintings, glass assemblages, sandblasted glass constructions, furniture designs, typography, photos and photo-collages and the famous series of abstract prints and paintings. The lucid texts do justice to this influential painter, poet, theoretician and teacher. 281 illustrations, 122 full colour.
[A481] Abrams hbk **£48.00**
WEBER, NICHOLAS FOX
The Drawings of Josef Albers
142 two colour reproductions and 12 colour.
[A482] Yale UP hbk **£21.00**

ANDRE, CARL (1935 -)
American minimalist artist whose provocative sculptures are constructed out of standard industrial materials and arranged in simple geometric units. 'I not only know better than the Daily Mirror and the Daily Mail but I also know better than the people at the Tate who bought a pile of bricks and called it art. I call it a pile of bricks; and that is what it is.' (Andre's sculpture reviewed by Bernard Levin in *The Times*, 1976)
Carl Andre: Whitechapel Catalogue 1978
[A483] Whitechapel pbk **£4.00**
FRAMPTON, HOLLIS
Carl Andre: Twelve Dialogues 1962 - 1963
[A484] Art Data pbk **£17.50**

BACON, FRANCIS (1909 -)
Francis Bacon started painting in 1929 but destroyed nearly all his early work during World War II. Disregarding international schools of art, Bacon fiercely pushed his own style to the fore, producing portraits and narrative sequences infused with an existentialist anxiety.
Brutality of Fact: Interviews with Francis Bacon
[A485] Thames & H pbk **£8.95**
Francis Bacon
Exhibition catalogue.
[A486] Tate Gall pbk **£15.95**
Francis Bacon `NEW`
Published to coincide with the artist's 80th birthday, this exceptional monograph emphasizes key paintings from Bacon's later period. Essays written by the major contemporary critics, Sir Lawrence Gowing and Sam Hunter, offer extensive insight into the work. 87 illustrations, 75 colour.
[A487] Thames & H hbk **£25.00**

Illustration from *Beardsley* by Simon Wilson
(Phaidon Press pbk £8.50)

ADES, DAWN & FORGE, ANDREW
Francis Bacon
This extensive catalogue documenting the Tate Gallery retrospective offers essays by prominent historians, a detailed description of Bacon's painting techniques and a bibliography. The publisher claims the book offers the most comprehensive survey of Bacon's paintings available.
[A488] Thames & H hbk **£30.00**
[A489] Thames & H pbk **£19.95**
BERNARD, BRUCE
About Francis Bacon `NEW`
With over 200 colour illustrations, this publication presents many works previously unpublished. Concludes with a review of Bacon's 1988 retrospective in Moscow.
[A490] Macdonald Orbis hbk **£35.00**
LEIRIS, MICHEL
Francis Bacon
[A491] Phaidon hbk **£50.00**
SYLVESTER, DAVID
Interviews with Francis Bacon 1962 - 1979
[A492] Thames & H hbk **£6.95**

BALTHUS (BALTHASAR KLOSOWSKI DE ROLA) (1908 -)
A French painter of Polish origin, Balthus was encouraged to develop his art by the poet Rainer Maria Rilke. Balthus's disorienting narratives camouflage a cool and objectified vision of reality. Balthus also designed theatre sets, the most famous being his creation for Albert Camus' *L'Etat de siege*, 1948.
CARANDENTE, GIOVANNI
Balthus: Drawings and Watercolours
A good introductory essay and selection of pictures, some rare, on this modern French painter of quiet subtle power.
[A493] Thames & H hbk **£15.00**
[A494] Thames & H pbk **£9.95**
REWALD, SABINE
Balthus
A catalogue from Museum of Modern Art NY and Centre Georges Pompidou including excellent colour plates.
[A495] Abrams hbk **£27.50**

BASELITZ, GEORG
Baselitz has been exhibiting his work since 1961. His figurative painting has contributed in a fundamental way to the International Movement. Almost violent in use of colour and employment of gesture, Baselitz's themes circle around the re-presentation of 'heroes' and 'new types', his most recognised motif being the upside-down figure.
FRANZKE, ANDREAS
Georg Baselitz: Ideas and Concepts `NEW`
Georg Baselitz is Germany's leading contemporary figurative painter. This monograph is a major comprehensive study of his *oeuvre* including interpretations of individual works, and discussions of themes and formal and technical strategies. 240 illustrations, 189 colour.
[A496] Prestel hbk **£41.50**
GOHR, SIEGFRIED (ED)
Georg Baselitz: Druckgraphik-Prints-Estampes
With texts in English, French and German, this book documents Baselitz's prolific career, focusing solely on his prints.
[A497] Prestel hbk **£23.00**

BEARDSLEY, AUBREY (1872 - 1898)
This English illustrator's *oeuvre* can be roughly divided into three phases: work executed under the influence of the Pre-Raphaelites; a highly decorative style influenced by Japanese prints; and a return to

greater naturalism. He illustrated Oscar Wilde's *Salome* in (1894) and Alexander Pope's *The Rape of the Lock* in 1896.

Aubrey Beardsley: Early Works
[A498] Dover pbk **£5.20**
Aubrey Beardsley: Later Work
[A499] Da Capo hbk **£16.50**
CLARK, KENNETH
The Best of Aubrey Beardsley
[A500] J Murray hbk **£12.50**
READE, BRIAN
Aubrey Beardsley
Definitive monograph from the organiser of the major Beardsley exhibition in the mid-1970s at the V & A.
[A501] Antique Coll Club hbk **£19.95**
WALKER, R.A. (ED)
Best of Beardsley
[A502] Spring Books hbk **£7.95**
WILSON, SIMON
Beardsley
[A502A] Phaidon pbk **£8.50**

BERNINI, GIANLORENZO (1598 - 1680)
Italian baroque painter, sculptor and architect who is most representative of the prolific artistic activity of the 17th century.
Bernini
[A504] Penguin pbk **£5.95**
BERN, G.
Bernini: New Aspects of His Art and Thought
[A505] Pennsylvania UP hbk **£33.60**
HIBBARD, HOWARD
Bernini
A clear study on the outstanding genius of the baroque style.
[A506] Penguin pbk **£3.95**
SUTHERLAND, ANN HARRIS
Gianlorenzo Bernini: Selected Drawings
[A507] Dover pbk **£5.55**
WITTKOWER, RUDOLPH
The Sculptor of the Roman Baroque
The 3rd edition of a major study.
[A508] Phaidon hbk **£27.50**

BEUYS, JOSEPH (1921 - 1986)
The artist as *shaman* best describes this experimental German artist who worked in performance, installation and more traditional art forms. His pieces embody a profound and highly unique poetic sensibility.
GRINTEN, FRANZ JOSEPH & GRINTEN, HANS VAN DER (ED)
Oil Colours 1936 - 1965
With texts in German and English, this special edition concentrates on Beuys' lesser known works. 100 colour plates.
[A509] Prestel hbk **£129.00**
MOFFITT
Joseph Beuys: Case of Occultism in Avant-Garde Art
[A510] UMI Research P hbk **£33.50**
SEYMOUR, ANNE
Joseph Beuys: Drawings
[A511] V & A pbk **£6.95**
THOMAS, KARIN (ED)
Joseph Beuys: Life and Works
[A512] Barrons pbk **£4.95**

BLAKE, WILLIAM (1757 - 1827)
English mystic, poet and engraver whose lavishly coloured illuminations integrated text and image, encompassing a visionary's view of the world.
Illustrated Catalogue of the Works in the Fitzwilliam Museum
[A514] Fitzwilliam hbk **£5.00**
William Blake and His Contemporaries
[A515] Fitzwilliam pbk **£6.95**

BINDMAN, DAVID
William Blake
[A516] Thames & H pbk **£14.95**
BUTLIN, MARTIN
William Blake 1757 - 1827   NEW
Redesigned in a new format and lavishly illustrated, this edition of the catalogue of Blake's works in the Tate Gallery is considerably enlarged and includes several recent acquisitions. The text includes a new article on the formation of the collection by Krzystof Cieszkowski, Assistant Librarian at the Tate Gallery.
[A517] Tate Gall hbk **£45.00**
LISTER, RAYMOND
The Paintings of William Blake
[A518] Cambridge UP hbk **£22.50**
[A519] Cambridge UP pbk **£11.95**
RAINE, KATHLEEN
Blake
An illustrated introduction to the life and work of Blake, by the acclaimed poet and revered Blakeophile.
[A520] Thames & H pbk **£4.95**

BOMBERG, DAVID (1890 - 1957)
Working on the periphery of art production, Bomberg suffered from neglect during his lifetime. Current reassessment identifies him as a leading figure in experimental painting.
CORK, RICHARD
David Bomberg
This publication served as the catalogue for the 1988 Tate Gallery Exhibition. In it, Richard Cork sensitively examines Bomberg's uneasy relationship with the art world of his day.
[A521] Yale UP hbk **£65.00**
[A522] Yale UP pbk **£24.95**

BONNARD, PIERRE (1867 - 1947)
Bonnard's acute sense of subdued colour make his paintings of quiet interiors, women bathing and family scenes highly intimate portrayals, concealing repressed emotions that account for the 'poetic excess' of his work.
BOUVET, FRANCIS
Bonnard: Complete Graphic Works
[A523] Thames & H hbk **£35.00**
COGNIAT, RAYMOND
Bonnard
[A524] Bonfini hbk **£7.50**
FERMIGIER, ANDRE
Bonnard
Library of Great Painters.
[A525] Thames & H hbk **£25.00**
[A526] Thames & H pbk **£12.95**
MIRBEAU, OCTAVE
Sketches of a Journey   NEW
Previously unpublished drawings accompanied by Mirbeau's imaginative account. 104 black and white line drawings.
[A527] Zwemmer hbk **£19.95**
TERRASSE, ANTOINE
Pierre Bonnard: Illustrator
[A528] Thames & H hbk **£38.00**
TERRASSE, MICHEL
Bonnard at Le Cannet
[A528A] Thames & H hbk **£18.00**

BOSCH, HIERONYMUS (1450 - 1516)
Bosch transformed his environment into grotesque, mythical representations mirroring the medieval world view.
GIBSON, WALTER S.
Bosch
[A529] Thames & H hbk **£10.95**
[A530] Thames & H pbk **£5.95**
LINFERT, CARL
Hieronymus Bosch   NEW
This new paperback edition by the distinguished German art critic provides a masterly account of

Bosch's *oeuvre*. Of the 40 colour illustrations included in this publication, 34 are details which magnify Bosch's richly populated world.
[A531] Thames & H pbk **£12.95**

BOTTICELLI, SANDRO (1444/45 - 1510)
One of the most respected Renaissance painters who formulated an independent style that gracefully combined the linear with the volumetric. Botticelli is best known for the *Birth of Venus* which was commissioned for the Medici villa in 1480.
Quattrocento Neo-Platonism and Medici Humanism in Botticelli's Paintings
[A532] America UP hbk **£20.45**
Sandro Botticelli: Complete Paintings
Classics of World Art
[A533] Penguin pbk **£7.95**

BOUCHER, FRANCOIS (1703 - 1770)
French rococo painter whose delicate style was reproduced to the extreme in the 18th century arts.
BRUNEL, GEORGES
Boucher
A study which includes a biographical account of Boucher setting him in the context of the *ancien régime*.
[A534] Trefoil hbk **£45.00**
[A535] Weidenfeld pbk **£15.00**
LAING, ALASTAIR; MARANDEL, J. PATRICE ET AL
François Boucher 1703 - 1770
Highly illustrated study.
[A536] Abrams hbk **£52.00**

BRANCUSI, CONSTANTIN (1876 - 1957)
Brancusi was interested in primitive sculptural forms and, in addition to his refined abstractions, produced works characterised by the sharply defined planes found in African carvings.
HULTEN, PONTUS; DUMITRESCO, NATALIA & ISTRATI, ALEXANDRE
Brancusi   NEW
Brancusi's innovative and highly original techniques influenced many contemporary sculptors. This much appreciated monograph incorporates 600 illustrations, over 60 in colour, and covers all of his artistic creations including his drawings, paintings and photographs.
[A537] Faber hbk **£60.00**

BRAQUE, GEORGES (1882 - 1963)
The French painter Georges Braque is closely linked with Picasso and his contribution to artistic development is equally impressive, yet for obscure reasons public access to his art is rare. Picasso and Braque together forged the angular style of the cubists and examined the implications of *re-presenting* form from an experiential perspective.
Conversations with, and Thoughts and Quotations by Georges Braque
[A538] Zwemmer hbk **£25.00**
Georges Braque: The Complete Graphics
This volume has been compiled with the aid of the artist's own collection. It includes a number of previously unpublished works and preparatory sketches, drypoints, lithographs and illustrated limited edition books. 138 illustrations, most in colour.
[A539] Alpine Fine Art hbk **£24.95**
COGNIAT, RAYMOND
Braque
Library of Great Painters. Covers Braque's early work in the Fauve manner (1906-7), the beginnings of Cubism (1909) through to his late work of the 1950s. 121 illustrations, 48 colour.
[A540] Thames & H hbk **£25.00**

FAUCHEREAU, SERGE
Georges Braque
[A541] Academy Ed hbk **£9.95**
LEYMARIE, JEAN (ED)
Georges Braque
With contributing essays by Jean Leymarie, Braque's close friend, this monograph presents the personal history of a critically important 20th century painter. Published to accompany the 1988 retrospective at the Guggenheim (New York), the book is the first to view the whole of Braque's *oeuvre* and to bring to the fore his innovative technical developments. The art of collage, incorrectly associated with Picasso, was introduced by Braque along with adding sand to oil paint in order to produce highly textured areas. 123 colour illustrations, 35 black and white.
[A542] Prestel hbk **£26.00**

BRUEGEL, PIETER (c.1525 - 1569)
Rejecting the dominant style of his time, Bruegel drew on the work of the primitives for inspiration. 'With his special ability to give pictorial shape to the flesh and blood, foibles and strengths of human existence, Bruegel remains an example of what art can be.' (*NY Times*).
The Age of Bruegel: Netherlandish Drawings in the 16th Century
In addition to more than 350 reproductions, this volume contains three in-depth essays which discuss from varying viewpoints the art of the period.
[A543] Cambridge hbk **£44.00**
GIBSON, WALTER S.
Bruegel
[A544] Thames & H hbk **£10.95**
[A545] Thames & H pbk **£4.95**
MARTIN, GREGORY
Bruegel
A concise summary of Bruegel's professional life. Detailed commentaries accompany the 40 colour illustrations.
[A546] Park South Books hbk **£6.95**
ROBERTS, KEITH & BROWN, CHRISTOPHER
Bruegel
[A547] Phaidon pbk **£7.50**
STECHOW, WOLFGANG
Bruegel
Library of Great Painters. The author brings to his subject an in-depth understanding of both the formal and iconographic elements in Bruegel's paintings. Literary works of the period are examined as source material. 144 illustrations, 48 colour.
[A548] Thames & H hbk **£25.00**

BULATOV, ERIC (1933 -)
Russian painter. *"The world around us is too active, too unstable for us to maintain any true belief in it; everything is in a state of flux, everything is changing. Only the picture is immutable."* (Bulatov).
Eric Bulatov: Paintings 1971 - 1988
Includes reproductions of the paintings, writings by Bulatov and a conversation with Ilya Kabakov.
[A549] ICA/Parkett pbk **£12.50**

CARAVAGGIO, MICHELANGELO MERISI DA (1571 - 1610)
A Milanese painter whose revolutionary use of light and shadow, termed *chiaroscuro*, was employed to great dramatic effect. His behaviour, no less theatrical than his art, led Caravaggio to murder in 1606.
Caravaggio: Complete Paintings
Classics of World Art.
[A551] Penguin pbk **£7.95**
HIBBARD, HOWARD
Caravaggio
[A552] Thames & H pbk **£18.95**

JARMAN, DEREK
Caravaggio
The text/image narrative recreates Jarman's film.
[A553] Thames & H hbk **£10.00**
MOIR, ALFRED
Caravaggio
Library of Great Painters.
[A554] Thames & H hbk **£25.00**

CARO, ANTHONY (1924 -)
Caro trained under Henry Moore but abandoned the *lump modeller* approach to sculpting forms and began experimenting in steel, forcing his practice and the English sculptural tradition to a new and exhilarating edge.
Anthony Caro: Table Sculptures
Includes an essay by Michael Fried, biographical summary and bibliography. 16 black and white illustrations, 4 colour.
[A555] British Council pbk **£3.50**
FENTON, TERRY
Anthony Caro
[A556] Thames & H hbk **£14.95**
RUBIN, WILLIAM
Anthony Caro
[A557] Thames & H hbk **£10.95**
[A558] MOMA hbk **£5.50**
WALDMAN, DIANE
Anthony Caro
Discusses both the artist's development and the relation of his work to that of his contemporaries. 340 illustrations, 90 colour.
[A559] Phaidon hbk **£50.00**

CASSATT, MARY (1845 - 1926)
An American impressionist and friend of Degas, Cassatt's portraits move away from the subject matter of her contemporaries and focus on representations of mothers with children.
BREESKIN (ED)
A Catalogue Raisonné of the Graphic Work
[A561] Smithsonian Inst hbk **£32.85**
BULLARD, JOHN E.
Mary Cassatt: Oils and Pastels
'Chronology of this wonderful Pennsylvania woman who was ahead of her time. Beautiful colour'. (*Art Bulletin*) 32 colour illustrations.
[A562] Phaidon hbk **£9.95**
MATHEWS, NANCY MOWLL
Cassatt and Her Circle
This selection of 208 letters - most published here for the first time - provides insight into the life of Cassatt and her contemporaries. Complementing the text are more than 50 illustrations of the work and her group of friends.
[A563] Abbeville pbk **£12.95**

'Entrance-No Entrance' from *Eric Bulatov: Paintings 1971 - 1988* (ICA/Parkett pbk £12.50)

CEZANNE, PAUL (1839 - 1906)
Cézanne prepared the way for all modern movements; he laid the groundwork for Cubism and was the first to present painting as autonomous, dependent on no other art or literary form.
Cézanne and the End of Impressionism
[A564] Chicago UP hbk **£23.95**
[A565] Chicago UP pbk **£15.25**
Cézanne: Complete Paintings
[A566] Penguin pbk **£8.99**
Cézanne: Drawings and Watercolours
[A567] Crown Pub hbk **£15.95**
Cézanne: The Early Years 1859 - 1872 `NEW`
Prepared by the Royal Academy to accompany an exhibition in 1988, this catalogue is an excellent source book and complements *The Late Work* published by MOMA. It includes essays by five leading historians on 'Literature, Music and Cézanne's Early Subjects', 'Parisian Writers and the Early Work of Cézanne' and 'Notes on Cézanne's Early Figure Scenes'. Beautiful colour reproductions depict many lesser known portraits of Cézanne's intimates.
[A568] Royal Academy pbk **£11.95**
Cézanne: Watercolours
[A569] Abrams hbk **£44.00**
Paul Cézanne: The Basel Sketchbook
[A570] Thames & H hbk **£25.00**
REWALD, JOHN
Cézanne and America: Dealers, Collectors, Artists and Critics `NEW`
The internationally recognised scholar describes how Cezanne became established in America between 1981 and 1921 and how some of the world's largest collections of his works were formed in the United States. 193 illustrations, 16 colour.
[A572] Thames & H hbk **£38.00**
Cézanne: A Biography
A highly enjoyable book for all levels of interest, not least because of its excellent plates.
[A573] Thames & H hbk **£40.00**
RILKE, RAINER MARIA
Letters on Cézanne `NEW`
The letters have been arranged to form a unique commentary on painting. 'It says more about art than any other book I know.' (*New Yorker*).
[A574] Cape hbk **£9.95**
RUBIN, WILLIAM
Cézanne: The Late Work `NEW`
The essays by nine prominent scholars focus with particular detail on the last 10 years of Cézanne's life. His image is re-assessed and popular myths which brand Cézanne a 'hermit' and 'non-intellectual' are deconstructed. Although issued by MOMA, the text is lengthy and the volume is less a picture book than a serious account of Cézanne's life. 427 illustrations, 50 colour.
[A575] Thames & H hbk **£33.00**
SCHAPIRO, DAVID
Cézanne
Library of Great Painters.
[A576] Thames & H hbk **£25.00**

CHADWICK, HELEN
The work of British artist Helen Chadwick has been widely exhibited, in venues which include the Tate Gallery, the Institute of Contemporary Art, the Hayward Gallery and the Victoria and Albert Museum. In 1987 she was shortlisted for the Turner Prize.
WARNER, MARINA
Enfleshings `NEW`
Covering Chadwick's many installation-based works, this book concentrates on the artist's use of the self as subject. Chadwick employs innovative techniques including photocopied images of her own body, slide

projections and computer generated imagery in an attempt to define her cultural core. 72 colour illustrations.
[A577] Secker hbk **£25.00**
[A578] Secker pbk **£15.00**

CHAGALL, MARC (1887 - 1985)
A French painter of Russian Jewish origin, he created narrative sequences of intense colour and pure vision. His *oeuvre* includes stained glass windows, tapestries, the new ceiling of the Paris Opera (1964) and murals for the facade of the Metropolitan Opera in New York (1966).
Marc Chagall: Arabian Nights
The volume, subtitled 'Four Tales From 1001 Arabain Nights', illustrates Chagall's fantastically beautiful lithographs inspired by Sheherazade's tales. The magical prints are published together with the tales Chagall chose to illuminate and the translation he himself used.
[A579] Prestel hbk **£51.00**
My Life
[A580] P Owen hbk **£13.95**
[A581] Oxford pbk **£5.95**
COMPTON, SUSAN
Chagall
Excellent catalogue of an exhibition.
[A582] Weidenfeld pbk **£10.95**
HAFTMANN, WERNER
Chagall
The author, formerly the Director of the Nationalgalerie Berlin, presents a thorough study of Chagall's art, complemented by personal insights into his life and art production. 140 illustrations, 49 colour.
[A583] Thames & H hbk **£25.00**
Marc Chagall: Gouaches, Drawings, Watercolours
[A584] Abrams hbk **£34.00**
KEMMENSKY, ALEKSANDR
Chagall: The Russian Years   **NEW**
Comprehensive assessment of the artist's *oeuvre* including translations of the articles written by Chagall at the time of the Russian Revolution and extracts from the interview the artist gave the author in Moscow in 1973. 403 illustrations, 192 colour.
[A585] Thames & H hbk **£60.00**

Self-portrait by Marc Chagall from *My Life* (Peter Owen hbk £13.95, Oxford pbk £5.95)

MAKARIUS, MICHEL
Chagall
This volume concentrates on Chagall's most influential canvases, executed between 1909 and 1980. Short explanatory texts accompany each illustration and an introduction provides notes of biographical interest.
[A586] Bracken Books hbk **£12.50**
WERNER, ALFRED
Chagall
Excellent quality colour (32 plates).
[A587] Phaidon pbk **£9.95**
Marc Chagall: Watercolours and Gouaches
[A588] Watson-Gupthill NY pbk **£10.50**

CHAMBERLAIN, JOHN (1927 -)
American abstract expressionist. Chamberlain emerged as a sculptor of immense importance in the early 1960s with assemblages constructed from crushed car bodywork. The more recent scuptures, relying on the same source material, are still regarded as influential.
John Chamberlain: A Catalogue Raisonné of the Sculpture 1954 - 1985
Exhaustively documented volume on all Chamberlain's work to date. 313 colour illustrations, 371 black and white.
[A589] Hudson Hills P hbk **£37.50**

CHARDIN, JEAN BAPTISTE SIMEON (1669 - 1779)
A French master of still-life painting, his domestic scenes of great intimacy pleased philistines and art lovers alike.
CONISBEE, PHILIP
Chardin
[A590] Phaidon hbk **£37.50**

CHRISTO (CHRISTO JARACHEFF) (1935 -)
Bulgarian-American artist. Christo's pivotal works involve wrapping objects, initially small in scale but gradually increasing in size to cars, momuments, buildings and natural forms: *"the packaging calls attention to the underlying form and thus is a temporary transformative act."*
Prints and Objects, Munich 1988
[A591] Schellman pbk **£19.95**

CLEMENTE, FRANCESCO
Contemporary Italian artist. Clemente's paintings are classified as *Neo-Expressionism* but his playful meandering through subjects, formats, mediums and sizes defies categorization. Generally favouring a palette reminiscent of early fresco painting, Clemente creates canvases diagrammatic in nature, incorporating symbolic and representational elements.
Francesco Clemente: India
[A592] Twin Palms US hbk **£30.00**
AUPING, MICHAEL
Francesco Clemente
Two lengthy essays: *Fragments* by Auping and *Through India to America* by Francesco Pollizzi. 71 colour illustrations.
[A593] Abrams hbk **£30.00**

COLLINS, HANNAH
Collins' largescale photographs are of intense poetic beauty, evoking a haunting sense of absence. One of Britian's representatives in the 1988 Venice Biennale.
Hannah Collins: Legends 1988 - 1989
[A594] ICA pbk **£10.95**

CONSTABLE, JOHN (1776 - 1837)
British landscape artist of remarkable talent whose depictions of the English countryside are to many matched only by Turner's, although there is a clear difference of style between them.

Constable Collection
[A595] V & A hbk **£12.00**
Landscape Watercolours and Drawings
[A596] Tate Gall hbk **£12.00**
Landscapes in Miniature
[A597] Lutt P hbk **£9.95**
CORMACK, MALCOLM
Constable
[A598] Phaidon hbk **£35.00**
FLEMING-WILLIAMS, IAN
Constable: Landscape Watercolours and Drawings
[A599] Tate Gall hbk **£12.00**
FLEMING-WILLIAMS, IAN & PARRIS, LESLIE
The Discovery of Constable
[A600] Hudson Hills P hbk **£25.00**
HILL, DAVID
Constable's English Landscape Scenery
[A601] J Murray hbk **£15.95**
REYNOLDS, GRAHAM
Constable's England
[A602] Weidenfeld hbk **£15.95**
ROSENTHAL, MICHAEL
Constable: The Painter and His Landscape
[A603] Yale UP hbk **£27.50**
[A604] Yale UP pbk **£10.95**
SUNDERLAND, JOHN
Constable
Colour Library.
[A605] Phaidon hbk **£12.50**
[A606] Phaidon pbk **£9.50**

CONSTRUCTIVISM
The Constructivist Manifesto was published in Moscow in 1920 by the brothers Naum Gabo and Antoine Pevsner. The term identifies the artists' desire to *construct* in art and, at its most extreme, describes a purely functional aesthetic, forefronting a refined geometry based exclusively on the relations of plane and mass, space and volume. See *Naum Gabo, Kasimir Malevich, Piet Mondrian,* and *Vladimir Tatlin.*
Malevich   **NEW**
Catalogue documenting the major retrospective, including paintings from Russian collections, theatre designs, architectural plans, and writings. All aspects of his life and art production are examined in detailed essasys.
[A607] Artdata hbk **£22.95**
LODDER, CHRISTINA
Russian Constructivism
The first detailed study of the movement in English, based on Soviet archives.
[A608] Yale UP hbk **£45.00**
[A609] Yale UP pbk **£14.95**
RUDENSTINE, ANGELICA ZANDER (ED)
Russian Avant-Garde Art
The George Costakis Collection
[A610] Thames & H hbk **£60.00**

COROT, JEAN BAPTISTE CAMILLE (1796 - 1875)
The French painter Corot foreshadowed the impressionists in favouring outdoor rather than indoor scenes and in his use of colour and light.
HOURS, MADELEINE
Corot
This volume presents Corot's lithographs and etchings and discusses his experiments with light in the oil paintings. 122 illustrations, 48 colour.
[A611] Thames & H hbk **£25.00**
LEYMARIE, JEAN
Corot
[A612] Rizzoli hbk **£26.00**
TAILLANDIER, YVON
Corot
A good general introduction. Reproduces oils, drawings, lithographs and woodcuts. 75 illustrations.
[A613] Bonfini hbk **£7.50**

COURBET, GUSTAVE (1819 - 1877)

Courbet rejected classicism, romanticism and all idealization in art, proclaiming that the only subject for the artist was the worker and the peasant.

Gustave Courbet

This catalogue documents a critical exhibition first held in the Grand Palais, Paris in 1977 and shown in London at the Royal Academy of Arts in 1978. The text is by Alan Bowness and includes a biography compiled by Marie-Therese de Forges.

[A614] South Bank Centre hbk **£8.00**

CLARK, TIMOTHY JAMES

Image of the People: Gustave Courbet and the 1848 Revolution

[A615] Thames & H hbk **£14.50**

[A616] Thames & H pbk **£7.95**

FAUNCE, SARAH & NOCHLIN, LINDA

Courbet Reconsidered **NEW**

The authors analyses the origins of Courbet's realism; illustrated with 70 black and white pictures, 112 colour.

[A617] Yale UP hbk **£29.95**

FOUCART, BRUNO

Courbet

[A618] Bonfini hbk **£7.50**

CRAGG, TONY (1949 -)

Cragg has worked from the start with found objects, developing a vocabulary of immense variety. His material sources are so diverse that it is difficult to link Cragg with a characteristic style, however he is perhaps most commonly associated with the 'mural series' begun in 1978, in which he re-created politically provocative sequences out of bits of brightly coloured plastic debris arranged in a mosaic-like style.

Tony Cragg: 1987

This publication serves as a good introduction to this important British sculptor. It includes an interview with Tony Cragg and an essay by Lynne Cooke, a list of exhibited works and chronology. 33 illustrations, 29 in colour.

[A619] South Bank Centre hbk **£12.00**

Tony Cragg: La Biennale di Venezia XLIII

Features include the 15 pieces which were exhibited at the Biennale, an illlustrated history of Cragg's sculpture from 1969 to 1987 and two critical essays. 73 illustrations.

[A620] Brit Council pbk **£8.60**

MORRIS, FRANCES

Tony Cragg

Tony Cragg won the 1988 Turner Prize for his singular contribution to British Art. This book documents the exhibition held to commemorate this impressive achievement. Beautifully designed, it contains 21 illustrations and excerpts from the artist's writings. The sculptures included in the exhibition represent a wide range of the materials employed by Cragg: found objects, industrial waste, cast bronze, plaster and stone.

[A621] Tate Gall hbk **£7.50**

CUBISM

Cubism marked a shift away from the purely surface concerns of Impressionism. Cézanne is historically acknowledged as the visionary who began to structure a new language based on a more metaphysical approach to describing landscapes and objects. Picasso and Braque furthered Cézanne's explorations, resulting in a style identified by fragmented objects displayed simultaneously from all angles, depicting the essence, rather than the surface, of our physical world. See *Georges Braque*, *Paul Cézanne*, *Ferdinand Léger*, and *Pablo Picasso*.

COOPER, DOUGLAS & TINTEROW, GARY

Essential Cubism 1907 - 20: Braque, Picasso and their Friends

[A622] Tate Gall hbk **£14.00**

FRY, ROGER

Cubism

[A623] Thames & H pbk **£5.95**

GOLDING, JOHN

Cubism: A History and an Analysis 1907 - 1914

The standard work on the subject now in its 3rd edition.

[A627] Faber pbk **£14.95**

GREEN, CHRISTOPHER

Cubism and Its Enemies **NEW**

Subtitled 'Modern Movements and Reaction in French Art 1916-1928', this volume examines the debates that revolved around Cubism. Winner of the 20th Century Mitchell Prize for an outstanding contribution to the history of art. 278 black and white illustrations, 28 colour.

[A624] Yale UP hbk **£24.95**

KOSINSKI, DOROTHY

Douglas Cooper and the Masters of Cubism

Published for the exhibition held at the Tate in 1988, this book gives an account of Cooper's collection of drawings, prints, gouaches and papier colles by the major exponents of the movement - Picasso, Braque, Léger and Gris. Cooper was not only a collector but also a scholar; his friendships with the artists lead to a unique understanding of their works. 101 illustrations, 35 colour.

[A625] Tate Gall pbk **£14.95**

RUBIN, WILLIAM

Picasso and Braque: Pioneering Cubism **NEW**

More than 500 illustrations provide a pictorial history of the movement and of the working relationship between two of the major proponents.

[A626] Thames & H hbk **£40.00**

DALI, SALVADOR (1904 - 1987)

Spanish surrealist. Through meticulous detail and photorealistic effects, Dali's paintings create a hallucinatory sense.

Hidden Faces

In rich visual language Dali describes the lives and loves of a group of aristocratic characters who symbolize the decadent Europe of the 1930s.

[A628] P Owen pbk **£7.95**

Salvador Dali's Muse: 'Wicked Lady'

[A629] Hutchinson hbk **£16.95**

Salvador Dali: Secret Life

[A630] Vision P hbk **£34.95**

The Dali Scandal: An Investigation

[A631] Gollancz hbk **£12.95**

ADES, DAWN

Dali

[A632] Thames & H hbk **£10.95**

[A633] Thames & H pbk **£5.95**

DE LA SERNA, RAMON G.

Dali

This was conceived as a tribute to the artist.

[A634] Macdonald hbk **£25.00**

DESCHARNES, ROBERT

Dali

Library of Great Painters.

[A635] Thames & H hbk **£25.00**

[A636] Thames & H pbk **£12.95**

LAINO, IGNACIO GOMEZ DE

Dali

[A637] Academy Eds pbk **£9.95**

SECREST, MERYLE

Salvador Dali: The Surrealist Jester

[A638] Weidenfeld hbk **£14.95**

DAUMIER, HONORE (1808 - 1879)

French caricaturist and political satirist.

120 Great Lithographs

[A639] Dover pbk **£5.90**

Drawings

[A640] Zwemmer pbk **£3.95**

DAVID, JACQUES LOUIS (1748 - 1825)

French neo-classical painter who became dictator of the arts during the Revolution and was imprisoned after the fall of Robspierre. After his release, he met Napoleon who used him as a propogandist, resulting in the execution of his well-known paintings: *Napolean Crossing the Alps* and the huge *Coronation*.

BROOKNER, ANITA

Jacques-Louis David

A classic work on David which places him in the context of French history painting as a whole. By the Booker Prize-winning novelist who is also a respected art historian.

[A641] Chatto hbk **£25.00**

[A642] Chatto pbk **£12.95**

NANTEUIL, ROBERT

David

Library of Great Painters.

[A643] Thames & H hbk **£25.00**

DE STIJL

A Dutch magazine, *De Stijl's* editorial panel was committed to promoting Neo-Plasticism and, more particularly, the art of Piet Mondrian. The theories represented by the publication took on its name and had a marked influence on the Bauhaus movement.

BLOTKAMP, CAREL, ESSER, HANS, ET AL

De Stijl: The Formative Years

Augmented by over 260 illustrations, this book exposes the relatively unexplored differences between the artists who founded the movement.

[A644] MIT Press hbk **£42.75**

FRIEDMAN, MILDRED (ED)

De Stijl: Visions of Utopia

Informative introduction to the artists and the social, philosophical and political forces that influenced them.

[A645] Phaidon pbk **£15.95**

JAFFE, H.L.C.

De Stijl 1917 - 1931

A history of the movement which describes the roles played by the key proponents.

[A646] Harvard UP pbk **£13.25**

TROY, NANCY J.

The De Stijl Environment

Nancy Troy offers a critical examination of a most significant 20th century movement and one that is currently arousing renewed interest.

[A647] MIT Press hbk **£17.50**

Tony Cragg, 'The Artist with Pebbles, 1988' (Photo: The Sunday Times)

DEGAS, EDGAR (1834 - 1917)

This French impressionist chose contemporary society, primarily dancers, working women and models in the act of dressing or bathing, as his principal subject matter. Instead of dissolving his forms in light, Degas accentuated them, often using the dramatic effects of artificial illumination rather than the natural light so favoured by his fellow Impressionists.

Degas: The Institute of Chicago

Issued as a catalogue for the 1984 exhibition at the Chicago Institute, this volume examines the Institute's major collection. The commentary is extensive, offering a thorough overview of the many narrative themes running through Degas' work. 90 illustrations.
[A648] Abrams hbk **£13.50**
ADHEMAR, JEAN & CACHIN, FRANCOISE

Degas: The Complete Etchings, Lithographs and Monotypes

Foreword by John Rewald.
[A649] Thames & H hbk **£28.00**
ADRIANI, R.

Degas: Pastels, Oil Sketches, Drawings

The best-presented book on Degas.
[A650] Thames & H hbk **£35.00**
BOGGS, JEAN SUTHERLAND ET AL

Degas `NEW`

This volume includes reproductions of paintings, pastels, drawings, monotypes, prints, photographs and sculpture from every period of this artist's prolific career. The essays are written by a distinguished group of critics and historians based on current research. 728 illustrations, 281 colour.
[A651] Abrams pbk **£35.00**
GORDON, ROBERT & FORGE, ANDREW

Degas

324 reproductions of Degas' paintings, pastels, drawings, monotypes and sculptures are arranged by theme, demonstrating Degas' great technical facility. The text is generously supported by excerpts from periodicals, letters and diaries of the period. This extensive monograph is classified as the most complete portrait of Degas.
[A652] Thames & H hbk **£40.00**
KENDALL, RICHARD (ED)

Degas by Himself: Drawings, Prints, Paintings and Writings

This monograph is introduced by the editor and then relies on Degas' texts to illustrate the different periods in his life: 'The Apprentice Years 1850-1870', 'The Impressionist Era 1870-1885', 'Late Maturity 1886-1912'. Over 250 colour illustrations.
[A653] Macdonald Orbis hbk **£35.00**
LIPTON, EUNICE

Looking into Degas: Uneasy Images of Women and Modern Life `NEW`

The author claims that for the 19th century audience, Degas' paintings and drawings exposed issues of class, sex and work. Lipton's sensitive reading and appreciation of Degas' oeuvre enrich our understanding of the artist and of his time.
[A654] California UP pbk **£14.95**
PICKVANCE & PECIRKA (ED)

Edgar Degas: Drawings

[A655] Hamlyn hbk **£12.95**
PICKVANCE, RONALD

Degas Drawings

Good reproductions.
[A656] Hamlyn hbk **£12.95**
REED, SUE WELSH & SHAPIRO, BARBARA STERN

Degas as Printmaker

[A657] Tiptree hbk **£40.00**
RICH, CATTON

Degas

[A658] Thames & H hbk **£12.95**
[A659] Thames & H hbk **£25.00**

ROUART

Edgar Degas: In Search of His Technique

[A660] Rizzoli pbk **£14.95**
TERRASSE, ANTOINE

Degas

[A661] Cassell pbk **£10.95**
THOMSON, RICHARD

Degas: The Nudes

This is the first full-scale study of the recurring theme of the nude in Degas' work. The author draws from recent art historical writings to re-contextualize Degas' artistic output. 226 illustrations, 50 in colour.
[A662] Thames & H hbk **£28.00**

The Private Degas

[A663] Herbert P hbk **£12.95**
WERNER, ALFRED

Degas Pastels

Excellent value for the 32 colour plates.
[A664] Phaidon pbk **£10.95**

DELACROIX, EUGENE (1798 - 1863)

Major painter of the Romantic movement.
"Continual caution in showing only what is shown in nature will always make the painter colder than the nature which he thinks he is imitating."
(Delacroix, 1853).
JOHNSON, LEE

The Paintings of Eugene Delacroix: The Public Decorations and Their Sketches

[A665] Clarendon P hbk **£90.00**

DINE, JIM (1935 -)

American pop artist. Dine is best known for his traditonal prints and graphic works, but in the the late 1960s and 1970s, he pioneered *process* or *performance art*, often collaborating with other prominent artists such as Claes Oldenburg.
GLENN (ED)

Jim Dine: Drawings

[A666] Abrams hbk **£55.00**
SHAPIRO, DAVID

Jim Dine

[A667] Abrams hbk **£45.00**

DONATELLO (1385 - 1466)

Not only classified as one of the greatest humanist sculptors of the Renaissance before Michelangelo, Donatello was also the most influential individual artist of the 15th century.
BENNETT, BONNIE A. & WILKINS, DAVID G.

Donatello

[A669] Phaidon hbk **£35.00**
GREENHALGH, M.

Donatello and His Sources

[A670] Duckworth hbk **£35.00**

DORE, GUSTAVE (1832 - 1883)

A most prolific French engraver who produced illustrations for books by Rabelais, Balzac and Dante, amongst others.

Dante's Divine Comedy

[A671] Dover hbk **£5.05**

Illustrations for Don Quixote

[A672] Dover hbk **£5.90**

The Doré Bible Illustrations

[A673] Dover hbk **£8.50**

The Rime of the Ancient Mariner

[A674] Dover pbk **£7.60**
DORE, GUSTAVE & JERROLD

London: A Pilgrimage

[A675] Dover pbk **£7.95**

DUCCIO DI BUONINSEGNA (c.1255 - 1315)

Sienese painter of the Early Renaissance who introduced a new humanism into painting.
WHITE, JOHN

Duccio

[A676] Thames & H hbk **£20.00**

DUCHAMP, MARCEL (1887 - 1968)

Now considered to be one of the most influential 20th century artists, Duchamp was instrumental in establishing the foundations for the conceptualist philosophy. A movement which has been incorporated into many current art forms, Conceptualism forefronts an intellectual rather than an emotional approach to art production.
ADCOCK

Marcel Duchamp's Notes from the Large Glass: An N-Dimensional Analysis

[A677] UMI Research Press hbk **£56.75**
ALEXANDRIAN, S.

Duchamp

The author, an authority on Surrealism, offers an accessible introduction to this complex artist. 42 colour illustrations, 29 black and white.
[A678] Clematis hbk **£7.50**
BAILLY

Marcel Duchamp

[A679] Art Data pbk **£6.95**
BONK, ECKE

Marcel Duchamp: Boite-en-Valise: An Inventory

Duchamp reproduced all of his artworks in miniature and designed a case to hold the collection, which he referred to as a 'portable museum'. The work is of inestimable importance; this publication presents each item individually with explanatory notes. 200 illustrations, 100 in colour.
[A680] Thames & H hbk **£55.00**
CABANE, PIERRE

Dialogues with Marcel Duchamp

With an appreciation by Jasper Johns.
[A681] Da Capo pbk **£9.95**
KUENZLI, RUDOLF E. & NAUMANN, FRANCIS M. (EDS)

Marcel Duchamp: Artist of the Century `NEW`

Although Marcel Duchamp was not a prolific artist, the meanings inherent in his work are dense and multi-layered. The 11 essays included in this edition investigate the complex structure of Duchamp's vitally important *oeuvre*.
[A682] MIT Press hbk **£22.50**
MOURE, GLORIA

Marcel Duchamp

This survey places Duchamp's works in the context of the artist's reaction to France and to America. 144 illustrations, 94 colour.
[A683] Thames & H pbk **£10.95**

DUFY, RAOUL (1877 - 1953)

Influenced by the fauvists, Dufy adopted a bold palette and a decorative style, well-suited to textile design and ceramics.
COGNIAT, RAYMOND

Dufy

[A684] Bonfini hbk **£7.50**
WERNER, ALFRED

Dufy

Library of Great Painters.
[A685] Thames & H hbk **£25.00**
[A686] Thames & H hbk **£12.95**

DURER, ALBRECHT (1471 - 1528)

Durer's enormous *oeuvre* consists of engravings, woodcuts, drawings, paintings and detailed essays on artistic theories and techniques. A highly skilled draughtsman, his style has become synonomous with German Realism.

Albrecht Dürer: Engravings and Etchings

[A687] Da Capo hbk **£27.50**

Complete Engravings

[A688] Dover pbk **£6.70**

Complete Woodcuts

[A689] Dover pbk **£7.45**

Dürer: Complete Paintings
[A690] Penguin pbk £7.95
Human Figure: A Dresden Sketchbook
[A691] Dover pbk £7.45
ANZELEWSKY
Durer: His Art and His Life
[A692] Gordon Fraser hbk £50.00

ENSOR, JAMES (1860 - 1949)
A Belgian expressionist painter and printmaker who had a particularly macabre outlook, frequently incorporating death masks and skeletons into his work.
The Prints of James Ensor
Reprint Geneva & Brussels 1952.
[A693] Da Capo hbk £27.50
JANSSENS, J.
James Ensor
[A694] Bonfini hbk £7.50

ERNST, MAX (1891 - 1976)
A founder of the Dadaist movement who moved on to embrace Surrealism becoming one of the school's leading artists.
Semaine de Dante: A Surrealist Novel in Collage
[A695] Dover pbk £5.95
RAINWATER, ROBERT ET AL (ED)
Max Ernst: Beyond Surrealism
[A696] Oxford hbk £35.00
[A697] Oxford pbk £13.50
SPIES, WERNER
Max Ernst: Frottages
[A698] Thames & H pbk £12.95
Max Ernst: Loplop
The Artist's Other Self.
[A699] Thames & H hbk £28.00

ESCHER, M.C. (1898 - 1971)
Dutch graphic artist whose use of overall patterns and spacial constructions involve sophisticated mathematical concepts. His work has sparked interest in the academic world and an exhibition of prints was held at the International Mathematical Congress, Amsterdam, in 1964.
Escher on Escher: Exploring the Infinite NEW
Through a variety of texts including the complete series of lectures he was scheduled to deliver in the States but cancelled due to illness, and excerpts from letters and magazine articles, this book exposes how Escher perceived his relationship to his art. A most illuminating source, complete with 120 illustrations, 30 in full colour.
[A700] Abrams pbk £12.25
ERNST
Magic Mirror of M.C. Escher
[A701] Tarquin Pubs pbk £6.50
LOCHER, J.L. & G.W. ET AL
The World of M.C. Escher
Includes four essays analysing Escher's work from the perspectives of both art and science. 300 illustrations, 8 in colour.
[A702] Abrams hbk £25.00
Twenty-Nine Prints of M.C. Escher
[A703] Abrams pbk £11.50

EXPRESSIONISM
As a movement, Expressionism is difficult to situate historically: its influence is still evident in contemporary art practice. The impetus to use art as an expressive rather than representational medium, grew out of dissatisfaction with the naturalism implicit in Impressionism. Thus the movement incorporates many diverse artists including *Van Gogh*, *Munch*, *Beckmann*, *Nolde* and *Kokoschka*, amongst others. Abstract Expressionism flourished after World War II, a 'movement' so flexible as to include all abstract art that is not pure geometric abstraction (*de*

Kooning, *Pollock*, *Rothko* and *Motherwell*). New Figurative Painting which emerged in the 1970s, most notably in Europe, demonstrates the lasting influence of Expressionism (see *Kiefer*, *Baselitz* and *Fischl*).
A New Spirit in Painting
Documents the major exhibition held at the Royal Academy, London in 1981. The work included covers every facet of current Expressionism. Ferdinand Leger, Francis Bacon, Anslem Kiefer and Andy Warhol are amongst the artists represented.
[A704] Weidenfeld hbk £17.95
German Expressionist Prints and Drawings Volume 1 NEW
The Robert Gore Rifkind Centre for German Expressionist Studies houses the world's most comprehensive collection of German expressionist prints, drawings, books and periodicals. This two-volume publication makes available for the first time the centre's magnificent holdings.
[A705] Prestel hbk £28.50
Volume 1 and II NEW
The second volume is available only in a set case with volume I.
[A706] Prestel hbk £95.00
BARRON, STEPHANIE
German Expressionism 1915 - 1925: The Second Generation NEW
The six essays in this book chart the development of expressionist art in Germany from the grouping together of artists with common political concerns, through the spread from the cities to the international market, and the end of the movement in the late 1920s. 516 illustrations, 89 colour.
[A707] Prestel hbk £28.50
BEHR, SHULAMITH
Women Expressionists
[A708] Phaidon pbk £11.95
DONALD & GORDON (ED)
Expressionism: Art and Idea
Art and Idea defines the spirit of Expressionism, covering its initial conception in 1905 through to its revival in the art of the 1970s. The list of artists represented is a comprehensive one and the inclusion of contemporary figures helps clarify the link between the original movement and the recent school of painting. Major artists covered include Kirchner, Kokoschka, Nolde, Schiele, Pollock and Kiefer.
[A709] Yale UP hbk £27.50

A drawing by Lucian Freud from *Lucian Freud: Works on Paper* by Nicholas Penny & R.F. Johnson (Thames & Hudson hbk £24.00, pbk £12.95)

DUBE, W.D.
Expressionists
[A710] Thames & H pbk £5.95
WHITFORD, FRANK
Expressionist Portraits
[A711] Thames & H hbk £20.00
ZWIETE, ARMIN (ED)
The Blue Rider in the Lenbachhaus, Munich NEW
'Der Blaue Reiter' was founded in Munich in 1911. Headed by Wassily Kandinsky and Franz Marc, they organized a seminal exhibition and published an almanac. The group also included such major contemporary 20th century figures as Klee, August Macke and Gabriele Munter, making an important contribution to the development of German Expressionism. 121 colour illustrations.
[A712] Prestel hbk £31.50

FISCHL, ERIC (1948 -)
The American artist Eric Fischl is one of the major painters of the new generation of figurative artists to emerge in the 1980s and has been described by critic Peter Schjeldahl as 'a national classic as special as Winslow Homer, Edward Hopper, Walt Whitman and Mark Twain'.
Eric Fischl
David Whitney, guest curator of Fischl's 1986 Whitney Museum Retrospective, offers extensive insight into the artist's life and paintings, in a text both illuminating and entertaining. Over 100 illustrations in colour.
[A713] Stewart & Tabori, US hbk £40.00

FLANAGAN, BARRY (1941 -)
The Welsh artist Barry Flanagan's cast bronze series of leaping hares brought him to the attention of the public and the critics alike. Each is perched atop an unexpected object which parodies the gallery pedestal. In 1982, Flanagan was Great Britain's representative at the Venice Biennale.
Barry Flanagan: A Visual Invitation, Sculpture 1967 - 1987
The 55 works reproduced in this catalogue represent every phase of Flanagan's career. Includes a full length essay by Lewis Biggs. 71 black and white illustrations, 7 colour.
[A714] British Council pbk £10.00
Barry Flanagan: New York 1984
A solid introduction to Flanagan's quirky sculptures.
[A715] Art Data hbk £18.00
Barry Flanagan: Prints 1970 - 1983
[A716] Tate Gall pbk £4.95

FRANKENTHALER, HELEN
American artist. Helen Frankenthaler was instrumental in negotiating a way through Abstract Expressionism to colour field painting.
CARMEAN ., E.A. JUN
Helen Frankenthaler: A Paintings Retrospective NEW
Documents an exhibition of 40 key paintings. Frankenthaler is quoted liberally, reinforcing the lucid overview presented by Carmean. 55 illustrations, 40 in colour.
[A717] Abrams hbk £25.00
ELDERFIELD, JOHN
Frankenthaler
Sadly, the price of this important monograph places this book outside the range of many art lovers. It is the only complete survey of Frankenthaler's career to date. Compiled by the the Director of the Department of Drawings and Curator in the Department of Painting and Sculpture at the MOMA, New York, this thorough analysis chronologically charts Frankenthaler's development and includes more than 400 illustrations with 250 in full colour.
[A718] Abrams hbk £115.00

FREUD, LUCIAN (1922 -)

British contemporary painter of dramatic realism. Freud favours a subdued palette, building up his delicate brushwork to an almost unbearable pitch. Subject matter includes nudes of disturbing eroticism.

GOWING, LAWRENCE

Lucian Freud

Fascinating monograph on this sometimes shocking and always prominent contemporary artist.

[A719] Thames & H hbk **£25.00**
[A720] Thames & H pbk **£14.00**

HUGHES, ROBERT

Lucian Freud Paintings `NEW`

Published to coincide with a major exhibition at the Haywood Gallery in Spring 1988.

[A721] Thames & H hbk **£24.00**
[A722] Thames & H pbk **£14.95**

PENNY, NICHOLAS & JOHNSON, R.F.

Lucian Freud: Works on Paper

All the works included were chosen by the artist.

[A723] Thames & H hbk **£24.00**
[A724] Thames & H pbk **£12.95**

FUTURISM

Although born in Paris, Futurism is the first modern movement to be independent of French influence. Perhaps as a consequence, the manifestos promote a violent sense of movement and an impetus to leap into new technology, brutally shedding the residue of the past. Artists include *Boccioni*, *Carra* and *Balla*.

APPOLLONIO, UMBRO

Futurist Manifestos

[A725] Thames & H hbk **£10.95**

CLOUGH, ROSA

Futurism: The Story of a Modern Art Movement

[A726] Greenwood hbk **£17.50**

TISDALL & BOZZOLLA

Futurism

[A727] Thames & H hbk **£10.95**
[A728] Thames & H pbk **£5.95**

GABO, NAUM (1890 - 1977)

A founding member of the Russian Constructivist movement, Gabo created staggeringly beautiful sculptures based on geometric form. His works speak of a purity and elegance derived from a complete understanding of source materials and linear precision.

Naum Gabo: The Constructive Idea

Introduced by Caroline Collier, this 1987 publication includes reproductions of Gabo's sculptures, drawings, paintings and monoprints, and extracts from statements by Gabo. 51 illustrations, 8 in colour.

[A729] South Bank Centre pbk **£7.95**

Sixty Years of Constructivism

[A730] Tate Gall pbk **£2.95**

FORGE

An Appreciation of Naum Gabo

[A731] Forin P hbk **£35.00**

NASH, STEVEN A. & MERKERT, JORN

Naum Gabo

[A732] Prestel hbk **£31.50**

READ, SIR HERBERT & MARTIN, LESLIE

Naum Gabo

[A733] Zwemmer hbk **£32.00**

GAINSBOROUGH, THOMAS (1727 - 1788)

English landscape and portrait painter. *"These odd scratches and marks which are so observable in Gainsborough's pictures,...this uncouth and shapeless appearance, by a kind of magic, at a certain distance, assumes form and all the parts seem to drop into their proper places."* (Sir Joshua Reynolds, *Discourses*).

HAYES, JOHN (ED)

The Landscape Paintings of Thomas Gainsborough

Critical text and *catalogue raisonné*. Two volumes.

[A734] Sotheby's hbk (slipcase) **£85.00**

Thomas Gainsborough: Catalogue

[A735] Tate Gall hbk **£6.50**
[A736] Tate Gall pbk **£4.50**

GAUGUIN, PAUL (1848 - 1903)

French painter, initially following the impressionist movement, but later abandoning Europe and settling in Tahiti where he turned to the non-naturalistic style of the Primitives.

Noa Noa

Gauguin's Tahiti: The Original Manuscript. This illustrated tale was designed to explain the artist's work to Parisians.

[A737] Phaidon hbk **£14.50**

The Intimate Journals of Paul Gauguin

[A738] Routledge pbk **£7.50**

GAUGUIN, POLA

My Father

[A739] Hacker Fine Art hbk **£31.50**

GOLDWATER, ROBERT

Gauguin

Library of Great Painters.

[A740] Thames & H hbk **£25.00**
[A741] Thames & H pbk **£12.95**

GRAY, CHRISTOPHER

Sculpture and Ceramics of Paul Gauguin

[A742] Hacker Fine Art hbk **£65.00**

HOOG, MICHAEL

Gauguin: Life and Works

[A743] Thames & H hbk **£75.00**

HUYGHE, RENE

Gauguin

[A744] Bonfini hbk **£7.50**

PICHON, YAN LE

Gauguin: Life, Art, Inspiration

Another superb study from Abrams with exceptional colour reproductions.

[A745] Abrams hbk **£35.00**

GIACOMETTI, ALBERTO (1901 - 1966)

Swiss sculptor whose bronze renditions of the human figure are of incomparable beauty. Giacometti elongated the natural form and arrived at a style which synthesizes the delicacy of linear drawing with the pitted and textural surface of ancient artefacts.

FLETCHER, VALERIE J.

Alberto Giacometti: 1901 - 1966 `NEW`

An extended analysis of Giacometti's *oeuvre* covering his early years while working under the influence of Brancusi and his return to more realistic single figures, extremely emaciated in form and moulded directly in plaster of Paris on a wire foundation. With essays by Reinhold Hohl and Dr Silvio Berthould. 40 colour and 75 black and white reproductions.

[A746] Lund Humphries hbk **£29.95**

LEIRIS

Alberto Giacometti: Thoughts and Quotations

[A747] Zwemmer hbk **£25.00**

LORD, JAMES

Giacometti

A biography.

[A748] Faber hbk **£25.00**
[A749] Faber pbk **£6.95**

MATTER, HERBERT & MERCEDES

Giacometti

Giacometti's finest works are reproduced here in a specially commissioned body of photographs taken over several years.

[A750] Thames & H hbk **£37.50**

GILBERT & GEORGE (1942 -) (1943 -)

Gilbert and George met at St Martins School of Art in London, and began the collaborative work for which they are now internationally known. Their art production includes videos, performances and the large scale photographic assemblages. They won the Turner Prize in 1986.

Gilbert and George: The Complete Pictures 1971 - 1985

Large catalogue for the 1985 exhibition.

[A751] Thames & H pbk **£14.95**

The Charcoal on Paper Sculptures 1970 - 1974

Produced by the *Capc Musee d'Art Contemporain de Bordeaux*, this catalogue surveys a lesser known body of work executed by Gilbert & George. With texts in English and French, it draws from the artists' own statements and writings and includes an interview with them from 1986. Over 120 illustrations, most in colour.

[A752] Musee d'Art pbk **£22.50**

The Paintings: 1971

[A753] Fruitmarket Gal pbk **£6.30**

JAHN, WOLF

The Art of Gilbert and George `NEW`

An extremely comprehensive textual and pictorial analysis of the controversial work of Gilbert & George. This monograph includes extensive documentation of their less familiar early experimentations in the fields of photography and performance art. The author looks at their large scale photo-collages in the context of their overall production rather than as an isolated body of work.

[A754] Thames & H hbk **£20.00**

GIOTTO DI BONDONE (1276 - 1337)

Early Renaissance Florentine painter who with Cimabue is historically regarded as the founder of modern painting. He broke away from the stylized forms of Byzantine art and sought to represent his subjects in a naturalistic way. The frescoes at Padua, near Venice, are well preserved and bear witness to Giotto's mastery.

BARACHE, MOSHE

Giotto and the Language of Gesture

[A755] Cambridge hbk **£37.50**

BAXANDALL, MICHAEL

Giotto and the Orators

[A756] Oxford pbk **£10.95**

STUBBLEBINE, J.H.

Giotto: The Arena Chapel Frescoes

[A757] Norton pbk **£8.00**

GOGH, VINCENT VAN (1853 - 1990)

Van Gogh's paintings register an acute sensibility expressed both in the rhythm of the brushwork and in his use of colour. An artist of inestimable influence, his canvases resonate with a poetic insight that is derived from his ability to continually expand his gestural vocabulary and from his understanding of the experiential.

Complete Letters of Van Gogh (3 Vols)

[A758] Thames & H hbk **£70.00**

Letters (Ed. Roskill, Mark)

[A759] Fontana pbk **£3.50**

Seven Sketchbooks of Vincent Van Gogh

The author exposes Van Gogh's working methods. 399 illustrations, 35 in colour.

[A760] Thames & H hbk **£30.00**

Vincent Van Gogh: Studies in the Social Aspects of His Work

[A761] Humanitites P hbk **£15.00**

BERNARD, BRUCE

Vincent by Himself

Combination of pictures and writings by the artist. Over 250 illustrations.

[A762] Macdonald hbk **£35.00**

BUMPUS, JUDITH

Van Gogh's Flowers `NEW`

The text draws heavily from Van Gogh's own writings, revealing the importance of nature in his work. 45 illustrations, 35 full-page colour plates.

[A763] Phaidon hbk **£17.50**

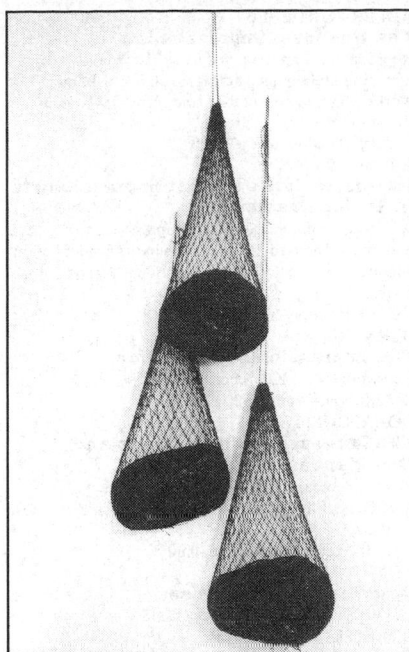

Untitled ('Three Nets') by Eva Hesse from *Eva Hesse: Sculpture* by Bill Barrette (Timken hbk £40.00)

DUNCAN
Sunflowers for Vincent Van Gogh
[A764] Rizzoli hbk **£19.95**
GRAEFE
Vincent Van Gogh: A Biographical Study
[A765] Greenwood P hbk **£24.50**
HAMMACHER, A.M.
Van Gogh: Documentary Biography
[A766] Thames & H hbk **£24.00**
Vincent Van Gogh: Genius and Disaster
[A767] Abrams hbk **£20.00**
LASSAIGNE, JACQUES
Van Gogh
[A768] Cassell pbk **£10.95**
SCHAPIRO, DAVID
Van Gogh
Library of Great Painters.
[A769] Thames & H hbk **£25.00**
UHDE, W.
Van Gogh
Colour Library.
[A770] Phaidon pbk **£9.50**
VAN UITERT, EVERT
Van Gogh Drawings
World of Art.
[A771] Thames & H pbk **£4.95**

GOLUB, LEON (1922 -)
'Golub has created the epic view of the 20th century. The dream of universal power and self-possessed stature, the nightmare of the use of power and the failure to secure well-being are brought together in totemic images of our plight and our hope.' (Barry Schwartz, 1974).
Leon Golub: Existential/Activist Painter
[A772] Rutgers UP hbk **£32.50**
[A773] Rutgers UP pbk **£7.95**
Leon Golub: Mercenaries and Interrogations 1982
[A774] ICA pbk **£3.95**

GOYA, FRANCISCO DE G.Y. LUCIENTES (1746 - 1828)
A Spanish Court painter by definition, Goya utilized his art to express his own political and psychological perspectives. His most widely known body of work is a series of etchings entitled *The Disasters of War*, which document the 1808 Spanish insurrection against the French.
Caprichos
[A775] Dover pbk **£3.70**
Tavroaquia and the Bulls of Bordeaux
[A776] Dover pbk **£5.95**
GUDIOL, JOSE
Goya
[A777] Thames & H hbk **£25.00**
SAYRE, ELEANOR & SANCHEZ, ALFONSO PEREZ
Goya and the Spirit of the Enlightenment **NEW**
Published as the primary catalogue for the major 1989 exhibition at the Museo del Prado in Madrid which will travel to the United States, this extensive monograph explores all aspects of Goya's work including his paintings, prints and drawings.
[A778] Mus of Art Boston hbk **£40.00**
SYMMONS, SARAH
Goya: In Pursuit of Patronage
[A779] Gordon Fraser hbk **£20.00**
WILLIAMS
Goya and the Impossible Revolution
[A780] Viking hbk **£7.95**

GRANT, DUNCAN
TURNBAUGH, DOUGLAS BLAIR
Private: The Erotic Art of Duncan Grant **NEW**
US art historian D.B. Turnbaugh compiled this introduction to Duncan Grant, the darling of the Bloomsbury set and friend of John Maynard Keynes and Lytton Strachey. 40 colour, 40 black and white plates.
[A781] GMP hbk **£20.00**

GRECO, EL DOMENIKOS THEOTOCOPOULOS (1541 - 1641)
Cretan painter who worked primarily in Italy and Spain. His work is characterised by elongated figures and an angular, distorted vision which anticipated later expressionist painters.
COSSIO
El Greco
[A782] Dolphin hbk **£18.00**
MANN, RICHARD G.
El Greco and His Patrons: Three Major Projects
[A783] Cambridge UP hbk **£37.50**

GROSZ, GEORGE (1893 - 1959)
German political and social satirist. *"The answer to the question, whether my work can be called art or not, depends on whether one believes that the future belongs to the working class."* (Grosz, 1924).
FLAVELL, KAY
George Grosz: A Biography
This book provides critical insight into the artist's commitment to social protest, arguing against the commonly held belief that Grosz became a conformist in his later years. 85 black and white illustrations, 20 colour.
[A784] Yale UP hbk **£29.95**
HESS, HANS
George Grosz
[A785] Yale UP hbk **£30.00**
[A786] Yale UP pbk **£14.95**
SCHNEEDE, UWE M.; BUSSMAN, G. & SCHNEEDE-SCZESNY, M.
George Grosz: His Life and Work
[A787] Gordon Fraser hbk **£9.95**

GUSTON, PHILIP (1913 - 1980)
Guston moved away from abstraction and into the figurative, inspiring the re-emergence of the figure in American art in the 1970s and 1980s. His style resembles cartoon drawings in that he uses a heavy black line to define form, but underlying the 'coarse' technique is a vital awareness of psychological states.
DABROWSKI, MAGDALENA
Drawings of Philip Guston
Published to accompany an exhibition at MOMA (New York), this collection establishes the drawings as autonomous works, quite separate from Guston's paintings. Executed in varying forms from the abstract to the linear, Guston's commitment to disrupting the accepted aesthetic and the art historical is consistent. 172 illustrations, 31 in colour.
[A788] MOMA hbk **£22.50**

HAACKE, HANS (1936 -)
German Experimental artist. Haacke's work reveals an interest in the spectator and the social function of art. His presentational format is inextricably linked with his conceptual concerns and thus varies from piece to piece.
WALLIS, BRIAN (ED)
Unfinished Business
Includes penetrating essays by critical writers and by Hans Haacke. The dialectic of meaning in Haacke's work rests in the self-conscious presentation of content and the understanding of how this 'message' is read. Co-published with the New Museum of Contemporary Art in New York.
[A789] MIT Press hbk **£13.50**

HALS, FRANS (c.1581 - 1666)
'When Hals' brush touches the canvas it creates drawing and painting, volume and colour simultaneously...Every brushstroke expresses at the same time relief, light, movement, material.' (N.S. Trivas, 1941).
BAARD, H P
Frans Hals
[A790] Thames & H hbk **£25.00**

HAMILTON, RICHARD (1922 -)
Hamilton promoted Pop Art and New Realism in Britain and was a founder member of the Independent Group in 1950. His more familiar works often utilize commercial photographs which are portrayed in a montage form, the image wholly subservient to the idea.
Richard Hamilton: Collected Works
[A791] Thames & H hbk **£18.00**

HEPWORTH, BARBARA (1903 - 1975)
Widely recognised British abstract sculptress.
Barbara Hepworth: Complete Sculpture 1960 - 69
[A792] Lund Humphries hbk **£30.00**
Barbara Hepworth: Pictorial Autobiography
[A793] Tate Gall pbk **£6.50**
HAMMACHER, A.M.
Barbara Hepworth
[A794] Thames & H hbk **£18.00**

HESSE, EVA (1936 - 1970)
Hesse's work represents a crucial intervention in the art production of her time. Historically situated within the minimalist tradition, Hesse disrupted the purity of form and the autonomy of the object by introducing potentially emotive content.
BARRETTE, BILL
Eva Hesse: Sculpture **NEW**
This meticulous study focuses on Hesse's artworks, utilizing biographical notes only when necessary to highlight the psychological thrust of her creativity.

Barrette's lucid commentary makes this volume an essential source book on this major 20th century artist. 176 illustrations.
[A795] Timken hbk **£40.00**

HOCKNEY, DAVID (1937 -)
'Hockney is...a fantasist with an entrancingly original imagination...His performance is as precarious as a tight-rope act: the balance is perfectly held but prentiousness and whimsicality seem to yawn on either side.' (*Times* critic, 1973).
David Hockney: A Retrospective
Assessing Hockney's *oeuvre* from every perspective, this accompanied the 1988 exhibition held in Los Angeles. 342 illustrations, 253 in colour.
[A796] Thames & H hbk **£29.95**
Hockney by Hockney
Autobiographical study augmented by many illustrations.
[A797] Thames & H hbk **£20.00**
Hockney: Paper Pools
[A798] Thames & H hbk **£14.95**
[A799] Thames & H pbk **£7.95**
Pictures by David Hockney
[A800] Thames & H pbk **£5.95**
FRIEDMAN
Hockney Paints the Stage
[A801] Thames & H hbk **£28.00**
HOCKNEY, DAVID & SPENDER, STEPHEN
China Diary
Jointly compiled by the artist and Steven Spender, this volume chronicles a three week trip, capturing the experiences through photographs, drawings and journal entries. 158 watercolours, drawings and photographs.
[A802] Thames & H hbk **£14.95**
LIVINGSTONE
David Hockney: Etchings and Lithographs
[A803] Thames & H hbk **£12.95**
WEBB, PETER
Portrait of David Hockney
[A804] Chatto hbk **£20.00**

HOFMANN, HANS (1880 - 1966)
German painter. Hofmann experimented with many styles but was most influential in the field of Abstract Expressionism.
Hans Hofmann: Late Paintings
[A805] Tate Gall pbk **£5.95**
GOODMAN, CYNTHIA
Hans Hofmann
[A806] Abbeville hbk **£18.95**
[A807] Abbeville pbk **£12.95**

HOGARTH, WILLIAM (1697 - 1764)
British painter and political satirist, Hogarth is famous for his series of engravings realistically depicting London's poor entitled *Gin Lane*.
BINDMAN, DAVID
Hogarth
[A808] Hogarth pbk **£4.95**
COWLEY, ROBERT
Marrriage à la Mode: A Review of Hogarth's Narrative Art
[A809] Manchester UP pbk **£12.95**
EINBERG, ELIZABETH
Manners and Morals: Hogarth and British Painting
[A810] Viking hbk **£30.00**
[A811] Penguin pbk **£12.95**

HOLBEIN, HANS (c.1497 - 1543)
With an international reputation during his lifetime as a portraitist, Holbein is historically classified as the most accomplished realist painter of the North.
Dance of Death
[A812] Dover pbk **£4.45**

DVORAK, FRANTISEK
Hans Holbein: Drawings
[A813] Crown Pub hbk **£15.95**
ROWLANDS, JOHN
Holbein
The author presents 'not just a synthesis of the latest research on Holbein but the most balanced and authoritative book on his paintings.' (*Daily Telegraph*).
[A814] Phaidon hbk **£55.00**

HOLZER, JENNY
Contemporary American artist whose work is primarily textually based. She re-presents 'truisms' in diverse forms and for a public audience, commandeering billboards and electronic signboards. Her work recently appeared in London, at Piccadilly Circus and on till receipts at Tower Records.
Jenny Holzer: Signs Under a Rock 1988 - 1989
[A815] ICA pbk **£12.95**

HOPPER, EDWARD (1882 - 1967)
Hopper's pictures are characterized by isolated figures in empty rooms, capturing the haunting loneliness of modern America.
HOBBS, ROBERT
Edward Hopper
Hobbs examines the recurring theme of fundamental loss experienced by the individual in reaction to technological changes. 102 illustrations, 55 in colour.
[A816] Abrams hbk **£25.00**
LEVIN, GAIL
Edward Hopper
[A817] Bonfini hbk **£7.50**
Edward Hopper: Complete Prints
[A818] Norton hbk **£11.30**
Edward Hopper: The Art and the Artist
Examines all aspects of Hooper's career; his oil paintings, watercolours, drawings, etchings and commercial illustrations are fully discussed.
[A819] Norton hbk **£35.30**
[A820] Norton pbk **£17.95**

HUNT, WILLIAM HOLMAN (1827 - 1910)
Pre-Raphaelite visonary painter most famous for his painting *The Light of the World* in Keble College Chapel, Oxford.
LANDOW, GEORGE
William Holman-Hunt and Typological Symbolism
[A821] Yale UP hbk **£35.00**
MAAS, JEREMY
Holman Hunt and 'The Light of the World'
[A822] Scolar P hbk **£12.50**
[A823] Scolar P pbk **£4.95**

IMPRESSIONISM
The impressionists radically altered the way in which form is described, focusing on the impermanency of the moment to suggest an ever-changing perception rather than definitive representation. Ethereal and fluid, their paintings rely on the use of light to blur and dissolve the real world rather than bringing it into sharp focus. See *Cassatt*, *Cézanne*, *Degas*, *Monet*, *Morisot*, *Pissarro* and *Renoir*.
Impressionism and Contemporary Russian Art `NEW`
[A824] Phaidon hbk **£25.00**
ADAMS, STEPHEN
The World of the Impressionists `NEW`
Special features of this survey include biographical notes on the leading figures of the movement, an examination of the social, cultural and political background and illustrated essays on key themes from the cityscapes of Paris to the influence of music on painting.
[A825] Thames & H hbk **£16.95**

ADLER, KATHLEEN
The Unknown Impressionists
Reproductions are arranged by subject matter, matching up famous paintings with lesser-known works which represent the same scene. 100 colour illustrations.
[A826] Phaidon hbk **£30.00**
BARSKAYA, ANNA
Impressionists and Post-Impressionists in Soviet Museums
A very large number of major impressionist pictures are housed in collections in the Soviet Union and are reproduced here in exceptionally good colour plates.
[A827] Phaidon hbk **£25.00**
BERNARD (ED)
The Impressionist Revolution
Foreword by Sir Lawrence Gowing.
[A828] Macdonald hbk **£25.00**
BONAFOUX, PASCAL
The Impressionists: Portraits and Confidences
Plentiful colour pictures and interesting text give a good idea of the atmosphere and personalities of these painters.
[A829] Weidenfeld hbk **£40.00**
BOYLE, RICHARD J.
American Impressionism
[A830] NY Graph Soc pbk **£12.95**
BRETTELL, RICHARD R.
French Impressionists in the Art Institute of Chicago
Excellent reproductions.
[A831] Abrams hbk **£21.50**
[A832] Abrams pbk **£13.50**
DENVIR, BERNARD
The Impressionists at First Hand
[A833] Thames & H pbk **£5.95**
FARR, DENNIS & HOUSE, JOHN ET AL
Impressionist and Post-Impressionist Masterpieces: The Courtauld
Samuel Court's collection of French impressionist painting is one of the most extensive in existence. This book highlights 48 works including both familiar and lesser-known paintings.
[A834] Yale UP hbk **£25.00**
[A835] Yale UP pbk **£9.95**
FLINT, KATE
Impressionists in England: The Critical Reception
[A836] Routledge hbk **£27.50**
GARB, TAMAR
Women Impressionists
A discussion of Berthe Morisot, Mary Cassatt and other artists.
[A837] Phaidon hbk **£11.95**
HERBERT, ROBERT L.
Impressionism: Art, Leisure and Parisian Society `NEW`
Herbert's book re-contextualizes this major movement by locating Impressionism within the social rather than the cultural milieu. The two themes - entertainment and leisure - dominated the seminal years of impressionist painting, 1865 - 1885, and emphasize how completely this art form was integrated into the life of its period.
[A838] Yale UP hbk **£29.95**
LACLOTTE, MICHEL & LUCIE-SMITH, EDWARD
Impressionist and Post-Impressionist Masterpieces: Musée d'Orsay
A survey of the collection in Paris's recently opened museum dedicated to the culture of the 19th century.
[A839] Thames & H hbk **£9.95**
LANGDON, HELEN
Impressionist Seasons
[A840] Phaidon pbk **£11.95**

Portrait of **T.E. Lawrence**, 1888 - 1935, by Augustus John (Picture: National Portrait Gallery)

LLOYD, CHRISTOPHER & THOMPSON, RICHARD
Impressionist Drawings
[A841] Phaidon hbk **£14.95**
[A842] Phaidon pbk **£9.95**
MCQUILLAN, MELISSA
Impressionist Portraits
[A843] Thames & H hbk **£18.00**
MOFFETT, CHARLES
The New Painting: Impressionism 1874 - 1886
A book with excellent colour pictures dating from the 1986 exhibition in Washington. The author has thoroughly researched his subject drawing on 19th century newspaper reports and criticism. 212 colour illustrations, 215 black and white.
[A844] Phaidon hbk **£38.00**
NOCHLIN, LINDA (ED)
Impressionism and Post-Impressionism 1874 - 1904
An excellent collection of letters and other source documents for the serious student.
[A845] Prentice-Hall pbk **£27.80**
POOL, PHOEBE
Impressionism
Very good introduction to the subject.
[A846] Thames & H pbk **£5.95**
REWALD, JOHN
Studies in Impressionism
A selection of essays from this master critic of the period.
[A847] Thames & H hbk **£25.00**
The History of Impressionism
A popular general survey.
[A848] Secker hbk **£30.00**
[A849] Secker pbk **£18.00**

JOHN, AUGUSTUS EDWIN
Welsh painter. Early in his career, John established himself as one of the leading draughtsmen in England and his work has been compared with that of Hogarth and Gainsborough. His portraits made fashionable the gypsy-type women of North Wales.
HOLROYD, MICHAEL
Augustus John - Vol 1: The Years of Innnocence
[A851] Heinemann hbk **£12.00**
Augustus John - Vol 2: The Years of Experience
[A852] Heinemann hbk **£12.00**
Augustus John: Vols 1 & 2
[A853] Penguin pbk **£5.25**

JOHN, GWEN (1876 - 1939)
Recent years have witnessed a renewed interest in the work of Gwen John. Her painting is characterized by its refined spirituality.
CHITTY, SUSAN
Gwen John
[A854] Hodder pbk **£8.95**
LANGDALE, CECILY
Gwen John NEW
The first significant study of the paintings of Gwen John. Langdale discusses John's life including her relationships with her brother, and with Whistler and Rodin, and concludes with a complete catalogue of her paintings and a selection of her drawings.
[A855] Yale UP pbk **£19.95**
LANGDALE, CECILY & FRASER, JENKINS DAVID
Gwen John: An Interior Life
[A856] Phaidon pbk **£9.95**
TAUBMAN, SUSAN
Gwen John
[A857] Scolar P hbk **£25.00**

JOHNS, JASPER (1930 -)
American artist who came to prominence in 1955 when he developed a style independent of the Abstract Expressionism then current. Johns began painting flags, targets, numbers and letters, separating his art from self-expression and posing questions about the nature of perception.
Jasper Johns: Prints 1970 - 1977
[A858] Petersburg P pbk **£12.50**
CASTLEMAN, RIVA
Jasper Johns: A Print Retrospective
[A859] Thames & H hbk **£25.00**
FRANCIS, RICHARD
Jasper Johns
[A860] Abbeville hbk **£18.95**
[A861] Abbeville pbk **£12.95**
ROSENTHAL, MARK
Jasper Johns: Work since 1974 NEW
Beginning with the cross-hatch paintings of 1974 and moving on to his more personal imagery of the 1980s, this volume documents a large body of work which has never been exhibited as a group. Generous commentary, with 75 illustrations, 36 in colour.
[A862] Thames & H hbk **£18.95**
SHAPIRO, DAVID
Jasper Johns
[A863] Abrams hbk **£53.95**

KABAKOV, ILYA
Contemporary Russian artist, who creates whole environments, transforming the gallery space in its entirety.
Ilya Kabakov: Ten Albums, Ten Characters NEW
Includes 20 loose pages designed by the artist and Kabakov's essays. 25 black and white reproductions.
[A864] Riverside Gal pbk **£4.00**
Ten Characters NEW
The highlight of this catalogue is the inclusion of the narrative texts which form an integral part of Kabakov's work. The short pieces of prose serve as titles for the installations and exist independently as politically provocative texts. Titles include 'The Man Who Flew into His Picture', 'The Man Who Collects the Opinions of Others', 'The Man Who Flew to Space From His Apartment', amongst others.
[A865] ICA pbk **£10.95**

KAHLO, FRIDA (1907 - 1954)
Kahlo is a prominent Mexican painter. *"Women painters are often forced to make exhibitions of themselves in order to mount exhibitions. Fame, notoriety, scandal, eccentric dress and behaviour - Rosa Bonheur, Meret Oppenheim, Leonor Fini, Georgia O'Keefe. Frida Kahlo. Fame is not an end in itself but a strategy. Being famous means she can stake out her own territory, can even determine wholly or in part the way her paintings will be looked at."* (Angela Carter).
Images of Frida Kahlo NEW
This unusual 'publication' is presented in the form of a box of postcards documenting Kahlo's paintings and including a booklet by Angela Carter introducing the artist. Other 'surprises' include a mini-poster of the artist taken from a 1952 photograph.
[A866] Redstone P hbk **£9.95**
HERRERA, HEYDEN
A Biography of Frida Kahlo
Heyden's biography reveals Kahlo as an extremely sensitive and imaginative artist. It explores the origins of her subject matter and links her art with her personal history.
[A867] Harper & R pbk **£12.95**

KANDINSKY, WASSILY (1866 - 1944)
This Russian painter was one of the founders of abstract art. His series of 'Improvisations' lent art language the spontaneity and flexibility of musical scores.
Concerning the Spiritual in Art
[A868] Dover pbk **£2.20**
Kandinsky: Complete Writings on Art
[A869] Faber hbk **£35.00**
Sounds
[A870] Yale UP hbk **£41.95**
[A871] Yale UP pbk **£14.95**
Watercolours and Paintings and Unpublished Texts
[A872] Zwemmer hbk **£32.00**
LACOSTE, MICHEL
Kandinsky
[A873] Clematis pbk **£7.50**
ROETHEL, HANS K. & BENJAMIN, JEAN K.
Kandinsky
Features 48 colour illustrations each with a full commentary, with excerpts from Kandinsky's writings and a biography. 150 black and white illustrations.
[A874] Phaidon hbk **£35.00**
BELLIDIO, RAMON TIO
The Masterworks NEW
Originally trained as a lawyer in Moscow, Kandinsky was almost 30 when, after seeing Monet's *Haystacks*, he decided to become an artist. This new volume concentrates on his pivotal paintings and writings, citing examples ranging from the representational landscapes of 1910, to the spiritual abstracts of the early 40s.
[A875] Bracken Bks hbk **£12.95**

KIEFER, ANSLEM (1945 -)
Kiefer's paintings attempt to *"make visible from the darkness of the lived moment"* the overwhelming presence of German history. Although his work was at first classified as part of New German Painting, the artist had been developing independently from the beginning. His extensive *oeuvre*, to which he is still adding, includes large scale mixed media painting, sculptures and books.
The High Priestess/ Zweistromland NEW
Large scale catalogue which does more than document the work of Kiefer: the photographs included are artpieces in themselves and not straightforward reproductions. A beautiful presentation.
[A876] Anthony d'Offay hbk **£50.00**
HARTEN, JURGEN
Anslem Kiefer NEW
This beautifully presented volume is a reproduction of one of Kiefer's book pieces entitled *Transition from Cool to Warm*. It is encased in a slip cover and includes full-colour illustrations documenting selected pages from Kiefer's book.
[A877] Thames & H hbk **£38.00**

ROSENTHAL, MARK
Anslem Kiefer **NEW**
This catalogue of the 1989 exhibition which toured to Chicago, Los Angeles, Philadelphia and New York offers a critical study of Kiefer. *Flash Art* magazine cites the publication as 'one of the main sources on this artist thanks to the depth of its documentation'.
[A878] Prestel pbk **£29.00**

KITAJ, R.B. (1932 -)
American-born British painter associated with Pop Art who describes his impetuts in the following terms: *"to do Cezanne and Degas and Kafka over again, after Auschwitz."*
LIVINGSTONE, MARCO
R.B. Kitaj
The author methodically examines Kitaj's early life, his first impressions of England, the Age of Mechanical Reproduction and his current practice. With a foreword by Kitaj and 172 illustrations, 50 in colour.
[A879] Phaidon hbk **£45.00**
SHANNON, JOE
Kitaj
[A880] Thames & H pbk **£10.95**

KLEE, PAUL (1879 - 1940)
Describing his free fantasy work as *"taking a line for a walk"*, Klee was associated with Kandinsky and the Blaue Reiter group. A dedicated theorist, he taught for many years at the Bauhaus.
Paul Klee on Modern Art
[A881] Faber pbk **£3.95**
Pedagogical Sketchbook
[A882] Faber pbk **£3.95**
CHEVALIER, DENYS
Klee
[A883] Bonfini pbk **£7.50**
GROHMANN, WILL
Klee
[A884] Thames & H hbk **£25.00**
[A885] Thames & H pbk **£12.95**
REWALD, SABINE
The Berggruen Klee Collection
90 works by Klee have recently been given to the Metropolitan Museum of Art in New York by Heinz Berggruen. Photographs of the Klee family and an inside view of the Bauhaus give an insight into his private life. Nearly all the 111 reproductions are in full colour and are accompanied by an extensive entry which includes quotations from Klee's letters, as yet unpublished in English.
[A886] Tate Gall hbk **£25.00**
[A887] Tate Gall pbk **£18.00**
SCHMALENBACH
Paul Klee
[A888] Prestel hbk **£18.95**
VERDI, RICHARD
Klee and Nature
[A889] Zwemmer hbk **£27.50**
[A890] Zwemmer pbk **£16.95**

KLIMT, GUSTAV (1862 - 1918)
An Austrian art nouveau painter.
BAUMER, ANGELICA
Gustav Klimt: Women
[A891] Weidenfeld hbk **£30.00**
COMINI, ALLESSANDRA
Gustav Klimt
[A892] Thames & H pbk **£9.95**
DOBAI
Gustav Klimt: Landscapes
[A893] Weidenfeld hbk **£30.00**
KALLIR, JANE
Gustav Klimt: 25 Masterworks **NEW**
Gustav Klimt is thought by some to be the only strong painter of the Art Nouveau movement. This critical commentary certainly supports the claim, providing both an art-historical assessment and new insight into the Viennese society at the turn of the century. Each of the 25 masterworks represents the highlight of the successive phases of Klimt's career; the full-page colour reproductions portray his spectacular paintings to great effect.
[A894] Abrams pbk **£12.95**
SABARSKY, SERGE
Klimt: Drawings
[A895] Gordon Fraser hbk **£15.00**

KOKOSCHKA, OSKAR (1886 - 1980)
Austrian British painter who remained uninfluenced by modern movements and techniques (Futurism, Cubism, Surrealism etc) and chose to represent a personal version of pre-1914 Expressionism.
Oskar Kokoschka 1886 - 1960
[A897] Tate Gall hbk **£25.00**
[A898] Tate Gall pbk **£17.95**
Oskar Kokoschka: My Life
[A899] Thames & H hbk **£8.95**
GOMBRICH, ERNST
Kokoschka in His Time
Essay based on a lecture given by Gombrich at the Tate Gallery.
[A900] Tate Gall pbk **£2.95**
WHITFORD, FRANK
Oskar Kokoschka: A Life
[A901] Weidenfeld hbk **£15.00**

KOLLWITZ, KATHE (1867 - 1945)
Kollwitz's work moves completely beyond the accidental and it is this feature, coupled with her intuive understanding of the tragic, which places her in line with modern German Expressionism. Her art expresses social and political protest in its purest form.
Kathe Kollwitz: Exhibition Catalogue
[A902] Kettle's Yard Gal hbk **£2.95**
Prints and Drawings
[A903] Dover pbk **£7.45**
FECHT, TOM
Kathe Kollwitz: Works in Colour **NEW**
[A904] Random House hbk **£30.00**

KOONING, WILLIAM DE (1904 -)
Born in Rotterdam, de Kooning has lived in the United States since 1926. Breaking away from the influence of De Stijl, he became one of the leading action painters.
CUMMINGS
William de Kooning
[A905] Norton hbk **£31.80**
GAUGH, HARRY F.
Willem de Kooning
[A906] Abbeville hbk **£18.95**
[A907] Abbeville pbk **£12.95**
WALDMAN, DIANE
Willem de Kooning
[A908] Thames & H hbk **£20.00**

KRUGER, BARBARA
Kruger's large scale photocollages appropriate images from magazines which are re-contextualized by the inclusion of texts written in the style of advertising slogans.
BARRY, LITA & HARPER, JENNY
Barbara Kruger 1988
[A909] Art Data pbk **£9.95**

LEGER, FERDINAND (1881 - 1955)
A French artist associated with the Cubist movement. His paintings interpret the human figure as robotic and integrate the worker with the machine.
DE FRANCIA, PETER
Ferdinand Léger
This highly acclaimed biography emphasizes Léger's own writings, stressing the social and political factors which informed his work.
[A910] Yale UP hbk **£35.00**

DIEHL, GASTON
Léger
[A911] Bonfini pbk **£7.50**
SEROTA, NICHOLAS (ED)
Ferdinand Léger: The Later Years 1940 - 1955
Lavishly illustrated, this monograph includes essays by five critics offering insight into an important phase in Léger's career covering the years spent in America and the execution of his monolithic painting cycles.
[A912] Prestel hbk **£27.50**

LEONARDO DA VINCI (1452 - 1519)
In his time, Leonardo's most decisive influence was in painting, yet his explorations in the fields of science and engineering occupied the greater part of his life. He left behind numerous unfinished canvases and, according to Vasari, *"he reproached himself with having offended God and man by his failure to do his duty in art"*. Sigmund Freud's writings on *Art and Literature* include a lengthy and most fascinating examination of Leonardo's enigmatic character.
Leonardo da Vinci: Complete Paintings
[A913] Penguin pbk **£7.95**
Leonardo da Vinci: The Notebooks (Ed. Richter, I.A.)
[A914] Oxford pbk **£3.50**
CLARKE, KENNETH
Leonardo da Vinci
[A915] Viking hbk **£15.95**
HEYDENREICH, LUDWIG
Leonardo Studies
This volume makes available fifteen essays by the internationally recognised scholar L.H. Heydenreich. The texts are represented in their original languages: English, French, German and Italian.
[A916] Prestel hbk **£65.00**
KEELE & ROBERTS (ED)
Leonardo da Vinci
Anatomical drawings from the Royal Library, Windsor Castle
[A917] Met Museum of Art hbk **£30.50**
KEMP, MARTIN & ROBERTS, JANE
Leonardo da Vinci **NEW**
Leonardo's notebooks are widely known but few authors have attempted to make their contents accessible. Considered chaotic and idiosyncratic, his complex recordings have frequently been classified as artistic rather than scientific. In this book, published to accompany the recent exhibition at the Hayward,

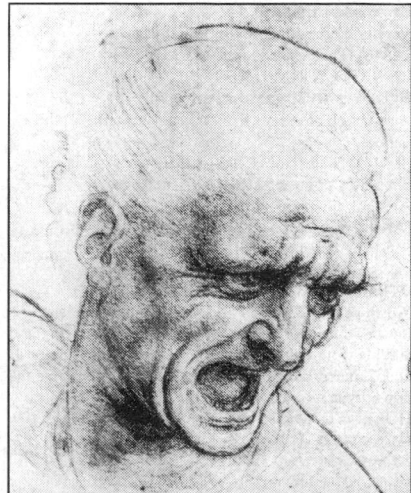

Study of a head of a warrior from the Battle of Anghiari c. 1504 by Leonardo da Vinci from *Leonardo da Vinci* by Kenneth Clarke (Viking hbk £15.95)

Martin Kemp and Jane Roberts work towards revealing the intellectual and artistic patterns behind Leonardo's work. 180 colour illustrations, 40 black and white.
[A918] Yale UP hbk **£30.00**
[A919] Yale UP pbk **£12.95**
KEMP, MARTIN (ED)
Leonardo da Vinci: The Marvellous Works of Nature and Man
[A920] Dent hbk **£25.00**
Leonardo on Painting: An Anthology of Writings by Leonardo da Vinci `NEW`
Kemp has organised Leonardo's creatively chaotic notes on painting into an accessbile documentary study. He has drawn material from the original texts, other manuscripts and contemporary sources. 238 black and white illustrations, 8 colour.
[A921] Yale UP hbk **£20.00**
[A922] Yale UP pbk **£6.95**
POPHAM, A.E.
Leonardo Drawings
[A923] Cape hbk **£9.95**
[A924] Cape pbk **£4.95**
WASSERMAN, JACK
Leonardo da Vinci
[A925] Thames & H hbk **£25.00**

LICHTENSTEIN, ROY (1923 -)
American pop artist best known for his large scale paintings of comic book scenes lifted directly from pulp romances.
ALLOWAY, LAWRENCE
Roy Lichtenstein
[A926] Abbeville hbk **£18.95**
[A927] Abbeville pbk **£12.95**
HENDRICKSON, JAMES
Lichtenstein `NEW`
Very informative survey which explores Lichtenstein's art in the context of traditional and contemporary art history. Over 100 illustrations.
[A928] Taschen pbk **£4.99**
ROSE, BERNICE
The Drawings of Roy Lichtenstein
Includes an extensive introduction which links the drawings with the paintings, statements by the artist and examines influential source. 165 illustrations, 80 in colour.
[A929] Thames & H hbk **£23.50**
TOMKINS
Roy Lichtenstein: Mural with Blue Brushstrokes
[A930] Abrams hbk **£14.50**

LONG, RICHARD (1945 -)
Long first used 'the walk' while a student, an activity that remains at the heart of his art production. Enacting a merging of art and nature by setting out on extensive journeys on foot, Long then translates these experiences into 'gallery-bound' works by laying out simple geometric constructions in stone, wood, slate or mud on the floor. Photo-documentation of his treks accompany the *earthworks*, lending specificity to a poetic gesture.
FUCHS, RUDI
Richard Long
Long represented Great Britain at the Venice Biennale in 1976 and was one of the six finalists for the Turner prize in 1984.
[A931] Thames & H pbk **£16.95**

LORRAIN, CLAUDE (1600 - 1682)
French landscape painter. The common comparison is with Poussin but the artist drew heavily from the earlier mannerists.
ASKEW, PAMELA (ED)
Claude Lorrain 1600 - 1682: A Symposium
[A932] NG Washington pbk **£14.00**

LANGDON, HELEN
Claude Lorrain `NEW`
Provides an account of the artist's times and examines his entire output including the drawings and etchings. 130 illustrations, 50 colour.
[A933] Phaidon hbk **£30.00**

LOWRY, L.S. (1887 - 1976)
Lowry lived throughout his life in Manchester and Salford. His pictures focus chiefly on industrial landscapes, including figures painted in the stick-like manner which has come to be associated with the artist.
LEBER, MICHAEL & SANDLING, JUDY
L.S. Lowry
[A934] Phaidon hbk **£19.95**
[A935] Phaidon pbk **£11.95**
ROHDE, SHELLEY
A Private View of L.S. Lowry
[A936] Methuen pbk **£6.95**
SPALDING, JULIAN
Lowry
[A937] Herbert P pbk **£8.95**

MAGRITTE, RENE (1898 - 1967)
A leading surrealist whose paintings moved far beyond disturbing portrayals of the unconscious world and into the complex field of meta-language. *"If the dream is the translation of waking life, then waking life is also a translation of the dream."* (Magritte).
CALVOCORESSI, RICHARD
Magritte
[A938] Phaidon hbk **£12.50**
[A939] Phaidon pbk **£9.50**
GABLIK, SUZY
Magritte
[A941] Thames & H pbk **£5.95**
HAMMACHER, A.M.
Magritte
In this extended and updated monograph, the author offers careful explanations of Magritte's symbolism and brief essays on his graphics, sculpture and the mural at Knokke. 138 illustrations, 48 colour.
[A942] Thames & H hbk **£25.00**
[A943] Thames & H hbk **£12.95**
TORCZYNER
Magritte: The True Art of Painting
[A944] Abrams hbk **£15.50**

MANET, EDOUARD (1832 - 1883)
French painter who is traditionally placed within the Impressionist movement, although he was unwilling to be included in their exhibitions. In 1863, he painted the controversial *Olympia* which offended the art public with its confrontational depiction of nudity.
Manet and Modern Paris
One hundred paintings, drawings, prints and photographs by Manet and his contemporaries.
[A945] Chicago UP hbk **£31.95**
Manet: Complete Paintings
[A946] Penguin pbk **£7.95**
The Paintings of Manet `NEW`
A solid introduction to the major works.
[A947] Hamlyn pbk **£7.95**
ADLER, KATHLEEN
Manet
Manet's themes are fully discussed in addition to the views of 19th century critics and historians. 220 illustrations, 50 in colour.
[A948] Phaidon hbk **£39.50**
BAREAU
Hidden Face of Manet
An investigation of the artist's working processes.
[A949] Burlington Mag pbk **£5.75**
BAZIN, GERMAIN
Manet
Examines Manet's works in relation to his

contemporaries. Includes introductory pieces by Proust and Zola. 167 illustrations, 56 colour.
[A950] Cassell hbk **£12.95**
COURTHION, PIERRE
Manet
[A951] Thames & H hbk **£20.00**
[A952] Thames & H pbk **£12.95**
FORGE, ANDREW & GORDON, ROBERT
The Last Flower Paintings of Manet
[A953] Thames & H hbk **£12.95**
HAMILTON, GEORGE HEARD
Manet and His Critics
[A954] Yale UP pbk **£8.95**
HANSON, ANNE COFFIN
Manet and the Modern Tradition
An illuminating comparative analysis of the body of criticism inspired by Manet's paintings.
[A955] Yale UP hbk **£39.95**
[A956] Yale UP pbk **£13.95**
MANET, JULIE
Growing Up with the Impressionists: The Diary of Julie Manet
[A957] Sotheby's hbk **£19.95**

MANTEGNA, ANDREA (c.1431 - 1506)
The Renaissance master of *sotto in su* (ceiling painting with perspective adapted to be seen from below).
Triumphs of Caesar by Andrea Mantegna
From the collection of Her Majesty the Queen at Hampton Court.
[A958] Harvey Miller hbk **£48.00**
LIGHTBROWN, RONALD
Mantegna
[A959] Phaidon hbk **£60.00**

MATISSE, HENRI (1869 - 1954)
French painter, principle artist of the Fauve group. *"I am unable to make a servile copy of nature...When I have worked out all my tonal relationships, the result should be a living harmony of colours, comparable to that of a musical composition."* (Matisse 1908).
Matisse in the Collection of the Museum of Modern Art, NY
[A960] MOMA hbk **£15.00**
CASTLEMAN, RIVA
Matisse Prints: From the Museum of Modern Art
[A961] Thames & H pbk **£8.25**
COWART, JACK & FOURCADE, D.
Henri Matisse: The Early Years in Nice 1916 - 1930
[A962] Abrams hbk **£35.00**
ELDERFIELD, JOHN
The Drawings of Henry Matisse
[A963] Thames & H pbk **£9.95**
FLAM, JACK D.
Matisse On Art
'An unrivalled book that will remain indispensable for a very long time' (Sir Lawrence Gowing). Flam has drawn upon previously neglected material - works of art, critical writings, letters and interviews with family and friends - to discuss Matisse's work in all mediums. 497 illustrations, 101 in colour.
[A964] Phaidon pbk **£7.50**
Matisse: The Man and His Art 1869 - 1918
[A965] Thames & H hbk **£60.00**
GUICHARD-MEILI, JEAN
Matisse: Paper Cut-Outs
[A966] Thames & H hbk **£60.00**
JACOBUS, JOHN
Matisse
[A967] Thames & H hbk **£25.00**
[A968] Thames & H pbk **£12.95**
LEGG, ALICE
Sculpture of Matisse
[A969] Thames & H pbk **£3.25**

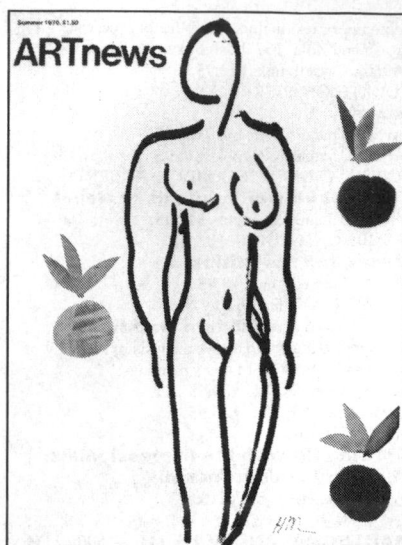

A Matisse drawing of the human figure from the front cover of ARTnews, 1970

SCHNEIDER, PIERRE
Matisse
[A970] Thames & H hbk **£85.00**
WATKINS, NICHOLAS
Matisse
[A971] Phaidon hbk **£25.00**

MICHELANGELO BUONARROTI

(1475 - 1654)
In his art production, Michelangelo has often gone to the utmost limit of what is expressible in visual terms. His statues and paintings reveal a psychological impetus, demonstrating a desire to isolate experiential moments rather than to illustrate historical themes. Many of his great works retain a vitality through his ability to contain strong emotions within a passive form.
Michelangelo and His Drawings
[A972] Yale UP hbk **£25.00**
Paintings of Michalangelo
[A973] Thames & H hbk **£25.00**
BALDINI, UMBERTO
Complete Sculpture of Michelangelo
[A974] Thames & H pbk **£25.00**
GOLDSCHEIDER, LUDWIG
Michelangelo: Paintings, Sculpture, Architecture
Contains reproductions of all the artist's work apart from the drawings. 400 illustrations, 10 colour.
[A975] Phaidon hbk **£17.50**
HARTT, FREDERICK
David by the Hand of Michelangelo: The Original Model Discovered
It is possible to gain valuable insight on an artist's entire *oeuvre* by studying in detail one work. Frederick Hartt bases his book on his discovery of the preparatory model of *David* executed by Michelangelo, takes the reader through to the final realization of a monumental piece of work.
[A976] Thames & H hbk **£28.00**
LIEBERT, ROBERT
Michelangelo: A Psychoanalytic Study of His Life and Images
Liebert expands our knowledge of one of art history's key figures through drawing in an incisive analysis of Michelangelo's early development and adulthood.
[A977] Yale UP hbk **£46.25**
[A978] Yale UP pbk **£16.95**

MURRAY, LINDA
Michelangelo
[A979] Thames & H pbk **£5.95**
Michelangelo: His Life, Work and Times
[A980] Thames & H hbk **£20.00**
PIETRANGELI, CARLO
The Sistine Chapel: Michelangelo Rediscovered
[A981] Muller hbk **£40.00**
WILDE, JOHANNES
Michelangelo: Six Lectures
[A982] Oxford pbk **£12.50**

MINIMALISM

The origins of Minimalism lie in Kasimir Malevich's *Black Square on a White Ground* (1913). The minimalists rejected painterly expression in favour of restraint, mechanical precision and all-over composition. The absence of the artist's gestural mark questioned notions of authorship. Donald Judd's aluminum cubes and Ellsworth Kelly's sharp-edged geometric compositions, executed in pure colours with immaculate surfaces characterise this movement.
Minimalism `NEW`
"Now the world is neither meaningful or absurd. It simply is. In place of this universe of 'meanings' one should try to construct a more solid immediate world." (Robbe-Grillet). Excellent introduction to Minimalism with key works represented, artists' biographies, quotes and an essay by Michael Craig-Martin.
[A985] Tate Gall pbk **£3.95**
KELLY, ELLSWORTH
The Prints of Ellsworth Kelly
A *catalogue raisonné* 1949-1985, edited by Richard Axsom. Kelly figures significantly in American non-gestural abstraction. This volume documents and reproduces virtually all the prints to date. The essay traces Kelly's career as printmaker and discusses points of contact with his painting.
[A986] Phaidon hbk **£35.00**
LEWISON, JEREMY
Sol LeWitt Prints 1970 - 1986
Printmaking has always been central to LeWitt's art and this book records an exhibition of his etchings, screen prints, lithographs, woodcuts and books made between 1970 and 1986. It also incudes a comprehensive list of all LeWitt's prints and a full bibliography. 48 illustrations, 16 colour.
[A987] Tate Gall pbk **£7.50**

MIRO, JOAN (1893 - 1983)

Classed as a Spanish surrealist, Miró's paintings transform line into a transitional device, less restraining than fluid and musical.
Drawings by Joan Miró: 'Captured Imagination'
From the Fundacio Miró, Barcelona
[A988] Pennsylvania UP hbk **£28.45**
Miró in the Collection of the Museum of Modern Art, NY
[A989] MOMA hbk **£10.95**
CATALA-ROCA, FRANCESCA & PERMANYER, LUIS
Miró: Ninety Years
[A990] Macdonald hbk **£19.95**
MALET, ROSA MARIA
Miró `NEW`
A new title in the Academy Editions series, this book provides a solid introduction to Miró. Illustrations include paintings executed before Miró entered the Exchange School of Fine Art through to a large public sculpture executed in 1982. The text is divided into sections covering separately each of the mediums he worked in.
[A991] Academy Editions pbk **£9.95**

ROWELL, MARGIT (ED)
Joan Miró: Selected Writings and Interviews
This collection is presented in a standard book format although it does include photographs of Miró's work and life. Essentially autobiographical, the writings describe Miró's struggle to transform his personal visions and conflicts into a universal language. The book focuses on Paris between the wars and Miró's involvement with Hemingway, Ernst, Picasso, Braque, Dubuffet, Matisse and others. The editor collaborated on this project with Miró before his death.
[A992] Thames & H hbk **£22.50**
WEELEN, GUY
Miró `NEW`
The most comprehensive survey to appear on Miró in the last 25 years, Weelen traces the artist's 65 year career, beginning with a drawing made at the age of eight to a sculpture completed five years before Miro's death. The author, a poet, curator and critic, looks at how Miro emerged from the surrealist movement with a strong painterly vocabulary of his own. Generously quoting the artist's statements, Weelen sensitively reveals Miró's poetic impulse. 267 illustrations, 54 in full colour.
[A993] Abrams hbk **£55.00**

MODIGLIANI, AMEDEO (1884 - 1920)

A major Italian artist whose stylised portraits and stone sculptures echo African sculpture and early cubist paintings.
HALL, DOUGLAS
Modigliani
[A994] Phaidon hbk **£12.50**
[A995] Phaidon pbk **£9.50**
MANN, CAROL
Modigliani
[A996] Thames & H pbk **£5.95**
ROY
Modigliani
[A997] Rizzoli hbk **£14.95**
WARNER, ALFRED
Modigliani `NEW`
New edition in the Masters of Art series. 94 illustrations, 40 colour.
[A998] Thames & H hbk **£12.95**
WERNER, ALFRED
Modigliani
[A999] Thames & H hbk **£25.00**

MONDRIAN, PIET (1872 - 1944)

A Dutch painter who went to New York in 1940 where he exerted great influence on American artists. His particular form of abstraction was an especially rigorous one termed *Neo-Plasticism* and consisted of canvases restricted to grid-like divisions with individual squares painted in primary colours or black and white.
Piet Mondrian: Theories and Thoughts
[A1000] Zwemmer hbk **£21.00**
HENKELS
Mondrian: From Figuration to Abstraction
[A1001] Thames & H hbk **£19.95**
HOLTMAN, HARRY ET AL
New Art, the New Life: Collected Writings of Piet Mondrian
[A1002] Thames & H hbk **£38.00**
JAFFE, HANS L.
Mondrian
A new edition in the Masters of Art series, this volume offers a comprehensive introduction to this complex artist. 108 illustrations, 40 colour.
[A1003] Thames & H hbk **£12.95**
LEMOINE
Mondrian and 'De Stijl'
[A1004] Art Data hbk **£6.95**

MONET, CLAUDE (1840 - 1926)

One of the leaders of the Impressionists, Monet's magnificent series of paintings entitled *Water Lilies* best characterise his ability to use light to astonishing effect. The paint shimmers on the canvas, creating a mirage-like vision, transparent and fleeting.
HOUSE, JOHN
Monet
[A1005] Phaidon pbk **£9.50**
Monet: Nature into Art
[A1006] Yale UP hbk **£24.95**
JOYES, CLAIRE
Claude Monet: Life at Giverny
The artist lived for 43 years at Giverny where he created an extravagant garden. The *Water Lilies* series was painted at this site, as were many other works of great influence. 134 illustrations, 62 colour.
[A1007] Thames & H hbk **£12.95**
KENDALL, RICHARD
Monet by Himself **NEW**
Original and exciting selection of paintings, drawings and pastels including many less familiar works, with numerous excerpts from Monet's correspondence. 200 illustrations most in colour.
[A1008] Macdonald Orbis hbk **£35.00**
REWALD & WEITZENHOFFER
Aspects of Monet
A symposium on the artist's life and times.
[A1009] Abrams hbk **£38.50**
SEITZ, WILLIAM E.
Monet
[A1010] Thames & H hbk **£25.00**
[A1011] Thames & H hbk **£12.95**
SKEGGS, DOUGLAS
Rivers of Light: Monet's Impressions of the Seine
The Seine was not only one of Monet's favourite subjects but also a 'testing ground' for his technical experiments. 147 illustrations.
[A1012] Gollancz hbk **£14.95**
STUCKEY, CHARLES F.
Water Lilies **NEW**
This publication is presented in a horizontal format admirably suited to the proportions of the paintings. Includes details of the canvases which reveal the artist's brushwork, producing breaktaking visuals. 65 superb colour illustrations, including fold-outs.
[A1013] Macmillan hbk **£45.00**
TUCKER, PAUL HAYES
Monet at Argenteuil
Monet spent six years at Argenteuil where he painted some of his most important works. The pictures are examined in the context of the town where he worked, taking into account events in the artist's life. 40 colour illustrations, 146 black and white.
[A1014] Yale UP hbk **£27.50**
[A1015] Yale UP pbk **£11.95**

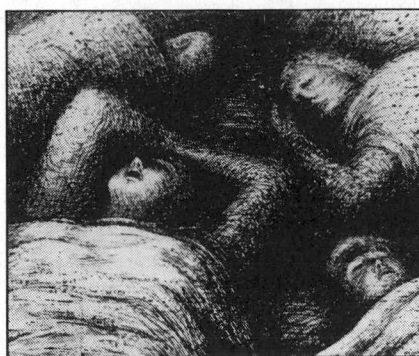
Illustration from *Henry Moore: Drawings* by Ann Garrould (Thames & Hudson hbk **£45.00**)

MOORE, HENRY (1898 - 1986)

Considered by many to be the most eminent British sculptor, Moore's large scale pieces emphasize man's relationship with nature, rejecting geometric form in favour of the organic. *"I would like my work to be thought of as a celebration of life and nature."*
Henry Moore
Catalogue of the Royal Academy Exhibition 1988.
[A1016] Weidenfeld hbk **£25.00**
[A1017] Weidenfeld pbk **£12.95**
Henry Moore
This catalogue accompanied the retrospective held at the National Gallery of Modern Art, New Delhi in 1987. 200 pieces are illustrated, 24 in colour, along with 23 photographs from Moore's life.
[A1018] British Council pbk **£25.00**
Henry Moore in India 1987/88
The 12 bronzes and 36 graphics which toured through India are illustrated in black and white. Includes 3 essays, one of which is written by a sculptor who lives and works in India.
[A1019] British Council pbk **£8.95**
Henry Moore: Etchings and Lithographs
Covering work executed between 1949 and 1984, this catalogue includes an essays by David Mitchinson (curator of the Henry Moore Foundation's collection) and 80 illustrations.
[A1020] British Council pbk **£8.95**
Moore's Sheep Sketchbook
[A1021] Thames & H hbk **£5.00**
BERTHOUD, ROGER
The Life of Henry Moore
Sources include interviews with Moore's friends, his former assistants and students, dealers, collectors, museum officials, and leading architects with whom he worked. 190 photographs.
[A1022] Faber hbk **£14.95**
BOWNESS, ALAN (ED)
Henry Moore: The Complete Works
Vol 2: 1949 - 54
[A1023] Lund Humphries hbk **£30.00**
Vol 3: 1955 - 64
[A1024] Lund Humphries hbk **£30.00**
Vol 4: 1964 - 73
[A1025] Lund Humphries hbk **£30.00**
Vol 5: 1974 - 80
[A1026] Lund Humphries hbk **£30.00**
Vol 6: 1981 - 86
[A1027] Lund Humphries hbk **£30.00**
CAREY, FRANCES (ED)
Henry Moore: A Shelter Sketchbook
This volume documents drawings executed by Moore during the Blitz in 1940, works which have subsequently influenced many of his major sculptural pieces. The sketches are accompanied by the artist's account of how they came to be made and a commentary by Frances Carey, an Assistant Keeper in the Department of Prints and Drawings at the British Museum. 67 colour reproductions.
[A1028] Brit Mus P hbk **£25.00**
GARROULD, ANN (ED)
Henry Moore: Drawings
[A1029] Thames & H hbk **£45.00**
HEDGECOE, JOHN
With Henry Moore: Artist at Work
[A1030] Sidgwick hbk **£12.95**
[A1031] Sidgwick pbk **£8.95**
HEDGECOE, JOHN & MOORE, HENRY
Henry Moore: My Ideas, Inspiration and Life as an Artist
Spanning the whole of Moore's lifetime from his childhood in Yorkshire mining villages to his student days, travel abroad and most recent practice, this monograph includes black and white photographs of the many places and subjects that have influenced the artist. 50 illustrations.
[A1032] Ebury P hbk **£12.95**

SPENDER, STEPHEN
In Irina's Garden: With Henry Moore's Sculpture
[A1033] Thames & H hbk **£12.50**
[A1034] Thames & H pbk **£8.50**

MORISOT, BERTHE (1841 - 1895)

Great-granddaughter of Fragonard, Morisot was the first woman to join the Impressionists.
Berthe Morisot and Joan Mitchell
[A1037] Hudson Hills P hbk **£35.00**
ADLER, KATHLEEN & GARB, TAMAR (EDS)
Berthe Morisot
[A1038] Phaidon hbk **£19.95**
Berthe Morisot: Correspondence
[A1039] Camden P pbk **£6.95**
REY, JEAN DOMINIQUE
Berthe Morisot
[A1040] Bonfini pbk **£7.50**

MOTHERWELL, ROBERT (1915 -)

Founder of the New York School and one of the orginators of Abstract Expressionism in the 1940s, this Amercian painter and critic creates large-scale canvases dominated by forceful, clearly defined symbols. His series, *Elegies to the Spanish Republic* is perhaps best known, incoporating massive forms painted in flat black.
Robert Motherwell: The Formative Years
[A1041] UMI Research Press hbk **£38.50**
ARNASON, H.H.
Robert Motherwell
[A1042] Abrams hbk **£55.00**
ASHTON, DORE & FLAM, JACK
Robert Motherwell
[A1043] Abbeville hbk **£25.00**
[A1044] Abbeville pbk **£16.95**
GLENN, CONSTANCE AND JACK
The Dedalus Sketchbooks
Motherwell's bold gestures are pared down to elegant lines in the drawings that take as their inspiration the work of James Joyce. Most of the drawings are lyrical sketches which further develop Motherwell's visual themes, but others are acute portraits of Joycean characters: Leopold and Molly Bloom and Stephen Dedalus himself. The images originally filled two notebooks which were dismantled and are now reproduced here for the first time in their entirety. A deluxe edition is available, limited to 105 copies, signed and numbered by the artist (£225.00).
[A1045] Abrams pbk **£18.50**
TERENZIO, STEPHANIE & BELKNAP, DOROTHY
The Prints of Robert Motherwell
[A1046] Phaidon hbk **£45.00**

MUNCH, EDVARD (1863 - 1944)

"One evening I was walking along a path...I stopped and looked out over the fjord - the sun was setting and the clouds turning blood red. I sensed a scream passing through nature...I painted this picture, painted the clouds as actual blood. The colour shrieked. This became 'The Scream'." (Munch,1889).
BISCHOFF, VLRICH
Edvard Munch **NEW**
Translated from German. This extremely informative introductory catalogue includes close to 90 large colour reproductions.
[A1047] Taschen pbk **£4.99**
HELLER, REINHOLD
Munch: His Life and Work
[A1048] J Murray hbk **£25.00**
HODIN, J.P.
Edvard Munch
[A1049] Thames & H pbk **£5.95**
MESSER, THOMAS M.
Munch
[A1050] Thames & H hbk **£12.95**

STANG, RAGNA
Edvard Munch
[A1051] Gordon Fraser hbk **£35.00**

TORJUSEN, BENTE
**Words and Images of Edvard
Munch** NEW
Through a unique interplay of poetic texts and
images, this book exposes Munch's tortured inner
vision and draws the reader into a personal encounter
with one of the leading expressionist painters. Munch
built up an autobiographical 'frieze of life' based on
his own writings and illustrations which records his
many painful transformations. Includes 55
illustrations (34 in colour) and 25 hand-lettered texts.
[A1052] Thames & H pbk **£12.95**

NAIVE ART

Naive or Primitive art developed outside the main
artistic currents of the Western tradition, placing
importance on high craft and on recording in minute
detail the everyday environment. Artists practising
this approach to painting rarely completed a formal
course of study. See *Rousseau*.
**Primitivism in 20th Century Art
Volumes I and II**
The introductory essay sketches the history of
Western attitudes to Primitivism and is followed by
chapters by specialists on African, Oceanic, American
Indian and Eskimo art. Over 1,000 illustrations.
[A1053] NY Graph Soc pbk **£27.50**

AYRES, JAMES
English Naïve Painting 1750 - 1900
Exciting and distinct images by artists who did not
follow the dominant movements of their time.
[A1054] Thames & H pbk **£6.95**

RUMFORD, BEATRIX & WEEKLEY, CAROLYN
Treasures of American Folk Art NEW
This catalogue documents all aspects of
American folk art including trade signs, quilts, toys,
paintings and sculptures.
[A1055] NY Graph Soc hbk **£20.00**

TOMASEVIC, NEBOJSA & MERIN, B.
World Encyclopedia of Naïve Art
Well-illustrated book on some 800 artists working in
the untrained style described as 'modern primitives'.
[A1056] Bracken Bks hbk **£21.95**

NASH, PAUL (1889 - 1946)
British painter, illustrator and designer whose work
moved across a whole range of styles.

CAUSEY, ANDREW
Paul Nash
[A1057] Oxford hbk **£55.00**

KING, JAMES
**Interior Landscapes: A Biography of
Paul Nash**
[A1058] Weidenfeld hbk **£16.95**

NAUMAN, BRUCE (1941 -)
American experimental artist most recognised for
paintings incorporating neon tubing.
Bruce Nauman Drawings 1965 - 1986
[A1059] Art Data hbk **£20.00**
Bruce Nauman Neons
[A1060] Art Data hbk **£17.50**

BRUGGEN, COOSJE VAN
Bruce Nauman NEW
A very thorough monograph with extensive text
which presents a detailed overview of Nauman's
career from 1965-1988. It includes early work in
fiberglass, wax, felt and rubber executed while a
graduate student, more recent sculptures in neon and
details of Nauman's films and videos. Over 100
illustrations in colour and black and white.
[A1061] Rizzoli hbk **£50.00**

NEVELSON, LOUISE (1899 -)
In 1944, the American artist Nevelson exhibited the
abstract wood reliefs that became her hallmark.

Painted in solid colours of black, white or gold
the huge constructions resemble collages of
geometrically shaped wooden 'cut-outs' mounted on
backdrops.
Nevelson's World
Presented in an extremely large format with a black
and gold embossed cover, this monograph is
beautifully put together. It includes biographical
notes, Nevelson's early work, the wood constructions,
transparent and metal sculptures, all accompanied by
excerpts from the artist's writings. Over 100
illustrations including installation and studio shots.
Published by the Whitney Museum of Art.
[A1062] Phaidon hbk **£50.00**
Skygates and Collages
[A1063] Art Data pbk **£9.50**

NOLDE, EMIL (1867 - 1956)
German expressionist painter.
Emil Nolde
[A1064] America UP hbk **£24.65**
[A1065] America UP pbk **£12.20**
**Emil Nolde and German Expressionism:
A Prophet in His Own Land**
[A1066] UMI Research P hbk **£38.50**
[A1067] UMI Research P pbk **£15.00**

URBAN, EMILE
**Emil Nolde: A Catalogue Raisoné of Oil
Paintings Vol 1: 1895 - 1914**
[A1068] Sothebys hbk **£97.50**

NUDE, THE
*"To me Art's subject is the human clay,/And
landscape but a background to a torso;/All Cézanne's
apples I would give away/For one small Goya or a
Daumier"* (W.H. Auden).
Veruschka: Trans-figurations NEW
This unique photographic album documents the
multiple transformations of Vera Lehndorff who
achieved international fame when she appeared in
Antonioni's film *Blow Up* in the 1960s. Adopting the
name of the film character, Veruschka experimented
with using her own body as a canvas, mimicking
other forms and foreshadowing the work of Cindy
Sherman. This disturbing yet provocative work is
reproduced in full colour and introduced by Susan
Sontag, a most respected and admired contemporary
critic.
[A1069] Thames & H pbk **£10.95**

HOBHOUSE, JANET
The Bride Stripped Bare NEW
Discusses the artists' relationship to the nude
in the 20th century. 250 illustrations, most in
colour.
[A1070] Cape hbk **£25.00**

LUCIE-SMITH, EDWARD
Life Class 1820 - 1920 NEW
This catalogue, introduced by Edward Lucie-Smith,
traces studies of the male nude. Colour and black and
white reproductions include work by Etty, Speed and
Millais.
[A1071] GMP pbk **£14.95**

SAUNDERS, GILL
The Nude: A New Perspective NEW
Published to coincide with an exhibition at the
Victoria and Albert Museum of the same title, this
book attempts to examine the history of the nude in
art from the perspective of the Eighties.
[A1072] Herbert Press hbk **£14.95**
[A1073] Herbert Press pbk **£10.95**

O'KEEFFE, GEORGIA (1887 - 1986)
American painter who reacted against the avant-garde
in the 1920s and loosely falls into the school of
'magical realism'. She lived in New Mexico for a
long period of time and was greatly influenced by the
landscape.
Georgia O'Keeffe
[A1074] Penguin pbk **£17.95**

CALLOWAY, NICHOLAS
Georgia O'Keeffe: One Hundred Flowers
Reproduces many works previously unpublished. 100
colour illustrations reproduced, in a large format.
[A1075] Phaidon hbk **£70.00**

CASTRO, JANE GARDEN
Art and Life of Georgia O'Keeffe
[A1076] Virago hbk **£27.50**

HOFFMAN
Art of Georgia O'Keeffe: Enduring Spirit
[A1077] Scarecrow Press hbk **£32.00**

LISLE, LAURA
**Portrait of an Artist: A Biography of
Georgia O'Keeffe**
[A1078] Heinemann hbk **£15.00**

MESSINGER, LAURA MINTZ
Georgia O'Keeffe
[A1079] Thames & H pbk **£12.95**

WEBB & TODD
**Georgia O'Keeffe: The Artist's
Landscape**
[A1080] Twelve Trees hbk **£40.00**

OLDENBURG, CLAES (1929 -)
American experimental artist. Oldenburg's first
preoccupation was with drawing which prefigures his
sculpture. *The Street* is a continuing theme, recurring
repeatedly in Oldenburg's graphic and installation-
based work and best exemplified in *Drainpipe*, a soft
sculpture executed in fabric, which hangs in the Tate
Gallery, London.

CELANT, GERMANO
**A Bottle of Notes and Some
Voyages** NEW
This book documents a recent installation conceived
by Oldenburg and his wife, Coosje van Bruggen, and
constructed at the Northern Centre for Contemporary
Art. It includes essays by the two artists and
additional notes by Celant and by Gehard Storck.
[A1081] NCCA pbk **£15.00**

PAOLOZZI, EDUARDO (1924 -)
Born in Edinburgh of Italian parents, Paolozzi
specializes in large abstract sculpture executed in
stone and bronze. In recent years the human figure
and the head have assumed considerable importance
in his work. An example of his versatility can be seen
in the tile mosaics which now decorate Tottenham
Court Road underground station in London.
Eduardo Paolozzi: Lost Magic Kingdoms
[A1082] Brit Mus P pbk **£8.50**
Eduardo Paolozzi: Underground Design
[A1083] Architectural Assoc hbk **£45.00**

GIBSON, ROBIN
Paolozzi Portraits NEW
This highly illustrated and annotated catalogue
contains a new essay on the theme of portraiture and
self-portraiture in Paolozzi's work by Gibosn who is
an authority on the artist and one of his close friends.
65 illustrations, 17 in colour.
[A1084] Nat Portrait Gal pbk **£5.95**

ROBINSON, MARLEE
Private Visions, Public Art
[A1085] Architectural Assoc pbk **£4.50**

WHITFORD, FRANK
Eduardo Paolozzi
Subtitled 'Sculptures from a Garden', this volume
documents work shown at the Serpentine Gallery in
1987.
[A1086] Serpentine Gal pbk **£8.00**

PICASSO, PABLO (1881 - 1973)
Picasso and Marcel Duchamp are considered to be the
two leading influences on the development of
contemporary art, Picasso's work representing the
emotive and the gestural, Duchamp's the conceptual.
Caisse à Remords
Forty-five etchings by Picasso.
[A1088] Edward Totah Gall pbk **£5.00**

Late Picasso 1953 - 1973

Issued to accompany the major exhibition at the Centre Georges Pompidou, Paris and the Tate Gallery, London, this book brings into sharp focus the bolder and more colourful paintings. With essays by Michael Leiris, Brigitte Bear et al.
[A1089] Tate Gall pbk **£17.95**

Late Picasso Paintings, Sculpture and Drawings

[A1090] Tate Gall hbk **£25.00**
[A1091] Tate Gall pbk **£17.95**

Pablo Picasso: A Retrospective

[A1092] MOMA hbk **£30.00**

Picasso's Linoleum Cuts

Prepared by MOMA, New York, this book documents the prints held in the Mr and Mrs Charles Kramer Collection. It commences with an essay by Philippe Montebello and then proceeds chronologically. 147 colour reproductions of the lino-cuts, 10 colour reproductions of his ceramic plaques.
[A1093] Random Ho hbk **£25.00**

Picasso's Vollard Suite

'The Vollard Suite is a majestic sequence combining a restless formal inventiveness within the limits of a completely open 'classical line'.' (*The Times*). 100 illustrations with an introduction by Hans Bolliger.
[A1094] Thames & H pbk **£4.95**

Picasso: Complete Paintings - Blue and Rose Period

[A1095] Penguin pbk **£7.95**

Picassos in Barcelona

[A1096] Alpine Fine Art hbk **£29.95**

The Musee Picasso, Paris Volume I

With six illustrations to the page, this set is not presented in the standard art book format, which normally offers a very few large scale full colour reproductions. The two volumes serve as invaluable *reference* books, documenting an extremely large number of works by the artist in all mediums. Volume I covers: paintings, papiers-colles, picture reliefs, sculptures and ceramics, with 871 illustrations, 58 in colour.
[A1097] Thames & H hbk **£35.00**

The Musee Picasso, Paris Volume II

Covers: drawings, watercolours, gouaches and pastels, 871 illustrations, 58 colour.
[A1098] Thames & H hbk **£35.00**

BOECK, WILHELM

Picasso: Linoleum Cuts

Subtitled 'Bacchanals, Women, Bulls and Bullfighters', this volume concentrates on the colourfully patterned prints executed in a medium used by Picasso for the first time at the age of 78. The short introtory text is by one of the leading authorities on Picasso. 45 full colour reproductions.
[A1099] Abrams hbk **£56.00**

BOUDAILLE, GEORGES

The Drawings of Picasso   NEW

In this collection of over 100 drawings executed in pencil, crayon, chalk and ink, the author has highlighted those most significant to Picasso's development. Chapters are arranged chronologically and the book concludes with sections examing specific subject matters: *The Smokers*, *The Muskateers*, *Eros Eternal*.
[A1100] Hamlyn hbk **£15.00**

CHIPP, HERSCHEL B.

Picasso's Guernica   NEW

'Far and away the most accurate, exhaustive and lucid account of Guernica', according to John Richardson, this rich documentary explores the history behind Picasso's large scale work, charting its many transformations and their complex meanings. 456 illustrations, 56 in colour, accompany this text-based work.
[A1101] Thames & H hbk **£28.00**

COOPER, DOUGLAS

Picasso Theatre

[A1102] Abrams hbk **£55.00**

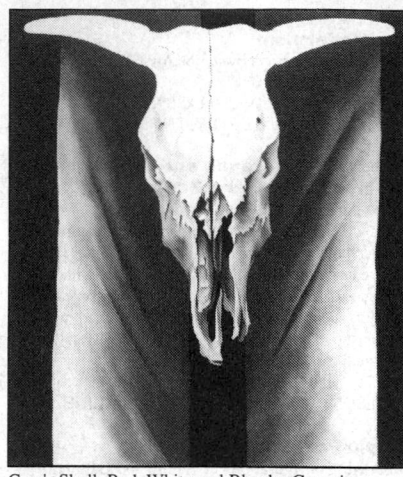

Cow's Skull: Red, White and Blue by Georgia O'Keeffe from *Georgia O'Keeffe* by Laura Mintz Messinger (Thames & Hudson pbk **£12.95**)

DAIX, PIERRE & QUINN, EDWARD

The Private Picasso

This photographic album documents the artist's life through intimate views of Picasso at work and with family and friends, complemented by colour reproductions of specific pieces. Short on text: the biographical history is pictorially-based. Daix and Quinn are both close friends of the artist. 384 large scale photographs, 90 colour.
[A1103] NY Graph Soc hbk **£35.00**

DAIX, PIERRE ET AL

Picasso: The Cubist Years 1907 - 1916

[A1104] Thames & H hbk **£65.00**

FAIRWEATHER, SALLY

Picasso's Concrete Sculptures

A study of the collaboration with Carl Nesjar. 104 illustrations, 6 in colour.
[A1105] Hudson Hills P hbk **£25.00**

FISCH, EBERHARD

Guernica   NEW

Fish re-examines the historical and philosophical context of this great work.
[A1106] Associated UP hbk **£18.00**

HOFFELD (ED)

The Late Drawings   NEW

Reproduces for the first time graphic works in pen, pencil, crayon, pastel and watercolour executed in the years between 1960 and 1973 when Picasso returned to his early influences. These small scale drawings center on his obsessive concern with themes of love and death. The text relates the drawings to the works in other mediums. 31 illustrations, 23 in colour.
[A1107] Abrams hbk **£18.50**

JAFFE, HANS LUDWIG

Picasso

Includes an extensive biographical outline, texts on drawings and prints and detailed commentaries on all works reproduced. 133 illustrations, 48 in colour.
[A1108] Thames & H hbk **£25.00**

LEAL, BRIGETTE (ED)

Demoiselles d'Avignon Sketchbook

The sketchbook reproduced here represents the most complete set of preparatory studies for all the characters appearing in the final work as well as the four figures that were eventually dropped. Brief introduction by Brigette Leal, with 102 colour illustrations.
[A1109] Thames & H hbk **£32.50**

O'BRIAN, PATRICK

Picasso   NEW

This volume was described by Kenneth Clarke as 'the best biography of Picasso'.
[A1110] Collins pbk **£9.95**

PALAU, JOSEP I. FABRE

Picasso 1881 - 1907

[A1111] Academy Eds hbk **£9.95**

RAMIE, GEORGES

The Ceramics of Picasso

Georges Ramie, himself an expert potter, has collaborated with Picasso on this documentation of the various but distinct phases in the artist's work. The volume is broken down into chapters: 'Challenge of the New Material', 'Mastery of the Technique', 'Research and Experiments', amongst others. 223 colour illustrations.
[A1112] Edicones Polligrafa hbk **£15.00**

RODRIGUEZ-AGUILERA, CESAREO

Picassos in Barcelona   NEW

This extremely comprehensive volume documents artpieces held in public and private collections in Barcelona, cataloguing all works by suject matter or medium. 128 colour illustrations, 1,000 black and white.
[A1113] Alpine Fine Art hbk **£25.00**

RUBIN & BOZO

Picasso: A Retrospective

[A1114] Thames & H hbk **£25.00**
[A1115] Thames & H pbk **£14.95**

PIERO DELLA FRANCESCA (c1410 - 1492)

Piero's rigorous mathematical precision and translucent colour place him at the fore of the Quattrocento painters. Much respected by Cézanne and the Cubists.

Piero della Francesca: Complete Paintings

[A1116] Penguin pbk **£7.95**

GINZBURG, CARLO

The Enigma of Piero

[A1117] Verso hbk **£7.95**

PISSARRO, CAMILLE (1831 - 1903)

French impressionist painter. *"We must approach nature with sincerity, using our modern sensibilities."*

Camille Pissaro

Produced in celebration of the 150th anniversary of the birth of Camille Pissaro, this publication includes 'Camille Pissaro: A Revision' by Richard Brettell, 'Looking at Pissaro' by Francois Cachin and an extensive chronology.
[A1118] South Bank hbk **£10.00**

LLOYD, C.H.

Studies on Camille Pissarro

[A1119] Routledge pbk **£19.95**

REWALD, JOHN

Pissarro

[A1120] Thames & H hbk **£25.00**

SHIKES & HARPER

Pissarro: His Life and Work

[A1121] Quartet hbk **£19.50**

THOMSON, RICHARD

Camille Pissarro: The Impressionist at Work   NEW

Themes covered include previously unexplored aspects of the artist's work, including his interpretation of the nude, his purely decorative projects and the interplay between his preparatory work and the finished paintings.
[A1122] Herbert Press hbk **£13.95**

POLLOCK, JACKSON (1912 - 1956)

With Pollock, American painting finally broke away from European influence and assumed a leading role in the international forum. *"Most of the paint I use is liquid, flowing...the brushes are used more as sticks and do not touch the surface...I am able to be more free and move about with greater ease. I deny the accident. I have a general notion of what I'm about and what the results will be."* (J. Pollock 1956).

Jackson Pollock's Visual Dynamics in Abstractions

Pollock's *action paintings* (paint dripped and poured)

pushed abstraction into new directions. This volume includes an extensive introductory essay with statements by the artist and excerpts from Michael Fried's analysis of Pollock's paintings. 70 illustrations, black and white and colour
[A1123] UMI Research Press hbk **£34.50**
ROSE, BERNICE
Jackson Pollock: Drawing into Painting
[A1124] Thames & H pbk **£11.75**

POP ART
Pop Art surfaced in New York in the late 1950s as a reaction to the predominance of European culture. Pop artists appropriated American signs and symbols from the everyday environment and re-constructed their meaning by placing them in a fine art context. Andy Warhol's silkscreen prints of coco-cola bottles exemplify the focus on both cultural simulacrum and mass production. See *Richard Hamilton*, *Jasper Johns*, *Robert Rauschenburg* and *Andy Warhol*.
FRITH & HORNE (EDS)
Art into Pop
Explores the links between Pop Art and pop music.
[A1125] Methuen pbk **£6.95**
LIPPARD, LUCY
Pop Art
Decisive illustrated history by the well-known American critic.
[A1126] Thames & H pbk **£5.95**
WALLIS, BRIAN ET AL (ED)
Modern Dreams: The Rise and Fall of Pop NEW
Modern Dreams compares and contrasts the theoretical and sociological distinction between art production in London in the 50s and New York in the 80s. 170 illustrations, 16 in colour.
[A1127] MIT pbk **£15.95**

POST IMPRESSIONISM
"A widespread plot to destroy the whole fabric of European painting." (Review of the first London Post-Impressionist exhibition, *Morning Chronicle* 1910)
Post-Impressionism: Cross-Currents in European Painting
Catalogue from the massive and distinguished 1979 exhibition at the Royal Academy which includes some very good essays.
[A1128] Weidenfeld hbk **£16.50**
BRETTELL, RICHARD R.
Post-Impressionists in the Art Institute of Chicago
Excellent reproductions.
[A1129] Abrams hbk **£21.50**
[A1130] Abrams pbk **£13.50**
REWALD, JOHN
Post-Impressionism
A classic bestselling survey from Van Gogh to Gaugin.
[A1131] Secker hbk **£40.00**
Studies in Post-Impressionism
A selection of essays from one of the foremost critics of the period
[A1132] Thames & H hbk **£25.00**

POST MODERNISM
Post modernism defies definition which is consistent with the deconstructed and fragmented vision it represents. J.F. Lyotard, one of its key theorists, describes one aspect: *"A post modern artist or writer is in the position of a philosopher: the text he writes, the work he produces are not in principle governed by pre-established rules and they cannot be judged according to a determining judgement...Those rules and categories are what the work of art itself is looking for."* See *Cragg*, *Clemente*, *Holzer*, *Kabakov* Additional titles appear in *Theory and Criticism*.

APPIGNANESI, LISA (ED)
Postmodernism
A collection of essays by major American and European critics.
[A1133] ICA/Free Assoc pbk **£9.95**
BOIS, YVE-ALAIN; CROW, THOMAS, FOSTER, HAL ET AL.
Endgame: Reference and Simulation in Recent Painting and Sculpture
An exciting publication presenting two groups of artists who have recently emerged amidst rigorous critical debate. Painters Ross Bleckner, Peter Halley, Sherrie Levine and Philip Taffe who appropriate the strategies of earlier modern artists are compared with sculptors General Idea, Jeff Koons and others who use consumer items and other found objects in their constructions.
[A1134] MIT Press hbk **£11.75**
JAMESON, FREDERIC & JARDINE, ALICE, ET AL.
Utopia Post Utopia NEW
Subtitled 'Configurations of Nature and Culture in Recent Sculpture and Photography', the publication takes a close look at the nature/culture dichotomy seen from the perspective of post modernism. It documents two prominent exhibitions: a sculptural installation including works by Robert Gober, Meg Webster and Richard Prince and a photographic installation by James Welling, Oliver Wasow, Dorit Cypis, Lorna Simpson, Jeff Wall and Larry Johnson.
[A1135] MIT hbk **£11.75**
KRENS, THOMAS; GOVAN, MICHAEL & THOMPSON, JOSEPH
Refigured Painting: The German Image 1960 - 88 NEW
A complex and diverse school of painting rose to the fore of the international scene in the late 1970s. Loosely termed *The New Spirit*, the artists placed in this group integrate both figurative and abstract styles in order to explore their historical relationship with the modernist and post modernist traditions. The list of artists included in this book is an impressive one: highlights include Georg Baselitz, Jiri Georg Dokoupil, Jorg Immendorf, Markus Lupertz, Sigmar Polke, Gerhard Richter and Rosemarie Trockel.
[A1136] Prestel hbk **£31.50**

POUSSIN, NICOLAS (1594 - 1665)
French allegorical painter. *"The grandest system of light and shadow in the collection at the Louvre."* (J.M.W. Turner on Poussin's *The Israelites Gather Manna*).
Poussin: The Early Years
Explores the origins of French classicism.
[A1137] Phaidon hbk **£45.00**
PACE, CLAIRE
Felibien's Life of Poussin
[A1138] Zwemmer pbk **£15.00**

PRE-RAPHAELITES
This short-lived association of English painters included *William Holman-Hunt*, *Millais* and *Rossetti*. The group collectively expressed dissatisfaction with the grandiloquent forms and sentiments found in Raphael's paintings and were drawn instead to the works by his predecessors, the Florentine and the Sienese primitives. The eminent Victorian critic, John Ruskin, backed the movement.
BENNET, MARY
The Artists of the Pre-Raphaelite Circle
[A1139] Lund Humph pbk **£18.50**
FAXON, ALICIA CRAIG
Dante Gabriel Rossetti NEW
The myths that surround the artist have masked his real contribution to British art. Dr Faxon brings the art, not the man, back into focus. 277 illustrations, 147 in colour.
[A1140] Phaidon hbk **£65.00**

HILTON, TIMOTHY
Pre-Raphaelites
[A1141] Thames & H pbk **£5.95**
LUTYENS, MARY
Millais and the Ruskins
An interesting biography.
[A1142] J Murray hbk **£13.95**
MARSH, JAN & GERRISH NUNN, PAMELA
Women Artists and the Pre-Raphaelite Movement NEW
The authors examine the movement from the female artists' perspective, presenting many of their pictures for the first time.
[A1143] Random Ho hbk **£15.95**
POINTON, MARCIA
Pre-Raphelites Reviewed NEW
Compilation of new thoughts on the ways in which the Pre-Raphaelites approached philosophical, political and social issues.
[A1144] Manchester UP pbk **£7.95**
ROSE, ANDREA
The Pre-Raphaelites
[A1145] Phaidon pbk **£9.50**
WHITELY, JON
Pre-Raphaelite Paintings and Drawings NEW
New addition to the Ashmolean-Christie's handbooks series, which emphasises the drawings. 35 colour illustrations.
[A1146] Phaidon hbk **£8.95**
WOOD, CHRISTOPHER
The Pre-Raphaelites
From the 1981 Royal Acadamy exhibition. The best illustrated book available.
[A1147] Weidenfeld pbk **£12.95**

RAPHAEL (RAFFAELLO SANZIO)
(1483 - 1520)
Raphael's classicism comprise some of the most serene and perfectly conceived works of the High Renaissance.
Drawings by Raphael
Exhibition catalogue, 1983.
[A1148] Brit Mus P pbk **£8.95**
Raphael: Complete Paintings
[A1149] Penguin pbk **£7.95**
AMES-LEWIS, FRANCIS
The Draughtsman Raphael
An invigorating study of Raphael's exquisite cartoons. 154 black and white illustrations, 31 colour.
[A1150] Yale UP hbk **£30.00**
BECK, JAMES A.
Raphael
[A1151] Thames & H hbk **£25.00**
CUZIN, JEAN PIERRE
Raphael NEW
With over 230 illustrations, this new monograph provides a very comprehensive study of Raphael's entire *oeuvre*.
[A1152] Montreaux Fine Art hbk **£22.50**
ETTLINGER, LEOPOLD & HELEN
Raphael
All aspects of the artist's life are examined including his tapestry designs, engravings and architecture. 206 illustrations, 41 colour.
[A1153] Phaidon hbk **£45.00**
JOANNIDES, PAUL
The Drawings of Raphael
The first full catalogue of the drawings. 690 illustrations, 8 colour plates.
[A1154] Phaidon hbk **£65.00**
JONES, ROGER & PENNY, NICHOLAS
Raphael
[A1155] Yale UP hbk **£35.00**
[A1156] Yale UP pbk **£12.95**
THOMPSON, DAVID
Raphael: The Life and the Legacy
[A1157] BBC hbk **£19.95**

RAUSCHENBURG, ROBERT (1925 -)

This American artist marked the transition between Abstract Expressionism of the 1950s and the new pop imagery. His canvases ignore the boundaries traditionally placed between art mediums and are termed 'combine paintings' because of the complex nature of the collage elements. An extremely influential 20th century figure.

Robert Rauschenburg: Photographs
[A1158] Thames & H hbk **£14.95**

REMBRANDT, HARMENSZ VAN RIJN (1606 - 1669)

Dutch painter. *"Rembrandt thought it more important to paint light than the objects that are seen by it."* (Sir Joshua Reynolds, *Discourses*).

Harmensz van Rijn Rembrandt
Paintings from Soviet museums. Translated from Russian by V. Pozner.
[A1159] Aurora hbk **£30.00**

Rembrandt and His Critics 1630 - 1730
[A1160] Hacker Fine Art hbk **£32.50**
ALPERS, SVETLANA

Rembrandt's Enterprise: The Studio and the Market
[A1161] Thames & H hbk **£20.00**
BOMBERG, DAVID; BROWN, CHRISTOPHER & ROY, ASHOK

Art in the Making **NEW**
Catalogue issued to accompany an intriguing exhibition at the National Gallery. The insights into Rembrandt's painting techniques are drawn from new technological processes employed by art historians.
[A1162] Tate Gall hbk **£9.95**
BOON, K.G.

Rembrandt: Complete Etchings
[A1163] Thames & H hbk **£15.00**
CASTER, SUSAN P. & PARKINSON, R. (EDS)

Richard Redgrave
[A1164] Yale UP hbk **£35.00**
CLARK, KENNETH

An Introduction to Rembrandt
[A1165] J Murray hbk **£10.95**
GILTAIJI, JEROEN

The Drawings of Rembrandt and His School **NEW**
A detailed examination of works from the Museum Boymans van Beuningen, Rotterdam.
[A1166] Thames & H hbk **£29.00**
HAAK, BOB

Rembrandt: Drawings
[A1167] Thames & H pbk **£4.95**
MUNZ, LUDWIG

Rembrandt
[A1168] Thames & H hbk **£25.00**
[A1169] Thames & H pbk **£12.95**
SCHWARTZ G.

Rembrandt: His Life, His Paintings
[A1170] Viking hbk **£25.00**
VELS HEIJN, ANNEMARIE

Rembrandt **NEW**
The first in a new series on great artists, this volume coincides with the National Gallery's exhibition and catalogue entitled 'Art in the Making' and makes available the recent findings of the Rembrandt Research Project in Amsterdam.
[A1171] Scala Books hbk **£12.50**
WHITE, CHRISTOPHER

Rembrandt
[A1172] Thames & H pbk **£5.95**
WRIGHT, CHRISTOPHER

Rembrandt: Self Portraits
[A1173] Weidenfeld hbk **£40.00**

RENOIR, PIERRE AUGUSTE (1841 - 1919)

Impressionist master famous for his vibrant paintings of public life. *"All true works of art have been conceived and carried out according to the principle of irregularity."* (Renoir, 1884).

Illustration from *The Drawings of Rembrandt and his School* by Jeroen Giltaiji (Thames & Hudson hbk **£29.00**)

Renoir: His Life, Art and Letters
[A1174] Abrams pbk **£22.50**
RENOIR, JEAN

Renoir: My Father
[A1175] Columbus pbk **£5.95**
DAULTE, FRANCOIS

Renoir
[A1176] Cassell pbk **£12.95**
GAUNT, WILLIAM

Renoir
[A1177] Phaidon hbk **£10.50**
HOUSE, JOHN & GOWING, SIR LAWRENCE ET AL

Renoir
[A1178] Abrams hbk **£26.95**
PACH, WALTER

Renoir
[A1179] Thames & H hbk **£25.00**
[A1180] Thames & H pbk **£12.95**
WHITE, BARBARA EHRLICH (ED)

Renoir: His Life, Art and Letters
[A1181] Abrams hbk **£60.50**

RIVERA, DIEGO (1886 - 1957)

Pioneer of the modern Mexican Muralist School who deliberately sacrificed his desire to experiment in order to develop an art suited to the political situation in post-revolutionary Mexico.

Diego Rivera: A Retrospective
[A1182] Norton hbk **£45.00**
ROCHFORT

Murals of Diego Rivera
[A1183] Journeymen P pbk **£7.95**

ROBBIA, LUCA DELLA (1400 - 1482)

Florentine Renaissance sculptor and ceramicist.
POPE-HENNESSY, JOHN

Luca della Robbia
Presents a detailed examination of the life and sylistic development of the artist. Winner of the Mitchell Prize for the History of Art 1981, this offers 232 illustrations, 32 in colour, in slipcase.
[A1184] Phaidon hbk **£60.00**

ROCKWELL, NORMAN (1894 - 1978)

American illustrator famous for his work on the *Saturday Evening Post*.

My Adventures as an Illustrator **NEW**
This autobiography charts Rockwell's rising career as

an illustrator, his relationship with his colleagues and models, and includes over 120 examples of his work.
[A1185] Abrams hbk **£29.50**

Norman Rockwell's America
[A1186] Abrams hbk **£17.50**

Norman Rockwell: Family Songbook
[A1187] Abrams hbk **£21.95**
BRECHNER, THOMAS S.

Norman Rockwell: Artist and Illustrator
[A1188] Abrams hbk **£35.00**

RODCHENKO (1891 - 1956)

Russian painter and designer. Rodchenko's originality is most evident in his photography which aimed at documenting and creating a visual record of the new Russia. His exploitation of perspectives and new angles greatly influenced significant Russian filmmakers.

Rodchenko and Stepanova **NEW**
Documents the 1989 exhibition of the work of Rodchenko and his wife.
[A1189] Serpentine pbk **£12.00**
QUILICI, VERI (ED)

Rodchenko: The Complete Work
[A1190] Thames & H hbk **£40.00**

RODIN, AUGUSTE (1840 - 1917)

The most prominent sculptor of the late 19th century, Rodin achieved fame during his own lifetime. Most recognised for his sculpture *The Thinker*, Rodin's mastery lay in his sensitive modelling combined with vigorous characterization.
CHAMPIGNEULLE, BERNARD

Rodin
[A1191] Thames & H pbk **£5.95**
ELSEN, ALBERT (ED)

Rodin Rediscovered
[A1192] NY Graph Soc hbk **£35.00**
GOLDSCHEIDER & STORY

Rodin: Sculptures
[A1193] Phaidon hbk **£15.00**
[A1194] Phaidon pbk **£7.95**
GRUNFELD, FREDERIC V.

Rodin: A Biography **NEW**
An exposé on Rodin's life counter-balanced by the new biography on fellow artist and lover, Camille Claudel.
[A1195] Hutchinson hbk **£30.00**
[A1196] Oxford pbk **£12.95**
GRUNFELD, FREDERICK V.

Rodin: Sculptures
[A1197] Hutchinson hbk **£14.95**
LAMPERT, CATHERINE

Rodin: Drawings and Watercolours
[A1198] Yale UP hbk **£30.00**
[A1199] Yale UP pbk **£14.95**
LAURENT, MONIQUE

Rodin **NEW**
Classified by the publisher as the best general introduction to Rodin, this monograph examines the sculptor's contemporaries, his reaction to them and subsequent development of an independent style, and his controversial relations with women. 108 colour and 283 black and white illustrations.
[A1200] Barrie & J pbk **£19.95**

ROTHKO, MARK (1903 - 1970)

Rothko was born in Russia and emigrated to America in 1913. His monumental paintings of profound but disturbing beauty epitomise the strength of abstraction. 'Rothko shares with composers of music an absence of explicit imagery and a correspondingly developed capacity to evoke content by association.' (Thomas Messer, Director, Guggenheim).

Mark Rothko: 1903 - 1970
[A1201] Tate Gall pbk **£7.95**
ASHTON, DORE

About Rothko
[A1202] Oxford hbk **£16.50**

CHAVE, ANNA C.
Mark Rothko: Subjects in Abstraction `NEW`
The author reassesses Rothko's form of abstraction, suggesting that the artist's images are as coded as other types of art but in a different way 'with more layered, indeterminate, shifting and unstable messages'. Chave offers a new methodology for interpreting abstract art. Text-based with 50 supporting illustrations.
[A1203] Yale UP hbk **£24.95**

CLEARWATER, BONNIE
Mark Rothko: Works on Paper `NEW`
[A1204] Phaidon hbk **£25.00**
[A1205] Phaidon pbk **£16.50**

COMPTON, MICHAEL
Mark Rothko: The Seagram Mural Project
The paintings included in the Seagram project hang in a specially created room at the Tate, London but have recently been on loan to the Tate, Liverpool. The installation in Liverpool aimed to recreate more accurately than ever before the space in the Four Seasons Restaurant, Seagrams Building, New York for which they were commissioned in 1958. Michael Compton researches Rothko's preparation for and ultimate rejection of the commission.
[A1206] Tate pbk **£7.50**

WALDMAN, DIANE
Mark Rothko
This major critical study analyses the progression of Rothko's work from the early figurative experiments of the 1920s to the achievements of his late canvases. Reproductions include photographs of the artist. 275 illustrations, 96 colour.
[A1207] Thames & H hbk **£35.00**

ROUSSEAU, HENRI (1844 - 1910)
"Rousseau has opened the way for the new possibilities for simplicity." (Wassily Kandinsky).
Art of Henri Rousseau: Portrait of a Primitive
[A1208] Omega Books hbk **£7.95**
Henri Rousseau
[A1209] Thames & H hbk **£25.00**
[A1210] Thames & H pbk **£9.95**

VALIER, DORA
Rousseau
[A1211] Clematis hbk **£7.50**

RUBENS, SIR PETER PAUL (1577 - 1640)
Major Baroque Dutch history and landscape painter.
Rubens: Old Testament Paintings `NEW`
The paintings included document Rubens' position as supporter of the Counter-Reformation. The associated drawings and engravings are also illustrated.
[A1213] Harvey Miller hbk **£62.00**

HELD, JULIUS S.
Rubens: Selected Drawings
The drawings are classified according to their relation to the artist's other work. Current research is used as source material. 255 illustrations, 8 colour.
[A1214] Phaidon hbk **£50.00**

VEREGARA, LISA
Rubens and the Poetics of Landscape
[A1215] Yale UP hbk **£44.75**

WHITE, CHRISTOPHER
Peter Paul Rubens: Man and Artist
Generously illustrated and wide-ranging, this volume explores Ruben's life from a social and historical viewpoint. 180 black and white illustrations, 157 colour.
[A1216] Yale UP hbk **£50.00**

RUSCHA, EDWARD
Contemporary American artist who emerged during the Pop Art movement in the 1960s and is characterised by his paintings of the Hollywood sign, the Standard petrol station and the 20th Century-Fox trademark. Ruscha has been described as 'the quintessential West Coast artist'. Unconventional in his approach, he has painted and drawn with gunpowder, chocolate paste and other organic substances.

CLEARWATER, KNIGHT & TRASOBARES
Edward Ruscha `NEW`
This is the catalogue of an exhibition of recent works by Ruscha held at the Lannan Museum in Florida, concentrating on the execution of his first public commission - the major rotunda mural and 45 smaller lunette murals installed in the Miami-Dade Public Library in 1985. The 126 foot mural is based on a quotation from *Hamlet* - 'Words Without Thoughts Never to Heaven Go' - and features each word on a separate panel painted over a tropical sky. A handsome book on a contemporary artist who continues to gain prominence. More than 100 illustrations, including 4 large fold-out pages.
[A1217] Abrams pbk **£18.50**

HICKEY, DAVE & PLAGENS, PETER
The Works of Edward Ruscha
Informative and detailed essays place Ruscha historically and discuss his work both from formal and conceptual perspectives. Includes the transcription of an extensive interview by Dave Hickey. Over 125 colour reproductions.
[A1218] Hudson Hills hbk **£25.00**
[A1219] Hudson Hills pbk **£16.50**

SARGENT, JOHN SINGER 1856 - 1925)
American painter and society portraitist. *"These portraits live in a way that great fictional characters exist - we want to know what happened to them next."* (Richard Dorement, *Literary Review*, 1986).
HILLS
John Singer Sargent
[A1220] Abrams hbk **£24.95**

HOOPES, DONELSON F.
Sargent: Watercolours
[A1221] Phaidon pbk **£10.50**

OLSON, STANLEY
John Singer Sargent: His Portrait
[A1222] Macmillan hbk **£16.95**

SCHIELE, EGON (1890 - 1918)
The third child of a railway official, Schiele developed into one of the major Austrian expressionist artists. He was greatly influenced by Freud and his paintings and drawings are acute psychological portraits often exhibiting a lonely eroticism.

SCHRODER & SZEEMAN
Egon Schiele and His Contemporaries
This book draws together works from the Rudolph Leopold collection focusing on painting in Vienna from 1900-1930. Schiele's influences and the effect of his work on other Austrian artists are documented by 100 works by 23 of his contemporaries. One of the authors is the Director of the Kunsthalle, Bern and a freelance curator.
[A1223] Prestel hbk **£31.50**

Egon Schiele: Eternal Child
A comparative analysis of Schiele's paintings and poems. 23 full page colour reproductions.
[A1224] Weidenfeld hbk **£14.95**

COMINI, ALESSANDRA
Schiele
This volume offers a good introduction to the artist and includes supporting notes and photographs of Schiele entitled *A Photographic Album*. 97 illustrations.
[A1225] Thames & H pbk **£9.95**

MITSCH, ERWIN
The Art of Egon Schiele `NEW`
This new monograph presents a balanced selection of Schiele's paintings and drawings arranged in chronological order. Texts explore the character and development of the artist and examine his relationships with Munch, Rodin, Klimt and other contemporaries. 80 full page reproductions, 81 black and white and 12 portrait photographs of Schiele.
[A1226] Phaidon hbk **£30.00**

NEBEHAY, CHRISTIAN
Egon Schiele Sketchbooks `NEW`
Twelve of the thirteen major sketchbooks dating from 1912-1918 are reproduced, presenting many works for the first time. 800 illustrations, 130 in colour.
[A1227] Thames & H hbk **£42.00**

WHITFORD, FRANK
Egon Schiele
[A1228] Thames & H hbk **£10.95**
[A1229] Thames & H pbk **£5.95**

SCHNABEL, JULIAN
This American artist drew the art world's attention with his large-scale paintings incorporating a surface of shattered plates which were painted over in a loose gestural style. *"I once said that style is the fringe benefit of intention. I think you do something in a certain way and out of that involvement with materials you find that different alternatives present themselves."* (Schnabel).
Julian Schnabel
[A1230] Tate Gall pbk **£2.50**
Julian Schnabel: Whitechapel Catalogue 1986
[A1231] Whitechapel Gal pbk **£10.75**

SCHWITTERS, KURT (1887 - 1948)
Schwitters was a pioneer of 'environmental art', working in a truly personal way. His paintings termed *Merz* incorporate many found objects - pieces of text ranging from bus tickets to extracts from newspapers, nails, bits of wood, string, rags etc. He extended this concept into *Merzbau* which took the form of complete environments.
Kurt Schwitters in Exile: The Late Work 1937 - 1948
Selection of essays including one by the artist's son, Ernst Schwitters. Additional reproductions include interior shots of the rooms and houses which Kurt converted into complete environments, and photographs of the artist with friends and contemporaries. 157 illustrations, most in colour.
[A1232] Marlborough pbk **£16.00**

ELDERFIELD, JOHN
Kurt Schwitters
This broad survey is divided into two sections: 'The Invention of Merz 1918-1921' and 'The Development of Merz 1922-1948'. Published as a catalogue for the retrospective held at the Tate and MOMA, New York in 1986, it includes extensive texts, 356 illustrations, 32 in colour, and won the 1986 Mitchell Prize for History of 20th Century Art.
[A1233] Thames & H hbk **£30.00**
[A1234] Thames & H pbk **£18.95**

SERRA, RICHARD (1939 -)
American sculptor. Serra's academic training was in painting, yet he exhausted its creative potential early on in his careeer, moving on to industrially produced sculptures of lead or hot rolled steel. Immense metal slab constructions, rigid in geometric precision, painterly in texture, they challenge the commercial system and the traditional art site, placing Serra in a provocatively political position that still retains its critical edge.
CRIMP, DOUGLAS
Richard Serra (1986, MOMA NY)
[A1235] Rizzoli hbk **£42.50**

KRAUSS, ROSALIND
Richard Serra: Sculpture
Edited and with an introduction by Laura Rosenstock, the texts trace Serra's passage through the gallery site to constructing sculpture for public places. Serra's films and videos are incorporated. 114 illustrations.
[A1236] MOMA hbk **£29.00**
[A1237] MOMA pbk **£16.95**

SEURAT, GEORGES (1859 - 1891)
Seurat's original interpretation of impressionist painting led to the development of the *pointilliste* technique. A highly disciplined approach to art production involved Seurat in a scientific exploration of his medium, resulting in invaluable research into colour theory.
COURTHION, PIERRE
Seurat
The reproductions represent a selection of Seurat's most important paintings produced during his short but prolific career. Numerous black and white illustrations demonstrate his extraordinary handling of charcoal and conté crayon. 84 illustrations, 40 in colour.
[A1238] Thames & H hbk **£20.00**
FRANZ, ERICH & GROWE, BERND
Georges Seurat: Drawings
[A1239] NY Graph Soc hbk **£35.00**
HOMER
Seurat and the Science of Painting
[A1240] Hacker Art Books hbk **£45.00**
RUSSELL, JOHN
Seurat
[A1241] Thames & H pbk **£4.95**
THOMSON, RICHARD
Seurat
Provides sustained analysis of Seurat's subject matter. 255 illustrations, 60 colour.
[A1242] Phaidon hbk **£45.00**

SICKERT, WALTER (1860 - 1942)
The most important artist associated with the Camden Town School, Sickert fell under the influence of Whistler and because of this is often classed as an impressionist. However his later works increasingly rely on the photograph as a source, creating a distancing and more abstracting effect.
SHONE, RICHARD
Walter Sickert
Summarizes the artist's life from his early association with the Impressionists to his later works. 101 illustrations, 40 in colour.
[A1243] Phaidon hbk **£25.00**
SHONE, RICHARD & CURTIS, PENELOPE
W.R. Sickert Drawings and Paintings 1890 - 1942
This book documents an exhibition of Sickert's painting covering early works from the end of the 19th century to paintings completed near the end of his career. The catalogue is divided into sections focusing on each of the European towns where Sickert lived.
[A1244] Tate Gall pbk **£5.95**

SMITH, DAVID (1906 - 1965)
Towards the end of his life, Smith completed the monumental work for which he is best known, bringing into sculpture the objectivity which characterised then current painting. These structures, resembling 'metal calligraphy', were as influential as the work of Caro in England, initiating a new era in American sculpture.
David Smith: Drawings of the Fifties (1988)
[A1245] Anthony d'Offay hbk **£8.00**
GRAY, CLEVE (ED)
David Smith by David Smith: Sculpture and Writing (1989)
[A1246] Thames & H pbk **£14.95**

MERKERT, JORN
David Smith: Sculpture and Drawings
An important monograph on one of America's most prominent sculptors. This volume traces Smith's development through careful examination of his drawings on paper and their translation into the three dimensional.
[A1247] Prestel hbk **£27.50**

STELLA, FRANK (1936 -)
A very prominent American artist who emerged on the international scene early in his career when he exhibited a series of black canvases in which parallel stripes echoed the edges of the painting. His more recent works abandon the frame altogether and are composed of complex sequences of overlapping geometric shapes painted in bright synthetic colours.
Frank Stella
[A1252] MOMA pbk **£11.95**
Frank Stella 1985
[A1253] ICA pbk **£16.95**
Frank Stella: Working Space
[A1254] Harvard UP hbk **£31.95**
[A1255] Harvard UP pbk **£15.95**
RUBIN, LAWRENCE
Frank Stella: Paintings 1958 - 1965
[A1256] Thames & H hbk **£26.95**
[A1257] Thames & H pbk **£13.95**

STEPANOVA, VARVARA (1894 - 1958)
Russian avant-garde artist. In addition to painting, Stepanova wrote, designed film sets, fabrics, theatre costumes, posters and book jackets. The designs themselves represent much more than an understanding of style: they reflect and merge with the major art and political movements of her time.
LAVRENTIEV, ALEXANDER
Varvara Stepanova: A Constructivist Life
Edited and introduced by John Bowlt, this volume spans the life of Stepanova and thus explores a moment of crucial importance in Russia's history. An extensive collection of photographs both of Stepanova's life and her work, many taken by Rodchenko, adds a vitality to this monograph. 342 illustrations, 72 in colour.
[A1258] Thames and H hbk **£28.00**

STUBBS, GEORGE (1724 - 1806)
"Fingering the margins, I think of the old Sway-backed and broken nags the pictures killed." (E. Lucie-Smith 'On Looking at Stubb's Anatomy of a Horse').
EGERTON, JUDY
George Stubbs 1724 - 1806
[A1262] Tate Gall hbk **£21.00**
[A1263] Tate Gall pbk **£12.95**
FOUNTAIN & GATES
Stubbs's Dogs
[A1264] Ackermann hbk **£14.95**

SURREALISM
The Surrealists focused their creative practice on freeing art from the constraints of the application of reason and aesthetic or moral preoccupation. Their primary objective was to devise an art language which allowed for a representation of the experiences that issue freely from the subconscious. Psychoanalytical and metaphysical theories informed cultural discourses resulting in a non-academic approach to the production of art. Shattered and fragmented images, startling juxtapositions and a disturbing sense of time and space describe key aspects of this pivotal art movement. See *Salvador Dali, Marcel Duchamp, Max Ernst, Paul Klee, Joan Miró, Pablo Piccasso.*

ADES, DAWN; SWEENEY, MICHAEL & BERNSTEIN, JOANNE
Surrealism in the Tate Gallery Collection
The Tate holds a strong collection of art from this period including major works by Max Ernst, de Chirico and Picasso. This catalogue includes illuminating essays by Dawn Ades and Michael Sweeny; Joanne Bernstein has compiled the notes on the works.
[A1265] Tate Gall pbk **£4.95**
ALEXANDRIAN, SARANE
Surrealist Art
[A1266] Thames & H pbk **£4.95**
CHADWICK, LYNN
In the Mind's Eye
[A1267] Abbeville hbk **£29.95**
Women Artists and the Surrealist Movement
The author examines the work of the women who exhibited in the international exhibitions of the 1930s and 1940s. 220 illustrations, 20 colour.
[A1268] Thames & H pbk **£16.50**
RICHTER, HANS
Dada
[A1269] Thames & H pbk **£4.95**
RUBIN, WILLIAM
Dada, Surrealism and their Heritage
[A1270] Thames & H pbk **£10.50**
WALDBERG, PATRICK
Surrealism
[A1271] Thames & H pbk **£4.95**
WILSON, SIMON
Surrealist Painting
[A1272] Phaidon hbk **£10.50**

SUTHERLAND, GRAHAM (1903 - 1980)
"It was in this country (Pembrokeshire) that I began to learn painting...I wish I could give you some idea of the exultant strangeness of this place." (Sutherland, 1934).
ALLEY, RONALD
Graham Sutherland
[A1273] Tate Gall pbk **£7.95**
BERTHOUD, ROGER
Graham Sutherland: A Biography
[A1274] Faber hbk **£15.00**
THUILLER
Graham Sutherland: Inspirations
[A1275] Lutter P hbk **£19.50**

TATLIN, VLADIMIR (1885 - 1953)
Tatlin's mounument to the Third International shown at the 1925 Paris World Exhibition has become the symbol of the Russian avant-garde. His many and varied creations move across a wide range of mediums including painting, theatre design, book illustration and writing.
MILNER, JOHN
Vladimir Tatlin and the Russian Avant Garde
[A1276] Yale UP hbk **£35.00**
[A1277] Yale UP pbk **£12.95**
ZHADOVA, ALEKSEEVNA
Tatlin
This impressive work of scholarship defines the full extent of Tatlin's artistic achievements and includes manifestos, letters and writings together with contemporary articles of all kinds, providing a valuable documentary reference. 426 illustrations, 76 colour.
[A1278] Thames & H hbk **£40.00**

TIEPOLO, GIAMBATTISTA (1696 - 1770)
Italian rococo painter. *"Tiepolo is the ideal artistic athlete. No stadium was too big or daunting for him to perform in."* (Michael Levey, *Observer*, 1986).

BARCHAM, WILLIAM
The Religious Paintings of Giambattista Tiepolo `NEW`
Subtitled 'Piety and Tradition in 18th Century Venice', this volume takes an academic look at specific works. 140 illustrations.
[A1279] Oxford hbk **£60.00**
LEVEY, MICHAEL
Giambattista Tiepolo: His Life and Art
A recent publication by the former Director of the National Gallery, London.
[A1280] Yale UP hbk **£55.00**

TINTORETTO, JACOPO (1818 - 1894)
Venetian painter, pupil of Titian.
PIGNATTI, TERISIO & VALCANOVER, FRANCESCO
Tintoretto
[A1281] Thames & H hbk **£25.00**

TISSOT, JAMES (1836 - 1902)
French painter who worked in England.
MATYJASZKIEWICZ, K. (ED)
James Tissot
Catalogue of the major exhibition held in London and Paris which prompted renewed interest in this artist of the Victorian social scene.
[A1282] Phaidon hbk **£17.50**
[A1283] Phaidon pbk **£6.95**
WENTWORTH, MICHAEL
James Tissot
[A1284] Oxford hbk **£70.00**
WOOD, CHRISTOPHER
Tissot
[A1285] Weidenfeld hbk **£10.95**

TITIAN (c.1487 - 1576)
Titian's unique artistic achievements set the course of European painting, influencing, amongst others, Rubens and Poussin.
FASOLO, UGO
Titian
[A1286] Constable pbk **£5.50**
ROSAND, DAVID
Titian
Written by a Professor of Art History at Columbia University, this volume traces Titian's development from his early training under Giovanni Bellini to his progress through the courts of Italy, becoming imperial painter to the Holy Roman Emperor Charles V. 138 illustrations, 48 in colour.
[A1287] Abrams hbk **£25.00**

TOULOUSE-LAUTREC, HENRI DE (1864 - 1901)
French impressionist painter and lithographer. *"The least touch of colour, the slightest pencil stroke expressed, through much that was animal, much that was human."* (Exhibition catalogue, 1914).
Toulouse-Lautrec: Complete Paintings
[A1288] Penguin pbk **£7.95**
CASTLEMAN, RIVA & WITTROCK, WOLFGANG (EDS)
Henri de Toulouse-Lautrec
[A1289] Thames & H hbk **£22.00**
COOPER, DOUGLAS
Toulouse-Lautrec
[A1290] Thames & H hbk **£25.00**
HUISMANN, PHILIPPE
Toulouse-Lautrec
[A1291] Cassell pbk **£10.95**
LUCIE-SMITH, EDWARD
Toulouse-Lautrec
[A1292] Phaidon pbk **£8.50**

TROCKEL, ROSEMARIE
Rosemarie Trockel `NEW`
A greatly appreciated monograph on this wonderfully eclectic and politically stimulating young German

artist, most famous for her large knitted paintings which have been exhibited at the Tate Gallery and at the ICA. Her work is also included in the 1989 title *Refigured Painting: The German Image 1960-1988*.
[A1293] ICA pbk **£5.95**

TURNER, JOSEPH MALLORD WILLIAM (1775 - 1851)
Turner was praised by Ruskin as *"the greatest in every branch of scenic knowledge"*.
J.M.W. Turner: The 'Ideas of Folkestone' Sketchbook 1845
[A1294] Tate Gall pbk **£8.95**
The Clore Gallery
One hundred and thirty six years after Turner's death, his paintings, drawings and watercolours are now on permanent exhibition in the Clore Gallery, an extension of the Tate. This book introduces the reader to the collection and in addition provides an account of the works on paper, and a guide to the use of the study room in which they can be examined. Over 75 illustrations, most in colour.
[A1295] Tate Gall pbk **£5.95**
Turner: The Second Decade 1800 - 1810 `NEW`
Watercolours and drawings from the Turner Bequest.
[A1296] Tate Gall pbk **£4.95**
With a Poet's Eye
[A1297] Tate Gall hbk **£9.95**
[A1298] Tate Gall pbk **£5.95**
BUTLIN, M. & WARRELL, I. & LUTHER, M.
Turner at Petworth `NEW`
This publication commemorates the exciting collaboration between the National Trust and the Tate Gallery over the collection of paintings by Turner at Petworth, his association with that house and the patronage of the third Earl of Egremont. In addition to the 20 paintings acquired by the Earl, this book also reproduces the complete set of 135 gouache drawings on blue paper executed in the summer of 1827.
[A1299] Tate Gall hbk **£30.00**
BUTLIN, MARTIN & JOLL, EVELYN
The Paintings of J.M.W. Turner
The two volume set provides a visual record of Turner's entire body of oil paintings with extensive commentary. Winner of the 1978 Mitchell Prize for Art History.
[A1300] Yale UP hbk **£165.00**
[A1301] Yale UP pbk **£39.95**
GAGE, JOHN
Turner: A Wonderful Range of Mind
The author, an acknowledged authority on Turner, offers a biographical exposé, organising his discussion thematically rather than chronologically. 150 black and white illustrations, 170 in colour.
[A1302] Yale UP hbk **£24.95**
GAUNT, WILLIAM
Turner
A solid introduction to Turner with brief notes accompanying each reproduction. 86 illustrations, 52 in colour.
[A1303] Phaidon pbk **£9.50**
HERRMANN, LUKE
Turner
Second Edition. Shows the rich variety of Turner's *oeuvre*. 190 illustrations, 48 colour.
[A1304] Phaidon hbk **£25.00**
HILL, DAVID
Turner's Birds
A slim volume but beautifully presented with reproductions of 20 of Turner's exquisite watercolours painted for Farnley Hall's Ornithological Collection.
[A1305] Phaidon hbk **£11.95**
[A1306] Phaidon pbk **£8.95**
POWELL, CECELIA
Turner in the South: Rome, Naples, Florence
Drawing excerpts from Turner's notes and drawings, the author re-traces Turner's journeys in Italy on his

two trips to Rome in 1819 and 1828. She compares his responses to the three cities of the title with the reactions of his contemporaries who were also influenced by Italy: Byron, Shelley, Dickens, Stendhal and Goethe. Winner of the 1987 Eric Mitchell Prize.
[A1307] Yale UP hbk **£26.25**
REYNOLDS, GRAHAM
Turner
[A1308] Thames & H pbk **£4.95**
SELZ, JEAN
Turner
A strong collection of images (50 reproductions, 27 black and white) in addition to general but informative texts. Includes biographical notes.
[A1309] Bonfini hbk **£7.95**
SHANES, ERIC
Turner's Human Landscape `NEW`
A monumental publication claimed by the publisher to be the most important book on Turner since Ruskin's *Modern Painters*. 110 colour illustrations, 127 black and white.
[A1310] Heinemann hbk **£30.00**
WALKER, JOHN
Turner
The reproductions present a selection of oil paintings, watercolours, engravings and drawings. Each illustration is accompanied by a brief text by the Director of the National Gallery, Washington. With introduction including biographical notes. 94 illustrations, 44 colour.
[A1311] Thames & H hbk **£25.00**
Turner `NEW`
[A1312] Thames & H hbk **£12.95**
WILKINSON, GERALD
Turner on Landscape: The 'Liber Studiorum'
[A1313] Barrie & J hbk **£7.95**
WILTON, ANDREW
J.M.W. Turner: The 'Wilson' Sketchbook `NEW`
Written by the Curator of the Turner Collection at the Clore Gallery, this sketchbook documents a critical stage in the development of Turner's practice as a draughtsman. In use when Turner was only 21 years old, it is a working notebook in which the formulation of Turner's art language is charted.
[A1314] Tate Gall hbk **£9.95**
Life and Work of Turner
The definitive monograph on Turner, surveying the whole of his output including some 500 oil paintings and sketches, many thousands of watercolours, numerous drawings as well as portraits and prints. Wilton's biographical notes focus on Turner's psychology and the essays explore his theoretical and technological development. 1,580 illustrations.
[A1315] Academy Ed hbk **£49.50**
Turner in His Time
Andrew Wilton, a Turner scholar of international repute, is the curator of the the Turner Collection at the Tate. Turner's writings, documented impressions by his contemporaries and reviews of his exhibited works are represented in this publication. 308 illustrations, 65 colour.
[A1316] Thames & H hbk **£28.00**

TWOMBLY, CY (1928 -)
Twombly was born in Lexington, Virginia and studied at Washington and Lee University in Lexington, the Boston Museum School, and the Art Students' League in New York. Between 1951 and 1953, he lived in N Africa, Spain and Italy, moving to Rome in 1957 where he still lives. *"Of writing Twombly retains the gesture...it is the undefined inexhaustible sum of the reasons and drives that surround the act with an atmosphere; Twombly produces an effect."* (Roland Barthes).
Cy Twombly
[A1317] Prestel hbk **£40.00**

BASTIAN, HEINER
The Printed Graphic Work of Cy Twombly 1953 - 1984
Generously illustrated. Texts in German and English.
[A1318] Artdata pbk **£19.50**

VELAZQUEZ, DIEGO RODRIGUEZ DE SILVA (1599 - 1660)
Spanish court painter. Velazquez's output was relatively small and it was not until the 19th century when his early work was given by the Spanish court to the Prado Museum that his influence began to be felt. Many artists since then cite him as a major inspiration including Goya, Manet and most recently Francis Bacon.
BROWN, JONATHAN
Velazquez: Painter and Courtier
[A1319] Yale UP hbk **£55.00**
FERRARI
Velaquez
[A1320] Rizzoli pbk **£14.95**
GUDIOL, JOSE
Velazquez
Arranged chronologically. Includes extensive essays defining the decisive moments in Velazquez's career. 122 colour illustrations, 120 black and white.
[A1321] Alpine Fine Art hbk **£34.95**
HARRIS, ENRIQUETA
Velazquez
[A1322] Thames & H hbk **£27.50**
[A1323] Phaidon hbk **£14.95**
[A1324] Thames & H pbk **£8.95**
SERULLAZ, MAURICE
Velazquez
[A1325] Thames & H hbk **£25.00**
WIND, EDGAR
Velazquez's 'Bodegones'
A study in 17th century genre painting.
[A1326] G Mason UP hbk **£21.50**

VERMEER, JAN (1632 - 1675)
Dutch religious and landscape painter. Vermeer transformed commonplace environments into scenes of poetic beauty. He created 'pictures within pictures' adding a complex dimension to otherwise straightforward representations.
AUILLARD
Jan Vermeer NEW
A much welcomed monograph on this Dutch interior and landscape painter famous for his moving light effects and ability to lend straightforward scenes an air of serenity and religiousity.
[A1327] Rizzoli hbk **£50.00**
BANCIONI (ED)
Vermeer: Complete Paintings
[A1328] Penguin pbk **£7.95**
WHEELOCK, ARTHUR K.
Vermeer
[A1329] Thames & H hbk **£25.00**
[A1330] Thames & H hbk **£12.95**

VERONESE, PAOLO (c.1528 - 1588)
Mannerist religious painter. Veronese, classified as the greatest colourist of all time, produced paintings of transcendental beauty that record the splendor of Venice's Golden Age.
COCKE, RICHARD
Veronese's Drawings
Dr Cocke relates Veronese's commitment to drawing, to contemporary art theory. Includes over 150 autographed drawings, many previously unpublished, and over 300 reproductions.
[A1331] Sotheby hbk **£60.00**
PIGNATTI, TERISIO
The Art of Paolo Veronese 1528 - 1588 NEW
Catalogue designed to accompany the exhibition held in Washington DC. This is the first publication to offer a comprehensive selection of Veronese's work.

Arranged chronologically with extensive test, and over 100 illustrations in colour.
[A1332] Cambridge UP hbk **£49.50**

VUILLARD, EDOUARD (1868 - 1940)
French painter. Vuillard pushed beyond the limits of Naturalism and Impressionism, laying the foundation for the development of Fauvism.
EASTON, ELIZABETH WAYNE NEW
Intimate Interiors of Edouard Vuillard
The text concentrates on the complex pictorial construction of the paintings. 85 illustrations, 65 in colour.
[A1333] Thames & H hbk **£32.00**
PRESTON, STUART
Vuillard
Includes an examination of the Parisian world of modern art, individual commentaries and documentary photos. 114 illustrations, 40 in colour.
[A1334] Thames & H hbk **£12.95**
THOMSON, BELINDA
Vuillard
Incorporates much material from the artist's as yet unpublished diaries. 141 illustrations, 76 colour.
[A1335] Phaidon hbk **£30.00**
WARNOD, JEANINE
Vuillard NEW
New edition of the Bonfini Series written by the art critic of *Le Figaro* newspaper. 47 colour illustrations, 47 black and white.
[A1336] Bonfini hbk **£7.95**

WARHOL, ANDY
American Pop Artist. *"The Pop Artists did images that anybody walking down Broadway could recognize in a split second - comics, picnic tables, men's trousers, celebrities, shower curtains, refrigerators, coke bottles - all the great modern things that the Abstract Expressionists tried so hard to forget."*
25 Cats Named Sam, One Blue Pussy, Holy Cats by Andy Warhol's Mother
[A1337] Chatto hbk **£15.00**
Andy Warhol: A Picture-Show by the Artist NEW
[A1338] Rizzoli hbk **£32.50**
Andy Warhol: A Retrospective NEW
A very thorough monograph which endeavours to dispel the destructive myths that surround Warhol. Included are essays, intimate profiles by the artist's friends and extensive documentation of Warhol's impressive body of work. Published as a catalogue to the major restrospective held at the Museum of Modern Art in New York, this is an informative and highly enjoyable book.
[A1339] MOMA hbk **£35.00**
Andy Warhol: The Collection
[A1340] Abrams hbk **£76.00**
Cars NEW
Catalogue for an exhibition held at the Guggenheim, New York. Includes introductory essay: 'Critique of Emotionless' plus an extensive interview with the artist. 50 fold-out colour reproductions
[A1341] Guggenheim pbk **£27.00**
Success is a Job in New York NEW
Catalogue documenting the 1989 New York exhibition on the early art and business of Warhol.
[A1342] Serpentine hbk **£13.95**
Warhol by Makos NEW
A pictorial monograph by the famous photographer.
[A1343] Virgin pbk **£14.95**
FINKELSTEIN, NAT
Andy Warhol: The Factory Years NEW
Andy Warhol's warehouse studio took on the name 'The Factory', a tag rich in connotative meaning. Warhol's crowd included many international figures; behind this star studded 'smokescreen', Warhol worked in an extremely serious and committed fashion, altering contemporary culture in a profound way.
[A1344] Sidgwick pbk **£9.95**

HACKETT, PAT (ED)
The Diaries of Andy Warhol NEW
Beginning in 1976, Warhol rang Hackett daily and reported on the events of the previous 24 hours. This publication records the conversations, presenting the next best thing to an autobiography.
[A1345] Simon & Sch hbk **£17.95**
SMITH, PATRICK
Andy Warhol's Art and Films
Thoroughly covers Warhol's controversial films.
[A1346] UMI Research Press pbk **£13.50**

WATTEAU, ANTOINE (1684 - 1721)
French painter of Fêtes Galantes.
PARKES, K. T.
Jean Antoine Watteau: Drawings
[A1347] Hacker Fine Art hbk **£42.50**
POSNER, DONALD
Antoine Watteau
[A1348] Weidenfeld hbk **£30.00**

WHISTLER, JAMES MCNEIL (1834 - 1903)
Whistler's work marks the beginning of American painting. His *Arrangement in Gray and Black* (Whistler's mother) was for many years the only painting by an American to hang in the Louvre.
FINE (ED)
Whistler NEW
A considered account of this controversial artist accompanied by a selection of his major paintings.
[A1349] Nat Gal Washington hbk **£12.00**
HOLDEN, DONALD
Whistler Landscapes and Seascapes
[A1350] Phaidon pbk **£9.95**
LOCHNAN, KATHERINE N.
Etchings of James McNeill Whistler
[A1351] Yale UP hbk **£35.00**
[A1352] Yale UP pbk **£12.95**
WALKER, JOHN
Whistler
Walker, Director of the National Gallery in Washington, examines Whistler's life and his points of contact with many well known contemporaries. Commentaries on the works include statements by the artist. 110 illustrations, 55 colour
[A1353] Abrams hbk **£25.00**

WYETH, ANDREW (1917 -)
American realist. Wyeth's carefully rendered detail is imbued with a visionary quality.
The Art of Andrew Wyeth
[A1354] NY Graph Soc hbk **£25.00**
[A1355] NY Graph Soc pbk **£14.95**
WILMERDINE, JOHN
Andrew Wyeth: The Helga Pictures
These sensitive portrayals of the woman Wyeth formed a deep relationship with were held back from public release for many years.
[A1357] Viking hbk **£25.00**

Illustration from *Andy Warhol: A Retrospective* (Thames & Hudson hbk £35.00)

Theory & Criticism

BARRELL, JOHN
Political Theory of Painting from Reynolds to Hazlitt: 'The Body of the Public'
'Barrell establishes a tradition of political discussion among British 18th and 19th century artists that has received, until now, scant critical attention'. (*The Listener*).
[A1370] Yale UP hbk **£20.00**

BECKETT, WENDY
Contemporary Women Artists
The author takes a critical look at 50 women artists including Cindy Sherman, Jenny Holzer and Barbara Kruger and many who are not widely represented in other publications.
[A1371] Phaidon hbk **£25.00**

BELL, QUENTIN
Bad Art NEW
The author explores how we distinguish between good and bad art, and why bad art becomes good and vice versa. 88 black and white illustrations.
[A1372] Chatto hbk **£19.95**

BERGER, JOHN
Permanent Red
Berger's uncompromising social commitment dominates his critique of art production. This first collection of writings provides the ideal introduction to his aesthetic philosophy.
[A1373] Writers & Readers pbk **£5.95**
Ways of Seeing
Essays on aesthetics, in which Berger examines the basis upon which we perceive and discuss art.
[A1374] Pelican pbk **£3.95**

BETTERTON, ROSEMARY
Looking On - Images of Femininity in the Visual Arts
Brings together critical perspectives by 23 major writers. 65 illustrations
[A1375] Pandora pbk **£7.95**

BUCHLOCH, BENJAMIN
Marcel Broodthaers: Writings, Interviews and Photographs NEW
An important publication covering the work of the late Belgian artist and poet. It analyses art production from the perspective of institutional conditions and is invaluable to current discourses on post modernism. Includes a selection of Broodthaers' writings, interviews with the artist, illustrations of his work and critical essays.
[A1378] MIT Press pbk **£11.25**

BURGIN, VICTOR
The End of Art Theory
A provocative analysis of the art establishment and its traditionally ambiguous relationship to theory by one of Britain's most influential post modern critics.
[A1379] Macmillan pbk **£8.50**

CELANT, GERMANO
Unexpressionism: Art Beyond the Contemporary NEW
A collaborative project carried out by the author and 32 artists of critical importance. Each artist presents informative and creative pages about their work. Includes Jeff Koons, Tony Cragg, Rosemarie Trockel, Richard Prince, amongst others.
[A1380] Rizzoli hbk **£35.00**

DERRIDA, JACQUES
The Truth in Painting NEW
Academically oriented. Four essays explore whether or not there is a truth *peculiar* to painting.
[A1381] Chicago UP pbk **£15.95**

DIJKSTRA, BRAM
Idols of Perversity NEW
Subtitled 'Fantasies of Feminine Evil in Fin-de-Siècle Culture', this is a thorough analysis of the disturbing eruption of misogyny at the turn of the century in works by central artists of that age. Illustrated throughout.
[A1382] Oxford pbk **£9.95**

DYER, GEOFF
Ways of Telling: The Work of John Berger
Examines Berger's output from a new and stimulating perspective.
[A1383] Pluto P pbk **£4.95**

FISCHER, ERNST
The Necessity of Art
Originally published in 1959 in Germany, this text has established itself as one of the most influential books on art, examining the history of artistic achievement from a Marxist perspective.
[A1384] Peregine P pbk **£4.99**

FOSTER, HAL (ED)
Post-Modern Culture (3rd edition, 1989)
[A1385] Pluto P pbk **£6.50**

FULLER, PETER
Art and Psychoanalysis
[A1387] Hogarth P pbk **£5.95**
Seeing through Berger
[A1388] Claridge P pbk **£8.95**
Theoria: Art and the Absence of Grace NEW
Peter Fuller has developed a strong but controversial position in the field of art criticism. *Theoria* examines Post Modernism from an unsympathetic viewpoint, perferring to look back at the older romantic tradition embodied in Ruskin's *Theoria*.
[A1389] Chatto hbk **£15.00**

GREENBERG, CLEMENT
Collected Essays and Criticism: Vol I Perceptions and Judgements 1939 - 1944
These early essays present Greenberg's influential critique of modernist art.
[A1390] Chicago UP pbk **£10.25**
Vol 2 Arrogant Purpose 1945 - 1949
[A1391] Chicago UP pbk **£10.25**

Barbara Kruger's work from *Unexpressionism: Art Beyond the Contemporary* by Germano Celant (Rizzoli hbk £35.00)

Clement Greenberg from *Clement Greenberg: The Collected Essays & Critcism* edited by John O'Brian (Chicago University Press pbk £10.25)

GREER, GERMAINE
The Obstacle Race: Fortunes of Women Painters and Their Work
Raises the question why so few women artists of rank are acknowledged within traditional art history.
[A1392] Picador pbk **£7.95**

GUILBAUT, SERGE
How New York Stole the Idea of Modern Art
Explores Abstract Expressionism in relation to the Cold War.
[A1393] Chicago UP pbk **£8.95**

HALPERIN, JOAN UNGERSMA
Félix Fénénon: Aesthete and Anarchist in Fin-de-Siècle Paris NEW
Fénénon was not only the most important critic of his time but edited and published the new symbolist writing and was an anarchist propogandist for workers' rights. This biography, focusing on his art criticism and colour theories, includes 140 black and white illustrations, 20 in colour.
[A1394] Yale UP hbk **£19.95**

KUSPIT, DONALD
Clement Greenberg: Art Critic
A critique of Greenberg by the well-known American critic and theorist.
[A1395] Wisconsin UP hbk **£20.00**

LESSORE, HELEN
A Partial Testament: Essays on Some Moderns in the Great Tradition
'...in the art of today...as a whole, there is no belief in anything beyond the evidence of the senses and of scientific instruments unless perhaps in chance'. (H. Lessore).
[A1396] Tate Gall pbk **£7.50**

MICHELSON; KRAUSS; CRIMP & COPJEC (EDS)
'October': The First Decade
The First Decade brings together a selection of out-of-print essays from *October*, the much respected journal of art criticism and theory.
[A1397] MIT Press hbk **£0.00**

MITCHELL, W.T.J.
The Language of Images
Leading figures in art criticism discuss the function

and meaning of imagery in painting, film and literature, and the psychology of perception.
[A1399] Chicago UP pbk **£7.25**

MULVEY, LAURA
Visual and Other Pleasures: Collected Writings NEW
The essays are organised in chronological order and cover a variety of subjects, including Mulvey's 'Visual Pleasure and the Narrative Cinema'.
[A1400] Macmillan pbk **£9.95**

NOCHLIN, LINDA
Women, Art and Power NEW
Seven essays by the scholar who is a pioneer in her field. Subjects discussed include Morisot's *Wet Nurse*, women realists and eroticism in the 19th century.
[A1401] Thames & H pbk **£6.95**

PANOFSKY, ERWIN
Meaning in the Visual Arts
Panofsky was one of the foremost art historians of this century, particularly in the field of iconography. This selection of his work is well illustrated.
[A1402] Penguin pbk **£7.95**

PARSONS, MICHAEL J.
How We Understand Art
In this account, meaning in art is taken as separate from meaning in other fields and therefore evolves along quite different lines. An excellent starting point and an enjoyable book with numerous quotes and written in non-specialist language.
[A1404] Cambridge pbk **£9.95**

PETERSON, KAREN & WILSON, J.J.
Women Artists
[A1405] Women's P pbk **£7.95**

PLEYNET, MARCELIN
Painting and System
Departs from traditional criticism and draws upon post-structuralist theories in order to place art in a more authentic historical and ideological context.
[A1406] Chicago UP hbk **£13.95**

RADFORD, ROBERT
Art for a Purpose: The Artists International Association 1933 - 1953
A reassessment of Modernism. 'We are now more ready to perceive Modernism as no more (or no less) than one of the major dynamic structures of art history and we no longer stand so much in awe of it.' (R. Radford).
[A1408] Winchester Art P pbk **£6.50**

READ, HERBERT
Philosophy of Modern Art
[A1409] Faber pbk **£4.95**
The Meaning of Art
Read's essays offer solid introductions to the sometimes complex aspects of art theory and criticism. In this volume, he examines how we construct meaning in art and how our perspectives have evolved.
[A1410] Faber pbk **£4.95**

SMITH, BERNARD
The Death of the Artist as Hero NEW
The central problem discussed in this collection is that of defining and developing a visual aesthetic suited to a democratic society.
[A1412] Oxford pbk **£12.95**

STAROBINSKI, JEAN
1789: The Emblems of Reason NEW
In this seminal text on the 18th century, Starobinski explores the connections between art and revolution.
[A1413] MIT Press pbk **£13.50**

STEINBERG, LEO
20th Century Art: Confrontations with Other Criteria
[A1414] Oxford pbk **£4.95**

VOLPE, GALVANO DELLA
Critique of Taste NEW
The work questions the inherently radical and intellectual nature of art, by examining the sociological reductionism that has adversely affected much of marxist aesthetics.
[A1416] Verso hbk **£17.95**

WALLIS, BRIAN
Blasted Allegories: An Anthology of Writings by Contemporary Artists
Published in 1987, this is an extremely valuable source book on a number of contemporary artists who are not subjects of monographs to date. Highlights include Laurie Anderson, Barbara Kruger, Martha Rosler, Jenny Holzer, Matt Mullican and Richard Prince.
[A1417] MIT Press hbk **£17.95**

WHITING, CECILE
Antifascism in American Art NEW
Between 1933 and 1945, Amercian painters used their art to protest against fascism. This study, the first of its kind, shows how the art functioned in relation to aesthetic and political theories and historical developments.
[A1418] Yale UP hbk **£27.50**

WOLFF, JANET
The Social Production of Art
[A1420] Macmillan pbk **£7.50**

WOLFFLIN, HEINRICH
Principles of Art History
The author discusses the problems affecting the development of style in later art.
[A1421] Dover pbk **£4.45**

WOLLHEIM, RICHARD
On Art and Mind
Some of the essays in this volume are well known although hard to find. Three previously unpublished works are presented: a study of Walter Pater, of Giovanni Morelli and an examination of pyschoanalytical influences on creativity.
[A1422] Harvard UP pbk **£8.75**
Painting as Art
Masterly explorations into the question 'What is Painting?'
[A1423] Thames & H hbk **£28.00**

WOOD, CHRISTOPHER S.
The End of Art History?
In two essays the author discusses the conceptual models that have shaped art discourse and the methodological issues informing study.
[A1424] Chicago UP hbk **£13.50**

Catalogues & Museum Collections

100 Great Paintings in the Victoria and Albert Museum
A chance to view all the V&A's paintings from the British school. Superb illustrations, although the text is only in catalogue form.
[A1425] V & A Mus P pbk **£5.95**

16th Century Tuscan Drawings from the Uffizi NEW
Reproduces 100 drawings, providing an overview of styles and functions. Descriptive entries.
[A1426] Oxford hbk **£48.00**

Art from Europe NEW
Documents work by major contemporary artists from the Netherlands and Germany including Ulay and Marina Abramovic, Réné Daniels, Marlene Dumas, Astrid Klein, Pieter Laurens Mol, Andreas Schulze and Rosemarie Trockel. 21 illustrations, 7 colour.
[A1427] Tate Gall pbk **£4.95**

Art of Our Time
New and ongoing series documenting the work of international artists held in the Saatchi collection, with feature essays on central issues in art since the '60's. Contributions by Peter Schjeldahl et al.
Volume 1
Artists: André, Judd, LeWitt, Hesse
[A1428] Lund Humphries pbk **£20.00**
Volume 2
Artists: Artschwager, Chamberlain, Samaras, Stella, Twombly, Warhol.
[A1429] Lund Humphries pbk **£20.00**
Volume 3
Artists: Baselitz, Guston, Kiefer, Morley, Polke, Schanbel.
[A1430] Lund Humphries pbk **£20.00**
Volume 4
Artists: Bartlett, Borofsky, Fischl, Golub, Shapiro, amongst others.
[A1431] Lund Humphries hbk **£20.00**

Art-Expo 88
Record of all major art events, exhibitions and debates in Europe and America. Special features include information on new museums and highlights of Christie's and Sotheby's art auctions.
[A1432] Phaidon hbk **£35.00**

Berlinart 1961 - 1987 NEW
A wide-ranging publication cataloguing an extensive body of work including paintings, sculptures, films and performance pieces executed in Berlin, a recognised centre of the international art market. 415 illustrations, 86 in full colour.
[A1433] Prestel hbk **£31.50**

British Art Show
This catalogue, subtitled 'Old Allegiances and New Directions 1979-1984', includes work by 82 artists selected by Marjorie Allthorpe-Guyton, Alexander Moffat and Jon Thomson. The publication serves as an excellent introduction to the contemporary British art community.
[A1434] South Bank Centre hbk **£15.00**

Carnegie International NEW
Catalogue of the major exhibition of contemporary work held for the 50th time in Pittsburgh 1988-89.
[A1435] Prestel pbk **£28.50**

Exhibition Road: Painters of the Royal College of Art
A catalogue of artists who trained at the Royal College. Features Paul Nash, John Piper, Bridget Riley and David Hockney, amongst others.
[A1440] Phaidon hbk **£19.95**

French Paintings from the USSR NEW
[A1441] Nat Gal hbk **£16.95**

Indian Art in the National Museum, Delhi NEW
A new edition to Scala's museum series, this is the first book to make accessible the immense collection held at the National Museum in Delhi. It offers an

invaluable introduction to Indian Art, including chapters on Indian prehistory, Gupta sculpture, medieval stone and bronze sculptures, Central Asian antiquities, Islamic art in India, illuminated manuscripts and more.
[A1443] Scala hbk **£14.95**

Italian Art of the 20th Century **NEW**
This publication, issued as an accompanying catalogue to the 1989 Royal Academy Exhibition of the same title, presents a thoroughly researched overview of major 20th century Italian painting and sculpture, moving across the schools of Futurism and Metaphysical painting, into the painting and sculpture of the Fascist period, through realism and abstraction and into the less familiar territory of Arte Povera and Transavanguardia.
[A1444] Prestel hbk **£36.00**

Masterworks from the Gemäldegalerie Berlin: Vol 1
Paintings from 13th-18th centuries are arranged alphabetically in this comprehensive volume.
[A1448] Weidenfeld hbk **£40.00**

Museums in Cologne
This extensive catalogue documenting twenty-six collections acts both as a guide to the treasures of Cologne and as a reference book.
[A1449] Prestel pbk **£12.00**

National Gallery of Scotland **NEW**
With an introduction by the gallery's director, Timothy Clifford, and texts by the Keepers. 187 colour illustrations.
[A1450] Philip Wilson hbk **£14.95**

National Portrait Gallery Collection **NEW**
This generously illustrated catalogue offers an overview of portraiture in Britain ranging from the Middle Ages to present day - from Richard III to Ian Botham. Compiled by four gallery curators, the volume includes short introductory essays to each section of the book.
[A1451] Nat Portrait Gal hbk **£27.50**
[A1452] Nat Portrait Gal pbk **£14.95**

'Autumn Crocus' by Kurt Schwitters from *Modern British Sculpture* (A Tate Gallery Publication)

National Portrait Gallery: Complete Illustrated Catalogue **NEW**
Compiled by the Registrar of the National Portrait Gallery, Kai Kin Yung, this catalogue documents every painting, drawing, engraving, photograph and sculpture in the main collection to the latest acquisition of 1989. Each artwork is represented by a black and white reproduction and includes acquisition number, sitter, artist, size and date of execution. The book is fully cross-referenced and includes an invaluable index of artists, engravers, and photographers. An indispensable handbook for art historians as well as picture researchers. 900 pages, 7,000 b/w illustrations.
[A1453] Nat Portrait Gal hbk **£40.00**
[A1454] Nat Portrait Gal pbk **£25.00**

New British Art in the Saatchi Collection **NEW**
Best known for their collection of American and European art, the Saatchis have recently focused on purchasing art produced by British and British-based artists. This is an 'of-the-moment' collection, offering a valuable guide to current art practice in this country. Reproductions of the works are accompanied by lucid commentaries, clarifying major British influences on the international art movements of the eighties. With 150 colour reproductions, this publication is the first to celebrate the achievements of the artists represented.
[A1455] Thames & H pbk **£14.95**

Paintings in the Louvre
Informative catalogue and a useful reference book.
[A1456] Thames & H hbk **£55.00**

Paintings in the Musee d'Orsay **NEW**
The well-known art historian and professor Robert Rosenblum has compiled this survey of famous paintings and great artists from the 19th and 20th centuries. Included are familiar names and lesser known works by artists from Australia, Canada, Hungary, Russia and Czechoslovakia demonstrating the extent of the museum's holdings. 800 colour reproductions.
[A1457] Little Brown hbk **£50.00**

Starlit Waters **NEW**
This catalogue was published to accompany the opening of a major exhibition of British sculpture at the Tate Gallery, Liverpool. It illustrates the work of 18 practising artists who have been the focus of attention on the international scene. An immensely important body of artists including Art & Language, Tony Cragg, Ian Hamilton Finlay, John Hilliard, Alison Wilding and Bill Woodrow are represented.
[A1459] Tate Gall pbk **£12.75**

The American Collections: Columbus Museum of Art **NEW**
Founded in 1878, The Columbus Museum of Art began its collection of American art in 1906. The Museum's impressive holdings include important works by Winslow Homer, Mary Cassatt, Georgia O'Keeffe, Louise Nevelson and Edward Hooper. The first section highlights 86 masterworks, each fully illustrated and accompanied by a critical and biographical commentary. The second section incorporates a listing of 800 works in the collection, concluding with a narrative summary of other American collections in the museum.
[A1460] Abrams hbk **£25.00**

The Kremlin and Its Treasures **NEW**
Documents the work housed in one of the largest monuments in the world. It offers Westerners a new perspective on the art treasures and buldings in the Kremlin. 278 illustrations, 252 in colour.
[A1462] Phaidon hbk **£55.00**

The Last Romantics: The Romantic Tradition in British Art **NEW**
This book is the companion volume to the exhibition held in 1989 at the Barbican Art Gallery. The theme of both the exhibition and the book is the interpretation of imaginative subjects in British art from the decline of Pre-Rapahelitism to the rise of the Neo-Romantics. Edited and with text by John Christian. Over 200 illustrations, 70 in colour.
[A1463] Lund Humphries pbk **£17.50**

The Latin American Spirit: Art and Artists in the United States 1920 - 1970 **NEW**
Almost every major art movement of this century has included Latin American artists and this exciting catalogue acknowledges their contribution for the first time. The authors who are critics, curators and art historians from North and South America introduce to the reader to a stunning variety of artists, documenting both local movements and their integration into the United States. 230 illustrations, 100 in colour.
[A1464] Abrams hbk **£33.50**

The Life of Christ: Images from the Metropolitan Museum of Art **NEW**
Renaissance painters dominate this illustrative narrative, although it also includes a selection of woodcuts and engravings from the Middle Ages to our own time. 75 colour illustrations.
[A1465] Barrie & J hbk **£14.95**

The Metropolitan Museum of Art Guide
[A1466] Abrams hbk **£21.50**

The Neue Pinakothek, Munich **NEW**
[A1467] Scala pbk **£12.50**

The Prado
An informative catalogue featuring 400 reproductions.
[A1468] Thames & H pbk **£5.95**

Treasures from the Fitzwilliam Museum **NEW**
A colour catalogue highlighting the marvellous permanent collection which is currently touring the United States.
[A1469] Cambridge hbk **£35.00**
[A14691] Cambridge pbk **£15.00**

Verve: The Ultimate Review of Art and Literature (1927 - 1960) **NEW**
The unique French magazine *Verve* provided an important platform for major artists and writers, printing experimental images and texts by Jean-Paul Sartre, James Joyce, Pierre Reverdy, Matisse, Picasso, Chagall, and Brawue, amongst others. The publication gained a wide-ranging reputation for the high-quality reproductions and its innovative juxtapostions of old and new, both reflecting and encouraging the development of the modern movement in art and literature.This new text prints excerpts from every issue and features all of *Verve's* covers. 689 illustrations, 100 in full colour.
[A1470] Abrams hbk **£70.00**

Within these Shores: A Selection of Works from the Chantrey Bequest **NEW**
This catalogue selects 55 works out of more than 500, which have been acquired for the nation and are now housed in the Tate Gallery. Includes commentary and biographical notes on all artists represented, who include Vanessa Bell, Victor Pasmore, L.S. Lowry and Sir Jacob Epstein.
[A1471] Tate Gall pbk **£6.95**

Reference

Arts Review Yearbook 1989 `NEW`
Illustrated annual reference publication which includes up-to-date listings of all aspects of the art world. The lists provide additional information including descriptive commentaries, special features and an editorial by Graham Hughes. [1480] Lund Humphries pbk **£11.95**

ALBERTI, LEON BATTISTA
On Painting
15th century treatise by the archetypal Renaissance man.
[A1481] Yale UP pbk **£5.95**

BADDELEY, ORIANA & FRASER, VALERIE
Drawing the Line: Art and Cultural Identity in Contemporary Latin America `NEW`
Growing interest in the works of Diego Rivera and Frida Kahlo has brought Latin America to the public's attention, but no one has confronted its continuing marginalization within art criticism. This volume is an attempt to address the issue.
[A1482] Verso pbk **£10.95**

BAUDELAIRE, CHARLES
Selected Writings on Art and Artists
Artistic society in 19th century France brought to life. The Symbolist poet Baudelaire was famous for his visual imagery.
[A1483] Cambridge UP pbk **£13.50**

BAXANDALL, MICHAEL
Paintings and Experiences in 15th Century Italy `NEW`
A primer in the social history of pictorial style.
[A1484] Oxford pbk **£4.95**
Patterns of Intention
An historical explanation of pictures, which attempts to reveal how we can discover the artists' initial impetus.
[A1485] Yale UP pbk **£7.95**

'A Young Breton' by Glyn Philpot from *Within these Shores* (The Tate Gallery pbk £6.95)

BELL, CLIVE
Art
New edition of a book which examines the Bloomsbury Group's theory of art.
[A1486] Oxford pbk **£5.95**

BRITT, DAVID (ED)
Modern Art: Impressionism to Post-Modernism `NEW`
This concise volume covers every dominant movement over the last 100 years. The history of modern art is related by seven young art historians and offers insight into masterworks of the 20th century. 420 colour illustrations.
[A1487] Thames and H hbk **£14.95**

CLARK, KENNETH
Landscape into Art
Solid introduction to the genre.
[A1488] J Murray pbk **£9.95**
Moments of Vision
Clark presents his aesthetic viewpoints.
[A1489] J Murray hbk **£10.95**
The Art of Humanism
A survey of the Renaissance through the work of Donatello, Uccello, Alberti, Mantegna, etc.
[A1490] J Murray hbk **£12.50**
The Nude
A serious and revealing study.
[A1491] Penguin pbk **£8.95**

COOK, CATHERINE (ED)
Street Art of the Revolution `NEW`
Subtitled 'Festivals and Celebrations in Russia: 1918 -1933', this volume draws together visual and literary documents produced during the formative years immediately following the Russian Revolution. Quotes are taken from Lenin's first decree, the personal archives of participating artists and newspaper reports. 200 illustrations, 75 in colour.
[A1492] Thames and H hbk **£30.00**

CORK, RICHARD
The Social Role of Art
34 essays in criticism for a newspaper public.
[A1493] Gordon Fraser hbk **£6.95**

CURRIE, GEORGE
An Ontology of Art `NEW`
Currie structures a unified theory of the exemplification of art works.
[A1494] Macmillan hbk **£29.50**

ELLIOTT, DAVID
New Worlds: Russian Art and Society 1900 - 1937 `NEW`
The changes that took place in Russia between 1900 and 1937 caused repercussions throughout the world This book integrates text with images to produce a carefully reconstructed backdrop which helps to contextualizes the crucial moment in history when modernism was born.
[A1495] Thames & H pbk **£9.95**

FRY, ROGER
Vision and Design
A leading member of the Bloomsbury Group, the interest of Fry's criticism is not restricted to Bloomsbury followers.
[A1496] Oxford pbk **£5.95**

GAGE, JOHN (ED)
Goethe on Art
The German Romantic poet, dramatist, novelist and scientist had a marked influence on the development of art, especially with his writings on colour theory.
[A1497] Scolar P hbk **£7.95**

ART

PUBLICATIONS

The Whitechapel, one of London's major public galleries, is internationally recognised for its important contemporary exhibitions and community education activities.

The Gallery publishes distinctive full-colour catalogues, as well as posters, cards and videos, and provides a world-wide personal mail order service.

For further details please contact the Publications Assistant (quote ref WA1) or send the form below:

I am interested in Whitechapel Publications. Please send details of (Please tick as appropriate)

Trade terms
Annual catalogues subscription
Catalogues in print
Videos
Posters and cards
Artists and Schools book
Gallery newssheet mailing list

Name

Business

Address

Zip/code

Whitechapel Art Gallery
Whitechapel High Street London E1 7QX
Telephone 01-377 5015 Telefax 01-377 1685

WHITECHAPEL

GOLDWATER & TREVES (EDS)
Artists on Art
A useful anthology, covering the 14th to 20th
centuries.
[A1498] J Murray pbk **£8.95**

GOMBRICH, ERNST
Aby Warburg: An Intellectual Biography
Aby Warburg's influence on art history, particularly
in the field of iconography, was profound.
[A1500] Phaidon hbk **£19.95**
**Art and Illusion: A Study in the
Psychology of Pictorial Representation**
Challenging and absorbing look at subjects such as
the role of tradition in art and the problem of
abstraction.
[A1499] Phaidon hbk **£14.95**
[A1501] Phaidon pbk **£9.95**
**Meditations on a Hobby Horse: Essays
on the Theory of Art**
A selection of essays centred on abstraction and
expression.
[A1502] Phaidon hbk **£7.95**
**Reflections on the History of Art: Views
and Reviews**
A collection of 33 book reviews by the great art
historian.
[A1503] Phaidon hbk **£17.50**

GREENHALGH, MICHAEL
The Classical Tradition in Art
Artists from Giotto in the 14th century to Ingres in
the 19th.
[A1504] Duckworth pbk **£6.95**

HARGROVE, JUNE
The French Academy **NEW**
The author identifies and defines the relationship
between the classical ideal and the institution over
three centuries.
[A1505] Associated UP hbk **£20.00**

HASKELL, FRANCIS
Past and Present in Art and Taste
Selected essays from this master historian on art and
society. Very readable.
[A1506] Yale UP hbk **£22.50**
Rediscoveries in Art
Some aspects of taste, fashion and collecting in
England and France. Justifiably prize-winning book
on patronage.
[A1507] Phaidon pbk **£4.95**

HAUSER, ARNOLD
Social History of Art Volume 1
From Prehistoric times to the Middle Ages.
[A1508] Routledge pbk **£8.95**
Volume 2
Renaissance, Mannerism and the Baroque.
[A1509] Routledge pbk **£8.95**
Volume 3
Rococo, Classicism and Romanticism.
[A1510] Routledge pbk **£8.95**
Volume 4
Naturalism, Impressionism and the Film Age.
[A1511] Routledge pbk **£8.95**

HELLER, NANCY G.
**Women Artists: An Illustrated
History** **NEW**
Well illustrated and informative.
[A1512] Virago pbk **£30.00**

HILTON, TIMOTHY
John Ruskin: The Early Years
This detailed biography incorporates the complete
text of Ruskin's diaries and literally thousands of
unpublished letters.
[A1513] Yale UP hbk **£15.95**

HOLT, ELIZABETH GILMORE
The Expanding World of Art 1874 - 1902
Subtitled 'Universal State Sponsored Fine Art
Exhibitions', this collection of essays by recognized
critics including John Ruskin, Henry James and
Emile Zola examines the effect of expositions on
changing attitutes towards the role of art and artist in
society.
[A1514] Yale UP hbk **£35.00**

HONOUR, HUGH
These two volumes reveal how white artists depicted
images of Blacks across a variety of mediums.
**The Image of the Black in
Western Art** **NEW**
Vol 1: Slaves and Liberators
[A1515] Harvard UP hbk **£34.95**
**Vol 2: Black Models and White
Myths**
[A1516] Harvard UP hbk **£34.95**

JOHNSON, SAMUEL
**Samuel Johnson's Attitude to
the Arts** **NEW**
Challenges the long-held view that Johnson 'knew
little and cared less about the fine arts'.
[A1517] Oxford hbk **£30.00**

KRULL, EDITH
**Women in Art: A History of Women
Artists**
From the Renaissance to the beginning of the 20th
century the number of women artists able to
participate in cultural production was extremely
limited. Yet women have always trained in studio
practice and in many areas have played a more critical
role than is generally acknowledged. This book
documents the artistic achievements of women in
Europe, Britain and America, presenting the work
from an historical perspective and contextualizing it
within the societal and political climate of the day.
100 black and white illustrations, 31 colour
[A1518] Studio Vista hbk **£16.95**

LIPSEY, ROGER
**An Art of Our Own: The Spiritual
in 20th Century Art** **NEW**
Lipsey assess how contemporary artists have
interpreted Kandinsky's '*Concerning the Spiritual
in Art*.
[A1519] Shambhala hbk **£32.00**

**LYNTON, N.; SMITH, A.; CUMMING, R. &
COLLINSON, D.**
Looking into Painting
The authors' work towards transforming the way in
which we read art, in order to promote a clearer and
more intimate understanding of the visual arts. The
book has been divided into three parts - narrative or
history painting, portrait painting, and landscape
and still-life painting - and concludes with a section
on the philosophy of art and aesthetics by Diane
Collinson.
[A1520] Faber pbk **£12.99**

MOSZYNSKA, ANNA
Abstract Art **NEW**
In this new volume in the *World of Art* series,
Moszynska presents a clear treatise on the
development of a highly provocative movement. She
identifies its origins and proceeds with a wide-ranging
exploration of key artists whose work represents the
many and diverse forms of abstraction. The text
incorporates the Russian Constructivists, the De Stijl
and Bauhaus artists, Abstract Expressionism and
finally the current trends, including the revived
abstraction practised by Ne-Geo and other artists of
the 1980s. 175 illustrations, 25 in colour.
[A1522] Thames & H pbk **£5.95**

Illustration from *Pierre Bonnard: Illustrator* by
Antoine Terrasse (Thames & Hudson hbk £38.00)

OWUZU, KUESI
Storms of the Heart
An anthology of Black arts and culture.
[A1523] Camden P pbk **£12.95**

PARKER, ROSZIKA & POLLOCK G.
**Framing Feminism: Art and the
Women's Movement 1970 - 1985**
[A1524] Pandora pbk **£10.95**

PAULSON, RONALD
**Representations of the Revolution
1789 - 1820**
Paulson examines the art community's reaction
to a unique moment in history - the French
revolution - in an attempt to define aesthetic
responses.
[A1525] Yale UP pbk **£12.95**

PHILLPOT, CLIVE AND HENDRICKS, JOHN
**Fluxus: Selections from the
Gilbert and Lila Silverman
Collections** **NEW**
Fluxus, which derives its name from a
magazine produced in the early 1960s, was one
of the most innovative and radical art movements
of that period. This volume includes photos of
Fluxus objects and documentations of
performances by Nam June Paik, George
Brecht, and Yoko Ono amongst others. 37
illustrations.
[A1526] Thames & H pbk **£5.50**

RABB, THEODORE
**Art and History: Images and Their
Meanings**
The essays in this collection define the points
of contact between historians and art
historians.
[A1527] Cambridge pbk **£8.95**

REYNOLDS, SIR JOSHUA
Discourses on Art
Facsimile of some of Reynolds's lectures on art to the
Royal Academy in the 18th century.
[A1528] Yale UP pbk **£10.95**

ROBINSON, HILARY (ED)
Visibly Female: Feminism and Art Today - An Ontology
Critique of feminist art including interviews with Mary Kelly, Judy Chicago and others.
[A1529] Camden P pbk **£6.95**

RUSKIN, JOHN
Modern Painters (Ed. David, Barrie) **NEW**
This new edition is less than half the original length. It presents the essence of Ruskin's argument with economy and clarity.
[A1530] Deutsch pbk **£9.95**
Ruskin Today: An Anthology
(Ed. Clark, Kenneth)
[A1531] Penguin pbk **£5.99**
The Stones of Venice (Ed. Links, J.G.)
[A1532] Da Capo hbk **£11.50**

SASLOW, JAMES
Ganymede in the Renaissance: Homosexuality in Art and Society
The first detailed study of a provocative Renaissance development, taking the love of Zeus for Ganymede as a starting point.
[A1533] Yale UP pbk **£9.95**

SHEPPARD, ANNE
Aesthetics: An Introduction to the Philosophy of Art **NEW**
The author discusses the common characteristics of all works of art, and what gives them their value. Includes chapters on form, beauty and aesthetic appreciation, and the relationship between art and morals.
[A1534] Oxford pbk **£5.95**

UPDIKE, JOHN
Just Looking **NEW**
A collection of essays by the well-known American author John Updike revealing his response to painting and sculpture, and the art of the cartoonist and illustrator. 60 black and white illustrations.
[A1535] Deutsch hbk **£19.95**

VASARI, GIORGIO
Lives of the Artists: Vol 1
Edited highlights from the *Lives*. Classic criticism from the 16th century art historian essential background reading.
[A1536] Penguin pbk **£4.50**
Lives of the Artists: Vol 2
[A1537] Penguin pbk **£3.95**

WHEELER, DANIEL
Art since Mid-Century **NEW**
This review of painting and sculpture since 1945 attempts to contextualize the enormous body of painting and sculpture produced since the Second World War. Art trends progress at a pace which can be overwhelming; movements overlap and appropriate images and ideas from contemporary and historical sources produce an immense and complex aesthetic. Wheeler first sums up the 19th century origins of modernism before embarking on a study of post-war art including less common movements - Environments and Assemblage, Conceptualism, Earth and Site works, New Image Art, Neo-Expressionism and Neo-Abstraction. 500 illustrations, 170 colour.
[A1538] Thames & H pbk **£18.95**

WILLETT, JOHN
The New Sobriety: Art and Politics in the Weimar Period 1917 - 1933
The author draws on wide-ranging material of German, French and Russian origin in this overview of an unprecedented period in cultural history.
[A1539] Thames & H pbk **£8.95**

WITTKOWER, RUDOLF
Sculpture
The author examines the representative processes and principles of the field.
[A1540] Peregrine pbk **£9.99**

WOLFFLIN, HEINRICH
Landmarks in Art History
German author, one of the founders of art history as an academic discipline.
[A1541] Phaidon pbk **£5.95**

YABLONSKAYA, M.N.
Women Artists of Russia's New Age **NEW**
Many of the artists included abandoned traditional techniques, and experimented with new forms in order to find a way to express their ideological commitment. Much of the work represented is unknown in the West.
[A1542] Thames & H hbk **£28.00**

YORKE, MALCOLM
The Spirit of the Place **NEW**
Examines the influence of the Neo-Romantics on three major artists: Paul Nash, John Piper and Graham Sutherland.
[A1543] Constable hbk **£20.00**

ARCHITECTURE

The selection of books in this section has been made with the interests of the general reader in mind, although many new academic and specialist titles have been included. Special attention should be drawn to the various series: Thames & Hudson's comprehensive *World of Art* list provide ideal paperbook introductions, offering general titles on architectural history as well as monographs on architects. The Faber *History of World Architecture* range provides an excellent general reference series and for more expensive, specialist titles, the various series produced as Academy Editions are to be recommended. As regards practical reference for British architecture, the revised Pevsners from Penguin remain unequalled.

Reference & Introductions

BLOOMER & MOORE
Body, Memory, Architecture
Interesting essays on the 'psychology' of space in architecture.
[AB2] Yale UP pbk **£11.95**

CHITHAM, ROBERT
The Classical Orders of Architecture
Foreword by Quinlan Terry. Detailed handbook particularly useful for architects wishing to use the orders accurately.
[AB3] Butterworth pbk **£14.95**

CROOK, J. MORDAUNT
The Dilemma of Style
An exploration of English architecture and architectural ideas, ranging over 200 years from the Georgian to the modern. The search is for an understanding of the concept 'style' and the complex mechanisms at work for its realization.
[AB4] J Murray hbk **£25.00**
[AB5] J Murray pbk **£15.95**

FLETCHER, SIR BANISTER
A History of Architecture
Recent 19th edition of the classic text, which now includes seven chapters on modern architecture, and much more information.
[AB6] Butterworth hbk **£50.00**

GRANT, DIANA
The World Atlas of Architecture
Foreword by John Julius Norwich. Good on non-European architecture.
[AB7] M Beazley hbk **£29.95**

GUIDONI, ENRICO
Primitive Architecture
[AB8] Faber pbk **£14.95**

KOSTOF, SPIRO
A History of Architecture: Settings and Rituals
A guided tour of world architecture and urbanism, from prehistoric caves to the post-modern, described in the context of world history.
[AB9] Oxford pbk **£19.50**
MAINSTONE, ROWLAND J.
Developments in Structural Form
[AB10] Penguin pbk **£14.95**

NUTTGENS, PATRICK
The Story of Architecture
Designed as a companion to Phaidon's *Story of Art* and *Story of Modern Art*. Well-chosen illustrations enliven a necessarily brief survey: a good beginner's book.
[AB11] Phaidon hbk **£15.95**
[AB12] Phaidon pbk **£10.95**

PEVSNER, SIR NIKOLAUS
History of Building Types
[AB13] Thames & H pbk **£15.95**
Outline of European Architecture
A classic first book on architectural history. Dense and stimulating.
[AB14] Penguin pbk **£5.99**

STRATTON, ARTHUR
Elements of Form and Design in Classical Architecture
[AB15] Studio Eds hbk **£12.95**
The Orders of Architecture
[AB16] Studio Eds pbk **£8.95**

SUMMERSON, SIR JOHN
Classical Language of Architecture
[AB17] Thames & H pbk **£5.95**

TRACHTENBERG, MARVIN & HYMAN, ISABELLE
Architecture: From Prehistory to Post-Modernism
[AB18] Academy Eds hbk **£35.00**

WALKER, D. (ED)
The Great Engineers
Spectacular survey of civil engineering masterworks.
[AB19] Academy Eds hbk **£35.00**

WATKIN, DAVID
A History of Western Architecture
A recent and attractively presented history which has a refreshing perspective on modern art and its relationship with tradition.
[AB20] Barrie & J hbk **£19.95**

YARWOOD, DOREEN
Chronology of Western Architecture
[AB21] Batsford hbk **£19.95**
Encyclopaedia of Architecture
[AB22] Batsford hbk **£25.00**

General

ATTFIELD & KIRKHAM
A View from the Interior   NEW
Discusses the work and the lives of women designers and architects.
[AB23] Women's P pbk **£8.95**

BACON, EDMUND N.
Design of Cities
[AB24] Thames & H pbk **£10.95**

BALDON, CLEO & MELCHIOR, I.B.
Steps and Stairways   NEW
A survey tracing the evolution of the stair from prehistoric times to today's high-tech escalators. This lavishly illustrated book discusses all types of stairs in all kinds of architectural contexts, and celebrates the practical and technical features as well as the aesthetic considerations, calling attention to an architectural form which is all too often taken for granted.
[AB25] Rizzoli hbk **£29.95**

BENEVOLO, LEONARDO
History of the City
An overview, with over 1,500 illustrations, of urban civilization from prehistoric villages to the cities of the 20th century.
[AB26] Scholar hbk **£65.00**

CANTAZUCINO, SHERBAN
Re/Architecture: Old Buildings, New Uses   NEW
With the aid of hundreds of illustrations and plans the author celebrates the successful adaptation of existing buildings to new uses. The book stresses the challenge to architects and developers to preserve the original character of buildings, to establish a creative fusion between old and new and to consider the social or cultural significance of the new use.
[AB27] Thames & H hbk **£25.00**

COLQUHOUN, ALAN
Essays in Architectural Criticism: Modern Architecture and Historical Change
An eloquent collection of writings on the importance of history and its validity in creating a truly significant architecture for the present.
[AB28] MIT pbk **£9.95**

ETLIN, RICHARD E.
The Architecture of Death
Subtitled 'The Transformation of the Cemetery in 18th Century Paris', this is a richly illustrated study and account of historical attitudes towards death and the environment of the dead.
[AB30] MIT pbk **£17.95**

GAY, JOHN
Cast Iron: Architecture and Ornament, Function and Fantasy
[AB31] J Murray pbk **£8.95**

GIROUARD, MARK
Cities and People
A leading architectural historian looks at the sociology of cities by examining the way that the building of towns reflect different societies.
[AB32] Yale UP hbk **£25.00**
[AB33] Yale UP pbk **£13.95**

HAAN, H. & HAAGSMA, I.
Architects in Competition
History of architectural competitions over 200 years.
[AB34] Thames & H hbk **£40.00**

HARVARD ARCHITECTURE REVIEW
Scholarly journals on architectural history and theory with contributions by leading theorists and architects, produced annually by the Harvard Graduate School of Design.
Vol 5: Precedent and Invention
[AB35] Rizzoli pbk **£18.95**
Vol 6: Patronage
[AB36] Rizzoli pbk **£18.95**
Vol 7: The Making of Architecture   NEW
[AB37] Rizzoli pbk **£19.95**

HERSEY, G.
The Lost Meaning of Classical Architecture
Ornament fom Vetruvius to Venutri. Very relevant to the work of many post-modern architects.
[AB38] MIT pbk **£8.95**

HILLIER, BILL & HANSON, JULIENE
The Social Logic of Space   NEW
An investigation into the different kinds of spatial patterns produced by buildings and towns.
[AB39] Cambridge pbk **£15.00**

KING, A.D.
Global Cities NEW
An intriguing and original investigation of global cities, using critical tools borrowed from social theory and art/architectural history.
[AB40] Routledge hbk £27.95

Urbanism, Colonialism and the World Economy NEW
Companion volume to *Global Cities* which attempts to trace the structural forces at work in the evolution of architectural and urban development.
[AB41] Routledge hbk £27.95

MILMAN, MIRIAM
Trompe-L'Oeil Painted Architecture
An overview of this illusionistic mural art through the ages, including many contemporary works.
[AB42] Rizzoli hbk £25.00

MUMFORD, LEWIS
The City in History
[AB43] Penguin pbk £8.95

NORBERG-SHULZ, CHRISTIAN
Concept of Dwelling
A philosophical, technical and aesthetic examination of the home in all its practical and symbolic uses.
[AB44] Rizzoli pbk £16.95

OLSEN, DONALD J.
The City as a Work of Art
A study of London, Paris and Vienna, in which the author surveys the various attempts to unify the architecture of these capitals and draws conclusions about national cultures.
[AB45] Yale UP hbk £20.95

PERSPECTA
Perspecta is the Yale architectural journal, and perhaps the most important of the university journals on architecture in America. These volumes are characterized by acute scholarship, with essays by leading international historians and practising architects.
Vol 22: Architectural Paradigm
[AB46] Rizzoli pbk £18.95
Vol 23: Principia
[AB47] Rizzoli pbk £18.95
Vol 24: Idea in Material
[AB48] Rizzoli pbk £18.95
Vol 25 NEW
[AB49] Rizzoli pbk £18.95

PRECIS
Edited by post-graduate students of architecture from Columbia University, these journals reflect, in both form and content, the cosmopolitan quality and urban atmosphere of New York.
Vol 2: Tradition; Radical and Conservative
[AB50] Rizzoli pbk £8.95
Vol 3: Architecture in the Public Realm
[AB51] Rizzoli pbk £8.95
Vol 5: Beyond Style
[AB52] Rizzoli pbk £8.95

SAINT, ANDREW
The Image of the Architect
[AB53] Yale UP hbk £17.50
[AB54] Yale UP pbk £6.95

TAFURI, MANFREDO
The Spheres and the Labyrinth NEW
Subtitled 'Avant-gardes and Architecture from Piranesi to the 1970s' this is an innovative theoretical examination of the role, compromises and the conditions in which the architectural avant-garde has operated.
[AB55] MIT hbk £31.50

TAYLOR, LISA (ED)
Housing, Symbol, Structure, Site NEW
An exploration of the concept of 'home' in the United States, with 60 essays and more than a dozen photo essays.
[AB56] Rizzoli pbk £12.95

TIGERMAN, STANLEY
The Architecture of Exile
A philosophical, theological, and historical investigation into sacred and secular architecture. Buildings are linked and rediscovered through their biblical antecedents. The author also attempts to define man's unremitting sense of exile and displacement, and charts the implication this has for architecture.
[AB57] Rizzoli hbk £27.50

History of Architecture by Period

Ancient & Classical

LAWRENCE, ARNOLD W.
Greek Architecture
[AB62] Penguin hbk £30.00

LLOYD & MULLER
Ancient Architecture
[AB63] Faber hbk £14.95

MACDONALD, WILLIAM
Architecture of the Roman Empire
Vol 1: An Introductory Study
[AB64] Yale UP pbk £15.95
Vol 2: An Urban Appraisal
[AB65] Yale UP pbk £16.95

ROBERTSON, D.S.
Greek and Roman Architecture
Comprehensive and thorough.
[AB66] Cambridge hbk £40.00
[AB67] Cambridge pbk £13.50

RYKWERT, JOSEPH
The Idea of a Town
From the renowned architectural historian, a revised edition of his famous book with a new preface reviewing developments in urbanism. The author focuses on the Roman town as a work of art and explains how, through the articulations of private and public spaces, the city provides a clearly defined universe for its citizens.
[AB68] MIT pbk £13.50

VICKERS, MICHAEL
Ancient Rome NEW
A survey of the great achievements of Rome from its humble beginings in the 9th century BC through to the first centuries of the Christian era.
[AB69] Phaidon pbk £9.95

WARD-PERKINS, JOHN B.
Roman Architecture
[AB70] Faber hbk £14.95
Roman Imperial Architecture
[AB71] Penguin pbk £18.95

Early Christian/ Byzantine/Medieval

BRANNER, ROBERT
Burgundian Gothic Architecture
Burgundian Gothic was a style of the first half of the 13th century, as manifested in the cathedral of Auxerre and related to that of Canterbury and Lausanne. This study includes a select catalogue and wonderfully clear black and white photographs.
[AB72] Zwemmer pbk £19.95

CONANT, KENNETH J.
Carolingian and Romanesque Architecture: 800 - 1200
[AB73] Penguin pbk £18.95

GRODECKI, LOUIS
Gothic Architecture
[AB74] Faber pbk £14.95

KUBACH, HANS ERICH
Romanesque Architecture
This term describes the dominant architectural style of Western Europe from the 10th to 12th centuries, characterized by pure, solid forms, rounded arches and superb relief sculpture. This is an authoritative study.
[AB75] Faber pbk £14.95

MANGO, CYRIL
Byzantine Architecture
'Byzantine' describes the early Christian art produced under the influence of the Byzantine Empire, between the founding of Constantinople in AD 330 and its fall to the Turks in 1453.
[AB76] Faber pbk £14.95

WILSON, CHRISTOPHER
The Gothic Cathedral NEW
The gothic cathedral is the most enduring example of medieval culture. This is the first serious study to emerge that incorporates new research on the subject of intellectual and religious ideas as background to the splendid gothic style. Tracing the history of gothic design from its origins in the north of France and its spread throughout Europe, it explains why certain areas were more receptive than others. Over 200 illustrations chart the chronology of the style and provide a pictorial tour of some of the greatest works of art ever created.
[AB77] Thames & H hbk £24.00

Renaissance

ALBERTI, LEON BATTISTA
On the Art of Building in Ten Books
A translation of the first architectural treatise of the Renaissance, influenced by Vitruvius's *De Architectura*. Essential.
[AB78] MIT hbk £40.50

BURCKHARDT, JACOB
The Architecture of the Italian Renaissance
Classic from the 19th century art historian.
[AB80] Secker hbk £35.00

LOTZ, WOLFGANG
Studies in Italian Renaissance Architecture
Evocative, scholarly essays on the architecture of the Renaissance and its cultural context.
[AB82] MIT pbk £9.95

MURRAY, PETER
The Architecture of the Italian Renaissance
[AB83] Thames & H pbk £5.95

WOLFFLIN, HEINRICH
Renaissance and Baroque
[AB85] Collins pbk £4.95

17th - 19th Centuries

ARGAN, GIULIO CARLO
The Baroque Age `NEW`
Baroque art and architecture are characterized by dynamic forms appealing to the emotions of the viewer. The artists and architects of the period aimed for a fusion of the arts in which architectural forms achieved the fluidity of sculpture, and sculpture displayed the intentional play of light and dark like the chiaroscuro techniques of painting. This authoritative study by one of Italy's most famous contemporary art historians, surveys the baroque age of the 17th and 18th centuries mainly in Italy, the movement's birthplace and stronghold, and examines how in all the arts, by the use of illusionism, light and movement acted in concert on the spectator.
[AB86] Skira pbk £14.95

BLUNT, ANTHONY
Baroque and Rococo: Architecture and Decoration
'Baroque' is the term given to the dramatic and illusionistic style of art and architecture from about 1600-1750, which reached its fullest expression in Rome and Germany. As the Baroque became more heavy and ornate, it gave way in the 18th century to the lighter, more decorative style of Rococo.
[AB87] Grafton pbk £12.50
Neapolitan Baroque and Rococo Architecture
One of Zwemmer's scholarly series of architecture studies. This is the first detailed examination of the flowering of architecture in Naples at the beginning of the 18th century.
[AB89] Zwemmer hbk £57.50

CLARK, KENNETH
The Gothic Revival
Effectively a sequel to *The Romantic Rebellion*, on an aspect of the revolt against classicism which involved a return to pre-Renaissance motifs in art and literature.
[AB91] J Murray pbk £10.95

HITCHCOCK, HENRY RUSSELL
Architecture: 19th and 20th Centuries
[AB94] Penguin pbk £18.95

MIDDLETON & WATKIN
Neo-Classical & 19th Century Architecture
[AB95] Faber pbk £14.95

MIDDLETON, ROBIN (ED)
Beaux-Arts and 19th Century French Architecture
Interesting exhibition catalogue which shows the richly coloured classical style of architecture under the influence of the Ecole des Beaux Arts.
[AB96] Thames & H pbk £14.00

NORBERG-SCHULZ, CHRISTAIN
Baroque Architecture
[AB97] Faber pbk £14.95

Late Baroque and Rococo Architecture
[AB98] Faber pbk £14.95

RYKWERT, JOSEPH
The First Moderns: The Architecture of the 18th Century
A wide-ranging study of architecture in Europe between 1660 and 1780, with over 260 illustrations.
[AB99] MIT pbk £22.50

VARRIANO, JOHN
Italian Baroque and Rococo Architecture
[AB101] Oxford hbk £26.00
[AB102] Oxford pbk £13.50

WATKINS & MELLINGHOFF
German Architecture and the Classical Ideal 1740 - 1840
[AB104] Thames & H hbk £30.00

WITTKOWER, RUDOLF
Architectural Principles in the Age of Humanism
[AB105] Academy Eds hbk £17.50
[AB106] Academy Eds pbk £12.50

Modern

ARCHITECTURAL DESIGN SERIES
Each new title in this series concentrates on a particular development, national school or on-going issue in architecture. They are copiously illustrated and written by various specialist contributors.
Contemporary Architecture
[AB107] Academy Eds pbk £7.95
Deconstruction in Architecture
[AB108] Academy Eds pbk £7.95
Imitation and Innovation
[AB109] Academy Eds pbk £7.95
Japanese Architecture
[AB110] Academy Eds pbk £7.95
Las Terrenas `NEW`
This issue is dedicated to a major design competition for a large seaside resort in the Dominican Republic.
[AB111] Academy Eds pbk £7.95
The New Classicism
[AB112] Academy Eds pbk £7.95
Urban Concepts: The Rise and Fall of Community Architecture `NEW`
Focuses on the aesthetics, community participation in and the socio-political aspects of American Urban Planning as practiced by Denise Scott Brown.
[AB113] Academy Eds pbk £7.95

BANHAM, R.
Megastructure
Urban features of the recent past.
[AB114] Thames & H pbk £7.50
Theory and Design in the First Machine Age
Stimulating examination of the formation of the modernist aesthetic.
[AB115] Architectural P pbk £12.50

BANHAM, REYNER & SUZUKI, HIROYUKI
Contemporary Architecture of Japan
A beautifully-produced book documenting the work of over 60 Japanese architects including Kange, Kurukawa, and Isozaki.
[AB116] Butterworth hbk £45.00

BAYER, HERBERT & GROPIUS, WALTER
Bauhaus 1919 - 1928
[AB117] Secker hbk £12.50

COLQUHOUN, ALAN
Essays in Architectural Criticism: Modern Architecture and Historical Change
[AB118] MIT hbk £33.75
Modernity and the Classical Tradition `NEW`
A collection of essays from the noted theorist and practicioner examining prevailing concepts in architecture over the past two centuries such as classicism, romanticism, historicism and rationalism followed by an investigation of Le Corbusier and the relationship between history and the avant-garde.
[AB119] MIT hbk £22.50

CURTIS, WILLIAM J.R.
Modern Architecture since 1900
[AB120] Phaidon pbk £12.95

DAVIES, COLIN
High-Tech Architecture `NEW`
Davies charts the brief history and origins of high-tech architecture with special prominence given to the British exponents of the phenomenon. Questions are raised about its relationship to other technologies and whether high-tech architecture is a style or a technique.
[AB121] Thames & H pbk £18.95

DE WITT, DENNIS & ELIZABETH R.
Modern Architecture in Western Europe
Comprehensive guide from the early 19th century to the present day.
[AB122] Weidenfeld pbk £12.95

DEARSTYNE, HOWARD
Inside the Bauhaus
The author, a Chicago architect who died in 1979, was one of the first to study at the Bauhaus under such masters as Albers and Klee.
[AB123] Architectural P pbk £17.50

DUNSTER, DAVID
Key Buildings of the 20th Century Volume 1: 1900 - 1944
A collection of plans and sections of 48 important and classic modern houses from throughout the world by modern masters and lesser-known architects.
[AB125] Butterworth pbk £10.95
Volume 2: Houses 1945 - 1987 `NEW`
The second volume covers more than 50 modern and post modern houses from all over the world. The work of Rossi, Eisenman, Graves and Le Corbusier is included here.
[AB126] Butterworth pbk £10.95

ETLIN, RICHARD A.
Modernism in Italian Architecture, 1890 - 1940 `NEW`
A scholarly overview of the modern movement in Italy starting with the neo-classicists in Milan through to Futurism and Rationalism.
[AB127] MIT hbk £35.95

FRAMPTON, KENNETH
Modern Architecture: 1851 - 1945
A splendid survey and pictorial tour of specific buildings which have contributed to the development of modern architecture. Each building is discussed aesthetically, structurally and in terms of its significance in the progressive delineation of the movement's character.
[AB128] Rizzoli hbk £50.00
Vol 1: 1851 - 1919
Paperback editions of the above title.
[AB129] Rizzoli pbk £22.50
Vol 2: 1920 - 1945
[AB130] Rizzoli pbk £22.50

Modern Architecture: A Critical History
[AB131] Thames & H pbk **£5.95**

HALL, P.
Cities of Tomorrow
An intellectual history of urban planning and design in the 20th century.
[AB132] Blackwell hbk **£25.00**

HARAGUCHI, HIDEAKI
A Comparative Analysis of 20th Century Houses NEW
A pictorial tour, including axonometric drawings, as well as a concise history and discussion of the detatched house, from the medieval manor to the present day, with a detailed examination of influential and outstanding houses of this century.
[AB133] Academy Eds pbk **£12.95**

HAYDEN, DOLORES
The Grand Domestic Revolution
Subtitled 'A History of Feminist Designs for American Homes, Neighborhoods, and Cities' this is an important work on the history of modern housing and its relation to feminist culture.
[AB134] MIT pbk **£26.95**

JENCKS, CHARLES
Architecture Today NEW
From the man who first defined 'Post Modernism', this is an up-to-date survey which encompasses all the current trends in architecture from late- and post-modernism to new-classicism and deconstruction. Lavishly illustrated.
[AB135] Academy Eds hbk **£45.00**
Bizarre Architecture
[AB136] Academy Eds pbk **£6.95**
Late-Modern Architecture
[AB137] Academy Eds pbk **£9.95**
Modern Movements in Architecture
Jencks writes more clearly than most about modern architecture.
[AB138] Penguin pbk **£7.99**
Post-Modernism: The New Classicism in Art and Architecture
A major, if biased, survey of latest trends in both art and architecture.
[AB139] Academy Eds hbk **£45.00**
Symbolic Architecture: The Thematic House
Jencks's own London house adheres to a close pattern of symbolism, which he reveals in this interesting study.
[AB140] Academy Eds pbk **£35.00**
The Language of Post-Modern Architecture
The most readable of Jencks's books analysing recent architecture. It provides a clearer account than that given by many architects themselves.
[AB141] Academy Eds pbk **£12.50**

KLOTZ, HEINRICH
The History of Post-Modern Architecture NEW
A history of significant architecture of the past 25 years which assesses the controversial aesthetic preoccupations of a wide range of architects, from the pioneers Mies and Kahn to Eisenman, Botta and Hollein. The author identifies and examines the aesthetic preoccupations of many architects which broke ground, long before the term 'post-modern' existed.
[AB142] MIT hbk **£39.95**

KLOTZ, HEINRICH & KRASE, WALTRAUD
New Museums
Some of the most exciting public architecture of modern times.
[AB143] Academy Eds pbk **£14.95**

KOPP, ANATOLE
Constructivist Architecture in the USSR
Architecture of the Soviet aesthetic in the 1920s, characterized by its utilitarian simplicity.
[AB144] Academy Eds hbk **£27.50**

LISSITSKY, EL
Russia: An Architecture for World Revolution
Excellent source-book for a greater understanding of the origins of modern architecture by the Russian painter, designer, typographer, theorist, architect and apostle of constructivism.
[AB145] MIT pbk **£7.95**

LOTUS INTERNATIONAL
Three editions are currently available of the learned and well-produced Milanese journal on architecture. Each issue is concerned with an important aspect of contemporary architectural practice and theory. Superbly illustrated.
No. 47 Architecture in Engineering
[AB146] Electra pbk **£14.95**
No. 48/9 Double Cross
[AB147] Electra pbk **£28.00**
No. 50
[AB148] Electra pbk **£14.95**

NORBERG-SCHULZ, CHRISTIAN
Architecture: Meaning and Place NEW
A collection of essays by one of the most influental theoreticians on architecture. The reflections range from the phenomenological and theoretical to the historical and finally to existing buildings and trends.
[AB149] Butterworth pbk **£19.95**

NORRIS, CHRISTOPHER & BENJAMIN, ANDREW
What is Deconstruction? NEW
The authors attempt a definition of the term *deconstruction* and its recent application to architecture tracing the origin of this critical term to Jacques Derrida and his analysis of literary and philosophical texts.
[AB150] Academy Eds pbk **£6.95**

PEHNT, WOLFGANG
Expressionist Architecture in Drawings
A history of the style, partly a continuation of Art Nouveau, which was dominant in Northern Europe 1905-1925. Includes drawings by Gaudi.
[AB153] Thames & H pbk **£12.95**

PEVSNER, SIR NIKOLAUS
Pioneers of Modern Design
Modern architecture and design through its leading figures. An excellent, if idiosyncratic, study.
[AB154] Penguin pbk **£5.99**
Sources of Modern Architecture and Design
[AB155] Thames & H pbk **£5.95**

TAFURI, MANFREDO
Architecture and Utopia: Design and Capitalist Development
A scholarly discussion of modernism, the avant-garde, and semiological approaches to architecture.
[AB156] MIT pbk **£6.25**
History of Italian Architecture, 1944 - 1985 NEW
A detailed exploration and description of the major movements and protagonists of architecture and town-planning in Italy since the Liberation.
[AB157] MIT hbk **£22.50**

TAFURI, MANFREDO & DAL, FRANCESCO
Modern Architecture Vol 1
[AB158] Faber pbk **£14.95**

Vol 2
[AB159] Faber pbk **£14.95**

VENTURI, ROBERT
Complexity and Contradiction in Architecture
Considered a key text of post-modernist thought.
[AB160] Architectural P pbk **£12.50**
Learning from Las Vegas
Subtitled 'The Forgotten Symbolism of Architectural Form', these are highly original essays invoking a new kind of building ethic which responds to speed, mobility, communication networks and changing lifestyles.
[AB161] MIT pbk **£10.75**

WATES, N. & KNEVITT, C.
Community Architecture
Covers the latest thinking in urban planning.
[AB162] Penguin pbk **£5.99**

WHITFORD, FRANK
Bauhaus
[AB163] Thames & H pbk **£5.95**

WIGGINTON, MICHAEL
Glass in Architecture NEW
An international survey of this exciting material, discussing the practicalities, chemistry and the architectural circumstances of glass and its applications.
[AB164] Butterworth hbk **£27.50**

WINES, JAMES & MUSCHAMP, HERBERT
Site NEW
This lavishly illustrated book surveys the work of the controversial 'narrative' architectural firm Site (Sculpture in the Environment), founded in the early 1970s and based in New York. The group is comprised of architects, artists, writers and technicians and dedicated to the pursuit of architecture as fine art, as opposed to practical design.
[AB165] Rizzoli hbk **£35.00**
[AB166] Rizzoli pbk **£25.00**

WOLFE, TOM
From Bauhaus to Our House
Stimulating comment on modern architecture by the well-known American journalist. Very popular.
[AB167] Sphere pbk **£2.95**

British Architecture

BARKER, FELIX & HYDE, WHITE
London as It Might Have Been
Fascinating book showing some of the bizarre and beautiful unexecuted plans for London's famous buildings, such as the Houses of Parliament.
[AB223] J Murray pbk **£10.95**

BETJEMAN, JOHN
First and Last Loves
Typically affectionate polemic on architectural taste by the former Poet Laureate.
[AB224] Hutchinson pbk **£5.95**

BRAUN, HUGH
A Short History of English Architecture
Good general survey.
[AB225] Faber pbk **£3.50**

BROWN, R.J.
Windmills of England
A celebration of the aesthetic and technical aspects of the windmill which was an essential part of village life before the advent of steam power. Reissue.
[AB226] Hale hbk **£12.95**

BRUNSKILL, R.W.
Illustrated Handbook of Vernacular Architecture
[AB227] Faber pbk **£7.50**
Timber Building in Britain
Early domestic to barns. Good on techniques of construction.
[AB228] Gollancz hbk **£14.95**

CLIFTON-TAYLOR, ALEC
This most popular historian of English vernacular architecture: these books successfully convey his immense enthusiasm.
English Stone Building
[AB230] Gollancz hbk **£14.95**
Six English Towns
Covers Ludlow, Chicester, Richmond (Yorkshire), Stamford, Tewkesbury and Totnes.
[AB231] BBC pbk **£8.95**
Six More English Towns
This second book covers Warwick, Berwick-upon-Tweed, Saffron Walden, Lewes, Bradford-upon-Avon and Beverly.
[AB232] BBC pbk **£8.95**
Another Six English Towns
Includes Bury St Edmunds, Cirencester, Devizes, Durham, Sandwich and Whitby.
[AB233] BBC pbk **£8.95**
The Pattern of English Building
Very good history of building technique and materials in Britain.
[AB234] Faber pbk **£14.95**

COLVIN, HOWARD
A Biographical Dictionary of British Architects 1600 - 1840
A major work of reference. The backbone of an architectural library.
[AB237] J Murray hbk **£45.00**
Unbuilt Oxford
Scholarly work, covering the various plans for buildings in Oxford which were never realized.
[AB235] Yale UP pbk **£11.95**

COLVIN, HOWARD & SIMMONS, J.S.G.
All Souls
An illustrated architectural history of the famous Oxford College.
[AB236] Oxford hbk **£17.50**

CRAIG, MAURICE
Architecture of Ireland
From the earliest times to 1880.
[AB238] Batsford hbk **£25.00**

CRUICKSHANK, DAN & WYLD, PETER
London: The Art of Georgian Building
[AB239] Architectural P pbk **£17.95**

DIXON & MUTHESIUS
Victorian Architecture
[AB241] Thames & H pbk **£5.95**

EDINBURGH NEW TOWN CONSERVATION COMMITTEE
The Care and Conservation of Georgian Houses
Revised third edition of a magnificent practical building handbook detailing all aspects of stone-built 18th century Georgian houses, suggesting practical strategies for their upkeep and with a new section on decoration.
[AB242] Butterworth pbk **£19.95**

FITZ-SIMON, CHRISTOPHER
The Irish Village
[AB243] Thames & H hbk **£9.95**

FRIEDMAN, JOE & APRAHAMIAN, PETER
Inside London: Discovering London's Period Interiors `NEW`
This sumptous book, with colour photographs throughout, shows some of London's finest period interiors, many of which are not generally accesssible. The author and photographer make it clear to us that these wonderful but vulnerable architectural decorations must be preserved.
[AB244] Phaidon hbk **£17.95**

GAY, JOHN & BARKER, FRANCIS
Highgate Cemetery: Victorian Valhalla
An appealing selection of black and white photographs of the cemetery where Marx and many other luminaries have been buried.
[AB245] J Murray pbk **£8.95**

GIROUARD, MARK
'Sweetness and Light': 'The Queen Anne' Movement 1860 - 1900
[AB246] Yale UP pbk **£14.95**
Victorian Pubs
[AB247] Yale UP pbk **£12.95**

GLANCEY, JOHNATHAN
New British Architecture `NEW`
British architecture and architects have gained considerable international acclaim in the 1980's. Glancey attempts to disentangle the cross-currents of contemporary ideas in architectural design, both in practice and in theory, and identifies two trends: one looking back to history and decoration, the other pushing modernism to new limits in design and technology. Generously illustrated with the architects' own drawings and the work of architectural photographers.
[AB248] Thames & H hbk **£24.00**

GOMME & WALKER
Architecture of Glasgow
A well laid-out and highly detailed guide.
[AB249] Lund Humphries pbk **£14.95**

GUINNESS
Georgian Dublin
Dublin's architecture in this period was among the finest in Europe.
[AB251] Batsford pbk **£12.95**

H.R.H. THE PRINCE OF WALES
A Vision of Britain `NEW`
Since his 1984 RIBA speech, Prince Charles has found himself a spokesman for a great number of people in Britain when he makes pronouncements on architecture. In this book the Prince expands on themes from the TV film which he subsequently wrote and directed, such as the importance of conservation, the duty of architects and planners to give the people the buildings they want and the brutality of certain post-war buildings in Britain.
[AB252] Doubleday hbk **£14.95**

HESSENBERG (ED)
London in Detail
A picture book of decorative details on the buildings and street furniture of London.
[AB253] J Murray pbk **£11.95**

HOWARD, EBENEZER
Garden Cities of Tomorrow
Classic manifesto of English suburban development.
[AB254] Attic pbk **£10.00**

JONES, EDGAR
Industrial Architecture in Britain: 1750 - 1939
[AB256] Batsford hbk **£25.00**

KERSTING, A.F.
Buildings of Edinburgh
The author is one of Britain's best and most experienced architectural photographers. A worthy appreciation of Edinburgh in pictures.
[AB257] Batsford hbk **£9.95**

KIDSON, MURRAY & THOMPSON
History of English Architecture
[AB258] Penguin pbk **£3.50**

LAKE, JEREMY
Historic Farm Buildings
A study of agricultural buildings, examining their use and their evolution and with a detailed discussion of the architecture.
[AB259] Blandford pbk **£12.95**

LLOYD, DAVID
Historic Towns of South-East England: Kent, Surrey, Sussex, Hampshire
[AB261] Gollancz hbk **£14.95**
The Making of English Towns
[AB262] Gollancz hbk **£14.95**

MELLER, HUGH
London Cemeteries
[AB263] Scolar P pbk **£12.50**

MORIARTY, DENIS
Buildings of the Cotswolds `NEW`
This is a richly-illustrated architectural guide to the historic buildings of the Cotswolds, with commentary on style and architectural features based on Alex Clifton-Taylor's notes, updated and elaborated upon by Moriarty.
[AB264] Gollancz hbk **£14.95**

NICHOLSON, ADAM & MORTER, PETER
Prospects of England: 2,000 Years Seen through 12 English Towns `NEW`
A collaborative project between author and illustrator exploring architecture and specific 'shaping moments' in the architectural history of 12 English towns.
[AB266] Weidenfeld hbk **£14.95**

QUINEY, ANTHONY
The English Country Town
Well-produced book with a better text than many on currently privileged aspects of English Architecture.
[AB271] Thames & H hbk **£12.95**

SAUNDERS, A.
Art and Architecture of London
An exhaustive guide and source-book to the buildings and art collections of the capital.
[AB273] Phaidon pbk **£12.95**

SERVICE, ALASTAIR
Edwardian Architecture
A *World of Art* handbook to building and design in Britain.
[AB274] Thames & H pbk **£5.95**

SMITH, EDWIN & COOK, OLIVE
English Cathedrals `NEW`
An intelligent and original assessment of the English cathedral from Norman times to the present day accompanied by 200 illustrations showing interiors, exteriors and details by the great architectural photographer, Edwin Smith.
[AB275] Herbert Press hbk **£25.00**

SUDJIC, DEYAN
Norman Foster, Richard Rogers, James Stirling: New Directions in British Architecture `NEW`
Highly individual in approach and style, each of these

three British architects has attracted both international admiration and passionate criticism. Sudjic examines the buildings of the architects in detail, situating them in the critical context surrounding modern architecture in this country.
[AB276] Thames & H pbk **£14.95**

SUMMERSON, SIR JOHN
Architecture in Britain: 1530 - 1830
An essential volume in Pelican *History of Art* series.
[AB277] Penguin pbk **£17.95**
Georgian London
[AB278] Barrie & J hbk **£19.95**
[AB279] Penguin pbk **£7.95**
London Building World of 1860s
[AB280] Thames & H pbk **£4.50**
Victorian Architecture in England
[AB281] Norton pbk **£3.95**

WATKIN, DAVID
English Architecture
[AB282] Thames & H pbk **£5.95**

WHIPPLE & ANDERSON
The English Pub
Very popular landcape-format picture book.
[AB283] Thames & H hbk **£9.95**

WRIGHT, GEOFFREY
Stone Villages of Britain
[AB284] David & Ch hbk **£15.00**

Domestic Architecture

Covers all domestic forms of architecture, from castles to country houses, and their associated structures. Since the publication of Girouard's classic *Life in the English Country House*, many high-quality titles have been published.

ASLET, CLIVE
The Last Country Houses
An attractive book with some sense of fun about the great houses built before the two World Wars.
[AB286] Yale UP hbk **£25.00**
[AB287] Yale UP pbk **£12.95**

ASLET, CLIVE & POWERS, ALAN
The National Trust Book of the English House
[AB288] Penguin pbk **£6.95**

BAILEY, BRIAN
English Manor Houses
[AB289] Hale hbk **£11.95**
The National Trust Book of Ruins
[AB290] Weidenfeld hbk **£12.95**

BARRETT, HELENA
Suburban Style - The British Home: 1840 - 1960
An attractive book on an increasingly popular subject.
[AB292] Macdonald hbk **£12.95**

BENCE-JONES, MARK
The National Trust Ancestral Houses
A brief look at over sixty National Trust houses.
[AB293] Weidenfeld hbk **£12.95**

COOK & SMITH
English Cottages and Farmhouses
Probably the best-value combination of text and pictures on this subject.
[AB296] Thames & H pbk **£6.95**

The English House through Seven Centuries
[AB297] Penguin hbk **£11.95**

COOK, OLIVE
The English Country House
Excellent value: a standard text.
[AB298] Thames & H pbk **£5.95**

CORNFORTH, JOHN
The Search for a Style: Country Life and Architecture 1897 - 1935 **NEW**
A sumptuously illustrated collection of *Country Life* articles on English Country houses - the journal initially chronicled the owners' taste in decor and lifestyle, and subsequently came to influence it.
[AB299] Deutsch hbk **£19.95**

DE BREFFNY & FOLLIOTT
Houses of Ireland
Domestic architecture from the medieval Castle to the Edwardian villa.
[AB300] Thames & H pbk **£5.95**

DE BREFFNY, BRIAN
Castles of Ireland
[AB301] Thames & H pbk **£6.95**

FORDE-JOHNSON, J.
A Guide to the Castles of England and Wales
Handy pocket-sized guide with plenty of text.
[AB316] Constable hbk **£5.95**

FOWLER, MARIAN
Blenheim **NEW**
Perhaps the grandest house in England, Blenheim Palace is both a historical as well as an architectural monument. Fowler recounts specific events taking place in the long history of Blenheim and in the process also offers detailed descriptions of the park, the development of the layout, the furniture and interior decoration.
[AB302] Viking hbk **£15.95**

GIROUARD, MARK
Life in the English Country House: A Social & Architectural History
The book that started it all. Girouard manages to create a type of domestic biography, with architectural and social detail.
[AB304] Penguin pbk **£5.95**
Robert Smythson and the Elizabethan Country House
Another excellent book from Girouard on a romantic Elizabethan architect. Most illuminating about the period as a whole.
[AB305] Yale UP pbk **£12.95**
The English Country House: A Celebration
[AB306] Pavilion hbk **£16.95**
The Victorian Country House
A most enjoyable survey from one of the leading contemporary architectural historians.
[AB307] Yale UP hbk **£30.00**
[AB308] Yale UP pbk **£14.95**

HARRIS, JOHN
The Artist and the Country House
A history of country house and garden view painting from 1540-1870. An enormous book that is as handsome as it is interesting.
[AB311] Sothebys hbk **£39.50**

HEADLEY & MEULENKAMP
Follies
A National Trust book, covering the history of the often fanciful form, commonly built within the

grounds of great houses in the 18th and 19th centuries.
[AB312] Cape hbk **£15.00**

HILL, OLIVER & CORNFORTH, JOHN
English Country Houses: Caroline 1625 - 1685
An invaluable survey of earlier country houses. This is a collection of *Country Life* features on 25 houses of the period - such as Wilton House.
[AB313] Antique Coll Club hbk **£19.95**

JOHNSON, PAUL
Castles of England, Scotland and Wales
Johnson traces the history of the castle from Norman times to the present and also examines the social, political and military significance of these structures.
[AB255] Weidenfeld hbk **£12.95**
The National Trust Book of British Castles
[AB318] Panther pbk **£4.95**

KETTON-CREMER, R.W.
Felbrigg: The Story of a House
Charming reprint of a 1962 personal memoir about a 17th Century Norfolk house as it develops in the care of four generations of the author's family.
[AB319] Century pbk **£5.95**

LLOYD, NATHANIEL
A History of the English House
Copiously-illustrated standard reference work, for architects and designers as well as enthusiasts.
[AB320] Butterworth pbk **£12.95**

MACAULAY, KAMES
The Classical Country House in Scotland 1660 - 1800
[AB321] Faber hbk **£25.00**

MILLS, JOHN FITZMAURICE
The Noble Dwellings of Ireland
[AB322] Thames & H hbk **£12.95**

MUTHESIUS, STEFAN
The English Terraced House
Now established as a standard work on British domestic architecture, this is an immensely scholarly yet unintimidating work.
[AB323] Yale UP pbk **£9.95**

PEARCE, DAVID
London's Mansions
The palatial houses of the nobility.
[AB325] Batsford hbk **£25.00**

PLATT, COLIN
The Castle in Medieval England and Wales
The best book on the functional aspects of castle design.
[AB326] Secker hbk **£15.95**

QUINEY, ANTHONY
House and Home
A history of small English houses from the 13th century to the present day.
[AB327] BBC pbk **£9.95**

SAUNDERS, MATTHEW
The Historic House-Owner's Companion
A practical guide to technical and aesthetic considerations, from the law to professional advisors and where to get materials such as slate tiles.
[AB329] Batsford hbk **£14.95**

SPROULE, ANNA
Lost Houses of Britain
Fascinating as a record of the houses which have

disappeared, offering some understanding of why this has happened at such a rate since the end of the last War.
[AB330] David & Ch hbk **£12.95**

STAMP, GAVIN & GOULANCOURT, ANDRE
The English House 1860 - 1914: The Flowering of English Domestic Architecture
This was written as a 1980s response to Hermann Muthesius's famous book *The English House*.
[AB331] Faber hbk **£30.00**

SYKES, CHRISTOPHER SIMON
Ancient English Houses
A beautifully produced and richly illustrated chronicle of some of England's least-known houses, built between 1240 and the early 17th century.
[AB333] Chatto hbk **£25.00**
[AB334] Chatto hbk **£12.95**
Private Palaces NEW
A lavishly illustrated re-creation of the lost and lesser-known world of the great town houses of the rich and influential: be they landed nobility in town for the season, or fabulously ostentatious millionaires.
[AB335] Chatto pbk **£12.95**

WEAVER, LAWRENCE (ED)
Small Country Houses of Today
Reprint of the Edwardian classic on the houses of the Arts and Crafts Movement.
[AB336] Antique Coll Club hbk **£19.95**

WOODEFORDE, JOHN
Period Houses and their Details
A useful guide for students, and those wishing to restore their house with historical accuracy.
[AB337] Architectural P pbk **£17.95**

Religious Architecture

The Great Cathedrals of Britain: An Archeological History NEW
[AB339] BBC hbk **£14.95**

CLIFTON-TAYLOR, ALEC
Cathedrals of England
[AB340] Thames & H pbk **£5.95**
English Parish Churches as Works of Art
Characteristically clear and enthusiastic account from this author.
[AB341] Batsford hbk **£12.95**
[AB342] Oxford pbk **£4.95**

COBB, GERALD
English Cathedrals: The Forgotten Centuries
[AB343] Thames & H pbk **£9.95**

COWEN, PAINTON
Guide to Stained Glass in Britain
[AB344] Thames & H pbk **£5.95**

CURL, JAMES STEVENS
A Celebration of Death
An introduction to some of the buildings, monuments and settings of funerary architecture in the Western European tradition.
[AB345] Constable hbk **£15.00**

DANZIGER, DANNY
The Cathedral: A Portait of Lincoln Cathedral NEW
A description of Lincoln Cathedral today: from the

craftsmen who work on the ancient fabric to the workers and volunteers of the modern administration; from the music, bells and flowers to the Cathedral as institution with social and spiritual significance.
[AB346] Viking hbk **£14.95**

FOSTER, RICHARD
Discovering English Churches
Illustrated study of the development of the English parish church.
[AB348] BBC hbk **£12.00**

HIBBERT, C. & BLACK, M.
London's Churches
Over 160 churches in the Greater London area are examined as the capital's finest example of medieval architecture at St Bartholemew the Great to the magnificent creations of Wren and Hawksmoor.
[AB351] Macdonald hbk **£17.50**

HOWELL, PETER & SUTTON, IAN (EDS)
The Faber Guide to Victorian Churches NEW
[AB352] Faber hbk **£29.95**
[AB353] Faber pbk **£14.99**

HUTTON, COOK & SMITH
English Parish Churches
[AB354] Thames & H pbk **£5.95**

JERMAN, JAMES & WEIR ANTHONY
Images of Lust
A study of the sexual carvings to be found in medieval churches.
[AB355] Batsford hbk **£19.95**

MORRIS, RICHARD
Churches in the Landscape NEW
A history and celebration of the English parish church, focusing on the church as institution and as instigator of social and demographic change, sketching a chronology of these sites of worship and the parish itself.
[AB356] Dent hbk **£16.95**

NEW, A.
A Guide to the Abbeys of England and Wales
[AB357] Constable hbk **£7.95**
A Guide to the Abbeys of Scotland
[AB358] Constable hbk **£9.95**

PENNY, NICHOLAS
Church Monuments in Romantic England
This is a serious study of works by sculptors such as Flaxman and Roubillac.
[AB359] Yale UP hbk **£32.50**

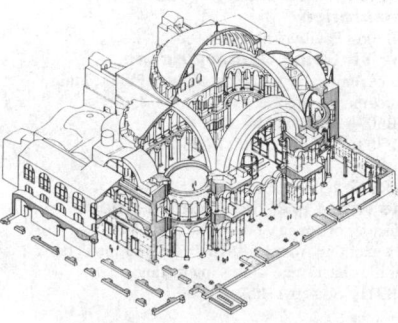

Illustration from *Architecture, Structure and Liturgy of Justinian's Great Church* (Thames & Hudson, currently unavailable)

PEVSNER, NIKOLAUS & METCALF, PRISCILLA
Selected text from Pevsner's Buildings of Britain series with good photographs. Recommended.
The Cathedrals of England: Midland, Eastern and Northern England
[AB360] Viking hbk **£12.50**
The Cathedrals of England: Southern
[AB361] Viking hbk **£25.00**

PLATT, COLIN
The Parish Churches of Medieval England
[AB362] Secker hbk **£15.95**

STALLEY, ROGER
The Cistercian Monasteries of Ireland
Over 30 monasteries were built in Ireland between 1142- 272 and many impressive ruins remain. The monasteries are discussed in terms of artistic achievement, and related to contemporary events in Ireland, England and France.
[AB364] Yale UP pbk **£27.50**

Pevsner: Buildings of England, Scotland, Wales & Ireland

An outstanding survey of the architecture of Britain: details of buildings of all types and dates are given, arranged by regional subsection. It is the product of decades of work by Pevsner himself - unless otherwise stated all volumes are written by him. The series is now being progressively up-dated by other distinguished architectural historians; all are hardbacks, published by Penguin.

Bedfordshire/County of Huntingdon £16.95
Berkshire £14.95
Buckinghamshire £14.95
Cambridgeshire £16.95
Cheshire (with Hubbard) £14.95
Clwyd (Hubbard) £17.95
Cornwall (revised Radcliffe) £14.95
County Durham (revised Williamson) £16.95
Cumberland/Westmoreland £14.95
Derbyshire (revised Williamson) £16.95
Devon £17.95
Dorset (with Newman) £16.95
Edinburgh (Gifford/McWilliam/Walker) £16.95
Essex (revised Radcliffe) £14.95
Fife (Gifford) £17.95
Gloucestershire: The Cotswolds (revised Verey) £14.95
Gloucestershire: The Vale & Forest of Dean (revised Verey) £16.95
Hampshire/The Isle of Wight (with Lloyd) £16.95
Herefordshire £16.95
Hertfordshire (revised Cherry) £16.95
Kent: North-East & East (revised Newman) £16.95
Kent: West & the Weald (revised Newman) £16.95
Lancashire: North £14.95
Lancashire: South £16.95
Leicestershire/Rutland (revised Williamson) £16.95
London 1: The Cities of London & Westminster (revised Cherry) £16.95
London 2: South (with Cherry) £17.95
Lothian, except Edinburgh (McWilliam) £16.95

Norfolk: North-East and Norwich £14.95
Norfolk: North-West and South £16.95
North-West Ulster: Counties of Londonderry, Donegal, Fermanagh & Tyrone (Rowan) £14.95
Northamptonshire (revised Cherry) £16.95
Northumberland (with Richmond) £14.95
Nottinghamshire (revised Williamson) £16.95
Oxfordshire (with Sherwood) £17.95
Powys (Haslam) £16.95
Shropshire £14.95
Somerset: North and Bristol £17.95
Somerset: South and West (with Cherry) £16.95
Staffordshire £14.95
Suffolk (with Radcliffe) £16.95
Surrey (with Nairn, revised Cherry) £16.95
Sussex (with Nairn) £17.95
Warwickshire (with Wedgwood) £16.95
Wiltshire (revised Cherry) £16.95
Worcestershire £14.95
Yorkshire: North Riding £12.95
Yorkshire: West Riding (revised Radcliffe) £17.95
Yorkshire: York and the East Riding (with Hutchinson) £16.95

World Architecture

American

BANHAM, REYNER
Los Angeles: The Architecture of Four Ecologies
[AB169] Penguin pbk £5.95

GENDROP, P. & HEYDEN, D.
Columbian Architecture of Meso-America
[AB170] Faber pbk £14.95

HANDLIN, D.P.
American Architecture
[AB171] Thames & H pbk £5.95

HEYDEN & GENDROP
Pre-Columbian Architecture of Meso-America
[AB172] Faber pbk £14.95

KEMP, JIM
American Vernacular
Subtitled 'Regional influences in architecture and interior design', this examines over 50 styles found in particular local forms through America.
[AB173] Viking hbk £25.00

MACRAE-GIBSON, GAVIN
The Secret Life of Buildings
Subtitled 'American Mythology for Modern Architecture', this is a scholarly analysis of 7 buildings completed in the 1980s, chosen as emblems of the fundamental changes in current US architecture.
[AB174] MIT hbk £26.90
[AB175] MIT pbk £12.50

MARDER, TOD A.
The Critical Edge: Controversy in Recent American Architecture
A detailed critical look at 12 of America's most controversial modern and post-modern buildings including Philip Johnson's AT&T headquarters, Michael Grave's Portland Building and Frank Gehry's house.
[AB176] MIT hbk £22.50

ROTH, LELAND M.
A Concise History of American Architecture
A good general introduction to American architecture written in a fresh, fluent style, assessing each period with contemporary concerns and conditions.
[AB177] Harper & R pbk £9.95

SCULLY, V.
The Shingle Style and Stick Style
An important book on American domestic style.
[AB178] Yale UP pbk £14.75

VAN LEEUWEN, THOMAS A. P.
The Skyward Trend of Thought
Subtitled the 'Metaphysics of the American Skyscraper', this is a historical and critical assessment of a truly American building type, celebrating the powerful aesthetics and resurrecting the ideological values.
[AB180] MIT hbk £22.50

European

ACTON & ZIELCKE
Villas of Tuscany
[AB182] Thames & H hbk £25.00

BORSI, FRANCO & GODOLI, EZIO **NEW**
Paris 1900: Architecture and Design
A spectacular overview of Art Nouveau architecture in Paris, which assumed distinctive undulatory characteristics. Extensively illustrated and expertly written.
[AB183] Rizzoli hbk £30.00

BUXTON, DAVID **NEW**
The Wooden Architecture of Russia
A great diversity of wooden buildings exist in the vast, forested regions of northern Russia. This study, with over 300 illustrations, examines the whole range of wooden structures in the region and describes construction methods as well as commenting on their aesthetic significance.
[AB184] Thames & H hbk £30.00
The Wooden Churches of Eastern Europe
Wood was the native building material of Russia for many centuries. For obvious reasons few buildings survive, but this study provides a fascinating parallel to European architecture.
[AB185] Cambridge hbk £65.00

DUNLOP, I.
Royal Palaces of France
A good comprehensive history.
[AB186] Hamilton pbk £9.00

FRIEDMAN, JOE & DARBLAY, JEROME
Inside Paris: Discovering Paris's Period Interiors **NEW**
A beautiful photographic record of some of Paris's finest architectural decoration, accompanied by texts that explain the historical and design interest of each period interior.
[AB187] Phaidon hbk £19.95

GOY, RICHARD
Venetian Vernacular Architecture **NEW**
A survey and assessment of the traditional domestic architecture in villages of the Venetian Lagoon.
[AB188] Cambridge hbk £37.50

HOWARD, DEBORAH
The Architectural History of Venice
[AB189] Batsford pbk £10.95

KENNETT & RUSSELL
Palaces of Leningrad
Stunning photographs of the Hermitage and other palaces.
[AB190] Thames & H hbk £20.00

VAN ZANTEN, DAVID
Designing Paris **NEW**
A study of the four French architects and main exponents of the Beaux-Arts school; Duban, Labrouste, Duc, and Vaudoyer.
[AB193] MIT hbk £31.50

WIT, WIM DE
The Amsterdam School: Dutch Expressionist Architecture, 1915 - 1930
The Amsterdam school produced buildings of great originality, led by the talented Michel De Klerk. This is a richly illustrated study.
[AB195] MIT hbk £29.95

Indian & Raj

DAVIES, PHILIP
Splendours of the Raj: British Architecture in India 1860 - 1947
[AB196] Penguin pbk £9.95

HERDIG, KLAUS
Formal Structure in Indian Architecture **NEW**
A primarily visual study of building typology, architectural detail and public spaces. Spiral-bound.
[AB198] Rizzoli pbk £27.50

IRVING
Indian Summer: Lutyens, Baker and Imperial Delhi
[AB200] Yale UP pbk £14.00

METCALF, THOMAS R.
An Imperial Vision: Indian Architecture and Britain's Raj **NEW**
By examining the political significance of imperial styles of architecture adopted by the English in India, Metcalf shows how such architecture helps to sustain the ideology of empire.
[AB265] Faber hbk £27.50

MORRIS, JAN & WINCHESTER SIMON
Stones of Empire: Buildings of the Raj
[AB202] Oxford pbk £8.95

MAHARAJAH OF BARODA & FASS, VIRGINIA
The Palaces of India
[AB203] Collins hbk £30.00

TILLOTSON, G.H.R.
The Rajput Palaces
The palaces of North-West India were built by the Hindu warrior rulers from 15th-18th centuries. This gives a glimpse into the extraordinary court life of the Princes and a rare detailed analysis of the diverse styles of their glorious buildings.
[AB204] Yale UP hbk £35.00
The Tradition of Indian Architecture **NEW**
Subtitled 'Continuity, Change, and the Politics of Style since 1850', the book examines the profound cultural transformation and the ensuing controversies in India due to British rule. The author discusses how events led to fears that indigenous design would become extinct and details late-19th century attempts to revive authentic Indian style. The book concludes with a description of Lutyens' New Delhi and Le Corbusier's work after Indian independence.
[AB205] Yale UP hbk £18.95

Islamic

Architecture of the Islamic World
[AB206] Thames & H hbk **£24.00**

FERRIER, R.W. (ED)
The Arts of Persia NEW
Persian art is renowned for its use of colour, ornamentation, intricacy and imagery. For the first time within a single volume are gathered together 20 experts considering all aspects of the arts of Persia, from prehistory to the Islamic period, discussing among other things, architecture, carpets, metalwork, the art of the book, glass and calligraphy.
[AB207] Yale UP hbk **£40.00**

GOODWIN, GODFREY
History of Ottoman Architecture
[AB208] Thames & H pbk **£18.95**

HERDIG, KLAUS
Formal Structure in Islamic NEW
Architecture of Iran and Turkestan
A primarily visual study of building typology, architectural detail and public spaces. Spiral-bound.
[AB209] Rizzoli pbk **£27.50**

HILLENBRAND, ROBERT
Islamic Architecture: Form,
Function and Meaning NEW
A survey of the architectural achievements of the Islamic world with a particular emphasis on the relationship between buildings, both sacred and secular, and society.
[AB210] Edinburgh UP hbk **£37.50**

HOAG, JOHN D.
Islamic Architecture
[AB211] Faber pbk **£14.95**

Oriental

BUSSAGLI, MARIO
Oriental Architecture Vol 1 NEW
A richly illustrated book tracing the history and evolution of architectre in Central Asia and the Far East.
[AB215] Faber pbk **£14.95**

CONNER, PATRICK
Oriental Architecture in the West
[AB216] Thames & H hbk **£18.00**

HIBI, SADAO
Japanese Detail: Traditional NEW
Architecture, Gardens and Interiors
A beautiful source-book of traditional Japanese interior design and architectural decoration presently enjoying a revival in Japan.
[AB217] Thames & H pbk **£12.95**

SSU-CH'ENG, LIANG
A Pictorial History of Chinese
Architecture
Subtitled 'A Study of the Devolopment of its Structural Systems and Evolution of Types', this is a richly illustrated discussion of one of the world's great building styles.
[AB218] MIT hbk **£40.50**

WARREN, WILLIAM
Thai Style
A beautifully produced book with full-colour illustrations showing the splendid and differing interiors of a selection of Thai homes.
[AB219] Thames & H hbk **£25.00**

YI WAN; WANG SHUOING & YANZHEN LU
Daily Life in the Forbidden City
The walled complex known as the Forbidden City stands in the centre of Peking. Comprising a multitude of splendid palaces, it is among the most significant examples of traditional Chinese architecture.
[AB220] Viking hbk **£50.00**

Architectural Monographs & Studies A - Z

AALTO, ALVAR (1898 - - 1976)
Finnish architect of the International Modern style, whose buildings often include exciting curved walls and rooflines.
Alvar Aalto
[AB409] Academy Eds pbk **£15.95**

ADAM, ROBERT (1728 - 1792) **& JAMES**
(1732 - 1794)
The Works in Architecture of Robert
and James Adam
Reprint of the architects' pattern book. 105 engravings of the work of these outstanding late 18th century British architects.
[AB410] Dover hbk **£51.00**
BOLTON, ARTHUR T.
The Architecture of Robert and James
Adam 1758 - 1794
2 Volumes. Classic reprint with photographs.
[AB411] Antique Coll Club hbk **£95.00**
ROWAN, ALISTAIR
Designs for Castles and Country Villas
by Robert & James Adam
[AB412] Phaidon hbk **£35.00**
RYKWERT, JOSEPH & ANNE
The Brothers Adam
[AB413] Collins hbk **£15.00**

ALBERTI, LEON BATTISTA (1404 - 1472)
BORSI, FRANCO
Leon Battista Alberti NEW
Scientist, painter, musician, athlete, author of the first architectural treatise of the Renaissance and, above all, a masterful architect, Alberti crystallised the current ideas on proportion, the orders, and ideal town planning. This illustrated study examines all of the activities of this 15th century humanist, thinker and architect and describes the buildings as well as the theoretical work in detail.
[AB414] Faber pbk **£25.00**
RYKWERT
Leon Battista Alberti
[AB415] Academy Eds pbk **£6.95**

ANDO, TADAO
FRAMPTON, KENNETH
Tadao Ando: The Yale Studio and
Current Works NEW
The first part of this book is a discussion by Ando, one of the foremost Japanese modernist architects, on his teaching at Yale University and his assignment to his students for the redesign of the art and architecture building, itself an icon of modernism. The second part is an examination of the architect's current work and his emphasis on tradition and modernist strategies.
[AB416] Rizzoli pbk **£16.95**
ZARDINI, MIRKO (ED)
Tadao Ando: Rokko Housing
Beautiful monograph documenting the Japanese architect's finest housing project and his philosophical vision for domestic architecture.
[AB417] Butterworth pbk **£16.00**

ARUP, OVE
Ove Arup
Glossy look at the famous partnership whose work includes the Sydney Opera House.
[AB418] Academy Eds hbk **£35.00**

ASPLUND, GUNNAR (1885 - 1940)
WIOLSON, COLIN ST
Gunnar Asplund 1885 - 1940: The
Dilemma of Classicism
Examines the highly distinctive classical character of Sweden's greatest modern architect.
[AB419] Architect Assn hbk **£30.00**
WREDE, STUART
The Architecture of Eric Gunnar
Asplund
[AB420] MIT pbk **£16.25**

BERLAGE, HENDRIK PETRUS (1856 - 1934)
POLANO, SERGIO
Hendrik Petrus Berlage: The
Complete Works NEW
The 19th century Dutch architect is noted for his lack of ornament, combined with bold patterns and moulded shapes. This monograph includes some of Berlage's own writings and a full catalogue of his buildings, assessing fully for the first time the architect's influence on later generations.
[AB421] Butterworth hbk **£27.50**

BERNINI, GIAN LORENZO (1598 - 1680)
BORSI, FRANCO
Bernini
Beautifully produced book on the baroque architect, sculptor and painter considered the dominant figure of Roman art of the 17th century. Bernini's sculpture and architecture are visible throughout Rome, and no other city bears so strong an imprint of one man's work and vision, from the daring Baldacchino erected under Michelangelo's dome in St Peter's to the enormous, oval colonnade of the piazza.
[AB422] Rizzoli hbk **£50.00**

BOTTA, MARIO
DAL CO, FRANCESCO
Mario Botta: Architecture 1960 - 1985
A sumptuously illustrated discussion and catalogue of the the Italian post modernist's work to 1985, documenting his elegant domestic and institutional architecture.
[AB424] Butterworth pbk **£26.00**

BROSSE, SALOMON DE (1571 - 1626)
COOPE, ROSALYS
Salomon de Brosse
The development of the classical style in French architecture from 1565 to 1630.
[AB425] Zwemmer hbk **£37.50**

BRUNELLESCHI, FILIPO (1327 - 1446)
BATTISTI, EUGENIO
Brunelleschi: The Complete Work
[AB426] Thames & H hbk **£42.00**
SAALMAN
Filipo Brunelleschi: The Cupola of
Santa Maria del Fiore
Thorough discussion of how the largest-ever eight-sided cloister vault was built.
[AB427] Zwemmer hbk **£67.50**

BUNSHAFT, GORDON (1909 -)
KRINSKY, CAROLE HERSELLE
Gordon Bunshaft of Skidmore,
Owens and Merrill NEW
The first complete monograph one of the major American modernists, whose buildings suggest a consummate understanding of Mies van der Rohe and Le Corbusier.
[AB428] MIT hbk **£44.95**

BURGES, WILLIAM (1827 - 1881)
CROOK, J. MORDAUNT
William Burges and the High Victorian Dream
First-class monograph on a major architect of the Gothic Revival who worked in Britain and America.
[AB429] J Murray hbk **£45.00**

CHAMBERS, SIR WILLIAM (1723 - 1796)
Sir William Chambers
Excellent study of the dominant Palladian architect and theorist.
[AB430] Zwemmer hbk **£30.00**

CHIATTONE, MARIO
GEROSA, PIER GIORGIO
Mario Chiattone: An Architectural Itinerary between Milan and Lugano
This profusely-illustrated monograph surveys the Italian architect's output subdividing it into 2 periods; beginning with his association with Futurism, it moves on to his cultural and regional investigation of architecture, town planning, painting and other arts in the canton of Ticino, in the north of Italy.
[AB431] Butterworth hbk **£25.00**

COCKERELL, C.R. (1788 - 1863)
WATKIN, DAVID
The Life and Work of C.R. Cockerell, RA
Cockerell is probably best known for the Ashmolean Museum Oxford.
[AB432] Zwemmer hbk **£37.50**

COLQUHOUN, ALAN & MILLER, JOHN
Colquhoun, Miller & Partners
A critical assessment of the English architectural practice by the main partners themselves. Colquhoun is a noted architect and theorist, dividing his time between England, where he is principal of the firm, and America, where he is a professor of architecture.
[AB433] Rizzoli pbk **£15.95**

CORREA, CHARLES
KHAN, HASAN-UDDIN
Charles Correa `NEW`
An overview of the Indian architect's projects, including urban planning, in the years 1958-1986. Recently Correa has emerged as a leading figure in contemporary architecture through his design approaches in a warm climate and his respect for the environment in planning. This fully revised monograph includes a chronological list of works and over 370 photographs and drawings.
[AB434] Butterworth hbk **£27.50**

ELDEM, SEDAD
BOZDOGAN & OZKAN & YENEL
Sedad Eldem `NEW`
Eldem, considered Turkey's most important architect, has practiced, taught and researched architecture for over 50 years. This beautiful and timely monograph includes a complete chronology of works and biographical detail.
[AB435] Butterworth hbk **£27.50**

FARRELL, TERRY
Terry Farrell
A brief paperback monograph on the contemporary architect best-known for his London buildings in a revived classical style.
[AB437] Academy Eds pbk **£12.95**

FATHY, HASSAN
RASTORFER, DARL
Hassan Fathy
The first monograph on the celebrated contemporary Egyptian architect, whose work has influenced architecture throughout the developing world.
[AB438] Butterworth hbk **£24.50**

FOSTER, NORMAN
WILLIAMS, S.
The Hong Kong Bank
Documents the controversial British architect's huge and inspiring post modern masterwork which houses the headquarters of the Hong Kong Bank.
[AB439] Cape hbk **£25.00**

FUJII, HIROMI
FRAMPTON, KENNETH
Architecture of Hiromi Fujii
A survey of the work of the contemporary Japanese architect whose graceful and yet forcefully modern structures reflect on traditional Japanese forms and also look forward to new developments.
[AB440] Rizzoli pbk **£16.95**

GABRIEL, ANGE-JACQUES
TADGELL, CHRISTOPHER
Ange-Jacques Gabriel
Thorough monograph.
[AB441] Zwemmer hbk **£57.50**

GAUDI, ANTONI Y CORNET (1852 - 1926)
Extraordinary Spanish architect whose loose, asymmetrical buildings, combining elements of gothic, moorish, and cubist design, dominate the Barcelona skyline and achieve a near-organic prescence which is quite unlike any other form of modern architecture.
MORALES, IGNASI DE SOLA
Gaudi
[AB442] Academy Eds pbk **£9.95**

GEHRY, FRANK
COBB, HENRY N.
The Architecture of Frank Gehry
A splendid monograph on the California-based architect and major exponent of the Deconstruction movement, which in Gehry's case translates into buildings and dwellings of extraordinary plastic articulation, with complex plans and oblique, witty references.
[AB444] Rizzoli pbk **£25.00**

GOFF, BRUCE
DE LONG, DAVID G.
Bruce Goff: Toward Absolute Architecture `NEW`
A detailed and richly illustrated examination of the American architect's highly idiosyncratic and original designs.
[AB445] MIT hbk **£44.95**

GRAVES, MICHAEL
NICHOLS, KAREN & BURKE, PATRICK
Michael Graves: Buildings and Projects 1982 - 1986 `NEW`
A new survey documenting recent commissions which include various buildings in America as well as paintings, murals, furniture designs and stage sets.
[AB446] Architectural Assn hbk **£26.00**
WHEELER; ARNELL & BICKFORD (EDS)
Michael Graves: Buildings and Projects 1966 - 1981
Copiously illustrated monograph of the controversial architect's buildings, murals and interior designs, from his early residences to the post-modernist Portland building in which ornamentation and classical motifs have created a structure of startling originality.
[AB447] Butterworth pbk **£26.00**

GUARINI, GUARINO (1624 - 1683)
MEEK, H.A.
Guarino Guarini
Innovative and rigorously intellectual master of the High Baroque style.
[AB448] Yale UP hbk **£35.00**

GUIMARD, HECTOR (1867 - 1942)
Hector Guimard
One of the most influential and daring of the Art Nouveau architects, responsible for the metal arches on the entrances to the Paris Metro.
[AB450] Academy Eds pbk **£12.95**

HARRISON, WALLACE K.
Wallace K. Harrison, Architect `NEW`
The architect-client combination of Harrison and Nelson Rockerfeller had extraordinary impact on the building pattern and development of New York. The author examines, in biographical and social detail, the life and work of the architect who masterminded monumental projects all over the city.
[AB452] Rizzoli hbk **£35.00**
[AB451] Rizzoli pbk **£19.95**

HAWKSMOOR, NICHOLAS (1661 - 1736)
DOWNES, KERRY
Hawksmoor
The standard work on Wren's greatest pupil and Vanbrugh's assistant, himself the architect of many fine London churches.
[AB453] Zwemmer hbk **£37.50**
Hawksmoor `NEW`
A brief introduction to Wren's work.
[AB454] Thames & H pbk **£5.95**

JONES, INIGO (1573 - 1652)
HARRIS, JOHN & HIGGOT, GORDON
Inigo Jones: The Complete Architectural Drawings
Over 90 architectural drawings, as well as other figurative drawings and stage designs form the bulk of this scholarly monograph which reassesses Jones's work by placing it in historical context and questions certain attributions and dates.
[AB455] Sotheby's hbk **£37.50**

KAHN, LOUIS I. (1901 -)
LOEBELL
Between Silence and Light: Spirit in the Architecture of Louis I. Kahn
This highly original book juxtaposes photos of buildings and architectual details with philosophical musings quoted from the architect himself on the nature and struggle of architecture. Kahn considers spaces for stillness and silence, and spaces for light where materials and structural form reveal themselves.
[AB456] Shambhala Pub pbk **£10.50**
WURMAN, RICHARD SAUL (ED)
What Will Be Has Always Been: The Words of Louis I. Kahn
A collection of thoughts on architecture and many other subjects drawn from taped conversations, notebooks and lectures by the architect. Kahn has assumed mythic proportions in modern architecture partly due to his writings and thinking, which always foreground a struggle for simplicity - childlike and clear, yet very obscure.
[AB457] Rizzoli pbk **£19.95**

LE CORBUSIER (1887 - 1966)
Journey to the East
The 24 year old architect's travel diary, kept during his first journey through Central and Eastern Europe, records his vivid impressions of buildings such as the Forum at Pompeii and the Parthenon in Athens.
[AB459] MIT hbk **£22.50**
Le Corbusier Sketchbooks
Vol 1: 1914 - 1948
[AB460] Thames & H hbk **£35.00**
Vol 2: 1950 - 1954
[AB461] Thames & H hbk **£35.00**
Vol 3: 1954 - 1957
[AB462] MIT hbk **£34.95**

Vol 4: 1957 - 1964
[AB463] MIT hbk £34.95
Selected Drawings
[AB464] Academy Eds pbk £12.50
The City of Tomorrow
[AB465] Architectural P pbk £10.95
The Decorative Art of Today
[AB466] Architectural P pbk £12.95
Towards a New Architecture
[AB467] Architectural P hbk £10.95
BAKER & GUBLER
The Villas of Le Corbusier: 1920 - 1930
[AB468] Yale UP hbk £30.00
BESSET, MAURICE
Le Corbusier: To Live with the Light
Paperback edition of a highly acclaimed monograph on Le Corbusier, discussing his most important buildings and other works, including plans, drawings and paintings. Demonstrating how, to a large extent, the French architect determined the course of modern architecture.
[AB469] Butterworth pbk £25.00
CURTIS, WILLIAM J.R.
Le Corbusier: Ideas and Form
Good study of arguably the greatest architect of the 20th century.
[AB470] Phaidon hbk £40.00
GANS, DEBORAH
The Le Corbusier Guide
A well documented guidebook to all the 69 existing buildings throughout the world including plans, elevations and descriptions for each building.
[AB471] Butterworth pbk £12.95
JENCKS, CHARLES
Le Corbusier and the Tragic View of Architecture
[AB472] Penguin pbk £7.95

LEDOUX, CLAUDE-NICHOLAS
(1736 - 1806)
Ledoux: L'Architecture
A fine edition of this work containing 300 plates which Ledoux had completed at the time of his death in 1806, including over 100 of his plans for a Utopian city.
[AB473] Architectural P hbk £57.50

LEONARDO DA VINCI (1452 - 1519)
PEDRETTI, CARLO
Leonardo Architect
Leonardo's reputation in architecture rests on some of his sketches, showing designs for simple, centralized churches, which later influenced Bramante.
[AB474] Thames & H hbk £45.00

LEWERENTZ, SIGURD
AHLIN, JANNE
Sigurd Lewerentz, Architect `NEW`
The first major work on this enigmatic Swedish architect, eclipsed by the fame of his partner and fellow countryman, Gunner Asplund.
[AB475] MIT hbk £44.95

LOOS, ADOLF (1869 - 1933)
Spoken into the Void: Collected Essays 1897-1900
A passionate and informed diatribe against applied design in *fin de siècle* Vienna from the very influential anti-ornamentalist modernist pioneer.
[AB476] MIT pbk £11.25

LUTYENS, SIR EDWIN (1869 - 1944)
Edwin Lutyens
Large paperback, offering a basic record of the architect's work.
[AB477] Academy Eds pbk £12.95
Houses and Gardens
[AB478] Antique Coll Club hbk £25.00

BUTLER, A.S.G.
The Domestic Architecture of Sir Edwin Lutyens `NEW`
A reprint of the first volume of the Lutyens memorial set, published six years after the architect's death in 1944. This is the most serious work on the domestic architecture of one of Britain's most famous architects: it is extensively illustrated and essential for architects and students interested in more traditional forms of building design.
[AB479] Antique Coll Club hbk £125.00
HUSSEY, CHRISTOPHER
The Life of Sir Edwin Lutyens
A first-class architectural biography. Readable and authoritative.
[AB480] Antique Coll Club hbk £25.00
LUTYENS, MARY
Edward Lutyens by his Daughter
An enjoyable personal memoir.
[AB481] J Murray hbk £13.95

MACHADO, RODOLFO & SILVETTI, JORGE
ROWE, PETER
Rodolfo Machado & Jorge Silvetti: Urban Design Work `NEW`
An illustrated documentation of 10 projects from this Boston-based architectural practice, including projects for Palermo, Sicily and a major transportation system.
[AB482] Rizzoli pbk £17.95

MACKINTOSH, CHARLES RENNIE
(1868 - 1928)
COOPER, J.; DUNSTER, D. & BERNARD, B.
Mackintosh Architecture
[AB483] Academy Eds pbk £12.95
GRIGG, J.
Charles Rennie Macintosh
[AB484] Drew pbk £5.95
HOWARTH, THOMAS
Charles Rennie Mackintosh and the Modern Movement
[AB485] Routledge hbk £35.00
MACLEOD, ROBERT
Charles Rennie Mackintosh
[AB486] Collins hbk £13.95

MCKIM, MEAD
ROTH, LELAND M.
McKim, Mead and White Architects
[AB487] Thames & H hbk £24.00

MEIER, RICHARD
RYKWERT, JOSEPH
Richard Meier, Architect
The acclaimed architectural historian traces the career of the award-winning modern architect whose buildings are seen as examples of economic solutions and deceptively simple designs.
[AB488] Rizzoli pbk £27.50

MENDELSOHN, ERICH (1887 - 1953)
ZEVI, BRUNO
Erich Mendelsohn
Mendelsohn was one of the masters and pioneers of the modern movement. This survey traces his career from Germany, where he was born and where he designed buildings of sculptural boldness, following him to London, Israel and finally the United States.
[AB489] Butterworth pbk £14.95

MICHELANGELO BUONARROTI
(1475 - 1564)
ACKERMAN, GERALD
Architecture of Michelangelo
[AB490] Zwemmer pbk £15.00

MICHELOZZO DI BARTOLOMMEO
(1396 - 1472)
Michelozzo and Donatello
An artistic partnership and its patrons in the early Renaissance.
[AB491] Miller hbk £45.00

MIES VAN DER ROHE, LUDWIG
(1886 - 1969)
JOHNSON, PHILIP
Mies van der Rohe
[AB492] Secker hbk £10.95
SPAETH, DAVID
Mies van der Rohe
Preface by Kenneth Frampton.
[AB493] Architectural P pbk £19.95
TEGETHOFF, WOLF
Mies van der Rohe: The Villas and Country Houses
A penetrating study of Mies's country house projects demonstrating the progressive realization of the famous modernist architect's goal to bring people, houses and nature into a greater unity.
[AB494] MIT hbk £53.95

MOLLINO, CARLO
BRINO, GIOVANNI
Carlo Mollino
A detailed monograph drawing on largely unpublished photographs.
[AB495] Thames & H pbk £18.95

MORPHOSIS
COOK, PETER `NEW`
Morphosis: Buildings and Projects
An asssessment of the influential avant-garde firm of Thom Mayne and Michael Rotondi based in California. This illustrated monograph documents the work of the past 15 years and comments on the architects' powerful use of ordinary materials and their clean, structurally sophisticated designs.
[AB496] Rizzoli pbk £25.00

NEUTRA, RICHARD
DREXLER, ARTHUR
Architecture of Richard Neutra
[AB497] Thames & H pbk £7.25
HINES, THOMAS
Richard Neutra and the Search for Modern Architecture
[AB498] Oxford pbk £19.50

OLBRICH, JOSEPH MARIA
HAIKO, PETER & KRIMMEL, BERND
Olbrich: Architecture `NEW`
The Austrian architect was one of the key representatives of the Vienna Secession. His reputation was established by the Secession Exhibition building, which is firm in its cubic and other basic shapes, as well as fanciful in its detail. This splendid monograph surveys all the work of the architect with a commentary on style and cultural context.
[AB499] Butterworth hbk £59.50

PALLADIO, ANDREA (1508 - 1580)
ACKERMAN, GERALD
Palladio
[AB500] Penguin pbk £5.99
CONSTANT, C.
The Palladio Guide
Very useful source-book.
[AB501] Architectural P pbk £14.95
PUPPI, LIONELLO
Andrea Palladio `NEW`
Inspired by the architecture of Ancient Rome, Palladio designed buildings of unrivalled harmony and beauty, and is widely considered to be one of Europe's greatest and most influential architects. This

richly illustrated book is regarded as the standard text on Palladio and offers a detailed critical and historical assessment of his work, as well as a chronological *catalogue raisonné*.
[AB502] Faber pbk **£25.00**

WITTKOWER, RUDOLF
Palladio and English Palladianism
A classic work.
[AB503] Thames & H pbk **£9.95**

PIANO, RENZO
DINI, MASSIMO
Renzo Piano: Projects and Buildings 1964 - 1983
A fully documented discussion, with many illustrations, of the architect's innovative and sophisticated buildings, which defy classification.
[AB504] Butterworth pbk **£19.95**

GOLDBERGER, PAUL
Renzo Piano: Buildings and Projects 1971 - 1989
Winner of this year's RIBA award, Piano is one of the most interesting architects of his generation combining high-tech sophistication with traditional craftsmanship. This splendidly illustrated monograph surveys the projects - beginning with the adventurous Centre George Pompidou in Paris - and examines his recent work in America and Europe, ending with the documentation for the future Kansai International airport in Japan.
[AB505] Rizzoli hbk **£37.50**

PIRANESI, GIOVANNI BATTISTA
(1720 - 1778)
ELY, JOHN WILTON
The Mind and Art of Giovanni Battista Piranesi
The essential monograph, profusely illustrated.
[AB507] Thames & H hbk **£18.95**

The Prisons
Reproduction of the drawings and engravings.
[AB509] Dover pbk **£5.55**

SCOTT, JONATHAN
Piranesi
[AB510] Academy Eds hbk **£35.00**

PLECNIK, JOZE
BURKHART, FRANCOIS
Joze Plecnick Architect, 1872 - 1957
A survey of the life and work of the Yugoslavian architect.
[AB511] MIT hbk **£35.95**

RICHARDSON H.H. (1838 - 1886)
OCHSNER, JEFFREY KARL
H.H. Richardson: Complete Architectural Works
With over 350 illustrations, this is the most complete overview of the influential 19th century American architect.
[AB512] MIT hbk **£26.95**

RIETVELD, GERRIT (1888 - 1964)
OVERY, PAUL
The Rietveld Schroder House
A documentation of the client-architect relationship which produced Rietveld's modern masterpiece in the outskirts of Utrecht. The house was completed in 1925 and has been recently restored and opened to the public.
[AB513] Butterworth hbk **£25.00**

ROCHE, KEVIN
DAL CO, FRANCESCO (ED)
Kevin Roche
This is the first monograph on the award-winning contemporary American architect. With over 350 illustrations.
[AB514] Butterworth hbk **£39.50**

ROGERS, RICHARD
APPLEYARD, BRYAN
Richard Rogers: A Biography
An excellent account of the life and work of one of Europe's most controversial architects, whose distinctive hi-tech style of modernism is seen to best advantage in huge functional buildings like the Centre Pompidou in Paris and the Lloyd's Building in London.
[AB515] Faber pbk **£9.95**

ROSSI, ALDO
A Scientific Autobiography
A critical assessment of the Italian post-modernist's own buildings and approaches to architecture in general.
[AB517] MIT pbk **£9.95**

Aldo Rossi Architect
[AB518] Architectural P pbk **£15.00**

Architecture of the City
A major critical reassessment of modernism from an inquisitive opponent and highly idiosyncratic architect which reminds us that the achievements of individual architects are less important than the cities themselves.
[AB519] MIT pbk **£10.95**

ARNELL
Aldo Rossi: Buildings and Projects
Aldo Rossi is one of Italy's pre-eminent contemporary architects, his buildings disquietingly evocative, purist designs with minimal intrusions of ornament, linked to Italian rationalism. This monograph documents the built and unbuilt works as well as the architect's influential and uncompromising ideas.
[AB520] Rizzoli pbk **£25.00**

SALVIN, ANTHONY
ALLIBONE, JILL
Anthony Salvin: Pioneer of Gothic Revival Architecture
[AB521] Lutterworth hbk **£19.50**

SANSOVINO, JACOB (1486 - 1916)
HOWARD, DEBORAH
Jacob Sansovino
Architecture and patronage in Renaissance Venice.
[AB522] Yale UP pbk **£9.95**

SANT' ELIA, ANTONIO (1888 - 1916)
CARAMEL, LUCIANO & LONGATTI, ALBERTO
Antonio Sant' Elia: The Complete Works **NEW**
Although no buildings are definitely attributed to the futurist architect, Sant' Elia has exerted considerable influence on modernism. This is a beautifully produced catalogue of drawings and writings from this enigmatic figure who extolled the virtues of technology and industrialism.
[AB523] Rizzoli hbk **£45.00**

SCARPA, CARLO
DAL CO, FRANCESCO & MAZZARIOL, GIUSEPPE
Carlo Scarpa: The Complete Works
A beautifully produced and complete account of the Italian architect's built and unrealized projects which are distinguished by a restrained and distilled elegance, and the subtle but forceful celebration of materials.
[AB524] Butterworth hbk **£39.50**

SEDDON, JOHN POLLARD
DARBY
John Pollard Seddon
The drawings of this wonderful Pre-Raphaelite/Gothic architect.
[AB525] V & A Mus P hbk **£11.95**

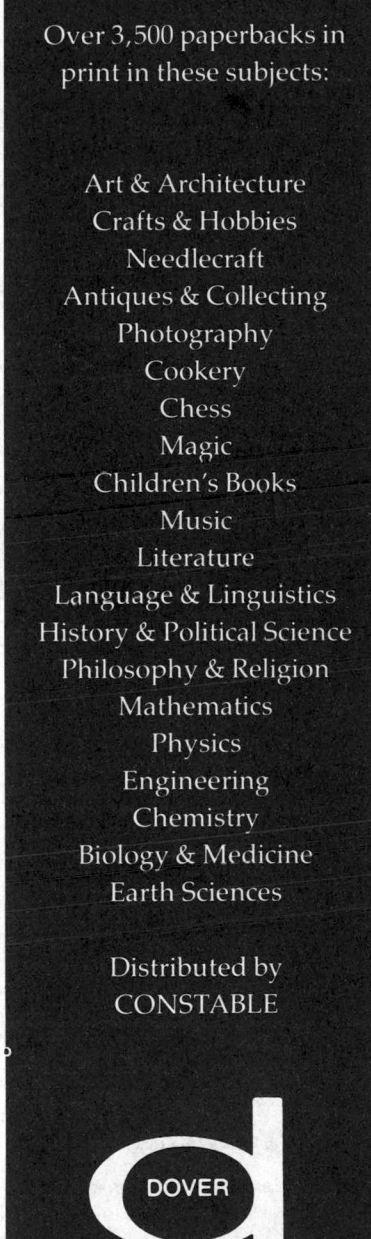

SHAW, RICHARD NORMAN (1831 - 1912)
SAINT, ANDREW
Richard Norman Shaw
[AB527] Yale UP pbk **£13.95**

SHUTZE, PHILIP TRAMMELL
DOWLING, ELIZABETH MEREDITH
American Classicist: Architecture of Philip Trammell Shutze NEW
Shutze spent 5 years in Italy meticulously studying Renaissance and Baroque architecture. Returning to America he designed over 750 buildings evolving an italianate classical style. His career spans the first half of this century and was marked by a determination to resist the rising tide of modernism.
[AB528] Rizzoli hbk **£35.00**
[AB529] Rizzoli pbk **£19.95**

SMITHSON, PETER (1923 -) **& ALISON** (1928 -)
A. & P. Smithson
[AB530] Academy Eds pbk **£9.95**
Heroic Period of Modern Architecture
[AB531] Thames & H pbk **£7.95**

SNOZZI, LUIGI
STRATHAUS & FRAMPTON & GREGOTTI
Luigi Snozzi: 1957-1984
Although only a few built works exist, Snozzi is one of Italy's most interesting contemporary architects. Including a brief text by the architect and illustrated with over 240 plans, models, drawings and photographs.
[AB532] Butterworth pbk **£25.00**

SOANE, SIR JOHN (1753 - 1837)
John Soane
A very attractive monograph with quality reproductions of Gandy's watercolours of Soane's work.
[AB533] Academy Eds pbk **£12.95**
STROUD, DOROTHY
Sir John Soane Architect
The best overall study of the architect.
[AB534] Faber hbk **£32.00**

STIRLING, JAMES
ARNELL, PETER & BICKFORD, TED
James Stirling: Buildings and Projects
A complete documentation, up to 1986, of the internationally acclaimed British architect's built and unbuilt works including his museums in Stuttgart and Cologne as well as the Clore extension housing the Turner collection of the Tate Gallery.
[AB535] Butterworth pbk **£29.50**

SULLIVAN, LOUIS H. (1856 - 1924)
TWOMBLY
Louis Sullivan: His Life and Work
[AB536] Chicago UP hbk **£13.50**
WEINGARDEN, LAUREN S.
Louis H. Sullivan: The Banks NEW
Louis Sullivan's buildings are noted for the brilliance of their ornamentation and functional expressionism. The author examines the architect's Mid Western banks and argues for their inclusion in the pantheon of masterworks.
[AB537] MIT hbk **£22.50**

TERRY, QUINLAN
Quinlan Terry
Leading contemporary British neo-classcist, and a disciple of Raymond Erith. Terry's rigorously traditional work has been championed by, among others, Roger Scruton.
[AB538] Academy Eds pbk **£5.95**
ASLET, CLIVE
Quinlan Terry
[AB539] Viking hbk **£40.00**

UNWIN, SIR RAYMOND (1863 - 1957)
The most important figure in the development of modern town planning, responsible for the successful implementation of the 'garden city' idea.
JACKSON, FRANK
Sir Raymond Unwin
[AB540] Zwemmer pbk **£15.95**

VANBRUGH, JOHN (1664 - 1726)
Vanbrugh was the outstanding English baroque architect, famous for the extravagances of Blenheim Palace and Castle Howard, as well as his literary achievements.
BEARD, GEOFFREY
The Work of John Vanburgh
[AB541] Batsford pbk **£12.95**
DOWNES, KERRY
Vanbrugh
[AB542] Zwemmer hbk **£57.50**

VELDE, HENRY VAN DE (1863 - 1957)
SEMBACH, KLAUS-JURGEN
Henry van der Velde NEW
The Belgian architect is noted for his influential architectural output which stressed honesty of design and the importance of line, as well as for his activity in other arts such as painting and metalware. Van de Velde was a pioneer of modernism in his rejection of 19th century historicism and a leading advocate of bringing good design to a wider public. With over 320 illustrations.
[AB543] Thames & H hbk **£30.00**

VENTURI, RAUCH & SCOTT BROWN
VON MOOS
Venturi, Rauch & Scott Brown
A survey of the important architectural firm headed by the theorist, historian and practising architect Robert Venturi.
[AB544] Rizzoli pbk **£25.00**

VITRUVIUS, POLLIO (active 46 - 30 BC)
Ten Books On Architecture
(Trans. Morgan)
[AB545] Dover pbk **£5.95**
MCKAY, ALEXANDER
Vitruvius: Architect and Engineer
The Roman architect of seminal influence in the Renaissance and afterwards.
[AB546] Bristol Classics pbk **£4.95**

WAGNER, OTTO (1841 - 1918)
Austrian architect whose impressive public architecture (including Vienna's Post Office Savings Bank) has a clarity and economy which was very modern in his own day.
Sketches, Projects & Executed Buildings
[AB547] Architectural P hbk **£59.50**

WREN, SIR CHRISTOPHER (1632 - 1723)
Usually described as England's greatest architect, Wren was a brilliant scientist and geometrician, who went on to design St Paul's Cathedral.
DOWNES, KERRY
The Architecture of Wren
A classic monograph.
[AB549] Redhedge pbk **£10.95**
WHINNEY, MARGARET
Wren
[AB550] Thames & H pbk **£5.95**

WRIGHT, FRANK LLOYD (1869 - 1959)
Frank Lloyd Wright: Preserving an Architectural Heritage
An illustrated source-book of design.
[AB551] Studio Vista hbk **£19.95**
Letters to Apprentices
[AB552] Architectural P pbk **£12.50**

Letters to Architects
[AB553] Architectural P pbk **£12.50**
Letters to Clients
[AB554] Architectural P pbk **£12.50**
GEBBHARD, DAVID
The California Architecture of Frank Lloyd Wright
A detailed analysis of Wright's 24 California NEW buildings, attempting to understand the design of site-specific works which aim at a perfect integration of indoors and outdoors, as well as determining the extent to which his personal interests in primitive forms and his defiant, uncompromising posturing manifest themselves in the buildings.
[AB555] Thames & H hbk **£20.00**
HEINZ, THOMAS A.
Frank Lloyd Wright
A perfect introduction to the work of America's most famous architect. The bulk of the book consists of 80 specially commissioned full-colour photographs of buildings and interiors, showing the diversity of plan, structure and texture. Includes an introductory essay and bibliography.
[AB556] Academy Eds pbk **£14.95**
JENCKS, CHARLES
Kings of Infinite Space: Frank Lloyd Wright and Michael Graves
A popular title in the Academy range of large-format paperbacks on architects.
[AB557] Academy Eds pbk **£12.50**
KAUFMAN, EDGAR JUN.
Fallingwater: A Frank Lloyd Wright Country House
A lavishly illustrated and detailed examination of perhaps the most famous modern house in America, an undoubted masterpiece of domestic architecture. Fallingwater's awesome cantilevered projections, glorious detailing, and placing in the natural setting are captured in this book.
[AB558] Butterworth hbk **£39.50**
LIPMAN, JONATHAN
Frank Lloyd Wright and the Johnson Wax Buildings
Considered among the architect's major achievements, the Johnson Wax buildings in Racine, Wisconsin, are masterfully streamlined structures with innovative use of materials including brick and glass tubing, and a grand interior space with reinforced concrete mushroom columns.
[AB559] Butterworth hbk **£29.50**
MUSCHAMP, HERBERT
Man about Town: Frank Lloyd Wright in New York City
An examination of Wright's built and unbuilt New York works.
[AB560] MIT pbk **£7.25**

WYATT, JAMES (1747 - 1813) **& THOMAS** (1807 - 1880)
ROBINSON, JOHN MARTIN
The Wyatts: An Architectural Dynasty
A very scholary work on the late 18th and early 19th century family of architects whose speciality was the neo-Gothic style.
[AB561] Oxford hbk **£45.00**

An illustration from *Piranesi* by Nicholas Penny (Oresko Books Ltd, currently unavailable)

Biographical Reference
Literary Biography
Historical & Political Biography
General Biography

Biography

A Treasury of Letters

Christopher Hibbert

"O ay, letters," says the coquettish Millamant in Congreve's *The Way of the World*, *"I had letters - I am persecuted with letters - I hate letters - nobody knows how to write letters; and yet one has 'em one does not know why - they serve one to pin up one's hair."*

Well, perhaps most letters deserve no better; but for my part I enjoy few books more than good thick volumes of correspondence written by such master hands as Horace Walpole or journals by such inquisitive and candid diarists as James Boswell. To see 17th century Venice, for example, through the discerning eyes of John Evelyn, or to go over Louis XV's Versailles in the company of Mrs Thrale or to visit Renishaw and meet Sir Osbert Sitwell's extraordinary father, or to be in Yugoslavia during the war with Evelyn Waugh exasperated by the 'appalling' Randolph Churchill, are pleasures for me that never pall. Then there is the delight of coming across a diarist unknown before; to have, for instance, life in an early 19th century village in Somerset vividly brought to life in the journal of a quarrelsome rector, John Skinner (*Journal of a Somerset Rector*). Some of my own favourite collections of letters and diaries are these:

SAMUEL PEPYS
The Diary of Samuel Pepys
A superb edition of the most entertaining of seventeenth-century diaries, a new and complete transcription with fascinating notes full of out-of-the-way information. From these beautifully printed pages emerge both a revealing self-portrait of a disarming hedonist and a fascinating picture of everyday life in London from the Restoration of Charles II until the diarist's failing sight brought his unique work to a close. For those alarmed by the cost of all eleven volumes (£190), there are well-chosen extracts in *The Illustrated Pepys*. (Bell & Hyman, pbk £8.95)

LORD BYRON
The Letters of Lord Byron
Another treasure trove, the marvellously readable correspondence of the poet who had so profound an influence upon the Romantic movement. Byron records with wonderful verve and wit his encounters with all kinds of men and women in England and on the Continent - his dramatic experiences and love affairs, in page after page of prose that seems to pour from the heart. There is also a one-volume selection edited by Leslie A. Marchand.
(John Murray, 12 vols hbk £155/selection hbk £12.50, Picador pbk £5.95)

LADY MARY WORTLEY MONTAGU
The Selected Letters of Lady Mary Wortley Montagu
The frank self-portrait of one of the most remarkable women of the 18th century, daughter of the Duke of Kingston, intimate friend of Addison and Pope, and wife of the British ambassador in Constantinople whom she abandoned for the Italian author, Francesco Algarotti. Lady Mary spent much of her life in Italy where Horace Walpole met her in Florence in 1740 when she had become an 'old, foul, tawdry, painted personage'. She was always certainly far from clean: when someone commented on the dirtiness of her hands, she airily replied, "If you call that dirty you should see my feet." But she was highly intelligent, amusing and a correspondent of rare insight. The complete three-volume edition of her letters is out of print. (Penguin, pbk £6.99)

EVELYN WAUGH
The Letters and Diaries of Evelyn Waugh
Candid, sometimes moving and often wildly funny, these diaries, beginning in 1911 when the author was seven and ending at Easter 1965, a year before his death, must surely be among the most revealing documents a great novelist has ever left behind him. Open them at any page and the attention is gripped immediately. The pen portraits of his friends and acquaintances are masterly. (The Diaries: Weidenfeld, hbk £14.95; The Letters: Penguin, pbk £8.95)

HAROLD NICOLSON
The Diaries & Letters of Harold Nicolson 1930 - 1964
The enthralling journals of a versatile and delightful man, Member of Parliament, junior Minister, journalist, broadcaster, friend of many of the leading figures of his day, and husband of Vita Sackville-West. Nicolson paints not only a brilliant picture of English society from the 1930s to the 1960s but a whole gallery of its inhabitants; he also tells us more about himself than perhaps he meant to do. His accounts of scenes in Parliament during the war are unforgettable. This one-volume selection is edited by Stanley Olson.
(Collins, hbk £12.95)

Evelyn Waugh, whose *Letters* are published by Penguin (pbk £8.95) (Photo: Methuen)

JOHN EVELYN
The Diary of John Evelyn

Anyone who enjoys Pepys should also like John Evelyn who left England after the outbreak of the Civil War and travelled on the Continent for four years before settling down at Sayes Court, Deptford. His style is more ponderous than that of Pepys but his interests range far and wide, and his descriptions of 17th century travel and sight-seeing, and of life in England under the later Stuarts, are absorbing.
(Oxford, pbk £5.95)

John Evelyn, whose Diary is published by Oxford University Press (pbk £5.95)

JAMES BOSWELL
The Journals of James Boswell

A compulsive writer's exact and vivacious record of people met, places visited, conversations enjoyed, and tireless pursuits of celebrated men and complaisant women. Everywhere the pushy, clever little Scotsman goes he is most carefully observant of clothes and accents, features and gestures down to the very length of a finger nail or the cut of a wig. He is at his most acute and entertaining in the *London Journal* but all the other journals are full of delights and of evidence of that practised expertise as a diarist which makes his *Life of Johnson* (Oxford, £8.95) the fresh, unique and indispensable work of art which it is. His diaries were, of course, an essential source not only for his biography of Johnson, but also for his own, which has been extremely well written by Frederick A. Pottle, (*The Earlier Years*) and Frank Brady, (*The Later Years*) and more succinctly, by Iain Finlayson, (*The Moth and the Flame*; only this is currently available, from Constable, hbk £9.95).

FANNY BURNEY
Journals and Letters

There were those who considered Boswell's imitations of Johnson's odd manner superior even to Garrick's. Fanny Burney thought them 'comical to excess', though 'far from caricature'. Miss Burney's own charming diaries contain delightful vignettes about the great man as well as endlessly entertaining stories of the life of a bluestocking, novelist and extremely harassed Keeper of the Queen's Robes whose duties were made all the more difficult by her not being allowed to wear spectacles, for this would have been a breach of court etiquette. The Burney diaries and letters are available in twelve, necessarily rather expensive volumes (Oxford, 12 vols hbk £594), but here again the publishers offer a selection (hbk, £19.50, pbk £5.95)

Lastly, two irresistible journals by two very different hands: the moving record of the quiet life of a country parson in Wales, Francis Kilvert's *Diary* (Cape three vols hbk £35; selected Penguin, pbk £4.99), and an effervescent evocation of literary life in Paris by those two most brilliant gossips, the brothers Goncourt: *Pages from the Goncourt Journal*, (Oxford, pbk £5.95).

Fanny Burney; a selection of her journals and letters are published by Oxford University Press (hbk £19.50, pbk £5.95)

An acclaimed popular historian, Christopher Hibbert is the author of a wide and varied range of works, including studies of Charles Dickens, Samuel Johnson and Benito Mussolini; his *The English: A Social History 1066-1945* appeared in 1987.

BIOGRAPHY

Reference

BULLOCK, ALLAN & WOODINGS, R.B.
The Fontana Biographical Companion to Modern Thought
An excellent companion to major 20th century thinkers.
[BB1] Fontana pbk **£9.95**

DICTIONARY OF NATIONAL BIOGRAPHY
This is the main historical source for biographical details about Britons. It is arranged alphabetically, each entry is prepared by a scholar distinguished in the subject's field, and the entries are regularly updated. The major historical work goes up to 1900, additional volumes covering those who died in the following decades are now published.
1951 - 1960
[BB2] Oxford hbk **£70.00**
1961 - 1970
[BB3] Oxford hbk **£70.00**
1971 - 1980
[BB4] Oxford hbk **£70.00**
Concise: From the Beginnings to 1900
[BB5] Oxford hbk **£75.00**
From the Earliest Times to 1900: 22 Volumes
[BB6] Oxford hbk **£850.00**

ISAACS & MARTIN
Longman Dictionary of 20th Century Biography
[BB7] Longman hbk **£13.95**

THORNE, J.O. (ED)
Chambers Biographical Dictionary
A recommended general work covering many figures in good detail.
[BB8] Chambers hbk **£25.00**
[BB9] Chambers pbk **£15.00**

LITERARY BIOGRAPHY

ACKERLEY, ROGER (1896 - 1967)
My Father and Myself
Ackerley describes his youth, which was soured by the complicated domestic arrangements of his bigamous father.
[B1] Penguin pbk **£3.50**
PARKER, PETER
Ackerley **NEW**
J.R. Ackerley was an editor, novelist, poet and autobiographer, whose life was as extraordinary as it was eventful. He was wounded on the Somme, and after the war went to Cambridge where he began a lifelong friendship with E.M. Forster. He travelled to India, an experience which inspired him to write the classic *Hindoo Holiday*. He was a gifted editor of *The Listener* and encouraged Virginia Woolf, amongst others. This biography also examines his less successful personal life. Here Ackerley is revealed as a promiscuous homosexual whose life ricocheted between tragedy and farce.
[B2] Constable hbk **£15.95**

PETRE, DIANA
The Secret Orchard of Roger Ackerley
This book, by the daughter of the other family of Roger Ackerley's father, attempts to redress the balance of the portrait painted by Ackerley.
[B3] H Hamilton pbk **£4.95**

ACTON, HAROLD (1904 -)
An art historian, now settled in Italy, Acton was a contemporary of Evelyn Waugh at Oxford, on whom the character of Anthony Blanche in *Brideshead Revisited* is popularly supposed to have been based. Written shortly after he was demobilised from the RAF, these memoirs cover the first 35 years of Acton's life. He wittily records an era in which the 'aesthete' still held his ground against the specialist and the politician.
Memoirs of an Aesthete
[B4] H Hamilton pbk **£5.95**
More Memoirs of an Aesthete
[B5] H Hamilton pbk **£6.95**

AKSAKOV, SERGEI (1791 - 1859)
Years of Childhood
Aksakov's sympathetic and lyrical childhood reminiscences give a fascinating insight into rural life in Russia at the close of the 18th and beginning of the 19th centuries. In this volume he recounts his life as a small boy on his father's country estate.
[B6] Oxford pbk **£3.95**
A Russian Schoolboy
Aksakov remembers his magical country boyhood, and its rural pursuits: hunting for mushrooms, shooting, and visits to mummers' revels. He goes on to compare this with his unhappy experiences at boarding school. Introduced by John Bayley.
[B7] Oxford pbk **£5.95**
A Russian Gentleman
The Russian novelist Sergei Aksakov, portrays Russian provincial life in the reign of Catherine the Great, and gives an intimate portrait of his grandfather, Stefan Mikhailovich.
[B8] Oxford pbk **£3.95**

ALAIN-FOURNIER, HENRI (1886 - 1914)
Towards the Lost Domain: Letters from London 1905
Fournier's postcards and letters back to France giving his impressions of London.
[B9] Carcanet hbk **£16.95**
ARKELL, DAVID
Alain-Fournier: A Brief Life
Alain-Fournier wrote one acknowledged masterpiece of French fiction, *Le Grand Meaulnes*, before he was killed in action during the First World War. This well-illustrated biography includes a portfolio of Alain-Fournier's own photographs. It tells, in his own words and those of his friends, of the cheerful, fragile, pre-war Parisian world he knew, and of the time he spent in London.
[B10] Carcanet hbk **£9.95**

ANGELOU, MAYA (1928 -)
Born in 1928 in St Louis, Missouri, Maya Angelou was raped at the age of eight by her mother's boy-friend. In a quite remarkable life she has been a wait-ress, a singer, an actress, a dancer, a Black Activist, an editor, as well as a mother. She describes it as 'a roller coaster life', and in her phenomenal autobiographical sequence, she renders the depths and the heights in forceful prose. The impression she creates is of an exhilarating journey through pleasure and pain.
I Know Why the Caged Bird Sings
This bestselling first volume of autobiography evokes Angelou's childhood in the American South in the 1930s, where she learns the power of the 'whitefolks' at the other end of the town. She finds escape in the pleasures of dance and drama.
[B11] Virago pbk **£3.95**

Maya Angelou, author of *I Know Why the Caged Bird Sings* (Virago pbk **£3.95**)

Gather Together in My Name
[B12] Virago pbk **£3.95**
Singin' and Swingin' and Gettin' Merry like Christmas
[B13] Virago pbk **£3.95**
The Heart of a Woman
Angelou moves to New York and becomes immersed in the world of black writers and artists in Harlem. She becomes involved with Martin Luther King and the Black Civil Rights movement and marries a South African freedom fighter.
[B14] Virago pbk **£3.95**
All God's Children Need Travelling Shoes
Angelou emigrates to Africa, where she experiences the joy of being black in a black country.
[B15] Virago pbk **£3.95**
ELLIOT, JEFFREY M.
Conversations with Maya Angelou **NEW**
Over two dozen interviews from British and American magazines, in which Angelou talks about her rich and varied life.
[B16] Virago pbk **£4.50**

APOLLINAIRE, GUILLAUME (1880 - 1918)
STEEGMULLER, FRANCIS
Apollinaire: Poet Among the Painters
Guillaume Apollinaire is celebrated as much for his unconventional life as for his writing. He was a Symbolist poet and champion of modernism, admired by Picasso, Braque and others. This biography is the standard life of an extraordinary figure.
[B17] Penguin pbk **£4.95**

ARCHER, JEFFREY (1940 -)
MANTLE, JONATHAN
In for a Penny
The unauthorised biography of Jeffrey Archer, champion runner, bestselling novelist and former Deputy Chairman of the Conservative Party. It details his rise as a politician, his subsequent decline into bankruptcy, and the manner in which he wrote himself out of disaster and became a hugely popular writer.
[B18] Sphere pbk **£3.50**

ARNIM, ELIZABETH VON (1822 - 1888)
USBORNE, KAREN
'Elizabeth'
A life of the Austrian-born cousin of Katherine Mansfield, who married into German aristocracy. She is best remembered for her novel *Elizabeth and her German Garden*.
[B19] Bodley hbk **£15.00**

AUBREY, JOHN (1626 - 1697)
Brief Lives
Aubrey's gossipy and intimate profiles of Elizabethan English personalities manage to sum up, despite their brevity, the most important characteristics of their subject. With great wit Aubrey portrays the human essences and excesses of people such as Francis Bacon, John of Gaunt, John Milton, Sir Walter Raleigh and Sir Kenelm Digby, a naval commander, of whom he says: *'No man became Grandeur better'.* This selection includes about one third of the complete *Brief Lives.*
[B20] Penguin pbk **£5.95**
POWELL, ANTHONY
John Aubrey and his Friends
A scholarly portrait of the great English eccentric, by the novelist Anthony Powell. Aubrey was a fascinating man who grew up in the shadow of the Civil Wars. His voluminous and acquisitive mind was interested in everything from heraldry to horticulture.
[B21] Hogarth pbk **£7.95**

AUDEN, WYSTAN HUGH (1907 - 1973)
CARPENTER, HUMPHREY
W.H. Auden: A Biography
This is an excellent and acclaimed biography of one of the greatest 20th century poets, providing the first full account of Auden's literary development. Using letters, manuscripts and journals, Carpenter shows how Auden found his poetic voice in the late 1920s. The book also explains many of the private jokes in the early poems, and shows how an intensely private crisis in Auden's homosexual love life brought him into the fertile period of his last three long poems.
[B22] Unwin Hyman pbk **£5.95**
ROWSE, A.L.
The Poet Auden: A Personal Memoir
[B23] Methuen hbk **£9.95**

AUSTEN, JANE (1775 - 1817)
AUSTEN-LEIGH, J.E.
Memoir of Jane Austen
First published in 1870, this is Austen-Leigh's revealing memoir of his aunt. It is the only published record by someone who actually knew Jane Austen and is worthy for that fact alone. This edition includes a new introduction by Fay Weldon.
[B24] Century pbk **£4.95**

Jane Austen (Picture: National Portrait Gallery)

CECIL, DAVID
A Portrait of Jane Austen
This superbly illustrated and enjoyable portrait has achieved almost classic status: it presents a careful blend of illustration, documentary, literary analysis and social history.
[B25] Constable hbk **£12.95**
[B26] Penguin pbk **£7.95**
HALPERIN, JOHN
Life of Jane Austen
A comprehensive and highly recommended critical biography which challenges the received view of Austen's life, revealing her feelings of social exclusion and her complicated relationships with men.
[B27] Harvester pbk **£8.95**
HONAN, PARK
Jane Austen: Her Life
Highly detailed and acclaimed recent biography, which includes much new material, some of it scandalous. This is the best biography of Austen available: Jonathan Keates wrote in the *Independent*: 'the best attempt yet at pinning down the elusive Jane.'
[B28] Weidenfeld hbk **£18.00**
[B28] Weidenfeld pbk **£8.95**
JENKINS, ELIZABETH
Jane Austen
This 1938 biography is for many the standard life of Jane Austen. It atmospherically evokes the world of Georgian England, the small circle of Jane Austen's friends, and shows how this was reflected in her novels. It carefully traces the development of Austen's writing from the early works to the great mature novels *Emma* and *Persuasion*.
[B29] Gollancz pbk **£4.95**
LASKI, MARGHANITA
Jane Austen
[B30] Thames & H pbk **£3.95**

BAGNOLD, ENID (1889 - 1981)
Autobiography
Bagnold was the author of the classic *National Velvet*. She describes her life from childhood in Jamaica, to 'coming out' in pre-war London, when she became part of the artistic circle in Chelsea in 1912, mixing with poets and painters such as Walter Sickert and Edward Thomas. Bagnold went on to become a grand hostess.
[B31] Century pbk **£4.95**
SEBBA, ANNE
Enid Bagnold: A Biography
[B32] Weidenfeld pbk **£8.95**

BARING, MAURICE (1874 - 1945)
Baring was a versatile writer, essayist, diplomat and reporter who is credited with helping to introduce Chekhov to the West. His autobiography describes his childhood in London, then Eton and Cambridge, followed by his studies in Russia just before the Revolution.
The Puppet Show of Memory
[B33] Cassell pbk **£6.95**

BARNES, DJUNA (1892 - 1982)
FIELD, ANDREW
**The Formidable Miss Barnes:
A Biography**
Biography of the American writer who lived in the Bohemian Greenwich Village of New York, and later became part of the expatriate community in Paris. She is best remembered for her extravagantly nightmarish novel *Nightwood*.
[B34] Secker hbk **£12.95**

BARRIE, J.M. (1860 - 1937)
BIRKIN, ANDREW
J.M. Barrie and the Lost Boys
It was whilst walking in Kensington Gardens that

J.M. Barrie first met the eldest three Llewellyn Davies boys, George, Jack and Peter. This illustrated book tells the unusual and moving story of Barrie's involvement with the family, which led to the creation of *Peter Pan*.
[B35] Constable pbk **£7.95**

BAUDELAIRE, CHARLES (1821 - 1867)
PICHOIS, CLAUDE
Baudelaire   **NEW**
This life of Baudelaire draws on a century's worth of research and scholarship, as well as Baudelaire's own writings. It analyses his fraught life, and his assault on the tastes of bourgeois readership, through his most famous work *Les Fleurs du Mal*.
[B36] H Hamilton hbk **£17.95**

BEACH, SYLVIA
FITCH, NOEL RILEY
Sylvia Beach and the Lost Generation
The first full portrait of Sylvia Beach and the multi-faceted goings-on at Shakespeare & Co, her celebrated bookshop in Paris.
[B37] Penguin pbk **£5.95**

BEAUVOIR, SIMONE DE (1908 - 1987)
Simone de Beauvoir was a giant in 20th century French culture. She will be remembered for the diversity of her influence on French life: as a pioneering feminist; for her unconventional relationship with the philosopher Jean-Paul Sartre; as the author of the ground-breaking study of women *The Second Sex* and the Prix Goncourt-winning novel *The Mandarins*; and for her courageously honest autobiography.
Memoirs of a Dutiful Daughter
The opening volume of de Beauvoir's autobiography, published in 1958, deals with her stiflingly respectable childhood. The book is remarkable for its depiction of her years of adolescence, between the ages of 13 and 17.
[B38] Penguin pbk **£4.95**
The Prime of Life
In this second volume (1960) de Beauvoir describes her life from the age of 21, through the uneasy 1930s, up to the war years. She writes with honesty of her struggle to become a writer.
[B39] Penguin pbk **£6.95**
Force of Circumstance
This volume, published in 1963, deals with de Beauvoir's unflinching political commitments to Vietnam, Suez, Cuba and Algeria, as well as her notoriety in middle age, and her relationships with Nelson Algren and Sartre.
[B40] Penguin pbk **£7.99**
All Said and Done
This final volume of autobiography covers the years 1962 to 1972. De Beauvoir reflects on the general course of her life, travels and relationships, as well as her commitment to feminism.
[B41] Penguin pbk **£6.95**
A Very Easy Death
[B42] Penguin pbk **£2.95**
Adieux: A Farewell to Sartre
This touching account of the loving relationship between de Beauvoir and Jean-Paul Sartre includes a frank account of his death. It also includes the transcript of a remarkable long conversation which they had in 1974, in which Sartre expresses himself fully on subjects which meant much to him: women, politics, religion and food.
[B43] Penguin pbk **£5.95**
CROSLAND, MARGARET
The Woman and Her Work
[B44] Heinemann hbk **£14.95**
FRANCIS, CLAUDE & GONTIER, FERNANDE
Simone de Beauvoir
The first full-scale biography of de Beauvoir confronts some of the paradoxes of her life. In

particular it attempts to reconcile her role as a major developer of feminist thought in the 20th century with her selfless devotion to Jean-Paul Sartre. It draws on 1,682 previously unpublished letters between de Beauvoir and Nelson Algren.
[B45] Sidgwick hbk **£16.95**

OKELY, JUDITH
Simone de Beauvoir
Looks at the changes in women's lives and in feminist thinking over the last 20 years, in order to assess how these have affected her own reponse to de Beauvoir.
[B46] Virago pbk **£4.95**

BEERBOHM, MAX (1872 - 1956)
CECIL, DAVID
Max
[B47] Constable pbk **£7.95**

HART-DAVIS, RUPERT (ED)
Letters of Max Beerbohm: 1893 - 1956
Beerbohm, *'the incomparable Max'* as Bernard Shaw called him, was a perfectionist, who tended to berate his abilities as a letter writer. This generous selection, however, shows flashes of his humour and delicate irony, whether defending *Zuleika Dobson* to Arnold Bennett, or writing to Edmund Gosse and Lytton Strachey.
[B49] J Murray hbk **£16.95**
[B48] Oxford pbk **£6.95**

BEHAN, BRENDAN (1923 - 1964)
Borstal Boy
Behan's notorious, provocative memoir of prison and borstal life. Kenneth Tynan said *"Behan sends language out on a swaggering spree, ribald, flushed and spoiling for a fight"*.
[B50] Corgi pbk **£3.50**
Confessions of an Irish Rebel
The final volume of his autobiography, published posthumously.
[B51] Arrow pbk **£2.95**
O'CONNOR, ULICK
Brendan Behan
[B52] Corgi pbk **£2.95**

BEHN, APHRA (1640 - 1689)
DUFFY, MAUREEN
The Passionate Shepherdess: Aphra Behn 1640 - 89   **NEW**
Aphra Behn was born in the 1640s, and by her mid-twenties she had travelled to South America, returned to England, been married and widowed. She was sent by Charles II to Antwerp as a spy, then on her return was imprisoned for debt. Once out of prison she became one of the most successful Restoration dramatists. Yet since then her reputation has been eclipsed. This biography sifts the life from the legend to restore this pioneering woman to contemporary attention.
[B53] Methuen pbk **£7.99**

BELL, CLIVE (1881 - 1964)
ARONSON, THEO
Old Friends
[B54] Cassell pbk **£5.95**

BELL, VANESSA (1879 - 1961)
SPALDING, FRANCES
Vanessa Bell
This first full-length biography of the painter Vanessa Bell (sister of Virginia Woolf) traces her emergence from a privileged but restricted background. It concentrates on the effects of her exposure to the radical art of the Post-Impressionists and the Bloomsbury intellectuals.
[B55] Macmillan pbk **£9.95**

BELLOC, HILAIRE (1870 - 1953)
MCCARTHY, DERMOD
Sailing with Mr Belloc
In 1931 Belloc acquired an ancient Channel Island

pilot cutter called *The Jersey*, and went to sea. Dermod McCarthy was one of the crew, and in his engaging memoirs he follows the ship and its crew over the next 15 years. The portrait of Belloc, robed in thick sweater, glass of wine in hand, shows a man of rugged and warm character.
[B56] Grafton pbk **£5.95**
WILSON, A.N.
Hilaire Belloc
Belloc was an MP, an accomplished writer and propagandist, yet nowadays he is chiefly remembered for his book of comic children's verse, *Cautionary Tales*. He was a noisy controversial figure with extreme religious views, and many enemies. Wilson's admirable and sympathetic biography restores Belloc to his proper place as a major literary figure.
[B57] H Hamilton hbk **£12.95**
[B58] Penguin pbk **£5.95**

BENNETT, ARNOLD (1867 - 1931)
DRABBLE, MARGARET
Arnold Bennett
Bennett, who is best known for the *Clayhanger* series of novels set in the Potteries of Staffordshire, is less popular now than in his own lifetime. He was quite a phenomenon in his day - a passionate cyclist, friend of H.G. Wells, and enemy of Ezra Pound. Drabble's enthusiastic study does much to reclaim Bennett's reputation and restore it to its rightful position: she shows us what a major writer and what a 'good', whole-hearted man he was.
[B59] Penguin pbk **£5.95**

BENSON, E.F. (1867 - 1940)
As We Were
Benson was one of six eccentric children born to Queen Victoria's Archbishop of Canterbury. E.F. is the best remembered of the family, primarily for his creation of the droll and whimsical *Mapp and Lucia* books. He was three times mayor of Rye in Sussex, where he lived in Henry James's former house. In this memoir, originally published in 1930, he looks back nostalgically to Queen Victoria's reign.
[B60] Hogarth pbk **£4.95**
Final Edition
This urbane volume of memoirs was completed ten days before Benson's death. In it he looks back to his youth as the son of the Archbishop of Canterbury, and his years in the dazzling literary London world of Somerset Maugham and Norman Douglas.
[B61] Hogarth pbk **£5.95**
Queen Victoria
Benson's tribute, first published in 1935, to the Victorian era.
[B62] Chatto hbk **£14.95**
PALMER, GEOFFREY & LLOYD, NOEL
E.F. Benson: As He Was
This first biography of Benson follows him from his youth at prep school, to Marlborough, Cambridge, Greece and high society in London and Rye. It traces his early friendship with Oscar Wilde and the development of his great comic fictional characters.
[B63] Lennard hbk **£12.95**

BETJEMAN, SIR JOHN (1906 - 1984)
Sir John Betjeman: A Life in Pictures
[B64] J Murray hbk **£11.95**
HILLIER, BEVIS
Young Betjeman
In this first major biography of the former Poet Laureate, Hillier poses the question: how did Betjeman 'become Betjeman'? Where did he find his poetic voice? The first volume covers the years 1906 to 1933 and deals with the poet's solitary childhood, his schooldays and his time as a Bright Young Thing at Oxford, before his expulsion.
[B65] J Murray hbk **£15.95**
[B66] Sphere pbk **£5.99**

Arnold Bennett (Picture: National Portrait Gallery)

BLAKE, WILLIAM (1757 - 1827)
GILCHRIST, ALEXANDER
The Life of William Blake
It is perhaps strange, given the perennial interest in Blake's life and work, that this is the only full biography in print. Gilchrist's **Life** dates from 1863, and includes personal reminiscences by those who actually knew the poet, giving the book a sense of freshness and immediacy. Mona Wilson's fine 1927 biography is currently out of print, so it is perhaps time for a new life.
[B67] Dent pbk **£4.50**

BLOOMSBURY
BELL, QUENTIN
Bloomsbury
When this book was first issued in 1968, the Bloomsbury Group was, to quote Quentin Bell, 'dead and stinking'. Now that the work of the circle has again found critical favour, this book stands out as one of the original sources.
[B68] Weidenfeld hbk **£9.95**
BELL, QUENTIN; GARNETT, ANGELICA & SHONE, RICHARD
Charleston: The Official Guide
An excellent illustrated celebration of the home of Duncan Grant and Vanessa Bell, where for over 50 years they entertained the likes of Virginia Woolf, Maynard Keynes and T.S. Eliot.
[B69] Hogarth pbk **£6.95**
EDEL, LEON
Bloomsbury: A House of Lions
An excellent and admiring book about the Bloomsbury phenomenon. It interweaves the lives of the nine principal characters: Virginia Woolf, Leonard Woolf, Lytton Strachey, John Maynard Keynes, Desmond McCarthy, Roger Fry, Clive Bell, Vanessa Bell and Duncan Grant.
[B70] Penguin pbk **£4.99**

BLUNDEN, EDMUND (1896 - 1974)
Undertones of War
The distinguished poet records his experiences as an infantrymen in France and Flanders during the First World War, where he took part in the disastrous battles of the Somme, Ypres and Passchendaele. This classic memoir, a mixture of prose and poetry, laments the futility of war, but finds hope in the qualities of rebirth in the natural landscape.
[B71] Penguin pbk **£3.95**

BLYTON, ENID (1897 - 1968)
MULLAN, BOB
The Enid Blyton Story
The story of Blyton's life is interspersed with
photographs of her family, along with a selection of
magnificent illustrations from editions of her books.
[B72] Boxtree hbk **£9.95**
STONEY, BARBARA
Enid Blyton: A Biography
This book reveals the two faces of Enid Blyton: the
hard-working, spellbinding storyteller, who could
hold an audience of children gripped; and the secret,
insecure, child-like individual, who found it difficult
to form relationships.
[B73] Hodder hbk **£7.95**

BOSWELL, JAMES (1740 - 1795)
FINLAYSON, IAIN
**The Moth and the Candle: The Life of
James Boswell**
[B74] Constable hbk **£9.95**
LUSTIG, IRMA A. & POTTLE, F.A. (EDS)
**Boswell: The English Experiment
1785 - 1789**
[B75] Heinemann hbk **£30.00**
**Boswell: The Great Biographer
1789 - 1795**   NEW
Publication of this final volume of Boswell's memoirs
marks the conclusion of a unique publishing project.
This volume covers the years between his wife's
death and his own. These were years of struggle, as
Boswell attempted to bring up five children. Yet
during this low point in his life, Boswell managed to
triumphantly complete his *Life of Johnson*.
[B76] Heinemann hbk **£25.00**

BOWEN, ELIZABETH (1899 - 1973)
Bowen's Court & Seven Winters
In the first of these memoirs, *Bowen's Court*,
Elizabeth Bowen describes the history of her Anglo-
Irish family in County Cork, from the Cromwellian
settlement up to 1959. The second memoir is a candid
account of her Dublin childhood.
[B77] Virago pbk **£8.99**
The Mulberry Tree
[B78] Virago hbk **£12.95**
CRAIG, PATRICIA
Elizabeth Bowen
Bowen was born into an Anglo-Irish family of the old
Protestant ascendancy. This brief study examines this
complex, independent, sociable novelist and her
heritage.
[B79] Penguin pbk **£2.95**
GLENDINNING, VICTORIA
Elizabeth Bowen: Portrait of a Writer
[B80] Weidenfeld hbk **£8.50**

Elizabeth Bowen (Photo: National Portrait Gallery)

BOWLES, JANE (1917 - 1973)
**Out in the World: Selected Letters
1935 - 1970**
[B81] Black Sparrow pbk **£11.95**
DILLON, MILLICENT
**A Little Original Sin: The Life and Work
of Jane Bowles**
An important biography of Bowles, author of *Two
Serious Ladies* and *In the Summer House*. It traces
her life from her youth in well-off New York
Bohemian circles, to her marriage to Paul Bowles and
their move to Tangiers. Dillon examines the growing
anxiety that undermined her confidence in herself,
which led to her passionate, destructive attachment to
an Arab woman, writer's block, and death at the age
of 56.
[B82] Virago pbk **£10.95**

BOWLES, PAUL (1910 -)
Without Stopping
Chiefly known as a brilliant, exotic and original
writer, Bowles considers himself primarily a musical
composer. Since the 1940s he has lived in Morocco,
where he has led a reclusive life. His 1972
autobiography reflects the many famous writers and
musicians he has known, including Gertrude Stein,
Aaron Copland, Christopher Isherwood, W.H. Auden,
Tennessee Williams and William Burroughs. He
evokes the artistic world of NY in the 1930s and 40s,
his life with Jane Bowles and their time in Morocco.
[B83] P Owen hbk **£18.50**
[B84] H Hamilton pbk **£7.95**
SAWYER-LAUCANNO, CHRISTOPHER
**An Invisible Spectator:
A Biography of Paul Bowles**   NEW
This first full-length biography of Bowles is based
upon extensive research and interviews, including
some conducted with the novelist himself. It pays
particular attention to his career as a composer and his
marriage to Jane Bowles.
[B85] Bloomsbury hbk **£14.95**

BRECHT, BERTOLT (1898 - 1956)
HAYMAN, RONALD
Brecht
The first book to put Brecht's complex political and
theatrical ideas in the context of his personal
experience. Hayman draws on a wealth of
unpublished material and interviews with Brecht's
acquaintances, describing Brecht's literary
development against a background of the violent
political upheavals of the 1930s, and tracing his life to
the point where he became the literary figurehead of
East Germany.
[B86] Weidenfeld hbk **£18.50**
[B87] Weidenfeld pbk **£8.95**

**BRONTE, CHARLOTTE, EMILY, ANNE &
BRANWELL**
Charlotte (1816-1855); Emily (1818-1848); Anne
(1820-1849) and Branwell (1817-1848).
The Illustrated Brontës of Haworth
[B88] Collins hbk **£12.95**
BENTLEY, PHYLIS
The Brontës
An illustrated introduction to the Brontë family and
the world of Haworth.
[B89] Thames & H pbk **£3.95**
CHITHAM, EDWARD
A Life of Charlotte Brontë
A recent biography which uses neglected material to
explore the origin of Charlotte's inspirations and
conflicts, emphasising the influence of her childhood
and her father's Irish background.
[B90] Blackwell hbk **£14.95**
FRASER, REBECCA
Charlotte Brontë
An outstanding new biography which shows
Charlotte's heroism to be far more robust than that

portrayed than Mrs Gaskell. Fraser shows Charlotte
beleaguered by death and disapproval, constantly
battling against ill-health and the shadow cast over
her life by the success of *Jane Eyre*. She emerges as a
complex and determined woman, deeply influenced
by the views of Victorian feminists such as Harriet
Martineau.
[B91] Methuen hbk **£14.95**
GASKELL, MRS ELIZABETH (1810 - 1865)
The Life of Charlotte Brontë
Elizabeth Gaskell became friends with Charlotte
Brontë in 1850, and their relationship culminated in
the publication of this, one of the greatest English
biographies, in 1857. The book initially offended
Victorian society on sexual and proprietorial grounds,
and had to be cut for the second and third editions.
Despite this, it remains a haunting portrait of a
tormented and tragic figure.
[B92] Penguin pbk **£3.99**
GERIN, WINIFRED
Emily Brontë: A Biography
[B93] Oxford pbk **£7.95**
LANE, MARGARET
The Brontë Story
A reconsideration and update of Mrs Gaskell's *Life*,
which adds information gleaned from recent
scholarship, and enriches our understanding of the
labyrinthine Brontë story.
[B94] Fontana pbk **£3.50**
MAURIER, DAPHNE DU
**The Infernal World of Branwell
Brontë**
Daphne du Maurier traces the story of the 'unknown'
Brontë, whose childhood promise never reached
fulfilment. Unable to sell his paintings or publish his
books he sank into addiction to laudanum and
alcohol, and finally death.
[B95] Penguin pbk **£3.95**
SPARK, MURIEL & STANFORD, D.
Emily Brontë: Her Life & Work
[B96] Arrow pbk **£3.95**

BROOKE, RUPERT (1887 - 1915)
Letters from America
A series of letters, written just before the outbreak of
the First World War, which Brooke sent during a trip
to New York, Boston and Canada. With a preface by
Henry James.
[B97] Sidgwick hbk **£9.95**
[B98] Sidgwick pbk **£7.95**
DELANEY, PAUL
The Neo-Pagans
A Canadian academic gives a critical appraisal of
Brooke and the milieu of sexual degeneracy and
decadence in which he moved. The book places
Brooke closer to the Bloomsbury group than has been
generally acknowledged in the past.
[B99] Macmillan hbk **£12.95**
[B100] H Hamilton pbk **£7.95**
HASSALL, CHRISTOPHER
Rupert Brooke: A Biography
The standard account of the 'young Apollo, golden-
haired', which reveals Brooke to be far more complex
and radical than is popularly supposed. He emerges as
a scholar and as the focus of the anti-Victorian
movement of the years leading up to 1914.
[B101] Faber pbk **£5.95**
LEHMANN, JOHN
Rupert Brooke
[B102] Quartet pbk **£2.95**

BROWNING, ELIZABETH BARRETT
(1806 - 1861)
DALLY, DR PETER
The Awful Lightning   NEW
This is a psychological biography of Browning which
reveals that the poet was dogged by anorexia nervosa
throughout her life.
[B103] Macmillan hbk **£16.95**

FORSTER, MARGARET
Elizabeth Barrett Browning
An important revisionary biography which challenges the received opinion of Elizabeth as a frail and terrified daughter. Forster's clearly written life shows us a woman as strong and determined as her tyrannical father, responsible in large part for her own incarceration in Wimpole Street. Elizabeth emerges as a dedicated poet and a complex, self-willed woman.
[B104] Chatto hbk **£14.95**
KARLIN, DANIEL
The Courtship of Robert Browning and Elizabeth Barrett
The story of Robert Browning and Elizabeth Barrett's secret courtship and elopement to Italy has become one of the most celebrated romances in history. Daniel Karlin's book gives a fresh account of the courtship and its principal figures.
[B105] Oxford pbk **£4.95**

BUCHAN, JOHN (1879 - 1940)
Memory Hold the Door
The autobiography of the author of *The Thirty Nine Steps* and the creator of the gentleman hero Richard Hannay.
[B106] Dent pbk **£4.95**
BUCHAN, WILLIAM
John Buchan: A Memoir
Drawn from the author's own memories and from unpublished sources, this is a revealing biography of the private face behind the public mask of a diverse character: writer, politician, soldier, scholar and Governor-General of Canada.
[B107] Harrap pbk **£5.95**
SMITH, JANET ADAM
Buchan and his World
[B108] Thames & H pbk **£2.95**
WEBSTER, JACK
Another Grain of Truth
[B109] Collins hbk **£11.95**

BURGESS, ANTHONY (1917 -)
Little Wilson and Big God
The first volume of Burgess's autobiography, which takes him up to his forties, has been gleefully received in the literary world. Burgess has led a very full life since his early days as a Manchester schoolboy, and this book is well-spiced with worldly anecdotes - as well as being a great fictional and verbal conjuror, Burgess is a vivid raconteur. John Carey memorably described it as 'the chaotic adventures of a cross-grained near genius'.
[B110] Heinemann hbk **£12.95**
[B111] Penguin pbk **£5.99**

BURNEY, FANNY (1752 - 1840)
Selected Letters and Diaries
A selection of acute observations from Fanny Burney's voluminous memoirs. They include impressions of great events, such as the flight of the Royalists during Napoleon's return from Elba, and her extraordinary account of the masectomy she underwent without anaesthetic.
[B112] Oxford pbk **£5.95**

BUTLER, LADY ELEANOR &
PONSONBY, SARAH
(1745 - 1829/1755 - 1831)
A Year with the Ladies of Llangollen
Extracts from their daybooks and journals arranged as a calendar.
[B113] Penguin pbk **£3.95**
MAVOR, ELIZABETH
The Ladies of Llangollen
A sympathetic study of the two reclusive Irish gentlewomen who settled in Wales in order to pursue their mutual devotion, where they received the visits of the aristocracy.
[B114] Penguin pbk **£3.95**

BYRON, GEORGE GORDON (1788 - 1824)
COOTE, STEPHEN
Byron: Making of a Myth
An illustrated review of Byron's life and his influence throughout subsequent history.
[B115] Bodley hbk **£14.95**
FOOT, MICHAEL
The Politics of Paradise
A challenging and provocative analysis of Byron's political faith. The examination begins with Hazlitt, one of Byron's fiercest critics, who ironically shared many of the same ideals and experienced the same enmity from the establishment. The book goes on to illuminate the terrible struggle Byron had to make his voice heard after his exile. Foot himself describes the book's thrust: *"The greatest writers in our history have always had a strong political bent and Byron's got stronger and stronger; indeed he himself was always emphasising the political character of what he wrote...He knew what he was doing, and would not allow anyone or anything to stop him. Such courage and such imagination can save us."*
[B116] Collins hbk **£17.50**
MARCHAND, LESLIE (ED)
Selected Letters and Journals of Lord Byron
This magnificent distillation of Byron's letters and journals, taken from the complete edition, is the best one-volume edition of Byron available. It is the best replacement for Byron's autobiography, which was reduced to ashes in the fireplace of his publisher.
[B117] J Murray hbk **£12.50**
[B118] Picador pbk **£3.95**
Collected Letters and Journals
Vol 1: 'In My Hot Youth' 1798 - 1810
[B119] J Murray hbk **£12.50**
Vol 2: 'Famous in My Time' 1810 - 1812
[B120] J Murray hbk **£12.50**
Vol 3: 'Alas the Love of Women!'
1812 - 1814
[B121] J Murray hbk **£12.50**
Vol 4: 'Wedlock's the Devil' 1814 - 1815
[B122] J Murray hbk **£12.50**
Vol 5: 'So Late Into the Night'
1816 - 1817
[B123] J Murray hbk **£12.50**
Vol 6: 'The Flesh is Frail' 1818 - 1819
[B124] J Murray hbk **£12.50**
Vol 7: 'Between Two Worlds' 1820
[B125] J Murray hbk **£12.50**
Vol 8: 'Born for Opposition' 1821
[B126] J Murray hbk **£12.50**
Vol 9: 'In the Wind's Eye'
1821 - 1822
[B127] J Murray hbk **£12.50**
Vol 10: 'A Heart for Every Fate'
1822 - 1823
[B128] J Murray hbk **£12.50**
Vol 11: 'For Freedom's Battle'
1823 - 1824
[B129] J Murray hbk **£12.50**
Vol 12: 'The Trouble of an Index'
[B130] J Murray hbk **£17.50**
MASSIE, ALLAN
Byron's Travels
Massie traces Byron's travels round Europe. He divides the book into three main parts: *The Adventurer* (Portugal, Spain, Malta, Greece and Turkey), *The Exile* (Switzerland, Venice and Rome) and *The Hero* (the last years in Greece). Throughout Massie quotes copiously from Byron's poems, letters and journals.
[B131] Sidgwick hbk **£14.95**
MAUROIS, ANDRE
Byron
This excellent 1930 biography offers many insights into Byron which remain unsurpassed.
[B132] Constable pbk **£7.95**

RAPHAEL, FREDERIC
Byron
A very lively biography, both serious and frivolous, which explores some controversial themes in depth. This is an unorthodox but entertaining account.
[B133] Sphere pbk **£4.99**

CAMPION, ST EDMUND (1540 - 1581)
WAUGH, EVELYN
Edmund Campion
A biography of the Elizabethan poet, scholar and gentleman. The book chronicles how Campion became a trapped and murdered priest, dying a horrifying traitor's death at Tyburn.
[B134] Cassell pbk **£4.95**

CANETTI, ELIAS (1905 -)
The Tongue Set Free
Canetti was born the son of proud, prosperous Jews and grew up in Bulgaria, Manchester, Vienna and Zurich. This book, the first in a three-volume autobiography, charts the development of his extraordinary multilingual mind and acute sensibility. It has been acclaimed as a masterpiece for its vivid evocation of an exotic, medieval Europe before the First World War.
[B135] Deutsch hbk **£12.95**
[B136] Pan pbk **£3.99**
The Torch in My Ear   **NEW**
The second volume of Canetti's memoirs is chiefly an account of his admiration for the first great mentor of his childhood, the Viennese writer Karl Kraus. He also portrays his first wife, Veza, and gives a clear account of the Vienna and Berlin of the 1920s.
[B1351] Deutsch hbk **£13.95**

CAPOTE, TRUMAN (1924 - 1984)
BRINNIN, JOHN MALCOLM
Truman Capote: A Memoir
Brinnin was a friend of Capote's for over 40 years, and in this memoir he charts their relationship through good times and bad. He writes with regret of Capote's steady dissolution into drug and alcohol abuse.
[B137] Sidgwick hbk **£11.95**
CLARKE, GERALD
Truman Capote: A Biography
Much of this major biography is culled from Capote's personal papers and writings, and from interviews with friends, enemies (of which there are a few...) and Capote himself. It recreates, with objectivity and sympathy, the glittering social world, details the writing of his major works, such as *In Cold Blood* and his tragic decline.
[B138] H Hamilton hbk **£16.95**
[B139] Sphere pbk **£6.99**

CARLYLE, JANE (1801 - 1866)
SURTEES, VIRGINIA
Jane Welsh Carlyle
A biography which reveals Carlyle's wife as a formidable woman in her own right. Their marriage (probably asexual) was one of intellectual striving and emotional strife.
[B140] Russell hbk **£12.95**

CARLYLE, THOMAS (1795 - 1881)
KAPLAN, FRED
Thomas Carlyle: A Biography
The fullest and most accurate account to date of the troubled writer. It draws heavily on published and unpublished documents.
[B141] Cambridge hbk **£30.00**

CARROLL, LEWIS (1832 - 1898)
HUDSON, DEREK
Lewis Carroll: An Illustrated Biography
Hudson's acclaimed biography was the first to appear after the publication of Lewis Carroll's diaries, and it includes much previously unpublished material. The

book is copiously illustrated with Carroll's own photographs and drawings, and with work by more recent illustrators.
[B142] Constable hbk **£10.00**
[B143] Constable pbk **£6.95**

CARY, JOYCE
BISHOP, ALAN
Joyce Cary: A Gentleman Rider
Alan Bishop illuminates the life of Joyce Cary, author of *The Horse's Mouth* and *Mister Johnson*, a writer whose comic vitality and vision hold a unique place in 20th-century literature.
[B144] Oxford pbk **£6.95**

CATHER, WILLA (1873 - 1947)
LEE, HERMIONE
Willa Cather: A Life Served Up **NEW**
Willa Cather is one of the great American writers of this century. Her imagination drew its inspiration from the prairie farmlands of Nebraska, a background combined in her work with new, female versions of pioneering heroism. This major new revisionary biography challenges the received opinion that Cather was a nostalgic celebrator of the American pastoral. Hermione Lee finds a stranger Cather: a writer of split personality and sexual conflicts.
[B145] Virago hbk **£12.99**

CAVENDISH, MARGARET, DUCHESS OF NEWCASTLE (1623 - 1673)
JONES, KATHLEEN
A Glorious Fame
Cavendish was the first woman to write specifically for publication and to consider herself primarily a writer. She was a feminist long before her time, believing in sexual equality and criticising the role that society assigned to women. She was so renowned that people, Samuel Pepys among them, queued in the streets of London to see her when she came to Court.
[B146] Bloomsbury hbk **£14.95**

CHANDLER, RAYMOND (1888 - 1959)
GARDIN, DOROTHY & WALKER, K.S. (EDS)
Raymond Chandler Speaking
A selection of letters and other writings on various themes. Sharply written and provocative, they include Chandler's thoughts on writing and on the creation of Philip Marlowe.
[B147] Penguin pbk **£4.95**
MCSHANE, FRANK
Selected Letters of Raymond Chandler
[B148] Cape hbk **£16.00**
[B149] Macmillan pbk **£6.95**
The Life of Raymond Chandler
"... a remarkable work of scholarship and those who considered that Chandler was a mere minor whodunnit man must now change their minds." - Anthony Burgess.
[B150] H Hamilton pbk **£6.95**

CHEEVER, JOHN
CHEEVER, BENJAMIN (ED)
The Letters of John Cheever **NEW**
Cheever's letters, edited by his son, cover every aspect of his writing, as well as his bisexuality and alcoholism. Among the correspondents are John Updike, Saul Bellow and Philip Roth. Surprisingly, the remarkable memoir of Cheever by his daughter Susan is out of print.
[B151] Cape hbk **£14.95**

CHEKHOV, ANTON (1860 - 1904)
HELLMAN, LILLIAN (ED)
Selected Letters of Anton Chekhov
A selection drawn from the definitive Soviet edition of Chekhov's complete works.
[B152] Pan pbk **£3.50**

HINGLEY, RONALD
A Life of Chekhov
Hingley is the pre-eminent translator of Chekhov into English, and his biography, based on much original research, shows his intimate awareness of the complexities of Chekhov's life and work. This book won the James Tait Black Prize for Biography.
[B153] Oxford pbk **£5.95**
PRITCHETT, V.S.
Chekhov: A Spirit Set Free
Pritchett's celebration of Chekhov is written out of a lifetime's admiration for the great Russian writer. This warm portrait shows Chekhov as a man of great complexity and courage, struggling to support his impoverished family, and working hard as a doctor to improve the lot of others. Pritchett also shows his intimate knowledge of Chekhov's short stories and gives some lucid analyses.
[B154] Hodder hbk **£12.95**
TROYAT, HENRI
Chekhov
Troyat is the acclaimed biographer of Tolstoy, Catherine the Great and Churchill, and an expert on 19th century Russian literature. His fine biography of the great Russian dramatist tells of Chekhov's childhood under a tyrannical father, his medical work, his literary success and his death, with a glass of champagne in his hand.
[B155] Macmillan hbk **£14.95**
[B156] H Hamilton pbk **£6.95**

CHESTERTON, G.K. (1874 - 1936)
Autobiography
First published posthumously in 1936, Chesterton's exuberant autobiography tells the story of his vivid life. Chesterton vividly recounts his friendships with H.G. Wells, Henry James and Hilaire Belloc.
[B157] H Hamilton pbk **£5.95**
COREN, MICHAEL
Gilbert: The Man Who Was G.K. Chesterton **NEW**
Whilst writing this book Coren decided to extend his research through appeals in the literary press, and received many fresh anecdotes and memories from Chesterton's friends and acquaintances. He presents a fresh picture of a man all too often seen as a Catholic apologist or right-wing man about town. Coren also exorcises the charge of anti-Semitism, often used against Chesterton, and shows a man whose approach to life was always full and robust.
[B158] Cape hbk **£12.95**
FINCH, MICHAEL
G.K. Chesterton
[B159] Weidenfeld pbk **£8.95**

CHRISTIE, AGATHA (1891 - 1976)
An Autobiography
Written over a 15 year period from 1950 onwards, this autobiography takes Christie up to the age of 75. She writes of the creation of Hercule Poirot, Miss Marple and of life with her archaeologist husband Sir Max Mallowan.
[B160] Fontana pbk **£3.50**
MORGAN, JANET
Agatha Christie
For this revealing biography, Morgan was given access to exclusive family papers. The result is much more revealing than anything Lady Mallowan would ever write about herself, but still leaves some enigmas.
[B161] Fontana pbk **£3.50**
OSBORNE, CHARLES
Life and Crimes of Agatha Christie
[B162] Collins hbk **£9.95**

CLARE, JOHN (1793 - 1864)
Autobiographical Writings
Clare, the son of a Northamptonshire labourer, was born near Peterborough, and the surrounding fens

provided much of the inspiration for his prose and poetry. This volume includes his impressions of childhood and of the London literary scene, where he mixed in the society of Hazlitt, Lamb and Coleridge. It has been described as 'one of the most valuable records we have of the mental, emotional and physical world of the English rural parson of the 19th century'. With wood engravings by John Lawrence.
[B163] Oxford pbk **£3.95**
STOREY, MARK (ED)
Selected Letters
Culled from the complete edition, this revealing selection retains Clare's idiosyncratic spelling and punctuation, and covers the whole of his adult life until a few years before his death. Many of the letters were written after his incarceration in various asylums, about which he says *"I am without Books or Amusements of any kind & have got nothing to kill time..."*
[B164] Oxford hbk **£25.00**
[B165] Oxford pbk **£6.95**

COCTEAU, JEAN (1889 - 1963)
Diaries Vol 1: Past Tense
Cocteau delighted in shocking the world through his artistic experiments in poetry, fiction, criticism, drama, film, ballet, painting, illustration and opera. However, little is known of the private man. These diaries, begun 13 years before his death, reveal a lonely and melancholy man. The first volume describes his life between 1951 and 1953, and in it he gives his opinions on Picasso, Stalin and the genesis of *Bacchus* and *Oedipus Rex*.
[B166] H Hamilton hbk **£15.00**
Le Livre Blanc
[B167] P Owen pbk **£6.95**
The Difficulty of Being
[B168] P Owen hbk **£10.95**
STEEGMULLER, FRANCIS
Cocteau: A Biography
Steegmuller's award-winning biography reveals the paradoxes and richness of Cocteau's life: the charm and nastiness, the generosity and egomania; the anguish of the opium addict; and the vitality of his avant-garde lifestyle.
[B169] Constable pbk **£9.95**

COLERIDGE, SAMUEL TAYLOR (1772 - 1834)
Selected Letters
Coleridge was a talker of great volubility, wit and gusto, and these qualities shine through in his correspondence. This selection includes letters to the Wordsworths, Charles Lamb and Thomas de Quincey. Important developments in his life, such as his troubled relationship with his wife, and his attachment to Sara Hutchinson are illuminated, as is his struggle against opium addiction.
[B170] Oxford hbk **£19.50**
[B171] Oxford pbk **£5.95**

Agatha Christie, whose autobiography is published by Fontana (pbk **£3.50**)

HOLMES, RICHARD
Coleridge: The Early Years `NEW`

Holmes looks afresh at the life of Coleridge, from his childhood in Devon, to his lonely departure for the Mediterranean in 1804. He also examines his formative literary experiences, such as his meeting the Wordsworths, and his interest in the French Revolution. Holmes has visited each Coleridge haunt and throws light on his complex emotional life, his opium addiction and his increasingly unhappy marriage. The result - as with Holmes's great biography of Shelley - enriches our vision of his subject.
[B172] Hodder hbk **£15.00**

COLERIDGE, SARA
LEFEBURE, MOLLY
The Bondage of Love: The Life of Mrs Samuel Taylor Coleridge

A corrective to the received opinion that Sara Coleridge was an ungenerous and unloving woman who drove her husband to take opium. This is a remarkable and convincing biography.
[B173] Gollancz hbk **£15.95**
[B174] Gollancz pbk **£4.95**

COLETTE, SIDONIE GABRIELLE
(1873 - 1954)
Journey For Myself: Selfish Memories
[B175] P Owen hbk **£12.95**
Looking Backwards: Recollections

Colette returns in 1941 to Paris from the safety of rural France. She is crippled by arthritis, yet finds hope in the prospect of liberation from Nazi occupation.
[B176] Womens P pbk **£4.95**
Evening Star: Recollections

The sequel to *Looking Backwards*, in which Colette offers up a tribute to Paris during the Nazi occupation. Restricted by illness as well as the Nazis, Colette travels freely in her imagination, portraying a generation of remarkable people and events.
[B177] Womens P pbk **£3.95**

COLLINS, WILKIE (1824 - 1889)
CLARKE, WILLIAM
Secret Life of Wilkie Collins
[B178] Allison & B hbk **£14.95**

COMPTON-BURNETT, IVY (1892 - 1969)
DICK, KAY
Ivy and Stevie

Includes a rare interview with Ivy Compton-Burnett, as well as reflections on her life.
[B179] Allison & B pbk **£1.95**
LIDDELL, ROBERT
Elizabeth and Ivy

A study of Ivy Compton-Burnett and Elizabeth Taylor.
[B180] P Owen hbk **£10.95**
SPURLING, HILARY
Ivy When Young: Early Life of Ivy Compton-Burnett 1884-1919

This is the first part of a brilliant 2-volume biography which uncovers the themes of Compton-Burnett's novels - strange developments within a family, emotional blackmail - in her own extraordinary life.
[B181] Allison & B pbk **£3.95**
Secrets of a Woman's Heart: Later Life of Ivy Compton-Burnett 1920-1969

Spurling sees the novelist's life as falling into two sharply delineated parts: pre- and post-First World War. After the war the settled life she previously knew was completely detroyed and the people who mattered to her most were dead. The biography shows what lay behind the split and how the pre-war experiences provided the material for the novels she wrote over the next 50 years.
[B182] Hodder hbk **£14.95**
[B183] Penguin pbk **£4.95**

CONNOLLY, CYRIL (1903 - 1974)
Enemies of Promise

First published in 1938, this is a semi-autobiographical enquiry into how one becomes a writer. Within this framework Connolly conducts a wide-ranging search into the *"theories and illusions common to our class, our race, our time"*. The enemies described are politics, conversation, drink, domesticity, journalism and worldly success. It is a landmark in the study of the interrelation between a writer's personal circumstances and his work.
[B184] Deutsch pbk **£5.95**
SHELDEN, MICHAEL
Friends of Promise: Cyril Connolly and the World of Horizon `NEW`

A new study showing how, with fervour and commitment, the young Cyril Connolly determined with two friends, Stephen Spender and Peter Watson, to establish a high quality literary magazine. *Horizon* first appeared in October 1939, and quickly established itself as a major platform for new literary talent. Shelden utilises much primary source material and pays particular attention to the role of Peter Watson, the publisher.
[B185] H Hamilton hbk **£14.95**
SKELTON, BARBARA
Tears Before Bedtime

Skelton, who was married to Connolly, retraces her life with him and with some of the demagogues of London's pre-war Bohemia: Augustus John, Feliks Topolski and Peter Quennell. As she reviews this peculiar era in British literary life she makes a few swingeing attacks on established reputations.
[B186] H Hamilton hbk **£12.95**
[B187] H Hamilton pbk **£7.95**
Weep No More `NEW`

In her second volume of memoirs, Barbara Skelton describes her disintegrating marriage to Cyril Connolly, and being wooed by publisher George Weidenfeld. She describes this, and her third marriage to millionaire physician Derek Jackson, with melancholy as well as a wicked sense of humour.
[B188] H Hamilton hbk **£14.95**

Samuel Taylor Coleridge, from *Coleridge: The Early Years* by Richard Holmes (Hodder & Stoughton hbk £15.00)

CONRAD, JOSEPH (1857 - 1934)
Collected Letters Vol 1: 1861 - 1897

The first of a projected eight-volume edition of all Conrad's letters, an extensive number of which have never yet been published.
[B189] Cambridge hbk **£25.00**
Vol 2: 1898 - 1902

The period covered by this volume includes the birth of Conrad's first son, an encounter with an early x-ray machine and the developing of a distinctively 'modern' quality in his work.
[B190] Cambridge hbk **£27.50**
Vol 3: 1903 - 1907
[B191] Cambridge hbk **£35.00**
BAINES, JOCELYN
Joseph Conrad: A Critical Biography

The definitive biography, acclaimed for its scholarly depth and for the manner in which it shows how Conrad's enormous range of experiences is revealed in his work. Baines shows Conrad's intense understanding of man's knowledge of solitude and longing for solidarity.
[B192] Penguin pbk **£5.95**

COWPER, WILLIAM (1731 - 1800)
CECIL, DAVID
The Stricken Deer

David Cecil's first book is a minor classic, which delves into the inner turmoil of the melancholic 18thcentury poet.
[B193] Constable pbk **£6.95**

CROMPTON, RICHMAL (1890 - 1969)
CADOGAN, MARY
Richmal Crompton: The Woman behind William

The enigmatic creator of the *Just William* books was for many years thought to have been a man. This biography shows us the real Richmal Crompton, a witty and talented woman, as well as celebrating her most famous creation.
[B194] Unwin Hyman pbk **£4.95**

DAHL, ROALD (1916 -)
Boy

Dahl's memoir of a magical boyhood, spent in Wales and Norway, is counterpoised against his barbaric experiences at an English public school. Dahl says of his often macabre experiences: *"Some are funny. Some are painful. Some are unpleasant...All are true."*
[B195] Cape hbk **£7.95**
[B196] Penguin pbk **£3.50**
Going Solo

The second part of his autobiography deals with Dahl's exotic experiences in Africa and with his time in the RAF during the Second World War, where he crashes a plane in the Western Desert. Throughout, Dahl shows his developing role as a connoisseur of the bizarre and extraordinary.
[B197] Cape hbk **£7.95**
[B198] Penguin pbk **£3.99**

DALEY, HARRY
This Small Cloud

A fascinating memoir by the Hammersmith policeman, who for a time was the lover of E.M Forster. He describes his relationship with the writer as well as his experiences pounding the beat.
[B199] Weidenfeld pbk **£6.95**

DAVIES, W.H. (1871 - 1940)
The Autobiography of a Super-Tramp

With a preface by George Bernard Shaw. Davies, whose nature poetry was admired by Bernard Shaw and Edward Thomas, was a tramp who was, as Shaw says, *'a true poet in his disregard for appearances'*. His autobiography (1908) is a classic account of his

adventures travelling around America and England at the turn of the century, amongst tricksters, down-and-outs and labourers.
[B200] Cape hbk **£9.95**
[B201] Oxford pbk **£3.95**
Later Days
Originally published in 1925, this is the sequel to *The Autobiography of a Super-Tramp*. In it Davies traces his experiences as the result of his literary success, before and after the First World War. Amongst the highlights of an engaging memoir are the descriptions of his relationships with Bernard Shaw, Max Beerbohm and Edward Thomas.
[B202] Oxford pbk **£3.50**

DE STAEL, MADAME (1766 - 1817)
HEROLD, J. CHRISTOPHER
Mistress to an Age: Life of Mme Staël
As a French writer, De Stael was the precursor of the French Romantic movement. She was also a friend of the famous: this biography recreates her life as a grand hostess of the most dazzling salon of intellectual life in Paris before the Revolution.
[B203] H Hamilton pbk **£7.95**

DICKENS, CHARLES (1812 - 1870)
ALLEN, MICHAEL
Charles Dickens' Childhood
An examination of Dickens' youth in the light of new documentary evidence.
[B204] Macmillan hbk **£29.50**
FORSTER, JOHN
Life of Charles Dickens Vol 1
The first major biography of Dickens was written by his friend John Forster. It is now considered to be too hagiographical in its treatment, but retains an immediacy that later studies inevitably lack.
[B205] Dent hbk **£8.95**
Life of Charles Dickens Vol 2
[B206] Dent hbk **£8.95**
HIBBERT, CHRISTOPHER
The Making of Charles Dickens
[B207] Penguin pbk **£4.50**
HOUSE, M. & STOREY, G. (EDS)
Selected Letters
[B208] Macmillan hbk **£35.00**
[B209] Macmillan pbk **£9.95**
JOHNSON, EDGAR
Charles Dickens: His Tragedy and Triumph
Acclaimed as the definitive biography, Edgar Johnson's monumental book draws on thousands of letters and portrays the rich Dickensian world, a world inhabited by writers such as Thackeray, Tennyson and Poe. As might be expected from a biography of Dickens, this entertaining account teems with life, colour and incident.
[B210] Penguin pbk **£5.95**
KAPLAN, FRED
Dickens: A Biography
Kaplan's recent biography has been hugely acclaimed both in Britain and America. For many people it has replaced the Edgar Johnson as the standard life of Dickens, and it of course has the advantage of being able to incorporate recent scholarship. It presents a vivid portrait of the Victorian world inhabited by Dickens, as well as offering a scholarly analysis of his works.
[B211] Hodder hbk **£16.95**
PEARSON, HESKETH
Dickens: His Character, Comedy and Career
Pearson's very competent 1949 biography tells the story of Dickens's life from his childhood in Portsmouth, through the periods of poverty when he saw the worst of London and its slums, on to his successful writing career. Pearson shows Dickens blazing his way through a richly crowded life.
[B212] Cassell pbk **£6.95**

WILSON, ANGUS
The World of Charles Dickens
A highly-illustrated examination of the imaginative aspects of Dickens' life and work.
[B213] Grafton pbk **£3.95**

DICKINSON, EMILY (1830 - 1886)
MCNEIL, HELEN
Emily Dickinson
A concise reassessment of the poet and her work which investigates the grounds for, and meaning of, her late recognition.
[B214] Virago pbk **£4.50**

DINESEN, ISAK (KAREN BLIXEN)
(1885 - 1962)
Letters from Africa 1914 - 1931
These letters are the raw material which Dinesen later used as the basis for her classic *Out of Africa*. They introduce us to a vulnerable woman and a life made miserable by the collapse of her coffee farm and the death of her lover. Despite these tragic circumstances, Dinesen's irrepressible spirit shines through.
[B215] Weidenfeld hbk **£12.95**
[B216] Pan pbk **£4.95**
Out of Africa
Karen Blixen lived in Kenya from 1913 to 1931, where she ran a coffee farm. She went home to Denmark after its failure and wrote this remarkable account of her experiences, a love letter to the people of the country.
[B217] Penguin pbk **£3.50**
Out of Africa/Shadows on the Grass
[B218] Penguin pbk **£3.95**
THURMAN, JUDITH
Isak Dinesen
A vivid biography of Karen Blixen, which details her exotic life in Africa, as well as giving insights into her mysterious fictional world.
[B219] Penguin pbk **£3.99**

DONNE, JOHN (1573 - 1631)
BALD, R.C.
John Donne: A Life
The definitive life of the Renaissance poet, published here in a revised edition.
[B220] Oxford pbk **£14.95**
PARFITT, GEORGE
John Donne: A Literary Life
[B221] Macmillan pbk **£7.95**

DOOLITTLE, HILDA (1886 - 1961)
The poet Hilda Doolittle, otherwise known as H.D., was a leading member of the Imagist movement. She was, at different times, the fiancée of Ezra Pound, lover of D.H. Lawrence and patient of Freud.
End to Torment: Memoir of Ezra Pound
[B222] Carcanet pbk **£4.95**
Tribute to Freud
An account of her analysis with Freud in 1933.
[B223] Carcanet pbk **£5.95**
GUEST, BARBARA
Herself Defined: The Poet H.D. and Her World
Given access to unpublished material, the poet Barbara Guest has written an intimate portrait of H.D. and her circle, which included Ezra Pound, Marianne Moore, D.H. Lawrence, T.S. Eliot and William Carlos Williams. Guest describes how H.D.'s lifelong attempt to 'define herself' led to explorations of the unconsciousness and to psychoanalysis with Freud.
[B224] Collins hbk **£15.00**

DOSTOEVSKY, FYODOR (1821 - 1881)
FRANK, JOSEPH
Dostoevsky: Vol 1: The Seeds of Revolt 1821 - 1849
A wide-ranging biography, detailed and scholarly, which examines Dostoevsky in minute detail, and

places him in the wider context of his times. This is the first of a projected five volumes. 'It is difficult to conceive terms of praise that would be too high for this masterly achievement' - Bernard Levin, *The Observer*.
[B225] Robson hbk **£10.50**
Vol 2: The Years of Ordeal 1850 - 1859
[B226] Robson hbk **£14.95**
Vol 3: The Stir of Liberation 1860 - 1865
[B227] Robson hbk **£14.95**
KJETSAA, GIER
Fyodor Dostoevsky: A Writer's Life
A scholarly one-volume biography by Professor Kjetsaa, who is an authority on Slavonic literature. He draws on recent scholarship to portray the tortuous and agonising events of Dostoevsky's life, such as epilepsy and gambling. He goes on to demonstrate how these are manifested in the writer's work.
[B228] Macmillan hbk **£16.95**
[B229] Macmillan pbk **£8.99**

DOUGLAS, KEITH (1920 - 1944)
GRAHAM, DESMOND
Keith Douglas 1920 - 1944
This biography of the Second World War poet is illustrated with photographs, facsimile manuscripts and drawings. Graham reveals the paradoxes of Douglas's personality, and of his arrogant, passionate yet generous nature.
[B230] Oxford pbk **£5.95**

DOYLE, SIR ARTHUR CONAN (1859 - 1930)
Memories and Adventures
The story of a richly lived and very full life in which Doyle, the man of action, tried many sports, including aeronautics and skiing (which he pioneered). In this memoir he also relates how he travelled to the Arctic and Africa and dabbled in the occult. Doyle says in his preface: *"I have had a life which, for variety and romance could hardly be exceeded...I have sampled every kind of human experience."*
[B231] Oxford pbk **£5.95**
PEARSON, HESKETH
Conan Doyle
Introduced by Graham Greene. Pearson's biography was first published in 1943 amidst a storm of controversy. It shows Doyle's life to have been as exciting as his fiction. In its course we are introduced to many of the originals for his fictional characters. Graham Greene says in his preface: *"It is one of Mr Pearson's virtues that he drives us to champion the subject against his biographer"*.
[B232] Unwin Hyman pbk **£6.95**

H.D. (Photo: Carcanet Press)

DRYDEN, JOHN (1631 - 1700)
WINN, JAMES ANDERSON
Dryden and His World
Dryden was a prolific writer who worked for Milton and Marvell as a translator for Cromwell's government. Later, on the return of Charles II he began writing for the re-opened theatre. This excellent biography gives us a fuller portrait of Dryden than any previously achieved. Here we see Dryden the poet, playwright and public figure, as well as Dryden the husband, father and friend. 'The most important biography of Dryden ever written.' - Pat Rogers, *New York Times*.
[B233] Yale pbk **£14.95**

DU MAURIER, DAPHNE (1907 - 1989)
Myself When Young: The Shaping of a Writer
An evocation of du Maurier's first 24 years, in London and the Home Counties.
[B234] Pan pbk **£2.50**

DURRELL, LAWRENCE (1912 -)
DURRELL, LAWRENCE & MILLER, HENRY
The Durrell/Miller Letters
The correspondence between the two literary giants began in 1935, when the young besotted Englishman wrote to the aged New Yorker. The latter realised he had found the perfect reader and responded with enthusiasm. Thus began a momentous correspondence which ended only with Miller's death, some 1,000,000 words later.
[B235] Faber hbk **£12.95**
[B236] Faber pbk **£7.95**

ELIOT, GEORGE (1819 - 1880)
Selections from George Eliot's Letters
(Ed. Haight, Gordon S.)
A fine and managcable selection from the nine-volume editon of Eliot's letters. The material included here forms a continuous narrative and commentary on Victorian life, as Eliot's eager intelligence searchingly examines many issues. There are also commentaries here on many of Eliot's contemporaries, Dickens, Carlyle, Tennyson and Browning amongst them.
[B237] Yale UP pbk **£16.95**
HAIGHT, GORDON
George Eliot
A detailed and near-definitive biography which analyses Eliot's 'need to be loved' and her 25-year non-marriage to G.H. Lewes. Haight evokes the emotional depth and warmth of Eliot whilst giving equal attention to her powerful intellect. The book also provides detailed analyses of Eliot's works, with chapters devoted to the creation of all the major works, from *Adam Bede* to *Daniel Deronda*.
[B238] Penguin pbk **£5.95**
LASKI, MARGHANITA
George Eliot
A lively illustrated introduction to Eliot and the Midlands of her upbringing.
[B239] Thames & H pbk **£3.95**
TAYLOR, INA **NEW**
George Eliot: Woman of Contradictions
In this scholarly recent biography, the result of new research, Ina Taylor emphasises Eliot's literary and social independence and originality. She describes how Eliot was a 'New Woman', well ahead of her time, one who courted atheism and avoided the trap of marriage until late in life.
[B240] Weidenfeld hbk **£16.95**
UGLOW, JENNIFER S.
George Eliot
A provocative reappraisal of Eliot which explores her ambivalent attitude to choice and change, especially for women. Uglow shows how Eliot consistently confronts the major tensions of Victorian life, such as class allegiance and the role of women.
[B241] Virago pbk **£3.95**

ELIOT, THOMAS STEARNS (1888 - 1965)
ACKROYD, PETER
T.S. Eliot
Being denied permission to reprint from Eliot's published or unpublished work, except for critical comment, would have daunted a lesser biographer. Ackroyd, however, has produced what many consider the best one-volume biography of Eliot. The result is a full and fluent portrait which shows Eliot's life and work to be inextricably bound together.
[B242] H Hamilton hbk **£12.50**
[B243] Sphere pbk **£5.99**
ELIOT, VALERIE (ED)
Letters Vol 1: 1898 - 1926
The first volume of Eliot's letters is the fruit of over 20 years of research. The period covered is from his childhood in Missouri, up until the end of 1922, when he had married, settled in England and published *The Waste Land*. Valerie Eliot has drawn heavily on her own archive in editing this collection. Eliot's letters do, however, bear out the sense derived from elsewhere of personal concealment.
[B244] Faber hbk **£25.00**
GORDON, LYNDALL
Eliot's Early Years
This book first established the autobiographical basis of Eliot's work. Drawing on many sources, it traces Eliot's life from his early American influences to his conversion to Anglo-Catholicism at the age of 38. 'The most valuable single book yet published about Eliot,' Jonathan Raban, *The Sunday Times*.
[B245] Oxford pbk **£4.95**
Eliot's New Life
In the sequel to *Eliot's Early Years*, Gordon further explores the ties between Eliot's life and work. Drawing on much unpublished material, she concentrates on Eliot's search for a 'new life' during the break-up of his first marriage, and his entry into the Anglican Church.
[B246] Oxford pbk **£5.95**
TOMLIN, E.W.F
T.S. Eliot: A Friendship
Written by a life-long acquaintance, this book gives a fresh insight into the private Eliot, previously seen only by his closest friends and admirers.
[B247] Routledge hbk **£19.95**

FAULKNER, WILLIAM
KARL, FREDERICK R. **NEW**
William Faulkner: American Writer
This huge and authoritative book looks at the way in which Faulkner wove the cultural forces which played upon him - his Southern heritage, family, marriage, drinking, and relations with women - into a single imaginative pattern.
[B248] Faber hbk **£25.00**

FIELDING, HENRY (1707 -1754)
BATTESTIN, MARTIN C.
Henry Fielding
The first biography of Fielding for seventy years. It looks at his literary work, particulary *Tom Jones* and *Joseph Andrews*, as well as his essays. Fielding was also a magistrate and he founded the Metropolitan Police. This biography looks at his professional accomplishments and his passionate and reckless private life.
[B2481] Routledge hbk **£29.50**

FITZGERALD, FRANCIS SCOTT KEY (1896 - 1940)
Letters of F. Scott Fitzgerald
[B249] Penguin pbk **£5.95**
BUTTITTA, TONY
Lost Summer
A personal memoir of conversations between Buttitta and F. Scott Fitzgerald.
[B250] Hodder pbk **£4.50**

MIZENER, ARTHUR
Scott Fitzgerald
[B251] Thames & H pbk **£3.95**

FITZROVIA
DAVID, HUGH
The Fitzrovians: A Portrait of Bohemian Society 1900 - 1955
A history of the Bohemian coterie of writers and artists that flourished during the early part of the century and included Augustus John, Walter Sickert and W.B. Yeats.
[B252] M Joseph hbk **£16.95**

FLAUBERT, GUSTAVE (1821 - 1880)
FLAUBERT, GUSTAVE & TURGENEV, IVAN
Friendship in Letters
The complete correspondence between Flaubert and Turgenev.
[B253] Athlone hbk **£20.00**
LOTTMAN, HERBERT R.
Flaubert: A Life **NEW**
In this scholarly recent biography, Lottman vividly portrays Flaubert's search for *le mot juste*, and his tormented writing life. He contrasts this life, when Flaubert was sequestered in the country, with the winter 'season', when he enjoyed the high society of the season in Paris.
[B254] Methuen hbk **£17.95**
STEEGMULLER, FRANCIS (ED)
Letters Vol 1: 1830 - 1857
Flaubert's celebrated and flamboyant letters constitute a major part of his oeuvre. They show the torments and thought processes of a great writer at work: *"Oh, I'm done for, my friend, done for!...Let me tell you confidentially that for the past month I've found it impossible to write. I can't find a single word. I'm horribly bored, and keep staring at the fire. Voilà."* (Letter to Ernest Feydeau, November 20th 1857, in Volume 2 of the *Letters*). The first volume details Flaubert's unhappy years at law school, his tumultuous affair with Louise Colet, and nights and days spent amongst the brothels and pyramids of Egypt.
[B255] Faber pbk **£8.95**
Letters Vol 2: 1857 - 1880
In this volume we see Flaubert in his maturity, collecting material for *Salammbo* in Tunisia, and summoning memories of the 1848 Revolution for *Sentimental Education*. He continues his correspondence with George Sand, endures the deaths of Louis Bouilhet and his mother, together with the prospect of financial ruin.
[B256] Faber pbk **£8.95**

FLEMING, IAN
PEARSON, JOHN
The Life of Ian Fleming
The fascinating life story of the creator of James Bond. Fleming was a newspaperman and a wartime Intelligence officer, a man who was devastatingly attractive to women: he always resented attempts to identify him with the character of 007, but the Bond novels turned out to be a form of undercover autobiography.
[B257] Hodder pbk **£4.50**

FORSTER, E.M. (1879 - 1970)
Selected Letters Vol 1: 1879 - 1920
[B258] Collins hbk **£15.95**
[B259] Arrow pbk **£4.50**
Selected Letters Vol 2: 1921 - 1970
[B260] Collins hbk **£17.50**
FURBANK, P.N.
E.M. Forster: A Life
The definitive life of Forster. Furbank, a close friend, was invited to write the book during the writer's later years. Forster's cosseted youth, during which his adoring mother constantly dressed him up, is seen as a

formative period, as is his subsequent emancipation at Cambridge. Furbank looks at the development of Forster's writing, culminating in the ambitious, metaphysical peak of *A Passage to India* in 1924, the last novel published in Forster's lifetime.
[B261] Secker hbk **£12.50**
[B262] Sphere pbk **£7.99**

FULLER, ROY (1912 -)
Memories of Childhood and Youth NEW
Memoirs by the underestimated poet, father of John Fuller and sometime Building Society Manager.
[B263] Collins pbk **£6.95**

GARNETT, ANGELICA
Deceived with Kindness: A Bloomsbury Childhood
The daughter of Vanessa Bell, and wife of David Garnett, as well as the niece of Virginia Woolf, Angelica Garnett was born in Charleston. She thus experienced from an early age the life and vitality of the Bloomsbury intellectual milieu, which she describes here with great sensitivity.
[B264] Chatto hbk **£12.95**
[B265] Oxford pbk **£3.95**

GASKELL, MRS ELIZABETH (1810 - 1865)
GERIN, WINIFRED
Elizabeth Gaskell: A Biography
Mrs Gaskell, the author of *Cranford* and *North and South*, spent much of her life, along with her husband, trying to alleviate the problems of the industrial poor in the North of England. This biography of her, by an authority on the period, describes her crusading life, as well as examining the writing of her novels. Gerin highlights her relationships with other 19th century figures, such as Dickens, Florence Nightingale, Thomas Carlyle and, of course, Charlotte Brontë.
[B266] Oxford pbk **£4.95**

GIBBON, EDWARD (1737 - 1794)
Memoirs
Based on recent research into the drafts of his unfinished memoirs, this book gives a full version of Gibbon's sickly childhood in London, and of the writing of the *Decline*. His intellectual passions and thorough thirst for knowledge, as well as his well-known ability to distil information, make this into a small masterpiece.
[B267] Penguin pbk **£3.95**

GIDE, ANDRE (1869 - 1951)
If It Die
André Gide, the French Nobel Prize-winning novelist, spent his life in revolt against convention. This autobiography is a record of his manhood up until his engagement to his cousin. In it he tells of friendships, travels and sexual awakening.
[B268] Penguin pbk **£5.95**

GINSBERG, ALLEN
MILES, BARRY
Allen Ginsberg: A Biography
A major biography which provides an intimate chronicle of the flamboyant American poet: it shows him as a major force in a group of visionaries which included William Burroughs, Tennessee Williams and Bob Dylan.
[B269] Viking hbk **£17.95**

GISSING, GEORGE (1857 - 1903)
HALPERIN, JOHN
Gissing: A Life in Books
Gissing was a brilliant scholar whose academic career was ruined when he was expelled for stealing in order to support his mistress, an alcoholic prostitute. This

engrossing biography, an essential introduction to Gissing, examines his subsequent career as husband and prolific novelist.
[B270] Oxford hbk **£18.50**
[B271] Oxford pbk **£6.95**

GODDEN, RUMER (1907 -)
A Time to Dance, No Time to Weep
The first part of the bestselling novelist's autobiography tells of her youth, divided between England and India. Her marriage to a stockbroker who abandoned her and their children left her with enormous debts, despite the success of her novel *Black Narcissus*. This volume tells the gripping story of how she learned to cope, and ends when she and her family go to live in Kashmir during WWII.
[B272] Macmillan hbk **£12.95**
[B273] Corgi pbk **£3.99**
A House With Four Rooms
The second volume of Godden's autobiography begins with her leaving India with her two small daughters in July 1945, and sailing to Liverpool on a troop ship.
[B2761] Macmillan hbk **£14.95**

GOETHE, JOHANN WOLFGANG VON (1749 - 1832)
FRIEDENTHAL, RICHARD
Goethe: His Life and Times
A classic study, first published in 1965. Richard Friedenthal examines the life, and shows how Goethe came closer than anyone else to the Renaissance ideal of the complete man.
[B274] Weidenfeld pbk **£10.95**

GOGOL, NIKOLAI (1809 - 1852)
NABOKOV, VLADIMIR (1899 - 1972)
Gogol
Nabokov relates the life of his fellow Russian novelist, beginning with Gogol's death (he starved himself) and ending with his birth. In between, Nabokov relates Gogol's works, such as *Dead Souls*, to his idiosyncratic life.
[B275] Oxford pbk **£5.95**

GOLLANCZ, VICTOR (1893 - 1967)
EDWARDS, RUTH DUDLEY
Victor Gollancz
A massive and admired prize-winning (James Tait Black Award) biography of the crusading publisher and socialist.
[B276] Gollancz hbk **£20.00**

GONCOURT, EDMOND DE & JULES DE (1822 - 1896); (1830 - 1870)
Pages from the Goncourt Journal
The Goncourt brothers' famous journal provides sensational and scandalous gossip concerning the lives of the rich and famous who visited their salon in Paris in the 19th century. Flaubert, George Sand, Victor Hugo, Oscar Wilde, Swinburne, Rodin, Degas, Baudelaire and Zola all stalk these pages, talking about art, money, sex and politics.
[B277] Penguin pbk **£4.95**
BALDICK, ROBERT (ED)
Pages from the Goncourt Journal
[B278] Oxford pbk **£5.95**

GORKY, MAXIM (1868 - 1936)
My Childhood
The first part of Gorky's great autobiographical trilogy documents his harsh and uncompromising upbringing. He tells how he was regularly beaten unconscious by his tyrannical grandfather. The redeeming feature of his early life, and the reason why he can remember it with tenderness, was his grandmother, who was a great storyteller and a tender woman.
[B279] Penguin pbk **£2.99**

My Apprenticeship
Gorky's encounters with the violent side of Russian 19th century life.
[B280] Penguin pbk **£4.95**
My Universities
The last part of the trilogy covers the years 1884 to 1888. The universities consist of discussions with revolutionaries in dark cellars, and passionate arguments with eccentrics and fanatics of all persuasions.
[B281] Penguin pbk **£3.99**
Fragments from My Diary
Gorky was a radical Russian writer, who supported the Revolution and who founded the style of socialist realism in literature. This book is a collection of fragments from his rich life, in which he was, at different times, revolutionary, traveller, tramp, baker and railwayman. These various elements combine to create a compelling vision of the Russia of the time.
[B282] Penguin pbk **£3.50**

GOSSE, EDMUND (1845 - 1928)
Father and Son
One of the most influential autobiographies ever written, *Father and Son* is a remarkable record of self-discovery. Gosse talks of his father having held him in a mental straitjacket, and he vividly recalls his childhood thoughts in response to this. As the book progresses, however, his objective account breaks down, and he presents us with a passionate and haunting portayal of his efforts to break free and come to terms with himself.
[B283] Penguin pbk **£2.95**
THWAITE, ANN
Edmund Gosse: A Literary Landscape
This admirable and highly-praised biography rescues Gosse's reputation from much of the prejudice that has surrounded it since his death. Gosse was a man of contradictions, both praised and reviled. Thwaite's biography examines him in this light, and looks at his friendships with Tennyson, Browning, Hardy and Henry James.
[B284] Secker hbk **£18.00**
[B285] Oxford pbk **£7.95**

GOYTISOLO, JUAN (1931 -)
Forbidden Territory NEW
The first volume of memoirs by the fine Spanish novelist, now belatedly achieving recognition in this country, thanks to Serpent's Tail, who publish his fiction. Goytisolo recalls a childhood overshadowed by the Civil War, his escape from Spain, and his search for an identity and a fatherland.
[B286] Quartet hbk **£15.00**

GRAVES, ROBERT (1895 - 1985)
Goodbye to All That
Graves's famous autobiography tells of his time at public school and as a young officer in the First World War. It is remarkable for its depiction of the war and its brutality, but also in showing the development of the young poet's mind.
[B287] Penguin pbk **£2.95**
GRAVES, RICHARD PERCEVAL
The Assault Heroic 1895 - 1926
The first volume of what could become the definitive biography of Graves. It documents the poet's formative years, including the bullying that he received at Charterhouse School, which kindled in him a hatred of British philistinism; and the devastating effect of the 1914-1918 war. This volume ends with Graves's flight from Britain to Egypt in 1926.
[B288] Weidenfeld hbk **£14.95**
[B289] Macmillan pbk **£8.95**
SEYMOUR-SMITH, MARTIN
Robert Graves: His Life and Work
A good one-volume life, written shortly before the poet's death, by a lifelong family friend. Seymour-

Smith naturally looks at the influence of the war on Graves's development, and how he later became a poet of a stature comparable to that of his friends Wilfred Owen and Siegfried Sassoon. The book then looks at his marriage to Laura Riding, during which he produced some of his most memorable love poems. In 1929 Graves went to Majorca, where he lived until his death.
[B290] Grafton pbk **£6.95**

GREENE, GRAHAM (1904 -)
A Sort of Life
The first volume of Greene's autobiography, written when he was 68, which closes *"with the years of failure which followed the acceptance of my first novel"*.
[B291] Penguin pbk **£3.95**
Ways of Escape
The second part of Greene's autobiography, in which he writes of Haiti, Vietnam, Kenya during the time of the Mau Mau, Hollywood during the making of *The Third Man*, and his time in the British Secret Service.
[B292] Penguin pbk **£3.95**
Getting to Know the General
[B293] Bodley hbk **£12.95**
[B294] Penguin pbk **£3.99**
Lord Rochester's Monkey
This biography of the notorious Restoration poet was written in the 1930s, but was left unpublished for forty years. It recreates the extraordinary atmosphere of Charles II's court and Rochester's pranks and erotic escapades.
[B295] Penguin pbk **£3.99**
GARLAND, NICHOLAS
Graham Greene Country
[B296] Pavilion pbk **£14.95**
MOCKLER, ANTHONY
Graham Greene: A Biography Volume 1: 1904 - 1945 **NEW**
The diversity of Greene's life provides rich pickings for biographers. He has been, at different periods, spy, journalist, francophile, propagandist and, of course novelist. This biography explores the complexities of the life and work of a very private man.
[B297] Collins hbk **£17.50**
SHERRY, NORMAN
The Life of Graham Greene: Vol 1 1904 - 1939 **NEW**
For his authorised biography of Greene, the result of 14 years of friendship, Norman Sherry was given complete access to his letters and diaries. At the heart of the book lies a remarkable correspondence between Green and his wife Vivien, for whose sake he became a Catholic. They show us a younger Greene, impassioned and romantic, struggling to find his feet as a novelist, and travelling to Mexico and West Africa.
[B298] Cape hbk **£17.50**

GURNEY, IVOR (1890 - 1937)
HURD, MICHAEL
The Ordeal of Ivor Gurney
Hurd describes the tragic career of Gurney, who was just beginning to be acknowledged as one of the finest poets and composers of his day, at the time of his death. His life, from his childhood in Gloucestershire, through his desolating experiences in the First World War, and his end in an asylum, forms a compelling and moving narrative.
[B299] Oxford pbk **£4.50**
THORNTON, ROBERT KELSEY (ED)
War Letters
An essential companion to Gurney's poetry, the letters describe his harrowing experiences in the First World War, and his developing mental instability. In contrast with this, he describes his life at home and evokes the artistic society of wartime England.
[B300] Carcanet hbk **£12.00**

HAGGARD, SIR HENRY RIDER
(1856 - 1925)
ELLIS, PETER BERRESFORD
H. Rider Haggard: A Voice from the Infinite
Haggard is best known as the author of *She* and *King Solomon's Mines*. This biography reveals little known aspects of his career: his early life in South Africa and his later years as a radical reforming squire in his native Norfolk.
[B301] Routledge pbk **£8.95**

HALL, RADCLYFFE (1883 - 1943)
BAKER, MICHAEL
Our Three Selves
Baker draws on unpublished material to throw light on the remarkable Radclyffe Hall, famous lesbian and author of the once-banned *The Well of Loneliness*. The biography recreates the colourful homosexual subculture of the 20s and 30s.
[B302] GMP pbk **£6.95**

HAMSUN, KNUT (1859 - 1952)
FERGUSON, ROBERT
Enigma: The Life of Knut Hamsun
Hamsun's fiction, particularly his novels *Pan*, *Hunger* and *Growth of the Soil*, is strikingly modern. His personal life, however, particularly his proto-Nazi sympathies during the war, has tended to overshadow his literary reputation. This biography explores Hamsun's literary and political development in depth.
[B303] Hutchinson hbk **£19.95**

HAN SUYIN (1917 -)
Han Suyin is a novelist and historian, who is widely regarded as one of the world's leading authorities on the history of modern China. She grew to maturity as her country was plunged through Revolution and Counter-Revolution. She describes these sweeping human events in her autobiographical works.
A Mortal Flower
[B304] Grafton pbk **£3.95**
A Share of Loving
[B305] Cape hbk **£9.95**
[B306] Grafton pbk **£2.95**
And the Rain My Drink
[B307] Grafton pbk **£2.95**
Birdless Summer
[B308] Grafton pbk **£3.50**

Ivor Gurney, whose letters are published by Carcanet (hbk **£12.00**). Photo: Gloucester County Library

Destination Chun-King
Han Suyin's first book is a devastating account of China's four-year war with Japan.
[B309] Grafton pbk **£2.95**
Four Faces
[B310] Grafton pbk **£2.99**
Morning Deluge Vol 1
[B311] Grafton pbk **£1.75**
Morning Deluge Vol 2
[B312] Grafton pbk **£1.75**
My House Has Two Doors
[B313] Grafton pbk **£3.95**
Phoenix Harvest
[B314] Grafton pbk **£3.50**
The Crippled Tree
[B315] Grafton pbk **£3.50**
Wind in the Tower
Mao Tse-Tung and the Chinese Revolution, 1949-75.
[B316] Grafton pbk **£1.75**

HANFF, HELENE
84 Charing Cross Road
The touching story of the love affair between Marks & Co, rare and secondhand booksellers of 84 Charing Cross Road (since turned into a record store) and Miss Helene Hanff of New York City. The relationship between the quirky American and the quirky bookshop evolves over a few years, beginning on the subject of books and subsequently developing into intimacy. It has been successfully filmed with Anne Bancroft and Anthony Hopkins.
[B317] Deutsch hbk **£6.95**
[B318] Futura pbk **£2.50**

HARDY, THOMAS (1840 - 1928)
Collected Letters Vol 1: 1840 - 1892
[B319] Oxford hbk **£37.50**
Vol 2: 1893 - 1901
[B320] Oxford hbk **£37.50**
Vol 3: 1902 - 1908
[B321] Oxford hbk **£37.50**
Vol 4: 1909 - 1913
[B322] Oxford hbk **£32.50**
Vol 5: 1914 - 1919
[B323] Oxford hbk **£27.50**
Vol 6: 1920 - 1927
[B324] Oxford hbk **£30.00**
GITTINGS, ROBERT
Young Thomas Hardy
The first part of the award-winning two-volume autobiography deals with Hardy's first 35 years and his struggles to become a writer.
[B325] Penguin pbk **£5.95**
The Older Hardy
[B326] Penguin pbk **£3.99**
MILLGATE, M.
Thomas Hardy: A Biography
This hugely detailed biography, the definitive one-volume life, gives a balanced view of Hardy. The author draws extensively on hitherto unknown material, including diaries, notebooks, letters, local records and contemporary newspapers.
[B327] Oxford pbk **£8.95**

HAWKINS, DESMOND
Hawkins, the son of a London ironmonger, evokes his life as an integral member of London literary society between the wars, when he was a friend of T.S. Eliot, Ezra Pound and Frieda Lawrence. He also describes his 1920s childhood, with its distractions of the music hall and the newly invented wireless.
When I Was
[B328] Macmillan hbk **£14.95**

HELLER, JOSEPH (1923 -)
HELLER, JOSEPH & VOGEL, SPEED
No Laughing Matter
The author of *Catch 22*'s account of his alarming experience of a disease which paralysed him

completely for a prolonged period. He recovered the use of his limbs gradually and ended up by marrying his nurse.
[B329] Cape hbk **£10.95**
[B330] Corgi pbk **£2.95**

HELLMAN, LILLIAN (1905 - 1984)
Pentimento
In the first volume of her bestselling memoirs Hellman describes her life, moving backwards and forwards between her Louisiana childhood and the present.
[B331] Quartet pbk **£2.95**
An Unfinished Woman
Hellman acerbically examines her life and the people in it: her love affair with Dashiell Hammett; her friendships with Dorothy Parker, Ernest Hemingway, F. Scott Fitzgerald and Norman Mailer. She also looks back to her time in the Spanish Civil War, and her opposition to the American witch-hunts.
[B332] Quartet pbk **£2.95**
Scoundrel Time
The third volume of memoirs tell of Hellman's involvement in the McCarthy witch-hunts in 1950s America, which she calls *'this sad, comic, miserable time of our history'*.
[B333] Quartet pbk **£2.95**
FEIBLEMAN, PETER
Lilly: Reminiscences of Lillian Hellman
Novelist Peter Feibleman first met Hellman when he was ten and she was thirty-five, and from that encounter developed an extraordinary relationship. This intimate and gossipy portrait includes anecdotes concerning Dashiell Hammett and Elizabeth Taylor, as well as an analysis of her lengthy feud with Mary McCarthy.
[B334] Chatto hbk **£14.95**
WRIGHT, WILLIAM
Lillian Hellman: The Image, the Woman
[B335] Sidgwick hbk **£15.00**

HEMINGWAY, ERNEST (1899 - 1961)
Selected Letters 1917 - 1961
Nearly 600 letters, providing a comprehensive insight into the man, the novelist of *A Farewell to Arms*, his dreams and the books he read.
[B336] Grafton hbk **£15.00**
[B337] Grafton pbk **£5.95**
BAKER, CARLOS
Ernest Hemingway
This celebrated 1968 biography has been for many years the standard life of Hemingway. It is a long and detailed analysis, which pieces together disparate elements: from his letters, manuscripts, interviews and correspondence. It debunks much of the myth surrounding Hemingway, portraying him as an ambitious, proud and freedom-loving man.
[B338] Penguin pbk **£7.95**
BRIAN, DENIS
True Gen: An Intimate Portrait of Ernest Hemingway
[B339] Grafton hbk **£11.95**
BURGESS, ANTHONY
Ernest Hemingway
An illustrated survey of Hemingway's life and his travels, particularly his Spanish sojourn.
[B340] Thames & H pbk **£3.95**
GRIFFIN, PETER
Along with Youth: Hemingway, the Early Years
With a wealth of new material, including some previously unpublished stories, this recent study brings the vigour and beauty of the young Hemingway to life.
[B341] Oxford pbk **£5.95**
HOTCHNER, A.E.
Hemingway and his World
An illustrated portrait of Hemingway and his milieu, including his exploits in the Great War, his years in

Paris with Joyce, Picasso and Gertrude Stein, the Spanish Civil War, the big-game hunting in Kenya and his part in the liberation of Paris during WWII.
[B342] Viking hbk **£25.00**
LYNN, KENNETH S.
Ernest Hemingway: His Life and Work
A highly-regarded biography, published in 1987, which traces Hemingway's literary influences, such as Henry James, and his obsessions, such as lesbianism. It presents Hemingway as a hero despite his many faults, and examines the contrasting viewpoints surrounding his reputation in the light of new discoveries, such as the recently published *Garden of Eden*. The most up-to-date life.
[B343] Simon & Schuster hbk **£16.00**
[B344] Sphere pbk **£7.99**
MEYERS, JEFFREY
Hemingway
Meyer's outstanding biography concentrates on the paradoxical nature of Hemingway: his progressively unpleasant yet generous personality; his cruel misrepresentations of former friends such as Gertrude Stein and F. Scott Fitzgerald; and the bookishness of the man of action, passionately engaging in worldly experience.
[B345] Macmillan hbk **£17.95**
[B346] Grafton pbk **£9.95**
REYNOLDS, MICHAEL
The Young Hemingway
A provocative literary biography which draws on family records. Reynolds reconstructs the cultural life of the pre- and post-war era, which is the essential background to the forging of the young writer's ideas.
[B347] Blackwell pbk **£7.95**

HESSE, HERMANN (1877 - 1962)
Autobiographical Writings
[B348] Grafton pbk **£2.95**
HESSE, HERMANN & MANN, THOMAS
The Hesse/Mann Letters 1910 - 1955
The correspondence between Hesse and Thomas Mann began in 1910 and ends with Hesse's memorial essay to Mann.
[B349] P Owen hbk **£11.95**

HILL, SUSAN (1942 -)
Family   NEW
At the core of this book is Susan Hill's moving account of the death of her daughter Imogen, who was born premature after 25 weeks' gestation. When she died, Susan Hill's one thought was that they must try again. Thus, when Clemency was born July 1985, when Susan was 43, there was jubilation from all connected with that long, traumatic journey: the family was complete.
[B350] M Joseph hbk **£12.95**

HOLMES, RICHARD
Footsteps: Adventures of a Romantic Biographer
"Without knowing it, my youthful journey through the Cevennes led me over the hills and far away into the undiscovered land of other men's and women's lives. It led me towards biography." This is a biographer's autobiography, but it is also Holmes's gripping exploration of his trade. He traces Robert Louis Stevenson's journey through the Cevennes, sleeping rough; he explains the strange world of Gérard de Nerval; and stalks Shelley and the Romantic idealists in Italy. This is a brilliant and acclaimed quest in search of the biographer's subject, through space and time.
[B351] Hodder hbk **£12.95**
[B352] Penguin pbk **£4.50**

HOPKINS, GERARD MANLEY (1884 - 1889)
KITCHEN, PADDY
Gerard Manley Hopkins: A Life   NEW
Kitchen says of her motivation for writing this

biography, published in 1989 for the first time in paperback: 'I loved his poetry. Hopkins had described those two states we feel - misery and ecstasy - to perfection. Hopkins packs a voltage unlike any other writer...' The book draws together the various and intricate strands of Hopkins's religion, sexuality and poetry.
[B353] Carcanet pbk **£6.95**

HURSTON, ZORA NEALE (1901 - 1960)
Dust Tracks on a Road
Hurston was one of the most prolific black women writers in America. This is her exuberant account of her life, her attitudes to racial politics and her quest for artistic expression.
[B354] Virago pbk **£5.99**

HUXLEY, ALDOUS (1894 - 1963)
BEDFORD, SYBILLE
Aldous Huxley Vol 1: The Apparent Stability 1894 - 1939
The definitive life of Huxley. Bedford was a friend of Huxley's for over 30 years and her fine biography utilises much first-hand observation, conversation and gossip. In this and the second volume, she traces Huxley's developing concern with the condition of man in the 20th century and his ability to destroy himself. She shows how these themes were worked into his great works (such as *Brave New World* and *Point Counter Point*). Bedford shows Huxley the great thinker as well as Huxley the private man.
[B355] Grafton pbk **£4.95**
Aldous Huxley Vol 2: The Turning Points 1939 - 1963
[B356] Grafton pbk **£4.95**
DUNAWAY, DAVID KING
Huxley in Hollywood   NEW
In 1937 Huxley went to America, as a result of his pacifism and rigid stand against engagement with Hitler. He became a well-paid Hollywood script writer, and wrote novels amidst a dazzling circle of exiles that included Charlie Chaplin, Thomas Mann, Christopher Ishwerwood, and fellow pacifist Marlene Dietrich. This book provides an enlightened portrait of Huxley's fate in the US.
[B357] Bloomsbury hbk **£14.95**
HUXLEY, ALDOUS
Grey Eminence
Huxley's biography of Father Joseph, Cardinal Richelieu's aide and inspirer in foreign policy. He was a man of contradictions, ruthlessly directing operations on the battlefield by day, and spending the night in prayer, composing spiritual guidance for the nuns in his charge.
[B358] Grafton pbk **£2.95**

IBSEN, HENRIK (1828 - 1906)
MEYER, MICHAEL
Ibsen
Excellent biography of the great Swedish dramatist by the distinguished translator of both Ibsen and Strindberg.
[B359] Penguin pbk **£5.95**

ISHERWOOD, CHRISTOPHER (1904 - 1985)
Christopher and His Kind
In 1929 Isherwood left England and went to stay for a week in Berlin. He remained there until 1939. In this exuberant account of his time spent there, he contrasts the fictional characters of his two 'Berlin' novels, with his friends, such as W.H. Auden and E.M. Forster.
[B360] Methuen pbk **£3.50**
My Guru and His Disciple
A humorous but moving account of Isherwood's search for spiritual truth in the Hollywood of the 1930s and 40s.
[B361] Methuen pbk **£1.95**

LEHMANN, JOHN
Christopher Isherwood: A Personal Memoir
Lehmann first met Isherwood in 1932, when the former was working for the Woolfs at the Hogarth Press. Lehmann took on Isherwood's novel *The Memorial* for publication. This memoir recalls their subsequent 35-year long relationship.
[B362] Weidenfeld hbk **£12.95**

JAMES, HENRY (1843 - 1916)
EDEL, LEON
The Life of Henry James
This is a shortened one-volume edition, taken from Edel's brilliant 5 volume *Life*. This edition is revised and updated to include much important new material. Edel has spent 50 years studying James, and this book is a distillation of a lifetime's research.
[B363] Collins hbk **£25.00**
EDEL, LEON (ED)
Complete Notebooks of Henry James
A marvellous collection of James's jottings and thoughts on writing and life. We catch a glimpse of the creative processes as he constructs his great sequence of novels, and see here the bare bones of the fictional and artistic processes at work, with all their difficulties, dead ends and hard-won glories.
[B364] Oxford hbk **£27.50**
NOWELL-SMITH, SIMON
The Legend of the Master
A fascinating, thematically-arranged glimpse of James both as man and legend. There are slightly unexpected revelations: James is seen to have a passion for motoring and a touch of the dandy about him.
[B365] Oxford pbk **£4.95**

JAMES, M.R. (1862 - 1936)
COX, MICHAEL
M.R. James: An Informal Portrait
M.R. (Monty) James wrote some of the finest ghost stories in the English language, as well as being a scholar of some repute. This biography looks at his academic achievements, his personal qualities and the atmospheric, lost world of 19th century public schools and universities which was his milieu.
[B366] Oxford pbk **£5.95**

JOHNSON, SAMUEL (1709 - 1784)
BATE, WALTER JACKSON
Samuel Johnson
This unsentimental life of Johnson presents him, not as the legendary figure of Boswell's *Life*, but as a writer of great relevance to the modern reader, who defined the literary and moral values of his age. This is the standard life after Boswell, which won the Pulitzer Prize in 1979.
[B367] Hogarth pbk **£7.95**
BOSWELL, JAMES
Boswell's Life of Johnson
Despite Johnson's polymathic pursuits (poet, essayist, dramatist, lexicographer and raconteur) his reputation in part survives because of the fortunate accident of having found the ideal biographer in Boswell. Boswell's devotion to Johnson, his constant companion, is reflected in this wonderfully anecdotal portrait. Johnson's wit and conversation shine, and Boswell portrays the social world of the 18th century in all its gossipy glory. *"I acquired a facility in recollecting, and was very assiduous in recording, his conversation, of which the extraordinary vigour and vivacity constituted one of the first features of his character...I have spared no pains in obtaining materials concerning him, from every quarter where I could."*
[B368] Oxford pbk **£8.95**
Life of Johnson
Manageable shortened version, based on the 1799 edition of the *Life*, the last in which the author had a hand; abridged and edited by Christopher Hibbert.
[B369] Penguin pbk **£3.99**

HIBBERT, CHRISTOPHER
Personal History of Samuel Johnson
[B370] Penguin pbk **£4.95**
PEARSON, HESKETH
Johnson and Boswell: The Story of Their Lives
An entertaining account of both Johnson and Boswell, which draws on contemporary accounts, as well as those by Mrs Thrale and Fanny Burney. The result is often more intimate and revealing than Boswell's *Life*.
[B371] Cassell pbk **£5.95**
PIOZZI, HESTER LYNCH
Dr Johnson by Mrs Thrale
[B372] Chatto hbk **£12.95**
WAIN, JOHN
Samuel Johnson
Winner of the James Tait Black Memorial Prize, this acclaimed critical biography discusses Johnson in all his aspects - his ideas, writings, loves and hates - and places him within the social and intellectual landscape of his day.
[B373] Macmillan pbk **£6.95**

JONSON, BEN
MILES, ROSALIND
Ben Jonson: His Life and Work
Jonson's literary career as a playwright, poet, writer of masques, and critic, was diverse and successful. Yet his life was as spectacular: as friend and then outcast of James I; as lover, libertine, undutiful husband; as honoured scholar and convicted murderer. This excellent biography, the fullest yet written, brings to light much that is new in relation to this Promethean character.
[B374] Routledge hbk **£27.50**

JOYCE, JAMES (1882 - 1941)
Selected Letters (Ed. Ellmann, Richard)
[B375] Faber hbk **£12.95**
ANDERSON, CHESTER G.
James Joyce
[B376] Thames & H pbk **£3.95**
ELLMANN, RICHARD
James Joyce
The definitive biography of Joyce. It is exhaustive in its detail, fluid in its narrative and scholarly in its literary analysis. Ellmann begins the book unassumingly: *"We are still learning to be James Joyce's contemporaries, to understand our interpreter. This book enters Joyce's life to reflect his complex, incessant joining of event and composition"*. Quoting copiously from Joyce's works and correspondence, he traces his life from his youth in Ireland to his death in Zurich. Proclaimed by Anthony Burgess as 'the greatest literary biography of the century', this is the 1982 version, revised by Ellmann before his death.
[B377] Oxford hbk **£25.00**
[B378] Oxford pbk **£9.95**

JOYCE, NORA
MADDOX, BRENDA
Nora: A Biography of Nora Joyce
A magnificent and enthralling biography of the earthy, lustful, sensuous and uninhibited Nora Barnacle. James Joyce was besotted with her, and it is said *Ulysses* would not exist without her. The story of her life, shaped by schizophrenia, emancipation and her marriage to a remarkable man, is fascinating both for itself, and for the insight it throws on the Joyce marriage.
[B379] H Hamilton hbk **£17.95**
[B380] Minerva pbk **£5.99**

KAFKA, FRANZ (1883 - 1924)
Diaries
[B381] Penguin pbk **£7.95**
Letters to Felice
Felice Bauer was Kafka's muse from 1912 to 1917 and she became the recipient of the outpourings of his

tortured soul. Their relationship was carried on through letters and they rarely met, intensifying the interest of this correspondence.
[B382] Penguin pbk **£6.95**
Letters to Friends
[B383] Calder hbk **£20.00**
Letters to Milena
Kafka's love for the cool and intelligent Milena Jesenska began in 1920. He became deeply attached to her and showed her his diaries, thus baring his heart and conscience to her. The letters are a moving tribute to their relationship.
[B384] Penguin pbk **£3.95**
CERNA, JANE
Kafka's Milena: The Life of Milena Jesenska
[B3861] Souvenir hbk **£12.95**
CITATI, PIETRO
Kafka   `NEW`
A major new biographical study of Kafka, already acclaimed in Italy. Citati gives major readings of the main works, *The Trial*, *The Castle*, *Metamorphosis*, and also explores the inner life of Kafka's mind, and the strange process by which Kafka lived his own stories.
[B385] Secker hbk **£14.95**
HAYMAN, RONALD
K: A Biography of Kafka
[B386] Weidenfeld pbk **£8.50**
PAWEL, ERNST
The Nightmare of Reason
Pawel reveals Kafka's life to be far more interesting than the myths that have arisen around it. He illuminates the interplay of Kafka's life and work and chronicles the Prague of affluent Germanised Jewry as well as the intellectual ferment of First World War Europe.
[B387] Collins pbk **£5.95**

KAVANAGH, P.J.
A Perfect Stranger
The early years of the poet's life made little sense to him until he met Sally, 'the perfect stranger'. This tender, funny and unsentimental celebration of their love is, despite its shocking conclusion, a tribute to human love.
[B388] Fontana pbk **£2.50**

KAZANTZAKIS, NIKOS
KAZANTZAKIS, HELEN
Nikos Kazantzakis: A Biography Based on his Letters
Kazantzakis, the author of *Zorba the Greek* and *The Last Temptation*, lived a full and intense life, during which he travelled constantly (Berlin in the twenties, Russia in the years following the Revolution, Spain in the Civil War, wartime in England). His passion and political commitment are here captured by Helen Kazantzakis, who interweaves many unpublished letters into her revealing biography.
[B389] B Sparrow pbk **£10.95**

KEATS, JOHN (1795 - 1821)
Letters
The letters of Keats contain, as well as his correspondence with other leading figures of his period, some of his most important critical reflections, such as his development of the idea of 'negative capability' in poetry.
[B390] Oxford pbk **£6.95**
GITTINGS, ROBERT
John Keats
This acclaimed biography won the W.H. Smith Literary Award. It is a scholarly and very detailed analysis of Keats's life, from his birth in London, through his relationships with the other Romantic poets, to his death in Rome.
[B391] Penguin pbk **£5.95**

KEROUAC, JACK (1922 - 1969)
NICOSIA, GERALD
Memory Babe: A Critical Biography of Jack Kerouac
An excellent, forthright analysis of Kerouac's sometimes tragic life. The book brings to life the whole era of the Beats, and analyses in some detail all of Kerouac's work. One of the best analyses of the era yet published.
[B392] Penguin pbk **£7.99**

KEYNES, JOHN MAYNARD (1883 - 1946)
HILL, POLLY & KEYNES, RICHARD (EDS)
Lydia and Maynard: Letters between Lydia Lopokova and John Maynard Keynes
A poignant collection of letters between Keynes and Lopokova, the great ballet dancer with whom he fell in love. They reveal much about the literary and theatrical world of London at the time.
[B393] Deutsch hbk **£14.95**

KILVERT, REVEREND FRANCIS
Kilvert's Diary: 1870 - 1879
[B394] Century hbk **£14.95**
PLOMER, WILLIAM (ED)
Diary Selections: 1870 - 1879
The Reverend Francis Kilvert kept a diary for nine years before his death. From it we gain a unique day-to-day documentary of mid-Victorian life in Wiltshire and on the Welsh Border. Kilvert is a delightful prose writer and a lively, gossipy, sociable and humorous commentator. This description of a ruined church from his diary entry of 6th August 1873 gives a flavour of his work: *"I ascended the tall rickety pulpit and several white owls disturbed from their day sleep floated silently under the crazy Rood Loft on their broad downy wings and sauntered sailing without sound through the frameless East and West windows to take refuge with a graceful sweep of their broad white pinions in the ancient yew that kept watch over the Church. It was a place for owls to dwell in and for satyrs to dance in."* Available in a full three-volume format, or in an abridged edition.
[B395] Cape hbk 3 vols **£35.00**
[B396] Cape hbk abridged **£10.95**
[B397] Penguin pbk abridged **£4.99**

KINGSMILL, HUGH (1889 - 1949)
INGRAMS, RICHARD
God's Apology: A Chronicle of Three Friends
Sensitive account of the friendship between writers Hugh Kingsmill, Hesketh Pearson and Malcolm Muggeridge.
[B398] H Hamilton pbk **£6.95**

KIPLING, RUDYARD (1865 - 1936)
Something of Myself
Kipling's 1936 autobiography recalls his childhood in India, his schooldays, and family life in the Pre-Raphaelite circle that included William Morris and Edward Burne-Jones. Critics have always found the book 'self-concealing' and 'reticent'. However in his introduction, Richard Holmes argues that Kipling reveals much of his secret emotional life in this book.
[B399] Penguin pbk **£3.95**
AMIS, KINGSLEY
Rudyard Kipling
An illustrated introduction to Kipling's life and the milieu in which he lived and worked.
[B400] Thames & H pbk **£3.95**
ANKERS, ARTHUR R.
The Pater: John Lockwood Kipling His Life and Times 1837 - 1911 **NEW**
A biography of Kipling's father, who was also an illustrator (of *Kim* and *The Jungle Books*). It reveals

much of Kipling's complicated relationship with his father as well as much about Rudyard's hitherto unknown sex life.
[B401] Hawthorn pbk **£9.95**
CARRINGTON, CHARLES EDMUND
Rudyard Kipling: His Life and Work
Carrington's biography looks beyond the controversial image of Kipling's 'Englishness' and his reputation as a supporter of British Imperialism. In this balanced portrait he concentrates on Kipling's literary craftsmanship and imagination. Graham Greene said of the book, in *The London Magazine*, *'we catch the pulse of the legend'*.
[B402] Penguin pbk **£4.95**

LAFORGUE, JULES (1860 - 1887)
ARKELL, DAVID
Looking for Laforgue
Arkell, a noted literary sleuth, has written a highly original biography of the French symbolist poet, which combines original research with a comprehensive review of the latest continental findings.
[B403] Carcanet pbk **£6.95**

LAMB, CHARLES (1775 - 1834)
CECIL, DAVID
A Portrait of Charles Lamb
An elegant introduction to the Romantic essayist, which describes his relationships with Wordsworth and Coleridge, as well as his involvement with family madness and murder.
[B404] Constable hbk **£9.95**
[B405] Constable pbk **£6.95**

LAMPEDUSA, GIUSEPPE DI (1896 - 1957)
GILMOUR, DAVID
The Last Leopard
Giuseppe Tomasi, Prince of Lampedusa, died in 1957, the last member of a great Sicilian family which traced its ancestry back to the early Byzantine Empire. He died childless, impoverished and unknown, leaving the manuscript of a novel, *The Leopard*. When this was published posthumously, it was received with great acclaim, and it has since come to be regarded as one of the greatest works of 20th-century fiction. Gilmour's biography is the first to have been based on access to Lampedusa's private papers, which have been unavailable for a quarter of a century. The many letters, diaries, notebooks and photographs (together with other papers dug out of the ruined Palazzo Lampedusa) provide a highly original biography.
[B406] Quartet hbk **£15.95**

LANCASTER, OSBERT (1908 -)
BOSTON, RICHARD
Osbert: A Portrait of Osbert Lancaster **NEW**
This biography of the celebrated cartoonist, by someone who knew him in the last ten years of his life, shows Lancaster as vivacious and multi-talented. We are shown the many sides of Sir Osbert: as a stylish writer; an under-rated painter; a perceptive historian and critic of architecture; a great dandy, bon viveur and public speaker. The portrait which emerges is of a warm-hearted and endearing man.
[B407] Collins hbk **£17.50**

LAWRENCE, D.H. (1883 - 1930)
Letters Vol 1: 1901 - 1913
[B408] Cambridge hbk **£37.50**
Letters Vol 2: 1913 - 1916
[B409] Cambridge hbk **£37.50**
Letters Vol 3: 1916 - 1921
[B410] Cambridge hbk **£37.50**
Letters Vol 4: 1921 - 1924
[B411] Cambridge hbk **£37.50**

BURGESS, ANTHONY
Flame into Being
A brisk and highly enjoyable introduction to Lawrence by Burgess, who is a committed disciple.
[B412] Heinemann hbk **£9.95**
[B413] Sphere pbk **£3.95**
CHAMBERS, JESSIE
D.H. Lawrence: A Personal Record
Jessie Chambers was the model for Miriam in *Sons and Lovers*. This remarkable account of their relationship is both a gloss on the novel, as well as a gripping story in itself.
[B414] F Cass hbk **£16.00**
MOORE, HARRY T.
The Priest of Love: A Life of D.H. Lawrence
A revised edition of *The Intelligent Heart*, which was acclaimed as the standard biography of Lawrence. Moore travelled and researched widely in order to gather information for the book. He devotedly follows Lawrence from his humble Midlands upbringing through his later restless wanderings across Europe and further. It may never be possible to achieve a definitive biography of such a complex and contradictory figure as Lawrence, but Moore's book, subsequently filmed, comes close. This revised edition incorporates much recent scholarship.
[B415] Penguin pbk **£4.95**
MOORE, HARRY T. & ROBERTS, WARREN
D.H. Lawrence
A revealing study which poses the question: did Lawrence's private life echo his writing or vice versa? The numerous illustrations provide a vivid survey of that life.
[B416] Thames & H pbk **£3.95**
SAGAR, KEITH
The Life of D.H. Lawrence
A richly illustrated pictorial biography which uses quotations from Lawrence's letters and those of his friends, as well as his paintings. This is an excellent book which reveals many hitherto unknown facets of the writer.
[B417] Methuen pbk **£5.50**

LEAR, EDWARD (1812 - 1888)
CHITTY, SUSAN
That Singular Person Called Lear
The first serious new biography of Lear for 20 years. Susan Chitty penetrates the complicated world of the

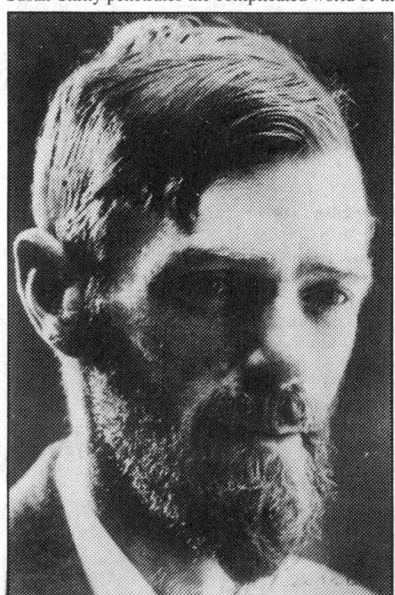

D.H Lawrence, the subject of *The Priest of Love* by Harry Moore (Penguin pbk **£4.95**)

writer, and examines aspects of it, such as the epilepsy that caused him to see literally a different world from other people. She also discusses his love for Edward Lushington, a young man whom Lear met in Corfu.
[B418] Weidenfeld hbk **£16.95**
NOAKES, VIVIEN (ED)
Selected Letters
As well as being a composer of delightful nonsense verse, Lear was a prolific letter writer. His circle of friends included the Pre-Raphaelites, the Tennysons, politicians, zoologists, peers and children. This selection also includes his vivid travel accounts along with sketches and pieces of nonsense.
[B419] Oxford hbk **£19.50**
[B420] Oxford pbk **£6.95**

LEE, LAURIE (1914 -)
A Rose for Winter
Lee returns to Andalucia 15 years after his first visit. He finds a country broken by the Civil War, but one which also survives through the eternal, indestructible elements of Spanish life: images of the Virgin in agony; the gypsy intensity; and the tradition of the bullfight.
[B421] Deutsch hbk **£10.95**
[B422] Penguin pbk **£2.50**
As I Walked Out One Midsummer Morning
Lee's classic account of his travels round Spain in 1934, earning his passage through playing the violin. Leaving behind the comfort of his Gloucestershire home, he first worked on a building site in London, then went to Spain, where he saw the signs of the impending Civil War. The writing is lyrical and evocative: *"Valladolid: a dark square city hard as its syllables - a shut box, full of pious dust and preserved breath of its dead..."*
[B423] Deutsch hbk **£9.95**
[B424] Penguin pbk **£2.50**
Cider with Rosie
First published in 1959, this is one of the most popular autobiographies ever written. It describes the rich, sensuous world of Lee's childhood in a remote Cotswold village, a world which has not quite vanished but may soon do so.
[B425] Chatto hbk **£10.95**
[B426] Penguin pbk **£2.99**
I Can't Stay Long
Miscellaneous impressions of Gloucestershire, Spain and the Caribbean. The writing is poetic, nostalgic and reflective.
[B427] Deutsch hbk **£8.95**
[B428] Penguin pbk **£2.95**

LEHMANN, ROSAMOND (1903 -)
Rosamond Lehmann's Album
[B429] Chatto pbk **£7.95**
The Swan in the Evening: Fragments of an Inner Life
Lehmann's fragmentary autobiography tells of the birth of her daughter and her tragic death at the age of 24. She goes on to describe the overwhelming psychic and mystical experiences she felt as a result of that loss.
[B430] Collins hbk **£8.95**
[B431] Virago pbk **£3.95**

LEVI, PETER (1931 -)
The Flutes of Autumn
The former Oxford Professor of Poetry's highly appraised and lyrical account of his life, first as a Jesuit priest, and later as a poet. He brings a poet's eye to all he sees, whether it be Harrow gasometers, Stonehenge or midsummer nights spent walking through the Chilterns.
[B432] Collins hbk **£8.95**
[B433] Arrow pbk **£2.95**

LEWIS, C.S. (1898 - 1963)
Letters
Lewis was a great letter writer, and his correspondence covers a vast range of subjects subjects: books, nature, people, places and every aspect of God.
[B434] Lion pbk **£5.95**
CARPENTER, HUMPHREY
The Inklings
Carpenter's enjoyable, Somerset Maugham Award-winning, study of the group that included C.S. Lewis, J.R.R. Tolkien and Charles Williams. The Inklings met every Tuesday to drink beer, and every Thursday to read to each other from the books that they were writing.
[B435] Unwin Hyman pbk **£5.95**
GRIFFIN, WILLIAM
C.S. Lewis: The Authoritative Voice
Brings the many facets of this energetic man to life.
[B436] Lion pbk **£5.95**
SAYER, GEORGE
Jack: C.S. Lewis and His Times
An affectionate biography of the versatile writer by a lifelong friend. It describes Lewis's complex life: his cruel and sadistic schooling; his terrible experiences in the Great War; his friendship with J.R.R. Tolkien and his moving marriage to Joy Davidman in his last years.
[B437] Macmillan hbk **£14.95**

LEWIS, NORMAN
Jackdaw Cake
Norman Lewis describes his early upbringing, poised between the care of three eccentric aunts in Wales and his spiritualist parents in Enfield. He goes on to relate how his life after this start became even more extraordinary with his marriage to the daughter of a Sicilian Mafia family, and shows how his experiences in the Intelligence Corps in Algeria prepared him for an unusual life of adventure and travel writing.
[B438] Penguin pbk **£3.95**

LONGFORD, ELIZABETH (1906 -)
The Pebbled Shore
Lady Longford, one of our foremost biographers, chronicles her own, very full life in which she has known a large number of the distinguished people of her generation. She talks of her active role in politics and of her marriage to Frank Pakenham (whom she converted to Socialism), and of the job of bringing up eight children.
[B439] Weidenfeld hbk **£14.95**
[B440] Hodder pbk **£4.95**

Norman Lewis, author of *The Missionaries* (Secker & Warburg hbk £10.95) & *Jackdaw Cake* (Penguin pbk £3.95)

LORCA, FEDERICO GARCIA (1898 - 1936)
Selected Letters
These letters reveal the complexity and charm of Lorca. This selection also includes many early drafts of his poems, giving a glimpse into the development of his writing. Lorca's passionate lyricism is never more evident than when he describes the landscape: *"Granada in the rain has the divine light of a pensive brow which reminds us of childhood."*
[B441] Boyars pbk **£7.95**
GIBSON, IAN
Federico Garcia Lorca: A Life `NEW`
Gibson, an acknowledged expert on Lorca, has produced the definitive life, based on a complete investigation of all the Lorca papers and hundreds of interviews with surviving friends and relatives. He builds on his earlier work on Lorca, and utilises much newly released material to portray the inner anguish and outer flamboyance of the great poet.
[B442] Faber hbk **£14.99**
The Assassination of Federico Garcia Lorca
A quite remarkable search for the truth about the assassination of Lorca by Spanish loyalists in August 1936. Gibson interviewed hundreds of people in the process of researching this gripping, scholarly and moving account. He brings to light much of the material that was suppressed by the Spanish government after the assassination.
[B443] Penguin pbk **£4.50**
LORCA, FRANCISCO GARCIA
In the Green Morning: Memories of Federico `NEW`
The poet's brother writes of the childhood he shared with his sisters and Federico in the Andalusian village of Fuente Vaqueros. He brings to life many of the characters featured in Lorca's poetry and plays.
[B444] P Owen hbk **£17.50**

LOWELL, ROBERT (1917 - 1977)
HAMILTON, IAN
Robert Lowell: A Biography
Despite its mixed reception, Hamilton's biography is an admirable and thoroughly researched life of the American 'confessional' poet. The book attracted controversy for its emphasis on Lowell's increasing wild bouts of insanity, but it gives at the same time a sensitive and detailed examination of the poetry, and provides a full analysis of Lowell's poetic development. Hamilton traces his life from his earnest youth as the favoured son of an aristocratic Bostonian family, when he read voraciously, then examines his abandonment of traditional forms and the publication of his landmark collection *Life Studies*.
[B445] Faber pbk **£7.95**

LOWRY, MALCOLM (1909 - 1957)
DAY, DOUGLAS
Malcolm Lowry: A Biography
Lowry's life was a mixture of heaven and hell, in which his writing was overshadowed by alcoholism and two tempestuous marriages. He travelled widely through Europe and America, constantly struggling to write, and creating his one undoubted masterpiece *Under the Volcano*. Until this biography was pub-lished, little was known of his life. Day uses anecdotes, many of them Lowry's own, to create a lucid portrait of this outrageous, brilliant but clumsy and murky man.
[B446] Oxford pbk **£5.95**

MACBETH, GEORGE (1932 -)
A Child of the War
Macbeth, a poet noted for violent imagery and themes, looks back to a childhood brutally altered by the Second World War. He records the tragic and comic events of his youth: the bomb which shattered

his family home in 1940, the death of his father in 1941, and his emerging sexuality.
[B447] Cape hbk **£10.95**

MACDIARMID, HUGH (1892 - 1978)
BOLD, ALAN
MacDiarmid
During a long career MacDiarmid revitalised the Scots language, and in such works as *The Drunk Man Looks at the Thistle*, created some of the greatest poetry of the 20th century. Alan Bold, a lifelong admirer, provides a clear view of his work and his life, during which he co-founded the National Party of Scotland and was expelled from the Communist Party.
[B448] J Murray hbk **£17.95**

MACKENZIE, COMPTON (1883 - 1972)
LINKLATER, ANDRO
Compton Mackenzie: A Life
When Compton Mackenzie published his first novel he was acclaimed as one of the bright hopes of 20thcentury fiction. Although this promise was never quite fulfilled, Mackenzie made up for it by living a life of breathtaking turbulence and variety - he was a spy running British Intelligence in Greece during the First World War, a Roman Catholic convert, a satirist prosecuted under the Official Secrets Act, a friend of Henry James, Scott Fitzgerald, D.H. Lawrence and Norman Douglas, and author of the bestselling *Whisky Galore*. Linklater portrays the contradictions of this flamboyant and complex figure, decribed by Raymond Mortimer as *"a perfectionist who has taken a wrong turning"*.
[B449] Chatto hbk **£20.00**

MAILER, NORMAN (1923 -)
MANSO, PETER
Mailer
An oral biography of the fast-talking, hard-drinking American novelist, which includes recollections from those who have loved and hated him, including Andy Warhol, Allen Ginsberg, and from Mailer himself.
[B450] Penguin pbk **£7.95**

MANDELSTAM, OSIP (1891 - 1938)
MANDELSTAM, NADEZHDA
Hope Abandoned
This complements *Hope Against Hope*. In it Nadezhda describes her youth in Kiev, her first meeting with Osip and the difficulties they encountered following his arrest. After his death Nadezhda sought to discover what had become of her husband and concentrated on keeping his memory alive for succeeding generations. She also portrays her contemporaries, including Anna Akhmatova and Boris Pasternak.
[B451] Collins pbk **£7.95**
Hope Against Hope
An exhilarating and courageous account of the last four years of the great Russian poet Osip Mandelstam's life, after he was arrested and sentenced to solitary confinement.
[B452] Collins pbk **£6.95**

MANLEY, MRS MARY DE LA RIVIERE
(1672 - 1724)
MORGAN, FIDELIS
A Woman of No Character: An Autobiography of Mrs Manley
[B453] Faber pbk **£3.95**

MANN, KLAUS (1906 - 1949)
The Turning Point
Klaus, the son of Thomas Mann, was born in 1906. He was a celebrated intellectual figure during the Weimar Republic in Germany, but, as a bitter opponent of fascism, left the country in 1933. This 1942 autobiography includes some controversial

portraits of prominent Germans, and gives a richly detailed account of the four preceding decades of European history. Despite acclaim for his great novel *Mephisto*, Mann committed suicide in 1949, desolated at the prospect of physical and intellectual exile.
[B454] Serpent's Tail pbk **£9.95**

MANN, THOMAS (1875 - 1955)
Diaries 1918 - 1939
The period covered by these informal diaries chronicles Mann's growing international reputation as a novelist and his reluctant emergence as the focus for intellectual opposition to Hitler abroad.
[B455] R Clark pbk **£7.95**
Letters 1889 - 1955
These letters form a personal record of his life in Germany and his years of exile in Switzerland and America. They chronicle his gradual shift from nationalism to his call for Hitler's defeat. The correspondents include Gide, Freud and Brecht.
[B456] Penguin pbk **£7.95**

MANSFIELD, KATHERINE (1888 - 1923)
Collected Letters Vol 1: 1903 - 1917
[B457] Oxford hbk **£22.50**
Collected Letters Vol 2: 1918 - 1919
[B458] Oxford hbk **£19.50**
Letters and Journals
These letters show Mansfield coming to terms with the problems of living with pain, fear and loneliness, and with the often anguished love she had for her own husband.
[B459] Penguin pbk **£5.95**
The Journal of Katherine Mansfield 1904 - 22
[B460] Constable pbk **£5.95**
The Memories of LM
The story of Katherine Mansfield's relationship with Ida Baker (LM), whom she met in 1903 and corresponded with until her death.
[B461] Virago pbk **£4.95**
ALPERS, ANTHONY
The Life of Katherine Mansfield
An authoritative biography which analyses how Mansfield revolutionised the English short story. It describes her relationship with D.H. Lawrence (who used her as the model for Gudrun in *Women in Love*) and with the London literary scene of the period.
[B462] Oxford pbk **£6.95**
BODDY, GILLIAN
Katherine Mansfield: The Woman and the Writer
An illustrated guide to Mansfield, which incorporates many rarely seen photographs and unpublished material.
[B463] Penguin pbk **£9.95**
HANKIN, CHERRY A.
The Letters of Katherine Mansfield to John Middleton Murry
A selection of letters which charts the unusual eleven-year relationship between Mansfield and Murry, which began in 1912 when they were both newcomers to the London literary scene. The letters brilliantly reflect the progress, actions and reactions of their relationship, and form a remarkable narrative in their own right.
[B464] Virago pbk **£12.95**
TOMALIN, CLAIRE
Katherine Mansfield: A Secret Life
An acclaimed, sympathetic and scholarly study. Tomalin describes the troubled life of the influential short story writer, and concludes that Mansfield was 'essentially a 20th-century character caught in a 19th-century trap of ignorance and prejudice' (Hilary Spurling, *Daily Telegraph*).
[B465] Viking hbk **£14.95**
[B466] Penguin pbk **£5.99**

MARLOWE, CHRISTOPHER
URRY, WILLIAM [NEW]
Christopher Marlowe and Canterbury
Marlowe's murder at a tavern in Deptford tavern in 1593 is one of the most famous events in English literature. It has been alleged that he was not murdered but was spirited away to the Continent, where he wrote a series of brilliant plays erroneously attributed to Shakespeare. It is also suggested that he was a spy working for the Netherlands. This remarkable book explores every known aspect of Marlowe's life in the search for the truth.
[B467] Faber hbk **£9.95**

MARTINEAU, HARRIET (1802 - 1876)
Autobiography Vol 1
Harriet Martineau was a controversial journalist, abolitionist and lifelong feminist. In 1855, thinking she was about to die, she produced her autobiography at breakneck speed. In the first volume she talks with passion of her childhood and middle years; of her life as a dutiful daughter and invalid, suffering under the constraints of Victorian society.
[B468] Virago pbk **£5.95**
Autobiography Vol 2
In this volume Martineau recounts the years when she became a national figure, through the writing of her *Illustrations of Political Economy*. These immensely popular tales explained, through fictional stories, the forms of political economy. She was lionised by literary society after their publication. She began to produce authoritative pamphlets on political reform, as well as working hard for the enfranchisement of women.
[B469] Virago pbk **£5.95**

MASEFIELD, JOHN (1868 - 1967)
Letters from the Front: 1915 - 1917
[B470] Constable hbk **£12.50**
BABINGTON-SMITH, CONSTANCE
John Masefield: A Life
John Masefield is best remembered as the Poet Laureate and the composer of long narrative sea poems such as *Cargoes* and *Sea Fever*. This biography tells how Masefield was apprenticed to a merchant sailing ship in 1894 at the age of 15, and how he thereafter developed a great love of the sea. This is a carefully constructed biography, based on a mass of archive material.
[B471] H Hamilton pbk **£6.95**

MAUGHAM, W. SOMERSET (1874 - 1965)
CALDER, ROBERT
Willie: The Life of W. Somerset Maugham [NEW]
Maugham's personality has always carried an aura of mystery about it. This scholarly biography, the product of 14 years of research, draws on a wealth of previously unavailable material and identifies the fundamental influences of his childhood and homosexuality on his writing. Calder reveals much interesting new material about Maugham, including his espionage activity in two world wars, and the destructive relationship he had with his daughter in his final years. Maugham emerges as generous, kind and difficult.
[B472] Heinemann hbk **£15.00**
RAPHAEL, FREDERIC
Somerset Maugham
When Raphael was in his twenties and Maugham was in his eighties, the two met at Maugham's famous Cap Ferrat home. That occasion provided Raphael with much material for this volume. The book explores Maugham's complicated personality: his childhood in France, miserable adolescence in England, and the pampered life he led at the famous watering-hole on the Riviera, where his guests included H.G. Wells and the Aga Khan.
[B473] Sphere pbk **£4.99**

MCCARTHY, MARY (1912 -)
How I Grew
McCarthy traces her life from girlhood in Seattle in the mid-1920s, to her graduation from Vassar and subsequent ill-matched marriage.
[B475] Penguin pbk **£4.99**
Memories of a Catholic Girlhood
An orphan at six, Mary McCarthy's youth was confused by the conflicting values of the Catholic, Jewish and Protestant relations who brought her up, traumas which she amusingly recounts here.
[B476] Penguin pbk **£3.99**
GELDERMAN, CAROL
Mary McCarthy: The Authorized Biography **NEW**
The first authorized biography, which details her Dickensian childhood when she was put into the care of an authoritarian aunt and uncle. The book goes on to discuss her four marriages, including her stormy union with Edmund Wilson, as well as her conflict with Stalinist intellectuals over the Moscow Trials.
[B477] Sidgwick hbk **£15.00**

MEHTA, VED (1934 -)
Daddyji and Mammaji
[B478] Picador pbk **£3.50**
Sound-Shadows of the New World
[B479] Collins hbk **£15.00**
[B480] Picador pbk **£4.95**
The Ledge Between the Streams
A beautifully composed evocation of India in the forties, up to the 1947 partition.
[B481] Collins hbk **£12.50**
[B482] Collins pbk **£3.95**
The Stolen Light **NEW**
Mehta takes us through his college years when, as a blind student in California, he set out to prove himself, and longed for all the experiences of a normal American life. This tender and lyrical narrative depicts his growing self-awareness, sexual awakening, and his growth as a writer.
[B483] Collins hbk **£17.50**
Vedi
Mehta describes the experiences of being sent to a boarding school for blind children, where no-one spoke his language, at the age of four. His blindness intensified his memory of the traumatic events, which are recalled with 'electrifying intensity'.
[B484] Picador pbk **£2.95**

MEW, CHARLOTTE (1869 - 1928)
FITZGERALD, PENELOPE
Charlotte Mew and Her Friends
A poet admired by Thomas Hardy, John Masefield and others, Charlotte Mew finally committed suicide after a life blighted by hopeless love, poverty, insanity and death in her family. This is a sympathetic study of the milieu by the Booker Prize-winning novelist.
[B485] Collins hbk **£12.95**

MILLER, ARTHUR (1915 -)
Timebends
Miller, one of the most influential 'committed' dramatists of the century, is an independent and tough-minded writer. His fine autobiography, published in 1987, shows his political and literary courage at its best. Within the structure of a basic linear narrative, Miller allows memories and associations to interlock and reflect upon one another. He inevitable deals with his marriage to Marilyn Monroe - in a candid way - and talks with great skill of his political affiliations and struggles during the McCarthy era.
[B486] Methuen hbk **£17.95**
[B487] Methuen pbk **£5.99**

MILNE, CHRISTOPHER
The Enchanted Places
Milne answers the questions readers of the *Pooh* books always ask him, such as 'what was it like being the original for Christopher Robin?'
[B488] Methuen pbk **£4.50**
The Hollow on the Hill
[B489] Methuen pbk **£4.50**
The Path through the Trees
Milne explores the need to outgrow his childhood influences and establish an identity of his own, a problem he faced quite acutely as the son of A.A. Milne. This autobiography traces the path he took, ending with the successful establishment of his bookshop in Dartmouth.
[B490] Methuen pbk **£4.50**

MILTON, JOHN (1608 - 1674)
WILSON, A.N.
The Life of John Milton
A.N. Wilson's terse, provocative, witty and short biography has been warmly received. It makes Milton accessible to the general reader and details the central events of his life, giving particular attention to the writing of the major works, **Samson Agonistes** and **Paradise Lost**, and his relationship with his family.
[B491] Oxford hbk **£9.95**
[B492] Oxford pbk **£5.95**

MISHIMA, YUKIO (1925 - 1970)
SCOTT-STOKES, HENRY
The Life and Death of Yukio Mishima
At the time of his ritual suicide in 1970, the day after he had completed his great work **The Sea of Fertility**, Mishima was Japan's most famous novelist. This book portrays the many sides of Mishima - the friend and family man; one of the most important post-war novelists, actors and playwrights; the homosexual narcissist, fanatical bodybuilder and self-styled Samurai - and ends with an examination of his final gesture.
[B493] P Owen hbk **£12.95**

MITFORD, JESSICA (1917 -)
Hons and Rebels
In her first volume of memoirs Jessica Mitford tells the story of her childhood and early life, up to the Second World War. She provides a portrait of a vanished era of English country life, and an insight into the world recreated by her sister Nancy in her fiction.
[B494] Gollancz pbk **£4.95**
A Fine Old Conflict
The second volume of Mitford's memoirs relates the story of her involvement with the American Communist Party, which she joined during the Second World War and which she left after the Hungarian uprising.
[B495] Quartet pbk **£2.95**
The Making of a Muckraker
A collection of Mitford's best articles, including *Let Us Now Appraise Famous Writers*, her near-fatal attack on the Famous Writers School.
[B496] Quartet pbk **£2.95**

MITFORD, NANCY (1904 - 1973)
ACTON, HAROLD
Nancy Mitford: A Memoir
[B497] H Hamilton pbk **£5.95**
HASTINGS, SELINA
Nancy Mitford: A Memoir
Nancy Mitford was perhaps the most talented of the Mitford sisters, remembered for comic novels such as **Love in a Cold Climate** and **The Pursuit of Love**. She was a witty observer of English upper-class life and a great letter writer, whose correspondents included Evelyn Waugh and Harold Acton. Selina Hastings's biography captures the gaiety as well as the unhappy truths of her life: her failed marriage and unfulfilled relationship with 'the Colonel'.
[B498] Macmillan pbk **£4.95**

Yukio Mishima, the subject of *The Life and Death of Yukio Mishima* by Henry Scott- Stokes (Peter Owen hbk £12.95)

MOLIERE, JEAN-BAPTISTE POQUELIN (1622 - 1673)
BULGAKOV, MIKHAIL
Molière: Life of Monsieur de Molière
A portrait of the great French satirist and dramatist by the Russian novelist, who felt a deep affinity for his outspoken subject.
[B499] Oxford pbk **£5.95**

MORTIMER, JOHN (1923 -)
Clinging to the Wreckage
Mortimer's touching and hilarious autobiography chronicles his life from school days, through Oxford, the development of his legal career, and his growth as a writer and creator of the one and only Rumpole of the Bailey. Brimming with gossip and anecdote, the book also provides a portrait of Mortimer's roguish father on a par with that given in his play **A Voyage Round My Father**.
[B500] Penguin pbk **£3.50**
In Character
The first series of Mortimer interviews with influential men and women, originally conducted for the *Sunday Times*. The subjects are from diverse backgrounds, and include Ken Livingstone, Tony Benn, Lord Denning and Angela Carter.
[B501] Penguin pbk **£2.99**
Character Parts
The second series of Mortimer's revealing interviews, including conversations with Christine Keeler, Lauren Bacall and Neil Kinnock.
[B502] Penguin pbk **£2.95**

MUIR, EDWIN (1887 - 1959)
An Autobiography
Muir's closely crafted poems were greatly admired by T.S. Eliot. His gentle and lyrical autobiography describes his upbringing on an unspoiled Orkney Island and his traumatic adolescence in industrial Glasgow, where his parents and brother died prematurely. This progress from rural idyll to urban nightmare was to haunt him for much of his life.
[B503] Hogarth pbk **£5.95**

NABOKOV, VLADIMIR (1899 - 1972)
Speak, Memory
Nabokov's extraordinary and beautiful autobiography

is a *"systematically correlated assemblage of personal recollections ranging geographically from St Petersburg to St Nazaire, and covering thirty-seven years, from August 1903 to May 1940, with only a few sallies into later space-time."* Into his memoirs of life in Russia, Nabokov weaves the story of his obsessions: young love, butterflies, literature and art.
[B504] Penguin pbk **£4.99**

FIELD, ANDREW
V.N.: The Life of Vladimir Nabokov
A controversial biography of Nabokov, which has elicited much criticism from the Russian writer's own family. Field reveals Nabokov as a narcissist and a sly slanderer, whilst acknowledging and examining the nature of his genius.
[B505] Futura pbk **£5.95**

NESBIT, E.
BRIGGS, JULIA
A Woman of Passion: The Life of E. Nesbit 1858 - 1924
A really excellent biography of the author of the children's books *The Phoenix and the Carpet* and *The Railway Children*. She is revealed as a woman of variable temper who, although devoted to her husband, had a string of young lovers, and an energetic character who, in addition to writing, helped to found the Fabian Society.
[B506] Penguin pbk **£5.99**

NOLAN, CHRISTOPHER (1965 -)
Under the Eye of the Clock
Nolan was severely brain-damaged at birth, but has learned how to communicate by typing with a unicorn stick attached to his forehead. He shows a remarkable facility for language, and his book of poems *Dam-Burst of Dreams* was acclaimed for its Joycean fecundity. His Whitbread Prize-winning autobiography describes his growth into language.
[B507] Pan pbk **£2.99**

O'BRIEN, FLANN (1911 - 1966)
COSTELLO, PETER & KAMP, PETER VAN DE
Flann O'Brien
A lively and unusual illustrated biography of one of Ireland's greatest comic geniuses, a man who was celebrated as much for his waspish tongue and capacity for drink as for his writing. The authors reveal the tragedy and personal courage that lay behind O'Brien's comic mask.
[B508] Bloomsbury hbk **£14.95**

CRONIN, ANTHONY   NEW
The Life and Times of Flann O'Brien
The first full-length biography of Brian O'Nolan, who was also known as Flann O'Brien and Myles Na Gopaleen. He was acclaimed in his lifetime as one of the best comic writers of the century, particularly for the unique and anarchic novels *The Third Policeman* and *At Swim Two Birds*. Little is known of him as a man, and this biography is a welcome addition to our knowledge.
[B509] Grafton hbk **£14.95**

O'CASEY, SEAN (1884 - 1964)
Autobiographies 1
Sean O'Casey, the Irish dramatist, whose best-known play is probably *Juno and the Paycock*, wrote his autobiography in six books, over more than twenty years. This volume includes the first three books.
[B510] Pan pbk **£2.50**
Autobiographies 2
The final three books of O'Casey's autobiography vividly recreates the period and personalities following his early triumphs at the Abbey Theatre, and his reasons for departure from Dublin to London in 1926. He writes about his friendships, especially with George Bernard Shaw, and of his enduring commitment to the people of Ireland.
[B511] Pan pbk **£3.95**

O'CONNOR, GARRY
Sean O'Casey: A Life   NEW
A recent life of the many-sided and antagonistic dramatist. O'Connor himself wrote: *"I attempt to show how Sean O'Casey, slum dramatist and guttersnipe, hobnail-booted labourer and communist freethinker, who disdained a tie and thumbed his nose at conventional bourgeois behaviour, painstakingly created himself out of the real-life John Casey."*
[B512] Hodder hbk **£17.95**
[B513] Grafton pbk **£5.99**

ORTON, JOE (1933 - 1967)
LAHR, JOHN (ED)
The Orton Diaries
Orton's candid and lurid diaries cover the period from December 1966 until he was murdered by his lover in August 1967. They trace periods of high and low life, during six months when the sixties were at their most exciting. Here we have Orton's riotous and sordid sexual escapades at his mother's funeral and with a dwarf in Brighton; his contact with the Beatles; and his relationship with Kenneth Halliwell.
[B514] Methuen hbk **£12.50**
[B516] Methuen pbk **£3.95**
LAHR, JOHN
Prick Up Your Ears
An acclaimed biography of the anarchic '60s dramatist, recently used as the basis for a film of Orton's life, which traces his progress from provincial playwright to fêted London dramatist. The main thrust of the book is Orton's 15-year love affair with Kenneth Halliwell, which ended in 1967 with Orton's murder.
[B515] Penguin pbk **£4.95**

ORWELL, GEORGE (1903 - 1950)
CRICK, BERNARD
George Orwell: A Life
Winner of the 1980 Yorkshire Post Book of the Year Award. Crick's biography supersedes all previous studies: he offers piercing political analyses of Orwell's work and its significance, emphasising his debt to writers such as Swift, and portrays Orwell's frequently contradictory nature, showing both his selfishness and his generosity. His greatest emphasis, however, is upon Orwell's honesty, and he suggests that this quality is an essential ingredient of his finest work, which he believes lies in the deeply-felt essays.
[B517] Penguin pbk **£7.95**
STANSKY, PETER & ABRAHAMS, WILLIAM
Orwell: The Transformation
A detailed study of the four crucial years in which Eric Blair became George Orwell
[B518] Grafton pbk **£2.95**
The Unknown Orwell
[B519] Grafton pbk **£2.95**

OSBORNE, JOHN (1929 -)
A Better Class of Person: An Autobiography 1929 - 1959
Osborne, one of the original 'angry young men' of 1950s drama, looks back at that crucial period in post-war British culture. He describes the transition from the world of his suburban upbringing to the backstage world of the theatre. 'Wonderfully funny about the horrors of digs, backstage skimble-skamble and awful Home Counties comedies or farces about maids compromised in their cami-knickers.' - John Barber, *Daily Telegraph*.
[B520] Penguin pbk **£4.99**

OWEN, WILFRED (1893 - 1918)
Selected Letters
This selection from the 1967 edition of Owen's letters includes some early examples of his poetry. The letters, almost all to his mother, constitute a self-portrait of the war poet from the age of five until the eve of his tragic death in 1918.
[B521] Oxford pbk **£6.95**

OWEN, HAROLD
Journey from Obscurity
Harold was Wilfred Owen's younger brother. His autobiography describes growing up in Birkenhead and Shrewsbury in a poor family. The portrait of Wilfred shows him as a poet in embryo, but also as the eldest son in a closely-knit family, a side of him not often revealed.
[B522] Oxford pbk **£5.95**
STALLWORTHY, JON
Wilfred Owen: A Biography
A widely-praised critical biography by the poet Jon Stallworthy, in which he examines the workings of his fellow writer's mind. The book includes drawings by Owen and facsimile manuscripts.
[B523] Oxford pbk **£5.95**

PARKER, DOROTHY (1893 - 1967)
FREWIN, LESLIE
The Late Mrs Dorothy Parker
Frewin shows Parker to be a fragile person with a deep seriousness which allowed her to address her sence of the pain and sorrow of being a woman.
[B524] Sidgwick hbk **£14.95**
KEATS, JOHN
You Might As Well Live: The Life and Times of Dorothy Parker
An acclaimed life which recaptures the serpent tongue and crackling wit of Dorothy Parker. Keats shows how the splendour of the surface of her life contrasted with the squalor of her lonely death.
[B525] Penguin pbk **£4.99**
MEADE, MARION
Dorothy Parker: What Fresh Hell is This?   NEW
This biography reveals the other side of the woman billed as the 'wittiest woman in America'. Two broken marriages, a series of lacerating love affairs, a string of attempted suicides and abortions led Parker to say of her life *"It was terrible"*.
[B526] Heinemann hbk **£12.95**
[B527] Mandarin pbk **£3.99**

PASTERNAK, BORIS (1890 - 1960)
HINGLEY, RONALD
Pasternak: A Biography
Hingley's major study unravels the elusive and secret Russian poet, drawing on newly available material to illustrate his life and work. Hingley shows Pasternak to be primarily a poet, despite his pre-eminence as the novelist of *Dr Zhivago*.
[B528] Weidenfeld hbk **£12.95**
[B529] Unwin Hyman pbk **£5.95**
PASTERNAK, BORIS; TSVETAYEVA, MARINA & RILKE, RAINER MARIA
Letters: Summer 1926
In the summer of 1926 these three literary giants indulged in a passionate correspondence in which they explored each others' poetry.
[B530] Oxford pbk **£5.95**

PATON, ALAN
Journey Continued   NEW
The second part of Paton's acclaimed autobiography chronicles his continued opposition to apartheid, including his defence of Nelson Mandela at the famous Rivonia trial.
[B531] Oxford pbk **£5.95**
Towards the Mountain
[B532] Penguin pbk **£4.99**

PEAKE, MERVYN (1911 - 1963)
PEAKE, SEBASTIAN
A Child of Bliss   NEW
Mervyn Peake's son remembers a childhoodod during which the family regularly received visits from literary figures such as Graham Greene and Louis MacNeice. As a child he was devoted to his father, and was the subject of some of his most exquisite

drawings. In this intimate portrait of Mervyn Peake he unflinchingly portrays his own failure to live up to his father's expectations.
[B533] Lennard hbk **£14.95**

PEPYS, SAMUEL (1633 - 1703)
The Diary of Samuel Pepys
Set of Eleven Volumes. Not the first English diarist, but the greatest. The diary covers only nine years of what was a very full and interesting career in an England of excitement and change. Pepys was Secretary to the Admiralty at a time of important changes and developments in naval matters, and was a founding member of the Royal Society.
[B534] Unwin Hyman hbk **£190.00**
The Illustrated Pepys: Extracts from the Diary
[B535] Unwin Hyman hbk **£9.95**
The Shorter Pepys
A very good condensed edition, containing approximately a third of the original.
[B536] Unwin Hyman hbk **£20.00**
[B537] Penguin pbk **£12.95**
BRYANT, SIR ARTHUR
Samuel Pepys: The Man in the Making 1633 - 1669
Bryant's is an acclaimed and vigorous biography of 'this many-sided great little man'. In this volume we see Pepys begin to write his diary, and chronicling the Great Fire of London; later editions show him as a rising Admiralty servant, laying the foundations for Britain's future seapower.
[B538] Grafton pbk **£3.95**
Samuel Pepys: The Years of Peril 1669 - 1683
[B539] Grafton pbk **£3.95**
Samuel Pepys: Saviour of the Navy 1683 - 1689
[B540] Grafton pbk **£3.95**
OLLARD, RICHARD
Samuel Pepys: A Biography
A succinct one-volume biography which traces out the character of Pepys and the times in which he lived.
[B541] Oxford pbk **£6.95**

PERELMAN, S.J. (1904 - 1979)
HERRMAN, DOROTHY
S.J. Perelman
Perelman was one of the century's wittiest and most sardonic humorists. This well-researched biography traces his life from his Russian-Jewish immigrant family background. It highlights his relationship with the Marx brothers and with his own family.
[B542] Simon & Schuster hbk **£12.95**
[B543] Macmillan pbk **£7.95**

PETERLEY, DAVID
Peterley Harvest: The Private Diary
This is purportedly the diary of a dilettante of the 1920s and 1930s. Originally published in 1960, its speedy withdrawal at that time led to the supposition that the document was a literary hoax rather than merely pseudonymous.
[B544] Penguin pbk **£4.50**

PLATH, SYLVIA (1932 - 1963)
PLATH, AURELIA SCHROBER (ED)
Letters Home: Correspondence 1950 - 1963
Plath's important letters to her mother document her anguish and mental striving, as well as revealing much of her poetic development. The correspondence has been subsequently dramatised.
[B545] Faber pbk **£8.95**
STEVENSON, ANNE
Bitter Fame: A Life of Sylvia Plath NEW
This biography of Plath is written with the co-operation of the family estate. It describes, often in the words of close friends who have not spoken before, her relentless drive towards perfection, and her struggle against the 'devils' that tormented her. Anne Stevenson paints a terrible story in all its true colours.
[B546] Viking hbk **£15.95**
WAGNER-MARTIN, LINDA
Sylvia Plath: A Life
Plath's life and work continue to fascinate readers and writers, nearly 30 years after her death: her *Collected Poems*, published in 1982, won the Pulitzer Prize. This timely reappraisal draws on much new material in discussing Plath as a writer and as a woman and mother. It inevitably focuses on Plath's marriage to fellow poet Ted Hughes, and brings much new information to light on the subject.
[B547] Chatto hbk **£13.95**

PLOMER, WILLIAM (1903 - 1973)
ALEXANDER, PETER F.
William Plomer: A Biography NEW
Plomer was born in South Africa, but moved to England in 1929, where he was befriended by the Woolfs and became a reader for publisher Jonathan Cape. During this time he edited and published *Kilvert's Diary* and discovered such well-known writers as Vladimir Nabokov and Ian Fleming. This well-received 1989 biography also describes his career as a poet and author of *Turbott Wolfe*.
[B548] Oxford hbk **£15.00**

POPE, ALEXANDER (1688 - 1744)
MACK, MAYNARD
Alexander Pope
The first full-scale portrait of Pope since 1900, written by the world's leading authority. This is a magnificent biography, widely acclaimed, by a writer gloriously obsessed with his subject (some said the book told you more about Mack and his obsessions than it did about Pope). Mack traces Pope's life in minute detail, from his Cockney origins, through the trials of tuberculosis, to the triumphs of his poetry.
[B549] Yale hbk **£19.95**
[B550] Yale pbk **£12.95**

POTTER, BEATRIX (1866 - 1943)
LANE, MARGARET
Tale of Beatrix Potter
A revealing biography of the creator of Peter Rabbit and other children's classics. It describes her lonely childhood and the cipher which she used to write her journals, and her later life in the Lake District.
[B551] Penguin pbk **£3.50**

POUND, EZRA (1885 - 1972)
Selected Letters 1907 - 1941
[B552] Faber pbk **£4.95**
ACKROYD, PETER
Ezra Pound
An illustrated introduction.
[B553] Thames & H pbk **£3.95**
CARPENTER, HUMPHREY
A Serious Character NEW
Carpenter's excellent and fully documented biography takes issue with the accepted valuations of Pound's life and work. He has examined Pound's vast correspondence and seen medical records and confidential American government memoranda relating to Pound's indictment and trial. This is probably the most comprehensive view of Pound to date.
[B554] Faber hbk **£20.00**
SCOTT, THOMAS L. & FRIEDMAN, MELVIN J.
The Little Review Correspondence: The Letters of Ezra Pound to Margaret Anderson NEW
The Little Review, edited by Margaret Anderson from 1914-1929, was one of the first magazines to be devoted to the new modernist writing, promoting the work of Joyce, Eliot, Hemingway, Yeats and Breton. In the magazine Pound felt he had found a vehicle for his strong literary views.
[B555] Faber hbk **£30.00**
STOCK, NOEL
Ezra Pound
Pound has always aroused feelings of controversy. His strong literary and extreme political opinions have made him both a revered and reviled figure. Against this background of opinion, Stock's biography presents a balanced account of the poet. Stock was a close friend of Pound and his meticulously detailed life, first published in 1970, offers the clearest first-hand view of a complex subject.
[B556] Penguin pbk **£5.95**
TYTELL, JOHN
Ezra Pound: The Solitary Volcano
An interpretive study which explores the myths behind Pound, relating tales of his ridicule when he visited London before going to Italy, and revealing the truth behind the poet's intentions. Tytell has had access to unpublished letters and psychiatric reports.
[B557] Bloomsbury hbk **£17.95**

PRIESTLEY, J.B. (1894 - 1984)
BROME, VINCENT
J.B. Priestley
The first authorised biography of the versatile writer. Born in working-class Bradford, Priestley achieved international fame in 1929 with his picaresque novel *The Good Companions*. He went on to become one of the most prolific novelists and dramatists of the century. This biography details his literary career as well as his three marriages and many affairs.
[B558] H Hamilton hbk **£16.95**

PROUST, MARCEL (1871 - 1922)
Selected Letters Vol 1 (1880 - 1903)
These letters trace Proust's formative years as a writer, his relationship with his parents, schoolfriends and literary figures.
[B559] Collins hbk **£15.95**
[B560] Oxford pbk **£4.95**
Selected Letters Vol 2: 1904 - 1909
The second volume covers the crucial period leading up to Proust's final discovery of his true vocation as a writer, a period overshadowed by his worsening health and his mother's death in 1905.
[B561] Collins hbk **£30.00**
FREMY, DOMINIQUE & MICHEL-THIRIET, PHILIPPE (EDS)
The Book of Proust
A comprehensive guide to all things Proustian, including maps, anecdotes, facts, figures and indexes.
[B562] Chatto hbk **£25.00**
MAUROIS, ANDRE
The Quest for Proust
[B563] Constable pbk **£6.95**
PAINTER, GEORGE D.
Marcel Proust
Undoubtedly one of the greatest biographies of the century, Painter's life of Proust concentrates on the parallels between Proust's masterpiece *A la Récherche du Temps Perdu*, and the life of its creator. The revelations of Proust's life are remarkable, and the scholarly care with which Painter shows how the fictional characters in *A la Récherche* were drawn from its author's life are enriching. This is a one-volume revision of the work, with a new preface.
[B564] Chatto hbk **£20.00**
[B565] Penguin pbk **£9.99**
SANSOM, WILLIAM
Proust
[B566] Thames & H pbk **£3.95**

PRYCE-JONES, ALAN
The Bonus of Laughter
The varied and entertaining autobiography of the former editor of the *Times Literary Supplement* and

book critic of the *New York Herald Tribune*. Throughout, Pryce-Jones lives up to his declared aim, that of enjoying himself.
[B567] H Hamilton pbk **£5.95**
PRYCE-JONES, ALAN (ED)
The Little Innocents
A collection of childhood reminiscences by John Betjeman, Harold Nicolson, Lord Alfred Douglas, Edward Blunden, Evelyn Waugh, Vita Sackville-West and others.
[B568] Oxford pbk **£3.95**

PYM, BARBARA (1930 - 1980)
A Very Private Eye
Despite her fame as a novelist, little was known of Barbara Pym's private life. This book collects together material from her diaries and notebooks. It describes her life from her Oxford days in the 1930s, through an unhappy love affair and her string of rejected novels, on to her final triumphs.
[B569] Grafton pbk **£2.95**

RANSOME, ARTHUR (1884 - 1967)
Autobiography of Arthur Ransome
[B570] Century pbk **£4.95**
BROGAN, HUGH
The Life of Arthur Ransome
An absorbing study of Arthur Ransome's adventurous life, which included two stormy marriages, as well as a journalistic career that gave him a first-hand view of the Russian Revolution. Brogan also examines closely the writing of Ransome's classic children's books, such as *Swallows and Amazons*.
[B571] H Hamilton pbk **£4.95**

RATUSHINSKAYA, IRINA (1954 -)
Grey is the Colour of Hope
This remarkable book tells the story of the Russian poet's incarceration in prison for 'anti-Soviet propaganda'. It is a story of great courage and defiance, not without humour. She tells of how she was determined to continue to compose poetry despite being forbidden to do so. She did this by writing the words down on bars of soap and memorising them.
[B572] Hodder pbk **£12.95**
[B573] Hodder pbk **£4.99**

RHYS, JEAN (1890 - 1979)
Letters 1931 - 1966
Jean Rhys spent many years in Paris during the early part of the century, a period memorably portrayed in her novel *Quartet*. After beginning a successful career as a novelist, she published nothing for twenty years until she made a remarkable comeback with *The Wide Sargasso Sea* in 1966. This fascinating collection of letters, begins when Rhys was in the first flush of literary success, and ends with her having just delivered the manuscript of *The Wide Sargasso Sea* to her publishers. In between she reveals the circumstances which led to her artistic silence, and her struggle to break it.
[B574] Deutsch hbk **£9.95**
[B575] Penguin pbk **£5.99**
Smile Please
Rhys's unfinished autobiography was published posthumously. It tells of her early days on Dominica and in the West Indies, and later life in bedsits in London and Paris.
[B576] Penguin pbk **£3.50**
ANGIER
Jean Rhys
[B577] Penguin pbk **£2.95**

RICHARDS, FRANK
CADOGAN, MARY
Frank Richards: The Chap Behind the Chums **NEW**
Frank Richards was a literary phenomenon. The most

prolific writer in the English language, he achieved a published output of at least 72 million words of fiction, the equivalent of 1,000 novels. This biography of the creator of Billy Bunter and Greyfriars School discusses the literary quality and social attitudes of the stories and their appeal.
[B578] Viking hbk **£14.95**

RILKE, RAINER MARIA (1875 - 1926)
Selected Letters 1902 - 1926
A major selection of Rilke's letters, introduced by John Bayley, which include some of his celebrated pieces on artists such as Cézanne. Also included are his passionate, warm and inspiring letters to his wife.
[B579] Quartet pbk **£7.95**
HENDRY, J.F.
Sacred Threshold: A Life of Rainer Maria Rilke
[B580] Carcanet hbk **£12.95**
PRATER
Ring of Glass: A Life of Rainer Maria Rilke
[B581] Oxford hbk **£30.00**

ROBBE-GRILLET, ALAIN (1922 -)
The Ghosts in the Mirror
In his autobiography, the French experimental novelist portrays his parents, whom he describes as extreme right-wing anarchists, and his life on the bleak Brittany coast. He openly reveals his erotic obsessions, as well as his emotional development.
[B582] Calder pbk **£5.95**

ROSSETTI, CHRISTINA (1830 - 1894)
BATTISCOMBE, GEORGINA
Christina Rossetti: A Divided Life
Rossetti has been acclaimed as one of the most important and underestimated 19th-century poets. Her life was one of physical and mental suffering. However Battiscombe explores her sadness and finds that it has roots which are deeper than her external troubles. She describes in particular Rossetti's spiritual and emotional crises in early adolescence.
[B583] Constable hbk **£9.50**
[B584] Constable pbk **£4.50**

ROTH, PHILIP **NEW**
The Facts: A Novelist's Autobiography
Roth, the master of shifting fictional and narrative voices, gives us his 'novelists's autobiography'. The title alone, however, indicates that we should be aware of the difficulty of the term autobiography. As Roth says: *"To my surprise, I now appear to have gone about writing a book backwards, taking what I had imagined and, as it were, desiccating it so as to restore my experience to the original, pre-fictionalised factuality."* The result is a highly original and entertaining examination of the relationship between Roth's life and his work.
[B585] Cape hbk **£11.95**

SACKVILLE-WEST, VITA (1892 - 1962)
Pepita
A biography of two of Vita Sackville-West's relatives: her grandmother Josefa Duran, the half-gypsy daughter of an old clothes pedlar from Malaga; and of her mother, Victoria.
[B586] Virago pbk **£3.95**
DESALVO, L. & LEASKA, M.A.
The Letters of Vita Sackville-West to Virginia Woolf
[B587] Macmillan pbk **£8.95**
GLENDINNING, VICTORIA
Vita: The Life of V. Sackville-West
Whitbread Award-winning biography of the complex aristocrat, poet, novelist, broadcaster and gardener, who transformed the ruins of Sissinghurst.
[B588] Weidenfeld hbk **£15.95**
[B589] Penguin pbk **£6.99**

NICOLSON, NIGEL
Portrait of a Marriage
A deeply revealing portrait of the marriage between Vita Sackville-West and Harold Nicolson, and their life at Sissinghurst.
[B590] Weidenfeld hbk **£12.95**
[B591] Futura pbk **£2.95**

SARTRE, JEAN-PAUL (1905 -1980)
Words
Sartre's famous autobiography looks back to his illusion-filled childhood, during which he developed a false conception of life and considers its effects on his later ideas and work. He talks of his life in these terms: *"I gave my entire self to the task of saving my entire self"*.
[B592] Penguin pbk **£3.99**
COHEN-SOLAL, ANNIE
Sartre: A Biography
Draws on much original research to show exactly how, and why, Sartre is such an influential figure.
[B593] Hogarth hbk **£14.95**
[B594] Heinemann pbk **£8.95**
HAYMAN, RONALD
Writing Against: A Biography of Sartre
[B595] Weidenfeld hbk **£18.95**
[B596] Weidenfeld pbk **£8.95**

SASSOON FAMILY
JACKSON, STANLEY
The Sassoons **NEW**
The Sassoons were bankers to successive Ottoman rulers, and leading citizens in Baghdad for centuries. The first Sassoon to wear Western dress arrived in England in 1858 and within a few years the family was established. Since then they have grown in stature and power: at one time a Sassoon simultaneously owned and edited both the *Sunday Times* and the *Observer*. The dynasty included the poet Siegfried as well as Sir Philip Sassoon. This richly detailed book gives a fascinating account of the great Jewish clan.
[B597] Heinemann pbk **£6.95**

SASSOON, SIEGFRIED (1886 - 1967)
Diaries 1920 - 1922
[B598] Faber hbk **£10.95**
Diaries 1923 - 1925
[B599] Faber hbk **£12.95**
Letters to Max Beerbohm with a Few Answers
[B600] Faber hbk **£9.95**
Siegfried's Journey 1916 - 1920
This intensely-written memoir examines Sassoon's life between 1916 and 1920, and evokes the literary people he knew: Wilfred Owen, Thomas Hardy, Robert Bridges. The most vivid portrayal, however, is that of himself.
[B601] Faber pbk **£2.95**
The Old Century
Sassoon's memoir of his first twenty-one years as a gentleman in late Victorian and early Edwardian England, before the Great War.
[B602] Faber pbk **£4.95**
The Weald of Youth
The sequel to *The Old Century*, which covers the years between 1909 and the Great War. Sassoon looks back at his life as a young poet and sportsman, and gives interesting pre-war glimpses of Edmund Gosse, Rupert Brooke and George Moore.
[B603] Faber pbk **£4.95**

SCHREINER, OLIVE
FIRST, RUTH & SCOTT, ANNE
Olive Schreiner
A well-received study of the South African feminist author of *The Story of an African Farm*. Foreword by Nadine Gordimer.
[B604] Women's P pbk **£5.95**

SCOTT, SIR WALTER (1771 - 1832)
BUCHAN, JOHN
Sir Walter Scott
[B605] Cassell pbk **£5.95**
PEARSON, HESKETH
Walter Scott: His Life and Personality
A thorough analysis which details the main events of
Scott's life: the torments of his infantile paralysis
when young; his huge success as a writer and in
rebuilding Abbotsford; and his financial ruin. 'Mr
Pearson's relish in human personality, in special
ideas, habits, characteristics and eccentricities which
express the essence of individuality, is contagious.' -
New York Times.
[B606] H Hamilton pbk **£6.95**
WILSON, A.N.
**The Laird of Abbotsford: A View of Sir
Walter Scott**
A subtle and provocative critical biography which
examines Scott's immense popularity in the 19th
century in contrast to his relative unpopularity in
the 20th.
[B607] Oxford hbk **£12.95**
[B608] Oxford pbk **£4.95**

SHAKESPEARE, WILLIAM (1564 - 1616)
HALLIDAY, F.E.
Shakespeare
[B609] Thames & H pbk **£3.95**
LEVI, PETER (1931 -)
**The Life and Times of William
Shakespeare**
A lively examination of Shakespeare's life and works
set against the background of Elizabethan England.
Levi brings together all the discoveries of scholars
from the last 50 years and places them in the context
of Shakespeare's life.
[B610] Macmillan hbk **£16.95**
OGBURN, CHARLES
The Mystery of William Shakespeare
[B611] Sphere pbk **£6.99**
PEARSON, HESKETH
Life of Shakespeare
A highly individual biography of Shakespeare in
which Pearson, despite the lack of hard facts about
the dramatist's life, draws a recognisable portrait and
even manages to tell us the colour of Shakespeare's
hair. With an introduction by Anthony Burgess.
[B612] H Hamilton pbk **£6.95**
SCHOENBAUM, S.
**William Shakespeare: A Compact
Documentary Life**
This book contains documentary evidence relating to
the events of Shakespeare's life, incorporating the
results of 400 years of Shakespeare scholarship.
[B613] Oxford pbk **£6.95**

SHAW, GEORGE BERNARD (1856 - 1950)
ELLIOTT, VIVIAN (ED)
Dear Mr Shaw
A selection of letters to Bernard Shaw.
[B614] Bloomsbury pbk **£7.95**
HOLROYD, MICHAEL
**Bernard Shaw Vol 1: The Search
for Love**
Holroyd's authorised three-volume biography of
Shaw has so far been 15 years in the making. It
provides a perfect matching of subject and author, in
a taut narrative that reads more like a novel than a
biography. This first volume covers Shaw's early life
from birth in Dublin to marriage in London at the age
of 41, detailing the years he spent gaining notoriety as
a political activist, controversial critic, censored
dramatist and, rather to his surprise, successful lover.
Holroyd says of the project *"As a non-Shavian I set
myself the task of saving him, in the most respectful
way possible, from the Old Guard. Most of them had
been quite happy to allow Shaw to continue in the
public imagination as a man with ink not blood in his*

*veins, who was born at the age of sixty with a white
beard, and who as a writer had become a feature of
interest on the horizon, well away from the approved
route of modern literature. I wanted to unsettle these
stereotypes, to show he was young once, that he made
human mistakes, that he couldn't work his
typewriter."*
[B615] Chatto hbk **£16.00**
Vol 2: The Pursuit of Power   NEW
Volume 2 starts at the beginning of Shaw's marriage
in 1898 and finishes at the end of the First World War.
This is the period of Shaw's great middle plays and of
his theatrical partnership with Granville-Barker at the
Royal Court, and his comradeship and rivalry with
H.G. Wells.
[B616] Chatto hbk **£18.00**
HYDE, MARY (ED)
**Bernard Shaw and Alfred Douglas: A
Correspondence**
Many years after the death of Oscar Wilde, Lord
Alfred Douglas asked George Bernard Shaw to write
a preface to his autobiography, a request which met
with a resounding 'no'. But this was the start of a
correspondence that turned into an enduring
friendship.
[B617] Oxford pbk **£5.95**
LAURENCE, DAN H. (ED)
Collected Letters Vol 1: 1874 - 1897
[B618] Reinhardt hbk **£30.00**
Collected Letters Vol 2: 1898 - 1910
[B619] Reinhardt hbk **£30.00**
Collected Letters Vol 3: 1911 - 1925
[B620] Reinhardt hbk **£30.00**
Collected Letters Vol 4: 1926 - 1950
[B621] Bodley hbk **£30.00**
PEARSON, HESKETH
Bernard Shaw
In one of his greatest biographies Pearson, very much
a fan of his subject, examines Shaw's wit, good
humour and diversity.
[B622] Unwin Hyman pbk **£8.95**
WILSON, COLIN
**Bernard Shaw:
A Reassessment**
Wilson's critical biography pinpoints two essential
characteristics in Shaw: that he was essentially a
romantic, but that he coupled this with a high degree
of objectivity.
[B623] Macmillan pbk **£6.95**

SHELLEY, MARY (1797 - 1851)
SPARK, MURIEL
Mary Shelley   NEW
A characteristically sharp investigation of Mary
Shelley, by the novelist Muriel Spark. She explores
Shelley's unconventional life as the daughter of
William Godwin, the radical, and Mary
Wollstonecraft, the pioneer feminist. At the age of 16
Mary eloped with the poet Percy Bysshe Shelley.
After only six years of marriage, however, Shelley
was drowned and Mary faced long decades of
widowhood. Spark throws light on Shelley's final
years when, with financial support from her family,
she set about editing an edition of her husband's
works.
[B624] Constable hbk **£14.95**
[B625] Sphere pbk **£3.99**

SHELLEY, PERCY BYSSHE (1792 - 1822)
HOLMES, RICHARD
Shelley: The Pursuit
This is a magnificent biography and has been
justifiably acclaimed. Holmes is like a detective
stringing together bits of evidence from Shelley's life
- he shows the poet warts-and-all, breaking down the
idealised portrait often seen, in order to investigate
Shelley's sometime cruelty and arrogance. As the
author says: *"There will always be Shelley lovers, but
this books is not for them."* By emphasising the poet's

political and philosophical concerns Holmes depicts a
richer, more considerable Shelley.
[B626] Weidenfeld hbk **£16.95**
[B627] Penguin pbk **£7.95**
MAUROIS, ANDRE
Ariel
[B628] Penguin pbk **£1.95**
ST. CLAIR, WILLIAM
The Godwins and the Shelleys   NEW
The first full account of one of the most extraordinary
families in the history of ideas. William Godwin's
great treatise on liberalism, *Political Justice*, brought
the ideas of the French Revolution to Britain, while *A
Vindication of the Rights of Women* by his wife,
Mary Wollstonecraft is one of the most important
books in the development of the modern women's
movement. Their daughter Mary, the author of
Frankenstein, eloped with the poet Shelley.
[B629] Faber hbk **£25.00**

SINGER, ISAAC BASHEVIS (1904 -)
Love and Exile
The formidable Jewish novelist describes his early
intellectual and emotional development. His youth
was spent avidly reading, during which period he
became spiritually rooted in the Middle Ages.
[B630] Cape hbk **£10.95**
[B631] Penguin pbk **£5.95**

SITWELL, EDITH (1887 - 1964)
English Eccentrics
[B632] Penguin pbk **£5.95**
GLENDINNING, VICTORIA
**Edith Sitwell: A Unicorn among the
Lions**
Dame Edith Sitwell, the sister of Sir Osbert and Sir
Sacheverell was a unique figure in 20th-century
English literature, both as a poet and as a grand
literary hostess. Her unconventional appearance and
behaviour was recorded by photographers and
painters such as Cecil Beaton and Wyndham Lewis.
This deeply-researched biography examines Sitwell
and her milieu, which included Aldous Huxley, T.S.
Eliot and Gertrude Stein.
[B633] Oxford pbk **£5.95**

SMITH, STEVIE (1902 - 1971)
BARARA, JACK & MCBRIEN, WILLIAM
Stevie: The Biography of Stevie Smith
A clearly-written biography of the inimitable novelist,
poet and doodler, which examines Stevie Smith's
writing and formative experiences, such as being
abandoned by her father at an early age. The book
draws on her work and that of friends and critics such
as Olivia Manning and Rosamond Lehmann.
[B634] Macmillan pbk **£7.95**
SPALDING, FRANCES
Stevie Smith   NEW
When Stevie Smith was asked to provide her own
biographical note, she gave the following eloquent
information: *"Born in Hull, but moved to London at
the age of three and has lived in the same house ever
since."* This biography reveals her to be far from the
recluse of popular legend. She emerges as a figure
actively involved with the intellectual and social life
of London in the 1930s. Spalding examines her public
and private life and the influence of her wide reading.
[B635] Faber hbk **£14.95**

SOLZHENITSYN, ALEXANDER (1918 -)
The Gulag Archipelago
An epic history and geography of the labour camps in
Russia.
[B636] Collins hbk **£15.00**
The Oak and the Calf
[B637] Collins hbk **£9.95**
SCAMMEL, MICHAEL
Solzhenitsyn
A monumental biography of the Russian exile and

Nobel Laureate, who was for many years imprisoned in a labour camp, where he developed stomach cancer. It shows how Solzhenitsyn's harsh experiences of imprisonment affected his work, and how this led to his outspoken criticism of the Soviet system.
[B638] Hutchinson hbk **£18.00**
[B639] Grafton pbk **£9.95**

SPENDER, STEPHEN (1909 -)
Journals 1939 - 1983
Spender's detailed journals chronicle events and observations from the politically committed 1930s to the present. They include drafts of poems, stories and travel notes, as well as the voices of his contemporaries, amongst whom were W.H. Auden, Christopher Isherwood, Virginia Woolf, Cyril Connolly, Guy Burgess and Henry Moore.
[B640] Faber hbk **£17.50**
Letters to Christopher
Letters to Christopher Isherwood 1929-1939.
[B641] B Sparrow hbk **£7.95**
World within World: Autobiography
[B642] Faber pbk **£4.95**

STAFFORD, JEAN (1915 - 1979)
ROBERTS, DAVID
Jean Stafford **NEW**
A much-needed life of the great American novelist, short story writer and critic. It describes her troubled marriage to Robert Lowell and her later one to A.J. Liebling.
[B643] Chatto hbk **£16.95**

STEIN, GERTRUDE (1874 - 1946)
Everybody's Autobiography
In her 1938 autobiography Gertrude Stein, the diverse American experimental writer, describes her life in Paris during the early part of this century. She recreates the coterie of writers and artists which she gathered around her, and her close relationship with painters such as Braque and Picasso, and recalls how in 1934 she returned to America with Alice B. Toklas to see her own opera produced to acclaim in NY.
[B644] Virago pbk **£6.95**
TOKLAS, ALICE B.
Autobiography of Alice B. Toklas
This is in reality the autobiography of Gertrude Stein, seen through the eyes of her great friend Alice B. Toklas. It describes her years in Paris, where she established her formidable artistic salon, whose adherents included Picasso, Matisse, Apollinaire, Hemingway and T.S. Eliot. This celebrated memoir has been highly influential in the development of American 20th-century prose writing.
[B645] Penguin pbk **£4.95**

STEINBECK, JOHN (1902 - 1968)
Travels with Charley
Steinbeck's journey through 40 American states with his poodle Charley.
[B646] Pan pbk **£1.95**
STEINBECK, ELAINE & WALLSTEN, ROBERT (EDS)
Steinbeck: A Life in Letters
This selection contains some 850 letters by the Nobel Prize-winning novelist. They show Steinbeck emerging as a man compelled to write, always planning new books, experimenting with ideas. In a letter in 1956 he says: *"Good God, I must have been writing for hundreds of years. But I must assure you that it fails to make me feel old or finished or fixed."*
[B647] Pan pbk **£3.95**

STEPHEN, LESLIE (1832 - 1904)
ANNAN, NOEL
Leslie Stephen: The Godless Victorian
Leslie Stephen was the first editor of the *Dictionary of National Biography*, but we probably know him

better as the father of Virginia Woolf and Vanessa Bell. He was responsible in large part for creating the cultivated atmosphere in which the Bloomsbury group came to flourish.
[B648] Weidenfeld hbk **£16.50**

STEVENSON, ROBERT LOUIS (1850 - 1894)
POPE-HENNESSY, JAMES
Robert Louis Stevenson **NEW**
An account of the great Scottish writer from his early life in Edinburgh to his death in Samoa.
[B649] Cassell hbk **£7.95**

STRACHEY, LYTTON (1880 - 1932)
Eminent Victorians
Strachey's celebrated study, first published in 1918, considers four of the priests of High Victorianism: Cardinal Manning, Florence Nightingale, Dr Arnold and General Gordon. In debunking the Victorian myth which they characterised, Strachey ushered in a new, fresh spirit of biographical writing.
[B650] Penguin pbk **£3.95**
HOLROYD, MICHAEL
Lytton Strachey: A Biography
This fine and exhaustive biography did much to re-kindle interest in the Bloomsbury group. Holroyd writes with great narrative skill in weaving together the interdependent lives of the Bloomsbury characters, amongst them the Woolfs and J.M. Keynes. Holroyd deals in detail with Strachey's relationship with the painter Dora Carrington. 'I am certain that this is one of the great biographies of our time' - C.P. Snow.
[B651] Penguin pbk **£8.99**
HOLROYD, MICHAEL & LEVY, PAUL (EDS)
The Shorter Strachey
A selection of refreshingly witty short pieces by Strachey, on subjects ranging from Gibbon to Sara Bernhardt, and Pope to Dostoyevsky.
[B652] Hogarth pbk **£7.95**

STRINDBERG, AUGUST (1849 - 1912)
Inferno/From an Occult Diary
An account of Strindberg's time as an alchemist in Paris, where he engaged in insane experiments to create gold out of base metal.
[B653] Penguin pbk **£5.95**
LAGERMANTZ, OLOF
August Strindberg
An interesting biography, which draws on many original Swedish sources. Lagermantz examines a view often held about Strindberg: that he was a stormy misogynist, and that his plays were merely the outpourings of a deranged mind. This book sweeps away these misconceptions to give a fresh perspective on Strindberg's life and work.
[B654] Faber hbk **£20.00**
MEYER, MICHAEL
Strindberg
An outstanding biography of the dark, pessimistic Swedish dramatist. It utilises unpublished letters and diary extracts in order to illustrate Strindberg's tormented life - his marriage breakdown, his friendships with Gauguin, Munch and Delius, and his recurrent bouts of madness.
[B655] Secker hbk **£25.00**
[B656] Oxford pbk **£8.95**

SUTCLIFF, ROSEMARY (1920 -)
Blue Remembered Hills
Rosemary Sutcliff is a leading children's writer. In this painful and touching memoir she recounts having a rare form of arthritis in her youth, which made it impossible for her to walk. She then goes on to describe how her writing developed in the aftermath of a long love affair.
[B657] Oxford pbk **£2.95**

SVEVO, ITALO (1861 - 1928)
GATT-RUTTER, JOHN
Italo Svevo: A Double Life **NEW**
This biography explores the dual life of Ettore Schmitz whose pen-name was Italo Svevo. His life embraced many contradictions: he was an anti-clerical Jew; a socialist who lived a bourgeois capitalist life; and a writer who was nurtured by his friend James Joyce, at the same time as being a father and a key member of the family firm.
[B658] Oxford hbk **£40.00**
SVEVO, LIVIA VENEZIANI
Memoir of Italo Svevo **NEW**
With a preface by P.N. Furbank. this is a memoir by Svevo's wife.
[B659] Libris hbk **£17.95**

SWIFT, JONATHAN (1667 - 1745)
DOWNIE, J.A.
Jonathan Swift: Political Writer
[B660] Routledge pbk **£10.95**
EHRENPREIS, IRVIN
Vol 1: Mr Swift and His Contemporaries
[B661] Methuen hbk **£27.50**
Vol 2: Dr Swift
[B662] Methuen hbk **£38.50**
Vol 3: Dean Swift
[B663] Methuen hbk **£47.50**
FOOT, MICHAEL
The Pen and the Sword
Subtitled 'Jonathan Swift and the Power of the Press', this gives a fascinating account of the 15-month period when the paths of Swift, the greatest journalist of his day, and the Duke of Marlborough, the greatest soldier, crossed. It traces the way in which the politicians of the time sought to control the press and how the pen was victorious over the sword.
[B664] Collins pbk **£6.95**
NOAKES, DAVID
Jonathan Swift: A Hypocrite Reversed
Winner of the James Tait Black Memorial Prize in 1985, this has become the standard one-volume life of Swift. It shows him in his multifarious roles as satirist, politician, churchman and friend.
[B665] Oxford hbk **£17.50**
[B666] Oxford pbk **£5.95**

TENNYSON, ALFRED LORD (1809 - 1895)
Tennyson: Interviews and Recollections
[B667] Macmillan pbk **£7.95**
MARTIN, ROBERT BERNARD
Tennyson: The Unquiet Heart
A major critical biography of the High Victorian poet, based on many unpublished primary sources. This highly-praised book won the Duff Cooper Memorial Prize, the Royal Society of Literature Award and the W.H. Heinemann Award.
[B668] Faber pbk **£5.95**
RICKS, CHRISTOPHER
Tennyson **NEW**
[B669] Macmillan pbk **£8.95**

THACKERAY, WILLIAM MAKEPEACE (1811 - 1863)
MONSARRAT, ANNE
Thackeray: An Uneasy Victorian
A portrait of the great 19th-century writer and author of *Vanity Fair*. Monsarrat shows him to be half-genius, half-child, and reveals how many of his fictional characters were drawn from real life.
[B670] Cassell pbk **£8.95**

THOMAS, D.M. (1935 -)
Memories and Hallucinations
An unusual 'autobiography' in which Thomas, novelist of *The White Hotel*, explores his inspirations and the evolution of his own fictions. Within a loose framework of an analytical session he weaves details

of his apparently serene Cornish childhood, his undergraduate days in Oxford and his relationships.
[B671] Gollancz hbk **£10.95**

THOMAS, DYLAN (1914 - 1953)
Collected Letters
Thomas devoted much energy to his correspondence, and in these letters to friends, lovers and literary contemporaries he displays his characteristic anguish, humour, energy, bawdiness, and gleeful love of language. The letters also document his struggle to find his poetic vocation and his often contradictory nature.
[B672] Dent hbk **£20.00**
[B673] Grafton pbk **£9.95**
FERRIS, PAUL
Dylan Thomas
Thomas was a complex and tormented man who was obsessed by his vocation as a poet. His reputation as a Bohemian and as a legendary drinker tends to preclude serious appraisals of his life. This acclaimed and prodigiously researched biography attempts to make sense of the Welsh bard's life - his rise to fame as a poet, his bawdiness and humour; his relationship with Caitlin, and his tragic decline and death.
[B674] Penguin pbk **£6.95**
GITTINGS, ROBERT
The Last Days of Dylan Thomas
[B675] Futura pbk **£3.95**
THOMAS, CAITLIN & TREMLETT, GEORGE
Caitlin: A Warring Absence
Dylan's wife's account of the disturbances of their married life.
[B676] Pan pbk **£3.95**

THOMAS, EDWARD (1878 - 1917)
The Childhood of Edward Thomas: A Fragment of Autobiography
When the poet Edward Thomas was killed in action at Arras in 1917, he left behind this fragment of autobiography in which he recalls his childhood. This edition also includes his war diary.
[B677] Faber pbk **£2.95**
THOMAS, HELEN
Under Storm's Wing
A collection of all Helen Thomas's memoirs of her husband: *As It Was*, *World Without End*, and *Time and Again*. Also included is Myfanwy Thomas's memoir of her father *One of These Fine Days*, as well as a substantial album of photographs.
[B678] Carcanet hbk **£14.95**
THOMAS, R. GEORGE
Edward Thomas: A Portrait
Before her death, Edward Thomas's widow gave her friend George Thomas access to all her papers. These include letters and unpublished documents relating to Edward Thomas, and they form the backbone of this fascinating recent biography of the poet.
[B679] Oxford pbk **£5.95**

THOMAS, LESLIE (1931 -)
In My Wildest Dreams
The energetic, comic author of *The Virgin Soldiers* here describes his time as an orphan in post-war Britain, his career as a journalist and his developing career as a novelist. Thomas is a great storyteller, and he includes many anecdotes in this frequently hilarious book.
[B680] Penguin pbk **£3.50**
This Time Next Week
Leslie Thomas and his brother were sent to a Dr Barnardo's home in Devon when their mother died of cancer. Their father had been killed in 1942 in a merchant ship in the South Atlantic. This vivid and humorous autobiography recalls how the two boys coped with being orphaned.
[B681] Pan pbk **£2.99**

THURBER, JAMES (1894 - 1961)
The Years with Ross
The American humorist's hilarious account of his years working for Harold Ross, editor of *The New Yorker*, who was a disastrous administrator and a brilliant but unpredictable editor.
[B682] H Hamilton pbk **£4.95**

TOKLAS, ALICE B. (1877 - 1967)
What is Remembered
Toklas would not write her own autobiography until after the death of Gertrude Stein. In this dry and humorous book she desribes her friendships with Apollinaire, Henri Rousseau, Lytton Strachey, Clive Bell and the Sitwells.
[B683] Sphere pbk **£4.99**

TOLKIEN, J.R.R. (1892 - 1973)
CARPENTER, HUMPHREY
J.R.R. Tolkien: A Biography
The first full-length biography of the author of *The Hobbit* and *The Lord of the Rings* draws on many private papers, diaries and manuscripts. Covers Tolkien's childhood, adolescence, war service and the painstaking process of writing *The Lord of the Rings*. Carpenter has also written on The Inklings, the group of which Tolkien was a member (see *C.S. Lewis*).
[B684] Unwin Hyman hbk **£12.50**
[B685] Unwin Hyman pbk **£4.95**

TOLSTOY, LEO (1828 - 1910)
Childhood, Boyhood, Youth
Written whilst Tolstoy was in his twenties, these sketches of his early life provide a self-portrait of the embryonic moralist and novelist.
[B686] Penguin pbk **£3.99**
Diaries: 1847 - 1910
[B687] Athlone hbk **£50.00**
Letters: 1828 - 1910
[B688] Athlone hbk **£60.00**
CRANKSHAW, EDWARD
Tolstoy: The Making of a Novelist
A brief but incisive critical commentary on Tolstoy's formative years, before he wrote *War and Peace* and *Anna Karenina*.
[B689] Macmillan pbk **£6.95**
TROYAT, HENRI
Tolstoy
Held by many to be the definitive life of Tolstoy, Troyat's biography is a triumph of narrative accessibility. In it he explores the contradictions of Tolstoy's character and the development of his writing and his philosophy.
[B690] Penguin pbk **£8.95**
WILSON, A.N.
Tolstoy NEW
Wilson's excellent book won the Whitbread Biography Award in 1988. He shows a Tolstoy full of super-abundant energy, manifested in all aspects of his life, whether as a dissolute layabout in the brothels of Moscow, or as an enlightened landowner educating his peasants. Tolstoy's paradoxical nature, as displayed in his tempestuous marriage, is carefully brought out by a biographer perfectly in sympathy with his subject.
[B691] H Hamilton hbk **£16.95**

TOLSTOY, SONYA
Diaries
[B692] Cape hbk **£35.00**
EDWARDS, ANNE
Sonya: The Life of Countess Tolstoy
The story of Tolstoy's long-suffering wife, whom he often treated with contempt.
[B693] Hodder pbk **£3.95**
SHOLUCHOWSKI, LOUISE
Lev and Sonya: The Story of the Tolstoy Marriage
[B694] Sidgwick hbk **£15.00**

TOYNBEE, PHILIP (1916 - 1981)
End of a Journey
This deeply moving autobiographical journal is the record of Philip Toynbee's final years. Part meditation on the prospect of death in the face of terminal illness, part exploration of the nature and demands of orthodox religion, it conveys with sharpness and precision his thoughts and feelings as he neared the end of his life.
[B696] H Hamilton pbk **£7.95**

TREFUSIS, VIOLET (1894 - 1972)
Don't Look Round NEW
Violet Trefusis is remembered as much for her scandalous affair with Vita Sackville-West and for being the daughter of Edward VII's mistress, as for her talent as a novelist. She never really assimilated herself into English society, and spent much of her time in France. This autobiography tells of her time in England and on the Continent, and of her relationships with Cocteau, Gide, Colette, Proust and Valéry.
[B697] H Hamilton pbk **£6.99**
Violet to Vita
[B697A] Methuen hbk **£14.95**
JULLIAN, PHILIPPE & PHILLIPS, JOHN
Violet Trefusis: A Biography NEW
Including her correspondence with Vita Sackville-West.
[B698] Methuen pbk **£5.95**

TRIOLET, ELSA (1896 - 1970)
MACKINNON, LACHLAN
The Lives of Elsa Triolet NEW
Born in Moscow, Triolet was the sister of Mayakovsky's mistress, the wife of Louis Aragon and the heroine of the 'Elsa' poems. She won the Prix Goncourt in 1945, wrote prolifically, was active in the Resistance, and became a Western Stalinist after the war. This is the first full-length biography.
[B699] Chatto hbk **£18.00**

TROLLOPE, ANTHONY (1815 - 1882)
An Autobiography
A work which damaged Trollope's reputation most unfairly by supposedly demystifying his creative processes.
[B700] Oxford pbk **£3.50**
An Illustrated Autobiography
[B701] Sutton hbk **£12.95**
POPE-HENNESSY, JAMES
Anthony Trollope
A critical biography which examines the reasons for Trollope's continuing popularity. James Pope-Hennessy also gives a fascinating account of Trollope's early life and his career as a junior clerk at the GPO.
[B702] Penguin pbk **£5.95**

TSVETAYEVA, MARINA (1892 - 1941)
FEINSTEIN, ELAINE
A Captive Lion: The Life of Marina Tsvetayeva
When Tsvetayeva published her first volume of poems in 1910, she was heralded as a major talent. Following this, however, her life was one of struggle and hardship. Exiled because her husband had fought with the White Russians, she was later ostracised by the émigré community for pro-Soviet views. This personal tragedy contrasted with her growing reputation as a poet as testified by her relationships with Boris Pasternak and Rainer Maria Rilke. Her feeling of isolation increased to the point where she took her own life in 1941. This is the first biography of one of the century's greatest poets, whost talent has not yet been fully appreciated.
[B703] Hutchinson hbk **£16.95**
[B704] Penguin pbk **£4.50**

RAZUMOVSKY, MARIA
Marina Tsvetayeva
Critical biography of the Russian poet translated from Russian and German editions by Aleksey Gibson. It draws on Tsvetayeva's autobiographical writings, letters and family memoirs.
[B705] Bishopgate pbk **£9.95**

UPDIKE, JOHN
Self-Consciousness **NEW**
The American novelist's long-awaited autobiography examines his inner life. In the course of six chapters we learn about his home town, his psoriasis, his stuttering, his religion, his discomfort during the Vietnam War and his sense of self. The book has received mixed reviews, some calling it the best and most beautiful thing he has ever written, others disappointing.
[B706] Deutsch hbk **£12.95**

VANBRUGH, SIR JOHN
DOWNES, KERRY
Sir John Vanbrugh
Vanbrugh was prolific in many fields: as soldier, playwright, architect, theatre manager and public servant. This biography looks at his achievements and the times he lived in, from the age of Pepys and the Great Plague, to the Revolution and the age of William and Mary.
[B707] Sidgwick hbk **£20.00**

VOLTAIRE, FRANCOIS (1694 - 1778)
AYER, A.J.
Voltaire
Poet, wit, philosopher, playwright, historian, biographer, pamphleteer and crusader against tyranny, there was hardly any important subject on which Voltaire did not speak during his life. In this intellectual biography Ayer examines the whole range of Voltaire's thought and its development, particularly the influence of England on him.
[B708] Faber pbk **£4.95**
MITFORD, NANCY
Voltaire in Love
An account of the famous love affair between Voltaire and the beautiful Marquise de Chatelet.
[B709] H Hamilton pbk **£4.95**

WAKEFIELD, TOM
Forties' Child
A tender account of a wartime Midlands childhood, by the novelist of *The Discus Throwers*.
[B710] Serpent's Tail pbk **£5.95**

WALPOLE, HUGH (1884 - 1941)
HART-DAVIS, RUPERT
Hugh Walpole
Hart-Davis's sensitive portrait of the author of *The Herries Chronicles* draws on Walpole's voluminous diaries, as well as his correspondence with leading contemporary writers such as Henry James and Joseph Conrad.
[B711] H Hamilton pbk **£7.95**

WARNER, SYLVIA TOWNSHEND
(1893 - 1973)
ACKLAND, VALENTINE
For Sylvia: An Honest Account
For over 40 years Valentine Ackland was Warner's closest friend and companion. This brief but powerful autobiographical essay reveals with harrowing frankness her unhappy lesbian relationships, as well as her battle against alcoholism, and her hopeless unconsummated marriage. Her love for Sylvia redeems all this.
[B712] Chatto pbk **£6.95**
HARMAN, CLARE
Sylvia Townshend Warner **NEW**
Warner became an idiosyncratic figure in London

literary life after the success of her novel *Lolly Willowes*. Claire Harman has written an excellent biography, based on previously unpublished material, including the diaries and those of the poet Valentine Ackland, with whom Warner lived for many years.
[B713] Chatto hbk **£16.95**

WAUGH, EVELYN (1903 - 1966)
A Little Learning
Waugh's memoir of his childhood in Hampstead and Lancing, and his hedonistic days at Oxford with Harold Acton and Cyril Connolly.
[B714] Penguin pbk **£3.95**
Diaries
[B715] Penguin pbk **£9.99**
Letters
Gossipy and malicious letters which are far more revealing about Waugh's opinions than anything else he wrote.
[B716] Weidenfeld hbk **£14.95**
[B717] Penguin pbk **£8.99**
CARPENTER, HUMPHREY
The Brideshead Generation
The members of the 'Brideshead' generation included Harold Acton, Graham Greene, John Betjeman, Cyril Connolly, Robert Byron, Anthony Powell and Lady Diana Cooper. This book examines their relationships with each other, and in particular to the most influential novelist of their generation, Evelyn Waugh.
[B718] Weidenfeld hbk **£20.00**
DONALDSON, FRANCES
Evelyn Waugh
An intimate portrait, first published in 1967, by a close, though not uncritical, friend and neighbour.
[B719] Weidenfeld hbk **£9.95**
[B720] Weidenfeld pbk **£4.95**
STANNARD, MARTIN
Evelyn Waugh: The Early Years 1903 - 1939
A detailed examination of Waugh's early years, which gets to the root of his elusive personality and snobbishness. The book utilises copious primary sources, including interviews with Harold Acton, John Betjeman, Graham Greene and Alec Waugh. Despite all this, Stannard honestly admits *"No biographer could 'capture' so elusive a character and I have not attempted to do so."*
[B721] Dent hbk **£14.95**
[B722] Grafton pbk **£6.95**
SYKES, CHRISTOPHER
Evelyn Waugh
[B723] Penguin pbk **£5.95**

WELCH, DENTON (1915 - 1948)
A Voice through a Cloud
Welch movingly relives the nightmare accident when, in 1935 at the age of 20, he fell off his bicycle, whilst on the way to visit his aunt; an accident which crippled him for life. He describes the hell of hospital life and his growing desire to live and to write.
[B724] Penguin pbk **£3.95**
Fragments of a Life Story
[B725] Penguin pbk **£5.95**
Journals 1942 - 1948
Welch's journals span the latter part of his life, until four months before his death. Often written whilst suffering intense pain from his accident, they nevertheless retain wit and freshness.
[B726] Penguin pbk **£4.95**
DE-LA-NOY, MICHAEL
Denton Welch: The Making of a Writer
A sympathetic biography of Welch's brief, eccentric life, which recovers his past reputation for modern readers. Although he died when he was only thirty-three, Welch had developed into a painter of startling originality, and had written three remarkable short novels. De-La-Noy utilises extensive source material and hundreds of unpublished letters.
[B727] Penguin pbk **£4.95**

WELLS, HERBERT GEORGE (1866 - 1946)
An Experiment in Autobiography Vol 1
[B728] Faber pbk **£8.95**
An Experiment in Autobiography Vol 2
[B729] Faber pbk **£8.95**
MACKENZIE, NORMAN & JEANNE
The Life of H.G. Wells: The Time Traveller
[B730] Hogarth hbk **£7.95**
SMITH, DAVID C.
H.G. Wells: Desperately Mortal
[B731] Yale hbk **£18.50**
WELLS, G.P.
H.G. Wells in Love
[B732] Faber pbk **£3.95**
WEST, ANTHONY
H.G.Wells
Anthony West, the son of H.G. Wells and Rebecca West, is well-equipped to profile the great man. His intimate portrait is prejudiced, scandalous and one of the most interesting studies of Wells published.
[B733] Penguin pbk **£4.95**

WEST, REBECCA (1892 - 1983)
Family Memories
An autobiographical memoir written in the last years of her life.
[B734] Virago pbk **£3.95**
GLENDINNING, VICTORIA
Rebecca West: A Life
This biography, commissioned by Rebecca West herself, tells the story of the influential feminist journalist and writer. Her love affair with H.G. Wells, whom she initially attacked, her subsequent life as an unmarried mother and her brilliant writing career, are all sympathetically detailed.
[B735] Weidenfeld hbk **£14.95**
[B736] Macmillan pbk **£7.95**
WELDON, FAY
Rebecca West
[B737] Penguin pbk **£2.95**

WHARTON, EDITH (1861 - 1937)
Backward Glance
[B738] Century pbk **£5.95**
Letters **NEW**
This collection of Wharton's letters span the period from the 1890s to a week before Wharton's death in 1937. They range across her friendships with Henry

Evelyn Waugh, author of *Brideshead Revisited* (Methuen hbk £10.95)

James, Bernard Berenson and Kenneth Clark, as well as her passionate correspondence with her lover Morton Fullerton.
[B739] Simon & Schuster hbk **£16.95**
LEWIS, R.W.B.
Edith Wharton
[B740] Constable pbk **£7.50**

WHITE, ANTONIA (1899 - 1979)
As Once in May
The early autobiography of Antonia White and other writings.
[B741] Virago pbk **£3.95**
CHITTY, SUSAN
Now to My Mother
[B742] Weidenfeld pbk **£4.95**
HOPKINSON, LYNDALL P.
Nothing to Forgive: A Daughter's Life of Antonia White `NEW`
Hopkinson was the only child of novelist Antonia White's third marriage. This is a compassionate, honest account of her complex mother.
[B743] Chatto hbk **£12.95**

WHITE, PATRICK (1912 -)
Flaws in the Glass
A forceful and emotional self-portrait by the great Nobel Prize-winning Australian novelist. White writes of his youth in Australia, his English boarding school, his life at Cambridge and in London during the Blitz. He goes on to describe meeting the man who was to become the main force in his life. *"Of course I am vain...If I have not yet lost my mind, I can sometimes feel it preparing to defect. But vanity is deeply rooted in me."*
[B744] Penguin pbk **£4.99**

WHITE, T.H. (1904 - 1964)
T.H. White: Letters to a Friend `NEW`
The correspondence between T.H. White and L.J. Potts.
[B745] Sutton hbk **£11.50**
WARNER, SYLVIA TOWNSHEND (1893 - 1973)
T.H. White
White, author of the celebrated Arthurian novel *The Book of Merlin*, was also a poet, falconer, ploughman and dog-lover. He was a man of many enthusiasms, and this biography, by his own favourite novelist, affectionately examines his life, vivid imagination and dependence on alcohol.
[B746] Oxford pbk **£5.95**

WHITMAN, WALT (1819 - 1891)
ZWEIG, PAUL
Walt Whitman: The Making of the Poet
Zweig's study concentrates on the Civil War years (1861-4) when Whitman's formative experiences led to him becoming the poet of sexual freedom, and the bardic voice of the American people.
[B747] Penguin pbk **£4.95**

WILDE, OSCAR (1854 - 1900)
Oscar Wilde's London
An illustrated look at the city in the age of Oscar Wilde.
[B749] O'Mara hbk **£15.00**
Selected Letters
Wilde's letters restore him to us in some of his original epigrammatic glory. This selection covers the whole of his life and includes those he wrote from prison, amongst them *De Profundis*.
[B750] Oxford pbk **£6.95**
More Letters
[B748] Oxford pbk **£4.95**
AMOR, ANNE CLARK
Mrs Oscar Wilde: A Woman of Some Importance
A fascinating portrait of Wilde's wife Constance, who stood by her husband throughout his notorious career,

despite his obvious preference for male company. Her courageous and stoical reaction to Oscar's trial and conviction are memorably related.
[B751] Sidgwick pbk **£7.95**
ELLMANN, RICHARD
Oscar Wilde
This is Ellmann's final great work, completed just before his death in 1987. It has generally been acclaimed as one of the greatest biographies of the century, and has been put on a par with his life of Joyce. The book marks the exorcism of a major obsession for Ellmann. *Oscar Wilde* at last does justice to Wilde's intellectual and literary development as well as his notorious public life. For Ellman, Wilde is a great writer, not simply a great personality. He analyses all the major works in detail and discovers Wilde's greatness particularly in *A Picture of Dorian Grey* and *The Importance of Being Earnest*. Ellmann quotes copiously from all manner of sources and he traces Wilde's life in minute detail. His account of the trial and Wilde's passionate defence of himself is extremely moving; his portrayal of Wilde's life after imprisonment and his death is aptly called the *Leftover Years*.
[B752] H Hamilton hbk **£17.95**
[B753] Penguin pbk **£6.99**
GOODMAN, JONATHAN
The Oscar Wilde File
Deals specifically with the infamous trial.
[B754] Allison & B hbk **£12.95**
HOLLAND, VYVYAN
Oscar Wilde
Wilde's own son Vyvyan steers a skilful course through the the maelstrom of public life and offers glimpses into Wilde's public and private personas.
[B755] Thames & H pbk **£3.95**
Son of Oscar Wilde
With a new foreword by Merlin Holland. After Wilde had been sent to prison he never saw his two sons, Vyvyan and Cyril, again. Cyril was killed in the First World War, but Vyvyan survived, and in 1954 produced these memoirs of the Oscar Wilde affair and its aftermath. This outstanding and emotional book recounts the family's struggle after the fall of Wilde, and the sudden change of name and environment that Cyril, Vyvyan and Constance underwent.
[B756] Oxford pbk **£4.95**
HYDE, H. MONTGOMERY
Oscar Wilde
This biography, first published in 1976, was acclaimed as the definitive life of Wilde, partly because of its revelations about Wilde's homosexuality.
[B757] Methuen pbk **£7.95**
PEARSON, HESKETH
Oscar Wilde
A well-balanced life which explores Wilde's controversial personality, but more importantly his skill as a wit and life-enhancer. Not as detailed as Ellmann's biography, but very readable.
[B758] Penguin pbk **£4.95**

WILLIAMS, TENNESSEE (1911 - 1983)
RADER, DOTSON
Tennessee Williams: An Intimate Memoir
Rader, a freelance New York writer, was the close confidant and frequent companion of Williams during the last 14 years of the playwright's life. Using anecdotes from people ranging from Marlon Brando to Fidel Castro, he presents an image of Williams as a man of charm and complexity.
[B759] Grafton hbk **£12.95**

WODEHOUSE, P.G. (1881 - 1975)
Wodehouse on Wodehouse
Comprising *Performing Flea*, *Bring on the Girls* and *Over Seventy*.
[B760] Penguin pbk **£6.99**

CONNOLLY, JOSEPH
Wodehouse
[B761] Thames & H pbk **£5.95**
MURPHY, N.T.P.
In Search of Blandings
An attempt to provide a key to the novels.
[B762] Penguin pbk **£6.95**

WOLFE, THOMAS (1900 - 1938)
DONALD, DAVID HERBERT
Look Homeward: A Life of Thomas Wolfe
This first full account of Wolfe's short but astonishing life. The author of *Look Homeward, Angel* and *Of Time and the River* is shown to have been a man of physical enormity and excessive appetites. The book also gives candid descriptions of his relationships with women and editors. David Donald won the Pulitzer Prize for this fascinating study, which Gore Vidal said was 'easily the best biography of an American novelist'.
[B763] Bloomsbury hbk **£16.95**
[B764] Bloomsbury pbk **£12.95**

WOLLSTONECRAFT, MARY (1759 - 1797)
TOMALIN, CLAIRE
Life and Death of Mary Wollstonecraft
Mary Wollstonecraft, the mother of Mary Shelley, was one of the most controversial women of her day. She lived through the Terror during the Revolution in France, where she witnessed the destruction of the incipient French feminist movement. This excellent and sympathetic biography of the author of *The Vindication of the Rights of Women*, portrays a radical who never reneged on her views, despite the difficult times she lived in.
[B765] Penguin pbk **£5.99**

WOOLF, LEONARD (1880 - 1969)
An Autobiography Vol 1: 1880 - 1911 Sowing and Growing
The autobiography of the colonial, civil servant, editor, journalist, politician, publisher, husband of Virginia Woolf, and central figure of the Bloomsbury Group. Introduced by Virginia Woolf's nephew, Quentin Bell.
[B766] Oxford pbk **£4.95**
An Autobiography Vol 2: 1911 - 1969 Beginning Again, Downhill All the Way
[B767] Oxford pbk **£6.95**

WOOLF, VIRGINIA (1882 - 1941)
DIARIES
A Moment's Liberty: The Shorter Diary
Woolf was one of the greatest diarists of the century. This admirable abridgement makes it available for the first time in a one-volume edition.
[B770] Hogarth hbk **£18.95**
Vol 1: 1915 - 1919
"More alive than most living voices...it is the map of a mind struggling against madness and reaching the equilibrium which made her great novels possible. On every page the sharp twin edges of intelligence and abnormally acute senses make their impress." (Claire Tomalin).
[B771] Chatto hbk **£20.00**
[B772] Penguin pbk **£5.99**
Vol 2: 1920 - 1924
[B773] Chatto hbk **£20.00**
[B774] Penguin pbk **£6.99**
Vol 3: 1925 - 1930
[B775] Chatto hbk **£20.00**
[B776] Penguin pbk **£6.95**
Vol 4: 1931 - 1935
[B777] Chatto hbk **£20.00**
[B778] Penguin pbk **£7.95**
Vol 5: 1936 - 1941
[B779] Chatto hbk **£20.00**
[B780] Penguin pbk **£7.50**

LETTERS
Vol 1: Flight of the Mind 1888 - 1912
[B781] Chatto hbk **£20.00**
Vol 2: Question of Things Happening 1912 - 1922
[B782] Chatto hbk **£20.00**
Vol 3: A Change of Perspective 1923 - 1928
[B783] Chatto hbk **£20.00**
Vol 4: A Reflection of the Other Person 1929 - 1931
[B784] Chatto hbk **£20.00**
Vol 5: The Sickle Side of the Moon 1932 - 1935
[B785] Chatto hbk **£20.00**
[B786] Chatto pbk **£8.95**
Vol 6: Leave the Letters Till We're Dead 1936 - 1941
[B787] Chatto hbk **£20.00**
[B788] Chatto pbk **£7.95**
Selected Letters
A good selection from the six-volume edition of Woolf's letters. Woolf was a great correspondent, and her letters discuss everything from the personal and domestic, to literature and art. Margaret Drabble said we are 'the richer for them'.
[B789] Chatto hbk **£16.95**
Moments of Being
A collection of autobiographical pieces which pinpoint luminous experiences in Woolf's childhood and her early days in Bloomsbury.
[B790] Grafton pbk **£4.99**
BELL, QUENTIN
Virginia Woolf 1882 - 1941
Winner of the James Tait Black Memorial Award and the Duff Cooper Prize. Acclaimed as the definitive life of Woolf, Bell's biography draws on much unpublished material to bring Virginia Woolf to life as a woman. Although he does not attempt a serious discussion of her work, he shows the processes and the life by which it was created it. 'So good a biographer is Quentin Bell that he makes his aunt seem quite a different person from the literary legend of Bloomsbury.' - John Bayley, *The Guardian.*
[B791] Grafton pbk **£7.95**
GORDON, LYNDALL
Virginia Woolf: A Writer's Life
This recent (1984) and highly-praised critical biography attempts to link Woolf's writing with her life, thus complementing the earlier biography by Quentin Bell.
[B792] Oxford hbk **£19.50**
[B793] Oxford pbk **£5.95**
LEHMANN, JOHN
Virginia Woolf
An illustrated introduction.
[B794] Thames & H hbk **£3.95**
NOBLE, JOAN RUSSELL
Recollections of Virginia Woolf by her Contemporaries
A collection of pieces from 28 contributors who talk about their friendships with Virginia Woolf. The book includes memoirs by T.S. Eliot, E.M. Forster, Stephen Spender, Vita Sackville-West. William Plomer remembers Virginia's teasing, and the Woolf's cook remembers how she talked to herself in the bath and baked perfect bread.
[B795] Sphere pbk **£4.50**
ROSE, PHYLLIS
Woman of Letters: A Life of Virginia Woolf
[B796] Pandora pbk **£3.95**

WORDSWORTH, DOROTHY (1771 - 1855)
Grasmere Journal
An illustrated edition of the most famous part of the *Journals.*
[B797] M Joseph hbk **£12.95**

Journals
Dorothy Wordsworth's celebrated journals cover the period of time spent at Alfreden in 1798 when Wordsworth and Coleridge were composing the *Lyrical Ballads*, as well as their time at Grasmere from 1800 to 1803, when Dorothy and William lived in Dove Cottage. The journals are particularly notable for their minute and enthusiastic observation of nature - witness this excerpt from a letter of November 1801: *"As we were going along we were stopped at once, at the distance perhaps of 50 yards from our favourite Birch tree. It was yielding to the gusty wind with all its tender twigs, the sun shone upon it and it glanced in the wind like a flying sunshiny shower. It was a tree in shape with stem and branches but it was like a spirit of water."*
[B798] Oxford pbk **£4.95**
Letters of Dorothy Wordsworth
The letters of Dorothy Wordsworth give us the most complete picture we have of the lives of William Wordsworth and Samuel Taylor Coleridge. Dorothy shared in the feelings and aims of the two poets and allows us to see an aspect of their creative processes. Her letters also detail the full and busy domestic life of the Wordsworths, their walks in the countryside, and the everyday arrangements surrounding the actual publishing of Wordsworth's poetry. This selection also includes letters written during Dorothy's final, tragic illness.
[B799] Oxford hbk **£14.95**
[B800] Oxford pbk **£3.95**
GITTINGS, ROBERT & MANTON, JO
Dorothy Wordsworth
The first biography to treat Dorothy Wordsworth as a person, rather than as simply an adjunct to her brother. The book shows her extraordinary devotion to running the Wordsworth household, and it explores aspects of her character as a woman of her day.
[B801] Oxford hbk **£17.50**
[B802] Oxford pbk **£4.95**

WORDSWORTH, WILLIAM (1770 - 1850)
Selected Letters
This selection of 162 letters takes us from Wordsworth's first flushes of enthusiasm at the French Revolution in the 1790s, through the Grasmere years, to his old age at Rydale Mount. The correspondents include Coleridge and De Quincey, and topics range across literature, politics, religion and the changing landscape of the Lakes.
[B803] Oxford hbk **£25.00**
[B804] Oxford pbk **£4.95**
GILL, STEPHEN
William Wordsworth: A Life   NEW
An authoritative new life of Wordsworth, based on considerable research into the poet's manuscripts. Gill considers Wordsworth's genius as a poet, and in particular examines Wordsworth's later years, traditionally assumed to have been a time of decline. Gill finds that Wordsworth remained true to his poetic gift in the face of critical scorn and the numbing death of three members of his family.
[B805] Oxford hbk **£17.50**
MCCRACKEN, DAVID
Wordsworth and the Lake District
An excellent guide to the poems and the places in which they are set. Good for both walkers and literary sleuths.
[B806] Oxford hbk **£12.50**
[B807] Oxford pbk **£4.95**
WORDSWORTH, WILLIAM & DOROTHY
Home at Grasmere: Extracts and Poems
[B808] Penguin pbk **£3.95**

YEATS, WILLIAM BUTLER (1865 - 1939)
Autobiographies
Yeats's own vivid portrayal of his Co. Sligo childhood, his involvement with the literary life of Victorian London, and his friendships with Oscar Wilde, Aubrey Beardsley and J.M. Synge. He also discusses his active engagement in the turbulent arena of Irish politics.
[B809] Macmillan hbk **£25.00**
[B810] Macmillan pbk **£11.95**
Collected Letters Vol 1: 1865 - 1895
[B811] Oxford hbk **£25.00**
Memoirs
The original text of Yeats's autobiography and journal, which was not intended for publication. It includes a frank account of his early sexual development.
[B812] Macmillan pbk **£8.95**
ELLMANN, RICHARD
Yeats: The Man and His Masks
This is Ellmann's first great biographical work, originally published in 1948, and revised in 1979. It describes Yeats's life and art with great subtlety, incorporating much unpublished material. Ellmann traces Yeats's life from the early pains of unrequited love, through the creation of the Abbey Theatre, his political involvements and his furious battle with impotence in old age.
[B813] Penguin pbk **£5.99**
JEFFARES, A. NORMAN
W.B. Yeats: A New Biography   NEW
When Jeffares first published this biography it was acclaimed as the definitive 'life'. This edition updates the book, and incorporates new material, both written and illustrative, including papers released by the poet's son and daughter. The result is a short but incisive biography which examines the three basic periods of Yeats's life, in the light of his work: up to 1903, from 1903 to 1917, and from 1917 until his death.
[B814] Hutchinson hbk **£16.95**
LIAMMOIR, MICHAEL MAC & BOLAND, EAVAN
W.B. Yeats
[B815] Thames & H pbk **£3.95**

ZWEIG, STEFAN (1881 - 1942)
The World of Yesterday: An Autobiography
Zweig - poet, dramatist, biographer and novelist of *Beware of Pity* - died by his own hand in Brazil in 1942. He left this remarkable autobiography in which he discusses his association and friendships with Freud, Brahms, Strauss, Rilke, Rodin and Yeats.
[B816] Cassell pbk **£6.95**

Mary Wollstonecraft (Picture: Hamish Hamilton)

Eleven Turn of the Century Literary Lives

Michael Holroyd

QUENTIN BELL
Virginia Woolf: A Biography
Quentin Bell's sympathetic account of his aunt Virginia Woolf is a perfect 'in house' biography. In succinct and witty style, he gives us a most reliable and authoritative picture of a life dedicated to writing.
(Grafton, pbk £7.95)

BERNARD CRICK
George Orwell: A Life
A rigorous biographical reappraisal of Orwell, written in reaction against the English impressionistic school of biography, that has established itself against strong competition as the standard Life. With his dual identity and false trails, Orwell seems to have the temperament of a perfect spy who here meets an unrelenting spycatcher.
(Penguin, pbk £6.95)

RICHARD ELLMAN
James Joyce
This is one of the masterworks of modern biography - a scholarly, ingenious and finally a moving recreation of a complex literary exile. It is an ideal marriage between biographer and subject.
(Oxford, hbk £25.00/pbk £9.95)

P.N. FURBANK
E.M. Forster: A Life
P.N. Furbank is like a sympathetic shadow as he takes us through Forster's life from its drab suburban beginnings over new horizons and new civilisations to international fame as the author of *A Passage to India*. He matches Forster's nimble wit with his own wry humour and allows Forster to collaborate posthumously in his own biography.
(Secker, hbk £12.50/Sphere, pbk £7.99)

VICTORIA GLENDINNING
Edith Sitwell, A Unicorn Among Lions
This is a wonderfully penetrating, yet protective, biography of a writer who famously concealed herself behind the glittering armour of a Plantagenet appearance. Ms Glendinning's achievement is to make us understand the need that drove Edith Sitwell to conduct such a picturesque refashioning of herself and make this part of the magic world she created with her poetry.
(Oxford, pbk £6.95)

NIGEL NICOLSON
Portrait of a Marriage
This book is one of the most original experiments in modern biography. Nigel Nicolson interleaves his mother, Vita Sackville-West's, posthumous autobiography with pages of his own biographical enquiry to uncover the truth of his parents' unconventional marriage. Like *Some People*, his father, Harold Nicolson's, non-fiction short stories, *Portrait of a Marriage* looks like becoming a classic.
(Futura, pbk £2.95)

HESKETH PEARSON
Conan Doyle
Pearson was the most popular biographer of the 1930s and 1940s. *Conan Doyle* is a fine example of his forthright skill. As Graham Greene writes in his introduction, it is 'an exciting story admirably told' which reveals Doyle to be more of a Dr Watson than a Sherlock Holmes.
(Unwin, pbk £6.95)

ROBERT SKIDELSKY
John Maynard Keynes: Hopes Betrayed
Robert Skidelsky shows Maynard Keynes as the man whom the Bloomsbury Group sent out from Cambridge University to represent their literary and aesthetic interests in the world of finance and politics. This is a most ambitious and impressive first volume of a work that, connecting literature and economics, politics with human relationships, charts an underlying pattern between Keynes's private and public life.
(Macmillan, hbk £14.95)

HILARY SPURLING
Hilary Spurling succeeds in cracking the code of Ivy Compton-Burnett's hypnotic but elusive novels. Her meticulous rediscovery of this strange life reads like a non-fiction version of a Compton-Burnett novel and makes her world accessible to a far wider readership.
Ivy When Young
The early life of Ivy Compton-Burnett. (Unfortunately this title is unavailable)
Secrets of a Woman's Heart
The later life of Ivy Compton-Burnett.
(Hodder, hbk £14.95/Penguin, pbk £4.95)

ANN THWAITE
Edmund Gosse: A Literary Landscape
A scrupulously researched, well structured biography that has altered our contemporary view of Gosse and shifted the whole landscape round him. Known primarily as the author of one masterpiece, *Father and Son*, Gosse now appears as a pivotal figure in late Victorian and Edwardian cultural history.
(Oxford, pbk £7.95)

CLAIRE TOMALIN
Katherine Mansfield: A Secret Life
Claire Tomalin's strengths as a biographer lie in her exceptional insight as a literary critic and her ability to place Katherine Mansfield in her cultural background. Making good use of previous biographies and adding new findings of her own, she balances sympathy with sharpness and presents her subject with a new clarity of focus.
(Viking, hbk £14.95/Penguin, pbk £4.99)

One of the most respected contemporary biographers, Michael Holroyd has written biographies of Lytton Strachey, Augustus John and Hugh Kingsmill. His most recent project is a three-volume life of George Bernard Shaw; the first volume of this massive undertaking, *The Search for Love*, was highly acclaimed on its publication in 1988, with its sequel *The Pursuit of Power* due in September 1989.

The James Tait Black Memorial Prizes

Founded as a memorial to one of the partners in the publishing house of A & C Black in 1918, the James Tait Black Memorial Prize is best known as Britain's most prestigious annual award for biography, although there is also an award given for fiction. Winners in both categories recieve £1,000, and the contest is traditionally adjudicated by the Professor of English Literature in the University of Edinburgh.

1919	H Festing Jones *Samuel Butler*	
	Hugh Walpole *The Secret City*	
1920	G M Trevelyan *Lord Grey of the Reform Bill*	
	D H Lawrence *The Lost Girl*	
1921	Lytton Strachey *Queen Victoria*	
	Walter de la Mare *Memoirs of a Midget*	
1922	Percy Lubbock *Earlham*	
	David Garnett *Lady into Fox*	
1923	Sir Ronald Ross *Memoirs*	
	Arnold Bennett *Riceyman Steps*	
1924	Rev William Wilson *The House of Airlie*	
	E M Forster *A Passage to India*	
1925	Geoffrey Scott *The Portrait of Zelide*	
	Liam O'Flaherty *The Informer*	
1926	H B Workman *John Wyclif*	
	Radcliffe Hall *Adam's Breed*	
1927	H A L Fisher *James Bryce*	
	Francis Brett Young *Portrait of Clare*	
1928	John Buchan *Montrose*	
	Siegfried Sassoon *Memoirs of a Fox-hunting Man*	
1929	Lord David Cecil *The Stricken Deer: The Life of Cowper*	
	J B Priestley *The Good Companions*	
1930	Francis Yeats Brown *Lives of a Bengal Lancer*	
	E H Young *Miss Mole*	
1931	J Y T Greig *David Hume*	
	Kate O'Brien *Without My Cloak*	
1932	Stephen Gwynn *The Life of Mary Kingsley*	
	Helen Simpson *Boomerang*	
1933	Violet Clifton *The Book of Talbot*	
	A G Macdonnell *England, their England*	
1934	J E Neale *Queen Elizabeth*	
	Robert Graves *I, Claudius & Claudius the God*	
1935	R W Chambers *Thomas More*	
	L H Myers *The Root and the Flower*	
1936	Edward SackvilleWest *A Flame in Sunlight: The Life and Work of Thomas de Quincey*	
	Winifred Holtby *South Riding*	
1937	Lord Eustace Percy *John Knox*	
	Neil M Gunn *Highland River*	
1938	Sir Edmund Chambers *Samuel Taylor Coleridge*	
	C S Forester *A Ship of the Line & Flying Colours*	
1939	David C Douglas *English Scholars*	
	Aldous Huxley *After Many a Summer Dies the Swan*	
1940	Hilda F M Prestcott *Spanish Tudor*	
	Charles Morgan *The Voyage*	
1941	John Gore *King George V*	
	Joyce Cary *A House of Children*	
1942	Lord Ponsonby of Shulbrede *Henry Ponsonby: Queen Victoria's Private Secretary*	
	Arthur Waley *Monkey by Wu Ch'eng-en*	
1943	G G Coulton *Fourscore Years*	
	Mary Lavin *Tales From Bective Bridge*	
1944	C V Wedgwood *William the Silent*	
	Forrest Reid *Young Tom*	
1945	D S MacColl *Philip Wilson Steer*	
	L A G Strong *Travellers*	
1946	R Alldington *Wellington*	
	G Oliver Onions *Poor Man's Tapestry*	
1947	REV C C E Raven *English Naturalists from Neckham to Ray*	
	L P Hartley *Eustace and Hilda*	
1948	Percy A Scholes *The Great Dr Burney*	
	Graham Greene *The Heart of the Matter*	
1949	John Connell *W E Henley*	
	Emma Smith *The Far Cry*	
1950	Mrs Cecil Woodham-Smith *Florence Nightingale*	
	Robert Henriquez *Along the Valley*	
1951	Noel G Annan *Leslie Stephen*	
	W C Chapman-Mortimer *Father Goose*	
1952	G M Young *Stanley Baldwin*	
	Evelyn Waugh *Men at Arms*	
1953	Carola Oman *Sir John Moore*	
	Margaret Kennedy *Troy Chimneys*	
1954	Keith Felling *Warren Hastings*	
	C P Snow *The New Men & The Masters*	
1955	R W Ketton-Kreimer *Thomas Gray*	
	Ivy Compton-Burnett *Mother and Son*	
1956	St John Greer Irvine *George Bernard Shaw*	
	Rose Macaulay *The Towers of Trebizond*	
1957	Maurice Cranston *Life of John Locke*	
	Anthony Powell *At Lady Molly's*	
1958	Joyce Hemlow *The History of Fanny Burney*	
	Angus Wilson *The Middle Age of Mrs Eliot*	
1959	Christopher Hassall *Edward Marsh*	
	Morris West *The Devil's Advocate*	
1960	Canon Adam Fox *The Life of Dean Inge*	
	Rex Warner *Imperial Caesar*	
1961	M K Ashby *Joseph Ashby of Tysoe*	
	Jennifer Dawson *The Ha-Ha*	
1962	Meriol Trevor *Newman: The Pillar and the Cloud & Light in Winter*	
	Ronald Hardy *Act of Destruction*	
1963	Georgina Battiscombe *John Keble: A Study in Limitations*	
	Gerda Charles *A Slanting Light*	
1964	Elizabeth Longford *Victoria R I*	
	Frank Tuohy *The Ice Saints*	
1965	Mary Moorman *William Wordsworth: The Later Years 1803 - 50*	
	Muriel Spark *The Mandelbaum Gate*	
1966	Geoffrey Keynes *The Life of William Harvey*	
	Christina Brooke-Rose *Such*	
	Aidan Higgins *Langrishe, Go Down*	
1967	Winifred Gérin *Charlotte Brontë: The Evolution of Genius*	
	Margaret Drabble *Jerusalem the Golden*	
1968	Gordon S Haight *George Eliot*	
	Maggie Ross *The Gasteropod*	
1969	Antonia Fraser *Mary, Queen of Scots*	
	Elizabeth Bowen *Eva Trout*	
1970	Jasper Ridley *Lord Palmerston*	
	Lily Powell *The Bird of Paradise*	
1971	Julia Namier *Lewis Namier*	
	Nadine Gordimer *A Guest of Honour*	
1972	Quentin Bell *Virginia Woolf*	
	John Berger *G*	
1973	Robin Lane Fox *Alexander the Great*	
	Iris Murdoch *The Black Prince*	
1974	John Wain *Samuel Johnson*	
	Lawrence Durrell *Monsieur, or the Prince of Darkness*	
1975	Karl Miller *Cockburn's Millenium* (Duckworth)	
	Brian Moore *The Great Victorian Collection* (Cape)	
1976	Ronald Hingley *A New Life of Chekhov* (Oxford)	
	John Banville *Doctor Copernicus* (Secker)	
1977	George Painter *Chateaubriand: Vol 1 The Longed-for Tempest* (Chatto)	
	John le Carré *The Honourable Schoolboy* (Hodder)	
1978	Robert Gittings *The Older Hardy* (Heinemann)	
	Maurice Gee *Plumb* (Faber)	
1979	Brian Finney *Christopher Isherwood: A Critical Biography* (Faber)	
	William Golding *Darkness Visible* (Faber)	
1980	Robert B Martin *Tennyson: The Unquiet Heart* (Oxford)	
	J M Coetzee *Waiting for the Barbarians* (Secker)	
1981	Victoria Glendinning *Edith Sitwell: Unicorn Among the Lions* (Weidenfeld)	
	Salman Rushdie *Midnight's Children* (Cape)	
	Paul Theroux *The Mosquito Coast* (Hamish Hamilton)	
1982	Richard Ellmann *James Joyce* (Oxford)	
	Bruce Chatwin *On the Black Hill* (Cape)	
1983	Alan Walker *Franz Liszt: the Virtuoso Years* (Faber)	
	Jonathan Keates *Allegro Postillions* (Salamander Press)	
1984	Lyndall Gordon *Virginia Woolf: A Writer's Life* (Oxford)	
	J G Ballard *Empire of the Sun* (Gollancz)	
	Angela Carter *Nights at the Circus* (Chatto)	
1985	David Nokes *Jonathan Swift: A Hypocrite Reversed* (Oxford)	
	Robert Edric *Winter Garden* (Deutsch)	
1986	D Felicitas Corrigan *Helen Waddell* (Gollancz)	
	Jenny Joseph *Persephone* (Bloodaxe)	
1987	Ruth Dudley Edwards *Victor Gollancz: A Biography* (Gollancz)	
	George Mackay Brown *The Golden Bird: Two Orkney Stories* (J Murray)	
1988	Brian McGuinness *Wittgenstein: A Life: Young Ludwig 1889 - 1921* (Duckworth)	
	Piers Paul Read *A Season in the West* (Secker)	

HISTORICAL & POLITICAL BIOGRAPHY

ALBERT, PRINCE (1819 - 1861)
JAMES, ROBERT RHODES
Albert Prince Consort
A man of outstanding ability, Albert, Queen Victoria's Consort and husband, has had a lasting influence upon the history of his time and on the development of the British constitutional monarchy. His achievements were innumerable: the reformation of Cambridge University, the organisation of the Great Exhibition of 1851, the building of Osborne and Balmoral, and his promotion of social and town planning amongst them. This detailed biography does full justice to this complex man.
[900] H Hamilton pbk **£4.95**

ALI, TARIQ
Street Fighting Years
One of the great radicals of our time describes his life, mostly during the sixties. He chronicles major events such as Phnom Penh, Vietnam and the Prague Spring, as well as personalities such as Lennon and Kissinger.
[B901] Collins hbk **£12.95**

AMERY, LEO (1873 - 1955)
Conservative politician, a tireless advocate of the British Commonwealth.
BARNES, JOHN & NICHOLSON, DAVID (EDS)
Diaries Vol 1 1896 - 1929
[B902] Hutchinson hbk **£30.00**
Diaries Vol 2 1929 - 1945
[B903] Hutchinson hbk **£19.95**

AMIN, IDI
CATO, WYCLIFFE **NEW**
Escape From Idi Amin's Slaughterhouse
Wycliffe Cato was involved in the raid on Entebbe in 1977, and was captured and imprisoned by Amin's forces.
[B904] Quartet hbk **£11.95**

ARENDT, HANNAH (1906 - 1975)
MAY
Hannah Arendt
A study of the great American political theorist.
[B905] Penguin pbk **£2.95**

ASQUITH, H.H. (1852 - 1928)
Liberal statesman, Prime Minister for eight years and eight months (a record recently supplanted by Margaret Thatcher).
Letters to Venetia Stanley
Asquith fell in love with Venetia Stanley in 1912, and wrote to her constantly for three years, sharing with her many political and military secrets. The correspondence ended abruptly on her engagement in 1915.
[B906] Oxford pbk **£8.95**
JENKINS, ROY
Asquith
[B907] Collins pbk **£10.95**
KOSS, STEPHEN
Asquith
[B908] H Hamilton pbk **£4.95**

ASQUITH, RAYMOND (1878 - 1916)
Son of H.H. Asquith and his first wife; a young man of great promise, who was killed in action in World War I.
Life and Letters
[B909] Century pbk **£5.95**

BACON, FRANCIS (1561 - 1626)
Essayist, philosopher, scientist, and in more practical matters a courtier and jurist infamous for sycophancy: *"the wisest, brightest, meanest of mankind"*.
DODD, ALFRED
Francis Bacon's Personal Life Story
Two volumes in one edition - *The Age of Elizabeth* and *The Age of James*.
[B910] Century hbk **£12.95**
MAURIER, DAPHNE DU
The Winding Stair: Francis Bacon - His Rise and Fall
[B911] Gollancz hbk **£12.95**

BENN, TONY (1925 -)
Out of the Wilderness: Diaries 1963 - 1967
[B912] Hutchinson hbk **£16.95**
[B913] Arrow pbk **£7.99**
Office without Power: Diaries 1968 - 1972
The second volume of diaries by the perennial *enfant terrible* of British politics covers the last years of Labour's increasingly demoralised and aimless government, up to the shattering defeat of 1970. He observes all the industrial and political dramas of the time: the Upper Clyde shipbuilders, Rolls-Royce and the long-standing controversial nuclear relationship with the USA. The events detailed here reveal why Benn has become one of the most controversial politicians of the 1980s.
[B914] Hutchinson hbk **£16.95**
[B915] Arrow pbk **£7.99**
Against the Tide: Diaries 1973-76 **NEW**
In the third volume of his diaries, Benn describes the defeat of Edward Heath, the surprise resignation of Harold Wilson and the rise of Jim Callaghan. At the time Benn himself was under attack, from the CBI, the Treasury, and an increasingly suspicious Number 10, as he attempted to pursue the radical policies in Labour's manifesto.
[B916] Hutchinson hbk **£20.00**

BEVAN, ANEURIN (1897 - 1960)
Labour politician and class warrior. As Minister of Health in the Attlee administration of 1945-51, he presided over the creation of the National Health Service. The recent Campbell book is objective, whilst the biography by Michael Foot is a monumental tribute by his political disciple.
CAMPBELL, JOHN
Nye Bevan
[B917] Weidenfeld hbk **£15.95**
FOOT, MICHAEL
Aneurin Bevan: Vol 1 1897 - 1945
[B918] Grafton pbk **£3.95**
Aneurin Bevan: Vol 2 1945 - 1960
[B919] Grafton pbk **£3.95**

BEVIN, ERNEST (1881 - 1951)
Labour statesman and Trade Unionist, Foreign Secretary in the Labour Government 1945-51.
BULLOCK, ALAN
Ernest Bevin: Foreign Secretary 1945 - 1951
[B920] Oxford pbk **£12.50**

BHUTTO, BENAZIR (1953 -)
Daughter of the East
The autobiography of the charismatic Pakistani leader, daughter of the President who was executed by General Zia in 1979. Benazir describes her upbringing as a member of one of Pakistan's richest families, her education at Oxford, and the traumatic events surrounding her father's death.
[B921] H Hamilton hbk **£12.95**
[B922] Mandarin pbk **£3.99**

BIELENBERG, CHRISTABEL
The Past is Myself
The moving autobiography of Christabel Bielenberg, a niece of Lady Northcliffe, who married a German lawyer in 1934. She lived through the war in Germany, under the horrors of Nazi rule and Allied bombings. She describes the conflicts and divided loyalties she encountered. The book has subsequently been adapted for television by Dennis Potter.
[B923] Corgi pbk **£3.50**

BIKO, STEVE
WOODS, DONALD
Biko
A study of the South African radical black activist who died while in police custody in 1977, written by the journalist and author of *Cry Freedom*.
[B924] Penguin pbk **£5.99**

BLOCH, MARC (1886 - 1944)
FINK, CAROLE
Marc Bloch: A Life in History **NEW**
This is the first ever biography of Marc Bloch, the French-Jewish patriot. Bloch was admired both as a historian, and as a soldier who fought in both world wars. As leader of the Resistance he was captured, tortured, and died a heroic death.
[B925] Cambridge hbk **£22.50**

BLUNT, ANTHONY
COSTELLO, JOHN
The Mask of Treachery
One of the most authoritative accounts of the Cambridge spies, which identifies Blunt not as the fourth man, but as the first - as the one who recruited everyone else into the net. The book had to wait for the outcome of a Lords ruling before it could be published, and it contains revelations about Blunt's secret missions for the Royal Family.
[B926] Pan pbk **£6.95**

BORGIA, LUCREZIA (1480 - 1519)
Italian noblewoman infamous for her extravagant vices and political intrigue. She died, however, a patroness of the arts in Ferrara, much respected and praised by poets such as Ariosto.
SHANKLAND, HUGH (TRANS)
Prettiest Love Letters
The love letters of Pietro Bombo and Lucrezia Borgia: a beautifully-produced book.
[B927] Collins hbk **£15.00**

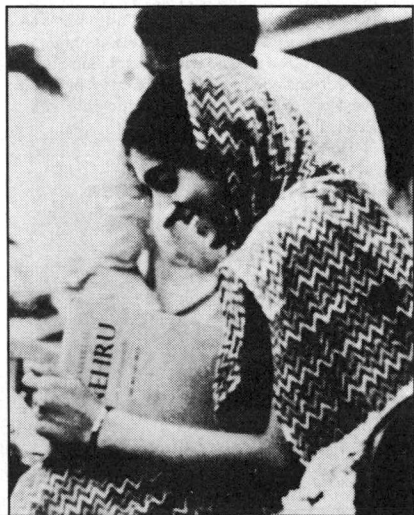

Indira Gandhi, whose biography is written by Inder Malhotra (Hodder & Stoughton hbk £16.95)

BURKE, EDMUND (1729 - 1897)
AYLING, STANLEY
Edmund Burke: His Life and Opinions
Burke, 'the father of English conservatism', was acknowledged to be without intellectual equal in the House of Commons. This is the first biography to appear for 50 years, and it is the first to be based on his full correspondence.
[B928] J Murray hbk **£16.95**

BUTLER, R.A. (1902 - 1982)
Conservative politician who served with distinction in several offices under different Prime Ministers, but never became leader himself. He will always be remembered for his forward-looking Education Act of 1944. The Howard biography is the official one, and has been much acclaimed.
BUTLER, MOLLIE
August and Rab: A Memoir
A memoir by his second wife.
[B929] Weidenfeld hbk **£12.95**
[B930] Weidenfeld pbk **£6.95**
HOWARD, ANTHONY
'Rab': The Life of R.A. Butler
[B931] Cape hbk **£16.00**
[B932] Macmillan pbk **£7.95**

CALLAGHAN, JAMES (1912 -)
Time and Chance
Callaghan's memoirs relate how he rose out of a deprived background to become one of Britain's most influential politicians. He became the only man this century to hold the four offices of Home Secretary, Foreign Secretary, Chancellor and Prime Minister.
[B933] Collins hbk **£15.95**
[B934] Fontana pbk **£5.95**

CARRINGTON, PETER (1919 -)
Reflect on Things Past
Lord Carrington, the former Foreign Secretary, who resigned at the time of the Falklands Crisis, looks at his distinguished political and diplomatic career.
[B935] Collins hbk **£17.50**

CASTRO, FIDEL (1927 -)
SZULC, TAD
Fidel: A Critical Portrait
The first portrait of the legendary Cuban leader written with his full co-operation. Szulc's book is a unique study of Castro's life and career, from his Jesuit-educated youth through his development as a revolutionary. The book relates how Castro survived CIA assassination attempts, and his role as prime mover in the Cuban missile crisis. Castro himself gives his personal views of the major crises of his day and reveals his opinions about his relationship with Jack Kennedy.
[B936] Hodder pbk **£8.99**

CHURCHILL, GEORGE SPENCER (1766 - 1840)
SOAMES, MARY
The Profligate Duke
Mary Soames relates the story of her 18th century ancestor, George Spencer Churchill, musician, bibliophile, collector and architect of the grounds at Blenheim.
[B937] Collins hbk **£17.50**

CHURCHILL, RANDOLPH (1849 - 1895)
FOSTER, R.F.
Lord Randolph Churchill: A Political Life
A scholarly political analysis of Churchill's life. Foster examines issues in which Churchill was involved, such as Home Rule, Protectionism, and Indian Nationalism.
[B938] Oxford pbk **£6.95**

JAMES, ROBERT RHODES
Lord Randolph Churchill
Lord Randolph Churchill was one of the greatest figures in late 19th century political life. In half a dozen years he rose from an obscure family seat to the Chancellorship of the Exchequer. His life was a turbulent one - he became involved in a famous scandal with the Prince of Wales and was obliged to leave England for a while. A legend by the time he was 33, he was the rising hope of the progressive element of the Tory Party until his early death. The author had access to Churchill private papers in order to write this portrait of the man and his times.
[B939] H Hamilton pbk **£7.95**

CHURCHILL, WINSTON LEONARD SPENCER (1874 - 1965)
My Early Life
[B940] Fontana pbk **£4.50**
CHURCHILL, RANDOLPH
Winston S. Churchill: A Life
Vol 1 Youth 1874 - 1900
This is the first part of a remarkable eight volume biography, begun by Winston Churchill's son Randolph, and taken over on his death by the Oxford historian Martin Gilbert, which has recently been completed. It portrays the unique proportions of its subject: the voluminous interests, the wit, the bravery and the unflinching dedication to the improvement of his country.
[B941] Heinemann hbk **£30.00**
Vol 2 The Young Statesman 1901 - 1914
[B942] Heinemann hbk **£30.00**
GILBERT, MARTIN
Vol 3 1914 - 1916
[B943] Heinemann pbk **£30.00**
Vol 4 1916 - 1922
[B944] Heinemann hbk **£30.00**
Vol 5 1922 - 1939
[B945] Heinemann hbk **£30.00**
Vol 6 The Finest Hour 1939 - 1941
[B946] Heinemann hbk **£30.00**
Vol 7 The Road to Victory 1941 - 1945
[B947] Heinemann hbk **£25.00**
[B948] Heinemann hbk uniform edition **£30.00**
[B949] Minerva pbk **£8.50**
Vol 8 Never Despair 1945 - 1965
The final volume of the great biography covers the 20 years from the end of the war in Europe to Churchill's death in 1965: from the pinnacle of his power as leader of a victorious Britain, through his fall from office, his efforts to return as Prime Minister and his retirement through ill health.
[B950] Heinemann hbk **£25.00**
[B951] Heinemann hbk uniform edition **£30.00**
[B952] Minerva pbk **£8.50**
GREEN, DAVID
The Churchills of Blenheim
A history of the nine generations of the Churchills of Blenheim Palace. It begins with Winston, father of John Churchill, first Duke of Marlborough, and ends with the great 20th century leader.
[B953] Constable pbk **£5.95**
HOUGH, RICHARD
Former Naval Person: Churchill and the Wars at Sea
[B954] Weidenfeld pbk **£6.95**
MANCHESTER, WILLIAM
The Caged Lion 1932 - 1940
This is the second part of Manchester's three-part biography of Churchill, the first volume of which was critically acclaimed. In this part Manchester suggests that it was the thirties, rather than the war years, that saw Churchill's finest hour, as he struggled to oppose Parliament's policy of appeasement towards Hitler.
[B955] M Joseph hbk **£17.95**
The Last Lion 1874 - 1932
[B956] Sphere pbk **£5.95**

Winston Churchill, the subject of *Memories and Adventures* by Winston S. Churchill (Weidenfeld & Nicolson hbk £14.95)

MORGAN, TED
Churchill: 1874 - 1915
[B957] Cape hbk **£12.50**
SMITH, F.E. (THE EARL OF BIRKENHEAD)
Churchill 1874 - 1922
As a long-time friend of Churchill, Lord Birkenhead draws on his intimate personal knowledge and upon private papers, in this major one-volume biography. As Churchill's godson he observed the great leader, warts-and-all, and at close quarters, from 1915 onwards.
[B958] Harrap hbk **£19.95**

CHURCHILL, WINSTON S.
Memories and Adventures
The grandson of Britain's great wartime leader sheds light on his distinguished family. He remembers his father Randolph, as well as Sir Winston in his dotage. He also portrays his own adventures as a war correspondent in Vietnam and the Middle East during the 1960s.
[B959] Weidenfeld hbk **£14.95**

CLARENDON, EDWARD HYDE, 1ST EARL OF (1609 - 1674)
OLLARD, RICHARD
Clarendon and His Friends
Clarendon was the architect behind the restoration of Charles II to the throne. He had an enormous impact on the society of his time and on the development of English politics. His other great achievement was as the chronicler of his own times in *History of the Rebellion*. This is the first biography to make use of Clarendon's own correspondence and to draw on original research in France and England.
[B960] H Hamilton hbk **£15.00**
[B961] Oxford pbk **£6.95**
Clarendon's Four Portraits `NEW`
Four more of Clarendon's portraits of historical figures which have remained untouched in an attic for 200 years. The subjects include George Digby, Earl of Bristol, and Sir John Berkeley of Stratton.
[B962] H Hamilton hbk **£14.95**
WORMALD, H.G.
Clarendon
A re-interpretation of Clarendon's work and attitudes.
[B963] Cambridge pbk **£10.95**

CLEOPATRA (?69 - 30 BC)
HUGHES-HALLETT, LUCY
Cleopatra `NEW`
A startling reappraisal of Cleopatra and what her

image has signified throughout the centuries. The book examines how her own life was re-invented by the propaganda of her enemies, and how her significance as a figure has been a mirror-image for the various cultures that have altered it according to their taste.
[B964] Bloomsbury hbk **£16.95**

COLUMBUS, CHRISTOPHER (1265 - 1321)
Explorer and official discoverer of America, who upset the medieval world view that the earth was flat. Columbus's nationality remains ambiguous: born in Genoa, resident in Portugal, he claimed America for Spain.
COLLIS, JOHN STEWART
Christopher Columbus
Columbus was a difficult man, and something of a religious extremist. All his life he refused to believe he had discovered America. Indeed, his original mission had been to travel to the East, in order to recover the Holy Sepulchre and to meet the Grand Khan. His life afterwards fluctuated between fame and failure, and he died in disgrace. Collis here gives a fresh sense of adventure to the complex story.
[B965] Sphere pbk **£3.99**
GRANZOTTO, GIANNI
Christopher Columbus: The Dream and the Obsession
Lively recent biography, which concentrates on the central events of Columbus's life.
[B966] Collins hbk **£13.95**
[B967] Grafton pbk **£4.95**

COLVILLE, SIR JOHN (1915 -)
As a high-ranking civil servant, and secretary to the cabinet during the premierships of Winston Churchill, Colville's Downing Street diaries offer a valuable insight into the conduct of state during the second World War, and through the early 1950s.
The Fringes of Power: Downing Street Diaries: 1939 - 55
[B967A] Hodder hbk **£25.00**
Vol 1
[B967B] Hodder pbk **£6.95**
Vol 2
[B967C] Hodder pbk **£5.95**
Footprints in Time
A more personal volumne of recollections.
[B967D] Century pbk **£4.95**

COOPER, LADY DIANA (1896 - 1987)
Daughter of the Duke of Rutland, wife of Duff Cooper, socialite and actress, ambassadress to France in the post-war years, Lady Diana was a great and enduring beauty.
The Rainbow Comes and Goes
The first volume of her autobiography, published in 1958. She describes her Edwardian childhood, culminating in her presentation at Court.
[B968] Century pbk **£4.95**
Light of Common Day
The second part, published in 1959, dwells on her career as an actress, and on Duff's political career.
[B969] Century pbk **£4.95**
Trumpets from the Steep
The third volume, published in 1960, describes the Second World War, and follows Duff's political career around the world.
[B970] Century pbk **£4.95**
COOPER, ARTEMIS
The Diana Cooper Scrapbook
Based on the numerous scrapbooks and albums kept by Cooper, this book reflects her taste for the outrageous and her amusement at her own public image.
[B971] H Hamilton hbk **£15.00**
ZIEGLER, PHILIP
Diana Cooper
[B972] H Hamilton hbk **£12.95**

COOPER, DUFF (1890 - 1954)
Old Men Forget: The Autobiography of Duff Cooper
[B973] Century pbk **£6.95**
CHARMLEY, JOHN
Duff Cooper: The Authorized Biography
A full life of Cooper which describes his wooing of Diana, one of the great beauties of the age. It also charts his political career, up to his resignation over the Munich Agreement and his subsequent dramatic recall to the Cabinet by Churchill.
[B974] Macmillan pbk **£7.95**
COOPER, ARTEMIS (ED)
A Durable Fire: The Letters of Duff and Diana Cooper 1913 - 1950
[B975] Collins hbk **£12.95**
[B976] H Hamilton pbk **£4.95**

CROSSMAN, RICHARD (1907 - 1974)
The Crossman Diaries
The controversial and revealing Crossman diaries cover the years 1964 - 1970, and form one of the most important political documents of the century. This condensed editon includes the three original volumes.
[B977] Methuen pbk **£6.95**
DALYELL, TAM
Dick Crossman: A Portrait   **NEW**
Crossman is one of the most important figures in the history of the Labour Party, whose intellectual eminence has left a powerful legacy. Dalyell, his former Parliamentary Private Secretary, knew him intimately, and draws on his knowledge, and the diaries, to explore the character of this unique man.
[B978] Weidenfeld hbk **£14.95**

CURZON, GEORGE NATHANIEL (1859 - 1925)
"My name is George Nathaniel Curzon,/I am a Most Superior Person,/My face is fat,/My hair is sleek,/I dine at Blenheim once a week." The Oxford undergraduate so described went on to become Viceroy of India.
ROSE, KENNETH
Curzon: A Most Superior Person
[B979] Macmillan pbk **£8.50**

DALTON, HUGH (1887 - 1962)
Labour politician, Chancellor of the Exchequer under Attlee, Dalton was forced to resign in 1947 over a budget leak to the press.
PIMLOTT, BEN
Hugh Dalton: A Biography
To the Tories, Dalton was a class traitor: son of a tutor to royal princes, he was educated at Eton and King's College, Cambridge, where he turned to Socialism. Hardened by the tragic death of his young daughter, he entered Parliament in 1924, becoming Chancellor of the Exchequer in 1945 and playing a major role in the setting up of the Welfare State by the Attlee Government. Using many sources, including private papers, and diaries, this magnificent and acclaimed book tells the story of the man some called a crusader, and others a traitor and conspirator.
[B980] Cape hbk **£30.00**
[B981] Macmillan pbk **£12.95**
PIMLOTT, BEN (ED)
The Diaries of Hugh Dalton: 1918 - 1940/1945 - 1960
[B982] Cape hbk **£40.00**
The Second World War Diary of Hugh Dalton: 1940 - 1945
[B983] Cape hbk **£40.00**

DEVEREUX, ROBERT, EARL OF ESSEX
STRACHEY, LYTTON
Elizabeth and Essex
Biography of the relationship between Elizabeth I and her ill-fated suitor.
[B987] Penguin pbk **£3.95**

EDEN, ANTHONY (1897 - 1977)
Conservative statesman and Prime Minister from 1955 to 1957, during which period he presided over the Suez crisis.
CARLTON, DAVID
Anthony Eden
[B988] Unwin Hyman pbk **£8.95**
JAMES, ROBERT RHODES
Anthony Eden
An authorised and revelatory biography, the chief importance of which is that it contains major new documents relating to the Suez Crisis. The book has been well received and has done something to restore Eden's stature.
[B989] Weidenfeld hbk **£16.95**
[B990] Macmillan pbk **£8.95**

EISENHOWER, DWIGHT D. (1890 - 1969)
General, commander of the Allied Forces in Europe after D-Day, and 34th President of the United States of America.
BRENDON, PIERS
Ike: The Life and Times of Dwight D. Eisenhower
[B991] Secker hbk **£12.95**

FOOT, MICHAEL (1913 -)
Another Heart and Other Pulses
Michael Foot is one of the most committed and learned politicians of his generation, very much in the radical intellectual tradition. He is a man of wide-ranging and passionately expressed views, who has never reneged on the basic principles of truth and democracy. He was cruelly vilified by the media during the 1983 election campaign, in which Labour suffered a major defeat. Throughout the campaign, however, Foot retained his dignity and subsequently some members of the media regretted the nature in which he seemed to have been framed. In this book, Foot gives his own forthright account of the election campaign, and offers his alternative to the Thatcher society.
[B992] Collins hbk **£8.95**
Loyalists and Loners
A series of portraits of contemporaries of Foot, including Jennie Lee, Barbara Castle, David Owen, Enoch Powell and George Orwell, who he describes as *"a model of courage as well as a master of the English language"*.
[B993] Collins hbk **£15.00**
[B994] Collins pbk **£6.95**

FRANCO, GENERAL (1892 - 1975)
FUSI, JUAN PABLO
Franco
An important re-assessment of the Spanish dictator, who overthrew the socialist government with Nazi and Fascist aid and established an authoritarian regime which lasted until his death.
[B995] Unwin Hyman hbk **£11.95**

FRANKLIN, BENJAMIN (1706 - 1790)
American statesman who played a considerable role in the final draft of the Declaration of Independence. He was also celebrated as a scientist: he experimented with lightning and electricity and invented a new kind of clock. His autobiography is a classic work, celebrated as much for its style as its content.
Autobiography and Other Writings
[B996] Penguin pbk **£2.95**
CLARK, RONALD W.
Benjamin Franklin: A Biography
[B997] Weidenfeld hbk **£18.50**

GANDHI, INDIRA (1917 - 1982)
MALHOTRA, INDER
Indira Gandhi: A Personal and Political Biography   **NEW**
Even now, after her death, Indira Gandhi evokes

fierce feelings of adoration or abuse in India. This biography of the former Indian Prime Minister explores her very private and complex personality, her marriage to Feroze Gandhi and her relationship with her sons, Rajiv and Sanjay. It also tells of how she sowed the seeds of her own downfall.
[B998] Hodder hbk **£16.95**

GANDHI, MAHATMA (1869 - 1948)
Autobiography
Gandhi's 1925 autobiography gives an account of his spiritual progress towards Absolute Truth, and his method of pursuing it through non-violent means. Gandhi believed that the result would be a federation of village republics, freed from British rule.
[B999] Penguin pbk **£5.99**
BROWN, JUDITH
Gandhi: Prisoner of Hope **NEW**
[B1000] Weidenfeld hbk **£16.00**
COPLEY, ANTONY
Gandhi
[B1001] Blackwell pbk **£3.50**
EDWARDES, MICHAEL
The Myth of the Mahatma: Gandhi, the British and the Raj
[B1002] Constable hbk **£12.95**
FISCHER, LOUIS
The Life of Mahatma Gandhi
[B1003] Grafton pbk **£3.95**
NANDA, B.R.
Mahatma Gandhi: A Biography **NEW**
A sensitive and exhaustive biography of Gandhi's life and philosophy.
[B1004] Oxford pbk **£3.95**

GAULLE, CHARLES DE (1890 - 1970)
COOK, DON
Charles de Gaulle: A Biography
[B984] Secker hbk **£22.95**
LACOUTURE, JEAN
Charles de Gaulle **NEW**
Lacouture's biography of Charles de Gaulle has been hailed in France as one of the most important contemporary biographies: a moving and balanced portrait of the great statesman. The original three-volume French edition has been rendered into two in English. The second will be published in 1990.
[B985] Collins hbk **£20.00**
WHITE, SAM
De Gaulle: A Reassessment
White lived in Paris in the years following the war, where he was ideally placed to understand de Gaulle and his entourage. This book consists of his reports on the French scene which were compiled for the *Evening Standard*.
[B986] Harrap hbk **£8.95**

GEMAYEL, BASHIR
NEWMAN, BARBARA & ROGAN, BARBARA
The Covenant: Love and Death in Beirut **NEW**
The extraordinary story of Bashir Gemayel, assassinated president of Lebanon. Barbara Newman, an ABC producer, was his lover during his rise to power. She used all her investigative skills to discover the truth behind his unsolved murder.
[B1005] Bloomsbury hbk **£13.95**

GORBACHEV, MIKHAIL (1931 -)
MURARKA, DEV
Gorbachev
A former *Observer* correspondent in Moscow discusses the rise to power of Gorbachev, and its implications for the future of the world.
[B1006] Hutchinson hbk **£12.95**
SCHMIDT-HAUER, CHRISTIAN
Gorbachev: The Path to Power
[B1007] Penguin pbk **£3.50**

GROMYKO, ANDREI (1909 - 1989)
Gromyko, who died this year, has held office under every leader from the past 50 years, from Stalin to Gorbachev, and, as his country's foreign minister he has met almost every foreign leader throughout the world, including Roosevelt and Churchill. His important and controversial memoirs give an insider's glimpse into the workings of the Kremlin and the major post-war global developments.
Memories **NEW**
[B1008] Hutchinson hbk **£16.95**

HAMILTON, LADY EMMA (1765 - 1815)
FRASER, FLORA
Beloved Emma: The Life of Emma, Lady Hamilton
A life of Nelson's mistress, famed for her beauty.
[B1009] Weidenfeld pbk **£8.95**

HEALEY, DENIS
The Time of My Life **NEW**
Healey is one of Britain's most universally-liked politicians. In this entertaining autobiography he describes his youth in Yorkshire, his wartime career and his life in politics, from winning his first in 1952 to becoming Chancellor of the Exchequer. Closely involved in much of British life over the last 50 years, he here describes the changes he has seen in Britain since 1945. He demonstrates his wide-ranging intelligence, particularly his passionate interest in literature and the arts.
[B1010] M Joseph hbk **£16.95**

HERVEY, CAPTAIN ALBERT
ALLEN, CHARLES (ED)
A Soldier of the Company: Life of an Indian Ensign 1833 - 1843
The frank memoirs of a young man who arrived as an eager cadet in Madras in 1833 to join the army of the East India Co. The memoirs concern his impressionable life in India before the Mutiny.
[B1011] M Joseph hbk **£15.95**

HERVEY, LORD (1696 - 1743)
Lord Hervey's Memoirs
The memoirs of Lord Hervey, who will always be remembered as the butt of Alexander Pope's satirical wit - he was bitterly attacked in *The Dunciad*, ridiculed in particular for his effeminacy.
[B1012] Penguin pbk **£4.95**

HERZEN, ALEXANDER (1812 - 1870)
Childhood, Youth and Exile
Alexander Herzen was a Russian 19th century radical thinker and political journalist. Chiefly remembered for his monumental autobiography, unambiguously titled *My Past and Thoughts*, in which he gives an unparalleled account of 19th century political life in Russia. One of the highlights of the first two volumes is his nurse's account of Napoleon's occupation of Moscow in 1812. He goes on to give an atmospheric account of his life at Moscow University, and his imprisonment for revolutionary opinions in 1834, and his subsequent departure from Russia.
[B1013] Oxford pbk **£3.95**
Ends and Beginnings
A selection from the later parts of *My Past and Thoughts*, in which Herzen displays his acute political and literary sensibility in describing 19th century Russia and Europe.
[B1014] Oxford pbk **£4.95**

HESELTINE, MICHAEL (1933 -)
CRITCHLEY, JULIAN
Heseltine
A balanced, if sometimes scathing portrait of the former Defence Secretary and his resignation over the Westland affair.
[B1015] Hodder pbk **£2.99**

Mikhail Gorbachev, whose biography, *Gorbachev*, is by Dev Murarka (Hutchinson hbk £12.95).

HIROHITO, EMPEROR (1901 - 1989)
BEHR, EDWARD
Hirohito **NEW**
Behr summons a large amount of evidence to support the view that Hirohito was a cunning waverer who skilfully concealed his own complicity in Japanese war crimes, as in his claims of innocence over plans for the attack on Pearl Harbor.
[B1016] H Hamilton hbk **£14.95**
HOYT, EDWIN P.
Hirohito: The Biography **NEW**
Hoyt draws on much original and unpublished material to shed new light on Hirohito: how he ended World War II against the wishes of his generals, his plans to introduce a constitutional monarchy, and his delicate relationship with the United States.
[B1017] Hutchinson hbk **£14.95**

HOLLIS, ROGER
DEACON, RICHARD
The Shadow of Roger Hollis **NEW**
Many attempts have been made to prove that Roger Hollis was the fifth man. In this first biography of Hollis, one man emerges as being the true fifth man in MI5 and MI6. He is a man of contrasting character to Hollis, who worked in Hollis's shadow and in partnership with Guy Burgess to destroy the British Empire.
[B1018] Century hbk **£12.95**

HOOVER, J. EDGAR
POWERS, RICHARD G.
Secrecy and Power: The Life of J. Edgar Hoover
A biography of the extraordinarily nasty and devious J. Edgar Hoover, which details his control of the labyrinthine interior world of the FBI.
[B1019] Hutchinson hbk **£17.95**

HYNES, SAMUEL
Flights of Passage
In World War II, Samuel Hynes flew over 100 missions against the Japanese. In this acclaimed war memoir he describes his transformation from untrained cadet to war-weary aviator, and from innocence to experience.
[B1020] Bloomsbury pbk **£4.99**

IGNATIEFF, PAUL (1832 - 1908)
IGNATIEFF, MICHAEL
The Russian Album
Ignatieff chronicles four generations of his family in Russia, beginning in the dazzling court of Tsar Alexander III, and traces the family's rise to power and influence in the imperial regime of Tsar Nicholas II. Through family albums and handed-down stories, Ignatieff poignantly attempts to come to terms with his roots and memories.
[B1021] Penguin pbk **£3.99**

JOHNSON, LYNDON (1908 - 1973)
CARO, ROBERT
Years of Lyndon Johnson: The Path to Power
Biography of the former American President (1963 - 1968) who took office after the assassination of John F. Kennedy. Johnson is now chiefly remembered as the man who prolonged the Vietnam War.
[B1022] Collins hbk **£15.00**

KEE, ROBERT
A Crowd Is Not a Company **NEW**
This compelling account of Kee's time in a Prisoner of War camp was first published in 1947, and describes how prisoners deceived themselves with fantastical plans for escape, or argued over such matters as who had the largest portion of margarine. After several false starts, Kee eventually managed to escape.
[B1023] Sphere pbk **£3.99**

KENNEDY, JOHN F. (1917 - 1963)
GOODWIN, DORIS KEARNS
The Fitzgeralds and the Kennedys: An American Saga
An account of the rise of the Kennedy family from obscurity in the Irish slums of Boston.
[B1024] Pan pbk **£5.99**

LOWE, JACQUES
Kennedy: A Time Remembered
[B1025] Quartet hbk **£20.00**
LOWE, JACQUES & SHEED, WILFRED
The Kennedy Legacy
A vibrant illustrated reminder of the Kennedy era, which discusses the legacy of John F. and Robert and their relevance today.
[B1026] Viking hbk **£15.95**
MANCHESTER, WILLIAM
One Brief Shining Moment
A good, well-illustrated survey of the magic of the Kennedy era.
[B1027] Little, Brown pbk **£9.95**

KERENSKY, ALEXANDER (1881 - 1970)
ABRAHAM, RICHARD
Alexander Kerensky
Kerensky was a lawyer and revolutionary, more moderate than the Bolsheviks, who became Premier of Russia's provisional government and was overthrown by the Bolshevik coup of 1917.
[B1028] Sidgwick hbk **£20.00**

KEYNES, JOHN MAYNARD (1883 - 1946)
SKIDELSKY, ROBERT
John Maynard Keynes Vol 1: 1883 - 1920 Hopes Betrayed
First volume of the definitive study of the economist, bibliophile and Bloomsbury aesthete. An important figure of the inter-war years, Keynes advocated the use of public expenditure to stimulate demand, thereby boosting employment.
[B1029] Macmillan hbk **£14.95**

KHOMEINI, AYATOLLAH
MOIN, BAQER
Khomeini: Sign of God **NEW**
This timely biography explores how a frail old man in the robes of a Muslim theologian overthrew the Shah of Iran. Moin investigates Khomeini's life and attempts to find out what changed a gentle, traditional theologian into a militant and vengeful radical.
[B1030] IB Tauris hbk **£12.95**

KING EDWARD VII (1841 - 1910)
ARONSON, THEO
The King in Love: Edward VII's Mistress
A study of the three loves of Edward VII: Lillie Langtry, Daisy Warwick and Alice Keppel. The book also evokes the colourful *fin de siècle* world and its characters, including Oscar Wilde and Sarah Bernhardt.
[B1031] J Murray hbk **£13.95**

KING EDWARD VIII, THE DUKE OF WINDSOR (1894 - 1972)
BLOCH, MICHAEL
The Secret File of the Duke of Windsor
Based on original research into the Duke's secret files, this tells the tragic story of the exile of the man who had been Edward VIII.
[B1033] Corgi pbk **£4.99**

KING GEORGE V (1865 - 1936)
ROSE, KENNETH
King George V
[B1034] Macmillan pbk **£7.95**

KING GEORGE VI (1895 - 1952)
BRADFORD, SARAH
King George VI
A full insider's account of the man who took over the throne when Edward VIII abdicated. This revealing biography is based on archive material, private correspondence and diaries.
[B1035] Weidenfeld hbk **£16.95**

HOWARTH, PATRICK
George VI
A major re-evaluation of a much-neglected monarch, which concentrates on his powerful influence on events in both peacetime and wartime.
[B1036] Hutchinson hbk **£12.95**

KOLLONTAI, ALEXANDRA (1872 - 1952)
PORTER, CATHY
Alexandra Kollontai
A study of the only woman member of the Bolshevik Central Committee: the USSR's first Minister of Social Welfare.
[B1037] Virago pbk **£6.95**

LASCELLES, ALAN
HART-DAVIS, DUFF (ED)
End of an Era: Letters and Journals 1887 - 1920
The first volume of Lascelles's writings describes his school and Oxford days and his WWI experiences.
[B1038] H Hamilton hbk **£16.95**
[B1039] H Hamilton pbk **£7.95**
In Royal Service: Letters and Journals 1920 - 1936 **NEW**
Lascelles was was 33 when he joined the staff of Edward, Prince of Wales, as assistant Private Secretary in 1920. He devoted eight years to trying to make the Prince fit to be king. From 1931 to 1935 he was Secretary to the Governor-General of Canada. He rejoined the royal staff in 1936 as Assistant Private Secretary to King George V, until the King's death threw him into the service of Edward VIII, with whom he later became disillusioned.
[B1040] H Hamilton hbk **£14.95**

LAWRENCE, T.E. (1888 - 1935)
Seven Pillars of Wisdom
Lawrence's classic memoir of the revolt in Arabia. 'He has brought to his task a fastidious scholarship...a profound distrust of himself, a still profounder faith.' - E.M. Forster.
[B1041] Cape hbk **£16.00**
[B1042] Penguin pbk **£6.99**
The Letters of T.E. Lawrence
(Ed. Brown, Malcolm)
This collection includes intimate letters with Mrs George Bernard Shaw on contentious subjects, such as the nature of his sexuality and the motives behind his retreat into relative obscurity.
[B1043] Dent hbk **£20.00**
The Mint
An unexpurgated edition of Lawrence's highly subjective account of his life in the RAF. It reflects the strange physical and mental state Lawrence was in after his war experiences and tells of his subsequent long struggle for the fulfilment of Government undertakings to the Arabs.
[B1044] Cape hbk **£12.95**
[B1045] Penguin pbk **£4.99**
BROWN, MALCOLM & CAVE, JULIA
A Touch of Genius: The Life of T.E. Lawrence
Lawrence has been an enigmatic figure since his death in 1935. This detailed biography reveals much about the legendary figure and includes interviews with Henry Williamson, E.M. Forster and with Lawrence's elder brother.
[B1046] Dent hbk **£14.95**
[B1047] Weidenfeld pbk **£8.95**
HYDE, H. MONTGOMERY
Solitary in the Ranks: Lawrence of Arabia as Airman and Private Soldier
A fascinating account of Lawrence's attempts to suppress his identity in the RAF and Royal Tanks Corps, after he had organised the Arab Revolt. The book is based on a revealing series of letters between Lawrence and Sir Hugh Trenchard.
[B1048] Constable pbk **£7.95**

STEWART, DESMOND
T.E. Lawrence
A refreshing and controversial 1977 biography, by a Middle East expert, which looks at the tensions of Lawrence's Oxford youth, his love of castles and chivalry, and his espionage activity in the desert.
[B1049] Grafton pbk **£3.95**
WILSON, JEREMY
Lawrence of Arabia: The Authorised Biography **NEW**
This scholarly biography is the result of prodigious research into previously unavailable government papers concerning the Arab Revolt, which were only released in 1975. It is the definitive work on one of the greatest Englishmen of the century.
[B1050] Heinemann hbk **£15.95**
T.E. Lawrence
An interesting and well-illustrated collection of material, which appeared as a catalogue to the recent National Portrait Gallery exhibition commemorating Lawrence's centenary.
[B1050A] Nat Portrait Gal hbk **£25.00**
[B1050B] Nat Portrait Gal pbk **£14.95**

LISTER, ANNE (1791 - 1840)
WHITBREAD, HELEN (ED)
I Know My Own Heart: The Diaries of Anne Lister
Lister was an outwardly conventional woman who lived in at Shibden Hall, Halifax. In these often painfully revealing diaries, written in code, she records her daily life: her studies, her domestic tasks, and her passionate love affairs with other women. Also included is a wonderful account of a trip to London and Paris with her father.
[B1051] Virago pbk **£8.99**

LLOYD, SELWYN
THORPE, D.R.
Selwyn Lloyd **NEW**
Lloyd is remembered as Chancellor of the Exchequer and principal victim of Harold Macmillan's 'Night of the Long Knives' on Friday 13 July 1962. Thorpe's meticulously researched biography is based on exclusive access to Lloyd's papers, and over 400 interviews, and reveals many unexpected aspects of an important, although outwardly less interesting, political figure.
[B1052] Cape hbk **£18.00**

LOUISE, PRINCESS
WAKE, JEHANNE
Princess Louise
An unusual royal biography, concerning Princess Louise, Queen Victoria's sixth child and most independent daughter, who travelled in 1871 to the Wild West, and later became a sculptor, moving easily in Bohemian circles.
[B1053] Collins hbk **£17.50**

LOVAT, SIMON FRASER, LORD
March Past
Lovat was a Scottish chieftain, the leader of the Lovat Scots, a renowned political intriguer.
[B1054] Weidenfeld pbk **£8.95**

LUCAN, LORD
MARNHAM, PATRICK
Trail of Havoc: In the Steps of Lord Lucan
The murder of Mrs Sandra Rivett, nanny to the Lucan family, and the subsequent disappearance of Lord Lucan in 1974 is one of the most extraordinary murder cases this century. It caused upheavals in the social and political life of the mid-1970s, including the libel case brought by James Goldsmith against *Private Eye*. Patrick Marnham explores the whole episode against Harold Wilson's last months in office.
[B1055] Penguin pbk **£2.99**

LUXEMBURG, ROSA HART (1870 - 1919)
ETTINGER, ELZBIETA
Rosa Luxemburg
The first new biography of the important socialist thinker for twenty years. It uses fresh material from unpublished letters and memoirs, and interviews with friends and relatives, putting her life into the context of her Polish background.
[B1056] Harrap hbk **£10.95**

MACDONALD, JOHN
Memoirs of an 18th Century Footman: 1745 - 1779
First published at the time of the French Revolution, these memoirs offer a delightful insight into the life of this Scottish highlander, his various masters, and his days in service all over the world.
[B1057] Century pbk **£4.95**

MACDONALD, RAMSAY (1866 - 1937)
COX, JANE (ED)
A Singular Marriage: The Letters of Ramsey and Margaret MacDonald
Ramsay MacDonald was a major force in the Labour Party in the first half of the century. He became Prime Minister in 1924, and served again from 1929 to 1935. This book covers the courtship and marriage of MacDonald and Margaret Gladstone, who died five years after he entered Parliament.
[B1058] Harrap hbk **£12.95**

MACLEAN, DONALD
CECIL, ROBERT
A Divided Life: A Biography of Donald MacLean
The first full-length biography of one of the last of the ideological spies, written by an associate from his Cambridge days. He breaks new ground in analysing MacLean and his access to American atomic secrets.
[B1059] Bodley hbk **£15.00**

MACMILLAN, HAROLD (1894 - 1987)
Conservative statesman, Prime Minister from 1957 to 1963, whose successful term of office was tagged with the catch-phrase *"You never had it so good"*. A member of the famous Macmillan publishing family, he was a voracious reader even whilst Prime Minister.
War Diaries: The Mediterranean 1943 - 1945
These diaries were written whilst Macmillan was Churchill's British Minister in North Africa, and responsible by the end of the war for British policy throughout the entire Mediterranean. The diaries began as letters to his wife, and offer a vivid picture of the crises of the time.
[B1060] Macmillan hbk **£18.50**
[B1061] Macmillan pbk **£9.95**
HORNE, ALISTAIR
Macmillan Vol 1: 1894 - 1957 The Road from the Isles
The acclaimed first volume of the official biography takes Harold Macmillan from his childhood, through Eton, Oxford, his five wounds in the trenches in Flanders and his entry into politics, and culminates with his arrival in Downing Street at the age of 62.
[B1062] Macmillan hbk **£16.95**
Macmillan Vol 2: 1957 - 1986 **NEW**
The second volume concentrates on Macmillan's period as Prime Minister, which began with the rapid restoration of the country's image, severely tarnished after the Suez affair. Horne then provides a detailed and scholarly analysis of the Profumo Affair and Macmillan's resignation, and finally examines his later years as Britain's elder statesman, when he became Lord Stockton.
[B1063] Macmillan hbk **£16.95**

MALCOLM X
Autobiography of Malcolm X
The autobiography of the hardline American Black Rights leader, whose extreme views led to his assassination in 1965.
[B1064] Penguin pbk **£2.95**

MANDELA, NELSON
BENSON, MARY
Nelson Mandela
This 1986 biography describes the jailed African Rights leader's life, work and ideas. It covers his childhood in the Royal Family of the Thembu people, his leadership of the African National Congress, and describes his imprisonment in 1962.
[B1065] Penguin pbk **£4.50**

MANLEY, MICHAEL
LEVI, DARRELL
Michael Manley: The Making of a Leader NEW
The only biography of the charismatic Jamaican leader, who swept back to power with a landslide victory in 1989. Drawing on Manley's personal papers and interviews, this book gives an insight into a remarkable man and the troubled world of Caribbean politics.
[B1066] Deutsch hbk **£17.95**

MARKIEWICZ, CONSTANCE (1868 - 1927)
An Irish nationalist, Markiewicz was the first woman elected to Parliament in 1918, although she never took her seat.
Prison Letters of Countess Markiewicz
[B1067] Virago pbk **£4.95**
HAVERTY, ANNE
Constance Markiewicz: An Independent Life
[B1068] Pandora hbk **£7.95**
NORMAN, DIANA
A Terrible Beauty: A Life of Constance Markiewicz
[B1069] Hodder hbk **£14.95**

MENZIES, STEWART
CAVE-BROWN, ANTHONY
The Secret Servant
The life of Sir Stewart Menzies, Head of British Intelligence 1939-1952.
[B1071] Sphere pbk **£5.99**

MONTAGU, LADY MARY WORTLEY
(1689 - 1762)
Selected Letters of Lady Mary Wortley Montagu
The correspondence of a brilliant English hostess and woman of letters, who accompanied her husband as Ambassador to Constantinople.
[B1072] Penguin pbk **£5.95**

MOUNTBATTEN OF BURMA, LORD LOUIS (1900 - 1979)
The most famous son of an illustrious family, and possibly the last of his kind: soldier, statesman and aristocrat. He was the last Viceroy of India and responsible for the transfer of power in 1947. His brutal murder by the IRA marked the end of an era.
HOUGH, RICHARD
Edwina: Countess Mountbatten of Burma
A biography of Countess Mountbatten (1901-1960) a formidable and independent woman.
[B1073] Sphere pbk **£3.95**
Mountbatten: Hero of Our Time
[B1074] Weidenfeld hbk **£12.95**
[B1075] Weidenfeld pbk **£6.95**

LAMBTON, ANTONY
The Mountbattens NEW
An examination of Mountbatten and his colourful forebears. Lambton claims that Mountbatten was so obsessed with his lineage that he actually concealed and glossed over aspects of it which were unacceptable to him.
[B1076] Constable hbk **£12.95**
ZIEGLER, PHILIP
Mountbatten
A highly-praised and well-balanced life of Mountbatten. It describes his distinguished career as Supreme Commander in South-East Asia, then as the Last Viceroy of India, and finally as Chief of Defence Staff. Ziegler uncovers the unconventional and complex character behind the official veneer, and shows the man who was a great intimate of the Royal Family, known to all his friends as Dickie. Ziegler goes on to describe Mountbatten's last years and his murder by the IRA.
[B1077] Collins hbk **£15.00**
[B1078] Fontana pbk **£5.95**
ZIEGLER, PHILIP (ED)
The Diaries Volume 1: 1920 - 1922
These diaries cover Mountbatten's tour of New Zealand and Australia in 1920, and India and Japan in 1921. During this time he was minder and confidant to his cousin the Prince of Wales. The diaries tell, in ribald detail, of the *contretemps* that went on behind the scenes of an apparently well-organised affair.
[B1079] Collins hbk **£15.00**
The Diaries Volume 2: 1943 - 1946
Frank and revealing journals, beginning in 1943 when Churchill asked Mountbatten if he would be prepared to go to South-East Asia as Supreme Commander of the Allied Forces.
[B1080] Collins hbk **£17.50**
The Diaries Volume 3: 1953 - 1979
From 1953 onwards Mountbatten used to dictate a long account of the day's proceeedings whenever he travelled abroad. His journals cover visits to India, Burma and Ceylon, Washington and NY, Sweden, Athens and West Africa. As he grew older he extended his diary to cover periods at home. Wherever he went he met people of consequence, and his diary records these events, along with entries on the Royal Family.
[B1081] Collins hbk **£18.00**

NEHRU, JAWAHARLAL (189 - 1964)
AKBAR, M.J. NEW
Nehru: The Making of Modern India
A perceptive examination of the social and cultural milieu in which Nehru grew up, giving a fascinating picture of the man behind the public figure. The book draws on a wealth of material only recently released from British Government records.
[B1082] Viking hbk **£17.95**
NEHRU, JAWAHARLAL & GANDHI, INDIRA
Freedom's Daughter: Letters Between Jawaharlal Nehru and Indira Gandhi
(Ed. Gandhi, Sonia)
The first volume of the famous correspondence between Nehru and his daughter covers the period when she was at school and at university in Oxford, and he was away on political business or in prison.
[B1083] Hodder hbk **£20.00**

NICOLSON, HAROLD (1886 - 1968)
Harold Nicolson's Diaries (Ed. Nicolson & Olson)
[B1084] Collins hbk **£12.95**
Some People
Nicolson's celebrated portrait of the English social and intellectual elite in the first part of this century has been hailed as a minor masterpiece of observation. The nine vignettes give an acute commentary on human behaviour and the social world of the time.
[B1085] Oxford pbk **£3.50**

LEES-MILNE, JAMES
Harold Nicolson Vol 1: 1886 - 1929
The first part of this biography traces Nicolson's life through his nomadic childhood in Budapest, Tehran, Constantinople and Bulgaria, and his education at Wellington and Balliol. After the war Nicolson joined the diplomatic service in Paris, where he met Cocteau, Gide and Proust. The volume ends when Nicolson leaves the Diplomatic Service to join the staff of the *Evening Standard*.
[B1086] H Hamilton pbk **£6.95**
Harold Nicolson Vol 2: 1930 - 1968
Part II opens with Nicolson's disillusionment with Oswald Mosley and his move to Sissinghurst with Vita Sackville-West. Both his political and literary careers began at this time. Lees-Milne draws an excellent portrait of this talented man.
[B1087] H Hamilton pbk **£5.95**

NIGHTINGALE, FLORENCE (1820 - 1910)
Letters from Egypt NEW
Nightingale visited Egypt in 1849-50. Her letters home describe her views on the country, and show her alive to every new experience and sensation.
[B1088] Barrie & J hbk **£14.95**
VICINUS, MARTHA & NERGAARD, BEA (EDS)
Letters of Florence Nightingale NEW
Florence Nightingale was adored by her public but loathed by politicians and army officers. This collection of letters presents Florence in her own words, revealing her troubled public and private self. The letters describe Florence's long search for religious peace; her anger at the constraints placed on upper-class women; and her preoccupation with major issues such as public health and the care of the ordinary soldier.
[B1089] Virago pbk **£15.99**
WOODHAM-SMITH, CECIL
Florence Nightingale
[B1090] Constable pbk **£7.50**

O'NEILL, TIP
O'NEILL, TIP & NOVAK, WILLIAM
Man of the House: The Life & Political Memoirs of Speaker Tip
O'Neill looks back over his career and recalls his involvement with such figures as Harry Truman and Ronald Reagan.
[B1091] Bloomsbury hbk **£15.00**

PHILBY, KIM (1912 - 1988)
KNIGHTLEY, PHILIP
Philby: The Life and Times of a Masterspy
Philby was one of the most remarkable spies in the history of espionage, at one point in line to become the head of British Intelligence, while working as a KGB agent. This biography of Philby is made more remarkable for the series of interviews which Knightley recorded with Philby in exile in Moscow, shortly before the latter's death.
[B1092] Deutsch hbk **£12.95**
[B1093] Pan pbk **£4.99**

PIN, MADAME DE LA TOUR DU
Memoirs of Madame de la Tour du Pin
The memoirs of an aristocrat who describes the days before and during the French Revolution, and her escape.
[B1094] Century pbk **£6.95**

POMPADOUR, MADAME DE (1721 - 1764)
MITFORD, NANCY
Madame de Pompadour
An evocation of the Court of Louis XV's court at Versailles and of his mistress.
[B1095] H Hamilton pbk **£6.95**

Enoch Powell, whose biography *The Lives of Enoch Powell* is by Patrick Cosgrave (Bodley Head hbk £16.00)

POWELL, ENOCH
COSGRAVE, PATRICK
The Lives of Enoch Powell   NEW
A powerful biography of one of the most controversial and intelligent politicians of recent times, whose 1968 speech on immigration was to change the face of British politics. Despite his dismissal from the Shadow Cabinet, he has remained an influential force on a range of issues, including defence, the EEC, Northern Ireland and immigration.
[B1096] Bodley hbk **£16.00**

PU YI
The last emperor of China, who ascended to the throne as a boy. His life was the subject of Bernardo Bertolucci's recent, sumptuous film.
BEHR, EDWARD
The Last Emperor
[B1097] Futura pbk **£3.95**
JOHNSTON, REGINALD F.
Twilight in the Forbidden City
The memoirs of Pu Yi's Scottish tutor present a fascinating picture of life at the imperial court at the turn of the century.
[B1098] Oxford pbk **£7.95**
POWER, BRIAN
The Puppet Emperor: A Life of Pu Yi, Last Emperor of China
[B1099] P Owen hbk **£13.95**

QUEEN VICTORIA (1819 - 1901)
STRACHEY, LYTTON
The Illustrated Queen Victoria
Strachey's biography evokes the Victorian era using carefully researched archive material, much of it in the Royal Archives at Windsor. These include advertisements, ephemera and drawings and watercolours by Queen Victoria herself.
[B1100] Bloomsbury hbk **£13.95**
WEINTRAUB, STANLEY
Victoria
This highly-praised biography illuminates Victoria's life and long reign. In lively fashion it examines her restricted childhood, her early years as queen, her tragic widowhood and triumphant old age.
[B1101] Unwin Hyman pbk **£8.95**

RASPUTIN, GRIGORII (1871 - 1916)
JONGE, ALEX DE
Life and Times of Grigorii Rasputin
A biography of the 'mad monk', the religious fanatic and womaniser who was the *eminence grise* of the last Tsar of Russia, Nicholas II.
[B1102] Fontana pbk **£2.95**

RICCI, MATTEO
SPENCE, JONATHAN D.
The Memory Palace of Matteo Ricci
Matteo Ricci was one of the most extraordinary merchants and missionaries who began to travel to the Far East in the late 16th century. A Jesuit, he left his native Italy in 1577 and journeyed first to India, then to China, where he lived from 1583 to 1610. This rich biography juxtaposes the worlds of Counter-Reformation Europe and Ming China.
[B1103] Faber pbk **£4.95**

ROOSEVELT, ARCHIE
For Lust of Knowing
The memoirs of an Intelligence Officer and Arabic scholar. He was the grandson of US President Theodore Roosevelt, and cousin of Franklin D.
[B1104] Weidenfeld hbk **£20.00**

ROOSEVELT, FRANKLIN D. (1882 - 1945)
American President, 1933 - 1935, famous for his 'New Deal' to counter the effects of the Depression.
LARRABEE, ERIC
Commander in Chief
A complete picture of how FDR ran the American side of World War II
[B1105] Deutsch hbk **£15.95**
MORGAN, TED
F.D.R.: A Biography
This first major one-volume biography of Roosevelt describes his family background, his childhood and youth, his marriage to his cousin Eleanor, and his transformation through illness from a charming and uncommitted patrician into one of the most determined, shrewd and powerful politicians of his time.
[B1106] Grafton hbk **£20.00**

ROOSEVELT, THEODORE (1858 - 1919)
American President 1901-1909.
MORRIS, EDMUND
The Rise of Theodore Roosevelt
[B1107] Collins hbk **£12.50**

SADAT, ANWAR (1918 - 1981)
SADAT, JEHAN
A Woman of Egypt
The courageous story of the wife of the assassinated former President of Egypt, Anwar Sadat. Jehan describes how she learned, throughout their life together, to live in daily fear of her husband's assassination, and tells of her attempts to rebuild her life in another country after his death.
[B1108] Hodder pbk **£4.99**

SCHARANSKY, ANATOLE
Fear No Evil   NEW
A leading Soviet dissident and Jewish activist Scharansky is world famous for his defiance of the Kremlin. This is the remarkable story of his nine harrowing years in KGB custody, told in detail and, for the first time, in his own words.
[B1109] Weidenfeld hbk **£14.95**
GILBERT, MARTIN
Scharansky: Hero of our Time
[B1110] Penguin pbk **£4.95**

SIDNEY, ALGERNON (1623 - 1683)
CARSWELL, JOHN
The Porcupine: A Life of Algernon Sidney   NEW
Sidney fought for the Parliamentary Cause, successively as soldier, MP, diplomat, conspirator, political thinker and finally martyr. With his great-uncle Sir Philip Sidney, he is among England's few military intellectuals. This biography assesses him as a key libertarian, and draws on much unpublished material, including the letters he wrote from the Tower of London during his last imprisonment.
[B1111] J Murray hbk **£17.95**

STANHOPE, LADY HESTER
HASLIP, JOAN
Lady Hester Stanhope
The extraordinary story of the arrogant young noblewoman who, as Pitt's niece and hostess at 10 Downing Street, queened it over Georgian London. She spent the end of her life abroad, travelling through the Near East.
[B1112] Cassell pbk **£6.95**

STEEL, DAVID
Against Goliath
The charismatic David Steel describes his twelve years as leader of the Liberal Party, how he became the country's youngest MP, his successful battle to reform Britain's abortion law, his fights against racism, for a Scottish parliament and a united Europe.
[B1113] Weidenfeld hbk **£14.95**

STEPHENSON, GEORGE (1781 - 1848) & ROBERT (1803 - 1859)
ROLT, L.T.C.
George and Robert Stephenson
[B1114] Penguin pbk **£5.95**

TAYLOR, A.J.P. (1906 -)
A Personal History
The frank and engaging memoirs of the unconventional British historian.
[B1115] Hodder pbk **£2.50**
An Old Man's Diary
'Extracts' originally published in literary magazines.
[B1116] H Hamilton hbk **£9.95**

THATCHER, MARGARET (1925 -)
ABSE, LEO   NEW
Margaret, Daughter of Beatrice
This book is gloriously subtitled *A Politician's Psycho-Biography of Margaret Thatcher*. Leo Abse, using his psychoanalytical scholarship and thirty years of parliamentary experience, here traces the continuing public consequences of Thatcher's earliest battles at the breast and on the pot. He gives us the untold story of how a bleak early life, and a far from empathetic mother have, to the detriment of the nation, left the Prime Minister a driven woman.
[B1117] Cape hbk **£12.95**
HARRIS, KENNETH
Thatcher
A good appraisal of how Mrs Thatcher reached her present position and how she maintains herself there. The author has interviewed many friends and colleagues and reveals how she has constantly wrong-footed commentators and politicians alike.
[B1118] Fontana pbk **£3.99**
MAITLAND, OLGA
Margaret Thatcher: The Great Decade
An admiring illustrated celebration of the Thatcher reign.
[B1119] Sidgwick hbk **£12.95**
YOUNG, HUGO   NEW
One of Us: A Biography of Mrs Thatcher
This is the first proper attempt at book-length to demystify a woman hitherto caught between the reverential effusions of her admirers and the blind anger of her enemies. Young analyses Thatcher's rise from being the daughter of a Grantham grocer to becoming Prime Minister. He describes her systematic destruction of the Conservatism of the 1950s, and her re-emergence as the senior statesperson of the Western world. Young says of the book's attitude: *"On re-reading it, the portrait is probably more appealing than one might expect...If you are writing a book about Mrs Thatcher you have to start from the fact that she has been in power for a very long time, so that by definition she is a phenomenon. It is futile to adopt a purely antagonistic slant."*
[B1120] Macmillan hbk **£16.95**

TOYNBEE, ARNOLD J. (1889 - 1975)
MCNEILL, WILLIAM H.
Arnold J. Toynbee: A Life `NEW`
An intimate biography of the author of the classic, but
controversial, 12 volume *A Study of History*. The
biography contemplates his enormously hard-working
life, as well as commenting on how history is written
and how it should be pursued.
[B1121] Oxford hbk **£16.95**

TRUMAN, HARRY (1884 - 1972)
American President from 1945 to 1952, who saw his
country through the McCarthy era and the Korean
War.
JENKINS, ROY
Truman
[B1122] Collins pbk **£6.95**

TZ'U HSI (1835 - 1908)
WARNER, MARINA
**The Dragon Empress: The Life and
Times of Tz'u-Hsi**
[B1123] H Hamilton pbk **£6.99**

VALLADARES, ARMANDO
Against All Hope
The diaries of a Cuban political prisoner.
[B1124] Hodder pbk **£3.95**

WALESA, LECH (1943 -)
A Path of Hope
Walesa, an electrician from a poor Catholic family,
won the Nobel Peace Prize for his attempts to found a
people's Poland. It was an heroic quest which began
when he scaled the railings at the Gdansk shipyard in
1980, and took control of the strike committee. In
1981 the trade union was banned and Walesa was
imprisoned. Walesa says of his attitude to life: *"If we
accept that we are only the temporary guardians of
life's various gifts, it's easier not to lose our heads or
give way to despair."*
[B1125] Collins hbk **£12.95**
[B1126] Pan pbk **£5.99**

WEINBERGER, CASPER
Fighting For Peace `NEW`
Weinberger was US Secretary of Defence to Reagan
for most of his presidency. He here gives the history
of the major defence and foreign policy problems of
the Reagan administration from the inside, including
crises in Nicaragua, El Salvador, Poland, the
Lebanon, NATO and the Falklands. A rare glimpse at
the inner machinations of power.
[B1127] M Joseph hbk **£16.95**

WHITELAW, WILLIAM
The Whitelaw Memoirs `NEW`
Lord Whitelaw has for long been a central figure in
Conservative politics, often regarded as the steadying
influence in a turbulent era. He served in government
and in opposition under Eden, Macmillan and
Douglas-Home, and as a cabinet minister under Heath
and Thatcher. In these memoirs he recalls the events
and moods of his day, along with dramas such as the
Iranian Embassy siege.
[B1128] Aurum hbk **£14.95**

WIESENTHAL, SIMON
Justice Not Vengeance: Memoirs
Wiesenthal, the world's most famous Nazi-hunter,
tells of a lifetime's struggle: his concentration camp
experiences, his near-miraculous survival of the
Holocaust, and his unswerving devotion to a single
sacred cause.
[B1129] Weidenfeld hbk **£14.95**

WILLENBERG, SAMUEL
Surviving Treblinka `NEW`
Between 1941 and 1943 some 900,000 Jews were

sent by the Nazis to the extermination camp at
Treblinka in Poland; a mere 70 survived. This is a
chilling memoir by one of those survivors. Willenberg
describes in compelling detail the physical conditions
of his journey to Treblinka, the brutality of the Nazis
and the heroism of the inmates. He also details the
grisly duties he performed as part of the camp labour
force, and the horrifyingly efficient killing methods of
the Nazis. The memoir culminates with the uprising
in 1943 when a group of prisoners set fire to the camp
and escaped.
[B1130] Yale hbk **£14.95**

WILLIAMS, ERIC
Tunnel
A celebrated memoir of escape from a German POW
camp.
[B1131] Penguin pbk **£1.95**

WILSON, HAROLD (1916 -)
**Memoirs: The Making of a Prime
Minister 1916 - 1964**
[B1132] M Joseph hbk **£14.95**

WILSON, HARRIETTE (1786 - 1834)
Courtesan who endeavoured to blackmail her lovers,
amongst them the Duke of Wellington, by threatening
to publish details of her affairs. *'Publish and be
damned'* they said. Luckily she did.
Harriette Wilson's Memoirs
[B1133] Century pbk **£4.95**

WYNNE, BETSY & EUGENIA
The Wynne Diaries
The diaries of two young ladies of fashion at the time
of the Napoleonic wars.
[B1134] Oxford pbk **£3.95**

YUSUPOV, PRINCE FELIX
DOBSON, CHRISTOPHER
**Prince Felix Yusupov: The Man
who Murdered Rasputin** `NEW`
The extraordinary story of Prince Felix Yusupov, the
man who boasted the smallest waist in pre-
revolutionary Russia, who murdered the 'Mad Monk',
Rasputin.
[B1135] Harrap hbk **£14.95**

Prince Felix Yusupov, 'The Man who Murdered
Rasputin', a biography by Christopher Dobson
(Harrap hbk £14.95)

GENERAL BIOGRAPHY

ABELARD & HELOISE
Letters of Abélard and Héloïse
In the 12th century, Peter Abélard was renowned all
over Europe as a theologian and teacher at the
University of Paris. He fell in love his landlord's
niece Héloïse, and the separation of the lovers
(including Abélard's violent castration) led to a
famous correspondence.
[B1136] Penguin pbk **£3.50**

ACKLAND, JOSS
Through the Looking Glass `NEW`
Joss Ackland is one of Britain's leading actors, and
possesses one of the richest, mellowest voices in the
theatre. He is best known for films such as *White
Mischief* and for his brilliant portrayal of C.S. Lewis
in *Shadowlands*. In his autobiography he describes
his early life in London and South Africa, and the
death of his son from drug addiction, as well as his
theatrical career in the West End and with the RSC.
[B1137] Hodder hbk **£14.95**

AGNELLI, GIOVANNI
FRIEDMAN, ALAN
Agnelli: The Network of Italian Power
Agnelli, owner of the giant Fiat industrial complex,
controls a quarter of the Italian stock exchange. This
biography reveals him as a glamorous socialite and as
a man whom key Italian politicians regularly consult.
[B1138] Harrap hbk **£12.95**

ALEXANDER, TANIA
An Estonian Childhood `NEW`
A remarkable memoir of pre-revolutionary Russia
which describes the Tsarist society at the beginning of
the century.
[B1139] Heinemann pbk **£6.95**

ANDERSEN, DAPHNE
The Toe-Rags `NEW`
The true account of an extraordinary 'rags-to-riches'
growing up in Southern Rhodesia (now Zimbabwe).
When Daphne Andersen was abandoned, along with
her brother and sister they were taken in by an aunt,
who banished them to the kitchen. There they were
befriended by the cook who was kind and sensitive.
[B1140] Deutsch hbk **£14.95**

ANNE, THE PRINCESS ROYAL (1950 -)
HOEY, BRIAN
The Princess Royal
An intimate, authoritative biography written with
Princess Anne's consent. She is perhaps the most
interesting and articulate member of the Royal Family
and has gained the admiration of many through her
Presidency of the Save the Children Fund and the
Riding for the Disabled Association.
[B1141] Grafton hbk **£14.95**
PARKER, JOHN
Princess Anne `NEW`
A frank and incisive book by a leading journalist,
which examines Princess Anne's uneasy relationship
with the press. Parker presents a view from both sides
that does not detract from Anne's established position
as a woman of courage, determination and drive. She
emerges as a woman of uncompromising beliefs, who
is both generous and caring.
[B1142] H Hamilton hbk **£12.95**

ARCHER, ROBYN
A Star is Torn
Contemporary musical revue of female artistes.
[B1143] Virago pbk **£10.99**

ASHCROFT, PEGGY (1907 -)
BILLINGTON, MICHAEL
Peggy Ashcroft
The first biography of Dame Peggy, by the distinguished drama critic, has been very well received. The book reverentially reflects on her key role in the development of the British theatre over the last 50 years, and her work with Lillian Baylis, Olivier, Gielgud and the National Theatre.
[B1144] J Murray hbk **£15.95**
TANITCH, ROBERT
Peggy Ashcroft
A pictorial record and full chronology of Ashcroft's career in film.
[B1145] Hutchinson hbk **£16.95**

ASPINALL, ANTHONY   NEW
The Misadventures of an Ageing Mule
The extraordinary memoirs of Anthony Aspinall, an eccentric drug smuggler who, at the age of seventy, was arrested at Damascus airport carrying 22 kilos of hashish and imprisoned for two and a half years. Six months later he was back in jail, in Amsterdam for smuggling cocaine. His story gives an insider's view of these two sharply opposing worlds.
[B1146] Deutsch hbk **£14.95**

ASPINALL, JOHN
MASTERS, BRIAN
The Passion of John Aspinall
After dropping out of Oxford Aspinall took to gambling, and later graduated from homely games to open the Claremont Club. In 1956 he took a capuchin monkey, a tigress and two Himalayan bears back to his surprised wife - this was the start of his extraordinary zoo, in which 600 animals came to depend on the gambling losses of a number of rich men. Brian Masters shows Aspinall in new and controversial light.
[B1147] Hodder pbk **£3.50**

ASTAIRE, FRED (1899 - 1987)
MUELLER, JOHN
Astaire Dancing
[B1148] H Hamilton hbk **£30.00**
SATCHELL, TIM
Astaire: The Definitive Biography
This tells the story of Frederic Austerlitz II, who became Fred Astaire, from his humble Mid West origins to his role as the world's most popular dancer.
[B1149] Arrow pbk **£4.50**

ATHILL, DIANA
After a Funeral
This is the moving story of how 'Didi', an Egyptian exile and the author of one novel, killed himself. He was a man of great personal charm, whose character was undermined by a self-destructive depression which wrecked all his relationships, apart from one. Diana Athill knew him in the last three years of his life. In this book she charts the complex, intense and variable course of their friendship, during which he fought his depression, before finally succumbing to it. A strange and compelling story.
[B1150] Cape hbk **£10.95**
[B1151] H Hamilton pbk **£5.95**
Instead of a Letter
Diana Athill wrote this autobiography in an attempt to discover what her life was for and why she enjoyed it so much, despite feeling that it had been a failure. She still receives letters from strangers, telling her how much the book means to them.
[B1152] R Clark pbk **£3.50**

AYER, ALFRED J. (1910 - 1989)
More of My Life
Ayer describes his life from his appointment as Professor of Philosophy at University College, London in 1946, up to the birth of his second son by his second marriage in 1963, with details of his rich private life and circle of friends, including E.E. Cummings, Bertrand Russell and J.B.S. Haldane.
[B1153] Oxford pbk **£4.95**
Part of My Life
[B1154] Oxford pbk **£5.95**

BADDELEY, HERMIONE (1906 - 1976)
The Unsinkable Hermione Baddeley
The witty autobiography of the queen of revue, who first came to prominence in the big Cochran extravaganzas with Noel Coward.
[B1155] Pan pbk **£2.95**

BAKER, JOSEPHINE
HAMMOND, BRYAN & O'CONNOR, PATRICK
Josephine Baker
A unique collection of memorabilia and photographs relating to the extraordinary Josephine Baker. Baker was most widely known as the black star of the *Folies Bergére*. She worked for the French Resistance during the war and adopted twelve children. This wonderful book celebrates every aspect of her life, from her poor childhood in St. Louis to her being awarded the Legion d'Honneur and a 21-gun-salute funeral.
[B1156] Cape hbk **£25.00**
ROSE, PHYLLIS
Jazz Cleopatra: The Story of Josephine Baker   NEW
An eloquent evocation of the truly remarkable, promiscuous, courageous and witty star. It details her life from her St Louis youth, through her first appearance, when, clad only in a skirt of feathers, she established herself as a potent symbol of sexuality. It goes on to look at her work for the Resistance and for the Civil Rights Movement.
[B1157] Chatto hbk **£16.00**

BALANCHINE, GEORGE (1904 - 1983)
BUCKLE, RICHARD
George Balanchine: Ballet Master
This biography describes Balanchine's career as Diaghilev's Ballet Master, his founding of the New York City Ballet Company and his role in choreographing films such as *On Your Toes*. Buckle portrays him as an ambitious man, a demanding teacher and an ardent lover.
[B1158] H Hamilton hbk **£20.00**

BANKS, JOSEPH (1743 - 1820)
O'BRIAN, PATRICK
Joseph Banks: A Life
Banks was a young botanist in Captain Cook's company when he circumnavigated the world and discovered Australia. He eventually went on to be President of the Royal Society for 40 years. Makes use of his letters, journals and private papers.
[B1159] Collins pbk **£5.95**

THE BEATLES
COLEMAN, RAY
Brian Epstein: The Man Who Made the Beatles   NEW
The definitive biography of Brian Epstein, who discovered the Beatles whilst he was the record department manager of his father's Liverpool store. Behind their subsequent unprecedented success lay consistent frustration and record company rejections, as Epstein struggled to get the group recognition. With the pressure increased by his determination to conceal his homosexuality, he resorted to pills, which resulted in violent mood swings. Epstein never found inner peace, and died in mysterious circumstances in 1967.
[B1160] Viking hbk **£12.95**
DAVIES, HUNTER
The Beatles
[B1161] Cape hbk **£12.95**
[B1162] Cape pbk **£7.95**

NORMAN, PHILLIP
Shout
[B1163] Transworld pbk **£2.50**

BEATON, CECIL (1904 - 1980)
VICKERS, HUGO
Cecil Beaton: The Authorized Life
The acclaimed official life of the great photographer.
[B1164] Weidenfeld pbk **£8.95**

BEAUMONT, BINKIE
HUGGETT, RICHARD   NEW
Binkie Beaumont: Eminence Grise of the West End Theatre 1933 - 1973
When Beaumont died in 1973 *The Times* was forced to admit that they didn't know anything about his parentage or even his real name. This biography reveals how he acquired the name 'Binkie', and portrays the huge empire that Beaumont built up, as co-founder of H.M. Tennant Ltd, and how in his heyday he had no less than fourteen West End productions running. It details how Beaumont kept stars such as John Gielgud, Vivien Leigh, Peggy Ashcroft, Edith Evans and Ralph Richardson permanently in work, and how he was always first in the queue for new plays by Coward and Rattigan.
[B1165] Hodder hbk **£16.95**

BEHRENS, T.
The Monument
A very unusual and beautiful book about the younger brother of the author who, when 16, met a mysterious Hungarian émigrée ten years his senior. The two spent the next sixteen years trying to elevate their lives into a work of art: the story ended in tragedy when both committed suicide within a year of each other.
[B1166] Sphere pbk **£4.50**

BELUSHI, JOHN
WOODWARD, BOB
Wired: The Short Life and Fast Times of John Belushi
Woodward, an investigative journalist, uses all his skills in exploring the sometimes shocking story of comedian John Belushi's life and death in Hollywood. He shows how Belushi's on-screen mayhem, most famously seen in *The Blues Brother*, had tragic parallels in real life.
[B1167] Faber pbk **£5.99**

BENOIS, ALEXANDRE
Memoirs
Benois was Diaghilev's associate at the Ballet Russe, and was responsible for designing sets for many of the outstanding ballet and opera productions, such as *Petrushka* and *The Rite of Spring*. This memoir features all the personalities of that glittering era, such as Stravinsky and Chagall.
[B1168] Columbus pbk **£6.95**

BENSON, MARY
A Far Cry   NEW
The autobiography of the dedicated South African human rights campaigner. Her early love of cinema took her to Hollywood, where she had a tempestuous affair with James Stewart, and subsequently worked for David Lean. The turning point in her life came when she met Alan Paton, author of *Cry, the Beloved Country*. From that time onwards she became intimately involved with the destiny of South Africa.
[B1169] Viking hbk **£12.95**

BERENSON, MARY (1864 - 1945)
STRACHEY, BARBARA
Mary Berenson
A self-portrait from her own letters and diaries, by the wife of the legendary art historian Bernard Berenson, in his day the foremost authority on Italian painting.
[B1170] H Hamilton pbk **£4.95**

BERGMAN, INGMAR (1918 -)
The Magic Lantern
Bergman, in this haunting and fiercely written autobiography, discusses his early life in Sweden, his many marriages and his film-making career. He recalls his deeply disturbing childhood, as a result of which he has found it increasingly difficult to separate dreams from reality. This has led him to value the imaginative world above the real, something which was partly revealed in his semi-autobiographical masterpiece *Fanny and Alexander*, which is also discussed here. Bergman also explores the relationship between actor and director, as well as his friendships with Charlie Chaplin and Greta Garbo.
[B1171] H Hamilton hbk **£14.95**
[B1172] Penguin pbk **£4.99**

BERGMAN, INGRID (1915 - 1982)
My Story
[B1173] Sphere pbk **£3.99**
LEAMER, LAURENCE
As Time Goes By: A Biography of Ingrid Bergman
The unvarnished truth about the ambitious and talented actress, star of *Casablanca*, who caused a scandal when she left her husband and daughter for her lover Roberto Rossellini, only to return later to be adored once more.
[B1174] H Hamilton hbk **£14.95**
[B1175] Sphere pbk **£3.99**

BERNHARDT, SARAH (1844 - 1923)
SAGAN, FRANCOISE
Dear Sarah Bernhardt   **NEW**
Whilst researching this intriguing and experimental life of the great actress, the author began visiting the Père Lachaise cemetery where Bernhardt's remains lie. From these experiences began a correspondence across time, in which Bernhardt's voice tells of her teenage years in the demi-bordello of her mother's home, as well as of her career as a star, and of all the men who were drawn to her in Paris.
[B1176] Macmillan hbk **£12.95**
STOKES, J. ET AL
Bernhardt, Terry, Duse: The Actress in Her Time
[B1177] Cambridge hbk **£15.00**

BERNSTEIN, LEONARD (1918 -)
The magnificent and extrovert American conductor and composer of *West Side Story*.
FREEDLAND, MICHAEL
Leonard Bernstein
[B1178] Harrap hbk **£12.95**
PEYSER, JOAN
Bernstein: A Biography
A warts-and-all account of this Renaissance man of the theatre.
[B1179] Bantam hbk **£12.95**

BESANT, ANNIE
DINNAGE, ROSEMARY
Annie Besant
Born in 1874, Besant was a phenomenon and a pioneer who, by the time she was 28, was notorious as a leader of militant atheism. During her life she embraced a variety of beliefs, from free-thought and socialism to theosophy; she was also a powerful advocate of women's rights, trade unionism and republicanism.
[B1180] Virago pbk **£3.95**

BOGARDE, DIRK (1921 -)
A Particular Friendship   **NEW**
In 1967 Bogarde received a long letter from a complete stranger in the United States. This was the start of a five-year correspondence, during which the two never met. Amongst the wide range of subjects discussed were the house and garden, the state of England. There are also cameo portraits of Vivien Leigh and Dame Edith Evans, amongst others, as well as a description of lunching with the Queen on the day that Robert Kennedy was shot.
[B1181] Viking hbk **£12.95**
A Postillion Struck by Lighting
The first volume of Bogarde's autobiography.
[B1182] Chatto hbk **£12.95**
[B1183] Penguin pbk **£3.50**
Snakes and Ladders
In his second book of autobiography Bogarde covers the years from the Second World War, up to the making of *Death in Venice* in the 1960s. These were years in which he transformed himself from the celebrity matinee idol of the *Doctor* films, into a great screen actor. He describes his friendships with Elizabeth Taylor, Jean Simmons and Judy Garland.
[B1189] Chatto pbk **£12.95**
[B1190] Penguin pbk **£3.99**
An Orderly Man
The third volume of Bogarde's memoirs describes the 15 years in which he has been living in an old farm house in Provence. He gives accurate portraits of acquaintances such as Visconti and Fassbinder.
[B1184] Chatto hbk **£12.95**
[B1185] Grafton pbk **£2.95**
Back Cloth
In this moving final volume of autobiography, Bogarde explores the patterns of pain and happiness that have made up his life since childhood.
[B1186] Viking hbk **£12.95**
[B1187] Penguin pbk **£3.99**
Omnibus: The Complete Autobiography
[B1188] Methuen hbk **£9.95**

BRANAGH, KENNETH
Beginning   **NEW**
Branagh is one of the most versatile and dynamic actors alive, whose performances with the RSC have included the youngest-ever Henry V. This passionate and forthright book tells of his youth in Belfast, his training at RADA and his astonishingly varied acting life, including his key relationship with the Renaissance Company.
[B1191] Chatto hbk **£12.95**

BRANDO, MARLON (1924 -)
CAREY, GARY
Marlon Brando: The Only Contender
[B1192] Hodder pbk **£2.50**
HIGHAM, CHARLES
Brando: The Unauthorized Biography
Higham investigates Brando's private life: his many affairs, marriages, the struggle for custody of his son, and his gay experiences.
[B1193] Grafton pbk **£3.99**
SHIPMAN
Marlon Brando
[B1194] Sphere pbk **£3.50**

BRANSON, RICHARD
BROWN, MICK
Richard Branson: The Inside Story
Mick Brown, *Sunday Times* journalist, looks at the uneven career of the tone-deaf son of a judge, who began Virgin Records, the first company to go public after the Big Bang.
[B1195] Headline pbk **£4.99**

BRITTAIN, VERA
Testament of Youth
In 1914 Vera Brittain won a scholarship to Oxford, but she abandoned her studies to go to work as a nurse in the First World War, throughout which she served. This moving 1933 autobiography tells of her provincial life as a girl in pre-1914 England, and of the horrors of the war that followed, in which she lost her lover, her brother and her closest friends.
[B1200] Virago pbk **£5.99**
Testament of Friendship
Vera Brittain's friendship with the novelist Winifred Holtby helped her survive the traumatic post-war years. This book records the close friendship of these two courageous women up until Winifred's untimely death at the age of 37.
[B1199] Virago pbk **£5.99**
Testament of Experience
Vera Brittain records her later years, during which she was a passionate and influential feminist, pacifist and author, constantly campaigning and writing.
[B1198] Virago pbk **£5.99**
Testament of a Peace Lover
A collection of courageous letters to peace campaigners during the Second World War.
[B1201] Virago pbk **£6.95**
Chronicle of Youth: War Diary 1913 - 1917
[B1197] Gollancz hbk **£16.95**
Chronicle of Friendship: Diaries of the Thirties 1932 - 1939
[B1196] Gollancz hbk **£16.95**
Wartime Chronicle: Diaries 1939 - 1945
(Ed. Bishop & Bennett)
Brittain's diary covers the period during the Second World War when she was a housewife, a pacifist and an enthusiastic writer of letters and articles. She gives some memorable descriptions of running the gauntlet of the Blitz, and of the fear she experienced when she heard a doodle-bug cut out.
[B1202] Gollancz hbk **£16.95**
BAILEY, HILARY
Vera Brittain
A sensitive appraisal for the general reader, of Vera Brittain's life up to the Second World War. It focuses on her struggle to achieve spiritual and intellectual autonomy.
[B1203] Penguin pbk **£3.95**
BERRY, PAUL & BOSTRIDGE, MARK
Vera Brittain: A Life   **NEW**
This first full-length biography of Brittain is written with the co-operation of her daughter Shirley Williams. It draws extensively on unpublished material to throw light on her harrowing First World War experiences and her friendship with Winifred Holtby.
[B1204] Chatto hbk **£16.95**

BROOK, PETER
The Shifting Point
Brook, described as 'the last authentic *enfant terrible* of stagecraft' by Kenneth Tynan, assesses the lessons of his pioneering work, from his brilliant début at Stratford and the West End in the 1960s, to the recent triumphant success of *The Mahabharata*.
[B1205] Methuen hbk **£14.95**
[B1206] Methuen pbk **£5.99**

BROOKS, LOUISE
Lulu in Hollywood
[B1207] H Hamilton pbk **£6.95**
JACCARD, ROLAND (ED)
Louise Brooks: Portrait of an Anti-Star
Brooks was one of the first actresses to turn her back on Hollywood's 'epic pretence'. This highly-illustrated book contains her own lucid reflections, which powerfully evoke the life of the undisputed queen of German expressionist cinema.
[B1208] Harrap pbk **£9.95**
PARIS, BARRY
Louise Brooks: Her Life, Death and Resurrection   **NEW**
The first full-length biography of one of the most beautiful women of the century, who shot to stardom with Ziegfeld's *Follies*, and became a symbol of defiant sexual liberation. At the peak of her fame, she threw away her film career and disappeared for a quarter of a century into a poverty-stricken, alcoholic existence. This lavishly-illustrated book utilises

Brooks' diaries and astonishing private correspondence to reveal much behind this cult actress.
[B1209] H Hamilton hbk **£25.00**

BRYNNER, YUL
BRYNNER, ROCK
Yul NEW
The dramatic story of Yul Brynner, who died of cancer nine months after declaring that he defeated the disease. The book also provides a moving account of Rock Brynner's love-hate relationship with his father.
[B1210] Collins hbk **£15.00**

BUNUEL, LUIS
My Last Breath
Reflections on a lifetime of film-making, as witty, cantankerous and unforgiving as the films themselves. Contains some wonderful anecdotes of Buñuel's early surrealist days with Dali and a truly inspirational recipe for the perfect dry martini.
[B1211] Fontana pbk **£4.95**

BURTON, RICHARD (1925 - 1985)
Burton was one of the greatest Shakespearean actors of his day, and became one of the most memorable screen performers of the century. He is also remembered for his tortuous relationship with Elizabeth Taylor, which came to a glorious artistic apex in *Who's Afraid of Virginia Woolf?*
BRAGG, MELVYN
Rich: The Life of Richard Burton
A gripping re-assessment of Burton, based on Bragg's extensive research into the actor's private papers. They reveal a man of exceptional qualities who suffered crippling melancholy and illness. Bragg says of Burton: *"He was a revelation to me. I think his achievements have been severely underrated, as both an artist and as a man."*
[B1212] Hodder hbk **£15.00**
FERRIS, PAUL
Richard Burton
[B1213] Hodder pbk **£2.50**
JENKINS, GRAHAM
Richard Burton: My Brother
With an introduction by Elizabeth Taylor. This is a controversial recent biography written by Burton's embittered younger brother.
[B1214] M Joseph hbk **£12.95**
JUNOR, PEGGY
Burton: The Man Behind the Myth
[B1215] Sphere pbk **£3.50**

BURTON, SIR RICHARD (1829 - 1900)
Victorian explorer, soldier, anthropologist and outstanding linguist who had a lifelong interest in erotic behaviour and literature.
BRODIE, FAWN M.
The Devil Drives: The Life of Sir Richard Burton
[B1216] Eland pbk **£6.95**
FARWELL, BYRON
Burton: A Life of Sir Richard Francis Burton NEW
A reissue of an acclaimed 1963 biography of the elusive explorer, which presents him as an eccentric who went on journeys that seldom reached a goal, who wrote books that had no market, and who had interests that led his wife to burn his papers.
[B1217] Viking hbk **£17.95**

BUSCETTA, THOMASO
YOUNG, MARTIN & SHAWCROSS, TIM
Men of Honour: The Confessions of Thomaso Buscetta
The memoirs of a high-ranking member of the Mafia who broke silence.
[B1218] Collins hbk **£12.95**

CALLAS, MARIA
CALLAS, JACKIE
Sisters NEW
Maria Callas was one of the century's greatest opera stars, a woman who gave much life to the art form, and gained for herself fame, wealth and public attention. But she suffered a price: a failed affair with Onassis, family trauma and loneliness. Her sister Jackie knew her intimately through these times, and she here provides an intimate and poignant portait of the great singer.
[B1219] Macmillan hbk **£14.95**

CALLOW, SIMON
Being an Actor
The versatile and energetic actor, director, playwright and writer describes the profession he loves and his life in it.
[B1220] Methuen hbk **£9.95**
[B1221] Penguin pbk **£4.50**

CAMERON, JAMES (1911 - 1985)
Cameron in 'The Guardian' 1974 - 84
[B1222] Grafton pbk **£3.50**
Point of Departure
James Cameron was pre-eminent amongst post-war journalists, having covered many of the major crises and events, from Bikini Atoll to Korea and Vietnam. His humorous and passionate autobiography tells the story of a man dedicated to the cause of humanity, written by one who saw many of its least attractive sides.
[B1223] Grafton pbk **£2.95**

CAMPBELL, MRS PAT (1865 - 1940)
PETERS, MARGOT
Mrs Pat: The Life of Mrs Patrick Campbell
Mrs Patrick Campbell was one of the first 'actress-managers', running her own repertory company. She was damned by many, however, because she presented such suspiciously modern playwrights as Ibsen, Bjornson and Maeterlinck. This superb biography captures the magnetism of this extraordinary woman.
[B1224] H Hamilton pbk **£7.95**

CAPRA, FRANK
MCBRIDE, FRANK
American Madness: The Life of Frank Capra NEW
A life of one of the greatest directors of Hollywood's golden age, which describes his immigration with his parents from Sicily, his hard childhood and his early persistent ambition.
[B1225] H Hamilton hbk **£25.00**

CARRINGTON, DORA
GERZINA, GRETCHEN NEW
Carrington: A Life of Dora Carrington
Early on the morning of March 11, 1932, Dora Carrington shot herself. Lytton Strachey, with whom she had a traumatic, unrequited relationship, had died a few weeks earlier. This excellent biography, the product of a number of years' research, examines the life of this mysterious painter, for whom both Aldous Huxley and D.H. Lawrence felt a profound attraction. Gerzina details her life both through her work and through her relationships with other members of the Bloomsbury Group.
[B1226] J Murray hbk **£17.95**

CATER, FRANK
TULLETT, TOM & CATER, FRANK
The Sharp End: Inside Scotland Yard's Flying Squad
The story of Frank Cater and his investigations into armed robbery, including the Brinks Mat robbery.
[B1227] Bodley hbk **£12.95**

Self-portrait by **Dora Carrington** from *Carrington: A Life of Dora Carrington* by Gretchen Gerzina (John Murray hbk £17.95)

CHALIAPIN, FEODOR (1873 - 1938)
BOROVSKY, VICTOR
Chaliapin
Chaliapin was one of the greatest operatic basses of the 20th century, as well as being an actor of great power, who developed a style of acting which was later to influence Stanislavsky and succeeding generations. This is an exhaustive, superbly illustrated biography.
[B1228] H Hamilton hbk **£20.00**
GORKY, MAXIM
Chaliapin
This fascinating account of the great Russian bass was told to his friend, the novelist Maxim Gorky. It tells of his early deprivation and subsequent progress to worldwide acclaim as an opera singer.
[B1229] Columbus pbk **£6.95**

CHANEL, COCO
CHARLES-ROUX, EDMOND
Chanel
An entertaining and gossipy life of the great fashion legend, a woman who revolutionised the way women looked. The book reveals the contradictions and confusions of her life, and her relationships with the Duke of Westminster, Stravinsky and Sam Goldwyn.
[B1230] Collins pbk **£7.95**
KENNETT, FRANCES
Coco: The Life and Loves of Gabrielle Chanel NEW
A sumptuously illustrated biography of the woman described by George Bernard Shaw as one of the *'two most influential women of the 20th century'*.
[B1231] Gollancz hbk **£16.95**

CHAPLIN, CHARLIE (1889 - 1977)
Autobiography
Chaplin tells his life story, from his poverty-stricken youth in London, to his Hollywood career. He describes acquaintances such as Randolph Hearst and Mahatma Gandhi, and ends with his marriage to Oona, daughter of Eugene O'Neill, describing their life together in Switzerland.
[B1232] Penguin pbk **£5.99**

BESSY, MAURICE
Charlie Chaplin
[B1233] Thames & H hbk **£20.00**
EPSTEIN, JERRY
Remembering Charlie   NEW
A first-hand account of Chaplin's turbulent
later years in Hollywood and Switzerland. The book
also includes a host of previously unpublished
photographs.
[B1234] Bloomsbury hbk **£20.00**
ROBINSON, DAVID
Chaplin: His Life and Art
An acclaimed biography which examines the way in
which Chaplin revolutionized the language of the
cinema. Robinson looks at how Chaplin's films drew
on his experience of immigrants and the urban poor,
and the way in which he utilised images from his own
childhood in the slums of Victorian Lambeth. This is
the only biography written with access to the Chaplin
archives.
[B1235] Collins hbk **£15.00**
[B1236] Grafton pbk **£8.95**

CHARLES, PRINCE OF WALES (1948 -)
CATHCART, HELEN
Charles: A Man of Destiny
An intimate biography by a long-term friend and
royal spokesperson, which follows Charles through
school and university, up to the present day.
[B1237] WH Allen hbk **£11.95**
HOLDEN, ANTHONY
Charles: A Biography
A much more interesting royal biography than is
usual, with Holden arguing that Charles is carving out
for himself a substantial role in a society where the
constitution fails to give him one.
[B1238] Weidenfeld hbk **£12.95**
[B1239] Fontana pbk **£3.95**
JUNOR, PENNY
Charles
[B1240] Pan pbk **£3.99**
MARTIN, RALPH GUY
Charles & Diana
[B1241] Grafton pbk **£6.95**

CHASE, TRUDI
When Rabbit Howls
The autobiography of Trudi Chase, a multiple
personality whose brain and body are inhabited by
over 90 different spirits. According to her doctor, she
will never find peace until these conflicting voices are
identified and reconciled with each other.
[B1242] Pan pbk **£3.99**

CHAUDHURI, NIRAD C. (1897 -)
A Passage to England
In 1955 Chaudhuri visited England for five weeks,
during which he delved into every crevice of English
life with great energy and pugnacity. Amongst the
highlights were a view of Churchill in the Commons
looking like a Toby-jug, and a visit to see the swans
on the Avon.
[B1243] Hogarth pbk **£5.95**
Autobiography of an Unknown Indian
[B1244] Hogarth pbk **£7.95**
**Thy Hand, Great Anarch!: India
1921 - 1952**
Chaudhuri's acclaimed self-portrait combines a
touching account of his private life with a sweeping
survey of Indian and Bengali politics in the years
leading up to Independence.
[B1245] Chatto hbk **£25.00**
[B1246] Hogarth pbk **£9.95**

CHIN, TSAI
Daughter of Shanghai
Autobiography of the Chinese actress who shot to
stardom in the 1960s through the musical *The World
According to Susie Wong*. Daughter of China's

greatest classical actor, she here chronicles her life
from her childhood in China to the present day,
including her time at RADA and her affair with
Kenneth Tynan.
[B1247] Chatto hbk **£12.95**

CLARE, GEORGE
Berlin Days   NEW
Clare writes about his service as a British Army
Officer in the Allied Commission in Berlin in 1946-7.
He portrays a city stunned by bombings and numbed
by defeat. Clare faces the larger question of how and
why was it possible for a nation to methodically
organise the destruction of the Jewish race.
[B1248] Macmillan hbk **£12.95**
Last Waltz in Vienna
The Destruction of a Family 1842-1942.
[B1249] Pan pbk **£2.95**

CLARK, KENNETH (1903 - 1983)
Another Part of the Wood
The great art historian's witty account of his eccentric
Edwardian upbringing and his success after leaving
Oxford.
[B1250] H Hamilton pbk **£4.95**
The Other Half
Clark continues his autobiography from the outbreak
of World War II to his outstanding achievement as
presenter of the TV series *Civilisation*.
[B1251] H Hamilton pbk **£6.95**
SECREST, MERYLE
Kenneth Clark
Written with Lord Clark's co-operation, this
biography describes the making of his brilliant
television series *Civilisation*, as well as his time as
Director of the National Gallery and as Chairman of
the Arts Council.
[B1252] Weidenfeld pbk **£5.95**

COBB, RICHARD (1917 -)
Still Life: A Tunbridge Wells Childhood
Cobb looks back to Tunbridge Wells in the 1920s and
1930s, showing a prosperous community, with its
middle classes and armies of servants and
shopkeepers.
[B1256] Hogarth pbk **£5.95**
A Classical Education
A bizarre blend of autobiography and entertainment,
with a brutal and bloody murder at its centre.
[B1253] Penguin pbk **£3.50**
**Something to Hold Onto:
Autobiographical Sketches**
In the third part of his engaging and acclaimed
memoirs, the distinguished Oxford historian begins in
the Colchester of his grandparents, moves through
years of research in Paris, to South Carolina, where he
was a visiting professor.
[B1255] J Murray hbk **£12.95**
People and Places
A collection of articles and reviews written over the
last 10 years. It includes recollections of old universty
friends such as Jack Gallagher and Christopher Hill,
as well as essays on authors and historians such as
Pierre Loti, Georges Lefevre and Georges Simenon.
[B1254] Oxford pbk **£4.95**

COFFEY, MARIA
Fragile Edge   NEW
The powerul and moving story of how Maria Coffey
retraced the last steps of her lover, climber Joe Tasker,
on his final journey up Mount Everest. It took her
through Tibetan villages and 21,000 feet up Everest.
[B1257] Chatto hbk **£12.95**

COHN, ROY
HOFFMAN, NICHOLAS VON
Citizen Cohn
Cohn was known as the toughest, most brilliant, and
most notorious lawyer in America. This biography

looks at his role as chief counsel to Senator Joseph
McCarthy during the senate hearings, and his
extraordinary friendship with J. Edgar Hoover, during
the latter's vendetta against Robert F. Kennedy, as
well as his secretive homosexuality.
[B1258] Harrap hbk **£12.95**

COLLINS, JOAN
Past Imperfect: Autobiography
[B1259] Hodder pbk **£3.99**
COLLINS, JOE
**A Touch of Collins: The Story of a
Showbusiness Dynasty**
[B1260] Headline pbk **£2.95**

COOKE, ALISTAIR
Six Men
The six men profiled by the pre-eminent journalist
and broadcaster are: Charlie Chaplin, Edward VIII,
H.L. Mencken, Adlai Stevenson, Humphrey Bogart
and Bertrand Russell.
[B1261] Penguin pbk **£3.99**

COPPOLA, FRANCIS FORD
COWIE, PETER
Coppola   NEW
The first major portrait of Coppola who, at the
age of 32, became a superstar in Hollywood with *The
Godfather*, and subsequently went on to make the
box-office smash *Apocalypse Now*. Cowie goes
behind the scenes to trace the creative and financial
turmoil involved in Coppola's films.
[B1262] Deutsch hbk **£15.95**

COTTEN, JOSEPH (1905 -)
**Vanity Will Get You Somewhere: An
Autobiography**
Orson Welles once said to Joseph Cotten: *"I'm afraid
you'll never make it as an actor. But as a star, I think
you might well hit the jackpot."* Cotten's early film
roles in *Citizen Kane* and *The Third Man* confirm
this. His generous, humorous portrait of himself is
both frank and revealing.
[B1263] Columbus hbk **£10.95**

COWARD, NOEL (1899 - 1973)
Autobiography
Introduced by Sheridan Morley, this contains the two
volumes of autobiography which Coward published
in his lifetime: *Present Laughter* and *Future
Indefinite*, as well as a portion of the third
unpublished volume, *Past Conditional*.
[B1264] Methuen hbk **£15.00**
Noël Coward Diaries
[B1265] Macmillan pbk **£11.95**
LESLEY, COLE
Life of Noël Coward
The definitive biography.
[B1266] Penguin pbk **£5.95**
LESLEY, COLE; GRAHAM, PAYN & MORLEY,
SHERIDAN
Noël Coward and his Friends
[B1267] Weidenfeld pbk **£8.95**
MORLEY, SHERIDAN
**A Talent to Amuse: Biography of Noël
Coward**
[B1268] Pavilion pbk **£9.95**

CRAWFORD, JOAN
WALKER, ALEXANDER
Joan Crawford
[B1269] Weidenfeld hbk **£12.50**
WAYNE, JAYNE ELLEN
**Crawford's Men: The Private Life
of Joan Crawford**   NEW
A new biography which offers some startling
revelations about Joan Crawford's relationships with
men such as Clark Gable and Douglas Fairbanks Jr.
[B1270] Robson hbk **£12.95**

CRISP, QUENTIN
The Naked Civil Servant
Crisp's funny, and frequently poignant, memoirs, speak revealingly of his homosexuality.
[B1271] Duckworth hbk **£9.95**
[B1272] Fontana pbk **£2.95**

CUNARD, NANCY
CHISHOLM
Nancy Cunard
Lady Cunard was a celebrated London literary hostess of the inter-war years: this biography tells of her varied life, and of the many artists she sponsored and lionised.
[B1273] Penguin pbk **£4.95**

CUSHING, PETER (1913 -)
An Autobiography
Cushing is best-known for his association with Hammer House horror films. His autobiography reveals him to be a gentle man, untainted by vampires and demons.
[B1274] Weidenfeld pbk **£5.95**
Past Forgetting
Memoirs of the Hammer Horror years and a sequel to his bestselling autobiography.
[B1275] Weidenfeld hbk **£9.95**

CUTTING, PAULINE
Children of the Siege
The moving story of the involvement of a British doctor in Beirut Palestinian refugee camps, and of the terrible conditions found there.
[B1276] Pan pbk **£3.50**

DALI, SALVADOR
MCGIRK, TIM
Wicked Lady: Salvador Dali's Muse `NEW`
The story of the extraordinary relationship between Gala and Salvador Dali. When they met she dragged him back from the edge of madness - during their 50 years together she nursed him through illnesses both real and imaginary. When Parkinson's disease prevented him from painting, she commissioned other artists to produce fakes in order to pay their enormous bills. She appears in hundreds of his paintings, yet she constantly cuckolded him: the story of their relationship sheds much light on the work of the great surrealist painter.
[B1277] Hutchinson hbk **£16.95**

DANIELS, LEROY
Tales of an Old Horse `NEW`
Memoirs by a 108-year old American pioneer.
[B1278] Carcanet hbk **£12.95**

DARLING, GRACE
MITFORD, JESSICA
Grace Had an English Heart `NEW`
The story of Grace Darling, who became a Victorian heroine when she and her father rescued nine survivors from the wrecked steamer *Forfarshire* off the Northumberland coast.
[B1279] Viking hbk **£14.95**

DARWIN, CHARLES (1809 - 1882)
Autobiography and Selected Letters
[B1280] Dover pbk **£5.35**
Correspondence: Vol 1 1821 - 1836
[B1281] Cambridge hbk **£32.50**
Correspondence: Vol 2 1837 - 1843
[B1282] Cambridge hbk **£30.00**
Correspondence: Vol 3 1844 - 1846
[B1283] Cambridge hbk **£30.00**
Correspondence: Vol 4 1847 - 1850
The latest volume of Darwin's correspondence shows him making exciting zoological discoveries in the relatively small field in which he was working. He continues his research on cirripedos and corresponds vigorously with fellow scientists. Throughout Darwin is both charming and accessible.
[B1284] Cambridge hbk **£32.50**
CLARK, RONALD W.
Survival of Charles Darwin
[B1285] Weidenfeld hbk **£14.95**

DASHWOOD, FRANCIS (1708 - 1781)
The Dashwoods of West Wycombe
West Wycombe was created by the 2nd Baronet, Sir Francis Dashwood. This energetic and fun-loving man is probably best known for having founded the Hell-Fire Club, whose revels at Medmenham Abbey, attended by John Wilkes, caused a minor scandal. Here the present Baronet, Sir Francis, tells the story of his charismatic ancestors.
[B1286] Aurum hbk **£14.95**

DAVIES, SCROPE
BURNETT, T.A.J.
The Rise and Fall of a Regency Dandy
[B1287] Oxford pbk **£3.50**

DAVIS, BETTE (1908 -)
This'n'That
Bette Davis, who has had to endure an ungrateful account of her life by her own daughter, puts the record straight about the pivotal moments and people in her life. What emerges is a portrait of human disappointment, endurance and survival.
[B1288] Sidgwick hbk **£12.95**
HYMAN, B.D.
My Mother's Keeper
The hostile biography.
[B1289] Sphere pbk **£3.99**
MOSELEY, ROY
Bette Davis: An Intimate Memoir
Roy Moseley, a devoted young admirer of Davis, formed a friendship with Davis that almost led them to the altar. This searching and funny memoir describes the 15 years which he spent with the star, as she filmed, and went to Oscar ceremonies and glittering show business parties.
[B1290] Sidgwick hbk **£12.95**
WALKER, ALEXANDER
Bette Davis: A Celebration
Pays tribute to the qualities which made Davis the personification of Hollywood glamour and bitchery.
[B1291] M Joseph hbk **£12.95**

DAVIS, SAMMY JR
Why Me? `NEW`
Sammy Davis Jr describes his richly varied life, from his birth in Harlem to his comeback in the 'rat-pack' reunion with Frank Sinatra and Dean Martin. He discusses his showbusiness career, beginning when he shared a vaudeville act with his father at the age of three. He also recalls the excesses and struggles of his life and his friendships with Martin Luther King and Jesse Jackson.
[B1292] M Joseph hbk **£14.95**

DAY, SIR ROBIN
Grand Inquisitor: Memoirs `NEW`
The foremost interviewer of the televison age describes his youth, his Oxford days, and his experiences as a barrister. He goes on to reveal how he made his way into television and how he made his name in the newly founded ITN. He recalls standing for Parliament, how he joined BBC's *Panorama* and his titanic clashes with six Prime Ministers.
[B1293] Weidenfeld hbk **£14.95**

DE SOUZA, DANIEL
Under a Crescent Moon
De Souza's account of his experiences in a Turkish prison where mass murderers and petty crooks rubbed shoulders.
[B1294] Serpent's Tail pbk **£5.95**

DEAN, JAMES (1931 - 1955)
Dean is still a much mythologised actor, and his image has often tended to obscure his genuine talent. His most powerful roles may be seen in *Rebel without a Cause* and *East of Eden*. His life was cut short in a car accident at the age of 24.
HOSKYNS, BARNEY
Jimmy Dean, Jimmy Dean `NEW`
An intelligent assessment of Dean's life and career, which seeks to explain why he reached the status of an icon and why his image is so important.
[B1295] Bloomsbury hbk **£16.95**
SCHATT, ROY
James Dean: A Portrait
A memoir as well as a photographic tribute to the special relationship between Dean and photographer Roy Schatt.
[B1296] Sidgwick pbk **£8.95**

DENCH, JUDI (1934 -)
Dench is one of the most outstanding English actresses of her generation, particularly notable for her magnificent performance in *Macbeth*, which she played with Ian McKellen, and a memorable Cleopatra at the National Theatre.
JACOBS, GERALD
Judi Dench: A Great Deal of Laughter
[B1297] Futura pbk **£1.95**

DEVAS, NICOLETTE
Devas's real father was Francis MacNamara, her adopted father was Augustus John: here are her tales of bohemian life.
Two Flamboyant Fathers
[B1298] H Hamilton pbk **£4.95**

DIAGHILEV, SERGEI (1872 - 1929)
Russian impresario of genius who founded the Ballet Russe company, which he directed until his death. He was responsible for bringing together an exceptionally talented group of artists, including Picasso, Matisse, Stravinsky, Ravel, Cocteau, Nijinsky and Chaliapin.
BUCKLE, RICHARD
Diaghilev
[B1299] H Hamilton pbk **£8.95**
SOKOLOVA, LYDIA
Dancing for Diaghilev
The moving story of an English girl who became a star of the Russian ballet.
[B1300] Columbus pbk **£5.95**

DIANA, PRINCESS OF WALES (1961 -)
BATTISCOMBE, GEORGINA
The Spencers of Althorp
The first known ancestors of the Princess of Wales were sheep farmers, and Althorp came into the family when successive John Spencers first tenanted and then brought the property at the end of the 15th century. This book describes the many ancestors of this prestigious family.
[B1301] Constable pbk **£6.95**
COURTNEY, NICHOLAS
Sisters-in-Law
[B1302] Futura pbk **£3.50**
SEWARD, INGRID
Diana
Seward knows Diana and her friends and she here looks at the woman and mother behind the public image.
[B1303] Grafton pbk **£3.99**

DIETRICH, MARLENE (1902 -)
My Life `NEW`
The great actress's autobiography begins with her childhood in war-torn Berlin, and moves on to her career in Hollywood, where she met and worked with Charlie Chaplin, Alfred Hitchcock and Orson Welles.
[B1304] Weidenfeld hbk **£12.95**

DISNEY, WALT (1901 - 1966)
MOSLEY, LEONARD
The Real Walt Disney
[B1305] Futura pbk **£3.95**
SCHICKEL, RICHARD
The Disney Version: The Life, Times, Art and Commerce of Walt Disney
[B1306] M Joseph hbk **£12.95**

DOUGLAS, KIRK (1916 -) **NEW**
The Ragman's Son: An Autobiography
Douglas was born into brutal poverty, the son of a Russian-Jewish ragman. In his revelatory autobiography he tells of his desire to succeed as an actor, and of the women in his life, such as Lauren Bacall and Marlene Dietrich.
[B1307] Simon & Schuster hbk **£14.95**
[B1308] Pan pbk **£3.99**

DU MAURIER, GERALD
HARDING, JAMES
Gerald du Maurier **NEW**
Gerald du Maurier entranced West End theatre audiences as the manager of Wyndham's Theatre, where his leading ladies included Mrs Patrick Campbell, Gladys Cooper, Tallulah Bankhead and Gertrude Lawrence. Yet he ended life a bitter and disappointed man. This biography explores why this was so. It also shows us a golden theatrical age, which ran from the Edwardian era to the twenties. Over it all broods the presence of Sir James Barrie, who gave du Maurier his greatest success with *Peter Pan*.
[B1309] Hodder hbk **£15.00**

DUCHESS OF YORK
MORTON, ANDREW
Duchess
The first biography of 'Fergie', the Duchess of York, shows how Sarah has changed from a woman hurt and alone, to a popular public figure, who has achieved a remarkable series of feats, including learning to fly planes and helicopters.
[B1310] O'Mara hbk **£10.95**

DUVEEN, JOSEPH (1869 - 1939)
Art dealer to the super-rich, in a collaboration with Bernard Berenson now seen as dubious. A significant benefactor of the national collections, he paid for the gallery which houses the Elgin Marbles.
BEHRMAN, S.N.
Duveen
[B1311] Deutsch pbk **£3.95**

DYLAN, BOB
SPITZ, BOB
Dylan: A Biography **NEW**
An above-average biography (there have been many below) of the self-styled guru of rock, who has deliberately fashioned for himself a shroud of mystery and obscurity. Spitz penetrates these obfuscations and portrays Dylan in his many guises: as rebel, poet, musical innovator, cultural demagogue and Christian fundamentalist.
[B1312] M Joseph hbk **£16.95**

EBERHARDT, ISABELLE
KOBAK, ANNETTE
Isabelle: A Biography of Isabelle Eberhardt **NEW**
The daughter of a Russian aristocrat, Isabelle Eberhardt dressed up as an Arab boy in the North African desert, joined a mystical Muslim sect and threw herself into Arab culture. Her writings are suffused with an Eastern sense of fate and personal destiny. This biography is based on Eberhardt's own diaries and a mass of previously unpublished letters.
[B1313] Chatto hbk **£14.95**

EDWARDS, ROBERT (1925 -)
Goodbye Fleet Street
An illuminating look at the newspaper world from one of its living legends. Edwards started out as a journalist just after the end of the Second World War. During his career he has been involved in several major controversies, amongst them his refusal to write leaders in support of the government during the Suez Crisis. He also put the head of Scotland Yard's Flying Squad behind bars and insisted that Lady Diana Spencer had visited Prince Charles on the Royal Train. His autobiography also contains portraits of the press barons he has known, such as Lord Beaverbrook and Robert Maxwell.
[B1314] Cape hbk **£12.95**
[B1315] Hodder pbk **£3.99**

EINSTEIN, ALBERT (1879 - 1955)
Nobel Prize-winning mathematician and physicist who published his revolutionary General Theory of Relativity in 1916. The consequences of his experiments in atomic energy are well known, though he campaigned passionately for international control of atomic weapons.
HOFFMANN, BANESH
Albert Einstein
[B1316] Grafton pbk **£3.95**
PAIS, ABRAHAM
Subtle is the Lord: The Science and Life of Albert Einstein
Pais is an award-winning scientist who knew Einstein during the last nine years of his life. His major scientific biography draws on unpublished papers and personal recollections.
[B1317] Oxford pbk **£8.95**

EISENSTEIN, SERGEI (1898 - 1948)
Immoral Memories: An Autobiography
The great eccentric Russian film pioneer, maker of masterpieces such as *The Battleship Potemkin* and *Ivan the Terrible*, wrote his autobiography in 1946, two years before his death. Its style is reminiscent of the montage effect he used in the cinema. He describes his life in Russia from the time of the Revolution, when he was a Bolshevik soldier, and his visits to the West, when he met such luminaries as Chaplin, Garbo and James Joyce.
[B1318] P Owen hbk **£20.00**
[B1319] P Owen pbk **£11.95**
SETON
Sergei Eisenstein: A Biography
[B1320] Dobson hbk **£17.50**

EVANS, HAROLD (1928 -)
Crusading journalist and former editor of *The Times*.
Good Times, Bad Times
[B1321] Hodder pbk **£3.50**

EVERAGE, DAME EDNA
My Gorgeous Life **NEW**
Dame Edna reveals all, including: how I met my future bridesmaid Madge Allsop; how I met Norm (was he the first?). Dame Edna says: *"I hope this publication does not cause me to lose my mystery but it is my way of saying 'thank you' to Dame Nature for making me a megastar. Buying it, reading it, and adoring it will be your way of saying 'thank you' to me"*. And there's more...
[B1322] Macmillan hbk **£12.95**

FEYNMAN, RICHARD P.
'What Do You Care What Other People Think?' **NEW**
Feynman, who died of cancer in 1988, was one of the greatest physicists of the 20th century. This book is partly a memoir of his father and his wife, and partly a behind-the-scenes account of the investigation following the space shuttle accident in 1986. We relive the moment when the cause of the 'Challenger' accident was revealed through a simple experiment, as Feynman dropped a rubber ring into a glass of cold water and pulled it out misshapen.
[B1323] Unwin Hyman hbk **£11.95**
'Surely You're Joking Mr Feynman!'
[B1323] Unwin Hyman pbk **£3.95**

FLEMING, PETER
Intrepid traveller (from the Brazilian jungle to Central Asia), also *Spectator* columnist and husband of the actress Celia Johnson.
HART-DAVIS, DUFF
Peter Fleming
[B1324] Oxford pbk **£5.95**

FORRESTER, HELEN (1920 -)
Forrester was brought up in Liverpool but now lives in America. She has written a popular series of memoirs of her poverty-stricken childhood in Liverpool during the Depression.
By the Waters of Liverpool
[B1325] Fontana pbk **£2.75**
Lime Street at Two
[B1326] Fontana pbk **£2.95**
Liverpool Miss
[B1327] Fontana pbk **£2.50**
Twopence to Cross the Mersey
[B1328] Fontana pbk **£2.50**

FOTHERGILL, JOHN
An Innkeeper's Diary
First published in 1931, but out of print for more than 30 years. Fothergill describes running the Spreadeagle in Thame, near Oxford, which was a mecca for the rich, powerful and famous. Fothergill was a provocative character and he shows his skills as a raconteur in recounting the many anecdotes from a bygone age.
[B1329] Faber pbk **£5.95**

FOUNTAINE, MARGARET (1882 - 1940)
Explorer and naturalist, particularly intrepid considering the restricted lives led by women of her generation.
Love Among the Butterflies
The Travels and Adventures of a Victorian Lady.
[B1330] Penguin pbk **£2.95**
Butterflies and Late Loves
Further Adventures of Margaret Fountaine.
[B1331] Collins hbk **£9.95**

FOX, ANGELA
Slightly Foxed by My Theatrical Family
[B1333] Fontana pbk **£2.95**
Completely Foxed **NEW**
The sequel to *Slightly Foxed* begins with the death of Angela's husband of 37 years, the theatre impresario Robin Fox. Through the painful years of widowhood she shows resilience, a quality reinforced by the support of her sons Edward, James and Robert, as well as friends like Dirk Bogarde and Rex Harrison.
[B1332] Collins hbk **£12.95**

FRANK, ANNE (1929 - 1945)
The tale of Anne Frank, who hid with her family from the Nazis, in a house in Amsterdam, is well known. After two years, 1942 - 1944, they were betrayed and sent to concentration camps, where Anne died. Anne's diary records the life of a normal middle class family coping under intolerable strain. It is a remarkable, moving and mature document, which traces in revealing detail, the emotional and physical problems of an adolescence spent in real and spiritual confinement.
The Diary of Anne Frank
[B1335] Pan pbk **£2.99**
Tales from the Secret Annexe
[B1334] Penguin pbk **£2.50**

FRASER, EUGENIE
The House by the Dvina: A Russian Childhood
A moving account of Russia before, during and after the Revolution. It tells the fascinating story of two families bound together by a Russian-Scottish marriage, and the purchase by the author's great grandfather of a Russian peasant girl.
[B1336] Corgi pbk **£3.95**

FRENCH, DOLORES
Working: My Life as a Prostitute NEW
Dolores French has worked as a prostitute for 10 years, since the age of 27. She loves her job but, incensed by the prejudices and injustices of the work, she campaigns and lectures on prostitutes' rights. She is married to a criminal defence lawyer.
[B1337] Gollancz hbk **£12.95**

FREUD, ANNA
YOUNG-BREUHL, ELISABETH
Anna Freud: A Biography NEW
When Anna Freud died in 1982 she left behind four trunks full of correspondence, manuscripts, dream interpretations and photographs. Elisabeth Young-Breuhl was granted access to this remarkable material in order to write an unparalleled account of the psychological and intellectual development of the youngest of the Freud children.
[B1338] Macmillan hbk **£18.95**

FREUD, SIGMUND (1856 - 1939)
GAY, PETER
Freud: A Life in Our Time
There is little that one could add to this massive, scholarly and engrossing one-volume biography of Freud. Gay gives a good overview of the working lives of early psychoanalysts, as well as a clear analysis of the details of Freud's life in a manner that is accessible to the general reader. He pays particular attention to Freud's relationship with Jung, his Jewishness, and is especially revealing on Freud's approach to women.
[B1339] Dent hbk **£16.95**
[B1340] Macmillan pbk **£8.99**
JONES, ERNEST
Life and Work of Sigmund Freud
[B1341] Penguin pbk **£7.99**

GAGE, NICHOLAS
Eleni
In 1948, in a Greek mountain village, Eleni Gatzoyiannis was arrested, tortured and shot. Her crime was that she had helped her children escape the Communist guerrillas during the Greek Civil War. Her son Nicholas Gage reached America, where he became one of the *New York Times*'s best investigative reporters. This passionate book is the result of his return to Greece in 1977. By the end of his search he was ready to confront his mother's executioners and his own memories.
[B1342] Collins pbk **£6.95**

GARRICK, DAVID (1717 - 1779)
A pupil of Dr Johnson at school, Garrick became a playwright, theatre manager and the leading actor of his day.
KENDALL, ALAN
David Garrick: A Biography
[B1343] Harrap hbk **£12.95**

GELDOF, BOB
Is That It?
Geldof's bestselling autobiography describes his childhood in Dublin and the birth of new wave music, in uncompromising terms. He describes the outrageous antics of the early Boomtown Rats, and his uneasy relationship with the press. The most important part of this energetic book, however,

concerns the inception and development of the unprecedented Band Aid and Live Aid charities in 1984/5.
[B1344] Penguin pbk **£4.99**

GIELGUD, JOHN (1904 -)
An Actor and his Time NEW
An updated edition of Gielgud's autobiography. He discusses his life in theatre and film, and the actors and actresses he has known, including James Mason, Marlon Brando, Richard Burton and Elizabeth Taylor. He also recalls the theatre of his youth and the great actor managers such as Tree and du Maurier as well as the star actresses, Eleanora Duse and Sarah Bernhardt.
[B1345] Sidgwick pbk **£9.95**
Backward Glances
A collection of Gielgud's portraits of the actors and actresses he has known, including Dame Edith Evans, Dame Sybil Thorndike and Sir Ralph Richardson.
[B1346] Hodder hbk **£14.95**
Early Stages 1921 - 1936
[B1347] Hodder pbk **£7.95**
HARWOOD, RONALD (ED)
Ages of Gielgud: An Actor at Eighty
[B1348] Hodder hbk **£9.95**
TANITCH, ROBERT
Gielgud
An excellent illustrated survey of Gielgud's career from the 1920s to the present day.
[B1349] Harrap hbk **£14.95**

GINGOLD, HERMIONE
How to Grow Old Disgracefully
[B1350] Gollancz hbk **£12.95**

GINZBURG, EUGENIA
Into the Whirlwind
In 1937 Eugenia Ginzburg was a model Communist, a teacher and a journalist. By 1939, when this volume ends, she had been falsely accused of terrorism and sent to hard labour camps, where she was to remain for 18 years. This book is a remarkable record of her human endurance, which caused a sensation on its publication in the west in 1967.
[B1351] Collins pbk **£7.95**
Within the Whirlwind
A sequel to *Into the Whirlwind*, in which Ginzburg describes falling in love with a doctor and fellow prisoner, and the redeeming joy of their relationship.
[B1352] Collins pbk **£7.95**

GISH, LILLIAN (1896 -)
The Movies, Mr Griffith and Me
Gish's autobiography tells the story of the birth of a great art form, and of one of its founding fathers, D.W. Griffith.
[B1353] Columbus pbk **£6.95**

GLASS, CHARLES
Tribes with Flags NEW
Charles Glass resigned his position as Chief Middle East Correspondent of ABC news in February 1987 to begin work on a book chronicling the land and its people. On 17 June 1987 he was kidnapped by pro-Iranian gunmen and held for 62 days. His daring escape in August made world headlines. This is the story of his involvement with the Middle East, one which gives an intimate portrayal of his life as a hostage.
[B1354] Secker hbk **£14.95**

GLASSER, RALPH
Growing Up in the Gorbals
[B1356] Pan pbk **£3.50**
Gorbals Boy at Oxford NEW
The first volume of Glasser's autobiography ended with Ralph preparing to take up his scholarship at Oxford before the Second World War. In this new

book he evokes the Oxford world of the 'boss class' progressives like Richard Crossman, and the Philip Toynbee circle of Communist 'soul mates'.
[B1355] Pan pbk **£3.95**

GLUCKSTEIN, HANNAH (1895 - 1978)
SOUHAMI, DIANA
Gluck: Her Biography
Born Hannah Gluckstein in 1895, into the family that created the Lyons catering company, Gluck rejected her wealthy background and flouted all conventions by dressing as a man. Her paintings drew considerable acclaim in the 1920s and 30s and a retrospective exhibition in 1973 revived interest in her work. This highly original biography traces her idiosyncratic life and troubled relationships.
[B1357] Pandora hbk **£19.95**

GOLDMAN, WILLY
East End: My Cradle
A re-issue of a much-praised account of Jewish working-class life.
[B1358] Robson hbk **£9.95**

GOLDWYN, SAM (1882 - 1974)
BERG, A. SCOTT
Goldwyn: A Biography NEW
The story of Warsaw-born Schmuel Gelbfisz who walked 500 miles to Hamburg, and from London to Liverpool, on his journey to America, where he became Sam Goldfish and established a company to produce and distribute films, eventually taking the name Sam Goldwyn. This portrait discusses the companies he built up, including MGM, and the actors and directors he discovered and helped, such as John Ford, Gary Cooper, David Niven and Merle Oberon.
[B1359] H Hamilton hbk **£16.95**

GRADE, LEW (1906 -)
Still Dancing
The autobiography of Lord Grade, the dynamic personality who founded Associated Television. The cast of his acquaintances includes Andrew Lloyd Webber, Edith Piaf and Laurence Olivier.
[B1360] Fontana pbk **£3.95**

GRAHAME, GLORIA
TURNER, PETER
Film Stars Don't Die in Liverpool
The story of the last days of Gloria Grahame, written by the man, an ex-lover, to whose home she came in the last stages of the illness which was responsible for her death.
[B1361] Penguin pbk **£2.95**

John Gielgud, author of *An Actor and his Time* (Sidgwick & Jackson pbk £9.95)

GRANT, CARY (1904 - 1986)
Debonair British-born actor, perhaps best known for his screwball comedies of the 1930s (such as *Bringing Up Baby*) and for his work with Alfred Hitchcock, notably *North by Northwest*.
DONALDSON, MAUREEN
An Affair to Remember: My Life with Cary Grant `NEW`
The story of Donaldson's four turbulent but intimate years with Grant, from 1973 to 1977. She reveals something of the mystery and eccentricity of the great man.
[B1362] Macdonald hbk **£12.95**
HIGHAM, CHARLES & MOSELEY, ROY
Cary Grant: The Unauthorised Biography `NEW`
This biography of the elusive actor pieces together aspects of his private life from interviews with Alfred Hitchcock, Mae West, Marlene Dietrich, Walter Matthau, Ingrid Bergman and Ginger Rogers, amongst others. The book reveals much about his tormented private self, as well as his life story from his youth in Bristol as Archibald Leach, the son of an alcoholic suit presser.
[B1363] NEL hbk **£14.95**

GREEN, MICHAEL
The Boy who Shot Down an Airship
The frequently hilarious autobiography of the author of *The Art of Coarse Acting-Drinking-Sailing* books and inventor of Squire Haggard.
[B1364] Bantam pbk **£3.95**

GRENFELL, JOYCE (1910 - 1979)
Darling Ma: Letters to Her Mother in America 1932 - 1944
Entertaining, gossipy and revealing letters from the comedienne to her mother (who was Nancy Astor's sister). They give an intriguing portrait of the English social scene of that time.
[B1365] Hodder hbk **£14.95**
The Time of My Life `NEW`
Beginning where *Darling Ma* left off, this book contains the journal which Joyce kept during the final months of the Second World War whilst travelling with the Entertainments National Service Association. Whether bathing in an inch of water in appalling quarters or dancing with the Aga Khan's playboy in Cairo, Joyce is revealed as a lively observer and raconteur.
[B1369] Hodder hbk **£15.00**
Joyce Grenfell Requests the Pleasure
The first volume of Grenfell's hilarious autobiography.
[B1367] Futura pbk **£3.50**
In Pleasant Places
In her second volume of memoirs, Grenfell describes her Broadway debut and her TV appearance with Elvis Presley.
[B1366] Futura pbk **£3.50**
Turn Back the Clock
[B1370] Futura pbk **£3.50**
Joyce, By Herself and Her Friends
A compilation of memoirs by people who knew the great comedienne.
[B1368] Futura pbk **£2.95**
GRENFELL, JOYCE & MOORE, KATHARINE
An Invisible Friendship: Correspondence 1957 - 1979
This intimate and witty correspondence between Grenfell and her great friend Katharine Moore, which was kept up until Joyce's death.
[B1371] Futura pbk **£3.50**

GRIMALDI, JOSEPH (1778 - 1837)
The creator of the English clown.
FINDLATER, RICHARD
Joe Grimaldi: His Life and Theatre
[B1372] Cambridge pbk **£9.50**

GUGGENHEIM, PEGGY (1898 - 1980)
American art collector, benificent sponsor and connoisseur of the Arts.
Out of This Century: Confessions of an Art Addict
[B1373] Deutsch pbk **£8.95**
WELD, JACQUELINE
Peggy: Wayward Guggenheim
[B1374] Bodley hbk **£15.00**

GUINNESS, ALEC (1914 -)
Blessings in Disguise
Guinness's brilliant and witty autobiography includes remarkable pen portraits of Ralph Richardson, Edith Evans, Sybil Thorndike, John Gielgud, Edith Sitwell and many others. He also writes of his conversion to Catholicism, and his wartime experiences.
[B1375] H Hamilton hbk **£12.95**
[B1376] Fontana pbk **£3.95**
HARWOOD, RONALD (ED)
Dear Alec: Guinness at Seventy-Five `NEW`
A celebration of Guinness's career, including assessments by John Gielgud, Simon Gray, Peggy Ashcroft and Franco Zeffirelli.
[B1377] Hodder hbk **£14.95**
TANITCH, ROBERT
Guinness
This biography gives a full pictorial record of Guinness's career, from the 1930s to the present day.
[B1378] Harrap hbk **£15.95**

GUTHRIE, TYRONE (1900 - 1971)
A Life in the Theatre
The memoirs of one of the 20th century's most important theatrical directors. Guthrie began his long connection with the Old Vic and Sadler's Wells Theatre in 1933, directing Laurence Olivier, Flora Robson and John Gielgud in many of their most memorable performances. He became administrator of both theatres, and was later made Chancellor of Queen's University in Belfast.
[B1379] Columbus pbk **£5.95**

HALDANE, J.B.S. (1892 - 1964)
Unorthodox British biologist, and committed Buddhist.
CLARK, RONALD
The Life and Works of J.B.S. Haldane
[B1380] Oxford pbk **£4.95**

HALL, PETER (1930 -)
Outstanding theatre and opera director, who took over from Olivier as the second Director of the National Theatre. His controversial diaries chronicle much of his time at the National, during which period he came into contact with the major theatrical figures of his generation.
Peter Hall's Diaries
[B1381] H Hamilton pbk **£5.95**

HAMNETT, NINA (1890 - 1956)
Hamnett was an artist and member of London's Bohemian society in the early part of the century. Denise Hooker's biography was a well-received, recent study.
Laughing Torso
[B1382] Virago pbk **£7.50**
HOOKER, DENISE
Nina Hamnett: Queen of Bohemia
[B1383] Constable pbk **£8.95**

HARE, AUGUSTUS (1834 - 1903)
English wit and bon viveur, famed for his classic comic work *Augustus Carp*.
The Years with Mother
A vivid and sometimes indiscreet record of social life in the upper strata of Victorian society.
[B1384] Century pbk **£4.95**

BARNES, MALCOLM
Augustus Hare: Victorian Gentleman
[B1385] Unwin Hyman hbk **£20.00**

HART-DAVIS, RUPERT & LYTTLETON, GEORGE
The celebrated correspondence between retired Eton schoolmaster George Lyttleton and one of his former pupils, publisher Rupert Hart-Davis. The letters between the two are diverse and humorous, covering a large range of serious and trivial subjects. The most interesting pieces occur where the two air their prejudices and opinions on the books they recommend for each other. George Lyttleton thus writes to Rupert Hart-Davis on 9th May 1956:
"The breakfast table this morning had that best of all objects - far better even than a dish of salmon kedgeree, or a headline in The Times *saying the atom bomb had been abolished, or that the price of coal was down - viz a fat little parcel of books...Life has, at all events at 73, no greater pleasure than that."*
The Lyttleton Hart-Davis Letters Vols 1 & 2
[B1386] J Murray pbk **£9.95**
The Lyttleton Hart-Davis Letters Vols 3 & 4
[B1387] J Murray pbk **£8.95**
The Lyttleton Hart-Davis Letters Vols 5 & 6
[B1388] J Murray pbk **£8.95**

HATTON, DEREK
Inside Left
Memoirs of the former Militant sympathiser and leader of Liverpool City Council, now a male model.
[B1389] Bloomsbury pbk **£3.95**

HAYDEN, TOM
Reunion: A Memoir
The memoirs of America's best-known radical student of the 1960s cover riots in the Deep South and the Vietnam War.
[B1390] H Hamilton hbk **£15.95**

HAYMON, SYLVIA
Opposite the Cross Keys: An East Anglian Childhood
A memoir of East Anglia in the 1920s and 30s.
[B1391] Sphere pbk **£3.50**

HAYWORTH, RITA (1918 - 1987)
LEAMING, BARBARA
If This Was Happiness: A Biography of Rita Hayworth `NEW`
The heartbreaking story of the legendary 'Love Goddess' of the silver screen. It describes the pathologically shy child who was thrust into the limelight as her father's dancing partner; her five failed marriages, including those to Orson Welles and Aly Khan; her brief affairs with David Niven and Howard Hughes; her compulsion to choose men who would exploit her; and her long decline with Alzheimer's disease. This first full biography draws on many sources, including medical reports and FBI files.
[B1392] Weidenfeld hbk **£14.95**

HEALEY, EDNA
Wives of Fame
The lives of the wives of the Victorian great men such as Mrs David Livingstone.
[B1393] Hodder pbk **£3.95**

HEPBURN, KATHARINE
Leading American actress perhaps best remembered for *The Philadelphia Story* and *The African Queen*. She was married for many years to Spencer Tracy, her partner in many films.

EDWARDS, ANNE
Katharine Hepburn
[B1394] Hodder pbk **£3.95**
MORLEY, SHERIDAN
Katharine Hepburn: A Celebration
[B1395] Pavilion hbk **£12.95**

HERCULES, TREVOR
Labelled a Black Villain   NEW
The powerful story of Trevor Hercules, who was
imprisoned for violent crime as a teenager and
labelled a black villain. He is now a freelance
journalist, and his excellent and troubling book
describes his struggle to win self-respect and dignity.
[B1396] Fourth Estate pbk **£4.95**

HILL, OCTAVIA
BARLEY, GILLIAN
Octavia Hill: A Life
This is the first new biography of Octavia Hill, the
founder of the National Trust, since 1942. It uncovers
much new information about this tireless social
reformer.
[B1397] Constable hbk **£14.95**

HILLARY, RICHARD
BOOKER, MARY
Mary and Richard
The story of the love affair between a young fighter
pilot and an older woman. Richard Hillary was a
dashing World War II pilot who survived a crash and
recovered with the aid of plastic surgery, only to go
up in the air once more and die at the age of 23.
[B1398] Deutsch hbk **£14.95**
[B1399] Mandarin pbk **£3.50**

HILLESUM, ETTY
Etty: A Diary 1941 - 1943
This remarkable book relates the experiences of a
young Dutch Jew in Amsterdam during 1941-43. It is
a profound document which relates Etty's personal
quest for liberation. As danger threatens and the
Nazis close in, Etty dedicates herself to the plight of
others. She retains her sense of a deeper reality even
as she stands on the platform at Westerbork, waiting
for the train to Auschwitz.
[B1400] Cape hbk **£10.95**
[B1401] Grafton pbk **£2.50**
Letters from Westerbork
[B1402] Cape hbk **£10.95**
[B1403] Grafton pbk **£2.95**

HITCHCOCK, ALFRED (1899 - 1980)
Probably the greatest craftsman popular film has ever
produced. Hitchcock remains a by-word for suspense
and psycho-sexual anxiety. His influence is
everywhere, but his instinct for entertainment with an
edge remains unequalled. His large oeuvre includes
such classics as *Rebecca*, *Vertigo* and *Psycho*.
SPOTO, DONALD
The Life of Alfred Hitchcock
[B1404] Collins hbk **£12.95**

HOGGART, RICHARD
A Local Habitation: Life and
Times Vol 1: 1918 - 1940   NEW
Hoggart, the author of the classic *The Uses of
Literacy*, recreates his Yorkshire childhood with wit
and accuracy. He evokes a vanished world of terraced
back-to-backs, potted meat sandwiches and
Morecambe holidays, of domineering aunts and the
bibulous Uncle Walter.
[B1405] Chatto hbk **£13.95**
[B1406] Oxford pbk **£5.95**

HOLLINGWORTH, CLARE
Front Line
Clare Hollingworth has been reporting upheavals
around the world for 50 years, having begun by

covering the outbreak of the Second World War in
Poland. Since then she has been amongst the handful
of journalists in China after the cultural revolution,
and during the Algerian War she went alone into the
dangerous Casbah in Algiers, in addition to breaking
the Kim Philby story on his disappearance to Russia.
Now in her seventies, this great professional tells the
story of her remarkable life.
[B1407] Cape hbk **£14.95**

HOLMAN-HUNT, DIANA
Descendant of the Pre-Raphaelite painter, herself a
biographer.
My Grandmothers and I
[B1408] H Hamilton pbk **£6.95**

HOPKINS, ANTHONY
FALK, QUENTIN   NEW
Anthony Hopkins: Too Good to Waste
Hopkins is one of Britain's greatest modern actors,
famous for a string of major roles on film, stage and
television, among them King Lear, Hitler and Pierre
in *War and Peace*. For this first ever biography,
Quentin Falk shadowed the actor for over a year,
during which he barely paused for breath. He profiles
Hopkins's lonely childhood, his struggle to become
an actor and his battles with alcohol.
[B1409] Columbus hbk **£14.95**

HORNEY, KAREN
QUINN, SUSAN
A Mind of Her Own   NEW
The portrait of a bold woman whose views were
influential in establishing the criteria of modern
feminism. Horney was a Berlin psychoanalyst in the
1920s, and was one of the first people to take issue
with Freud's ideas about women. This biography
draws on her diaries, papers and letters.
[B1410] Macmillan hbk **£16.95**

HOUSEMAN, JOHN (1902 - 1989)
Primarily a producer, Houseman's career later
broadened to include various acting roles, including
the role of the English academic in the TV soap about
American college kids, *The Paper Chase*.
Unfinished Business: A Memoir
[B1411] Chatto hbk **£14.95**

HU, JOHN
SPENCE, JONATHAN
The Question of Hu   NEW
The highly unusual story of Chinaman John Hu, who
accompanied a French missionary from Canton to
France in 1721. In France he became deranged by the
Western world he saw, and reacted to everything with
wildness. He was imprisoned, but escaped and
thereafter roamed the streets, preaching
incomprehensible sermons to astonished Parisians.
[B1412] Faber hbk **£12.99**

HUGHES, M.V.
A classic series of suburban domestic histories.
A London Child of the 1870s
[B1413] Oxford pbk **£3.95**
A London Girl of the 1880s
[B1414] Oxford pbk **£3.95**
A London Home in the 1890s
[B1415] Oxford pbk **£3.95**
A London Family between the Wars
[B1416] Oxford pbk **£3.95**

HUSTON, JOHN
An Open Book   NEW
Huston, veteran director of 36 films, including *The
Treasure of the Sierra Madre* and *Key Largo*, tells
his life story, including details of his time as a down-
and-out in London, and of his compelling love for
Ireland and his delight in animals.
[B1417] Columbus pbk **£5.95**

HUXLEY, JULIETTE (1896 -)
Governess at Garsington, the home of Lady Ottoline
Morrell of the Bloomsbury group, later married to
Julian Huxley.
Leaves of the Tulip Tree
[B1418] Oxford pbk **£4.95**

IONIDES
LANE, MARGARET
The Snake Man
An acclaimed biography of a solitary and eccentric
man. Ionides spent most of his life in Africa as a great
hunter and game warden. He later became an
authority on poisonous snakes which he collected for
museums.
[B1419] H Hamilton pbk **£6.95**

IRELAND, JILL
Lifewish
[B1421] Arrow pbk **£3.50**
Lifeline   NEW
The follow-up to *Lifewish* describes Jill Ireland's
miscarriage and adoption of a son, Jason, as well as
her disintegrating marriage to actor David McCallum.
She goes on to provide a touching portrait of her
subsequent husband Charles Bronson.
[B1420] Century hbk **£12.95**

IRVING, HENRY
IRVING, LAURENCE
Henry Irving
Irving brings his illustrious actor-manager grandfather
to life, and gives us a rich and vivid portrait of the
Victorian stage.
[B1422] Columbus pbk **£6.95**

ISAACS, JEREMY   NEW
Storm Over Four: A Personal Account
When the long-awaited fourth television channel
began in 1982 a critical storm arose over its chief
executive, Jeremy Isaacs, and its programmes were
continually denounced. There were calls for Isaacs to
resign. He weathered the storm, however, and saw the
channel's performance rise in the ratings. In this
major book, Isaacs discusses his entirely laudable
aims and why he thinks Channel Four should survive.
[B1423] Weidenfeld hbk **£14.95**

JAIPUR, MAHARANI OF
DEVI, GAYATRI & RAU, SANTHA RAMA
A Princess Remembers
This is the story of the daughter of the Maharajah of
Cooch Behar and the widow of the Maharajah of
Jaipur. Raised in a sumptuous palace staffed with 500
servants, she shot her first panther at the age of 12. In
later life she won a seat in the Indian Parliament, and
has apppeared on lists of the world's most beautiful
women.
[B1424] Century pbk **£5.95**

JAMESON, DEREK
Bestselling autobiography of the inimitable former
newspaper editor, now turned TV personality.
Touched by Angels
[B1425] Penguin pbk **£3.50**

JENKINS, ROY
Gallery of 20th Century Portraits
The experienced politician and diplomat distils the
essences of major public figures, such as Lloyd
George, Nancy Astor, Kurt Waldheim, Ernest Bevin
and F.D. Roosevelt.
[B1426] David & Ch hbk **£12.95**

JENNINGS, CHRISTIAN
Mouthful of Rocks
A bizarre account of life in the Foreign Legion:
Jennings was rejected by the British Army and went
to join the Amphibious Warfare Company. Sent to

John Huston, author of *An Open Book* (Columbus pbk £5.95)

East Africa, he deserted, only to be recaptured by native bounty hunters and gaoled. Featuring African brothels and parachute jumps over the deserts, this book exposes the myths and truths of this legendary Corps.
[B1427] Bloomsbury hbk **£12.95**

JERMAIN, CLIVE
SNODIN, DAVID
Clive: A Brief Life   NEW
The tragic story of Clive Jermain, who was killed by a spinal tumour at the age of 22. Fired by the knowledge that he was dying Clive wrote an acclaimed television play *The Best Years of Your Life*, and subsequently became the figure-head of the Cancer Charity Search '88. This book is based on frank and moving conversations with his family.
[B1428] Viking hbk **£10.95**

JOHN, CASPAR
JOHN, REBECCA
Caspar John
The memoirs of Augustus John's son, Caspar, who grew up in the Bohemian society frequented by his father, and went on to become an influential member of the Air Force.
[B1429] Collins hbk **£12.95**

JUNG, CARL GUSTAV (1875 - 1946)
Swiss psychiatrist who worked with Freud until 1912 when he severed his connection with the psychoanalysis movement, and founded his own school of analytical psychology. This led him into a diverse series of studies including religion, folklore, mythology, astrology and mysticism. His current popularity rests on his pioneering work with mental disorders and his writings on occultism and astrology. The Vincent Brome biography is the definitive life, and is complemented by Jung's own reflections on his life and work.
BROME, VINCENT
Jung: Man and Myth
[B1430] Grafton pbk **£3.95**
VAN DER POST, LAURENS
Jung and the Story of Our Time
[B1431] Penguin pbk **£4.95**

KAZAN, ELIA (1909 -)
A Life
Kazan is one of this century's greatest directors, whose evocative memoirs show why this poor son of Anatolian emigrants became one of the key figures of the American stage. He describes his close collaboration with Arthur Miller and Tennessee Williams, and his major Hollywood triumphs: *On the*

Waterfront, *A Streetcar Named Desire* and *East of Eden* amongst them. He also gives insights into his relationships with Natalie Wood and Marilyn Monroe.
[B1432] Deutsch hbk **£17.95**
[B1433] Pan pbk **£8.99**

KEELER, CHRISTINE
Scandal   NEW
The inside story of the Profumo Affair by one of its chief protagonists. The story which brought the downfall of the Macmillan administration blew up when it transpired that the same woman had slept with a top government minister and a Russian spy. Keeler's version of the events is set against a backdrop of a London sub-culture of violent drug-dealers and playboys.
[B1434] Xanadu pbk **£3.99**

KEMPSON, RACHEL
A Family and its Fortunes
Rachel Kempson, Lady Redgrave, chronicles her own acting career and that of her husband, Michael Redgrave. She goes on to describe the remarkable acting family that they created, which has now spawned two generations, from Vanessa Redgrave to Natasha Richardson.
[B1435] Duckworth hbk **£12.95**

KENDAL, GEOFFREY (1909 -)
Shakespeare Wallah
Both Geoffrey Kendal and his wife Laura are fine actors, and their daughters Jennifer and Felicity are equally well known on stage and screen. This autobiography presents an exotic picture of the 20 years he spent playing Shakespeare, first in India, then with the Shakespeare Company he and his wife formed together.
[B1436] Penguin pbk **£3.95**

KENNEDY, LUDOVIC
On My Way to the Club   NEW
The popular writer and broadcaster recalls his life with humour and frankness: his years at Oxford, his war years with the navy when he took part in forays against German battleships such as the *Bismarck*, and his increasingly successful career in television.
[B1437] Collins hbk **£15.00**

KEYNES, SIR GEOFFREY
Brother of Maynard, surgeon and distinguished bibliophile. This is a distinguished autobiography, with emphasis on the years of his childhood.
Gates of Memory
[B1438] Oxford pbk **£4.95**

KING HUSSEIN
LUNT, JAMES
Hussein of Jordan   NEW
Lunt first met King Hussein 36 years ago, when he had just come to the throne as a boy. His biography is a balanced account of one of the most influential figures of the region.
[B1439] Macmillan hbk **£16.95**

KINGSLEY, MARY
FRANK, KATHERINE
Voyager Out: Life of Mary Kingsley   NEW
Mary Kingsley gave up her youth in order to look after her invalid mother, until, at the age of 30, desperate for adventure, she set off for Africa, the 'heart-shaped continent'. In the short years before her tragically early death she explored vast areas, collecting specimens for the British Museum. This biography recounts her adventures, and describes her voyage of self-exploration.
[B1440] H Hamilton hbk **£14.95**

KNOX, RONALD
WAUGH, EVELYN
Ronald Knox
Waugh's biography of the noted religious figure, who was recieved into the Roman Catholic Church in 1917, first appeared in 1959.
[B1441] Cassell pbk **£6.95**

KRAUS, KARL
TIMM, EDWARD
Karl Kraus: Apocalyptic Satirist   NEW
A study of the great Austrian satirist, whose critiques of the mass media, the growth of military and industrial complexes and technology running out of control, have earned him a growing reputation in the 50 years since his death.
[B1442] Yale pbk **£10.95**

KRAY, REG & RON
Our Story
The candid and controversial story of two of Britain's most notorious criminals. They talk of their East End upbringing, their loving mother and their collisions with the law.
[B1443] Pan pbk **£3.99**

KRISHNAMURTI, J.
LUTYENS, MARY
Krishnamurti: The Years of Fulfilment
[B1445] J Murray hbk **£15.00**
Krishnamurti: The Open Door
This is the final volume of the official life of Krishnamurti. Krishnamurti had been identified as a boy as the potential vehicle for a reincarnation of the World Teacher. Later he disclaimed the role of Messiah, claiming that organized religions were barriers to truth. But he continued for the rest of his life to teach a religion of great subtlety, which attracted eminent people from all fields, such as Bernard Shaw and Nehru. Mary Lutyens knew Krishnamurti, and she interweaves the narrative of his later years with the words of his teaching, in this sensitive account.
[B1444] J Murray hbk **£13.95**

LAMBERT FAMILY
MOTION, ANDREW
The Lamberts: George, Constant & Kit
A remarkable and award-winning biography of three generations of the Lambert family. George (1873-1930) was a successful painter, Constant (1905-1951) was a well-known composer, and Kit (1935-1981) was a pop group manager. A consistent theme runs through this portrait: that of self-destructive inheritance, and remarkable promise and achievement cut short by drink, drugs and Bohemian behaviour.
[B1446] Hogarth pbk **£7.95**

LAPOTAIRE, JANE
Grace and Favour   NEW
A fine autobiography by the actress: looking back to her childhood, she vividly evokes the England of the 1950s and the confusion of growing up illegitimate.
[B1447] Macmillan hbk **£12.95**

LAUGHTON, CHARLES (1899 - 1962)
CALLOW, SIMON
Charles Laughton
Callow's acclaimed assessment of Laughton is based on testimonies of surviving friends and lovers. He explores Laughton's lifelong struggle to come to terms with his homosexuality, and concludes that Laughton was a great actor, despite his own assessment that his career had been a failure.
[B1448] Methuen hbk **£14.95**

LAWRENCE, GERTRUDE (1898 - 1952)
English actress best known for her appearances opposite Noel Coward.

MORLEY, SHERIDAN
A Bright Particular Star
[B1449] Pavilion pbk **£7.95**

LEE, PEGGY   NEW
Miss Peggy Lee: An Autobiography
At 14, Peggy Lee was running her father's railway
depot while he got drunk. Her tough childhood only
improved when she left to work for Benny Goodman,
and from this point her singing career took off. This
book includes stories behind such classic songs as
Johnny Guitar and *Black Coffee*, and she recalls her
friends, among whom were Frank Sinatra, Bing
Crosby, Nat King Cole and Paul McCartney.
[B1450] Bloomsbury hbk **£13.95**

LEES-MILNE, JAMES
Ancestral Voices
The first volume of a wartime diary.
[B1451] Faber pbk **£4.95**
Prophesying Peace
This volume describes inspecting houses that were on
offer to the National Trust during the war, and their
often bizarre and amusing owners. The last volume,
Midway on the Waves, describes his post-war career
with the Trust.
[B1452] Faber pbk **£4.95**
Caves of Ice
This part of the diary chronicles the years
immediately after the war, during the bitter winter of
1946-47. It offers a fascinating glimpse of life in
London with the Nicolsons and the Mitfords.
[B1453] Faber pbk **£3.95**
Midway on the Waves
[B1454] Faber pbk **£4.95**
Another Self
This short autobiographical work looks back to
Lees-Milne's Edwardian childhood and the civilising
effects of the 1920s and 1930s. Michael Holroyd
called it a 'minor masterpiece'.
[B1455] Faber pbk **£4.95**

LEIGH, VIVIEN (1913 - 1967)
EDWARDS, ANNE
Vivien Leigh
[B1456] Hodder pbk **£2.50**
MCBEAN, ANGUS
Vivien: A Love Affair in Camera   NEW
Angus McBean first met Vivien Leigh in 1936, when
he spotted her on a London stage, and asked her to
model for him. This book traces the history of their
relationship in a series of remarkable photographs.
[B1457] Phaidon hbk **£19.95**
VICKERS, HUGO
Vivien Leigh
A fascinating account of the volcanic actress, much of
it centred on her stormy relationship with Laurence
Olivier and her subsequent bouts of tuberculosis and
manic depression.
[B1458] H Hamilton hbk **£16.95**
WALKER, ALEXANDER
Vivien Leigh
In this best-selling biography, the film critic of the
Evening Standard traces the life of the iron-willed
actress from her early days in India, through her first
marriage and overnight stage fame, her impulsive
desertion of husband and baby for Olivier, her manic-
depressive illness and her quieter relationship with
Jack Merivale.
[B1459] Methuen pbk **£3.95**

LEIPMAN, FLORA (1918 -)
Scottish-born woman who moved with her Russian
mother back to the Soviet Union in 1932. Accused of
being a British spy, her mother spent ten years in
labour camps. Flora finally returned to Britain in
1984.
The Long Journey Home
[B1460] Corgi pbk **£3.95**

LENNON, JOHN (1940 - 1979)
GOLDMAN, ALBERT
John Lennon
When Lennon was shot he was revered as the guru of
rock and roll. This energetic and controversial
biography dusts off the received image of the pop star,
to present a piercing analysis of his bizarre and
contradictory life, from his tough childhood in
Liverpool, through the crazy Beatle years, to Yoko
Ono, drugs and doom. Goldman pulls no punches in
this frequently irreverent book.
[B1461] Bantam pbk **£3.95**

LENYA, LOTTE
SPOTO, DONALD
Lenya: A Life   NEW
Lotte Lenya's life spanned most of the great
intellectual and artistic currents of the 20th century.
This biography describes how she graduated to the
clubs and cabaret of pre-war Berlin and then to a
world of stardom on Broadway, and examines her
infamous marriage to Kurt Weill and her subsequent
relationships with a series of self-destructive
homosexual men. This is a major biography of the
woman who, in later life came to be seen as the living
embodiment of Weimar Germany.
[B1462] Viking hbk **£15.95**

LEONARD, HUGH
Out After Dark   NEW
The celebrated Irish playwright's humorous memoir
of late adolescence in a small Irish town. He recalls
the comic ups and downs of his first sexual
encounters, his first taste of theatrical life and his
attempts to break away from his demanding mother.
[B1463] Deutsch hbk **£10.95**

LEWIS, C. (1898 -)
Follower of the modern spiritual leader Gurdjieff, and
a long-term traveller. *Sagittarius Rising* is a classic
account of flying during the First World War.
Sagittarius Rising
[B1464] Penguin pbk **£2.95**

LINCOLN, TREBITSCH
WASSERSTEIN, BERNARD
The Secret Lives of Trebitsch Lincoln
This book unravels the career of an extraordinary
figure in a considerable feat of historical detective
work. Lincoln was a juvenile criminal in his native
Hungary, then emigrated to Canada in 1900 where he
became a missionary and then, successively, a curate,
Member of British Parliament, German agent (in both
world wars), an outlaw in the USA, member of the
1920 German government, adviser to warlords in
China, and Buddhist abbot in Shanghai.
[B1465] Yale hbk **£16.95**
[B1466] Penguin pbk **£4.99**

LONGDEN, DERIC
Diana's Story   NEW
Six years ago Deric Longden's wife fell ill with ME, a
mysterious disorder which is still not recognised as an
official disease. For Diana it meant years of chronic
pain and hospital visits. For Deric it meant
abandoning his career as a broadcaster and
scriptwriter, in order to look after his wife. Despite
her subsequent death, this is a frequently hilarious and
moving account of her illness and of their loving
relationship.
[B1467] Bantam hbk **£12.95**

LOY, MYRNA (1905 -)
LOY, MYRNA & KOTSILIBAS-DAVIS, JAMES
Being and Becoming
*"There ought to be a law against any man who
doesn't marry Myrna Loy"* declared Jimmy Stewart
who, along with the rest of America, was smitten by
the enchanting film star. From Montana pioneer stock,

she came to Hollywood with a talent for dancing, and
a face which the cameras adored. Now in her eighties,
she looks back with candour and gusto at her
glamorous film career and her friendships with
leading actors and actresses.
[B1468] Bloomsbury hbk **£14.95**

LUMLEY, JOANNA
Stare and Smile Back: Memoirs   NEW
Lumley looks back to her childhood in tropical
Malaya with her army parents, and remembers having
her long black hair laquered with boiled-up gum by
two Chinese amahs. She goes on to recreate her life in
London as a model and actress during the sixties, and
her later complete change of direction working for the
Chiswick Women's Refuge.
[B1469] Viking hbk **£12.95**

LUTYENS, EDWIN (1869 - 1944)
The Letters of Edwin Lutyens
Edwin Lutyens wrote to his wife at least once
every day that they were apart. The letters of this
brilliant architect - his best known works are the
Cenotaph in London and the Viceroy's house in
New Delhi - reveal an extraordinary and likeable
man.
[B1470] Collins hbk **£17.50**
[B1471] H Hamilton pbk **£7.95**

LUTYENS, EMILY
**A Blessed Girl: Memoirs of a
Victorian Childhood 1887 - 1896**   NEW
The author was the daughter of Bulwer-Lytton and
married Edwin Lutyens the architect. When she was
thirteen she began a correspondence with an old
family friend, 71 year-old Reverend Whitewell
Elwin, an enlightened man in Victorian Britain. In
these letters she poured out all her youthful thoughts
and stories of schooling and politics. She also records
her first meeting with the brilliant but penniless
Lutyens.
[B1472] Heinemann pbk **£5.95**

MACLAINE, SHIRLEY (1934 -)
American actress and dancer, sister of Warren Beatty.
Don't Fall off the Mountain
The first volume of MacLaine's memoirs. She takes
the reader on a voyage through her inner self, from
her Virginia roots, to stardom, marriage and
motherhood.
[B1473] Transworld pbk **£2.99**
You Can Get There from Here
She describes the flowering of her political and social
consciousness, her developing role in the international
women's movement and the trip to China in the 1970s
which changed her life.
[B1474] Bantam pbk **£2.95**
Out on a Limb
MacLaine describes a journey to Stockholm where
she meets a trance channeller who opens a door to
her past.
[B1475] Bantam pbk **£3.50**
Dancing in the Light
MacLaine describes her search for a new
understanding with her parents, and delves into her
past. She describes the compulsion to perform that
she felt as a child, and what this means to her today,
both physically and emotionally.
[B1476] Bantam hbk **£10.95**
[B1477] Bantam pbk **£3.50**
It's All in the Playing
In her most recent book MacLaine casts herself
in the role of a seeker after personal and
metaphysical truths. Describing her own personal
quest, from Malibu, to London, to Peru, she proposes
that we all have the power to design the world we
live in.
[B1478] Bantam hbk **£12.95**
[B1479] Bantam pbk **£3.99**

MACNEE, PATRICK
Blind in One Ear
Macnee, probably best known as John Steed in *The Avengers*, describes his strange upbringing with his lesbian mother and his hilarious and unpredictable life as an actor.
[B1480] Harrap hbk **£12.95**

MAHMOODY, BETTY
Not without My Daughter
American Betty Mahmoody describes how she had to escape on foot from Tehran with her young daughter, when she discovered that her Iranian husband and his family intended to prevent their return to America.
[B1481] Corgi pbk **£3.95**

MAKEBA, MIRIAM
MAKEBA, MIRIAM & HALL, JAMES
Makeba: My Story
A dramatic memoir by the black South African singer. It begins in poverty amid the cruelties of the apartheid system. Afraid of her celebrity status, the Government exiled her from South Africa, a move which has only increased the admiration of her fellow performers and audiences throughout the world.
[B1482] Bloomsbury hbk **£13.95**

MANNIX, DAN
Memoirs of a Swordswallower
A unique first-hand account of the circus in the first half of this century, a world that has now vanished forever.
[B1483] Columbus pbk **£5.95**

MARKHAM, BERYL
West with the Night
[B1485] Virago pbk **£5.50**
[B1486] Penguin pbk **£2.95**
The Illustrated West with the Night
The extraordinary Beryl Markham was brought up in Africa in the early 1900s, and spent her childhood hunting with warriors and running wild. In 1936 she made world headlines by becoming the first person to fly solo across the Atlantic from east to west. This is an illustrated edition of her classic autobiography. It depicts the life in Kenya in the 1920s and 30s of this legendary beauty and pioneering aviator.
[B1484] Virago hbk **£14.95**
LOVELL, MARY S.
Straight On Till Morning: The Biography of Beryl Markham
Lovell draws on her personal association with Markham, as well as family papers and interviews, to tell the full astonishing story of her life.
[B1487] Hutchinson hbk **£15.95**
[B1488] Arrow pbk **£3.99**

Richard Meinertzhagen, whose biography, *Soldier, Scientist, Spy* by Mark Cocker is published by Secker & Warburg (hbk £14.95)

MARX, GROUCHO (1890 - 1977)
With his three brothers, Chico, Harpo and Zeppo, Groucho began his stage career in vaudeville, before making the great zany comic films, such as *Duck Soup* and *A Night at the Opera*.
Groucho and Me
[B1489] Columbus pbk **£5.95**
CHANDLER, CHARLOTTE
Hello I Must Be Going: Groucho and his Friends
[B1490] Sphere pbk **£4.99**
MARX, ARTHUR
My Life with Groucho
A revised and expanded edition of Arthur Marx's memoir of his father. It includes an intimate view of the Marx family, and a controversial account of Groucho's relationship with his secretary.
[B1491] Robson hbk **£12.95**

MASON, JAMES
DE ROSSO, DIANA
Mason: A Personal Biography
[B1492] Lennard hbk **£12.95**
MORLEY, SHERIDAN
James Mason: Odd Man Out NEW
Written with the co-operation of the actor's widow, Morley's penetrating biography reveals Mason as a craftsman actor ill-at-ease with his star status. This is a detailed and well-researched book, based on hundreds of interviews. It delves into the personality of Mason, an essentially private man.
[B1493] Weidenfeld hbk **£12.95**

MASTERS, BRIAN
Gary NEW
Masters, author of *Killing for Company*, an account of the mass murderer Dennis Nielsen, recounts how he took under his protection and into his home a disturbed and violent teenager who had been abandoned by his father. This honest account of their complicated relationship portrays the battle of wills that took place - on the one hand the frightening but pathetically vulnerable Gary, and on the other the journalist, driven to examine his own motives.
[B1494] Cape hbk **£10.95**

MAY, SOMETH
Cambodian Witness
This remarkable autobiography tells the story of Someth May and his life in Cambodia after the Khmer Rouge took over the country in 1975. May's family originally numbered 14, but only four survived the era of the Khmer Rouge. This powerful story recounts May's survival and desperate escape from the country: it is a tribute to human endurance and courage. Edited and introduced by James Fenton.
[B1495] Faber pbk **£4.95**

MEINERTZHAGEN, RICHARD
COCKER, MARK
Richard Meinertzhagen: Soldier, Scientist, Spy NEW
A portrait of one of the most extraordinary Englishmen of the century, a man who attracted controversy throughout his long and varied career. As a soldier in East Africa he gained a reputation for bloodthirstiness, and he played a major part in the victorious campaign in Palestine during the First World War. With T.E. Lawrence he attended the Paris Peace Conference, where he was active in support of Zionist aspirations. After retiring at the age of 48, he devoted the rest of his life to the more sedate occupation of ornithology.
[B1496] Secker hbk **£14.95**

MERRICK, WILLIAM
HOWELL & FORD
True History of the Elephant Man
Merrick suffered from a rare condition, which woefully deformed his body, and led to him being used as a spectacle at fairgrounds. He was, however, a man of delicate sensibilities who was rescued and cared for by a doctor.
[B1497] Penguin pbk **£3.50**

METTERNICH, PRINCESS TATIANA
Tatiana: Five Passports in a Shifting Europe
Memoirs of a childhood in Russia before the Revolution, followed by the horrors of life in Nazi Germany and the deprivation of post-war Vienna.
[B1498] Century pbk **£5.95**

MEYER, MICHAEL
Not Prince Hamlet NEW
Meyer, an acknowledged scholar of the theatre, has known many of the leading literary and theatrical figures of the last 40 years. His contemporaries at Oxford included Philip Larkin, Keith Douglas, John Mortimer and Kenneth Tynan, and he met Bernard Shaw and Max Beerbohm, and was a close friend of George Orwell, Graham Greene, Mervyn Peake and Ralph Richardson. He supplements these revealing and hilarious pen portraits with memoirs of his own failure as a wartime scientist.
[B1499] Secker hbk **£14.95**

MILLER, CHRISTIAN
A Childhood in Scotland
A reissue, particularly memorable for its haunting account of Miller's life in her youth in her father's freezing cold castle.
[B1500] Canongate pbk **£2.95**

MILNE, ALASDAIR (1930 -)
The former Director General of the BBC who was dismissed by the Board of Governors during a period of strained relations between the government and the BBC.
DG: The Memoirs of a British Broadcaster
[B1501] Hodder pbk **£4.50**

MITFORD FAMILY
GUINNESS, CATHERINE & JONATHAN
The House of Mitford
A lively portrait of the Mitford clan, the six daughters and one son who were the offspring of the second Lord Redesdale. Among them were Nancy, the novelist and historian; Diana, who married the fascist leader Sir Oswald Mosley; Unity, friend and supporter of Hitler; Jessica who became a communist and then an investigative journalist in America; and Deborah, Duchess of Devonshire and mistress of Chatsworth House.
[B1502] Fontana pbk **£6.95**

MONROE, MARILYN (1926 - 1962)
Marilyn Monroe and the Camera NEW
A selection of 150 of the best photographs of Monroe, taken from archives, photographers and private collections. Includes previously unpublished material.
[B1503] Bloomsbury hbk **£40.00**
ARNOLD, EVE
Marilyn Monroe: An Appreciation
Eve Arnold developed a strong friendship with Marilyn Monroe during the long photo sessions they had together, which spanned most of her career. This book contains the photographs that Arnold believes reveal the real Marilyn.
[B1504] Pan pbk **£9.95**
DE DIENES, ANDRE
Marilyn Mon Amour: The Private Album of André de Dienes
André de Dienes first met Marilyn Monroe in 1945 when she was 19. He was captivated by her beauty

and wanted to marry her. These photographs, taken between 1945 and 1953, show her changing from an exuberant young beauty into a star.
[B1505] Sidgwick pbk **£10.95**
GUILES, FRED LAWRENCE
Norma Jean: The Life and Death of Marilyn Monroe
[B1506] Grafton pbk **£3.99**
JORDAN, TED
Norma Jean: A Hollywood Love Story
A memoir of Monroe by her former lover and friend, who met her when she was 17 and he was 19. She often turned to him in later life for friendship, and this book reveals their intimate relationship.
[B1507] Sidgwick hbk **£13.95**
SHAW, SAM & NOSTAN, NORMAN
Marilyn Among Friends
[B1508] Bloomsbury pbk **£9.95**
SHEVEY, SANDRA
The Marilyn Scandal
An interesting book, based on interviews with Monroe's surviving friends. It reveals, amongst other things, that Monroe was president of her own production company by the time she was thirty.
[B1509] Arrow pbk **£3.95**
SPADA, J. & ZENO, G.
Marilyn Monroe: Her Life in Pictures
[B1510] Sidgwick pbk **£10.95**
SPERIGLIO, MILO
The Marilyn Conspiracy
[B1511] Transworld pbk **£2.50**
STEINEM, GLORIA
Marilyn
The feminist editor of *MS* magazine presents a portrayal of Monroe as a woman exploited by men.
[B1512] Penguin pbk **£7.95**
SUMMERS, ANTHONY
Goddess: The Secret Lives of Marilyn Monroe
Summers, a top investigative journalist, spent more than two years researching this book. He examines Monroe's life and mysterious death at the age of 36, making a serious and provocative investigation of the long-rumoured Kennedy involvement. He also examines Monroe's preoccupation with childbearing, and chronicles the heartbreak of her final years through the correspondence of her psychiatrist.
[B1513] Sphere pbk **£4.50**

MORRIS, JAN
Conundrum
The story of how James Morris became Jan Morris is a subtle and moving account of an event, or series of events, of immense complexity and heartbreak. Jan Morris is candid about her motivation and the problems she faced. 'Her depiction of the scene in the clinic in which the operation was performed is a fittingly superb climax to a book which is throughout fascinating in its shrewdness, warmth and honesty' (*The Observer*).
[B1514] Penguin pbk **£3.99**

MORTON, JELLY ROLL
LOMAX, ALAN
Mr Jelly Roll
A classic of jazz literature about the man 'who invented jazz', with a foreword by Kingsley Amis.
[B1515] Columbus pbk **£5.95**

MUNTHE, AXEL
The Story of San Michele
Axel Munthe, born in 1857, was a Swedish doctor: this book describes how he devoted his life to rebuilding the Tiberian Villa of San Michele which stood in ruins on the island of Capri. Munthe also worked tirelessly to help the poor people he loved, and he was mobbed by fans in the streets after the publication of this book in 1927. *The Story of San*

Michele is a magical account of one man's quest to restore a great building: it has sold in its millions since it was first published.
[B1516] Grafton pbk **£2.95**

NEAL, PATRICIA (1926 -)
As I Am
A moving autobiography by the former Hollywood star, who had a stroke when she was married to Roald Dahl. She recounts anecdotes about Reagan, Hemingway, Gary Cooper and other friends, as well as describing the miraculous way in which she recovered from her illness.
[B1517] Arrow pbk **£3.99**

NEILL, A.S.
A Dominie's Log
Autobiography by the founder of Summerhill, the progressive school. He tells of his experiences as headmaster of Gretna Green school, from where he was dismissed in 1915.
[B1518] Hogarth pbk **£3.95**
CROALL, JONATHAN
Neill of Summerhill
[B1519] Ark pbk **£4.95**

NGOR, HAING S.
Surviving the Killing Fields
Dr Haing Ngor won an Academy Award for his extraordinary portrayal of the suffering Cambodian hero in the film *The Killing Fields*. His performance closely reflected his own experiences under the Khmer Rouge. As a doctor Ngor was a prime target for their atrocities: his wife died of starvation in his arms, and he himself was forced to escape through war-torn Cambodia. This is a simply told but deeply affecting story.
[B1520] Pan pbk **£4.99**

NICHOLS, PETER (1927 -)
Contemporay British dramatist best known for *Joe Egg*, which centres around a couple's struggle to look after their handicapped daughter Joe.
Feeling You're Behind
[B1521] Penguin pbk **£3.95**

NIVEN, DAVID (1909 - 1983)
Bring on the Empty Horses
[B1522] Hodder pbk **£3.99**
The Moon's a Balloon
[B1523] Hodder pbk **£3.99**
The Moon's a Balloon/Bring on the Empty Horses
In one volume.
[B1524] Hodder pbk **£7.95**
MORLEY, SHERIDAN
Other Side of the Moon: The Authorized Biography of David Niven
Niven's memoirs offer a selective, often inaccurate account of his life. This biography, written with the full co-operation of the Niven family, shows his life in greater detail. We learn of Niven's affairs with Rita Hayworth and Merle Oberon; of his barbaric prep-school days; the lasting effects of his first wife's death, and of his two-year losing battle with motor neurone disease.
[B1525] Weidenfeld hbk **£10.95**
[B1526] Hodder pbk **£2.95**

OLIVIER, LAURENCE (1907 - 1989)
Olivier is generally agreed to be the greatest British actor of the 20th century. Most of his best performances were on the stage, but some great moments were captured in films such as *Henry V*, *Wuthering Heights* and *Richard III*. His directorship of the National Theatre was pioneering and, if at times controversial, successful. His recent death was greeted by the dimming of the lights on Shaftesbury Avenue, and applause at the RSC in Stratford, since it

was said that that would have been his wish.
Confessions of an Actor
Olivier's bestselling autobiography.
[B1527] Hodder pbk **£4.99**
On Acting
[B1528] Weidenfeld hbk **£12.95**
[B1529] Sphere pbk **£3.95**
HOLDEN, ANTHONY
Olivier `NEW`
The definitive biography of Olivier, which complements the actor's own autobiography. It reveals the many different strands of the actor's career, as well as examining the various 'performances' that Olivier has given as a human being. *"Holden's Olivier provokes questions, stimulates speculation, offers tantalising glimpses of the character behind the make-up." - TLS.*
[B1530] Weidenfeld hbk **£15.95**
[B1531] Sphere pbk **£6.99**
TANITCH, ROBERT
Olivier: The Complete Career
A detailed pictorial record of Olivier's film and stage performances.
[B1532] Thames & H hbk **£12.95**

ONASSIS, ARISTOTLE (1906 - 1975)
DAVIS, L.J.
Onassis and Christina
The story of the daughter of Aristotle Onassis, and how she tried to fill her father's shoes, often to be greeted with ridicule from the press. Davis does reveal, however, that she had a strong head for business.
[B1533] Grafton pbk **£3.95**
EVANS, PETER
Ari: The Life and Times of Aristotle Socrates Onassis
A portrait of the ruthless and manipulative Greek shipping tycoon, who is as famous for his affairs - with Jackie Onassis, Maria Callas and Gloria Swanson - as for his business deals.
[B1534] Penguin pbk **£3.50**

ONASSIS, CHRISTINA
DEMPSTER, NIGEL
Christina: The Last Onassis `NEW`
The tragic story of the pampered, glittering, jet-setting life of the daughter of Aristotle Onassis.
[B1535] Weidenfeld hbk **£14.95**

ONASSIS, JACKIE
HEYMANN, C. DAVID
A Woman Named Jackie `NEW`
The first full-length and fully-documented biography

Marilyn Monroe from *Marilyn Monroe: An Appreciation* by Eve Arnold (Pan pbk **£9.95**)

of one of the world's most photographed women: Jacqueline Kennedy Onassis. Chronicles her childhood, her marriages to Jack Kennedy and Aristotle Onassis, and her current career in publishing. Heymann has interviewed over 600 people and has had access to secret CIA and FBI files.
[B1536] Heinemann hbk £12.95

ORIGO, IRIS
Images and Shadows
A fascinating account of life in three worlds: the author's American grandparents' New York 'Brownstone' house, her grandparents in Ireland, and her mother's villa in Italy.
[B1537] Century pbk £5.95
Need to Testify
[B1538] J Murray hbk £12.50
War in Val D'Orcia
[B1539] Century pbk £4.95

PAGE, TIM
Page after Page
The searing autobiography of one of the greatest contemporary war photographers, who made his name with his daring exploits during the Vietnam War.
[B1540] Sidgwick hbk £14.95

PAGNOL, MARCEL **NEW**
My Father's Glory & My Mother's Castle
The first two volumes of the early memoirs of Marcel Pagnol cover his sunlit Provençal youth, and are imbued with the same warmth and appreciation of the French landscape that characterised *Jean de Florette* and *Manon of the Springs*.
[B1541] Deutsch hbk £11.95
[B1542] Deutsch pbk £6.95

PARKER, PETER **NEW**
The Memoirs of Sir Peter Parker
At the heart of Sir Peter Parker's lively memoirs is the story of his chairmanship of British Rail, and his confrontation with the unions. He also gives a lively account of his childhood in India, and his acting career at Oxford. From his experience as chairman of many City companies, he also offers unique insights into the problems of industry and society.
[B1543] Cape hbk £18.00

PASOLINI, PIER PAULO (1922 - 1975)
SICILIANO, ENZO
Pasolini: A Biography
An excellent biography of the controversial filmmaker and poet, director of *The Decameron* and *Theorem*, which gives particular coverage to the intellectual content of his life and work.
[B1544] Bloomsbury pbk £9.95

PICASSO, PABLO (1881 - 1973)
STASSINOPOULOUS, ARIANNA
Picasso: Creator and Destroyer
An extravagant biography of the great painter which, despite being heavily slated by critics, became a bestseller. It portrays a man who, from his teenage passion for a gypsy boy, to his decline into old age, was unconventional in his desires and unable to love.
[B1545] Weidenfeld hbk £14.95
[B1546] Pan pbk £4.99

PITSTONE, JOSEPH D.
Donnie Brasco: My Undercover Life in the Mafia
Pitstone was the first and most important undercover FBI agent to infiltrate the Mafia. He posed as jewel thief Donnie Brasco and stayed underground for six years, during which over 100 Mafia men were convicted. He describes his extraordinary experiences in this book. Pitstone now lives under the threat of a $500,000 contract on his life.
[B1547] Pan pbk £3.99

Sir Laurence Olivier by Clive Francis from *Blessings in Disguise* by Alec Guinness (Hamish Hamilton hbk £12.95, Fontana pbk £3.95)

POLANSKI, ROMAN (1933 -)
Film-maker of Polish origin now living in France. His films, such as *Macbeth* and *Tess*, are visually exotic, and have also attracted controversy.
Roman by Polanski
[B1548] Pan pbk £3.95

POPE JOHN PAUL I
CORNWELL, JOHN
A Thief in the Night: The Death of Pope John Paul I **NEW**
On the night of 28 September, 1978 John Paul I, the 'smiling Pope', died unexpectedly after a reign of only 33 days. The official diagnosis was a heart attack. This investigation, written with the cooperation of the Vatican, tells a different story.
[B1549] Viking hbk £14.95

POST, LAURENCE VAN DER
Yet Being Someone Other
The great writer, explorer and anthropologist's classic autobiography describes his travels and his life amongst the rich, famous and eccentric.
[B1550] Penguin pbk £4.99

POWELL, MICHAEL (1905 -)
A Life in Movies
In the first part of his autobiography, Powell, one of the greatest British film directors of the century, relates the story of his career in cinema. This is a marvellously anecdotal book, in which Powell indulges his feel for atmosphere, sense of place and his talent for storytelling.
[B1551] Heinemann hbk £18.00
[B1552] Methuen pbk £7.95
Million Dollar Movie **NEW**
The first volume of Michael Powell's memoirs was ecstatically reviewed. In this second part he tells the complicated story of how he and Pressburger parted ways, and of how he went on to make *Peeping Tom*. He tells of happy marriages, and of the reinstatement of his reputation by the younger Hollywood directors, such as Scorcese and Coppola.
[B1553] Heinemann hbk £15.00

QUEEN ELIZABETH II (1926 -)
LACEY, ROBERT
Majesty: Elizabeth II & the House of Windsor
[B1554] Sphere pbk £4.95
LONGFORD, ELIZABETH
Elizabeth R
[B1555] Weidenfeld hbk £10.95
MORROW, ANN
The Queen
[B1556] Grafton pbk £2.50

QUEEN ELIZABETH, THE QUEEN MOTHER (1900 -)
HOLDEN, ANTHONY
The Queen Mother
[B1557] Sphere pbk £2.95
LLOYD, IAN
Crown Jewel: A Year in the Life of the Queen Mother **NEW**
Lloyd has been photographing the Queen Mother for over 10 years, and has her personal favour, as well as that of the staff at Clarence House. Provides an intimate journal of Her Majesty's life and her public engagements throughout 1988.
[B1558] Bloomsbury hbk £14.95
MORROW, ANN
Queen Mother
[B1559] Grafton pbk £2.95

QUEEN MARY
WARWICK, CHRISTOPHER
Queen Mary's Photograph Albums **NEW**
Queen Mary started her photograph album in 1880 and from then until her death she chronicled the life of the Royal Family in 33 albums. This collection of photographs, formal and informal, includes pictures of her sons, George VI and Edward VIII. Published with the permission of Her Majesty the Queen.
[B1560] Sidgwick hbk £15.00

RAVERAT, GWEN
Engraver and book illustrator. She was the granddaughter of Charles Darwin and was therefore familiar with the great Cambridge families.
Period Piece: A Cambridge Childhood
[B1561] Faber pbk £3.95

RAWLINSON, PETER
A Price Too High **NEW**
In these candid memoirs Lord Rawlinson, the former Attorney General, remembers many of the controversial cases he has been involved in. He prosecuted the Hosein brothers for the kidnap and murder of a woman that they mistook for Mrs Rupert Murdoch, as well as IRA bombers and spies. He was also involved in the Ruth Ellis case. Because of his controversial work, however, he and his family have had to live constantly in the shadow of police protection.
[B1562] Weidenfeld hbk £16.00

RAY, SATYAJIT
ROBINSON, ANDREW
Satyajit Ray: The Inner Eye **NEW**
The first ever biography of one of the greatest cinema directors of the century. Ray was brought up in Calcutta and struggled to achieve international acclaim, until the world-wide success of his first film *Pather Panchali*. This biography gives profound insight into his artistic and technical achievements as well as his great personal charisma.
[B1563] Deutsch hbk £17.95

REID, BERYL
So Much Love
The inimitable Beryl Reid describes her life from the great days of radio comedy with *Educating Charlie*, to her brilliant roles in *Entertaining Mr Sloane*, *The Killing of Sister George* and *Smiley's People*.
[B1564] Arrow pbk £2.50

REISNER, LARISSA
Writer, revolutionary fighter and diplomat who became the first Bolshevik commissar.
PORTER, CATHY
Larissa Reisner
[B1565] Virago pbk £6.50

REITSCH, HANNA
LOMAX, JUDY
Hanna Reitsch: Flying for the Fatherland
The first major biography of Hanna Reitsch, associate of Hitler and flying heroine of Germany. She was the last person to fly out of Berlin at the end of the Second World War, and was with Hitler in the bunker until only a few hours before the Fuhrer's death.
[B1566] J Murray hbk **£14.95**

RENOIR, PIERRE AUGUSTE (1841 - 1919)
RENOIR, JEAN
Renoir, My Father
A biography of the great Impressionist painter by his son, who was himself a great film-maker. The book was begun in 1915 in Renoir senior's flat in Montmartre.
[B1567] Columbus pbk **£6.95**

RICHARDSON, RALPH (1902 - 1983)
O'CONNOR, GARRY
Ralph Richardson: An Actor's Life
A lively and well-received biography, completed before Sir Ralph's death. It details the full and extraordinary life of the roguish and eccentric actor.
[B1568] Hodder hbk **£9.95**
[B1569] Hodder pbk **£2.50**

ROBERTS, RACHEL (1927 - 1980)
WALKER, ALEXANDER (ED)
No Bells on Sunday: The Journals of Rachel Roberts
During the last 18 months of her life, before she committed suicide in 1980, Rachel Roberts kept a journal. In it she reviewed her life and what it meant: her Welsh childhood, her stern upbringing by her minister father, her schooldays as a struggling actress. Two main themes then dominate: her marriage to and divorce from Rex Harrison, and her addiction to alcohol.
[B1570] Sphere pbk **£3.50**

RODRIGUEZ, HELEN
Helen of Burma: The NEW
Autobiography of a Wartime Nurse
The story of Helen Rodriguez, the daughter of a Scottish nurse and a Portuguese surgeon, who was brought up in the Civil station of Taunggyi, Burma. It was here that she served as a nurse during the war. She refused to abandon her patients as the Japanese approached. Bayoneted, starved and tortured, she faced each crisis with fortitude, even humour.
[B1571] Corgi pbk **£4.50**

ROLPH, C.H.
London Particulars
[B1572] Oxford pbk **£4.95**
Further Particulars NEW
The second volume of Rolph's memoirs describes his 21 years in the City Police at the end of the First World War, and his career as a journalist, during which he worked for the *New Statesman*. He also recounts his time at the BBC, which brought him into contact with Danny Kaye, Raymond Chandler and Rebecca West.
[B1573] Oxford pbk **£4.95**

ROOK, JEAN
The Cowardly Lioness NEW
Jean Rook, known as 'The First Lady of Fleet Street' has always been renowned for speaking her mind. This autobiography reveals the vulnerability that lies behind the tough public image. Rook describes the horror of discovering she had breast cancer, and the traumatic and humorous events on the road to recovery. She also describes the night that she and her

husband were subjected to an armed robbery, and his subsequent death from a brain tumour. Despite this, Jean retains her zest for living.
[B1574] Sidgwick hbk **£12.95**

ROTHSCHILD FAMILY
WILSON, DEREK
The Family: A Story of Wealth NEW
and Power
A history of the Rothschild family, written with the use of original source material and interviews with family members. Wilson shows in particular how their energy and determination has brought them through repeated crises, including those caused by anti-Semitism and the Holocaust. He shows how they operated an official diplomatic service relied on by Metternich, Disraeli, Bismarck and Churchill.
[B1575] Deutsch hbk **£14.95**

RUSSELL, KEN NEW
A British Picture: An Autobiography
The autobiography of one of Britain's most controversial film directors, the maker of *The Boyfriend*, *The Music Lovers* and *Women in Love*. He recounts his life from his thirties childhood and his first sexual experience (watching *Pinocchio*), through his career in the Royal Air Force to his first film-making assignment, interviewing Huw Wheldon. The book is frank and liberally sprinkled with witty anecdotes.
[B1576] Heinemann hbk **£12.95**

SCHLOSS, EVA
Eva's Story
Eva Schloss survived the horrors of Auschwitz, where she had been deported by the Gestapo in 1942. Her mother also survived and subsequently married Otto Frank, father of Anne.
[B1577] WH Allen hbk **£11.95**

SHACKLETON, ERNEST
HUNTFORD, ROLAND
Shackleton NEW
Shackleton, known as 'Great Shack', was a member of Scott's *Discovery* expedition of 1900, but was invalided home. Throughout his life he and Scott were rivals, both explorers competing in the race for wealth, fame and success. This enthralling biography recounts Shackleton's three expeditions to the Pole, and his rise and subsequent fall as a national hero.
[B1578] Sphere pbk **£6.99**

SHER, ANTHONY (1949 -)
Year of the King
Sher is one of the most versatile actors of his generation, and has enjoyed tremendous success in recent years, particularly with the RSC and with Fierstein's *Torch Song Trilogy*. His bestselling book recounts his preparation for playing the part of Richard III in the acclaimed RSC production of Shakespeare's play. It gives a remarkable insider's view into an actor's intense development of a role, and is illustrated with Sher's own vigorous drawings.
[B1579] Chatto hbk **£12.95**
[B1580] Methuen pbk **£5.95**

SINATRA, FRANK (1915 -)
KELLEY, KITTY
His Way: The Unauthorized Biography of Frank Sinatra
Kelley, a celebrated investigative journalist, spent years gaining access to government doucuments, including Mafia-related material, in order to provide an arresting and controversial account of the great entertainer.
[B1581] Bantam hbk **£12.95**
[B1582] Bantam pbk **£3.95**

SINATRA, NANCY
Frank Sinatra: My Father
A warm account of the relationship between Nancy and Frank, complemented by many rare and previously unpublished photographs
[B1583] Hodder pbk **£3.50**

SMEDLEY, AGNES (1892 - 1950)
MACKINNON, JANICE & STEPHEN, R.
Agnes Smedley: The Life and Times of an American Radical
An American writer and a committed socialist whose political activity culminated in her work with the Fourth Army during the Chinese Communist Revolution. After a life dogged by romantic difficulties, she died, a victim of McCarthyism. Drawing on FBI files, this book offers a compelling portrait of an extraordinary woman.
[B1584] Virago hbk **£17.95**

SPIEGEL, SAM
SINCLAIR, ANDREW NEW
Spiegel: The Man Behind the Pictures
A powerful portrait of Spiegel, from his early days as an illegal immigrant passing dud cheques, to the apex of his career, when he produced four great films *On the Waterfront*, *The African Queen*, *Bridge on the River Kwai* and *Lawrence of Arabia*.
[B1585] Weidenfeld hbk **£14.95**

STALKER, JOHN
Stalker
In 1984, the Deputy Chief Constable of the Manchester Police, John Stalker, was asked to undertake an enquiry into the deaths of six men, killed by the Royal Ulster Constabulary in 1982, whose deaths provoked enormous controversy and allegations that the RUC had a 'shoot to kill' policy in Northern Ireland against suspected members of the IRA. The investigation remained unfinished after two years when Stalker was dramatically relieved of his duties, at the very moment when he was about to gain access to material that would be embarrassing to the RUC. In this book Stalker tells the full story of these events.
[B1586] Harrap hbk **£12.95**
[B1587] Penguin pbk **£3.50**

STAMP, TERENCE (1940 -)
Stamp Album
The first volume of Stamp's autobiography.
[B1592] Grafton pbk **£2.95**
Coming Attractions
In the second volume of his memoirs Stamp describes winning a scholarship to the Webber Douglas Academy. He gains his first professional role and tours, where he is confronted by a blonde young actor called Michael Caine.
[B1589] Grafton pbk **£3.50**
Double Feature NEW
Terence Stamp turns his attention to the seething 1960s. For Stamp, it was the time when his dreams came true: starring in *Billy Budd*, mixing with the stars and great directors in Hollywood, becoming a well-known face on the swinging London scene, but above all, meeting the great love of his life, Jean Shrimpton.
[B1590] Bloomsbury hbk **£12.95**

STANLEY, SIR HENRY MORTON
MCLYNN, FRANK NEW
The Making of an African Explorer
Stanley, one of the 19th century's greatest explorers, is known for his celebrated meeting with David Livingstone, but is also a key figure in the story of European penetration into Africa. This biography explores his psychological complexity, as it traces his life from his early days in a Welsh workhouse. His celebrated meeting with Livingstone brought him

fame and fortune and gave him the opportunity to cross the African continent from east to west, one of greatest single feats in the history of African exploration. Yet, as this book shows, he was also a pathological liar, with sado-masochistic tendencies.
[B1593] Constable hbk **£14.95**

STOTT, MARY
Before I Go
[B1594] Virago pbk **£5.99**
Forgetting's No Excuse
The autobiography of Mary Stott, one of the major journalists, campaigners and feminists of the 20th century. With a new introduction by the author.
[B1595] Virago pbk **£6.99**

TELFORD, THOMAS (1754 - 1834)
Scottish civil engineer who built some 1,200 bridges and 1,000 miles of road.
ROLT, LIONEL T.C.
Thomas Telford
[B1596] Penguin pbk **£4.95**

TEMPLE, SHIRLEY (1928 -)
EDWARDS, ANNE
An American Princess
A revealing look at the child star and the disappointments that followed her meteoric rise to fame. The book goes on to discuss her subsequent resurgence as a world figure in her role of US Ambassador to the United Nations.
[B1597] Collins hbk **£15.00**

THERESE OF LISIEUX (1873 - 1897)
FURLONG, MONICA
Thérèse of Lisieux
A profile of the 15th-century Carmelite nun known as 'The Little Flower'. She died young, but not before writing an account of her experiences which gave her a cult following throughout France.
[B1599] Virago pbk **£4.99**

THOMPSON, JOSIAH **NEW**
Gumshoe: Reflections in a Private Eye
The extraordinary story of a philosophy professor who, rejecting the prospect of a conventional and safely mapped out life, decided to become a private detective earning £5 an hour. Thompson became obsessed with his new profession, and brings to his discussion of it insights into the human condition, its weaknesses and strengths.
[B1600] Macmillan hbk **£12.95**

THOMSON, DAVID (1914 -)
In Camden Town
[B1601] Penguin pbk **£2.95**
Nairn in Darkness and Light
Thomson recalls his boyhood on the Moray Firth, on the borders between the Highlands and the Lowlands. He sensitively recreates the divided population of Nairn, with its fisher community and its townfolk in the 1920s.
[B1602] Hutchinson hbk **£14.95**
[B1603] Arrow pbk **£3.99**
Woodbrook
[B1604] Penguin pbk **£3.95**

TOWNLEY, RALPH
The Brides of Enderby: A Lincolnshire Childhood
An autobiographical account of a young boy growing up in a traditional Quaker household in rural Lincolnshire during the late 1920s.
[B1605] Century hbk **£12.95**

TREE, HERBERT BEERBOHM
PEARSON, HESKETH
Beerbohm Tree: His Life and Laughter
Before he found fame as a biographer, Pearson

worked for Beerbohm Tree as an actor. This book is his unique portrait of the stage colossus and great eccentric, who was half-brother to Max Beerbohm.
[B1606] Columbus pbk **£6.95**

TREMAYNE, PENELOPE
A Writer or Something **NEW**
This is the autobiography of a fearless and independent woman, whose active life has led her into many fields: as a military intelligence officer, nurse, social correspondent for the *Sunday Times* and Red Cross worker. Her adventurous instincts also led her to be kidnapped for five weeks by Tamil terrorists in 1986, an experience she describes in *Nor Iron Bars a Cage*.
[B1607] Unwin Hyman hbk **£12.95**
Nor Iron Bars a Cage
[B1608] Fontana pbk **£2.95**

TRUFFAUT, FRANCOIS
Letters: Volume 1 **NEW**
The 500 letters collected here trace the evolution of this great filmmaker from the age of 12 up until his death in 1984. The correspondents include Alfred Hitchcock and Louis Malle, and the book also contains the details of his famous rupture with Jean-Luc Godard.
[B1609] Faber hbk **£16.99**
ALLEN, DON
Finally Truffaut
[B1610] Grafton pbk **£4.95**

TURNER, LANA (1920 -)
Hollywood actress of *Peyton Place* fame.
CRANE, CHERYL
Detour: A Hollywood Tragedy: My Life with Lana Turner
An unhappy memoir by the daughter who killed her mother's lover.
[B1611] Sphere pbk **£3.99**

TUTU, ARCHBISHOP DESMOND (1931 -)
Outspoken critic of the South African regime, campaigner for Black Rights and the first black Archbishop of Cape Town.
BOULAY, SHIRLEY DU
Tutu
[B1612] Hodder hbk **£12.95**
[B1613] Penguin pbk **£4.50**

TYNAN, KENNETH (1927 - 1980)
Influential drama critic, aesthete and wit who championed the cause of 'kitchen sink' realist dramatists such as John Osborne, in preference to the drawing-room comedies of Coward and Rattigan.
TYNAN, KATHLEEN
The Life of Kenneth Tynan
A riveting biography of one of the greatest theatre critics of the century, written by his wife, which reveals, amongst other things, his extravagant sexuality. This acclaimed and intimate life deals with Tynan's relationships with all the great actors and directors of his day, including Laurence Olivier and Sam Spielberg.
[B1614] Weidenfeld hbk **£16.95**
[B1615] Methuen pbk **£5.95**

USTINOV, PETER (1921 -)
Dear Me
Ustinov is a diverse personality - actor, author, designer, director, film star and playwright. His bestselling autobiography describes his first acting lessons from a parrot, his first stage role as a pig, and the comic events of his life amongst the rich and famous. Throughout it all he shows his lifelong search for honesty.
[B1616] Penguin pbk **£4.50**

VISCONTI, LUCHINO (1906 - 1976)

An important Italian post-war director, whose films range in style from the early neo-realistic *La Terra Trema* to the sumptuous *Death in Venice*.
SERVADIO, GAIA
Luchino Visconti
[B1617] Weidenfeld hbk **£12.95**

WARHOL, ANDY
ULTRA VIOLET
Famous for Fifteen Minutes: My Life With Andy Warhol **NEW**
After being expelled from her French convent. Isabelle Dusfresne moved to New York, where she took the social world by storm, attracting the attention of Richard Nixon, Howard Hughes and Salvador Dali. It was Dali who introduced her to Andy Warhol in 1963. Before long Isabelle had metamorphosed into Ultra Violet, becoming an intimate of Warhol's underground scene - the Factory, where drugs, orgies and film-making went on 24 hours a day. Ultra Violet describes the Factory and its glittering visitors, such as Bob Dylan, Truman Capote and John Lennon.
[B1618] Methuen hbk **£12.95**

WEBB, BEATRICE (1858 - 1953)
Social reformer in the Fabian Group who formed a life-long partnership of socialist activity with her husband Labour MP Sidney Webb.
MACKENZIE, NORMAN & JEANNE (EDS)
Diary
Vol 1 1873 - 1892 Glitter Around and Darkness Within
[B1619] Virago pbk **£11.50**
Vol 2 1892 - 1905 All the Good Things of Life
[B1620] Virago pbk **£11.50**
Vol 3 1905 - 1924 The Power to Alter Things
[B1621] Virago hbk **£22.50**
Vol 4 1924 - 1943 The Wheel of Life
[B1622] Virago hbk **£25.00**

WEBBER, ANDREW LLOYD
MANTLE, JONATHAN
Fanfare: The Unauthorised Biography of Andrew Lloyd Webber **NEW**
Webber is the creator of the mega-musical, a genre which includes such hugely successful works as *Cats* and *Evita*. Although a popular figure of fun, Webber's story is much more interesting than many people would believe. This biography describes his middle class semi-Bohemian upbringing and the private world of music and theatre into which he and his brother Julian retreated.
[B1623] M Joseph hbk **£14.95**
WALSH, MICHAEL
Andrew Lloyd Webber: His Life and Works **NEW**
Walsh's book discusses Webber's musical accomplishments in depth, as well as examining his life.
[B1624] Viking hbk **£20.00**

WELLES, ORSON (1916 - 1986)
HIGHAM, CHARLES
Orson Welles
[B1625] Hodder pbk **£3.95**
LEAMING, BARBARA
Orson Welles
Orson Welles was one of the most volcanic and original talents of the 20th-century cinema. Leaming delves behind the many myths to show his complex personality. *'Childish, charming, tyrannical, impossible, unreliable, unfaithful, and almost always over the top, Welles remained a child at heart...Barbara Leaming has successfully captured that overwhelming personality.'* (The Spectator)
[B1626] Weidenfeld hbk **£14.95**
[B1627] Penguin pbk **£5.99**

WESTON, SIMON
Walking Tall **NEW**
Simon Weston is familiar to millions as the Welsh Guardsman who suffered horrific burns in the attack upon the *Sir Galahad* during the Falkland War. In this book he describes what actually happened to him on board the ship, the deep despair that followed this horrific experience, and the memory of his dead friends, which pushed him to the brink of suicide. It concludes with his finding the strength to start a new life, and describes how he set up a charity for unemployed teenagers in Liverpool.
[B1628] Bloomsbury hbk **£13.95**

WHARTON, MICHAEL (1913 -)
The Missing Will
The hilarious autobiography of 'Peter Simple' of *The Daily Telegraph*, which describes the making of a great satirist.
[B1629] Hogarth pbk **£5.95**

WHISTLER, LAURENCE (1912 -)
British glass engraver and writer.
Laughter and the Urn: The Life of Rex Whistler
Rex Whistler was one of the most gifted artists of the inter-war years. He was still developing his own distinctive style when he was killed in action in Normandy in 1944, aged 39. Here, his brother Laurence gives us a poignant, objective but heartfelt account of his life.
[B1630] Weidenfeld pbk **£8.95**
The Initials in the Heart: A Celebration of Love
A reissue of the classic and moving account, first published in 1964, of Whistler's marriage to the actress Jill Furse, before her sudden and early death.
[B1631] Weidenfeld pbk **£6.95**

WIGHTON, SUZY **NEW**
Beirut Lines: The Diary of Suzy Wighton
In January 1988 the *Sunday Times* published an interview with the young Glaswegian nurse working in Bourj-al-Barajneh, one of the refugee camps in Beirut. She talked of what it was like living in a besieged Palestinian camp, with the memory of the massacre at the neighbouring Shatila camp, knowing that few outsiders realised the full extent of the human suffering. In this diary Suzy records the feelings and hopes of the people in the camp, so that their suffering and death would not pass unnoticed.
[B1632] Hutchinson hbk **£16.95**

Andy Warhol (Photo: Christopher Markos, New York)

WILLIAMS, KENNETH (1926 - 1988)
Acid Drops
[B1633] Dent pbk **£2.95**
Just Williams: An Autobiography
Kenneth Williams tells his life story from his days as a child growing up in London in the 1930s, through the barrack-room life in Singapore during the Second World War, to his career in comedy and the classic *Carry On* films.
[B1634] Fontana pbk **£3.50**

WINDSOR FAMILY
HOUGH, RICHARD
Born Royal: The Lives and Loves of the Young Windsors
This book contains biographies and pictures of the Prince and Princess of Wales and the Duke and Duchess of York.
[B1635] Deutsch hbk **£14.95**
LONGFORD, ELIZABETH
Royal House of Windsor
[B1636] Weidenfeld hbk **£12.95**

WINDSOR, DUCHESS OF
HIGHAM, CHARLES
Wallis: The Secret Lives of the Duchess of Windsor
This exhaustive biography of the Duchess of Windsor contains a number of quite extraordinary revelations about her life and activities. Higham claims that the Duchess was at some point a Soviet spy, a German spy and had affairs with the Italian fascist Count Galeazzo and Von Ribbentrop, Hitler's foreign minister.
[B1637] Sidgwick hbk **£14.95**
[B1638] Pan pbk **£4.99**

WOODFORDE, JAMES (1740 - 1803)
Woodforde was a Norfolk rector from 1774 until his death. His *Diary* covers details of his domestic life and that of his friends, and describes in particular Woodforde's love of food and drink.
Diary of a Country Parson: 1758 - 1802
[B1639] Oxford hbk illus **£12.95**
[B1640] Oxford pbk abridged **£6.95**

WRIGHT BROTHERS, WILBUR & ORVILLE (1867 - 1912/1871 - 1948)
HOWARD, FRED
Wilbur and Orville
A biography which follows the brothers from childhood to the peak of their achievements and beyond, illustrated with rare photographs of their early life.
[B1641] Hale hbk **£15.95**

WYNDHAM, JOAN
Two books of amusing and honest autobiography about a young girl growing up in pre-war Chelsea before and during the Second World War.
Love Lessons
[B1642] Fontana pbk **£3.95**
Love is Blue: A Wartime Diary
[B1643] Fontana pbk **£3.50**

YEAGER, CHUCK
YEAGER, CHUCK & JANOS, LEO
Yeager
The autobiography of the man who inspired *The Right Stuff*.
[B1644] Arrow pbk **£3.95**

ZEFFIRELLI, FRANCO (1922 -)
Italian theatre and opera director celebrated for his exuberant visual style. His *Romeo and Juliet* is one of the classic film versions of Shakespeare.
Zeffirelli: An Autobiography
[B1645] Weidenfeld hbk **£14.95**

General Reference
General Business
Personal Finance
Practical Business & Enterprise
Corporate Business

BUSINESS

General Reference

Listed here is a selection of the best general reference books: they provide excellent sources of information for a wide range of businesses.

'Business Traveller' Guide to the Business Cities of the World
[C1] Simon & Sch hbk **£9.95**

Abbey Financial Rights Handbook
[C2] Rosters pbk **£5.99**

Business Factfinder
[C3] Kogan Page hbk **£12.95**

Chambers' Book of Business Quotations
[C4] Chambers hbk **£12.95**

Chambers' Office Oracle
Sponsored by the Royal Mail, this is an indispensable mine of information.
[C5] Chambers hbk **£8.95**

Dictionary of British Qualifications, Abbreviations and Qualifying Bodies
[C6] Kogan Page hbk **£12.50**

Dictionary of Information Technology
(3rd Edition)
[C7] Macmillan pbk **£10.95**

Harrap's Dictionary of Business and Finance
The most recent up-to-date business dictionary.
[C8] Harrap hbk **£8.95**
[C9] Harrap pbk **£6.95**

Longman Dictionary of Business English
Essential guide to correct terminology.
[C10] Longman hbk **£10.45**
Longman Concise Dictionary of Business English
[C11] Longman pbk **£5.95**

CHAMBERS COMMERCIAL REFERENCE SERIES
A successful and expanding list, offering a variety of definitive and practical handbooks.
Book-keeping & Accounting Terms
[C12] Chambers pbk **£2.50**
Business Law Terms
[C13] Chambers pbk **£2.50**
Business Terms
[C14] Chambers pbk **£2.50**
Commerce and Business   `NEW`
[C15] Chambers pbk **£3.95**
Information Technology   `NEW`
[C16] Chambers pbk **£3.95**
Marketing Terms
[C17] Chambers pbk **£2.50**
Office Practice Terms
[C18] Chambers pbk **£2.50**
Office Procedures
[C19] Chambers pbk **£3.95**
Office Technology Terms
[C20] Chambers pbk **£2.50**
Printing and Publishing Terms
[C21] Chambers pbk **£2.50**

DAVIS, WILLIAM
The World's Best Business Hotels
Over 500 of the best hotels for business travellers in over 80 countries throughout the world.
[C22] Bloomsbury pbk **£14.95**

ECONOMIST BUSINESS TRAVELLER'S GUIDES
A reliable and practical series, essential for those working abroad.
Arabian Peninsula
[C23] Collins hbk **£12.95**
Britain
[C24] Collins hbk **£12.95**
France
[C25] Collins hbk **£12.95**
Japan
[C26] Collins hbk **£12.95**
China
[C27] Collins hbk **£12.95**
South East Asia
[C28] Collins hbk **£12.95**
USA
[C29] Collins hbk **£12.95**
West Germany
[C30] Collins hbk **£12.95**

ECONOMIST GUIDES
Authoritative series sponsored by *The Economist*.
Pocket Accountant
[C31] Blackwells pbk **£5.95**
Pocket Banker
[C32] Blackwells pbk **£5.95**
Pocket Economist
[C33] Blackwell pbk **£5.95**
Pocket Employer
[C34] Blackwells hbk **£15.00**
Pocket Entrepreneur
[C35] Blackwell hbk **£15.00**
Pocket Guide to Advertising
[C36] Blackwells hbk **£15.00**
Pocket Guide to Business Taxes
For self-employed, highly-taxed individuals and companies.
[C37] E Arnold hbk **£14.95**
Pocket Guide to Marketing
[C38] Blackwell hbk **£15.00**
Pocket Guide to the New City
[C39] Blackwell hbk **£15.50**
Pocket Lawyer
[C40] Blackwell hbk **£15.00**
Pocket Negotiator
[C41] Blackwell hbk **£15.00**

GREENER
Business Dictionary
[C42] Penguin pbk **£5.95**
Dictionary of Commerce
[C43] Penguin pbk **£5.95**

JANNER, GREVILLE
An MP for many years, Janner has established himself as the most reliable writer on business reference matters.
Janner on Communication
[C44] Hutchinson hbk **£17.95**
Janner on Meetings
[C45] Gower hbk **£18.50**
[C46] Wildwood H pbk **£5.95**
Janner on Presentation
[C47] Hutchinson pbk **£5.95**
Janner's Complete Letter Writer
A new edition providing the harrassed executive with fail-safe formula letters for all possible occasions.
[C48] Business bks hbk **£19.95**
Janner's Complete Presentation Skills
Cased set comprising: Janner's Complete Letter Writer, Complete Speechmaker and Janner on Presentation.
[C49] Hutchinson pbk **£17.95**

Janner's Complete Speechmaker
A new guide which takes the trauma out of public speaking.
[C50] Hutchinson pbk **£7.95**

KEMPNER
Handbook of Management
Encyclopaedic A-Z guide to management.
[C51] Penguin pbk **£7.95**

LAMMING, R. & BESSANT, J.
Dictionary of Business and Management
[C52] Macmillan hbk **£30.00**
[C53] Macmillan pbk **£10.95**

STEWART, I.
The Business Writing Workbook
[C54] Kogan Page pbk **£3.95**

Directories

The Listings and Yearbooks featured here offer invaluable information for businesses involved in corporate finance or marketing.

CICI Directory of UK Information Services and Products
[C55] Longman hbk **£35.00**

City Directory 1989
A comprehensive guide to more than 6,000 companies and institutions operating within the City of London.
[C56] Director Bks hbk **£75.00**

Crawford's Directory of City Connections
[C57] Economist hbk **£135.00**

Directory of Directors 1989
An A-Z listing of directors and their appointments, and major companies and their directors.
[C58] T Skinner 2 vols hbk **£95.00**

Kelly's Business Directory 1989
Contains details of over 88,000 companies.
[C59] Reed hbk **£90.00**

Mergers & Acquisitions Yearbook
The guide to who owns whom: bidders, targets, announcements, terms, financial statistics and financial advisers of past years, as well as several articles.
[C60] Macmillan hbk **£150.00**

The International Corporate 1000
[C62] Graham & Tr pbk **£95.00**

The International Stock Exchange Official Yearbook 1988 - 89
The most comprehensive guide to all the companies traded on the stock exchange.
[C63] Macmillan hbk **£125.00**

The Times 1,000 1988 - 89: The World's Top Companies
Comprehensive listings of banks, building societies and British companies as well as the top 1,000 world companies.
[C64] Times hbk **£25.00**

Unquoted Companies 1989
Financial profiles of Britain's top ten thousand unquoted companies.
[C65] Macmillan hbk **£115.00**

BROOKS, M.J.
Sources of Free Business Information
Excellent reference work.
[C66] Kogan Page pbk **£5.95**

CLEMENTSON
London International Finance Futures Yearbook 1989
[C67] Macmillan hbk **£150.00**

REYNOLDS, BOB
The 100 Best Companies to Work for in the UK
Aimed primarily at the job hunter, this is a fascinating survey in its own right.
[C68] Fontana pbk **£5.95**

General Business

Listed here are some of the most interesting books on various aspects of the UK and international economies, with an emphasis on titles which have practical relevance to people in business today.

CLUTTERBUCK, DAVID & CRAINER, STUART
The Decline and Rise of British Industry
A penetrating and detailed analysis of the challenge facing British industy, which asks a simple question: 'are we to be driven by tomorrow's global economy, or are we going to be one of the countries driving it?'
[C69] WH Allen hbk **£15.00**

COGGAN, PHILIP
The Money Machine
'Coggan gives a marvellously clear account of the city and all the modern financial developments, from the credit card, via the Big Bang to the Euromarket' (*Business Review*).
[C70] Penguin pbk **£4.99**

DALEY, SHERRI
High Cotton: Love and Death on Wall Street
An account of the high pressure world of Wall Street futures traders.
[C71] Weidenfeld hbk **£12.95**

DONALDSON, PETER & FARQUHAR, JOHN
Understanding the British Economy
The authors have successfully reduced many complex business issues into a single readable, introductory text.
[C72] Penguin pbk **£4.95**

FALLON, IVAN & SRODES, JAMES
Takeovers
Dawn Raids, White Knights, Poisoned Pills, and Boardroom Battles to the death!
[C73] Pan pbk **£4.99**

GRAY, S.J & MCDERMOTT, M.C.
Mega-Merger Mayhem: Takeover Strategies, Battles and Controls NEW
A fascinating account of corporate drama and intrigue, covering seven key takeover battles of recent years, as well as their context in relation to government policy.
[C74] P Chapman hbk **£19.95**

GREEN, EDWIN
Banking: An Illustrated History NEW
A beautifully illustrated book that serves as a scholarly and stylish history of an important profession.
[C75] Phaidon hbk **£25.00**

HILTON, ANTHONY
City Within a State: A Portrait of Britain's Financial World
[C76] IB Tauris hbk **£14.95**

JAMES, BARRIE G.
Trojan Horses: The Ultimate Japanese Challenge to Western Industry NEW
This controversial book is critical of the placing of assembly plants in Britain and the United States and suggests that they are of benefit mostly to Japan.
[C77] Mercury hbk **£15.00**

KINDLEBERGER, CHARLES P.
Manias, Panics and Crashes
Prophetic account of modern day economy written before Black Monday.
[C78] Macmillan hbk **£29.50**

MADRICK, JEFF
Marrying for Money
An accessible guide to the evolution of the modern merger phenomenon, insider trading and the Boesky scandal.
[C79] Bloomsbury hbk **£12.95**

PARKINSON, C.N.
Parkinson's Law
A classic humorous look at the underlying laws of business organisation.
[C80] Penguin pbk **£3.99**

PLENDER, JOHN & WALLACE, PAUL
The Square Mile: A Guide to the City Revolution
Originating from a television series, this is a non-technical book that serves as a very good introduction to the financial sector.
[C81] Century pbk **£4.95**

PUGH; HICKSON, HININGS
Writers on Organisations
A good review of various modern opinion makers and their theories.
[C82] Penguin pbk **£4.95**

REID, MARGARET
Anatomy of the City
Detailed study of the City of London after the Big Bang.
[C83] Macmillan hbk **£25.00**

ROSE, MICHAEL
Industrial Behaviour
A review of 'Industrial Sociology', providing much valuable information of interest to anyone concerned with society, work, managers and the managed.
[C84] Penguin pbk **£7.99**

SAMPSON, ANTHONY
The Changing Anatomy of Britain
The classic readable social and economic history that provides a good introductory look at Britain and its institutions.
[C85] Hodder pbk **£5.99**

SOBEL, ROBERT
Inside Wall Street
An American institution examined.
[C86] Norton pbk **£5.65**

VELJANOVSKI, CENTO
Selling the State: Privatisation in Britain
A general assessment of an aspect of government economic policy.
[C87] Weidenfeld hbk **£14.95**

VINER, ARON
The Financial Samurai: The Emerging Power of Japanese Money
A startling look at the pervasive influence of Japanese financial power.
[C88] Kogan Page hbk **£12.95**

WEST, H.
Fraud: The Growth Industry
[C89] Kogan Page hbk **£8.95**

WILTSHIRE, KENNETH
Privatisation: The British Experience
An academic look at the pros and cons of privatisation.
[C90] Longman pbk **£7.50**

WINANS, R. FOSTER
Trading Secrets: Seduction and Scandal on Wall Street
A racy read describing the setting up of a 'deal', how it worked, how much money was made, and how the perpetrators were caught.
[C91] Hodder pbk **£3.99**

Companies & Individuals

To improve the performance of one's business it is best to study the methods of successful operations Listed here, in alphabetical order of company / individual, are new and established books, whose common factor is their ability to encourage and educate the reader to new heights of business success.

APPLE COMPUTER
ROSE, FRANK
West of Eden: The End of Innocence at Apple Computer NEW
Controversial and enlightening study of how Apple Computer was transformed from a large garage operation into a disaster-prone, publicly-traded corporation that drove out its founders.
[C92] Hutchinson hbk **£14.95**

Anthony Sampson, author of *The Changing Anatomy of Britain* (Hodder & Stoughton pbk £5.99)

ARCHIER, GEORGE & SERIEYX, HERVE
The Type Three Company
This book looks at a number of 'excellent' companies in several countries concerned with the management of people, products, processes and relationships. It has already made a big impact in France, where it has won two business awards.
[C93] Gower hbk **£18.50**

BOONE, PICKENS T.
Boone
This man turned a $2,500 investment into Mesa Petroleum, the largest independent oil company in the US . Full of fascinating anecdotes.
[C94] Hodder hbk **£12.95**

BRUCE, ROBERT
Winners
A study of some winners of the Industrial Achievement Awards: it looks at what makes a successful company, and what lessons can be learned from them.
[C95] Sphere pbk **£3.99**

THE SULTAN OF BRUNEI
BARTHOLEMEW, JAMES
The Richest Man in the World:
The Sultan of Brunei `NEW`
The history and sumptuous lifestyle of the man whose wealth is beyond most people's imagination is described in this well-written biography.
[C96] Viking hbk **£12.95**

CARLZON, JAN
Moments of Truth
In this clear, anecdotal book, Carlzon explains how to restructure an organization so that customer needs take priority, how to utilize those employees who deal most closely with customers, and how to unleash employee motivation by delegating responsibility.
[C97] Harper & R pbk **£5.50**

CLORE
CLUTTERBUCK, DAVID & DEVINE, MARION
Clore
An interesting biography of a successful entrepreneur.
[C98] Weidenfeld pbk **£7.95**

EDWARDES, MICHAEL
Back from the Brink
An important case-study (from the ex-boss of British Leyland) of how to effect change in a large organisation. Still of practical interest today.
[C99] Pan pbk **£3.50**

EZRA, DEREK & OATES, DAVID
Advice from the Top `NEW`
12 business strategies from Britain's corporate leaders, ranging from de Savary to Conran.
[C100] David & Ch hbk **£12.95**

FAY, STEPHEN
Portrait of an Old Lady: Turmoil at the Bank of England
A candid look at our most famous financial institution.
[C101] Penguin pbk **£7.99**

FERRIS, PAUL
Gentlemen of Fortune
A well-written account of successful achievers.
[C102] Weidenfeld pbk **£6.95**

FIELD, MICHAEL
The Merchants: The Big Business Families of Arabia
The authoritative account of the Arabian commercial dynasties.
[C103] J Murray hbk **£17.95**

FORD, HENRY
LACEY, ROBERT
Ford
An excellent writer, Lacey's study of Ford is business biography at its best.
[C104] Pan pbk **£2.50**

FORTE, CHARLES
Forte: The Autobiography of Charles Forte
The great businessman, by himself.
[C105] Pan pbk **£4.99**

GARFIELD, CHARLES A.
Peak Performers: The New Heroes of American Business
A key text in the study of American business successes of recent years.
[C106] Hutchinson pbk **£5.95**

GEDDES, PHILIP
Inside the Bank of England
[C107] Boxtree hbk **£12.95**

GETTY, J. PAUL
LENZNER, ROBERT
Getty: The Richest Man in the World
A rare glimpse at the reclusive Getty.
[C108] Grafton pbk **£3.50**

GOLDSMITH, WALTER & RITCHIE, BERRY
The New Elite
Ten of Britain's top Chief Executives reveal the secrets of their success, talking with frankness about their careers, companies and British politics.
[C109] Penguin pbk **£6.95**

GOLDSMITH, WALTER & CLUTTERBUCK, DAVID
The Winning Streak
An important, stimulating analysis of the UK's most successful companies.
[C110] Penguin pbk **£4.50**
The Winning Streak Workout Book
An exercise-oriented follow-up to the above.
[C111] Penguin pbk **£3.50**

GUCCI
MCKNIGHT, GERALD
Gucci: A House Divided
An insight into business, ambition and fame.
[C112] Pan pbk **£3.99**

HARVEY-JONES, SIR JOHN
Making it Happen: Reflections on Leadership
Beginning with his experiences after the war supervising the transfer of a naval dockyard - every bolt of it - from Germany to Russia, this fascinating memoir traces Harvey-Jones's career to the top of ICI and into retirement. Full of inspiration and practical advice on running an organization as well as one's own life, it was regarded by many as the best business book of 1988.
[C113] Fontana pbk **£3.95**

HURST, MARGERY
Walking Down Brook Street
This inspirational book, the story of the efforts of one woman in creating the Brook Street Bureau.
[C114] Weidenfeld hbk **£10.95**

IACOCCA, LEE
Iacocca
Quite a classic of recent years, this is an excellent example of an entrepreneur writing an inspirational and practical book.
[C115] Bantam pbk **£4.95**

Sir John Harvey-Jones, author of *Making it Happen* (Fontana pbk £3.95)

WYDEN, PETER
The Unknown Iacocca
A personal look at the successful businessman.
[C116] Sidgwick hbk **£12.95**

IBM
CHOPOSKY, JAMES & LEONIS, TED
Blue Magic
Subtitled 'The People, the Power and the Politics behind the IBM Personal Computer', this is the first complete account of a most spectacular success story.
[C117] Grafton hbk **£14.95**
DELAMARTER, R.T.
Big Blue - IBM's Use and Abuse of Power
Of the books written about IBM, this is most critical.
[C118] Pan pbk **£4.99**
MAISONROUGE, JACQUES
Inside IBM: A European's Story
An account of the growth of IBM, a perspective from within the company.
[C119] Fontana pbk **£3.50**
MERCER, DAVID
IBM: How the World's Most Successful Corporation is Managed
Emphasizes the practical lessons to be drawn from its success.
[C120] Kogan Page hbk **£12.95**
RODGERS, BUCK & SHOOK, ROBERT L.
The IBM Way: Insights into the World's Most Successful Marketing Organisation
Of all the books about IBM, this one has made the most impact in terms of offering inspiration to companies who wish to emulate IBM's success.
[C121] Harper & R pbk **£6.95**

KAY, WILLIAM
Battle for the High Street
A topical look at some of Britain's major retailers and the way they are changing the face of our high streets.
[C122] Corgi pbk **£3.99**

KHASHOGGI
KESSLER, RONALD
Khashoggi: The Story of the World's Richest Man
An interesting look at the controversial and wealthy Khashoggi.
[C123] Bantam hbk **£10.95**

LEVINE, DENNIS
FRANTZ DOUGLAS
Mr Diamond
The story of Wall Street's most infamous
insider trader.
[C124] Pan pbk **£4.99**

LEWIS, MICHAEL M.
Liar's Poker `NEW`
A leading bond salesman for the world's most
profitable investment bank - Salomon Brothers -
Lewis looks back on his career at the Golden
Age of banking, at the company he worked for,
and at the spectacle of the financial boom which
marks the 1980s - a spectacle of greed, fear
and human folly.
[C125] Hodder hbk **£12.95**

MACDONALD'S
LOVE, JOHN F.
McDonald's: Behind the Arches
The story of how a single hamburger stand
was turned into a multi-million dollar
international corporation.
[C126] Bantam pbk **£4.95**

MAXWELL, ROBERT
BOWER, TOM
Maxwell: The Outsider
A controversial study - this is the book Maxwell tried
to ban.
[C127] Sphere pbk **£3.99**
HAINES, JOE
Maxwell
The official biography.
[C128] Futura pbk **£3.99**

MCLACHLAN SANDY
The National Freight Buy-Out
[C129] Macmillan hbk **£35.00**

MORITA, AKIO
Made in Japan:
Akio Morita & Sony
A thoroughly readable autobiography, and one
of the few books in English about Japanese
management methods actually written by a Japanese
chief executive.
[C130] Fontana pbk **£3.50**

NOMURA
ALLETZHAUR, ALBERT
The House of Nomura `NEW`
Tells the inside story of the rise to power of the most
powerful company in the world. Nomura Securities is
a firm so wealthy that it could buy up every stock-
broking firm in London.
[C131] Bloomsbury hbk **£12.95**

RAMSEY, DOUGLAS K.
The Corporate Warriors
A revealing exploration of some of the bitterly-fought
struggles of the 70s and 80s, including Penthouse
v. Playboy, General Motors v. the Japanese, and
Coke v. Pepsi.
[C132] Grafton pbk **£4.95**

ROBINSON, JEFFREY
Minus Millionaires
A colourful selection of stories about the world's
most extravagant failures.
[C133] Grafton pbk **£3.99**

ROWLAND, TINY
HALL, RICHARD
My Life with Tiny
A personal account of the career of 'Tiny' Rowland
by a former employee.
[C134] Faber pbk **£4.95**

SAATCHI AND SAATCHI
FALLON, IVAN
The Brothers: Rise and Rise of the
Saatchis
Illuminating look at the Saatchis, whose rise has not
been so meteoric since its publication.
[C135] Hutchinson hbk **£14.95**

SAMPSON, ANTHONY
Writing in an accessible, journalistic style, Anthony
Sampson has brought his perceptive mind to bear on
many aspects of the business world. The resulting
works are examples of investigative business writing
at its best.
Black and Gold
[C136] Hodder pbk **£3.95**
Empire of the Sky
[C137] Hodder pbk **£2.50**
The Arms Bazaar
[C138] Hodder pbk **£4.50**
The Midas Touch `NEW`
Published in association with BBC Books, this
is about money in the 1980s: why people
want it, how they use it, how it changes them and
connects them together. A companion to the BBC
series, the book includes much original and
additional material.
[C139] Hodder hbk **£16.95**
The Moneylenders
[C140] Hodder pbk **£4.50**
The Seven Sisters: The Great Oil
Companies and the World They Made
[C141] Hodder pbk **£4.50**

SCULLEY, JOHN
Odyssey: Pepsi to Apple
Personal and practical account of one of the world's
most successful marketing executives.
[C142] Fontana pbk **£4.95**

SIEFF, MARCUS
Don't Ask the Price
The life of the President of Marks and Spencer
in his own words. An inspiring story of determination
and success.
[C143] Fontana pbk **£3.95**

SINCLAIR, CLIVE
ADAMSON, IAN & KENNEDY, RICHARD
Sinclair and the Sunrise Technology
A not wholly sympathetic account of one of Britain's
dynamic entrepreneurs.
[C144] Penguin pbk **£3.95**

SLOAN, ALFRED P.
My Years with General Motors
A story of inspiration, leadership and triumph. Sloan
uses his 20 years as Chief Executive of GM to
illustrate the key strategies of successful management.
[C145] Penguin pbk **£5.95**

THOMSON, SIR ADAM
High Risk `NEW`
In this book, subtitled 'The Full Story of the
Rise and Fall of British Caledonian Airways',
Sir Adam Thomson here writes for the first time
about his business success story and the high
drama in the boardroom following the British
Airways takover. An entertaining and instructive
autobiography.
[C146] Sidgwick hbk **£15.00**

TRUMP, DONALD J.
Trump - The Art of the Deal
The doyen of New York society, and one of the
world's most successful businessman, Trump has
written a punchy autobiography that highlights his no-
nonsense negotiating methods.
[C147] Arrow pbk **£3.99**

SHEIKH YAMANI
ROBINSON, JEFFREY
Yamani: The Inside Story
A controversial book about one of the world's most
powerful men.
[C148] Fontana pbk **£4.50**

YAMASHITA, TOSHIKA
The Panasonic Way `NEW`
The autobiography of the man who made Panasonic
one of the most successful companies in the world.
[C149] Kodansha Int hbk **£11.95**

Personal Finance

We list here a selection of practical books on tax,
insurance and investment for the non-specialist. All
are regularly updated.

Check Your Tax: Money and Facts
[C150] Foulsham pbk **£2.75**

Sunday Telegraph 101 Ways of
Saving Tax
[C151] Sunday Telegraph pbk **£1.95**

Tolley's Tax Efficient Personal
Investment
[C152] Tolley's pbk **£11.95**
Tolley's Tax Guide
[C153] Tolley's hbk **£15.95**

With Government Approval
[C154] Sunday Telegraph pbk **£1.95**

ALLIED DUNBAR GUIDES
Capital Taxes and Estate Planning
Guide
[C155] Longman hbk **£13.50**
Expatriate Tax and Investment Guide
[C156] Longman hbk **£13.50**
Guide to Buying Your Home
[C157] Longman pbk **£4.95**
Guide to Investing in Shares
[C158] Longman pbk **£5.50**
Guide to Managing Your Finances
[C159] Longman pbk **£5.50**
Investment Guide 1989 - 90
[C160] Longman hbk **£13.95**
Leaving Your Money Wisely
[C161] Longman pbk **£4.95**
Pay, Perks and Employment `NEW`
Looks at the entire employment process, and
covers: seeking and applying for a job; remuneration;
pensions; sick pay; unions and equal opportunities;
and leaving work. Intended for both employer and
employee.
[C162] Longman pbk **£4.95**
Planning School and College Fees
[C163] Longman pbk **£4.95**
Tax Guide 1989 - 90 `NEW`
Facts, figures and expert guidance on every aspect of
personal and business taxation in jargon-free
language, with the emphasis on paying less tax.
[C164] Longman hbk **£13.95**

BOSE, MIHIR
Insurance: Are You Covered?
A thorough, practical look at insurance.
[C165] Longman pbk **£4.95**

BRETT, MICHAEL
How to Read the Financial Pages
Very reliable and easy-to-read guide to the
financial world.
[C166] Hutchinson pbk **£5.95**

BURGESS, JOHN
Personal Financial Planning: How to Manage Your Money Effectively
[C167] Kogan P pbk **£2.50**

BURR, ROSEMARY
100 Money Saving Ideas
[C168] Rosters pbk **£2.00**
Prudential Book of Money: Unlock Your Profit Potential Today
[C169] Rosters pbk **£3.50**
Sticky Fingers: How to Get Ripped Off and Enjoy It
[C170] Rosters pbk **£2.95**
The Share Book
A complete guide to shares, for novices and old hands alike.
[C171] Rosters pbk **£5.95**
Unit Trusts Explained: The Easy Way to Buy Shares
[C172] Rosters pbk **£3.99**

BYLAND, TERRY
Understanding Finance with 'The Financial Times'
The workings of the financial world are here explained for the executive, the new investor and the student.
[C173] Harrap pbk **£5.95**

CHAPMAN, COLIN
How the New Stock Exchange Works
Buying and selling stocks and shares in the new stockmarket.
[C174] Hutchinson pbk **£5.95**

CUMMINGS, GORDON
Investor's Guide to the Stock Market
[C175] Financial Times pbk **£9.50**

DAILY TELEGRAPH GUIDES
Daily Telegraph Guide to Income Tax 1989 - 90
In which money-saving and tax advice are combined with details of the 1989 budget and its implications for the public.
[C176] Daily Telegraph pbk **£2.95**

DELOITTE TAX DEPARTMENT
Reducing Your Personal Tax Bill
Clear advice, with examples, on the variety of allowances and reliefs which can help to keep one's tax bill to a minimum.
[C177] Deloitte HS pbk **£4.95**

ELKINGTON, WENDY
How to Beat the Money Sharks
A member of the Daily Mail's 'Money Mail' team gives advice in the light of the Financial Services Act.
[C178] Rosters pbk **£5.95**

GARTLAND, PETER
Dumenil Guide to International Investment
Will prove useful to all UK investors interested in finding out more about the wider opportunities which changing global markets offer them.
[C179] Rosters pbk **£5.95**

HARDMAN, ROGER
Stocks and Shares
[C180] Daily Telegraph pbk **£5.95**

JOHNSON, LUKE & ROBERTS, RICHARD
The Key to Making Money in the New Stock Market
An authoritative, highly readable and eminently practical book, not just for the city professional.
[C181] Weidenfeld pbk **£5.95**

LEVENE, TONY
The Daily Mail Guide to Insurance
A clear and comprehensive guide to the wide array of insurance policies now available.
[C182] Sidgwick pbk **£6.95**

MADDOCKS, TOM & ASHWORTH, ANNE
The Investor's Survival Guide: How to Cope with the Stock Market Jitters
[C183] Rosters pbk **£4.95**

MITCHELL, ALISON
The Penguin Personal Finance Guide
The author guarantees that if you take her advice you will: get more interest, pay less tax, sell your house for more, and get a better retirement deal etc.
[C184] Penguin pbk **£8.99**

PRIDHAM, HELEN
Managing Your Finances
The second edition of this very reliable book will be appearing in December 1989.
[C185] Longman pbk **£4.95**

REES-MOGG, WILLIAM & DAVIDSON, JAMES DALE
Blood in the Streets
A fascinating look at the relationship between political events and the money markets, with a view to a practical application of these insights towards making money oneself.
[C186] Sidgwick pbk **£9.95**

ROSE, SIMON
Fair Shares: The Post Big Bang Edition
Useful and readable guide by the editor of *The Shareholder* magazine. One of the best on the subject.
[C187] Mercury pbk **£5.95**
The Shareholder
Rather than concentrating on the buying and selling of shares, this looks at the majority of Britons who own, but do not trade them. It is peppered with pertinent and often hilarious anecdotes.
[C188] Mercury hbk **£10.95**

STOPP, CHRISTINE
More Shares for Your Money
A guide to buying investment trust shares.
[C189] Rosters pbk **£5.95**

WALTERS, MICHAEL
How to Make a Killing from Penny Shares
[C190] Sidgwick pbk **£5.95**
How to Make a Killing in New Issues
[C191] Sidgwick pbk **£5.95**
How to Make a Killing in the Share Jungle
[C192] Sidgwick pbk **£6.95**
How to Profit from your Personal Equity Plan
[C193] Sidgwick pbk **£5.95**

WHICH?
How to Make Your Own Will
New style action-pack full of information, advice and practical loose-leaf aids.
[C194] Hodder pbk **£6.95**
Which? Book of Tax
[C195] Hodder pbk **£9.95**
Which? How to Buy, Sell and Own Shares
[C196] Hodder pbk **£7.95**

WILLIAMS, DAVID
Tax for the Self-Employed   **NEW**
The second edition of this authoritative guide, due to appear at the end of 1989.
[C197] Longman pbk **£4.95**

WILLIAMS, SARA & WILLMAN, JOHN
The Lloyds Bank Tax Guide 1989/90
Written for anyone who has to deal with personal tax: a concise and popular handbook.
[C198] Penguin pbk **£4.99**

WRIGHT, DIANA
'Sunday Times' Book of Personal Finance
[C199] David & Ch pbk **£5.95**

WULLSCHLAGER, JACKIE
'Financial Times' Guide to Alternative Investments   **NEW**
A new and interesting book that includes information on collecting and speculating in Fine Arts. Covers the tax, valuation, insurance, and storage of a wide range of artefacts, from porcelain to pictures, cars to musical instruments.
[C200] Financial Times pbk **£14.50**

Living Abroad

A selection of books offering practical advice to anyone considering living or working abroad.

Expatriate Survival Kit
A comprehensive kit providing all the information and paperwork needed for a smooth transition from life at home to life abroad.
[C201] Financial Times other **£13.50**

Retiring Abroad
A step-by-step guide to making a success of settling overseas. A very informative book.
[C202] Financial Times hbk **£14.50**

BARKER, PHILIP
Retiring in Spain
[C203] Blandford pbk **£6.95**

BROWN, HARRY
Retiring Abroad?
Excellent guide to the financial dos and don'ts of being an expatriate.
[C204] Northcote pbk **£8.95**
Working Abroad?
This fifth edition of the classic handbook guide to the fiscal and financial dos and don'ts is full of more hardhitting advice on tax and money matters.
[C205] Northcote pbk **£7.95**

HALE
Invaluable and comprehensive guides, dealing with every conceivable aspect of each country for the potential resident.
Living in Italy
[C206] Hale hbk **£11.95**
Living in Portugal
[C207] Hale hbk **£10.95**

JONES, ALAN
How to Get a Job Abroad
Written by a recruitment consultant with first hand experience, this is an eminently practical book on how to succeed.
[C208] Northcote pbk **£6.95**

LONGMAN
Good, informative, and brief guides.
Your Home in France
[C209] Longman pbk **£4.95**
Your Home in Italy
[C210] Longman pbk **£4.95**
Your Home in Portugal
[C211] Longman pbk **£4.95**

Your Home in Spain
[C212] Longman pbk **£4.95**

NORTHCOTE
How to Live and Work in America
[C213] Northcote pbk **£7.95**
How to Live and Work in Australia
[C214] Northcote pbk **£6.95**
How to Live and Work in Belgium
[C215] Northcote pbk **£7.95**
How to Live and Work in Germany
[C216] Northcote pbk **£7.95**
How to Live and Work in Japan
[C217] Northcote pbk **£7.95**
How to Live and Work in Saudi Arabia
[C218] Northcote pbk **£7.95**

WARREN & NOLLET
Setting Up in France
An up-to-date, comprehensive guide.
[C219] Merehurst hbk **£9.95**

YOUNG, DAVID
Working Abroad - The Expatriate's Guide
A practical handbook covering the financial aspects of working abroad.
[C220] Financial Times pbk **£8.95**

Pensions & Retirement

Successful retirement and an adequate pension can only come about through careful long-term planning. These books are some of the best guides available and provide help in making the correct decisions.

Good Retirement Guide
[C223] Bloomsbury pbk **£10.95**

AGE CONCERN
Your Taxes and Savings 1989 - 90
Leads readers through the complexities of the tax system, and examines potential forms of investment in relation to the needs of older people.
[C224] Age Concern pbk **£2.50**

ALLIED DUNBAR
Financial Planning for the Over-50s
Explains how various pension and investment schemes work, and how to make best use of all the opportunities available.
[C225] Longman pbk **£4.95**
Pensions Guide
[C226] Longman hbk **£13.50**
Guide to Planning Your Pension
Revised edition covering the new personal pension plans and how they work.
[C221] Longman pbk **£4.95**
Retirement Planning Guide
[C222] Longman hbk **£13.95**

BURR, R.
Make Your Pension Work
How to choose the best pension to suit your needs. Recommended.
[C227] Rosters pbk **£5.95**

LEVENE, TONY
Planning Your Retirement
Sets out all the legal, financial and practical matters that ought to be to be considered when approaching retirement.
[C228] Daily Telegraph pbk **£5.95**

LEWIS, DAVID
Your Pension: The Norwich Union Guide
[C229] Penguin pbk **£4.95**

REARDON, TONY
Planning Your Pension
The revised second edition, available from the end of 1989.
[C230] Longman pbk **£4.95**

SPILL, RON
Investing in Pensions
Easy to understand, and well-informed guide to pension schemes, legislation, mortgage-linked pensions, married women's rights etc.
[C231] Ward Lock pbk **£4.99**

WHICH?
Approaching Retirement
Excellent guide to planning ahead for retirement - particulary on financial matters.
[C232] Hodder pbk **£6.95**
How to Choose Your Pension
A new manual offering information, advice and practical aids such as looseleaf worksheets, forms and directories.
[C233] Hodder pbk **£7.95**
Where to Live After Retirement
Describes how a wider range of accommodation may be available on retirement, through correct financial planning at earlier stages.
[C234] Hodder pbk **£5.95**

WILSON, JOHN & CARMEL
A Guide to Pensions and Life Assurance
A simple explanation of how life assurance can be the cheapest and most efficient way to meet most personal and financial needs, from savings and family protection to buying a house and building up a pension for retirement.
[C235] Kogan Page pbk **£13.95**

Practical Business & Enterprise

To improve personal business effectiveness, whether for oneself or for the company one works for, is the ultimate aim of the titles featured in this section: Whether practical or inspirational, many have received enormous acclaim for actually changing the work patterns of those who have read them.

ADAIR, JOHN
Effective Decision Making
[C236] Pan pbk **£3.95**
How to Manage Your Time
[C237] McGraw-Hill hbk **£13.95**

ADAMS, JOHN L.
Conceptual Blockbusting
This book describes how to develop more effective business strategies through broadening the scope of one's thinking.
[C238] Penguin pbk **£5.95**

ANTHONY, WILLIAM P.
Managing your Boss
Survival strategies and techniques for career advancement.
[C239] Amacon pbk **£9.95**

ATKINSON, GERALD
Negotiating the Best Deal   **NEW**
A new book that offers a systematic approach for preparation, and face-to-face negotiation. Case studies

and examples of working documents are included.
[C240] Director Bks hbk **£16.95**

BACK, KEN & KATE
Assertiveness at Work
A concise well-written and practical book.
[C241] McGraw-Hill hbk **£12.95**

BENTLEY
Report Writing in Business
[C242] Kogan Page pbk **£4.95**

BERNSTEIN, DAVID
Put it Together, Put it Across: The Craft of Business Presentation
A practical book that offers guidance for speech planning and preparation, and for its most effective delivery.
[C243] Cassell pbk **£9.95**

BONO, EDWARD DE
Conflicts: A Better Way to Resolve Them
[C244] Harrap hbk **£10.95**
[C245] Penguin pbk **£4.50**
Opportunities: Handbook of Business Opportunities
[C246] Penguin pbk **£4.50**
Tactics: The Art and Science of Success
[C247] Collins hbk **£9.95**
[C248] Fontana pbk **£4.95**

BOSTICCO, MARY
Instant Business Letters
[C249] Wildwood H pbk **£6.95**
Personal Letters for Business People
A new edition, revised and expanded, with hundreds of actual specimens to cover a wide variety of occasions and opportunities.
[C250] Gower pbk **£6.95**

BURKE, JOHN
The Management of Luck
How to make the element of luck work for you in your career, by the Chairman of Glaxo Pharmaceuticals Ltd.
[C251] Macdonald hbk **£11.95**

CAPEL, IFOR & GUMSEY, JOHN
Managing Stress
A straightforward guided to dealing with work-related stress.
[C252] Constable pbk **£6.95**

DENING, JIM
Ready-made Business Letters
[C253] Kogan Page pbk **£7.95**

EMDEN, JOAN VAN & EASTEAL, JENNIFER
Report Writing
[C254] McGraw-Hill pbk **£4.95**

FARNSWORTH, TERRY
On the Way Up
The author provides some good practical advice for the upwardly mobile.
[C255] Mcgraw-hill pbk **£9.50**
Power Plays: The 22 Point Executive Jungle Survivor's Guide
A combination of sound advice and humour makes this an invaluable book for survival in the executive jungle.
[C256] Arrow pbk **£2.99**

FISHER, MARK
The Instant Millionaire
A clear guide to financial and personal growth.
[C257] Sidgwick hbk **£9.95**

FISHER, ROGER
Getting to Yes (with William Ury)
A useful, well-established book on the skills of
negotiation.
[C258] Arrow pbk **£5.95**
Getting Together (with Scott Brown) **NEW**
A sequel to *Getting to Yes*, this book aims to show
how to build working relationships that really work.
[C259] Hutchinson hbk **£15.95**

FRANCIS, DAVE
Managing Your Own Career
Strategies for success and advancement.
[C260] Fontana pbk **£3.95**

FRANCIS, DAVE & WOODCOCK, MIKE
The Unblocked Manager: A Practical
Guide to Self-Development
Written for managers who wish to improve their
personal effectiveness. A well-established book.
[C261] Wildwood H pbk **£7.95**

GARRATT, SALLY
Managing Your Time
Concise volume that explains clearly the principles of
time management.
[C262] Fontana pbk **£3.50**

GELB, MICHAEL
Present Yourself
Demonstrates how one can strengthen one's
personality and skills to reach a dramatically higher
level of performance in the essential art of public
presentation.
[C263] Aurum P pbk **£5.95**

GOLZEN, GODFREY & PLUMBLEY, PHILIP
Changing Your Job After 35
[C264] Kogan Page pbk **£6.95**

GOODWORTH, CLIVE
How to Do More in Less Time
[C265] Hutchinson hbk **£13.95**
How to be a Super-Effective Manager
[C266] Hutchinson pbk **£6.50**
Taking the Strain: Managing Stress
at Work
[C267] Business Bks pbk **£6.95**

HAMPSHIRE, SHEILA & JAAP, TOM
How to Realise Your Potential
This short book is aimed at inspiring confidence in
oneself, and offers practical advice on achieving
success.
[C268] IPM pbk **£3.25**

HOPKINS, TOM
The Official Guide to Success
A popular handbook on personal effectiveness.
[C269] Grafton pbk **£2.99**

HUGHES, CHARLES L.
Goal Setting: The Key to Individual and
Organisational Effectiveness
A useful book about a useful concept.
[C270] Amer Man Ass pbk **£6.95**

JAMES, KIM & ARROBA, TANYA
Pressure at Work: A Survival Guide
Explains strategies for coping with stress.
[C271] McGraw-Hill hbk **£9.95**

KARP, H.B.
Personal Power: An Unorthodox Guide
to Success
An instructive book on the nature of power and the
constructive uses to which it can be put in both
business and personal relationships.
[C272] Amer Man Ass pbk **£7.95**

KARRASS, GARY
Negotiate to Close:
How to Make More Successful Deals
A popular and practical guide which teaches how to
come out on top.
[C273] Fontana pbk **£4.95**

KELLY, FRANCIS & HEATHER
What They Really Teach You at Harvard
Business School
Summarizes the Harvard approach to getting on in
business.
[C274] Grafton pbk **£3.99**

KENNEDY, ALAN
Managing Negotiations
[C275] Arrow pbk **£6.95**

KENNEDY, GAVIN
Everything is Negotiable
[C276] Arrow pbk **£3.99**
Negotiate Anywhere
[C277] Arrow pbk **£5.95**

KHADEM & LORBER
One Page Management
One of the most critical issues of management
is having instant, easy access to information, and
the ability to appreciate quickly and accurately
what is happening. *One Page Management*
shows how.
[C278] Sidgwick pbk **£7.95**

KIAM, VICTOR
Going for It !
Hard-hitting advice from the Remington razor man
who 'bought the company!'
[C279] Fontana pbk **£3.50**

KORVING, MARGARET
Running Your Own Office
A welcome little book on self- and office-
management.
[C280] BBC pbk **£3.95**

MCCORMACK, MARK
Success Secrets **NEW**
One of the most powerful business writers gives us
the street-smart executive's guide to how to beat the
competition.
[C281] Collins hbk **£12.95**
What They Don't Teach You at Harvard
Business School
Well-established as a modern classic, this book is a
tour-de-force of instruction on what are the best
attitudes to develop to make oneself, and one's
business, the best.
[C282] Fontana pbk **£4.95**
What They Don't Teach You at Harvard
Law School
Originally titled 'The Terrible Truth About Lawyers',
McCormack here gives timely advice on the pitfalls
of legal aspects of business.
[C283] Fontana pbk **£6.95**

PEDLER, MIKE & BOYDELL, TOM
Managing Yourself
A concise guide to organising one's life.
[C284] Fontana pbk **£3.95**

POPPLEWELL & WILDSMITH
Becoming the Best **NEW**
[C285] Gower hbk **£12.95**

PRICE, FRANK
Right First Time:
Using Quality Control for Profit
A key text on the subject.
[C286] Wildwood H pbk **£6.95**

Victor Kiam, author of *Going For It !* (Fontana pbk
£3.50)

RAWLINSON, J. GEOFFREY
Creative Thinking and Brainstorming
A good explanation of some techniques aimed at
developing one's potential.
[C287] Wildwood H pbk **£5.95**

ROBERTS, PAT
Living Images:
Styling Yourself for Success **NEW**
A useful guide that looks at the importance of
one's physical presentation and how ultimately it
can lead to career success. Particularly helpful for
women who may be considering a return to work
after a break.
[C288] Mercury hbk **£9.95**

RODGERS, BUCK
Getting the Best out of Yourself and
Others
A very instructive book from the author of *The IBM*
Way.
[C289] Harper & R hbk **£12.95**

SMILES, SAMUEL
Self-Help
The classic Victorian text that vividly portrays the
entrepreneurial spirit. The book that helped to launch
a thousand enterprises.
[C290] Penguin pbk **£3.95**

STUBBS, DAVID R.
How to Use Assertiveness
at Work
A straightforward, practical book.
[C291] Gower hbk **£12.50**

THORN, JEREMY
How to Negotiate Better Deals **NEW**
A well-arranged and thorough treatment of
negotiation. A handy reference manual.
[C292] Mercury hbk **£10.95**

TURLA, PETER & HAWKINS, KATHLEEN L.
Time Management Made Easy
A good introduction to some Time Management
practices.
[C293] Grafton pbk **£2.99**

WEISS, DONALD H.
Get Organised!
Advice on managing one's individual performance at work.
[C294] Kogan page pbk **£2.95**
Managing Stress
Clearly written handbook for anyone in stressful situations.
[C295] Kogan Page pbk **£2.95**

Women in Business

A selection of titles, offering inspiration and practical advice for women, particularly in terms of personal career success.

BAILEY, ROBERTA
Travelling Alone: A Guide for Working Women
This guide shows how careful planning and a few simple rules can ensure successful and enjoyable business trips.
[C296] Macdonald pbk **£5.95**

BEARD, MARY
Good Working Mother's Guide
A practical guide covering everything a prospective working mother needs to know: from maternity rights to breast-feeding, and employing help.
[C297] Duckworth pbk **£4.95**

BRYCE, LEE
The Influential Woman NEW
Subtitled 'How to Achieve Success Without Losing Your Feminity', this inspirational and helpful book gives advice on finding the qualities within that make for success, and the inner blocks and conditioning that cause women to hold themselves back.
[C298] Piatkus hbk **£12.95**

CAMERON, JANET
The Competitive Woman
A survival guide for the woman who aims to be boss - business from the woman's angle.
[C299] Mercury hbk **£9.95**

CHAPMAN, JANE
Women Working it Out
A good, concise reference book with practical advice and lots of useful information.
[C300] Careers & Occ pbk **£2.95**

DAVIDSON, MARILYN
Reach for the Top
A readable, practical guide to women's career success.
[C301] Piatkus pbk **£5.95**

GALLESE, LIZ ROMAN
Women Like Us
[C302] Grafton pbk **£3.95**

GROOCOCK, VERONICA
Women Mean Business
A guide to survival and success based on interviews with top business women.
[C303] Ebury pbk **£5.95**

HERTZ, LEAH
The Business Amazons
[C304] Deutsch hbk **£9.95**

MACDONALD, JANET
Climbing the Ladder: How to be a Woman Manager
Straightforward advice on women's career strategies.
[C305] Methuen pbk **£4.95**

How to be a Successful Business Woman: Working for Yourself
This book is of particular interest for women keen to start, or in the process of starting up a new business.
[C306] Methuen pbk **£4.95**
The Super Saleswoman
This book aims to show women how to get into selling, and how to develop one's career, as well as showing those already in selling how to improve their techniques.
[C307] Mandarin pbk **£4.99**

MOORE, DEBBIE
When a Woman Means Business
A challenging autobiography from a successful woman - the first to be admitted to the floor of the London Stock Exchange, following the flotation of Pineapple Dance Studios. An accessible and indispensable guide for every woman of ambition.
[C308] Pavilion hbk **£12.95**

O'CONNOR, GEMMA
Back to Work: A Guide for Women
Whether you are planning to return to a former career, start a new one, set up your own business, or go back to full-time education, this book provides advice and support with a touch of humour, and will help to pave the way.
[C309] Optima pbk **£5.99**

PRIDHAM, HELEN
Tax and Financial Planning for Women: The Allied Dunbar Money Guide NEW
The ever-increasing financial independence of women has meant new approaches and considerations for them in the area of tax and financial planning. This book looks at the woman's position and covers the whole range of financial aspects that she must consider, whether single or married.
[C310] Longman pbk **£4.95**

ROUCHE, JANICE LA & RYAN, REGINA
Strategies for Women at Work
Some good personal and career advice for the working woman.
[C311] Unwin Hyman pbk **£4.95**

SKINNER, JANE & FRITICHIE, RONNIE
Working Choices:
A Life Planning Guide for Women Today
[C312] Dent pbk **£4.50**

STEELE, MAGGIE & THORNTON, ZITA
Women Can Achieve
Career Success
Aimed at helping women who need to re-assess their strengths and abilities before returning to working life. Offers advice on confidence-building, bridging the career gap, changing direction and many other subjects.
[C313] Thorsons pbk **£4.99**

WARD, TERRY
Working the System NEW
Newly-published in the UK, this book has the subtitle 'Twelve ways to achieve career breakthroughs'. It adopts a very good goal-minded approach.
[C314] Columbus pbk **£5.95**

WATSON, SOPHIA
Winning Women:
The Meaning of 'Success' for Women
A well-written, thoughtful look at what career 'success' can bring.
[C315] Weidenfeld hbk **£12.95**

Small Businesses

The titles included here are purpose-written to offer guidance to the first-time entrepreneur, and to those who wish to improve the performance of their business.

Allied Dunbar Guide to Running Your Own Business
[C316] Longman pbk **£4.95**

The Guardian Guide to Running a Small Business
[C317] Kogan Page pbk **£6.95**

BARROW, COLIN
Financial Management for the Small Business
Practical advice on proper financial planning and control.
[C318] Kogan Page pbk **£8.95**
The New Small Business Guide NEW
Contains details of all the sources of practical information and help needed by anyone who runs, or who wants to start, their own business. A key resource book.
[C319] BBC pbk **£9.95**

BLACKWELL, EDWARD
How to Prepare a Business Plan
A straightforward book of great use to those raising finance for small businesses.
[C320] Kogan Page pbk **£5.95**

CHISNALL, DR PETER
Small Firms in Action:
Case Histories in Entrepreneurship
Telling the stories of 12 small firms, this book provides some valuable insights into the 'spirit of enterprise'.
[C321] McGraw-Hill pbk **£7.95**

FARRELL, PETER
How to Buy a Business: The 'Daily Telegraph' Guide
The second (updated and revised) edition considers why and when to buy, how to evaluate assets, how to finance a purchase, and sources of finance.
[C322] Kogan Page pbk **£6.95**

FOLEY, PAUL & GREEN, HOWARD
Small Business Success NEW
A look at the attributes, characteristics and strategies of a range of small businesses; aimed at the managers/owners who want their businesses to succeed.
[C323] P Chapman hbk **£12.95**

KNELL, ANNE
Employment Law for the Small Business
A brief but comprehensive guide for those who have become employers for the first time.
[C324] Kogan Page pbk **£7.99**

MASON, S.
The Small Business Finance Raiser
A straightforward, but very reliable guide to raising finance.
[C325] Hutchinson pbk **£5.95**

MORRIS, M.J.
Starting a Successful Small Business
The second edition of a highly acclaimed guide that covers all the important aspects of small business success.
[C326] Kogan Page pbk **£6.95**

Successful Expansion for the Small Business
[C327] Kogan Page pbk **£3.95**

PATTEN, DAVE
Successful Marketing for the Small Business: The 'Daily Telegraph' Guide
A new edition of this most instructive book.
[C328] Kogan Page pbk **£8.95**

PITMAN/NATWEST SMALL BUSINESS BOOKSHELF
A Business Plan
[C329] Pitman/NatWest pbk **£5.95**
Managing Growth `NEW`
Aimed at business owners needing guidance on managing change in the form of expansion.
[C330] Pitman/NatWest hbk **£12.95**
Small Business Survival `NEW`
A guide to DIY Management consultancy, this book contains hard-headed advice on overcoming practical crises.
[C331] Pitman/NatWest pbk **£5.95**
Starting Up
[C332] Pitman/NatWest pbk **£5.95**

SAUNDERS, PETER
The Cranfield New Entrepreneur `NEW`
Written in association with the Cranfield School of Management, this is a book which reveals how to spot good business ideas, and turn them into profitable and successful ventures.
[C333] Sidgwick hbk **£12.95**

STERRETT, P.W. & P.F.
Marketing Ideas for the Small Business `NEW`
Ideas, advice and guidance on successfully promoting one's wares including examples of modestly budgeted promotional schemes.
[C334] Mercury hbk **£10.95**

WINCKLES, KENNETH
Funding Your Business
Explains how to provide for and meet the financial demands of a business.
[C335] Kogan Page hbk **£15.95**

WOODCOCK, CLIVE
Raising Finance: The 'Guardian' Guide for the Small Business
Looks at the advantages and disadvantages of a wide range of sources of finance open to small businesses.
[C336] Kogan Page pbk **£8.95**

1992 & the European Market

The EEC celebrated its 30th anniversary in 1988. As we move towards 1992, it will play an increasingly important role in the 'deregulation' of European business, and a knowledge of its workings will be a distinct advantage for the Business manager. The best books currently available are featured below.

BREBNER & CO
Setting Up a Company in the European Community: A Country by Country Guide `NEW`
Compiled by a company of international solicitors, and published in association with the London Chamber of Commerce, this handbook covers detailed guidelines on legislation, capital requirements, management structures, documentation, registration and taxation.
[C337] Kogan Page hbk **£16.95**

CECCHINI, PAOLO
1992: The European Challenge - The Benefits of a Single Market
A readable and practical guide to the changes due in 1992, this has already proved itself a popular guide.
[C338] Wildwood pbk **£6.95**

DUDLEY, JAMES W.
1992: Strategies for the Single Market `NEW`
Investigates strategic and operational options open to managers preparing for 1992, and focuses on coping with changes, and taking advantage of the openings.
[C339] Kogan Page hbk **£19.92**

LEONARD, DICK
Pocket Guide to the European Community `NEW`
A highly informative overview of the economic, political and social issues which have shaped the EC today. Institutions and activities are explained in clear and concise language, cutting through the bureaucratic veil that surrounds the commission, and giving a valuable guide to how it actually *works*.
[C340] Blackwell hbk **£15.00**

OWEN, RICHARD & DYNES, MICHAEL
The 'Times' Guide to 1992
A highly recommended and popular guide.
[C341] Times Bks pbk **£5.95**

TAYLOR, CATHERINE & PRESS, ALISON
1992: The Facts and Challenges
Succinct, well-argued practical book on what 1992 could mean to businesses, and how companies can 'gear up' to a single European market.
[C342] Industrial Soc pbk **£5.00**

Corporate Business

This section is comprised of titles that help professional businessmen, in particular managers, to improve their expertise in more specialist areas. Whether providing introductions to the untrained, or revision for the trained, they are all reliable texts.

Accounting

These books are chosen particularly for the general professional without Accounting qualifications.

BIRD, PETER
Understanding Company Accounts
(2nd edition)
This is a new edition of the widely acclaimed text; it assumes no previous knowledge.
[C344] Pitman pbk **£6.95**

BROCKLINGTON, A.
Concise Dictionary of Accounting and Finance
1,200 entries covering all the main aspects of accounting and finance.
[C345] Pitman pbk **£4.95**

GRIFFITHS, IAN
Creative Accounting
In this excellent book Griffiths combines technical expertise with an elegant writing style.
[C346] Unwin Hyman pbk **£3.95**

JAMESON, MICHAEL
A Practical Guide to Creative Accounting
Company reports are not always all they seem; often

the figures on a balance sheet or profit and loss account have been adjusted in the interest of 'public image' or to gain tax benefits. This book offers a complete guide to such uses of creative accounting.
[C347] Kogan Page pbk **£6.95**

JOHNSON, W.L.
Baffled by Balance Sheets? Understanding Company Accounts Quickly and Easily
A good guide for the perplexed businessman.
[C348] Kogan Page pbk **£5.95**

MOTT, GRAHAM
Accounting for Non-Accountants
A well-established, introductory book that is among the best in its field.
[C349] Pan pbk **£3.95**

NOBES, DAVID
Accountancy Explained `NEW`
A detailed explanation in clear English of what accountants do, the structure of the profession, the training, pleasures and pitfalls, and the standard accounting terms which so often defeat non-accountants.
[C350] Penguin pbk **£3.99**

PARKER, R.H
Understanding Company Financial Statements
Another easy to understand guide for non-accountants.
[C351] Penguin pbk **£4.95**

ROCKLEY, L.E.
The Meaning of Balance Sheets and Company Reports
A readable reference work: among the best in this area.
[C352] Hutchinson pbk **£6.95**

SIZER, JOHN
An Insight into Management Accounting
A completely new edition of Professor Sizer's best-selling book - the standard introduction to the techniques, processes and rules of preparing and understanding management accounts.
[C353] Penguin pbk **£6.99**

WALKER, T.
Management Accountancy for the Company Executive
Guidance for those involved in financial planning, but who are without accountancy training.
[C354] Kogan Page pbk **£7.95**

Advertising

The advertising of one's product or service is essential amd the titles listed here offer a wide range of approaches to suit the needs of anyone in business.

The Complete Book of Advertising
Excellent glossy introduction to advertising - good both as a career guide and for anyone with a passing interest.
[C355] Macmillan pbk **£11.95**

ADAMS, J.
Media Planning
The author provides a number of strategies for those needing to organise publicity and / or advertising campaigns.
[C356] Hutchinson pbk **£6.95**

BROADBENT, S.
Leo Burnett Book of Advertising
A comprehensive description of effective approaches
to advertising.
[C357] Hutchinson hbk **£9.95**
Spending Advertising Money (4th edition)
Established text showing how managers can get value
for money from their advertising budget.
[C358] Hutchinson pbk **£7.95**

CARTER, H.C.
Effective Advertising
A good, practical book aimed at the small to medium-
sized businesses.
[C359] Telegraph pbk **£6.95**

CHANNON, CHARLES
Twenty Advertising Case Histories
Covers winning and commended entries in the IPA's
'Effectiveness in Advertising Awards'.
[C360] Cassell pbk **£7.95**

CLARK, ERIC
The Want Makers
A critical view of the advertising world from
investigative journalist Eric Clark.
[C361] Hodder hbk **£14.95**

CORKE, A.
Advertising and Public Relations
A short, basic introduction from the excellent *Pan
Management Guides* series.
[C362] Pan pbk **£2.95**

COWLEY, DON
How to Plan Advertising
The author draws together eight essays providing an
authoritative reference source for each stage of the
advertising planning process.
[C363] Cassell pbk **£9.95**

David Ogilvy, author of *Ogilvy on Advertising* (Pan
pbk £7.50)

CROMPTON, ALASTAIR
Two useful books on advertising for managers of
small to medium-sized businesses.
Do Your Own Advertising
[C364] Hutchinson pbk **£6.95**
The Craft of Copywriting
[C365] Hutchinson pbk **£6.95**

DAVIS, M.P.
The Effective Use of Advertising Media
A comprehensive, up-to-date text for planning an
advertising campaign.
[C366] Hutchinson pbk **£9.95**

HARRISON, T.
A Book of Advertising Techniques
A practical book with an emphasis on the creative
side of advertising.
[C367] Kogan Page hbk **£14.95**

HART, N. & O'CONNOR, JAMES
The Practice of Advertising (2nd edition)
Part of *The Marketing Series*, published on
behalf of the Institute of Marketing, and therefore
well-recommended.
[C368] Heinemann pbk **£14.95**

JEFKINS, FRANK
Dictionary of Advertising
Provides an ideal reference work for anyone working
in advertising, or students working towards exams.
[C369] Pitman pbk **£9.95**

KLEINMAN, P.
The Saatchi and Saatchi Story
The inside story of the phenomenal rise of the Saatchi
brothers' agency. The author's friendship with the
brothers does not prevent him from being critical.
[C370] Pan pbk **£3.99**

OAKLEY, M.   **NEW**
Creating and Producing Advertising
A textbook for the CAM Foundation with wider
appeal - an up-to-date and authoritative study.
[C371] Heinemann pbk **£14.95**

OGILVY, DAVID
Confessions of an Advertising Man
[C372] Pan pbk **£3.95**
Ogilvy on Advertising
The classic account by the most renowned of all
advertising men. Absolutely essential reading.
[C373] Pan pbk **£7.50**
The Unpublished David Ogilvy
96 fascinating excerpts from the private and public
papers of the most famous advertising man of our
time, including his own theories on what leads to
success in business.
[C374] Sidgwick pbk **£7.95**

QUINN, P.
The Secrets of Successful Copywriting
A 'know-how' manual for everyone who writes
advertising copy with practical exercises at the end of
each chapter.
[C375] Heinemann pbk **£5.99**
**The Secrets of Successful Low Budget
Advertising**
Aimed at small to medium-sized businesses which
spend less than £15,000 per annum. Will help
managers who know their businesses well, but who
are not achieving the results they expect from
advertising.
[C376] Heinemann pbk **£5.95**

ROMAN, K. & MAAS, J.
How to Advertise
A good introductory text.
[C377] Kogan Page pbk **£8.95**

WHITE, P.
**Advertising:What it is and How
to Do It**
A detailed look at the theory and practice of
advertising, for managers.
[C378] McGraw-Hill pbk **£8.95**

WILMSHURST, J.
The Fundamentals of Advertising
The author comprehensively covers the whole
business of advertising and promotion, and uses
plenty of clear examples, guidelines and checklists
throughout.
[C379] Heinemann pbk **£12.95**

WINNER, P.
Effective PR Management
Serving both the student and the businessman, this is
a well-recommended handbook for those who wish to
investigate public relations.
[C380] Kogan Page pbk **£12.95**

Law

A small selection of books for the professional
who needs only to assimilate a good working
understanding of the law as it relates to business
without having to grasp the finer points of the
substantive law or the machinations of the legal
system as a whole.

Business Law Made Simple
Like all the *Made Simple* series, this is a reliable
introductory handbook.
[C381] Heinemann pbk **£3.95**

CLAYTON, P.
**Consumer Law for Small Business
Managers**
An important reference book which is both readable
and reliable.
[C382] Kogan Page pbk **£5.95**

EVANS, A.
**The Data Protection Act:
A Guide for Personnel Managers**
A concise handbook covering aspects of the
law with specific relevance to Personnel
departments.
[C383] IPM pbk **£7.20**

JANNER, GREVILLE
Know Your Law
A handy reference work for those beginning in
business.
[C384] Hutchinson pbk **£5.95**

MOZLEY & WHITELEY
Law Dictionary
A particularly useful guide to those unfamiliar with
the subject, this dictionary is sufficiently
comprehensive to be virtually a miniature
encyclopaedia of the law in itself.
[C385] Butterworth hbk **£6.50**

PRICE, T.
Practical Business Law
Easy to understand book for the general business
reader.
[C386] Pan pbk **£3.95**

SUTER, E.
Contracts at Work
The Institute of Personnel Management's
recommended guide.
[C387] IPM hbk **£14.95**

Paul Winner, author of *Effective PR Management* (Kogan Page pbk £12.95)

Management

This section complements the Practical Business section in that it offers texts designed to improve one's practical skills but particularly the skills of managing other people. Also included are more advanced theoretical works that are nonetheless accessible to anyone motivated to improve their managerial know-how and the performance of their company.

ADAIR, JOHN
Action Centred Leader
[C388] Kogan Page hbk **£14.95**
Developing Leaders:
10 Key Principles
[C389] McGraw Hill hbk **£13.95**
Effective Leadership
[C390] Pan pbk **£2.95**
Effective Team Building
[C391] Pan pbk **£4.50**
The Skills of Leadership
[C392] Gower pbk **£6.95**

ALLAN, JANE
How to Solve Your
People Problems **NEW**
A workbook for the busy manager, offering advice on solving the inevitable, day-to-day personnel problems.
[C393] Kogan Page pbk **£7.99**

ATTWOOD, M.
Personnel Management
A good introductory book to an undeniably important area.
[C394] Pan pbk **£2.95**

BELL, WALLACE D. & HANSON, CHARLES
Profit Sharing and Profitability
How profit sharing promotes business success: based on extensive research this book examines the correlation between profit sharing and economic performance.
[C395] Kogan page hbk **£17.95**

BIRD, M.
A Better Way to Manage
Covering the major aspects of what management involves, this book is of use to those new to management, or those in need of new ideas.
[C396] Sphere pbk **£3.99**

BLANCHARD, KENNETH
Leadership and the One Minute Manager (with Zigarmi, Patricia & Drea)
[C397] Collins hbk **£6.95**
[C398] Fontana pbk **£3.50**
Putting the One Minute Manager To Work (with Lorber, R.)
[C399] Collins hbk **£6.95**
[C400] Fontana pbk **£3.50**
The One Minute Manager
(with Johnson, Spencer)
The first, and best, of the *One Minute* series, this book caused a sensation when first published. Every page is full of thought-provoking but practical ideas: essential reading for the new and the experienced manager.
[C401] Collins hbk **£6.95**
[C402] Fontana pbk **£2.95**

BLANCHARD, K & PEALE, NORMAN VINCENT
The Power of Ethical
Management **NEW**
The author of *The One Minute Manager* has worked with the author of *The Power of Positive Thinking* to make a punchy, uplifting book that gets to the heart of morality in business. Subtitled 'You Don't Have to Cheat to Win'.
[C403] Collins hbk **£9.95**

BONO, EDWARD DE
Atlas of Management Thinking
[C404] Penguin pbk **£4.99**
Lateral Thinking for Management
[C405] Penguin pbk **£4.99**

BREWSTER, C.
Industrial Relations
A useful handbook for managers.
[C406] Pan pbk **£2.95**

BURST, A.
The Management Game
An actual game in which readers test their ability to run a complex division of a large corporation.
[C407] Sidgwick hbk **£12.95**

CARMICHAEL, SHEENA & DRUMMOND, JOHN
Good Business: A Guide to Running an Ethical Organisation
An interesting and challenging guide to corporate responsibility, and the benefits of correct business ethics. A British book, supported throughout with case histories, such as the example of Marks & Spencer
[C408] Hutchinson pbk **£7.95**

COLEMAN, DR VERNON
Stress Management Techniques
Written for the manager, this explains how, why and when stress causes problems and, more importantly, how to minimise and control the stress experienced by your company.
[C409] WH Allen pbk **£9.95**

COURTIS, J.
Managing by Mistake
Subtitled 'The 44 most common management mistakes and how to avoid them', this book is about the process of learning to avoid future failings.
[C410] Kogan Page pbk **£7.95**

DRUCKER, PETER F.
Drucker is one of the most highly regarded business

'gurus' and provides challenging insights into today's management problems.
Frontiers of Management: Where Tomorrow is Being Made Today
[C411] Heinemann hbk **£14.95**
Innovation and Entrepreneurship
[C412] Heinemann pbk **£9.95**
Management: Tasks, Responsibilities, Practices
[C413] Heinemann hbk **£25.00**
Managing for Results
[C414] Pan pbk **£2.95**
Managing in Turbulent Times
[C415] Heinemann hbk **£10.95**
[C416] Pan pbk **£2.95**
The Effective Executive
[C417] Pan pbk **£2.95**
The New Realities **NEW**
[C418] Heinemann hbk **£16.95**
The Practice of Management
[C419] Heinemann hbk **£15.00**
[C420] Pan pbk **£4.95**

FLAMHOLTZ & RANDLE
The Inner Game of Management **NEW**
Shows ambitious managers how to manage themselves and therefore their careers.
[C421] Hutchinson hbk **£12.95**

FOSTER, N.
Innovation: The Attacker's Advantage
A highly-acclaimed business book on management strategy.
[C422] Pan pbk **£3.95**

GENEEN, H.
Managing
Slim, easy-to-read introduction to basic principles.
[C423] Grafton pbk **£3.95**

GOODWORTH, CLIVE
Two useful reference works for the new manager in need of instruction, or the experienced one in need of revision.
Effective Delegation
[C424] Hutchinson pbk **£5.95**
Effective Interviewing
[C425] Hutchinson pbk **£4.95**

HANDY, CHARLES
Age of Unreason **NEW**
The latest from Britain's leading expert on the future of work, showing us how best to succeed into the 1990s.
[C426] Century hbk **£14.95**

HANDY, J.
Understanding Organizations
A readable, theoretical work on organizational behaviour for managers.
[C427] Penguin pbk **£5.99**

HELLER, ROBERT
A leading management journalist, Heller has written an impressive series of books, full of acute observations, on Business and management today.
Naked Market
[C428] Sidgwick pbk **£8.95**
Superman: The Art and Science of Life Management
[C429] Sidgwick hbk **£9.95**
Supermanagers
[C430] Sidgwick pbk **£9.95**
Supermarketers
[C431] Sidgwick pbk **£8.95**
The Age of the Common Millionaire
Twenty-four of the most popular methods used to make a million.
[C432] Hodder pbk **£3.95**

The Best of Robert Heller NEW
All in one volume, Heller's best 'keys' to management, understanding business, and recognizing the potential in oneself.
[C433] Sidgwick hbk **£12.95**

The Business of Winning
[C434] Sidgwick pbk **£7.95**

The New Naked Manager
[C435] Hodder pbk **£2.95**

The Pocket Manager: An Alphabetical Reference Guide to Management
[C436] Hodder pbk **£2.95**

Unique Success Proposition
There is usually one overriding reason why a business or an individual is successful - what Heller describes as the 'unique success proposition'. How we identify it, and use such knowldege to our advantage, is explained through an analysis of successful individuals and businesses.
[C437] Sidgwick hbk **£12.95**

JENKS, J.
Don't Do, Delegate
An excellent thesis and antidote to the current fashion for 'hands-on' management.
[C438] Kogan Page pbk **£5.95**

KEMPNER, THOMAS
Penguin Management Handbook
An encyclopaedic A-to-Z guide to management.
[C439] Penguin pbk **£7.95**

KENT, ROBERT
Managing People: 25 Steps to Improving Employee Performance
A concise, practical guide to achieving the best performance from your staff, featuring a unique 25-step problem diagnosis flowchart.
[C440] Sidgwick pbk **£7.95**

LEEDS, D.
Smart Questions for Successful Managers
A handbook for further development.
[C441] Piatkus hbk **£14.95**

LESSEM, R.
Roots of Excellence
A popular book to help managers work out strategies for attaining quality management.
[C442] Fontana pbk **£3.95**

LLOYD, TOM & SVEIBY, KARL ERIK
Managing Know-How: Value Creativity - The New Business Challenge
Every business uses know-how; this book explores how it can be most effectively used.
[C443] Bloomsbury pbk **£7.99**

MAITLAND, IAIN
Successful Recruitment: A Guide for Managers
An invaluable step-by-step guide that summarizes the procedures, and makes copious use of checklists.
[C444] Kogan Page pbk **£7.99**

MAJARO, SIMON
The Creative Gap: Managing Ideas for Profit
A dynamic approach to creative management.
[C445] Longman hbk **£12.95**

MARCH, ROBERT M.
The Japanese Negotiator: Subtlety and Strategy Beyond Western Logic NEW
Shows how the Japanese negotiate among themselves, and examines case studies, providing advice to give the Western executive the edge.
[C446] Kodansha hbk **£12.95**

MILLS, G.
On the Board
A practical guide to being a Board member.
[C447] Unwin Hyman pbk **£7.95**

OAKLAND, JOHN
Total Quality Management NEW
Aims to show managers how to implement a total quality management strategy to improve effectiveness and flexibility, and get a company working together to eliminate errors and prevent waste.
[C448] Heinemann hbk **£20.00**

OHMAE, M.
Mind of the Strategist
Excellent exposition of the Japanese business philosophy and its practical applications.
[C449] Penguin pbk **£4.99**

OLINS, WALLY NEW
Corporate Identity: Making Business Strategy Visible through Design
In this supremely readable and well-illustrated design analysis, supported by many illustrations, Olins reveals how identity works for companies today - from Sony to Coca-Cola - and examines the practice of creating identity, how to manage it, and how to communicate it inside and outside the organisation.
[C450] Thames & H hbk **£16.95**

PETER, DR. LAWRENCE J.
The Peter Principle
A variety of aphorisms are used to analyse an individual's performance in an organization. A very perceptive book.
[C451] Pan pbk **£3.50**

PETERS, THOMAS
A Passion for Excellence
(with Nancy Austin)
Continuing the themes introduced in his earlier work.
[C452] Collins hbk **£12.95**
[C453] Fontana pbk **£5.95**

In Search of Excellence
(with Robert Waterman)
Several years after publication, this remains one of the most highly regarded books in its field. It is both a practical and inspirational look at how excellence has been achieved by a number of successful businesses.
[C454] Harper & R pbk **£7.95**

Thriving on Chaos: Handbook for a Management Revolution
To be constantly re-defining a company's aims towards quality and competitiveness is the only way to survive, let alone achieve excellence, in the ever-changing economic, social and technological climate. Here Peters offers his usual inspiring advice.
[C455] Macmillan hbk **£16.95**

RANDELL; PACKARD & SLATER
Staff Appraisal: A First Step to Effective Leadership
Authoritative analysis of the theory and practice of staff reviews. Covers a great breadth in 113 pages.
[C456] IPM pbk **£4.95**

REGESTER, MICHAEL
Crisis Management NEW
This new book deals with turning business crises into opportunities.
[C457] Hutchinson hbk **£6.95**

ROBERTS, WESS
Leadership Secrets of Attila the Hun NEW
A humorous look at the way Attila's principles of leadership can be applied to management and business situations today.
[C458] Bantam hbk **£8.95**

Robert Heller, author of *The Pocket Manager* (Hodder & Stoughton pbk £2.95)

ROWAN, ROY
The Intuitive Manager
A clearly-written book on the subject of widening the scope of one's thinking to include the intuitive side, from which the most creative thought can originate.
[C459] Wildwood pbk **£6.95**

SCOTT, BILL
The Skills of Communicating
A thorough treatise on one of the essential skills for managers at any level.
[C460] Wildwood pbk **£6.95**

SETSUO, MITO
The Honda Book of Management NEW
Subtitled 'A Leadership Philosophy for High Industrial Success', this book will serve as a key work of reference for management and industry, and all interested in Japan's industrial success.
[C461] Athlone hbk **£19.95**

SILVA, M. & HICKMAN, C.
The Future 500: Creating Tomorrow's Organisations Today
A future view based on the format of the Fortune 500 list.
[C462] Unwin Hyman pbk **£5.95**

STALLWORTHY, ERNEST & KHARBANDA, O.P.
Takeovers, Acquisitions and Mergers
When faced with a hostile takeover bid, will your company survive? There are many lessons to be learned from the experience of Guinness, Westland and Hanson in this practical book, showing managers how to recognise when a company is in trouble, and how to set it on the road to recovery.
[C463] Kogan Page hbk **£16.95**

STEWART, ROSEMARY
Choices for the Manager
[C464] McGraw-Hill pbk **£14.95**

Contrasts in Management
[C465] McGraw-Hill hbk **£11.95**

The Reality of Management
[C466] Pan pbk **£3.99**

The Reality of Organisations
[C467] Pan pbk **£3.95**

TAYLOR, W.
The Basic Arts of Management
(2nd edition)
A comprehensive, reliable introductory text outlining all the major areas that should command a manager's attention.
[C468] Hutchinson pbk **£5.95**

TOFFLER, ALVIN
The Adaptive Corporation
Cult sociologist Alvin Toffler takes a close look at the structures of companies.
[C469] Pan pbk **£2.95**

TOWNSEND, ROBERT
Further up the Organisation
A classic exposé of office politics.
[C470] Hodder pbk **£2.50**

WATERMAN, R.
The Renewal Factor:
Building and Maintaining the
Company's Competitive Edge
By the co-author of *In Search of Excellence*.
[C471] Bantam hbk **£14.95**

WATTS, B.
Creating the Hands-On Manager
A good explanation of the 'hands-on' business strategy.
[C472] Mercury hbk **£13.50**

WOODS, M.
The New Manager
By a managerial consultant to Shell, BP and GKN, this thought-provoking book looks at the type of managers needed in today's society.
[C473] Element pbk **£6.95**

Sales & Marketing

Whether in Sales, Marketing or General Management, anyone can benefit from the expertise represented in the titles offered below.

ADAMS, TONY
The Secret of Successful Sales
Management
A close look at the ins and outs of running a sales force - a 'must' for all budding sales managers.
[C474] Heinemann pbk **£5.95**
The Secret of Successful Selling
Combines autobiography with useful sales and marketing tips in an amusing style.
[C475] Heinemann pbk **£5.95**

ALLEN, P.
Selling
Part of the *Small Business Bookshelf* series, sponsored by National Westminster Bank.
[C476] Pitman pbk **£5.95**

BAKER, M.J.
The Marketing Book
[C477] Heinemann pbk **£14.95**

BEER, MICHAEL
The Joy of Selling
A detailed look at the sort of selling best suited to the reader, and how to develop it successfully.
[C478] Mercury pbk **£5.99**

BOLT, GORDON J.
Market and Sales Forecasting:
A Total Approach
Good presentation of a practical forecast plan that can

be adapted to any company's forecasting situations.
[C479] Kogan Page pbk **£10.95**

CHISNALL, P.M.
Two titles from the McGraw-Hill marketing series for professionals already practising marketing.
Marketing Research
[C480] McGraw-Hill pbk **£13.95**
Marketing: A Behavioural Analysis
[C481] McGraw-Hill pbk **£11.95**

CLUTTERBUCK, D. & MCBURNIE, T.
The Marketing Edge
Reveals vital strategies used by British companies to beat competition.
[C482] Penguin pbk **£3.95**

COOL, LISA COLLIER
Phone Power
This practical handbook is of wider application than the subtitle 'Telephone Techniques to Increase Your Profits and Performance' suggests.
[C483] Hale pbk **£6.50**

DAVIDSON, A.
Offensive Marketing
From the Penguin *Business Library*, a series aimed at the non-professional business person.
[C484] Penguin pbk **£5.99**

DAVIS, M.
Business to Business Marketing
and Promotion   **NEW**
The first book of its kind specifically of help to those offering services and goods to other businesses.
[C485] Hutchinson pbk **£12.95**

FAIRLIE, R.
Direct Mail
Reliable text explaining direct mail techniques.
[C486] Kogan Page hbk **£13.95**

FENTON, JOHN
101 Ways to Boost Your Business
Performance
Fenton's latest book, offering practical advice for improving executive effectiveness.
[C487] Heinemann hbk **£14.95**
How to Double Your Profits within
a Year
[C488] Pan pbk **£3.50**
How to Sell Against Competition
[C489] Pan pbk **£4.99**
The A-Z of Sales Management
[C490] Pan pbk **£2.95**

FOWLER, D.
Selling and Marketing for Small
Businesses
A good introductory book.
[C491] Sphere pbk **£3.95**

HAGUE, D.
Do Your Own Market Research
A step-by-step, practical guide covering consumer and industrial market research.
[C492] Kogan Page hbk **£16.95**

HART, N.A.
Glossary of Marketing Terms (3rd edition)
[C493] Heinemann pbk **£10.95**

HARVEY, CHRISTINE
Secrets of the World's Top Sales
Performers   **NEW**
Internationally-acclaimed sales and motivation guru Christine Harvey reveals how top achievers manage to crash through sales targets year after year.
[C494] Hutchinson pbk **£6.95**

HENZELL-THOMAS, NIGEL
Supercharge Your Selling:
60 Tips in 60 Minutes
[C495] Hutchinson pbk **£2.99**

HOLMES, GEORGE
Sales Force Incentives:
How to Use Them to Increase Sales
Motivations and rewards explained for the Sales manager, in a practical book.
[C496] Heinemann pbk **£12.95**

JAY, ANTONY
Effective Presentation
Concise and informative.
[C497] BIM pbk **£4.50**

JEFKINS, FRANK
Secrets of Successful Direct
Response Marketing
An excellent, practical book that covers all aspects of how direct marketing can help to improve business.
[C498] Heinemann hbk **£14.95**

JOHNSON, SPENCER & WILSON, LARRY
One Minute Sales Person
The *One-Minute* business guides are best-sellers because they offer quick, no-nonsense, informative advice that is easily accessible. They should always be on hand.
[C499] Collins hbk **£6.95**
[C500] Fontana pbk **£3.50**

KATZ, S.
How to Win More Business by Phone,
Telex and Fax
A recommended, practical book.
[C501] Hutchinson pbk **£5.95**

MARKS, P.
The Telephone Marketing Book
How to get the most from your telephone. Another excellent Hutchinson handbook.
[C502] Hutchinson pbk **£5.95**

MCDONALD, MALCOLM H.B.
Marketing Plans: How to Prepare Them,
and How to Use Them
[C503] Heinemann pbk **£15.95**

MCIVER, C.
The Marketing Mirage
[C504] Heinemann hbk **£17.50**

MILLER; HEIMAN & TULEJA
Strategic Selling:
Secrets of the Complex Sale
High-powered, high-level advice on selling.
[C505] Kogan Page pbk **£10.95**

RANDALL, GEOFFREY
Trade Marketing
[C506] Heinemann pbk **£15.00**

ROBINSON, NICK
Marketing Toolkit   **NEW**
Outlines strategies for more effective advertising, profitable direct marketing and improved direct mail responses.
[C507] Mercury hbk **£12.95**

SEWELL, M.K.
Retail Marketing
[C508] Heinemann hbk **£15.95**

THOMAS, M.J.
The Marketing Digest
[C509] Heinemann hbk **£25.00**

TURNER, H.
So You Want to be a Sales Manager
Serious lessons on sales management taught in a
lively, humorous style.
[C510] Arrow pbk **£2.99**

WALKER, H.
Marketing
Slim, readable, introductory text.
[C511] Pan pbk **£2.95**

WILSON, LARRY
**Changing the Game: The New Way
to Sell**
[C512] Simon & Sch pbk **£6.95**

WINTER, CHRIS DE
**The Secrets of Successful Telephone
Selling**
An indispensable guide which assumes no great
knowledge of this important selling method.
[C513] Heinemann hbk **£14.95**

Taxation

ALLIED DUNBAR
Business Tax and Law Guide   `NEW`
A guide to tax and the law as it affects one's business.
[C514] Longman hbk **£13.95**

BROOKS, JOHN & COPP, ANDREW
How to Live with VAT
A book (primarily for small and medium-sized
businesses) by two men who worked in the Customs
& Excise VAT offices.
[C515] McGraw Hill pbk **£6.75**

BUTTERWORTHS
Orange Tax Handbook
Popular annual handbook, dealing with inheritance
tax, VAT, NI contributions and stamp duty.
[C516] Butterworths pbk **£18.00**
Yellow Tax Handbook
Companion volume dealing with income, capital
gains and corporation tax.
[C517] Butterworths pbk **£20.00**

ECONOMIST
Pocket Guide to Business Tax
A guide useful for both small and large businesses.
[C518] E Arnold hbk **£15.50**

PACKER, BILL
**Touche Ross: VAT - A Business by
Business Guide**
Refreshingly practical occupation-based guide to
VAT, useful to most high street businesses.
[C519] Butterworths hbk **£23.95**

PRITCHARD, BILL
Taxation 1989-90
Recommended by many professional bodies; ideal for
students, practitioners and anyone who wants to
understand the fundamental concepts of taxation.
[C520] Pitman pbk **£9.50**

SOMERVILLE, IAN & ARNOLD, JOHN
**Trouble with the Taxman?
VAT Survival**   `NEW`
Alerts executives and financial advisers to problems,
and provides practical advice on how to avoid them.
[C521] Deloite pbk **£6.95**

WALTERS, R.
Managing Tax in Your Business
An easy to understand guide for managers.
[C522] Hutchinson hbk **£14.95**

Nursery Rhymes
Fairy & Folk Tales
Myths & Legends
Books for Pre-School
Children
Age 4 & Up
Age 6 - 9
Children's Classics
Age 8 - 12
Age 12 & Up

Children's

CHILDREN'S

Nursery Rhymes

Nursery rhymes, like folk tales, are part of every child's oral heritage. *"Tiny masterpieces of word craftsmanship,"* de la Mare called them, *"that free the fancy, charm tongue and ear, and delight the inward eye"*. Street cries, folk songs, remnants of custom or proverb polished into perfect form over the years, nursery rhymes lay the foundation of a child's joy in words and provide an early and satisfying experience of form in language. Their music, beat, bouncing rhythm and rhyme extend an irresistible invitation to the senses and elicit an active physical response. No matter that children don't always understand the words: it is the feeling for language and the pleasure in sound that matter, and the variety and surprise of subject, mood and character. Here all human life is distilled into a sharp, original form that leads naturally to nonsense verse and poetry, and to every sort of literary experience. As Dorothy Butler writes in *Babies Need Books* 'Don't even consider facing parenthood without a really good collection'.

BAYLEY, NICOLA
Working in the decorative-domestic tradition of Kate Greenaway and Willebeek le Mair, Nicola Bayley brings a vivid, slightly eccentric sensibility to her nursery rhyme interpretations. Her paintings, executed with the precision, detail and subtle use of colour of a miniaturist, are at once beautiful, magical, and brimful of fun.
Nicola Bayley's Bedtime Rhymes **NEW**
[D1] Walker pbk **£2.50**
Nicola Bayley's Book of Nursery Rhymes
[D2] Cape hbk **£5.95**
[D3] Puffin hbk **£1.95**
Nicola Bayley's Nonsense Rhymes **NEW**
[D4] Walker pbk **£2.50**

BLAKE, QUENTIN
Nursery Rhymes
Terrence McDiddler (the three-stringed fiddler) and William McTrimbletoe are just two of the singular characters in this sequence of 16 little-known rhymes. Children delight in the unusual language and

A was an apple pie

The Alphabet Pie from *The Nursery Treasury* selected by Sally Emerson, illustrated by Moira & Colin Maclean (Kingfisher hbk £7.95)

preposterous situations of the verse and in Blake's exuberant, idiosyncratic interpretations of them.
[D5] Collins pbk **£1.50**

BRIGGS, RAYMOND
Mother Goose Treasury
Briggs highlights the earthy, knock-about humour and inconsequence of the nursery rhyme in this collection of over 400 rhymes, each individually illustrated. Winner of the 1966 Kate Greenaway Medal, he plays out the eccentric comedy of the rhymes in a looking-glass world where rustics and wayward animals up-end accepted norms.
[D6] H Hamilton hbk **£9.95**

BROWN, MARC
Hand Rhymes
[D7] Collins pbk **£1.95**

CROWTHER, ROBERT
POP Goes the Weasel!
'Hooked' on Surrealism and Magritte, Crowther uses the pop-up to express this 'odd way of thinking about' and looking at things. His pop-up collection of 25 favourite rhymes, painted in watercolour, is surprisingly but divertingly traditional.
[D8] Walker hbk pop-up **£8.95**

DUDLEY & WALLNER
Old Macdonald Had a Farm - Musical Book
[D9] Collins hbk **£5.95**

EDENS, COOPER (ED)
The Glorious Mother Goose **NEW**
A collector's collection of 42 popular nursery rhymes illustrated by past masters such as Arthur Rackham, Randolph Caldecott and Kate Greenaway.
[D10] Macmillan hbk **£7.95**

EMERSON, SALLY
The Nursery Treasury
(Illus. Moira & Colin Maclean)
A bumper collection of baby games, action and memory rhymes, nursery songs and lullabies with cheerful illustrations that are both contemporary and traditional.
[D11] Kingfisher hbk **£7.95**

HAWKINS, COLIN & JACQUI
The Hawkinses bring their quirky humour to two favourite nursery rhymes, whose storyline is enhanced by their felicitous use of the flap device.
I Know an Old Lady Who Swallowed a Fly
[D12] Methuen pbk **£3.50**
Old Mother Hubbard
[D13] Methuen pbk **£3.50**

HAYES, SARAH & GOFFE, TONI
Clap Your Hands: Finger Rhymes
[D14] Walker pbk **£2.50**
Stamp Your Feet: Action Rhymes
[D15] Walker pbk **£2.50**

HENNESSEY, B.G.
The Missing Tarts **NEW**
(Illus. Tracey Campbell Pearson)
A new nursery verse collection that extends an old one, as the Queen of Hearts searches for her tarts helped by Jack and Jill who look 'over' the hill, Old Mother Hubbard who looks into her cupboard, and a host of other nursery rhyme characters. Pearson's pen and wash illustrations capture the slapdash fun.
[D15A] Viking hbk **£6.95**

KING, KAREN
Oranges & Lemons (Illus. Ian Beck)
[D16] Oxford pbk **£2.50**

J jumped for it

The Alphabet Pie from *The Nursery Treasury* selected by Sally Emerson, illustrated by Moira & Colin Maclean (Kingfisher hbk £7.95)

LINES, KATHLEEN
Lavender's Blue
A classic collection, first published in 1954, and beautifully, if nostalgically, illustrated by Harold Jones. His pen and ink drawings and muted water-colours highlight the strange, dream-like quality of the cradle songs, nursery rhymes, story rhymes and riddles.
[D17] Oxford hbk **£7.95**
[D17A] Oxford pbk **£5.95**

LOBEL, ARNOLD
Mother Goose
Like Briggs, Lobel emphasizes the broad, earthy humour of the rhymes. His pen and wash rustics, however, clad in mock-Regency costume, are cosier and funnier.
[D18] Walker hbk **£10.95**

MAIR, HENRIETTA WILLEBEEK LE
A Dutch Kate Greenaway, trained by the French artist Boutet de Monvel, le Mair paints with a delicacy given edge by her stunning sense of design. Her two delightful collections of words and music were first published in 1911 and 1912.
Little Songs of Long Ago
[D19] Blackie hbk **£4.95**
Our Own Nursery Rhymes
[D20] Blackie hbk **£4.95**

MATTERSON, ELIZABETH
This Little Puffin
The 'mother's godsend and playgroup's bible', this is *the* definitive collection of finger play and action rhymes, complete with diagrams and single-note music. For picture book collections suitable for sharing with the very youngest, see *Marc Brown*, *Sarah Hayes*, *Karen King* and *Sarah Williams*.
[D21] Puffin pbk **£2.50**

OPIE, IONA
Tail Feathers from Mother Goose: The Opie Rhyme Book
Drawn from the Opie archives, this is a rich anthology not only of unpublished rhymes (whose origins are entertainingly noted), but also of contemporary children's illustrative styles, including work by over 60 top artists.
[D22] Walker hbk **£12.95**

OPIE, IONA & PETER
"The need to understand the international exchange and flow of children's rhymes, songs and stories" lies

at the heart of Iona and Peter Opie's work. Their research into the folklore of childhood, which has resulted in their unrivalled collection of early and rare 'Childlife and Literature' was inspired by the birth of their first child in 1944. A rare combination of scholarship and humour informs their work, which includes *The Lore and Language of School Children* (1959) and *Children's Games in Street and Playground* (1969). Anthologies of verse and rhyme grew out of this work, which has been continued by Iona Opie since her husband's death in 1982.

The Oxford Dictionary of Nursery Rhymes
The definitive study of the origins and meanings of nursery rhymes. It gives the histories and texts - now regarded as standard - of more than 500 rhymes and songs.
[D23] Oxford hbk **£15.95**

The Oxford Nursery Rhyme Book
A classic indispensable collection of 800 rhymes and 600 illustrations - a fine blend of traditional engravings and modern pen and ink drawings by Joan Hassall.
[D24] Oxford hbk **£10.95**

The Puffin Book of Nursery Rhymes
The paperback equivalent of the above. An ideal memory booster for adults as the emphasis is on words rather than pictures.
[D25] Puffin pbk **£2.50**

OXENBURY, HELEN
Nursery Rhyme Book
Oxenbury's inventive crayon illustrations capture the rumbustious humour and absurdity of the rhymes in this varied collection.
[D26] Heinemann hbk **£6.95**

PAOLA, TOMIE DE
Tomie de Paola's Mother Goose
An exuberant, comprehensive Mother Goose for the very young, illustrated with humour in de Paola's characteristic folk style.
[D27] Methuen hbk **£9.95**

PELHAM, DAVID & MESSENGER, JANET
Twinkle Twinkle Little Star - Musical Book
[D28] Collins hbk **£5.95**

PIENKOWSKI, JAN
Fancy That! **NEW**
A pop-up version of an old favourite: *"There was an old lady who swallowed a fly"*.
[D29] Orchard hbk pop-up **£5.95**

Illustration from *Mother Goose* by Tomie de Paola (Methuen hbk £9.95)

POOLEY, SARAH
A Day of Rhymes
Rhymes for every moment of the day from breakfast to bedtime. Pooley's delightfully busy pen and wash illustrations place the rhymes in a contemporary multi-cultural world.
[D30] Bodley hbk **£5.95**

STONES, ROSEMARY & MANN, ANDREW
Mother Goose Comes to Cable Street
(Illus. Dan Jones)
New interpretations of old rhymes pictured in contemporary East London surroundings, which provide a valuable contrast to more traditional collections.
[D31] Puffin pbk **£1.95**

VOAKE, CHARLOTTE
Over the Moon
A good-humoured collection of largely familiar rhymes. Voake sets her nursery verse in the rural 18th century in spidery ink drawings and watercolours which, beneath their delicate colour, suggest the influence of Raymond Briggs.
[D32] Walker hbk **£7.95**
[D33] Walker pbk **£4.95**

WILDSMITH, BRIAN
Mother Goose
A painterly, unconventional Mother Goose - as brashly modern in feel now as when it first appeared in 1964. Its impact lies in Wildsmith's now characteristic use of geometric shapes and lavish colour.
[D34] Oxford hbk **£5.95**
[D35] Oxford pbk **£2.95**

WILLIAMS, SARAH
Pudding and Pie (Illus. Ian Beck)
[D36] Oxford hbk **£6.95**
Ride-a-Cock Horse (Illus. Ian Beck)
[D36A] Oxford pbk **£2.50**
Round & Round the Garden (Illus. Ian Beck)
[D37] Oxford pbk **£2.50**

YEOMAN, JOHN & BLAKE, QUENTIN
The subversive notion that fairy tale or nursery rhyme characters can be given a life beyond that of the original is splendidly conveyed in these modern sequels to the traditional nonsense rhyme. Here Old Mother Hubbard's Dog, a classic trickster, continues to take his mistress's advice literally: mischief and mayhem result.
Old Mother Hubbard's Dog Dresses Up
[D38] Walker hbk **£2.95**
Old Mother Hubbard's Dog Learns to Play **NEW**
[D39] Walker hbk **£2.95**
Old Mother Hubbard's Dog Needs a Doctor **NEW**
[D40] Walker hbk **£2.95**
Old Mother Hubbard's Dog Takes Up Sport **NEW**
[D41] Walker hbk **£2.95**

Fairy & Folk Tales, Myths & Legends

It is in folk and fairy tales, and later in the more complex myths which seek to explain the origins and nature of existence, and in the legendary epics which celebrate heroism and ideas that children, safely, begin 'to be at home in the world', and to explore fully the possibilities of life. These stories are the universal literature not just of childhood, but of

mankind - a common cultural heritage. They release the imagination and nourish the spirit, revealing and satisfying, through fantasy, the common hopes, fears and needs for security, competence and love in us all. Thus children who have 'entered the life of a story where there are giants and monsters to be feared in safety, younger sons to be admired for their wit and enterprise, and heroes to be imitated...know about wishes fulfilled, promises kept, testing times, dark days, and, above all, chance'. They have encountered too characters, situations, themes, story structures and patterns that they will meet, in a variety of guises, for the rest of their reading lives. And most of all they will have engaged with age-old stories that 'will initiate them fully into the kind of *meanings* that reading makes possible as the extension of "let's pretend"' (Margaret Meek, *Learning to Read*). Fairy and folk tales, myths and legends, like nursery rhymes, are a literature that no child should miss. Where titles are more suitable for particular age-ranges, these are given in brackets after the title.

Fairy Tales

AESOP
Aesop is said to have been a slave who lived in Greece in the mid 6th century BC; of the fables attributed to him, many may be of Greek and Far Eastern origin. Whatever their source, once included in Aesop's collection, they assumed the Aesop form: a brief story in which inanimate objects or stylized animals embody human characteristics, their actions pointing an obvious moral lesson. 'Aesop has always had the affection and regard of ordinary people', the poet James Reeves wrote, 'because the virtues he praises are not the heroic ones...they are the peasant virtues of discretion, prudence, moderation and forethought.'
Aesop's Fables (Illus. Michael Hague)
A baker's dozen beautifully illustrated in Hague's mannered, slightly Rackhamesque style.
[D42] Methuen hbk **£6.95**
Aesop's Fables (Illus. Heidi Holder)
Nine of the original tales illustrated with rich and intricately detailed patterns.
[D43] Macmillan pbk **£2.95**
Aesop's Fables (Illus. Lizbeth Zwinger)
[D43A] Picture Book St hbk **£6.95**
Once in a Wood (Illus. Eve Rice)
Ten familiar tales imaginatively adapted and illustrated with young readers in mind. The tellings are simple and rhythmic, the elegant black and white drawings dramatic and slyly humorous.
[D44] Collins pbk **£1.50**
MICHIE, JAMES
Aesop's Fables (Illus. John Vernon Lord)
A comprehensive collection, freshly translated and idiosyncratically illustrated.
[D358] Cape hbk **£12.95**
ROSS, TONY
Foxy Fables **NEW**
Six of Aesop's fables illustrated with characteristic Ross humour.
[D45] Puffin pbk **£1.95**

AIKEN, JOAN
The Kingdom under the Sea
(6 +, illus. Jan Pienkowski)
A magnificent and fresh retelling of 11 traditional East European folktales - startlingly illustrated by Pienkowski's silhouette-based paintings, which won the Kate Greenaway Medal for 1971.
[D46] Puffin pbk **£1.95**

ANDERSEN, HANS CHRISTIAN
Andersen (1805-1875) was a Danish shoemaker's son whose extraordinary imagination brought him lasting

fame not as the playwright and novelist he longed to be, but as the creator of an original genre: the invented fairy tale for children. His stories (over 150) have a freshness and range as astonishing to modern readers as they were to his own contemporaries. The majority are his own invention, and reflect his particular experience (Andersen, his friends and enemies appear in many roles). His inspired blend of fantasy and the everyday - in particular his ability to make any human scene come to life, by imagining a teapot or a darning needle as living characters in poignant dramas, or creating a metaphoric world as in 'The Snow Queen', is underpinned by a sharp observation of human nature, and a quizzical sense of humour.

Eighty Fairy Tales
[D47] Random H pbk **£8.95**
CORRIN, STEPHEN (TRANS)
Tales from Hans Christian Andersen
(Illus. Edward Ardizzone)
Corrin's translation of 14 of Andersen's tales, including 'The Little Mermaid', 'The Princess and the Pea' and 'The Steadfast Tin Soldier', is crisp and pithy - catching exactly the different note and voice of each story. Ardizzone's traditional line drawings might have graced the original editions.
[D48] Deutsch hbk **£7.95**
[D49] Deutsch pbk **£4.50**
EHRLICH, AMY
The Wild Swans (Illus. Susan Jeffers)
Andersen's brooding tale of the bewitched swan brothers and the untiring devotion of their sister Elisa is splendidly interpreted in meticulously executed paintings that evoke the darkness, anguish and love at its centre.
[D50] Macmillan pbk **£3.99**
HAUGAARD, ERIK (TRANS)
Hans Andersen: His Classic Fairy Tales
(Illus. Michael Foreman)
Haugaard, himself a Dane, translates 18 of Andersen's tales (including 'The Emperor's New Clothes' and 'The Little Match Girl'), retaining the vigour, directness and listener appeal of the great storyteller. It is *the* best introduction to these invented fairytales; their humour, drama and lyric beauty magnificently interpreted by Foreman in both colour and black and white.
[D51] Gollancz hbk **£7.95**
[D52] Gollancz pbk **£3.95**
LEWIS, NAOMI
The Flying Trunk & Other Stories from Andersen
A baker's dozen - including 'The Tinder Box'. 'The Emperor's New Clothes', 'The Jumping Competition'

Illustration from *Foxy Fables* by Tony Ross (Puffin pbk **£1.95**)

and 'The Snowman'. Each is chosen and illustrated by contemporary artists such as Ruth Brown, Michael Foreman, David McKee and Ralph Steadman.
[D53] Beaver pbk **£2.99**
The Snow Queen (Illus. Errol le Cain)
A lucid retelling of Andersen's masterpiece. Text and dramatic paintings chronicle Gerda's travels through a dream world of strange beauty to save Kay from the Snow Queen - a journey that is also a passage from childhood to maturity.
[D54] Puffin pbk **£1.95**

ARABIAN NIGHTS

A collection of exotic tales collected over many centuries from ancient India, North Africa and Persia, and bound together in the story of Scheherazade, who avoids execution by her royal husband by telling him a fresh story each night for 1,001 nights, never revealing the ending until the following evening. Aladdin, Ali Baba and Sinbad the Sailor appear in her tales, which were first introduced to Europe by the French translator and storyteller Antoine Galland between 1704-17.
DAWOOD, N.J.
Aladdin and Other Tales from the Arabian Nights NEW
[D55] Puffin pbk **£1.99**
Sinbad the Sailor and Other Tales from the Arabian Nights NEW
[D56] Puffin pbk **£1.99**
LANG, ANDREW
Aladdin and the Wonderful Lamp
(Illus. Errol Le Cain)
A picture book interpretation of Aladdin's strange magical story in le Cain's stylized variation on the Persian miniature.
[D57] Puffin pbk **£2.50**
LEWIS, NAOMI
Stories from the Arabian Nights
(Illus. Anton Pieck)
Lewis retells 30 of the 1,001 tales in a leisurely, romantic, read-aloud voice that varies with the type of narrative. Sinbad and Ali Baba are here, but so too are the less familiar tales such as 'The Prince and the Tortoise', an unusual Cinderella variant. Pieck's illustrations match Lewis's interpretation.
[D58] Methuen hbk **£12.95**
MCCAUGHREAN, GERALDINE
1001 Arabian Nights (Illus. Stephen Louis)
An outstanding recreation of 35 of the tales, notable for its vigour and immediacy, and for the humour and suspense with which Scheherazade's personal story is told.
[D59] Oxford hbk **£7.95**

BENNETT, JILL
Teeny Tiny (3 - 7, illus. Tomie de Paola)
One day a teeny, tiny woman finds a teeny, tiny bone in a teeny, tiny grave and takes it home. De Paola's atmospheric illustrations build neatly to the surprise ending.
[D60] Oxford pbk **£1.95**

BLEGVAD, ERIK
The Three Little Pigs (4 - 7)
The classic tale of how one clever pig outwits the wicked wolf, with delicately coloured and wonderfully detailed new pen and wash illustrations.
[D61] Collins pbk **£1.75**

BRADMAN, TONY
Look Out, He's Behind You!
(Illus. Margaret Chamberlain)
A light-hearted retelling of *Little Red Riding Hood* in which the wolf hides behind a flap on every page, waiting to gobble her up.
[D62] Mammoth pbk **£2.50**

Illustration by Raymond Briggs for *The Fairy Tale Treasury* edited by Virginia Haviland (Hamish Hamilton hbk **£9.95**)

Who's Afraid of the Big Bad Wolf? NEW
(3 +. illus. Margaret Chamberlain)
A delectable flap-book version of *The Three Pigs*.
[D356] Methuen hbk **£5.95**

CORRIN, SARA & STEPHEN
The Faber Book of Favourite Fairy Tales (Illus. Juan Wijngaard)
A family treasury of 26 well-loved fairy tales, many translated by the Corrins themselves, from the first published editions of Perrault, Grimm, Afanasiev and Andersen - exquisitely illustrated by Juan Wijngaard.
[D63] Faber hbk **£9.95**

CROSSLEY-HOLLAND, KEVIN
British Folk Tales
(11 +, illus. Peter Nelhyczuk)
A folklore scholar, poet and storyteller, Crossley-Holland offers 'new versions' of 55 old tales - reworked sometimes in new settings and in new voice. An outstanding collection, whose impact is deepened by the notes on the sources and background to each tale.
[D64] Orchard hbk **£12.95**
Folk Tales of the British Isles
(11 +, illus. Hannah Firmin)
An essential collection of the varied and rich folk tales of the British Isles - retold in every kind of voice from Robert Southey to Augustus Hare, and W.B. Yeats to Alan Garner. Arranged thematically - the headings of Fairies, Origins and Causes, Nursery and Jocular themes, Ghosts, Saints and Devils and so on defining the range of our native heritage - with introductions placing the stories in their historical and literary contexts.
[D65] Faber hbk **£9.95**

DE LA MARE, WALTER
Molly Whuppie (4 +, illus. Errol le Cain)
De la Mare's romantic literary prose, atmospherically matched by le Cain's glowing illustrations, make this a distinguished version of the folk tale in which resourceful Mollie outwits a fierce giant and wins a royal husband.
[D66] Puffin pbk **£2.25**

GARNER, ALAN
A Bag of Moonshine
(7 - 12, illus. Patrick James Lynch)
Garner attempts to convey the oral storyteller's voice in written text. In this splendid collection of 22 jocular tales, he succeeds in versions that are immediate, colloquial and robust. These reworkings of stories of enchantments, outwittings, and come-

uppances are matched by Lynch's award-winning colour and black and white illustrations.
[D67] Collins pbk **£4.95**

Book of British Fairy Tales
(10 +, illus. Derek Collard)
Garner's potent reworkings of familiar and lesser-known fairy tales are for older children and adults, keen to share his scholarship and rediscover folk tales, and pass them on as storytellers themselves.
[D68] Collins pbk **£4.95**

GRIMM
Jacob and Wilhelm Grimm began their collections of oral traditional literature, recording meticulously the imaginative household tales recounted to them by their acquaintances and relatives, not with children in mind, but as part of a scholarly study of the roots and development of the German language. Their tales range from the sheer nonsense of 'drolls' like 'Clever Elsie' to the romantic, and the sombre and harrowing ('The Juniper Tree') - although the darker tales are softened by magic. Rhythmic and patterned in language, structure and image, these stories have offered generations of readers, young and old, an essential and imaginative window on human behaviour.

Grimm's Fairy Tales
(Illus. George Cruikshank)
Cruikshank (1792-1878) was a satirist and cartoonist for *Punch*. His humorous, lively illustrations for the first English translation of Grimm are reproduced here.
[D69] Puffin pbk **£1.95**

The Fisherman & His Wife
(Illus. Mark Southgate)
Grimm's tragi-comic tale of avarice is aptly interpreted in Southgate's increasingly frenzied pictures.
[D70] Corgi pbk **£2.25**

The Twelve Dancing Princesses
(Illus. Errol Le Cain)
Le Cain's beautiful picture book interpretations of this classic tale, and of *Thorn Rose*, are characteristically theatrical and bejewelled.
[D71] Puffin pbk **£1.50**

Thorn Rose (Illus. Errol Le Cain)
[D72] Puffin pbk **£0.95**

ALDERSON, BRIAN (TRANS)
Popular Folk Tales (Illus. Michael Foreman)
An inspired colloquial translation of 31 of Grimm's most popular folk tales - including 'Hansel and Gretel', 'Snow White' and 'The Juniper Tree'. Foreman's beautiful, suggestively Freudian illustrations reveal the emotional core of each tale in haunting visual images.
[D73] Gollancz hbk **£7.95**

COLUM, PADRAIC & CAMPBELL, JOSEPH (EDS)
The Complete Grimm Fairy Tales
210 of Grimm's tales, translated in 1948 into formal but accessible prose.
[D74] Routledge pbk **£6.95**

MANNHEIM, RALPH (TRANS)
Dear Mili (Illus. Maurice Sendak)
Newly discovered, this haunting story was told by Wilhelm in 1816 in a letter of condolence to a young girl whose mother had just died. It concerns a girl, sole surviving child of a widow, sent into a magical forest to escape death from War. Sendak's illustrations, in the reflective mode of *Outside Over There*, miss the darkness of the girl's sojourn but glowingly capture her return.
[D75] Puffin pbk **£5.99**

QUARRIE, ELEANOR (TRANS)
Hansel & Gretel (Illus. Anthony Browne)
Browne's modern setting gives a chilling relevance to this dark tale of parental abandonment and childhood survival. Each detail in his characteristic illustrations

- a naked lightbulb, the children's patched clothes, their stepmother's fur and make-up - freshly illuminates this story for the perceptive older reader.
[D76] Magnet pbk **£1.95**

ZIPES, JACK (TRANS)
The Complete Fairy Tales of the Brothers Grimm (Illus. John Gruelle)
This collection, containing many stories appearing for the first time in English, and a fascinating introduction which reveals how the 'strict Protestant brothers reworked the stories for moral and political ends', is an 'essential source book' for adults.
[D77] Bantam hbk **£12.95**

HAVILAND, VIRGINIA (ED)
The Fairy Tale Treasury
(4 +, illus. Raymond Briggs)
First published in 1972 and still unsurpassed, this is a fairy tale treasury to grow up on. Thirty two stories from around the world range from nursery favourites to Grimm and Andersen, and tales from Japan, Jamaica and Africa. Briggs' illlustrations in black and white and colour on every page are consistently inventive. An essential collection.
[D78] H Hamilton hbk **£9.95**
[D79] Puffin pbk **£5.95**

HOWE, JOHN
Jack and the Beanstalk   **NEW**
Retold and illustrated by Howe, this is a vivid and immediate picture book interpretation of the classic fairy tale - notable for its use of unusual perspectives and arrestingly visualised characters.
[D80] Little Brown hbk **£6.95**

JACOBS, JOSEPH
Jacobs (1854-1916) was a folklorist who collected fairy tales by country and culture. His retellings are vivid and lively - displaying his keen ear for dialect and speech rhythms. They are classics of their kind, and the main source of our folk and fairy lore: each collection reflects Jacobs' preference for knockabout humour and rustic mischief-making over enchantment and mystery.

Celtic Fairy Tales (8 +, illus. Victor Arbus)
[D81] Bodley pbk **£5.95**

English Fairy Tales (7 +, illus. Margery Gill)
[D82] Bodley pbk **£4.95**

English Fairy Tales (Illus. Edward Ardizzone)
[D83] Deutsch pbk **£2.95**

Illustration by Raymond Briggs for *The Fairy Tale Treasury* edited by Virginia Haviland (Hamish Hamilton hbk £9.95)

KENT, JACK
Fat Cat (4 +)
A cumulative Danish folk tale about a cat who eats everyone he meets until a woodcutter comes in sight. A favourite.
[D84] Puffin pbk **£1.75**

LANG, ANDREW
Best known for his collections of Colour Fairy books begun in 1889 with the *Blue Fairy Book*, and extended over 11 more volumes to the final *Lilac Fairy Book* (1910). These two volumes, freshly edited by Brian Alderson, who has revised, reordered and occasionally removed Lang's texts, breathe new life into these classic collections.

Blue Fairy Book (7 +)
[D85] Puffin pbk **£2.95**
Yellow Fairy Book (7 +)
[D86] Puffin pbk **£2.95**

LURIE, ALISON
Clever Gretchen and Other Forgotten Folk Tales (Illus. Margot Tomas)
A reissue of a feminist collection of 'forgotten' folk tales about strong-minded heroines, like Molly Whuppie and Kate Crackernuts.
[D87] Heinemann hbk **£7.95**

MARSHALL, JAMES
Red Riding Hood (6 - 9)
A stylish, wickedly funny retelling of the classic tale that mixes traditional and contemporary ingredients in pictures and telling. *"Care to stop for a little chat?"* inquires the wolf.
[D88] Collins pbk **£2.25**

MCGARRY, M.
Great Fairy Tales of Ireland
[D89] Muller pbk **£2.95**
Great Folk Tales of Ireland
[D90] Muller pbk **£2.95**

MONTGOMERIE, NORAH & WILLIAM
The Well at the World's End
(8 +)
A classic collection of Scottish folk and fairy tales, including 'Molly Whuppie', 'Cuchulain', 'Finn MacCoull' and 'Childe Roland' - vigorously retold, often through the device of dialogue between the characters.
[D91] Canongate pbk **£1.80**

O'SHEA, PAT
Finn MacCool and the Small Men of Deeds   **NEW**
(8 - 12, illus. Stephen Lavis)
Comedy and fantasy rub shoulders in this spirited retelling of a traditional Irish folktale about one of the 'High Deeds' (the rescue of three children from a giant king) of the tallest, wisest and bravest of warriors.
[D92] Puffin pbk **£2.25**

OXENBURY, HELEN
The Helen Oxenbury Nursery Story Book (3 - 7)
Ten favourite fairytales for the nursery age child - 'Henry Penny', 'Goldilocks and the Three Bears', the 'Three Billy Goats Gruff' amongst others - generously and robustly illustrated.
[D93] Collins pbk **£3.95**

PAOLA, TOMIE DE
Tomie de Paola's Favourite Nursery Tales (4 - 8)
A big, handsome, richly illustrated collection of 17 favourite fairy stories, nine of Aesop's fables, and four poems.
[D94] Methuen hbk **£9.95**

QUAYLE, E.
The Magic Ointment & Other Cornish Legends (7 +, illus. Michael Foreman)
Author and illustrator, both inhabitants of Cornwall, almost 'landscape' these twelve tales of giants, piskies, witches, spriggins and little folk. Quayle's brisk, spirited, concrete prose and Foreman's superb pen and wash illustrations localize these tales of terror and humour in a landscape of stark granite outcrops, 'ancient stone hedges' and wild, empty moor.
[D95] Macmillan pbk **£4.95**

RACKHAM, ARTHUR
Fairy Tales from Many Lands
Tales from around Europe, gathered together and illustrated by the classic Edwardian artist.
[D96] Heinemann hbk **£7.95**

RANSOME, ARTHUR
Old Peter's Russian Tales
Ransome retells folktales he heard and enjoyed when in Russia, in the guise of 'Old Peter' - a grandfather passing on the folklore of his generation to his grandchildren Vanya and Sasha in and around his winter-bound forest home. A classic collection which evokes a Tzarist Russian world of superstition, magnificence, fear and comedy.
[D97] Puffin pbk **£2.95**

ROCKWELL, ANNE
The Three Bears and Fifteen Other Stories (3 - 6)
An indispensable collection for the nursery, expressively illustrated in colour on every page.
[D98] H Hamilton hbk **£7.95**
[D99] Puffin pbk **£4.50**

SPIRIN, GRENNADY
The Enchanter's Spell
Russian artist Spirin interprets five classic tales - 'The Nutcracker', 'The Emperor's New Clothes', 'The Princess and the Seven Brothers' (Pushkin), 'Little Daylight' (MacDonald) and 'The Beautiful Kitchen Maid' (Cervantes) - with paintings of exceptional beauty.
[D100] Macmillan pbk **£4.95**

TOLSTOY, ALEXIE
The Great Big Enormous Turnip (3 - 5, illus. Helen Oxenbury)
The classic cumulative tale of the little old man who calls on the little old woman, little girl, little cat and little mouse to help him pull up his 'great big enormous turnip'. Oxenbury's detailed vigorous illustrations add to the humour of this favourite nursery story.
[D101] Collins pbk **£1.95**

WATTS, BERNADETTE
Goldilocks & the Three Bears (3 - 6)
A comfortable nursery version of an old favourite, with friendly dungaree clad bears.
[D102] North-South pbk **£2.95**

WILDE, OSCAR
Wilde wrote his two collections of fairy tales - *The Happy Prince* (1888) and *A House of Pomegranates* (1891) - early in his career. Simple yet subtle, polished and adult (Wilde claimed his allegorical tales were *"not for children, but for childlike people"*), these strange invented fairy stories which owe much to Andersen are loved as much for their underlying melancholy as for their gentle humour and wisdom.
Fairy Tales (7 +, illus. Charles Mozley)
An elegant edition with delicate drawings and designs by Charles Mozley.
[D103] Bodley hbk **£5.95**
Stories for Children (Illus. P.J. Lynch)
Six of Wilde's fairytales - including 'The Happy

Prince', 'The Remarkable Rocket' and 'The Selfish Giant' - illustrated with haunting and dramatic watercolours.
[D359] Simon & Sch hbk **£7.95**
The Fairy Stories of Oscar Wilde
(7 +, illus. Harold Jones)
A popular edition in which Harold Jones' fine pen and ink drawings match Wilde's eccentric dreamlike imagination.
[D104] Gollancz hbk **£6.95**
[D105] Gollancz pbk **£3.50**
The Happy Prince and Other Stories (7 +)
[D106] Puffin pbk **£1.50**
The Selfish Giant
(5 +, illus. Foreman & Wright)
Wilde's story of the selfish giant who learns to love is perhaps his most famous. Foreman and Wright's interpretation uses traditional fairytale images of the ferocious giant and enormous castle.
[D107] Picture Book St pbk **£1.75**
The Selfish Giant (Illus. Lisbeth Zwerger)
Zwerger's delicate interpretation humanizes Wilde's story. She shows a tall, thin, introverted Victorian gentleman, lively Victorian children and a small boy who, at last, touches the old man's heart.
[D108] Picture Book St pbk **£3.50**

WILLIAMS-ELLIS, AMABEL
The Enchanted World Part 1
(7 - 12, illus. Moira Kemp)
A folklorist, Williams-Ellis chose her favourite tales from the collections she made throughout her life of stories from around the world. 'Childe Roland' rubs shoulders with little-known African tales in this varied and exquisitely illustrated anthology - newly available in two picturebook paperbacks.
[D109] Macmillan pbk **£3.95**
The Enchanted World Part 2
(7 - 12, illus. Moira Kemp)
[D110] Macmillan pbk **£3.95**

WILLIAMSON, DUNCAN
Williamson is a Scottish traveller who grew up listening to stories around the campfire at night and has spent his adult life retelling them. These two 'great' collections about the strange and enchanted creatures and folk of Scottish folklore are transcribed from readings, so that 'the spoken word is so alive that the type only just holds it down on the page' (*Signal Review 2*).
Fireside Tales of the Traveller Children (10 +)
[D111] Canongate pbk **£3.95**
The Broonies, Silkies & Fairies: Traveller's Tales (10 +)
[D112] Canongate pbk **£3.95**

WILLIAMSON, DUNCAN & LINDA
The Genie and the Fisherman and Other Tales from the Travelling People
[D113] Cambridge pbk **£3.95**

ZEMACH, MARGOT
The Little Red Hen (3 - 6)
An eccentric interpretation of an old favourite in which the fussy Little Red Hen defies her idle friends (here depicted playing cards): *"Then I'll do it myself"*. And she did.
[D114] Puffin pbk **£1.75**

Modern Fairy Tales

AIKEN, JOAN
Aiken is a born storyteller and master of the modern fairytale, as her five collections of short, mysterious, occasionally tall stories ably demonstrate. Many are

Illustration by Raymond Briggs for *The Fairy Tale Treasury* edited by Virginia Haviland (Hamish Hamilton hbk **£9.95**)

set in motion by a spark of traditional magic (a bedtime story or lullaby in *Past Eight O'Clock*), but subsequently develop a vein of fantasy peculiar to this author. The beauty of her language and the richness of her tellings are particularly well matched by Jan Pienkowski's silhouette pictures. They are suitable for 5 to 9 year olds.
A Necklace of Raindrops
(Illus. Jan Pienkowski)
[D115] Puffin pbk **£1.95**
Foxhounds Wind Cat Sea Mice
(Illus. John Lawrence)
[D116] Piccolo pbk **£1.75**
Past Eight O'Clock: Goodnight Stories
(Illus. Jan Pienkowski)
[D117] Cape hbk **£7.95**
Tale of a One-Way Street
(Illus. Jan Pienkowski)
[D118] Puffin pbk **£2.50**
The Last Slice of Rainbow
(Illus. Margaret Walty)
[D119] Puffin pbk **£2.50**

CORBALIS, JUDY
The Wrestling Princess & other Stories (7 - 10)
A popular collection of light, 'non-sexist' fairy tales, in which a queen runs away to be a racing driver, a princess rescues a prince, and another wrestles and drives a fork-lift truck.
[D120] Hodder pbk **£1.95**

CORRIN, STEPHEN & SARA
The Puffin Book of Modern Fairy Tales
A discerningly chosen and varied collection of fifteen original fairytales, all written during the last one hundred years, that includes Anstey, Laurence Housman, Thurber, Hughes and Aiken.
[D121] Puffin pbk **£2.50**

JONES, TERRY
Fairy Tales (6 - 10, illus. Michael Foreman)
In more than 30 tales, Jones of *Monty Python* fame takes all the ingredients of the traditional fairytale - its characters (witches, ogres, dragons, fools), motifs (rhymes, riddles and wishes), style and ever-present morality - to create his own idiosyncratic and brilliant stories.
[D122] Pavilion hbk **£7.95**
[D123] Puffin pbk **£4.99**

MUNSCH, ROBERT N.
The Paperbag Princess (4 - 7)
A modern favourite in which Princess Elizabeth up-ends tradition to rescue her fiancée Prince Ronald from a fearsome dragon. 'You are a mess - come back

when you are dressed like a real princess' says ungrateful Ronald. And they didn't get married!
[D124] Hippo pbk **£1.95**

WILLIAMS, JOY
The Practical Princess & Other Liberating Fairy Tales (8 - 10)
A gently feminist reversal of traditional fairy tale roles provides the tongue-in-cheek humour in this witty collection. Here it is the princess who sorts out the dragon, decides to marry the enchanter (instead of the dis-spelled prince) and generally wreaks havoc in the hitherto well-ordered world of magic.
[D125] Hippo pbk **£1.25**

Greek Myths

CONNOLLY, PETER
The Legends of Odysseus (12 +)
Storyteller, archaeologist, artist and historian, Connolly brings all these skills to bear in his award-winning *The Legends of Odysseus*. His vigorous adaptation of Homer's story in five sections is supported by notes, diagrams, maps, site reconstructions and photographs which explain the background to the epic, and enable readers to appreciate its cultural origins.
[D126] Oxford pbk **£3.95**

GIBSON, MICHAEL
Gods, Men & Monsters from Greek Mythology (10 +, illus. Giovanni Caselli)
A popular, strikingly illustrated collection of 27 stories covering the principal myths of Ancient Greece. Told in clear prose and concentrating on the dramatic action, it is a fine introduction for 8-10s.
[D127] P Lowe hbk **£6.95**

GREEN, ROGER LANCELYN
Green, a historian and critic, retells the Greek myths and epics in atmospheric, well-paced prose. His versions are comprehensive (attempting to thread the myths together as history), dramatic, action-packed and highly readable. In these tellings, myth becomes adventure.
Tales of the Greek Heroes (9 - 12)
[D128] Puffin pbk **£1.50**
The Luck of Troy (9 - 12)
[D129] Puffin pbk **£1.95**
The Tale of Troy (9 - 12)
[D130] Puffin pbk **£1.95**

LANG, ANDREW
Tales of Troy and Greece (9 - 12)
A classic retelling of the Homeric legends, first published in 1907 by the folklorist, notable in its time for the way in which Lang used his knowledge of Greek history and current archaeological finds to enrich and set his versions.
[D131] Faber pbk **£2.50**

LINES, KATHLEEN (ED)
The Faber Book of Greek Legends
(10 +, illus. Faith Jacques)
25 stories, some the best retellings of the past, others newly minted for this volume, from authors including A.J. Church, Charles Lamb, Andrew Lang and Rosemary Sutcliff.
[D132] Faber pbk **£4.95**

Norse Myths

BRANSTON, BRIAN
Gods & Heroes from Viking Mythology
(10 +, illus. Giovanni Caselli)
Drawing from original sources, Branston retells the

Norse myths in simple, vigorous prose to reconstruct a clear account of the Viking world and its beliefs.
[D133] P Lowe hbk **£7.50**

CROSSLEY-HOLLAND, KEVIN
Axe-Age, Wolf-Age: A Selection from Norse Myths (11 +, illus. Hannah Firmin)
Crossley-Holland chooses 22 of the myths from his *Norse Myths*, setting them in the framework of the rise and fall of the gods. A colloquial, pounding, atmospheric retelling. Firmin's woodcuts capture the rough-and-tumble side of the sagas.
[D134] Faber pbk **£4.50**

GREEN, ROGER LANCELYN
Myths of the Norsemen (9 - 12)
A compact, highly readable and interestingly arranged collection of the Norse myths.
[D135] Puffin pbk **£1.95**

British & Celtic Myths

CROSSLEY-HOLLAND, KEVIN
Beowulf (10 +, illus. Charles Keeping)
An 'electrifying' retelling of the Anglo-Saxon epic poem, which retains the rhythms and structures of the oral bardic tradition. The alliterative prose and dramatic illustrations capture the grim confrontation of Beowulf and the monstrous Grendel, and the sorrow and ceremony of the hero's death in a picture book of great distinction.
[D136] Oxford pbk **£2.50**

GREEN, ROGER LANCELYN
King Arthur & the Knights of the Round Table (10 +)
A retelling of the Arthurian legend, based on Malory's *Morte d'Arthur*, presents Camelot as a world that never was. Its dominant themes are the unification of Britain by chivalric ideals, and the quest for the Holy Grail.
[D137] Puffin pbk **£2.50**
The Adventures of Robin Hood (9 - 12)
A straightforward, active retelling of the story of Robin Hood and his Merry Men.
[D138] Puffin pbk **£2.25**

HASTINGS, SELINA
Two magnificent picture book editions of the adventures of Sir Gawain, illustrated by Juan Wijngaard. The first is a retelling of the great 14th century alliterative poem and concerns Gawain's contest with the superhuman Green Knight; the second, how he honours chivalric code by marrying the misshapen 'Loathly Lady'. Wijngaard's beautiful illustrations, reminiscent of a medieval manuscript, capture the faitytale quality of Camelot, while emphasizing that Arthur and his knights were ordinary mortals, surounded by uncontrollable sorcery and magic.
Sir Gawain & the Green Knight (9 - 12)
[D139] Walker pbk **£2.25**
Sir Gawain & the Loathly Lady (9 - 12)
[D140] Walker pbk **£2.50**

JONES, GWYN
Welsh Legends & Folk Tales
[D141] Puffin pbk **£2.50**

MCCOUGHREAN, GERALDINE
Saint George and the Dragon   `NEW`
(7 +, illus. Nicki Palin)
A dramatic retelling of the story of England's patron saint - illustrated in powerful, atmospheric paintings.
[D142] Oxford hbk **£5.95**

MCGOWRAN, HUGH
Leprechauns, Legends and Irish Tales
(11 +, illus. Peter Haigh)
A comprehensive selection of Irish folk tales - handsomely produced and strikingly illustrated.
[D143] Gollancz hbk **£10.95**

MOCKLER, ANTHONY
King Arthur & His Knights
(11 - 14, illus. Nick Harris)
A vigorous, straightforward retelling of the Arthurian legend.
[D144] Oxford hbk **£8.95**

PHILIP, NEIL
The Tale of Sir Gawain
(12 +, illus. Charles Keeping)
A retelling of the Arthurian legend by Sir Gawain on his deathbed. The individuality of Philip's voice is matched by Keeping's powerful illustrations of the disaster that ultimately overwhelms Camelot.
[D145] Beaver pbk **£2.50**

PYLE, HOWARD
The Adventures of Robin Hood (9 - 12)
First published in 1883, Pyle's version of *Robin Hood* is romantic and elegant. Pyle was his own artist, and his illustrations are outstanding amongst the work of the late 19th century in America. His Pre-Raphaelite style, based on the Arts and Crafts medievalism then popular at the time, is distinctive.
[D146] Collins hbk **£4.95**

SUTCLIFF, ROSEMARY
Sutcliff uses her unique skills as a historian to enrich these great English myths - her voice and prose always echoing the originals. In her trilogy, she merges the ancient myths of *The Mabinogion* with Malory's *Morte d'Arthur* and its Christian imagery to create an openly romantic version of the Arthurian legends, told in bardic style - rich, measured and pictorial.
1: The Light Beyond the Forest (11 +)
The stories of the knights Lancelot, Gawain, Galahad, Perceval and Bors, whose quest for the grail finally reaches 'the light beyond the forest'.
[D147] Hodder pbk **£1.75**
2: The Sword & the Circle (11 +)
An account of the 'shining time between the Dark and the Dark' when the fellowship of the Round Table grew.
[D148] Hodder pbk **£2.50**
3: The Road to Camlann (11 +)
The downfall of Camelot and the final dispersal of Arthur's knights is seen here as the result both of Lancelot's love for Guinevere and Mordred's treachery.
[D149] Hodder pbk **£1.95**
Dragon Slayer: The Story of Beowulf
(10 +)
The old epic in a bleak, dark, resonant prose telling.
[D150] Puffin pbk **£1.50**
Tristan and Iseult (12 +)
The tragic romance of the Celtic legend about the warrior Tristan's love for his uncle's bride to be is starkly but simply told.
[D151] Puffin pbk **£1.95**

THOMAS, GWYN & CROSSLEY-HOLLAND, KEVIN
Highly individual and richly poetic translations of the great Celtic myths: the quest of Culhwah for Olwen and the four branches of the Mabinogion. The tales are offered in full versions - no effort being made to dilute the complexities and conventions of plot. The vigour, drama, and poetry of the originals is thus preserved. Illustrated by Margaret Jones.
Tales from the Mabinogion (11 +)
[D152] Gollancz pbk **£5.95**

The Quest for Olwen (11 +)
[D153] Lutterworth hbk **£8.95**

WHITE, T.H.
White's extraordinary *The Once and Future King*, which he spent more than half his life writing and re-writing, is set in a kind of 'alternative Middle Ages', cluttered with anachronisms. Arthur establishes the Round Table and its chivalric code to disprove the notion that 'Might Equals Right'.
The Once and Future King (12 +)
[D154] Collins hbk **£10.95**
The Sword in the Stone (10 +)
Telling the story of a hero's apprenticeship - in particular, 'Wart's' education by Merlyn; the knockabout comedy of this first book darkens in subsequent volumes, when Arthur grows up to sombre manhood, and the love of Lancelot and Guinevere begins.
[D155] Collins hbk **£4.95**
[D156] Collins pbk **£2.25**

World Myths, Legends & Folk Tales

AARDEMA, VERNA
Bringing the Rain to Kapiti Plain (5 - 8)
A traditional and dramatic Kenyan tale about a drought retold by Aardema in cumulative rhyming verse, reminiscent of 'The House that Jack Built'.
[D157] Macmillan pbk **£2.95**
Oh Kojo! How Could You!
(5 - 8, illus. Marc Brown)
An entertaining Ananse story from Ashantiland, in which Ananse tricks Kojo out of all his mother's gold - 'Oh Kojo! How Could You!' - but is outwitted in the end.
[D158] Macmillan pbk **£2.95**

AL-SALEH, KHAIRET
Fabled Cities, Princes & Jinn from Arab Myths & Legends
(10 +, illus. Rashed N. Salim)
A facinating collection of Middle Eastern legends and stories, from the ancient myths of pre-Islamic times to folk tales from the Golden Age of the Arab Muslim world.
[D159] P Lowe hbk **£6.50**

APPIAH, PEGGY
Appiah herself collected these West African tales about Kwaku Ananse, the Spiderman, and other Ghânaian people and animals. Her retellings have the verve and wit of the original oral tales, and demonstrate clearly their link with Caribbean folk tales.
Tales of an Ashanti Father (7 +)
[D160] Deutsch pbk **£3.95**
The Pineapple Child and Other Tales from Ashanti (7 +)
[D161] Deutsch pbk **£3.95**

CHARLES, FAUSTIN (ED)
Under the Storyteller's Spell: Caribbean Folk Tales **NEW**
(8 +, illus. Rosetta Woolf)
Charles represents the range of Caribbean folk traditions in a new collection of stories told by West Indian writers - Grace Nicholls, James Berry and Petronella Breinberg. There is one story from each of the main Caribbean countries, covering the English, Dutch, French and Spanish traditions.
[D162] Viking hbk **£6.95**

COHEN, MARK (ED)
Don't Count Your Chickens and Other Fabulous Fables (7 +, illus. Mark Southgate)
A lively collection of fables from all over the world - some favourites from Aesop and La Fontaine; others from the Indian *Fables of Bidpai*, and some newly discovered.
[D163] Viking hbk **£6.95**

HADITHI, MWENYE & KENNEWAY, ADRIENNE
Three humorous cumulative African *pourquoi* or creation narratives - how the animals got their colours and the Zebra his stripes, how the Hippo lives in water by day and on land by night, and how the Chameleon outwitted Leopard and Crocodile by changing colour - illustrated in rich Matisse-like shapes and colours.
Crafty Chameleon (5 - 8)
[D164] Hodder pbk **£2.50**
Greedy Zebra (5 - 8)
[D165] Hodder pbk **£2.50**
Hot Hippo (5 - 8)
[D166] Hodder pbk **£2.50**

HADLEY, ERIC & TESSA
Two beautifully illustrated and unusual picture book collections of legends from around the world - all concerned with the forces of nature. The stories, each occupying a double page spread, include tales from the Aboriginal, Polynesian, Chinese, Maori, Bantu, Mexican and North American Indian oral heritages.
Legends of Earth, Air, Fire & Water
(8 - 12, illus. Bryna Wildman)
[D167] Cambridge hbk **£6.95**
Legends of the Sun & Moon
(8 - 12, illus. Jan Nesbitt)
[D168] Cambridge pbk **£3.50**

HALLWORTH, GRACE
A gifted storyteller, whose collections recall the Caribbean folk tales she heard as a child in Trinidad and has collected as an adult. Her tellings retain the 'feel of the spoken word', and use West Indian speech patterns and dialect to add colour and humour to the stories.
Cric Crac: A Collection of West Indian Stories **NEW**
(7 +, illus. Avril Turner)
A new collection of West Indian folk tales - rich in source and variety. There are familiar Anansi stories here along with less familiar creation stories and ghost stories.
[D169] Heinemann pbk **£3.95**
Listen to This Story: Tales from the West Indies (6 - 9, illus. Dennis Ronston)
A read-aloud collection of ten Anansi stories.
[D170] Methuen pbk **£1.50**
Mouth Open, Story Jump Out
(10 - 14, illus. Art Derry)
Supernatural stories based on Trinidadian folklore.
[D171] Methuen pbk **£1.75**

HAMILTON, VIRGINIA
The People Could Fly: American Black Folk Tales (10 +, illus. Leo and Diane Dillon)
A fine collection of Black American folk tales - 'John' tales, slave tales, 'Brer Rabbit' tales - stirringly retold by a black writer. Hamilton's introductions and notes place them in their historic context, making this book a moving testament to the indomitability of the human spirit in the face of slavery and oppression.
[D172] Walker hbk **£9.95**

HARRIS, G.
Gods & Pharaohs from Egyptian Mythology (10 +, illus. David O'Connor)
Harris, an Egyptologist, has collected Egyptian myths and legends from scattered fragments recorded only in hieroglyphics to introduce readers to the gods and heroes of ancient Egypt.
[D173] P Lowe hbk **£6.50**

HOROWITZ, ANTHONY
The Kingfisher Book of Myths & Legends (9 +)
A lively introduction to over 50 legends from around the world.
[D174] Kingfisher hbk **£5.95**

JAFFREY, MADHUR
Seasons of Splendour
(9 - 12, illus. Michael Foreman)
A splendid collection of Indian tales, myths and legends about Krishna, Hanuman and others, arranged according to the sequence of Hindu Festivals throughout the year. Jaffrey introduces each section, personalizing it by relating it to the celebrations and happenings in her own family home in India.
[D175] Penguin pbk **£5.95**

KANAWA, KIRI TE
Land of the Long White Cloud: Maori Myths, Tales and Legends **NEW**
(illus. Michael Foreman)
Te Kanawa, herself a Maori, retells the tales she heard as a child, interspersed with reminiscences of her early life in New Zealand. These stories, beginning with the birth of Maui, the mischievous fish god, and including creation, heroic and romantic tales, will be new to most readers.
[D176] Pavilion hbk **£9.99**

KNAPPERT, JAN
Kings, Gods & Spirits from African Mythology (10 +, illus. Francesca Palizzoli)
A selection of myths and legends, collected from all Africa. The book includes tales of gods, spirits and ghosts; heroic sagas, and fables about magical animals.
[D177] P Lowe hbk **£6.50**

LESTER, JULIUS
The Tales of Uncle Remus
(6 +, illus. Jerry Pinkey)
Julius Lester removes the framework of the slave story teller, Uncle Remus, and tells the classic 'Brer

Illustration from *The Golden Treasury of Poetry* edited by Louis Untermeyer (Collins hbk **£8.95**)

Rabbit' stories directly to his readers. His voice is conversational - without use of dialect. The tales emerge freshly minted, tough and funny.
[D178] Bodley hbk **£9.95**

LIYI HE (TRANS)
The Spring of Butterflies & Other Chinese Folk Tales
(10 - 14, illus. Pan Aiping and Li Zhao)
An unusual collection of 14 tales from the cultures of the minority peoples of Communist China, translated by a Chinese schoolmaster and illustrated by Chinese artists living in Belai City. Themes common to the folklore of the world abound, but the stories have an individuality and originality that springs from the cultures from which they are derived.
[D179] Collins hbk **£7.95**

MCKISSACK, PATRICIA
Flossie and the Fox (Illus. Rachel Isadora)
In this humorous variant on an African folk tale set in the American South, Flossie uses her knowledge of folklore to outwit a wily fox 'who will do almost anything' to get at the eggs she is taking to a neighbour.
[D179A] Penguin pbk **£2.25**

QUAYLE, ERIC
The Shining Princess and Other Japanese Legends (Illus. Michael Foreman)
A splendid introduction to the folklore of Japan.
[D180] Andersen hbk **£8.95**

RIORDAN, JAMES
The Woman in the Moon and Other Tales of Forgotten Heroines
(11 - 14, illus. Angela Barrett)
A reissue of a stimulating collection of world folk tales whose heroines are positive, not passive.
[D181] Hutchinson pbk **£4.95**

SANDERS, TAO TAI LIU
Dragons, Gods & Spirits from Chinese Mythology (10 +, illus. Johnny Pau)
A rich and varied selection of Chinese myths.
[D182] P Lowe hbk **£6.50**

SHERLOCK, PHILIP
A distinguished Jamaican scholar retells twenty-one tales - some Anansi, some from the Caribs and Waraus who first inhabited the Caribbean Islands. All stem from the African heritage of many West Indians.
West Indian Folk Tales (8 - 12)
[D183] Oxford pbk **£2.95**

SINGH, RANI
The Indian Storybook
(7 - 12, illus. Bryan Orion)
A storyteller and theatre performer of Indian folk tales, Singh retells eight favourites, remembered from her childhood. Orion's traditional-style Indian illustrations are a delight.
[D184] Heinemann pbk **£3.95**

TROUGHTON, JOANNA
Troughton has retold many of the creation stories of the non-European world, in picture book versions notable for their lively, direct prose and often humorous illustrations that derive from the original culture of each.
How Stories Came into the World: Folk Tales from West Africa (5 - 9) **NEW**
[D185] Blackie hbk **£6.95**
Tortoise's Dream (5 - 9)
An African cumulative tale in which Tortoise dreams of an Omumbo-Rombonga tree which will contain all the fruits on earth.
[D186] Blackie hbk **£6.50**

What Made Tiddalick Laugh? (5 - 9)
A funny, cumulative Aborigine dreamtime story about Tiddalick the Frog and the coming of the first rains.
[D187] Blackie hbk **£6.50**

VAUTIER, GHISLAINE
Two beautifully illustrated picture book collections of legends for star gazers; the first tells the stories of the star signs of the Zodiac; the second, how the constellations were named.
The Shining Stars (8 - 12)
[D188] Cambridge pbk **£3.50**
The Way of the Stars (8 - 12)
[D189] Cambridge pbk **£3.50**

WOLKSTEIN, DIANE
The Magic Orange Tree and Other Haitian Folktales (11 +) **NEW**
An unusual and arresting collection of Haitian folktales by a gifted American storyteller. Her introduction and prefatory notes to each tale reveal the customs, beliefs and practices of Haitian culture.
[D190] Cambridge pbk **£3.95**

WOOD, MARION
Spirits, Heroes and Hunters from North American Mythology
(10 +, illus. John Sibbick)
A fine introduction to the myths of the many tribes of North American Indians.
[D191] P Lowe hbk **£6.50**

YOLEN, JANE
Favourite Folk Tales from Around the World
[D192] Random House hbk **£13.50**

Poetry

Poets are wordsmiths: so too are children, who are fascinated by words and their sounds, and often invent and experiment with their own. Verse that introduces children to the limitless possibilities for rhyme, rhythm, metre, sound and mood that spring from the crafting of poetry is essential. Poetry offers a unique way of seeing and hearing, and an invitation to participate in experiences - to actually *live* more fully, richly, and with enhanced awareness, through its compressed and patterned forms, created by the inventive use of words, the power of rhythms and music of sounds. Children come naturally to this patterned and layered way of using words, as their early delight in the invented and original language of nursery rhymes and songs and nonsense verse readily attests. At every level, children need to have their horizons extended and their experience deepened: thus, they move with ease from Lear's 'The Owl and the Pussycat' to Rosen's *Wouldn't You Like to Know?*, Causley's 'Mary Magdalene' and Hughes' *Season Songs*.

AGARD, JOHN
A Guyanese poet whose closely observed verse for, and about, younger children, whether set in England or the Caribbean, in everyday English or dialect, displays a keen ear for language forms and rhythms and a totally engaging sense of humour.
I Din Do Nuttin (5 +, Illus. Susanna Gretz)
A funny, rumbustious collection of poems about the everyday lives of children in the West Indies and Britain.
[D193] Methuen pbk **£1.75**
Laughter is an Egg (9 +) **NEW**
An original collection of verse about laughter.
[D194] Viking hbk **£6.50**

Life Doesn't Frighten Me At All (12 +)
Edited by Agard, this is a teenage anthology of contemporary multi-cultural verse with poems by Maya Angelou, Benjamin Zephaniah, Dory Previn, Bob Marley, Grace Nicholls and Agard himself, amongst others.
[D195] Heinemann pbk **£3.95**
Say It Again, Granny!
(5 +, illus. Susanna Gretz)
Dedicated to *"our ancestors who old-talked for our children to new-talk these proverbs"*, this collection is built around conversations between a granny and grandaughter about 20 Caribbean proverbs. An original way of transcribing an oral culture.
[D196] Methuen pbk **£1.95**

AHLBERG, ALLAN
Ahlberg is as versatile a poet as he is a story-maker and teller, and draws on the same sources - fairytale and contemporary children's culture - for inspiration.
Heard It in the Playground **NEW**
(8 - 10, illus. Fritz Wegner)
A further collection of poems and songs about life in a contemporary primary school including 'The Mrs Butler Blues', 'The Longest Kiss' and 'The Boy without a Name'.
[D197] Viking hbk **£5.95**
Please Mrs Butler (7 +, illus. Fritz Wegner)
An established favourite, this generous collection of poems is a witty, aptly observed compendium of modern school life, written by a former teacher. Not to be missed.
[D198] Puffin pbk **£1.50**
The Mighty Slide (8 +, illus. Charlotte Voake)
A delightful collection of five story poems, subtly varied in subject, background, form and style. The title poem concerns the temporary community a group of children form to preserve an ice patch to slide on.
[D199] Puffin pbk **£1.99**

BELLOC, HILAIRE
Belloc's *Cautionary Tales*, first published in 1940, are parodies of the moral tales of the Victorian Era and of their more alarming German counterpart - *Struwelpeter*. The continuing appeal of his tongue-in-cheek stories (that of Matilda 'who told lies and was burned to death' is a particular favourite) lies in his skill as a poet, his wit, and his imaginative and verbal dexterity.
Cautionary Tales for Children (7 - 11)
[D200] Duckworth pbk **£3.95**
Cautionary Verses
Complete illustrated edition with memorable line drawings by Nicolas Bentley.
[D201] Duckworth hbk **£12.95**
Selected Cautionary Verses
[D202] Puffin pbk **£2.25**

BENNETT, JILL (ED)
A Pot of Gold (8 - 12, illus. Paddy Mounter)
A fresh, wide-ranging collection from an accomplished anthologist - strongly slanted in favour of unanthologized verse.
[D203] Corgi hbk **£7.95**
Noisy Poems (5 +)
A thematic collection of onomatopoeic pieces by poets such as Farjeon, McCord and Milligan, which emphasizes the pleasure in sound that is one of the delights of poetry.
[D204] Oxford pbk **£2.50**
Packet of Poems (5 +)
A delicious collection of poems all about food.
[D205] Oxford pbk **£2.50**
Roger Was a Razorfish (4 - 7)
A 'day-in-the-life-of' collection compiled, designed, and laid out by Jill Bennett and her pupils.
[D206] Hippo pbk **£1.95**
Singing in the Sun (5 +)
[D207] Puffin pbk **£2.50**

Tiny Tim (3 - 6, illus. Helen Oxenbury)
An irresistible picture book collection of first verse - mostly strong, funny poems - splendidly illustrated by Helen Oxenbury.
[D208] Collins pbk **£1.95**

BERRY, JAMES
A major collection from the Jamaican poet, which recently won him the 1988 Signal Poetry Prize: 'rhythmically live to the tips of their toes...many of the poems are in Caribbean dialect, but their verbal invention and imaginative generosity exclude nobody. Sensuous, streetwise, candid in their acute understanding of teenage frustration and the preciousness of private worlds, they jump from the page with rare immediacy' (*TES*).
When I Dance (12 +)
[D209] H Hamilton hbk **£6.95**

BLEGVAD, LEONOR ERIC (ED)
This Little Pig-a-Wig (4 - 8)
For pig lovers, a picture book collection of porcine verse - mainly traditional American and English.
[D210] Puffin pbk **£1.95**

BLISHEN, EDWARD (ED)
Oxford Book of Poetry for Children
(Illus. Brian Wildsmith)
A now standard 'literary' anthology; particularly strong on ballads and narrative verse, but with unfamiliar lyrics by poets such as Lewis Carroll and Thomas Hardy.
[D211] Oxford hbk **£8.95**

CARROLL, LEWIS
Jabberwocky (Illus. Graeme Base)
Carroll's nonsense masterpiece brought to surreal life in Australian artist Base's picture book interpretations.
[D212] Hodder pbk **£3.95**

CAUSLEY, CHARLES
A Cornishman, and one of Britain's finest adult poets, Causley's children's verse, firmly in the English tradition, is notable for its apparent simplicity ('experience first, explanation after'), its sharp, dark eye, and its spaces - there for the reader to fill and inhabit.
Early in the Morning
(3 +, illus. Michael Foreman)
Winner of the 1987 Signal Poetry Award, this is an original collection of fresh-minted 'traditional' verse for the youngest.
[D213] Puffin pbk **£1.50**

The pig from *Dirty Beasts* by Roald Dahl, illustrated by Quentin Blake (Cape hbk £5.95, pbk £2.95)

Figgie Hobbin
Causley's first published book of poetry for children (1970) is extraordinarily wide ranging in subject, language, form and mood. It includes the much quoted 'I Saw a Jolly Hunter' and the haunting 'Mary Magdalene'.
[D214] Puffin pbk **£1.99**
Jack the Treacle Eater
(Illus. Charles Keeping)
[D214A] Macmillan pbk **£3.99**

CAUSLEY, CHARLES (ED)
Causley's three anthologies are among the finest available today, displaying the 'mystery and magic' he sees as 'poetry', and which he achieves in his own verse.
Puffin Book of Magic Verse (8 +)
[D215] Puffin pbk **£2.50**
Puffin Book of Salt-Sea Verse (8 +)
[D216] Puffin pbk **£2.95**
The Sun Dancing: Anthology of Christian Verse (8 +)
[D217] Puffin pbk **£3.50**

COLE, WILLIAM
Humour is often a way into verse (and literature) for children. American anthologist Cole offers readers a feast of comic poems in each of these collections. Illustrated by Tomi Ungerer in sharp-edged line drawings which capture their exuberant dottiness perfectly, they are suitable for children from the age of 6 upwards.
Beastly Boys and Ghastly Girls
[D218] Methuen pbk **£1.50**
Oh How Silly!
[D219] Methuen pbk **£1.50**
Oh Such Foolishness!
[D220] Methuen pbk **£1.50**
Oh That's Ridiculous!
[D221] Methuen pbk **£1.50**

COPE, WENDY (ED)
Is That the New Moon? (13 +) `NEW`
An invigorating collection of funny, sad, tender, moving poems from leading modern women poets about their own and other women's experience.
[D222] Collins pbk **£2.25**

CORRIN, S. & S.
Once upon a Rhyme (5 - 10)
A 'kaleidoscope' of 101 poems for young children containing a solid mix of old and new - often in surprising juxtaposition.
[D223] Puffin pbk **£1.95**

COUZYN, JENI (ED)
Singing Down the Bones (14 +) `NEW`
Couzyn invites readers to sing the poems of 'women who would not accept the narrow territory the bone-man cast for them', in this exhilarating collection of poems - old and new, familiar and unexpected - by, and about, women from around the world.
[D223A] Women's P pbk **£3.50**

DAHL, ROALD
Enormously popular collections of raucous, colloquial, subversive verse. Exceptionally illustrated by Quentin Blake.
Dirty Beasts (7 - 12)
[D224] Cape hbk **£5.95**
[D225] Puffin pbk **£2.95**
Revolting Rhymes (7 - 12)
Dahl takes traditional fairy tales and up-ends, up-dates and generally tampers with them with wit and humour. Good debunking stuff.
[D226] Cape hbk **£5.95**
[D227] Puffin pbk **£2.95**
Rhyme Stew (8 +) `NEW`
[D227A] Cape hbk **£7.50**

DAVIS (ED)
A Single Star (8 - 14)
A fine collection of Christmas poetry.
[D228] Puffin pbk **£1.75**

DE LA MARE, WALTER
De la Mare's poetry - particularly *Peacock Pie* - was considered to be the finest for children of his generation: his fluent, rhythmically inventive verse was described by Auden 'as a revelation of the wonders of the English language'. Some find his poems too whimsical; others respond to their magic, romance and mystery.
Collected Rhymes & Verses (7 +)
[D229] Faber pbk **£5.99**
Peacock Pie (9 +, illus. Louisa Brierley)
[D230] Faber hbk **£9.95**
Peacock Pie (Illus. Edward Ardizzone)
[D231] Faber pbk **£3.95**

Illustration by Edward Ardizzone from *Peacock Pie* by Walter de la Mare (Faber pbk £3.95)

EDWARDS, RICHARD
A 'child-poet' in the tradition of R.L. Stevenson, A.A. Milne and Eleanor Farjeon, who works experimentally within a well-known framework. His voice is original and contemporary.
If Only...(6 - 10, illus. Alison Darke) `NEW`
[D232] Viking hbk **£5.95**
The Word Party (Illus. John Lawrence)
[D233] Puffin pbk **£1.50**
Whispers from the Wardrobe `NEW`
(Illus. John Lawrence)
[D234] Puffin pbk **£1.75**

ELIOT, T.S.
'Masterpieces of their kind' that, despite the popularity of the musical *Cats*, should be introduced in their original form, with Bentley's essential illustrations, at about 9.
Growl Tiger's Last Stand & Other Poems
(9 +, illus. Errol le Cain)
[D235] Faber hbk **£5.95**
Old Possum's Book of Practical Cats
(Illus. Nicolas Bentley)
[D236] Faber hbk **£7.95**
[D237] Faber pbk **£3.95**

FARJEON, ELEANOR
Kings & Queens (8 +, illus. Robin Jacques)
The histories of the Kings and Queens of England written in elegant, amusing verse.
[D238] Puffin pbk **£1.50**
Something I Remember
A poet in the tradition of R.L. Stevenson whose language is that of a 'bygone age' - but an age where

young readers may still find themselves at
home.
[D239] Penguin pbk **£2.95**

FISHER, ROBERT (ED)
Pet Poems NEW
(9 +, illus. Sally Lindberg)
A wide-ranging anthology of verse celebrating pets
from the household cat and dog to the exotic hippo
and yak.
[D240] Faber hbk **£6.99**

FOSTER, JOHN (ED)
A popular series of anthologies - primarily of
contemporary verse - arranged so that one poem leads
on to the next, and lavishly illustrated with black and
white drawings, colour paintings, and photographs.
A Very First Poetry Book (5 - 7)
[D241] Oxford pbk **£2.95**
A First Poetry Book (7 - 8)
[D242] Oxford pbk **£2.95**
A Second Poetry Book (8 - 10)
[D243] Oxford pbk **£2.95**
A Third Poetry Book (9 - 11)
[D244] Oxford pbk **£2.95**
A Fourth Poetry Book (10 - 12)
[D245] Oxford pbk **£2.95**
A Fifth Poetry Book (11 - 13)
[D246] Oxford pbk **£2.95**
Let's Celebrate (8 +)
An anthology of 'festival' verse from around the
world.
[D246A] Oxford pbk **£3.95**

GRAHAM, ELEANOR (ED)
Two 'literary' collections, now classics of their kind.
Puffin Book of Verse (8 - 14)
[D247] Puffin pbk **£2.95**
Puffin Quartet of Poets (9 - 14)
Not a traditional anthology, but an interestingly
balanced selection of the work of four writers of
children's, as opposed to the currently fashionable
'kid's', verse: Eleanor Farjeon, James Reeves,
E.V. Rieu and Ian Serraillier.
[D248] Puffin pbk **£1.95**

GROSS, PHILIP NEW
Manifold Manor (10 +, illus. Chris Riddell)
A poetic, privately conducted tour of Manifold
Manor, a haunted ruin.
[D249] Faber pbk **£3.99**

HARRIS, ROSEMARY (ED)
Love & the Merry-Go-Round (13 +)
Poems of relationships, love, war, death and renewal
from the 19th and 20th centuries.
[D250] H Hamilton hbk **£6.95**

**HARRISON, MICHAEL & CLARK,
CHRISTOPHER STUART (EDS)**
An Oxford Book of Christmas Poems
(7 +)
[D251] Oxford pbk **£3.95**
New Dragon Book Of Verse (12 +)
A popular anthology. Handsome double page
illustrations by various artists open each section:
landscapes, seascapes, creatures, childhood, war and
so on.
[D252] Oxford pbk **£2.95**
**The Oxford Treasury of Children's
Poems**
An illustrated collection of tried and tested favourites
that take readers from nursery rhymes and limericks
to the work of poets such as Rossetti, Lear, Milne,
Nash, Causley and Rosen.
[D253] Oxford hbk **£7.95**
The Young Dragon Book of Verse NEW
(10 +)
[D253A] Oxford hbk **£5.95**

HARVEY, ANNE (ED)
A fine anthologist whose thematically based
collections have a richness, density and pluralism that
is reflected in their telling arrangements, and is often
enhanced by the added dimension of introductory
essays and biographical notes on the poets included.
**Faces in a Crowd: Poems About
People** (10 +) NEW
[D254] Viking hbk **£6.95**
In Time of War (12 +)
An exceptional anthology of poems, songs, slogans
and popular verse from both World Wars - made to
'echo the moods of war: patriotism and pacifism,
enthusiasm and disillusionment' and the heightened
emotions that the 'threat of conflict, separations,
hardship and death' engenders.
[D255] Puffin pbk **£2.99**
**Of Caterpillars, Cats and Cattle: An
Anthology of Animal Poems**
(10 +, illus. William Geldart)
An 'elegant' and indispensable collection of over 200
poems about animals.
[D256] Puffin pbk **£2.99**
Poets in Hand: A Puffin Quintet of Poets
(9 - 14)
A companion volume to Eleanor Graham's *A Puffin
Quartet*. The five poets are John Walsh, Charles
Causley, Elizabeth Jennings, Vernon Scannell and
John Fuller.
[D257] Penguin pbk **£2.95**
**Six of the Best: A Puffin Sextet of
Poets** NEW
[D258] Puffin pbk **£3.50**
The Language of Love (13 +) NEW
[D259] Blackie hbk **£7.50**

HOBERMAN, MARY ANN'
A House is a House for Me (5 +)
This mind-bending book expands all our notions
about homes: *"A box is a house for a teabag/A
teapot's a house for some tea/If you pour me a cup
and I drink it all up/Then the teahouse will turn
into me"*.
[D259A] Puffin pbk **£2.50**

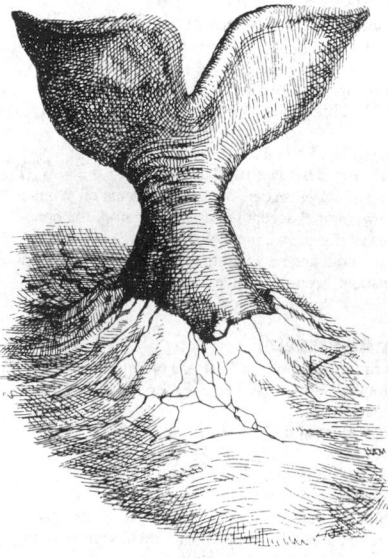

Illustration by Chris Riddell from *Moon Whales* by
Ted Hughes (Faber hbk **£7.50**)

Illustration from *The Oxford Treasury of Children's
Poems* edited by Michael Harrison & Christopher
Stuart-Clark (Oxford University Press hbk **£8.95**)

HOLBROOK, DAVID (ED)
Iron, Honey, Gold (11 - 14)
A reissue of the first volume of an anthology of
classic poetry, first published in 1961. Holbrook's
selection is wide-ranging, often exotic, and includes
poems from the Chinese, folksongs and ballads as
well as verse from poets such as Hardy, Wordsworth,
Crabbe, Frost and Clare. The unexpectedness of its
arrangement provokes new awareness.
[D260] Cambridge hbk **£6.95**

HUGHES, TED
Except for his early *Meet My Folks* (1961), a
collection of comic portraits of the poet's family and
relations, Hughes' poetry for children bears all the
marks of his adult verse. 'It too', writes Aidan
Chambers in *Poetry for Children*, 'grapples with
emotion through stingingly accurate and often
unexpected images, precisely placed words, and ideas
usually fixed in individualized animals'. His eye is
'merciless' - able to empathize with prey and
predator alike.
Meet My Folks (8 +)
[D261] Faber hbk **£2.95**
Moon Bells and Other Poems
(10 +)
Winner of the 1979 Signal Poetry Prize. A marvellous
startling collection about real and mythical animals -
some creatures of the Moon.
[D262] Bodley hbk **£5.95**
Moon Whales (8 +, illus. Chris Riddell)
Hughes first explored the flora and fauna of an
imagined moon world in *The Earth Owl and Other
Moon People* (1963). This recent collection contains
almost all of *Earth Owl* plus later poems about this
'spine chilling', inhospitable planet.
[D263] Faber hbk **£6.95**
Poetry in the Making
The key book for anyone interested in the writing,
reading and teaching of poetry. An anthology with a
linking commentary based on a BBC radio series for
9-14 year olds.
[D264] Faber pbk **£2.95**
Season Songs (12 +)
One of the finest collections of children's poetry ever
published. 'What it offers,' writes Aidan Chambers,
'is sometimes thought of as nature poetry, but it is
utterly modern, unsentimental, vivid, alive -
sometimes uncomfortably so - and always powerful.
You *have* to attend...'
[D265] Faber hbk **£7.95**
[D266] Faber pbk **£2.95**
The Coming of the Kings
[D267] Faber pbk **£3.95**

What is the Truth? A Farmyard Fable for the Young (9 +)
Winner of the Guardian Award for Children's Fiction as well as the Signal Poetry Award, this collection of poems, linked by a prose narrative, concerns God's son and his curiosity about earth and the nature of truth. God and his son come to Earth, and summon the inhabitants of an English farm who tell them in verse a story about life as they have lived it, and about truth.
[D268] Faber pbk **£4.95**

HUGHES, TED & HEANEY, SEAMUS (EDS)
The Rattle Bag
The poetry anthology of the 80s. Arranged alphabetically by title or first line, this wide-ranging collection provocatively mixes classics (Blake, Shakespeare, Hardy, D.H. Lawrence) and modern verse with the unfamiliar and the unusual (hunter's prayers, incantations, charms).
[D269] Faber hbk **£10.00**
[D270] Faber pbk **£5.95**

HUTH, ANGELA (ED)
Island of the Children (8 +, illus. Jane Ray)
An inspired anthology of new, unpublished work by contemporary writers, specially commissioned for this volume.
[D271] Orchard hbk **£9.95**

IRESON, BARBARA (ED)
Over and Over Again (3 +)
[D272] Beaver pbk **£1.50**
The Faber Book of Nursery Verse
(3 - 12)
The title and cover suggest a younger readership than this splendid collection deserves. Hundreds of traditional and more recent poems are enticingly arranged - sometimes by subject, sometimes by form.
[D273] Hutchinson pbk **£4.95**
The Young Puffin Book of Verse (4 - 8)
An excellent 'dip-in' anthology first published in 1970, and unrivalled for many years.
[D274] Puffin pbk **£1.95**

KOCH, KENNETH & FARRELL, JANE (EDS)
Talking to the Sun (10 +)
A beautiful, invigorating and unusual anthology in which poems from around the world are matched by reproductions of paintings, sculpture, and other art objects from the collection of the Metropolitan Museum of Art in New York.
[D275] Viking hbk **£10.95**

LEAR, EDWARD
Equally famous as an artist and painter of birds and landscapes, and as a writer of children's nonsense verse, Lear published his **Book of Nonsense** - a collection of limericks - in 1846, introducing entertainment and fun into a Victorian 'nursery' literature heavy with moral didacticism. His later poems include such classics as 'The Owl and the Pussycat' and 'The Jumblies'. They are made vivid by his imagination, inspired word play and invention, but are touched too with the melancholy from which he suffered all his life. His illustrations are an inspired and intrinsic part of the text, bringing his characters to an idiosyncratic, oddly bird-like life.
A Book of Bosh (Ed. Brian Alderson)
[D276] Puffin pbk **£2.95**
Complete Nonsense of Edward Lear
(Ed. Holbrook Jackson)
[D277] Faber hbk **£7.95**
The Owl and the Pussycat
(Illus. Paul Galdone)
[D278] Heinemann hbk **£6.95**
The Quangle Wangle's Hat
(Illus. Helen Oxenbury)
[D279] Puffin pbk **£1.50**

LEWIS, NAOMI (ED)
Messages (12 +)
A personal anthology of poets (Clare, Dickinson, Stevie Smith, Leyland) who have, as children's book critic, writer and poet Lewis states in her introduction 'the kind of imagination that sees to the other side of experience'.
[D280] Faber pbk **£3.95**

LITTLE, JEAN
'Hey World, here I am!' announces Kate Bloomfield - 'author' of the wry, child-eyed poems and pieces of prose about *everything* - school, babies, her best friend - in this lively and original collection.
Hey World, Here I Am! (8 +, illus. Sue **NEW** Truesdall)
[D280A] Oxford hbk **£4.95**

LIVINGSTONE, MYRA COHN (ED) **NEW**
Cat Poems (6 +, illus. Trina Schart Hyman)
A celebration of the feline - kittens, alley cats, jellicle cats - in verse and line.
[D280B] Oxford hbk **£5.95**

LONGFELLOW, HENRY WADSWORTH
Longfellow's narrative poem, first published in Boston in 1855 and immensely popular in its day, is an invented American Indian myth, based on contemporary accounts of Indian life, customs, legend and oral tradition. Told in the incantatory, almost hypnotic, metre and often in the same spirit as the Finnish epic *The Kalevala*, it is a classic story of the birth, apprenticeship, superhuman feats and death of the godlike hero and leader, Hiawatha. Artists le Cain and Jeffers offer rich picture-book interpretations of extracts from Hiawatha's childhood, each based on the traditional art of the American Indians, and suitable for younger children.
Hiawatha (6 +, illus. Susan Jeffers)
[D281] Macmillan pbk **£3.95**
Hiawatha's Childhood
(6 +, illus. Erroll le Cain)
[D282] Puffin pbk **£1.75**
Song of Hiawatha (Illus. J. Kiddell Monroe)
[D283] Dent hbk **£7.50**

MACBAIN (ED)
Book of a Thousand Poems
[D284] Bell & Hyman hbk **£7.95**

MACKAY, DAVID (ED)
A Flock of Words (12 +)
A reissue of a fine, eclectic collection of verse from around the world (it includes translations from Russian, Japanese, Chinese, Czech as well as verse by Chaucer, Rilke, Yevtushenko, Rimbaud and others). Its arrangement is subtle and reveals new aspects of the poems, while the notes and introduction provide suggestions for exploring poetry further.
[D285] Bodley hbk **£6.95**

'There was an Old Man of the Nile' from *Complete Nonsense of Edward Lear* (Faber hbk **£7.95**)

Illustration from *The Kingfisher Book of Comic Verse* selected by Roger McGough (Kingfisher hbk **£7.95**)

MAGEE, WES (ED)
Madtail, Mini Whale and Other Shape Poems (7 - 10, illus. Caroline Crossland)
An original anthology in which the shape of the poem reflects its subject, and forms a picture.
[D286] Viking hbk **£6.95**

MCCORD, DAVID
An introduction to the work of an American poet whose verse ranges from pure, word-playing nonsense to quiet meditations.
Mr Bidery's Spidery Garden **NEW**
(6 +)
[D286A] Puffin pbk **£1.99**

MCGOUGH, ROGER
One of the original Liverpool 'Beat' poets, McGough has been called a '*nouveau* poet version of Causley'. His range is wide, from jokey, light verse to concrete poems, and surprisingly dark and serious lyric verse.
An Imaginary Menagerie
(8 +, illus. Tony Blundell)
Short poems based on word play about a variety of real and invented animals: a 'teapet', a 'caterpillow', newts playing flutes.
[D287] Viking hbk **£6.95**
Helen Highwater (8 - 12)
A narrative poem - witty and action-packed, about Helen Highwater and her epic swim to save the town of Chucklewick.
[D288] Viking hbk **£5.95**
Nailing the Shadow
(9 +, illus. Marketa Prachaticka)
An amusing volume of original poems. The bizarre and original illustrations set off the surreal jokes and puns of the poems.
[D289] Puffin pbk **£1.99**
Sky in the Pie
(9 - 14, illus. Satoshi Kitamura)
A 'live-wire' collection of McGough at his best - demonstrating his 'mood-swinging versatility' (matched by Kitamura's quirky pen and ink drawings and lino cuts), and his ability to write unconventional humorous and serious verse. The arrangement of the poems makes it own point.
[D290] Puffin pbk **£1.50**
You Tell Me (7 +)
A companion volume to *Sky in the Pie*, written with Michael Rosen.
[D291] Puffin pbk **£1.10**

MCGOUGH, ROGER (ED)
The Kingfisher Book of Comic Verse
(11 +)
A well-designed bumper collection of modern comic verse.
[D292] Kingfisher hbk **£7.95**

Strictly Private (11 +)
A fine anthology of modern verse - much of it
performance poetry grouped thematically under
poems of McGough's: 'Being in Love', 'First Day of
School' and 'He's Behind Her'.
[D293] Puffin pbk **£2.50**

MCNAUGHTON, COLIN
**There's an Awful Lot of Weirdoes in Our
Neighbourhood**
Picture artist McNaughton describes his first book of
poetry as a collection of 'rather silly' kid's verse. It is
a humorous, sometimes poignant, sometimes
outrageous exploration of neighbourhood life and the
problems of being small and surviving.
[D294] Walker pbk **£4.95**

MILLIGAN, SPIKE
The zany, fantastical humour of this ex-Goon as well
as his pro-child, anti-establishment stance make his
verse immediately appealing to children.
Book of Milliganimals (8 +)
[D295] Puffin pbk **£1.50**
Silly Verse for Kids (8 +)
[D296] Puffin pbk **£1.25**
Startling Verse for all the Family
[D297] Puffin pbk **£1.99**
Unspun Socks (10 +)
[D298] Puffin pbk **£1.10**

MILNE, A.A.
Milne's poetry celebrates the dreams and nonsense
and ordinary events of childhood in narrative verse.
Dated though its whimsical and sentimental tone now
seems, it survives because Milne's voice is a strong,
individual and recognizable one. Children (and

'The Sugar Lady' from *Tomie de Paola's Book of
Poems* (Methuen hbk **£8.95**)

adults) still rejoice in its Arcadian quality and in its
wit, ingenuity and sophisticated mastery of rhythm
and rhyme. All of these editions have the original
illustrations of Ernest Shepard, the more expensive
editions of *Now We Are Six* and *When We Were Very
Young* being illustrated in colour.
Christopher Robin Verse Book
An ideal introduction to Milne's verse with 24 poems
and many illustrations.
[D299] Methuen pbk **£2.99**
Now We Are Six
[D300] Methuen hbk **£8.95**
[D301] Methuen hbk **£5.50**
[D302] Methuen pbk **£1.75**
The World of Christopher Robin
A collection of *When We Were Very Young* & *Now
We Are Six*.
[D303] Methuen hbk **£7.95**
When We Were Very Young
[D304] Methuen hbk **£8.95**
[D305] Methuen hbk **£5.50**
[D306] Methuen pbk **£1.75**

MOORE, CLEMENT C.
First published in 1822 in New York, Moore's
Christmas Eve fantasy, while not great verse, has
become a seasonal classic.
The Night before Christmas
(5 -8, illus. Anita Lobel)
Lobel gives a Victorian New York setting to this
evergreen narrative poem.
[D307] Corgi pbk **£1.95**
The Night before Christmas
(5 - 8, illus. Tomie de Paola)
De Paola sets the work in his own 19th century
farmhouse in a small New Hampshire village. Each
page is bordered with brightly coloured New England
quilt patterns.
[D308] Oxford pbk **£2.95**

NASH, OGDEN
Custard and Company (8 +)
A fine introduction to the work of the great American
wordsmith and writer of humorous verse.
[D309] Puffin pbk **£1.50**

NICHOLLS, GRACE
Come into My Tropical Garden
This first collection of verse for children by Guyanese
poet Nicholls is rich in rhythm, sound and idiomatic,
dialectic language, and memorably evokes a
Caribbean childhood.
[D310] A & C Black hbk **£4.95**

NICHOLLS, JUDITH (ED)
**What on Earth..? Poems with a
Conservation Theme** (8 +, illus. Alan Baker)
A topical wide-ranging anthology.
[D311] Faber pbk **£3.99**
Wordspells (6 +, illus. Alan Baker)
Nicholls weaves 'wordspells' in this rich, lyrical
collection of original verse - wide ranging in time and
place from ancient China to medieval Ireland, and
from 19th century to present day America.
[D312] Faber hbk **£7.95**

NICOLL, HELEN (ED)
Poems for 7-Year Olds and Under
(5 +, illus. Michael Foreman)
A fine popular anthology of verse, mostly light, some
by children's poets and some by adult. Yeats, T.S.
Eliot, Keats and Stevie Smith are included.
[D313] Puffin pbk **£1.95**

NOYES, ALFRED
The Highwayman (10 +, illus. Charles Keeping)
A picture book version of Noyes' narrative tale of the
highwayman who came *"riding, riding, riding up to
the old inn door"* and his faithful love, accompanied

by Keeping's expressive and idiosyncratic line
drawings.
[D314] Oxford pbk **£2.50**

OPIE, PETER & IONA
Oxford Book of Children's Verse
Evergreen classic packed with enduringly popular
modern and classic children's verse.
[D315] Oxford hbk **£12.95**

OWEN, GARETH
Owen's verse is contemporary in subject, theme and
treatment, but traditional in manner. His *Song of the
City*, winner of the Signal Poetry Award in 1986, has
a range of style and subject 'unusual' in verse for the
very young. The same is true of *Salford Road* - a
nostalgic collection of poems about a city-based
childhood.
Salford Road (10 - 14)
[D316] Collins pbk **£1.75**
Song of the City (6 +)
[D317] Collins pbk **£1.95**

PAOLA, TOMIE DE
Book of Poems (5 - 12)   **NEW**
A generous book of poems, traditional and
modern, illustrated in de Paola's glowing colour and
assured line.
[D318] Methuen hbk **£8.95**

PATTEN, BRIAN
Gargling with Jelly (8 +)
An enormously popular collection of original verse
that appeals initially for its silly, occasionally vulgar,
nonsensical verse, but offers serious, thought-
provoking poems too.
[D319] Puffin pbk **£1.50**

PRELUTSKY, JACK (ED)
Walker Book of Poetry for Children
(Illus. Arnold Lobel)
An inviting collection of 572 poems arranged in 14
thematic sections. The emphasis is on humour and
light verse. Lobel's illustrations, in colour and
monochrome, deepen the impact.
[D320] Walker hbk **£10.95**

REEVES, JAMES
A poet in the tradition of Stevenson and de la Mare,
Reeves is a consummate craftsman whose poetry,
magical, mysterious and filled with delightful
characters - Old Moll, Dr Hearty and some of his
'pre-fabulous animals' - evokes a gentler era.
**Wandering Moon & Other
Poems**
(7 +, illus. Edward Ardizonne)
[D321] Puffin pbk **£2.50**

REGNIERS, BEATRICE SCHENK DE (ED)
Sing a Song of Popcorn (8 +)
A splendid collection of 130 poems arranged
thematically - nonsense, story, people and so on. Each
section is illustrated by top American picture book
artists, including Marcia Brown, Arnold Lobel and
Maurice Sendak.
[D322] Hodder hbk **£8.95**

ROSEN, MICHAEL
When Mike Rosen appeared on the poetry scene in
the 1970s, his funny, child-centred, conversational
performance pieces offended purists. His verse is built
around slice of life family incidents and escapades -
often autobiographical. Rosen, writes Aidan
Chambers in *Poetry for Children*, has 'extended the
definition and the form of 'poetry' for children, and in
doing so has extended its audience.'
Don't Put Mustard in the Custard
(7 +, illus. Quentin Blake)
[D323] Collins pbk **£2.50**

Ticklish Tom from *A Light in the Attic* by Shel
Silverstein (Cape hbk £6.95)

Mind Your Own Business
(7 +, illus. Quentin Blake)
[D324] Collins pbk **£1.50**
Quick, Let's Get Out of Here
(Illus. Quentin Blake)
[D325] Puffin pbk **£1.75**
The Hypnotiser (7 +, illus. Tony Tiffen)
[D326] Deutsch hbk **£5.95**
When Did You Last Wash Your Feet?
(12 + illus. Tony Pinchuck)
A marvellous, streetwise collection for teenagers,
about the unromantic side of growing up. Pinchuck's
tough, zany comic-strip illustrations are just right.
[D327] Collins pbk **£2.95**
Wouldn't You Like to Know
(7 +, illus. Quentin Blake)
[D328] Puffin pbk **£1.50**
You Can't Catch Me
(5 - 8, illus. Quentin Blake)
[D329] Puffin pbk **£1.75**

ROSEN, MICHAEL (ED)
Two standard, well-chosen anthologies of poems
Rosen has himself shared with children.
A Spider Bought a Bicycle
(3 - 10, illus. Inga Moore)
[D330] Kingfisher hbk **£6.95**
Kingfisher Book of Children's Poetry
(8 +)
[D331] Kingfisher hbk **£7.95**

RUMBLE, ADRIAN (ED)
Is a Caterpillar Ticklish? **NEW**
(6 - 10)
A chunky, amiable collection of poems old and new.
[D332] Puffin pbk **£2.50**

SCANNELL, VERNON
The Clever Potato (8 - 12)
A collection of comic verse about the potato and
other edible items.
[D333] Beaver pbk **£1.99**

SILVERSTEIN, SHEL
A Light in the Attic (7 - 11)
Described as an 'Ogden Nash for juveniles',
Silverstein is an American Michael Rosen. His zany

verse, complimented by his Lear-like pen and ink
drawings, focuses on the comic side of growing up.
[D334] Cape hbk **£6.95**

SMITH, JANET ADAM (ED)
Faber Book of Children's Verse (9 +)
A good general literary anthology.
[D335] Faber pbk **£3.95**

STEVENSON, ROBERT LOUIS
First published in 1885 and never out of print,
Stevenson's verse, based on memories of his
childhood and its wonders, real and imagined, has
been often imitated but never bettered. The most
notable illustrated editions are: Eve Garnett's delicate
thirties version, Wildsmith's colour-rich sixties
edition, and Foreman's subtle pen and wash eighties
interpretation, set in a Cornish landscape. Suitable for
all ages from 5 up.
A Child's Garden of Verses
(Illus. Brian Wildsmith)
[D336] Oxford hbk **£6.95**
[D337] Oxford pbk **£4.95**
A Child's Garden of Verses
(Illus. Eve Garnett)
[D338] Penguin pbk **£1.50**
A Child's Garden of Verses
(Illus. Michael Foreman)
[D339] Gollancz pbk **£4.95**

STYLES, MORAG & COOK, HELEN (EDS)
There's a Poet Behind You (9 +)
A novel introduction to the work of five
contemporary poets for children: Grace Nicholls,
Adrian Mitchell, Gillian Clarke, Michael Rosen and
John Agard. All introduce themselves, their writing
and their ideas in insightful commentaries which
accompany a selection of their verse.
[D340] A & C Black hbk **£6.95**

STYLES, MORAG (ED)
Two stimulating anthologies drawn from many
cultures around the world, in a variety of forms -
haiku, folk song, free verse.
I Like That Stuff (8 - 12)
[D341] Cambridge hbk **£5.25**
You'll Love This Stuff (8 - 12)
[D342] Cambridge hbk **£5.25**

The Pobble Who Has No Toes from *The Golden
Treasury of Poetry* edited by Louis Untermeyer
(Collins hbk £8.95)

Illustration from *The Golden Treasury of Poetry*
edited by Louis Untermeyer (Collins hbk £8.95)

THOMSON, PAT
Rhymes Around the Day
(3 - 8, illus. Jan Ormerod)
A 'day-in-the-life-of' picture book collection of
traditional verse set in a pictorial narrative of
Ormerod's subtly detailed pastels.
[D343] Puffin pbk **£2.25**

UNTERMEYER, LOUIS (ED)
The Golden Treasury of Poetry
(8 +)
The best general anthology available. A wonderful
compendium of the poetic riches of our common
English-speaking heritage.
[D344] Collins hbk **£8.95**

WEBB, KAY (ED)
I Like This Poem (6 - 16)
An enormously popular, surprisingly traditional,
anthology of favourite verse chosen by children for
children - enlivened by their own commentaries on
their choices.
[D345] Puffin pbk **£2.95**

WILSON, RAYMOND (ED)
A poet himself, Wilson has edited many fine thematic
anthologies.
Every Poem Tells a Story
A wide ranging, indispensable collection of
contemporary and traditional narrative verse.
[D346] Viking hbk **£5.95**
Nine O'Clock Bell (8 +)
A collection of poems about school.
[D347] Puffin pbk **£1.95**
**Out and About: Poems of the
Outdoors** (9 +)
[D348] Puffin pbk **£2.25**

WORTH, VALERIE
All the Small Poems **NEW**
(6 +, illus. Natalie Babbitt)
An original American collection of 'small' poems
about big subjects.
[D349] Faber pbk **£2.99**

WRIGHT, KIT
A 'kid's poet' whose subject is everyday experience.
His verse is funny, fast-moving and occasionally
tender and thought-provoking. These three collections
are illustrated by Posy Simmonds, and are suitable for
children from the age of 8 up.
Cat among the Pigeons
[D350] Puffin pbk **£1.99**
Hot Dog and Other Poems
[D351] Puffin pbk **£1.50**
Rabbiting On and Other Poems
[D352] Collins pbk **£1.95**

WRIGHT, KIT (ED)
Two fine thematically arranged anthologies,
illustrated by Michael Foreman - a balanced mix of
old and new.
Poems for 9-Year Olds and Under
[D353] Puffin pbk **£2.25**
Poems for Over-10 Year Olds
[D354] Puffin pbk **£1.95**

The Library Association Kate Greenaway Medal

The Library Association Kate Greenaway Medal is intended to recognise the importance of illustration in children's books. It is awarded to the artist who, in the opinion of The Library Association, has produced the most distinguished work in the illustration of children's books first published in the United Kingdom during the preceding year.

GENERAL FICTION

Books for Pre-School Children

Board Books

It is never too early to begin sharing books with children, and they can play a crucial role right from birth. The board book, whose chief justification is its indestructability, enables books to be handled by children early in their first year. Babies who are busy learning about their world by looking, listening and touching, and by having the objects, people and activities in it named, can discover books as a natural extension of this activity. At first they see clearly-drawn objects; then, at around one, they recognise and name familiar domestic activities and situations - such as getting up and eating - in thematic stories; finally they respond to pictures accompanied by a brief, uncondescending text, which tells a real, sustained story with the simplest of plots, often about characters such as Spot or Mog, whom they will meet later in picture books.

AWDRY, REV. W. & AWDRY, CHRISTOPHER
In these cheerful, simply-drawn, chunky board books, young readers can enjoy the mini-adventures of four of the most famous trains that they will meet later in Awdry's much loved 'Railway Series' (cf. *Picture Books 4 & Up*).
Henry Pulls the Express
[D360] Heinemann board **£1.99**
James and the Rescue Train
[D361] Heinemann board **£1.99**
Percy the Seaside Train
[D362] Heinemann board **£1.99**
Thomas and the Goods Train
[D363] Heinemann board **£1.99**

BOYNTON, SANDRA
The judicious blend of rhythm, rhyme, repetition and nonsense which will later endear **Dr. Seuss** and the *Berenstains* (cf. *Learning to Read*) to children finds an early precursor in Sandra Boynton's work. Well-produced, deftly and clearly drawn, these titles are consistently original and funny. Their humour is just right for the over-ones, who are ready for real stories, and all last beyond the age of 18 months.
A - Z
[D364] Methuen pbk **£1.95**
Blue Hat, Green Hat
A getting dressed story in which the humour derives from a repeated joke: three animals dress correctly in 'blue shirt, red shirt, green shirt' and one mistakenly - 'oops!'.
[D365] Methuen hbk **£1.95**
But Not the Hippopotamus
[D366] Methuen boards **£1.95**
Doggies
A first counting book. Pleasure derives from the built up cacophony of different dog barks and from the anticipation of finding one cat at the end.
[D367] Methuen boards **£1.95**
Horns to Toes
[D368] Methuen boards **£1.95**
Moo Baa La La La
[D369] Methuen boards **£1.95**
Opposites
[D370] Methuen boards **£1.95**

The Going to Bed Book
Animals on an ark engage in familiar bedtime routines.
[D371] Methuen boards **£1.95**

BRUNA, DICK
First wordless thematic board books of the utmost simplicity in which Dutch artist Dick Bruna introduces a new object, painted in bright primary colours and outlined in black on a white background for each page, for baby to identify and talk about.
Families   NEW
[D371A] Methuen boards **£1.99**
Good Morning
[D372] Methuen boards **£1.50**
Good Night
[D373] Methuen boards **£1.50**
In My House
[D374] Methuen boards **£1.95**
In My Toy Cupboard
[D375] Methuen boards **£1.95**
My Farmyard
[D376] Methuen baords **£1.95**
My Toybox
[D377] Methuen boards **£1.95**
Noisy   NEW
[D377A] Methuen boards **£1.99**
On My Walk
[D378] Methuen boards **£1.95**
On the Farm
[D379] Methuen boards **£1.95**

CAMPBELL, ROD
These die-cut, delightfully illustrated board books are shaped so as to allow them to fold out and stand up in front of a baby. The youngest reader is introduced to the animal world.
Baby Animals
[D380] Campbell Bks boards **£1.95**
Countryside Animals
[D381] Campbell Bks boards **£1.95**
Farm Animals
[D382] Campbell Bks boards **£1.95**
Wild Animals
[D383] Campbell Bks boards **£1.95**

CURRY, PETER
Curry, like Dick Bruna, uses flat, brightly-coloured, one-dimensional shapes outlined in black to convey the essence of each object drawn. In these concertina-shaped books - ideal for object identification - the strong visual appeal is heightened by using cut-out pages.
I Like Driving
[D384] Heinemann boards **£1.99**
I Like Eating
[D385] Heinemann boards **£1.99**
I Like Playing
[D386] Heinemann boards **£1.99**
I Like Wearing
[D387] Heinemann boards **£1.99**

HILL, ERIC
First tales in which the irrepressible and universally-loved puppy Spot is incidentally introduced to various concepts. A fuller listing appears in *Pre-School Picture Books*.
Play with Spot
[D388] Heinemann boards **£1.99**
Spot Counts from 1 to 10
[D389] Heinemann boards **£1.99**
Spot Looks at Colours
[D390] Heinemann boards **£1.99**
Spot Looks at Opposites
[D391] Heinemann boards **£1.99**
Spot Looks at Shapes
[D392] Heinemann boards **£1.99**
Spot Looks at the Weather
[D393] Heinemann boards **£1.99**

Spot at the Fair
[D394] Heinemann boards **£1.99**
Spot at the Farm
[D395] Heinemann boards **£1.99**
Spot's First Words
[D396] Heinemann boards **£1.99**

KERR, JUDITH
Board book introductions to Mog, one of the most engaging picture book cats (cf. *Picture Books 4 & Up*).
Mog and Me
A day in the life of 'Mog and Me' as cat and child eat, wash, play and sleep together.
[D397] Collins boards **£1.75**
Mog's Family of Cats
Mog's relations - shop cats, farm cats, cats with kittens - celebrate Mog's birthday.
[D398] Collins boards **£1.75**

MORRIS, ANN & ROFFEY, MAUREEN
These four comfortably square books are ideal for playing the 'naming' game. Each book contains a collection of thematically linked objects, with one brightly-coloured and named article to each page.
Animals
[D399] Methuen boards **£1.99**
Clothes
[D400] Methuen boards **£1.99**
Home
[D401] Methuen boards **£1.99**
Toys
[D402] Methuen boards **£1.99**

OXENBURY, HELEN
Since her first **Baby Board** books were published in 1981, Helen Oxenbury's work has been much imitated but never bettered. She observes the inevitable pains and pleasures of infancy and the snags of early childhood with affection and humour.
All Fall Down
[D403] Walker boards **£2.50**
Animals
[D404] Walker boards **£1.95**
Bedtime
[D405] Walker boards **£1.95**
Clap Hands
[D406] Walker boards **£2.50**
Dressing
[D407] Walker boards **£1.95**
Family
[D408] Walker boards **£1.95**
Friends
[D409] Walker boards **£1.95**
Helping
[D410] Walker boards **£1.95**
Holidays
[D411] Walker boards **£1.95**
Playing
[D412] Walker boards **£1.95**
Say Goodnight
[D413] Walker boards **£2.50**
Shopping
[D414] Walker boards **£1.95**
Tickle Tickle
[D415] Walker boards **£2.50**
Working
[D416] Walker boards **£1.95**

ZEFF, CLAUDIA & CARTWRIGHT, STEPHEN
In each of these wordless board books small children are invited to play one of their favourite games. While hunting for clues, some easily apparent, some harder to spot, the child is introduced to various new environments; the lively illustrations combine the fun of playing the looking game with discoveries which stimulate the child to discussion.
Find the Bird
[D417] Usborne boards **£1.75**

Find the Duck
[D418] Usborne boards **£1.75**
Find the Kitten
[D419] Usborne boards **£1.75**
Find the Piglet
[D420] Usborne boards **£1.75**
Find the Puppy
[D421] Usborne boards **£1.75**
Find the Teddy
[D422] Usborne boards **£1.75**

Early Learning

Alphabet and counting books are often shared with the smallest readers as 'naming' books, but their greatest use comes during the early school years, when children are learning to count and recognise letters. Because ABCs, counting and first concept or information books have the circumscribed purpose of providing pleasurable learning, they need to be chosen with care. Clarity without condescension is essential, as is effectiveness, accessibility, aesthetic quality and originality. The best often provide children with their first experience of art appreciation and of the art of looking. Some are like beautifully executed (sometimes humorous) catalogues of objects, both animate and inanimate, and of letter and number identification (*Burningham*, *Oxenbury* or *Wildsmith*); others incorporate the alphabet or numerals into a narrative, either as an ingenious story (*Gretz*, *Hutchins* and *Kerr*), or as a provocative one for older readers which seeks to extend their ideas about letters and numbers, along with their use and value (*Anno* and *Kitamura*).

ANNO, MITSUMASA
A Japanese artist whose work is unique in its evocation of spatial and temporal relationships. His mathematical books, such as *Anno's Hat Tricks*, challenge and extend our understanding of numbers and of concepts such as logic.
Anno's Counting Book
Anno takes an empty winter landscape (Zero) through different seasons and periods of time, into a village teaming with people, homes and animals, where the presence of 12 reindeer announce Christmas. A distinguished counting book that is also an introduction to the passing of time and the cycle of the seasons.
[D423] Macmillan pbk **£2.50**
Anno's Counting House
[D424] Bodley hbk **£4.95**
Anno's Hat Tricks
[D425] Bodley hbk **£6.95**

BANG, MOLLY
Ten, Nine, Eight
Count down to bedtime as a black father helps his daughter in a nightime ritual: from '10 small toes all washed and warm' to '1 big girl all ready for bed'.
[D426] Puffin pbk **£1.50**

BARTON, BYRON
A splendid introduction to the world of moving vehicles for pre-school readers. Barton's texts are minimal but his illustrations, while Bruna-esque in colour, clarity and design, are full of absorbing, extending detail.
Aeroplanes
[D427] Walker pbk **£1.99**
Boats
[D428] Walker pbk **£1.99**
Trains
[D429] Walker pbk **£1.99**
Trucks
[D430] Walker pbk **£1.99**

BLAKE, QUENTIN
Quentin Blake's ABC **NEW**
Like Lear and Cruickshank, Blake is an inspired master of the cartoon technique. His leaping 'freeze-frame' animation, robust comedy and warmth inspire this ABC, in which young and old together engage in a variety of activities - some familiar, some outlandish - as suggested by the rhyming, deadpan text.
[D431] Cape hbk **£6.95**

BOON, EMILIE
Dutch artist Emilie Boon invests these delectable counting books, illustrated in blurred line and soft flat paint with a warmth and gentle humour just right for the very young.
123 How Many Animals Can You See?
Count the animals 1 to 10 as they make their way to school through a varied landscape.
[D432] Corgi pbk **£2.25**
A Bun for Barnie
Text by Joyce Dunbar. A diminishing tale with a rhyming alliterative text about a bear who sets off home to eat an iced bun, but is accosted by a host of greedy animals on his way.
[D433] Corgi pbk **£2.50**

BRUNA, DICK
Brilliant blocks of primary colour focus attention on the object and the letter or number depicted: these arresting books are suitable for use with the very youngest.
B Is for Bear
[D434] Methuen hbk **£4.95**
I Can Count
[D435] Methuen hbk **£1.95**
I Can Count More
[D436] Methuen hbk **£1.95**
I Know about Numbers
[D437] Methuen hbk **£1.95**
I Know More about Numbers
[D438] Methuen hbk **£1.95**
Miffy's Book of Colours
[D439] Methuen board **£2.95**

BURNINGHAM, JOHN
Absurd comedy, implausible situation and a delight in unusual words characterize Burningham's diverting concept books, illustrated in delicate wash and crayon.
ABC
[D440] Cape hbk **£6.50**
Alphabet Book
[D441] Walker pbk **£1.99**

Illustration from *Quentin Blake's ABC*
(Cape hbk £6.95)

Colours Book
[D442] Walker pbk **£1.99**
Numbers Book
[D443] Walker pbk **£1.99**
Opposites
[D444] Walker pbk **£1.99**
Seasons
[D445] Cape hbk **£6.95**
The Shopping Basket
A simple shopping trip becomes a battle of wits as small, bespectacled Stephen is accosted by a bear, a monkey and other greedy animals as he tries to return home with 'six eggs, five bananas...'. A funny story that is also a visible lesson in subtraction.
[D446] Collins pbk **£2.25**

CARLE, ERIC
The possibilities of paper, collage and colour are an integral part of Carle's narrative sequences, as well as providing strong visual patterns for his work. His inventive use of these materials gives fresh life and originality to stories of common natural phenomena.
123 to the Zoo
[D447] H Hamilton hbk **£6.95**
A House for Hermit Crab
A cumulative story about a year in the life of a hermit crab who moves into a new shell in January. As the months pass, he decorates it with the flora and fauna he discovers on the sea bed, only to find that he must move into a bigger shell again...
[D448] Hodder hbk **£6.95**
Brown Bear, Brown Bear What do You See?
Text by Bill Martin. A book about colour in which Brown Bear is the first in a succession of animals to answer the repeated title question.
[D449] Collins pbk **£1.95**
Rooster's Off to see the World
Early one morning Rooster sets off to see the world. He is soon joined by two cats, three frogs, and so on. When evening comes he realizes he has made no plans for food and shelter...
[D449A] Hodder pbk **£2.50**
The Bad-Tempered Ladybird
The bad-tempered ladybird picks fights with bigger and better insects and animals until a whale's tail provides her come-uppance. Clever page-cutting and enlarging type-faces emphasize the central joke about size, as well as the underlying sequence of the sun's rising and gradual setting.
[D450] Puffin pbk **£1.75**
The Mixed-Up Chameleon
A chameleon visits a zoo and, discovering that it can change not only colour but also shape and size, takes on the characteristics of all the zoo animals at once.
[D451] Puffin pbk **£1.95**
The Tiny Seed
[D452] Hodder pbk **£2.50**
The Very Hungry Caterpillar
Already a modern classic, this book is simultaneously a counting and colour book, a lesson in metamorphosis and in the days of the week. A superb story in which a caterpillar gnaws his way (literally, as the holes in the page demonstrate) through one apple on Monday, two pears on Tuesday, and so on until he finally spins a cocoon and emerges as a beautiful butterfly.
[D453] H Hamilton hbk **£6.95**
[D454] Puffin pbk **£1.95**

CARTER, DAVID A.
How Many Bugs in a Box (Pop-Up)
Lift the flaps in this witty counting book and up jump a 1 to 10 sequence of comical bugs.
[D455] Orchard hbk **£6.95**

CROWTHER, ROBERT

The pop-up applied with wit and ingenuity to simple and sturdy ABC and counting books. Pull up a tab, open a flap, and from behind each of the huge letters and numbers leaps an ape, bear, and crocodile...

The Most Amazing Hide-and-Seek Alphabet Book
[D456] Viking hbk £8.95

The Most Amazing Hide-and-Seek Counting Book
[D457] Viking hbk £8.95

DUPASQUIER, PHILIPPE

The detailed cartoon-like illustrations of this French artist invite readers to scrutinize and speculate on the workers, users and activities of each site.

The Airport
[D458] Walker pbk £1.99

The Building Site
[D459] Walker pbk £1.99

The Factory
[D460] Walker pbk £1.99

The Garage
[D461] Walker pbk £1.99

The Harbour
[D462] Walker pbk £1.99

The Railway Station
[D463] Walker pbk £1.99

GRETZ, SUSANNA

Gretz's perennially popular teddy bears engage in innovative numerical and alliterative alphabetical adventures.

Teddybear's 1 to 10
[D464] Collins pbk £1.95

Teddybear's ABC
[D465] Collins pbk £1.95

HAWKINS, COLIN & JACQUI

When I Was One

A delectable introduction to counting in which two young children make their plans for what they'll do when they're four, five, six and seven... and discover numbers in the process.
[D466] Viking hbk £6.95

This Old Car: A Counting Book
[D466A] Orchard Books hbk £5.95

HOWELL, LYNN & RICHARD

Winifred's New Bed

When Winifred moves from her cot into a new bed, it feels huge until all her toy animals move in. The simple joke - from too big to too small - develops with a clever use of the split page device. An incidental introduction to time and to the days of the week, as well as size.
[D467] Macmillan pbk £2.99

HUGHES, SHIRLEY

One of Britain's best-loved illustrators and an artist who consistently confounds expectations. Children first encounter her work in the alphabetical and numerical *Lucy & Tom* narratives, and in her seven wonderfully undidactic concept books. She has found new and imaginative ways of approaching traditional material, taking and expanding the circumscribed worlds of childhood and the daily routine.

All Shapes & Sizes
[D468] Walker pbk £1.50

Bathwater's Hot
[D469] Walker pbk £1.50

Colours
[D470] Walker pbk £1.50

Lucy & Tom's 123
[D471] Gollancz hbk £4.95
[D472] Penguin pbk £2.50

Lucy & Tom's ABC
[D473] Gollancz hbk £4.95
[D474] Penguin pbk £1.95

Illustration from *This Old Car: A Counting Book* by Colin & Jacqui Hawkins
(Orchard Books hbk £5.95)

Noisy
[D475] Walker pbk £1.50

Out & About

A little girl and her baby brother romp through mud, water, sand and snow as they go 'out and about' in the changing seasons.
[D476] Walker hbk £7.95

Two Shoes, New Shoes
[D477] Walker pbk £1.50

When We Went to the Park
[D478] Walker pbk £1.50

HUTCHINS, PAT

Clocks and More Clocks

Mr Higgins wants to know if his clock is telling the right time. He fills his house with more clocks but whenever he checks them, each one gives a different hour. A typical Hutchins joke about the passage of time.
[D479] Penguin pbk £1.50

One Hunter

More than a counting book, this is also an adventure spoof: the hunter stalks his prey, but the reader notices that the prey is in fact stalking *him*.
[D480] Penguin pbk £1.75

KERR, JUDITH

Mog's Amazing Birthday Caper

An ingenious and rousing alphabetical adventure story that begins when Mog bursts an alligator-shaped balloon at a birthday party. Disgraced, she falls asleep and enjoys a dream, filled with 'Mad Mouse Monsters' and 'Nightmare Nibblers', that is funny, scary, poetic and surreal.
[D481] Collins pbk £2.75

KITAMURA, SATOSHI

A Japanese artist much influenced by Surrealism, who provides older children with a provocative and original alphabet book and a wonderful joke of a counting book.

What's Inside? The Alphabet Book

An extraordinary trip in free association through the alphabet as the reader guesses the contents of the alphabetical container on each page.
[D482] Beaver pbk £2.95

When Sheep Cannot Sleep

Woozy, an insomniac sheep, takes a night time walk searching for objects to count until finally, worn out, he starts to count the members of his own family and starts to fall asleep.
[D483] Beaver pbk £2.50

LINDBERG, REEVE

The Midnight Farm (Illus. Susan Jeffers)

A tender, reassuring book in verse that is at once an exploration of darkness and a mother's dissolving of her child's fear of it, *and* a counting book. Jeffers' delicately cross-hatched drawings of dusky interiors and a silvered farm world outside capture beautifully the unfamiliarity of the familar at night.
[D483A] Puffin pbk £2.50

MACDONALD, SUSE

Alphabatics

A novel alphabet book in which the letters are transformed (from, for example, A to an ark and B to a balloon) by performing a series of visual acrobatics.
[D484] Macmillan pbk £3.99

MARIS, RON

In My Garden

Ron Maris uses the split page device to explore a garden and discover there are 'two birds in my birdbath', 'three blackbirds and a thrush', and so on.
[D485] Walker pbk £1.99

MCGOUGH, ROGER

Counting Book　　　　**NEW**

(6 +, illus. Markéta Prachatická)

An offbeat variant on the traditional counting book by poet McGough.
[D486] Viking hbk £3.95

MCNAUGHTON, COLIN

A welcome re-issue of two early, original McNaughton picture books. The *ABC* is an alphabet of colloquialisms, illustrated literally: a burglar surfs on a 'crime wave', children swim 'in the soup'. The rhyming *123* is equally unexpected, from the dream sequence of 'One on the run from a vast cream bun' to the soccer extravaganza of '50,084 could not believe just what they saw'.

123 (6 +)
[D487] Macmillan hbk £3.95

ABC (6 +)
[D488] Macmillan hbk £3.95

MILLER, JANE

Beautifully designed photographic essays on farm life.

Farm Alphabet Book
[D489] Dent hbk £4.50

Farm Counting Book
[D490] Dent hbk £5.50

Seasons on the Farm
[D491] Dent hbk £4.50

ORMEROD, JAN

Joe Can Count

Joe, a small black boy, is looking for a pet. He counts from one fish up to ten puppies and then, to his delight, 'one puppy chooses Joe for its very own'.
[D492] Walker pbk £1.99

OXENBURY, HELEN

The ingenious grouping of a number of unlikely 'things' for each letter of the alphabet - the wedding of a weasel and a wolf, attended by a wasp - gives Oxenbury's *ABC* a sharp, original comedy that is echoed in her more conventional but equally entertaining *Numbers of Things*.

ABC of Things
[D493] Collins pbk £2.75

Numbers of Things
[D494] Collins pbk £2.25

PIENKOWSKI, JAN
Like Dick Bruna, Pienkowski uses flat, brightly coloured shapes to great effect. The books make complex concepts clear and immediately accessible to the very young, and are now available in board as well as in picturebook form.
123
[D495] Heinemann boards £1.50
[D496] Puffin pbk £1.50
ABC
[D497] Heinemann boards £1.50
[D498] Puffin pbk £1.99
Colours
[D499] Heinemann boards £1.50
[D500] Puffin pbk £1.50
Faces
[D501] Puffin pbk £1.75
Farm
[D502] Heinemann boards £1.50
[D503] Puffin pbk £1.50
Food
[D504] Puffin pbk £1.75
Homes
[D505] Heinemann boards £1.50
[D506] Puffin pbk £1.50
Shapes
[D507] Heinemann boards £1.50
[D508] Puffin pbk £1.25
Sizes
[D509] Puffin pbk £1.50
Time
[D510] Puffin pbk £1.50
Weather
[D511] Heinemann boards £1.50
[D512] Puffin pbk £1.25
Zoo
[D513] Heinemann boards £1.50
[D514] Puffin pbk £1.50
LITTLE MONSTERS PLUS
Pienkowski's absurd *Little Monsters* reappear in these enchanting rhyming stories which introduce the fundamental mathematical concepts of number, grouping, shape and spatial relationship with clarity, imagination and wit.
Eggs for Tea NEW
[D515] Orchard hbk £2.95
Home Sweet Home NEW
[D516] Orchard hbk £2.95
Pet Food NEW
[D517] Orchard hbk £2.95
Race You! NEW
[D518] Orchard hbk £2.95

RODGERS, PAUL
Rhyming introductions to the range of weather experienced at the same time in different parts of the world, and to geometric shape, for the pre-school child. Stunningly captured in Kazuko's bright collage folk artwork, and in the design and patterns of Tucker's paintings.
The Shapes Game NEW
(Illus. Sian Tucker)
[D519] Orchard hbk £5.95
What Will the Weather Be Like Today? (Illus. Kazuko) NEW
[D520] Orchard hbk £6.95

SALT, JANE
Two large format naming and talkabout books in which words and numbers are presented in scenes of everyday life - arranged thematically (at school, at the shops etc) and filled with Pooley's characteristic absorbing and amusing detail.
The Kingfisher Number Book NEW
(Illus. Sarah Pooley)
[D521] Kingfisher £5.95

The Kingfisher Picture Word Book NEW
(Illus. Sarah Pooley)
[D522] Kingfisher hbk £5.95

SENDAK, MAURICE
The Nutshell Library
Four cased, minute books: an alphabet book, a counting book, a book of months and a cautionary tale. Vintage Sendak, witty and original.
[D523] Collins hbk £5.95

SNOW, ALAN
Alan Snow may be a Richard Scarry for the 1990s. Concise, simple texts and bright comic illustrations, complete with diagrams, offer intelligent explorations of the worlds of nature, social studies and geography, concepts and transport.
Animals, Birds, Bees and Flowers NEW
[D524] Collins Carnival hbk £3.95
Colours, Words, Shapes and Numbers NEW
[D525] Collins Carnival hbk £3.95
Holidays, Parties, Peoples and Places NEW
[D526] Collins Carnival hbk £3.95
Machines, Cars, Trucks and Tractors NEW
[D527] Collins Carnival hbk £3.95

WILD, JOCELYN
Childhood play is the underlying subject of these delectable stories in which three bears experiment with objects found in a rubbish dump - an axe (too dangerous), a bike, a broken car; take on Goldilock's role and enter *1* empty house, and investigate its contents (*2* chairs, *3* beds and so on); and play 'I Spy' in a storm-swept meadow.
The Bear's ABC Book
[D528] Methuen pbk £2.50
The Bear's Counting Book
[D529] Methuen pbk £2.50
The Bears' Book of Colours NEW
[D530] Heinemann £5.95

WILDSMITH, BRIAN
Brian Wildsmith's *ABC*, *123*, his books of collective nouns and names of wildlife and his book of opposites framed in a discussion between Sun and Moon are as much picture books about the act of painting as they are mind-stretching concept books. All Wildsmith's work celebrates the possibilities of paint in creating richly textured and contrasting surfaces of colour, and affirms his belief *"that beautiful picture books are vitally important in forming a child's visual appreciation"*.
123
[D531] Oxford hbk £4.95
ABC
Published in 1962, this landmark book was the first children's picture book in which the artist used the full range of his palette, without having to make arduous colour separations by hand.
[D532] Oxford pbk £4.95
Birds
[D533] Oxford pbk £2.50
Fishes
[D534] Oxford pbk £2.50
The Circus
[D535] Oxford pbk £2.50
What the Moon Saw
[D536] Oxford pbk £2.50
Wild Animals
[D537] Oxford pbk £2.50

YEOMAN, JOHN & BLAKE, QUENTIN
Sixes and Sevens
Yeoman's deadpan text tells a cumulative counting story of Barnaby who poles his raft up the river to

Limber Lee, collecting passengers as he goes: one kitten, two mice and so on... The resulting mayhem is depicted in Blake's increasingly farcical pictures.
[D538] Macmillan pbk £2.50

Picture Books

From 18 months, children are ready for their first real books. For this early age range, publishers provide mainly 'series' - often built around situations occurring in the everyday lives of toddlers (who are sometimes lightly disguised as toys or animals). These thematic books are essentially descriptive, presented in texts and images in accordance with the limited understanding and imaginative grasp of the toddler. Between the ages of two and four children move on to explore with intense curiosity the world outside the home, at least partly through stories. These first picture books are experienced primarily through visual images; until recently their illustrations were largely descriptive, illuminating and expanding the all-important text. In 1968, however, Pat Hutchins introduced a new story-telling technique in *Rosie's Walk*, a modern classic of just 32 words. The text is simple, describing a quiet, uneventful walk, but the combined story of words and pictures (in which a fox, never once mentioned in the text, appears) is quite different, subtler, more complex and, above all, more fun. In contemporary picture books, children read both words *and* pictures, which are incomplete when separate, but together tell a whole tale.

AHLBERG, JANET & ALLAN
The Ahlbergs are dedicated and brilliant artists whose work has continually extended the possibilities of the picture book form, their stories offering reading experiences drawn from their insight into the role of traditional lore and games in children's lives. Each book uses a game of early childhood to engage the imagination as well as to initiate children into the rules of the reading game.
Bye Bye Baby NEW
'A sad story with a happy ending' about a baby who has no mummy and lives by himself, until one day he sets off down the road - 'Bye Bye Baby' - to find one. Classic Ahlberg.
[D539] Heinemann hbk £5.95
Each Peach Pear Plum
An 'I Spy' book in which characters from well-known nursery rhymes and tales get into each other's stories and lie hidden in the pictures waiting to be 'spied' by the reader.
[D540] Viking hbk £5.95
[D541] Puffin pbk £2.50
Peepo!
"Here's a little baby/One, two, three/Stands in his cot/What does he see? Peepo!" Through the cut-out holes, baby in the book and baby reader see mother, father, and events in the life of a 1940s family.
[D542] Viking hbk £5.95
[D543] Puffin pbk £2.50
Starting School
From playhouse to playground, from stories to school dinners, readers can follow the fortunes of eight newcomers as they learn school routines, are introduced to the three Rs, and act in a nativity play.
[D544] Viking hbk £6.95
The Baby's Catalogue
The youngest can play the 'naming' game in this pictorial compendium of everyday objects and people which babies learn to love and identify. Older readers can play 'Spot the Family' as they trace five separate families through the book (a device also used in *Starting School*).
[D545] Viking hbk £6.50
[D546] Puffin pbk £2.25

ALIKI

Cock-a-Doodle-Do
Written with Fritz Brandenberg. An ideal picture book for the very young. The text consists of animal noises. Aliki's warm, expansive pictures reveal the early morning life of a waking farm - from milking and feeding the animals to breakfast preparations for the family
[D547] Piper pbk **£2.50**

Welcome, Little Baby
Perfect for new parents or a 'big' new brother or sister, an enchantingly realistic book in which a mother introduces her new baby to the world into which it has been born.
[D548] Piper pbk **£2.99**

ALLEN, PAMELA

Who Sank the Boat?
Echoes of John Burningham's *Mr Grumpy's Outing* underpin this cumulative tale about a disastrous boat ride. The absurdity of Allen's anthropomorphised animals, however, gives it a flavour all its own.
[D549] H Hamilton pbk **£2.95**

ASCH, FRANK

Th delight of small children in the adventures of Bear and Little Bird lies in the fact that they do not share Bear's misunderstandings about shadows, echoes, the moon, or rainbows.

Bear Shadow
[D550] Corgi pbk **£2.50**

Goodbye House
The Bears are moving. Little Bear has forgotten something. As he searches the strange, empty rooms, he remembers: he wanted to say 'Good-bye'! A simple, satisfying exploration of a common childhood experience.
[D551] Corgi pbk **£2.50**

Happy Birthday, Moon
[D552] Corgi pbk **£2.25**

Mooncake
[D553] Corgi pbk **£1.75**

Moongame
[D554] Corgi pbk **£2.25**

Skyfire
Bear, seeing a rainbow for the first time, thinks the sky is on fire and rushes to the emergency with a honey pot filled with water.
[D555] Corgi pbk **£2.25**

The cushion is soft.

Illustration from *The Baby's Catalogue* by Janet & Allan Ahlberg (Puffin pbk **£2.25**)

BARTON, BYRON

I Want to be an Astronaut **NEW**
An imaginary journey into space by a small girl who wants 'to be an astronaut'.
[D555A] Simon & Sch hbk **£5.95**

BAUM, LOUIS

Are We Nearly There? (Illus. Paddy Bauma)
Children from divided homes will find this story about Simon's train trip to Mum after a day out with Dad particularly reassuring.
[D556] Methuen pbk **£1.95**

I Want to See the Moon (Illus. Niki Daly)
[D557] Methuen pbk **£1.75**

BRIGGS, RAYMOND & VIPONT, ELFRIDA

The Elephant and the Bad Baby
A bad baby who never once says 'Please' is taken for a ride through town by an elephant. Along the way they steal ice-cream, buns and apples and are hotly pursued by an ever-increasing cast of irate shopkeepers. The racy text, the neat and unexpected moral, and the spirited early Briggs illustrations have firmly established the book as a favourite with children.
[D558] H Hamilton hbk **£6.95**
[D559] Puffin pbk **£1.75**

BROWNE, ANTHONY

The pictorial joke is central to Browne's work. It provides these simplest of picture books with a sense of visual fun, and points up the underlying message about the positive power of the imagination.

Bear Hunt
The first of three stories about Little Bear who uses his magic pencil to draw himself out of trouble when pursued by hunters or confronted with dangerous jungle beasts and fairytale witches, goblins, dragons and giants.
[D560] Hippo pbk **£1.95**

I Like Books **NEW**
An irresistible chimp celebrates his love of books and invites readers to share with him funny books, scary books, comic books, colouring books and strange books. A gem.
[D561] Julia MacRae hbk **£3.95**

The Bear-y Tale Book **NEW**
[D562] H Hamilton hbk **£2.99**

The Little Bear Book
[D563] H Hamilton hbk **£2.99**

BRUNA, DICK

Simple thematic stories illustrated in characteristic Bruna style in which Miffy - a small rabbit - engages in both familiar and unusual childhood activities.

Miffy
[D564] Methuen hbk **£1.95**

Miffy at School
[D565] Methuen hbk **£1.95**

Miffy at the Playground
[D566] Methuen hbk **£1.95**

Miffy at the Seaside
[D567] Methuen hbk **£1.95**

Miffy at the Zoo
[D568] Methuen hbk **£1.95**

Miffy goes Flying
[D569] Methuen hbk **£1.95**

Miffy in Hospital
[D570] Methuen hbk **£1.95**

Miffy in the Snow
[D571] Methuen hbk **£1.95**

Miffy's Bicycle
[D572] Methuen hbk **£1.95**

Miffy's Birthday
[D573] Methuen hbk **£1.95**

Miffy's Dream
[D574] Methuen hbk **£1.95**

The Little Bird
[D575] Methuen hbk **£1.95**

Miffy, one of Dick Bruna's most loved creations. Bruna's books are published by Methuen Children's Books

BURNINGHAM, JOHN

Two comic tales about Mr. Grumpy and his outings in an ancient boat and motor car with an irresponsible group of child and animal friends. Told in a folk-tale style that cumulatively builds up to an inevitable catastrophe, each of these apparently simple stories is full of subtle word-play.

Mr Grumpy's Motor-Car
[D576] Penguin pbk **£1.50**

Mr Grumpy's Outing
[D577] Penguin pbk **£1.50**

LITTLE BOOKS
Burningham's eight 'Little Books' humorously depict simple domestic happenings from a toddler's viewpoint.

The Baby
[D578] Cape hbk **£1.95**

The Blanket
[D579] Cape hbk **£1.95**

The Cupboard
[D580] Cape hbk **£1.95**

The Dog
[D581] Cape hbk **£1.95**

The Friend
[D582] Cape hbk **£1.95**

The Rabbit
[D583] Cape hbk **£1.95**

The School
[D584] Cape hbk **£1.95**

The Snow
[D585] Cape hbk **£1.95**

BUTLER, DOROTHY

A reviewer, children's bookseller, and author of the indispensable *Babies Need Books*, Butler has a deep understanding of children and the crucial role that books can play in their lives.

My Brown Bear Barney **NEW**
(Illus. Elizabeth Fuller)
Wherever she goes - to the shops, the beach, to her friends - the narrator takes a number of people and things *and* her 'brown bear Barney' - but not to school: 'We'll see about that'. Fuller's warm, carefully built-up pictures reveal the security provided by a beloved toy as a child goes out into the world - a security implied in the simple, patterned text.
[D586] Hodder hbk **£5.95**

BUTTERWORTH, NICK & INGPEN, MIKE

Just Like Jasper **NEW**
"Jasper (the cat) is going to the toyshop with his

birthday money. What will he buy?" The smallest reader will enjoy helping Jasper make his choice as he tries out the different toys in the shop. This is a delightful 'naming', 'I Spy' book; by placing its minimal text and brilliant colour against a white background, it achieves a remarkable clarity.
[D587] Hodder hbk **£5.95**

CAMPBELL, ROD
Like Eric Hill, Campbell is an artist who invites readers to participate in the telling of his stories by lifting flaps and opening doors. The repetition and cumulative nature of each story enables children to discover patterns in their telling and to anticipate what will happen next - two essential reading skills.
Buster Gets Dressed
[D588] Campbell Bks hbk **£2.95**
Buster Keeps Warm
[D589] Campbell Bks hbk **£2.95**
Buster's Day
A 'touch' book in which the reader, like toddler Buster, can actually feel the objects encountered in a day's play, such as a furry toy, a mirror, a towel.
[D590] Campbell Bks hbk **£5.50**
Dear Zoo
A series of unsuitable pets are sent from the zoo but returned, until finally the perfect pet arrives.
[D591] Campbell Bks hbk **£5.50**
[D592] Penguin pbk **£3.50**
My Day
A simple 'naming' book of objects painted in bright colour and clear line that thematically takes a reader through a typical toddler day.
[D593] Collins pbk **£2.25**
Oh Dear!
Buster, sent to find an egg on his grandmother's farm, looks in the homes of a host of barnyard animals before he finally lifts the flap of the henhouse and finds his breakfast.
[D594] Pan pbk **£2.50**

CARLE, ERIC
See *Early Learning*.
Have You Seen My Cat?
An introduction to the world of cats in which a small boy circles the globe in search of his lost pet, only to find her waiting at home with an unexpected surprise.
[D595] Hodder pbk **£2.50**
The Very Busy Spider
A determined spider spins a web on a fence and, despite the effort of the farmyard animals to distract her, catches a fly. Spider, web and fly are embossed so that the reader not only sees but also *feels* the story developing.
[D596] H Hamilton hbk **£10.95**

DODD, LYNLEY
Pleasure in the sounds and rhythms of language is infectiously communicated to readers in these comic tales about Hairy Maclary - a loveable mongrel - and a bear who, despite the animals' attempts to rouse him from his winter's sleep, carries on snoring until a bee buzzes by.
Hairy Maclary from Donaldson's Dairy
[D597] Puffin pbk **£1.75**
Hairy Maclary's Bone
[D598] Puffin pbk **£1.75**
Hairy Maclary's Caterwaul Caper
[D599] Puffin pbk **£2.50**
Hairy Maclary's Scattercat
[D600] Puffin pbk **£1.75**
Wake Up Bear
[D601] Puffin pbk **£1.95**

DUNBAR, JOYCE
I Wish I Liked Rice Pudding **NEW**
(Illus. Carol Thompson)
A catalogue of one small girl's spirited objection to the things she doesn't like, and her relish for the

things she does. Thompson's pen and wash illustrations, which have Charlotte Voake's energy and Sarah Garland's perceptiveness, capture quirky individuality and everyday experience alike.
[D601A] Simon & Sch hbk **£5.50**

FOREMAN, MICHAEL
Ben's Baby
A semi-autobiographical story in which Foreman's son Ben, who wants a baby for his birthday, gets his wish.
[D602] Beaver pbk **£2.50**

GARLAND, SARAH
Four appparently simple but intriguing and humorous books about an endearingly fraught Mum, her energetic toddler and their mongrel, as they do the washing, go shopping, have a picnic in the park, and entertain unexpected visitors for tea.
Coming to Tea
[D603] Puffin pbk **£1.95**
Doing the Washing
[D604] Puffin pbk **£1.75**
Going Shopping
[D605] Puffin pbk **£1.75**
Having a Picnic
[D606] Puffin pbk **£1.75**
Polly's Puffin
A chase through town by Mum and children begins when baby Jim throws Polly's Puffin into the hood of a duffle-coated gentleman... An innovative treatment of the 'lost and found' theme in which author and reader share a joke.
[D607] Bodley hbk **£5.95**
All Gone! **NEW**
For the youngest, two characteristic picture books built with humour and perception around expressions that punctuate a baby's day: 'All Gone' and 'Oh, No'.
[D607A] Reinhardt hbk **£5.99**
Oh, No! **NEW**
[D607B] Reinhardt hbk **£5.99**

GORDON, MARGARET
Deadpan prose counterpoints crazy pictures in these delectable tales of a small bear's outings.
Wilberforce Goes Shopping
[D608] Puffin pbk **£1.75**
Wilberforce Goes on a Picnic
[D609] Puffin pbk **£1.75**
Wilberforce Goes to Playgroup
[D610] Puffin pbk **£2.25**
Wilberforce Goes to a Party
[D611] Puffin pbk **£1.75**

GRAHAM, BOB
Working in the line of Quentin Blake, Australian Bob Graham affectionately chronicles the highlights and hazards of pre-school life for two-year old William, an incorrigible wanderer, and Julia, whose most treasured possession - a red woolen blanket - grows smaller as she gets bigger.
Has Anyone Here Seen William?
[D612] Walker pbk **£1.99**
The Red Woolen Blanket
[D613] Walker pbk **£1.99**

GRETZ, SUSANNA
Mischievous multi-coloured teddybears move house, go to the seaside, or spend a rainy day inside flying to the moon in these arresting and enduringly popular picture books.
Teddybears & the Cold Cure
[D614] Hippo pbk **£1.75**
Teddybears Moving Day
[D615] Hippo pbk **£1.75**
Teddybears go Shopping
[D616] Hippo pbk **£1.50**
The Bears who Stayed Indoors
[D617] Hippo pbk **£1.75**

The Bears who Went to the Seaside
[D618] Puffin pbk **£1.50**

GRETZ, SUSANNA & SAGE, ALISON
Teddybears Take the Train
[D619] Hippo pbk **£1.95**

GRINDLEY, SALLY
Stories for the Very Young **NEW**
A read-aloud collection of classic, fairy and modern stories.
[D620] Kingfisher **£7.95**

HAYES, SARAH
A black English family copes with Baby Gemma's eating problems and celebrates Christmas in these warm, amusing stories. Sensitively illustrated by Jan Ormerod in rich colour, reminiscent of the work of Ezra Jack Keats.
Eat Up, Gemma (Illus. Jan Ormerod)
[D621] Walker pbk **£1.99**
Happy Christmas Gemma
[D622] Walker pbk **£1.99**

HEDDERWICK, MAIRI
Peedie Peeble's Summer or
Winter Book **NEW**
A Scottish artist working in pen and wash, Hedderwick uses the flap device to great effect in this absorbing story of a mischievous toddler and his activities, summer and winter. Her cluttered, alternately chaotic and peaceful, scenes reflect traditional family life.
[D623] Bodley hbk **£4.95**

HEWITT, ANITA & BROOMFIELD, ROBERT
Mrs Mopple's Washing Line
An old favourite built around a repeated joke: a boisterous wind whips Mrs Mopple's washing off the line and entertainingly re-arranges it on farmyard animals and objects.
[D624] Puffin pbk **£2.25**

HILL, ERIC
Tales about the irrepressible, universally loved puppy Spot, which use the flap both to involve the reader and to move the story on. The texts are primarily dialogue, with narratives often built around a simple search: 'Where's Spot?' asks Mum in the first book. As the reader lifts lids, opens doors, looks under bedspreads, a host of other animals are discovered, until finally the puppy is discovered where he should be - in his basket. Essential pre-school and beginning-to-read stories.
Where's Spot?
[D640] Heinemann hbk **£5.95**
[D641] Puffin pbk **£3.95**
(In Sign Language)
[D642] Nat Deaf Inst hbk **£5.95**
Spot Goes on Holiday
[D625] Puffin pbk **£3.95**
Spot Goes to School
[D626] Heinemann hbk **£5.95**
[D627] Puffin pbk **£3.95**
Spot Goes to the Circus
[D628] Heinemann hbk **£5.95**
[D629] Puffin pbk **£3.99**
Spot Goes to the Farm
[D630] Heinemann hbk **£5.95**
Spot's Baby Sister **NEW**
[D631] Heinemann hbk **£5.95**
Spot's Big Book of Words
[D632] Heinemann boards **£5.95**
Spot's Birthday Party
[D633] Heinemann hbk **£5.95**
[D634] Puffin pbk **£3.95**
Spot's First Christmas
[D635] Heinemann hbk **£5.95**
[D636] Puffin pbk **£3.95**

Spot's First Easter
[D637] Heinemann hbk **£5.95**
Spot's First Walk
[D638] Heinemann hbk **£5.95**
[D639] Puffin pbk **£3.95**
Spot Looks at Opposites
[D639A] Heinemann hbk **£1.99**

HUGHES, SHIRLEY
Shirley Hughes has a rare ability to see the extraordinary in the ordinary and to translate everyday family life into fresh picture book life. She is an acute observer of modern childhood: her pen and tempera illustrations depict, according to Dorothy Butler in *Babies Need Books*, 'children's outsides in a way which leaves no doubt about her knowledge of their insides.'
ALFIE
In her stories about the energetic Alfie and his little sister Annie Rose, Hughes provides small children with a real flesh and blood hero and an early experience of fictional drama.
Alfie Gets In First
[D643] Bodley hbk **£5.25**
[D644] Collins pbk **£2.25**
Alfie Gives a Hand
[D645] Bodley hbk **£5.25**
[D646] Collins pbk **£1.95**
Alfie's Feet
[D647] Collins pbk **£2.25**
An Evening at Alfie's
[D648] Bodley hbk **£5.25**
[D649] Collins pbk **£1.95**
The Big Alfie and Annie Rose Storybook
[D650] Bodley hbk **£7.95**
LUCY & TOM
Hughes takes the circumscribed world of childhood and recreates it in simple thematic narrative sequences about Lucy and her little brother Tom.
Lucy & Tom Go to School
[D651] Corgi pbk **£2.25**
Lucy & Tom at the Seaside
[D652] Corgi pbk **£2.25**
Lucy & Tom's Christmas
[D653] Puffin pbk **£1.95**
Lucy & Tom's Day
[D654] Puffin pbk **£1.95**

Illustration from *Spot Looks at Opposites* by Eric Hill (Heinemann hbk **£1.99**)

HUTCHINS, PAT
Since the publication of her now classic **Rosie's Walk** in 1968, Pat Hutchins' inventiveness as a picture-bookmaker has continued unabated. Although her pared down, stylized illustrations are immediately recognizable, each of her books has a different feel to it. In many she invites the reader to share a joke, which may be verbal or may lie in the disparity between words and pictures. In all, she builds up cumulative verbal and visual patterns which offer the reader the chance to anticipate what will happen next, and an adventure in reading which will continue to delight for years to come.
Don't Forget the Bacon!
A shopping story in which the humour, as in *The Surprise Party*, springs from a message that becomes hilariously garbled.
[D655] Puffin pbk **£1.50**
Goodnight, Owl!
A noise book about Owl who tries to sleep all day, but 'the bees buzzed, buzz, buzz... The cuckoo called, cuckoo, cuckoo.. ' So when night comes...
[D656] Puffin pbk **£1.75**
Happy Birthday Sam
The frustrations of being small, but feeling old enough to switch on lights and get dressed, are solved by Grandpa's birthday present.
[D657] Puffin pbk **£1.50**
One-Eyed Jake
A greedy pirate gets his come-uppance when his ill-gotten gains sink his ship.
[D658] Puffin pbk **£2.25**
Rosie's Walk
A pictorial joke in which Rosie the hen goes for a walk around the farmyard. Unmentioned in the 32 word text is a fox who appears in the pictures, eager to catch her.
[D659] Bodley hbk **£5.50**
[D660] Puffin pbk **£1.25**
The Door Bell Rang
There were enough biscuits for tea until the doorbell rang. A diminishing tale with a surprise ending.
[D661] Puffin pbk **£1.95**
The Silver Christmas Tree
Squirrel finds the perfect Christmas present for his friends.
[D662] Puffin pbk **£2.50**
The Surprise Party
[D663] Puffin pbk **£1.50**
The Very Worst Monster
Hazel determines to be the 'worst monster in the world' when her brother Billy is born. A funny, perceptive story about sibling rivalry continued in *Where's the Baby*.
[D664] Puffin pbk **£1.75**
The Wind Blew
Winner of the 1984 Kate Greenaway Medal, this is a cumulative tale about a capricious wind that whips away hats, scarves and umbrellas, and leaves in its wake a growing crowd of people pursuing their belongings.
[D665] Puffin pbk **£1.75**
Titch
The problems of being the smallest are explored in this story and its sequel, *You'll Soon Grow into Them, Titch*, in which Titch passes on his role (and his hand-me-down clothes) to the new baby.
[D666] Puffin pbk **£1.50**
Tom and Sam
Tom and Sam are best friends until the day Tom digs a lake in his garden, and Sam becomes jealous.
[D667] Puffin pbk **£1.95**
Where's the Baby
[D668] Bodley hbk **£5.50**
You'll Soon Grow into Them, Titch
[D669] Puffin pbk **£1.75**

KEATS, EZRA JACK
Collage and vivid colour are strikingly combined in the work of this American artist which conveys a small black boy's delight in the pleasures of playing in newly fallen snow, and at learning how to whistle for his dog 'Willie'.
The Snowy Day
[D670] Penguin pbk **£2.25**
Whistle for Willie
[D671] Penguin pbk **£2.25**

LLOYD, DAVID
Duck
(Illus. Voake, Charlotte)
An engaging, acutely observed first story about a little boy, helped by his grandmother, learning the names of things in the world around him.
[D672] Walker pbk **£2.50**

MARIS, RON
Ron Maris uses the split page technique, like the flap, to take his readers on journeys of searching and discovery. Simple, clearly thought-out and enormously satisfying.
Are You There Bear?
A torchlight hunt for teddy in a dark room, where bear-shaped objects are revealed in the light to be a dog, a doll, and so on.
[D673] Puffin pbk **£1.95**
Better Move On Frog!
Finding a home isn't easy - until Frog discovers a pond.
[D674] Collins pbk **£1.95**
Is Anyone Home?
A search for Grandma and Grandpa on a tea-time visit.
[D675] Puffin pbk **£1.75**
My Book
A guided tour of a tabby's home.
[D676] Puffin pbk **£1.95**

MOSS, ELAINE
Polar
(Illus. Baker, Jeannie)
A welcome re-issue of a nursery favourite about a teddy bear who toboggans down the snow-white dustsheets - 'numb, dumb bear' - in a cardboard box, and predictably comes to grief. The strong, simple text and beautifully conceived collage pictures chart Polar's recovery.
[D676A] Deutsch pbk **£1.95**

MURPHY, JILL
Children and parents everywhere recognize themselves in these acutely perceived parodies of domestic life. Memorable texts, which demand reader participation, cumulative narratives, and the absurd spectacle of bears and elephants dressed as humans and involved in familiar domestic dramas, help to make these long-term favourites.
A Piece of Cake **NEW**
[D677] Walker hbk **£5.95**
All in One Piece
[D678] Walker pbk **£2.50**
Five Minutes Peace
Harrassed Mrs Large, an elephant, retires to the bath for 'five minutes peace' from her boisterous children in this first 'Large' tale. In subsequent stories, she endeavours to get ready 'all in one piece' for an evening out, and goes on a diet.
[D679] Walker pbk **£2.50**
Peace at Last
A perfect picture book about insomniac Mr Bear, who tries sleeping in one place after another, only to find that each is too noisy.
[D680] Macmillan hbk **£5.95**
[D681] Macmillan pbk **£2.95**
Whatever Next
[D682] Macmillan pbk **£2.50**

NICOLL, HELEN & PIENKOWSKI, JAN

Favourites long past the nursery years, these stories have everything children love: three sharply drawn comic characters (Meg the witch, Mog the cat and Owl), boldly coloured illustrations, hand-lettered texts, comic strip presentation, delight in language and plots built around spells that go wrong or jokes the reader - but not the characters - are aware of.

Meg and Mog
[D683] Puffin pbk **£1.95**

Meg at Sea
[D684] Puffin pbk **£1.95**

Meg on the Moon
[D685] Puffin pbk **£1.95**

Meg's Car
[D686] Puffin pbk **£1.75**

Meg's Castle
[D687] Puffin pbk **£1.75**

Meg's Eggs
[D688] Puffin pbk **£1.95**

Meg's Veg
[D689] Puffin pbk **£1.75**

Mog at the Zoo
[D690] Puffin pbk **£1.75**

Mog in the Fog
[D691] Puffin pbk **£1.75**

Mog's Box
[D692] Puffin pbk **£2.25**

Mog's Mumps
[D693] Puffin pbk **£1.75**

Owl Goes to the Vet   NEW
[D694] Heinemann hbk **£5.95**

Owl at School
[D695] Puffin pbk **£1.75**

NILSSON, ULF

Four delectable stories, illustrated by Eva Eriksson, about an independent Little Bunny who sorts out her quarrelsome friends, gets lost and then found, goes swimming against her brother's advice, and meets a bad fox. Eriksson's wispy pen and wash illustrations capture bunny-as-child with humour and sensitivity.

Little Bunny Gets Lost   NEW
[D696] Canongate hbk **£3.50**

Little Bunny and Her Friends   NEW
[D697] Canongate hbk **£3.50**

**Little Bunny and the Hungry
Fox**   NEW
[D698] Canongate hbk **£3.50**

Little Bunny at the Beach   NEW
[D699] Canongate hbk **£3.50**

ORMEROD, JAN

101 Things to Do with a Baby
An essential first guide, for all the family, to living with a new baby. Told in strip form, from no. 1 "Say good-morning", to 101 "and a kiss goodnight".
[D700] Puffin pbk **£1.75**

Kitten Day   NEW
A day of discovery for a little girl and her new Burmese kitten is chronicled in delicately coloured and imaginatively arranged strip sequences.
[D701] Walker hbk **£5.95**

Moonlight
[D702] Puffin pbk **£1.95**

Sunshine
Ormerod makes innovative use of strip sequencing in two companion books which wordlessly chronicle the beginning and end of a family day. The quiet, naturalistic artwork makes a strong, positive statement about family life.
[D703] Puffin pbk **£1.75**

DAD & ME
Touchingly simple books which celebrate the special relationship of father and baby.

Dad's Back
[D704] Walker pbk **£1.50**

Illustration from *Peace at Last* by Jill Murphy (Macmillan pbk £2.95)

Messy Baby
[D705] Walker pbk **£1.50**

Reading
[D706] Walker pbk **£1.50**

Sleeping
[D707] Walker pbk **£1.50**

OXENBURY, HELEN

The understated dialogue of these texts reflects a child'-eye view of the situations depicted, humorously counterpointed by pictures which frequently offer a different interpretation of events.

Eating Out
[D708] Walker pbk **£1.50**

Gran and Grandpa
[D709] Walker pbk **£1.50**

Our Dog
[D710] Walker pbk **£1.50**

Playschool
[D711] Walker pbk **£1.50**

The Birthday Party
[D712] Walker pbk **£1.50**

The Check-Up
[D713] Walker pbk **£1.50**

The Dancing Class
[D714] Walker pbk **£1.50**

The Drive
[D715] Walker pbk **£1.50**

The Visitor
[D716] Walker pbk **£1.50**

TOM & PIPPO
This recent series recounts the adventures of Tom and his long-suffering companion Pippo, a toy monkey, who shares all Tom's good times, but takes the blame when things go wrong.

Tom & Pippo Get Lost   NEW
[D717] Walker pbk **£1.99**

Tom & Pippo Go Shopping
[D718] Walker pbk **£1.99**

Tom & Pippo Go for a Walk
[D719] Walker pbk **£1.99**

Tom & Pippo Make a Friend   NEW
[D720] Walker pbk **£1.99**

Tom & Pippo Make a Mess
[D721] Walker pbk **£1.99**

Tom & Pippo Read a Story
[D722] Walker pbk **£1.99**

Tom & Pippo See the Moon
[D723] Walker pbk **£1.99**

Tom & Pippo and the Dog   NEW
[D724] Walker pbk **£1.99**

Tom & Pippo and the Washing Machine
[D725] Walker pbk **£1.99**

Tom & Pippo in the Garden
[D726] Walker pbk **£1.99**

Tom & Pippo in the Snow   NEW
[D727] Walker pbk **£1.99**

Tom & Pippo's Day
[D728] Walker pbk **£1.99**

ROSE, GERALD

'Ahhh!' Said Stork
When Stork finds an egg to eat, he can't break the shell, so the other animals try: 'Hippopotamus rolled on it...'etc. A splendid cumulative tale with a surprise ending.
[D729] Macmillan pbk **£2.50**

ROSEN, MICHAEL

We're Going on a Bear Hunt   NEW
(Illus. Oxenbury, Helen)
A family of five (including the baby, but not the dog) set out on a bear hunt in this retelling of a traditional tale. Oxenbury's illustrations, in alternating black and white and colour double spreads, match the pace and humour of Rosen's poetic performance text. They have an added dramatic intensity, and show her as an accomplished landscape artist.
[D730] Walker **£9.95**

SCARRY, RICHARD

Endless entertainment combined with incidental instruction are the key to the popularity of these enormous picture books in which a huge animal cast dressed as humans busily encircle the globe, engaged in every conceivable kind of work and play.

Busy, Busy World
[D731] Hamlyn pbk **£3.95**

Cars & Trucks & Things that Go
[D732] Collins hbk **£3.95**

Cars, Boats, Trains & Planes
[D733] Hamlyn hbk **£3.50**

Great Big Schoolhouse
[D734] Collins hbk **£3.95**

The Busiest People Ever
[D735] Collins hbk **£3.95**

What Do People Do All Day?
[D736] Collins hbk **£3.95**

WADDELL, MARTIN

Can't You Sleep, Little Bear?
(Illus. Firth, Barbara)
Already hailed as a contemporary classic, this is an enchanting, cumulative tale of a Little Bear who is afraid of the dark, and Big Bear's attempts to reassure him. Firth's pen and wash illustrations glow with the shadowy lantern light of the bear's cave, and with the secure and affectionate relationship of lovable, impish Little Bear and studious, kind Big Bear.
[D737] Viking hbk **£6.95**

ZACHARIAS, THOMAS & WANDA

But Where is the Green Parrot?
A game of 'hide and seek' as the reader hunts for a missing green parrot in various settings. A brilliantly imaginative picture book about names and colours of things, and about looking, which effortlessly involves the young child in the act of reading.
[D738] Bodley hbk **£5.25**
[D739] Piper pbk **£2.50**

Illustration from *Thomas and the Goods Train* by Rev W. Awdrey & Ken Stott (Heinemann Board Books £1.99)

D dealt it

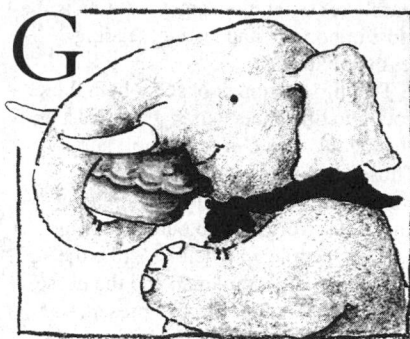

G got it

Learning to Read: Reading to Learn?

Margaret Meek

Books are at the heart of all matters related to children learning to read and reading to learn. They are linked to children's curiosity, excitement and growth in understanding their world (unless something in childhood happens to spoil them). Adults who know what books are good for want the young to grow up enjoying them and putting their reading skills to profitable use. Those who wish they'd given more attention to reading at an earlier age themselves try to make sure that their children don't miss any reading chances. There has never been more genuine concern about reading, nor a greater variety of good children's books. And, despite those who persist in spreading gloom, official reports show that children are actually reading better than at any time in the past.

Before they go off to school, most children become familiar with many forms of print and all of them have some idea about reading itself: advertising, television, magazines and junk mail see to that. But many don't encounter books so casually, nor can they discover what grown-ups do when they read just by watching them. So when adults deliberately read to children, sitting beside them, looking at the pictures and talking, they discover both a splendid kind of story-sharing and also what a book is, how it feels and smells and

works. This early view of the prospect of becoming a reader also conveys the possibility of success: *"I think I'll learn to do this."*

Reading begins as a special kind of play-as-looking-and-saying. With school in mind, parents want to be sure as soon as possible that the words will come right, and so they sometimes miss both the fun and the subtlety of what modern artists devise for new readers. They also read children's books too fast. They know how to play hide and seek with Spot, and that the Very Hungry Caterpillar combines new words for exotic foods with the sequencing of the days of the week and the delicate daring of a hole in the page. The secret of *Rosie's Walk* has been made plain. But they are sometimes uneasy about Anthony Browne's surrealism: is he serious? To see exactly what Nicola Bailey and Janet Ahlberg do is to gaze with a child's intensity at the details. Early encounters with books have a firstness about them to be savoured by both child and adult, and every year brings a shoal of new artists and storytellers whose intent is to capture the innocent eye and to revive the older, more jaded glance worn down by soap commercials.

In a society saturated with images which children interpret before they learn to speak, the young learn more significant and lasting reading lessons from books

than just word-recognition. They discover alternative worlds they can enter and be more themselves. They also discover reading as a complete

Part of what books are good for is to let us discover what we needn't remember as quickly as we can find out

production, something they make with the teller of the story. This is the first step to the essential discovery that, to be a reader, each of us has to become both the *teller* and the *told*, and that reading is about making meaning, including the important meanings at the edge of sense and nonsense. Language, for good readers, is a plaything.

Not everything about children is small. Their emotions and feelings, pleasures and anxieties are always full-sized. Until they discover the predictability of events - something language teaches them - they respond to each incident as a separate event. In stories, the absolute bedrock of children's reading, there are sequences and consequences, so that the reader looks for 'what happens next' with effective expectation. Authors like Maurice Sendak and Shirley Hughes count on this when they make the strange familiar and the familiar strange. In *Where the Wild Things Are* and *Alfie Gets in First*, the reader discovers that the world the adults call 'real' has alternative existences in what is already imagined. A book like *Can't You Sleep Little Bear* not only dispels a young child's fear of the dark, it also provides a place to confront it, safely.

In school, where children officially become literate, reading and writing are changing. Books, papers and texts are now supplemented by all the other forms in which information is made available in our highly technologised society. Craft, Design and Technology, where other kinds of notation besides writing loom large, are only some of the new subjects in the National Curriculum. The official document that discusses school reading sets the attainment target for all children as 'the development of the ability to read, understand and respond to all types of writing' and 'the development of reading and information-retrieval strategies for

the purposes of study'. These are more explicit literary standards than we have ever had before, and they come primed with tests at ages 7, 11 and 14. More than at any time in the past, parents and teachers are asking: 'what, then, are the important reading lessons, not only for children, but also for those who choose books for them to read in school and outside?'

Not all useful information comes from books; we actually get most of what we immediately need from talking to each other and asking questions. But part of what books are good for is to let us discover what we needn't remember as quickly as we can find out. Children need to know how reference books work, but I've never known them to enjoy using them for invented purposes and dummy runs. A sense of intellectual independence comes when they pursue their own curiosity, or a need to know is awakened in them by someone who interests them or something they discover. There is nothing small about children's knowing; they learn with passion when teaching opens up understanding and lets them take hold of it. We often underestimate what children can learn from books because we assume too easily that difficulty is a function of age and development and that progress is linear. Most children who appear not to 'know' things, in the school sense, are neither ignorant nor stupid. They are often bored because they haven't had their kind of knowing confirmed or extended by text or conversation. There are more young experts (on fishing, cars, aeroplane engines, pop music and football) than schools are prepared to find books for. I wish they knew more booksellers.

Not all important understanding comes from books of information. It is difficult to persuade adults (even with the help of Jerome Bruner's **Actual Minds, Possible Worlds**) that narrative is a way of knowing. We expect the young to read novels for recreation, forgetting that stories show how we turn experience into meaning. What's more, to read a novel is to find a thread of meaning through a spectrum of possible meanings. Books like Philippa Pearce's **The Way to Sattin Shore** shows how the imaginative construction of possibilities is common to both literature and science. In our hurry to turn learning to read into reading to

learn, we sometimes forget that this is the most important, and lasting, reading lesson of all.

The information books that help the young to this understanding are, alas, and despite this fine **Guide**, in short supply. Those for younger children mostly confirm in writing what they already know: the words for colours, counting and 'the people who help us', like the postman and the milkman and the nurse. In middle childhood, books present double-page segments of subject matter, free floating, attractively presented and loosely related to topics of current concern in our multi-faith and multi-cultural community. History is crumbled into fragments to be reassembled as 'topics'. Publishers work on in good faith, often abetted by teachers, who themselves need the information, to present books in series from astronomy to zoology. Competent readers know how to turn the brightly coloured pages where restricted vocabulary impedes rather than helps their encounter with complicated ideas - they select what they think they need. But inexperienced readers 'retrieve' information with nowhere to put it, from books that don't help them. We need fewer 'beginner' books at every level in schools. But we won't know what to put in their place until we discover more about how children learn from the interaction of words, pictures and diagrams. At present, writers, publishers and booksellers are all just guessing because we don't take the time (or, in research, don't afford it) to learn better.

In secondary schools, nothing simple or straightforward can be said about books and reading: except, perhaps, that adolescents, like younger children, discover more of what they want to know about (the important topics are origins, sex and death) from novels than from handbooks. Young adults openly read what their peers approve of and keep what they *want* to explore as a more private enquiry. By this stage some young people have decided that reading comes low on their list of preferred occupations outside school. To revive their interest in it needs both knowledge and tact on the part of parents. Teenagers who learned earlier the change of consciousness that comes with being 'lost in a book' will still return to reading as a

Illustration from *Jackanory Stories* by Joan Aiken, drawing by Quentin Blake (BBC/Cape hbk £5.95)

part of living. Others need a combination of comradely encouragement and tolerance of their preferences to get that far.

Persistent readers know reading as a kind of deep play, where the act of reading is itself part of the experience of the text. Aidan Chambers, Robert Cormier and others introduce elements of risk, in both subject and style, so that the reader has to work a little harder and the pleasure is in the effect. These books anticipate both modern adult novels and the student who will discover **Tristram Shandy** as a lifelong friend. The irony is, the same quality of 'writerliness' is the stock-in-trade of artists like Anthony Browne, John Burningham and the Ahlbergs, whose works have the constant quality of surprise which distinguishes the all-age appeal of their picture books.

From the lists presented here (and I have never discovered anything more useful), we may be inclined to say that whatever children read becomes a book for children; from comics (the genre remains, the examples change), to classics (books that look after themselves), and everything between. I have long since given up predicting what children will like. How can they know till they try? But I'm still prepared to explore on their behalf. I know that I'd rather they had good adult reference books than simplified accounts of history or science or geography, for then they'd discover

that none of these 'subjects' exists by itself. The fairy tales are every child's birthright, but once in a lifetime is too brief an encounter. They have to be rediscovered in adolescence if our readers are to understand why there are so many versions of *Cinderella*, what feminism in literature is all about, and what Fay Weldon is up to. Margaret Mahy, who writes some of the best comic verse and stories for the young that I have ever read, also hollows out the pulpy interiors of romantic fiction and replaces them, in fine prose, with startling metaphors for the complexities and ambiguities of growing up. When I began reading children's books, there was nothing like *The Changeover*.

The problem for concerned adults remains keeping up with what's happening to childhood and to reading. Children's books are as good a guide as anything else: the only present certainty is difference.

An educationalist and academic, Margaret Meek has written widely on children and reading, in works such as *Learning to Read* and *How Texts Teach What Readers Learn*.

Years 4 & Up

Picture Books

Picture books for four to six year olds range from the realistic tales of everyday life - the familiar domestic stories of the pre-school years - to wild excursions into the imaginative, the fanciful and the ridiculous. This broadening of literal and literary horizons reflects both children's move from home to school, and the burgeoning of their imaginations. Picture books for this age group need to be dramatic, funny, well-rounded and peopled with recognisable universal characters, and with heroes and heroines (child or otherwise) who satisfyingly overcome the obstacles or hurdles confronting them. Texts, if rhythmic or repetitive, give children the chance to anticipate and to predict what comes next - two fundamental skills of reading. Good illustrations not only extend text, but visually convey complex ideas - often those about feelings - that are not yet possible to explain in words. Essential for a child's literary growth at this stage, they lead into a fuller appreciation of language and the subtle relationship between word and image, opening doors to experiences, thoughts and feelings that otherwise might not be encountered or understood.

AHLBERG, JANET & ALLAN
The Ahlbergs again use the popular culture of childhood - its games, rhymes, jokes and comics - to invite readers into four ingenious and original picture books.
Burglar Bill
Bungling Burglar Bill accidentally steals a baby in a box, and is then burgled by the baby's mother - Burglar Betty. Love blossoms, the couple wed, reform, and return all their stolen loot. A much-loved, riotous send-up of criminal life.
[D740] Mammoth pbk **£2.50**
Cops and Robbers
The game of Cops and Robbers is given the Ahlberg treatment in a hilarious tongue-in-cheek verse saga about upstanding Officer Pugh, and his arch-enemies, the villainous robbers of London Town.
[D741] Mammoth pbk **£2.50**
Funny-bones
The Ahlbergs use a familiar rhyme - 'In a dark, dark...' to create a comic, mock-scary story told in strip about the night time hi-jinks of a big skeleton, a little skeleton and a dog skeleton.
[D742] Heinemann hbk **£5.95**
[D743] Picture Lion pbk **£2.25**
Old Joke Book
The comic strip adventures of a host of 'Oddbod' characters are told in this glorious compendium of corny jokes, both visual and verbal: young children love them.
[D744] Viking hbk **£5.95**
[D745] Puffin pbk **£2.95**

ALLEN, PAMELA
An Australian artist distinguished for the virtuosity of her pictures, in particular for her assured use of the cartoonist's line and exaggerated figure, her sense of design, colour and drama, and impeccable comic timing.
A Lion in the Night
A rousing nightmare (dream?) chase with echoes of Sendak and Briggs, in which an angry baby rides off on a lion, hotly pursued by the King, Queen and Admiral...
[D746] H Hamilton hbk **£5.95**

Bertie and the Bear
'Because a bear was chasing Bertie', the queen chased the bear, the king chased the queen... each would-be rescuer making a new noise to frighten the bear before he eats Bertie up. A cumulative noisy romp, with a delectable surprise at its end.
[D747] Puffin pbk **£2.50**
I Wish I Had a Pirate Suit   NEW
Peter and his patient crew sail the seas in search of adventure in this rhyming extravaganza.
[D748] H Hamilton hbk **£6.95**

AWDRY, REV. W.
The Rev. Awdry's fascination with railways dates from his childhood: his father had a two-and-a-half inch gauge railway in the garden. He started his 'Railway' stories in 1943 to amuse his son, who was ill with measles. Already convinced that each steam engine had a personality, Awdry developed this notion in 26 tales in which trains assume human characteristics, exploiting in his illustrations the full comic potential of each engine's 'face'.
Station Book Box
A presentation box containing all 26 of Awdry's stories, each one of which is available separately, priced at £2.50 for each hardback edition. They comprise: *Branch Line Engines, Duck and the Diesel Engine, Duke the Last Engine, Edward the Blue Engine, Eight Famous Engines, Enterprising Engines, Four Little Engines, Gallant Old Engine, Gordon the Big Engine, Henry the Green Engine, James the Red Engine, Little Old Engine, Main Line Engines, Mountain Engines, Oliver the Western Engine, Percy the Small Engine, Small Railway Engines, Stepney the Bluebell Engine, Tank Engine Thomas Again, Thomas the Tank Engine, Three Railway Engines, Toby the Tram Engine, Tramway Engines, Troublesome Engines, Twin Engines, Very Old Engines* .
[D766] Heinemann box set **£70.00**

BARKLEM, JILL
Nostalgia for a rustic past is evoked in these popular hedgerow tales that invite comparison with the work of Beatrix Potter, but, although charming, lack her spare, selective prose.
Autumn Story
[D776] Collins hbk **£3.50**
Spring Story
[D777] Collins hbk **£3.50**
Summer Story
[D778] Collins hbk **£3.50**
The Four Seasons of Brambly Hedge
[D779] Collins hbk **£13.95**
The High Hills   NEW
[D780] Collins hbk **£3.50**
The Secret Staircase   NEW
[D781] Collins hbk **£3.50**

Babar and Queen Celeste from *Babar the King* by Jean de Brunhoff (Methuen hbk £5.95, pbk £1.95)

Winter Story
[D782] Collins hbk **£3.50**

BAYLEY, NICOLA
Tiny fantasy adventures in which a cat imagines life as a crab on the seashore, a bear in the attic, and so on - exquisitely captured in Bayley's jewel-like miniatures.
Crab Cat   NEW
[D783] Walker pbk **£1.25**
Elephant Cat   NEW
[D784] Walker pbk **£1.25**
Parrot Cat   NEW
[D785] Walker pbk **£1.25**
Polar Bear Cat   NEW
[D786] Walker pbk **£1.25**
Spider Cat   NEW
[D787] Walker pbk **£1.25**

BLAKE, QUENTIN
Mister Magnolia
A nonsense rhyme worthy of Lear, about Mr Magnolia whose life would be perfect except that he 'has only one boot'. Winner of the 1980 Kate Greenaway Award for its joyous, leaping illustrations.
[D788] Picture Lion pbk **£1.95**

BLISHEN, EDWARD & NANCY
A Treasury of Stories for Five Year Olds   NEW
[D789] Kingfisher hbk **£7.95**

BOYD, LIZI
The Not-So-Wicked Stepmother
A small girl discovers that her father's new wife isn't as wicked, mean and ugly as fairytale stepmothers might be, in this re-assuring tale about the aftermath of divorce.
[D790] Puffin pbk **£2.25**

BRIGGS, RAYMOND
A picture book artist of unparalleled inventiveness who turns to past and present folk culture for inspiration.
The Complete Father Christmas
In his two filmic strip-cartoons about crusty but love-able Father Christmas, his Christmas Eve workload, and his attempts to go on holiday without being detected by over-observant children, Briggs irrevently and comically challenges all our assumptions about this folk hero without once diminishing his appeal.
[D791] H Hamilton hbk **£7.95**
[D792] Puffin pbk **£4.99**
Father Christmas
[D793] H Hamilton hbk **£6.95**
[D794] Puffin pbk **£2.99**
Father Christmas Goes on Holiday
[D795] H Hamilton hbk **£6.95**
[D796] Puffin pbk **£2.50**
Jim & the Beanstalk
In a hilarious variant on the traditional Jack and the Beanstalk tale, Jim, son of Jack, climbs the beanstalk to find a bald, harmless, short-sighted, toothless giant. Jim enterprisingly provides him with a wig, spectacles and teeth, but unfortunately, the giant then decides to eat him...
[D797] Puffin pbk **£2.25**
The Snowman
Wordless and haunting, this story of a boy and his mysteriously come-to-life snowman explores the magic of a dream journey.
[D798] H Hamilton hbk **£6.95**
[D799] Puffin pbk **£2.99**

BROWN, RUTH
The naturalistic paintings of Ruth Brown have an intensity, beauty, focus and atmospheric feel which derive from a powerful use of light and dark, of sun and shade rarely found in picture books. In all her

work, she consistently uses language and images to rivet and stretch children's imagination.

A Dark Dark Tale
An eerie variant on an old rhyme.
[D800] Hippo pbk **£1.95**

If At First You Do Not See . . .
A hungry caterpillar story which tells one tale if read conventionally, and another if turned upside down. The form and content of the book demand that the reader looks and looks again.
[D801] Beaver hbk **£2.50**

Ladybird, Ladybird
A picture book which explores the Ladybird's life beyond that of the original nursery rhyme.
[D802] Beaver pbk **£2.50**

Our Cat Flossie
A series of framed stills of a cat's life as she 'helps' with the knitting, pursues her 'hobbies' of birdwatching and fishing... and 'sleeps and sleeps'. The dry humour of the text adds to the pleasure of this affectionate study.
[D803] Beaver pbk **£2.50**

Our Puppy's Holiday
A companion volume chronicles a puppy's wonder as it explores a new landscape of seashore and countryside on the first day of a family holiday.
[D804] Beaver pbk **£2.50**

BRUNHOFF, J. DE
Originally told to entertain his children, de Brunhoff's first story about Babar the elephant - his life in Africa and abroad -.crossed the Channel in 1934 at the behest of A.A. Milne. Its impact on the development of the picture book was profound: the artistic daring of de Brunhoff's illustrations - their size, use of white space, colour and detail, and their superb reproduction - set the standard, along with the work of Edward Ardizzone, for post-war publications. Children respond to Babar as an imaginative hero and delight in the comic spectacle of elephants masquerading as humans.

Babar & Father Christmas
[D805] Methuen hbk **£5.95**
[D806] Methuen pbk **£1.95**
Babar at Home
[D807] Methuen hbk **£5.95**
[D808] Methuen pbk **£1.95**
Babar the King
[D809] Methuen de luxe hbk **£9.95**
[D810] Methuen hbk **£5.95**
[D811] Methuen pbk **£1.95**
Babar's Friend Zephyr
[D812] Methuen hbk **£5.95**
[D813] Methuen pbk **£1.95**
Babar's Travels
[D814] Methuen de luxe hbk **£9.95**
[D815] Methuen hbk **£5.95**
[D816] Methuen pbk **£1.95**
The Story of Babar the Little Elephant
[D817] Methuen deluxe hbk **£7.50**
[D818] Methuen hbk **£5.95**
[D819] Methuen pbk **£1.50**

BURNINGHAM, JOHN
Avocado Baby
A non-eating weakling is transformed into a cot-lifting, burglar-routing Goliath in this riotous spoof of the 'magic potion' tale.
[D820] Cape hbk **£5.95**
[D820A] Picture Lion pbk **£2.50**

Borka: The Adventures of a Goose with No Feathers
A tall tale about the adventures of a jumper-wearing goose that quietly explores the problems of being different - an 'original'. Burningham's first picture book, it won the Kate Greenaway Award in 1963.
[D821] Puffin pbk **£2.50**

CARTER, PETER
Captain Teachum's Buried **NEW**
Treasure (Illus. Paul, Korky)
'Captain Teachum was a pirate,' he said, 'the terror of the seven seas'. But he had three secrets... a spoof (or is it?) adventure.
[D822A] Oxford hbk **£5.95**

CECIL, LAURA
Two splendidly varied read-aloud collections, drawn from folk tales, riddles and the work of writers such as Richard Hughes, Philippa Pearce and Margaret Mahy; strikingly illustrated in rich pen and wash by Emma Chichester-Clark.
Listen to This
[D822] Bodley hbk **£7.95**
Stuff and Nonsense **NEW**
An imaginative selection of fantastical stories and poems about objects which 'come to life' - sometimes with alarming results: a wicked pumpkin; a lonely skyscraper; forty performing bananas; walking, talking macaroni and many more oddities.
[D823] Bodley hbk **£7.95**

COLE, BABETTE
A quartet of zany books about a Mum, Dad, Gran and Grandad who are not quite ordinary: Mum is a witch, Dad an eccentric inventor, Gran an alien, and Grandad an over-zealous vegetable-grower. From these outrageous beginnings, Babette Cole weaves four hilarious tales which make serious points about the value of eccentricity, ingenuity and difference.
The Trouble with Dad
[D824] Picture Lion pbk **£2.25**
The Trouble with Gran
[D825] Picture Lion pbk **£2.25**
The Trouble with Grandad
[D826] Mammoth pbk **£2.50**
The Trouble with Mum
[D827] Picture Lion pbk **£2.25**

CUNLIFFE, JOHN
In these lastingly popular stories, Cunliffe uses the device of the postman to introduce readers to the inhabitants, life and adventures of an English rural village. Illustrated by Celia Berridge.
Postman Pat & the Mystery Thief
[D828] Hippo pbk **£1.75**

Illustration from *Avocado Baby* by John Burningham (Cape hbk **£5.95**, Picture Lion pbk **£2.50**)

Postman Pat Goes Sledging
[D829] Hippo pbk **£1.75**
Postman Pat's Summer Storybook
[D830] Hippo pbk **£2.50**
Postman Pat Takes a Message
[D831] Hippo pbk **£1.75**
Postman Pat to the Rescue
[D832] Hippo pbk **£1.75**
Postman Pat's Breezy Day
[D833] Hippo pbk **£1.75**
Postman Pat's Difficult Day
[D834] Hippo pbk **£1.75**
Postman Pat's Foggy Day
[D835] Hippo pbk **£1.75**
Postman Pat's Letters on Ice
[D836] Hippo pbk **£1.75**
Postman Pat's Rainy Day
[D837] Hippo pbk **£1.75**
Postman Pat's Secret
[D838] Hippo pbk **£1.75**
Postman Pat's Thirsty Day
[D839] Hippo pbk **£1.75**
Postman Pat's Tractor Express
[D840] Hippo pbk **£1.75**
Postman Pat's Treasure Hunt
[D841] Hippo pbk **£1.75**
Postman Pat's Winter Storybook
[D842] Deutsch hbk **£4.95**

Illustration from *Avocado Baby* by John Burningham (Cape hbk **£5.95**, Picture Lion pbk **£2.50**)

DUPASQUIER, PHILIPPE
A French artist continually alert to the possibilities of the narrative picture strip as a medium for pointing out the drama in, and offering fresh perceptions on, ordinary domestic and workaday life.
Dear Daddy
A wordless picture book that depicts simultaneously the life of a small girl at home and that of her sailor father at sea.
[D843] Puffin pbk **£1.75**
I Can't Sleep **NEW**
A textless autobiographical account of a family's sleepless night as the father creeps out of bed to his studio, and is joined by one family member after another. Detailed strip in pen and atmospheric colour capture a rich nightime experience.
[D844] Walker hbk **£6.95**

GAG, WANDA
Millions of Cats
The classic tale of a little old man who sets out in search of the cat for which his wife longs, only to find: *"Cats here, cats there/Cats and kittens everywhere..."*
[D845] Puffin pbk **£2.25**

HEDDERWICK, MAIRI
Spirited Katie Morag and her dungareed, tractor-driving Gran sort out each of her problems - mischief making cousins, jealousy of her new baby brother, and a muddled postal delivery, while the reader is

introduced - in Hedderwick's delicate watercolours, to life on a small Scottish island: to its inhabitants, its flora and fauna, and its economy.

Katie Morag & the Big Boy Cousins
[D846] Bodley hbk **£5.50**
Katie Morag & the Tiresome Ted
[D847] Bodley hbk **£5.25**
[D848] Picture Lion pbk **£2.25**
Katie Morag & the Two Grandmothers
[D849] Picture Lion pbk **£2.25**
Katie Morag Delivers the Mail
[D850] Bodley hbk **£5.50**
[D851] Picture Lion pbk **£1.95**

HERRIOT, JAMES
Bonny's Big Day (Illus. Brown, Ruth)
[D852] Piper pbk **£2.50**
Moses the Kitten (Illus. Barrett, Peter)
[D853] Piper pbk **£2.99**
Only One Woof (Illus. Barrett, Peter)
[D854] Piper pbk **£2.99**
The Christmas Day Kitten (Illus. Brown, Ruth)
[D855] Piper pbk **£2.99**
The Market Square Dog **NEW**
(Illus. Ruth Brown)
[D856] M Joseph hbk **£6.99**

HISSEY, JANE
Three delightful tales of nursery life. Hissey's artwork, in meticulous crayon, has the accuracy, texture and impact of photographic illustration.
Little Bear Lost **NEW**
The nursery toys are playing hide and seek, but Little Bear hides himself so well that he can't be found at all.
[D857] Hutchinson hbk **£5.95**
Little Bear's Trousers
Little Bear goes in search of his missing trousers, which the toys have borrowed and put to some disconcerting uses.
[D858] Beaver pbk **£2.50**
Old Bear
The nursery toys ingeniously manage to rescue the forgotten Teddy from the attic where he has been discarded.
[D859] Beaver pbk **£2.50**

HOBAN, RUSSELL
This American writer's delight in language and its possibilities (which reached subversive heights, in his futuristic adult novel *Riddley Walker*) was apparent in his first published stories: the endearing and humorous domestic tales of Frances the verse-making Badger, who faces competition in the form of a baby sister, and food fads, but always comes out on top. In his 'Hungry Three' stories about children's dressing-up fantasy play, he invents a riddling language to transform home into imaginary worlds: the planet 'Aargh', for instance, which a 'Mummosaurus' invades to announce lunch.
A Baby Sister for Frances (Illus. Lillian Hoban)
[D860] Hippo pbk **£1.50**
Bread and Jam for Frances (Illus. Lilian Hoban)
[D861] Puffin pbk **£1.75**
The Great Fruit Gum Robbery (Illus. Colin McNaughton)
[D862] Walker pbk **£1.99**
They Came from Aargh! (Illus. Colin McNaughton)
[D863] Walker pbk **£1.99**

HUGHES, SHIRLEY
Perhaps the greatest dramatist of the perennial hazards of childhood. Hughes recognizes the enormity of childhood concerns - the loss and retrieval of a stuffed toy (*Dogger*); the ordeal of

moving house (*Moving Molly*); or building an extension (*The Great Big Concrete Lorry*); the arrival of a new baby (*Angel Mae*); or the trouble with young siblings (*The Trouble with Jack*) - and the importance of their successful resolution.
Angel Mae **NEW**
[D865] Walker hbk **£5.95**
Dogger
[D866] Bodley hbk **£5.50**
[D867] Picture Lion pbk **£2.25**
Helpers
[D868] Picture Lion pbk **£2.25**
Moving Molly
[D869] Picture Lion pbk **£2.25**
Sally's Secret
[D870] Puffin pbk **£1.75**
The Great Big Concrete Lorry **NEW**
[D871] Walker hbk **£5.95**
The Trouble with Jack
[D872] Corgi pbk **£2.25**
Up & Up
A wordless fantasy told in inventive strip about a small girl who yearns to fly, and finally does.
[D873] Picture Lion pbk **£1.95**

KERR, JUDITH
Mog must be one of the most engaging and best-known picture book cats. She continually creates mayhem because she isn't very bright and forgets things: that she can't fly, for instance, or that she has a cat flap, or how to get off the roof. 'Bother that cat' cry her owners, until she inadvertently foils a burglar, and saves the baby, and all is forgiven.
Mog & Bunny
Mog is given, and loses, a toy bunny. The book treats the drama of love, loss and reconciliation with sensitivity and, as always, with humour.
[D874] Collins hbk **£4.95**
Mog & the Baby
[D875] Picture Lion pbk **£1.95**
Mog in the Dark
[D876] Picture Lion pbk **£2.95**
Mog the Forgetful Cat
[D877] Collins hbk **£4.95**
[D878] Picture Lion pbk **£2.25**
Mog's Christmas
[D879] Picture Lion pbk **£1.95**
Tiger who Came to Tea
A delicious variant on the greedy, unexpected guest theme.
[D880] Collins hbk **£4.95**
[D881] Picture Lion pbk **£2.25**

KITAMURA, SATOSHI
Lily Takes a Walk
Lily is never scared when taking a walk if her dog Nicky is with her. But Nicky is! A pictorial joke in which the 'spooky surprises' that turn Lily's

Samuel Whiskers from *The Tale of Samuel Whiskers* of the Roly-Poly Pudding by Beatrix Potter (F Warne hbk £3.99)

excursion into a disquieting one for Nicky leap out of Kitamura's surreal town and country landscapes, but are unmentioned in the text.
[D882] Corgi pbk **£2.50**

KRASILOVSKY, PHYLLIS
The Cow Who Fell in the Canal (Illus. Peter Spier)
First published in 1959, this is a classic story about Hendrika, a Dutch cow bored with life in the field, who falls into the canal, climbs on a raft and drifts down to the city. Spier's detailed panoramas of the Dutch landscape capture the absurdity and pleasure of Hendrika's adventure.
[D883] Puffin pbk **£1.75**

LIONNI, LEO
Frederick
The simplest of allegories about the value of stories in life. Frederick, a field mouse, gathers not food but stories, colours and dreams to sustain his family through the long harsh winter.
[D884] Hodder pbk **£2.50**

MAHY, MARGARET
See also *Fiction 6 - 9, 9 - 12* and *12 & Up*.
A Lion in the Meadow (Illus. Williams, Jenny)
A little boy 'makes up' stories, but so does his mother, and hers come true! The lion who might or might not be in the meadow, and the dragon in the matchbox, are early images of this New Zealand writer's long concern with the double-edged nature of the imagination.
[D885] Dent hbk **£5.95**
[D886] Puffin pbk **£2.50**
The Boy with Two Shadows (Illus. Jenny Williams)
A boy looks after his own shadow so well (he knows it must last a lifetime) that a witch asks him to take care of her's too. Shadow-sitting proves to be an alarming responsibility.
[D887] Picture Lion pbk **£2.25**
The Man Whose Mother Was a Pirate (Illus. Margaret Chamberlain)
The hilarious story of a man and his mother who abandon convention-bound work and domesticity for the wild life of the sea.
[D888] Puffin pbk **£1.95**

MAYNE, WILLIAM
The Patchwork Cat (Illus. Nicola Bayley)
A cat's-eye view underpins this book in which some 'snatchwork' on Tabby's beloved 'patchwork' sends her on an alarming journey on a rubbish truck. The text is subtle and onomatopoeic, and the paintings of Tabby in action retrieving her quilt are exquisite.
[D889] Cape hbk **£6.95**
[D890] Puffin pbk **£1.95**

MORRISON, BLAKE
The Yellow House (Illus. Craig, Helen)
A small girl, fascinated by an abandoned yellow house, climbs over the gate when her mother's back is turned, and meets a gnome-like boy who introduces her to the wonders of the garden, and then vanishes. Poet Morrison's mysterious, multi-layered text - his first for children - is about the 'transformational power of the imagination'; his fantasy world beautifully realized in Craig's aqua-tint etchings.
[D892] Walker pbk **£1.99**

PIENKOWSKI, JAN
Dinner Time (Pop-Up)
A 'scary' cumulative story in which one animal after another snaps his jaws and says 'I'm going to eat you for my dinner', until shark has the last word.
[D893] Orchard hbk **£5.95**

Little Monsters (Pop-Up)
A different mischievous monster pops out of each double spread until a twist at the end of the rhyming text, and a mirror, confront the reader with himself.
[D894] Orchard hbk **£5.95**
Small Talk (Pop-Up)
[D895] Orchard hbk **£5.95**

POTTER, BEATRIX
A self-taught artist, Potter (1866-1943) began to draw plants and animals on childhood holidays in the Lake District. She developed into an accomplished watercolour artist, but also began placing the animals in her naturalistic studies in imaginary situations, masquerading as humans, but without losing their basic animal instincts. In 1893 she began writing picture-letters to the children of her former governess. It was here that many of her characters were born. *Peter Rabbit* was published privately in 1901, and the rest of her work followed in the years up to 1913, when she married. The unchallenged success of Potter's stories lies in her sure sense of audience; the economy of her artwork; her precise elegant prose with its dry humour and delight in the sharp new word; and in her ability to transmit the real life of small animals.
Beatrix Potter's Mouse Tales NEW
[D897] Warne hbk **£7.50**
Complete Adventures of Peter Rabbit
[D898] Warne hbk **£6.95**
[D899] Penguin pbk **£4.50**
Complete Adventures of Tom Kitten
[D900] Warne hbk **£6.95**
[D901] Penguin pbk **£3.95**
Complete Tales of Beatrix Potter NEW
The full set of 23 tales, reset in a single-volume format.
[D902] Warne hbk **£20.00**
Fairy Caravan
[D903] Warne hbk **£5.95**
[D904] Penguin pbk **£1.95**
Hill Top Tales
[D905] Warne hbk **£6.95**
The Tale of Mrs Tittlemouse & Other Mouse Stories
[D906] Warne hbk **£6.95**
The Tales from Beatrix Potter
[D907] Warne hbk **£5.95**
More Tales from Beatrix Potter
[D908] Warne hbk **£5.95**
Complete Beatrix Potter Set
A full presentation set of 23 titles, each of which is also available individually at **£3.99**. Together they comprise: *Appley Dapply's Nursery Rhymes, Cecily Parsley's Nursery Rhymes, The Story of Miss Moppet, The Story of a Fierce Bad Rabbit, The Tailor of Gloucester, The Tale of Benjamin Bunny, The Tale of the Flopsy Bunnies, The Tale of Ginger & Pickles, The Tale of Jemima Puddle-Duck, The Tale of Mr Jeremy Fisher, The Tale of Johnny Town-Mouse, The Tale of Little Pig Robinson, The Tale of Mr Tod, The Tale of Mrs Tiggy-Winkle, The Tale of Mrs Tittlemouse, The Tale of Peter Rabbit, The Tale of Pigling Bland, The Tale of Samuel Whiskers, The Tale of Squirrel Nutkin, The Tale of Timmy Tiptoes, The Tale of Tom Kitten, The Tale of Two Bad Mice, The Tale of the Pie and the Patty-Pan.*
[D909] Warne hbk **£92.95**
Complete Peter Rabbit Books
Presentation box of 12 Titles.
[D910] Warne hbk **£48.95**

RAYNER, MARY
The Big Bad Wolf in a variety of guises - baby sitter, ice-cream vendor - seeks the little pigs in modern settings in these suspense-laden and funny tales.
Bath Time for Garth Pig NEW
[D934] Picture Lion pbk **£2.25**

Garth Pig & the Ice Cream Lady
[D935] Macmillan pbk **£2.95**
Mr and Mrs Pig's Evening Out
[D936] Macmillan pbk **£2.50**
Mrs Pig Gets Cross
[D937] Fontana Lion pbk **£1.95**
Mrs Pig's Bulk Buy
[D938] Macmillan pbk **£2.99**

ROSS, TONY
Tony Ross's picture books rarely take his readers where they think they are going. His quirky, irreverent sense of humour ensures that each one is a kind of carefully constructed joke that sets us (and sometimes his characters) up for a final glorious twist or punchline. From the come-uppance of *Naughty Nigel* and *Super Dooper Jezebel*, a perfect child, to the discovery that Oscar's imaginary friend is, well, real, to the revelation that the monster from outer space coming to get Tommy Brown is, in fact, minute, Ross's books not only delight, but also raise questions about perception and the artistic manipulation of the imagination.
I Want a Cat NEW
When Jess is denied a cat, she makes herself a catsuit, and wears it *all* the time, until her parents give in - but too late! Jess has decided she'd rather have a dog!
[D939] Andersen hbk **£5.95**
I Want my Potty
[D940] Fontana pbk **£1.95**
I'm Coming to Get You
[D941] Puffin pbk **£2.25**
Naughty Nigel
[D942] Puffin pbk **£1.95**
Oscar Got the Blame
[D943] Beaver pbk **£2.50**
Super Dooper Jezebel
[D944] Picture Lion pbk **£2.25**

RYLANDS, LJILJANA
Teddy's Friend NEW
A teddy searches for a friend among the crowds of cut-out teddy bears dancing, playing, roller-skating through this enchanting novelty book.
[D945] Orchard hbk **£5.95**

SCHUBERT, DIETER
Where Is Monkey?
A beautiful and eloquent treatment of the lost toy theme.
[D946] Beaver pbk **£2.50**

SENDAK, MAURICE
One of the great illustrators of all time, whose unique vision has profoundly altered the scope and landscape of contemporary picture book art. Strongly influenced by Freud and psychoanalysis, he opened the way for picture books to explore the interior world of the child, and the way in which imagination, fantasy and dream help to resolve and heal childhood traumas. He has said of his own work: *"What is too often overlooked is the fact that, from their earliest years, children live on familiar terms with disrupting emotions, that fear and anxiety are an intrinsic part of their everyday life... it is through fantasy that children achieve catharsis. It is the best means they have for taming the Wild Things"*.
In the Night Kitchen
Mickey's night time dream journey to the Night Kitchen (run by Oliver Hardy look-alikes) is a complex, sensual and endlessly fascinating celebration of food, flight, night and much more, told in bold inventive strip, bubble and narrative.
[D947] Bodley hbk **£5.95**
[D948] Penguin pbk **£2.50**
Where the Wild Things Are
The circular story about Max who rampages in his wolf suit and is sent to bed without his supper for being 'a wild thing', sets the reader on a fantasy

voyage with him to the land where the Wild Things are. This book broke boundaries on its publication in 1963 for its account of children's inner life.
[D949] Bodley hbk **£8.95**
[D950] Puffin pbk **£2.95**

STEIG, WILLIAM
Doctor de Soto
An ingenious story, in which a mouse dentist accepts a hungry fox with toothache as a patient: it reworks the traditional fairy-tale theme of the small and resourceful outwitting the strong and wily.
[D951] Beaver pbk **£2.50**
Solomon the Rusty Nail
A sparky, inventive anthropomorphic tale about Solomon - a rabbit who can transform himself into a rusty nail at will. Hilarious hijinks result until, over-confident, he finds himself in the power of a one-eyed cat with a penchant for bunny stew.
[D951A] Gollancz pbk **£3.50**

THOMAS, VALERIE
Winnie the Witch (Illus. Korky Paul)
Trying to find a black cat in a totally black house poses problems even if you aren't a witch. Winnie decides to experiment with the magic of colour (power and its uses are an underlying theme) with hilarious results.
[D952] Oxford pbk **£2.95**

UTTLEY, ALISON
A science teacher whose first work was published in magazines in the 1920s, Alison Uttley (1884 - 1976) was a prolific writer. Her best loved stories are about Little Grey Rabbit and her friends. Based on a sound knowledge of the natural world as are Beatrix Potter's tales, Uttley's stories are not as strictly naturalistic. Her small animals lead woodland lives, based on the domestic customs, and spiced with the superstition and lore of the old Derbyshire farm where Uttley herself grew up. Margaret Tempest captures this rural environment in delicate watercolours that firmly establish the characters of Grey Rabbit, Squirrel and Hare.
Fuzzypeg Goes to School
[D953] Collins hbk **£2.95**
Hare & Guy Fawkes
[D954] Collins hbk **£2.95**
Hare & the Easter Eggs
[D955] Collins hbk **£2.95**
Little Grey Rabbit & the Circus
[D956] Collins hbk **£2.95**
Little Grey Rabbit Goes to Sea
[D957] Collins hbk **£2.95**
Little Grey Rabbit Makes Lace
[D958] Collins hbk **£2.95**
Little Grey Rabbit and the Wandering Hedgehog
[D959] Collins **£2.95**
Little Grey Rabbit to the Rescue
[D960] Collins **£2.95**
Little Grey Rabbit's Birthday
[D961] Collins **£2.95**
Little Grey Rabbit's Christmas
[D962] Collins **£2.95**
Little Grey Rabbit's May Day
[D963] Collins hbk **£2.95**
Little Grey Rabbit's Paint Box
[D964] Collins hbk **£2.95**
Little Grey Rabbit's Pancake Day
[D965] Collins hbk **£2.95**
Little Grey Rabbit's Party
[D966] Collins hbk **£2.95**
Little Grey Rabbit's Story Book
[D967] Collins hbk **£7.95**
Little Grey Rabbit's Valentine
[D968] Collins hbk **£2.95**
Little Grey Rabbit's Washing Day
[D969] Collins hbk **£2.95**

Moldy Warp the Mole
[D970] Collins hbk **£2.95**
Squirrel Goes Skating
[D971] Collins hbk **£2.95**
The Knot Squirrel Tied
[D972] Collins hbk **£2.95**
The Speckledy Hen
[D973] Collins hbk **£2.95**
Water Rat's Picnic
[D974] Collins hbk **£2.95**
Wise Owl's Story
[D975] Collins hbk **£2.95**

VARLEY, SUSAN
Badger's Parting Gift
Susan Varley won the 1985 Mother Goose award for her delicate Ardizzone-like pen and wash illustrations in this moving story of how Badger's friends learn to accept the death of someone they love, and realise that he still lives on in their memory.
[D976] Picture Lion pbk **£1.95**

WELLS, ROSEMARY
The children who populate these gently humorous stories disguised as small furry creatures deal triumphantly with a series of problems: aggression in *Benjamin and Tulip*; the need for attention in *Noisy Nora*; the problems of being big brother to mischievous young Rhoda in *Stanley & Rhoda*; the feelings of inferiority that a popular but beastly child can cause a newcomer at school in *Timothy Goes to School*; and getting lost and being bullied in *Hazel's Amazing Mother*.
Benjamin and Tulip
[D977] Puffin pbk **£2.25**
Hazel's Amazing Mother
[D978] Picture Lion pbk **£2.25**
Morris's Disappearing Bag
[D979] Puffin pbk **£1.95**
Noisy Nora
[D980] Picture Lion pbk **£1.95**
Stanley & Rhoda
[D981] Picture Lion pbk **£1.95**
Timothy Goes to School
[D982] Puffin pbk **£2.25**

WILDSMITH, BRIAN
While Wildsmith's gifts as a story-teller are not as great as his ability to catch natural life or to visualise conceptual ideas in paint, his picture-books, nonetheless, offer readers deeply satisfying stories made memorable by the extravagant colour and beauty of his illustrations.
Bear's Adventure
The wildly improbable adventures of a bear who falls asleep in the basket of a balloon.
[D983] Oxford pbk **£2.50**
Professor Noah's Spaceship
Wildsmith gives a new twist to the biblical tale when Noah and his animals leave polluted earth to find a new home in outer space.
[D984] Oxford pbk **£2.50**
The Lazy Bear
Loveable, lazy Bear learns a lesson when his friends, tired of pushing him uphill on a wood-cutter's trolley so he can joyride down, push him *over* the hill instead.
[D985] Oxford pbk **£2.50**

WILLIAMS, MARCIA
When I Was Little   `NEW`
Whenever Granny comes to stay, she talks about the time 'when she was little'. Through her memories, a little girl discovers how some things change, while others never change at all. Homes past and present, games, toys, jokes, family relationships, and much more are explored in a delightful book for all grandparents and grandchildren to share.
[D986] Walker hbk **£6.95**

WILLIS, JEAN
The Long Blue Blazer (Illus. Susan Varley)
When Wilson, the mysterious new boy in class who refuses to take off his blazer (even for PE), is not collected at the school gates, everyone thinks he has been abandoned. But his Mum beams in for him from Outer Space - wearing, of course, a blue blazer.
[D987] Beaver pbk **£2.50**
The Monster Bed (Illus. Susan Varley)
A monster's mother tells her son not to believe in humans. When a small boy appears in his bedroom both are frightened out of their wits.
[D988] Beaver pbk **£2.50**

WINTHROP, ELIZABETH
Maggie and the Monster   `NEW`
(Illus. Tomie de Paola)
When Maggie's bedroom is invaded each night by a monster in search of something, Maggie solves the mystery. A humorous mock-scary story enlivened by de Paola's atmospheric pictures.
[D989] Beaver pbk **£2.50**

YORINKS, ARTHUR
Hey Al (Illus. Richard Egielski)   `NEW`
A thought-provoking fantasy about the nature of happiness. Al, a janitor, and Eddie, his faithful dog, share a dull monochrome life in a one-room, monochrome apartment, until the day a mysterious bird offers them a change of fortune. But is life on brightly-coloured Bird Island what they really want?
[D990] H Hamilton hbk **£6.95**

Learning to Read

'How can I best help my child learn to read?' is one of the questions a children's bookseller is most frequently asked. Margaret Meek in her invaluable and practical *Learning to Read* asserts that 'literature makes readers in a way that reading schemes never do'. The message for parents is clear. First, continue to read aloud and discover and enjoy together as many kinds of book as possible. Return to the well-loved pre-school picture books, but explore too those books and stories which your child is mature enough to appreciate but cannot yet read with ease. Remember that reading aloud acts as a foretaste of the literary delights that await the apprentice reader once the basic reading skills are mastered. Second, encourage your child to read to you by providing easy reading books to practise on at home. These may be familiar picture books, such as the *Meg and Mog* or *Spot* books, or they may be stories from the series listed here, which act as a bridge between more formal school reading schemes and more substantial storybooks. In school schemes unity of format and limitations on language level have often resulted in dull, artificial and meaningless tales: here they have inspired stories which are funny, inventive and re-readable. These series beat reading schemes at their own game, and are worth a place on any child's bookshelf.

Beginner Books

BERENSTAIN, STAN & JAN
Berenstain Bears & the Missing Dinosaur Bone
[D991] Collins pbk **£1.95**
The Bear Detectives
[D992] Collins pbk **£1.95**
The Bear Scouts
[D993] Collins pbk **£1.95**

BROWN, MARC
Spooky Riddles
[D994] Collins pbk **£1.75**

EASTMAN, P.D.
Go Dog Go
[D995] Collins pbk **£1.95**
The Best Nest
[D996] Collins pbk **£1.95**

LOPSHIRE, ROBERT
I Want to Be Somebody New!
[D997] Collins pbk **£1.95**
Put Me in the Zoo
[D998] Collins pbk **£1.95**

SEUSS, DR.
When Theodore Geisel - better known as Dr Seuss, or Theo le Sieg - published *The Cat in the Hat* in 1957, he was the first to cock a snook, in a subversive way, at the 'Cat Sat on the Mat' of the stodgy class reader. In these rhyming stories, Geisel's ingenuity with plot, inventiveness with language, and absurd animal characters who parody people, provide readers with a wonderful introduction to the possibilities and richness of language. Colourful, rough-drawn, cartoon-like illustrations are an essential part of his books' appeal.
Fox in Socks
[D999] Collins pbk **£1.95**
Green Eggs & Ham
[D1000] Collins pbk **£1.95**
Hop on Pop
[D1001] Collins pbk **£1.95**
My Book about Me
[D1002] Collins pbk **£1.95**
Oh Say Can You Say?
[D1003] Collins pbk **£1.95**
The Cat in the Hat
[D1004] Collins pbk **£1.95**
The Cat in the Hat Comes Back
[D1005] Collins pbk **£1.95**

Knox in Sox from *Fox in Socks* by Dr Seuss (Collins pbk **£1.95**)

SIEG, THEO LE
One Fish, Two Fish, Red Fish, Blue Fish
[D1006] Collins pbk **£1.95**
Please Try to Remember the First of Octomber
[D1007] Collins pbk **£1.75**
Ten Apples up on Top!
[D1008] Collins pbk **£1.95**

Bright & Early Beginners

A judicious blend of rhythm, rhyme, repetition and nonsense is the key to the popularity of these zany stories, which precede the *Beginner Books*. The Berenstain's saga of a bear who 'went to town/Inside, outside, upside down' uses only eighteen different words, and is typical of the vigorous doggerel that makes this series so irresistible.

BERENSTAIN, STAN & JAN
Bears in the Night
[D1009] Collins pbk **£1.95**
Bears on Wheels
[D1010] Collins pbk **£1.75**
Berenstain Bears & the Spooky Old Tree
[D1011] Collins pbk **£1.75**
Berenstain Bears on the Moon
[D1012] Collins pbk **£1.95**
He Bear, She Bear
[D1013] Collins pbk **£1.75**
Old Hat, New Hat
[D1014] Collins pbk **£1.75**

BROWN, MARC
Wings on Things
[D1015] Collins pbk **£1.75**

SEUSS, DR.
Mr Brown Can Moo, Can You?
[D1016] Collins pbk **£1.75**
The Foot Book
[D1017] Collins pbk **£1.95**
There's a Wocket in My Pocket
[D1018] Collins pbk **£1.95**

SIEG, THEO LE
The Eye Book
[D1019] Collins pbk **£1.95**

Cat on the Mat Books

WILDSMITH, BRIAN
The first of these very simple stories with a minimalist text and repetitive vocabulary plays games with the reading scheme 'cat'. Other books play jokes, either verbal or visual, on the reader: a tree trunk for climbing proves to be an elephant's trunk for sliding in *The Trunk*; an island, a hippo's back in *The Island*. Whichever, these short tales with their luminous, painterly illustrations are a delight.
All Fall Down
[D1020] Oxford pbk **£0.95**
Cat on the Mat
[D1021] Oxford pbk **£0.95**
Giddy Up
[D1022] Oxford pbk **£0.95**
If I Were You
[D1023] Oxford pbk **£0.95**
My Dream
[D1024] Oxford pbk **£0.95**
The Apple Bird
[D1025] Oxford pbk **£0.95**
The Island
[D1026] Oxford pbk **£0.95**
The Nest
[D1027] Oxford pbk **£0.95**
The Trunk
[D1028] Oxford pbk **£0.95**

Toot Toot
[D1029] Oxford pbk **£0.95**
What a Tale
[D1030] Oxford pbk **£0.95**
Whose Shoes?
[D1031] Oxford pbk **£0.95**

WOOD, LESLIE
A Dog Called Mischief
[D1032] Oxford pbk **£0.95**
Bump, Bump, Bump
[D1033] Oxford pbk **£0.95**
Dig Dig
[D1034] Oxford pbk **£0.95**
My House
[D1035] Oxford pbk **£0.95**
Sam's Big Day
[D1036] Oxford pbk **£0.95**
The Frog & the Fly
[D1037] Oxford pbk **£0.95**
Tom & his Tractor
[D1038] Oxford pbk **£0.95**

Fun to Read Picture Books

New in paperback, the excellent design, layout, production, illustration and clear, well-spaced text make these books infinitely approachable. The stories are entertaining and varied, ranging from the nursery-rhyme inspired 'This is the bear/Who fell in the bin/This is the dog/Who pushed him in', a variant on the lost pet/toy theme, to the nonsense verse of Colin West, and the racy *The Tough Princess*, in which the reader's expectations of a fairy tale princess are up-ended.

DALE, PENNY
Bet You Can't
[D1039] Walker pbk **£1.99**

GRINDLEY, SALLY
Four Black Puppies (Illus. Clive Scruton)
[D1040] Walker pbk **£1.99**

HAWKINS, COLIN & JACQUI
The Terrible Terrible Tiger
[D1041] Walker pbk **£1.99**

HAYES, SARAH
This Is the Bear
[D1042] Walker pbk **£1.99**
This Is the Bear & The Picnic Lunch
(Illus. Helen Craig)
[D1043] Walker pbk **£1.99**

KING-SMITH, DICK
A Prince (Illus. Martin Honeyscott)
[D1044] Walker pbk **£2.50**

LLOYD, DAVID
Cat and Dog (Illus. Clive Scruton)
[D1045] Walker pbk **£1.99**
The Stopwatch
(Illus. Penny Dale)
[D1046] Walker pbk **£2.50**

WADDELL, MARTIN
The Tough Princess (Illus. Patrick Benson)
[D1047] Walker pbk **£1.99**

WEST, COLIN
'Have You Seen the Crocodile?'
[D1048] Walker pbk **£1.99**
'Hello Great Bullfrog!'
[D1049] Walker pbk **£1.99**

'Not Me!' Said the Monkey
[D1050] Walker pbk **£1.99**
'Pardon?' said the Giraffe
[D1051] Walker pbk **£1.99**

Happy Families

The *Happy Families* books, based on updated characters from the traditional card games, are firm favourites. Allan Ahlberg acknowledges the robust, music hall nature of children's humour in plot and text while his cast of characters reflects a multi-cultural and non-sexist view of our society. The subjects and situation comedy in these easy-to-read stories appeal across the entire primary range.

AHLBERG, ALLAN & JANET
Master Bun the Baker's Boy
[D1052] Puffin pbk **£1.95**
Master Money the Millionaire
[D1053] Puffin pbk **£1.99**
Master Salt the Sailor's Son
[D1054] Puffin pbk **£1.75**
Miss Brick the Builder's Baby
[D1055] Puffin pbk **£1.95**
Miss Dose the Doctor's Daughter
[D1056] Puffin pbk **£1.95**
Miss Jump the Jockey
[D1057] Puffin pbk **£1.99**
Mr Biff the Boxer
[D1058] Puffin pbk **£1.95**
Mr Buzz the Beeman
[D1059] Puffin pbk **£1.95**
Mr Cosmo the Conjuror
[D1060] Puffin pbk **£1.99**
Mr Creep the Crook
[D1061] Puffin pbk **£1.95**
Mr Tick the Teacher
[D1062] Puffin pbk **£1.95**
Mr and Mrs Hay the Horse
[D1063] Puffin pbk **£1.75**
Mrs Jolly's Joke Shop
[D1064] Puffin pbk **£1.95**
Mrs Plug the Plumber
[D1065] Puffin pbk **£1.95**
Mrs Wobble the Waitress
[D1066] Puffin pbk **£1.95**

Hippo Solos

Hippo Solos are drawn from a variety of beginning-to-read sources and have no overall series unity. They range from an early reading series about the ever popular *Postman Pat* to Wilson Gage's gently humorous tales of old Mrs Gaddy trying to outwit a pesky crow and a resident ghost, to Anita Lobel's modern folk tale in which a spirited girl gives three robbers their come-uppance, and Anne Rockwell's jolly ghost story.

CUNLIFFE, JOHN
Postman Pat & the Christmas Puddings
[D1067] Hippo pbk **£1.50**
Postman Pat & the Greendale Ghost
[D1068] Hippo pbk **£1.50**
Postman Pat Makes a Splash
[D1069] Hippo pbk **£1.50**
Postman Pat Plays for Greendale
[D1070] Hippo pbk **£1.50**
Postman Pat and the Dinosaur Bone
[D1071] Hippo pbk **£1.50**
Postman Pat and the Pet Show
[D1072] Hippo pbk **£1.50**

Postman Pat's Day in Bed
[D1073] Hippo pbk **£1.50**
Postman Pat's Messy Day
[D1074] Hippo pbk **£1.50**
Postman Pat's Safari
[D1075] Hippo pbk **£1.50**
Postman Pat's Spring Cleaning Day
[D1076] Hippo pbk **£1.50**
Postman Pat's Washing Day
[D1077] Hippo pbk **£1.50**
Postman Pat's Wet Day
[D1078] Hippo pbk **£1.50**

GAGE, WILSON
Mrs Gaddy & the Ghost
[D1079] Hippo pbk **£1.75**
The Crow & Mrs Gaddy
[D1080] Hippo pbk **£1.75**

LOBEL, ANITA
The Straw Maid
[D1081] Hippo pbk **£1.50**

ROCKWELL, ANNE
The Bump in the Night
[D1082] Hippo pbk **£1.75**

I Can Read

The long-established *I Can Read* series has a freshness, simplicity and artistic and literary vigour that makes it one of the best of this genre. Indeed, two of its authors - Else Minarik and Arnold Lobel - have risen above the constraints of working with a limited vocabulary to create books of great warmth and humour that already stand as classics.

CHORAO, KAY
Oink & Pearl
[D1083] Puffin pbk **£1.75**

HOFF, SYD
Danny & the Dinosaur
[D1084] Puffin pbk **£1.95**
Grizzwold
[D1085] Puffin pbk **£2.25**

LOBEL, ARNOLD
A wordsmith and artist whose inventive use of language and superb, restrained colour and design make his beautifully crafted books amongst the finest currently in print for children.
Days with Frog & Toad
These books of very short stories about touchy, endearingly thick Toad and buoyant, decisive Frog provide one of the funniest, most moving accounts of the give-and-take of friendship to be found in children's literature.
[D1086] Puffin pbk **£1.95**
Frog & Toad All Year
[D1087] Puffin pbk **£2.50**
Frog & Toad Are Friends
[D1088] Puffin pbk **£1.25**
Frog & Toad Together
[D1089] Puffin pbk **£1.95**
Mouse Soup
[D1090] Heinemann pbk **£2.95**
Mouse Tales
An outstanding book. Papa Mouse tells seven surprising and 'dotty' stories, one to each child at bedtime.
[D1091] Puffin pbk **£1.75**
Owl at Home
Owl isn't wise: he lets the snow in, is frightened of the 'bumps' at the bottom of his bed, and tries to be upstairs and downstairs at the same time. But his

misadventures and misunderstandings endear him to readers who know better.
[D1092] Heinemann pbk **£2.95**

MINARIK, ELSE HOLMELUND
These collections of stories about Little Bear, his family friends and his irresistible antics (flying to the moon or overcoming hiccups) are amongst the happiest, most reassuring tales a young child or a beginning reader can encounter. The essential Sendak illustrations develop pictorially the psychological ambience of childhood, play and relationships.
Father Bear Comes Home
[D1093] Puffin pbk **£1.95**
Little Bear
[D1094] Puffin pbk **£1.95**
Little Bear Stories
[D1095] Heinemann hbk **£5.95**
Little Bear's Visit
[D1096] Heinemann pbk **£2.95**

SCHWARTZ, ALVIN
In a Dark, Dark Room (Illus. Dirk Zimmer)
Seven scary stories - wide-ranging in scope and appeal, from a variant on the classic 'in a dark, dark...' to the heart-stopping 'The Green Ribbon'.
[D1097] Heinemann pbk **£2.95**

Red Nose Readers

The very title of this series indicates its subversive character. The comic invention and the power to stretch, or even confound, the reader's imagination of the author/illustrator team of Allan Ahlberg and Colin McNaughton rarely flags. Ahlberg's texts are deceptively simple.

1: RED BOOKS
In these simplest of stories, Ahlberg builds whole fairy stories or mini-dramas from phrases and the before/after notion: 'before the witch/after the witch' or 'before the haircut/after the haircut'. The space between is gloriously filled by McNaughton's robust and humorous illustrations.
Bear's Birthday
[D1098] Walker pbk **£1.25**
Big Bad Pig
[D1099] Walker pbk **£1.25**
Fee Fi Fo Fum
[D1100] Walker hbk **£2.50**
Happy Worm
[D1101] Walker hbk **£2.50**
Help!
[D1102] Walker hbk **£2.50**
Make a Face
[D1103] Walker pbk **£1.25**
So Can I
[D1104] Walker pbk **£1.25**

2: BLUE BOOKS
The verse stories of the Blue Books have a boisterous nursery rhyme flavour: *"Blow me down!/Says Burglar Bert/Someone's pinched/My football shirt"*.
Blow Me Down
[D1105] Walker hbk **£2.50**
Look Out for the Seals!
[D1106] Walker hbk **£2.50**
One, Two, Flea!
[D1107] Walker pbk **£1.25**
Tell Us a Story
[D1108] Walker pbk **£1.25**

3: YELLOW BOOKS
Each Yellow book contains one complete nonsensical tale with a picture dictionary to help explain key words.

Crash! Bang! Wallop!
[D1109] Walker hbk **£2.50**
Me and My Friend
[D1110] Walker hbk **£2.50**
Push the Dog
[D1111] Walker pbk **£1.25**
Shirley's Shops
[D1112] Walker pbk **£1.25**

Share-a-Story

Based on the premise that the initial stages of the learning to read process can be helped along if parent and child actually share the reading, Pat Thompson's books are ingeniously designed so that parent and child share the conversations that make up each story, the parent initially reading the harder dialogue on the left, and the child the easier right hand page. The conversations are entertaining and full of word play and jokes.

THOMSON, PAT
Best Pest (Illus. Peter Firmin)   NEW
[D1113] Gollancz hbk **£4.95**
Can You Hear Me, Grandad? (Illus. Jez Alborough)
[D1114] Gollancz pbk **£1.95**
Good Girl Granny (Illus. Faith Jacques)
[D1115] Gollancz pbk **£1.95**
My Friend Mr Morris (Illus. Satoshi Kitamura)
[D1116] Gollancz pbk **£1.95**
No Trouble at All (Illus. Jocelyn Wild)   NEW
[D1117] Gollancz hbk **£4.95**
One of those Days (Illus. Bob Wilson)
[D1118] Gollancz pbk **£1.95**
Thank You for the Tadpole (Illus. Mary Rayner)
[D1119] Gollancz pbk **£1.95**
The Treasure Sock (Illus. Tony Ross)
[D1120] Gollancz pbk **£1.95**

Illustration from *My Naughty Little Sister* by Dorothy Edwards, illustrated by Shirley Hughes (Methuen hbk **£4.95**, Mammoth pbk **£1.99**)

The Duke's Oak *Arthur Rackham*

Stories in Pictures
Shirley Hughes

A story told in pictures will always be a necessary feature of our lives, one way or another. In earlier times artists were required to develop their narrative skills to communicate the stories of the Bible to a largely unlettered populace. Now, in the late twentieth century, a picture-book illustrator is concerned with exactly the same kind of challenge: to involve someone who cannot yet read in a story through their enjoyment of the imagery.

In this first introduction to fiction the words (read aloud in this case) carry the thread; but the characterisation, the background, much of the humour and drama of the plot is there to be discovered in the pictures. A delightful and

satisfying dialogue emerges. Young children like to discuss what is happening and point out the details in the illustrations (they are very good at this). In responding to the story they are flexing their own verbal and visual muscles and reinforcing their personal experiences of life. If a story captures their imagination they take it to their hearts and make it their own in an astonishing number of ways, using it as a starting point for their own stories, pictures and imaginings. They can memorise an entire text with ease, and become highly indignant if a single word or phrase is skipped by the reader. They are also capable of making their own leisurely exploration of drawing styles and can readily recognise their

favourite illustrators. As anyone who has had the pleasure of sharing in this experience knows, the aesthetic responses of non-readers are not necessarily crude or un-developed. Far from it: our visual memories are probably better before the age of seven than at any other time of our lives.

Sadly there are not so many illustrated books for older children around these days. The kind I loved as a child were the classic editions with plenty of line drawings set in the text and tipped-in colour plates which were always printed on a different kind of high-gloss paper. These were a great thrill, but if they did not coincide exactly with the right moment in the narrative ('See p.182') one felt sold short. Some of my favourite illustrators were the Brock brothers, Ernest Shepard, Edmund Dulac and the incomparable Will Heath Robinson, one of the great classic illustrators in both colour and black and white until he turned

The kind I loved as a child were the classic editions with plenty of line drawings set in the text and tipped-in colour plates

to comic magazine invention. Rackham, though undoubtedly wonderful, always created some unease, especially with those gnarled tree roots like creeping, grasping hands. And Kay Neilson was a little too coldly stylish for comfort.

Modern children may find some of the classics which we enjoyed (but by no means all) less interesting than the very high standard of contemporary fiction which is on offer. Fortunately some intrepid publishers, such as Victor Gollancz, are keeping going those classics which do still appeal in fine style, offering new visual interpretations as well as fully-illustrated modern novels by authors of the calibre of Peter Dickinson.

Comics, probably the most potent visual influence of childhood before Walt Disney swept all before him, have naturally influenced many illustrators. You can spot the power of the *Beano* style in the work of Colin McNaughton and Tony Ross. The young Maurice Sendak must surely have pored over the

American newspaper 'Funnies', with special attention to George MacManus and the brilliant Winsor McCay, as is evident from *In the Night Kitchen*. Personally, I belong to the far off era of *Pip, Squeak and Wilfred*, *Japhet and Happy* and *The Bruin Boys*; not such sophisticated draughtsmanship perhaps, but an innocent world in which we could linger with pleasure. For some reason the art of strip-cartoon tends to be regarded in this country as rubbishy, inferior stuff (certainly some recent developments are depressing). But on the continent, masters of *bande désinée* such as Hergé and Uderzo (of *Tintin* and *Asterix* fame) are highly regarded, and rightly, as consummate graphic artists. To tell a story using no words at all represents a kind of Mount Everest to many illustrators, but not many have scaled the heights with such success as Raymond Briggs with *The Snowman*.

In the abundance of children's books available today colour rules. The art of

> *On the continent, masters of bande désinée such as Hergé and Uderzo are highly regarded, and rightly, as consummate graphic artists*

black and white line illustrations does not often pull in the big print-runs. But for me the most inspiring illustrators will always be masters of line like Edward Ardizzone and Ernest Shepard. They both developed highly individual styles, instantly recognisable yet capable of adapting to a very wide range of texts, able to create a perfect balance between word and image on a page, and enhance each story with their dazzling drawing skills.

Children's Book Choice

The cream of the *Babar* stories are the ones by Jean de Brunhoff, drawn with spacious simplicity and a wealth of eloquent detail. The full-size hardcover editions are well worth saving up for.

Rosemary Wells' *Noisy Norah*, Gabrielle Vincent's beautifully illustrated *Ernest and Celestine* stories and Charlotte Voake's nursery rhyme collection *Over the Moon* are all very good bets for the under-sixes. Edward Ardizzone's heroic adventures of *Little Tim* illustrated in his inimitable pen and wash style, are still some of the most original picture-books around. (The paperbacks are of an excellent printing standard). For fairy-tale illustration at its most sophisticated watch out for the brilliant Russian illustrator Grennady Spirin. His pictures for *The Mysterious Tale of Gentle Jack and the Bumblebee* by George Sand are in the finest European tradition.

James Reeves ranks with Charles Causley in the exacting art of writing poetry for children. His language is simple and full of imagery, funny but never facetious. His *Complete Poems*, superbly illustrated in line by his old friend Ardizzone, represents word and image in complete rapport. Robert Louis Stevenson's *Treasure Island*, surely the best adventure story ever written, has had many illustrators. My favourite are the bravura colour-plates by N.C. Wyeth (father of the painter Andrew Wyeth and big daddy of classic American illustration). And, for me, no interpretation of Kenneth Graham's magical *The Wind in the Willows* gets so close to the heart of the story or its characters than Ernest Shepard's intimate, atmospheric line drawings.

Adult Book Choice

Norman Rockwell: Artist and Illustrator, text by Thomas S. Brechner, celebrates probably the last illustrator to achieve rock-star status. His public of the 1930s and 40s waited with bated breath to see what he would do with the next cover of *The Saturday Evening Post*. A direct heir to Victorian narrative painting, every picture told a clear story, packed with details of social history, and reinforcing all the myths of small town America, rocking-chairs on the front porch and Mom's apple-pie, in which my generation firmly believed.

Kenneth Clark's lectures when he was Slade Professor in Oxford were packed to

the doors and opened up a visual world which I for one never knew existed. He never allowed his erudition to overlay his own personal response to beauty, which he communicated in lucid, elegant prose. His *Civilization* still remains one of the best possible books to put into the hands of anyone, young or old, who is contemplating a trip to Europe with eyes wide open.

Bonnie Bennett and David G. Wilkins' book on *Donatello*, one of the greatest and most unpredictable giants of the Italian Renaissance, has the advantage of an intelligent and accessible text. The excellent photography illuminates details which it is often hard to see when confronting the originals, especially the astonishing San Lorenzo reliefs.

Simon Schama's highly enjoyable interpretation of the Dutch culture in the Gold Age, *The Embarrassment of Riches*, is brilliantly written, scholarly but without assumption of any but the most passing prior knowledge of the subject on the part of the reader. He makes you want to look again with a fresh eye at Dutch paintings, and draws some clever analogies with other pioneering cultures which expanded, became rich, and 'invented' their own creative life within the period of a hundred years or so.

Renowned for her children's books and for the illustration which accompanies them, Shirley Hughes is one of the most distinguished contemporary children's writers. Her work includes the ever popular *Lucy & Tom* and *Alfie* books; she is a committed advocate of the importance of illustration in story books and her own style of line drawing is distinctive.

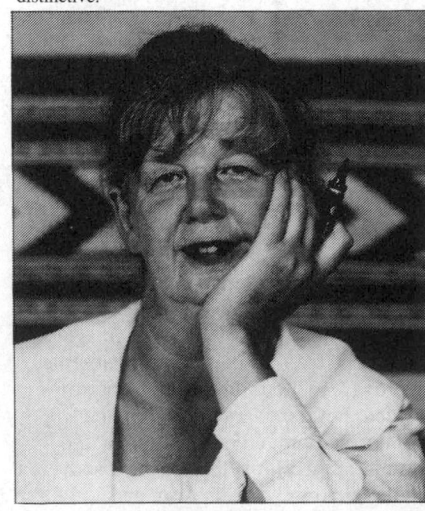

Age 6 - 9

At some point between six and nine, children meet their first extended stories, and discover the pleasure of being able to read a 'proper' book by themselves. They are gradually weaned off pictures with words onto words with some pictures (to help the story along, and break up pages into manageable chunks of text) and finally to words alone. The books we offer need to be as exciting an invitation as the infinitely varied, often subversive, picture books they already know and will continue to encounter. Indeed, picture books for this age explore increasingly complex ideas - not yet expressable in words alone - whose mind-stretching meaning is unlocked by an understanding of the subtle interplay, often ironic, between text and visual image.

In fiction, narratives need to be compulsive - the desire to know what happens next, and how, is what keeps children reading and turning the pages. As for content, the big events of childhood at home and at school are still central - explored both realistically and fantastically through animals, toys and magical creatures. Relationships - in particular, how to deal with adults and the outside world,- emerge as a theme, while children's appetite for farcical and knockabout humour and for wordplay and verbal and pictorial wit develops, paralleled by their growing ability to reflect thoughtfully on what they have read. For parents anxious to encourage their children as readers, no better guidance can be found than that offered by Nancy Chambers in *Fiction 6 to 9*, or by Dorothy Butler's more expansive and anecdotal *Five to Eight*.

Picture Books

AHLBERG, JANET & ALLAN
The Jolly Postman; or Other People's Letters
The Jolly Postman goes on his rounds (a tale told in verse) and delivers actual letters, inside envelope pages, to various fairy-tale characters. Among them are some of the funniest letters in fiction: solicitors Meeny, Miny & Mo write to B.B. Wolf about his harassment of Miss Red Riding Hood's grandmother; Goldilocks apologises to the Three Bears for breaking and entering. The Ahlberg's invention is unsurpassed in this extraordinary adventure in reading.
[D1130] Heinemann hbk **£6.95**

ARDIZZONE, EDWARD
The seagoing adventures of Tim, Ardizzone's most famous creation, have endured because they embody (in text and picture) that central fantasy of childhood: the independent child who steps out into the world, and faces danger and hardship before returning safely and triumphantly home. Ardizzone's wash drawings reflect 'the world he knew as a child illuminated by his sympathy as a parent' (Margery Fisher, *Intent upon Reading*).
Little Tim and the Brave Sea Captain
[D1131] Viking hbk **£6.50**
[D1132] Puffin pbk **£2.50**
Tim and Charlotte
[D1133] Oxford pbk **£2.50**
Tim and Ginger
[D1134] Oxford pbk **£2.50**
Tim All Alone
[D1135] Oxford pbk **£2.50**
Tim in Danger
[D1135A] Oxford pbk **£2.50**
Tim to the Lighthouse
[D1136] Oxford pbk **£2.50**
Tim to the Rescue
[D1137] Puffin pbk **£1.95**
Tim's Friend Towser
[D1138] Oxford pbk **£2.50**
Tim's Last Voyage
[D1139] Macmillan pbk **£2.95**

BAKER, JEAN
Where the Forest Meets the Sea
In this eloquent picture book worked in vibrant collage, the reader explores an Australian rain forest threatened by civilization, with a young boy who imagines the wilderness as it was in primeval times, and as it might be if vandalized by man.
[D1140] Walker pbk **£2.50**

BANKS, KATE
Alphabet Soup (Illus. Peter Sis) **NEW**
A boy doesn't want his alphabet soup - but its letters provide him with the ingredients for an extraordinary 'alphabetical' adventure. Sis converts the objects on a kitchen table into a surreal dreamscape (a cup becomes a boat, a peppergrinder an ogre, and so on), where anything is possible; his fresh, subtle line reveals the transformational power of words, only hinted at in Banks' rich, rhythmic text.
[D1140A] Heinemann hbk **£6.95**

BLAKE, QUENTIN
The Story of the Dancing Frog
Bereaved Great Aunt Gertrude, when young, dedicates her life to the theatrical career of George, her amazing 'Dancing Frog'. The comic fantasy of this story within a story, told by a young widow to her son, is an allegory of poignancy and depth.
[D1141] Picture Lion pbk **£2.50**

BROWNE, ANTHONY
Anthony Browne uses the surreal in his picture books to grab his readers' attention, engage their imagination and extend their understanding of the values and relationships of the world around them. While his visual absurdities initially provoke games of 'I Spy', each pictorial joke is related to theme: class and snobbery in *A Walk in the Park*; material possessions versus the imagination in *Look What I've Got*; and the power of imagination in *Through the Magic Mirror*.
A Walk in the Park
[D1142] Macmillan pbk **£2.50**
Look What I've Got
[D1143] Magnet pbk **£1.95**
Through the Magic Mirror
[D1144] Macmillan pbk **£2.50**

BURNINGHAM, JOHN
Burningham has both explored and extended the dynamic imaginative life of 6 to 9 year olds in his innovative picture books. In *Would You Rather...*, a book of distinctly alarming possibilities, he takes children's imaginative questioning to the limit, while the more complex Shirley and Julius stories look at the interplay between our inner and outer lives.
Come Away from the Water, Shirley
While her parents sit, sleep, eat on the beach, and address various admonishments to her on the left of each doublespread, Shirley, in glorious technicolour on the right, transforms an ordinary day at the seaside into a swashbuckling piratical adventure.
[D1145] Picture Lion pbk **£1.95**
Granpa
Burningham extends the narrative techniques used in his *Shirley* books. Here, in fragments of conversation and experience, he simultaneously depicts the inner and outer worlds and the shared surface life of a little girl and her grandfather as they garden, play and explore, until, after a snowy outing, we find the young girl pondering Granpa's empty chair. A remarkable book as interesting for the way it is made as for the ideas about time, memory and relationship that it explores.
[D1145A] Cape pbk **£3.95**
Oi, Get Off My Train **NEW**
Another Burningham adventure of the imagination: this time involving a small child, a mysteriously enlarged toy train and a host of endangered animals wanting a ride.
[D1146] Cape hbk **£6.95**
Time to Get Out of the Bath, Shirley
[D1147] Picture Lion pbk **£1.95**
Where's Julius?
Julius is too busy 'travelling' to eat but his parents, unlike Shirley's, actually collaborate in his imaginative journeys.
[D1148] Piper pbk **£2.50**
Would You Rather...
[D1149] Picture Lion pbk **£2.50**

CARTWRIGHT, ANN
Hedgehog (Illus. Reg Cartwright) **NEW**
Rich, rhythmic text and clear bright, Rousseauesque pictures tell the tale of the 'smallest' hedgehog who slips away to look for winter when his family hibernates.
[D1149A] Hutchinson hbk **£6.95**

COLE, BABETTE
Babette Cole, with riotous anarchy, subverts fairy tale and ancient myth as she chronicles the adventures of a wayward Cupid who shoots his arrows at Gods and Policemen alike; a feminist princess who wants to remain a Ms.; and a prince who cleans up after his bullying brothers who won't let him go to the Palace Disco.
Cupid **NEW**
[D1150] H Hamilton hbk **£7.50**
Prince Cinders
[D1151] Picture Lion pbk **£2.25**
Princess Smartypants
[D1152] Collins pbk **£2.25**

DAHL, ROALD
The Enormous Crocodile (Illus. Quentin Blake)
[D1153] Puffin pbk **£2.50**
The Giraffe, the Pelly & Me (Illus. Quentin Blake)
[D1154] Puffin pbk **£2.95**

DALLAS-SMITH, PETER
Trouble for Trumpets (Illus. Peter Cross)
A glorious 'hotch potch' of a book in which a familiar storyline - the battle between the affable 'Trumpets' and the sharp, prune-faced 'Grumpets' - is interlarded with vignettes of their respective lives, including nature drawings, joke maps, hieroglyphic alphabets and secret messages to decode. This original comic fantasy offers the reader hours of absorption.
[D1155] Walker pbk **£3.99**

FOREMAN, MICHAEL
Foreman's early picture books display an original and extravagant imagination, able to explore social and political issues in a child-appealing way. Rich, punning humour subtly conveys serious intent in text and watercolours that echo both the comics of Foreman's youth and Eastern Art.
All the King's Horses
A welcome re-issue of Foreman's up-ended fairy-tale about an Asian princess who isn't 'a milk-white, golden-haired, pink little number the way princesses are supposed to be', but is 'BIG' and outwrestles all her suitors. An ironic comment on folk tales and feminism.
[D1156] H Hamilton hbk **£6.95**

Dinosaurs & All that Rubbish
A parable about conservation, in which dinosaurs return to a vandalised, deserted Earth and clear it up.
[D1157] Puffin pbk **£2.25**

Moose
An 'amoosing' satire of the Cold War. Eagle and Bear hurl abuse, and more, at each other. Peace-loving Moose, caught between, collects their sticks and stones, and, with the other animals, builds a new world - complete with 'Mooseum' and 'Amoosement Park'.
[D1158] Puffin pbk **£1.75**

Panda's Puzzle
Panda sets out to discover whether he is a black bear with white bits, or a white bear with black bits. What he learns is that it doesn't matter: living is more important.
[D1159] Puffin pbk **£1.95**

War & Peas
Skeletal King Lion leaves his desert home to ask the Fat King for economic aid in this satiric swipe at the problems of the starving Third World and the glutted West, played out against a collage landscape composed of skyscraper sundaes and food.
[D1160] Puffin pbk **£1.95**

FOX, MEM
Wilfred Gordon Macdonald Partridge
(Illus. Julie Vivas)
A poignant tale about Wilfred who lives next door to an old people's home where he develops a special relationship with Miss Nancy, because they both have four names. When Miss Nancy loses her memory, Wilfred sets out to discover what memories are, so he can restore hers.
[D1161] Puffin pbk **£1.95**

FURTADO, JO
Sorry Miss! (Illus. Frederic Joos)
Miss Folio is a librarian, and this book is a compendium of the ever more improbable excuses a child dreams up to explain his missing library book.
[D1162] Beaver pbk **£2.50**

GRAY, NIGEL
A Country Far Away
(Illus. Philippe Dupasquier)
Despite great differences in culture and environment, two boys - one in an African village, the other in a British town - lead similar lives. Gray's first-person narrative records everyday events, while Dupasquier's characteristic narrative strips simultaneously capture the contrasts.
[D1163] Andersen hbk **£5.95**

HAZEN, BARBARA SHOOK
The Knight Who Was Afraid of the Dark (Illus. Tony Ross) **NEW**
A tongue-in-cheek spoof in which a 'bold and much loved' knight overcomes the 'one crack' in his armour - his 'knee-bumping, heart-thumping fear of the dark' - to win his love.
[D1163A] Andersen hbk **£6.95**

HOBAN, RUSSELL
How Tom Beat Captain Najork and His Hired Sportsmen
Quick thinking and tomfoolery save Tom from his authoritarian iron-hatted aunt and from Captain Najork and his hired sportsmen in Hoban's comic masterpiece. An inventive look at adult-child relationships.
[D1164] Cape hbk **£5.95**
[D1165] Piper pbk **£1.50**
Monsters (Illus. Quentin Blake) **NEW**
A hilarious and monstrous - extravaganza about a boy whose drawings of monsters get out of hand.
[D1165A] Gollancz hbk **£5.95**

HUGHES, FRIEDA
The Meal a Mile Long **NEW**
A sailor, imprisoned for picking a flower, escapes with the aid of some starving rats and a 'meal a mile long'. Rich text and comic quirky illustrations combine in this first picture book by the poet laureate's daughter.
[D1165B] Simon & Sch hbk **£6.95**

INGPEN, ROBERT
The Idle Bear **NEW**
An unusual, mind-stretching book about two battered teddy bears - one a realist, the other a philosopher - whose conversation explores such ideas as 'the power of names, the wish to be valued for our own sake, the natural comfort we derive from the imperfections of others, and the discomforts of being old' (*Signal Selection 1986*).
[D1166] Blackie hbk **£5.95**
[D1167] Blackie hbk/miniature **£1.95**

KING, DEBORAH
Cloudy **NEW**
"I am a little grey cat called Cloudy. I am the colour of thunder and rain..." The shadowy secret world of the author's own cat is revealed in brief poetic text and remarkable, naturalistic yet mysterious watercolours.
[D1167A] Hutchinson hbk **£5.95**

KITAMURA, SATOSHI
UFO Diary **NEW**
A little boy befriends an unseen spaceman, who takes him on a mind-expanding trip through space. Kitamura's skyscapes dazzle the imagination, his message about acceptance, the heart.
[D1168] Andersen hbk **£5.95**

MAYNE, WILLIAM
A House in Town (Illus. Sarah Fox-Davies)
Spare, poetic, naturalistically true, Mayne's story tells of a family of town foxes growing up and learning about danger when a demolition team destroys their earth. Their flight to safety from an ever-increasing pack of dogs is breath-takingly rendered in prose and paint.
[D1169] Walker pbk **£2.50**

MCKEE, DAVID
McKee, like Anthony Browne, introduces the surreal into his illustrations to jolt children into paying attention. The everyday and the bizarre meet in his comic picture books which operate on many levels, and can be read in many ways: this is ably demonstrated by *I Hate My Teddy Bear*, about fantasy games, and *Snow Woman*, about gender.
I Hate My Teddy Bear
[D1170] Beaver pbk **£2.50**
Not Now, Bernard
Bernard, ignored by his preoccupied parents ('*not now, Bernard*'), is eaten by a monster. A seemingly simple story that evokes a response from absorbed parent and attention-needing child alike.
[D1171] Beaver pbk **£2.50**
Snow Woman
[D1172] Beaver pbk **£2.50**
The Monster and the Teddybear **NEW**
"I don't like teddy bears... I want a monster" says Angela. But when a monster climbs through her bedroom window one night, it isn't quite the playmate she expected. Teddy unexpectedly comes to the rescue... Vintage McKee that echoes *Not Now, Bernard*, but has a different twist.
[D1172A] Andersen hbk **£5.95**
The Sad Story of Veronica Who Played the Violin
An ironic moral tale about Veronica, a child prodigy, whose soulful violin playing moves everyone to tears,

until she sets off for the jungle where a deaf lion eats her up.
[D1173] Beaver pbk **£2.50**

MCNAUGHTON, COLIN
Football Crazy
A 'Boy's Own Story' in inventive strip, with echoes of the old 'Rainbow' comics, about Bruno bear, who becomes a hero when he saves the local football team from defeat.
[D1173A] Mammoth pbk **£5.95**

MURPHY, JILL
On the Way Home
'On the way home' a little girl invents ever taller tales (told in bubble strip) to explain to friends how she grazed her knee. With sympathy and humour, text and picture capture story-making in process.
[D1174] Macmillan pbk **£2.50**

OAKLEY, GRAHAM
Oakley is a satirist who pokes fun at space programmes, advertising, scientific research, and a host of other topics in his richly humorous tales about Arthur the Church Mouse and Sampson the Church Cat, who are friends because Sampson has listened to so many sermons about the meek being blessed. His texts are superb, as are his detailed mouse-eye view watercolours of life in and around vestry and parish.
Church Cat Abroad
[D1175] Macmillan pbk **£2.99**
Church Mice Adrift
[D1176] Macmillan pbk **£2.99**
Church Mice Spread Their Wings
[D1177] Macmillan pbk **£2.99**
Church Mice at Bay
[D1178] Macmillan pbk **£2.99**
Church Mice at Christmas
[D1179] Macmillan pbk **£2.99**
Church Mice in Action
[D1180] Macmillan pbk **£2.99**
Church Mice on the Moon
[D1181] Macmillan pbk **£2.99**
Church Mouse
[D1182] Macmillan pbk **£2.99**
Diary of a Church Mouse
[D1183] Macmillan pbk **£2.99**
The Church Mice Chronicles
[D1184] Macmillan hbk **£5.95**

ORAM, HAIWYN
In the Attic (Illus. Satoshi Kitamura)
Surrounded by a million toys, but bored, a small boy climbs the ladder of his toy fire engine into the attic where he goes on an extraordinary adventure of the imagination. Kitamura's startling, poetic and surreal paintings illuminate this intriguing story.
[D1185] Beaver pbk **£2.50**

PIENKOWSKI, JAN
Robot
[D1186] Heinemann hbk pop-up **£7.95**
The Haunted House
[D1187] Heinemann hbk pop-up **£7.95**

PRICE-THOMAS, BRIAN
The Magic Ark
An enigmatic fantasy in which a young boy is taken by the mysterious Mr Antrobus over the world on a magic dream trip in a Noah's Ark, releasing the animals Mr Antrobus has carved, into their natural habitats, where they come alive.
[D1188] Macmillan pbk **£2.95**

SENDAK, MAURICE
The Sign on Rosie's Door
A subtle, funny evocation of the fantasy-play of a group of backstreet children led by Rosie Calios Alinda, the lovely lady singer, as they dress up, put on

a show, and pretend to be firecrackers. An early Sendak exploration of the way fantasy enriches children's lives.
[D1189] Puffin pbk **£2.25**

SIMMONDS, POSY
Fred
Told in characteristic strip, *Guardian* cartoonist Simmonds' first book for children concerns the death of Fred the cat and the revelation to his child mourners, in a wonderful night-time fantasy, of his existence as the Tom Jones of Tom Cats.
[D1190] Puffin pbk **£2.50**
Lulu and the Flying Babies
A boring trip to the museum is transformed for a reluctant Lulu when a winged Cupid leans out of a painting and takes her on a guided 'inside' tour of its masterpieces.
[D1191] Cape hbk **£5.95**

Illustration from *Lulu and the Flying Babies* by Posy Simmonds (Cape hbk £5.95)

TURNBULL, ANN & FOREMAN, MICHAEL
The Sandhorse NEW
The haunting story of a sand horse, sculpted by an artist on the beach at St Ives, who yearns to join the white horses prancing out at sea. Foreman's luminous pen and wash illustrations distil the experience of a windy summer's day in his native St Ives, and chronicle a longing mysteriously fulfilled.
[D1192] Andersen hbk **£5.95**

VELTHUIJS, MAX
Frog in Love
Frog is in love with Duck. *"You can't be - you're green and she's white"* said Piglet. But Frog didn't let that bother him... An enchanting, delectably comic anthropomorphic tale, with an important message.
[D1192A] Andersen hbk **£5.95**

WADDELL, MARTIN
The Great Green Mouse Disaster (Illus. Philippe Dupasquier)
A troupe of performing mice escape in a hotel in this wordless picture book, and a series of stories begins. Dupasquier presents the whole hotel, from basement to attic, on each doublespread. Page by page, from room to room and floor to floor, readers delightedly follow the fortunes of each mouse as mayhem ensues.
[D1193] Beaver pbk **£2.99**

H.R.H. THE PRINCE OF WALES
The Old Man of Lochnagar (Illus. Sir Hugh Casson)
[D1194] H Hamilton pbk **£3.95**

YEOMAN, JOHN
Beatrice and Vanessa (Illus. Quentin Blake)
Beatrice the ewe and Vanessa the nanny goat venture beyond their familiar field in search of adventure and a holiday.
[D1195] Macmillan pbk **£2.50**
The Wild Washerwomen (Illus. Quentin Blake)
Sexual politics is the underlying theme of this absurd tale of the anarchic liberation of seven demure washerwomen.
[D1196] Puffin pbk **£1.25**
The Young Performing Horse (Illus. Quentin Blake)
A rags-to-riches tale about Victorian twins who buy a young performing horse, which wins them all fame and fortune at the pantomime.
[D1197] Methuen pbk **£1.50**

Fiction

AHLBERG, JANET & ALLAN
Some of the richest and most inventive stories for 6 to 9 year olds have their roots in folk and fairy tales and in popular contemporary culture. The Ahlberg's ever fertile imaginations remake these elements in all their books into something original and new: these three tongue-in-cheek extravaganzas are no exception.
Jeremiah in the Dark Woods
Jeremiah Obadiah Jackanory Jones goes in search of the no-good thief who stole his grandma's tarts and encounters a motley crew of storybook characters (Goldilocks, a Mad Hatter, a grandma-eating Wolf) in the dark woods.
[D1198] Viking hbk **£6.95**
[D1199] Puffin pbk **£2.99**
Ten in a Bed (Illus. André Amstutz)
One evening a little girl named Dinah Prince kisses her Mum and Dad goodnight, climbs the stairs to her room - and finds three bears in her bed. Eight other fairy tale characters appear on subsequent nights - each demanding a bedtime story.
[D1200] Viking hbk **£6.95**
The Clothes Horse
A collection of stories about everyday expressions made literal: a 'clothes horse' made entirely of clothes, a 'night train' that brings the night, etc.
[D1201] Viking hbk **£6.95**
[D1202] Puffin pbk **£2.99**

ARKLE, PHYLLIS
Humorous episodic stories about Alfie, a station cat whose curiosity continually gets him into scrapes which incur the wrath of Hack, the station porter.
The Railway Cat
[D1203] Puffin pbk **£1.75**
The Railway Cat & Digby
[D1204] Puffin pbk **£1.50**
The Railway Cat & the Horse
[D1205] Puffin pbk **£1.99**
The Railway Cat's Secret
[D1206] Puffin pbk **£1.75**

ASHLEY, BERNARD
Ashley translates his own experiences as headmaster of a large multi-racial London school into powerful, acute and sometimes humorous stories of school and city life.
Dinner Ladies Don't Count
Jason is blamed for something he didn't do while

Linda tells a lie - just a little one - and is horrified to see how it grows.
[D1207] Puffin pbk **£1.75**
I'm Trying to Tell You
Four children tell their own misinterpreted stories.
[D1208] Puffin pbk **£1.50**

BARRY, MARGARET STUART
The stories of Simon and his best friend, who happens to be a witch and in each book the witch causes chaos in the neighbourhood. Children love the knockabout comedy and racy dialogue of these madcap stories.
Simon and the Witch
[D1209] Collins pbk **£1.75**
Simon and the Witch in School
[D1210] Collins pbk **£1.75**
The Return of the Witch
[D1211] Collins pbk **£1.75**
The Witch VIP
[D1212] Collins pbk **£1.95**
The Witch and the Holiday Club
[D1213] Collins pbk **£1.75**
The Witch of Monopoly Manor
[D1214] Collins pbk **£1.75**
The Witch on Holiday
[D1215] Collins pbk **£1.75**

BERG, LEILA
A Box for Benny
"You keep on giving love. And one day you'll get the thing you want", the ragman tells Benny. As Benny makes swops, trying to get a shoebox to keep his hazlenuts in, so he can join in the spring nut games, he discovers the rich and diverse community around him. An enduring favourite, deep in understanding, from a master storyteller.
[D1216] Magnet pbk **£1.25**
My Dog Sunday
A gritty, powerful story with an inner city setting about Ben who longs for a dog and briefly realizes his dream when he finds a stray (or so he thinks) in the park.
[D1217] Puffin pbk **£1.75**

BIEGEL, PAUL
The King of the Copper Mountain
The ancient device of a tale within a tale provides the framework for this rich and satisfying fantasy about an ancient, dying King who must be kept alive by intriguing stories until the Wonder Doctor arrives. Each day an animal recounts his history, as all work against time to save him. A wonderful read-aloud.
[D1218] Collins pbk **£2.25**

BLACKER, TERENCE
Ms Wiz Spells Trouble
When hippy Ms Wiz takes over Class Three - the 'problem class' - strange things start to happen. The comic potential of a feminist witch as teacher is fully exploited in this outrageous school story.
[D1218A] Pan pbk **£1.99**

BOND, MICHAEL
After Winnie-the-Pooh, Paddington must be the best known bear in British children's fiction. Arriving from 'Darkest Peru' at Paddington Station, he is found and taken home by the Browns. The marmalade-eating bear gets his new 'family' into endless embarrassing fixes, as he struggles to master the routines of modern urban life. The comedy of bear as innocent, disaster-prone child is irresistible.
A Bear Called Paddington
[D1219] Collins hbk **£5.95**
[D1220] Collins pbk **£1.75**
More about Paddington
[D1221] Collins pbk **£4.95**
[D1222] Collins pbk **£1.75**
Paddington Abroad
[D1223] Collins pbk **£1.75**

Paddington Goes to Town
[D1224] Collins pbk **£1.75**
Paddington Helps Out
[D1225] Collins pbk **£1.75**
Paddington Marches On
[D1226] Collins pbk **£1.75**
Paddington Takes the Air
[D1227] Collins pbk **£1.75**
Paddington Takes the Test
[D1228] Collins pbk **£1.75**
Paddington at Large
[D1229] Collins pbk **£1.75**
Paddington at Work
[D1230] Collins pbk **£1.75**
Paddington on Screen
[D1231] Collins pbk **£1.75**
Paddington on Top
[D1232] Collins pbk **£1.75**

BRISLEY, JOYCE LANKESTER
Milly-Molly-Mandy was first introduced to young
readers in 1928. While the stories are comfortably
old-fashioned in feel, Milly's adventures
(blackberrying, having tea in a tree-house, or giving a
party) are those of some children today, innocently
and humorously told.
Milly-Molly-Mandy Stories
[D1233] Puffin pbk **£1.50**
Further Doings of Milly-Molly-Mandy
[D1234] Puffin pbk **£1.99**
Milly-Molly-Mandy Again
[D1235] Puffin pbk **£1.99**
More of Milly-Molly-Mandy
[D1236] Puffin pbk **£1.50**

BROWN, JEFF
Two original comic fantasies about Stanley
Lambchop and his family. In one Stanley is
squashed flat when his bulletin board falls on him in
the night, and has some novel adventures in his new
shape. In the other, the family's straight-faced
response to the unexpected consequences of wishes
granted by a visiting genie generates another funny
tale.
A Lamp for the Lambchops
[D1237] Magnet pbk **£1.75**
Flat Stanley
[D1238] Magnet pbk **£1.50**

CAMERON, ANN
In each of these episodic books about family life
and childhood friendship, Julian's father deals
with his son's mischief-making and imagination
with an originality (and understanding) that Julian
has clearly inherited. He weaves 'magical'
solutions to disaster and disappointment just as
Cameron weaves rich, poetic and distinctive
tales.
The Julian Stories
[D1239] Collins pbk **£1.75**
Julian's Glorious Summer
[D1240] Gollancz hbk **£5.95**
More Stories Julian Tells
[D1241] Collins pbk **£1.75**

CHERRINGTON, CLARE
**Sunshine Island, Moonshine
Baby**
Listening to the members of her Grandmother's
sewing circle share memories of their Caribbean
childhoods, Sara learns, like the reader, to 'read' the
influence of childhood, place, culture and time on
character.
[D1242] Collins pbk **£1.75**

CLEARY, BEVERLEY
Ramona Quimby, the ebullient five-year old whose
plans often misfire, is one of the best developed
characters in young fiction. Readers three or four

years older than her delight in these finely-observed
episodic stories, and view her behaviour with the
indulgence of hindsight, while recognising her fears
and problems.
Beezus and Ramona
[D1243] Puffin pbk **£1.75**
Ramona Forever
[D1244] Puffin pbk **£1.75**
Ramona Quimby, Age Eight
[D1245] Puffin pbk **£1.50**
Ramona and Her Father
[D1246] Puffin pbk **£1.25**
Ramona and Her Mother
[D1247] Puffin pbk **£1.50**
Ramona the Brave
[D1248] Puffin pbk **£1.25**
Ramona the Pest
[D1249] Puffin pbk **£1.25**
Henry and Risby   `NEW`
Nine-year old Henry Huggins tackles life with the
same impetuous ardour as Ramona - with similar
results, in these humorous chronicles of a 1950s
American childhood.
[D1250] Puffin pbk **£1.75**
Henry and the Clubhouse   `NEW`
[D1251] Puffin pbk **£1.75**

COLWELL, EILEEN
A well-known children's librarian who told stories on
Play School and *Jackanory*, Colwell has gathered
short stories, rhymes and finger games which she has
used successfully with children in these popular
collections.
Bad Boys
[D1252] Penguin pbk **£1.95**
High Days and Holidays
[D1253] Puffin pbk **£2.50**
More Stories to Tell
[D1254] Penguin pbk **£1.95**
Tell Me a Story
[D1256] Penguin pbk **£1.95**
Tell Me Another Story
[D1255] Penguin pbk **£2.95**
Time for a Story
[D1257] Penguin pbk **£1.95**

CORRIN, SARA & STEPHEN (EDS)
Storytellers who believe that certain stories are best
encountered at particular ages, the Corrins have
collected a wide range of both traditional and modern
tales in their rich, read-aloud anthologies.
A Time to Laugh
[D1258] Faber pbk **£1.99**
Round the Christmas Tree
[D1259] Penguin pbk **£1.99**
Stories for Under-Fives
[D1260] Penguin pbk **£1.99**
More Stories for Under-Fives
[D1261] Penguin pbk **£1.99**
Stories for Five-year-olds
[D1262] Penguin pbk **£2.25**
Stories for Six-year-olds
[D1263] Penguin pbk **£2.25**
Stories for Seven-year-olds
[D1264] Penguin pbk **£2.50**
More Stories for Seven-year-olds
[D1265] Penguin pbk **£2.50**
Stories for Eight-year-olds
[D1266] Penguin pbk **£2.50**

COUNSEL, JUNE
The comic potentials of a dragon in school is
exploited fully in these two sprightly episodic stories
about Scales, who is visible to his classmates but not
to the teacher.
A Dragon in Class 5
[D1267] Corgi pbk **£1.75**
A Dragon in Spring Term
[D1268] Corgi pbk **£1.95**

CRESSWELL, HELEN
A Gift from Winklesea
The everyday is uproariously transformed by magic
when the souvenir of a school trip to the seaside - a
beautiful, egg-shaped stone - hatches the Gift!
[D1269] Puffin pbk **£1.50**
Dragon Ride
A dream (or is it?) fantasy in which a small girl rides
into adventure on the back of the dragon in her
favourite poster.
[D1270] Puffin pbk **£1.99**
Two Hoots
Cresswell takes the cliché - *wise as an owl* - and
deliciously subverts it in this tale of two owl brothers,
'the Hoots' who are 'as daft as Coots'. One of an
innovative new series - *Jets* - in which each page is
broken up into words and pictures in just the way the
story demands, in a dynamic interaction of text,
speech balloon and illustration (for others in the series
see *Firmin*, *Impey*, *Taylor*, *Thomson* and *Wilson*).
[D1271] Collins 'Jets' pbk **£1.75**

CROSSLEY-HOLLAND, KEVIN
Storm
In this poetic introduction to the literary ghost story, a
young girl conquers fear and rides across storm-
wracked fenland with a ghostly horseman, to fetch the
doctor for her sister's unborn child.
[D1272] Heinemann hbk **£2.50**

DAHL, ROALD
Fantastic Mr Fox
One of Dahl's best stories about Mr Fox's fight to
feed his starving family and outwit his enemies,
farmers Boggis, Bunce and Bean. All the best-loved
Dahl ingredients are here: a racy, suspense-filled
storyline, revolting 'baddies' and sympathetic
'goodies', empathy with the underdog, and subversive
humour.
[D1273] Puffin pbk **£1.75**
The Magic Finger
Another tale of hunters and hunted in which the
young narrator puts his 'magic finger' on the trigger-
happy Mr Gregg and his boys and turns them into
ducks.
[D1274] Puffin pbk **£1.50**

DAVIES, EVELYN
Joseph's Bear
In this unusual story set in frontier America Joseph's
longings for a pet are fulfilled when he rescues a
dancing bear from its cruel owner. But the bear is
wild, and in the spring Joseph must lose him...
[D1275] Puffin pbk **£1.75**

EDWARDS, DOROTHY
The archetypal pre-schooler of these stories is one of
the best-loved heroines of this type of fiction.
Children relish the escapades of this spirited child,
and her companion in crime, Bad Harry. Enjoyment
springs from contemplation of behaviour readers have
long since outgrown.
My Naughty Little Sister
[D1276] Methuen hbk **£4.95**
[D1277] Mammoth pbk **£1.99**
All About My Naughty Little Sister
[D1278] Methuen pbk **£6.95**
More Naughty Little Sister Stories
[D1279] Mammoth pbk **£1.99**
My Naughty Little Sister & Bad Harry
[D1280] Magnet pbk **£1.75**
My Naughty Little Sister's Friends
[D1281] Magnet pbk **£1.75**
**When My Naughty Little Sister Was
Good**
[D1282] Magnet pbk **£1.75**
King Dicky Bird and the Bossy Princess
"Anyone can marry a husband...I want a career" says
the bossy Princess who rejects all suitable suitors until

she meets her match in a barefoot beggar. A primary *Taming of the Shrew*, the fun springs from the parody and the reader's slow realization of who the beggar *really* is.
[D1283] Methuen pbk **£1.75**

FIRMIN, PETER
Nina's Machines
A funny, subversive tale in which a 'Renaissance' Italian girl literally invents her way out of domesticity. The transformation of Nina's increasingly ingenious versions of modern machines (vacuum cleaner, washing machine, bicycle, lift & flying machine) from design board into active life will delight all would-be inventors.
[D1284] Collins 'Jets' pbk **£1.75**

GARDAM, JANE
Writer of perfectly crafted short stories, imbued with the nature of the countryside.
Bridget and William
Bridget and William - her pony - save Mum and a premature baby by riding for the doctor over a frozen moor.
[D1285] Puffin pbk **£1.75**
Kit in Boots
Kit discovers new ways of seeing from the artist who lives near her farm, and learns to value both his brain and her farmer father's brawn.
[D1286] Puffin pbk **£1.75**

GERAS, ADELE
Apricots at Midnight NEW
An enchanting collection of reminiscences of an Edwardian childhood told by Aunt Pinny, an old dressmaker, to a young visitor. Each story is inspired by a patchwork piece in the quilt on the child's bed: bringing back memories of St Giles Fair, a puppet theatre and a ball where Pinny shared 'apricots at midnight' with the host.
[D1287] Collins pbk **£2.25**

GODDEN, RUMER
Perfectly realized, beautifully imagined domestic dramas scaled to the miniature world of the doll's house: from *Candy Floss*, a coconut-shy mascot; to *Impunity Jane*, a pocket-sized Victorian doll who longs to go out into the world and have adventures; to *Holly*, who dreams of a home other than the toyshop, and humble *Tottie*, who wins through against an unwelcome newcomer to the doll's house. Each of Godden's heroines is a distinctive personality: like children they are vulnerable, their movements controlled by child-owners who misunderstand or mistreat them. Godden explores issues and truths fundamental to human experience, and sets children on a literary path that leads to *The Borrowers*, another study of human nature in miniature.
Candy Floss and Impunity Jane
[D1288] Puffin pbk **£1.99**
Little Plum
[D1289] Puffin pbk **£1.75**
Miss Happiness and Miss Flower
[D1290] Puffin pbk **£1.75**
Rocking Horse Secret
[D1291] Puffin pbk **£1.75**
Story of Holly & Ivy (Illus. Barbara Cooney)
[D1292] Macrae hbk **£6.95**
[D1293] Puffin pbk **£1.75**
The Dragon of Og
[D1294] Magnet pbk **£1.50**
Tottie: The Story of a Doll's House
[D1295] Puffin pbk **£1.95**

GRAVES, ROBERT
The Big Green Book
Jack uses some magic from the Big Green Book to get the better of a stuffy aunt and uncle.
[D1296] Puffin pbk **£1.25**

GRAY, NIGEL
Carrot Top NEW
A set of crisp, zesty stories about ginger-haired Melinda, her family - Mum who can never find her purse, loving 'cack-handed' Dad, and baby - and her friends. City children will recognise themselves here in the comfortable way they do in Leila Berg's *A Box for Benny*.
[D1297] Collins pbk **£1.75**

HALL, WILLIS
The Last Vampire
A spoof in which the Hollins family, on a camping holiday somewhere in Europe, encounter more than they had bargained for in an ancient castle: wolves, suspicious villagers and a vegetarian vampire!
[D1298] Collins pbk **£1.95**

HEIDE, FLORENCE PARRY
The Shrinking of Treehorn
A black comedy about adult-child relationships in which Treehorn begins to shrink. His mother thinks he's pretending; his teacher says *"We don't shrink in this class"*. On his own, he must save himself: how he does so makes very funny reading.
[D1299] Puffin pbk **£1.75**
Treehorn's Treasure
A sequel in which the focus is on Treehorn's cashflow and its sudden augmentation by a dollar-producing tree, which the adults fail to notice.
[D1300] Puffin pbk **£1.50**

HOBAN, RUSSELL
Dinner At Alberta's
Mannerless Arthur Crocodile undergoes a transformation when he is invited to dinner by the delectable Alberta Sourian.
[D1301] Puffin pbk **£1.25**
Jim Hedgehog's Supernatural Christmas NEW
Jim Hedgehog is addicted to food, relaxation and TV - until the day he is sucked inside it by the 'Revolting Blob', the monster in his favourite film, who slips out and makes himself comfortable in Jim's house. How Jim escapes makes for very funny reading.
[D1302] H Hamilton hbk **£6.95**
Ponders NEW
In characteristic Hoban style, the title for this set of eight tales of pondside life suggests multiple meanings. These are 'sharp', metaphoric 'little meditations-in-stories', built around common human

Paddington from *Paddington at the Station* by Michael Bond (Collins pbk **£0.99**)

experiences: Charlie Meadows, mouse and newsboy, confronts fear in the shape of Ephraim Owl; Jim Frog recovers from depression.
[D1303] Walker pbk **£1.99**
The Marzipan Pig
A frothy but haunting Andersen-like tale of consuming love and misapprehension between animate and inanimate. A greedy mouse gobbles up a marzipan pig, lost behind the sofa, and precipitates a circular chain of events involving a grandfather clock, an owl, and a taxi meter... A comic fantasy whose bitter-sweet nature is revealed through word play and dialogue.
[D1304] Puffin pbk **£1.75**

HOFFMAN, MARY
Readers' expectations are comically up-ended when, in one, a fairy tale princess abandons her traditional role and, in the other, the Batty's adopted daughter grows second teeth that are sharp and pointed..
Beware Princess!
[D1305] Heinemann hbk **£2.50**
Dracula's Daughter
[D1306] Heinemann hbk **£2.50**

HOWE, JAMES & DEBORAH
These sophisticated spoofs of the horror genre, set in suburban America, involve Bunnicula, a vampire rabbit who attacks vegetables, and Howard the dog and Chester the cat who attempt to restrain his 'natural' instincts.
Bunnicula
[D1307] Collins pbk **£1.95**
Howliday Inn
[D1308] Collins pbk **£1.95**
The Celery Stalks at Midnight
[D1309] Collins pbk **£1.95**

HUGHES, SHIRLEY
Shirley Hughes combines the cartoon-strip format with conventional narrative and illustrations, and creates a set of poignant and comic adventures about two friends, in a way very different from what the formula leads the reader to expect.
Another Helping of Chips
[D1310] Collins pbk **£1.75**
Chips & Jessie
[D1311] Collins pbk **£1.75**

HUGHES, TED
Hughes's two books of creation tales and his enthralling fable *The Iron Man* are absorbing as much for their event-filled surfaces as they are for their mysterious and mythic implications and rich poetic language.
How the Whale Became & Other Stories
[D1312] Faber pbk **£1.99**
Tales of the Early World
A retelling of the creation myth with God as an artist sometimes surprised by his own handiwork.
[D1313] Faber hbk **£6.50**
The Iron Man: A Story in Five Nights
(Illus. Alan Davidson)
"Taller than a house, the Iron Man stood at the top of the cliff, on the very brink, in the darkness" and stepped over. So begins this gripping fable of a misunderstood giant who initially terrorizes man, but eventually saves him from an invading space bat. Hughes' child-appealing, dramatic images - the surreal self-reassembly of the broken giant; the bizarre parody of his feast in the scrapmetal yard - are magnificently illuminated in Davidson's tinted woodcuts.
[D1314] Faber hbk **£7.95**
[D1315] Faber pbk **£1.99**

HUTCHINS, PAT
Children reared on Pat Hutchins' picture book jokes will now savour the broader humour of her slapstick

farces about six-year old Morgan, his family, his school class, and Sam and his pet rat, Nibbles. These are seeing-but-not-believing tales in modern dress: the knockabout comedy of disguise, pursuit, and the improbable event works like a Max Sennett film in print.

Follow That Bus!
[D1316] Collins pbk **£1.95**

King Henry's Palace/The Tale of Thomas Mead
Two simpler jokes for children beginning to read: one about Good King Henry who outwits Bad King Boris; the other, a cautionary tale in verse about 'Thomas Mead who never ever learned to read'.
[D1317] Pan pbk **£1.50**

Rats!   **NEW**
[D1318] Bodley hbk **£5.95**

The Curse of the Egyptian Mummy
[D1319] Collins pbk **£1.95**

The House That Sailed Away
[D1320] Collins pbk **£2.25**

The Mona Lisa Mystery
[D1321] Collins pbk **£1.95**

IBBOTSON, EVA
The Worm and the Toffee-Nosed Princess
Five stories in which folk-tale characters and situations are treated with comic irreverence.
[D1322] Piper pbk **£1.75**

IMPEY, ROSE
The childhood longing for a pet, and the joy of its fulfillment, underpin these stories in which two sisters, 'desperate for a dog', try to persuade their parents to buy them one; having succeeded, they explore possible names for it (such as 'Houdini' because she keeps on escaping, and 'Dustbin' because she eats everything).

Desperate for a Dog   **NEW**
[D1323] Collins 'Jets' pbk **£1.75**

Houdini Dog   **NEW**
[D1324] Collins 'Jets' pbk **£1.75**

KAYE, GERALDINE
The Beautiful Take-Away Palace
Kai-Cheng must learn to read a new language when he arrives in England after his grandmother's death in Hong Kong. Kaye delicately and movingly chronicles his displacement, grief, and the prejudice he encounters at school which inhibit the process, until he ingeniously performs the funeral rites necessary for his grandmother's spirit to rest in peace.
[D1325] Methuen pbk **£1.50**

KING-SMITH, DICK
Friends and Brothers
A fine collection of short stories, enlivened by puns and word play, about William and his younger brother Charlie. The ups and downs of their relationship are explored with realism and gentle humour.
[D1326] Mammoth pbk **£1.99**

George Speaks
The wonderfully funny story of a baby who learns to speak like an adult at the age of four weeks.
[D1327] Puffin pbk **£1.99**

Sophie's Snail
Six enchanting, acutely observed stories about Sophie, a self-possessed four-year old of endearing but determined character, who loves snails and plans to be a 'lady' farmer when she grows up.
[D1328] Walker pbk **£1.99**

The Hodgeheg
This story of the 'First Crossing' tells how ordinary Max the Hedgehog becomes the heroic Victor Maximillian St George when he pioneers a new method for hedgehogs to cross the road in safety.
[D1329] Puffin pbk **£1.99**

LAVELLE, SHEILA
The misadventures of two girlfriends - Angela, whose bright ideas inevitably lead to disaster, and long-suffering, gullible Charlie who often, but not always, takes the blame for her 'best friend's' shenanigans.

Holiday with the Fiend
[D1330] Collins pbk **£1.95**

My Best Fiend
[D1331] Collins pbk **£1.95**

The Fiend Next Door
[D1332] Collins pbk **£1.95**

Trouble with the Fiend
[D1333] Collins pbk **£1.95**

LEAF, MUNRO
The Story of Ferdinand
The classic story of a Spanish bull who prefers sitting peacefully in his meadow to fighting in the bullring.
[D1334] Puffin pbk **£1.50**

LEESON, ROBERT
Never Kiss Frogs!
An 'alternative' fairy tale in which ordinary Gail's extraordinary habit of kissing frogs doesn't produce quite the prince she had longed for. A splendid spoof.
[D1334A] H Hamilton hbk **£2.99**

MAHY, MARGARET
A writer of unique ability and astonishing range, Mahy is able to tune her story-making and telling to the nature and needs of whatever age she writes for. Her collections of short stories deal with creatures of the imagination, witches, ghosts and characters from this world; the worlds created are poetic and full of a rare understanding of, and joy in, the unpredictability of human nature. Wonderful for reading aloud.

Leaf Magic & Five Other Favourites
[D1335] Magnet pbk **£1.50**

Nonstop Nonsense
[D1336] Methuen pbk **£1.75**

The Boy who Bounced & Other Magic Tales
[D1337] Puffin pbk **£1.95**

The Great Piratical Rumbustification
[D1338] Puffin pbk **£1.75**

The Little Witch & 5 Other Favourites
[D1339] Puffin pbk **£1.75**

MATTHEWS, ANDREW
Wolf Pie
"Take two ripe, greedy Monarchs, a bold dash of Tax Police Chief, one fresh woodcutter's son, and three wolves" and *"a sprinkling of apprentice chefs"* and you have the beginnings of a recipe for 'Wolf Pie'. Subversive, funny and rude in the style of Dahl, with essential Tony Ross illustrations.
[D1340] Methuen pbk **£1.50**

MCCABE, BERNARD
Bottle Rabbit
An original fantasy in which the innocent Bottle Rabbit wins a Magic Bottle as a Kindness Prize. It can bring him benefits (lunch, dinner, even a private aeroplane), but also trouble (in the shape of the Confidence Pig, the Vulture Crad and the monstrous Grumble). The delicate comedy (and pathos) is caught in Alex Scheffler's highly individual line drawings.
[D1341] Faber pbk **£1.99**

MCGOUGH, ROGER
McGough plays to the verbal wit and televisual, street-wise culture of his readers in these two spoof adventure stories. Tony Blundell's cartoons are an integral part of the fun.

The Great Smile Robbery
Emerson foils the plots of the Stinker gang to steal his collection of smiles in order to win a National Smile Competition.
[D1342] Puffin pbk **£1.10**

The Stowaways
Two Liverpool lads search for adventure (running away to sea on the Mersey Ferry), but their efforts always come to hilarious, unconventional ends.
[D1343] Puffin pbk **£1.75**

MILLER, MOIRA
Hamish and the Wee Witch
Miller makes new folk tales in these six stories, set in Scotland, in which Hamish, his wife Mirren and his old mother outwit a host of intruders to their croft - from a Big Wind who steals two haystacks, to a Wee Witch who robs them of milk and wool.
[D1344] Methuen pbk **£1.75**

MORGAN, ALISON
Bright Eye
The relationship of a child and a wild duck lies at the heart of this moving story which examines (without sentimentality) the problems in raising a pet that is, by nature, wild.
[D1345] Puffin pbk **£1.50**

MORGAN, HELEN
Satchkin Patchkin
Eight poetic tales in which a poor widow with the aid of a little green magic man outwits her greedy landlord. With its patterned and repetitive language, it's a wonderful tale to read aloud.
[D1346] Puffin pbk **£1.75**

MURPHY, JILL
The racy humour of these tales about an incompetent young witch, Mildred Hubble, stems in part from Murphy's clever transposition of familiar classroom types, routines and situations to Miss Cackle's Academy for Witches.

The Worst Witch
[D1347] Puffin pbk **£1.75**

A Bad Spell for the Worst Witch
[D1348] Puffin pbk **£1.75**

The Worst Witch Strikes Again
[D1349] Puffin pbk **£1.75**

PEARCE, PHILIPPA
Mrs Cockle's Cat
The gently humorous story of Old Mrs Cockle, a London balloon seller, who pines when her cat Peter vanishes and becomes so thin that she is swept out to sea with her balloons, and subsequently finds him aboard a fisherman's boat.
[D1350] Puffin pbk **£1.50**

Illustration from *Chips and Jessie* by Shirley Hughes (Collins pbk **£1.75**)

Old Belle's Summer Holiday NEW
(Illus. William Geldart)
For cat lovers, the closely observed story of Old Belle who leaves her home in the mill for a 'holiday' in the empty family house. Only the reader knows that the threatening cat who sends her home was her own reflection in the wardrobe mirror.
[D1350A] Deutsch hbk **£3.95**

The Battle of Bubble & Squeak
One of the finest pieces of fiction for young readers by a writer whose rare honesty ensures that this is not just a one-sided story about young Sid's conflict with his mother over his inherited gerbils, but a deeply moving account of family relationships.
[D1351] Puffin pbk **£1.25**

POWLING, CHRIS
"It's a rather strange story. To tell you the truth I'm not sure I believe it myself - and I'm telling it". This is the voice of a storyteller who knows how to take his readers straight into his fantasies, and keep them there.

Fingers Crossed: Stories for Nine-Year Olds (Ed. Powling)
[D1352] Hodder pbk **£1.99**

The Conker as Hard as a Diamond
When Alpesh finds a conker with extraordinary powers he develops an ambition to become conker champion of the world.
[D1353] Puffin pbk **£1.50**

The Phantom Carwash
A poetic Christmas Eve adventure about Lenny who longs for a carwash and finds one with magical powers that transforms a rag-and-bone man into a Santa Claus, in whom Lenny no longer really believes.
[D1354] Heinemann hbk **£2.50**

Ziggy and the Ice Ogre
When the fountains of ice cream in Fountain City stop, Ziggy sets out to find the missing ice ogre.
[D1355] Heinemann hbk **£2.50**

ROGERS, PAUL
Rain and Shine
Make-believe and the everyday mingle in these seven delightful stories about three children's secret play and daily misadventures in the overgrown garden and open fields behind their country home.
[D1356] Collins pbk **£1.75**

ROSEN, MIKE
Hairy Tales and Nursery Crimes
Poet Mike Rosen plays subversive games with traditional tales and rhymes here. The anarchic humour and wordplay in these retellings of such favourites as 'Goldisocks and the Wee Bears' and 'Pushing Boots' delights young readers.
[D1357] Collins pbk **£1.95**

SENDAK, MAURICE
Higglety Pigglety Pop!
Based on an old nursery rhyme this modern fairy tale concerns Jennie, a terrier who packs her bags and leaves home, because 'there must be more to life than having everything'. Jennie eats her way through a series of adventures to find true happiness as the star of the World Mother Goose Theatre.
[D1358] Puffin pbk **£1.95**

STEVENS, CARLA
Anna, Grandpa & the Big Storm
Trapped with her grandfather in an overhead train in a snow storm that really happened in New York in 1888, Anna listens to the passengers sharing stories of their lives. A beautifully judged adventure that is also about the storytelling that is an everyday part of our lives.
[D1359] Puffin pbk **£1.50**

Alice at the Queens's Croquet Ground from *Alice's Adventures in Wonderland* by Lewis Carroll, illustrated by Arthur Rackham (Heinemann hbk **£9.95**)

STORR, CATHERINE
In the *Polly* books Storr, a professional psychologist, takes the 'big bad wolf' and turns him with rich comic implausibility into the persistent but inept marauder of Polly's suburban life. Just as Polly uses her knowledge of fairytales to outwit the wolf, so readers can apply theirs to spot his latest blunder.

Clever Polly and the Stupid Wolf
[D1360] Puffin pbk **£1.75**

Polly and the Wolf Again
[D1361] Puffin pbk **£1.75**

Tales of Polly and the Hungry Wolf
[D1362] Puffin pbk **£1.99**

TAYLOR, LISA
The Pesters of the West NEW
Esther and Hester Pester, the terrible twins of Chipmunk Creek, are hot on the trail of escaped bank robber, Burnt Bottom Bert. But maybe he's in disguise... A rip-roaring slapstick farce.
[D1363] Collins 'Jets' pbk **£1.75**

THOMSON, PAT
Jacko NEW
New boy Dan makes a friend who tells him about her fantastic family as they walk home from school: her Granny's a tightrope walker; her Dad's an inventor, and they have a wolf for a pet. Is it a tall tale?
[D1364] Collins pbk **£1.75**

Trouble in the Cupboard
There's trouble in the toy cupboard when Jimmy the Guinea Pig is carried away by a wild dog. Can the toys and local cats rescue her?
[D1365] Corgi pbk **£1.95**

TOMLINSON, JILL
Gentle, sharply observed cumulative stories about animals in the kind of awkward situations all children know. Her tale about Plop, the baby owl who is afraid of the dark, is a particular favourite.

Penguin's Progress
[D1366] Magnet pbk **£1.50**

The Aardvark Who Wasn't Sure
[D1367] Magnet pbk **£1.50**

The Cat Who Wanted to Go Home
[D1368] Magnet pbk **£1.50**

The Gorilla Who Wanted to Grow Up
[D1369] Magnet pbk **£1.75**

The Hen Who Wouldn't Give Up
[D1370] Magnet pbk **£1.50**

The Otter Who Wanted to Know
[D1371] Magnet pbk **£1.50**

The Owl Who Was Afraid of the Dark
[D1372] Puffin pbk **£1.75**

UTTLEY, ALISON
Lavender Shoes: Eight Tales of Enchantment
[D1373] Faber pbk **£1.99**

WADDELL, MARTIN
Starting school is always a watershed: for Billy and his best friend 'Owl' it's an unsettling prospect, especially when they can play with Mr Bennet, alias 'the Spaceman', at the 'Old Folks' down the street. Using the device of the toy as alter ego, this is a gem of a story about the way in which children discover the world as a positive place through play, especially when adults know when and how to collude in their imaginings.

Owl and Billy
[D1374] Methuen pbk **£1.75**

Owl and Billy and the Space Days
In an inventive sequel, Mr Bennett introduces Billy to word play in a half-term romp running from 'Moon-day' and 'Chooseday' to 'Sat-on-day' and 'Funday'.
[D1375] Methuen pbk **£1.75**

WILLIAMS, URSULA MORAY
Gobbolino the Witch's Cat
The adventures of Gobbolino, a witch's cat who would much prefer to be an ordinary house cat.
[D1376] Puffin pbk **£1.99**

Adventures of the Little Wooden Horse
An epic quest story on a miniature scale in which a toy horse bravely ventures into the world beyond the toyshop, in order to save his master Uncle Peder. He encounters violence, death and evil before his final joyous reconciliation with the old toymaker.
[D1377] Puffin pbk **£1.99**

The Further Adventures of the Little Wooden Horse
[D1378] Puffin pbk **£1.99**

WILSON, BOB
Ging, Gang, Goolie It's an Alien!
A brilliant science fiction send-up about the hilarious confrontation between the 3rd Balsawood Scout Troop and an alien space monster, larded with jokes, puns, an invented inverted language and many more visual and verbal delights.
[D1379] Collins 'Jets' pbk **£1.75**

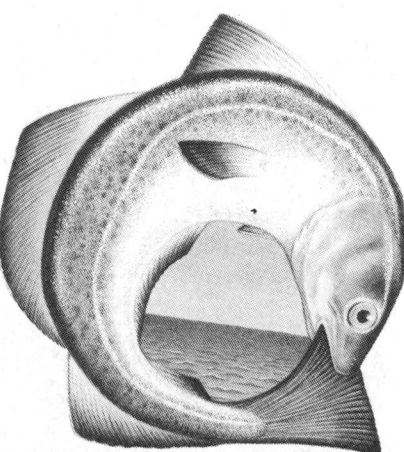

Illustration from *Alice's Adventures in Wonderland* by Lewis Carroll, illustrated by Anthony Browne (Julia MacRae Books hbk **£12.95**)

Guardian Children's Fiction Award

This prize of £500 goes to an outstanding work of fiction for children by a British or Commonwealth author, first published in the UK in the preceding year. Some of the classics of modern children's fiction can be found amongst the prizewinners, with works by authors such as *Leon Garfield, Alan Garner, Joan Aiken, Richard Adams* and *Nina Bawden*. Since 1982, the winners have been:

1982
MICHELLE MAGORIAN
Goodnight Mister Tom

Powerful and moving exploration of the blossoming relationship between a half-starved, maltreated evacuee and Mister Tom, a lonely old widower with whom he is billetted.
(Puffin pbk £2.50)

1983
ANITA DESAI
The Village by the Sea

Two teenagers faced with an unemployed father, a seriously ill mother and two young sisters take on the responsibility of looking after their family. Contrasting lifestyles and experiences of poverty on the Indian subcontinent are explored in this absorbing and extending novel.
(Penguin pbk £1.95)

1984
DICK KING-SMITH
The Sheep-Pig

Prolific writer who explores the reaction of ordinary people and animals to extra-ordinary creatures. In his humorous animal fantasies, King-Smith flies in the face of nature and asks the reader to consider various unlikely possibilities such as a pig who wants to fly but discovers instead he can swim.
(Puffin pbk £1.75)

1985
TED HUGHES
What is the Truth?

Subtitled 'A Farmyard Fable for the Young', this modern classic by the Poet Laureate combines vivid evocation of the natural world with a sense of myth and fantasy. It is two o'clock in the morning, and God and his son look down from a grassy hilltop on the spire and roofs of a village. Summoned in their sleep, the inhabitants one by one describe truly an animal they know well, in many different styles of verse.
(Faber pbk £4.95)

1986
ANNE PILLING
Henry's Leg

Henry has a passion for collecting all kinds of junk: wire coat hangers, copper tubing, a gas mask, even dead hedgehogs. By chance, he finds a leg from an old fashion dummy - and his possession of this object begins to land him in some dark and dangerous places. A story which combines adventure, humour and warmth.
(Puffin pbk £1.75)

1987
JAMES ALDRIDGE
The True Story of Spit MacPhee

The story of young Spit MacPhee who goes to live with his crazed grandfather in the Australian country town of St Helen. When the old man dies, there are people in the town who think Spit should be sent to an orphanage - but Spit is desperate to keep his freedom, and determine his own destiny. An adventure story with urgency and pace.
(Puffin pbk £1.95)

1988
RUTH THOMAS
The Runaways

'It is a book about two not-very-likeable London children, Julia (white) and Nathan (black), who, rejected by their peers, find comradeship and adventure together. Their experiences [on the run across the country to Exmoor where they finally give themselves up] bring out the best in them and eventually they become much more pleasant people.' *(Ruth Thomas)* (Beaver pbk £1.99)

1989
GERALDINE MCCAUGHREAN
A Pack of Lies

A series of brilliantly contrived pastiche short stories. Stephanie Nettell, chairman of this year's judging committee and Children's Book editor for the *Guardian* commented on *A Pack of Lies*: 'Here is a splendid introduction to the riches of style that lie waiting in books but more - it is an exuberant celebration of fiction's spell, a tribute to the power of story, a smiling surrender to the grip of the unruly imagination.'
(Oxford hbk £7.95)

Children's Classics

ALCOTT, LOUISA MAY

Set in New England against the background of the
Civil War, *Little Women*, published in England in
1868, was the first American children's novel to
become a classic. The characters' domestic trials, of
growing up and experiencing of first love, are based
on those of the four Alcott sisters themselves. The
novels' strengths lie in their masterly flesh and blood
characterization, and fine perception of what is real
and true in family relationships.

Good Wives
[D1391] Dent hbk **£7.50**
[D1392] Puffin pbk **£2.25**

Jo's Boys
[D1393] Dent hbk **£7.50**
[D1394] Puffin pbk **£2.25**

Little Men
[D1395] Dent hbk **£7.50**
[D1396] Puffin pbk **£1.75**

Little Women
[D1397] Collins hbk **£4.95**
[D1398] Dent hbk **£7.50**
[D1399] Puffin pbk **£1.75**

'B B'

Artist, naturalist and fisherman, 'B B', pseudonym
of D.J. Watkins-Pitchford, was an art master at Rugby
School. His books, written with a naturalist's
accuracy, are celebrations of the threatened
Northamptonshire countryside.

Brendon Chase
'BB' invites readers to identify with a whole
woodland environment in his matchless story of three
boys who run away to the forest of Brendon Chase,
pretend to live like Robin Hood and his Merrie Men,
but discover that open-air living has its
disadvantages.
[D1400] Methuen hbk **£7.95**

The Little Grey Men
Written in the form of the ancient quest tale, 'BB's
stories about the Little Grey Men - the last gnomes in
England are a classic mix of fantasy, country lore and
humour, and naturalist observation. In this, the first
novel, three gnomes - Baldmoney, Sneezewort and
Dodder - leave their Warwickshire home in an oak-
root to find their brother Cloudberry; in the sequel,
they seek a new home.
[D1401] Methuen hbk **£7.50**

**The Little Grey Men Go Down the
Bright Stream**
[D1402] Methuen hbk **£7.50**
[D1403] Methuen pbk **£1.95**

BAGNOLD, ENID

A British novelist and playwright, whose
extraordinarily successful story of a girl who wins a
horse in a raffle, and rides it to victory in the Grand
National, helped establish the 'pony story' as a
popular genre.

National Velvet
[D1404] Pan pbk **£1.99**

BALLANTYNE, R.M.

Apprenticed when sixteen to the Hudson Bay
Company, and sent to Canada, Ballantyne lived a
rough, remote life which gave him a taste for
writing adventure stories. Among his many books,
Coral Island is considered the finest, although he
had no specific knowledge of its Pacific Island
setting. Its emphasis is on episodic action, calling for
his young characters to show courage and
determination in confronting the events which face
them.

Coral Island (Abridged)
[D1405] Puffin pbk **£1.75**

J.M. Barrie, author of *Peter Pan in Kensington
Gardens* (Hodder & Stoughton hbk £7.95)

BARRIE, J.M.

Barrie's most famous creation, *Peter Pan* was based
on Barrie's view of himself as a 'boy who wouldn't
grow up'. First written as a play in 1904, the novel
appeared in 1911. One of the great myths of the 20th
century, it dramatizes the secure child's dream of
danger, of wild distances, and freedom from adult
rules. Readers play out the game of adventure in
'Never Never Land', before returning home like
Wendy, John and Michael to begin the more
complicated adventure of growing up.

Nursery Peter Pan (Illus. Mabel Lucie Attwell)
Easy reading edition.
[D1406] Hodder hbk **£4.95**

Peter Pan
[D1407] Bell & Hyman hbk **£8.95**

Peter Pan (Illus. Michael Hague)
Different artists have interpreted the complex figure
of Peter in different ways: from Attwell's popular but
inappropriately sentimentalized drawings which
suggest a nursery fantasy, to Foreman's view of Peter
as a puckish adventurer and Ormerod's as a kind of
'changling', to Hague's vision of Peter as an
adolescent, full of bravado but moody, displaying a
darker streak

Peter Pan (Illus. Jan Ormerod)
[D1408] Methuen hbk **£9.95**

Peter Pan (Illus. Jan Ormerod)
[D1409] Viking hbk **£7.95**
[D1410] Puffin pbk **£1.95**

Peter Pan and Wendy (Illus. Michael
Foreman)
[D1411] M Joseph hbk **£8.95**

Peter Pan and Wendy (Illus. Shirley Hughes)
Retold by Mary Byron.
[D1412] Hodder hbk **£4.95**

Peter Pan and Wendy (Illus. Mabel Lucie
Attwell)
[D1413] Hodder hbk **£16.95**

Peter Pan and Wendy (Illus. Michael
Foreman)
[D1414] M Jospeh pbk **£5.99**

Peter Pan in Kensington Gardens (Illus.
Arthur Rackham)
[D1415] Hodder hbk **£7.95**

BAUM, FRANK

In 1900, newspaperman Baum wrote a children's
novel based on a bedtime story he had told his sons.
The Wonderful Wizard of Oz was the first full-length
original American fantasy, and its fame has been
appropriately immortalized in film. Baum's modern
fairytales place traditional characters and their
modern counterparts (the Tin Man) in a distinctly
American landscape and contemporary social setting.
Despite stylistic inadequacies, his subversive stories
of the Kingdom of Oz delight with their mix of good
humour, excitement, magic and mystery.

Dorothy & the Wizard in Oz
[D1416] Puffin pbk **£1.95**

Emerald City of Oz
[D1417] Puffin pbk **£2.25**

Marvellous Land of Oz
[D1418] Puffin pbk **£1.99**

Ozma of Oz
[D1419] Puffin pbk **£1.99**

Patchwork Girl of Oz
[D1420] Puffin pbk **£1.99**

Road to Oz
[D1421] Puffin pbk **£1.75**

The Wizard of Oz
[D1422] Pavilion hbk **£9.95**
[D1424] Puffin pbk **£1.50**
(Illus. Michael Hague)
[D1423] Methuen hbk **£6.95**

Tik-Tok of Oz
[D1425] Puffin pbk **£1.75**

BURNETT, FRANCES HODGSON

Born in Manchester, Frances Hodgson emigrated with
her family to America, where in 1873 she married Dr
Swan Burnett. Her first domestic drama, *Little Lord
Fauntleroy*, was widely acclaimed on publication in
1885, but later this 'rags-to-riches' story was subject
to ridicule for the 'beauty' of its young hero. Sarah
Crewe in *A Little Princess* (1905) suffers a reversal
of Fauntleroy's fortunes. The question asked by both
books is 'What is a noble? What is a *true* princess?',
and their answer speaks to all young readers.

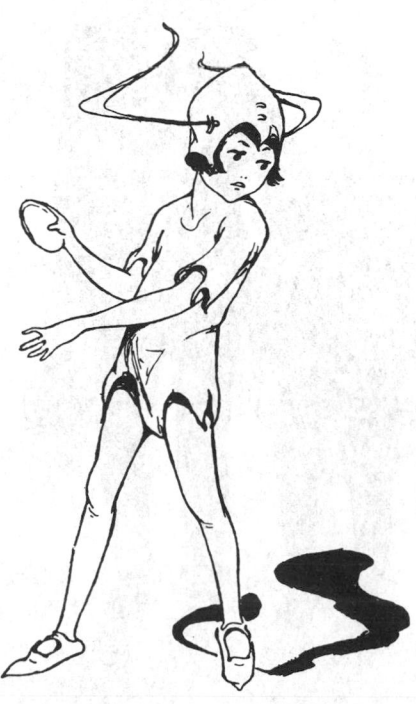

Peter Pan and his shadow from *Peter Pan and
Wendy* by J.M. Barrie, illustrated by Mabel Lucie
Attwell (Hodder & Stoughton hbk £16.95)

A Little Princess
[D1426] Puffin pbk **£1.95**
A Little Princess (Illus. Graham Rust) **NEW**
[D1427] M Joseph hbk **£12.95**
Little Lord Fauntleroy
[D1428] Dent hbk **£7.50**
[D1429] Puffin pbk **£1.95**
The Lost Prince
[D1430] Puffin pbk **£1.75**
The Secret Garden
Written in 1911, Hodgson's most memorable novel is a richer, more complex book; indeed a subversive one. Its emphasis on self-reliance rather than obedience was a distinctly modern ideal for children. Its central image, of the Arcadian walled garden, has always exerted a powerful hold on children's imaginations, as has its theme of transformation. Here, the growth of a neglected garden matches that of the main characters, from disagreeable, spoilt and lonely children into a true hero and heroine.
[D1431] Collins hbk **£4.95**
[D1432] Puffin pbk **£1.75**
(Illus. Graham Rust)
[D1433] M Joseph hbk **£10.95**
(Illus. Shirley Hughes)
[D1434] Gollancz hbk **£9.95**

CARROLL, LEWIS
At whatever age these stories are read (and they can be spoiled if introduced too soon), and at whatever level - as fairytale, inspired nonsense, political satire; as an exploration of violence, death or nothingness, or an attack on Christianity, they can enrich the imagination. First told by mathematician Rev. Charles Dodgson to the three Liddell girls on a boat-trip up the river Cherwell in 1862, the *Alice* books were of revolutionary importance in children's literature - opening up an imaginative new vein of fantasy and turning the accepted moral tale upside down.

Illustration from *The Secret Garden* by Frances Hodgson Burnett, illustrated by Shirley Hughes (Gollancz hbk £9.95)

Alice in Wonderland (Illus. Anthony Browne)
Controversial winner of the 1988 Kurt Maschler award, Browne's work delights in surrealism and the pictorial joke, in a way which perfectly captures the illogIcality, puns, conundrums and jokes of Carroll's text.
[D1435] Julia MacRae hbk **£12.95**
Alice in Wonderland (Illus. Arthur Rackham)
[D1435A] Hutchinson hbk **£9.95**
Alice in Wonderland (Illus. Tenniel)
Many modern artists have attempted fresh interpretations, but John Tenniel's original wood engravings provide a never-surpassed vision of Wonderland and its fantastic characters (the more expensive editions reproduce the Victorian texts in facsimile).
[D1436] Macmillan hbk/facsimile **£9.95**
[D1437] Macmillan hbk **£6.50**
[D1438] Puffin pbk **£1.25**
Through the Looking Glass (Illus. Tenniel)
[D1439] Macmillan hbk/facsimile **£10.95**
[D1440] Macmillan hbk **£6.50**
[D1441] Puffin pbk **£1.10**
Alice in Wonderland/Through the Looking Glass (Illus. Tenniel)
[D1442] Macmillan hbk/facsimile **£21.00**
[D1443] Puffin pbk **£1.95**
Alice's Adventures in Wonderland (Illus. Peter Weevers)
An original interpretation of 'Alice' in beautiful, watercolour paintings, which focus with great sensitivity on character; in particular, that of Alice, modelled on Weever's own eight-year old daughter.
[D1444] Hutchinson hbk **£12.95**

COLLODI, CARLO
After founding an Italian satirical magazine, Collodi turned to writing for children, as *"grown-ups are hard to satisfy"*. In *Pinocchio* - the story of a roguish puppet carved by a childless toymaker Gepetto for company - Collodi created an early version of the 'personified toy' story. Pinocchio yearns to become human but, despite his good resolutions, is given to misbehaviour and wickedness; finally, chastened by his adventures, his wish comes true.
Pinocchio (Illus. Roberto Innocenti)
[D1445] Cape hbk **£8.95**
[D1446] Puffin pbk **£1.75**

COOLIDGE, SUSAN
A nurse during the American Civil War, Susan Coolidge (the pen name of Sarah Chauncy Woolsey) was a prolific writer and poet. She created the inimitable Katy from memories of her own childhood, basing the fictional Carr family on her own brothers, sisters and cousin. The moral undertones of the three books - particularly evident in her disablement and recovery in *What Katy Did*, are countered by a popular, irrepressible heroine who has *"so many delightful schemes rioting in her brains, that all she wished for was ten pairs of hands to carry them out"*.
What Katy Did
[D1447] Dent hbk **£7.50**
[D1448] Puffin pbk **£1.25**
What Katy Did Next
[D1449] Puffin pbk **£1.75**
What Katy Did at School
[D1450] Puffin pbk **£1.10**

CROMPTON, RICHMAL
Crompton's William Brown has remained eleven years old throughout his existence; he has outlived innumerable fictional bad boys, due to her skill as a storyteller and appeal both to 'adult nostalgia' and the 'glee of children vicariously creating chaos' (*Signal Review 2*). All the stories are brilliantly contrived farcical melodramas of village life in the 1920s - a life disrupted by one well-intentioned but unruly boy. As social commentary and as a chronicle of a boy's

rebellion against the adult world, the stories are exceptionally funny with a satiric bite reminiscent of P.G. Wodehouse. Only a selection of the full range appears here.
Just William
[D1451] Macmillan pbk **£1.95**
Just William's Luck
[D1452] Macmillan pbk **£2.50**
Trust William's Luck
[D1455] Macmillan pbk **£1.95**
William
[D1456] Macmillan pbk **£1.95**
William Again
[D1459] Macmillan pbk **£1.25**
William and the Brain's Trust
[D1462] Macmillan pbk **£2.50**
William in Trouble
[D1463] Macmillan pbk **£1.95**
William the Bad
[D1464] Macmillan pbk **£1.95**
William the Conquerer
[D1465] Macmillan pbk **£1.95**
William the Detective
[D1466] Macmillan pbk **£1.99**
William the Dictator
[D1467] Macmillan pbk **£1.75**
William the Gangster
[D1469] Macmillan pbk **£1.50**
William the Good
[D1470] Macmillan pbk **£1.95**
William the Outlaw
[D1471] Macmillan pbk **£1.95**
William the Pirate
[D1472] Macmillan pbk **£1.50**
William the Rebel
[D1473] Macmillan pbk **£1.50**

DICKENS, CHARLES
An enduring classic, Dickens's *A Christmas Carol* (1843), best read aloud to children from the age of ten or so, has done much to explain the meaning of Christmas to young and old alike. A tale of extremes and disconcerting images, it tells the story of the miser Scrooge, who experiences a change of heart one Christmas Eve when the spirits of Christmas Past, Present and Future visit him and reveal to him his withered spirit and selfishness. Michael Foreman's pen and ink and full colour paintings capture the grotesque exaggeration of the characters; their desolation and joy, with rare emotional power.
A Christmas Carol
[D1477] Puffin pbk **£1.50**
(Illus. Michael Foreman)
[D1478] Gollancz pbk **£4.95**

FALKNER, J. MEADE
Originally written for adults, *Moonfleet* (1848) is today a classic children's adventure story. A tale of obsession set in Dorset, and encompassing treasure, smugglers, prison and shipwreck, it concerns John Trenchard, the fifteen-year old narrator, his determination to find a lost family diamond, and his growth to manhood through black and painful experience.
Moonfleet
[D1479] Puffin pbk **£1.50**

FORTESCUE, J.W.
A military historian, Fortescue wrote his *Story of a Red Deer* in 1897 to introduce his grandson to the wildlife of Devon through the story of the life and death of an Exmoor stag. While he reproduces the social hierarchy of his local parish quite naturally in the dialogue and relationships of the animals, it is his naturalist's sure eye and feel for the animal world and landscape which make his story memorable.
The Story of a Red Deer
[D1480] Canongate pbk **£1.95**

GRAHAME, KENNETH

The riverside adventures of the impossible, preposterous Toad and his long-suffering friends - Ratty, Mole and Badger - make Grahame's *Wind in the Willows* rich in humour, detail and language, and full of wisdom. Beneath its timeless daydream surface lies a complex tale that reveals much: not only about human nature (human quirks being comfortably housed in Grahame's animal heroes) but also about the virtues of the natural world as opposed to the mechanized one.

The Wind in the Willows (Illus. Shepard)
Interpreted by many artists, the original light-hearted illustrations of E.H. Shepard, and those of Arthur Rackham (his last work in 1939) who personalized Rat, Mole and Toad more effectively than Shepard, and more recently of American artist Michael Hague, who hints at the deeper meaning of the text in his Rackhamesque paintings, are the most popular.
[D1481] Methuen hbk/colour illus **£9.95**
[D1482] Methuen hbk/b&w illus **£5.95**
[D1483] Puffin pbk **£1.50**
[D1484] Methuen pbk **£1.95**
The Wind in the Willows (Illus. Rackham)
[D1485] Methuen hbk **£12.95**
[D1486] Methuen hbk **£8.95**
The Wind in the Willows (Illus. Michael Hague)
[D1487] Methuen hbk **£9.95**
The Wind in the Willows (Pop-Up)
[D1488] Methuen hbk **£6.95**
The Reluctant Dragon (Illus. E.H. Shepard)
A retelling of the legend of St George and the Dragon only this time neither protagonist wants to fight. The boy who acts as an intermediary saves their reputations by arranging a mock fight.
[D1489] Deutsch hbk **£4.95**
[D1490] Collins pbk **£1.75**

HAGGARD, H. RIDER

An outstanding writer of adventure stories, Haggard's far-flung locations, strong narratives and haunting images (who can forget the sudden aging of She in the Fire of Life?) have earned him an enduring readership.
King Solomon's Mines
Written for 'boys young and old', Haggard's adventure yarn tells of an English expedition to find the legendary wealth of King Solomon; an instant bestseller when published in 1885, it has remained popular ever since.
[D1491] Puffin pbk **£1.75**
She
Published in 1887, *She* is an 'exotic fantasy' about a mysterious priestess Ayesha, an apparently immortal woman of blinding beauty who rules a secret tribe in Africa, and her long-dead lover Kalikrates, re-incarnated as a handsome Englishman Leo.
[D1492] Methuen pbk **£1.99**

HOPE, ANTHONY

Hope gave a name - 'Ruritanian' - to the special kind of romantic adventure story he created in *The Prisoner of Zenda* (1894). The story of an Englishman who saves the throne of Ruritania by impersonating its young king, it was an immediate success, as was its sequel. Often imitated, but never bettered, these adventures are told with narrative speed, well-paced dialogue and an enticingly light touch.
Rupert of Hentzau
[D1493] Puffin pbk **£1.95**
The Prisoner of Zenda
[D1494] Puffin pbk **£1.50**

IRVING, WASHINGTON

The early 19th century revival of interest in the folktale in Europe and America led Washington Irving to retell traditional continental folktales set in the Hudson River valley. *Rip Van Winkle* (1819) is the story of a farmer who falls asleep on a hillside before the War of Independence, and wakes up 20 years later.
Rip Van Winkle (Illus. John Howe)
[D1495] Little, Brown hbk **£6.95**
Rip Van Winkle (Illus. Thomas Locker)
[D1496] Cape hbk **£6.95**
[D1497] Puffin pbk **£1.75**

JEFFERIES, RICHARD
Bevis, A Boy (Abridged)
A 'playing at adventure' and delight in nature story, and an ancestor of 'BB's *Brendon Chase*, this splendid novel of two boy's holiday experiences is semi-autobiographical and is set in a countryside similar to that of Jefferies' childhood home near Swindon in Wiltshire.
[D1498] Puffin pbk **£2.50**

KINGSLEY, CHARLES

However adults may read Rev. Kingsley's *The Water Babies* - as an attack on child labour and on pedagogic books of instruction, or as an almost 'Dantean' account of a soul's spiritual path to redemption, children read it for the infectious energy and power of his storytelling. This fairy-tale adventure tells the allegorical story of a runaway chimney-sweep, who plunges into a river, to find that he has been turned into an immortal 'water baby'. Kingsley's account of his magical/moral lessons and his dangerous underwater quest was unlike anything previously written for children.
The Water Babies (Abridged, illus. S. Rowe)
[D1499] Dragon World hbk **£9.95**
[D1500] Puffin pbk **£1.50**
The Water Babies (Illus. Harold Jones)
[D1501] Gollancz pbk **£3.95**

KIPLING, RUDYARD

Kipling's published work spans the two great genres of British children's literature: the 'realistic' adventure story, with its emphasis on action, heroism, and love of country, and fantasy, which comments on contemporary life through a 'fairy', or magical looking glass. Kipling's successive homes - India, a Devon boarding school, New England, and later the Sussex Downs, provide the settings for many of his books, each evoked with his intense and rich prose. The resonance and rhythm of his writing is such that it is often better heard, and then read.
Just So Stories
These mock-evolutionary tales of the 'Time of the Very Beginnings' reveal a poet's ear for nuances of sound and rhythm. The rich, riddling humour of Kipling's prose and its mystery are perfectly caught in his own witty black and white silhouette drawings.
[D1502] Macmillan hbk **£7.95**
[D1503] Puffin pbk **£1.95**
Just So Stories (Illus. Sophia Salter)
[D1504] Pavilion hbk **£7.95**
[D1505] Pavilion pbk **£5.99**
Just So Stories (Illus. Michael Foreman)
[D1506] Viking hbk **£7.95**
Kim
Like *Huckleberry Finn* this book is popular amongst adults and children of all ages. Kim passes through a series of adventures set against the most vivid and authentic picture we have of India, as Kipling knew it a century ago.
[D1507] Puffin pbk **£2.50**
Puck of Pook's Hill
Set in Kipling's own county of Sussex this book and its sequel, *Rewards and Fairies*, unfold across the span of English History from the Iron Age to the Edwardian present. Kipling's strong belief in the continuity of the nature of England, its history and inhabitants, is constantly revealed.
[D1508] Puffin pbk **£1.95**

Illustration from *The Lion, the Witch and the Wardrobe* by C.S. Lewis (Collins hbk **£6.95**, pbk **£2.25**)

Rewards & Fairies
[D1509] Puffin pbk **£2.50**
Stalky & Co
[D1510] Puffin pbk **£1.95**
The Jungle Book
The Jungle Book, "best beloved' of children's books, is a set of short stories, concerned primarily with the growth to manhood of the boy Mowgli, reared by wolves and taught jungle-lore and law by Baloo the Bear and Bagheera the Black Panther. Mowgli's jungle world is the human jungle too - the animals have personality as well as speech.
[D1511] Macmillan hbk **£7.50**
[D1512] Puffin pbk **£1.75**
(Illus. Michael Foreman)
[D1513] Viking hbk **£8.95**
Second Jungle Book
[D1514] Macmillan hbk **£7.50**
[D1515] Puffin pbk **£1.95**

LAMB, CHARLES
Tales From Shakespeare (10 +)
[D1516] Dent hbk **£7.50**
[D1517] Puffin pbk **£2.50**

LEWIS, C.S.

Influenced by his friend Tolkien, Lewis began his seven book cycle, *The Chronicles of Narnia*, after World War II; it tells the story of four children staying in a strange house, who find their way through a wardrobe into the snowbound land of Narnia. They are drawn into the struggle for power between the White Witch and Aslan the Lion, which re-enacts the story of Christianity through fantasy. For all their symbolism and Christian zeal, what remains in the reader's mind is the feeling of noble deeds, far distances, mysterious and magical places and events, and the sure division of right and wrong.

THE CHRONICLES OF NARNIA
(in reading order)
The Lion, the Witch & the Wardrobe
[D1518] Collins hbk £6.95
[D1519] Collins pbk £2.25
Prince Caspian
[D1520] Collins hbk £6.95
[D1521] Collins pbk £2.25
The Voyage of the Dawn Treader
[D1522] Collins hbk £6.95
[D1523] Collins pbk £2.25
The Silver Chair
[D1524] Collins hbk £6.95
[D1525] Collins pbk £2.25
The Horse & His Boy
[D1526] Collins hbk £6.95
[D1527] Collins pbk £2.25
The Magician's Nephew
[D1528] Collins hbk £6.95
[D1529] Collins pbk £2.25
The Last Battle
[D1530] Collins hbk £6.95
[D1531] Collins pbk £2.25

LOFTING, HUGH
The eccentric character of Dr Doolittle first appeared in the letters Lofting sent to his children during active service in World War I. Doctor turned vet / explorer / naturalist of Puddleby-on-the-Marsh, Doolittle is an 'animalinguist': this ability to converse with his animal patients sends him on adventures into worlds inconceivable to others. Lofting's black and white pen drawings, described as 'comic Japanese prints', perfectly match the unique invention and gravity with which the deadpan texts treat both serious and preposterous events.
Introducing Doctor Doolittle
[D1532] Puffin pbk £2.25
Doctor Doolittle & the Green Canary
[D1533] Puffin pbk £2.50
Doctor Doolittle & the Secret Lake
[D1534] Cape hbk £6.95
Doctor Doolittle in the Moon
[D1535] Cape hbk £6.95
Doctor Doolittle's Caravan
[D1536] Puffin pbk £2.25
Doctor Doolittle's Circus
[D1537] Puffin pbk £1.95
Doctor Doolittle's Garden
[D1538] Puffin pbk £2.25
Doctor Doolittle's Puddleby Adventures
[D1539] Puffin pbk £2.25
Doctor Doolittle's Return
[D1540] Puffin pbk £1.95
The Voyages of Doctor Doolittle
[D1541] Cape hbk £6.95

LONDON, JACK
An American who grew up in poverty, London took part in the Klondike gold rush in 1897, and drew on his experiences in his writing. His two most popular adventures tell the same story in reverse: in *Call of the Wild* Buck, a Saint Bernard, reverts to the untamed life of the wild north, while in *White Fang* a wild wolf is domesticated.
Call of the Wild
[D1542] Puffin pbk £1.99
White Fang
[D1543] Puffin pbk £1.50

MACDONALD, GEORGE
Magic and mysticism, fear and wonder, lie at the heart of the great Victorian fairytales of George Macdonald, a Scottish congregationalist minister turned author. Religious allegories, his stories are filled with beautiful images that remain in the mind: Irene's mysterious great-great grandmother forever spinning in her turret while wicked goblins tunnel beneath the mountain castle in *The Princess and the Goblin*, or

Diamond's dream adventures travelling to the land 'at the back of the North Wind'.
At the Back of the North Wind
[D1544] Puffin pbk £2.25
The Light Princess
[D1545] Canongate pbk £1.95
The Princess and the Curdie
[D1546] Puffin pbk £1.95
The Princess and the Goblin
[D1547] Puffin pbk £1.75

MARRYAT, CAPTAIN FREDERICK
After a colourful career at sea, Marryat began writing historical adventures for the general public, based on his experiences but also influenced by *Robinson Crusoe* and *Swiss Family Robinson*. Even *Children of the New Forest*, built around a Roundheads and Cavaliers theme, has Crusoesque elements: the Beverley children escape from their mansion destroyed by Cromwell's soldiers to a forester's cottage.
The Children of the New Forest
[D1548] Dent hbk £7.50
[D1549] Puffin pbk £2.25

MASEFIELD, JOHN
Poetic language, skilful plotting, and a real sense of magic as a mover and shaper of people and time, distinguish poet laureate Masefield's two fantasy 'boxes of delight'. The helter-skelter quest of the orphan Kay Harker to find his great grandfather's lost treasure before Abner Brown and his governess's witch gang is richly inventive, as is its wintry sequel: best read in the full hardback versions.
Midnight Folk
[D1550] Heinemann hbk £7.50
[D1551] Collins pbk £2.25
The Box of Delights
[D1552] Heinemann hbk £7.50
[D1553] Collins pbk £2.50

MILNE, A.A.
The continuing popularity of his children's books, based to some extent on nostalgia, has overshadowed Milne's other achievements. Drawn from life, the animals in his 'nursery' tales were based on toys from the well-stocked 1920s nursery of his son, the idealized Christopher Robin. Set in an Arcadian Hundred-Acre Wood, the 'Pooh' stories personify human character in the engaging Pooh, Piglet, Tigger et al. Milne's short, humorous episodes delight because 'with unparalleled dedication, they go nowhere in particular and return happily'. All editions are illustrated by E H Shepard; the more expensive editions are illustrated in colour.
Pooh Bear's Box (Four Paperbacks)
[D1554] Methuen pbk £6.90
Pooh Gift Box (Four Hardbacks)
[D1555] Methuen hbk £24.95
The House at Pooh Corner
[D1556] Methuen hbk £5.95
[D1557] Methuen hbk/colour illus £8.95
[D1558] Methuen pbk £1.95
Winnie-the-Pooh
[D1559] Methuen hbk £5.95
[D1560] Methuen hbk/colour illus £8.95
[D1561] Methuen pbk £1.95
The World of Pooh
Winnie-the-Pooh & *The House at Pooh Corner* with 8 colour plates.
[D1562] Methuen hbk £7.95
The House at Pooh Corner (Pop-Up)
[D1553] Methuen hbk £7.95
Winnie Ille Pu (Latin)
[D1564] Methuen hbk £6.95

MONTGOMERY, L.M.
A Canadian writer whose character was much like that of her plucky heroine in *Anne of Green Gables*, a

headstrong orphan who is sent by mistake to an elderly couple who expect a boy. Many sequels appeared in the first half of this century, and together they make an enduring collection of classic girl's stories.
Anne of Green Gables
[D1566] Puffin pbk £2.50
Anne of Avonlea
[D1565] Puffin pbk £2.50
Anne of Ingleside
[D1567] Puffin pbk £2.50
Anne of the Island
[D1568] Puffin pbk £2.50
Anne of the Windy Willows
[D1569] Puffin pbk £2.50
Anne's House of Dreams
[D1570] Puffin pbk £2.50
Rilla of Ingleside
[D1571] Harrap hbk £3.95

NESBIT, E.
A radical free-thinker and journalist, Nesbit described herself as a child in a grown-up world. She wrote, like the Mother in *The Railway Children*, to keep her family from starvation. Her humorous stories, whether 'fantasy' or 'family', reflect not only her theories but an Edwardian view of children and, however fantastic, are rooted in character, circumstance and period.
Five Children & It
The first of three stories (the others are *The Phoenix and the Carpet* and *The Story of the Amulet*) in which a magical character or object lift a family of five children from ordinary life and rush them, through time and space, from one richly-imagined adventure to another.
[D1572] Puffin pbk £1.50
House of Arden
[D1573] Puffin pbk £2.50
Last of the Dragons
[D1574] Puffin pbk £1.25
The Enchanted Castle
[D1575] Puffin pbk £1.95
The New Treasure-Seekers
[D1576] Puffin pbk £1.75
The Phoenix and the Carpet
[D1577] Puffin pbk £2.25
The Railway Children
This realistic story, packed with incident and adventure, of a city family living out a year in the country in straitened circumstances, is given emotional tension by the mysterious absence of the father.
[D1578] Dent hbk £6.95
[D1579] Puffin pbk £1.50
The Story of the Amulet
[D1580] Puffin pbk £1.95
The Story of the Treasure-Seekers
The three stories about the Bastable children - the others being *The New Treasure Seekers* and *The Wouldbegoods* - are splendid comic set-pieces in which the children's efforts to go treasure seeking 'to restore the fallen fortunes of the House of Bastable' have unpredictable outcomes.
[D1581] Puffin pbk £1.50
The Wouldbegoods
[D1582] Puffin pbk £1.95

NORTON, MARY
In the *Borrowers* Mary Norton (herself very short-sighted) creates a perfectly proportioned and realized world of tiny people who live under the floor of a country house, a Lilliputian race in danger of extinction, which exists by 'borrowing' from 'human beans'. The adventures of the Clock family - Pod, Homily and daughter Arietty - in the nightmare world which is our everyday reality, are rivettingly described as, forced to escape the disaster of being 'seen', they emigrate. Fused with tenderness and

poetry, the stories sustain absolute belief in these miniature beings, 'snipped off human edges, who are completely themselves and yet, comically and sadly, images of human nature.'

The Borrowers
[D1583] Dent hbk **£6.95**
[D1584] Puffin pbk **£1.75**
The Borrowers Afield
[D1585] Puffin pbk **£1.75**
The Borrowers Afloat
[D1586] Puffin pbk **£1.75**
The Borrowers Aloft
[D1587] Puffin pbk **£1.75**
The Borrowers Avenged
[D1588] Puffin pbk **£1.95**
The Complete Borrowers Stories
[D1589] Puffin pbk **£6.95**

RANSOME, ARTHUR
Set in the Lake District, the Norfolk Broads and other vividly drawn locations, Ransome's holiday stories about the Walker (Swallow), Blackett (Amazon) and 'Two Ds' families continue to enthrall children. They are the kind of heady, self-sufficient adventures about which all children day-dream, combined with meticulous descriptions of the practical details of the camping, sailing and fishing needed to undertake them.

Big Six
[D1590] Cape hbk **£8.95**
[D1591] Puffin pbk **£2.99**
Coot Club
[D1592] Cape hbk **£8.95**
[D1593] Puffin pbk **£2.95**
Coots in the North and Other Stories
[D1594] Cape hbk **£6.95**
Great Northern
[D1595] Cape hbk **£8.95**
[D1596] Puffin pbk **£2.95**
Missee Lee
[D1597] Cape hbk **£8.95**
[D1598] Puffin pbk **£2.95**
Peter Duck
[D1599] Cape hbk **£8.95**
[D1600] Puffin pbk **£2.50**
Picts & the Martyrs
[D1601] Cape hbk **£7.95**
[D1602] Puffin pbk **£2.95**
Pigeon Post
[D1603] Cape hbk **£8.95**
[D1604] Puffin pbk **£2.50**
Secret Water
[D1605] Cape hbk **£7.95**
[D1606] Puffin pbk **£2.50**
Swallowdale
[D1607] Cape hbk **£8.95**
[D1608] Puffin pbk **£2.50**
Swallows & Amazons
[D1609] Cape hbk **£8.95**
[D1610] Puffin pbk **£2.50**
Swallows & Amazons Forever
[D1611] Puffin pbk **£2.50**
We Didn't Mean to Go to Sea
[D1612] Cape hbk **£8.95**
[D1613] Puffin pbk **£2.50**
Winter Holiday
[D1614] Cape hbk **£7.95**
[D1615] Puffin pbk **£1.95**

SEWELL, ANNA
Written to protest against the serious cruelties to which horses and other animals were subjected, *Black Beauty* (1877) - which draws on the author's own experiences - tells the story of a horse whose life on a country estate and as a London cab horse, reveals unbearable hardship, degradation and tragedy before a joyous ending.

Black Beauty (Illus. Charles Keeping)
Keeping's inspired black-and-white, or brown and green-tinted illustrations with their assured sense of period (essential in a story that comments on Victorian society) depict horse and man with unique intensity.
[D1616] Gollancz hbk **£9.95**
[D1617] Puffin pbk **£1.25**
Black Beauty (Adapted by Robin McKinley, illus. Susan Jeffers)
[D1618] Macmillan pbk **£4.99**

ST EXUPERY, ANTOINE DE
This poetic tale of wonder and love was the masterpiece of its French writer and illustrator. *The Little Prince* is a touching and profound fable about the nature of existence, explored through the adventures and discoveries of a solitary, child prince. St Exupery's delicate wash drawings are as simple and as lovely as his verbal images.

The Little Prince
[D1621] Heinemann hbk **£6.95**
[D1622] Pan pbk **£1.50**
[D1623] Pan pbk illus. **£4.99**

STEVENSON, R.L.
The adventure stories of this prolific Scottish author have never gone out of fashion, even though he himself denigrated them. *Treasure Island* (1883), his masterpiece, forever ousted the didactic from the adventure yarn, and through its powerful characterization blurred conventional notions of right and wrong. Stevenson's sure sense of his audience is as evident in these swashbuckling tales as in his *Child's Garden of Verses*, where children played at adventure.

Kidnapped
[D1624] Collins hbk **£4.95**
[D1625] Puffin pbk **£1.75**
The Strange Case of Dr Jekyll & Mr Hyde / The Suicide Club
[D1626] Puffin pbk **£1.50**
Treasure Island
[D1628] Puffin pbk **£1.50**
(Illus. N.C. Wyeth)
[D1627] Gollancz hbk **£9.95**

TOLKIEN, J.R.R.
The Hobbit
One of this century's outstanding fantasy adventures, *The Hobbit* is an infinitely 'expandable' book. Heroism is its subject; the quest structure provides its shape; the creation of a sharply realized secondary world, Middle Earth, its fascination, and its moral themes, its reverberating quality. Bilbo Baggins, a sort of 'Hornblower with fur', is persuaded by the Wizard Gandolf to try to destroy the Dragon Smaug, and sets out to do so...
[D1629] Unwin deluxe hbk **£20.00**
[D1630] Unwin hbk **£8.95**
[D1631] Unwin hbk **£2.50**
(Illus. Michael Hague)
[D1632] Unwin hbk **£14.95**
LORD OF THE RINGS (in reading order)
Fellowship of the Ring
A broader and darker work than *The Hobbit*, *The Lord of the Rings* was written during the Second World War, and further champions the survival of the small and ordinary against impossible odds and deadly evil.
[D1633] Unwin pbk **£3.50**
The Two Towers
[D1634] Unwin pbk **£3.50**
Return of the King
[D1635] Unwin pbk **£3.50**
The Trilogy
[D1636] Unwin pbk **£8.95**

TRAVERS, P.L.
A professional dancer and actress, P.L. Travers came to England from Australia at the age of seventeen.

The first of what became a series, *Mary Poppins* was written while she was recovering from an illness in the early 1930s.
Mary Poppins
The eccentric character of Mary Poppins, visually established in Mary Shepard's pen and ink drawings, dominates the books: predictably unpredictable, magic but respectable, Nannie and 'God' at once, she whisks the Banks children to wild, fantastic worlds which mirror, or make a nonsense of, our own.
[D1637] Collins hbk **£5.95**
[D1638] Puffin pbk **£1.75**
Mary Poppins Comes Back
[D1639] Puffin pbk **£2.25**
Mary Poppins Opens the Door
[D1640] Puffin pbk **£1.95**
Mary Poppins and the House Next Door
[D1641] Collins hbk **£5.95**
Mary Poppins in Cherry Tree Lane
[D1642] Puffin pbk **£1.50**
Mary Poppins in the Park
[D1643] Puffin pbk **£2.50**

TWAIN, MARK
Set on the Mississippi, childhood home of S.L. Clemens, *Tom Sawyer* (1876) and its brilliant sequel have an almost mythic position in the American consciousness. Both are adventure stories, but their heroes are children, and their morality is subversively unconventional. *Tom Sawyer* recounts the boyish pranks of Tom and Huck Finn (based on the Clemens boyhood), while the darker *Huckleberry Finn* charts Huck's and the runaway slave Jim's journey on the Mississippi river.
Adventures of Huckleberry Finn
[D1644] Puffin pbk **£1.75**
The Adventures of Tom Sawyer
[D1645] Dent hbk **£6.95**
[D1646] Puffin pbk **£1.50**
The Prince and the Pauper
[D1647] Puffin pbk **£1.95**

VERNE, JULES
Although not written for children, Verne's 'speculative adventures' were immediately popular with young readers. These early Science Fiction stories were suggested to Verne by the scientific adventures of the day, but their science was at least partly Verne's own invention.
Around the World in Eighty Days
[D1648] Dent hbk **£7.50**
Journey to the Centre of the Earth
[D1649] Puffin pbk **£1.95**
Twenty Thousand Leagues under the Sea
[D1650] Puffin pbk **£2.50**

WILLIAMS, MARGERY
The Velveteen Rabbit (Illus. William Nicholson)
This poetic toy fantasy of friendship and devotion between a boy and his 'velveteen rabbit' develops a theme popular in 'nursery' stories: the notion that, loved long enough, a toy will become 'real'. There is a perfect fusion between text and the illustrations of William Nicholson: colour lithographs on stone.
[D1651] Heinemann hbk **£5.95**
The Velveteen Rabbit (Illus. Michael Hague)
[D1652] Mammoth pbk **£2.50**

WYSS, J.D.
Swiss Family Robinson
Robinson Crusoe was the inspiration for the Swiss Pastor J.D. Wyss's adventure story. Now a period piece, it recounts the experiences of a shipwrecked family as they adapt to desert island life, and put its resources (often hilariously) to their use.
[D1653] Dent hbk **£7.50**
[D1654] Puffin pbk **£1.95**

Age 8 - 12

At this age almost all of the riches of children's literature are now within the grasp of young readers. Picture books are of a very high quality: here you will find a delight in language and its possibilities (look at the virtuosity of Briggs' and Goscinny's punning), brilliant adaptations of sophisticated literary genres, conventions and narrative technique in an immediately accessible format (the detective novel in Hergé, satire in Briggs, and irony and farce in Wilson), and an innovative use of the strip format. Such works can be crucial in the process of children becoming independent readers, and in their moving away from pictures and on to text.

In children's fiction we find, according to Joan Aitken, 'everything that is in adult writing, but squeezed into smaller compass, in a form suited to children's capacities'. The emotional range is wide - the remaining differences lie in viewpoint, and the need for a happy ending. By journeying imaginatively into the experiences of others, children return better able to understand their own - the journeys offered here may be familiar, fantastical, funny, or gripping, but they provide the chance to grow up through fiction, and learn more of the world.

Picture Books

BRIGGS, RAYMOND
In his work for older children (and adults) Briggs creates picture books that have been described as 'satirical novels in strip'. Certainly readers need enough literary experience to appreciate his satire: not only the anarchic pastiche of literary genre and conventions, the misquotations, puns, dictionary definitions, footnotes, and adaptable book titles, but also the Briggs version of 'the many languages through which we fail to communicate with each other in Britain - official bureaucratic, journalistic advertisement, "high-faluting" legal...' (Moss, *Picture Books for Young People*). His artistry is elaborate, precise and calculated, and uses the strip format in unconventional ways to give a comic, approachable appearance to stories which both entertain readers, and offer a challenging critique of contemporary Britain.

Fungus the Bogeyman (10 +)
Briggs' 'cult' guide to Bogeydom invites the reader into the dank green alternative underground world of the Bogeyman, whose life mirrors our own with riotous comic anarchy. Fungus has a wife ('Drear'), eats 'Flaked Corns' for breakfast, reads 'The Expurge' and 'Cider with Bogey', visits the Odeum, and 'works' on the 'surface' raising night-time mayhem (and boils) among humans. Beneath the scatological jokes, word play, and invention lies a provocative challenge to 'civilised life'.
[D1660] H Hamilton pbk **£3.50**
[D1661] H Hamilton pop-up **£8.95**
Gentleman Jim (10 +)
The heart-rending but comic story of Jim Bloggs, an uneducated lavatory attendant, who decides to better himself by putting his Mittyesque fantasies into practice, as Gentleman Jim the highway robber. But when he holds up a police car on the M1, he lands in prison.
[D1662] H Hamilton pbk **£2.95**
When the Wind Blows (13 +)
This disturbingly bleak and (literally) devastating strip explores the possible results of a nuclear holocaust for those who blindly follow Government cant and instructions. Dramatic use of colour and underplayed comic dialogue emphasise the pathetic bewilderment of old Jim Bloggs and his wife. The

title - a phrase from the nursery rhyme 'Rock-a-bye Baby' - makes its own ironic comment.
[D1663] Penguin pbk **£3.95**

BROWNE, ANTHONY
Surreal imagery, visual jokes, and symbolic use of colour characteristically provide a comic, attention-grabbing pictorial framework for each of these thought-provoking picture books. Each explores serious, painful contemporary issues in an extraordinary way: how to cope with a newly single and self-absorbed parent (*Gorilla*); male chauvinism (*Piggybook*); and the modern obsession with body culture and self-image (*Willy the Wimp* and *Willy the Champ*). See also *Picture Books: Pre-School & 6-9*.
Gorilla
Lonely Hannah, obsessed with Gorillas, longs to see them in the Zoo as a birthday treat with her father. She does just this in a haunting nightime fantasy with a gorilla father, and awakens, on her birthday, to find her wish come true.
[D1664] Magnet pbk **£1.95**
Piggybook
[D1665] Magnet pbk **£1.95**
The Tunnel NEW
An original fairytale in the vein of Browne's modern *Hansel and Gretel*. It takes danger and possible loss to connect a brother and sister, fractiously and stereotypically opposed in character and action. Jack vanishes down a tunnel, and Rose follows into a threatening fairy tale forest to find him turned to stone. Powerful images of fantasy, fear and fairy story mirror Rose's inner and outer worlds as she frees him.
[D1666] Julia MacRae hbk **£5.95**
Willy the Champ
[D1667] Magnet pbk **£1.95**
Willy the Wimp
[D1668] Magnet pbk **£1.95**

CUTLER, IVOR
Herbert: Five Stories
Sometimes it's easier to pretend you are something else than to face up to growing up. Herbert tries out life at home and at school in a variety of animal guises - chicken, elephant, kangaroo and finally a Herbert - before deciding to be himself. Beneath the quirky, preposterous surface of poet Cutler's text lies a deeper message about the value of fantasy play; Patrick Benson's richly humorous cross-hatched pen and ink illustrations display a matching exuberant imagination.
[D1669] Walker pbk **£2.99**

GOSCINNY & UDERZO
The popularity of these French comic strips about Asterix the Gaul and his companions Obelix, Getafix and Vitalstatix, is universal. Goscinny's satirical cops and robbers approach to the Gallic wars, his irreverent jibes at the history of the Roman Empire, and the perpetual theme of the clever little fellow outwitting brute force makes for irresistible reading. The wit of Goscinny's texts - notable for their punning and word-play - is matched by the knockabout humour of Uderzo's cartoons. For older readers there are literary and artistic allusions to pick up. Editions are also available in Latin and other languages.
Asterix & Caesar's Gift
[D1670] Hodder pbk **£2.95**
Asterix & Cleopatra
[D1671] Hodder pbk **£2.95**
Asterix & Son
[D1672] Hodder pbk **£2.95**
Asterix & the Big Fight
[D1673] Hodder pbk **£2.95**
Asterix & the Black Gold
[D1674] Hodder pbk **£2.95**
Asterix & the Cauldron
[D1675] Hodder pbk **£2.95**

Asterix & the Chieftain's Shield
[D1676] Hodder pbk **£2.95**
Asterix & the Golden Sickle
[D1677] Hodder pbk **£2.95**
Asterix & the Goths
[D1678] Hodder pbk **£2.95**
Asterix & the Great Crossing
[D1679] Hodder pbk **£2.95**
Asterix & the Great Divide
[D1680] Hodder pbk **£2.95**
Asterix & the Laurel Wreath
[D1681] Hodder pbk **£2.95**
Asterix & the Magic Carpet
[D1682] Hodder pbk **£2.95**
Asterix & the Normans
[D1683] Hodder pbk **£2.95**
Asterix & the Olympic Games
[D1684] Hodder pbk **£2.95**
Asterix & the Roman Agent
[D1685] Hodder pbk **£2.95**
Asterix & the Soothsayer
[D1686] Hodder pbk **£2.95**
Asterix & the Banquet
[D1687] Hodder pbk **£2.95**
Asterix in Belgium
[D1688] Hodder pbk **£2.95**
Asterix in Britain
[D1689] Hodder pbk **£2.95**
Asterix in Corsica
[D1690] Hodder pbk **£2.95**
Asterix in Spain
[D1691] Hodder pbk **£2.95**
Asterix in Switzerland
[D1692] Hodder pbk **£2.95**
Asterix the Gaul
[D1693] Hodder pbk **£2.95**
Asterix the Gladiator
[D1694] Hodder pbk **£2.95**
Asterix the Legionary
[D1695] Hodder pbk **£2.95**
Asterix versus Caesar
[D1696] Hodder pbk **£2.95**
How Obelix Fell in the Magic Potion When He Was a Little Boy NEW
[D1696A] Hodder hbk **£4.99**
Obelix & Co
[D1697] Hodder pbk **£2.95**
The Mansions of the Gods
[D1698] Hodder pbk **£2.95**
The Twelve Tasks of Asterix
[D1699] Hodder pbk **£2.95**
UDERZO, ALBERT
Carnet de Croquis NEW
A 'sketchbook' by Uderzo, illustrator of the *Asterix* strip narratives, which gives a unique insight into how an Asterix book takes shape from research to reference documentation, to working methods and techniques. In French.
[D1700] Hodder hbk **£30.00**

HERGE
A Belgian cartoonist whose exceptional skills as a storyteller and artist met in his strip 'detective' stories about Tintin, the boy detective. Tintin was an inspired creation: a resourceful, courageous, kind, fresh-faced, independent youth - a 'modern folk hero' (like Ardizzone's 'Tim', only older), who always overcomes his (more powerful) adversaries through a combination of ingenuity, wit, bravery and good fortune. In a series of adventures around the globe (each country evoked with brilliant and memorable exactness), he is accompanied by his faithful, ironical dog Snowy, salty 'Blustering Barnacles' Captain Haddock and other recurring and unforgettable characters, such as the absent-minded Professor Calculus, and the impossibly foolish Thompson twins. The virtuoso dialogue, fast-moving plots and perfectly controlled pictorial pace of Hergé's mysteries have delighted readers for over 60 years.

Illustration from Hergé's *Adventures of Tintin*
(Methuen pbk £2.50)

Cigars of the Pharaoh
[D1701] Methuen pbk **£2.25**
Destination Moon
[D1702] Methuen pbk **£2.50**
Explorers on the Moon
[D1703] Methuen pbk **£2.25**
Flight 714
[D1704] Methuen pbk **£2.25**
King Ottokar's Sceptre
[D1705] Methuen pbk **£2.50**
Lake of Sharks
[D1706] Methuen pbk **£2.25**
Land of Black Gold
[D1707] Methuen pbk **£2.50**
Prisoners of the Sun
[D1708] Methuen pbk **£2.50**
Red Rackham's Treasure
[D1709] Methuen pbk **£2.50**
The Black Island
[D1710] Methuen pbk **£2.25**
The Blue Lotus
[D1711] Methuen pbk **£2.50**
The Broken Ear
[D1712] Methuen pbk **£2.50**
The Calculus Affair
[D1713] Methuen pbk **£2.50**
The Castafiore Emerald
[D1714] Methuen pbk **£2.50**
The Crab with the Golden Claws
[D1715] Methuen pbk **£2.50**
The Making of Tintin
A bumper edition containing the complete and
unabridged volumes of *The Secret of the Unicorn*
and *Red Rackham's Treasure*, together with a final
chapter explaining Hergé's detailed research for each
story. Early sketches show the development of the
Tintin character.
[D1716] Methuen hbk **£9.95**
**The Making of Tintin in the World
of the Inca** NEW
Another special edition of two Tintin favourites - *The
Seven Crystal Balls* and *Prisoners of the Sun*.
[D1717] Methuen hbk **£9.95**
**The Making of Tintin: Mission to
the Moon** NEW
[D1717A] Methuen hbk **£10.95**
The Red Sea Sharks
[D1718] Methuen pbk **£2.50**
The Secret of the Unicorn
[D1719] Methuen pbk **£2.50**
The Seven Crystal Balls
[D1720] Methuen pbk **£2.50**

The Shooting Star
[D1721] Methuen pbk **£2.50**
The Tintin Companion NEW
How do you tell the difference between the
Thompson twins? What did Tintin get up to in
Moscow? Which character did Hergé himself most
want to be? Find the answers to these and hundreds
more questions in this first guide for Tintin readers,
illustrated with sketches and strip never seen in
Britain before.
[D1722] Methuen hbk **£7.95**
The Tintin Poster Book NEW
Twenty plates from the first seven Tintin
stories enlarged and ready to hang on the wall.
[D1722A] Methuen pbk **£12.95**
Tintin & the Picaros
[D1723] Methuen pbk **£2.50**
Tintin in America
[D1724] Methuen pbk **£2.25**
Tintin in Tibet
[D1725] Methuen pbk **£2.25**
Tintin's Moon Adventures
[D1726] Methuen pbk **£2.95**
PEETERS, BENOIT
Tintin and the World of Hergé NEW
An authoritative account of Hergé's artistic life and
his development of the character of Tintin from his
first appearance in 1929.
[D1726A] Methuen hbk **£12.95**

MCAFEE, ANNALENA & BROWNE, ANTHONY
Kirsty Knows Best
[D1727] Magnet pbk **£1.95**
The Visitors Who Came to Stay
An exploration of how Kate, who lives alone with her
introverted father, reacts to the arrival of a new
parental partner and her son. Katy's changing
response from disturbed to delighted is recorded in
Browne's characteristic illustrations.
[D1728] H Hamilton pbk **£3.50**

SENDAK, MAURICE
Outside Over There
While 'Papa was away at sea, and Mama in the
Arbor', Ida adventures in her daydreams 'outside over
there' to rescue her baby sister, stolen by goblins
when she played her wonder horn 'but never
watched'. Music is the key to the baby's loss and retrieval in this haunting third story in Sendak's trilogy
exploring childhood fantasy. 'Flowing romantic
pictures' counter and capture its darker undertones.
[D1729] Bodley hbk **£5.95**
[D1730] Puffin pbk **£3.95**

WADDELL, MARTIN
Going West (Illus. Philippe Dupasquier)
A serious exploration in strip format of a pioneer
family's trek West. The flat statements of the child
narrator are counterpointed by Dupasquier's dramatic
narrative illustrations which chronicle the family's
struggle to survive (not always successfully, for a
child dies) against the elements, illness and Indians.
[D1731] Puffin pbk **£2.50**

WILSON, BOB
Straight-faced farces, recounted in Stanley Holloway-
type rhyming monologues (interrupted by bubble talk)
and strip, about the improbable adventures of young
Stanley in Huddersgate 'up North where it's boring
and slow'. Riotously funny.
**Stanley Bagshaw and the
Fourteen-Foot Wheel**
[D1732] Puffin pbk **£1.75**
**Stanley Bagshaw and the Mafeking
Square Cheese Robbery**
[D1733] Puffin pbk **£2.25**
**Stanley Bagshaw and the Rather
Dangerous Miracle Cure**
[D1734] Puffin pbk **£2.25**

**Stanley Bagshaw and the Short-Sighted
Football Trainer**
[D1735] Puffin pbk **£2.25**
**Stanley Bagshaw and the Twenty-Two
Ton Whale**
[D1736] Puffin pbk **£1.75**

Fiction

AHLBERG, ALLAN
Son of a Gun
A 'Wild West' spoof.
[D1737] Puffin pbk **£1.75**
Woof
Comic complications follow a boy's discovery that he
can turn into a dog.
[D1738] Puffin pbk **£1.99**

AIKEN, JOAN
HISTORICAL FANTASIES (in reading order)
The Wolves of Willoughby Chase
Rich in language, riotously funny, and highly
idiosyncratic, Aiken's gothic historical fantasies re-
invent history: set in an England in which the
Hanoverian succession did not happen, and Good
King James came to the throne, also one ravaged by
wolves who have migrated through the Channel
Tunnel. In this tale of double-dyed villainy two
children, aided by loyal servants, foil the plots of their
wicked governess.
[D1739] Puffin pbk **£1.99**
Black Hearts in Battersea
Aiken's brave ingenious heroine Dido Twite, a
cockney waif, is first introduced in this Dickensian
tale of a Hanoverian conspiracy against the
Tudor-Stuart monarchy: a subject pursued in later
books.
[D1740] Puffin pbk **£2.50**
Night Birds on Nantucket
[D1741] Puffin pbk **£2.50**
The Stolen Lake
[D1742] Puffin pbk **£2.95**
The Cuckoo Tree
[D1743] Puffin pbk **£2.95**
Dido and Pa
[D1744] Cape hbk **£7.95**
HISTORICAL NOVELS (in reading order)
Bridle the Wind
Set in the 19th century, these three thrilling novels
concern the picaresque quest of the orphaned Felix
Brooke to uncover the identity of his unknown father,
a quest which takes him from Spain to England and
back again.
[D1745] Puffin pbk **£2.95**
Go Saddle the Sea
[D1746] Puffin pbk **£2.50**
Teeth of the Gale
[D1747] Cape hbk **£6.95**

ALCOCK, VIVIEN
The Cuckoo Sister
The 'cuckoo sister' is Emma, snatched from her pram
before Kate was born and now thirteen and streetwise,
newly returned to her middle-class home.
[D1748] Collins pbk **£1.95**
The Haunting of Cassie Palmer
An original ghost story in which the daughter of an
unsuccessful clairvoyant raises a spirit (malign or
benevolent?) from the local cemetery, who offers to
save the family's dwindling fortunes - or does he?
[D1749] Collins pbk **£1.95**
The Monster Garden
A touching variant on the Frankenstein theme in
which Frankie, determined to prove to her scientist
father that she is brighter than he thinks, takes some
tissue from his laboratory and, to her surprise, breeds
a monster with human emotions. Favouritism, gender

and the dangers of genetic engineering are themes broached by Alcock's compelling narrative.
[D1750] Collins pbk **£1.95**

The Mysterious Mr Ross
Who is the mysterious Albert Ross rescued by Felicity from a rock in the sea? He transforms the lives of all he meets in a seaside town, and then vanishes. Beneath the light surface of this unusual story, Alcock explores complex concerns: favouritism, hero-worship, and a first boy-girl relationship.
[D1751] Collins pbk **£1.95**

The Stone Walkers
An eerie fantasy leavened with humour about a temporarily fostered girl whose only friend is a statue. When the statue mysteriously comes to life as a stonewalker, friendship turns to menace.
[D1752] Collins pbk **£1.95**

The Trial of Anna Cotman   **NEW**
When new girl Anna challenges the rules of the school Society of Masks, originally set up to combat bullying, but now a sinister power group run by bullies, she is put 'on trial'. A dark, chilling study of childhood corruption and abuse of power.
[D1753] Methuen hbk **£7.95**

ALEXANDER, LLOYD
Based on the Welsh Mabinogion legend and built around the traditional quest, this rich, funny fantasy sequence chronicles a hero's apprenticeship, as Taran grows from assistant pigkeeper to High King of Prydain. In reading order:

The Book of Three
[D1754] Collins pbk **£1.95**

The Black Cauldron
[D1755] Collins pbk **£1.95**

The High King
[D1756] Collins hbk **£1.95**

The Castle of Llyr
[D1757] Collins pbk **£1.95**

Taran Wanderer
[D1758] Collins pbk **£2.25**

ALLEN, JUDY
Travelling Hopefully
Clare learns that there are many kinds of 'travelling' when she is sent on a breakneck tour of Devon with her Aunt Maggie, a travel writer. Convinced that this 'holiday' is a cover for something alarming happening to her mother, who is about to have a late baby, Clare journeys uneasily. Beneath the sharp comedy, Allen explores how we learn to live with one another.
[D1759] Corgi pbk **£1.99**

ARMSTRONG, WILLIAM H.
Sounder
The indomitable spirit of a black sharecropper jailed for stealing food for his starving family is mirrored by his wounded hunting dog who hangs on to life until his return. A powerful story of injustice, hardship and the endurance neccessary to survive.
[D1760] Puffin pbk **£1.25**

ASHLEY, BERNARD
The Trouble with Donovan Croft
Ashley draws on his experience as a headmaster in a large multi-racial London school in this powerful story of a fostered West Indian boy, whose power of speech has been affected by the shock of being removed from home and parents.
[D1761] Puffin pbk **£1.50**

BABBITT, NATALIE
An American author-illustrator who draws on folk and fairy tales for her storylines, patterns and themes, but adapts them to her own ends, and for modern times.

The Eyes of Amaryllis
A gripping ghost story filled with memorable characters, living and dead, which begins when a sea-captain's widow sends her granddaughter to search the beach for a message from her husband, lost at sea with his crew thirty years before.
[D1762] Faber pbk **£2.99**

The Search for Delicious
A witty poetic fantasy that touches lightly on the place of myth, story and song in our lives, and on the power of words. In a country that has long forgotten its fairytale origins and whose concerns are superficial, a courtly squabble over the meaning of the word 'delicious' brings the kingdom to the brink of Civil War.
[D1763] Faber pbk **£2.95**

Tuck Everlasting
Enlightenment and release from childhood come to Winnie Foster when she is kidnapped by the rustic Tuck family and, discovering their unearthly secret - a fountain of eternal youth - must make a profound moral choice.
[D1764] Faber pbk **£2.95**

BANKS, LYNNE REID
Omri, a nine year old boy, accidentally brings to life his three-inch-high plastic Indian brave by placing him in what proves a magic cupboard. Responsibilities and problems beset him as he learns to care for a miniature human from another place and time. In two equally exciting sequels, Omri is tempted to travel through time himself to provide his Indian and his tribe with modern weapons, and then to bring them medical help after a terrible battle.

Return of the Indian
[D1765] Collins pbk **£1.95**

The Indian in the Cupboard
[D1766] Collins pbk **£1.95**

The Secret of the Indian   **NEW**
[D1766A] Collins hbk **£5.95**

BAWDEN, NINA
A highly literate writer, whose work is also very accessible. She focuses with great acuteness on child-adult politics, and the more difficult sides of growing up, but always from the child's point of view.

A Handful of Thieves
[D1767] Puffin pbk **£1.50**

Carrie's War
Told as a flashback to the dramatic events of the War years, when Carrie and her brother are evacuated to a Welsh village to live with a narrow, bigoted shopkeeper and his kindly, but brow-beaten sister. Bawden presents readers with a portrait of a whole community and its goings-on, seen through the half-comprehending eyes of children.
[D1768] Puffin pbk **£1.50**

Keeping Henry
The growth of a pet squirrel towards freedom, and its inevitable return to the wild, parallels that of the young heroine in this perceptive story of a family evacuated to a Welsh farm during the Second World War, and the injured squirrel who comes to live with them.
[D1769] Puffin pbk **£1.99**

On the Run
[D1770] Puffin pbk **£1.95**

Rebel on a Rock
[D1771] Puffin pbk **£1.50**

Squib
A story about an abused child, which takes as its subject not the child's actual plight, but the fantasies that a group of children create to explain his state to themselves.
[D1772] Puffin pbk **£1.25**

The Finding
[D1773] Puffin pbk **£1.75**

The Outside Child   **NEW**
A finely-drawn quest story of a girl - an 'outside'

child - living with aunts, who sets out to find her little-known father and unknown younger half-brother and sister, to see if she can at last be part of a proper family.
[D1773A] Gollancz hbk **£7.95**

The Peppermint Pig
A small masterpiece in the tradition of E. Nesbit about the enforced sojourn in the country of a suddenly impoverished Edwardian family, when the father leaves for America to seek his fortune.
[D1774] Puffin pbk **£1.50**

The Robbers
[D1775] Puffin pbk **£1.50**

The Runaway Summer
On one level, an adventure story about two children who harbour an illegal immigrant, and on another, an examination of a child's response to her parents' divorce.
[D1776] Puffin pbk **£1.75**

The Secret Passage
[D1777] Puffin pbk **£1.50**

The White Horse Gang
[D1778] Puffin pbk **£1.25**

The Witch's Daughter
[D1779] Puffin pbk **£1.75**

BERRY, JAMES
A Thief in the Village and Other Stories
A magical collection of stories by Jamaican poet James Berry about the longings and fears of children growing up in Jamaica today.
[D1780] Puffin pbk **£1.75**

BLUME, JUDY
Super Fudge
[D1781] Pan pbk **£2.25**

Tales of a Fourth Grade Nothing
[D1782] Pan pbk **£2.25**

BLYTON, ENID
A prolific and perennially popular writer, who has survived charges of racism, sexism and small-mindedness. The literary drawbacks of her books - their formula plots, stereotyped characters, questionable motivation and values, stilted dialogue and 'aesthetically anaemic' prose - are precisely what attracts children to them. As Margaret Meek writes: 'Inexperienced readers feel safe in this limited world of predictable events, and familiar words and phrases'. Secured by such stories in the reading habit, a child, with adult guidance, is more likely to go on to richer, more rewarding books. Blyton's most successful series include the school books (*Malory Towers* and *St Clare's*), her adventure books (the *Famous Five* and *Secret Seven*) and her detective/mystery books (*Five Find Outers*). Only a selection of her many works appears here.

FAMOUS FIVE

Five Are Together Again
[D1783] Hodder pbk **£1.95**

Five Get into Trouble
[D1784] Hodder pbk **£1.95**

Five Go Down to the Sea
[D1785] Hodder pbk **£1.95**

Five Go Off in a Caravan
[D1786] Hodder pbk **£1.95**

Five Go on a Hike Together
[D1787] Hodder pbk **£1.95**

Five Go to Mystery Moor
[D1788] Hodder pbk **£1.95**

Five Go to Smuggler's Top
[D1789] Hodder pbk **£1.95**

Five Have a Mystery to Solve
[D1790] Hodder pbk **£1.95**

Five on Finniston Farm
[D1791] Hodder pbk **£1.95**

Five on a Treasure Island
[D1792] Hodder pbk **£1.95**

FIVE FIND OUTERS

The Ragamuffin Mystery
[D1793] Collins pbk **£1.95**
The Rat-a-Tat Mystery
[D1794] Collins pbk **£1.95**
The Rilloby Fairy Mystery
[D1795] Collins pbk **£1.95**
The Ring O'Bells Mystery
[D1796] Collins pbk **£1.95**
The Rockingdown Mystery
[D1797] Collins pbk **£1.95**
The Rub-a-Club Mystery
[D1798] Collins pbk **£1.95**

MALORY TOWERS

First Term at Malory Towers
[D1799] Armada pbk **£1.95**
In the Fifth at Malory Towers
[D1800] Armada pbk **£2.25**
Last Term at Malory Towers
[D1801] Armada pbk **£1.95**
Second Form at Malory Towers
[D1802] Armada pbk **£1.95**
Third Year at Malory Towers
[D1803] Armada pbk **£1.95**
Upper Fourth at Malory Towers
[D1804] Armada pbk **£1.95**

SECRET SEVEN

Fun for the Secret Seven
[D1805] Hodder pbk **£1.75**
Good Old Secret Seven
[D1806] Hodder pbk **£1.50**
Look Out Secret Seven
[D1807] Hodder pbk **£1.50**
Puzzle for the Secret Seven
[D1808] Hodder pbk **£1.50**
Secret Seven Mystery
[D1809] Hodder pbk **£1.50**
Shock for the Secret Seven
[D1810] Hodder pbk **£1.50**
The Secret Seven
[D1811] Hodder pbk **£1.50**
Well Done Secret Seven
[D1812] Hodder pbk **£1.50**

ST CLARE'S

Claudine at St Clare's
[D1813] Armada pbk **£1.95**
Fifth Formers at St Clare's
[D1814] Armada pbk **£1.95**
Second Form at St Clare's
[D1815] Armada pbk **£2.25**
Summer Term at St Clare's
[D1816] Armada pbk **£1.95**
The O'Sullivan Twins
[D1817] Armada pbk **£1.95**
The Twins at St Clare's
[D1818] Armada pbk **£1.95**

BOSTON, LUCY

The magic of place dominates the Greene Knowe books, which are based on the author's ancient manor house in Huntingdon. The children who visit the mysterious Mrs Oldknow there encounter old inhabitants (ghosts, or creations of the imagination?), and get involved in extraordinary adventures in the present. Strange, powerful and utterly compelling to readers, who respond to the atmosphere of a secretive house where memory is suspended in time.

A Stranger at Green Knowe
[D1819] Puffin pbk **£1.95**
An Enemy at Green Knowe
[D1820] Puffin pbk **£1.95**
The Children of Green Knowe
[D1821] Puffin pbk **£1.75**
The Chimneys of Green Knowe
[D1822] Puffin pbk **£1.95**
The River at Green Knowe
[D1823] Puffin pbk **£1.75**
The Stones of Green Knowe
[D1824] Puffin pbk **£1.75**

BRENT-DYER, ELINOR M.

A writer of girls' stories, Brent-Dyer, herself a headmistress, is best-known for her series about the 'Chalet School', an international school in the Tyrol. The old-fashioned atmosphere of the books, with their bazaars and the tame mischief-making of the girls, remained unchanged from *The School at the Chalet* (1925) to *Prefects of the Chalet School* (1970). The cast list was huge, but event, and not character, were important to Brent-Dyer: the ordinary, average girl, rather than the exceptional one, being a typical heroine. Only a selection of her many works appears here.

A Rebel at the Chalet School
[D1825] Collins pbk **£1.95**
A United Chalet School
[D1826] Collins pbk **£1.95**
Bride Leads the Chalet School
[D1827] Collins pbk **£2.25**
Excitements at the Chalet School
[D1828] Collins pbk **£1.95**
Jo of the Chalet School
[D1829] Collins pbk **£1.95**
Rivals of the Chalet School
[D1830] Collins pbk **£1.95**
Shocks for the Chalet School
[D1831] Collins pbk **£1.95**
The Chalet School and the Lintons
[D1832] Collins pbk **£1.95**
The Chalet School at War
[D1833] Collins pbk **£1.95**
The Chalet School in Exile
[D1834] Collins pbk **£1.95**
The Chalet School in the Oberland
[D1835] Collins pbk **£2.25**
The Coming of Age of the Chalet School
[D1836] Collins pbk **£1.95**
The Feud in the Chalet School
[D1837] Collins pbk **£1.95**
The Princess of the Chalet School
[D1838] Collins pbk **£1.95**
The School at the Chalet
[D1839] Collins pbk **£1.95**
The Wrong Chalet School
[D1840] Collins pbk **£1.95**
Trials for the Chalet School
[D1841] Collins pbk **£2.25**

BRIGGS, K.M.

Best known for her work on folklore, Briggs wove material gathered in her studies into two fine children's fantasies: *Hobberdy Dick* about a hobgoblin who guards a 17th century country manor, and *Kate Crackernuts*.

Hobberdy Dick
[D1842] Canongate pbk **£1.95**
Kate Crackernuts
[D1843] Canongate pbk **£1.95**

BUCKERIDGE, ANTHONY

Newly re-issued, Buckeridge's stories about affable Jennings, his friend Darbishire, and the other boarders at Linbury Court Preparatory School have remained popular because his small boys are individuals, not types, in speech and action, and their adventures and escapades are not only funny, but also credible.

Especially Jennings
[D1844] Macmillan pbk **£2.25**
Jennings Goes to School
[D1845] Macmillan pbk **£2.25**
Jennings in Particular
[D1846] Macmillan pbk **£2.25**
Speaking of Jennings
[D1847] Macmillan pbk **£2.50**
Thanks to Jennings
[D1848] Macmillan pbk **£2.25**
Trust Jennings
[D1849] Macmillan pbk **£2.50**

BURNFORD, SHEILA

The Incredible Journey
A Siamese cat, an English bullterrier and a labrador retriever make their way painfully over hundreds of miles of Canadian wilderness to find their master and home again. A book about comradeship, courage and loyalty, that is deeply moving, and totally riveting after a slow start.
[D1850] Hodder pbk **£1.95**

BYARS, BETSY

An immensely popular American author concerned with the problems of growing up today. Byars sets her stories on the fringes of society, with characters who are often offbeat or 'outsiders', placed in complex and powerful situations. The immediacy and pull of her televisual style, however, takes readers through unfamiliar, desperately funny experiences, that speak tellingly of survival and growth, but hint too at mortality and human limitation.

After the Goat Man
[D1851] Puffin pbk **£1.50**
Cracker Jackson
When Cracker learns that his one-time babysitter is being abused by her husband, he and his friend Goat attempt to rescue her.
[D1852] Puffin pbk **£1.75**
Goodbye Chicken Little
[D1853] Puffin pbk **£1.25**
The Animal, the Vegetable and John D. Jones
[D1854] Puffin pbk **£1.25**
The Cartoonist
[D1855] Puffin pbk **£1.25**
The Cybil War
[D1856] Puffin pbk **£1.25**
The Eighteenth Emergency
One of Byars' best novels, in which Benjie Fawley, nicknamed 'Mouse', must face up to the consequences of insulting the school bully, Marv Hammerman - the 'Neanderthal' boy. Benjy reaches a solution to his predicament through his killingly funny inner monologues (a device used frequently by Byars), in which he explores his way out of 17 other emergencies.
[D1857] Puffin pbk **£1.50**
The Glory Girl
[D1858] Puffin pbk **£1.50**
The House of Wings
Sammy is frightened of his grandfather whose house is filled with flying birds. But the old man's concern for and care of an injured crane bring grandparent and grandchild together.
[D1859] Puffin pbk **£1.50**
The Midnight Fox
A city boy under protest spends a summer at his uncle's farm. He is convinced 'animals hate him', until he sees a black fox and becomes involved in a desperate attempt to save the vixen from his uncle's gun.
[D1860] Puffin pbk **£1.75**
The Night Swimmers
[D1861] Puffin pbk **£1.25**
The Pinballs
Three children fostered in the same home find security and genuinely meaningful relationships.
[D1862] Puffin pbk **£1.50**

BLOSSOM FAMILY (in reading order)

The Not-Just-Anybody Family
The first of four stories about three generations of the Blossom family: innocent outsiders whose eccentricity and resourcefulness are both a virtue and a vice. Each book is built around the troubles that Junior's homemade inventions and his grandfather's impetuous nature unexpectedly land them in.
[D1863] Pan pbk **£1.99**
The Blossoms and the Green Phantom
[D1864] Pan pbk **£1.99**

The Blossoms meet the Vulture Lady
[D1865] Pan pbk **£1.99**
A Blossom Promise
[D1866] Pan pbk **£1.99**

CHAMBERS, AIDAN (ED)
Ghost After Ghost
[D1867] Puffin pbk **£1.95**
Ghosts That Haunt You
[D1868] Puffin pbk **£1.99**

COOPER, SUSAN
Apart from her semi-autobiographical *Dawn of Fear*, Susan Cooper is a writer of fantasy. In the *Dark is Rising* quintet, named after the magnificent second book (one of the most chilling accounts of evil in children's fiction), the countering of ancient and worldly evils by children in modern England provides a linking theme. She draws on myth, legend (the second coming of King Arthur) and religion, in an action which moves about in time and space, and is characterised by the continual eruption of the supernatural into the everyday. Cooper's strong grasp of character makes her novels as much about young people coming to terms with maturity, as about the unending struggle between dark and light.
Dawn of Fear
Set in London during the Blitz, a young boy plays battlegames with his best friend in a home-made fort, and fights with a gang of bullies: these wars more real than the war above him. It is only when tragedy intervenes that he begins to understand what war is, and fear dawns.
[D1869] Puffin pbk **£1.75**
THE DARK IS RISING (in reading order)
Over Sea, Under Stone
Children on holiday in Cornwall find themselves caught up in a dangerous quest for the Holy Grail, helped by their mysterious Uncle Merryweather who is as 'old as the hills', and has a strange affinity with the ancient figure Merlin.
[D1870] Puffin pbk **£1.95**
The Dark is Rising
[D1871] Puffin pbk **£1.95**
Greenwitch
[D1872] Puffin pbk **£1.75**
The Grey King
Set in an isolated Welsh farming community this is the most haunting of Cooper's books. Young Will Stanton, last of the Old Ones, discovers his mysterious lineage with the ancient Arthurian sleepers, and, his time at hand, engages in a trial of faith and courage against the evil power of the Grey King.
[D1873] Puffin pbk **£1.75**
Silver on the Tree
[D1874] Puffin pbk **£1.95**
The Dark is Rising Sequence
[D1875] Puffin pbk **£5.95**

CORRIN, SARA & STEPHEN (EDS)
Puffin Book of Christmas Stories (10 +)
[D1876] Puffin pbk **£2.50**
Puffin Book of Pet Stories (10 +)
[D1877] Puffin pbk **£2.50**
Stories for Nine-year-olds
[D1878] Penguin pbk **£2.25**
Stories for Tens and Over
[D1879] Penguin pbk **£2.50**

CRESSWELL, HELEN
A writer of unusual idiosyncratic fantasies, sometimes comic, sometimes sinister, which defy categorisation.
Ellie and the Hagwitch
A chilling, atmospheric tale in which Ellie discovers that only she has the power to defeat the wicked Hagwitch and save an entire race from becoming Nomen.
[D1880] Corgi pbk **£1.75**

Lizzie Dripping
[D1881] Puffin pbk **£1.25**
Moondial
[D1882] Puffin pbk **£2.25**
The Beachcombers
[D1883] Puffin pbk **£1.50**
The Bongleweed
[D1884] Puffin pbk **£1.75**
The Night Watchmen
Who are the night watchmen: two eccentric tramps who camp by a hole in the road and are pursued by the jealous Greeneyes? Was a magic train really whistled up to help them escape, or was the magic the product of a lonely child's imagination?
[D1885] Puffin pbk **£1.50**
The Piemakers
A rustic extravaganza about the Roller family of Darby Dale, who compete to make the biggest and best pie in a competition to be judged by the king.
[D1886] Puffin pbk **£1.75**
The Secret World of Polly Flint
Polly, who has the dubious gift of being able to see things other people can't, meets a family who has slipped through the net of time, and helps them to return to their own age and time.
[D1887] Puffin pbk **£1.95**
Time Out
A comic time-slip fantasy in which Tweeny, her butler father and housemaid mother, are transported by a 'hundred year's spell', from their lives in a respectable Victorian house to the same house in the 1980s.
[D1888] Corgi pbk **£1.95**
Up the Pier
[D1888A] Faber pbk **£1.99**
BAGTHORPE SAGA
Absolute Zero
The first of Cresswell's sophisticated and comic Bagthorpe sagas about a brilliant, slightly mad, accident-prone family.
[D1889] Puffin pbk **£2.25**
Bagthorpes Abroad
[D1890] Puffin pbk **£1.95**
Bagthorpes Haunted
[D1891] Puffin pbk **£1.95**
Bagthorpes Liberated   NEW
[D1892] Faber hbk **£7.95**
Bagthorpes Unlimited
[D1893] Puffin pbk **£1.95**
Bagthorpes v. the World
[D1894] Puffin pbk **£1.95**
Ordinary Jack
[D1895] Puffin pbk **£1.95**

CROSS, GILLIAN
Comic but chilling fantasies about an evil hypnotist whose fiendish plans to take over Britain and 10 Downing Street are thwarted by ordinary schoolchildren.
The Demon Headmaster
[D1896] Puffin pbk **£1.50**
The Prime Minister's Brain
[D1897] Puffin pbk **£1.99**

DAHL, ROALD
The most widely-read contemporary children's author whose popularity stems, in part, from his ability to realise in fiction children's innermost dreams, and to offer subversive, gruesomely satisfying, sometimes comic solutions to their nightmares. He eschews a firm, if simplistic, moral line: his heroes tend to be underdogs - the poor, the bullied, the hunted, the orphans - whose lives are transformed by the fantastic, sometimes disconcerting events of the stories.
Charlie and the Chocolate Factory
An ebullient send-up of a Victorian moral tale in which a gallery of unsavoury children, spoiled Veronica Salt, greedy Augustus Gloop - all winners

of a tour around the immense chocolate factory of Willie Wonka - get their just desserts. Deserving, impoverished Charlie Bucket gets his reward when he is named heir to the factory.
[D1898] Unwin Hyman hbk **£7.95**
[D1899] Puffin pbk **£2.25**
Charlie and the Great Glass Elevator
More adventures with Willy Wonka.
[D1900] Puffin pbk **£1.95**
Charlie: The Complete Adventures
[D1901] Unwin Hyman hbk **£9.95**
Danny the Champion of the World
This book, full of poignancy and understanding, examines the close relationship between a boy and his widowed father, and their role in a plan by the whole villlage to sabotage a local shooting party.
[D1902] Puffin pbk **£1.95**
George's Marvellous Medicine
[D1903] Puffin pbk **£1.95**
James and the Giant Peach
James is a poor orphan who lives with his two grotesque spinster aunts, one very fat and one very thin. When a giant peach grows in the back garden, James escapes inside it into an exciting new world of adventure.
[D1904] Puffin pbk **£1.75**
Matilda
[D1905] Cape hbk **£8.50**
[D1906] Penguin pbk **£3.50**
The BFG
BFG stands for 'Big Friendly Giant' and he, small bespectacled orphan Sophie and Queen Elizabeth II join together to overthrow his repulsive, child-eating brethren - Bonecruncher, Childchewer, Maidmasher et al. An inventive fantasy in which Dahl's use of language is superb: the giant, never having been to school, speaks an 'almost English' full of malapropisms and incredible word-play.
[D1907] Puffin pbk **£2.50**
The Twits
[D1908] Puffin pbk **£1.75**
The Witches
[D1909] Puffin pbk **£2.50**

DANN, COLIN
A popular sequence of tales about animals driven from their Farthing Wood home by man, as they establish themselves in a new territory on the White Deer reserve. In reading order:
The Animals of Farthing Wood
[D1910] Mammoth pbk **£2.50**
In the Grip of Winter
[D1911] Beaver pbk **£2.50**
Fox's Feud
[D1912] Beaver pbk **£1.99**
The Fox Cub Bold
[D1913] Beaver pbk **£1.99**
The Siege of White Deer Park
[D1914] Beaver pbk **£1.99**
The King of the Vagabonds
[D1915] Beaver pbk **£1.99**

DAVIES, ANDREW
Conrad's War
A thought-provoking book for younger war-game enthusiasts about a boy, like themselves, whose war-gaming lands him in the battlefields of World War I.
[D1916] Hippo pbk **£1.75**

DAVIES, HUNTER
When Flossie Teacake tries on her sister's fur coat, she unexpectedly becomes the teenager of her dreams in these episodic fantasies whose broad comedy stems from Flossie's inappropriate, nine year old response to the adult situation she finds herself in.
Flossie Teacake Again
[D1917] Collins pbk **£1.95**
Flossie Teacake Strikes Back
[D1918] Collins pbk **£1.95**

Flossie Teacake's Fur Coat
[D1919] Collins pbk £1.95

DEJONG, MEINDERT
The Wheel on the School
When storks desert a tiny Dutch fishing village, it is Lira, the village's only schoolgirl, who succeeds in mobilising her friends, teacher, and eventually the whole community to lure them back, despite storm and high winds. An unusual story which gives a remarkably detailed picture of village life and of a society - young and old - working together.
[D1920] Puffin pbk £2.25

DOHERTY, BERLIE
How Green You Are!
In this book and its sequel, *The Making of Fingers Finnigan* - a set of closely observed, semi-autobiographical stories about incidents in the lives of a group of children who live on the same street - Doherty builds up a realistic and entertaining picture of a neighbourhood and its characters.
[D1921] Collins pbk £1.75
The Making of Fingers Finnigan
[D1922] Collins pbk £1.50
Children of Winter
A time-slip novel offering readers a telling evocation of country life threatened by the plague in 17th-century Derbyshire.
[D1923] Collins pbk £1.75
Spellhorn **NEW**
A haunting fantasy with an unusual heroine: a blind girl who 'sees' with her 'mind's eye'. Laura's life becomes entwined with that of a silver unicorn, pursued by the Wild Ones who need him to lead them back to the Wilderness.
[D1924] H Hamilton hbk £7.50

DUNBAR, JOYCE
Mundo and the Weather Child
Drawing on her own experience and that of her younger son, Dunbar enters inside the imagination of an isolated, misunderstood child in this strange, lyric chronicle of a young boy's adapting to sudden deafness through a fantasy spun round a neglected garden.
[D1925] Pan pbk £1.95

DUNLOP, EILEEN
The House on the Hill
An atmospheric mystery in which two cousins, sent to stay at their Great Aunt Jane's gloomy mansion in Glasgow, discover a secret room upstairs - apparently empty for years but inexplicably lit up at night. Intrigued, Susan and Philip begin digging into their Aunt's past, and gradually unravel the house's unexpected secrets.
[D1926] Canongate pbk £1.95

FARMER, PENELOPE
A writer who uses fantastical happenings, such as time-slips, to explore common human pre-occupations, questions about identity, reality and illusion, and even the nature of time.
A Castle of Bone
A magic cupboard which can time-change anything placed in it provides the point of entry into various fantasy worlds from which its owner, Hugh, emerges satisfied, having finally completed a quest that ends in self-knowledge.
[D1927] Puffin pbk £1.95
Charlotte Sometimes
An intriguing time-shift novel in which Charlotte on her first night at boarding school slips back in time to change places with Clare in 1918.
[D1928] Puffin pbk £1.95
The Summer Birds
[D1929] Bodley pbk £3.95

FINE, ANNE
In stories remarkable for their comic invention and delicate tuning of pain, anger and complex experience to a young audience, Anne Fine treats common family dilemmas, such as care of the elderly or the 'new' man in a divorced mother's life. These are stories to grow up on.
Crummy, Mummy and Me
Parent-child relationships are hilariously upended in this irreverent collection of stories about an endearingly unconventional family (Mum is un-domesticated, punk and unpredictable, and daughter Miranda just the opposite) and their adventures.
[D1930] Puffin pbk £1.99
Goggle-Eyes (11 +) **NEW**
Narrated by school-girl Kitty, this wry, sure-footed exploration of the difficulties two girls experience with their mother's new partners - 'Toad-Shoes' and 'Goggle-Eyes' - is also a refreshingly funny (although sympathetic) send-up of Greenham Common's 'mores and manoeuvres'.
[D1931] H Hamilton hbk £7.95
The Granny Project (11 +)
There are two 'Granny Projects' in this splendid novel. One is theoretical and academic: a school sociology project on the elderly; the other a realistic one, as four children decide to fight their parents' decision to put their aging, demanding grandmother in a home.
[D1932] Methuen pbk £1.75

FISK, NICHOLAS
A writer of provocative, eerie, futuristic tales which, beneath action-packed surfaces and colloquial style, touch on disturbing possibilities. Might over-exploited nature show up a 'flip side' to the world? Might robots be capable of unprogrammed and sinister action?
Grinny
The chilling tale of an apparently benevolent old lady who turns out to be an alien robot.
[D1933] Puffin pbk £1.25
On the Flip Side
[D1934] Puffin pbk £1.50
Robot Revolt
[D1935] Puffin pbk £1.50
Trillions
An exciting, thought-provoking adventure sparked off by a heavy rainfall of strange, glittering metallic objects which the children of Harbour town call 'trillions'.
[D1936] Puffin pbk £1.00

FITZHUGH, LOUISE
An American writer whose funny, refreshing novels celebrate individualism and offer readers a set of 'highly idiosyncratic' child characters, unbound by convention.
Harriet the Spy
Eleven year old New Yorker, Harriet M. Welsh, knows that writing is in her blood, and carries around a notebook in which she records her acid, but devastatingly honest, remarks about her neighbours and classmates. When it is stolen, she has some explaining to do to regain her friendships in the class.
[D1937] Collins pbk £2.25
The Long Secret
Harriet and her best friend, Beth Ellen, determine to solve a mystery in the equally funny sequel to *Harriet the Spy*.
[D1938] Collins pbk £1.25
Nobody's Family Is Going to Change (11 +)
Parental prejudice, sexual stereotyping and children's rights are the targets of this funny perceptive book. Eleven year old black Emma wants to be a distinguished lawyer like her father, while Willie her brother hopes to be a dancer.
[D1939] Collins pbk £2.25

FLEISCHMAN, SID
A writer of picaresque folktales with loosely 'historical' setttings. These are accomplished comic pieces seasoned with trickery, villainy and hair-breadth escapes; a gallery of larger than life and stock comic characters; clever plotting, joy in language and rich visual imagery.
McBroom's Wonderful One-Acre Farm
Hillbilly idiom and a hilarious deadpan narrative characterise these tall tales in which the resourceful McBroom family, who have moved West to begin a new life on an eighty acre farm that proves to be eighty acres *deep*, triumph over man and nature.
[D1940] Puffin pbk £1.75
The Ghost in the Noonday Sun
The voyage of 'The Bloody Hand' is chronicled in this rip-roaring 'pirate' spoof, in which young Oliver Finch is pressganged by the villainous Captain Scratch, who thinks Oliver's supernatural powers will lead him to treasure.
[D1941] Puffin pbk £1.50
The Whipping Boy
Fleischman builds this gem of an adventure story around an outrageous historical practice - that of a palace keeping a 'whipping boy' to be educated with a prince, but punished in his stead. When Prince Brat runs away, it is Jemmy, his whipping boy, who saves him from two notorious villains.
[D1942] Methuen pbk £1.99

FOX, PAULA
One-Eyed Cat
Guilt and its consequences are the subject of this magnificent novel in which 11 year old Ned Willis, having disobeyed his father one night and shot his air-rifle at a moving shadow, discovers a one-eyed cat.
[D1943] Piper pbk £1.99

GARDAM, JANE
A Few Fair Days
Jane Gardam's originality is apparent in this first book: a remarkable collection of linked stories based on her Yorkshire childhood. Seen through the eyes of young Lucy, they are filled with the kind of endearing eccentrics, sharp insight, wry humour, and polished prose, which is to be found in her later works.
[D1944] Walker pbk £1.99
Through the Doll's House Door
A chronicle of the separate but inextricably linked lifetimes of four dolls - Trojan, Dutch Miss Bossy, Sad Cry and Sigger - and their owners, as they grow from girls to grandmothers. Abandoned, the dolls, whose existence depends on being remembered, tell each other stories of better days (Homeric, Dutch, Eygptian) until they are, at last, rediscovered. The effects of time, growing-up, love, and the power of the imagination in the human world and its miniature counterpart, are explored in this funny, poignant and unforgettable novel, that can be read in many ways and at many diferent ages.
[D1945] Walker pbk £1.99

Jane Gardam, author of *A Few Fair Days* (Walker Books pbk £1.99)

GARFIELD, LEON

A British writer of idiosyncratic and flamboyant 'historical' novels, set mainly in an 18th century of his own making, whose rich, naturalistic style, dark humour, and concern with themes of dark and light, and deception and enlightenment have earned him comparison with Dickens and R.L. Stevenson. Garfield's child heroes are often the displaced or terrorised, who survive adventures of Gothic complexity, relying on their wits and innate goodness.

Black Jack
[D1946] Puffin pbk **£2.75**

Devil in the Fog
[D1947] Puffin pbk **£1.75**

Jack Holborn
In Garfield's first novel (1964), Jack, a foundling, runs away to sea and falls into the hands of pirates. A classic adventure ensues complete with murder, shipwreck, treasure, and a villain - Mister Solomon Trumpet - as ambiguous and memorable as Long John Silver.
[D1948] Puffin pbk **£2.25**

John Diamond
The murky slums and underworld of early Victorian London provide the historical and metaphoric backdrop for this story of light and dark, puzzles of identity, menace and mystery in which a young country lad sets out to right a family wrong to the mysterious 'Jack Diamond'. At the end of his search he discovers not an elusive gold 'treasure' but the treasure of friendship with 'Shot-in-the-Head', a roof-dwelling urchin who lives by 'snick-and-lurk' (pickpocketing).
[D1949] Puffin pbk **£1.50**

Revolution (11 +)   NEW
[D1949A] Collins pbk **£2.50**

Shakespeare Stories
(11 +, illus. Michael Foreman)
Rich, idiosyncratic retellings of 12 of Shakespeare's best-known plays that retain the poetry, spirit and meaning of the originals, distilled for a younger audience.
[D1950] Gollancz pbk **£6.95**

Smith
Smith, an illiterate 18th century pickpocket - *"a sooty spirit of the violent and ramshackle town"* - finds a document, witnesses a murder, and, in strange partnership with a blind Justice whose 'eyes' he becomes, unravels a mystery, unmasks villainy, and wins a fortune.
[D1951] Puffin pbk **£1.95**

The Apprentices
Garfield's masterpiece is a series of twelve short novels - one for each month of the year - set amongst the lowlife of an 18th century London coloured by poverty and injustice. Each story, linked by recurring characters, concerns the life, trade and hopes of one apprentice. The book's mood and focus encompass the grimly macabre, the farcical and the tender.
[D1952] Puffin pbk **£2.95**

The December Rose
[D1953] Puffin pbk **£2.25**

The Empty Sleeve
The interdependent lives of twin brothers, whose souls are mysteriously mirrored in the bottled ships given them at birth, are the focus of Garfield's most recent period 'thriller'.
[D1954] Puffin pbk **£2.25**

The Ghost Downstairs
A highly imaginative variant on the Faust theme.
[D1955] Puffin pbk **£1.95**

GARNER, ALAN

If the 1960s in British fantasy were dominated by Garner's early work, the 1970s reached a 'literary peak' with the publication of his autobiographical 'prose-poems' to craftsmanship, *The Stone Book Quartet*. In it the imaginatively invigorating tensions of a working-class boy educated at Manchester Grammar School and Oxford (which underpinned his fantasies) were resolved, as he reforged his broken links with his family and past. Since finishing this unique work in 1978, Garner has sought to 're-negotiate the role of oral tradition in a society where story-telling has become a minority art', producing reworkings of folk and fairy tales in which, according to *Signal Selection 1986*, 'the printed text may sing'.

Elidor
Two worlds meet in a derelict church explored by 4 children in the back streets of Manchester: the world of today and the parallel doomed world of Elidor which the children are to be instrumental in saving.
[D1956] Collins pbk **£1.95**

The Stone Book Quartet
The height of Garner's achievement, these four short novels portray five generations of Garner's own Cheshire family from the mid-19th century to World War II. Each has a child at its centre, and is 'concerned with the transmission of a craftsman's skills, the wisdom that resides in work and the continuity of life in an intricately known environment' (Townsend, *Written for Children*).
[D1957] Collins hbk **£6.95**
[D1958] Collins pbk **£4.95**

The Weirdstone of Brisingamen
The characteristic eruption of ancient myth and magic into a modern setting appeared in Garner's first novel. Two children exploring Alderley Edge in Cheshire (Garner's home) find themselves taking part in a long-suppressed battle between good and evil forces, which involves them in the loss and recovery of a stone of power. An even higher order of imagination and poetry appears in the sequel *The Moon of Gomrath*.
[D1959] Collins pbk **£2.25**

The Moon of Gomrath
[D1960] Collins pbk **£2.25**

GEORGE, JEAN

Julie of the Wolves
Lost in the Alaskan wilderness 13 year old Julie is found by a pack of wolves, who help her to survive.
[D1961] Puffin pbk **£1.75**

GLANVILLE, BRIAN

Goalkeepers Are Different
Picked up by a club scout on the look-out for new talent, Ronnie Blake rises to stardom as Borough goalkeeper. Glanville chronicles his career with just the right mixture of off- and on-field events: highlighting the glamour and excitement, as well as the loneliness and tensions, of a life lived for football.
[D1962] Puffin pbk **£1.75**

GODDEN, RUMER

The Diddakoi
A half-gipsy child, wrenched from her familiar way of life, struggles to maintain her identity against the children who torment her.
[D1963] Puffin pbk **£1.50**

GRANT, GWEN

Gwen Grant has been described as 'the Beryl Cook of children's literature'. These three stories, set in the late 1940s, are about a spirited Nottinghamshire lass and her working-class family. Written in colloquial diary form, they are both gritty and extremely funny.

Knock and Wait
[D1964] Collins pbk **£1.95**

One Way Only
[D1965] Collins pbk **£1.95**

Private - Keep Out!
[D1966] Collins pbk **£1.95**

GRAY, NICHOLAS STUART

Grimbold's Other World
Grimbold's 'other world' is a night one: magical, mysterious, alarming and exciting. When the black farm cat introduces Muffler to it, the foundling boy's life is never the same again. In this strange, haunting fantasy Gray creates a moonlight landscape populated with the lost princes, sorcerers, dwarves and talking beasts of fairytale and myth.
[D1967] Faber pbk **£1.99**

GRICE, FREDERICK

The Bonny Pit Laddie
Set in the early 20th century in a Durham mining village, this story of a boy fighting his way out of the pits was one of the first children's books to depict the hardships of pit and working-class life.
[D1968] Puffin pbk **£1.50**

HARNETT, CYNTHIA

Cynthia Harnett grafts her own convincing children's fiction on to historical fact and artefact. Her interest is not in major historical events, but rather in creating a panorama of the domestic life of a particular period. In *The Wool Pack* she builds her adventure around the Wool Trade in the Cotswolds after Henry VII's accession to the throne, while *The Load of Unicorn* focuses on William Caxton and the introduction of printing. Her line drawings, not of action, but of objects, clothes and buildings, provide delightful pictorial footnotes that educate and entertain, and are always germane to the plot.

The Load of Unicorn
[D1969] Puffin pbk **£2.50**

The Wool Pack
[D1970] Puffin pbk **£2.25**

HARRIS, ROSEMARY

The Moon in the Cloud
Winner of the Carnegie Award, Harris's first novel mixes an Ancient Eygpt of her own making with a funny and irreverent retelling of the Biblical flood. Reuben, an itinerant animal trainer, agrees to assemble the animals for Noah, in return for a place on the Ark. Accompanied by a lazy dog, a jealous camel and a socially mobile cat - all of whom talk - he sets out to accomplish this...
[D1971] Faber pbk **£1.99**

The Shadow on the Sun
In this compelling sequel Reuben, the voyage of the Ark completed, returns to Egypt where he becomes involved in the loves and troubles of King Merenkere.
[D1972] Faber pbk **£1.99**

HUNTER, MOLLIE

A Pistol in the Greenyards
A powerful story built around the brutal eviction of tenant farmers from Greenyards in the Scottish Highlands in 1854.
[D1973] Canongate pbk **£1.95**

Escape from Loch Leven
An exciting, dramatic novel constructed around the planned escape of Mary Queen of Scots from her island prison.
[D1974] Canongate pbk **£1.95**

The Spanish Letters
A tale of espionage and intrigue set in 16th century Edinburgh.
[D1975] Canongate pbk **£1.50**

HUNTER, NORMAN

Hunter's stories about the absent-minded Professor Branestawm and his misadventures with a series of home-made devices (magnetic suspenders, burglar-catching and potato-peeling machines etc) have entertained children for over 50 years. While they have elements of the nightmare, it is their absurdity and brilliantly exaggerated notion of ordinary things gone wrong that appeals. Heath Robinson's illustrations for *The Incredible Adventures* capture Branestawm's world perfectly.

Professor Branestawm Round the Bend
[D1976] Puffin pbk **£1.95**

Professor Branestawm's Perilous Pudding
[D1977] Puffin pbk **£1.50**
The Incredible Adventures of Professor Branestawm
[D1978] Puffin pbk **£2.25**

IBBOTSON, EVA
The Haunting of Hiram C. Hopgood
A breathless, farcical replay of *The Ghost Goes West*, which satirises literary and cinematic clichés.
[D1979] Pan pbk **£1.99**
Which Witch?
When the wizard Arrimen decides to marry he carries out a Witchcraft/Beauty contest to decide 'which witch' will be his wife. An irreverently funny, tongue-in-cheek parody.
[D1980] Pan pbk **£1.99**

IRESON, BARBARA (ED)
Never Meddle with Magic: Story Chest 1
[D1981] Puffin pbk **£2.99**
Runaway Shoes: A Puffin Bedtime Story Chest **NEW**
[D1982] Puffin pbk **£2.99**

JANSSON, TOVE
Like Lewis Carroll, Finnish writer Tove Jansson uses the literary nonsense of the looking-glass world to poke fun at human types. Her Moominvalley (pictured in her own idiosyncratic illustrations), home of the music-making Snufkin, the Snow Maiden, the Hattifatteners, the Freezing Gonk and other invented creatures, is an absurd, satiric, poetic creation, at once funny and melancholic.
Comet in Moominland
[D1983] Puffin pbk **£1.50**
Finn Family Moomintroll
[D1984] Puffin pbk **£1.50**
Moomin Summer Madness
[D1985] Puffin pbk **£1.50**
Moominland Midwinter
[D1986] Puffin pbk **£1.50**
Moominvalley in November
[D1987] Puffin pbk **£1.75**
Tales from Moominvalley
[D1988] Puffin pbk **£1.75**
The Exploits of Moominpappa
[D1989] Puffin pbk **£1.50**

JONES, DIANA WYNNE
An original and dazzlingly inventive British storyteller who blends comedy and the supernatural (a heady mixture of magic, myth, folk and fairytale) to explore metaphorically the significance and changes faced in growing up and achieving self-knowledge. At once lyric, muscular, funny and deeply perceptive, her work is endlessly entertaining and rewarding.
Archer's Goon
[D1990] Methuen pbk **£1.75**
Dogsbody (11 +)
A breathtaking mix of magic, myth, quest, coming of age, and classic animal story (the love of a lonely, ill-treated child for an unwanted pet). The pet here is Sirius the fiery dogstar, exiled to Earth as a puppy until he can regain his heavenly status by retrieving a lost 'zoi' - an object of great magical power.
[D1991] Methuen pbk **£1.99**
The Homeward Bounders (11 +)
War gaming is the subject of this tense and thought-provoking fantasy, in which a twelve year old boy is doomed to exile from his own time when he becomes a 'Random Factor' in the 'Real and Ancient Game' played by sinister gamers with real people and overlapping worlds.
[D1992] Methuen pbk **£1.50**
The Ogre Downstairs
[D1993] Puffin pbk **£1.75**

HIT THE VICAR IN THE WAISTCOAT

The Vicar from *The Incredible Adventures of Professor Branestawm* by Norman Hunter (Puffin pbk £2.25)

Wild Robert **NEW**
'Wild Robert' was buried 350 years ago, but he returns to transform Heather's life and that of the tourists who invade Castlemaine.
[D1993A] Methuen hbk **£6.95**
Witch Week
[D1994] Methuen pbk **£1.95**
THE 'CHRESTOMANCI' NOVELS
(in reading order)
A Charmed Life
Chrestomanci, an enchanter of great power, appeared first in this Carnegie Award winning novel. When orphaned Cat Chant and his obnoxious sister Gwendolyn are adopted by him, Cat thinks it is because his sister is a witch. However, Gwendolyn abuses her magic powers, while Cat unexpectedly discovers his.
[D1995] Puffin pbk **£2.25**
The Magicians of Caprona
Chrestomanci travels to a Renaissance-like Italy to unravel a mystery when the spells of the feuding *Magicians of Caprona* lose their strength.
[D1996] Beaver pbk **£1.95**
Lives of Christopher Chant
The enchanter's own apprenticeship and coming of age are chronicled in another story of magical skulduggery, involving Twelve Related Words and a Living Goddess.
[D1997] Mammoth pbk **£1.99**

JONES, TERRY
A gifted storyteller, whose imagination is equally at home creating *Monty Python* scripts and modern fairytales and mythic sagas. Both these novels are built around the classic quest: two children set out to find the land of Dragons in one, while Erik and his warriors seek the fabled land in which the sun goes down in the other. Jones treats traditional ingredients - adventure, danger, puzzles, fantastic men and beasts, humour and morality - with an unmistakable personal touch.
Nicobobinus
[D1998] Puffin pbk **£2.25**
The Saga of Erik the Viking
[D1999] Puffin pbk **£2.25**

JUSTER, NORTON
The Phantom Tollbooth
A wonderful piece of Carrollesque nonsense in which the boy Milo, passes through a magic tollbooth into

Dictionopolis (the kingdom of words), where he is sent on a quest to Digitopolis (the kingdom of numbers) to find the missing princesses Rhyme and Reason who can restore harmony. A book to make readers think about words, their power, meaning and value.
[D2000] Collins pbk **£2.50**

KASTNER, ERICH
A left-wing German writer, whose work was banned and burnt by the Nazis, Kastner is best known for *Emil and the Detectives*, a prototype children's adventure story, in which a gang of Berlin boys catch the thief who stole Emil's money when he fell asleep in a train.
Emil and the Detectives
[D2001] Puffin pbk **£1.75**
Emil and the Three Twins
[D2002] Puffin pbk **£1.99**

KEMP, GENE
A former teacher, British author Gene Kemp is best known for her comic but poignant stories set in and around Cricklepit Combined School. Her sharp and earthy writing displays a fine ear for contemporary primary dialogue, and her characters, drawn from life, and gutsy in the face of disturbing difficulties, are unforgettable.
Charlie Lewis Plays for Time
Charlie Lewis, the son of an absentee concert pianist, is determined that he will be as successful as she is, and survives by writing contemporary songs in the company of the large Moffat family next door.
[D2003] Puffin pbk **£1.75**
Gowie Corbie Plays Chicken
Quick-fingered, quick-tongued Gowie Corby is at odds with schoolmates and authority, until he is transformed by the friendship of a new neighbour - Black American Rosie.
[D2004] Puffin pbk **£1.50**
Jason Badger & the Priory Ghost
An hilarious time-slip yarn, set in motion during a school trip to an old Priory where Jason Badger, the endearing class terror, first sees the ghost of the spirited novice Matilda, born 800 years earlier. Kemp's version of medieval history is not to be missed.
[D2005] Puffin pbk **£1.75**
Juniper
While the 'cops and robbers' in this mystery are stereotypical, its young heroine with a thalidomide arm is not. This is a modern and moving reworking of Grimm's *The Juniper Tree*.
[D2006] Puffin pbk **£1.75**
The Prime of Tamworth Pig
[D2007] Faber pbk **£1.99**
The Turbulent Term of Tyke Tiler
An unforgettable account of Tyke Tiler's last term at primary school - the term in which this ever-resourceful child shields a slow classmate, Danny Pryce, from disaster at home and at school. Kemp's skill with characterisation and dialogue makes this a very funny story, whose biggest joke is saved for the wonderful surprise ending.
[D2008] Puffin pbk **£1.75**
The Well
A junior version of *Cider with Rosie*, this autobiographical story nostalgically evokes a pre-war country childhood when time moved slower (or does memory make it seem to?), and life was simpler.
[D2009] Puffin pbk **£1.75**

KERR, JUDITH
Seen through the eyes of Anna as she grows up, these novels form a moving, and largely autobiographical, trilogy which chronicles the escape of a prosperous Jewish family from Nazi Germany; the hardships of their refugee life on the continent, and during the London Blitz; and finally Anna's adolescence and

marriage to an Englishman, and her realisation that she can never escape her past. Listed in reading order.
When Hitler Stole Pink Rabbit
[D2010] Collins pbk **£2.50**
The Other Way Round (11 +)
[D2011] Collins pbk **£4.95**
A Small Person Far-Away (11 +)
[D2012] Collins pbk **£4.95**

KING, CLIVE
Stig of the Dump
A hugely popular book among children: a lonely boy finds a Stone-Age dweller in a rubbish dump, and they start up a friendship based on their mutual fascination with each other.
[D2013] Puffin pbk **£1.75**

KING-SMITH, DICK
The reaction of ordinary people and animals to extraordinary creatures is the comic focus of many of these humorous animal fantasies, in which King-Smith flies in the face of nature, and asks the reader to consider various unlikely possibilities - such as a pig who wants to fly but discovers instead that he can swim (in *Daggie Dogfoot*), and another pig who runs away to join the army in *Saddlebottom*.
Daggie Dogfoot
[D2014] Puffin pbk **£1.50**
Dodos Are Forever NEW
The extinct dodo survives in this desert island spoof, in which a colony of dodos are invaded by sailors and rats, and forced to make a daring escape.
[D2015] Viking hbk **£6.95**
Magnus Powermouse
[D2016] Puffin pbk **£1.25**
Martin's Mice
Martin the kitten defies tradition when, instead of catching mice, he decides to keep them as pets.
[D2017] Puffin pbk **£1.99**
Saddlebottom
[D2018] Puffin pbk **£1.50**
The Fox Busters
[D2019] Puffin pbk **£1.75**
The Mouse Butcher
[D2020] Puffin pbk **£1.50**
The Queen's Nose
Harmony Parker, denied a pet, disconcertingly comes to see family and friends as animals.
[D2021] Puffin pbk **£1.50**
The Sheep-Pig
A piglet fostered by a sheep dog becomes champion sheep-pig. Original, improbable, funny, but grounded in farm life and animal behaviour and eschewing a firm moral line about the need for manners.
[D2022] Puffin pbk **£1.75**

Dick King-Smith, author of *The Toby Man* (Gollancz hbk £5.95)

The Toby Man NEW
An hilarious chronicle of the exploits of a would-be highwayman, and his four faithful animal friends.
[D2023] Gollancz hbk **£5.95**
Tumbleweed
[D2024] Puffin pbk **£1.99**

KINGFISHER STORY LIBRARY
Each collection, compiled by a well-known children's writer (including Robert Westall, Jan Mark and Michael Rosen) and illustrated with line drawings, features an original selection of tales on a particular theme, combining favourite classics with stories by modern authors.
Adventure Stories
[D2025] Kingfisher hbk **£6.95**
Funny Stories
[D2026] Kingfisher hbk **£6.95**
Ghost Stories
[D2027] Kingfisher hbk **£6.95**
School Stories NEW
[D2028] Kingfisher hbk **£6.95**
Science Fiction Stories
[D2029] Kingfisher hbk **£6.95**

KONIGSBURG, E.L.
From the Mixed-Up Files of Mrs Basil E. Frankweiler
An original comedy about two children who run away from home and spend a week hiding in the Metropolitan Museum of Art in New York.
[D2030] Macmillan pbk **£3.50**

L'ENGLE, MADELEINE
A Wrinkle in Time
A science fiction thriller in which the Murray children voyage to another planet to rescue their scientist father from the evil powers of IT, which reduces people to conformist robots.
[D2031] Puffin pbk **£1.75**

LAIRD, ELIZABETH
Red Sky in the Morning
When twelve year old Anna's mother gives birth to a longed-for baby brother, he is handicapped. The effect of his brief life on her family is movingly chronicled in this splendid tragic-comic novel.
[D2032] Piper pbk **£1.99**

LE GUIN, URSULA
The Earthsea Trilogy, le Guin's finest children's work, is one of the most convincing fictional accounts of magic and its place in the human world. It follows the adventures of Ged, who is destined to be the most famous sage on Earthsea; three qualities particularly distinguish it - an adroit use of Jungian psychology, the plausibility of Earth as a secondary world, and its fine narrative style.
THE EARTHSEA TRILOGY (in reading order)
A Wizard of Earthsea
[D2033] Puffin pbk **£1.75**
The Farthest Shore
[D2034] Puffin pbk **£1.95**
The Tombs of Atuan
[D2035] Puffin pbk **£1.95**
The Earthsea Trilogy
[D2036] Puffin pbk **£5.95**

LEESON, ROBERT
Hilarious modern variants on the traditional genie tale, in which a boy's curiosity releases an incompetent mischief-making genie from an empty, yet unopened, beer-can into a tension-filled Inner City environment.
Genie on the Loose
[D2037] Collins pbk **£1.95**
The Third Class Genie
[D2038] Collins pbk **£1.95**

LEWIS, C. DAY
The Otterbury Incident
Popular since its publication in 1948, Lewis's story follows the adventures of a group of boys in outwitting a trio of criminals.
[D2039] Puffin pbk **£1.75**

LILLINGTON, KENNETH
The Halloween Cat
Reprimanded unfairly, Mike curses his teacher. A curse made at Halloween is 'likely to work', Meg the Witch tells him: then Miss Gratwick breaks an arm. Beneath the Halloween shenanigans and suspense, Lillington explores guilt and the way in which irrational fears grow, when you don't know if magic is real or in the mind. Unputdownable!
[D2040] Faber pbk **£1.99**

LIMB, SUE
China Lee
When China Lee, as part of a school voluntary project, begins visiting Mr Jupiter - who may or may not be the aged eccentric recluse he appears to be - she encounters more than she expected: an Earth-destruct machine, burglary and the nature of deity. An unusual first novel that poses moral questions while taking a sharp funny look at modern family life.
[D2041] Collins pbk **£1.95**

LINDGREN, ASTRID
A Swedish writer, best-known in Britain for her comic, wildly imaginative fantasies about nine year old Pippi Longstocking. Pippi, a heroine for any child longing for independence, is a tomboy who lives on her own, free of adult rules, with a monkey and a horse in a little house in a Swedish village.
Pippi Longstocking
[D2042] Puffin pbk **£1.75**
Pippi Goes Abroad
[D2043] Puffin pbk **£1.75**
Pippi in the South Seas
[D2044] Puffin pbk **£1.50**

LINKLATER, ERIC
The Wind on the Moon
An inventive fantasy about two sisters who, when 'there is a wind on the moon', turn into kangaroos in the zoo.
[D2045] Canongate pbk **£1.95**

LIVELY, PENELOPE
Lively mixes comedy, adventure, time travel and history in a set of children's novels which explore the effect of the past on the present, and illuminate her concern with continuity and historical and personal memory: *"Children need to sense that we live in a permanent world, that reaches away behind and ahead of us...that the span of a lifetime is something to be wondered at and thought about, and that - above all - people evolve during their own lives"*.
A House Inside Out
In this inventive, gently ironic comedy, Lively, in unexpected mode, introduces the animal inhabitants of a house, who are invisible except to all-seeing Baby and Dog Willie: Nat the woodlouse (whose purpose in life is to climb the bath), spider, mice and a sardonic cat! Each tells a tale of adventure and daring that makes readers wonder who really runs *A House Inside Out*.
[D2046] Puffin pbk **£1.75**
A Stitch in Time
[D2047] Puffin pbk **£1.95**
Astercote
[D2048] Puffin pbk **£1.75**
Going Back
The wartime childhood of a brother and sister in a Somerset manor house is lovingly remembered by the grown-up sister when she returns to visit years later.
[D2049] Puffin pbk **£1.50**

The Driftway
[D2050] Puffin pbk **£1.75**

The Ghost of Thomas Kempe
What, or who, is responsible for the peculiar happenings in James's new home in an old Oxfordshire cottage? The ghost of a 17th century sorcerer emerges as a poltergeist and tries to make the boy his apprentice. How James lays Thomas Kempe to rest makes for a funny, absorbing read.
[D2051] Puffin pbk **£1.95**

The Revenge of Samuel Stokes
[D2052] Puffin pbk **£1.75**

The Wild Hunt of Hagworthy
[D2053] Puffin pbk **£1.99**

Uninvited Ghosts
[D2054] Puffin pbk **£1.50**

LOWRY, LOIS
Anastasia Krupnik is a totally engaging heroine: A Ramona Quimbly for the 8 to 12s. Her prodigious sense of self occasionally lands her in trouble, but invariably enables her to come out on top of the world. Life in these books has the content and pace of a television situation comedy, but is often under-pinned by the enigmas (the way in which memory and time distort the past), complexities (death), and pains (bullying) encountered in growing up. As Anastasia works out the world and her place in it, so do her readers. The 7 titles are listed in reading order.

Anastasia Krupnik
Ten year old Anastasia grows to understand the older generation (her grandmother) and finds the maturity to accept a new generation (her baby brother).
[D2055] Collins pbk **£1.95**

Anastasia Again!
[D2056] Collins pbk **£1.95**

Anastasia at Your Service
[D2057] Collins pbk **£1.95**

Anastasia Ask Your Analyst
Anastasia decids to overcome her imagined complexes by secretly undergoing a course of therapy with a plaster bust of Freud.
[D2058] Collins pbk **£1.95**

Anastasia On Her Own
When her mother takes an unprecedented business trip to California, Anastasia smugly volunteers to run the house: an experiment in adulthood which goes predictably but hilariously wrong!
[D2059] Collins pbk **£1.95**

Anastasia Has the Answers `NEW`
[D2060] Puffin pbk **£1.95**

Anastasia's Chosen Career `NEW`
[D2061] Collins **£1.95**

The Woods at the End of Autumn Street (11 +)
When Elizabeth moves to her grandparents' country house 'because of the war', she makes friends with the grandson of the family's black housekeeper. As the two explore this new world, they are inexorably drawn to the forbidden house at the end of the street - the scene of an 'abrupt tragedy as wounding to the little girl as the war is to the world outside'. A beautiful story.
[D2062] Collins pbk **£1.95**

MACLACHLAN, PATRICIA
Sarah Plain and Tall
An intense, moving but never sentimental story about Sarah, the mail order bride whom a motherless family of settlers hope will bring beauty, song and joy into their lives again.
[D2063] Puffin pbk **£1.75**

MAGORIAN, MICHELLE
Back Home (11-14)
Back home after her evacuation to the United States a young girl learns to cope with the austerity of life in post-war England.
[D2064] Puffin pbk **£2.99**

Goodnight Mister Tom
Powerful, occasionally sentimental exploration of the blossoming relationship between a half-starved, maltreated evacuee and Mister Tom, the lonely old widower with whom he is billeted.
[D2065] Puffin pbk **£2.99**

MAHY, MARGARET
The Haunting
A chilling and unconventional ghost story in which a boy is haunted by a great-uncle, who proves to be not only very much alive, but a necromancer too.
[D2066] Methuen pbk **£1.95**

MARK, JAN
An exceptionally fine writer of short stories, whose biting wit and incisive depiction of character and situation work best within this smaller compass. Her novels too, while thin on plot, are richly observed slices of life which often focus on new relationships, and moments of discovery and apprehension.

Dream House (11 +) `NEW`
[D2067] Penguin pbk **£1.99**

Hairs in the Palm of the Hand
Two hilarious short stories set in school.
[D2068] Puffin pbk **£1.50**

Handles
In this jewel of a book city-bred Erica, on an unwanted country holiday with dreadful relatives, discovers the value of 'handles', the nicknames that define identity. Hers is 'Dreaded Yellow Jelly Mould', which stands for her delight at being allowed to work as the mechanic she longs to be in a local motorbike repair shop.
[D2069] Puffin pbk **£1.75**

Man in Motion `NEW`
A new town, a new house, a new school...and new friends? When Lloyd moves, to his surprise, he becomes a 'man in motion', but eventually must choose one sport and friends...Jan Mark, in mordant, witty form.
[D2069A] Viking hbk **£7.50**

Nothing to Be Afraid Of
Ten startling short stories built around common childhood fears, and containing one of the finest, funniest short stories in print, *William's Version*, in which Granny's traditional re-telling of 'The Three Pigs' is countered by small William's subversive 'personal' version which reflects his anxiety about the arrival of a new baby.
[D2070] Puffin pbk **£1.50**

Thunder and Lightnings
Two boys become friends because of their shared passion for aeroplanes.
[D2071] Puffin pbk **£1.50**

Trouble Half-way
Amy's journey round Britain with her stepfather, a lorry driver, turns out to be a journey of discovery.
[D2072] Puffin pbk **£1.50**

MAYNE, WILLIAM
One of Britain's most eminent children's writers, Mayne is also one of the most 'controversial': does he write children's book for children, or for adults? His work is certainly unclassifiable, and has always extended literary boundaries, taking readers in new ways, and to new places which have little to do with conventional notions of what is acceptable in children's literature. His prose is masterly - precise, intriguing and delicately tuned to layers of mood and feeling beneath the surface. Any child who accepts the challenge of his work will be richly rewarded.

Antar and the Eagles `NEW`
Antar, captured by eagles, has been chosen to carry out the most important mission in eagle history. But first the boy must learn to survive, eagle-fashion. A gripping fantasy that calls for a mind-expanding reversal of perception.
[D2073] Walker hbk **£8.95**

Drift
Mayne charts the odyssey of a white boy lost in the American wilderness and the Indian girl who helps him to survive, telling the story first through the eyes of Rafe, and then through Tawena's, in a way which modifies our perception of their experience. A fine study of the clash and interaction of two differing cultures.
[D2074] Puffin pbk **£1.75**

Gideon, Ahoy (11 +)
For all children there comes a rite of passage to independence. For brain-damaged Gideon, it is the summer when he begins work on a river-boat and encounters near disaster. Told from the viewpoint of his younger, twelve year old sister, this is a magnificent family story which charts a 'time when family love ceases to be compatible with the absolute duty to protect' (*Signal Selection 1987*).
[D2075] Puffin pbk **£2.25**

Kelpie
Does the legendary monster Kelpie really exist in the Scottish loch which Lucy's school class visit on a hostelling trip? Only if you believe he does. A richly imagined and funny adventure story that poses questions about appearance and reality, imagination and truth, and much more.
[D2076] Puffin pbk **£1.99**

MCCAUGHREAN, GERALDINE
A Little Lower Than the Angels
To escape his brutal treatment as an apprentice mason, Gabriel joins a band of travelling players presenting mystery plays across Medieval England. As the Archangel Gabriel, will his life be any more secure - caught betwen 'God' and 'the Devil'? In a world of more than one kind of illusion, Gabriel learns that people are not what they seem. A compelling, powerful novel.
[D2077] Puffin pbk **£1.99**

A Pack of Lies
[D2077A] Oxford hbk **£7.95**

MCCAUGHREN, TOM
A gripping saga of the foxes of the land of Sinna - their lives, adventures, the education of their young - which is played out against a richly detailed Irish landscape, captured in Jeanette Duane's fine naturalistic drawings, which illustrate these volumes.

Run Swift, Run Free
[D2078] Wolfhound pbk **£3.95**

Run to Earth
[D2079] Wolfhound pbk **£3.95**

Run with the Wind
[D2080] Wolfhound pbk **£3.95**

NAUGHTON, BILL
The Goalkeeper's Revenge and Other Stories
Gritty, funny, occasionally touching tales filled with incident about working class boys.
[D2081] Puffin pbk **£1.50**

NIMMO, JENNY
Ancient Celtic magic mingles with the harsh tensions of three domestic dramas in this mystical, lyrical trilogy set in modern rural Wales. Each story charts a rite of passage: in *The Snow Spider*, young Gwyn learns to use his five gifts of magic wisely; in *Emlyn's Moon* he uses his powers to save a boy seeking his lost mother in the world beyond, while in *The Chestnut Soldier* he comes of age through facing the mysterious Evan Llyr, who seems to have leapt out of old legends, in a battle in which one of them must perish.

The Snow Spider
[D2082] Methuen pbk **£1.75**

Emlyn's Moon
[D2083] Methuen pbk **£1.75**

The Chestnut Soldier
[D2084] Methuen hbk £7.95   **NEW**

O'BRIEN, ROBERT C.
Mrs Frisby and the Rats of Nimh
Super-rats, given heightened intellects in laboratory experiments, escape and come to the aid of a dead colleague's sickly mouse child and his anxious mother. Can they use their new intelligence to achieve a higher morality in the society they intend to build? A futuristic fantasy that comments tellingly on the ways of our society.
[D2085] Puffin pbk £2.25

O'HARA, MARY
Three established favourites set in Wyoming, about the McLaughlin family and their relationship with the horses of Goose Bar Ranch.
Green Grass of Wyoming
[D2086] Methuen pbk £1.95
My Friend Flicka
[D2087] Methuen pbk £2.50
Thunderhead
[D2088] Methuen pbk £1.95

O'SHEA, PAT
The Hounds of the Morrigan
Knockabout comedy and the mythic battle of good and evil mingle in this splendid fantasy in which two Irish children are sent on a quest into Tir-na-nog pursued by the evil Morrigon.
[D2089] Puffin pbk £2.95

PEARCE, PHILIPPA
Regarded as one of the finest British 20th century writers for children, Pearce's writing is spare, lyrical, child-eyed, painfully honest and brimming with a strong sense of people and place. In narratives distinguished by a 'breathless detective pull', she focuses on the gap between imagined promise and sober reality, and on children's ability 'to accept two sorts of truth at the same time' (Margaret Meek, *The Cool Web*), as well as on relationships between adults and children, and past and present.
A Dog So Small
Ben wants a dog so badly that he becomes preoccupied with an imaginary chihuahua, 'a dog so small you can only see it with your eyes shut', with catastrophic results. In the final scenes he must learn to live with the real dog he is given, rather than the dog of his dreams.
[D2090] Puffin pbk £1.50
Minnow on the Say
Pearce's first novel, published in 1955, is the story of two boys, their canoe - the *Minnow* - and their search on the River Say for an Elizabethan treasure lost 'over the water'.
[D2091] Puffin pbk £2.25
The Way to Sattin Shore
An atmospheric, closely plotted mystery in which young Kate gradually uncovers her family's closely guarded conspiracy of silence about her apparently dead father.
[D2092] Puffin pbk £1.95
Tom's Midnight Garden
One of the landmarks of English post-war fantasy, this compelling novel is concerned with time, dreams, loneliness and old age, and the relationship between them. A lonely boy, staying with childless relatives, hears the clock strike thirteen, and, opening the back door, finds himself in a Victorian garden.
[D2093] Puffin pbk £1.95

PEPPER, DENNIS (ED)
An Oxford Book of Christmas Stories
[D2094] Oxford pbk £3.95

PRICE, SUSAN
Winner of the 1987 Carnegie Award. This unusual fantasy concerns Chingis, a witch girl who lives in a house that runs on chicken legs, and Safa, prisoner son of the Czar whom she saves. A strange compelling tale of a struggle for power between witchcraft and tyranny.
The Ghost Drum
[D2095] Faber pbk £1.99

RHODDA, EMILY
Pigs Might Fly
Sick, bored, and hoping that 'something would happen', Rachel is transported by unicorn to a country where UEF (Unlikely Events Factor) storms, or Grunters, cause pigs to fly and all manner of peculiar events to occur - events deliciously upending Rachel's known world. A fantasy of the 'looking glass' sort.
[D2096] Puffin pbk £1.75

RICHTER, HANS PETER
Richter offers two alternative versions of life in pre-war Nazi Germany, seen through the eyes of Friedrich who is Jewish, and those of two boys who join the Hitler Youth movement.
Friedrich
[D2097] Puffin pbk £1.95
I Was There
[D2098] Puffin pbk £1.95

RODGERS, MARY
A single bizarre alteration to the ordinary - in this case parent and child swopping places - provides the springboard for two original and funny fantasies which give those involved (and the reader) the chance to see life through the other's eyes.
Freaky Friday
[D2099] Puffin pbk £1.99
Summer Switch
[D2100] Puffin pbk £1.95

RODOWSKY, COLBY
P.S. Write Soon
Narrative and letters to an unmet pen-pal offer alternative versions of the same events in the life of Tanner, newly-fitted with a leg brace after a car accident. The narrative records Tanner's displacement - life as it is; the letters, her reworking of inadmissable reality - life as it should be - until the moment when she must write the truth.
[D2101] Faber pbk £2.95

ROSEN, BILLI
Andi's War
Set in the 1940s during the Greek Civil War this first novel, winner of the 1987 *Faber/Guardian/Jackanory* Children's Writers competition, chronicles young Andi's slow realisation that her own private battles cannot be separated from the conflict outside.
[D2102] Faber pbk £1.99

ROSEN, MIKE & GRIFFITHS, JOAN (EDS)
That'll Be Telling
A thought-provoking collection of stories, songs and riddles from many cultures, grouped under themes such as trickery, greed, chases, weddings and ghosts.
[D2103] Cambridge hbk £4.95

SERRAILLIER, IAN
The Silver Sword
The wanderings of a family of Polish children across war-torn Europe in search of their parents, based on true events. An absorbing tale about the courage of the human survivors and casualties of war.
[D2104] Puffin pbk £1.95

SINGER, ISAAC BASHEVIS
Singer is a distinguished Jewish author and a great storyteller. In each of these collections, originally written in Yiddish, he draws on the folktales of his Polish childhood to create richly imagined new tales which reflect the humour and pathos of European Jewish life.
Naftali the Storyteller and his Horse, Sus
[D2105] Faber pbk £2.95
When Shlemiel Went to Warsaw
[D2106] Faber pbk £2.95

SLEIGH, BARBARA
The ordinary black cat and broomstick Rosemary buys from sinister old Mrs. Cantrip turn out to be extraordinary, involving their new owner in an exciting quest. An inviting blend of witchcraft, magic and humour.
Carbonel
[D2107] Puffin pbk £2.25
Carbonel & Colidor
[D2108] Puffin pbk £2.50
The Kingdom of Carbonel
[D2109] Puffin pbk £2.50

SMITH, DODIE
101 Dalmations
The classic tale of Pongo and Missus saving their puppies from the evil clutches of the ink-swilling Cruella de Ville.
[D2110] Pan pbk £1.99
Starlight Barking
[D2111] Puffin pbk £1.50

SMITH, DORIS BUCHANAN
A Taste of Blackberries
A boy's grief and guilt following the tragic death of his close friend are sensitively explored in this honest, unsentimental story.
[D2112] Puffin pbk £1.50

STEIG, WILLIAM
A *New Yorker* cartoonist whose forte is double-edged satire. Beneath the comedy of his elegant word-loving anthropomorphic sagas (whose storylines, patterns and themes rework old tales) lies a moral seriousness about choice and values and a life-enhancing optimism just right for readers longing to test themselves against the unknown. Steig's animal heroes are refreshing models: *Dominic*, whose doggy optimism enables him to overcome the marauding Domesday gang when he sets out along life's highway; *Abel*, the Edwardian dandy mouse marooned Crusoe-like on a river islet, who discovers what is of value in surviving today; *Gawain* the Goose, Chief Guard of the Royal Treasury, falsely accused of stealing rubies. Each odyssey is a gem, of which Steig's cartoons are an integral part.
Abel's Island
[D2113] Faber pbk £2.95
Dominic
[D2114] Faber pbk £2.95
The Real Thief
[D2115] Faber pbk £2.99

STORR, CATHERINE
Marianne Dreams
A 'psycho-fantasy' in which Marianne, convalescing, draws a house and a boy who turn out to be real, but whom she only meets in her dreams. In this other world, Marianne's acquaintance first endangers, and then saves the 'real' boy. Powerful, disturbing, yet ultimately reassuring.
[D2116] Puffin pbk £1.95

STREATFEILD, NOEL
An enduringly popular author, whose early *Ballet Shoes* about life at a Ballet School initiated a new genre of the career-story after its appearance in 1936. Subsequent books, all based on detailed research, perceptively explore young careers in the theatre (*Curtain Up*), the circus, music (*Apple Bough*), the

ice-rink (*White Boots*) and films (the *Gemma* stories, *The Painted Garden*).

Apple Bough
[D2117] Puffin pbk **£2.50**
Ballet Shoes
[D2118] Puffin pbk **£2.50**
Ballet Shoes for Anna
[D2119] Collins pbk **£1.95**
Gemma
The first in a series of family stories.
[D2120] Collins pbk **£1.95**
Gemma & Sisters
[D2121] Collins pbk **£1.95**
Gemma Alone
[D2122] Collins pbk **£1.95**
Goodbye Gemma
[D2123] Collins pbk **£1.95**
The Circus Is Coming
[D2124] Puffin pbk **£2.95**
The Growing Summer
[D2125] Puffin pbk **£2.25**
The Painted Garden
[D2126] Puffin pbk **£2.95**
When the Siren Wailed
[D2127] Collins pbk **£1.95**
White Boots
[D2128] Puffin pbk **£2.25**

SUTCLIFF, ROSEMARY
A British writer who has dominated the post-war development of the historical novel, Sutcliff is concerned with themes of dark and light, as symbolising the turbulent changes which characterise her favourite period, the Late Roman Empire. The dilemmas of the individuals of whom she writes so compassionately, as they respond to the social and political pressures of the past, have direct relevance for readers today, proving her stated belief that *"the disintegration of the Roman Empire and the onset of the Dark Ages contains truths for our own time"*.

Blood Feud
[D2129] Puffin pbk **£2.50**
Bonnie Dundee
[D2130] Puffin pbk **£2.50**
Dawn Wind
[D2131] Puffin pbk **£2.99**
Flame-Coloured Taffeta
[D2132] Puffin pbk **£1.99**
Frontier Wolf
[D2133] Puffin pbk **£2.50**
Outcast
[D2134] Puffin pbk **£2.50**
Song for a Dark Queen
[D2135] Hodder pbk **£1.95**
The High Deeds of Finn MacCool
[D2136] Puffin pbk **£2.50**
The Mark of the Horselord
The making of a leader - a frequent Sutcliff theme - lies at the heart of this novel about Phaedrus, a gladiator and freed slave who becomes king of the Gaelic 'horse people'.
[D2137] Puffin pbk **£2.50**
Warrior Scarlet
To become a 'Warrior Scarlet', one-armed Drem, a Bronze Age boy, must kill a wolf - a rite of passage he fails. Cast out, he lives as a shepherd until he finally does kill a wolf, and proves himself a hero.
[D2138] Puffin pbk **£2.50**
THE THREE LEGIONS TRILOGY
(in reading order)
The Eagle of the Ninth
The first book of the trilogy, chronicling the history of one family during the Roman occupation of Britain. In this story a young centurion, discharged from the Roman Army with a damaged leg, embarks on a quest to the north in search of the Eagle standard of the lost Ninth Legion, to which his father belonged.
[D2139] Puffin pbk **£2.99**

The Silver Branch
[D2140] Puffin pbk **£2.95**
The Lantern Bearers
[D2141] Puffin pbk **£2.50**
The Three Legions Trilogy
[D2142] Puffin pbk **£4.95**

THURBER, JAMES
The 13 Clocks and The Wonderful 'O'
Two brilliantly comic fairy tales for those who delight · in verbal gymnastics, by the well-known American humorist. Time has frozen (literally) in *The 13 Clocks*, while in *The Wonderful O*, pirates, disappointed in treasure hunting, set about removing the letter 'O' from all the words which contains it. Ridiculous and funny.
[D2143] Puffin pbk **£1.95**

TOMLINSON, TERESA
The Water Cat
Tomlinson's first novel, set in a Northern steel town, is built around a strange 'water cat' found by two children near their new home. A shape-changer, the cat is a merman, cut off from the sea by the hostile metal of the steel works. As the children unravel the cat's identity, they discover links between their village's past and present *and* themselves. A haunting debut.
[D2144] Walker pbk **£1.99**

TOWNSEND, JOHN ROWE
Gumble's Yard
An early example of a novel with an inner-city, working-class background, about two children who make a home for themselves in a deserted warehouse, and uncover a gang of criminals.
[D2145] Puffin pbk **£1.75**

TREASE, GEOFFREY
Cue for Treason
An exciting story of a plot against Queen Elizabeth's life which is foiled by two child actors.
[D2146] Puffin pbk **£2.50**

TREECE, HENRY
Legions of the Eagle
Reflecting Treece's fascination with crossroads in history, this book takes place as the Romans are leaving Britain.
[D2147] Puffin pbk **£2.50**
The Children's Crusade
[D2148] Puffin pbk **£1.95**
The Viking Saga
[D2149] Puffin pbk **£4.50**

Jenny Nimmo, author of *The Chestnut Soldier* (Methuen hbk **£7.95**)

UTTLEY, ALISON
A Country Child
A memoir of a country childhood.
[D2150] Puffin pbk **£2.50**
A Traveller in Time
One of Uttley's finest works, concerning a girl who moves in time between her life on a Derbyshire farmhouse, and a drama involving Mary Queen of Scots.
[D2151] Puffin pbk **£2.25**

VON STOCKUM, HILDA
The Winged Watchman
The 'Winged Watchman', a non-electrified polder mill, broods over the action of this story set in Holland in the final months of the German occupation, becoming the centre of the alarming events into which the miller's two sons, working for the Underground, are drawn. Von Stockum offers readers not only an adventure, but an evocation of a way of life under threat.
[D2152] Faber pbk **£2.95**

WEBB, KAYE (ED)
I Like This Story
An introduction to 50 favourite children's novels that should send readers to the originals.
[D2153] Puffin pbk **£2.95**

WHITE, E.B.
Charlotte's Web
Charlotte, an intelligent and perceptive spider, with the aid of Fern the farmer's daughter contrives a brilliant publicity stunt to save her friend Wilbur the pig from looming butchery. An American classic, this comic and profound barnyard fantasy is rooted firmly in the natural world and depicts a natural order that includes birth and death, destruction and survival.
[D2155] Puffin pbk **£1.95**

WILDER, LAURA INGALLS
Among historical sagas offering a genuine portrait of American pioneer life in the late 19th century, Wilder's *Little House* books are unexcelled. Told as a third-person narrative, the ten stories follow Laura's actual life from early childhood in a log cabin in the 'Big Woods' of Wisconsin through moves westward to the prairies and Dakota territory, where she marries Almanzo Wilder (whose story is told in *Farmer Boy*) at eighteen. While the Ingall's life is filled with danger and hardship (they nearly starve to death in the magnificent *The Long Winter*), it is rich in love and unity. As Laura grows up, the books grow with her - their evolving style reflecting her growing maturity. The 7 titles of the series are listed in reading order.
Little House in the Big Woods
[D2156] Methuen hbk **£5.95**
[D2157] Puffin pbk **£1.95**
Little House on the Prairie
[D2158] Puffin pbk **£2.25**
On the Banks of Plum Creek
[D2159] Puffin pbk **£2.50**
By the Shores of Silver Lake
[D2160] Puffin pbk **£2.25**
The Long Winter
[D2161] Puffin pbk **£2.50**
Little Town on the Prairie
[D2162] Puffin pbk **£2.50**
These Happy Golden Years
[D2163] Puffin pbk **£2.25**
Farmer Boy
[D2164] Puffin pbk **£2.50**
The First Four Years
[D2165] Puffin pbk **£1.50**

WILLIAMS, URSULA MORAY
Jeffy, the Burglar's Cat
An hilarious story about the efforts of Jeffy the cat to reform his owner, old Miss Amity, who is a burglar.
[D2166] Puffin pbk **£1.99**

Age 12 & Up

Trying to come to terms with a self that is no longer, either physically or emotionally, the familiar comfortable fit that it was in childhood, and with feelings and relationships that have become unexpected and sometimes disturbing, teenagers look for books which provide a growing awareness of the world as a complex, often confusing and ambiguous place in which to live. They read for the pleasure of unbounded experience which books offer, not just in the here and now, but in time and space (see the *History* and *Fantasy and Science-Fiction* sections below), but also for information; books like Judy Blume's 'do-it-yourself' guides to growing up, or Barbara Wersba's 'Fat' trilogy, John Rowe Townsend's *Downstream*, Paul Zindel's self-absorbed stories of adolescent angst, and Robert Cormier's bleak studies of corruption appeal precisely because they examine areas of life that are unknown and perhaps frightening.

Growing Up

BLUME, JUDY
A teenage cult figure on both sides of the Atlantic, Blume is an American writer whose subject matter (variations on the onset of puberty theme), values (an unquestioning acceptance of conformity and consumerism) and style (slangy, adolescent first-person narratives) excite controversy among adults. Her suburban comedies have been variously described: as a highly accessible 'rite of passage' literature that 'gives information and independence without risks'; as 'frank', 'funny' and 'morally responsible'; as teenage 'Blyton'; and as 'bibliotherapy' in which 'navel-gazing stereotypes' and the 'facsimile realism' of *Neighbours* are offered to readers in 'anorexic, emotionally impoverished narratives'. Whatever adults feel, the young universally believe that they cannot do without these upbeat, reassuring stories in which their contemporaries ultimately get what they want.
Are You There God? It's Me Margaret (11 +)
An eleven year old prays for puberty: *"I just told my mother I wanted a bra. Please help me to grow God. You know where."*
[D2170] Pan pbk **£2.25**
Deenie (11 +)
[D2171] Pan pbk **£2.25**
Forever (14 +)
The romance of two seventeen year olds from first date to first sexual encounter (a fumbling, clinically described consummation) to realisation that their relationship is not going to last 'forever'.
[D2172] Pan pbk **£2.50**
Its Not the End of the World (10 +)
12 year old Karen, her brother and sister discover that their parents' divorce is 'not the end of the world'.
[D2173] Pan pbk **£2.25**
Just as Long as We're Together (10 +)
[D2174] Pan pbk **£2.25**
Otherwise Known as Sheila the Great (10 +)
[D2175] Pan pbk **£2.25**
Starring Sally J. Freedman as Herself (10 +)
[D2176] Pan pbk **£2.25**
Then Again, Maybe I Won't (11 +)
A middle school *Catcher in the Rye* which chronicles the indignities suffered by Tony when his Italian-American working class family 'strike it rich' and move to suburbia.
[D2177] Pan pbk **£2.25**

BROOKS, BRUCE
The Moves Make the Man
The 'moves' in this ambitious and original first novel about sport, survival, truth and 'fictions' are the 'trickster' ones of Basketball, and are both focus and metaphor for the story's action. The players are the black narrator, Jerome Foxworthy, and Bix, a white athlete whose narrow definition of truth prevents him from using 'fakes' in basketball *and* in life.
[D2178] Pan pbk **£2.25**

CASEY, MAUDE
Over the Water (14 +)
The traumatic events of a summer holiday in Ireland after her grandfather's death bring the young heroine closer to understanding and accepting her own roots and nature, as well as the unhappiness of her mother with English life. Powerful, gritty, and funny.
[D2179] Women's P pbk **£2.95**

CHAMBERS, AIDAN
A writer of challenging novels that are experimental in both form and content.
Breaktime (14 +)
A young man's rite of passage into adulthood by way of his first (fantasy?) love affair is sensitively recounted in a narrative that includes strip cartoons, quotes from Dr. Spock, and uses different typefaces.
[D2180] Bodley pbk **£4.50**
Dance on My Grave (14 +)
Newspaper headlines at the start and finish of this powerful, extending and funny novel state its plot: 'Grave Damage: Youth Charged' - 'Youth's Pact to Dance on Friend's Grave'. In between Chambers explores the first homosexual relationship that resulted in this act of disrespect, in a text woven out of current literacies (socialwork reports, press clippings, jokes, footnotes) with strong echoes of Vonnegut.
[D2181] Pan pbk **£1.95**

CHAMBERS, AIDAN (ED)
A Sporting Chance: Stories of Winning and Losing (14 +)
The theme of taking a chance in life, of winning and losing, links these eight original stories by well-known writers, including Jan Mark, Peggy Woodford, and K.M. Peyton, set against a background of sport.
[D2182] Bodley pbk **£3.95**
Love All (14 +)
A fine collection of eight new stories from established contemporary writers such as Jan Mark, John Gordon, Hunter Davies and the compiler himself, about first love. In each, as the title suggests, love is seen as a game or contest.
[D2183] Bodley pbk **£4.50**

CHICK, SANDRA
Push Me, Pull You (14 +)
An angry brooding first-person narrative in which a sexually abused fourteen year old searches for understanding of her stepfather's shattering behaviour.
[D2184] Women's P pbk **£2.95**

COONEY, CAROLINE B.
I'm Not Your Other Half
As the title suggests, this love story, told from a girl's point of view, examines the conflict between commitment and independence that is a part of any romantic relationship.
[D2185] Methuen pbk **£1.95**

CORLETT, WILLIAM
The Secret Line
A complex, strikingly original story, whose televised narrative technique reflects its troubled heroine's inner and outer worlds, as Joanna Carson travels on 'the secret line' - a private extension of the London

Underground - inside her head. Her adventures finally enable her to grow into her 'mixed skin', and accept herself and her home.
[D2185A] Walker pbk **£1.99**

CORMIER, ROBERT
8 Plus 1
Nine short stories, uncharacteristically touching and personal, about relationships or moments of change or revelation: a first love, departure from home to college, a boy's discovery that his father is all too human.
[D2186] Collins pbk **£2.50**

DANEMAN, MEREDITH
Francie and the Boys
Actress Daneman's first novel for teenagers, this wise, amusing stage story chronicles the experiences of fourteen year old Francie - endearing, funny and forthright - who learns a lot about drama, boys and life itself when she unexpectedly lands a part in a local boys' school play.
[D2187] Walker pbk **£1.99**

DANZIGER, PAULA
An American writer in the Blume mould, but better. Her comic chronicles of adolescent angst in urban America are unusual for their 'authentic' teenage voice.
Can You Sue Your Parents for Malpractice?
When your older glamorous sister and comic younger sister always get their own way, and you get the washing-up, it's time to learn your 'rights'. That's why fourteen year old Lauren takes a law course at school. She discovers more than she bargained for: a younger boy who likes her.
[D2188] Pan pbk **£1.99**
It's an Aardvark Eat Turtle World
[D2189] Pan pbk **£1.99**
Remember Me to Harold Square
[D2190] Pan pbk **£2.25**
The Cat Ate My Gymsuit
A book about ways of seeing in which a teenage girl with a negative self-image learns to think positively about herself with the help of a refreshing new teacher and boy friend. When Ms Finney is suspended because of her controversial teaching methods, Marcy finds the courage to fight for her re-instatement.
[D2191] Pan pbk **£1.99**
The Divorce Express
[D2192] Pan pbk **£1.75**
The Pistachio Prescription
Thirteen year old hypochondriac Cassie is the odd one out in her appalling family, until she decides to try the

Robert Cormier, author of *8 Plus 1* (Collins pbk £2.50)

'pistachio prescription' and assert herself by standing for class president.
[D2193] Pan pbk **£1.99**
There's a Bat in Bunk 5
[D2194] Pan pbk **£1.99**

DARKE, MAJORIE
Comeback
Tough, determined Gail Knight, abandoned as a baby and brought up in council homes, has two burning ambitions: to win the Gold Medal for gymnastics, and to find her natural parents. An unromanticised look at the gruelling, competitive world of gymnastics and at the life of a black girl in Britain: loosely linked to *The First of Midnight* and *A Long Way to Go* (see *History*), accounts of Gail's ancestors.
[D2195] Puffin pbk **£2.50**

DESAI, ANITA
The Village by the Sea
Two teenagers faced with an unemployed, drunken father, a seriously ill mother and two young sisters, take on the responsibility for their family. Twelve year old Hari seeks work in corrupt Bombay, leaving Lisa in charge in their small Indian village. Contrasting lifestyles, values and kinds of poverty in India are explored in this rich, extending novel, based on fact.
[D2196] Puffin pbk **£1.99**

DOHERTY, BERLIE
Doherty tellingly puts the case for historical fiction in these two novels, linked by her concern to transmit the way in which binding family ties and a knowledge of family history enable the young to discover who they are, to learn from the experience of their elders, and to go out confidently into the world.
Granny Was a Buffer Girl
The histories Jess hears on the eve of her departure to study in France are the personal ones of three generations of her plucky Sheffield family. These shared stories, interwoven with the life and death of the town's mills, reveal to her family secrets, the complex relationships and changing ambitions of its women, enabling her to 'celebrate' her past and future.
[D2197] Collins pbk **£1.95**
White Peak Farm
Jeannie, teenage daughter of a Derbyshire sheepfarmer, introduces her family - their quirks, adventures, and tragedies - and explores their relationship with the land itself, as she moves towards maturity and leaves for university.
[D2198] Collins pbk **£1.75**

EDGE, TERRY
Fanfare for a Teenage Warrior in Love
'Passion and principle…collide' in a refreshingly funny first novel built around a series of sixth form debates in which the narrator and his best friend participate, but which they also use as an opportunity to run a school betting shop on their results.
[D2199] Corgi pbk **£1.95**

FINE, ANNE
Madame Doubtfire
Divorce is played for laughs in this black comedy in which three children are pawns in a grim emotional battle between their divorced parents. When their father - disguised as 'Madame Doubtfire' - becomes his ex-wife's housekeeper, the children but not the wife recognise him, and uproarious comedy ensues.
[D2200] Puffin pbk **£2.50**

FOX, PAULA
One of America's finest children's novelists, Fox writes with the measured clarity, honesty and richness of felt experience of a Philippa Pearce. The child isolated from family, peers, and surroundings by

his/her own actions or situation is often her subject. In these two layered and sharply challenging novels, she explores modern variations on an age-old theme - parental abandonment.
The Lost Boy
A spare account of a Greek island holiday in which two American families - one solid and caring, the other rootless - briefly and unforgettably meet. The arrival of young Jack Hemmings - morally abandoned by his shiftless, divorced father - disrupts an idyllic summer for the Careys, and leads to a tragic climax.
[D2201] Pan pbk **£1.99**
The Moonlight Man (14 +)
A fifteen year old girl, for whom her parents' divorce has been 'the main fact of her life', spends a transforming summer with her little-known father. From him she learns to take nothing for granted, and that to love is to accept frailty. A fine, deeply moving novel.
[D2202] Pan pbk **£1.95**

GERAS, ADELE
Happy Endings
Sixteen year old Mel looks back over a summer spent rehearsing and performing the part of Natasha in a youth theatre production of *The Three Sisters* and finds echoes of its characters' longings and loves in the highly charged atmosphere of company relationships. Her compassionate but naive narrative recognises but does not fully understand the parallel adult dramas.
[D2203] Collins pbk **£2.25**

GREENWALD, SHEILA
It All Began with Jane Eyre
Fiction for Franny is where her 'real life' takes place. When she begins acting out *Jane Eyre*, her mother buys her some teenage problem novels as a 'healthy' alternative. Like the heroines she now meets, Franny begins a diary and an investigation of the problems of her own family and friends - real and imagined. A sharp, funny spoof.
[D2204] Puffin pbk **£1.95**

GREGORY, SUSAN
Two perceptive, entertaining short story collections, the first about life in a comprehensive and the other about teenage life in a multi-racial urban setting.
Kill-a-Louise Week
[D2205] Puffin pbk **£2.25**
Martini-on-the-Rocks
[D2206] Puffin pbk **£1.50**

HOLMAN, FELICE
Slake's Limbo
A minor masterpiece about Aremis Slake, one of life's natural victims, who lives for 121 days in a refuge in New York's subway. He survives on his wits and imagination, and finally emerges with a new sense of achievement and dignity, which enables him to deal with his fears and face life as a survivor.
[D2207] Collins pbk **£1.95**

HOWKER, JANNI
Badger on the Barge
A memorable collection of short stories about encounters and relationships between gritty youth and the troubled old.
[D2208] Collins pbk **£2.25**

HUNTER, MOLLIE
A Sound of Chariots
Bridie is desolate on the death of her father, from whom she absorbed a love of books and language. With the help of a perceptive teacher and her mother, she emerges from her grief, realising that through her own writing she can make her father live again.
[D2209] Collins pbk **£2.25**

Berlie Doherty, author *Granny Was a Buffer Girl* (Collins pbk £1.95)

The Dragon Fly Years
Bridie's struggles to achieve her ambition to become a writer are movingly chronicled in this sequel to Hunter's autobiographical *A Sound of Chariots*.
[D2210] Collins pbk **£2.25**
I'll Go My Own Way
When Cat McPhie, only child of a traveller family, is taught her father's skills, she learns to go her own way by reconciling this unorthodox role with tradition. An absorbing and dramatic portrait of modern tinker life in a world that no longer has room for them.
[D2211] Collins pbk **£2.25**

KLEIN, ROBIN
Games
The games played by three teenage girls at an illicit party in an apparently empty house in the Australian bush are many: malicious bullying and a simulated séance that causes menacing spirits, dominate. Beneath the suspense, Klein tellingly charts a rites of passage that reveals an uncertain outsider's real nature and exposes that of her tormentors.
[D2212] Puffin pbk **£1.99**

LE VERT, JOHN
The Flight of the Cassowary (14 +)
An ambitious first novel - fresh, funny and challengingly ambiguous - of teenage metamorphosis miscarried. The cause of Paul's identity crisis - paternal disapproval and scorn - is not unique. It's manifestation is: Paul, with nods to Kafka and his school biology lessons, develops the habit of becoming any animal whose characteristics he can assume, for safety in stressful situations.
[D2213] Collins pbk **£2.50**

MAHY, MARGARET
Memory
A moody self-obsessed teenager learns to take responsibility not only for himself and his past actions but also for an old woman who he finds wandering in the streets.
[D2214] Puffin pbk **£2.50**

Anne Fine, author of *Madame Doubtfire*
(Puffin pbk £2.50)

The Catalogue of the Universe
Two teenagers try to work out their odd-ball relationship while one pursues the father she has never met.
[D2215] Methuen pbk **£1.95**

MARK, JAN
Two collections of a master short storyteller whose mordant wit pokes fun at a range of contemporary teenage pre-occupations and situations, from classroom routine, to teenage mothers and unsuitable love.
Feet and Other Stories
[D2216] Puffin pbk **£1.75**
Frankie's Hat
[D2217] Puffin pbk **£1.95**

OLDHAM, JUNE
Enter Tom
Shy Tom is the refreshingly unlikely hero of this funny novel which charts his attempts to understand women: his feminist mother, his classmates at school, and a glamorous new physics teacher.
[D2218] Puffin pbk **£1.95**
Grow up Cupid
"When I say I'm giving up men I do not refer to a single sample, but the whole species". When you're writing a romantic novel and a possible romantic hero with rainbow coloured hair is interested in you, it's not that easy, Meg discovers. An 'anti-romance' that subverts and makes fun of the romantic genre.
[D2219] Puffin pbk **£2.25**

PATERSON, KATHERINE
Jacob Have I Loved
A rich, deeply satisfying story which explores the jealousy of a despised (or so she thinks) elder twin for her favoured sister, and her recognition, when her sister leaves home, that she too is loved.
[D2220] Puffin pbk **£1.95**

PEYTON, K.M.
Three gripping novels about a gifted young working-class lad, who fights his way from delinquency to become a world-class concert pianist, with the help of a sympathetic and long-suffering girlfriend.

Pennington's Heir
[D2221] Methuen pbk **£1.95**
Pennington's Seventeenth Summer
[D2222] Methuen pbk **£1.95**
The Beethoven Medal
[D2223] Methuen pbk **£1.95**

PRINCE, ALISON
Nick's October
The story of a boy at a crisis point who feels that nobody is prepared to let him live the life he wants.
[D2224] Methuen pbk **£1.95**

SACHS, MARILYN
The Fat Girl
The unlikely relationship between handsome, popular, talented Jeff and the class 'fat girl' Ellen, whom Jeff tries to mould into his own preferred image, provides the springboard for a skilful exploration of the connection between love and power.
[D2225] Corgi pbk **£1.95**

SCHWARTZ, JANE
Caught (14 +)
A love of pigeons ignites the unlikely friendship of a ten year old New York girl and Casey, a middle-aged law-breaking failure. A master only of pigeon flying, Casey makes Louie his apprentice. She tells the story of their partnership, her naive vision only half-comprehending the despair of Casey's impoverished life beyond the rooftop world they share. Rich and demanding.
[D2226] Virago pbk **£3.95**

SMITH, DODIE
I Capture the Castle
A sensitive, beautifully written classic about the pain of first love and a young girl's desire to become a writer.
[D2227] Bodley pbk **£4.95**

STONES, ROSEMARY (ED)
More to Life than Mr Right
A varied, gritty collection of feminist stories.
[D2228] Fontana pbk **£1.95**

TAYLOR, ANDREW
The Coal House
A moving story about a thirteen-year-old trying to get over her mother's death, come to terms with the loneliness of moving to a new town.
[D2229] Collins pbk **£2.25**

TOWNSEND, JOHN ROWE
Downstream (14 +)   **NEW**
A highly charged novel, literally and metaphorically, about moving 'downstream'. It is built around three emotive subjects: a sixteen year old boy's relationship with his domineering father, the notion of father and son as rivals in love, and a child's dawning realisation that his parents are individuals.
[D2230] Walker pbk **£1.99**
The Intruder
Townsend's finest work, this is a tense thriller about a sinister intruder of the same name who invades Arnold Haithwaite's life and attempts to displace him and take over his identity.
[D2231] Puffin pbk **£2.50**

URE, JEAN
A Proper Little Nooryeff
A comical story about a working-class boy who thinks ballet is 'alright for girls' until he meets Anita and starts taking ballet lessons for her sake. In a sequel, *You Win Some, You Lose Some*, Jamie knows he has a talent for dancing, but isn't sure if he has one for girls. A witty challenge to male sex-stereotyping.
[D2232] Puffin pbk **£2.25**

You Win Some, You Lose Some
[D2233] Corgi pbk **£1.75**
See You Thursday
For Marianne - unhappy at home and at her 'snob' school, a romance with her mother's new lodger - a young, blind musician - breaks through her sullen self-absorption, and enables her to discover talents, feelings and friends she hadn't known before.
[D2234] Puffin pbk **£2.25**

VOIGT, CYNTHIA
An outstanding American novelist who explores the modern American landscape in rich and satisfying narratives infused with perception and honesty about feelings and relationships, of a sort rare in fiction for any age. Her stature has grown with each addition to her remarkable saga of books about the singular and invincible Tillerman family. The six titles are listed in reading order.
Homecoming (11 +)
The first of the 'Tillerman' novels describes a modern odyssey: the long, desperate and enthralling journey from Connecticut to Maryland of four children abandoned by their mentally-ill mother. Led by thirteen year old Dicey - a tough, resilient modern heroine, determined to keep her family together - they find a home with their unknown, reclusive grandmother on her run-down farm. Each subsequent book continues their story, with the focus shifting from child to child, and to friends and relatives. The resulting chronicle, spanning three generations, is rich beyond measure: each story illuminating the others and charting the way a damaged family mends, changes and grows.
[D2235] Collins pbk **£2.50**
Dicey's Song (11 +)
[D2236] Collins pbk **£2.25**
A Solitary Blue
[D2237] Collins pbk **£2.25**
The Runner
[D2238] Collins pbk **£2.25**
Come a Stranger
[D2239] Collins pbk **£2.50**
Son from Afar
[D2240] Collins pbk **£2.50**
Izzy, Willy, Nilly
A penetrating life-affirming novel which chronicles the courageous, un-selfpitying struggle of a 'Sweet Valley Highish' teenage girl - pretty, popular, conventional - to learn to lead a life she never contemplated, when she loses a leg in a car crash.
[D2241] Collins pbk **£2.50**
Tell Me if the Lovers Are Lovers (14 +)
Forced together as roommates at college, three young women with three distinct backgrounds share one common interest: volleyball. The game provides a centre for their developing friendship and unity as team members, and gives each of them strength and purpose when a teammate dies tragically.
[D2242] Collins pbk **£2.50**

WEBSTER, JEAN
Daddy Long Legs
An established favourite, written in 1912, about an orphan sent to college by an unknown benefactor known to Judy as 'Daddy Long Legs' because her only glimpse of him is of his elongated shadow. The book consists of her letters to him: tender, humorous and full of fun.
[D2243] Hodder pbk **£1.95**

WELCH, SANDY
Breaking Training
A collection of stories about modern teenage girls.
[D2244] Collins pbk **£1.95**

WERSBA, BARBARA
Unconventional but sound teenagers are Wersba's subjects; her targets - the pre-occupied parents,

unthinking prejudices, and obsession with fitness of contemporary America. Wersba approaches Zindel country 'in the eccentricity and articulateness of her characters', but her wry, ironic humour lacks 'the Zindel edge of hysteria' (*Signal Selection 1987*). Funny, reflective and honest.

Crazy Vanilla
Like his entry to the ice-cream naming contest, Tyler's account of a boy-girl friendship that alters his perspectives and enables him to contemplate renewed friendship with his brother whose homosexuality has come as a betrayal, is imaginative and wholesome. Wersba chronicles Tyler's loss of naiveté and romantic vision, and subsequent growth, with humour and care.
[D2245] Pan pbk **£2.25**

Tunes for a Small Harmonica
Incidents in the funny life of an unorthodox teenage girl who dresses like a boy, chain-smokes, is sent to a psychiatrist by her anxious, conventional mother, and falls in love with her poetry teacher.
[D2246] Pan pbk **£1.95**

THE 'FAT' TRILOGY (in reading order)

Fat - A Love Story
First in an hilarious trilogy about overweight Rita and her search for true love.
[D2247] Pan pbk **£2.50**

Love is a Crooked Thing
Romance blossoms between Rita and Arnold, a delightful but impractical dreamer, twice her age. When Arnold agrees with Rita's parents that he is too old for her and departs for Zurich, Rita has two choices: chocolate cake, or the chase!
[D2248] Pan pbk **£2.50**

Beautiful Losers
While Arnold writes his biography of Bach, Rita works to support them in this satisfying conclusion to her quest.
[D2249] Pan pbk **£2.50**

WOODFORD, PEGGY
Please Don't Go
There is more than one kind of love, as fifteen year old Mary discovers, in this romantic novel in which she develops a crush on an older man, and falls in love, on an exchange holiday in France, with a boy who dies tragically.
[D2250] Corgi pbk **£1.75**

ZINDEL, PAUL
An American writer whose work takes readers into the painfully absurd country of Holden Caulfield and Adrian Mole: a contemporary landscape of teenage disorientation, alienation and disillusionment with home, adults and society. Beneath the now familiar ingredients of neurosis, an apparently unbridgeable generation gap, zappy titles and dazzlingly articulate, fast-talking first-person narratives, Zindel's novels for older readers, at once funny and sad, have important messages, and are perennially popular.

A Begonia for Miss Applebaum   **NEW**
Zelda and Henry alternately tell the story of the last three months in the life of their beloved biology teacher, Miss Applebaum - affectionately known as 'the Shocker' because she 'loved to surprise her classes'.
[D2251] Bodley pbk **£2.95**

Confessions of a Teenage Baboon
[D2252] Collins pbk **£2.25**

Harry and Hortense of Hormone High
[D2253] Collins pbk **£1.95**

I Never Loved Your Mind
[D2254] Collins pbk **£2.25**

My Darling My Hamburger
Zindel explores the contrasting relationships of plain Maggie and pretty Liz with boyfriends and parents in a funny, inventive story that includes school assignments, posters and handwritten letters.
[D2255] Collins pbk **£2.25**

Pardon Me You're Stepping on My Eyeballs
The story of two teenage misfits whose oddball relationship begins at a group session run by the school psychiatrist.
[D2256] Collins pbk **£1.95**

The Amazing and Death-Defying Diary of Eugene Dingman
The title says it all: on his fifteenth birthday, Eugene Dingman begins a diary in which he records the hang-ups and humiliations suffered during a summer spent working as a waiter at a holiday resort.
[D2257] Collins pbk **£2.25**

The Pigman
Two teenagers befriend a lonely old man (nicknamed 'the Pigman' because he collects piggy-banks), but their mindless misuse of his kindness has tragic results.
[D2258] Collins pbk **£2.25**

The Pigman's Legacy
[D2259] Collins pbk **£2.25**

Contemporary Issues

ANDERSON, RACHEL
The War Orphan
Based on the author's own experience, this is a compelling and unusual account of the developing relationship of a young English boy and his adopted, handicapped Vietnamese brother, explored in part through their shared dreams of each other's lives.
[D2260] Richard Drew pbk **£2.25**

BANKS, LYNNE REID
One More River
The relationship of an Arab boy and a Jewish girl leads to an inevitable conflict of loyalties, both personal and political.
[D2261] Puffin pbk **£2.50**

BLUME, JUDY
Tiger Eyes
In this topical novel about teenage Davey and her family's response to her father's murder, Blume moves beyond her usual subject matter to confront serious social and political issues: teenage alcoholism, death (by violence and disease) and the morality of producing weapons of death.
[D2262] Pan pbk **£2.25**

CARTER, PETER
Bury the Dead
Carter grimly documents the way in which the past has the power to destroy the present. When Uncle Karl, a Nazi presumed dead, and now pursued by police, invades the lives of the East German Norden family, his reappearance, initially welcomed, ultimately lays waste to their lives and their daughter Erika's promising career as a high jumper. A taut thriller which probes the tensions and insecurities of life behind the Iron Curtain and in world athletics.
[D2263] Collins pbk **£2.75**

Under Goliath
This thought-provoking exploration of the problems inherent in the secret friendship of a Protestant drummer and a Catholic piper in Belfast is ultimately a plea for the abolition of 'borders without meaning except that they divide the hearts of men'.
[D2264] Puffin pbk **£1.75**

CORMIER, ROBERT
An American writer of compelling but disturbing, even shocking novels, whose subject is the destruction of the innocent and humane by a corrupt, morally bankrupt and oppressive world. Cormier has

been accused of cynicism and despair (evil inevitably triumphs in his work), but the moral and political dilemmas he confronts are not as extreme as his critics aver, and lead readers on to books such as Orwell's *1984*. For mature readers, Cormier's novels come as a 'jolting revelation'.

The Chocolate War
Ironically set in an American school run by monks, this bleak story of corruption, violence and abuse of power concerns the brave stand of one boy against the atrocities of the manipulative Brother Leon and the Vigils, a secret student society. The impotence of the individual who resists mob rule is brutally dramatised in a setting that mirrors institutional evil at all levels.
[D2265] Collins pbk **£2.50**

Beyond the Chocolate War
[D2266] Collins pbk **£2.25**

After the First Death
The terrorist hijack of a busload of school children and its tragic consequence provide the narrative framework for this chilling study of bravery, cowardice, innocence and guilt, and the disturbing notion that the potential to do evil resides in us all.
[D2267] Collins pbk **£2.50**

I am the Cheese
Adam's odyssey to visit his father in hospital is shockingly revealed as a double-edged one: an arduous bike ride and a sinister psychological journey to unlock a past that must not be remembered if he is to survive. A gripping but pessimistic thriller about the destruction of a boy's mind under political interrogation.
[D2268] Collins pbk **£2.25**

The Bumblebee Flies Anyway
Cormier confronts determinism and healers-turned-killers who reduce humans to specimens, in this disturbing story set in an experimental hospital for the terminally ill.
[D2269] Collins pbk **£2.25**

DHONDY, FARRUKH
Come to Mecca & Other Stories
Six pungent, often funny, short stories about teenagers, black, white and Asian, growing up in London today: stories edged with the energy, insecurities and tensions of the young in an urban society that celebrates carnival but puts them to work in machinist sweatshops, and subjects them to National Front abuse. Dhondy's ear for distinct, colourful, colloquial speech patterns distinguishes his vibrant prose.
[D2270] Collins pbk **£1.95**

DICKINSON, PETER
Green politics and terrorism, exploitation of a 'healer's gift', and a political kidnapping are the subjects of these taut many-layered thrillers.

Annerton Pit
[D2271] Puffin pbk **£1.95**

Healer
[D2272] Puffin pbk **£2.25**

The Seventh Raven
[D2273] Puffin pbk **£2.25**

GORDON, SHEILA
Waiting for the Rain
A fine, penetrating study of apartheid explored through the changing relationship of Frikki, grandson of a white Afrikaner farmer, and Tengo, son of the grandfather's 'boss-boy' - once friends, now fated to become enemies.
[D2274] Collins pbk **£2.50**

GUY, ROSA
A Trinidadian now living in New York City, where she is the President of the Harlem Writers' Guild, Guy is an astute, if harsh, chronicler of contemporary black experience in urban America. Harlem is her setting, with its inner city tenements, burnt out

buildings, brutalising poverty, violence and oppression. Her characters - streetwise Imamu Jones, Phyllisia Cathy and the Jackson sisters - are survivors: their search for identity and love as they emerge, however painfully, into adulthood, speaking directly to mature teenagers. 'Disturbing', realistic, raw and racy.

The Disappearance
A powerful novel about young Imamu Jones, released on probation from a detention centre, who tries to make a success of living with his new wealthy foster family. When the Aimsley's eight year old daughter disappears, Imamu's criminal record makes him a prime suspect. A chilling thriller that is also the story of a resilient teenager winning his place in the world.
[D2275] Puffin pbk £1.95

New Guys Around the Block
Back home in Harlem, an older Imamu becomes involved with two 'new guys' - brothers from New Orleans whose sophistication hides their cruel, destructive nature. A fast-paced mystery in which Imamu learns a painful lesson about appearance and reality.
[D2276] Puffin pbk £2.50

The Friends
The first book in a loose trilogy, this is a story of friendship, trust and betrayal. West Indian Phyllisia Cathy, newly brought to live in Harlem where her rigid, demanding father works, suffers abuse at school and strife at home. Befriended by ugly dynamic Edith who copes with desperate family responsibilities and poverty, Phyllisia finds her feet - but at Edith's expense.
[D2277] Puffin pbk £2.50

Edith Jackson
Edith, now seventeen and living with her sisters in a foster home, has struggled to keep her family together since her mother's death. As her sisters individually find solutions to their problems, Edith too must learn to make decisions for herself alone. A deeply moving story of a young person's growing awareness of herself as a woman and as a Black.
[D2278] Puffin pbk £2.25

Ruby
Like an older *The Friends*, this novel is about Edith's elder sister and is a sympathetic and perceptive study of lesbian love.
[D2279] Puffin pbk £2.50

The Ups and Downs of Carl Davis the Third   NEW
Carl Davis the Third (super-intelligent and the apple of his parents' eyes) is sent down South to stay with his grandmother. What has he done? Tragic news from his parents reveals what he didn't understand, in a powerful novel that explores themes of race, status, trust and betrayal.
[D2279A] Gollancz hbk £8.95

HARRIS, ROSEMARY
Zed
A gripping but compassionate account of the siege of the London offices of a Lebanese firm by Arab terrorists, recollected seven years later for his school magazine by 'Zed', one of the hostages, who was then aged eight. Terrorism and related political issues are addressed in this thriller, whose 'recall' device results in an unusual and moving study of a father/son relationship profoundly altered by the siege.
[D2280] Methuen pbk £1.75

HENTOFF, NAT
The Day They Came to Arrest the Book
Censorship is the subject of a compelling story built around an attempt to ban *Huckleberry Finn* from an American school because of its alleged racism.
[D2281] Puffin pbk £1.95

HINTON, S.E.
An American writer whose novels, like Judy Blume's, excite controversy. Gang warfare, violence, class differences, conflicting loyalties, teenage alienation, and the relationship between brothers are Hinton's subjects. Their treatment has been variously described as 'tough', 'hard-hitting', 'starkly realistic'; as 'genuine' studies of 'raw youth, rawly described'; and as a 'sort of Mills and Boon' for boys; her 'greaser' heroes as middle class 'sheep in wolves' clothing'. Explosive and enormously popular.

Rumble Fish
[D2282] Collins pbk £2.25

Tex
During the long absence of their feckless father, two brothers - one a 'goer' and the other a 'stayer' and potential delinquent - find their relationship strained to breaking point.
[D2283] Collins pbk £2.25

That Was Then This is Now
[D2284] Collins pbk £1.95

The Outsiders
Written when the author was seventeen, this thrilling novel is narrated by orphaned Ponyboy, a fourteen year old rebel from the wrong side of the town. His tale of class warfare between his gang, 'the Greasers', and 'the Socs', moneyed middle-class thugs, raises important questions about justice, prejudice and the way people respond to poverty.
[D2285] Collins pbk £2.25

HOWKER, JANNI
The Nature of the Beast
The 'beast' is both a real and dangerous animal and a creation of the narrator's imagination. It is a metaphor for the injustices that enforced unemployment brings to a small Northern community. A harsh, illuminating book about the realities of life in Britain today.
[D2286] Collins pbk £2.25

JONES, TOECKEY
Go Well, Stay Well
Apartheid and the racist attitudes of Whites and Blacks towards each other are the subject of this honest book which documents the developing friendship between two teenage girls, one black, one white, who are determined not to give up the right to share each other's company.
[D2287] Collins pbk £2.25

Skindeep
An exploration of growing up in a racially segregated society. The focus is on a mixed-race love story.
[D2288] Pan pbk £2.50

KENNEMORE, TIM
The Fortunate Few
A chilling tale, set in the not-too-distant future, about the exploitation of child gymnasts, in a Britain where gymnastics has replaced football as the main spectator sport.
[D2289] Puffin pbk £1.75

LESTER, JULIUS
The Basketball Game
Set in Nashville, Tennessee in the 1950s, this sensitive but hard-hitting novel chronicles the growing friendship of a black boy and a white girl that breaks the unwritten rules of friendship in this segregated city - and is doomed to failure.
[D2290] Puffin pbk £1.75

LINGARD, JOAN
The love story of Protestant Sadie and Catholic Kevin begins in Belfast, and follows them to England, in this popular series which sets their personal saga against the conflicts in Northern Ireland. The five titles are listed in reading order.

The Twelfth Day of July
[D2291] Puffin pbk £1.99

Across the Barricades
[D2292] Puffin pbk £1.99

Into Exile
[D2293] Puffin pbk £1.99

A Proper Place
[D2294] Puffin pbk £1.99

Hostages to Fortune
[D2295] Puffin pbk £1.99

The Guilty Party
When Josie embarks on a determined struggle against the building of a nuclear power station near her home, she jeopardises her relationship with her family and boyfriend.
[D2296] Puffin pbk £2.25

MARSHALL, JAMES VANCE
Walkabout
An adolescent girl and her brother survive an air crash in the Australian Outback and are helped to stay alive by an aboriginal boy. Young people from two entirely different cultures meet, but misunderstanding between them ultimately results in tragedy.
[D2297] Puffin pbk £1.50

NEEDLE, JAN
My Mate Shofiq
Bernard defends Shofiq, a Pakistani boy in his class, and is ostracised by his gang as a 'Paki-lover'. Set in a Northern mill town, this hard-hitting, often funny book, tackles racism head on.
[D2298] Collins pbk £1.95

O'BRIEN, ROBERT
Z for Zachariah
Written in diary form this novel tells the story of two holocaust survivors.
[D2299] Collins pbk £2.50

PAUSEWANG, GUDRUN
The Last Children   NEW
Life - or at least the struggle for life - after a nuclear explosion is the subject of this compelling story that has already had a profound effect on attitudes in Germany, where it was first published in 1983.
[D2299A] Julia MacRae hbk £7.95

SEBESTYEN, OUIDA
The Girl in the Box   NEW
"To anyone who finds this: My name is Jackie McGee. I am kidnapped". Abducted and imprisoned in a small, always dark cellar, with her typewriter and some paper, Jackie courageously sustains herself by tapping out a series of letters, autobiographical sketches and 'talking to myself' musings. A brilliant, often claustrophobic story that illuminates what are probably Jackie's last hours.
[D2300] H Hamilton hbk £7.95

SEFTON, CATHERINE
Catherine Sefton is the pseudonym of Martin Waddell, a writer whose work is enormously varied and spans all ages. Winner of the 1988 Smarties Prize for Children's Books for his picture book *Can't You Sleep Little Bear?*, Waddell, himself from Northern Ireland, aims to show the effects of the political and social situation there on young people and their lives in this trilogy of books.

Frankie's Story
A fast-moving, taut story in which Catholic Frankie's domestic and inner conflicts (her father has deserted her family, her boyfriend is Protestant) not only mirror the political and social ills and misery around her, but put her in danger from the resulting rigid, narrow viewpoint they encourage.
[D2301] Methuen pbk £1.99

Starry Night
A moving story set on the Irish Republican border, of a fifteen year old's loss of innocence - of 'the starry nights' of her childhood. When the truth behind a

Joan Lingard, author of *The Guilty Party* (Puffin pbk £2.25)

family crisis is revealed, Kathleen learns what everyone else knows: that her beloved 'sister' Rose is her mother, disgracefully pregnant again.
[D2302] Methuen pbk **£1.95**

The Beat of the Drum   **NEW**
Can anyone escape the 'beat of the drum' in Northern Ireland? The response of Brian Hanna, trapped on the 'British' side of the conflict and one of its victims, and that of his friends and uncle who seccumb to the unremitting beat, is explored in this bleak conclusion to Sefton's powerful trilogy.
[D2303] H Hamilton hbk **£7.95**

SMITH, RUKSHANA
Rainbows of the Gutter
During a summer of rioting a young West Indian artist, with dreams of a united multi-racial society, must face up to the realities of being black in Britain today.
[D2304] Methuen pbk **£1.95**

Salt on the Snow
A young girl helping out at a local volunteer bureau is shocked to discover that her first assignment is to teach English to Rashmi, a middle-aged Asian woman. Gradually the two grow closer together, despite opposition from both families.
[D2305] Bodley pbk **£2.95**

Sumitra's Story
A semi-documentary novel about the plight of a young Ugandan Asian girl who finds it difficult to conform to her parents' traditional way of life in modern Britain.
[D2306] Bodley pbk **£3.95**

SWINDELLS, ROBERT
Two fine novels from a committed anti-nuclear campaigner which explore the involvement of young people in anti-nuclear protest, and life in a post-nuclear Britain.
A Serpent's Tooth
[D2307] Puffin pbk **£1.99**
Brother in the Land
[D2308] Puffin pbk **£1.99**

WATSON, JAMES
A British writer of topical political thrillers.
Talking in Whispers
Set in a Junta-controlled Chile, Watson's tale of sixteen year old Andres, wanted by the secret police as a dissident, pits the resistance struggle for human rights against the oppression of a military dictatorship.
[D2309] Collins pbk **£2.25**
Where Nobody Sees
Another story of establishment corruption which sets a young country couple and their family and friends, against an authority conspiracy of silence and intimidation, over the construction of a nuclear waste dump near their village.
[D2310] Collins pbk **£2.25**

Historical Fiction

AVERY, GILLIAN
A Likely Lad
Set in Manchester at the turn of the century and full of social comedy, this is a finely observed study of family conflicts and class values.
[D2311] Bodley pbk **£4.50**
The Greatest Gresham
Julia Gresham living in a London suburb in the 1890s longs for greatness but does not know how to achieve it - until she meets the unsuitable Holt children.
[D2312] Bodley pbk **£4.55**
The Warden's Niece
Maria runs away from her hated school to her uncle, the Warden of an Oxford college, and develops an ambition to become a professor of Greek.
[D2313] Bodley pbk **£3.95**

CARTER, PETER
The Sentinels
A gripping adventure story in which the passage to manhood of two youths - one an orphaned volunteer in the British navy, the other a West African youth captured to be sold into slavery - is set against the backdrop of the British naval anti-slavery patrols of 1840.
[D2314] Richard Drew pbk **£2.25**

CONRAD, PAM
Prairie Songs
A haunting evocation of turn-of-the-century pioneer life in Nebraska. Louisa, the young narrator, knows only the wide, empty spaces, isolation, endurance, small triumphs and big defeats of prairie life, until a fragile and beautiful New Yorker arrives bringing books and glimpses of a different world. But not eveyone can live up to the demands of prairie life…
[D2315] Penguin pbk **£2.25**

DARKE, MARJORIE
The historical struggle of courageous young individuals for important social and political causes - freedom from slavery and oppression, women's rights, equal opportunities - is Darke's subject in each of these rich, loosely linked novels.
A Long Way to Go
A vivid unusual story of a young conscientious objector, Luke, great grandson of Midnight and Jess of *The First of Midnight*, facing conscription in the Great War. Set against the background of the suffragette movement and the struggle in the munitions factories for equal rights.
[D2316] Puffin pbk **£2.25**
A Question of Courage
When Emily, a young working-class seamstress, joins the Suffragettes and moves to London to become one of Mrs Pankhurst's bodyguards, she learns about the courage needed to endure police brutality, imprisonment and force feeding in the fight for a just cause.
[D2317] Collins pbk **£1.95**
The First of Midnight
Revolving around the illicit slave trade in 18th-century Bristol, this powerful Dickensian novel chronicles the developing love between Jess, an ignorant, orphaned servant girl and Midnight, an educated Ibo slave, as both seek liberation from their 'chattel' status. The child Jess bears after Midnight returns to Africa to realise his dreams for his people becomes his symbol of personal freedom.
[D2318] Puffin pbk **£1.95**

FRANK, RUDOLF
No Hero for the Kaiser (14 +)
A fine, grimly humorous, anti-war novel published in Germany in 1931 and burnt by the Nazis. It charts the growing perception of a fourteen year old Polish boy,

adopted by invading German soldiers and taken to the Russian and Western fronts, of war as a battlefield of deceit.
[D2319] Richard Drew pbk **£2.25**

GERAS, ADELE
The Girls in the Velvet Frame
The fatherless Bernstein sisters in pre-World War I Jerusalem pine for their elder brother who has migrated to America to seek his fortune, but hasn't written. Will their portrait in a 'velvet frame', sent to a New York Rabbi, find him? An evocative family story.
[D2320] Collins pbk **£1.95**
Voyage
The moving story of the steerage voyage of a group of Jewish emigrants from the poverty and pogroms of their Eastern European homelands to a new life in New York in the early 1900s.
[D2321] Collins pbk **£1.95**

GREENE, BETTE
The Summer of My German Soldier
A devastating but powerful story set in America during World War II. A disturbed, abused Jewish girl living in a racist, anti-semitic Arkansas town, Patty defies the values of her family and her culture in befriending her black nurse and, ironically, an escaped German POW, whom she daringly but disastrously shelters. A bleak, compelling study of prejudice, parental cruelty and friendship.
[D2322] Puffin pbk **£2.25**

HARRIS, RUTH ELWIN
The Quantocks Quartet (three have been published) is an acclaimed sequence - 'a *Little Women* of our times' - which follows the fortunes of the four Purcell sisters, and their neighbours the Mackenzie family, from their mother's death in 1910 through the Great War and its aftermath. Each book is told from a different sister's viewpoint, and each story illuminates the others. A vivid, substantial, compelling chronicle.
The Silent Shore
This is the story of Sarah - a child when her mother dies, but determined, like her older sisters, to stay on in their country house - and the years before she takes up an Exhibition at Oxford in the early twenties.
[D2323] Walker pbk **£1.99**
The Beckoning Hills
The love story of the outspoken eldest sister Frances who defies convention to study at the Slade School of Art, and Gabriel, the Mackenzies' Byronic eldest son. Will marriage compromise her talent? War changes her perspectives.
[D2324] Walker pbk **£1.99**
The Dividing Sea   **NEW**
Julia lives in the shadow of her mercurial, gifted sister Frances. When war breaks out, she joins the VAD to follow Geoffrey, her childhood love, to France. This is the story of their doomed love. •
[D2325] Julia MacRae hbk **£8.95**

HAUTZIG, ESTHER
The Endless Steppe
A fresh, buoyant autobiographical survival story of a ten year old Polish girl and her Jewish family, exiled to a labour camp in Siberia during World War II.
[D2326] Puffin pbk **£2.25**

HOLM, ANNE
I Am David
A boy escapes from a concentration camp and makes his way across Europe to Denmark. His fear of capture and delight in his unknown freedom give a sharp, emotional edge to an escape story that is more than a thriller.
[D2327] Methuen pbk **£1.75**

LEESON, ROBERT
Candy for King (14 +)
Orphaned, earnest Candleford Kitchener is a born
innocent. Expelled from school and branded as a
troublemaker, Candy enlists in the army and is sent to
the Middle East. His increasingly funny, picaresque
adventures are born from his attempts to put the
hollow cant of those in authority in the 1950s into
idealistic practice.
[D2328] Collins pbk **£1.75**

LESTER, JULIUS
Lester offers a rare black perspective in these two
collections which explore the injustices, pains,
miseries and pride of life as a slave in the years
preceding the American Civil War. His short stories
of slaves and ex-slaves in *Long Journey Home* are
based on factual material. Slaves tell what it felt like
To Be A Slave in their own words in Lester's
poignant history.
Long Journey Home
[D2329] Puffin pbk **£1.50**
To Be a Slave
[D2330] Puffin pbk **£1.95**

NEWTH, METTE
The Abduction (14 +)   **NEW**
Newth explores ageless ills - greed, ignorance,
prejudice, superstition - against an unusual
background. Set in the late 16th century, *The
Abduction* tells the story of an Inuit girl and her
intended husband, a shaman, kidnapped by traders
and taken from Greenland to Norway as freaks.
Humiliated, falsely accused of murder and witchcraft,
the pair plan their escape...
[D2331] Simon & Sch pbk **£3.95**

O'DELL, SCOTT
Island of the Blue Dolphins
Set in the 19th century, this is the true story of an
Indian girl, abandoned by her tribe, who survived
alone on an island off the Californian Coast for 18
years.
[D2332] Puffin pbk **£1.50**
Streams to the River
The true story of Sacagawea, the Indian girl who
acted as interpreter to explorers Lewis and Clark on
their epic journey into the uncharted American West.
[D2333] Puffin pbk **£2.50**

ORGEL, DORIS
The Devil in Vienna   **NEW**
A semi-autobiographical novel about the doomed
friendship of two girls - Inge, a Jew, and Liese, a
member of the Hitler Youth - in Vienna in 1938.
[D2334] Simon & Sch pbk **£3.95**

OVERTON, JENNY
The Ship from Simnel Street
The ballads and bakehouse rituals of 150 years ago
blend in this fine novel which sets Sussex domestic
history against the background of the Peninsular War.
It follows the story of the baker's two daughters:
Polly who defies convention, dresses as a soldier, and
follows her love to war, and Susannah who stays
behind to run the bakehouse and mastermind the
baking of 1,200 cakes of forgiveness to be sent to
Polly's husband's regiment.
[D2335] Puffin pbk **£1.95**

PEYTON, K.M.
A family saga set in the early 1900s at the Essex
manor house Flambards. When the orphaned heroine
Christina first arrives, she encounters a way of life
that is still Victorian in social outlook and custom. As
she grows she sheds these values, and gradually
moves into the 20th century.
Flambards
[D2336] Puffin pbk **£2.50**

The Edge of the Cloud
An oily insight into the harsh realities behind the
glamour of early flying.
[D2337] Puffin pbk **£2.50**
Flambards in Summer
[D2338] Puffin pbk **£2.50**
Flambards Divided
[D2339] Puffin pbk **£2.50**

ROSTOWSKI, MARGARET
After the Dancing Days
For thirteen year old Annie, her father's return from
World War I is the beginning of her confrontation
with war and its continuing effect - for, as a doctor, he
decides to work in a veterans' hospital for the
wounded. Annie's growing friendship with one of his
patients mirrors the complex feelings of a community
coming to terms with the casualties of war. An
impressive first novel.
[D2340] Pan pbk **£2.25**

SEBESTYEN, OUIDA
Words by Heart
Lena, hungry for books and learning, memorises most
of the Bible, and wins a Sunday School contest. It is
then that she confronts the handicap of her blackness
for the first time as the Jim Crowism her family
moved West to escape emerges in Scatter Creek in
1910. A powerful story about finding oneself in a
prejudiced world and remaining true to the words
learned 'by heart'.
[D2341] Pan pbk **£2.25**

TAYLOR, MILDRED D.
Roll of Thunder Hear My Cry
A powerful novel depicting the struggles and
hardships of a black family in Mississippi in the
1930s, as they stand up against racism and oppression
to retain their land and dignity.
[D2342] Puffin pbk **£2.50**
Let the Circle Be Unbroken
The sequel.
[D2343] Puffin pbk **£2.95**

VOIGT, CYNTHIA
In a different voice from her *Tillerman* books, Voigt
has written a fine period piece - New England 1894 -
that is also a gripping mystery. When twelve year old
Jean Wainwright goes to work for Mr Thiel,
cataloguing business and personal papers of his late
wife's family, she begins to unravel clues to a terrible
story involving her employer, his brother-in-law, and
her own identity.
The Callender Papers   **NEW**
[D2344] Collins pbk **£2.25**

WALSH, JILL PATON
A Parcel of Patterns
The grim chronicle of the village of Eyam which
voluntarily quarantined itself during the Great Plague
of 1665, and lost most of its 350 inhabitants, is
unforgettably told in a moving fictionalised account
by sixteen year old Moll.
[D2345] Puffin pbk **£1.95**
Fireweed
Two runaway evacuees from different classes
return to London during the Blitz and set up home in
the cellar of a destroyed house. Their innocent
romance is shattered by a bomb. Poignant and
haunting.
[D2346] Puffin pbk **£1.75**
The Dolphin Crossing
Two young boys steal a boat to help save British
soldiers stranded at Dunkirk.
[D2347] Puffin pbk **£1.99**

WESTALL, ROBERT
Echoes of War   **NEW**
A collection of short stories in which Westall looks at

the way war shapes and changes lives.
[D2347A] Viking hbk **£4.99**
Fathom Five
[D2348] Puffin pbk **£2.50**
The Machine Gunners
Set on Tyneside in World War II, this realistic, often
funny adventure tells the story of Chas and his
teenage mates, who think of war as a kind of game,
until they steal a machine gun from a crashed
German plane, hide it from the authorities in a
dugout, and finally, with the help of a Nazi airman
on the run, make their own dangerous contribution
to Tyneside's defence. An uncompromising
exploration of violence, its corrupting power, and
morality.
[D2349] Puffin pbk **£2.50**

WILLARD, BARBARA
The *Mantlemass* sequence of novels chronicles
the history of two landowning families from the
15th to the 17th centuries. Willard's work is small-
scale and domestic, but great events intrude and
often endanger this settled rural life. The stories
are all set in Ashdown Forest, and a strong sense
of place and feel for season and weather pervade
the books. The nine titles are listed in reading
order.
The Lark and the Laurel
[D2350] Macdonald pbk **£2.50**
Sprig of Broom
[D2351] Macdonald pbk **£2.50**
A Cold Wind Blowing
[D2352] Macdonald pbk **£2.50**
The Iron Lily
[D2353] Macdonald pbk **£2.50**
Harrow and Harvest
[D2354] Macdonald pbk **£2.50**
The Eldest Son
[D2355] Macdonald pbk **£2.50**
A Flight of Swans
[D2356] Macdonald pbk **£2.50**
The Miller's Boy
[D2357] Macdonald pbk **£2.50**
The Keys of Mantlemass
[D2358] Macdonald pbk **£2.50**

Fantasy & Science-Fiction

ADAMS, RICHARD
Watership Down
A vision of doom starts a band of rabbits on an epic
adventure in search of a new home, when their warren
is endangered by property developers. A sustained
and compelling fantasy saga remarkable for its
portrayal of a rabbit society which, despite having its
own language, politics and customs, remains true to
life.
[D2359] Puffin pbk **£3.50**

CHRISTOPHER, JOHN
The Prince in Waiting Trilogy
A novel sequence set in a fragmented warring Britain
plunged into a medieval limbo following an industrial
accident. The hero Luke spearheads a new scientific
Renaissance and attempts to unite the country but,
after personal loss, turns this new technology against
his people.
[D2360] Puffin pbk **£4.50**
The Tripods Trilogy
A gang of young resistance fighters seek to
overthrow the tyrannical tripods, three-legged metal
monsters from outer space who have destroyed
technology and control mens' minds by brain
implants.
[D2361] Puffin pbk **£3.50**

CLARKE, ARTHUR C.
Of Time & Stars
A varied and fascinating collection of Clarke's best science fiction stories, including 'The Nine Billion Names of God' and 'The Sentinel', on which the film *2001* was based.
[D2362] Puffin pbk **£1.99**

DAHL, ROALD
The Wonderful Story of Henry Sugar
Seven characteristically off-beat tales about people who possess unlikely powers, including 'The Boy Who Talked to Animals'.
[D2363] Puffin pbk **£2.50**

DALTON, ANNIE
Out of the Ordinary
When Mollie scribbles an ad for a holiday job - *'Quests undertaken, lost things found, enchantments broken'* - her 'ordinary' life with a single mother is transformed. Three mysterious visitors appear to tell her that she has been chosen to hide a small, silent, bewitched child from an evil wizard. A poetic blend of fantasy and family story, and a vigorous debut novel.
[D2364] Methuen pbk **£1.99**

DICKINSON, PETER
The *Changes* trilogy - novels linked by situation rather than character - is set in England in the near future in the time of the Changes: a period when man has turned his back on machinery and retreated into a new dark age of ignorance and brutality. Quirky, intellectually challenging, inventive and entertaining.
THE CHANGES TRILOGY (in reading order)
The Weathermonger
Two young people set off in an antique car from the Beaulieu motor museum to find the cause of the Changes. A 'revived but drug-sick Merlin' is the incongruous source.
[D2365] Puffin pbk **£1.99**
The Devil's Children
Set at the beginning of *The Changes*, this story concerns Nicky, an abandoned London girl who joins a group of Sikhs in search of a good place to live.
[D2366] Puffin pbk **£1.25**
Heartsease
Three children find a 'witch' who has been stoned and left for dead, and contrive his escape.
[D2367] Puffin pbk **£1.99**
The Trilogy
[D2368] Puffin pbk **£3.99**

DUNLOP, EILEEN
A Flute in Mayferry Street
Set in a shabby town house in Edinburgh, this novel concerns three members of the once prosperous Ramsay family: the chance discovery of an old letter sets them on a search through the house for clues to the past, which dramatically alter their straitened present.
[D2369] Richard Drew pbk **£2.25**
Robinsheugh
Sent to spend the summer with a favourite aunt at Robinsheugh in the Scottish borders, 12 year old Elizabeth finds her relative unaccountably withdrawn - until she too begins to succumb to the past life of the house, and starts to slip in time between the 20th and the 18th centuries.
[D2370] Richard Drew pbk **£2.25**

FARMER, PENELOPE
Thicker than Water `NEW`
A mysterious SOS message for her mother on Radio Four from an unknown aunt has disturbing social consequences for Becky.
[D2370A] Walker hbk **£8.95**

FISK, NICHOLAS
A Rag, a Bone and a Hank of Hair
The triumph of free will over social determinism is the subject of Fisk's ingenious and compelling science-fiction story - set in the 23rd century after nuclear accidents have disastrously reduced the birth rate. Brin, one of the 'rare' young people, is entrusted with the task of monitoring the 'reborns' - genetically engineered children on whom human survival depends.
[D2371] Puffin pbk **£1.25**

GARNER, ALAN
In these masterly novels Garner finds 'new terms of reference' for contemporary adolescence in metaphor, symbol and speech. Each is a three-layered narrative - 'intersected by image, place, repeated phrase, echoing event' and characterised by a pared-down 'elliptical mode of speech…piercing in its capacity for expressing the *changing* emotions of his characters'. This structure and poetic compression, with its resulting complexity, makes considerable demands on the reader, but offers in return great rewards.
Red Shift
A controversial book in which the stories of two young men from different periods of time - a Roman legionary, whose violence begets violence, and a villager who brings death to his community in the Civil War - frame and enlarge a contemporary love story: that of Tom whose inability to reconcile tenderness and violence leads him to 'murder' love.
[D2372] Collins pbk **£2.25**
The Owl Service
A spare, emotional novel, winner of the Carnegie Medal and Guardian Award, set in a Welsh Valley in which the potential tragedy of a local mythological love triangle is re-enacted by three contemporary youngsters.
[D2373] Collins pbk **£1.75**

GORDON, JOHN
The Giant under the Snow (11 +)
A supernatural fantasy built around an ancient brooch of power, which involves modern children in the re-workings of myth, as mysterious natural forces are unexpectedly awakened from their slumber.
[D2374] Puffin pbk **£1.75**
The House on the Brink
An atmospheric chiller in which the fens are as much a character as the two teenagers who try to unearth the mystery of an unnameable log-like object which rises from the mud of the tidal estuary.
[D2375] Puffin pbk **£2.25**

HOBAN, RUSSELL
The Mouse and His Child
A clockwork mouse and his child face each other, holding hands, and set out on a journey through a naturalistic world to escape from the villainous Manny Rat and to discover the key to 'self-winding'. This multi-layered fantasy may be read as either a richly comic adventure story or as a savage, satirical, philosophical journey.
[D2376] Puffin pbk **£1.75**

HUGHES, MONICA
Keeper of the Isis Light
The first in a trilogy of books built around a popular sci-fi theme: escape from an unsatisfactory environment to seek a better world. Set on the distant planet of Isis, they concern the struggle of settlers from Earth to establish a sound community. The two following titles are listed below.
[D2377] Methuen pbk **£1.95**
The Guardian of Isis
[D2378] Methuen pbk **£1.95**
The Isis Pedlar
[D2379] Methuen pbk **£1.50**

Devil on My Back
[D2380] Methuen pbk **£1.75**
Sandwriter
[D2381] Methuen pbk **£1.95**

JACQUES, BRIAN
Mattimeo `NEW`
Eight seasons after the great Redwall War, the legendary warrior Matthies sets out to free his young son Mattimeo - captured by a band of slave traders. When he is away, general Iron Beak and his crows, cast a greedy eye on the peaceful Well-Stock Abbey. Another epic confrontation between good and evil.
[D2382] Hutchinson hbk **£9.95**
Mossflower
The prequel to *Redwall*, telling how the legendary mouse Martin rids Mossflower Wood of a demonic wildcat and her minions.
[D2383] Beaver pbk **£2.99**
Redwall
A compelling rumbustious animal fantasy, in which the mice of Redwall Abbey are assailed by a vicious warring gang of rats and are saved only when the central character finds his birthright.
[D2384] Beaver pbk **£2.95**

JONES, DIANA WYNNE
Jones uses her unique and intellectually challenging blend of fantasy and comedy to explore the significance and changes faced as adolescents grow older: her protagonists, who often *feel* ordinary, find themselves 'catapaulted' into magic worlds which reveal them to be extraordinary. The magical transformations in these three stories are powerful metaphors for the transition from uncertain youth to potent adulthood, as well as for the dislocations of personality and shifting nature of reality which can occur along the way.
A Tale of Time City
In a dazzling tale of astonishing complexity, Jones recounts the adventures of Vivian Smith, kidnapped from her English home in 1939 by two boys, and taken through a time lock into Time City, a place outside time.
[D2385] Methuen pbk **£1.99**
Fire and Hemlock
In this modern re-enactment of the legendary imprisonment of Tam Lyn, the rhymer, by fairies, Polly grows to womanhood and independence as she helps the cellist Thomas Lynn escape his ex-wife Laurel, using a series of extraordinary games, in which the pair invent heroic roles for one another that take them in and out of the real world.
[D2386] Methuen pbk **£1.95**
Howl's Moving Castle
Timid Sophie Hatter, Jones's spellbound heroine, is not the ancient crone she appears to be: neither is her employer, the Wizard Howl, a latter-day Bluebeard. In this wonderfully funny romance they discover their true, unstereotypical roles, and find love.
[D2387] Methuen pbk **£1.95**

LILLINGTON, KENNETH
An Ash-Blonde Witch
When the beautiful daughter of a 22nd century researcher arrives out of nowhere in the isolated 'conservation' community of Urstwhile, her scientific skills and 'rare powers' suggest she is a witch. An hilarious mix of science fiction/fantasy, romance and 'mock political intrigue'.
[D2388] Puffin pbk **£1.99**

MAHY, MARGARET
Like Diana Wynn Jones, Mahy uses fantasy and the supernatural in equally original ways to explore similar terrain. In her complex, beautifully crafted novels, the intrusion of the supernatural into the real world occurs at a point of 'changeover' and of fresh awareness in her character's lives: the transition from

childhood to adolescence, adolescence to maturity, from denial of love or responsibility to acceptance of it.

The Changeover
A blend of supernatural thriller, romance and family story, this fine, multi-layered novel concerns a teenage girl's 'changeover' into a witch in order to save her possessed brother, and the resulting 'supernatural romance' she experiences.
[D2389] Methuen pbk **£1.95**

The Tricksters
A compelling mix of coming-of-age and family story, which is as much about finding identity as it is about appearance and reality. Here it is not just the mysterious Carnival brothers - humans, ghosts, fictitious characters? - who are 'tricksters', but also the apparently happy Hamilton family whose lives they invade during a New Zealand Christmas holiday.
[D2390] Puffin pbk **£2.50**

NORTON, ANDRE
One of America's finest writers of adventure stories with a science fiction setting. Particularly popular amongst young teenage boys.

Catseye
In both *Catseye* and *The Iron Cage* Norton constructs powerful thought-provoking novels around the ancient kinship of beast and man, and its potential subversion by men who believe in their 'right' to exploit fellow creatures. The animals here, extraordinary and convincingly realised, are as intelligent as man, if not more so.
[D2391] Puffin pbk **£1.95**

The Beast Master
[D2392] Puffin pbk **£1.95**

The Iron Cage
[D2393] Puffin pbk **£2.50**

SLEATOR, WILLIAM
Interstellar Pig
"The only survivor is the one who holds the Piggy at the end of the game" : a new neighbour instructs Barney as he tries to master the complex rules of the board game Interstellar Pig - the game, however, is a real one with Barney as the human element in an interstellar struggle. A fast-paced, inventive exploration of the nature of competition and the power a game can exert over the player.
[D2394] Methuen pbk **£1.95**

ST GEORGE, JUDITH
Haunted
A boy comes into contact with supernatural forces while looking after an empty mansion.
[D2395] Methuen pbk **£1.95**

WESTALL, ROBERT
A British writer of 'disturbing brilliance', Westall writes with increasing anger about violence and conflict of all kinds - often using super-normal forces or a futuristic or science fiction setting to give an extra edge to the situations he describes.

Break of Dark
A collection of eerie short stories in which the supernatural intrudes into the natural world, with chilling results.
[D2396] Puffin pbk **£1.50**

Futuretrack 5
A bleak, hard, compelling futuristic novel about a desolate computerised conformist 20th century Britain, where those who do not fit in are lobotomised. The story concerns one young man's revolt against the system.
[D2397] Puffin pbk **£1.95**

Ghosts and Journeys
[D2398] Pan pbk **£1.99**

The Call & Other Stories   NEW
[D2399] Viking hbk **£6.95**

The Cats of Seroster
Set in a vividly realised medieval world, this is a perilous swords-and-sorcery quest adventure: a search for the legendary Seroster and his great golden cats.
[D2400] Pan pbk **£1.95**

The Devils on the Road
A time-slip novel in which a young motorcyclist is hurled back in time.
[D2401] Puffin pbk **£1.50**

The Haunting of Chas McGill
[D2402] Puffin pbk **£1.75**

The Scarecrows
An eerie psychological supernatural thriller, with echoes of *Hamlet*, in which Simon's anger and resentment at his mother's happy second marriage, and his deep hatred for his stepfather, releases the ominous, destructive powers of the scarecrows - remnants of an ancient love triangle.
[D2403] Puffin pbk **£1.75**

The Watch House
[D2404] Puffin pbk **£2.25**

The Wind Eye
A fantasy account of the impact on a modern family of St. Cuthbert, a ferocious old saint.
[D2405] Puffin pbk **£1.75**

Urn Burial
When Ralph, a slow eighteen year old shepherd, discovers the corpse of an unusual cat entombed beneath the cairns of the Cumbrian fells, he unwittingly unleashes an extra-terrestrial struggle that threatens his own community.
[D2406] Puffin pbk **£1.99**

Crafts

CRAFTS & PRACTICAL ART

Widely considered the poor cousin of fine art, craft used to be seen as the domain solely of artisans and housewives, but increased leisure time has now made many crafts popular recreational pursuits. Talented practitioners such as Kaffe Fassett have inspired a renaissance of the former domestic pastimes, elevating them to the status of art. Today, shelves groan with the vast range of titles available - everything from fairytale knits to woodturned candlesticks. Enthusiasts will find detailed instructions in specific projects, while beginners can explore the fundamentals of hobbies that interest them. Batsford and Macdonald Orbis produce particularly lucid manuals, but all the titles below have been chosen for their clarity and accessibility.

General

ANDREWS, H.
The Batsford Encyclopaedia **NEW**
Nearly 150 crafts are described: country, traditional and experimental processes in modern media.
[E0] Batsford pbk **£12.99**

CARTER, JENNY & RAE, JANET
Chambers Guide to the Traditional Crafts of Scotland
Both traditional cottage industry and modern multi-enterprise ventures reveal high quality craftsmanship in curling stones, kilts, fiddles etc.
[E1] Chambers hbk **£10.95**

ELINOR, GILLIAN
Women & Craft
Documents the work of countless women who have passed on essential skills regarded as 'women's work'.
[E2] Virago pbk **£9.95**

A saddler stuffing the collar from *Forgotten Household Crafts* by John Seymour (Dorling Kindersley hbk £12.95)

PARKER, ROZSIKA
The Subversive Stitch
A thought-provoking history of sewing in women's lives from a feminist point of view.
[E3] Women's P hbk **£14.95**
[E4] Women's P pbk **£8.95**

SEYMOUR, JOHN
Forgotten Household Crafts
Describes the largely unsung crafts of the home, celebrating a lost way of life.
[E5] D Kindersley hbk **£12.95**
The Forgotten Arts
Published in association with the National Trust.
[E6] D Kindersley hbk **£12.95**

SMITH-SHAW, DAVID
Ireland's Traditional Crafts
An important record of the disappearing crafts of Ireland: harp making, stonework, glassware and textiles.
[E7] Thames & H pbk **£9.95**

Major Crafts A - Z

Basketry

BARRATT, ELTON
Rushwork
Suitable for beginners, this manual covers all aspects from selecting materials to creating table mats, baskets and rush seating. It includes a useful bibliography and a list of suppliers.
[E8] Dryad hbk **£6.95**

BROWN, MARGERY
Cane & Rush Seating
The techniques involved in re-seating are clearly explained and are supported by illustrations and photographs.
[E9] Batsford pbk **£6.99**

SANDFORD, LETTICE
Straw Work & Corn Dollies
Traditionally the corn dolly was made from the last sheaf of the harvest field. This book includes the making of straw jewellery, animals, marquetry and collage.
[E10] Batsford pbk **£5.95**

SILER, LYN
The Basket Book
Stunning watercolours make this an attractive and instructive tool for reproducing traditional American baskets.
[E11] Sterling Lark pbk **£7.95**

WALPOLE, LOIS
Creative Basket Making **NEW**
This book presents a new approach to making and designing baskets. The author mixes natural and man-made materials to create twelve imaginative projects, enhanced by step-by-step illustrations and original designs.
[E12] Collins hbk **£14.95**

WRIGHT, DOROTHY
The Complete Book of Baskets & Basketry
A history of regional and national styles, materials, techniques, care and repair.
[E13] David & Ch pbk **£8.95**

Dress-Making

'French Style' Children's Clothes
Zany patchwork parkas, vibrant jumpsuits, wool blousons, classic sailor dresses and other easy-to-make examples of junior chic.
[E14] Conran Octopus pbk **£4.99**

COLES, MYRA
The Complete Computer Sewing Book
Cotton on to hi-tech sewing with this guide to computerised machines. Ideal for showing beginners how to make the best of the many stitches now available.
[E15] Heinemann pbk **£6.95**

FOSTER, BETTY
Fashionmaker
Adapt a simple T-shape into 28 different garments, including trousers, cowl-neck dress, and kimono jacket.
[E16] Heinemann hbk **£12.95**

GREENHOWE, JEAN
Party Costumes for Kids
Create a South Seas sarong, Cleopatra's robe and other fun-time wear from just one metre of fabric.
[E17] David & Ch hbk **£9.95**

GYNTHER, ELSEBETH
Easy Style
Pattern drafting and sewing guides for the new classics.
[E18] Sterling pbk **£7.95**

LADBURY, ANN
Complete Pattern Designing **NEW**
Separate sections cover collars, sleeves, trouser and shirt shapes, blouses, coats and jackets, lingerie, nightwear and beachwear. Clear illustrations and easy-to-follow instructions are interspersed with the common-sense sewing tips for which Ann Ladbury is famous.
[E19] Sidgwick hbk **£15.95**
The Simplicity Pocket Guide to Home Sewing
A compact guide to repairs and alterations.
[E20] Mitchell Beazley hbk **£4.95**

LENKER, SANDRA
'Vogue' Fitting
Fundamentals of fitting, adjustment and alteration make this an essential manual for tailoring.
[E21] Harper & R pbk **£10.95**

PYMAN, KIT
Every Kind of Smocking
Patterns, photographs and step-by-step instructions for traditional children's garments, decorative textiles, cushions, and fashion wear.
[E22] Search P pbk **£7.95**

READER'S DIGEST
Reader's Digest Complete Guide to Sewing
Every home should have one. A practical, well-illustrated manual showing techniques of pattern design and construction, sewing collars, zips, button holes and much more.
[E23] Hodder hbk **£15.95**

SHOBEN, MARTIN
Patterns from Your Favourite Clothes
Adapting old favourites to suit new images and shapes. Seven basic garments are shown with a set of

style variations, all within the grasp of inexperienced pattern-makers.
[E24] Heinemann pbk **£9.95**

STUBBS, UNA
A Stitch in Time
A family sewing survival guide with other household titbits from the popular comedy actress.
[E25] Ward Lock pbk **£9.95**

Embroidery & Needlework

ANDREW, ANNE
Smocking `NEW`
A guide to basic methods, with valuable sections on more experimental techniques, such as reverse smocking, ruching, Portuguese smocking and the use of machine embroidery and appliqué before smocking.
[E26] Merehurst hbk **£9.95**

BEANEY, JAN
The Art of the Needle `NEW`
Colour photographs and drawings show how to achieve successful results in techniques as diverse as embroidery, appliqué and quilting.
[E27] Century hbk **£16.95**

BECK, THOMASINA
Embroiderer's Garden `NEW`
Re-interpreting the patterns, textures and colours of gardens. Lavish photographs and diagrams translate herbals, hedges and Tudor knots into needlecraft.
[E28] David & Ch hbk **£16.50**

COPELAND, SANDRA
Embroidery and Needlepoint: An Information Sourcebook `NEW`
Annotated bibliography of more than 1,500 titles.
[E29] Oryx pbk **£32.85**

DAWSON, BARBARA
White Work Embroidery
Many stitches are shown for working in white thread on a white ground.
[E30] Batsford hbk **£17.95**

DE DILLMONT, THERESE
Encyclopaedia of Needlework `NEW`
Specially commissioned drawings and colour plates supplement the original 19th century text detailing all aspects of needlework.
[E31] Bracken hbk **£24.50**

EATON, JAN
'French Style' Embroidery
A collection of delightfully unusual designs which can be used for anything from T-shirts to tablecloths.
[E32] Octopus pbk **£4.99**
Mary Thomas's Dictionary of Embroidery Stitches `NEW`
A classic work of reference, first published in 1934, now fully revised and illustrated. Contains over 400 stitches - over 100 of them new - with an individual colour illustration to show the working method in detail. Essential for the serious embroiderer.
[E33] Hodder hbk **£12.95**

FASSETT, KAFFE
Glorious Needlepoint
Glowing colour plates illustrate the author's sources of inspiration and their development into working sketches, charts and instructions, and the completed items.
[E34] Century hbk **£16.95**

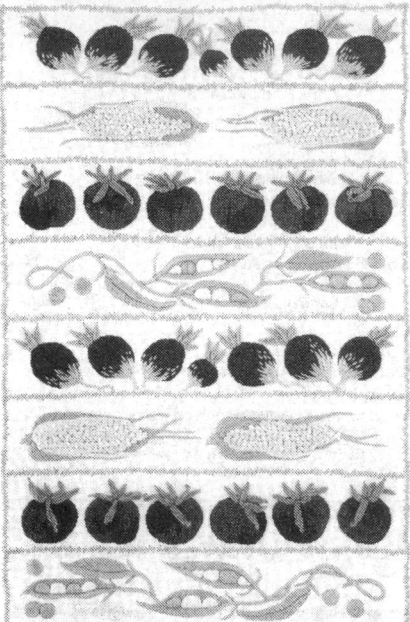

An example of stumpwork technique from *The Needlework Garden* by Jane Iles (Century Hutchinson hbk £15.95)

FORSTNER, REGINA
Traditional Samplers `NEW`
Origins, history and advice.
[E35] Thorsons pbk **£5.99**

HIGGINSON, SUSAN
Needlepoint Stitch Directory `NEW`
A handy pocket-book which features 89 stitches, each on separate page, accompanied by a colour photograph and a numbered diagram showing the different stages of working.
[E36] A & C Black hbk **£7.95**

HOWARD, CONSTANCE
Twentieth Century Embroidery in Great Britain Vol 1: To 1939
Charting the course of British embroidery: techniques, tools, personalities and events.
[E37] Batsford hbk **£25.00**
Vol 2: 1940 - 1963
[E38] Batsford hbk **£25.00**
Vol 3: 1964 - 1977
[E39] Batsford hbk **£25.00**
Vol 4: From 1978
[E40] Batsford hbk **£29.95**
Vols 1 - 4 (Set)
[E41] Batsford hbk **£79.95**

ILES, JANE
Learn Embroidery
Simple step-by-step instructions and diagrams to encourage beginners.
[E42] Collins pbk **£4.95**
The Needlework Garden `NEW`
Inspired by English gardens, two traditional pastimes are combined in 20 projects.
[E43] Century hbk **£15.95**

JONES, NORA
Canvaswork
One in a series on needlecraft, this book covers all the major canvas work stitches.
[E44] Search P pbk **£1.10**

KENNETT, FRANCES & SCARLETT, BELINDA
Country House Needlepoint `NEW`
Flemish tapestries and 18th century nursery samplers are a part of the needlework heritage, here displayed in stately settings. Charts and instructions show how to recreate traditional patterns for modern homes.
[E45] Conran Octopus hbk **£14.95**

MCNEILL, MOYRA
Machine Embroidery
Lace and see-through techniques using a domestic sewing machine.
[E46] Batsford hbk **£10.95**

PASCOE, MARGARET
Blackwork Embroidery
History and application of this 16th-century counted thread technique.
[E47] Batsford hbk **£12.95**

PEARSON, ANNA
First Steps in Needlepoint
A chapter is devoted to each of the five main stitch varieties. Projects are in categories for beginners, advanced, and accomplished.
[E48] Macdonald hbk **£14.95**

PYMAN, KIT
Gold and Silver Embroidery
Ornate decorative styles incorporating lettering, beads and sequins.
[E49] Search P pbk **£6.95**

READER'S DIGEST
Reader's Digest Complete Guide to Needlework
No nonsense, comprehensive manual with step-by-step instructions for techniques ranging from lacemaking and embroidery to macramé and crochet.
[E50] Hodder hbk **£15.95**

SPRINGALL, DIANA
Design for Embroidery `NEW`
A fine art approach concentrating on shape, line, texture, colour, pattern and form.
[E51] Pelham hbk **£16.95**

STUBBS, UNA
In Stitches
'I'm not a technically perfect needlewoman, just a friend with an urge to push you into having a go.'
[E52] Ward Lock hbk **£9.95**
[E53] Ward Lock pbk **£5.95**

WEIR, SHELAGH & SHAHID, SERENE
Palestinian Embroidery
The elaborate patterns and vibrant colours of village craft translated into vivid cushions and textiles.
[E54] Brit Mus P pbk **£3.50**

Flower Arranging

BLACK, PENNY
Complete Book of Pressed Flowers
This is a very attractive book with clear step-by-step photographs. It demonstrates the many uses of pressed flowers as pictures, greeting cards and as detail on furniture.
[E55] D Kindersley hbk **£9.95**

BURGESS, LINDA & INNES, MIRANDA
A Sense of the Country `NEW`
A beautifully produced seasonal guide to flower arranging which uses fresh and dried flowers, fruits,

vegetables and natural objects to create imaginative and harmonious still lifes for the home.
[E56] Macdonald hbk **£14.95**

COE, STELLA
Ikebana: Practical Guide to Japanese Flower Arrangement
Shows how to adapt Western flowers and equipment to create the unique styles of the Orient. Explains the detailed philosophy behind the art of flower arranging in the East.
[E57] Conran Octopus pbk **£5.95**

CONDER, SUSAN
Terence Conran's 'Plants At Home'
Offers a vast range of imaginative and practical ideas for displaying flowers to their best advantage. Also shows how to use plants as an integral part of a decorative scheme.
[E58] Conran Octopus hbk **£9.95**

COWLES, FLEUR
Flower Decorations
Sweeps away the restrictive conventions and paraphernalia of traditional flower arrangements, showing how flowers can be used in stunningly simple yet original ways.
[E59] Conran Octopus hbk **£10.95**

GUILD, TRICIA
Designing with Flowers
An up-market interior decorator's approach.
[E60] M Beazley hbk **£12.95**

HAMILTON, ANNE & WHITE, KATHLEEN
Silk Flowers **NEW**
Making and arranging birds of paradise, roses and other flowers from silk ribbon.
[E61] Merehurst hbk **£13.95**

HILLIER, MALCOLM
Flowers **NEW**
Colour, season, scent, composition and occasion are the themes in this beautifully photographed book. Also included are tips and information on care, preparation, and wiring. Published in conjunction with the National Trust.
[E62] D Kindersley hbk **£14.95**

A woodland arrangement from *Flowers for All Seasons* by Jane Packer (Pavilion hbk **£9.99**)

HILLIER, MALCOLM & HILTON, COLIN
The Complete Book of Dried Flowers
Beautiful photographs and lots of practical advice make this the most attractive and comprehensive book about dried flowers currently available.
[E63] D Kindersley hbk **£12.95**

MCNICHOL, PAM & COOKE, DOROTHY
The History of Flower Arranging **NEW**
Published in association with the National Association of Flower Arrangement Societies, and illustrated with drawings and photographs.
[E64] Heinemann hbk **£14.95**

PACKER, JANE
Celebrating with Flowers
The author was responsible for the floral arrangements for the wedding of the Duke and Duchess of York. This book takes us through her much-praised natural designs.
[E65] Pavilion hbk **£12.95**
Flowers for All Seasons: Autumn **NEW**
Combines sound practical advice on keeping blooms fresh, preserving flowers and combining the rich palette of autumnal colours to best effect, with specific projects, such as a Hallowe'en apple wreath, an autumn bridal bouquet, and fruit and flower baskets to celebrate the harvest.
[E66] Pavilion hbk **£9.99**
Flowers for All Seasons: Spring
Contains a variety of arrangements suitable for spring weddings, St Valentine's Day and other springtime occasions, presented with clear instructions and lists of materials.
[E67] Pavilion hbk **£9.99**
Flowers for All Seasons: Summer
The second in the series, expressly tailored to reflect the moods, festivals and flowers associated with summer.
[E68] Pavilion hbk **£9.99**

PEPLOW, REGINALD
Pot Pourri and Other Scented Delights
Reviving the art of a sweetly scented past with pot pourri, pomanders, sleep pillows and other treats. Published in association with the National Trust.
[E69] Unwin Hyman hbk **£4.95**

PIERCY, HAROLD
Constance Spry Book of Flower Arranging
A traditional approach that follows the celebrated Constance Spry method.
[E70] Conran Octopus pbk **£3.95**
Constance Spry Creative Ideas in Floristry & Flower Arranging **NEW**
The Director of the Constance Spry Flower School here provides a comprehensive practical guide to growing and preparing fresh flowers for decoration, with excellent chapters on wiring, dried and artificial flowers and flowers for special occasions.
[E71] C Helm hbk **£13.95**

ROGERS, BARBARA RADCLIFFE
The Dried Flower Encyclopaedia
Beautifully illustrated with watercolours, the alphabetically arranged listings include useful guidelines for growing and preserving a huge variety of flowers.
[E72] Simon & Sch hbk **£10.95**

WALDEN, HILARY
Flower Works **NEW**
'Flower power' is what this beautiful book is all about. It shows how flowers can meet contemporary concerns for beauty without cruelty, alternative medicines and healthy foods, through their use in teas, cuisine, face creams and other treatments.
[E73] Windward hbk **£12.95**

WESTCOTT, JEANNE
Paper Flower Sculpture
Instructions illustrated by line drawings which show the beginner how to make paper blooms and foliage.
[E74] Blandford hbk **£10.95**

WESTLAND, PAMELA
Creative Flower Craft
As well as giving ideas on arranging fresh and dried flowers, this informative guide also shows how flowers can be used as beauty products and in food and drink.
[E75] David & Ch hbk **£10.95**

Glass

CARPENTIER, DIDIER
Painting on Glass
A demonstration of easy and accessible methods for decorating glass.
[E76] A & C Black pbk **£3.00**

CASCIANI, PAUL
The Technique of Decorative Stained Glass
Leading, painting, staining and fusing decorative panels, mirrors and lamps.
[E77] Batsford hbk **£12.95**

KLEIN, DAN
Glass: A Contemporary Art
Written by the director in charge of 20th century decorative arts at Christie's, this book gives a world-wide insight into the contemporary glass scene, combining a history of the art with a selection of superb colour photographs.
[E78] Collins hbk **£30.00**

PEACE, DAVID
Glass Engraving: Lettering & Design
One of England's leading glass engravers examines the history of the letter forms, the techniques used to achieve them and the general delights and problems of working with glass.
[E79] Batsford hbk **£14.95**

REYNTIENS, PATRICK
Technique of Stained Glass
An authoritative technical handbook by a craftsman whose work is found in many churches and cathedrals.
[E80] Batsford hbk **£14.95**

Jewellery

BAGLEY, PETER
The Encyclopedia of Jewellery Techniques
Tried and tested techniques for amateurs and professionals alike.
[E81] Batsford hbk **£19.95**

EDWARDS, ROD
Technique of Jewellery
[E82] Batsford pbk **£8.95**

PERKIN, LYNDA & DEWHURST, HEATHER
Jazzy Jewellery **NEW**
Make earrings, brooches, bracelets, necklaces and hair accessories from readily available materials. Great for young people.
[E83] Arrow pbk **£2.50**

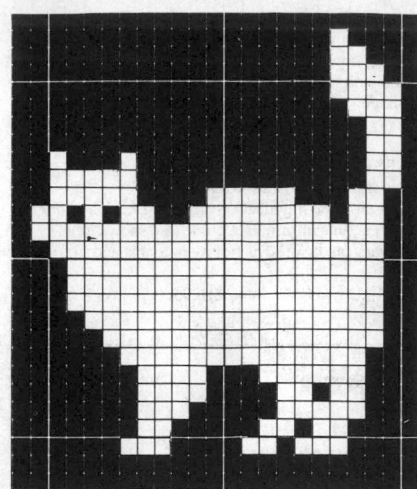

Part of a pattern design for a 'meow' Fair Isle sweater from *Cat Knits* by Melinda Coss (Aurum Press hbk £10.95)

Knitting & Crochet

'French Style' Baby Knits
These designs combine a sense of colour and style with common sense and practicality.
[E84] Conran Octopus pbk **£4.99**

'French Style' Family Knits
Co-ordinated knitwear lifts family knits into the designer category. Colourful ski jumpers and first day at school outfits feature among designs suitable for beginners and experienced knitters alike.
[E85] Conran Octopus pbk **£4.99**

'French Style' Fashion Knitting
From thick rustic wool jumpers to airy cotton knits...c'est bon!
[E86] Conran Octopus pbk **£3.99**

Ward Lock Guide to Knitting Stitches
An economical handbook.
[E87] Ward Lock pbk **£5.95**

BRADLEY, SUE
Stitches in Time
Historical designs inspired this collection, which includes an Egyptian sweater, medieval leggings and an art deco jacket.
[E88] Macdonald hbk **£14.95**
The Cotton Collection
Easy to knit, easy to wear cotton T-shirts and sweaters.
[E89] Bloomsbury hbk **£10.95**

CASH, SYLVIA
The Crochet Sweater Book
Iridescent butterflies inspired one design in this collection of high-fashion patterns.
[E90] D Kindersley hbk **£9.95**

COMPTON, JO
The Knitting Book
Aims to show knitters how to adapt patterns and design professional-looking garments. Contains advice on choosing yarns and stitches.
[E91] A & C Black pbk **£9.95**

COSS, MELINDA
Cat Knits
Feline sweaters inspired by the author's five pets. Colour graphs and diagrams show cat-lovers how to make their own motifs.
[E92] Aurum hbk **£10.95**

COSS, MELINDA & ROBINSON, DEBBY
Knitting with Mohair
Soft, sensual knits for day wear or glamorous, glittering evening wear.
[E93] Sidgwick hbk **£10.95**

DUCKWORTH, SUSAN
Knitting
'New Wave' knitting pioneer presents over 30 designs in her first published collection.
[E94] Century hbk **£16.95**

ELLIOT, SALLY ANNE
Creative Machine Knitting
Pattern writing, design, yarn selection techniques, and avoiding mistakes are the themes of this useful guide.
[E95] Windward hbk **£12.95**

FASSETT, KAFFE
Glorious Knitting
A bestselling knitting book: excellent photography captures the glorious colours incorporated in Fassett's designs, made popular by the 'nearly knit' kits available in craft shops throughout the country. A marvellous book even if you don't know your plains from your purls!
[E96] Century hbk **£14.95**
[E97] Century pbk **£8.95**
Kaffe Fassett at the V & A
Islamic textiles and oriental pottery at the V & A inspired Fassett to create his own sumptuous museum pieces for the first exhibition of a contemporary textile artist at the museum. Beautiful colour plates follow the artist's development and 17 new designs are presented with charts and instructions.
[E98] Century hbk **£16.95**

HARDING, SALLY
Crochet Style
Low-back sweaters and delicate halternecks bring crochet to the forefront of fashion.
[E99] Windward hbk **£9.95**

HARRISON, ERIKA
Sweaters for Men
Hefty knits in Arran and fishermen's rib to suit all activities and seasons.
[E100] WH Allen hbk **£10.95**
[E101] WH Allen pbk **£4.99**

JAGO, JILL & EVANS, JACQUES
Classic Knitting for Country Living
Traditional leisurewear for outdoor stalwarts.
[E102] Penguin pbk **£6.95**

KEE, JENNY
Winter Knits
Exuberant and colourful knits inspired by the vivid landscape, flora and fauna of Australia.
[E103] Century hbk **£12.95**

KENT, MURIEL
Exciting Crochet
Classic designs featuring broomstick and Tunisian crochet.
[E104] David & Ch hbk **£12.95**

KOGAN, SASHA
Big and Little Sweaters
Witty and whimsical, posies and petals, flashes and splashes, geometric and figurative are the subject of these adult and children's knits.
[E105] D Kindersley hbk **£9.95**

MATTHEWS, ANNE
'Vogue' Dictionary of Crochet Stitches
A concise guide.
[E106] David & Ch hbk **£10.95**

MENCHINI, PAT
The Beatrice Potter Knitting Book
Peter Rabbit, Mrs Tittlemouse and the Lakeland landscape provide themes for this range of patterns, many of which are suitable for adults as well as children.
[E107] F Warne hbk **£11.95**

PEARSON, MICHAEL
Traditional Knitting
The author has scoured the British Isles to create this celebration of the great tradition of British craft knitting. The book includes authentic patterns for Guernsies, Fair Isle and Arrans.
[E108] Collins pbk **£6.95**

POPE, HAZEL
The Machine Knitter's Handbook
Choice of machines, stitch tension, yarns, patterns, and pitfalls.
[E109] David & Ch hbk **£10.95**

ROBERTS, PATRICIA
Patricia Robert's Knitting Book
[E110] WH Allen hbk **£9.95**
[E111] Star pbk **£6.95**
Patricia Robert's Second Knitting Book
[E112] WH Allen hbk **£9.95**

ROBINSON, DEBBY
The Encyclopaedia of Knitting Techniques
A - Z from angora to yarn, and from armholes to yokes.
[E113] M Joseph pbk **£9.95**
The Odd-Ball Knitting Book
Creative and fashionable ways to use up left-over yarn in landscape gloves, socks, an entrelac jacket and even shoulder pads.
[E114] Bloomsbury hbk **£9.95**

Kaffe Fassett, author of *Glorious Knitting* (Century Hutchinson hbk £14.95, pbk £8.95)

A pattern design from *Glorious Knitting* by Kaffe Fassett (Century Hutchinson hbk £14.95, pbk £8.95)

RUTT, RICHARD
A History of Hand Knitting
Richard Rutt, the Bishop of Leicester, was taught to knit when he was seven years old, by his grandfather. He later knitted garments for wartime soldiers. This personal interest has spawned the first full history of the craft, including the development of tools and techniques.
[E115] Batsford hbk **£17.95**

TURNER, PAULINE
The Technique of Crochet
Written for more adventurous needlewomen, complex processes and variations are explained for those who wish to experiment.
[E116] Batsford hbk **£12.95**

PROBERT, CHRISTINE
Vogue Knitting Library:
Children's Knits
[E117] Angell pbk **£2.95**
Classic Knits
[E118] Angell pbk **£2.95**
Cotton & Silk Knits
[E119] Angell pbk **£2.95**
Fair Isle & Textured Knits
[E120] Angell pbk **£2.95**
Men's Knits
[E121] Angell pbk **£2.95**
Thick Knits
[E122] Angell pbk **£2.95**

Lace-Making

COOK, BRIDGET
The Torchon Lace Book   NEW
A course of lacemaking with prickings and diagrams for 27 projects.
[E123] Batsford hbk **£9.95**

EARNSHAW, PAT
Needle Made Lace
Featuring 12 types of lace including previously neglected Hollie point, Halas, Buratto and Bebilla.
[E124] Ward Lock pbk **£14.95**

HOARE, LADY
The Art of Tatting
Shuttle lace has been a companion in illness and in health to Lady Hoare. She demonstrates its possibilities for endless adaption and design. The book also features examples of the work of the Queen of Roumania.
[E125] Batsford hbk **£17.95**

LEWIS, ROBIN
101 Torchon Patterns
A colour diagramming method which eliminates lengthy descriptions of technique.
[E126] Dryad hbk **£16.95**

STEVENS, AGNES
Starting Zele Lace   NEW
Jewellery made from an unusual type of needle lace.
[E127] Dryad hbk **£8.95**

WITHERS, JEAN
Lace to Use
Easy-to-care-for lace for household use, handkerchiefs and bridal veils.
[E128] Dryad hbk **£9.95**

Model Work

CAKET, COLIN
Model a Monster
Prehistoric creatures made from coathangers, papier mâché and other accessible materials. Cartoons, riddles, recipes and quips help make the book amusing as well as practical.
[E129] Blandford hbk **£9.95**
[E130] Blandford pbk **£5.95**

EVANS, MARTIN
The Model Steam Locomotive
A complete treatise on design and construction.
[E131] Argus pbk **£11.50**

GOODCHILD, GRAHAM
Radio-Controlled Models: Design &
Construction
Full working plans for battery and solar cell models made from simple materials.
[E132] Batsford hbk **£9.95**

JOHNSON, PETER
Clay Modelling for Everyone
Pottery sculpture and miniatures made without a wheel.
[E133] Batsford hbk **£10.95**

SMEED, VIC
Boat Modelling
Building and operating power and sail model boats.
[E134] Argus pbk **£5.50**
Model Magic
A beginner's guide to modelmaking: cars, boats, planes and trains.
[E135] Argus pbk **£3.95**

Patchwork

'French Style' Quilting, Patchwork and
Appliqué
The projects range from a witty appliqué cushion to a simple Irish tweed patchwork spread and a dinosaur-shaped sleeping bag.
[E136] Conran Octopus pbk **£4.99**

BROWN, PAULINE
Appliqué
Excellent introduction to this ancient and versatile craft. Detailed instructions are provided for beginners; more difficult methods - 3-D, inlay and reverse, Hawaiian and Persian - are also covered,with chapters on colour, texture, painting and dyeing fabrics, and the use of beads and ribbons.
[E137] Merehurst hbk **£9.95**

COLBY, AVERIL
Patchwork Quilts
Needlecraft historian Colby adapts traditional approaches to present day materials and designs.
[E138] Batsford pbk **£6.95**

FAIRFIELD, HELEN
Patchwork From Mosaics
Venetian paved church floors are translated into geometric templates for bags, cushions, quilts and clothing.
[E139] Batsford pbk **£6.95**

LOGAN, DIANN
Designs in Patchwork   NEW
Something old, something new - 30 bright new quilts for machine piecing.
[E140] Oxmoor hbk **£12.95**

MARTIN, PEGGI & YOUNG, SUSAN
Imaginative Patchwork
Illustrated with line drawings,this covers nine quilting methods and gives projects to suit, including a 'Japanese' quilt.
[E141] Little Hills P hbk **£12.95**

PYMAN, KIT
Every Kind of Patchwork
American, block, applied, border, crazy, log cabin, medallion and other styles are demonstrated with comprehensive instructions.
[E142] Pan pbk **£7.95**

Pottery

CARDEW, MICHAEL
A Pioneer Potter
Initially aiming to 'make pots which could be used for the purposes of daily life and to make them cheap...', Cardew went on to be one of Britain's leading potters. This autobiography describes his formative years working with Bernard Leach, and his own special period of creativity in the 1930s.
[E143] Oxford pbk **£6.95**

CLARK, KENNETH
Potter's Manual
Practical and informative text with step-by-step illustrations.
[E144] Macdonald pbk **£9.95**

COLBECK, JOHN
Pottery Materials
Composition, preparation and use of the various raw

A black slipware cider jug from *A Pioneer Potter* by Michael Cardew (Oxford pbk £6.95)

materials used in pottery, and the principles on which mixtures may be compounded.
[E145] Batsford hbk **£25.00**

COOPER, EMMANUEL
Potter's Book of Glaze Recipes
Just as a good cook starts with a recipe and adapts it, a good potter learns to control and develop a glaze. Over 500 recipes are included.
[E146] Batsford pbk **£9.95**

EVETTS, ECHO
China Mending
Restoration advice for collectors.
[E147] Faber pbk **£4.95**

FOURNIER, ROBERT
Illustrated Dictionary of Pottery Decoration
From celadon and etching to fluting, glazing and impasto.
[E148] Prentice Hall hbk **£29.95**

·HAMILTON, DAVID
Manual of Pottery & Ceramics
History, hand and mechanical methods, firing and final surface treatment.
[E149] Thames & H pbk **£5.95**

LEACH, BERNARD
A Potter's Book
West meets East in Leach's classic treatise on Japanese raku, English slipware, stoneware and oriental porcelain. 'Really there is no East, no West, where then is the South and North? Illusion makes the world close in, Enlightenment opens it on every side' (Soyetsu Yaragi).
[E150] Faber pbk **£5.95**
Beyond East & West
Memoirs, portraits and essays by Britain's most influential modern potter.
[E151] Faber pbk **£5.95**

LUMM, RUDOLF
Painting on Porcelain
Techniques for overglaze painting.
[E152] Costello pbk **£3.95**

OLSEN, FREDERICK
The Kiln Book
Materials, specifications and construction details for electric and fuel-burning kilns.
[E153] A & C Black hbk **£12.00**

RHODES, DANIEL
Clay & Glazes for the Potter
Raku, salt glazing, metallic salts, overglaze processes and the use of fibreglass in clay are included in this revised edition.
[E154] A & C Black hbk **£19.95**

Spinning, Weaving & Dyeing

BRYANT, DAVID
Wheels & Looms: Making Equipment for Spinning & Weaving
Aimed at woodworkers, but of interest to spinners and weavers who wish to make their own equipment.
[E155] Batsford hbk **£14.95**

CHETWYND, HILARY
The Weaver's Handbook
The complete process from drafting to finishing, focusing on types of weave.
[E156] R Hale hbk **£17.95**

DALBY, GILL & CHRISTMAS, LIZ
Spinning & Dyeing: An Introductory Manual
Step-by-step instructions on carding, spinning, preparation for dyeing, dyeing techniques, and over 140 dye recipes.
[E157] David & Ch hbk **£12.95**

DYRENFORTH, NOEL
The Technique of Batik
Background, tools and techniques for wax resist and dye decoration.
[E158] Batsford hbk **£17.95**

FREEMAN, SUE
Feltcraft **NEW**
Instructions from fleece to finished projects using man's oldest textile.
[E159] David & Ch hbk **£10.95**

Illustration from *Dolls* by Marco Tosa (Batsford hbk £29.95)

ROSS, MABEL
Encyclopaedia of Handspinning
Factual and technical information covering animal, vegetable and man-made fibres.
[E160] Batsford hbk **£17.95**

SANDBERG, GOSTIA **NEW**
Indigo Textiles: Technique & History
History and application of the oldest dye in use.
[E161] A & C Black pbk **£9.95**

SPYROU, MARY & SINGER, MARGO **NEW**
Textile Arts: Multicultural Traditions
Fascinating practical guide to a variety of fabric decorating skills: embroidery and mirror work from India, appliqué from Chile, mola work from Panama, tie and dye and tritik from West Africa, batik from Indonesia and many fabric folding, gathering and bias techniques from 19th century Europe.
[E162] A & C Black pbk **£12.95**

Toy Making

BLIZZARD, RICHARD
Wooden Action Toys
A treasury of sturdy wooden toys.
[E163] Unwin Hyman hbk **£11.95**

BRADSHAW, ENID
Dolls' Houses
Build and furnish a house; make and dress its tiny residents.
[E164] Blandford hbk **£10.95**

BUCKLAND, RALPH S.
Toymaker's Wooden Vehicles
Projects and plans for a steam engine, snow plough, cars and more.
[E165] Sterling pbk **£8.95**

CHURCHILL, E. RICHARD
Instant Paper Toys
Flying gizmos, snappers and crackers and toys to pop, spin and whirl.
[E166] Sterling pbk **£5.95**

COXON, JOHN
Easy to Make Learning Toys
Information on wood selection, tools, and techniques for making skill development puzzles and toys.
[E167] Sterling pbk **£7.95**

EARNSHAW, NORA
Collecting Dolls' Houses and Miniatures **NEW**
A new edition to the acclaimed Collins *Collecting* series, this book takes a detailed look at the history of the dolls' house, combining sound pre-purchase advice for collectors with photographs from previously unseen private collections.
[E168] Collins hbk **£14.95**

GAMMON, JOY
Knitted Dogs
Lovable mutts to make.
[E169] Search P pbk **£1.95**

GRAHAM, PETER
The Junk Book
Throwaway disposable products provide a valuable resource for those with imagination.
[E170] Blandford pbk **£3.95**

GREENHOWE, JEAN **NEW**
Jean Greenhowe's Character Dolls
Easy-to-follow instructions for over 30 small dolls,

from Cinderella, Santa Claus and Robin Hood to a gypsy, a pop star and a tennis player.
[E171] Batsford hbk **£9.95**

JANITCH, VALERIE
The Kate Greenaway Doll Book
Dainty moppets in highwaisted dresses and romantic four-poster beds feature in this nostalgic collection.
[E172] David & Ch hbk **£9.95**

MACLENNAN, JENNIFER
Simple Puppets You Can Make
Snip, stitch and stuff to make a host of colourful finger and mouth puppets.
[E173] Sterling hbk **£8.95**

PEAKE, PAMELA
Little Grey Rabbit's Pattern Book
Make and dress five characters from Alison Uttley's popular books.
[E174] Collins hbk **£8.95**

RATH, ERNA
The Splendid Soft Toy Book
Fierce squashy trolls and traditional teddies feature in this practical toybox.
[E175] Pan pbk **£7.95**

ROWLANDS, JIM
Making and Flying Modern Kites **NEW**
Novice kitefliers and enthusiasts will enjoy this survey and construction guide to kite styles.
[E176] Dryad hbk **£9.95**

STREETER, TAL
The Art of the Japanese Kite
Soaring and sweeping birds and insects, legendary heroes, kabuki actors and sumo wrestlers all take form in Japanese kites. The 'tako-kichi' (kite-crazy) author introduces many kites from the workshops of six famous kitemakers. 'The tiny kites are the size of the nail of my little finger. I fly them over the rising hot air of a charcoal brazier with a flying line of human hair.'
[E177] Weatherhill pbk **£11.50**

Woodwork

CAMPKIN, MARIE
The Technique of Marquetry
Introduction to veneers, designs, cutting and finishing.
[E178] Batsford pbk **£6.95**

CHILD, PETER
The Craftsman Woodturner
A standard guide to woodturning skills and projects.
[E179] Unwin Hyman pbk **£9.95**

CHIPPENDALE, THOMAS
The Gentleman & Cabinet-Maker's Director
A facsimile reprint of the 1762 edition by England's celebrated furniture maker.
[E180] Dover pbk **£9.30**

EDLIN, HERBERT L.
What Wood is That?
A manual of wood identification.
[E181] Stobart hbk **£13.50**

HAYWARD, CHARLES H.
Cabinet-Making for Beginners
A basic introduction to handling tools and cutting joints.
[E182] Unwin Hyman pbk **£8.95**

Complete Book of Woodwork
An excellent introduction to woodworking for beginners with projects including a small workshop.
[E183] Unwin Hyman pbk **£7.50**
Staining & Polishing
A detailed look at French polishing and other traditional and modern wood finishes.
[E184] Unwin Hyman pbk **£7.50**

HEPPLEWHITE, GEORGE
The Cabinet-Maker & Upholsterer's Guide
A classic reprint of the 1794 edition.
[E185] Dover pbk **£6.25**

JACKSON, ALBERT & DAY, DAVID
Collins Complete Woodworker's Manual **NEW**
Written by the best-selling authors of the *Collins DIY Manual*, this manual gives a clear introduction to woodworking, illustrating the process of design, the selection of tools and with useful advice for the novice and the accomplished woodworker.
[E186] Collins hbk **£19.95**

LEACH, NOEL
Wood Finishing
Waxing, bleaching, stripping, staining, polishing and veneering are detailed, with advice on care and maintenance.
[E187] Argus pbk **£9.95**

LEGGAT, ALEX & SANDRA
Carpentry for the Home
Busy householders will appreciate this guide to using minimal equipment and simple techniques.
[E188] Batsford pbk **£7.95**

MARTENSSON, ALF
The Woodworker's Bible
Complete guide to equipment and techniques needed to set up and run a workshop.
[E189] A & C Black pbk **£10.95**

OUGHTON, F.
Grinling Gibbons & the English Woodcarving Tradition
Offering exceptional scholarship and inspiration for all carvers, this illustrated book looks at the work of British carvers from medieval times to the present day.
[E190] Stobart hbk **£21.50**

SAINSBURY, JOHN
The Router Workshop
How to make the most of your router, whether amateur or professional.
[E191] David & Ch hbk **£14.95**

SELF, CHARLES
Wood Fences and Gates
Plans, designs and construction details for picket, post and rail, board and panel and other types of fence.
[E192] Sterling pbk **£7.95**

SHERATON, THOMAS
The Cabinet-Maker & Upholsterer's Drawing Book
Reprint taken from various editions of 1793 to 1802 from this classic furniture maker.
[E193] Dover pbk **£10.75**

SMITH, ALAN
How to Restore & Repair Furniture
Not only is wooden furniture featured but metal and plastic furniture as well.
[E194] Ward Lock hbk **£12.95**

TAYLOR, VIC
The Woodworker's Dictionary
Terms and practices relating to all aspects of woodcraft.
[E195] Argus pbk **£12.95**

VASS, GOSTA
The Wood Worker's Manual
Breadboards for beginners and an ambitious writing-desk are among projects with step-by-step instructions.
[E196] Macdonald pbk **£6.95**

WHEELER, WILLIAM & HAYWARD, CHARLES H.
Practical Woodcarving & Gilding
Traditional techniques, patterns, and projects.
[E197] Unwin Hyman pbk **£7.50**

Miscellaneous Crafts A - Z

BOOKBINDING
HARLEY-LEWIS, ROY
Fine Bookbinding in the Twentieth Century
The only recent survey of a fascinating and much underrated art. It is full of interest and well worth reading.
[E198] David & Ch pbk **£20.00**
HARTHAN, JOHN
Bookbinding
Coptic, Islamic and European treasures of the Victoria & Albert Museum.
[E199] HMSO pbk **£6.95**
JOHNSON, ARTHUR
Bookbinding
All stages of preparation, different binding styles and the finer points of finishing.
[E200] Thames & H pbk **£5.95**

ENAMELLING
BARNHART, STROSAHL & STROSAHL
A Manual of Cloisonné & Champlevé Enamelling
Straightforward information with illustrations.
[E201] Thames & H hbk **£16.00**
CLARKE, GEOFFREY
Technique of Enamelling
A handbook of contemporary enamelling methods.
[E202] Batsford pbk **£6.95**

LEATHER
ATTWATER, W.A.
Technique of Leathercraft
Types of leather, tools and construction methods.
[E203] Batsford pbk **£14.95**
WILCOX, DONALD
Modern Leather Design
Make your own designs in leather, from shoes and belts to furniture and sculpture.
[E204] Watson Guptill pbk **£4.95**

MACRAME
SCMID-BURLESON, BONNY
The Technique of Macramé
Elementary knots and more elaborate patterns and braids.
[E205] Batsford pbk **£6.99**

METALWORK
CUZNER, BERNARD
A Silversmith's Manual
Basic processes for silver work.
[E206] NAG Press hbk **£9.95**

GEORGE, MIKE
The Complete Guide to Metalworking
Anyone can start with a few simple tools and a small working surface.
[E207] Crowood hbk **£14.95**

HULL, CHARLES
The Complete Guide to Pewtersmithing
In the 17th century, pewter was second only to cloth in the value of its exports. Hull's family were making pewter as early as 1451, so he is well-informed to present this clear resource book.
[E208] Batsford hbk **£14.95**

SMITH, ERNEST
Working in Precious Metals
Types and structures of metals and alloys, annealing, chemical treatments, soldering, polishing, enamelling and treatment of waste are examined.
[E209] NAG Press hbk **£10.95**

MOSAIC
GOODWIN, ARTHUR
The Technique of Mosaic
Collecting and storing tesserae and other stones, designing and creating mosaic, and the history of the medium.
[E210] Batsford hbk **£14.95**

MUSICAL INSTRUMENTS
BUCHANAN, GEORGE
The Making of Stringed Instruments
A workshop guide to making a violin, guitar, mandolin and others.
[E211] Batsford hbk **£19.95**

PAPER
AARON, ELIZABETH
Quilling: The Art of Paper Scroll Work
Paper filigree is used to make cards, brooches, jewellery and mobiles.
[E212] Batsford pbk **£6.99**

CAPON, ROBIN
Papier Mâché
Demonstrates how sculptures, furniture, costumes and ornaments can be made from recycled paper with glue.
[E213] Davis Pub hbk **£8.00**

CHAMBERS, ANNE
The Practical Guide to Marbling Paper
The definitive guide, it explains all you need to know about this fascinating and decorative craft, with colour photographs and patterns described in the text.
[E214] Thames & H pbk **£6.95**

GLASSBARROW, JILLY (ED)
The Creative Christmas Book   NEW
A bestselling guide to imaginative and memorable Christmas decorations, now available in this new edition.
[E215] Salamander Bks pbk **£4.95**

KHAN, ARONA
Wrap It Up
Innovative ideas for wrapping.
[E216] Ward Lock hbk **£8.95**

SCHEELE, ZAYTURE
The Great Origami Book
Includes dragons, eagles, snowflakes and sailing boats. Perfect decorations for parties, gift packages and Christmas trees.
[E217] Cassell pbk **£7.95**

SHANNON, FAITH
Paper Pleasure
Celebrating the beauty of paper in association with the Florentine marbling firm of Il Papino.
[E218] M Beazley pbk **£12.95**

TURNER, SYLVIE
Home Made Paper Today
A worldwide survey of mills, papers, techniques and uses.
[E219] Lund Humphries hbk **£35.00**

PICTURE FRAMING
CUNNING, ROBERT
Picture Framing
Function, history and types of frames and basic instructions for cutting, assembling and finishing.
[E220] Ward Lock hbk **£7.95**

LISTER, MARK
Picture Framing Techniques
A good basic guide to framing anything from a tapestry to a bunch of dried flowers.
[E221] Ebury hbk **£5.95**

RIBBON CRAFT
BAWDEN, JULIET
The Ribbon Book
Exciting ways to transform your clothes and home with ribbon.
[E222] Piatkus **£2.95**

RIBBON ART PUBLISHING COMPANY
Old Fashioned Ribbon Art
Ideas and designs for accessories and decorations.
[E223] Dover pbk **£2.65**

RUG MAKING
BENARDOUT, DAVID
Care & Repair of Rugs & Carpets
This is a very useful handbook geared towards the repair of commercial products.
[E224] Ebury hbk **£5.95**

COSS, MELINDA & SOUDAN, SYLVIE
Magic Carpets
Features thirty original rug designs based on a variety of artistic themes, with full instructions and simple colour graphs to follow for an interested beginner.
[E225] Collins **£12.95**

GOOD HOUSEKEEPING
Rugs & Wall Hangings
Over fifty rug designs and the techniques used to make them: hooked, punch, needle, needlepoint, prodded, braided and woven.
[E226] Ebury hbk **£4.95**

MOSHIMER, JOAN
The Complete Rug Hooker
A complete and very detailed guide to making hooked rag rugs in the classic American tradition. Patterns for beginners and lots of inspiring ideas.
[E227] NY Graphic Soc pbk **£7.95**

Practical Art

Books on contemporary techniques, including airbrushing and computer graphics, are included here, along with design reference 'epics' and guides to more traditional painting and drawing methods. Macdonald and Collins provide cheap and excellent series covering practical aspects; they are complemented by more expensive volumes on specialist areas by Watson Guptill and Phaidon.

General Techniques

Illustrators' Figure Reference Manual
Clothed and nude figures in an exhaustive range of poses to solve illustrators' problems with live models.
[E229] Bloomsbury hbk **£14.95**

BORGMAN, HARRY
Art & Illustration Techniques
Step-by-step instructions on the use of different media: pencil, ink, tone markers, designer colours, watercolours, acrylic and mixed media.
[E230] Watson Guptill pbk **£14.95**

BUTLER, DAVID
Making Ways
The visual artist's guide to surviving and thriving.
[E231] Artic pbk **£7.95**

EASLEY, THOMAS
The Figure in Motion
Male and female figures in suspended action poses, showing line, lighting and muscle structure in positions unsustainable by models.
[E232] Watson Guptill hbk **£19.50**

FABRI, RALPH
Artist's Guide to Compostition
How to achieve symmetry - a summary of dos and don'ts.
[E233] Watson Guptill pbk **£14.95**

GILL, ROBERT
Creative Perspective
Short-cut methods to understanding perspective provide a valuable tool for designers and draughtsmen.
[E234] Thames & H pbk **£3.95**

HEBBLEWHITE, IAN
Artist's Materials
Lists and gives detailed descriptions of materials currently available from all the major manufacturers with, where applicable, an assessment of quality and suitability.
[E235] Phaidon hbk **£16.95**

JACOBS, TED SETH
Light for the Artist
Light effects applied to figure, still life and landscape renditions.
[E236] Phaidon hbk **£19.50**

MAYER, RALPH
The Artist's Handbook of Materials & Techniques
Complete and up-to-date accounts of materials and methods for practising artists.
[E237] Faber hbk **£18.50**
[E238] Faber pbk **£12.50**

SMITH, RAY
The Artist's Handbook
An excellent guide to all aspects of painting and drawing. Good advice on choice of equipment and materials.
[E239] D Kindersley hbk **£14.95**

ZELANSKI, PAUL
Colour   NEW
Understanding and use of colour are explained with reference to the theories of Newton, Goethe and others. Includes useful details on composition, mixing colours, computer graphics, video and holography.
[E240] Herbert pbk **£12.95**

Calligraphy

ATKINS, KATHRYN
Masters of the Italic Letter   NEW
A survey of twenty masters of the italic letter from the 16th century.
[E241] Viking hbk **£20.00**

BRIEM, GUNNLAUGUR SE
Sixty Alphabets
Diverse lettering styles from a leading calligrapher.
[E242] Thames & H pbk **£5.95**

The letter 'A' from *Masters of the Italic Letter* by Kathryn Atkins (Viking hbk £20.00)

FURBER, ALAN
Layout & Design for Calligraphers
Balance, format, headings and borders for harmonious layouts.
[E243] Dryad hbk **£7.95**

GARDNER, WILLIAM
Book of Calligraphy NEW
Structure, spacing and practice for those who have mastered the basics.
[E244] Wildwood hbk **£17.95**

GOURDIE, TOM
The acknowledged expert in this field.
Basic Calligraphic Hands
[E245] A & C Black pbk **£4.95**
Calligraphic Styles
[E246] Studio Vista pbk **£5.95**
Gothic Scripts
[E247] A & C Black pbk **£5.95**
Italic Handwriting
[E248] Cassell pbk **£3.50**

LYNSKEY, MARIE
Creative Calligraphy
A complete course in decorative lettering from a basic foundation hand to colour and illustrative styles.
[E249] Thorsons pbk **£6.99**

MARTIN, JUDY
The Complete Guide to Calligraphy
Styles, history and practical hints about pens and letter forms.
[E250] Phaidon hbk **£10.95**

SOGEN, OMORI
Zen & the Art of Calligraphy
Explains how a balanced mind and body control the pen.
[E251] Routledge pbk **£4.95**

Collage

DIGBY, JOHN & JOAN
The Collage Handbook
An overview of the techniques developed by Braque and Picasso, concentrating on the work of modern collage artists.
[E252] Thames & H hbk **£12.95**

Drawing

BORGESON, BEK
Coloured Pencil Fast Techniques
Methods and strategies for gaining speed and improving your work.
[E253] Phaidon hbk **£19.50**

EDWARDS, BETTY
Drawing on the Artist Within
This excellent book is the companion volume to the classic *Drawing on the Right Side of the Brain*. Fully illustrated, it demonstrates how to unlock the subliminal artist within each of us.
[E254] Collins hbk **£12.95**
[E255] Fontana pbk **£6.95**
Drawing on the Right Side of the Brain
Tune into the creative side of the brain to heighten awareness of colour, shape and forms.
[E256] Fontana pbk **£7.95**

GILL, ROBERT M.
Manual of Rendering with Pen & Ink
Pen drawing for architects, engineers, draughtsmen and technicians.
[E257] Thames & H pbk **£5.95**

GORDON, LOUISE
Drawing the Human Head
Anatomy and lighting for beginners and advanced artists.
[E258] Batsford pbk **£6.99**

HAYES, COLIN
The Complete Guide to Painting & Drawing
An encyclopaedic guide to popular painting and drawing techniques, materials, framing and mounting.
[E259] Phaidon hbk **£14.95**
[E260] Phaidon pbk **£9.95**

MACDONALD ACADEMY OF ART SERIES
An excellent series of inexpensive paperbacks, covering all aspects of learning to paint and draw. The painting titles are listed in the *Paint & Pastel* section.
How to Draw & Paint the Figure
[E261] Macdonald pbk **£2.50**
How to Draw & Paint the Nude
[E262] Macdonald pbk **£2.50**
How to Draw & Sketch
[E263] Macdonald pbk **£2.50**
How to Draw with Pastels
[E264] Macdonald pbk **£2.50**

MCKENZIE, ALAN
How to Draw & Sell Comic Strips for Newspapers & Comic Books
Practical advice for all those who want to draw and create their own cartoons.
[E265] Macdonald hbk **£12.95**

NICOLAIDES, KIMON
The Natural Way to Draw NEW
If you are going to draw something well: identify with it, feel it, connect with it, rather than concentrate on technique, Nicolaides told his students. Although he died in 1938, his distinctive methods are still vigorously practised.
[E266] Deutsch pbk **£8.95**

SHEPPARD, JOSEPH
Drawing the Living Figure
Describes how bones and muscles create the forms of the living figure; a complete guide to surface anatomy.
[E267] Watson Guptill hbk **£19.50**

SMITH, STAN
Drawing and Sketching
[E463] Ebury P pbk **£8.95**

WEST, KEITH
How to Draw Plants: Techniques of Botanical Illustration
Provides detailed advice on the techniques of botanical illustration. This book is aimed at both professionals and those who wish to draw plants as a hobby.
[E268] A & C Black pbk **£8.95**

Graphic Art Techniques & Design

The Methuen Handbook of Colour NEW
Ready-reference for technicians and designers, featuring 1,266 colour samples and a glossary of colour names.
[E269] Methuen hbk **£30.00**

ALDERSLEY-WILLIAMS, HUGH
New American Design NEW
Focusing on graphics and products for a post-industrial age; the book also includes interviews and illustrations.
[E270] Rizzoli hbk **£22.50**

BAYLEY, STEPHEN (ED)
20th Century Style & Design
Source book featuring all the major trends in the West during this century. Of interest to layman and art historian alike.
[E271] Thames & H hbk **£22.50**
The Conran Directory of Design
An authoritative and spirited guide to the history of well-designed consumer goods of the last hundred years.
[E272] Conran Octopus hbk **£16.95**

BEAUMONT, MICHAEL
Type & Colour
This is an important aspect of graphic design. The book gives practical advice on choosing the most suitable typeface and colour to achieve successful designs.
[E273] Phaidon hbk **£12.95**

CHARLESWORTH, ANDY
Airbrushing the Human Form NEW
Elements of the human body, image styles, materials and techniques.
[E274] Studio Vista hbk **£14.95**

DALLEY, TERENCE
Complete Guide to Illustration & Design
Aimed at the professional and amateur alike, this is a comprehensive guide to the techniques, tools and materials used in illustration and graphic design today.
[E275] Phaidon hbk **£17.50**
[E276] Phaidon pbk **£11.95**

DEAN, MARTYN
The Guide to Fantasy Art NEW
An insider's view of the creative processes behind the mystic landscapes and futuristic visions of eight contemporary fantasy artists.
[E277] Paper Tiger **£6.95**

DELL, FRED & CHARLESWORTH, ANDY
Airbrush Artist's Handbook: Equipment, Maintenance & Materials
Technical information for the practising artist.
[E278] Macdonald hbk **£9.95**

DUCKETT, GRAHAM
Creative Air Brushing
A step-by-step course in techniques, skills and equipment for home hobbyists and serious art students.
[E279] Ebury pbk **£7.95**

GUILD, TRICIA
Design and Detail   NEW
'Design, style - whatever you choose to call it - arises out of a feeling, an intuition for colour, scale and pattern.' Guild has it; if you aren't afraid of colour, this beautiful book is for you.
[E280] Conran Octopus hbk **£17.95**

HELLER, STEVEN & CHWAST, SEYMOUR
Graphic Style   NEW
A time-line of 150 years of design styles, from Victorian to post-modern. Colourfully illustrated with prints, labels, posters, shopping bags and book illustrations.
[E281] Thames & H hbk **£24.95**

HICKS, ROGER
The Airbrushing Book
Using the Aztek airbrush, this manual covers safety, colour, propellants, grounds, tools and technique.
[E282] Broadcast hbk **£15.95**

ISOSAKI, ARATA
International Design Year Book 1988/89
National trends and the state of design are showcased in this collection of contemporary work.
[E283] Thames & H hbk **£36.00**

LEWELL, JOHN
Computer Graphics
A clearly laid out book covering all aspects of this new art form, without relying too heavily on computer double speak.
[E284] Macdonald hbk **£12.95**

LOEWY, RAYMOND
Industrial Design   NEW
Coca-Cola bottles, Concorde and toothbrushes are among the consumer items designed by Loewy. This retrospective looks at the man and his vision.
[E285] Fourth Estate pbk **£15.95**

MCQUISTON, LIZ
Women & Design   NEW
Classic and controversial women designers expanding a traditionally male discipline.
[E286] Trefoil hbk **£16.95**

MORGAN, JACQUI
Watercolour for Illustration
A workshop of techniques for commercial illustration and a guide to marketing your work.
[E287] Watson Guptill hbk **£19.50**

MULHERIN, JENNY
Presentation Techniques for the Graphic Artist
How to sell your ideas effectively.
[E288] Phaidon hbk **£12.95**

ROBERTSON, BRUCE
Techniques of Fantasy Art
Aimed at the complete beginner, this book presents clear instructions on how to create striking images of your own in the fantasy art style.
[E289] Macdonald hbk **£11.95**

SPARKE, PENNY
Design Source Book
[E290] Macdonald hbk **£14.95**
Design in Context
Designers are said to be the mediators between consumers and industry. This book puts the history, application and development of design in a socio-political context.
[E291] Bloomsbury hbk **£16.95**

SWANN, ALAN
Basic Design & Layout
This practical and informative book shows how to choose the right combination of elements such as headings, text and illustrations to create successful designs.
[E293] Phaidon hbk **£12.95**

TROTMAN, FELICITY (ED)
How to Write and Illustrate Children's Books
Includes an examination of picture books and illustrations in successful children's books.
[E294] Macdonald hbk **£12.95**

TURNER, MARK
Silver Studio of Design   NEW
English furniture, decorating, and style over the last 100 years, with many examples taken from the Silver Studio, established in 1880.
[E295] Webb & B hbk **£15.95**

VELARDE, GILES
Designing Exhibitions   NEW
How to provide information, excitement and pleasure to audiences at shows and exhibitions.
[E296] Design Council pbk **£14.95**

WHITE, TONY
The Animator's Workbook
Steps to hand-drawn animation by an award-winning animator.
[E297] Phaidon pbk **£12.95**

WOOLERY, LEE
Marker Techniques   NEW
A series of projects with marker pens.
[E298] North Light pbk **£6.99**

Paint & Pastel

BROWNING, COLLEEN
Working Out a Painting   NEW
Adventures in transforming your oils into mature works.
[E299] Watson Guptill hbk **£19.50**

CRAWSHAW, ALWYN
The Half-Hour Painter   NEW
A new book for all artists and leisure painters aiming to paint a complete work of art within a limited time and offering progressive hints on improving techniques.
[E300] Collins hbk **£12.95**

CRESPO, MICHAEL
Experiments in Watercolour
20 ways to learn by doing.
[E301] Phaidon hbk **£19.50**
Watercolour Day by Day
An innovative course in transparent watercolour.
[E302] Phaidon hbk **£18.50**

GALTON, JEREMY
Choosing and Mixing Colours for Painting   NEW
Avoid muddy messes with these tips for selecting

pigments, mixing, glazing and dry brushing.
[E303] Studio Vista hbk **£12.95**

GREENE, DANIEL E.
Pastel
A survey of materials and techniques.
[E304] Phaidon hbk **£14.95**

HUNTLY, MOIRA
Painting in Mixed Media
Imaginative combinations of traditional materials: acrylic, oil, watercolour, ink and wash, roller techniques, marbling and collage. Covers both abstract and representational painting.
[E305] A & C Black pbk **£9.95**

JOHNSON, CATHY
Watercolour Tricks and Techniques
Tin foil, cooking spray, candle wax and straws are among the unusual materials used to create textured painting effects.
[E306] Collins hbk **£12.95**

KATCHEN, CAROLE
Planning Your Paintings
This book explains how to plan paintings effectively to make better watercolours, oils and pastels.
[E307] Phaidon hbk **£19.50**

KOMINSKY, NANCY
Nancy Kominsky's Painting with Pastels
[E308] Collins pbk **£6.95**

LONG, JEAN
Practical Chinese Painting
Symbolism, composition, techniques and materials for this ancient art form are explained with prolific illustrations.
[E309] Blandford hbk **£12.95**

MACDONALD ACADEMY OF ART SERIES
An excellent series of inexpensive paperbacks, covering all aspects of learning to paint and draw.
How to Paint Flowers & Plants
[E310] Macdonald pbk **£2.50**
How to Paint Landscapes in Oils
[E311] Macdonald pbk **£2.50**
How to Paint Landscapes with Watercolours
[E312] Macdonald pbk **£2.50**
How to Paint Nature
[E313] Macdonald pbk **£2.50**
How to Paint Portraits
[E314] Macdonald pbk **£2.50**
How to Paint Portraits in Oils
[E315] Macdonald pbk **£2.50**
How to Paint Still Life in Oils
[E316] Macdonald pbk **£2.50**
How to Paint Still Life with Acrylics
[E317] Macdonald pbk **£2.50**

MASIAS, MARIE-THERESE & PINHAS-MASSIN, AGNES
Painting on China
A well-laid out and informative cheap guide.
[E318] Hobby Craft S pbk **£3.50**

MILLIARD, DAVID
Impasto
Impasto is the technique of laying on paint thickly. David Milliard demonstrates how to make paintings more interesting by using different textures of impasto.
[E319] Watson Guptill hbk **£19.50**

PARSONS, JOY
Wildlife Painting
A spider in its web first inspired the author to paint

wildlife. Contains useful information on techniques and materials.
[E320] Batsford hbk **£10.95**

ROURKES, NICHOLAS
Acrylics Bold & New
Innovative ideas and techniques.
[E321] Watson Guptill hbk **£19.50**

SCHAFFER, S. ALLYN
The Oil Painter's Guide to Painting Water
50 lessons in painting oceans, rivers, lakes, marshes and beaches.
[E322] Watson Guptill hbk **£19.50**

SELIGMAN, PATRICIA
Step-by-Step Art School Oils `NEW`
Fundamental techniques and materials in easy-to-follow sections.
[E323] Hamlyn hbk **£8.95**

SMITH, RAY
How to Draw & Paint What You See
A complete practical course.
[E324] D Kindersley hbk **£12.50**

Printing

BIGGS, JOHN E.
Classic Woodcut Art & Engraving `NEW`
An international collection and practical handbook.
[E325] Blandford pbk **£10.95**

BRETT, SIMON
Engravers: A Handbook for the Nineties
An arresting portfolio of contemporary British wood engravers.
[E326] Silent Bks pbk **£7.95**

CHAMBERLAIN, WALTER
Woodcut Printmaking
Simple methods and inexpensive materials are outlined.
[E327] Thames & H pbk **£3.95**

JAFFE, PATRICIA
Women Engravers `NEW`
Many of the finest exponents of this art in the twentieth century have been women, and it continues to flourish in their hands.
[E328] Virago hbk **£15.00**

SENEFELDER, ALOIS
A Complete Course of Lithography
As well as being a personal account of the author's struggles to popularise his medium, this is also a technical manual to all aspects of the craft.
[E329] Da Capo pbk **£12.95**

SIMMONS, ROSEMARY
The Complete Manual of Relief Printmaking
Well-laid-out guide to tools and techniques of lino-cutting, woodcutting and wood engraving.
[E330] D Kindersley hbk **£12.95**

House & Home

Pressure on people to buy their own homes, sky-rocketing costs for professional tradespeople, and the leisure to explore design ideas have led to a flourishing interest in DIY, decorating and renovation.

The publishing industry has responded with many excellent practical manuals on DIY and some stunning, colourful titles on interior decoration. This selection includes a balance of straightforward guides and inspirational reference books on interiors and exteriors, chosen for their practicality, cost and enthusiastic approach.

Do-It-Yourself

BREMNER, MOYRA
Enquire Within Upon Everything: The Complete Home Expert
[E332] Century hbk **£16.95**

DO IT
An excellent Collins series with clear instructions and illustrations.
Fence It `NEW`
[E333] Collins pbk **£2.25**
Frame It
[E334] Collins pbk **£1.25**
Glaze It
[E335] Collins pbk **£1.25**
Mirror It
[E336] Collins pbk **£1.25**
Paint It
[E337] Collins pbk **£1.25**
Paper It
[E338] Collins pbk **£1.25**
Pave It `NEW`
[E339] Collins pbk **£2.25**
Plumb It
[E340] Collins pbk **£1.25**
Shelve It
[E341] Collins pbk **£1.25**
Strip It
[E342] Collins pbk **£1.25**
Tile It
[E343] Collins pbk **£1.25**
Wire It
[E344] Collins pbk **£1.25**

ENTWHISTLE, RICHARD
DIY Designer Furniture
Chic and classic Italian-inspired furniture to make at home.
[E345] Ebury hbk **£9.95**

FRANKS, BETH
Very Small Living Spaces `NEW`
Fitting all your needs into a confined area while maintaining taste and style is the problem addressed in this imaginative guide.
[E346] Colombus hbk **£9.95**

GUINNESS
Step by Step DIY
Colour-coded sections cover electrics, plumbing, electric, decorating, central heating and insulation, and indoor and outdoor repairs.
[E347] Guinness hbk **£14.95**

HOLLOWAY, DAVID
The 'Which' Book of Do-It-Yourself
An excellent general guide which shows how to make a professional-looking job of repairs and home improvement.
[E348] Hodder hbk **£14.95**

LAWRENCE, MIKE
Straightforward repairs and maintenance.
The Complete Home Plumber
[E349] Macdonald hbk **£8.95**
The Complete Home Electrician
[E350] Macdonald hbk **£7.95**

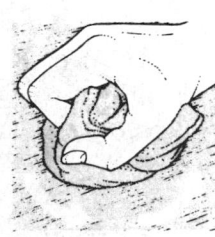

An illustration from *The Daily Mail Book of Hints and Household Tips* by Barty Phillips (Dorling Kindersley pbk £9.95)

MORRIS, IAN
Bazaar Property Doctor `NEW`
TV's property doctor and surveyor explains the symptoms of household ills and offers remedies to everything from rising damp to falling roof tiles.
[E351] BBC pbk **£2.95**

PHILLIPS, BARTY
The 'Daily Mail' Book of Household Hints `NEW`
[E462] D Kindersley pbk **£9.95**

READER'S DIGEST
New DIY Manual
Tested techniques are clearly illustrated in this guide to everything remotely connected with home improvement. It comes in a sturdy plastic folder. Recommended.
[E352] Hodder hbk **£23.95**

TRAINI, ROBERT
Home Security and Protection
Protecting your home, its occupants and possessions, whether in an inner city flat or country house.
[E353] Collins hbk **£4.95**

Interior Decoration

ASHLEY, LAURA
Laura Ashley at Home `NEW`
The *doyenne* of interior decoration shows off her distinctive style in the homes of six members of her family.
[E354] Weidenfeld hbk **£16.00**

BURNS, MARK & DIBONIS, LOUIS
Fifties Homestyle `NEW`
Fifties America revisited - the age of rock'n'roll, TV, plastic, advertising, and the automobile.
[E355] Thames & H pbk **£6.95**

CHESHIRE, JANE
The Country Diary Book of Stencilling `NEW`
Watercolours from Edith Holden's diary inspired this rustic collection. Includes suggestions for projects to copy.
[E356] Webb & B hbk **£14.95**

CONRAN, TERENCE
Terence Conran's New House Book
The complete guide to home design. It effectively combines creative stimulation with easy-to-use information providing hundreds of decorating ideas. Tackles everything from restructuring an entire house to creating delightful rooms for children.
[E357] Conran Octopus hbk **£17.95**

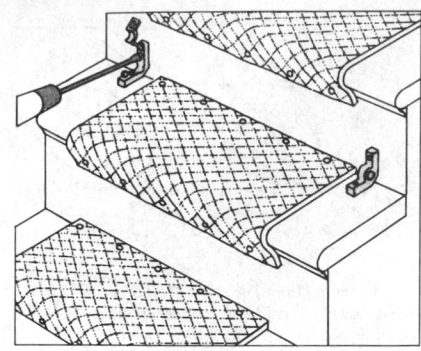

Diagram from *The Conran Beginner's Guide to Decorating* by Jocasta Innes and Jill Blake (Conran Octopus hbk £12.95)

DICKSON, ELIZABETH
Colefax & Fowler: The Best in English Interiors
A handsomely illustrated account of the interior decorating style of Colefax & Fowler, the legendary firm whose work over the last fifty years has included Buckingham Palace, Badminton and many of the most prestigious English country houses.
[E358] Barrie & J hbk **£16.95**

GILLIAT, MARY
New Guide to Decorating NEW
Author of *Dream Houses* and design consultant to Debenham's and Liberty's, Gilliat uses charts, checklists and time-saving tips to guide you through budgets, structural changes, classic and contemporary styling and practical decorating techniques.
[E359] Conran Octopus hbk **£16.95**

GRAY, LINDA & INNES, JOCASTA
The Complete Book of Decorating Techniques
Gone are the days when home decorating meant a swift flick through the wallpaper catalogues. Here the whole spectrum of decorative effects - both basic and designer - is covered.
[E360] Macdonald hbk **£12.95**

HICKS, DAVID
Style & Design
'Taste' is a subjective term, but Hicks has 30 years of experience on which to base his advice.
[E361] Viking hbk **£17.95**

HOGG, MIN & HARRAP, WENDY
The World of Interiors NEW
Celebrating interior decor, exploring 8 major decorative styles and including many colour photos.
[E362] Conran Octopus hbk **£20.00**

INNES, JOCASTA
Innes' books on the finer details of decorating are enormously popular and easy to use; they include a wide range of colour, diagrams and ideas.
Paint Magic
[E363] Windward hbk **£14.95**
Paintability
[E364] Weidenfeld hbk **£12.95**
[E365] Weidenfeld pbk **£8.95**

INNES, JOCASTA & BLAKE, JILL
The Conran Beginner's Guide to Decorating
[E464] Conran Octopus hbk **£12.95**

LE GRICE, LYN
The Stencilled House NEW
Room by room, the author demonstrates how

stencilling can be adapted to individual settings. Published in conjunction with the National Trust.
[E366] D Kindersley **£14.95**

PFEIFFER, WALTER
In the Houses of Ireland NEW
Glowing photographs open doors to warm, rich rooms, which reflect a living history.
[E367] Thames & H hbk **£25.00**

PLANT, TIMOTHY
Painted Illusions
Murals, trompe l'oeil techniques, and wall preparation are explained alongside guidance on emphasising or hiding architectural features.
[E368] Ward Lock hbk **£14.95**

RUST, GRAHAM
The Painted House NEW
A beautifully illustrated source book for figurative and abstract trompe l'oeil and murals.
[E369] Macmillan hbk **£30.00**

SABINO, CATHERINE
Italian Country Living NEW
La dolce vita at home in the fields, vineyards, mountains and coasts of Italy.
[E370] Thames & H hbk **£25.00**

SAINT GEORGE, AMELIA
The Stencil Book
Includes 30 stencils to pull out or trace.
[E371] Conran Octopus hbk **£14.95**

SLESIN, SUSAN & STAFFORD, CLIFF
English Style
The best of British, from the comfortably traditional to the provocatively modern.
[E372] Thames & H hbk **£25.00**

Template from *The Stencil Book* by Amelia Saint George (Conran Octopus hbk £14.95)

SPENCER, STUART
The Art of Marbling
Opulent marble can be replaced with a thin film of paint. Step-by-step instructions show exactly how.
[E373] Macdonald hbk **£10.95**

STEFANIDIS, JOHN
Rooms: Design & Decoration NEW
Shows off the skills of one of London's top interior designers.
[E374] Weidenfeld hbk **£30.00**

WARRENDER, CAROLYN
The Book of Stencilling NEW
The founder of the first specialist stencilling store shows how she extended the decorations of the pilgrim settlers into an immensely popular contemporary medium.
[E375] Deutsch hbk **£30.00**

WILSON, ALTHEA
Paint Works
Sponging, marbling, and crumbling palazzo are among the decorative paint techniques featured.
[E376] Century hbk **£16.95**

Furnishings

'French Style' Decorative Home Embroidery
Charming designs for cushions, table and bed-linen, chair covers and rugs. The motifs include sprays of flowers, classic Italian villas and scatterings of herbs.
[E377] Conran Octopus pbk **£4.99**

'French Style' Decorative Home Sewing
A superb collection of things to sew for the home: cushions, covers, curtains, rugs, bed and table-linen.
[E378] Conran Octopus pbk **£4.99**

CONRAN, TERENCE
The Soft Furnishings Book
Inspirational as well as practical. Includes the most beautiful and widely appealing range of soft furnishings. Covers doors, windows, chairs and beds.
[E379] Conran Octopus hbk **£15.00**

GRAY, LINDA
The Window Style Book NEW
Dress up your windows, inside and out. Glass, frames, security, and techniques for making curtains and blinds are examined.
[E380] Merehurst hbk **£15.95**

PAINE, MELANIE
Fabric Magic
Stitching, layering or handpainting can transform an everyday fabric into something individual.
[E381] Windward hbk **£14.95**

PEVERILL, SUE
The Fabric Decorator: Colouring Fabrics for the Home
Furnishing fabrics become an artist's canvas: dyed, sponged, splattered and painted to make curtains, furniture and floor coverings.
[E382] Macdonald hbk **£14.95**

SUDJIC, DEYAN
The Lighting Book
[E383] M Beazley hbk **£10.95**

THOMERSON, CAROLE
The Complete Upholsterer: A NEW
Practical Guide to Upholstering Traditional Furniture
An indispensable handbook which gives

comprehensive instructions on restoring upholstered furniture to its proper shape and outline, as well as a richly detailed history of styles and techniques.
[E384] F Lincoln hbk **£14.95**

WATKINS, CHARMIAN
Decorating with Fabric Liberty Style
Rich colours and textures make drapes, covers and table sets in the distinctive Liberty style.
[E385] Ebury hbk **£12.95**

WRAY, CHRISTOPHER
Guide to Decorative Lighting
Useful ideas on how to enhance a room by incorporating lighting into your design.
[E386] Webb & B hbk **£14.95**

Renovation & Restoration

ARTLEY, ALEXANDRA
Putting Back the Style
A dictionary of authentic renovation. How to restore your period home cheaply yet with true historical accuracy.
[E387] Ward Lock pbk **£8.95**

DAVIS, KENNETH
Restoring Furniture
Basic craftsmanship demonstrated by one of Britain's leading furniture restorers.
[E388] Macdonald pbk **£6.95**

GRAY, LINDA
Room for Change
Innovative and exciting ideas for transforming your home. An insight into the way professional interior designers work.
[E389] Macdonald hbk **£12.95**

JOHNSON, ALAN
Converting Old Buildings
Adapting barns, churches, warehouses, stations and mills into stylish, spacious houses.
[E390] David & Ch hbk **£15.00**

MACK, LORRAINE & HAYLEY, GEOFFREY
Restoring Upholstered Furniture
Simple techniques for professional-looking home restorations.
[E391] Macdonald hbk **£5.00**

MCGOWAN, JOHN
Book of Home Restoration
Time-honoured techniques and materials to maintain older houses, gardens and possessions.
[E392] Sidgwick pbk **£7.95**

MILLER, JUDITH & MARTIN
Period Details
A pictorial source book of structural and decorative styles, fixtures and fittings, period by period.
[E393] M Beazley hbk **£14.95**

ORCHARD, JAN
Room for Improvement
Clever schemes for adding on, adapting, and finding hidden spaces in small houses.
[E394] Windward hbk **£12.95**

PHILLIPS, BARTY
Doing up a Dump
Mainly for young people, this book includes down-to-earth advice on tenancy obligations, finding money, painting, storage and appliances.
[E395] Macdonald pbk **£5.95**

QUINEY, ANTHONY
Period Houses NEW
Invaluable source of ideas and information for anyone thinking of buying or restoring a period house. The book examines medieval, Tudor, Jacobean, Georgian, Victorian and Edwardian houses, covering every aspect of their construction and placing them in their broader social context.
[E396] George Philip hbk **£15.95**

REED, J. RONALD
Authentic Craftsmanship in Design NEW
After years of mass production and a decline in craftsmanship, authentic techniques are again being valued. Conservator Reed discusses methods and materials.
[E397] Simon & Sch hbk **£12.95**

SANDERS, MATTHEW
A Historic Home Owner's Companion
Anyone planning to maintain or restore their period home will benefit from this companion to sympathetic restoration.
[E398] Batsford hbk **£14.95**

SUDJIC, DEYAN
House Style Book
[E399] M Beazley hbk **£16.95**

Fashion

The magical world of fashion has spawned a glamorous written and visual vocabulary: Chanel and Dior star among those captured in expansive (and expensive) photographic masterpieces; while Batsford tracks back over centuries of costume history in comprehensive, cheaper series. See *Practical Fashion* and *Dressmaking* for further titles.

Costume History & Reference

BAILEY, ADRIAN
The Passion for Fashion NEW
The period from 1700 to 1950 is unparalleled in the wild swings of its fashion. This interesting reference work reviews the trends in their social contexts.
[E401] Dragon's World hbk **£16.95**

BATSFORD COSTUME ACCESSORIES
1: Shoes
[E402] Batsford hbk **£10.95**
2: Bags & Purses
[E403] Batsford hbk **£10.95**
3: Hats
[E404] Batsford hbk **£10.95**
4: Gloves
[E405] Batsford hbk **£10.95**
5: Fans
[E406] Batsford hbk **£10.95**
6: Jewellery
[E407] Batsford hbk **£10.95**
7: Umbrellas & Parasols
[E408] Batsford hbk **£10.95**
8: Shawls, Stoles & Scarves
[E409] Batsford hbk **£10.95**

BATSFORD COSTUME REFERENCE
A very good series systemically covering all periods.
SICHEL, MARION
1: Roman Britain & the Middle Ages
[E410] Batsford hbk **£8.95**
2: Tudors & Elizabethans
[E411] Batsford hbk **£8.95**

3: Jacobean Stuart & Restoration
[E412] Batsford hbk **£8.95**
4: The Eighteenth Century
[E413] Batsford hbk **£8.95**
5: The Regency
[E414] Batsford hbk **£8.95**
6: The Victorians
[E415] Batsford hbk **£8.95**
7: The Edwardians
[E416] Batsford hbk **£8.95**
8: 1918 - 1939
[E417] Batsford hbk **£8.95**
9: 1939 - 1950
[E418] Batsford hbk **£8.95**
10: 1950 - 1978
[E419] Batsford hbk **£8.95**

BATSFORD NATIONAL COSTUME REFERENCE
1: Japan
[E420] Batsford hbk **£8.95**
2: Russia
[E421] Batsford hbk **£8.95**
3: Scandinavia
[E422] Batsford hbk **£8.95**
4: South America
[E423] Batsford hbk **£8.95**

COX, JAMES
An Illustrated Dictionary of Hairdressing & Wigmaking
Names and details of wigs, beards, moustaches and hairstyles of all periods.
[E424] Batsford hbk **£25.00**

DE MARLY, DIANE
Fashion for Men: An Illustrated History
The rise and decline of the codpiece, the kilt and other high points of male fashion.
[E425] Batsford hbk **£17.95**

FERRAGAMO, SALVATORE
The Art of the Shoe 1927 - 1960
Ferragamo, 'The Shoemaker of Dreams', has become synonymous with innovation and glamour in the modern shoe. This catalogue celebrates the shoe as art.
[E426] V & A Mus P pbk **£27.50**

HOLLANDER, ANNE
Seeing Through Clothes
Details how clothes and art have contributed to our visualisation of the human body.
[E427] Penguin pbk **£7.99**

MCDOWELL, COLIN
A Hundred Years of Royal Style
Behind the Royal image, protocol and PR determine dress requirements.
[E428] Muller hbk **£14.95**
Shoes: Fashion and Fantasy NEW
Brogues, brothel-creepers, clogs, cowboy boots, platforms, Doc Martens, sneakers, loafers, sandals and slingbacks all feature in this fascinating celebration of the shoe as cultural fetish. Preface by Manolo Blahnik.
[E429] Thames & H hbk **£24.00**

RACINET, ALBERT
The Historical Encyclopaedia of Costume NEW
Originally published in France in 1876-88, the scope and detail of this, one of the earliest books on the subject, have never been surpassed. Illustrated with photographs, traveller's reports and sketches of collections of the time. Re-edited and re-designed for this new edition.
[E430] Studio Eds hbk **£19.95**

ROBINSON, JULIAN
The Fine Art of Fashion: An Illustrated History `NEW`
[E460] Bay Bks hbk £29.95

ROTHSTEIN, NATALIE (ED)
Barbara Johnson's Album of Fashion & Fabrics
The painstaking record of an 18th-century lady's changing wardrobe.
[E431] Thames & H hbk **£35.00**

SAINT LAURENT, CECIL
A History of Women's Underwear
Radical changes in women's nether garments have mirrored the great wheel of fashion and the place of women in society. From Egyptian G-strings to lacy girdles and spotted boxers, this is a fascinating and colourful history.
[E432] Academy hbk **£25.00**

SICHEL, MARION
Costume of the Classical World
[E433] Batsford hbk **£8.95**
History of Children's Costume
[E434] Batsford hbk **£7.95**
History of Men's Costume
[E435] Batsford hbk **£7.95**
History of Women's Costume
[E436] Batsford hbk **£8.95**

STEELE, VALERIE
Paris Fashion
For 300 years Paris has been the international capital of style. Steele focuses on the city and culture of Paris to show the development of modern urban fashion.
[E437] Oxford hbk **£35.00**

WALKER, RICHARD
The Savile Row Story
'A man's first duty is to his tailor. What his second is, nobody has yet discerned' (Oscar Wilde). Synonymous with sartorial excellence, the street contains the world's most famous concentration of bespoke tailors, all of whom are detailed in this definitive history.
[E438] Multimedia Bks hbk **£14.95**

20th Century Fashion

BAINES, BARBARA BURMAN
Fashion in the Twentieth Century
This book charts the changing styles of fashion and explores the way fashion affects our everyday lives.
[E439] Batsford hbk **£14.95**

BEATON, CECIL
The Glass of Fashion `NEW`
A facsimile of Beaton's classic examination of fashion and style in the first half of the 20th century.
[E440] Cassell hbk **£14.95**

COLERIDGE, NICHOLAS
The Fashion Conspiracy
From the catwalks in Paris to the sweatshops of South Korea, this book offers a fascinating insight into the opulent world of international fashion in the 1980s.
[E441] Heinemann hbk **£12.95**

MARTIN, RICHARD
Fashion & Surrealism
Traces the fruitful dialogue that has developed between high fashion and the often shocking techniques of experimental art developed by the Surrealists.
[E442] Thames & H hbk **£27.50**

Illustration from *The Fine Art of Fashion: An Illustrated History* by Julian Robinson (Bay Books hbk £29.95)

MULVAGH, JANE
Costume Jewellery in Vogue `NEW`
'It doesn't matter if its real, as long as it looks like junk!' said Chanel. This book follows the fads of paste and plastic, using informative text and illustrations.
[E443] Thames & H pbk **£12.95**
Vogue History of 20th Century Fashion `NEW`
Why did flappers imitate adolescent boys? Have Japanese designers cocked a snook at Western style? This book uses diaries, interviews, memoirs and photographs to bring *Vogue*'s archives alive.
[E444] Viking hbk **£30.00**

O'HARA, GEORGINA
The Encyclopaedia of Fashion
An A-Z listing from 1840 to the present day, which offers an invaluable source of information for designers, students, collectors and fashion enthusiasts.
[E461] Thames & H pbk £12.95

STEELE, H. THOMAS
The Hawaiian Shirt
'You know you are in Hawaii when her muu-muu matches his shirt.' A gallery of exotic, vibrant Polynesian print shirts.
[E445] Thames & H pbk **£7.95**

Fashion Designers & Illustrators

BARNES, COLIN & WOLFE, MARY LEE
Fashion Illustration: A Source Book for the Student
Over 100 stunning examples from the work of the best fashion illustrators past and present, including Zandra Rhodes, Bruce Oldfield, and Dior.
[E446] Macdonald hbk **£14.95**

DESLANDRES, YVONNE
Paul Poiret
'Dress is an industry whose raison d'être is novelty.' A tribute to the designer who many consider the inventor of the 20th century woman.
[E447] Thames & H hbk **£75.00**

GIROUD, FRANÇOISE
Dior
The life and times of the 'New Look'.
[E448] Thames & H hbk **£75.00**

LAURENT, YVES SAINT
Yves Saint Laurent & The Photography of Fashion
Photographs by Irving Penn, Helmut Newton, Jean Loupp Sieff, David Bailey and others. With an introduction by Marguerite Duras.
[E449] Ebury hbk **£60.00**

LEYMARIE, JEAN
Chanel
'Chanel is an everlasting bomb that not one of us can defuse,' said a rival. An excellent overview of Chanel's life and work.
[E450] Skira hbk **£70.00**

LLOYD, VALERIE
The Art of Vogue Photographic Covers `NEW`
The best photographs in *Vogue* from the time of its first printing through to the present day. The pictures chosen reflect the changes in fashion and beauty over the fifty years of the magazine's history.
[E451] Conran Octopus hbk **£11.95**

PACKER, WILLIAM
Fashion Drawing in 'Vogue'
A selection of *Vogue*'s best illustrations.
[E452] Thames & H hbk **£24.00**

PENN, IRVING
Issey Miyake
Combined project from a leading American photographer and the spearhead of the Japanese fashion revolution.
[E453] NY Graphic Soc hbk **£25.00**

PIAGGI, ANNA
Karl Lagerfeld: A Fashion Journal
Including a preface by Lagerfeld himself.
[E454] Thames & H hbk **£30.00**

ROSS, JOSEPHINE
Beaton in 'Vogue'
'The man who would have run *Vogue* single-handedly was Cecil Beaton. He was a superb photographer, wrote and drew beautifully and had all the right contacts. He'd redraw on the proofs, or yell "slice the lips, that sag must go" and the retouchers worked overtime so that his subjects would ring up and say "The most divine pictures - I'll have 12 more prints."'
[E455] Thames & H hbk **£25.00**

Practical Fashion

ALLEN, JEANNE
Showing Your Colours
Enhance your colouring by choosing the right clothes.
[E456] Angus & R pbk **£6.95**

FAUX, SUSIE
Wardrobe `NEW`
'There is no excellent beauty that hath not some strangeness in the proportion,' said Sir Francis Bacon. But with wise shopping and this book, you can make the most of your shape and lifestyle.
[E457] Piatkus hbk **£12.95**

JAQUES, BARBARA
The Colour and Style File
A step-by-step guide to building up an accurate picture of your colouring, figure, image and fashion look.
[E458] Piatkus hbk **£10.95**

Drama

Shakespeare: Texts
Shakespeare: Criticism

British & Irish Drama: By Period
American Drama
Classical Drama: Greek & Roman
European & World Drama

Drama Studies

Shakespeare Around Us
Stanley Wells

F our hundred years ago, though
William Shakespeare was in his
mid-twenties - he had been born in
1564 - his name had not appeared in
print, none of his work had been
published, and for all we know he may
not have written a line. He was a slow
starter. Yet within twenty-five years he
was to write close on forty plays without
which the world we live in would be a
very different, and much poorer, place.
Shakespeare is constantly around us.

He has become a mainstay of our
educational system. At primary,
secondary and tertiary levels, both at
home and overseas, his works are read
and studied, taught and examined.
Schoolchildren learn speeches from
them, read them round the class, act out
extracts from them. Undergraduates
attend lectures and seminars on
Shakespeare, write essays and suffer
examinations on him. Postgraduates
write theses on him and are awarded
degrees purely for studying his works.
University teachers think up
examination questions, lecture, and
write articles about him. Scholars devote
large parts of their lives to the study of
his works. There are Shakespeare
Conferences and Summer Schools,
annual Shakespeare lectures - in

London, in Stratford, in Washington -
Shakespeare reference libraries,
Shakespeare Institutes, a Shakespeare
Birthplace Trust, and at least one
professorial chair (mine) in Shakespeare
Studies. Educational publications are
devoted solely to Shakespeare: in
England, *Shakespeare Survey* and
Shakespeare and Schools; in America,
Shakespeare Quarterly, *Shakespeare
Newsletter*, *Shakespeare on Film
Newsletter*, and *The Upstart Crow*; both
West Germany and East Germany
publish a *Shakespeare Jahrbuch*; there
are annual publications of Shakespeare
societies in Hungary, Japan, in South
Africa; in India there is a journal,
Hamlet Studies, devoted to a single play.

Shakespeare is a major figure of
international theatre. Annual festivals are
devoted to his plays, theatre buildings are
constructed especially for them - in
Stratford-upon-Avon, in Stratford,
Ontario, in Stratford, Connecticut, in
Texas and Australia and Tokyo. Great
efforts are being made by theatre folk, by
scholars, and by fund-raisers to
reconstruct Shakespeare's Globe Theatre
on Bankside, close to where it originally
stood. Actors and actresses create reputations by playing major roles in his plays
- "Hamlet", wrote Max Beerbohm, is "a

hoop through which every very eminent
actor must, sooner or later, jump" - and
win awards for doing so. Translated into
all the world's major languages and most
of the minor ones, the plays are
performed in Bangladesh and Tibet, in
Moscow and Peking, in Helsinki and
Kyoto.

Shakespeare is a mainstay of the
publishing industry. Editions of his plays
and poems appear with dizzying
frequency - plain texts, annotated texts,
simplified texts, parallel texts,
modernized texts, old-spelling texts,
facsimiles, Shakespeare for scholars, for
students, for children, for overseas
readers, for actors. There are
concordances to Shakespeare, reference
books, dictionaries of quotations, quiz
books, anthologies of and about
Shakespeare, books about the flowers he
mentions, the birds and beasts, the places
and people, the sports, the weapons, the
coins and the clothes. There are studies of
his language, the metaphors and the
similes, the prose and the verse, the hard
words and the rude words. There are
textual studies, historical studies,
philosophical studies, critical studies, and
sociological studies. There are
guidebooks, bibliographies, biographies,
sourcebooks, books about Shakespeare in
the theatre, on film, and on television.
And there is an entire sub-industry of
publications attempting to prove that
Shakespeare's works were written by
someone else.

No one interested in the arts can remain
untouched by Shakespeare. There are
great Shakespeare operas by Nicolai and
Verdi, Rossini and Britten. He turns up in
the concert hall, in orchestral music by
Mendelssohn and Tchaikovsky, Prokofiev
and Walton, in songs by Schubert and
Sullivan, Warlock and Finzi. Berlioz was
obsessed by him. Creative artists are
inspired by his works in musical such as
Cole Porter's **Kiss Me, Kate,** in films
such as Kurosawa's **Throne of Blood** and
Ran, in plays such as Tom Stoppard's
**Rosencrantz and Guildenstern Are
Dead**, in poems such as W.H. Auden's
'The Sea and the Mirror', in novels such
as Iris Murdoch's **The Black Prince**,
in detective stories such as Michael
Innes's **Hamlet, Revenger!** and in
paintings by Hogarth and Fuseli, Blake
and Millais.

Even people with little or no interest in
the arts can scarcely evade Shakespeare's

presence. They may speak of a Shylock, a Romeo, or a Hamlet while knowing nothing of the plays in which these characters figure. They may quote Shakespeare without realizing it, claiming to be more sinned against than sinning, to speak more in sorrow than in anger, to be cruel to be kind. They may suspect foul play, ask "what's in a name?", talk about the funeral baked meats, the crack of doom, murder most foul, the milk of human kindness, and the primrose path. They may exhort friends to be bloody, bold and resolute, complain of customs more honoured in the breach than in the observance, and declare brevity to be the soul of wit. They may drink Shakespeare Ale in the Froth and Elbow bar of the Shakespeare Hotel, or smoke a Hamlet cigar. They will hear Shakespeare quoted by politicians and sent up by comedians. They will be invited to buy figurines of Shakespearean characters, and they will see Shakespeare's image twinkling in the hologram on their credit cards and imprinted on their banknotes and on postage stamps.

William Shakespeare was his parent's third child and the first to survive infancy. If he too had died as a baby, how different life would be!

Anthony Sher's acclaimed account of the experience of Playing the part of Richard III. *Year of the King*, is published by Methuen (pbk £4.95)

Bookchoice

As things stand, readers are faced with bewildering problems of choice, so let me make a few suggestions.

The best biographical study is S. Schoenbaum's *William Shakespeare: A Compact Documentary Life*, which conveys encyclopaedic scholarship and discerning judgement in sparkling prose. A.J. Gurr's *The Shakespearean Stage 1574-1642* will tell you all you need to know about the theatrical conditions of Shakespeare's time. If you want straightforward, short introductions to all the plays, you'll find them in John Wilders's *New Prefaces to Shakespeare*, written originally for the editions accompanying the BBC television series. For more detailed critical studies of groups of plays, you could go to Alexander Leggatt's *Shakespeare's Comedy of Love*, Kenneth Muir's *Shakespeare's Tragic Sequences* and

Ernst Honigmann's *Shakespeare: Seven Tragedies* (along with A.C. Bradley's classic *Shakespearean Tragedy*), and E.M.W. Tillyard's *Shakespeare's History Plays* - dated in some respects, but still valuable. For serious students, *The Cambridge Companion to Shakespeare Studies* surveys the field in a series of essays by various hands, and readers interested in the application of current critical approaches to Shakespeare will value Dollimore and Sinfield's *Political Shakespeare* and Drakakis's *Alternative Shakespeares*.

Shakespeare belongs in the theatre, and happily directors and actors are becoming increasingly articulate about their work. Antony Sher's entertaining *The Year of the King*, based on his diaries during the year he was preparing and rehearsing the role of Richard III for the Royal Shakespeare Company, will appeal even to readers with no special interest in Shakespeare. John Barton's *Playing Shakespeare* distils the wisdom of one of our finest directors along with the actors he worked with on the successful television series of the same name. Individual actors write about some of their best roles in Cambridge's series *Players of Shakespeare*, and standards of performance are acutely examined in Richard David's *Shakespeare in the Theatre*.

When I want to look up a quick

reference, I make unashamed use of my own *Shakespeare: An Illustrated Dictionary*; and if you want to give young people a taste of (and for) Shakespeare before they're ready for the real thing, you can't do better than put them on to Leon Garfield's *Shakespeare Stories*.

Stanley Wells is Professor of Shakespeare Studies and Director of the Shakespeare Institute at the University of Birmingham. *The Oxford Shakespeare*, of which he was an editor, appeared in 1986.

DRAMA

Shakespeare

Texts

COMPLETE WORKS
ALEXANDER, PETER (GENERAL ED)
The Complete Works
From 1951, popularly known as the 'Alexander' text. A paperback edition appeared in 1985 and is easily the best version available in soft cover format.
[FA1] Collins hbk **£8.95**
[FA2] Collins pbk **£4.95**
WELLS, STANLEY & TAYLOR, GARY
(GENERAL EDS)
The Oxford Shakespeare
Based on eight years of full-time research by a team of British and American scholars, who have undertaken the most thorough examination ever of the nature and relative authority of the early documents. Published in 1986, it will remain the standard complete works for many years to come.
The Complete Works
Contains a general introduction and brief factual introductions to each play by Stanley Wells.
[FA3] Oxford hbk **£25.00**
[FA4] Oxford leather **£50.00**
The Complete Works: Original-Spelling Edition
The first ever critical edition of the complete works in old spelling and punctuation. Contains a general introduction and brief factual introductions to each play by Stanley Wells and an essay on Shakespeare's language by Vivian Salmon.
[FA5] Oxford hbk **£75.00**
The Complete Works : Compact Edition
The modern spelling edition in its entirety but produced in a smaller format.
[FA6] Oxford hbk **£9.95**
[FA7] Oxford blue/red leather **£29.50**
The Complete Oxford Shakespeare: Histories, Comedies, Tragedies
The modern-spelling edition (complete with introductions) in a handy three-volume presentation format.
[FA8] Oxford hbk **£32.50**

INDIVIDUAL PLAYS
The Oxford Shakespeare
General editor: Stanley Wells. Ten plays available, in compact editions, with illustrations and indexes and emphasis in the notes on language and staging. All the plays should eventually be available in this series.
The New Cambridge Shakespeare
General Editor: Philip Brockbank. One of the largest format editons with detailed, illustrated introductions that contain plenty of useful information for staging. A new series, gradually being made complete.
The Penguin Shakespeare
General Editor: T.J.B. Spencer. The least expensive of the pocket size editions, with introductions and useful commentaries collected at the back of the book.
The Arden Shakespeare
Generally regarded as the best indivuidual texts available, with scholarly introductions and detailed annotation on each page. Published by Routledge, each play is also available in a hardback edition at £20.00.

A Midsummer Night's Dream
[FA12] Routledge-Arden pbk **£3.95**
[FA13] Cambridge pbk **£3.50**
[FA14] Penguin pbk **£1.99**
All's Well That Ends Well
[FA15] Routledge-Arden pbk **£3.95**
[FA16] Cambridge pbk **£3.50**
[FA16A] Penguin pbk **£2.50**
Antony and Cleopatra
[FA17] Routledge-Arden pbk **£3.95**
[FA18] Penguin pbk **£2.25**
As You Like It
[FA19] Routledge-Arden pbk **£3.95**
[FA20] Penguin pbk **£1.99**
Coriolanus
[FA21] Routledge-Arden pbk **£3.95**
[FA22] Penguin pbk **£2.99**
Cymbeline
[FA23] Routledge-Arden pbk **£3.95**
Hamlet
[FA24] Routledge-Arden pbk **£5.50**
[FA25] Oxford pbk **£4.50**
[FA26] Cambridge pbk **£3.50**
[FA27] Penguin pbk **£2.25**
Julius Caesar
[FA28] Routledge-Arden pbk **£3.95**
[FA29] Oxford pbk **£3.50**
[FA29A] Cambridge pbk **£3.50**
[FA30] Penguin pbk **£2.25**
King Henry IV Part I
[FA31] Routledge-Arden pbk **£3.95**
[FA32] Oxford pbk **£3.95**
[FA33] Penguin pbk **£1.99**
King Henry IV Part II
[FA34] Routledge-Arden pbk **£3.95**
[FA35] Penguin pbk **£2.99**
King Henry V
[FA36] Routledge-Arden pbk **£3.95**
[FA37] Oxford pbk **£3.50**
[FA38] Penguin pbk **£2.50**
King Henry VI Part I
[FA39] Routledge-Arden pbk **£4.95**
[FA40] Penguin pbk **£2.95**
King Henry VI Part II
[FA41] Routledge-Arden pbk **£4.95**
[FA42] Penguin pbk **£3.50**
King Henry VI Part III
[FA43] Routledge-Arden pbk **£4.95**
[FA44] Penguin pbk **£2.99**
King Henry VIII
[FA45] Routledge-Arden pbk **£4.95**
[FA46] Penguin pbk **£3.99**
King John
[FA47] Routledge-Arden pbk **£4.95**
[FA48] Oxford pbk **£3.95**
[FA49] Penguin pbk **£3.50**
King Lear
[FA50] Routledge-Arden pbk **£3.95**
[FA51] Penguin pbk **£2.25**
Love's Labour's Lost
[FA52] Routledge-Arden pbk **£3.95**
[FA53] Penguin pbk **£2.50**
Macbeth
[FA54] Routledge-Arden pbk **£3.95**
[FA55] Penguin pbk **£1.99**
Measure for Measure
[FA56] Routledge-Arden pbk **£3.95**
[FA57] Penguin pbk **£1.99**
Much Ado About Nothing
[FA58] Routledge-Arden pbk **£3.95**
[FA59] Penguin pbk **£1.99**
[FA59A] Cambridge pbk **£3.50**
Othello
[FA60] Routledge-Arden pbk **£3.95**
[FA61] Cambridge pbk **£3.50**
[FA62] Penguin pbk **£2.25**
Pericles
[FA63] Routledge-Arden pbk **£4.95**
[FA64] Penguin pbk **£2.95**

Richard II
[FA65] Routledge-Arden pbk **£3.95**
[FA66] Cambridge pbk **£3.50**
[FA67] Penguin pbk **£1.99**
Richard III
[FA68] Routledge-Arden pbk **£3.95**
[FA69] Penguin pbk **£1.99**
Romeo and Juliet
[FA70] Routledge-Arden pbk **£3.95**
[FA71] Cambridge pbk **£3.50**
[FA72] Penguin pbk **£2.50**
The Comedy of Errors
[FA73] Routledge-Arden pbk **£3.95**
[FA73A] Cambridge pbk **£3.50**
[FA74] Penguin pbk **£2.50**
The Merchant of Venice
[FA75] Routledge-Arden pbk **£3.95**
[FA76] Cambridge pbk **£3.50**
[FA77] Penguin pbk **£1.99**
The Merry Wives of Windsor
[FA78] Routledge-Arden pbk **£4.25**
[FA79] Penguin pbk **£2.99**
The Taming of the Shrew
[FA80] Routledge-Arden pbk **£3.95**
[FA81] Oxford pbk **£3.75**
[FA82] Cambridge pbk **£3.95**
[FA83] Penguin pbk **£2.50**
The Tempest
[FA84] Routledge-Arden pbk **£3.95**
[FA85] Oxford phk **£3.95**
[FA86] Penguin pbk **£1.99**
The Two Gentlemen of Verona
[FA87] Routledge-Arden pbk **£4.95**
[FA88] Penguin pbk **£3.50**
The Winter's Tale
[FA89] Routledge-Arden pbk **£3.95**
[FA89A] Penguin pbk **£1.99**
Timon of Athens
[FA90] Routledge-Arden pbk **£4.95**
[FA91] Penguin pbk **£3.95**
Titus Andronicus
[FA92] Routledge-Arden pbk **£4.95**
[FA93] Oxford pbk **£3.95**
Troilus & Cressida
[FA94] Routledge-Arden pbk **£3.95**
[FA95] Oxford pbk **£3.50**
[FA96] Penguin pbk **£2.50**
Twelfth Night
[FA97] Routledge-Arden pbk **£3.95**
[FA98] Penguin pbk **£1.99**
Two Noble Kinsmen
[FA99] Oxford pbk **£4.50**
[FA100] Penguin pbk **£3.95**

SPECIAL EDITIONS
The History Plays: An Illustrated Edition NEW
The first volume of a new series of collected Shakespeare.
[FA101] Barrie & J hbk **£19.95**

Illustration from *Rebuilding Shakespeare's Globe* by Andrew Gurr with John Orrell (Weidenfeld & Nicolson hbk £15.95)

DRAMA

The Plantagenets `NEW`
The text from the epic Barbican production which was adapted from Shakespeare's *Henry VI Parts I, II, III* and *Richard III*. Introduced by Adrian Noble.
[FA102] Faber pbk **£7.99**

POEMS
The Arden Shakespeare:
Poems (Rd. Prince F.T.)
[FA103] Methuen pbk **£4.95**
The Oxford Shakespeare:
Shakespeare's Sonnets (Ed. Wells, Stanley)
Also contains 'A Lover's Complaint' and little-known alternative versions of four of the sonnets.
[FA104] Oxford pbk **£3.95**
The Penguin Shakespeare:
Narrative Poems
Contains *Venus and Adonis* and *The Rape of Lucrece*.
[FA105] Penguin pbk **£4.99**
The Sonnets & A Lover's Complaint
[FA106] Penguin pbk **£4.99**
BOOTH, STEPHEN (ED)
Shakespeare's Sonnets
The standard academic text, with parallel 1609 facsimile/modern spelling versions and exhaustive textual notes and critical commentaries. A masterpiece of modern scholarship.
[FA107] Yale UP pbk **£14.75**
SEYMOUR-SMITH, MARTIN (ED)
The Sonnets
A useful student edition with an excellent introduction and lucid notes.
[FA108] Heinemann pbk **£3.95**

Criticism

Reference & Introductions

BARTLETT, J.
Concordance to the Works of Shakespeare
[FA115] Macmillan pbk **£65.00**

CLARK, SANDRA & LONG, T.H. (EDS)
Hutchinson Shakespeare Dictionary
An A-Z guide to Shakespeare's plays, characters and contemporaries.
[FA116] Hutchinson pbk **£4.95**

FOX, LEVI
The Shakespeare Handbook
An introduction to the plays, with background detail; it is noted here for its extensive and well-chosen illustrations.
[FA117] Bodley pbk **£9.95**

LAMB, CHARLES & MARY
Tales from Shakespeare
The Lambs' well-crafted and very popular versions of the stories from the major plays.
[FA119] Dent pbk **£2.50**

ONIONS, C.T.
A Shakespeare Glossary
[FA120] Oxford pbk **£6.50**

ROWSE, A.L.
Shakespeare's Characters: A Complete Guide
A definitive work, with over 1,000 entries.
[FA121] Methuen hbk **£9.50**

WELLS, PROFESSOR STANLEY
An Oxford Anthology of Shakespeare (1987)
A finely-balanced selection of some 200 passages, from a few lines in length to complete scenes.
[FA123] Oxford hbk **£12.95**
Shakespeare: An Illustrated Dictionary (1985)
A compact and informative guide, with entries on Shakespeare's life and influences, and on the performance history of his works.
[FA124] Oxford pbk **£4.95**

Critical Series

Macmillan Casebooks
Collections of some of the most interesting and illuminating essays that have been written on individual plays, from actors and directors, as well as critics and scholars. Each casebook is designed to raise the main issues of the play, at a level suitable for students or general readers. They are available for the following plays:
Antony and Cleopatra, Coriolanus, Hamlet, Julius Caesar, Henry IV Part I & II, King Henry V, King Richard II, King Lear, Macbeth, Measure for Measure, The Merchant of Venice, A Midsummer Night's Dream, Much Ado About Nothing & As You Like It, Othello, The Tempest, Titus Andronicus, Troilus & Cressida, Twelfth Night, The Winter's Tale.
[FA109] Macmillan pbk **£7.95**

Harvester New Critical Introductions
Accessible studies, conversant with the most recent critical ideas and trends, examining the plays from a variety of perspectives. They also include selective guides for further reading. Available for the following plays:
All's Well That Ends Well, Coriolanus, Hamlet, Henry IV, King Lear, Macbeth, Measure for Measure, The Merchant of Venice, The Tempest, Titus Andronicus, Timon of Athens, Troilus & Cressida, The Winter's Tale.
[FA110] Harvester pbk **£7.95**

Shakespeare Survey
An annual publication which collects a wide variety of new articles on the study and production of Shakespeare. The range of back numbers is also available.
Volume 40: Current Approaches to Shakespeare through Language, Text, Theatre & Ideology
[FA111] Cambridge hbk **£27.50**
Volume 41: Shakespearean Stages and Staging `NEW`
[FA112] Cambridge hbk **£30.00**

Major Studies

ADAMSON, JANE
Othello as Tragedy (1980)
A detailed study, which examines several earlier interpretations of the play. Adamson discusses *Othello* as a profound tragedy, which raises complex moral questions for both the characters and the spectators.
[FA125] Cambridge pbk **£9.95**

BARTON, JOHN
Playing Shakespeare (1984)
A discussion with RSC actors, led by the experienced

director John Barton, debating approaches to performances. He emphasizes the importance of verbal projection, paying close attention to Shakespeare's use of language.
[FA126] Methuen pbk **£5.95**

BAYLEY, JOHN
Shakespeare and Tragedy (1981)
This memorable, much acclaimed book rejects arbitrary theories and reaffirms the connections between literature and life. Bayley detects and describes the complex sets of oppositions upon which he believes Shakespeare's tragedies are founded.
[FA127] Routledge pbk **£7.95**

BLAKE, N.F.
Shakespeare's Language (1983)
An exploration of the way in which Shakespeare created words and expanded the range of expression available to him as an Elizabethan Englishman. Blake suggests a rich variety of possible linguistic interpretations.
[FA128] Macmillan pbk **£6.95**

BRADBROOK, M.C.
Shakespeare: The Poet in His World (1978)
Bradbrook is an authority on Elizabethan literature, and has written several books on Shakespeare. This study relates specific, known incidents from his life and from the period of history in which he lived, to events and themes in the plays.
[FA129] Weidenfeld hbk **£8.95**
[FA130] Routledge pbk **£2.95**

BRADLEY, A.C.
Shakespearean Tragedy (1904)
Sometimes criticized for a detective-like interest in the character's motivations, Bradley's study nevertheless remains a compelling account of the four main tragedies. He offers great insight into the structure and language of the plays and has exerted a considerable influence on 20th century Shakespeare criticism in general.
[FA131] Macmillan pbk **£5.95**

BRATCHELL, D.F.
Shakespearean Tragedy `NEW`
Part of an excellent new series of critical introductions to major topics in English literature, this book offers a clear guide to the changing critical perceptions of Shakespeare's work, from the Renaissance to modern times. The selection of critical responses covers both Shakespearean tragedy in general and the individual plays.
[FA131A] Routledge pbk **£6.95**

BROCKBANK, PHILIP (ED)
Players of Shakespeare 1 (1985)
12 essays in which leading RSC players describe approaches to roles and their realization in performance. Includes Sinead Cusack on Portia, Michael Pennington on Hamlet, and David Suchet on Caliban.
[FA132] Cambridge pbk **£7.95**

BURTON, S.H.
Shakespeare's Life and Stage (1989) `NEW`
An introduction to Shakespeare, offering an account of his life in Stratford and London, particularly strong in describing the working conditions he faced: the various demands of the audiences, the actors, the theatres and the stages themselves.
[FA133] Chambers pbk **£4.99**

CHARLTON, H.B.
Shakespearean Comedy (1938)
A selection of lectures - one of the first studies of the comedies - which traces Shakespeare's developing mastery of comic form.
[FA134] Routledge pbk **£9.95**

CLEMEN, WOLFGANG H.
Shakespeare's Soliloquies (1987)
Examines 27 soliloquies in context. Clemen is always keenly sensitive to Shakespeare's manipulation of audience response.
[FA135] Methuen pbk **£7.95**
The Development of Shakespeare's Imagery (1951)
An influential study of the verbal imagery that is at the heart of the major plays, examining the progressive stages in which the use of imagery evolves, from the early plays to the great tragedies.
[FA136] Methuen pbk **£9.95**

COLERIDGE, SAMUEL TAYLOR
Shakespearean Criticism (Ed. Foukes, 1989)
The lectures Coleridge gave on Shakespeare between 1808 and 1819 were awaited with some fervour in his time. This selection brings them together, along with many random, characteristically idiosyncratic notes. Coleridge gives his assessment of Shakespeare as a dramatist and as a poet, along with some influential and most original considerations of the major plays.
[FA137] Athlone hbk **£25.00**

COOK, JUDITH
At the Sign of the Swan (1986)
Not a book focused specifically on Shakespeare, but it does provide some insight into his artistic environment, with a series of intriguing biographical details concerning his contemporaries.
[FA138] Harrap pbk **£6.95**

DANBY, JOHN F.
Shakespeare's Doctrine of Nature
A classic study which looks at 'natural bonds', a theme that dominated Renaissance views of society. Danby focuses on *King Lear*, where those bonds are under immense strain, as Albion is fraught with divisions.
[FA139] Faber pbk **£2.95**

DAWSON, ANTHONY B.
Watching Shakespeare: A Playgoer's Guide (1988)
A lively study of 18 plays, which describes the key decisions that actors and directors face, and the consequences of those decisions for the spectator in interpreting and assessing specific productions.
[FA140] Macmillan pbk **£11.95**

DEAN, LEONARD F. (ED)
Shakespeare: Modern Essays in Criticism
[FA141] Oxford pbk **£7.95**

DOLLIMORE, JONATHAN & SINFIELD, ALAN (EDS)
Political Shakespeare - New Essays in Cultural Materialism (1985)
A selection of diverse and informative essays. The first half look at Shakespeare within his own time, examining issues such as colonialism and sexuality. The remainder investigate the presentation of Shakespeare today, in film, theatre and education.
[FA142] Manchester UP pbk **£6.95**

DRAKAKIS, J. (ED)
Alternative Shakespeares (1985)
A collection of essays which challenge 'traditional' readings of Shakespeare based on ideas of aesthetic coherence. Various approaches are applied -

semiotics, psychoanalysis, feminism, marxism - in an attempt to deconstruct the texts and emphasize plurality of meaning.
[FA143] Routledge pbk **£7.95**

DUTTON, RICHARD
William Shakespeare: A Literary Life (1989) `NEW`
Avoiding many of the now contentious conventions of literary biography, be it traditional or theoretical, Dutton attempts to trace the professional and social contexts that shaped Shakespeare's literary career.
[FA144] Macmillan pbk **£7.95**

EAGLETON, TERRY
William Shakespeare (1986)
A brief but precise study, from Eagleton's characteristically marxist perspective. Stimulating and enthusiastic, the book offers much that will surprise and challenge.
[FA145] Blackwell pbk **£6.95**

EDWARDS, PHILIP
Shakespeare: A Writer's Progress (1987)
An informative work which stresses the continuities and developing vision in everything that Shakespeare wrote. It also contains a detailed bibliography of critical works on Shakespeare.
[FA146] Oxford pbk **£5.95**

EMPSON, WILLIAM
Essays on Shakespeare (1986)
A subtle, idiosyncratic collection from an innovative critic and poet. Included are discussions of *Hamlet* and *Macbeth* and an agile entertaining piece on Falstaff, as well as essays on Shakespeare's last plays and the architecture of the Globe.
[FA147] Cambridge pbk **£8.95**

FERMOR, UNA ELLIS
Shakespeare's Drama (1980)
Edited by Kenneth Muir, collected essays from the 1940s and 50s by the first editor of the Arden Shakespeare. Fermor places emphasis on the study of plot, character and imagery, paying particular attention to the elements which form the delicate equilibrium of tragedy.
[FA148] Routledge pbk **£8.95**

FRYE, NORTHROP
On Shakespeare (1986)
In a genial study, Frye presents lucid expositions of ten major plays, relating each work to others in the Shakespeare canon to build a complex and suggestive picture of his dramatic output.
[FA150] Yale pbk **£5.95**

GOLDBERG, S.L.
An Essay on King Lear (1974)
A study of the moral questions raised by *King Lear*. Goldberg places emphasis on character presentation, allowing an overall interpretation to develop as the play, and the study of it, unfolds.
[FA151] Cambridge pbk **£8.95**

GREER, GERMAINE
Shakespeare (1986)
A concise and balanced introduction to the life and work, centring on Shakespeare's presentation of ethical and political issues.
[FA152] Oxford pbk **£3.95**

GURR, ANDREW
Playgoing in Shakespeare's London
An entertaining and thorough investigation of the various backgrounds and changing tastes of the audiences, which also describes the theatres and playhouses of Shakespeare's time.
[FA153] Cambridge pbk **£10.95**

HALLIDAY, F.E.
Shakespeare: A Literary Life
A brief and illustrated account.
[FA154] Thames & H pbk **£3.95**

HARRISON, G.B.
Introducing Shakespeare (1939)
A useful illustrated introduction to Shakespeare studies, giving an outline of his life and era, describing the development of his style, and an account of critical approaches to the plays.
[FA155] Penguin pbk **£4.50**

HAWKES, TERENCE
That Shakespeherian Rag (1986)
A provocative survey of the various and sometimes loaded ways Shakespeare has been 'used' by English society. Hawkes examines in particular the influence of four exceptional critics: Sir Walter Raleigh, A.C. Bradley, T.S. Eliot and John Dover Wilson.
[FA156] Routledge pbk **£5.95**

HUSSEY, S.S.
The Literary Language of Shakespeare (1982)
An introduction, especially detailed in explaining the variety of linguistic styles Shakespeare used to create different dramatic effects and suggestions.
[FA157] Longman pbk **£7.95**

JACKSON, RUSSELL & SMALLWOOD, ROBERT (EDS)
Players of Shakespeare 2 `NEW`
The second volume of essays by actors with the RSC. Fourteen actors describe the Shakespearean roles they played in productions between 1982 and 1987. The contributors include Kenneth Branagh, Ben Kingsley, Fiona Shaw, Frances Barber, and Anthony Sher.
[FA118] Cambridge pbk **£7.95**

JOHNSON, SAMUEL
Selections from Johnson on Shakespeare (Ed. Bronson)
Some thoughts and insights from the leading 18th century poet and critic, who himself edited Shakespeare's works. Johnson reveals a rare and encyclopaedic knowledge of the plays.
[FA158] Yale pbk **£10.50**

JONES, PROFESSOR EMRYS
Scenic Form in Shakespeare (1971)
One of the first studies to discuss Shakespeare's dramatic techniques, as opposed to character and theme. Jones describes the ways in which each scene in a play is constructed as a unit, and in the second half of the book, relates this mastery of organization to specific moments in *King Lear*, *Macbeth*, *Othello* and *Antony and Cleopatra*.
[FA159] Oxford pbk **£8.95**

KEATS, JOHN
Keats as a Reader of Shakespeare (Ed. White, R.S.)
Keats is particularly inspired when euphorically describing Shakespeare's language and expression; his own talent for word-creation may well be second only to that of Shakespeare.
[FA160] Athlone hbk **£25.00**

KNIGHT, G. WILSON
One of the most original 20th century critics of Shakespeare, his work is distinguished by his imaginative sense of Shakespeare's poetic vision.
The Crown of Life (1947)
Considerations of the late plays, which Wilson Knight feels are too easily dismissed. Essays on *Pericles*, *The Winter's Tale*, *Cymbeline*, *The Tempest* and *Henry VIII*.
[FA161] Routledge pbk **£8.95**

The Imperial Theme (1931)
Essays on the Roman tragedies, along with studies of *Macbeth* and *Hamlet*.
[FA162] Routledge pbk **£8.95**
The Wheel of Fire (1930)
Perhaps his most influential book, including some memorable essays on the major tragedies.
[FA163] Routledge pbk **£8.95**

KOTT, JAN
Shakespeare Our Contemporary (1967)
A popular book, which suggests many relevant contemporary parallels in particular plays. These essays have had much impact on Shakespearean production, notably the austere, minimal *King Lear* directed by Peter Brook, who introduces this volume.
[FA164] Routledge pbk **£7.95**

LEGGATT, ALEXANDER
Shakespeare's Comedy of Love (1974)
Leggatt is particularly sensitive to the practical demands of theatre in this cogent study. He examines the internal variety of nine comedies, and while acknowledging the links between the plays, he describes each as a new experiment with new possibilties.
[FA165] Routledge pbk **£8.95**

LERNER, LAURENCE (ED)
Shakespeare's Tragedies: An Anthology of Modern Criticism (1963)
A collection of essays examining specific plays, which also examines Shakespeare's overall vision and presentation of tragedy.
[FA166] Penguin pbk **£4.95**

LEVI, PETER
The Life and Times of William Shakespeare (1988)
A recent biography, with particularly detailed accounts of relevant 16th century English history. Levi also offers a critical reading of each play.
[FA167] Macmillan hbk **£16.95**

MACKINNON, LACHLAN
Shakespeare the Aesthete (1988)
A study of the 'problem plays': *All's Well That Ends Well*, *Troilus and Cressida* and *Measure for Measure*, which also discusses *Macbeth* and *The Winter's Tale*. Mackinnon examines Shakespeare's understanding of contemporary aesthetics, linked to the use of allegory, symbolism and genre in the plays.
[FA168] Macmillan hbk **£29.50**

MUIR, KENNETH (ED)
Interpretations of Shakespeare (1985)
Academy lectures from between 1942 and 1975, with a finely balanced variety of contributors, edited by a leading contemporary authority on Shakespeare.
[FA169] Oxford pbk **£8.95**

OGBURN, CHARLES
The Mysterious William Shakespeare
An investigation which has sparked heated recent debate, attempting to prove that the author of the major plays was not William Shakespeare, but Edward de Vere.
[FA170] Cardinal pbk **£7.99**

PARTRIDGE, ERIC
Shakespeare's Bawdy
A list of expressions capable of bawdy intepretation, with appropriate allusions. The glossary is prefaced by an essay on 'The sexual, the homosexual and the non-sexual bawdy in Shakespeare'.
[FA171] Routledge pbk **£6.95**

RUTTER, CAROL
Clamourous Voices (1988)
With Sinead Cusack, Paola Dionisitti, Fiona Shaw, Juliet Stevenson and Harriet Walter. Five leading actresses discuss current theatrical practices, and describe with intelligence and feeling their readings of Shakespeare's most challenging female roles.
[FA172] Women's P pbk **£6.95**

RYAN, KIERNAN
Shakespeare `NEW`
A brief compelling study, which argues against both the 'traditional' and the 1980s 'alternative' approaches to Shakespeare.
[FA122] Harvester pbk **£7.95**

SCHOENBAUM, SAMUEL
William Shakespeare: A Compact Documentary Life
Generally acknowledged as the finest scholarly biography, a fascinating book, with reproductions and facsimiles of 50 letters, manuscripts and drawings.
[FA122A] Oxford pbk **£6.95**

SEN GUPTA, S.C.
Shakespearean Comedy (1950)
Traces Shakespeare's development in mastering comic forms, focusing on the presentation of particular characters.
[FA173] Oxford pbk **£4.50**

SPURGEON, CAROLINE F.E.
Shakespeare's Imagery and What It Tells Us (1935)
A pioneeering study of imagery in the plays, suggesting ways in which Shakespeare develops themes and characters with subtle and sustained patterns of imagery. Spurgeon provides some pointed comparisons in the works of Shakespeare's contemporaries, notably Marlowe and Jonson.
[FA174] Cambridge pbk **£13.95**

STYAN, J.L.
Shakespeare's Stagecraft (1967)
Places Shakespeare's dramatic skills within the context and conventions of his time, looking in particular at the actor's movements and speech delivery.
[FA175] Cambridge pbk **£10.95**
The Shakespeare Revolution: Criticism and Performance in the 20th Century
An unusual and valuable study, which looks at the relationship between scholar and director, critical ideas and theatrical practice. Styan examines this complex interaction, looking at productions from the turn of the century to those of Peter Brook.
[FA176] Cambridge pbk **£8.50**

TAYLOR, GARY
Reinventing Shakespeare `NEW`
An energetic and informed account of the 'Shakespeare industry' by one of its most brilliant young exponents. Taylor describes the way each age invents a version of 'Shakespeare' to suit its own ends, debating the many contradictions raised by these changing versions, which in turn leads the author to question the changing criteria of literary judgement.
[FA177] Hogarth hbk **£20.00**

TILLYARD, E.M.W.
Shakespeare's History Plays (1944)
Regarded as a classic study of the history plays, outlining the philosophical, historical and artistic background, and linking this to the plays themselves.
[FA178] Penguin pbk **£4.95**

Shakespeare's Problem Plays (1950)
Contains chapters on *Hamlet*, *Troilus and Cressida*, *All's Well That Ends Well* and *Measure for Measure*. Tillyard traces common links between the four, comparing and contrasting their final effects.
[FA179] Penguin pbk **£3.99**

WELLS, STANLEY (ED)
The Cambridge Companion to Shakespeare Studies (1986)
A collection of 17 essays from an impressive range of contributors. There are discussions of most aspects of Shakespearean studies, the emphasis being on 20th century approaches. Includes essays on Shakespeare adapted for film and television, and on the new critical methods of the 1980s.
[FA180] Cambridge pbk **£8.95**
William Shakespeare: A Textual Companion (1987)
Written with Gary Taylor, who co-edited the *Oxford Complete Works* with Wells, this is a useful companion to that volume, describing the editorial problems Shakespeare presents, and explaining the decisions, and their implications, in the Oxford edition.
[FA181] Oxford hbk **£50.00**

WILDERS, JOHN
New Prefaces to Shakespeare (1988)
Some thoughts on each play from the literary adviser to the recent BBC productions of Shakespeare.
[FA182] Blackwell pbk **£7.95**

WILSON, JOHN DOVER
What Happens in Hamlet (1935)
A careful analysis of the play, with Wilson's distinctive sensitivity and maverick humour. It contains chapters discussing old Hamlet's Ghost, the 'antic disposition', the play-within-the-play, and a study of the catastrophe which overwhelms the characters in the last act.
[FA183] Cambridge pbk **£10.95**

Shakespeare, the Droeschoudt engraving made for the publication of Shakespeare's plays in 1623. An illustration from *Rebuilding Shakespeare's Globe* by Andrew Gurr with John Orrell (Weidenfeld & Nicolson hbk £15.95)

British & Irish Drama by Period

Medieval Drama

Medieval drama originated with the Church's realization that doctrine was often better understood by a popular audience when presented in dramatic form rather than through a sermon. It survives in the mystery (or miracle) play and the morality play. The plays quickly developed from the Latin of the liturgy into a rich vernacular language, and allowed considerable opportunity to incorporate the comic and spectacular within the didactic framwork. Performed and revised through the 14th and 15th centuries, they were presented out of doors, usually on movable pageant wagons, over a period of between one and three days. Texts survive of the cycles from Coventry, Chester, Lincoln, Wakefield and York. They allowed considerable experiment with elements strictly outside the divine narrative - seen on the one hand in the harsh language and brutal stage action of the York *Crucifixion*, on the other in the comedy of the Wakefield *Second Shepherd's Pageant*.

MYSTERY
English Mystery Plays
[FB1] Penguin pbk **£6.95**
Everyman & Medieval Miracle Plays
[FB2] Dent pbk **£1.95**
Seven Miracle Plays
[FB3] Oxford pbk **£2.50**
York Mystery Plays
[FB4] Oxford pbk **£6.95**

MORALITY
The other major form of the period, the best known of the Morality plays was *Everyman*; these were allegorical dramas in which vices and virtues were personified and set in conflict, allowing complicated issues of doctrine, such as original sin and atonement, to be presented to an audience which was largely illiterate.
Four Morality Plays
Castle of Perseverance/Magnyfycence/King Johan/Ane Satire of the Three Estaitis.
[FB5] Penguin pbk **£5.95**
Three Late Medieval Morality Plays
Everyman/Mankind/Mundus et Infans.
[FB6] A & C Black pbk **£3.95**

Elizabethan & Jacobean Drama

A Book of Masques
[FB7] Cambridge pbk **£15.00**

Early 17th Century Drama
[FB8] Dent hbk **£8.95**

Elizabethan and Jacobean Comedy
The Old Wives' Tale/The Shoemaker's Holiday/Eastward Ho!/Bartholomew Fair/The Malcontent/A Trick to Catch the Old One.
[FB9] A & C Black pbk **£5.95**

Elizabethan and Jacobean Tragedies
The Spanish Tragedy/Doctor Faustus/Sejanus, His Fall/Women Beware Women/The White Devil/'Tis Pity She's A Whore.
[FB10] A & C Black pbk **£5.95**

Four Jacobean City Comedies
The Dutch Courtesan/A Mad World, My Masters/The Devil is an Ass/A New Way to Pay Old Debts.
[FB11] Penguin pbk **£4.95**

Jacobean Tragedies
The Malcontent/The Revenger's Tragedy/The Atheist's Tragedy/The Changeling/Women Beware Women.
[FB12] Oxford pbk **£6.95**

Jacobean and Caroline Comedies
[FB13] Dent pbk **£8.95**

Three Elizabethan Domestic Tragedies
Arden of Faversham/A Yorkshire Tragedy/A Woman Killed with Kindness.
[FB14] Penguin pbk **£3.95**

Three Jacobean Tragedies
The Changeling/The Revenger's Tragedy/The White Devil.
[FB15] Penguin pbk **£3.95**

Three Jacobean Witchcraft Plays
[FB16] Manchester UP pbk **£4.95**

Three 16th Century Comedies
Gammer Gurton's Needle/Roister Doister/The Old Wives' Tale.
[FB17] A & C Black pbk **£4.95**

ANON
A Yorkshire Tragedy
Attributed to both Middleton and Shakespeare, *A Yorkshire Tragedy* was based on the story of a father's murder of his two children. Described by Swinburne as 'unsurpassable for the pure potency of its horror', it is one of the best examples of the Jacobean 'domestic tragedy'.
[FB18] Manchester UP pbk **£9.95**
Arden of Faversham
Attributed to Shakespeare, *Arden of Faversham* is an early domestic tragedy and tells the story, based on an actual murder committed in 1551, of a faithless wife's attempts to kill her husband, and of her own execution when the crime was discovered.
[FB19] A & C Black pbk **£3.95**

BEAUMONT, FRANCIS (1584 - 1616) & FLETCHER, JOHN (1579 - 1625)
Beamont and Fletcher collaborated on a number of works, most of which appeared between 1605 and 1615. *The Knight of the Burning Pestle* is a burlesque of knight-errantry, taking the form of a play-within-a-play. A grocer and his wife interrupt the drama they are about to watch to insist that their apprentice have a part in it. He joins the play as the Grocer Errant, with a Burning Pestle emblazoned on his shield, and becomes involved in a series of absurd adventures.
The Knight of the Burning Pestle
[FB20] A & C Black pbk **£3.95**

CHAPMAN, GEORGE (1560 - 1634)
Chapman was involved in the theatre from 1598 to 1610, afterwards turning to the work for which he is best known, the translation of Homer's *Odyssey*. For his part in *Eastward Ho!* a play that was seen as critical of James I, Chapman suffered a prison sentence, along with Ben Jonson. The powerful tragedy *Bussy D'Ambois* (1607) tells of an impoverished, brave man caught and eventually destroyed by the intrigues of the French court; it contains some of Chapman's finest poetry. It has been suggested that he is the 'rival poet' mentioned in Shakespeare's sonnets.
Bussy D'Ambois
[FB21] A & C Black pbk **£3.95**
[FB22] Manchester UP pbk **£7.95**

Eastward Ho!
[FB23] Manchester UP hbk **£35.00**

DEKKER, THOMAS (1570 - 1632)
Dekker worked mainly in collaboration, with writers such as Marston, Middleton and Rowley. Many of his plays were lost, together with some by Ford and Massinger, when John Warburton's manuscript collection of about 60 Elizabethan and Jacobean plays was inadvertently destroyed by his cook in the 18th century. Dekker's work shows the daily life of London in close detail, notably in the genial comedy *The Shoemaker's Holiday* (1599) in which, amidst various romantic intrigues, a master shoemaker rises to become the Lord Mayor of London.
The Shoemaker's Holiday
[FB24] A & C Black pbk **£3.95**

FORD, JOHN (1586 - 1640)
A poet of 'the silent griefs which cut the heartstrings', Ford's most memorable work is the tragedy of incestuous love *'Tis Pity She's A Whore* (c.1631). One of the last of the Jacobean dramatists, he shows the influence of Shakespeare. His verse, however, has much originality, and he offers some sublime insight into character.
'Tis Pity She's A Whore
[FB25] A & C Black pbk **£3.95**
Three Plays
[FB26] Penguin pbk **£5.95**
[FB27] Cambridge pbk **£13.50**

HEYWOOD, THOMAS (1573 - 1641)
Heywood is believed to have written over 200 works, many of which are now lost. *A Woman Killed With Kindness* (1603) is one of the best of the domestic tragedies of the time, telling the story of a husband who takes revenge on his unfaithful wife not by violence, but by isolating her until she dies of remorse. *The Fair Maid of the West* is an extraordinary picaresque comedy, featuring a most resourceful heroine who rescues her lover from the Spaniards, written in two parts between 1610 and 1630.
A Woman Killed with Kindness
[FB28] A & C Black pbk **£3.95**
The Fair Maid of the West
[FB29] Methuen/Swan Theatre pbk **£3.95**

JONSON, BEN (1572 - 1637)
Involved in literary and political controversy throughout a turbulent life, Jonson was twice imprisoned for involvement in plays which were considered seditious. His undisputed masterpieces are *Volpone* (1605) and *The Alchemist* (1610). The first is set in Venice, where characters compete to 'gull' or swindle one another in an intoxicating atmosphere of greed and lust. *The Alchemist* is set in Blackfriars, where the charlatan Subtle uses the promise of creating gold from base metal as a lure to rook a variety of characters betrayed by their greed. Jonson's command of language is agile, his taut control of plot and staging immaculate. An acute awareness of the surfaces of things runs through his work, repeatedly setting the tangible against the cosmetic, in a world where personal and political duplicity are paramount. T.S. Eliot's influential essay on him, written in 1919, was instrumental in rekindling interest in Jonson's work.
Bartholomew Fair
[FB30] A & C Black pbk **£3.95**
Ben Jonson's Plays and Masques
[FB31] Norton pbk **£6.75**
Epicoene
[FB32] A & C Black pbk **£3.95**
Every Man in His Humour
[FB33] A & C Black pbk **£3.95**
Five Plays
[FB34] Oxford pbk **£4.95**

Ben Jonson, from Samuel Coleridge's copy of his *Dramatic Works, 1811*

Selected Works (Oxford Authors)
[FB35] Oxford hbk **£21.50**
[FB36] Oxford pbk **£8.95**
The Alchemist
[FB37] A & C Black pbk **£3.95**
The Complete Plays Vol 1
A Tale of a Tub/The Case Is Altered/Every Man in
His Humour/Every Man out of His Humour.
[FB38] Oxford hbk **£67.50**
The Complete Plays Vol 2
Cynthia's Revels/Poetaster/Sejanus, His
Fall/Eastward Ho!
[FB39] Oxford hbk **£77.50**
The Complete Plays Vol 3
Volpone/Epicoene/The Alchemist/Catiline.
[FB40] Oxford hbk **£77.50**
The Complete Plays Vol 4
Bartholomew Fair/The Devil Is an Ass/
The Staple of News/The New Inn/The Magnetic
Lady.
[FB41] Oxford hbk **£77.50**
The New Inn
[FB42] Methuen/Swan Theatre pbk **£3.95**
Three Comedies
Volpone/The Alchemist/Bartholemew Fair.
[FB43] Penguin pbk **£3.95**
Volpone, or The Fox
[FB44] A & C Black pbk **£3.95**

KYD, THOMAS (1558 - 1594)
The Spanish Tragedy was perhaps the most popular
and frequently performed play in the time between its
appearance in the late 1580s and the theatre
closures of 1642. It is an intricately constructed,
bloody tale of incurable grief, laying the foundations
for the 'Revenge tragedy' form of drama. Little is
known of Kyd, although it is believed he wrote a
version of *Hamlet* as a revenge play, now lost, on
which Shakespeare drew for his more famous
work.
The Spanish Tragedy
[FB45] A & C Black pbk **£3.95**

MARLOWE, CHRISTOPHER (1564 - 1593)
Swinburne described Marlowe as the 'father of
English tragedy and the creator of English blank
verse', while to T.S. Eliot, he was the 'poet of
torrential imagination'. A key figure of the early
Elizabethan stage, his greatest plays, among them
Tamburlaine (1587) and *Doctor Faustus* (two

versions from 1604 & 1616), were crucial in
developing drama from its medieval roots. The
'overreaching heroes' of these two plays seem to
strangely mirror the vast energy and expansion of
England in Marlowe's time. After a whirlwind life, he
died young, stabbed in a tavern brawl, possibly
assassinated for his secret service activities.
Cambridge offers the complete works in two volumes,
edited by F. Bowers, published in 1981.
Complete Plays
[FB46] Penguin pbk **£4.50**
Complete Poems and Plays
[FB47] Dent pbk **£3.50**
Edward II
[FB48] A & C Black pbk **£3.95**
[FB49] Oxford pbk **£3.50**
Tamburlaine
[FB50] A & C Black pbk **£3.95**
The Complete Works Vol 1
[FB51] Cambridge hbk **£45.00**
The Complete Works Vol 2
[FB52] Cambridge hbk **£45.00**
The Jew of Malta
[FB53] A & C Black pbk **£3.95**
**The Tragical History of Doctor
Faustus**
[FB54] A & C Black pbk **£3.95**
[FB55] Manchester UP pbk **£5.95**

MARSTON, JOHN (1576 - 1634)
The Malcontent (1604) is a tragi-comedy which
exploits aspects of the revenge play, but in which the
status quo is reasserted, as the banished duke is
restored, casting aside his disguise as the malcontent
Malevole. It gives a harsh picture of court life,
crumbling and rotten with corruption.
The Malcontent
[FB56] A & C Black pbk **£3.95**
**The Selected Plays of John
Marston**
[FB57] Cambridge pbk **£13.95**

MASSINGER, PHILIP (1583 - 1640)
Massinger's two comedies *A New Way to Pay Old
Debts* and *The City Madam* have remained in the
general repertoire ever since their first performances
in 1628 and 1632. In the first, the part of the
villainous Sir Giles Overreach seems to have held a
particular fascination and appeal for actors, most
notably Edmund Kean.
A New Way to Pay Old Debts
[FB58] A & C Black pbk **£3.95**
**The Selected Plays of Philip
Massinger**
[FB59] Cambridge pbk **£10.95**

MIDDLETON, THOMAS (1580 - 1627)
Middleton was a charismatic figure in late Jacobean
theatre. His reputation mainly rests on the tragedies
Women Beware Women (1621) and *The Changeling*
(1622), which was written with William Rowley. In
both, the tragedy of the characters is that they come to
self-awareness too late. In *The Changeling*, Beatrice
uses the repulsive servant De Flores to murder a
suitor, only to find her complicity allows him a
control over her that is total, and eventually fatal.
Women Beware Women is set at an Italian court,
where an innocent wife falls for the power and wealth
of the state's ruler in a celebrated seduction scene,
running parallel to a game of chess being played in
the same room. The catastrophe in the last scene is
one of the most striking set-pieces of Renaissance
drama.
A Chaste Maid in Cheapside
[FB60] A & C Black pbk **£3.95**
A Game at Chess
[FB61] A & C Black pbk **£3.95**
A Trick to Catch the Old One
[FB62] A & C Black pbk **£3.95**

Five Plays
[FB63] Penguin pbk **£4.95**
**The Selected Plays of Thomas
Middleton**
[FB64] Cambridge pbk **£10.95**
Women Beware Women
[FB65] A & C Black pbk **£3.95**
[FB66] Manchester UP pbk **£5.95**
Women Beware Women (Adapted by Barker,
Howard)
[FB67] Calder pbk **£2.95**
With ROWLEY, WILLIAM (1585 - 1626)
A Fair Quarrel
[FB68] A & C Black pbk **£3.95**
The Changeling
[FB69] A & C Black pbk **£3.95**

SHIRLEY, JAMES (1596 - 1666)
Shirley's comedies provide the link between the work
of Jonson and the theatre of the Restoration. He was
the leading dramatist in London at the time of the
closure of the theatres in 1642; his plays survived, and
were performed again in the 1660s. Pepys writes of
having seen a production of *Hyde Park* which
brought live horses onto the stage. Shirley himself
died of exposure during the great fire of London.
Hyde Park
[FB72] Methuen/Swan Theatre pbk **£3.95**
The Cardinal
[FB73] Manchester UP pbk **£8.95**
The Lady of Pleasure
[FB74] Manchester UP pbk **£8.95**

TOURNEUR, CYRIL (1575 - 1626)
"When the bad bleeds, then is the tragedy good." The
ominous words of Vindice, the villain-hero of *The
Revenger's Tragedy* (1607), characterize what is
perhaps the most extreme and intense play of that
genre. Little is known of Tourneur, and the feebleness
of the other surviving plays credited to him has led
many to suspect the guiding hand of Middleton in
The Revenger's Tragedy.
The Atheist's Tragedy
[FB75] A & C Black pbk **£3.95**
The Plays of Cyril Tourneur
[FB76] Cambridge hbk **£15.00**
The Revenger's Tragedy
[FB77] A & C Black pbk **£3.95**

WEBSTER, JOHN (1580 - 1634)
Webster was less concerned with characterization
than with creating convincing worlds in which his
characters could exist, described with richly textured
poetic dialogue, framed within dramatic structures
which suggest the influence of Shakespeare. *The
White Devil* (1612) and *The Duchess of Malfi* (1613)
are both set in the Machiavellian world of
Renaissance Italy, both achieving a sense of
compassion for characters broken by corruption, most
apparent with the Duchess of Malfi herself, who
seems to grow in tragic stature as her death
approaches. The rhetoric, pace and dramatic spectacle
of Webster's work has made him a popular
dramatist for revival; there have been several
successful productions of his work over the last few
decades.
**Selected Plays (John Webster & John
Ford)**
[FB78] Dent pbk **£2.50**
The Devil's Law-Case
[FB79] A & C Black pbk **£3.95**
The Duchess of Malfi
[FB80] A & C Black pbk **£3.95**
[FB81] Manchester UP pbk **£5.95**
The White Devil
[FB82] A & C Black pbk **£3.50**
[FB83] Manchester UP pbk **£5.95**
Three Plays
[FB84] Penguin pbk **£3.95**

Restoration & 18th Century Drama

Female Wits
A collection of Restoration drama from women writers, including Behn's *The Lucky Chance*, Manley's *Royal Mischief* and Pix's *The Innocent Mistress*.
[FB94A] Virago pbk **£16.95**

Five Restoration Comedies
The Man of Mode/The Plain Dealer/Love for Love/The Provok'd Wife/The Recruiting Officer.
[FB85] A & C Black pbk **£5.95**

Four English Comedies
The Way of the World/She Stoops to Conquer/The School for Scandal/Volpone.
[FB86] Penguin pbk **£3.99**

Love and Thunder   NEW
A new anthology of plays by women from the age of Queen Anne, including Pix's *The Spanish Wives*, Trotter's *Love at a Loss*, Wiseman's *Antiochus the Great* and Cent Livre's *Adventures of Venice*.
[FB86A] Methuen pbk **£5.99**

Restoration and 18th Century Plays
The Country Wife/The Man of Mode/The Way of the World/The Conscious Lovers/The School for Scandal.
[FB88] Norton pbk **£8.50**

The Beggar's Opera and Other 18th Century Plays
Includes Addison's *Cato*, Rowe's *Jane Shore*, Lillo's *The London Merchant*, Colman and Garrick's *The Clandestine Marriage* and Cumberland's *The West Indian*.
[FB106] Dent pbk **£2.95**

Three Restoration Comedies
The Man of Mode/The Country Wife/Love for Love.
[FB89] Penguin pbk **£4.99**

BEHN, APHRA (1640 - 1689)
Virginia Woolf described Aphra Behn as the first English woman to succeed as a professional writer. A prolific dramatist, and most successful with spirited comedies of intrigue, which often centre upon marriages of expedience, her work has enjoyed a considerable revival in the 1980s.

Five Plays   NEW
A new collection of Behn's best work, published to mark the tercentenary of her death.
[FB90] Methuen pbk **£4.99**

The Rover
[FB91] Methuen/Swan Theatre pbk **£3.95**

CONGREVE, WILLIAM (1670 - 1729)
The master of the 'comedy of manners', Congreve's plays appeared in the seven years between 1693 and 1700. One of the last of these was *The Way of the World*, and although not a popular success at first, it has been generally acknowledged as one of the finest examples of Restoration comedy, with a verbal touch of great subtlety, particularly effective in the dialogue between the lovers, Mirabell and Millamant.

Comedies
[FB92] Penguin pbk **£4.95**

Love for Love
[FB93] A & C Black pbk **£3.95**

The Comedies of William Congreve
[FB94] Cambridge pbk **£11.95**

The Double Dealer
[FB95] A & C Black pbk **£3.95**

The Way of the World
[FB96] A & C Black pbk **£4.95**

DRYDEN, JOHN (1631 - 1700)
Dryden was the major poet and satirist of the Restoration. His prolific dramatic output, however, is now the most neglected aspect of his work, possibly because the form he pioneered - the 'Heroic Tragedy' - died with him. His best known play is *All for Love* (1678), a blank-verse version of *Antony and Cleopatra*.

All for Love
[FB97] A & C Black pbk **£3.95**

ETHEREGE, GEORGE (1635 - 1691)
Etherege was among the first writers to structure plays with multiple plot lines. His first work, *The Comical Revenge* (1664), alternates scenes of rhymed heroic verse with a comic sub-plot in prose. His last play, *The Man of Mode* (1676), is perhaps his best; it reveals a society living for pleasure, where characters are caught in a web of love affairs. It also featured one of the most memorable Restoration characters, the 'prince of fops', Sir Fopling Flutter.

The Man of Mode
[FB98] A & C Black pbk **£3.95**
[FB99] Methuen/Swan Theatre pbk **£4.50**

The Plays of Sir George Etherege
[FB100] Cambridge pbk **£10.95**

FARQUHAR, GEORGE (1677 - 1707)
Farquhar is remembered for three plays: *The Constant Couple*, which was a popular triumph for him in 1699, *The Recruiting Officer* (1706) based on his own experience of that job, and *The Beaux' Stratagem* (1707), still his most popular play. The country settings of the last two mark a movement away from the urban, interior atmosphere that prevailed in Restoration Comedy.

The Beaux' Stratagem
[FB103] A & C Black hbk **£3.95**

The Constant Couple
[FB104] Methuen/Swan Theatre pbk **£4.50**

The Recruiting Officer
[FB101] A & C Black pbk **£3.95**
[FB102] Manchester UP pbk **£7.95**

GAY, JOHN (1685 - 1732)
The Beggar's Opera (1728) was the most frequently performed play of the period. It mixes a burlesque of Italian opera with political satire, largely at the expense of Walpole, who promptly banned the sequel. It was the inspiration for *The Threepenny Opera* by Brecht and Weill.

The Beggar's Opera
[FB105] Penguin pbk **£3.50**

GOLDSMITH, OLIVER (Irish, 1730 - 1774)
Goldsmith, also a poet and a novelist, has won considerable acclaim for the play *She Stoops To Conquer* (1773). A satire of city snobbery, with which Goldsmith mocks the sentimental tone adopted by many of his predecessors, it advocates a return to comedy of sharper wit.

Poems and Plays
[FB107] Dent pbk **£8.95**

She Stoops to Conquer
[FB108] A & C Black pbk **£3.95**

MILTON, JOHN (1608 - 1674)
Samson Agonistes is one of Milton's later works, written between 1666 and 1670. It was never intended for performance, though Kenneth Tynan presented a controversial adaptation in the 1950s, casting himself as the Angel of the Lord. Close to classical drama in form and Christian in content, it shows Samson in the period before his final triumph, as he reasserts his strength in dialogues with his father, Dalila, and Harapha, the strong man of Gath.

Samson Agonistes
[FB109] Oxford pbk **£2.75**
[FB110] Macmillan pbk **£3.95**

OTWAY, THOMAS (1652 - 1685)
Otway's career as an actor ended after one performance, overwhelmed with stage-fright in Aphra Behn's *The Forced Marriage*. He turned to writing, and in *Venice Preserv'd* (1682) he shows a keener interest in characterization than many of his contemporaries, with expressions of unfeigned emotion that were at odds with the fashions of his time.

Venice Preserv'd
[FB111] Arnold pbk **£4.95**

SHERIDAN, RICHARD BRINSLEY (1751 - 1816)
Sheridan was born in Dublin, and is remembered for *The Rivals* (1775) and *The School for Scandal* (1777). Both derive from the 'comedy of manners', retaining the pointed wit, but without the more scurrilous content of earlier plays. He was also a co-manager of the Drury Lane Theatre until it was destroyed by fire in 1809, a scene which Sheridan watched from a nearby window.

Plays
[FB112] Oxford pbk **£7.95**

The Critic
[FB113] A & C Black pbk **£3.95**

The Rivals
[FB114] A & C Black pbk **£3.95**

The School for Scandal
[FB115] A & C Black pbk **£3.95**
[FB116] Penguin pbk **£3.99**

VANBRUGH, SIR JOHN (1664 - 1726)
The celebrated architect of Castle Howard and Blenheim Palace, Vanbrugh was also a dramatist. His best work bears comparison with that of Congreve, though his comedy and characters have a more earthy quality than those of his contemporary.

The Provok'd Wife
[FB117] A & C Black pbk **£3.95**

The Relapse
[FB118] A & C Black pbk **£3.95**

WYCHERLEY, WILLIAM (1640 - 1716)
Wycherley's comedies describe a world of coarseness and vitality. *The Country Wife* (1765) tells of a jealous husband's efforts to keep his young and naturally wayward wife from the temptations of London. *The Plain Dealer* (1676) is an ominous version of Molière's *The Misanthrope*, after which, despite its success, Wycherley began a strange, unhalting slide, and never wrote another word.

The Country Wife
[FB119] A & C Black pbk **£3.95**

The Plain Dealer
[FB120] A & C Black pbk **£3.95**
[FB121] Methuen/Swan Theatre pbk **£3.95**

The Plays of William Wycherley
[FB122] Cambridge pbk **£10.95**

19th Century Drama

19th Century Plays
Contains: Jerrold, *Black Ey'd Susan*; Bulwer-Lytton, *Money*; Taylor & Reade, *Masks and Faces*; Boucicault, *The Colleen Brawn*; Hazlewood, *Lady Audley's Secret*; and other plays.
[FB123] Oxford pbk **£6.95**

BARRIE, J.M. (1860 - 1937)
Recent interest in Barrie has centred more on his life than his work; however, he is remembered for the social comedy *The Admirable Crichton* (1902), and for the extraordinary fantasy *Peter Pan* (1904).

The Admirable Crichton
[FB124] Hodder pbk **£2.60**

BOUCICAULT, DION (Irish, 1820 - 1890)
Perhaps the most popular dramatist of the last half of the 19th century, Boucicault worked with great energy (and sometimes devious imagination) as an actor-manager, touring England and America most of his career. His skill in characterization and fine sense of dramatic timing is strongly evident in *London Assurance* (1841), a huge success when it opened at Covent Garden.
London Assurance
[FB124A] A & C Black pbk **£3.95**
Plays by Dion Boucicault
[FB125] Cambridge pbk **£12.50**

GALSWORTHY, JOHN (1867 - 1933)
Nobel Prize for Literature 1932. A novelist, Galsworthy also found success as a dramatist. His play about prison life, *Justice* (1910), is credited with inspiring a campaign for prison reform.
Five Plays
Strife/Justice/The Eldest Son/The Skin Game/Loyalties.
[FB126] Methuen pbk **£3.50**
Ten Best Plays
[FB127] Duckworth hbk **£18.00**

GILBERT, W.S. (1836 - 1911)
Best known for the libretti to accompany Sullivan's music in the 'Savoy Operas', Gilbert was also a stage dramatist of burlesques and extravaganzas. Some of his plays have a sharper, satirical edge, notably *Sweethearts* (1874) and *Engaged* (1877).
Plays
The complete texts of the 14 Gilbert & Sullivan Operas.
[FB128] Norton pbk **£8.95**
Plays by W.S. Gilbert
[FB129] Cambridge pbk **£8.50**

JONES, HENRY ARTHUR (1851 - 1929)
A leading turn-of-the-century dramatist, Jones' work presents social and moral issues in a naturalistic setting. Some plays are coloured by elements of melodrama, vividly illustrated by *The Silver King* (1882), which was highly successful in its day.
Plays by Henry Arthur Jones
[FB132] Cambridge pbk **£9.95**

PINERO, SIR ARTHUR WING (1855 - 1934)
Pinero's first significant plays were the Royal Court farces, starting with *The Magistrate* (1885), which were more popular at the time than the work of his contemporaries Wilde and Shaw. His later work moves towards a more serious social drama, notably *The Second Mrs Tanqueray*, the story of a 'woman with a past', which caused controversy when first seen in 1893.
Plays by A.W. Pinero
[FB133] Cambridge pbk **£10.95**
Three Plays
The Magistrate/The Second Mrs Tanqueray/Trelawny of the Wells.
[FB134] Methuen pbk **£3.95**

ROBERTSON, TOM (1829 - 1871)
Robertson abandoned the traditions of the old theatre in which he had been fostered, and founded what has been described as the 'cup-and-saucer' school of theatre. With plays such as *Caste* (1867), for which he gave elaborate instructions for 'realistic' scenery and costume, along with detailed stage directions, Robertson foreshadows the drama of the end of the century.
Plays by Tom Robertson
[FB135] Cambridge pbk **£8.50**
Six Plays
Society/Ours/Caste/Progress/School/Birth.
[FB136] Amber Lane pbk **£6.95**

SHAW, GEORGE BERNARD
(Irish, 1856 - 1950)
Nobel Prize for Literature 1925. Shaw's awareness of the possibilities offered by the stage as a platform for debating contemporary issues, along with his regard for the work of Ibsen, led to the production of *Widowers' Houses*, his first play, in 1892. The dexterity of his thought and his characteristic sharp wit were a dominating influence in the early part of this century, gaining momentum after the popular success of *Pygmalion* in 1914.
Androcles and the Lion
[FB137] Penguin pbk **£2.95**
Back to Methusaleh
[FB138] Penguin pbk **£5.95**
Caesar and Cleopatra
[FB139] Longman pbk **£2.50**
Candida
[FB140] Longman pbk **£2.50**
Getting Married/Press Cuttings
[FB141] Penguin pbk **£3.95**
Heartbreak House
[FB142] Penguin pbk **£2.95**
John Bull's Other Island
[FB143] Penguin pbk **£3.99**
Last Plays
[FB144] Penguin pbk **£4.99**
Major Barbara
[FB145] Penguin pbk **£2.99**
Man and Superman
[FB146] Penguin pbk **£3.95**
Misalliance & The Fascinating Foundling
[FB147] Penguin pbk **£4.50**
Plays
[FB148] Norton pbk **£6.95**
Plays Extravagant
[FB149] Penguin pbk **£3.95**
Plays Pleasant
[FB150] Penguin pbk **£3.99**
Plays Political
[FB151] Penguin pbk **£4.95**
Plays Unpleasant
[FB152] Penguin pbk **£3.99**
Pygmalion
[FB153] Penguin pbk **£2.50**
Saint Joan
[FB154] Penguin pbk **£2.99**
Selected Shorter Plays
[FB155] Penguin pbk **£5.95**
Showing Up Blanco Posnet/Fanny's Last Play
[FB156] Penguin pbk **£3.95**
The Apple Cart
[FB157] Penguin pbk **£3.50**
The Devil's Disciple
[FB158A] Longman pbk **£2.50**
The Doctor's Dilemna
[FB159] Penguin pbk **£3.99**
Three Plays for Puritans
[FB160] Penguin pbk **£4.99**

TAYLOR, TOM (1817 - 1880)
Taylor combined his work as a prolific and popular playwright with various demanding careers - he was successively a Professor of English, barrister, civil servant, and editor of *Punch*. Four plays are collected in this volume, of which the best known is a melodrama of low-life, *The Ticket-of-Leave Man* (1863).
Plays by Tom Taylor
[FB161] Cambridge pbk **£10.95**

THOMAS, (WALTER) BRANDON
(1856 - 1914)
Only the farce *Charley's Aunt* (1892) remains from Thomas' dozen or so plays. It has proved a favourite with professional and amateur companies the world over, and apparently at one time could be seen in over

twenty languages, including Chinese, Gaelic, Russian and Zulu.
Charley's Aunt
[FB162] Heinemann pbk **£2.75**

WILDE, OSCAR (1854 - 1900)
The finest example of Wilde's genius at work in the theatre is often cited as *The Importance of Being Earnest* (1895), distinguished by its sparkling comic dialogue, and its rare agility in handling plot conventions. Some of the other plays, notably *The Ideal Husband* (also 1895), move closer to the current of the 'problem comedy' of the time, an element strongly evident in the recent Glasgow Citizens' Theatre production.
Lady Windemere's Fan
[FB163] A & C Black pbk **£3.95**
Plays
[FB164] Methuen pbk **£2.95**
Salome
[FB165] Quartet pbk **£5.95**
The Complete Works of Oscar Wilde
[FB166] Collins pbk **£5.95**
The Importance of Being Earnest
[FB167] A & C Black pbk **£3.95**
[FB168] Methuen pbk **£3.95**
[FB169] Penguin pbk **£2.25**
The Importance of Being Earnest: 4 Act Version
[FB170] Sangam pbk **£2.25**
Two Society Comedies
An Ideal Husband/A Woman of No Importance.
[FB171] A & C Black pbk **£3.95**

20th Century Drama

Classic Irish Drama
Yeats, *The Countess Cathleen*; Synge, *Playboy of the Western World*; O'Casey, *Cock-a-Doodle-Dandy*.
[FB175] Penguin pbk **£3.95**

Landmarks of Modern British Theatre Vol 1: The Sixties
Wesker, *Roots*; Arden, *Serjeant Musgrave's Dance*; Pinter, *The Caretaker*; Osborne, *A Patriot for Me*, Bond, *Saved*; Orton, *Loot*; Barnes, *The Ruling Class*.
[FB178] Methuen hbk **£14.95**
[FB178A] Methuen pbk **£6.99**
Vol 2: The Seventies
Ayckbourn, *Just Between Ourselves*; Brenton, *Weapons of Happiness*; Stoppard, *Every Good Boy Deserves Favour*; Shaffer, *Amadeus*; Nichols, *Passion Play*; Gray, *Quartermaine's Terms*, Churchill, *Top Girls*.
[FB177] Methuen hbk **£14.95**
[FB179] Methuen pbk **£6.99**

John Arden, whose fiction and controversial stage work, much of it written with his Margaretta D'Arcy, is published by Methuen Paperbacks.

Landmarks of Irish Theatre
Yeats, *On Baile's Strand*; Shaw, *John Bull's Other Island*; Synge, *The Playboy of the Western World*; O'Casey, *The Silver Tassie*; Behan, *The Quare Fellow*; Beckett, *All That Fall*; Johnson, *The Old Lady Says 'No'*.
[FB180] Methuen hbk **£14.95**
[FB181] Methuen pbk **£6.99**

Plays of the Sixties
Peter Shaffer, *The Royal Hunt of the Sun*; Waterhouse and Hall, *Billy Liar*; Rattigan, *Ross*; Lessing, *Play with a Tiger*.
[FB184] Pan pbk **£3.95**

First Run
An annual publication, this volume features five plays from authors who made their breakthrough in 1988: Simon Donald, *Prickly Heat*; Winsome Pinnock, *Leave Taking*; Clare McIntyre, *Low Level Panic*; Billy Roche, *A Handful of Stars*; Paul Godfrey, *Inventing a New Colour*.
[FB176] N Hern pbk **£6.95**

Methuen New Theatre Scripts
A collection of the most recent editions of Methuen's anthologies of drama from groups which are otherwise frequently under-represented in contemporary selections. Previous volumes remain available.
Black Plays Colour & Space Vol 2 NEW
[FB176A] Methuen pbk **£5.95**
Gay Plays Colour & Space Vol 4 NEW
[FB176B] Methuen pbk **£5.95**
Lesbian PlaysVol 2 NEW
[FB176C] Methuen pbk **£5.95**
Plays by Women Vol 7 NEW
[FB176D] Methuen pbk **£5.95**

Plays Introduction
A collection from 1984, featuring: *In Kanada* by Nick Darke, *Babylon Has Fallen* by John Fletcher, *Ladies in Waiting* by Ellen Fox, *Trial and Error* by Lennie James, and *New Anatomies* by Timberlake Wertenbaker.
[FB183] Faber pbk **£3.95**

Young Playwright's Festival
Plays broadcast in October 1988 as part of BBC Radio's Young Playwrights Festival, featuring Benjamin Zephaniah and Jeanette Winterson, among others.
[FB185] BBC pbk **£4.95**

ARDEN, JOHN & D'ARCY, MARGARETTA
Arden's drama celebrates the Dionysian attitudes of 'noise, disorder, drunkenness, lasciviousness, nudity, generosity, corruption, fertility and ease.' A social dramatist of the 1960s, he draws strongly on conflict and myth, punctuating his dialogue with poetry and song. In 1960 he began working on plays with his wife, Margaretta D'Arcy. Since then, they have moved increasingly away from mainstream theatre, often drawing on Irish history for their polemical dramas. Their latest work, *Whose Is the Kingdom?* (1989) is set between the time of Christ and the death of Constantine in AD 337, and explores the relationship of Church to society.
Plays: One
Serjeant Musgrave's Dance/The Workhouse Donkey/Armstrong's Last Goodnight.
[FB186] Methuen pbk **£3.95**
Pearl
[FB187] Methuen pbk **£4.50**
Serjeant Musgrave's Dance
[FB187A] Methuen pbk **£4.50**
The Island of the Mighty
[FB188] Methuen pbk **£5.95**

The Little Gray Home in the West
[FB189] Methuen pbk **£3.95**
The Non-Stop Connolly Show
[FB190] Methuen pbk **£6.95**
The Royal Pardon
[FB191] Methuen pbk **£3.95**
Three Plays
Waters of Babylon/Live Like Pigs/Happy Haven.
[FB192] Penguin pbk **£4.95**
Vandaleur's Folly
[FB193] Methuen pbk **£3.95**
Whose Is the Kingdom?
[FB194] Methuen pbk **£6.95**

AUDEN, W.H. (1907 - 1973) & ISHERWOOD, CHRISTOPHER (1904 - 1986)
Auden and Isherwood collaborated on these verse dramas in the 1930s, early in their respective careers. The plays are elusive, characterized by secret manoeuvres in strange, derelict places, and evoke a sense of confusion and disaster.
The Ascent of F6 & On the Frontier
[FB195] Faber pbk **£3.95**
The Dog Beneath the Skin
[FB196] Faber pbk **£3.95**

AYCKBOURN, ALAN (1939 -)
One of England's most popular contemporary dramatists, Ayckbourn's territory is middle-class suburbia, where he manoeuvres comic situations masterfully, with an increasingly acerbic insight into marital relationships.
A Small Family Business
[FB197] Faber pbk **£3.95**
Chorus of Disapproval
[FB198] Faber pbk **£3.95**
Confusions
[FB199] Methuen pbk **£2.95**
Henceforward
Opened in the West End in 1988, this is the story of a composer who attempts to win access to his beloved daughter by hiring an actress to pose as his wife, with unfortunate results.
[FB200] Faber pbk **£3.95**
Joking Apart & Other Plays
[FB201] Penguin pbk **£4.99**
Norman Conquests
[FB202] Penguin pbk **£3.99**
Three Plays
Bedroom Farce/Absent Friends/Absurd Person Singular.
[FB203] Penguin pbk **£4.99**
Woman in Mind (December Bee)
[FB204] Faber pbk **£3.95**

BARKER, HOWARD (1946 -)
Since Barker's plays first appeared in the early 1970s, he has developed an inventive, uncompromising body of work. His plays often view contemporary Britain from an outsider's perspective, turning on jagged contradictions, continually reversing expectations. *"Nothing in my plays is incredible. It is the world which is incredible"*.
Collected Plays Vol 1
Claw/No End of Blame/Scenes from an Execution/Victory/The Castle.
[FB205] Calder pbk **£5.95**
The Bite of the Night
A six-hour epic, examining the story of Helen of Troy. Tragic in tone, the text is illuminated by interludes of scabrous wit.
[FB206] Calder pbk **£4.95**
The Hang of the Gaol
[FB207] Calder pbk **£4.95**
The Last Supper
A quasi-religious work, set in a ravaged Eastern Europe, this examines themes of alienation and submission.
[FB208] Calder pbk **£3.95**

The Possibilities
A collection of ten short plays with political themes.
[FB209] Calder pbk **£4.95**

BARNES, PETER (1931 -)
While delighting in the grotesque, Barnes seems to find a perverse optimism in detailing a world he sees moving towards a final sunset.
Plays: One
The Ruling Class/The Bewitcher/Leonardo's Last Supper/Noonday Demons/Laughter!/Eight Monologues.
[FB211] Methuen pbk **£4.99**
Lulu: A Sex Tragedy
A 1970 adaptation of Wedekind's powerful dramas about destructive sexuality, *Earth Spirit* and *Pandora's Box*, first published this year.
[FB210] Methuen pbk **£4.50**
The Real Long John Silver & Other Plays
[FB212] Faber pbk **£5.50**

BECKETT, SAMUEL (Irish, 1906 -)
Nobel Prize for Literature 1969. In 1952, Samuel Beckett caused a sensation with the Paris production of his first play, *Waiting for Godot*: no other work has had such a dynamic influence on theatre since the war. For Beckett, it set into motion a chain of themes which had been at the heart of his novels - an uneasy sense of loneliness and futility, the always elusive nature of memory. His ideas are eloquently alive in the extraordinary images of his plays - the two clowning tramps fruitlessly waiting by the tree, or Winnie up to her neck in scorched earth in *Happy Days*, or the dustbins that are homes in *Endgame*. With compassionate irony Beckett explores what a curious thing it is to be set in time; despite the apparent desolation of his situations, his plays are bizarrely exhilarating.
All That Fall: A Play for Radio
[FB213] Faber pbk **£1.95**
Collected Shorter Plays
[FB214] Faber pbk **£4.95**
Endgame: A Play in One Act & Act without Words
[FB215] Faber pbk **£2.50**
Footfalls
[FB216] Faber pbk **£1.10**

Samuel Beckett; *File on Beckett*, a critical compilation on the influential playwright, is published by Methuen Paperbacks (£4.99)

Happy Days: A Play in Two Acts
[FB217] Faber pbk **£2.95**
Krapp's Last Tape and Embers
[FB218] Faber pbk **£2.50**
Three Occasional Pieces
[FB219] Faber pbk **£1.50**
Waiting for Godot
[FB220] Faber pbk **£2.95**

BEHAN, BRENDAN (Irish, 1923 - 1964)
Extrovert, alcoholic Irish writer, imprisoned in 1939
for carrying IRA explosives, and then again in 1942
for shooting at a policeman. His robust comedies are
sparked by immense energy, several of them enjoying
continuous success since they first appeared in the
late 1950s. He is best known for the dark comedy
The Quare Fellow, set in a prison on the eve of a
hanging, and *The Hostage*, a lively tale of the Dublin
underworld, concerning an English soldier held IRA
hostage in a brothel.
The Complete Plays
The Hostage/The Quare Fellow/Richard's Cork
Leg/Moving Out/A Garden Party/The Big House.
[FB221] Methuen pbk **£4.95**

BENNETT, ALAN (1934 -)
An actor as well as playwright, Bennett's sharp obser-
vation and laconic wit has distinguished his work for
stage, television and screen since the early 1960s.
Forty Years On & Other Plays
Forty Years On/Habeus Corpus/Getting On.
[FB222] Faber pbk **£4.95**
Objects of Affection
[FB223] BBC pbk **£5.95**
Single Spies
A double bill staged at the National Theatre in 1988-
89, featuring an adaptation of Bennett's very
successful television play about Guy Burgesss, *An
Englishman Abroad*, and a companion piece *A
Question of Attribution*, which concerns Anthony
Blunt.
[FB224] Faber pbk **£3.99**
Talking Heads
Six brilliantly crafted monologues for television.
[FB225] BBC pbk **£4.95**
The Old Country
[FB226] Faber pbk **£2.50**
The Writer in Disguise & Other Plays
The Writer in Disguise/Me! I'm Afraid of Virginia
Woolf/The Old Crowd/Afternoon Off/One Fine Day.
[FB227] Faber pbk **£4.95**
Two Kafka Plays
Contains *Kafka's Dick* and *The Insurance Man*.
[FB228] Faber pbk **£4.95**

BERKOFF, STEVEN (1937 -)
Iconoclastic dramatist, best known for his Kafka
adaptations in the late 1960s (*The Trial* and
Metamorphosis), and for the richness of his linguistic
experimentation in *East*.
Decadence/Greek/East/West
[FB229] Faber pbk **£5.99**
Kvtech/Acapulco
[FB230] Faber pbk **£3.95**
Sink the Belgrano!
Verse statire which parodies *Henry V*, directed by
Berkoff himself in 1986, examines some of the
complex social and political issues arising from the
Falklands War.
[FB231] Faber pbk **£3.99**
The Trial/Metamorphosis
[FB232] Amber Lane pbk **£4.50**
**Three Plays by Steven Berkoff: West,
Harry's Christmas and Lunch**
[FB233] Faber pbk **£3.95**

BLEASDALE, ALAN (1946 -)
A Northern king of deadpan humour, Bleasdale's
touch can be savage, as he displayed in the despairing

comedy in the television series *The Boys from the
Blackstuff*.
Are You Lonesome Tonight?
Story of the decaying Elvis Presley, contrasting his
decline with younger, more glorious days.
[FB234] Faber pbk **£3.95**
Having a Ball/It's a Madhouse
[FB235] Faber pbk **£4.95**

BOLT, ROBERT (1924 -)
A Man for all Seasons
A grave and sympathetic portrait of Sir Thomas
More, centred on the questions of faith which
confronted him in his relationship with Henry VIII.
[FB236] Heinemann pbk **£2.75**

BOND, EDWARD (1934 -)
Bond has drawn inspiration from a variety of sources,
combining a wide range of dramatic techniques with a
rare imagination. The strength of his contribution to
contemporary drama is undeniable, although the
impassioned social protest of some of his plays has
sparked controversy.
Plays: One
Saved/Early Morning/The Pope's Wedding. The three
1960s plays for which Bond is perhaps most
notorious; each centres on the deprived and
disaffected, displaying a hard edge of violence which
he believes to be provoked by social isjustice.
[FB238] Methuen pbk **£3.95**
Plays: Two
Lear/The Sea/Narrow Road to the Deep North/Black
Mass/Passion. A diverse collection, featuring his
powerful version of *King Lear* with a companion
comedy *The Sea*, a Japanese parable and two short
pieces for the Anti-Apartheid movement and CND
respectively.
[FB240] Methuen pbk **£3.95**
Plays: Three
Bingo/The Fool/The Woman. Three works set in the
distant past, concerning the last days of Shakespeare,
the poet John Clare, and a re-working of Greek
myths.
[FB239] Methuen pbk **£3.95**
A-A-America! & Stone
[FB237] Methuen pbk **£4.50**
Restoration & The Cat
[FB241] Methuen pbk **£4.50**
Summer
[FB242] Methuen pbk **£4.95**
The Bundle
[FB243] Methuen pbk **£4.50**
The War Plays: Vol 1
A nightmarish vision of England in the wake of a
nuclear war. The trilogy is published in two volumes,
the first containing *Red, Black and Ignorant* and *The
Tin Can People*, the second *Great Peace*.
[FB244] Methuen pbk **£3.50**
The War Plays: Vol 2
[FB245] Methuen pbk **£3.50**
The Worlds
[FB246] Methuen pbk **£4.50**
Theatre Poems and Songs
[FB247] Methuen pbk **£4.50**

BRENTON, HOWARD (1942 -)
Brenton is determined that his theatre should be
disruptive, and often addresses loaded contemporary
issues, such as political imprisonment or urban
terrorism. He has also earned his share of controversy,
notably with *The Romans in Britain*, which drew
parallels between Julius Caesar's invasion and British
involvement in Ireland.
Plays: One
Christie in Love/Magnificence/The Churchill
Play/Weapons of Happiness/Epsom Downs/Sore
Throats: a selection of Brenton's most interesting
plays from the 1970s.
[FB250] Methuen pbk **£3.95**

Edward Bond, whose plays are published by
Methuen Paperbacks

Plays: Two
The Romans in Britain/Thirteenth Night/The
Genius/Bloody Poetry/Greenland: a selection of
works from the 1980s, including his most recent play
Greenland, which turns on a 700-year time shift,
contrasting contemporary Utopian dreams of Britain
with their future realization.
[FB251] Methuen pbk **£4.99**
Hitler Dances
[FB248] Methuen pbk **£4.50**
Plays for the Poor Theatre
The Saliva Milkshake/Christie in Love/Gum and
Goo/Heads/The Education of Skinny Spew. A series
of intense short dramas, intended for small casts with
minimal staging resources.
[FB249] Methuen pbk **£4.50**
Revenge
[FB252] Methuen pbk **£4.50**
with ALI, TARIQ
Iranian Nights
A short play staged by the Royal Court in 1989,
which was a swift reaction to the 'appalling
predicament' faced by Salman Rushdie, attempting to
provide insight into Islamic culture.
[FB253] N Hern pbk **£3.50**
with HARE, DAVID (1947 -)
Brassneck
[FB254] Methuen pbk **£4.50**
Pravda
An investigation into seedy Fleet Street practices,
Pravda has proved one of the most popular plays seen
at the National Theatre, where it was first staged in
1985.
[FB255] Methuen pbk **£4.50**
with IKOLI, TUNDE
Sleeping Policeman
Innovative play from 1983, which intercuts two
separate stories involving the same six contemporary
South London characters.
[FB256] Methuen pbk **£3.50**

BYRNE, JOHN (Irish, 1926 -)
Creator of the television series *Tutti Frutti*, Byrne's
reputation was made by his earlier trilogy of plays,
portraying the life and times of a group of factory
workers in Paisley, set between 1957 and 1972. John
Byrne is the pseudonym of Hugh Leonard.

The Slab Boys Trilogy
[FB257] Penguin pbk **£3.95**
Tutti Frutti
[FB258] BBC pbk **£3.95**

CARTWRIGHT, JIM
Bed NEW
A surreal burlesque, produced by the National
Theatre in 1989, of a long night in a vast bed shared
by seven elderly people. The play links strange,
fragmented dreams with their memories of the past.
[FB259] Methuen pbk **£4.99**
Road
A wild and innovative play from 1986, looking
behind the doors of a derelict Lancashire street. The
original promenade production presented each
household's scenario simultaneously to great dramatic
effect. The bitter kaleidoscope of poverty and
violence at times threatens to overwhelm, but
Cartwright tempers the despair with moments of
genuine lyricism, communicating a battered dignity to
the lives of his bruised characters.
[FB260] Methuen pbk **£4.99**

CHURCHILL, CARYL (1938 -)
A popular and prominent contemporary playwright,
much of Churchill's early work in the 1970s was
written for left-wing and feminist companies, such as
Joint Stock and Monstrous Regiment. Her plays
disrupt conventional theatrical modes with ingenuity,
often featuring complex explorations of gender roles.
Plays: One
Owners/Vinegar Tom/Traps/Light Shining in
Buckinghamshire/Cloud Nine. Five plays from 1972-
79, introduced by the author, including *Cloud Nine*,
her first international success, which explores sexual
and colonial oppression.
[FB263] Methuen pbk **£3.95**
Plays: Two NEW
Five plays from 1982-87, including *Objections to
Sex and Violence*, an energetic polemic from 1975;
the major hit of 1987, *Serious Money*, a satire on the
sharp practices of brokers in the vacuous boom world
of the City; also *Softcops*, *Top Girls* and *Fen*.
[FB264] Methuen pbk **£4.99**
Ice Cream NEW
First staged in summer 1989 at the Royal Court, a
story of the intertwining lives of an English and an
American couple, examining the fragile affection
each holds for the other's country.
[FB261] N Hern pbk **£4.50**
Mouthful of Birds (with Lan, David)
[FB262] Methuen pbk **£3.95**
Shorts NEW
Diverse collection of short plays from the 1970s.
[FB265] N Hern pbk **£3.95**

CLARK, BRIAN (1932 -)
Whose Life is it Anyway?
The story of a disabled sculptor facing life on a
support machine, and debating his right to suicide.
[FB266] Amber Lane pbk **£3.95**

COWARD, NOEL (1899 - 1973)
Actor, playwright and composer who was for many
years one of the most flamboyant and celebrated
talents of British theatre and society. His first play,
The Vortex (1925), was uncharacteristically tragic,
centred around the torments of a young drug addict
who suffers from his mother's adulteries; it enjoyed a
successful West End revival in 1989. The brilliant
light comedies for which he is generally remembered
shine with sparkling wit and sophisticated cynicism,
often treating marital relationships with a brittle
amorality which found immediate popularity with
pre-War audiences.
Plays: One
Hay Fever/The Vortex/Fallen Angels/Easy Virtue.
[FB269] Methuen pbk **£3.95**

Plays: Two
Private Lives/Bitter Sweet/The Marquise/Post
Mortem.
[FB271] Methuen pbk **£3.95**
Plays: Three
Design for Living/Cavalcade/Conversation
Piece/Hands Across the Sea/Still Life/Fumed Oak
from Tonight at 8.30.
[FB270] Methuen pbk **£3.95**
Plays: Four
Blithe Spirit/This Happy Breed/Present
Laughter/Ways and Means/The Astonished Heart/Red
Peppers from Tonight at 8.30.
[FB268] Methuen pbk **£3.95**
Plays: Five
Relative Values/Look After Lulu/Waiting in the
Wings/Suite in Three Keys.
[FB267] Methuen pbk **£3.95**

DELANEY, SHELAGH (1939 -)
A Taste of Honey
Delaney's first play, staged in 1958 while she was still
a teenager, tells of the energetic, eccentric moves a
young woman makes to bring to life her drab
existence in Manchester.
[FB272] Methuen pbk **£4.50**

EDGAR, DAVID (1948 -)
One of the most prolific and successful of the wave of
dramatists emerging after 1968, Edgar is often
described as a political playwright, or as a realist with
political leanings. He has worked with the RSC,
notably on the epic 1980 adaptation of *Nicholas
Nickleby*.
Plays: One
Five major works from the 1970s: *The Jail Diary of
Albie Sachs*, *Mary Barnes*, *Saigon Rose*, *O Fair
Jerusalem*, *Destiny*. Edgar develops his ideas around
an emotive image or theme - for example, South
Africa in *Jail Diary*, or the rise of fascism in Britain
in *Destiny*.
[FB275] Methuen pbk **£3.95**
Entertaining Strangers (NT Version)
Originally a Dorchester community play, which Edgar
then adapted for the National Theatre in 1987: it
offers a panoramic view of a 19th century market
town facing a cholera epidemic.
[FB273] Methuen pbk **£4.50**
Maydays
[FB274] Methuen pbk **£4.50**
Teen Dreams & Our Own People
[FB276] Methuen pbk **£4.50**
That Summer
Edgar's most recent stage work, centred on the
culture clashes which arise when the family of an
Oxford don play summer hosts to the daughters of
miners involved in the 1984 strike.
[FB277] Methuen pbk **£4.50**
Wreckers
[FB278] Methuen pbk **£3.50**

ELIOT, T.S. (1888 - 1965)
Nobel Prize for Literature 1948. Eliot advocated a
return to poetic drama, seen most memorably in his
play with chorus, *Murder in the Cathedral* (1935),
based on the martyrdom of Thomas à Becket. He
wrote several verse plays with contemporary settings,
attempting to combine West End conventions with
more profound dramatic traditions. Thus *The Family
Reunion* (1939) is a drawing room drama with
elements of Greek tragedy, and *The Cocktail Party*
(1949), with a plot based on Euripides' *Alcestis*,
combines the London party circuit with the heroine's
eventual crucifixion on an ant-hill. The balance of
elements in these plays remains uneasy, but they have
excited much critical attention, and have run
successfully both in London and New York.
Complete Poems and Plays
[FB279] Faber hbk **£14.95**

Murder in the Cathedral
[FB280] Faber pbk **£2.50**
The Cocktail Party
[FB281] Faber pbk **£5.95**
The Confidential Clerk
[FB282] Faber pbk **£5.95**
The Elder Statesman
[FB283] Faber pbk **£2.95**
The Family Reunion
[FB284] Faber pbk **£2.95**

FRAYN, MICHAEL (1933 -)
Frayn was known as a newspaper wit and comic
novelist until his comedies for the stage began to
appear in the 1970s. He scored particular success in
1982 with his farce of theatre life *Noises Off*. He is
also noted for his translations and adaptations of
Chekhov's works, the most recent of these being *The
Sneeze*, which appeared in 1988.
Plays: One
Noises Off/Alphabetical Order/Donkeys
Years/Clouds/Make and Break.
[FB287] Methuen pbk **£3.95**
Balmoral
[FB285] Methuen pbk **£4.50**
Benefactors
[FB286] Methuen pbk **£4.50**

FRIEL, BRIAN (Irish, 1929 -)
Friel is one of the leading Irish dramatists of the last
twenty years. His strength lies in his ability to probe
the conditions of individual lives, with an awareness
of the historical and political forces which shape
them.
Fathers and Sons
[FB288] Faber pbk **£3.95**
Making History NEW
Friel's most recent work, from 1988, which tells of
the Earl of Tyrone's attempts to drive the armies of
Elizabeth I out of Ireland. It is as much concerned
with the various ways in which history is made and
told, as with the historical events at its centre.
[FB289] Faber pbk **£3.95**
Selected Plays
Includes *Philadelphia, Here I Come!*, which
established his name in 1964, focusing on the
experiences which brought a man to the brink of
exile. *Translations* explores themes of
communication and change, with an elaborate play of
contrasts between Gaelic culture and English
influences. Also featured in this volume: *The
Freedom of the City*, *Living Quarters*, *Aristocrats*
and *Faith Healer*.
[FB290] Faber pbk **£4.95**

Caryl Churchill, whose plays are available from
Methuen Paperbacks

The Enemy Within
Friel's first significant play, produced by the Abbey Theatre in 1962, based on the exile of St Columba.
[FB291] Gallery P pbk **£4.50**
Translations
[FB292] Faber pbk **£3.95**

FRY, CHRISTOPHER (1907 -)
Fry enjoyed considerable acclaim during the 1940 for his verse dramas, which some compared to the work of T.S. Eliot. *The Lady's Not for Burning* is regarded as his most considerable work.
Selected Plays
Boy with a Cart/A Phoenix Too Frequent/The Lady's Not for Burning/A Sleep of Prisoners/Curtmantle.
[FB293] Oxford pbk **£5.95**

GEMS, PAM (1925 -)
Gems' work is characterized by exuberant celebrations of womanhood, most notably in *Piaf*, a portrait of the great French *chanteuse*, which the RSC staged in the West End and on Broadway in 1980 and 1981.
Three Plays
Piaf/Camille/Loving Women.
[FB294] Penguin pbk **£4.95**

GODBER, JOHN
Five Plays
As artistic director of the Hull Truck Theatre Company, Godber has scored notable successes with *Bouncers*, *Teechers* and *Up'n'Under*, which he describes as 'Rocky set in Yorkshire'. These three are included here, along with *Happy Jack* and *September in the Rain*.
[FB295] Penguin pbk **£5.99**

GRAY, SIMON (1936 -)
Gray's plays often focus on men of letters - academics or publishers - and the various traumatic dilemmas they face. Their air of loneliness and inadequacy, underscored by recurring themes of sexual uncertainty, is frequently rendered with Gray's distinctively dry sense of irony.
Plays: One
Butley/The Common Pursuit/Otherwise Engaged/The Rear Column/Quartermaine's Terms. *Butley* (1971) was Gray's first success, and involves an academic caught between his crumbling marriage and a younger man. In *The Common Pursuit*, adultery divides a set of ex-Cambridge liberals who move in literary circles.
[FB298] Methuen pbk **£3.95**
Close of Play & Pig in a Poke
[FB296] Methuen pbk **£4.50**
Dog Days
[FB297] Methuen pbk **£3.95**
Stage Struck
[FB299] Methuen pbk **£4.50**
The Rear Column and Other Plays
The Rear Column/Molly/Man in a Side-Car.
[FB300] Methuen pbk **£4.50**

GREENE, GRAHAM (1904 -)
Collected Plays
Greene's plays share strong thematic affinities with his novels and screenplays. This volume contains all of his plays, which appeared between 1953 and 1980.
[FB301] Penguin pbk **£5.95**

GRIFFITHS, TREVOR (1935 -)
A dramatist of the left whose work combines incisiveness with heart, and whose commitment to political change is driven by his search for the way forward.
Comedians
A painful and at times savage piece from 1975, perhaps Griffiths' most ambitious and effective work, which tells of a fading comic preparing some students for auditions.
[FB302] Faber pbk **£3.95**

Occupations
[FB303] Faber pbk **£3.99**
Oi for England
[FB304] Faber pbk **£3.25**
Real Dreams
[FB305] Faber pbk **£4.95**
The Party
[FB306] Faber pbk **£3.99**

HALL, WILLIS (1929 -)
The Long, the Short and the Tall (1958)
Popular play which follows a small group of soldiers through the Malayan jungle, facing the extreme question at the heart of war - should they kill another man, should they murder their Japanese captive?
[FB307] Heinemann pbk **£2.75**

HAMPTON, CHRISTOPHER (1946 -)
Hampton is an elegant and sophisticated writer, who seems to move effortlessly through an impressive array of settings, be it 1940s Hollywood or contemporary South America. A skilled linguist, he has adapted and translated several classic European plays, his versions of Ibsen being perhaps his most successful.
George Steiner's Portage to San Christobal of A.H.
[FB308] Faber pbk **£3.25**
Les Liaisons Dangereuses
A chilling portrayal of aristocratic decadence, the play has enjoyed an unbroken run in the West End since 1986, with a Hollywood film version appearing recently.
[FB309] Faber pbk **£3.95**
Savages
[FB310] Faber pbk **£2.95**
Tales from Hollywood
[FB311] Faber pbk **£3.50**
Total Eclipse
One of Hampton's first plays, from 1968, this is an absorbing story of the love affair between Paul Verlaine and the 17 year old poetic genius, Arthur Rimbaud.
[FB312] Faber pbk **£2.95**

HARE, DAVID (1947 -)
Hare has ably walked the uncertain line between 'alternative' and 'established' theatre. He is both a founder of the innovative Joint Stock Company, and was associate director of the National Theatre, where he had huge success with his production of *Pravda*. More recently, he has worked in cinema, as both writer and director of the psychological dramas *Wetherby* and *Paris By Night*.
Plenty
[FB313] Faber pbk **£3.95**
Racing Demon   **NEW**
[FB314] Faber pbk **£3.99**
The Asian Plays
Fanshen/Saigon/A Map of the World.
[FB315] Faber pbk **£4.95**
The Bay at Nice/Wrecked Eggs
[FB316] Faber pbk **£3.95**
The History Plays
Knuckle/Licking Hitler/Plenty.
[FB317] Faber pbk **£3.95**
The Secret Rapture (1988)
Hare's latest stage-work, which some have described as his best play, is a strange twisting of the conventions of social comedy, exploring the different responses of two sisters to their father's death. It was also hailed as a major statement on the state of Thatcherite England at the end of the 1980s.
[FB318] Faber pbk **£3.95**

HARRISON, TONY (1937 -)
The only contemporary poet to have made an impact on the theatre, Harrison's adaptations have breathed life into plays which had seemed inaccessible.

Dramatic Verse: Theatre Works 1973-85
Includes versions of *The Misanthrope*, *Phaedra*, *The Oresteia* and *Medea*.
[FB319] Penguin pbk **£4.95**
The Mysteries
Exhilarating versions of the Medieval Mystery cycles.
[FB320] Faber pbk **£4.95**

HARWOOD, RONALD (1934 -)
J.J. Farr
[FB321] Amber Lane pbk **£2.95**
The Dresser (1980)
Harwood's best known work, an affectionate and at times uneasy portrait of a charismatic but tyrannical actor-manager facing the last curtain, seen through the eyes of his devoted and desperate assistant.
[FB322] Amber Lane pbk **£3.95**

HEGGIE, IAIN
An emerging, gifted comedy writer, Heggie has exploited the concerns and language of his native Glasgow with spirited abandon, his conjured mayhem tempered by a measured irony.
American Bagpipes
[FB323] Penguin pbk **£4.99**

HUGHES, DUSTY
Futurists/Commitments
Futurists, first staged in 1986, is Dusty Hughes best-received work. Set in post-1917 Petrograd, with characters that include many of the major Russian writers of the time, it describes some of the expectations and betrayals encountered in the wake of the Revolution.
[FB324] Faber pbk **£4.95**
Jenkin's Ear (1987)
A political thriller, centred on the moral dilemmas faced by a British journalist working in Central America.
[FB325] Faber pbk **£3.95**

JELLICOE, ANN (1927 -)
Dramatist, director and actress, Jellicoe has been especially active in community theatre. She made her name when the Royal Court staged her first play, *The Sport of My Mad Mother*, in 1958. It defies dramatic conventions, basing itself on fragmented speech patterns which sometimes have an air of free-form improvisation.
The Knack/The Sport of My Mad Mother
[FB326] Faber pbk **£4.50**

JOHNSON, TERRY
Insignificance
Johnson, once described as 'that rare creature: a moralist with wit', is still probably best known for this play, later filmed by Nic Roeg, in which Einstein discusses the Theory of Relativity with Marilyn Monroe in a hotel room.
[FB327] Methuen pbk **£2.95**
Unsuitable for Adults
[FB328] Faber pbk **£3.95**

KEATLEY, CHARLOTTE
My Mother Said I Never Should (1987)
A play which examines the bonds between four generations of women, moving subtly through different times and locations, and presenting the characters and their lives with unerring warmth.
[FB329] Methuen pbk **£2.95**

KEEFFE, BARRIE (1945 -)
At his best, Keeffe provides some of the most stormy and immediate protest theatre of the 1970s and 80s.
A Mad World, My Masters
[FB330] Methuen pbk **£4.50**
Barbarians
Killing Time/Abide With Me/In the City.
[FB331] Methuen pbk **£4.50**

Gimme Shelter
Gem/Gotcha/Getaway.
[FB332] Methuen pbk **£4.50**
King of England & Bastard Angel
[FB333] Methuen pbk **£4.99**
My Girl and Frozen Assets   **NEW**
[FB334] Methuen pbk **£5.50**

KUREISHI, HANIF
Kureishi is one of the most talented new writers with
a particular strength in dramatizing racial pressures
and conflicts, often set in a city wasteland, where
prospects are slim and family ties strained. He writes
with great depth of feeling for his characters and their
situations, often piercing the gloom with touches of
the absurd, exemplified in his script for the film *My
Beautiful Laundrette*.
Birds of Passage
[FB335] Amber Lane pbk **£3.50**
Borderline
[FB336] Methuen pbk **£2.95**
My Beautiful Laundrette
[FB336A] Faber pbk **£3.95**
**Outskirts (The King and Me/
Tomorrow - Today)**
[FB337] Calder pbk **£3.95**

LEIGH, MIKE (1943 -)
Abigail's Party/Goosepimples
Two of the best examples of Leigh's stagework; like
many of his plays, both were developed by improvising with actors. The outcome is a form of social
comedy that is extremely acute and at times cruel.
[FB338] Penguin pbk **£3.95**

LEONARD, HUGH (Irish, 1926 -)
A Dubliner who has been writing comedies since the
1950s, his major successs came in 1978 with
Broadway awards for his poignant comedy *Da*. It was
filmed in 1988 with Martin Sheen in the lead.
Da/A Life/Time Was
[FB339] Penguin pbk **£3.95**

LOCHHEAD, LIZ
A poet and dramatist from Scotland, whose plays are
beginning to make an impact outside her native land.
She is committed to taking her work beyond
established institutions, believing passionately that
drama can play an important role in communicating
ideas and information to the wider community.
**Mary Queen of Scots Got Her
Head Chopped Off/Dracula**   **NEW**
[FB340] Penguin pbk **£3.99**

LUCIE, DOUG
Lucie's plays dissect the style obsessions of the
privileged, often contrasting their gruesome power
games with the deeper issues facing the world beyond
their doors. *Fashion*, centred on the world of
advertising, was first staged by the RSC in 1987.
Fashion
[FB341] Methuen pbk **£3.50**
Progress/Hard Feelings
[FB342] Methuen pbk **£4.50**

MACDONALD, SHARMAN
**When I Was a Girl, I Used to Scream
and Shout**
A West End success from 1984, which reviews with
wry sympathy the various difficulties and sexual
misadventures of a girl growing up in 1950s Scotland,
her life made all the more impossible by a repressive,
possessive mother.
[FB343] Faber pbk **£3.95**

MACDONALD, STEPHEN
Not About Heroes
Intriguing two-man play which has been produced
many times since its Edinburgh debut in 1982,

including versions for television and radio. It
concentrates on the friendship which grew up
between Siegfried Sassoon and Wilfred Owen during
a period of the First World War when both were in an
Edinburgh hospital.
[FB344] Faber pbk **£4.95**

MCGRATH, JOHN (1935 -)
Founder of the influential touring companies 7:84,
McGrath developed a style of popular theatre
involving song, dance and story in an attempt to reach
an audience beyond the margins of institutional
theatre. An unusual figure, his forceful manifesto *A
Good Night Out* is of considerable interest.
**The Cheviot, the Stag and the Black,
Black Oil**
First performed in 1973, a celebrated touring play
which describes the social experiences and
exploitation of the Highlands from the time of the
clearances to the North Sea boom.
[FB349] Methuen pbk **£4.50**

MARCHANT, TONY
Speculators (1987)
Entertaining attack on City whizz-kids, and their
world of greed, Porsches and nervous breakdowns.
[FB345] Amber Lane P pbk **£3.95**
The Attractions
An old man running a declining horror museum on
the South Coast is disturbed by the appearance of a
sinister young man with extreme ideas.
[FB346] Amber Lane pbk **£3.95**

MATHIAS, SEAN
Two plays from an award-winning writer who has
also made considerable impact in recent years as both
director and producer.
A Prayer for Wings
Studies the close bonds between mother and daughter,
both trapped in different ways by the mother's
multiple sclerosis.
[FB347] Amber Lane pbk **£3.95**
Infidelities
A dark, elaborate comedy with echoes of Joe Orton.
Married life is torn apart when a violent young
homosexual appears in the couple's home, claiming to
be their long-lost son.
[FB348] Amber Lane pbk **£3.95**

MERCER, DAVID (1928 - 1980)
A prolific writer and idiosyncratic Marxist, much
of Mercer's early work was for television, though
he was often associated with the RSC from the mid-
1960s onwards. His plays are fraught with
class conflict and social alienation, forces which
drive his characters to acts of eccentricity or
rebellion.
After Haggerty
[FB350] Methuen pbk **£4.50**
**Cousin Vladimir & Shooting the
Chandelier**
[FB351] Methuen pbk **£4.50**
Duck Song
[FB352] Methuen pbk **£4.50**
No Limits to Love
[FB353] Methuen pbk **£4.50**
**The Monster of Karlovy Vary/
Then and Now**
[FB354] Methuen pbk **£4.50**

MINGHELLA, ANTHONY
Interior: Room, Exterior: City   **NEW**
Two plays from 1988, *Cigarettes and Chocolate* and
Hang Up, with the earlier acclaimed television play,
What If It's Raining?, concentrating on a familiar
Minghella theme of sexual irresponsibility.
[FB355] Methuen pbk **£4.99**
Made in Bangkok (1986)
Dramatized indictment of Western attempts to exploit

the East which follows a group of Westerners as they
tour the brothels of Bangkok.
[FB356] Methuen pbk **£3.50**
Whale Music
[FB357] Methuen pbk **£4.95**

MITCHELL, JULIAN (1935 -)
Another Country (1982)
Mitchell's best known play examines the various
pressures experienced by two 'misfits' within a 1930s
English public school - one a homosexual, and one a
committed Marxist - and how it finally leads to
treachery.
[FB358] Amber Lane pbk **£3.95**

MORTIMER, JOHN (1923 -)
Barrister, novelist and dramatist, Mortimer offers wry
critiques of bourgeois England.
A Voyage Round My Father (1971)
A semi-autobiographical portrait of Mortimer's blind
barrister father, memorably played by Sir Alec
Guinness in the original stage production, and then by
Laurence Olivier in an excellent television adaptation.
Also contains: *What Shall We Tell Caroline?* and
Dock Brief.
[FB359] Penguin pbk **£3.95**
**Edwin/Bermondsey Marble Arch/Fear of
Heaven/Prince of Darkness**
[FB360] Penguin pbk **£3.50**

MURPHY, TOM (Irish, 1935 -)
A leading figure in contemporary Irish drama,
Murphy's first significant play was *A Whistle in the
Dark* (1961) told in sometimes harrowing terms of the
despair faced by a group of Irish immigrants in
England. The three plays included in *After Tragedy*
are among his finest works; among them is the poetic
Bailegangaire, in which the mad, rambling memories
of an old women are set against those of her
granddaughters, who struggle to leave behind the pain
that the past holds for them.
**A Whistle in the Dark and Other
Plays**   **NEW**
[FB361] Methuen pbk **£4.95**
After Tragedy
[FB362] Methuen pbk **£4.95**

NICHOLS, PETER (1927 -)
Nichols' work often focuses on painful domestic
situations, as in his best known play, *A Day in the
Death of Joe Egg* (1967), where a couple struggle to
look after their handicapped child. He also has a talent
for more extravagant works which mix various styles,
such as *Poppy* (1983), a pantomime parody, complete
with horses, about the Chinese opium wars.
Plays: One
Forget-Me-Not Lane/Hearts and Flowers/Neither Up
Nor Down/Chez Nous/Privates on Parade.
[FB366] Methuen pbk **£4.99**
A Day in the Death of Joe Egg
[FB363] Faber pbk **£2.95**
A Piece of My Mind
[FB364] Methuen pbk **£4.50**
Passion Play
[FB365] Methuen pbk **£4.50**
Poppy
[FB367] Methuen pbk **£4.50**
The National Health
[FB368] Faber pbk **£3.50**

O'CASEY, SEAN (Irish, 1880 - 1964)
Born into a poor Protestant family, O'Casey was self-
educated, working as a manual labourer for many
years before revealing his talents as a dramatist. A
nationalist, he took part in the Easter Rebellion of
1916 and remained committed to political causes all
his life. His greatest work is the Dublin trilogy, *The
Shadow of a Gunman* (1923), *Juno and the Paycock*
(1924) and *The Plough and the Stars* (1926), all

produced by the Abbey Theatre. The popularity of his first two plays provided valuable funds for the Abbey, while *The Plough and the Stars* sparked riotous scenes, provoked by the critical stance it took on the 1916 uprising. The trilogy offers an eloquent diagnosis of Ireland's troubles, combining elements of wild comedy with tragic insight. O'Casey's later work was of a formal nature, experimental and expressionistic, and though often dismissed, these plays have been successfully produced by the Abbey in recent years.

Seven Plays of Sean O'Casey
[FB369] Macmillan hbk **£35.00**
[FB370] Macmillan pbk **£10.95**
Three Plays
Juno and the Paycock/The Shadow of a Gunman/The Plough and the Stars.
[FB371] Pan pbk **£3.99**

ORTON, JOE (1933 - 1967)
A writer of mercurial brilliance, Orton has perhaps become better known for the impetuosity of his brief life, and the brutal manner of his death, described in the absorbing biography and film, *Prick Up Your Ears*. His most popular play is *Entertaining Mr Sloane*, which enjoyed both success and scandal when first staged in 1964. Orton's love of the grotesque, his sudden flights of outrageous excess, are finely balanced by the intricacy of his plays' construction, exemplified in his last stage-work, the much-underrated burlesque, *What the Butler Saw*, not produced until 1969, two years after his death.

The Complete Plays
Entertaining Mr Sloane/Loot/What the Butler Saw/The Ruffian on the Stair/The Erpingham Camp/Funeral Games/The Good and Faithful Servant.
[FB372] Methuen pbk **£5.99**

OSBORNE, JOHN (1929 -)
Perhaps the most famous 'Angry Young Man' of the 1950s, Osborne's drama introduced a radical departure from the stylized elegance of Coward and Rattigan, which had dominated the English theatre of his youth. Although he may be best known for the direct, gritty 'realism' of his plays, one of his main strengths has been his ability to constantly create challenging characters at the heart of his work.

A Patriot for Me & A Sense of Detachment
[FB373] Faber pbk **£3.95**
A Subject of Scandal and Concern
[FB374] Faber pbk **£0.60**
Epitaph for George Dillon
[FB375] Faber pbk **£0.60**
Inadmissable Evidence
[FB376] Faber pbk **£2.95**
Look Back in Anger
Introduced the first 'angry young man', Jimmy Porter, in 1956; it now survives as a play which successfully reflects personal rather than more political concerns.
[FB377] Faber pbk **£2.50**
Luther
[FB378] Faber pbk **£2.95**

Harold Pinter, whose plays are published by Methuen Paperbacks

Strindberg's 'The Father' & Ibsen's 'Hedda Gabler'
[FB379] Faber pbk **£5.99**
The Entertainer
Centred on a seedy comic, Archie Rice, who features in desperate revues, immortalized on stage and screen by Laurence Olivier.
[FB380] Faber pbk **£2.95**

PAGE, LOUISE
Contemporary playwight who has a growing following all over Europe.
Diplomatic Wives   NEW
Like many of Page's plays, its theme dwells on the nature of female ambition, as a woman faces a crisis, choosing between her undynamic husband and a challenging diplomatic post overseas.
[FB381] Methuen pbk **£4.50**
Golden Girls
Much acclaimed play, staged by the RSC in 1984, charting the pressures faced by a women's Olympic relay team, where drugs, racism, and sexism move in perilous harness with the women's burning determination to succeed.
[FB382] Methuen pbk **£4.50**

PARKER, STEWART
Three Plays: Northern Star, Heavenly Bodies, Pentecost   NEW
Three plays from 1983-87, set in different periods of Irish history: '…a freewheeling lunatic sense of invention, harnessed to a cultivated, literary imagination.' (John Peter).
[FB383] Oberon pbk **£6.50**

PINTER, HAROLD (1930 -)
A former actor, born and educated in London's East End, Pinter's singular style has been a dominating influence on contemporary British drama. His early, and perhaps still most celebrated plays, such as *The Birthday Party* (1957), and *The Caretaker* (1960) share many affinities with Samuel Beckett, although, unlike Beckett, Pinter choses naturalistic, easily recognizable settings for his ominous dramas which serve to heighten their sense of menace and alarm. He has a remarkable ear for the speech rhythms of English, and his careful control of pause and silence help to reveal the ambiguities and various implications of seemingly bland dialogue.

Plays: One
The Birthday Party/The Room/The Dumb Waiter/The Hothouse/A Slight Ache/A Night Out.
[FB389] Methuen pbk **£3.95**
Plays: Two
The Caretaker/Night School/The Dwarfs/The Collection/The Lover/Fire Revue Sketches.
[FB391] Methuen pbk **£3.95**
Plays: Three
The Homecoming/Tea Party/The Basement/Landscape/Silence/Six Revue Sketches.
[FB390] Methuen pbk **£3.99**
Plays: Four
Old Times/No Man's Land/Betrayal/Monologue/Family Voices.
[FB388] Methuen pbk **£3.95**
A Slight Ache and Other Plays
A Slight Ache/A Night Out/The Dwarfs/Revue Sketches.
[FB384] Methuen pbk **£4.50**
Mountain Language   NEW
[FB385] Faber pbk **£2.95**
One for the Road
[FB386] Methuen pbk **£4.50**
Other Places
Family Voices/Victoria Station/A Kind of Alaska.
[FB387] Methuen pbk **£4.50**
Tea Party and Other Plays
Tea Party /Night School /The Basement.
[FB392] Methuen pbk **£4.50**

The Birthday Party
[FB393] Methuen pbk **£4.50**
The Caretaker
[FB394] Methuen pbk **£4.50**

POLIAKOFF, STEPHEN (1952 -)
Breaking the Silence (1984)
This play, an exciting story set just before the Russian revolution, marked a turning point for Poliakoff, realizing the promise which had sometimes been clouded in his earlier plays of urban malaise and alienation. Its first performance by the RSC was one of the great successes of 1984.
Plays One   NEW
Clever Soldiers/Hitting Town/City Sugar/Shout Across the River/American Days/Strawberry Fields.
[FB398] Methuen pbk **£4.99**
Breaking the Silence
[FB396] Methuen pbk **£4.50**
Coming in to Land
[FB396] Methuen pbk **£4.50**
Playing with Trains   NEW
[FB397] Methuen pbk **£4.99**

POTTER, DENNIS (1935 -)
Few television dramas have enjoyed the controversy and acclaim of Potter's *The Singing Detective*, a bizarre mix of popular song, hospital beds and pulp fiction heroes, which moves effortlessly between the past, the present and the imagined.
Sufficient Carbohydrate
[FB399] Faber pbk **£3.50**
The Singing Detective
[FB400] Faber pbk **£4.95**
Waiting for the Boat
Blue Remembered Hills/Joe's Ark/Cream in My Coffee
[FB401] Faber pbk **£3.50**

PRIESTLEY, J.B. (1894 - 1984)
Priestley's dramatic output was varied, ranging from satire, such as *Laburnum Grove* (1933), to more experimental plays like *Dragon's Mouth* (1952). He is probably best known, however, for his series of 'Time' plays from the 1930s, of which *I Have Been Here Before* and *Time and the Conways* are fine examples, both using surprising shifts of time as an entertaining theatrical device. His most consistently popular play remains the psychological mystery, *An Inspector Calls* (1947).
An Inspector Calls
[FB402] Heinemann pbk **£2.75**
Time and the Conways
With *I Have Been Here Before*, *An Inspector Calls*, *Linden Tree*.
[FB403] Penguin pbk **£3.99**

RATTIGAN, TERENCE (1911 - 1977)
French Without Tears was Rattigan's first play and the best example of his early light comedies; it made him a celebrity when it first appeared in 1936. The plays written immediately after the war have a more sombre tone, as can be seen in his scathing treatment of an unjust naval establishment in *The Winslow Boy* (1946), or in the various levels of personal failure detailed in *The Browning Version* (1948). Nevertheless, his popularity reached its height at this time, and despite the sometimes bitter criticisms he faced from the new wave of writers in the 1950s, his work has endured, distinguished by a fine sense of timing and psychological subtlety.
Plays: One
French Without Tears/The Winslow Boy/The Browning Version/Harlequinade.
[FB404] Methuen pbk **£3.95**
Plays: Two
The Deep Blue Sea/Separate Tables/In Praise of Love.
[FB405] Methuen pbk **£3.95**

REID, GRAHAM (Irish, 1945 -)

Two volumes of television plays set in Reid's native Belfast describing family lives torn by psychological disturbance and sectarian tensions. The stage-play *Remembrance* (1984) tells of a love affair across the Belfast divide, and the impact it has on two families.

Billy: Three Plays for Television
[FB406] Faber pbk **£5.95**

Remembrance
[FB407] Faber pbk **£3.95**

Ties of Blood
[FB408] Faber pbk **£4.95**

RUSSELL, WILLY (1947 -)

Educating Rita/ Blood Brothers/ Stags and Hens
Educating Rita (1980), filmed with Julie Walters and Michael Caine, tells of an intelligent Liverpool woman's hunger for education, while *Blood Brothers* (1983) is an unusual musical which, avoiding the conventional trappings, centres on twin brothers growing up in different circumstances.
[FB409] Methuen pbk **£4.50**

Shirley Valentine & One for the Road
Shirley Valentine (1988) has won awards both in the West End and on Broadway. It is an entertaining one-woman play focusing on a Liverpool housewife's desire to rattle the chains of her drab life.
[FB410] Methuen pbk **£4.95**

SHAFFER, ANTHONY

Twin brother of Peter, his crafty suspense thriller *Sleuth* (1970) has enjoyed huge popular success over the years.

Murderer
[FB411] Boyars pbk **£3.95**

Sleuth
[FB412] Boyars pbk **£4.50**

This Savage Parade
[FB413] Amber Lane pbk **£3.95**

SHAFFER, PETER (1926 -)

Shaffer has provided the National Theatre with some of its most successful productions of contemporary plays - notably *The Royal Hunt of the Sun* (1964), an epic account of the conquest of Peru, and then later with his two masterpieces *Equus* (1973) and *Amadeus* (1979). His latest play, *Lettice and Lovage* (1987), an elegant comedy which originally starred Maggie Smith, has enjoyed a lengthy West End run.

Amadeus
[FB414] Penguin pbk **£3.50**

Equus
[FB415] Penguin pbk **£2.99**

Equus/Shrivings/Five Finger Exercises
[FB416] Penguin pbk **£4.95**

Four Plays
[FB417] Penguin pbk **£4.95**

Lettice & Lovage/Yonnadab NEW
[FB418] Penguin pbk **£4.99**

The Royal Hunt of the Sun
[FB419] Penguin pbk **£3.50**

SHERIFF, R.C. (1896 - 1975)

An insurance clerk who served in World War I and was wounded at Flanders, Sheriff is remembered for one work, his powerful anti-war play, *Journey's End*. It was first staged in 1928 and made an almost immediate world-wide impact.

Journey's End
[FB420] Penguin pbk **£2.95**

SIMPSON, N.F. (1919 -)

Two surreal and strangely anarchic plays, which enjoyed much popularity in their Royal Court productions of the 1950s.

A Resounding Tinkle
[FB421] Faber pbk **£2.25**

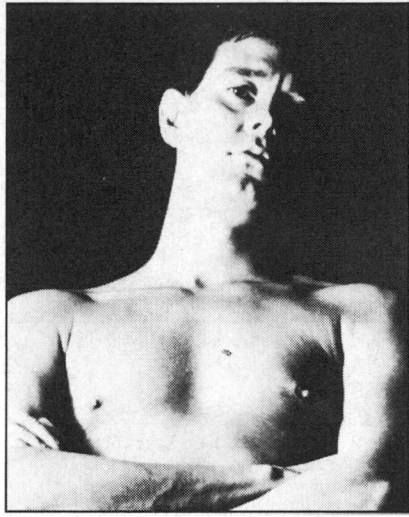

Joe Orton, whose *Complete Plays* are published by Methuen (pbk **£5.99**)

One Way Pendulum
Successfully revived by Jonathan Miller at the Old Vic in 1988.
[FB422] Faber pbk **£3.95**

STOPPARD, TOM (1937 -)

Stoppard won instant fame with *Rosencrantz and Guildenstern Are Dead* (1966), and his later plays have confirmed his ingenious talent for combining levity and seriousness. A highly conceptual dramatist, Stoppard has enjoyed considerable success in commercial theatre all over the world. He combines complex philosophical speculation with extravagant wit and remarkable theatrical invention.

After Magritte
[FB423] Faber pbk **£2.95**

Dalliance & Undiscovered Country
[FB424] Faber pbk **£2.95**

Dirty Linen & New-Found Land
[FB425] Faber pbk **£2.99**

Dogg's Hamlet, Cahoot's Macbeth
[FB426] Faber pbk **£3.95**

Enter A Free Man
[FB427] Faber pbk **£3.50**

Every Good Boy Deserves Favour/Professional Foul
[FB428] Faber pbk **£2.95**

Hapgood
[FB429] Faber pbk **£3.95**

Jumpers
[FB430] Faber pbk **£3.95**

Night and Day
[FB431] Faber pbk **£2.50**

On the Razzle
[FB432] Faber pbk **£2.95**

Rosencrantz and Guildenstern are Dead
[FB433] Faber pbk **£2.50**

Rough Crossing
[FB434] Faber pbk **£3.95**

Squaring the Circle/Professional Foul/Every Good Boy Deserves Favour
[FB435] Faber pbk **£4.95**

The Dog It Was That Died & Other Plays
[FB436] Faber pbk **£3.95**

The Real Inspector Hound
[FB437] Faber pbk **£2.50**

The Real Thing
[FB438] Faber pbk **£3.95**

Travesties
[FB439] Faber pbk **£2.95**

STOREY, DAVID (1933 -)

In his novels and plays Storey combines an understated realism with a subtle use of allegory. *Home* (1970) and *Early Days* (1980) are fine examples of his work; both starred Ralph Richardson in the original productions and, like many of Storey's sharpest and most affecting plays, both were directed by Lindsay Anderson.

Early Days/Sisters/Life Class
[FB440] Penguin pbk **£4.95**

Home/The Changing Room/Mother's Day
[FB441] Penguin pbk **£3.95**

SYNGE, J.M. (Irish, 1871 - 1909)

Synge was a leading figure in the Abbey Theatre which stimulated the revival of Irish drama from 1904. He is best known for his rich comedy *The Playboy of the Western World* (1907), and for the notorious riots provoked by the indecorous picture of Irish life he presented in the play. His writing often expresses his strong feeling for rural Ireland and its dialects, transposing its sound and rhythm in his lyrical dialogue, inspired by his visits to the Aran Islands at the turn of the century.

The Complete Plays
The Playboy of the Western World/The Tinker's Wedding/In the Shadow of the Glen/Riders to the Sea/The Well of the Saints/Deirdre of the Sorrows.
[FB442] Methuen pbk **£2.95**

The Playboy of the Western World
[FB443] A & C Black pbk **£3.95**

TAYLOR, CECIL P. (Scottish, 1928 - 1981)

A prolific dramatist, with over 70 plays to his credit, Taylor was closely associated with the Live Theatre Company in Newcastle and wrote many plays for performance in the North East and Edinburgh. Whether the plays were local community projects or West End productions such as *Good* (1981), a vital energy runs through his work that charms even the most unpromising material to life.

And A Nightingale Sang
[FB444] Methuen pbk **£4.50**

Good
[FB445] Methuen pbk **£4.50**

North: Six Plays
[FB446] Methuen pbk **£5.95**

TERSON, PETER (1932 -)

Strippers
Set in a depressed North East, *Strippers* sympathetically describes a group of women who take to stripping to supplement social security. It provoked much debate when staged in 1984, some feeling it celebrated a dubious form of entertainment.
[FB447] Amber Lane pbk **£3.50**

Zigger Zagger/Mooney and His Caravans
An immense success when first staged by the National Youth Theatre in 1967, *Zigger Zagger* looks at football fans and hooligans through their rituals and passions, displaying Terson's fine command of large ensemble scenes.
[FB448] Penguin pbk **£3.50**

THOMAS, DYLAN (1914 - 1953)

Under Milk Wood
The celebrated radio play, from 1953, carried all the magical power for which his poetry is renowned. It is filled with extraordinary images and rich wit, weaving evocatively through the lives of an unforgettable array of characters who live, love, die and dream in a small Welsh coastal town.
[FB449] Dent pbk **£1.25**

WALL, MICHAEL

Amongst Barbarians NEW
An award-winning play staged in 1989, this is Wall's first major work for the stage, although he is also

known for his radio drama. *Amongst Barbarians* concerns the plight of two Englishmen sentenced to death in Malaysia for drug-trafficking.
[FB450] N Hern pbk **£4.50**

WERTENBAKER, TIMBERLAKE
A French-born dramatist, now living in London. Her plays have been seen since the early 1980s, her breakthrough coming in 1988, with the award-winning *Our Country's Good*; based on the Thomas Keneally novel, *The Playmaker*, it tells the story of a production of *The Recruiting Officer* staged by convicts in Australia at the end of the 18th century.

Our Country's Good
[FB451] Methuen pbk **£3.50**

The Love of the Nightingale & The Grace of Mary Traverse
[FB452] Faber pbk **£5.99**

WESKER, ARNOLD (1932 -)
Wesker is one of the key figures responsible for implanting a radical, optimistic socialism into British drama in the 1950s.

The Journalists/The Wedding Feast/The Merchant
[FB453] Penguin pbk **£3.50**

The Wesker Trilogy
Three linked plays (*Chicken Soup with Barley*, *Roots*, *I'm Talking About Jerusalem*) which begin with a Jewish family in 1930s Hackney, where Wesker was born. *Roots* (1959), which follows a young woman in pursuit of education, was revived in 1989.
[FB454] Penguin pbk **£3.95**

Volume 5: One Woman Plays **NEW**
Five plays which appeared between 1982 and 1988, they bring into focus Wesker's rare ability to craft intelligent and affecting monologues for women. Includes: *Yardsale*, *Whatever Happened to Betty Lemon?*, *Four Portraits - of Mothers*, *The Mistress*, *Annie Wobbler*.
[FB455] Penguin pbk **£5.99**

WHITEMORE, HUGH (1936 -)
Breaking the Code (1986)
Centres on Alan Turing, the brilliant mathematician who deciphered the German Enigma codes in World War II.
[FB456] Amber Lane pbk **£3.95**

Arnold Wesker, author of *The Merchant* (Photo: Methuen)

Pack of Lies (1983)
A big West End success, this is a story of betrayal set against the 1960 Portland spy case.
[FB457] Amber Lane pbk **£3.95**

Stevie (1977)
Whitemore's first stage play, based on the life of Stevie Smith.
[FB458] Amber Lane pbk **£3.50**

The Best of Friends (1988)
A curious portrait of an elderly George Bernard Shaw, focusing on two occasionally eccentric friendships.
[FB459] Amber Lane pbk **£3.95**

WRIGHT, NICHOLAS
Mrs Klein **NEW**
Wright's first play for the National Theatre, where he was literary manager, centres on Melanie Klein, still a controversial figure in psychoanalysis. The play describes her response to her son's death in a climbing accident and was well received when it appeared in the West End at the end of 1988.
[FB461] N Hern pbk **£3.95**

YEATS, W.B. (Irish, 1865 - 1939)
Yeats's blank verse drama, *The Countess Cathleen* (1899) heralded the modern revival in Irish drama. He drew from Irish myth and folklore to create a tale of a woman attempting to help the poor in time of famine, eventually selling her own soul to demons to protect herself. Yeats believed that the flat realism of the 19th century had failed to inspire audiences, and in response he founded the National Theatre of Ireland - the Abbey - with Lady Gregory in 1904. Although his own plays are steeped in the beautiful 'sovereignty of words' for which his poetry is celebrated, they failed to reach a popular audience. The Abbey Theatre, however, introduced many new writers, among them Synge and O'Casey, and with Yeats as a guiding light, it became a vital forum for the Irish cultural revival at the beginning of the century.

Collected Plays
[FB462] Macmillan pbk **£11.95**
Selected Plays
[FB463] Pan pbk **£2.95**

W.B. Yeats in 1935, drawn by I. Opfer (Picture: National Portrait Gallery)

American

Four American Plays
Four plays from the early 1960s, with an introduction by Charles Marowitz. Albee, *American Dream*; Richardson *Gallows Humour*; Schisgal, *Typist*; Miller, *Incident at Vichy*.
[FB466] Penguin pbk **£4.95**

Plays from the New York Shakespeare Festival (Ed. Papp, Joseph)
The New York Shakespeare Festival was founded by Joseph Papp in 1954, and every summer gives productions of Shakespeare, while also staging new works from America and Europe. This collection includes *Necessary Ends* by Marvin Cohen (produced 1983), *The Time Trial* by Jack Gilhooey (1975), *Short Eyes* by Miguel Piñero (1974), *Streamers* by David Rabe (1976), *The Least People* by Dennis Reardon (1975), and *For Colored Girls…* by Ntozake Shange (1976).
[FB467] Ianmead pbk **£9.50**

ALBEE, EDWARD (1928 -)
Who's Afraid of Virginia Woolf?
Albee emerged explosively in the early 1960s with a series of dramas, torn by violent conflicts. His reputation was crowned by the Broadway production of *Who's Afraid of Virginia Woolf?* in 1962, in which, over the course of a drunken night, a husband and wife cruelly strip their marriage of all protective illusions, with tragic consequences.
[FB469] Penguin pbk **£2.95**

ASHBERY, JOHN (1927 -)
Three Plays
Experimental New York poet, who won the Pulitzer Prize in 1975, Ashbery began his writing career with these plays. Includes: *The Heroes*, *The Compromise*, and *The Philosopher*.
[FB470] Carcanet hbk **£10.95**

FIERSTEIN, HARVEY
Torch Song Trilogy
Three linked plays which describe the life and loves of a New York drag queen, swaying between wild comedy and anguish. Fierstein won great acclaim when the play opened in 1983; he has successfully repeated his starring role in the 1989 film version.
[FB471] Methuen pbk **£3.95**

HWANG, DAVID HENRY
M Butterfly NEW
The winner of four major awards for best American play of 1988, *M Butterfly* tells the story of a French diplomat's love for a Chinese diva, who is in fact a man. Hwang attempts to expose a chain of misconceptions with this play, undermining a complex series of sexual and cultural myths.
[FB472] Penguin pbk **£3.99**

KAUFMAN, GEORGE S. (1889 - 1961) & HART, MOSS (1904 - 1961)
Once in a Lifetime/You Can't Take It With You/The Man Who Came to Dinner
Three popular comedies from the 1930s, set against the backdrop of the Depression, introduced by the authors.
[FB473] Methuen pbk **£4.50**

KOPIT, ARTHUR (1937 -)
Indians
First staged in 1968, combining elements of circus and vaudeville, the play is a critical study of the treatment, and eventual genocide, of North American Indians by white settlers.
[FB474] Methuen pbk **£4.50**

Wings
[FB475] Methuen pbk **£4.50**

KRAMER, LARRY
The Normal Heart
The Normal Heart tells of a man's passionate determination to break through the silent hostility and fear with which AIDS sufferers were initially treated.
[FB476] Methuen pbk **£4.50**

MAMET, DAVID (1947 -)
David Mamet is one of the most distinctive and original writers to have emerged in American theatre during the 1970s. His tightly-paced, dark visions of city life are filled with the often violent, subtly shifting voices of the Chicago streets. Recently he has worked in cinema, both as writer and director; his latest play, *Speed-the-Plow*, staged by the National Theatre in 1989, is a tough satire on modern Hollywood dreams.
A Life in the Theatre NEW
[FB477] Methuen pbk **£4.99**
American Buffalo
[FB478] Methuen pbk **£4.50**
Edmond
[FB479] Methuen pbk **£2.95**
Glengarry Glen Ross
[FB480] Methuen pbk **£4.50**
Speed-the-Plow NEW
[FB481] Methuen pbk **£4.50**
The Shawl & Prairie du Chien NEW
[FB482] Methuen pbk **£4.99**

MEDOFF, MARK
Children of a Lesser God
Medoff's most popular play, first performed in 1979, concerns the troubled relationship between a teacher for the deaf and one of his students.
[FB483] Amber Lane pbk **£3.95**

MILLER, ARTHUR (1915 -)
Arthur Miller was the dominating presence in American theatre from the late 1940s to the 1960s. He developed a dramatic form steeped in realism, skilfully counterpointed by his characters' frustrated desires for poetic expression. 1987 saw the publication of his excellent autobiography, *Timebends*.
Collected Plays: Vol 1 NEW
All My Sons/Death of a Salesman/The Crucible/ A Memory of Two Mondays/A View from the Bridge.
[FB487] Methuen pbk **£4.50**
Collected Plays: Vol 2 NEW
The Misfits/After the Fall/Incident at Vichy/The Price/The Creation of the World and Other Business/Playing for Time.
[FB488] Methuen pbk **£4.95**
A View from the Bridge/All My Sons
First performed in 1955, and a recent hit in the West End, *A View From the Bridge* tells the tragic story of a hard-working, illiterate Sicilian's attempts to escape from his oppressive social environment and his fatal transgression of the unwritten law of silence which surrounds illegal immigrants.
[FB484] Penguin pbk **£2.95**
After the Fall
[FB485] Penguin pbk **£3.50**
An Enemy of the People NEW
Miller's poweful adaptation of Ibsen's play was recently staged at the Young Vic.
[FB486] N Hern pbk **£4.50**
Danger: Memory!
[FB489] Methuen pbk **£4.50**
Death of a Salesman
Miller's masterpiece, first seen in 1949, is one of the most important modern American plays. Willy Loman, sixty year old Brooklyn salesman, is doomed

to speak in worn clichés which can never express the weight of his aspirations; his insecurities and vain delusions are painfully laid bare as the play charts his downfall.
[FB490] Penguin pbk **£2.50**
Golden Years/The Man Who Had All the Luck NEW
[FB491] Methuen pbk **£4.95**
Incident at Vichy
[FB492] Penguin pbk **£2.50**
The American Clock
[FB493] Methuen pbk **£4.50**
The Archbishop's Ceiling
[FB494] Methuen pbk **£4.50**
The Crucible
Perhaps Miller's most immediate and powerful play, it centres on the Salem witchcraft trials of the 17th century. Written at the height of the McCarthy era in the 1950s, it is a savage indictment of the superstitious malice that gripped both 'witch-hunts'.
[FB495] Penguin pbk **£2.95**
Two Way Mirror: A Double Bill of Elegy for a Lady & Some Kind of Love
[FB496] Methuen pbk **£4.50**

NELSON, RICHARD
A playwright from Chicago whose work has been regularly seen in England. Nelson's most recent play, *Some Americans Abroad*, sets a group of tourists against various English landmarks, from Shakespeare's birthplace to a London hamburger bar, raising a curious interplay of ideas.
Sensibility and Sense
[FB497] Faber pbk **£4.95**
Some Americans Abroad
[FB498] Faber pbk **£3.95**

NORMAN, MARSHA
Night, Mother
Marsha Norman won the Pulitzer Prize in 1983 for this play, a distressing two-hander which focuses on the last hours of a woman planning suicide. The night has been prepared meticulously, even down to providing her mother's favourite sweets…
[FB499] Faber pbk **£3.95**

O'NEILL, EUGENE (1888 - 1953)
Nobel Prize for Literature 1936. Eugene O'Neill was the first great, and perhaps the greatest, American playwright. His work crafted new forms for American drama, depicting contemporary life in surroundings rich in symbolism and myth, giving the often crude vernacular speech of his characters a strange, halting lyricism.
Collected Plays
Excellent volume, which includes 45 plays, from his failures to his greatest work.
[FB500] Cape hbk **£40.00**
Long Day's Journey Into Night
The story of an exhausted actor's decline into alcoholism, and its effect on his family, for which O'Neill drew on his own experience of his father. It is an intense, personal play, not seen until 1956, three years after O'Neill's death.
[FB501] Cape pbk **£3.95**
Mourning Becomes Electra
An extraordinary trilogy lasting six hours, first staged in 1931, transposing the story of Aeschylus' *Oresteia* to Puritan New England.
[FB502] Cape pbk **£6.95**
The Iceman Cometh
A group of dead-beat drunks play out their delusions in a whiskey bar, driven - like so many of O'Neill's characters - to the edge of ruin by their destructive passions. The play had a long run on Broadway in 1946.
[FB503] Cape pbk **£5.95**

ODETS, CLIFFORD (1906 - 1963)
Six Plays
Waiting for Lefty/Awake and Sing!/Till the Day I Die/Paradise Lost/Golden Boy/Rocket to the Moon. These six plays from the leading social protest dramatist of the Depression era were all staged during the 1930s by the Group Theatre, of which Odets was a founder. They gave voice to the anger and sorrow of classes dispossessed by the economic recession.
[FB504] Methuen pbk **£4.95**

SHANGE, NTOZAKE
For colored girls who have considered suicide/when the Rainbow is enuf
A hypnotic prose poem, involving words, music and dance, exploring the experiences of seven Black women. It had immediate impact when first performed in 1974 to an audience of twenty; the play developed, and reached Broadway just two years later.
[FB505] Methuen pbk **£4.50**
Spell Number Seven
[FB506] Methuen pbk **£3.50**

SHEPARD, SAM (1943 -)
Shepard's vast American landscape is a lonely one, where characters seem haunted by a kind of rootless desolation. The sense of despair broken by sudden flights of optimism was captured particularly strongly in the film *Paris, Texas*, written by Shepard for the director Wim Wenders.
A Lie of the Mind
[FB507] Methuen pbk **£4.50**
Fool for Love/The Sad Lament of Bill Pecos on the Eve of Killing His Wife
[FB508] Faber pbk **£3.95**
Seven Plays
Includes *Buried Child*, *Curse of the Starving Classes*, *The Tooth of Crime*, *La Turista*, *Savage Love*, *Tongues*, *True West*. Introduction by Richard Gilman.
[FB509] Faber pbk **£4.95**

SHERMAN, MARTIN
Martin Sherman, an American now living in London, is probably best known for the play *Bent*; set in 1930s Nazi Germany, *Bent* describes the brutal treatment, and ultimate defiance, of a homosexual couple.
A Madhouse in Goa   **NEW**
[FB510] Amber Lane pbk **£4.50**
Bent
[FB511] Amber Lane pbk **£3.95**
Messiah
[FB512] Amber Lane pbk **£3.50**
When She Danced
[FB513] Amber Lane pbk **£3.95**

WILDER, THORNTON (1897 - 1975)
Our Town/The Skin of Our Teeth/The Matchmaker
Our Town, a picture of a small-town life in New Hampshire, opened on Broadway in 1938; it proved both popular and provocative, introducing many of the formal experiments and narrative techniques that Wilder also developed in his novels.
[FB514] Penguin pbk **£4.50**

WILLIAMS, TENNESSEE (1911 - 1983)
In the period between his first Broadway success, *The Glass Menagerie* in 1945, and *The Night of the Iguana* in 1961, Tennessee Williams produced his most original and exciting work. Suffused with an air of Southern decadence, his plays are charged with erotic tension, his characters frequently tortured by desires which promise both release and ruin. Although the quality of his later work somewhat clouded his reputation, in recent years there has been a resurgence of interest: *The Glass Menagerie, A*

Streetcar Named Desire, and *Cat on a Hot Tin Roof* are frequently revived, and are acknowledged masterpieces of American drama.
Baby Doll/Something Unspoken/Suddenly Last Summer
[FB515] Penguin pbk **£3.95**
Cat on a Hot Tin Roof & Other Plays
[FB516] Penguin pbk **£4.50**
Five Plays
Cat on a Hot Tin Roof/The Rose Tattoo/Something Unspoken/Suddenly Last Summer/Orpheus Descending.
[FB517] Secker hbk **£12.95**
Period of Adjustment/Summer and Smoke/Small Craft Warnings
[FB518] Penguin pbk **£3.95**
Rose Tattoo/Camino Real/Orpheus Descending
[FB519] Penguin pbk **£5.95**
Sweet Bird of Youth/A Streetcar Named Desire/The Glass Menagerie
[FB520] Penguin pbk **£3.99**

WILSON, AUGUST
Fences/Ma Rainey's Black Bottom
Since the 1984 production of *Ma Rainey's Black Bottom*, August Wilson has become a prominent figure in contemporary theatre. His plays address the central issues American Blacks have faced this century. *Ma Rainey* is set in 1920s Chicago and concerns a group of musicians, or more particularly their music, the Blues. *Fences*, which won the Pulitzer Prize in 1987, centres on a Black family trying to settle into an inhospitable industrial urban sprawl, set in the 1950s.
[FB521] Penguin pbk **£4.95**

WOLFE, GEORGE C.
The Colored Museum
Wolfe's satirical play lampooning Black and White America was successfully transferred from New York's Public Theater to London's Royal Court in 1987.
[FB522] Methuen pbk **£4.50**

Classical Drama

Greek Drama

It seems that Greek theatre evolved within a relatively short period in Athens in the 5th century BC, and is represented by the two forms of tragedy and comedy. Theatre was an integral part of Athenian life, presented as part of religious festivals in large, open-air auditoria. There was no scenery, and the actors - all male - wore masks; considering the distances across which their voices had to be projected, they must have adopted a grandiose style of delivery. Watling's Sophocles in the Penguin series is probably the standard translation, while Fagels' *Oresteia* contains a useful introduction on the myth behind the play. The colloquial style of Aristophanes makes him a difficult author to translate, and David Barrett in the Penguin series achieves an especially good version. In addition to these there are translations by writers famous in their own right, such as Stephen Spender, Ezra Pound and Wole Soyinka, who adapt the works more freely.

Classical Comedy: An Anthology
A series of comedies by four classical authors. Includes Aristophanes: *Lysistrata*, *The Birds* (Trans. Sutherland/Kerr); Menander, *The Grouch* (Trans. D'Attri); Plautus: *The Menaechmi*, *The Haunted*

House (Trans. Bovie); and Terence, *The Self-Tormenter* (Trans. Bovie).
[FB523] Applause pbk **£6.95**
Classical Tragedy: An Anthology
A series of tragedies by three classical authors; supplemented by commentaries and stimulating critical essays from a wide range of authors (eg. T.S. Eliot, Jan Kott, Peter Brook). Includes: Aeschylus: *Prometheus Unbound*, *The Oresteia* (Trans. Greene/Harrison); Euripides: *Medea*, *The Bacchae* (Trans. Townsend/Bagg); Seneca: *Oedipus*, *Medea* (Trans. Ahl); Sophocles, *Antigone*, *Oedipus the King* (Trans. Fitts & Fitzgerald/Carander).
[FB524] Applause pbk **£6.95**

AESCHYLUS (525 - 456 BC)
Aeschylus was distinguished both as a soldier and playwright, and is remembered as the first figure of importance in Athenian drama. He is said to have added a second actor to the existing form of protagonist and chorus, and to have reduced the size of the chorus from about 50 to 15. It seems likely that all his surviving plays formed parts of closely-linked trilogies, except for *The Persians*, which was also unique in treating a historical rather than a mythical subject; only the three plays of *The Oresteia* have survived intact. Here the complexity of poetic thought is matched by a strength of dramatic technique, creating what is unquestionably one of the great masterpieces of world literature.
The Agamemnon (Trans. Jones, H.L.)
[FB525] Duckworth pbk **£2.95**
The Agamemnon of Aeschylus (Trans. MacNeice, Louis)
[FB526] Faber pbk **£0.95**
The Oresteia (Trans. Fagels, R.)
[FB527] Penguin pbk **£3.95**
The Oresteia (Trans. Harrison, Tony)
This is the translation succesfully used by the National Theatre, both in London and on their visit to the ancient theatre at Epidaurus, where they gave the first performance by a non-Greek company.
[FB528] R Collings pbk **£3.50**
The Oresteia (Trans. Jones, H.L.)
[FB529 Duckworth pbk **£9.95**
The Oresteia (Trans. Raphael, F. & McLeish, K.)
[FB530] Cambridge pbk **£8.95**
Oresteian Trilogy (Trans. Vellacott, P.)
[FB531] Penguin pbk **£2.99**
Prometheus Bound/Suppliants/Seven Against Thebes/Persians
(Trans. Vellacott, P.)
[FB532] Penguin pbk **£2.99**

SOPHOCLES (496 - 406 BC)
If to Aeschylus the argument of the play was ultimately more important than the presentation of the individual, in the work of Sophocles this equation is reversed. His language is clearer, and his tendency is to show powerful individuals - such as Oedipus in plague-ridden Thebes, or Antigone in her insistence on burying her dead brother - at moments of crisis. The climaxes of these works provide some of the most powerful moments of world drama, and achieve a sense of serenity through triumph. This is vividly apparent the last play which Sophocles wrote, *Oedipus at Colonus*, in which the blind Oedipus, after years of remorse and blind wandering, finds tranquility in death. Aristotle based his analysis of tragedy on the work of Sophocles, and his influence has been felt throughout European literature.
Electra/Antigone/Philoctetes
(Trans. McLeish, K.)
[FB551] Cambridge pbk **£3.75**
Electra/Women of Trachis/Philoctetes/Ajax
(Trans. Watling, E.F.)
[FB552] Penguin pbk **£2.99**

King Oedipus/Oedipus at Colonus/Antigone (Trans. Watling, E.F.)
[FB553] Penguin pbk **£2.50**
Oedipus the King (Trans. Berg, S. & Clay, D.)
[FB554] Oxford pbk **£5.96**
Oedipus Trilogy (Ed. Spender, Stephen)
[FB555] Faber hbk **£12.50**
Theban Plays (Trans. Taylor, Don)
[FB556] Methuen pbk **£1.95**
Three Theban Plays (Trans. Fagels, R.)
[FB557] Penguin pbk **£4.95**
Three Theban Plays (Trans. Banks, T.H.)
[FB558] Oxford pbk **£5.50**

EURIPIDES (484 - 406 BC)
Euripides is the last and most individualistic of the great tragedians. His approach to any of the traditional subjects of legend involved a new edge of cynicism which was controversial in its time, examining extremes of behaviour, often seen in the situation of women in love, such as Medea and Hecuba, or like Electra, in search of vengeance. The use of the chorus is significantly reduced in some of his work, and the boundaries of tragedy itself are widened to include elements of tragi-comedy and melodrama.
Plays: One `NEW`
(Trans. Walton, J.M)
[FB543] Methuen pbk **£2.95**
Alcestis/Iphigenia in Tauris/ Hippolytus
(Trans. Vellacott, Philip)
[FB537] Penguin pbk **£2.95**
The Bacchae (Adapt. Soyinka, Wole)
[FB538] Methuen pbk **£4.50**
The Bacchae/Ion/Women of Troy/Helen
(Trans. Vellacott, P.)
[FB539] Penguin pbk **£3.50**
Medea/Hecabe/Electra/Heracles
(Trans. Vellacott, Philip)
[FB540] Penguin pbk **£2.99**
Orestes/The Children of Heracles/Andromache/The Suppliant Women (Trans. Vellacott, Philip)
[FB542] Penguin pbk **£5.99**
Trojan Women/Helen/The Bacchae
(Trans. Curry, N.)
[FB544] Cambridge pbk **£3.95**

ARISTOPHANES (c.448 - 380 BC)
Aristophanes's influence on subsequent drama is slight, since the form of comedy with chorus was soon to disappear. As a popular dramatist, his plays include elements of slapstick as well as literary parody and political satire, needing performance to bring out much of the humour. The fusion he achieved between commentary on contemporary issues - such as the war with Sparta in *The Acharnians* - and a fantastic use of language and disguise, is unique, revealing much about the public life of Athens at the time.
The Birds/The Knights/Peace/ Wealth/The Assembly of Women
[FB533] Penguin pbk **£4.99**
Lysistrata/The Acharnians/ The Clouds
[FB535] Penguin pbk **£4.50**
Wasps/Poet and the Woman/Frogs
[FB536] Penguin pbk **£2.95**

MENANDER (c.342 - 293 BC)
Menander's comedies of manners set against the background of the city are the only significant Greek drama of the Hellenistic age. His influence on the Roman dramatists Plautus and Terence was immense, and it is through them that the 'comedy of manners' developed in Western Europe.
Plays and Fragments
[FB545] Penguin pbk **£4.95**

Roman Drama

The subjects of the Roman theatre were largely those of the Greek 'new' comedy, involving intrigue, deception, swindling, and a range of stock characters: miserly old men, extravagant youths, jealous wives, treacherous pimps and intriguing slaves. Similar borrowings were made from Greek tragedy, concentrating on the more melodramatic aspects, the flamboyant and the gruesome, and developing rhetoric at the expense of truth.

PLAUTUS (c.254 - 184 BC)
Plautus freely adapted from the Greek 'new' comedy, using vigour of language and flowing wit to make up for what he lacked in subtlety. He was the most popular Roman playwright and his plots achieved great variety within the narrow framework which he inherited. Later dramatists who were loosely influenced by him include Shakespeare in *The Comedy of Errors* and Molière in *The Miser*.
Pot of Gold/Prisoners/Brothers/ Menaechemus/Swaggering Soldier/Pseudodolus (Trans. Watling, E.F.)
[FB546] Penguin pbk **£3.95**
Rope/Amphitryo/Ghost/Three Dollar Day
(Trans. Watling, E.F.)
[FB547] Penguin pbk **£3.99**
Rudens/Curculia/Casina (Trans. Stace, C.)
[FB548] Cambridge pbk **£3.75**

TERENCE (c.190 - 159 BC)
Less vigorous and more polished than Plautus, Terence's plays are set in indefinable environments, neither specifically Greek nor Roman. They lack the comic sureness of Plautus, but have proved widely influential since the Middle Ages.
Comedies
[FB559] Penguin pbk **£5.95**

SENECA, LUCIUS ANNAEUS
(c.4 BC - AD 65)
Seneca was a statesman, philosopher and dramatist, and at one time tutor to the Emperor Nero, who was later responsible for his death. Seneca's tragedies (and the *Octavia*, formerly attributed to him but now ascribed to an unknown author) are the only surviving examples of drama from the Roman Empire, and were written to be read rather than performed. The world in which they are set is one of brutality, treachery and political intrigue - close to that in which Seneca himself must have lived. Its tyrants, witches and 'the ghost-strewn stage' reappear in Elizabethan drama with Heywood's translation of *Thyestes*, and its influence is apparent on Shakespeare in *Titus Andronicus* and *Richard III*, and on Jonson in his two Roman political tragedies, *Catiline* and *Sejanus*.
Four Tragedies & Octavia
[FB549] Penguin pbk **£5.99**
Thyestes (Trans. Heywood, Thomas)
[FB550] A & C Black pbk **£3.95**

European & World Drama

Absurd Drama
A phrase coined by Martin Esslin to describe a style of theatre that emerged in the 1950s, which was to successfully expand many outmoded theatrical conventions. This volume includes: Ionesco's *Amédée*, Adamov's *Professor Taranne*, Arrabal's *The Two Executioners* and Albee's *The Zoo Story*.
[FB570] Penguin pbk **£3.95**

Contemporary Drama Series
Excellent collections, originating from America, of contemporary and recent plays, which are otherwise very difficult to obtain.
France
Includes: Duras, *Véra Baxter*; Saurette, *Over Nothing at All*; Vinaver, *Chamber Theatre*; Bourder, *The Gas Station*; Cormann, *Exiles*; Grumberg, *The Work Room*.
[FB571] Ianmead pbk **£8.95**
Latin America
Includes: Puig, *Kiss of the Spider Woman*; Skármeta, *Burning Patience*; Vargas Llosa, *Kathie and the Hippopotamus*; Fuentes, *Orchids in the Moonlight*.
[FB572] Ianmead pbk **£8.95**
Spain
Includes: Buero-Vallejo, *The Foundation*; Recuerda, *The Inmates of the Convent*; Salon, *The Cock's Short Flight*; Nieva, *Coronada and the Bull*.
[FB573] Ianmead pbk **£8.95**

New French Plays `NEW`
Vinever, *Portrait of a Woman*; Cousse, *These Childish Things*; Demarcy, *Stranger in the House*, Koltes, *The Struggle of the Dogs and the Black*.
[FB574] Methuen pbk **£5.99**

Noh Plays of Japan (Trans. Waley, Arthur)
Waley's 1921 translations had a stimulating impact on 20th century Western drama. The traditional Japanese Noh plays, founded on elaborate patterns of declamatory gestures and symbols, suggested all kinds of theatrical possibilities to dramatists as diverse as Yeats and Brecht.
[FB575] Unwin pbk **£7.95**

Plays for Today
From the Longman Caribbean Writers Series, this 1986 collection includes Walcott's *Ti Jean and his Brothers*, Scott's *Echo in the Bine* and Hill's *Man Better Man*.
[FB576] Longman pbk **£3.95**

Seven Expressionist Plays
This volume contains work from Kokoschka, Kafka, Barlach, Kaiser, Stramm, Brust and Gall, covering the years from 1907 to the mid-1920s. Expressionism was influential not only for its emphasis on emotional states, but also for developing a fragmentation of coherent linear narrative, along with suggestions of many extravagant visual possibilities in theatrical presentation.
[FB577] Calder pbk **£4.95**

Six Yuan Plays
The 130 or so plays that survive from the Yuan dynasty (AD 1280-1368) represent the beginnings of Chinese drama. The authors were rarely of a high social rank, and these carefully-structured plays, usually centred on a single man and woman, appear to have been the basis of a people's theatre.
[FB578] Penguin pbk **£4.95**

Stars in the Morning Sky `NEW`
A collection of Soviet plays from the 1980s, describing subjects considered 'untouchable' before *glasnost*. Includes: Galin, *Stars in the Morning Sky*; Chervinsky, *Heart of a Dog*; Gorin, *Forget Herostratus*; Petrushevskaya, *Three Girls in Blue*; Gelman, *A Man with Connections*.
[FB579] N Hern pbk **£6.95**

Three Great Jewish Plays
Includes *The Dybbuk*, a play version by S. Anski of the classic Jewish Story, along with Leivick's *The Golem* and Asch's *God of Vengeance*.
[FB580] Applause pbk **£3.95**

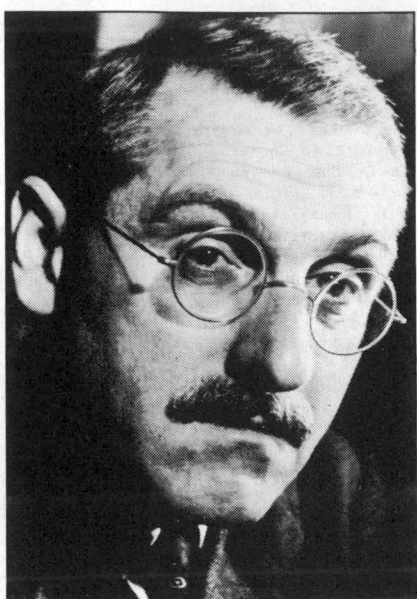

Jean Anouilh; the distinguished French playwright's work is published by Methuen Paperbacks.

ADAMOV, ARTHUR (Armenian, 1908 - 1970)
Adamov was born in Armenia, but emigrated to Paris, where he was associated with the Surrealists in the 1920s. His later plays, such as *Professor Taranne* (1953), which can be found in the anthology *Absurd Drama*, are often associated with the 'theatre of the absurd', although his exposure of various levels of corruption in French society in *Paolo Paoli* (1957) moves closer to the political theatre of Brecht.
Paolo Paoli
[FB581] Calder hbk **£4.95**

ANOUILH, JEAN (French, 1910 - 1987)
The most popular entertainer of modern French theatre, Anouilh's work combines racy dialogue with bitter-sweet comic invention, re-working classical myths, as in *Antigone* (1944) or drawing from history, as in *The Lark* (1953), his version of Joan of Arc.
Becket
[FB582] Methuen pbk **£4.50**
Five Plays
Antigone/Poor Bitos/The Lark/Leocadia/Waltz of the Toreadors.
[FB583] Methuen pbk **£4.99**

ARRABAL, FERNANDO (1932 -)
A Spanish/French dramatist, Arrabal's plays mix dream, poetry and violence with arresting effect. He achieved notoriety with *The Labyrinth* (1967), and has since been prolific, attempting to shock and disturb audiences with his 'Panic Theatre'.
Plays: One
The Car Cemetery/Orison/Fando & Lids/The Two Executioners.
[FB584] Calder hbk **£5.95**
Plays: Two
Guernica/The Labyrinth/The Tricycle/Picnic on the Battlefield/The Condemned Man's Bicycle.
[FB585] Calder hbk **£5.95**

ATAIE, IRAJ JANNATE (Iranian)
Ataie is one of Iran's foremost playwrights, now living in exile. This volume contains *Our Wounds*, a mythical story in which an uprising deposes a King in league with the Devil, and *Prometheus in Evin*, centred on a poet being broken by military torture, recently staged at the Young Vic Theatre.

The Night Sun   **NEW**
[FB586] Methuen pbk **£5.99**

BEAUMARCHAIS, PIERRE-AUGUSTIN CARON DE (French, 1732 - 1799)
Beaumarchais's comedies of intrigue share with the author's extraordinary life remarkable ingenuities of plot: in early life he was a financial speculator and brilliant opportunist, becoming a confidential agent for both Louis XV and Louis XVI. One of his last schemes was a fairly disastrous plot to supply arms to the rebels in America. These two comedies, both of which ran into censorship troubles, are tightly paced and rich in devious stratagems, forming the basis of operas by Rossini and Mozart.
Barber of Seville/The Marriage of Figaro
[FB587] Penguin pbk **£3.50**

BRECHT, BERTOLT (German, 1898 - 1956)
Brecht is a dominant figure in the theatre of this century, and both as writer and director, his influence on politically engaged dramatists everywhere has been immense. He abandoned the expressionist influences of his early work to develop a new form of drama - 'epic theatre' - using parable and song and other devices to keep the audience critical of issues raised by the play. Brecht continued to develop these ideas all his life, although his first big success using the new techniques came with *The Threepenny Opera* (1928). He left Germany in 1933 for exile in Scandinavia, and between 1938 and 1941 wrote some of his greatest plays, among them *The Life of Galileo* and *The Resistable Rise of Arturo Ui*. He founded the influential Berliner Ensemble with his wife Helene Wiegel in 1948, and the versions of his work which resulted - usually directed by Brecht himself - confirmed his pre-eminent position in world theatre.
Plays: One
Baal/The Threepenny Opera/The Mother.
[FB598] Methuen pbk **£4.99**
Plays: Two
Fear and Misery of the Third Reich/Mother Courage & Her Children/The Good Person of Szechwan.
[FB600] Methuen pbk **£3.95**
Plays: Three
Life of Galileo/The Resistable Rise of Arturo Ui/The Caucasian Chalk Circle.
[FB599] Methuen pbk **£3.95**
A Respectable Wedding & Other One Act Plays
[FB588] Methuen pbk **£4.50**
Drums in the Night
[FB589] Methuen pbk **£4.50**
Fear and Misery of the Third Reich & Senora Carrar's Rifles
[FB590] Methuen pbk **£4.50**
Happy End (with Weill & Lane)
[FB591] Methuen pbk **£4.50**
In the Jungle of the Cities
[FB592] Methuen pbk **£4.50**
Life of Galileo (Adapt. Brenton, Howard)
[FB593] Methuen pbk **£4.50**
Man Equals Man & The Elephant Calf
[FB594] Methuen pbk **£4.50**
Mother Courage and her Children
[FB595] Methuen pbk **£4.50**
Mr Puntila and His Man Matti
[FB596] Methuen pbk **£4.50**
Parables for the Theatre
Good Woman of Setzuan/Caucasian Chalk Circle.
[FB597] Penguin pbk **£3.95**
Poems and Songs from the Plays   **NEW**
[FB597A] Methuen hbk **£15.00**
Schweyck in the Second World War/ The Vision of Simone Machard
[FB601] Methuen pbk **£4.50**
The Caucasian Chalk Circle
[FB602] Methuen pbk **£4.50**

The Life of Galileo
[FB603] Methuen pbk **£4.50**
The Messingkauf Dialogues
[FB604] Methuen pbk **£4.50**
The Mother
[FB605] Methuen pbk **£4.50**
The Resistable Rise of Arturo Ui
[FB606] Methuen pbk **£4.50**
The Rise and Fall of the City Mahagonny & The Seven Deadly Sins
[FB607] Methuen pbk **£4.50**
The Threepenny Opera
[FB608] Methuen pbk **£4.50**

BROOK, PETER & CARRIERE, JEAN-CLAUDE (Adapt.)
The Mahabharata
An already legendary adaptation of the sacred Indian epic poem of the Hindus, performed as an exhilarating visual spectacle in Glasgow in 1988, with a television version appearing in 1989. It is a daunting 9 hour work which has been described as the most significant production of contemporary theatre, redefining, as Brook has always tried to do, the bounds of theatrical possibility.
[FB609] Methuen pbk **£4.95**

BUCHNER, GEORG (German, 1813 - 1837)
Büchner completed three plays in his brief life, none of which were performed until sixty years after his death. *Danton's Death* (1835) was written while Büchner faced arrest by German authorities for conspiracy to revolution; he depicts the fall of Danton, whose fate seems inevitable, owing to forces Büchner describes as the 'terrible fanaticism of history'. *Woyzeck* (1837) tells of a small man who is cast aside by society, the series of elliptical, disconnected scenes communicating a sense of grotesque tragedy.
Complete Plays
[FB610] Methuen pbk **£3.95**
Danton's Death/Woyzeck/Leonce and Lena
[FB611] Oxford pbk **£3.95**

BULGAKOV, MIKHAIL (Russian, 1891 - 1940)
Russian novelist and dramatist, Bulgakov adapted his novel *The White Guard*, a story of the civil war set in the Ukraine in 1919, for the Moscow Arts Theatre, where it ran from 1926 until it was banned in 1929. He continued to work through the 1930s, but suffered increasingly from censorship restrictions imposed by the Soviet authorities.
The White Guard
[FB612] Methuen pbk **£4.50**

CALDERON DE LA BARCA, PEDRO (Spanish, 1600 - 1681)
Spain's greatest dramatist was writing at a time of waning Spanish power, and the nation he depicts is one in decline. He was prolific, writing over 200 plays, and although half of these were comedies, he is most often described as a serious, religious dramatist. His most famous play is the poetic *Life is a Dream* (1635), in which the Prince Segismondo has to learn how to distinguish the transient from the eternal elements in his experience, a recurring theme in Calderon's work. He achieved immense popularity during his lifetime and many of his plays were seen in England in the 17th century. Unfortunately, contemporary productions are rare outside Spain.
Life is a Dream
[FB613] Applause pbk **£4.95**

CAMUS, ALBERT (French, 1913 - 1960)
Nobel Prize for Literature 1957. Although Camus's dramatic works are less successful than his brilliant essays and novels, he has said that the only places he was truly happy were on the football field and in the

theatre. His plays, like much of his work, use the dramatic narrative as a forum for philosophical speculation and debate.

Caligula/Cross Purpose/The Just/The Possessed
[FB614] Penguin pbk **£4.95**

CAPEK, KAREL (Czech, 1890 - 1938)
Capek is one of the few Czech dramatists to make an impact outside the country. His plays are characterized by their portrayal of the horror of totalitarian aggression, and by Capek's interest in scientific progress - he coined the term 'robot', and foresaw the coming of the atom bomb. He wrote the comedy *Insect Play* (1922) with his elder brother Josef, who was also a Cubist painter.

R.U.R. and The Insect Play
[FB615] Oxford pbk **£4.95**

CHEKHOV, ANTON (Russian, 1860 - 1904)
Chekhov trained as a doctor but supported himself at first precariously as a writer of short stories, and then of plays. His first dramas were failures with audiences, but when the Moscow Arts Theatre revived *The Seagull* in 1898, it proved a success. His later works were all presented there under Stanislavski's direction. They are intricate, elegant constructions which demonstrate an unusually wide range of influences, and an unrivalled feel for the complexities of Russian middle-class life, trapped in nostalgia on the eve of dispossession by revolution.

Five Plays
Ivanov/The Seagull/Uncle Vanya/The Three Sisters/The Cherry Orchard.
[FB616] Oxford pbk **£2.95**

Plays
Ivanov/The Cherry Orchard/The Seagull/Uncle Vanya /The Three Sisters/The Bear, Proposals and Jubilee.
[FB617] Penguin pbk **£3.99**

Plays
The Seagull/Uncle Vanya/Three Sisters/The Cherry Orchard, with four 'vaudevilles'.
[FB618] Methuen pbk **£4.99**

The Cherry Orchard
A new adaptation by Trevor Griffiths.
[FB619] Faber pbk **£3.99**

The Sneeze **NEW**
[FB620] Methuen pbk **£4.50**

CORNEILLE, PIERRE (French, 1606 - 1684)
One of the pioneers of French classical drama, Corneille created a grand, tragic theatre, where heroic figures grapple with problems of epic proportion. *The Cid* (1637) was his first major triumph, an involved tragicomedy set in medieval Spain, and still regularly staged in Paris.

The Cid/Cinna/Theatrical Illusion
[FB621] Penguin pbk **£4.95**

DURAS, MARGUERITE (French,1914 -)
French experimental novelist who has written for stage and screen. Her plays have been adapted for radio, where her beautiful, flowing dialogue, elliptical and evocative, is particularly effective.

Suzanna Adler/La Musica/L'Amante Anglaise
[FB622] Calder hbk **£6.95**

DURRENMATT, FRIEDRICH (Swiss, 1921 -)
A Swiss essayist, novelist and dramatist who believes grotesque comedy is the only way to express the despair and chaos of modern times. His two best known plays are both uncompromisng satires on the themes of power and responsibility.

The Physicists
Describes the fragile power in the hands of scientists with atomic secrets, the uncertain division between responsibility and madness remaining blurred.
[FB623] Macmillan pbk **£5.50**

The Visit
A dark and inventive parable in which an aging millionairess offers money to the people of a bankrupt town on condition that they kill her ex-lover.
[FB624] Cape pbk **£3.50**

FASSBINDER, RAINER WERNER (German, 1945 - 1982)
Film director with a predilection towards disruptive elements, in pieces for both the cinema and theatre. His plays are passionate and raw, but usually founded on strong, coherent narratives.

The Bitter Tears of Petra Von Kant/Blood on the Neck of the Cat
[FB625] Amber Lane pbk **£4.50**

FILIPPO, EDUARDO DE (Italian, 1900 - 1985)
De Filippo was a prolific and popular dramatist, although the finest productions of his plays appear to be those which he directed himself, and in which he led his own troupe. *Inner Voices* is a farce, richly threaded with the dialects and manners of his native Naples.

Inner Voices
[FB626] Amber Lane pbk **£3.95**

FO, DARIO (Italian, 1926 -)
A leading contemporary Italian dramatist who has attempted to reconcile his Marxist ideals with the demands of mainstream popular theatre. Fo first gained international recognition with his political satires in the 1970s.

Accidental Death of an Anarchist
Very popular high speed comedy, focused on a serious exposé of Italian police corruption.
[FB627] Methuen pbk **£4.50**

Archangels Don't Play Pinball
[FB628] Methuen pbk **£4.50**

Can't Pay, Won't Pay
A bizarre farce, which describes the protests of housewives to exaggerated supermarket prices.
[FB629] Methuen pbk **£4.50**

Elizabeth
[FB630] Methuen pbk **£4.50**

Mistero Buffo
An ingenious contemporary political satire distilled from elements of Italian medieval mystery plays.
[FB631] Methuen pbk **£4.50**

Trumpets & Raspberries
[FB632] Methuen pbk **£4.50**

FRISCH, MAX (Swiss, 1911 -)
A much-acclaimed Swiss dramatist who has also worked as an architect and written novels. His plays are constructed with a clear and direct visual strength, the two most popular being *The Fireraisers* (1958) and *Andorra* (1961). Both cry out against Swiss complacency, manifested in its underlying hostility towards 'outsiders', be they the two tramps who are practically obliged to become arsonists in *The Fireraisers*, or the Blacks and Jews, who are feared and victimized by the racist characters of *Andorra*, to their irrevocable shame.

Andorra
[FB633] Methuen pbk **£4.50**

The Fire Raisers
[FB634] Methuen pbk **£4.50**

Triptych
[FB635] Methuen pbk **£4.50**

FUGARD, ATHOL (South African, 1932 -)
From his earliest work, Fugard has dramatized the turmoil of South Africa, describing the devastating effect the political system has had on the various peoples of the country. This tragic history serves as a powerful backdrop to his stories of personal isolation and pain.

A Place with the Pigs
Fugard has directed this 'personal parable' around the world; it tells of an army deserter, who has hidden in a pigsty for 41 years, providing the playwright with sublime metaphors for the human condition at its most basic.
[FB636] Faber pbk **£3.95**

Dimetos & Two Early Plays
[FB637] Oxford pbk **£2.50**

Selected Plays
Master Harold and the Boys/Boesman and Lena/Hello and Goodbye/revised version of The Blood Knot.
[FB638] Oxford pbk **£5.95**

Statements: Three Plays
[FB639] Oxford pbk **£4.95**
Sizwe Bansi/The Island/Statements After an Arrest.

The Road to Mecca
[FB640] Faber pbk **£3.95**

GELMAN, ALEXANDER (Russian, 1933 -)
A Man with Connections **NEW**
One of the most popular recent plays at the Moscow Arts Theatre, this is a sharp attack on the values and bureaucracy of the current Soviet system, centred on a darkly comic portrait of a strained marriage. Staged in Edinburgh and London in 1989.
[FB641] N Hern pbk **£3.95**

GENET, JEAN (French, 1910 - 1986)
Iconoclastic French writer, whose work has provoked much stormy debate - notably with *The Screens*, a taut, ritualistic avant-garde drama concerning the Algerian War, published at the height of the conflict in 1961, but considered too controversial to stage until 1966. In his plays, Genet offers a strange contrast between grim, often sordid circumstances, and the beauty of poetic language with which the characters describe them.

The Balcony
[FB642] Faber pbk **£4.99**

The Maids/Deathwatch
[FB643] Faber pbk **£4.99**

The Screens
[FB644] Faber pbk **£5.95**

GOETHE, JOHANN WOLFGANG VON (German, 1749 - 1832)
A pioneering mind in many fields - poet, scientist and statesman - Goethe's theatrical career began under the influence of 'Sturm und Drang' with free verse dramas of protest, rejecting social constraint and centred on titanic individuals. His most effective stage works, however, rejected these tendencies in favour of the new classicism. This is exemplified in *Torquato Tasso* (1789), based on the life of the persecuted Italian poet, with its inclination towards harmony, balance and synthesis. His masterpiece, *Faust*, perhaps never intended for the theatre, has proved formidably difficult to stage. Goethe began the first part in 1770, and the second was completed just before his death in 1832.

Faust
[FB645] Norton pbk **£8.50**

Faust, Part 1
[FB646] Penguin pbk **£2.99**

Faust, Part 2
[FB647] Penguin pbk **£3.99**

Torquato Tasso
[FB649] Angel pbk **£5.95**

GOGOL, NICOLAI (Russian, 1809 - 1852)
The Government Inspector
A strange satire of small-town corruption from this extraordinary Russian novelist. The severe condemnation with which the play was greeted in 1836 was perhaps less disturbing to the author than the extravagantly inappropriate burlesque elements which characterized the first productions.
[FB650] Heinemann pbk **£2.75**

GORKY, MAXIM (Russian, 1868 - 1936)

Gorky became a kind of bohemian folklore hero in pre-revolutionary Russia. He educated himself after a hard and unhappy childhood, and his twelve plays present an uneasy friction between bitterness and idealism. They are emphatically rhetorical, often founded on basic class conflicts, with Gorky championing the causes of the down-and-out. After 1917, he was hailed as a hero of Soviet art.

Five Plays
Enemies/The Lower Depths/Summerfolk/Children of the Sun/Barbarians.
[FB651] Methuen pbk £5.95

HANDKE, PETER (Austrian, 1942 -)

Austrian novelist and dramatist, who recently wrote the screenplay for Wim Wender's *Wings of Desire*. His work in the theatre has been characterized by a fascination with experimentation.

Kaspar
A variation on the (true) story of Kaspar Hauser, the 'natural man' who cannot speak until he is an adult; the play shows him slide into incoherence, frustrated by the limitations language places on his thought.
[FB652] Methuen pbk £4.50

The Long Way Round   NEW
A story of Europe in the 1980s, contrasting the breaking-up of traditional village life with the alienation of the modern city.
[FB653] Methuen pbk £4.99

HAUPTMANN, GERHART

(German, 1862 - 1946)
Nobel Prize for Literature 1912. Hauptmann introduced naturalism to German drama with *The Weavers* (1892); he later developed a more symbolic, poetic style, away from the harshness of the early 1890s plays, although it is those early works which now seem his most exciting.

The Weavers
An epic drama of human suffering and endurance in the industrial age, based on an 1844 revolt by Silesian workers; it is a play with a collective hero, the weavers themselves.
[FB654] Methuen pbk £4.50

HAVEL, VACLAV (Czech, 1936 -)

Havel was associated with the Czech avant-garde of the 1960s and, with Kundera, was prominent in the Prague Spring of 1968. He has written under an unrelenting state of pressure, imprisoned several times, his plays only seen abroad after 1969.

Largo Desolato (1985)
[FB655] Faber pbk £4.95

Temptation (1986)
An extraordinary comic play, a strange version of Dr Faustus transposed to give a picture of life in Eastern Europe.
[FB656] Faber pbk £3.95

The Memorandum (1965)
Staged many times around the world, the play gives a satirical view of a bureaucratic organization which adopts a synthetic language that few employees can comprehend.
[FB657] Methuen pbk £4.50

IBSEN, HENRIK (Norwegian, 1828 - 1906)

Ibsen broke with the romantic obsession with the past that was current in Norwegian art, to create powerful and original dramas of contemporary life, distinguished by their psychological conflicts. He described himself as a poet rather than as a social reformer, and his poetic sensibility can be felt in all his work from the early plays such as *Peer Gynt* (1867). But social themes are often a strong undercurrent - the role of women in *A Doll's House* (1879), for example, or sexual disease in the domestic realist drama *Ghosts* (1881). His last play, *When We Dead*

Awaken (1899), which he described as his 'Epilogue', draws together many themes and images that had echoed through his work.

Plays: One
Ghosts/The Wild Duck/The Master Builder.
[FB667] Methuen pbk £2.95

Plays: Two
A Doll's House/An Enemy of the People/Hedda Gabler.
[FB670] Methuen pbk £2.95

Plays: Three
Rosmersholm/Little Eyolf/The Lady from the Sea.
[FB669] Methuen pbk £3.50

Plays: Four
John Gabriel Borkman/The Pillars of Society/When We Dead Awaken.
[FB666] Methuen pbk £2.50

Plays: Five
Brand/Emperor and Galilean.
[FB665] Methuen pbk £2.95

Plays: Six
Peer Gynt/The Pretenders.
[FB668] Methuen pbk £2.95

A Doll's House/The League of Youth/The Lady from the Sea
[FB658] Penguin pbk £3.99

Four Major Plays
A Doll's House/Ghosts/Hedda Gabler/The Master Builder.
[FB659] Oxford pbk £3.50

Ghosts/A Public Enemy/When We Dead Awaken
[FB660] Penguin pbk £2.95

Hedda Gabler/A Doll's House   NEW
(Trans. Hampton, Christopher)
[FB661] Faber pbk £4.99

Hedda Gabler/The Pillars of the Community/The Wild Duck
[FB662] Penguin pbk £3.99

Peer Gynt
[FB663] Penguin pbk £2.95
[FB664] Oxford pbk £2.95

The Master Builder/Rosmersholm/Little Eyolf/John Gabriel Borkman
[FB671] Penguin pbk £3.95

The Wild Duck
[FB672] Norton pbk £5.59

IONESCO, EUGENE (1912 -)

Chief architect and major exponent of the Theatre of the Absurd, whose characters struggle to survive in an incomprehensible and hostile universe; his major successes came in the 1960s. His plays are characterized by a hallucinatory quality, and by his wild, anarchic humour.

Rhinoceros/Chairs/The Lesson
[FB673] Penguin pbk £4.99

Three Plays: The Killer/The Chairs/Maid to Marry
[FB674] Calder pbk £4.95

JARRY, ALFRED (1873 - 1907)

Ubu Roi was first staged in 1896, and presents the grotesque puppet creation, the lazy, ruthless Ubu, in violent pursuit of the Polish throne. Jarry wrote two more plays describing this character, *Ubu Cuckolded* and *Ubu Enchained* - though neither could match the shock impact of the first. The three plays are often cited as forerunners of Surrealism and Dada.

The Ubu Plays
[FB675] Methuen pbk £4.50

LORCA, FEDERICO GARCIA

(Spanish, 1898 - 1936)
Spanish poet and dramatist of rare lyrical intensity and passion. His plays from the 1920s present a fantastic puppet-like theatre, but it is for the powerful tragedies of the 1930s that he is celebrated: *Blood Wedding* (1933), *Yerma* (1934) and *The House of*

Bernarda Alba (1936). Each play is centred on a strong, passionate woman, suffocated by life in rural Spain, and their attempts to break through the circle of jealousy and frustration.

Plays: One
Blood Wedding/Dona Rosita the Spinster/Yerma.
[FB677] Methuen pbk £3.95

Plays: Two   NEW
The Shoemaker's Wonderful Wife/The Love of Don Perlimplin/When Five Years Pass/The Puppet Play of Don Christobal/The Butterfly's Evil Spell.
[FB678] Methuen pbk £4.99

Five Plays
[FB676] Penguin pbk £5.95

Three Tragedies
Blood Wedding/Yerma/The House of Bernarda Alba.
[FB679] Penguin pbk £4.50

MARIVAUX, PIERRE CARLET CHAMBLAIN DE (French, 1688 - 1763)

Marivaux's prose comedies were extremely popular in their day, and have survived by virtue of their romantic charm, and for their subtle nuances of dialogue.

Plays
The first and only selection in English contains 10 of Marivaux's plays.
[FB680] Methuen pbk £5.95

MATURA, MUSTAPHA (West Indian)

An acclaimed dramatist from Trinidad, Matura currently lives in England. His plays are perceptive contemplations of post-colonial Trinidad, and the problems and pressures opened up by independence. Since his early success with *As Time Goes By* (1963), his work has been regularly staged in London and New York.

As Time Goes By & Black Pieces
[FB681] Boyars pbk £3.95

Play Mas/Independence/Meetings
[FB682] Methuen pbk £4.50

MAYAKOVSKY, VLADIMIR

(Russian, 1893 - 1930)
A wild, eccentric poet and dramatist who put his euphoric talents and vision at the service of Soviet culture after the Revolution. The plays included here are his finest, and were all originally directed by Meyerhold: *Mystery-Bouffe* (1918), a curious satire in which heaven is made on earth, and two works written in the years just before he committed suicide, both expressing disillusion with the progress of the revolution - *The Bed Bug*, a comic extravaganza, and *The Big Clean Up*, also known as *The Bathhouse*, a drama with circus and fireworks.

Plays/Articles/Essays
[FB683] Raduga hbk £8.95

MOLIERE (Jean-Baptiste Poquelin, French, 1622 - 1673)

Perhaps the most frequently performed of all French dramatists, Molière transformed social comedy with his ingenious satires on 17th century manners and fashion. He blends robust clowning with close observation of human absurdity and weakness, creating a gallery of mischievous rogues, perhaps most notably the grovelling priest Tartuffe. His work had a considerable influence on Restoration comedy in England.

Five Plays
The Misanthrope/Tartuffe/The School for Wives/The Miser/The Hypochondriac.
[FB684] Methuen pbk £3.95

The Misanthrope & Other Plays
Includes *Sicilian*, *Tartuffe*, *Doctor in Spite of Himself*, and *The Imaginary Invalid*.
[FB685] Penguin pbk £3.95

The Miser & Other Plays
Includes *The Would-Be Gentleman, Scoundrel Scapin, Love's the Best Doctor.*
[FB686] Penguin pbk **£3.99**

NGUGI WA THIONGO (Kenyan, 1938 -)
I Will Marry When I Want
Ngugi is a key figure in African literature. *I Will Marry When I Want* was first performed by workers and peasants, in defiance of the exclusive atmosphere surrounding the Kenyan National Theatre, and introduced a theatre based in the community. It was suppressed by the authorities, and Ngugi subsequently imprisoned for a year without trial.
[FB687] Heinemann pbk **£4.15**

PHILLIPS, CARYL (West Indian)
Novelist and dramatist from St Kitts, West Indies, whose plays revolve around culture clashes, most especially those faced by West Indians living in Britain. Phillips's writing tempers anguish with a cool eloquence, strongly evident in his most recently published stage work, an evocative pair of linked two-handers, *The Shelter* (1983), both describing a bond between a black man and a white woman.
Strange Fruit
[FB688] Amber Lane pbk **£3.50**
The Shelter
[FB689] Amber Lane pbk **£3.50**
Where There is Darkness
[FB690] Amber Lane pbk **£3.50**

PIRANDELLO, LUIGI (Italian, 1867 - 1936)
Pirandello's innovative theatre has had much influence on modern drama, and although he became a dramatist late in his career, it is his plays that have gained him world renown. With provocative irony and scepticism, they present puzzling ideas and situations, experimenting with the relationship of art to life. They still evoke uncertainty and debate today, while retaining the power to disturb and inspire: the first performance of *Six Characters in Search of an Author* (1921) was greeted with uproar in Rome.
Collected Plays Vol 1
[FB691] Calder pbk **£6.95**
Collected Plays Vol 2
[FB692] Calder pbk **£6.95**
Six Characters in Search of an Author
[FB693] Methuen pbk **£4.50**
Three Plays
Six Characters in Search of an Author/Henry IV/ The Rules of the Game.
[FB694] Methuen pbk **£3.99**

PUIG, MANUEL (Argentinian, 1932 -)
Argentinian novelist whose plays have begun to make an impact around the world in recent years.
Kiss of the Spider Woman
Puig's novel, which he adapted for the stage, was later made into a very successful film. It explores the relationship between a revolutionary and a flam-boyant homosexual, set in a South American prison.
[FB695] Amber Lane pbk **£3.95**
Mystery of the Rose Bouquet (1987)
Another two-hander centred on an uneasy alliance described with the use of fantasy and dream. It tells of the friendship which develops with difficulty between a rich, cantankerous old woman and her much-abused nurse.
[FB696] Faber pbk **£4.95**

RACINE, JEAN (French, 1639 - 1699)
A leading figure in French drama, Racine's plays re-defined the conventions of neo-classical tragedy, producing sophisticated works of unusual evocative power. He gives profound, at times merciless, insights into his characters' feelings and weaknesses, often showing their aspirations doomed by the folly of their passions.

Andromache/Britannicus/Bérénice
[FB697] Penguin pbk **£4.50**
Iphigenia/Phaedra/Athaliah
[FB698] Penguin pbk **£3.95**

SARTRE, JEAN-PAUL
(French, 1905 - 1980)
In his dramatic work Sartre tempers his existentialism with human sympathy. He was always more drawn towards a theatre of ideas, where actions and situation are of more concern than motivation or emotional states. Several of his best plays were written in the late 1940s, when popular interest in his work was most keen.
Crime Passionel (Les Mains Sales) (1948)
A story of the seemingly inevitable moral compromises experienced by a young bourgeois convert to the Communist Party.
[FB699] Methuen pbk **£4.50**
Three Plays
Altona/Men without Shadows/The Flies.
Altona (1959) is the tragic story of a young German's belief in free-will devastated by the rise of Nazism.
[FB700] Penguin pbk **£5.99**
Three Plays
Kean/Nekrassov/The Trojan Women.
Includes an exciting version of Euripides's *The Trojan Women*, first staged in 1965.
[FB701] Penguin pbk **£4.95**

SCHILLER, JOHANN CHRISTOPH FRIEDRICH VON (German, 1759 - 1805)
Schiller's profound contribution to German drama began with *The Robbers* (1781), a passionate rejection of social corruption which strongly echoed the turbulent Romantic spirit of the 'Sturm und Drang' movement of the 1770s. With *Don Carlos*, he began to temper the rebellious intensity of his work, developing a more elevated form of historical tragedy in verse of mighty resonance, particularly evident in the *Wallenstein* trilogy. These plays, along with *Mary Stuart* (1800) and *William Tell* (1804), suggest a romantic belief in social change and liberty chastened by the lessons of the French Revolution, and a drama which comes to concentrate on a more personal search for spiritual freedoms.
Don Carlos
[FB702] Oberon pbk **£3.95**
The Robbers & Wallenstein
[FB703] Penguin pbk **£5.95**
Wilhelm Tell
[FB704] Chicago UP pbk **£7.25**

SCHNITZLER, ARTHUR
(Austrian, 1862 - 1931)
An innovator in the technique of interior monologue, Schnitzler scorned the psychological stance of contemporary naturalist plays. *Anatol* (1893) and *La Ronde* (1900) view sceptically the sophisticated veneer and casual sexual values of Vienna at the turn of the century. Schnitzler's conclusions, along with his treatment of the unconscious, suggest several parallels with Freud.
Anatol   **NEW**
[FB705] Absolute P pbk **£4.50**
La Ronde
[FB706] Methuen pbk **£4.50**

SOBOL, JOSHUA (1939 -)
Ghetto   **NEW**
First staged in Israel in 1984, and at the National Theatre in 1989, *Ghetto* is based on diaries written as the Nazis began their policy of extermination, which tell the story of a theatre flourishing in a Jewish ghetto. Songs and music are included, along with extracts from the original diaries.
[FB707] N Hern pbk **£4.50**

SOYINKA, WOLE (Nigerian, 1934 -)
Nobel Prize for Literature 1986. Soyinka was educated in his native Nigeria and in England, where his plays were first performed, and where he joined the Writer's Group at the Royal Court Theatre in the late 1950s. He has mixed the traditions of African and European drama to create, with innovative stagecraft, a unique theatrical language dense with symbols and metaphysical elements, developing dialogue that combines both African and English vernacular. He has involved himself deeply in African political life, and at some personal cost - he was imprisoned in the 1960s for attempting to negotiate a truce in the Biafran War. His work exposes hypocrisy and corruption, both within African government and in the attitudes to developing countries of the superpowers.
A Play of Giants
[FB708] Methuen pbk **£4.50**
Collected Plays One
A Dance of the Forests/The Swamp Dwellers/The Strong Breed/The Road/The Bacchae of Euripides.
[FB709] Oxford pbk **£4.95**
Collected Plays Two
The Lion and the Jewel/Kongi's Harvest/The Trials of Brother Jero/Jero's Metamorphosis/Madmen and Specialists.
[FB710] Oxford pbk **£4.95**
Six Plays
The Trials of Brother Jero/Jero's Metamorphosis/Camwood on the Leaves/Death and the King's Horsemen/Madmen and Specialists/Opera Wonyosi.
[FB711] Methuen pbk **£4.50**

STRINDBERG, AUGUST
(Swedish, 1849 - 1912)
A Swedish dramatist, and one of the key figures in modern world theatre, Strindberg's work is distinguished by his powerful sense of visual dramatic images, and by his foregrounding the unconscious inner lives of his characters. He wrote in a range of forms, from the idiosyncratic naturalism of *The Father* (1887) and *Miss Julie* (1888), through the Swedish historical dramas, to the strange, mystical later work, particularly *A Dream Play* (1902), which stands at the threshold of many developments in 20th century drama.
Motherly Love/Pariah/The First Warning
[FB712] Amber Lane pbk **£3.95**

August Strindberg, whose plays are published by Secker & Warburg (Picture: John Freeman & Co)

Plays: One
The Father/Miss Julie/The Ghost Sonata.
[FB713] Secker hbk £15.00
[FB714] Methuen pbk £2.99
Plays: Two
A Dream Play/The Dance of Death/The Stronger.
[FB715] Secker hbk £15.00
[FB716] Methuen pbk £3.95
Three Plays
The Father/Miss Julie/Easter.
[FB717] Penguin pbk £2.50
Thunder in the Air `NEW`
[FB718] Absolute P pbk £4.50

VEGA, LOPE DE (Spanish, 1562 - 1635)
Vega claimed authorship of over 1,500 plays,
although only 314 of the 500 that remain are
undoubtedly his work. He developed a form of
drama known as the 'three-act *commedia*', flouting
the classical unities of place and time, and using
two or more plots to combine tragic and comic
elements. *Fuenteovejuna* (1614), like many of his
plays, sets a peasant community against a tyrannical
overlord, whom they eventually kill. The
townspeople, despite torture, will only tell the King
that the assassin was 'Fuenteovejuna', the name of
the town.
Fuenteovejuna
[FB719] Absolute P pbk £5.95

WALCOTT, DEREK (St Lucia, 1930 -)
A celebrated poet, Walcott has also had a long
career in drama. His plays were first performed by
the St Lucia Arts Guild, which he founded with
his brother Roderick in 1950. Since then he has
regularly worked in West Indian theatre, with
characteristic energy and vision. The plays included
here are *The Last Carnival* (1983), *Beef, No
Chicken* (1982) and *A Branch of the Blue Nile*
(1983) - together they span four decades of Trinidad's
history.
Three Plays
[FB720] Faber pbk £6.95

WEDEKIND, FRANK (German, 1864 - 1918)
A pioneer of German expressionism, his first major
play *Spring Awakening* (1891) sparked a furore when
it was eventually seen in 1906, with its scathing
picture of a repressive German society, centred on an
overt theme of sexual awakening in children. He
caused more disturbance with the *Lulu* plays (1895,
1904), ruthless portraits of greed and social
corruption, revolving around the ambiguous and
sexually destructive figure of Lulu.
Spring Awakening
[FB721] Methuen pbk £4.50
**The Lulu Plays & Other Sex
Tragedies**
[FB722] Calder pbk £6.95

WEISS, PETER (German, 1916 - 1982)
A radical German dramatist, whose work experiments
with the formal mechanics of theatre, often disturbing
audiences with the fragmented nature of his social
critiques.
The Investigation (1966)
Weiss's recreation of the 1964 Auschwitz trials,
without plot or conventional characterization: the
careful selection and juxtaposition of documentary
facts undermines the objective tone with which they
are related to the audience.
[FB723] Boyars pbk £4.95
The Marat/Sade (1964)
Focused on Marat's assassination by Charlotte
Corday, this is an extraordinary, innovative play,
which fuses the disparate influences of Artaud, Brecht
and Beckett. It was first seen in Britain in Peter
Brook's influential production.
[FB724] Boyars pbk £4.95

Drama Studies

Reference

BANHAM, MARTIN (ED)
**The Cambridge Guide to World
Theatre**
An excellent reference book, finely balanced and
presented with great precision. First published in
1988.
[FB725] Cambridge hbk £25.00

FLETCHER, S. & JOPLING, N.
The Book of 1,000 Plays `NEW`
A guide to the most frequently performed plays, with
plot outlines and full *dramatis personae*.
[FB726] Harrap hbk £12.95

GRIFFITHS, TREVOR R. & WODDIS, CAROLE
The Bloomsbury Theatre Guide `NEW`
Illustrated, with extensive and surprising
cross-references.
[FB727] Bloomsbury hbk £12.95

HARTNOLL, PHYLLIS
**The Oxford Companion to the
Theatre**
Regarded as a standard, invaluable reference work; it
presents balanced and concise opinions on all figures
and themes of world drama.
[FB728] Oxford hbk £25.00
**The Concise Oxford Companion to the
Theatre**
[FB729] Oxford pbk £6.95

HAY, PETER (ED)
Theatrical Anecdotes `NEW`
Some curious glimpses into life in the theatre, from
actors' eccentricities to some awesome calamities.
[FB730] Oxford hbk £12.95

LEMMON, DAVID (ED)
British Theatre Yearbook 1989 `NEW`
Illustrated record of professional productions seen in
1988, with cast lists.
[FB731] Helm pbk £9.95

History & Theory

ARDEN, JOHN
Awkward Corners `NEW`
(with D'Arcy, Margaretta)
Essays centred on the artist's role and the 'Matter
of Ireland'.
[FB732] Methuen pbk £7.95
To Present the Pretence
A collection of diverse pieces, first published between
1966 and 1977.
[FB733] Methuen pbk £7.50

BASSNETT, SUSAN
**The Magdalena Experiment:
International Women's Theatre** `NEW`
An illustrated account of the first International
Festival of Women in Theatre.
[FB735] Berg hbk £12.95

BENTLEY, ERIC (ED)
Theory of the Modern Stage
An anthology of writings from figures such as Artaud,
Brecht and Stanislavski, which presents their theories
on modern theatre.
[FB736] Penguin pbk £6.99

BRAUN, EDWARD
The Director and the Stage
From Naturalism to Grotowski.
[FB755] Methuen pbk £5.95

DEVLIN, DIANA
Mask and Scene `NEW`
A recent concise introduction to theatre history.
[FB736A] Macmillan pbk £7.95

ESSLIN, MARTIN
The Field of Drama
A careful analysis of the use of semiotics in the study
of cinema, television and theatre.
[FB737] Methuen pbk £5.95
Theatre of the Absurd
Regarded as a classic study of the new theatre which
emerged in the 1950s.
[FB738] Penguin pbk £5.95

EVANS, G. BLAKEMORE
Elizabethan-Jacobean Drama `NEW`
Selection of writings, including extracts from letters
and diaries, which provide a social and cultural
context for the theatre of the period.
[FB739] A & C Black pbk £9.95

HARTNOLL, PHYLLIS
The Theatre: A Concise History
From the authoritative *World of Art* series.
[FB740] Thames & H pbk £5.95

JACKSON, RUSSELL
Victorian Theatre `NEW`
Anthology of documents, collection writings and
thoughts from those most closely involved in
Victorian drama.
[FB741] A & C Black pbk £12.50

LEACROFT, RICHARD & LEACROFT, HELEN
Theatre and Playhouse
An illustrated survey of theatre buildings, from
Ancient Greece to the present day.
[FB742] Methuen pbk £8.99

MCGRATH, JOHN
A Good Night Out
From the founder of 7: 84, a persuasive polemic,
examining the role of popular theatre in the
community.
[FB743] Methuen pbk £5.50

PETER, JOHN
**Vladimir's Carrot: Modern Drama and
the Imagination**
A collection of essays from the Drama critic of the
Sunday Times; using *Waiting for Godot* as a particular
example, he develops ideas on the modern theatre and
the differences in relation to the audience between
'open' and 'closed' texts.
[FB743A] Methuen pbk £6.95

ROBERTS, P. (ED)
Two volumes which reprint the best items from the
major British monthly theatrical magazine.
**The Plays and Players Reader
Vol 1: 1953 - 1968**
[FB743B] Methuen pbk £8.99
Vol 2: 1969 - 1983 `NEW`
[FB743C] Methuen hbk £15.99

ROOSE-EVANS, JAMES
**Experimental Theatre from
Shakespeare to Peter Brook**
One of Britain's most experienced and influential
directors surveys the history of the avant-garde
in theatre, from its origins to most recent
developments.
[FB744] Routledge pbk £9.95

STYAN, J.L.
A prolific critic with a subtle and sure grasp of his material. *The Dramatic Experience* attempts to explain theatrical practices through the ages to those who have little or no opportunity to go to the theatre.
The Dramatic Experience
[FB745] Cambridge pbk **£10.95**
The Elements of Drama
Explores the complex links between author, actor, producer and the audience.
[FB746] Cambridge pbk **£10.95**

TAYLOR, JOHN RUSSELL
Anger and After
A Guide to British drama post-Osborne.
{FB746A} Methuen pbk **£7.95**

TYNAN, KENNETH
A View of the English Stage
A collection of Tynan's reviews from 1944 to 1965: they are both highly entertaining reading and provide a valuable history of the drama of that period.
[FB747] Methuen pbk **£5.95**
Profiles **NEW**
An A-Z of star profiles - actors, directors, authors - Tynan's gallery of 'high definition performers'.
[FB804] N Hern hbk **£14.95**

WANDOR, MICHELENE
Look Back in Gender
A recent study of some well-known plays of the last 30 years, suggesting a number of unstated gender assumptions.
[FB748] Methuen pbk **£6.99**

WILLIAMS, RAYMOND
Drama from Ibsen to Brecht
A short study of modern drama, particularly concerned with the social aspects of art.
[FB749] Hogarth pbk **£6.95**

Criticism

Methuen 'Writer-Files'
These volumes assemble often unavailable material on many of this century's major dramatists, and are not strictly critical in intention. They include comprehensive checklists of the writer's work, with detailed performance histories, excerpts of reviews, and extracts from the writer's own essays, interviews and letters. General Editor: Simon Trussler.
Available for:
Arden, *Ayckbourn*, *Beckett*, *Bond*, *Brenton*, *Chekhov*, *Churchill*, *Coward*, *Dario Fo*, *Ibsen*, *Miller*, *O'Casey*, *Osborne*, *Pirandello*, *Shaffer*, *Shaw*, *Shepard*, *Stoppard*, *Strindberg*, *Wesker*, *Tennessee Williams*.
[FB749A] Methuen pbk **£4.99**

Methuen Modern Theatre Profiles
These works give an up-to-date view of contemporary and recent playwrights, and are well-illustrated.
Beckett Fletcher, John & Spurling, John **£5.95**
Bond: A Study of His Plays Hay, Malcolm & Roberts, Philip **£4.95**
Brecht: A Choice of Evils
Esslin, Martin **£5.95**
Chekhov Magarshack, David (hbk) **£9.95**
Churchill Cousins, Geraldine **£5.99**
Coward Lahr, John **£5.95**
Miller Welland, Dennis **£5.95**
Odets Weales, Gerald **£5.95**
Pinter Esslin, Martin **£5.95**
Stoppard Billington, Michael **£5.50**
Wesker Leeming, Glenda **£5.50**
[FB749B] Methuen pbk **£4.95 - £5.95**

Theatre Studies

ARTAUD, ANTONIN (1896 - 1946)
The Theatre and Its Double
A collection of some influential essays. Includes the Manifestos of the Theatre of Cruelty.
[FB750] Calder pbk **£4.95**
ESSLIN, MARTIN
Antonin Artaud: The Man and His Work
[FB751] Calder hbk **£5.95**
SCHUMACHER, CLAUDE (ED)
Artaud on Theatre **NEW**
A major new selection of Artaud's writings, taken from the full 24-volume French edition.
[FB751A] Methuen hbk **£25.00**

AYCKBOURN, ALAN
Conversations with Ayckbourn
(with Watson, Ian)
New edition published 1988.
[FB752] Faber pbk **£5.95**

BECKETT, SAMUEL
MCMILLAN, DOUGALD & FEHSENFELD, MARTHA
Beckett in the Theatre
Detailed study, with some particularly good photographs from productions, and diagrams from Beckett's notebooks and production plans.
[FB753] Calder hbk **£18.95**

BERKOFF, STEVEN
I Am Hamlet **NEW**
Scene by scene observations of *Hamlet*, expressed with Berkoff's characteristic originality and rich imagination.
[FB754] Faber pbk **£5.99**

BRECHT, BERTOLT (1898 - 1956)
Diaries 1920 - 1922
[FB756] Methuen pbk **£7.95**
Letters 1913 - 1956 **NEW**
The first comprehensive selection of Brecht's letters to be published in English, this covers the whole of his adult life, and reveals much about his private and public concerns.
[FB756] Methuen hbk **£17.99**
BENTLEY, ERIC
The Brecht Commentaries 1943 - 1980
[FB757] Methuen pbk **£7.95**
WILLETT, JOHN
Brecht on Theatre
[FB758] Methuen pbk **£5.95**
The Theatre of Bertold Brecht
[FB759] Methuen pbk **£5.95**

BROOK, PETER (1925 -)
The Empty Space
A key text for modern theatre production, which draws together thoughts on a wide variety of performances witnessed by Brook.
[FB760] Penguin pbk **£3.95**
The Shifting Point
Brook describes the ideas and events which have shaped his innovative career, from early success in the 1940s to the epic version of *The Mahabharata*.
[FB761] Methuen pbk **£5.99**
HEILPERN, JOHN
Conference of Birds **NEW**
An absorbing account of Brook's trek through Africa with a troupe of actors in 1973. Newly re-issued.
[FB762] Methuen pbk **£5.95**
O'CONNOR, GARRY
The Making of the Mahabharata **NEW**
The only writer to observe the filming of *The Mahabharata* for television in an old Paris studio, O'Connor presents interviews with Peter Brook, the production team and the cast, as well as insights into

the meaning of the work itself. Illustrated with production photographs.
[FB763] Hodder hbk **£14.95**
[FB764] Hodder pbk **£9.95**
SELBOURNE, DAVID
The Making of A Midsummer Night's Dream
[FB765] Methuen pbk **£7.50**
WILLIAMS, DAVID (ED)
Peter Brook: A Theatrical Casebook
[FB766] Methuen pbk **£6.95**

CALLOW, SIMON
Notes from a successful English actor, who has recently turned to writing and directing.
Being an Actor
[FB767] Penguin pbk **£4.50**

COLE, TOBY (ED)
Playwrights on Playwriting
Articles from 27 key playwrights of the last 100 years.
[FB768] Methuen pbk **£5.50**

COOK, JUDITH
Directors' Theatre **NEW**
Collected interviews with 16 leading directors.
[FB769] Hodder pbk **£6.95**

CRAIG, EDWARD GORDON
(1862 - 1961)
A highly original designer, theorist and director, Craig's work ushered in a new approach to the possibilities of theatre, advocating a non-naturalistic aesthetic.
BABLET, DENIS
The Theatre of Edward Gordon Craig
[FB770] Methuen pbk **£5.95**
WALTON, J. MICHAEL
Craig on Theatre
[FB771] Methuen pbk **£5.95**

DEVINE, GEORGE (1910 - 1965)
Founder of the influential English Stage Company in 1956.
WARDEL, IRVING (ED)
The Theatre of George Devine
[FB772] Methuen pbk **£8.95**

EDGAR, DAVID
The Second Time as Farce
Subtitled 'Reflections on the Drama of Mean Times', this collects Edgar's writing on theatre from recent years.
[FB773] Lawrence & W hbk **£12.95**

FUGARD, ATHOL (1932 -)
"Everything is reflected here. My plays come from life and from encounters with actual people".
Notebooks 1960 - 1977
[FB774] Faber pbk **£4.95**

GASKILL, WILLIAM
A Sense of Direction
An autobiography from the distinguished Royal Court director, with some unusual perspectives on the people and practices of his craft.
[FB775] Faber pbk **£4.95**

GRANVILLE-BARKER, HARLEY
(1877 - 1946)
KENNEDY, DENNIS
The Dream of the Theatre **NEW**
The first detailed study of this key figure in early 20th century British theatre. The book includes some facsimiles of original documents, as well as contemporary press reports.
[FB776] Cambridge pbk **£9.95**

GRAY, SIMON
How's That for Telling 'Em, Fat Lady?
A rueful account of the sublime tortures suffered by
the author during the preparations for the 1986
American production of *The Common Pursuit*.
[FB777] Faber pbk **£5.95**

GROTOWSKI, JERZY (1933 -)
With the 'Theatre Laboratory' which he established at
Wroclaw, Grotowski has developed a concept of
'poor theatre', withdrawing inessentials of setting and
costume, and staging plays in cellars. His manifesto
Towards a Poor Theatre has had much influence
since its publication in 1968.
Towards a Poor Theatre
[FB778] Methuen pbk **£6.99**
KUMIEGA (ED)
The Theatre of Grotowski
[FB779] Methuen pbk **£10.99**

IONESCO, EUGENE (1912 -)
Ionesco was the pioneering figure of the 'Theatre of
the Absurd' in France, with plays rejecting the
traditions of dramatic realism. In this volume he
develops a number of the ideas presented in his plays.
Notes and Counternotes
[FB780] Calder pbk **£5.95**

KANTOR, TADEUSZ (1915 -)
Kantor emerged as an experimental director in post-
War Cracow, making use of the unplanned
'happening', and a technique which included mime,
group actions, dummies and marionettes.
**Wielopole/Wielopole: Thoughts on the
Theatre**
[FB781] Boyars hbk **£18.00**

MAMET, DAVID
Mamet's first collection of essays cover a wide range
of subjects, from *The Cherry Orchard* to Hollywood,
and poker-playing to dramatic realism.
Writing in Restaurants
[FB783] Faber pbk **£3.95**

MAROWITZ, CHARLES (1934 -)
**Prospero's Staff: Acting and Directing
in the Contemporary Theatre**
A personal, articulate study of the relationship
between actor and director.
[FB784] Boyars hbk **£17.95**

MEYERHOLD, VSEVOLOD (1874 - 1940/3)
A Russian director, Meyerhold was a dominant figure
in early 20th century drama. He developed a theatre
with an emphasis on movement, and his use of actors
as 'puppets' resulted in rifts with Stanislavski.
BRAUN, EDWARD
**The Theatre of Meyerhold: Revolution
on the Modern Stage**
[FB785] Methuen pbk **£9.95**
BRAUN, EDWARD (ED)
Meyerhold on Theatre
[FB786] Methuen pbk **£7.95**

MILLER, ARTHUR (1915 -)
Miller's diary of the 1983 production of *Death of a
Salesman* in Peking, linking random thoughts in a
sustained comparison of East and West.
'Salesman' in Beijing
[FB787] Methuen pbk **£7.50**

MILLER, JONATHAN (1934 -)
Miller brings together ideas, arguments and
experiences from over 20 years in theatre.
Subsequent Performances
[FB788] Faber pbk **£6.95**

PISCATOR, ERWIN (1893 - 1966)
Piscator worked with Brecht in Berlin in the 1920s,

and both used theatre to endorse their strongly-held
socialist beliefs. Piscator's experimental use of the
stage included the introduction of film projections.
The Political Theatre
[FB789] Methuen pbk **£6.50**
WILLETT, JOHN (ED)
The Theatre of Piscator
[FB790] Methuen pbk **£9.95**

SCHNEIDER, ALAN
Entrances
An excellent autobiography from the director largely
responsible for bringing the work of Beckett, Albee
and Pinter to the American stage.
[FB791] Ianmead pbk **£12.95**

STAFFORD-CLARK, MAX
Letters to George `NEW`
The curious relationship between a leading director in
modern theatre and the Restoration dramatist George
Farquhar, author of Stafford-Clark's recent
production, *The Recruiting Officer*. The letters offer
insights into the play itself, and into the state of
contemporary theatre.
[FB793] N Hern hbk **£10.95**

STANISLAVSKI, CONSTANTIN (1863-1938)
Enormously influential as an actor, director and
teacher, Stanislavski was responsible for the 'Method'
school of acting which taught the actor to exploit an
intense psychological absorption in building up
character. He established the Moscow Arts Theatre in
1898, where many of Chekhov's works were first
performed.
An Actor Prepares
[FB794] Methuen pbk **£5.95**
Building a Character
[FB795] Methuen pbk **£5.95**
Creating a Role
[FB796] Methuen pbk **£5.95**
My Life in Art
[FB797] Methuen pbk **£8.95**
Stanislavski on the Art of the Stage
[FB798] Faber pbk **£5.95**
Stanislavski's Legacy
[FB799] Methuen pbk **£5.95**
BENEDETTI, JEAN
Stanislavski: A Life `NEW`
As the translations of many of his own works are far
from satisfactory, Benedetti's new biographical study
of offers an excellent insight into his character and
methods.
[FB800] Methuen hbk **£16.95**
Stanislavski: An Introduction
A brief but bold study, which goes to the roots of
Stanislavski's acting system.
[FB801] Methuen pbk **£4.50**

STOPPARD, TOM
JENKINS, ANTHONY
The Theatre of Tom Stoppard `NEW`
An accessible study, examining the continuities in all
Stoppard's work, particularly sensitive to the practical
stage values of the plays.
[FB802] Cambridge pbk **£7.95**

STRASBERG, LEE
Strasberg describes the inspiration he drew from
Stanislavski, which led to his development of an
acting system known as the 'Method'.
A Dream of Passion
[FB803] Methuen pbk **£5.99**

**Cambridge 'Directors in Perspective'
Series**
An excellent series of studies which concentrate on
the achievements and methods of directors who have
made major contributions to the state of modern
theatre. Their key productions have been recreated

from promptbooks, reviews, scene-designs,
photographs, diaries, correspondence, and interviews.
Adolphe Appia: Theatre Artist Beacham,
Richard C. hbk **£30.00**
Ingmar Bergman Marker & Lona pbk **£9.50**
Roger Blin Aslan, Odette pbk **£10.95**
Brecht Fuegi, John pbk **£10.95**
Joseph Chaikin Blumenthal, Eileen pbk **£9.50**
Jaques Copeau Rudkin, John pbk **£8.95**
Edward Gordon Craig Innes, C. pbk **£9.50**
Erwin Piscator's Political Theatre Innes,
C. pbk **£9.50**
Harold Prince Hirsch, Foster pbk **£10.95**
Max Reinhardt Styan, J.L. pbk **£9.95**
Peter Stein Patterson, Michael pbk **£9.95**
Andrzej Wajda Karpinski, Maciej hbk **£30.00**
[FB804A] Cambridge hbk/pbk **£8.95 - 30.00**

Practical Guides

BERRY, CICELY
Valuable guidance from the Voice Director of the
RSC.
The Actor and the Text
[FB804A] Harrap pbk **£5.95**
The Voice and the Actor
[FB804B] Harrap pbk **£4.50**

BLUHM, ANNIKA (ED)
Two superb collections of audition speeches selected
from British plays of the last 20 years. Each volume
contains over 45 speeches, with suitable pieces for
every kind of audition, and notes and advice drawn
from interviews with experienced casting directors.
Audition Book for Men `NEW`
[FB805] Methuen pbk **£5.99**
Audition Book for Women `NEW`
[FB806] Methuen pbk **£5.99**

HOGGETT, CHRIS
Stagecrafts
Includes chapters on the acting arena, costume,
design, lighting, make-up, painting and properties.
[FB807A] A & C Black hbk **£15.00**

MCCALLION, MICHAEL
The Voice Book
By the voice teacher at RADA for nearly 12 years.
[FB807B] Faber pbk **£5.95**

PHAIDON 'THEATRE MANUAL' SERIES
A series of five volumes, well-illustrated and versed
in recent developments, these offer guidance at a
number of levels to the subjects considered.
Costume and Make-Up
[FB808] Phaidon pbk **£7.95**
Directing a Play
[FB809] Phaidon pbk **£7.95**
Lighting and Sound
[FB810] Phaidon pbk **£7.95**
Stage Design and Properties
[FB811] Phaidon pbk **£7.95**
**Stage Management and Theatre
Administration**
[FB812] Phaidon pbk **£7.95**

PISK, LITZ
The Actor and His Body
Influential guide from a most experienced director of
movement in the theatre.
[FB813] Harrap pbk **£4.25**

TURNER, BARRY
The Actor's Handbook
A very useful source book with over 5,000 contacts
from all areas of drama.
[FB814] Bloomsbury pbk **10.95**

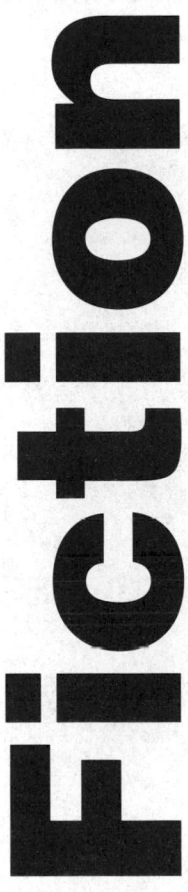

Classic Fiction & Prose
20th Century British & Irish Fiction

African & Caribbean Fiction
North American Fiction
Australasian Fiction
European Fiction
Latin American Fiction
World Fiction

Adventure Fiction
Crime Fiction
Science Fiction

CLASSIC FICTION & PROSE

Including novelists from Defoe to the end of the 19th century, as well as the great prose writers of that period, from Sir Thomas Browne to Lamb, Hazlitt and de Quincey.

AUSTEN, JANE (1775 - 1817)

"Charming as were all of Mrs Radcliffe's works, it was not in them perhaps that human nature, at least in the midland counties of England, was to be looked for...among the English, she believed, in their hearts and habits, there was a general though unequal mixture of good and bad." So Catherine Morland, heroine of Austen's early *Northanger Abbey*, defines her author's fictional territory against the gothic novels which that work so hilariously parodies. The world she portrays may be limited, but it is probed and appraised in intricate detail, and her irony shows a technical and moral sophistication that has seldom been matched. Her subtle comedy remains highly valued, as are her insights into the emotional life of her heroines. The novels are newly available in the 'Virago Classics' list, each one with an introduction by Margaret Drabble.

Emma (1816)
The most ambitious and accomplished of Austen's novels, it follows the moral development of Emma Woodhouse, a pretty and initially self-satisfied young woman. The creation of a morally charged landscape imbues every social nicety with unexpected significance.
[GA1] Chatto hbk **£9.95**
[GA2] Oxford pbk **£1.50**
[GA3] Penguin pbk **£1.75**
[GA4] Virago pbk **£4.99**

Lady Susan/The Watsons/Sanditon
[GA5] Penguin pbk **£2.95**

Mansfield Park (1814)
This belies Austen's reputation as a creator of charming heroines, for Fanny is a shy, drab girl who must set her face against her environment and wait for the man she loves to do the same. In some ways the converse of *Emma*, it is about the necessity of retreat from society. Both, however, show the same moral sophistication and a powerful use of landscape and architecture to signify moral states.
[GA6] Chatto hbk **£9.95**
[GA7] Oxford pbk **£1.35**
[GA8] Penguin pbk **£1.75**
[GA9] Virago pbk **£4.99**

Northanger Abbey
(1798 - 1803, published 1818)
This first work, a satire on the Gothic novel, went unpublished until after Austen's death. As with the best spoofs, it rises above its limitations to become an enjoyable if slight work in its own right. The Oxford edition includes her juvenilia and the unfinished *Sanditon*.
[GA10] Chatto hbk **£9.95**
[GA11] Penguin pbk **£1.75**
[GA12] Oxford pbk **£1.25**
[GA13] Virago pbk **£4.99**

Oxford Illustrated Jane Austen
(Boxed Set)
[GA14] Oxford 6 vols hbk **£50.00**

Persuasion (1818)
Her last completed work, published posthumously, has a rather different viewpoint, for the heroine is twenty-nine, and the plot centres on the re-instatement of an engagement that had been broken off some years before. Anne Elliot's story of romantic love is expressed with greater emotional intensity than is allowed in the earlier,

more oblique works.
[GA15] Chatto hbk **£9.95**
[GA16] Oxford pbk **£1.50**
[GA17] Penguin pbk **£1.95**
[GA18] Virago pbk **£4.99**

Pride and Prejudice (1813)
The best loved of Austen's works, its popularity depends on the charm of the heroine, Elizabeth, the rich comedy of the incidental characters, and the subtleties of the plot. It is all too easy to take the title at face value and presume the pride lies with Darcy and the prejudice with Elizabeth, but this novel is too clever for such black and white conclusions.
[GA19] Chatto hbk **£9.95**
[GA20] Oxford pbk **£1.50**
[GA21] Penguin pbk **£1.50**
[GA22] Virago pbk **£4.99**

Sense and Sensibility (1811)
Austen's first major novel is a gentle satire on late 18th century fiction's cult of extreme sensibility. The title suggests the opposing temperaments of the sisters Elinor and Marianna Dashwood. Elinor's powers of discernment act as a check on Marianna's impulsive emotional outpourings, but in order to survive each must adopt qualities from the other.
[GA23] Chatto hbk **£9.95**
[GA24] Oxford pbk **£1.60**
[GA25] Penguin pbk **£1.75**
[GA26] Virago pbk **£4.99**

AUSTEN, JANE & BRONTE, CHARLOTTE

Juvenilia of Jane Austen & Charlotte Bronte
[GA27] Penguin pbk **£2.95**

BAGE, ROBERT (1720 - 1801)

Hermsprong, or Man as He is Not (1796)
Influenced by Rousseau's notion of the 'Noble Savage', this is a story of the possibilities of a 'natural' man.
[GA28] Oxford pbk **£3.95**

BECKFORD, WILLIAM (1754 - 1844)
Beckford was a man of immense wealth, builder of Fonthill Abbey (a Gothic extravaganza) and author of *Vathek*, which follows the sins of the cruel and sensual Caliph Vathek. Exotic and with a homo-erotic subtext, it was one of the most successful of the 'oriental tales' then in fashion.

Vathek (1784)
[GA29] Oxford pbk **£2.25**

Aphra Behn, author of *Love Letters Between a Nobleman and His Sister* (Virago pbk **£6.95**)

BEHN, APHRA (1640 - 1689)
"All women together ought to let flowers fall upon the tomb of Aphra Behn, for it was she who earned them the right to speak their mind" (*Virginia Woolf*). As well as being a spy, a political satirist (arrested for making 'abusive reflections upon persons of quality') and a prolific playwright, she was the first professional authoress in Britain.

Love Letters Between a Nobleman and His Sister (1683)
The first epistolary novel in English, it recounts the contemporary scandal of Lord Grey and his sister-in-law Lady Berkeley in familiar Restoration style.
[GA30] Virago pbk **£6.95**

Oroonoko & Other Stories (1688)
Oroonoko is a heroic, passionate tale of black rebellion against slavery.
[GA31] Methuen pbk **£3.95**

BLACKMORE, R.D. (1825 - 1900)
Who immortalised Hardy country before Hardy? Why, R.D. Blackmore of course, although his work is more in the Scott tradition of Historical Romance.

Lorna Doone (1869)
A much loved classic of murder, kidnapping, outlaws, revenge, highwaymen and finally requited love on 17th century Exmoor. The emotions are not complex, but the action is great fun.
[GA32] Pan pbk **£4.50**

BORROW, GEORGE (1803 - 1881)

Lavengro (1851)
"The reader is aware of a monstrous misuse of co-incidence," commented one critic on this energetic, part-autobiographical tale of an educated man who joins a gypsy band. A loose, picaresque celebration of life beyond the pale.
[GA33] Oxford pbk **£3.50**

BRADDON, MARY E. (1837 - 1915)
The chief writer of the Sensational novel, Braddon was queen of the circulating libraries and very popular across Victorian society. Only her 'two bigamy novels' remain in print from over 80 that she published.

Aurora Floyd (1863)
"If I could plot like Miss Braddon," said Thackeray, *"I should be the greatest novelist that ever lived."* This mysterious tale of murder, arson, blackmail and seduction shows why.
[GA34] Virago pbk **£5.95**

Lady Audley's Secret (1862)
Her first novel was as popular as it was controversial, being attacked for the sensuality of its unscrupulous heroine. It was *"a skilful combination of bigamy, arson, murder and insanity"* for Henry James who deemed it *"indecent but not immoral"*.
[GA35] Oxford pbk **£4.95**

BRONTE, ANNE (1820 - 1849)
Anne's work is direct, passionate and unfairly under-rated. In her two novels a sincere religious framework endeavours to accommodate romantic love and demonic self-hatred.

Agnes Grey (1847)
A restrained tale of disillusionment and longing as a governess (clearly Anne herself) copes with being in love and looking after nasty children.
[GA36] Chatto hbk **£8.95**
[GA37] Penguin pbk **£2.99**

Tenant of Wildfell Hall (1848)
A love story, but with more desire, guilt and desperation than was thought proper at the time. The much maligned structural shift, when a long flashback occurs through the heroine's diary, is more endearing and innovative than clumsy.
[GA38] Chatto hbk **£8.95**
[GA39] Penguin pbk **£2.95**

BRONTE, CHARLOTTE (1816 - 1855)

Although all the Brontës spent time away from Haworth, Charlotte's wider experience is evident in her novels. Structurally they are varied and inventive, as she grapples to include both personal and political dimensions. Charlotte felt novelists should be 'social regenerators', and she chose plain, typical girls as heroines to illustrate the restrictions on women, particularly those rendered unmarriageable by choice or penury. There is also a proud provincialism in her work, and a concern to document real emotion rather than make trite gestures towards it. For this she drew on her own experiences, particularly two years learning to be a teacher in Brussels (her unrequited love for the school director surfaces in **The Professor** and **Villette**). Acclaimed in her lifetime, by Thackeray and Mrs Gaskell among others, her high standing can be seen in the many biographies of her, the most recent being Rebecca Fraser's.

Jane Eyre (1847)

The first Brontë success which could serve as an archetype of their collective strengths. A strong first-person narrative, with wild and Gothic elements (the madwoman in the attic), charts the heroine's troubled discoveries of the depths of desire. We follow Jane from a cruel, terrorised childhood to her post as governess at the house of the dark, handsomely Byronic Mr Rochester. Intense descriptions, both of emotions and environment, underpin a gripping plot.
[GA40] Chatto hbk **£8.95**
[GA41] Oxford pbk **£1.60**
[GA42] Penguin pbk **£1.99**

Shirley (1849)

A brave change in direction after **Jane Eyre**. As Charlotte says in chapter one, "something real, cool and solid lies before you, something unromantic as Monday morning." A social, historical novel set in West Yorkshire as the Industrial Revolution, the Napoleonic wars, and widespread Luddite rioting in the North threatened social stability.
[GA43] Chatto hbk **£8.95**
[GA44] Oxford pbk **£2.95**
[GA45] Penguin pbk **£3.50**

The Professor (1857)

Toned down for fear of being accused of melodrama and daydreaming (as her poetry had been) this first novel was rejected for being insufficiently exciting. An autobiographical account of her time in Brussels.
[GA46] Chatto hbk **£8.95**
[GA47] Penguin pbk **£2.99**

Villette (1853)

A dense and difficult book. Lucy Snowe is the narrator who goes to teach in a girls' school in a provincial European town. The humdrum details and claustrophobia of solitude give way to a desperate, unrequited attraction. A mature and innovative work.
[GA48] Chatto hbk **£8.95**
[GA49] Penguin pbk **£3.50**

BRONTE, EMILY (1818 - 1848)

"A native and nursling of the moors...her native hills were far more to her than a spectacle; they were what she lived in, and by, as much as the wild birds, their tenants, or as the heather they produce" (Charlotte Brontë). This image of Emily, the most solitary and uncommunicative of the sisters, is enforced by her early death from TB (she refused to convalesce despite repeated warnings) and by her one extraordinary novel.

Wuthering Heights (1847)

The novel that really is as gripping and as good as everyone says it is. Its fame lies in its dark celebration of the obsessive and destructive love between Heathcliffe and Cathy, who grow up together but are separated by Cathy's marriage to the genteel Edgar Linton. The novel has a wilfulness and confidence all its own. Its splintered narrative, pieced together from reported conversations, dreams and surmises, creates a unique intensity of reader involvement. Recent

criticism has focused on Emily as 'Milton's daughter', writing within a stark but liberating Puritan tradition while reacting against its misogynistic foundations.
[GA50] Chatto hbk **£8.95**
[GA51] Oxford pbk **£1.75**
[GA52] Penguin pbk **£1.99**

BROUGHTON, RHODA (1840 - 1920)

Of an ancient and well-connected family, her novels served as a mild form of sex education for girls in the 1870s and 1880s. Broughton began as a Sensation novelist, but, tarred by the brush of immorality already applied to Mary Braddon, changed to social comedies. **Belinda** is a sharp satire of Oxford university and of one academic and former friend in particular.

Belinda (1883)

[GA53] Virago pbk **£5.95**

BROWNE, SIR THOMAS (1605 - 1682)

One of England's finest and most memorable prose stylists, Browne's most famous works are the **Religio Medici** (in which a doctor discusses his faith), the haunting and solemn elegy **Hydrotaphia**, and **The Garden of Cyrus**, a joyous celebration of the impalpable connections of the universe.

Major Works

[GA54] Penguin pbk **£7.95**

Religio Medici, Hydrotaphia & The Garden of Cyrus

[GA55] Oxford pbk **£5.95**

BRUNTON, MARY (1778 - 1818)

Brunton is neither stern nor straightforward, despite her titles. An important influence on Jane Austen, her heroines seek passion and independence within restrictive man-made codes of behaviour.

Discipline (1815)

[GA56] Pandora pbk **£4.95**

Self Control (1810/11)

[GA57] Pandora pbk **£4.95**

BUNYAN, JOHN (1628 - 1680)

A tinker by trade, Bunyan's conversion to evangelical Protestantism led him to a life of preaching and writing. His novelty to our eyes lies in a direct, resonant prose style coupled to a lively imagination. This springs partly from a heritage of native English Protestant (as opposed to Latinate Anglo-Catholic) writing, and partly from his lowly, unlearned origins. Although careful to distance himself from more radical Protestant elements (remnants from the Diggers and Ranters of the Civil War) Bunyan was deemed seditious enough to be jailed for 12 years, a period from which most of his writing comes.

Grace Abounding & Mr Badman

A standard and unpromising form, the autobiographical testimony is enthused into life by Bunyan's energetic and unpretentious prose (his discussion of the sins of bell ringing is particularly instructive). **Mr Badman** is a later based on dialogue and more self-conscious in literary style.
[GA58] Dent pbk **£3.50**

Pilgrim's Progress (1678 - 84)

This tale of the Pilgrimage of Mr Christian (and later of his wife and children) is one of the most celebrated pieces of English prose. Its influence and wide appeal led E.P. Thompson the historian to rank it 'one of the two founding texts of the English working class movement'. It is not hard to see why. The reader is drawn into an allegorical journey through life: common experiences such as friendship and self-doubt are translated into epic set pieces and given life by an extraordinary visual imagination. In general the writing is powerful and sparse but the book also contains visionary and rapturous descriptions, in

which Bunyan's prophetic voice is given glorious flow.
[GA59] Oxford pbk **£2.25**
[GA60] Penguin pbk **£2.25**

BURNEY, FANNY (1752 - 1840)

The first acclaimed female novelist, her books deal humorously with the development of young women into the perilous society of men. Never before had the domestic, women's world been armed with a satirical pen.

Camilla (1796)

"I mean this work to be sketches of characters and morals put in action - not a romance". Contains in Edgar Mandlebert one of the great prigs of English literature.
[GA61] Oxford pbk **£4.95**

Cecilia (1782)

A single woman tries to keep her inherited fortune from the clutches of suitors, guardians and rogues. Unusual for the time in having an assertive, well-written heroine.
[GA62] Virago pbk **£6.95**

Evelina (1778)

Written in secret as a teenager and published anonymously, this first novel was a roaring success and its satirical malice is still undimmed.
[GA63] Oxford pbk **£3.95**

BUTLER, SAMUEL (1835 - 1902)

Butler was a theologian, natural historian, travel writer, composer, psychologist and literary scholar as well as author of a varied collection of fiction. His particular concerns were Darwinism and exposing humbug.

Erewhon (1872)

Although this should be Nowhere (spelt backwards), it is in fact New Zealand which has been strained through a Swiftian sieve to emerge as a merciless satire on contemporary society and hypocrisy.
[GA64] Penguin pbk **£2.50**

The Way of All Flesh (1903)

Published after his death, this was something of a therapeutic mould-breaker in its day, with its autobiographical rubbishing of traditional institutions, particularly the family. A cold-blooded dissection comedy.
[GA65] Penguin pbk **£3.95**

CARLYLE, THOMAS (1795 - 1881)

The man who had the misfortune to have the only manuscript of his first volume of **A History of the French Revolution** used accidentally as a fire lighter by J.S. Mill. In his day he was very influential as a social prophet, critic, occasional philosopher and master prose stylist. **Sartor Resartus** is an early piece, concerning an imaginary German Professor's Philosophy of Clothes.

Sartor Resartus

[GA66] Oxford pbk **£3.95**

Selected Writings

[GA67] Penguin pbk **£5.95**

CARROLL, LEWIS (1832 - 1898)

The Alice books must be high on most people's lists of wonderful literature, even if unhealthy tendencies have since been unearthed in Charles Dodgson's character. Many editions are in print, but for the adult or questioning child Martin Gardner's **The Annotated Alice** offers, as well as the full text and many of Tenniel's illustrations, an enlightening introduction to Dodgson's thought. (See also **Children's Classics**).

Alice in Wonderland/Through the Looking Glass

[GA68] Oxford pbk **£2.50**

The Annotated Alice

[GA69] Penguin pbk **£4.99**

CLELAND, JOHN (1709 - 1789)

Subtitled 'Memoirs of a Woman of Pleasure', *Fanny Hill* is a shamelessly indecent work in which Cleland documents both the joys and physiology of sexual experience, through his breathless narrator Fanny Hill.

Fanny Hill (1749)

Published to mark Cleland's bi-centenary, this hardback edition is lavishly illustrated with the work of artists of the period, including Hogarth, Fragonard, Boucher and Watteau.

[GA70] Sidgwick hbk **£14.95**
[GA71] Oxford pbk **£2.95**
[GA72] Penguin pbk **£2.95**

COLLINS, WILLIAM WILKIE (1824 - 1889)

Collins learned his trade as a literary apprentice to Dickens but went on to develop the detective novel genre as we know it. His gripping, ingenious plots are all the more remarkable for being written for weekly serialisation; equally remarkable is his private life, the subject of a recent biography, *The Secret Life of Wilkie Collins* by William Clarke. In all he wrote 21 novels; his Sensation novels are still popular but he also produced social novels with a propagandist edge.

Armadale (1866)

Lydia Guilt was *"one of the most hardened female villains whose devices and desires have ever blackened fiction"* for one contemporary.

[GA73] Dover pbk **£7.95**

Basil (1852)

His first attempt at melodrama. A young man is infatuated with a worthless girl of inferior social status. When she is seduced (somewhat graphically for the period), Basil takes revenge.

[GA74] Dover pbk **£4.75**

Haunted Hotel (1878)

Although Swinburne called this short novel *"a hideous fiction"*, the ghosts and disembodied heads are as convincing as ever.

[GA75] Dover pbk **£2.80**

Hide and Seek (1854)

A light tumble through lower-class life. Collins claimed his deaf-mute Madonna was the first disabled character to be treated sympathetically in fiction.

[GA76] Dover pbk **£4.75**

Little Novels

Fourteen stories written for Dickens' periodicals.

[GA77] Dover pbk **£4.75**

No Name (1862)

An audacious novel written under Dickens' influence. Its treatment of two orphaned, illegitimate daughters (their parents had refused to marry) has greater resonance now more is known of Collins' own marital status.

[GA78] Oxford pbk **£4.95**

Tales of Terror and the Supernatural

Twelve macabre stories in the Edgar Allan Poe tradition, written between 1850-59.

[GA79] Dover pbk **£5.20**

The Biter Bit & Other Stories

[GA80] Sutton pbk **£2.50**

The Dead Secret (1857)

A tentative move in the direction of the Sensation novel.

[GA81] Sutton pbk **£3.95**

The Moonstone (1868)

The first detective novel in English. Dorothy Sayers called it 'impeccable' but it is the blend of a novelist's depth of characterization with a crime writer's delight in suspense and surprise which makes it work so well.

[GA82] Oxford pbk **£2.95**
[GA83] Penguin pbk **£2.95**

The Woman in White (1860)

Collins proved himself to be the Alfred Hitchcock of the Sensation novel in this gripping tale, told in alternating diary narratives, of a young woman who is deprived of her inheritance and identity when she is drugged, put in an asylum, and replaced by a double. Can she prove who she really is? The dastardly Count Fosco was created a foreigner because Collins felt his crime 'too ingenious' for an English villain.

[GA84] Oxford pbk **£2.95**
[GA85] Penguin pbk **£2.95**

DEFOE, DANIEL (1660 - 1731)

Credited with 560 books, pamphlets and journals, Defoe is commonly hailed England's first novelist. He began in commerce (selling wool, bricks, oysters, ship insurance and breeding civet cats) before being imprisoned and then becoming a government spy. This heady blend of capitalism, political opportunism and a journalist's eye for vivid detail, produces energetic and diverse novels.

Captain Singleton (1720)

"His life, adventures and pyracies…"

[GA86] Sutton pbk **£2.95**

Journal of the Plague Year (1722)

A powerful but detached account of the 1665 plague told with vivid circumstantial detail. Defoe's own Providential religious views make this a slippery, intriguing work. It inspired Camus' *La Peste*.

[GA87] Penguin pbk **£2.95**

Moll Flanders (1722)

An 'Everywoman' tale of a destitute, spirited woman making it in a man's world. Defoe's narrative is a 'Pilgrim's Progress' while also being acutely aware of economic forces and the thrills of being resourceful in the face of them.

[GA88] Oxford pbk **£1.50**
[GA89] Penguin pbk **£1.75**

Robinson Crusoe (1719)

It is not unfair to call this the first capitalist and colonialist myth, and definitely worth reading to discover why. Crusoe's isolation combines adventure and rich detail with an epic sense of European progress from 'savagehood'.

[GA90] Penguin pbk **£1.95**
[GA91] Penguin pbk **£1.50**

Roxana (1724)

A purported biography of prosperous wickedness, which leads the heroine to prison and finally penitence.

[GA92] Oxford pbk **£2.80**
[GA93] Penguin pbk **£2.50**

The Complete Tradesman (1726)

A guide to all aspects of business from apprenticeship to partnership, book-keeping to fraud, with contributions also on marriage and 'innocent diversions'. Not a novel, but then thankfully not a Victor Kiam guide to entrepreneurship either.

[GA94] Sutton pbk **£5.95**

Tour Through the Whole Island of Great Britain

[GA95] Penguin pbk **£5.95**

DICKENS, CHARLES (1812 - 1870)

Enormously successful in his own day, Dickens enjoyed a close relationship with his reading public: so much so that he would happily change a plot in mid-novel (as with *Martin Chuzzlewit* or the conclusion of *Great Expectations*), if his monthly sales fell. His work is a great deal more complex than the popularly held view of him admits, and his concerns developed throughout his career. Early experience of poverty (he worked in a blacking warehouse at the age of 12) adds bite to even his most wooden characters, and his descriptive powers (as in the opening of *Bleak House*) make the later novels even darker.

A December Vision: Dickens's Social Journalism

[GA96] Collins hbk **£10.95**

American Notes (1842)

The result of Dickens' American trip. It didn't live up to his high expectations, and he returned disillusioned, as can be seen in the American scenes of *Martin Chuzzlewit*.

[GA97] Penguin pbk **£5.99**

American Notes & Pictures from Italy (1842)

[GA98] Oxford hbk **£4.95**

Barnaby Rudge (1841)

Scott's influence on this Historical Novel, dealing with the Gordon Riots in London, did not make it entirely successful, nor is his portrayal of the mad Barnaby, although the riots themselves are furious and vivid.

[GA99] Oxford hbk **£4.95**
[GA100] Penguin pbk **£4.50**

Bleak House (1852 - 3)

A long, dark tale whose atmosphere is set by the fog-bound city and the claustrophobic Chancery court of the opening chapter. One of Dickens' finest hours, the range of characters and machinations is astounding, and the use of two narrators innovative and unsettling.

[GA101] Oxford hbk **£4.95**
[GA102] Penguin pbk **£3.95**

Christmas Books

Dickens intended these five stories to *"awaken loving and forebearing thoughts"*. *A Christmas Carol* with Scrooge, Marley and the Ghosts is justifiably the most celebrated.

[GA103] Oxford hbk **£4.95**

Christmas Books: Vol 1

[GA104] Penguin pbk **£2.99**

Christmas Books: Vol 2

[GA105] Penguin pbk **£3.99**

Christmas Stories

[GA106] Oxford hbk **£4.95**

David Copperfield (1849 - 50)

Said to be Dickens' favourite novel, David is the helpless (and autobiographical) child growing into a familiar world of melodrama, savage comedy and tenderness. As well as other popular characters like Mr Micawber, Peggoty, Em'ly and David's eventual wife Agnes, it contains Uriah Heep *"the epitome of slimy hypocrisy, of malevolent, rancorous envy, masking itself under professions of duty and humility"*.

[GA107] Oxford hbk **£4.95**
[GA108] Oxford pbk **£2.50**
[GA109] Penguin pbk **£2.95**

Dombey and Son (1848)

"Papa, what's money? It isn't cruel, is it?" Dombey, the rich head of a shipping house, is given the chance to find out when his son Paul dies, he alienates his daughter Florence, and his company fails. Genuinely moving, the novel is famous for its plea that children

Charles Dickens (Picture: Mary Evans Picture Library)

be treated as individuals, and for being the first work of fiction to feature railways.

[GA110] Oxford hbk **£4.95**
[GA111] Oxford pbk **£2.95**
[GA112] Penguin pbk **£3.95**

Great Expectations (1860 - 1)

The predictable plot of Pip, a young man climbing socially to maturity and responsibility, was Dickens' penultimate work. The haunting figures of Miss Havisham and Abel Magwitch, both straight from Sensation novels, provide colour, and Pip himself has his moments.

[GA113] Oxford hbk **£4.95**
[GA114] Penguin pbk **£1.99**

Hard Times (1854)

A visit to Preston produced Dickens' most socially critical work, as emphasised in Terry Eagleton's Methuen edition. Gradgrind and Bounderby are effective satires on the tyranny of Utilitarianism and Facts although Dickens is equally critical of the working class. Gissing, a more committed political novelist, found it unconvincing, but F.R. Leavis rated it his best novel.

[GA115] Oxford hbk **£4.95**
[GA116] Penguin pbk **£1.75**
[GA117] Oxford pbk **£1.95**
[GA118] Methuen pbk **£4.95**

Little Dorrit (1855 - 7)

Following the sombre tone of *Hard Times*, this complex tale begins with Dorrit senior in Marshalsea prison for debt (recalling Dickens' own father). It tells of the psychological damages of poverty and wealth while also containing in the relationship of Amy Dorrit and Arthur Clennam one of Dickens' most powerful love stories. Shaw rated it *"a masterpiece among masterpieces"*.

[GA119] Oxford hbk **£4.95**
[GA120] Penguin pbk **£3.99**
[GA121] Oxford pbk **£3.50**

Martin Chuzzlewit (1843)

Part of this work is set in America to which Martin travels to make his fortune. Dickens' comic picture of the country caused great offence at the time. The book is about selfishness: Martin loses his scant resources (to the fraudulent Eden Land Company) and his egocentricity, but his memorably unctuous teacher Mr Pecksniff does not.

[GA122] Oxford hbk **£4.95**
[GA123] Penguin pbk **£4.50**
[GA124] Oxford pbk **£3.95**

Mudfog Papers

[GA125] Sutton pbk **£2.50**

Mystery of Edwin Drood (1870)

Written to rival the success of Wilkie Collins' Sensation novels but unfinished on Dickens death, the plot concerns the disappearance of Edwin just as he has become estranged from his childhood sweetheart Rosa. No solution to the mystery exists, though at 280 pages (in the Penguin) it is still a good read.

[GA126] Oxford hbk **£4.95**
[GA127] Penguin pbk **£2.95**
[GA128] Oxford pbk **£2.50**

Nicholas Nickleby (1838 - 9)

His third novel, a broad mixture of melodrama and a splendid comedy of manners, is famous for Wackford Squeers the school teacher and his awful family, and for Smike, Nicholas' devoted friend. As anyone who saw the Royal Shakespeare Company's adaption in the early 1980s will testify, the power and pathos of this work has remarkable stamina.

[GA129] Oxford hbk **£4.95**
[GA130] Penguin pbk **£3.99**
[GA131] Oxford pbk **£2.95**

Oliver Twist (1837 - 8)

This shorter novel has passed into folklore and is a fine example of Dickens' strengths - his larger-than-life characterisation and his deft manipulation of the reader's sensibilities. Oliver is born in a workhouse but flees from the cruelty of the local beadle, Mr

Bumble, to London's teeming underworld. It may be short on catchy tunes, but the novel more than compensates with the gore and glamour of Fagin's gang.

[GA132] Oxford hbk **£4.95**
[GA133] Penguin pbk **£2.25**
[GA134] Oxford pbk **£1.95**

Our Mutual Friend (1864 - 5)

Henry James felt this final novel to be so laboured as to have been *"dug out with spade and pick axe"* (which is ironic given the nature of James' own late novels). A more charitable interpretation would be that it is a complex, mature work. John Harman, returning from exile to claim his inheritance and his wife by arranged marriage, survives an attempted murder but finds that everyone believes him to be dead. It *is* a demanding novel, but its range of settings and descriptions (particularly the pervasive use of money-dirt symbolism) are familiar strengths.

[GA135] Oxford hbk **£4.95**
[GA136] Penguin pbk **£4.50**

Selected Short Fiction

Comprising *Tales of the Supernatural*, *Impressionistic Sketches* and *Dramatic Monologues*, the pieces span Dickens' literary career.

[GA137] Penguin pbk **£4.95**

Sikes and Nancy & Other Public Readings

It is not well known that Dickens both wrote and acted in plays, and that from 1854 he also gave charity readings of his own works, sometimes impersonating as many as 20 characters in one item. Then in 1858, stung by poor reviews for *Little Dorrit* and with his marriage breaking up, he began to do paid public reading tours. In all he gave over 450 performances, the most popular items being 'The Trial from Pickwick' and 'A Christmas Carol'.

[GA138] Oxford pbk **£2.95**

Sketches by Boz (1836)

Early articles from various periodicals, praised for their Hogarthian scenes of misery and despair, offset by brightly coloured pictures of mass jollification.

[GA139] Oxford hbk **£4.95**

Tale of Two Cities (1859)

The two cities are Paris at the time of the Revolution, and London where Romance is blossoming between disguised French nobleman Charles Darnay, and Lucie Manette, daughter of an exiled French physician. Charles returns to Paris to try and save a faithful servant who is on trial - a dangerous move it transpires.

[GA140] Oxford hbk **£4.95**
[GA141] Penguin pbk **£1.95**
[GA142] Oxford pbk **£1.95**

The Old Curiosity Shop (1840 - 1)

Dickens at his most sentimental, notably in the much discussed tear-jerking death of Little Nell. The shop is Nell's grandfather's who, forced into penury by family troubles, has borrowed money from the odious dwarf Mr Quilp in the hope of gambling it back again. When the shop is repossessed, Nell and her grandfather are at the mercy of Victorian England.

[GA143] Oxford hbk **£4.95**
[GA144] Penguin pbk **£3.99**

The Pickwick Papers (1836 - 7)

"It appears to have been written in a series of jerkily spasmodic bouts of inane euphoria" said an unkind modern critic, referring to the unusual origins of this first novel. It was originally commissioned to supply text for a series of illustrations, but the characters of the Pickwick Club rapidly usurped their minor role to produce an enduring comic and sentimental triumph.

[GA145] Oxford hbk **£4.95**
[GA146] Penguin pbk **£3.50**
[GA147] Oxford pbk **£3.50**

The Uncommercial Traveller (1860)

Journalistic articles, essays and reminiscences.

[GA148] Oxford hbk **£4.95**

DISRAELI, BENJAMIN (1804 - 1881)

He became the most powerful politician in the land but was also an original political novelist. The chivalric and idealistic Coningsby trilogy (*"to believe in the heroic makes heroes"*) are his only books still in print. Written to ingratiate himself with the 'Young England' faction of the Tory Party, they also have sympathy for the poorer elements of society.

Coningsby (1844)

A remarkable picture of the actual workings of politics at the the time of the first Reform Bill.

[GA149] Oxford hbk **£3.50**
[GA150] Penguin pbk **£3.99**

Sybil, or The Two Nations (1845)

Aimed to show the 'Two Nations of England, Rich and Poor' whose division results in a Chartist rising, this was the first novel to expose the appalling conditions of the urban working class.

[GA151] Penguin pbk **£4.95**
[GA152] Oxford pbk **£3.95**

Tancred, or The New Crusade (1847)

The hero renounces Christianity and certain social and political success to explore Judaism in the Holy Land. Reflects Disraeli's own concerns as a Jew brought up in the Anglican tradition as his father attempted to assimilate English culture.

[GA153] Greenwood hbk **£24.75**

EDEN, EMILY (1797 - 1869)

In which we enter a world where everybody is impertinent or indignant. More Oscar Wilde than Jane Austen, Eden's dialogue sparkles with wit. Her letters from Upper India, where she spent 6 years, were addressed to her sister.

The Semi-Attached Couple/The Semi-Detached House (1859 - 60)

[GA154] Virago pbk **£5.50**

Up the Country: Letters from India

[GA155] Virago pbk **£5.95**

Early Women Novelists

The poet Southey is probably famous now only for his advice to Charlotte Brontë: *"Literature cannot be the business of a woman's life, and it ought not to be. The more she is engaged in her proper duties, the less leisure will she have for it, even as an accomplishment and a recreation"*. Yet women had been producing novels to support themselves for 100 years before he said this. Despite being deprived of formal education, and belonging to a world where they were still the disposable property of men, women wrote the majority of early novels, and for a reading public that was itself predominantly female. Fanny Burney, Maria Edgeworth and Eliza Heywood were among those highly praised in their day, and there is even evidence that men posed as women in order to be published. Both Virago and Pandora have made a concerted effort to reprint classic women's fiction: two good background books are Virginia Woolf's seminal *A Room of One's Own* and Dale Spender's recent *Mothers of the Novel*.

EDGEWORTH, MARIA (1767 - 1849)

Highly paid and respected in her day, Edgeworth's lasting fame is that she initiated the Regional Novel, and made gestures towards the embryonic Historical Novel form. Until *Castle Rackrent*, novels had been set in Society: ie. London, Bath or unspecified country houses. She rooted her narratives in actual places where the feel of a specific landscape has shaped opinions and desires. Scott credited her influence in *Waverley*. Her other style dealt with contemporary British society, and it is to this category that *Belinda*, *Helen* and *Patronage* belong.

Belinda (1801)

[GA156] Pandora pbk **£4.95**

Castle Rackrent (1800)
[GA157] Oxford pbk **£2.95**
Helen (1834)
[GA158] Pandora pbk **£5.95**
Patronage (1814)
[GA159] Pandora pbk **£6.95**
The Absentee (1812)
Though set in Ireland this has a Russian flavour with its decaying aristocrats and obstructive peasantry.
[GA160] Oxford pbk **£4.95**

ELIOT, GEORGE (1819 - 1880)
"The only effect I ardently long to produce by my writing, is that those who read them should be better able to imagine and feel the pains and the joys of those who differ from themselves in everything but the broad fact of being struggling, erring human beings." Although she was no doubt a sympathetic, compassionate woman, Eliot's strengths as a writer come from her philosophical militancy. She was a Free Thinker, a cohabitor with a married man who believed in free love, and a translator of two works of Liberal Theology (by Strauss and Feuerbach) which sought to deregulate religious experience. Her books are driven by the tragedy of mankind's perfectability, and the ease with which that potential is dented. Without a hard intellectual sympathy, such feelings would lapse into sentimentality, but Eliot's strength, as Virginia Woolf commented, was to write novels 'for grown-up people'.
Adam Bede (1859)
Mrs Gaskell said of this first novel: *"I have never read anything so complete and beautiful in fiction in my whole life before."* The influences are Wesleyan and Pastoral. The hope of redemption, by nature, love or salvation, shapes the tale of Hetty Sorel's trial for infanticide, Adam's unrequited love for her, and the emptiness at the heart of Dinah, the Methodist preacher. This is Eliot at her most enthusiastic - even the flaws are joyous.
[GA161] Chatto hbk **£9.95**
[GA162] Penguin pbk **£3.95**
Brother Jacob (1860)
This novella enjoys its first reprint since 1906 this year, thanks to Virago. It is a tale of 'moral dinginess', featuring the squalid villain David Faux's quest for colonial bliss and a confectionery fortune.
[GA163] Virago pbk **£3.50**
Daniel Deronda (1874 - 6)
Her final and most complex novel foregrounds two plots. Gwendolen Harleth, shamelessly pirated by Henry James in *A Portrait of a Lady*, is the familiar high-spirited but egocentric young woman, but it is poverty as much as ambition which drives her to marry the cruel, languid aristocrat Grandcourt. The descriptions of her increasingly bitter and frenzied thoughts as the marriage collapses are Eliot's finest hour. Lewes, Eliot's partner, read the penultimate chapter *"with hot eyes and a sense of having been beaten all over"*.
[GA164] Chatto hbk **£9.95**
[GA165] Penguin pbk **£4.50**
[GA166] Oxford pbk **£3.95**
Felix Holt, The Radical (1866)
Set in developing England on the eve of the first Reform Bill (1832) this is noted for being her 'political novel' although as ever her understanding is of the powers of circumstance and social interaction to dictate character. (*"This history is chiefly concerned with the private lot of a few men and women: but there is no private life which has not been determined by a wider public life."*) Here character is rooted in history and an organically developed culture at odds with newer materialist values. The plot is unconvincing but the characterization, particularly of the suffering Mrs Transome and the Dissenting Minister Mr Lyon, is as acute as ever.
[GA167] Penguin pbk **£2.95**

George Eliot by L.C. Dickinson (Picture: National Portrait Gallery)

Middlemarch: A Study of Provincial Life (1871 - 2)
Middlemarch is Coventry in the 1820s just before the first Reform Bill, and the town is the novel's centre. *"My design"*, Eliot wrote, *"is to show the gradual action of ordinary causes rather than exceptional"* and it is these social causes - gossip, flirtation, pride and a rigid class structure - that warp the novel's bright young things (Ladislaw, Lydgate and Dorothea). The compassion and fluid irony with which the omniscient narrator treats the characters have made this a paradigm Realist novel. The reader is constantly appealed to as judge and arbitrator, which makes the book a flattering experience quite apart from its manifold other strengths.
[GA168] Chatto hbk **£9.95**
[GA169] Penguin pbk **£2.95**
[GA170] Oxford pbk **£2.95**
Romola (1863)
An unexpected excursion into 15th century Florence, with philosophic intent built into its historical structure.
[GA171] Penguin pbk **£4.50**
Scenes of Clerical Life (1858)
Eliot's first fictional work comprised three tales. The final story 'Janet's Repentance' details the persecution of an evangelical vicar in an industrial town. 'Mr Gilfil's Love Story' prefigures *Adam Bede* with its atmosphere of intrigue, thwarted love and selfless devotion. 'The Sad Fortunes of the Rev. Amos Barton' is a portrait of the unglamorous Reverend, treated in a restrained way to form an effective plea for tolerance and sensitivity.
[GA172] Oxford pbk **£3.95**
[GA173] Penguin pbk **£3.99**
Silas Marner, the Weaver of Raveloe (1861)
A moving and intense short novel. Silas is a miserable, reclusive weaver who spends his hours accumulating money and avoiding human contact. The money is stolen by the reckless son of the local squire, but in its place enters Eppie, an orphan child walking in from the snow. Although it sounds like a fairy tale, and its conclusion is a delightful fiction, the evocation of depression in Silas is unsettling.
[GA174] Chatto hbk **£8.95**
[GA175] Penguin pbk **£2.50**
The Lifted Veil (1859)
Written in the first person, this unusual novella has death as its theme, and a sensationalist edge. Latimer is a barren artist searching for inspiration. Instead he receives a bizarre vision of Prague with zombie-like inhabitants, and then as the veil lifts further, a vision

of Bertha, a faery death figure. Written during the composition of *Middlemarch*, this reworking of the Faust myth was not published until 1878.
[GA176] Virago pbk **£2.95**
The Mill on the Floss (1860)
A fine novel of contrasting halves. The first is a glorious easy-paced evocation of childhood with Maggie Tulliver impetuously growing up, admiring her older but less worthy brother Tom. The second is an epic tragedy governed by passion, both in Mr Tulliver's response to his bankruptcy and in Maggie's attraction to her cousin's fiancé Stephen Guest. Eliot's emotional realism is relentless throughout, until the impressionistic ending which has been much criticized despite being consistent with a fatalism evident elsewhere in the book. Maggie was D.H. Lawrence's favourite (fictional) woman.
[GA177] Chatto hbk **£9.95**
[GA178] Oxford pbk **£2.50**
[GA179] Penguin pbk **£2.99**

FERRIER, SUSAN (1782 - 1854)
Scottish comic novelist with a keen sense of the ludicrous and a shrewd social and moral sensibility. She was much admired by Walter Scott.
Marriage (1818)
A high-spirited farce in which an affected young English lady sacrifices all for the love of a disinherited Scottish officer.
[GA180] Oxford pbk **£3.95**
[GA181] Virago pbk **£5.50**

FIELDING, HENRY (1707 - 1754)
First a playwright, then a lawyer, Fielding is now regarded as the writer of the first recognisably modern novel, *Tom Jones*. He saw his work as burlesque fiction - a manly slapstick where characters' mock-heroic pretensions are continually undermined by the wiser but still fallible author. The comic potential this offers is exploited to the full but it is up to the reader whether such irony constitutes an accurate reflection on some brutal facts of life, or a canny evasion of them.
Amelia (1752)
Fielding's last (and his own favourite) novel changes tone to provide an extended critique of corruption and poverty, influenced by his experience as magistrate and legal reformer at Bow St. Court. 'Good' no longer triumphs as Amelia suffers from society's neglect of its duty.
[GA182] Dent hbk **£7.95**
[GA183] Penguin pbk **£3.95**
Jonathan Wild (1743)
An unstable mock-heroic satire on 'greatness', with Jonathan as the hypocritical, manipulative thief turned gentleman, attempting to corrupt the gullible but good Mr and Mrs Heartfree. As with his other works, much of the fun for the reader lies in deciding whether the intended satire works or rebounds onto itself.
[GA184] Penguin pbk **£2.95**
Jonathan Wild/The Voyage to Lisbon
A lively account of the journey the ailing writer took to regain his health, although it turned out to be his last.
[GA185] Dent hbk **£8.95**
[GA186] Dent pbk **£1.95**
Joseph Andrews (1742)
A buoyant, merciless parody of Richardson's *Pamela*. Joseph, a servant, labours under all Richardson's moral pedantry as he wards off the vampish widow Lady Booby and journeys to find Fanny, his true love. He remains relatively loyal throughout his travels, assisted by the bumbling Parson Adams and an outrageous picaresque plot.
[GA187] Penguin pbk **£2.99**
[GA188] Methuen pbk **£5.95**
Joseph Andrews & Shamela
Shamela was Fielding's first prose piece, a hilarious

short parody of *Pamela* written in drastically pruned epistolary form. Clever and bursting with vitality.
[GA189] Oxford pbk **£2.50**

Tom Jones (1749)
A comic picaresque novel on a grand scale, centred on the contrasting experiences of the reptilian Blifil and the decent and dashed handsome Tom, who grow up together as rivals for the lovely Sophie. Compromised by alternative attractions and his own illegitimacy, Tom is banished and so begins his pursuit of Sophie across the country to prove his love. A host of colourful characters and the author's mischievous irony make this his finest work.
[GA190] Dent hbk **£7.95**
[GA191] Penguin pbk **£3.99**

FIELDING, SARAH (1710 - 1768)
Henry's sister has been neglected by critics, but as Samuel Richardson said: *"What a knowledge of the human heart! Well might a critical judge (Samuel Johnson) say your late brother's knowledge of it was not (fine writer as he was) comparable to yours. His was but a knowledge of the outside of a clockwork machine, while yours was that of the finer springs and movements of the inside."*

The Adventures of David Simple (1744)
The unwordly Simple journeys around England unwittingly revealing society's double standards. The heroine Cynthia experiences this from a woman's perspective.
[GA192] Oxford pbk **£4.95**

The Governess or The Little Female Academy (1749)
This follows a *Canterbury Tales* format as pupils in a girls' boarding school tell their life history and an adventure or fairy story. The pivot is the moral Mrs Teachum.
[GA193] Pandora pbk **£4.95**

GALT, JOHN (1770 - 1839)
A Scot who wrote national historical novels noted for their broad comedy and hard realism, substantiated by a wealth of detail.

Annals of the Parish (1821)
This first novel impresses as an authentic and vivid account of a small village's development (Dalmailing in Ayrshire) during the Industrial Revolution. The New Industrialists are depicted with particular cunning.
[GA194] Oxford pbk **£2.95**

The Ayreshire Legatees (1821)
A social satire, largely epistolary in form, as a Scottish minister and his family comment with quiet irony on their experiences in London.
[GA195] Mercat P pbk **£3.95**

The Entail (1823)
An ambitious novel following three generations of one family as they attempt to regain family land. Comparable in tone to Gogol and Dostoyevsky, according to a modern critic.
[GA196] Oxford pbk **£3.95**

The Provost (1822)
Exposes the self-importance and hypocritical manipulations of a small town politician and self-made man.
[GA197] Oxford pbk **£2.95**

GASKELL, MRS ELIZABETH (1810 - 65)
The first effective social novelist, Mrs Gaskell depicted industrial society, and particularly class and gender conflicts with an unprecedented boldness and psychological breadth. She was based in Manchester where she had first-hand experience of relief work during times of recession and famine, but each novel has a different, carefully researched regional setting. This grasp of different classes and cultures is allied to a dramatic sense of plot to create memorable, innovative novels.

Mrs Elizabeth Gaskell, author of *North and South* (Oxford pbk **£3.50**, Penguin pbk **£3.99**)

Cousin Phillis and Other Tales (1865)
The title piece is a fine novella with her characters as usual exhibiting varied and absorbing psychologies.
[GA198] Oxford pbk **£2.95**

Cranford (1853)
An episodic collection of experiences, hopes and resentments among a group of middle-class ladies in a quiet Cheshire town. Famed for its charm, humour and pathos, its careful naturalism is also impressive.
[GA199] Oxford pbk **£2.25**

Cranford and Cousin Phillis
[GA200] Penguin pbk **£2.95**

Four Short Stories (1847 - 58)
Independent women of lower middle-class origins form the subjects of these stories, two of which were for Dickens' *Household Words* journal. Her handling of her unmarried mother, her seamstress and her disabled heroine is confident and perceptive, despite being controversial at the time.
[GA201] Pandora pbk **£3.95**

Mary Barton, A Tale of Manchester Life (1848)
Written in part to channel her suffering on the death of her child, this is a passionate and at times crude social novel which dramatises Chartism and the deep divisions between employer and worker in the figure of Mary herself. When her rich admirer is killed suspicion falls on her poor lover Jem Wilson. This sensitive first novel broke new ground for its forceful portrayal of working-class living conditions and poverty.
[GA202] Penguin pbk **£3.50**
[GA203] Oxford pbk **£2.95**

My Lady Ludlow (1851)
A swiftly written minor novel compounded from various stories she had contributed to *Household Words* (Dickens' journal), and based on Eliot's *Scenes from Clerical Life*.
[GA204] Sutton pbk **£2.95**

North and South (1855)
A remarkable novel, held to be her best. Margaret Hale moves from Pastoral Hampshire to Darkshire, a cotton town where Thornton is an autocratic mill owner. For both, prejudices and insensitivities break down through a wide range of experiences and emotions. Gaskell allows her social critique to develop organically from these experiences.
[GA205] Penguin pbk **£3.99**
[GA206] Oxford pbk **£3.50**

Ruth (1853)
Members of her husband's congregation burned copies of this second novel because its heroine was an unmarried mother. In fact it is a *Tess* type fable of the noble, fallen woman.
[GA207] Oxford pbk **£2.95**

Sylvia's Lovers (1853)
A glorious love story set in the whaling town of Whitby, as it is garrisoned by the press gang trapping men for the Napoleonic Wars. Sylvia's isolation on a farm necessitates an intense courtship, the intricacies of which have a Lawrentian fury, but social concerns are also present, particularly in the fate of her patriot father. Although the moral stamina exhibited by the characters seems questionable now, the book has a compelling emotional realism.
[GA208] Oxford pbk **£3.95**

The Manchester Marriage (1858)
The title piece is a short story in which a marriage develops from being a business agreement to a relationship of mutual respect.
[GA209] Sutton pbk **£3.95**

Wives and Daughters (1866)
Molly Gibson is the last of Gaskell's well-drawn heroines, and although unfinished this novel has all the feeling and social astuteness of its predecessors. It is, however, her most constructed and conventional work, dealing with a rural community and various complications of love and status.
[GA210] Penguin pbk **£3.95**
[GA211] Oxford pbk **£3.95**

GISSING, GEORGE (1857 - 1903)
Generally seen as a difficult, nihilist writer, his unusual private life and early familiarity with poverty produced gritty, angry novels where 'fiction cries loud as the mouthpiece of social reform'. While at Manchester University he stole to support a young prostitute and was expelled. The resulting unhappy marriage was followed by a second with a woman he met casually in the street, which was just as disastrous. Respect for his work has revived recently owing to its pioneering naturalism and social realism. If England *has* ever had a poor, alienated Romantic artist, it is Gissing.

A Life's Morning (1888)
A romantic melodrama interesting for the psychology of its heroine Emily Hood, who is disgraced in her position as governess for having an affair with a social superior.
[GA212] Harvester pbk **£6.95**

Born in Exile (1892)
A man of humble origins but outstanding ability sees the only way to a rich wife lies in becoming a parson. A satire on opportunism that becomes a more fundamental critique of social hypocrisy and charlatanism.
[GA213] Harvester pbk **£7.95**
[GA214] Hogarth pbk **£3.95**

Demos (1886)
A jumbled bitter book in which the by now disillusioned socialist condemns attempts at social reform because the workers have become too selfish and mean-spirited to take any action other than vandalism. The plot follows a worker turned gentleman and his attempts to form a workers' community.
[GA215] Harvester pbk **£6.95**

In the Year of the Jubilee (1894)
[GA216] Hogarth pbk **£4.95**

New Grub Street (1891)
Poverty again, but this time it is an autobiographical investigation into its effects on the artist. What sort of fiction should the socially aware novelist produce and how should he live? Gissing's best known work.
[GA217] Penguin pbk **£3.95**

Sleeping Fires (1895)
[GA218] Harvester pbk **£9.95**

The Crown of Life (1899)
[GA219] Harvester pbk **£6.95**

The Emancipated (1890)
A change in style sees Gissing in Italy concerned with

the spiritual impact of conformity on a sensitive mind.

[GA220] Harvester pbk **£4.95**

The Nether World (1889)

Written after his first wife's pitiful death from drink this is a grim, thorough onslaught on the poverty and inescapability of slum life. The characters are firm and convincing, and well-drawn scenes of popular high spirits on holidays highlight the otherwise unrelieved miseries of illness, violence and pointlessness.

[GA221] Harvester pbk **£4.95**

The Odd Women (1893)

Builds on a lifetime concern with the emancipation of women to present five 'odd' (ie. unmarried) women and their fates. Its naturalism has been praised.

[GA222] Virago pbk **£4.50**

The Private Papers of Henry Ryecroft (1903)

"More of an aspiration than a memory," said Gissing of this partly autobiographical, reflective work which looks back on his earlier suffering via the distancing technique of Ryecroft's 'literary remains'.

[GA223] Harvester pbk **£6.95**
[GA224] Oxford pbk **£3.95**

The Unclassed (1884)

His second attempt at a novel of social protest has a number of people attempting to opt out of society's conventions.

[GA225] Harvester pbk **£6.95**

The Whirlpool (1897)

The whirlpool is materialism, which removes all meaning from love, aspirations and justice. Henry Rolfe tries to cope with this sombre metaphor.

[GA226] Harvester pbk **£5.95**

Thyrza (1887)

A more sympathetic work based around a workers' education institute where love and melodrama interfere.

[GA227] Harvester pbk **£7.95**

Will Warburton (1905)

A lighter work, published posthumously, with hints of absurdist comedy and an emergent conservatism.

[GA228] Hogarth pbk **£4.95**

Workers in the Dawn (1880)

Indignation and horror fill this long first novel in which contemporary political and philosophical theories are tested against the Hell of London slums (where Gissing lived at this stage) and found wanting.

[GA229] Harvester pbk **£9.95**

GODWIN, WILLIAM (1756 - 1836)

Important anarchist political philosopher in the troubled 1790s, married to Mary Wollstonecraft; their daughter Mary wrote *Frankenstein* and married the poet Shelley.

Caleb Williams (1794)

A psychological detective thriller cum political propagandist novel unique in British fiction. As Hazlitt said, *"no one has ever begun Caleb Williams that did not read it through"*.

[GA230] Oxford pbk **£4.50**
[GA231] Penguin pbk **£4.95**

GOLDSMITH, OLIVER (1730 - 1774)

Anglo-Irish in origin, Goldsmith wrote plays and poetry as well as a novel which has always been popular for its gentle humour and the romanticised goodness of the hero.

The Vicar of Wakefield (1766)

[GA232] Oxford pbk **£1.95**
[GA233] Penguin pbk **£2.50**

GROSSMITH, GEORGE & WEEDON

The Diary of a Nobody (1892)

A slick irony undermines the life of the diligent mediocre clerk Mr Pooter. One of the greatest comic

masterpieces in English, it possesses obsessional powers to enslave its readers to a lifetime of 'Pootering'.

[GA234] Dent hbk **£8.95**
[GA235] Dent pbk **£1.50**

HAMILTON, MARY (1736 - 1816)

Munster Village (1778)

[GA236] Pandora pbk **£3.95**

HARDY, THOMAS (1840 - 1928)

His emerging popularity as a poet now threatens to eclipse his fame as a novelist but Hardy's novels, often undersold as tragic love stories, have a poetic feel too. He described them as *"an endeavour to give shape and coherence to a series of seemings or personal impressions"*. These 'seemings' make him a writer of images, with a sense of the grotesque (from his work as a church restorer) and of an inevitable decay which sets in quite apart from man's hopes and intentions. His characters are ordinary rustic people, facing tragic situations they can do little about, their tragedies intensified by vivid descriptions of 'Hardy Country' (Wessex) which seems to inhabit their minds and express their moods. The result is powerful, even in his earlier, lighter works.

A Changed Man and Other Tales (1913)

Twelve short stories.

[GA237] Sutton pbk **£3.95**

A Group of Noble Dames (1891)

Ten short stories, chiefly romances.

[GA238] Sutton pbk **£2.50**

A Laodicean (1881)

A minor romance, dictated to his wife during a long illness. The title refers to the vacillating heroine, Paula Powers.

[GA239] Macmillan hbk **£7.95**

A Pair of Blue Eyes (1873)

Early tragic tale of unconsummated passion and rivalry in love. A stonemason working on a church falls in love with the vicar's daughter and they elope together but Elfride Swancourt is Hardy's first inconstant heroine.

[GA240] Macmillan hbk **£10.95**
[GA241] Macmillan pbk **£2.50**
[GA242] Penguin pbk **£2.95**
[GA243] Oxford pbk **£2.50**

Desperate Remedies (1871)

His first published novel is an unrepeated attempt at the Sensation novel in the Wilkie Collins vein. A preposterous plot does not obliterate some powerful and sensual writing.

[GA244] Macmillan pbk **£2.95**

Thomas Hardy by William Strang (Picture: National Portrait Gallery)

Far From the Madding Crowd (1874)

Bathsheba is the capricious but passionate heroine. She has three men to choose from - the dependable Oak, the wayward but spirited Troy, and the stern obsessional Boldwood. A sense of bold, buoyant inevitability grips this piece of classic Hardy as it races to a fine finale.

[GA245] Macmillan hbk **£10.95**
[GA246] Macmillan pbk **£1.50**
[GA247] Penguin pbk **£1.50**

Jude the Obscure (1895)

Criticised bitterly at the time (*"simply one of the most objectionable books we have read in any language whatsoever,"* said one reviewer) for its gloom and adultery, this last novel now seems capably modern. Jude is a sensitive stonemason, the victim of his own weakness, fate, and the 'deadly war between flesh and spirit.'

[GA248] Macmillan hbk **£10.95**
[GA249] Macmillan pbk **£1.95**
[GA250] Oxford pbk **£1.95**
[GA251] Penguin pbk **£1.99**

Life's Little Ironies (1894)

Nine short stories.

[GA252] Sutton pbk **£2.95**

Our Exploits at West Poley (1883)

A children's story.

[GA253] Oxford pbk **£2.95**

Selected Stories

[GA254] Macmillan pbk **£2.50**

Stories Vol 1

[GA255] Macmillan hbk **£7.50**

Stories Vol 2

[GA256] Macmillan hbk **£5.50**

Stories Vol 3

[GA257] Macmillan hbk **£5.50**

Tales from Wessex

[GA258] Pan pbk **£1.95**

Tess of the d'Urbervilles (1891)

A defiant and frank tragedy whose attempts to elevate the lowborn and eventual murderess Tess to a 'Pure Woman' of epic status caused a furore when published. Tess is the victim of two men: her cold, wordly seducer Alec and the pure, ascetic Angel Clare, whose idealism prevents him from seeing her independent womanhood. But she is also a triumphant creation, whose feelings Hardy writes into the landscapes around her: after she is abandoned by Angel her desolation becomes the frozen, barren brown earth of the turnip fields. This is Hardy at his best.

[GA259] Macmillan hbk **£10.95**
[GA260] Penguin pbk **£1.95**
[GA261] Oxford pbk **£1.95**

The Distracted Preacher and Other Tales

The title piece is a smuggling story and one of his earliest published works.

[GA262] Penguin pbk **£2.99**

The Hand of Ethelberta (1875)

A comic novel of high society.

[GA263] Macmillan hbk **£12.95**
[GA264] Macmillan pbk **£2.95**

The Mayor of Casterbridge (1886)

A dark tale of obsession and insecurity in which Hardy succeeds in giving his own fatalism credible psychological life. The mayor has sold his wife and child while a frustrated and inebriated tinker, for which he has atoned by grim industry and become a self-made man. But it has not cured his self-destructive paranoia…

[GA265] Macmillan hbk **£10.95**
[GA266] Penguin pbk **£1.99**
[GA267] Oxford pbk **£1.75**

The Return of the Native (1878)

The protagonist is the sombre beauty of Egdon Heath, which provides a constant reminder of a life alien to the social ways of men. Against this

backcloth unfolds the tragedies of two women and their loves.

[GA268] Macmillan hbk **£10.95**
[GA269] Macmillan pbk **£1.75**
[GA270] Penguin pbk **£1.75**

The Trumpet-Major (1880)
Set in the Napoleonic Wars this is a reworking of the *Far From the Madding Crowd* theme, save with genial comic intent. Anne Garland has to choose one of three men.

[GA271] Macmillan hbk **£10.95**
[GA272] Penguin pbk **£1.95**

The Well-Beloved (1897)
His penultimate novel, serialised in 1892 but not published until 1897, is a mature, anti-realistic treatment of the psychology of loving. Jocelyn Pierston loves three generations of the same family, but in each woman love's spirit departs *"like the nest of some beautiful bird from which the inhabitant has departed and left it to fill with snow"*.

[GA273] Macmillan hbk **£9.95**
[GA274] Macmillan pbk **£2.50**
[GA275] Oxford pbk **£2.25**

The Woodlanders (1887)
Hardy's personal favourite - the setting is gentler but the story of thwarted love and ruined lives is the familiar one.

[GA276] Macmillan hbk **£10.95**
[GA277] Oxford pbk **£1.95**
[GA278] Penguin pbk **£1.95**

Two on a Tower (1882)
[GA279] Macmillan pbk **£10.95**
[GA280] Macmillan pbk **£2.50**

Under the Greenwood Tree (1872)
His second novel has a lighter tone. A traditional story of love rivalry is set against the arrival of a new organ for the village church, which ousts the musicians and prompts the 'rustics' to revolt.

[GA281] Macmillan hbk **£8.95**
[GA282] Oxford pbk **£1.25**
[GA283] Penguin pbk **£1.50**

HAYS, MARY (1760 - 1843)
A close friend of Mary Wollstonecraft and William Godwin, her other writings included the six volume 'Female Biography or Memoirs of Illustrious and Celebrated Women of all Ages and Countries'. *Emma Courtney* describes a woman's need for sexual, intellectual and financial autonomy and incorporates her own letters into the text.

Memoirs of Emma Courtney (1796)
[GA284] Pandora pbk **£4.95**

HAYWOOD, ELIZA (1693 - 1756)
Swift called her a *"stupid, scribbling woman"*, such was her productivity and versatility.

The History of Miss Betsy Thoughtless (1751)
A feminist *Tom Jones* without Fielding's indulgent conservatism.
[GA285] Pandora pbk **£5.95**

HAZLITT, WILLIAM (1778 - 1830)
A great romantic essayist, involved with all the key issues of his day, and one of the first professional literary critics, whose essays on Shakespeare were vital in forming contemporary ideas on the plays.

Selected Writings
[GA286] Penguin pbk **£6.95**

HOGG, JAMES (1770 - 1835)
Known in his life as the 'Ettrick Shepherd', Hogg really was a shepherd before his discovery by Scott. His lasting fame rests on the masterpiece *Confessions*.

The Private Memoirs and Confessions of a Justified Sinner (1824)
Technically sophisticated - the book opens with the deeds of the Sinner and concludes with his

confessions, found when his grave is opened 100 years later - this is a famous and convincing account of psychological and religious delusion. The 'Sinner' tells, with extreme self-righteousness, how a young man persuades him to murder and rape in the Lord's name, for he is predestined for salvation.

[GA287] Penguin pbk **£2.95**
[GA288] Oxford pbk **£2.95**

INCHBALD, ELIZABETH (1753 - 1821)
A Simple Story (1791)
The story is of the love affair between the sober Catholic priest Mr Doniforth and Miss Milner, an impressionable, fashionable young woman. Highly regarded for its 'realistic' handling of a relationship and its machinations.
[GA289] Pandora pbk **£4.95**

JEFFERIES, RICHARD (1848 - 1887)
A naturalist and rural writer whose few novels have a mystical bent. (See the *Natural History* chapter for a more extensive listing of his work.)

After London (1885)
In a savage vision of the future, London is a poisonous swamp inhabited by cruel dwarfs.
[GA290] Oxford pbk **£2.50**

Bevis, the Story of a Boy (1882)
A childhood idyll, celebrating a boy's imagination as he invents his own exciting worlds.
[GA291] Dent pbk **£2.75**

JEROME, JEROME K. (1859 - 1927)
After Supper Ghost Stories (1891)
[GA292] Sutton pbk **£2.95**

Idle Thoughts of an Idle Fellow (1886)
"What readers ask nowadays in a book is that it should improve, instruct and elevate. This book wouldn't elevate a cow. I cannot conscientiously recommend it for any useful purpose whatsoever'.(J.K. Jerome)
[GA293] Sutton pbk **£2.50**
[GA294] Dent pbk **£1.50**

Miscellany of Sense and Nonsense
[GA295] Sutton pbk **£2.95**

My Life and Times (1926)
A lighthearted autobiography.
[GA296] Sutton pbk **£3.50**

Second Thoughts of an Idle Fellow (1898)
[GA297] Sutton pbk **£2.50**

Three Men in a Boat (1889)
All the misadventures that can befall three innocents (and dog) on what should have been a pleasure cruise on the Thames. His finest work.
[GA298] Dent hbk **£8.95**
[GA299] Penguin pbk **£2.50**
[GA300] Sutton pbk **£2.50**

Three Men in an Omnibus
[GA301] Methuen pbk **£4.95**

Three Men on the Bummel (1900)
[GA302] Dent hbk **£8.95**
[GA303] Sutton pbk **£2.50**
[GA304] Penguin pbk **£2.25**

Tommy & Co.
[GA305] Sutton pbk **£2.95**

KINGSLEY, CHARLES (1819 - 1875)
An energetic Rector, History Professor, social reformer and early socialist, he wrote confidently philistine lower-middle-class broadsides against a hypocritical Establishment. His lasting fame rests on the seminal children's book *The Water Babies*, and posterity has buried his jingoistic excesses.

Alton Locke, Tailor and Poet (1850)
A social propagandist novel, immersed in Chartism and the London sweat shops from which Locke tries to escape by education but is finally rescued by Christian Socialism and emigration.
[GA306] Oxford pbk **£3.95**

Christmas in the West Indies
[GA307] Writers & R pbk **£8.95**

Yeast (1848)
Intended to shatter myths of pastoral bliss this first novel takes the reader among the rural poor. The moral hectoring is crude but effective and *Yeast* extended the boundaries of what was then seen as fiction's domain.
[GA308] Dent hbk **£8.95**

LAMB, CHARLES (1775 - 1834)
Lamb was an essayist who collaborated with his sister to produce popular prose renderings of Shakespeare, and, with Hazlitt, the most distinguished critic of the Romantic age.

Elia & The Last Essays of Elia
[GA309] Oxford pbk **£4.95**

Selected Prose
[GA310] Penguin pbk **£5.95**

Tales from Shakespeare (1807)
[GA311] Dent pbk **£2.50**

LE FANU, SHERIDAN (1814 - 1873)
Le Fanu specialised in tales of the supernatural, and was one of the bestselling authors of the 1860-80s: as M.R. James has acknowledged, he was in many ways the father of the modern ghost story.

Best Ghost Stories
[GA312] Dover pbk **£6.35**

Guy Deverell (1865)
[GA313] Dover pbk **£5.55**

In a Glass Darkly (1872)
[GA314] Sutton pbk **£3.50**

Rose & the Key (1871)
[GA315] Dover pbk **£5.55**

Uncle Silas (1864)
His most respected work now, but its extravagant excesses of horror and incident did much to bring the Sensation tradition into disrepute.
[GA316] Oxford pbk **£4.95**

LENNOX, CHARLOTTE (1727 - 1804)
Samuel Johnson was her literary agent, Richardson her printer and Henry Fielding thought her work better than Cervantes', but still Lennox has fallen from our literary heritage.

The Female Quixote (1752)
The racy comedy of Arabella who, because she is brought up with books of Romantic fiction, is incapable of seeing any situation except in fictionally Romantic terms. Thus gardeners, highwaymen or dark strangers in church are all potential princes come to chivalrously carry her away. Will she recognise the honest love of plain Mr Glanville before it is too late?
[GA317] Pandora pbk **£4.95**

The Cult of Sensibility

The Novel of Sentiment, or Sensibility was the most influential literary form of the 1760-80s, its intention being to foreground the emotions. A 'good' character had to combine noble virtue with acute displays of feeling and sympathy. This led to excesses of insane tender-heartedness and flowing tears such as can be seen in Mackenzie's *Man of Feeling*. Richardson and Fielding, with their more detailed analysis of emotional nuance, bear more modest signs of its influence, as do Smollett and Sterne in his *Sentimental Journey*. The Cult reached its peak in the extremes of feeling of the Gothic novels, while Jane Austen's *Sense and Sensibility* (1811) is an attempt to restrain the genre's extreme tendencies and use Sentiment's positive elements to attain a psychological balance.

FICTION

LEWIS, MATTHEW (1775 - 1818)
The Monk (1795)
One of the more extravagant Gothic Romances which were in vogue at the end of the 18th century. A monk breaks his vows to embark on a life of sexual obsession, rape and murder.
[GA318] Oxford pbk **£4.95**

MACKENZIE, HENRY (1745 - 1831)
The Man of Feeling (1771)
Burns called it the book *"I prize most next to the Bible"*, for this is the most successful novel inspired by the 18th century cult of Sensibility. Mackenzie himself was a hard-headed Edinburgh lawyer but his book, which follows an innocent's experiences in a Babylonic London, created a fashion for pathos and quantities of weeping.
[GA319] Oxford pbk **£2.95**

MALORY, SIR THOMAS (d. 1471)
Malory wrote his *Morte d'Arthur* in prison: it is the most complete and memorable treatment of the Arthurian legends, recorded in a distinctively simple prose style, but articulating a modern, and questioning, attitude to its traditional subject. One of the great works of early English prose.
Malory: Works
[GA320] Oxford pbk **£8.95**
Morte D'Arthur Vol 1
[GA321] Penguin pbk **£4.50**
Morte D'Arthur Vol 2
[GA322] Penguin pbk **£4.50**

MARRYAT, CAPTAIN (1792 - 1848)
Admired by Conrad, his exuberant adventure stories based on his own navy career formed only part of a varied (but now unprinted) writing repertoire. Later he confined himself to children's stories such as *Children of the New Forest*.
Children of the New Forest (1847)
[GA323] Penguin pbk **£2.95**
Peter Simple
[GA324] Sutton pbk **£2.95**

MARTINEAU, HARRIET (1802 - 1876)
A political economist, journalist and feminist; *Deerbrook* was her only novel although her autobiography, also by Virago, is eventful enough to read like one.
Deerbrook (1839)
The two Ibbotson sisters move to a rural village and inhabit the world of a Jane Austen novel.
[GA325] Virago pbk **£5.95**

MAURIER, GEORGE DU (1834 - 1896)
Trilby (1894)
A curiosity of a novel from a man more renowned as an artist; it gave a new stock character to English fiction in Svengali, the mentor and mesmeric guardian of the heroine. The singer Trilby has also enriched the language with her form of headgear.
[GA326] Dent pbk **£2.50**

MEREDITH, GEORGE (1828 - 1909)
It is strange that so poetic and intelligent a writer as Meredith should have become so neglected. His style teems with a Modernist delight in detail and shifting emotional nuances, and he pre-empted Henry James with his detached ironic control. Oscar Wilde paid him a fitting compliment when he wrote: *"To him belongs philosophy in fiction. His people not merely live, but they live in thought."*
Beauchamp's Career (1876)
An unexpected journey into politics. Beauchamp is a naval officer, patronised by his rich aristo-cratic uncle but possessing progressive views on social issues. His quest for love and honour form the plot.
[GA327] Oxford pbk **£5.95**

Diana of the Crossways (1885)
An effective story of a woman's heart and her spiritual growth which gestures towards feminism as she becomes estranged from her husband.
[GA328] Virago pbk **£4.95**

The Egoist (1879)
The most accomplished rehearsal of his philosophical optimism. Sir Willoughby Patterne is the man deviating from Nature's intended altruism. As a result, he is both romantically unsuccessful and mocked by Meredith's careful irony. A fine, if challenging, novel.
[GA329] Penguin pbk **£4.95**
The Ordeal of Richard Feverel (1859)
His first novel displays a harsher comic irony than usual in representing an embittered father depriving his son of any knowledge of sexual desire, because his own marriage has collapsed.
[GA330] Oxford pbk **£4.95**
The Shaving of Shagpat (1856)
An early oriental tale with opaque allegorical intent, based on **The Arabian Nights** and Beckford's **Vathek**.
[GA331] Lake pbk **£6.95**

MOORE, GEORGE (1852 - 1933)
A tireless self-publicist (a man who *"didn't kiss, but told"* according to one woman) and writer, Moore imported Naturalism to Britain, his models being Turgenev and Zola.
Esther Waters (1894)
His most popular novel, due partly to its warm descriptions of life in a racing stables. It is a harrowing tale though, as a poor servant girl is seduced and has to rear her child in great hardship.
[GA332] Oxford pbk **£3.95**
The Lake (1905)
A short novel written following his return to Ireland from Paris.
[GA333] C Smythe pbk **£4.25**
Untilled Field (1903)
[GA334] C Smythe hbk **£8.95**

MORGAN, LADY (SYDNEY OWENSON) (1776 - 1859)
An Irish Nationalist and by stages actress, governess, socialite and physician's wife, she became so successful that Sir Charles Morgan retired to assist his wife's research and accompany her on speaking tours. Both novels remaining in print are 'political Romances', pleading for the emancipation of Catholics.
The O'Briens and the O'Flahertys (1827)
[GA335] Pandora pbk **£8.95**
The Wild Irish Girl (1805)
[GA336] Pandora pbk **£4.95**

MORRIS, WILLIAM (1834 - 1896)
Influential socialist artist and designer who also wrote historical sagas, poetry and propagandist romances.
News from Nowhere/John Ball/Pilgrims of Hope (1885 - 91)
Pilgrims of Hope is a verse tale, while *John Ball*, as leader of the 1381 Peasants' Revolt, is an ideal mouthpiece for Morris to celebrate the communal elements of the medieval world he so admired. Both emerged from his reading of Marx and are attempts to present the dialectical workings of history.
[GA337] Lawrence & W pbk **£4.95**
News from Nowhere/Selected Writings and Designs (1891)
Utopian fantasy in a dream setting portraying London transformed into a communist paradise.
[GA338] Penguin pbk **£4.95**
Novel on Blue Paper (1872)
Unfinished, partly due to the difficult emotional circumstances of its writing as his wife's affair with Rossetti had become public.
[GA339] Journeyman pbk **£1.95**

NASHE, THOMAS (1567 - 1601)
The Unfortunate Traveller & Other Works
The Unfortunate Traveller (1594) defies categorisation. A historical fantasy, cum travel narrative, cum rhetorical parody, and posturing, it has far more energy than the other leaden works emerging at the time.
[GA340] Penguin pbk **£5.95**

NEWMAN, JOHN HENRY (1801 - 1890)
Loss & Gain (1848)
Cardinal Newman's first novel tells of a young man's search for faith and certainty amid the competing loyalties of Victorian Oxford. As befits one of England's most accomplished prose stylists it is written with consummate elegance.
[GA341] Oxford pbk **£3.95**

OLIPHANT, MRS MARGARET (1828 - 1897)
The necessity to write to support her own three children (and those of her brother) diluted Margaret Oliphant's talent over almost 100 novels, quite apart from her reviewing and translating. Nonetheless there is a spirited irony and social comedy to her works which, although anachronistic in their day, shine with surprising freshness now. Virago have just completed reprinting her most famous series of novels, *The Chronicles of Carlingford*.
A Beleaguered City and Other Stories (1880)
Mrs Oliphant produced tales of the supernatural later in her career, of which the title piece was her first.
[GA342] Oxford pbk **£4.95**
Curate in Charge (1875)
Focuses on the curate's two daughters Cicely and Mab, and on the dearth of opportunities for women having others to care for.
[GA343] Sutton pbk **£2.95**
Hester (1883)
Deals with the fraught relationship between two independent women, the young woman of the title and the elderly second cousin, Catherine. The polemical feminism which seems inconsistent with her earlier beliefs reveals the frustrations Mrs Oliphant came to feel as an underpaid lady novelist without the regular salary given to men of her trade.
[GA344] Virago pbk **£4.95**
The Doctor's Family and Other Stories
[GA345] Oxford pbk **£2.95**
The Perpetual Curate (1864)
[GA346] Virago pbk **£4.95**

Mrs Oliphant, author of *Hester* (Virago pbk **£4.95**) and *Salem Chapel* (Virago pbk **£4.95**)

THE CHRONICLES OF CARLINGFORD
Miss Marjoribanks (1866)
[GA347] Virago pbk **£5.95**
Phoebe Junior (1876)
[GA348] Virago pbk **£5.50**
Salem Chapel (1863)
Dissenting Minister Arthur Vincent dreams of social stardom in the modest town of Salem but meets the darker side of life as 'Sensation novel' melodrama creeps into the plot.
[GA349] Virago pbk **£4.95**
The Rector & The Doctor's Family (1863)
The first two short novels of the Chronicles.
[GA350] Virago pbk **£4.50**

OPIE, MRS AMELIA (1769 - 1853)
Part of the free-thinking groups in London in the 1790s which included William Godwin, Mary Wollstonecraft and Elizabeth Inchbald. Opie's third novel, loosely based on Wollstonecraft's life, focuses on the institution 'marriage', and the social ostracism experienced by those who chose to live together outside it.
Adeline Mowbray (1804)
[GA351] Pandora pbk **£4.95**

PATER, WALTER H. (1839 - 1894)
Influential *fin de siècle* figure (admired by Wilde, Yeats and Joyce among others) famous for his emphasis on sensation (*"to burn always with this hard gem-like flame, to maintain this ecstasy is success in life"*) and his scepticism as to whether ultimate truths and values could exist in art (or indeed in anything). In life he was a timid Oxford Classics scholar.
Marius the Epicurean (1885)
Pater's elaborate prose style and philosophical musings usurp Marius as the novel's centre, as a high-minded pleasure seeker contemplates early Christian practices.
[GA352] Oxford pbk **£4.95**
[GA353] Penguin pbk **£4.95**
[GA354] Soho pbk **£7.95**

PEACOCK, THOMAS LOVE (1785 - 1866)
Writer of unusual prose satires. According to Virginia Woolf, *"Peacock bends over heaven and earth one fantastic distorting mirror in which a tea-cup may be Vesuvius or Vesuvius a tea-cup."*
Gryll Grange (1860)
[GA355] Sutton pbk **£1.95**
Headlong Hall/Gryll Grange (1816 & 1860)
[GA356] Oxford pbk **£4.95**
Nightmare Abbey/Crotchet Castle (1818 & 1831)
[GA357] Penguin pbk **£3.99**

QUINCEY, THOMAS DE (1785 - 1859)
Friend of Coleridge and Wordsworth, de Quincey was a magnificent essayist, whose cumulative, labyrinthine style is majestic in exploring subjects such as childhood and dreams. The *Confessions*, together with other essays such as 'The English Mail Coach' are among the high points of imaginative prose writing.
Confessions of an English Opium Eater
[GA358] Oxford pbk **£2.50**
[GA359] Penguin pbk **£2.95**

RADCLIFFE, ANN (1764 - 1823)
The most successful Gothic novelist, her compelling portrayal of rapture and terror set in subliminal landscapes is genuinely sensuous.
Romance of the Forest (1791)
Her third novel, full of Gothic conventions (dungeons, shattered abbeys and mouldy manuscripts) but with the sophisticated concern for the sublime that can be found in Shelley's poetry.
[GA360] Oxford pbk **£4.95**

The Italian (1797)
[GA361] Oxford pbk **£4.95**
The Mysteries of Udolpho (1794)
Brought her an advance of £500 (where Jane Austen received only £10 for satirising it in *Northanger Abbey*), it has been praised ever since. The most compact Gothic horror story.
[GA362] Oxford pbk **£5.95**

RICHARDSON, SAMUEL (1681 - 1761)
Although one of England's most important and pioneering novelists, Richardson's reputation suffers from the length and high moral tone of his works. In fact they display surprising psychological and political penetration. They are dramatic, and the tension between his role as moral pedagogue and as imaginative explorer of feelings allows for some unintentionally hilarious moments.
Clarissa (1747-8)
In which the dramatic novel comes of age. *Clarissa* is a sophisticated study of greed (her family are pooling assets to buy a peerage and so force Clarissa into an unwanted marriage which starts the problems), psychology (in Lovelace, the rake, and Clarissa's own pride and later madness) and of relationships lived in the real world (i.e. politics). By expanding the number of correspondents, the epistolary form permits ever-expanding insights and interpretations: the penalty is that the book is immense. The Penguin edition is based on the first edition; the Dent edition presents a longer text still.
[GA363] Viking hbk **£19.95**
[GA364] Dent hbk (4 vols) **£35.80**
[GA365] Penguin pbk **£12.95**
Pamela (1739 - 40)
This first novel became a sensation. *"Fashionable ladies displayed copies in public places and held fans painted with pictures of their best loved scenes, Pamela became a play, an opera, even a waxwork"* (Mark Kinkead-Weekes); and although the book's conclusion is crudely moralistic there is still much to admire. Its form is epistolary, with Pamela writing most of the letters. This gives an immediacy to her harassment by her master and would-be seducer Mr B and more angles to the action than might be expected. Fielding parodied it mercilessly in *Shamela*.
[GA366] Penguin pbk **£3.99**
[GA367] Dent pbk **£2.75**
Pamela Vol 2 (1741)
A lesser work charting Pamela's behaviour as the perfect, obedient wife.
[GA368] Dent pbk **£2.75**
Sir Charles Grandison (1753-4)
A novel of domestic manners anticipating Jane Austen who dramatised this work herself. It was requested by aristocratic women friends who wanted to see a 'Good Man' portrayed, and who participated in its composition. Sir Charles is the man, but he faces a test of integrity when in love with two women.
[GA369] Oxford pbk **£9.95**

RUTHERFORD, MARK (W.H. WHITE) (1831 - 1913)
A political and religious Dissenter trapped in his own mid-Victorian Crisis of Faith. *The Revolution* is a historical novel of radical Dissenter politics set around the 1819 Peterloo massacre.
The Revolution in Tanner's Lane (1887)
[GA370] Hogarth pbk **£5.95**

SALZMAN, PAUL (ED)
An Anthology of Elizabethan Prose Fiction
Contains five of the more important and varied works of the time, including Gasgoine's *Adventures of Master F.J.*, Lyly's *Euphues*, Greene's *Pandosto* (source for *A Winter's Tale*), and Deloney's *Jack of Newbury*
[GA371] Oxford pbk **£4.95**

SCOTT, SARAH
Millenium Hall (1762)
The Hall is a utopian, all-women community, so good and pure it is as if the millenium has already arrived. Although indebted to the Richardsonian tradition of instructive moral novels, the six female characters have independence, and are permitted to think.
[GA372] Virago pbk **£4.95**

SCOTT, SIR WALTER (1771 - 1832)
In his day Scott was confidently compared to Shakespeare. His imaginative empathy with past generations created the Historical Novel form, while his innovative use of dialogue to advance a plot and his celebration of low-life characters and dialects influenced British and European fiction for many years. Modern readers may prefer the political ambiguities his histories uncover, or delight in the wealth of detail propping up even his worst written characters. Endearingly honest about his own limitations, Scott even submitted anonymous reviews of his work to journals. His lasting strengths lie in his energetic commitment to 'Scottishness' and his sheer delight in story-telling, which he likened to *"a dog merrily chasing its own tale"*.
Guy Mannering (1815)
A clash of Gothic Romance and Social Realism, Scott's second novel tells how a ruined aristocrat's son, Harry Bertram, regains his estates from the social climber Glossin (motto - *'he who takes it, makes it'*).
[GA373] Soho pbk **£5.95**
Ivanhoe (1819)
Anglo-Saxons face Normans in this much loved but also much underrated early Medieval Romance.
[GA374] Dent hbk **£8.95**
[GA375] Penguin pbk **£3.95**
Old Mortality (1816)
Fact and fiction are blurred as Scott whitewashes the Covenantors' Rebellion of 1679. However, his attempts to override the resulting contradictions by talking in a loud, dramatic voice make this a vivid work.
[GA376] Penguin pbk **£4.95**
Redgauntlet (1824)
He returned to firmer ground for his last great novel, contrasting Ancient Traditions with the emerging Edinburgh middle class in an imaginary sequel to the '45 rebellion.
[GA377] Dent hbk **£8.95**
[GA378] Oxford pbk **£4.95**
Rob Roy (1817)
This thrilling tale of Highland clan life under the Old Pretender earned Scott £1,700 and confirmed his status as the most popular novelist of his day.
[GA379] Collins hbk **£4.95**
The Abbot (1820)
Ever faithful to Historical Romance, Scott plumps for Mary Queen of Scots and tells of her escape from Lochleven castle aided by the brave page Roland Graeme.
[GA380] Dent hbk **£8.95**
The Bride of Lammermoor (1819)
Dictated during a prolonged, painful illness, the book surprised Scott who couldn't remember composing most of it. The resulting extravagance of tone made it 'a masterpiece of Gothic fiction' for one critic.
[GA381] Dent pbk **£3.50**
The Heart of Midlothian (1818)
Rated by many as his best novel, Scott's occasionally gross historical appetites are restrained by Jeanie Deans, his unglamorous Puritan peasant heroine, and the moral dilemmas she faces to save her sister. Deliberately recalling *Measure for Measure*, it is subtle enough in its treatment of 'Justice' to keep both moralist and Marxist happy.
[GA382] Dent hbk **£8.95**
[GA383] Oxford pbk **£4.95**

The Talisman (1825)
This Crusader novel tells how the honourable Saladin saves the dishonoured David, Prince of Scotland from King Richard's wrath. For Hazlitt, *"all is spontaneous, bold and original in this beautiful and glowing design"*.
[GA384] Dent pbk **£2.50**

The Two Drovers & Other Stories (1827)
The title piece features low-life characters in a dark tale of two cattle-droving friends, a Yorkshireman and a Highlander, who fall into dispute.
[GA385] Oxford pbk **£3.95**

Waverley (1814)
The 1745 Rebellion sets the Highland Clans (romantic but doomed) against the enlightened Hanoverians (boring but triumphant). This first novel recreated his country's immediate past well, although the brutality of Culloden is forgotten in Waverley's convenient marriage at the end.
[GA386] Oxford pbk **£3.50**
[GA387] Penguin pbk **£4.50**

SHELLEY, MARY (1797 - 1851)
Considering she was the only child of William Godwin and Mary Wollstonecraft and married P.B. Shelley when 19, it is remarkable Mary Shelley was not awed into silence. In fact she produced much highly original work, of which two novels remain in print.

Frankenstein (1818)
Written when she was only 19 at Byron's prompting this has endured not only because it can *"awaken thrilling horror… to curdle the blood and quicken the beatings of the heart"*, but because it is subtle enough to have varied interpretations placed upon it. Very different to the film!
[GA388] Oxford pbk **£3.50**
[GA389] Penguin pbk **£3.50**

The Last Man (1826)
An unusual hybrid, formed of the domestic Romance, Gothic and social reform novels, pictures the world in the grip of an incurable plague in the 22nd century. Its twin themes of social progress and the individual's ultimate isolation echo her husband's concerns, and he appears thinly disguised as Adrian, Earl of Windsor.
[GA390] Hogarth pbk **£4.95**

SHERIDAN, FRANCES (1724 - 1766)
Playwright mother of Richard, who borrowed many of her scenes for his own work.

Memoirs of Miss Sidney Biddulph (1761)
The heroine marries to please her mother, only to face life with a boorish, bigoted husband.
[GA391] Pandora pbk **£5.95**

SIDNEY, SIR PHILIP (1554 - 1586)
An Elizabethan soldier, courtier, diplomat, lover and poet who produced the most important work of Renaissance literary theory in English *The Apology for Poetry*, and a Petrarchan sonnet sequence *Astrophel and Stella* as well as *The Arcadia*, the most important prose fiction of its day. This exists in two forms, the *New Arcadia* being an unfinished extension and revision. Both weave together oracles, songs, poems, lyrical description, melodramatic incident and tangled love situations, with the *New Arcadia* being the more complex.

The Old Arcadia (1581)
[GA393] Oxford pbk **£4.95**

The New Arcadia (1583-4)
[GA392] Penguin pbk **£7.95**

SMITH, CHARLOTTE (1749 - 1806)
Unhappily married at 15, she left her husband to support herself and 8 children by writing 10 novels in as many years. Her heroines are mature women who undergo some of the bitter experiences she herself faced and come to see the need for social justice. Her

style was praised by an early critic for *"delighting in the internal woman, that mystery which man has rarely fathomed"*.

Emmeline (1788)
[GA394] Pandora pbk **£7.95**

The Old Manor House (1793)
[GA395] Pandora pbk **£5.95**

SMOLLETT, TOBIAS (1721 - 1771)
This Scottish naval surgeon is noted for his cantankerous moral satires, accompanied by detailed descriptions of the character's anatomical shortcomings. In fact his picaresque comic novels are packed with incident and a rich gallery of attendant characters, all presented with considerable if imprecise irony.

Adventures of Roderick Random (1748)
[GA396] Oxford pbk **£3.95**

Expedition of Humphrey Clinker (1771)
His last and best tempered novel is an epistolary travelogue in which a family group, with assorted hangers-on, tell of their eventful and finally reconciliatory journey around Britain.
[GA397] Penguin pbk **£3.50**
[GA398] Oxford pbk **£2.95**

Life and Adventures of Sir Launcelot Greaves
[GA399] Penguin pbk **£3.95**

Peregrine Pickle (1751)
[GA400] Oxford pbk **£4.95**

Travels through France and Italy
[GA401] Oxford pbk **£4.95**

STERNE, LAURENCE (1713 - 1768)
By profession a priest in North Yorkshire, Sterne recognised the flexibility of the novel form long before the 'Modernists' of this century to produce the genuinely original *Tristram Shandy*.

Life & Opinions of Tristram Shandy (1760 - 67)
This was the comic sensation of its day and has remained technically unsurpassed up to ours. Two concerns run beneath its boundless clowning and trickery - Sensibility and Perception. Although absurd at times, the book proclaims 'the pleasures of the feeling heart' in a credible way, while it owes its digressional style to Locke's theory of perception ('the product of things operating on the mind in a natural way') and questions just what 'natural' means. The result is a teasing, influential playground of a book, idiosyncratic and compassionate, although one

Laurence Sterne, from the 1783 edition of his *Complete Works*

of the least successful attempts at autobiography in history (Tristram is not born until Book Four).
[GA402] Oxford pbk **£3.95**
[GA403] Penguin pbk **£3.99**

Sentimental Journey through France and Italy (1768)
Based on a journey undertaken to ease his ill health, this is narrated by Parson Yorrick from *Tristram Shandy*, whose 'sensibility' enables him to appreciate all that he encounters. Sterne stated the book's intention was to *"teach us how to love the world and our fellow creatures"*.
[GA404] Penguin pbk **£2.25**

Sentimental Journey/The Journal to Eliza/A Political Romance
A Political Romance is an early work satirising local ecclesiastical courts, while *Journal to Eliza* records his unconsummated love for Elizabeth Draper and was unpublished while he lived.
[GA405] Oxford pbk **£1.95**

STEVENSON, ROBERT LOUIS (1850 - 1894)
Scotsman whose adventure stories and Jacobite novels mark him as a natural successor to Scott. Unlike Scott however he was unconventional, anti-authoritarian and travelled constantly in search of happiness in life. His powerful stories and characters have passed into popular consciousness, but he also explores psychological and personal conflicts with skill.

Dr Jekyll and Mr Hyde (1886)
Classic story of the division of good and evil in a man. A doctor discovers, with the aid of a drug, how to allow his baser instincts free reign (as Hyde), to discover that he can no longer finally separate the two sides of his personality.
[GA406] Penguin pbk **£2.99**
[GA407] Oxford pbk **£2.95**

Island Landfalls
Three imaginative tales, with letters and essays from his stay in the South Seas.
[GA408] Canongate pbk **£3.95**

Kidnapped/Catriona (1886 & 1893)
Along with its lesser sequel *Catriona*, the theme is the Jacobite rising of 1745 and its sad aftermath. Although told by a Whig who becomes involved, it revels in all the romantic excesses of the lost cause.
[GA409] Oxford pbk **£3.50**

The Black Arrow
[GA410] Blackie pbk **£2.95**

The Lantern Bearers & Other Essays
A valuable, recent collection of Stevenson's prose writings.
[GA411] Chatto hbk **£16.95**

The Master of Ballantrae (1889)
An extravagant tale of family feuding in the years following Culloden with the main action in Scotland and the climax in America: the Master himself is a memorably Satanic double-figure.
[GA412] Oxford pbk **£3.95**

Treasure Island (1883)
Often classed as a children's book this is gripping stuff, whose real appeal is for day-dreaming adventurers of all ages.
[GA413] Oxford pbk **£2.95**

STOKER, BRAM (1847 - 1912)
An Irishman who ran Sir Henry Irving's theatre company for many years before publishing his famous novel.

Dracula (1897)
The seminal Gothic horror story, with a fine plot spanning Old Transylvania and modern Whitby.
[GA414] Oxford pbk **£2.95**

SURTEES, ROBERT S. (1805 - 1864)
A Durham gentleman whose forte was vigorous comic novels of provincial, hunting society with

Illustration from *Mr Sponge's Sporting Tour* by R.S. Surtees (Oxford University Press pbk £3.95)

masterful caricatures such as the newly arrived London grocer, Mr Jorrocks, or Mr Pigg, the huntsman. Thanks to the activities of the R.S. Surtees Society, many of his books are in print in superb facsimiles of the Victorian editions.

Ask Mama (1858)
[GA415] Surtees Soc hbk **£14.95**
[GA416] Sutton pbk **£3.95**
Handley Cross (1854)
[GA417] Surtees Soc hbk **£14.95**
Hawbuck Grange (1847)
[GA418] Surtees Soc hbk **£16.95**
Hillingdon Hall (1848)
[GA419] Surtees Soc hbk **£14.95**
Jorrock's Jaunts and Jollities (1838)
[GA420] Surtees Soc hbk **£14.95**
Mr Facey Romford's Hounds (1865)
[GA421] Surtees Soc hbk **£14.95**
[GA422] Sutton pbk **£3.95**
[GA423] Oxford pbk **£3.95**
Mr Sponge's Sporting Tour (1853)
[GA424] Surtees Soc hbk **£14.95**
[GA425] Oxford pbk **£3.95**
[GA426] Sutton pbk **£3.95**
Plain or Ringlets? (1860)
[GA427] Surtees Soc hbk **£14.95**
Young Tom Hall (1851)
[GA428] Surtees Soc hbk **£16.95**

SWIFT, JONATHAN (1667 - 1745)
A Tale of a Tub & Other Stories (1704)
Ostensibly written by a Modern hack writer who is paid by the word and so pads the book out by ever more irrelevant digressions, the *Tale* is a polemic allegory of church history. Peter, Martin and Jack (the Catholic, Anglican and Dissenting Traditions) are each given identical coats by their dying father. Although ordered not to alter them the Catholics over elaborate while the Dissenters pull theirs to pieces. A later, merciless digression has the Dissenters prophesying by their body wind, which they believe to be God's breath. The accompanying *Battle of the Books* describes a mock-heroic battle between Ancients and Moderns fought in St James library.
[GA429] Oxford pbk **£2.95**
Gulliver's Travels (1726)
This parody of travel literature for philosophic ends is so successful it can be read on any number of different levels from child to scholar. The gullible Gulliver has three main travels, to the charming but vicious Lilliputians, the huge Brobdingnags, and his more confused and disturbing final journey during

which he visits the bestial Yahoos (humans) and the noble horse-like Houyhnhnms.
[GA430] Dent hbk **£8.95**
[GA431] Penguin pbk **£1.99**
Portable Swift
[GA432] Penguin pbk **£5.95**

THACKERAY, WILLIAM MAKEPEACE
(1811 - 1853)
In his day a literary giant competing with Dickens as a blustering social critic, his irony now is more difficult to fathom. As he said himself he was an 18th century novelist born too late, but such skills as lampoonery, clever plotting and an urbane but principled insight into snobbery and hypocrisy never age.
History of Henry Esmond (1852)
Historical novel set in Queen Anne's reign memorable for its virtuoso descriptions, coloured by the hero's nostalgia as he looks back on his life as soldier and lover.
[GA433] Penguin pbk **£4.95**
History of Pendennis (1848-50)
A complex plot reined in by Thackeray's commensurate irony, follows 'Pen's' life from boyhood ardour to spendthrift adolescence and imprudent romance.
[GA434] Penguin pbk **£5.95**
The Luck of Barry Lyndon (1834)
Lyndon is a roguish Irish adventurer whose account of his varied exploits is undermined by Thackeray the parodist.
[GA435] Oxford pbk **£3.95**
Vanity Fair (1847)
Becky Sharpe, English fiction's greatest woman, is just one of the many fine portraits in this, his greatest novel. Thackeray sustains momentum by maintaining a distance of powerless wisdom, leaving his ponderous good characters and spirited bad ones to tussle for the reader's sympathy. A great read.
[GA436] Dent hbk **£7.95**
[GA437] Oxford pbk **£3.50**
[GA438] Penguin pbk **£3.50**

TROLLOPE, ANTHONY (1815 - 1882)
Trollope's posthumously published autobiography - a fascinating mixture of candour and reticence - revealed the methodical working habits which enabled him to publish 47 novels as well as lead a busy public life. It also shows how important his fictional characters were to him - no novelist of his time shows greater psychological penetration, especially of human relationships centred on marriage. His two greatest achievements are the series

Illustration from *Vanity Fair* by William Thackeray (Oxford University Press pbk £3.50)

of *Barsetshire* and *Palliser* novels: the first, set in the cathedral city of Barchester, shows a society dominated by the clergy and caught up in the turmoil of mid-19th century religion. The second, more mature series, also called the Political novels, depicts the lives of characters involved in government, centred on the Palliser family and the career of Phineas Finn; characters such as Planty Pall and Lady Glencora are among the most fully developed in English fiction.
BARSETSHIRE NOVELS
1: The Warden (1855)
Warden Harding has enjoyed a comfortable sinecure, and done much good, until reforming voices attack his position, and a misdirection of charitable funds. He feels bound by conscience to step down.
[GA439] Chatto hbk **£8.95**
[GA440] Penguin pbk **£1.95**
[GA441] Oxford pbk **£1.75**
2: Barchester Towers (1857)
The appointment of a new bishop to Barchester brings not only himself but his wife Mrs Proudie and his wonderfully odious chaplain Mr Slope. Against the conflicts of the different factions of the church are set the more personal ones of powerful personalities in a small society.
[GA442] Chatto hbk **£9.95**
[GA443] Oxford pbk **£2.50**
[GA444] Penguin pbk **£2.50**
3: Doctor Thorne (1858)
A conventional Victorian plot of illegitimacy and missing heirs, with a counter-plot in which pompous aristocracy is forced to adopt the stratagems it condemns in others.
[GA445] Chatto hbk **£9.95**
[GA446] Oxford pbk **£4.95**
4: Framley Parsonage (1861)
One of Trollope's first stories of the problems of impatient ambition, as a young curate gets into debt as a result of trying to obtain preferment by influence: his problems are solved because of the worth of his sister.
[GA447] Chatto hbk **£9.95**
[GA448] Oxford pbk **£3.95**
[GA449] Penguin pbk **£3.95**
5: The Small House at Allington (1864)
A moving story of disappointed love in which the hero does not win the lady of his heart, despite reforming and bettering himself, because she insists on regarding herself as eternally promised to a man who has jilted her and married someone else.
[GA450] Chatto hbk **£9.95**
[GA451] Oxford pbk **£4.95**
6: The Last Chronicle of Barset (1867)
Often accepted as Trollope's greatest novel, it portrays the terrible plight of a very poor but highly educated curate with a family, who is accused of having stolen a cheque, and who in his mentally disturbed state cannot properly account for it. His accusation and trial polarise opinions, and all the conflicts in the county rise to the surface.
[GA452] Chatto hbk **£9.95**
[GA453] Penguin pbk **£4.95**
[GA454] Oxford pbk **£4.50**
PALLISER NOVELS
1: Can You Forgive Her? (1864)
While the story is mainly about the amatory problems of Alice Vavasour, young Lady Glencora is also introduced as an heiress pressured into an unwelcome but splendid marriage with Plantagenet Palliser, the heir to the Duke of Omnium and a rising politician. He puts his personal life above his political fortunes when he takes his wife abroad on a long journey in order to bring them closer together.
[GA455] Oxford pbk **£4.95**
[GA456] Penguin pbk **£3.95**
2: Phineas Finn (1869)
The career and love problems of a capable and attractive Irish politician, whose first love marries

another. He has to face an election without funds after his principles over an Irish bill have cost him his government stipend, but he chooses to give up his political career rather than accept the fortune (and hand) of Marie Goesler, a rich widow.
[GA457] Oxford pbk **£4.95**
[GA458] Penguin pbk **£4.99**
3: The Eustace Diamonds (1873)
Lizzie Eustace owes something to the heroines of the Sensation novels of the previous decade, but her machinations are designed not to save her name but to keep control of the family diamonds which she has misappropriated.
[GA459] Oxford pbk **£3.95**
[GA460] Penguin pbk **£4.50**
4: Phineas Redux (1876)
Mr Finn's return to politics is honourable, but his path is by no means smooth, and as well as a political imbroglio he is shot at by a jealous husband, and charged with the murder of the President of the Board of Trade. Marie Goesler finds the evidence to free him, and he marries her and takes up his political career again.
[GA461] Oxford pbk **£4.95**
5: The Prime Minister (1876)
Palliser, now Prime Minister (of a coalition) is burdened by the care of the country despite his wife's support. When Lady Glencora is embroiled by Lopez, an unscrupulous adventurer, into promises of electoral help which the Duke cannot in conscience support, there is personal and political embarrassment.
[GA462] Oxford pbk **£4.95**
6: The Duke's Children (1880)
After the death of Lady Glencora, Trollope's concern moves to the next generation, and the problems of getting the ducal children settled down. The happy ending involves the heir, daringly, marrying an American.
[GA463] Oxford pbk **£4.95**
TROLLOPE'S OTHER WORKS
An Old Man's Love (1884)
Trollope's last completed novel; an elderly bachelor gives up the girl who has promised to marry him, to her young but long absent lover.
[GA464] Sutton pbk **£2.95**
Ayala's Angel (1881)
A comic novel of the coming-to-earth of a young lady whose romantic notions falter when confronted with the reality of her matrimonial choice.
[GA465] Oxford pbk **£4.95**
Castle Richmond
Contains some moving scenes portraying the Irish famine, which Trollope had seen at first hand.
[GA466] Oxford pbk **£5.95**
Cousin Henry (1879)
[GA467] Oxford pbk **£3.95**
Dr Wortle's School (1881)
Dr Wortle runs a fashionable school, and defies his bishop when his assistant master is accused of bigamy.
[GA468] Oxford pbk **£3.95**
Harry Heathcote of Gangoil (1874)
A tale of Australian bush life.
[GA469] Sutton pbk **£3.50**
He Knew He Was Right (1869)
An impressive study of marital disharmony, admired by Henry James, accompanied by several other plots, some in lighter vein.
[GA470] Oxford pbk **£4.95**
Is He Poppenjoy? (1878)
An inheritance plot allows Trollope to feature a socially ambitious Dean, a dissolute Marquis, and his stuffy younger brother.
[GA471] Oxford pbk **£5.95**
Kept in the Dark (1882)
A late study of a husband's obsession with his wife's past.
[GA472] Sutton pbk **£2.95**

Illustration from *Phineas Redux* by Anthony Trollope (Oxford University Press pbk **£4.95**)

Lady Anna (1874)
The daughter of an Earl loves the son of a tailor, to her mother's intense and violent dismay.
[GA473] Sutton pbk **£3.95**
Miss Mackenzie (1865)
[GA474] Oxford pbk **£4.95**
Mr Scarborough's Family (1883)
On his death-bed, Mr Scarborough tries to outwit the law by proving both his sons illegitimate in turn, so as to save his estate from the money-lenders.
[GA475] Sutton pbk **£3.95**
Orley Farm (1862)
A long tale of disputed inheritance, where the winner in the legal battle finally admits her moral guilt and does the decent thing.
[GA476] Oxford pbk **£5.95**
Rachel Ray (1863)
A small-scale, mildly satirical comedy of parish life.
[GA477] Oxford pbk **£4.95**
Ralph the Heir (1871)
An old squire is frustrated in his wish to leave his estate to his illegitimate son. The novel also reflects Trollope's unhappy experiences as a Parliamentary candidate.
[GA478] Dover pbk **£5.95**
Sir Harry Hotspur of Humblethwaite (1871)
[GA479] Dover pbk **£4.75**
The American Senator (1877)
An examination of English mores by a visiting outsider, with some fox- and husband-hunting involved.
[GA480] Oxford pbk **£4.95**
The Belton Estate (1866)
[GA481] Oxford pbk **£3.95**
The Bertrams (1859)
[GA482] Sutton pbk **£3.95**
The Claverings (1867)
The vacillating hero is let off lightly when the relatives who stand between him and a fortune are drowned.
[GA483] Oxford pbk **£4.95**
The Kellys & The O'Kellys (1848)
An early tale of Irish life, subtitled 'Lords and Tenants'.
[GA484] Oxford pbk **£4.95**
The Macdermots of Ballycloran (1847)
Trollope's first novel.
[GA485] Dover pbk **£7.15**
The Spotted Dog and Other Stories
[GA486] Sutton pbk **£2.95**
The Three Clerks (1857)
The contrasting personalities and stories of three clerks who marry three sisters, with some

autobiographical detail from Trollope's own experience of the Civil Service.
[GA487] Sutton pbk **£3.95**
The Vicar of Bullhampton (1870)
The Vicar is also a detective who clears up a murder mystery and brings respectability to a fallen woman.
[GA488] Oxford pbk **£4.95**
The Way We Live Now
Conceived as an attack on the 'commercial profligacy of the age', this wide-ranging novel is now regarded as one of Trollope's most important works, and is different in tone to most of his others.
[GA489] Oxford pbk **£5.95**

WALPOLE, HORACE (1719 - 1797)
A major English exponent of Gothic taste in all its manifestations, from architecture to this, the first Gothic novel.
The Castle of Otranto (1764)
[GA490] Oxford pbk **£1.95**

WALPOLE, HORACE ET AL
Three Gothic Novels
The Castle of Otranto with Mary Shelley's *Frankenstein* and Beckford's *Vathek*.
[GA491] Penguin pbk **£3.95**

WARD, MRS HUMPHRY (1851 - 1920)
A major literary figure of her day producing 25 novels on social and religious subjects. She was a tireless social reformer but drew the line at women's suffrage.
Helbeck of Bannisdale (1898)
Describes tensions between an independent, free-thinking young woman and her aloof, conventional catholic lover, recalling Brontë's *Villette* in the process.
[GA492] Penguin pbk **£4.99**
Marcella (1894)
A young philanthropic art student with socialist views falls for a rural gentleman and local Tory candidate. The love interest is played against realistic descriptions of brutal rural and urban poverty.
[GA504] Virago pbk **£4.95**
Robert Elsmere (1888)
The moving story of a young clergyman, whose decision to abandon the cloth to do social work in London's East End alienates his evangelical wife. On the strength of this novel Tolstoy praised her as among the greatest of English novelists.
[GA493] Oxford pbk **£4.95**

WILDE, OSCAR (1854 - 1900)
Now that he is back in the literary limelight following Richard Ellmann's valedictory biography, the time may have come to proclaim that Wilde's fiction sparkles as much as his peerless comic drama and mischievous essays.
Lord Arthur Savile's Crime and Other Stories (1891)
The hero has to commit murder before marrying his sweetheart, so beginning the search for disposable relatives.
[GA494] Penguin pbk **£2.25**
Teleny
An unusual piece of predominantly homosexual Victorian pornography accepted to be at least partly by Wilde.
[GA495] GMP pbk **£4.95**
The Complete Shorter Fiction
His incomparable children's stories dominate this collection which also includes *Lord Arthur Savile's Crime* and his late prose poems. Although charming they are never sentimental for as Wilde knew - *"the sentimentalist is always a cynic at heart. Indeed sentimentality is merely the bank-holiday of cynicism"*.
[GA496] Oxford hbk **£9.95**
[GA497] Oxford pbk **£3.50**

Oscar Wilde from a biography by Richard Ellmann
(Hamish Hamilton hbk £17.95, Penguin pbk £6.99)

The Picture of Dorian Gray (1890)
An unsettling exploration of *fin de siècle* perversity.
Dorian is a handsome image of perfectability, who
becomes corrupted by his own temptations. While he
remains beautiful and successful, his portrait bears the
scars of an addiction to depravity.
[GA498] Oxford pbk **£1.95**
[GA499] Penguin pbk **£1.95**

WILLIAMS (ED)
Book of English Essays
[GA500] Penguin pbk **£4.95**

WOOD, MRS HENRY (ELLEN) (1814 - 1887)
With about 40 novels to her credit, Mrs Henry Wood
was one of the most prolific writers of her time. Her
first work relied heavily on Sensation techniques, and
proved immediately successful; the close plotting of
her later works relates them to the detective story
which was evolving at the time.
East Lynne (1861)
The quintessence of Victorian melodrama, with an
erring wife so changed after an accident that she can
return to her children's home as their governess. It is,
however, sad that the line: *"Dead! Dead! - and never
called me mother!"* is not in the novel but comes
from a stage adaption.
[GA501] Dent pbk **£3.95**

YONGE, CHARLOTTE MARY (1823 - 1901)
Her novels are devout and rather romantic, and seek
to teach young women the joys of family life.
The Clever Woman of the Family (1865)
[GA502] Virago pbk **£5.95**
The Daisy Chain (1856)
[GA503] Virago pbk **£6.95**

Michael Moorcock

My tendency to recommend out of print books to people is fairly notorious so I'll merely mention *The Amazing Marriage* by George Meredith, *Maude Em'ly* by W. Pett Ridge, *Fowler's End* by Gerald Kersh and *One Last Mad Embrace* by Jack Trevor Story as four of the books which conscienceless publishers refuse to put back into print!

I'd like to recommend all the work I've enjoyed by friends and acquaintances… J.G. Ballard, Brian Aldiss, Thomas M. Disch, Colin Greenland, Norman Spinrad, Rob Holdstock, Alfred Bester, M. John Harrison, Joanna Russ, Pamela Zoline, Lisa Tuttle, John Sladek, Peter Ackroyd, Angus Wilson, Robert Nye, Andrea Dworkin, Mervyn Peake, Harlan Ellison, Eudora Welty, Barrington Bayley, Lisa Goldstein, Angela Carter, Edward Blishen, Ellen Gilchrist, Louise Erdrich, David Hughes, Terry Pratchett, Don DeLillo, Harvey Jacobs, Judith Merrill, Leigh Brackett, John Stoltenburg among them.

Then there's my list of childhood enthusiasms including the William books, E. Nesbit, Edgar Rice Burroughs and, for some weird reason, George Bernard Shaw. I'd like to celebrate my teenage years with Aldous Huxley, George

Orwell, H.G. Wells, Colin MacInnes, John Steinbeck and Fritz Leiber, my relish for the early 'magic realists' or for Camus or, for that matter, John Buchan. There was a time when an enjoyment of Raymond Chandler or Dashiell Hammett seemed rather rarefied, like a taste for Jazz, when science fiction was thought to be the idiot child of Verne and Wells and you had to read Spanish to enjoy Borges (I first *heard* Borges recounted by a Spanish-speaking Swede while trying to hitch a lift outside Copenhagen in the 1950s). There was a time, too, when publishers weren't mere departments of some international conglomerate in the whacky, wonderful land of Thatcheria.

I decided in the end to choose ten of the books I am most enthusiastic about that are in print, in English and, with one exception, of the 20th century, and resist airing my enduring passion for Smollett, Austen, Dickens, Eliot, Conrad, Mann, Faulkner and others who are, inevitably, on every syllabus, and to recommend easily-obtained books that are possibly unfamiliar to many readers. I'd like to offer them in the spirit of sheer delight with which I first read them.

GEORGE MEREDITH
Diana of the Crossways
This is one of Meredith's great books, exhibiting all his admiration for women of spirit - his books are full of women of spirit - challenging the fundamental coarseness of Victorian Society. It's on a par with *The Amazing Marriage*, whose heroine outdoes Diana in taking charge of her own destiny. Meredith really liked women, though he'd been hurt by his first wife (Peacock's daughter Mary who ran off with Wallis the painter, who used Meredith as a model for Chatterton) and was obsessed by the injustice of Woman's position in the mid- to late-19th century. His best work ranks with George Eliot's. (Virago, pbk £5.99)

ISAAC BABEL
The Collected Stories
A master of the short story, Babel wrote little. Before he reached maturity Stalin had begun to impose the rules of 'socialist realism' on Soviet writers and the accuracy of Babel's stories of Cossacks during the Russian civil war (Babel had been a Chekist officer with Trotski's cavalry - a Jewish intellectual amongst

traditionally anti-semitic fighting men) had become political wrong-thinking. As an undisputed hero of the Revolution, Babel led something of a charmed life when all around him the Terror progressed. He did what he could for his fellow artists and indeed was more than once successful in saving a life, but he flirted with danger, it was said, by courting the wife of Yezhov, until 1938 boss of the NKVD and chief orchestrator of Stalin's purges. Whatever the truth - and we'll never know the whole of it - Babel was arrested, his work in progress destroyed, and he died in a labour camp, probably in 1941. These stories, which include his joyful, clever Odessa tales based on his own youth in his hometown, are his enduring monument.
(Penguin, pbk £4.99)

ELIZABETH BOWEN
The Death of the Heart
Simple and unsensational as this story is, it is for me Bowen's masterpiece. The tension generated by the tale of a girl's innocent falling in love with a selfish young man had me close to tears and on the edge of my bunk (I read it at sea in a storm - oblivious to giant waves and howling winds!). Bowen is a wonderfully subtle writer who sometimes can be a little unforgiving in the matter of plot. This book provides the delicious, old-fashioned anguish we usually only find in Dickens or a Brontë.
(Cape, hbk £9.95/Penguin, pbk £4.99)

Elizabeth Bowen, author of *The Death of the Heart* (Cape hbk £9.95, Penguin pbk £4.99) (Photo: Methuen) (Photo: National Portrait Gallery)

EUDORA WELTY
Collected Short Stories

Welty is probably the greatest living American novelist, but for all that I admire her novels, it's her short stories I return to frequently for that sweet, measured, stiletto-sharp descriptive prose which echoes all the melodies and witty ironies of good Southern conversation. There's melancholy as well as outright comedy here and perhaps the best companion to this volume is Welty's *One Writer's Beginnings* which provides an illuminating context for those readers unfamiliar with the Deep South of Faulkner or O'Connor.
(Boyars, hbk £15, pbk £8.95)

ALFRED BESTER
Tiger! Tiger!

Gully Foyle's rise from illiterate space hand to master of the universe. This is the book that turned me on to SF - and I've never read a better. I spent most of my teenage years buying it in the hope it would match this in style, invention, sophistication, political attitude, pace and character - and never succeeded. It remains, if I had to choose, the only modern SF book I'd want to keep.
(Penguin, pbk £3.95)

MARGERY ALLINGHAM
The Tiger in the Smoke

Of her 'classic' detective stories, Margery Allingham's *Dancers in Mourning* is probably the most perfect, but after the War, with its revelations of impossible cruelties, her work darkened and deepened and she produced her masterpieces, including *More Work for the Undertaker* and *Hide My Eyes*. *Tiger in the Smoke* has an astonishing sense of pervasive, sickening evil spreading out like the London fog itself to touch all but the purest of heart like gentle old Canon Avril who in the end confronts Jack Havoc, the Tiger, in a church and, essentially, destroys the evil in him. I am no lover of English detective fiction. Allingham, like Chandler and Hammett, stands high above her contemporaries.
(Hogarth, pbk £3.95)

ANGUS WILSON
Late Call

It's hard to select one Wilson, especially when the *Collected Stories* are now available, but I think for sheer observation, wit and quiet compassion *Late Call* has to be the book I would pick. His picture of England in the late 1950s is perfect and captures both the atmosphere of the time as well as the poignancy of the old woman, Sylvia Calvert, who has been powerful and independent all her life and now, through the inevitability of age, becomes dependant and is condescended to by a son for whom she feels a sort of gentle contempt. A beautifully constructed book, probably the finest of Wilson's pre-experimental novels.
(Secker & Warburg, hbk £10.95/Granada, pbk £2.95)

J.G. BALLARD
The Empire of the Sun

In many ways this is Ballard's apotheosis, possessing the visual intensity and density of metaphor of his early trilogy which began with *The Drowned World*. Basing the book firmly on his own experience as a child prisoner of the Japanese, Ballard is at his most inspired and most subtle in depicting all the various ways in which his characters learn to survive the horrors of conquest and occupation. The Japanese are viewed as sympathetically as the English and Americans, which caused some unseemly complaints and admonitions from Bournemouth and points West, where many retired colonials failed to see how an English prisoner could even want to understand the point of view of a war-crazed enemy. Read this Ballard in conjunction with *High Rise* or *The Crystal World* and take pleasure in the imagination of this country's most original and creative writer.
(Gollancz, hbk £9.95/Granada, pbk £3.50)

ELLEN GILCHRIST
Drunk with Love

Good as they are, Gilchrist's novels have yet to achieve what she achieves in her short stories *In the Land of Dreamy Dreams*, *Victory Over Japan* and this one. The adventures of her determinedly free-spirited character Rhoda take up much of this, and other, books. This is a funny, sardonic, joyful break with the tradition of Southern US fiction, as optimistic, tolerant and contradictory as the New South itself.
(Faber, pbk £3.95)

ANDREA DWORKIN
Letters from a War Zone

I admire Dworkin inordinately for all her books - *Our Blood*, *Pornography*, *Right Wing Women*, *Woman-Hating*, *Ice and Fire*, *The New Woman's Broken Heart* - but *Letters* is probably the best introduction to her brand of fierce, idealistic, humane, often humorous and profoundly-reasoned feminism. Dworkin is almost the last unsilenced voice of her generation, who has provided the women's movement with a polemic of hope and helped keep the flame of anger and radicalism blazing in a world where authority is busily trying to drown all dissent. Her courage in the face of positive threats (including death threats) is an example to everyone who believes in the cause of justice and egalitarianism. Read her and, yes, you will weep!
(Secker & Warburg, pbk £5.95)

J.G. Ballard, author of *The Empire of the Sun* (Gollancz hbk £9.95, Granada pbk £3.50)

One of the most prolific authors of Science and Fantasy Fiction of the post-war era, Moorcock has also written acclaimed 'mainstream' fiction, including the complex and panoramic *Mother London* (1988). This year he has published a new novel in the Elric series, *The Fortress of the Pearl*, with a collection of short stories and non-fiction pieces, *Casablanca*, due out in December to coincide with his fiftieth birthday.

BRITISH & IRISH FICTION

Short Stories

English Short Stories of Today
(Ed. Shattuck, Roger)
[GBA1] Oxford pbk **£2.50**
Modern English Short Stories
(Ed. Hudson, Derek)
From the period 1900-1935.
[GBA2] Oxford pbk **£2.95**
**The Penguin Book of English Short
Stories** (Ed. Dolley, Christopher)
[GBA3] Penguin pbk **£3.99**
**The Second Penguin Book of English
Short Stories** (Ed. Dolley, Christopher)
[GBA4] Penguin pbk **£2.95**
**The Penguin Book of Modern British
Short Stories** (Ed. Bradbury, Malcolm)
[GBA5] Penguin pbk **£4.99**

CLASSIC ENGLISH SHORT STORIES
A recent series from Oxford which reflects the best of
20th century writing in the language.
The Dragon's Head
Stories from 1900-1945.
[GBA6] Oxford pbk **£3.95**
Charmed Lives (Ed Dorsch, T.E.)
The Killing Bottle (Ed. Davin, Dan)
Stories from the 1930s and 1940s.
[GBA7] Oxford pbk **£3.95**
Stories from the 1950s and 1960s.
[GBA8] Oxford pbk **£3.95**
The Green Man Revisited
(Ed. Sharrock, Roger)
Stories from the 1960s and 1970s.
[GBA9] Oxford pbk **£3.95**

Modern Scottish Short Stories
(Ed. Urquhart & Gordon)
[GBA11] Faber pbk **£3.99**
**The Grafton Book of Scottish Short
Stories** (Ed. Campbell, James)
[GBA12] Grafton pbk **£2.95**
**The Penguin Book of Scottish Short
Stories** (Ed. Hendry, J.F.)
[GBA13] Penguin pbk **£3.95**
**The New Penguin Book of Scottish
Short Stories** (Ed. Murray, Ian)
[GBA14] Penguin pbk **£4.99**
**The Red Hog of Colima: Scottish
Short Stories 1989** **NEW**
17 new short stories by Scottish writers. Introduction
by John Linklater.
[GBA15] Collins hbk **£10.95**

A New Book of Dubliners (Ed. Forkner, Ben)
A collection of stories set in Dublin in this century,
including Joyce's 'Ivy Day in the Committee Room'.
[GBA16] Methuen pbk **£4.95**
Classic Irish Short Stories
(Ed. O' Connor, Frank)
[GBA17] Oxford pbk **£4.95**
Irish Short Stories (Ed. Marcus, David)
[GBA18] Hodder pbk **£3.50**
Modern Irish Short Stories (Ed. Forkner)
[GBA19] Futura pbk **£5.99**
The Penguin Book of Irish Short Stories
[GBA21] Penguin pbk **£4.50**
**The Oxford Book of Irish Short
Stories** (Ed. Trevor, William) **NEW**
Excellent new collection: from Sheridan Le Fanu and

Sean O'Faolain to James Joyce and Elizabeth Bowen.
[GBA22] Oxford hbk **£15.00**

Penguin Book of Welsh Stories
(Ed. Richards, Alun)
[GBA23] Penguin pbk **£4.50**

Writers A-Z

ACKROYD, PETER (1949 -)
Prize-winning biographer, poet and novelist, Ackroyd
writes a probing form of historical fiction in which he
combines the past and the present, creating intriguing
'dialogues with the dead'. He achieved enormous
popular and critical success with his metaphysical
thriller *Hawksmoor*.
Chatterton (1987)
A multi-layered reconstruction of the life of the
legendary 18th century poet-forger Chatterton,
involving three separate time sequences.
[GB1] Sphere pbk **£3.99**
First Light (1989) **NEW**
A Hardyesque novel set in the West Country,
marrying together an archaeological dig and an
astronomer's investigations. Positively reviewed as a
meditation upon the nature of history, time and the
English landscape.
[GB2] H Hamilton hbk **£12.95**
Hawksmoor (1985)
A chilling and highly original tale centring around
the construction of Nicholas Hawksmoor's seven
churches, half of which is written in a pastiche of
18th century prose, which brilliantly evokes that
lost London.
[GB3] Sphere pbk **£3.99**
The Diversions of Purley (Poems)
[GB4] H Hamilton hbk **£8.95**
The Great Fire of London (1982)
[GB5] Sphere pbk **£3.99**
The Last Testament of Oscar Wilde
(1983)
Ayckroyd presents a carefully reconstructed and
extremely moving account of Wilde's last years
in Paris.
[GB6] Sphere pbk **£3.99**

ADAMS, RICHARD (1920 -)
Since the enormous success of *Watership Down*,
Adams has written other powerful epics featuring
animals as narrators or central subjects. His novels are
characterized by their exoticism and imaginative
scope.
Girl on a Swing (1980)
[GB7] Penguin pbk **£3.95**
Iron Wolf
[GB8] Penguin pbk **£2.99**
Maia (1984)
[GB9] Penguin pbk **£7.95**
Shardik (1974)
[GB10] Penguin pbk **£5.99**
The Legend of Te Tuna (1986)
[GB11] Sidgwick hbk **£8.95**
The Plague Dogs (1977)
[GB12] Penguin pbk **£3.95**
Traveller (1989) **NEW**
Richard Adams' first animal protagonist in ten
years is the narrator of this rather revisionist
version of the American Civil War, but then he is
General Robert E. Lee's horse, and does not care
to admit defeat.
[GB13] Hutchinson hbk **£12.95**
Watership Down (1972)
The terrors and rewards of life within a community of
wild rabbits.
[GB14] Viking hbk illus **£12.95**
[GB15] Penguin pbk **£3.99**

Peter Ayckroyd, author of *First Light* (H Hamiton
hbk £12.95)

ALDINGTON, RICHARD (1892 - 1962)
A writer and poet connected with the Imagist
movement, a friend and apologist for D.H. Lawrence,
and the husband of Hilda Doolittle (HD).
Death of a Hero (1921)
His first and most successful novel, written from his
experiences in the First World War. One of the most
powerful and horrifying novels of war.
[GB16] Hogarth pbk **£5.95**
The Colonel's Daughter (1931)
[GB17] Hogarth pbk **£5.95**

AMIS, KINGSLEY (1922 -)
Amis has written in a variety of forms, his work
invariably characterized by comic outrage and
irreverence. His fictional landscape has broadened
since the social and sexual satires that made his name,
of which *Lucky Jim* and *Take a Girl Like You* were
his most notable successes. He is still writing at the
height of his powers, as witnessed by his 1986
Booker Prize.
Collected Short Stories (1987)
[GB18] Hutchinson hbk **£11.95**
[GB19] Penguin pbk **£3.95**
Difficulties with Girls (1988)
Amis is still in sparkling form, as this tale of marital
infidelity and sexual neurosis, set in the swinging
London of the 1960s, amply demonstrates.
[GB20] Hutchinson hbk **£11.95**
Ending Up (1974)
[GB21] Penguin pbk **£2.50**
Girl, 20 (1971)
A deliciously wicked tale of vile Sylvia, seventeen
and mistress to part-time composer and full-time
lecher Sir Roy.
[GB22] Penguin pbk **£2.95**
I Like it Here (1958)
[GB23] Penguin pbk **£2.99**
I Want it Now
[GB24] Penguin pbk **£2.95**
Jake's Thing (1978)
[GB25] Penguin pbk **£2.99**
Lucky Jim (1954)
The quintessential 1950s 'angry young man' novel,
and perennial comic classic, relating the trials of
redbrick academic Jim Dixon.
[GB26] Gollancz hbk **£9.95**
[GB27] Penguin pbk **£2.99**

One Fat Englishman (1963)
[GB28] Penguin pbk **£2.95**
Russian Hide and Seek (1980)
[GB29] Penguin pbk **£2.95**
Stanley and the Women (1984)
Stanley's well-ordered life is disrupted by a series of events and women; the novel angered many feminists for its unsympathetic portrayal of their sex.
[GB30] Penguin pbk **£3.50**
Take a Girl Like You (1960)
[GB31] Penguin pbk **£3.50**
That Uncertain Feeling (1955)
[GB32] Penguin pbk **£2.99**
The Alteration (1976)
[GB33] Penguin pbk **£2.50**
The Anti-Death League
[GB34] Penguin pbk **£3.50**
The Crime of the Century
Amis has written written two crime novels, this and *The Riverside Villas Murder*.
[GB34a] Dent pbk **£2.95**
The Green Man
Amis's only supernatural novel, centring around the haunted Herefordshire pub of the title.
[GB35] Penguin pbk **£2.99**
The Old Devils (1986)
A beautifully written, Booker Prize-winning tragicomedy about a group of middle-aged Welsh men and women approaching old age and sobriety.
[GB36] Hutchinson hbk **£9.95**
[GB37] Penguin pbk **£3.95**
The Riverside Villas Murder (1973)
[GB38] Penguin pbk **£2.95**

AMIS, MARTIN (1949 -)
Kingsley's son, but from a different school of writing. His novels are sophisticated and often sordid comedies making satirical comment on the spirit of our times, increasingly in the manner of certain famous American novelists, Amis's stylistic mentors. More recent work reveals a developing seriousness of purpose yoked to a confident narrative style.
Dead Babies (1975)
[GB39] Penguin pbk **£2.99**
Einstein's Monsters (Stories, 1987)
Five tales preceded by a swingeing polemic on the folly of maintaining nuclear weapons.
[GB40] Penguin pbk **£3.50**
London Fields (1989)   **NEW**
Again Amis plumbs the depths of depravity in a tale of murder and deception, with a feckless darts champ and failed criminal Keith Talent. Fans of *Money* won't be disappointed by this loveless *tour de force*.
[GB41] Cape hbk **£11.95**
Money (1984)
The hapless and debauched John Self gives us an account of his jet-set lifestyle in New York and London. Paints a compellingly awful picture of 20th century decay, related in an original comic language.
[GB42] Cape hbk **£9.95**
[GB43] Penguin pbk **£3.99**
Other People (1981)
[GB44] Penguin pbk **£2.95**
Success (1978)
[GB45] Penguin pbk **£2.95**
The Rachel Papers (1973)
His award-winning first novel, which details adolescent lust with canny humour.
[GB46] Penguin pbk **£2.99**

ANGADI, PATRICIA (1914 -)
Having begun writing at the age of 70, Angadi has been well received as a writer of highly individual novels broadly based in the English tradition.
Sins of the Mothers (1989)   **NEW**
Before her 80th birthday, Iffey the 17-stone night-club singer and sometime prostitute recalls her life, friends and former clients, some of whom overlap...
[GB47] Gollancz hbk **£12.95**

The Done Thing (1986)
[GB48] Transworld pbk **£4.95**
The Governess (1985)
[GB49] Transworld pbk **£3.95**
The Highly Flavoured Ladies (1987)
The heroine inhabits both the world of a poor woman in 1870s England who falls in love with a curate, and that of a woman alive a century later.
[GB50] Transworld pbk **£3.95**

ARNIM, ELIZABETH VON (1866 - 1941)
Australian-born cousin of Katherine Mansfield who married a German aristocrat, Count von Arnim-Schlaganthen.
Elizabeth and Her German Garden (1898)
The author's family life and her garden in Prussia.
[GB51] Virago pbk **£4.99**
Enchanted April (1923)
[GB52] Virago pbk **£5.00**
Fraulein Schmidt and Mr Anstruther
[GB53] Virago pbk **£5.50**
Pastor's Wife (1912)
[GB54] Virago pbk **£5.50**
Vera (1921)
[GB55] Virago pbk **£4.99**

BAGNOLD, ENID (1889 - 1981)
After a childhood in Jamaica, Bagnold lived as a painter and journalist before working in hospitals during the First World War. Her novels draw upon her acquaintance with many of the prominent social and political figures of her day. She is also remembered for her children's novel, *National Velvet*.
The Happy Foreigner
[GB56] Virago pbk **£4.99**
The Loved and Envied (1931)
The heroine of this novel was based upon her friend Diana Cooper.
[GB57] Virago pbk **£4.99**
The Squire (1938)
Whilst the squire is away, the mistress waits, heavy with child. This sensuous novel explores the themes of childbirth, motherhood and maturity.
[GB58] Virago pbk **£5.50**

BAILEY, HILARY (1936 -)
A writer of satires attacking the hypocrisy and corruption of the middle class.
A Stranger to Herself (1989)   **NEW**
A good dramatic novel on a wide canvas. A woman is employed to research the biography of a legendary female politician, and unearths some interesting details about her early life during the war.
[GB59] Macmillan hbk **£11.95**
All the Days of My Life (1985)
[GB60] Pan pbk **£3.99**
As Time Goes By
The dark but comic story of a woman's involvement with a strange wealthy man.
[GB61] Pan pbk **£3.99**
Hannie Richards (1985)
A pastiche of Buchanesque, *Boys' Own* writing.
[GB62] Virago pbk **£3.95**
Mrs Mulvanney (1978)
[GB63] Pan pbk **£2.95**

BAILEY, PAUL (1937 -)
Novelist of acute sensitivity, twice shortlisted for the Booker Prize, who writes of the pains of both youth and age with eloquence and compassion. His earlier books are delightfully compact; *Gabriel's Lament*, with its combination of rich humour and incurable grief, represents the true flowering of his genius.
A Distant Likeness (1973)
[GB64] Cape hbk **£7.95**
At the Jerusalem (1980)
Stories from the nursing home that recurs in Bailey's writing, exploring loss, hope and patience.
[GB65] Penguin pbk **£3.95**

Gabriel's Lament (1986)
Abandoned by his mother at a tender age, Gabriel is left in the hands of his authoritarian father, whose voice is brilliantly captured in this wonderful novel that has been called Dickensian - both for its human sympathy and its atmospheric re-creation of London.
[GB66] Cape hbk **£9.95**
[GB67] Penguin pbk **£3.95**
Old Soldiers (1980)
Fine, short novel about two aging men who become unlikely companions.
[GB68] Penguin pbk **£3.50**
Peter Smart's Confessions (1977)
[GB69] Cape hbk **£8.95**

BAINBRIDGE, BERYL (1934 -)
Critic, columnist, and author of both novels and non-fiction, Bainbridge is a popular literary figure hailing from Liverpool. Her novels touch upon the unwitting cruelty in personal relations, and brilliantly exhibit the potential horror of our everyday world. Twice shortlisted for the Booker Prize, her writing is lucid, stylish, and often very funny.
A Quiet Life (1976)
[GB70] Fontana pbk **£3.95**
An Awfully Big Adventure (1989)   **NEW**
It is 1950 and the Liverpool Repertory Company is rehearsing its Xmas production of *Peter Pan*. O'Hara has come from London to play Captain Hook, but finds that stage-hand Stella is more diverting...
[GB71] Duckworth hbk **£10.95**
Another Part of the Wood (1979)
[GB72] Fontana pbk **£2.95**
Filthy Lucre (1986)
The remarkably assured novel that Bainbridge wrote at the age of 13.
[GB73] Fontana pbk **£3.50**
Harriet Said (1973)
[GB74] Fontana pbk **£3.50**
Injury Time (1977)
One of her best-regarded works; a terse black comedy delivered in immaculately measured prose.
[GB75] Fontana pbk **£2.50**
Mum and Mr Armitage (1984)
[GB76] Fontana pbk **£2.95**
Sweet William (1975)
[GB77] Fontana pbk **£3.95**
The Bottle Factory Outing (1974)
[GB78] Fontana pbk **£3.50**
The Dressmaker (1973)
[GB79] Fontana pbk **£3.50**
Watson's Apology (1984)
[GB80] Fontana pbk **£2.95**
Weekend with Claude (1967)
[GB81] Fontana pbk **£1.50**
Winter Garden (1980)
[GB82] Fontana pbk **£3.50**
Young Adolf (1980)
This novel imagines Hitler growing up in Liverpool.
[GB83] Fontana pbk **£2.50**

BALLARD, J.G. (1930 -)
Although best known for his unique and provocative brand of imaginative fiction (see under *Science Fiction*), these two novels have brought Ballard well-deserved attention from a wider audience.
Empire of the Sun (1984)
This moving, semi-autobiographical account of a child's life in a Japanese prison camp during the last war was shortlisted for the Booker Prize and has also been filmed.
[GB84] Gollancz hbk **£9.95**
[GB85] Grafton pbk **£2.99**
The Day of Creation (1987)
An imaginative fable of a doctor in drought-stricken Africa, trying to find the source of the mysterious river he believes runs beneath the dry earth.
[GB86] Gollancz hbk **£10.95**
[GB87] Grafton pbk **£2.99**

BANKS, IAIN

Banks received immediate attention for his first novel's notable desire to shock. His bizarre novels are cleverly constructed and frequently threatening - some critics feel that the psycho-sexual violence so central to his work is, at times, gratuitous. (See *Science Fiction* for other novels).

Canal Dreams (1989) **NEW**
Banks' latest work is a chilling premonition of a future war. A famous cellist, travelling by steamer to Europe, finds herself the hostage of sinister guerrillas...
[GB88] Macmillan hbk **£11.95**

Espedair Street (1988)
[GB89] Futura pbk **£4.99**

The Bridge (1986)
After a car crash, the central character finds himself in a strange comatose state.
[GB90] Futura pbk **£3.99**

The Wasp Factory (1984)
An emotionally isolated youth experiments with life and death, until his lunatic brother interrupts, leading to a stunning and sinister climax.
[GB91] Futura pbk **£3.99**

Walking on Glass (1985)
[GB92] Futura pbk **£3.99**

BANKS, LYNNE REID (1929 -)

Achieved enormous success with *The L-Shaped Room*, which caught the mood of the 1960s.

An End to Running (1962)
[GB97] Penguin pbk **£2.95**

Backward Shadow (1970)
[GB93] Penguin pbk **£2.99**

Casualties (1986)
[GB94] Penguin pbk **£3.50**

Children at the Gate (1968)
[GB95] Penguin pbk **£3.50**

Dark Quartet (1976)
[GB96] Penguin pbk **£3.99**

The L-Shaped Room (1962)
The story of an unmarried but pregnant woman whose personal and spiritual rejuvenation leads to a more fruitful existence.
[GB98] Chatto hbk **£8.95**
[GB99] Penguin pbk **£2.99**

Two is Lonely (1974)
[GB100] Penguin pbk **£2.95**

Warning Bell (1984)
[GB101] Penguin pbk **£3.50**

BANVILLE, JOHN (Irish, 1945 -)

One of the most acclaimed novelists to appear in the 1970s, now literary editor of the *Irish Times*. His reputation is based on his award-winning metaphysical and speculative 'science' novels, the style of which is dense and rich, with an evocative Gothic atmosphere.

Birchwood (1973)
An evocation of Ireland in chaos which is centred on a large country house.
[GB102] Grafton pbk **£3.50**

Doctor Copernicus (1976)
The work of Copernicus shattered the medieval view of the Universe, and in this novel Banville magnificently evokes the life of the haunted genius.
[GB103] Grafton pbk **£3.95**

Kepler (1980)
Winner of the 1981 *Guardian* Fiction prize and considered by many to be Banville's best novel, this tells of the astronomer's life and dreams, set amid the splendour and squalor of Renaissance Europe.
[GB104] Grafton pbk **£2.50**

Long Lankin (Stories, 1970)
This is his first collection, here published in a new edition.
[GB105] Gallery P pbk **£4.95**

Mefisto (1986)
[GB106] Grafton pbk **£3.95**

The Book of Evidence (1989) **NEW**
An exquisitely written and often hilarious novel of the highest order, this is the monologue of a murderer trying to come to terms with forty years of dissolute living. A remarkable blend of tragedy and farce.
[GB107] Secker hbk **£10.95**

The Newton Letter (1982)
Trying to complete a book on Isaac Newton in a rented cottage in Ireland, a writer becomes obsessed by the family in the big house nearby.
[GB108] Grafton pbk **£1.95**

BARBER, NOEL (1909 - 1988)

A great foreign correspondent who translated personal experiences in the Middle East and elsewhere into very well-researched, exotic romances and thrillers.

A Farewell to France (1983)
[GB109] Hodder pbk **£4.50**

A Woman of Cairo (1984)
[GB110] Hodder pbk **£3.99**

Tanamera (1981)
[GB111] Hodder pbk **£3.99**

The Daughters of the Prince **NEW**
Barber's last book opens in June 1936. Three young men are in love with the Italian Prince's three daughters, but are separated by the war. Like Barber's other novels, this is a rich and colourful story.
[GB112] Hodder hbk **£12.95**

The Other Side of Paradise (1987)
[GB113] Hodder pbk **£3.95**

The Weeping and the Laughter (1988)
The heroes of this novel are Russian aristocrats who were scattered throughout Europe in the aftermath of the October Revolution.
[GB114] Hodder pbk **£3.99**

BARKE, JAMES (Scottish, 1905 - 1958)

The Land of the Leal (1939)
A Lewis Grassic Gibbon-influenced epic of Galloway life.
[GB115] Canongate pbk **£4.95**

BARKER, A.L. (1918 -)

A writer much admired by Rebecca West, Barker explores the way in which odd, eccentric people possess the capacity to experience the world about them in exact, sharp detail.

Gooseboy (1987)
An aging film idol employs the eponymous boy, who finds himself the centre of attention when the star's agent and sister come visiting.
[GB116] Arrow pbk **£3.99**

John Brown's Body
[GB117] Arrow pbk **£3.99**

No World of Love (1985)
[GB118] Chatto hbk **£9.50**

Relative Successes (1984)
[GB119] Chatto hbk **£9.95**

The Woman who Talked to Herself **NEW**
The latest work from this highly-praised writer is an intriguing account of a middle-aged female writer whose fictional creations are invariably sexually unfulfilled. Eventually we discover the connection between these stories and the narrator's marriage.
[GB120] Hutchinson hbk **£12.95**

BARKER, PAT (1943 -)

A passionate and committed writer who attempts to convey both the difficulties of working-class women's lives as well as their great resources.

Blow Your House Down (1984)
[GB122] Virago pbk **£4.50**

The Century's Daughter (1986)
[GB123] Virago pbk **£4.99**

The Man who Wasn't There (1988)
An optimistic novel about the bridging of barriers between ages, classes and individuals, related in Barker's vivid and realistic style.
[GB124] Virago hbk **£10.95**

Union Street (1982)
[GB125] Virago pbk **£4.50**

'Stanley and Iris' **NEW**
A film tie-in edition of *Union Street*, now filmed as *Stanley and Iris* starring both Jane Fonda and Robert de Niro.
[GB121] Virago pbk **£4.99**

BARNES, JULIAN (1946 -)

Critics have claimed that Barnes' work embodies the experimental attitudes and multi-cultural resonance necessary for truly international success, though in fact his novels display quintessentially English poise and ironic humour, as well as an intriguing inventiveness.

A History of the World in 10 1/2 Chapters (1989) **NEW**
As the title suggests, this is no ordinary history, but a kaleidoscope of narrative voices which slowly but compellingly come into focus, interlocking in unexpected ways. An audacious and entertaining book.
[GB126] Cape hbk **£10.95**

Before She Met Me (1982)
A voyeuristic story of one man's obsessional jealousy of his girlfriend's former life as a sleazy film star.
[GB127] Cape hbk **£8.95**
[GB128] Picador pbk **£3.50**

Flaubert's Parrot (1984)
An award-winning novel which centres on the narrator's absorbing obsession with Flaubert and with his own past. An intriguing blend of fact and fiction.
[GB129] Cape hbk **£9.95**
[GB130] Picador pbk **£3.95**

Metroland
[GB131] R Clark pbk **£3.95**

Staring at the Sun (1986)
A work of limpid understatement and original wit, exploring a woman's life from her wartime youth onwards.
[GB132] Cape hbk **£9.95**
[GB133] Picador pbk **£3.95**

BARR, PAT

Popular author of exotic sagas with well-researched period detail and fast-paced plots.

Jade (1984)
Combining two of Barr's Chinese novels: *Chinese Alice*, and its sequel, *Uncut Jade*.
[GB134] Transworld pbk **£3.95**

BARRY, SEBASTIAN (Irish, 1955 -)

One of Ireland's up-and-coming young poets.

The Engine of Owl Light (1987)
An ambitious and lyrical work about a journey across America in a stolen car.
[GB135] Grafton pbk **£4.50**

BARSTOW, STAN (1928 -)

Realistic North country novelist, whose accurate portrayal of provincial domestic life earned him a distinctive reputation in the 1960s.

A Kind of Loving (1960)
His first and most famous novel, which was also filmed. An office worker is pressed into marriage and thereafter has to suffer the non-stop verbal barrages of an overbearing mother-in-law.
[GB136] Transworld pbk **£3.99**

B-Movie (1987)
[GB137] Transworld pbk **£3.95**

Brother's Tale
[GB138] M Joseph hbk **£8.95**

Desperadoes (1961)
[GB139] Transworld pbk **£3.95**

Give Us This Day (1989) **NEW**
An evocative novel of civilian life during the Second World War, featuring the enchanting, forthright Ella from *Just You Wait and See*. Her husband is at war,

and in his absence, she befriends the wayward widow of her dead brother.
[GB140] M Joseph hbk **£11.95**
Glad Eye (Stories, 1984)
[GB141] Transworld pbk **£3.50**
Joby (1964)
[GB142] Transworld pbk **£2.95**
Just You Wait and See (1986)
[GB143] Transworld pbk **£3.99**
Raging Calm (1968)
[GB144] Transworld pbk **£4.95**
Watchers on the Shore (1966)
[GB145] Transworld pbk **£3.99**

BATES, H.E. (1905 - 1974)
Extremely popular and prolific novelist and short story writer whose sensitive, unadorned style is perfectly suited to the pastoral simplicity of the lives of rural English families - a subject he made very much his own with his creation of the inimitable Larkins.
Fair Stood the Wind for France (1944)
His famous and moving wartime novel.
[GB152] Penguin pbk **£2.99**
Feast of July (1944)
[GB153] Penguin pbk **£2.99**
Four Beauties (1968)
[GB154] Penguin pbk **£2.50**
Golden Oriole (1962)
[GB155] Penguin pbk **£2.50**
Grapes of Paradise (1964)
[GB156] Penguin pbk **£3.99**
Jacaranda Tree (1949)
[GB159] Penguin pbk **£2.99**
Love for Lydia (1954)
[GB160] Penguin pbk **£3.50**
Moment in Time (1964)
[GB161] Penguin pbk **£2.99**
My Uncle Silas
[GB162] Oxford pbk **£3.95**
Nature of Love (1953)
[GB163] Penguin pbk **£2.50**
Perfick, Perfick!
Includes: *A Breath of French Air*, *A Little of What You Fancy*, *The Darling Buds of May*, *Oh! To Be in England* and *When the Green Woods Laugh*. A full collection of Bates's comic masterpieces, famous for their rollicking comedy, and the memorable characters of Pop Larkin and his family.
[GB165] Penguin pbk **£6.99**
Purple Plain (1947)
[GB166] Penguin pbk **£3.50**
Seven by Five (1963)
[GB167] Penguin pbk **£5.99**
Sleepless Moon
[GB168] Penguin pbk **£3.50**
Song of the Wren (1972)
[GB169] Penguin pbk **£1.95**
Triple Echo (1970)
[GB171] Penguin pbk **£1.95**
Wild Cherry Tree (1968)
[GB174] Penguin pbk **£2.99**

BAWDEN, NINA (1925 -)
Successful children's writer who is also a respected novelist.
Circles of Deceit (1987)
Shortlisted for the 1987 Booker Prize, this is a subtle comedy related by a professional copier of paintings who is brought into collusion with three powerful women.
[GB175] Penguin pbk **£3.99**

BAYLEY, JOHN (1925 -)
In Another Country
When war ends, a different struggle - to live a normal life - begins. A sensitive and observant novel by a distinguished literary critic.
[GB176] Oxford pbk **£3.95**

BEAUMAN, SALLY
Destiny (1987)
This lucrative and much-publicized novel is the very paradigm of the modern sex and society blockbuster, set in French chateaux and on Hollywood couches.
[GB177] Transworld pbk **£3.95**

BECKETT, MARY (Irish, 1926 -)
A deceptively simple writer with a brilliant ear for the cadences of speech, often producing striking interior monologues.
A Belfast Woman (Stories, 1980)
Eleven finely crafted stories of ordinary life in Northern Ireland.
[GB178] Poolbeg pbk **£3.95**
Give Them Stones (1987)
An old woman recounts her troubled and courageous life in Ulster.
[GB179] Bloomsbury pbk **£3.95**

BECKETT, SAMUEL (Irish, 1906 -)
Nobel Prize for Literature 1969. Beckett became famous overnight with *Waiting for Godot*, although he had been writing fiction for many years prior to his theatrical success. As with his plays (see under *Drama*), Beckett has distilled his fiction over the years into a remarkably pure and poetic form. Despite the apparent sparseness of these later works, they display Beckett's linguistic brilliance, black humour and acute pathos more cogently than ever.
All Strange Away (1979)
[GB180] Calder pbk **£2.95**
Collected Shorter Prose 1945 - 80 (1984)
Including four novellas, as well as *The Expelled* and *The End*.
[GB181] Calder hbk **£9.95**
[GB182] Calder pbk **£5.95**
Company (1980)
The narrator is lying on his back in the dark, reviewing his life. From this situation Beckett builds a work that is moving, lyrical and comic.
[GB183] Calder hbk **£5.95**
Disjecta (1983)
[GB184] Calder pbk **£5.95**
For to End Yet Again and Other Fizzles
[GB185] Calder pbk **£3.95**
How It Is (1961)
Two narrators attempt to create some kind of sense out of life as they crawl through mud. The book is both characteristically bleak and comic.
[GB186] Calder pbk **£4.95**
Ill Seen, Ill Said (1981)
[GB187] Calder pbk **£3.95**
Imagination Dead Imagine (1966)
[GB188] Calder pbk **£2.50**
Malone Dies (1951)
[GB189] Calder hbk **£6.95**
[GB190] Calder pbk **£4.95**
Mercier and Camier (1970)
The first novel that Beckett wrote in French, close in style to *Watt*.
[GB191] Picador pbk **£2.95**
Molloy (1950)
[GB192] Calder hbk **£9.95**
More Pricks than Kicks (Stories, 1934)
Early works which contain elements of later Beckett heroes in embryo.
[GB193] Calder pbk **£4.95**
Murphy (1938)
This, Beckett's earliest novel, is a tragi-comic account of an Irishman in West London who becomes a nurse in a mental hospital as he tries to escape from himself.
[GB194] Calder hbk **£9.95**
[GB195] Picador pbk **£3.95**
No's Knife (1967)
Collected shorter prose 1945-66.
[GB196] Calder hbk **£7.95**

Nohow On (1989) **NEW**
A volume bringing together *Company*, *Ill Seen, Ill Said* and *Worstward Ho*.
[GB197] Calder hbk **£10.95**
Samuel Beckett Reader
A valuable collection, edited by John Calder.
[GB198] Picador pbk **£3.95**
Texts for Nothing (1947 - 52)
Thirteen highly-concentrated monologues.
[GB199] Calder hbk **£5.95**
The Beckett Trilogy (1950 - 52)
This trilogy, comprising *Molloy*, *Malone Dies*, and *The Unnameable*, is one of Beckett's major achievements. *"I can't go on, I'll go on"*: despite the apparently terminal pessimism of these novels, their mercurial shifts of tone - from black humour to elegiac remembrance - make for exhilarating reading.
[GB200] Calder hbk **£9.95**
[GB201] Picador pbk **£4.95**
The Expelled (1980)
These four wonderful interlinked novellas are among Beckett's most accessible prose works, and provide an excellent starting point.
[GB202] Penguin pbk **£3.50**
The Unnameable (1952)
[GB203] Calder hbk **£8.95**
Watt (1953)
Written mostly during the war, this is Beckett's second novel. It provides a hilariously idiosyncratic portrait of a man suffering from profound epistemological confusion. A memorable comedy on the incongruity of existence.
[GB204] Calder hbk **£9.95**
[GB205] Picador pbk **£3.95**
Worstward Ho (1983)
[GB206] Calder pbk **£3.50**

BEDFORD, SYBILLE (1911 -)
Her three novels written in the 1950s and '60s and her biography of Aldous Huxley earned Bedford lavish praise, as has her return to fiction after a silence of twenty years, with *Jigsaw*.
A Legacy (1956)
The life of a German family before the First World War.
[GB207] Fontana pbk **£2.50**
Compass Error (1968)
[GB208] Virago pbk **£4.99**
Favourite of the Gods (1962)
[GB209] Virago pbk **£5.50**
Jigsaw: An Unsentimental Education (1989) **NEW**
A fascinating and enjoyable autobiographical novel about a young girl's solitary childhood in Germany, with interludes in Italy, France and England.
[GB210] H Hamilton hbk **£11.95**

BEERBOHM, MAX (1872 - 1956)
Flamboyant essayist and illustrator who wrote one memorable novel.
Zuleika Dobson (1911)
The classic comic Oxford novel for which he will always be remembered, dominated by the beautiful Zuleika who breaks all the young men's hearts.
[GB211] Yale hbk illus **£14.95**
[GB212] Penguin pbk **£4.50**

BEHAN, DOMINIC (Irish, 1928 -)
Brother of Brendan, former folk singer (he wrote 'The Patriot Game') and active Trade Unionist, this is Dominic Behan's first novel.
The Public World of Parable Jones **NEW**
A picaresque novel of Dublin life that is sure to be a hit. By way of homage to Joyce, the wanderings of this biographer of the man himself take place in the course of one day, from pub to pub, misadventure to misadventure. Very much in the modern Irish tradition.
[GB213] Collins hbk **£11.95**

FICTION

BELL, ADRIAN (1901 -)
Classic rural tales dealing with farming life in the
Suffolk countryside. Bell's joyous series of novels
vividly re-creates the bygone agricultural age, and
reflect the author's own departure from London to
begin a new life of farming.
Corduroy (1930)
First volume of Bell's autobiographical account of his
farming life; continued in the two volumes below.
[GB214] Oxford pbk **£3.95**
Silver Ley (1931)
[GB215] Oxford pbk **£3.95**
The Cherry Tree (1932)
[GB216] Oxford pbk **£3.95**

BELL, QUENTIN (1910 -)
Novel by the son of Clive and Vanessa Bell, who has
written several acclaimed Bloomsbury biographies.
The Brandon Papers (1985)
[GB217] Grafton pbk **£2.95**

BELLAMY, GUY
Witty parodist who writes what could be called
'designer sex comedies' that take place within the
circles of the smart set.
The Nudists (1986)
[GB221] Penguin pbk **£2.95**
The Secret Lemonade Drinker (1977)
[GB222] Penguin pbk **£2.95**
The Tax Exile (1989)　　　**NEW**
Another frolic in the sun: penniless Fred Carton finds
that a stay in Monte Carlo will save him a tax bill of
£600,000. Whilst there a friend's wife appears with a
revoltingly smooth young man in tow...
[GB223] Viking hbk **£11.95**

BELLOC, HILAIRE (1870 - 1953)
Most celebrated for his vicious *Cautionary Tales*, but
Belloc was a prolific writer who turned out more than
100 books. This is his only novel currently available.
Four Men (1911)
[GB224] Oxford pbk **£3.50**

BENNETT, ARNOLD (1867 - 1931)
Versatile novelist, short story writer, playwright and
journalist (one-time assistant editor of *Woman*
magazine). His sympathetic depiction of obscure and
ordinary lives in the *Five Towns* owes a great deal to
the French realists, whom he much admired. He also
wrote lighter books about the Edwardian high life,
such as *The Card*. Conrad admired him, as did the
young D.H. Lawrence.
Anna of the Five Towns (1902)
Bennett's first major achievement, set in the
Staffordshire Potteries of his childhood.
[GB225] Penguin pbk **£3.99**
Clayhanger (1910)
One of the best of English regional novels, in the
tradition of *Middlemarch* and Hardy.
[GB226] Penguin pbk **£5.99**
Elsie and the Child (Stories)
[GB227] Sutton pbk **£2.95**
Grand Babylon Hotel (1902)
A comedy thriller about a millionaire's problems.
[GB228] Penguin pbk **£3.50**
Grim Smile of the Five Towns (1907)
[GB229] Penguin pbk **£3.50**
Journals (Non-fiction, 1932-3)
Begun in 1896, Bennett's journals were inspired by
those of the Goncourt brothers.
[GB230] Penguin pbk **£4.95**
Pretty Lady (1918)
[GB232] Sutton pbk **£3.95**
The Card (1911)
[GB233] Penguin pbk **£3.50**
The Old Wives' Tale (1908)
[GB231] Penguin pbk **£3.95**
Whom God Hath Joined
[GB234] Sutton pbk **£2.95**

BENSON, E.F. (1867 - 1940)
Creator of the recently televised 'Mapp and Lucia'
books - among the funniest social comedies written
this century - he was three times mayor of Rye
(renamed 'Tilling' in the novels).
As We Were (Non fiction, 1930)
[GB235] Hogarth pbk **£5.95**
Autumn Sowing (1917)
[GB236] Hogarth pbk **£4.95**
David Blaize
A delightfully nostalgic novel of public school life,
from midnight feasts at prep school to cricket and
waxy beaks at Marchester College (Marlborough).
[GB237] Hogarth pbk **£4.95**
Dodo Omnibus (1893)
[GB238] Hogarth pbk **£5.95**
Freaks of Mayfair (1916)
[GB239] Hogarth pbk **£4.95**
Luck of the Vails (1901)
[GB240] Hogarth pbk **£4.95**
Mrs Ames (1912)
[GB241] Hogarth pbk **£4.95**
Paying Guests (1929)
[GB242] Hogarth pbk **£4.95**
Secret Lives
[GB243] Hogarth pbk **£4.95**
The Blotting Book
[GB244] Hogarth pbk **£4.95**
THE MAPP & LUCIA BOOKS
Queen Lucia (1920)
[GB245] Transworld pbk **£3.95**
Lucia in London (1927)
[GB246] Transworld pbk **£3.99**
Miss Mapp (1922)
[GB247] Transworld pbk **£3.95**
Mapp and Lucia (1935)
[GB248] Transworld pbk **£3.95**
Lucia's Progress (1935)
[GB249] Transworld pbk **£3.99**
Trouble for Lucia (1939)
[GB250] Transworld pbk **£3.95**

BENSON, PETER
A Lesser Dependency (1989)　　**NEW**
Elegiac account of the destruction of a community on
an island in the Indian Ocean, which is brought about
by the arrival of unsympathetic outsiders.
[GB251] Macmillan hbk **£11.95**
The Levels (1987)
Winner of the 1987 *Guardian* Fiction award.
[GB252] Penguin pbk **£3.99**

BERGER, JOHN (1926 -)
Known for his grasp of the complexities of visual
perception he is a Marxist art-critic as well as a writer
G (1972)
Winner of the 1972 Booker Prize; a strenuously
thoughtful blend of narrative, political treatise,
personal reflection and historical reconstruction.
[GB253] Hogarth pbk **£6.95**
Pig Earth (1979)
Simple and poetic novel of rural life, arising out of
Berger's new life in a French farming community.
[GB254] Hogarth pbk **£5.95**

BERRIDGE, ELIZABETH
A writer of crisp, delicate and feminine English
novels. The quiet brilliance of her writing was
admired in the 1960s, and is now enjoying a revival.
Across the Common (1964)
[GB255] Sphere pbk **£2.75**
Rose Under Glass (1961)
Set in a colony of London writers and artists in the
late '50s, this novel centres on Penelope, a young
woman recently and unexpectedly widowed.
[GB256] Sphere pbk **£2.95**
Sing Me Who You Are (1967)
Two cousins come together when their aunt dies....
[GB257] Sphere pbk **£2.95**

Sybille Bedford, author of *Jigsaw: An Unsentimental Education* (Hamish Hamilton hbk £11.95)

BILLANY, DAN
The Trap (1950)
An outstanding war novel, written before the author's
mysterious death in 1944 while on active service.
[GB258] Faber pbk **£4.95**

BILLINGTON, RACHEL (1942 -)
A novelist who specializes in witty insights into men
and women and the games they play. Her modern
comedies of manners often feature acerbic portrayals
of the glamorous world of night-clubs, chic hotels and
expensive restaurants.
Garish Day (1985)
[GB259] Penguin pbk **£3.50**
Loving Attitudes (1988)
A grown-up foster child traces her real mother: it
changes her life and those of the people around her.
[GB260] Penguin pbk **£2.99**
Occasion of Sin (1982)
[GB261] Penguin pbk **£2.95**
Woman's Age (1979)
[GB262] Penguin pbk **£4.50**

BINCHY, MAEVE (Irish, 1940 -)
An ex-journalist who often sets her novels in the
earlier part of this century, focusing on the domestic
troubles of ordinary people. She has won particular
acclaim for her richly-cadenced Irish dialogue.
Dublin 4 (1983)
[GB263] Arrow pbk **£2.50**
Echoes (1985)
[GB264] Hodder pbk **£3.95**
Firefly Summer
A novel following the exploits of teenagers in an
empty seaside resort.
[GB265] Hodder pbk **£4.50**
Light a Penny Candle (1982)
[GB266] Hodder pbk **£3.99**
Lilac Bus (1986)
Short stories around the theme of a group of
passengers who regularly use a local country bus.
[GB267] Arrow pbk **£2.99**
The Silver Wedding (1988)
A series of brilliantly interlinked stories relating Anna
O'Hagan's troubles in arranging her parents' silver
wedding celebration, culminating in the party itself.
[GB268] Arrow pbk **£2.99**
Victoria Line & Central Line
Also known as 'London Transports'.
[GB269] Hodder pbk **£2.99**

BINGHAM, CHARLOTTE (1942 -)
Principally a television writer - responsible for *Upstairs, Downstairs* - Bingham is also the author of several witty novels about country matters and the well-to-do.
At Home (1986)
[GB270] M Joseph hbk **£9.95**
The Business (1989)　　**NEW**
A novel of power, corruption and lies set in the world of stage and screen. The heroine, starting at the bottom, works her way up to the unprecedented (for a woman) position of studio head, from where she can revenge herself upon her ex-husband...
[GB271] M Joseph hbk **£12.95**
To Hear a Nightingale (1988)
An evocative saga of a woman deprived and rejected as a child, who becomes a top Irish horse breeder.
[GB272] M Joseph hbk **£11.95**

BIRCH, CAROL
The Fog Line (1989)　　**NEW**
The new novel from last year's winner of the David Higham Award is a passionate and unsentimental tale of life on the margins of society. Gloria is raped and made pregnant: thus ends her childhood, and begins many years of wandering in 'the fog' with her new daughter. This is the tale of how she silences the insistent voices from her past that she hears in her head.
[GB273] Bloomsbury hbk **£12.95**

BLACKWOOD, CAROLINE (1931 -)
Award-winning novelist and journalist who was married to the poet Robert Lowell.
Good Night Sweet Ladies
[GB274] Penguin pbk **£3.99**
The Fate of the Mary Rose (1981)
[GB275] Penguin pbk **£3.99**

BLAKEMORE, MICHAEL
Next Season
A novel of theatre life from the Australian-born actor.
[GB276] Faber pbk **£4.95**

BLISS, ELIOT (1903 -)
Born in Jamaica, the daughter of an officer in the English Army, Eliot Bliss left for England in 1925, where she became an astute observer of the 1930s literary scene.
Luminous Isle
[GB277] Virago pbk **£5.50**
Saraband
[GB278] Virago pbk **£5.50**

BOGARDE, DIRK (1921 -)
The English actor who began as a matinée idol, but later developed his range and gradually made a name as an author. His novels will often take second place to his superb autobiographies, but the writing is finely-tuned, evocative and effortlessly graceful.
A Gentle Occupation (1981)
[GB279] Grafton pbk **£3.50**
Voices in the Garden (1983)
[GB280] Grafton pbk **£2.95**
West of Sunset (1984)
[GB281] Penguin pbk **£2.50**

BOOTH, MARTIN
Dreaming of Samarkand (1989)　　**NEW**
A fictional account of the relationship between the poet James Elroy Flecker and T.E. Lawrence, who were both active in the Middle East before the Great War.
[GB282] Hutchinson hbk **£11.95**
Hiroshima Joe (1985)
A poetic and moving novel about a boy growing up during the Second World War.
[GB283] Arrow pbk **£2.95**

BOWEN, ELIZABETH (1899 - 1973)
Anglo-Irish author who explored upper middle-class life with sharp insight, in novels which show a debt to Henry James. A faintly eccentric stylist, her writing, with its memorable and impressionistic descriptions of landscapes, urban and rural, has a fine edge to it.
Collected Stories (1980)
[GB284] Cape hbk **£15.00**
[GB285] Penguin pbk **£7.99**
Eva Trout (1969)
[GB286] Penguin pbk **£4.50**
Friends and Relations (1931)
[GB287] Penguin pbk **£3.99**
Last September (1929)
[GB288] Penguin pbk **£3.95**
Little Girls (1964)
Impressionistic re-creation of a childhood incident, seen through the eyes of a young girl.
[GB289] Penguin pbk **£4.50**
The Death of the Heart (1938)
One of her best-known works, this is a sensitive account of a young girl's adolescence.
[GB290] Cape hbk **£9.95**
[GB291] Penguin pbk **£4.99**
The Heat of the Day (1949)
Her most acclaimed work, this is a tragic love story set in wartime London.
[GB292] Penguin pbk **£4.50**
The Hotel (1927)
[GB293] Penguin pbk **£3.50**
The House in Paris (1935)
[GB294] Penguin pbk **£4.99**
To the North (1932)
[GB295] Penguin pbk **£3.95**
World of Love (1955)
[GB296] Penguin pbk **£3.95**

BOYD, WILLIAM (1952 -)
A clever, comic writer who has taken up where Waugh and Amis *père* left off. His themes are often familiar - the English abroad, colonial life - but they are given freshness and resonance by being placed in an acutely modern environment.
A Good Man in Africa (1981)
Morgan Leafy, Her Majesty's representative in Kinjaja, becomes embroiled in lascivious political adventures.
[GB297] Penguin pbk **£3.50**
An Ice-Cream War (1982)
A ridiculous and little-reported war is still being waged in East Africa after the Armistice - simply because noone told them to stop.
[GB298] Penguin pbk **£3.50**
On the Yankee Station (1981)
[GB299] Penguin pbk **£2.99**
School Ties (1985)
[GB300] Penguin pbk **£3.95**
Stars and Bars (1984)
Henderson Dores, an Englishman of gentle manners, faces the torments of brash New York.
[GB301] Penguin pbk **£3.50**
The New Confessions (1987)
Boyd's most recent novel signalled an increasing seriousness and ambition. These are the memoirs of a veteran film director: thus the novel spans his career, with impressive period detail, from his early newsreel work through to Hollywood during the McCarthy era.
[GB302] H Hamilton hbk **£11.95**
[GB303] Penguin pbk **£3.99**

BOYLAN, CLARE (Irish, 1948 -)
Wry and sometimes devastating comic novelist with a deep feel for language, and a recurrent preoccupation with religion and the loss of innocence.
Black Baby (1988)
A comic fairy story about a 'black baby', sold to a woman by nuns, who appears 50 years later displaying some strange predilections.
[GB304] H Hamilton hbk **£10.95**

Concerning Virgins (1989)　　**NEW**
'Now concerning virgins, I have no commandment of the Lord', St Paul wrote to the Corinthians, and in this collection of stories, the young men and women are indeed lacking guidance. Their adventures and misadventures are recounted with wit and affection.
[GB305] H Hamilton hbk **£11.95**
Holy Pictures
Dublin: 1925 the advent of cinema offers to rescue Nan from the confines of her Catholic upbringing.
[GB306] Penguin pbk **£2.50**
Last Resorts
A vigorous and witty work. Harriet has brought up her three children alone and taken on a succession of lovers in order to feed her desires.
[GB307] Penguin pbk **£2.50**
Nail on the Head
Collection of short stories about disappointed love.
[GB308] Penguin pbk **£2.50**

BOYT, ROSE
Sexual Intercourse (1989)　　**NEW**
Promising first novel about the relationship between a son and a daughter, one of whom has an over-protective mother, the other a resentful father, by the great-granddaughter of Sigmund Freud.
[GB625] Cape hbk **£10.95**

BRACEWELL, MICHAEL (1958 -)
Divine Concepts of Beauty (1989)　　**NEW**
A suburban comedy of manners which traces the lives of five young people starting out in the 1970s, who are reunited in the London of the '80s.
[GB309] Secker hbk **£11.95**
The Crypto-amnesia Club (1988)
A novel of London night-life that attempts to do for the English novel what *Bright Lights, Big City* does for the American.
[GB310] Serpent's Tail pbk **£4.95**

BRADBURY, MALCOLM (1932 -)
Ever since the publication of his first book, Bradbury has been hailed as a witty satirist who delights in the misunderstandings between people. An academic by profession, much of his fiction takes place within a campus setting, although some of his recent work is set in a wider cultural context.
All Dressed Up and Nowhere to Go
[GB311] Arrow pbk **£2.95**
Cuts (1987)
A novella with a political theme.
[GB312] Arrow pbk **£3.95**
Eating People is Wrong (1959)
A middle-aged, aging don and a pushy undergraduate both fall in love with a desirable post-grad: the result is a hilarious triangle.
[GB313] Arrow pbk **£3.95**
Mensonge (1987)
A humourous, semi-philosophical fiction parodying the convolutions of structuralism.
[GB314] Arrow pbk **£2.99**
Rates of Exchange (1983)
At a conference in Eastern Europe the hapless Dr Petworth finds himself embroiled in events beyond his control.
[GB315] Arrow pbk **£3.50**
Stepping Westward (1965)
[GB316] Arrow pbk **£3.99**
The History Man (1975)
Classic comic novel (later televised) about the manipulative academic Dr Howard Kirk and his dubious (s)exploits in a 1970s redbrick university.
[GB317] Arrow pbk **£3.50**
Who Do You Think You Are? (1976)
[GB318] Arrow pbk **£2.99**
Why Come to Slaka? (Non fiction, 1986)
A guide to the imaginary Eastern European state created for *Rates of Exchange*.
[GB319] Arrow pbk **£2.95**

BRADFORD, BARBARA TAYLOR
Highly popular 'rags to riches' novels which trace the rise of women in traditionally masculine worlds of business and commerce. Emma Harte's story begins in *A Woman of Substance*, and continues in *Hold the Dream* and *To Be the Best*.

A Woman of Substance
[GB320] Grafton pbk **£3.50**
Act of Will
[GB321] Grafton pbk **£3.95**
Hold the Dream (1985)
[GB322] Grafton pbk **£3.95**
To Be the Best (1988)
[GB323] Grafton pbk **£3.99**
Voice of the Heart (1983)
[GB324] Grafton pbk **£4.50**

BRAGG, MELVYN (1939 -)
Known as a cultural impresario and TV presenter, Bragg is also a novelist. Drawing on his childhood in Cumbria, and his affection for writers such as Hardy and Wordsworth, his books are very much in an English 'rural' tradition, with a strong sense of landscape.

A Hired Man (1969)
[GB325] Hodder pbk **£1.95**
Cumbrian Trilogy (1969-80)
[GB326] Hodder pbk **£6.99**
For Want of a Nail (1964)
Re-issue of Bragg's first novel, a vivid tale of growing up in Cumberland.
[GB328] Hodder pbk **£5.99**
Josh Lawton (1972)
A tale of love, betrayal and tragedy in a small rural community.
[GB329] Hodder pbk **£3.99**
The Maid of Buttermere (1987)
Erudite historic tale set in the Lake District, based on a true story. A fraudulent man finds himsel falling for and eventually marrying a beautiful young woman.
[GB330] Hodder pbk **£4.95**

BRAHMS, CARYL & SIMON, S.J.
Bullet in the Ballet (1937)
A minor comic classic - a murder in the Ballet Stroganoff investigated by Inspector Quill - that has been described affectionately as 'inspired nonsense'.
[GB331] Hogarth pbk **£4.95**
Casino for Sale (1938)
[GB332] Hogarth pbk **£4.95**
Don't Mr Disraeli
[GB333] Hogarth pbk **£4.95**
Envoy on Excursion
[GB334] Hogarth pbk **£4.95**
No Bed for Bacon (1941)
[GB335] Hogarth pbk **£4.95**

BRAINE, JOHN (1928 - 1986)
Famous for his 'angry young man' stance of his first novel *Room at the Top*, which very much reflected the mood of the late 1950s. His radical views waned in later years, but Braine's fiction proves him to be an assured, and under-rated, craftsman.

Queen of a Distant Country (1972)
[GB337] Methuen hbk **£9.95**
Room at the Top (1957)
The rise of Joe Lampton, working-class hero; the story continues in *Life at the Top*.
[GB339] Penguin pbk **£2.50**
Life at the Top (1962)
[GB340] Methuen pbk **£2.50**
The Vodi (1959)
[GB341] Methuen pbk **£1.25**
These Golden Days (1985)
[GB342] Methuen pbk **£2.50**
Two of Us (1985)
[GB343] Methuen pbk **£1.95**
Waiting for Sheila (1976)
[GB344] Methuen pbk **£1.95**

BRAYFIELD, CELIA
Pearls (1987)
Another extremely well-marketed 'sex and shopping' blockbuster.
[GB344] Penguin pbk **£3.95**

BRODERICK, JOHN (Irish, 1927 - 1989)
Born in Athlone, and self-educated, Broderick has written a powerful series of provincial novels set in the Irish midlands. He was the winner of the 1975 Irish Academy of Letters Award.

A Prayer for Fair Weather (1984)
A bleakly realistic spy story very much in the style of le Carré.
[GB345] Boyars hbk **£8.95**
Ross Tree (1985)
[GB346] Boyars hbk **£8.95**
The Flood (1987)
[GB347] Boyars hbk **£14.95**
Trial of Father Dillingham (1981)
[GB348] Boyars hbk **£8.95**

BROOKE, JOCELYN (1908 - 1966)
The Orchid Trilogy (1948 - 50)
Brooke's celebrated work was based on his experiences as a medical orderly in World War II.
[GB349] Penguin pbk **£4.99**

BROOKNER, ANITA (1938 -)
Brookner's renown as an art critic has now been overtaken by her success as a novelist. Her books are subtle and exquisite, with a keen eye for place and a sharp ear for dialogue. Many of her heroines are lonely single women facing crucial mid-life decisions; Brookner excels at gently unravelling their complex hopes and fears.

A Friend from England (1987)
The complex relationship between a single woman and a wealthy, apparently reassuring, family is probed by Brookner with her usual blend of intelligence and accessibility.
[GB350] Cape hbk **£9.95**
[GB351] Grafton pbk **£2.99**
A Misalliance (1986)
The story of the search for, and discovery of, a new alliance when the heroine is deserted by her husband.
[GB352] Cape hbk **£9.95**
[GB353] Grafton pbk **£2.95**
A Start in Life (1981)
Brookner's first novel, which opens with the immortal sentence, *"Dr Weiss at forty knew that her life had been ruined by literature"*.
[GB354] Cape hbk **£9.95**
[GB355] Grafton pbk **£2.95**
Family and Friends (1985)
[GB356] Cape hbk **£8.95**
[GB357] Grafton pbk **£2.99**
Hotel du Lac (1984)
Booker Prize-winning tale of a lonely romance novelist on holiday in Switzerland, and the man she meets.
[GB358] Cape hbk **£8.95**
[GB359] Grafton pbk **£2.99**
Latecomers (1988)
Something of a breakthrough for Brookner, in that this novel focuses upon the shared lives of two men. A refugee from Nazi Europe forms a lasting friendship with an English orphan, but 40 years later has to come to terms with the gaps in their relationship.
[GB360] Cape hbk **£10.95**
[GB361] Grafton pbk **£2.99**
Lewis Percy (1989)   **NEW**
Each successive new novel from Brookner enhances her reputation. *Lewis Percy* is no exception: it is an ironic but loving portrait of a man out of step with his times, whose unreal, cosy married world collapses when he meets another woman.
[GB362] Cape hbk **£11.95**

Look at Me (1983)
[GB363] Cape hbk **£8.95**
[GB364] Grafton pbk **£2.99**
Providence (1982)
[GB365] Cape hbk **£8.95**
[GB366] Grafton pbk **£2.99**

BROPHY, BRIGID (1929 -)
Critic and novelist who is noted for her elegant comedies which explore character and relationships through startling fictional techniques. She is also an accomplished essayist, as the collection *Baroque'n'Roll* demonstrates.

Baroque'n'Roll & Other Essays
[GB367] Abacus pbk **£5.95**
Finishing Touch (1963)
[GB368] GMP pbk **£3.50**
Flesh (1962)
[GB369] Allison & B pbk **£1.95**
Hackenfeller's Ape (1953)
[GB370] Allison & B pbk **£1.95**
In Transit
[GB371] GMP pbk **£4.95**

BROSTER, D.K. (Scottish)
The Jacobite Trilogy (1925 - 1929)
Popular trilogy, comprising *The Flight of the Heron*, *The Gleam in the North* and *Dark Mile*, based on the Jacobite Uprisings.
[GB372] Penguin pbk **£5.99**

BROWN, CHRISTY (Irish, 1932 - 1981)
Born a spastic into a family of 23 in a slum district of Dublin, Brown found he was able to type with his toe. His resulting works are effective in their portrayal of his struggles, and marvellously rich in humour, while his observations of Dublin life reveal his gift for poetic description. Watch out for the new film based on his life.

Down All the Days
[GB373] Secker hbk **£10.95**
Shadow on Summer
[GB374] Secker hbk **£8.95**

BROWN, GEORGE DOUGLAS
(Scottish, 1869 - 1902)
The House with Green Shutters (1901)
Written as a reaction to what he saw as the cloying sentimentality of the Kailyard school, Brown's only novel is a marvellous study of smalltown greed and selfishness: a landmark in modern Scottish fiction writing.
[GB375] Penguin pbk **£3.99**

BROWN, GEORGE MACKAY
(Scottish, 1921 -)
A highly-respected writer who has produced poetry, plays, novels and short stories, nearly all of whose work is centred on his native Orkney. Brown draws inspiration from the myth and folklore of the islands, and his elegiac evocation of a disappearing world is haunting and poetic.

A Calendar of Love (1988)
Stories set amidst the rugged landscape of the Orkney Islands.
[GB376] Grafton pbk **£3.50**
A Time to Keep (1969)
[GB377] Chatto hbk **£6.95**
Christmas Stories
[GB378] Perpetua P pbk **£3.00**
Hawkfall (1974)
[GB379] Grafton pbk **£1.75**
Magnus (1973)
[GB380] R Drew pbk **£3.95**
The Golden Bird (1987)
Two novellas exploring the life of an isolated fishing community before its simplicity is destroyed by encroaching civilization.
[GB381] Grafton pbk **£2.99**

The Masked Fisherman & Other Stories (1989) NEW
A varied collection of 21 new stories from the 1st century to Viking times many of them set in Orkney.
[GB382] J Murray hbk **£11.95**
Time in a Red Coat (1984)
[GB383] Penguin pbk **£3.95**

BURGESS, ANTHONY (1917 -)
Born and educated in Manchester, but later stationed in the East as an educational officer, Burgess sprang to notice with the Waugh-like descriptions of racial disharmony and misunderstanding in his *Malayan Trilogy*. He has since become a diverse and prolific writer. displaying linguistic virtuosity and great erudition. Not all of his works are in print.
1985 (1980)
[GB384] Arrow pbk **£1.95**
A Clockwork Orange (1962)
The celebrated novel set in a violent and futuristic world, written in its own bizarre, debased language.
[GB385] Heinemann hbk **£9.95**
[GB386] Penguin pbk **£3.50**
Abba, Abba (1977)
[GB387] Faber pbk **£2.95**
Any Old Iron (1989) NEW
Excellently reviewed earlier this year, this substantial novel imagines what the cynical modern world would make of the miraculous rediscovery of Excalibur. Spanning many years and encompassing many serious themes, this is nonetheless a remarkable comic novel.
[GB388] Hutchinson hbk **£12.95**
Doctor is Sick (1960)
[GB389] Penguin pbk **£3.95**
Earthly Powers (1980)
Huge and ambitious look at the 20th century through the eyes of an aging, successful homosexual writer; it includes much humour at the expense of major literary figures. Shortlisted for the Booker Prize.
[GB390] Penguin pbk **£5.95**
Enderby Omnibus (1963, 1968)
Richly entertaining pair of novels about the poet Enderby, whose carnal and cultural career spans England, Rome, Tangiers and New York.
[GB391] Penguin pbk **£5.99**
Enderby's Dark Lady (1984)
Enderby's return, due to popular demand, long after he was originally dispatched by Burgess.
[GB392] Sphere pbk **£1.95**
Eve of Saint Venus (1964)
[GB393] Arrow pbk **£2.95**
Honey for the Bears (1963)
[GB394] Penguin pbk **£3.99**
Nothing like the Sun (1964)
A novel about Shakespeare.
[GB395] Arrow pbk **£1.95**
The Devil's Mode & Other Stories NEW
His first collection is a strong one, which includes a 110-page novella about Attila the Hun, an imagined meeting between Shakespeare and Cervantes, and a story based on Débussy's 1889 journey to Ireland.
[GB396] Hutchinson hbk **£12.95**
The End of the World News (1982)
[GB397] Penguin pbk **£4.99**
The Kingdom of the Wicked (1985)
A rumbustious re-creation of the early years of Christianity, featuring many well-known and loved apostles and Roman emperors.
[GB398] Sphere pbk **£3.99**
The Long Day Wanes (1956-59)
Originally published as *The Malayan Trilogy*.
[GB399] Heinemann hbk **£12.95**
[GB400] Penguin pbk **£5.95**
The Pianoplayers (1986)
A semi-autobiographical novel.
[GB401] Arrow pbk **£2.50**
The Wanting Seed (1962)
[GB402] Arrow pbk **£2.25**

BURTON, RICHARD
A Christmas Story (1989) NEW
A re-issue of the famous actor's only published work, a short account of a Welsh childhood that is clearly modelled on his own. Introduced by his widow, Sally Burton, it is illustrated with contemporary photographs of the Welsh valleys.
[GB403] Hodder hbk **£7.95**

BURTON, SALLY
The Barren Patch (1988)
First novel by the actor's widow tells the humorous story of two women on the lookout for men.
[GB404] Penguin pbk **£2.99**

BUTLIN, RON (Scottish, 1949 -)
This poet's elegant skill with words is reflected in his fiction.
The Sound of My Voice (1987)
Short, finely-crafted novel charting the career of a successful but alcoholic businessman who has to struggle with his disintegrating sense of identity.
[GB405] Grafton pbk **£3.99**
The Tilting Room (Stories, 1983)
[GB406] Canongate pbk **£2.95**

BYATT, A.S. (1936 -)
An ambitious novelist whose settings are frequently academic, Byatt's books are dense and allegorical, rich in intricate detail and character, and unafraid of literary allusion.
The Virgin in the Garden (1978)
The start of her account of contemporary British middle-class society.
[GB410] Penguin pbk **£4.95**
Still Life (1985)
The continuation of a projected series of novels which started with *The Virgin in the Garden*, chronicling the life of a Northern family in the 1950s.
[GB407] Penguin pbk **£4.99**
Sugar & Other Stories (1987)
[GB408] Penguin pbk **£3.95**
The Game (1967)
[GB409] Penguin pbk **£3.95**

CAMERON, DAVID KERR (Scottish)
A Kist of Sorrows (1987)
A sometimes nostalgic novel of the North-East, which echoes the style of Lewis Grassic Gibbon.
[GB411] Flamingo pbk **£3.95**

CARR, J.L.
As a preface to one of his novels, Carr has placed a quotation from Dr Johnson's Dictionary: *"A Novel - a small tale, generally of love"*. It serves as an illuminating definition of Carr's own work.
A Month in the Country (1980)
An elegiac novel set in the 1920s: two young men meet in a Yorkshire village amid the sense of loss which pervaded post-war England.
[GB412] Penguin pbk **£3.50**
Season in Sinji (1962)
Three military men in love with the same woman in West Africa. Even the soothing formalities of their cricket cannot hide or prevent the tragedy to come.
[GB413] Penguin pbk **£3.99**
The Battle of Pollocks Crossing (1985)
Booker Prize shortlisted, this novel delightfully combines comedy with the serious. Set in 1929, a young teacher exchanges his job in Bradford for one in the Wild West of his dreams: the trouble is that it really is wild.
[GB414] Penguin pbk **£3.99**
The Harpole Report (1972)
[GB415] Penguin pbk **£2.50**
What Hetty Did (1988)
Carr proved himself delightfully eccentric in the best sense when he decided to publish this novel, which he claims will be his last, himself. A shoebox became his accounts department, and the book sold healthily, thereby giving the lie to many of publishing's received wisdoms.
[GB416] Quince Tree P pbk **£3.95**

CARRE, JOHN LE (1931 -)
Since the 1963 publication of his third novel, *The Spy Who Came in from the Cold*, le Carré has written some of the finest post-war fiction, often nominally placed within the 'thriller' genre for the frequency of their espionage situations. By any terms he is a fine novelist, examining the dilemmas of characters caught up by a loss of personal belief, in a public context where dreams of the past - particularly of Britain's greatness - are qualified by post-war decline. Noted for the considerable intricacy of his plots, and the human pessimism inherent in much of his work, le Carré's most recent novel, *The Russia House*, has a humour and optimistic tone which marks new ground.
A Perfect Spy (1986)
A breakthrough novel for le Carré, who incorporated elements of his own life - his relationship with his beguiling but fraudulent father, and his own involvement with espionage - into the story of the personal crisis of Magnus Pym. Stylistically more complicated than earlier works, it was acclaimed by Philip Roth as 'the best English novel since the war'.
[GB427] Hodder hbk **£10.95**
[GB428] Hodder hbk **£3.95**
A Small Town in Germany (1968)
[GB429] Heinemann hbk **£9.95**
[GB430] Pan pbk **£3.50**
Smiley's People (1980)
[GB432] Hodder hbk **£9.95**
[GB433] Pan pbk **£3.50**
The Honourable Schoolboy 1977)
[GB434] Hodder hbk **£9.95**
[GB435] Pan pbk **£3.95**
The Little Drummer Girl (1983)
A development towards the political marks le Carré's novel about the Palestine conflict; it caused some controversy among the Jewish community in America, but is in fact a finely balanced and non-partisan work.
[GB436] Hodder hbk **£9.95**
[GB437] Pan pbk **£3.99**
The Looking Glass War (1965)
[GB438] Heinemann hbk **£10.50**
[GB439] Pan pbk **£3.50**
The Naive and Sentimental Lover (1971)
[GB440] Hodder hbk **£10.95**
[GB441] Pan pbk **£3.50**

John le Carré, author of *The Russia House* (Hodder & Stoughton hbk **£12.95**)

The Quest for Karla
A collection of the three major Smiley novels - *Tinker, Tailor, Soldier, Spy*, *The Honourable Schoolboy* and *Smiley's People* - which follow the fortunes of George Smiley in his battle of wits with Karla from Europe and the Far East, and ends on a memorable note of hollow victory.
[GB442] Hodder hbk **£12.95**

The Russia House (1989) **NEW**
Two visits to the Soviet Union post-*glasnost* produced a profound effect on le Carré. As in *The Spy Who Came in from the Cold*, the central character is a man drawn reluctantly into espionage, the difference being that Barley Blair - a jazz-loving, alcohol-softened publisher - finally chooses the course of action which accords with his private belief. Atmospheric scenes of Russia and a new quality of humour make it among his best works.
[GB443] Hodder hbk **£12.95**

The Spy Who Came in from the Cold (1963)
A bleak tale of deceit, this was le Carré's first work to earn wide-scale popular and critical success; it was later memorably filmed, starring Richard Burton.
[GB444] Gollancz hbk **£9.95**
[GB445] Pan pbk **£2.95**

Tinker, Tailor, Soldier, Spy (1974)
[GB446] Hodder hbk **£9.95**
[GB447] Pan pbk **£3.50**

CARSON, MICHAEL
Friends and Infidels (1989) **NEW**
In remote Ras-Al-Surra, electricity has come and peace has broken out. A naive English inspector arrives, but neither he nor Ibrahim, the fisherman's son, is prepared for the terrible events they will encounter in this last corner of Arabia.
[GB448] Gollancz hbk **£11.95**

Sucking Sherbet Lemons (1988)
This first novel from an original and very funny writer portrays the teenage agony of boys trying to establish their own sexual identity against the strictures of the Catholic faith.
[GB449] Transworld pbk **£3.99**

CARSWELL, CATHERINE
(Scottish, 1879 - 1946)
Known for her biographies of Burns and D.H. Lawrence, Carswell also wrote these two novels of great sensitivity and intelligence.
Open the Door! (1920)
[GB450] Virago pbk **£5.50**
The Camomile Lawn (1922)
[GB451] Virago pbk **£5.50**

CARTER, ANGELA (1940 -)
A leading exponent of what has been termed 'magical realism', Carter characteristically gives free reign to incongruous leaps of the imagination, whilst retaining an ostensibly realistic surface to the narrative. Her novels are daring and inventive, drawing diverse cultural references from both past and present. She often manipulates well-known fairy and folk tales into new and powerfully resonant pieces, in prose which is atmospheric, exotic, and highly-charged.
Black Venus (1985)
[GB452] Chatto hbk **£9.95**
[GB453] Picador pbk **£2.95**
Fireworks (1987)
[GB454] Chatto hbk **£10.95**
[GB455] Virago pbk **£2.95**
Heroes and Villians (1969)
A combination of post-apocalyptic romance and gripping adventure story, showing a world divided between Professors and the Barbarians.
[GB456] Penguin pbk **£3.95**
Love (1987)
[GB457] Chatto hbk **£10.95**
[GB458] Picador pbk **£3.95**

Nights at the Circus (1984)
Carter's masterpiece concerns itself with Fevvers, a 19th century trapeze artist who is half-woman, half-bird.
[GB459] Chatto hbk **£11.95**
[GB460] Picador pbk **£4.95**
The Bloody Chamber (Stories, 1979)
[GB461] Penguin pbk **£3.95**
The Infernal Desire Machines of Doctor Hoffman (1972)
[GB462] Penguin pbk **£3.95**
The Magic Toyshop (1967)
A conventional middle-class girl is orphaned and sent to live with her mysterious, sinister uncle in London who lives in a twilight world of toymaking. The story of the peculiar conditions of her new life is accompanied by her growing emotional and erotic awareness.
[GB463] Virago pbk **£3.50**
The Passion of New Eve (1977)
[GB464] Virago pbk **£3.50**

CARY, JOYCE (Irish, 1888 - 1957)
Cary served in the Nigerian political service before becoming a full-time writer in 1920. His exotic professional experiences no doubt encouraged his celebrated flair for vivid characterization, and all his novels are peopled by an extensive gallery of 'characters'.
Mister Johnson (1939)
Set in West Africa, this novel explores the confrontation between tribal culture and British administration.
[GB466] M Joseph hbk **£11.95**
The Captive and the Free (1959)
An unfinished novel with a religious theme.
[GB467] Penguin pbk **£3.95**
The Horse's Mouth (1944)
Cary's best-known work tells the story of an impoverished painter so preoccupied with his art that he is willing to endure any privation for its sake. Thus the only morality he practises is the devotion he gives to painting.
[GB468] Penguin pbk **£4.95**
Triptych (1941 - 1944)
His most important trilogy, this volume comprises *Herself Surprised*, *To Be a Pilgrim*, and *The Horse's Mouth*.
[GB469] Penguin pbk **£6.99**

CASEY, JUANITA (Irish, 1925 -)
Casey's mother, an Irish tinker, died giving birth to her while her father, an English gypsy, abandoned her a year later. Casey was then sent to private boarding schools by benefactors between periods of circus life; she draws on these experiences in the two novels below.
Horse of Selene (1971)
[GB470] Dolmen P pbk **£4.95**
The Circus (1974)
[GB471] Calder hbk **£6.95**

CASEY, KEVIN (Irish, 1940 -)
Critic, novelist and dramatist, Casey is married to the poet Eavan Boland.
Dreams of Revenge (1977)
[GB472] Wolfhound pbk **£3.95**
Sense of Survival (1974)
[GB473] Wolfhound pbk **£3.50**

CHAND, MEIRA
English writer living in Japan whose elegant novels thoughtfully portray the often violent emotion dwelling beneath that country's 'collective personality'.
House of the Sun **NEW**
[GB476] Hutchinson hbk **£12.95**
The Gossamer-Fly
[GB477] Arrow pbk **£3.50**

CHAPLIN, SID
In Blackberry Time (1987)
Introduced by Stan Barstow, this is a selection of stories which mirror Chaplin's life, published as a tribute to a man who influenced a generation of Northern writers.
[GB478] Bloodaxe pbk **£5.95**

CHATWIN, BRUCE (1940 - 1989)
All of Chatwin's work sprung from his enormous appetite for people, places and ideas, in the pursuit of which he claimed he left two jobs - first at Sothebys and subsequently at the *Sunday Times*. With *In Patagonia* (see the *Travel* section) he breathed new life into the travel book, and he displayed a similarly original approach to writing fiction: *The Songlines* is a work which can only be called a *roman d'idées*. By the time of his premature death earlier this year he was regarded as one of our most consistently original and interesting writers.
On the Black Hill (1982)
Award-winning novel about a pair of brothers living in a Welsh farming community. A beautifully English novel.
[GB480] Cape hbk **£9.95**
[GB481] Picador pbk **£3.99**
The Songlines (1987)
Chatwin's travels in Australia provided the basis for this magnificent work, which explores the Aborigines' nomadic way of life and meditates on the very nature of human rootlessness.
[GB482] Cape hbk **£10.95**
[GB483] Picador pbk **£3.99**
The Viceroy of Ouidah
Part novel, part travel book, part biography, this economical tale concerns the Brazilian peasant who sailed to Africa to make his fortune in the slave trade and father his heirs. It was made into a film starring the inimitable Klaus Kinski.
[GB484] Cape hbk **£8.95**
[GB485] Picador pbk **£3.95**
Utz (1988)
A novella, nominated for the 1988 Booker Prize, this relates the story of Utz, collector of Meissen porcelain, and an enigma in the post-war world of Communist Prague.
[GB486] Cape hbk **£9.95**
[GB486A] Picador pbk **£3.99**
What Am I Doing Here? (Non fiction) **NEW**
A collection of Chatwin's essays and journalism, describing many of the places and people encountered in the course of his many and varied travels and his writing career. The book reflects Chatwin's interest in a wide range of subjects.
[GB486B] Cape hbk **£12.95**

CHESTERTON, G.K. (1874 - 1936)
A prolific Catholic writer and associate of Hillaire Belloc, Chesterton is best known for his Father Brown crime novels (see *Crime Fiction*). His other work is more eccentric, and tends generally to side with the individual in his struggle against the state.
Daylight and Nightmare
[GB487] Xanadu hbk **£9.95**
Spirit of Christmas
Stories, poems and essays.
[GB488] Xanadu hbk **£2.50**
The Club of Queer Trades (1905)
[GB489] Penguin pbk **£2.95**
The Essential G.K. Chesterton
[GB490] Oxford pbk **£5.95**
The Man Who Was Thursday (1908)
[GB491] Penguin hbk **£3.95**
The Napoleon of Notting Hill (1904)
A political fantasy which reflects Chesterton's distaste for the modern world of business in its celebration of an earlier, pre-industrial world.
[GB492] Penguin pbk **£3.95**

CHOLMONDLEY, MARY (1859 - 1925)
Red Pottage (1899)
This novel caused a scandal on its publication for its attack on the pretensions and complacency of the middle classes. It explores the ways in which two women search for fulfillment in a society bound by convention.
[GB493] Virago pbk **£6.50**

CLARKE, LINDSAY
Sunday Whiteman (1987)
Clarke's first novel.
[GB494] Cape hbk **£10.95**
The Chymical Wedding (1989) **NEW**
A compelling tale of emotional and intellectual passion that interweaves two narratives set over a century apart in the same remote Norfolk village. A Victorian alchemist and his latter-day researcher are the main protagonists in this suggestive, near-mystical work that announces Clarke as a major new writer.
[GB495] Cape hbk **£11.95**

CLEMENT, AERON
Cold Moons (1988)
A story about badgers in the tradition of *Watership Down*, which has won wide praise and popular success.
[GB496] Penguin pbk **£3.99**

CLEWLOW, CAROL **NEW**
A Woman's Guide to Adultery (1989)
A wonderfully funny but moving look at one woman's choice between sin and celibacy - she chooses sin, but it doesn't solve any problems. A novel very much in tune with the reality of women's lives.
[GB497] M Joseph hbk **£11.95**

COCKBURN, CLAUD (1904 - 1981)
Ballantyne's Folly (1970)
[GB498] Hogarth pbk **£4.95**
Beat the Devil (1953)
A cult novel which was made into a well-known film starring Humphrey Bogart. It concerns a group of people stranded in the South of France.
[GB499] Hogarth pbk **£4.95**

COE, JONATHAN
A Touch of Love (1989) **NEW**
A novel that bravely tries to tackle the problem of depression, and how it affects a lonely student. When the recluse in the room above him offers him a touch of love, it is all too possible that it has come too late.
[GB500] Duckworth hbk **£9.95**
The Accidental Woman (1987)
The first novel from an interesting new writer who contributes excellent book reviews to the *Guardian*.
[GB501] Hodder pbk **£3.99**

COLEGATE, ISABEL (1931 -)
A novelist with a real feel for the Edwardian period, excellently reconstructed in her novels, which are graceful and thoughtful.
Deceits of Time (1988)
Colegate's first novel for eight years finds its heroine trying to write the authorized biography of a politician of the 1930s. However, someone is hiding information from her, and she is caught up in tragedy.
[GB502] H Hamilton hbk **£11.95**
Glimpse of Sion's Glory (1985)
[GB503] Penguin pbk **£2.95**
News from the City of the Sun (1970)
[GB504] H Hamilton hbk **£8.95**
Orlando Trilogy (1968-73)
[GB505] Penguin pbk **£4.95**
Statues in a Garden (1964)
[GB506] Penguin pbk **£2.25**
The Shooting Party (1980)
A deceptively simple account of a shooting weekend;

the style is graceful and distant, but the book achieves a vivid critical statement on pre-World War I England.
[GB507] Penguin pbk **£3.99**
Three Novels (1984)
Comprising *Blackmailer*, *Man of Power* and *Great Occasion*.
[GB508] Penguin pbk **£5.95**

COLLIER, JOHN (1901 - 1980)
His Monkey Wife (1930)
Minor cult novel about an explorer who marries his monkey...
[GB509] Oxford pbk **£3.95**
John Collier Reader (Stories)
[GB510] Souvenir P hbk **£8.95**

COLLINS, JACKIE
Feisty tales of a steamy, glamorous world inhabited by film-stars, designer labels and scheming philanderers, played out against an endless parade of locations. This cartoon existence, aptly symbolized by sister Joan, has proved irresistible the world over.
Chances
[GB511] Pan pbk **£3.99**
Hollywood Husbands
[GB512] Pan pbk **£3.99**
Hollywood Wives
[GB513] Pan pbk **£3.99**
Lady Boss (1989) **NEW**
Lucky Santangelo is back - and how. In *Chances* she grew up in a top crime family; in *Lucky* she tore through three husbands. Here she tackles Hollywood, becoming the head of a major studio, clearly a huge power trip in US terms (see Danielle Steele's latest).
[GB514] Heinemann hbk **£12.95**
Lovers and Gamblers
[GB515] Pan pbk **£3.99**
Lucky
[GB516] Pan pbk **£3.99**
Rock Star
[GB517] Pan pbk **£3.99**
Sinners
[GB518] Pan pbk **£3.99**
The Bitch
[GB519] Pan pbk **£2.99**
The Stud
[GB520] Pan pbk **£2.95**
The World is Full of Divorced Women
[GB521] Pan pbk **£3.50**
The World is Full of Married Men
[GB522] Pan pbk **£2.99**

COMPTON-BURNETT, IVY (1884 - 1969)
Writing of enclosed domestic worlds with Austen-like objectivity, Compton-Burnett uncovers the disturbed emotions beneath the surface veneer of polite Edwardian society. Her books, which rarely move beyond this chosen territory, are characterized by their moody, sombre and secretive atmosphere.
A Family and a Fortune (1939)
[GB523] Penguin pbk **£4.95**
A House and its Head (1935)
[GB524] Penguin pbk **£4.95**
Brothers and Sisters (1929)
[GB525] Gollancz hbk **£7.95**
God and his Gifts (1939)
[GB527] Penguin pbk **£3.99**
Manservant and the Maidservant (1947)
[GB528] Oxford pbk **£3.95**
Men and Wives (1931)
[GB529] Allison & B pbk **£2.95**
More Women than Men (1933)
[GB530] Allison & B pbk **£2.95**
Parents and Children (1941)
[GB531] Penguin pbk **£3.95**
The Last and the First (1971)
[GB532] Penguin pbk **£3.95**
The Present and the Past
[GB533] Gollancz hbk **£7.95**

COMYNS, BARBARA (1909 -)
An original, often eccentric writer with a macabre sense of humour. Her books and characters have a quirky, sometimes magical feel, like her creation, Sophia, who carries a newt in her coat pocket.
A Touch of Mistletoe
[GB534] Virago pbk **£3.95**
House of Dolls (1989) **NEW**
[GB535] Methuen hbk **£11.95**
Mr Fox (1987)
A destitute, single young mother turns, in desperation, to a local spiv for help. The ensuing scenario is both grim and highly comic.
[GB536] Methuen pbk **£3.95**
Our Spoons Came from Woolworths
[GB537] Virago pbk **£4.50**
Sisters by a River (1947)
[GB538] Virago pbk **£4.50**
The Juniper Tree (1985)
[GB539] Methuen pbk **£3.50**
The Skin Chairs (1962)
[GB540] Virago pbk **£3.95**
Vet's Daughter (1959)
[GB541] Virago pbk **£4.50**
Who Was Changed and Who Was Dead
[GB542] Virago pbk **£4.99**

CONNOLLY, CYRIL (1903 - 1974)
Epicurean man of letters who failed to live up to his early promise, and thus made a career of underachievement.
The Rock Pool (1936)
Connolly's only novel is a satirical tale of a young man's disintegration at the hands of an artistic group in France.
[GB543] Oxford pbk **£2.95**

CONRAD, JOSEPH (1857 - 1924)
Born Jozef Konrad Korzeniowski in the Ukraine of exiled Polish nobles, Conrad was orphaned at an early age; in his youth he began a sea career that lasted 20 years, much of it in the East. Surviving a reckless suicide attempt, and later settling in England, he became one of our most vigorous and formidable novelists, a remarkable achievement considering that English was originally his third language. Not only was this master story-teller gifted with a singular understanding of structure, but also with phenomenal insight into human nature and psychology. His distinguished revitalization of the English novel, with his frequently dark vision, stands at the threshold of modern literature.
Almayer's Folly (1895)
His first novel, set in the East Indies.
[GB544] Penguin pbk **£2.50**
An Outcast of the Islands (1896)
[GB545] Penguin pbk **£2.95**
Chance (1913)
[GB546] Penguin pbk **£3.95**
Heart of Darkness (1902)
The best introduction to Conrad's work: an account of a steam-boat journey up the Congo River away from civilization and into the depths of human depravity. The sense of disquiet it creates is profound.
[GB547] Penguin pbk **£1.50**
Lord Jim (1900)
The story of the remarkable Jim, filtered through the consciousness of Marlow, Conrad's recurrent narrator. A major novel, and a remarkable analysis of guilt.
[GB548] Oxford pbk **£2.50**
[GB549] Penguin pbk **£2.50**
Nostromo (1904)
Conrad's fullest and most complex work, famous for its pessimism, is set in a turbulent small South American republic.
[GB550] Oxford pbk **£2.50**
[GB551] Penguin pbk **£2.99**
Sea Stories
[GB552] Grafton pbk **£5.95**

Selected Literary Criticism/The Shadow Line
[GB553] Methuen pbk **£5.95**
Tales of Unrest (1898)
[GB554] Penguin pbk **£2.50**
The Mirror of the Sea/A Personal Record (1906, 1912)
Two volumes of impressionistic memoirs, principally of his life at sea, and his early influences as a writer.
[GB555] Oxford pbk **£4.95**
The Nigger of the 'Narcissus' (1897)
[GB556] Oxford pbk **£2.50**
The Nigger of the 'Narcissus', Typhoon & Other Stories
[GB557] Penguin pbk **£2.95**
The Rescue (1920)
One of Conrad's later, more traditional novels, and a good sea-yarn.
[GB558] Penguin pbk **£4.99**
The Rover (1923)
[GB559] Greenhill hbk **£8.95**
The Secret Agent (1907)
In this wonderfully atmospheric depiction of minor revolutionaries at work in London at the turn of the century, Conrad's irony is given fullest rein. A blackly comic tale.
[GB560] Oxford pbk **£1.75**
[GB561] Penguin pbk **£2.25**
The Shadow Line (1917)
A semi-autobiographical novel; a sea captain on his first command has to cross the 'shadow line' between youth and manhood.
[GB562] Oxford pbk **£2.50**
[GB563] Penguin pbk **£1.95**
'Twixt Land and Sea
[GB564] Penguin pbk **£2.95**
Typhoon & Other Tales (1902)
[GB565] Oxford pbk **£1.95**
Under Western Eyes (1911)
Conrad's range is another marvellous aspect to his work. Here he crafted a brilliant Russian novel, a Dostoevskian tale of a revolutionary who betrays his fellow men.
[GB566] Oxford pbk **£1.95**
[GB567] Penguin pbk **£2.50**
Victory: An Island Tale (1915)
[GB568] Oxford pbk **£1.95**
[GB569] Penguin pbk **£3.50**
Youth/Heart of Darkness/The End of the Tether
Three of his best short works.
[GB570] Oxford pbk **£2.95**
Youth/The End of the Tether (1902)
[GB571] Penguin pbk **£2.99**

CONRAN, SHIRLEY (1932 -)
Author of the *Superwoman* books who later tapped a rich vein of gold with her racy modern blockbusters.
Lace: The Complete Story
The two volumes of the blockbusting novel.
[GB572] Penguin pbk **£4.99**
Savages (1987)
[GB573] Pan pbk **£3.95**

COOK, DAVID (1940 -)
Probably one of Britain's most underrated novelists, Cook is unusual in his consistent and skilful ability to tackle potentially agonizing or sentimental subjects such as Walter, the brain-damaged boy, who features in his two best-known works.
Crying Out Loud (1988)
With his latest, Whitbread Award-shortlisted novel, Cook embraces a topical but unfashionable subject: child abuse. From a sordid scenario involving two generations of abusers and abused he draws out a novel of great compassion and insight. Cook tackles his subject head-on and builds it up to an uncomfortable but moving conclusion.
[GB1060] Secker hbk **£10.95**

Missing Persons (1986)
A compassionate and hilarious tale of two enterprising elderly women who begin new lives as private investigators.
[GB574] Arrow pbk **£2.99**
Sunrising (1984)
[GB575] Arrow pbk **£2.99**
Walter (1978)
Moving and award-winning novel about a brain-damaged boy.
[GB576] Arrow pbk **£3.50**
Winter Doves (1979)
[GB578] Arrow pbk **£3.50**
Walter and June (1989) **NEW**
Walter and *Winter Doves* re-issued in a single volume, thus telling the entire tale of Walter's childhood, his time in institutions, his meeting with June and their life together. With a new introduction by the author.
[GB577] Secker hbk **£12.95**

COOKSON, CATHERINE (1906 -)
A North-Eastern author whose romantic novels, which number more than 60, are usually set in the Tyneside area, and sympathetically portray working-class poverty past and present. Many feature strong women characters, who triumph against, or endure adversity. Only a selection of her work appears here, including the 'Mallen', 'Mary Ann' and 'Tilly Trotter' series.
Bill Bailey
[GB579] Transworld pbk **£2.95**
Bill Bailey's Lot
The second part of a contemporary trilogy.
[GB580] Transworld hbk **£10.95**
Fifteen Streets
Recently made into a successful stage musical.
[GB581] Transworld pbk **£1.95**
The Black Candle (1989) **NEW**
A vibrant tale from Cookson's pen, with another strong female heroine. When Bridget inherits her father's businesses at the age of 19 - and this is 1880 - she knows she has a hard path to tread.
[GB582] Bantam hbk **£12.95**
The Cultured Handmaiden
Set in Tyneside against the background of the 'winter of discontent'.
[GB583] Transworld pbk **£3.50**
The Moth
[GB584] Transworld pbk **£3.50**
MALLEN SERIES
Mallen Streak
[GB585] Transworld pbk **£2.75**
The Mallen Girl
[GB586] Transworld pbk **£2.95**
The Mallen Litter
[GB587] Transworld pbk **£2.95**
The Mallen Novels
[GB588] Heinemann hbk **£10.95**
MARY ANN SERIES
Grand Man
[GB589] Transworld pbk **£1.99**
Lord and Mary Ann
[GB590] Transworld pbk **£2.50**
Devil and Mary Ann
[GB591] Transworld pbk **£2.50**
Love and Mary Ann
[GB592] Transworld pbk **£1.95**
Life and Mary Ann
[GB593] Transworld pbk **£2.50**
Marriage and Mary Ann
[GB594] Transworld pbk **£1.95**
Mary Ann's Angels
[GB595] Transworld pbk **£2.50**
Mary Ann and Bill
[GB596] Transworld pbk **£1.75**
Mary Ann Omnibus
[GB597] Macdonald hbk **£12.95**

Catherine Cookson, author of *The Black Candle* (Bantam hbk £12.95)

TILLY TROTTER SERIES
Tilly Trotter
[GB598] Transworld pbk **£3.50**
Tilly Trotter Wed
[GB599] Transworld pbk **£2.95**
Tilly Trotter Widowed
[GB600] Transworld pbk **£2.99**

COOPER, JEREMY
Ruth (1986)
This promising first novel from the art critic was critically acclaimed on its publication in 1986: set in Somerset, it is the story of the heroine's mental illness.
[GB601] Transworld pbk **£3.50**

COOPER, JILLY (1937 -)
Jilly Cooper's early books were essentially love stories featuring a series of upper middle-class heroines and set mainly in the 1960s. They are amusing, if far-fetched, entertainments about a mythical world of Oxbridge innocents, Scottish castles, artists and glamorous socialites all engaged in amorous play.
Bella
[GB602] Transworld pbk **£2.50**
Emily
[GB603] Transworld pbk **£2.50**
Harriet
[GB604] Transworld pbk **£2.50**
Imogen
[GB605] Transworld pbk **£2.50**
Lisa and Co
[GB606] Transworld pbk **£2.50**
Octavia
[GB607] Transworld pbk **£2.50**
Prudence
[GB608] Transworld pbk **£2.50**
Riders
With this novel, Cooper moved into the blockbuster market.
[GB609] Transworld pbk **£4.50**
Rivals (1988)
In this recent sequel to the commercially successful *Riders*, the hero becomes embroiled in a battle over the television franchise for rural Gloucestershire.
[GB610] Transworld pbk **£4.50**

COOPER, LETTICE (1897 -)

Her first novel was published in 1925 and her most recent in 1986. In between, Cooper, a lifelong socialist, has helped found the Writer's Action Group and was instrumental in establishing Public Lending Rights for authors.

Fenny (1953)
[GB611] Virago pbk **£5.50**
National Provincial
[GB612] Gollancz pbk **£5.95**
The New House (1936)
[GB613] Virago pbk **£5.50**
Unusual Behaviour (1986)
[GB614] Gollancz hbk **£8.95**

COOPER, WILLIAM (1910 -)

A novelist whose fifth book, *Scenes from Provincial Life*, proved to be a valuable influence on writers such as John Braine and the entire brigade of Angry Young Men. This and its three sequels tell the story of Joe Lunn, Cooper's cynical and pragmatic lower-middle-class hero.

Scenes from Later Life (1983)
[GB615] Methuen pbk **£2.95**
Scenes from Married Life (1961)
[GB616] Methuen pbk **£2.95**
Scenes from Metropolitan Life (1982)
[GB617] Methuen pbk **£2.95**
Scenes from Provincial Life (1950)
[GB618] Methuen pbk **£3.95**

CORDELL, ALEXANDER (Welsh)

A popular historical novelist who dramatizes his native Wales' history.

Novels of Wales
Comprising three novels: *Fire People*, *Land of My Father* and *This Sweet and Bitter Earth*.
[GB619] Hodder pbk **£6.95**
Rape of the Fair Country (1976)
[GB620] Hodder pbk **£2.95**
Requiem for a Patriot (1988)
[GB621] Weidenfeld pbk **£10.95**
This Proud and Savage Land (1987)
Opening in 1800, this novel portrays a troubled Wales divided between rich and poor, and moving irreversibly towards the Chartist Rebellion.
[GB622] Sphere pbk **£3.50**
Traitor Within (1974)
[GB623] Heinemann pbk **£2.95**
Tunnel Tigers
[GB624] Sphere pbk **£2.99**

COWARD, NOEL (1899 - 1973)

Multi-talented actor, playwright and composer who was for many years one of the most flamboyant and celebrated thespians of English theatre. He also wrote verse, short stories and one novel, *Pomp and Circumstance*, that, like his plays, are characterized by their sparkling wit and sophisticated cynicism.

Complete Stories
[GB626] Methuen hbk **£12.95**
[GB627] Methuen pbk **£4.95**
Pomp and Circumstance (1960)
[GB628] Methuen pbk **£2.95**

CRACE, JIM (1946 -)

A relatively new writer who has already garnered quite a collection of plaudits.

Continent (1986)
This first novel won a remarkable three prizes. It is in fact made up of seven loosely-connected stories set in an imaginary land, but the theme is clear: our exploitation of the Third World.
[GB632] Picador pbk **£3.95**
The Gift of Stones (1988)
A highly imaginative tale set among a community of tool-makers in the Stone Age, recounted in vivid and poetic language.
[GB633] Picador pbk **£3.99**

CRONIN, A.J. (Scottish, 1896 - 1981)

Cronin was a doctor and physician by profession but he gave up practising medicine after the success of his first novel. His books, of which *Hatter's Castle* and *The Citadel* are probably the best and most well-known, are either set in his native Scotland or his beloved Wales.

A Pocketful of Rye (1969)
[GB636] Hodder pbk **£2.50**
Adventures in Two Worlds
(Non fiction)
His autobiography, from 1952.
[GB637] Hodder pbk **£2.95**
Grand Canary (1933)
[GB638] Hodder pbk **£2.50**
Green Years (1944)
[GB639] Hodder pbk **£2.95**
Hatter's Castle (1931)
[GB640] Hodder pbk **£4.50**
Keys of the Kingdom (1942)
[GB641] Hodder pbk **£3.50**
Northern Light (1958)
[GB642] Hodder pbk **£2.50**
Shannon's Way (1948)
[GB643] Hodder pbk **£2.95**
Song of Sixpence (1964)
[GB644] Hodder pbk **£2.95**
The Citadel (1937)
A solid and enjoyable tale of the trials and tribulations that test a young doctor practising in a small Scottish town.
[GB645] Hodder pbk **£3.50**
The Judas Tree (1961)
[GB646] Hodder pbk **£2.95**

CRONIN, ANTHONY (Irish, 1926 -)

Anthony Cronin is well-known both as a critic and as a poet.

The Life of Riley (1983)
The comic progress of Patrick Riley, poet and professional scrounger, as he travels from Dublin to London via various pubs and doss houses. Cronin's story is hilarious.
[GB647] Faber pbk **£3.25**

DAHL, ROALD (1916 -)

The most successful contemporary children's writer, and a highly popular adult one too, famous for his *Tales of the Unexpected*. Dahl is a master at building familiar and believable situations to which he then gives a devilish twist; he is sophisticated, macabre black comedy.

Ah, Sweet Mystery of Life (1989) **NEW**
This new book collects all Dahl's famous country stories together with the title story, a new one. Illustrated throughout by John Lawrence, this is an affectionate portrait of a vanishing world of rustic cunning, with the characteristic twists we have come to expect from Dahl.
[GB648] M Joseph hbk **£11.95**
Best of Roald Dahl (1978)
[GB650] Penguin pbk **£4.99**
Kiss Kiss (1959)
[GB651] Penguin pbk **£2.99**
My Uncle Oswald (1979)
[GB653] Penguin pbk **£2.99**
Over to You (1945)
[GB654] Penguin pbk **£2.99**
Roald Dahl's Completely Unexpected Tales
Includes *Tales* and *More Tales*.
[GB655] Penguin pbk **£3.99**
Selected Works
[GB656] Heinemann hbk **£9.95**
Someone Like You (1953)
[GB657] Penguin pbk **£2.99**
Switch Bitch (1974)
Tales of sexual intrigue and nastiness.
[GB658] Penguin pbk **£2.25**

DALY, ITA (Irish, 1955 -)

Daly is representative of the new wave of young Irish writers whose exploration of form and voice connects them to a much wider influence.

Dangerous Fictions (1989) **NEW**
Ita Daly's third novel looks behind the façade of Martina's marriage to where she harbours dark passions. Life in her tall Georgian house goes on 'as normal', but she is treading a thin line between sanity and madness. A strange and transfixing tale.
[GB660] Bloomsbury hbk **£12.95**
Ellen (1986)
Ellen was a strange and solitary girl until she met Myra, who opens up a whole new world for her. A deft and promising first novel.
[GB661] Transworld pbk **£2.95**
Singular Attraction (1987)
[GB662] Transworld pbk **£2.95**

DAWSON, JENNIFER (1929 -)

Judasland (1989) **NEW**
[GB665] Virago hbk **£11.95**
The Ha-Ha (1961)
A lucid and highly amusing classic novel of madness: a young woman is removed from her Oxford college and is committed to an asylum. Winner of the James Tait Black Memorial Prize in 1962.
[GB666] Virago pbk **£4.99**
Upstairs People (1988)
[GB667] Virago hbk **£11.95**

DE LA MARE, WALTER (1873 - 1956)

Chiefly known as a lyric poet, de la Mare also wrote short stories which are distinguished by their feel for the mysterious, odd and fantastic aspects of ordinary life, and for their disarming ability to shift abruptly from the gently elegiac to the grotesque.

Best Stories
[GB668] Faber pbk **£4.95**

DELAFIELD, E.M. (1890 - 1943)

The pen-name of Edmée Elizabeth Monica Dashwood, novelist, journalist, magistrate, and pillar of the Women's Institute.

Diary of a Provincial Lady (1930)
A gentle satire on English middle-class life, written from the inside.
[GB669] Virago pbk **£4.99**
Thank Heaven Fasting! (1932)
[GB670] Virago pbk **£4.99**
The Way Things Are (1927)
[GB671] Virago pbk **£4.99**

DELDERFIELD, R.F.

A prolific novelist who manages to write with touching sentiment. His sagas are imaginative and dramatic, and have lent themselves easily to television adaptation.

To Serve Them All My Days
[GB672] Hodder pbk **£4.50**
A HORSEMAN RIDING BY
Long Summer Day
[GB673] Hodder pbk **£4.50**
Post of Honour
[GB674] Hodder pbk **£3.95**
Green Gauntlet
Follows Paul Craddock and his family after his return from the Boer War up to the 1950s.
[GB675] Hodder pbk **£3.50**
SWANN SAGA
God is an Englishman
The story of Adam Swann who lives through the latter half of the 19th century.
[GB676] Hodder pbk **£4.50**
Theirs Was the Kingdom
[GB677] Hodder pbk **£4.50**
Give Us This Day
[GB678] Hodder pbk **£4.99**

THE AVENUE SAGA
The Dreaming Suburb
[GB679] Hodder pbk **£3.50**
The Avenue Goes to War
[GB680] Hodder pbk **£3.95**

DEVLIN, ANNE (Irish)
Talented and powerful playwright.
The Way Paver (Stories, 1986)
A well-received book of nine short stories,
depicting scenes of everyday personal life set
against the tense and volatile political
background of Northern Ireland.
[GB681] Faber pbk **£3.50**

DICKENS, MONICA (1915 -)
The great-granddaughter of Charles Dickens,
Monica Dickens is a wide-ranging, observant and
funny writer. She writes what could be called
typically English novels, often inspired by her
personal experiences.
Dear Doctor Lily (1988)
Two women rush to escape their past and exchange
England for the US. However, the dream fades, and
things go wrong...
[GB683] Penguin pbk **£3.99**
Enchantment (1989)   **NEW**
Her second adult work in 10 years, a compassionate
novel detailing the relationship between a young man
in his 20s and an autistic child and its mother.
[GB684] Viking hbk **£11.95**
Flowers on the Grass (1949)
[GB685] Penguin pbk **£2.95**
Kate and Emma (1964)
[GB686] Penguin pbk **£2.95**
Man Overboard (1958)
[GB687] Penguin pbk **£2.50**
Mariana (1940)
[GB688] Penguin pbk **£2.99**
No More Meadows (1953)
[GB689] Penguin pbk **£2.95**
Thursday Afternoons (1945)
[GB690] Penguin pbk **£3.50**

DILLON, EILIS (Irish, 1920 -)
Born in Galway, Dillon has written over 40 books. As
a historical novelist he portrays his fellow
countrymen with compassion: this is his best-known
work.
Across the Bitter Sea
[GB691] Hodder pbk **£3.95**

DISKI, JENNY (1947 -)
Diski gained attention for her controversial first
novel, *Nothing Natural*; her work is often
challenging in its subject matter.
Like Mother (1988)
A characteristically eerie and unsettling tale of the
symbiotic relationship between a mother and her
(literally) brainless baby.
[GB694] Bloomsbury hbk **£12.95**
Nothing Natural (1986)
A chilling account of a sado-masochistic relationship.
Very powerful.
[GB695] Methuen pbk **£2.50**
Rain Forest (1987)
A scientist, who has had a breakdown, attempts to
reconstruct her life and sense of self.
[GB696] Penguin pbk **£3.99**

DOYLE, RODDY (Irish)
Young writer and dramatist whose book below had
the undeniable honour of being the first unsolicited
manuscript to be published by Heinemann for many
years.
The Commitments (1988)
Joyful first novel about a band - the Commitments -
who bring the Gospel of Soul to Dublin.
[GB697] Heinemann pbk **£3.95**

DRABBLE, MARGARET (1939 -)
Popular and highly-skilled writer whose characters
generally experience discontent over a broad
spectrum of human needs. Drabble's novels are
entertaining to read and are often touched by light
comedy, but ultimately address serious issues of
social change which confront families and marriages.
She is also a respected literary critic.
A Natural Curiosity (1989)   **NEW**
A sequel to *The Radiant Way*, continuing the story of
Alix, Liz and Esther, with the scene now shifting from
London to Yorkshire. Very much a novel of the late
1980s, it searchingly asks what ten years of
Thatcherism have done to this country: are we now
better or worse off?
[GB698] Viking hbk **£12.95**
Jerusalem the Golden (1967)
[GB699] Weidenfeld hbk **£10.95**
[GB700] Penguin pbk **£2.95**
Realms of Gold (1975)
[GB701] Weidenfeld hbk **£10.95**
[GB702] Penguin pbk **£3.95**
Summer Bird-Cage (1963)
An early novel, from early in her career, that
expresses many of her later themes in polished and
accessible prose.
[GB703] Weidenfeld hbk **£11.95**
[GB704] Penguin pbk **£2.95**
The Garrick Year (1964)
[GB705] Weidenfeld hbk **£8.95**
[GB706] Penguin pbk **£2.95**
The Ice Age (1977)
[GB707] Weidenfeld hbk **£8.95**
[GB708] Penguin pbk **£3.50**
The Middle Ground (1980)
[GB709] Weidenfeld hbk **£11.95**
[GB710] Penguin pbk **£3.50**
The Millstone (1965)
Her most renowned work, about a young woman with
an unwanted pregnancy.
[GB711] Weidenfeld hbk **£10.95**
[GB712] Penguin pbk **£2.50**
The Needle's Eye (1972)
[GB713] Weidenfeld hbk **£8.95**
[GB714] Penguin pbk **£3.99**
The Radiant Way (1987)
After seven years' silence, Drabble clearly returned to
form with this account of the various struggles of
three middle-aged women in 1980s London. Set under
an always overcast sky, the novel is rich with political
allusion.
[GB715] Weidenfeld hbk **£10.95**
[GB716] Penguin pbk **£3.99**
The Waterfall (1969)
A tale of the complicated, fleeting passions of
adultery.
[GB717] Weidenfeld hbk **£10.95**
[GB718] Penguin pbk **£2.95**

DUFFY, MAUREEN (1933 -)
A writer much respected for her frank and dignified
accounts of homosexual life. Her major work has
been her naturalistic triptych of London life:
Londoners, *Wounds* and *Capital*.
Capital (1975)
[GB719] Methuen pbk **£2.95**
Change (1987)
A mosaic of different characters' lives which builds a
moving picture of war-time life.
[GB720] Methuen pbk **£3.95**
Gor Saga (1981)
[GB721] Methuen hbk **£9.50**
I Want to Go to Moscow (1973)
[GB722] Methuen pbk **£3.50**
Londoners (1983)
A sardonic but poignant novel of London life seen
through the eyes of a sexually ambivalent writer-
narrator who lives in a bedsit in Earls Court.
[GB723] Methuen pbk **£3.50**

The Microcosm (1966)
A novel of women on the margins of society.
[GB724] Virago pbk **£4.99**
Wounds (1962)
[GB725] Methuen pbk **£2.95**

DUNN, DOUGLAS (Scottish, 1942 -)
Award-winning poet whose understated, descriptive
writing is distinguished by images of peculiar
emotional power which lifts it beyond realism into
something more haunting.
Secret Villages (1985)
Sharply observant book of short stories.
[GB726] Faber pbk **£3.95**

DUNN, NELL (1936 -)
Novelist and playwright (she wrote the memorable
Steaming) who, in these two re-issued novels,
displays her keen ear for dialogue and considerable
sympathy for working-class life. They were
controversial at the time for their sexual candour, and
both were later filmed.
Poor Cow (1967)
[GB727] Virago pbk **£3.99**
Up the Junction (1963)
[GB728] Virago pbk **£3.99**

DUNNETT, DOROTHY (1923 -)
Writer of well-researched and creative historical
novels, the best known of which are in the *Lymond
Saga*.
LYMOND SAGA
Game of Kings
A sequence of novels about Frances Crawford of
Lymond, a 16th century soldier of fortune.
[GB733] Century pbk **£3.95**
Queen's Play
[GB734] Arrow pbk **£3.95**
Disorderly Knights
[GB735] Century pbk **£3.95**
Pawn in Frankincense
[GB736] Century pbk **£3.95**
Ringed Castle
[GB737] Century pbk **£3.95**
Checkmate
[GB738] Century pbk **£3.95**
THE HOUSE OF NICCOLO SERIES
Niccolo Rising
The beginning of a new series about Renaissance
politics and personalities.
[GB739] Penguin pbk **£4.95**
Spring of the Ram
The continuation of the above.
[GB740] Penguin pbk **£4.99**
Race of Scorpions (1989)   **NEW**
The third volume in this popular series finds Niccolo
embarking on a campaign against Zacco, the
illegitimate brother of the Queen of Cyprus, who will
turn out to be his toughest adversary yet.
[GB741] M Joseph hbk **£12.95**

DURRELL, LAWRENCE (1912 -)
The brother of the naturalist Gerald, Lawrence
Durrell first came to notice as a poet. His reputation
as a novelist rests upon his *Alexandria Quartet*,
which approaches the same set of events from
different angles. Originally inspired by Henry Miller,
Durrell's writing is exotic, ornate and sensual, and is
actually more highly regarded abroad than in
Britain.
Antrobus Complete (1985)
Hilarious tales of diplomatic misadventure.
[GB743] Faber pbk **£4.99**
Nunquam (1970)
[GB754] Faber pbk **£4.95**
The Black Book (1938, revised 1973)
[GB745] Faber pbk **£3.95**
The Dark Labyrinth (1961)
[GB746] Faber pbk **£3.95**

Tunc (1968)
[GB747] Faber pbk **£4.95**
White Eagles Over Serbia (1957)
[GB748] Penguin pbk **£2.50**
The Alexandria Quartet (1957-60)
Comprising *Justine*, *Balthazar*, *Mountolive* and
Clea. Set in Alexandria before the Second World War,
it details the sexual and political intrigues of a set of
central characters. Durrell called it his 'investigation
into modern love'.
[GB749] Faber hbk **£14.95**
[GB750] Faber pbk **£5.95**
THE AVIGNON QUINTET
Constance (1982)
[GB751] Faber pbk **£3.95**
Livia (1978)
[GB752] Faber pbk **£3.95**
Monsieur (1974)
[GB753] Faber pbk **£2.50**
Quinx (1985)
[GB755] Faber pbk **£3.95**
Sebastian (1983)
[GB756] Faber pbk **£3.95**

DYER, GEOFF
The Colour of Memory   **NEW**
Modestly experimental first novel, which portrays life
in South London with gritty and compassionate
realism.
[GB756A] Cape hbk **£10.95**

EDWARDS, DOROTHY (1903 - 1934)
Quintessentially English tales of rambling walks and
afternoon teas from the famed children's writer.
Rhapsody (1927)
[GB757] Virago pbk **£4.99**
Winter Sonata (1928)
A delicate, near-perfect minor classic, dealing with
loneliness.
[GB758] Virago pbk **£4.99**

EGREMONT, MAX
Painted Lives (1989)   **NEW**
Egremont's tale of art world rivalries and powerful
emotion set in an English country house has been
very well received and seems assured of success.
'This is a novel to be savoured: superbly written and
complete with a sparkling plot and a cast of cultivated
eccentrics' (*Literary Review*).
[GB759] H Hamilton hbk **£11.95**

ELLIOTT, JANICE (1931 -)
Dr Gruber's Daughter (1986)
[GB760] Hodder pbk **£3.99**
Sadness of the Witches (1988)
The curious tale, set in the West Country, of a couple
who find there is a witch living across the estuary
from their house.
[GB761] Hodder pbk **£3.99**
The Italian Lesson
An excellent 'Forsterian' novel about the English in
Italy.
[GB762] Hodder pbk **£3.50**

ELLIS, A.E.
The Rack (1958)
Widely acclaimed and classic novel about life in a TB
sanatorium.
[GB763] Penguin pbk **£4.95**

ELLIS, ALICE THOMAS (1932 -)
Critic, columnist (Ellis writes 'Home Life' in *The
Spectator*) and popular novelist whose highly
inventive social comedies are coloured by bizarre and
mysterious events with portentous overtones.
Birds of the Air (1980)
[GB765] Penguin pbk **£3.99**
The Clothes in the Wardrobe (1987)
A young girl finds herself trapped in a married life of

suburban convention. When her friends from Egypt
visit, new possibilities open up...
[GB766] Duckworth hbk **£9.95**
[GB767] Penguin pbk **£3.99**
The Skeleton in the Cupboard (1988)
The sequel, in which old Mrs Munro watches
helplessly as her son's wedding approaches.
[GB768] Duckworth hbk **£9.95**
The Other Side of the Fire (1983)
[GB769] Penguin pbk **£3.50**
The Sin Eater (1977)
[GB771] Penguin pbk **£3.99**
The Twenty Seventh Kingdom (1982)
Shortlisted for the Booker Prize in 1982.
[GB772] Penguin pbk **£3.99**
Unexplained Laughter (1985)
In this, her best-known novel, a wordly journalist has
to escape from London to recover from a broken
heart.
[GB773] Duckworth hbk **£9.95**
[GB774] Penguin pbk **£3.99**

ELLISON, JANE
A Fine Excess (1985)
A raffish and racy comedy centred on the publishing
and media world.
[GB775] Transworld pbk **£3.95**
Another Little Drink (1987)
[GB776] Arrow pbk **£3.99**

EMERSON, SALLY
The Fire Child (1987)
Uncontrollable desire, murder and revenge combine
in this chilling tale of an enigmatic and fatally
attractive young woman.
[GB777] Sphere pbk **£2.99**

ENRIGHT, D.J. (1920 -)
Academic Year (1955)
A wry and exactly observed campus novel by the
celebrated poet and critic.
[GB778] Oxford pbk **£3.95**

EVANS, CARADOC (Welsh, 1878 - 1945)
Journalist, playwright and novelist, this was Evans's
first novel, a memorable and realistic depiction of
Welsh valley life at the beginning of the century; his
characters have been compared to those of Faulkner,
for the manner in which personality emerges through
speech.
Nothing to Pay (1930)   **NEW**
[GB778A] Carcanet hbk **£12.95**

FAIRBAIRNS, ZOE (1948 -)
An interesting author, who is committed to
examining the position and role of women in
contemporary society.
Benefits (1979)
Futuristic look at women's lives under a crushing
bureaucracy, related with irony and realism.
[GB781] Virago pbk **£4.50**
Closing (1987)
An ambitious novel linking together the lives of
several businesswomen which gained Fairbairns a
wider audience.
[GB782] Methuen pbk **£3.50**
Here Today (1984)
[GB783] Methuen pbk **£3.50**
Stand We at Last (1983)
[GB784] Virago pbk **£4.95**

FALLOWELL, DUNCAN (1955 -)
Witty and unusual writer with a distinct penchant for
the sordid.
Satyrday (1986)
Satirical, blackly funny tale of urban excesses.
[GB789] Grafton pbk **£3.95**
The Underbelly (1987)
[GB790] Grafton pbk **£4.50**

FAQIR, FADIA (1956 -)
Born in Amman, *Nisanit* is a powerful novel set in
the context of the current Arab-Israeli conflict. Faqir
has recently completed the Creative Writing course at
the University of East Anglia, and is now working on
a second novel.
Nisanit
Penguin pbk **£3.99**

FARMER, PENELOPE (1939 -)
Novelist, children's writer and researcher.
Away from Home (1987)
A novel forming a mosaic of multi-cultural female
experience; 10 chapters told from 10 parts of the
world.
[GB791] Sphere pbk **£3.99**
Eve: Her Story (1985)
A witty and irreverent look at the Garden of Eden.
[GB792] Sphere pbk **£3.95**
Glasshouses (1988)
This novel is a compelling and magical work; five
glassblowers tell their different tales as they work. It
earned consistently good reviews last year.
[GB793] Gollancz hbk **£11.95**
Standing in the Shadow (1984)
[GB794] Gollancz hbk **£9.95**

FARRELL, J.G. (1935 - 1979)
A novelist of quite considerable talent who died
prematurely at the height of his powers. His three
best-known works (*Troubles*, *The Singapore Grip*
and *The Siege of Krishnapur*) form a loose trilogy -
they share some characters - dealing with the persis-
tent, occasionally heroic, refusal of his characters to
recognize the waning of the British Empire.
A Girl in the Head (1967)
The voyeuristic yearnings of an ironic, acerbic man at
a seaside resort.
[GB795] Fontana pbk **£1.95**
The Hill Station (1981)
His last novel, left unfinished at the time of his
drowning.
[GB796] Fontana pbk **£3.95**
The Siege of Krishnapur (1973)
Farrell won the Booker Prize for this ironic and comic
novel based on the Indian Mutiny.
[GB797] Fontana pbk **£3.95**
The Singapore Grip (1973)
A near-epic and partly-factual account of the fall of
Singapore to the Japanese which, in Farrell's book,
dealt a death-blow to the Empire.
[GB798] Fontana pbk **£4.95**
Troubles (1970)
A fine, substantial novel set in the decaying Majestic
Hotel during the Irish Troubles.
[GB799] Fontana pbk **£5.95**

FARRELL, M.J. (Irish, 1905 -)
Molly Keane took the name M.J. Farrell from a pub
sign and used it as her pen-name. She became a
successful comic novelist and playwright, but gave up
writing for twenty years after her last play was
savagely attacked in the 1950s by the 'angry young
men' of British theatre. See under *Molly Keane* for
her excellent return to form.
Devoted Ladies (1934)
A well-received work, acclaimed by, amongst others,
Compton Mackenzie.
[GB800] Virago pbk **£4.99**
Full House (1935)
One of her most intuitive works, exposing the
precariousness and insecurity of a family in an Irish
mansion.
[GB801] Virago pbk **£4.99**
Loving without Tears (1951)
Angel, warm-hearted but selfish, awaits her son's
return. She must sharpen her wits in order to retain
her tyranny...
[GB802] Virago pbk **£4.99**

Mad Puppetstown (1931)
In the 1900s Easter lives with her cousins and aunts
in her country house, Puppetstown, enjoying a
carefree life.
[GB803] Virago pbk **£4.99**
Taking Chances (1929)
A novel that perfectly captures the leisured Anglo-
Irish life of the era in which it was written.
[GB804] Virago pbk **£4.99**
The Rising Tide (1937)
[GB805] Virago pbk **£4.99**
Two Days in Aragon (1941)
The Georgian house of Aragon is a testament to years
of gracious living. But things are changing: one of its
inhabitants is a member of Sinn Fein.
[GB806] Virago pbk **£4.99**
Young Entry (1928)
[GB807] Virago pbk **£4.99**

FARRELL, MICHAEL (Irish, 1900 - 1962)
A doctor who worked in the Belgian Congo before
retiring to the Wicklow hills to devote himself to his
legendary novel.
Thy Tears Might Cease (1963)
Farrell's life's work became the archetypal Irish novel
- endlessly talked about, but never finished. It grew to
such an unmanageable length that only after his death
was it edited by a friend and published to tremendous
acclaim on both sides of the Atlantic.
[GB808] Arrow pbk **£3.95**

FEINSTEIN, ELAINE (1930 -)
An accomplished poet, biographer and recent
translator of Marina Tsvetayeva, the Russian poet.
Her work is characterized by unusual imagery and
explorations into perception.
All You Need (1989) **NEW**
A wry and satirical look at life in London. Nell's
husband is sent to gaol, but his absence allows her to
realize her own worth. However, surviving the world
of TV programme makers and feminist groups is not
easy.
[GB809] Hutchinson hbk **£11.95**
Mother's Girl (1988)
A complex novel which explores interwoven
family relationships.
[GB810] Arrow pbk **£3.99**
The Border (1984)
A passionate story of pain and betrayal in Hitler's
pre-war Europe.
[GB811] Arrow pbk **£3.99**

Ford Madox Ford, author of *The Good Soldier*
(Penguin pbk £3.99)

FERGUSON, RACHEL (1893 - 1957)
Ferguson worked in the theatre and as a journalist, in
addition to writing nine novels, of which this is the
best known. Her talent for depicting the domestic
comedy of well-to-do Victorian life is here combined
with a fantastic and more imaginative perspective.
The Brontës Went to Woolworths (1931)
Introduced by A.S.Byatt.
[GB814] Virago pbk **£4.50**

FERMOR, PATRICK LEIGH (1915 -)
The Violins of Saint-Jacques (1953)
Masterful short novel about an island in the Antilles,
by the celebrated travel writer who walked right
across pre-war Europe on foot.
[GB815] Oxford pbk **£2.95**

FIGES, EVA (1932 -)
Currently one of the more interesting of British
women writers, whose work shows a strong feminist
awareness.
Ghosts (1988)
An unsettling but highly lyrical novel about a
mysterious woman with an ambivalence towards her
past.
[GB816] Fontana pbk **£3.95**
Nelly's Version (1985)
[GB817] Fontana pbk **£3.95**
The Seven Ages (1986)
A passionate and panoramic account of 1,000 years of
women's history (or herstory), as narrated by seven
different women. According to Tillie Olsen, 'Virginia
Woolf would have welcomed this book'.
[GB818] Fontana pbk **£3.95**

FIRBANK, RONALD (1886 - 1926)
Dandy and aesthete who travelled widely and whose
books often have exotic settings; Firbank's novels are
witty and frequently bizarre, drawing imaginatively
upon the decadent atmosphere of the 1890s. He is
now credited with being a major liberating force in
the development of the novel.
New Rhythm and Other Pieces
[GB821] Duckworth hbk **£12.95**
The Complete Firbank
Contains the major novels - *Valmouth*, *Prancing
Nigger* and *Concerning the Eccentricities of
Cardinal Pirelli*, as well as a number of lesser works.
[GB823] Picador pbk **£4.95**
The Flower Beneath the Foot (1923)
'I think there would be something wrong with an
elderly man who could enjoy Firbank.' (Evelyn
Waugh).
[GB824] Penguin pbk **£2.95**
Three More Novels
Vainglory (1915); *Inclinations* (1916); *Caprice*
(1917).
[GB825] New Directions pbk **£7.75**
Valmouth (1918)
Set in a watering hole dominated by a manipulative
Black masseuse. Regarded as one of the best comic
novels of this century.
[GB826] Penguin pbk **£4.50**

FITZGERALD, PENELOPE (1916 -)
A very English author who won the Booker Prize in
1979, Fitzgerald's novels are notable for her exquisite
prose style and for a certain purity of feeling; in their
cultural diversity, they reflect the range and quality of
her learning.
At Freddie's (1982)
[GB827] Fontana pbk **£3.99**
Human Voices (1980)
Acclaimed evocation of life at the BBC during the
war.
[GB829] Fontana pbk **£3.95**
Innocence (1986)
A novel set in Italy.
[GB830] Fontana pbk **£3.50**

Offshore (1979)
Her Booker Prize winning story is set among a
houseboat community on the Thames.
[GB831] Fontana pbk **£3.95**
The Beginning of Spring (1988)
Her most recent novel, shortlisted for the Booker
Prize, concerns an English family living in Russia in
the years immediately preceding the Revolution. It is
a delicately suggestive book, with intimations of huge
events lurking beneath the surface lives of the
characters. Her evocation of Moscow is atmospheric
and historically accurate.
[GB832] Fontana pbk **£3.95**
The Bookshop (1978)
Shortlisted for the Booker Prize. An account of a
middle-aged widow's attempts to run a bookshop in a
small East Anglian town.
[GB833] Flamingo pbk **£3.99**

FLEETWOOD, HUGH
The Witch (1989) **NEW**
At the heart of Fleetwood's latest novel is a love
triangle involving two men and a woman who are
working on a film in Italy. Their fun is disrupted by
the arrival of the sinister Nora, who increasingly
dominates them, propelling this powerful satire on
film-making towards a tragic end.
[GB834] H Hamilton hbk **£11.95**

FORD, FORD MADOX (1873 - 1939)
The grandson of Ford Madox Brown, Ford grew up in
Pre-Raphaelite circles, which he later claimed
influenced him unduly. He became a prolific and
diverse writer, who is sometimes only remembered
for *The Good Soldier* and his collaborations with, and
influence on, his friend Conrad. While it is true that
his encouragement and publication of authors such as
Joyce, Pound, Cummings and Lawrence in his
pioneering magazine the *Transatlantic Review* did
much to shape the course of 20th century writing, his
own work is of the highest order, and currently
undervalued.
A Call
[GB835] Carcanet pbk **£4.95**
A Ford Madox Ford Reader (1986)
[GB836] Grafton pbk **£5.95**
A History of Our Times (Non fiction) **NEW**
Projected as a three-volume study of the history of his
own times, Ford completed only this, the first volume,
covering 1870-1895. Published now for the first time,
it aims to 'present what a normally cultured reader
should know as a minimum of the history of his own
day', and serves as a valuable commentary to the
period and to Ford's own work, particularly *Parade's
End*.
[GB836A] Carcanet hbk **£25.00**
A Rash Act
[GB837] Carcanet pbk **£3.95**
Ladies whose Bright Eyes
[GB838] Carcanet hbk **£12.95**
Parade's End (1924 - 28)
[GB839] Penguin pbk **£7.99**
The Fifth Queen (1907- 8)
[GB839] Oxford pbk **£4.95**
The Good Soldier (1915)
Ford's one undisputed masterpiece, and a technical
tour de force. It is the story of the intertwined lives
and relationships of two Edwardian couples; only
slowly does the truth emerge.
[GB840] Penguin pbk **£3.99**
COLLECTED WORKS
**Vol 1: The Good Soldier/Selected
Memories/Poems**
[GB841] Bodley hbk **£12.95**
Vol 2: The Fifth Queen Trilogy (1907 - 08)
An ornate and colourful historical romance describing
the fate of Catherine Howard, one of the wives of
Henry VIII.
[GB842] Bodley hbk **£12.95**

Vol 3: Parade's End I (1924 - 26)
Inspired by his experiences in World War I, this epic work is a satire in which Ford undermines all aspects of the narrative voice. A classic formalist novel.
[GB843] Bodley hbk **£12.95**
Vol 4: Parade's End II (1926 - 28)
[GB844] Bodley hbk **£12.95**

FORSTER, E.M. (1879 - 1970)
The framework for most of Forster's novels is that of the Edwardian social comedy of manners, but in his hands it becomes a tool to expose and satirize the prejudices and inadequacies of the English. Forster's symbolic structures may now appear somewhat contrived, but his combination of delicate, close scrutiny of character with far-reaching, sometimes metaphysical universality made him a distinctive and influential novelist who is still widely enjoyed.
A Passage to India (1924)
This masterful work was to be the last of Forster's novels. Born of two extended stays in the country, it mixes elements of almost Austenesque social comedy with altogether more serious themes.
[GB851] Arnold hbk **£35.00**
[GB852] Penguin pbk **£4.99**
A Room with a View (1908)
One of his lighter novels, satirising the English aptitude for snobbery and self-denial; it was recently adapted onto the screen.
[GB853] Arnold hbk **£30.00**
[GB854] Penguin pbk **£4.50**
Arctic Summer & Other Fiction
[GB855] Arnold hbk **£35.00**
Aspects of the Novel (Criticism, 1927)
Informal discussion of the narrative art including the celebrated comment - *"Yes - oh dear yes - the novel tells a story."*
[GB856] Penguin pbk **£3.99**
Collected Short Stories
[GB857] Penguin pbk **£3.50**
Commonplace Book
[GB858] Scolar P hbk **£25.00**
Howard's End (1910)
Second only to *A Passage to India* in quality, this tells the story of the interaction between two deeply different families, and an attempt to reconcile Forster's Bloomsbury values with a sense of economic realities.
[GB859] Arnold hbk **£27.00**
[GB860] Penguin pbk **£2.95**
Maurice (1971)
Completed in 1913 but published posthumously (although Forster circulated it privately during his lifetime), this has the most overtly homosexual theme of all his novels.
[GB861] Arnold hbk **£30.00**
[GB862] Penguin pbk **£3.99**
New Collected Short Stories
[GB863] Sidgwick hbk **£11.95**
[GB864] Sidgwick pbk **£7.95**
The Hill of Devi (Non fiction, 1953)
[GB865] Penguin pbk **£3.99**
The Life to Come & Other Stories (1927)
[GB866] Arnold hbk **£30.00**
[GB867] Penguin pbk **£3.95**
The Longest Journey (1907)
Forster's own favourite novel, and his most autobiographical.
[GB868] Arnold hbk **£45.00**
[GB869] Penguin pbk **£2.95**
Two Cheers for Democracy (Essays, 1951)
[GB870] Arnold hbk **£30.00**
Where Angels Fear to Tread (1905)
An English woman marries an Italian man with tragi-comic results. The novel is evocatively set in Tuscany.
[GB871] Arnold hbk **£30.00**
[GB872] Penguin pbk **£2.99**

FORSTER, MARGARET (1938 -)
Popular novelist sometimes best remembered for *Georgy Girl* and the famous film of that book, although currently very highly regarded as a result of her two recent novels and her biography of Elizabeth Barrett Browning.
Georgy Girl (1965)
[GB873] Penguin pbk **£3.50**
Have the Men Had Enough? (1989) **NEW**
Forster's finest work to date: a story of female courage and a compelling portrait of an indomitable grandmother whose final fight for her rights, blackly funny at first, develops a disturbing pathos.
[GB874] Chatto hbk **£12.95**
Mother Can You Hear Me?
[GB875] Penguin pbk **£3.95**
Private Papers (1986)
[GB876] Penguin pbk **£4.50**
Travels of Maudie Tipstaff (1967)
[GB877] Secker hbk **£9.95**

FOWLES, JOHN (1926 -)
One of the more interesting of contemporary English writers, Fowles employs a variety of fictional strategies in his novels, from the pastiche Victorian of his best-known work, *The French Lieutenant's Woman* to the quasi-magic realism of *The Magus*. A complex writer, he gives the nature and status of fiction as an art form considerable thought.
A Maggot (1985)
[GB878] Cape hbk **£9.95**
[GB879] Pan pbk **£3.50**
Daniel Martin (1977)
A wide-ranging and humane *bildungsroman*, which chronicles Daniel's long search for himself.
[GB881] Cape hbk **£10.95**
[GB882] Picador pbk **£5.99**
Mantissa (1982)
[GB883] Cape hbk **£8.95**
[GB884] Grafton pbk **£2.50**
The Aristos (Non fiction, 1964)
An idiosyncratic collection of notes and aphorisms which form Fowles' personal philosophy.
[GB885] Cape hbk **£8.95**
[GB880] Grafton pbk **£2.99**
The Collector (1963)
Fowles's astonishingly assured début is a macabre tale of a repressed clerk and butterfly collector who then entraps a human specimen.
[GB886] Cape hbk **£9.95**
[GB887] Pan pbk **£2.95**
The Ebony Tower (1974)
A collection of novellas exploring the nature of art.
[GB888] Cape hbk **£9.95**
[GB889] Pan pbk **£3.99**
The French Lieutenant's Woman (1969)
A semi-historical novel set in Lyme Regis in 1867, shot through with authorial comment and insight, and thus a fascinating critique of the Victorian novel.
[GB890] Cape hbk **£9.95**
[GB891] Grafton pbk **£3.99**
The Magus (1966, revised 1977)
Hailed as one of the outstanding achievements in post-war British fiction. Set mainly on a Greek island, it is highly modern in its conviction in the plurality of truth. Complex and mythological.
[GB892] Cape hbk **£10.95**
[GB893] Picador pbk **£4.95**

FRAME, RONALD (Scottish, 1953 -)
A modern master of crisp, sinister but funny short stories, who now also writes excellent novels.
A Long Weekend with Marcel Proust (1986)
Seven stories and a novel.
[GB894] Hodder pbk **£3.50**
A Woman of Judah (1987)
A novel and 15 stories.
[GB895] Hodder pbk **£4.99**

Penelope's Hat (1989) **NEW**
Fitzgerald's latest novel is a fictional biography of novelist Penelope Milne: born in Borneo, reared in wartime London, she achieved literary success in the 1960s, and finally went to live in Australia. An engrossing and emotional read.
[GB896] Hodder hbk **£12.95**
Sandmouth People (1987)
Uncannily precise dissection of the many characters to be found in a seaside resort on one day in the 1950s. An incisive look at what lies beneath the classic British exterior.
[GB897] Hodder pbk **£3.95**
Watching Mrs Gordon (Stories, 1985)
[GB898] Grafton pbk **£2.95**
Winter Journey (1984)
[GB899] Grafton pbk **£2.50**

FRANKAU, PAMELA (1907 - 1967)
An accomplished novelist of women's experience whose work has recently been rediscovered and reissued by Virago.
Willow Cabin (1949)
[GB900] Virago pbk **£5.50**
Winged Horse
[GB901] Virago pbk **£5.50**
Wreath for the Enemy (1954)
[GB902] Virago pbk **£4.95**

FRASER, GEORGE MACDONALD
Author of the extremely popular Flashman series, centred on the character Harry Flashman (borrowed from *Tom Brown's School Days*), who is apparently a winner of the VC but is in fact a base coward and charlatan.
Flash for Freedom: From the Flashman Papers
[GB903] Fontana pbk **£3.50**
Flashman (1970)
[GB904] Fontana pbk **£3.50**
Flashman and the Dragon (1985)
[GB905] Fontana pbk **£3.50**
Flashman at the Charge (1974)
[GB906] Fontana pbk **£3.50**
Flashman in the Great Game
[GB907] Fontana pbk **£3.50**
Flashman's Lady (1979)
[GB908] Pan pbk **£2.50**
McAuslan in the Rough (1976)
[GB909] Fontana pbk **£2.95**
Royal Flash (1981)
[GB910] Fontana pbk **£3.50**
The General Danced at Dawn (1972)
[GB912] Fontana pbk **£2.95**

FRAYN, MICHAEL (1933 -)
Although he is now better-known as an award-winning playwright, Frayn produced intelligent and uproariously comic novels in his earlier years. His new novel, *The Trick of It* is his first for sixteen years.
A Very Private Life (1968)
[GB913] Fontana pbk **£2.50**
The Russian Interpreter (1966)
[GB914] Fontana pbk **£2.50**
Sweet Dreams (1973)
Perhaps his most popular novel.
[GB915] Fontana pbk **£2.95**
The Tin Men (1965)
[GB916] Fontana pbk **£2.50**
The Trick of It (1989) **NEW**
A gleefully witty epistolary novel about the creative process. A minor English academic finally meets the female novelist on whom he has built his career, and seduces her. What follows is a series of mishaps and missives.
[GB917] Viking hbk **£11.95**
Towards the End of Morning (1967)
[GB918] Fontana pbk **£2.95**

FRIEL, BRIAN (Irish, 1929 -)
A dramatist and short story writer whose strength lies in his ability to probe the conditions of individual lives as well as the historical and political forces that shape them.
The Diviner (Stories, 1983)
A selection from his two previous collections.
[GB925] O'Brien P pbk **£3.45**

FRIEL, GEORGE & JANE
(Scottish, 1910 - 1963/1866 - 1946)
Against a usually depressing Glasgow landscape, the Friels create sensitive, alienated characters struggling for ideals and contentment.
An Empty House (1975)
[GB926] Calder hbk **£6.95**
Grace and Miss Partridge (1969)
[GB927] Calder pbk **£4.95**
Mr Alfred, M.A. (1972)
[GB928] Canongate pbk **£3.95**
The Boy Who Wanted Peace (1964)
[GB929] Polygon pbk **£4.95**

FULLER, JOHN (1937 -)
The son of Roy Fuller whose reputation rests chiefly on his elegant poetry, Fuller lives in Oxford, where he is as an English don.
Flying to Nowhere (1983)
Highly poetic novel set in an island monastery. Shortlisted for the Booker Prize.
[GB931] Penguin pbk **£2.99**
Tell it Me Again (1988)
[GB932] Chatto hbk **£10.95**
The Adventures of Speedfall (1985)
Comic stories of Oxford academic life.
[GB933] Penguin pbk **£2.50**
The Burning Boys (1989) **NEW**
A disfigured fighter pilot and a motherless boy meet in wartime Lancashire. As boy and man are brought into temporary and fragile conjunction, each undergoes his own painful rite of passage. An evocative tale of growing up in wartime.
[GB934] Chatto hbk **£10.95**

FULLER, ROY (1912 -)
A very highly regarded poet, Fuller employs the same ironic detachment in his novels.
Image of a Society (1956)
An account of a Northern building society written out of personal experience; a brilliant portrait of professional and personal conflict.
[GB935] Hogarth pbk **£4.95**
Roy Fuller Crime Omnibus
Three of his crime novels in one volume.
[GB936] Carcanet hbk **£12.95**
The Ruined Boys (1959)
[GB937] Hogarth pbk **£4.95**

GALE, PATRICK (1962 -)
An impressively prolific young writer whose books have received very positive reviews.
Ease (1986)
[GB938] Sphere pbk **£3.50**
Facing the Tank (1988)
Fluent tragi-comedy about a historian who unearths more than he bargains for.
[GB939] Hutchinson hbk **£9.95**
Kansas in August (1987)
[GB940] Arrow pbk **£2.99**
Little Bits of Baby (1989) **NEW**
Returning to London from an eight year sojourn at an island monastery, Robin finds that the world he knew has changed substantially. However when he falls in love at a christening, he little suspects the extraordinary effect this will have on those around him.
[GB942] Chatto hbk **£11.95**
The Aerodynamics of Pork (1986)
[GB943] Sphere pbk **£3.95**

GALSWORTHY, JOHN (1867 - 1933)
Nobel Prize for Literature 1932. Popular novelist and playwright who often portrayed the divide between the rich and the poor, displaying a strong feel for social justice. Although Galsworthy never received strong critical acclaim, the Forsyte stories have proved enduringly popular.
Country House (1907)
[GB944] Sutton pbk **£3.95**
The Forsyte Saga (1906-22)
The first half of the famous 'saga' (Galsworthy used the word with irony) chronicles the acquisitive and sometimes brutal urges of Soames Forsyte.
[GB945] Penguin pbk **£6.99**
A Modern Comedy (1924-29)
The second half of the Forsyte chronicles. Together, these books formed the basis for one of the most famous television series ever produced.
[GB946] Penguin pbk **£5.99**

GARDAM, JANE (1928 -)
An award-winning novelist and short story writer whose books are consistently good; Gardam has now earned a considerable band of admirers with her poignant tales.
A Long Way from Verona (1971)
[GB947] Sphere pbk **£3.99**
Bilgewater (1977)
A delightful and moving novel; the story of an adolescent girl's loneliness and longing for fulfillment told with pathos and humour.
[GB948] Sphere pbk **£3.99**
Black Faces, White Faces (1975)
[GB949] Sphere pbk **£3.50**
Crusoe's Daughter (1985)
Bewitching study of a six year old girl who visits her aunt and remains there, in isolation, for 81 years.
[GB950] Sphere pbk **£3.99**
God on the Rocks (1978)
Shortlisted for the Booker Prize.
[GB951] Sphere pbk **£3.50**
Showing the Flag & Other Stories **NEW**
This fine collection of short stories is the first from Gardam to focus exclusively on England - and why the English still wave their flags so much.
[GB952] H Hamilton hbk **£11.95**
The Pangs of Love (Stories, 1983)
[GB953] Sphere pbk **£3.50**
The Sidmouth Letters (1980)
[GB954] Sphere pbk **£3.50**

GARNETT, DAVID (1892 - 1981)
Husband of Angelica Garnett (the niece of Virginia Woolf), and a close associate of the Bloomsbury Group.
Aspects of Love (1955)
A delicate account of a love triangle, which has recently been turned into a West End musical.
[GB956] Hogarth pbk **£2.95**
Lady into Fox/Man in the Zoo (1922)
Two bizarre fables - one tells the story of a woman who turns into a fox, the other of a thwarted lover who donates himself to a zoo for exhibition as a specimen of *homo sapiens*.
[GB957] Hogarth pbk **£4.95**
The Grasshoppers Come/Beany-Eye
Two novellas: a tale of disaster on a record-breaking 1920s air flight, and a bizarre adventure with a tramp.
[GB958] Hogarth pbk **£4.95**

GARNETT, HENRIETTA
The great niece of Virginia Woolf whose literary début was praised for its ingenuity and restraint.
Family Skeletons (1986)
Set against the beautiful but crumbling backdrop of Malabay, this is the tale of how Catherine's solitary childhood is disrupted by her handsome cousin with whom she has long been in love.
[GB959] Hodder pbk **£3.95**

GEBLER, CARLO (Irish, 1954 -)
The son of Edna O'Brien who has won considerable praise as a promising young novelist and screenwriter. Perhaps, with the publication of his fourth novel, the time has come to drop the 'promising' tag and acknowledge how accomplished he already is.
August in July (1986)
An exploration of spiritual exile; a Polish immigrant in London finds himself estranged from other people by his shyness.
[GB970] Penguin pbk **£3.50**
Malachy and His Family (1989) **NEW**
When Malachy discovers that his real father was an Irish immigrant who now lives in London, he leaves New York to find him. He ends up spending the summer with him, his Hungarian wife and their daughter, who Malachy is increasingly drawn to. A bitter-sweet tale of sons, fathers and families.
[GB971] H Hamilton hbk **£11.95**
The Eleventh Summer (1985)
[GB972] Penguin pbk **£2.50**
Work and Play (1987)
Gebler's third novel tackles a range of contemporary issues - law and order, racism, drugs - with anger and compassion.
[GB973] Penguin pbk **£3.50**

GEE, MAGGIE (1948 -)
Maggie Gee was voted one of the Best of Young British novelists a few years ago. Her writing is experimental, but also lyrical, and she deals with politically charged subjects, mainly concerned with nuclear issues.
Dying, in Other Words (1981)
An ingenious mystery tale - a young woman is found murdered in the street - in which anyone could have done it.
[GB974] Grafton pbk **£3.95**
Grace (1988) **NEW**
A fictional reworking of the considerable mystery surrounding Hilda Murrell's death, and thus a novel dealing with the threatening forces within our society.
[GB975] Heinemann hbk **£10.95**
Light Years (1985)
The breakup of a marriage expressed in terms of cosmic despair; the husband buys a telescope and turns it on the stars...
[GB976] Faber pbk **£3.95**

John Fowles, author of *The French Lieutenant's Woman* (Cape hbk £9.95)

The Burning Book (1983)
An evocative, experimental tale with the shadow of nuclear war hanging over it.
[GB977] Faber pbk **£3.95**

GERHARDIE, WILLIAM (1895 - 1977)
Born in St Petersburg of English parents, Gerhardie was partly raised in Russia. His work was admired by Wells and Waugh among others. His major novel *Futility* is unfortunately unavailable.
Of Mortal Love (1936)
A tale of love in the 1920s. Oblique but often lyrical.
[GB978] Penguin pbk **£3.95**
The Polyglots (1925)
Autobiographical tragi-comedy about an officer's relationship with a Belgian family, set in the Far East.
[GB979] Oxford pbk **£4.95**

GIBBON, LEWIS GRASSIC
(Scottish, 1901 - 1935)
Like so many Scottish writers, James Leslie Mitchell died very young, having produced a large number of books both under his real name and his pseudonym, Gibbon. His influential novels, he said, *"moulded the English language into the rhythms and cadences of Scots spoken speech."*
A Scots Quair: Sunset Song/Cloud Howe/Grey Granite (1932 - 1934)
Gibbon's trilogy is this century's most famous Scots work of fiction, and charts the parallel development of its heroine's life and the transition from rural to urban living in Scotland. A magnificent, lyrical work, inspired by Gibbon's Communist beliefs.
[GB981] Pan pbk **£4.99**

GIBBONS, STELLA (1902 -)
Cold Comfort Farm (1932)
The famous comic novel which parodies the earthy regional fiction of the period as found in Mary Webb and D.H. Lawrence. Flora Poste visits the Starkadders down on their farm seething with gloom and intrigue.
[GB985] Penguin pbk **£2.99**
Ticky
[GB986] Sutton pbk **£2.95**

GILLIATT, PENELOPE (1932 -)
Shrewd and witty writing in the best English tradition of close, sharp psychological observation.
Mortal Matters (1983)
[GB987] Macmillan hbk **£8.95**
What's It Like Out?
[GB988] Virago pbk **£4.50**
Woman of Singular Occupation (1988)
A novel set in wartime Europe. A young woman flees Paris on the Orient Express to Istanbul, only to meet further danger.
[GB989] Weidenfeld hbk **£10.95**

GLENDINNING, VICTORIA
The Grown-Ups (1989) **NEW**
The first novel from the well-established biographer is a witty and warmly entertaining chronicle of the irresistible Leo's sexual involvements. In him, Glendinning has created a memorable figure of male vanity who well deserves his nemesis.
[GB990] Hutchinson hbk **£10.95**

GLOAG, JULIAN (1930 -)
Author of some remarkably original novels who has perhaps never received the wider success he deserves; his novel *Our Mother's House* is quite a cult classic.
Blood for Blood (1985)
[GB991] Grafton pbk **£2.95**
Only Yesterday (1986)
Humorous account of old age which touches on many issues common to all of us, related with sincerity, and an admirable sureness of touch which never topples into sentimentality.
[GB992] Grafton pbk **£3.50**

Our Mother's House (1982)
A bizarre exploration of mother worship: seven children conceal their mother's death by burying her in the garden. Superbly filmed by Jack Clayton.
[GB993] Penguin pbk **£3.95**
Sleeping Dogs Lie
[GB994] Grafton pbk **£3.50**

GODDARD, ROBERT
A new writer of 'quality' blockbusting novels, who has been heavily promoted by his publishers.
In Pale Battalions (1988)
World War I murder story.
[GB995] Transworld pbk **£3.99**
Past Caring (1986)
[GB996] Transworld pbk **£3.95**

GODDEN, RUMER (1907 -)
Successful as both a children's and adult writer, Godden's settings reflect her childhood in Asia, which she has also described in volumes of autobiography.
Black Narcissus (1939)
Her most famous novel, perhaps because of the 1947 Powell and Pressburger film, which charts the progress of a group of nuns and their repressed eroticism in a remote Himalayan village.
[GB997] Penguin pbk **£3.95**

GOGARTY, OLIVER S. JOHN (Irish, 1878 - 1957)
A poet whose escape from death during the Irish Civil War is legendary, Gogarty was a contemporary of Yeats and Joyce. It is widely supposed that the 'stately, plump Buck Mulligan' of *Ulysses* is a fairly malicious portrait of Gogarty.
Sackville Street & Other Stories
Reminiscences and stories. The title piece gave rise to a famous libel case.
[GB1003] Sphere pbk **£5.99**

GOLDING, LOUIS (1895 - 1958)
Outstanding novelist of Jewish life in early 20th century England.
Five Silver Daughters (1934)
[GB1004] Gollancz pbk **£5.95**
Magnolia Street (1931)
Classic novel of Jewish immigrant life in Manchester following the battles between poor Jews on one side of the street and shabby genteel Gentiles on the other.
[GB1005] Gollancz pbk **£5.95**

GOLDING, WILLIAM (1911 -)
Nobel Prize for Literature 1983. One of our most ambitious contemporary novelists, Golding achieved international recognition when he was awarded the Nobel Prize. He tends to write about people in extreme situations, and through his use of symbol and allegory, creates fables of the human condition - as much in his remarkable début, *Lord of the Flies*, as in his latest work, the nautical Edmund Talbot trilogy.
A Moving Target (Non fiction, 1982)
Lectures and essays.
[GB1006] Faber pbk **£4.95**
The Brass Butterfly (Play, 1958)
[GB1007] Faber pbk **£3.50**
Darkness Visible (1979)
This novel marked Golding's return to fiction after an absence of many years. It is notable for its most powerful of openings.
[GB1011] Faber pbk **£3.50**
Free Fall (1968)
[GB1013] Faber pbk **£2.95**
Lord of the Flies (1954)
This justly famous tale of schoolboys wrecked on an island and their descent into bestial behaviour is a grotesque parody of Ballantyne's *Coral Island*, and a richly suggestive fable of civilization.
[GB1014] Faber hbk **£10.95**
[GB1015] Faber pbk **£2.95**

Pincher Martin (1956)
One of Golding's more difficult novels, and a fierce look at the egotism of the human heart.
[GB1016] Faber pbk **£2.95**
Rites of Passage (1980)
The first part of the much-praised trilogy, set on an emigrant ship travelling to Australia in the last century. In this Booker Prize-winning novel Golding shows a remarkable eye for detail and a mastery of sea-faring language.
[GB1017] Faber hbk **£9.95**
[GB1018] Faber pbk **£2.95**
Close Quarters (1987)
The second part of his trilogy. Talbot is now an older and wiser man than the youth who started the voyage.
[GB1008] Faber hbk **£10.95**
[GB1009] Faber pbk **£3.95**
Fire Down Below (1989) **NEW**
The conclusion of the great sea trilogy. Her decrepit timbers now held together with rope, the old ship, with her cosmos of human cargo, lumbers towards Sydney Cove.
[GB1012] Faber hbk **£11.99**
The Inheritors (1955)
This unusually visual novel charts the passing of the innocent Neanderthal people and their strangely beautiful world due to the emergence of the predatory Homo Sapiens, and thus further develops Golding's vision of corrupt humanity.
[GB1019] Faber pbk **£2.95**
The Paper Men (1983)
[GB1020] Faber pbk **£2.95**
The Pyramid (1967)
An apparently 'realistic' novel set in the provincial England of the 1930s tinged with eerie unease.
[GB1022] Faber pbk **£2.95**
The Scorpion God (1973)
Three short novels.
[GB1023] Faber pbk **£3.50**
The Spire (1964)
Acclaimed as Golding's most visionary novel, and one with the rich simplicity of fable. In medieval England, one man has a burning ambition: to erect the spire of Salisbury cathedral.
[GB1024] Faber pbk **£3.50**

GOUDGE, ELIZABETH (1900 - 1984)
An enchanting, magical writer who will be remembered for her classic children's novels such as *The Little White Horse*. All her work is pervaded by a sense of supernatural mystery and unutterable joy, just beyond reach.
Bird in the Tree
[GB1025] Duckworth hbk **£9.95**
Castle on the Hill
[GB1028] Duckworth hbk **£9.95**
Cathedral Trilogy
Comprising *City of Bells, Towers in the Mist* and *Dean's Watch*.
[GB1026] Hodder hbk **£5.95**
Make Believe
[GB1027] Duckworth hbk **£9.95**
White Wings
[GB1029] Duckworth hbk **£12.95**

GRAHAM, BARRY
Of Darkness and Light (1989) **NEW**
Taut, vivid tale of horror, both psychological and physical set in the seedy side of Glasgow, illustrated, unusually, with broodingly suggestive drawings.
[GB1035] Bloomsbury hbk **£10.95**

GRAHAM, WINSTON
Best-known for the *Poldark* novels which are set in 18th century Cornwall, Graham has also written other historical and suspense novels, several of which have been filmed, most notably *Marnie* by Hitchcock.
Angell, Pearl and Little God
[GB1036] Fontana pbk **£2.95**

Cameo (1988)
A dead woman found in a London house during the Blitz leads to the discovery of a lethal network of enemy agents.
[GB1037] Fontana pbk **£2.95**
Fortune is a Woman
[GB1039] Fontana pbk **£1.50**
Green Flash
[GB1040] Fontana pbk **£3.50**
Marnie
[GB1042] Fontana pbk **£1.75**
Walking Stick
[GB1044] Fontana pbk **£2.50**
POLDARK SERIES
Ross Poldark
[GB1046] Fontana pbk **£3.95**
Demelza
[GB1047] Fontana pbk **£3.95**
Jeremy Poldark
[GB1048] Fontana pbk **£3.50**
Warleggan
[GB1049] Fontana pbk **£2.75**
Black Moon
[GB1050] Fontana pbk **£3.95**
Four Swans
[GB1051] Fontana pbk **£3.95**
Angry Tide
[GB1052] Fontana pbk **£3.50**
Stranger from the Sea
[GB1053] Fontana pbk **£3.95**
Miller's Dance
[GB1054] Fontana pbk **£2.95**
Loving Cup
[GB1045] Fontana pbk **£3.95**

GRAVES, ROBERT (1895 - 1985)
A prolific and idiosyncratic poet, essayist and novelist, who spent much of his life in Majorca, Graves is remembered for his volume of autobiography arising out of his experiences in the trenches, *Goodbye to All That*. His knowledge of ancient history and mythology make his historical novels enduringly readable.
Antigua, Penny, Puce (1936)
[GB1055] Penguin pbk **£3.95**
Claudius the God (1934)
Graves' most famous fictional creation. The wily Emperor Claudius weaves his way through the labyrinths of the Roman World.
[GB1057] Penguin pbk **£3.95**
I, Claudius (1934)
[GB1062] Penguin pbk **£3.95**
I, Claudius/Claudius the God (Omnibus)
[GB1063] Penguin pbk **£7.50**
Collected Short Stories (1932)
[GB1058] Penguin pbk **£4.99**
Count Belisarius
Historical novel with a Byzantine theme.
[GB1059] Penguin pbk **£4.95**
King Jesus (1946)
[GB1064] Arrow pbk **£4.99**
Seven Days in Crete
[GB1065] Oxford pbk **£3.95**
Wife to Mr Milton (1943)
Fictional re-creation of John Milton's strange marriage.
[GB1066] Penguin pbk **£5.95**

GRAY, ALASDAIR (Scottish, 1934 -)
The most prominent member of what has been called the 'new wave' of Scottish writing (see also James Kelman and Agnes Owens), Gray originally trained as an illustrator, which is reflected in the beautiful and often eccentric production of his hardbacks. His first two novels are picaresque tales which show the influence of Sterne and Joyce, and delight in the breaking of convention in style, layout and plot.
1982, Janine (1984)
Gray's other homage to Glasgow, but also the tale of

one man's drunken collapse as he bewails the loss of his lover. Typographically challenging and experimental.
[GB1067] Penguin pbk **£4.50**
Lanark (1981)
Set in Gray's native Glasgow, this sprawling novel ranges from telling descriptions of that city to fantastical adventures.
[GB1068] Canongate hbk **£15.00**
[GB1069] Grafton pbk **£4.99**
The Fall of Kelvin Walker (1985)
[GB1070] Canongate hbk **£7.95**
[GB1071] Penguin pbk **£3.99**
Unlikely Stories, Mostly (Stories, 1984)
[GB1072] Penguin pbk **£5.99**

GRAY, JOHN
Park, A Fantasy (1966)
The legendary fantasy novel about a futurist world, it became a cult classic and has recently been reissued.
[GB1073] Carcanet pbk **£3.50**

GRAY, SIMON (1936 -)
Gray's preoccupations with the dilemmas of English middle-class life can as well be found in this, his only novel, as in his plays.
Little Portia (1967)
[GB1074] Faber pbk **£4.95**

GREEN, HENRY (1905 - 1973)
Born Henry Vincent Yorke, Green wrote deft social comedies and was a considerable literary stylist. Admired by Auden and Updike among others, his novels are notable for their intricacy of design, use of dialogue and vernacular speech.
Back (1946)
[GB1075] Chatto hbk **£10.95**
Caught (1943)
[GB1076] Chatto hbk **£10.95**
Concluding (1948)
[GB1077] Chatto hbk **£10.95**
Loving/Living/Party Going (1945/29/39)
Living is Green's vivid re-creation of life on a Birmingham factory floor; *Loving*, perhaps his most admired work, is a portrait of life above and below stairs in an Irish country house during the war. Introduced by John Updike.
[GB1078] Picador pbk **£4.95**
Nothing/Doting/Blindness (1950/52/26)
The first two novels are written almost entirely in dialogue, Green's particular skill. *Blindness*, his first novel, was published while he was still a student.
[GB1079] Picador pbk **£2.95**
Pack My Bag (1940)
His autobiography.
[GB1080] Oxford pbk **£5.95**

GREENE, GRAHAM (1904 -)
Considered by many to be the greatest living English novelist, Greene enjoys the rare combination of critical acclaim and wide popular success. He spent much of his early life working as a journalist, and travelling widely, factors reflected in his novels' economy and frequently exotic locations. Much of his fiction operates within the conventions of the thriller, but Greene's exceptional flair for narrative and his persistent preoccupation with moral dilemmas make him at once an immediately accessible and deeply serious writer. (The Bodley Head hardbacks are the Collected Editions, many with specially written prefaces).
A Burnt Out Case (1961)
[GB1081] Bodley hbk **£12.95**
[GB1082] Penguin pbk **£2.95**
A Gun for Sale (1936)
A thriller, and a remarkable dissection of the criminal mind.
[GB1083] Bodley hbk **£12.95**
[GB1084] Penguin pbk **£2.99**

A Sense of Reality (Stories, 1963)
[GB1085] Penguin pbk **£2.25**
Author's Choice
Four novels: *The Power and the Glory*; *The Quiet American*; *Travels with My Aunt* and *The Honorary Consul*.
[GB1087] Penguin pbk **£5.95**
Brighton Rock (1938)
Set in the seedy Brighton underworld, this psychological thriller introduces the callous juvenile gangster Pinkie, who marries a witness to one of his murders.
[GB1088] Bodley hbk **£12.95**
[GB1089] Penguin pbk **£2.99**
Collected Essays (1969)
[GB1090] Bodley hbk **£12.95**
[GB1091] Penguin pbk **£5.99**
Collected Plays
[GB1092] Penguin pbk **£5.99**
Collected Short Stories
[GB1093] Penguin pbk **£4.99**
Collected Stories (1972)
[GB1094] Bodley hbk **£12.95**
Dr Fischer of Geneva, or, The Bomb Party (1980)
Memorable novella in which an eccentric millionaire forces his dinner guests to risk their lives in order to satisfy their greed.
[GB1095] Bodley hbk **£9.95**
[GB1096] Penguin pbk **£2.50**
England Made Me (1935)
Early stream-of-consciousness novel.
[GB1097] Bodley hbk **£12.95**
[GB1098] Penguin pbk **£2.99**
It's a Battlefield (1934)
[GB1102] Bodley hbk **£12.95**
[GB1103] Penguin pbk **£2.99**
Loser Takes All (1955)
[GB1106] Penguin pbk **£2.50**
May We Borrow Your Husband?
(Stories, 1967)
[GB1107] Penguin pbk **£2.50**
Monsignor Quixote (1981)
One of Greene's most delightful and amusing novels, following the travels of a Catholic priest and a Marxist mayor around Spain.
[GB1108] Bodley hbk **£12.95**
[GB1109] Penguin pbk **£2.99**
Our Man in Havana (1958)
[GB1110] Bodley hbk **£12.95**
[GB1111] Penguin pbk **£2.99**
Stamboul Train (1932)
Greene's first commercial success, an entertaining thriller set on an Ostend-Constantinople train.
[GB1112] Bodley hbk **£12.95**
[GB1113] Penguin pbk **£2.99**
The Captain and the Enemy (1988)
His latest work is a short, almost fable-like tale, notable for an attractively eccentric central character, and final betrayal.
[GB1114] Reinhardt hbk **£10.95**
[GB1115] Penguin pbk **£3.50** .
The Comedians (1966)
[GB1116] Bodley hbk **£12.95**
[GB1117] Penguin pbk **£2.99**
The Confidential Agent (1939)
An extremely successful thriller with a central character - a former lecturer in Romance languages on a mission in England for a troubled continental government - whose inner conflicts are as interesting as the swiftly-paced plot.
[GB1118] Bodley hbk **£12.95**
[GB1119] Penguin pbk **£2.99**
The End of the Affair (1951)
Brilliant account of a semi-mystical adulterous love affair set in London during the Blitz. One of his best novels, and certainly his most romantic.
[GB1120] Bodley hbk **£12.95**
[GB1121] Penguin pbk **£2.99**

The Heart of the Matter (1948)
Set in Africa, the story of Harry Scobie, deputy police commissioner and would-be suicide, is one of Greene's most admired novels.
[GB1122] Bodley hbk **£12.95**
[GB1123] Penguin pbk **£2.99**
The Honorary Consul (1973)
[GB1124] Bodley hbk **£12.95**
[GB1125] Penguin pbk **£2.99**
The Human Factor (1978)
A novel about the Secret Service, this thriller of espionage and intrigue is centred around a love story.
[GB1126] Bodley hbk **£12.95**
[GB1127] Penguin pbk **£2.99**
The Lawless Roads (Non fiction, 1939)
Greene went to Mexico in 1938 to report on the religious persecution there, out of which came both this book and *The Power and the Glory*.
[GB1128] Bodley hbk **£12.95**
[GB1129] Penguin pbk **£3.95**
The Man Within (1929)
His first novel, a historical thriller.
[GB1130] Bodley hbk **£12.95**
[GB1131] Penguin pbk **£2.99**
The Ministry of Fear (1943)
[GB1132] Bodley hbk **£12.95**
[GB1133] Penguin pbk **£2.99**
The Power and the Glory (1940)
Perhaps Greene's most famous novel. Set in Mexico, it combines elements of a pacy thriller with an exploration of the spiritual dilemmas of a burnt-out, boozy Catholic priest.
[GB1134] Bodley hbk **£12.95**
[GB1135] Penguin pbk **£2.99**
The Quiet American (1955)
Set in Vietnam, this is a lyrical and elegiac picture of a country on the verge of terrible mutilation by war. Certainly one of Greene's finest works.
[GB1136] Bodley hbk **£12.95**
[GB1137] Penguin pbk **£2.99**
The Tenth Man (1985)
Rediscovered film script from the 1950s.
[GB1138] Bodley hbk **£8.95**
[GB1139] Penguin pbk **£2.50**
The Third Man/Fallen Idol (1950)
[GB1140] Penguin pbk **£2.50**
The Third Man/Loser Takes All (1950)
[GB1141] Bodley hbk **£12.95**
Travels with My Aunt (1969)
[GB1142] Bodley hbk **£12.95**
[GB1143] Penguin pbk **£3.50**
Twenty-One Stories (1954)
[GB1144] Penguin pbk **£2.99**

GREENWOOD, WALTER (1903 - 1974)
A Salford novelist who was born of radical working-class parents.
Love on the Dole (1933)
Classic depiction of a northern town in the midst of the 1930s Depression.
[GB1146] Penguin pbk **£3.95**

GREGORY, PHILIPPA
Wideacre (1987)
A big bestseller from a new author. It concerns one woman's determined attempt to retain possession of her ancestral home, despite having no rights of inheritance as a woman in the 18th century.
[GB1147] Penguin pbk **£3.99**

GRIFFITHS, PAUL
Myself and Marco Polo (1989) **NEW**
This first novel from *The Times* art critic is an unusual and kaleidoscopic retelling of Polo's voyage from Venice to Peking, as told by the scribe who records and embellishes the great traveller's words. This is a book which should be read alongside Calvino's *Invisible Cities*.
[GB1150] Chatto hbk **£11.95**

GUNN, NEIL (Scottish, 1891 - 1973)
A prolific output over 30 years was followed by two decades in which Gunn, disappointed by critics who misunderstood the deep symbolism of his writing, wrote nothing new. Today much of his work is back in print and attracts a large following. For Gunn, the Highlands' enduring features are Gaelic and pre-commercial, and he manages to convey this with a sensitivity which is more potent than mere nostalgia.
Highland River (1937)
His renowned evocation of boyhood.
[GB1151] Arrow pbk **£1.95**
Morning Tide (1930)
[GB1152] Souvenir pbk **£3.95**
Second Sight (1940)
[GB1153] R Drew pbk **£3.95**
Selected Letters
[GB1154] Polygon hbk **£12.95**
The Atom of Delight (1956)
Autobiographical work giving insights into his life philosophies and the recurrent themes of his fiction.
[GB1155] Polygon pbk **£4.95**
The Lost Chart (1949)
[GB1156] R Drew pbk **£3.95**
The Lost Glen (1932)
[GB1157] R Drew pbk **£3.95**
The Other Landscape (1954)
[GB1158] R Drew pbk **£3.95**
The Silver Bough (1948)
[GB1159] R Drew pbk **£3.95**
The Silver Darlings (1941)
Perhaps his most popular work, this is an epic evocation of the hard lives of the herring fishers of Caithness and Sunderland, displaced by the clearances and forced to make the sea their livelihood.
[GB1160] Faber pbk **£4.95**
Whisky and Scotland (1935)
His appraisal of an intimate relationship.
[GB1161] Souvenir hbk **£6.95**

HAAN, TOM DE
Child of Good Fortune **NEW**
From the author of the widely praised *A Mirror for Princes*, another complex allegorical fantasy set in the imaginary land of Brychmachrye.
[GB1170] Cape hbk **£11.95**

HALL, RADCLYFFE (1883 - 1943)
Powerful and strident writer, who caused a scandal in her day for the then controversial nature of her (lesbian) subject matter. She is now buried in the mausoleum at Highgate cemetery.
A Saturday Life (1925)
[GB1171] Virago pbk **£4.50**
Adam's Breed (1926)
[GB1172] Virago pbk **£4.95**
The Unlit Lamp (1924)
[GB1173] Virago pbk **£4.50**
The Well of Loneliness (1928)
Originally banned for its depiction of lesbianism, it was championed by Forster and Woolf, amongst others, and finally republished in 1949.
[GB1174] Hutchinson hbk **£11.95**
[GB1175] Virago pbk **£4.50**

HAMILTON, IAN (ED)
Soho Square II **NEW**
The second annual Bloomsbury anthology draws together a wide range of styles and forms. Above all else, it seeks to explore lesser-known writers.
[GB1176] Bloomsbury pbk **£9.95**

HAMILTON, PATRICK (1904 - 1962)
Hamilton wrote about the twilight side of urban life, depicting with great compassion and humour a range of low life characters who inhabit, in J.B. Priestley's words, 'a kind of No-Man's-Land of shabby hotels, dingy boarding-houses and all those saloon bars where the homeless can meet'.

Hangover Square (1941)
An atmospheric thriller set in Earls Court.
[GB1178] Penguin pbk **£3.95**
Mr Stimpson and Mr Gorse (1953)
The book upon which the TV series *The Charmer* was based.
[GB1179] Penguin pbk **£2.95**
Slaves of Solitude (1947)
[GB1180] Oxford pbk **£3.95**
The West Pier (1951)
[GB1182] Penguin pbk **£3.95**
Twenty Thousand Streets Under the Sky (1935)
A trilogy of Hamilton's early novels, comprising *The Midnight Bell*, *The Siege of Pleasure* and *The Plains of Cement*.
[GB1183] Hogarth pbk **£5.95**

HAMPSON, JOHN
Saturday Night at the Greyhound (1931)
A story of the darker undercurrents connecting a group of labourers drinking the night away at a remote pub.
[GB1184] Hogarth pbk **£3.95**

HANDL, IRENE (1908 - 1987)
Although better known as an actress, these eccentric and exuberant novels were recently republished with great success.
The Gold Tip Pfitzer (1973)
[GB1185] Fontana pbk **£3.50**
The Sioux (1965)
[GB1186] Fontana pbk **£3.95**

HARDING, ALISON
Also Georgiana (1986)
Deftly constructed story of a young illegitimate Victorian woman who discovers her own history through some of her mother's letters.
[GB1187] Grafton pbk **£3.95**

HARRIS, HELEN
Angel Cake (1987)
This novel concerns the developments which take place when a young woman invites herself into the life of an elderly and retired actress.
[GB1188] Futura pbk **£3.99**

HARRIS, MARTYN
Do it Again **NEW**
Millionaire socialist Alec Smith is tired of London, life, the eighties. But having an affair doesn't help…
[GB1189] Viking hbk **£11.95**

HARTLEY, L.P. (1895 - 1972)
Highly regarded novelist, who at his best stands comparison with Henry James. His talent matured late: *The Shrimp and the Anemone* (part of the *Eustace and Hilda* trilogy), his first significant novel, was not published until 1944. Childhood and the legacy it bequeathes on adult life is a recurrent theme in his work.
Eustace and Hilda Trilogy (1947)
A beautifully realized account of a brother and sister, strong-minded Hilda and impressionable Eustace, who are doomed to destroy each other.
[GB1190] Faber pbk **£7.50**
Facial Justice (1940)
A dystopian society emerges after World War III, based on a collective sense of guilt. Within this setting, a woman begins her struggle to reassert the rights of the individual.
[GB1191] Oxford pbk **£3.95**
The Go-Between (1953)
His most famous novel, in which an old man recalls a summer holiday in 1900, and the way in which it shaped the rest of his life.
[GB1192] H Hamilton hbk **£9.95**
[GB1193] Penguin pbk **£3.95**

The Hireling (1957)
[GB1194] Penguin pbk **£3.95**
The Travelling Grave (1951)
[GB1195] Dent pbk **£2.50**

HARVEY, ANDREW (1952 -)
Stylish and amusing travel writer and novelist who
was born in India and now lives in Paris. All his
writing has a strong autobiographical streak,
reflecting his homosexuality and his interest in
Buddhism.
Burning Houses (1986)
[GB1196] Fontana pbk **£3.50**
One Last Mirror (1985)
[GB1197] Cape hbk **£8.95**
The Web (1985)
[GB1198] Cape hbk **£11.95**

HAY, JAMES MACDOUGALL
(Scottish, 1881 - 1919)
Like George Douglas Brown's, *House with the
Green Shutters*, Hay's novel is a grim portrait
of power struggles and revenge in a small fishing
village in Argyll. Himself a minister, Hay believed
that capitalistic materialism was a vehicle of
human evil.
Gillespie (1914)
[GB1200] Canongate pbk **£4.95**

HEALY, DERMOT (Irish, 1947 -)
Banished Misfortune (Stories)
[GB1201] Allison & B pbk **£2.95**
Fighting With Shadows
This is a tragi-comic novel dealing with a family
caught between the violence of the conflict in the
North and its shadow in the South.
[GB1202] Allison & B pbk **£3.95**

HEMINGWAY, MAGGIE
The Bridge (1986)
[GB1204] Pan pbk **£2.95**
Stop House Blues (1988)
A dense and well-written novel charting the spiritual
journey of the boy Robert through situations of which
he can make little sense.
[GB2147] Penguin pbk **£3.99**

HENDRY, J.F. (Scottish, 1912 - 1986)
A central figure of the 1940s 'New Apocalypse'
movement, Hendry's novel is a portrait of a young
man's awakening, which echoes James Joyce's
Portrait of the Artist as a Young Man.
Fernai Brai
[GB1205] Polygon pbk **£3.95**

HEPPENSTALL, RAYNER (1911 - 1985)
Neglected experimental novelist, known as the
'master eccentric' for his sometimes perverse literary
pronouncements; one of the few English writers to
assimilate the aims of the French 'nouveau roman'
movement, his best work - *Two Moons* - is complex,
but rewarding.
Greater Infortune (1960)
[GB1206] P Owen pbk **£5.50**
The Blaze of Noon
[GB1207] Allison & B pbk **£2.50**
The Pier
[GB1208] Allison & B pbk **£3.95**
The Woodshed (1960)
[GB1209] Calder pbk **£3.95**
Two Moons
[GB1210] Allison & B pbk **£2.95**

HERBERT, A.P. (1890 - 1971)
The Secret Battle (1919)
Although well known as a comic writer, this is a
moving account of the horrors of war based upon his
own experiences.
[GB1211] Oxford pbk **£3.95**

HIGGINS, AIDAN (Irish, 1927 -)
A novelist influenced by his experiences of living in
England and South Africa.
Asylum (Stories)
[GB1229] Calder pbk **£3.95**
Balcony of Europe
[GB1230] Calder pbk **£4.95**
Bornholm Night Ferry
[GB1231] Allison & B hbk **£9.95**
Langrishe, Go Down
[GB1232] Grafton pbk **£3.50**
Scenes from a Receding Past
[GB1233] Calder hbk **£6.95**

HILL, SUSAN (1942 -)
Hill's writing is firmly rooted in the traditions of
Dickens and Hardy, and like the latter has a powerful
sense of the symbolic potential of the English
landscape. Her sharp prose cuts through apparent
conventionality of character and narrative to reveal
underlying tensions, even madness, as seen in her war
novel *Strange Meeting* and the powerful drama of
conflict *I'm the King of the Castle*.
Albatross (1971)
[GB1234] Penguin pbk **£3.95**
Bird of Night (1972)
[GB1235] Penguin pbk **£3.99**
Bit of Singing and Dancing (1983)
[GB1236] Penguin pbk **£3.99**
Change for the Better (1969)
[GB1237] Penguin pbk **£3.99**
Gentlemen and Ladies (1968)
[GB1238] Penguin pbk **£3.99**
I'm the King of the Castle (1970)
[GB1239] Penguin pbk **£3.99**
In the Springtime of the Year (1974)
[GB1240] Penguin pbk **£3.99**
Strange Meeting (1971)
[GB1241] Penguin pbk **£3.99**
Woman in Black (1973)
A chilling ghost story which has recently been
dramatized.
[GB1242] Penguin pbk **£3.99**

HIND, ARCHIE (Scottish, 1928 -)
The Dear Green Place (1966)
'Proletarian romanticism' has been a heartfelt and
successful theme of much modern Scottish fiction; in
this novel, the idealistic hero works by day in a
Glasgow slaughterhouse and by night writing a novel.
[GB1243] Polygon pbk **£4.95**

HINES, BARRY (1939 -)
An author who engages the troubled existence of
modern urban communities with humour and
compassion. His work has been adapted successfully
to film, particularly *A Kestrel for a Knave*, the story
of a boy who finds fulfilment in his relationship with
a bird of prey.
Blinder (1966)
[GB1244] Penguin pbk **£2.99**
Kestrel for a Knave (1968)
[GB1245] M Joseph hbk **£9.95**
[GB1246] Penguin pbk **£2.50**
Looks and Smiles (1981)
[GB1247] Penguin pbk **£2.95**
The Gamekeeper (1975)
[GB1248] Penguin pbk **£2.99**
The Price of Coal (1979)
[GB1249] Penguin pbk **£2.50**

HOCKING, MARY (1921 -)
Acclaimed for her successful trilogy *Good
Daughters*, *Indifferent Heroes* and *Welcome
Strangers*, domestic novels which explore the lives of
the Fairley family from the 1930s to the aftermath of
World War II.
An Irrelevant Woman (1988)
[GB1254] Sphere pbk **£3.99**

Good Daughters (1984)
[GB1250] Sphere pbk **£3.95**
Indifferent Heroes (1985)
[GB1251] Sphere pbk **£3.95**
Welcome Strangers (1986)
[GB1252] Sphere pbk **£3.99**
A Particular Place **NEW**
The new vicar in a small West Country town meets
resistance and adversity everywhere he turns.
[GB1253] Chatto hbk **£12.95**

HOGAN, DESMOND (Irish, 1951 -)
Hogan is one of the most exciting writers to have
emerged from Ireland in recent years. His prose is
dense and lyrical, and his plots involve the haunting
use of myth and time shifts. His short stories are
particularly acclaimed, but his excellent novel, *A
Curious Street* is sadly out of print.
A New Shirt
[GB1259] Faber pbk **£3.95**
Lebanon Lodge (1988)
This haunting and melancholic collection of stories
concerns dispossession and disenchantment. The
subjects include Irish exiles in London and travelling
players on the fair greens of Ireland.
[GB1260] Faber pbk **£3.99**
The Ikon Maker (1979)
[GB1261] Pulsifer pbk **£3.95**
The Mourning Thief & Other Stories
An excellent selection of twelve stories taken from his
first two collections *The Children of Lir* and *The
Diamonds at the Bottom of the Sea*.
[GB1262] Faber pbk **£4.95**

HOLDEN, URSULA
Noted for her strong characterization, Holden
combines humour with powerful undercurrents of
horror.
Bubble Garden (1988)
The trilogy that began with *Tin Toys* and *Unicorn
Sisters* is brought to a disturbing conclusion.
[GB1263] Methuen hbk **£10.95**
Cloud Catchers (1979)
[GB1264] Methuen pbk **£3.50**
Eric's Choice (1942)
[GB1265] Methuen pbk **£3.50**
Tin Toys
[GB1266] Methuen pbk **£3.95**
Unicorn Sisters (1988)
[GB1267] Methuen hbk **£9.95**

HOLLINGHURST, ALAN
Deputy Editor of the *TLS*, Hollinghurst is also a poet.
The Swimming Pool Library (1988)
Vivid and widely acclaimed portrayal of a
homosexual world which no longer exists, centred on
the wordly lifestyle of a young gay aristocrat and his
meeting with an elderly lord in search of a biographer
and protégé.
[GB1268] Penguin pbk **£3.99**

HOLT, VICTORIA
Prolific and enormously successful author of
historical romances, Holt also writes under the names
Jean Plaidy and Philippa Carr. Her new novel tells the
story of a woman's plunge into bizarre and dangerous
adventure, after a quiet and protected life in her
father's Bloomsbury home. A full list of her other
works is available on request.
The Captive **NEW**
[GB1284] Collins hbk **£11.95**

HOLTBY, WINIFRED (1989 - 1935)
Friend and companion of Vera Brittain, and like her a
committed and vocal feminist, Holtby was a prolific
writer, whose achievement is commemorated in
Brittain's *Testament of Friendship*.
Anderby Wold (1923)
[GB1286] Virago pbk **£4.50**

Crowded Street (1924)
[GB1287] Virago pbk **£4.50**
Land of Green Ginger (1927)
[GB1288] Virago pbk **£4.50**
Mandoa, Mandoa! (1923)
[GB1289] Virago pbk **£4.50**
Poor Caroline (1931)
[GB1290] Virago pbk **£4.50**
South Riding (1936)
Holtby's best novel is a realistic portrayal of life in her native Yorkshire, centred around its heroine, a powerfully-minded headmistress.
[GB1291] Collins hbk **£10.95**
[GB1292] Virago pbk **£4.50**
[GB1293] Fontana pbk **£2.95**

HOOD, STUART (Scottish, 1915 -)
Hood was head of the BBC World Sertvice, before establishing himself as a freelance scriptwriter and film producer; in addition to his novels, he is a distinguished translator from various European languages. His new work echoes the themes of earlier novels, in its mixing of the larger patterns of modern history with the individual lives of his characters.
A Storm from Paradise (1985)
[GB1294] Grafton pbk **£3.95**
Brutal Heart `NEW`
A story of conflicting loyalties during the political turmoil of 1968.
[GB1295] Carcanet hbk **£12.95**
The Upper Hand (1987)
[GB1296] Carcanet hbk **£10.95**

HORWOOD, WILLIAM
Acclaimed for his stories of animal civilizations.
Callanish
[GB1297] Penguin pbk **£2.50**
Duncton Quest (1988)
[GB1298] Arrow pbk **£3.99**
Duncton Wood
[GB1299] Arrow pbk **£3.50**
Skallagrigg
[GB1300] Penguin pbk **£4.50**
Stonor Eagles
[GB1301] Arrow pbk **£3.50**

HOWARD, ELIZABETH JANE
Well respected novelist who centres upon the domestic and public lives of educated modern women. She has been praised for her accurate portrayal of the vicissitudes of love and marriage.
After Julius (1965)
[GB1302] Penguin pbk **£2.95**
Beautiful Visit (1950)
[GB1303] Penguin pbk **£3.95**
Getting it Right (1982)
[GB1304] Penguin pbk **£3.50**
Long View (1956)
[GB1305] Penguin pbk **£3.50**
Mr Wrong (1975)
[GB1306] Penguin pbk **£2.95**
Odd Girl Out (1972)
[GB1307] Penguin pbk **£3.95**
Sea Change (1959)
[GB1308] Penguin pbk **£3.95**
Something in Disguise (1969)
[GB1309] Penguin pbk **£2.95**

HOWATCH, SUSAN (1940 -)
English writer of panoramic and detailed historical sagas (of which the most popular *Penmarric* and *Cashelmara* are included here) and of lighter contemporary suspense novels.
Cashelmara
[GB1312] Penguin pbk **£4.50**
Glamorous Powers
[GB1315] Fontana pbk **£3.95**
Penmarric
[GB1317] Penguin pbk **£4.99**

The Rich Are Different
[GB1319] Penguin pbk **£4.50**
Ultimate Prizes `NEW`
A very respectable Archdeacon in the Church of England, married with family and a successful career, one day meets an attractive woman and suddenly finds himself entangled in the dangers of adultery, hypocrisy and obsession.
[GB1320] Collins hbk **£12.95**

HUGHES, DAVID (1930 -)
An award-winning writer, widely acclaimed for the imaginative fictional strategies he has adopted in recent novels.
But for Bunter (1985)
Based on the infamous cartoon character.
[GB1323] Grafton pbk **£3.50**
Imperial German Dinner Service (1983)
Highly entertaining novel which depicts life in England in 1914 and tells of a race to find the Kaiser's thousand-piece dinner service.
[GB1324] Grafton pbk **£2.95**
The Pork Butcher (1984)
Short, tense, award-winning novel about wartime France.
[GB1325] Penguin pbk **£3.50**

HUGHES, GLYN (1935 -)
A writer of historical fiction, often set in the North of England. He is both lyrical and hard-edged and creates a distinctive 'period' feel.
The Hawthorn Goddess (1984)
[GB1326] Penguin pbk **£3.95**
The Rape of the Rose (1987)
[GB1327] Penguin pbk **£4.99**

HUGHES, RICHARD (1900 - 1976)
A singular and highly imaginative writer who travelled widely before the war, notably in the West Indies. He began an ambitious sequence called *The Human Predicament* in 1961, which remained unfinished at his death. Hughes was to describe it as *"an historical novel of my own times"*.
A High Wind in Jamaica (1929)
A nightmarish classic in which children are kidnapped by pirates.
[GB1329] Chatto hbk **£9.95**
Fox in the Attic (1961)
The first volume of *The Human Predicament*, in which a naïve young Welshman travels to the Germany of the post-war Weimar Republic and meets a range of historical personages, including Hitler and Goering.
[GB1330] Chatto hbk **£8.95**
The Wooden Shepherdess (1973)
The sequel to the above, this contains a famous account of 'The Night of the Long Knives', depicting the Nazis' rise to power in the Berlin of the 1930s.
[GB1328] Grafton pbk **£2.50**

HUMPHREYS, EMYR (1930 -)
Contemporary Welsh novelist, most of Humphreys' works are set in Wales in the 1920s and 30s.
Absolute Hero (1986)
[GB1332] Sphere pbk **£2.99**
Best of Friends (1978)
[GB1333] Sphere pbk **£3.50**
Flesh and Blood (1974)
[GB1334] Sphere pbk **£3.50**
Jones (1984)
[GB1335] Dent hbk **£8.95**
Man's Estate
[GB1336] Dent pbk **£3.95**
Open Secrets
[GB1337] Dent pbk **£3.95**
Outside the House of Baal
[GB1338] Dent pbk **£4.95**
Salt of the Earth (1985)
[GB1339] Sphere pbk **£2.95**

HUNTINGTON, GLADYS
Madam Solario (1956)
A novel set in Edwardian England and published anonymously. The author died shortly afterwards and has only recently been identified.
[GB1340] Penguin pbk **£3.95**

HUTCHINSON, R.C. (1907 - 1975)
Author of historical novels, often tragic in tone, most of which are sadly out of print. He had a gift for writing convincing descriptions of foreign locations, which he had never visited: an under-rated figure.
Collected Stories
[GB1341] Carcanet hbk **£8.95**
Testament (1938)
Set in Russia at the time of the October Revolution.
[GB1342] Duckworth hbk **£12.95**

HUXLEY, ALDOUS (1894 - 1963)
His early writing consists of elegant, fashionable and satirical novels, sometimes glib in their detachment. In the years following *Brave New World*, he became more seriously fixated upon the notion that despair was humanity's perpetual condition. At his best he was a novelist of ideas, adept at cataloguing the difficulties of faith or vision in an increasingly secular age, and a prose stylist of great accomplishment, who never lost his Waugh-like gift for satire.
After Many a Summer (1939)
[GB1343] Grafton pbk **£2.95**
Antic Hay (1923)
Together with *Chrome Yellow*, the major work of Huxley's early period. Like Eliot's *Waste Land*, it is a pessimistic portrayal of the post-war world, written out of some personal despair.
[GB1344] Grafton pbk **£2.95**
Ape and Essence (1948)
[GB1345] Grafton pbk **£1.95**
Brave New World (1932)
Infamous prophetic novel about genetic engineering.
[GB1346] Grafton pbk **£2.50**
Brave New World Revisited (Non fiction, 1958)
[GB1347] Grafton pbk **£2.50**
Brave New World/Brave New World Revisited
[GB1348] Chatto hbk **£12.95**
Brief Candles
[GB1349] Grafton pbk **£1.95**
Chrome Yellow (1921)
[GB1350] Chatto hbk **£9.95**
[GB1351] Grafton pbk **£1.95**
Ends and Means
[GB1352] Chatto hbk **£8.95**
Eyeless in Gaza
His last English novel is another insight into personal and public depair; soon after its publication he moved to California.
[GB1353] Chatto hbk **£9.95**
Genius and the Goddess
[GB1354] Grafton pbk **£2.50**
Giaconda Smile and Other Stories (1922)
[GB1355] Grafton pbk **£2.95**
Grey Eminence
[GB1356] Grafton pbk **£1.95**
Island (1962)
[GB1357] Chatto hbk **£9.95**
[GB1358] Grafton pbk **£2.95**
Music at Night (1931)
[GB1359] Grafton pbk **£2.50**
The Perennial Philosophy (Non fiction, 1946)
[GB1361] Grafton pbk **£2.95**
Point Counter Point (1928)
[GB1362] Grafton pbk **£2.95**
Texts and Pretexts
[GB1363] Grafton pbk **£2.95**
The Devils of Loudon (Non fiction, 1952)
[GB1364] Grafton pbk **£1.95**

The Doors of Perception/Heaven and Hell (Non fiction, 1954/56)
Two works resulting from his experimentation with altered states of consciousness, and use of mescalin.
[GB1365] Grafton pbk **£2.50**
The Human Situation
[GB1366] Grafton pbk **£1.95**
Those Barren Lives
[GB1367] Grafton pbk **£1.95**
Time Must Have a Stop
[GB1368] Grafton pbk **£2.50**

ILLIS, MARK
A Chinese Summer
[GB1368A] Bloomsbury pbk **£4.99**
The Alchemist   `NEW`
A subtle and richly-layered tale of a child's troublesome quest for truth.
[GB1369] Bloomsbury hbk **£12.95**

IRWIN, ROBERT (1946 -)
Irwin is a curious writer whose exoticism and eccentricity has been highly praised of late.
An Arabian Nightmare (1987)
A story told with relentless energy, comprising a veritable bombardment of philosophies and fantastic visions, set in 15th century Cairo.
[GB1375] Penguin pbk **£3.95**
Limits of Vision (1986)
[GB1376] Penguin pbk **£2.95**
Mysteries of Algiers (1988)
A uniquely unpredictable political thriller set in the final months of French rule in Algeria.
[GB1377] Viking hbk **£11.95**

ISHERWOOD, CHRISTOPHER (1904 - 1986)
His friendship with W.H. Auden and experiences of living in Berlin in the 1930s formed the basis of his most famous book *Goodbye to Berlin*, and its well-known 'I am a Camera' technique of reportage. He emigrated to the United States in 1939 and lived in California for the rest of his life, developing an interest in Indian philosophy and religion, as is described in his volumes of autobiography.
A Single Man (1964)
The best of Isherwood's later works, this is a frank and movingly humorous story of a homosexual English academic living alone in California after the death of his lover.
[GB1379] Methuen pbk **£3.50**
All the Conspirators (1928)
[GB1380] Methuen pbk **£2.95**
Down There on a Visit (1962)
[GB1382] Methuen pbk **£3.50**
Exhumations (Stories/articles)
[GB1384] Methuen pbk **£4.95**
Goodbye to Berlin (1939)
[GB1385] Methuen pbk **£3.99**
Goodbye to Berlin & Mr Norris Changes Trains
[GB1386] Chatto hbk **£12.95**
Lions and Shadows (1938)
[GB1387] Methuen hbk **£9.95**
Meeting By the River (1967)
[GB1389] Methuen pbk **£2.95**
Mr Norris Changes Trains (1935)
Affecting picture of pre-Hitler Germany: a society sliding towards dissolution, centred on a delightful flabby, rogue.
[GB1390] Methuen pbk **£3.50**
Prater Violet (1946)
[GB1392] Methuen pbk **£2.50**
The Memorial (1932)
Held by many to be one of Isherwood's best books, this tells of two generations struggling to escape the shadow of the First World War.
[GB1393] Methuen pbk **£3.95**
World in the Evening (1954)
[GB1395] Methuen pbk **£3.50**

ISHIGURO, KAZUO (1954 -)
The subtlety of Ishiguro's reflections on the nature of the artist's profession, and the delicate and suggestive poise of his descriptions are unique in contemporary fiction. His first two novels are set in Japan, and his highly individual view of the social intercourse of that country is so plausible that it has been assumed he is describing a society he knows well, the fact that Ishiguro has lived in the UK since the age of six being ignored. In his new novel he has broken new ground, writing a convincing first-person narrative around that most English of characters, the butler.
An Artist of the Floating World (1986)
Whitbread Award winner/Booker Prize shortlisted. It is a tale woven around the life of a painter in the process of reviewing his life, and most particularly his role as a war artist.
[GB1396] Faber hbk **£8.95**
[GB1397] Faber pbk **£3.95**
A Pale View of Hills (1982)
[GB1398] Faber hbk **£9.95**
[GB1399] Penguin pbk **£3.95**
The Remains of the Day (1989)   `NEW`
Stevens, a butler in the twilight of his career, embarks on a rare motoring holiday around the West Country. As he reflects back on his life he comes to some startling and moving conclusions about society, his role within it, and about love This is a brilliantly controlled narrative, in which the central character's comic lack of self-knowledge masks a sub-text of great depth and gravity.
[GB1400] Faber hbk **£10.95**

JACOBSON, DAN (1929 -)
Born in Johannesburg, Jacobson has lived in Britain for more than 30 years. His fiction reveals both his country of origin - in the early stories such as *The Trap* - and his Jewish religion: *The Rape of Tamar* adapts Old Testament material in a distinctly modern way.
Her Story (1987)
A profound and impressive novel set in the future, where a woman's life is reconstructed from an old manuscript.
[GB1420] Fontana pbk **£3.50**
Price of Diamonds (1956)
[GB1402] Deutsch pbk **£3.95**
The Rape of Tamar (1970)
[GB1403] Deutsch pbk **£3.95**
The Trap & A Dance in the Sun (1955/56)
[GB1404] Oxford pbk **£3.95**

JACOBSON, HOWARD (1942 -)
Australian-born Jewish novelist who satirizes English literature, contemporary sexual mores, Antipodean oafishness, and everything else in sight.
Coming from Behind (1983)
[GB1405] Transworld pbk **£3.95**
Peeping Tom
[GB1406] Transworld pbk **£3.95**
Redback
[GB1407] Transworld pbk **£3.95**

JAMESON, STORM (1891 - 1986)
Jameson is best-known for her two trilogies which depict, from the mid-19th century through to the 1920s, the fortunes of a Yorkshire family, which, like Jameson's own, derived their wealth from ship-building; only one is currently available - it consists of *Company Parade*, *Love in Winter* and *None Turn Back*.
Company Parade (1934)
[GB1416] Virago pbk **£5.50**
Love in Winter (1935)
[GB1417] Virago pbk **£5.50**
None Turn Back (1936)
[GB1418] Virago pbk **£5.50**
Women Against Men (Stories, 1933)
[GB1419] Virago pbk **£3.95**

Christopher Isherwood pictured with W.H. Auden, from *Camera Portraits*, National Portrait Gallery

JENKINS, ROBIN (Scottish, 1912 -)
A consistently fine writer, Jenkins is at last earning the recognition he deserves. He is best-known for the comic masterpiece *Fergus Lamont* and the early *The Cone-Gatherers*, which reflects his own experience as a conscientious objector during the War, during which period he worked in forestry.
Dust on the Paw (1961)
[GB1421] R Drew pbk **£3.95**
Fergus Lamont (1979)
[GB1422] Canongate pbk **£3.95**
Just Duffy (1988)
[GB1423] Canongate hbk **£10.95**
The Awakening of George Darrock (1985)
[GB1424] Penguin pbk **£3.95**
The Cone-Gatherers (1955)
[GB1425] Penguin pbk **£3.95**

JESSE, F. TENNYSON
Grand-niece of the poet Tennyson and a forceful novelist in her own right. *A Pin to See the Peepshow*, based on a real-life murder in the 1920s, is her best known novel.
A Pin to See the Peepshow (1924)
[GB1426] Virago pbk **£4.95**
Moonraker (1927)
[GB1427] Virago pbk **£3.50**
The Lacquer Lady (1929)
Fanny Morrow leaves her dull English school to return to Mandalay in the 1880s, the last years of the opulent, decaying Kingdom of Burma.
[GB1428] Virago pbk **£4.50**

JOHNSON, ALISON FINDLAY (Scottish)
Children of Disobedience   `NEW`
A love story set in a crofting community in the Outer Hebrides.
[GB1429] Deutsch hbk **£11.95**

JOHNSTON, JENNIFER (Irish, 1930 -)
All her novels are set in Ireland during different periods of this century, and many continue the tradition of the 'Big House' novel, examining the decline of the Protestant gentry. They are rendered in an elegant and discerning prose style that has led to her present reputation as one of Ireland's finest writers.
Captains and the Kings (1972)
Her first novel deals with the relationship between an old man, the relic of a past age, and a young boy.
[GB1432] Fontana pbk **£2.50**

Fool's Sanctuary (1979)
[GB1434] Penguin pbk **£3.50**
Gates (1985)
[GB1435] H Hamilton hbk **£8.50**
How Many Miles to Babylon? (1974)
[GB1437] Penguin pbk **£3.99**
Old Jest (1984)
Winner of the Whitbread Award in 1979.
[GB1439] Penguin pbk **£3.99**
Shadows On Our Skin (1977)
When Joe Logan's elder brother returns home to
Derry with a gun in his pocket, Joe's childhood is
suddenly over. Although Johnston lives in Northern
Ireland, it is only in this novel that she examines the
state of the North, looking at the effect of the
Troubles on a 'normal' family.
[GB1441] Fontana pbk **£2.95**
The Christmas Tree (1981)
Constance sits and waits for the father of her child to
arrive home longing to bring the situation to a head
on her own terms.
[GB1442] H Hamilton hbk **£8.50**
The Railway Station Man (1986)
[GB1444] Penguin pbk **£3.99**

JORDAN, NEIL (Irish, 1950 -)
Successful director of films acclaimed for their
singular visual flair, including *Angel*, *The Company
of Wolves* and *Mona Lisa*.
Dream of a Beast
[GB1448] Chatto pbk **£2.95**
Night in Tunisia (stories)
[GB1449] Chatto pbk **£3.95**

JOYCE, JAMES (Irish, 1882 - 1941)
Among this century's most influential writers of
fiction, Joyce's comedy and sense of life is too often
buried under scholarly exegesis. His first two books -
the most accessible works - *Dubliners* and *A
Portrait of the Artist*, remain vivid depictions of turn-
of-the-century Dublin, the city he recreated with such
extraordinary detail in *Ulysses*. All of Joyce's works
have a vigour and demonstrate an impeccable ear for
the music of speech. Richard Ellmann's
comprehensive biography is recommended as
essential background to understanding Joyce's work.
**A Portrait of the Artist as a
Young Man** (1916)
Exuberant and impressionistic autobiographical first
novel about Joyce's Catholic upbringing in Dublin,
instantly recognized as a classic on publication.
[GB1450] Cape hbk **£10.95**
[GB1451] Grafton pbk **£3.95**
Dubliners (1914)
Short stories, including the majestic 'The Dead'.
[GB1452] Cape hbk **£10.95**
[GB1453] Grafton pbk **£3.99**
Exiles (Play, 1918)
[GB1454] Grafton pbk **£2.95**
Finnegan's Wake (1939)
Joyce's last experimental novel, taking 17 years to
write and now more often studied than read, due to its
fearsome complexity. Its use of language, however, is
highly poetic, and wholly unique in effect.
[GB1455] Faber pbk **£7.50**
Finnegan's Wake (Abridged)
Edited by Anthony Burgess.
[GB1456] Faber pbk **£4.95**
Giacomo Joyce
Delightful, word-perfect piece of fictionalized
autobiography set in Trieste. With facsimile pages
and an introduction by Richard Ellmann.
[GB1457] Faber pbk **£2.95**
Stephen Hero (1944)
Early draft of *A Portrait of the Artist as a Young
Man* reveals much about the development of that
work.
[GB1458] Cape hbk **£10.95**
[GB1459] Grafton pbk **£2.50**

The Essential James Joyce
Includes *Dubliners*, *A Portrait* and the play *Exiles*
with selections from *Ulysses* and *Finnegan's Wake*.
[GB1460] Grafton pbk **£3.99**
Ulysses (1922)
This new edition of the once-banned, now universally
celebrated masterpiece of experimental fiction,
corrects many textual errors, as well as including an
introduction by Richard Ellmann. Many of the
emendations have, however, given rise to a fierce
academic debate which has been raging for a year in
the *New York Review of Books*.
[GB1461] Bodley hbk **£18.00**
[GB1462] Penguin pbk **£7.99**

KAVANAGH, PATRICK (Irish, 1906 - 1967)
An acclaimed poet well known for his celebrations of
rural Ireland, Kavanagh was also an Inniskeen farmer
and shoemaker. His evocation of provincial Ireland
was never sentimental and he was sharply critical of
the stifling frustration of small communities.
Tarry Flynn (1948)
Tarry Flynn's responsibilities of family farm, poetic
inspiration and his own unyielding lust, are heavy....
[GB1464] Penguin pbk **£3.95**
The Green Fool (1938)
The Green Fool is Kavanagh's autobiography and,
like *Tarry Flynn* gives a delightful evocation of life
as it was lived in Ireland earlier this century
[GB1465] Penguin pbk **£3.99**

KAYE, M.M.
Brought up in India, Kaye's most accomplished work
is the romantic novel *The Far Pavilions*, a story of
clashing cultures set against the final years of the Raj.
The Far Pavilions
[GB1475] Penguin pbk **£5.95**

KEANE, MOLLY (Irish, 1905 -)
See also *M.J. Farrell*. These three novels marked
Keane's return to writing after a silence of twenty
years, and have been rapturously received.
Good Behaviour (1981)
This caused a publishing sensation, even though
Keane claimed she wrote it 'just for herself'. It is a
masterful and elegant black comedy about an
aristocratic Anglo-Irish family sinking into a state of
decaying grace.
[GB1479] Sphere pbk **£3.99**
Loving and Giving (1988)
Nicandra's marriage prospers, wavers, and crashes,
but by a brilliant, tragic twist, she becomes blissfully
happy… Another highly entertaining comic novel
from the irrepressible Keane.
[GB1480] Deutsch hbk **£10.95**
Time after Time (1983)
Into the lives of three sisters comes a beguiling cousin
from the past.
[GB1481] Sphere pbk **£3.95**

KEATES, JONATHAN
The Strangers' Gallery (1987)
Strong first novel, set in Italy in 1847, which sees an
Englishman reluctantly involved in a local imbroglio.
[GB1482] Sphere pbk **£3.99**

KELLY, MAEVE (Irish)
Florrie's Girls **NEW**
Florrie is Florence Nightingale, and her girls the
young women who have chosen nursing: some soon
realize that life can be good and bad.
[GB1483] M Joseph hbk **£11.95**
Necessary Treasons (1985)
Her most acclaimed work. Eve Gleeson joins the
Women's Movement in Limerick as a hobby, but it
becomes an issue of central importance in her life.
[GB1484] Methuen pbk **£3.95**
Resolution (1986)
[GB1485] Blackstaff P pbk **£4.95**

KELMAN, JAMES (Scottish, 1946 -)
Kelman is uncompromising in his realist style: *"I live
in Glasgow. This is what I write"*. Whether in his
short story miniatures or in the more expansive
proletarian stream-of-consciousness novels, his
articulation of the monotony and the greyness - and
humour and resilience - of working-class life is
unique.
A Chancer
[GB1486] Picador pbk **£4.50**
A Disaffection **NEW**
Another honest examination of culture and character
in which a teacher, suffering the disaffection of the
title, decides to change the way he lives. Acclaimed
as a modern masterpiece on its publication.
[GB1487] Secker hbk **£11.95**
Greyhound for Breakfast (Stories, 1987)
Acclaimed volume of bizarre and angry short stories.
[GB1488] Picador pbk **£3.95**
Not, Not While the Giro & Other Stories
[GB1489] Polygon pbk **£4.95**
The Busconductor Hines (1984)
[GB1490] Dent pbk **£2.95**

KENNEDY, MARGARET (1896 - 1967)
Author of a number of novels, as well as plays and a
biography of Jane Austen, Kennedy is remembered
today for *The Constant Nymph*, the story of a family
devoted to music.
The Constant Nymph (1924)
[GB1491] Virago pbk **£3.95**
The Ladies of Lyndon (1923)
[GB1492] Virago pbk **£4.50**
Troy Chimneys (1952)
[GB1493] Virago pbk **£4.50**

KESSON, JESSIE (Scottish, 1915 -)
Beautifully written, unsentimental novels of hard life
in the towns and country of the North East.
Another Time, Another Place (1983)
[GB1494] Hogarth pbk **£3.95**
Glitter of Mica
[GB1495] Hogarth pbk **£4.95**
The White Bird Passes (1985)
[GB1496] Hogarth pbk **£4.95**
Where the Apple Ripens (Stories, 1985)
[GB1497] Hogarth pbk **£4.95**

KIELY, BENEDICT (Irish)
A Letter to Peachtree (Stories, 1987)
'There are fine things all over this collection... he
should be preserved in aspic or crowned high king or
just bought in huge numbers.' *(Sunday Independent)*
[GB1498] Methuen pbk **£3.95**
Nothing Happens in Carmincross (1985)
[GB1499] Methuen pbk **£3.95**
Proxopera (1977)
[GB1500] Methuen pbk **£3.50**

KILWORTH, GARY **NEW**
In the Hollow of the Deep Sea Wave
A novel set on an island in the Indian Ocean. Its
central theme of responsibilities deferred is
augmented by the accompanying short stories.
[GB1501] Bodley hbk **£11.95**

KING, FRANCIS (1923 -)
A sensitive and delicate writer whose recent novels
have won wide praise for their evocation of chilling
and mysterious forces, most notably in *Acts of
Darkness*, set in India.
Acts of Darkness (1983)
[GB1502] Penguin pbk **£2.50**
Custom House (1986)
[GB1503] Hutchinson hbk **£8.95**
Domestic Animal (1970)
[GB1504] GMP pbk **£3.95**
Frozen Music (1987)
[GB1505] Arrow pbk **£2.50**

FICTION

Man on the Rock (1957)
[GB1506] GMP pbk **£3.95**
One is a Wanderer (Stories, 1985)
[GB1507] Hutchinson hbk **£9.95**
Punishments   NEW
A student travels to post-war Germany where he
struggles to understand a people coping with the
aftermath of horror.
[GB1508] H Hamilton hbk **£11.95**
The Firewalkers (1956)
[GB1509] GMP pbk **£3.95**
The Needle (1975)
[GB1510] Penguin pbk **£2.95**
Woman Who Was God (1988)
Tense and vivid account of a woman who travels to
Africa to investigate the circumstances which
surrounded her son's death and finds herself
exploring a strange cult of mother worship.
[GB1511] Hutchinson hbk **£10.95**

KIPLING, RUDYARD (1865 - 1936)
Kipling was born and brought up in India, which acts
as the setting for much of his work. A journalist by
trade, he based his books on meticulous research,
which gives his fiction a vivid authenticity. In 1907
he became the first English writer to be awarded the
Nobel Prize, reflecting the esteem with which he was
held during his own lifetime. After his death Kipling
went out of fashion, criticized for his flag-waving
jingoism - but more recently he has been reassessed
as a major writer whose psychological insights prove
a good deal more complex than at first they appear.
Choice of Prose
[GB1513] Faber pbk **£6.95**
Complete Supernatural Stories
[GB1514] WH Allen hbk **£12.95**
Day's Work (1898)
[GB1515] Penguin pbk **£3.50**
[GB1516] Oxford pbk **£2.95**
Debits and Credits (1926)
[GB1519] Penguin pbk **£2.95**
Diversity of Creatures (1917)
[GB1522] Penguin pbk **£2.95**
Just So Stories (1894)
First told to Kipling's children these incantory animal
fables reveal a poet's ear for the nuances of sound and
rhythm.
[GB1524] Penguin pbk **£1.95**
Kim (1901)
Generally considered to be his masterpiece. Like
Huckleberry Finn, this book is popular amongst
adults and children of all ages. Kim passes through a
series of adventures set against one of the more vivid
and authentic literary pictures of India, as Kipling
knew it a century ago.
[GB1525] Oxford pbk **£2.95**
[GB1526] Penguin pbk **£2.95**
Life's Handicap
[GB1527] Oxford pbk **£2.95**
[GB1528] Penguin pbk **£2.95**
Limits and Renewals
[GB1530] Penguin pbk **£2.95**
Man Who Would Be King
[GB1531] Oxford pbk **£2.95**
Plain Tales From the Hills
[GB1532] Oxford pbk **£2.95**
[GB1533] Penguin pbk **£2.95**
Puck of Pook's Hill
[GB1534] Penguin pbk **£2.50**
Selected Stories
[GB1536] Dent pbk **£3.95**
Short Stories: Vol 1
[GB1537] Penguin pbk **£4.95**
Short Stories: Vol 2
[GB1538] Penguin pbk **£1.95**
Soldiers Three
[GB1539] Surtees Soc pbk **£2.95**
Something of Myself
[GB1540] Penguin pbk **£3.95**

Stalky and Co.
[GB1541] Oxford pbk **£2.95**
The Jungle Book (1894)
Tells how the child Mowgli was brought up by the
wolves and taught, by Baloo the bear and Bagheera
the black panther, the law and business of the jungle.
Filmed in cartoon form by Disney, this is a classic.
[GB1542] Oxford pbk **£1.95**
Second Jungle Book
[GB1535] Oxford pbk **£1.95**
Jungle Books 1 & 2
[GB1523] Penguin pbk **£2.50**
The Light That Failed (1891)
[GB1529] Penguin pbk **£2.99**
Thy Servant a Dog
[GB1543] Macmillan pbk **£3.95**
Traffics and Discoveries
[GB1544] Penguin pbk **£2.95**
Wee Willie Winkie (1895)
[GB1545] Penguin pbk **£3.95**

LAMBERT, ANGELA
Love Among the Single Classes   NEW
Fiction début concerning the attempts of a woman in
her mid-forties to build a relationship with a Polish
refugee.
[GB1546] Bodley hbk **£11.95**

LARKIN, PHILIP (1922 - 1985)
Larkin said that writing fiction seemed to him harder
than writing poetry. His two novels are remarkably
accomplished considering the age at which he wrote
them, and show a more romantic, sensitive and
vulnerable side to his personality (particularly the
yearning of *A Girl in Winter*) than is immediately
apparent in the poetry.
A Girl in Winter (1947)
A day in the life of librarian Katherine Lind in a grey
provincial town, with a flashback to a brief broken
romance in her past.
[GB1547] Faber pbk **£4.95**
Jill (1946)
Set in wartime Oxford, with identifiable references to
his own college, St John's, Larkin's first novel centres
on John Kemp, who feels lonely and isolated from his
privileged fellow students and invents an imaginary
friend 'Jill' for company.
[GB1548] Faber pbk **£3.95**

LASSALLE, CAROLINE
Breaking the Rules
The story of a woman in retreat from her past lives.
She hides out on a Mediterranean island hoping to
come to an understanding of her predicament.
[GB1549] Penguin pbk **£3.95**

LAVERTY, MAURA (Irish, 1907 - 1966)
Laverty spent much of her early life in Spain as a
governess and journalist, before returning to Ireland
in 1928. Spain features as a place of escape and self-
realization in both of the novels listed here, which
appear in writing order.
Never No More (1942)
[GB1550] Virago pbk **£3.95**
No More Than Human (1944)
[GB1551] Virago pbk **£3.95**

LAVIN, MARY (Irish, 1912 -)
Since her first book appeared in 1942, Lavin has
received many of Ireland's most prestigious literary
awards and is acknowledged as one of the best writers
of her generation.
A Family Likeness (1985)
[GB1552] Constable hbk **£7.95**
Mary O'Grady (1950)
One of her best books, this is a sensitive novel about a
woman who leaves the countryside and moves to
Dublin, where she puts down new roots. As her
family grows up she realizes that her love cannot

protect her children from the horrors and tragedies
which surround them.
[GB1554] Virago pbk **£4.50**
Stories: Vol 1
'Mary Lavin is a great artist: we are excited by her
acute knowledge of the heart, her truthfulness and,
above all, by the controlled revelation of untidy,
powerful emotion.' (V.S. Pritchett).
[GB1556] Constable hbk **£10.95**
Stories: Vol 2
[GB1557] Constable hbk **£10.95**
Stories: Vol 3
[GB1558] Constable hbk **£10.95**
Collected Stories
Vols 1, 2 and 3 in a gift set.
[GB1553] Constable hbk **£25.00**
The House in Clewe Street (1945)
An absorbing family saga which reveals the
poignancies of an Irish Catholic upbringing.
[GB1559] Virago pbk **£4.95**

LAWRENCE, D.H. (1885 - 1930)
One of the finest lyric and symbolist novelists of the
20th century, Lawrence's work developed from his
uneasy but intensely moving early writing, such as
Sons and Lovers, into a highly original and ambitious
symbolic system in the great mature novels, notably
Women in Love. His work has inspired passionate
attacks for its supposed proto-fascist, misogynist,
immoral and racist undercurrents, and in some aspects
of his thought he was decidedly eccentric; at its best his
work celebrates the potential and the possibilities of
the human spirit.
Aaron's Rod (1922)
[GB1560] Heinemann hbk **£10.95**
[GB1561] Penguin pbk **£3.50**
Apocalypse (Non fiction, 1931)
[GB1562] Grafton hbk **£8.95**
[GB1564] Penguin pbk **£3.50**
Collected Short Stories: Vol 1
[GB1566] Heinemann hbk **£10.95**
Collected Short Stories: Vol 2
[GB1567] Heinemann hbk **£10.95**
Collected Short Stories: Vol 3
[GB1568] Heinemann hbk **£10.95**
Complete Short Stories
[GB1569] Penguin pbk **£3.95**
England, My England (1922)
[GB1570] Penguin pbk **£2.50**
Fantasia of the Unconscious/
Psychoanalysis and the Unconscious
(Non fiction, 1922)
[GB1571] Penguin pbk **£3.95**
John Thomas and Lady Jane (1954)
[GB1572] Heinemann hbk **£10.95**
[GB1573] Penguin pbk **£3.50**
Kangaroo (1923)
[GB1574] Heinemann hbk **£9.95**
[GB1575] Penguin pbk **£3.50**
Lady Chatterley's Lover (1928)
[GB1576] Heinemann hbk **£10.95**
[GB1577] Penguin pbk **£3.99**
Love Among the Haystacks
[GB1578] Penguin pbk **£2.50**
Mr Noon (1985)
[GB1581] Cambridge pbk **£8.95**
[GB1582] Grafton pbk **£2.95**
Princess & Other Stories
[GB1583] Penguin pbk **£2.95**
Selected Essays
[GB1584] Penguin pbk **£5.95**
Selected Literary Criticism
[GB1585] Heinemann hbk **£6.95**
Selected Short Stories
[GB1586] Penguin pbk **£3.50**
Short Novels: Vol 1
[GB1587] Heinemann hbk **£10.95**
Short Novels: Vol 2
[GB1588] Heinemann hbk **£10.95**

Sons and Lovers (1913)
Lawrence's most popular and accessible work is a re-creation of his own childhood, and in particular his restrictive relationships with his ambitious mother and Miriam, his first love.
[GB1589] Heinemann hbk £10.95
[GB1590] Penguin pbk £3.99
St Mawr & Other Stories
[GB1591] Cambridge hbk £35.00
[GB1592] Grafton hbk £8.95
[GB1593] Grafton pbk £1.95
St Mawr/The Virgin and the Gypsy
[GB1594] Penguin pbk £2.95
Stories, Essays and Poems
[GB1595] Dent hbk £8.95
Studies in Classic American Literature (1924)
[GB1596] Penguin pbk £3.50
Study of Thomas Hardy & Other Essays
[GB1598] Grafton hbk £10.95
[GB1597] Cambridge pbk £11.95
The First Lady Chatterley (1944)
There are three versions of this controversial work, which show its development from a symbolist to a realistic novel.
[GB1599] Heinemann hbk £10.95
[GB1600] Penguin pbk £2.95
The Great Stories and Short Novels of D.H. Lawrence
Contains, among others, *The Prussian Officer, The Woman Who Rode Away, The Daughters of the Vicar, The Fox, Odour of Chrysanthemums, The Man Who Loved Islands, St Mawr* and *The Virgin and the Gypsy*.
[GB1601] Robinson pbk £8.99
The Lost Girl (1920)
[GB1603] Cambridge pbk £12.95
[GB1605] Penguin pbk £3.95
The Mortal Coil & Other Stories
[GB1606] Penguin pbk £3.95
The Plumed Serpent (1926)
[GB1607] Heinemann hbk £10.95
[GB1608] Penguin pbk £3.95
The Prussian Officer & Other Stories (1914)
[GB1609] Cambridge hbk £35.50
[GB1611] Grafton pbk £2.50
[GB1612] Penguin pbk £2.99
The Rainbow (1915)
Originating from the sprawling ambition of *The Sisters*, this is one of Lawrence's finest achievements. It describes the emotional struggle within three generations of the Brangwen family. It contains one of the most powerful descriptions of young married life in English literature.
[GB1613] Heinemann hbk £10.95
[GB1614] Penguin pbk £2.95
The Trespasser (1912)
[GB1616] Cambridge pbk £11.95
[GB1618] Penguin pbk £2.50
The Virgin and the Gypsy (1930)
[GB1619] Penguin pbk £1.99
The White Peacock (1911)
[GB1621] Cambridge pbk £12.95
[GB1623] Penguin pbk £2.95
The Woman Who Rode Away (1928)
[GB1624] Penguin pbk £2.99
Three Novellas (1923)
[GB1625] Penguin pbk £2.95
Women in Love (1920)
Lawrence's great novel is one of the most powerful expressions of the modernist aesthetic. It is conceived in grand terms but its roots are the minutiae of social behaviour and the intense relationship between man and his surroundings. A remarkable statement of the insecurities of his age.
[GB1627] Heinemann hbk £10.95
[GB1628] Cambridge pbk £19.50
[GB1629] Penguin pbk £3.99

LEHMANN, BEATRIX (1903 - 1979)
The sister of Rosamond, she was one of the most successful stage actresses of her era.
The Rumour of Heaven (1934)
[GB1635] Virago pbk £4.50

LEHMANN, JOHN (1907 - 1987)
Brother of the better-known Rosamond, John Lehmann was a prominent man of letters who enjoyed the friendship of several generations of significant English writers.
In the Purely Pagan Sense (1976)
[GB1636] GMP pbk £3.95

LEHMANN, ROSAMOND (1901 -)
Writer who handled her main theme - the sufferings of women in love - with pioneering frankness. The new wave of feminist criticism has encouraged a revival of her work.
A Dusty Answer (1927)
[GB1637] Penguin pbk £4.50
A Note in Music (1930)
[GB1638] Virago pbk £4.99
An Invitation to the Waltz (1923)
[GB1639] Virago pbk £4.50
Gypsy's Baby (Stories, 1946)
[GB1640] Virago pbk £4.50
The Ballad and the Source (1944)
[GB1641] Virago pbk £4.50
The Echoing Grove (1953)
[GB1642] Penguin pbk £4.50
The Sea-Grape Tree (1976)
A sensitively devised novel of a woman, betrayed by her husband, who travels to the Caribbean in the 1930s and encounters voices from the past.
[GB1644] Virago pbk £4.99
The Weather in the Streets (1936)
Sequel to *An Invitation to the Waltz*, it shocked readers by taking the heroine through a failed marriage, an adulterous love affair and an abortion.
[GB1645] Virago pbk £4.50

LESSING, DORIS (1919 -)
One of the most important post-war authors, born in Rhodesia. Her main concerns are political, often dealing with the appeals and pitfalls of Marxism, the insidiousness of racial hatred and the destiny of women from a range of different angles. Her *Children of Violence* quintet and *The Golden Notebook* are her most substantial works. See *Science Fiction* for her *Canopus in Argos* sequence.
A Habit of Loving (Stories, 1957)
[GB1653] Grafton pbk £2.50
A Man and Two Women (1965)
[GB1654] Grafton pbk £2.50
A Proper Marriage (1954)
[GB1656] Grafton pbk £3.50
Black Madonna (1964)
[GB1657] Grafton pbk £2.95
Briefing for a Descent into Hell (1971)
[GB1658] Grafton pbk £2.95
Diaries of Jane Somers (1984)
[GB1660] Penguin pbk £4.99
Doris Lessing Reader
A fine introduction to her work with extracts from the great novel sequences *Children of Violence* and *Canopus in Argos*, along with other stories and essays.
[GB1661] Cape hbk £13.95
Five (1953)
[GB1662] Grafton pbk £3.50
Four-Gated City (1969)
[GB1663] Grafton pbk £3.99
Going Home (Non fiction, 1957)
[GB1664] Grafton pbk £2.50
In Pursuit of the English (Non fiction, 1960)
[GB1666] Grafton pbk £1.95
Landlocked (1965)
[GB1667] Grafton pbk £2.50

Martha Quest (1952)
[GB1669] Grafton pbk £2.50
Memoirs of a Survivor (1974)
[GB1670] Pan pbk £3.50
Particularly Cats (Non fiction, 1967)
[GB1671] Grafton pbk £2.50
Ripple from the Storm (1958)
[GB1672] Grafton pbk £2.50
Story of a Non-Marrying Man (Stories)
[GB1674] Penguin pbk £3.95
Temptation of Jack Orkney (1978)
[GB1675] Grafton pbk £2.50
The Fifth Child (1988)
Chilling recent novella about a happy family destroyed by one of its members.
[GB1676] Grafton pbk £3.95
The Golden Notebook (1962)
Generally accepted to be her major work, it is a key statement about women in the 20th century. It is written as a series of notebooks which are juxtaposed against each other to make up a complex picture of breakdown and renewal.
[GB1677] M Joseph hbk £11.95
[GB1678] Grafton pbk £3.95
The Good Terrorist (1985)
[GB1679] Cape hbk £9.95
[GB1680] Grafton pbk £2.95
The Grass is Singing (1950)
[GB1681] M Joseph hbk £8.95
[GB1682] Grafton pbk £2.50
The Summer Before the Dark (1973)
[GB1683] Cape hbk £9.95
[GB1684] Penguin pbk £3.95
The Sun Between Their Feet (Stories, 1973)
[GB1685] M Joseph hbk £9.95
[GB1686] Grafton pbk £2.95
This Was the Old Chief's Country (Stories, 1978)
[GB1687] M Joseph hbk £9.95
[GB1688] Grafton pbk £2.95
To Room Nineteen (Stories, 1978)
[GB1689] Cape hbk £9.95
[GB1690] Grafton pbk £2.50
Winter In July (Stories, 1966)
[GB1691] Grafton pbk £2.50

LEVERSON, ADA (1862 - 1933)
A friend of celebrities such as Oscar Wilde, she wrote this witty trilogy about fashionable London society.
The Little Ottleys (1908 - 16)
[GB1692] Virago pbk £4.95

LEVEY, MICHAEL (1927 -)
Husband of the novelist Brigid Brophy, Levey is a past director of the National Gallery and author of several prestigious works on the history of art.
Men at Work
The story of a retired civil servant intent on building a stable relationship before it is too late. Levey gives a moving account of the man's unlikely involvement with one of the workmen redeveloping his house and with the latter's seven year old daughter.
[GB1693] H Hamilton hbk £11.95

LEVI, PETER (1931 -)
To the Goat (1988)
Novella concerned with the destructively wild and bohemian lifestyle of a university tutor, by the former Professor of Poetry at Oxford.
[GB1694] Hutchinson hbk £8.95

LEVY, DEBORAH
Beautiful Mutants
A disturbing first novel, part of the *Cape New Writers* series.
[GB1695] Cape hbk £9.95
Ophelia and the Great Idea (Stories)
[GB1689] Cape hbk £9.95

LEWIS, NORMAN (1908 - 1957)

A wonderfully fluent prose writer, well-known for his travel and non-fiction work. He often sets his novels in Sicily and Italy, and brings in elements of history, thriller writing and a vivid sense of place to animate his fiction. *The Day of the Fox* is an acclaimed classic in the Hemingway vein.

A Suitable Case For Corruption (1984)
[GB1696] Penguin pbk **£3.95**
The Day of the Fox (1955)
[GB1697] Robinson pbk **£3.95**
The March of the Long Shadows (1987)
[GB1698] Arrow pbk **£3.99**

LEWIS, WYNDHAM (1882 - 1957)

Wyndham Lewis considered himself an artist first and writer second, but the collision of styles in his writing was ranked highly by his contemporaries, particularly T.S. Eliot. The range of his fictional writing - not to mention his criticism - is broad: from the early, dynamic and biting comedy *Tarr*, currently unavailable, to the long satire on the Bloomsbury Group and other 1930s figures, *The Apes of God*, the *Childermass* trilogy, and Lewis's late and most autobiographical novel, *Self-Condemned*.

Apes of God (1930)
[GB1699] Penguin pbk **£7.50**
Revenge for Love (1937)
[GB1702] Penguin pbk **£4.95**
Rotting Hill (1951)
[GB1703] B Sparrow pbk **£11.95**
Self-Condemned (1954)
[GB1704] Carcanet hbk **£12.95**
The Essential Wyndham Lewis **NEW**
An excellent collection, edited by Julian Symons, which includes work from the range of Lewis's writing, with good representation from his non-fiction.
[GB1705A] Deutsch hbk **£17.95**
The Childermass (1928)
The first novel of Lewis's fantasy trilogy, set outside the gates of Heaven; the two novels listed immediately below continue the story, which is effectively a philosophical enquiry, and one of the more notable of Lewis's later works.
[GB1705] Calder pbk **£4.95**
Monstre Gai (1955)
[GB1701] Calder pbk **£4.95**
Malign Fiesta (1955)
[GB1700] Calder pbk **£4.95**
The Vulgar Streak (1941)
[GB1706] B Sparrow pbk **£11.95**

LINDSAY, DAVID (Scottish, 1878 - 1945)

Writer of fantastical and supernatural works which investigate, like much modern fantasy writing, moral questions of good and evil.
The Haunted Woman (1922)
[GB1707] Canongate pbk **£3.95**

LINKLATER, ERIC (Scottish, 1899 - 1974)

His mock-heroic stories can be as entertaining as Compton Mackenzie's more riotous output: *Juan* may fairly be called a comic masterpiece.
Juan in America (1931)
[GB1710] Penguin pbk **£3.95**
The Merry Muse (1959)
[GB1711] R Drew pbk **£3.95**

LITVINOV, IVY (1889 - 1977)

Born in London and married to one of Stalin's foreign ministers, she was the only Englishwoman amongst top-ranking Soviet personnel.
His Master's Voice
[GB1712] Virago pbk **£4.50**
She Knew She Was Right (Stories, 1971)
[GB1713] Virago pbk **£4.50**

LIVELY, ADAM
Blue Fruit (1987)
An acclaimed first novel from the son of Penelope Lively.
[GB1714] Hodder pbk **£3.50**
Burnt House (1989) **NEW**
Adam Lively's new book is a vivid novel of contemporary London, concerning the bitter-sweet experiences of American TV anchorman Bob Morton and his daughter Laura, as they renovate a gutted house and attempt to immerse themselves in London life.
[GB1709] Simon & Sch hbk **£12.95**

LIVELY, PENELOPE (1933 -)

Lively wrote novels for children with great success from 1970, and only in 1977 was her first adult novel published, *The Road to Lichfield*. Like her children's books, her novels often reflect the influence which the past exerts on the present, and are concerned with memory and the creation of personal and collective histories.
According to Mark (1984)
[GB1716] Penguin pbk **£3.99**
Judgement Day (1980)
[GB1717] Penguin pbk **£3.99**
Moontiger (1987)
This novel, in which an elderly woman recalls her affair with a young officer in wartime Cairo, was winner of the Booker Prize.
[GB1718] Deutsch hbk **£9.95**
[GB1719] Penguin pbk **£3.99**
Next to Nature, Art (1982)
[GB1720] Penguin pbk **£3.99**
Pack of Cards (Stories, 1986)
[GB1722] Penguin pbk **£4.99**
Passing On **NEW**
A middle-aged brother and sister are released by the death of their domineering mother.
[GB1723] Deutsch hbk **£10.95**
Perfect Happiness (1983)
[GB1724] Penguin pbk **£3.99**
The Road to Lichfield (1977)
[GB1725] Penguin pbk **£3.99**
Treasures of Time (1979)
[GB1726] Penguin pbk **£3.99**

LLEWELLYN, RICHARD (Welsh)
How Green Was My Valley (1939)
Classic story of a family in a mining community, in Wales; an immediate bestseller on publication.
[GB1732] Hodder pbk **£3.95**

LODGE, DAVID (1935 -)

Lodge's reputation is that of an accomplished comic novelist who specializes in satirical portraits of the self-absorbed, trans-cultural world of academic game-playing and sexual intrigue. There is, however, an underlying seriousness to his work and, as befits a progressive literary theorist, much of his fiction embodies ideas drawn from traditional religion, sociology and contemporary philosophical and linguistic theory.
Changing Places (1975)
Along with its sequel, *Small World*, this witty, satirical and occasionally farcical novel offers splendid glimpses of the academic rat race.
[GB1735] Secker hbk **£10.95**
[GB1736] Penguin pbk **£2.99**
Ginger, You're Barmy (1962)
[GB1737] Secker hbk **£10.95**
[GB1738] Penguin pbk **£2.99**
How Far Can You Go? (1980)
[GB1739] Secker hbk **£10.95**
[GB1740] Penguin pbk **£2.99**
Nice Work (1988)
Bringing together a businessman and a feminist university lecturer in a sharply observed comedy of class misunderstandings this takes the Victorian 'two

worlds' novel (cf. *North and South*) as its model.
[GB1741] Secker hbk **£10.95**
[GB1742] Penguin pbk **£3.99**
Out of the Shelter (1970)
[GB1743] Secker hbk **£10.95**
[GB1744] Penguin pbk **£2.99**
Small World (1984)
Booker Prize-shortlisted novel which charts the quest for true love of a naïve young Irish scholar. A deceptively complex book that reworks the Grail legend to great comic effect.
[GB1745] Secker hbk **£10.95**
[GB1746] Penguin pbk **£3.50**
The British Museum is Falling Down (1965)
Lodge's first major novel combines spirited parodies of major modernist writers such as Joyce and Woolf with a more serious examination of the particular influence of Catholicism on family life.
[GB1747] Secker hbk **£10.95**
[GB1748] Penguin pbk **£2.50**

LOWNDES, NATALYA
Angel in the Sun **NEW**
A historical novel set in revolutionary Russia, with a plot that parallels many real events.
[GB1760] Hodder hbk **£12.95**
Chekago
A novel of Moscow life centred on the strangely innocent character of a dustman, Sasha, during the brief rule of Yuri Andropov.
[GB1761] Hodder pbk **£4.99**

LOWRY, MALCOLM (1909 - 1957)

Self-destructive, alcoholic novelist whose literary reputation rests on his masterpiece, *Under the Volcano*. As a youthful admirer of Conrad and Melville, he went to sea after leaving school, an experience reflected in his first novel *Ultramarine*. He was never able to settle, travelling restlessly in South America and Europe, and after spending years in Canada, returned to England. The two other titles listed here were collected from work left unfinished at Lowry's death.
Dark as the Grave Wherein My Friend is Laid (1968)
[GB1762] Penguin pbk **£4.95**
October Ferry to Gabriola (1971)
Set in Canada.
[GB1763] Penguin pbk **£3.99**
Ultramarine (1933)
[GB1764] Penguin pbk **£3.95**

Penelope Lively, author of *Passing On* (Deutsch hbk £10.95)

Under the Volcano (1947)
His Mexican-inspired masterpiece is an ambitious and unusual piece of writing, charting the confused and seemingly endless ruminations of an alcoholic British consul. The action takes place on a single day in 1939 - the Day of the Dead - and ends with the consul's death amid a growing sense of doom and menace.
[GB1765] Cape hbk **£9.95**
[GB1766] Penguin pbk **£4.99**

LUARD, NICHOLAS
Gondar (1988)
A blockbusting first novel based on an historical event - the battle for control of an Abyssinian city in the late 19th century.
[GB1767] Arrow pbk **£3.99**

LUCAS, RUSSELL
Evenings at Mongini's   **NEW**
A warm, fictional introduction to the characters who people the streets of modern Bombay, the city in which the author grew up.
[GB1768] Heinemann hbk **£10.95**

MACAULAY, ROSE (1889 - 1958)
A popular novelist of the 1920s and '30s, Macaulay's work is notable for a distinctive provincial period feel; sometimes menacing in tone, it also ranges through works of greater compassion.
Crewe Train (1926)
[GB1772] Methuen pbk **£3.95**
Dangerous Ages (1921)
[GB1773] Methuen pbk **£3.95**
Keeping Up Appearances (1928)
[GB1774] Methuen pbk **£3.95**
They Were Defeated (1932)
[GB1775] Oxford pbk **£3.95**
Told by an Idiot (1923)
[GB1776] Virago pbk **£3.95**
Towers of Trebizond (1956)
Her most famous work is a bitter-sweet comedy about a woman who travels to Turkey to escape an affair.
[GB1777] Futura pbk **£2.95**
World My Wilderness (1950)
[GB1778] Virago pbk **£3.95**

MACDONALD, SHARMAN (1931 -)
Better-known as a playwright, her novels cast a penetrating eye over domestic battlegrounds in suburbia.
Night Night
[GB1781] Collins hbk **£10.95**
The Beast
[GB1782] Fontana pbk **£2.95**

MACDONNELL, A.G. (1895 - 1941)
England, Their England (1933)
Classic comedy about English life, and the noble game of cricket in particular.
[GB1783] Pan pbk **£2.95**

MACINNES, COLIN (1914 - 1976)
The son of Angela Thirkell, he is now famous for the atmospheric **London Novels**, which offer a powerful, realistic evocation of fringe life in the capital during the 1950s.
Absolute Beginners (1959)
[GB1784] Penguin pbk **£2.99**
Absolute MacInnes: The Best of Colin McInnes
[GB1785] Allison & B pbk **£4.95**
All Day Saturday (1966)
[GB1786] Hogarth pbk **£3.95**
City of Spades (1957)
[GB1787] Penguin pbk **£2.50**
England, Half English (Non fiction, 1961)
[GB1788] Hogarth pbk **£4.95**
June in Her Spring
[GB1789] Hogarth pbk **£3.95**

Mister Love and Justice (1960)
[GB1790] Penguin pbk **£2.99**
Omnibus: Absolute Beginners/City of Spades/Mr Love and Justice
[GB1791] Allison & B pbk **£6.95**
To the Victors the Spoils
[GB1792] Allison & B pbk **£4.95**

MACKAY, COLIN
The Song of the Forest
Widely praised allegory of modern times constructed out of folklore, myth, history and the supernatural.
[GB1793] Fontana pbk **£3.50**

MACKAY, SHENA (1944 -)
Mackay's stories dredge the everyday misery of thwarted lives and present the results with the blackest comedy, in a style which can include elements of high Gothic floridness.
Advent Calendar
[GB1794] Bloodaxe pbk **£2.95**
Babies in Rhinestones
[GB1795] Sphere pbk **£2.75**
Bowl of Cherries (1984)
[GB1796] Sphere pbk **£3.99**
Dreams of Dead Women's Handbags (1987)
[GB1797] Sphere pbk **£3.95**
Music Upstairs (1988)
[GB1798] Virago pbk **£4.50**
Redhill Rococo (1986)
A hilarious novel about Luke Ribbons, a failed Post Office robber, and the eccentric goings on among the people of Redhill. 'If England has to sink giggling into the sea, Shena Mackay contributes a great deal to the cruel comedy of decomposition.' (*TLS*).
[GB1799] Sphere pbk **£3.50**

MACKEN, WALTER (Irish, 1916 - 1967)
Macken worked both at Abbey and at Galway's Gaelic Language Theatre, writing plays for both. He is, however, best known for his fiction, particularly the historical trilogy, *Seek the Fair Land*, *The Silent People* and the *The Scorching Wind*, which deal respectively with the Cromwellian invasion, the Famine and the Easter Rising.
Flight of the Doves (1971)
[GB1800] Pan pbk **£1.50**
Quench the Moon (1974)
[GB1801] Pan pbk **£2.95**
Rain on the Wind (1970)
[GB1802] Pan pbk **£2.50**
Scorching Wind (1969)
[GB1803] Pan pbk **£2.95**
Seek the Fair Land (1968)
[GB1804] Pan pbk **£3.50**
Sunset on the Window-Panes (1978)
[GB1806] Pan pbk **£2.50**
The Bogman (1972)
[GB1807] Pan pbk **£2.95**
The Silent People (1968)
[GB1805] Pan pbk **£3.50**

MACKENZIE, COMPTON
(Scottish, 1883 - 1972)
Considering the success and acclaim he enjoyed during his long and prolific life, Mackenzie now seems strangely neglected. His comedies are much more than patronizing tartan kitsch: they can be hilarious and, coming from the pen of an ardent nationalist, subtly parodic of the Scottish myths they appear to sustain.
Buttercups and Daisies
[GB1808] Sutton pbk **£3.95**
Extraordinary Women (1928)
[GB1809] Hogarth pbk **£4.95**
Highland Omnibus: Monarch of the Glen/Whisky Galore/Rival Monster
[GB1810] Penguin pbk **£5.95**

Sinister Street (1914)
[GB1811] Penguin pbk **£5.95**
Sublime Tobacco
[GB1812] Sutton pbk **£5.95**
Vestal Fire (1927)
[GB1813] Hogarth pbk **£4.95**
Whisky Galore (1947)
[GB1814] Penguin pbk **£3.95**

MACLAVERTY, BERNARD (Irish, 1942 -)
He sets his work in his native Belfast, and writes sensitively and tenderly of the difficulties of family relationships, set against the violence of the Troubles.
A Time to Dance (Stories, 1982)
Touching and surprising short stories.
[GB1815] Penguin pbk **£3.50**
Cal (1983)
A troubled love story set against the societal fear and violence of Ulster.
[GB1816] Penguin pbk **£2.50**
Lamb (1980)
His first novel. In an attempt to discover happiness a borstal official and a young boy escape together.
[GB1817] Penguin pbk **£3.99**
Secrets & Other Stories (1984)
[GB1818] Blackstaff P pbk **£3.95**
The Great Profundo & Other Stories
A collection of short stories from 1987, ranging from Ireland to Portugal, about people on the fringes of society.
[GB1819] Cape hbk **£9.95**

MACNAMARA, BRINSLEY
(Irish, 1890 - 1963)
The Clanking of Chains (1920)
The account of an Irish nationalist disillusioned and embittered by the struggle for freedom.
[GB1821] Anvil pbk **£2.95**
Valley of the Squinting Windows (1918)
The novel based on his birthplace in Westmeath that caused great controversy when published.
[GB1822] Anvil pbk **£3.95**

MADDEN, DEIRDRE (Irish)
Hidden Symptoms (1987)
A careful and moving novel that explores a woman's crisis of faith following the murder of her twin brother.
[GB1823] Faber pbk **£3.50**
The Birds of the Innocent Wood (1988)
Winner of the 1989 Somerset Maugham Award.
[GB1824] Faber hbk **£9.95**

MAITLAND, SARA (1950 -)
Maitland's work is intense and lyrical, dealing with emotional and spiritual events, but everywhere leavened by a robust feminism and an engaging sense of humour.
A Book of Spells (1987)
[GB1826] Methuen pbk **£3.95**
Daughter of Jerusalem (1987)
[GB1827] Pan pbk **£2.95**
Telling Tales
[GB1828] Journeyman pbk **£3.75**
Three Times Table (1989)   **NEW**
Maitland's new novel interweaves the lives of three women, one of whom flies on a dragon, and mixes mild fantasy with observations of everyday life.
[GB1839] Chatto hbk **£12.95**
Virgin Territory
[GB1829] Pan pbk **£2.95**

MAITLAND, SARA & WANDOR, MICHELENE
Arky Types (1987)
Flamboyant feminism, wild wit, stirring stories and an impassioned examination of writing; all in an unorthodox letter form.
[GB1830] Methuen pbk **£3.95**

MANNING, FREDERIC
Her Privates We
Classic war novel originally published under a
pseudonym.
[GB1831] Hogarth pbk **£4.95**

MANNING, OLIVIA (1911 - 1980)
Her experiences in Eastern Europe during the war
formed the basis for her *Balkan Trilogy*, which
vividly evokes the time and the effects the war had
upon the people. Both this and its sequel, the *Levant
Trilogy*, are notable for their fine period feel, and
their impressive array of boldly drawn characters.
Artist Among the Missing (1949)
[GB1832] Heinemann hbk **£9.50**
**Balkan Trilogy: Great Fortunes/Spoilt
City/Friends and Heroes** (1960 - 65)
[GB1833] Heinemann hbk **£14.95**
[GB1834] Penguin pbk **£5.95**
Different Face (1978)
[GB1835] Heinemann hbk **£9.50**
Doves of Venus (1977)
[GB1836] Virago pbk **£4.95**
**Levant Trilogy: Danger Tree/Battle Lost
and Won/Sum of Things** (1977 -78)
[GB1837] Penguin pbk **£4.95**
Play Room (1969)
[GB1838] Virago pbk **£3.50**
Rain Forest (1974)
[GB1840] Penguin pbk **£3.95**
School for Love (1981)
[GB1841] Penguin pbk **£3.99**
Wind Changes (1937)
[GB1842] Virago pbk **£4.95**

MANSFIELD, KATHERINE (1888 - 1923)
New Zealand-born author educated in London, who
eventually settled permanently in Europe. Her
reputation rests on her stories, of which the earliest
are impressionistic vignettes based on her childhood;
the later ones become more profound and tragic,
foreshadowing her early death from tuberculosis. She
is now acknowledged as one of the greatest modern
exponents of the short story.
Bliss & Other Stories (1921)
[GB1843] Penguin pbk **£2.95**
Collected Short Stories (1945)
[GB1844] Penguin pbk **£7.95**
Dove's Nest & Other Stories
[GB1845] Hutchinson pbk **£3.95**
In a German Pension (1911)
[GB1846] Penguin pbk **£2.99**
Selected Stories
[GB1847] Oxford pbk **£2.95**

Olivia Manning, author of *The Levant Trilogy*
(Penguin pbk **£4.95**)

Short Stories
[GB1848] Dent pbk **£2.50**
Stories (1953)
[GB1849] Oxford hbk **£17.50**
The Aloe (1937)
[GB1850] Virago pbk **£4.50**
The Garden Party (1922)
[GB1851] Penguin pbk **£2.95**

MANTEL, HILARY (1952 -)
Comic novelist whose books are characterized by an
explosive mixture of lust, social satire, low comedy
and suburban mayhem.
**Eight Months on Ghazzah
Street** (1988)
A women who becomes bored with her life as
an expatriate, eventually falls victim to her
own curiosity.
[GB1852] Penguin pbk **£3.99**
Every Day is Mother's Day (1985)
[GB1853] Penguin pbk **£2.50**
Fludd (1989)   **NEW**
Fetherhoughton, an industrial town in the North, is
visited by Fludd, whose effect on the spiritually low
town leads to profound changes.
[GB1854] Viking hbk **£11.95**
Vacant Possession (1986)
[GB1855] Penguin pbk **£2.50**

MARCUS, DAVID (Irish, 1924 -)
Writer of powerful historical novels set in Cork.
A Land Not Theirs (1986)
[GB1864] Transworld pbk **£3.50**
Land in Flames (1987)
[GB1865] Transworld hbk **£10.95**

MARS-JONES, ADAM (1954 -)
Extremely gifted and intelligent young writer, who
won the Somereset Maugham Award for these
satirical short stories, which includes a scathing satire
on royalty.
Lantern Lecture (1981)
[GB1445] Pan pbk **£2.50**

MARS-JONES, ADAM &
WHITE, EDMUND
The Darker Proof (1987)
A collection of short stories which gives the AIDS
crisis a humane and personal dimension. '*The Darker
Proof* distils the cruelty of the disease and the defiant
heroism it can evoke, in writing so beautiful that it
haunts.' (*The Sunday Times* .).
[GB1446] Faber pbk **£3.95**

MASON, ANITA (1942 -)
Booker Prize shortlisted novelist who fuses biblical
and magical themes.
The Illusionist (1983)
[GB1868] Sphere pbk **£1.95**
The War Against Chaos
[GB1869] Sphere pbk **£3.99**

MASSIE, ALLAN (Scottish, 1938 -)
A skilful novelist who stands aloof from the political
identifications (socialist/nationalist) perhaps too
frequently associated with the 'Scottish' writer.
Massie is a leading exponent of that form of fiction
wherein literary art is at least as important as any
'message' it may contain.
Augustus (1986)
[GB1870] Hodder pbk **£3.99**
Change and Decay in All I See (1978)
[GB1871] Bodley hbk **£6.95**
One Night in Winter (1984)
[GB1872] Bodley hbk **£9.95**
The Death of Men (1981)
[GB1873] R Clark pbk **£2.95**
The Last Peacock (1980)
[GB1874] R Clark pbk **£2.95**

MATHEWS, AIDAN CARL
Adventures in a Bathyscope (Stories, 1988)
Written in light, balanced prose, these dark comedies
and absurd tragedies reveal a refreshing irreverence
for narrative convention.
[GB1875] Secker hbk **£10.95**

MAUGHAM, ROBIN
Wrong People
Gay classic that raised eyebrows on first publication.
[GB1876] GMP pbk **£3.95**

MAUGHAM, W. SOMERSET (1874 - 1965)
One of the best known English novelists, short story
writers and playwrights Maugham has been
immensely popular with the reading public, although
critics have been divided as to his merits.
Ah King & Other Stories (1933)
[GB1877] Oxford pbk **£4.95**
Cakes and Ale (1930)
One of his best known books, this is a warm-hearted
comedy which satirizes literary circles. One of the
characters is allegedly based on Thomas Hardy.
[GB1878] Heinemann hbk **£9.95**
[GB1879] Pan pbk **£3.99**
Casuarina Tree & Other Stories (1926)
[GB1880] Oxford pbk **£3.95**
Catalina (1948)
[GB1881] Pan pbk **£2.50**
Collected Short Stories: Vol 1
[GB1882] Pan pbk **£4.99**
Collected Short Stories: Vol 2
[GB1883] Pan pbk **£4.99**
Collected Short Stories: Vol 3
[GB1884] Pan pbk **£3.50**
Collected Short Stories: Vol 4
[GB1885] Pan pbk **£4.99**
Complete Short Stories: Vol 1
[GB1886] Heinemann hbk **£10.95**
Complete Short Stories: Vol 2
[GB1887] Heinemann hbk **£10.95**
Complete Short Stories: Vol 3
[GB1888] Heinemann hbk **£10.95**
Creatures of Circumstance (1947)
[GB1889] Heinemann hbk **£9.95**
Mrs Craddock
[GB1892] Pan pbk **£2.50**
Narrow Corner (1932)
[GB1893] Heinemann hbk **£9.95**
[GB1894] Pan pbk **£2.50**
Of Human Bondage (1915)
An important novel, largely autobiographical, about
the life of a partially handicapped boy, his training as
a doctor and his life as an artist in Paris.
[GB1895] Heinemann hbk **£9.95**
[GB1896] Pan pbk **£3.95**
Ten Novels and their Authors
[GB1897] Pan pbk **£2.95**
The Magician (1908)
[GB1898] Pan pbk **£2.50**
The Moon and Sixpence (1919)
[GB1899] Heinemann hbk **£9.95**
[GB1900] Pan pbk **£2.99**
The Painted Veil (1925)
[GB1901] Heinemann hbk **£9.95**
[GB1902] Pan pbk **£2.99**
The Razor's Edge (1944)
[GB1903] Heinemann hbk **£9.95**
[GB1904] Pan pbk **£3.99**
Theatre (Non fiction)
[GB1905] Heinemann hbk **£9.95**
[GB1906] Pan pbk **£3.99**
Up at the Villa (1953)
[GB1907] Heinemann hbk **£9.95**
Vagrant Mood (Essays)
[GB1908] Heinemann hbk **£9.95**
Writer's Notebook (Non fiction)
[GB1909] Heinemann hbk **£9.95**
[GB1910] Pan pbk **£2.95**

FICTION

MAURIER, DAPHNE DU (1907 - 1989)
Popular English writer whose best works are suspense classics, often with historical settings, elegant and powerful evocations of a bygone era, mysterious and charming. Du Maurier is one of a few English writers to find romance and adventure in Cornish settings.
Blue Lenses & Other Stories
[GB1911] Penguin pbk **£2.95**
Classics of the Macabre
[GB1913] Gollancz hbk **£10.95**
Don't Look Now & Other Stories
[GB1914] Penguin pbk **£2.99**
Flight of the Falcon
[GB1916] Penguin pbk **£2.95**
Four Great Cornish Novels
[GB1917] Gollancz hbk **£9.95**
Frenchman's Creek
[GB1919] Pan pbk **£3.50**
Hungry Hill
[GB1922] Penguin pbk **£3.95**
I'll Never Be Young Again
[GB1923] Pan pbk **£3.50**
Jamaica Inn
[GB1924] Gollancz hbk **£9.95**
[GB1925] Pan pbk **£3.99**
Mary Anne
[GB1927] Pan pbk **£3.99**
My Cousin Rachel
[GB1929] Pan pbk **£2.99**
Rebecca
Outstanding gothic novel about an innocent young woman caught up in the sinister mystery of her aristocratic husband's previous, beautiful, dead wife.
[GB1931] Gollancz hbk **£9.95**
[GB1932] Pan pbk **£3.99**
Rendezvous & Other Stories
[GB1933] Gollancz hbk **£9.95**
Rule Britannia
[GB1935] Pan pbk **£2.95**
The Birds & Other Stories
[GB1936] Pan pbk **£3.50**
The Glass Blowers
[GB1937] Penguin pbk **£3.99**
The House on the Strand
[GB1939] Pan pbk **£3.99**
The King's General
[GB1941] Pan pbk **£2.95**
The Loving Spirit
[GB1942] Pan pbk **£2.95**
The Parasites
[GB1944] Penguin pbk **£3.50**
The Scapegoat
[GB1947] Pan pbk **£2.95**

MAYOR, F.M. (1872 - 1932)
The Rector's Daughter (1924)
A rediscovered masterpiece, giving a tender and honest portrayal of marriage and middle-aged desire.
[GB1949] Virago pbk **£3.95**
The Squire's Daughter (1929)
[GB1950] Virago pbk **£3.95**
The Third Miss Symons (1913)
[GB1951] Virago pbk **£3.50**

MCARTHUR, ALEXANDER & LONG, KINGSLEY (Scottish)
No Mean City (1956)
The standard Glasgow novel of razor gangs and dance-hall violence; the title is a phrase coined long before Glasgow's recent renaissance.
[GB1952] Corgi pbk **£2.95**

MCCABE, PATRICK (Irish)
McCabe, now living in London, has set his first novel in the Irish border town of Carn, where the inevitable conflict of a divided Ireland weighs heavily on its residents. **NEW**
Carn
[GB1954] Aidan Ellis hbk **£11.50**

MCCRUM, ROBERT
McCrum is well-known as a publishing editor and as the author of the series *The Story of English*. His early novels are taut and assured but more substantial work is promised for the future.
In the Secret State
Espionage thriller characterized by an atmosphere of nameless suspicion.
[GB2148] Fontana pbk **£2.25**
The Fabulous Englishman
A fictional chronicle of the personal drama of an Englishman, set against a backdrop of the events of Prague in 1968.
[GB2150] Fontana pbk **£3.50**

MCEWAN, IAN (1948 -)
McEwan's early work made an immediate impression for its presentation of derelict and perverted lives. It achieves a suprising lyricism, despite the lean, clipped prose and thematic exploration of the more sinister sides of human nature.
First Love, Last Rites (Stories, 1975)
[GB1955] Cape hbk **£8.95**
[GB1956] Picador pbk **£3.50**
In Between the Sheets (Stories, 1978)
[GB1957] Picador pbk **£2.95**
Or Shall We Die? (Poetry)
[GB1958] Cape hbk **£4.95**
The Cement Garden (1978)
After concealing the death of their mother, a group of children experience a bizarre but temporary liberation from their programmed course into adulthood. The concerns of McEwan's earlier stories are here streamlined into what many believe to be his finest novel.
[GB1959] Cape hbk **£8.95**
[GB1960] Picador pbk **£2.95**
The Child in Time (1987)
A young couple have their child snatched from them and are driven apart by despair. The underlying compassion of earlier work is here brought to the surface, and McEwan explores the political and social dimensions of the story with admirable directness.
[GB1961] Cape hbk **£10.95**
[GB1962] Picador pbk **£3.95**
The Comfort of Strangers (1981)
[GB1963] Cape hbk **£8.95**
[GB1964] Picador pbk **£3.50**
The Imitation Game (1981)
[GB1965] Cape hbk **£8.95**
[GB1966] Picador pbk **£2.95**

MCGAHERN, JOHN (Irish, 1935 -)
School teacher and writer who caused a scandal with his controversial novel *The Dark*.
Getting Through (1978)
[GB1967] Faber pbk **£3.95**
High Ground (1985)
This is an award winning collection of short stories. 'A scrupulously lyrical collection from an artist in his prime,' according to Paul Bailey, writing in *The Observer* .
[GB1968] Faber pbk **£3.99**
The Barracks (1963)
His first novel. After years of freedom a woman returns to the enclosed Irish village of her upbringing.
[GB1970] Faber pbk **£3.95**
The Dark (1965)
His second novel deals with the problems of adolescence and clerical celibacy in a way that aroused much controversy until the book was banned outright.
[GB1971] Faber pbk **£3.95**
The Leavetaking (1974)
A day in the life of a young Catholic schoolteacher who faces dismissal by his authorities for having married an American divorcee.
[GB1972] Faber pbk **£3.99**

MCGAUGHREAN, GERALDINE
The Maypole **NEW**
McGaughrean's first work for adults is set in the Middle Ages. Rendered in spare and elegant prose, it is a complex tale of the dark days of feudalism and the cruel sovereignty of the church.
[GB1974] Secker hbk **£9.95**

MCGINLEY, PATRICK (Irish, 1937 -)
McGinley's novels are rich in suspense and riddles and celebrate 'the Irish lust for fantasy and disorder'.
Bogmail (1978)
In true McGinley fashion *Bogmail* answers such questions as why an ex-priest turned pub-owner should cook a poisonous omelette for his barman and then hit him over the head with Volume 25 of the *Encyclopedia Britannica*.
[GB1975] Fontana pbk **£2.95**
Foggage (1984)
This is a comic and sexual farce about the farm that Kevin and Maureen Hurley run together.
[GB1976] Fontana pbk **£2.95**
The Fantasist
Patricia Teeling, a girl raised among farmers, goes to Dublin to be confronted by many mysterious happenings.
[GB1978] Fontana pbk **£2.95**
The Red Men (1987)
On his 75th birthday Gulban gives each of his four sons £10,000. The one who uses it best will inherit his fortune.
[GB1979] Fontana pbk **£3.95**
The Trick of the Ga Bolga (1985)
[GB1980] Fontana pbk **£3.50**
The Devil's Diary (1988)
Father Jerry, a devout and idealistic priest, has to contend with the ravages of venal property developer Arty Brennan and, even more disturbing, the oafish, libidinous brother who has returned to torment him with memories of their childhood.
[GB19801] Cape hbk **£10.95**

MCILVANNEY, WILLIAM (Scottish, 1936 -)
Heroes holding traditional (and, it must be said, male) working-class values, which are also held with conviction and honesty by McIlvanney himself, are confronted by circumstances which test them to the limit.
Docherty (1975)
[GB1981] Hodder pbk **£3.95**
Laidlaw
[GB1982] Hodder pbk **£2.50**
Remedy is None
[GB1983] R Drew pbk **£4.95**

William McIlvanney, author of *Walking Wounded* (Hodder hbk **£10.95**)

The Big Man (1985)
[GB1984] Hodder pbk **£3.50**
The Papers of Tony Veitch
[GB1985] Hodder pbk **£2.50**
Walking Wounded   **NEW**
[GB1986] Hodder hbk **£10.95**

MCLAVERTY, MICHAEL (Irish, 1907 -)
Distinguished short story writer who evokes the
wholeness of the Irish landscape, from its remote hill
farms to the streets of Belfast.
Call My Brother Back (1979)
[GB1988] Poolbeg pbk **£3.25**
Truth in the Night (1985)
[GB1989] Poolbeg pbk **£3.45**

MCWILLIAM, CANDIA
McWilliam's novels blend superior elegance and
savagery while coldly dissecting the lives of their
erring protagonists.
A Case of Knives
[GB1992] Sphere pbk **£3.99**
A Little Stranger (1989)   **NEW**
A parable of domestic horror involving a woman on
the brink of losing all because she has relied on the
imagined ordinariness of everything in her life.
[GB1993] Bloomsbury hbk **£11.95**

MIDDLETON, STANLEY (1919 -)
A prolific novelist, most of whose work is set in the
Potteries of the Midlands. His style is noted for its
obliqueness, giving his descriptions of work-a-day
existence an interest as documents of suburban life.
After a Fashion
[GB1994] Arrow pbk **£3.50**
After Dinner's Sleep (1986)
[GB1995] Methuen pbk **£3.95**
Entry into Jerusalem (1983)
[GB1996] Methuen pbk **£2.95**
Holiday (1974)
[GB1997] Arrow pbk **£3.50**
Recovery
[GB1998] Hutchinson hbk **£10.95**
Valley of Decision (1985)
Examines a perennial theme of modern fiction - the
struggle between self-fulfilment and relationships,
between individual growth and empathy.
[GB1999] Methuen pbk **£3.95**

MILLAR, MARTIN
Born in Glasgow, Millar currently lives in Brixton in
which his books are set. He writes post-punk comic
fantasies about petty criminality amid the young in
deprived urban communities.
Lux the Poet (1988)
During a riot in Brixton the self-obsessed, would-be
poet Lux, stumbles in and out of danger, pursued by
gangs and the police.
[GB2000] Fourth Estate pbk **£4.95**
Milk, Sulphate and Alby Starvation
A paranoid drug pusher and comic collector finds
himself pursued by Kung-Fu mafia and the Milk
Marketing Board in low-life South London.
[GB2001] Fourth Estate pbk **£4.95**
Ruby and the Stone Age Diet   **NEW**
[GB2002] Fourth Estate pbk **£4.95**

MITCHISON, NAOMI (Scottish, 1897 -)
With over 70 books to her credit, her literary output
matches her extraordinarily diverse life. Leaving
aside autobiographical, historical and cultural
writings, and a lifelong commitment to Black Africa,
her work ranges through history, prehistory, the future
and fantasy, exploring feminism, environmentalism
folklore, and politics - all with energy and sensitivity.
Beyond this Limit (Stories)
[GB2006] Scottish Acad P pbk **£4.95**
Early in Orcadia (1987)
[GB2007] R Drew pbk **£3.95**

Memoirs of a Spacewoman (1962)
[GB2008] Womens P pbk **£1.95**
The Bull Calves (1947)
[GB2009] R Drew pbk **£4.95**
Travel Light (1952)
[GB2010] Virago pbk **£3.50**

MITFORD, NANCY (1904 - 1973)
The most talented of the 'famous Mitford sisters',
Nancy's ever-popular comic novels are celebrated as
minor masterpieces, depicting the reckless and
'amusing' world of pre- and post-war aristocratic
indulgence with dialogue that is pitch perfect.
Best Novels
*The Pursuit of Love/Love in a Cold Climate/The
Blessing/Don't Tell Alfred.*
[GB2011] H Hamilton hbk **£10.95**
[GB2014] Penguin pbk **£5.95**
Don't Tell Alfred (1960)
[GB2012] Penguin pbk **£2.50**
Love in a Cold Climate (1949)
[GB2013] Penguin pbk **£3.99**
Pudding and Pie
[GB2016] Arrow pbk **£5.95**
The Blessing (1951)
[GB2018] Penguin pbk **£2.95**
The Pursuit of Love (1945)
Her first major success, this follows the amatory
progress of the six Radlett cousins, in particular the
prolific love life of the beautiful Linda, who finally
falls victim to a premature death.
[GB2017] Penguin pbk **£3.99**

MO, TIMOTHY (1950 -)
A major novelist who has twice been shortlisted for
the Booker Prize. The son of an English mother and a
Cantonese father, he was born in Hong Kong and
attended an English university. A writer of diverse
interests, Mo also writes regularly for *Boxing News*.
An Insular Possession (1986)
Mo received considerable acclaim for this ambitious
historical novel in which he unfolds the founding of
Hong Kong.
[GB2019] Chatto hbk **£10.95**
[GB2020] Pan pbk **£5.95**
Sour Sweet (1982)
A refreshing comic novel about the Chinese
community in 1960's London.
[GB2021] Deutsch hbk **£7.95**
[GB2022] Sphere pbk **£3.99**
The Monkey King (1978)
[GB2023] Sphere pbk **£3.99**

MOGGACH, DEBORAH (1948 -)
A talented novelist who has written wittily about love,
emotional corruption and the controversial subject of
surrogate motherhood.
Close to Home (1979)
[GB2024] Penguin pbk **£2.25**
Driving in the Dark (1988)
Hilarious and compassionate account of a man
travelling around in a bus on a frantic chase to find
his estranged eleven year old son.
[GB2025] H Hamilton hbk **£11.95**
Hot Water Man (1982)
[GB2026] Penguin pbk **£2.99**
Porky (1983)
[GB2027] Penguin pbk **£2.99**
Smile (Stories, 1987)
[GB2028] Penguin pbk **£2.50**
To Have and to Hold (1986)
[GB2029] Penguin pbk **£2.95**

MOONEY, BEL
Mooney's work looks at the way in which people's
well-ordered lives are disrupted when confronted with
conflicting emotions.
Anderson Question (1985)
[GB2030] Pan pbk **£2.95**

Fourth of July (1988)
[GB2031] H Hamilton hbk **£10.95**
Windsurf Boy (1983)
[GB2032] Pan pbk **£2.95**

MOORCOCK, MICHAEL (1939 -)
Although his reputation rests chiefly on his fantsay
writing (see *Science Fiction*), Moorcock has also
written dynamic historical novels, such as *Gloriana*,
his treatment of the Elizabethan age, which form huge
tapestries and combine fact with imaginative
speculation.
Byzantium Endures (1981)
[GB2033] Fontana pbk **£3.95**
Casablanca (1989)   **NEW**
Moorcock's latest collection, consisting of six new
stories, a miscellany of articles, and a long novella.
[GB2034] Gollancz hbk **£11.95**
Gloriana (1978)
[GB2035] Fontana pbk **£4.95**
Mother London (1988)
This major work connects the blitz era with the
present day and also links a group of misfits, both
with each other and with strange, neglected parts of
the capital. It is a vast panoramic view of the
endlessly mutating and complex urban landscape - a
phenomenon, Moorcock suggests, comprised more of
human souls than the buildings they inhabit.
[GB2036] Secker hbk **£11.95**
[GB2037] Penguin pbk **£3.99**
The Laughter of Carthage (1984)
[GB2038] Fontana pbk **£4.50**

MOORE, BRIAN (Irish, 1921 -)
Born in Belfast, Moore emigrated to Canada in 1948
and has now settled in California. Many of his novels
deal with the theme of displacement and migration,
which he treats in a carefully understated style. His
books are strongly imaginative, often involving
bizarre plots, but his fictional landscapes are always
carefully evoked and fully realized.
Black Robe (1985)
A highly acclaimed and imaginative work.
Accompanying Father Paul Laforgue on his mission
to relieve an isolated priest in danger, Daniel Davost
is torn between the need to serve God and the power
of the native Indian way of life.
[GB2039] Grafton pbk **£3.95**
Catholics (1972)
[GB2041] Grafton pbk **£2.50**
Cold Heaven (1983)
[GB2043] Grafton pbk **£2.50**
Fergus (1971)
Fergus Fadden has come to Hollywood to seek his
fortune and to escape the ghosts of his past.
[GB2044] Grafton pbk **£2.50**
I am Mary Dunne (1968)
A vivid picture of one day in the life of Mary Dunne.
[GB2045] Grafton pbk **£1.50**
The Answer from Limbo (1963)
Moore's fourth novel concerns the clash of two
cultures and two systems of morality which occur
when Brendan Tierney brings his mother from Ireland
to his home in New York.
[GB2046] Deutsch pbk **£3.95**
The Colour of Blood (1987)
His most recent novel, shortlisted for the Booker
Prize, is a brilliant, sustained narrative about an East
European priest who becomes embroiled in the
politics of the state.
[GB2047] Cape hbk **£10.95**
[GB2048] Grafton pbk **£3.95**
The Doctor's Wife (1976)
Shortlisted for the Booker Prize.
[GB2050] Grafton pbk **£3.95**
The Emperor of Ice Cream (1965)
During World War II in Belfast a young Republican
joins the ARP, but finds it as irksome as school.
[GB2051] Grafton pbk **£3.95**

The Feast of Lupercal (1957)
[GB2052] Grafton pbk **£2.50**
The Great Victorian Collection (1975)
[GB2054] Grafton pbk **£3.95**
The Lonely Passion of Judith Hearne (1955)
Reality and fantasy become mix when Judith Hearne moves into new lodgings and meets James Madden. Is it too late for love in her life? Now filmed.
[GB2055] Deutsch hbk **£9.95**
[GB2056] Grafton pbk **£3.50**
The Luck of Ginger Coffey (1960)
The story of a man who emigrates from Ireland to Canada but finds no outlet for his many talents.
[GB2057] Grafton pbk **£3.95**
The Mangan Inheritance (1979)
[GB2058] Cape hbk **£9.95**
The Temptation of Eileen Hughes (1981)
Moore has been acclaimed by critics for his understanding of women. He shows his characteristic skill in this work about a young shop assistant and her employers who take her to London.
[GB2059] Grafton pbk **£3.50**

MORGAN, CHARLES (1894 - 1958)
One of the most popular writers of the 1930s and 1940s, rated higher than Evelyn Waugh by some of his contemporaries.
The Fountain
[GB2060] Robson pbk **£5.95**
The Judge's Story
A retired judge faces the hardest verdict of his life, the verdict on himself.
[GB1987] Robson pbk **£6.95**
The River Line (1949)
A young airman shot down in Belgium during the Second World War is saved by the underground network known as the 'River Line'. When he meets again some of the people involved in his escape, he relives those days and wonders why one of their party had to be sacrificed.
[GB2061] Robson pbk **£5.95**

MORRIS, JAN (1926 -)
Last Letters From Hav (1985)
Morris is a fine prose stylist, renowned for her non-fiction and travel works. This is an extraordinary *tour de force*, in which she creates an imaginary city, in the tradition of fantastical utopian novels such as *Erewhon* and *News from Nowhere*.
[GB2063] Penguin pbk **£2.95**

MORTIMER, JOHN (1923 -)
Barrister, novelist, screenwriter and dramatist, Mortimer offers sharp and witty critiques of the English middle class. A comic novelist very much in the English tradition, he has created his own alter ego in the unforgettable barrister Horace Rumpole.
Charade (1947)
[GB2064] Penguin pbk **£2.99**
Like Men Betrayed (1953)
[GB2066] Penguin pbk **£2.99**
Paradise Postponed (1985)
His most serious novel to date presents a vivid panorama of English life from 1945 to the present , assessing the changing mores of the post-war decades.
[GB2067] Penguin pbk **£3.95**
Summer's Lease (1988)
An English woman brings her family to a small Italian community for their holidays, providing another vehicle for Mortimer's wit and Dickensian flair for character, as well as his more serious concern with notions of personal honesty and fulfilment.
[GB2075] Viking hbk **£10.95**
[GB2076] Penguin pbk **£3.50**
First Rumpole Omnibus
[GB2065] Penguin pbk **£5.99**
Second Rumpole Omnibus
[GB2074] Penguin pbk **£5.99**

MORTIMER, PENELOPE (1918 -)
A novelist whose *The Pumpkin Eater* made an important contribution to the development of women's fiction in the 1960s. She writes frankly about the passion and despair of everyday life, and female experience in particular.
Home (1971)
[GB2078] Hutchinson hbk **£9.95**
My Friend Says It's Bullet Proof (1967)
[GB2079] Virago pbk **£4.99**
Saturday Lunch with the Brownings
[GB2080] Penguin pbk **£2.95**
The Pumpkin Eater (1962)
[GB2081] Penguin pbk **£2.95**

MOSCO, MAISIE
Manchester playwight turned novelist. Her *Between Two Worlds* trilogy is a Jewish family saga set in her native North of England.
Almonds & Raisins
Set in the cold world of Manchester in 1905, the Sandberg family found the good things of life scarce and the hardships as bitter as the chill northern winds.
[GB2083] Hodder hbk **£12.95**
Out of the Ashes `NEW`
The story of a modern Jewish matriach who, following in her recently-deceased grandmother's footsteps, tries to keep the family together while meeting outside demands.
[GB2086] Collins hbk **£11.95**
Scattered Seed
[GB2088] Hodder pbk **£3.50**

MOTION, ANDREW
Pale Companion (1989) `NEW`
The renowned poet's new novel - the first part of a proposed sequence - describes the confusions and intensities of growing up, and early attempts to reconcile interior and exterior realities.
[GB2093] Viking hbk **£11.95**

MUIR, EDWIN (Scottish, 1887 - 1959)
The Marionette (1927)
The earliest of three novels by the celebrated Orkney poet and critic.
[GB2094] Hogarth hbk **£4.50**

MUIR, HELEN
Nothing For You, Love (1988)
Sharp and funny book about a woman who absents herself from her family and returns to Liverpool to clear her mind while comforting a dying relative.
[GB2095] Gollancz hbk **£10.95**

MUIR, WILLA (Scottish, 1890 - 1970)
Imagined Corners (1936)
A better novelist than her husband Edwin, Willa Muir, in her first novel, shows the effects of moral and sexual repression on the inhabitants, particularly the women, of a small coastal town in the North East.
[GB2096] Canongate pbk **£3.95**

MULKERNS, VAL (Irish, 1925 -)
The Summer-House (1984)
The voices of five separate but intertwined characters tell the story, dominated by the central image of the crumbling summer house, a symbol of failure and decay.
[GB2097] Futura pbk **£1.95**
Very Like a Whale (1986)
[GB2098] Futura pbk **£3.50**

MURDOCH, ANNA
Family Business
A wealthy woman, attempting to build a communications empire, tries to balance her drive for power with her love for a prominent, charismatic politician.
[GB2099] Fontana pbk **£3.99**

MURDOCH, IRIS (1919 -)
One of the most popular contemporary English novelists, Iris Murdoch continues to defy classification: she has created her own genre, elaborate love stories with a streak of philosophy which explore the emotional, sexual and spiritual malaise of contemporary Britain. She has won many awards throughout her long career, remaining unrivalled in contemporary British fiction for her fearless moral seriousness and for the magnanimity of her compassion.
A Fairly Honourable Defeat (1970)
[GB2100] Chatto hbk **£9.95**
[GB2101] Penguin pbk **£3.95**
A Severed Head (1961)
[GB2102] Chatto hbk **£12.95**
[GB2103] Penguin pbk **£3.99**
A Word Child (1975)
[GB2104] Chatto hbk **£9.95**
[GB2105] Penguin pbk **£3.95**
An Accidental Man (1971)
[GB2106] Chatto hbk **£12.95**
[GB2107] Penguin pbk **£4.50**
An Unofficial Rose (1962)
[GB2108] Chatto hbk **£12.95**
[GB2109] Penguin pbk **£4.50**
Bruno's Dream (1979)
[GB2110] Chatto hbk **£9.95**
[GB2111] Penguin pbk **£3.50**
Henry and Cato (1976)
[GB2112] Chatto hbk **£12.95**
[GB2113] Penguin pbk **£3.95**
Nuns and Soldiers (1980)
[GB2114] Chatto hbk **£9.95**
[GB2115] Penguin pbk **£3.95**
The Bell (1958)
Her most famous and acclaimed novel. Set in an idealistic lay religious community in the country, the book explores the moral, spiritual and erotic tensions beneath an apparently peaceful surface.
[GB2116] Chatto hbk **£12.95**
[GB2117] Penguin pbk **£3.99**
The Black Prince (1973)
A dramatic love story between a middle-aged man and much younger woman, which develops into an ambiguous murder story.
[GB2118] Chatto hbk **£12.95**
[GB2119] Penguin pbk **£4.50**
The Book and the Brotherhood (1987)
Booker Prize-shortlisted novel about a group of old students who meet at an Oxford ball, many years after their youthful pact to help one of them, now estranged, write a dissertation on a radical new society for Britain.
[GB2120] Chatto hbk **£11.95**
[GB2091] Penguin pbk **£4.99**
The Flight from the Enchanter (1956)
[GB2121] Chatto hbk **£12.95**
[GB2122] Penguin pbk **£2.95**
The Good Apprentice (1985)
Booker Prize shortlisted. The story of two brothers: Stuart, with a religious temperament but no God; and Edward, who is tormented by guilt. One of the very best of her long and elaborate later novels, with an intricate formal pattern.
[GB2123] Chatto hbk **£9.95**
[GB2124] Penguin pbk **£3.95**
The Italian Girl (1964)
[GB2125] Chatto hbk **£12.95**
[GB2126] Penguin pbk **£3.99**
The Message to the Planet (1989) `NEW`
Murdoch's 24th novel concerns the pursuit of a fundamental secret to the human condition. The secret is in the possession of one Professor Marcus Vallar, but is Vallar genius or madman?
[GB2127] Chatto hbk **£12.95**
The Nice and the Good (1968)
[GB2128] Chatto hbk **£9.95**
[GB2129] Penguin pbk **£4.99**

FICTION

The Philosopher's Pupil (1983)
[GB2130] Chatto hbk £9.95
[GB2131] Penguin pbk £4.95
The Red and the Green (1965)
A fictionalized account of a group involved in the Easter Rising.
[GB2132] Chatto hbk £12.95
[GB2133] Penguin pbk £3.95
The Sacred and Profane Love Machine (1974)
[GB2134] Chatto hbk £12.95
[GB2135] Penguin pbk £4.50
The Sandcastle (1957)
[GB2136] Chatto hbk £12.95
[GB2137] Penguin pbk £3.95
The Sea, the Sea (1978)
Booker Prize winner. A theatre director retires to a lonely house by the sea, and there discovers that his whole life has been governed by a woman he knew in his youth. This is one of Murdoch's most moving and elegiac love stories.
[GB2138] Chatto hbk £12.95
[GB2139] Grafton pbk £3.95
The Unicorn (1963)
[GB2140] Chatto hbk £9.95
[GB2141] Penguin pbk £3.95
Time of the Angels (1966)
[GB2142] Chatto hbk £12.95
[GB2143] Penguin pbk £3.95
Under the Net (1954)
[GB2144] Chatto hbk £9.95
[GB2145] Penguin pbk £3.95

MURPHY, ROBERTA
The Enchanted **NEW**
A young girl in South Wales becomes entranced by a fantasy echoing the lore of the local hills, created partly by herself and partly by her late grandfather.
[GB21451] Heinemann pbk £11.95

MYERS, L.H. (1881 - 1944)
The Root and the Flower
Distinguished novel about India in the 19th century, part of a tetralogy which highlights the poverty of contemporary society.
[GB2146] Oxford pbk £5.95

NAUGHTON, BILL
Reissues of the famous books which wittily evoke working-class life.
Alfie
Bestseller, later made into a successful film, starring the young Michael Caine as the eponymous hero.
[GB2158] Allison & B pbk £3.99
Late Night on Watling Street (Stories)
[GB2159] Allison & B pbk £3.99
One Small Boy
[GB2160] Allison & B pbk £4.99

NEWBY, P.H. (1918 -)
Booker Prize winning novelist, acclaimed for his taut, accomplished comic novels.
Feelings Have Changed (1981)
[GB2161] Faber hbk £6.95
Leaning in the Wind (1986)
[GB2162] Faber hbk £9.95

NORTH, JOSEPH
Diary of a Misplaced Philosopher **NEW**
A masterful comic novel, depicting the eccentric household and acquaintance of an unemployed philosopher, stuck in a shabby London suburb.
[GB2169] Bloomsbury hbk £11.95

NORTH, SAM
Automatic Man **NEW**
A first novel with an imaginative treatment of the paranoia of modern urban life.
[GB2170] Secker hbk £11.95

NYE, ROBERT (1939 -)
Robert Nye uses mythical or real characters from the past as the starting point for some ingenious discursive novels.
Faust (1980)
[GB2171] Penguin pbk £2.95
Merlin (1978)
[GB2172] Penguin pbk £3.95
The Memoirs of Lord Byron **NEW**
In a delicious mix of truth and fiction, history and invention, Nye here provides a provocative, engrossing portrait of the inner life of the 'mad, bad' Romantic poet.
[GB21721] H Hamilton hbk £12.95
Voyage of the Destiny (1982)
[GB2173] H Hamilton hbk £9.95

O'BRIEN, EDNA (Irish, 1932 -)
Born in the West of Ireland, Edna O'Brien's subject is often the transition between a state of innocence and a state of experience, revealed in her series *The Country Girls*. She writes of female sensuality and male treachery, and is adept at describing the pains and pleasures of country life.
A Pagan Place (1970)
[GB2175] Penguin pbk £2.95
A Scandalous Woman & Other Stories
[GB2177] Penguin pbk £2.25
August is a Wicked Month (1965)
Ellen, separated from her husband and alone, is in London. She then heads South in search of sun and sex.
[GB2178] Penguin pbk £2.50
Casualties of Peace (1966)
[GB2179] Penguin pbk £2.50
High Road (1988)
[GB2180] Weidenfeld hbk £10.95
Johnny I Hardly Knew You (1977)
A desperate woman is driven to exact revenge by murdering her lover - he is also her son's best friend.
[GB2182] Penguin pbk £2.50
Mrs Reinhardt and Other Stories (1978)
[GB2184] Penguin pbk £2.50
Night (1972)
[GB2186] Penguin pbk £2.25
Returning: Tales (1982)
[GB2188] Penguin pbk £2.50
The Fanatic Heart (Stories, 1985)
The best of the stories from her previous collections together with four new pieces, and a foreword by Philip Roth.
[GB2189] Weidenfeld hbk £10.95
[GB2190] Penguin pbk £5.95
The Love Object & Other Stories (1968)
[GB2191] Penguin pbk £2.99
Some Irish Loving: A Selection
O'Brien edited this anthology of pieces by authors ranging from J.M. Synge to Samuel Beckett, on the Irish attitude to love.
[GB2198] Penguin pbk £3.95
THE COUNTRY GIRLS TRILOGY
Country Girls (1960)
Her famous trilogy opens with the escape of two girls from the countryside and their convent to the alluring lights of Dublin.
[GB2193] Penguin pbk £2.95
The Girl with Green Eyes (1962)
Comic sequel in which one of the girls finds romance in Dublin.
[GB2194] Penguin pbk £2.50
Girls in their Married Bliss (1964)
[GB2195] Penguin pbk £2.25
Country Girls Trilogy (with epilogue)
[GB2196] Cape hbk £15.00
[GB2197] Penguin pbk £5.95

O'BRIEN, FLANN (Irish, 1916 - 1966)
Flann O'Brien worked for much of his life in the Irish Civil Service and his work explores Irish culture on a variety of levels, both comic and naturalistic, and acknowledges the influence of James Joyce. He is probably best remembered for *The Third Policeman* and *At Swim-two-birds*, both comic masterpieces which develop amid complex, lampooning plot structures.
At Swim-two-birds (1939)
A brilliant impressionistic jumble of a novel incorporating plots within plots and giving full reign to O'Brien's Celtic wit.
[GB2199] Penguin pbk £3.95
Best of Myles Na Gopaleen
For many years of his life O'Brien contributed weekly a satirical column to *The Irish Times*. The best of those columns are presented here in an illustrated collection.
[GB2201] Grafton pbk £5.95
Myles Away from Dublin
[GB2204] Grafton pbk £4.95
Myles Before Myles
[GB2205] Grafton pbk £6.95
Further Cuttings from Cruiskeen Lawn
[GB2202] Grafton pbk £5.95
Hair of the Dogma
[GB2203] Grafton pbk £4.95
Stories and Plays
[GB2206] Grafton pbk £4.95
The Dalkey Archive (1965)
Science fiction-like collage featuring 'characters' such as St. Augustine, James Joyce, and a man who is in danger of turning into a bicycle.
[GB2207] Grafton pbk £4.95
The Hard Life (1967)
The hilarious story of two boys who come into the house of Mr Collopy.
[GB2208] Grafton pbk £4.95
The Poor Mouth (1941)
'Putting on the poor mouth' means pretending to be poor in order to gain advantage from creditors. Its practitioners are satirized in this witty account of rural hardship in a Gaelic-speaking region in the south of Ireland. *The Poor Mouth* is also a hilarious satire on the revival of the Irish language. Illustrated by Ralph Steadman.
[GB2209] Grafton pbk £3.95
The Third Policeman (1940, published 1967)
A wonderfully bizarre combination of murder thriller, comic satire, surrealistic vision and an inevitably unrequited love affair between a man and his bicycle.
[GB2210] Grafton pbk £4.95
The Various Lives of Keats, Chapman and the Brother
[GB2211] Grafton pbk £5.95

O'BRIEN, KATE (Irish, 1897 - 1974)
Her main interest was Spain, which is reflected in her best known novel, *That Lady*.
Ante-Room
[GB2213] Virago pbk £4.99
Land of Spices
[GB2214] Virago pbk £4.50
Mary Lavelle (1936)
In 1922 Mary Lavelle leaves her home in Ireland to become a governess in Spain. Little by little she loses her heart to the Spanish landscape.
[GB2215] Virago pbk £3.95
That Lady (1946)
The tragic love story of Philip II's mistress who was referred to as 'that lady' after her fall.
[GB2216] Virago pbk £3.95
Without My Cloak (1931)
This, her first novel, won the Hawthornden and James Tait Black Prizes. It is a stirring family saga opening in 1789. Introduced by Desmond Hogan.
[GB2217] Virago pbk £4.50

O'CONNOR, FRANK (Irish, 1903 -1966)
O'Connor has for many years been regarded as one of the great masters of the short story. His work shows the life of the middle and working classes of Ireland in a warmly humorous style.
My Oedipus Complex (Stories)
[GB2219] Penguin pbk **£3.95**

O'DONNELL, PEADAR (Irish, 1893 -)
His sympathies were always left-wing and his deepest interest was in the welfare of the farmers of the North West of Ireland, exploited first by the landlords and then apparently no better off under the Free State.
The Knife (1930)
After capture in the battle of Four Courts Dublin O'Donnell was sentenced to death by the Free State for fighting against the Republican side in the Civil War. He escaped and this novel is based on his experiences which included a forty-one-day hunger strike.
[GB2220] O'Brien P pbk **£4.50**

O'FAOLAIN, JULIA (Irish, 1932 -)
No Country for Young Men (1980)
Shortlisted for the Booker Prize, this is a devastating story of human and political relations in contemporary Ireland. Four generations of families attempt to come to terms with the after-effects of the Civil War.
[GB2221] Penguin pbk **£3.95**
The Irish Signorina (1984)
A love story set in Ireland and Italy.
[GB2222] Penguin pbk **£2.50**
Women in the Wall (1973)
O'Faolan's second novel is a rich and vivid portrait of 6th century Gaul, based on original chronicles from the time.
[GB2223] Virago pbk **£4.50**

O'FAOLAIN, SEAN (Irish, 1900 -)
Politically active during the Civil War, O'Faolain returned to Ireland in 1933. His novels deal in part with the frustrations of the Irish nationalists, and a sense of loss and limitation colours his stories, which owe something to those of Chekhov.
A Nest of Simple Folk (1934)
The story of the Hussey family and the deep-seated conflicts of an Irish middle-class family in the early parts of this century.
[GB2224] Constable hbk **£10.95**
And Again?
[GB2225] Constable hbk **£5.95**
Bird Alone (1936)
Introduced by Benedict Kiely. A man reviews his past life: growing up in late 19th century Cork in a family marked by pride and poverty.
[GB2226] Oxford pbk **£3.95**
Collected Stories
Vol 1: Midsummer Night Madness
'One of the most accomplished living exponents of the short story.' (John Fowles).
[GB2228] Penguin pbk **£4.95**
Vol 2: The Heat of the Sun
[GB2230] Penguin pbk **£4.95**
Vol 3: Foreign Affairs
[GB2232] Penguin pbk **£4.95**

O'FLAHERTY, LIAM (Irish, 1897 - 1984)
A nationalist better known for his short stories which deal unsentimentally with life and death, loss of faith and devotion, the tenacity of old age and the need for 'freedom'.
Black Soul (1924)
[GB2233] Wolfhound hbk **£8.95**
Ecstasy of Angus (1931)
[GB2234] Wolfhound pbk **£2.95**
Famine (1937)
One of the classic works of 20th century Irish literature, this is the story of three generations of the Kilmartin family set mainly in the period of the Great Famine of the 1840s.
[GB2235] Wolfhound pbk **£4.95**
Insurrection
[GB2236] Wolfhound pbk **£3.95**
Short Stories
[GB2238] Hodder pbk **£3.50**
Skerrett
[GB2239] Wolfhound pbk **£3.25**
The Assassin (1928)
A political thriller which captures a particular time and facet of Dublin life.
[GB2240] Wolfhound pbk **£2.95**
Wilderness
[GB2241] Wolfhound pbk **£3.95**

OAKLEY, ANN
The Men's Room (1988)
Challenging love story chronicling the extra-marital affair between two sociology lecturers, which exposes the fantasies and weaknesses of both sexes.
[GB2243] Virago hbk **£11.95**
[GB2244] Fontana pbk **£3.99**

OBERMAN, WENDY
Mothers and Other Loves
A mother's obsessive love for her son has far-reaching effects on his adult life.
[GB2245] Heinemann hbk **£10.95**

OLDHAM, JUNE
Flames (1986)
'Has an almost Lawrentian theme in its exploration of the marriage between an uneducated labourer and a sensitive, introverted schoolmistress.' (Jane Gardam). Winner of the Virago First Fiction Prize.
[GB2256] Virago pbk **£3.50**

OLDHAM, MARK
New Values
Horror story from a new novelist, about an autocratic German nursemaid in a crumbling English country home during the run up to World War II.
[GB2257] Hodder hbk **£12.95**

ORWELL, GEORGE (1903 - 1950)
Orwell's reputation rests chiefly on two political allegories of the 1940s (*Animal Farm* and *1984*). He is, however, equally celebrated for his essays which are constantly entertaining. His identification with the society's displaced and disenfranchized has earned him accusations of false consciousness and inverted snobbery; but, his non-conformism is peculiarly British, a radical puritanism that links plain living and language with honesty, freedom and social justice.
A Clergyman's Daughter (1935)
[GB2260] Secker hbk **£12.95**
[GB2261] Penguin pbk **£2.95**
Animal Farm (1945)
As a political fable, *Animal Farm* has lost none of its bite. Economy of prose, clarity of theme, structure and imaginative vision combine to form the modern parable *par excellence*.
[GB2262] Secker hbk **£5.95**
[GB2263] Penguin pbk **£1.95**
Burmese Days (1934)
[GB2264] Secker hbk **£12.95**
[GB2265] Penguin pbk **£2.95**
Collected Essays, Journalism and Letters
Volume 1
[GB2267] Secker hbk **£12.50**
[GB2271] Penguin pbk **£6.95**
Volume 2
[GB2268] Secker hbk **£12.50**
[GB2272] Penguin pbk **£6.99**
Volume 3
[GB2269] Secker hbk **£12.50**
[GB2273] Penguin pbk **£6.95**

Volume 4
[GB2270] Secker hbk **£12.50**
[GB2274] Penguin pbk **£7.95**
Coming Up for Air (1939)
[GB2275] Secker hbk **£12.95**
[GB2276] Penguin pbk **£2.50**
Complete Longer Non-Fiction
[GB2277] Penguin pbk **£5.95**
Complete Novels
[GB2278] Penguin pbk **£6.95**
Decline of the English Murder
(Non fiction)
[GB2279] Penguin pbk **£2.95**
Down and Out in Paris and London
(1933)
[GB2280] Secker hbk **£12.95**
[GB2281] Penguin pbk **£2.99**
Essays
[GB2282] Penguin pbk **£4.95**
Homage to Catalonia (Non fiction, 1939)
[GB2283] Penguin pbk **£4.95**
Inside the Whale (Essays)
[GB2284] Penguin pbk **£2.99**
Keep the Aspidistra Flying (1936)
The novel which most clearly exemplifies Orwell's obsessive conviction that the quality of life is determined by money.
[GB2285] Secker hbk **£12.95**
[GB2286] Penguin pbk **£2.95**
Lion and the Unicorn (Essays)
[GB2287] Penguin pbk **£2.50**
Nineteen Eighty-four (1949)
A nighmarish and Kafkesque vision of a totalitarian world, whose implications and wider significance remain wholly relevant today.
[GB2288] Secker hbk **£12.95**
[GB2289] Penguin pbk **£2.99**
The Road to Wigan Pier (Non fiction, 1937)
[GB2290] Secker hbk **£12.95**
[GB2291] Penguin pbk **£2.95**
War Broadcasts (Non fiction)
[GB2292] BBC hbk **£12.95**
War Commentaries (Non fiction)
[GB2293] BBC hbk **£14.95**
[GB2294] Penguin pbk **£4.95**

PARGETER, EDITH
As well as being author of these books of medieval historical fiction, Edith Pargeter also writes the famous 'Brother Cadfael' mysteries under the pseudonym Ellis Peters (see *Crime*).
Marriage of Meggotta
[GB2298] Futura pbk **£3.50**
THE BROTHERS OF GWYNEDD
1: The Sunrise in the West
[GB2299] Headline pbk **£2.95**
2: The Dragons at Noonday
[GB2300] Headline pbk **£2.95**
3: Hounds of Sunset
[GB2301] Headline pbk **£2.95**
4: Afterglow & Nightfall
[GB2302] Headline pbk **£3.50**
The Brothers of Gwynedd Quartet `NEW`
[GB2327] Headline pbk **£6.95**

THE HEAVEN TRILOGY
1: The Heaven Tree
[GB2303] Futura pbk **£2.95**
2: The Green Branch
[GB2304] Futura pbk **£2.95**
3: The Scarlet Seed
[GB2305] Futura pbk **£2.95**

PARK, CHRISTINE
Househusband `NEW`
A love story centring on the despair of a man burdened with his children, who finds relief and friendship in his meetings with a young girl.
[GB2306] Heinemann hbk **£10.95**

PARKS, TIM
Wry and often powerful observer of contemporary life and its attendant passions.
Family Planning **NEW**
[GB2309] Collins hbk **£11.95**
Home Thoughts (1988)
[GB2310] Fontana pbk **£3.95**
Loving Roger
[GB2311] Fontana pbk **£3.95**
Tongues of Flame (1985)
[GB2312] Fontana pbk **£1.95**

PATTERSON, GLENN (Irish, 1961 -)
Burning Your Own (1988)
First novel about the rite of passage of ten year old Mal Martin through the streets of Belfast in the summer of 1969.
[GB2313] Chatto hbk **£11.95**
[GB2314] Sphere pbk **£3.99**

PEAKE, MERVYN (1911 - 1968)
He is celebrated both as an artist and as the author of an extravagant and grotesque gothic fantasy - the *Gormenghast* trilogy. His writing is elaborate and sustained: a triumphant combination of Dickens and Kafka.
Mr Pye (1953)
[GB2315] Penguin pbk **£3.95**
Gormenghast
[GB2316] Eyre & S hbk illus **£12.95**
[GB2317] Methuen pbk **£3.50**
Titus Alone
[GB2318] Eyre & S hbk illus **£10.95**
[GB2319] Methuen pbk **£2.95**
Titus Groan
[GB2320] Eyre & S hbk illus **£12.95**
[GB2321] Methuen pbk **£3.50**

PHIPPS, CONSTANTINE
Among the Thin Ghosts **NEW**
A restless Englishwoman marries a slightly suspect Italian whom she does not even love. Why? Things of course go wrong and her descent into Hell is the subject of this elegant examination of human behaviour.
[GB2325] Bloomsbury hbk **£12.95**

PICKERING, PAUL
Blue Gate of Babylon **NEW**
In this novel a spy finds his sanity hanging in the balance when events from his distant past catch up with him.
[GB2326] Chatto hbk **£12.95**

PILCHER, ROSAMUND
The Shell Seekers (1988)
A novel of traditional values with insight into the frailties and strengths of family relationships.
[GB2328] Hodder pbk **£3.99**

PIZZEY, ERIN (1939 -)
The founder of Women's Aid (a refuge for battered women) now writing novels in which she expounds the values of home and family, as opposed to the attractions of power and influence.
Consul General's Daughter
[GB2330] Collins hbk **£11.95**
First Lady
[GB2331] Fontana pbk **£2.95**
In the Shadow of the Castle
[GB2332] Transworld pbk **£2.50**
The Snow Leopard of Shanghai **NEW**
Pizzey's new novel tells the story of two sisters who flee from Tsarist Russia to China, and the fates which await them. An evocative portrait of 'exotic' ways of life, and of the different characters of the two women.
[GB2333] Collins hbk **£12.95**
The Watershed
[GB2334] Transworld pbk **£2.95**

PLATER, ALAN
Accomplished playwright with a particular flair for television drama. These are an extremely entertaining group of comic thrillers, which have recently been televised.
Beiderbecke Affair
[GB2352] Methuen pbk **£2.95**
Beiderbecke Tapes
[GB2353] Methuen pbk **£2.95**
Misterioso (1987)
[GB2354] Methuen pbk **£2.95**

PLOMER, WILLIAM (1903 - 1973)
A South African, educated in England, who wrote poetry and collaborated with Benjamin Britten on the librettos of his operas.
Turbott Wolfe (1926)
A savage satire on life in South Africa, this was Plomer's first novel: little that he wrote afterwards achieved the same power.
[GB2355] Oxford pbk **£4.50**

PLUNKETT, JAMES (Irish, 1920 -)
His most acclaimed novel, *Strumpet City*, describes life in Dublin in the early years of this century.
Collected Short Stories (1977)
[GB2356] Poolbeg pbk **£1.95**
Strumpet City (1969)
[GB2357] Arrow pbk **£3.99**
The Farewell Companions (1977)
[GB2358] Arrow pbk **£3.99**

POST, LAURENS VAN DER (1906 -)
Van der Post is a travel and adventure writer, as well as a distinguished anthropologist, whose knowledge of the diversity of human culture and society is reflected in the wide-ranging nature of his fiction. *The Seed and the Sower*, about a Japanese prisoner of war camp during World War II, formed the basis for Oshima's film, *Merry Christmas, Mr Lawrence*.
A Far Off Place (1974)
[GB2359] Penguin hbk **£4.95**
Flamingo Feather (1955)
[GB2360] Penguin pbk **£4.50**
In a Province (1934)
[GB2361] Penguin pbk **£3.99**
Story Like the Wind (1972)
[GB2362] Penguin pbk **£4.95**
The Hunter and the Whale (1967)
[GB2363] Penguin pbk **£4.50**
The Seed and the Sower (1963)
[GB2364] Penguin pbk **£3.95**

POTTER, DENNIS (1935 -)
One of the best known and most controversial of contemporary screenwriters, acclaimed for his ambitious television serials, *Pennies from Heaven* and *The Singing Detective*. His work weaves together elements of memory, voyeuristic fantasy, reality, pulp fiction and popular music to create worlds of compelling psychological urgency.
Blackeyes (1987)
An aging novelist enjoys a vicarious sex life through listening to the promiscuous exploits of a young model.
[GB2365] Faber pbk **£3.95**
Ticket to Ride (1986)
[GB2366] Faber pbk **£3.95**

POWELL, ANTHONY (1905 -)
Powell is the creator of one of the greatest novel sequences of this, or any century, the twelve-volume *A Dance to the Music of Time*. To read it is to witness the events and moods of the 1930s and 1940s through the kaleidoscopic impressions of one man, Nicholas Jenkins. These stylish and engaging *tableaux vivants* deal with minutiae rather than melodrama, and are frequently hilarious. But the reader is cumulatively aware of the relentless passage of time and the shaping of personal destinies amid an all pervading, tragic view of England in decline and decay.
A DANCE TO THE MUSIC OF TIME
(in series order)
A Question of Upbringing (1951)
[GB2380] Heinemann hbk **£9.95**
[GB2381] Fontana pbk **£2.95**
A Buyer's Market (1952)
[GB2382] Heinemann hbk **£11.95**
[GB2383] Fontana pbk **£2.95**
The Acceptance World (1955)
[GB2384] Heinemann hbk **£9.95**
[GB2385] Fontana pbk **£2.50**
At Lady Molly's (1957)
[GB2386] Heinemann hbk **£9.95**
[GB2387] Fontana pbk **£2.95**
Casanova's Chinese Restaurant (1960)
[GB2388] Heinemann hbk **£9.95**
[GB2389] Fontana pbk **£2.95**
The Kindly Ones (1962)
[GB2390] Heinemann hbk **£9.95**
[GB2391] Fontana pbk **£2.95**
Valley of Bones (1964)
[GB2392] Heinemann hbk **£9.95**
[GB2393] Fontana pbk **£2.95**
The Soldier's Art (1966)
[GB2394] Heinemann hbk **£9.95**
[GB2395] Fontana pbk **£2.95**
The Military Philosophers (1968)
[GB2396] Heinemann hbk **£9.95**
[GB2397] Fontana pbk **£2.95**
Books Do Furnish A Room (1971)
[GB2374] Heinemann hbk **£9.95**
[GB2375] Fontana pbk **£2.95**
Temporary Kings (1973)
[GB2376] Heinemann hbk **£9.95**
[GB2377] Fontana pbk **£2.95**
Hearing Secret Harmonies (1975)
[GB2378] Heinemann hbk **£9.95**
[GB2379] Fontana pbk **£2.95**
OTHER NOVELS
Agents and Patients (1955)
[GB2367] Penguin pbk **£2.95**
From a View to a Death (1933)
[GB2368] Heinemann hbk **£9.95**
Oh! How the Wheel Becomes It (1983)
[GB2369] Penguin pbk **£3.95**
The Afternoon Men (1931)
[GB2370] Heinemann hbk **£9.95**
The Fisher King (1986)
[GB2371] Hodder pbk **£3.95**
Venusberg (1932)
[GB2372] Penguin pbk **£3.50**
What's Become of Waring (1932)
[GB2373] Fontana pbk **£1.50**

POWYS, JOHN COWPER (1872 - 1963)
Brother of Llewellyn and T.F. Powys, he did not become a serious novelist until his late fifties. His grandiose and supernatural historical novels have acquired a cult following, though critics remain divided as to their merits.
Romer Mowl & Other Stories
[GB2398] Toucan pbk **£3.00**
Three Fantasies
[GB2399] Grafton pbk **£3.50**
Weymouth Sands (1963)
[GB2400] Picador pbk **£3.50**
Wolf Solent (1929)
[GB2401] Penguin pbk **£5.99**

POWYS, T.F.
Mr Weston's Good Wine (1927)
An ironic allegory in which God appears in Dorset in the form of a wine merchant, this is Weston's best-known novel.
[GB2402] Hogarth pbk **£4.95**

POYSER, JAMES
In a Lonely Place `NEW`
An old man, born at the dawn of a new century, looks back to his past and tries to account for what has happened to him over the years.
[GB24011] H Hamilton hbk **£11.95**

PRANTERA, AMANDA
An imaginative new novelist, whose work is imbued with elements of the Gothic novel.
The Cabalist (1985)
[GB2403] Sphere pbk **£3.50**
Conversations with Lord Byron on Perversion (1987)
[GB2404] Sphere pbk **£3.99**
Strange Loop (1984)
[GB2405] Sphere pbk **£2.95**

PRIEST, CHRISTOPHER (1943 -)
Strangely haunting novelist who pares back the surface of his narratives, allowing oblique and disturbing connections to emerge.
Dreams of Wessex
[GB2406] Sphere pbk **£3.95**
The Affirmation (1981)
[GB2407] Gollancz pbk **£2.99**
The Glamour (1984)
[GB2408] Sphere pbk **£2.95**

PRIESTLEY, J.B. (1894 - 1984)
Novelist, dramatist and man of letters, Priestley's output was so varied that his writing is impossible to categorize neatly. His novels range from the energetic, picaresque tale of theatre travellers in *The Good Companions*, to the gritty urban realism of his London novel, *Angel Pavement*. A Yorkshireman who liked to present a cantankerous image of himself, several of his other novels evoke vivid northern settings.
Angel Pavement (1930)
[GB2409] Heinemann hbk **£9.95**
Lost Empires (1965)
[GB2410] Grafton pbk **£2.95**
Shapes of Sleep
[GB2411] Dent pbk **£3.95**
The Good Companions (1929)
[GB2412] Heinemann hbk **£8.95**
[GB2413] Grafton pbk **£3.50**
The Image Men (1929)
[GB2414] Allison & B pbk **£4.95**
Three Men in New Suits
[GB2415] Allison & B pbk **£2.95**

PRITCHETT, V.S. (1900 -)
Renowned as a modern master of the English short story, Pritchett's work is noted for its irony and precision across a wide range of subjects, and for its delicate and subtle delineations of character.
A Careless Widow & Other Stories `NEW`
A fine collection of short stories which display all Pritchett's great hallmarks: melancholy, comedy and sensitive portraiture. A hairdresser on holiday finds, to his horror, that his garrulous London neighbour is staying in the same hotel, and a carpet salesman is put firmly in his place by a former employee.
[GB2416A] Chatto hbk **£12.95**
Collected Stories (1982)
[GB2416] Chatto hbk **£12.50**
[GB2417] Penguin pbk **£5.95**
Dead Man Leading (1937)
[GB2418] Oxford pbk **£3.95**
Man of Letters (Essays)
[GB2419] Chatto hbk **£12.95**
More Collected Stories (1983)
[GB2420] Chatto hbk **£12.50**
Mr Beluncle (1951)
[GB2421] Oxford pbk **£3.95**
The Other Side of the Frontier
[GB2422] R Clark pbk **£5.95**

PROFUMO, DAVID
Sea Music (1988)
Promising début in which an eleven year old boy spends a school holiday on a remote Scottish island. Written with subtlety and power, it is notable for its strong awareness of folklore, and for its sense of the pervasive presence of the ocean.
[GB2423] Hodder pbk **£4.50**

PYM, BARBARA (1913 - 1980)
English high comedy and middle-class satire at its best. Her books are subtle, Austen-like comedies of manners, often gently poking fun at the clergy. Philip Larkin and A.N. Wilson both declared her a favourite.
A Glass of Blessings (1958)
[GB2424] Penguin pbk **£2.95**
An Academic Question
[GB2426] Grafton pbk **£2.95**
An Unsuitable Attachment (1942)
[GB2427] Macmillan hbk **£7.95**
Civil to Strangers & Other Writings
[GB2428] Macmillan hbk **£10.95**
Crampton Hodnet (1985)
[GB2429] Grafton pbk **£2.50**
Excellent Women (1952)
[GB2430] Penguin pbk **£2.95**
A Few Green Leaves (1980)
[GB2431] Grafton pbk **£2.95**
Jane and Prudence (1953)
[GB2432] Grafton pbk **£2.99**
Less Than Angels (1955)
[GB2433] Grafton pbk **£2.99**
No Fond Return of Love (1961)
[GB2434] Grafton pbk **£2.99**
Quartet in Autumn (1977)
[GB2435] Grafton pbk **£2.95**
Some Tame Gazelle (1950)
[GB2436] Grafton pbk **£2.95**
Sweet Dove Died (1978)
[GB2437] Grafton pbk **£2.50**

QUICK, RICHARD
Simon's Bug (1988)
Comic novel about a man who taps the family phone.
[GB2438] Penguin pbk **£4.99**

RABAN, JONATHAN (1942 -)
Foreign Land
A fine novel about a man who takes to the sea. It employs Raban's renowned skills as a travel writer in its sharp observations of contemporary England.
[2450] Picador pbk **£4.95**
Soft City (Non fiction)
His acclaimed early travel book about London.
[GB2451] Collins Harv pbk **£4.95**

RAE, HUGH (Scottish, 1935 -)
Skinner (1965)
Rae has described his early novel as a 'criminal roman', which uses an act of violence as a tool with which to delve into closed areas of the Scottish character.
[GB2452] R Drew pbk **£3.95**

RAPHAEL, FREDERIC (1931 -)
Witty social novelist, best known for his glamorous tales of Oxbridge life.
After the War (1988)
A conscience-ridden English artist living in comfort muses on the uselessness of middle-class guilt.
[GB2453] Fontana pbk **£3.95**
Glittering Prizes (1976)
[GB2454] Penguin pbk **£2.95**
Heaven and Earth (1985)
[GB2455] Penguin pbk **£3.95**
Oxbridge Blues (1980)
[GB2456] Penguin pbk **£3.50**
Think of England (Stories, 1986)
[GB2457] Cape hbk **£8.95**

RAVEN, SIMON (1927 -)
Alms for Oblivion is a series of English class comedies, often set in the world of academia. They are splendidly bibulous and full of a hearty rancour, as Raven, with scores of his own to settle, depicts a rambling social panorama.
Blood of My Bone
[GB2458] Blond hbk **£11.95**
Fortunes of Fingel
[GB2459] Blond hbk **£7.95**
Inch of Fortune
[GB2460] Blond hbk **£7.95**
Roses of Picardie
[GB2461] Blond hbk **£7.95**
September Castle
[GB2462] Grafton pbk **£2.50**

ALMS FOR OBLIVION (in writing order)
Fielding Gray
[GB2464] Grafton pbk **£1.95**
Sound the Retreat
[GB2465] Grafton pbk **£1.95**
The Sabre Squadron
[GB2466] Grafton pbk **£1.95**
The Rich Pay Late
[GB2467] Grafton pbk **£1.95**
Friends in Low Places
[GB2468] Grafton pbk **£1.95**
The Judas Boy
[GB2469] Grafton pbk **£1.95**
Places Where They Sing
[GB2470] Grafton pbk **£1.95**
Come Like Shadows
[GB2471] Grafton pbk **£1.95**
Bring Forth the Body
[GB2472] Grafton pbk **£1.95**
The Survivors
[GB2463] Grafton pbk **£1.95**

THE FIRST BORN OF EGYPT (in writing order)
His new series which follows on from *Alms for Oblivion*.
Morning Star
[GB2473] Grafton pbk **£2.50**
The Face of the Waters
[GB2474] Grafton pbk **£3.50**
Before the Cock Crow
[GB2475] Grafton pbk **£3.50**
New Seed for Old
[GB2476] Muller hbk **£10.95**

RAWLINSON, JANE
Cargo
[GB2477] Grafton pbk **£5.99**
Cradle Song
Subtle, restrained account of the whims and fantasies of a young mother in the stuffy atmosphere of colonial Kenya.
[GB2478] Grafton pbk **£3.50**
The Lion and the Lizard
Highly-charged tale of women in post-revolutionary Iran.
[GB2479] Grafton pbk **£3.95**

RAYNER, CLAIRE (1931 -)
More renowned as an 'agony aunt' than as a creative writer, Rayner has also produced a series of racy London sagas.
Clinical Judgments `NEW`
Her new novel is set in a modern London hospital, seen through the lives of its staff and the various crises and dilemmas they meet every day.
[GB2483] M Joseph hbk **£12.95**

READ, MISS
Chronicles of Fairacre (1964)
Combines the first three Miss Read novels, written in the 1950s: *Village School*, *Village Diary* and *Storm in the Village*.
[GB2497] M Joseph hbk **£14.95**

Mrs Pringle
Mrs Pringle, the lugubrious school cleaner, receives the honour of her own book. She is observed with the usual Miss Read blend of wry perception and humorous irony.
[GB2498] M Joseph hbk **£11.95**

READ, PIERS PAUL (1941 -)
Read has won both critical acclaim and wide popular success for his sharp, sophisticated novels which combine taut narrative interest with subtle explorations of the moral and spiritual dilemmas of his characters, who are generally Catholic and middle class.
A Married Man (1979)
A married man with a mid-life crisis is the central focus of this intriguing exploration of the political, social and religious unease of affluent middle class Britain.
[GB2499] Pan pbk **£2.95**
A Season in the West (1988)
An acclaimed novel in which a defecting Czech writer is helped in London by a married English woman, with complications.
[GB2500] Secker hbk **£10.95**
[GB2501] Pan pbk **£3.95**
Game in Heaven with Tussy Marx (1974)
[GB2502] Secker hbk **£10.95**
Monk Dawson (1969)
[GB2503] Secker hbk **£10.95**
Polonaise (1976)
[GB2504] Secker hbk **£10.95**
Professor's Daughter (1971)
[GB2505] Secker hbk **£10.95**
The Free Frenchman (1986)
An acclaimed historical novel-cum-psychological thriller, which was praised for its sure narrative skill, sustained through a wide range of events and locations.
[GB2506] Secker hbk **£10.95**
[GB2507] Pan pbk **£3.50**
The Junkers (1968)
[GB2508] Secker hbk **£10.95**
The Upstart (1976)
[GB2509] Secker hbk **£10.95**
The Villa Golitsyn (1981)
[GB2510] Hodder pbk **£3.95**

REED, JEREMY (1951 -)
Blue Rock
A flamboyant first novel by the gifted lyric poet.
[GB2511] Cape hbk **£9.95**
Red Eclipse
Beneath the fabric of carefully wrought prose is a study of isolation and of the unforeseen external forces which disrupt people's lives.
[GB2512] Cape hbk **£10.95**

RENAULT, MARY (1905 - 1983)
After her early autobiographical novels and her successful story of homosexual life in wartime, *The Charioteer*, Renault found her true *métier* in a series of novels set in classical Greece.
Bull from the Sea (1962)
[GB2513] Penguin pbk **£2.95**
Friendly Young Ladies (1944)
[GB2515] Virago pbk **£3.95**
Nature of Alexander (Non fiction)
[GB2517] Penguin pbk **£4.50**
The Charioteer (1953)
[GB2519] Hodder pbk **£4.50**
The King Must Die (1958)
[GB2520] Hodder pbk **£4.95**
The Last of the Wine (1956)
[GB2521] Hodder pbk **£3.95**
The Mask of Apollo (1966)
Perhaps her most successful single novel - the story of an actor in the great days of Ancient Greek drama.
[GB2522] Hodder pbk **£4.50**

THE ALEXANDER TRILOGY
Fire from Heaven (1970)
The first part tells of Alexander's childhood with a terrifying mother, his education and his friendship with Hephaiston.
[GB2514] Penguin pbk **£4.50**
The Persian Boy (1972)
In the second part, the conqueror is at the height of his empire, seen through the eyes of his Persian catamite; the third tells of how his successors divide, squabble over and lose their inheritance.
[GB2523] Penguin pbk **£3.99**
Funeral Games (1981)
[GB2516] Penguin pbk **£3.95**
The Alexander Trilogy
[GB2518] Penguin pbk **£7.99**

RHYS, JEAN (1890 - 1979)
Born in Dominica, many of Rhys's novels are set in Paris between the wars and have a doomed, bitter-sweet quality. She wrote almost nothing between 1939 and 1966 when *The Wide Sargasso Sea* appeared, reviving interest in her work. She is now acknowledged as one of the prominent novelists of this century, with a prose style of unrivalled grace and clarity. She commented in 1966, upon receipt of an award: 'It has all come too late!'
After Leaving Mr Mackenzie (1930)
[GB2524] Penguin pbk **£3.99**
Early Novels
[GB2525] Deutsch hbk **£9.95**
Good Morning, Midnight (1939)
[GB2526] Penguin pbk **£3.99**
Quartet (1928)
[GB2527] Penguin pbk **£3.99**
Sleep It Off Lady (Stories, 1976)
[GB2528] Penguin pbk **£3.99**
The Wide Sargasso Sea (1966)
An extremely powerful and original work which retells the story of the mad Mrs Rochester in *Jane Eyre*.
[GB2529] Penguin pbk **£3.99**
Tigers are Better Looking (1968)
[GB2530] Penguin pbk **£3.95**
Voyage in the Dark (1934)
[GB2531] Penguin pbk **£3.95**

RICHARDSON, DOROTHY (1873 - 1957)
Pilgrimage (1915-38) is a twelve-volume novel sequence, recently republished in four volumes, after being championed by Anthony Burgess and notable feminist critics. It has been said that her work is similar to Joyce's, employing as it does, a form of 'interior monologue' or 'stream of consciousness' to relate the complex narrative.
Pilgrimage 1
[GB2532] Virago pbk **£5.95**
Pilgrimage 2
[GB2533] Virago pbk **£5.95**
Pilgrimage 3
[GB2534] Virago pbk **£5.95**
Pilgrimage 4
[GB2535] Virago pbk **£5.95**

RILEY, JOAN
Romance (1988)
A novel which follows the lives of two Black sisters in urban Britain.
[GB2536] Women's P pbk **£4.95**
Waiting in the Twilight (1987)
[GB2537] Women's P pbk **£3.95**

ROBERTS, MICHELE (1949 -)
A fine feminist writer who often uses and reinterprets biblical themes. She is also well known as a poet and this is reflected in the charged and figurative quality of her fiction.
A Piece of the Night (1978)
[GB2538] Women's P pbk **£3.95**

Michele Roberts, author of *The Book of Mrs Noah* (Methuen pbk **£3.95**)

Mirror of the Mother
[GB2539] Methuen pbk **£3.95**
The Book of Mrs Noah (1987)
[GB2540] Methuen pbk **£3.95**
The Visitation (1983)
[GB2541] Women's P pbk **£3.95**
The Wild Girl (1984)
[GB2542] Methuen pbk **£2.95**

ROBERTSON, E. ARNOT (1903 - 1961)
One of the most popular novelists of the '30s and '40s, her heroines are independent and broad-minded, most particularly with *Four Frightened People*.
Four Frightened People
[GB2545] Virago pbk **£4.99**
Ordinary Families
[GB2545A] Virago pbk **£4.99**

ROBINSON, RONY
The Beano (1987)
A bottle factory outing to Scarborough, planned by Britlings Brewery, is marred by tragedy and overshadowed by the approach of World War I.
[GB2546] Faber pbk **£3.95**

ROGERS, JANE (1952 -)
An exciting young author who faces up to the complexities of feminism and motherhood, using various inventive fictional approaches.
Her Living Image (1984)
[GB2548] Fontana pbk **£3.95**
Separate Tracks (1983)
[GB2549] Fontana pbk **£2.50**
The Ice is Singing (1987)
The story of a woman on the run from her husband, her children and herself, through the freezing landscape of Northern England.
[GB2550] Faber pbk **£3.95**

ROLFE, FREDERICK (1860 - 1913)
A Londoner by birth (the title 'Baron Corvo' was spurious), he aspired in vain to the Roman Catholic priesthood. His work reflects a bizarre obsession with a particularly ostentatious form of Catholicism.
Desire and Pursuit of the Whole (1934)
Fictional account of Rolfe's declining years in Venice.
[GB2551] Oxford pbk **£3.95**
Hadrian the Seventh (1904)
Autobiographical fantasy about a failed ordinand who is elected Pope and proceeds to take his revenge on the Church.
[GB2552] Picador pbk **£3.95**

FICTION

ROSS, IAN **NEW**
Rocking the Boat
A humorously harrowing tale of transplanting a bit of American culture into 'frumpy' London.
[GB25521] Heinemann hbk **£11.95**

RUBENS, BERNICE (1928 -)
Extremely popular prize-winning novelist, noted for her bizarre comic touch, and for her deft ability to suggest the complex undercurrents of human behaviour hidden within a story.
Birds of Passage (1987)
[GB2555] Sphere pbk **£3.99**
Brothers (1983)
[GB2556] Sphere pbk **£4.95**
Five Year Sentence (1978)
[GB2557] Sphere pbk **£3.50**
I Sent a Letter to My Love (1975)
[GB2558] Sphere pbk **£3.99**
Kingdom Come (1989) **NEW**
An audacious novel, set in the 17th century, concerning the life (and death) of a false Jewish Messiah.
[GB2558A] H Hamilton hbk **£12.95**
Madame Sousatzka (1962)
[GB2559] Sphere pbk **£3.99**
Mr Wakefield's Crusade (1985)
[GB2560] Sphere pbk **£3.99**
Our Father (1987)
[GB2561] Sphere pbk **£3.99**
Set on Edge (1960)
[GB2562] H Hamilton hbk **£11.95**
Spring Sonata (1979)
[GB2563] Sphere pbk **£3.50**
Sunday Best (1971)
[GB2564] Sphere pbk **£3.99**
The Elected Member (1970)
Booker Prize winner. It is the story of an East End Jewish boy prodigy who rises to become a barrister, but gradually loses his grip on life and ends up in a mental institution.
[GB2565] Sphere pbk **£3.50**

RUMENS, CAROL (1944 -)
Plato Park (1987)
A first novel by the well-known poet and critic, it portrays love and separation in the diplomatic milieu, set in Moscow and London.
[GB2566] Fontana pbk **£3.95**

RUSH, CHRISTOPHER (Scottish)
A Twelvemonth and a Day
A fusion of autobiography, family tradition and social comment, recalling a childhood in the fishing communities of the East Neuk of Fife.
[GB2567] Aberdeen UP pbk **£4.95**
Peace Comes Dropping Slow
[GB2568] Ramsay Head P hbk **£8.50**

RUSHDIE, SALMAN (1947 -)
Rushdie is of Indian origin, but he is now considered one of the most original voices in contemporary British fiction. His early highly imaginative work *Grimus* was attacked by critics; he re-emerged strongly in 1981 with his Booker Prize-winning *Midnight's Children*, which was hailed all over the world as one of the greatest 'Indian' novels of the century. It brought him into conflict with Indira Gandhi and her family, and his follow-up novel *Shame* (also shortlisted for the Booker Prize) caused a similar furore in Pakistan. This inflammatory quality in his work has of course come to a ghastly head in the protests surrounding the publication of *The Satanic Verses*. This and the other controversies draw attention away from Rushdie's brilliance as a narrator, inventor, and intellectual *agent provocateur*.
Grimus (1975)
[GB2569] Grafton pbk **£2.95**

Midnight's Children (1981)
Rushdie's great Indian novel is a mixture of history, imagination, satire and autobiography, surrounding the long-nosed hero Saleem Sinai, born in the hour of India's independence.
[GB2570] Cape hbk **£10.50**
[GB2571] Picador pbk **£4.95**
Shame (1983)
[GB2572] Cape hbk **£9.95**
[GB2573] Picador pbk **£2.95**
The Satanic Verses (1988)
The controversy surrounding *The Satanic Verses* has affected the impact of what is certainly a *literary* achievement. Epic in both form and subject matter, it is a 'great wheel of a book', eschewing linear narrative to incorporate examinations of faith and identity, of good and evil. Rushdie utilizes themes taken from his university study of Islamic history, exploring the process of metamorphosis and how the revelation of a 'divine' truth can be interpreted by a secular world. Despite these deeply serious themes, the book is characterized by bawdy humour and an undeniable irreverence.
[GB2574] Viking hbk **£12.95**

RUTHERFORD, EDWARD
Sarum
Mammoth, and well-researched saga of five families during 10,000 years of history in Wiltshire. Packed with human interest and a strong sense of place.
[GB2575] Arrow pbk **£4.95**

SACKVILLE-WEST, VITA (1892 - 1962)
An intriguing literary figure whose unusual life has been the subject of many studies. Born and brought up in Kent, Sackville-West was a confidante and lover of Virginia Woolf, wife of diplomat Harold Nicolson, and amorous friend of Violet Trefusis. She was also a sharp writer, and her novels are period classics.
All Passion Spent (1931)
[GB2576] Virago pbk **£4.99**
Family History (1932)
[GB2577] Virago pbk **£4.99**
Heritage (1918)
[GB2578] Futura pbk **£2.50**
No Signposts in the Sea (1961)
[GB2580] Virago pbk **£3.99**
Pepita (1937)
[GB2580A] Virago pbk **£5.99**
Seducers in Ecuador/The Heir (1922)
[GB2581] Virago pbk **£2.95**
The Edwardians (1930)
[GB2582] Virago pbk **£4.99**

SAKI (H.H.MUNRO) (1870 - 1916)
Taking his name from the cup-bearer in *The Rubaiyat of Omar Khayyam*, Saki became a master of the short story, although he also wrote two novels, which appear in the *Complete Works*. After a brief spell in the Burma police he worked as a foreign correspondent in Poland, Russia and Paris, and died on the Western Front.
Best of Saki (Ed. Greene, Graham)
Saki's stories are whimsical and light-hearted but with a certain darkness and cynicism, informed probably by his own unhappy childhood with two spinster aunts.
[GB2583] Picador pbk **£3.99**
Chronicles of Clovis (1911)
[GB2584] Penguin pbk **£3.99**
Complete Saki
[GB2585] Penguin pbk **£7.99**
The Unbearable Bassington (1912)
[GB2590] Oxford pbk **£3.95**

SASSOON, SIEGFRIED (1886 - 1967)
Sassoon made his name in the First World War with his angry and satirical poems, and also as Wilfred

Jean Rhys, author of *The Wide Sargasso Sea* (Penguin pbk **£3.99**

Owen's mentor and, later, editor. After the war he wrote, and published anonymously, some important autobiographical prose works, the best of which is the trilogy listed below.
Complete Memoirs of George Sherston (1928 - 36)
The trilogy in one volume.
[GB2591] Faber pbk **£7.95**
Memoirs of a Fox Hunting Man (1928)
[GB2592] Faber pbk **£3.95**
Memoirs of an Infantry Officer (1930)
Sassoon's hero, George Sherston, has left behind the privileged life of leisure he formerly led, and finds himself thrown into the complete horror of the trenches.
[GB2593] Faber pbk **£3.50**
Sherston's Progress (1936)
[GB2594] Faber pbk **£4.95**

SCOTT, PAUL (1920 - 1978)
The only time that Paul Scott went to the subcontinent was serving in the army during World War II, but he set virtually all of his subsequent novels in India or Malaya. He will be best remembered for his Conrad-influenced *Raj Quartet*, a magnificent series of novels that only gained a prominent place after Scott's death.
A Male Child (1956)
[GB2599] Grafton pbk **£2.50**
Alien Sky (1953)
[GB2600] Grafton pbk **£2.50**
Chinese Love Pavilion (1960)
[GB2601] Grafton pbk **£2.50**
Johnnie Sahib (1952)
His first novel.
[GB2602] Pan pbk **£3.99**
Mark of the Warrior (1958)
[GB2603] Grafton pbk **£2.50**
Staying On (1977)
Booker Prize-winning coda to the *Raj Quartet*. Two of the minor characters have stayed on after Independence, and must come to face the reality of growing old in an alien country.
[GB2604] Pan pbk **£3.99**
The Birds of Paradise (1962)
The best of Scott's earlier novels.
[GB2605] Grafton pbk **£2.50**
The Corrida at San Feliu (1964)
[GB2606] Grafton pbk **£2.50**

THE RAJ QUARTET
The Jewel in the Crown (1966)
These four novels tell the story of the last five years of the British in India, 1942-47. The multiple narrative angles slowly build up a complex and symbolic picture; and the novel's long, slow movement brilliantly re-creates the processes of history.
[GB2608] Pan pbk **£4.99**
The Day of the Scorpion (1968)
[GB2609] Pan pbk **£3.99**
The Towers of Silence (1971)
[GB2610] Pan pbk **£3.99**
A Division of the Spoils (1975)
[GB2611] Pan pbk **£4.50**
The Raj Quartet (1966 - 75)
[GB2607] Heinemann hbk **£16.00**

SELINCOURT, HUGH DE
Game of the Season (1982)
A humorous cricket novel.
[GB2612] Oxford pbk **£3.95**
The Cricket Match (1980)
[GB2613] Oxford pbk **£4.95**

SHAKESPEARE, NICHOLAS
The Vision of Elena Silves (1989)   **NEW**
Three old men pass their days in the main square of a city in the heart of Peruvian Amazonia; they tell the story of Elena, who has spent the last twenty years in a convent because of her vision, which broke her lover's heart. Yet one day she disappears... a fine 'Latin American' novel from the literary editor of the *Daily Telegraph*.
[GB2615] Collins Harv hbk **£11.95**

SHARP, ALAN (Scottish, 1934 -)
A Green Tree in Gedde (1965)
Ambitious and idealistic novel of an odyssey, with Greenock as the point of departure.
[GB2616] R Drew pbk **£3.95**

SHARPE, TOM (1928 -)
An outrageous and frequently satirical comic novelist, Sharpe's already immense popularity has increased with recent television adaptations of his work.
Ancestral Vices (1980)
[GB2617] Pan pbk **£2.99**
Blott on the Landscape (1975)
[GB2618] Pan pbk **£3.50**
Great Pursuit (1977)
[GB2619] Pan pbk **£3.50**

Paul Scott, author of the *Raj Quartet* (Heinneman hbk £16.00)

Indecent Exposure (1973)
[GB2620] Pan pbk **£2.99**
Porterhouse Blue (1974)
Hilarious satire on a dinosaur of an Oxbridge college, where the dons dine on roast swan. Memorably televised.
[GB2621] Pan pbk **£2.99**
Riotous Assembly (1971)
[GB2622] Pan pbk **£3.50**
Selected Works
[GB2623] Heinemann hbk **£9.95**
The Throwback (1978)
[GB2624] Pan pbk **£3.50**
Vintage Stuff (1982)
[GB2625] Pan pbk **£3.50**
Wilt (1976)
[GB2626] Pan pbk **£3.50**
Wilt Alternative (1979)
[GB2627] Pan pbk **£3.50**
Wilt on High (1984)
[GB2628] Pan pbk **£3.50**

SHAW, GEORGE BERNARD
(Irish, 1856 - 1950)
One of Ireland's timeless literary figures, Shaw needs little introduction as a man of many talents with a highly active mind (and pen). The works below were among his first published writings, but were wholly unsuccessful at the time; Shaw later claimed that his first nine years in London netted him less than £10.
An Unsocial Socialist
[GB2629] Virago pbk **£4.95**
Black Girl in Search of God & Other Tales
[GB2630] Penguin pbk **£4.95**
Cashel Byron's Profession
[GB2631] Penguin pbk **£4.99**

SHEEHAN, CANON (Irish, 1852 - 1913)
Glenanaar
This is one of Canon Sheehan's 19th century novels which achieved enormous success in its day.
[GB2632] Mercier P pbk **£3.25**

SHEPHERD, NAN (Scottish, 1928 -)
The Quarry Wood
Long neglected, Shepherd's novels focus on women's individual development and quest for self-knowledge. This is her first novel.
[GB2633] Canongate pbk **£3.95**
The Weatherhouse
[GB2634] Canongate pbk **£3.95**

SHER, ANTHONY
Middlepost (1988)
Sher's first novel has been a resounding critical and commercial success. It explores the history of his ancestors and tells the tale of Smous, a new arrival in South Africa in 1902.
[GB2635] Chatto hbk **£11.95**
[GB2636] Hodder pbk **£4.99**

SILLITOE, ALAN (1928 -)
Born and bred in Nottingham, the son of an illiterate labourer, Sillitoe started his wide reading and writing while in hospital with TB after the war. Although his reputation rests chiefly upon his first two books, which found fame alongside those of other such as Cooper, Braine and Barstow, Sillitoe remains a sturdy and skilful writer.
Death of William Posters (1965)
[GB2637] Grafton pbk **£2.50**
Down from the Hill (1965)
A lyrical evocation of 1945.
[GB2638] Grafton pbk **£2.50**
Flame of Life (1974)
[GB2639] Grafton pbk **£2.95**
Guzman Go Home (1960)
[GB2640] Grafton pbk **£2.50**

Her Victory (1982)
[GB2641] Grafton pbk **£2.50**
Key to the Door (1978)
[GB2642] Grafton pbk **£2.95**
Life Goes On (1985)
[GB2643] Grafton pbk **£3.95**
Lost Flying Boat (1983)
[GB2644] Grafton pbk **£1.95**
Men, Women and Children (1973)
[GB2645] Grafton pbk **£2.50**
Out of the Whirlpool (1987)
[GB2646] Arrow pbk **£2.50**
Ragman's Daughter (1963)
[GB2647] Grafton pbk **£2.50**
Raw Material (1972)
[GB2648] Grafton pbk **£2.50**
Saturday Night and Sunday Morning (1958)
The novel that made Sillitoe's name. The young, anti-social Arthur Seaton, factory worker and hedonist, is often bracketed with other, similar '50s rebels, yet he alone among them is actually working-class.
[GB2649] WH Allen hbk **£10.95**
[GB2650] Grafton pbk **£2.50**
Second Chance (1981)
[GB2651] Grafton pbk **£1.50**
Start in Life (1970)
[GB2652] Grafton pbk **£2.95**
The General (1960)
[GB2653] Grafton pbk **£1.95**
The Loneliness of the Long Distance Runner (1959)
The title story of this collection is narrated by an anarchic borstal boy who refuses to win the races he has been entered.
[GB2654] WH Allen hbk **£10.95**
[GB2655] Grafton pbk **£2.50**
The Open Door (1989)   **NEW**
Birmingham, 1949. Enter Brian Seaton, Arthur's older brother, bursting with energy but dogged by TB. Thirty years after *Saturday Night and Sunday Morning*, here is a triumphant sequel.
[GB2656] Grafton hbk **£11.95**
The Storyteller (1979)
[GB2657] Grafton pbk **£2.50**
Travels in Nihilon (1971)
[GB2658] Grafton pbk **£2.95**
Tree on Fire (1979)
[GB2659] Grafton pbk **£2.95**
Widower's Son (1976)
[GB2660] Grafton pbk **£2.95**

SINCLAIR, ANDREW (1935 -)
These partly autobiographical novels depict a world of privileged high life and parties, based on the author's experience at public school and at Cambridge.
Beau Bumbo (1985)
[GB2666] Weidenfeld hbk **£8.95**
Breaking of Bumbo (1958)
[GB2667] Faber pbk **£2.95**
My Friend Judas (1960)
[GB2668] Faber pbk **£2.95**

SINCLAIR, CLIVE (1948 -)
An important British, and Jewish, writer, Sinclair's books combine great compassion with an eccentric, even frightening, comic style.
Bedbugs (Stories, 1982)
[GB2669] Penguin pbk **£2.95**
Blood Libels (1985)
[GB2670] Picador pbk **£3.95**
Cosmetic Effects (1989)   **NEW**
Sinclair's new novel is as outrageous as ever. A philandering lecturer loses his left arm in an accident, and gets involved in a film intended to be the breakthrough Israeli Western, backed by his wife's uncle. A mad, hilarious novel.
[GB2671] Deutsch hbk **£10.95**

SINCLAIR, MAY (1863 - 1946)

A former suffragette and Red Cross worker, Sinclair was influenced by Freud and Jung, and thus her novels have been labelled 'psychological'. However she owed her literary style more to Dorothy Richardson's *Pilgrimage*, and became a leading exponent of the stream-of-consciousness technique.

Mary Olivier, A Life (1919)
An intense study of a mother-daughter relationship which is clearly autobiographical.
[GB2672] Virago pbk **£5.50**

The Life and Death of Harriet Frean (1922)
[GB2673] Virago pbk **£4.50**

SITWELL, OSBERT (1892 - 1969)

Brother of Edith, Osbert first produced satirical and pacifist war poetry before writing the novel included here. However, he is remembered above all for his entertaining volumes of autobiography.

Before the Bombardment (1926)
This novel describes the shelling of Scarborough in 1914, and its effect on the genteel female population.
[GB2674] Oxford pbk **£3.95**

Collected Short Stories
[GB2675] Duckworth hbk **£18.00**

SLAUGHTER, CAROLYN

Author of Anglo-African novels which draw on her African childhood.

Banquet (1983)
An intense portrait of obsessional love.
[GB2676] Penguin pbk **£2.95**

Perfect Woman
[GB2677] Penguin pbk **£2.95**

The Innocents (1986)
An exploration of the psychology of a suppressed passion, at the heart of a story set in South Africa.
[GB2678] Penguin pbk **£2.95**

The Widow (1989)   **NEW**
Psychological suspense story: Joseph, a specialist in criminology finds that the brain surgeon with whom he is involved is not quite what she seems. Soon he is in a battle of wits that leads to a shocking climax.
[GB2679] Heinemann hbk **£10.95**

SMITH, DODIE (1896 -)

The creator of *101 Dalmatians*, whose romantic novel listed here is a minor comedy classic.

I Capture the Castle (1949)
Two sisters live in an old crumbling castle. Enter a young American claiming it as his inheritance...
[GB2680] Bodley pbk **£4.95**

George Bernard Shaw, from Michael Holroyd's biography *The Search for Love* (Chatto hbk £16.00)

SMITH, IAIN CRICHTON (Scottish, 1928 -)

Prose works from the much-admired Hebridean poet.

Consider the Lilies (1968)
A justly acclaimed work of great sensitivity, a re-telling of the Highland Clearances from the point of view of an old woman being evicted.
[GB2681] Canongate **£2.95**

In the Middle of the Wood (1987)
[GB2682] Gollancz hbk **£9.95**

The Last Summer (1969)
A portrait of adolescence in the dual Gaelic-English context of a Lewis lad about to go to college, with strong autobiographical overtones.
[GB2683] R Drew pbk **£3.95**

SMITH, PAUL (Irish, 1932 -)

Smith is a man of many roles, having seen employment as a factory worker, waiter, dancer and costume designer. Dorothy Parker compared his writing to that of Sean O'Casey.

Annie (1972)
Twelve year old Annie Murphy is forced to slum a living in the swarming streets of Dublin.
[GB2684] Picador pbk **£3.50**

The Countrywoman (1962)
[GB2685] Picador pbk **£3.50**

SMITH, STEVIE (1902 - 1971)

Although she was born in Hull, Smith spent all but the first three years of her life in Palmers Green, London, working later for Newnes-Pearson, the magazine publishers. Her three novels are as full of her sad but irrepressible sense of life as her generally better-known poetry.

Novel on Yellow Paper (1936)
Pompey Casmilus works as a secretary to the splendid magazine publisher, Sir Phoebus Ullwater, and scribbles her romantic, imaginative yearnings on office paper.
[GB2686] Virago pbk **£4.50**

Over the Frontier (1938)
[GB2687] Virago pbk **£4.99**

The Holiday (1949)
[GB2688] Virago pbk **£4.50**

SNOW, C.P. (1905 - 1980)

A contemporary of Greene and Powell, Snow rose from humble beginnings, pursuing a scientific career at Cambridge before joining the upper echelons of the Civil Service and finally receiving a life peerage under Harold Wilson. In the early 60s he occupied a seminal position in the 'Two Cultures' debate, decrying the schism between the arts and sciences. His writing eschews modernist experiment for the relaxed and digressive style of his beloved Trollope.

A Coat of Varnish (1979)
[GB2690] Penguin pbk **£3.95**

Corridors of Power (1964)
Snow's novel of Westminster life, which gave us the now well-worn phrase. One of his best-known works.
[GB2691] Penguin pbk **£3.95**

Death Under Sail (1932)
His first novel, a conventional detective story.
[GB2692] Penguin pbk **£3.99**

Strangers and Brothers Vol 1
First volume in the three-volume series, which is a re-issuing of the 11 linked novels written between 1940 and 1970; they follow the career of Lewis Eliot along a similar route to Snow's, and beyond into political eminince Not currently available in paperback.
[GB2693] Macmillan hbk **£9.95**

Strangers and Brothers Vol 2
[GB2694] Macmillan hbk **£9.95**
[GB2695] Penguin pbk **£4.95**

Strangers and Brothers Vol 3
[GB2696] Macmillan hbk **£9.95**
[GB2697] Penguin pbk **£4.95**

The New Men (1954)
[GB2698] Penguin pbk **£2.95**

SOMERVILLE, EDITH & ROSS, VIOLET (Irish, 1858 - 1949/1862 - 1915)

Somerville and Ross were second cousins who wrote more than 30 books between them, their *Irish R.M.* series being the best known of them. These feature Major Yeates, with a capacity to attract calamity at every turn, as often as not on the hunting field.

Further Experiences of an Irish R.M. (1908)
[GB2699] Surtees Soc hbk **£7.95**

In Mr Knox's Country (1915)
[GB2700] Surtees Soc hbk **£7.95**

Irish R.M. (1899)
A new edition of *The Complete Experiences of an Irish R.M.*.
[GB2701] Sphere pbk **£3.99**

Real Charlotte (1894)
[GB2702] Hogarth pbk **£4.95**

Some Experiences of an Irish R.M. (1899)
[GB2703] Surtees Soc hbk **£7.95**
[GB2704] Dent pbk **£2.50**

SPARK, MURIEL (Scottish, 1918 -)

Celebrated post-war novelist who has also published plays, poems and short stories. Her novels are short, carefully poised, and often contain a distinct vein of irony or black humour. The quality of fable which some of her novels possess gives them the feel of cautionary tales: she is adept at pricking vanities.

A Far Cry From Kensington (1988)
Mrs Hawkins, the large and overweight narrator of this novel, is one of Spark's great comic creations. She looks back nostalgically on her bedsitter life in 1950s South Kensington, particularly on her work for a publisher and her conflict with hack writer Hector Bartlett, whom she calls a *'pisseur de copie'*. The results of her clash with Hector and his editor are dire. This short novel is rendered in a prose that shows consummate skill, with a characteristic delicacy of comic touch.
[GB2705] Penguin pbk **£3.99**

Bang Bang You're Dead (Stories)
[GB2706] Grafton pbk **£1.25**

Driver's Seat (1970)
[GB2708] Penguin pbk **£3.50**

Girl of Slender Means (1963)
A short novel set in a hostel in 1945, coloured by eccentricity and pain.
[GB2709] Penguin pbk **£3.99**

Go-Away Bird (Stories, 1958)
[GB2710] Penguin pbk **£3.95**

Going Up to Sotheby's (Poetry, 1982)
[GB2711] Grafton pbk **£1.25**

Loitering with Intent (1981)
[GB2712] Grafton pbk **£1.25**

Memento Mori (1959)
A comic and macabre study of old age.
[GB2713] Penguin pbk **£3.95**

Robinson (1958)
[GB2714] Penguin pbk **£3.95**

The Abbess of Crewe (1975)
Conspiratorial intrigue in a convent; complete with 'phone bugging, this is a thinly-veiled satire on Watergate.
[GB2715] Grafton pbk **£1.95**

The Bachelors (1960)
[GB2716] Penguin pbk **£3.95**

The Ballad of Peckham Rye (1960)
A highly comic novel about the London underworld.
[GB2717] Penguin pbk **£3.99**

The Collected Stories of Muriel Spark (1987)
[GB2718] Bodley hbk **£14.95**

The Comforters (1957)
[GB2719] Penguin pbk **£3.95**

The Mandlebaum Gate (1965)
Uncharacteristically long novel about a pilgrimage to Jerusalem, featuring much exotic comedy.
[GB2720] Penguin pbk **£3.95**

The Only Problem (1984)
[GB2721] Grafton pbk **£2.50**
The Prime of Miss Jean Brodie (1961)
Spark's most famous work: a haunting portrait of an
Edinburgh schoolmistress and her corrupting
influence on her pupils.
[GB2722] Penguin pbk **£2.50**
The Public Image (1968)
[GB2723] Penguin pbk **£3.95**
The Take Over (1976)
[GB2724] Grafton pbk **£1.95**

SPENCE, ALAN (Scottish, 1945 -)
Its Colours They Are Fine
Brilliant and touching semi-autobiographical stories
about growing up in Glasgow, linked by a search for
truth and contentment which Spence later found in
Zen-Buddhism.
[GB2725] Corgi pbk **£2.50**

SPENDER, STEPHEN (1909 -)
The Temple (1988)
Written in 1929 but unpublished until recently, this is
a thinly disguised account of a trip the young Spender
made to Weimar Germany with appearances by
friends Auden and Isherwood. The book captures
their optimistic hopes for a radical new world.
[GB2726] Faber hbk **£10.95**
[GB2727] Faber pbk **£4.99**

SPROAT, ROBERT (1944 -)
A new writer with a sense of black humour, Sproat
has been praised for his sharp portrayals of modern
urban life, particularly high-rise living.
Chinese Whispers (1988)
[GB2728] Faber pbk **£4.99**
Stunning the Punters (1985)
A well-received collection of short stories.
[GB2729] Faber pbk **£4.95**

SPURLING, JOHN
The Ragged End (1989)   **NEW**
The first novel from the accomplished playwright
takes in a broad sweep of history. Four men find that
they are drawn back into the mess they left behind in
Africa when the Empire wound down: this novel
examines the way their lives are bound up in this
particular denouement in British history.
[GB2730] Weidenfeld hbk **£11.95**

STEPHENS, JAMES (Irish, 1882 - 1950)
A writer famous for his fairy-tale *The Crock of Gold*,
one of the classic prose fantasies of Ireland, Stephens
was also a poet and novelist, and an important figure
in the early 20th century revival of Gaelic culture and
language.
The Charwoman's Daughter
[GB2733] Gill & Macmillan pbk **£2.20**
The Crock of Gold (1912)
[GB2734] Picador pbk **£2.95**
The Demi-Gods
[GB2735] Butler Sims pbk **£1.95**

STEWART, MARY (1916 -)
Writer of excellent traditional popular fiction
upholding old-fashioned values. Most of her books
are historical sagas or modern semi-thrillers, with
good characterization and well-paced plots.
Airs Above the Ground
[GB2736] Hodder pbk **£2.99**
Madam, Will You Talk?
[GB2737] Hodder pbk **£2.50**
My Brother Michael
An exciting thriller set in Greece, combining elements
of a modern adventure story with overtones of
classical Greek mythology.
[GB2738] Hodder pbk **£2.50**
Nine Coaches Waiting
[GB2739] Hodder pbk **£2.95**

The Gabriel Hounds
[GB2741] Hodder pbk **£2.99**
The Moonspinners
[GB2744] Hodder pbk **£2.50**
Thunder on the Right
[GB2746] Hodder pbk **£2.50**
Wildfire at Midnight
[GB2747] Hodder pbk **£2.95**
THE ARTHURIAN NOVELS
The Crystal Cave
First of her four Arthurian novels, probably her best
work. The other three follow below in reading order.
[GB2740] Hodder pbk **£3.99**
The Hollow Hills
[GB2742] Hodder pbk **£3.99**
The Last Enchantment
[GB2743] Hodder pbk **£3.95**
The Wicked Day
[GB2745] Hodder pbk **£3.99**

STOPPARD, TOM (1937 -)
Lord Malquist and Mr Moon (1966)
The only novel from the well-known playwright is a
blend of inventive speculation and extravagant wit.
[GB2748] Faber pbk **£2.95**

STOREY, DAVID (1933 -)
A significant contemporary novelist as well as a
successful playwright, Storey's work shows a
preoccupation with the social issues of class conflict
and alienation. He was born in Wakefield, the son of a
miner, and this, along with his combination of brutal
realism and subtle symbolism, prompts comparisons
with Lawrence.
A Prodigal Child (1982)
[GB2749] Cape hbk **£9.95**
Present Times (1984)
[GB2750] Penguin pbk **£3.95**
Radcliffe (1963)
Perhaps his best-known work, a sombre, almost
gothic tale of destructive relationships and
homosexual passion.
[GB2751] Penguin pbk **£3.99**
Saville (1976)
[GB2752] Penguin pbk **£3.95**
This Sporting Life (1960)
Storey's first novel tells of a Rugby League player
whose external success is set against a dark sense of
loneliness. Storey himself played professional Rugby
and this is set in a bleakly realistic landscape which
was to become characteristic of his work.
[GB2753] Penguin pbk **£3.95**

SWIFT, GRAHAM (1949 -)
Acclaimed as a leading member of the 'younger'
generation of British writers, Swift's reputation rests
chiefly with the magnificently detailed *Waterland*,
which has proved a hard act to follow. In this and his
other works he reveals an interest in different forms
of narratives, exploring in particular the way in which
historical events affect the present.
Learning to Swim (1982)
[GB2758] Picador pbk **£3.99**
Out of this World (1988)
Swift achieves a profound exploration of this century
and its failure to perceive itself, through the story of
an ex-photojournalist turned aerial photographer.
[GB2759] Penguin pbk **£3.99**
Shuttlecock (1981)
[GB2760] Penguin pbk **£3.99**
The Sweet Shop Owner (1980)
[GB2761] Penguin pbk **£4.50**
Waterland (1983)
Booker Prize shortlisted. A sophisticated narrative
interweaving several generations of local and family
history in East Anglia, encompassing wide-ranging
reflections on history and landscape. This is a tightly
organized novel, and a *tour de force* of storytelling.
[GB2762] Picador pbk **£3.99**

SWINNERTON, FRANK (1884 - 1932)
A now much neglected novelist and literary figure.
The novel that is listed here, set in London,
represents the best of his essentially English brand
of social realism.
Nocturne (1917)
[GB2763] Oxford pbk **£3.95**

TANNAHILL, REAY
Also a distinguished social historian, author of books
on the role of food and sex in history. These two
novels are set in the 19th century Scottish highlands
and 15th century France respectively.
Dark and Distant Shore
[GB2765] Penguin pbk **£4.50**
The World, the Flesh and the Devil
[GB2766] Penguin pbk **£3.95**

TAYLOR, ELIZABETH (1912 - 1975)
An understated, shrewd observer of middle-class life
and manners, Taylor's reputation is undergoing
something of a revival: in a recent promotion, *Angel*
was voted one of the best post-war novels.
A View of the Harbour (1949)
[GB2767] Virago pbk **£4.99**
A Wreath of Roses (1950)
[GB2768] Penguin pbk **£3.95**
Angel (1957)
[GB2769] Virago pbk **£4.99**
At Mrs Lippincote's
[GB2770] Virago pbk **£4.99**
Game of Hide and Seek (1951)
A respectable young woman is emotionally torn
between two men.
[GB2771] Virago pbk **£4.99**
Hester Lilly & Other Stories (1954)
[GB2772] Virago pbk **£4.99**
In a Summer Season (1961)
[GB2773] Virago pbk **£4.99**
Mrs Palfrey at the Claremount (1972)
[GB2774] Virago pbk **£4.99**
Palladian (1947)
Cassandra becomes a governess at a manor - a latter-
day Jane Eyre.
[GB2775] Virago pbk **£4.99**
The Blush (Stories, 1958)
[GB2776] Virago pbk **£4.99**
The Devastating Boys (1972)
Collection of some of her best short stories. The title
story concerns a middle-aged couple who take two
Black children from the East End on holiday.
[GB2777] Virago pbk **£4.99**
The Sleeping Beauty (1953)
The gentle tale of how a middle-aged man falls in
love for the first time.
[GB2778] Virago pbk **£4.99**
The Soul of Kindness (1964)
[GB2779] Virago pbk **£4.99**
The Wedding Group (1968)
[GB2780] Virago pbk **£4.99**

TEMPLETON, EDITH (1916 -)
A cosmopolitan author, born in Prague of a wealthy
family, whose novels dwell on the hatred and
ambition underlying beau monde society in Bohemia.
Living on Yesterday (1951)
Her best novel, a comedy of manners involving the
loss of innocence of its young heroine, Francesca.
[GB2781] Hogarth pbk **£4.95**
Summer in the Country (1950)
[GB2782] Hogarth pbk **£4.95**
The Island of Desire (1952)
[GB2783] Hogarth pbk **£4.95**

TENNANT, EMMA (1937 -)
An unusual and diverse writer whose novels often
explore psychological states and different levels of
reality. To this end, Tennant's style is characterized by
her use of dream sequences, fantasy and stream-of-

consciousness, although her recent books have revealed an increasingly conventional narrative style.

A Wedding of Cousins (1988)
[GB2784] Viking hbk **£11.95**
Black Marina (1985)
[GB2785] Faber pbk **£2.95**
Hotel de Dream (1967)
[GB2786] Faber pbk **£3.50**
The Adventures of Robina: By Herself
[GB2787] Faber pbk **£3.95**
The Bad Sister
[GB2788] Faber pbk **£3.99**
The Colour of Rain (1963)
[GB2789] Faber pbk **£3.95**
The Crack (1973)
[GB2790] Faber pbk **£2.95**
The House of Hospitalities (1988)
Vigorous and entertaining tale of a middle-class girl in a country house where the incumbents' behaviour is both highly civilized and perverse; a *Brideshead*-like trip into the 'otherness' of the aristocracy.
[GB2791] Penguin pbk **£3.99**
The Last of the Country House Murders
[GB2792] Faber pbk **£3.50**
The Magic Drum (1989)   **NEW**
Set in the Welsh borders, where two cousins run a creative writing course, his new novel is an unusual work about the enigmatic power of Muriel, a major 20th century poet, and how the enigmatic power of her personality and poetry linger on after her death.
[GB2792A] Viking hbk **£11.95**
Two Women of London (1989)   **NEW**
Striking reworking of the Jekyll and Hyde story - here, two women who live in West London. A haunting, modern crime novel.
[GB2793] Faber hbk **£10.99**
Women Beware Women/Wild Nights
Two of the best of Tennant's earlier works now in one volume: a chilling account of amorous obsession, and 'a whirlwind of pure imagination' (J.G. Ballard).
[GB2794] Faber pbk **£4.99**

TERAN, LISA ST AUBIN DE (1953 -)
Stylish word magician and self-confessed train addict whose exotic novels of love and exile draw largely on her own extraordinary experiences in South America and on her wide-ranging travels.
Black Idol (1987)
Wonderful period novel set in 1920s New York about the life, loves and death of poet Harry Crosby.
[GB2795] Pan pbk **£3.99**
Keepers of the House (1982)
Somerset Maugham Award-winning tale of the 17 year old girl who leaves England to manage her husband's estate in the Andes.
[GB2796] Penguin pbk **£3.95**
The Bay of Silence (1986)
[GB2797] Pan pbk **£2.95**
The High Place (Poetry, 1985)
[GB2798] Cape hbk **£6.95**
The Marble Mountain & Other Stories (1989)   **NEW**
Her first collection of stories; with a variety of settings, both exotic and mundane.
[GB2799] Cape hbk **£10.95**
The Slow Train to Milan (1983)
[GB2800] Penguin pbk **£3.95**
The Tiger (1984)
A terrible grandmother rules Lucien's world; a fine portrait of the tyranny of love.
[GB2801] Penguin pbk **£4.50**

THIRKELL, ANGELA
A popular writer of cultured English novels in the 1930s, she was the mother of Colin McInnes.
Three Houses (1931)
[GB2802] R Clark hbk **£8.95**
Trooper to the Southern Cross (1934)
[GB2803] Virago pbk **£4.50**

THOMAS, D.M. (1935 -)
A poet and translator of Russian verse, D.M. Thomas has an evident feel for language, and interest in the Freudian poles of love and death. His novels have met with less success, perhaps due to his taste in explicit eroticism, although *The White Hotel* won considerable acclaim on publication, and was shortlisted for the Booker Prize.
Ararat (1983)
[GB2804] Sphere pbk **£3.99**
Birthstone (1980)
[GB2805] Penguin pbk **£3.95**
Sphinx (1986)
[GB2806] Sphere pbk **£3.99**
Summit (1987)
Thomas's most recent novel is a satire on global politics, particularly the relationship between the USSR and the US.
[GB2807] Sphere pbk **£3.99**
Swallow (1984)
[GB2808] Sphere pbk **£3.99**
The Flute Player (1979)
[GB2809] Picador pbk **£2.95**
The White Hotel (1981)
An atmospheric and experimental novel in which Freudian psychoanalytic ideas are mixed with both erotic fantasy and episodes from modern history to startling effect.
[GB2810] Penguin pbk **£4.50**

THOMAS, DYLAN (Welsh, 1914 - 1953)
Although Dylan Thomas's reputation rests principally upon his complex and sensual poetry, he wrote prolifically in a variety of forms throughout his life: he started as a reporter, working for the BBC as a scriptwriter and broadcaster during the war years. His fiction is, for the most part, both comic and celebratory, and is marked by his effervescent love of language.
A Portrait of the Artist as a Young Dog (Stories, 1955)
[GB2811] Dent pbk **£2.95**
A Prospect of the Sea (1955)
[GB2812] Dent pbk **£3.95**
Adventures in the Skin Trade (1955)
A partly autobiographical and highly comic novel, it was left incomplete at Thomas's tragically early death.
[GB2813] Dent pbk **£2.95**
Collected Stories
[GB2814] Dent hbk **£10.50**
[GB2815] Dent pbk **£3.50**
Quite Early One Morning (1954)
[GB2820] Dent pbk **£3.95**
The Outing
[GB2821] Dent pbk **£5.95**
The Visit to Grandpa's and Other Stories
[GB2822] Dent hbk **£5.95**

THOMAS, LESLIE (1931 -)
Enduring and endearingly English light novelist. His most popular works, based on his own experiences, recount the sexual adventures of National Service conscripts; they have become durable comic classics. All his work is characterized by a warm heart and good humour.
Adventures of Goodnight and Loving
[GB2824] Penguin pbk **£3.99**
Bare Nell
[GB2825] Pan pbk **£3.99**
Come to the War
[GB2826] Pan pbk **£3.99**
Dangerous Davies: The Last Detective
[GB2827] Pan pbk **£3.50**
Dangerous in Love
[GB2828] Penguin pbk **£2.99**

Dearest and the Best
[GB2829] Penguin pbk **£3.99**
His Lordship
[GB2830] Pan pbk **£3.99**
Magic Army
[GB2831] Penguin pbk **£3.99**
Onward Virgin Soldiers
[GB2832] Pan pbk **£3.99**
Orange Wednesday
[GB2833] Pan pbk **£3.50**
Orders for New York (1989)   **NEW**
Thomas's latest novel takes historical fact as its starting point: the betrayal by their leader of eight Nazi saboteurs off Long Island in 1942. An English journalist is lured to the States years later to find this leader, and becomes embroiled in an adventure, which is alarming, comic and romantic by turns.
[GB2834] Methuen hbk **£12.99**
Ormerod's Landing
[GB2835] Pan pbk **£2.95**
Stand Up Virgin Soldiers
[GB2836] Methuen hbk **£9.50**
The Love Beach
[GB2837] Pan pbk **£2.95**
The Man with the Power
[GB2838] Pan pbk **£3.50**
The Virgin Soldiers
[GB2839] Pan pbk **£3.99**
Tropic of Ruislip
[GB2840] Pan pbk **£2.99**

THOMSON, RUPERT (1958 -)
His first novel, listed here, is so full of ideas, energy and humour that Thomson is undoubtedly a name to watch.
Dreams of Leaving (1987)
The tale of Moses Highness and his search for his origins leads him from the London underworld to the bizarre rural police state of Little Egypt.
[GB2852] Transworld pbk **£4.99**

THUBRON, COLIN (1939 -)
A prize-winning travel writer, Thubron is also an extremely accomplished novelist; his book *A Cruel Madness* is a highly poetic novel set in a mental institution.
A Cruel Madness (1984)
[GB2861] Heinemann hbk **£9.95**
Falling (1989)   **NEW**
Thubron's third novel is an unusual tale of a journalist's unstoppable attraction for a trapeze-artist, told from the prison cell where he now resides. A moving investigation into self-oppression, love and loss.
[GB2862] Heinemann hbk **£10.95**

TINDALL, GILLIAN (1938 -)
Biographer and broadcaster as well as a novelist. Her most recent novel was favourably received by critics.
Give Them All My Love (1989)   **NEW**
Tindall's latest has been hailed as her best yet: it is a powerful examination of a murder, narrated by a former judge, now in prison. As the action shifts back in time, we come to understand how his daughter died. A compelling *tour de force*.
[GB2864] Hutchinson hbk **£11.95**
To the City (1988)
On a skiing holiday, one man prepares himself for a return to his birthplace, Vienna, and the unwelcome memories that await him there.
[GB2865] Dent pbk **£3.95**

TOWNSEND, SUE
The playwright and creator of the inimitable *Adrian Mole* stories (see the *Children's* chapter).
Rebuilding Coventry (1988)
The first adult novel from Townsend offers implicit social criticism of present-day England.
[GB2866] Methuen pbk **£3.50**

FICTION

TRANTER, NIGEL (Scottish)

Author of lengthy and popular historical sagas, reminiscent of Walter Scott. But where Scott created weak heroes in contact with real historical figures, Tranter focuses on the kings, and saints themselves.

Flowers of Chivalry
[GB2867] Hodder hbk **£11.95**

James, by the Grace of God
[GB2868] Hodder pbk **£2.95**

Lord of the Isles
[GB2869] Hodder pbk **£3.50**

Macbeth the King
[GB2870] Hodder pbk **£3.50**

Mail Royal   **NEW**
[GB2871] Hodder hbk **£11.95**

Margaret the Queen
[GB2872] Hodder pbk **£3.50**

Riven Realm
[GB2873] Hodder pbk **£2.95**

Rough Wooing
[GB2874] Hodder pbk **£3.50**

The Bruce Trilogy
Novels about Robert the Bruce, comprising *Steps to the Empty Throne*, *Price of the King's Peace* and *Path of the New King*.
[GB2875] Hodder pbk **£6.95**

The MacGregor Trilogy
[GB2876] Hodder pbk **£6.95**

The Stewart Trilogy
Comprising *Lords of Misrule*, *Folly of Princes* and *The Captive Crown*.
[GB2877] Hodder pbk **£6.95**

The Wisest Fool
[GB2878] Hodder pbk **£3.99**

Warden of the Queen's March   **NEW**
The well-known drama of Mary Queen of Scots told from a different angle: that of her Protector, Thomas Kerr of Ferniehirst.
[GB2879] Hodder hbk **£11.95**

TREFUSIS, VIOLET (1894 - 1972)

Through the fortunes of literary history, Trefusis is more famous for her liaison with Vita Sackville-West than for her own output.

Broderie Anglaise (1935)
Fictionalized account of the author's affair with Sackville-West. Originally written in French, it only appeared in English in 1986.
[GB2880] Methuen pbk **£3.50**

Echo (1931)
A young Parisian leaves her husband for a spell in her aunt's Scottish castle.
[GB2881] Methuen hbk **£10.95**

Hunt the Slipper (1937)
[GB2882] Virago pbk **£4.50**

TREMAIN, ROSE (1943 -)

Award-winning and highly acclaimed novelist and short story writer.

Garden of the Villa Mollini (Stories, 1987)
[GB2883] Hodder pbk **£2.95**

Letter to Sister Benedicta (1979)
[GB2884] Arrow pbk **£2.50**

Restoration (1989)   **NEW**
Merivel is enjoying all the excesses of the court of Charles II when he commits the unspeakable crime of falling in love with the King's wife. Helped by a Quaker friend, and working with the insane, he finds he must now effect a personal 'restoration'. A very boisterous but thought-provoking work of the imagination.
[GB2885] H Hamilton hbk **£12.95**

The Colonel's Daughter (Stories, 1984)
[GB2886] Hodder pbk **£3.50**

The Swimming Pool Season (1985)
A beautifully written love story that alternates between Oxford and France, examining a myriad of intricate relationships.
[GB2887] Hodder pbk **£2.95**

TRESSELL, ROBERT (c.1870 - 1911)

Pen-name of Robert Noonan, a vagrant house-painter of Irish extraction, who left behind this classic and still highly readable socialist novel, published posthumously.

The Ragged Trousered Philanthropists (1914)
A tough and unsentimental look at the political implications of the industrial age for the working man. Still a bestseller.
[GB2888] Grafton pbk **£4.50**

TREVOR, WILLIAM (Irish, 1928 -)

Strictly speaking William Trevor is an Anglo-Irish writer, and his knowledge of both of those countries informs his work. His subjects are often deliberately low-key or unglamorous: he has written with poignant insight about the lives of the lonely and the elderly, and is an acknowledged master of the short story.

A Standard of Behaviour (1958)
[GB2889] Sphere pbk **£1.95**

Angels at the Ritz & Other Stories (1975)
[GB2890] Bodley hbk **£10.95**

Ballroom of Romance (1972)
[GB2891] Bodley hbk **£9.95**

Beyond the Pale (1981)
[GB2892] Bodley hbk **£9.95**

Elizabeth Alone (1973)
[GB2893] Bodley hbk **£10.95**
[GB2894] Penguin pbk **£3.95**   **NEW**

Family Sins & Other Stories (1989)
The latest collection of short stories from a master of the genre contains themes that will be familiar to his established readership: the temptation of compromise, the comic nature of our foibles and the poverty of life without love.
[GB2895] Bodley hbk **£11.95**

Fools of Fortune (1983)
With this novel Trevor became the only writer to have won the Whitbread Award twice. 'To my mind William Trevor's best novel.' (Graham Greene).
[GB2896] Bodley hbk **£10.95**
[GB2897] Penguin pbk **£3.95**
Miss Gomez and the Brethren (1971)
[GB2898] Grafton pbk **£1.95**
Mrs Eckdorf in O'Neill's Hotel (1969)
[GB2899] Penguin pbk **£3.50**
Nights at the Alexandra (1987)
Excellent illustrated novella.
[GB2900] Arrow pbk **£2.50**
Other People's Worlds (1980)
[GB2901] Penguin pbk **£4.50**
Stories (1983)
A highly acclaimed omnibus volume containing all the stories from five collections. 'All of these are *tour de force* stories.' (Malcolm Bradbury in *The Observer*).
[GB2902] Penguin pbk **£6.99**
The Boarding House (1965)
William Bird filled his boarding house with people no one would miss from society. He created a unique atmosphere - until, that is, he died...
[GB2903] Bodley hbk **£10.95**
[GB2904] Penguin pbk **£4.99**
The Children of Dynmouth (1976)
Shortlisted for the Booker Prize, this novel won the Whitbread Award.
[GB2905] Bodley hbk **£10.95**
[GB2906] Penguin pbk **£3.95**
The Distant Past & Other Stories (1979)
A selection by of Trevor's best Irish stories.
[GB2907] Poolbeg pbk **£3.75**
The Love Department (1966)
[GB2908] Penguin pbk **£3.95**
The News from Ireland & Other Stories (1986)
'This may well be his best collection yet.' (Alan Massie, *The Scotsman*)
[GB2909] Bodley hbk **£10.95**
[GB2910] Penguin pbk **£3.99**
The Old Boys (1964)
Winner of the Hawthornden Prize.
[GB2911] Penguin pbk **£3.99**
The Silence in the Garden (1988)
Trevor's latest novel opens in the early 20th century with Sarah Pollexfen longing to return to the ancient family seat. When she learns about her ancestry, she discovers how and why its magic became tarnished.
[GB2912] Bodley hbk **£10.95**

TROCCHI, ALEXANDER (Scottish)
A cult writer associated with the Beat movement.
Cain's Book
[GB2913] Calder pbk **£4.95**
Man at Leisure
[GB2914] Calder pbk **£4.95**
Young Adam
[GB2915] Calder pbk **£4.95**

TROLLOPE, JOANNA
A Village Affair (1989)
An enlightened and beautiful novel that relates how the love between two women shocks their beloved country village. Not only a novel about breaking conventions, it is also a perceptive look at modern rural life.
[GB2916] Bloomsbury hbk **£12.95**

TWEEDIE, JILL (1936 -)
The well-known columnist from *The Guardian*, originator of the 'Fainthearted Feminist', writes perceptive, gentle comedies about the genuine difficulties of adhering to one's feminist beliefs in middle-class Britain today.
Internal Affairs
[GB2917] Penguin pbk **£2.95**

UNSWORTH, BARRY (1930 -)
Unsworth is best-known for *Stone Virgin*, an acclaimed multi-layered novel about the mystery surrounding a statue of the Madonna. *Pascali's Island* was recently filmed.
Pascali's Island
[GB2918] Penguin pbk **£3.99**
Stone Virgin (1985)
[GB2919] Penguin pbk **£2.95**
Sugar and Rum (1988)
[GB2920] H Hamilton hbk **£11.95**

UPWARD, EDWARD (1903 -)
An associate of Isherwood in the 'thirties, Upward became an important political novelist, whose fine trilogy *The Spiral Ascent* is sadly out of print.
The Railway Accident & Other Stories
[GB2921] Penguin pbk **£4.50**

USTINOV, PETER
The justly famous actor is also a brilliant raconteur, both on and off the page. The pair of novellas are his first works of fiction for some years, and to celebrate it two of his earlier works have been re-issued.
Krumnagel
[GB2922] M O'Mara hbk **£11.95**
The Comedy Collection NEW
Ustinov edited this up-to-the-minute anthology of much-loved comedy, with stories, cartoons, as well as limericks, one-liners and poems.
[GB2923] M O'Mara hbk **£11.95**
The Disinformer/A Nose by Any Other Name NEW
A pair of novellas. The first is the timely tale of retired spy who sets a trap for two Arabs and gets caught up in his own web. In the second a girl rebels against her greatest family inheritance: a big nose.
[GB2925] M O'Mara hbk **£10.95**
The Loser
[GB2926] M O'Mara hbk **£11.95**

WAIN, JOHN (1925 -)
Better known as one of the 'Movement' poets who went on to become Professor of Poetry at Oxford, Wain has also known some success as a novelist.
Hurry on Down (1953)
Rebellious novel in the tradition of Kingsley Amis and John Braine about a university graduate's escape from the life that has been prepared for him.
[GB2927] Penguin pbk **£3.50**
Where the Rivers Meet (1988)
This long-awaited novel from Wain is the first part of a projected trilogy spanning five decades of life in Oxford, exploring the confluence of academia and industry, and evoking the broader spirit of the age.
[GB2928] Hutchinson hbk **£10.95**

WAKEFIELD, TOM
Accomplished gay novelist 'who knows exactly what he's doing and does it resoundingly well' (Peter Ackroyd).
Drifters (1984)
His second novel explores gay existence with irony, sympathy and quiet anger.
[GB2929] GMP pbk **£3.95**
Lot's Wife (1984) NEW
The final, prophetic opinions of Henry Checket and Peggy Thurston, two people forgotten in an old people's home, develop as they measure the broader implications of their relegation.
[GB29291] Serpent's Tail pbk **£5.95**
Mates (1983)
[GB2930] GMP pbk **£3.95**
The Discus Throwers (1985)
[GB2931] GMP pbk **£4.50**
Variety Artistes (1988)
Intense portrayal of a woman rejecting the stifling constraints of her family.
[GB2932] Serpent's Tail pbk **£6.95**

WALPOLE, HUGH (1884 - 1941)
Unfairly lampooned by Maugham in *Cakes and Ale* as a literary careerist, Walpole was an immensely popular writer in his day. Despite being a close friend of Virginia Woolf, his style owes more to the 19th century than to the 20th.
The Herries Chronicles Vol 1 (1930 - 32)
An ambitious fictional project about a family in the Lake District; originally published as *Rogue Herries* and *Judith Paris*.
[GB2935] Pan pbk **£3.95**
The Herries Chronicles Vol 2 (1932 - 1933)
Comprising *The Fortress* and *Vanessa*.
[GB2936] Pan pbk **£6.99**

WARNER, MARINA (1946 -)
An established art critic and the author of major art historical works such as *Monuments and Maidens*, Warner is now winning equal recognition as a novelist.
The Lost Father (1988)
Warner's third novel was highly praised and also shortlisted for the 1988 Booker Prize. It is a magnificently rich saga of an Italian family history through this century.
[GB2939] Picador pbk **£4.99**
The Skating Party (1982)
This novel was compared to work by Elizabeth Bowen and Rosamond Lehmann.
[GB2940] Methuen pbk **£3.50**

WARNER, SYLVIA TOWNSEND (1893 - 1978)
Yeats praised her early poetry, but it is for her novels that Warner is now best remembered, since it is in them that one finds the strongest expression of her original voice. Her work, which is currently enjoying a popular resurgence, manages to combine a leaning towards myth and the supernatural with a lifelong affection for the English countryside.
After the Death of Don Juan (1938)
The supposed death of the corrupt noble Don Juan gives hope to the oppressed peasants of a remote Spanish village in the 1860s: this 'historical' novel is Warner's own investigation into the roots of the Spanish Civil War.
[GB2941] Virago pbk **£4.99**
Lolly Willowes (1926)
A spinster discovers her calling as a witch.
[GB2942] Women's P pbk **£3.95**
Mr Fortune's Maggot (1927)
The story of an unsuccessful South Seas missionary.
[GB2943] Virago pbk **£4.95**
One Thing Leading to Another
[GB2944] Women's P pbk **£3.95**
Selected Stories
Many of these stories first appeared in the *New Yorker*, which helped Warner to develop a popular following in the US.
[GB2945] Chatto hbk **£13.95**
Summer Will Show (1936)
[GB2946] Virago pbk **£4.95**
The True Heart (1929)
A love story set in the Essex marshes; Warner at her imaginative and lyrical best.
[GB2947] Virago pbk **£4.95**

WATERHOUSE, KEITH (1929 -)
Born and educated in Leeds, Waterhouse is a well-known comic writer who still writes as a journalist. His most celebrated creation is *Billy Liar* .
Billy Liar (1959)
Brilliant and moving tale of a young man's escape from his drab life into fantasy, and how he returns to earth.
[GB2948] Penguin pbk **£2.50**
Billy Liar on the Moon (1975)
Belated sequel to the earlier novel.
[GB2949] Penguin pbk **£2.95**

Bimbo (1989) **NEW**
A highly entertaining confessional novel rendered throughout in tabloid-speak: page 3 celebrity Debra Chase finally tells the truth behind her outrageous newspaper exposés.
[GB2950] Hodder hbk **£11.95**
Collected Letters of a Nobody (1986)
[GB2951] Grafton pbk **£3.95**
Jubb (1963)
[GB2952] Grafton pbk **£2.99**
Maggie Muggins (1981)
[GB2953] Grafton pbk **£2.99**
Mrs Pooter's Diary (1983)
The Diary of a Nobody rewritten from Mrs, not Mr, Pooter's point of view.
[GB2954] Transworld pbk **£3.95**
Office Life (1978)
[GB2955] Grafton pbk **£2.99**
Our Song (1988)
A middle-aged former advertising executive reflects on his astonishing affair with a far younger woman.
[GB2956] Hodder pbk **£3.99**
There is a Happy Land (1957)
[GB2957] Longman pbk **£2.95**
Thinks (1984)
[GB2958] Grafton pbk **£2.99**

WAUGH, ALEC (1898 - 1981)
The brother of Evelyn, he is remembered chiefly for his autobiographical works, although his novel, *The Loom of Youth*, caused a furore when published for its portrayal of homosexuality in public schools.
A Spy in the Family (Autobiography)
[GB2959] WH Allen pbk **£9.95**
The Loom of Youth (1917)
[GB2960] Methuen pbk **£3.95**

WAUGH, DAISY
What's the Matter With Daisy Jane (1987)
A first novel bravely tackling the subject of anorexia nervosa.
[GB2966] Heinemann hbk **£10.95**

WAUGH, EVELYN (1903 - 1966)
The spectacular success of his first novel *Decline and Fall* allowed Waugh, a London publisher's son, to forsake his unhappy teaching career and establish himself as a journalist, travel writer and novelist. His talent for comedy and social satire enabled him, in his earlier books, to capture the brittle and cynical frivolity of his post-war generation. With his later novels and their increasing devotion to the Catholic faith, Waugh communicates a deeper set of values.
A Handful of Dust (1934)
Regarded by many as one of Waugh's best, this is a heartless and amoral story of adultery and lost love. A very dark and bitter work.
[GB2968] Methuen hbk **£9.95**
[GB2967] Penguin pbk **£2.99**
A Little Learning (Non fiction, 1964)
[GB2969] Methuen hbk **£10.95**
[GB2970] Penguin pbk **£3.95**
Black Mischief (1932)
Famous satire set in Africa.
[GB2971] Methuen hbk **£10.95**
[GB2972] Penguin pbk **£2.95**
Brideshead Revisited (1945)
Baroque and elegiac evocation of youthful summer days in Oxford with a nostalgic portrait of a doomed Catholic aristocratic family. Although Waugh later came to view it as overly sentimental, it has lasted better than many of his works.
[GB2973] Methuen hbk **£10.95**
[GB2974] Penguin pbk **£3.50**
Decline and Fall (1928)
A hilarious romp through high society and upper-class craziness.
[GB2976] Methuen hbk **£10.95**
[GB2975] Penguin pbk **£2.95**

Helena (1950)
Unusual experiment with the historical novel.
[GB2977] Penguin pbk **£3.95**
Put Out More Flags (1942)
[GB2978] Penguin pbk **£2.99**
Scoop (1938)
Waugh's most joyous comic novel; a guileless naturalist is sent, by mistake, to report on a war somewhere in Ethiopia. A fine Fleet Street satire.
[GB2979] Methuen hbk **£11.99**
[GB2980] Penguin pbk **£2.99**
The Loved One (1948)
Set in California, this is a blackly funny look at the excesses of the American funeral industry.
[GB2981] Methuen hbk **£8.50**
[GB2982] Penguin pbk **£2.99**
The Ordeal of Gilbert Pinfold (1957)
Based on Waugh's own nervous breakdown, this is a rarely revealing novel.
[GB2983] Methuen hbk **£10.95**
[GB2984] Penguin pbk **£2.95**
Vile Bodies (1930)
[GB2986] Methuen hbk **£9.95**
[GB2987] Penguin pbk **£2.99**
Work Suspended, Charles Ryder & Other Stories
[GB2988] Penguin pbk **£3.95**

THE SWORD OF HONOUR TRILOGY
Men at Arms (1952)
Drawing upon his own experiences, this trilogy follows Guy Crouchback's inglorious war career with a mixture of sympathy and scorn. Perhaps Waugh's most considerable overall achievement, memorable for its economic evocations of life during wartime.
[GB2989] Methuen hbk **£10.95**
[GB2989A] Penguin pbk **£2.95**
Officers and Gentlemen (1955)
[GB2990] Methuen hbk **£10.95**
[GB2990A] Penguin pbk **£2.99**
Unconditional Surrender (1961)
[GB2991] Methuen hbk **£10.95**
[GB2991A] Penguin pbk **£2.95**
The Sword of Honour Trilogy (1952 - 61)
[GB2985] Penguin pbk **£5.95**

WAUGH, TERESA
An Intolerable Burden
[GB2993] H Hamilton hbk **£10.95**
Painting Water
[GB2994] Penguin pbk **£2.95**
Song at Twilight (1989)
A retired French teacher sits down to write her memoirs, but tells instead of how she befriended one of her earlier pupils. But from her daily diary, disturbing correspondences with that earlier story begin to emerge. A clever novel about self-delusion.
[GB2995] H Hamilton hbk **£11.95**
Waterloo, Waterloo
[GB2996] Penguin pbk **£2.95**

WEBB, MARY (1881 - 1927)
Opinions differ about Mary Webb. While many prefer Stella Gibbons's satire of Webb's brooding, unhumorous style in *Cold Comfort Farm*, others enjoy her descriptions of life in her native Shropshire for their Lawrentian, lyrical intensity. Among the latter was Stanley Baldwin, whose praise of her most famous work, *Precious Bane*, ensured its popularity.
Armour Wherein He Trusted (1929)
[GB2997] Virago pbk **£4.99**
Gone to Earth (1917)
[GB2998] Virago pbk **£4.99**
House in Dormer Forest (1920)
[GB2999] Virago pbk **£4.99**
Precious Bane (1924)
A memorable portrait of a strong woman, unhappy with her harelip who strives after a fuller life. Highly praised by Rebecca West.
[GB3000] Virago pbk **£4.99**

WELDON, FAY (1933 -)
In her former career as a copywriter Weldon gave us the 'Go to work on an egg' slogan, but since then she has produced many successful television plays and a series of inventive novels. Her books generally articulate contemporary feminist concerns within a tragi-comic domestic world.
Down Among the Women (1971)
[GB3001] Penguin pbk **£3.99**
Fat Women's Joke (1967)
[GB3002] Hodder pbk **£1.95**
Female Friends (1975)
[GB3003] Pan pbk **£3.50**
Hearts and Lives of Men (1987)
[GB3004] Fontana pbk **£3.95**
Leader of the Band (1988)
The wild life and exploits of a vociferous and *outré* heroine, who leaves her barrister husband and elopes to the South of France with a jazz player.
[GB3005] Hodder pbk **£2.99**
Letters to Alice on First Reading Jane Austen (Non fiction, 1984)
[GB3006] Hodder pbk **£2.50**
Little Sisters (1977)
[GB3007] Hodder pbk **£2.50**
Polaris (Stories, 1985)
[GB3008] Hodder pbk **£2.50**
Praxis (Stories, 1978)
Shortlisted for the Booker Prize.
[GB3009] Hodder pbk **£3.50**
Puffball (1980)
[GB3010] Hodder pbk **£2.95**
Remember Me (1976)
[GB3011] Hodder pbk **£2.50**
The Cloning of Joanna May (1989) **NEW**
Joanna May's husband has created four younger clones of his wife. The disturbing ramifications of this, springing from his misguided love for her, make this an imaginatively speculative work.
[GB3012] Collins hbk **£11.95**
The Heart of the Country (1987)
Part farce, part tragedy, this is the brilliant story of a hopelessly dependent woman who is abandoned by her husband and then saved by his first wife.
[GB3013] Arrow pbk **£2.50**
The Life and Loves of a She Devil (1984)
Weldon's best-known work on account of its fine transition onto the TV screen. It is a macabre tale of an ugly woman struggling to survive in a world hooked on female beauty.
[GB3014] Hodder pbk **£2.95**
The President's Child (1982)
[GB3015] Hodder pbk **£2.50**
The Rules of Life (1987)
[GB3016] Arrow pbk **£2.50**
The Shrapnel Academy (1986)
[GB3017] Hodder pbk **£2.50**
Watching Me, Watching You (1981)
[GB3018] Hodder pbk **£2.50**

WELLS, H.G. (1866 - 1946)
Determination and prolific output enabled Wells to overcome his humble origins and unsuccessful early life to become one of the most popular authors of his day. Wells was a vigorous and provocative thinker, and in keeping with his unconventional, 'scandalous' attitude to sexual emancipation, he was a great popularizer of ideas. His novels can usefully be divided into those with scientific preoccupations like *The Time Machine*, and his more comic, realistic depictions of the lower middle-class world that he once knew, as in *Kipps*.
Ann Veronica (1909)
The story of a woman who defies convention and runs off with the man she loves, this a novel considered scandalous in its day.
[GB3019] Virago pbk **£4.95**
Christina Alberta's Father (1925)
[GB3020] Hogarth pbk **£5.95**

Dame Rebecca West, author of *The Return of the Soldier* (Virago pbk £4.95) (Photo: Jerry Bauer)

Complete Short Stories
[GB3021] Black hbk **£9.95**
Kipps (1905)
The story of a haberdasher's assistant whose life falls apart when he inherits a fortune, this is one of Wells' most sustained novels.
[GB3022] Oxford pbk **£4.95**
Man with a Nose (Uncollected Stories)
[GB3023] Athlone hbk **£12.50**
Marriage (1912)
[GB3024] Hogarth pbk **£5.95**
Mr Britling Sees It Through (1916)
Moving novel written at the height of the First World War, exploring the pain of those left behind.
[GB3025] Hogarth pbk **£5.95**
Passionate Friends (1913)
[GB3026] Hogarth pbk **£5.95**
Selected Short Stories
[GB3027] Penguin pbk **£3.95**
The Dream (1924)
Perceptive and romantic scientific fiction novel in which the hero is swept from the 40th century back into the gaslit streets of Edwardian England.
[GB3028] Hogarth pbk **£5.95**
The History of Mr Polly (1910)
The eponymous shopkeeper burns down his ill-run business and starts a new life - a recurring theme in Wells' fiction.
[GB3029] Pan pbk **£2.50**
The Invisible Man (1897)
[GB3030] Pan pbk **£2.50**
The Island of Doctor Moreau (1896)
Chilling tale of the naturalist who splices humans and animals. Can still be read as a warning against genetic engineering.
[GB3031] Heinemann hbk **£11.95**
The New Machiavelli (1911)
Wells' brilliant defence of his views on politics, science, feminism and art.
[GB3032] Penguin pbk **£4.99**
The Time Machine (1895)
The fable of a future world divided between workers and the leisured ruling class.
[GB3033] Pan pbk **£2.99**
The War of the Worlds (1898)
Brilliantly imaginative account of a Martian invasion.
[GB3034] Pan pbk **£2.99**
Tono-Bungay (1909)
Once again Wells' foresight is remarkable, as proved by this vision of an England declining at the hands of a meretricious entrepreneurial class.
[GB3035] Pan pbk **£2.50**
Wheels of Chance (1896)
[GB3036] Dent pbk **£2.50**

Wife of Sir Isaac Harman (1914)
[GB3037] Hogarth pbk **£5.95**
World Set Free
[GB3038] Hogarth pbk **£4.95**

WENDORF, PATRICIA
Popular author of well-crafted, satisfying novels with a touch of the 'saga' about them.
Bye Bye, Blackbird
[GB3039] Futura pbk **£3.50**
Double Wedding Ring (1989)
This is the tale of Rhoda, born in the late 19th century to a Somerset farmer, and her adventures in the new world after her old flame asks her to join him in the American Midwest. An absorbing story told with real vigour.
[GB3040] H Hamilton hbk **£12.95**
Leo Days
[GB3041] Futura pbk **£3.50**
Peacefully, in Berlin
[GB3042] Futura pbk **£3.50**
Larksleve
With its sequel *Blanche*, this follows the fortunes of the Greypaull family in Victorian England, largely based on the author's family history in the West Country.
[GB3043] Futura pbk **£2.50**
Blanche
The heroine of this novel escapes from the squalor of her unhappy childhood to the London of 1881, but despite a prestigious marriage, finds she cannot forget the young gypsy she once knew.
[GB3044] Futura pbk **£3.50**

WESLEY, MARY (1912 -)
Although she did not start writing novels until she was in her seventies, Mary Wesley has rapidly gained a wide and devoted following. Her novels are warm, humorous and vividly paced.
Harnessing Peacocks (1985)
[GB3045] Transworld pbk **£3.99**
Jumping the Queue (1983)
[GB3046] Transworld pbk **£3.50**
Not that Sort of Girl (1987)
[GB3047] Transworld pbk **£3.99**
Second Fiddle (1988)   **NEW**
Another highly entertaining contemporary tragi-comedy from Wesley: a middle-aged woman, meeting a struggling young writer, thinks she can fit him into her well-ordered life. What she doesn't foresee is that *she* may end up playing second fiddle.
[GB3048] Macmillan hbk **£11.95**
The Camomile Lawn (1984)
A fast-moving novel which follows a group of young people between Cornwall and London during the war. It explores their developing relationships with wit and insight.
[GB3049] Transworld pbk **£3.99**
The Vacillations of Poppy Carew (1986)
[GB3050] Transworld pbk **£3.99**

WEST, REBECCA (1892 - 1983)
Cecily Fairfield adopted this name from an Ibsen heroine at the age of nineteen, when she started writing combative feminist journalism. For many years she was involved with H.G. Wells and they eventually bore a son. Her novels are still admired for their fine craftsmanship and unconventional heroines.
A Celebration
[GB3051] Macmillan hbk **£8.50**
Cousin Rosamund
[GB3052] Virago pbk **£4.95**
Harriet Hume (1929)
A passionate feminist tale set in London, this recounts the triumph of love over man's apparent desire for dominance and destruction.
[GB3053] Virago pbk **£4.95**
Sunflower (1986)
First paperback publication of West's fictionalized

account of her love for Lord Beaverbrook and her affair with H.G. Wells, suppressed during her own lifetime.
[GB3054] Virago pbk **£5.50**
The Birds Fall Down (1966)
An eighteen year old girl witnesses the momentous events leading up to the Russian Revolution.
[GB3055] Virago pbk **£4.99**
The Essential Rebecca West (1978)
[GB3056] Penguin pbk **£6.95**
The Fountain Overflows (1956)
[GB3057] Virago pbk **£4.99**
The Harsh Voice (1935)
Four novellas set in America, England and Paris.
[GB3058] Virago pbk **£4.95**
The Judge (1922)
A vigorous portrait of a suffragette and the relationship she has with her mother.
[GB3059] Virago pbk **£5.50**
The Real Night (1984)
[GB3060] Virago pbk **£4.95**
The Return of the Soldier (1918)
West's first novel is perhaps her best known. A shell-shocked soldier returns from the Great War to the various loving women waiting for him.
[GB3061] Virago pbk **£4.95**
The Thinking Reed (1936)
[GB3062] Virago pbk **£4.95**

WHITE, ANTONIA (1899 - 1980)
The translator of many of Colette's works, White shared a similar love of the sensuous and the bohemian. She started her first novel when she was 16, later allegedly completing it as *Frost in May* in six weeks. With the exception of *Strangers*, the novels below form a semi-autobiographical quartet.
Beyond the Glass (1954)
Her descent into mental illness and confinement in an asylum.
[GB3071] Virago pbk **£4.99**
Frost in May (1933)
Her Catholic, convent childhood.
[GB3072] Virago pbk **£4.99**
The Lost Traveller (1950)
Her experiences as an actress in provincial repertory theatre.
[GB3074] Virago pbk **£4.99**
The Sugar House (1952)
[GB3075] Virago pbk **£4.99**
Strangers (1953)
[GB3073] Virago pbk **£4.99**

WILLIAMS, NIGEL (1948 -)
An author who is gaining increasing critical recognition for his clever, comic novels and plays, noted for their sense of the absurd.
Black Magic (1988)
A novella mixing fable with realism.
[GB3082] Hutchinson hbk **£3.95**
Jack Be Nimble (1984)
A novel of distinctly Pythonesque humour.
[GB3084] Faber pbk **£3.50**
My Life Closed Twice (1977)
[GB3085] Faber pbk **£3.50**
Star Turn (1985)
Story of two East End boys told by Amos from his desk in the Ministry of Information in World War II.
[GB3086] Faber pbk **£2.95**
Witchcraft (1987)
A witty exploration of sexual obsession.
[GB3087] Faber pbk **£4.95**

WILLIAMS, RAYMOND (Welsh, 1921 - 1988)
The greatly admired thinker and critic was also an accomplished novelist. Williams' concern for social and political questions is reflected in his fiction, although his last work delves into Welsh pre-history.
Border Country
Set during the General Strike, this is the powerful

story of a Welshman returning to his homeland to bury his father, which gives rise to inner conflict about his roots.
[GB3088] Hogarth pbk **£5.95**
Loyalties
[GB3089] Hogarth pbk **£5.95**
People of the Black Mountains (1989)   **NEW**
The first part of an epic work left unpublished on Williams' death. A young man is searching for his grandfather in the Black Mountains, and is suddenly pulled back over the rim of time to before the Ice Age. He follows the tracks of his ancestors across the ages up until the Roman invasion. A second part will follow.
[GB3090] Chatto hbk **£12.95**
Second Generation
[GB3091] Hogarth pbk **£5.95**
The Fight for Manhood
A gripping and emotional battle on the Welsh borders, as local men attempt to stop redevelopment.
[GB3092] Hogarth pbk **£4.95**
The Volunteers (1978)
[GB3093] Hogarth pbk **£4.95**

WILLIAMSON, HENRY (1895 - 1977)
After seeing active service in the trenches and an unhappy spell as a Fleet Street journalist, Williamson retreated to Devon in 1921. It was there that he wrote his best-known 'nature' works like *Tarka the Otter* and his two huge novel sequences which are almost completely out of print, perhaps reflecting the permanent damage to his reputation caused by his support for Hitler.
Linhay on the Downs
[GB3094] Sutton pbk **£4.95**
Lone Swallows
[GB3095] Sutton pbk **£4.95**
Salar the Salmon (1935)
[GB3096] Webb & Bower hbk illus **£14.95**
[GB3097] Faber pbk **£3.95**
Tarka the Otter (1927)
The perenially popular story, which reveals Williamson's great debt to the 19th century naturalist, Richard Jefferies.
[GB3098] Webb & B hbk **£14.95**
[GB3098A] Penguin pbk **£2.95**

WILSON, A.N. (1950 -)
Wilson's early novels are very much in the English tradition of ironic social comedy as typified by Evelyn Waugh, but his more recent works are intricately plotted tragicomedies. Wilson's High Church sympathies are increasingly evident, adding a further dimension to his incisive explorations of contemporary middle-class life.
Incline Our Hearts (1988)
A quintessentially English comic novel relating Julian Ramsey's progress through life in the post-war years, with a large assortment of eccentric characters and a serious sub-plot.
[GB3099] H Hamilton hbk **£11.95**
Love Unknown (1986)
This novel follows the love lives of three women who originally lived together in North London, introducing a rich gallery of incidental characters on the way.
[GB3100] Penguin pbk **£3.95**
Scandal (1983)
[GB3101] Penguin pbk **£2.95**
The Healing Art (1980)
[GB3102] Penguin pbk **£3.95**
The Sweets of Pimlico (1977)
[GB3103] Penguin pbk **£3.99**
Who Was Oswald Fish? (1981)
[GB3104] Penguin pbk **£3.95**
Wise Virgin (1982)
[GB3105] Penguin pbk **£3.95**

WILSON, ROBERT MCLIAM
Ripley Bogle (1989)   **NEW**

Ripley is a tramp who lives within sight of Buck House. Going over his life, he wonders how he ended up here; but his litany of woes is infused with lively self-mockery, making this an entertaining first novel from a new Irish writer.
[GB3106] Deutsch hbk **£10.95**

WILSON, SIR ANGUS (1913 -)
One of our most gifted satirical writers, Wilson has worked in the Foreign Office, the British Library and as a lecturer. Although misleadingly compared to Forster, he is a sharp critic of human foibles. Yet his novels and short stories, which display his taste for macabre farce, also reveal considerable compassion.
A Bit off the Map (1957)
[GB3107] Grafton pbk **£1.50**
Anglo-Saxon Attitudes (1956)
One of his best-known books, concerning the historian whose attempts to reconstruct his life are bound up within an archaeological mystery.
[GB3108] Grafton pbk **£3.50**
As If by Magic (1973)
[GB3109] Grafton pbk **£3.50**
Collected Stories (1987)
His first three volumes of highly-acclaimed stories collected together.
[GB3110] Secker hbk **£14.95**
Hemlock and After (1952)
[GB3111] Grafton pbk **£2.95**
Late Call (1964)
[GB3112] Grafton pbk **£2.95**
The Middle Age of Mrs Eliot (1958)
[GB3113] Grafton pbk **£2.95**
No Laughing Matter (1967)
[GB3114] Grafton pbk **£3.95**
Setting the World on Fire (1980)
[GB3115] Secker hbk **£10.95**
Such Darling Dodos (Stories, 1958)
[GB3116] Secker hbk **£10.95**
The Old Men at the Zoo (1961)
Another noted satirical novel, which uses the different world of London Zoo as a metaphor for the state of civilized man. Rather a dark work.
[GB3117] Grafton pbk **£1.95**
The Wrong Set (Stories, 1949)
[GB3118] Grafton pbk **£1.95**

WINTERSON, JEANETTE (1959 -)
Gore Vidal called her 'the most interesting young writer I have read in 20 years', and many would agree. A vigorous and poetic novelist, Winterson has quickly won critical recognition, two prizes and a devoted following. *The Passion* remains her most notable book to date, and should not be missed.
Boating for Beginners (1985)
A light, Biblical skit.
[GB3119] Methuen pbk **£3.95**
Oranges are Not the Only Fruit (1985)
Winner of the 1985 Whitbread Prize for best first novel. Hilarious autobiographical account of a Pentecostal upbringing in Lancashire that proved hostile to her sexuality.
[GB3120] Pandora Pan pbk **£3.99**
Sexing the Cherry (1989)   **NEW**
Another highly inventive high-wire act from Winterson, set in the 17th century. A mountainous woman who lives with fifty dogs, fishes a small boy out of the river: so this magical tale begins, giving us glimpses of the Civil War, the Plague and the Great Fire of London along the way.
[GB3121] Bloomsbury hbk **£12.95**
The Passion (1987)
Winner of the 1987 John Llewelyn Rhys Memorial Prize. A brilliant, interwoven tale bringing together Napoleon's chicken-server and a Venetian cross-dresser. An evocative exploration of love, war and chance.
[GB3122] Bloomsbury hbk **£11.95**
[GB3123] Penguin pbk **£3.99**

WODEHOUSE, P.G. (1881 - 1975)
A much-loved comic genius, whose first novel was published in 1902 and who eventually wrote more than 120 books, the incomparable duo of Bertie Wooster and his butler, Jeeves, first appearing in 1917. Although Wodehouse settled in America after the war, he remained the most English of writers, and was knighted only a number of weeks before his death. A necessarily small selection of his many works is offered here: details of the full range are available on request.
Adventures of Sally (1922)
[GB3129] Penguin pbk **£2.99**
Aunts Aren't Gentlemen (1974)
[GB3130] Penguin pbk **£2.99**
Bachelors Anonymous (1973)
[GB3131] Penguin pbk **£2.50**
Big Money (1931)
[GB3132] Penguin pbk **£2.99**
Blandings Castle (1935)
[GB3133] Penguin pbk **£2.99**
Carry on Jeeves (1925)
[GB3134] Penguin pbk **£2.99**
Code of the Woosters (1938)
[GB3136] Penguin pbk **£2.95**
Damsel in Distress (1919)
[GB3138] Penguin pbk **£2.99**
Do Butlers Burgle Banks? (1968)
[GB3139] Penguin pbk **£2.25**
Doctor Sally (1932)
[GB3140] Penguin pbk **£2.50**
Four Plays
The pick of Wodehouse's considerable theatre work: two social comedies from the 1920s, along with a Psmith and a Jeeves play.
[GB3141] Methuen pbk **£4.95**
Life at Blandings
Includes *Something Fresh/Summer Lightning/Heavy Weather*.
[GB3141A] Penguin pbk **£5.99**
Life with Jeeves
Includes *Right Ho, Jeeves/The Inimitable Jeeves/Very Good, Jeeves*.
[GB3141B] Penguin pbk **£5.99**
Mating Season (1949)
[GB3143] Penguin pbk **£2.95**
Meet Mr Mulliner (1927)
[GB3145] Penguin pbk **£2.50**
Money in the Bank (1942)
[GB3146] Penguin pbk **£2.99**
Much Obliged, Jeeves (1971)
[GB3147] Penguin pbk **£2.99**
Mulliner Nights (1933)
[GB3148] Penguin pbk **£2.95**
Pelican at Blandings (1969)
[GB3149] Penguin pbk **£2.99**
Piccadilly Jim (1917)
[GB3150] Penguin pbk **£2.95**
Pothunters & Other School Stories
[GB3152] Penguin pbk **£4.95**
Psmith Journalist (1915)
[GB3153] Penguin pbk **£2.50**
Psmith in the City (1910)
[GB3154] Penguin pbk **£2.99**
Sam the Sudden (1972)
[GB3157] Penguin pbk **£2.95**
Service with a Smile (1961)
[GB3158] Penguin pbk **£2.99**
Spring Fever (1948)
[GB3161] Penguin pbk **£2.95**
Stiff Upper Lip, Jeeves! (1963)
[GB3162] Penguin pbk **£2.95**
Summer Moonshine (1937)
[GB3164] Penguin pbk **£2.99**
Sunset at Blandings
Wodehouse's last and unfinished novel, decorously resolved by Richard Usborne on the basis of the author's detailed notes.
[GB3164A] Hutchinson hbk **£12.95**

The Aunts Omnibus
This collection of novels, short stories and extracts includes the redoubtable Aunt Agatha, the amiable Aunt Dahlia, and a host of other aunts *"lashing their tails and glaring at you out of their red eyes"*.
[GB3165] Hutchinson pbk **£9.95**

The Jeeves Omnibus
An omnibus of Jeeves novels and stories including: *Thank You, Jeeves*, *The Code of the Woosters* and *The Inimitable Jeeves*.
[GB3166] Hutchinson pbk **£9.95**

The Parrot & Other Poems
Alan Coren draws together a selection of Wodehouse's best comic verse ranging from political satires to poems about the 'county set'.
[GB3167] Hutchinson pbk **£5.95**

The Unknown Wodehouse Omnibus
A new omnibus of lesser-known favourites selected by well-known humorous writers. **NEW**
[GB3168] Hutchinson pbk **£9.95**

Ukridge (1924)
[GB3169] Penguin pbk **£2.99**

Uncle Fred in Springtime (1939)
[GB3124] Penguin pbk **£2.95**

Vintage Wodehouse (1977)
[GB3126] Penguin pbk **£4.99**

Young Men in Spats (1936)
[GB3127] Penguin pbk **£2.99**

WOOLF, VIRGINIA (1882 - 1941)
One of the truly great Modernist writers, Woolf's reputation has grown consistently since her 'rediscovery' as a prototypical feminist. She was a key member of the Bloomsbury Group and a talented *TLS* critic; Woolf put a lot of thought into the creative process, often suffering from extreme mental stress as a result, finally drowning herself after completing *Between the Acts*. Her best novels, those written between 1922-31, combine her lyrical, fluid style with remarkable impressionistic detail. See *Biography* and *Women's Studies* for her voluminous diaries, letters and criticism.

Between the Acts (1941)
Published posthumously, this is an experimental account of an interval in a play being performed in a rural town, entering into the minds of actors and audience alike.
[GB3170] Chatto hbk **£10.95**
[GB3171] Grafton pbk **£2.50**

Captain's Death Bed
[GB3172] Chatto hbk **£8.95**

Complete Shorter Fiction
A new edition which includes a recently discovered tale, and some previously unpublished, unfinished pieces.
[GB3173] Chatto hbk **£20.00**
[GB3174] Grafton pbk **£4.95**

Flush (Non fiction)
A 'biography' of Mrs Browning's spaniel; a good example of some of the lighter work that Woolf also produced.
[GB3175] Chatto hbk **£10.95**

Haunted House (Stories, 1943)
[GB3177] Grafton pbk **£2.50**

Jacob's Room (1922)
This is a fluid portrayal of the life and death of a young intellectual in World War I, and is thought to have been based on her brother Thoby Stephen; it also signalled Woolf's departure from conventional fiction.
[GB3178] Grafton pbk **£2.50**

Mrs Dalloway (1925)
The first of Woolf's three undisputed masterpieces, the other two being *To the Lighthouse* and *The Waves*. It blends the mental processes of the eponymous society lady with a shell-shocked war victim.
[GB3179] Grafton pbk **£2.99**

Night and Day (1919)
A beautiful evocation of Edwardian life in London, the city which held an endless fascination for Woolf.
[GB3180] Grafton pbk **£3.50**

Orlando (1928)
This is another one of her more playful works of fiction.
[GB3181] Grafton pbk **£2.99**

The Pargiters
[GB3182] Chatto hbk **£10.95**

The Voyage Out (1915)
Her first and most traditional novel, it tells the tragic story of a young woman's voyage to South America. Only 125 copies of the book were sold on its original publication.
[GB3183] Grafton pbk **£2.95**

The Waves (1931)
An intensely poetic novel, quite possibly Woolf's crowning achievement. The external forces of nature are woven into the interior monologues of six characters, as they progress from youth to late middle-age.
[GB3184] Chatto hbk **£10.95**
[GB3185] Grafton pbk **£2.99**

The Years (1938)
The longest, and definitely the most successful of her novels specifically during her own lifetime; it is a family saga covering the period from 1880 to 1936.
[GB3186] Grafton pbk **£3.50**

Three Guineas (1938)
[GB3187] Hogarth pbk **£5.95**

To the Lighthouse (1927)
Probably her most popular novel. Set at one family's summer house in the Hebrides, it is exquisitely evocative of the rhythms of their lives, tempered by an elegiac sense of loss.
[GB3188] Dent hbk **£8.95**
[GB3189] Grafton pbk **£2.99**

WYNDHAM, FRANCIS
Mrs Henderson & Other Stories (1985)
[GB3190] Cape hbk **£9.95**
The Other Garden (1987)
His first novel proved a critical success. Village life
during wartime is narrated by a young boy.
[GB3191] Arrow pbk **£3.99**

YATES, PAULA
Good Times with Bad Boys (1989) **NEW**
Acid House, warehouse, your house, mine; the
Chelsea world of music, parties, drugs and sex forms
the backdrop of Paula Yates's first foray into fiction.
[GB3192] Bloomsbury pbk **£7.99**

YEATS, W.B. (Irish, 1865 - 1939)
Yeats's spearheading of an Irish cultural rebirth in the
first half of the century had much to do with his love
for his native country's lore, a preoccupation which is
reflected in these two books.
The Secret Rose & Other Stories (1897)
Rich retelling of traditionally inspired tales.
[GB3193] Macmillan pbk **£6.95**
Fairy and Folk Tales of Ireland
Edited by the poet.
[GB3194] Picador pbk **£3.95**

YOUNG, E.H. (1880 - 1949)
Novelist who sets her work mainly in Bristol, and is
undergoing a revival as a result of Virago's efforts.
Young offers exquisite and witty portraits of class,
love and provincial life in 1920s England.
Celia
[GB3195] Virago pbk **£4.99**
Chatterton Square (1947)
[GB3196] Virago pbk **£4.99**
Curate's Wife (1934)
[GB3197] Virago pbk **£4.95**
Jenny Wren (1932)
[GB3198] Virago pbk **£4.95**
Miss Mole (1930)
[GB3199] Virago pbk **£4.95**
Misses Mallett (1922)
[GB3200] Virago pbk **£4.95**
William (1925)
[GB3201] Virago pbk **£4.95**

General Short Stories

Best Short Stories 1989 **NEW**
(Ed. Gordon & Hughes)
Stories that were published last year in various
periods; by such names as Peter Carey, Angela Carter,
Adam Mars-Jones, Ruth Rendell and William Trevor.
[GBB1] Heinemann hbk **£12.95**

**Best Short Stories from 'Strand'
Magazine** (Ed. Tracy, Lorna)
[GBB2] Methuen pbk **£3.95**

Introduction 8: Stories by New writers
Faber's 'Introduction' series is dedicated to
introducing the work of young writers to a wider
readership.
[GBB3] Faber pbk **£2.95**
First Fictions: Introduction 9
[GBB4] Faber pbk **£3.95**
First Fictions: Introduction 10
[GBB5] Faber pbk **£4.99**

Mae West Is Dead (Ed. Mars-Jones, Adam)
Contemporary lesbian and gay stories from Britain
and America.
[GBB6] Faber pbk **£4.95**

The Art of the Tale
An international anthology of short stories from
1945-85, with many of the finest post-war authors,
such as Camus, Kundera, Marquez, Nabokov and
Greene.
[GBB7] Viking hbk **£17.95**

The Oxford Book of Short Stories
(Ed. Pritchett, V.S.)
Short stories from the 19th and 20th centuries.
[GBB8] Oxford pbk **£5.95**

**The World of the Short Story: A 20th
Century Collection** (Ed. Faidman, Clifton)
62 stories from a vast array of writers, including
Nobel Prize winners and bestsellers.
[GBB9] Pan pbk **£7.95**

WOMEN'S STORIES
Any Woman's Blues (Ed. Washington, Mary)
Contemporary Black writers, including Alice Walker
and Toni Morrison.
[GBB10] Virago pbk **£4.95**

Close Company (Ed. Park & Heaton)
Stories by Colette, Jane Gardam, Jeanette Winterson
and Sylvia Plath on the theme of mothers and
daughters.
[GBB11] Virago pbk **£4.95**

Deep Down (Ed. Chester, Laura)
New sensual writing by women.
[GBB12] Faber hbk **£12.95**

Indiscreet Journeys
(Ed. Teran, Lisa St Aubin de) **NEW**
Virago hbk **£12.95**

One Whale Singing (Ed. Macleod & Wevers)
Stories from New Zealand, including work by Janet
Frame and Keri Hulme, and many new writers.
[GBB13] Women's P pbk **£4.95**

**Other Fires Stories from Latin
American Women** (Ed. Manguel, A.)
[GBB14] Picador pbk **£3.50**

Passion Fruit (Ed. Winterson, Jeanette)
Subtitled 'Romantic Fiction with a Twist', it includes
Marge Piercy, Angela Carter and Fay Weldon.
[GBB15] Pandora pbk **£4.95**

Storia I
Contemporary writers from around the world.
[GBB16] Pandora pbk **£5.95**

**The Secret Self: Short Stories by
Women Writers** (Ed. Lee, Hermione)
Stories drawn from the some of the best 20th century
woman writers in English, reflecting a variety of
cultural backgrounds and psychological moods.
[GBB17] Dent pbk **£4.95**
The Secret Self II (Ed. Lee, Hermione)
[GBB18] Dent pbk **£4.95**

Tales I Tell My Mother
[GBB19] Journeyman pbk **£5.95**
More Tales I Tell My Mother
[GBB20] Journeyman pbk **£5.95**

The Seven Deadly Sins
Seven women writers look at the oldest sins of
all, with Kathy Acker ('Lust') and Leslie Dick
('Envy').
[GBB21] Serpent's Tail pbk **£7.00**

Wayward Girls and Wicked Women
(Ed. Carter, Angela)
[GBB22] Virago pbk **£4.95**

FICTION

FICTION AND FANTASY · FOOD AND COOKERY · HEALTH AND FITNESS · HUMOUR · GAMES AND PUZZLES · CRI
AND THRILLERS · PHILOSOPHY AND POLITICS · PSYCHOLOGY AND SCIENCE · TRAVEL WRITING AND GUIDE BOC
· REVISION NOTES AND STUDY AIDS · RELIGION AND REFERENCE · ECONOMICS AND ENVIRONMENT · LANGUAG
AND LINGUISTICS · TWENTIETH CENTURY CLASSICS · NEW AGE AND SHORT STORIES · AUTOBIOGRAPHY AND
BIOGRAPHY · POLITICS AND CURRENT AFFAIRS · CONTEMPORARY FICTION · PENGUIN CLASSICS · GIFT BOOKS
AND GARDENING · ART AND AR[...]CIENCE FICTION AND FANTASY
FOOD AND COOKERY · HEALT[...]CRIME AND THRILLERS · PH
LOSOPHY AND POLITICS · PSYC[...]IDE BOOKS · REVISION NOTES
AND STUDY AIDS · RELIGION A[...]LANGUAGE AND LINGUISTICS

PENGUIN
BOOKS

All your reading needs

TWENTIETH CENTURY CLASSIC[...]IY AND BIOGRAPHY · POLITIC
AND CURRENT AFFAIRS · CONT[...]OOKS AND GARDENING · ART
ARCHITECTURE · HISTORY · P[...]Y · FOOD AND COOKERY ·
HEALTH AND FITNESS · HUMOU[...]· PHILOSOPHY AND POLITICS
PSYCHOLOGY AND SCIENCE · TRAVEL WRITING AND GUIDE BOOKS · REVISION NOTES AND STUDY AIDS · RELIG
AND REFERENCE · ECONOMICS AND ENVIRONMENT · LANGUAGE AND LINGUISTICS · TWENTIETH CENTURY CLA
SICS · NEW AGE AND SHORT STORIES · AUTOBIOGRAPHY AND BIOGRAPHY · POLITICS AND CURRENT AFFAIRS ·
CONTEMPORARY FICTION · PENGUIN CLASSICS · GIFT BOOKS AND GARDENING · ART AND ARCHITECTURE · HI
TORY · POETRY AND PLAYS · SCIENCE FICTION AND FANTASY · FOOD AND COOKERY · HEALTH AND FITNESS ·
HUMOUR · GAMES AND PUZZLES · CRIME AND THRILLERS · PHILOSOPHY AND POLITICS · PSYCHOLOGY AND
SCIENCE · TRAVEL WRITING AND GUIDE BOOKS · REVISION NOTES AND STUDY AIDS · RELIGION AND REFERENC
ECONOMICS AND ENVIRONMENT · LANGUAGE AND LINGUISTICS · TWENTIETH CENTURY CLASSICS · NEW AGE A
SHORT STORIES · AUTOBIOGRAPHY AND BIOGRAPHY · POLITICS AND CURRENT AFFAIRS · CONTEMPORARY FICT
· PENGUIN CLASSICS · GIFT BOOKS AND GARDENING · ART AND ARCHITECTURE · HISTORY · POETRY AND PLA
SCIENCE FICTION AND FANTASY · FOOD AND COOKERY · HEALTH AND FITNESS · HUMOUR · GAMES AND PUZZ
· CRIME AND THRILLERS · PHILOSOPHY AND POLITICS · PSYCHOLOGY AND SCIENCE · TRAVEL WRITING AND
GUIDE BOOKS · REVISION NOTES AND STUDY AIDS · RELIGION AND REFERENCE · ECONOMICS AND ENVIRONME

Jeanette Winterson

I like to read widely and although I'm not looking for anything specific, I know that those books that continue to matter to me share a particular quality: they free me from the problems of Gravity.

They are escapist in the just sense of the word, in the same way that Shakespearean comedy is escapist. In all those plays the characters, and therefore the audience, find themselves in a semi-magical world, (for instance the Forest of Arden in *As You Like It*) where their prejudices are challenged and where they must laugh at themselves or live miserably. The things they had thought so important are not at all, and the things they had overlooked shine like precious stones.

On returning to the real world, which they always do, they are no longer so defeated by it, no longer so at the mercy of society's weight.

They have learned a little Zen.

ITALO CALVINO
Invisible Cities
A novel constructed of short paragraphs, each describing a fabulous city, supposedly for the benefit of Kublah

Khan and related to him by Marco Polo. All of Calvino's work, fiction and non-fiction, feeds the imaginative life of the reader. He is the proper antidote to the fatty acids of modern prose. Wonderfully translated by William Weaver, it is the most perfect work of fiction I have yet read.
(Secker, hbk £10.95/Picador, pbk £3.50)

VICKI HEARNE
Adam's Task: Calling Animals by Name
A book about training animals but through that discipline, a philosophic enquiry into the nature of our souls. Hearne is a top-notch trainer and also a philosopher who teaches English at Yale. This amalgam of talents has produced a book to exercise the most thoughtful or the least used of minds. She is accessible, funny and never pretentious. Please read this book.
(Unfortunately this title is currently unavailable)

ROBERT GRAVES
Collected Poems
For me, the finest 20th century poet, even though Eliot's *The Four Quartets* remains my favourite modern poem. I love Graves's work because he is literary without being elitist and a great magician of words without endlessly showing you how clever he is. (I wonder if Anthony

Italo Calvino, author of *Invisible Cities* (Secker & Warburg hbk £10.95, Picador pbk £3.50)

Burgess has read him?). The other great thing in his favour, is that he loves women and writes about them with ardour and awe. I doubt that even the most radical feminist, determined to shoot any Muse in the foot, would feel offended or boxed-in by his work.
(Cassell, hbk £18.95)

THE BROTHERS GRIMM
Grimm's Fairy Tales
I've been reading these since I was a child. In those days they gave me hope because the one who wins the treasure or the Kingdom or the princess, is not the well-connected obvious choice, but the little person overlooked and maligned. These are tales of great hope and instruction and definitely not only for children. Try them with a mug of hot chocolate last thing at night.
(Routledge & Oxford, pbk £7.95)

GASTON BACHELARD
Poetics of Space
A study of language and imagination through the spaces those intangibles occupy: drawers, houses, forests, shells, attics, all the tiny and vast recesses of the mind, actually lived in and continually used as metaphors for the things we hardly know how to talk about. Within all this is another question: what is it about imaginative reality that allows a person whom we have never met and whose experiences have not been ours, to write in such a way that his or her work enters our minds and resonates in our hearts, perhaps forever?
(Beacon, pbk £6.95)

VIRGINIA WOOLF
A Room of One's Own
Mrs Woolf's writing is always clear and sharp, so when I feel bogged down by trivia I turn to her, and what matters comes clearly into focus again. This book, her most famous piece of non-fiction, examines the conditions a woman needs to think and to write. Sadly, for most women those conditions remain a hope, not a reality.
(Chatto, hbk £12.95/Panther, pbk £2.99)

SUE TOWNSEND
The Diary of Adrian Mole aged 13 3/4; The Growing Pains of Adrian Mole
These two books, both screamingly funny, touching and sad, saved me from

Sue Townsend, author of *The Diary of Adrian Mole Aged 13 3/4* (Methuen pbk £2.50)

utter madness when I was writing my latest novel. I thoroughly recommend them for manic depressives, misery guts, people in hospital (though not with stitches) and anyone broken-hearted by three terms of Thatcherism. Children can read them too.
(Methuen, pbks £2.50 & £1.95/together, hbk £7.95)

JONATHAN SWIFT
Gulliver's Travels
There's a lot of rubbish talked about Magic Realism these days, but the weaving of the fabulous and the everyday into an indivisible strand is not new, nor did it come out of Latin America. For an older example, try Swift's biting satire on the way we live now, complete with floating islands and talking horses, and, of course, little people who live in thimbles on Lilliput.
(Oxford, pbk £1.95/Penguin, pbk £1.99)

EMILY BRONTE
Wuthering Heights
Not the best told story, nor the most sympathetic characters. Stumbling and crude in parts and full of emotional clichés, and yet it remains one of the most powerful novels we know. It releases a peculiar fiery energy that continues undiminished with time. It is truly metaphysical, not in what it contains but in what it releases in the reader. The present vanishes and the moor is our home and then we find the moor is our heart (a most astonishing essay on this

work can be found in Andrea Dworkin's collection *Letters from a War Zone*).
(Chatto, hbk £9.95/Penguin, pbk £1.99/Oxford, pbk £1.95)

SHARI BENSTOCK
Women of the Left Bank
A much needed, too little read, corrective to the barrage of partially sighted male scholarship on the writers we think of as the Modernist Movement. If you wondered what happened to the likes of HD, Gertrude Stein, Natalie Barney, Djuna Barnes, Sylvia Beach et al, then this book will tell you. It's sobering reading but I returned from it with a kind of joy, knowing that as usual, the women were there, and they were important and they should be still. Necessary reading for women who want to discover their literary ancestors and for men who'd rather they didn't.
(Virago, pbk £9.99)

Emily Brönte (Picture: National Portrait Gallery)

One of the most interesting new voices in British Fiction of the decade, Jeannette Winterson won a Whitbread Award for her first novel *Oranges Are Not the Only Fruit* (1985), an original and grimly humorous account of a girl's adolescence, growing up within a strongly fundamental Pentecostalist family; in *The Passion* (1987) her new novel, *Sexing the Cherry*, she has moved towards a more allegorical and highly imaginative style.

The Booker Prize

This is Britain's best-known literary prize, awarded each year to a novel written in English by citizens of the British Commonwealth, Republic of Ireland, Pakistan, Bangladesh or South Africa, and published for the first time in the UK by a British publisher. The prize was created in 1968 to make the author more prominent in the eyes of the public and to increase the sale of books. The winner recieves £15,000 and since 1981 the prize-giving ceremony has been televised live, stimulating enormous press and radio coverage. The choice of judges has been attractively eclectic ranging from figures of international literary stature (Saul Bellow, Philip Larkin, Cyril Connolly, Rebecca West) to newscasters (Trevor McDonald), actresses (Joanna Lumley), politicians (Norman St John-Stevas, Michael Foot), critics (Frank Kermode, John Carey) and even a philosopher (A.J. Ayer).

'The Booker Prize has been good for fiction: it is honestly judged in that the judges read all the submitted books without sifters, and it has, over the past 20 years, shortlisted a large number of consistently good books.'
A.S. Byatt
Chairman, Society of Authors

Winners of the prize from its inception until 1977 are as follows:

1969 PH Newby *Something to Answer For* (Faber)
1970 Bernice Rubens *The Elected Member* (Eyre & Spottiswoode)
1971 V S Naipaul *In a Free State* (Deutsch)
1972 John Berger *G* (Weidenfeld)
1973 J G Farrell *The Siege of Krishnapur* (Weidenfeld)
1974 Nadine Gordimer *The Conservationist* (Cape) Stanley Middleton *Holiday* (Hutchinson)
1975 Ruth Prawer Jhabavala *Heat & Dust* (J Murray)
1976 David Storey *Saville* (Cape)
1977 Paul Scott *Staying On* (Heinemann)

The following are the complete shortlists for the last ten years:

1978
Iris Murdoch *The Sea, The Sea* (Chatto)
Kingsley Amis *Jake's Thing* (Hutchinson)
André Brink *Rumours of Rain* (W H Allen)
Penelope Fitzgerald *The Bookshop* (Duckworth)
Jane Gardam *God on the Rocks* (Hamish Hamilton)
Bernice Rubens *A Five-Year Sentence* (W H Allen)

1979
Penelope Fitzgerald *Offshore* (Collins)
Thomas Keneally *Confederates* (Collins)
V S Naipaul *A Bend in the River* (Deutsch)
Julian Rathbone *Joseph* (Michael Joseph)
Fay Weldon *Praxis* (Hodder)

1980
William Golding *Rites of Passage* (Faber)
Anthony Burgess *Earthly Powers* (Hutchinson)
Anita Desai *Clear Light of Day* (Heinemann)
Alice Munro *The Beggar Maid* (Allen Lane)
Julia O'Faolain *No Country for Young Men* (Allen Lane)
Barry Unsworth *Pascali's Island* (Michael Joseph)
J L Carr *A Month in the Country* (Harvester)

1981
Salman Rushdie *Midnight's Children* (Cape)
Molly Keane *Good Behaviour* (Deutsch)
Doris Lessing *The Sirian Experiments* (Cape)
Ian McEwan *The Comfort of Strangers* (Cape)
Anne Schlee *Rhine Journey* (Macmillan)
Muriel Spark *Loitering with Intent* (Bodley Head)
D M Thomas *The White Hotel* (Gollancz)

1982
Thomas Keneally *Schindler's Ark* (Hodder)
John Arden *Silence Among the Weapons* (Methuen)
William Boyd *An Ice-Cream War* (Hamish Hamilton)
Lawrence Durrell *Constance or Solitary Practices* (Faber)
Alice Thomas Ellis *The 27th Kingdom* (Duckworth)
Timothy Mo *Sour Sweet* (Deutsch)

1983
J.M. Coetzee *Life and Times of Michael K* (Secker)
Malcolm Bradbury *Rates of Exchange* (Secker)
John Fuller *Flying to Nowhere* (Salamander Press)
Anita Mason *The Illusionist* (Hamish Hamilton)
Salman Rushdie *Shame* (Cape)
Graham Swift *Waterland* (Heinemann)

1984
Anita Brookner *Hotel du Lac* (Cape)
J.G. Ballard *Empire of the Sun* (Gollancz)
Julian Barnes *Flaubert's Parrot* (Cape)
Anita Desai *In Custody* (Heinemann)
Penelope Lively *According to Mark* (Heinemann)
David Lodge *Small World* (Secker)

1985
Keri Hulme *The Bone People* (Hodder)
Peter Carey *Illywacker* (Faber)
J.L. Carr *The Battle of Pollocks Crossing* (Viking)
Doris Lessing *The Good Terrorist* (Cape)
Jan Morris *Last Letters from Hav* (Viking)
Iris Murdoch *The Good Apprentice* (Chatto)

1986
Kingsley Amis *The Old Devils* (Hutchinson)
Margaret Atwood *The Handmaid's Tale* (Cape)
Paul Bailey *Gabriel's Lament* (Cape)
Kazuo Ishiguro *An Artist of the Floating World* (Faber)
Timothy Mo *An Insular Possession* (Chatto)
Robertson Davies *What's Bred in the Bone* (Viking)

1987
Penelope Lively *Moon Tiger* (Deutsch)
Chinua Achebe *Anthills of the Savannah* (Heinemann)
Peter Ackroyd *Chatterton* (Hamish Hamilton)
Nina Bawden *Circles of Deceit* (Macmillan)
Brian Moore *The Colour of Blood* (Cape)
Iris Murdoch *The Book and the Brotherhood* (Chatto)

1988
Peter Carey *Oscar and Lucinda* (Faber)
Bruce Chatwin *Utz* (Cape)
Penelope Fitzgerald *The Beginning of Spring* (Collins)
Davis Lodge *Nice Work* (Secker)
Salman Rushdie *The Satanic Verses* (Viking)
Marina Warner *The Lost Father* (Chatto)

The Whitbread Literary Awards

Almost equal to the Booker in terms of prestige and publicity, these annual awards are now given in five categories: Novel, First Novel, Biography, Children's Novel and Poetry. The winner of each category receives a nomination award of £1,500 and the five nominations then go forward to be judged for the Whitbread Book of the Year. The overall winner of the award receives £22,000, currently the richest literary prize of all. As far as the Fiction award is concerned, the Whitbread seems almost to run in tandem with the Booker: books hotly - but sometimes mistakenly - tipped for the Booker are often subsequent winners of the Whitbread (*The Satanic Verses* is the most recent example).

Here is the full list of previous winners with the Book of the Year, where awarded, indicated in bold.

1971
Novel *The Destiny Waltz* Gerda Charles (Eyre & Spottiswoode)
Biography *Henrik Ibsen* Michael Meyer (Hart-Davis)
Poetry *Mercian Hymns* Geoffrey Hill (Deutsch)

1972
Novel *The Bird of Night* Susan Hill (Hamish Hamilton)
Biography *Trollope* James Pope-Hennessey (Cape)
Children's Book *The Diddakoi* Rumer Godden (Macmillan)

1973
Novel *The Chip Chip Gatherers* Shiva Naipaul (Deutsch)
Biography *CB: A Life of Sir Henry Campbell-Bannerman* John Wilson (Constable)
Children's Book *The Butterfly Ball & the Grasshopper's Feast* Alan Aldridge & William Plomer (Cape)

1974
Novel *The Sacred and Profane Love Machine* Iris Murdoch (Chatto)
Biography *Poor Dear Brendan* Andrew Boyle (Hutchinson)
Children's Book *How Tom Beat Captain Najork & His Hired Sportsmen* Russell Hoban & Quentin Blake (Cape)
The Emperor's Winding Sheet Jill Paton Walsh (Macmillan)
First Book *The Life and Death of Mary Wollestonecraft* Claire Tomalin (Weidenfeld)

1975
Novel *Docherty* William McIlvanney (Allen & Unwin)
Autobiography *In Our Infancy* Helen Corke (Cambridge)
First Book *The Improbable Puritan: A Life of Bulstrode Whitelock* Ruth Spalding (Faber)

1976
Novel *The Children of Dynmouth* William Trevor (Bodley Head)
Biography *Elizabeth Gaskell* Winifred Gérin (Oxford)
Children's Book *A Stitch in Time* Penelope Lively (Heinemann)

1977
Novel *Injury Time* Beryl Bainbridge (Duckworth)
Biography *Mary Curzon* Nigel Nicolson (Weidenfeld)
Children's Book *No End to Yesterday* Shelagh Macdonald (Deutsch)

1978
Novel *Picture Palace* Paul Theroux (Hamish Hamilton)
Biography *Lloyd George: The People's Champion* John Grigg (Methuen)
Children's Book *The Battle of Bubble and Squeak* Philippa Pearce (Deutsch)

1979
Novel *The Old Jest* Jennifer Johnston (Hamish Hamilton)
Autobiography *About Time* Penelope Mortimer (Allen Lane)
Children's Novel *Tulku* Peter Dickinson (Gollancz)

1980
Novel *How Far Can You Go ?* David Lodge (Secker)
Biography *On the Edge of Paradise: A C Benson the Diarist* David Newsome (J Murray)
Children's Novel *John Diamond* Leon Garfield (Kestrel)

1981
Novel *Silver's City* Maurice Leitch (Secker)
Biography *Monty: The Making of a General* Nigel Hamilton (Hamish Hamilton)
Children's Novel *The Hollow Land* Jane Gardam (McRae)
First Novel *A Good Man in Africa* William Boyd (Hamish Hamilton)

1982
Novel *Young Shoulders* John Wain (Macmillan)
Biography *Bismarck* Edward Crankshaw (Macmillan)
Children's Novel *The Song of Pentecost* W J Corbett (Methuen)
First Novel *On the Black Hill* Bruce Chatwin (Cape)

1983
Novel *Fools of Fortune* William Trevor
Biography *Vita* Victoria Glendinning
King George V Kenneth Rose
Children's Novel *The Witches* Roald Dahl
First Novel *Flying to Nowhere* John Fuller

1984
Novel *Kruger's Alp* Christopher Hope
Biography *T S Eiot* Peter Ackroyd
Children's Novel *The Queen of the Pharisees' Children* Barbara Willard
First Novel *A Parish of Rich Women* James Buchan
Short Story *Tomorrow is Our Permanent Address* Diane Rowe

1985
Novel *Hawksmoor* Peter Ackroyd
Biography *Hugh Dalton* Ben Pimlott
Children's Novel *The Nature of the Beast* Janni Howker
First Novel *Oranges are Not the Only Fruit* Jeanette Winterson
Poetry *Elegies* Douglas Dunn

1986
Novel *An Artist of the Floating World* Kazuo Ishiguro
Biography *Gilbert White* Richard Mabey
Children's Novel *The Coal House* Andrew Taylor
First Novel *Continent* Jim Crace
Poetry *Stet* Peter Reading

1987
Novel *The Child in Time* Ian McEwan
Biography *Under the Eye of the Clock* Christopher Nolan
Children's Novel *A Little Lower than the Angels* Geraldine McCaughren
First Novel *The Other Garden* Francis Wyndham
Poetry *The Haw Lantern* Seamus Heaney

1988
Novel *The Satanic Verses* Salman Rushdie
Biography *Tolstoy* A.N. Wilson
Children's Novel *Awaiting Developments* Judy Allen
First Novel *The Comforts of Madness* Paul Sayer
Poetry *The Automatic Oracle* Peter Porter

Ngugi wa Thiong'o: An Interview

Ngugi wa Thiong'o is something of a legend in Africa. There his name stands high as one of those awkward people no régime can silence. Here most booksellers would struggle to pronounce it. Yet for 25 years he has fought against the evils inflicted on his continent, and grafted on the frontiers of World Literature consistently breaking new ground. The resulting 6 novels (plus theoretical writings, short stories and plays) form one of the cornerstones of Heinemann's African Writers Series and were honoured last year with a large format and more cheery covers. The release of his latest novel, *Matigari* should set his British record straight. A deceptively simple fable - of an old man searching for his family - turns and turns on the reader, tricking him variously from laughter to outrage, and all the while allows nothing to escape a cool satirical embrace. A purer synthesis of myth, socialism and national pride would be hard to find.

Ngugi's own story begins in Limuru, in Kenya's 'White' Highlands, renowned among colonials for its hunt, its golf course and its bacon. For the son of a polygamous household, landless and earning their living picking tea, coffee and pyrethrum, the contrast could not have been greater. When Ngugi writes of the Mau Mau, and detention camps in his first published novel *Weep Not Child*, there is little fiction present. His mother was detained for 3 months in 1955 after his brother joined the bush fighters. When the young Ngugi returned from his first term at secondary school, he found his home village razed to the ground by British and Home Guard soldiers.

His first novels reflect this embattled history. *The River Between*, written in 1961, puts the question of female circumcision in the context of the history and origins of the Gikuyu nation. The novel's heart is the community itself, and the strange, symbiotic relationship of landscape and history with personal psychology. By *Weep Not Child* (1964), this sense of communal belonging has been shattered. The land is owned by whites, the history re-written by missionaries and the psychology twisted by numerous humiliations and deprivations. Njoroge, the young protagonist, still dreams of fulfilment as his ancestors did, but the symbols pointing the way are all but gone. What remains is education, Christianity, or solidarity with the Mau Mau armed struggle.

Both novels portray people whose culture is wrenched from their control. A certain tragic powerlessness seems to set in. Is this how Ngugi remembers them?

"No, it wasn't meant to make the reader feel the characters were being crushed by these opposing forces. There is always an element of hope. Whether this is borne out by the novels is for the reader to decide of course, but something is left, something to go with or by. In *Weep Not Child*, the main character is on the brink of suicide when he makes a resolution that life has to go on. In any case the dream-like qualities of his conception of life is criticised. And the same is true of *The River Between*. The main character's obsession with education divorced from political struggle is criticised."

As with the best literature, these novels possess room for manoeuvre and debate. If comparisons are needed, they stand with Thomas Hardy and the lyricism of Lawrence's early short stories. How does he rate them now? "Of course there are serious weaknesses. In terms of the polemical or social vision guiding the works, it's not as mature as my later writing. And they are very traditional in terms of having a linear, biographical kind of approach."

By 1967, and *A Grain of Wheat*, Ngugi's artistic and social vision had sharpened. Of that work, he admits: "clearly it was important in my ideological and artistic development. Where before the plot development is linear, I break from that and use multiple narratives, flashbacks and stream of consciousness." The title, with its Biblical undercurrent, suggests a new literary cunning, and sure enough the books opens into dialogue with contemporary Kenyan politics. His literary vehicle is myth, particularly Biblical myths. The messages are coded, but the values under debate clear: myth is set loose to worry reality. The reality in *A Grain of Wheat* is Independence and the competing meanings of the word. Kenyan history was unique in that a large settler population faced a determined, organised guerilla army. The Mau Mau not only terrified white settlers (Elspeth Huxley compared Jomo Kenyatta to Hitler, and he wasn't even part of the rising): it set a radical black agenda before the world.

"There's no way you can divorce the impact of Mau Mau from the overall evolution of colonial policy in Africa and elsewhere. It played a very, very important part in the de-colonisation process."

It was these values which the new Kenyan government, reliant then as now upon overseas goodwill and investment, set out to bury.

"The new government was very ambivalent. On the one hand there was no way it could deny the actual contribution of Mau Mau in making possible even that type of independence. At the same time the new government was very keen to show the western world that Mau Mau had nothing to do with them. At the level of slogans it appealed and paid homage to Mau Mau, but at the level of real politics they denied the role of Mau Mau."

A Grain of Wheat tackles this ambivalence: "In my preface I drew attention to the fact that although names and places in the book were fictional, the situation was only too real for the peasants who fought against the British, yet could now see all they fought for being put on one side." It is Ngugi's first literary hybrid - the African political myth commenting on contemporary events - a development which led later to his complete rejection of the 'Afro-European' novel in *Caitaani Mutharabaini* (*Devil on the Cross*, 1979) and *Matigari Ma Njiruungi* (*Matigari*, 1987).

Before this came *Petals of Blood* (1977) and the controversial play *Ngaahika Ndeenda* (*I Will Marry When I Want*). "*Petals of Blood* was very important. It took a long time - 6 years - but it also grew out of historical times when I too was growing. There are some events mentioned which were not there in the opening. So the novel grew with the times."

Once again Ngugi's literary inventiveness excels. It is really a detective novel: three prominent men have been killed and four people have motives. But the motives are religious, political, sexual...and suddenly we are

Feature

321

back on familiar territory, where versions of the truth conflict, and the reader is in the jury's place. By weaving in the 'events' referred to, Ngugi neatly merges 'personal' justice with 'political' justice. Who are the real criminals?

Petals of Blood, although the most sophisticated African novel of its day, did not satisfy its restless author. As he says in his book **Decolonizing the Mind**:

"I was becoming increasingly uneasy about the English language. I knew whom I was writing about, but whom was I writing for? The peasants, whose struggles fed the novel, would never read it."

The solution came from a delegation from Kamiriithu, a village of 10,000 people near Limuru, who said to him: "We hear you have a lot of education and that you write books. Why don't you and others of your kind give some of that education to the village? We don't want the whole amount, just a little of it, and a little of your time."

The result was Ngugi's first work in his native tongue and a crucial break in approach, "even more important than the change in writing style between my first and last novels in English." The whole community mobilised itself. An auditorium designed with matchsticks on the ground by a group led by an office messenger, was built to hold over 2,000 people. A peasant and worker cast re-moulded Ngugi's tentative script, using their own experiences from the fields and the local BATA shoe factory. Surprisingly, in a village noted for its drunken brawls, those months of activity saw no drunken incidents. The rehearsals alone attracted huge crowds. For Ngugi, "the six months between June and November 1977 were the most exciting in my life and the true beginning of my education. I learnt my language anew. I re-discovered the creative nature and power of collective work."

If anyone doubts the power of theatre they need only look at the Kamiriithu experience (A new book, **Mother Sing For Me** by I Bjorkman is a good place to start). Within two months of opening the play had been banned and on December 31st 1977, Ngugi found himself in Kamiti Maximum Security Prison, detained without trial and without a release date. It is practically inconceivable (at least it was until Rushdie) that a British writer would say anything of enough

consequence to get him or herself into the headlines, let alone prison. But with Ngugi it was not only what he said, but the way he said it. His response came in his two Gikuyu novels: **Devil on the Cross** (written on toilet paper in detention) is ferocious, **Matigari** genuinely funny, and both were read aloud in bars and at firesides throughout Kenya. The police even set out to arrest a man called Matigari, who was heard to be roaming the countryside in search of truth and justice, only to find it was a book. They 'arrested' it all the same. Ngugi's last three novels are now banned in Kenya.

The decision to write in Gikuyu has clearly been a liberating one. He hopes it will inspire a 'symphony' of African works, with each community tongue offering its contribution. Only in this way, he believes, will African literature be truly free. His own late works are unlike anything in English literature, except perhaps a mischievous **Pilgrims Progress**, or an ireful William Blake. In fact Ngugi quotes Blake with some pride:

"The prophets Isaiah and Ezekiel dined with me and I asked them how they dared so roundly to assert that God spoke to them: and whether they did not think at the time that they would be misunderstood. Isaiah answered: 'I saw no God, nor heard any in a fine organical perception: but my senses discovered the infinite of everything, and as I was then persuaded and remained confirmed, that the voice of indignation is the voice of God, I cared not for consequences, but wrote.'"

Ngugi is now based in London, but not even exile has dimmed the voice of outrage.

A new prize awarded annually to the best work of fiction written in English by a citizen of the Commonwealth, established by the Commonwealth Foundation in 1987. The First Prize is £10,000; the runner-up receives £1,000; and there are four regional winners who each receive £1,000.

1987
Winner: *Summer Lightning* Olive Senior (Longman)
Runner-Up: *The Matriarch* Witi Ihimaera (Heinemann)
Africa:
Incidents at the Shrine Ben Okri (Heinemann)
A Forest of Flowers Ken Saro-Wiwa (Saros International)
Caribbean & Canada:
The Handmaid's Tale Margaret Atwood (Cape)
Eurasia:
Plans for Departure Nayantara Saghal (Heinemann)
South East Asia & South Pacific:
Winter in Jerusalem Blanche D'Alpuget (Heinemann)

1988
Winner: *Heroes* Festus Iyayi (Longman)
Runner-Up: *The Sea and Summer* George Turner (Faber)
Africa:
The Setting Sun and the Rolling World Charles Mungoshi (Henemann)
Caribbean & Canada:
The Honorary Patron Jack Hodgins (McClelland & Stewa)
Inspecting the Vaults Eric McCormack (Penguin)
Eurasia:
The Songlines Bruce Chatwin (Cape)
The Passion Jeanette Winterson (Bloomsbury)
South East Asia & South Pacific:
Oracles and Miracles Stevan Eldred Grigg (Penguin)

Feature

AFRICAN & CARIBBEAN FICTION

"Haven't we heard critics who demand of African writers that they stop writing about colonialism, race, colour and exploitation and simply write about human beings?" (Ngugi wa Thiong'o). African fiction has been slow to gain popularity in this country, although this may change with the international recognition of two of its finest exponents, Soyinka and Achebe, but why should it have happened in the first place? Black African fiction *is* alien to the British/Western mind, but this is partly because we attempt to yoke it within the Western tradition of the novel, where it does not belong. This is why it is such an exciting body of literature - every African writer is an innovator, moulding imported literary forms around traditional ones, particularly a long-established oral tradition. This remains worthily represented by collections from Diop (Senegal), Niane (Mali) and p'Bitek (Uganda). But when it is brought to face contemporary issues (as in Achebe's *Anthills of the Savannah* or Ngugi's *The Devil on the Cross*), the writing has a vitality and commitment which can make European work seem tired and predictable. African writers often have a national 'responsibility', which makes their opinions interesting. Many have been jailed for their writing and beliefs (La Guma and Breytenbach in South Africa, Xitu and Vieira in Angola, Ngugi in Kenya, Iyayi in Nigeria) or have been active politicians (Plaatje in South Africa, Lopes in Congo) or trade union leaders (Ousmane in Senegal). Such writers and nations have faced unprecedented upheavals in their culture, and it has been their task to make sense of this, from both a personal and political perspective. This is the stuff of good literature, but it may also be our sticking point as British/Western readers. As Achebe has written: *"An African creative writer who tries to avoid the big social and political issues of contemporary Africa will end up being completely irrelevant, like that absurd man in the proverb who leaves his house burning to pursue a rat fleeing from the flames"*. But this is not to say it is all strident ranting: there are many ways of being political, and one of African fiction's finest recommendations is that it is varied and skilled enough to encompass most of them. For newcomers to the subject, the 'big' novels have been re-issued by Heinemann in a more attractive, larger format; these include works by Achebe, Bessie Head, Ngugi, Ousmane and Soyinka's *The Interpreters*. Short story collections are always a useful introduction, and Tlali's *Soweto Stories* and Makoso's *Man Pass Man* are two good new collections, while the work of the London-based Nigerian writer, Ben Okri, reveals him as a new writer of great promise.

ABRAHAMS, PETER (South Africa, 1919 -)
His career spans early realistic novels in his native South Africa (*Mine Boy*, *A Wreath for Udomo*, and the autobiography *Tell Freedom*) to more determined political and black consciousness writing following his move to Jamaica (*This Island Now*). He returned to writing in the 1980s: *The View From Coyaba* documents 150 years of Black history beginning with the emancipation of Jamaican slaves in 1833, while *Hard Rain* was recently acclaimed on its British publication.
A Wreath for Udomo (1956)
[1] Faber pbk **£2.95**
Hard Rain (1988)
[GC2] NEL hbk **£11.95**

Mine Boy (1946)
[GC3] Heinemann pbk **£3.15**
Tell Freedom (1954)
[GC4] Faber pbk **£3.95**
The View from Coyaba (1985)
[GC5] Faber pbk **£4.99**
This Island Now (1966)
[GC6] Faber pbk **£3.95**

ACHEBE, CHINUA (Nigeria, 1930 -)
The father of modern anglophone African literature, who has produced consistently innovative work, combining keen sympathy for the individual with a critical social edge. Achebe's narratives and dialogues move through proverbs, pidgin and the bold use of tribal idioms to build up a coherent politically-charged world. A long silence followed his work in the 1960s until the increasingly corrupt and confused state of his country under Shagari prompted an open letter to the Nigerian electorate in 1983 (*The Trouble with Nigeria*).
Anthills of the Savannah (1987)
A gentle irony puts the finishing touches to this mature tragedy of post-colonial Africa. Achebe rewrites Soyinka's early masterpiece *The Interpreters* to view the delicate politics of Kangan (a mythical state) through two school friends, now Minister for Information and Editor of the National Gazette. A third friend, the Sandhurst educated military leader, threatens to become a despot. What values can be called upon to oppose him? Achebe's strength lies in his ability to foreground his own limitations (as an educated man) and give space to the thoughts of an oppressed population, particularly women, in this elegant plea for tolerance and humanity.
[GC7] Picador pbk **£3.95**
Arrow of God (1964)
Set in 1920s Eastern Nigeria, unsympathetic white officialdom tries to change traditional culture and an African priest leads the resistance.
[GC8] Heinemann pbk **£3.95**
Beware Soul Brother (Poetry, 1972)
[GC9] Heinemann pbk **£3.15**
Girls at War & Other Stories (1972)
[GC10] Heinemann pbk **£4.15**
Man of the People (1966)
A sustained satire on the corruption of opportunistic Nigerians following independence. The humour

Chinua Achebe, author of *Things Fall Apart* (Heinemann pbk £3.50)

comes thick and fast until the bitter irony of the fraudulent Hon. M.A. Nango MP catches up with the innocent narrator and election opponent Odili.
[GC11] Heinemann pbk **£3.95**
No Longer at Ease (1960)
Obi, grandson of the protagonist of *Things Fall Apart* is the hero of this second novel set in modern Lagos. He is an educated civil servant given responsibility for running his own country but corrupted by the pressures of superstition and prejudice.
[GC12] Heinemann pbk **£3.95**
The African Trilogy
Comprises *Things Fall Apart*, *No Longer at Ease* and *Arrow of God*.
[GC13] Picador pbk **£6.95**
The Trouble with Nigeria (1983)
[GC14] Heinemann pbk **£3.25**
Things Fall Apart (1958)
This masterpiece has become the African literary standard and sold over 3 million copies to date. Colonizing missionaries and taxmen arrive and threaten the traditional village life. Although this may seem alien to western readers the plot emerges effectively through the proud hero Okwonkwo, as he is exiled from his village and tries to regain the respect of his ancestors in a gripping conclusion.
[GC15] Heinemann pbk **£3.50**

ACHEBE, CHINUA & INNES, C.L.
African Short Stories
[GC16] Heinemann pbk **£3.95**

AIDOO, AMA ATA (Ghana, 1942 -)
Also a noted playwright.
No Sweetness Here (Stories, 1970)
Eleven short stories dramatizing the conflicts and confusions of post-colonial Ghana.
[GC17] Longman pbk **£3.95**
Our Sister Killjoy (1977)
Explores the thoughts and experiences of a Ghanaian girl on a voyage of self-discovery in Europe.
[GC18] Longman pbk **£3.95**

AKARE, THOMAS (Kenya, 1950 -)
The Slums (1980)
Eddy is an unglamourous, misogynist slum dweller and soft drug addict, who earns a living cleaning cars: Akare resists sensationalism to produce a grim, politically aware insider's story of poverty.
[GC19] Heinemann pbk **£3.15**

ALFREY, PHYLLIS SHAND
The Orchid House (1953)
One of the early novels of the post-war West Indian literary renaissance, by the Dominican novelist and journalist; it combines a romantic moodiness (in the manner of Jean Rhys) with acute political insight.
[GC20] Virago pbk **£4.99**

ALKALI, ZAYNAB (Nigeria)
The Stillborn
Unusual in being by a woman from the Muslim north of Nigeria, this tells of three women raised in a male-dominated society and their efforts to realize themselves.
[GC21] Longman pbk **£3.95**

AMADI, ELECHI (Nigeria, 1934 -)
A novelist who has also served as soldier and teacher. His experiences fighting on the government side in the civil war are memorably described in *Sunset in Biafra* while his latest work *Estrangement* deals with the experiences of ordinary people, both soldiers and refugees, returning after the war.
Estrangement (1986)
[GC22] Heinemann pbk **£3.95**
Sunset in Biafra: A Civil War Diary (1973)
[GC23] Heinemann pbk **£3.50**

Thomas Akare, author of *The Slums* (Heinemann pbk £3.15)

The Concubine (1966)
First part of his trilogy (continued with *The Great Ponds* and *The Slave*) dwelling in fascinating and episodic detail on the lives of a traditional village people in Eastern Nigeria before colonial interference.
[GC24] Heinemann pbk **£3.15**
The Great Ponds (1969)
[GC25] Heinemann pbk **£3.15**
The Slave (1978)
[GC26] Heinamann pbk **£3.15**

ANTHONY, MICHAEL (1932 -)
Trinidadian novelist and story writer, much of whose work is concerned with childhood and adolescence, often set in the physical environments in which he himself grew up. *The Year in San Fernando*, which tells the story of a boy's growing insight into the workings of the adult, urban world, is a classic of post-war Caribbean literature.
All That Glitters (1981)
[GC27] Heinemann pbk **£3.15**
Cricket in the Road & Other Stories (1973)
[GC28] Heinemann pbk **£2.75**
Green Days by the River (1967)
[GC29] Heinemann pbk **£2.75**
The Games Were Coming (1963)
[GC30] Heinemann pbk **£3.15**
The Year in San Fernando (1965)
[GC31] Heinemann pbk **£2.75**

ARMAH, AYI KWEI (Ghana, 1939 -)
Armah has lived and worked in every region of Africa, which is reflected in his stylistic sophistication. *The Healers* is a historical novel telling of the fall of the Ashanti empire, which is used to symbolize African disunity. His first novel *The Beautyful Ones Are Not Yet Born* is a realistic portrayal of a man struggling to resist endemic corruption.
Fragments (1970)
[GC32] Heinemann pbk **£4.85**
Beautyful Ones Are Not Yet Born (1968)
[GC33] Heinemann pbk **£4.25**

The Healers (1978)
[GC34] Heinemann pbk **£4.15**
Two Thousand Seasons (1973)
[GC35] Heinemann pbk **£4.15**
Why Are We So Blest? (1972)
[GC36] Heinemann pbk **£4.25**

BA, MARIAMA (Senegal, 1929 - 81)
Her death shortly after the success of her first novel, *So Long a Letter* (acclaimed as 'a cry from the heart of a Muslim woman'), robbed West African literature of its most effective feminist voice.
Scarlet Song (1981)
A tragic study of a marriage against all odds - between Mireille, sensitive daughter of a French diplomat, and Ousmane, a polygamous peasant from a poor Muslim family. Their attempts to live on his home territory are described with terse emotional realism.
[GC37] Longman pbk **£3.95**
So Long A Letter (1981)
[GC38] Virago pbk **£3.50**

BETI, MONGO (Cameroon, 1932 -)
Noted for his accomplished social satires where the targets are the colonists and their henchmen, in *King Lazarus* the traditional culture also gets a quiet knock as clan members squabble over a terminally ill but stubbornly alive chief. A political concern underwrites all his novels. *Remember Ruben*, written after a long silence, reasseses the West African independence movements of the 1950s. He has been exiled from Cameroun since 1959.
King Lazarus (1958)
[GC39] Heinemann pbk **£3.15**
Mission to Kala (1957)
[GC40] Heinemann pbk **£3.15**
Perpetua and the Habit of Unhappiness (1974)
[GC41] Heinemann pbk **£4.15**
Remember Ruben (1974)
[GC42] Heinemann pbk **£4.85**
The Poor Christ of Bomba (1956)
[GC43] Heinemann pbk **£4.15**

BISSOONDATH, NEIL (1955 -)
The nephew of V.S. Naipaul, Bissoondath was born in Trinidad but emigrated to Canada in 1973. His work captures the rootlessness of characters who have left their origins behind, without fully settling into a new environment. *A Casual Brutality* established him as a promising young novelist.
A Casual Brutality
The story of a Canada-trained doctor, Ramsingh, and his return to his native island of Casquemada; Bissoondath presents an acute picture of the effects of a false economic boom, and of the social instability it engenders.
[GC44] Minerva pbk **£4.50**
Digging up the Mountains
An acclaimed first collection of stories.
[GC45] Penguin pbk **£3.95**

BREYTENBACH, BREYTEN (South Africa, 1939 -)
The leading poet in Afrikaans and an accomplished painter, who has been hailed as 'unique' among Afrikaner intellectuals for his independent, passionate voice. After a clandestine return from Europe in 1975 he was arrested and imprisoned for seven years on a charge of 'treason', a searing experience which has affected everything he has written since.
A Season in Paradise (1985)
[GC46] Faber pbk **£4.95**
End Papers (1986)
[GC47] Faber hbk **£12.50**
Judas Eye (1988)
A moving collection of prose fragments and poems describing his years in prison.
[GC48] Faber hbk **£9.95**

Memory of Snow and of Dust **NEW**
A two part novel: the first deals with the interactions of three characters of different races, the second records the experiences of a Black political prisoner as he faces the death sentence.
[GC49] Faber hbk **£11.99**
Mouroir: Mirror Notes of a Novel (1983)
Nadime Gordimer wrote of this collection (written in jail): *"Prison irradiates this book with dreadful enlightenments - the dark and hidden places of the country from which the book arises are phosphorescent with it."*
[GC50] Faber pbk **£4.95**
True Confessions of an Albino Terrorist (Non-fiction, 1984)
[GC51] Faber pbk **£4.95**

BRINK, ANDRE (South Africa 1935 -)
A Professor of Literature and Drama, his work (written in both Afrikaans and English), has won numerous prizes in South Africa and has twice been runner-up for the Booker Prize. He has been a consistent critic of the apartheid regime.
A Dry White Season (1979)
The story of a decent man's involvement in the process of opposition after the death of his friend in police hands; once labelled a rebel, he can't turn back.
[GC52] Fontana pbk **£3.95**
An Instant in the Wind (1983)
[GC53] Fontana pbk **£3.50**
Chain of Voices (1982)
An historical novel set in 1825, about the hopes of freedom offered to slaves by their master, and the events which result when these are refused.
[GC54] Fontana pbk **£2.95**
Looking on Darkness (1984)
Nadime Gordimer wrote that this book broke 'political taboos', and it was the first novel in Afrikaans to be banned by the authorities.
[GC55] Fontana pbk **£3.95**
Map Makers: Writing in a State of Siege (1983)
[GC56] Faber pbk **£3.95**
Rumours of Rain (1984)
[GC57] Fontana pbk **£3.95**
States of Emergency (1987)
Three stories set against a series of documentary accounts of contemporary South Africa present, in a fascinating patchwork of opinion, fiction and history, Brink's insight into the state of the country.
[GC58] Fontana pbk **£3.95**
The Ambassador (1958)
[GC59] Fontana pbk **£3.95**
The Wall of the Plague (1984)
[GC60] Fontana pbk **£3.95**

BRINK, ANDRE & COETZEE, J.M.
A Land Apart: A South African Reader
[GC61] Faber pbk **£4.95**

COETZEE, J.M. (South Africa, 1940 -)
Afrikaner writer willing to face the realities of his society; his best novel is *Waiting for the Barbarians*, an allegory on the South Africans in Namibia. Against a vision which is frequently bleak, Coetzee's style is beautiful, haunting and poetical.
Dusklands (1974)
Two novellas concerned with racial abuse of power, one dealing with American involvement in Vietnam, the second with a Boer settler in the 18th century.
[GC62] Penguin pbk **£2.95**
Foe (1986)
A subtle reworking of *Robinson Crusoe*. Daniel Foe (the author) is approached by a woman who tells the story of a shipwreck she has been in with Crusoe, and requests he record it from her point of view.
[GC63] Penguin pbk **£3.95**
In the Heart of the Country (1975)
[GC64] Penguin pbk **£3.95**

Life and Times of Michael K (1983)
This Booker Prize winner, a stark and powerful allegory, owes much to Kafka and his portrayal of state absurdity. Michael K progresses through modern Southern Africa and its persecutions but retains an inner freedom unassailable by those who imprison him.
[GC65] Penguin pbk **£3.99**
Waiting for the Barbarians (1980)
[GC66] Penguin pbk **£3.95**

CONDE, MARYSE
A Season in Rihata   **NEW**
[GC67] Heinemann pbk **£3.95**

DANGAREMBGA, TSITSI (Zimbawe)
Nervous Conditions (1988)
This promising first novel is set in colonial Rhodesia. A schoolgirl is rescued from her poor village by a worldly, wealthy cousin, but only on condition she conforms to white expectations.
[GC68] Women's P pbk **£3.95**

DIOP, BIRAGO (Senegal, 1906 -)
Tales of Amadou Koumba (1966)
Dubbed 'the poet of the African bush' his concern with the Oral Tradition had the political aim of honouring the culture of rural, pre-colonial society. Amadou Koumba was his family's *griot* or storyteller, from a long line of guardians of traditional folklore and values. Diop's interpretations stay loyal to their originals, which have a surreal and mysterious quality far removed from the childish tales we know in the Western tradition.
[GC69] Longman pbk **£3.95**

DJOLETO, AMU (Ghana, 1929 -)
Hurricane of Dust (1987)
Post-revolution Ghana spins out of control as seen through the eyes of a small time thief and hustler.
[GC70] Longman pbk **£3.95**
The Strange Man (1968)
[GC71] Heinemann **£3.50**

ECHEWA, T. OBINKARAM (Nigeria, 1940 -)
The Crippled Dancer (1986)
A tale of inter-tribal conflict, dealt with in the traditional manner of Igbo society. A grandson, tarred by his grandfather's long standing rivalry with the village chief, faces possible disinheritance.
[GC72] Heinemann pbk **£3.95**

J.M. Coetzee, author of *Life and Times of Michael K*. (Penguin pbk £3.99)

EGBUNA, OBI (Nigeria, 1938 -)
Former Black Power activist (for which the British authorities imprisoned him in 1971) and noted playwright who spent some time as a journalist in this country.
Elina (1964)
His first novel: a young beautiful woman is orphaned and therefore fair game for both traditional (Ojukwu) and modern (Councillor Ogidi) predatory patriachs. But both their plans are thwarted when the son of the judge deciding her fate falls in love with her.
[GC73] Fontana pbk **£1.50**
Emperor of the Sea (Stories, 1974)
[GC74] Fontana pbk **£1.00**
The Madness of Didi (1980)
[GC75] Fontana pbk **£1.95**
The Minister's Daughter (1975)
[GC76] Fontana pbk **£1.50**

EKWENSI, CYPRIAN (Nigeria, 1921 -)
Described as the 'Nigerian Defoe', he is a pioneering and influential documentor of African city life, with a sure populist touch. Like Achebe he supported Biafra in the civil war and his most committed novel, *Survive the Peace* is set at the end of that conflict.
Beautiful Feathers (1963)
[GC77] Heinemann pbk **£3.15**
Burning Grass (1962)
A rural novel following the nomadic Fulani, a tribe of pastoralist farmers.
[GC78] Heinemann pbk **£3.15**
Jagua Nana (1961)
The original African urban novel describing the promiscuous decline of an ageing good time girl in Lagos.
[GC79] Heinemann pbk **£3.95**
Lokotown & Other Stories (1966)
[GC80] Heinemann pbk **£3.15**
Survive the Peace (1976)
[GC81] Heinemann pbk **£4.50**

EMECHETA, BUCHI (Nigeria, 1944 -)
Notable for her female characters who find themselves caught between tradition and a desire for independence, Emecheta also writes well of her experience in the Biafran War, in which members of her family perished.
Adah's Story (1983)
A one-volume collection of *Second Class Citizen* and *In the Ditch*, telling of a young Nigerian woman coming to London, and her struggles to maintain her independence in an alien country, while bringing up her children.
[GC82] Allison & B pbk **£2.95**
Bride Price (1976)
[GC83] Fontana pbk **£1.75**
Destination Biafra (1981)
[GC84] Fontana pbk **£1.95**
Double Yoke (1982)
[GC85] Fontana pbk **£1.95**
Gwendolen   **NEW**
Emecheta's new novel moves from Jamaica to England, and draws on the experience of three continents; it tells the story of a girl's harsh experience of growing-up, and her later struggle to maintain her identity in a hostile and strange environment.
[GC86] Collins hbk **£10.95**
Head Above Water
[GC87] Fontana pbk **£3.50**

EQUIANO, OLAUDAH
The Life of Olaudah Aquiano (1789)
Classic autobiography of an African slave, telling of his capture and eventual emancipation.
[GC88] Longman pbk **£4.50**

Cyprian Ekwensi, author of *Survive the Peace* (Heinemann pbk £4.50)

ESSOP, AHMED (South Africa)
Hajii Musa and the Hindu Fire Walker
This collection, dominated by the novella 'The Visitation' has its roots in Indian life in Johannesburg under apartheid, but a varied cast of racial and psychological types passes under his ironic wit.
[GC89] Readers Int pbk **£4.95**

FALL, AMINATA SOW (Senegal)
The Beggars' Strike (1979)
A satire on the conflicting values of an African state. As the beggars are removed to keep the city attractive for tourists, the Vice-President is ruined because they go on strike.
[GC90] Longman pbk **£3.95**

FARAH, NURUDDIN (Somalia, 1945 -)
Stylish and acclaimed writer who deals with contemporary African issues such as female circumcision (*Sardines*, now given an attractive new cover) and civil war (*Maps*). The latter novel charts the development of the guerilla Askar, through a unique fusion of African and English literary traditions.
Maps (1986)
[GC91] Picador pbk **£3.50**
Sardines (1981)
[GC92] Heinemann pbk **£4.15**

FUGARD, ATHOL (South Africa, 1932 -)
Tsotsi (1979)
An internationally successful playwright, this is his one novel, which was written in 1959-60. It is a white man's vision of the former Black township Sophiatown, described as 'scarifyingly realistic'.
[GC93] Penguin pbk **£3.95**

FUGARD, SHEILA (South Africa, 1932 -)
A Revolutionary Woman (1983)
Set in the 1920s as a European woman arrives to teach in a remote coloured school in South Africa, only to face racial and sexual tensions.
[GC94] Virago pbk **£3.50**

Nadine Gordimer, author of *A Guest of Honour* (Penguin pbk **£4.95**)

GORDIMER, NADINE (South Africa, 1923 -)

"I have come to the abstraction of politics through the flesh and blood of individual behaviour. I didn't know what politics was about, until I saw it happening to people". Gordimer's honesty and consistent opposition to apartheid bear fruit in her vivid tales, which deal in the everyday 'small horrors and tendernesses' of ordinary people under oppression.

A Guest of Honour (1970)
A major work set outside South Africa in an imaginary, newly-indepedent nation. The 'guest' is an Englishman, expelled from his post as a colonial administrator ten years before for siding with Black nationalist leaders. Returning for Independence celebrations, he sees his friend becoming a dictator, and is asked to help in a plot against him.
[GC95] Penguin pbk **£4.95**
A Soldier's Embrace (Stories, 1975)
[GC96] Penguin pbk **£3.50**
A Sport of Nature (1987)
[GC97] Penguin pbk **£4.99**
A World of Strangers (1976)
[GC98] Penguin pbk **£4.99**
Burger's Daughter (1979)
[GC99] Penguin pbk **£4.99**
July's People (1981)
[GC100] Penguin pbk **£3.99**
Occasion for Loving (1970)
[GC101] Virago pbk **£4.50**
Selected Stories (1975)
Graham Greene described this volume as 'a magnificent collection worthy of all hommage'. Much of her best work is here.
[GC102] Penguin pbk **£5.95**
Six Feet of the Country (Stories, 1982)
[GC103] Penguin pbk **£3.50**
Some Monday for Sure (1976)
[GC104] Heinemann pbk **£4.15**
Something Out There (1984)
[GC105] Penguin pbk **£3.99**
The Conservationist (1972)
[GC106] Penguin pbk **£3.99**
The Late Bourgeois World (1966)
[GC107] Penguin pbk **£2.99**
The Lying Days (1978)
[GC108] Virago pbk **£4.99**

HARRIS, WILSON (Caribbean, 1921 -)
The Guyana Quartet (1960 - 63)
Presenting a picture of Guyana's present state as well as an analysis of its myth and history, Harris's series is one of the richest and most complex pieces of Caribbean fiction.
[GC109] Faber pbk **£5.95**

HAVEMANN, ERNST (South Africa)
Bloodsong (1988)
Mature writer who produced his first book, a collection of short stories, last year. Their concern is with the ordinary, humiliating facts of apartheid, as experienced by both oppressor and oppressed.
[GC110] H Hamilton pbk **£5.95**

HEAD, BESSIE (South Africa, 1937 - 1986)
Although born in Pietermaritzburg, Bessie Head spent most of her life in exile in Botswana where her novels and stories are set.
A Question of Power (1973)
Powerful novel of the psychological effects of exile and assimilation.
[GC111] Heinemann pbk **£3.95**
Collector of Treasures and Other Botswana Village Tales (1977)
[GC112] Heinemann pbk **£4.15**
Maru (1971)
"With all my South African experience I longed to write an enduring novel on the hideousness of racial prejudice. But I also wanted the novel to be so beautiful and so magical that I, as the writer, would long to read and re-read it". That novel was *Maru*.
[GC113] Heinemann **£3.95**
Serowe: Village of the Rain Wind (1981)
Fine observation of 100 years in the life of a Botswanaian village.
[GC114] Heinemann pbk **£4.85**
When Rain Clouds Gather (1969)
[GC115] Heinemann pbk **£3.95**

HEARNE, JOHN (1926 -)
Hearne is one of the younger generation of Caribbean novelists; born in Jamaica, he has worked there as an academic, and for the island's Broadcasting Corporation.
The Sure Salvation
[GC116] Faber pbk **£3.95**
Voices Under the Window (1955)
[GC117] Faber pbk **£3.95**

HEATH, ROY A.K. (1926 -)
Born in Guyana, Heath has worked both as a barrister and teacher, and his lived for some time in London.
From the Heat of the Day (1979)
First of a trilogy (including *One Generation* and *Genetha*), which presents a memorable picture of family life over two generations in Georgetown, Guyana, and of a world full of sad intrigues and personal tragedies.
[GC118] Fontana pbk **£1.95**
Genetha (1981)
[GC119] Fontana pbk **£1.95**
Kwaku (1982)
[GC120] Fontana pbk **£2.95**
One Generation (1981)
[GC121] Fontana pbk **£1.95**
Orealla (1984)
[GC122] Fontana pbk **£3.95**
The Murderer (1978)
[GC123] Fontana pbk **£1.95**
The Shadow Bride
Heath's latest novel portrays the Indian community in Guyana, and is a powerful testimony to the limits of human hope and suffering.
[GC124] Fontana pbk **£4.95**

HOPE, CHRISTOPHER (South Africa, 1944 -)
Born in Johannesburg of white Irish-Catholic parents, Hope has lived in London since 1976. His work is characterized by an angry, satirical, intelligent and often sad attack on the immorality of his country.
Black Swan (1987)
[GC125] Arrow pbk **£2.50**
Kruger's Alp (1984)
[GC126] Sphere pbk **£2.95**
My Chocolate Redeemer   **NEW**
A funny and ironic novel, telling of the effect of the arrival of a deposed African emperor (exiled amid rumours of embezzlement and cannibalism) in a small French village, and on a teenage chocolate junkie, Bella, in particular. Hope's best novel to date.
[GC127] Heinemann hbk **£10.95**
The Hottentot Room (1986)
[GC128] Sphere pbk **£3.99**
White Boy Running: A Book About South Africa (1988)
Hope writes of his return to South Africa in the election year of 1987, after an absence of 12 years.
[GC129] Sphere pbk **£3.99**

IKE, CHUKWUEMEKA (Nigeria, 1931 -)
Unaffected social comedies form the main body of his work, such as *Naked Gods* which deals with the tensions between progressive science and witchcraft in a West African university, or *Toads for Supper* where a dissolute student who has engaged himself to three girls and been kicked out of university, has to face the wrath of the community which has funded him. *Sunset at Dawn* reveals a more serious side as Ike recounts his experiences in the Biafran war.
Chicken Chasers (1980)
[GC130] Fontana pbk **£1.75**
Expo '77 (1980)
[GC131] Fontana pbk **£1.75**
Naked Gods (1970)
[GC132] Fontana pbk **£1.95**
Sunset at Dawn (1976)
[GC133] Fontana pbk **£1.95**
The Potter's Wheel (1973)
[GC134] Fontana pbk **£1.95**
Toads for Supper (1965)
[GC135] Fontana pbk **£1.95**

Bessie Head, author of *Maru* (Heinemann pbk **£3.95**)

IROH, EDDIE (Nigeria)
Forty-Eight Guns For The General (1977)
Biafran based thriller in which European mercenaries
(the 48 guns) enlist to fight for the Biafran side but
prove uncontrollable.
[GC136] Heinemann pbk **£3.15**

IYAYI, FESTUS (Nigeria, 1948 -)
A gritty social realist writer who was detained in 1988
by the military government for protesting at human
rights abuses. His first novel *Violence* follows a
couple in extreme poverty who come to recognize the
many levels of exploitation which cause their
experience. In *Heroes* (his third work) a journalist
becomes politically active but only after his
girlfriend's father has been shot.
Heroes (1986)
[GC137] Longman pbk **£3.50**
Violence (1979)
[GC138] Longman pbk **£4.50**

KARODIA, FARIDA (South Africa)
Like her many compatriot writers, Karodia deals with
the economic, psychological and physical
consequences of apartheid. Although now based in
Canada, her concerns remain those of ordinary
people, as shown in the powerful novella *Coming
Home*, and by Meena, daughter of a 'coloured'
mother and Indian father, whose life is the subject of
Daughters.
Coming Home and Other Stories (1988)
[GC139] Heinemann pbk **£3.95**
Daughters of the Twilight (1986)
[GC140] Women's P pbk **£3.95**

KATIYO, WILSON (Zimbabwe)
A Son of the Soil
[GC141] Longman pbk **£3.50**

KINCAID, JAMAICA
Born in Antigua, Kincaid now lives in New York. Her
work draws on the environment in which she grew up,
giving a vivid feeling of the Caribbean landscape, in
stories which often recall the memories and
experiences of children growing up.
Annie John (1985)
[GC142] Picador pbk **£2.95**
At the Bottom of the River (1984)
[GC143] Picador pbk **£1.95**
Small Place
[GC144] Virago pbk **£3.50**

LA GUMA, ALEX (South Africa, 1925 - 1985)
A leading activist who was among the accused in the
1956 Treason Trial (which followed the 'People's
Charter' declaration) and was detained many times
before going into exile, to become ANC
representative in Cuba. His determination to pinpoint
real details of community life under severe repression
keeps his work authentic and persuasive, and his
social realism influenced the new generation of
African writers led by Achebe and Ngugi.
A Walk in the Night (1962)
His first and best-known work, a taut thriller set in the
Coloured Cape Town slum, District 6.
[GC145] Heinemann pbk **£3.50**
In the Fog of the Season's End (1972)
Tells the story of everyday life in the underground
Black resistance movement.
[GC146] Heinemann pbk **£4.15**
Time of the Butcherbird (1979)
A savage indictment of the 'Homelands' policy,
which follows both community and individual
opposition to forced resettlement.
[GC147] Heinemann pbk **£3.95**

LAING, KOJO (Ghana, 1946 -)
Laing is a technically acomplished young Ghanaian
writer, whose first novel *Search Sweet Country* was

an important attempt to define contemporary
Ghanaian, and African, identity - it deserves to be re-
issued. This novel is more of a fantasy, but with a
strong vein of underlying humanity.
Women of the Aeroplanes
[GC148] Picador pbk **£4.95**

LAMMING, GEORGE (1932 -)
A Barbadian novelist, Lamming has spent much of
his life in London. His work shows a fantastic and
exciting imagination, and a vivid prose style.
In the Castle of My Skin (1953)
A partly-autobiographical early work, which is one of
Lamming's finest; it tells of a village boy's evolving
consciousness as he grows up in colonial Barbados,
and observes the rapid social change taking place
around him.
[GC149] Longman pbk **£3.95**
Natives of My Person (1972)
[GC150] Allison & B pbk **£4.95**
Of Age and Innocence
[GC151] Allison & B pbk **£4.50**
Pleasures of Exile
[GC152] Allison & B pbk **£3.50**
Season of Adventure
[GC153] Allison & B pbk **£3.95**
The Emigrants (1954)
[GC154] Allison & B pbk **£3.50**

LAYE, CAMARA (Guinea, 1924 - 1980)
Perhaps the most important francophone African
writer, Laye was born into a traditional environment
which he saw to be vanishing, and in which he
located his own identity. His vision of Africa is
poitically non-partisan, but he remained firmly
committed to the definition of a Black identity on
terms which escape those imposed by colonialism.
A Dream of Africa (1966)
[GC155] Fontana pbk **£1.50**
The African Child (1954)
A new edition of Laye's best work; written in Paris, it
evokes in loving detail his own childhood among the
Malinké tribe, surrounded by ritual, magic and
superstition.
[GC156] Fontana pbk **£2.50**
The Guardian of the Word (1978)
[GC157] Fontana pbk **£1.95**
The Radiance of the King (1954)
Laye's second work is an allegory in the colloquial
griot style of a white man's search for God in Africa,
both comic and serious.
[GC158] Fontana pbk **£1.95**

LOPES, HENRI (Congo, 1937 -)
An ex-Prime Minister of Congo, which gives his
short-story collection *Tribaliks* a unique insight into
the world of politics and the abuse of power. His
subjects are educated people who often find
themselves both victim and oppressor as they balance
modern allegiances.
**Laughing Cry: An African Cock &
Bull Story**
[GC159] Readers Int pbk **£4.95**
**Tribaliks: Contemporary Congolese
Stories** (1971)
[GC160] Heinemann pbk **£3.95**

LOVELACE, EARL (1935 -)
Trinidadian novelist and playwright, whose fiction
explores contemporary issues in a fluent, humorous
and vivid narrative style, often showing the effects of
social change in rural environments.
**A Brief Conversation and Other
Stories**
[GC161] Heinemann pbk **£3.95**
Jestina's Calypso and Other Plays
[GC162] Heinemann pbk **£2.70**
The Dragon Can't Dance (1979)
[GC163] Longman pbk **£3.95**

The Schoolmaster (1968)
[GC164] Heinemann pbk **£2.75**
The Wine of Astonishment (1982)
[GC165] Heinemann pbk **£3.50**
While Gods Are Falling (1965)
[GC166] Longman pbk **£3.95**

MACGOYE, MARJORIE OLUDHE
Coming to Birth (1986)
Acclaimed story of a young woman's arranged
marriage, its failure, and her new life in post-Uhuru
Kenya. Political events, beginning with the 1956
Mau-Mau Emergency, complement her 'coming to
birth'.
[GC167] Virago pbk **£3.95**

MACKAY, CLAUDE (1890 - 1948)
The first West Indian novelist of importance, Mackay
travelled extensively in America and England, and
also wrote poetry.
Banana Bottom (1933)
Described as 'the first classic of West Indian prose',
Banana Boat shows Jamaican village and urban life,
and a woman's liberation from social and racial
fear.
[GC168] Serpent's Tail pbk **£5.95**
Long Way from Home
[GC169] Serpent's Tail pbk **£5.95**

MAIS, ROGER (1905 - 1955)
Mais wrote his three novels in England in the three
years before his death: they depict his native Jamaica
with vigour and clarity, and show a strong social
conscience, testimony to his activity in the Nationalist
movement.
Brother Man (1954)
[GC170] Heinemann pbk **£3.15**
Listen the Wind
A selection of stories, including hitherto unpublished
as well as better-known works.
[GC171] Longman pbk **£3.50**
Porte Ouverte
[GC172] Heinemann pbk **£4.25**
The Hills Were Joyful Together (1953)
[GC173] Heinemann pbk **£3.15**

MAJA-PEARCE, ADEWALE (Nigeria)
Loyalties (1987)
A collection of short stories evoking a society in
transition which threatens to go out of control.
[GC174] Longman pbk **£3.50**

MARECHERA, DAMBUDZO (Zimbabwe)
An intense and experimental writer, by turns
passionate, obscene and lyrical, but certainly unique.
Black Sunlight (1980)
[GC175] Heinemann pbk **£4.15**
The House of Hunger (Stories, 1979)
[GC176] Heinemann pbk **£4.15**

MATSHOBA, MTUTUZELI (South Africa)
Conceived in heady days of the 1976 Soweto riots,
and the emergence of 'Black Consciousness' (under
Biko), these are confident, documentary tales of
Black experience, secured by a formidable writer's
receptiveness. Particularly strong are the stories
where the urban narrator visits rural areas, either to a
'homeland' or as prisoner on a work farm.
Call Me Not A Man and Other Stories
(1979)
[GC177] Longman pbk **£3.95**

MOFOLO, THOMAS (South Africa, 1877 - 1948)
Chaka the Zulu (1925)
Classic tale of the founder of the Zulu nation, written
in the Sesotho language in a vivid, epic form. This
new edition sites both myth and writer in South
African history.
[GC178] Heinemann pbk **£3.15**

MOKOSO, NDELEY (Cameroon)
Man Pass Man & Other Stories (1987)
13 short stories ranging in subject from witchcraft to wife-battering, goal-keepers to coup leaders.
[GC179] Longman pbk **£2.95**

MPHAHLELE, ES' KIA (South Africa, 1919 -)
The elder statesman of Black South African writers, his critical book *The African Image* (1962) was the first study of Black African literature, and the treatment of black characters by white authors. His fame also rests on his angry autobiography *Down Second Avenue* and his short stories (*Renewal Time* is a selection from these, with two accompanying essays).
Down Second Avenue (Autobiography, 1959)
[GC180] Faber pbk **£3.50**
Renewal Time (1981)
[GC181] Readers Int pbk **£4.95**

MPHAHLELE, EZEKIEL & KOMEY, E.A. (EDS)
Modern African Stories
[GC182] Faber pbk **£1.95**

MULWA, DAVID
Master and Servant
A novel of adolescent discovery set in Kenya at the end of colonial rule, in which Mulwa explores the levels of society in his country.
[GC183] Longman hbk **£3.95**

MUNONYE, JOHN (Nigeria, 1929 -)
A sympathetic chronicler of the perplexing changes brought about by Western intervention. *The Only Son* follows a widow whose life falls apart when her son is taken to a Catholic Mission school; *The Oil Man of Obange* details a poor man's fight to support his family (the oil being the cans of palm oil he sells, not the crude stuff that wreaked havoc on the Nigerian economy in the 1970s). In *Obi* a Christian couple return to their home village, and face traditional expectations which try their deepest loyalties.
A Dancer of Fortune (1974)
[GC184] Heinemann pbk **£3.15**
Bridge to a Wedding (1978)
[GC185] Heinemann pbk **£4.15**
Obi (1969)
[GC186] Heinemann pbk **£3.15**
Oil Man of Obange (1971)
[GC187] Heinemann pbk **£4.15**
The Only Son (1966)
[GC188] Heinemann pbk **£3.15**

MWANGI, MEJA (Kenya)
Exciting urban thriller writer with a sharp line in plots of felony and treachery; he was recently involved with the film 'The Kitchen Toto'.
Going Down River Road (1976)
[GC189] Heinemann pbk **£3.15**
Kill Me Quick (1973)
[GC190] Heinemann pbk **£3.15**

MZAMANE, MBULELO (South Africa)
The Children of Soweto (1982)
[GC191] Longman pbk **£3.95**

MZAMENE, MBULELO (ED)
Hungry Flames and Other Black South African Short Stories
[GC192] Longman pbk **£3.95**

NAGENDA, JOHN (Uganda)
The Seasons of Thomas Tebo
[GC193] Heinemann pbk **£3.50**

NAIPAUL, SHIVA (1945 - 1985)
Like his brother, Naipaul wrote novels about the Caribbean from the distance of abroad, recording the decline of the traditional culture among Trinidadians

of Indian origin. The tenor of his work is dark, a mood leavened by his humane insight into human lives and by some humour. He is also known for his political and travel studies.
A Hot Country (1983)
[GC194] Sphere pbk **£2.95**
Beyond the Dragon's Mouth (1984)
A retrospective collection of some of Naipaul's work since his departure from the Caribbean in 1964, including stories, non fiction and an autobiographical piece.
[GC195] Abacus pbk **£4.99**
Fireflies (1970)
[GC196] Longman pbk **£3.95**
The Chip-Chip Gatherers (1973)
[GC197] Longman pbk **£3.95**

NAIPAUL, V.S. (1932 -)
A distinguished novelist and non-fiction writer, Naipaul has lived in England since 1950; his extensive travels, and their resulting narratives, have provided both a mood and sense of environment for his fiction, notably in *In a Free State*, and his pessimistic view of emergent Africa, *A Bend in the River*. After the more genial comedy of his first three works, which culminated in the masterpiece *A House for Mr Biswas*, his mood has progressively darkened, in a way which is both personal and public.
A Bend in the River (1979)
[GC198] Penguin pbk **£2.99**
A Flag on the Island (1967)
[GC199] Penguin pbk **£2.95**
A House for Mr Biswas (1961)
Naipauls's first major work tells of the passage of a mild-mannered man from life to death, and his effort to achieve personal independence, as symbolized by the house which he acquires shortly before his death. At the same time it observes the gradual dissolution of traditional Indian ways of life, an insight developed in his later work, as well as in that of his younger brother, Shiva.
[GC200] Deutsch hbk **£9.95**
[GC201] Penguin pbk **£3.99**
Guerillas (1975)
[GC202] Penguin pbk **£3.50**
In a Free State (1971)
[GC203] Penguin pbk **£2.95**
Miguel Street (1959)
[GC204] Penguin pbk **£2.50**
Mr Stone and the Knight's Companion (1963)
[GC205] Penguin pbk **£2.50**
Mystic Masseur (1957)
[GC206] Penguin pbk **£2.95**
The Enigma of Arrival (1987)
Naipaul's most recent novel is a largely autobiographical masterpiece, bleak in tone, but lyrical and elegaic in its record of a particular English landscape (and the characters who populate it) through the changing patterns of the seasons and years. A moving sense of growing old permeates the book.
[GC207] Viking hbk **£11.95**
[GC208] Penguin pbk **£4.95**
The Mimic Men (1967)
[GC209] Penguin pbk **£2.95**
The Suffrage of Elvira (1958)
[GC210] Penguin pbk **£2.50**

NDEBELE, NJABULO SIMAKHALE (South Africa, 1948 -)
Fools and Other Stories
[GC211] Longman pbk **£4.50**

NGUGI WA THIONGO (Kenya, 1938 -)
Socialist, literature teacher and patriot, Ngugi's popularising of progressive opinions through drama and his later novels led to his detention by Mzee Kenyatta, and prudent self-exile under President Moi.

He has moved from early, relatively imitative work to a bold rejection of Western forms, and now attempts to authenticate peasant and worker experiences in novels written in his own toungue, Gikuyu. Equally at home describing rural or urban life, his volumes of theoretical writing also deserve attention.
A Grain of Wheat (1967)
A tale of betrayal based around a pre-independence village where the local hero has just been hanged by a colonial administration.
[GC212] Heinemann pbk **£4.50**
Decolonizing the Mind (Non fiction)
A volume of critical and theoretical writing, in which Ngugi explains, among other subjects, his decision to write in African languages.
[GC213] J Currey pbk **£4.95**
Detained: A Writer's Prison Diary (1981)
[GC214] Heinemann pbk **£4.95**
Devil on the Cross (1982)
Originally written on toilet paper in Gikuyu during his year-long detention in 1978, this powerful allegory balances a European/biblical mythical form and traditional African rules of song and riddle to savage the hypocritical heart of global capitalism.
[GC215] Heinemann pbk **£3.95**
Matigari (1989) **NEW**
Matigari ma Njiiruungi (the patriot who survived the bullets) is a bruised old fighter who returns from the bush to find his family and enjoy his country's independence. The resulting blend of farce and realism, traditional and Christian legend, with solid political tragedy, is one of the cleverest of modern novels; his fictional cavortings only underline the craziness of neo-colonialism and restate Ngugi's faith in a people's right to self-determination.
[GC216] Heinemann hbk **£10.95**
[GC217] Heinemann pbk **£4.95**
Petals of Blood (1977)
A unique hybrid of national epic, crime thriller and vivid social realism make this the most ambitious and successful piece of anglophone African writing. In the development of Ilmorog from a neglected bush village to a bustling jewel of capitalism, Ngugi captures Kenyan life since Uhuru with his usual accuracy, using the four main characters to probe the origins of Black exploitation of Black.
[GC218] Heinemann pbk **£3.95**
Secret Lives (Stories, 1975)
Summarizes his writing prior to *Petals of Blood*. The depiction of individuals struggling to create fulfilling lives from their environment links the early village and Mau-Mau stories with the later 'Secret Lives' section, and its urban struggles for identity.
[GC219] Heinemann pbk **£3.15**
The River Between (1965)
The river separates a Gikuyu people in conflict, mission-led condemnations of female circumcision having polarized Christians and traditionalists. This bold debut, set in the 1920s, has Waiyaki, a mission-educated son of a traditional seer attempting to fulfil an ancient prophesy, and unite the warring parties.
[GC220] Heinemann pbk **£3.15**
Weep Not Child (1964)
Njoroge is the prototype mission-educated boy for whom schooling holds the key to fulfilment. But with his brothers in the Mau-Mau, and his father a humiliated squatter on his own land, he is forced to question what 'fulfilment' means.
[GC221] Heinemann pbk **£3.95**

NIANE, D.T.
Sundiata: An Epic of Old Mali
Retold by the *griots*, the oral tradition of Mali has been handed down from the 13th century, and captures the mystery and majesty of the medieval African kingdoms.
[GC222] Longman pbk **£3.95**

NWANKWO, NIKEM (Nigeria, 1931 -)
Spirited satirist of modern Nigeria, whether of
traditional communities (*Danda* - a picaresque novel
of a chief's attempts to subdue the frivolous young
men of his tribe), or of urban superficiality (*My
Mercedes*), where a PR man covers his unfortunate
lack of personality with a shiny new car.
Danda (1964)
[GC223] Fontana pbk **£1.75**
My Mercedes is Bigger Than Yours
(1975)
[GC224] Fontana pbk **£1.50**

NWAPA, FLORA (Nigeria, 1931 -)
Noted for her effective, strong women characters
whose loyalties are not those you might expect.
Efuru (1966)
[GC225] Heinemann pbk **£3.15**
Idu (1970)
[GC226] Heinemann pbk **£3.15**

OKARA, GABRIEL (Nigeria, 1921 -)
Leading West African poet (his collection *The
Fisherman's Invocation* is still available), who used
his concern with language to create a unique novel.
The Voice is a politically conceived parable where the
syntax and idiom of Ijaw kneads English prose into a
convincing reflection of African thought and feeling.
The Voice (1964)
[GC227] Heinemann pbk **£3.15**

OKPEWHO, ISIDORE (Nigeria)
The Last Duty (1976)
Showing the ties which unite a group of six
individuals, this is a successful reconstruction of the
time of the Nigerian Civil War.
[GC228] Longman pbk **£4.50**
Victims (1970)
A powerful novel about a polygamous household in
Nigeria, in which mounting tensions culminate in
tragedy.
[GC229] Longman pbk **£3.95**

OKRI, BEN (Nigeria, 1961 -)
The greatest discovery in recent African literature,
Okri won the 1987 Commonwealth Writers Prize. He
is now based in England, which provides the setting
for a fine story 'A Hidden History' in his collection
Incidents at the Shrine. His strength is a rich, almost
hallucinatory prose, coupled to an unsettling
imagination. *Stars of the New Curfew*, his latest
novel, is set in a Nigeria held under military curfew.
Flowers and Shadows (1980)
[GC230] Longman pbk **£4.50**
Incidents at the Shrine (1987)
[GC231] Fontana pbk **£3.50**
Landscapes Within (1981)
[GC232] Longman pbk **£3.95**
Stars of the New Curfew (1988)
[GC233] Penguin pbk **£3.99**

OUOLOGUEM, YAMBO (Mali, 1940 -)
Bound to Violence (1968)
A history of Black domination by feudal lords, Arab
invaders, and finally Europeans, told with an
unhinged delight in black magic, eroticism and
unnatural death.
[GC234] Heinemann pbk **£4.15**

OUSMANE, SEMBENE (Senegal, 1923 -)
A leading African film-maker and novelist whose
varied history includes spells as a French soldier,
docker, trade union leader, fisherman, plumber and
mason.
God's Bits of Wood (1960)
Powerful modern classic of the great 1947-48 Dakar-
Niger railstrike, which the African labour force
eventually won.
[GC235] Heinemann pbk **£3.95**

Last of the Empire (1981)
A punchy tale of political machinations in a de-
stabilized ex-French colony.
[GC236] Heinemann pbk **£4.85**
The Black Docker (1956)
His first book, straight from his own experience, is an
angry exposure of the treatment of immigrant workers
in France.
[GC237] Heinemann pbk **£3.95**
The Money Order/White Genesis
(Novellas, 1965)
[GC238] Heinemann pbk **£3.95**
Xala (1973)
A rich businessmen is struck with the Xala
(impotence) as he marries his third wife. What can
save him from everlasting humiliation? Also an
acclaimed film.
[GC239] Heinemann pbk **£4.15**

OWEN, DAVID (Zimbabwe/South Africa, 1956 -)
Venter and Son is set in a general store in the heart of
the Afrikaaner veld, while *Eden* is a lighter tale of a
multi-racial area threatened by the government.
Eden/Venter and Son (1988)
[GC240] Bloomsbury pbk **£4.99**

OYONO, FERDINAND (Cameroon, 1929 -)
Oyono's work combines satire, humour and pathos.
His first novel, *Houseboy*, written in Paris, is a story
of a young and innocent boy in an African mission,
whose belief in his teachers is undercut by authorial
irony. *The Old Man and the Medal* is a similar story
of the 'good African' rewarded for his services, who
changes his mind about his masters when he receives
it.
Houseboy (1956)
[GC241] Heinemann pbk **£3.15**
Old Man and the Medal (1956)
[GC242] Heinemann pbk **£3.15**

P'BITEK, OKOT (Uganda, 1932 -1982)
The Hare and the Hornbill (1978)
A selection of myths from the Oral Tradition
expressed by Africa's most famous poet.
[GC243] Heinemann pbk **£2.50**

PATON, ALAN (South Africa, 1903 - 1988)
Paton was involved with the South African Liberal
Party throughout his life, and was a committed
churchman. The strength of his early works,
especially the widely-known *Cry, the Beloved
Country* is undeniable, although his idealism came to
seem increasingly out-of-place as the country's
political situation worsened.
Ah, But Your Land Is Beautiful (1981)
[GC244] Penguin pbk **£3.99**

Ben Okri, author of *Stars of the New Curfew* (Secker
& Warburg hbk £10.95) (Photo: Andrew Douglas)

Caryl Phillips, author of *Higher Ground* (Viking
hbk £11.95) (Photo: Tara Heinemann)

Cry, the Beloved Country (1948)
The first book to tell a world-wide audience of the
iniquities of apartheid, it tells the story of a father's
search for his son through a labyrinth of violence and
racial hatred; the ending may be idealistic, but it is is
a novel full of passion.
[GC245] Cape hbk **£8.95**
[GC246] Penguin pbk **£2.99**
Debbie Go Home (1965)
[GC247] Penguin pbk **£3.50**
Too Late the Phalarope
[GC248] Penguin pbk **£3.95**

PATTERSON, H. ORLANDO (1926 -)
The Children of Sisyphus (1964)
A vivid and sympathetic fictional account of the
Rastafarian movement by the renowned Jamaican
sociologist.
[GC249] Longman pbk **£3.95**

PETERS, LENRIE (Gambia, 1932 -)
A surgeon as well as a novelist, Peters is more
renowned as a poet.
The Second Round (1965)
A melancholy tale of a bright young man returning
home from England to begin his career who finds
himself unable to cope.
[GC250] Heinemann pbk **£3.15**

PHILLIPS, CARYL
Brought up and educated in England, Phillips writes
of the sense of displacement caused by living in an
alien country, as well as (in *A State of Independence*)
of the loss of identity with the area or country initially
left behind. He is an accomplished playwright, and
has also written *The European Tribe*, an account of a
journey around Europe.
A State of Independence (1986)
[GC251] Faber pbk **£3.95**
Higher Ground   **NEW**
A novel in three parts, telling stories of entrapment
and abandonment, set in Africa in the days of the
slave trade, an American gaol and post-war England
for a refugee from Poland; the characters of each face
external hostility and the difficult struggle to preserve
self-dignity.
[GC252] Viking hbk **£11.95**

The Final Passage (1985)
[GC253] Faber pbk **£3.95**

PLAATJE, SOLOMON TSHEKISHO (South
Africa, 1877 - 1932)
As secretary of the South African National Congress
(founded in 1912), Plaatje is a significant political
figure as well as a leading early novelist.
Mhudi (1930)
Written in 1917 in response to the 1913 Native's Land
Act, the first step on the road to apartheid, it is both a
historical story of the war between the Matabele and
the Barolong, and a subtle attack on white invasion of
a stable, sophisticated African culture.
[GC254] Heinemann pbk **£3.95**
Native Life in South Africa (Non fiction,
1916)
*"Awakening on Friday morning, June 20 1913, the
South African Native found himself...a pariah in the
land of his birth"*. Vehement polemic against the
1913 act which confined African land ownership to a
tiny part of the country.
[GC255] Longman pbk **£3.95**

REID, V.S.
New Day (1973)
[GC256] Heinemann pbk **£4.15**
The Leopard (1980)
[GC257] Heinemann pbk **£2.75**

RIVE, RICHARD (South Africa, 1931 -)
Buckingham Palace: District Six (1986)
Vignettes of coloured slum life, following 15 years in
the life of a community.
[GC258] Heinemann pbk **£3.50**

ROUMAIN, JAQUES
Masters of the Dew (1944)
[GC259] Heinemann pbk **£4.10**

SALKEY, ANDREW (ED)
West Indian Stories
[GC260] Faber pbk **£1.95**

SAMKANGE, STANLAKE
(Zimbabwe, 1922 -)
Fascinating elder statesman of Zimbabwean literature,
who writes imaginative historical novels with a
political bite. *On Trial for My Country* reconstructs
Cecil Rhodes's battle with the Matabele King
Lobengula, in the form of a folk tale, using Rhodes's
actual letters; while *Year of the Uprising* is based
around the great rebellion of the Matabele and
Mashona of 1896.
On Trial for My Country (1966)
[GC261] Heinemann pbk **£3.15**
The Mourned One (1975)
[GC262] Heinemann pbk **£4.15**
Year of the Uprising (1978)
[GC263] Heinemann pbk **£3.15**

SCHREINER, OLIVE (South Africa, 1855 -
1920)
A tireless feminist, socialist and anti-colonialist, who
is bestknown for her first novel *The Story of an
African Farm*, which influenced D.H. Lawrence
among others. It tells of two cousins growing up
on a remote ostrich farm, and mixes poetic realism
with vigorous social preaching. Pandora have
collected her political and imaginative writing in their
fine *Reader*.
From Man to Man (1926)
[GC264] Virago pbk **£5.95**
Olive Schreiner Reader
[GC265] Pandora pbk **£5.95**
The Story of an African Farm
(1883)
[GC266] Virago pbk **£4.95**
[GC267] Penguin pbk **£3.95**

SELVON, SAM (1923 -)
Born in Trinidad of Indian descent, Selvon spent
much of his life in London, moving finally to Canada.
His books tell of the West Indian experience in
London (*Lonely Londoners* and the two Moses
novels); his first two, *A Brighter Sun* and its sequel
Turn Again, Tiger, concern a married couple of
Indian origin in Trinidad, their growth together and
into their Creole surroundings.
A Brighter Sun (1952)
[GC268] Longman pbk **£3.50**
Moses Ascending (1975)
[GC269] Heinemann pbk **£4.15**
Moses Migrating (1983)
[GC270] Heinemann pbk **£3.95**
The Lonely Londoners (1956)
[GC271] Longman pbk **£3.50**
Turn Again, Tiger (1958)
[GC272] Heinemann pbk **£3.15**
Ways of Sunlight (Stories)
[GC273] Longman pbk **£3.50**

SENIOR, OLIVE
Winner of the Commonwealth Writers Prize, this is a
collection of stories set in Jamaica, told mainly from a
child's point of view.
**Summer Lightning and Other
Stories**
[GC274] Longman pbk **£3.50**

SEROTE, MONGANE (South Africa, 1944 -)
Renowned as a poet exiled in Botswana for his
political beliefs, this is Serote's first novel, set in
Alexandra Township, Johannesburg.
To Every Birth Its Blood (1981)
[GC275] Heinemann pbk **£4.15**

SOYINKA, WOLE (Nigeria, 1934 -)
Better known as a poet and playwright, Soyinka's
novel *The Interpreters* beats European modernism at
its own game. Beneath the sophistication and foolery
lies a sobering, critical assessment of early post-
independence Nigeria, as seen through the internal
monologues of the 'interpreters', young
graduates returning from study overseas. Highly
recommended.
Ake: The Years of Childhood (1981)
Soyinka's autobiography tells of his childhood with
great power and insight.
[GC276] Arrow pbk **£2.95**
Man Died: Prison Notes
[GC277] Arrow pbk **£2.95**
Season of Anomy (1973)
[GC278] Arrow pbk **£3.99**
The Interpreters (1965)
[GC279] Heinemann pbk **£4.15**

STOCKENSTROM, WILMA (South Africa)
The Expedition to the Baobab Tree
(1983)
Translated by J.M. Coetzee, this is an intense, poetic
exploration of womanhood, 'dramatic in concept and
epic in scope, a wonderful spiral moving,
unflinchingly, ever more deeply inwards' according to
André Brink.
[GC280] Faber pbk **£2.95**

TLALI, MIRIAM (South Africa)
Worthy successor to Bessy Head as chronicler of the
inner thoughts and hopes of black South African
women, but translated to a harsh, urban context.
Miriam, typist in a furniture store for poor whites, is
typical of her carefully-drawn, unpolemical but
clearly oppressed charcaters, who recur in her new,
and much recommended *Soweto Stories*.
Muriel at Metropolitan (1979)
[GC281] Longman pbk **£3.95**
Soweto Stories   **NEW**
[GC282] Pandora pbk **£3.95**

TUTUOLA, AMOS (Nigeria, 1920 -)
A Yoruba novelist who, despite the simplicity of
his style, achieves a real power and oral directness
in his best work; he received little formal education
and derives his writing and style from village
tales.
My Life in the Bush of Ghosts (1954)
[GC283] Faber pbk **£2.95**
Pauper, Brawler and Slanderer (1987)
[GC284] Faber pbk **£3.95**
The Palm-Wine Drinkard (1952)
Among the earliest African novels to be widely
read in the West. Essentially a collection of folk-
tales united by a first-person narrator, it refashions
English to suit the thought patterns and speech of
West Africa.
[GC285] Faber pbk **£2.95**
**The Witch-Herbalist of the Remote
Town** (1981)
[GC286] Faber pbk **£2.95**

VIEIRA, JOSE LUANDINO (Angola, 1935 -)
White MPLA activist imprisoned for 11 years by
the Portugese authorities. *Luuanda* is a collection
of three stories capturing the oral tradition of the
Kimbundu language, which was banned until
the overthrow of Portugal's fascist government in
1974.
Luuanda (1964)
[GC287] Heinemann pbk **£4.15**
The Real Life of Domingos Xavier
(1978)
[GC288] Heinemann pbk **£2.25**

WANGUSA, TIMOTHY (Uganda)
A poet and lecturer in literature, this is Wangusa's
first novel.
Upon This Mountain   **NEW**
[GC289] Heinemann pbk **£4.25**

WORKU, DANIACHEW (Ethiopia, 1936 -)
Resonant work following a young radical's uneasy
relationship with Ethiopia's ancient Christian
rituals.
The Thirteenth Son (1973)
[GC290] Heinemann pbk **£4.15**

XITU, UANHENGA (Angola)
Written while in a Portugese prison, Xitu resisted the
temptation to revise his work; what remains is a
spontaneous gem of a book. Varied episodes are
linked by the bombastic, irreverent Tamoda, while the
racy, colloquial translation keeps the incidents
coming.
The World of 'Mestre' Tamoda (1974)
[GC291] Readers Int pbk4.95

Wole Soyinka, author of *Ake: The Years of
Childhood* (Arrow pbk £2.95) and *The Interpreters*
(Heinemann pbk £4.15) (Photo: Jane Brown)

NORTH AMERICAN

Includes the fiction of the United States and Canada.

ABBEY, EDWARD
The Fool's Progress (1989) **NEW**
One of those delightfully funny *and* sad picaresque, rambunctious novels that could only come out of God's own country. During the course of an immense journey across America, Henry Holyoak Lightcap recounts his life story - a series of madcap adventures and mishaps. The US critics loved it.
[GD1] Bodley Head hbk **£11.95**

ACKER, KATHY
A cult author much associated with American underground publishing, but now resident in the UK. Her books are startling collages, employing cut up and bricolage, often appropriating the language of violence and pornography for her own subversive ends.
Blood and Guts in High School Plus Two (1984)
[GD2] Picador pbk **£4.50**
Don Quixote (1986)
[GD3] Grafton pbk **£2.95**
Empire of the Senseless (1988)
'An orgy of disgust which also contains fresh, funny statements about Western society...the effect is like being held at knife point' (*The Listener*).
[GD4] Picador pbk **£3.95**
Young Lust (1989) **NEW**
Three early works springing from Acker's inside knowledge of the sex industry.
[GD5] Pandora pbk **£4.95**

AGEE, JAMES (1909 - 1955)
Southern-born Agee worked most of his life in New York as a journalist and film critic for *Time* and *The Nation*. He collaborated with John Huston on the script for *The African Queen*, and wrote filmscripts of his own. However, it is for the wonderful *Let Us Now Praise Famous Men* that he will always be remembered.
A Death in the Family (1957)
A partly autobiographical novel which won the Pulitzer Prize on its posthumous publication. It is a

Paul Auster, author of *Moon Palace* (Faber hbk £11.99)

moving and poetic account of how a secure family is shattered by the loss of its father.
[GD6] Picador pbk **£3.95**
Let Us Now Praise Famous Men (Non fiction, 1941)
Originally commissioned but then rejected (for its unconventionality) by *Fortune* magazine, this is the product of Agee's collaboration with Walker Evans, whose timeless photographs make up much of the book. It is a tribute to the plight of rural Alabama families during the Depression, and is now recognised as a classic.
[GD7] Picador pbk **£6.95**

ALGREN, NELSON (1909 - 1981)
Born in Detroit, Algren was reared in Chicago, and subsequently became another of that city's great naturalistic writers. Most of his many novels have been out of print for some time, but it is quite possible that his portaits of urban drifters and their frequently amoral activities will find a new audience with these re-issues.
Never Come Morning (1942)
A Polish hoodlum dreams of a better life as a prizefighter, but in desperation turns to murder.
[GD8] Fourth Estate pbk **£5.95**
Somebody in Boots
[GD9] Thunder's Mouth P pbk **£5.95**

ALTHER, LISA (1944 -)
An energetic and intelligent writer who writes of women's lives and their involvement with feminism with great humour.
Kinflicks (1976)
Her first novel, hilarious and mournful by turns, that took 12 years to find a publisher.
[GD10] Penguin pbk **£4.50**
Original Sins (1981)
[GD11] Penguin pbk **£3.95**
Other Women (1984)
[GD12] Penguin pbk **£3.50**

ANDERSON, SHERWOOD (1876 - 1941)
Often undervalued and overlooked, Anderson left his stamp on many American writers. His belief that our instinctive urges are all too often suppressed made him rather ahead of his time.
Winesburg, Ohio (1919)
Anderson's most celebrated work relates the experiences of a disillusioned young reporter preparing to take his leave from this small town. A landmark of American writing.
[GD13] Picador pbk **£3.95**

APPLE, MAX
Although essentially a satirical and humorous writer, Apple's work resonates with timeless American themes.
Free Agents (1987)
His first novel.
[GD14] Faber **£9.95**
The Oranging of America (1976)
An excellent collection of amusing short stories with a humane touch.
[GD15] Faber pbk **£3.95**

ATWOOD, MARGARET (Canada, 1939 -)
Poet and novelist, Atwood is one of Canada's most prominent writers. Her poetry is an exposure of the power politics of nationality and gender; it features a sharp and witty idiom, where the prosaic and the surreal interact. Her fiction is thematically unified, displaying great control over effect and direction.
Bluebeard's Egg (Stories, 1983)
A collection of short stories about the state of relationships for women in the prime of life.
[GD16] Virago pbk **£3.95**

Bodily Harm (1981)
In plot something of a departure for Atwood - a young journalist leaves Canada to work in the Caribbean, and unwittingly plays a part in a network of corruption, intrigue and betrayal. A sublime, if unexpected, cautionary tale.
[GD17] Virago pbk **£3.95**
Cat's Eye (1989) **NEW**
In this, her most recent novel, Atwood returns squarely to home territory, examining through the painter, Elaine, the many layers of her past. Lifting the cover off both time and place, these 'revisions' churn up the memories of people, once central, who are before her again, and test the comfortably fused components of her life.
[GD18] Bloomsbury hbk **£12.95**
Dancing Girls and Other Stories (Stories, 1977)
A collection of witty and incisive short stories which look at the range of human motivation that lies under the surface of so-called ordinary people.
[GD19] Virago pbk **£3.95**
Lady Oracle (1976)
From fat girl to thin, from London to Toronto, the quixotic story of a young woman utterly and at times happily confused by her life of multiple identities. Escape to an Italian seaside resort may be an answer, but first she must plan her 'death'…
[GD20] Virago pbk **£3.95**
Life before Man (1979)
Elizabeth, unpleasant yet pitiable; Nate, her disillusioned, eclectic husband; and Lesje, the natural history buff who loves men and dinosaur's equally. Three people become involved in a tragicomic love triangle, with no clear way out.
[GD21] Virago pbk **£3.95**
Omnibus: The Edible Woman, Surfacing, Lady Oracle
[GD22] Deutsch hbk **£12.95**
Surfacing (1972)
The narrator, unnamed, travels to the Québec wilderness in search of her father, reported missing. She endeavours to link up with her past, with the wilderness both as a psychological and literal retreat, in which she feels compelled to re-evaluate cultural systems. In particular, Atwood re-examines Western ways of interpreting nature.
[GD23] Virago pbk **£3.95**
The Edible Woman (1969)
The very ordinary Marian is not really that normal at all. She likes most of the elements in her life but, as we learn, finds *marriage à la mode* a little too hard to stomach.
[GD24] Virago pbk **£3.95**
The Handmaid's Tale (1985)
A futuristic and science-fictional parable focusing on systematic political oppression and ensuing rebellion. Allowed only to breed, Offred resists the Republic's attempts to obliterate desire.
[GD25] Virago pbk **£3.95**

AUSTER, PAUL
Essayist, novelist, poet and translator, Auster has found greater popularity here than in his native New York. His work has been labelled post-modern, since it tends towards the abstract and elliptical, privileging style over content. He is a skilled and original writer.
In the Country of Last Things (1988)
A short, futuristic tale of a woman's search for her brother in an ugly city of the imagination.
[GD26] Faber pbk **£3.99**
Moon Palace (1989) **NEW**
Auster's latest is an allegorical Western and the story of Marco Stanley Fogg and his search for love, the father he never knew, and ultimately, the key to life.
[GD27] Faber hbk **£11.99**

The Invention of Solitude (1989) **NEW**
A meditation on fatherhood and death springing from
the personal circumstances of the author's own loss.
[GD28] Faber pbk **£3.99**
The New York Trilogy (1987)
An intriguing reworking of the American detective
novel which has got much more to do with the search
for meaning and identity than tracking killers.
[GD29] Faber hbk **£10.95**
[GD30] Faber pbk **£3.99**

BALDWIN, JAMES (1924 - 1987)
Essayist, playwright, and political activist as well as
novelist, Baldwin's death robbed American literature
of one of its leading lights. His work expresses the
anger of both the gay and Black communities in prose
of quiet, controlled rage.
Another Country (1962)
His most celebrated novel. 'An almost unbearable,
blood-pounding experience' (*Washington Post*).
[GD31] Transworld pbk **£4.95**
Giovanni's Room (1956)
Intense and violent tale of gay love set in the Parisian
underworld.
[GD32] Transworld pbk **£3.95**
Go Tell It On the Mountain (1953)
Frightening tale examining the stifling power of the
Church.
[GD33] Transworld pbk **£3.95**
Going to Meet the Man (Stories, 1965)
[GD34] Transworld pbk **£2.50**
Notes from a Native Son (Essays, 1955)
Includes Baldwin's remarkable account of his time
spent in a Paris jailhouse.
[GD35] Pluto pbk **£4.50**
The Fire Next Time (Non fiction, 1963)
[GD36] Penguin pbk **£2.95**
The Price of the Ticket (Essays, 1985)
Collected non-fiction 1948-1986.
[GD37] M Joseph hbk **£14.95**

BARNES, DJUNA (1892 - 1982)
Eccentric modernist contemporary of Joyce and
Beckett whose hedonist lifestyle in Europe is
mirrored in her writings.
Djuna Barnes's New York (Non fiction)
Published in newspapers and magazines from 1911 to
1931, and collected here for the first time, this
presents a personal and unforgettable perspective on
NY from an intrepid reporter of the life around her.
[GD38] Virago pbk **£8.99**
Nightwood (1936)
A charged and poetic novel of psychopathic
Americans in Paris in the 1920s.
[GD39] Faber pbk **£3.95**
Smoke and Other Early Stories (1982)
Strange tales of Greenwich Village decadence.
[GD40] Virago pbk **£4.50**

BARTH, JOHN (1930 -)
An inventive novelist, Barth is a confident and
deliberately self-conscious story-teller.
Sabbatical (1982)
[GD41] Grafton pbk **£2.50**
The Sot-Weed Factor (1960)
Fantastical, bawdy and baroque parody of the 18th
century picaresque novel.
[GD42] Grafton pbk **£3.95**
The Tidewater Tales (1988)
Cruising around Chesapeake Bay, a couple tell each
other stories.
[GD43] Minerva pbk **£4.99**

BARTHELME, DONALD (1931 -)
New York humorist best known for his
irrational and fantastical short stories. 'Looking
up from the page, you'll have undergone a
peculiar alteration of vision. Life, for a while, will
hold more promise.' (Anne Tyler).

Dead Father (1975)
[GD44] Routledge hbk **£12.95**
Forty Stories (1988)
[GD45] Secker hbk **£10.95**
Sixty Stories (1989)
A companion volume to *Forty Stories* **NEW**
containing many previously unpublished pieces.
Barthelme's stories are in turns funny, obsessively
learned and always original and inventive.
[GD46] Secker hbk **£14.95**

BARTHELME, FREDERICK (1943 -)
A short story writer of some distinction, Barthelme
(no relation to Donald) uses a deceptively simple style
to eavesdrop on the bizarre, almost surreal, world of
anonymous urban suburbia and its eerily unfamiliar
inhabitants.
Chroma (Stories, 1988)
[GD47] Penguin pbk **£3.99**
Moon Deluxe (Stories, 1983)
A collection that captures the true strangeness of his
America.
[GD48] Penguin pbk **£3.95**
Second Marriage
[GD49] Dent hbk **£9.95**
Tracer
[GD50] Dent hbk **£9.95**
Two Against One (1989) **NEW**
Set in the new suburbia that Barthelme has
made peculiarly his own, this is a portrait of a
marriage gone awry. It is Edward's 40th birthday, and
his estranged wife appears unannounced. A novel
both funny and sad.
[GD51] Viking hbk **£11.95**

BEATTIE, ANN (1947 -)
Long recognised as an important contributor to the
recent renaissance of the American short story,
Beattie remains curiously underpublished here. She
has no easily definable terrain, and she consciously
draws her characters from a wide panorama of
American life.
Love Always (1985)
A wry and humorous novel.
[GD52] Penguin pbk **£2.95**
Where You'll Find Me (Stories, 1987)
[GD53] Pan pbk **£3.99**

BELL, MADISON SMARTT (1957 -)
A highly-praised and talented young novelist who
captures the dangerous brutality and arbitrary
nastiness of New York and the modern world.
Straight Cut (1987)
[GD54] Sphere pbk **£3.99**
Waiting for the End of the World (1985)
The tale of the epileptic, drunk drifter Larkin and a
sardonic vision of a contemporary Hell.
[GD55] Sphere pbk **£4.95**
Year of Silence (1987)
[GD56] Sphere pbk **£4.50**
Zero db (Stories, 1987)
[GD57] Sphere pbk **£3.99**

BELLOW, SAUL (1915 -)
Winner of the Nobel Prize for Literature in 1976,
Bellow's work addresses the chaos of 20th century
man's public and private lives with rare virtuosity.
Born of Russian Jewish parents and raised in the Mid
West, he is prolifically diverse in his cultural
references. Many of his novels are united by their
heroes' robust attempts to retain their individuality
and delicacy of feeling in a world increasingly hostile
to such endeavours.
A Theft **NEW**
Something of a novelty from Bellow: his latest work
is a graceful novella with a woman as the central
character, made immediately available in paperback.
[GD58] Secker hbk **£10.95**
[GD59] Penguin pbk **£3.50**

Dangling Man (1944)
[GD60] Secker hbk **£10.95**
[GD61] Penguin pbk **£3.99**
Henderson the Rain King (1959)
His most consistently underrated novel is, in fact, his
most entertaining, being partly a parody of the
Hemingway pose.
[GD62] Secker hbk **£10.95**
[GD63] Penguin pbk **£4.95**
Herzog (1964)
Bellow's prizewinning bestseller dramatises one
crumbling man's stand against his past and his
intellectual mentors.
[GD64] Secker hbk **£10.95**
[GD65] Penguin pbk **£4.95**
**Him with His Foot in His Mouth & Other
Stories** (1984)
A major work; Bellow returns to favourite themes
with remarkable poise.
[GD66] Secker hbk **£10.95**
[GD67] Penguin pbk **£4.99**
Humboldt's Gift (1975)
Pulitzer Prize Winner.
[GD68] Secker hbk **£10.95**
[GD69] Penguin pbk **£4.99**
More Die of Heartbreak (1987)
[GD70] Secker hbk **£10.95**
[GD71] Penguin pbk **£4.99**
Mosby's Memoirs & Other Stories (1969)
[GD72] Penguin pbk **£4.50**
Mr Sammler's Planet (1970)
[GD73] Secker hbk **£10.95**
[GD74] Penguin pbk **£4.95**
Seize the Day (1956)
Perhaps Bellow's most controlled work, and the one
cited in the Nobel Prize award: Tommy's disastrous
day is a *tour de force* that is both moving and
amusing.
[GD75] Secker hbk **£8.95**
[GD76] Penguin pbk **£3.50**
The Adventures of Augie March (1953)
A great, sprawling picaresque novel; the novel that
announced Bellow's stature and ambition.
[GD77] Secker hbk **£10.95**
[GD78] Penguin pbk **£5.95**
The Dean's December
Bucharest and Chicago provide dual, contrasting
backdrops to this controversial novel. Its roots as a
work of non-fiction show, but indicate Bellow's
concern for the way we actually live.
[GD79] Secker hbk **£10.95**
[GD80] Penguin pbk **£4.99**

James Baldwin, author of *The Price of the Ticket*
(Michael Joseph hbk £14.95)

The Victim (1948)
[GD81] Secker hbk **£10.95**
[GD82] Penguin pbk **£3.99**
To Jerusalem and Back (Non fiction, 1976)
[GD83] Penguin pbk **£3.95**

BIERCE, AMBROSE (1842 - 1914?)
Brilliant and bitter journalist who also wrote strange gothic tales reminiscent of Poe, now celebrated for his macabre war stories. Tired of America, he disappeared into war-torn Mexico, and was never seen again.
Collected Writings
[GD84] Picador pbk **£6.95**

BLAIS, MARIE-CLAIRE (Canada, 1939 -)
Blais rose to prominence as a prodigy, publishing *La Belle Bête* at 20, in pre-Quiet Revolution Québec, which was to set in motion a powerful and sustained creative *oeuvre*, which examines personal torment and microcosmic societal discord. Especially in her early works, parents figure as evil or perverted, priests insidious, nuns cruel: all of these build up her consistent theme of rampant wrong-doing and innocence flagrantly abused.
Nights in the Underground (1979)
A study of lesbians, here ostracized from the 'mainstream', which deftly combines English and French colloquial in extremely long, winding paragraphs. Set in a tired, vaguely sleezy lesbian bar in Montréal.
[GD85] General Publ Co pbk **£2.95**

BOWLES, PAUL (1910 -)
Born in New York, Bowles spent his early life as a composer for ballet, film and opera before expatriating himself to Morocco, and attracting something of a cult following. He is celebrated for the detached coolness and precision of his prose, which purports to be a free flowing of ideas, bypassing the intellect.
A Distant Episode (Stories, 1988)
[GD86] P Owen hbk **£11.95**
A Thousand Days for Mokhtar   **NEW**
Sixteen tales of alienation and travel set in the US, South America and Morocco.
[GD87] P Owen hbk **£11.95**
Call At Corazon (Stories, 1988)
Stories set in Latin America, Mexico, the US and Morocco spanning fifty years.
[GD88] P Owen hbk **£11.95**
Collected Stories (1979)
Introduced by Gore Vidal.
[GD89] B Sparrow pbk **£8.95**
Let It Come Down (1952)
[GD90] Arrow pbk **£2.95**
Midnight Mass (Stories, 1985)
'His short stories are among the best ever written.' (Gore Vidal).
[GD91] P Owen hbk **£9.95**
Pages from Cold Point (Stories)
[GD92] Arrow pbk **£2.95**
Points in Time (Non-fiction, 1982)
[GD93] P Owen pbk **£8.95**
The Sheltering Sky (1949)
His best known work, considered by many a masterpiece, recording the violent destruction of an American couple in highly controlled prose.
[GD94] Grafton pbk **£2.95**
The Spider's House (1955)
[GD95] Arrow pbk **£3.95**
Their Heads Are Green (Travel, 1963)
A chronicle of his journeys through Hindu, Mohammedan, Buddhist and Central American lands.
[GD96] P Owen hbk **£11.95**
Up Above the World (1966)
A couple holidaying in Latin America are taken on a terrifying and dangerous journey by a young man they meet.
[GD97] Arrow pbk **£2.25**

BOYLE, T. CORAGHESSAN
An inventive and fantastical writer with a distinct penchant for the world of drugs and bikers.
Greasy Lake (Stories, 1985)
[GD98] Penguin pbk **£3.95**
World's End (1988)
A big, pyrotechnical novel that intertwines the destinies of three families over three centuries of Hudson Valley history.
[GD99] Picador pbk **£5.99**

BRODKEY, HAROLD
The Abundant Dreamer (Stories)   **NEW**
Brodkey has been publishing stories for the past three decades to great critical acclaim; collected for the first time in book form, they reveal a writer of great talent, creator of a remarkable fictional world.
[GD100] Cape hbk **£11.95**

BROWNMILLER, SUSAN
Author of the classic feminist polemic *Against Our Will*.
Waverley Place (1989)   **NEW**
A fictional recreation of the story behind the recent NY infanticide and wife battery that was as shocking for the sadistic husband's behaviour - he was a successful lawyer - as the battered wife's complicity. A US bestseller already, this is a challenging book.
[GD101] H Hamilton hbk **£12.95**

BUCK, PEARL (1892 - 1973)
Nobel Prize for Literature 1938. Buck spent her childhood in China, the daughter of missionaries, and later returned there as a missionary and teacher herself. Her best work was based on her knowledge of China, about which she wrote with sympathy and understanding. She remains to date the only American woman writer to have been awarded the Nobel Prize.
Dragon Seed (1942)
[GD102] Methuen pbk **£1.95**
Letter From Peking (1957)
When the communist revolution breaks in China, Elizabeth returns home without her husband. Alone, she awaits a letter from him...
[GD103] Methuen pbk **£1.95**
The Mother (1934)
[GD104] Methuen pbk **£1.95**
Three Daughters of Madame Liang (1973)
[GD105] Methuen pbk **£1.95**

BUKOWSKI, CHARLES (1920 -)
Born in Andermach, Germany, Bukowski is an obsessive outsider, contemptuous of the literary world. Rarely sober, his imagery occasionally reels into the surreal. Deceptively literate and unfailingly honest, his deliberately disgusting prose is an expression both of a desire for freedom and joyful scorn for the straight world.
Bring Me Your Love (1983)
[GD106] B Sparrow pbk **£3.95**
Dangling in the Tournefortia (1981)
[GD107] B Sparrow pbk **£8.50**
Factotum (1975)
[GD108] Allison & B pbk **£3.99**
Ham on Rye (1982)
Intense autobiographical novel of a painful, isolated childhood. All Bukoskwi's themes - drink, women, solitude and overwhelming anger - are well represented here.
[GD109] B Sparrow pbk **£7.95**
Hollywood (1989)   **NEW**
His first novel for seven years. Of this account of Henry Chinaski's adventures as a screenwriter Bukowski has said: *"Hollywood is at least 400 times worse than anybody has ever written about it. Of course I'll probably get sued, but it's true"*.
[GD110] B Sparrow hbk **£18.95**
[GD111] B Sparrow pbk **£9.95**

Hot Water Music (1983)
[GD112] B Sparrow pbk **£8.50**
Notes of a Dirty Old Man
[GD113] City Lights pbk **£5.95**
Post Office
[GD114] Allison & B pbk **£3.99**
South of No North (1973)
[GD115] B Sparrow pbk **£6.95**
Tales of Ordinary Madness (1967)
'Horrible and holy, you cannot read them and ever come away the same again.' (*New York Times*).
[GD116] City Lights pbk **£5.95**
The Most Beautiful Woman in Town
[GD117] City Lights pbk **£5.95**
There's No Business (1984)
[GD118] B Sparrow pbk **£3.95**
Women
[GD119] Allison & B pbk **£4.99**

BURROUGHS, WILLIAM S. (1914 -)
Surreal, caustic, experimental and witheringly funny, Burroughs is the lone frontiersman of American literature, continually re-defining and inventing its boundaries. With Brion Gysin, he rediscovered the Dadaist 'cut up' prose technique, and turned it into something more than automatic writing. In his later books, one can 'discern an anti-authoritarian voice so articulate and vicious that his continued survival seems to prove that the CIA cannot read.' (Chris Challis).
A William Burroughs Reader (1982)
Edited by John Calder.
[GD120] Picador pbk **£3.95**
Ah Pook Is Here & Other Texts (1979)
[GD121] Calder pbk **£6.95**
Cities of the Red Night (1981)
The first and best received volume of a trilogy that continues in *The Place of the Dead Roads*, and is completed with his most recent work, *The Western Lands*.
[GD122] Picador pbk **£3.95**
Exterminator! (1973)
[GD123] Calder pbk **£4.95**
Interzone   **NEW**
A new collection, including pieces relating to the *Cities of the Red Night* trilogy, and previously unpublished fragments.
[GD124] Picador hbk **£11.95**
Junky (1953)
One of the most powerful books ever written about drug addiction.
[GD125] Penguin pbk **£3.99**
Port of Saints (1980)
A quasi-autobiographical novel.
[GD126] Calder pbk **£4.95**
Queer (1986)
Finally published after three decades, this is Burroughs' second novel. It is a story of seduction and romantic agony in New Mexico.
[GD127] Picador pbk **£2.95**
The Adding Machine (Essays, 1985)
Burrough's collected essays provide a fascinating insight into his own work and that of other writers, as well as covering a wide range of other subjects. With a microscopic eye he dissects human folly, ambition and vice.
[GD128] Calder hbk **£10.95**
[GD128A] Calder pbk **£6.95**
The Job (1971)
Recorded interviews detailing Burroughs' philosophy.
[GD129] Calder pbk **£4.95**
The Last Words of Dutch Schultz (1975)
Fictive tale of real gangster, which records his deathbed talk.
[GD130] Calder pbk **£4.95**
The Naked Lunch (1959)
His most renowned novel, which documents the life of a drug addict in fantastic and surreal detail.
[GD131] Grafton pbk **£3.50**

The Place of the Dead Roads (1984)
A foray into the Western, where he grapples with the most powerful of all American myths.
[GD132] Grafton pbk **£3.50**

The Soft Machine (1961)
The sequel to *The Naked Lunch*, employing the radical 'cut up' technique.
[GD133] Grafton pbk **£3.50**

The Ticket That Exploded (1962)
[GD134] Grafton pbk **£3.50**

The Western Lands (1988)
This is Burroughs' Book of the Dead: the title refers to the final state to which the souls of the dead must travel if they are to find true immortality. Completes his trilogy.
[GD135] Picador pbk **£3.95**

The Wild Boys (1972)
A fantasy about revolutionary homeosexuals.
[GD136] Calder pbk **£4.95**

CALDER, JOHN (ED)
The New American Writing   NEW
A collection of American writing from outside the commercial mainstream - writers include David Applefield, John Green, Susan Ludwigson and Claudia Menza.
[GD136A] Calder pbk **£6.95**

CALDWELL, TAYLOR
Imaginative author of more than thirty books. Historical settings range from contemporary and 19th century America to the golden age of Athens and the legendary Atlantis.
Ceremony of the Innocent
[GD137] Fontana pbk **£2.95**

Dear and Glorious Physician
[GD138] Fontana pbk **£4.95**

Sound of Thunder
[GD139] Fontana pbk **£3.50**

The Answer as a Man
[GD140] Fontana pbk **£3.50**

The Beautiful Is Vanished
[GD141] Fontana pbk **£3.50**

The Great Lion of God
A fictional life of St Luke, this is perhaps his most interesting work along with *The Answer As A Man*, itself a life of St Paul.
[GD142] Fontana pbk **£4.95**

CANIN, ETHAN
Not yet thirty, Canin is a student at Harvard Medical School who writes in his spare time.
Emperor of the Air (Stories, 1988)
This debut collection of stories met with great acclaim both sides of the Atlantic.
[GD143] Picador pbk **£3.99**

CAPOTE, TRUMAN (1924 - 1984)
Born in New Orleans, Capote shot to fame with his first novel *Other Voices, Other Rooms* and thereafter became a friend and confidant of New York high society. Much of the time he worked as a journalist, which led him into 'inventing' the non-fiction novel with *In Cold Blood*. While his early work is riveting, in later years he spent more time keeping the reputation alive than the writing.
A Truman Capote Reader (1987)
A compendious selection of Capote's short stories, travel sketches, portraits, and essays, with his two novellas.
[GD144] Sphere pbk **£6.99**

Answered Prayers (1986)
The only surviving fragment of Capote's legendary (but in reality non-existent) society novel.
[GD145] Sphere pbk **£3.99**

Breakfast at Tiffany's (1958)
Wonderfully bittersweet tales of Holly Golightly and other carefree New Yorkers.
[GD146] Sphere pbk **£3.99**

In Cold Blood (1966)
His magnum opus, a non-fiction novel about a mass murderer.
[GD147] Sphere pbk **£3.99**

Music for Chameleons (1980)
Fourteen journalistic pieces that stretch the boundaries of artistic licence.
[GD148] Sphere pbk **£3.99**

Other Voices, Other Rooms (1948)
Dreamlike first novel, in the tradition of Southern Gothic, which charts young Joel's emerging sexuality.
[GD149] Sphere pbk **£4.99**

The Grass Harp (1951)
Two old women and a boy take up residence in a tree-house, with riotous consequences.
[GD150] Penguin pbk **£3.99**

CARVER, RAYMOND (1939 - 1988)
The death of Raymond Carver from cancer last year was an unquestionable tragedy. He was one of the very finest of writers whose later work exhibits an almost saintly sensitivity. That he was so often compared to Chekhov is a fitting testament. Both were true story-tellers of the heart.
A New Path to the Waterfall   NEW
A courageous book of last poems interspersed with passages from Chekhov and Milosz among others. These poems are about Carver's work, his alcoholism and his loves. Most movingly, there are poems about his illness and the sure knowledge that he was going to die. In her introduction, Carver's widow, Tess Gallagher, recounts their last days together.
[GD151] Collins hbk **£11.00**

Elephant & Other Stories (1988)
These stories exist in the same mysterious and dangerous everyday world as his earlier work. The quiet beauty of his prose comes to suggest a release from life's burden.
[GD152] Collins hbk **£10.95**
[GD153] Collins pbk **£4.95**

Fires (1985)
Assorted essays, poems and stories.
[GD154] Collins hbk **£10.95**
[GD155] Picador pbk **£3.50**

The Stories of Raymond Carver (1982)
Three former collections in one volume: a treasure house of truthful stories set in a world inhabited by everyday people on the edge of some unnameable darkness. Indispensable.
[GD156] Picador pbk **£4.99**

Paul Bowles, author of *A Thousand Days for Mokhtar* (Peter Owen hbk £11.95)

CATHER, WILLA (1873 - 1947)
Brought up in the pioneer country of Nebraska, Cather's novels express her commitment to the emancipation of women, as well as an emotional attachment to her background. A groundbreaking and important early American novelist who remains highly readable due to her grace of style and emotional command of subject matter.
A Lost Lady (1923)
The life of a beautiful and charming woman in a Mid Western town whose fine qualities set her apart from her grasping neighbours.
[GD157] Virago pbk **£4.50**

Death Comes for the Archbishop (1927)
Her most famous novel, a celebration of the spiritual pioneering of the Catholic Church in New Mexico.
[GD158] Virago pbk **£5.50**

Lucy Gayheart (1935)
The tragic story of a Mid Western girl whose life is marred by misfortune despite her essential goodness of spirit.
[GD159] Virago pbk **£5.50**

My Antonia (1918)
[GD160] Virago pbk **£5.50**

My Mortal Enemy (1926)
[GD161] Virago pbk **£4.50**

O Pioneers! (1913)
An idealistic rendering of the heroic and creative qualities of the passing frontier.
[GD162] Virago pbk **£5.50**

One of Ours (1922)
Pulitzer Prize winner.
[GD163] Virago pbk **£5.99**

Sapphira and the Slave Girl (1940)
[GD164] Virago pbk **£5.50**

Shadows on the Rock (1931)
A historical novel set in 17th century Québec, centred on the French Catholic community.
[GD165] Virago pbk **£5.50**

The Professor's House (1925)
[GD166] Virago pbk **£5.50**

The Short Stories of Willa Cather   NEW
(1989)
The first English publication of many of Cather's beguiling short stories, spanning her entire life as a writer. Introduced by Hermione Lee.
[GD167] Virago pbk **£9.99**

The Song of the Lark (1915)
Perhaps the most autobiographical of Cather's novels, in which the heroine finds eventual fulfillment in the determined pursuit of artistic success.
[GD168] Virago pbk **£6.50**

CHEEVER, JOHN (1912 - 1982)
Cheever was a fine novelist, but a wonderful and definitive short story writer too; so good, in fact, that his novels are often critically neglected. Some of his stories combine striking originality in construction with a cutting edge that goes straight to the heart of America. It remains unfortunate, in the year that sees the English publication of his letters, that his stories, as well as his last work, the novella *Oh What A Paradise It Seems*, remain out of print.
Falconer (1977)
A departure from his traditional themes: a searing account of one man in prison.
[GD169] Penguin pbk **£3.50**

The Wapshot Chronicle (1957)
Winner of a National Book Award, this is a lively and humorous novel centred on a wealthy and eccentric family in affluent Massachusetts suburbia.
[GD171] Sphere pbk **£3.99**

The Wapshot Scandal (1964)
The sequel charts the family's strange decline.
[GD172] Sphere pbk **£3.99**

CHOPIN, KATE (1851 - 1904)
Chopin was a respected writer by the time she wrote the novel below, but its publication and ensuing

scandal wrecked her career and led to her eclipse for most of this century, until her rehabilitation in the hands of the feminist movement.
The Awakening & Other Stories (1899)
A married woman awakens to the emotional and sexual needs unfulfilled by her marriage, and willingly becomes adulterous.
[GD173] Penguin pbk **£4.99**

COHEN, MATT (Canada, 1942 -)
Cohen's body of work is voluminous and diverse, frequently delving into situations in which seemingly ordinary individuals are psychologically imperilled, though not overtly threatened. A diversion from a central, conventional course, in which characters and situations border on but never actually merge with the predictable - a consistent theme in Canadian literature - is prominent.
Colours of War (1977)
Canada and the US are in a state of civil disorder. At the plot's centre, Theodore Bean, journeying by train across Canada, allows his mind to float through its childhood memories and experiences.
[GD174] Penguin pbk **£3.95**
Disinherited
[GD175] Penguin pbk **£3.95**
Flowers of Darkness (1981)
Annabelle and Allen Jamieson move from the big city to occupy an old stone house in rural Ontario, where after a time, they adjust to the area's muted rhythms. Cohen offers access to his characters, respecting them, and allows himself to be moved by them.
[GD176] Penguin pbk **£3.95**
Intimate Strangers
[GD177] Penguin pbk **£3.95**
Living on Water (Stories, 1989)   **NEW**
Nine short stories, diverse in plot. Cohen sifts through the ephemeral ties that exist between control and happiness, pyschological anarchy and everyday whimsy, as they play upon the ordinary, half-suspecting people of imaginary settings.
[GD178] Viking hbk **£11.95**
Nadine
[GD179] Penguin pbk **£2.95**
Sweet Second Summer of Kitty Malone (1979)
Two lives are inextricably mixed. Kitty Malone and Pat Frank have been loving, hating and ignoring each other for twenty years and have now reached the point of no return.
[GD180] Penguin pbk **£3.95**

CONNELL, EVAN S. (1924 -)
Essayist, novelist, short story writer and poet, Connell is also an astute archaelogist of his country's past.
Mrs Bridge/Mr Bridge (1959, 1969)
Classic evocation of a Protestant marriage and middle- age, performed with great irony and subtlety.
[GD181] Picador pbk **£4.95**
Notes from a Bottle Found on the Beach at Carmel (1963)
[GD182] North Point P pbk **£7.95**
Points for a Compass, Rose (1973)
[GD183] North Point P pbk **£9.50**
Saint Augustine's Pigeon (Stories, 1980)
[GD184] North Point P pbk **£7.95**
Son of the Morning Star (Non fiction, 1986)
A fine, fascinating account of General Custer's Big Horn Campaign.
[GD185] Picador pbk **£4.50**

COOPER, JAMES FENIMORE (1789 - 1851)
One of the great mythologisers of the pioneer spirit, Cooper's most famous novels, here listed in their chronological order of action, trace the exciting and dangerous life of the heroic frontiersman Natty Bumppo and his association with the Indians. An emormously popular author in his day, Cooper was

very concerned with the loss of personal freedom that accompanied the evolution of his society with its often corrupt values.
THE LEATHERSTOCKING TALES
1: The Deerslayer (1841)
[GD186] Penguin pbk **£4.95**
2: The Last of the Mohicans (1826)
[GD187] Penguin pbk **£3.95**
3: The Pioneers (1823)
[GD188] Penguin pbk **£4.99**
4: The Prairie (1827)
[GD189] Penguin pbk **£4.95**

COOPER, RAND RICHARDS
The Last To Go: A Family Chronicle (1989)   **NEW**
In telling the story of the Slatterys from their romantic marriage to troubled middle-age, Cooper has produced a most memorable novel that captures all the joy and pain of these lives with luminous, unsentimental simplicity.
[GD190] Bloomsbury hbk **£13.95**

COOVER, ROBERT (1932 -)
A predominantly satirical writer who fuses fantasy and realism to produce mercurial, many-layered fiction, often with half an eye on the surreal world of American politics.
Gerald's Party (1985)
'Takes on all the queasy affluence of Reagan's America...murderously funny.' (Angela Carter).
[GD191] Grafton pbk **£3.95**
Spanking the Maid (1982)
[GD192] Grafton pbk **£2.95**
Whatever Happened to Gloomy Gus of the Chicago Bears? (1988)
This is the wonderfully funny account of Gloomy Gus, also known as Iron Butt, who learns the secrets of seduction and football by rote. An often hilarious political fable (Gus as Nixon) that is also a serious examination of the masculinity of power.
[GD193] Minerva pbk **£3.99**

CRANE, STEPHEN (1871 - 1900)
Despite his early death at 29 from the tuberculosis that had frequently interrupted his journalistic career, Crane left behind a distinguished body of work. He was much admired by his contemporaries, including Henry James and Joseph Conrad.
Maggie/The Red Badge of Courage/Stories, Sketches, Poetry & Journalism
Almost all of Crane's work that one might want, including his grimly realistic first novel.
[GD194] Cambridge **£7.95**
The Red Badge of Courage (1895)
Set during the American Civil War, this justly famous novel vividly contrasts one inexperienced soldier's heroic ideals with the gruesome reality he encounters in battle.
[GD195] Penguin pbk **£1.99**
The Red Badge of Courage & Other Stories
[GD196] Oxford pbk **£4.95**

CRUMLEY, JAMES
The author of perhaps the definitive modern American crime novel *The Last Good Kiss*.
Whores (1989)   **NEW**
His collected short fiction, most notably the wonderful title story, plus non-fiction and a long interview.
[GD197] D McMillan pbk **£6.30**

CUMMINGS, E.E. (1894 - 1962)
This only novel from the renowned experimental poet was a response to his wrongful incarceration in a French detention centre while he was serving on ambulance duty in World War I.

The Enormous Room (1922)
Cummings' fellow prisoners come to embody exceptional human virtues in contrast to the inhumanity of their captors.
[GD198] Penguin pbk **£4.95**

DAVIES, ROBERTSON (Canada, 1913 -)
Davies started as a playwright in Toronto just after World War II, and in the 1950s turned to the writing of novels. His themes of education and the expansion of learning, closely juxtaposed with the humorous idiosyncrasies of small-town Ontario (in which he was reared), identify him closely with early 20th century semi-rural Canada.
Salterton Trilogy (1951-58)
The first Davies trilogy, comprising *Tempest-Tost*, *Leaven of Malice*, and *A Mixture of Frailties*. In an early example of his hybrid style, mixing humour with extreme irony, Davies guides us through the many and various aspirations of the people in the dreamy fictional Ontario town of Salterton.
[GD199] Penguin pbk **£6.95**
Deptford Trilogy (1970-75)
The second Davies trilogy, comprising *Fifth Business*, *The Manticore*, *World of Wonders*. Starting with the mysterious death of Boy Staunton, Davies' saga follows the various lives of the sons and daughters of fictional Deptford, his evocation of Eastern Canada, through the first half of this century.
[GD200] Penguin pbk **£7.99**
High Spirits
[GD201] Penguin pbk **£3.99**
The Papers of Samuel Marchbanks (1987)
Samuel Marchbanks was the fictional respondent to all the unpleasant letters received by the editor of a small-town paper.
[GD202] Viking hbk **£12.95**
THE CORNISH TRILOGY
Rebel Angels (1981)
Davies' Cornish trilogy is his richest yet: in this the first part an unpublished manuscript by Rabelais is discovered among some private papers, leading to an erudite and highly entertaining debate about what should be done.
[GD203] Penguin pbk **£4.99**
What's Bred in the Bone (1986)
Part two: Davies philosophises about art and its role in life, and follows with light-hearted, witty prose the life of the eccentric and at times mysterious Francis Cornish through the greater part of this century and its rich history. Nominated for the 1986 Booker Prize.
[GD204] Penguin pbk **£4.99**
Lyre of Orpheus (1988)
In the concluding volume, Davies' academicians debate lucidly about the morals and genius of a young female musician and the creation of a libretto.
[GD205] Viking hbk **£11.95**

DELILLO, DON (1936 -)
A marvellously inventive writer often compared to Pynchon, although Delillo is more accessible. His black sense of humour touches upon all that concerns him about the modern world, posing questions of disturbing pertinence.
Libra (1988)   **NEW**
Delillo's latest novel is a fictional life of Kennedy's assassin, Lee Harvey Oswald.
[GD206] Viking hbk **£11.95**
The Names (1983)
[GD207] Picador pbk **£3.95**
White Noise (1984)
Jack Gladney, chairman of Hitler studies at a small American college, is obsessed with his own mortality. Delillo's combination of social comedy and ecological disaster is thus, not surprisingly, hilarious.
[GD208] Picador pbk **£3.95**

DEXTER, PETE
Paris Trout (1988)
Winner of the 1988 American National Book Award. A violent and shocking tale of a psychopathic and racist murderer set in the Deep South of the 1950s.
[GD209] Flamingo pbk **£3.99**

DIDION, JOAN (1934 -)
One of contemporary America's sharpest observers, Didion's style is variously described as unsparing, lucid, ironic and razor-sharp. Her two collections of essays and reflections are paragons of modern prose writing and should not be missed, while her four novels are acerbic tales of Californian women coping with disintegration.
Democracy (1984)
[GD210] Pan pbk **£2.95**
Play It As It Lays (1970)
[GD211] Penguin pbk **£3.95**
Run, River (1963)
[GD212] Penguin pbk **£3.95**
Slouching Towards Bethlehem (Non fiction, 1968)
The book about America in the throes of the sixties that established her name as a formidable essayist.
[GD213] Penguin pbk **£3.95**
The Book of Common Prayer (1970)
Charlotte arrives in Boca Grande, two marriages the worse for wear, and grieving over a daughter turned revolutionary.
[GD214] Penguin pbk **£4.99**
The White Album (Non fiction, 1979)
Brave, often personal attempts to get to grips with the full picture of American life.
[GD215] Penguin pbk **£3.95**

DOCTOROW, E.L. (1931 -)
A New York writer who interweaves elements of 20th century culture into kaleidoscopic narratives. His novels are both funny and critical, with a moving commitment to social issues.
Billy Bathgate (1989)   **NEW**
This is the life story of a 1930s Huck Finn, protégé of the Dutch Schultz gang and apprentice mobster, as told by himself. Ecstatically reviewed in the US as a richly entertaining mixture of fact, fiction and narrative mastery, the culmination of Doctorow's talents.
[GD216] Macmillan hbk **£11.95**
Lives of the Poets (1984)
A novella and six short stories.
[GD217] Picador pbk **£2.95**
Loon Lake (1980)
A novel set in the 1930s Depression.
[GD218] Picador pbk **£2.50**
Ragtime (1975)
Doctorow's marvellous evocation of the Jazz era, with a rich array of character (including Henry Ford and Scott Joplin) and incident. His most successful book, and perhaps his best.
[GD219] Picador pbk **£3.95**
The Book of Daniel (1971)
[GD220] Picador pbk **£3.99**
World's Fair (1985)
A triumphant recreation of a 1930s New York Jewish boyhood seen through the eyes of a child and the adult he becomes.
[GD221] Picador pbk **£3.50**

DONLEAVY, J.P. (1926 -)
Born in Brooklyn, Donleavy served in the Navy before attending Trinity College, Dublin, and he has now made his home in Ireland. His work is characterized by its bawdy comedy, and inventive linguistic wit. His first novel *The Ginger Man* remains his best-known; the rest of his work seems currently undervalued.
A Singular Man (1961)
[GD222] Penguin pbk **£4.99**

Are You Listening, Rabbi Low?
[GD223] Viking hbk **£11.95**
De Alfonce Tennis
[GD224] Fontana pbk **£2.95**
Destinies of D'Arcy Dancer, Gentleman (1977)
[GD225] Penguin pbk **£4.99**
Fairy Tale of New York
[GD226] Penguin pbk **£5.95**
Leila (1983)
[GD227] Penguin pbk **£4.95**
Meet My Maker, the Mad Molecule (Stories, 1964)
[GD228] Penguin pbk **£3.95**
Onion Eaters (1971)
[GD229] Penguin pbk **£3.95**
Schulz
[GD230] Penguin pbk **£3.99**
The Beastly Beatitudes of Balthazar B. (1968)
[GD231] Penguin pbk **£4.95**
The Ginger Man (1955)
Donleavy's most famous novel concerns the exploits of a GI and his wife in London and Ireland, and drew on his own experiences of Dublin literary life.
[GD232] Penguin pbk **£3.95**
The Saddest Summer of Samuel K
[GD233] Penguin pbk **£1.25**

DOOLITTLE, HILDA (H.D.) (1886 - 1961)
Born in Pennsylvania, and best known as a poet, Doolittle also wrote fiction which reveals her interest in psychoanalysis and philosophy. Her novels are coloured by her Imagist flair for clear, sharp vision, with moments of heightened awareness achieved through richly figurative language.
Bid Me To Live (1960)
Stream-of-consciousness Bloomsbury novel and *roman à clef*, featuring a striking portrait of D.H. Lawrence.
[GD234] Virago pbk **£5.50**
Hedlys (1928)
Set on the isle of Samos, between the Athens of intellect and the Alexandria of imagination.
[GD235] Carcanet pbk **£4.95**
Her
[GD236] Virago pbk **£5.50**
The Gift
[GD237] Virago pbk **£4.50**

DOS PASSOS, JOHN (1896 - 1970)
A revolutionary writer both in form and content, concerned with the conflicting demands of capitalists and workers, and the opposing forces of reform and conservatism in society. His conclusions are, ultimately, pessimistic: Dos Passos came to believe that the materialism and rigidity of society can only lead to personal unhappiness.
Manhattan Transfer (1925)
A portrait of the sprawling, diversified life of New York in hundreds of fictional episodes. A unique fictional experiment, and a great novel of the city.
[GD238] Penguin pbk **£4.99**
U.S.A. (1938)
Dos Passos' trilogy of novels in one volume - *The 42nd Parallel*, *1919* and *The Big Money* - telling the interconnected stories of numerous Americans in the first thirty years of this century, mixed in with non-fictional characters and period material.
[GD239] Penguin pbk **£7.95**

DREISER, THEODORE (1871 - 1945)
Dreiser's novels offer heady social criticism of his times. One of the fathers of American naturalism, he championed the dignity and humanity of those subjected to the cruelties of the capitalist system which he came wholeheartedly to oppose. According to Saul Bellow, 'he somehow conveys depths of

feeling we usually associate with Balzac or Shakespeare.'
An American Tragedy (1925)
A young man becomes increasingly trapped by the circumstances of his poverty and is finally executed for murder. A harrowing but humane work.
[GD240] Collins pbk **£1.20**
Sister Carrie (1900)
His first novel, initially received with greater acclaim in England than in America, where its realism caused offence.
[GD241] Penguin pbk **£3.99**

ELLISON, RALPH (1914 -)
Invisible Man (1952)
One of the great post-war American novels, tracing the growing self-awareness of a young Black and his search for a place in society.
[GD242] Penguin pbk **£3.95**

ENGEL, MARIAN (Canada, 1933 - 1985)
Engel's prose style is simple, as is the construction of her plots. She wrote about women, not from a distinctly feminist viewpoint, but rather about humanity through the eyes of modern women with modern pressures. Thematically, her works follow the lives of independent, embattled women who cannot meet the demands of society's expectations, questioning finally the justification for their doing so. In many of her works the women act to save themselves, often fleeing untenable situations only to face the ensuing confusion with unclear emotions.
Bear
[GD243] Pandora pbk **£3.95**
Monodromos (1984)
Audrey Moore, her life quietly disintegrating, travels on a whim to a Mediterranean island and unwittingly becomes part of the eccentric circle of expatriates, yet remains the innocent 'outsider' looking in.
[GD244] Penguin pbk **£3.95**

ERDRICH, LOUISE (1954 -)
One of the rising stars among young American novelists, Erdrich is a true original. Of German-American and Chippewa Indian descent, her three interlinked novels combine Mid West family drama with Indian myth and magic, together forming a compelling trilogy, soon to become a quartet.
Love Medicine (1984)
A multi-layered tale of sexual obsession with a distinct vein of humour.
[GD245] Futura pbk **£2.50**
The Beet Queen (1987)
Spanning forty years of this century with breath-taking confidence and a wide array of narrators, this novel is electrifying in the clarity of its vision.
[GD246] H Hamilton hbk **£11.95**
[GD247] Pan pbk **£3.50**
Tracks (1988)
The story of Fleur Pillager as told by the elderly Nanapush and the gossipy Pauline; set in the grim years between 1912 and 1924, chronologically this is the earliest of Erdrich's trilogy.
[GD248] H Hamilton hbk **£11.95**
[GD249] Picador pbk **£4.50**

FANTE, JOHN (1911 - 1983)
A realist whose best writing is set in the 1930s Depression years, chronicling American family life with an unflinching eye.
Ask the Dust (1939)
A novel about Italian American workers in California.
[GD250] Grafton pbk **£2.50**
Dreams from Bunker Hill (1982)
[GD251] Grafton pbk **£2.50**
The Road to Los Angeles
[GD252] B Sparrow pbk **£8.95**
The Wine of Youth (1940)
[GD253] Grafton pbk **£3.50**

Wait Until Spring, Bandini (1938)
[GD254] Grafton pbk **£2.50**

FARRELL, JAMES T. (1904 - 1979)
Vastly prolific naturalist writer much influenced by
Joyce, Dreiser and Proust, and a self-professed
Marxist.
Studs Lonigan (1932 - 1935)
The outstanding naturalistic trilogy set amidst the
urban squalor of Chicago, drawing on Farrell's Irish
Catholic background, and written in the stream-of-
consciousness style.
[GD255] Picador pbk **£5.95**

FAULKNER, WILLIAM (1897 - 1962)
Nobel Prize for Literature 1950. Faulkner's
reputation as one of this century's great novelists
now rests secure. His series of interlinked
Yoknapatawpha novels utilize multiple narrative
points of view to render complex family sagas
embedded in Southern history, with its legacy of
violence, racism and miscegenation. His best books,
written between 1929 and 1942, marry the mythic and
tragic elements of his work to a remarkable gift for
black humour and psychological realism.
Absalom, Absalom! (1936)
This majestic novel charts the rise and fall of Thomas
Sutpen, filtered through the latter-day consciousness
of Quentin Compson. Considered by many to be
Faulkner's most comprehensive vision of the South's
doom.
[GD256] Penguin pbk **£5.95**
As I Lay Dying (1930)
The blackly comic and bleak tale of the hillbilly
Bundrens' efforts to transport their mother's coffin to
its final resting place.
[GD257] Penguin pbk **£4.50**
Collected Stories
[GD258] Penguin pbk **£7.95**
Go Down, Moses (1942)
Seven brilliantly interlinked stories make up this
fragmented history of the McCaslin family.
[GD259] Penguin pbk **£4.99**
Intruder in the Dust (1948)
[GD260] Penguin pbk **£3.99**
Light in August (1932)
A powerful and gripping study of how mixed-
blood Joe Christmas is hounded by racist
society.
[GD261] Penguin pbk **£4.99**
Mosquitoes (1927)
Faulkner's second, Pulitzer Prize-winning
novel.
[GD262] Picador pbk **£4.99**
Requiem for a Nun (1951)
The sequel to *Sanctuary*: Temple Drake's painful
redemption.
[GD263] Penguin pbk **£3.95**
Sanctuary (1931)
The sensational novel that made Faulkner's name. A
lurid tale of sex, rape, murder and vengeance, with a
keen moral edge.
[GD264] Penguin pbk **£3.95**
Sartoris (1929)
[GD265] Chatto **£10.95**
Soldier's Pay (1926)
His first novel tells the story of the return home of a
dying soldier.
[GD266] Penguin pbk **£3.95**
The Mansion (1959)
[GD267] Chatto **£10.95**
The Portable Faulkner
Malcolm Cowley, who almost single-handedly
rescued Faulkner from utter obscurity in the forties,
edited this selection of Yoknapatawpha material,
arranged in its fictional chronology.
[GD268] Penguin pbk **£5.95**
The Reivers (1962)
[GD269] Penguin pbk **£4.99**

The Sound and the Fury (1929)
Written at the peak of Faulkner's powers and a key
modern novel. Told in four parts, three of which are
memorable interior monologues - including one from
the 'idiot' Benjy - it artfully relates the dissolution of
the Compson family.
[GD270] Chatto hbk **£10.95**
[GD271] Penguin pbk **£4.95**
The Town (1957)
[GD272] Chatto **£10.95**
The Unvanquished (1938)
A series of short stories distilled into a novel, tracing
the history of the Sartoris family.
[GD273] Penguin pbk **£3.95**
The Wild Palms (1939)
Technically adventurous novel yoking two
unconnected stories together.
[GD274] Penguin pbk **£3.95**

FINDLEY, TIMOTHY (Canada, 1930 -)
As a child Findley was emotionally and intellectually
influenced by the violence and destruction of World
War II, although he had no direct experience of it.
Thus, the theme of the apparently settled society
descending into madness plays at least some part in
each of his novels. He consistently destroys the hope
that might be offered by man's spiritual enlightment,
building characters who are both victim and
victimiser in situations ensconced within sometimes
dense political metaphor.
Famous Last Words (1981)
Hugh Selwyn Mauberley is borrowed from the Ezra
Pound poem and proceeds to tell his version of the
last days of 1930s Fascism. His story, scrawled on the
decaying walls of a hotel room, alludes to the
destructive relationship between aestheticism and
fascism.
[GD275] Arrow pbk **£3.99**
Not Wanted on the Voyage
An allegorical retelling of the Great Flood.
[GD276] Arrow pbk **£3.95**
Telling of Lies
[GD277] Macmillian hbk **£11.95**

FITZGERALD, F. SCOTT (1896 - 1940)
Fifty years after his death, Fitzgerald remains one of
the mythical figures of American literature - the man
who charted and defined the Jazz Age. Although his
output was small, he wrote what is certainly one of
the finest of American novels, *The Great Gatsby*,
which like most of his enduringly popular novels, can
be read as both a haunting romance and a critique of
the American Dream.

F. Scott Fitzgerald, author of *Tender is the Night*
(Bodley Head hbk £10.95, Penguin pbk £3.95)
(Picture by Gordon Bryant, with permission of
Hodder & Stoughton)

**Bernice Bobs Her Hair & Other
Stories**
[GD278] Penguin pbk **£3.50**
Collected Stories
[GD279] Penguin pbk **£6.95**
Tender is the Night (1934)
His other major novel, which explores the slow
decline of an expatriate community in the South of
France.
[GD280] Bodley Head hbk **£10.95**
[GD281] Penguin pbk **£3.95**
The Beautiful and the Damned (1921)
His second novel and perhaps his weakest, although it
enjoyed considerable popularity on publication. It
concerns the decline of a fashionable young couple.
[GD282] Bodley Head hbk **£10.95**
[GD283] Penguin pbk **£3.95**
The Crack-Up & Other Stories (1935)
Mainly autobiographical pieces written after
Fitzgerald's breakdown.
[GD284] Penguin pbk **£3.99**
**The Diamond as Big as the Ritz & Other
Stories**
[GD285] Penguin pbk **£3.95**
The Great Gatsby (1925)
Fitzgerald's consummately formal novel; the story of
his most memorable creation, Jay Gatsby, and his
obsessive love for Daisy.
[GD286] Penguin pbk **£2.50**
The Last Tycoon (1941)
His last novel, incomplete at his death, set in the
'great' days of Hollywood; the central character of
Monroe Stahr captures the contradictory brilliance of
that age.
[GD287] Penguin pbk **£3.95**
The Lost Decade & Other Stories
[GD288] Penguin pbk **£3.50**
The Pat Hobby Stories
Seventeen late stories about an unsuccessful
Hollywood script writer.
[GD289] Penguin pbk **£2.95**
This Side of Paradise (1920)
His first novel, based on his time at Princeton, which
made him rich and famous overnight.
[GD290] Penguin pbk **£3.95**
THE BODLEY HEAD COLLECTED F. SCOTT
FITZGERALD
1: The Great Gatsby/The Last Tycoon
A uniform edition of six volumes; vols two and four
are *Tender is the Night* and *The Beautiful and the
Damned*.
[GD291] Bodley Head hbk **£10.95**
3: This Side of Paradise/The Crack-Up
[GD292] Bodley Head hbk **£10.95**
**5: Early Success: Glamour &
Disillusionment**
[GD293] Bodley Head hbk **£10.95**
6: Retrospective: Basil & Josephine
[GD294] Bodley Head hbk **£10.95**

**FITZGERALD, SCOTT & ZELDA
Bits of Paradise**
Ten stories from either half of the marriage.
[GD295] Penguin pbk **£3.95**

FORD, RICHARD (1944 -)
A true ear for dialogue, resonant cinematic prose and
versatility as a story-teller have won Ford high praise.
His novels and stories deal with men and women on
the edges of post-Vietnam America.
A Piece of My Heart (1976)
Ford's first novel is emphatically a Southern tale; the
Faulknerian gallows humour is deliberate, the cast
traditionally grotesque.
[GD296] Collins hbk **£10.95**
[GD297] Flamingo pbk **£3.95**
Rock Springs (1988)
An inspired collection of stories written over the last
eight years. Ford's quiet voice amongst the modern

desolation he describes is steady and reassuring; he has become a major story-teller.
[GD298] Collins hbk **£10.95**
[GD299] Flamingo pbk **£3.95**
The Sportswriter (1986)
Wonderfully elegiac study in suburban alienation and self-realization, rightly hailed as one of the finest novels of 1986. Beautifully understated and haunting.
[GD300] Collins hbk **£10.95**
[GD301] Flamingo pbk **£3.95**
The Ultimate Good Luck (1989)   **NEW**
Collins have now completed their publication of Ford's three novels to date, this being his second. Set in Mexico, it involves a prison break, and is an atmospheric meditation on love and luck.
[GD302] Collins hbk **£11.95**

FRENCH, MARILYN (1929 -)
Fired by the possibilities of liberation, French has, in both her fiction and non-fiction, written powerful works dissecting and celebrating modern women's lives.
Her Mother's Daughter (1987)
[GD303] Pan pbk **£4.99**
The Bleeding Heart (1980)
[GD304] Sphere pbk **£4.99**
The Women's Room (1978)
The novel that many would term classic, since it crystallized the experiences of a whole generation of women. 'The kind of book that changes lives' (Fay Weldon).
[GD305] Sphere pbk **£4.99**

GADDIS, WILLIAM (1922 -)
One of the most respected post-war American writers. His densely structured experimental novels show an agile fascination with ideas, coupled with a devastating satirical wit.
Carpenter's Gothic (1986)
A book crammed with ideas, and a satire on modern American politics.
[GD306] Picador pbk **£3.95**
JR (1976)
A rich and complex parody of American capitalism, focussing on the meteoric business career of a yuppie.
[GD307] Penguin pbk **£7.95**

GALLAGHER, TESS
A distinguished poet and professor at Syracuse University.
The Lover of Horses (1989)   **NEW**
A wonderful first collection of stories that render the ordinary remarkable. The simplicity of the truths she reveals is, like all truths, hard-won.
[GD308] H Hamilton hbk **£11.95**

GALLANT, MAVIS (Canada, 1922 -)
Gallant takes people out of their natural setting and examines the strain of exposure to alien cultures, as they construct defences against the perceived threats of living in the other, foreign situation. As events deteriorate her characters are seldom saved, not even by the satires in which they find themselves, which should and could be optimistic. Ultimately, she draws the conclusion that in real life people will not necessary be guided.
Overhead in a Balloon
[GD309] Cape hbk **£10.95**
Paris Notebooks: Essays and Reviews
Essays on various aspects of modern France by one of the world's great short-story writers.
[GD310] H Hamilton pbk **£6.95**

GALLICO, PAUL (1897 -)
Born in New York of Austrian and Italian parents, Gallico worked as a sports editor and a gunner's mate before settling in Monaco. His fiction shows a wide range of interest and sensibility, from the pathos and delicacy of *The Snow Goose* to his portraits of boxers and his gripping disaster story, *The Poseidon Adventure*.
Flowers for Mrs Harris
[GD311] Penguin pbk **£2.25**
Jennie (1950)
[GD312] Penguin pbk **£2.95**
Love of Seven Dolls
[GD313] Penguin pbk **£2.25**
Ludmilla and the Lonely (1955)
[GD314] Penguin pbk **£2.50**
The Adventures of Miriam Holliday (1939)
[GD315] Penguin pbk **£2.50**
The Best of Paul Gallico
[GD316] M Joseph hbk **£11.95**
The Poseidon Adventure (1969)
An ocean liner is toppled by a tidal wave; this novel charts the desperate efforts of the passengers to survive.
[GD317] Penguin pbk **£2.95**
The Snow Goose/The Small Miracle (1941, 1951)
His most enduring and popular tale, based on the retreat from Dunkirk, coupled with a moving tale of a small girl who works for a cruel puppet master.
[GD318] Penguin pbk **£1.95**

GARDNER, JOHN (1933 - 1982)
A prolific ex-professor of English and an enormous influence on Raymond Carver, Gardner often explored his themes through allegory and myth. He mourned the lack of moral fibre in contemporary fiction, and his own writing is much concerned with moral problems and dilemmas.
Mickelsson's Ghosts (1982)
A professor is caught up in a web of erotic, emotional and philosophical conflicts, his problems darkened by a terrible Mormon murder.
[GD319] Arrow pbk **£4.95**
Stillness and Shadows (1987)
[GD320] Secker hbk **£12.95**

GELLHORN, MARTHA
As a novelist, Gellhorn shows the same independence and strength of spirit in her writing as she did in her experience as a war correspondent.
Liana (1944)
A long neglected, disturbing novel concerning the sadness and inhumanity of oppression.
[GD321] Virago pbk **£4.50**
Stricken Field (1942)
The story of an American woman in Prague during the early 1940s, a city transformed by fear.
[GD322] Virago pbk **£4.50**
The Weather in Africa (1980)
Three novellas set in Africa: 'a stunningly good book' (Victoria Glendinning).
[GD323] Eland pbk **£3.95**
Travels With Myself and Another (Travel)
[GD324] Eland pbk **£4.95**

GILCHRIST, ELLEN
A distinctive and original writer whose evocative tales of Southern women around New Orleans searching for satisfaction have earned her much praise. Her writing is tender and lyrical.
Drunk with Love (Stories, 1987)
[GD325] Faber pbk **£3.95**
Falling through Space: An Author's Journal (Non fiction, 1988)
[GD326] Faber hbk **£14.95**
In the Land of Dreamy Dreams (Stories, 1984)
Memorable short tragedies set in New Orleans.
[GD327] Picador pbk **£3.95**
The Anna Papers (1989)   **NEW**
A successful writer, learning she has cancer, walks into the sea. She leaves her sister some private papers, which at first shock her, and then start to exert a curious influence. Thus this is the tale of a writer whose death brings a legacy of life.
[GD328] Faber hbk **£12.99**
The Annunciation (1983)
Her first novel.
[GD329] Faber pbk **£2.95**
Victory Over Japan (Stories, 1985)
Southerners in search not so much of happiness as satisfaction.
[GD330] Faber pbk **£3.50**

GILMAN, CHARLOTTE PERKINS (1860 - 1935)
Probably the most influential woman thinker in the pre-World War I generation of Americans, Gilman has come to provide important intellectual backing for the women's rights movement.
Charlotte Perkins Gilman Reader
Although she called herself a humanist, Gilman combined socialism with feminism to create a coherent theory of women's oppression.
[GD331] Women's P pbk **£4.95**
Herland
A feminist dystopia, as envisioned 80 years ago.
[GD332] Women's P pbk **£1.95**
The Yellow Wallpaper (1892)
The awakening of a woman to whom a room of her own meant a prison-like attic nursery created by her husband.
[GD333] Virago pbk **£3.50**

GLASGOW, ELLEN (1874 - 1945)
Born of an aristocratic Southern family, Glasgow revolted against the sentimental tradition of the Southern novel by depicting the genteel code of the Old South threatened by encroaching industrialisation. Keenly interested in the social and political problems of her day, she was also quite a proto-feminist.
Barren Ground (1925)
The story of a country girl who runs away and works in New York before returning to the farm which provides her with a reason to endure.
[GD334] Virago pbk **£5.99**
The Sheltered Life (1932)
A bleak and realistic tale of passion ending in death.
[GD335] Virago pbk **£5.50**
Virginia (1913)
Another jilted and forlorn heroine, deserted by her now successful husband and emancipated daughters.
[GD336] Virago pbk **£5.99**

William Gaddis, author of *JR* (Penguin pbk £7.95) (Photo: Jerry Bauer)

FICTION

GODWIN, GAIL (1937 -)

An author with a great gift for story-telling whose novels present detailed pictures of domestic life. Her books have been compared to those of Jane Austen, since she describes family life with insight and clarity.

A Mother and Two Daughters (1982)
[GD337] Pan pbk **£3.99**
Mr Bedford and the Muses (1983)
[GD338] Pan pbk **£2.95**
Odd Woman (1974)
A Ph.D., a stimulating job and an affair with a married man leave Jane Clifford, with her 19th century sensibility, wanting more.
[GD339] Pan pbk **£3.50**
The Finishing School (1984)
[GD340] Pan pbk **£2.95**
The Perfectionists (1970)
[GD341] Pan pbk **£2.95**
Violet Clay (1978)
Violet yearns to be a real painter although she pays her rent illustrating the covers of Gothic novels.
[GD342] Pan pbk **£3.50**

GORDON, MARY (1940 -)

A humane and intelligent novelist who has been widely praised for her powerful rendering of delicately observed situations. With her morally invigorating themes, Gordon is a fine prose stylist.

Final Payments (1978)
'A little like Mary McCarthy, a little like Margaret Drabble, yet really, like nothing but itself.' (Susan Hill).
[GD343] Penguin pbk **£3.99**
Men and Angels (1985)
A novel about maternal love charged with dark imaginings.
[GD344] Penguin pbk **£2.95**
Temporary Shelter (Stories, 1987)
[GD345] Penguin pbk **£3.99**
The Company of Women (1981)
[GD346] Transworld pbk **£3.95**
The Other Side (1989) **NEW**
An Irish-American family undergo a nerve-wracking reunion as their matriarch, one-time campaigner for FDR and the trade unions, prepares to die. Once again Gordon proves herself an intriguingly lucid observer of human mores.
[GD347] Bloomsbury hbk **£12.95**

GOYEN, WILLIAM (1915 -)

Like his contemporaries O'Connor and McCullers, Goyen's work is deeply rooted in the Southern tradition, but with a black humour and hyper-charged lyricism of his own.

Arcadio
[GD348] Serpent's Tail pbk **£6.50**
Had I a Hundred Mouths: Short Stories 1947 - 1983
'Among the great short stories of the century.' (*New York Times*).
[GD349] Serpent's Tail pbk **£7.95**

GURGANUS, ALLAN
Oldest Living Confederate Widow Tells All (1989) **NEW**
Magnificently frank and funny account of the American Civil War seen through the eyes of a wife and mother. Already much-hyped, but deservedly so.
[GD350] Faber hbk **£12.99**

HARRIS, JOEL CHANDLER (1848 - 1908)

It was in Alice Walker's hometown of Eatonton, Georgia, that Harris wrote the first of his Uncle Remus books, thereby appropriating timeless African fables and making himself a hugely popular and wealthy author.

Joseph Heller, author of *Catch 22* (Cape hbk £9.95, Transworld pbk £4.95)

Uncle Remus: His Songs & His Sayings
This edition is worth buying for the introduction alone, which argues convincingly that Harris' appeal lay in the comforting picture of slavery that his work depicted.
[GD351] Penguin pbk **£3.95**

HARRISON, JIM
Dalva (1989) **NEW**
Harrison's wonderful new novel is the story of Dalva's search for the son she gave away. It is also the history of her pioneer family as told by her great-grandfather, whose diary relates the dispossession of the American Indian.
[GD352] Cape hbk **£12.95**
Sundog (1986)
A compelling tale of the enigmatic recluse Strang, a man free from 'the bondage of the appropriate'.
[GD353] Penguin pbk **£3.95**

HAWTHORNE, NATHANIEL (1804 - 1864)

A direct descendant of one of the Salem witch trial judges, Hawthorne was deeply preoccupied with the impact harsh Puritanism had on the guilty New England conscience. The profound undercurrents of his seemingly artless stories have led him to being acclaimed as one of America's major early writers.

Collected Novels
Includes *Fanshawe* (1828), his semi-autobiographical first novel, and *The Marble Faun* (1860), a romance set amongst the art students of Rome, as well as his three other classics.
[GD354] Cambridge hbk **£7.95**
Selected Tales & Sketches
32 of his best.
[GD355] Penguin pbk **£5.95**
Tales and Sketches
A voluminous selection in the beautifully produced Library of America series. Incredibly good value - 1,493 (acid-free paper) pages.
[GD356] Cambridge hbk **£7.95**
The Blithedale Romance (1852)
This satirical novel was the result of his involvement with an idealistic co-operative community with an unscrupulous leader.
[GD357] Penguin pbk **£3.95**
The House of the Seven Gables (1851)
A gothic romance exposing the hypocrisy of the Puritan Judge Pyncheon.
[GD358] Penguin pbk **£3.50**

The Scarlet Letter (1850)
His most important work, set in the 17th century. Hester Prynne does public penance for her adultery.
[GD359] Penguin pbk **£3.50**
The Scarlet Letter & Selected Tales
Includes a small selection of Hawthorne's best stories (of which he wrote a great many).
[GD360] Penguin pbk **£3.50**

HEINEMANN, LARRY (1944 -)

Gutsy Chicago writer whose two novels about Vietnam, written out of personal experience, are a cut above the rest.

Close Quarters (1987)
Philip Dosier is plunged from High School into the surreal violence of Vietnam. A gripping rites of passage tale.
[GD361] Faber pbk **£3.95**
Paco's Story (1987)
Narrated by a ghost of the marine company of which Paco is the sole survivor, this is the masterful story of how Paco comes home, mutilated inside and out, to find he is valued only as a curiosity. Shattering and wholly convincing.
[GD362] Faber pbk **£3.95**

HELLER, JOSEPH (1923 -)

Singularly original novelist noted for his black humour, who explores the absurdity and madness of the modern world. Fearsomely intelligent, Heller's aim is consistently true when spearing his victims.

Catch 22 (1961)
The devastating tale of the dangerously sane Yossarian; a savage, memorable indictment of military madness and stupidity.
[GD363] Cape hbk **£9.95**
[GD364] Transworld pbk **£4.95**
God Knows (1984)
The ranting memoirs of King David.
[GD365] Transworld pbk **£3.95**
Good as Gold (1979)
A comic view of Jewish family life.
[GD366] Cape hbk **£9.95**
Picture This (1988)
A daring tale of rewritten history in which Rembrandt brings Aristotle back to life by painting his portrait.
[GD367] Picador pbk **£4.99**
Something Happened (1971)
A promising executive finds that maintaining the pretence of happiness that society demands increasingly difficult.
[GD368] Cape hbk **£9.95**

HELWIG, DAVID (Canada, 1938 -)

Something of a social realist, Helwig gives his individuals a web of mixed feelings; he often sets attempts to find safety within modern life against the natural aggressiveness that characterises the manifold avarices all too common in the actions of 'modern people'. This personal bifurcation he takes to extremes, pitting spiritual calm against madness, good against evil. This is found both in his clear, unstinting poetry and in his many novels.

Only Son (1984)
Walter grows up on a rich man's estate. In adulthood, he turns his back on the structure in which he was reared, only to learn the true nature of power and how it manifests itself.
[GD369] Penguin pbk **£3.95**
Postcard from Rome **NEW**
[GD370] Viking hbk **£11.95**
The Bishop (1986)
A Bishop lies immobile, paralyzed by a stroke, and is tended by an Inuit shaman. People from his past re-surface, and within the sympathetic, taut narrative, reconstruct the sick man's remarkable life.
[GD371] Penguin pbk **£3.95**

HEMINGWAY, ERNEST (1899 - 1961)
Nobel Prize For Literature 1954. His revolutionary and 'bespattered' prose coupled with enormous gifts as a story-teller make Hemingway central to the American novel. His public image of the hard-drinking, womanizing 'Papa' all too often obscures the qualities of his work: like none other, Hemingway has the genius to evoke a time and place for the reader, be it Spring in Montparnasse, or a trout breaking the water of a Michigan river. The fear that his art was slipping away led him to suicide by shotgun in 1961.
A Farewell to Arms (1929)
The arbitrary nature of death, both in war and in peace, is a central theme to this novel born of Hemingway's traumatic experiences in World War I.
[GD372] Cape hbk **£8.95**
[GD373] Grafton pbk **£2.99**
A Moveable Feast (Non-fiction, 1964)
The writer in later life reflecting on, and beautifully evoking, the Paris he remembers from the 1920s.
[GD374] Cape hbk **£9.95**
[GD375] Grafton pbk **£2.95**
Across the River and into the Trees (1950)
Despite the beauty of its opening, this World War II novel never convinces or holds as *A Farewell To Arms* does.
[GD376] Grafton pbk **£2.99**
Death in the Afternoon (1932)
Bullfighting as tragic art is the theme, which Hemingway pursues with admirable attention to detail. Includes the justly famous, elegiac final chapter.
[GD377] Grafton pbk **£3.50**
Fiesta (The Sun Also Rises) (1926)
The novel which made both him and the Pamplona festival famous. Splendidly evokes the decadent 1920s and the expatriate life in Paris.
[GD378] Cape hbk **£8.95**
[GD379] Grafton pbk **£2.95**
For Whom the Bell Tolls (1940)
This novel of love and death in the Spanish Civil War is a carefully constructed study in heroism and self-sacrifice.
[GD380] Cape hbk **£9.95**
[GD381] Grafton pbk **£3.50**
Islands in the Stream (1970)
[GD382] Penguin pbk **£3.95**
Men without Women (Stories, 1927)
Marvellous collection of stories; Hemingway's gift for understatement is perfectly suited to the form.
[GD383] Grafton pbk **£2.50**
On Writing (Non fiction)
[GD384] Grafton pbk **£2.50**
The Dangerous Summer (Non fiction)
[GD385] H Hamilton hbk **£12.95**
[GD386] Grafton pbk **£2.95**
The Essential Hemingway
Containing all of *Fiesta* and many fine short stories.
[GD387] Grafton pbk **£3.95**
The Fifth Column (Play, 1938)
[GD388] Grafton pbk **£2.50**
The First Forty-Nine Stories
All the stories from his first five collections.
[GD389] Cape hbk **£9.95**
The Garden of Eden (1987)
This published version is half the size of the unfinished manuscript Hemingway worked on for many years, yet is nonetheless an intriguing study of sexual games. As might be expected, the countryside of the Mediterranean is unforgettably drawn.
[GD390] H Hamilton hbk **£11.95**
[GD391] Grafton pbk **£2.95**
The Green Hills of Africa (1935)
Accounts of big game hunting in Africa.
[GD392] Grafton pbk **£2.95**

The Old Man and the Sea (1952)
A word perfect study of 'grace under pressure', it stands as Hemingway's masterpiece.
[GD394] Cape hbk **£9.95**
[GD393] Grafton pbk **£2.50**
The Snows of Kilimanjaro (Stories, 1936)
[GD395] Grafton pbk **£2.50**
The Torrents of Spring (1926)
An early novel satirizing Sherwood Anderson.
[GD396] Grafton pbk **£2.50**
To Have and Have Not (1937)
The flawed but exciting adventures of Harry Morgàn, rum, gun, and man-running between Florida and Cuba.
[GD397] Grafton pbk **£2.99**
Winner Take Nothing (Stories, 1933)
[GD398] Grafton pbk **£2.95**

HEMLEY, ROBIN
All You Can Eat (1989) `NEW`
A sparkling collection of stories for American short story addicts, that take a bracing, off-beat look at the oddities of our lives.
[GD399] Heinemann hbk **£9.95**

HOBAN, RUSSELL (1925 -)
A remarkable contemporary novelist of outstanding imagination and range. He can weave myth and allegory together as in *Riddley Walker*, or create a perfectly understated comedy of manners like *Turtle Diary*. Also known for his children's books.
Kleinzeit (1974)
[GD400] Picador pbk **£2.95**
Pilgermann (1983)
An extraordinary vision of the Biblical age as a grotesque, hellish world where bodies are boiled and human heads used as cannonballs, shot through with Hoban's characteristic metaphysical thought.
[GD401] Picador pbk **£3.50**
Riddley Walker (1980)
The celebrated novel set in a post-holocaust England in which language has returned to an oral primitivism. Rich in linguistic and intellectual invention.
[GD402] Cape hbk **£9.95**
[GD403] Picador pbk **£3.99**
The Medusa Frequency (1987)
A witty and moving account of an erudite writer's compulsive sense of loss.
[GD404] Picador pbk **£3.95**
Turtle Diary (1975)
A touching tale of two loners who decide to free the sea turtles from London Zoo.
[GD405] Picador pbk **£3.95**

HOWELLS, WILLIAM DEANE (1837 - 1920)
Like so many 19th century American writers, Howells' training was as a journalist, which led him to becoming concerned with the social problems of an industrializing society. Although he became the pre-eminent man of American letters in his day, he is little read now.
Indian Summer (1886)
An elegiac and charming love story, one of the first novels to depict Americans in Europe.
[GD406] Oxford pbk **£4.95**
The Rise of Silas Lapham (1885)
The Boston life of the *nouveau riche* Colonel Lapham, a self-made man. Generally considered Howells' best book.
[GD407] Penguin pbk **£4.95**

HUMPHREY, WILLIAM
No Resting Place (1989) `NEW`
A moving recreation of the shameful removal of the Cherokee nation from Georgia, as seen through the eyes of a young Indian boy. A fine novel.
[GD408] Secker hbk **£11.95**

HURSTON, ZORA NEALE (1901? - 1960)
One of the great figures of the Harlem Renaissance, Hurston's work has recently undergone a revival in popularity thanks to Alice Walker's avowed debt to her. She trained as an anthropologist, doing pioneering work on Black folk traditions, before later becoming a novelist and critic.
I Love Myself: A Reader
An anthology of Hurston's best writings edited by Alice Walker.
[GD409] Feminist P pbk **£7.95**
Jonah's Gourd Vine (1934)
Fast moving first novel about a sinning pastor.
[GD410] Virago pbk **£4.99**
Spunk!
Celebrations of Black culture and experience.
[GD411] Camden P pbk **£4.95**
Their Eyes Were Watching God (1937)
Hurston's triumphant and poetic novel of a woman's search for self-fulfilment, written in prose of a unique, musical quality.
[GD412] Virago pbk **£4.99**

INGALLS, RACHEL (1940 -)
Predominantly a short story writer whose work has a unique fairy-tale quality; the calm manner in which Ingalls relates her often horrifying subject matter makes these modern parables strangely powerful.
Binstead's Safari (1983)
[GD413] Dent pbk **£2.95**
Four Stories (1987)
[GD414] Faber pbk **£2.95**
Mrs Caliban & Other Stories (1982)
[GD415] Dent pbk **£2.95**
The End of Tragedy (1987)
[GD416] Faber hbk **£10.95**
Theft (1970)
[GD417] Faber pbk **£2.95**

IRVING, JOHN (1942 -)
A very popular novelist whose books are lively and packed with bizarre situations and hectic madcap adventures. Immensely satisfying not only for their fast-paced narratives but in their attention to detail.
158lb Marriage (1974)
Two couples intertwined by adultery.
[GD418] Transworld pbk **£3.95**
A Prayer For Owen Meany (1989) `NEW`
This is John Irving at what can only be called his Dickensian best. Shot through with flamboyantly staged set pieces and peopled with characters larger than life (like Hester the Molester), this prodigious novel is not a page too long. The ending is also quite tremendous.
[GD419] Bloomsbury hbk **£12.95**
Hotel New Hampshire (1981)
An exotic family caught in a web of domestic intrigue. Elements of high farce and perversity are blended with a more serious intent.
[GD420] Transworld pbk **£4.95**
Setting Free the Bears (1968)
A novel about an attempt to free the bears from Vienna Zoo.
[GD421] Transworld pbk **£4.95**
The Cider House Rules (1985)
Off-beat tale which follows the fortunes of Homer Wells, an orphan too old and awkward to be adopted, who becomes instead an apprentice abortionist and maker of cider.
[GD422] Transworld pbk **£3.95**
The Water Method Man (1972)
The fantastical exploits of an Iowa student.
[GD423] Transworld pbk **£4.95**
The World According to Garp (1978)
Irving's most popular book, the glorious, fanciful tale of the imaginative novelist who is killed by one of his dissatisfied readers.
[GD424] Transworld pbk **£4.95**

JAMES, HENRY (1843 - 1916)

Since James lived most of his adult life in England, he is perhaps best termed an Anglo-American writer, the great part of his work being concerned with the rival claims of the two cultures: American and European. However, it was literature itself that remained his over-riding passion, and his late fiction has earned him an almost legendary position in the history of the novel; they manage to express nuances in our perceptions and reactions to others which are beyond the reach of any other art form. (The Bodley Head hbk editions present James' work in the final form in which he published it in 1907-9, with the celebrated prefaces).

A London Life & The Reverberator
[GD425] Oxford pbk **£5.95**
An International Episode & Other Stories (1879)
[GD426] Penguin pbk **£2.95**
Complete Notebooks
These provide valuable insights into the development of James' craft, and a unique sense of the patterns of his creative impulse.
[GD427] Oxford hbk **£25.00**
Daisy Miller & Other Stories (1878)
The truly innocent Daisy and her entrancing personality has always made this one of the more popular shorter novels.
[GD428] Oxford pbk **£1.75**
English Hours (Travel, 1905)
[GD429] Oxford pbk **£2.95**
In The Cage & Other Stories
[GD430] Penguin pbk **£3.99**
Novels 1871 - 1880: Watch and Ward/Roderick Hudson/The American/The Europeans
[GD431] Cambridge hbk **£30.00**
Roderick Hudson (1876)
An early novel that appears to carry the rather harsh moral that an artist, in this case a young American sculptor, must put his art before his emotions.
[GD432] Oxford pbk **£2.50**
[GD433] Penguin pbk **£3.95**
Selected Tales
[GD434] Dent pbk **£2.75**
The Ambassadors (1903)
One of the last three major novels, and James' personal favourite. Lambert Strether is sent to Paris to secure a fellow American's return to his family in New England.
[GD435] Bodley hbk **£10.95**
[GD436] Penguin pbk **£3.95**
[GD437] Oxford pbk **£3.50**
The American (1877)
[GD438] Penguin pbk **£3.99**
The American Scene (Travel, 1907)
[GD439] Granville pbk **£5.95**
The Aspern Papers & Other Stories (1888)
James wrote about 200 stories, and the title story to this collection is one of the most successful.
[GD440] Oxford pbk **£1.95**
The Aspern Papers/The Turn of the Screw (1888, 1898)
[GD441] Penguin pbk **£2.99**
The Awkward Age (1899)
[GD442] Bodley hbk **£10.95**
[GD443] Penguin pbk **£3.95**
[GD444] Penguin pbk **£3.95**
The Bostonians (1886)
The central character of this novel, unusually set in America, is a beautiful and gifted young girl who finds herself torn between the attractions of marriage and the feminist cause.
[GD445] Bodley hbk **£10.95**
[GD446] Penguin pbk **£2.99**
[GD447] Oxford pbk **£2.95**

The Critical Muse: Selected Literary Criticism
[GD448] Penguin pbk **£6.95**
The Europeans (1878)
Reversing James' usual formula, this short novel finds the sophisticated Europeans in mid-19th century New England, where their presence creates certain problems.
[GD449] Penguin pbk **£1.99**
[GD450] Oxford pbk **£1.50**
The Europeans/Washington Square (1878, 1880)
[GD451] Bodley hbk **£10.95**
The Figure in the Carpet & Other Stories (1896)
[GD452] Penguin pbk **£4.95**
The Golden Bowl (1904)
Graham Greene hailed this, James' last completed novel, a 'poetic masterpiece'. The subtle exploration of the intricacies of two couples' intertwined relationships shows a major novelist writing at the height of his powers.
[GD453] Bodley hbk **£9.95**
[GD454] Penguin pbk **£3.95**
[GD455] Oxford pbk **£3.50**
The Great Short Novels of Henry James
Ten of James' best short novels, including *The Turn of the Screw* and *Daisy Miller*.
[GD456] Robinson pbk **£7.99**
The Portable Henry James
A useful selection of James' various writings, including stories, letters and criticism.
[GD457] Penguin pbk **£5.95**
The Portrait of a Lady (1881)
Probably the finest work of James' middle period, and one of the few with which he achieved contemporary success. A substantial and satisfying novel.
[GD458] Bodley hbk **£9.95**
[GD459] Penguin pbk **£3.50**
[GD460] Oxford pbk **£3.50**
The Princess Casamassima (1886)
[GD461] Bodley hbk **£7.50**
[GD462] Penguin pbk **£5.99**
The Spoils of Poynton (1897)
A relatively short novel about the corrupting effects of an excessive commitment to beauty.
[GD463] Bodley hbk **£10.95**
[GD464] Oxford pbk **£2.95**
[GD465] Penguin pbk **£2.95**
The Tragic Muse (1890)
[GD466] Penguin pbk **£6.95**
The Turn of the Screw (1898)
The famous tale of the ghostly haunting of two children; mysterious and impressive.
[GD467] Dent pbk **£2.95**
The Wings of the Dove (1902)
The third of James' final masterpieces, as intricate as the other two in its depiction of the complexities of human relationships, but a more accessible tale of the evils of human manipulation.
[GD468] Bodley hbk **£10.95**
[GD469] Oxford pbk **£2.95**
[GD470] Penguin pbk **£3.95**
Washington Square (1881)
A fine short novel, and a rather melancholy one too; plain but rich Catherine Sloper has only one suitor, who her father refuses to accept is anything other than an opportunist.
[GD471] Penguin pbk **£2.25**
[GD472] Oxford pbk **£1.95**
What Maisie Knew (1897)
In modern parlance, Maisie is a 'tug-of-love' child, and this artfully ambiguous short novel is told from her point of view.
[GD473] Bodley hbk **£10.95**
[GD474] Oxford pbk **£1.95**
[GD475] Penguin pbk **£2.99**

The Tales of Henry James Vol 1: 1864 - 1869
Unfortunately the middle volume is now out of print.
[GD476] Oxford hbk **£30.00**
Vol 2: 1875 - 1879
[GD477] Oxford hbk **£45.00**

JOHNSON, JOYCE

Author of the classic *Minor Characters*, an account of her love affair with Jack Kerouac.
In the Night Cafe (1989) **NEW**
A tale of lost sons and absent fathers told from a woman's point of view. In 60s Greenwich Village, Joanna meets the love of her life, an artist separated from his own children. He tells her his tale of New York in the 20s, the time of his own abandonment. A spirited and affecting love story.
[GD478] Collins hbk **£11.95**

KAUFFMAN, JANET

Collaborators (1989) **NEW**
The collaborators of the title are the extraordinary Andrea and her capricious mother, who live in a rural Pennsylvanian religious community. When Andrea's mother is silenced by a stroke, their roles appear to reverse.
[GD479] Cape hbk **£10.95**

KEILLOR, GARRISON (1942 -)

'The best humorous writer to come out of America since James Thurber', according to Paul Bailey. Keillor perfected his very own laconic style through years of live radio work, which lends his writing a touching, conversational tone.
Happy To Be Here (1987)
A wonderfully funny collection of short pieces originally written for the *New Yorker*, the best of them radiating Keillor's wry love for common humanity.
[GD480] Faber pbk **£3.95**
Lake Wobegon Days (1985)
The novel of life in a Minnesotan small-town inspired by his radio show, a fantastic bestseller both here and in the US; justly so, for it is a masterpiece.
[GD481] Faber hbk **£9.95**
[GD482] Faber pbk **£3.99**
Leaving Home (1988)
A collection of Lake Wobegon stories.
[GD483] Faber hbk **£10.95**
[GD484] Faber pbk **£3.99**
We Are Still Married (1989) **NEW**
A further collection of what can only be called vintage Keillor: tales of love lost and found, letters on marriage, and reflections on the art of sitting.
[GD485] Faber hbk **£11.99**

John Irving, author of *A Prayer for Owen Meany* (Bloomsbury hbk £12.95)

KENNEDY, WILLIAM (1928 -)
Kennedy is one of those American novelists who has made a part of the US entirely his own by immersing himself in its history, and recreating it in his novels.
Quinn's Book (1988)
The memorable journal of a man living in mid-19th century Albany.
[GD486] Picador pbk **£4.99**
The Ink Truck (1975)
His first novel about an unsuccessful newspaper strike.
[GD487] Penguin pbk **£3.99**
THE ALBANY TRILOGY
Legs (1976)
The first of the cycle evokes the career of the legendary gangster Jack 'Legs' Diamond.
[GD488] Penguin pbk **£3.95**
Billy Phelan's Greatest Game (1983)
The story of Billy Phelan, pool hustler and poker player.
[GD489] Penguin pbk **£3.95**
Ironweed (1984)
Pulitzer Prize winner. An ex-ball player, hitting rock bottom, returns to Albany to make peace with his ghosts.
[GD490] Penguin pbk **£3.95**

KEROUAC, JACK (1922 - 1969)
Kerouac was the 'new Buddha of American prose' whose pursuit of joy and saintliness made him a legend and led to his early death. Recorded in the Duluoz Legend (the name he gave to his interlinked novels) are the spiritual adventures of a generation. His wonderfully melodic novels are celebratory tales of the joy of life, unexpected and fleeting.
Increasingly disillusioned by the world, Kerouac's later work deals beautifully with his search for spiritual peace.
Big Sur (1962)
Possibly Kerouac's finest achievement. A harrowing account of a public, wounded man seeking privacy and peace. The opening account of his arrival at Ferlinghetti's Big Sur cottage is quite unlike anything else in American literature.
[GD491] Grafton pbk **£2.50**
Book of Dreams (1961)
Revealing record of Kerouac's dreams and nightmares, composed on waking.
[GD492] City Lights pbk **£2.95**
Desolation Angels (1965)
[GD493] Grafton pbk **£2.95**
Doctor Sax (Faust Part III) (1959)
[GD494] Grafton pbk **£1.95**
Lonesome Traveller (1960)
[GD495] Grafton pbk **£2.50**
Maggie Cassidy (1974)
[GD496] Deutsch hbk **£6.95**
On the Road (1957)
The classic expression of beat, a journey in search of meaning and fulfilment. Jack's wandering trail across America with Neal Cassady becomes a moving tale of self-discovery, at once joyous and sad.
[GD497] Deutsch hbk **£7.95**
[GD498] Penguin pbk **£3.95**
The Dharma Bums (1965)
Poetic account of Kerouac's pursuit of Zen truths with poet Gary Snyder.
[GD499] Grafton pbk **£2.99**
Vanity of Duluoz (1968)
[GD500] Grafton pbk **£1.95**

KESEY, KEN (1935 -)
Involved in the drug scene throughout the sixties after the US Government gave him his first taste of LSD (for experimental purposes), Kesey has always been a maverick character (see Tom Wolfe's account of their trip across the States in Kesey's Magic Bus, *The Electric Kool-Aid Acid Test*), now apparently reformed.

Demon Box (1986)
The life story of Devlin Deboree told in a succession of linked stories, poems and essays.
[GD501] Methuen pbk **£3.95**
One Flew Over the Cuckoo's Nest (1962)
Celebrated and moving novel about the liberation of the inmates from a mental institution, and from the repressive tyranny of the staff; later filmed
[GD502] Boyars hbk **£8.95**
[GD503] Picador pbk **£3.99**
Sometimes a Great Notion (1964)
His second novel, a macabre comedy centred around a logging community in Oregon.
[GD504] Methuen pbk **£4.95**

KING, FLORENCE (1936 -)
Confessions of a Failed Southern Lady (1985)
Her grandmother's determination to bring her up a perfect Southern Lady is foiled by her own daughter's addiction to baseball, cigarettes and sinful language. A wonderfully comic novel, straight from the horse's mouth.
[GD505] Transworld pbk **£3.99**
Southern Ladies and Gentlemen NEW (1989)
Further humorous escapades.
[GD506] Transworld pbk **£3.99**

KINGSTON, MAXINE HONG (1940 -)
Award-winning Chinese American writer from California.
China Men
[GD507] Picador pbk **£3.95**
The Woman Warrior
[GD508] Picador pbk **£3.95**
Tripmaster Monkey: His Fake Book (1989) NEW
Wittman Ah Sing is a Chinese American hipster poet who wanders the streets of San Francisco in the 60s, quoting Rilke, falling in love, and dreaming of literary celebrity. This word-spinning novel is his chronicle: an alternative American Dream.
[GD509] Picador hbk **£12.95**

KINSELLA, W.P. (Canada, 1935 -)
Kinsella inserts real events into subtle fantasies in which he tries to correct wrongs of the past, symbolizing his immense sympathy for the 'underdog'. This is visible in his early works, where the narrator is often a North American Indian who grows up to understand the omnipotent white man's humourless, repressive and, compared with his own, spiritless culture.
Shoeless Joe
[GD510] Allison & B hbk **£11.95**

KITTREDGE, WILLIAM
Kittredge turned to writing after the Oregon farm that he grew up on and subsequently managed was sold. He is a fine and much admired story-teller, concerned with the American West and its inhabitants.
We Are Not in This Together (Stories)
Introduced by Raymond Carver.
[GD511] Graywolf pbk **£5.95**

KORDA, MICHAEL
The Fortune (1989) NEW
Another blockbusting novel of family intrigue, centering around the vast legacy of one of the super-rich, Arthur Bannerman.
[GD512] Collins hbk **£12.95**

KOSINSKI, JERZY (1933 -)
Born in Poland and raised in Russia, Kosinski came to New York without being able to speak English. The world he found and portrays in his writing is the one we often choose not to see.

Being There (1971)
The fable of the mild-mannered and uneducated gardener who becomes a national leader wholly by chance, beautifully portrayed in the cinema by Peter Sellers.
[GD513] Transworld pbk **£2.95**
Cockpit (1975)
An ex-spy's lonely search for intimacy through sex.
[GD514] Arrow pbk **£1.60**

KRAMER, LARRY
Faggots (1980)
Hilarious gay novel from the author of the acclaimed play *The Normal Heart*.
[GD515] Methuen pbk **£3.95**

KRANTZ, JUDITH
Bestselling author of blockbusters set in the glamorous world of big business.
I'll Take Manhattan
[GD516] Transworld pbk **£3.99**
Mistral's Daughter
[GD517] Transworld pbk **£2.95**
Princess Daisy
[GD518] Transworld pbk **£3.99**
Scruples
[GD519] Futura pbk **£3.99**

LARDNER, RING (1885 - 1933)
Initially a journalist, Lardner's first works drew on his sportswriting background. He went on to write a large number of short stories whose groundbreaking use of vernacular American English fills them with deadpan humour, and strongly influenced both Hemingway and Salinger.
The Best Short Stories of Ring Lardner
Perhaps the better of the two selections available.
[GD520] Picador pbk **£4.95**
The Best of Ring Lardner
Introduced by David Lodge.
[GD521] Dent pbk **£2.95**

LARSEN, NELLA (1893 - 1963)
Quicksand/Passing (1928, 1929) NEW
The two ground-breaking novels that made Larsen the toast of the Harlem Renaissance, now re-issued. "Novels that I will never forget." (Alice Walker)
[GD522] Serpent's Tail pbk **£7.95**

LAURENCE, MARGARET (Canada, 1926 - 1987)
Laurence at first appears to be Canada's prairie novelist, but in fact transcends the borders of Manitoba, and indeed, in her African stories, the whole of Canada. Her four Canadian novels are all linked to the town of Manawaka, which is a fusion of the many prairie towns overshadowed by their Scots-Presbyterian founders. Central to each is a strongly-conceived woman character who battles against societal forces and bad marriages to arrive at a fuller, but by no means simple, realization of life's meaning.
A Jest of God (1966)
Rachel is lonely, spiritually trapped by her demanding, invalid mother. She grows desperate to move, in any way: emotionally, or socially. The film *Rachel, Rachel* (Joanne Woodward, Paul Newman) was based on this novel.
[GD523] Virago pbk **£4.99**
The Diviners (1974)
Morag Gunn looks back on the many incidents of her life: a painful adolescence on the Manitoba prairies; flight from marriage to writing fiction; time in England and Scotland; and finally, to a final realization about someone she dearly loves.
[GD524] Virago pbk **£5.99**
The Fire-Dwellers (1969)
Stacey, forty-ish, finds herself wanting out: initially, out of her marriage to a salesman, but then out of the nagging indecision over whether she should throw

away her present incarnation and flee. Will it be self-rescue, will she one day understand herself?
[GD525] Virago pbk **£4.99**
The Stone Angel (1964)
The aged Hagar Shipley surveys her long, full life, retreating from the present, endless bickering between her son and his wife. She looks back on her failures, past thoughts and experiences, and slowly comes to terms with her own impending mortality.
[GD526] Virago pbk **£4.99**

LEACOCK, STEPHEN (Canada, 1869 - 1944)
Central to Leacock's work was the belief that Anglo-Saxon humour was the irrefutable sign of society's progress, a clear indication of his place among Victorians. He wrote many kind, but gently prodding short stories depicting the idiosyncrasies of small-town Ontario society. But he also wrote more serious collections which, though still humorous, remain more soberly critical, one in particular directed at the United States.
Moonbeams from a Larger Lunacy (1915)
[GD527] A Sutton pbk **£2.95**
Penguin Stephen Leacock
[GD528] Penguin pbk **£2.95**

LEAVITT, DAVID
A young writer who is becoming increasingly popular, not the least for his depiction of homosexual relationships in the context of family life.
Equal Affections (1989)   **NEW**
An intimate portrait of a family struggling to come to terms with the death of their matriach Louise, as observed by Danny, her homosexual son and successful lawyer. Leavitt once again proves himself a master dissector of domestic life.
[GD529] Viking hbk **£11.95**
Family Dancing (1985)
This first collection of stories was acclaimed for its assurance and maturity in confronting what lies beneath the veneer of domestic life.
[GD530] Penguin pbk **£3.95**
The Lost Language of Cranes (1987)
Set in New York, this is a story of a young man's struggle to get his parents to accept his gay sexuality, and of the problems of their own relationship.
[GD531] Penguin pbk **£4.99**

LERNER, JONATHON
Caught in a Still Place (1989)   **NEW**
A quiet and thoughtful account of four survivors of an America destroyed by plague.
[GD532] Serpent's Tail pbk **£5.95**

LEVINE, NORMAN (Canada, 1923 -)
Levine has written for forty years about the 'underside' of Canadian life, deliberately ignoring the superficial changes during the period in which Canada 'grew up'. He attacks the complacency brought on by the immense wealth which has carried this change, and often creates lone figures (in many instances writers), who move under the surface of the urban monolith, delving deeply into the nature of simple, isolating poverty.
Thin Ice (Stories, 1979)
Semi-autobiographical fiction in which he examines both the ease and difficulty of close family life, using in detail the patterns of day-to-day existence to show how life perpetually involves the impulse to decipher the past.
[GD533] Wildwood Ho hbk **£5.95**

LEWIS, SINCLAIR (1885 - 1951)
The first American writer to win the Nobel Prize for Literature (in 1930), Lewis is known for his satirical critiques of Mid Western life. He was a life-long socialist with a keen political awareness and a loathing of hypocrisy.

Babbitt (1922)
The eponymous hero of this minor classic finds himself trapped by his own success as a small businessman: an examination of middle American values.
[GD534] Penguin pbk **£4.99**
Elmer Gantry (1927)
Introduced by Paul Bailey. A remarkable novel attacking revivalist preachers that still hits home.
[GD535] Oxford pbk **£3.95**
Main Street (1920)
Introduced by Malcolm Bradbury. Perhaps Lewis' most universal novel, as the smalltown pettiness that he satirises is not a peculiarly American phenomenon.
[GD536] Penguin pbk **£5.99**

LONDON, JACK (1876 - 1916)
Another great American writer whose canonization has obscured his active socialism. Although his depictions of the rugged outdoor life are justly famous for their universal appeal, his other works reveal a man troubled by his times, and by his own journey from lawless vagrant to millionaire author.
Martin Eden (1909)
A semi-autobiographical novel of a poor writer struggling to win the love of a woman by winning fame and fortune.
[GD537] Penguin pbk **£3.95**
Tales of the Pacific   **NEW**
[GD538] Penguin pbk **£4.99**
The Call of the Wild & Other Stories (1903)
[GD539] Penguin pbk **£2.99**
The Call of the Wild/White Fang/The Sea-Wolf/Klondike & Other Stories (1903 - 06)
The first two novels are both about dogs, one wild who becomes domesticated, the other reversing this process. *The Sea-Wolf* is a sealing adventure with an ambitious theme.
[GD540] Cambridge hbk **£7.95**
The People of the Abyss/The Road/The Iron Heel/Martin Eden/John Barleycorn (1903 - 13)
A fine selection of London's varied work at a bargain price. The first came out of London's trip to London and is a study of the slum conditions he found. *The Iron Heel* is a futuristic novel about resistance to socialism in America, and *John Barleycorn* an autobiographical plea for temperance.
[GD541] Cambridge hbk **£7.95**
The Sea-Wolf & Other Stories   **NEW**
[GD542] Penguin pbk **£4.99**
The Star Rover (1914)
A murderer imprisoned for life transports himself backwards into history through self-induced trances.
[GD543] Sutton pbk **£3.95**

LOOS, ANITA (1893 - 1981)
Fate Keeps On Happening
[GD544] Harrap hbk **£9.95**
Gentlemen Prefer Blondes/But Gentlemen Marry Brunettes (1925, 1928)
Celebrated satirical novel satirizing the Jazz Age, and its sequel.
[GD545] Picador pbk **£3.99**

LURIE, ALISON (1926 -)
A professor herself, Lurie frequently writes sparkling and subtle novels about academics and writers. She receives extravagant acclaim for her work, which has been compared to that of Jane Austen and Truman Capote amongst others.
Foreign Affairs (1985)
Pulitzer Prize Winner. Two American academics visit London and become disorientated in different ways.
[GD546] Sphere pbk **£3.99**

Imaginary Friends (1967)
Two sociologists investigate a religious cult and become more involved than they anticipated.
[GD547] Sphere pbk **£3.99**
Love and Friendship (1962)
[GD548] Sphere pbk **£3.99**
Nowhere City (1965)
[GD549] Sphere pbk **£3.99**
Only Children (1979)
[GD550] Penguin pbk **£3.95**
Real People (1970)
A comic account of the ways of artists.
[GD551] Sphere pbk **£3.99**
The Truth about Lorin Jones (1988)
Her latest work, and probably her best to date, it is a kind of detective novel. An art historian delves into the life of a neglected woman artist, and uncovers some startling information.
[GD552] Sphere pbk **£3.99**
The War between the Tates (1974)
One family's civil war between the sexes and the generations. One of Lurie's best novels.
[GD553] Sphere pbk **£3.99**

MAILER, NORMAN (1923 -)
A Brooklyn child, ex-Army man, Reichian existentialist and public brawler, Mailer made his name and notoriety as much from his defiantly political poses as from his stylistic innovations. Much of his polemic is out of date now, as is his hyper-masculine stance: his best works remain his earliest.
An American Dream (1965)
A lurid and violent depiction of a disintegrating marriage and a corrupt society.
[GD554] Grafton pbk **£3.50**
Ancient Evenings (1983)
Ten years' research went into this massive reconstruction of the age of Rameses IX.
[GD555] Picador pbk **£6.99**
The Deer Park (1955)
A bitter look at America through the lens of Hollywood, memorable for its portrayal of Eitel, the radical film director.
[GD556] Grafton pbk **£2.95**
The Executioner's Song (1979)
Semi-fictional account of the life and death of Gary Gilmour.
[GD557] Arrow pbk **£3.50**
The Naked and the Dead (1948)
Deservedly famous World War II novel.
[GD558] Grafton pbk **£3.95**
Tough Guys Don't Dance (1984)
[GD559] Sphere pbk **£2.99**
Why Are We In Vietnam? (1967)
[GD560] Oxford pbk **£4.95**

MALAMUD, BERNARD (1914 - 1986)
The son of Russian immigrants, Malamud became one of the foremost American Jewish novelists, often using the Jewish experience as a metaphor for the human condition.
A New Life (1961)
[GD561] Penguin pbk **£4.50**
God's Grace (1982)
His last book and a comic masterpiece. One man survives the nuclear holocaust and founds a new civilisation among the chimpanzees.
[GD562] Chatto hbk **£11.95**
[GD563] Penguin pbk **£2.99**
Pictures of Fidelman (1969)
[GD564] Penguin pbk **£3.95**
Selected Stories (1969)
[GD565] Penguin pbk **£4.95**
The Assistant (1957)
This tale of a gentile who works for a Jewish grocer explores a recurring theme in Malamud's work: the longing to start a new life.
[GD566] Chatto hbk **£10.95**
[GD567] Penguin pbk **£3.95**

The Fixer (1966)
Pulitzer Prize Winner. A murder trial set in pre-war Kiev, with anti-semitism in the air.
[GD568] Chatto hbk **£10.95**
[GD569] Penguin pbk **£3.95**
The Natural (1952)
His first novel, which depicts baseball as a realm of American heroism and myth. Much better than the film.
[GD570] Chatto hbk **£10.95**
[GD571] Penguin pbk **£3.95**
The Tenants (1971)
The last tenant in a condemned NY tenement races against time to finish the book he began 10 years ago.
[GD572] Chatto hbk **£10.95**
[GD573] Penguin pbk **£3.99**

MALONE, MICHAEL (1942 -)
Handling Sin (1986)
A huge, rambunctious picaresque novel that has won over many readers with its infectious humour.
[GD574] Sphere pbk **£4.99**
Time's Witness (1989) **NEW**
The irrepressible duo from *Uncivil Seasons* are back, with Cuddy as narrator. A serio-comic thriller and courtroom drama.
[GD575] Chatto hbk **£12.95**
Uncivil Seasons (1984)
A wisecracking detective novel featuring the unlikely duo of Cuddy Mangum, the redneck, and Justin Savile, the gentleman.
[GD576] Sphere pbk **£3.99**

MARKSON, DAVID
Wittgenstein's Mistress (1989) **NEW**
An experimental novel that has attracted rave reviews in the States, narrated by an utterly engaging but mad woman. 'An absolute masterpiece' (Ann Beattie).
[GD577] Cape hbk **£10.95**

MARSHALL, PAULE (1929 -)
Fine contemporary Black writer whose books are often about the experience of growing up.
Brown Girl, Brownstones (1954)
[GD578] Virago pbk **£5.50**
Merle (1983)
A novella and some short stories.
[GD579] Virago pbk **£3.95**
Praisesong for the Widow (1983)
[GD580] Virago pbk **£4.99**

MASON, BOBBIE ANN (1940 -)
Originally a Pennsylvanian, Mason writes of rural Kentucky with moving simplicity and realism. The appearance of two new works this autumn seems set to raise the profile in this country of a sympathetic chronicler of the emotional life of small-town America.
In Country (1986)
Gentle, understated tale of a young girl's reconciliation with her father's death in Vietnam.
[GD581] Flamingo pbk **£3.50**
Love Life (Stories) **NEW**
[GD582] Chatto hbk **£11.95**
Shiloh (1982)
Sixteen remarkably even stories; an impressive debut.
[GD583] Flamingo pbk **£3.95**
Spence + Lila **NEW**
Cancer forces a new perspective on the forty-year marriage of a Southern couple: memories of past life are interwoven with haunting intimations of mortality and surprising flashes of humour, to evoke a deep, largely unspoken, love.
[GD584] Chatto·hbk **£11.95**

MASTERTON, GRAHAM
Blockbusters set in turbulent periods of American history by an author otherwise known for his horror fiction.

Family Portrait
[GD585] Arrow pbk **£3.50**
Famine
[GD586] Sphere pbk **£3.50**
Lady of Fortune
[GD587] Sphere pbk **£3.95**
Maiden Voyage
[GD588] Sphere pbk **£3.99**

MATTHEWS, HARRY
An experimental writer who first made his name in the 1960s with his novel of esoteric riddles, *The Conversions*, subsequently compared with Pynchon, Vonnegut and Barth. He has lived in France for many years.
Cigarettes (1988)
His first novel in a dozen years: a witty, stylish, serio-comic tale.
[GD589] Carcanet hbk **£12.95**
The Conversions (1962)
[GD590] Carcanet pbk **£4.95**
The Sinking of the Odradek Stadium (1984)
[GD591] Grafton pbk **£3.50**
The Way Home: Collected Prose **NEW** (1989)
A collection of Matthews' unpublished writing of the last decade, including his memoir of his close friend George Perec.
[GD592] Atlas pbk **£5.50**
Tlooth
[GD593] Carcanet pbk **£4.95**

MATTHIESSEN, PETER (1927 -)
Better known for his work as a naturalist and travel-writer now, Matthiessen was previously a successful novelist.
At Play in the Fields of the Lord (1966)
A novel that details the despoliation of an Amazon tribe and their culture by missionaries from the Mid West.
[GD594] Collins pbk **£5.95**
Far Tortuga (1975) **NEW**
A resonant and mythical sea-novel, excellently received in the US fourteen years ago, finally published here.
[GD595] Collins pbk **£6.95**
On the River Styx (1989) **NEW**
The first British publication of this ever interesting writer's short stories, spanning his entire writing career from 1951 - 1988 and reflecting his manifold pursuits.
[GD596] Collins hbk **£11.95**

MAUPIN, ARMISTEAD (1944 -)
Developed from his cult series in *The San Francisco Chronicle*, Maupin's delightful novels, published as a sequence, depict the full range of experience available in that city, and show the alterations in mood of a decade in the changing lives of his characters. He writes sensitively about relationships, both straight and gay.
Tales from the City (1978)
The first in the series.
[GD602] Transworld pbk **£3.95**
More Tales of the City (1980)
[GD600] Transworld pbk **£3.95**
Further Tales of the City (1982)
[GD599] Transworld pbk **£3.95**
Babycakes (1984)
[GD598] Transworld pbk **£4.95**
Significant Others (1988)
The latest in Maupin's bittersweet series finds Michael getting over his lover's death, and the devoted lesbian couple Dede and D'Or falling out over another woman.
[GD601] Transworld pbk **£4.99**

An Omnibus: Tales of the City/More Tales/Further Tales **NEW**
The first three books of the remarkable *Tales* series, the sixth and last of which, titled *Sure of You*, will be a novel to look forward to later in 1990.
[GD597] Chatto hbk **£14.95**

MCCARTHY, CORMAC (1933 -)
A highly acclaimed Southern writer who is often compared to Faulkner, McCarthy writes lyrically and beautifully of madness, violence, and dignified solitude. These three novels mark the first appearance of his work in this country. 'Cormac McCarthy very well may, I believe, be America's greatest writer.' (Stanley Booth).
Blood Meridian, or, The Evening Redness in the West (1989) **NEW**
The bloody story of 'the Kid', who joins a band of mercenaries journeying across the American West. Starting in some legitimacy, the travellers' excesses lead finally to a Hellish descent into violence.
[GD603] Picador hbk **£11.95**
Child of God (1974) **NEW**
This is the truly horrifying tale of Lester Ballard who, psychologically unbalanced, haunts the backwoods of East Tennessee.
[GD604] Picador pbk **£3.99**
Suttree (1979) **NEW**
Cornelius Suttree chooses to live his life on a ramshackle houseboat by Knoxville, Tennessee, in an outcast community of misfits. A prodigious novel, *Suttree* is long and stunningly written (in turns blackly comic and unbearably sad), and is the closest to autobiography McCarthy has come.
[GD605] Picador pbk **£5.99**

MCCARTHY, MARY (1912 -)
Best known for her satirical social commentaries, McCarthy is also a learned and witty campus novelist. Look under *Biography* for her highly amusing volumes of autobiography.
Birds of America (1971)
Strained relations between a mother and her son.
[GD606] Weidenfeld hbk **£8.95**
The Group (1963)
Perhaps her most famous novel; the misadventures of eight Vassar graduates.
[GD607] Penguin pbk **£4.50**
The Groves of Academe (1952)
A satirical portrait of life at a liberal women's college.
[GD608] Weidenfeld hbk **£8.95**

MCCLOY, KRISTIN
Velocity (1989) **NEW**
A powerful tale of sexual obsession set in North Carolina, this first novel was fought over by British publishers, perhaps for its unusually frank and skilled writing about sex.
[GD609] Hutchinson hbk **£11.95**
[GD610] Hutchinson pbk **£5.95**

MCCORMACK, ERIC (Canada)
A new writer now making a name for himself, with great rapidity, as an imaginative and Borgesian storyteller.
Inspecting the Vaults (Stories, 1988) **NEW**
Shortlisted for the Commonwealth Writers' Prize, this is a collection of 18 bizarre, often macabre stories.
[GD611] Bloomsbury pbk **£4.99**
The Paradise Motel (1989) **NEW**
A fantastical novel of tall tales within tall tales that has earned McCormack high praise.
[GD612] Bloomsbury hbk **£12.95**

MCCULLERS, CARSON (1917 - 1967)
Highly gifted contemporary of Tennessee Williams and Faulkner. Her poetic, finely tuned tales of suffering and loneliness make her an almost unbearably sensitive storyteller, a sensivity born of a

long, wasting illness. Her Georgia landscapes are peopled by a collection of misfits with whom she clearly identified.

Clock without Hands (1961)
[GD613] Penguin pbk **£3.95**
Reflections in a Golden Eye (1941)
A macabre story set in a Southern army camp before the war.
[GD614] Penguin pbk **£3.99**
The Ballad of the Sad Café (1951)
Along with six short stories, here is a word-perfect novella of love and revenge in a small town.
[GD615] Penguin pbk **£3.95**
The Heart is a Lonely Hunter (1940)
Her famous first novel is an atmospheric, moving story of a disparate group of misfits and their responses to a gentle deaf mute, in whom McCullers fashioned one of the most endearing yet sad free spirits in American fiction.
[GD616] Hutchinson hbk **£11.95**
[GD617] Penguin pbk **£4.99**
The Member of the Wedding (1946)
Humorous and delicate novel of one weekend in the life of a 12 year old tomboy.
[GD618] Penguin pbk **£3.95**
The Mortgaged Heart (Non fiction, 1971)
[GD619] Penguin pbk **£3.95**

MCGRATH, THOMAS
This Coffin Has No Handles (1947)
A classic novel of the struggle between capital and labour, never before published. Set on the New York waterfront, it is both a magnificent document of social history and a moving celebration of ordinary people's lives.
[GD620] Thundermouth pbk **£6.95**

MCGUANE, THOMAS (1939 -)
One of the finest contemporary novelists in America but unfortunately badly under-represented here. He is fêted for the dazzling virtuosity of his prose style, as displayed in his earlier novels.
Something To Be Desired (1985)
McGuane's sixth novel is the story of Lucien who abandons his family and job to come to the aid of an old sweetheart hoping that this will fill the emptiness of his life.
[GD621] Arena pbk **£2.95**
To Skin a Cat (Stories, 1987)
[GD622] Secker hbk **£10.95**

MCINERNEY, JAY
The first, and the best, of the 'brat-pack' writers, as famous for his fame as for his books.
Bright Lights, Big City (1985)
The quintessential comic novel of trendy NY nightlife, fêted and filmed.
[GD623] Flamingo pbk **£3.50**
Ransom (1986)
The 'serious' second novel, set in Japan.
[GD624] Flamingo pbk **£3.50**
Story of My Life
The world of the young rich - sex, drugs and credit cards - is laid bare by one of its own in a hilarious monologue.
[GD625] Penguin pbk **£3.99**

MCMURTRY, LARRY
Highly successful Texan writer of very readable cowboy stories now being republished here. Later responsible for *Terms of Endearment*.
Anything for Billy **NEW**
This wholly satisfying and amusing new novel from McMurtry tells the story of Billy (the Bone) kid and his adventures, in the words of Sippy, a dime novelist who has forsaken his family for a taste of the 'real' Wild West. However, he finds more than he had bargained for...
[GD626] Collins hbk **£11.95**

Horseman, Pass By (1961)
The inspiration for the classic Paul Newman film *Hud*.
[GD627] Pan pbk **£3.50**
Leaving Cheyenne (1963)
Three interlocked friends, three interlinked narratives.
[GD628] Pan pbk **£3.50**
Lonesome Dove (1985)
The gigantic Western epic set in the 1880s, the film of which has been the surprise smash of Hollywood this year.
[GD629] Pan pbk **£5.95**
Texasville (1987)
'This is oil country and McMurtry gushes crude.' (*The New Yorker*)
[GD630] Pan pbk **£4.99**
The Last Picture Show
[GD631] Pan pbk **£3.99**

MCPHERSON, WILLIAM
Testing the Current (1985)
The ordered, pre-war world of a Mid Western childhood, lovingly evoked.
[GD632] Grafton pbk **£3.95**
To the Sargasso Sea (1988)
A partial continuation of McPherson's first novel finds a couple embarking on a second honeymoon.
[GD633] Heinemann hbk **£10.95**

MELVILLE, HERMAN (1819 - 1891)
Although now considered one of the truly great figures of American literature, Melville spent most of his life in public disfavour if not total obscurity (he worked as an outdoor customs inspector for the last 19 years of his life). The novels he published during the 1840s did win him considerable acclaim, but it was the neglect of the triumphant *Moby-Dick* that hastened his disaffection for the novel; he turned instead to short stories and poetry. His adventurous early life aboard whaling ships and in the South Seas formed the inspiration for much of his early work.
Billy Budd & Other Stories
The famous novella was written just before Melville's death, and remained unpublished until the reappraisal of his work began in the 1920s. His short stories are amongst his best work after *Moby-Dick*.
[GD634] Penguin pbk **£3.99**
Moby-Dick, or, The Whale
Dedicated to his friend Hawthorne, Moby Dick is truly innovative in its stylistic departures. The adventure narrative is spliced throughout with Melville's knowledge of whale lore, making it a compelling and intellectual work.
[GD635] Oxford pbk **£3.95**
[GD636] Penguin pbk **£4.99**
Omoo: Adventures in the South Seas (1847)
A fictionalized account of Melville's time in Tahiti.
[GD637] Routledge pbk **£6.95**
Redburn (1849)
The experiences, often harrowing, of a boy on his first sea voyage and in London.
[GD638] Penguin pbk **£4.95**
Redburn/White-Jacket/Moby-Dick
Some 1,500 pages of Melville's best in the beautiful Library of America series, now vastly reduced in price. *White-Jacket* (1850) is an account of his time on a man-of-war, and a criticism of the conditions he endured.
[GD639] Cambridge hbk **£7.95**
Typee (1846)
His first novel that was based on his experiences among the savage and cannibalistic Marquesas islanders.
[GD640] Penguin pbk **£3.99**

Typee/Omoo/Mardi
Mardi (1849) is one of Melville's more complex works, being a mixture of South Seas adventure and an allegorical exploration of the mid-19th century world.
[GD641] Cambridge hbk **£7.95**

MICHENER, JAMES (1907 -)
International author of immensely popular historical novels; massive in length, they are the fruit of extensive research.
Alaska (1988)
[GD642] Transworld pbk **£4.99**
Centennial
[GD643] Transworld pbk **£4.95**
Chesapeake (1978)
The story of the history, people and wildlife of Chesapeake Bay.
[GD644] Transworld pbk **£4.95**
Hawaii (1959)
[GD645] Transworld pbk **£4.95**
Journey (1989) **NEW**
Five men attempt to make the hazardous trip to the Klondike Gold Rush in 1897 across the most inhospitable terrain.
[GD646] Secker hbk **£12.95**
Poland (1983)
Still topical, this is the story of the union leader pitted against the politicians.
[GD647] Transworld pbk **£4.95**
Sayonara (1954)
[GD648] Transworld pbk **£2.50**
Space
[GD649] Transworld pbk **£3.95**
Tales of the South Pacific (1947)
Pulitzer Prize Winner that formed the basis of the Rodgers and Hammerstein musical.
[GD650] Transworld pbk **£2.95**
Texas
[GD651] Transworld pbk **£4.95**
The Caribbean (1989) **NEW**
Another of Michener's massive and triumphant blends of fact and fiction spanning six hundred years of the Caribbean from Columbus to Castro.
[GD652] Secker hbk **£14.95**
The Covenant
South African history forms the fabric for this, one of Michener's best books.
[GD653] Transworld pbk **£3.95**

MILLER, ARTHUR (1915 -)
The only novel by the influential American dramatist.
Focus (1945)
A gentile who looks like a Jew discovers how prevalent anti-semitic prejudice is.
[GD654] Penguin pbk **£3.95**

MILLER, HENRY (1891 - 1980)
Miller's work, first and best appreciated in Europe, is a fearless quest for personal and literary freedom, marked for their explicit sexuality and grotesque humour. As a result, many of his books were banned for decades in Britain and the US. Although early critics such as Orwell acclaimed his writing, recognition as a major writer came late.
A Henry Miller Reader
Edited by John Calder.
[GD655] Picador pbk **£3.95**
Black Spring (1936)
[GD656] Grafton pbk **£2.99**
Nexus (1960)
The last part of *The Rosy Crucifixion* trilogy based on his early life.
[GD657] Grafton pbk **£3.50**
Opus Pistorum
[GD658] Star pbk **£2.25**
Plexus (1953)
Second part of the trilogy.
[GD659] Grafton pbk **£2.95**

Arthur Miller, author of *Focus* (Penguin pbk £3.95)

Quiet Days in Clichy
[GD660] Allison & B pbk **£3.99**
Sexus (1949)
First part of the trilogy.
[GD661] Grafton pbk **£3.50**
The Air Conditioned Nightmare
(1945)
A travelogue of Miller's travels in America, showing the full and hilarious nature of his disgust for the falsity and 'cleanliness' of his homeland.
[GD662] Grafton pbk **£2.50**
Tropic of Cancer (1934)
The first part of Miller's intense personal narrative in the form of the emotional and intellectual life of an American expatriate in Paris in the 1920s.
[GD663] Grafton pbk **£3.50**
Tropic of Capricorn (1939)
[GD664] Grafton pbk **£3.50**

MILLER, RICHARD
Squed (1989)   NEW
A delirious black comedy in which the hero finds himself on the Other Side; while his fate hangs in the balance, he witnesses some of the more bizarre goings-on of this alternative world. An outlandish satire on America.
[GD665] Bloomsbury pbk **£7.99**

MILLER, SUE (1943 -)
Inventing the Abbotts (Stories, 1987)
[GD666] Gollancz hbk **£10.95**
The Good Mother (1986)
A very gifted novel that examines (far better than did the film) the conflicting desires - erotic and maternal - of a divorced woman with a young child and a new lover.
[GD667] Pan pbk **£3.99**

MINER, VALERIE
A powerful and compelling feminist author.
All Good Women (1987)
[GD668] Methuen pbk **£3.95**
Blood Sisters (1981)
A powerful political tale about the IRA.
[GD669] Methuen pbk **£3.95**
Movement (1982)
A decade of feminist agitation in four different countries.
[GD670] Methuen pbk **£3.50**
Winter's Edge (1984)
[GD671] Methuen pbk **£2.95**

MINOT, SUSAN
Monkeys (1986)
The luminous prose of this minimalist novel poetically evokes a Mid Western childhood.
[GD672] Flamingo pbk **£3.50**

MITCHELL, MARGARET (1900 - 1949)
Georgia journalist whose sole book made publishing history; 50,000 copies were sold in one day. The subsequent film version only enhanced the book's unparalleled popularity.
Gone with the Wind (1936)
Pulitzer Prize Winner. One of the earliest and best of the blockbusters: the Civil War seen from the point of view of the middle class of the Old South.
[GD673] Macmillan hbk **£14.95**
[GD674] Pan pbk **£5.95**

MONROE, MARY
A new Afro-American writer who began picking cotton at the age of four and writing one year later.
The Upper Room   NEW
A vivid tale of healer Mama Ruby's life in the Deep South.
[GD675] Allison & B pbk **£3.99**

MOORE, LORRIE (1957 -)
Another of the rising stars in the modern literary firmament to have made her mark with skilful short stories. Moore has a rare talent for achieving humour and pathos within a single line, which suggests a superior writer in the making.
Anagrams (1987)
The bruised heroine of this clever first novel tilts at love and loss with wisecracks and witty word-play, but cannot hide her tender heart.
[GD676] Faber pbk **£3.95**
Self-Help (1985)
Nine wry stories that take an ironic and compassionate look at the plight of the single woman. Highly recommended.
[GD677] Faber pbk **£3.95**

MORRISON, TONI (1931 -)
Immensely popular and acclaimed, Morrison is a poet of the Black experience. Her deep sense of the community of the Deep South is conveyed in a highly original and resonant prose style which always carries a powerful emotional charge.
Beloved (1987)
Pulitzer Prize winning novel about the terrors of slavery and the struggle for freedom. Based on a true story, this is a passionate work of unquestionable greatness.
[GD678] Chatto hbk **£12.95**
[GD679] Picador pbk **£3.99**
Sula (1974)
Two young Black girls grow up together sharing their secrets until Sula breaks away to roam the cities of America.
[GD680] Chatto hbk **£11.95**
[GD681] Grafton pbk **£2.95**
Tar Baby (1981)
A Black graduate and a criminal on the run enter a white millionaire's mansion...
[GD682] Chatto hbk **£10.95**
[GD683] Grafton pbk **£2.95**
The Bluest Eye (1979)
The tragic, torn lives of a poor Black family in 1940s Ohio.
[GD684] Chatto hbk **£10.95**
[GD685] Grafton pbk **£2.95**
The Song of Solomon (1978)
[GD686] Chatto hbk **£10.95**
[GD687] Picador pbk **£4.99**

MUKHERJEE, BHARATI
Middleman and Other Stories   NEW
[GD688] Virago hbk **£11.95**

MUNRO, ALICE (Canada, 1931 -)
Primarily a writer of short stories, Munro could be placed among social realists were it not for the absence of political comment. She uncovers with some intensity the complex web of emotions which accompanies even the most simple lives. The main instrument of this revelation is usually a young female who secretly wants to be an artist, but lives where such aspirations are met with hostility - belief in her difference is not accompanied by sufficient self-assurance, and she continues to fear 'discovery' and the ensuing mockery of her provincial peers. Munro's older women evolve further into an isolation of sorts, while still fighting for identity.
Dance of the Happy Shades
(Stories, 1968)
A collection of short stories, thematically connected by the problems of communication between separate groups of similar people.
[GD689] Penguin pbk **£3.95**
Lives of Girls and Women (1971)
A novel in which a young woman grows up trying to come to terms with social awkwardness and the effects it has on her own life.
[GD690] Penguin pbk **£3.95**
Moons of Jupiter and Other Stories
(Stories,1982)
Further observations of women seeking identity while trying to avoid compromise in social situations.
[GD691] Penguin pbk **£4.50**
Progress of Love (1986)
[GD692] Fontana pbk **£3.95**
Something I've Been Meaning to Tell You (Stories, 1974)
[GD693] Penguin pbk **£3.95**
The Beggar Maid (Stories, 1978)
A collection of short stories in which the very competent and seemingly independent Rose finds difficulty escaping from her dependency on men and the easy identity she derives from active sexuality.
[GD694] Penguin hbk **£3.95**

NABOKOV, VLADIMIR (1899 - 1977)
Chess master, lepidopterist and translator as well as novelist, Nabokov was born in St Petersburg, the son of a liberal politician. Following the Revolution, he spent twenty years of his life in Europe, before making America his home in 1940. His novels (many of them originally written in Russian) are sophisticated and stylish forays into eroticism, morality and modern thought.
A Russian Beauty (Stories, 1973)
[GD695] Penguin pbk **£4.50**
Ada (1969)
A man's obsessional love for his sister Ada.
[GD696] Penguin pbk **£5.95**
Bend Sinister (1947)
His most political novel; a rising tyrant state seeks to destroy all freedom of thought under the slogans of Equality and Community.
[GD697] Penguin pbk **£4.50**
Despair (1965)
[GD698] Penguin pbk **£3.95**
Details of a Sunset (Stories)
[GD699] Weidenfeld **£6.50**
Glory (1932, trans. 1971)
[GD700] Penguin pbk **£3.95**
King, Queen, Knave (1928, trans. 1968)
[GD701] Oxford pbk **£3.95**
Laughter in the Dark (1933, trans. 1938)
[GD702] Penguin pbk **£3.95**
Lolita (1955)
Originally published by Maurice Girodia's Olympia Press in Paris, *Lolita* became an enormous bestseller in the US, having created a furore on publication for its sexual content. It remains one of the most eloquent novels of obsesssional love.
[GD703] Weidenfeld hbk **£8.95**
[GD704] Penguin pbk **£3.50**

Look at the Harlequins (1974)
[GD705] Penguin pbk **£4.50**
Mary (1926, trans. 1970)
His first and most gentle novel is unmistakably
autobiographical, infused with the nostalgia of recent
emigration.
[GD706] Penguin pbk **£3.50**
Nabokov's Dozen (Stories, 1958)
[GD707] Penguin pbk **£3.95**
Pale Fire (1962)
An elaborate and lucid novel which consists of a
poem in four cantos by a famous and recently
murdered American poet with preface, notes and
index by his posthumous editor.
[GD708] Penguin pbk **£4.99**
Pnin (1957)
[GD709] Penguin pbk **£3.95**
Speak, Memory
A glorious evocation of Nabokov's childhood in
Imperialist Russia.
[GD710] Penguin pbk **£4.99**
The Defence (1930, trans. 1964)
A skilfully manipulative and poetic novel based on a
chess defence.
[GD711] Oxford pbk **£3.95**
The Enchanter (1987)
A recently discovered early novella which bears
considerable similarity to the fanciful eroticism of
Lolita.
[GD712] Picador pbk **£2.95**
The Gift (1937, trans. 1963)
The story of a young writer living in Berlin in the
1920s.
[GD713] Penguin pbk **£4.95**
Transparent Things (1971)
[GD714] Penguin pbk **£3.50**
Tyrants Destroyed (Stories, 1981)
[GD715] Weidenfeld hbk **£5.50**

NAYLOR, GLORIA
A young Black writer who has won acclaim for her
insight into the experience of Black people.
Linden Hills (1985)
[GD716] Methuen pbk **£3.95**
Mama Day (1988)
An 80 year old descendent of an African slave
inherits strange insights into the past and the future.
[GD717] Hutchinson hbk **£10.95**
The Women of Brewster Place (1983)
This collection of linked short stories won the 1983
American Book Award.
[GD718] Methuen pbk **£3.95**

NICHOLS, JOHN
The Milagro Beanfield War (1974)
Now filmed by Robert Redford, a novel of conflict
between Mexican workers and American capitalists.
[GD719] Arrow pbk **£3.95**

NIN, ANAIS (1903 - 1977)
Poetic and sensual novelist, remembered for her
erotic descriptions of women's sexuality and her
study of relationships. She lived in Paris between the
wars, traning as a psychoanalyst, associating with
other writers such as Henry Miller and Lawrence
Durrell, in a full life recorded in her voluminous
diaries. The collection of stories *Under a Glass Bell*
provides a good introduction to the quality and tone
of her writing, now undergoing re-appraisal.
A Woman Speaks (1975)
[GD720] Star pbk **£1.60**
Cities of the Interior (1965)
[GD721] P Owen pbk **£15.95**
Collages (1964)
[GD722] Quartet Pbk **£1.50**
Delta of Venus (1968)
[GD723] Star pbk **£2.99**
Henry and June
[GD724] Star pbk **£2.99**

In Favour of the Sensitive Man (Essays)
[GD725] Star pbk **£1.50**
Little Birds (1979)
[GD726] Star pbk **£2.50**
Novel of the Future (1968)
[GD727] P Owen hbk **£11.95**
Spy in the House of Love (1954)
[GD728] Penguin pbk **£3.50**
Under a Glass Bell (1944)
[GD729] P Owen hbk **£10.95**
[GD730] Penguin pbk **£3.50**
Winter of Artifice (1961)
[GD731] Quartet pbk **£1.50**

NORRIS, FRANK (1870 - 1902)
Strongly influenced by Zola, Norris believed that the
naturalistic novel was a powerful tool for showing
mankind to itself. His *Epic of Wheat* trilogy,
unfinished at his early death, aimed to show the
disparate areas connected by a single commodity.
McTeague: A Story of San Francisco
(1899)
A dramatic story of love and revenge, this must be
one of the only novels to have a dentist (albeit
unlicensed) as a hero. Filmed by von Stroheim as
Greed.
[GD732] Penguin pbk **£4.99**
Novels and Essays
[GD733] Cambridge hbk **£7.95**
The Octopus (1901)
The first part of Norris' unfinished trilogy; a bitter
and realistic tale of how the powerful state railroad -
the Octopus - strangles the wheat farmers of
California.
[GD734] Penguin pbk **£4.99**

O'BRIEN, DAN
Spirit of the Hills (1989)   `NEW`
A gutsy first novel that intertwines the fortunes of
three characters, a Vietnam vet, a wolf trapper, and a
Sioux girl, in a tale of murder and revenge set in the
mysterious Black Hills of South Dakota.
[GD735] Collins hbk **£11.95**

O'BRIEN, TIM
A young novelist of much promise, who has written
powerfully of contemporary issues, including the
Vietnam war.
Going After Cacciato (1988)
Winner of the National Book Award. This novel
springs from O'Brien's own experiences in the
Vietnam war, and is a remarkable journey through
war and peace.
[GD736] Fontana pbk **£3.95**
If I Die in a Combat Zone (1973)
The Vietnam war and nuclear age provide this
powerful drama with its frightening background.
[GD737] Grafton pbk **£2.50**
Northern Lights (1976)
[GD738] Boyars pbk **£4.95**
The Nuclear Age (1986)
[GD739] Fontana pbk **£3.95**

O'CONNOR, FLANNERY (1925 - 1964)
Despite a short life affected by illness, O'Connor left
an indelible mark upon the literature of the Deep
South with her vivid depictions of the absurd and
violent margins of society. She writes with grotesque
humour, irony, and a vision of our spiritual
impoverishment: her stories are particularly
outstanding.
A Good Man is Hard to Find (Stories, 1955)
[GD740] Women's P pbk **£4.95**
Everything That Rises Must Converge
(Stories, 1965)
Her last collection of short stories explores in detail
the familiar tensions of the Deep South. Introduced by
Hermione Lee.
[GD741] Faber pbk **£3.95**

Mystery and Manners (1969)
Her prose writings on the art of fiction.
[GD742] Faber pbk **£3.95**
The Violent Bear it Away (1960)
Her second novel is a compelling tale of obsession
and religious conflict centred around an orphan who
lives with his uncle in Tennessee. Introduced by Paul
Bailey.
[GD743] Faber pbk **£3.95**
Wise Blood (1952)
A blackly comic first novel that satirizes the
South's eccentric religiosity. Introduced by V.S.
Pritchett.
[GD744] Faber pbk **£3.95**

O'HARA, JOHN (1905 - 1970)
A brutal realist, currently neglected. His books expose
the unpleasantness behind the glossy lives of the
smart middle classes.
Appointment in Samarra (1934)
His successful first novel.
[GD745] Faber pbk **£3.95**
Collected Stories (1986)
[GD746] Pan pbk **£4.95**
**Omnibus: Pal Joey/Hope of
Heaven/Sermons and Soda Water** (1940,
1938, 1960)
[GD747] Ravette pbk **£5.95**
Ten North Frederick (1955)
[GD748] Hutchinson hbk **£10.95**

OATES, JOYCE CAROL (1938 -)
A prolific and diverse author, Oates' writing is
abrasive, often exploring situations of murder and
violence.
All the Good People I've Left Behind
(1979)
[GD749] B Sparrow pbk **£4.95**
American Appetites (1989)   `NEW`
A domestic row in affluent suburbia ends with a wife
dead. In the ensuing court case it seems that it isn't
just the husband who is on trial, but his society's
values too.
[GD750] Macmillan hbk **£12.95**
Cybele (1979)
[GD751] B Sparrow pbk **£5.95**
Marya: A Life (1987)
Marya is an Everywoman for the 1980s: intellectual
and successful, but still beset by doubt.
[GD752] Pan pbk **£3.99**
Mysteries of Winterthurn (1984)
Oates' appropriation of the form of Victorian
melodrama.
[GD753] Cape hbk **£9.95**
Solstice (1985)
[GD754] Pan pbk **£2.95**
Unholy Loves (1980)
A wickedly funny campus novel.
[GD755] Dent pbk **£3.50**
Wild Saturday (Stories, 1984)
[GD756] Dent pbk **£3.50**
You Must Remember This (1988)
Set in the 1950s, this is the story of the relationship
between a 15 year old girl and her uncle twice her
age.
[GD757] Macmillan hbk **£10.95**

OLSEN, TILLIE (1913 -)
The demands of work, marriage and motherhood
prevented Olsen from ever realizing her literary
ambitions, but gave her keen insight into the
oppression of women. A writer whose political beliefs
are underscored by personal experience.
Silences (Essays, 1978)
Analyses of why the oppressed rarely get to become
writers.
[GD758] Virago pbk **£5.95**
Tell Me a Riddle (Stories, 1962)
[GD759] Virago pbk **£3.50**

Vladimir Nabokov, author of *Lolita* (Weidenfeld hbk £8.95, Penguin pbk £3.50) and *The Enchanter* (Picador pbk £2.95)

Yonnondio: From the Thirties (1974)
A reconstruction of Olsen's unfinished novel from the 30s; a young girl's search for an escape from poverty.
[GD760] Virago pbk **£2.95**

OLSHAN, JOSEPH
A Warmer Season (1987)
[GD761] Pan pbk **£4.50**
Clara's Heart (1986)
Olshan won the Times/Cape New Writer's award with this comic and humane novel about the effect on a Long Island household of an imposing Black woman.
[GD762] Pan pbk **£2.95**
The Waterline (1989)   **NEW**
The delicate and moving tale of how a seven year old is held to blame for the drowning of an unattended toddler. Olshan proves himself once again a master of domestic nuance.
[GD763] Bloomsbury hbk **£12.95**

ONDAATJE, MICHAEL (Canada, 1943 -)
Ondaatje's writing owes little to indigenous Canadian influences but rather feeds from a diversity of writers such as Wallace Stevens and also from several major writer-directors in contemporary cinema. The potency and flexibility of his narrative, as well as the cyclical, bouncing 'instability' of themes, compel readers to revise their acceptance of the existence of only one reality.
Coming through Slaughter (1976)
The fictionalized life of the jazz musician Charles 'Buddy' Bolden, whom Ondaatje admires because to Bolden life and creativity are one and the same.
[GD764] Picador pbk **£3.95**
In the Skin of the Lion (1987)
In early 20th century Toronto, the disappearance of a 'society' fraudster is interspersed with the allegorical building of a bridge by brave immigrants.
[GD765] Picador pbk **£4.50**
Running in the Family (1982)
A fictionalized portrait of Ondaatje's ancestral life in Ceylon which draws on photographs and linked sketches to quietly dissolve the normally solid line between autobiography and fiction.
[GD766] Picador pbk **£2.95**
The Cinnamon Peeler (Poetry)
A book of recent poetry.
[GD767] Picador pbk **£3.99**

The Collected Works of Billy the Kid
The 19th century American outlaw is placed in unusual situations. All manner of forms are included, such as disrupted narrative, photographs, deliberately blank pages, as well an intricate mix of poetry and prose.
[GD768] Picador pbk **£3.50**

PALEY, GRACE (1922 -)
A distinctive short story writer with a remarkable ear for dialogue. Her work vividly evokes post-war NY.
Enormous Changes at the Last Minute (1975)
Tragi-comic short stories set in a New York of too little money, too many kids and husbands gone off for good.
[GD769] Virago pbk **£3.95**
Later the Same Day (1985)
Paley's newest collection displays her mastery of the dramatic monologue.
[GD770] Penguin pbk **£3.95**
The Little Disturbances of Man (1960)
[GD771] Virago pbk **£3.95**

PARKER, DOROTHY (1893 - 1967)
The renowned creator of the perfect one liner will always be remembered for her acid wit. The range of her satirical writing was broad, including sketches, reviews, poems and gossip columns.
Best of Dorothy Parker
[GD772] Duckworth hbk **£6.95**
Collected Works
[GD773] Duckworth hbk **£9.80**
Penguin Dorothy Parker (1976)
[GD774] Penguin pbk **£5.99**

PERCY, WALKER (1916 -)
A Southern novelist who always portrays his characters' yearnings and disappointments with compassion. He is less well known here than in his homeland.
Lancelot (1977)
One man's quest to discover the extent of his wife's infidelity.
[GD775] Grafton pbk **£3.95**
The Last Gentleman (1966)
A young Southerner in New York is drifting into a dangerous ocean of loneliness when he buys a telescope and starts to spy on two women...
[GD776] Grafton pbk **£2.95**
The Moviegoer (1961)
[GD777] Grafton pbk **£2.95**
The Second Coming (1980)
The sequel to *The Last Gentleman*.
[GD778] Grafton pbk **£2.95**
The Thanatos Syndrome (1987)
A doctor uncovers a criminal experiment to 'impose' behaviour patterns on a parish of America. Percy's best novel to date.
[GD779] Grafton pbk **£4.99**

PHILLIPS, JAYNE ANNE (1952 -)
A startling and innovative writer who is justly praised for her stories of the drifting and disillusioned - stories of 'crooked beauty' (Carver) - that reveal her faith in the strength of ordinary people.
Black Tickets (Stories, 1985)
Her first dazzling collection of short stories.
[GD780] Penguin pbk **£3.95**
Fast Lanes (Stories, 1987)
Visions of America as seen by its wanderers.
[GD781] Faber pbk **£3.50**
Machine Dreams (1985)
Phillips' wonderful and bestselling first novel of graceful and visionary power, relating the experiences of a smalltown family between World War II and Vietnam. A tone of lost innocence is recalled with heartbreaking clarity.
[GD782] Faber pbk **£3.95**

PIERCY, MARGE (1937 -)
A powerful and energetic writer who dramatizes the political, self-searching and liberating impulses of modern women.
Braided Lives (1982)
Two friends who come together at college and never let go.
[GD783] Penguin pbk **£3.95**
Fly Away Home (1984)
[GD784] Pan pbk **£3.50**
Gone to Soldiers (1987)
A large and ambitious war novel.
[GD785] Penguin pbk **£3.95**
High Cost of Living (1979)
[GD786] Women's P pbk **£4.95**
My Mother's Body (1985)
[GD787] Pandora pbk **£4.95**
Small Changes (1972)
[GD788] Penguin pbk **£4.50**
Summer People (1989)   **NEW**
Piercy has produced another substantial and satisfying book in this tragic tale of a hitherto happy *ménage a trois* disrupted from within, as one of the three artists tires of the remoteness of their Cape Cod retreat, and gives reign to her longing for the city.
[GD789] M Joseph hbk **£12.95**
Vida (1980)
[GD790] Penguin pbk **£3.95**
Woman on the Edge of Time (1979)
Her celebrated futuristic novel about a world where the balance between the sexes is startlingly subverted.
[GD791] Women's P pbk **£3.95**

PINDER, LESLIE HALL (Canada)
Under the House (1987)
Successful first novel which deals with the secrecy and corruption, endemic in the lives of the Rathbones of Saskatchewan.
[GD792] Faber pbk **£4.99**

PLANTE, DAVID (1940 -)
An elegant writer whose books, which are often about adolescence, are harrowing and poetic.
The Catholic (1985)
[GD793] Grafton pbk **£3.50**
The Foreigner (1984)
'A superb account of late adolescent dislocation' (New Statesman).
[GD794] Grafton pbk **£3.95**
The Francoeur Family: The Family/The Woods/The Country (1984)
[GD795] Chatto pbk **£5.95**
The Native (1987)
[GD796] Grafton pbk **£3.99**

PLATH, SYLVIA (1932 - 1963)
Poet and novelist noted for her presentation of acute moods, often of suffering, and (particularly in the poetry) for her sharp and vivid language. She married the British poet Ted Hughes in 1956; only after her suicide was her reputation established, in particular with the collection of poems *Ariel*.
Johnny Panic and the Bible of Dreams
A posthumous collection of shorter works.
[GD797] Faber pbk **£3.95**
The Bell Jar (1963)
Plath's only novel is a semi-autobiographical and intense work about late adolescence and mental breakdown, depicted in Winthrop, US and written years later in Devon.
[GD798] Faber pbk **£2.95**

PLIMPTON, GEORGE
The Curious Case of Sidd Finch (1988)
Charming tale of an English Buddhist monk whose ability to pitch a baseball at 168 mph threatens to upset the balance of the game. A delightful first novel from the editor of the *Paris Review*.
[GD799] Bloomsbury pbk **£4.95**

POE, EDGAR ALLEN (1809 - 1849)
Until this century, Poe suffered from his notoriety as the writer of morbid tales who married his 13 year old cousin and died a poverty-stricken drunk. However, his originality as an imaginative story-teller and his skill as a lyric poet are now justly celebrated.

Comedies and Satires
[GD800] Penguin pbk **£4.99**

Complete Tales and Poems
This collection has all the classics in many genres such as 'The Pit and the Pendulum' and 'The Murders in the Rue Morgue'.
[GD801] Penguin pbk **£7.95**

Essays and Reviews
[GD802] Cambridge **£7.95**

Tales of Mystery & Imagination
[GD803] Dent hbk **£8.95**
[GD804] Dent pbk **£2.95**

The Fall of the House of Usher & Other Writings
Poe's classic tale with a selection of other stories, poems and articles.
[GD805] Penguin pbk **£4.50**

The Narrative of Arthur Gordon Pym (1838)
Mutiny, shipwreck and famine on the high seas.
[GD806] Penguin pbk **£3.99**

The Portable Poe
Letters, tales, poems and criticism.
[GD807] Penguin pbk **£5.95**

The Science Fiction of Edgar Allen Poe
Sixteen of Poe's lesser known speculative tales.
[GD808] Penguin pbk **£3.99**

PORTER, KATHERINE ANNE (1890 - 1980)
Southern writer who specialized in the short story.

Collected Stories (1965)
Pulitzer Prize-winning collection.
[GD809] Virago pbk **£5.95**

The Ship of Fools (1962)
This bitter allegory, set on board a 1931 passenger ship, took Porter twenty years to write.
[GD810] Secker hbk **£10.95**

POTOK, CHAIM
Noted Jewish writer, originally a rabbi, who dramatizes the dilemmas shared alike by orthodox and reformed Jew.

Book of Lights (1981)
His most ambitious novel to date, pitting the Kabbelah against the nuclear bomb, by way of the Korean War.
[GD811] Penguin pbk **£3.50**

In the Beginning (1975)
[GD812] Penguin pbk **£3.95**

My Name is Asher Lev (1972)
[GD813] Penguin pbk **£3.99**

The Chosen (1967)
A Hasid and a modern Jew struggle to remain friends in the shadow of the Holocaust.
[GD814] Penguin pbk **£3.50**

The Promise (1969)
The sequel to *The Chosen*.
[GD815] Penguin pbk **£3.95**

POWERS, J.F. (1917 -)
A great comic writer whose stories about the clergy, with their piercing analyses of human frailty, have earned him an almost cult-like following.

Look How the Fish Live
[GD816] Hogarth pbk **£5.95**

Morte D'Urban (1962)
His comic masterpiece featuring Father Urban Roche: priest, golfer, fisherman and raconteur.
[GD817] Hogarth pbk **£5.95**

Presence of Grace (1956)
[GD818] Hogarth pbk **£5.95**

The Prince of Darkness (1947)
[GD819] Hogarth pbk **£5.95**

Wheat that Springeth Green (1988)
His long-awaited new novel transports us to the American Middle West. Joe enters the priesthood intent on becoming a saint but instead submits to the lure of the bottle.
[GD820] Hogarth hbk **£12.95**

PRAGER, EMILY

A Visit from the Footbinder (1983)
A highly praised first collection of short stories of black humour and fierce irony.
[GD821] Chatto pbk **£3.95**

Clea and Zeus Divorce (1988)
[GD822] Chatto hbk **£11.95**

PULLINGER, KATE (Canada, 1959 -)
Canadian writer, resident in London, whose politicized evocations of everyday urban life show a subtle insight into the workings of the psychology of human motivation.

Tiny Lies (Stories, 1987)
Intense stories which frequently show people at their most vulnerable. The lies are those used by mankind at its most self-deceiving.
[GD823] Picador pbk **£3.99**

When the Monster Dies (1989) `NEW`
Pullinger's first novel, set in South London, where her characters are both hemmed in and released by the paradoxes of their alternative, quietly defiant lifestyles.
[GD824] Cape hbk **£10.95**

PURDY, JAMES (1923 -)
Frequently bizarre and startling, Purdy is an underrated writer, too often marginalized by his homosexuality. His novels are powerful examinations of sexual passion that can turn violent and destructive.

Garments the Living Wear (1989) `NEW`
A satirical vision of New York in the 1980s - a city scourged by the HIV virus, criminal conspiracies, the super-rich and modern evangelists.
[GD825] P Owen hbk **£11.95**

I am Elijah Thrush (1972)
Hilarious fantasy set in a wholly unfamiliar New York.
[GD826] GMP pbk **£3.50**

In A Shallow Grave (1988)
A hideously scarred Vietnam vet finds himself drawn into a mesmerizing relationship.
[GD827] P Owen pbk **£4.95**

In the Hollow of His Hand (1988)
Set in the Mid West of the 1920s, this new novel has all the baroque intensity and humour that characterize Purdy's writing.
[GD828] P Owen hbk **£11.95**

Narrow Rooms (1978)
[GD829] GMP pbk **£3.95**

On Glory's Course (1985)
[GD830] P Owen hbk **£11.95**

The Candles of Your Eyes (Stories, 1988)
[GD831] P Owen hbk **£11.95**

The House of the Solitary Maggot (1974)
[GD832] P Owen hbk **£11.95**

PYNCHON, THOMAS (1937 -)
Adopting the stance of mysterious recluse, Pynchon has won both extravagant critical acclaim and a following devoted to decoding his work. His two huge and labyrinthine novels (*V* and *Gravity's Rainbow*) certainly invite vigorous interpretation, depicting as they do a world so fragmented into innumerable systems of knowledge that overall comprehension remains tantalizingly out of reach. Undoubtedly one of literature's true originals.

Gravity's Rainbow (1973)
A prodigiously dense and referential novel of great complexity and imaginative power, concerning the British Special Operations Directive during WW II.
[GD833] Picador pbk **£6.95**

Low-lands
A single short story.
[GD834] Aloes pbk **£1.00**

Mortality and Mercy in Vienna
[GD835] Aloes pbk **£1.00**

Secret Integration
[GD836] Aloes pbk **£1.50**

Slow Learner (1985)
Collected early stories, with a revelatory essay on his early influences and writing.
[GD837] Picador pbk **£2.95**

Small Rain
[GD838] Aloes pbk **£1.50**

The Crying of Lot 49 (1966)
A short novel, and a good introduction to Pynchon's bizarre world.
[GD839] Picador pbk **£3.50**

V (1963)
Astounding first novel in which Pynchon's imagination is let loose in New York, Cairo, Alexandria and Malta.
[GD840] Picador pbk **£5.95**

RAND, AYN (1905 - 1982)
Russian-born novelist deeply preoccupied with the concept of 'enlightened self-interest'.

The Fountainhead (1943)
Her cult novel apparently based on the life of the innovative architect Frank Lloyd Wright.
[GD841] Grafton pbk **£3.95**

RASKIN, BARBARA

Hot Flashes (1987)
The female *Big Chill*; a hugely successful novel of female friendship.
[GD842] Bantam pbk **£3.99**

REED, ISHMAEL (1938 -)
Wilfully subversive satirist whose varied works have all long been out of print. Reed is the only writer to have been nominated for America's National Book Award in both fiction and poetry. This publication of two of his novels is welcome if overdue.

Mumbo Jumbo (1972) `NEW`
Surrealist journey through America in the company of philosopher-detectives Papa La Bas and Black Herman.
[GD843] Allison & B pbk **£3.99**

Reckless Eyeballing `NEW`
Satirical *tour-de-force* that looks behind the scenes of NY theatre through the eyes of an out-of-favour Black playwright.
[GD844] Allison & B pbk **£3.99**

RICHLER, MORDECAI (Canada, 1931 -)
From a working-class Jewish ghetto in Montréal, Richler rigorously dissects human hypocrisy and attempts to dissolve the many myths shrouding the Jew in Diaspora; he has been accused of anti-semitism because of his refusal to treat all of Judaism with unquestioning respect. His incisive wit and dogged determination to uncover falsity in all its forms have placed him among the more effective satirists of his generation.

The Apprenticeship of Duddy Kravitz (1959)
The story of a raucous, avaricious and at times morally contemptible young man living in the Jewish ghetto in Montréal. He lusts after land and money in order to escape from what seems to be a closed destiny.
[GD845] M Vallentine hbk **£9.95**

RIDING, LAURA (1901 -)
Best known as a poet, and for her association with Robert Graves (she worked with him in Majorca for many years), Riding is a writer of rigorous intelligence.

A Progress of Stories (1935)
A series of 17 stories, and an essay on storytelling.
[GD846] Carcanet pbk **£5.95**
A Trojan Ending (1937)
[GD847] Carcanet hbk **£10.95**
Lives of Wives (1939)
An examination of the women behind such figures as
Aristotle, Alexander the Great and Herod.
[GD848] Carcanet hbk **£12.95**

ROBBINS, HAROLD (1916 -)
One-time commodity broker and shipping clerk who
became the originator and most popular purveyor of
blockbuster fiction-fantasy. Character is not of great
importance to Robbins, whose novels are the product
of ingenious plots, much explicit sex, and impressive
business sense.
Lonely Lady
[GD849] Hodder pbk **£3.99**
The Adventurers
[GD850] Hodder pbk **£4.50**
The Betsy
[GD851] Hodder pbk **£3.95**
The Carpetbaggers
[GD852] Hodder pbk **£3.95**
The Inheritors
[GD853] Hodder pbk **£3.50**
The Pirate
[GD854] Hodder pbk **£3.50**

ROBINSON, MARILYNNE
Housekeeping (1981)
The sad, haunting tale of two sisters' unconventional
upbringing in the remote mountains of Idaho. Filmed
by Bill Forsyth.
[GD855] Penguin pbk **£3.95**

ROTH, HENRY (1906 -)
Roth only wrote this one autobiographical novel, re-
issued to great acclaim in the 60s, before going on to
become a turkey farmer. It is something of a classic
however, and a wonderful evocation of a child's life
with immigrant parents in turn-of-the-century New
York.
Call it Sleep (1934)
[GD856] Penguin pbk **£4.95**

ROTH, PHILIP (1933 -)
Much fêted chronicler of Jewish-American life, Roth
is a comic writer with deeply serious concerns. His
use of his own life as material for his fiction
(principally in the Zuckerman books) makes him
endlessly examine the identity and role of the writer
in a series of novels that are becoming increasingly
inventive and politically aware.
A Philip Roth Reader (1981)
[GD857] Penguin pbk **£5.95**
Goodbye Columbus (1959)
His prize-winning first book of five short stories and
a novella.
[GD858] Penguin pbk **£4.50**
Letting Go (1962)
His second novel, a realistic tale of 1950s America.
[GD859] Penguin pbk **£5.99**
My Life as a Man (1974)
[GD860] Penguin pbk **£4.99**
Portnoy's Complaint (1969)
A masterpiece of comic bawdry about the pressures a
young Jew suffers, and the various means by which
he attempts to escape.
[GD861] Cape hbk **£9.95**
[GD862] Penguin pbk **£3.99**
Reading Myself and Others
(Non fiction, 1975)
[GD863] Penguin pbk **£3.95**
The Anatomy Lesson (1983)
Third part of the Zuckerman Trilogy.
[GD864] Cape hbk **£9.95**
[GD865] Penguin pbk **£4.99**

The Breast (1972)
[GD866] Penguin pbk **£2.99**
The Counterlife (1987)
The return of Zuckerman, and perhaps Roth's best
novel. In an astonishing display of fictional turns
and shifts, the novel spans England, Israel and
America, encompassing many versions of the
'truth'.
[GD867] Cape hbk **£10.95**
[GD868] Penguin pbk **£4.50**
The Facts: A Novelist's
Autobiography (1989)   **NEW**
As we would expect from Roth, this is no
conventional autobiography, but a candid exploration
of the relationship between his life and his fiction.
Even more surprisingly, he allows his own creation,
Zuckerman, a word or two in the matter. Very
favourably reviewed.
[GD869] Cape hbk **£11.95**
The Ghost Writer (1979)
The first part of his unique and endlessly creative
Zuckerman Trilogy.
[GD870] Penguin pbk **£3.50**
The Great American Novel (1973)
[GD871] Cape hbk **£9.95**
[GD872] Penguin pbk **£4.95**
The Prague Orgy (1985)
A surreal and powerful coda to the Zuckerman
Trilogy centred in Prague.
[GD873] Cape hbk **£7.95**
[GD874] Penguin pbk **£2.50**
The Professor of Desire (1977)
[GD875] Cape hbk **£9.95**
[GD876] Penguin pbk **£3.95**
When She Was Good (1967)
[GD877] Penguin pbk **£4.99**
Zuckerman Unbound (1981)
The rumbustious and hilarious second part of
the Zuckerman Trilogy in which successful
novelist Nathan Zuckerman tries to shake off his
alter-ego.
[GD878] Cape hbk **£9.95**
[GD879] Penguin pbk **£3.50**

RULE, JANE (Canada, 1931 -)
Rule is probably best known for writing that does not
shy away from supposedly controversial issues,
though she does not tend toward extremes. Her novels
often look at the lives and concerns of lesbians,
although there is usually a 'complete' society
intertwined with her central concerns.
After the Fire (1989)   **NEW**
Rule's latest novel.
[GD880] Pandora hbk **£12.95**
Against the Season
[GD881] Pandora pbk **£4.50**
Deserts of the Heart (1964)
Two women meet in the desert gambling town of
Reno, Nevada. They fall in love and are eventually
able to give each other the strength to override
prejudice and their own fears and so begin living
together.
[GD882] Pandora pbk **£3.95**
Memory Board
[GD883] Pandora pbk **£4.95**
This Is Not for You (1970)
A reworking of the epistolary novel, in which a
women writes a long letter that is never meant to be
mailed. It portrays a woman trapped by convention,
who is unable to unleash her love for another
woman.
[GD884] Pandora pbk **£4.50**

RUNYON, DAMON (1884 - 1946)
The NY underworld of petty gangsters in loud
suits, fast-talking gamblers and deft bookies was
inimitably brought to life, some say created, by
newspaperman Runyon, whose short stories are rich
in vernacular and slang.

On Broadway (1950)
All the banditry and bawdiness of *Guys and Dolls* is
here, with characters such as Waldo Winchester, Ickey
the Pig and Dave the Dude.
[GD885] Picador pbk **£5.95**
Trials and Other Tribulations
[GD886] Xanadu hbk **£10.99**

RUSSO, RICHARD
Brilliant, up-and-coming writer who deftly mixes the
comic with the tragic. His two novels of 'ordinary'
American life, while owing something to the much-
vaunted 'Dirty Realism', belong to an earlier and
stronger tradition, of which Russo is a worthy heir.
Mohawk (1987)
The intertwined lives of the residents of smalltown
Mohawk, already a minor classic. Highly
recommended.
[GD887] Hodder pbk **£4.95**
The Risk Pool (1989)   **NEW**
Also set in Mohawk, and with a similarly loveable
cast of characters, Russo's second novel focuses upon
the moving trials of young Ned, whose ne'er-do-well
father abandons him and his mother on his return
from World War II.
[GD888] Chatto hbk **£12.95**

SALINGER, J.D. (1919 -)
One of the great mystery men of contemporary
literature, Jerome David Salinger has published
nothing since 1965, yet remains as popular now as
then. His books are very much celebrations of youth,
with their cast of precocious but always loveable
characters such as Franny, Buddy and Zooey Glass, in
whose mouths Salinger places his idiosyncratic,
homespun philosophy.
Catcher in the Rye (1951)
One of the bestselling books of this century, and
Salinger's only novel, it stands alongside *Le Grand
Meaulnes* as a faultless evocation of a time and a
place in boyhood, as Holden Caulfield makes his
stand against the 'phoniness' of the adult world.
[GD889] H Hamilton hbk **£12.95**
[GD890] Penguin pbk **£2.99**
For Esmé: With Love and Squalor (1953)
Nine gems of shortstory writing, and the elusive
Seymour Glass' only appearance.
[GD891] H Hamilton hbk **£11.95**
[GD892] Penguin pbk **£2.99**
Franny and Zooey (1962)
Two charming novellas featuring the younger
members of the Glass family.
[GD893] Heinemann hbk **£9.95**
[GD894] Penguin pbk **£2.99**
Raise High the Roof Beam,
Carpenters/Seymour (1963)
Buddy Glass - Salinger's 'alter-ego and collaborator'
- remembers his dead brother Seymour.
[GD895] Heinemann hbk **£9.95**
[GD896] Penguin pbk **£2.50**

SALTER, JAMES
A much neglected writer whose name is frequently
invoked as an influence upon other writers. Most
often commented upon is his prose style, which is as
clear as Cheever's.
A Sport and a Pastime (1988)
Salter's erotic masterpiece, a classic love story which
has become a key cult novel told in his
characteristically luminous prose.
[GD897] Picador pbk **£3.95**
Dusk & Other Stories (1989)   **NEW**
[GD898] North Point Press hbk **£9.95**

SANDLIN, TIM
Sex and Sunsets (1988)
A warm and comic novel of love at first sight in
Wyoming.
[GD899] Fontana pbk **£3.95**

SARTON, MAY (1912 -)
Known also as a poet, Sarton's heroines are often old or middle-aged women looking back over their lives.
A Reckoning (1978)
The unhappy memories of a woman dying of cancer.
[GD900] Women's P pbk **£4.95**
As We Are Now (1973)
The diary of a retired schoolteacher coping with life in an old people's home: 'I am not mad, only old'.
[GD901] Women's P pbk **£3.95**
Journal of a Solitude (1973)
Reflections of one year.
[GD902] Women's P pbk **£3.95**
The Magnificent Spinster (1985)
[GD903] Women's P pbk **£4.95**

SAVAN, GLENN
White Palace (1987)
Recently widowed but upwardly mobile Max finds himself drawn into an obsessive sexual passion - for a hard-drinking waitress from his local diner.
[GD904] Bantam pbk **£4.95**

SCHAEFER, FRANK
The Scapeweed Goat (1989)   NEW
A debut novel from a new Texan writer which mixes Crusoe with fable. It is a bitter and haunting tale of two pioneers' harsh lives, and the damage wrought by unwelcome, wandering fanatics.
[GD905] H Hamilton hbk **£11.95**

SCHAEFFER, SUSAN FROMBERG
(1941 -)
Anya (1974)
A middle-aged woman looks back to her life in Poland before and during World War II.
[GD906] Pan pbk **£3.95**
Buffalo Afternoon (1989)   NEW
Schaeffer's eighth novel is a portrait of one man, Pete Bravado, whose escape from his overbearing father takes him into the army and consequently the horror of the Vietnam War, which changes him forever.
[GD907] H Hamilton **£11.95**
Mainland (1985)
[GD908] Pan pbk **£2.95**
The Injured Party (1986)
[GD909] Pan pbk **£3.95**
The Madness of a Seduced Woman
(1984)
A passionate and comic feminist novel about the love of a woman for a man who will never make her happy.
[GD910] Pan pbk **£4.99**

SCHULBERG, BUDD
On the Waterfront (1956)
Elia Kazan memorably filmed this story of NY stevedores.
[GD911] Allison & B pbk **£3.99**
The Disenchanted (1950)
The famous, poignant novel about Hollywood in the 1930s and a writer down on his luck (based on Scott Fitzgerald).
[GD912] Allison & B pbk **£3.99**

SEGAL, ERICH
American academic and writer of immensely popular lachrymose tragedies of campus life.
Doctors (1989)   NEW
The latest blockbuster from Segal follows the traumas and dramas of a group of young medical students and their subsequent careers.
[GD913] Bantam hbk **£12.95**
Love Story
How Oliver forsakes his inheritance for the lowly-born love of his life, only to lose her to leukaemia. Filmed with Ryan O'Neal as Ollie
[GD914] Hodder pbk **£1.95**

Oliver's Story
The sequel to *Love Story*, with Oliver now as a widower.
[GD915] Hodder pbk **£1.95**
The Class
[GD916] Transworld pbk **£2.95**

SELBY, HUBERT (1928 -)
An uncompromising writer whose books are drawn from his experience at the bottom of the social ladder.
Last Exit to Brooklyn (1964)
Prosecuted here for obscenity, these stories powerfully depict the brutal Brooklyn of illicit sex and violent crime.
[GD917] Grafton pbk **£3.95**
Requiem for a Dream (1978)
[GD918] Grafton pbk **£3.95**
Song of the Silent Snow (Stories, 1986)
[GD919] Grafton pbk **£3.95**
The Demon (1973)
Explores the dark recesses and erotic fixations of a promising young businessman.
[GD920] Boyars pbk **£3.50**
The Room (1971)
A nameless psychopath awaits his trial; this is his story.
[GD921] Grafton pbk **£3.95**

SETH, VIKRAM
The Golden Gate (1986)
The celebrated novel of Californian yuppies and protestors - written entirely *in verse*.
[GD922] Faber pbk **£3.95**

SHAINBERG, LAWRENCE
Memories of Amnesia (1989)   NEW
A fascinating black comedy about how a top American neurosurgeon who develops amnesia finds himself fighting a losing battle against this disease.
[GD923] Collins hbk **£10.95**

SHANGE, NTOZAKE
Shange writes vibrant, rhythmic fiction about racial confrontation and Black American culture. Her books (she has also written poetry and a play) map the expanding horizons of the Black imagination today.
A Daughter's Geography (1983)
[GD924] Methuen pbk **£3.95**
Betsey Brown (1985)
[GD925] Methuen pbk **£3.50**
For Coloured Girls Who Have Considered Suicide... (1978)
...When the Rainbow is Enuf.
[GD926] Methuen pbk **£4.50**
Sassafrass, Cypress and Indigo (1983)
[GD927] Methuen pbk **£3.95**

SHAW, IRWIN
Prolific and perenially popular novelist, most famous for his *Rich Man, Poor Man* saga.
Acceptable Losses (1982)
[GD928] Hodder pbk **£2.95**
Bread Upon the Waters (1981)
[GD929] Hodder pbk **£3.50**
Evening in Byzantium (1973)
[GD930] Hodder hbk **£2.95**
Five Decades (Stories, 1978)
[GD931] Pan pbk **£5.95**
Nightwork
An innocent man finds himself seduced by a crisp, cool Washington lawyer; when she becomes pregnant she wants to marry him.
[GD932] Weidenfeld hbk **£8.95**
Rich Man, Poor Man
Long and compelling saga about the different members of a working-class family trying to make it in America, from the Depression to the present.
[GD933] Hodder pbk **£4.50**

The Top of the Hill (1979)
[GD934] Hodder pbk **£3.50**
The Troubled Air (1951)
[GD935] Hodder pbk **£3.95**

SHEPARD, SAM
Motel Chronicles and Hawk Moon (1982)
Short fictions set in Shepard's typically desolate landscapes, and the inspiration for Wenders' *Paris, Texas*.
[GD936] Faber pbk **£3.95**

SIMPSON, MONA
Anywhere But Here (1987)
Substantial first novel from a young writer to watch, memorable for its depiction of a remarkable mother/daughter relationship.
[GD937] Sphere hbk **£4.50**

SINCLAIR, UPTON (1878 - 1968)
A passionate and committed believer in social reform, Sinclair was also a vastly prolific writer who has suffered the indignity of only having one of over a hundred of his books available in this country.
The Jungle (1906)
This exposure of the corruption of Chicago's stockyards was a major literary event, causing as it did immediate legislative reform.
[GD938] Penguin pbk **£3.95**

SINGER, ISAAC BASHEVIS (1904 -)
Nobel Prize for Literature 1978. Singer fled the Polish ghettos in the 30s, and has lived in New York ever since. His books draw upon the mystical traditions of his Jewish heritage, and are richly woven with myth and folklore.
Collected Stories (1982)
[GD939] Penguin hbk **£6.95**
Death of Methusaleh & Other Stories
[GD939A] Cape hbk **£11.95**
Enemies (1970)
[GD940] Penguin pbk **£4.99**
Family Moskat (1950)
[GD941] Penguin pbk **£4.99**
Passions (stories)
[GD942] Cape hbk **£8.95**
Shosha (1978)
[GD943] Penguin pbk **£4.99**
The Estate (1969)
A sequel to *The Manor*.
[GD944] Penguin pbk **£4.95**

Philip Roth, author of *The Facts: A Novelist's Autobiography* (Cape hbk £11.95)

The King of the Fields (1989) **NEW**
Singer's latest work is an unusual fictional explor-ation of man's primitive history set in the mythical Vistula valley, and a dissection of human perversity.
[GD945] Cape hbk **£10.95**
The Magician of Lublin (1960)
[GD946] Penguin pbk **£3.99**
The Manor (1967)
Chronicles the dilemmas of Jews in 19th century Poland.
[GD947] Penguin pbk **£4.95**
The Penitent (1984)
Joseph Shapiro feeling spiritually impoverished, returns to his traditional Jewish community, and becomes a penitent.
[GD948] Penguin pbk **£2.95**
The Slave (1962)
A powerful drama and love story set against the background of 17th century Poland, and rooted in the rich folklore of the period.
[GD949] Penguin pbk **£3.95**

SMART, ELIZABETH (1913 -)
By Grand Central Station I Sat Down and Wept (1945)
Classic novel which charts the main character's self-discovery with poetry and passion.
[GD950] Grafton pbk **£2.50**

SMITH, LEE
Three novels set in the mountains of Virginia (published here for the first time) from a woman writer already well established in the US: Smith recently won the John Dos Passos Prize for Literature, and has been compared to Flannery O'Connor and Eudora Welty.
Fair and Tender Ladies (1989) **NEW**
Smith's latest novel displays her continuing interest in the private history (and its documentation) of 'ordinary' lives: this is Ivy Rowe's life story as told through the letters she is forever writing to friends, loved ones and family. A novel that is inspiringly real and warm-hearted.
[GD951] Macmillan hbk **£11.95**
Family Linen (1985) **NEW**
A comic novel that explores the mysteries of family history. Undergoing hypnosis, Sybill learns that she witnessed, in early childhood, her mother murdering her father with an axe.
[GD952] Picador pbk **£3.99**
Oral History (1983) **NEW**
A young student moves to her mother's backwoods hometown to create an oral history of her family. The tales she records are vividly captured in this skilful novel that offsets its serious themes with a sure comic sense.
[GD953] Picador pbk **£3.99**

SORRENTINO, GILBERT (1929 -)
Celebrated NY poet and novelist, author of whacky and humorous experimental fiction.
Aberration of Starlight (1980)
[GD954] Boyars pbk **£3.95**
Crystal Vision (1981)
An early, previously unpublished, comic novel.
[GD955] Boyars pbk **£3.95**
Mulligan Stew (1979)
Highly inventive and self-conscious comic novel about writing.
[GD956] Boyars pbk **£4.50**

STAFFORD, JEAN (1915 - 1979)
A great short story writer, Stafford's work is restrained and precise, often dealing with innocence, corruption and the loneliness of young women.
Boston Adventure (1946)
An excellent novel about Boston snobbery and its conflict with the new Jazz Age.
[GD957] Hogarth pbk **£5.95**

Collected Stories (1969)
Pulitzer Prize winner.
[GD958] Hogarth pbk **£5.95**
The Mountain Lion (1947)
Her second novel.
[GD959] Hogarth **£5.95**

STEEL, DANIELLE
An ex-PR 'Supergirl', Steel describes this image-conscious world with authority, and some ambivalence. In true blockbuster fashion, her plots are elaborate and well-researched.
Changes
[GD960] Sphere pbk **£3.50**
Crossings
[GD961] Sphere pbk **£3.50**
Daddy (1989) **NEW**
The story of how Oliver copes with his three children, one of whom becomes a father himself, when his wife walks out on him.
[GD962] Bantam hbk **£11.95**
Full Circle
[GD963] Sphere pbk **£3.50**
Love Poems
[GD964] Sphere pbk **£2.99**
Now and Forever
[GD965] Sphere pbk **£3.50**
Remembrance
[GD966] Sphere pbk **£3.99**
Star (1989) **NEW**
The sweeping romance of a rich lawyer trapped in a loveless marriage and a Hollywood star accused of murder, set in California in the 50s and 60s.
[GD967] M Joseph hbk **£12.95**
To Love Again
[GD968] Sphere pbk **£2.99**

STEIN, GERTRUDE (1874 - 1946)
Experimental writer whose own version of the stream-of-consciousness technique became very influential among her circle of friends in 20s Paris, including Hemingway, whose prose style owes much to Stein.
Autobiography of Alice B. Toklas (1933)
A fictionalized account of Stein's own life, as narrated by her lifelong companion Alice B. Toklas.
[GD969] Penguin pbk **£4.95**
Blood on the Dining Room Floor (1948)
An unusual foray into detective fiction with a difference.
[GD970] Virago pbk **£2.95**
Brewsie and Willie (1946) **NEW**
Her last book; an account of American soldiers in Paris during the war.
[GD971] Brilliance pbk **£4.95**

John Steinbeck, author of *The Grapes of Wrath* (Heinemann hbk £11.95, Picador pbk £4.95)

How to Write
[GD972] Dover pbk **£4.45**
Lectures in America (1989) **NEW**
[GD973] Virago pbk **£6.95**
Paris, France (1933)
Personal recollections.
[GD974] Brilliance pbk **£2.50**
Three Lives (1909)
Stein's 'first definite step away from the 19th century and into the 20th'.
[GD975] Penguin pbk **£4.50**
Wars I Have Seen
[GD976] Brilliance pbk **£3.95**
Yale Gertrude Stein (Selections, 1980)
[GD977] Yale pbk **£11.50**

STEINBECK, JOHN (1902 - 1968)
Nobel Prize for Literature 1962. Forsaking marine biology at Stanford for the life of a writer, Steinbeck rapidly made his name as the novelist of the rural proletariat in the years of the depression. Although he wrote in a variety of styles, his best work belongs to the tradition of American novelists who utilize their formidable journalistic talents to write dramatic social realism.
Cannery Row (1945)
The popular tale of a group of essentially hopeless but good-hearted misfits who make a shambles out of arranging a party at Tortilla Flats.
[GD978] Heinemann hbk **£9.95**
[GD979] Pan pbk **£2.99**
East of Eden (1952)
A vigorous, epic novel and a family saga, revealing Steinbeck's more overt symbolic tendencies, though undoubtedly one of his best.
[GD980] Heinemann hbk **£10.95**
[GD981] Pan pbk **£4.99**
In Dubious Battle (1936)
[GD982] Heinemann hbk **£9.95**
[GD983] Pan pbk **£2.99**
Of Mice and Men (1937)
The memorable tale of migrant farm workers and their search for a home.
[GD984] Heinemann hbk **£9.95**
[GD985] Pan pbk **£2.50**
Sweet Thursday (1954)
[GD986] Pan pbk **£2.50**
The Grapes of Wrath (1939)
Pulitzer Prize winning classic, and justifiably his most popular book.
[GD987] Heinemann hbk **£11.95**
[GD988] Picador pbk **£4.95**
The Long Valley (Stories, 1938)
[GD989] Pan pbk **£2.95**
The Moon is Down (1942)
A short novel about the Norwegian resistance to the German invasion.
[GD990] Pan pbk **£2.50**
The Pastures of Heaven (Stories, 1933)
[GD991] Arrow pbk **£2.95**
The Pearl (1948)
[GD992] Pan pbk **£1.99**
The Portable Steinbeck
Two complete novels and generous selections from the others.
[GD993] Penguin pbk **£5.95**
The Short Novels of John Steinbeck
[GD994] Heinemann hbk **£10.95**
The Wayward Bus (1947)
[GD995] Arrow pbk **£3.50**
The Winter of Our Discontent (1961)
[GD996] Pan pbk **£3.99**
To a God Unknown (1933)
[GD997] Pan pbk **£2.50**
Tortilla Flat (1935)
His first great popular success: the gentle comedy of the paisanos in Monterey.
[GD998] Heinemann hbk **£9.95**
[GD999] Pan pbk **£2.99**

FICTION

Travels With Charley: In Search of America (1962)
Charley was the poodle with whom he travelled through the States, discovering his own country.
[GD1000] Heinemann hbk £9.95

STONE, IRVING
Each of his books is a fictionalized biography of a different artist, respectively Camille Pissarro, Vincent Van Gogh and Michelangelo. They are very entertaining, with a fine feel for the periods described.
Depths of Glory
[GD1001] Methuen pbk £2.95
Lust for Life
[GD1002] Methuen pbk £3.99
The Agony and the Ecstasy
[GD1003] Methuen pbk £2.95

STONE, ROBERT (1937 -)
A novelist of urgent social convictions whose terrain is politics, corruption and modern war.
A Flag for Sunrise (1982)
An ambitious adventure story set in Central America characterized by intense moral outrage.
[GD1004] Picador pbk £3.95
A Hall of Mirrors (1967)
[GD1005] Picador pbk £3.95
Children of Light (1986)
[GD1006] Penguin pbk £3.95
Dog Soldiers (1974)
A violent novel of drugs and Vietnam.
[GD1007] Picador pbk £3.95

STOWE, HARRIET BEECHER (1811 - 1896)
The daughter of a Calvinist preacher, and a friend of George Eliot and Elizabeth Barrett Browning, Stowe became a household name as a result of the controversy provoked by *Uncle Tom's Cabin*.
Uncle Tom's Cabin (1852)
The biggest-selling novel of the 19th century, and a sentimental polemic against slavery. In the midst of the Civil War ten years later, Abraham Lincoln called it 'the book that made this great war'.
[GD1008] Penguin pbk £3.95
Uncle Tom's Cabin/The Minister's Wooing/Oldtown Folks (1852, 1859, 1869)
Her famous novel, a slight historical romance, and a delightful New England tale.
[GD1009] Cambridge hbk £7.95

STYRON, WILLIAM (1925 -)
A great story-teller who has won many readers with his fictions based on controversial historical subjects, often based in the South.
Confessions of Nat Turner (1967)
Pulitzer Prize winner and his most critically acclaimed work; it tells the story of the 1831 Black uprising.
[GD1010] Transworld pbk £4.95
Lie Down in Darkness (1951)
[GD1011] Transworld pbk £4.95
Set This House on Fire (1960)
[GD1012] Transworld pbk £3.95
Sophie's Choice (1979)
His most popular novel (as a result of its filming): it tells the story of one woman's dark past in Nazi Germany.
[GD1013] Transworld pbk £3.95
The Long March (1953)
[GD1014] Transworld pbk £3.95
This Quiet Dust and Other Writings (1982)
[GD1015] Transworld pbk £4.95

SUSANN, JACQUELINE
An ex-actress who died of cancer, Susann created quite a stir with her (pre-brat pack) cynical and would-be expose of her world of drugs, sex and decadent ennui.

Once Is Not Enough
[GD1016] Transworld pbk £3.95
The Love Machine
[GD1017] Transworld pbk £3.95
Valley of the Dolls
[GD1018] Transworld pbk £3.95

TAN, AMY
The Joy Luck Club (1989) `NEW`
The Chinese-American novel that has been a surprise superseller Stateside. Four émigré women gather regularly to relate tales from their pasts. Forty years later one of the four has died, and only then does her daughter discover her mother's lifelong wish. An unforgettable tale of the joys and heartbreaks these Chinese women experience in their new lives in the West.
[GD1019] Heinemann hbk £11.95

TAYLOR, PETER (1919 -)
An under-rated master of the short story, now finally receiving recognition. Taylor is an acute observer of Southern life and its complex undercurrents.
Summons to Memphis (1987)
Pulitzer Prize winner. From a small story - how one man and his two sisters try to prevent their father from remarrying - Taylor creates a tale of family relationships and the legacy of the South which carries great resonance.
[GD1020] Chatto hbk £12.95
The Old Forest (Stories, 1985)
[GD1021] Penguin pbk £4.95

TEXIER, CATHERINE
Editor of the underground NY magazine of experimental writing *Between C and D*.
Love Me Tender (1989) `NEW`
A raw novel of sexual passion and experimentation set in the unglamorous Lower East Side of New York.
[GD1022] Grafton pbk £3.99

THEROUX, PAUL (1941 -)
An accomplished travel writer and journalist as well as novelist, Theroux is a voracious man of letters. His novels frequently reflect the global scale of his interests and experiences, as witnessed by their often exotic locations.
Doctor Demarr (1988)
An eerie novella about two identical twins who hate each other from childhood.
[GD1023] Hutchinson hbk £8.95
Doctor Slaughter (1984)
[GD1024] Penguin pbk £2.50
Girls at Play (1969)
[GD1025] Penguin pbk £2.99
Jungle Lovers (1971)
Hilarious comedy about an insurance salesman who is taken prisoner by a ruthless terrorist and then attempts to sell him a policy.
[GD1026] Penguin pbk £3.50
London Embassy (1982)
Sequel to *The Consul's File*.
[GD1027] Penguin pbk £2.99
My Secret Life (1989) `NEW`
This large and populous novel describes the life and secrets of André Parent from his beginnings as an altar boy to his successful later life and marriage. Yet underneath his outward respectability are a few interesting secrets. An ambitious and comic novel, quite possibly Theroux's best yet.
[GD1028] H Hamilton hbk £11.95
O-Zone (1987)
[GD1029] Penguin pbk £4.50
Picture Palace (1978)
[GD1030] Penguin pbk £3.95
Saint Jack (1977)
[GD1031] Penguin pbk £2.95
The Black House (1974)
[GD1032] Penguin pbk £2.95

The Consul's File (1972)
[GD1033] Penguin pbk £2.95
The Family Arsenal (1976)
A thriller about anarchists that brilliantly evokes South London.
[GD1034] Penguin pbk £3.50
The Mosquito Coast (1981)
Acclaimed as his best novel. It is a terrifying book about the clash of Western technology and jungle civilization.
[GD1035] H Hamilton hbk £10.95
[GD1036] Penguin pbk £3.99
World's End (1980)
[GD1037] Penguin pbk £2.95

THOMAS, MARIA
Antonia Saw the Oryx First (1988)
'A complex and finely wrought portrait of two women, one black, one white, picking their way through the débris of shattered colonialism in Africa' (Margaret Atwood).
[GD1038] Serpent's Tail pbk £7.95
Come to Africa and Save Your Marriage (1989) `NEW`
A collection of stories about expatriates in Africa. 'Brilliant with light and darkness, smells and people' (Grace Paley).
[GD1039] Serpent's Tail pbk £7.95

THOMPSON, HUNTER S.
The legendary *Rolling Stone* journalist whose heyday was in the seventies.
Fear and Loathing in Las Vegas (1972)
Not one for understatement, Thompson subtitled this account of his drug-crazed adventures in the gambling capital 'A Savage Journey to the Heart of the American Dream'.
[GD1040] Grafton pbk £3.50
Generation of Swine (Essays, 1988) `NEW`
The Gonzo Papers vol 2: the collected columns from the *San Francisco Examiner*, and a demented commentary on American life.
[GD1041] Picador pbk £4.95
Hell's Angels (Non fiction, 1966)
Thompson hung loose with the Angels for a year in order to write this account of their disturbing habits.
[GD1042] Penguin pbk £3.95
The Great Shark Hunt (Essays, 1979)
Twenty years of journalistic excess and political dissent.
[GD1043] Picador pbk £5.95

TOOLE, JOHN KENNEDY (1937 - 1969)
Toole sent his novel to almost every American publisher and committed suicide after its universal rejection. However, it is now recognized as a comic masterpiece.
Confederacy of Dunces (1980)
A classic satire of American life set in New Orleans, notable for its rich cast of eccentric characters.
[GD1044] Penguin pbk £4.99

TOURETTE, AILEEN/AMELIE LA (1946 -)
Interesting and amusing feminist author.
Cry Wolf (1986)
[GD1045] Virago pbk £4.50
Ice Dancing (1986)
Four women reply to the following advertisement: 'Dancers wanted, no experience necessary, salary plus room and board. Alaska.'
[GD1046] Pandora pbk £3.95
Nuns and Mothers (1984)
[GD1047] Virago pbk £4.50

TRAVEN, BEN (1890?/ 1901? - ?)
A mysterious writer who has managed to maintain almost total anonymity, quite possibly of German origin since some of his works were first written in

that language. His adventure-style novels are usually set in Central America, or during the Mexican Revolution.

Cotton Pickers (1969)
[GD1048] Allison & B pbk **£2.95**
General from the Jungle
[GD1049] Allison & B pbk **£3.50**
Government
[GD1050] Allison & B pbk **£2.95**
March to the Monteria (1971)
[GD1051] Allison & B pbk **£2.95**
Rebellion of the Hanged (1952)
[GD1052] Allison & B pbk **£2.95**
The Carreta
[GD1053] Allison & B pbk **£2.95**
The Death Ship (1940)
A seething anti-capitalist novel of the seaways.
[GD1054] Picador pbk **£4.95**
The Treasure of the Sierra Madre (1934)
The classic novel of greedy gold-hunters in Mexico, filmed by John Huston.
[GD1055] Picador **£3.95**

TWAIN, MARK (1835 - 1910)
Born Samuel Langhorne Clemens and brought up on the Mississippi River, Twain made his part of America internationally famous through the immortal characters of Tom Sawyer and his friend Huck Finn. An immensely popular writer during his own lifetime, Twain's reputation has only increased with time as one of the key American vernacular prose stylists.
A Connecticut Yankee at King Arthur's Court (1889)
A satirical fantasy that turns into something altogether darker.
[GD1056] Penguin pbk **£4.50**
Innocents Abroad (The New Pilgrim's Progress) (1869)
Twain's first success; the humorous narrative of a shrewd American travelling in the Old World.
[GD1057] Century pbk **£4.95**
Life on the Mississippi (1883)
The mixture of history, memoir, travelogue and anecdote makes this one of Twain's best works.
[GD1058] Penguin pbk **£4.99**
Pudd'nhead Wilson (1894)
A tale of mistaken identity and murder that revolves around Twain's perennial theme of racial identity.
[GD1059] Penguin pbk **£3.50**
Roughing It (1872)
A travelogue of Twain's adventures in the American West related with unfailing humour, if not total veracity.
[GD1060] Penguin pbk **£4.95**
The Adventures of Huckleberry Finn (1884)
The triumphant sequel to *Tom Sawyer*, narrated with great élan by Huck himself: *the* seminal American novel, according to Hemingway.
[GD1061] Penguin pbk **£2.50**
The Adventures of Tom Sawyer (1876)
Nostalgic and humorous recreation of Tom and Huck's life on the river.
[GD1062] Penguin pbk **£2.50**
The Portable Twain
[GD1063] Penguin pbk **£5.95**
Tom Sawyer/Life on the Mississippi/Huckleberry Finn/Pudd'nhead Wilson
[GD1064] Cambridge hbk **£7.95**

TYLER, ANNE (1941 -)
An increasingly popular and well-regarded author, Tyler explores the disruptions and irrationality of family life in novels which are both acidly funny and sad: she is often very aware of the isolation of the individual.
A Slipping Down Life (1970)
[GD1065] Arrow pbk **£2.50**

Breathing Lessons (1989) **NEW**
On her way to her best friend's husband's funeral, Maggie Moran, thickening at the waist and approaching fifty, opens her heart. Met with excellent reviews earlier this year.
[GD1066] Chatto hbk **£11.95**
Celestial Navigation (1975)
[GD1067] Pan pbk **£2.95**
Dinner at the Homesick Restaurant (1973)
The loneliness and grief of a deserted wife.
[GD1068] Penguin pbk **£3.50**
Earthly Possessions (1977)
[GD1069] Arrow pbk **£2.95**
Morgan's Passing (1980)
[GD1070] Arrow pbk **£1.65**
Searching for Caleb (1976)
[GD1071] Pan pbk **£4.50**
The Accidental Tourist (1985)
A glorious tragi-comedy about how a man addicted to routine - he even flosses his teeth before making love - tries to cope with the chaos of everyday life.
[GD1072] Penguin pbk **£3.50**
The Clock Winder (1973)
[GD1073] Arrow pbk **£2.95**
The Tin Can Tree (1966)
[GD1074] Arrow pbk **£3.50**

UPDIKE, DAVID
Out on the Marsh (1989) **NEW**
Careful, quiet stories that tempt comparisons to his father, John, but marked with a humour and sensibility of his own.
[GD1075] Constable hbk **£10.95**

UPDIKE, JOHN (1932 -)
The great chronicler of marital upset and reconciliation, Updike couches his views on human relationships in simple, elegant prose. Alongside his novels, he is also a celebrated short story writer, having begun writing for *The New York Times* and later *The New Yorker*.
A Month of Sundays (1975)
[GD1076] Deutsch pbk **£4.95**
Bech: A Book (1970)
A celebrated Jewish novelist loses the knack of writing.
[GD1077] Penguin pbk **£2.50**
Bech is Back (1982)
[GD1078] Penguin pbk **£2.95**
Couples (1968)
The stylish young couples in Tarbox, Mass., feel almost obliged to take part in adulterous musical chairs.
[GD1079] Penguin pbk **£4.99**
Forty Stories (1987)
A special selection from his four collections.
[GD1080] Penguin pbk **£5.95**
Hugging the Shore (Essays, 1984)
A compendious volume of essays, book reviews and journalism.
[GD1081] Penguin pbk **£8.95**
Marry Me (1976)
[GD1082] Penguin pbk **£3.99**
Of the Farm (1965)
[GD1083] Deutsch pbk **£4.95**
Rabbit, Run (1960)
The first novel in the 'Rabbit' trilogy: ex-basketball player Rabbit deserts his family to rediscover the excitement of his heroic youth.
[GD1084] Penguin pbk **£3.95**
Rabbit Redux (1971)
Second 'Rabbit' novel: 36-year-old Rabbit struggles to keep a grip on his disintegrating life.
[GD1085] Penguin pbk **£3.50**
Rabbit is Rich (1981)
Pulitzer Prize winner, third novel in the series.
[GD1086] Penguin pbk **£4.99**

Roger's Version (1986)
A divinity dean is involved in a struggle to prove the existence of God. The best of his recent works.
[GD1087] Penguin pbk **£4.50**
S (1988)
An epistolary novel that satirizes America's religious communities.
[GD1088] Penguin pbk **£3.99**
Self-Consciousness: Memoirs **NEW**
Six meditations upon topics as diverse as Updike's hometown, his psoriasis and stuttering, his experience of Vietnam and his sense of self, rendered as sensitively and amusingly as we have come to expect from this fine writer.
[GD1089] Deutsch hbk **£12.95**
The Centaur (1963)
[GD1090] Deutsch pbk **£4.95**
The Coup (1978)
[GD1091] Penguin pbk **£2.99**
The Poorhouse Fair (1958)
His first novel.
[GD1092] Penguin pbk **£3.99**
The Witches of Eastwick (1984)
Three divorced women form a coven and are lured into the evil Darryl Van Horne's mansion.
[GD1093] Penguin pbk **£3.50**
Trust Me (1987)
22 new stories of trust betrayed or fulfilled, told in prose of characteristic elegance and clarity.
[GD1094] Penguin pbk **£3.99**
Your Lover Just Called (1979)
[GD1095] Penguin pbk **£3.95**

URIS, LEON (1924 -)
Ambitious and immensely popular historical novelist.
Armageddon (1964)
Set in Berlin in 1945.
[GD1096] Transworld pbk **£3.99**
Exodus (1957)
The birth of modern Israel.
[GD1097] Transworld pbk **£3.99**
Mila 18 (1961)
Powerful story of the uprising of the Jews in Warsaw in 1944.
[GD1098] Transworld pbk **£3.50**
Mitla Pass (1989) **NEW**
Billed as Uris' 'most personal novel yet', this is the story of the successful author and US marine who escapes from the destructive clutches of Hollywood; he travels to Israel to research a book and find his own roots.
[GD1099] Doubleday hbk **£12.95**
The Haj (1984)
[GD1100] Transworld pbk **£2.95**

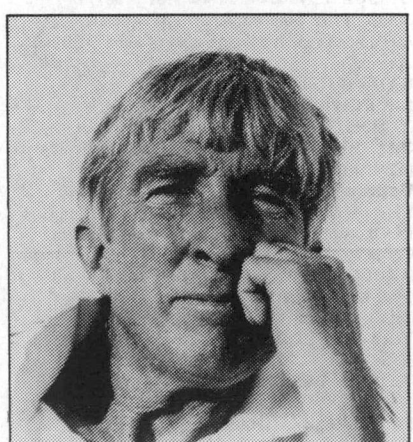

John Updike, author of *Self-Consciousness: Memoirs* (Deutsch hbk **£12.95**)

Gore Vidal, author of *Hollywood* (Deutsch hbk £12.95)

Topaz (1968)
Factually based novel about the Cuban missile crisis.
[GD1101] Transworld pbk **£2.95**
Trinity (1976)
The history of Ireland: from the 1840's famine to the 1916 Easter Rising.
[GD1102] Transworld pbk **£3.99**

VASSI, MARCO
The Erotic Comedies (1981)
An underground classic in the US, this is a hilarious and outrageous collection of erotic short stories.
[GD1103] Black Spring pbk **£4.95**

VIDAL, GORE (1925 -)
One of the giants of contemporary American letters, Vidal is a noted satirist and essayist as well as novelist. Coming from a famous Democrat family, he is a penetrating critic of America past as well as present; his sequence of novels (*Washington DC*, *Burr*, *1876*, *Lincoln* and *Empire*) form a political history of the US from the end of the 19th century.
1876 (1976)
[GD1104] Grafton pbk **£2.95**
Armageddon? (Essays, 1987)
His latest collection of incisive essays on modern America.
[GD1105] Grafton pbk **£3.99**
Burr (1973)
[GD1106] Grafton pbk **£3.99**
Creation (1981)
A characteristically ambitious novel set in Byzantine times, which takes in the whole of the history of Western civilization.
[GD1107] Grafton pbk **£3.95**
Dark Green, Bright Red (1950)
A US army officer in a Latin American revolution.
[GD1108] Grafton pbk **£1.25**
Duluth (1983)
A glittering satire on suburbia.
[GD1109] Grafton pbk **£1.95**
Empire (1987)
Vidal's fictional history of America reaches the 20th century.
[GD1110] Grafton pbk **£4.99**
Hollywood (1989) **NEW**
The latest instalment in Vidal's epic and engrossing series continues the story of Caroline Sanford as she becomes involved in the new motion picture business, becoming a star herself in the process.
[GD1111] Deutsch hbk **£12.95**

In a Yellow Wood (1947)
[GD1112] Grafton pbk **£1.25**
Kalki (1978)
A satire on feminism in the post-Vietnam world.
[GD1113] Grafton pbk **£2.50**
Lincoln (1984)
[GD1114] Grafton pbk **£4.95**
Messiah (1954)
In California, where strange cults flourish, there arose a new Messiah who knew that mankind yearned for death...
[GD1115] Grafton pbk **£2.50**
Myra Breckenridge/Myron (1968, 1974)
A new edition, with an introduction by the author, of his satirical novel about transexuality and its sequel.
[GD1116] Grafton pbk **£4.50**
The Judgement of Paris (1952)
[GD1117] Grafton pbk **£3.50**
Washington DC (1967)
Classic evocation of the American political scene.
[GD1118] Grafton pbk **£2.50**
Williwaw (1946)
Outstanding World War II novel.
[GD1119] Grafton pbk **£2.50**

VOLLMAN, WILLIAM T. (1959 -)
This young Californian writer is making a name for himself as the new Pynchon, principally on the strength of his sprawling and eclectic first novel.
The Rainbow Stories (1989) **NEW**
The stories in this book are drawn from real life stories of prostitutes, skinheads, drug addicts, derelicts and war heroes interviewed by the author in the course of his research, but subsequently filtered through his own weird consciousness.
[GD1120] Deutsch hbk **£12.95**
You Bright and Risen Angels (1987)
An unusually imaginative first novel that has become quite a cult book on both sides of the Atlantic.
[GD1121] Picador pbk **£6.95**

VONNEGUT, KURT (1922 -)
A novelist with a strong cult following, Vonnegut weaves together elements of fantasy, science fiction and philosophical speculation into a style wholly of his own making. He has an urgent concern about the way we live; his books are often eloquent pleas for compassion.
Bluebeard (1988)
The autobiography of abstract painter Rabo Karabekian, who first appeared in *Breakfast of Champions*.
[GD1122] Grafton pbk **£4.50**
Breakfast of Champions (1973)
One of his most popular novels; a sharp critique of contemporary society exposed through the wild, zany adventures of several Americans.
[GD1123] Grafton pbk **£2.95**
Cat's Cradle (1963)
Chilling black comedy of global destruction.
[GD1124] Penguin pbk **£3.95**
Deadeye Dick (1983)
[GD1125] Grafton pbk **£2.50**
Galapagos (1985)
A blistering satire on Natural Selection. 'It makes the reader sweat with pleasure.' (Martin Amis)
[GD1126] Grafton pbk **£2.99**
God Bless You, Mr Rosewater (1965)
[GD1127] Grafton pbk **£2.50**
Happy Birthday, Wanda June (Play, 1970)
Vonnegut's only play follows the lives of the 'heroes' who dropped the bomb on Nagasaki.
[GD1128] Grafton pbk **£2.50**
Jailbird (1979)
The fanciful life of a fictitious participant in the Watergate scandal.
[GD1129] Grafton pbk **£2.50**
Mother Night (1961)
[GD1130] Grafton pbk **£1.95**

Palm Sunday (Essays, 1981)
[GD1131] Grafton pbk **£2.95**
Player Piano (1952)
Drawing on his experience of working for General Electric, this novel satirizes the extent to which humans are subjected to the demands of machines.
[GD1132] Grafton pbk **£2.50**
Sirens of Titan (1959)
[GD1133] Gollancz pbk **£3.50**
Slapstick (1976)
[GD1134] Grafton pbk **£3.99**
Slaughterhouse 5 (1969)
Working underground in Dresden when it was firebombed, Vonnegut emerged to find 135,000 Germans had been 'baked like gingerbread men'. The experience of this atrocity inspired this, probably his best novel.
[GD1135] Cape hbk **£9.50**
[GD1136] Grafton pbk **£3.99**
Wampeters, Foma and Granfalloons (1974)
[GD1137] Grafton pbk **£2.95**
Welcome to the Monkey House (Stories & essays, 1968)
[GD1138] Grafton pbk **£2.50**

VRIES, PETER DE (1910 -)
Humourist and parodist who writes fantastical comedies of manners.
Slouching towards Kalamazoo (1983)
[GD1139] Gollancz hbk **£7.95**
The Mackerel Plaza (1958)
A wickedly funny critique of the prejudices and complacencies of American suburbia in the Eisenhower era. Introduced by Frederic Raphael.
[GD1140] Oxford pbk **£3.95**

WALKER, ALICE (1944 -)
A leading contemporary Black poet, novelist, essayist and activist who shot to fame with her poignant and controversial novel *The Colour Purple*. Born in Georgia, Walker has taught at Yale and has long been associated with the magazine *Ms* (she describes herself as a 'womanist'). Her writing is as vivid and poetic as any currently coming out of the States.
Horses Make a Landscape More Beautiful (Poetry, 1985)
[GD1141] Women's P pbk **£2.95**
In Love and Trouble (Stories, 1984)
Thirteen angry and loving tributes to the Black women of the rural South.
[GD1142] Women's P pbk **£3.95**
In Search of Our Mothers' Gardens (Prose, 1984)
An inspirational collection of memories, essays and interviews.
[GD1143] Women's P pbk **£6.95**
Living By The Word (Essays, 1988) **NEW**
A further collection of essays, as ever brilliantly blending the political and the personal.
[GD1144] Women's P pbk **£5.95**
Meridian (1976)
Her second novel, and a celebration of civil rights campaigning.
[GD1145] Women's P pbk **£4.95**
Once (Poetry, 1968)
Dealing with the civil rights movement and her experiences of living in Africa.
[GD1146] Women's P pbk **£2.95**
The Colour Purple (1982)
Her celebrated epistolary novel about the love between two sisters who become separated. Pulitzer Prize winner.
[GD1147] Women's P pbk **£4.95**
The Temple of My Familiar **NEW**
The eagerly awaited new novel from Walker turns out to be a highly unconventional meditation upon,

and celebration of, women's role through time and space, with a huge array of characters. Powerfully poetic.
[GD1148] Women's P hbk **£11.95**
The Third Life of Grange Copeland (1970)
[GD1149] Women's P pbk **£4.95**
You Can't Keep a Good Woman Down (1982)
Fourteen short stories displaying Walker's range of subjects and styles.
[GD1150] Women's P pbk **£3.95**

WEBB, CHARLES
The Graduate (1963)
Famous story of the graduate seduced by Mrs Robinson; his life is complicated when he falls in love with her daughter.
[GD1151] Penguin pbk **£2.50**

WELTY, EUDORA (1909 -)
One of the great short story writers and novelists of the South, Welty's work is centred around the lives of the people of the Mississippi, and employs the full rich speech of the area to maximun effect. *One Writer's Beginnings* provides a marvellous account of the environment in which she grew up, and of her writing development. While her novels are somewhat in the tradition of Southern Gothic, her stories have a quality of life which, at its best, is without parallel.
Collected Stories
[GD1152] Boyars hbk **£15.00**
[GD1153] Boyars pbk **£8.95**
Delta Wedding (1945)
A subtle examination of the attitudes of a plantation family.
[GD1154] Virago pbk **£4.99**
Losing Battles (1970)
A Mississippi family in the 1930s who feel their old familiar world slipping away from them.
[GD1155] Virago pbk **£4.99**
One Writer's Beginnings (Non fiction)
[GD1156] Faber pbk **£2.95**
The Eye of the Story (Essays, 1978)
[GD1157] Virago pbk **£6.99**
The Optimist's Daughter (1972)
Pulitzer Prize winner. Acclaimed by many as her masterpiece, this novel explores the tensions between a judge's daughter and his second wife.
[GD1158] Virago pbk **£4.50**
The Ponder Heart (1954)
A delightful and humorous evocation of life in a small Mississippi town.
[GD1159] Virago pbk **£4.50**

Alice Walker, author of *The Colour Purple* (Women's Press pbk **£4.95**)

Edith Wharton, Christmas 1905 from *Edith Wharton* by R.W.B. Lewis (Constable hbk **£7.50**)

The Robber Bridegroom (1942)
A fairy-tale novella which tells the story of an unusual Mississippi romance between a planter's daughter and a robber.
[GD1160] Virago pbk **£4.50**

WEST, NATHANIEL (1903 - 1940)
Although largely ignored during his own lifetime, West is now widely admired for his crisp, sardonic wit; his four novels are famous as bitter satires of American life.
The Complete Works
Includes: *The Dream Life of Balso Snell* (1931); *Miss Lonelyhearts* (1933), in which an agony aunt columnist despairs of ever solving the petty human problems, let alone the big ones; *A Cool Million* (1934), a savage attack on the American rags-to-riches dream; and *The Day of the Locust* (1939), which exposes the sordid reality beneath the veneer of Hollywood.
[GD1161] Secker hbk **£12.95**
[GD1162] Picador pbk **£4.95**

WHARTON, EDITH (1862 - 1937)
Along with Willa Cather, Wharton was one of the most important of America's early women writers, although her territory - of moneyed New York with its fine distinctions of class - is very different. Born into a wealthy New York family, she married early, and it took her many years to attain her independence, her experiences making her an acute social critic of her class. She was later honoured for her wartime relief work, and lived the later part of her life in France.
Ethan Frome (1911)
[GD1163] Penguin pbk **£3.50**
Ethan Frome/Summer (1911, 1917)
Both these novels are well away from Edith Wharton's usual society settings, being realistic rural tragedies.
[GD1164] Oxford pbk **£3.95**
Hudson River Bracketed (1929)
[GD1165] Virago pbk **£4.95**
Madame de Treymes (1907)
[GD1166] Virago pbk **£4.50**
Old New York (1924)
[GD1167] Virago pbk **£4.50**
Roman Fever and Other Stories
[GD1168] Virago pbk **£3.95**
The Age of Innocence (1920)
Wharton became the first woman to be awarded the Pulitzer Prize with this novel, arguably the last of her great works; set in the 1870s, it concerns a young man torn between two women.
[GD1169] Penguin pbk **£4.95**

The Children (1928)
[GD1170] Virago pbk **£4.50**
The Custom of the Country (1913)
The conscience-free quest of a social-climbing woman who variously marries an aristocratic New Yorker, a French Count, and an American billionaire, it is nonetheless a work of great sympathy.
[GD1171] Penguin pbk **£4.95**
The Fruit of the Tree (1907)
[GD1172] Virago pbk **£5.50**
The Gods Arrive (1932)
[GD1173] Virago pbk **£5.50**
The House of Mirth (1905)
Wharton's first undisputed masterpiece was also her most widely popular novel; it records the disastrous social career of Lily Bart, and is a moving depiction of the restrictions placed upon women in early American society.
[GD1174] Penguin pbk **£4.95**
The Mother's Recompense (1925)
[GD1175] Virago pbk **£4.50**
The Reef (1912)
Of all Edith Wharton's novels this one most shows the influence of her life-long friend, Henry James.
[GD1176] Virago pbk **£4.50**
The Stories of Edith Wharton Vol 1
Chosen and introduced by Anita Brookner.
[GD1177] Simon & Sch pbk **£5.95**
The Stories of Edith Wharton Vol 2 `NEW`
A further selection of stories, many of them minor classics, again introduced by Anita Brookner.
[GD1178] Simon & Sch hbk **£12.95**

WHARTON, WILLIAM (1925 -)
A bewitching writer whose novels are remarkable not only for their profound insights into the human heart, but also for their singular originality and gentle humour.
A Midnight Clear (1982)
Tragi-comic novel set in the Ardennes at Christmas. A tense work of taut emotions.
[GD1179] Penguin pbk **£3.50**
Birdy (1979)
Strange and memorable first novel about a young man obsessed with flight, who enjoys an almost erotic relationship with his pet birds.
[GD1180] Penguin pbk **£3.99**
Dad (1981)
A profound exploration of fathers and sons stirring in its affirmation of the power of love.
[GD1181] Penguin pbk **£4.95**
Franky Furbo `NEW`
Set in a remote Italian village, Wharton's new novel focuses on an attempt to prove the truth of what seems a fantasy; Franky Furbo is a fox, the subject of stories told by the main character, William, to his children over many years. The imaginative quest which results involves a journey back forty years into the past, and over 50,000 forward into the future.
[GD1182] Cape hbk **£12.95**
[GD1183] Cape pbk **£8.95**
Pride (1986)
A charming and imaginative tale wherein two worlds collide: that of a lion in a carnival, and a young boy's 1930s childhood.
[GD1184] Penguin pbk **£4.50**
Scumbler (1984)
Scumbler spends his life in Paris on his Honda. But he has to face up to urgent intimations of mortality.
[GD1185] Cape hbk **£8.95**
Tidings (1988)
Emotional and intimate study of family life.
[GD1186] Cape hbk **£10.95**

WHITE, EDMUND (1940 -)
Fine and sensitive gay novelist who has won wide acclaim for his two autobiographical novels about growing up gay in America.

A Boy's Own Story (1983)
The bestselling account of an adolescent boy's realization of his gay sexuality.
[GD1187] Picador pbk **£3.95**

The Beautiful Room is Empty (1988)
Impressive sequel to *A Boy's Own Story* which charts the narrator's life up to the birth of the gay liberation movement.
[GD1188] Picador pbk **£3.95**

Caracole (1985)
A young man is introduced to the great rites of adulthood: sexual desire, social intrigue, and political power.
[GD1189] Picador pbk **£3.95**

Forgetting Elena/Nocturnes for the King of Naples (1978)
Two early works of homoerotic love.
[GD1190] Picador pbk **£2.95**

States of Desire: Travels in Gay America (Non-fiction, 1986)
[GD1191] Picador pbk **£3.95**

WIDEMAN, JOHN EDGAR (1941 -)
A writer whose work is by turns poetic, nightmarish and realistic, Wideman paints convincing portraits of Black communities.

Brothers and Keepers
[GD1192] Fontana pbk **£4.95**

Damballah
[GD1193] Fontana pbk **£2.95**

Hiding Place
[GD1194] Fontana pbk **£2.95**

Sent For You Yesterday
[GD1195] Fontana pbk **£2.95**

WIGGINS, MARIANNE (1947 -)
Herself in Love   `NEW`
Her acclaimed 1987 collection, re-issued with four new stories.
[GD1196] Secker hbk **£11.95**

John Dollar (1989)   `NEW`
Rangoon, 1918. A war widow meets John Dollar and falls in love. Their journey to chart a nearby island, and the ensuing catastrophe, form a compelling narrative that deftly weaves symbol and reality together.
[GD1197] Secker hbk **£10.95**

Separate Checks (1985)
[GD1198] Fontana pbk **£3.50**

WILDER, THORNTON (1897 - 1975)
Born in Wisconsin but reared in China, Wilder became a professor of English before winning wide popularity with his brilliant novella, *The Bridge of San Luis Rey*. However, his real name and fortune was subsequently made in the theatre, with plays such as *Our Town*.

Mr North, or, Theophilus North (1973)
The entertaining and poignant adventures of a language tutor set loose in a wealthy resort in the 20s. Recently filmed.
[GD1199] Penguin pbk **£3.99**

The Bridge of San Luis Rey (1927)
Wilder won the Pulitzer Prize for this exquisitely written exploration of the role of providence in the sudden death of five travellers in Peru in 1714.
[GD1200] Penguin pbk **£2.95**

The Eighth Day (1967)
A novel centred around a murder case in the Mid West: Wilder's last novel seems very much out-of-place in the late 60s.
[GD1201] Penguin pbk **£4.95**

The Ides of March (1948)
A multi-directional look at the end of Caesar's life.
[GD1202] Penguin pbk **£3.95**

WILEY, RICHARD (1944   )
Fools' Gold (1989)   `NEW`
Alaska in the 19th century, and the gold rush is on:

Wiley's second novel charts the collisions between the different prospectors and cultures with profound sympathy and perception.
[GD1203] Chatto hbk **£11.95**

Soldiers in Hiding (1986)
Winner of the PEN/Faulkner Award for the best American novel of 1986.
[GD1204] Picador pbk **£3.50**

WILLIAMS, JOY
A very highly regarded member of the 'new' school of 'realist' writing. This is the first of her three novels to be published here.

Breaking and Entering (1987)
Willie and Liberty are two drifters who break into Florida vacation homes while their owners are away. Another of those sparse, hauntingly plain stories rendered in perfect prose.
[GD1205] Flamingo pbk **£3.99**

WILLIAMS, TENNESSEE (1911 - 1983)
Born and bred in the South, Williams became a noted and successful playwright. He also wrote poetry, novels and stories, these latter often providing the germ for his plays, and dealing with the same themes of loss, desperation and guilt.

Collected Stories (1986)
Introduced by Gore Vidal.
[GD1206] Picador pbk **£6.99**

Three Players of a Summer Game (1984)
[GD1207] Dent pbk **£3.50**

WILLIAMS, WILLIAM CARLOS (1883 - 1963)
New Jersey paediatrician, better known for his Imagist and Objectivist poetry, and his epic poem *Paterson*.

In the American Grain (Essays, 1925)
The classic volume of impressionistic literary criticism is at last published here in the UK. It is a fascinating analysis of how early Americans forged themselves a new cultural language.
[GD1208] Penguin pbk **£4.99**

The Doctor Stories
An amusing series of partly autobiographical stories.
[GD1209] Faber pbk **£3.95**

WILSON, EDMUND (1895 - 1972)
Celebrated critic and man of letters.

Memoirs of Hecate County (1946)
Stories of wealthy New Yorkers, this is Wilson's only work of fiction.
[GD1210] Hogarth pbk **£5.95**

WISTER, OWEN (1860 - 1938)
The Virginian (1902)
The epic novel of the American West that inspired a million films and earned itself a permanent place in American mythology. It tells of the tall, silent stranger who one day rides into town...
[GD1211] Penguin pbk **£3.95**

WOLFE, THOMAS (1900 - 1938)
Wolfe's powerful talent and passionate style has to be balanced with a lack of discipline and tendency to overwrite. There are elements of autobiography throughout his work, most notably in his first, and best, novel, *Look Homeward Angel*, which tells the story (continued in *Of Time and the River*) of the childhood and growth to manhood of Eugene Gant. The other two novels were edited from material left unfinished at his death.

Look Homeward, Angel (1929)
[GD1212] Penguin pbk **£6.95**

Of Time and the River (1935)
[GD1213] Penguin pbk **£6.99**

The Web and the Rock (1939)
[GD1214] Penguin pbk **£5.99**

You Can't Go Home Again (1940)
[GD1215] Penguin pbk **£5.99**

WOLFE, TOM (1931 -)
Without doubt America's foremost social commentator, who started life as the King of 'New Journalism', and has now crossed over into overt fiction, using the same baroque prose style.

Radical Chic (Non-fiction, 1971)
A searing attack on 1970s radicalism.
[GD1216] Sphere pbk **£3.99**

The Bonfire of the Vanities (1988)
This first work of fiction by Wolfe has been a runaway success, both critical and commercial. Celebrated for its Dickensian sweep and reviled for its racism, it presents the spectacular fall from grace of Wall Street whizz Sherman McCoy.
[GD1217] Cape hbk **£12.95**
[GD1218] Picador pbk **£4.99**

The Electric Kool-Aid Acid Test (Non fiction, 1968)
[GD1219] Transworld pbk **£4.99**

The Painted Word (Non fiction, 1976)
A bitter exposé of the art world.
[GD1220] Transworld pbk **£3.50**

The Pump House Gang (1969)
A racy collection of stories and incidents.
[GD1221] Transworld pbk **£4.99**

The Purple Decades (Essays, 1983)
[GD1222] Penguin pbk **£5.99**

The Right Stuff (Non fiction, 1984)
Wolfe's account of the space-race astronauts: all-American heroes with vulnerable private lives.
[GD1223] Cape hbk **£12.50**
[GD1224] Transworld pbk **£4.99**

WOLFF, TOBIAS (1945 -)
Very much the contemporary of Ray Carver and Richard Ford, Wolff's reputation rests upon his mastery of the short story form, which in his hands is often used to reveal people's habitual self-deceit in their dealings with others.

Back in the World (1985)
His second collection.
[GD1225] Cape hbk **£8.95**

Collected Stories (1988)
Contains all the stories from his two collections, as well as his powerful novella.
[GD1226] Picador pbk **£5.95**

The Barracks Thief (1984)
Winner of the 1985 PEN/Faulkner Award. A marvellous novella about a triad of relationships between three young army recruits in the 60s.
[GD1227] Cape hbk **£9.95**

This Boy's Life (1989)   `NEW`
Wolff's first full-length book is an astonishing and revealing memoir of his far-from-model teenage years. It confirms his emergence as a major writer.
[GD1228] Bloomsbury hbk **£13.95**

WOLITZER, WILMA
Silver (1989)   `NEW`
The near-permanent breakdown of a middle-class marriage is, unusually, related by both husband and wife in this engaging new novel. How they find the best way of living together - or apart - is the subject of a moving tale.
[GD1229] Hutchinson hbk **£11.95**

WOUK, HERMAN (1915 -)
His best and most popular work is set in the South Pacific during World War II, a period which he evokes through strong narrative and accumulated detail.

Don't Stop the Carnival (1965)
[GD1230] Fontana pbk **£3.50**

Inside Outside (1985)
[GD1231] Fontana pbk **£3.95**

The Caine Mutiny (1951)
Pulitzer Prize winner: the tale of passions on board a World War II minesweeper.
[GD1232] Fontana pbk **£4.50**
War and Remembrance (1978)
[GD1233] Fontana pbk **£3.50**
Winds of War (1971)
[GD1234] Fontana pbk **£3.95**

WRIGHT, RICHARD (1908 - 1960)
One of the major Black writers of his generation, Wright used the naturalistic tradition to dramatize the plight of the negro in the prejudiced South. His work reflects his interest and involvement in, as well as eventual rejection of, communism as a solution to Black problems.
Black Boy (1945)
His memorable volume of autobiography.
[GD1235] Picador pbk **£4.95**
Native Son (1940)
Powerful and defiant novel of one man's growing self-awareness as he awaits his trial.
[GD1236] Penguin pbk **£4.95**

YOURGRAU, BARRY
'I can never remember my own dreams, so Mr Yourgrau's stories are a pretty good substitute.' (David Byrne).
A Man Jumps Out of an Airplane/Wearing Dad's Head (1988)
Over one hundred and fifty bizarre and magical short-shorts.
[GD1237] Grafton pbk **£3.95**

The American Short Story

"While short stories often tell us things we don't know anything about - and this is good, of course, - they should also, and maybe more importantly, tell us what everybody knows, but no-one is talking about. At least not publicly - except for the short story writers" (Raymond Carver). The American short story has had an illustrious history and, of all the literary genres, it is one the US has made very much its own. In the last century, Hawthorne and Poe found the form particularly suited to their own inimitable imaginations, but it was not until earlier this century that the real roots of this strong tradition were formed. All too often the English short story rests upon its ending; but the best of American short stories, with their tradition of remarkable compression, have the ability to read like novels in miniature. Indeed, one of the fathers of the tradition, Sherwood Anderson, made his best book, **Winesburg, Ohio** (1919), a collection of linked stories suggestive of a larger work. Faulkner took this interesting mini-tradition a stage further with his fragmented but interwoven collection **Go Down, Moses** (1942), and a modern counterpart can be found in Alice Munro's **The Beggar Maid** (1971), a collection of stories that share the same female protagonist (from a writer who is most at home in the short story form).
The writer who crystallized the genesis of the American short story as a separate tradition was Hemingway. He took Ring Lardner's rugged use of the vernacular, and along with Anderson's thoughtful style and Gertrude Stein's literary guidance, wrote his best work in this form. **In Our Time** (1925) remains a milestone. Since Hemingway, almost every American novelist of note has produced an obligatory volume of short stories. Three notable collections from the fifties are J.D. Salinger's **For Esmé, With Love and Squalor** (1953), Truman Capote's **Breakfast at Tiffany's** (1958) and Carson McCullers' **The Ballad of the Sad Café** (1951); the last two of these, with their longer pieces, making explicit the relation between such writing and the novel.

The *New Yorker* has for a long time nurtured (some would say shaped) the talents of many a short story writer. Since Salinger, it has supported two of the classic writers of their 'school', John Updike and John Cheever. However, in the last ten years it has been America's regional and Mid Western writers who have been responsible for the form's renaissance: suddenly all the best young writers were pouring their energies into the genre. Six years ago *Granta* caught the moment and christened it with their subsequently unparalleled **Dirty Realism** collection. Since then Richard Ford, Tobias Wolff and Jayne Anne Phillips have all won the respect and praise they deserve for their stories, but all three would undoubtedly reserve pride of place for their now sadly dead mentor, Raymond Carver. To read him is to discover how infinitely supple the form can be in the hands of a master story-teller, and to appreciate the finest flowering of the tradition. It is unlikely that anyone will surpass his achievement for a very long time indeed.

American Short Stories
(Ed. Cournos)
[GD001] Dent pbk **£2.50**
American Short Stories
(Ed. Tayor, Barry)
[GD002] Longman pbk **£1.75**
Major American Short Stories
[GD003] Oxford pbk **£9.95**
American Short Stories of Today
(Ed. Jones, E.)
[GD004] Penguin pbk **£2.95**
Penguin Book of American Short Stories (Ed. Cochrane, James)
[GD005] Penguin pbk **£3.99**
The Year's Best American Short Stories 1984 (Ed. Tyler, Anne)
[GD006] Severn H hbk **£7.95**
The Year's Best American Short Stories 1985 (Ed. Updike, John)
[GD007] Severn H pbk **£4.95**
Twenty under Thirty: The Best of America's Young Writers
[GD008] Penguin pbk **£4.99**
American Short Stories of the 19th Century
[GD009] Dent pbk **£2.50**
Old Maids: Short Stories by US Women
[GD0010] Pandora pbk **£4.95**

William Faulkner, author of *Go Down, Moses*, seven short stories written in 1942 (Penguin pbk £4.99) (Photo: Camera Press)

FICTION

AUSTRALASIAN FICTION

Despite the title of this section, there is no such thing as an Australasian literature. The two antipodean nations Australia and New Zealand, separated by more than a thousand miles of sea (further than from London to Russia) and just as much history, have a homogeneity that is only perceivable from half a world away. Though their literatures share a common language, they have an icy disrespect for one another. It often seems that for a writer from one country to break into the other, they must first succeed in the cultural hub centers of the north. Fiction from the early years often deals with the discontinuity between the traditions of Europe and the experience of a new land and even younger culture. Preoccupations with physical space became a hallmark of such work, often being depicted as a confrontation of the self with a harsh and unforgiving land. Australian literature sought to come to an understanding of the overwhelming sense of space and solitude in the dusty 'Outback' hinterland. This is the so called 'dead center' that Patrick White explores in his novel *Voss*, an impressive allegory of the poverty of the human condition. This mysterious mythic interior is of course anything but empty or dead - as Bruce Chatwin's masterly novel *The Songlines* shows (although ironically this will be found in the 20th century British Fiction section). In New Zealand the idea of writing a sense of place became enmeshed in a self-conscious desire for national identity. This is articulated in both cultures as a kind of dry naturalism, earthy and rich but often appallingly dull and worthy. Frank Sargeson's stories are a wonderful antidote. Though working within this tradition, these gothic and ironic masterpieces capture the essence of small-minded New Zealand in the 1930s, with an underlying ambiguous eroticism. Contrary to European perceptions, there is now a considerable body of sophisticated experimental fiction - work that has gained a wider popular acceptance in their own countries than might be expected in Britain. These novels question the nature of the form as much as perceptions about nation or place - as can be seen in the recent work of C.K. Stead and Janet Frame in New Zealand, and David Ireland and David Malouf in Australia; or the sprawling, heterogeneous works of the Booker prize winners Keri Hulme and Peter Carey.

BAIL, MURRAY (ED)
Faber Book of Contemporary Australian Short Stories
Bail's provocative and original selection shows the remarkable vigour of contemporary Australian short fiction.
[GE1] Faber pbk **£5.95**

BROOKS, DAVID
An editor and poet as well as novelist, Brooks has been pivotal in introducing modern North American poetry to Australia.
The Book of Sei (Stories, 1987)
The first British publication of this book had Brooks compared with Borges, Calvino and Kundera. His work is deeply sensual, precise, and intellectual.
[GE2] Faber pbk **£3.99**

CAMBRIDGE, ADA
Following a childhood in Norfolk, Ada Cambridge left for Victoria where she became known as a writer of romantic fiction. Her best work transcends this genre, offering delicate explorations of the social constraints facing colonial women complemented by splendid evocations of the landscapes of Australia.

A Marked Man (1890)
Considered her finest novel and her first financial success, this novel concerns the rise to colonial prosperity of two generations of the Delavel family, and subtly explores the tensions between radicalism and convention.
[GE3] Pandora pbk **£5.95**
The Three Miss Kings (1891)
[GE4] Virago pbk **£5.99**

CAREY, PETER (1943 -)
The most prominent young Australian novelist, and winner of the 1988 Booker Prize for his novel *Oscar and Lucinda*. His works daringly mix many elements of fiction: weaving together vivid realism and social history with veins of surrealism and dark, macabre comedy.
Bliss (1981)
A Brisbane advertising agent called Harry Joy dies three times and awakens after each death to new kinds of experience, half nightmare and half bliss. A splendidly savage satire, now made into a feature film.
[GE5] Faber hbk **£6.50**
[GE6] Picador pbk **£3.99**
Exotic Pleasures (Stories, 1981)
A new edition of *The Fat Man in History*, the story of a fat man's persecution, after a revolution in which obesity has been made a crime.
[GE7] Picador pbk **£3.99**
Illywhacker (1985)
A dazzlingly comic narrative related by a 139 year old con-man, set on the outskirts of the bush and the city, concerning parents, planes, cars, disappearing acts, rust and lust. A hilarious *tour-de-force*.
[GE8] Faber hbk **£10.95**
[GE9] Faber pbk **£4.99**
Oscar and Lucinda (1988)
Winner of the 1988 Booker Prize, this vast work sprawls over a century of murky Australian history, and describes the bizarre results of a love affair between an Oxford seminarian with a passion for gambling and a Sydney heiress with a fascination for glass.
[GE10] Faber hbk **£10.95**
[GE11] Faber pbk **£4.99**

Peter Carey, author of *Oscar and Lucinda* (Faber hbk £10.95, pbk £4.99)

Miles Franklin, author of *My Brilliant Career* (Virago pbk £4.99)

FRAME, JANET (1924   )
New Zealand's most distinguished living novelist, Janet Frame's work is noted for its lyrical intensity, linguistic control and stunning originality. Her recently completed three-volume autobiography has been described as one of the finest in recent years, offering an evocative exploration of her memories of emergence as a writer and an artist, set against a personal history of strife and difficulty.
Faces in the Water (1961)
[GE12] Women's P pbk **£4.95**
Living in the Maniototo
An exploration of an uncharted land in the imagination, this is Frame's most exciting and fictionally creative work to date.
[GE13] Women's P pbk **£3.95**
Owls Do Cry (1957)
Her first published novel, about an educated and impoverished family, notable for the freshness of its description and its enchanting evocation of a child's point of view.
[GE14] Women's P pbk **£4.95**
The Carpathians
Strange happenings disturb the comfortable suburban lives of a fictional New Zealand town, as a wealthy New York writer journeys to discover the Maori legend of the Memory Flower, only to discover it drastically alters the logic and physicality of her world.
[GE15] Pandora pbk **£3.95**
You Are Now Entering the Human Heart
[GE16] Women's P pbk **£4.95**
AUTOBIOGRAPHY
1: To the Is-land: An Autobiography (1954)
The first volume of her autobiography, this is both a haunting account of childhood and adolescence in the 1920s and 30s, and an exploration of the nature and function of memory.
[GE17] Grafton pbk **£3.95**
2: Angel at My Table
Second volume of her autobiography, telling of her incarceration in a mental asylum and the writing of her first book.
[GE18] Grafton pbk **£3.50**
3: The Envoy from Mirror City
[GE19] Grafton pbk **£3.95**

FRANKLIN, MILES (1879 - 1954)

Pseudonym of Stella Maria Sarah Miles. Descendant of a convict and the eldest of seven children, Miles Franklin's family squatted on a property in a remote area of New South Wales in the 1840s, an experience of which she wrote in her fiction. After leaving her family she became a nurse, housemaid, journalist, editor and feminist.

My Brilliant Career (1901)

One of Australia's most famous novels, written when the author was only 16, it vividly describes the drudgery of an outback upbringing and the rites of passage of a girl who longs to become a writer.
[GE20] Virago pbk **£4.99**

My Career Goes Bung (1946)

Written as a sequel to *My Brilliant Career* at the turn of the century, it was considered too outspoken and remained unpublished for ten years.
[GE21] Virago pbk **£4.50**

Some Everyday Folk and Dawn

Life in a drab Australian town Penrith, subtly exploring ideas of female suffrage.
[GE22] Virago pbk **£4.99**

GEE, MAURICE (1931 -)

New Zealand writer whose work evocatively portrays the lives of ordinary people with uncommon intimacy and convincing intensity. His major work is a densely textured trilogy comprising *Plumb* (currently unavailable), *Meg*, and *Sole Survivor* - describing the history of one family for more than 70 years.

Meg (1981)

The second part of the trilogy, telling the story of Meg, a woman dominated by her father who was a Presbyterian minister entangled in a trial of conscience.
[GE23] Faber hbk **£5.95**

Prowlers (1987)
[GE24] Faber pbk **£4.95**

Sole Survivor (1983)
[GE25] Faber hbk **£7.95**

HALL, RODNEY (1935 -)

English-born, and Australia-bred, Hall has worked in theatre, television and academia, and is active in aboriginal affairs.

Captivity Captive

The confession, set on a farm homestead in 1868, tells with sparse language and intense feelings of an unsolved triple murder.
[GE26] Faber pbk **£4.95**

Clive James, author of *The Remake* (Picador pbk £3.95)

Just Relations   NEW

Entertaining and imaginative portrayal of the close and distant relations of the residents of an old gold-mining town.
[GE27] Faber pbk **£5.99**

Kisses of the Enemy   NEW
[GE28] Faber hbk **£12.95**

HULME, KERI (1947 -)

Born in Christchurch, New Zealand, of mixed Scottish, English and Maori descent, Hulme identifies most strongly with her Kai Tahu Maori origins. She has won international acclaim as a novelist over recent years, and is also a painter and a poet.

The Bone People (1984)

Controversial winner of the Booker Prize in 1985, this intriguing and often disturbing work poetically links Maori myth with Christian symbolism in a fable of often passionate emotion and shocking physical violence.
[GE29] Picador pbk **£4.99**

The Windeater: Te Kaihau (Stories)

A collection of early short stories.
[GE30] Sceptre pbk **£3.99**

IHIMAERA, WITI (1944 -)

Tangi (1973)

The first and foremost Maori novel, Tangi is a poem in prose about a funeral and its aftermath.
[GE31] Methuen pbk **£5.95**

The Matriarch (1988)

A boldly original work marrying Maori legend to contemporary reality - with a good measure of Italian opera to help it along.
[GE32] Heineman hbk **£10.95**

IRELAND, DAVID (1927 -)

After working as a gamekeeper and on an oil-refinery, Ireland has become an acclaimed experimental novelist. His often politically critical fiction employs discontinuous narrative, surrealism and a range of metafictional techniques, to eccentric and humorous effect.

Bloodfather

A rich and inventive novel centered on a character known as David, the only survivor of a pair of twins and inheritant of the cumulative eccentricity of his bizarre family, as he becomes both a writer and an artist of prodigious creativity.
[GE33] Penguin pbk **£5.99**

City of Women (1981)

Set in a futuristic city of Sydney without any men, the novel follows the adventures of ex-engineer and lesbian Billie Shockley.
[GE34] Penguin pbk **£2.95**

JAMES, CLIVE (1939 -)

The ubiquitous and ebullient critic and wit, who made his name in Britain as a writer on the media for *Punch* and the *Observer*, and is now, as a provocative presenter, literally all over television. His fiction is self-consciously concerned with the fashionable life of media people.

Brilliant Creatures (1983)

The travails of a publishing executive who conquers literary London.
[GE35] Picador pbk **£3.95**

Falling Towards England (1985)

The story that tells of his early years in London - of his adventures with his landlady, the literati, the heating system and his girlfriend.
[GE36] Picador pbk **£3.99**

Flying Visits (1984)
[GE37] Picador pbk **£3.95**

From the Land of Shadows (Essays)
[GE38] Picador pbk **£3.99**

Snake Charmers in Texas (Essays)
[GE39] Picador pbk **£4.99**

The Remake (1987)

The tale of what happens when the hero thinks he is Ian Fleming, initiates an identity crisis, and develops a middle-age spread.
[GE40] Picador pbk **£3.95**

Unreliable Memoirs: Autobiography (1980)
[GE41] Picador pbk **£3.50**

JOLLEY, ELIZABETH (1923 -)

A sophisticated, witty writer who probes society with a sharp sense of its absurd and farcical elements, combining delightful playfulness with subtle moral discernment.

Foxybaby (1985)

A comic portrayal of the disastrous consequences of love, set on a residential summer school in a remote country district that teaches writing and fat reduction.
[GE42] Penguin pbk **£3.95**

Milk and Honey
[GE43] Penguin pbk **£3.99**

Mr Scobie's Riddle (1982)
[GE44] Penguin pbk **£3.99**

Palomino (1980)
[GE45] Penguin pbk **£4.99**

The Newspaper of Claremont Street

A novel that follows the fortunes of its heroine, a cleaning lady, the gatherer and disseminator of all local gossip, and an unlikely sage.
[GE46] Penguin pbk **£3.50**

The Sugar Mother   NEW
[GE47] Viking hbk **£11.95**

The Well
[GE48] Penguin pbk **£3.95**

Woman in a Lampshade (1983)
[GE49] Penguin pbk **£4.50**

KENEALLY, THOMAS (1935 -)

Though educated for the law, Keneally has become a major international novelist. His work covers a wide range of subjects, often away from his Australian home, and always showing a great deal of captivating and memorable research. His dramatizations of human dilemmas have been consistently compelling, revealing a preoccupation with social violence (particularly war) and combining an accessible vernacular style with larger ideas and influences. He has won many major awards, including the Booker Prize for *Schindler's Ark*.

Blood Red, Sister Rose (1974)

A novel based around the story and concept of Joan of Arc.
[GE50] Hodder pbk **£2.95**

Chant of Jimmie Blacksmith (1972)

A fictional recreation of the Jimmy Governor murders, provoked by racism in rural Australia.
[GE51] Fontana pbk **£2.50**

Cut-Rate Kingdom (1979)

Set in Australia and New Guinea during World War II.
[GE52] Penguin pbk **£3.95**

Schindler's Ark (1982)

Based on the real-life story of a German industrialist who protected his Jewish workers in wartime Poland. Winner of the Booker Prize in 1982.
[GE53] Hodder pbk **£4.99**

The Playmaker (1987)

Set in Sydney Cove convict settlement in 1789, this novel tells the story of the first production of a play in Australia, Farquhar's *The Recruiting Officer*. Combining the play's own contradictions with the ironies of its production by convicts, Keneally develops a captivating novel about the nature of imprisonment, and race relations in early Australia.
[GE54] Sceptre pbk **£3.99**

The Survivor (1969)
[GE55] Penguin pbk **£3.95**

Thomas Keneally, author of *Towards Asmara*
(Hodder hbk £12.95) (Photo: Stuart Windsor)

Towards Asmara   `NEW`
Set against the forgotten civil war in Ethiopia
and Eritrea, this new novel charts the experiences of a
group of travellers aiming for Asmara, once the
cultural capital of the region.
[GE56] Hodder hbk **£12.95**

KOCH, C.J. (1932 -)
Tasmanian-born writer and radio producer who has
lived in Europe and Asia. He came to the fore with
Patrick White as a novelist attempting to provide an
antidote to the naturalism which dominated
Australian fiction until the 1950s. His prose is
meticulously crafted and dense to the point of
poetry.
The Doubleman (1985)
An exploration of a Catholic childhood, based on the
author's own education at a Christian Brothers school
in Hobart.
[GE57] Grafton pbk **£2.95**
The Year of Living Dangerously (1978)
Generally regarded as his finest work, and filmed by
Peter Weir, it is set in Indonesia in 1965 just before
the fall of President Sukarno. The events are seen
through the eyes of a foreign correspondent
captivated by the erotic charge of the tropics and a
fascination with power.
[GE58] Grafton pbk **£2.99**

LINDSAY, LADY JOAN (1896 - 1984)
Picnic at Hanging Rock (1967)
An evocative and elegantly written story of the
disappearance of a group of girls from a school
picnic. Their mysterious departure, from the
repressive constraints of their school life into the eerie
emptiness of the great rock formations has strange
and mythic overtones.
[GE59] Penguin pbk **£2.99**

MALOUF, DAVID (1934 -)
Acclaimed as one of the most interesting and
thoughtful Australian novelists and poets of today,
Malouf explores a wide range of subjects with a sure
grasp of the formal possibilities of the novel. His
fiction is noted for its allusive, poetic quality and for
its clear sense of theme.

12 Edmonstone Street (Autobiography, 1985)
[GE60] Chatto hbk **£11.95**
[GE61] Penguin pbk **£2.95**
Antipodes (Stories)
[GE62] Penguin pbk **£2.95**
Child's Play (1982)
With *Eustace & The Prowler*. A documentary-like
account of an Italian terrorist meticulously planning
the assassination of a great writer. As he plots the
killing, he feels uncannily caught up in the
machinations of the writer's plot.
[GE63] Chatto hbk **£10.95**
Fly Away Peter (1982)
Set in Queensland in the 1930s, this novel explores
what happens to Jim Saddler, a birdwatcher, when he
comes into contact with the brutalities of war.
[GE64] Penguin pbk **£3.50**
Harland's Half Acre (1984)
Spanning most of this century, the novel is an account
of an artist's attempt to regain the land lost by his
ancestors, a goal he achieves not by repossession but
by capturing the land through his painting.
[GE65] Penguin pbk **£3.95**
The Great World   `NEW`
Malouf's new novel is a meditation on the
young Australian dead, who perished in other
people's wars, from Gallipoli to North Africa; it
ranges across five decades and many lives, and is a
fine and moving testament.
[GE65A] Chatto hbk **£12.95**

MCCULLOUGH, COLLEEN (1937 -)
Bestselling historical and romantic writer, whose
novels show a particular sensitivity towards her
country. Born of Irish Catholic parents, she worked
variously as a schoolteacher, journalist and
neurophysiologist before becoming a bestselling
author.
A Creed for the Third Millennium
[GE66] Futura pbk **£3.99**
An Indecent Obsession (1981)
A novel set in the psychiatric wing of a South Pacific
hospital for war veterans, combining elements of sex
and romance with violence and paranoia.
[GE67] Futura pbk **£3.50**
Ladies of Missalonghi
Set in the early 1900s in a small town in the Blue
Mountains, this is a story of genteel poverty and male
vanity.
[GE68] Arrow pbk **£2.50**
The Thorn Birds (1977)
A vivid and compelling novel that follows the
fortunes of several generations of the Cleary family
on a sheep station in New South Wales.
[GE69] Futura pbk **£3.25**
Tim (1974)
The relationship between a middle-aged spinster and
an unskilled labourer with a retarded mind.
[GE70] Pan pbk **£2.95**

NEW ZEALAND SHORT STORIES
An anthology of New Zealand short stories now in its
fourth series, painting an expansive portrait of the
changes in New Zealand literature from the 19th
century to the present day. Edited by Dan Davin, C.K.
Stead and Lydia Wevers respectively.
1st Series
[GE71] Oxford pbk **£6.50**
2nd Series
[GE72] Oxford pbk **£3.75**
4th Series
[GE73] Oxford pbk **£8.95**

PRAED, ROSA (1851 - 1935)
Praed began writing as the young wife of a station
owner, in order to tell of her isolation. After settling
in England she became more celebrated, although
some found in her novels a sentimental awe of the
English. Her work often dramatizes the encounter of a

refined European with a more earthy, and ultimately
more enduring, Australian.
Bond of Wedlock
[GE74] Pandora pbk **£4.95**
Lady Bridget in the Never-Never Land
(1915)
Thrown together during drought in Queensland at the
turn of the century, Lady Bridget O'Hara, an Irish
aristocrat, and Colin McKeith, a bushman, are forced
to confront the issues of unionized labour, the plight
of aborigines and the significance of marriage.
[GE75] Pandora pbk **£4.95**
Outlaw and Lawmaker (1893)
A love story in a country where the roles of lawmaker
and lawbreaker at times overlapped, using the
technique of the thriller to highlight the conflict that
ensues when passion and justice meet.
[GE76] Pandora pbk **£6.95**

RICHARDSON, HENRY HANDEL (1870 -
1946)
Pseudonym of the novelist Ethel Florence Richarson,
she is one of Australia's most famous early writers.
Born in Melbourne, she spent most of her life in
Europe.
Maurice Guest (1908)
Published under a pseudonym and praised by
Somerset Maugham, this early novel is the story of a
musician frustrated by the limits of his talent, who
develops an obsessive self-destructive love for an
older woman.
[GE77] Virago pbk **£4.95**
The Getting of Wisdom (1910)
Described by the author as a 'merry little book', and
acclaimed by many as a classic account of childhood.
It is the story of an artistic girl's painful inner growth
during her boarding school days, aged 13 to 17, where
she feels isolated and withdrawn, and forms an
intense attachment to an older girl.
[GE78] Virago pbk **£3.50**

SARGESON, FRANK (1903 - 1984)
A major influence on the development of an
indigenous New Zealand literature, Sargeson's work
captured a colloquial feel in witty and satiric portraits
of New Zealand. His best work, the early short
stories, is collected in many anthologies, and presents
a humorous and sardonic criticism of middle class
values, in eccentrically short but disturbingly gothic
vignettes.
Sunset Village (1979)
Excellent social comedy with a sharp use of the
vernacular.
[GE79] MB & O'Keefe hbk **£4.95**
AUTOBIOGRAPHY
1: Once is Enough (1972)
[GE80] MB & O'Keefe hbk **£5.95**
2: More Than Enough: A Memoir (1974)
[GE81] MB & O'Keefe hbk **£5.95**
3: Never Enough! (1977)
[GE82] MB & O'Keefe hbk **£5.95**

STEAD, C.K. (1932 -)
An internationally celebrated New Zealand critic and
poet, Stead has now produced three novels. The finest
and most ambitious is *The Death of a Body*, a
metafictional murder tale set in New Zealand and
Europe, notable for both its humour and its evocative
descriptions of Auckland.
All Visitors Ashore (1984)
[GE83] Picador pbk **£2.95**
The Death of a Body (1986)
[GE84] Collins pbk **£10.95**
Sister Hollywood   `NEW`
A young boy, confused and hurt by his elder sister's
abrupt departure, travels to Hollywood to search for
her. A gently paced and affectionate portrait of
Tinseltown in the 1940s.
[GE84A] Collins hbk **£11.95**

STEAD, CHRISTINA (1902 - 1983)

Probably the most prominent Australian woman novelist, a formidable writer whose semi-autobiographical masterpiece *The Man Who Loved Children* has been acclaimed as one of the masterworks of 20th century fiction. Although born in Australia, her urge to travel has meant that she has lived much of her life abroad. Her works offer intense and imaginative portrayals of the inner lives of her characters, concentrating on powerful subconscious currents of emotion.

A Little Tea, A Little Chat (1948)
[GE85] Virago pbk **£5.50**
Cotters' England (1966)
Set in 1950's England, this novel is dominated by the chain-smoking highly strung heroine Nellie, who works for a socialist newspaper.
[GE86] Virago pbk **£4.95**
For Love Alone (1944)
A love story ranged between Sydney and London, about a woman who idealizes a shallow young man for years; she finally learns how to love another man by accepting the compromises necessary for a successful relationship.
[GE87] Virago pbk **£4.95**
I'm Dying Laughing
[GE88] Penguin pbk **£5.99**
Letty Fox: Her Luck (1946)
Based on her experiences in America, this satirical account of one woman's sexual adventuring testifies to Stead's independant spirit.
[GE89] Virago pbk **£5.50**
Ocean of Story: Uncollected Stories
[GE90] Penguin pbk **£4.95**
Puzzleheaded Girl (1967)
A volume of four novellas.
[GE91] Virago pbk **£5.50**
Salzburg Tales (1934)
Her first published work, a group of experimental tales with echoes of the *Canterbury Tales*; by turns romantic, macabre, supernatural and satirical.
[GE92] Virago pbk **£5.50**
The Beauties and Furies (1936)
Set in Paris, the story is centred around a student community.
[GE93] Virago pbk **£4.95**
The Man Who Loved Children (1940)
Her most powerful work, this is a semi-autobiographical exploration of the trials of family life, sympathetic to the difficulties experienced by both children and adults.
[GE94] Penguin pbk **£5.95**

WEDDE, IAN

A gifted young New Zealand writer and poet, breaking the mould of New Zealand fiction with the urban settings and postmodern metaphysical playfulness of his novels.
Survival Arts (1987)
A bizarre tale set on the outskirts of Wellington involving a writer embalmed in his own fictions, a stolen army tank and a ransomed seven foot Black basketball star.
[GE95] Faber pbk **£3.95**
Symme's Hole (1986)
A wild and often hilarious collision of MacDonald's corporation, contemporary culture and the myth of the great white whale.
[GE96] Faber pbk **£5.95**

WENDT, ALBERT (1939 -)

The one writer from the South Pacific with an international reputation, this Western Samoan novelist, academic and poet was educated in New Zealand and has taught in Samoa and Auckland. His best known work is *The Leaves of the Banyan Tree* (1979), a three generation saga of Samoan life.
Shaman of Visions
[GE97] Oxford pbk **£7.95**

Christina Stead, author of *For Love Alone* (Virago pbk £4.95)

WHITE, PATRICK (1912 -)

The most considerable figure in modern Australian literature, awarded the Nobel Prize in 1973. The great poet of Australia's landscape, he has turned its vast empty spaces into mythic landscapes of the soul. Educated at Cambridge, his understanding of the world was formed by journeys to Greece and Germany and friendships with modernists in London. Technically brilliant, his novels probe the hinterlands of consciousness, and embrace Nietzschean philosophy and the writings of Jung on symbol. Ambivalence, both for his country and its people, has always been a central feature of his work, whose aim he descibes as the desire to *"convey a splendour, a transcendence which is... there above human realities."*

A Fringe of Leaves (1976)
Ellen Gluyas, an artless farm-girl, marries an educated gentleman Austin Roxburgh. Their quiet and inhibited life, broken by disaster and enslavement, awakes to spiritual fulfillment.
[GE98] Penguin pbk **£4.95**
Flaws in the Glass (Autobiography, 1981)
[GE99] Penguin pbk **£4.99**
Memoirs of Many in One (1986)
[GE100] Penguin pbk **£3.95**
Riders in the Chariot (1961)
Set in White's imaginary suburbs of Sarsaparilla and Paradise East, this novel explores the inner and outer lives of four visionaries who finally come together in a spiritual union. Social satire is mixed with strong mythic overtones.
[GE101] Penguin pbk **£4.95**
The Aunt's Story (1948)
An exploration of a spiritual journey charting the inner life of Theodora Goodman, a maiden aunt who goes mad. The novel at first maintains a realistic representation, but gradually the form begins to echo the very movement of Theodora's life through surreal, imagistic fragments.
[GE102] Penguin pbk **£4.95**
The Burnt Ones (Stories, 1964)
Four stories set in Greece, and seven in Australia.
[GE103] Penguin pbk **£4.95**
The Cockatoos (Stories, 1974)
Six novellas and stories, darker in tone than *The Burnt Ones*.
[GE104] Penguin pbk **£4.95**
The Eye of the Storm (1973)
Elizabeth Hunter, an ex-socialite in her eighties, has a mystical experience during a summer storm in

Sydney which transforms all her relationships, and her existence becomes charged with new meaning.
[GE105] Penguin pbk **£5.99**
The Living and the Dead (1941)
An early work and a conventional novel of manners set in 1920s England. The novel centres around the distinction between those who have learned to live a full life and those who do no more than exist.
[GE106] Penguin pbk **£4.95**
The Solid Mandala (1966)
Dramatic tale of the relationship between twin brothers Arthur and Waldo Brown.
[GE107] Penguin pbk **£5.95**
The Tree of Man (1955)
Epic in attitude this novel draws from Genesis in its efforts to trace the nature of existence through the lives of an ordinary man and woman, pioneers Stan and Amy Parker.
[GE108] Penguin pbk **£5.50**
The Twyborn Affair (1979)
A fascinating exploration of sexual identity: the novel is divided into three parts, each with its own chief protagonist (a Greek mistress, a military hero, and a London brothel madam), who turn out to be the same person.
[GE109] Penguin pbk **£5.95**
The Vivisector (1970)
Hurtle Duffield is the vivisector: a painter who treats all aspects of his life, including his relationships with people, as material to be cut up for his art. A hilarious satire directed against the follies of artistic genius and the patrician system, the novel is also a barbed attack on Sydney 'society' culture.
[GE110] Penguin pbk **£5.99**
Three Uneasy Pieces
White's latest work is a collection of three long stories.
[GE111] Cape hbk **£7.95**
Voss (1957)
White's most celebrated novel which sets his habitual story of spiritual quest in the vast mythic landscapes of the Australian hinterland, and against a satirised vision of the 'society' of coastal life: the doomed visionary and pioneer Johann Voss attempts to cross Australia in 1848, a Nietzschean figure pitting his will against a vast, unknown desert.
[GE112] Penguin pbk **£5.95**

WINTON, TIM (1960 -)

Born in Perth, Winton has already received the Miles Franklin Award in 1984 for his spare, evocative fiction.
In the Winter Dark   **NEW**
[GE113] Weidenfeld hbk **£10.95**
Minimum of Two (1988)
[GE114] Weidenfeld hbk **£10.95**
Shallows (1986)
[GE115] Weidenfeld hbk **£9.95**
That Eye the Sky (1986)
[GE116] Sceptre pbk **£3.50**

Patrick White, author of *Voss* (Penguin pbk £5.95)

40 Years of Independent Publishing

John Calder

Creative literary publishing is totally different from general publishing and is more like running an art gallery. It needs the capital to endure a small and slow return, enough knowledge and energy to function effectively with little outside help, a small staff able to do anything and a missionary belief that the effort is worthwhile. It also needs a flair to publicise a personal taste so that the author one is trying to build up gets some benefit and recognition in his lifetime. Because a literary publisher starts with little competition, making his own discoveries, it is usually some time before he has to worry about larger, predatory publishers seducing his authors, and he must use that honeymoon period to get the confidence and affection of his writers. Then, provided he does his job well, he has a good chance of keeping his authors once they are established and profitable. He should also have the good luck to find at least one really unusual and important new talent whose name will become synonymous with the imprint; this will give him the energy and pride to ride the waves of adversity that will inevitably attack him periodically.

After forty years as a literary publisher I write with hindsight, not having always followed that prescription, but I have come near enough to it to survive. The follies have been the result of stepping outside my special field, taking on titles in which I did not believe but hoped would be profitable - they seldom are, but might be with another publisher - or in getting out of my financial depths with too grandiose ideas, or by publishing books in which I believed but where the libel risks were imperfectly thought out. One has to be lucky enough to have the occasional bestseller, but it must not be too obvious a bestseller or you pay too much for it and whatever the sales you will end with a loss.

My list is founded partly on an interest from childhood in serious reading - I had intended to be a writer, which I occasionally am in a minor way - and on the accident of a family disagreement that sent me to Zürich University where I studied, quite unofficially, several languages, world literature in those languages, philosophy, music and art, all of which remain my major interests today. When I started publishing in 1949 with a (to me) useless degree in economics, my list reflected those interests and I was able to progress from neglected classics in

Samuel Beckett, author of *Waiting for Godot* (Photo: Methuen)

translation to modern writers who few other publishers could read or liked. I found my lucky genius in the middle fifties in Samuel Beckett, who became a friend and a guru as well as a much-prized author. With persistence, I was able to establish the *nouveau roman* of Robbe-Grillet, Sarraute, Pinget, Duras and Claude Simon, the latter the most recent of the fourteen Nobel Prize winners who have graced the list; also many important German and East European writers and such British writers

---

I found my lucky genius in the middle fifties in Samuel Beckett, who became a friend and a guru as well as a much-prized author

---

as Aidan Higgins, Alexander Trocchi, Alan Burns and Ann Quin who in the late fifties and early sixties were doing something new in the novel. The reason some of these are not with me today is because in 1975, after fourteen years of partnership with Marion Boyars, we separated, and having bought half the company, she acquired half the list.

We also have an American list and our two most eminent US authors, Henry Miller and William Burroughs, brought us acclaim, notoriety and profit in the 1960's. Another American, Hubert Selby, brought us to the Old Bailey, and, although we won our obscenity case on appeal, two creative years went into fighting that battle and I have little doubt that our more notorious iconoclastic authors cost us our Arts Council grant - very necessary to sustain an often slow-selling list - when that body became party-politicised.

In the fifties, we introduced absurdist theatre to Britain through the work of Eugène Ionesco, Fernando Arrabal, Robert Pinget, René de Obaldia and some British writers. We still continue to publish British, American and European plays, most notably today Howard Barker, who has emerged as a radical innovator who looks at the world's problems with a poetic but jaundiced eye. If literature can be thought of as a chain linked by ideas and influences, we have followed that

chain, going back in time to pick up the unpublished predecessors of our current writers and those who carry on their outlook to a new generation. We have expressionist and surrealist series of literature, among others. Literature is an art, or should be: it is influenced by, and influences in its turn, the other arts. This chain of ideas has led into a deeper investigation of music, drama, philosophy and politics, all of which has expanded the list with books on these arts, on new

The very growth of the publishing megaliths has made it easier for an independent publisher to continue without being a dinosaur

ideas and into new critical approaches. My own forthcoming book on literature explores these links in what I believe is a new way.

Little by little we have abandoned general publishing for a more specialised list of books of and on literature and the related arts, with a large section devoted to opera, a special love. Most publishers produce books that they expect to die in a year or so, possibly with an extended sale as a paperback, but we on the contrary expect each new book, unless on a topical subject, to continue to sell for many years, being regularly reprinted and with sales increasing as both academic and general interest grows. The risks we now take are on new unknown authors, especially on those who look to us to provide them with an income that will enable them ultimately to write full-time. Part of our past ability to survive depended on being able to obtain grants for writers to provide most of their income. The only answer today must lie in ways of selling more books. That means getting reviews, finding new methods of responsible publicity and having the support of bookshops, such as Waterstone's.

One of the welcome changes of recent years has been the coming of good bookshops employing enthusiastic and knowledgeable book-lovers in place of the old, shabby, philistine shops that had never heard of any author published in the previous half-century, where

prejudice went from generation to generation, and the bookseller always knew what *wouldn't* sell, which was whatever he was offered by the likes of myself. Waterstone's have been in the vanguard of this new development and other chains have had to become more adventurous to compete. Waterstone's courage and willingness to please every kind of customer, as well as their brilliance in getting the right staff, cannot be overpraised. Nothing could be more encouraging for a publisher like myself at a time when libraries decline, universities are forced to abandon culture and newspapers increasingly avoid the intellectual in their review coverage.

To remain a literary publisher, I have had to spend much time in related fields, organising literary festivals and events, writing for journals of every kind and on many subjects, lecturing, debating and even performing. I founded the *Theatre of Literature* which tours the country giving readings; it consists of a company of actors, some of them well-known television names, who read Beckett and other modern authors in a dramatic context. It sells books, expands reputations and entertains in a creative and lively way.

The very growth of the publishing megaliths has made it easier for an independent publisher to continue without being a dinosaur: it is the happy combination of writers, publisher and booksellers, working together to spread the joy of reading and learning, on which so much of our culture and civilisation is based, which provides an alternative to lives and values based on greed and ignorance, and enhances, rather than diminishes, what is best and most promising in the human character.

A publisher since 1949, John Calder has been active in promoting literature and culture in the post-war era, through his support of many important English, Continental and American writers. He has written plays, stories and criticism himself as well as editing selections of Samuel Beckett, Henry Miller, William Burroughs and the Nouveau Roman. His forthcoming book is *The Defence of Literature*.

JOHN CALDER
40th Anniversary

Recent fiction

SAMUEL BECKETT
Nohow On. A trilogy of three important late novellas (*Company, Ill Seen Ill Said, Worstward Ho*) in one volume. £10.95.

L.F. CÉLINE
Journey to the End of the Night and *Death on Credit*. Two large, masterly novels. 'the most blackly humorous and disenchanted voice in all of French literature' *London Review of Books*. Each £14.95.

ALAIN ROBBE-GRILLET
Ghosts in the Mirror. A fascinating autobiography and self-examination by the most discussed French writer: £12.95. Reprinted in paperback: *The Erasers* £5.95 *Jealousy* £3.95.

JULIAN SEMYONOV
Tass is authorized to announce... pits KGB agent Slavin against his CIA counterpart in an African coup. £9.95. *17 Moments of Spring* is a spy thriller set in Berlin in the last months of the war. £12.95. Semyonov is the USSR's most popular novelist.

CLAUDE SIMON
The Georgics is perhaps the literary masterpiece of the decade, a brilliant multi-level look at war and the contrast of peace by a brilliant and original stylist. £15.95.

Theatre Books

ANTONIN ARTAUD
The Theatre and its Double. One of the key books on modern drama. £4.94 pb.

HOWARD BARKER
Recent plays include *The Last Supper* £3.95, *The Possibilities* £3.95, *The Bite of the Night* £4.94. Poems: *Lullabies for the Impatient* £3.95. Barker writes brilliant political parables.

JOHN CALDER (Publishers) LTD
18 Brewer Street, London W1R 4AS

EUROPEAN FICTION

ADAM, VILLIERS DE L'ISLE-
(French, 1838 - 1889)
An impoverished aristocrat and Symbolist writer, Adam's works are poetic and often obscure. His symbolic drama of morbid romanticism, *Axel*, had a profound influence on writers such as W.B. Yeats.
Axel (Play, 1890)
[GF1] Soho pbk **£4.95**
Cruel Tales
[GF2] Oxford pbk **£3.95**

AITMATOV, CHINGIZ (Russian, 1928 -)
A foremost Soviet writer of recent years, Aitmatov spent much of his early life as a rural shepherd, absorbing the ancient culture of the Kirgiz people. With this folk-lore for inspiration he addresses vital contemporary issues, such as drug abuse, corruption, the planned economy, environmental policy and the role of religion in Soviet society today.
Mother Earth & Other Stories **NEW**
Written between 1958 and 1963, the stories are set in the rugged mountains and parched steppes of Kirgizia. Against the background of the pastoral, nomadic, illiterate Kirgiz, we witness revolution, war and cultural change.
[GF3] Faber hbk **£12.99**
The Place of the Skull **NEW**
A major work of recent Soviet literature: young Avidy Kallistratov finds himself working with a gang of wild antelope hunters, but cannot reconcile his high ideals of religion and love with the destruction of the environment that he is forced to witness.
[GF4] Faber hbk **£12.99**

ALAIN-FOURNIER, HENRI (1886 - 1914)
Tragically killed in World War I, Alain-Fournier left an undisputed masterpiece. A classic novel of adolescence, it tells of a young man who stumbles across what seems to be an enchanted world, which is abruptly and devastatingly destroyed.
Le Grand Meaulnes
[GF5] Oxford illus hbk **£12.95**
[GF6] Penguin pbk **£3.95**

ALAS, LEOPOLDO (Spanish, 1852 - 1901)
The only full-length work by Alas, a 19th century critic and lawyer from Northern Spain; similar to Flaubert's *Madame Bovary*, it tells the story of a sensitive woman's attempts to find fulfilment through marriage, adultery and religion.
La Regenta (1884)
[GF7] Penguin pbk **£14.95**

ALEICHEM, SHOLEM (Yiddish, 1859 - 1916)
Aleichem's development of Yiddish as a living literature was crucial at the turn of the century; these stories' humour made his work well-known - written in a unique and colloquial idiom, they are said to have helped the modern Jew to laugh at his predicament.
Tevye the Diaryman & the Railroad Stories **NEW**
[GF8] Random House pbk **£7.95**

ALLAIN, MARCEL & SOUVESTRE, PIERRE (French)
After its publication in 1911, the detective novel *Fantomas* rapidly became a cult success, caused a scandal across Europe, and resulted in 31 sequels. James Joyce described it as 'enfantomastic'.
Fantomas (1911)
[GF9] Picador pbk **£3.50**
The Silent Executioner
[GF10] Picador pbk **£3.95**

APOLLINAIRE, GUILLAUME
(French, 1880 - 1918)
Better known as a poet and critic associated with the Cubist painters, Apollinaire's fiction is an important aspect of his work.
Exploits of a Young Don Juan
[GF11] Star pbk **£2.50**
Les Onze Milles Verges, or the Amorous Adventures of Prince Mony
[GF12] P Owen pbk **£7.95**
The Poet Assassinated & Other Stories
[GF13] Grafton pbk **£3.50**

APPELFELD, AHARON (Israeli, 1932 -)
Born in Bukovina, Appelfeld is a highly religious writer whose vision of contemporary Israel is conditioned by his awareness of Jewish history. He has written with great power about the Holocaust and its impact on society.
Badenheim, 1939 (1975)
[GF14] Dent pbk **£2.95**
The Age of Wonders (1982)
Described as 'the most remarkable prose ever to come out of Israel', this is Appelfeld's masterpiece to date. It is divided into two parts - the first, told by a boy in the first person, the story of an Austrian family on the eve of the Second World War, the second of a man's (perhaps imaginary) return to his Austrian home town in 1970, narrated in the third person.
[GF15] Weidenfeld hbk **£11.95**
The Immortal Bartfuss
[GF16] Weidenfeld hbk **£10.95**
The Retreat
[GF17] Quartet pbk **£3.95**
To the Land of the Reeds
[GF18] Weidenfeld hbk **£9.95**

ARAGON, LOUIS (French, 1897 - 1982)
Paris Peasant
An hallucinatory, surrealist novel which is outwardly a guided tour of the byways of 1920s Paris. As well as being Aragon's best novel, it is perhaps the most important prose fiction to emerge from surrealism.
[GF19] Picador pbk **£3.50**

BABEL, ISAAC (Russian, 1894 - 1941)
The son of a Jewish shopkeeper in Odessa, Babel rose to fame in 1924 with a series of short stories, later collected and published as *Red Cavalry* and *Tales of Odessa*. He was arrested in the purges of the late 1930s, and died in a Siberian labour camp in 1941. His taut, economical and powerful short stories - many drawing on personal experience - are often considered the first classics of Soviet literature.
Collected Stories
[GF20] Penguin pbk **£4.99**

BALZAC, HONORE DE (French, 1799 - 1850)
Honoré de Balzac's great series of loosely-connected novels, which he characterized as *La Comédie Humaine*, follows French society from the Consulate to the July Monarchy. The range of characters, and the closeness of Balzac's observation of them, is unique, and combines a strain of rare fantsay with one of realism.
A Harlot High and Low (1838-47)
[GF21] Penguin pbk **£5.99**
A Passion in the Desert (Stories)
[GF22] Sutton pbk **£2.50**
Black Sheep
[GF23] Penguin pbk **£4.99**
Chouans (1829)
[GF24] Penguin pbk **£4.99**
Cousin Pons (1847)
[GF25] Penguin pbk **£4.95**
Cousine Bette (1846)
[GF26] Penguin pbk **£4.50**
Eugènie Grandet (1833)
[GF27] Penguin pbk **£3.50**

History of the Thirteen
[GF28] Penguin pbk **£4.95**
Lost Illusions (1837-43)
[GF29] Penguin pbk **£4.95**
Murky Business
[GF30] Penguin pbk **£4.50**
Old Goriot
Deriving its plot partly from *King Lear*, this is a masterful study of the relations between a father and his daughters, showing how greed sours 'natural' human relations; it presents a notable picture of Paris and the complications of city life.
[GF31] Penguin pbk **£3.50**
Selected Short Stories
[GF32] Penguin pbk **£4.50**
The Wild Ass's Skin
[GF33] Penguin pbk **£4.99**
Ursule Mirouet (1841)
[GF34] Penguin pbk **£4.99**

BARANSKAYA, NATALYA (Russian, 1908 -)
A Week Like Any Other
A collection of a novella and short stories, telling of women's everyday life in the Soviet Union.
[GF35] Virago pbk **£4.95**

BARBUSSE, HENRI (French, 1874 - 1935)
Barbusse's World War I novel tells the story of a doomed squad of men in the perpetual winter of the trenches - exploited creatures fighting a war that can in no way benefit them.
Under Fire: Story of a Squad
[GF36] Dent pbk **£3.50**

BARILLE, ELIZABETH (French, 1965 -)
Body of a Girl **NEW**
A first novel which explores, largely through interior monologue, the growing self-awareness of a young woman, and her realization of her attractiveness to men.
[GF37] Quartet hbk **£9.95**

BASSANI, GIORGIO (Italian, 1916 -)
The Garden of the Finzi-Continis (1962)
Set in the Jewish community of Ferrara, Bassani writes of how a wealthy family continues with the traditional pattern of their lives within their garden walls, while outside hostility and inhumanity are increasing as war approaches.
[GF38] Quartet pbk **£6.95**

Honoré de Balzac. Picture: The Mansell Collection

FICTION

BATAILLE, GEORGES (French, 1897 - 1962)
A controversial essayist and novelist of a distinct brand of mystical, erotic anti-fiction, Bataille's work has at best a sophisticated quality, which shows the influence of Freud and Nietzsche. His erotic novels - *L'Abbé C* and *Story of the Eye* - parody 18th and 19th century pornography.
Blue of Noon
[GF39] Grafton pbk **£3.95**
Eroticism (Non fiction)
A complex study of the underlying sexual basis of religion and philosophy especially in its relationship with ritual.
[GF40] Boyars hbk **£8.95**
L'Abbé C (1950)
[GF41] Boyars pbk **£5.95**
Literature and Evil (Non fiction)
[GF42] Grafton pbk **£3.95**
My Mother, Madam Edwarda/
The Dead Man NEW
[GF43] Boyars hbk **£12.95**
Story of the Eye (1928)
[GF44] Penguin pbk **£2.95**

BEAUVOIR, SIMONE DE
(French, 1908 - 1986)
De Beauvoir's best novels are perhaps the first two she wrote, *The Blood of Others* and *She Came to Stay*; for her other work, see the *Biography* and *Women's Studies* chapters.
Les Belles Images (1969)
[GF45] Fontana pbk **£3.95**
Old Age (1972)
[GF46] Penguin pbk **£6.95**
She Came to Stay (1949)
An analysis of a *ménage à trois* that ends in murder.
[GF47] Fontana pbk **£4.50**
The Blood of Others (1944)
A girl discovers through love her ability to die for freedom: having at first accepted the Nazis, she finally dies fighting with the Maquis.
[GF48] Penguin pbk **£3.95**
The Mandarins (1957)
A partly autobiographical *roman à clef*, featuring portraits of Sartre, Camus and others.
[GF49] Fontana pbk **£5.95**
The Woman Destroyed (Stories, 1969)
[GF50] Fontana pbk **£3.95**
When Things of the Spirit Come First
[GF51] Fontana pbk **£3.50**

BELY, ANDREI (Russian, 1880 - 1934)
Symbolist writer, poet and critic, Bely's *Petersburg* is a highly complex, rhythmical and allusive novel set in the 1905 revolution, with a strangely haunting dream-like evocation of the landscapes of St Petersburg, acclaimed by Nabokov as one of the four major novels of the 20th century.
Petersburg: A Novel (1913-16)
[GF52] Penguin pbk **£4.95**

BERNHARD, THOMAS (Austrian, 1931 - 1989)
Born in Holland, Bernhard was raised in Austria; although he wrote poetry, his major achievements remain his novels. He survived what was believed to be a terminal illness to create fiction set in an often nihilistic and despairing world, related in an uncomfortably cool and uncompromising style. Regarded by some as a truly great writer, his is a bleak vision, surveying man's attempts to reach a meaningful conception of his own existence.
Concrete
[GF53] Quartet pbk **£5.95**
Cutting Timber (1988)
[GF54] Quartet hbk **£9.95**
Old Masters NEW
[GF55] Quartet hbk **£11.95**
Wittgenstein's Nephew (1987)
[GF56] Quartet hbk **£8.95**

BERNLEF, J. (Dutch)
A moving story of the impact on a couple's long-established relationship of the husband's gradual but increasing loss of memory, and strikingly portrays his new existence in a world in which, all of a sudden, the certainties of time and space begin to crumble; from one of Holland's most important writers.
Out of Mind
[GF57] Faber pbk **£3.99**

BALESTRINI, NANNI (Italian, 1935 -)
Following the events of 'Autonomy', the group which arose between 1976-77, combining together the forces of the victims of Italian society, and which drew down a draconian and repressive response from the authorities, this centres around the progress of its protagonist from high-school rebellion to eventual imprisonment.
The Unseen NEW
[GF58] Verso pbk **£8.95**

BOCCACCIO, GIOVANNI
(Italian, 1313 - 1375)
The Decameron
A masterpiece of imaginative narrative, *The Decameron* is a collection of 100 short stories, or *novelle*, which in turn influenced Chaucer. The work is set against the Florentine plague of 1348, from which the narrators escape, to pass their time telling one another stories in a secure castle.
[GF59] Penguin pbk **£5.99**

BOLL, HEINRICH (German, 1917 -)
Winner of the Nobel Prize for Literature in 1972. Among the most influential European writers of the last 40 years, Böll deals compassionately with ordinary people facing inevitable moral compromise, in works set both during the war and the ensuing reconstruction. A Catholic by birth, he came to symbolise liberalism in post-war German literature, significantly adopting many features of American style; his fiction is distinguished by a union of informal language and political stridency, frequently including humour.
Absent Without Leave (Stories, 1967)
[GF60] Boyars pbk **£5.95**
And Never Said a Word (1953)
[GF61] Secker hbk **£9.95**
[GF62] Routledge pbk **£4.95**
And Where Were You, Adam? (1974)
[GF63] Secker hbk **£9.95**
[GF64] Penguin pbk **£3.99**
Billiards at Half Past Nine (1961)
An extremely profound look at one man's efforts to flee his war-time experiences, a maze of guilt and innocence, until the return of a friend shatters his new-found peace.
[GF65] Boyars pbk **£5.95**
Children Are Civilians Too (1973)
[GF66] Secker hbk **£9.95**
Group Portrait with Lady(1971)
A metaphorical walk through the range and diversity of German feelings, this dense novel deals mordantly with Böll's painful dislike of the present and hatred of the past.
[GF67] Penguin pbk **£4.99**
Lost Honour of Katharina Blum (1975)
An oblique and timely novel in the form of an official report criticizing police tactics in dealing with early 1970s terrorism.
[GF68] Secker hbk **£9.95**
[GF69] Penguin pbk **£3.50**
Missing Persons & Other Essays
[GF70] Secker hbk **£9.95**
Soldier's Legacy
[GF71] Secker hbk **£9.95**
Stories
60 stories, ranging from short monologues to delicate

sketches, and including three of Böll's short novellas.
[GF72] Secker hbk **£15.95**
[GF73] Sphere pbk **£7.99**
The Casualty
[GF74] Hogarth pbk **£4.95**
The Clown (1963)
Perhaps his best novel, a compelling and warm study of a small-time performer in turmoil, battling against his own dissolving sense of purpose, losing faith both with his Church and with his private circle.
[GF75] Boyars pbk **£5.95**
The Safety Net (1982)
A lucid and dry examination of a wealthy industrialist caged in by the newly-arrived threat of a terrorist kidnap. Böll at his best towards the end of his life.
[GF76] Secker hbk **£9.95**
The Train Was on Time (1949)
[GF77] Secker hbk **£9.95**
What's to Become of the Boy?
[GF78] Secker hbk **£9.95**
Women in a River Landscape NEW
Published posthumously, this is Böll's last novel, and one of his finest. It is a powerful, experimental tale about the insatiable quest for power, influence and money in high government circles in Bonn.
[GF79] Secker hbk **£10.95**

BORCHERT, WOLFGANG (German, 1921 - 47)
Borchert died young having written a number of short stories; he is best-known for *Man Outside*, a bleak description, owing much to Expressionism, of a soldier's return from the Second War to a Germany in ruins, in which his home and family have been lost.
Man Outside (1952)
[GF80] Boyars pbk **£4.95**
Sad Geraniums
[GF81] Boyars pbk **£4.95**

BORODIN, LEONID (Russian, 1938 -)
Born in Irkutsk, Siberia, Borodin trained as a teacher and taught in a village school near Leningrad until he was arrested in 1967 and sentenced to hard labour for being a member of the Social Christian Union, and because the publication of his work in the West was considered as 'anti-Soviet propaganda'. Freed in 1973, Borodin was re-arrested in 1982 and sentenced to a further 10 years, but was finally released after pressure from the West in 1987.
Partings
[GF82] Collins Harv pbk **£4.95**
The Third Truth NEW
Set in the forest lands of Siberia, this is a powerful story of the effect wrought on one of the central characters by 25 years of detention in the *gulag*, and how, on release, he is helped to reconstruct his life.
[GF83] Collins Harv hbk **£11.95**
Year of Miracle and Grief
A beautiful tale of a young boy growing up on the shores of Lake Baikal, in which the real world of breathtaking landscape and nature is interwoven with an imaginary one of myth, legend and fairytale.
[GF84] Quartet pbk **£4.95**

BOVE, EMMANUEL (French, 1898 - 1945)
With the encouragement of Colette, Bove became a popular writer, dividing his time between potboilers, and the serious novels for which he is remembered. He claimed to have created a genre, the novel of 'impoverished solitude', and his work is a rare combination of comedy and sadness - he has been described as the 'Monsieur Hulot of fiction'.
A Man Who Knows NEW
[GF85] Carcanet hbk **£12.95**
Armand
[GF86] Carcanet hbk **£9.95**
My Friends
[GF87] Grafton pbk **£3.50**

BRECHT, BERTOLT (German, 1898 - 1956)
Collected Short Stories (1984)
37 brief tales drawn from the most important years of his literary life, 1921-1946.
[GF88] Methuen pbk **£3.95**
The Threepenny Novel (1929)
Adapted from Gay's 18th century play, Brecht contemporarizes themes of greed and corruption in late Victorian London; his only major novel, it complements *The Threepenny Opera*.
[GF89] Penguin pbk **£4.95**

BROCH, HERMANN (German, 1886 - 1951)
A powerful and profound writer, described by George Steiner as 'the greatest novelist European literature has produced since Joyce'; Broch turned to literature late in his life (*The Sleepwalkers* trilogy was his first work), having worked until the age of 41 in his father's textile business. Although a Jew, he was allowed to leave Europe after the National Socialist invasion of Austria, and settled in America, where his best-known work *The Death of Virgil* appeared in 1945. Broch's concern throughout his work is with the ethical bases of society, and he explores with deep insight the decline of culture which he witnessed in Weimar Germany.
The Death of Virgil (1945)
[GF90] Oxford pbk **£4.95**
The Guiltless   NEW
[GF91] Quartet pbk **£6.95**
The Sleepwalkers (1932)
[GF92] Quartet pbk **£9.95**
The Spell (1952)
[GF93] Picador pbk **£5.95**

BUFALINO, GESUALDO (Italian)
Set in Sicily in the summer of 1951,Gesualdo Bufalino's novel tells of the complicated patterns of love which spring up between different characters, and how they are resolved: told in retrospect, the narrator, now on the edge of death, looks back on the passions of his youth with painful clarity and a pervasive self-mockery.
Blind Argus   NEW
[GF94] Collins Harv hbk **£10.95**

BULGAKOV, MIKHAIL (Russian, 1891 - 1940)
Born in Kiev, Mikhail Bulgakov achieved fame and recognition early in his career as a playwright, but as Soviet censorship became harsher, his plays ceased to be performed. With the publication of *The Master and Margarita* and *The White Guard*, some 26 years after his death, Bulgakov again achieved acclaim. The latter is among the most imaginative and exciting novels ever to have emerged from the Soviet Union.
Black Snow (1937)
[GF95] Fontana pbk **£2.95**
The Heart of a Dog   NEW
An absurd and superbly comic story, which can also be read as a parable of the Russian Revolution, this combines grotesque ideas with a narrative of deadpan naturalism.
[GF96] Collins Harv pbk **£4.95**
The Master and Margarita (1940)
A unique blend of many genres - philosophical novel, magical fantasy of Satanic misdemeanours, a witty satire on the cowardice of the Soviet system - this is Bulgakov's masterpiece, which he finished in the three years before his death, despite increasing blindness.
[GF97] Collins Harv pbk **£5.95**
The White Guard
This grimly realistic novel is apparently unique in Soviet literature as it deals sympathetically with the fate of Russian intellectuals and officers in the Tsarist army who are caught up in both revolution and Civil War.
[GF98] Collins Harv pbk **£5.95**

BUNIN, IVAN (Russian, 1870 - 1953)
Nobel Prize for Literature 1933. The last significant representative of 19th century Russian literature, Bunin wrote of the Russia described by Tolstoy, Goncharov and Chekhov. He spent much of his life in Europe, and, bitterly opposed to the Revolution, emigrated to Paris in 1917.
Long Ago: Selected Stories
[GF99] Angel pbk **£5.95**
The Gentleman from San Francisco & Other Stories
[GF100] Penguin pbk **£3.95**

BUSI, ALDO (Italian)
Less shocking for its content than for the accomplishment with which it displays a world in which traditional values are inverted, and self-advancement becomes man's dominant motivation, Busi's work has been acclaimed for its 'raucous vitality'. His first novel, *Seminar on Youth*, tells of the struggle forced on an Italian peasant who becomes a male prostitute, and of how he prospers in a society brutalized by the ethic of survival.
Seminar on Youth
[GF101] Faber pbk **£4.99**
The Standard Life of a Temporary Pantyhose Salesman   NEW
A dense, but nonetheless acclaimed work: Angelo Basarovi writes his thesis by day, by night he cruises the homosexual beaches of Lake Garda. He is also employed as a salesman by a magnate of the underwear trade. Together the two embark on a series of sales trips during which they have adventures as improbable as those of Don Quixote and Sancho Panza.
[GF102] Faber hbk **£12.95**
[GF103] Faber pbk **£5.99**

BUTOR, MICHEL (French, 1926 -)
Associated with the *nouveau roman*, Butor's work retains a closer contact with human emotion than some of his contemporaries: *Passing Time* tells of a young Frenchman's attempts to preserve his identity in a large English industrial town.
Passing Time (1957)
[GF104] Calder pbk **£4.95**

BUZZATI, DINO (Italian, 1906 - 1972)
Born in Northern Italy, Buzzati worked in Milan as a journalist, novelist, playwright and painter. His fiction shows the influence of Kafka, often contrasting a flat and unvarnished style with a disturbing subject; in his early work, such as *The Tartar Steppe*, the story of a frontier garrison waiting for an opportunity to prove its gallantry which never arises, this allowed him to express truths indirectly which could not be directly stated in pre-war Italy.
A Love Affair (1962)
[GF105] Carcanet hbk **£9.95**
Restless Nights: Selected Stories
[GF106] Carcanet pbk **£4.95**
The Tartar Steppe (1940)
[GF107] Carcanet pbk **£3.95**

CALASSO, ROBERTO (Italian, 1941 -)
The Ruins of Kasch (1983)   NEW
Calasso adapts a legend recounted by Bedouin tribesmen, in order to question the legitimacy of power, tyranny and sacrifice. A complex tale, which revolves around the arrival of a stranger in the African kingdom of Kasch, and the fatal disruption which this causes.
[GF108] Carcanet hbk **£14.95**

CALVINO, ITALO (Italian, 1923 - 1985)
One of the greatest post-war writers, Calvino moved from an early neo-realism, as seen in work such as the collection of stories *Difficult Loves*, towards the increasingly complex, fantastic and imaginative style of *If On a Winter's Night*. He has used the fable form and science fiction to illuminate the realities of human existence.
Adam, One Afternoon & Other Stories
[GF109] Picador pbk **£3.95**
Cosmicomics (1965)
Together with *Time and the Hunter*, Calvino's two excursions into science fiction and fantasy, for which he was described as an 'Edward Lear of the Space Age'.
[GF110] Sphere pbk **£3.99**
Difficult Loves (Stories, 1954)/**Smog** (1971)/**A Plunge into Real Estate** (1964)
The collection of stories, *Difficult Loves*, presents a sad picture of the malaise of post-war Italy, with quiet but poignant insight into trapped and unfulfilled human emotions.
[GF111] Picador pbk **£3.95**
If On a Winter's Night a Traveller (1979)
A complex, funny masterpiece of modernism, in which the book you are reading changes at the beginning of every chapter: far more than a literary game, it has been acclaimed as the major work of Calvino's late period.
[GF112] Picador pbk **£3.95**
Invisible Cities (1972)
A 'Baedeker of the Imagination', *Invisible Cities* is a collection of stories and descriptions told by Marco Polo to his master Kublai Khan.
[GF113] Secker hbk **£10.95**
[GF114] Picador pbk **£3.50**
Italian Folk Tales
An anthology of tales gathered from every region of Italy, and retold in Calvino's own language, this forms the first full attempt by a major writer to 'reunite the modern Italian sensibility and its popular roots'.
[GF115] Penguin pbk **£9.99**
Marcovaldo (1963)
[GF116] Picador pbk **£3.95**
Mr Palomar (1983)
[GF117] Picador pbk **£3.50**
Our Ancestors
Includes *The Cloven Viscount* (1951), *Baron in the Trees* (1957), *The Non-Existent Knight* (1959). The first works in which Calvino turned away from 'realism' to 'romance', or as he described it - *"Instead of writing the book I ought to write, I conjured up the book I would have liked to read."*
[GF118] Picador pbk **£4.95**
The Castle of Crossed Destinies
[GF119] Picador pbk **£3.99**
The Literature Machine (Essays)
[GF120] Picador pbk **£4.99**
Time and the Hunter (1967)
[GF121] Sphere pbk **£3.50**

CAMUS, ALBERT (French, 1913 - 1960)
Nobel Prize for Literature 1957. Born in Algeria, Camus became famous as a novelist and essayist in the 40s and 50s, capturing the mood of those decades in much of his work. His first novel, *The Outsider*, defines the territory of much of his work, which advances from a sense of alienation and absurdity in a search for human dignity, rebelling against the human predicament, yet remaining stoic in the face of it.
A Happy Death
[GF122] Penguin pbk **£2.95**
American Journals   NEW
[GF123] H Hamilton hbk **£11.95**
Collected Fiction: The Outsider/The Plague/The Fall/Exile and the Kingdom
[GF124] H Hamilton hbk **£12.50**
Exile and the Kingdom (1957)
Six short stories, each written in a different style.
[GF125] Penguin pbk **£3.50**
Myth of Sisyphus (Non fiction, 1942)
[GF126] Penguin pbk **£3.95**
Selected Essays & Notebooks
[GF127] Penguin pbk **£3.95**

The Fall (1956)
The last novel Camus published, and arguably his most powerful, pitting creative subversion against intellectual social conscience.
[GF128] H Hamilton hbk **£10.95**
[GF129] Penguin pbk **£2.99**
The Outsider (1942)
Camus's most widely-read work, a short work of spare, strangely poetic prose, about a Frenchman in Algiers who kills an Arab in a moment of blankness on a hot day; through his own indifference and the incompetence of his lawyer, he is sentenced to death.
[GF130] H Hamilton hbk **£10.95**
[GF131] Penguin pbk **£2.95**
The Plague (1948)
[GF132] H Hamilton hbk **£11.95**
[GF133] Penguin pbk **£3.99**
The Rebel
[GF134] Penguin pbk **£4.50**
Youthful Writings
[GF135] Penguin pbk **£4.95**

CANETTI, ELIAS (Austrian, 1905 -)
Nobel Prize for Literature 1981. Canetti left Vienna in 1938, and settled in London. Iris Murdoch has called *Auto Da Fé*, first published in German in 1935, 'one of the few great novels of the century, savage, subtle, beautiful, mysterious and very large'. It tells of the decline into madness of a great scholar and individualist, and explores the theme of Canetti's other major work *Crowds and Power*, the relation of the individual to the mass, an issue especially relevant to any survey of fascism.
Auto Da Fé (1935)
[GF136] Picador pbk **£4.95**
Crowds and Power (Non fiction)
[GF137] Penguin pbk **£7.95**

CARPELAN, BO (Finnish, 1926 -)
Axel NEW
Baron Axel Carpelan was Bo Carpelan's great-uncle. Jean Sibelius found in him his most responsive listener, dedicating his Second Symphony to him. This fictional 'diary of a life', unfolds the story of these gifted men.
[GF138] Carcanet hbk **£14.95**

CARTANO, TONY (French)
After the Conquest NEW
A multi-layered novel from a French writer with a growing reputation. It concerns an American resident in London who is obsessed with the identity of a man who he believes to be his father.
[GF139] Secker hbk **£10.95**

CAVAZZONI, ERMANNO (Italian, 1947 -)
The Voice of the Moon NEW
Ermanno Cavazzoni's first novel is about madness, and in particular the madness to which residents of Padua succumb. It is currently being made into a film by Fellini.
[GF140] Serpent's Tail pbk **£7.95**

CELINE, LOUIS FERDINAND
(French, 1894 - 1967)
Journey to the End of the Night (1932)
This important novel is a bitter and graphic picture of World War I and its aftermath. Both autobiographical and horrifying, its compelling force comes not only from the author's compulsion to seek the truth under society's veneer of civility, but also from the muscular strength of his prose style.
[GF141] Calder hbk **£14.95**
Death on Credit *(1936)
A sequel to *Journey to the End of the Night*, which follows the career of the author's *alter ego*, Bardamu, as a suburban doctor in France and abroad during the thirties.
[GF142] Calder hbk **£12.95**

CERVANTES, MIGUEL DE
(Spanish, 1547 - 1616)
Spain's greatest writer experimented in every literary style, except epic poetry, but is remembered now for his great novel. Behind its comic, picaresque surface, the book raises the most profound questions about reality and illusion, life and art, and at its conclusion reaches the rare height where comedy and tragedy are indistinguishable.
Don Quixote (Trans. Smollett, Tobias)
Perhaps the best translation, even if not the most accurate, made by a novelist who was himself deeply indebted to Cervantes.
[GF143] Deutsch hbk **£15.00**
[GF144] Deutsch pbk **£8.95**
Don Quixote (1605 - 18)
[GF145] Penguin pbk **£4.95**
Exemplary Stories
[GF146] Penguin pbk **£4.50**

CHAREF, MEHDI
Charef's first novel, *Tea in the Harem*, was made into a prize-winning film and became a rallying-point for second-generation Algerians and Moroccans.
Tea in the Harem NEW
This poignant new novel concerns Madjid, a second-generation Algerian growing up in a housing estate in Paris, caught between two cultures.
[GF147] Serpent's Tail pbk **£6.95**

CHEDID, ANDREE
A novelist, poet and playwright who was born in Cairo, but is now resident in Paris. She writes in French.
From Sleep Unbound
[GF148] Serpent's Tail pbk **£5.95**
The Return to Beirut NEW
This is Chedid's atmospheric hymn for the Lebanon. Sybil, a 12-year old American, meets her grandmother, Kalya, for the first time. It is Beirut in 1975, and Lebanon is on the verge of civil war.
[GF149] Serpent's Tail pbk **£6.95**
The Sixth Day
[GF150] Serpent's Tail pbk **£5.95**

CHEKHOV, ANTON (Russian, 1860 - 1904)
The contribution Chekhov made to drama is only eclipsed by his outstanding contribution to the development of the short story as an international art form. Within the limitations of the genre, Chekhov probes and analyses the petty failings and great expectations of human nature, and although each story is firmly set in the context of late 19th century Russia, the observations are equally relevant in the cynical 1980s.
Lady with Lapdog & Other Stories
The title story has been described as 'the most beautiful short story in the world' by Frank O'Connor, and its restrained, delicate lyricism is characteristic of Chekhov's fading pastoral world of yearning, frustration and pathos.
[GF151] Penguin pbk **£3.50**
The Black Monk & Other Stories
[GF152] Sutton hbk **£2.95**
The Duel & Other Stories
[GF153] Penguin pbk **£2.95**
The Fiancée & Other Stories
[GF154] Penguin pbk **£3.50**
The Kiss & Other Stories
Another ten short masterpieces including the trilogy 'Man in a Case', 'Gooseberries' and 'Concerning Love'. The title story is remarkable for its incredibly sharp psychological analysis and flawless construction.
[GF155] Penguin pbk **£2.99**
The Party & Other Stories
[GF156] Penguin pbk **£2.99**
The Russian Master & Other Stories
[GF157] Oxford pbk **£2.95**

The Shooting Party
Chekhov's only novel-length story.
[GF158] Deutsch pbk **£4.95**
The Steppe
[GF159] Sutton pbk **£2.95**
Viking Portable Chekhov
[GF160] Penguin pbk **£5.95**
Ward Number Six & Other Stories
[GF161] Oxford pbk **£2.95**
Woman's Kingdom & Other Stories
[GF162] Oxford pbk **£2.95**

COCTEAU, JEAN (French, 1889 - 1963)
Renowned as a film-maker, illustrator, poet and novelist, Cocteau's best-known fiction is *Les Enfants Terribles*, a study of the complex and strangely destructive relationship between a brother and sister, enclosed within an unreal world which moves inevitably towards collapse.
Les Enfants Terribles (1929)
[GF163] Penguin pbk **£3.95**
The Imposter
[GF164] P Owen hbk **£10.95**
The Miscreant
[GF165] P Owen hbk **£10.95**
[GF166] Brilliance pbk **£3.95**

COLETTE, SIDONIE-GABRIELLE
(French, 1873 - 1954)
The Claudine novels, which were among Colette's early work, are an enchantingly fresh and humorous study of schoolgirl life in the country at the turn of the century. In the rest of her work she writes about romantic love, nature, animals, life in the country and on the music hall stage, with an ease which is deceptive, and with an understanding of her female characters and of domestic life which is instinctive and rarely sentimental. Her early novels were written under the direction of her husband, who then published them under his own name.
Break of Day
[GF167] Women's P pbk **£1.50**
Chance Acquaintance/
Julie de Carneilhan
[GF168] Penguin pbk **£3.99**
Chéri/The Last of Chéri
[GF169] Penguin pbk **£3.95**
Claudine Novels
[GF170] Penguin pbk **£6.95**
Collected Stories
[GF171] Secker hbk **£14.95**
[GF172] Penguin pbk **£8.95**

Drawing of **Collette**, author of *Break of Day*
(Women's P pbk **£1.50**) by Jacqueline Morreau

Duo & Le Toutounier (1934)
[GF173] Women's P pbk **£1.50**
Evening Star: Recollections
[GF174] Women's P pbk **£3.95**
Gigi & the Cat (1944)
[GF175] Penguin pbk **£3.95**
Looking Backwards: Recollections
[GF176] Women's P pbk **£4.95**
My Mother's House & Sido
[GF177] Penguin pbk **£3.95**
Omnibus: Six Novels
The Vagabond/Chéri/The Last of Chéri/The Ripening Seed/The Cat/Gigi.
[GF178] Secker hbk **£12.95**
The Captive
[GF179] Penguin pbk **£3.95**
The Innocent Libertine (1909)
[GF180] Penguin pbk **£3.99**
The Pure and the Impure
[GF181] Penguin pbk **£2.95**
The Ripening Seed
[GF182] Penguin pbk **£3.50**
The Vagabond (1911)
[GF183] Penguin pbk **£3.50**

CONSTANT, BENJAMIN (French, 1767 - 1830)
Constant's one work of fiction, *Adolphe*, is an early novel of psychological analysis, following the course of a young man's involvement with an older woman.
Adolphe (1807)
[GF184] Penguin pbk **£3.50**

CRESCENZO, LUCIANO DE (Italian)
Quirky bestseller from Naples, Crescenzo's novel speaks volumes about the city. Professor Bellavista, a modern day Zarathustra with an ample Italian love of life, debates on most subjects under the sun.
Thus Spake Bellavista
[GF185] Picador pbk **£3.99**

DAGERMAN, STIG (Swedish, 1923 - 1954)
Dagerman was regarded as the most talented writer of post-war Sweden. His work reflects the anxieties of a generation of collapsing myths, as well as a debt to Kafka. The collection of stories *Games of the Night* contains his best work, and mixes a dark humour with the bleakness characteristic of his vision.
Games of the Night (1947)
[GF186] Quartet pbk **£4.95**
German Autumn (Essays & Articles)
This collection was the fruit of Dagerman's travels in Germany in 1946, and records the broken state of the country immediately after the war.
[GF187] Quartet pbk **£5.95**

DAUDET, ALPHONSE (French, 1840 - 1897)
Lettres de Mon Moulin
Delicately sentimental and humorous sketches of Provençal life.
[GF188] Penguin pbk **£4.99**
Sappho
[GF189] Soho pbk **£5.95**
Tartarin de Tarascon/
Tartarin of the Alps
Daudet's most popular works: Tartarin is a genial caricature of the Frenchman of the Midi, exuberant and boastful, who gets involved in a string of misadventures.
[GF190] Soho pbk **£5.95**

DEL GIUDICE, DANIELE (Italian)
Lines of Light **NEW**
A young Italian physicist and an aging German writer who is renouncing fiction and seeking a new way to perceive and feel, meet at an airfield. A sense of being abandoned in a world where the past, present and future are unknown brings the two together.
[GF191] Viking hbk **£11.95**

DELEDDA, GRAZIA (Italian, 1871 - 1936)
Nobel Prize for Literature 1927. Sardinia dominates Deledda's work, rather in the way that Sicily does that of Verga. Her writing moves from an early romanticism towards a more realistic study of characters struggling against an often primitive background, with a superb evocation of the traditions and folklore of the Sardinian people.
After the Divorce (1902)
[GF192] Quartet pbk **£4.95**
Woman and the Priest (La Madre) (1920)
[GF193] Dedalus pbk **£4.95**

DER NISTOR (Yiddish, 1884 - 1950)
'Der Nistor', meaning literally 'the occult one', was the pseudonym of Pinchas Kahonovitch, a writer who spent most of his life in Russia, and died in a forced labour camp there. *The Family Mashber* is his major work, a cycle of novels which combine elements of fictional realism with the older and more allusive traditions of Hasidism.
The Family Mashber (1939 - 48)
[GF194] Fontana pbk **£5.95**

DIDEROT, DENIS (French, 1713 - 1784)
More famous as the editor of the *Encyclopédie*, Denis Diderot's prose fiction manages to combine both satire and moral debate in a vivid and discursive style.
Irresistible Diderot
[GF195] Quartet hbk **£15.00**
Jacques the Fatalist (1796)
Inspired by the experimental form and philosophical speculation of Tristram Shandy, and based round the peregrinations and conversations of the indefatigable Jacques and his master.
[GF196] Penguin pbk **£4.95**
Rameau's Nephew/D'Alembert's Dream
[GF197] Penguin pbk **£4.50**
The Nun (1796)
[GF198] Penguin pbk **£3.95**

DINESEN, ISAK (Danish, 1885 - 1962)
Born into an aristocratic Danish family, Dinesen spent seventeen years of her life in Kenya, where she farmed coffee, a period described in her autobiography *Out of Africa*; she is also much admired for her short stories, which show a sophisticated and discerning wit, as well as a richly imaginative gift for story-telling.
Anecdotes of Destiny (1958)
[GF199] Penguin pbk **£3.95**
Angelic Avengers (1947)
[GF200] Penguin pbk **£4.50**
Carnival: Entertainments/
Posthumous Tales
[GF201] Grafton pbk **£3.50**
Ehrengard (1963)
[GF202] Penguin pbk **£3.99**
Last Tales (1957)
[GF203] Penguin pbk **£4.99**
Seven Gothic Tales (1934)
Exaggeratedly gothic to the point of pastiche, Dinesen's stories are full of mystery, richness and sadness, told in a memorable and direct style.
[GF204] Grafton pbk **£4.50**
Shadows on the Grass (1960)
[GF205] Penguin pbk **£3.50**
Winter's Tales (1942)
[GF206] Penguin pbk **£3.95**

DOBLIN, ALFRED (German, 1878 - 1957)
By training a doctor and psychologist, Döblin was a Socialist and prominent intellectual of Weimar Berlin. Described by Kafka as 'one of the great names among German novelists', his books were banned in 1933, and from then until the end of the war, he lived abroad, at first in France and later in America. His finest work is *Berlin Alexanderplatz* which is most

interesting as a powerful portrayal of the life of the proletariat, and one of the great novels of the city.
Berlin Alexanderplatz (1931)
[GF207] Penguin pbk **£4.95**
November 1918
Döblin presents a huge panorama of post-War Germany, which features both the makers of history - such as Rosa Luxemburg and Karl Liebknecht - as well as anonymous men and women.
1: A People Betrayed
[GF208] Fromm pbk **£11.95**
2: Karl & Rosa
[GF209] Fromm pbk **£9.95**

DODERER, HEIMITO VON
(Austrian, 1896 - 1966)
Doderer's monumental novel shows the influence of Proust, in its attempt to recapture the virtues of pre-World War I Austria through an examination of the later social history of the country.
The Demons:
Vol 1 **NEW**
[GF210] Quartet pbk **£8.50**
Vol 2 **NEW**
[GF211] Quartet pbk **£8.50**
Vol 3 **NEW**
[GF212] Quartet pbk **£8.50**

DOMBROVSKY, YURY (Russian)
Set in 1937, Dombrovsky's novel tells how the keeper of antiquities in a provincial museum is sucked into the turmoil of Stalin's Russia; when he learns that the town's cathedral is to be demolished and replaced by a museum of glass, he commits himself to the future survival of the culture whose past he has been guarding.
The Keeper of Antiquities (1964)
[GF213] Carcanet hbk **£12.95**

DORRIE, DORIS (German)
Love, Pain and the Whole
Damn Thing **NEW**
Literary debut by the young German film-maker. In these four stories she tells us how to get a man (dye your hair blue and play the saxophone); how to get rid of him (try an electric hair-dryer at bathtime) and how to protect your dignity when lying in the bushes.
[GF214] Viking hbk **£11.95**

DOSTOEVSKY, FYODOR
(Russian, 1821 -1881)
One of the most powerful and influential writers in European literature, Dostoevsky is best known for his four great novels *Crime and Punishment*, *The Idiot*, *The Devils* and *The Brothers Karamazov*, in all of which he undertakes a profound and intricate analysis of human nature. His protagonists, such as Raskolnikov, Stavrogin, Myshkin and the Karamazov brothers, are often driven by extremes of emotion or obsession, caught in spiritual and moral dilemmas which are probed with exceptional insight. Celebrated for his almost hallucinatory depiction of cities and dark places, Dostoevsky creates haunting landscapes which are expressive of his characters' profound spiritual crises, and the dark recesses of the human soul.
Crime and Punishment (1866)
In 1865, when Dostoevsky began writing the novel that was to bring him international recognition, he was so encumbered by debt as the hero he created. Raskolnikov, an impoverished student, decides to murder an old woman moneylender for gain. After the murder, he is unable to come to terms with his growing sense of guilt. Dostoevsky influenced a whole generation of European writers with his powerful psychological analysis and his unerring sense of the dramatic.
[GF215] Oxford pbk **£2.95**
[GF216] Penguin pbk **£3.50**

Memoirs from the House of the Dead
[GF217] Oxford pbk **£2.95**
Netochka Nezvanova
[GF218] Penguin pbk **£2.95**
**Notes from the Underground/
The Double**
[GF219] Penguin pbk **£3.50**
Poor Folk & Other Stories
[GF220] Penguin pbk **£3.99**
The Brothers Karamazov (1879 - 80)
Dostoevsky's last novel, completed in 1880 shortly before his death, draws together all the themes of his mature work. This many faceted work of parricide and fraternal jealousy contains the much analysed Legend of the Grand Inquisitor, considered to be the clearest exposition of Dostoevsky's world view.
[GF221] Penguin pbk **£5.99**
The Devils (1871 - 72)
[GF222] Penguin pbk **£4.95**
The Double
[GF223] Collins Harv pbk **£5.95**
The Gambler/Bobok/A Nasty Story
[GF224] Penguin pbk **£2.95**
The House of the Dead (1860 - 62)
[GF225] Oxford pbk **£2.95**
[GF226] Penguin pbk **£3.99**
The Idiot (1868 - 69)
[GF227] Penguin pbk **£4.50**
The Insulted and Injured
[GF228] Grafton pbk **£4.95**
Uncle's Dream & Other Stories
[GF229] Penguin pbk **£4.50**
Village of Stepanchikovo
[GF230] Angel pbk **£5.95**
Winter Notes on Summer Impressions
[GF231] Quartet hbk **£7.50**

DROUIN, CECILE (French)
Child of the Red Land
First novel by a Hanoi-born novelist. It is a story of a little girl's search for love set in French Indochina, and of her reactions on returning to France.
[GF232] Pan pbk **£2.99**

DUMAS, ALEXANDRE (French, 1802 - 1870)
Dumas *père* wrote historical novels from 1839 with phenomenal success: *The Three Musketeers*, set in Richelieu's time, is his greatest, and shows his gift for narrative and dialogue, and for finding the dramatic scene in any story - his fiction is not complicated by psychology, and follows a belief that, as in life, it is *'l'action et l'amour'* which are important.
The Three Musketeers
[GF233] Penguin pbk **£2.95**

DUMAS, ALEXANDRE (French, 1824 - 1895)
Dumas the Younger became one of the leading playwrights of the Second Empire; he wrote *Lady of the Camelias* as a novel, subsequently dramatised it, and won rapid fame with the story of the doomed passion of Marguerite Gautier and Armand Duval.
Lady of the Camelias (1848)
[GF234] Oxford pbk **£3.95**

DURAS, MARGUERITE (French, 1914 -)
Contemporary novelist associated with the *nouveau roman*, whose work is distinguished by a fine ear for suggestive dialogue. She wrote the screenplay for Alain Resnais's *Hiroshima Mon Amour*, and reached a wide audience with a powerful, semi-autobiographical, award-winning novella *The Lover*.
Blue Eyes, Black Hair
[GF235] Fontana pbk **£3.95**
Emily L **NEW**
A tale of two couples, which meditates on love, art and the ruin wrought by time, and achieves its effect through a subtle blurring of the distinctions between reality and imagination.
[GF236] Collins hbk **£10.95**

La Douleur
[GF237] Fontana pbk **£3.95**
Moderato Cantabile
[GF238] Calder pbk **£4.95**
Outside: Selected Writings
[GF239] Fontana pbk **£3.95**
The Little Horses of Tarquinia
[GF240] Calder pbk **£4.95**
The Lover (1971)
[GF241] Fontana pbk **£3.50**
The Sea Wall (1959)
[GF242] Faber pbk **£4.95**
The Square (1955)
[GF243] Calder pbk **£3.95**
Trilogy: The Square/Ten Thirty on a Summer Night/The Afternoon of M Andesmas
[GF244] Calder hbk **£7.95**
Whole Days in the Trees
[GF245] Calder pbk **£4.95**

DURRENMATT, FRIEDRICH (Swiss, 1921 -)
An ingenious writer better known for plays such as *The Physicists* and *The Visit*; among his more interesting, perhaps least ambitious work, is the series of five thriller novels first published in the 1950s, which have been described as 'paradoxical detective stories with a touch of Kafka'.
The Assignment
[GF246] Cape hbk **£12.95**
The Execution of Justice **NEW**
In 1955 a distinguished German councilman walks into a restaurant full of politicians, businessmen and artists and shoots a university professor. For his crime he is sentenced to 20 years in prison.
[GF247] Cape hbk **£11.95**
The Novels of Friedrich Dürrenmatt
[GF248] Picador pbk **£3.95**

EBERHARDT, ISABELLE (French)
A remarkable adventurer who dressed as an Arab boy to travel in the North African desert, these two titles are a collection of stories and vignettes and a vivid picaresque novel, both evoking North Africa.
The Oblivion Seekers
[GF249] P Owen pbk **£4.50**
Vagabond
[GF250] Hogarth pbk **£4.95**

ECA DE QUEIROZ, JOSE MARIA
(Portuguese, 1845 - 1900)
Eça's novels expose the vices and corruption of the Portuguese bourgeoisie; in an objective, straightforward style which allowed his radical, reforming beliefs their most specific statement.
The Maias (1888)
[GF251] Dent pbk **£4.95**

ECO, UMBERTO (Italian, 1932 -)
A semiotician and examiner of the surfaces and appearances of our society, Eco is an academic in Bologna, whose recent collection of essays *Travels in Hyperreality* revealed the passage of his mind over a wide range of subjects. *The Name of the Rose* is a fascinating blend of metaphysical speculation and semiological inquiry, framed within the context of a medieval thriller.
Foucault's Pendulum **NEW**
Eco's first work of fiction since *The Name of the Rose* has become a remarkable literary bestseller in Italy. It is a fascinating intellectual thriller, which ranges back and forth across the centuries, full of startling plot shifts and self-reference. '*Foucault's Pendulum* exemplifies what postmodernist fiction is about, with its learning - real and bogus - its concern with books talking to books, its elements of self-mockery, its semiological obsession...This is the way the European novel is going...' (Anthony Burgess).
[GF252] Secker hbk **£14.95**

Reflections on the Name of the Rose
(Non fiction)
[GF253] Secker hbk **£5.95**
The Name of the Rose
[GF254] Secker hbk **£12.95**
[GF255] Picador pbk **£5.95**
Travels in Hyperreality: Essays
[GF256] Picador pbk **£3.95**

EMANTS, MARCELLUS (Dutch, 1848 - 1923)
An important figure of 19th century literature in Holland, a champion of Zola, and an interesting naturalistic novelist, Emants's work often describes the squalor of human existence: his masterpiece, *A Posthumous Confession*, is an account of a man who has murdered his wife, and a pioneering psychological novel.
A Posthumous Confession (1894)
[GF257] Quartet pbk **£4.95**

ENDE, MICHAEL (German, 1929 -)
Ende's early career was spent as an actor and painter; his novels were written for children, but are appropriate for all ages - *Momo* is a modern fairy-story, and *The Never-Ending Story*, a haunting work of the imagination, headed the German bestseller lists for over three years.
Mirror in the Mirror (1986)
[GF258] Viking hbk **£11.95**
Momo (1973)
[GF259] Penguin pbk **£2.50**
The Never-Ending Story (1979)
[GF260] Penguin pbk **£3.50**

FABRE, FERNAND (French, 1827 - 1898)
The Abbé Tigrane
A satiric novel charting the quarrels and intrigues amongst the clergy of a country diocese over the appointment of a new bishop, by an author acclaimed as a French equivalent of Trollope.
[GF261] P Owen hbk **£10.95**

FALDBAKKEN, KNUT (Norwegian) **NEW**
Adam's Diary
The compelling story, set in Oslo, of three lovers - each representing an aspect of the male psyche - who love, fear and hate the same woman.
[GF262] P Owen hbk **£12.95**
The Sleeping Prince
Written by one of Norway's leading writers, this novel tells of a middle-aged woman's experience of unrequited love.
[GF263] P Owen hbk **£11.95**

FALLADA, HANS (German, 1893 - 1947)
Fallada was one of the great socialist realist novelists of his period, sharing with Brecht a concern with the victims of his society, those defeated by the inflation and corruption of the post-First World War world. His best-known work, *Little Man, What Now?*, is currently unavailable.
The Drinker (1950) **NEW**
A documentary, autobiographical novel charting a man's steady descent into alcoholism and self-destruction, this was published after Fallada's death: it remains a powerful depiction of mental and physical anguish.
[GF264] Libris pbk **£9.95**

FEUCHTWANGER, LION
(German, 1884 - 1958)
Feuchtwanger was a prominent socialist and Jewish intellectual, a collaborator with Brecht on *Edward II* and other works, who emigrated to the United States in the 1930s. *Jew Suss* is a memorable historical novel portraying Germany in the 18th century, which shows strong left-wing sympathy.
Jew Suss (1986)
[GF265] Grafton pbk **£3.95**

FINK, IDA (Polish, 1921 -)
This is a haunting collection of stories about life in Poland at the time of the Holocaust; Fink herself survived the events which she describes, and now lives in Israel; she presents a picture of a world where ordinary human decency is lost, and life becomes little more than a daily struggle to survive and hope.
A Scrap of Time & Other Stories
[GF266] P Owen hbk **£10.95**

FLAUBERT, GUSTAVE (French, 1821 - 1880)
Never 'realistic' in the manner of Zola, Gustave Flaubert reveals sympathetically but unblinkingly the circumscribed existence of all of his central characters. Apart from the exquisite perfection of his closely crafted prose style, the quality that most clearly distinguishes Flaubert's fiction is his vision: through a careful, exact and frequently lyrical observation of detail, he builds up pictures which linger in the mind long after the novel is finished. Aside from *Madame Bovary*, his major works are *A Sentimental Education*, the uncompleted *Bouvard and Pécuchet* and the story 'A Simple Heart' in the *Three Tales*.
A Sentimental Education (1869)
[GF271] Penguin pbk **£4.50**
Bouvard and Pécuchet (1881)
[GF267] Penguin pbk **£4.95**
Madame Bovary (1856)
Flaubert paints a devastating picture of the small-mindedness of provincial life in this, his greatest novel; Emma Bovary is his most memorable character, a beautiful but frustrated egotist, both better than the world she longs to escape, and unavoidably a part of it.
[GF268] Oxford pbk **£2.95**
[GF269] Penguin pbk **£2.99**
Salammbo
[GF270] Penguin pbk **£4.50**
Temptation of St Anthony
[GF272] Penguin pbk **£4.99**
Three Tales
[GF273] Penguin pbk **£2.99**

FONTANE, THEODOR (German, 1819 - 1898)
Theodor Fontane supported himself as a journalist through most of his life, only publishing his first novel, *Before the Storm*, in his fifties. Acclaimed as one of the greatest historical novels in German, it is set in 1812/1813 at the time of the arrival of the French army retreating from Moscow. *Effi Briest*, the story of a woman's adultery, establishes him as a realist in the same league as Flaubert and Zola.
Before the Storm: A Novel of the Winter of 1812 - 1813 (1878)
[GF274] Oxford pbk **£6.95**
Effi Briest (1895)
[GF275] Penguin pbk **£3.95**

FRISCH, MAX (Swiss, 1911 -)
Together with Dürrenmatt, Frisch is perhaps the most eminent European playwright of the post-war era, famous for works such as *The Fire Raisers* and *Andorra*. His best novel is *I'm Not Stiller*, the story of a man in prison who refuses to acknowledge his past identity, in tone somewhere between Kafka and Camus.
Bluebeard (1982)
[GF276] Penguin pbk **£3.50**
Gantenbein (1964)
[GF277] Methuen hbk **£9.50**
Homo Faber (1957)
[GF278] Penguin pbk **£3.95**
I'm Not Stiller (1954)
[GF279] Penguin pbk **£4.50**
Man in the Holocene (1979)
[GF280] Methuen hbk **£8.50**

FROMENTIN, EUGENE (French, 1811 - 1872)
Dominique (1863)
An early work of psychological analysis, it is a semi-autobiographical study of disappointment in love and life. The narrator has missed supreme happiness in love and work, and has to accept the second best.
[GF281] Soho pbk **£4.95**

FUST, MILAN (Hungarian)
The Story of My Wife `NEW`
For seven years up to 1942 Milan Fust, an unemployed Jewish Hungarian schoolmaster and poet, averted his eyes from the threatening world to create this extraordinary confessional novel. It maps out the mind and emotions of Captain Storr as he focuses on a crucial question - is his young wife Lizzie unfaithful or not?
[GF282] Cape hbk **£11.95**

GADDA, CARLO EMILIA (Italian, 1893 - 1973)
Gadda's best known work, *That Awful Mess on Via Merulana*, is formally a detective story, but one in which the solution is teasingly withdrawn from the reader rather than brought closer. Its elements of social satire, showing the state of Rome in 1927, an increasingly sick society of profiteers and bureaucrats, are combined with a fully modernistic approach to language, to form 'a philosophical as well as a murder novel'.
Acquainted with Grief (1963)
[GF283] P Owen hbk **£12.95**
That Awful Mess on Via Merulana (1957)
[GF284] Quartet pbk **£7.95**

GALDOS, BENITO PEREZ
(Spanish, 1843 - 1920)
The leading realistic novelist of 19th century Spain, Galdós wrote vast cycles of contemporary Spanish life, creating sumptuously realised environments and a wealth of rounded charcters; Anthony Burgess praised him for 'his creation of a world which does for a dead Madrid what Balzac did for Paris, and Dickens for London'.
Fortunata and Jacinta (1886)
[GF285] Penguin pbk **£6.99**
Torquemada
This tetralogy portrays middle-class Madrid with a keen eye and relentless irony. In sardonic fashion Galdós follows the rise from obscurity to great fortune of a Madrid moneylender.
[GF286] Deutsch hbk **£15.95**
[GF287] Deutsch pbk **£8.95**

GAUTIER, THEOPHILE (French, 1811 - 1872)
One of the most important Romantics of the mid-19th century, noted for his passion for visual description, and for his articulation of the aesthete's position. *Mademoiselle de Maupin* is a long, diffuse novel which is prefaced by Gautier's famous passage on '*l'art pour l'art*'. Its sensuous descriptive writing scandalized the public of the day.
Mademoiselle de Maupin (1835)
[GF288] Penguin pbk **£4.50**

GENET, JEAN (French, 1910 - 1987)
Iconoclastic writer whose reputation rests chiefly on his 'absurd' dramas. Genet's novels are interesting for their evocation of a squalid and vicious world using pure, lyrical language, drawing on his experience in the Paris underworld.
Funeral Rites (1969)
[GF289] Panther pbk **£2.95**
Our Lady of the Flowers (1942)
[GF290] Grafton pbk **£3.95**
Prisoner of Love (Non fiction) `NEW`
Autobiographical account of the last phase of his life, and of his unusual involvement with the Palestinian cause, with which he felt a close sympathy.
[GF291] Picador hbk **£12.95**

Querelle of Brest (1947)
[GF292] Grafton pbk **£3.95**
The Miracle of the Rose (1946)
[GF293] Penguin pbk **£4.99**
Thief's Journal (1948)
Genet's autobiography describes the milieu of criminals, prostitutes and homosexuals in which he lived, and which provides the background to his fiction.
[GF294] Penguin pbk **£4.95**

GIDE, ANDRE (French, 1869 - 1951)
Nobel Prize for Literature 1947. A major novelist who concerned himself with demonstrating his liberation from the conventions - moral and sexual - in which he was brought up, and of transferring this disturbance to his readers.
Corydon (Non fiction, 1923)
[GF295] GMP pbk **£3.95**
Fruits of the Earth
[GF296] Penguin pbk **£4.50**
La Symphonie Pastorale/Isabelle
[GF297] Penguin pbk **£3.95**
Strait is the Gate (1909)
[GF298] Penguin pbk **£3.50**
The Counterfeiters (1926)
Gide himself regarded this as his major work, describing it with the term *roman*, as opposed to *sotie* or *récit* with which he described his other shorter novels and short tales.
[GF299] Penguin pbk **£4.95**
The Immoralist (1902)
[GF300] Penguin pbk **£3.95**
The Vatican Cellars (1914)
[GF301] Penguin pbk **£2.95**

GINZBURG, NATALIA (Italian, 1916 -)
Born in Sicily, Ginzburg grew up in Turin. She has been active throughout her life in politics, and in recent years a senator in Rome; the success of her work, written in an extremely personal style, a mixture of the everyday and the lyrical, has made her perhaps the best-known woman writer in Italy today.
All Our Yesterdays (1952)
[GF302] Carcanet pbk **£3.95**
Dear Michael
[GF303] P Owen hbk **£10.95**
Family & Borghesia
[GF304] Carcanet hbk **£10.95**
Family Sayings (1963)
[GF305] Grafton pbk **£3.50**
Little Virtues
[GF306] Carcanet hbk **£8.95**
The City and the House (1984)
[GF307] Carcanet hbk **£8.95**
The Manzoni Family (1983)
Using letters, diaries and contemporary accounts, this is a full and novelistic study of Alessandro Manzoni, author of *The Betrothed*, and of those around him.
[GF308] Carcanet hbk **£12.95**
[GF309] Grafton pbk **£3.99**
**The Road into the City &
The Dry Heart** `NEW`
The Road into the City, Ginzburg's first novel, is centred on a young peasant girl who longs for the city and silk stockings. She gets there by devious methods but leaves a wake of human destruction. *The Dry Heart* is a novella about a simple woman who fools herself into believing she is in love.
[GF310] Carcanet hbk **£10.95**
Valentino & Sagittarius (1951, 1957)
[GF311] Carcanet hbk **£10.95**
Voices in the Evening (1961) `NEW`
Republished in English, this tells the story of the effect of the Second World War on a Piedmont family which has risen from nothing to prosperity, their subsequent collapse, and the new beginning for some who had depended on it.
[GF312] Carcanet hbk **£10.95**

GIONO, JEAN (French, 1895 - 1970)
A prolific writer, he set his best novels in the Midi, depicting in rich poetic language a way of life that is simple and idyllic but also harsh and close to nature.
The Man Who Planted Trees   **NEW**
In the figure of Elzéard Bouffier and his story - both parable and manual - of reafforestation, Giono shows us the best in man's relationship with nature, and his fellow men. Illustrated with Michael McCurdy's beautiful woodcuts.
[GF313] P Owen pbk **£5.95**

GIOVENE, ANDREA (Italian, 1904 -)
Born into an aristocratic, though down-at-heel, Neapolitan family; his monumental series of five novels, here published in two volumes, is partly autobiographical, telling of the travels of a dispossessed nobleman around pre-war Europe, his return to Mussolini's Italy, his refusal to serve under the occupying German regime (which sends him to a prisoner-of-war camp), and the final resurgence of Italy in the post-war years.
Sansovero: Vol 1 (1966-1970)
[GF314] Quartet pbk **£6.95**
Vol 2
[GF315] Quartet pbk **£6.95**

GOETHE, JOHANN WOLFGANG VON
(German, 1741 - 1832)
The greatest literary figure of his time, Goethe's early novel *The Sorrows of Young Werther* was enormously influential in shaping and defining the tastes of the last decades of the 18th century. It is a classic story of unrequited love: the hero, Werther, is a sensitive artist, in love with Charlotte, who is engaged to another, and the novel ends with the hero's suicide; the presentation of Werther's despair, both with society and with himself, is memorable and helped to develop a popular image of the 'romantic', which still survives, in some forms, to this day.
Elective Affinities (1809)
An exploration of adulterous passions without moralisation about the feelings presented.
[GF316] Penguin pbk **£4.95**
Kindred by Choice
[GF317] Calder pbk **£4.95**
The Sorrows of Young Werther (1774)
[GF318] Dedalus pbk **£4.95**
Wilhelm Meister
Written between 1777 and 1829, this series of novels is the prototype of the *bildungsroman*, or novel of emotional and intellecual development; it shows the hero's wanderings and encounters, combining a picaresque form with a philosophical content as he learns to understand himself and the world about him.
Vol 1
[GF319] Calder hbk **£6.95**
Vol 2
[GF320] Calder hbk **£6.95**
Vol 3
[GF321] Calder hbk **£6.95**
Vol 4
[GF322] Calder pbk **£3.95**
Vol 5
[GF323] Calder pbk **£3.95**
Vol 6
[GF324] Calder pbk **£3.95**

GOGOL, NIKOLAI VASILIEVICH
(Russian, 1809 - 1852)
Gogol's reputation as Russia's greatest satirist rests on a handful of completed works: two collections of stories, including the masterpieces 'The Nose' and 'The Overcoat', a play, *The Government Inspector*, and part of a three-novel trilogy, *Dead Souls*.
Dead Souls (1842)
[GF325] Penguin pbk **£3.99**
Diary of a Madman
[GF326] Penguin pbk **£2.95**

GOMBROWICZ, WITOLD
(Polish, 1903 - 1969)
An early member of the Polish avant-garde, a novelist as well as playwright, Gombrowicz's work first appeared in the 1930s, but remained unappreciated until its republication in French in 1958. *Pornografia* is his best-known novel, dealing with the problem of 'submission to youth'.
Ferdydurke (1937)
[GF327] Boyars pbk **£4.95**
Pornografia (1960)
[GF328] Boyars pbk **£4.95**
Possessed (1939)
[GF329] Boyars pbk **£6.95**

GOMEZ-ARCOS, AUGUSTIN (Spanish)
A Spanish-born writer, who now lives in France and writes in French. His novels explore the cruelty - both domestic and political - of Franco's Spain.
A Bird Burned Alive
[GF330] Chatto hbk **£11.95**
Carnivorous Lamb
[GF331] GMP pbk **£4.95**

GONCHAROV, IVAN (Russian, 1812 - 1891)
The creator of one of the chief archetypes of Russian literature, Ilya Oblomov: an intellectual and a member of the lesser nobility, Oblomov is not only introspective, contemplative and visionary, but also, ultimately, indolent, impotent and emotionally bankrupt. His profound ennui has influenced modern writers all over the world.
Oblomov (1859)
[GF332] Penguin pbk **£4.95**

GONCOURT, EDMOND & JULES
(French, 1822 - 1896/1830 - 1970)
Together with Balzac, Flaubert and Zola, the brothers Goncourt are masters of the 19th century French novel; this is the first translation of this work since the 1880s, and begins a new series of their work.
Germinie Lacerteux
Written on learning the truth about the life of their apparently exemplary servant, Rose, - *"a woman in whom vice and depravity co-exist with pure love and selfless devotion"* - this was the Goncourts' fourth novel, and an acclaimed work of realism.
[GF333] Penguin pbk **£3.95**
Sister Philomene   **NEW**
A vivid record of life in a public hospital in 19th century Paris, this novel also tells a poignant love story.
[GF334] Chatto hbk **£12.95**

GOYTISOLO, JUAN (Spanish, 1931 -)
Spain's most celebrated modern writer, for many years exiled in Paris and a bitter opponent of the Franco regime. The distinguishing mark of all of Goytisolo's fiction is hatred: he hates the betrayals, suppressions and moral fecklessness of modern Spain. As with Buñuel, his work is revolutionary, driven by Marxist analysis, but also darkly comic, powerfully erotic and entirely independent. Ultimately he is an affirmative voice - championing the suppressed heritage of Moorish Spain, less for its exoticism than the perception central to all his fiction: that unless a culture can admit the past in its entirety then genuine change and renewal remains impossible.
Marks of Identity
[GF335] Serpent's Tail pbk **£8.95**
Count Julian   **NEW**
A Spanish exile in Tangiers fulminates bitterly against his homeland, invoking Julian, the Great Traitor, a legendary figure who was reputed to have opened the nation's gates to the Moorish invaders. First published in 1970, this is the second of Goytisolo's trilogy, due to be completed in 1990 with the publication of *Juan the Landless* in English.
[GF336] Serpent's Tail pbk **£7.95**

Landscapes after the Battle
Goytisolo's satiric portrait of the condition of exile is assembled from fragments of different details - from newspapers, dialogue, narratives.
[GF337] Serpent's Tail pbk **£7.95**

GRAB, HERMANN (Czech, 1903 - 1949)
Born in Prague, Grab spent the last ten years of his life in exile, and died in the United States. *The Town Park* (1934) is the story of a boy's adolescence in First World War Prague, and of his growing away from the bourgeois world in which his family lives. Together with the ten stories which accompany it, this comprises the complete body of Grab's work.
The Town Park & Other Stories
[GF338] Verso hbk **£10.95**

GRASS, GUNTER (German, 1927 -)
An important, popular and at times controversial figure in the post-war generation of German writers, Grass seeks to unravel collective guilt and the problems of a ubiquitous past in modern society. His most famous novel, *The Tin Drum*, is distinguished by the grotesque, grim playfulness and combination of disparate tones which characterises all his work.
From the Diary of a Snail (1974)
[GF339] Picador pbk **£4.95**
Headbirths: or, The Germans Are Dying Out (1982)
[GF340] Penguin pbk **£3.50**
Local Anaesthetic (1969)
[GF341] Penguin pbk **£3.95**
Meeting at Telgte (1981)
[GF342] Penguin pbk **£2.95**
On Writings and Politics (Essays)
[GF343] Penguin pbk **£3.95**
The Flounder (1978)
[GF344] Picador pbk **£5.95**
The Rat (1986)
[GF345] Picador pbk **£4.50**
The Danzig Trilogy: The Tin Drum/ Cat and Mouse/Dog Years
[GF346] Secker hbk **£25.00**
The Tin Drum (1962)
This dazzling masterpiece established Grass as a major social and political voice of his age. A compassionate and humanistic epic, it follows concurrently the life of a Danzig family and the historical events which intrude upon them. The central character is the dwarf, Oskar, who uses special powers to control his fate until political events consume him.
[GF347] Picador pbk **£6.99**
Cat and Mouse
[GF348] Picador pbk **£3.95**
Dog Years
[GF349] Picador pbk **£5.95**

GREEN, JULIEN (French, 1900 -)
Born in Paris of American parents, Green should be considered a French writer, who is now a member of the Académie Française. Deeply religious, he writes sombre novels charting the conflicts between carnal and spiritual desire.
Each in his Darkness
[GF350] Quartet pbk **£6.95**
Moira
[GF351] Quartet pbk **£6.95**

GRIMMELSHAUSEN, JOHANN JAKOB VON (German, c.1625 - 1676)
Grimmelshausen wrote one of the literary masterpieces of 17th century German literature: telling the story of one man's life from peasant boyhood to middle-aged retirement from the world, *Simplicissimus* is a rare combination of pessimism, humour and remarkable human sympathy.
Adventurous Simplicissimus (1669)
[GF352] Dedalus pbk **£5.95**

GROSSMAN, DAVID (Israeli)
A highly regarded writer whose non-fiction book about the Israeli-Palestine dilemma, *The Yellow Wind*, was published to acclaim in 1988.
See Under: Love `NEW`
Momik, the protagonist of *See Under: Love*, is the only child of survivors of the Holocaust. He is determined to try and understand the Nazi beast and to shield himself from all feeling and attachment. Yet Momik becomes 'infected with humanity', and with the love which exists alongside the horrors of human history.
[GF353] Cape hbk **£13.95**

GROSSMAN, VASILY (Russian, 1905 - 1964)
War novels are a neglected genre in the West but in the Soviet Union some of the most imaginative literature has developed from incidents in the Great Patriotic War. Grossman, for a long time highly regarded in the Soviet Union, has found belated recognition in the West with the epic *Life and Fate*. In the great naturalist tradition of *War and Peace*, this enormous novel has at its heart the tragic struggle for Stalingrad, one of the great episodes of recent Russian history.
Forever Flowing
[GF354] Collins Harv pbk **£4.95**
Life and Fate
[GF355] Fontana pbk **£5.95**

HACKL, ERICH (German)
Aurora's Motive `NEW`
A prize-winning first novel, based on an actual, much-publicised murder case about a mother compelled to kill her 18 year old daughter.
[GF356] Cape hbk **£10.95**

HAMSUN, KNUT (Norwegian, 1859 - 1952)
Nobel Prize for Literature 1920. Hamsun was born of peasant stock, and worked at a variety of jobs, including four years spent in America in the 1880s, before the publication of his first novel *Hunger*. His view of human life is complicated, and includes a very negative and actively 'unpleasant' strain; yet much of his work reveals an outstanding poetic imagination, with a powerful grasp of symbolism and imagery expressed in richly figurative language; *Mysteries* has been acclaimed as one of the ten great novels of the century (despite ante-dating it by eight years).
Growth of the Soil (1917)
[GF357] Souvenir pbk **£5.95**
Hunger (1888)
Hamsun's first novel tells strikingly of the mental perceptions of a friendless wanderer, and is an example of his work at its most uncompromising.
[GF358] Picador pbk **£3.50**
Mysteries (1892)
The story of a young man who spends the summer in a small resort town, and of the contacts which he makes before he kills himself; these contacts, through which he discovers something of himself and of his motivations, are the 'mysteries' of the book's title.
[GF359] Picador pbk **£3.99**
Pan
[GF360] Souvenir pbk **£5.95**
The Wanderer (1922)
[GF361] Souvenir pbk **£3.95**
Victoria (1898)
[GF362] Picador pbk **£3.50**
Wayfarers (1930)
[GF363] Souvenir pbk **£4.50**
Women at the Pump
[GF364] Souvenir pbk **£3.95**

HANDKE, PETER (German, 1942 -)
Also a playwright, Handke has produced fiction that is intense and complex. Often situated amid the unnerving, frequently with a single character

challenged by a metaphysical need, Handke's novels are intelligent examples of contemporary philosophical fiction, and he has been described by John Updike as 'widely regarded as the best young writer, and by many as the best writer altogether, in his language'.
A Slow Homecoming (1983)
[GF365] Methuen pbk **£3.95**
Across
[GF366] Methuen pbk **£3.95**
Left-Handed Woman (1980)
[GF367] Methuen pbk **£2.95**
Repetition
[GF368] Methuen hbk **£10.95**
Short Letter, Long Farewell (1974)
[GF369] Methuen pbk **£5.50**
The Goalie's Anxiety at the Penalty Kick (1977)
[GF370] Methuen pbk **£4.95**

HANSEN, MARTIN A. (Danish, 1909 - 1955)
Born and brought up in a traditional rural community near Copenhagen, similar to that of which he writes in *The Liar*, Martin Hansen was an important Nationalist and Christian writer, with a vigorous and vivid prose style. His reputation has grown since his death.
The Liar (1950)
[GF371] Quartet pbk **£4.95**

HASEK, JAROSLAV (Czech, 1883 - 1923)
Subversive and anti-authoritarian, Hasek published a number of short stories before the First World War, in which he was taken prisoner on the Eastern front, and spent several years in Russian prison camps; but his masterpiece is *The Good Soldier Schweik*, which he wrote in the last two years of his life, completing only four out of an intended six books.
The Good Soldier Schweik (1921)
Schweik has been described as the archetypal Czech hero, the 'little man' who fights against officialdom and bureaucracy with his native subterfuge and wit. This caused it to be banned in several countries as detrimental to discipline.
[GF372] Penguin pbk **£7.99**
The Red Commissar
[GF373] Sphere pbk **£2.95**

HAVIARIS, STRATIS (Greek)
The Heroic Age
Set in Greece in the late 1940s, *The Heroic Age* tells the story of a small band of children who decide to leave their village during the Civil War to try to escape to Albania, and is a masterful study of how war can affect children. Haviaris wrote the novel in English.
[GF374] Penguin pbk **£4.95**

HESSE, HERMANN (German, 1897 - 1962)
Nobel Prize for Literature 1946. Best known as the novelist of *Steppenwolf*, Hesse's mystical novels chart a spiritual quest which he described as 'a sublime alchemy, an approach to the spirit that is unified in itself beyond all images'. Following a callow romantic phase, he was transformed by the 1914-1918 war and rose to be a widely-read humanist and pacifist. He investigated diverse approaches to spiritual self-awareness, maintaining a strong if sometimes idiosyncratic faith in Christianity, and inclined to political neutrality in a politically treacherous era.
Demian (1919)
[GF375] Grafton pbk **£3.99**
Gertrude (1910)
[GF376] Penguin pbk **£3.95**
Hours in the Garden (Poetry)
[GF377] Cape pbk **£3.95**
If the War Goes On (Non fiction)
[GF378] Grafton pbk **£2.50**

Journey to the East (1956)
A profound and lucid novella which ignores the conventional boundaries of time and place, this is Hesse's spiritual summing-up.
[GF379] Grafton pbk **£3.50**
Klingsor's Last Summer
[GF380] Grafton pbk **£2.50**
Knulp (1915)
[GF381] Grafton pbk **£2.95**
My Belief (Essays on Life and Art)
[GF382] Grafton pbk **£5.99**
Narziss and Goldmund (1930)
[GF383] Penguin pbk **£3.99**
Peter Camenzind (1904)
Hesse's first novel and the most important of his pre-Eastern period, in which a youth travels to Switzerland in search of inner peace.
[GF384] Penguin pbk **£3.95**
Poems (Poetry)
[GF385] Cape pbk **£3.95**
Prodigy (1957)
[GF386] Penguin pbk **£3.50**
Rosshalde (1914)
[GF387] Grafton pbk **£2.95**
Siddhartha (1922)
Set in a timeless East, a series of events lead the main character to a greater spiritual fulfilment.
[GF388] Picador pbk **£3.50**
Steppenwolf (1927)
The major result of his psychoanalytic investigations, this stands as his most magical, surrealistic effort to represent the world; Hesse said it was the 'most often and most violently misunderstood' of his novels, but it is the one for which he will be remembered.
[GF389] Penguin pbk **£3.95**
Stories of Five Decades
[GF390] Grafton pbk **£2.95**
Strange News from Another Star & Other Tales
[GF391] Penguin pbk **£3.50**
The Glass Bead Game (1943)
Set in the future, this is a mystical allegory: a group of intellectuals contemplate threats to their homeland; it captures the quintessence of his life's philosophy.
[GF392] Picador pbk **£5.95**
Wandering
[GF393] Grafton pbk **£3.99**

HOFFMAN, E.T.A. (German, 1776 - 1822)
Writer and composer, famed for his *Tales*, which exploit the bizarre and grotesque in a way unmatched by his contemporaries, in a way not dissimilar to Poe.
Tales of Hoffman
[GF394] Penguin pbk **£4.95**
The King's Bride
[GF395] Calder pbk **£3.95**

HOFMANN, GERT (German)
Gert Hofmann, father of the poet Michael, is one of Germany's most important post-war novelists. His reputation as a highly individual writer, whose books encompass highly-coloured imagery, comedy and the grotesque, is gradually growing in this country.
Balzac's Horse `NEW`
A dazzling collection of hallucinatory stories. In the title piece, Balzac is led from an opulent box at a theatre into a nightmarish world beneath the city.
[GF396] Secker hbk **£10.95**
Our Conquest
[GF397] Carcanet hbk **£9.95**
The Parable of the Blind `NEW`
A remarkable novel written from the perspective of the blind characters in Breughel's 16th century painting *The Parable of the Blind*. It explores their lives on the day they are to be painted.
[GF398] Secker hbk **£10.95**
[GF399] Minerva pbk **£3.99**
The Spectacle at the Tower
[GF400] Carcanet pbk **£4.95**

HORVATH, ODON VON
(Austrian, 1901 - 1938)
A dramatist and novelist who had settled in Vienna, Horvath was famous for plays such as *Tales from the Vienna Woods*. *The Age of the Fish*, his only novel in print, is an attempt to understand the fascist mentality, telling the story of an adolescent growing up in a world in which individuality is not tolerated.
The Age of the Fish (1938)
[GF401] Penguin pbk **£2.95**

HRABAL, BOHUMIL (Czech, 1914 -)
One of this century's leading Czech writers, best known for the film *Closely Observed Trains* made from an earlier work, has been described by Kundera as 'one of our very best writers, full of strength and talent, a joyous incarnation of the Czech spirit'.
I Served the King of England
Witty and energetic story of a sharp-witted **NEW** waiter who has a way with women, set in pre-war Prague.
[GF402] Chatto hbk **£12.95**

HUGO, VICTOR (French, 1802 - 1885)
The greatest of the French Romantics, with a passion for social justice, Hugo was a prominent poet, dramatist and novelist, as well as an active politician in the Third Republic. His two major novels are *Les Miserables*, a panorama of post-Waterloo France and *Notre-Dame Of Paris*, an historical novel set in the 15th century.
Les Miserables
[GF403] Penguin pbk **£5.99**
Notre-Dame of Paris
[GF404] Penguin pbk **£4.99**

HUYSMANS, JORIS KARL (1848 - 1907)
French novelist of Dutch descent, whose name and work - particularly *Against Nature* - has become synonymous with the decadent movement of the end of the 19th century. This story of the pursuit of sensual satisfaction in an attempt to overcome boredom was admired by Oscar Wilde.
Against Nature
[GF405] Penguin pbk **£4.50**
[GF406] Dedalus pbk **£4.95**

IONESCO, EUGENE (French, 1912 -)
Famous as a dramatist, Ionesco is a major exponent of the Theatre of the Absurd. This is one of his rare novels. See also *Drama*.
The Hermit
[GF407] Calder pbk **£4.95**

JAPRISOT, SEBASTIEN (French)
Award-winning novelist, screenwriter and film-director who published his first novel at the age of 17. His work will also be found in *Crime Fiction*.
Women in Evidence
A young man staggers onto a beach at sunset clutching the spreading stain on his shirt. But who shot him? And on what beach? All the evidence expands and conflicts, and even the lawyer seems to be involved.
[GF408] Secker hbk **£11.95**

JELINEK, ELFRIEDE (Austrian, 1946 -)
Jelinek was awarded the 1986 Heinrich Böll Prize for her distinguished contribution to German literature. This is the first English publication of her work.
The Piano Teacher **NEW**
By day, Erika Kohut teaches piano at the Conservatory. By night, she trawls the Vienna of immigrant workers, porn shows and quick sex. This Jekyll and Hyde existence is disturbed by Walter Klemmer, a handsome student out to revenge sexually Erika's less than fulsome appreciation of his musical skills.
[GF409] Serpent's Tail pbk **£7.95**

JONSSON, REIDAR (Swedish)
My Life as a Dog **NEW**
The novel upon which the internationally acclaimed film was based. It is a poignant tale set in 1950s Sweden about a young boy who tries to come to terms with life in spite of his mother's terminal illness and his separation from his pet dog Sickan.
[GF410] Faber hbk **£9.99**

JUNGER, ERNST (German, 1895 - 1985)
Treating a fantastical situation realistically, in a way similar to some of Hesse's work, *On the Marble Cliffs* is a semi-allegorical study of tyranny, telling of the rise, and predicting the fall, of the Nazis; it was eventually banned by them, after having sold more than 250,000 copies.
On the Marble Cliffs (1939)
[GF411] Penguin pbk **£1.95**

KADARE, ISMAIL (Albanian, 1936 -)
Kadare is the only Albanian writer known widely outside his own country. He has written powerfully of the effect of the Second World War, in *A Chronicle in Stone* and *The General of the Dead Army*.
A Chronicle in Stone
[GF412] Serpent's Tail hbk **£9.95**
Broken April **NEW**
[GF413] Saqi hbk **£10.95**
Doruntine
[GF414] Saqi hbk **£10.95**
The General of the Dead Army (1963)
Called Albania's 'first real novel', this was translated into 14 languages; a story of the absurdity of war, it tells of the meeting in Albania of a German and an Italian general, each sent to repatriate the remains of their troops killed in the war which had ended twenty years before.
[GF415] Quartet pbk **£6.95**

KAFKA, FRANZ (Czech, 1885 - 1924)
Kafka's vision has been amongst the most influential of the 20th century, developing a distorted world, half fable, half allegory, in which, according to Jorge Luis Borges, 'reality is a continuous sequence of melancholy nightmares'. Born in Prague, the son of a rich Jewish merchant, he wrote in German, leaving much of his major work in an unfinished state, and bequeathing it to his friend Max Brod, with the instructions that all should be destroyed (which were fortunately ignored). The heroes of his novels, Joseph K in *The Trial* and K in *The Castle*, are products of a truly modern paranoia, and his short stories, such as 'Metamorphosis', echo these themes.
America (written 1911-14 published 1927)
[GF416] Secker hbk **£10.95**
[GF417] Penguin pbk **£3.99**
Collected Novels
[GF418] Penguin pbk **£6.95**
Collected Short Stories
[GF419] Penguin pbk **£6.95**
Description of a Struggle & Other Stories
[GF420] Secker hbk **£10.95**
[GF421] Penguin pbk **£3.95**
Metamorphosis & Other Stories
Gregor Samsa wakes one morning to find himself alarmingly transformed into an enormous insect; the story, written in minute detail, tells of the metamorphosis itself and the reactions of Gregor's family.
[GF422] Penguin pbk **£3.99**
Short Stories 1904 - 1924
A selection of Kafka's greatest short works translated by J.A. Underwood, with a foreword by Jorge Luis Borges.
[GF423] Futura pbk **£3.99**
The Castle (written 1921-2 published 1926)
The story of a stranger's arrival at the village below the Castle, which seems to rule the place, reflects on

Franz Kafka, from *The Modern World: Ten Great Writers* by Malcolm Bradbury (Secker hbk £12.95) (Photo: BBC Hulton Picture Library)

the pathos of human isolation, and man's quest for freedom and responsibility.
[GF424] Secker hbk **£10.95**
[GF425] Penguin pbk **£3.95**
The Trial (written 1914-15 published 1925)
The story of Josef K, from the morning he wakes up to find himself inexplicably arrested, and his progress through a labyrinth of bureaucratic procedure, culminating in his execution; telling of the individual's struggle against an inexplicable and ubiquitous superior power, this is one of the most disturbing visions of the 'absurdity' of human life.
[GF426] Secker hbk **£10.95**
[GF427] Penguin pbk **£3.99**
[GF428] Pan pbk **£3.99**

KANTURKOVA, EVA (Czech)
Winner of the Tom Stoppard Prize, Kanturkova's novel is set in the prison of Ruzynen outside Prague, where a group of women await trial.
My Companions in the Bleak House **NEW**
[GF429] Quartet hbk **£12.95**

KASTNER, ERICH (German, 1899 - 1974)
Kastner's autobiographical novel from the end of the Weimar republic, (1931) shows the crumbling Berlin world depicted by Christopher Isherwood, but with a deeper and more tragic tone to it.
Fabian, the Story of a Moralist **NEW**
[GF430] Libris pbk **£9.95**

KAZANTZAKIS, NIKOS (Greek, 1885 - 1957)
Greek poet and writer, whose monumental epic, *The Odyssey*, was a modern retelling of the Homeric original. Kazantzakis grew up on the island of Crete, at the time of its bloody uprisings against Ottoman rule, and his perception of the life of the island and its ancient culture informs much of his work. His novels, written later in life, are notable for the flamboyance with which they treat their heroes, and for the vital and evocative environments in which they are set.
At the Palace of Knossos
[GF431] P Owen hbk **£12.95**
Christ Recrucified
[GF432] Faber pbk **£4.95**

Freedom and Death (1953)
The most revealing and personal of his novels, this illustrates that he could never reconcile his Western and Cretan heritages.
[GF433] Faber pbk **£4.95**
God's Pauper: St Francis of Assisi
[GF434] Faber pbk **£4.95**
Report to Greco (1961)
[GF435] Faber pbk **£5.95**
The Fratricides (1967)
[GF436] Faber pbk **£4.95**
The Last Temptation (1961)
[GF437] Faber pbk **£4.50**
Zorba the Greek (1946)
[GF438] Faber pbk **£4.95**

KELLER, GOTTFRIED (Swiss, 1819 - 1890)
Keller wrote most successfully of the small societies with which he was familiar, often displaying a finely honed satirical wit. *Green Henry* is a *bildungsroman* in the tradition of Goethe's *Wilhelm Meister*.
Green Henry (1846-55)
[GF439] Calder pbk **£9.95**
Martin Salander (1866)
[GF440] Calder hbk **£4.95**

KEMAL, YASHAR (Turkish, 1922 -)
The most internationally famous contemporary Turkish writer, Kemal is committed to realistic depictions of the harshness of peasant life, at his best achieving a powerful epic sweep in works such as *Mehmed, My Hawk*.
Iron Earth, Copper Sky
[GF441] Collins Harv pbk **£5.95**
Mehmed, My Hawk
[GF442] Fontana pbk **£2.95**
The Birds Have Also Gone
[GF443] Methuen pbk **£3.95**
The Sea-Crossed Fisherman
[GF444] Methuen pbk **£3.95**
The Undying Grass NEW
[GF445] Collins Harv pbk **£6.95**
The Wind from the Plain NEW
[GF446] Collins Harv pbk **£6.95**

KIHLMAN, CHRISTER
The Downfall of Gerdt Bladh NEW
This novel by one of Finland's best-known writers charts the downfall of Gerdt Bladh, established family man and a pillar of the Helsinki business community, who cracks under the strain of his wife's unfaithfulness.
[GF447] P Owen hbk **£12.95**

KIS, DANILO (Yugoslav)
Kis is an acclaimed novelist, whose *Garden Ashes* is a haunting account of his childhood, the story of a boy growing up in the shadow of a brilliant but destructive father figure.
Encyclopaedia of the Dead NEW
A collection of eight lyrical stories, ranging from the revelations of the surviving lover of the Yiddish poet Mendel Osipovich, to the lavish funeral rights accorded to a prostitute in 1920s Hamburg. All intertwine death with love.
[GF448] Faber hbk **£11.99**
Garden Ashes (1965)
[GF449] Faber pbk **£3.95**
Tomb for Boris Davidovich (1978)
[GF450] Faber pbk **£3.95**

KLEIST, HEINRICH VON
(German, 1777 - 1811)
Kleist turned to writing after an intellectual and personal crisis beset him in 1801, and in the 10 years before his suicide in 1811, produced the dramatic works, for which he is best known, eight stories, and various minor writings. His prose describes, with an almost clinical objectivity strikingly different from the passionate engagement of his plays, alternating moods of lyrical beauty and frenzied brutality.
Six German Romantic Tales
[GF451] Angel pbk **£4.95**
The Marquise of O & Other Stories
[GF452] Penguin pbk **£4.50**

KLIMA, IVAN (Czech, 1931 -)
Unlike his compatriots Kundera and Skvorecky, Klima has remained in Czechoslovakia, having returned there from America in 1970, although all his work is banned by the Czech authorities. His lyrical fiction has been said to explore 'the boundaries of consciousness and the awakenings of conscience'.
A Summer Affair
[GF453] Chatto hbk **£11.95**
My First Loves
[GF454] Chatto hbk **£10.95**
My Merry Mornings: Stories from Prague
[GF455] Readers Int pbk **£4.95**

KOESTLER, ARTHUR (1905 -1983)
Of Hungarian extraction, Koestler's best novel, *Darkness at Noon*, is the story, written with outstanding psychological insight, of an old guard Communist who falls victim to Stalin's purges, yet attains a personal freedom in his destruction. Together with *Arrival and Departure*, it was part of a trilogy, concerned with what Koestler has called the 'ethics of revolution'.
Arrival and Departure (1943)
[GF456] Penguin pbk **£3.95**
Darkness at Noon (1940)
[GF457] Penguin pbk **£2.99**

KOLLONTAI, ALEXANDRA
(Russian, 1873 - 1952)
One of the most remarkable figures of the Revolution, Alexandra Kollontai was the only woman member of the Bolshevik Central Committee; she later lost favour with Stalin, and moved to Oslo, where she began her collection of stories *Love of the Worker Bees*.
A Great Love
[GF458] Virago pbk **£4.99**
Love of the Worker Bees (1923)
[GF459] Virago pbk **£5.50**

KONWICKI, TADEUSZ (Polish, 1926 -)
One of Poland's most important film directors as well as prose writers, Tadeusz Konwicki's acute examination of himself and of the state of modern Poland has meant that his novels are banned in his own country.
A Minor Apocalypse
[GF460] Faber pbk **£4.95**
Moonrise, Moonset
[GF461] Faber hbk **£11.95**

KRLEZA, MIROSLAV (Yugoslav, 1893 - 1981)
A controversial figure and a dedicated Communist, Krleza was the grandest figure in Yugoslavia's cultural life, and a giant of Croatian literature; he was a playwright, poet and novelist, and throughout his life defied what he saw as the confining forces of authority, whether those of the old Austrian empire, or the post-war Serbian regime, and was among the first writers who rebelled against the confines of Socialist Realism.
On the Edge of Reason
[GF462] Quartet pbk **£4.95**
The Return of Philip Latinowicz (1932)
In this novel Krleza writes of the problem of retaining creative freedom in the deadly and corrupt world of the dictatorial inter-war monarchy.
[GF463] Quartet pbk **£5.95** NEW

KUNDERA, MILAN (Czech, 1929 -)
Acknowledged as the most prominent Czech writer, Kundera's early novel *The Joke*, with its satire on the false Communism of the Stalinists, was briefly prominent in the few months of the Prague Spring of 1968. In 1975 he left for Paris, and now writes in both Czech and French. His work combines erotic tragicomedy with metaphysical debate in a manner unique in modern fiction.
Jacques and His Master (Play)
[GF464] Faber pbk **£3.95**
Laughable Loves (Stories)
[GF465] Penguin pbk **£4.99**
Life Is Elsewhere
[GF466] Faber pbk **£3.95**
The Art of the Novel (Essays)
[GF467] Faber pbk **£9.95**
The Book of Laughter and Forgetting (1978)
[GF468] Faber hbk **£9.95**
[GF469] Penguin pbk **£4.50**
The Farewell Party
[GF470] Penguin pbk **£3.99**
The Joke (1967)
[GF471] Penguin pbk **£4.50**
The Unbearable Lightness of Being (1984)
Kundera's most acclaimed novel to date. Set in Prague around the time of the Russian invasion in 1968, it explores the relationship of two lovers, developing from the particular a profound and broad discourse, based on the opposition of the fundamental polarities of lightness and heaviness.
[GF472] Faber hbk **£12.50**
[GF473] Faber pbk **£3.95**

KUZNETSOV, ANATOLI
(Russian, 1929 - 1979)
Babi-Yar
Based on his own childhood experience, Kuznetsov describes the Nazi atrocities perpetrated in occupied Kiev, incorporating first hand accounts of people who survived mass executions in the ravine at Babi-Yar.
[GF474] Penguin pbk **£3.95**

LACLOS, PIERRE CHODERLOS DE
(French, 1741 - 1803)
This story of a professional seducer's relationship with his evil accomplice is written in epistolary form; it charts the machinations whereby he selects his victims, until the final moral end with his repentance. Laclos hoped to be seen as a moralist, but it is the portraits of the protagonists which are memorable.
Les Liaisons Dangereuses
[GF475] Penguin pbk **£4.99**
[GF476] Routledge pbk **£3.95**

LAFAYETTE, COMTESSE DE
(French, 1634 - 1693)
Lafayette's romance has been described as the first French character novel, taking over from previous romances of adventure and grandiloquence. It tells of the regretful obligations of duty over passion.
Princesse de Cleves
[GF477] Penguin pbk **£3.95**

LAGERKVIST, PAR (Swedish, 1891 - 1974)
Nobel Prize for Literature 1951. Influenced by expressionism, Lagerkvist's work has been described as centred around 'man's search for meaning, the problem of love and destructiveness, and the enigma of man's soul'. It is often set in the past, as in *The Dwarf*, the story of a dwarf attendant on an Italian Renaissance Court, who follows his master like a shadow, and reflects the opposite sides of his virtues.
Guest of Reality
[GF478] Quartet pbk **£5.95**
The Dwarf (1944)
[GF479] Quartet pbk **£4.95**

LAMPEDUSA, GUISEPPE TOMASI DI
(Italian, 1896 - 1957)

A remarkable literary phenomenon: the only significant work of a cultured Sicilian aristocrat, and one of the most acclaimed works of Italian literature since the war. *The Leopard* is both a story of the decline of the old order as embodied in the history of one noble family, and a profound, if nostalgic, insight into the problems of Sicily itself.

The Leopard (1958)
With two short stories and a memoir of Lampedusa's life.
[GF480] Collins Harv hbk **£10.95**
[GF481] Collins Harv pbk **£4.95**

LANDOLFI, TOMMASO (Italian, 1908 - 1979)
Tommaso Landolfi led a mysterious, reclusive existence, and his work has been compared to that of Joyce, Kafka, Borges and Poe; in the 24 stories collected here, he depicts a world of mixed fact and fantasy.

Words in Commotion & Other Stories
[GF482] Penguin pbk **£4.50**

LARBAUD, VALERY (French, 1881 - 1957)
Fermina Márquez
A wonderful study of the ferment caused in an exclusive boy's boarding school by the presence in the locality of the Spanish American sisters of a new pupil.
[GF483] Quartet pbk **£4.95**
Barnabooth NEW
[GF484] Quartet pbk **£5.95**

LE CLEZIO, J.M. (French, 1940 -)
Mondo NEW
A short novel, with a number of stories, from one of the most widely admired and yet puzzling of modern French writers. His writing shows remarkable descriptive powers, and is close to the *nouveau roman*.
[GF485] Calder hbk **£10.95**

LEDUC, VIOLETTE (French, 1907 - 1972)
Encouraged in her writing by Simone de Beauvoir, Leduc is remembered for this honest, autobiographical account of her upbringing and lesbianism.
La Batarde
[GF486] Virago pbk **£5.95**

LENZ, SIEGFRIED (German, 1926 -)
A contemporary of Günter Grass, Lenz writes on the similar subject of Germany's immediate war-time past, although he is is less of a visionary, more an intellectual novelist. His most powerful work is *The German Lesson*, a re-appraisal of the War years, presented through the eyes of a young boy imprisoned in reform school.

The German Lesson (1968)
[GF487] Methuen pbk **£3.95**
The Heritage (1978)
[GF488] Methuen pbk **£4.95**
The Lightship (Stories, 1960)
[GF489] Methuen pbk **£2.95**

LERMONTOV, MIKHAIL YUREVICH
(Russian, 1814 - 1841)

Lermontov's reputation as a Russian version of Byron is based on the wildly extravagant tale of Pechorin's adventures in the Caucasus, *A Hero of Our Time*. His romantic exploits and untimely death - in a duel - have given his life the status of myth, and he remains one of the most widely-read Russian authors.

A Hero of Our Time (1840)
[GF490] Oxford pbk **£2.25**
[GF491] Penguin pbk **£3.95**

LESKOV, NIKOLAI (Russian, 1831 - 1895)
Unlike his illustrious contemporaries, Leskov was not of noble birth - he claimed that he came to know the common people by growing up among them. A talented short story writer, his 'Lady Macbeth of Mtsensk' is a small masterpiece.

Five Tales
[GF492] Angel pbk **£5.95**
Lady Macbeth of Mtsensk & Other Stories
[GF493] Penguin pbk **£4.95**
The Enchanted Wanderer
[GF494] Deutsch pbk **£4.95**

LEVI, CARLO (Italian, 1902 - 1975)
Levi was an accomplished journalist, who in this, his best novel, provides a remarkable insight into the way of life of Southern Italy; based on his experience in remote Lucania, to which he was exiled by the Fascists, it tells of a village so remote that Christianity has never reached it, having instead stopped at Eboli.

Christ Stopped at Eboli (1945)
[GF495] Penguin pbk **£4.50**

LEVI, PRIMO (Italian, 1919 - 1987)
Having formed a band of partisans to resist the occupying German forces, Levi was captured and sent to Auschwitz; he survived the camp because his training as a chemist was useful to the authorities, and at the time of the final evacuation he was sick and unable to move. The experience of those years has appeared throughout his work, and there have been few more humane interpreters of this terrible period of history.

Collected Poems
[GF496] Faber pbk **£4.95**
If Not Now, When? (1982)
A story of Jewish partisans fighting together with Russians and Poles against the German forces on the Eastern front, and of their attempts to survive and remain concealed while continuing their resistance.
[GF497] Sphere pbk **£3.99**
If This Is A Man/The Truce (1958, 1963)
Levi's first work is his most direct, non-fictional account of his time in Auschwitz, described by Philip Roth as 'one of the century's truly necessary books'; together with *The Truce*, in which he describes his flight away from the hell in which he had been incarcerated, it is matchless in its consideration of a subject which seemed for a long time too terrible for literature.
[GF498] Sphere pbk **£4.50**
Moments of Reprieve (1981)
Short works which Levi described as *"about the human figures who stood out against the tragic background...the few, the different, the ones in whom I recognised the will and capacity to react, and hence a rudiment of virtue."*
[GF499] Sphere pbk **£3.99**
Other People's Trades (Non fiction) NEW
Levi's essays cover a wide range of subjects, including the house in which he lived throughout his life, butterflies, imaginary creatures dreamed up by children, Rabelais, writing a novel, playing games, returning to school at the age of sixty, and the need for fear.
[GF500] M Joseph hbk **£12.95**
The Drowned and the Saved (1986)
[GF501] Sphere pbk **£3.99**
The Periodic Table (1975)
A work arranged around twenty-one chemical elements of the Periodic Table, this novel attempts the widest breadth of subject of all Levi's books, as he writes of nationality, history, nature and of his own past.
[GF502] Sphere pbk **£3.99**
The Wrench (1978)
[GF503] Sphere pbk **£3.99**

LIND, JAKOV (German, 1927 -)
Lind fled Vienna as an eleven year old child, escaping to Holland, Palestine and a life in exile, and has written in both German and English. His stories describe the horror and human degradation of the Camps in a bleak, macabre style, portraying a world, like that of Kafka, which becomes a 'wild nightmare, from which one wakes up laughing'.

Soul of Wood (1962, written in German)
[GF504] Methuen pbk **£3.50**
Travels to the Enu (1982, written in English)
[GF505] Methuen pbk **£2.95**

LINDGREN, TORGNY (Swedish)
In *Bathsheba* Lindgren retells the biblical Bathsheba legend in an accessible style, treating it as a tale of desire, violence and sexual passion; the novel won the French *Prix Femina*. *Merab's Beauty* is a collection of stories.

Bathsheba (1984)
[GF506] Collins Harv pbk **£5.95**
Merab's Beauty NEW
[GF507] Collins Harv hbk **£11.95**

LUSTIG, ARNOST (Czech, 1926 -)
Lustig grew up in Prague, but since 1979 has been a naturalized American citizen; detained in concentration camps during the War, he was one of the few Jewish writers to survive. His work frequently celebrates the strength of the individual against society, depicting characters who may be physically damaged, but retain a mental dignity.

Diamonds of the Night (Stories) NEW
[GF508] Quartet pbk **£5.95**
Night and Hope (Stories) NEW
[GF509] Quartet pbk **£5.95**
Darkness Casts No Shadow (1976)
[GF510] Quartet pbk **£5.95** NEW

MALRAUX, ANDRE (French, 1901 - 1976)
A left-wing intellectual throughout the early part of his life, Malraux was always politically committed. Like one of his heroes he saw himself as 'a man capable of acting - when necessary' and was prominent both in the Spanish Civil War, and later in the French Resistance. His novels are meditations on the human condition, aware of its frequent absurdity, and reflect his liberal humanism. He spent the 1920s in the Far East, and both *Man's Estate* and *Conquerors* are set in China.

Conquerors
[GF511] Journeyman pbk **£3.75**
Man's Estate
[GF512] Penguin pbk **£3.95**

MANN, HEINRICH (German, 1871 - 1950)
A more overtly political writer than his brother Thomas, Heinrich Mann explores in a similar way the predicament of the artist within a bourgeois society.
Man of Straw (1918)
[GF513] Penguin pbk **£4.95**

MANN, KLAUS (German)
Mephisto
The rise of an actor playing Faust to Nazism's Mephistopheles, whose realization of the true situation in which he has placed himself comes too late.
[GF514] Penguin pbk **£3.95**

MANN, THOMAS (German, 1875 - 1955)
Nobel Prize for Literature 1929. The major German novelist of the 20th century, Mann is widely known for his perfectly formed novella *Death in Venice*, though it is his ambitious long novel *The Magic Mountain* which has been acclaimed as his master-work. Although his work presents a steadily deepening portrayal of the developing evils of Germany in the 1920s and 30s, unlike his brother

Heinrich, he was never a pacifist. In voluntary exile from 1933, Mann's frequently long and ironic novels capture the mood and troubles of the European bourgeoisie in the first half of the 20th century.

Buddenbrooks (1901)
The novel which brought Mann his first major success, an epic saga tracing the decline of the Buddenbrooks, a once successful industrial family.
[GF515] Penguin pbk **£6.95**

Confessions of Felix Krull, Confidence Man (1954)
[GF516] Penguin pbk **£4.95**

Death in Venice/Tristan/Tonio Kröger
The story of a respected author who is locked in a quest to put art and beauty above all else, with tragic results, as he develops an irrational, obsessive passion for a beautiful Polish boy, Tadzio.
[GF517] Penguin pbk **£3.95**

Doctor Faustus (1947)
[GF518] Penguin pbk **£5.99**

Joseph and His Brothers (1933-43)
Mann's ambitious reworking of Genesis chapters 12-50, in which he displays much historical and tribal knowledge of the Near East.
[GF519] Secker hbk **£15.00**
[GF520] Penguin pbk **£10.95**

Little Herr Friedman & Other Stories
[GF521] Penguin pbk **£4.50**

Lotte in Weimar (1939)
[GF522] Penguin pbk **£4.99**

Mario and the Magician & Other Stories
[GF523] Penguin pbk **£5.95**

Royal Highness
[GF524] Penguin pbk **£4.95**

The Holy Sinner
[GF525] Penguin pbk **£3.95**

The Magic Mountain (1924)
Set in a Swiss sanatorium, a cocooned environment away from the outside world, Mann's novel creates characters who in their eccentricity and extremism mirror the confusion and imbalance of the world which they have left.
[GF526] Secker hbk **£15.00**
[GF527] Penguin pbk **£7.50**

MANZONI, ALESSANDRO
(Italian, 1785 - 1873)
The Betrothed (1823)
Set in the province of Milan during the 17th century, the story tells of two young peasants in love, whose marriage is prevented by the local lord's infatuation for the bride. Its insight into character and broad picture of society make it one of the great works of Italian fiction, described as 'a national institution'.
[GF528] Penguin pbk **£6.95**

MAUPASSANT, GUY DE
(French, 1850 - 1893)
Influenced by Flaubert, Maupassant shares many of his master's preoccupations, including a strong vein of pessimism, disgust at bourgeois complacency, and a certain despair at the possibility of any human relationship. His short stories present a rich canvas of experience, from realistic presentation of the Normandy in which he had grown up, to excursions into the fantastic and supernatural.
A Woman's Life (1883)
[GF529] Penguin pbk **£2.99**

Bel-Ami
[GF530] Penguin pbk **£4.50**

Pierre and Jean (1888)
His best novel, with an important preface. It charts the mistrust and jealousy that grows in a family when one of the sons inherits a fortune.
[GF531] Penguin pbk **£2.50**

Selected Short Stories
[GF532] Penguin hbk **£3.95**

Short Stories
[GF533] Dent pbk **£3.95**

MAURIAC, FRANCOIS
(French, 1885 - 1970)
Nobel Prize for Literature 1952. A Catholic writer whose central theme was the meaninglessness of existence without God. His early novels are particularly powerful, although gloomy. They reveal the guilty obsessions and uneasy passions that lie beneath the veneer of respectable people. His most powerful work *A Knot of Vipers* is a partly autobiographical study of the conflict of family life.
A Knot of Vipers (1932)
[GF534] Penguin pbk **£3.95**

A Woman of the Pharisees (1941)
[GF535] Penguin pbk **£3.95**

Desert of Love
[GF536] Penguin pbk **£3.99**

The Frontenac Mystery (1933)
[GF537] Penguin pbk **£3.50**

Thérèse (1935)
[GF538] Penguin pbk **£4.50**

MERIMEE, PROSPER (French, 1803 - 1870)
An active figure in 19th century France, Mérimée treated historical themes with a characteristic interest in extremes of passion, as seen in his best-known work, *Carmen*, on which Bizet's opera was based.
Carmen & Other Stories
[GF539] Oxford pbk **£4.95**

MEYRINK, GUSTAV (German, 1868 - 1932)
A contemporary of Kafka in Prague, Meyrink's *The Golem* is an attack on the values of the Austro-Hungarian bourgeoisie, using the legends of the Old Testament and the Cabbalah.
The Golem (1915)
[GF540] Dedalus pbk **£4.95**

MILOSZ, CZESLAW (Polish, 1911 -)
Nobel Prize for Literature 1980. Better known as a poet and essayist (he wrote the classic critique of culture under Communism, *The Captive Mind*), Milosz was born in Lithuania and now lives in America. His novel *Issa Valley* recalls his childhood in the Lithuanian countryside.
Issa Valley (1955)
[GF541] Carcanet hbk **£7.95**

Seizure of Power
[GF542] Faber hbk **£7.95**

MINCO, MARGA (Dutch)
The Glass Bridge
A huge success in Holland, where it has sold almost half a million copies, this book tells of the fate of Dutch Jews in the last world war. Its sequel, *An Empty House*, tells of how, after the end of the war, the narrator emerges from hiding and returns to Amsterdam, where she begins to reconstruct her life.
[GF543] P Owen hbk **£9.95**

An Empty House NEW
[GF544] P Owen hbk **£10.95**

MITGUTSCH, ANNA (Austrian, 1948 -)
An Austrian writer whose first novel, a study of the lives of women of three generations, shows the ways in which children suffer at the hands of their parents, and how patterns of oppression and cruelty are repeated from generation to generation.
Punishment
[GF545] Virago pbk **£5.50**

MONTALBAN, MANUEL VAZQUEZ
(Spanish, 1939 -)
A leading literary figure in post-Franco Spain, Montalban is best known for his detective stories featuring Pepe Carvalho.
Murder in the Central Committee
[GF546] Serpent's Tail pbk **£5.50**

Southern Seas
[GF547] Serpent's Tail pbk **£5.50**

The Angst-Ridden Executive NEW
Antonio Jaume, an old acquaintance, dies desperately wanting to get in touch with Pepe Carvalho. Jauma's widow has good reason to believe that her husband's death is not what it seems. And who better to find the truth than Carvalho, a private eye with a CIA past and contacts with the Communist Party?
[GF548] Serpent's Tail pbk **£5.95**

The Pianist NEW
[GF549] Quartet hbk **£12.95**

MONTHERLANT, HENRI DE
(French, 1896 - 1972)
Novelist and essayist acclaimed as an impassioned moralist and fine prose stylist; he was also a controversial figure, well known for the arrogance of his pronouncements, and for his fascist preferences.
The Bachelors
[GF550] Quartet pbk **£4.95**

The Girls
[GF551] Pan pbk **£4.95**

MORALES, ADELAIDA GARCIA (Spanish)
Morales's second novel won her the Herralde prize for fiction in Spain; it tells the story of the meeting of two women in a hillside village of Southern Spain, and of their different attitudes to the society in which they find themselves - the one, a schoolteacher, shocked by the primitive rites of the place, the other, caught up in its magic, but with fatal consequences.
The Silence of the Sirens
[GF552] Fontana pbk **£3.95**

MORANTE, ELSA (Italian, 1917 - 1985)
Morante's best-known work is *History*, telling the story of everyday life in Rome during the Second World War, and acclaimed as one of the greatest studies of Italy's involvement in the war.
Arturo's Island (1959)
A novel in eight sections which tell of a youth growing up largely alone on an island close to Ischia.
[GF553] Carcanet hbk **£12.95**

History: A Novel (1974)
[GF554] Penguin pbk **£4.95**

MORAVIA, ALBERTO (Italian, 1907 -)
A writer of great intelligence and integrity, whose early work was censored by the Fascists, causing him to turn to fables to disguise criticisms of society which would have been unacceptable if directly expressed. His central insight is into the ennui and emptiness of his world, of human beings who have sex with one another to disguise the utter lack of love in their relations; at their best, his novels succeed in penetrating the heart of human solitude, while at their least successful they themselves seem infected with the barrenness which is their theme.
1934
[GF555] Secker hbk **£10.95**

Conjugal Love (1949)
[GF556] Secker hbk **£10.95**

Empty Canvas (1960)
[GF557] Futura pbk **£2.95**

Erotic Tales (1983)
[GF558] Secker hbk **£10.95**
[GF559] Futura pbk **£2.95**

Roman Tales
[GF560] Oxford pbk **£3.95**

The Fancy Dress Party (1941)
[GF561] Secker hbk **£10.95**

The Voice of the Sea & Other Stories
[GF562] Secker hbk **£10.95**
[GF563] Grafton pbk **£1.95**

The Voyeur
[GF564] Grafton pbk **£3.99**

Time of Desecration (1929)
[GF565] Secker hbk **£10.95**

Woman of Rome (1947)
Moravia's most successful novel and one of his

FICTION

warmest; his depiction of the life of a Roman prostitute, and of the vitality of the city, and its characters who surround her, is achieved with insight and in sensual detail.
[GF566] Secker hbk **£10.95**

MORCH, DEA TRIER (Danish, 1941 -)
Morch is a successful artist as well as writer. *Winter's Child*, her best known novel, is set in the maternity ward of a Copenhagen hospital, and tells the story of eighteen women facing labour, and of the relationships which develop between them. Her most recent novel, *Evening Star* is a moving story of a family coming to terms with cancer.
Evening Star
[GF567] Serpent's Tail pbk **£6.95**
Winter's Child (1976)
[GF568] Serpent's Tail pbk **£4.95**

MORSELLI, GUIDO (Italian, 1912 - 1973)
Born in Bologna, Morselli was the author of seven novels, all published after his suicide in 1973. His work undermines historical objectivity, highlighting the absurdity of real events.
Divertimento 1889
[GF569] Chatto hbk **£9.95**
Past Conditional **NEW**
This novel rewrites the story of the Great War. When a Viennese *dilettante* builds a tunnel through the Alps, linking Austria and Italy, the trench-bound, stagnant war of attrition is transformed into a thrilling conflict.
[GF570] Chatto hbk **£12.95**

MULISCH, HARRY (Dutch, 1927 -)
A Dutch novelist whose book *The Assault* won awards and high praise. Set in the Second World War, it expresses the impact of war on the formation of a child's consciousness with considerable force.
Last Call (1987)
[GF571] Collins hbk **£16.95**
The Assault
[GF572] Penguin pbk **£3.95**
Two Women
[GF573] Calder pbk **£6.95**

MULLER, HERTA (Romanian)
Müller comes from the German-speaking minority of Romania; *The Passport* is a surrealistic novel telling of a community living a life of spiritual and cultural dislocation.
The Passport
[GF574] Serpent's Tail pbk **£5.50**

MUSIL, ROBERT (Austrian, 1880 - 1942)
Musil's reputation rests on this one magnificent work, a massive novel which tells of a year in the life of a Viennese intellectual, and portrays a society on the brink of an abyss, seen through the eyes of Ulrich, the man who has cast off the 'qualities' which convention demands. He is recruited to prepare imperial anniversary celebrations planned for 1918, an event fore-doomed by the ironies of history. Musil worked on the novel from the 1920s until his death in 1942, and left it unfinished.
Man Without Qualities: Vol 1
[GF575] Picador pbk **£4.99**
Man Without Qualities: Vol 2
[GF576] Picador pbk **£5.95**
Man Without Qualities: Vol 3
[GF577] Picador pbk **£5.95**
Tonka & Other Stories
[GF578] Picador pbk **£3.99**
Young Torless
Musil's only other full-length novel was completed while he was a student; it tells of life in a military academy on the Eastern frontier, and is a parable of the corruption of power.
[GF579] Picador pbk **£3.99**

MYRIVILIS, STRATIS (Greek, 1892 - 1969)
Myrivilis drew on his own experiences of war in his great novel, *Life in the Tomb*; an effective work of realism, it is written in the form of letters home from a sergeant in the trenches of the Macedonian front.
Life in the Tomb
[GF580] Quartet pbk **£5.95**

NAVARRE, YVES (French)
Cronus' Children
This *Prix Goncourt* winning novel depicts a family dominated by a self-centred patriarch, who, 20 years before the day when the action is set, had his youngest son, a brilliant homosexual student poet, lobotomised.
[GF581] Calder pbk **£6.95**
The Little Rogue in Our Flesh **NEW**
[GF582] P Owen hbk **£10.95**

NYIRI, JANOS (Hungarian)
Battlefields and Playgrounds **NEW**
Nyiri left Hungary after the 1956 uprising, and settled in London. This autobiographical novel describes the fortunes of a Jewish family in Hungary during World War II, the story seen through the eyes of a child. Achieving a sense of the comic in the face of tragedy, it is a rare document of the Holocaust.
[GF583] Macmillan hbk **£12.95**

OZ, AMOS (Israeli, 1939 -)
Oz has been acclaimed as Israel's finest living writer. Born into a family which, he has written, 'dreamed in Yiddish, conversed in Russian and Polish, read books in German and French', he was taught to write in Hebrew. He has lived on a kibbutz in Israel, and is a spokesman for the more moderate aspects of his nation. In much of his work there exists a tension between the brilliance of his style and the desperation of the situation he portrays when writing about the position of modern Israel.
A Perfect Peace
[GF584] Fontana pbk **£3.95**
Black Box
[GF585] Fontana pbk **£3.99**
Elsewhere Perhaps (1966)
[GF586] Fontana pbk **£3.99**
My Michael
Oz's most famous book, narrated by an unhappy woman, demonstrates the effect of siege mentality on mental stability.
[GF587] Fontana pbk **£2.50**
The Hill of Evil Council
[GF588] Fontana pbk **£2.50**
Touch the Water, Touch the Wind
[GF589] Fontana pbk **£2.50**
Unto Death: Two Stories
[GF590] Fontana pbk **£2.50**

PAGNOL, MARCEL (French, 1895 - 1974)
The only novels by this great film-maker, together these form the epic tale of family pride, greed, cruelty and remorse inspired by a Provençal legend of a mysterious shepherdess who exacted vengeance on an entire village.
Jean de Florette/Manon des Sources
[GF591] Deutsch hbk **£12.95**
[GF592] Picador pbk **£5.99**

PASOLINI, PIER PAOLO (Italian, 1922 - 1975)
Pasolini's two novels of urban life, *The Ragazzi* and *A Violent Life*, achieved controversy with their depiction of the slums of Rome, showing the hunger, theft, betrayal, and prostitution involved in life there, and combine standard Italian with the distinctive Roman dialect.
A Dream of Something (1962)
Set in the more pastoral world of the northern province of Friuli in which he himself grew up, Pasolini's third novel tells of a period in the lives of three boys as they look for work, explore the country, and approach adulthood and political awareness.
[GF593] Quartet pbk **£4.95**
A Violent Life (1959)
[GF594] Carcanet pbk **£4.95**
The Ragazzi (1955)
[GF595] Carcanet hbk **£9.95**

PASTERNAK, BORIS (Russian, 1890 - 1960)
Pasternak's whole career as a writer, beginning with his first collection of poetry in 1913, until the publication of *Doctor Zhivago* in Europe in 1957, was one of continual conflict with the State. In 1958 he became the second Russian to be awarded the Nobel Prize for Literature. Under extreme pressure from the Party and from the Union of Writers he was forced to refuse the award. Barely two years later he was dead.
Doctor Zhivago (1957)
Banned in the Soviet Union and an enormous bestseller in the West, this is an epic novel of enormous power, and a profoundly moving love story. One critic accurately described it as 'a series of brilliant fragments, the study of the disintegration of an intellectual who died...after having welcomed the Revolution and been disillusioned by its aftermath.'
[GF596] Collins Harv hbk **£10.95**
[GF597] Collins Harv pbk **£5.95**
The Last Summer
[GF598] Penguin pbk **£2.50**
Zhenia's Childhood
[GF599] Allison & B pbk **£2.95**

PAVESE, CESARE (Italian, 1908 - 1950)
Novelist, poet and translator whose suicide, coming at the end of a period of political disillusionment and personal depression, shocked Italy. A novelist of great sensitivity, who confronted the contrasts facing him bravely, his last novel *The Moon and the Bonfire* is a poignant tale of the necessity of coming to terms with the past, telling the story of an exile's return to his native village after years away in America.
Among Women Only (1953)
[GF600] Quartet pbk **£2.50**
Devil in the Hills (1954)
[GF601] P Owen hbk **£10.95**
Festival Night
[GF602] P Owen hbk **£10.95**
House on the Hill
[GF603] P Owen hbk **£11.95**
Leather Jacket
[GF604] Quartet pbk **£2.50**
Political Prisoner (Journals)
[GF605] P Owen hbk **£10.95**
Summer Storm and Other Stories
[GF606] P Owen hbk **£9.95**
The Moon and the Bonfire (1950)
[GF607] Quartet pbk **£3.50**
This Business of Living (Diaries, 1952)
[GF608] Quartet pbk **£3.95**

PAVIC, MILORAD (Yugoslav, 1935 -)
Really three books in one, Pavic's ludic novel concerns the vanished race of the Khazars, who lived near the Black Sea until late in the 9th century. From a historical event Pavic constructs a mesmerising detective story, where a lost culture is intimated through stories, guesses, lies and, above all, dreams. Available in male and female versions (a vital paragraph is different), the reader eventually becomes the most important participant in the quest.
The Dictionary of the Khazars
[GF609] H Hamilton hbk **£11.95**

PEREC, GEORGES (French, 1936 - 1982)
Georges Perec's fiction experimented with almost every element of the language, both playful in manner and serious in intent, combining frivolity with personal scrutiny and wide-ranging

Alexander Pushkin, author of *Eugene Onegin* (Penguin pbk £3.99) by Hippins (Photo: The Mansell Collection)

philosophical speculation. *Life: A User's Manual* was published in Britain in 1987, some ten years after its appearance in France, and for vastness of scale and complexity of style, has been compared to Joyce's *Ulysses*.

Life: A User's Manual
[GF610] Collins Harv pbk **£9.95**

W, or The Memory of Childhood
[GF611] Collins Harv pbk **£5.95**

PERUCHO, JUAN (Spanish, 1920 -)
The first work by a distinguished Catalan writer to be published outside his native Spain, *Natural History* recalls the work of Borges and Calvino in tone. Set in the 1830s, the book tells of one man's attempts to defeat a vampire which
pursues him across the country. Combining imagination, myth and history, this is an intriguing philosophical thriller.

Natural History `NEW`
[GF612] Secker hbk **£11.95**

PERUTZ, LEO (Czech, 1882 - 1957)
Born in Prague, Leo Perutz later moved to Vienna, before finally emigrating to Israel in 1938. After a long period of neglect, his historical novels are only now being rediscovered, and have attracted the admiration of Calvino, Borges and Graham Greene; the two which appear here are set respectively in Renaissance Italy and Spain during the years of the Peninsular War.

Leonardo's Judas `NEW`
[GF613] Collins Harv hbk **£10.95**

The Marquis of Bolibar `NEW`
[GF614] Collins Harv hbk **£10.95**

PIRANDELLO, LUIGI (Italian, 1867 - 1936)
Nobel Prize for Literature 1934. Pirandello explores in his fiction themes similar to those which dominate his plays - the ambiguous balance between reality and illusion in human life, and the contrast of man's outer and inner worlds. *The Late Mattia Pascal* is an early investigation into a man who loses his identity in the terms which society sets, and is unable to reconstruct himself. In addition, Pirandello wrote more than 200 short stories, of which 21 of the best are included in this new selection.

Short Stories
[GF615] Quartet pbk **£5.95**

The Late Mattia Pascal (1904)
[GF616] Dedalus pbk **£4.95**

POMBO, ALVARO (Spain, 1939 -)
The Hero of the Big House
Within the walls of a seemingly respectable house a darkly erotic fable of loyalty and betrayal is enacted. A servant's theft has tragic results ....
[GF617] Chatto hbk **£11.95**

The Resemblance `NEW`
Pombo here mercilessly exposes the hypocrisy and corruption of middle class society. By day, the port of Leton appears sedate enough, but with the death of a wealthy young man in a motorcycle accident the city erupts into gossip and rumour.
[GF618] Chatto hbk **£12.95**

POPESCU, DMITRIU (Romanian, 1935 -)
The Royal Hunt (1973)
A physician remembers adolescence in a community where agents of the state manipulate the reactions and lives of people terrified by the unusual; driven back on their instincts, they run wild. A startling study of the psychology of mass terror, newly translated, from Romania's most prominent living writer.
[GF619] Quartet pbk **£4.95**

PREVOST, ABBE (French, 1697 - 1763)
Manon Lescaut
The story of the passionate love of des Grieux for the unworthy Manon. He loses all sense of honour and dignity, and in his passion even overlooks her repeated infidelity. The couple go through desperate adventures, to a tragic end. The simple and realistic description of the story, in contrast to the fashions of the time, made it a huge success.
[GF620] Soho pbk **£5.95**
[GF621] Penguin pbk **£3.99**

PROUST, MARCEL (French, 1871 - 1922)
Proust's series of novels *The Remembrance of Things Past* is now seen as one of the major works of fiction this century. The narrator sets out to recall his past life from childhood to middle age, realizing that this is possible through repeating sensory perceptions which stimulate the powers of memory, or through the agency of works of art. No other novelist has ever captured the mystery and power of memory so fully, and his extraordinary psychological insight is an achievement which ranks with the founding fathers of psychoanalysis, Freud and Jung. The work includes much social comedy, as Proust analyses the classes in which he himself had lived the early years of his life.

Against St Beuve & Other Essays
[GF622] Penguin pbk **£5.95**

Albertine `NEW`
Before his death in 1922, Proust completed a revised version of *Albertine Disparue*, the penultimate volume of his great work, making changes which have dramatic implications for the rest of the work. Discovered in 1986 on the death of his niece, it is translated by Terence Kilmartin, who was responsible for the revised edition of *A La Recherche*.
[GF623] Chatto hbk **£11.95**

By Way of St Beuve
[GF624] Hogarth pbk **£5.95**

Jean Santeuil
Posthumously published fragment: the germ of his masterpiece.
[GF625] Penguin pbk **£6.99**

Pleasures and Regrets
[GF626] Grafton pbk **£3.95**

The Remembrance of Things Past
Vol 1
[GF627] Chatto hbk **£25.00**
[GF628] Penguin pbk **£9.95**
Vol 2
[GF629] Chatto hbk **£25.00**
[GF630] Penguin pbk **£9.95**
Vol 3
[GF631] Chatto hbk **£25.00**
[GF632] Penguin pbk **£9.95**

PUSHKIN, ALEXANDER SERGEVICH
(Russian, 1799 - 1837)
Better known as a poet, in a handful of his stories, Pushkin provided a model for Russian prose which was to influence the development of Russia's greatest writers. 'The Captain's Daughter' and 'The Queen of Spades' should be ranked alongside the best of Tolstoy and Dostoevsky.

Complete Prose Tales
[GF633] M Russell pbk **£7.50**

Eugene Onegin
Classic story in verse and a precursor of the great 19th century naturalist novel.
[GF634] Penguin pbk **£3.99**

The Queen of Spades & Other Stories
[GF635] Penguin pbk **£3.99**

Tales of Belkin/The History of the Village of Goryukhino
[GF636] Angel pbk **£5.50**

QUEFFELEC, YANN (French)
The Wedding
Winner of the *Prix Goncourt* and enormously successful in France where it sold over a million copies. A gothic, violent tale of obsessional love, it tells of the relationship between an unwanted child and his adored mother.
[GF637] Hodder pbk **£3.99**

QUENEAU, RAYMOND (French, 1903 - 1976)
After an early involvement with surrealism, Queneau's later fiction attempted to bring the spoken language back into literature. Few writers are more stylistically aware, and his *Exercises In Style* achieves the unique feat of retelling a story in 99 different versions.

Bark Tree
[GF638] Calder pbk **£4.95**

Exercises in Style
[GF639] Calder pbk **£6.95**

Flight of Icarus
[GF640] Calder pbk **£4.95**

Sunday of Life
[GF641] Calder pbk **£4.95**

We Always Treat Women Too Well
[GF642] Calder pbk **£4.95**

Zazie in the Metro
[GF643] Calder pbk **£4.95**

RABELAIS, FRANCOIS
(French, c.1494 - c.1553)
French humanist who combined in these fictions an unusual blend of satire, storytelling, propaganda and outrageous comedy. Enormously influential throughout Europe, he was sometimes criticized for obscenity.

Gargantua and Pantagruel
[GF644] Penguin pbk **£4.95**

RADIGUET, RAYMOND (French, 1903 - 1923)
A precocious genius, saluted by Cocteau, who wrote two novels before his death at the age of 20. *The Devil in the Flesh* is the marvellous story of an adolescent love the narrator feels for an older woman, conveyed with a sensitivity matched by few. It caused a sensation, partly because it was semi-autobiographical, and partly because it showed a wife being unfaithful while her husband was away at war.

Comte d'Orgel
[GF645] Boyars pbk **£3.95**

The Devil in the Flesh
[GF646] Boyars pbk **£4.95**

REMARQUE, ERICH MARIA
(German, 1898 - 1970)
All Quiet on the Western Front (1929)
Remarque's powerful story of one soldier's experience in the First War sold two and a half million copies in the eighteen months after

publication, translated into 25 languages, but by 1933 was burned in Berlin as 'defeatist'. One of the great novels of man at war of all time, it was also powerfully filmed by Lewis Milestone.
[GF647] Picador pbk **£3.99**
Arch of Triumph (1946)
One of Remarque's later novels, this tells the story of a man fleeing Germany and his experience in the pre-war Concentration Camps, searching Europe for his torturer. Set in Paris in the months leading up to September 1939, it reflects Remarque's own experiences of being driven out of Germany.
[GF648] Picador pbk **£4.99**

RILKE, RAINER MARIA
(German, 1875 - 1926)
The most important German lyric poet of the 20th century, the father of modern 'existential' poetry. The semi-autobiographical *Notebook* tells of an impoverished Danish nobleman and poet, leading a solitary existence in Paris; for its record of his impressions of the city, and for the memories of childhood it contains, it is Rilke's prose masterpiece.
Notebook of Malte Laurids Brigge (1910)
[GF649] Oxford pbk **£4.50**
[GF650] Picador pbk **£3.95**
Rilke's Early Prose `NEW`
[GF651] Quartet pbk **£5.95**
Rodin & Other Prose Pieces
[GF652] Quartet pbk **£4.95**

ROBBE-GRILLET, ALAIN (French, 1922 -)
An important exponent of the *nouveau roman*, Robbe-Grillet, in rejecting the conventions of character and plot, has presented instead a world where the reassurances of a believed reality are withdrawn, or altered in such a way as to disorientate the reader. He is also the author of the magnificent brooding screenplay for Alain Resnais's masterpiece, *Last Year at Marienbad*.
A Regicide `NEW`
An early novel, about a man who dreams of fame by killing the king.
[GF653] Calder hbk **£10.95**
Djinn
[GF654] Calder pbk **£4.95**
Immortal One (1971)
[GF655] Calder pbk **£3.95**
In the Labyrinth
[GF656] Calder pbk **£4.95**
Jealousy
[GF657] Calder pbk **£3.95**
Project for a Revolution in New York
[GF658] Calder hbk **£6.95**
Reflections of the Golden Triangle
[GF659] Calder pbk **£4.95**
The Erasers
[GF660] Calder pbk **£5.95**
The House of Assignation
One of Robbe-Grillet's most important novels, it utilizes many of the virtuoso techniques of the thriller: agents and counter-agents, drug trafficking, and erotic extravagances in the East.
[GF661] Calder pbk **£6.95**
The Voyeur
[GF662] Calder pbk **£4.95**
Topology of a Phantom City
[GF663] Calder pbk **£4.95**

ROCHE, HENRI-PIERRE (French)
The delightful and sad story of a love triangle, filmed memorably by François Truffaut.
Jules & Jim
[GF664] Pan pbk **£2.95**

ROTH, JOSEPH (Austrian, 1894 - 1939)
Roth's short and troubled life was set against the background of the collapse of the Austro-Hungarian Empire, and as a journalist he was one of the central figures of the intellectual opposition to Nazism, leaving Germany in 1933 and committing suicide in Paris in 1939. His semi-autobiographical fiction has been greatly undervalued; it charts as dispassionately as was possible for him the end of the established order, never falling into a simple nostalgia for the past.
Confessions of a Murderer (1936)
[GF665] Picador pbk **£3.50**
Flight Without End (1927)
Roth here most exactly shows the parallels between the decline of the Empire under which he was born and the degeneration of an Army officer, and reflects his own experiences of poverty and anti-semitism.
[GF666] Dent pbk **£2.95**
Hotel Savoy
[GF667] Picador pbk **£3.95**
Job: The Story of a Simple Man (1931)
[GF668] Chatto pbk **£4.95**
Silent Prophet
[GF669] P Owen hbk **£10.95**
Tarabas: A Guest on Earth
[GF670] Picador pbk **£4.95**
The Emperor's Tomb
[GF671] Chatto pbk **£4.95**
The Legend of the Holy Drinker `NEW`
Roth's last novel concerns Andreas, a down-and-out alcoholic and convicted murderer whose death is strangely blessed by earthly miracles.
[GF672] Chatto pbk **£7.95**
The Radetzky March (1932)
The story of three generations of the Trotta family in the years preceding the 1918 collapse of the Austro-Hungarian Empire, told to the accompaniment of Strauss's Radetzky March, the signature tune of that Empire.
[GF673] Penguin pbk **£3.95**
The Spider's Web/Zipper and the Father
[GF674] Chatto pbk **£11.95**
Weights and Measures
[GF675] Dent pbk **£2.50**

RYBAKOV, ANATOLI (Russian, 1911 -)
Rybakov was himself a child of the Arbat, the environment described in his acclaimed novel, recently made available with the impact of *glasnost*. Suppressed in the Soviet Union for over 20 years, it is a classic of historical fiction; set in 1934, it presents a chilling portrayal of Stalin and the beginnings of his reign of terror, and its impact on a circle of young friends who live in Moscow's intellectual and artistic centre, the Arbat. 'This is a great book, a great moment in our literature. After this it will be impossible to have the same history books in our libraries and schools.' (Yevgeny Yevtushenko).
Children of the Arbat
[GF676] Hutchinson hbk **£12.95**
[GF677] Pan pbk **£4.50**
Heavy Sand
A warm, but ultimately tragic tale of a large and closely-knit Jewish family in the Ukraine.
[GF678] Penguin pbk **£4.99**

SABA, UMBERTO (Italian, 1883 - 1957)
Saba is better known as a poet, who spent most of his life in Trieste; behind the lyric surface of his work there lies a melancholy intelligence.
Ernesto
[GF679] Grafton pbk **£3.99**

SAGAN, FRANCOISE (French, 1935 -)
Best-selling novelist, whose first work *Bonjour Tristesse*, written when Sagan was only 18, earned her much acclaim and some scandal, with its cynically amoral and pessimistic picture of love.
A Certain Smile
[GF680] Penguin pbk **£2.95**
Aimez-Vous Brahms?
[GF681] Penguin pbk **£2.95**

Bonjour Tristesse
[GF682] Penguin pbk **£3.50**
Engagements of the Heart
[GF683] Allison & B pbk **£3.99**
Incidental Music
[GF684] Allison & B pbk **£3.99**
Painting in Blood ?
[GF685] A Ellis hbk **£11.95**
Still Storm
[GF686] Star pbk **£1.95**
Those Without Shadows `NEW`
[GF687] Allison & B pbk **£3.99**
Unmade Bed
[GF688] A Ellis pbk **£4.50**
With Fondest Regards
[GF689] Allison & B pbk **£3.99**

SAINT-EXUPERY, ANTOINE DE
(French, 1900 - 1944)
Called the 'poet of the air', Saint-Exupéry's stories tell of his early experiences as a pilot, and convey a sense of the mystery and wonder inspired in him by flying.
Le Petit Prince
[GF690] Pan pbk **£4.95**
Southern Mail/Night Flight
[GF691] Penguin pbk **£3.50**
War-Time Writings
[GF692] Picador pbk **£4.95**
**Wind, Sand and Stars/
Flight to Arras**
[GF693] Picador pbk **£3.95**

SALTYKOV, M.E. SHCHEDRIN-
(Russian, 1826 - 1889)
Shchedrin-Saltykov is chiefly remembered for his 1876 novel *The Golovlevs*, a series of linked stories detailing the inevitable decline and fall of a provincial family of almost unrelieved selfishness and greed.
The Golovlevs (1826 - 1889)
[GF694] Penguin pbk **£4.95**
[GF695] Oxford pbk **£4.95**

SAND, GEORGE (French, 1804 - 1876)
Best known now for her friendships with many of the leading artistic figures of her time, including Chopin, Flaubert and de Musset, Sand's novels have lost the wide popularity they gained among her contemporaries, but remain interesting for their assertion of a woman's right to love and need for independence.
Lettres d'un Voyageur
[GF696] Penguin pbk **£4.95**
Marianne
[GF697] Methuen pbk **£3.95**

SANDEL, CORA (Norwegian, 1880-1974)
The theme of much of Sandel's fiction is the attempt by a heroine, an artistically gifted girl or woman, to realise herself in a hostile environment. She is sensitive in her understanding of women, as well as sharp in her condemnation of male selfishness, especially in the Alberta trilogy.
Alberta Alone (1939)
[GF698] Women's P pbk **£2.50**
Alberta and Freedom (1931)
[GF699] Women's P pbk **£2.50**
Alberta and Jacob (1926)
[GF700] Women's P pbk **£2.50**
Krane's Cafe (1945)
Sandel's masterpiece tells the story of the consequences of a woman's act when she breaks the conventions of society.
[GF701] Women's P pbk **£3.50**
Silken Thread (Stories and Sketches)
[GF702] Women's P pbk **£3.95**
The Leech (1958)
[GF703] Women's P pbk **£3.95**

SARAMAGO, JOSE (Portuguese)

Saramago is one of Portugal's foremost contemporary writers; the first of his novels to be translated into English, this is a human black comedy, the story of a love affair set in 18th century Portugal against a background of the final years of the Inquisition.

Baltasar & Blimunda
[GF704] Cape hbk **£11.95**

SARRAUTE, NATHALIE (French, 1900 -)

A leading exponent of the *nouveau roman*. *Tropisms* defined the area of sensations on the borders of consciousness which she believes influence human behaviour and her novels, if not easy, are rewarding raising questions about the status of the novel itself.

Childhood
[GF705] Calder pbk **£5.95**
Do You Hear Them?
[GF706] Calder pbk **£5.95**
Fools Say
[GF707] Calder pbk **£5.95**
Martereau
[GF708] Calder pbk **£4.95**
The Planetarium
[GF709] Calder pbk **£4.95**
Tropisms/Age of Suspicion
[GF710] Calder pbk **£5.95**
Use of Speech
[GF711] Calder pbk **£4.95**

SARTRE, JEAN-PAUL (French, 1905 - 1980)

One of the century's major intellectual figures and the chief exponent of existentialism. His novels come from the early part of his writing life: *Nausea* (1938) charts the degrees of disengagement which man can achieve, while the trilogy *The Roads to Freedom* (1945-1949), (comprising the other books listed here) tells of one intellectual's move towards political and social commitment, against a background extending from Munich in 1938 to the Fall of France in 1940.

Iron in the Soul
[GF712] Penguin pbk **£4.95**
Nausea
[GF713] Penguin pbk **£3.50**
The Age of Reason
[GF714] Penguin pbk **£4.50**
The Reprieve
[GF715] Penguin pbk **£4.50**

SCHULZ, BRUNO (Polish, 1862 - 1942)

Living for most of the inter-war years in the Polish oil-town of Drohobycz, Schulz was murdered in the Jewish Ghetto in 1942. His stories are both pictures of this local landscape, and more surreal indictments of the barbarism approaching his civilization.

The Fictions of Bruno Schulz
[GF716] Picador pbk **£4.95**

SCHWARTZ-BART, ANDRE (Polish, 1928 -)

Born a Polish Jew, Schwarz-Bart escaped the concentration camps, and survived the War. He started writing in the 1950s in France; *A Woman Named Solitude* is a semi-autobiographical picture of Europe under Nazi occupation.

A Woman Named Solitude
[GF717] Picador pbk **£3.50**
Last of the Just
[GF718] Penguin pbk **£3.95**

SCIASCIA, LEONARDO (Italian, 1921 -)

Sciascia evokes his native Sicily more acutely than any of his contemporaries, examining both its history and current political situation, and exposing the extent to which the Mafia has become the major force on the island. He is a master of the detective genre, and one of the most acute commentators on the political and literary scene in which he lives.

1912 + 1   `NEW`
All through the year 1913 the Italian poet Gabriele

D'Annunzio wrote the date '1912 + 1' because he was suspicious of writing 1913. But in fact the year was lucky for him. Sciascia traces the career of the poet from this point, linking him to the eventual advent of Fascism.
[GF719] Carcanet hbk **£10.95**
Candido (1977)
[GF720] Carcanet pbk **£3.95**
Cronachette
[GF721] Carcanet hbk **£10.95**
Day of the Owl (1961)/**Equal Danger** (1971)
Two masterful detective stories set in Sicily.
[GF722] Grafton pbk **£3.95**
Moro Affair/Mystery of Majorana
Half-fictional, half-factual pieces, including an essay on the kidnapping and murder of Aldo Moro.
[GF723] Carcanet hbk **£9.95**
One Way or Another (1974)
[GF724] Carcanet hbk **£9.95**
Sicilian Uncles (1958)
[GF725] Grafton pbk **£3.95**
The Wine Dark Sea (1973)
[GF726] Grafton pbk **£3.95**
To Each His Own
A meditation on the nature of Sicilian truth concerning the shooting of Manno, the pharmacist and his friend Dr Roscio, whilst they are out hunting.
[GF727] Carcanet hbk **£10.95**

SEMYONOV, JULIAN (Russian, 1931 -)

An almost unique phenomenon in Soviet literature, Semyonov is a crime and thriller writer. His debut novel *Petrovka 38*, a cops and robbers story set in Moscow, made him a bestseller overnight, and later works have spread his reputation in the West, as well as broadening the scope of his writitng.

Intercontinental Knot   `NEW`
Another spy thriller from the bestselling Soviet writer, featuring Vitaly Slavin as the KGB hero who has to suss out and defeat the dirty tricks of the other side.
[GF728] Calder hbk **£12.95**
Reporter   `NEW`
A political novel in which Semyonov looks at Soviet Russia under Gorbachev, with its new opportunities.
[GF729] Calder hbk **£12.95**
Seventeen Moments of Spring
[GF730] Calder hbk **£12.95**
Tass Is Authorised to Announce
[GF731] Calder hbk **£9.95**

SHOLOKOV, MIKHAIL (Russian, 1905 - 1984)

Nobel Prize for Literature 1965. One of the few internationally recognised exponents of 'Socialist Realism', Sholokhov's *Don* epics provide the authorised version of Soviet society in the Ukraine from the Civil War to the collectivisation of the Five Year Plans.

And Quiet Flows the Don
[GF732] Penguin pbk **£6.95**
Harvest on the Don
[GF733] Penguin pbk **£4.50**
One Man's Destiny & Other Stories
[GF734] Sphere pbk **£2.95**
Tales from the Don
[GF735] Sphere pbk **£2.95**
The Don Flows Home to the Sea
[GF736] Penguin pbk **£7.95**
Virgin Soil Upturned
[GF737] Penguin pbk **£4.95**
[GF738] Picador pbk **£5.95**

SILONE, IGNAZIO (Italian, 1900 - 1978)

Born in the Marisca region of Central Italy, which has provided the background to his fiction, Silone escaped from the Fascists into exile in Switzerland; *Bread and Wine* was first published there in German, and Silone did not return to Italy until 1944.

Bread and Wine (1936)
[GF739] Dent pbk **£4.95**

Fontamara (1933)
The story of how the villagers of Fontamara are driven by the sufferings they receive at the hands of their landlords to a useless and tragic revolt against the state.
[GF740] Dent pbk **£4.50**

SIMON, CLAUDE (French, 1913 -)

Nobel Prize for Literature 1985. Influenced by the *nouveau roman*, Simon writes of characters whose emotional obsessions provide the novels with their own narrative order and tension. At its best, as in *Flanders Road*, his technique achieves great power, and recalls the work of William Faulkner.

Flanders Road
[GF741] Calder pbk **£5.95**
The Georgics   `NEW`
This novel won Simon the Nobel Prize. Three characters at such different but important historical dates as 1789, 1940, 1792, 1937, 1799 (periods of tumult, war and revolution) live through events and help to make them happen.
[GF742] Calder hbk **£12.95**
The World About Us
This novel is a montage of diverse elements: a remnant of French cavalry about to be overrun by Germans, a group of people from an Impressionist painting strolls along a sea cliff, and an adulterous affair being consummated under the night sky.
[GF743] P Owen hbk **£11.95**
Triptych
[GF744] Calder pbk **£4.95**

SKVORECKY, JOSEF (Czech, 1924 -)

A major Czech novelist in exile who now lives in Canada, the publication of Skvorecky's first novel, *The Cowards*, resulted in his losing his job; he published several of his subsequent works under the name of a friend, only recovering greater artistic freedom in the cultural relaxation of the mid-1960s. His recent work powerfully describes the effects of separation on the human soul.

Dvorak in Love: A Light-Hearted Dream
[GF745] Hogarth pbk **£5.95**
Miss Silver's Past
[GF746] Picador pbk **£2.95**
Sins for Father Knox   `NEW`
The second in Skvorecky's series of detective stories; featuring the melancholy detective, they are an acute parody of the 'standard' detective mystery.
[GF747] Faber hbk **£11.99**
Talkin' Moscow Blues (Essays)   `NEW`
The fruit of a life lived both under Nazi and Soviet oppression, and now in exile in the West, this is a collection of pieces: ranging from personal stories about friends to re-examinations of the nature of art, politics and freedom, and reviews of writers and film makers such as Faulkner, Kafka and Coppola.
[GF748] Picador pbk **£6.99**
The Bass Saxophone
[GF749] Picador pbk **£3.50**
The Cowards
[GF750] Penguin pbk **£4.99**
The Engineer of Human Souls
Subtitled 'An entertainment on the old themes of Life, Women, Fate, Dreams, the Working Class, Secret Agents, Love and Death', and hailed by Milan Kundera as 'Magnificent - a Magnum Opus', this massive novel is Skvorecky's most acclaimed work. He draws high comedy out of the tragic but farcical world of the police state which he left behind, and exposes the shallowness of the safe world to which he has come.
[GF751] Picador pbk **£3.99**
The Mournful Demeanour of Lieutenant Boruvka
[GF752] Faber pbk **£3.99**
The Swell Season
[GF753] Picador pbk **£3.99**

SOLZHENITSYN, ALEXANDER
(Russian, 1918 -)

Nobel Prize for Literature 1974. Solzhenitsyn burst onto the literary scene in Russia during the 1960s with the brilliant short novel *One Day in the Life of Ivan Denisovich*. As an exposé of the Stalinist Gulag system it was unique, and as a work of art it has been acclaimed as his best. This was followed by *Cancer Ward*, *The First Circle*, *August 1914* and his masterpiece of documentary journalism *The Gulag Archipelago*. In 1974, he was expelled from the Writers' Union and deported from the Soviet Union. Solzhenitsyn's style is blunt, often crusading, and very uneven in quality, but all his writing has a compelling volcanic power, and he remains one of the most distinctive voices of modern letters.

August 1914
Conceived as part of a cycle of historical novels which remains unfinished, *August 1914* is in the great tradition of the 19th century epic. A vast panorama of war, it blends the lives of historical and fictional characters, and explores the tragedy and heroism of a nation heading inexorably towards defeat. This is a revised and expanded edition, newly translated.
[GF754] Bodley hbk **£18.00**
[GF755] Bodley pbk **£9.95**

Cancer Ward (1971)
[GF756] Penguin pbk **£5.95**

One Day in the Life of Ivan Denisovich
Authorised for publication in 1962, this is an exceptional novel in many ways. A lowly Zek recounts a better than average day in a forced labour camp, north of the arctic circle. The subject was unique and daring in 1962, as was the novel's style. Written in the camp vernacular, this short novella contravened all the laws of Socialist Realism and paved the way for the greater freedom in subject matter and experimentalism of style that typifies the period of 'The Thaw'.
[GF757] Penguin pbk **£3.50**

Stories and Prose Poems
[GF758] Bodley hbk **£8.95**

The First Circle
[GF759] Collins Harv pbk **£6.95**

The Gulag Archipelago (abbreviated)
[GF760] Collins Harv hbk **£15.00**
[GF761] Collins Harv pbk **£6.95**

STENDHAL (French, 1783 - 1842)
One of the greatest novelists of his period, Stendhal's typical hero is essentially a loner, whose ironic curiosity about society impels him into uneasy involvement; youthful purity and ambition are transmuted into hypocrisy, and happiness comes often only at the moment of fall.

Armance
[GF762] Soho pbk **£5.95**

Henri Beyle Stendahl, (Photo:Mary Evans Picture Library)

Charterhouse of Parma
A novel of intrigues set at the court of Parma between 1815 and 1830. The story centres on the exploits of the young Fabrice and his relationship with the Duchess.
[GF763] Chatto hbk **£9.95**
[GF764] Penguin pbk **£3.95**

Love
[GF765] Penguin pbk **£4.99**

Pink and the Green
[GF766] H Hamilton hbk **£10.95**

Red and the Black
A portrait of the unpopular but mercurial Julien Sorel, who overcomes his disadvantages of birth, only to be executed for attempting to murder the only woman he loved. One of the great studies of a flawed individual.
[GF767] Penguin pbk **£3.95**

To the Happy Few: Letters
[GF768] Soho pbk **£6.95**

SUSKIND, PATRICK (German, 1949 -)
Suskind's most acclaimed novel, *Perfume*, is an atmospheric story of murder set in 18th century Paris; it tells the story of a dwarf - a genius of scent - with the 'finest nose in Paris', who aspires to create a perfume which will render him instantly loveable. Filled with detail, it touches on profound issues of desire and need.

Perfume
[GF769] Penguin pbk **£4.99**

The Double Bass
[GF770] Penguin pbk **£2.99**

The Pigeon
[GF771] Penguin pbk **£3.50**

SVEVO, ITALO (Italian, 1861 - 1928)
Italo Svevo produced his comic-psychological masterpiece *The Confessions of Zeno* in 1923; it was originally unacknowledged in Italy, but when Larbaud acclaimed the French translation a masterpiece, his own country belatedly recognised his achievement. Svevo's work is hard to characterise; his characters have been called 'trapped self-analysts', whose only solution to their solitude and impotence lies in fantasy, though this does not deprive the works of a certain comedy.

A Life (1892)
[GF772] Penguin pbk **£3.95**

As A Man Grows Older (1898)
[GF773] Penguin pbk **£4.99**

The Confessions of Zeno (1923)
[GF774] Penguin pbk **£5.95**

TABUCCHI, ANTONIO (Italian)

Indian Nocturne
Winner of the *Prix Médicis Etranger* for 1987. This atmospheric novel, concerning the tantalising search for the mysterious and elusive Xavier in India, subtly mixes past and present, appearance and reality, to great effect.
[GF775] Chatto hbk **£10.95**

Little Misunderstandings of No Importance
[GF776] Chatto hbk **£10.95**

Vanishing Point **NEW**
A Calvino-esque novel about a young man whose unidentified body is delivered to the mortuary of an Italian town one morning. The newspapers report that he was killed by the police, but no-one knows who he was.
[GF777] Chatto hbk **£11.95**

TANER, HALDUN (Turkish)
A varied collection of stories, that give a vivid flavour of what life was like in Turkey during the 1930s.

Thickhead & Other Stories **NEW**
[GF778] Forest Bks pbk **£7.95**

TIMM, UWE (German, 1940 -)

The Snake Tree
The story of an engineer, escaping from his failing marriage to a job in Latin America; instead of finding himself, he must confront military dictatorship, bureaucracy, and superstition.
[GF779] Picador pbk **£4.95**

TISMA, ALEXSANDAR (Yugoslav)

The Use of Man **NEW**
Four friends are growing up in Yugoslavia, during and after the Second World War. The horror of their daily lives during the war is almost matched by the stultifying boredom of living in their town when it is over.
[GF780] Faber hbk **£12.99**

TOLSTOY, LEO (Russian, 1828 - 1910)
One of the indisputable giants of European culture, there are few people who would deny that *War and Peace* and *Anna Karenina* rank among the major works of world literature. In these novels, he brought the 19th century psychological novel to a climax, setting the personal dilemmas, thoughts and emotions of his major characters against a vast sweep of society, landscape and history. For those who may find the size of these novels too daunting, *Childhood, Boyhood, Youth*, *The Cossacks* and *The Kreutzer Sonata* provide a wonderful introduction.

A Confession and Other Religious Writings
[GF781] Penguin pbk **£3.99**

A Landowner's Morning (Stories)
[GF782] Quartet hbk **£7.95**

Anna Karenina (1873 - 77)
[GF783] Penguin pbk **£3.99**
[GF784] Oxford pbk **£3.95**

Childhood, Boyhood, Youth
[GF785] Penguin pbk **£3.99**

Master and Man & Other Stories
[GF786] Penguin pbk **£3.50**

Resurrection (1899)
The third and least successful of Tolstoy's long novels, *Resurrection* was published over 20 years after *Anna Karenina*. Despite certain weaknesses of structure, it does contain some of the most penetrating satire Tolstoy ever wrote.
[GF787] Penguin pbk **£4.99**

Sebastopol Sketches
[GF788] Penguin pbk **£2.99**

The Cossacks & Other Stories
[GF789] Penguin pbk **£3.95**

The Death of Ivan Illyich & Other Stories
[GF790] Penguin pbk **£3.99**

The Kreutzner Sonata & Other Stories
[GF791] Penguin pbk **£3.50**

The Raid & Other Stories
[GF792] Oxford pbk **£2.95**

War and Peace (1863 - 69)
Not only an epic retelling of Napoleon's invasion of Russia in 1812, it is also a brilliant reconstruction of life in early 19th century Russia. Drawing heavily on his own family and acquaintances, Tolstoy creates a cast of characters unparalleled in world literature.
[GF793] Oxford 2 vols pbk **£5.90**
[GF794] Penguin pbk **£5.99**

TOLSTAYA, TATYANA (Russian)

On the Golden Porch **NEW**
An acclaimed volume of short stories by one of the most original contemporary voices in Russian literature. A descendant of Leo, Tolstaya's stories are strikingly unusual and imaginative explorations of the heart and soul, set in a finely-realized environment and including a memorable range of characters, sympathetically portrayed.
[GF795] Virago hbk **£12.95**

TOMEO, JAVIER (Spanish) **NEW**
The Coded Castle & Dear Monster
Tomeo has been described as 'the Iberian Kafka'. *The Coded Castle* takes the form of a job interview for the post of nightwatchman at a bank, during which interviewee and interviewer discover that they share a problem. *Dear Monster* involves the delivery of a letter to a mysterious castle, a place of history and power.
[GF796] Carcanet hbk **£12.95**

TOURNIER, MICHEL (French, 1924 -)
Although he began writing late in life, Tournier has earned considerable popular acclaim. His novels often sparkle with intelligence and metaphysical meditation, though he has also been censured for a certain precociousness in his wit and cleverness.
Four Wise Men
[GF797] Methuen pbk **£3.95**
Gemini
[GF798] Methuen pbk **£4.50**
Gilles & Jeanne
[GF799] Methuen pbk **£3.99**
The Erl King
[GF800] Methuen pbk **£4.50**
The Fetishist
[GF801] Methuen pbk **£3.95**
The Golden Droplet
[GF802] Methuen pbk **£3.95**
The Wind Spirit
[GF803] Collins hbk **£15.00**

TOUSSAINT, JEAN-PHILIPPE (French)
An international bestseller, this is a quirky philosophical novel, which sets the imaginative world of a young man against the banality of the environment in which he lives.
The Bathroom
[GF804] Boyars hbk **£11.95**

TOZZI, FEDERICO (Italian, 1883 - 1920)
Eyes Shut **NEW**
The first English translation in 60 years of this acclaimed Italian writer, placed on a par with Pirandello and Italo Svevo. Tozzi's novels have a strong autobiographical streak. *Eyes Shut* is based on his early years, his conflict with a bullying father and his infatuation with a young country girl.
[GF805] Carcanet hbk **£12.95**

TREFUSIS, VIOLET (French, 1894 - 1972)
Trefusis's best-known novel, originally written in French, is *Broderie Anglaise*, a fictionalized account of her affair with Vita Sackville-West, which serves as a riposte to Virginia Woolf's *Orlando*.
Broderie Anglaise
[GF806] Methuen pbk **£3.50**
Hunt the Slipper
[GF807] Virago pbk **£4.50**

TUCHOLSKY, KURT (German, 1890 - 1935)
Tucholsky was one of the most uncompromising satirists of the inter-war period, whose work was left-wing in tone and written in the colloquial slang of Berlin.
Castle Gripsholm
[GF808] Chatto hbk **£8.95**
Germany? Germany **NEW**
A Tucholsky reader which reveals the full range of his work, from essays and newspaper columns to poetry and cabaret songs, and shows him as a bitter but honest voice of the inter-war years.
.[GF809] Carcanet hbk **£18.00**

TURGENEV, IVAN SERGEEVICH
(Russian, 1818 - 1883)
The most Western of the great Russian writers, he is best known for his series of polished novels depicting the lives of the 19th century gentry and intelligentsia.

Turgenev lived for many years outside his natural land and developed close ties with Flaubert, Henry James and George Sand.
A House of Gentlefolk
[GF810] Grafton pbk **£3.95**
Fathers and Sons (1862)
Generally considered Turgenev's best novel, the hero Bazarov is one of the most remarkable characters in Russian literature. Turgenev's creation of the first literary nihilist and his demonstration of the failure of communication between generations succeeded in enraging both fathers and sons in the Russia of his time.
[GF811] Penguin pbk **£3.50**
First Love
[GF812] Penguin pbk **£2.50**
First Love & Other Stories
[GF813] Oxford pbk **£3.95**
Home of the Gentry
[GF814] Penguin pbk **£3.99**
On the Eve (1862)
[GF815] Penguin pbk **£3.50**
Rudin
[GF816] Penguin pbk **£3.95**
Sketches from a Hunter's Album
Published in 1852, the sketches are among the most successful and satisfying of all Turgenev's works. This loose series of lyrical stories of rural life under serfdom, retain their freshness and beauty to the 20th century reader.
[GF817] Penguin pbk **£3.50**
Smoke
[GF818] Sutton pbk **£2.95**
Spring Torrents ?
[GF819] Penguin pbk **£4.50**

UNDSET, SIGRID (Norwegian, 1882 - 1949)
Along with Hamsun, Undset is one of Norway's great novelists - *Kristin Lavransdatter* is her classic work, an epic trilogy of 14th century Norway, in which Christianity clashes with the twilight world of the Norse Sagas.
Kristin Lavransdatter (1920-22)
[GF820] Picador pbk **£6.95**

VASSALLI, SEBASTIANO (Italian, 1941 -)
Born in Genoa, Vassalli has written several novels and experimental prose works and has been associated with the avant-garde 'Gruppo 63'. This novel, his first to be translated into English, recreates the life of the poet Dino Campana, a man of genius in a world impatient of genius, a radical imagination visited upon a torpid culture.
The Night of the Comet **NEW**
[GF821] Carcanet hbk **£12.95**

VERGA, GIOVANNI (Italian, 1840 - 1922)
Verga's best work studies the position of individuals, often the underprivileged peasantry of Sicily, in relation to their communities. He created a vernacular language based on the Sicilian dialect, understandable to outside readers, but expressing fully the thought-patterns of his characters, and thus successfully creates the personal and physical landscape of the country he describes. He described his own view of the world thus: *"The fateful, endless and often wearisome and agitated path trod by humanity to achieve progress is majestic in its end result, seen as a whole and from afar."*
Cavalleria Rusticana & Other Stories
(Trans. D.H. Lawrence)
[GF822] Dedalus pbk **£4.50**
House by the Medlar Tree (1881)
Heralded by some as the first modern novel in Italy, this story of Sicilian fishermen set in the 1860s was the first of a projected series showing contemporary social history. Only the second, *Maestro Don Gesualdo* was completed.
[GF823] Dedalus pbk **£4.95**

Maestro Don Gesualdo
[GF824] Dedalus pbk **£4.95**
Short Sicilian Novels
(Trans D.H. Lawrence)
[GF825] Dedalus pbk **£3.95**

VIAN, BORIS (French, 1920 - 1959)
A distinctive writer, Vian was a jazz trumpeter who wrote hard-boiled American-style popular fiction under a pseudonym, as well as various more serious novels (including these listed here) which went unrecognised during his own life. His fiction mixes fantasy, surrealism and lyricism with a cruel, sharp macabre strain.
Froth on the Daydream
[GF826] Quartet pbk **£5.95**
Heartsnatcher
[GF827] Quartet pbk **£6.95**

VILLALONGA, LLORENC
(Spanish, 1897 - 1980)
Villalonga wrote mainly in Catalan, and lived for much of his life on the island of Mallorca, of which he writes in *The Dolls' Room*: a story of the provincial aristocracy in decline, it is similar in theme to Lampedusa's *The Leopard* (which Villalonga translated into Catalan).
The Dolls' Room (1961)
[GF828] Deutsch hbk **£11.95**

VITTORINI, ELIO (Italian, 1908 - 1966)
Conversation in Sicily (1939)
The hero of Vittorini's novel has returned to his Sicilian home after fifteen years away; the journey represents a rite of passage, and the novel's vision of Italy's descent into Fascism, and the resulting rottenness which afflicted the country, is expressed poetically and subtly, as was neccessary for a work which was published on the eve of the Second World War.
[GF829] Quartet pbk **£5.95**

VOINOVICH, VLADIMIR (Russian, 1932 -)
One of a long line of talented Soviet satirists, he was expelled from the Writers' Union in 1974 for his continued support of Solzhenitsyn. This novel is a complex dystopia, and has been described as 'a work of both historical pain and massive comic ebullience'.
Moscow 2042
[GF830] Picador pbk **£4.99**

VOLPONI, PAOLO (Italian, 1924 -)
Volponi's *The World-Wide Machine* is an interesting study of man's mis-use of knowledge, telling the story of an ignorant peasant who creates a false religion out of books; stylistically, he juxtaposes a sense of the absurdity of human life, familiar from Pirandello, with a more personal and lyrical streak.
The Memorandum
[GF831] Boyars pbk **£3.95**
The World-Wide Machine (1965)
[GF832] Boyars hbk **£6.95**

VOLTAIRE, FRANCOIS MARIE AROUET DE (French, 1694 - 1778)
Formal, precise, lucid and elegant, Voltaire's work epitomises the Enlightenment of the 18th century. He is best known as a satirist, particularly for his philosophical tale *Candide*, but he was also a poet, dramatist, historian, moralist, polemicist and critic.
Candide
[GF833] Penguin pbk **£2.50**
Candide & Other Tales
[GF834] Dent pbk **£2.25**
Zadig & L'Ingenu
[GF835] Penguin pbk **£3.95**

VOZNESENSKAYA, JULIA (Russian, 1933 -)
Her international debut as a novelist *The Women's Decameron* was an immediate bestseller. Combining humour and blunt realism, it compares and contrasts the lives of ten women in contemporary Soviet society, brought together in the labour ward of a Moscow hospital. Her latest novel addresses the awful tragedy at Chernobyl in 1986.
The Star Chernobyl
[GF836] Methuen pbk **£3.95**
The Women's Decameron
[GF837] Methuen pbk **£4.50**

WAGNER, RICHARD (Romanian, 1952 -)
Wagner's first novel portrays the oppressive and absurd world of Ceaucescu's Romania, and in particular the Swabian minority of the Banat, from which he has now emigrated. It is a fine, stark work which depicts an environment of claustrophobia and human desolation.
Exit
[GF838] Verso pbk **£8.95**

WALSER, MARTIN (German, 1927 -)
German writer and radio producer, whose work is important for its social criticism of the materialism of post-war Germany. Often placed on a level with Grass and Frisch, he is one of the most articulate and socially aware writers of his generation.
Breakers (1988)
[GF839] Deutsch hbk **£12.95**
Rabbit Race Detour (1962)
[GF840] Boyars pbk **£3.95**
The Inner Man (1986)
[GF841] Methuen pbk **£3.95**
The Unicorn (1966)
[GF842] Boyars pbk **£4.50**

WALSER, ROBERT (Swiss, 1878 - 1956)
Walser spent the last part of his life in a mental hospital, and behind what his translator (the poet Christopher Middleton) has described as a 'charmed ironic clownishness', his work displays a disturbing vision of spiritual nightmare which certainly influenced Kafka, and which makes his fiction unfairly neglected today.
Selected Stories
[GF843] Carcanet hbk **£8.95**
The Walk & Other Stories
[GF844] Calder hbk **£4.95**

WEISS, PETER (German, 1916 - 1964)
Conversation of the Three Walkers/The Shadow of the Coachman's Body
[GF845] Boyars hbk **£6.95**
Leavetaking/Vanishing Point (1961/62)
Two autobiographical pieces covering the years 1916-1947 which illuminate the alienation Weiss felt (which itself delayed the start of his writing) and describe in lucid detail the realities and circumstances in which he grew up.
[GF846] Boyars pbk **£3.95**

WITKIEWICZ, STANISLAW IGNACY
(Polish, 1885 - 1939)
Insatiability (1930)
Insatiability is a complex anti-utopian novel and satire, tracing the adventures of a young man whose fate parallels the inevitable collapse of Western civilization following a Chinese invasion from the East.
[GF847] Quartet pbk **£7.50**

WOLF, CHRISTA (German, 1929 -)
A committed Socialist, Wolf has been described as 'East Germany's most formidable woman of letters'. Her work examines the present state of Germany, as well as remembering existence under the Nazis, preoccupied with the imposed 'personal suppressions

and official silences'. In *A Model Childhood*, the story of a child growing up in the years following 1933, the opening reads - *"What is past is not dead; it is not even past. We cut ourselves off from it; we pretend to be strangers"*, and the theme of much of her fiction is to show how the two, past and present, can never be entirely separated.
A Model Childhood (1977)
[GF848] Virago pbk **£5.50**
Accident: A Day's News   NEW
[GF849] Virago pbk **£5.99**
Cassandra: A Novel & Four Essays (1983)
[GF850] Virago pbk **£5.99**
No Place on Earth (1979)
[GF851] Virago pbk **£6.95**
The Quest for Christa T (1968)
[GF852] Virago pbk **£4.50**

YEHOSHUA, ABRAHAM (Israeli, 1937 -)
Yehoshua's early work is in the form of novellas - only in *A Late Divorce* and his most recent novel *The Five Seasons*, does he write at greater length: his recurrent subjects are the complications of close emotional relationships, especially when interrupted by divorce or death.
A Late Divorce
[GF853] Collins Harv hbk **£10.95**
The Continuing Silence of the Poet: The Collected Stories
[GF854] P Halban hbk **£12.95**
The Five Seasons   NEW
[GF855] Collins hbk **£11.95**

YOURCENAR, MARGUERITE
(French, 1903 - 1987)
In 1980 Yourcenar became the first woman to be elected to the Académie Française. She has lived since the Second War in America, though continuing to write in French. Her novels reflect her wide learning and travel, in particular her classical scholarship, as shown in *Memoirs of Hadrian*, a meticulously researched novel about the celebrated humanist Emperor which brought her international renown.
Alexis
[GF856] A Ellis hbk **£8.95**
Coin in Nine Hands
[GF857] Transworld pbk **£2.50**
Coup de Grace
[GF858] Transworld pbk **£2.50**
Dark Brain of Piranesi (Essays)
[GF859] A Ellis hbk **£9.50**
Fires
[GF860] Transworld pbk **£2.50**
Memoirs of Hadrian
[GF861] Penguin pbk **£4.95**
Mishima (Non fiction)
[GF862] A Ellis hbk **£8.95**
That Mighty Sculptor Time
[GF863] A Ellis hbk **£12.50**
The Abyss
[GF864] Transworld pbk **£3.95**
Two Lives and a Dream
[GF865] Transworld pbk **£4.50**

ZAMYATIN, YEVGENY (Russian, 1884 - 1937)
Vilified by the Soviet establishment for his unique brand of satire, Zamyatin is best remembered as the author of the utopian novel *We*. His vision of a totalitarian state precedes both Orwell's *1984* and Huxley's *Brave New World* by several years and undoubtedly influenced them both.
Dragon & Other Stories
[GF866] Penguin pbk **£4.50**
Islanders/Fishers of Men
[GF867] Fontana pbk **£2.50**
We (1929)
[GF868] Penguin pbk **£3.95**

ZINOVIEV, ALEXANDER (Russian, 1922 -)
A philosopher by training, Alexander Zinoviev was expelled from the Soviet Union in 1978. His novels are written in a distinctive and somewhat unusual style, and present a mixture of dialogue, interior monologue, verse, pastiche, parody and dramatic sketch.
The Madhouse
[GF869] Grafton pbk **£5.95**

ZOLA, EMILE (French, 1840 - 1902)
Zola's adherence to fictional 'naturalism' led him to treat documentation as the start of fiction-making, and his interest in science is revealed in a quasi-sociological concern with environment and heredity as the foundations of character. His concern was with a truth which often proved unpalatable to the primarily bourgeois reader of his time. In *Thérèse Raquin*, with its compelling, although brutal, analysis of criminal passion, he achieved an enduring masterpiece.
Attack on the Mill (Stories)
[GF870] Oxford pbk **£3.95**
Beast in Man (1890)
[GF871] Penguin pbk **£3.95**
[GF872] Grafton pbk **£2.95**
Earth (1887)
[GF873] Penguin pbk **£4.95**
Fortune of the Rougons
This was the first of the Rougon-Macquart series of twenty novels written to illustrate Zola's theories of the naturalist novel. It traces the Rougon-Macquart family in its various different branches through several generations of the Second Empire in France.
[GF874] Sutton pbk **£3.95**
Germinal (1885)
[GF875] Penguin pbk **£3.99**
L'Assomoir (1877)
[GF876] Penguin pbk **£3.99**
Nana (1880)
[GF877] Penguin pbk **£3.99**
Restless House
[GF878] Grafton pbk **£2.95**
The Debacle
[GF879] Penguin pbk **£3.99**
The Kill
[GF880] Grafton pbk **£2.95**
The Masterpiece
[GF881] Sutton pbk **£3.95**
Thérèse Raquin
[GF882] Penguin pbk **£2.95**

ZWEIG, ARNOLD (German, 1887 - 1968)
Born a Silesian Jew, Zweig was expelled from Germany in 1933; his best novel traces the pitiful nature of bureaucracy on the individual, and shows the monstrous destructiveness of war. J.B. Priestley described it as 'the greatest novel on a war theme from any country'.
The Case of Sergeant Grischa (1927)
[GF883] Penguin pbk **£4.95**

ZWEIG, STEFAN (Austrian, 1881 - 1942)
One of the generation of international intellectuals of the 1920s, Zweig was an ardent advocate of a new international order for the post-war world. His small body of work, the short stories and one novel, *Beware of Pity*, neglected for too long, has now been republished to great acclaim. A writer of sophisticated simplicity and rare insight, he wrote the exquisite and lyrical love story used for the Max Ophül's film *Letter from an Unknown Woman*.
Beware of Pity (1939)
[GF884] Penguin pbk **£4.95**
The Royal Game & Other Stories
[GF885] Penguin pbk **£3.95**

Boris Pasternak 1890 - 1960

D.M. Thomas

I remember, like a first, passionate love affair, my first encounter with Boris Pasternak. It was summer, 1958; a student, I was at home in my Cornish village on vacation. I had a holiday job at a library a couple of miles away, and would set off walking in the sunny morning, my eyes buried in a pristine, red hardback, my steps finding their way automatically. This book, *Doctor Zhivago*, was like nothing I had ever read; I was drunk on its poetic power and beauty. Its hero was a poet, and one didn't have to take it on trust - his actual poems formed the novel's conclusion, related back to the events in the narrative. Driving through Moscow on a snowy night, the young Zhivago sees that a candle has burned a hole in the ice of an upstairs window. And here is the poem: *"The candle on the table burned,/The candle burned"*. Inside the upstairs room is Zhivago's future mistress, Lara. They will be separated by revolution and civil war, but will meet again in a provincial

library. Their reunion haunted me as I got to work among the shelves of my own small-town public library. Life *was* poetry, the book proclaimed: everything interrelated, like a poem's metaphor.

Doctor Zhivago had been first published in Milan, an event which created a storm in the Soviet Union. Zhdanov, the leading cultural administrator, said that to compare a pig with Pasternak would be unfair to the pig. Awarded the Nobel Prize for Literature, Pasternak was forced to refuse it, fearing the creative death of exile if he travelled to the West to receive his award. He who had miraculously survived Stalinism was broken in health by the persecution and abuse, and died not long after. His grave at Peredelkino, the writers' village near Moscow, became a place of pilgrimage. His most famous work was widely read in *samizdat*, but not until 1988 did it become openly available, published by *Novy Mir*. It was a stunning success. The Moscow bestseller list for May, 1989, makes

interesting reading: Pasternak's novel headed a distinguished list - the poems of Gumilev, executed in 1921; Nabokov's *Lolita*; *We and Other Stories* by Zamyatin, forced into exile in 1931; and Vasili Grossman's anti-Stalinist epic *Life and Fate*. Comparison with the British bestseller list of that period is salutary.

Now even that arch exponent of Cold War communism, Andrei Gromyko, can boast in his autobiography, *Memories*, of

---

Its publication at this time is one of the most significant events of glasnost: a person who can freely read Doctor Zhivago is no longer enslaved

---

having met Pasternak socially, and expresses regret that *Doctor Zhivago* was not published thirty years ago and that its author was so abused. Gromyko allows himself the complaint that Zhivago is not an admirable character in that he is weak-willed - thus showing, unsurprisingly, that he completely fails to understand the novel's import. Pasternak is demonstrating that man cannot impose his will on creation. Systems, ideologies, are born and pass away; the candle goes on burning, the snows in Russia - evoked in marvellous passages as Zhivago travels by train across his country's immense space - go on tumultuously melting in the Spring. Re-birth is a recurrent theme; we are bidden to awake, to look up, to listen. The novel is profoundly though unorthodoxly Christian; the love-story of Yury and Lara is counterpointed by references to Christ and Mary Magdalene. Just as Christ died that others might live, Yury serves creation by letting himself drift, under providence. *"In me are people without names,/Children, stay-at-homes, trees./I am conquered by them all/And this is my only victory"*. In his writing too, he finds his greatest rapture when he has no will of his own, but submits to the power of language itself.

To those who truly understand it, *Doctor Zhivago* is the antithesis of Marxism-Leninism, with its conviction that the last word has been said about life. By their own lights, the Soviet authorities were wise to ban the novel; its publication

at this time is one of the most significant events of *glasnost*: a person who can freely read **Doctor Zhivago** is no longer enslaved.

Pasternak was born into a highly-cultured *milieu*. His father was the artist Leonid Pasternak, his mother a concert pianist, Rozaliya Kaufman. Boris studied musical composition for six years, then philosophy at Moscow University and, briefly, Marburg. But in this time of cultural and political turbulence, the century's first decade, poetry became his vocation. **Twin in the Storm Clouds**, his first verse collection, appeared in 1914; and for his second collection, **My Sister Life**, he was acclaimed. In its exhilarating rhythms and tumult of imagery and metaphor his readers recognised a unique vision, as much at home in the urban excitement of revolutionary Moscow as in nature. His contemporary and friend, Anna Akhmatova, eloquently suggests the creative energy - almost like a natural force - of Pasternak: *"He who compared himself to the eye of a horse,/Peers, looks, sees, recognises,/And instantly puddles shine, ice/Pines away, like a melting of diamonds"* ('Boris Pasternak').

At first, like his character Yury Zhivago, Pasternak welcomed the Revolution. Everything, he felt, was revived and re-formed. Trying to believe and to belong, he turned to longer

---

Fearless in standing up for artistic independence, he ought to have been destroyed, like so many other, more conformist, artists

---

narrative forms, more in tune with the times: **The Year 1905** (1926), **Lieutenant Schmidt** (1927), and **Spektorsky** (1924-30). But as the age darkened towards the Stalinist Terror, he returned to lyricism in his collection **Second Birth** (1932), strongly influenced by a journey to the Caucasus.

A passage in **Doctor Zhivago** records an encounter 'at the corner of Silver Street and Silent Street'. In its characteristically symbolic way this is describing what happened when the creative fountain of Russia's Silver Age

(Blok, Bely, Akhmatova, Mandelstam, Gumilev) became frozen by Stalinism. Pasternak was creatively silent in the second half of the thirties; he published only translations. Fearless in standing up for artistic independence, he ought to have been destroyed, like so many other,

---

In the Khrushchevian thaw there appeared to be a chance that it might be published in his own country. It was not to be

---

more conformist, artists. Perhaps his Georgian translations persuaded Stalin to spare him. Or it has been suggested that a note, hinting at clairvoyance, which he appended to a group-letter condoling Stalin for his wife's suicide, frightened the superstitious Georgian. But there was seldom a rationale for Stalin's life-or-death decisions. A shadowy figure in **Doctor Zhivago**, Yury's half brother Yevgraf, appears now and again 'out of the blue' to save him. Through Yevgraf, it would seem, Pasternak was acknowledging his own good fortune.

War brought some easing of the cultural atmosphere - "How ironic," said Akhmatova in besieged Leningrad, "that these are the happiest days of our lives!" Pasternak was able to publish two new collections, **On Early Trains** and **Breadth of Earth**. Then the terror was renewed; he returned to translations, and also worked on the novel which had been simmering in his mind for the past twenty years. In the Khrushchevian thaw there appeared to be a chance that it might be published in his own country. It was not to be. And he was harried beyond the grave. At the end of **Doctor Zhivago** he describes how "one day Lara went out and did not come back. She must have been arrested in the street, as so often happened in those days, and she died or vanished somewhere, forgotten as a nameless number on a list which later was mislaid, in one of the innumerable mixed or women's concentration camps in the north." The woman on whom Lara was based, Olga Ivinskaya, was arrested for currency offences and imprisoned. She has written movingly of her joyful and perplexed relationship with him in *A*

Captive of Time (Collins, 1978).

After his death there was no official announcement of his funeral; yet handwritten notices appeared in Moscow giving the time and place, and many thousands crowded into the Peredelkino cemetery. KGB agents mingled, taking photographs. 'No more speeches!' someone cried, as the lid was put on the coffin, but the mourners would not be silenced. A workman in a coloured, open-neck shirt started to speak: 'Sleep peacefully, dear Boris Leonidovich! We do not know all of your works, but we swear to you at this hour: the day will come when we shall know them all.'

The day has come.

Novelist (best known for **The White Hotel**), poet and translator (of Pushkin and Akhmatova), D.M. Thomas's interest in Russia is long-established (he lists 'Russia and other myths' as a recreation in his entry in 'Who's Who'). It has influenced his own work, most notably in the series of novels **A Russia Quartet**.

D.M. Thomas (Photo: Mark Gerson)

LATIN AMERICAN

ALLENDE, ISABEL (Chilean, 1942 -)
Of Chilean birth (she is the niece of the late President), and now living in voluntary exile, Allende has achieved immense popularity in recent years. Like many Latin American writers her work is necessarily political, in so far as it concerns the effect of politics upon people. Of greater resonance is the idea, now familiarly known as 'magic realism', that 'reality' has a magical dimension - exemplified in a phrase of Alejo Carpentier, applicable to Allende and to many other writers of the continent: *"What is the story of Latin America if not a chronicle of the marvellous in the real?"*

Eva Luna NEW
Conceived on her father's death bed, Eva Luna grows up surrounded by squalor and bizarre people. She is befriended by a Lebanese emigré who fulfils her sexual desires, and by a transsexual cabaret artist who teaches her the ways of the world. She eventually finds 'the other half of her being' in Rolf Carlé, a gucrilla leader, but it is a relationship fraught with danger. A sensitively written and powerfully evocative novel.
[GG1] H Hamilton hbk **£11.95**

Of Love and Shadows (1987)
[GG2] Corgi pbk **£3.50**

The House of the Spirits (1985)
A masterful saga spanning four generations, featuring a cast of memorable and eccentric characters.
[GG3] Cape hbk **£9.95**
[GG4] Corgi pbk **£3.95**

ALMEIDA, JOSE AMERICO DE (Brazilian, 1887 -)
Trash (1929)
Almeida's first-hand experience of Brazilian politics inform this, his most important novel, which portrays and analyses the social problems that beset his native land in 1915.
[GG5] P Owen hbk **£7.50**

AMADO, JORGE (Brazilian, 1912 -)
Involved with the Brazilian Communist Party, Amado's best work overcomes any tendency to stereotype characters according to their social position: *The Violent Land* is his most powerful work, written while the author was in exile in Uruguay.

Dona Flor and Her Two Husbands (1970)
A comic-epic novel, set in Bahia, about the amorous life of the recently-widowed Flor.
[GG6] Serpent's Tail pbk **£7.95**

Gabriela: Clove and Cinnamon (1973)
[GG7] Souvenir hbk **£9.95**

Isabel Allende, author of *Eva Luna* (Hamish Hamilton hbk £11.95) & *The House of the Spirits* (Cape hbk £9.95, Corgi pbk £3.95)

Pen, Sword, Camisole
[GG8] Avon pbk **£3.95**
Tent of Miracles
[GG9] Collins Harv pbk **£5.95**
Tereza Batista (1982)
[GG10] Souvenir hbk **£9.95**
The Violent Land/Shepherd of the Night
[GG11] Collins Harv pbk **£5.95**
Tieta (1982)
[GG12] Souvenir hbk **£7.95**

ANJOS, CYRO DOS (Brazilian)
Diary of a Civil Servant
A Brazilian novel set in the social and political turmoil of 1935-36 chronicling the life of an introspective state employee with literary pretensions.
[GG13] Associated UP hbk **£18.50**

ARGUEDAS, JOSE MARIA
(Peruvian, 1911 - 1969)
One of the most celebrated of Peruvian writers, whose Spanish conveys the essence of Quechua, the language of the Incas, and conveys something of the older culture of the indigenous people.

Yawar Fiesta (1941)
Accessible short novel which examines the tensions between different social groups in a small town in the Andes when the annual bullfight is banned by central government.
[GG14] Quartet hbk **£8.95**

ARGUETA, MANLIO (El Salvadorian)
Cuzcatlan
A rich and lyrical evocation of El Salvador, told through fifty years in the life of one family, and its quiet but heroic defiance of a brutal military regime.
[GG15] Chatto hbk **£11.95**

One Day of Life
[GG16] Chatto pbk **£3.95**

ASSIS, MACHADO DE (Brazilian, 1839 - 1908)
Machado was the first truly great novelist to come out of Brazil, one of the major writers in Portuguese, and a figure far ahead of his time. His pose of ironic comedy hides a deep concern, often becoming despair, for the Brazil which he both condemns and loves.

Devil's Church (Stories)
[GG17] Grafton pbk **£3.95**
Epitaph of a Small Winner
[GG18] Hogarth pbk **£3.95**
Esau and Jacob
[GG19] P Owen hbk **£10.95**
Yaya Garcia
[GG20] P Owen hbk **£10.95**

ASTURIAS, MIGUEL ANGEL (Guatemalan, 1839 - 1974)
Nobel Prize for Literature 1964. From the many novels of Asturias only one is currently available in English. His writing presents a strong indictment of economic, social and political injustice, often with reference to the Indians and the impact of western civilisation on their culture.

Men of Maize (1949)
This combination of fantasy and realism in semi-automatic writing heavily influenced by Jung, is a difficult but rewarding read. It tells of the shattering impact of colonialism on the Mayans. The first experiment in what is now known as 'Magic Realism'.
[GG21] Verso hbk **£12.95**

BALCARE, ALBERTO (Argentinian)
A Long Night of Death
Set in Argentina during the reign of terror and its aftermath, this novel is a passionate account of one man's survival.
[GG22] Calder pbk **£5.95**

Jorge Luis Borges, author of *Book of Sand* (Penguin pbk £3.95) & *Fictions* (Calder pbk £3.95)

BASTOS, AUGUSTO ROA
(Paraguayan, 1917 -)
I, the Supreme (1974)
This novel is a portrait of a dictator who controlled Paraguay for the early part of the 19th century. It is a massive rumination on the uses and abuses of power, rich in texture and language.
[GG24] Faber pbk **£4.95**

BORGES, JORGE LUIS (Argentinian, 1899 - 1986)
Borges's metaphysical short stories and essays are crammed with polymathic learning: he thought of himself as an Alexandrian, and worked much of his life as a librarian. The 'fictions' he produced are unique and influential, and he has been attributed with establishing 'magic realism' as a form. This preoccupation with the boundaries of fiction and reality, and with the identity of 'self' and the 'other' pervades his work, seen to particular effect in the collection of short stories *Labyrinths*.

Atlas
[GG26] Viking hbk **£12.95**
Book of Imaginary Beings (1969)
[GG27] Penguin pbk **£3.95**
Book of Sand (1979)
[GG28] Penguin pbk **£3.95**
Doctor Brodie's Report (1972)
[GG29] Penguin pbk **£3.50**
Dreamtigers (1973)
[GG30] Souvenir hbk **£6.95**
Fictions (1944)
[GG31] Calder pbk **£3.95**
Labyrinths (1962)
[GG32] Penguin pbk **£3.95**
Other Inquisitions (1973)
[GG33] Souvenir hbk **£7.95**
Selected Poems (1985)
[GG34] Penguin pbk **£5.95**
Seven Nights (Essays, 1986)
[GG35] Faber pbk **£3.95**
Universal History of Infamy (1975)
[GG36] Penguin pbk **£2.95**

BORGES & CASARES
Extraordinary Tales (1973)
[GG25] Souvenir hbk **£6.95**

CAISTOR, NICK (ED)
The Faber Book of Latin American Short Stories
The 20 stories contained in this volume include works by Isabel Allende, Joao Ubaldo Ribeiro and other, as yet unfamiliar names. Many are published here in English for the first time. They are exciting proof of the enduring vitality of a literature that continues to defy categorisation and to enjoy a world-wide appeal.
[GG37] Faber hbk **£11.99**

CORTAZAR, JULIO (Argentinian, 1914 - 1984)
Argentinian novelist and story writer who is, like Borges (who influenced him), preoccupied with metaphysical speculation rather than with exploration of character. His work is difficult and intellectual, but rewarding.
62: A Model Kit (1968)
[GG38] Boyars pbk **£6.95**
All Fires the Fire (Stories, 1979)
[GG39] Boyars pbk **£6.95**
Change of Light (Stories, 1984)
[GG40] Arrow pbk **£2.95**
Cronopias and Famas (1978)
[GG41] Boyars pbk **£8.95**
We Love Glenda So Much (1984)
[GG42] Arrow pbk **£2.50**
Winners
[GG43] Allison & B pbk **£4.95**

DOURADO, AUTRAN (Brazilian)
Bells of Agony
A tale of crime, passion, treason and punishment, strongly threaded with suspense, set in 18th century Brazil.
[GG44] P Owen hbk **£12.95**
Pattern for a Tapestry (1984)
[GG45] P Owen hbk **£10.95**
[GG46] Penguin pbk **£2.95**
Voices of the Dead (1980)
[GG47] P Owen hbk **£10.95**

FUENTES, CARLOS (Mexican, 1928 -   )
Probably the Mexican novelist best known in the West, Fuentes has also worked in the film industry with Buñuel. He explores the dissatisfaction in Mexican society which has followed the failure of the Revolution, and its growing social evil. *The Death of Artemio Cruz* is his finest novel.
Change of Skin (1968)
[GG48] Deutsch pbk **£6.95**
Christopher Unborn (1989)   **NEW**
[GG48A] Deutsch hbk **£12.95**
Distant Relations (1982)
[GG49] Sphere pbk **£2.95**
Myself with Others (Essays, 1988)
[GG50] Picador pbk **£3.99**
Terra Nostra (1977)
The life and times of Philip II, encapsulating both the New World's future and the corrupt decline of Spanish glory.
[GG51] Penguin pbk **£6.99**
The Death of Artemio Cruz (1964)
One of the most important of the recent books from Latin America. Cruz is a vastly wealthy Mexican magnate on his death bed, a man who rose through and then betrayed the Revolution. As the novel progresses, the crucial events of his life are revealed, and a complex picture of Mexican society emerges.
[GG52] Secker hbk **£10.95**
The Good Conscience (1959)
[GG53] Deutsch pbk **£3.95**
The Old Gringo (1986)
Based on the real case of an American journalist who travelled into the Chichuhuaha desert and disappeared. Fuentes vowed that this was his last novel.
[GG54] Picador pbk **£3.50**
Where the Air is Clear (1960)
[GG55] Deutsch pbk **£4.95**

Carlos Fuentes, author of *Myself with Others* (Picador pbk £3.99)

GALEANO, EDUARDO
Days and Nights of Love and War
[GG56] Pluto pbk **£5.50**
MEMORY OF FIRE
Genesis
The first part of his extrordinary trilogy: a stunning fusion of history and imagination.
[GG57] Methuen pbk **£3.95**
Faces and Masks
[GG58] Minerva pbk **£4.99**
Century of Wind   **NEW**
[GG59] Quartet hbk **£14.95**

HOWES, BARBARA (ED)
The Eye of the Heart
42 short stories by some of South America's finest writers.
[GG60] Allison & B pbk **£6.99**

INFANTE, GUILLERMO CABRERA
(Cuban, 1929 -   )
Infante is one of the great modernists writing in Spanish today. He has a densely allusive punning style, and a particular quality of wit that distinguishes him from other Latin American writers. He left Cuba in 1965, and a central preoccupation of his books is the vitality of pre-revolutionary Cuba, compared to its present sterility.
Holy Smoke (Non fiction, 1985)
This idiosyncratic book is an extravagant compendium of miscellaneous information inspired by Infante's love of cigars.
[GG61] Faber pbk **£4.95**
Infante's Inferno (1984)
Semi-autobiographical and sensual novel set in Cuba, charting the narrator's upbringing in a densely-realised Havana of the 1950s.
[GG62] Faber pbk **£4.95**
Three Trapped Tigers
The fond, wondering recollections of a double exile, a man separated by circumstances from his country and by a decade or more from his youth. This is Infante's legendary novel about Havana before Castro's revolution. It has long been recognised as a classic of Latin American fiction.
[GG63] Faber hbk **£11.99**

View of Dawn in the Tropics
[GG64] Faber hbk **£10.95**

IVO, LEDO (Brazilian)
Snake's Nest   **NEW**
A party political allegory: Ivo explores the nature of good and evil, setting his novel in a provincial port in North Eastern Brazil during the Second World War.
[GG65] P Owen hbk **£10.95**

LISPECTOR, CLARICE (Brazilian, 1924 -   )
A Brazilian of Russian origin, Lispector first gained acclaim for her short stories; her major breakthrough came with the publication of *Apple in the Dark*, which painstakingly studies the birth and abandonment of a human consciousness.
Apple in the Dark
[GG66] Virago pbk **£4.95**
Family Ties (Stories, 1985)
[GG67] Carcanet pbk **£3.50**
Foreign Legion (1986)
[GG68] Carcanet hbk **£8.95**
Hour of the Star (1986)
[GG69] Grafton pbk **£2.95**

LLOSA, MARIO VARGAS (Peruvian, 1936 -   )
A former political leftist, Llosa has emerged as a potential conservative Presidential candidate. As he has employed various contemporary literary devices to portray a negative vision of his homeland, Llosa has been described as a pessimist. However underlying his *oeuvre*, are the moralist's hope for reform and the sentimentalist's yearning for resolution. *Aunt Julia and the Scriptwriter* is probably the best introduction to Llosa's complicated framework.
Aunt Julia and the Scriptwriter (1983)
His comic masterpiece juxtaposes the life of a soap-opera writer with the narrator's shocking affair with his cousin who is twenty years older.
[GG70] Faber hbk **£7.95**
[GG71] Picador pbk **£3.95**
Captain Pantoja and the Special Service
[GG72] Faber pbk **£3.95**
The Green House (1966)
[GG73] Picador hbk **£3.95**
The Perpetual Orgy (Non fiction, 1987)
An enlightening study of Flaubert.
[GG74] Faber hbk **£10.95**
The Real Life of Alejandro Mayta (1986)
The narrator is researching an amateurish and bungled attempt at revolution in the 1950s against the backdrop of increasing political anarchy. A powerful vision of the fate which may await Peru.
[GG75] Faber hbk **£9.95**
[GG76] Faber pbk **£3.95**
The War of the End of the World (1985)
This monumental novel based on fact tells of the growth of an apocalyptic sect in North Eastern Brazil in the late 19th Century.
[GG77] Faber hbk **£9.95**
[GG78] Faber pbk **£3.95**
Time of the Hero (1962)
Llosa's first novel, set in a military academy in Lima tells of the 'education' of the first year students by their superiors.
[GG79] Picador pbk **£4.95**
Who Killed Palomino Molero? (1988)
A murder mystery set in Latin America, this is both a witty detective story and a social study.
[GG80] Faber hbk **£9.95**
[GG81] Faber pbk **£3.95**

MALLEA, EDUARDO (Argentinian, 1903 -   )
An important novelist, who has scrupulously avoided any involvement in the political movements that have overrun his country. A most accomplished technician, who at his best allows his deep-seated humanism to assert itself.

All the Green Shall Perish (1941)
His masterpiece, a study of loneliness and disappointment in a woman, with a tragic ending. It has a sense of nostalgia worthy of Proust.
[GG82] Boyars hbk **£5.95**
Chaves & Other Stories
[GG83] Boyars hbk **£5.95**
Fiesta in November (1939)
A protest against fascism, taking place in Mallea's native Buenos Aires. One of his best novels.
[GG84] Boyars pbk **£5.95**

MANGUEL, ALBERTO (ED)
Other Fires: Stories from the Women of Latin America
[GG85] Pan pbk **£3.50**

MARQUEZ, GABRIEL GARCIA
(Colombian, 1928 -)
Since the award of the Nobel Prize in 1982 Marquez has become the best known writer of his continent. His masterwork, *One Hundred Years of Solitude*, like his earlier short stories, is set in Macondo. This fictional town, isolated from reality, is a rough-and-tumble Eden where nothing is impossible. Marquez's dual purposes are to describe its beauty and enchantment and the savage results when outsiders break through to 'civilise' it. Due to his radical politics and friendship with Castro, Marquez is presently banned from entering the US. His most recent novel, as yet untranslated, is a fictional life of Simon Bolivar.
Chronicle of a Death Foretold (1982)
A short oblique novel which charts the inevitable murder of a stranger who is presumed to be responsible for seducing a young girl. It analyses the harsh unwritten laws of Latin America.
[GG86] Cape hbk **£9.95**
[GG87] Picador pbk **£3.50**
Clandestine in Chile (Non fiction)   **NEW**
Marquez writes about the Chilean film director Miguel Littin, who risked his freedom to bring the world a truer picture of life under Pinochet, by returning in disguise to the country he had fled in 1973. Marquez wrote this study on the basis of 18 hours of taped interviews: it presents a valuable insight both into the writer himself, and the state of Latin America today.
[GG87A] Viking hbk **£10.95**
In Evil Hour (1966)
The inhabitants of Macondo are driven into a frenzy by a series of anonymous scandalous posters.
[GG88] Cape hbk **£9.95**
[GG89] Picador pbk **£3.95**
Innocent Erendira (Stories, 1979)
The title-story of this collection is one of the most powerful of all Marquez's stories. It tells of a girl who, by mistake, burns down her Grandmother's house; her Grandmother then takes her round the country as a prostitute until she can pay off the debt.
[GG90] Cape hbk **£9.95**
[GG91] Picador pbk **£3.50**
Leaf Storm (1955)
A portrayal of the rottenness and ruin of Macondo in a series of interior reminiscences.
[GG92] Picador pbk **£3.95**
Love in the Time of Cholera (1988)
Dr. Juvenal Urbino, the most distinguished physician along the Caribbean coast, dies when he falls from a tree trying to catch a parrot. His wife, enraged at the emptiness before her, recoils from the one hand extended to comfort her, that of Florentino Ariza whose vigil of devotion had begun half a century earlier.
[GG94] Cape hbk **£11.95**
[GG93] Penguin pbk **£3.99**
No One Writes to the Colonel (1961)
His first short novel, set in Macondo, is about an eccentric old colonel who waits for a pension that never arrives.
[GG95] Picador pbk **£3.99**

One Hundred Years of Solitude (1970)
[GG96] Cape hbk **£11.95**
[GG97] Picador pbk **£4.95**
The Autumn of the Patriarch (1977)
Written in a dense allusive style, this portrays a crazy but all-powerful South American dictator. Though intimidating because of the scarceness of punctuation, it is a compelling work.
[GG98] Cape hbk **£9.95**
[GG99] Picador pbk **£3.50**
The Story of a Shipwrecked Sailor (1986)
[GG100] Cape hbk **£8.95**

MOYANO, DANIEL (Argentinian)
The Devil's Trill
The first novel to be published in this country by this Argentinian novelist, who has been influenced by Borges. It is the story of a prodigious violinist whose music threatens the silence imposed by the dictatorship.
[GG101] Serpent's Tail pbk **£6.95**

NUNEZ, RAUL
The Lonely Hearts Club (1986)
An original and humorous novel, telling of a night porter in a sleazy Barcelona hotel, whose only advantage is his resemblance to Frank Sinatra.
[GG102] Serpent's Tail pbk **£6.95**

PUIG, MANUEL (Argentinian)
Since the success of *Kiss of the Spider Woman*, Puig's work has gone from strength to strength: Faber have recently made available two more works, both stories involving sexual passion and violence.
Blood of Requited Love (1988)
Puig paints a fascinating and disturbing picture of a lover's quest for satisfaction, passion and violence.
[GG104] Faber pbk **£4.99**
Kiss of the Spider Woman (1984)
The relationship of a criminal and a homosexual in prison. The success of the film, directed by Hector Babenco, brought Puig's work to a wider audience.
[GG105] Arrow pbk **£2.95**
Pubis Angelical (1987)
A *tour de force* of sexual obsession and paranoia.
[GG106] Faber hbk **£9.95**
The Buenos Aires Affair (1988)
A gripping thriller which involves the abduction of a woman, an insidious threat of sexual violence and passion.
[GG107] Faber pbk **£4.99**

RAMIREZ, SERGIO (Nicaraguan)
Currently vice-president of Nicaragua and an established poet. *To Bury Our Fathers* is an ambitious panoramic novel set in the early Somoza era showing the deep-seated corruption of the military regime.
Stories (1986)
[GG108] Reader's Int pbk **£3.95**
To Bury Our Fathers (1985)
[GG109] Reader's Int pbk **£5.95**

RAMOS, GRACILIANO (Brazilian, 1892 - 1953)
A major Brazilian novelist, and successor to Machado de Assis, Ramos writes with remarkable psychological penetration and formidable intelligence; his involvement in, or at least knowledge of, the 1936 coup against Vargas, led to his imprisonment and torture, and the wrecking of his health, so that he wrote little except short stories in the latter part of his life.
Childhood
[GG110] P Owen hbk **£10.95**
Sao Bernardo (1934)
A comic but disturbing story of a man's inability to change himself, prevented from responding to others

because of the rigidity of his social position, and unable to create anything which comes spontaneously from himself.
[GG111] P Owen hbk **£9.95**

RIBEIRO, JOAO UBALDO (Brazilian)
An Invincible Memory   **NEW**
An epic best-seller in Brazil. It involves a family saga, covering nearly four hundred years, from the arrival of the Portuguese in Brazil to the present day. Jorge Amado has written of it: 'I don't know of any Brazilian novel published in the last 20 years more beautifully written or more important...Altogether universal.'
[GG112] Faber hbk **£12.99**
Sergeant Getulio (1986)
[GG113] Faber pbk **£3.95**

RIVABELLA, OMAR (Argentinian)
Requiem for a Woman's Soul (1987)
Recent and powerful story of prison experiences under the Argentinian military regime. It tells of the tortures a woman must witness before her own death.
[GG114] Penguin pbk **£3.50**

ROSA, RODRIGO REY (Guatemalan)
Dust on Her Tongue   **NEW**
A new collection of stories, which hauntingly evoke disturbing events in the lives of ordinary people.
[GG115] P Owen hbk **£8.95**
The Beggar's Knife
26 stories from one of Guatemala's most talented young writers. Peopled with sorcerers, ghosts and assassins, they are at once brutal and strongly lyrical. Translated by Paul Bowles.
[GG116] P Owen pbk **£4.50**

SORIANO, OSVALDO
Funny Dirty Little War (1986)
[GG117] Reader's Int hbk **£3.95**

VALENZUELA, LUISA (Argentinian)
The Lizard's Tail
The fictional biography of one of Peron's ministers, the 'minister for well being', who ruled through sorcery and butchered his compatriots. Valenzuela lives in New York, in exile from her native Argentina.
[GG118] Serpent's Tail pbk **£7.95**

Mario Vargas Llosa, author of *The War at the End of the World* (Faber hbk £9.95, pbk £3.95) (Photo: Jerry Bauer)

WORLD FICTION

ABE, KOBO (Japanese, 1924 -)
Japan's foremost living novelist; his most famous work *Woman of the Dunes* won him the Yomiori prize for literature, and has been made into a successful film. His most recent novel, *The Ark Sakura*, was described by one critic as 'a cross between Kafka and Alice in Wonderland'.
Secret Rendezvous
[GH1] Secker hbk **£8.95**
The Ark Sakura
[GH2] Secker hbk **£11.95**
Woman in the Dunes
[GH3] Oxford pbk **£3.95**

ANG, LI (Chinese)
The Butcher's Wife `NEW`
Li Shi, a young peasant women, is forced into an arranged marriage with a sadistic pig butcher. Brutalized by her husband, she is driven to madness and finally to homicide. The novel's appearance in 1930 aroused controversy for its vivid portrayal of sexual violence and emotional cruelty.
[GH4] P Owen hbk **£10.95**

ANON (Japanese)
The Tale of the Lady Ochikubo
The first Japanese novel, a 10th Century classic.
[GH5] P Owen hbk **£10.95**

ANYI, WANG (Chinese, 1954 -)
Baotown `NEW`
Written in 1984, *Baotown* is now recognized as one of the best post-revolutionary works of Chinese literature: it portrays life in an isolated village of central China through a series of short, detailed vignettes.
[GH6] Viking hbk **£11.95**

BANERJI, BHIBHUTIBHUSAN (Indian)
Pather Panchali
This classic tale of Bengali peasant life was the basis for Satyajit Ray's great film trilogy.
[GH7] Lokamaya P pbk **£4.95**

CAO XUEQIN (Chinese, c.1716 - 64)
The Dream of Red Mansions
An abridged edition of *The Story of the Stone*.
[GH10] Unwin pbk **£7.95**
The Story of the Stone Vol 1
This great 18th Century Chinese novel of manners is the story of the greatness and decline of the Jia family, with an extended analysis of their many relationships. A rich tapestry of humour and poetry, which benefits from an excellent translation.
[GH11] Penguin pbk **£6.95**
Vol 2
[GH12] Penguin pbk **£6.95**
Vol 3
[GH13] Penguin pbk **£5.95**
Vol 4
[GH14] Penguin pbk **£5.95**
Vol 5
[GH15] Penguin pbk **£5.95**

CHATTERJEE, UPAMANYU (Indian)
English, August: Agastya Sen
The funny and observant story of a civil servant sent for a year to a small Indian provincial town, and of the way the experience changes his character and view of the world.
[GH16] Faber pbk **£4.95**

DESAI, ANITA (Indian, 1937 -)
Desai is a widely-acclaimed Indian novelist whose works, since the publication of her first novel *Cry the Peacock* in 1963, have described the changing position of women in a society which is itself developing rapidly (*In Custody*, her first novel centred on a male character, is less successful). She has twice been shortlisted for the Booker Prize; her best work includes *Clear Light of Day* and her most recent novel *Baumgartner's Bombay*.
Baumgartner's Bombay
[GH17] Penguin pbk **£4.50**
Clear Light of Day (1980)
[GH18] Penguin pbk **£3.95**
Cry the Peacock
[GH19] Vision pbk **£2.95**
Fire on the Mountain (1977)
[GH20] Penguin pbk **£3.50**
Games at Twilight (1978)
[GH21] Penguin pbk **£3.50**
In Custody (1984)
[GH22] Penguin pbk **£3.95**
Village by the Sea (1982)
[GH23] Penguin pbk **£3.50**

DESANI, G.V. (Indian, 1909 -)
All About H Hatterr (1948)
Desani's single novel tells of the quixotic life and behaviour of its hero, like Desani himself an Anglo-Malay who lives as an Indian. Acclaimed by Saul Bellow as a great 'forgotten' book.
[GH24] Penguin pbk **£4.95**

DESHPANDE, SHASHI (Indian)
That Long Silence
On a retreat into the country near Bombay a middle-class Indian woman is haunted by self-questioning about her past.
[GH28] Virago pbk **£5.50**

ENDO, SHUSAKU (Japanese, 1923 -)
Outside his native Japan Endo's books have been published in 25 languages. His Catholicism - unusual for Japan - has influenced his work, which manages to fuse the literary traditions of East and West in a way rarely achieved by others. *Scandal*, which appeared in English in 1988, was singled out for special praise in the West.
A Life of Jesus (Non fiction) `NEW`
[GH29] P Owen hbk **£13.95**
Foreign Studies `NEW`
This early novel works through three thematically linked narratives set in different periods of history: a student in France in the 1950s, a Japanese Catholic in 17th century Rome and a Japanese de Sade scholar in France after the Second World War.
[GH30] P Owen hbk **£11.95**
Golden Country
[GH31] Tuttle hbk **£5.25**
Scandal
[GH32] P Owen hbk **£12.95**
Silence
[GH33] Quartet pbk **£1.50**
Stained Glass Elegies (Stories)
[GH34] Penguin pbk **£3.99**
The Golden Country (Play) `NEW`
Endo's three-act play, set in 1633, concerns a Jesuit missionary who chooses to apostasize rather than face an agonizing death. It recalls themes of faith and commitment found in earlier novels, such as *Silence*, because of which Endo's work has often been compared to that of Greene.
[GH35] P Owen hbk **£11.95**
The Samurai
[GH36] Penguin pbk **£3.95**
The Sea and Poison
[GH37] Quartet pbk **£1.95**
Volcano
[GH38] Quartet pbk **£2.50**
When I Whistle
[GH39] Quartet pbk **£2.95**
Wonderful Fool
[GH40] Quartet pbk **£2.25**

Anita Desai, author of *Village by the Sea* (Penguin pbk **£3.50**)

GHOSE, ZULFIKAR (Indian, 1935 -)
The only fictional work available in England by the Indian critic and novelist, whose work, centred around an international nexus of India-England-America, mirrors his own experience - having left India for England, he now lives in the United States.
Figures of Enchantment (1986)
[GH41] Hutchinson hbk **£11.95**

INOUE, YASUSHI (Japanese)
The Counterfeiter collects three stories by one of Japan's leading contemporary writers, in which he explores with subtlety and compassion the lives and preoccupations of his characters. *The Hunting Gun*, a short novel set at the end of WWII, describes, from alternating points of view, the complexities of a man's relationship with three women.
The Counterfeiter `NEW`
[GH42] P Owen hbk **£10.95**
The Hunting Gun `NEW`
[GH43] P Owen hbk **£8.95**

JELLOUN, TAHAR BEN (Moroccan)
Jelloun's new novel, *The Sacred Night*, won the Prix Goncourt in 1987, and is the sequel to *The Sand Child*. In a dream-like narrative, Jelloun releates the adult life of Zahra, who in a corrupt, unjust and enslaving society struggles to be reborn and purified.
The Sand Child
[GH44] Quartet pbk **£11.95**
The Sacred Night `NEW`
[GH45] Quartet hbk **£11.95**

JHABVALA, RUTH PRAWER
(Indian, 1927 -)
"To live in India and be at peace, one must to a very considerable extent become Indian and adopt Indian attitudes, beliefs and habits...How is this possible? And, if it is possible, is it desirable?" Jhabvala has lived in India for many years, and her work charts, often with an element of satire, the irrationality of human behaviour - both of Indians and Europeans, and the strange manners in which the two races have interacted. She has worked with consistent success as a scriptwriter for Merchant-Ivory. Her novel *Heat and Dust* won the Booker Prize in 1975.
Backward Place (1965)
[GH46] Penguin pbk **£3.95**
Esmond in India
[GH47] Penguin pbk **£3.95**
Get Ready for Battle
[GH48] Penguin pbk **£3.50**
Heat and Dust (1975)
[GH49] J Murray hbk **£9.95**
[GH50] Futura pbk **£2.99**
Householder
[GH51] Penguin pbk **£2.95**
How I Became a Holy Mother
(Stories, 1976)
[GH52] Penguin pbk **£3.95**

Ruth Prawer Jhabvala, author of *Three Continents* (Penguin pbk £4.99)

In Search of Love and Beauty
[GH53] Penguin pbk **£3.95**
Like Birds Like Fishes
[GH54] Grafton pbk **£2.50**
Nature of Passion
[GH55] Penguin pbk **£3.95**
New Dominion
[GH56] Grafton pbk **£2.50**
Out of India (Stories)
[GH57] Penguin pbk **£4.50**
Stronger Climate
[GH58] Grafton pbk **£2.50**
Three Continents
The story of a group of wealthy Indians drawn into a small religious cult, this is Jhabvala's most recent work.
[GH59] Penguin pbk **£4.99**
To Whom She Will (1985)
[GH60] Penguin pbk **£3.95**

KAIKO, TAKESHI (Japanese)
Darkness in Summer
A tender and haunting novel about the attempts of two re-united former lovers to rekindle their mutual passion and overcome their present unhappiness.
[GH61] P Owen hbk **£12.95**
Five Thousand Runaways   NEW
[GH62] P Owen hbk **£11.95**

KAWABATA, YASUNARI
(Japanese, 1899 - 1972)
Four years after becoming Japan's only Nobel Prize winner, Kawabata took his own life. A leading New Perceptionist, he represents a rare combination of tradition and modernity, exploring the more bizarre extremes of erotic behaviour.
Beauty and Sadness
[GH63] Secker pbk **£10.95**
Izu Dancer (1926)
[GH64] Tuttle pbk **£5.95**
Lake
[GH65] P Owen hbk **£9.95**
Master of Go
[GH66] Penguin pbk **£3.50**

LUBIS, MOCHTAR (Indonesian, 1922 -)
An Indonesian writer, whose episodic novel *Twilight in Djakarta* presents a harshly critical analysis of that country under Sukarno.

The Outlaw & Other Stories
[GH67] Oxford pbk **£8.95**
Twilight in Djakarta
[GH68] Oxford pbk **£8.50**

MAHFOUZ, NAGIB (Egyptian, 1912 -)
Winner of the 1988 Nobel Prize for Literature. Although relatively unknown in the West, Mahfouz is one of the most important and well-respected of contemporary Arab writers. His trilogy (1956 - 57) chronicling life in Cairo between the wars laid the foundations for the urban Egyptian novel, though in recent years his own work has become more openly experimental.
Children of Gebelawi
[GH69] Heinemann pbk **£4.25**
Midaq Alley
[GH70] Heinemann pbk **£3.50**
Miramar
[GH71] Heinemann pbk **£3.50**

MANTO, SAADAT HASAN
(Indian, 1912 - 1955)
One of the most popular short story writers in India and Pakistan, Manto brings a humane irony to his tales of outsiders and social outcasts.
Kingdom's End & Other Stories
[GH72] Verso hbk **£11.95**

MARUYA, SAIICHI (Japanese)
'One of the major comic novelists of our day, a revealer of essences, a universal voice...' (Anthony Burgess)
Singular Rebellion
This story of a middle-aged businessman's marriage bursts with comic characters and provides a warm and tolerant portrait of modern Japan.
[GH73] Deutsch hbk **£12.95**

MEHTA, GITA (Indian)
Raj   NEW
The remarkable story of an Indian princess who grows up in the ancient traditions of the Royal House of Balmer but is gradually forced to re-evaluate the traditions of her forefathers, becoming an admirer of Gandhi and finally arriving at the heart of India's bloody struggle for independence.
[GH74] Cape hbk **£11.95**

MISHIMA, YUKIO (Japanese, 1925 - 70)
Long before his ritual suicide, Mishima had established himself as the first Japanese writer whose fame was world-wide. His work shows a high degree of Western influence, mixed with an obsession with homo-erotic fantasies, extreme right-wing politics and a view of the contemporary decline of Japan. The novel *Confessions of a Mask*, and the stories *Death in Midsummer*, provide a good introduction to his work.
Confessions of a Mask (1949)
[GH75] P Owen hbk **£10.50**
[GH76] Grafton pbk **£2.95**
Death in Midsummer (Stories)
[GH77] Penguin pbk **£3.95**
Forbidden Colours
[GH78] Penguin pbk **£4.95**
Sailor Who Fell from Grace with the Sea (1963)
A child tortures a sailor who wants to marry his mother, secure in the knowledge that as a minor he will not be held responsible.
[GH79] Penguin pbk **£3.95**
Temple of Dawn
[GH80] Secker hbk **£10.95**
Temple of the Golden Pavilion (1956)
A trainee-priest burns down the temple he is studying in. A powerful psychological exploration.
[GH81] Penguin pbk **£3.95**

The Sea of Fertility (1965-71)
Mishima's magnum opus, a four-novel work which builds up a magnificent view of 20th century Japan.
[GH82] Secker hbk **£18.00**
[GH83] Penguin pbk **£9.95**
Thirst for Love (1950)
[GH84] Penguin pbk **£3.50**

MRABET, MOHAMMED (Moroccan, 1940 -)
Born in the Rif Mountains of North Africa, Mrabet has lived for much of his life in Tangier. His work, originally in the Moghrebi dialect, is told orally, to be taped and subsequently translated by his friend and collaborator, the expatriate American novelist Paul Bowles.
Beach Cafe/The Voice (1980)
[GH85] B Sparrow pbk **£3.95**
Harmless Poisons Blameless Sins (1976)
[GH86] B Sparrow hbk **£8.50**
Look and Move On   NEW
[GH87] P Owen hbk **£12.95**
M'Hashish
[GH88] P Owen pbk **£4.50**
The Big Mirror   NEW
[GH91] P Owen pbk **£4.95**
The Lemon (1969)
[GH89] P Owen hbk **£9.95**
[GH90] City lights pbk **£5.95**

MURARI, T.N. (Indian)
Born in Madras, Murari divides his time betwen India and London. His two most recent works, *The Imperial Agent* and *The Last Victory*, continue the story of Kimball O'Hara - more famous as the hero of Kipling's *Kim*.
Lovers Are Not People (1978)
[GH93] Sphere pbk **£2.99**
Taj
[GH94] Hodder pbk **£3.50**
The Imperial Agent
[GH95] Hodder pbk **£3.95**
The Last Victory
[GH96] Hodder hbk **£12.95**
The Shooter
[GH97] Hodder pbk **£1.95**

MURASAKI, LADY (Japanese, 980 - 1030)
An early Japanese novelist and diarist, whose experiences at court provided material for her masterpiece, *Tale of Genji*.
Tale of Genji
The most important work of classical Japanese literature; it is a long and magnificent tale of the amorous adventures of Prince Genji, told in a subtle and allusive style and set against an imaginary court background.
[GH98] Secker hbk **£35.00**
[GH99] Penguin pbk **£14.95**

NAMJOSHI, SUNITI (Japanese)
Namjoshi is renowned as a poet, satirist and artful feminist fabulist: *The Blue Donkey Fables* provide the best introduction to her work.
Conversations of Cow
[GH100] Women's P pbk **£2.95**
The Blue Donkey Fables
[GH101] Women's P pbk **£3.95**

NARAYAN, R.K. (Indian, 1906 -)
A Hindu novelist writing in English whose best works (such as *The Vendor of Sweets*) encompass a power and finesse which make him at least an equal to Naipaul. The fictitious town and community which he creates, Malgudi, extends over a series of loosely connected novels .
Bachelor of the Arts
[GH102] Chicago UP pbk **£6.95**
Dark Room
[GH103] Chicago UP pbk **£3.50**

English Teacher (1945)
[GH104] Chicago UP pbk **£7.95**
Financial Expert (1952)
[GH105] Chicago UP pbk **£7.25**
Gods, Demons and Others
[GH106] Vision pbk **£4.95**
Malgudi Days
[GH107] Penguin pbk **£3.95**
Man-Eater of Malgudi (1961)
[GH108] Penguin pbk **£3.50**
Mr Sampath and the Printer of Malgudi
[GH109] Chicago UP **£3.50**
Painter of Signs
[GH110] Penguin pbk **£3.50**
Swami and Friends
[GH111] Chicago UP pbk **£5.50**
Talkative Man
[GH112] Penguin pbk **£3.50**
The Guide (1958)
The tragi-comic story of a con-man. One of Narayan's best and most complex novels.
[GH113] Penguin pbk **£3.95**
The Vendor of Sweets
[GH114] Penguin pbk **£3.50**
Tiger for Malgudi
[GH115] Penguin pbk **£3.99**
Under the Banyan Tree
[GH116] Penguin pbk **£3.99**

OE, KENZABURO (Japanese)
One of the new generation of Japanese writers who has gained notoriety for involvement in radical causes. His writing focuses on themes of madness and idiocy, in the light of the aftermath of Hiroshima and Japan's post-war economic miracle.
Fire from the Ashes: Short Stories about Hiroshima & Nagasaki `NEW`
[GH117] Readers Int hbk **£8.95**
[GH118] Readers Int pbk **£3.50**
Teach Us to Outgrow Our Madness
[GH119] Boyars hbk **£8.95**
The Silent Cry
The narrator attempts to find a new life in the countryside, only to be haunted by the urban ghosts of the past.
[GH120] Serpent's Tail pbk **£7.95**

RAY, SATYAJIT (Indian, 1921 -)
Stories (1987)
Ray is one of Bengal's bestselling authors, as well as a great film director. His stories are mainly imaginative, and show a rare gift of fantasy.
[GH121] Penguin pbk **£3.99**

SAADAWI, NAWAL EL- (Egyptian, 1930 -)
Egyptian novelist, doctor and militant writer on Arab women's problems and their struggle for liberation, whose work has evoked the antagonism of highly-placed political and theological authorities - Saadawi lost first her job with the Ministry of Health, and then her liberty, under the Sadat régime.
Death of An Ex-Minister (1987)
[GH122] Methuen pbk **£2.95**
God Dies by the Nile (1985)
[GH123] Zed pbk **£3.95**
Memoirs of a Woman Doctor (1957)
Saadawi's first novel not translated until thirty years after its publication.
[GH124] Saqi pbk **£3.50**
She Has No Place In Paradise (1987)
[GH125] Methuen pbk **£3.95**
The Fall of the Imam
Saadawi's most recent novel presents a devastating vision of the structures of authority in an imaginary Arab country.
[GH126] Methuen hbk **£10.95**

The Hidden Face of Eve (Non fiction)
A classic study of women in Islam.
[GH127] Zed pbk **£5.95**
Two Women in One (1985)
[GH128] Zed pbk **£3.95**
Woman at Point Zero (1975)
[GH129] Zed pbk **£3.95**

SAHGAL, NAYANTARA (Indian, 1927 -)
The niece of Nehru, Sahgal writes perceptively on Indian politics and society. Her more recent work, *Plans for Departure* and *Mistaken Identity* (1988) has brought a new sweep to her work.
Mistaken Identity
In 1929, an Indian playboy is arrested and while waiting for trial tells his life story.
[GH130] Heinemann hbk **£10.95**
Plans for Departure
[GH131] Heinemann hbk **£9.95**
Rich Like Us
[GH132] Hodder pbk **£3.95**

SEI SHONAGAN (Japanese)
Little is known about this female writer whose work flourished around 1000 AD. Her book is a collection of scathing comments about individuals and other observations, which are still entertaining today.
Pillow Book of Sei Shonagan
[GH133] Penguin pbk **£4.95**

SOSEKI, NATSUME (Japanese, 1867 - 1916)
The greatest of Japanese novelists, Soseki embodies a yearning for calm and resignation, as well as a realisation that such states were, for him, unlikely. The treatment of his characters is subtle and original, and the bitterness inspired in him by isolation is tempered by an inherent gentleness. His novels offer intensely moving portraits of the fundamental loneliness of humans.
Botchan (1906)
[GH134] Tuttle pbk **£6.95**
I am a Cat
[GH135] P Owen hbk **£13.95**
Kokoro ('Heart') (1914)
[GH136] Arrow pbk **£2.95**
Light and Darkness (1916)
[GH137] P Owen hbk **£12.95**
Mon (1910)
[GH138] P Owen hbk **£12.95**
Three Cornered World
[GH139] Arrow pbk **£1.95**

SUYIN, HAN (Chinese)
Chinese historian and biographer, whose epic novels are convincing and intelligent.
A Many Splendoured Thing
[GH140] Grafton pbk **£2.95**
And the Rain My Drink
[GH141] Grafton pbk **£2.95**
Four Faces
[GH142] Grafton pbk **£2.95**
The Enchantress
[GH143] Bantam pbk **£2.95**
The Mountain Is Young
[GH144] Grafton pbk **£3.95**
Till Morning Comes
[GH145] Bantam pbk **£3.50**

TAGORE, RABINDRANATH
(Indian, 1861 - 1941)
Novelist, poet, painter, dramatist and musician, Tagore was a major Bengali writer, and the first Asian winner of the Nobel Prize for literature, in 1913.
Home and the World
Setting domestic conflict between husband and wife against a background of regional strife, Tagore's novel was the basis for one of Satyajit Ray's greatest films.
[GH146] Penguin pbk **£4.95**

Hungry Stones and Other Stories
[GH147] Macmillan pbk **£1.25**

TANIZAKI, JUNICHIRO
(Japanese, 1886 - 1965)
Tanizaki's novels reflect a fondness for the past, set against the losses suffered in the course of modernization, the transition betweeen the two often being explored in psychological-sexual terms. The implications of his work in the first half of the century evoked wide attention.
Diary of a Mad Old Man (1962)
[GH148] Oxford pbk **£3.95**
Naomi
[GH149] Pan pbk **£2.95**
Some Prefer Nettles/The Secret History of the Lord of Mushashi/Arrowroot
[GH150] Picador pbk **£3.95**
The Key (1960)
[GH151] Fontana pbk **£2.50**
The Makioka Sisters (1943-8)
[GH152] Picador pbk **£3.95**

TOGAWA, MASAKO (Japanese)
An essayist who has been described as the P.D. James of Japan. *The Lady Killer* lifts the lid on modern Japanese nightspots and their habitués.
Kiss of Fire
[GH153] Chatto hbk **£11.95**
The Lady Killer
[GH154] Penguin pbk **£2.50**

TSHUSHIMA, YUKO (Japanese)
Tshushima's reputation as one of Japan's most remarkable young writers is based on her short fiction. Her stories look at the frustrations and unhappiness of women in Japan.
Child of Fortune
[GH155] Women's P pbk **£3.95**
The Shooting Gallery & Other Stories
[GH156] Women's P pbk **£3.95**

XIANLIANG, ZHANG (Chinese)
Half of Man is Woman
The story of a man's experiences in an agricultural labour camp in the north-west of China, this caused tremendous controversy when published in 1985, for its political content as well as its explicit sexual material.
[GH157] Viking hbk **£11.95**

YEH, CHUN-CHAN (Chinese)
Quiet Are the Mountains Vol 1: The Mountain Village `NEW`
A remarkable trilogy, *Quiet Are the Mountains* is set in rural China at the beginning of the Communist Revolution; in this and the second volume, the consciousness of the protagonist Chun-Sheng, and his fellow villagers, once docile, develops towards action.
[GH158] Faber pbk **£4.99**
Vol 2: The Open Fields `NEW`
[GH159] Faber pbk **£4.99**
Vol 3: A Distant Journey `NEW`
Takes the reader up to the start of the Long March, and completes the retelling of the origins of the Chinese Revolution.
[GH160] Faber pbk **£4.99**

ZHANG JIE (Chinese)
One of China's most popular writers, whose stories satirise the abuses and hypocrisies of contemporary Chinese society.
As Long as Nothing Happens, Nothing Will (1988)
[GH161] Virago pbk **£4.50**
Leaden Wings
[GH162] Virago pbk **£3.95**

The Nobel Prize

The most prestigious international prize of all, the Nobel Prize was established by Alfred Nobel (1833 - 1896), a distinguished Swedish chemist who stipulated in his will that prizes be awarded annually in the fields of Literature, Science and to the person who has most promoted 'the fraternity of nations' - the Nobel Peace Prize. The Nobel Prize for Literature is conferred on anyone judged to have produced 'the most outstanding work of an idealistic tendency' over the previous year, with reference to an author's *oeuvre* as a whole, rather than one particular work. Winning a Nobel Laureate is perhaps the highest accolade any living author can receive, and ensures world recognition. However, a look at the list of Laureates reveals that there have been some unexpected winners alongside the more obvious literary giants like W.B. Yeats and Thomas Mann, and there have been some curious omissions including Marcel Proust and James Joyce.

Winners of the prize for literature since its inception have been as follows:

1901	Réné-Francois-Armand Sully-Prudhomme (Switzerland)
1902	Theodor Mommsen (Germany)
1903	Bjørnstjerne Bjørnson (Norway)
1904	José Echegaray (Spain)/Frédéric Mistral (France)
1905	Henryk Sienkiewicz (Poland)
1906	Giosué Carducci (Italy)
1907	Rudyard Kipling (Great Britain)
1908	Rudolf Eucken (Germany)
1909	Selma Lagerlöf (Sweden)
1910	Paul Heyse (Germany)
1911	Maurice Maeterlinck (Belgium)
1912	Gerhart Hauptmann (Germany)
1913	Rabindranath Tagore (India)
1914	No award
1915	Romain Rolland (France)
1916	Verner von Heidenstam (Sweden)
1917	Karl Gjellerup (Denmark)/Henrik Pontoppidan (Denmark)
1918	No award
1919	Carl Spitteler (Switzerland)
1920	Knut Hamsun (Norway)
1921	Anatole France (France)
1922	Jacinto Benavente y Martinez (Spain)
1923	William Butler Yeats (Ireland)
1924	Wladyslaw Reymont (Poland)
1925	George Bernard Shaw (Great Britain)
1926	Grazia Deledda (Italy)
1927	Henri Bergson (France)
1928	Sigrid Undset (Norway)
1929	Thomas Mann (Germany)
1930	Sinclair Lewis (United States)
1931	Erik Axel Karlfeldt (Sweden)
1932	John Galsworthy (Great Britain)
1933	Ivan Bunin (stateless)
1934	Luigi Pirandello (Italy)
1935	No award
1936	Eugene O'Neill (United States)
1937	Roger Martin du Gard (France)
1938	Pearl S. Buck (United States)
1939	F.E. Sillanpää (Finland)
1940-3	No awards
1944	Johannes V. Jensen (Denmark)
1945	Gabriela Mistral (Chile)
1946	Herman Hesse (Switzerland)
1947	André Gide (France)
1948	T.S. Eliot (Great Britain)
1949	William Faulkner (United States)
1950	Bertrand Russell (Great Britain)
1951	Pär Lagerkvist (Sweden)
1952	François Mauriac (France)
1953	Winston S. Churchill (Great Britain)
1954	Ernest Hemingway (United States)
1955	Halldór Laxness (Iceland)
1956	Juan Ramón Jiménez (Spain)
1957	Albert Camus (France)
1958	Boris Pasternak (USSR; declined prize)
1959	Salvatore Quasimodo (Italy)
1960	Saint-John Perse (France)
1961	Ivo Andric (Yugoslavia)
1962	John Steinbeck (United States)
1963	George Seferis (Greece)
1964	Jean-Paul Sartre (France)
1965	Mikhail Sholokhov (USSR)
1966	Shmuel Y. Agnon (Israel)/Nelly Sachs (Germany)
1967	Miguel Angel Asturias (Guatemala)
1968	Yasunari Kawabata (Japan)
1969	Samuel Beckett (Ireland)
1970	Alexander Solzhenitsyn (USSR)
1971	Pablo Neruda (Chile)
1972	Heinrich Böll (Federal Republic of Germany)
1973	Patrick White (Australia)
1974	Eyvind Johnson (Sweden)/Harry Martinson (Sweden)
1975	Eugenio Montale (Italy)
1976	Saul Bellow (United States)
1977	Vincente Aleixandre (Spain)
1978	Isaac Bashevis Singer (United States)
1979	Odysseus Elytis (Greece)
1980	Czeslaw Milosz (Poland/United States)
1981	Elias Canetti (Austria)
1982	Gabriel García Márquez (Colombia)
1983	William Golding (Great Britain)
1984	Jaroslav Seifert (Czechoslovakia)
1985	Claude Simon (France)
1986	Wole Soyinka (Nigeria)
1987	Joseph Brodsky (USSR)
1988	Naguib Mahfouz (Egypt)

The Hawthornden Prize

The oldest British literary prize, the Hawthornden was founded by Alice Warrender in 1919 and is awarded annually for a work of imaginative literature published by a British author under forty-one years of age. It is one of the few prizes for which books do not have to be specially submitted and the 'imaginative' category is wide enough to include biography (Waugh's *Edmund Campion*), history (Horne's *The Price of Glory*), essays (Sacks's *Awakenings*) and travel literature (Chatwin's *In Patagonia*) as well as fiction and verse.

1919	Edward Shanks *The Queen of China*
1920	John Freeman *Poems New and Old*
1921	Romer Wilson *The Death of Society*
1922	Edmund Blunden *The Shepherd*
1923	David Garnett *Lady into Fox*
1924	Ralph Hale Mottram *The Spanish Farm*
1925	Sean O'Casey *Juno and the Paycock*
1926	Vita Sackville-West *The Land*
1927	Henry Wil'iamson *Tarka the Otter*
1928	Siegfried Sassoon *Memoirs of A Fox-Hunting Man*
1929	Lord David Cecil *The Stricken Deer*
1930	Geoffrey Dennis *The End of the World*
1931	Kate O'Brien *Without My Cloak*
1932	Charles Morgan *The Fountain*
1933	Vita Sackville-West *Collected Poems*
1934	James Hilton *Lost Horizon*
1935	Robert Graves *I, Claudius*
1936	Evelyn Waugh *Edmund Campion*
1937	Ruth Pitter *A Trophy of Arms*
1938	David Jones *In Parenthesis*
1939	Christopher Hassall *Penthesperon*
1940	James Pope-Hennessy *London Fabric*
1942	John Llewellyn-Rhys *England is My Village*
1943	Sidney Keyes *The Cruel Solstice and the Iron Laurel*
1944	Martyn Skinner *Letters to Malaya*
1958	Dom Moraes *A Beginning*
1960	Alan Sillitoe *The Loneliness of the Long Distance Runner*
1961	Ted Hughes *Lupercal*
1962	Robert Shaw *The Sun Doctor*
1963	Alistair Horne *The Price of Glory: Verdun 1916*
1964	V S Naipaul *Mr Stone and the Knight's Companion*
1965	William Trevor *The Old Boys*
1967	Michael Frayn *The Russian Interpreter*
1968	Michael Levey *The Early Renaissance*
1969	Geoffrey Hill *King Log*
1970	Piers Paul Read *Monk Dawson*
1974	Oliver Sacks *Awakenings*
1975	David Lodge *Changing Places*
1976	Robert Nye *Falstaff*
1977	Bruce Chatwin *In Patagonia*
1978	David Cook *Walter*
1979	P S Rusforth *Kindergarten*
1980	Christopher Reid *Arcadia*
1981	Douglas Dunn *St Kilda's Parliament*
1982	Timothy Mo *Sour Sweet*
1983	Jonathan Keates *Allegro Postillions*
1988	Colin Thubron *Behind the Wall*
1989	Alan Bennett *Talking Heads*

PRIZES

ADVENTURE FICTION

AELLEN, RICHARD
Red Eye **NEW**
Journalist Paul Stafford's world is turned upside-down when he discovers that the dream-inspired murder stories he has written are factual recountings of real-life hits on American intelligence agents.
[GJ1] H Hamilton **£11.95**

ALLEBURY, TED
During and after the Second World War, Ted Allebury served as an officer in the Intelligence Corps. This inside knowledge has added authenticity and realism to his classic espionage thrillers.
A Choice of Enemies
[GJ2] Grafton pbk **£2.50**
A Wilderness of Mirrors
A loyal SIS officer is ordered to carry out the kidnapping of a girl from the other side of the Wall. But the operation collapses when he discovers what his superiors plan to do with the girl.
[GJ3] Hodder hbk **£11.95**
All Our Tomorrows
[GJ4] Grafton pbk **£2.50**
Alpha List
[GJ5] Grafton pbk **£1.95**
Children of Tender Years
On an apparently routine mission to Germany, Jake Malik finds himself confronted by a terrible past. His memories of Auschwitz are rekindled when he discovers a small, fanatic group of Israelis and Germans with their own answer to the Soviet threat.
[GJ6] Hodder pbk **£2.50**
Consequence of Fear
In 1956 a major nuclear explosion shook the Urals. Thousands were killed. Was it an accident?
[GJ7] Grafton pbk **£1.95**
Deep Purple
Hoggart and Fletcher are intrepid MI6 investigators. Their field of expertise, predictably enough, is the Soviet Union. Two Russian defectors are telling them remarkably similar stories, yet each prove the other to be a fraud. But who is telling the truth? Hoggart and Fletcher investigate.
[GJ8] Hodder hbk **£10.95**
Moscow Quadrille
[GJ9] Grafton pbk **£1.50**
Palomino Blonde
[GJ10] Grafton pbk **£1.95**
Pay Any Price
[GJ11] Grafton pbk **£1.95**
Secret Whispers
[GJ12] Grafton pbk **£1.50**
Shadow of Shadows
[GJ13] Grafton pbk **£1.50**
Snowball
[GJ14] Grafton pbk **£1.95**
The Choice
[GJ15] Hodder pbk **£2.95**
The Girl from Addis
Johnny Grant returns to Ethiopia. The last time he was there, as an MI6 agent, his cover was blown. But now he has a war to win, as well as the heart of the beautiful Aliki, the girl from Addis.
[GJ16] Grafton pbk **£1.95**
The Judas Factor
Intelligent espionage novel which explores parallels between intelligence services the world over.
[GJ17] Hodder pbk **£2.50**
The Lantern Network
[GJ18] Grafton pbk **£2.50**
The Man with the President's Mind
[GJ19] Grafton pbk **£1.50**
The Only Good German
[GJ20] Grafton pbk **£1.95**
The Other Side of Silence
[GJ21] Grafton pbk **£2.95**
The Reaper
[GJ22] Grafton pbk **£2.50**
The Special Collection
In 1945 British agent Stephen Felinski is parachuted into Hitler's fast-collapsing Empire. His brief is to reorganize a group of Soviet agents abandoned by Moscow. Forty years later a top cabinet minister defects to the Russians and Felinski is called out of retirement.
[GJ23] Grafton pbk **£2.50**
The Twentieth Day of January
[GJ24] Grafton pbk **£1.95**
Where All the Girls are Sweeter **NEW**
Violence and adventure in Santa Margherita.
[GJ25] Firecrest hbk **£9.95**

AMBLER, ERIC
Set in the shadowy world of espionage and counter-espionage, where nothing is what it seems, these popular thrillers possess realism and a swift pace.
A Kind of Anger
[GJ26] Fontana pbk **£3.50**
Dirty Story
[GJ27] Fontana pbk **£3.50**
Doctor Frigo
[GJ28] Fontana pbk **£3.50**
Epitaph for a Spy
Classic 1938 spy thriller set in France on the eve of World War II. Josef Vadassy is an unlikely spy but the gendarmes have their suspicions and he must prove his innocence by tracking down a real spy.
[GJ29] Dent pbk **£2.50**
Journey into Fear
[GJ30] Fontana pbk **£3.50**
Judgement on Deltchev
[GJ31] Fontana pbk **£3.50**
Passage of Arms
[GJ32] Fontana pbk **£3.50**
Send No More Roses
[GJ33] Fontana pbk **£3.50**
The Levanter
[GJ34] Fontana pbk **£3.50**
The Light of Day
[GJ35] Fontana pbk **£2.50**
Uncommon Danger
[GJ36] Fontana pbk **£3.50**

ANTHONY, EVELYN
Tremendously popular writer of historical wartime thrillers, with an emphasis on espionage.
Albatross
[GJ37] Arrow pbk **£2.99**
Avenue of the Dead
[GJ38] Arrow pbk **£2.50**
Company of Saints
[GJ39] Arrow pbk **£2.50**
Grave of Truth
[GJ40] Arrow pbk **£2.50**
Imperial Highness
[GJ41] Hodder pbk **£2.95**
Malaspiga Exit
[GJ42] Arrow pbk **£2.50**
No Enemy but Time
The tragic story of a divided family. Clare Fraser returns to Ireland to discover that her beloved half-brother has disappeared.
[GJ43] Arrow pbk **£2.95**
Poellenberg Inheritance
[GJ44] Arrow pbk **£2.50**
The Assassin
[GJ45] Arrow pbk **£2.50**
The Defector
[GJ46] Arrow pbk **£2.95**

Jeffrey Archer, author of *A Twist in the Tale* (Hodder & Stoughton pbk **£3.50**)

The Legend
Bored with conventional life, Peter Arundsen longs for the days when he was a spy with the SIS. When he learns that one of their members has defected, he is drawn into a complicated and dangerous investigation.
[GJ47] Arrow pbk **£2.50**
The Occupying Power
[GJ48] Arrow pbk **£2.50**
The Rendezvous
[GJ49] Arrow pbk **£2.50**
The Return
[GJ50] Arrow pbk **£2.50**
The Scarlet Thread **NEW**
A tale of love, jealousy and betrayal, set in Sicily and New York.
[GJ51] Hutchinson hbk **£11.95**
The Silver Falcon
A wealthy racing owner dies, leaving his widow to carry out his life's wish: to win the Derby.
[GJ52] Arrow pbk **£2.50**
The Tamarind Seed
[GJ53] Sphere pbk **£2.99**
Voices on the Wind
[GJ54] Arrow pbk **£2.95**

ARCHER, JEFFREY
These phenomenally successful thrillers combine fast-paced narratives with clear characterization, providing little psychological insight but plenty of entertainment. Jeffrey Archer was born in 1940 and educated at Wellington School and Oxford, before becoming the youngest member of the House of Commons in 1969.
A Matter of Honour
[GJ55] Hodder pbk **£3.50**
A Twist in the Tale
Twelve short stories, each with a peculiar twist at the end.
[GJ56] Hodder pbk **£3.50**
First Among Equals
The tale of four ambitious new MPs who take their seats in Westminster for the first time in the early 1960s.
[GJ57] Hodder pbk **£3.50**
Kane and Abel
[GJ58] Hodder pbk **£3.50**
Not a Penny More, Not a Penny Less
His first novel, written in 1974. Harvey Metcalfe thinks he has committed the perfect crime when he

swindles four eminent men out of one million dollars with a non-existent oil well.
[GJ59] Hodder pbk **£2.50**
Quiver Full of Arrows
Archer's first collection of short stories.
[GJ60] Hodder pbk **£2.95**
Shall We Tell the President?
A classic modern thriller, now revised and updated to carry the saga of Florentyna Kane into the 1990s.
[GJ61] Hodder pbk **£2.50**
The Prodigal Daughter
The story of the making of the first woman President of the United States.
[GJ62] Hodder pbk **£3.50**

ARMSTRONG, CAMPBELL
Fandango
Frank Pagan finds himself confronted by two strange problems. A German terrorist held in Britain has escaped and a murky conspiracy is taking shape in the underworld of émigré Cuban politics.
[GJ63] Hodder hbk **£11.95**
Jig
Frank Pagan is a British counter-terrorist agent, hot on the trail of Jig, a young American assassin, entrusted by the IRA with tracking down a hijacked shipment of funds.
[GJ64] Hodder pbk **£3.95**
Mazurka
Frank Pagan, Scotland Yard rebel and hero of *Jig* is back. On a visit to Edinburgh, the First Secretary of the Estonian Communist Party is murdered. Pagan investigates.
[GJ65] Hodder hbk **£11.95**

BAGLEY, DESMOND
Prolific and extremely popular thriller writer who died in 1983. His novels usually have a wartime setting and his heroes are the old-style macho men.
Bahama Crisis
[GJ66] Fontana pbk **£2.95**
Flyaway
[GJ67] Fontana pbk **£2.95**
High Citadel
[GJ68] Fontana pbk **£2.95**
Juggernaut
[GJ69] Fontana pbk **£3.50**
Landslide
[GJ70] Fontana pbk **£2.95**
Night of Error
[GJ71] Fontana pbk **£3.50**
Running Blind
[GJ72] Fontana pbk **£2.95**
The Enemy
[GJ73] Fontana pbk **£2.95**
The Freedom Trap
[GJ74] Fontana pbk **£2.50**
The Golden Keel
[GJ75] Fontana pbk **£2.50**
The Snow Tiger
[GJ76] Fontana pbk **£2.95**
The Spoilers
[GJ77] Fontana pbk **£2.95**
Tightrope Men
[GJ78] Fontana pbk **£2.95**
Vivero Letter
[GJ79] Fontana pbk **£2.95**
Windfall
[GJ80] Fontana pbk **£2.95**
Wyatt's Hurricane
[GJ81] Fontana pbk **£2.50**

BALDWIN, MICHAEL
Exit Wounds
Charles Kay is an expert on snakes. He has an attractive daughter, Ginerra. Mossad kidnap Kay, but kill the wrong girl...
[GJ82] Futura pbk **£3.50**

Holofernes
Patrick Mason, hero of *Exit Wounds*, is involved in a violent hijack. So too is the Israeli Secret Service.
[GJ83] Macdonald hbk **£11.95**

BELL, SIMON
Heaven's Empire
A gripping thriller about the fast-moving, high-flying world of international money markets.
[GJ84] Heinemann hbk **£10.95**

BENCHLEY, PETER
Highly sophisticated thrillers set in, or near, the dangerous world of the sea. *The Deep* and, most famously, *Jaws*, were made into successful films.
Jaws
[GJ85] Hutchinson pbk **£2.95**
The Deep
[GJ86] Hodder pbk **£2.95**
The Island
[GJ87] Pan pbk **£2.50**

BERNAU, GEORGE
Promises to Keep
It is November 22, 1963 in Dallas, Texas. The young charismatic President of the United States, beloved by his beautiful wife, his country and the world, has everything to live for. Then, driving in a motorcade through the crowded streets, he is shot in the head by an unknown gunman. And he survives the assassination attempt...
[GJ88] Pan pbk **£3.99**

BLACK, JONATHAN
Power and corruption in the world of big business and high finance are the focus of these authentic thrillers by an ex-investigative journalist.
Megacorp
[GJ89] Grafton pbk **£3.50**
Oil
[GJ90] Grafton pbk **£2.95**
Ride the Golden Tiger
[GJ91] Grafton pbk **£2.95**
The House on the Hill
[GJ92] Grafton pbk **£2.50**
The Plunderers
[GJ93] Grafton pbk **£3.95**

BOULLE, PIERRE
The Bridge on the River Kwai
The remarkable story of three men who survived the hell of the Japanese war camps on the Burma-Siam railway.
[GJ94] Fontana pbk **£2.95**

BROWN, DALE
Day of the Cheetah
Sophisticated, high-tech aerial combat story. The 'Cheetah' is an experimental aircraft, America's secret weapon. But the project has been infiltrated by a KGB agent.
[GJ95] Grafton hbk **£12.95**
Silver Tower
[GJ96] Grafton pbk **£3.50**

BUCHAN, JOHN
The modern thriller begins with John Buchan whose adventures are set on a grand scale, encompassing national security and global travel. Their hero, Richard Hannay, is a paragon of moral rectitude, a far cry from the amoral spies of today.
Best Short Stories 1
[GJ97] Grafton pbk **£1.95**
Best Short Stories 2
[GJ98] Grafton pbk **£1.95**
Castle Gay
[GJ99] Dent pbk **£2.50**
Courts of the Morning
[GJ100] Dent pbk **£3.50**

Greenmantle
Sequel to *The Thirty-Nine Steps*. It is 1915, a crisis point in the First World War for England. The spirit of Islam threatens to be harnessed to the German war machine. Only Hannay can save the day.
[GJ101] Penguin pbk **£2.95**
House of the Four Winds
[GJ102] Dent pbk **£2.50**
Island of Sheep
[GJ103] Penguin pbk **£2.95**
John Macnab
[GJ104] Penguin pbk **£2.95**
Mr Standfast
[GJ105] Penguin pbk **£2.95**
Power House
[GJ106] Dent pbk **£2.50**
Prester John
[GJ107] Penguin pbk **£2.95**
Sick Heart River
[GJ108] Macdonald hbk **£6.95**
The Dancing Floor
[GJ109] Penguin pbk **£2.95**
The Thirty-Nine Steps
Richard Hannay finds himself in the classic thriller predicament, hounded by the police and pursued by criminals.
[GJ110] Chatto hbk illus **£10.95**
[GJ111] Pan pbk **£2.99**
Three Hostages
[GJ112] Penguin pbk **£2.95**

CALLISON, BRIAN
Realistic naval stories, usually set during World War II. Noted for their suspense and harsh realism, they glorify both the nobility and humour of war.
A Flock of Ships
[GJ113] Fontana pbk **£2.50**
A Frenzy of Merchantmen
[GJ114] Fontana pbk **£2.50**
A Plague of Sailors
[GJ115] Fontana pbk **£1.75**
A Ship Is Dying
[GJ116] Fontana pbk **£2.50**
A Thunder of Crude
[GJ117] Fontana pbk **£1.95**
A Web of Salvage
[GJ118] Fontana pbk **£1.95**
Spearfish
[GJ119] Fontana pbk **£1.75**
The Auriga Madness
[GJ120] Fontana pbk **£1.95**
The Bone Collectors
[GJ121] Fontana pbk **£2.50**
The Dawn Attack
[GJ122] Fontana pbk **£2.50**
The Judas Ship
[GJ123] Fontana pbk **£2.50**
The Sextant
[GJ124] Fontana pbk **£1.95**
Trapp and World War Three
[GJ125] Fontana pbk **£2.95**
Trapp's Peace
[GJ126] Fontana pbk **£1.50**
Trapp's War
[GJ127] Fontana pbk **£2.50**

CHILDERS, ERSKINE
The Riddle of the Sands
An entertaining classic and one of the very first spy thrillers. It was written before the First World War to alert Britain to the German menace. A German officer and an accomplice are cruising around the Frisian Islands. Why are they so interested in the channels and sandbanks? What is the riddle of the sands?
[GJ128] Grafton hbk **£7.95**
[GJ129] Penguin pbk **£3.50**

FICTION

CHORLTON, WINDSOR

Rites of Sacrifice **NEW**

A spectacular thriller set in the icy wastes of Tibet. Walter Melville is an American anthropologist, one of life's natural observers. He is an unlikely recruit for a daring scheme to smuggle a defecting Chinese general out of Tibet.
[GJ130] WH Allen hbk **£11.95**

CLANCY, TOM

Thrillers with authentic contemporary settings, all phenomenal bestsellers. Tom Clancy ranks alongside Wilbur Smith, Alistair Maclean and Hammond Innes as one of the masters of the genre. As well as being an independent businessman, Tom Clancy is a war games and computer enthusiast.

Cardinal of the Kremlin

The superpowers are developing their Star Wars missile defence systems, but their respective agents are weaving a web of danger and deceit. The sky is no longer the limit, but the ultimate battlefield.
[GJ131] Fontana pbk **£3.95**

Clear and Present Danger

At what point does ordinary criminal activity threaten national security? When can a nation respond to it as to an outside enemy? These are the difficult questions Jack Ryan must ponder when he hears the awful news that Columbian drug lords have assassinated the US Ambassador to Columbia, as well as the visiting head of the FBI. And that is just the beginning.
[GJ132] Collins hbk **£11.95**

Patriot Games

A stranger saves the lives of the Prince and Princess of Wales, and earns the enmity of the deadly Ulster Liberation Army.
[GJ133] Fontana pbk **£3.95**

Red Storm Rising

Moslem fundamentalists have bombed their oilfields and the Russians need another source of supply. The Persian Gulf provides the answer.
[GJ134] Fontana pbk **£3.95**

The Hunt for Red October

Russia's ultra secret missile submarine is heading West. The Americans want her, the Russians want her back, and World War III is only seconds away.
[GJ135] Fontana pbk **£3.95**

CLAVELL, JAMES

James Clavell's phenomenally successful Asian series is a vast historical tapestry. The periods the books cover run chronologically as follows: *Shogun*, 1600; *Tai-Pan*, 1841; *King Rat*, 1945; *Noble House*, 1963; *Whirlwind*, 1979.

King Rat

During the Second World War the fall of Singapore resulted in the capture of 150,000 men: only 1 in 15 survived to VE Day. Set in Changi, the notorious Asian POW camp, this account is based on Clavell's own experience.
[GJ136] Hodder pbk **£3.50**

Noble House
[GJ137] Hodder pbk **£4.95**

Shogun: A Novel of Japan
[GJ138] Hodder pbk **£4.95**

Tai-Pan
[GJ139] Hodder pbk **£3.95**

Whirlwind

February 1979. The Shah has fled from Tehran - a group of Western pilots is embroiled in the ensuing chaos.
[GJ140] Hodder pbk **£4.95**

CLEARY, JON

Australian writer of crime and some general fiction. His plots usually focus on family intrigue within a wider landscape of history and nationality.

Babylon South

Two murders, twenty years apart, take place in Sydney's 'yuppie' community, known locally as the Silvertails. Scobie Malone investigates.
[GJ141] Collins hbk **£11.95**

City of Fading Light
[GJ142] Fontana pbk **£2.95**

Phoenix Tree
[GJ143] Fontana pbk **£2.25**

Sundowners
[GJ144] Fontana pbk **£2.95**

The Beaufort Sisters
[GJ145] Fontana pbk **£3.50**

CONDON, RICHARD

Richard Condon began writing in 1957, when he retired from the film industry. *The Manchurian Candidate*, *Winter Kills* and *Prizzi's Honour* have all been successfully filmed.

A Trembling Upon Rome
[GJ146] Arrow pbk **£1.95**

Oldest Confession
[GJ147] Arrow pbk **£2.99**

Prizzi's Family
[GJ148] Arrow pbk **£2.95**

Prizzi's Glory

Don Corrado Prizzi, head of the largest and most powerful Mafia family in the United States, wants to fulfil a life-long ambition: to be respectable.
[GJ149] M Joseph hbk **£11.95**

Prizzi's Honour
[GJ150] Arrow pbk **£2.95**

The Entwining
[GJ151] Arrow pbk **£1.95**

The Manchurian Candidate
[GJ152] Arrow pbk **£2.95**

CORNWELL, BERNARD

Cornwell's hero, Sharpe, is a leader in the mould of Forester's Hornblower. Set during the Napoleonic Wars, the Sharpe series charts the rise of his fortunes.

Redcoat
[GJ153] Sphere pbk **£3.50**

Sea Lord

A contemporary maritime thriller. Sea gypsy John Stowey returns to England where he becomes involved in a series of violent events involving his family's inheritance.
[GJ154] M Joseph hbk **£11.95**

Sharpe's Company
[GJ155] Fontana pbk **£2.95**

Sharpe's Eagle
[GJ156] Fontana pbk **£2.95**

Sharpe's Enemy
[GJ157] Fontana pbk **£2.95**

Sharpe's Gold
[GJ158] Fontana pbk **£3.25**

Sharpe's Honour
[GJ159] Fontana pbk **£2.95**

Sharpe's Regiment
[GJ160] Fontana pbk **£2.95**

Sharpe's Rifles

Soon to be a major Central television series.
[GJ161] Fontana pbk **£3.50**

Sharpe's Siege
[GJ162] Fontana pbk **£3.50**

Sharpe's Sword
[GJ163] Fontana pbk **£2.95**

Wildtrack
[GJ164] Sphere pbk **£3.50**

COYLE, HAROLD

Sword Point

An intriguing story of war between the superpowers, set in Iran in the near future.
[GJ165] Viking hbk **£11.95**

CUNNINGHAM, PETER

The Bear's Requiem

Gripping financial thriller set in the hectic world of Wall Street.
[GJ166] M Joseph hbk **£12.95**

CUSSLER, CLIVE

Maritime thrillers, centred on trails of action-packed global adventure.

Cyclops
[GJ167] Sphere pbk **£3.50**

Deep Six
[GJ168] Sphere pbk **£3.50**

Iceberg
[GJ169] Sphere pbk **£3.50**

Mayday!
[GJ170] Sphere pbk **£3.50**

Night Probe
[GJ171] Sphere pbk **£3.50**

Pacific Vortex
[GJ172] Sphere pbk **£2.99**

Treasure
[GJ173] Grafton hbk **£11.95**

Vixen
[GJ174] Sphere pbk **£3.50**

DALEY, ROBERT

One-time New York Deputy Chief Commissioner whose knowledge of the workings of the New York City Police Department informs his work.

Dangerous Edge
[GJ175] Hodder pbk **£2.95**

Hands of a Stranger
[GJ176] Hodder pbk **£2.95**

Man With A Gun
[GJ177] Hutchinson hbk **£10.95**

Year of the Dragon
[GJ178] Hodder pbk **£2.95**

DEIGHTON, LEN

1: Berlin Game

The first part of the *Game, Set and Match* trilogy, introducing Bernard Samson. Its sequels are *Mexico Set* and *London Match*.
[GJ179] Grafton pbk **£3.50**

2: Mexico Set
[GJ180] Grafton pbk **£3.50**

3: London Match
[GJ181] Grafton pbk **£3.50**

Game, Set and Match in 1 Volume

Contains a new preface, written specially for the omnibus edition.
[GJ182] Hutchinson hbk **£12.95**

An Expensive Place to Die

His fifth novel, about a CIA plan to leak nuclear fall-out data to the Chinese Embassy in Paris.
[GJ183] Grafton pbk **£2.95**

Billion Dollar Brain

The tale of an anti-communist spy ring run by a Texan billionaire. Filmed by Ken Russell.
[GJ184] Grafton pbk **£2.95**

Bomber

The story of a routine RAF raid on the Rühr that goes disastrously wrong.
[GJ185] Grafton pbk **£3.95**

Close-Up

His eighth novel, set in the film business.
[GJ186] Grafton pbk **£3.50**

Declaration of War

Deighton's only collection of short stories.
[GJ187] Grafton pbk **£2.95**

Funeral in Berlin

Successfully filmed, with Michael Caine as Harry Palmer.
[GJ188] Grafton pbk **£2.50**

Goodbye Mickey Mouse

Wartime thriller, Deighton's 14th novel, about US fighter pilots flying escort missions over Germany.
[GJ189] Grafton pbk **£3.50**

Horse Under Water
[GJ190] Grafton pbk **£2.95**
SS-GB
[GJ191] Grafton pbk **£3.50**
Spy Hook
Bernard Samson, a shadow of his former self, plods through a snow blizzard in Washington DC. Old friends and colleagues are not as confiding as they used to be. Ignoring all warnings, Bernard pursues his own investigation into his wife's defection.
[GJ192] Grafton pbk **£3.50**
Spy Line **NEW**
The second part of the *Hook, Line and Sinker* trilogy: Bernie Samson is on the run in Berlin.
[GJ193] Hutchinson hbk **£11.95**
Spy Story
[GJ194] Grafton pbk **£2.95**
The Ipcress File
Deighton's celebrated first novel, later filmed with Michael Caine as Harry Palmer.
[GJ195] Grafton pbk **£2.95**
Twinkle, Twinkle, Little Spy
[GJ196] Grafton pbk **£2.95**
Winter
A detailed portrait of a Berlin family as it develops during the early 20th century. Considered the pinnacle of Deighton's writing.
[GJ197] Grafton pbk **£3.99**
XPD
[GJ198] Grafton pbk **£3.50**
Yesterday's Spy
[GJ199] Grafton pbk **£2.95**

DOBBS, MICHAEL
House of Cards **NEW**
Post-Thatcher political intrigue is the backdrop of this fast-paced tale of power and ruthlessness.
[GJ200] Collins hbk **£11.95**

DIEHL, WILLIAM
Thai Horse
A superspy searches for his friend who was supposedly killed in Vietnam 15 years before.
[GJ201] Corgi pbk **£3.99**

DUCKWORTH, COLIN
Steps to the High Garden
Fast-paced thriller which explores the theory of reincarnation.
[GJ202] J Calder hbk **£12.95**

EASTERMAN, DANIEL
The Brotherhood of the Tomb
Action packed adventure thriller set in the dangerous world of hostage-taking and assassinations.
[GJ203] GRAFTON hbk **£12.95**
The Last Assassin
[GJ204] Hodder pbk **£2.95**
The Ninth Buddha **NEW**
Set in Britain and Mongolia during the 1920s, this is the story of a deadly game in which the Russians, Tibetans and Chinese have high stakes.
[GJ205] Grafton hbk **£10.95**
The Seventh Sanctuary
[GJ206] Grafton pbk **£3.95**

EGLETON, CLIVE
Contemporary thrillers informed by Egleton's considerable expertise in Arabic and Islamic studies.
Death of a Sahib
Jack Henderson is in India to investigate a simple case which rapidly becomes complicated and violent.
[GJ207] Hodder hbk **£10.95**
Gone Missing
[GJ208] Hodder hbk **£10.95**
Picture of the Year
[GJ209] Hodder pbk **£2.95**

ENGEL, ALAN
Variant
A super-charged medical thriller written by a renowned doctor. A disease called progeria accelerates ageing. A Russian boy, Ivan, contracts the disease and turns up at a Paris hospital. He dies within 3 weeks and US intelligence officials are intrigued by his extraordinary strength. The Russians will do everything within their powers to prevent research on Ivan's brain.
[GJ210] WH Allen hbk **£9.95**

ERDMAN, PAUL
Fast-moving financial thrillers set in the international money markets and the global business environment. Terrifying stories which erode the boundaries between fact and fiction.
Billion Dollar Killing
[GJ211] Arrow pbk **£1.75**
Panic of '89
[GJ212] Sphere pbk **£3.50**
The Crash of '79
[GJ213] Secker pbk **£10.95**
The Last Days of America
[GJ214] Sphere pbk **£3.50**
The Palace
The world of big-time gambling and international banking is the setting of this gripping thriller.
[GJ215] Sphere pbk **£3.50**

FLEMING, IAN
James Bond 007 is for many the ultimate secret agent and Ian Fleming's many novels, on which the films are loosely based, have enjoyed enormous success, although they present a world, as John le Carré has pointed out, which relies on a picture of an 'absolutely evil enemy'. *Casino Royale* was the first Bond novel, and the series has been continued since Fleming's death by John Gardner.
Casino Royale
[GJ216] Grafton pbk **£2.50**
Diamonds Are Forever
[GJ217] Grafton pbk **£2.50**
Doctor No
[GJ218] Grafton pbk **£1.95**
For Your Eyes Only
[GJ219] Hodder pbk **£2.50**
From Russia with Love
[GJ220] Hodder pbk **£2.50**
Goldfinger
[GJ221] Hodder pbk **£2.50**
Live and Let Die
[GJ222] Hodder pbk **£2.50**
Moonraker
[GJ223] Hodder pbk **£2.50**
Octopussy/Living Daylights
[GJ224] Grafton pbk **£1.95**
On Her Majesty's Secret Service
[GJ225] Hodder pbk **£2.50**
The Man With The Golden Gun
[GJ226] Hodder pbk **£2.50**
Thunderball
[GJ227] Hodder pbk **£2.50**
You Only Live Twice
[GJ228] Hodder pbk **£2.50**

FLEMING, THOMAS
Time and Tide
Set on board the USS Jefferson City, a warship on the cutting edge of the combat zone in the months following Pearl Harbour.
[GJ229] Pan pbk **£3.99**

FOLLETT, KEN
Cardiff-born philosophy graduate who became a journalist and began to write books in his spare time. Ken Follett has written thrillers, children's books, non-fiction, short stories and scripts, many under pseudonyms.

Eye of the Needle
[GJ230] Futura pbk **£2.95**
Lie Down with Lions
[GJ231] Corgi pbk **£3.50**
On Wings of Eagles
[GJ232] Corgi pbk **£3.50**
Swift
[GJ233] Methuen pbk **£2.50**
The Key to Rebecca
[GJ234] Corgi pbk **£2.99**
The Man from St Petersburg
[GJ235] Corgi pbk **£2.95**
The Pillars of the Earth **NEW**
[GJ236] Macmillan hbk **£13.95**
Triple
[GJ236] Futura pbk **£2.95**

FORBATH, PETER
The Last Hero
A vivid recreation of Stanley's expedition into the heart of undiscovered Africa. A classic adventure story.
[GJ237] Heinemann hbk **£11.95**

FORBES, COLIN
Prolific English writer of war thrillers. These exciting tales owe their realism to his own wartime experiences.
Avalanche Express
[GJ238] Pan pbk **£3.50**
Cover Story
[GJ239] Pan pbk **£3.99**
Deadlock
A fully-trained master planner of the Soviets has turned maverick. He must be tracked down before he causes chaos.
[GJ240] Pan pbk **£3.99**
Double Jeopardy
[GJ241] Pan pbk **£2.99**
Heights of Zervos
[GJ242] Pan pbk **£3.50**
Palermo Ambush
[GJ243] Pan pbk **£3.50**
Target Five
[GJ244] Pan pbk **£2.99**
Terminal
The barbed wire surrounding a clinic in Berne conceals a dreadful secret. Bob Newman and the British SIS are trying to find out more about 'Terminal' but anyone who talks to them ends up murdered.
[GJ245] Pan pbk **£3.50**
The Janus Man
[GJ246] Pan pbk **£2.95**
The Leader and the Damned
[GJ247] Pan pbk **£3.99**
The Stockholm Syndicate
[GJ248] Pan pbk **£3.50**
The Stone Leopard
[GJ249] Pan pbk **£3.50**
Tramp in Armour
[GJ250] Pan pbk **£3.50**
Year of the Golden Ape
[GJ251] Pan pbk **£2.99**

FORESTER, C.S.
Horatio Hornblower is the hero of many of these naval adventures, set during the Napoleonic Wars. He makes his first appearance in *The Happy Return* and through a sequence of adventures rises to the rank of admiral.
Death to the French
[GJ252] Bodley Head hbk **£4.50**
Hornblower and the 'Hotspur'
[GJ253] Penguin pbk **£3.50**
Lord Hornblower
[GJ254] Penguin pbk **£2.99**
Mr Midshipman Hornblower
[GJ255] Penguin pbk **£2.99**

C.S. Forester, author of *Death to the French* (Bodley Head hbk £4.50) & *The African Queen* (Penguin pbk £2.99)

Ship of the Line
[GJ256] Penguin pbk **£2.99**
The African Queen
[GJ257] Penguin pbk **£2.99**
The Happy Return
[GJ258] Penguin pbk **£2.95**
The Ship
[GJ259] Penguin pbk **£2.99**

FORSYTH, FREDERICK
One of the greatest of modern thriller writers. Packed with details and sophisticated characterization, his many novels enjoy tremendous popularity. They usually focus on distinctive features of post-war history and tend to blur the distinction between fact and fiction. His books have been filmed with great success.
No Comebacks
A collection of short stories, each full of suspense and bearing all the hallmarks of his longer fiction.
[GJ260] Hutchinson hbk **£10.95**
[GJ261] Corgi pbk **£2.95**
Omnibus: Day of the Jackal/The Odessa File/The Fourth Protocol
[GJ262] Hutchinson hbk **£12.95**
The Day of the Jackal
'The Jackal' is a professional killer employed to assassinate President de Gaulle in the spring of 1963. He works his way towards his target with relentless and deadly efficiency.
[GJ263] Hutchinson hbk **£10.95**
[GJ264] Corgi pbk **£2.95**
The Devil's Alternative
An appalling choice faces the President of the United States and other statesmen; whatever they choose to do, people will die.
[GJ265] Hutchinson hbk **£9.95**
[GJ266] Corgi pbk **£2.95**
The Dogs of War
The discovery of a $10 billion mountain of platinum in a remote African republic causes tycoon Sir James Manson to hire an army of mercenaries to topple the government.
[GJ267] Hutchinson hbk **£10.95**
[GJ268] Corgi pbk **£3.50**
The Fourth Protocol
Plan Aurora is hatched in a forest outside Moscow. It is a brilliant and daring plan to breach the secret Fourth Protocol. As a Soviet agent under cover in an English town works furiously towards a deadline, MI5 try to stop him.
[GJ269] Hutchinson hbk **£10.95**
[GJ270] Corgi pbk **£3.95**

The Negotiator NEW
In the 1990s the growing world shortage of oil and the imminent ratification of the Nantucket arms reduction treaty cause two right-wing factions in America to prepare a ruthless plan to force the President of the United States out of office. Their success would push the superpowers to the brink of war.
[GJ271] Bantam hbk **£12.95**
The Odessa File
The Odessa is the secret organisation of former members of the SS. Peter Miller is a journalist committed to tracking them down.
[GJ272] Hutchinson hbk **£10.95**
[GJ273] Corgi pbk **£2.99**
The Shepherd
It is Christmas Eve 1957 and a pilot is flying home on leave from Germany. Suddenly a fog closes in and out of the mist appears a World War II bomber.
[GJ274] Hutchinson hbk **£5.95**
[GJ275] Corgi pbk **£2.50**

FRANCIS, CLARE
Romantic adventure thrillers which combine Clare Francis' first-hand knowledge of life at sea with genuine insight into human relationships.
Night Sky
[GJ276] Pan pbk **£3.99**
Red Crystal
[GJ277] Pan pbk **£3.99**
Wolf Winter
[GJ278] Pan pbk **£3.99**

FRASER, DAVID
A Candle for Judas
Political treachery in the world of high finance. For young Simon Marlow, growing up in Gloucestershire after the war, a kind gesture to an old tramp proves to be an astonishing quirk of fate.
[GJ279] Collins hbk **£11.95**

FREEMANTLE, BRIAN
Brian Freemantle has created the classic anti-hero, the spy Charlie Muffin. He is a crumpled, perpetually hungover, middle-aged loser whose only aim and greatest ability is to survive.
Blind Run
[GJ280] Arrow pbk **£2.50**
Charlie Muffin
[GJ281] Arrow pbk **£2.50**
Charlie Muffin's Uncle Sam
[GJ282] Arrow pbk **£2.50**
Clap Hands, Here Comes Charlie
[GJ283] Arrow pbk **£2.50**
Madrigal for Charlie Muffin
[GJ284] Arrow pbk **£2.50**
The Fix
[GJ285] Arrow pbk **£2.50**
The Inscrutable Charlie Muffin
[GJ286] Arrow pbk **£2.50**

FULLERTON, ALEXANDER
These wartime adventure stories owe their authenticity to Alexander Fullerton's own experiences. He once worked in Germany with Red Army units.
Special Deception
[GJ287] Macmillan hbk **£10.95**
Special Deliverance
[GJ288] Sphere pbk **£2.99**
Special Dynamic
[GJ289] Macmillan hbk **£10.95**
The Gatecrashers
[GJ290] Pan pbk **£2.50**

GALL, SANDY
Salang NEW
Exciting traditional adventure story by the well known TV news reporter. Set during the Russian withdrawal of troops from Afghanistan.
[GJ291] Bodley Head hbk **£10.95**

GARDNER, JOHN
Best known for his Boysie Oakes stories, with their blundering special agent hero, and for his recent additions to the James Bond canon, which now number eight.
Dancing Dodo
[GJ292] Hodder pbk **£2.95**
Garden of Weapons
[GJ293] Hodder pbk **£2.95**
Icebreaker
[GJ294] Hodder pbk **£2.50**
Licence Renewed
[GJ295] Hodder pbk **£2.50**
Nobody Lives Forever
[GJ296] Hodder pbk **£2.50**
Nostradamus Traitor
[GJ297] Hodder pbk **£2.75**
Quiet Dogs
[GJ298] Hodder pbk **£2.75**
Role of Honour
[GJ299] Hodder pbk **£2.50**
Scorpius
[GJ300] Hodder hbk **£10.95**
The Secret Families
The last installment of the Secret Generations trilogy. It is December 1964, fourteen years after the close of *The Secret Houses* - Caspar Railton is dead, but witnesses and documents surface which suggest that he was a traitor.
[GJ301] Bantam hbk **£12.95**
The Secret Generations
[GJ302] Corgi pbk **£3.95**
Traitor's Exit
[GJ303] Star pbk **£1.60**
Werewolf Trace
[GJ304] Hodder pbk **£2.50**
Win, Lose or Die
John Gardner's eighth Bond novel. Bond is back in the Navy, relieved of his Foreign Office duties.
[GJ305] Hodder hbk **£10.95**

GEDDES, PAUL
Geddes' own experience of working for the government, in London and abroad, is apparent in these detailed and authentic political thrillers.
A Special Kind of Nightmare
[GJ306] Bodley Head hbk **£10.95**
A State of Corruption
[GJ307] Grafton pbk **£2.95**
Goliath
[GJ308] Grafton pbk **£2.95**

Sandy Gall, author of *Salang* (Bodley Head hbk £10.95)

GERSON, JACK
Death Squad London
Maurice Korel is summoned to a police station in the East End one foggy evening in September 1936. He is there to identify the body of his only daughter, Beth. Was it suicide, or is there a more sinister cause?
[GJ309] WH Allen hbk **£11.95**

GOLDMAN, WILLIAM
Goldman's background is in screenwriting (see his excellent *Adventures in the Screen Trade*). His novels show the same strengths as his films: they are taut, intelligent thrillers, filled with suspense.
Brothers
[GJ310] Grafton pbk **£2.95**
Edged Weapons
[GJ311] Grafton pbk **£2.95**
The Colour of Light
[GJ312] Grafton pbk **£3.50**

GRAHAM, WINSTON
Cameo
Gripping thriller set during the Blitz.
[GJ313] Fontana pbk **£3.50**

GREY, ANTHONY
Ambitious and well-informed thrillers with contemporary settings.
Peking
[GJ314] Pan pbk **£3.99**
Saigon
[GJ315] Pan pbk **£3.95**
The Chinese Assassin
[GJ316] Pan pbk **£1.95**

HAILEY, ARTHUR
Author of a celebrated series of theme novels, each set in a particular environment, and usually incorporating the threat of disaster.
Airport
[GJ317] Pan pbk **£3.99**
Hotel
[GJ318] Pan pbk **£3.99**
In High Places
[GJ319] Pan pbk **£3.99**
Overload
[GJ320] Pan pbk **£3.50**
Strong Medicine
[GJ321] Pan pbk **£3.99**
The Final Diagnosis
[GJ322] Pan pbk **£3.99**
The Moneychangers
[GJ323] Pan pbk **£4.50**
Wheels
[GJ324] Pan pbk **£3.99**

HALL, ADAM
A prolific author who also writes under his real name of Elleston Trevor. His books have been translated into 18 languages. He is a black belt in karate and lives in the Arizona desert.
Mandarin Cypher
[GJ325] Fontana pbk **£2.25**
Ninth Directive
[GJ326] Fontana pbk **£2.50**
Northlight: A Quiller Mission
[GJ327] Star pbk **£2.95**
Quiller KGB NEW
Quiller is to be briefed on his new mission by Colonel Yassler of the KGB. Quiller must work with Yassler to foil an attempt on Gorbachev's life. But can the KGB be trusted?
[GJ328] WH Allen hbk **£11.95**
Scorpion Signal
[GJ329] Fontana pbk **£1.95**
Sinkiang Executive
[GJ330] Fontana pbk **£2.75**
Striker Portfolio
[GJ331] Fontana pbk **£2.50**

Tango Briefing
[GJ332] Fontana pbk **£1.95**
Warsaw Document
[GJ333] Fontana pbk **£2.50**

HAY, HEATHER & HEARN, BARRY
The Business
A tough, authentic and fast-paced thriller set in the snooker halls of the 1970s.
[GJ334] Penguin pbk **£3.50**

HEYWOOD, JOSEPH
The Berkut
[GJ335] Penguin pbk **£3.99**

HIGGINS, JACK
Prolific and versatile writer, who is probably most at home in wartime Europe with the Allies outmanoeuvring the Germans. *The Eagle Has Landed* was made into a successful film.
A Fine Night for Dying
[GJ336] Arrow pbk **£2.25**
A Prayer for the Dying
[GJ337] Pan pbk **£2.95**
A Season in Hell
An American widow and an SAS veteran in pursuit of a murderous drugs baron.
[GJ338] Collins hbk **£10.95**
Confessional
[GJ339] Pan pbk **£3.50**
Dark Side of the Street
[GJ340] Hodder pbk **£1.95**
Day of Judgment
[GJ341] Pan pbk **£2.99**
East of Desolation
[GJ342] Hodder pbk **£1.95**
Exocet
[GJ343] Pan pbk **£3.50**
Hell is Always Today
[GJ344] Pan pbk **£2.50**
In the Hour before Midnight
[GJ345] Hodder pbk **£1.95**
Luciano's Luck
[GJ346] Pan pbk **£3.50**
Memoirs of a Dance Hall Romeo
A new departure for Jack Higgins. This is the story of Oliver Shaw, who returns to the Yorkshire town of Manningham in 1949, and struggles to become a writer.
[GJ347] Collins hbk **£10.95**
Night Judgment at Sinos
[GJ348] Hodder pbk **£2.50**
Night of the Fox
[GJ349] Pan pbk **£3.50**
Solo
[GJ350] Pan pbk **£2.99**
Storm Warning
[GJ351] Pan pbk **£3.50**
The Dark Side of the Island
[GJ352] Hodder pbk **£1.95**
The Eagle Has Landed
[GJ353] Pan pbk **£3.50**
The Iron Tiger
[GJ354] Hodder pbk **£1.95**
The Keys of Hell
[GJ355] Hodder pbk **£1.95**
The Last Place God Made
[GJ356] Pan pbk **£2.99**
The Savage Day
[GJ357] Pan pbk **£3.50**
The Testament of Caspar Schultz
[GJ358] Hodder pbk **£1.95**
The Violent Enemy
[GJ359] Hodder pbk **£1.75**
Toll for the Brave
[GJ360] Arrow pbk **£2.25**
Touch the Devil
[GJ361] Pan pbk **£3.50**

Wrath of the Lion
[GJ362] Hodder pbk **£1.95**

HOOVER, THOMAS
Caribbee
[GJ363] Sphere pbk **£3.50**
The Moghul
[GJ364] Sphere pbk **£3.95**
The Samurai Strategy
[GJ365] M Joseph hbk **£11.95**

HOUSEHOLD, GEOFFREY
Published in 1939, *Rogue Male* was a topical and frightening contemporary classic thriller. The standard has not dropped and *Rogue Justice* is a particularly worthy successor.
Escape into Daylight
[GJ366] Heinemann pbk **£2.75**
Face to the Sun
[GJ367] M Joseph hbk **£10.95**
Rogue Justice
[GJ368] Penguin pbk **£2.50**
Rogue Male
[GJ369] Penguin pbk **£2.50**
Watcher in the Shadows NEW
A tale of revenge and suspense.
[GJ370] Firecrest hbk **£9.95**

HUNTER, MATTHEW
Schiller NEW
A story about the secrets trade in an era of East-West co-operation and détente. Features one of the most exciting chases in recent fiction.
[GJ371] Heinemann hbk **£10.95**

HUNTER, STEPHEN
The Day before Midnight
Armed fanatics, the Provisional Army of the United States, take over the only independent nuclear missile base in the world, situated in Maryland. A menacing thriller on a grand scale.
[GJ372] Grafton hbk **£12.95**

HYDE, ANTHONY
The Red Fox
[GJ373] Pan pbk **£2.95**

IGNATIUS, DAVID
Agents of Innocence
Gripping tale of espionage in the Middle East. A convincing thriller with a ring of authenticity.
[GJ374] Star pbk **£3.50**

INNES, HAMMOND
Colourful and action-packed, these highly successful novels follow a central character through foreign locations and numerous close shaves.
Air Bridge
[GJ375] Fontana pbk **£2.95**
Angry Mountain
[GJ376] Fontana pbk **£2.95**
Atlantic Fury
[GJ377] Fontana pbk **£2.95**
Attack Alarm
[GJ378] Fontana pbk **£2.95**
Big Footprints
[GJ379] Fontana pbk **£2.95**
Black Tide
[GJ380] Fontana pbk **£3.50**
Blue Ice
[GJ381] Fontana pbk **£2.95**
Campbell's Kingdom
[GJ382] Fontana pbk **£2.95**
Dead and Alive
[GJ383] Fontana pbk **£2.50**
Golden Soak
[GJ384] Fontana pbk **£2.95**
High Stand
[GJ385] Fontana pbk **£2.95**

Adam Hall, author of *Quiller KGB* (WH Allen hbk £11.95)

Levkas Man
[GJ386] Fontana pbk **£2.95**
Maddon's Rock
[GJ387] Fontana pbk **£2.95**
Medusa
A group of misfits and a worn-out frigate battle to prevent an attempted coup.
[GJ388] Fontana pbk **£3.50**
North Star
[GJ389] Fontana pbk **£2.95**
Solomon's Seal
[GJ390] Fontana pbk **£2.95**
Strange Land
[GJ391] Fontana pbk **£2.95**
Strode Venturer
[GJ392] Fontana pbk **£2.95**
The Doomed Oasis
[GJ393] Fontana pbk **£2.50**
The Killer Mine
[GJ394] Fontana pbk **£2.95**
The Land God Gave to Cain
[GJ395] Fontana pbk **£2.95**
The Last Voyage: Captain Cook's Lost Diary
[GJ396] Fontana pbk **£2.95**
The Lonely Skier
[GJ397] Fontana pbk **£2.95**
The Trojan Horse
[GJ398] Fontana pbk **£2.95**
The White South
[GJ399] Fontana pbk **£2.95**
Wreck of the 'Mary Deare'
[GJ400] Fontana pbk **£2.95**
Wreckers Must Breathe
[GJ401] Fontana pbk **£2.50**

JAKES, JOHN
California Gold   NEW
The story of Mark Chance, a penniless young drummer who makes his fortune in California: it's monumental in scope and weaves fictional and historical characters in a rich tapestry.
[GJ402] Collins hbk **£12.95**

JAMES, IAN ST
Contemporary thrillers, large in scope and ambition. Ian St James is a subtle and intelligent master of the genre: this year sees the launch of the Ian St James Award, Britain's most valuable literary prize in any fiction category.
Cold New Dawn
[GJ403] Fontana pbk **£2.95**

Justice
Jack Webb is charismatic, a winner, who protects his friend Peter Mortlake from the excesses of a bullying father. But when a beautiful young American brings her talent for music to London, everything changes...
[GJ404] Fontana pbk **£4.50**
The Balfour Conspiracy
[GJ405] Fontana pbk **£2.95**
The Killing Anniversary
[GJ406] Fontana pbk **£3.95**
The Money Stones
[GJ407] Fontana pbk **£2.95**
Winner Harris
[GJ408] Fontana pbk **£2.95**

JENKINS, GEOFFREY
Sailing thrillers with an emphasis on complicated political intrigue, and scientifically accurate sea technology.
A Bridge of Magpies
[GJ409] Fontana pbk **£2.95**
A Cleft of Stars
[GJ410] Collins hbk **£10.95**
A Grue of Ice
[GJ411] Fontana pbk **£2.50**
A Ravel of Waters
[GJ412] Fontana pbk **£2.75**
Fireprint
[GJ413] Fontana pbk **£2.50**
Hunter Killer
[GJ414] Fontana pbk **£2.25**
South Trap
[GJ415] Fontana pbk **£2.95**
The Unripe Gold
[GJ416] Fontana pbk **£1.75**

JUDD, ALAN
An intelligent and witty writer, whose first novel, *A Breed of Heroes*, is a fascinating war story which transcends the conventions of most English descriptions of army life. It was nominated for the Booker Prize.
A Breed of Heroes
[GJ417] Fontana pbk **£2.50**
Noonday Devil
[GJ418] Hutchinson hbk **£9.95**
Short of Glory
[GJ419] Hodder pbk **£2.50**

KELLERMAN, JONATHAN
Los Angeles-born, Kellerman is an accomplished writer of political thrillers: his recent novel *The Butcher's Theatre*, set in Jerusalem, was particularly acclaimed.
Blood Test
[GJ420] Futura pbk **£2.95**
Over the Edge
[GJ421] Futura pbk **£3.50**
Silent Partner   NEW
[GJ422] Macdonald hbk **£11.95**
The Butcher's Theatre
[GJ423] Futura pbk **£3.99**
When the Bow Breaks
[GJ424] Futura pbk **£3.50**

KENT, ALEXANDER
Another incarnation of the prolific Douglas Reeman, Alexander Kent has written a series of tremendously popular novels set in the Napoleonic Wars.
Colours Aloft!
[GJ425] Arrow pbk **£2.99**
Command a King's Ship
[GJ426] Arrow pbk **£2.99**
Enemy in Sight
[GJ427] Arrow pbk **£2.95**
In Gallant Company
[GJ428] Arrow pbk **£2.50**
Midshipman Bolitho/The 'Avenger'
[GJ429] Arrow pbk **£1.95**

Passage to Mutiny
[GJ430] Arrow pbk **£2.95**
Richard Bolitho, Midshipman
[GJ431] Arrow pbk **£3.25**
Signal-Close Action!
[GJ432] Arrow pbk **£2.99**
Sloop of War
[GJ433] Arrow pbk **£2.50**
Stand into Danger
[GJ434] Arrow pbk **£2.95**
Success to the Brave
[GJ435] Arrow pbk **£2.99**
The Flag Captain
[GJ436] Arrow pbk **£2.95**
The Inshore Squadron
[GJ437] Arrow pbk **£2.50**
Tradition of Victory
[GJ438] Arrow pbk **£2.99**

KERRIGAN, PHILIP
Public Burning   NEW
The story of a young man's search for the Nazi criminal who slaughtered his family.
[GJ439] Grafton hbk **£12.95**

KILCOMMON, DENIS
Serpent's Tooth   NEW
An IRA major must work with the British authorities to uncover a ruthless terrorist plot.
[GJ440] Bantam hbk **£11.95**

KYLE, DUNCAN
Intriguing political thrillers, usually involving the KGB.
A Cage of Ice
[GJ441] Fontana pbk **£2.50**
A Raft of Swords
[GJ442] Fontana pbk **£2.95**
Black Camelot
[GJ443] Fontana pbk **£2.95**
Flight into Fear
[GJ444] Fontana pbk **£2.50**
Green River High
[GJ445] Fontana pbk **£2.50**
Stalking Point
[GJ446] Fontana pbk **£2.95**
Terror's Cradle
[GJ447] Fontana pbk **£2.50**
The Back of Bourke
[GJ448] Collins hbk **£10.95**
The Dancing Men
[GJ449] Fontana pbk **£2.50**
The King's Commissioner
[GJ450] Fontana pbk **£2.75**
The Semonov Impulse
[GJ451] Fontana pbk **£2.50**
Whiteout
[GJ452] Fontana pbk **£2.95**

LAMBERT, DEREK
Inventive thrillers with a strong sense of history, often focusing on political intrigue on a global scale.
Golden Express
[GJ453] Sphere pbk **£3.95**
I, Said the Spy
[GJ454] Sphere pbk **£1.95**
Red Dove
[GJ455] Sphere pbk **£1.95**
The Judas Code
[GJ456] Sphere pbk **£2.95**
The Man Who Was Saturday
[GJ457] Sphere pbk **£1.95**
Trance
[GJ458] Sphere pbk **£1.75**

LAWRENCE, CURT
Zecan Termination   NEW
A Black ex-green beret, an alcoholic lesbian and a

burnt-out CIA agent are just some of the characters in this innovative thriller.
[GJ459] Hale hbk **£10.95**

LEASOR, JAMES
Frozen Assets **NEW**
Dr Jason Love was one of the most successful fictional characters of the late '60s and '70s, immortalised on the screen by the late David Niven. In *Frozen Assets* he returns in a new adventure, reaching from London to Moscow, Pakistan and Afghanistan.
[GJ460] Grafton hbk **£11.95**

LUDLUM, ROBERT
One of the most popular thriller writers today. His many novels, usually set in an indeterminate present, explore various unthinkable political scenarios.
Omnibus: Holcroft Covenant/Matarese Circle/Bourne Identity
[GJ461] Grafton hbk **£12.95**
Selected Works: Scarlatti Inheritance/Osterman Weekend
[GJ462] Octopus hbk **£9.99**
The Aquitaine Progression
[GJ463] Grafton pbk **£3.99**
The Bourne Identity
[GJ464] Grafton pbk **£3.99**
The Bourne Supremacy
[GJ465] Grafton pbk **£3.95**
The Chancellor Manuscript
[GJ466] Grafton pbk **£3.50**
The Gemini Contenders
[GJ467] Grafton pbk **£3.50**
The Holcroft Covenant
[GJ468] Grafton pbk **£3.50**
The Icarus Agenda
[GJ469] Grafton pbk **£4.50**
The Matarese Circle
[GJ470] Grafton pbk **£3.50**
The Matlock Papers
[GJ471] Grafton pbk **£2.95**
The Osterman Weekend
[GJ472] Grafton pbk **£2.99**
The Parsifal Mosaic
[GJ473] Grafton pbk **£3.99**
The Rhinemann Exchange
[GJ474] Grafton pbk **£3.50**
The Road to Gandolfo
[GJ475] Grafton pbk **£2.99**
The Scarlatti Inheritance
[GJ476] Grafton pbk **£2.95**
Trevayne
Written at the time of Watergate, this is a tale of mendacity and lust for power. Trevayne enters government, and comes to head one of the biggest foundations in the US - so powerful is he that no one could touch him, or so he thought.
[GJ477] Grafton pbk **£2.95**

LUSTBADER, ERIC VAN
The author of big, powerful, passionate books, van Lustbader has established himself as a splendid storyteller for men and women alike. According to Robert Ludlum, 'he is a man who understands both the Western and the Oriental mind'.
Beneath an Opal Moon
[GJ478] Grafton pbk **£2.95**
Black Heart
[GJ479] Grafton pbk **£3.95**
French Kiss **NEW**
Set in Europe, Vietnam and America, this is the story of two brothers, their experience in the aftermath of war, and the trail of death they leave in their wake.
[GJ480] Grafton hbk **£12.95**
Jian
[GJ481] Grafton pbk **£3.95**
Shallows of Night
[GJ482] Star pbk **£3.50**

Shan
[GJ483] Grafton pbk **£3.95**
Sirens
[GJ484] Grafton pbk **£3.50**
The Miko
[GJ485] Grafton pbk **£3.99**
The Ninja
[GJ486] Grafton pbk **£3.50**
Zero
[GJ487] Grafton pbk **£3.99**

LYALL, GAVIN
Ingenious thrillers. Their settings cover the entire globe, and their subject matter reflects a sharp sense of future possibilities.
Blame the Dead
[GJ488] Pan pbk **£2.50**
Midnight Plus One
[GJ489] Pan pbk **£2.50**
The Conduct of Major Maxim
[GJ490] Pan pbk **£2.99**
The Crocus List
[GJ491] Pan pbk **£3.50**
The Most Dangerous Game
[GJ492] Pan pbk **£2.99**
The Secret Servant
[GJ493] Pan pbk **£2.99**
The Shooting Script
[GJ494] Pan pbk **£2.99**
The Wrong Side of the Sky
[GJ495] Pan pbk **£2.99**
Uncle Target
The Ministry of Defence's war-prototype tank vanishes in the desert near the Gulf of Aquaba.
[GJ496] Pan pbk **£3.50**
Venus with Pistol
[GJ497] Pan pbk **£2.50**

MACINNES, HELEN
Popular, fast-paced thrillers, often with a romantic element, by the 'Queen of spy writers'.
Above Suspicion
[GJ498] Fontana pbk **£2.50**
Agent in Place
[GJ499] Fontana pbk **£2.95**
Assignment in Brittany
[GJ500] Fontana pbk **£2.95**
Cloak of Darkness
[GJ501] Fontana pbk **£1.95**
Decision at Delphi
[GJ502] Fontana pbk **£3.50**
Friends and Lovers
[GJ503] Fontana pbk **£2.95**
Horizon
[GJ504] Fontana pbk **£2.95**
I and My True Love
[GJ505] Fontana pbk **£2.95**
Message from Malaga
[GJ506] Fontana pbk **£3.50**
Neither Five Nor Three
[GJ507] Fontana pbk **£2.95**
North from Rome
[GJ508] Fontana pbk **£2.95**
Pray for a Brave Heart
[GJ509] Fontana pbk **£2.95**
Prelude to Terror
[GJ510] Fontana pbk **£2.95**
Rest and be Thankful
[GJ511] Fontana pbk **£2.75**
Ride a Pale Horse
[GJ512] Fontana pbk **£3.50**
The Double Image
[GJ513] Fontana pbk **£2.95**
The Hidden Target
[GJ514] Fontana pbk **£2.95**
The Salzburg Connection
[GJ515] Fontana pbk **£2.95**
The Snare of the Hunter
[GJ516] Fontana pbk **£1.75**

The Unconquerable
[GJ517] Fontana pbk **£3.50**
The Venetian Affair
[GJ518] Fontana pbk **£2.95**

MACLEAN, ALASTAIR
One of the most popular and prolific contemporary thriller writers, whose keen sense of history reflects his own experience. The son of a Scots minister, he was brought up in the Highlands, and joined the Navy in 1941, spending two and a half years aboard a cruiser. He died in 1977, having written 30 books.
Athabasca
[GJ519] Fontana pbk **£2.95**
Bear Island
[GJ520] Fontana pbk **£2.50**
Breakheart Pass
[GJ521] Fontana pbk **£2.95**
Caravan to Vaccares
[GJ522] Fontana pbk **£2.50**
Circus
[GJ523] Fontana pbk **£2.50**
Fear is the Key
[GJ524] Fontana pbk **£2.95**
Floodgate
[GJ525] Fontana pbk **£2.95**
Force Ten from Navarone
[GJ526] Fontana pbk **£2.50**
Goodbye California
[GJ527] Fontana pbk **£2.95**
H.M.S. Ulysses
[GJ528] Fontana pbk **£2.95**
Ice Station Zebra
[GJ529] Fontana pbk **£2.50**
Night without End
[GJ530] Fontana pbk **£2.95**
Puppet on a Chain
[GJ531] Fontana pbk **£2.95**
River of Death
[GJ532] Fontana pbk **£2.95**
San Andreas
[GJ533] Fontana pbk **£2.25**
Santorini
[GJ534] Fontana pbk **£2.95**
Seawitch
[GJ535] Fontana pbk **£2.50**
South by Java Head
[GJ536] Fontana pbk **£2.95**
The Golden Gate
[GJ538] Fontana pbk **£2.95**
The Golden Rendezvous
[GJ539] Fontana pbk **£2.95**

Robert Ludlum, author of *Trevayne* (Grafton Books hbk **£12.95**)

FICTION

The Guns of Navarone
[GJ540] Fontana pbk £2.95
The Last Frontier
[GJ541] Fontana pbk £2.95
The Lonely Sea: Collected Sea Stories
[GJ542] Fontana pbk £2.95
The Partisans
[GJ543] Fontana pbk £2.95
The Way to Dusty Death
[GJ544] Fontana pbk £2.95
When Eight Bells Toll
[GJ545] Fontana pbk £2.95
Where Eagles Dare
[GJ546] Fontana pbk £2.95

MACLEAN, ALASTAIR & STUART, IAN
The Dark Crusader
[GJ547] Fontana pbk £2.95
The Satan Bug
[GJ548] Fontana pbk £2.50

MACNEILL, ALASTAIR
Macneill has developed two of Alastair Maclean's
unfinished story outlines. His most recent tells the
story of how Rembrandt's 'Night Watch' is
dispatched on a tour of the world's art galleries - by
the time it arrives in New York, it has been swopped
with a forgery.
Alastair Maclean's Death Train
[GJ549] Fontana pbk £3.99
**Alastair Maclean's The
Rembrandt Affair**   NEW
[GJ550] Collins hbk £11.95

MASON, ALFRED EDWARD WOODLEY
The Four Feathers
Classic adventure story of a man accused of
cowardice who seeks to redeem himself in the eyes of
his friends.
[GJ551] Dent pbk £3.95

MASTERS, JOHN
Adventure stories set during the twilight of the
British Empire. With *Bhowani Junction*, he achieved
a solid presentation of the last years of the Raj,
long before such subject matter became widely
popular. *The Nightrunners of Bengal* is a
classic.
Bhowani Junction
[GJ552] Sphere pbk £3.99
Man of War
[GJ553] Sphere pbk £3.50
The Deceivers
[GJ554] Sphere pbk £3.99
The Nightrunners of Bengal
[GJ555] Sphere pbk £3.50
LOSS OF EDEN
Now, God Be Thanked
A highly acclaimed trilogy depicting the Great War as
it affected England.
[GJ556] Sphere pbk £4.50
Heart of War
[GJ557] Sphere pbk £3.99
By the Green of the Spring
[GJ558] Sphere pbk £3.95
SAVAGE NOVELS
Lotus and the Wind
[GJ559] Sphere pbk £1.95
Far, Far the Mountain Peak
[GJ560] Sphere pbk £2.50
Ravi Lancers
[GJ561] Sphere pbk £3.99
Venus of Konpara
[GJ562] Sphere pbk £2.25

MELVILLE-ROSS, ANTHONY
Wartime thrillers set on board submarines.
Command
[GJ563] Fontana pbk £2.50

Lohengrin
[GJ564] Fontana pbk £2.95
Shaw's War
[GJ565] M Joseph hbk £10.95
Talon
[GJ566] Fontana pbk £1.75

MEREK, JACK
Target Stealth   NEW
A world-threatening terrorist plot culminating in a
fighter-plane dogfight.
[GJ567] Sidgwick hbk £12.95

MILLE, NELSON DE
Huge sprawling thrillers with a loyal following.
By the Rivers of Babylon
[GJ568] Grafton pbk £3.50
Cathedral
[GJ569] Grafton pbk £3.95
Talbot Odyssey
[GJ570] Grafton pbk £3.95
Word of Honour
[GJ571] Grafton pbk £3.95

MONTSERRAT, NICHOLAS
A prolific writer of classic sea stories, Montserrat
rose to the rank of Lieutenant-Commander in World
War II. His experience brings a sharp authenticity to
all his novels, but *The Cruel Sea* is a particular
classic.
H.M.S. Marlborough Will Enter Harbour
[GJ572] Pan pbk £2.50
Richer than All His Tribe
[GJ573] Pan pbk £1.95
Running Proud
[GJ574] Pan pbk £1.50
The Cruel Sea
[GJ575] Penguin pbk £3.50
The Kappillan of Malta
[GJ576] Pan pbk £3.95
The Pillow Fight
[GJ577] Pan pbk £1.95
The Ship that Died of Shame
[GJ578] Pan pbk £1.95
The Tribe that Lost Its Head
[GJ579] Pan pbk £2.50
Three Corvettes
[GJ580] Pan pbk £2.50

O'BRIAN, PATRICK
Captain Jack Aubrey is the hero of these naval
adventures in the Hornblower tradition.
Desolation Island
[GJ581] Fontana pbk £3.50
H.M.S. Surprise
[GJ582] Fontana pbk £2.50
Post Captain
[GJ583] Fontana pbk £3.50
The Far Side of the World
[GJ584] Fontana pbk £3.50
The Fortune of War
[GJ585] Fontana pbk £2.50
The Ionian Mission
[GJ586] Fontana pbk £2.50
The Mauritius Command
[GJ587] Fontana pbk £2.95
The Reverse of the Medal
[GJ588] Fontana pbk £2.95
The Surgeon's Mate
[GJ589] Fontana pbk £2.50
The Thirteen-Gun Salute   NEW
Aubrey's career seems at last to be entering harbour.
All his life he has triumphed over the dangers of the
sea, and the violence of the enemy. But his rashness
and indiscretion have time and again enabled his
rivals to prevent him from reaping his just rewards.
[GJ590] Collins hbk £11.95
Treason's Harbour
[GJ591] Fontana pbk £2.50

ORCZY, BARONESS
The Scarlet Pimpernel
A classic spy story, set in the French Revolution. The
League of the Scarlet Pimpernel attempts to rescue
victims of the reign of terror.
[GJ592] Hodder hbk £7.95

PALLISER, PETER
The Bid   NEW
Financial thriller set in the world of take-overs.
[GJ593] Penguin pbk £3.99

PARKER, GERRARD
Prism   NEW
A Second World War thriller involving the Mafia,
Interpol and the Kennedy family. Gerrard Parker is
the *nom de plume* of two well-known thriller writers
who prefer to remain anonymous.
[GJ594] Sidgwick hbk £11.95

PATTERSON, HARRY
The alter ego of *Jack Higgins*.
Brought in Dead
[GJ595] Arrow pbk £1.95
Comes the Dark Stranger
[GJ596] Arrow pbk £2.50
Graveyard Shift
[GJ597] Arrow pbk £2.50
The Cry of the Hunter
[GJ598] Arrow pbk £2.50
The Sad Wind from the Sea
[GJ599] Arrow pbk £2.50
The Thousand Faces of Night
[GJ600] Arrow pbk £2.50
The Valhalla Exchange
[GJ601] Arrow pbk £2.50

POPE, DUDLEY
The most popular of all maritime adventure
novelists. The eponymous hero of the *Ramage* novels
is a British Naval Captain in the Napoleonic
Wars.
Admiral
[GJ602] Arrow pbk £2.50
Buccaneer
[GJ603] Arrow pbk £2.50
Corsair
[GJ604] Secker hbk £10.95
Decoy
[GJ605] Arrow pbk £2.95
Galleon
[GJ606] Arrow pbk £2.50
Governor Ramage RN
[GJ607] Fontana pbk £2.95
Ramage
[GJ608] Fontana pbk £2.95
Ramage and the Dido   NEW
Ramage has a new command, the Dido, one of the
most formidable war machines in the Royal Navy.
This is vintage Ramage - the colourful characters and
gripping battle scenes will be welcomed by new
readers and *aficionados* alike.
[GJ609] Secker hbk £11.95
Ramage and the Drumbeat
[GJ610] Fontana pbk £2.95
Ramage and the Freebooters
[GJ611] Fontana pbk £3.50
Ramage and the Guillotine
[GJ612] Fontana pbk £2.95
Ramage and the Rebels
[GJ613] Fontana pbk £2.95
Ramage and the Renegades
[GJ614] Fontana pbk £2.95
Ramage at Trafalgar
[GJ615] Fontana pbk £2.95
Ramage's Challenge
[GJ616] Fontana pbk £2.95
Ramage's Devil
[GJ617] Fontana pbk £2.95

Ramage's Diamond
[GJ618] Fontana pbk **£2.95**
Ramage's Mutiny
[GJ619] Fontana pbk **£2.95**
Ramage's Prize
[GJ620] Fontana pbk **£2.95**
Ramage's Signal
[GJ621] Fontana pbk **£2.95**
Ramage's Trial
[GJ622] Fontana pbk **£2.95**
The Ramage Touch
[GJ623] Fontana pbk **£3.25**

PORTER, ANNA
Mortal Sins   `NEW`
Strange things are happening in downtown Toronto:
an expensively dressed, shoeless corpse is found
outside Brandy's Restaurant, journalist Judith Hayes
is granted an interview by the reclusive
multimillionaire Paul Zimmerman. Is there more to
him than meets the eye?
[GJ624] WH Allen hbk **£11.95**

PRICE, ANTHONY
One of the very best contemporary thriller
writers. Price was educated at King's School,
Canterbury and studied history at Oxford; until his
retirement in 1988, he was editor of the *Oxford
Times*.
A New Kind of War
[GJ625] Grafton pbk **£3.50**
A Prospect of Vengeance   `NEW`
The discovery of Philip Masson's body in old Mrs
Griffin's pond launches the investigative team of Ian
Robinson and Jenny Callaghan on a trail of discovery
that leads them back to the end of the
Wilson/Callaghan era.
[GJ626] Futura hbk **£2.95**
For the Good of the State
[GJ627] Grafton pbk **£2.95**
Gunner Kelly
[GJ628] Grafton pbk **£2.50**
Here Be Monsters
[GJ629] Grafton pbk **£2.50**
October Men
[GJ630] Futura pbk **£2.95**
Old Vengeful
[GJ631] Grafton pbk **£2.95**
Other Paths to Glory
[GJ632] Futura pbk **£2.25**
Our Man in Camelot
[GJ633] Futura pbk **£1.95**
Sion Crossing
[GJ634] Grafton pbk **£2.50**
Soldier No More
[GJ635] Grafton pbk **£3.50**
The '44 Vintage
[GJ636] Futura pbk **£2.95**
The Alamut Ambush
[GJ637] Grafton pbk **£2.95**
The Labyrinth Makers
[GJ638] Grafton pbk **£2.95**
The Memory Trap   `NEW`
David Audley finds himself pig-in-the-middle
in a bizarre sequence of events in Germany, Italy and
on the Welsh border. Terrorism is changing
the rules of his familiar Cold War world of
espionage.
[GJ639] Gollancz hbk **£11.95**
Tomorrow's Ghost
[GJ640] Futura pbk **£2.95**
War Game
[GJ641] Futura pbk **£2.25**

PUZO, MARIO
Fools Die
[GJ642] Pan pbk **£3.99**
Fortunate Pilgrim
[GJ643] Hodder pbk **£2.25**

The Fourth K   `NEW`
The first Mario Puzo novel for four years: its
publishers say that so astonishing and controversial is
its subject matter, that nothing can be printed about its
plot or characters.
[GJ644] Heinemann hbk **£12.95**
The Godfather
An epic novel, which was the basis for one of the
most successful films of the 70s.
[GJ645] Pan pbk **£4.50**
The Sicilian
[GJ646] Bantam pbk **£3.95**

QUINNELL, A.J.
Complex thrillers set in exotic locations.
Blood Ties
[GJ647] Hodder pbk **£2.95**
Man on Fire
[GJ648] Futura pbk **£2.95**
Siege of Silence
The new American ambassador to San Canbo
becomes involved in a Communist-directed plot.
[GJ649] Hodder pbk **£2.95**
Snap Shot
[GJ650] Futura pbk **£1.95**
The Mahdi
[GJ651] Futura pbk **£2.95**

REEMAN, DOUGLAS
Classic wartime thrillers which focus on some
of the horrific features of modern warfare. Variously
set during both world wars, Reeman writes
perceptive novels which have a reputation for
intelligence and sensitivity, as well as being
tremendously popular.
A Prayer for the Ship
[GJ652] Arrow pbk **£2.50**
A Ship Must Die
[GJ653] Arrow pbk **£2.50**
Badge of Glory
[GJ654] Arrow pbk **£2.95**
Dive in the Sun
[GJ655] Arrow pbk **£2.95**
Go in and Sink
[GJ656] Arrow pbk **£2.95**
High Water
[GJ657] Arrow pbk **£2.50**
Hostile Shore
[GJ658] Arrow pbk **£2.50**
In Danger's Hour
[GJ659] Pan pbk **£2.50**
Path of the Storm
[GJ660] Arrow pbk **£2.25**
Rendezvous South Atlantic
[GJ661] Arrow pbk **£2.50**
Send a Gunboat
[GJ662] Arrow pbk **£1.95**
Strike from the Sea
[GJ663] Arrow pbk **£2.95**
Surface with Daring
[GJ664] Arrow pbk **£1.95**
The Destroyers
[GJ665] Arrow pbk **£2.50**
The First to Land
[GJ666] Arrow pbk **£2.50**
The Iron Pirate
[GJ667] Pan pbk **£2.95**
The Last Raider
[GJ668] Arrow pbk **£2.95**
The Volunteers
[GJ669] Arrow pbk **£2.75**
The White Guns   `NEW`
VE Day, 1945. Most are rejoicing, but not Lieutenant
Vere Marriott.
[GJ670] Heinemann hbk **£10.95**
To Risks Unknown
[GJ671] Arrow pbk **£2.50**
Torpedo Run
[GJ672] Arrow pbk **£2.50**

Winged Escort
[GJ673] Arrow pbk **£2.95**
With Blood and Iron
[GJ674] Arrow pbk **£2.50**

RYAN, CHARLES
Panjang Incident   `NEW`
A Trident missile is sunk by terrorists. Soviet and US
teams race to the site before a tidal wave wipes out
the leaders of the Western world at their summit
conference. Charles Ryan is a commercial airline pilot
living in California.
[GJ675] Hodder hbk **£7.95**

RYDER, JONATHAN
Pseudonym of Robert Ludlum.
The Cry of Halidon
[GJ676] Grafton pbk **£3.50**
Trevayne
[GJ677] Grafton pbk **£2.95**

SAPPER
Pseudonym of Herman Cyril McNeile, who
served with the Royal Engineers during the First
World War. These are gripping adventure yarns,
full of heroic deeds and nationalism. Classics of the
genre.
Best Short Stories
[GJ678] Dent hbk **£9.50**
[GJ679] Dent pbk **£3.50**
Bulldog Drummond
[GJ680] Penguin pbk **£2.95**
The Black Gang
[GJ681] Dent pbk **£2.95**
The Final Count
[GJ682] Dent pbk **£3.50**
Third Round
[GJ683] Dent pbk **£2.50**

SEBASTIAN, TIM
Spy Shadow   `NEW`
Another topical spy story from the first BBC
correspondent in Moscow. He was expelled in 1985
after being accused of spying.
[GJ684] Simon & Sch hbk **£11.95**
The Spy in Question
[GJ685] Bantam pbk **£3.50**

SEYMOUR, GERALD
A former ITN news reporter, Seymour has become an
exciting writer of thrillers.
A Song in the Morning
[GJ686] Fontana pbk **£2.95**
Archangel
[GJ687] Fontana pbk **£2.95**
At Close Quarters
[GJ688] Fontana pbk **£3.50**
Field of Blood
[GJ689] Fontana pbk **£2.95**
Harry's Game
[GJ690] Fontana pbk **£2.95**
Home Run   `NEW`
A new thriller set in the Middle East. For two
decades, spanning the Shah's rule and the regime of
Ayatollah Khomeini, Matthew Furniss has run the
British agents in Tehran. In the wake of the Islamic
revolution, Furniss is ordered to the Middle East to
fortify his agents.
[GJ691] Collins Harv hbk **£12.95**
In Honour Bound
[GJ692] Fontana pbk **£3.50**
Kingfisher
[GJ693] Fontana pbk **£2.95**
Red Fox
[GJ694] Fontana pbk **£2.95**
The Contract
[GJ695] Fontana pbk **£2.95**
The Glory Boys
[GJ696] Fontana pbk **£2.95**

SHELDON, SIDNEY
American bestselling thriller writer.
Bloodline
[GJ697] Pan pbk **£3.95**
If Tomorrow Comes
[GJ698] Pan pbk **£3.99**
Master of the Game
[GJ699] Pan pbk **£3.99**
Other Side of Midnight
[GJ700] Pan pbk **£3.99**
Rage of Angels
[GJ701] Pan pbk **£3.99**
Stranger in the Mirror
[GJ702] Pan pbk **£3.99**
The Sands of Time   `NEW`
Four nuns become embroiled in the Basque
revolutionary struggle.
[GJ703] Collins hbk **£11.95**
Windmills of the Gods
[GJ704] Fontana pbk **£3.95**

SHUTE, NEVIL
Born in 1899, Nevil Shute was educated at
Shrewsbury School and Balliol College, Oxford, and
wrote his first novel, *Marazan*, in 1926. His books
provide classic story-telling in a fine tradition of
romantic adventure novels. He has also given us fine
descriptions of Australia (most notably in *A Town
Like Alice*), where he lived from 1948 until his death
in 1960.
A Town Like Alice
[GJ705] Pan pbk **£2.99**
An Old Captivity
[GJ706] Pan pbk **£3.50**
Beyond the Black Stump
[GJ707] Pan pbk **£2.95**
In the Wet
[GJ708] Pan pbk **£3.50**
Landfall
[GJ709] Pan pbk **£2.50**
Lonely Road
[GJ710] Pan pbk **£2.50**
Marazan
[GJ711] Pan pbk **£2.50**
Most Secret
[GJ712] Pan pbk **£2.99**
No Highway
[GJ713] Pan pbk **£3.99**
**Omnibus: A Town Like Alice/On the
Beach/No Highway**
[GJ714] Heinemann hbk **£9.95**
On the Beach
[GJ715] Pan pbk **£3.50**
Pastoral
[GJ716] Pan pbk **£2.99**
Pied Piper
[GJ717] Pan pbk **£3.50**
Requiem for a Wren
[GJ718] Pan pbk **£3.50**
Round the Bend
[GJ719] Pan pbk **£2.95**
Ruined City
[GJ720] Pan pbk **£3.50**
So Disdained
[GJ721] Pan pbk **£2.50**
Stallion Gate
[GJ722] Pan pbk **£2.95**
Stephen Morris
[GJ723] Heinemann hbk **£9.95**
The Chequer Board
[GJ724] Pan pbk **£2.95**
The Far Country
[GJ725] Pan pbk **£3.50**
The Rainbow and the Rose
[GJ726] Pan pbk **£2.99**
**Three of a Kind: An Old
Captivity/Pastoral/Requiem for a
Wren**
[GJ727] Heinemann hbk **£10.95**

Trustee from the Toolroom
[GJ728] Pan pbk **£2.99**
What Happened to the Corbetts
[GJ729] Pan pbk **£2.50**

SILVERMAN, DOV
Fall of the Shogun
[GJ730] Grafton pbk **£3.99**
The Shishi   `NEW`
Continues the story of John Mungi: an epic saga in
the great tradition of James Michener and James
Clavell.
[GJ731] Grafton hbk **£12.95**

SMITH, MARTIN CRUZ
Serious and authentic thrillers. *Gorky Park* is a
classic.
Gorky Park
[GJ732] Pan pbk **£3.50**
Nightwing
[GJ733] Pan pbk **£2.95**
Polar Stars   `NEW`
The long-awaited sequel to *Gorky Park*. Former
Moscow Police Inspector Arkady Renko is a fugitive,
imprisoned in a psychiatric hospital for political
unreliability upon his return to Russia at the end of
Gorky Park, escapes to Siberia and goes
underground, working on a Russian factory-ship.
[GJ734] Collins hbk **£12.95**

SMITH, WILBUR
Prolific bestselling author who has lived all his life in
Africa. Born in Zambia, he was educated at Rhodes
University: he is passionately committed to the
continent, and has set the majority of his novels there.
Cry Wolf
[GJ735] Pan pbk **£3.50**
Eagle in the Sky
[GJ736] Pan pbk **£2.95**
Gold Mine
[GJ737] Pan pbk **£2.99**
Hungry as the Sea
[GJ738] Pan pbk **£3.50**
Shout at the Devil
[GJ739] Pan pbk **£2.99**
The Dark of the Sun
[GJ740] Pan pbk **£3.50**
The Diamond Hunters
[GJ741] Pan pbk **£2.99**
The Eye of the Tiger
[GJ742] Pan pbk **£3.50**

Wilbur Smith, author of *A Time To Die* (Heinemann
hbk **£12.95**)

The Sunbird
[GJ743] Pan pbk **£3.99**
Wild Justice
[GJ744] Pan pbk **£3.50**
THE BALLANTYNE NOVELS
A Falcon Flies
[GJ745] Pan pbk **£3.99**
Men of Men
[GJ746] Pan pbk **£3.99**
The Angels Weep
[GJ747] Pan pbk **£3.99**
The Leopard Hunts in Darkness
[GJ748] Pan pbk **£3.99**
THE COURTNEY NOVELS
When the Lion Feeds
[GJ749] Pan pbk **£3.99**
The Sound of Thunder
[GJ750] Pan pbk **£3.99**
A Sparrow Falls
[GJ751] Pan pbk **£3.99**
The Burning Shore
[GJ752] Pan pbk **£3.99**
The Power of the Sword
[GJ753] Pan pbk **£3.99**
Rage
[GJ754] Pan pbk **£3.99**
A Time to Die   `NEW`
Sean Courtney, professional hunter and veteran
guerrilla fighter, is swept into the savage tide of a new
war.
[GJ755] Heinemann hbk **£12.95**

SOHMER, STEVE
Favourite Son
Chilling political thriller about the US presidency.
[GJ756] Bantam pbk **£3.99**

STANLEY, GUY
Death in Tokyo
A thriller set in modern Japan, involving organized
crime, drugs, high finance and murder.
[GJ757] Bantam pbk **£3.99**

STONEHOUSE, JOHN
The Baring Fault
[GJ758] Calder pbk **£7.95**
Who Sold Australia?   `NEW`
A story of international intrigue from the late John
Stonehouse.
[GJ759] Hale hbk **£10.95**

TEVIS, WALTER
A versatile popular writer, whose novels defy
categorization: *The Queen's Gambit* is set in the
tension-filled world of chess, while *The Colour of
Money* and *The Hustler* (both filmed) depict,
realistically and memorably, the seedy world of pool-
halls.
Queen's Gambit
[GJ760] Pan pbk **£2.50**
Steps of the Sun
[GJ761] Gollancz hbk **£7.95**
The Colour of Money
[GJ762] Pan pbk **£2.50**
The Hustler
[GJ763] Pan pbk **£1.95**

THOMAS, CRAIG
All the Grey Cats
Kenneth Aubrey arranges the defection of the son of
his most bitter enemy, General Brigitte Winterbach of
East German Intelligence. But when the defection
goes wrong, Aubrey finds himself the victim of
Brigitte's violent revenge.
[GJ764] Fontana pbk **£3.99**
Bear's Tears
[GJ765] Sphere pbk **£3.50**
Firefox
[GJ766] M Joseph hbk **£10.95**

Firefox Down
[GJ767] Sphere pbk **£3.50**
Jade Tiger
[GJ768] Sphere pbk **£3.50**
Rat Trap
[GJ769] Sphere pbk **£2.99**
Sea Leopard
[GJ770] Sphere pbk **£3.50**
Snow Falcon
[GJ771] Sphere pbk **£3.50**
Winter Hawk
[GJ772] Fontana pbk **£3.50**
Wolfsbane
[GJ773] Sphere pbk **£3.50**

THOMAS, MICHAEL M.
An ex-banker, whose financial thrillers show a strong
knowledge of the world of political finance. Soviet
infiltration is one of his major themes.
Green Monday
[GJ774] Arrow pbk **£2.95**
Hard Money
[GJ775] Arrow pbk **£2.95**
Someone Else's Money
[GJ776] Arrow pbk **£2.95**
The Rosespinner Conspiracy
[GJ777] Corgi pbk **£2.95**

THOMAS, ROSS
American mystery and thriller writer, particularly
adept at slick dialogue, whose novels inhabit the
traditional thriller world of international espionage.
Briar Patch
[GJ778] Penguin pbk **£2.95**
Chinaman's Chance
[GJ779] Penguin pbk **£2.50**
Missionary Stew
[GJ780] H Hamilton hbk **£8.95**
Out on the Rim
[GJ781] Mysterious P hbk **£9.95**
Singapore Wink
[GJ782] Firecrest hbk **£6.95**
The Backup Men
[GJ783] Firecrest hbk **£7.95**

THORP, RODERICK
Die Hard
The bestselling book of the blockbusting film. Twelve
terrorists take over a 40 storey office block: their
hostages include Joe Leland's family. So Joe goes to
save them.
[GJ784] Penguin pbk **£2.99**

TOLKIN, MICHAEL
The Player
Unusual thriller set in Hollywood.
[GJ785] Faber pbk **£3.95**

TONKIN, PETER
The Coffin Ship   **NEW**
Officers of a supertanker plan to sell the cargo and
sink the ship.
[GJ786] Headline hbk **£12.95**

TREHERNE, JOHN
The Galapagos Affair
[GJ787] Grafton pbk **£3.50**
The Mangrove Chronicle
[GJ788] Grafton pbk **£2.95**
The Trap
[GJ789] Grafton pbk **£2.50**

TRENHAILE, JOHN
Espionage, high finance and political intrigue set, in
particular, in contemporary Russia and China.
Krysalis   **NEW**
Fast-moving, action-packed thriller which tells the
story of three people caught in a trap.
[GJ790] Collins hbk **£11.95**

Kyril
[GJ791] Sphere pbk **£2.95**
Nocturne for the General
[GJ792] Sphere pbk **£2.50**
The Gates of Exquisite View
[GJ793] Fontana pbk **£3.95**
The Mahjong Spies
[GJ794] Fontana pbk **£3.50**
The Scroll of Benevolence
In 1997 Hong Kong will return to China. The
commercial empires have made plans to leave, their
assets telexed to safety in a brilliant scheme,
codenamed the scroll of benevolence.
[GJ795] Fontana pbk **£3.99**
View from the Square
[GJ796] Fontana pbk **£2.95**

TREW, ANTHONY
The world of oil tankers, shipwrecks and lost treasure
brought to life by a sailor and business executive.
Bannister's Chart
[GJ797] Fontana pbk **£2.50**
Death of a Supertanker
[GJ798] Fontana pbk **£1.50**
Running Wild
[GJ799] Fontana pbk **£1.50**
Sea Fever
[GJ800] Fontana pbk **£1.50**
Yashimoto's Last Dive
[GJ801] Fontana pbk **£2.95**

WALLACE, IRVING
Intricately plotted bestsellers, whose complicated
succession of events requires a good deal of
suspension of disbelief. They rely on the ever-popular
stock tricks of doubles, double-agents and the innate
stupidity of world leaders. Escapist fun.
Celestial Bed
[GJ802] Sphere pbk **£2.99**
Second Lady
[GJ803] Arrow pbk **£2.99**
Seven Minutes
[GJ804] Hodder pbk **£3.50**
Seventh Secret
[GJ805] Sphere pbk **£2.95**
The Almighty
[GJ806] Sphere pbk **£3.50**
The Chapman Report
[GJ807] Sphere pbk **£3.50**
The Guest of Honour   **NEW**
The gripping tale of a disillusioned US president and
his involvement with his attractive female counterpart
in a communist-besieged South East Asian state.
[GJ808] M Joseph hbk **£12.95**
Three Sirens
[GJ809] Hodder pbk **£3.95**

WEST, MORRIS
Well-crafted, rather old-fashioned thrillers, set in
exotic places, often with dilemmas of faith,
specifically Catholic, at their centre.
Cassidy
[GJ810] Hodder pbk **£2.95**
Children of the Sun
[GJ811] Hodder pbk **£2.50**
Daughter of Silence
[GJ812] Hodder pbk **£1.95**
Harlequin
[GJ813] Fontana pbk **£2.50**
Naked Country
[GJ814] Hodder pbk **£2.99**
Second Victory
[GJ815] Hodder pbk **£1.95**
Shoes of the Fisherman
[GJ816] Hodder pbk **£2.50**
Summer of the Red Wolf
[GJ817] Hodder pbk **£2.99**
The Ambassador
[GJ818] Hodder pbk **£2.95**

The Devil's Advocate
[GJ819] Fontana pbk **£2.95**

WINTON, JOHN
Polaris   **NEW**
A young submarine officer is forced to come to terms
with the nuclear issue.
[GJ820] M Joseph hbk **£11.95**

WOODMAN, RICHARD
Historical novels set during the Napoleonic Wars and
featuring Captain Nathaniel Drinkwater.
1805
[GJ821] Sphere pbk **£2.95**
A King's Cutter
[GJ822] Sphere pbk **£2.99**
Baltic Mission
[GJ823] Sphere pbk **£2.99**
Bomb Vessel
[GJ824] Sphere pbk **£2.99**
Brig of War
[GJ825] Sphere pbk **£2.99**
Eye of the Fleet
[GJ826] Sphere pbk **£2.99**
The Corvette
[GJ827] Sphere pbk **£2.99**

YATES, DORNFORD
The pseudonym of Cecil Mercer (1885-1960), an
accomplished barrister who later turned to writing.
His numerous thrillers were particularly popular in
the inter-war years, and inspired a large following.
Blind Corner
[GJ828] Dent pbk **£2.50**
Blood Royal
[GJ829] Dent pbk **£2.50**
Cost Price
[GJ830] Dent pbk **£3.95**
Gale Warning
[GJ831] Dent pbk **£3.50**
Perishable Goods
[GJ832] Dent pbk **£2.50**
Red in the Morning
[GJ833] Dent pbk **£3.95**
She Fell Among Thieves
[GJ834] Dent pbk **£2.95**

Morris West, author of *The Ambassador*
(Hodder & Stoughton pbk **£2.95**) & *Harlequin*
(Fontana pbk **£2.50**)

Sherlock Holmes and Dr Watson from *The Return of Sherlock Holmes* (Michael O' Mara Books hbk £12.00)

The Geniuses and the Plodders : The Early Detectives

Julian Symons

It seems reasonable to suppose that detectives could not have appeared in fiction until they existed in fact, but that is not quite true. The Oxford Dictionary traces the word 'detective' back to 1843, just after a Detective Office had been set up at Scotland Yard, and a little later New York appointed its first chief of police, but genius had anticipated reality. It was in 1841 that Edgar Allan Poe's Chevalier C. August Dupin appeared on the scene, solving the mysteries of the two women found murdered on the fourth storey of an apparently inaccessible room, in 'The Murders in the Rue Morgue'.

Dupin owed something to the *Mémoires* of Eugène François Vidocq, the former criminal who became the first chief of the Sûreté. It was no doubt reading Vidocq's extravagant account of his own life and achievement that led Poe to make Dupin a Parisian, but the detective himself is a wholly original creation. He is moody, egotistical, anti-

Sir Arthur Conan Doyle from *The Return of Sherlock Holmes*, illustrated by Frederic Dorr Steele (Michael O'Mara Books hbk £12.00)

social, with extraordinary powers of analytical deduction plus flashes of intuitive genius, as in a passage where he exactly interprets his companion's thoughts. Rather more than half a century

later, Conan Doyle used the same device, when Sherlock Holmes broke in on Watson's reverie about the American Civil War, and said: "You are right, it does seem a most preposterous way of settling a dispute."

Dupin appeared in only three short stories, but he set the pattern for many Great Detectives, all amateurs and

> *He is moody, egotistical, anti-social, with extraordinary powers of analytical deduction plus flashes of intuitive genius*

variously eccentric, many of them masters of disguise like Vidocq. But the workaday down-to-earth professional flourished in Victorian fiction too, most notably through Dickens and Wilkie Collins. Dickens was fascinated by police work, and in *Oliver Twist* introduced two of the Bow Street Runners who were replaced by the Metropolitan and other police forces, but his true admiration was reserved for the Detective Department, and in particular for one of its two Inspectors, Frederick Field. He spent nights out with Field and other detectives, when they visited thieves' lairs or went down to the river, and wrote articles praising the detectives' unusual intelligence, and remarking how in one haunt Field's "roving eye searches along every corner of the cellar as he talks". Field was the model for 'Inspector Bucket of the Detective' in *Bleak House*. Bucket is able to disguise himself when necessary, but is a bloodhound rather than a genius. A decade later, Dickens' friend Wilkie Collins produced in *The Moonstone* a counterpart to Bucket in Sergeant Cuff, whose face is sharp as a hatchet, its skin "yellow and dry and withered as an autumn leaf". Cuff has a nice line in enigmatic observations, as when he says blandly that nobody has stolen the missing moonstone. And in a sense he is right.

But it was Dickens' example that spawned a host of imitators, like the apparently authentic but actually fictional *Recollections of a Detective Police-Officer* by "Waters", and in the United States the similarly fictional *Leaves from*

Illustration from *Tales of Mystery and Imagination* by Edgar Allan Poe, illustrated by Harry Clarke (Michael O'Mara Books hbk £12.00)

the Note-Book of a New York Detective. The remarkable *Notting Hill Mystery* by Charles Felix introduced another variation, an investigator for a life assurance company as detective, and had

---

The head of Scotland Yard's Detective Department and three of his Inspectors were found guilty of taking bribes, and the popularity of pseudo-authentic memoirs faded

---

other novel features like a map and a facsimile letter. In the 1870s however, the head of Scotland Yard's Detective Department and three of his Inspectors were found guilty of taking bribes, and the popularity of pseudo-authentic memoirs faded.

Collins admired the novels of Emile Gaboriau, and the French writer's Monsieur Lecoq did more original work of a practical kind than any of his predecessors. He was the first detective in fiction to make a plaster cast of footprints, and to show how a striking clock may be used misleadingly by a criminal. *Monsieur Lecoq* (1869) is the one to read, though *L'Affaire Lerouge* and *Le Crime d'Orcival* are also interesting, at least to the student of detection. For others it has to be said that Gaboriau is often pretty hard going.

None of these professionals - Bucket,

Cuff, Lecoq - had any pretensions to gentility, and the same applies to Ebenezer Gryce, the creation of the American Anna Katharine Green, who does some very creditable detecting in *The Leavenworth Case* (1878). There are other Gryce novels, and Ms Green (in fact Mrs Rohlf) also gave us one of the earliest amateur woman detectives, Amelia Butterworth, who acts sometimes as Gryce's assistant. She was very likely based on one of the pseudo-authentic memoirs of the 1860s, *The Experiences of a Lady Detective*.

And thus to Sherlock. He is so justly famous that Conan Doyle's casual borrowings are forgotten, though he acknowledged them handsomely enough. Poe's Dupin is the model for Holmes as a personality, eccentric, egotistical, anti-social, a drug-taker and a misogynist - although the portrait was much softened in the later stories. From Gaboriau came details about plaster casts and the possibility of leaving misleading clues, although Conan Doyle improved on everything he borrowed. The passion for detective fiction that has lasted for a century was created above all by the Sherlock Holmes short stories, as they began to appear in the nineties and caused a clamour for the *Strand* magazine at bookstalls "worse than anything at a bargain sale", as an eye-witness put it. Other interesting detectives were Holmes' early contemporaries, among them Arthur Morrison's Martin Hewitt, and M. McDonnell Bodkin's under-estimated Paul Beck, 'the Rule of Thumb Detective', but these more prosaic characters could never compete in popularity with Sherlock Holmes.

By the end of the century the two very different kinds of detective were firmly

---

What is the psychological reason behind this passion for appearing to be somebody else?

---

established. The eccentric amateur, who plays the detective game for love rather than money, had a host of 20th century followers - Hercule Poirot, Miss Marple, Lord Peter Wimsey, Philo Vance and Nero Wolfe only head the long list. And

plodding in the wake of Inspector Bucket came Superintendents French and Wilson, and Inspector Richard Queen. But one aspect of the early amateur is unique: his capacity for disguise. What is the psychological reason behind this passion for appearing to be somebody else, one equalled only by the need many writers of detective stories feel to hide behind pseudonyms? No doubt it exists, but all we can be certain of is the pleasure we feel when Holmes deceives the credulous Watson in the guise of an elderly deformed book collector, or an addict in an opium den. The same pleasure was felt by thousands of Victorians when watching Tom Taylor's immensely popular melodrama *The Ticket-of-Leave Man*, at the moment when the hero pulled off the wig and whiskers he was wearing while pretending to be a drunken navvy, and cried triumphantly: *"I am Hawkshaw the Detective."*

As a writer, editor and archivist, Julian Symons has contributed much to the development of the modern crime story; he has written a number of classic novels, including *The Colour of Murder* and *The Narrowing Circle*, and a range of critical studies and histories.

CRIME FICTION

Statistics can be dull, but one market research company recently claimed to have discovered what women do in bed: apparently they read paperbacks, and the chances are (one in four, or 26%) that they will read crime, murder or mystery stories. As a category, crime fiction now equals romance in British paperback sales, being purchased by 12% of the adult population.

Naturally enough publishers have responded to this trend by promoting their major authors - recent examples include Ruth Rendell, Dorothy Simpson, P.D. James and Margaret Yorke. But what was also discovered in the survey was that by far and away the most popular type of crime story remained the 'classical/traditional', otherwise known as the 'Golden Age', centred on writers such as Allingham, Sayers and Christie. Thus, when sales of Fontana's Agatha Christie titles actually began to decline a year ago, the situation was deemed sufficiently serious to call in - what else? - a market research company. Inappropriate covers were soon identified as the culprit (they suggested horror rather than crime) and sales quickly picked up again. No doubt mindful of such trends, Gollancz, with a long tradition of yellow-jacketed crime novels behind them (including Michael Innes and Emma Lathen), and Oxford University Press, with rather less of a track record, have recently launched paperback crime series. Oxford's approach is characteristically purist: their first three titles, Frank Arthur's *Who Killed Netta Maul?*, James Hilton's *Was It Murder?* and *The Eye of Osiris* by Austin R. Freeman, are all golden age gems that have languished out of print for years. Hogarth, with a list which includes Carter Dickson's *The Skeleton in the Clock*, continues to reprint the best from this era, as do, occasionally, Penguin with their 'Classic Crime' series, but in general the field is wide open for plundering.

The continued emphasis on American 'hard-boiled' fiction (which accounts for a mere 5% of crime readership) is therefore surprising, but no less welcome, since it guarantees the availability of a variety of literary styles. Of the major publishers, Chatto have launched a hardback crime series, which includes Michael Malone, a name to watch, while, among the small independents, No Exit Press (an Oldcastle imprint) have already established an impressive list. Their 'Vintage Crime' includes Paul Cain and Raoul Whitfield, both contributors to the legendary hard-boiled pulp magazine *Black Mask*, and the eccentric Jonathan Latimer. Their 'Contemporary Crime' series offers the first real opportunity to read Arthur Lyons, Michael Collins and Michael Lewis in paperback. Perhaps most interesting is their decision to introduce a 'European Crime' list, a field most unjustly ignored by British publishers, which opens with Sebastien Japrisot's *The Lady in the Car with Glasses and a Gun*. There are many other novelists, including the Swiss Friedrich Dürrenmatt, the French team Boileau-Narcejac and Sweden's Peter Wahlöo, who deserve a wider exposure. Maybe they should bring the market researchers in on that one too.

Anthologies & Studies

ASIMOV, ISAAC (ED)
The Best Crime Stories of the 19th Century `NEW`
An intriguing mixture of early detection (Holmes and Poe's C. Auguste Dupin are the best known characters) and criminal tales by more mainstream novelists such as Wilkie Collins, Thomas Hardy and Nathaniel Hawthorne. A strong sense of period pervades these stories, not least in Mark Twain's 'The Man That Corrupted Hadleyburg'.
[GK1] Robson hbk **£11.95**

BARNES, MELVYN
Murder in Print
A critical guide to two centuries of Crime Fiction. Recommended.
[GK2] Barn Owl Books hbk **£14.50**

BINYON, T.J.
Murder Will Out:
The Detective in Fiction from Poe to the Present Day `NEW`
Binyon, who reviews Crime Fiction for the *TLS*, has produced a stimulating overview of the genre with particular reference to its central character, the detective. Useful also as a guide to 'who did what to whom, and how'.
[GK3] Oxford hbk **£12.95**

GORMAN, EDWARD (ED)
The Black Lizard Anthology of Crime Fiction
Reprinted gems and contemporary interpretations of the American *roman noir*, including Estleman, Thompson and Whittington.
[GK4] Creative Arts pbk **£6.95**
The Second Black Lizard Anthology of Crime Fiction
More *noir* originals and classics ranging from Spillane and Willeford to McBain and Westlake, plus a novelette from the neglected Peter Rabe.
[GK5] Creative Arts pbk **£10.95**

GREENBERG & PRONZINI (EDS)
Locked-Room Puzzles
Includes the famous John Dickson Carr puzzle, 'The Third Bullet'.
[GK6] Academy pbk **£3.95**
Mammoth Book of Private Eye Stories `NEW`
Short novels and stories, cunningly chosen, from Chandler, McBain, Frederic Brown, Joseph Hanson and 22 others.
[GK7] Robinson pbk **£4.95**
Mammoth Book of Short Crime Stories
[GK8] Robinson pbk **£4.95**
Police Procedurals
[GK9] Academy pbk **£3.50**

GREENE, H. & G. (EDS)
Victorian Villanies
An anthology of stories featuring more rivals of Sherlock Holmes.
[GK10] Penguin pbk **£5.95**

JAKUBOWSKI, MAXIM (ED)
New Crime `NEW`
The first of an annual showcase for modern British and American crime fiction, including specially commissioned or unpublished work by George V. Higgins, James Crumley, David Goodis and Cornell Woolrich.
[GK11] Robinson pbk **£4.99**

KEATING, H.R.F. (ED)
The Bedside Companion to Crime `NEW`
An illustrated miscellany of fact and foible from the world of crime writing. Keating draws on his unrivalled storehouse of knowledge to delight the *aficionado* once again.
[GK12] M O'Mara hbk **£9.95**

PEYTON, RICHARD (ED)
Deadly Odds: Crime & Mystery Stories of the Turf
23 related short stories, including 'The Day of the Losers' by Dick Francis and the 'Grand National Case' by Julian Symons. Doyle, Kipling, Wallace, Innes and Charteris also feature.
[GK13] Pan pbk **£2.95**

QUEEN, ELLERY
Queen's Quorum
A history of the Short Crime story, including the 'best' 125 titles from 1845 - 1967.
[GK14] Greenhill hbk **£15.00**

RADICE, LISANNE
The Way to Write Crime Fiction
Plotting, pacing, false clues and other techniques are all examined, with examples from Rendell, Chandler, le Carré etc, and interviews with Colin Dexter and Anthony Price. A broad list of recommended titles rounds off a useful primer for the aspiring writer of crime fiction.
[GK15] Elm Tree hbk **£10.95**

REILLY, JOHN M. (ED)
20th Century Crime & Mystery Writers (2nd Ed)
A vast and comprehensive critical bibliography listing nearly every English and American crime writer (and some foreign language ones too) with contributing essays by many of the authors themselves. Needs updating to include many of the recent stars in the field.
[GK16] St James P hbk **£45.00**

SYMONS, JULIAN
Bloody Murder
A stimulating critical history of the Crime Novel.
[GK17] Penguin pbk **£3.95**

SYMONS, JULIAN (ED)
Classic Crime Omnibus
Carefully chosen selection of less well known stories by famous crime writers (Sayers, Rendell, Faulkner, Chesterton) and 21 others.
[GK18] Penguin pbk **£4.99**

WATSON, COLIN
Snobbery With Violence: English Crime Stories & Their Audience
Discusses the English 'Golden Age' Crime Story and its sociological implications.
[GK19] Methuen pbk **£4.95**

Crime Writers A - Z

AIRD, CATHERINE (British, 1930 -)
'Whodunnit' specialist whose mysteries remain consistently and genuinely baffling, until solved by Inspector Sloan of the Calleshire County Police. The mythical locale, combined with set piece plots and innocent characterisation are features more reminiscent of the so-called 'Golden Age'.
A Dead Liberty
[GK20] Collins hbk **£9.95**
A Late Phoenix
[GK21] Corgi pbk **£1.95**
Henrietta Who?
[GK22] Corgi pbk **£2.50**
Parting Breaths
[GK23] Corgi pbk **£2.50**
The Complete Steel
[GK24] Corgi pbk **£2.50**

ALLINGHAM, MARGERY (British, 1904 - 1966)
With Sayers and Christie, Allingham epitomized the

Golden Age of English crime writing. Less intense than Sayers, more credible than Christie, her books combined the best qualities of both. She produced consistently well-written and entertaining mysteries, especially those featuring her gentlemanly hero, Albert Campion, played with just the right degree of eccentricity by Peter Davison in the recent TV series.

Beckoning Lady
[GK25] Hogarth pbk **£3.95**

Black Plumes
[GK26] Dent pbk **£3.95**

Cargo of Eagles
[GK27] Hogarth pbk **£3.95**

China Governess
[GK28] Hogarth pbk **£3.95**

Coroner's Pidgin
[GK29] Dent pbk **£3.95**

Dancers in Mourning
[GK30] Penguin pbk **£3.95**

Death of a Ghost
[GK31] Penguin pbk **£3.95**

Flowers for the Judge
[GK32] Penguin pbk **£3.95**

Hide My Eyes
[GK33] Hogarth pbk **£3.95**

Look to the Lady
[GK34] Penguin pbk **£3.95**

More Work for the Undertaker
[GK35] Penguin pbk **£3.99**

Mr Campion and Others
[GK36] Penguin pbk **£3.95**

No Love Lost
[GK37] Penguin pbk **£3.95**

Police at the Funeral
[GK38] Penguin pbk **£3.95**

Sweet Danger
[GK39] Penguin pbk **£3.95**

The Allingham Case-Book
[GK40] Hogarth pbk **£3.95**

The Case of the Late Pig
Although one of her shorter novels, this is quintessential pre-war Allingham in which Campion is in commanding form as he searches for missing corpses and, with the aid of his rough diamond of a manservant, Magarsfontein Lugg, finds the solution to the village crime.
[GK41] Penguin pbk **£3.50**

The Fashion in Shrouds
[GK42] Dent pbk **£3.95**

The Mind Readers
[GK43] Penguin pbk **£3.95**

The Return of Mr Campion NEW
A collection of 'lost' short stories (including non-crime ones), many featuring Campion, published for the first time.
[GK44] Hodder hbk **£10.95**

Tiger in the Smoke
Her most famous book, justly praised for its evocation of urban unease, and the pure evil embodied in the character of Jack Havoc.
[GK45] Hogarth pbk **£3.95**

Traitor's Purse
[GK46] Dent pbk **£2.95**

ARTHUR, FRANK
Who Killed Netta Maul?
[GK46A] Oxford pbk **£3.99**

BARDIN, JOHN FRANKLIN (US, 1916 - 1981)
Recently given a much-publicized plug by Denis Healey, Bardin is set to be 'rediscovered' in a big way. These three novels, all written in less than two years, reveal an extraordinary imagination at work, and are closer to the psychological horror story than to conventional crime fiction. Penguin deserve credit for reprinting them.

Deadly Percheron
[GK47] Penguin pbk **£3.99**

Devil Take the Blue-Tail Fly
Especially terrifying, *Devil Take the Blue-Tail Fly* explores the themes of music and madness in a thoroughly convincing way.
[GK48] Penguin pbk **£3.99**

Last of Philip Bantea
[GK49] Penguin pbk **£3.99**

BARNARD, ROBERT
Increasingly popular practitioner of the classical British detective story, Barnard favours satire over shotguns, and grim reality over capers, in settings as diverse as Norway and Australia. His dialogue is witty, intelligent and darkly humorous.

Bodies
[GK50] Corgi pbk **£2.50**

Death and the Chaste Apprentice NEW
The author's two great joys, opera and English literature, are combined in this urbane story of an Arts Festival, a Jacobean play and an unknown opera by Donizetti. Murder stalks the stage.
[GK51] Collins hbk **£10.95**

Death of a Salesperson NEW
A collection of short stories with hard centres.
[GK52] Collins hbk **£10.95**

Out of the Blackout
[GK53] Corgi pbk **£2.50**

Political Suicide
[GK54] Corgi pbk **£2.50**

Sheer Torture
[GK55] Corgi pbk **£2.50**

The Disposal of the Living
[GK56] Corgi pbk **£2.50**

Unruly Son
[GK57] Mysterious P pbk **£2.50**

BEEDING, FRANCIS
Death Walks in Eastrepps
Written in 1931, *Eastrepps* (a fictional English coastal town) has been hailed as one of the greatest detective stories of all time. This highly suspenseful story of multiple murder and the subsequent scenes in the Old Bailey culminate in a surprise ending plausible enough to satisfy the most hardened cynic.
[GK58] Dover pbk **£4.05**

BENTLEY, E.C. (British, 1875 - 1956)
Trent's Last Case, Bentley's first book, features scruffy Philip Trent, and is one of the world's best known detective novels. It generated three films and many radio dramatisations, and revitalised a weary genre on publication in 1913. It is still an excellent read today, *"the finest detective story of modern times"* according to G.K. Chesterton.

Trent Intervenes
[GK59] Dent pbk **£3.95**

Trent's Last Case
[GK60] Hale hbk **£10.50**

BERKELEY, ANTHONY (British, 1893 - 1971)
Pseudonym of A.B. Cox. Witty and intelligent stories featuring amateur detective Roger Sheringham, a Wimsey-like figure who, in the manner of the times, solved complex cases that were beyond the competence of the Police. Cox also wrote as *Francis Iles* (qv).

Dead Mrs Stratton
[GK61] Hogarth pbk **£3.95**

Piccadilly Murder
[GK62] Dover pbk **£5.55**

The Poisoned Chocolates Case
Members of a 'Crime Circle' produce alternative solutions to a murder. Berkeley's most ingenious and cleverly constructed novel, which has become a classic.
[GK63] Penguin pbk **£3.95**

BLAKE, NICHOLAS (British, 1904 - 1972)
The pseudonym of C. Day Lewis, Blake, like Michael Innes, introduced an erudite and literary element to the genre, causing what had usually been met with critical disdain to be re-appraised. Often featuring his amateur detective Nigel Strangeways, his stories are down-to-earth and topical, and lack the whimsical flavour of Innes's work.

End of a Chapter
[GK64] Dent pbk **£3.95**

Head of a Traveller
[GK65] Dent pbk **£3.95**

Sad Variety
[GK66] Dent pbk **£5.50**

Smiler with a Knife
[GK67] Hogarth pbk **£3.95**

The Beast Must Die
A crime writer hunts down the motorist who killed his son: one of the first and best 'psychological' portraits of a would-be killer's mind, this is Blake's most famous novel.
[GK68] Hogarth pbk **£3.95**

The Private Wound
[GK69] Dent pbk **£3.95**

BLOCK, LAWRENCE (US)
Prolific, multi-faceted author who wrote Rex Stout pastiches (*Topless Tulip Caper*), downbeat procedurals featuring the alcoholic ex-cop Matt Scudder, and Westlake-style capers which chronicle the exploits of bungling burglar Bernie Rhodenbarr.

Burglars Can't Be Choosers
[GK70] Oldcastle P pbk **£1.99**

Eight Million Ways to Die
[GK71] Hodder pbk **£3.50**

Five Little Rich Girls
[GK72] Allison & B pbk **£2.95**

Topless Tulip Caper
[GK73] Allison & B pbk **£2.95**

When the Sacred Gin Mill Closes
Scudder is back doing favours for friends in sleazy New York bars - favours which go sour in the face of murder.
[GK74] Mysterious P pbk **£2.99**

BRAMAH, ERNEST (British, 1868 - 1942)
Best Max Carrados Detective Stories
The first blind detective of note, Carrados was able to solve cases without leaving his armchair. Always ingenious, occasionally unconvincing.
[GK75] Dover pbk **£4.20**

BRAND, CHRISTIANNA (British, 1907 -)
A versatile and individual writer, with something of the English 'Golden Age' atmosphere to her work; her series detective, Inspector Cockrill, is in the best tradition of the English eccentric hero.

Green for Danger
[GK76] Pandora pbk **£3.95**

London Particular
[GK77] Pandora pbk **£3.95**

BRETT, SIMON (British, 1945 -)
Brett specialises in theatrical whodunnits, giving actor/sleuth Charles Paris plenty of scope to debunk Amateur Dramatics and solve the crime. Preposterous scenarios but welcome depth of character, cynically related. Currently a very popular mixture.

A Comedian Dies
[GK78] Futura pbk **£1.75**

A Nice Class of Corpse
[GK79] Hodder pbk **£2.50**

A Series of Murders NEW
While Paris is filming a TV mystery series, one of its stars is 'accidentally' crushed to death, enabling Charles, flask in pocket, to don the figurative deer-stalker.
[GK80] Gollancz hbk **£10.95**

Dead Giveaway
[GK81] Futura pbk **£1.95**

Dead Romantic
[GK82] Dent pbk **£3.95**
Murder Unprompted
[GK83] Futura pbk **£1.95**
Murder in the Title
[GK84] Futura pbk **£1.95**
Not Dead, Only Resting
[GK85] Futura pbk **£1.95**
Shock to the System
[GK86] Dent pbk **£3.95**
Situation Tragedy
[GK87] Futura pbk **£1.95**
What Bloody Man Is That?
[GK88] Futura pbk **£2.95**

BURLEY, W.J. (British, 1945 -)
The West Country based Superintendent Wycliffe approaches his cases with the doggedness of a Columbo, although he is rather more anti-authoritarian. Born in 1914, Burley began writing in the 1960s after discovering Simenon, whose close, dry style he has inherited.
Wycliffe and the Beales
[GK89] Corgi pbk **£2.50**
Wycliffe and the Four Jacks
[GK90] Corgi pbk **£2.50**
Wycliffe and the Pea Green Boat
[GK91] Corgi pbk **£2.50**
Wycliffe and the Quiet Virgin
[GK92] Corgi pbk **£2.50**
Wycliffe and the Scapegoat
[GK93] Corgi pbk **£2.50**
Wycliffe and the Tangled Web   **NEW**
Wycliffe's speciality is tying together the seemingly unconnected strands of a case, and the ingredients here - a pregnant schoolgirl missing from a Cornish fishing village, an anonymous corpse, a Lewis Carroll *aficionado* and an art historian's crippled wife - provide the threads of the tangled web.
[GK94] Gollancz hbk **£10.95**
Wycliffe and the Wild Goose Chase
[GK95] Corgi pbk **£2.50**
Wycliffe in Paul's Court
[GK96] Corgi pbk **£2.50**

BURNETT, W.R. (US, 1899 - 1982)
Little Caesar
The classic tale of Chicago gangsters that spawned a generation of imitations.
[GK97] Oldcastle P pbk **£1.99**

BYRD, MAX (US)
Intelligent private-eye stories in the Hammett mould, featuring Mike Haller and the environs of San Francisco. 'Max Byrd is in the first rank of American crime writing' (*The Times*).
California Thriller
[GK98] Allison & B pbk **£2.95**
Finders Weepers
[GK99] Allison & B pbk **£2.95**
Fly Away Jill
[GK100] Allison & B pbk **£3.50**
Target of Opportunity   **NEW**
[GK101] M Joseph hbk **£10.95**

CAIN, JAMES M.
(US, 1892 - 1977)
Raymond Chandler once described Cain as the 'offal of literature' because he wrote about 'dirty things in a dirty way'. In fact, Cain was an astute writer who realised how much misery resulted from human sexual greed: this is the theme which dominated his best work, notably *The Postman Always Rings Twice* (already filmed three times) and *Double Indemnity* (for which Chanlder ironically wrote the screenplay). He wrote in a spare, vernacular style about characters whose fates were sealed but it isn't appropriate to call him a 'hard-boiled' writer, for beneath the incidental violence lies a good deal of sensitivity.

Cloud Nine
[GK102] Dent pbk **£3.95**
Five Great Novels of James M. Cain
[GK103] Picador pbk **£5.95**
Magician's Wife
[GK104] Dent pbk **£3.95**

CAIN, PAUL (US, 1902 - 1966)
Pseudonym of George Sims. Described by Chandler as *"some kind of high-point in the hard-boiled school"*, Cain's **Fast One** is more sickening than slick with its relentless descriptions of brutality and violence. Useful as a yardstick of the genre, or as an historical curiosity.
Fast One
[GK105] Oldcastle pbk **£1.99**
Seven Slayers
[GK106] Oldcastle pbk **£3.99**

CAMPBELL, ROBERT (US)
US award-winner who specialises in the seamier side of crime (decapitations, ODs etc) from New Orleans to Los Angeles, the latter chosen as the setting for his recent **Whistler** series; 'one of the most stylish crime writers in the business' (*New York Times*).
Alice in La-La Land
[GK107] Mysterious P pbk **£2.99**
In La-La Land We Trust
[GK108] Mysterious P pbk **£2.99**
Sweet La-La Land   **NEW**
A vicious killer is released to prowl the neon streets of Whistler's La-La Land: uppermost in his mind are the cops who put him away fifteen years ago. Very tough excursion into depravity and Satanism, in the third of this series.
[GK109] Mysterious P hbk **£10.95**
The Junkyard Dog
[GK110] Mysterious P pbk **£2.50**

CARR, JOHN DICKSON (US, 1906 - 1970)
Prolific American author of the 'puzzle' school of crime writing, especially the so-called 'locked-room' mystery. Gregarious Dr Gideon Fell, reputedly based on G.K. Chesterton, appeared in 23 novels and Sir Henry Merrivale in almost as many under the **Carter Dickson** (qv) byeline. Given the quality and quantity of Carr's output, there is far too little currently available.
Hollow Man
[GK111] Penguin pbk **£3.95**
The Crooked Hinge
[GK112] Xanadu pbk **£3.99**

CARRE, JOHN LE (British, 1931 -)
Le Carré's first two works, written while he was still in the Foreign Office (hence his adoption of a pseudonym), are more conventional detective stories, with George Smiley investigating the murders of a schoolmaster's wife and Foreign Office official respectively. His renowned plot complexity foreshadows the later novels.
Call for the Dead
[GK113] Penguin pbk **£2.25**
Murder of Quality
[GK114] Penguin pbk **£2.25**

CHANDLER, RAYMOND (US, 1888 - 1959)
Chandler represents the height of achievement in the crime novel. Gumshoe Philip Marlowe, modern White Knight of the mean streets, has already passed into folklore, and his creator is the yardstick by which all similar writers are measured. His work excels for its ability to convey both the exotic seediness of Los Angeles and the conflicting emotions of his moral and idealistic (some would say even sentimental) hero, in an inimitable style of quick-fire dialogue.
Farewell My Lovely
[GK115] H Hamilton hbk **£11.95**
[GK116] Penguin pbk **£3.99**

Raymond Chandler: 1888 - 1959

Of all the tributes and celebrations which Chandler's recent centenary brought, Byron Preiss' collection of 'Marlowe Stories' (*Raymond Chandler's Philip Marlowe*) has struck some Chandler *aficionados* as sacrilege, while others have enjoyed its playful imitations of the great writer's style. Chandler might have despised its commercial motivations, but a more important reason lies in the peculiarly close and personal relationship that the author had with his leading character Marlowe: the incorruptible private-eye and modern knight of the city, who embodied an ideal to which Chandler himself could only aspire, but which his writing has lent a unique fervour.

Much psychoanalysis has been practised on Raymond Chandler, focusing mainly on his time at Dulwich College, the public school which rendered him forever an English gentleman in exile, and on his unusual marriage to Cissy, his senior by many years, who represented mother more than wife to him; his novels, meanwhile, have been endlessly trawled for clues to the significance of Marlowe in relation to his creator. For those who wish to know what made Chandler tick, there is no better source than in the *Collected Letters*, superbly edited by Frank McShane. What constantly emerges from these is his fury at the low regard in which 'mystery writing' was held in the United States, or more accurately, the accepted wisdom that it was not even *possible* to achieve literary excellence through the medium of the crime story. Thus motivated, and after years of practice and imitation (of Hammett , Gardner and others), Chandler found a style which could not be ignored on any level - the hyperbolic simile (*"he breathed like an old Ford with a leaky head gasket"*) and quick-witted dialogue satisfied the dime novel reader, while Marlowe's musings touched a core in those who wanted more from a book than cheap thrills.

Chandler was always delighted that Britain considered him a novelist first, and crime writer second, and there are many amusing exchanges in the letters between him and his British publishers Hamish Hamilton (who have now re-issued his work in an attractive new hardcover format). There was much sadness in his last years, following the death of his wife, and a fast decline into alcoholism - in the final Marlowe novel (unfinished, but about to be completed by Robert Parker who has, for some, inherited Chandler's mantle, with his stories featuring Spenser) the hero of the mean streets is married, but directionless. The private-eye figure which Chandler did so much to create may, with Humphrey Bogart's help, have become a cliché, but imitation is often flattery: the exploits attributed to Marlowe in Preiss' collection, of which Jonathan Valin's and Sara Paretsky's are the most skilful, and Roger Simon's the most fun, stand both as pastiche and tribute to a master of the genre.

John le Carré, author of *The Russia House* (Hodder & Stoughton hbk **£12.95**)

Killer in the Rain
[GK117] H Hamilton hbk **£12.95**
Pearls Are a Nuisance
[GK118] Penguin pbk **£3.99**
Playback
[GK119] H Hamilton hbk **£11.95**
[GK120] Penguin pbk **£3.99**
Raymond Chandler Speaking
A selection from Chandler's letters and other sources, presenting his views on a number of subjects (including Hollywood and his fellow writers), in his own words.
[GK121] Penguin pbk **£4.95**
The Big Sleep
[GK122] H Hamilton hbk **£11.95**
[GK123] Penguin pbk **£3.95**
The High Window
[GK124] H Hamilton hbk **£11.95**
[GK125] Penguin pbk **£3.99**
The Lady in the Lake
[GK126] H Hamilton hbk **£11.95**
[GK127] Penguin pbk **£3.99**
The Little Sister
[GK128] H Hamilton hbk **£11.95**
[GK129] Penguin pbk **£3.99**
The Long Goodbye
[GK130] H Hamilton hbk **£11.95**
[GK131] Penguin pbk **£4.99**
The Smell of Fear
[GK132] H Hamilton hbk **£12.95**
Trouble is My Business
[GK133] Penguin pbk **£3.99**
PREISS, BYRON (ED)
Raymond Chandler's Philip Marlowe: A Celebration
[GK134] Bloomsbury pbk **£7.99**

CHARTERIS, LESLIE (British, 1926 -)
Not quite as stereotyped in outlook as Bulldog Drummond, the Saint nevertheless dealt out his own brand of private justice to the 'enemies of England' in ways that would get him locked up pretty swiftly today. These entertaining mystery adventures were successfully televised with Roger Moore as the dapper hero.
Count on the Saint
[GK135] Hodder pbk **£0.95**
Enter the Saint
[GK136] Dent pbk **£3.50**
The Saint in New York
[GK137] Dent pbk **£3.50**

CHASE, JAMES HADLEY (British, 1906 -)
Steeped in the American 'hard-boiled' school, Chase has written over eighty novels, formulaic and widely popular novels. *No Orchids for Miss Blandish*, about the kidnapping of an heiress, is the first and most notorious (currently only available in a large print edition). However, in the final analysis, there is little to tell them all apart, entertaining as they are.
Dead Stay Dumb
[GK138] Corgi pbk **£1.95**
No Orchids for Miss Blandish
[GK139] Magna hbk **£7.95**
There's a Hippy on the Highway
[GK140] Grafton pbk **£1.95**
This Way for a Shroud
[GK141] Grafton pbk **£1.95**
Try This One for Size
[GK142] Corgi pbk **£1.95**
You Must Be Kidding
[GK143] Corgi pbk **£1.95**

CHESTERTON, G.K. (British, 1874 - 1936)
The Father Brown stories are but a tiny part of Chesterton's enormous body of work, but are undoubtedly the most widely read. As 'puzzles to be solved', many of the stories are ingenious, while others disappoint in their predictability. Their major strength lies in the 'little priest from Essex' himself and his delightful sermons on the 'overlooking of the commonplace'.
Best of Father Brown
[GK144] Dent pbk **£3.95**
Complete Father Brown
[GK145] Penguin pbk **£5.95**
Innocence of Father Brown
[GK146] Penguin pbk **£3.95**
Secret of Father Brown
[GK147] Penguin pbk **£2.50**
Seven Suspects   **NEW**
On the theme of people under suspicion, this collection includes some rare, previously unpublished stories and the newly-discovered 'The Man Who Shot the Fox'.
[GK148] Xanadu hbk **£10.95**
The Incredulity of Father Brown
[GK149] Penguin pbk **£2.95**
The Scandal of Father Brown
[GK150] Penguin pbk **£2.95**
Wisdom of Father Brown
[GK151] Penguin pbk **£3.95**

CHEYNEY, PETER (British, 1896 - 1951)
British writer of American style 'gangster' novels which sold millions world-wide in the '30s and '40s. Quite violent and risqué in their day, they now seem comparatively quaint, although those featuring his tough-talking private eye Callaghan are still a good, quick read.
Dangerous Curves
[GK152] Fontana pbk **£2.95**
It Couldn't Matter Less
[GK153] Fontana pbk **£2.95**
The Urgent Hangman
[GK154] Fontana pbk **£2.95**
Uneasy Terms
[GK155] Fontana pbk **£2.95**

CHRISTIE, AGATHA (British, 1880 - 1976)
The undisputed master of the extended conundrum: some have claimed that aspects of character, context and motivation are sacrificed to the central determing factor of 'Whodunnit?' (and 'Howdunnit?' too), but her books represent the greatest flowering of the genre, and have done much to pave the way for later writers. The ingenuity and complexity of her plots is unrivalled, and her two inimitable sleuths, Hercule Poirot and Miss Jane Marple, have achieved legendary status. Included here is a selection from the wide range of her writings.

Death Comes as the End
[GK156] Fontana pbk **£2.50**
Murder at the Vicarage
[GK157] Fontana pbk **£2.50**
Murder of Roger Ackroyd
[GK158] Fontana pbk **£2.95**
N or M?
[GK159] Pan pbk **£2.99**
Secret of Chimneys
[GK160] Fontana pbk **£2.95**
Sparkling Cyanide
[GK161] Fontana pbk **£2.95**
The Pale Horse
[GK162] Fontana pbk **£2.50**
Why Didn't They Ask Evans?
[GK163] Fontana pbk **£2.50**
MISS MARPLE
4.50 from Paddington
[GK164] Fontana pbk **£2.95**
Body in the Library
[GK165] Fontana pbk **£2.50**
Pocket Full of Rye
[GK166] Fontana pbk **£2.50**
POIROT
Hickory Dickory Dock
[GK167] Fontana pbk **£2.95**
Lord Edgware Dies
[GK168] Fontana pbk **£2.50**
Murder on the Orient Express
[GK169] Fontana pbk **£2.50**
The Mysterious Affair at Styles
[GK170] Fontana pbk **£2.95**

COLLINS, MICHAEL
Act of Fear
[GK170A] Oldcastle P pbk **£2.99**

CONSTANTINE, K.C. (US)
Small-town stories featuring Mario Balzic, police chief of Rocksburg, Pennsylvania; the crime element is secondary to the characters.
Always a Body to Trade
[GK171] Allison & B pbk **£2.95**
Joey's Case   **NEW**
Balzic is forced to deal with the father of a boy shot dead by someone who escapes justice through the incompetence of the prosecuting officer.
[GK172] Hodder hbk **£10.95**
The Man Who Liked to Look at Himself
[GK173] Allison & B pbk **£2.95**
The Rocksburg Railroad Murders
[GK174] Coronet pbk **£2.99**
Upon Some Midnight Clear
[GK175] Hodder pbk **£2.50**

CRISPIN, EDMUND (British, 1921 - 1978)
Part of the 'farceur' school of crime fiction (cf *Michael Innes*) Crispin's output was relatively small, and consequently of the highest quality. Professor Gervase Fen, his 'flaxen-haired' amateur detective, is in many ways impossibly able, but there is much intended humour in these country and community tales; the subordinate characters have real flesh and blood, and their emotions are described with a degree of pathos unusual in this type of mystery novel.
Beware of the Trains
[GK176] Penguin pbk **£2.95**
Fen Country
[GK177] Penguin pbk **£3.50**
Frequent Hearses
[GK178] Penguin pbk **£3.50**
Glimpses of the Moon
[GK179] Penguin pbk **£3.95**
Long Divorce
[GK180] Mysterious P pbk **£2.50**
Love Lies Bleeding
[GK181] Mysterious P pbk **£2.50**
The Moving Toyshop
[GK182] Penguin pbk **£3.95**

CROFTS, FREEMAN WILLS (Irish, 1897 - 1937)

The 'railway timetable as alibi' became Croft's hallmark in these meticulously fashioned 'whodunnits' and 'howdunnits'. Inspector French, however, wins no marks for personality.

Inspector French and the Starvel Tragedy
[GK183] Hogarth pbk **£3.95**
Inspector French's Greatest Case
[GK184] Hogarth pbk **£3.95**
The Cask
[GK185] Dover pbk **£5.35**

CRUMLEY, JAMES (US)

Cult American private-eye novelist, also a fine poet, whose limited output has hindered a wider reputation. Crumley's heroes are often disillusioned veterans at war with the violence of their own country.

Dancing Bear
[GK186] Penguin pbk **£2.50**

DEXTER, COLIN (British, 1930 -)

Television was relatively slow to spot the potential in Dexter's pair of Oxford policemen, Detective Chief Inspector Morse (cerebral, rueful) and Sergeant Lewis (sensible and sporty), but the recent series starring John Thaw was expertly realised.

Dead of Jericho
[GK187] Pan pbk **£2.99**
Last Bus to Woodstock
[GK188] Pan pbk **£2.99**
Last Seen Wearing
[GK189] Pan pbk **£2.99**
Secret of Annexe 3
[GK190] Pan pbk **£2.99**
Service of All the Dead
[GK191] Pan pbk **£2.99**
The Riddle of the Third Mile
[GK192] Pan pbk **£2.99**
The Silent World of Nicholas Quinn
[GK193] Pan pbk **£2.99**
The Wench is Dead   NEW
Inspector Morse returns in a convoluted case of murder committed over a hundred years ago. The Inspector has lost none of his endearingly irascible qualities.
[GK194] Macmillan hbk **£11.95**

DIBDIN, MICHAEL (British)

A highly original and disturbing writer who does not conform to the conventions of the mystery story, but is adding new dimensions to it. *Ratking* won the 1988 Gold Dagger for the year's best Crime Novel.

A Rich Full Death
[GK195] Faber pbk **£3.95**
Ratking
A tangled tale of pain and passion, set in Italy: strong psychological forces lurk just below the surface of the narrative. Much recommended.
[GK196] Faber pbk **£3.99**
The Last Sherlock Holmes Story
[GK197] Faber pbk **£3.99**
The Tryst   NEW
Young Gary Dunn, mentally unstable and witness to murder, is treated by Aileen Macklin, a psychiatrist who is curiously drawn to him when she discovers a link with her own scarred past.
[GK198] Faber hbk **£10.99**

DICKINSON, PETER (British, 1927 -)

Eccentric Englishman, also a successful children's author, whose locations are usually exotic and peopled by larger than life characters such as Superintendent Pibble. Clues and suspects abound, but Dickinson writes with genuine insight. A real oddity.

Death of a Unicorn
[GK199] Mysterious P pbk **£3.50**

Glass-Sided Ants' Nest
[GK200] Mysterious P pbk **£2.25**
King and Joker
[GK201] Mysterious P pbk **£2.50**
Lizard in the Cup
[GK202] Mysterious P pbk **£2.50**
One Foot in the Grave
[GK203] Mysterious P pbk **£2.50**
Perfect Gallows
[GK204] Mysterious P pbk **£2.50**
Tefuga
[GK205] Mysterious P pbk **£2.50**

DICKSON, CARTER (US, 1906 - 1970)

The pseudonym of *John Dickson Carr* (qv), for his novels featuring Sir Henry Merivale.

Lord of the Sorcerers
[GK206] Hogarth pbk **£3.95**
The Skeleton in the Clock
[GK207] Hogarth pbk **£3.95**

DOBYNS, STEPHEN (US)

Suitably-named American newcomer invariably billed as the man to make Dick Francis look to his many laurels, since the Saratoga racetrack is the setting for his stories. Tough, laconic and packed with horseracing lore.

Saratoga Bestiary   NEW
Private Eye Charlie Bradshaw returns in a case with many seemingly unrelated strands, all of which lead to the nether world of illegal gambling - and to a particularly nasty criminal.
[GK208] Mysterious P hbk **£10.95**
Saratoga Headhunter
[GK209] Allison & B pbk **£2.95**
Saratoga Longshot
[GK210] Mysterious P pbk **£2.50**
Saratoga Swimmer
[GK211] Allison & B pbk **£2.95**

DOYLE, SIR ARTHUR CONAN (British, 1859 - 1930)

More has been written and more films made about Sherlock Holmes than any other fictional character in the world. The stories, which don't actually stand up very well to individual stylistic or structural analysis, nevertheless have a unique quality which makes one want to continue re-reading them time and time again. The bygone age, not too far distant from the present, has romantic attractions for the modern reader, but the satisfaction one derives from stories which often contain weak plots and repetitive dialogue is much more difficult to explain and is most likely attributable to the complex character of Holmes himself.

Adventures of Sherlock Holmes
[GK212] J Murray/Cape hbk **£9.95**
[GK213] Penguin pbk **£2.99**
Casebook of Sherlock Holmes
[GK214] J Murray/Cape hbk **£9.95**
[GK215] Penguin pbk **£2.50**
Complete Sherlock Holmes
[GK216] Secker hbk **£15.00**
[GK217] Penguin pbk **£6.99**
His Last Bow
[GK218] J Murray/Cape hbk **£9.95**
[GK219] Penguin pbk **£2.50**
Memoirs of Sherlock Holmes
[GK220] J Murray/Cape hbk **£9.95**
[GK221] Penguin pbk **£2.50**
Return of Sherlock Holmes
[GK222] Penguin pbk **£3.50**
Sign of Four
[GK223] Penguin pbk **£2.50**
Study In Scarlet
[GK224] Penguin pbk **£2.25**
The Hound of the Baskervilles
[GK225] J Murray/Cape hbk **£9.95**
[GK226] Penguin pbk **£2.50**

The Valley of Fear
[GK227] J Murray/Cape hbk **£8.95**
[GK228] Penguin pbk **£2.50**

ELLROY, JAMES (US, 1948 -)

More L.A. locations, another tough Private Investigator (Lloyd Hopkins). If you like Byrd, Campbell or Estleman, James Ellroy can match them all for punchy dialogue and street realism.

Because the Night
[GK229] Mysterious P pbk **£2.50**
Black Dahlia   NEW
[GK230] Mysterious P hbk **£11.95**
Suicide Hill
[GK231] Mysterious P pbk **£2.99**

ENGEL, HOWARD (Canadian)

Workmanlike private-eye novels set in Canada and featuring the dogged Benny Cooperman. Engel sets the mood with admirable economy.

A Victim Must Be Found   NEW
Benny Cooperman's sixth case, in which he uncovers a network of corruption within the Art World, when a list of paintings, on loan to local VIPs, goes missing.
[GK232] Gollancz hbk **£10.95**
City Called July
[GK233] Penguin pbk **£2.99**
Murder on Location
[GK234] Penguin pbk **£2.25**
Ransom Game
[GK235] Penguin pbk **£1.95**

ESTLEMAN, LOREN D. (US, 1952 -)

Young American writer who started out as a Sherlock Holmes parodist, then found his niche in the exploits of Amos Walker, Detroit private-eye. Now in the vanguard of US crime fiction, Estleman's Motown is already something of a literary legend.

Any Man's Death   NEW
Amos Walker accepts a case he soon begins to wish he had turned down: ninth in the Detroit-based series.
[GK236] Mysterious P hbk **£10.95**
Downriver
[GK237] Macmillan pbk **£3.99**
Every Brilliant Eye
[GK238] Penguin pbk **£2.95**
Kill Zone
[GK239] Mysterious P pbk **£2.50**
Lady Yesterday
[GK240] Macmillan pbk **£3.95**
Roses Are Dead
[GK241] Mysterious P pbk **£2.50**
Sugartown
[GK242] Penguin pbk **£2.50**
The Glass Highway
[GK243] Macmillan pbk **£3.95**
The Midnight Man
[GK244] Macmillan pbk **£3.95**

FRANCIS, DICK (British, 1920 -)

Once a National Hunt champion jockey, Francis has used his racetrack experience to create a microcosm of human toughness and greed; and unlike most 'hard-boiled' authors who describe only the physical violence, Francis gives the impression of having actually taken the knocks himself, lending his work a rare compassion. As a stylist he is sparing of vocabulary, and his narrative timing is excellent; he is not afraid of making moral judgments, nor of raising dilemmas which beg tough moral questions.

Banker
[GK245] Pan pbk **£2.99**
Blood Sport (1967)
[GK246] Pan pbk **£2.99**
Bolt (1986)
[GK247] Pan pbk **£3.50**
Break In (1985)
[GK248] Pan pbk **£3.50**

Dick Francis, author of *Straight* (Michael Joseph hbk £11.95)

Dead Cert (1962)
[GK249] Pan pbk **£3.50**
Forfeit (1969)
[GK250] Pan pbk **£2.95**
Hot Money (1987)
[GK251] Pan pbk **£3.50**
Nerve (1964)
[GK252] Pan pbk **£2.99**
Proof (1984)
[GK253] Pan pbk **£3.50**
Risk (1977)
[GK254] Pan pbk **£2.99**
Slay Ride (1973)
[GK255] Pan pbk **£3.50**
Smokescreen (1972)
[GK256] Pan pbk **£2.99**
Sport of Queens
A personal view of racing and the history of the sport.
[GK257] M Joseph hbk **£12.95**
Straight   NEW
Derek Franklin, a steeplechase jockey whose career is
coming to an end, is shattered by the death of his
older brother, a gem importer. Once again Francis
explores the themes of honesty and courage in a
crooked world, as the beleaguered jockey tries to
identify his brother's mysterious enemy.
[GK258] M Joseph hbk **£11.95**
The Edge (1988)
Jockey Club investigator Tom Kelsey has one brief:
to rid racing of the villainous Julius Apollo Filmer,
who is among a party of racehorse owners on a
luxurious train junket through Canada. A closely-
plotted adventure story of corruption and conspiracy
to murder.
[GK259] M Joseph hbk **£11.95**
[GK260] Pan pbk **£3.99**
Trial Run (1978)
[GK261] Pan pbk **£2.99**
Twice Shy (1981)
[GK262] Pan pbk **£2.99**
Whip Hand (1979)
[GK263] Pan pbk **£2.99**

FRASER, ANTONIA (British, 1932 -)
Respected historian who turned her attention to the
light-weight detective novel, and whose entertaining
clutch of Jemima Shore stories were quickly made
into a television series.
Cool Repentance
[GK264] Methuen pbk **£2.95**

Jemima Shore's First Case & Other Stories
[GK265] Methuen pbk **£2.95**
Oxford Blood
[GK266] Methuen pbk **£2.50**
Quiet As A Nun
[GK267] Methuen pbk **£2.50**
Splash of Red
[GK268] Methuen pbk **£2.95**
Your Royal Hostage
[GK269] Methuen pbk **£2.95**

FREELING, NICHOLAS (British, 1927 -)
Strasbourg-based writer best known for the stories
(some televised) featuring Dutch Police Inspector Van
der Valk, but equally at home with other European
detectives, notably the French Henri Castang. Like
those of Simenon, his tales are characterized by the
patient investigation of a sordid crime, very much in
the tradition of the 'roman policier'.
Because of the Cats
[GK270] Penguin pbk **£2.50**
City Solitary
[GK271] Penguin pbk **£2.99**
Cold Iron
[GK272] Penguin pbk **£2.99**
Double-Barrel
[GK273] Penguin pbk **£2.50**
Dressing of Diamond
[GK274] Penguin pbk **£2.95**
Gun before Butter
[GK275] Penguin pbk **£2.50**
King of the Rainy Country
[GK276] Penguin pbk **£1.95**
Lady Macbeth
[GK277] Penguin pbk **£2.99**
Long Silence
[GK278] Penguin pbk **£2.99**
Night Lords
[GK279] Penguin pbk **£2.95**
No Part in Your Death
[GK280] Penguin pbk **£2.50**
Not as far as Velma   NEW
The latest Henri Castang novel in which a young
widow disappears from a town in Northern France.
[GK281] Deutsch hbk **£10.95**
Sand Castles   NEW
Van der Valk returns after a long absence, pursuing
racketeers and spies around the islands and estuaries
of the Dutch seaboard. A story with more adventure
than usual for the Amsterdam Inspector.
[GK282] Deutsch hbk **£10.95**
Tsing Boum
[GK283] Penguin pbk **£2.50**

FREEMAN, AUSTIN R. (British, 1862 - 1943)
British creator of Dr Thorndyke, the first (and only)
really convincing fictional scientific detective.
Freeman's dry style does not detract from the
considerable suspense even of those 'inverted' stories
in which the murderer's identity is known at the
beginning.
Mr Pottermack's Oversight
[GK284] Hogarth pbk **£3.50**
The Eye of Osiris
A chilling Golden Age tale of buried bones and
Eygptian mummies launches Oxford's new paperback
series, called (rather unimaginatively) *Classic Crime*.
[GK285] Oxford pbk **£3.95**

GASH, JONATHAN (British, 1933 -)
Pseudonym of John Grant. In compelling stories of
punters and pocket-watches, Gash's over-sexed anti-
hero Lovejoy sits nicely with Minder's Arthur Daley
as a modern example of the dodgy English rogue. The
antiques trade is well researched and provides a
perfect setting for these high camp tales of low life.
Firefly Gadroon
[GK286] Mysterious P pbk **£2.50**

Gold from Gemini
[GK287] Mysterious P pbk **£2.50**
Gondola Scam
[GK288] Mysterious P pbk **£2.50**
Grail Tree
[GK289] Mysterious P pbk **£2.50**
Jade Woman
[GK290] Collins hbk **£9.95**
Judas Pair
[GK291] Mysterious P pbk **£2.50**
Moonspender
[GK292] Mysterious P pbk **£2.50**
Pearlhanger
[GK293] Mysterious P pbk **£2.50**
Sleepers of Erin
[GK294] Mysterious P pbk **£2.50**
Spend Game
[GK295] Mysterious P pbk **£2.50**
Tartan Ringers
[GK296] Mysterious P pbk **£2.50**
The Very Last Gambado   NEW
In which Lovejoy attempts the ultimate: to rob the
British Museum. The narrative is set in London and
East Anglia.
[GK297] Collins hbk **£10.95**
Vatican Rip
[GK298] Mysterious P pbk **£2.99**

GILBERT, MICHAEL (British, 1912 -)
A lawyer who has succeeded with a variety of sub-
genres, all containing complex plots and well-rounded
character, amongst whom Inspector Petrella in the
police procedurals, and the entertaining counter-
intelligence officers Calder and Behrens are the best
known. *Smallbone Deceased* is generally reckoned to
be his chef d'oeuvre.
Blood and Judgement
[GK299] Mysterious P pbk **£2.50**
Close Quarters
[GK300] Mysterious P pbk **£2.50**
Death Has Deep Roots
[GK301] Mysterious P pbk **£2.50**
Death in Captivity
[GK302] Mysterious P pbk **£2.50**
Death of a Favourite Girl
[GK303] Mysterious P pbk **£2.99**
Etruscan Net
[GK304] Mysterious P pbk **£2.50**
Long Journey Home
[GK305] Mysterious P pbk **£2.50**
Mr Calder and Mr Behrens
[GK306] Penguin pbk **£2.50**
Night of the Twelfth
[GK307] Mysterious P pbk **£2.50**
Paint, Gold and Blood   NEW
Ever-reliable storytelling from Gilbert, on the themes
of art theft by Nazi exiles in Argentina, and the covert
funding of Iranian Freedom Fighters, all made
completely plausible.
[GK308] Hodder hbk **£10.95**
Smallbone Deceased
Described by many as a masterpiece, the central
puzzle revolves around life in the solicitor's office of
Horniman, Birley and Craine: Gilbert's legal
background ensures absolute authenticity.
[GK309] Dent pbk **£3.95**
The Dust and the Heat
[GK310] Mysterious P pbk **£2.99**

GILL, B.M. (British, 1921 -)
Pseudonym of Barbara M. Trimble. Mystery novelist
of immense skill, who deserves a wider readership.
Her books deal with the emotional violence that
erupts in small, close communities such as schools,
hospitals and weekend seminars.
Death Drop
[GK311] Hodder pbk **£2.50**
Dying to Meet You
[GK312] Hodder pbk **£2.50**

Nursery Crimes
[GK313] Hodder pbk **£2.50**
Seminar for Murder
[GK314] Hodder pbk **£2.50**
Time and Time Again **NEW**
The fall and fall of a respectable accountant who befriends another woman from a different social background after their release from prison, and is implicated in murder.
[GK315] Hodder hbk **£10.95**
Twelfth Juror
[GK316] Hodder pbk **£2.50**
Victims
[GK317] Hodder pbk **£2.50**

GOODIS, DAVID (US, 1917 - 1967)
US pulp writer of the 1940s and 1950s who specialised in tales of losers and fugitives, many of them filmed - *Dark Passage*, *Moon in the Gutter*, *Shoot the Piano Player* - all of them darkly powerful. His books are currently enjoying a considerable revival of interest.
Black Friday
[GK318] Creative Arts pbk **£2.95**
Cassidy's Girl
[GK319] Creative Arts pbk **£2.95**
Nightfall
[GK320] Creative Arts pbk **£2.95**
Shoot the Piano Player
[GK321] Creative Arts pbk **£2.95**
Street of No Return
[GK322] Creative Arts pbk **£2.95**
The Burglar
[GK323] Simon & Sch pbk **£3.50**

GOSLING, PAULA (US, 1939 -)
American suspense writer who crosses over into 'thriller' territory, not least through the emphasis on her characters' love affairs. Very fast-paced action.
A Running Duck
[GK324] Pan pbk **£2.50**
Backlash **NEW**
The sequel to the award-winning *Monkey Puzzle*. Here her character Jack Stryker is faced with a killer who appears to be randomly shooting policemen.
[GK325] Macmillan hbk **£10.95**
Hoodwink **NEW**
[GK326] Pan pbk **£3.50**
Loser's Blues
[GK327] Pan pbk **£2.50**
Monkey Puzzle
[GK328] Pan pbk **£2.50**
The Woman in Red
[GK329] Pan pbk **£2.50**
Wychford Murders
[GK330] Pan pbk **£2.50**

GRAFTON, SUE (US, 1940 -)
Creator of the sparky but cynical private-eye, Kinsey Mulhone. The alphabetical titles may be a gimmick but the series is very well written, and undeniably successful.
A is for Alibi
[GK331] Macmillan pbk **£3.95**
B is for Burglar
[GK332] Macmillan pbk **£3.95**
C is for Corpse
[GK333] Macmillan pbk **£3.95**
D is for Deadbeat
[GK334] Macmillan pbk **£3.99**
E is for Evidence
[GK335] Macmillan hbk **£9.95**
F is for Fugitive **NEW**
An escaped convict, recaptured after 20 years, professes innocence to the crime of murder: Mulhone's task, identifying the real perpetrator, is the basis for the sixth in this increasingly popular series.
[GK336] Macmillan hbk **£10.95**

GRANT-ADAMSON, LESLEY (British)
Young British writer who has already justified Faber's faith in her with five mystery novels of great merit. Refreshingly uncontrived, they are quintessentially English without being quaint. Definitely a star of the future.
Face of Death
[GK337] Faber pbk **£2.95**
Guilty Knowledge
[GK338] Faber pbk **£2.95**
Patterns in the Dust
[GK339] Faber pbk **£2.95**
The Threatening Eye **NEW**
Two men's lives linked by tragedy: one, seedy and haunted, whose double life is threatened with exposure, the other in the process of rebuilding his life following the discovery of a secret in the local churchyard.
[GK340] Faber hbk **£10.95**
[GK341] Faber pbk **£3.99**
Wild Justice
[GK342] Faber pbk **£3.99**

GRIERSON, EDWARD (British, 1914 - 1975)
A one-book reputation for Grierson, whose brilliant story of domestic murder and courtroom sophistry became a classic.
Reputation for a Song
[GK343] Penguin pbk **£3.95**

GRIMES, MARTHA (British)
Superior, sophisticated detective stories already popular in the US and increasingly in her own country. Each title is named after a real pub and features series character Richard Jury.
Deer Leap
[GK344] Headline pbk **£3.99**
Help the Poor Struggler **NEW**
Richard Jury tries to connect the strands of an unsolved murder with the recent killings of three children in a 'modern gothic landscape' where everyone is under suspicion.
[GK345] M O'Mara hbk **£10.95**
I am the Only Running Footman
[GK346] Headline pbk **£2.50**
Jerusalem Inn
[GK347] Headline pbk **£2.99**
The Anodyne Necklace **NEW**
The Detective Superintendant features again, with his dilettante partner Melrose Plant: they find themselves in a village 40 miles from London, among an extraordinary cast of characters. The seventh in this amusing, suspenseful series.
[GK348] M O'Mara hbk **£10.95**
The Dirty Duck
[GK349] Headline pbk **£2.50**
The Five Bells and Bladebone
[GK350] Headline pbk **£2.99**

GULICK, ROBERT VAN (Dutch, 1910 -)
Dutch author who rewrote certain classical Chinese folk stories as modern detective tales, seen through the eyes of Judge Dee. Original plots followed and the books have enjoyed worldwide success, due mainly to strong characterisation and their fascinating insight into Chinese custom. The two hardback re-issues from Michael Joseph include new line drawings.
Celebrated Cases of Judge Dee
[GK351] Dover pbk **£4.95**
Haunted Monastery/Chinese Maze Murders
[GK352] Dover pbk **£5.00**
The Chinese Bell Murders
[GK353] M Joseph hbk **£11.95**
[GK354] Sphere pbk **£2.99**
The Chinese Gold Murders
[GK355] Sphere pbk **£2.99**
The Chinese Lake Murders
[GK356] Sphere pbk **£2.99**

The Chinese Nail Murders
[GK357] M Joseph hbk **£11.95**
[GK358] Sphere pbk **£2.99**

HAMMETT, DASHIELL (US, 1894 - 1961)
Hammett was the originator of the realistic, tough crime story in which characters used dialogue as it was actually spoken and were themselves an honest reflection of real people in the real world: the term 'hard-boiled' is hardly an adequate expression of this idea, but it has stuck and Hammett is considered its king. All Hammett's books, including the short stories, are highly recommended.
Big Knockover & Other Stories
[GK359] Penguin pbk **£3.95**
Red Harvest
[GK360] Pan pbk **£1.95**
The Continental Op
[GK361] Pan pbk **£3.50**
The Dain Curse
[GK362] Pan pbk **£1.95**
The Four Great Novels
The Dain Curse/The Glass Key/The Maltese Falcon/Red Harvest.
[GK363] Picador pbk **£6.99**
The Glass Key
The Glass Key is perhaps his most compassionate and ambitious novel; dealing with corruption and human relationships in the context of American society at that time, it would be afforded a different reputation if the writer had been, say, Hemingway.
[GK364] Pan pbk **£1.95**
The Maltese Falcon
[GK365] Pan pbk **£2.99**
Thin Man
[GK366] Penguin pbk **£3.50**
Woman in the Dark **NEW**
This novella has not been published in Britain before: compared to Hammett's major novels and short stories, it is a relatively slight effort, somehow more Romance than Crime Story. However, it does contain some elements of mystery and the blunt dialogue for which Hammett was renowned. A collectable curiosity.
[GK367] Headline hbk **£7.95**

HARE, CYRIL (British, 1900 - 1958)
Currently enjoying something of a revival, Cyril Hare's elegant detective stories are escapist, cosy and quintessentially English. Of his two series characters, bumbling barrister Francis Pettigrew is perhaps a more entertaining proposition than the Yard's plodding Inspector Mallett but both exist in a world as endearing as the made-up place names that characterised the crime fiction of earlier decades (Markshire, Didford Parva, etc) and both of them have their devoted followers (notably P.D. James). Perfect for riverbank reads while waiting for the fish to rise.
An English Murder
[GK368] Hogarth pbk **£3.95**
Best Detective Stories of Cyril Hare
[GK369] Faber pbk **£3.95**
Death Is No Sportsman
[GK370] Faber pbk **£3.95**
Suicide Excepted
[GK371] Hogarth pbk **£2.95**
Tenant for Death
[GK372] Faber pbk **£2.95**
That Yew Tree's Shade
[GK373] Faber pbk **£3.95**
Tragedy at Law
[GK374] Faber pbk **£2.95**
Untimely Death
[GK375] Hogarth pbk **£3.95**
Wind Blows Death
[GK376] Faber pbk **£2.95**
With a Bare Bodkin
[GK377] Faber pbk **£2.95**

HEALD, TIM (British, 1944 -)

Creator of Simon Bognor, the rather undignified special investigator from the Board of Trade, ex-journalist Heald has continued in the tradition of the 'farceur' school, merciless in his exposure of the absurdities of self-serving bureaucracy.

Brought to Book

Dirty dealings in the world of publishing pit Bognor against characters called Vernon Hemlock, Andover Strobe and Rosemary Flange: shades of Tom Sharpe here, the social satire at least as acute.

[GK378] Macmillan pbk **£3.99**

Red Herrings

[GK379] Macmillan pbk **£3.95**

HEYER, GEORGETTE

(British, 1902 - 1974)

As well-known for her Romantic/Historical Novels, Heyer's detective stories have stood up well since the 1930s, given that they are formulaic and escapist in the manner of the Golden Age (settings are Country House, London Party or Theatrical Company). Superintendent Hannasyde is unremarkable but some of the peripheral characters are very amusing.

Blunt Instrument

[GK380] Grafton pbk **£2.95**

Detection Unlimited

[GK381] Grafton pbk **£2.95**

Duplicate Death

[GK382] Grafton pbk **£2.95**

No Wind of Blame

[GK383] Grafton pbk **£3.50**

Unfinished Clue

[GK384] Grafton pbk **£2.95**

Why Shoot a Butler?

[GK385] Grafton pbk **£2.95**

HIGGINS, GEORGE V. (US, 1939 -)

American novelist who dislikes the tag of crime writer, claiming instead that his books are about the ordinary people of Boston who simply happen to lead criminal lives. Higgins tries to highlight the broader political milieu in which his corrupt characters move, and his skill has been to make them recognizable, believable and memorable. Widely praised for dialogue "as polished as a gem-collector's specimens".

A Choice of Enemies

[GK386] Robinson pbk **£3.95**

Cogan's Trade

[GK387] Robinson pbk **£3.99**

Impostors

[GK388] Sphere pbk **£3.95**

Judgement of Deke Hunter

[GK389] Robinson pbk **£3.95**

Kennedy for the Defense

[GK390] Sphere pbk **£3.95**

Outlaws

[GK391] Sphere pbk **£3.99**

Patriot Game

[GK392] Robinson pbk **£3.99**

Penance for Jerry Kennedy

[GK393] Sphere pbk **£3.95**

The Friends of Eddie Coyle

[GK394] Robinson pbk **£3.50**

The Rat on Fire

[GK395] Robinson pbk **£2.95**

The Sins of the Fathers

[GK396] Robinson pbk **£3.99**

Wonderful Years, Wonderful Years

Higgins once again takes us on a journey through the legal and political process in the story of Ellen Farley, about to be released from a mental institution and convinced that her husband wants her dead. This is a powerful story of corrupting ambition, marriage and madness.

[GK397] Deutsch hbk **£11.95**

HIGHSMITH, PATRICIA (US, 1921 -)

The term 'Highsmithian' has come to embody the idea of suspense in its purest form - a mundane life transformed by one small slip into a tortured existence, in which everyday situations become unbearable dilemmas, and her characters slide relentlessly towards destruction - nowhere more masterfully done than in *The Blunderer*, one of her earliest books. The *Ripley* stories established her as an international bestselling author, and she is still a prolific contributor of macabre and socially-aware short stories to magazines.

Cry of the Owl (Stories)

[GK398] Penguin pbk **£3.50**

Deep Water

[GK399] Penguin pbk **£2.99**

Dog's Ransom

[GK400] Penguin pbk **£2.95**

Found in the Street

[GK401] Penguin pbk **£3.50**

Game for the Living

[GK402] Penguin pbk **£2.95**

Glass Cell

[GK403] Penguin pbk **£2.99**

People who Knock on the Door

[GK404] Penguin pbk **£3.50**

Strangers on a Train

The classic plot, filmed by Hitchcock (and screenplayed by Chandler), in which tennis pro Guy Haines disastrously agrees to 'swop murders' with the effete psychopath Bruno. A definite *folie à deux*.

[GK405] Penguin pbk **£2.95**

Suspension of Mercy

[GK406] Penguin pbk **£2.95**

Tales of Natural and Unnatural Catastrophes (Stories)

[GK407] Methuen pbk **£2.95**

The Blunderer

[GK408] Penguin pbk **£3.50**

The Tremor of Forgery

A suspense novel with dreamlike qualities, set in Tunisia where a film-maker waits for a friend who never arrives. An original work in which knowledge and uncertainty collide and fact becomes illusion. Antonioni's film *The Passenger* is its closest cinematic equivalent.

[GK409] Penguin pbk **£2.95**

This Sweet Sickness

[GK410] Penguin pbk **£2.95**

Those Who Walk Away

[GK411] Penguin pbk **£2.99**

Two Faces of January

[GK412] Penguin pbk **£2.95**

Patricia Highsmith, author of *Strangers on a Train* (Penguin pbk £2.95)

THE RIPLEY CANON

1: The Talented Mr Ripley

The essential difference between the books which feature Tom Ripley, an expatriate American layabout living in France, and many of her other works, is that Ripley is a survivor, despite the criminal and amoral nature of his actions. He is one of the great psychopaths of post-war literature, a cultured and calculating man whose exploits are described in a spare, chilling, matter-of-fact style. Many have found it shocking and distasteful that such a man is 'allowed' to cheat justice, yet it is undoubtedly the very reason for the books' tremendous popularity.

[GK413] Penguin pbk **£2.95**

2: Ripley Underground

[GK414] Penguin pbk **£2.95**

3: Ripley's Game

[GK415] Penguin pbk **£2.95**

4: The Boy who Followed Ripley

[GK416] Penguin pbk **£3.50**

The Mysterious Mr Ripley

A collection of *The Talented Mr Ripley*, *Ripley Underground* & *Ripley's Game*.

[GK417] Penguin pbk **£5.99**

HILL, REGINALD (British, 1936 -)

Hill's first book *A Clubbable Woman* (1970) introduced the bluff Yorkshireman Inspector Dalziel to his dour Sergeant Peter Pascoe. These early stories, as well as the non-Dalziel crime novels, are distinguished by a verbal wit which never becomes overbearing, and an unusually keen attention to plot. Hill deals with real issues in a serious way, and yet his best books (*A Killing Madness* and *An Advancement of Learning*) are also full of humour. Grafton have begun to raise his profile in paperback with further reprints and new covers.

A Clubbable Woman

[GK418] Grafton pbk **£2.95**

A Killing Kindness

[GK419] Grafton pbk **£2.95**

A Pinch of Snuff

[GK420] Grafton pbk **£2.95**

An Advancement of Learning

[GK421] Grafton pbk **£2.95**

An April Shroud

[GK422] Grafton pbk **£2.95**

Child's Play

[GK423] Grafton pbk **£2.95**

Dead Heads

[GK424] Grafton pbk **£2.95**

Exit Lines

[GK425] Grafton pbk **£2.99**

Ruling Passion

[GK426] Grafton pbk **£2.99**

The Collaborators

[GK427] Grafton pbk **£3.99**

Underworld

[GK428] Grafton pbk **£3.50**

HILLERMAN, TONY (US, 1925 -)

Former wire-service reporter and college professor domiciled in New Mexico, Hillerman has created a thoroughly original and convincing pair of Navajo Tribal Policemen, Jim Chee and Joe Leaphorn, in elegantly-written stories, praised for their hauntingly beautiful sense of place. An unusual combination of mystery and mysticism.

A Thief of Time　　　　**NEW**

Already highly acclaimed in America, the latest Chee and Leaphorn story revolves around a dig at an ancient Anasazi burial ground, where a volatile archaeologist has been posted missing. The tribal policemen have to unearth the past in order to solve a mystifying series of murders.

[GK429] M Joseph hbk **£11.95**

People of Darkness

[GK430] Sphere pbk **£2.99**

Skinwalkers
[GK431] M Joseph hbk £10.95
The Dark Wind
[GK432] Sphere pbk £2.99
The Ghostway
[GK433] Sphere pbk £2.99

HILTON, JAMES
Was it Murder?
[GK433A] Oxford pbk £3.95

HIMES, CHESTER (US, 1909 - 1948)
Chester Himes's marvellously lucid and darkly humorous tales of murder and petty larceny in Harlem are unrivalled in their ability to convey the atmosphere of a black, urban community. Coffin Ed Johnson and Grave Digger Jones do not follow standard police procedure in their efforts to bring a felon to book. Very funny repartee, much mayhem.
A Rage in Harlem
[GK434] Allison & B pbk £3.50
All Shot Up
[GK435] Allison & B pbk £3.99
Blind Man with a Pistol
[GK436] Allison & B pbk £2.95
Cotton Comes to Harlem
[GK437] Allison & B pbk £3.50
Real Cool Killers
[GK438] Allison & B pbk £3.50
The Big Gold Dream
[GK439] Allison & B pbk £3.99
The Crazy Kill
[GK440] Allison & B pbk £3.50
The Heat's On
[GK441] Allison & B pbk £3.99

HORNUNG, E.W. (British, 1866 - 1921)
A.J. Raffles, the Gentleman Cracksman, who played cricket for England in the daytime and kleptomaniac for himself at night, is an enduring literary hero. Hornung was Conan Doyle's brother-in-law.
Collected Raffles
[GK442] Dent pbk £3.50
Complete Short Stories of Raffles,
Amateur Cracksman
[GK443] Penguin pbk £4.95

HUME, FERGUS (British, 1859 - 1932)
Prolific author (over 150 novels) doomed to be remembered for **Hansom Cab**, his first title, alone. Although indeed a classic, **Hansom Cab's** plot is convoluted to say the least, in the tradition of the Victorian novel.
Mystery of a Hansom Cab
[GK444] Hogarth pbk £3.95

HUXLEY, ELSPETH (British, 1907 -)
Straight 'whodunnits' with a 1930s British African setting, described by one critic as a cross between P.G. Wodehouse and Evelyn Waugh.
African Poison Murders
[GK445] Dent pbk £3.95
Murder at Government House
[GK446] Dent pbk £3.95
Murder on Safari
[GK447] Dent pbk £3.95

ILES, FRANCIS (British, 1893 - 1971)
Pseudonym of Anthony Cox, who also wrote under the name **Anthony Berkeley** (qv). As Iles, he dispensed with the Golden Age form to produce two masterful studies of a murderous mind (the other, **Before the Fact**, is currently unavailable).
Malice Aforethought
[GK448] Dent pbk £3.95

INNES, MICHAEL (British, 1916 -)
Novelist (as **J.I.M. Stewart**) and English don, Innes has been a leading light in what Julian Symons has

called the 'farceur' school of detective fiction, in that his stories are urbane and erudite, self-consciously literary, slightly fantastic and often whimsical. Many feature the stolid policeman John Appleby, and the more substantial ones (such as **Death at the President's Lodging**) must be acknowledged as cornerstones of the genre.
Appleby on Ararat
[GK449] Gollancz pbk £3.50
Appleby's Answer
[GK450] Penguin pbk £1.95
Awkward Lie
[GK451] Penguin pbk £1.95
Carson's Conspiracy
[GK452] Penguin pbk £2.25
Death at the Chase
[GK453] Penguin pbk £1.95
Death at the President's Lodging
Innes' first (and some say still best) work, which launched Appleby on his career of detection. The Master of St Anthony's College, Umpleby, has been murdered: none of the dons liked him...The story is crammed with Shakespearian quotations and literary one-upmanship, but there is real substance to the writing, and Appleby, in the early books, has not yet become stodgy. Considered the most intelligent detective novel even when it first appeared in 1936.
[GK454] Penguin pbk £3.95
Hare Sitting Up
[GK455] Mysterious P pbk £2.50
Lord Mullion's Secret
[GK456] Penguin pbk £1.95
Second Michael Innes Omnibus:
Journeying Boy/Operation Pax/Man
from the Sea
[GK457] Penguin pbk £4.95
Seven Suspects
[GK458] Penguin pbk £1.95
Silence Observed
[GK459] Mysterious P pbk £2.50
The New Sonia Wayward
[GK460] Gollancz pbk £2.99
There Came Both Mist and Snow
[GK461] Mysterious P pbk £2.99

JAMES, BILL (British)
Already showered with plaudits for the uncompromising realism of his police procedurals, Bill James deals in the blurred line between copper and villain, raising vital questions of ethics associated with the way in which the British police force sets about fighting serious crime.
Come Clean **NEW**
Sarah Iles, the wealthy wife of an Assistant Chief Constable, becomes involved with a young lover on the edge of petty crime. Against a background of gang warfare and drugs, Iles pursues a private and professional vendetta.
[GK462] Constable hbk £10.95
Halo Parade
[GK463] Penguin pbk £2.99
Protection
[GK464] Penguin pbk £2.99
The Lolita Man
[GK465] Penguin pbk £2.50

JAMES, P.D. (British, 1920 -)
The leading writer of detective fiction in Britain, James has brought the 'educated' crime story as practised by Sayers and Allingham into the modern age, resulting in a new level of literary sophistication and a far higher degree of realism. Her detective Cordelia Gray is if anything an even more interesting personality than the poeticising Adam Dalgliesh (sympathetically portrayed on television by Roy Marsden) and, like James herself, she approaches the case with a refreshingly detached eye. P.D. James is one of the few who actually give credence to the old cliché about 'transcending the genre'.

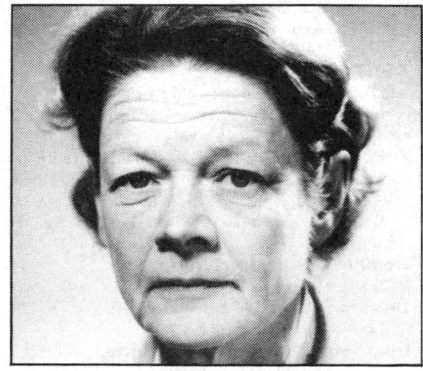

Elspeth Huxley, author of *Murder on Safari* (Dent pbk £3.95)

Innocent Blood (1980)
[GK466] Sphere pbk £2.95
P.D. James Omnibus: Unnatural
Causes/Shroud for a Nightingale/
An Unsuitable Job
[GK467] Faber pbk £8.95
CORDELIA GRAY
An Unsuitable Job for a Woman (1972)
[GK468] Sphere pbk £2.99
The Skull Beneath the Skin (1982)
[GK469] Sphere pbk £3.50
INSPECTOR DALGLIESH
A Taste for Death (1986)
[GK470] Faber hbk £9.95
[GK471] Sphere pbk £3.99
Black Tower (1975)
[GK472] Sphere pbk £3.50
Cover Her Face (1962)
[GK473] Sphere pbk £3.50
Death of an Expert Witness (1977)
[GK474] Sphere pbk £3.50
Devices and Desires **NEW**
Dalgliesh finds a comforting solitude in the converted windmill left to him by his aunt. It is situated on a remote Norfolk headland and is an ideal refuge from the publicity attendant upon his latest book of poetry, until a particularly ingenious and horrifying local murder calls him back to duty.
[GK475] Faber hbk £11.99
Mind to Murder (1963)
[GK476] Sphere pbk £2.99
Shroud for a Nightingale (1971)
[GK477] Sphere pbk £3.50
Unnatural Causes (1967)
[GK478] Sphere pbk £2.99

JAPRISOT, SEBASTIEN
The Lady in the Car with Glasses and a
Gun
Oldcastle P pbk £2.99

KAVANAGH, DAN (British)
Otherwise known as novelist Julian Barnes, Kavanagh has already achieved cult status with these tawdry tales of London's seamier side and his bi-sexual detective, Duffy, who encounters some seriously nasty characters in his investigations into Soho sleaze, London Airport, or the local football club. Modern and authentic, these stories are highly recommended.
Duffy
[GK479] Penguin pbk £2.99
Fiddle City
[GK480] Penguin pbk £2.50
Going to the Dogs
[GK481] Penguin pbk £2.99

Putting the Boot In
[GK482] Penguin pbk **£2.50**

KEATING, H.R.F. (British)
Keating has been chairman of the Crimewriters' Association, crime fiction reviewer for *The Times* and author of many anthologies and critical guides to the genre. But it is his Inspector Ghote novels, featuring the likeable and tenacious Bombay policeman, which have ensured Keating's lasting fame as one of the great post-war practitioners of the classical detective story.
Body in the Billiard Room
[GK483] Mysterious P pbk **£2.50**
Dead on Time
[GK484] Mysterious P pbk **£2.99**
Inspector Ghote Draws a Line
[GK485] Mysterious P pbk **£2.95**
Inspector Ghote Hunts a Peacock
[GK486] Mysterious P pbk **£2.50**
Inspector Ghote Plays a Joker
[GK487] Mysterious P pbk **£2.50**
Inspector Ghote's Good Crusade
[GK488] Mysterious P pbk **£2.50**
Murder of the Maharajah
[GK489] Mysterious P pbk **£2.95**
Sheriff of Bombay
[GK490] Mysterious P pbk **£2.95**
The Perfect Murder
[GK491] Mysterious P pbk **£2.50**

KNIGHT, ERIC (British, 1897 - 1943)
Pseudonym of Richard Hallas. Hallas was British but in 1938 he managed to write the classic American 'hard-boiled' crime novel (his only one). Critics raved but the book became a 'lost' masterpiece. Newly reprinted, this mixture of Hemingway and James M. Cain is a ferocious 'at-a-sitting' read.
You Play the Black and the Red Comes Up
[GK492] Creative Arts pbk **£2.95**

LATHEN, EMMA
Pseudonym of Martha Henissart and Mary Latsis. Altogether the Lathen team has now written 20 books featuring the Wall Street banker/detective John Putnam Thatcher, each one a fascinating insight into the world of high finance (not as apocalyptic as Paul Erdman). These well-researched stories, with their quite brilliant characterisation, are amusing, clever and well-plotted - an irresistible mixture.
Accounting for Murder
[GK493] Penguin pbk **£2.50**
Banking on Death
[GK494] Penguin pbk **£2.99**
Going for Gold
[GK495] Gollancz pbk **£2.99**
Murder without Icing
[GK496] Penguin pbk **£2.99**
Something in the Air   NEW
The pilot of a small airline is murdered during a dispute between management and employees, enabling Thatcher to investigate embezzlement, fraud and drug-running in Boston.
[GK497] Simon & Sch hbk **£10.95**
When in Greece
[GK498] Penguin pbk **£2.50**

LATIMER, JONATHAN (1906 - 1983)
Hard-boiled but highly amusing stories featuring private detective Bill Cane and his whisky bottle. Currently a cult author.
Headed for a Hearse
[GK499] Oldcastle P pbk **£3.99**
Lady in the Morgue
[GK500] Oldcastle P pbk **£3.99**
Murderer in the Madhouse
[GK501] Oldcastle P pbk **£3.99**

Red Gardenias
The fifth and final Bill Crane mystery, in which he teams up with his old ally Doc Williams.
[GK502] Oldcastle P pbk **£2.99**
The Dead Don't Care
[GK503] Oldcastle P pbk **£3.95**

LEONARD, ELMORE (US, 1925 -)
Although Leonard has been writing tough, realistic crime stories for almost twenty years, it is only recently that he has become a bestselling author on both sides of the Atlantic. He does for Florida and the East Coast what George V. Higgins has done for the Boston Irish, absorbing and accurately representing the vernacular dialogue of real petty crooks and policemen through his vivid characters. It is to be hoped that his newly-won fame does not cause future books to lose the sharp edge of, for example, *La Brava*.
52 Pick-Up
[GK504] Penguin pbk **£2.50**
Bandits
[GK505] Penguin pbk **£3.50**
City Primeval
[GK506] Penguin pbk **£2.99**
Freaky Deaky
Explosive (literally) epitaph for the Sixties, as two ageing Flower Children play with dynamite. Labyrinthine plot, unbearable suspense.
[GK507] Viking hbk **£11.95**
Glitz
[GK508] Penguin pbk **£2.99**
Gold Coast
[GK509] Penguin pbk **£2.50**
Hunted
[GK510] Penguin pbk **£2.50**
Killshot   NEW
Two men try to put the squeeze on a Canadian real estate operator only to find he's the toughest customer they've yet encountered. A chilling new novel from Leonard, at the top of his form.
[GK511] Viking hbk **£12.95**
La Brava
[GK512] Penguin pbk **£3.50**
Mr Majestyk
[GK513] Penguin pbk **£2.50**
Stick
[GK514] Penguin pbk **£2.95**
Swag
[GK515] Penguin pbk **£2.99**
Switch
[GK516] Penguin pbk **£2.50**
Touch
[GK517] Penguin pbk **£2.99**
Unknown Man No. 89
[GK518] Penguin pbk **£2.95**

LOVESEY, PETER (British, 1936 -)
Detective novelist whose best work has usually featured the Victorian Police Sergeant Cribb and his assistant Constable Thackery, as well as a wealth of fascinating historical detail expertly researched.
Abracadaver
[GK519] Mysterious P pbk **£2.50**
Bertie and the Tinman
[GK520] Mysterious P pbk **£2.50**
False Inspector Dew
[GK521] Mysterious P pbk **£2.50**
Invitation to a Dynamite Party
[GK522] Mysterious P pbk **£2.50**
Keystone
[GK523] Mysterious P pbk **£1.95**
On the Edge   NEW
Two ex-WAAF plotters meet up again after the War, both married to husbands they wished were dead. Antonia has a scheme, and if Rose keeps her nerve, they could get away with murder.
[GK524] Mysterious P hbk **£10.95**

H.R.F. Keating, author of *Inspector Ghote's Good Crusade* (Mysterious Press pbk **£2.50**) Picture: Michael O'Mara Books

Rough Cider
[GK525] Mysterious P pbk **£2.50**
The Detective Wore Silk Draws
[GK526] Mysterious P pbk **£2.50**
Waxwork
[GK527] Mysterious P pbk **£2.50**

LYONS, ARTHUR
Castles Burning
[GK527A] Oldcastle P pbk **£2.99**
Dead Ringer
[GK527B] Oldcastle P pbk **£2.99**
Hard Trade
[GK527C] Oldcastle P pbk **£2.99**
Killing Floor
[GK527D] Oldcastle P pbk **£2.99**
Three with a Bullet
[GK527E] Oldcastle P pbk **£2.99**

MACDONALD, JOHN DANN
(US, 1916 -)
Crime readers are most familiar with John MacDonald's 'colour title' series, which chronicles the exploits of a lone operator Travis Magee, an investigator who works to a strict code of ethics. The books are violent, but they deal with violence in a responsible way and the character of Magee gives them a moral centre. A much better writer than his pulp origins might suggest.
Cinnamon Skin
[GK528] Pan pbk **£2.50**
Deep Blue Goodbye
[GK529] Pan pbk **£2.50**
Dreadful Lemon Sky
[GK530] Pan pbk **£2.50**
Empty Copper Sea
[GK531] Pan pbk **£2.50**
Free Fall in Crimson
[GK532] Pan pbk **£2.50**
Green Ripper
[GK533] Pan pbk **£2.50**
Nightmare in Pink
[GK534] Pan pbk **£2.50**
The Turquoise Lament
[GK535] Pan pbk **£2.50**

MACDONALD, ROSS (US, 1915 - 1983)
Often labelled 'Chandler's natural successor', Ross MacDonald is a master of intriguing plots which employ faintly gothic elements, involving perverse secrets from the past and skeletons in the family closet. His private eye Lew Archer does resemble Philip Marlowe (and works the same West Coast

territory), but the stories generally lack Chandler's inventiveness.

Barbarous Coast
[GK536] Allison & B pbk **£3.99**
Black Money
[GK537] Allison & B pbk **£2.95**
Blue City
[GK538] Fontana pbk **£2.95**
Blue Hammer
[GK539] Allison & B pbk **£3.50**
Far Side of the Dollar
[GK540] Allison & B pbk **£3.99**
Goodbye Look
[GK541] Allison & B pbk **£3.99**
Meet Me at the Morgue
[GK542] Allison & B pbk **£3.99**
Moving Target
[GK543] Allison & B pbk **£2.95**
The Chill
[GK544] Allison & B pbk **£3.50**
The Drowning Pool
[GK545] Allison & B pbk **£3.99**
The Galton Case
[GK546] Allison & B pbk **£3.99**
The Three Roads
[GK547] Allison & B pbk **£3.99**

MACLEOD, CHARLOTTE (US, 1922 -)
Clever plotting and liberal helpings of humour and romance characterize MacLeod's escapist crime stories, an effective antidote to the ultra-realism that is currently so fashionable. Her two protagonists, Professor Shandy and Sarah Kelling, are delightful creations.

The Family Vault
[GK548] Mysterious P pbk **£2.99**
The Recycled Citizen
[GK549] Mysterious P pbk **£2.99**
The Withdrawing Room
[GK550] Mysterious P pbk **£2.99**
Vane Pursuit `NEW`
Peter Shandy in a battle with demented survivalists as priceless weathervanes disappear in Balaclava County.
[GK551] Collins hbk **£10.95**

MALONE, MICHAEL
Handling Sin
[GK551A] Sphere pbk **£4.99**
Time's Witness `NEW`
[GK551B] Chatto hbk **£12.95**
Uncivil Seasons
[GK551C] Sphere pbk **£3.99**

MARSH, NGAIO (New Zealand, 1899 - 1982)
Marsh is one of the four great 'Queens of Crime'. Her central character, the intellectual Superintendent Roderick Alleyne, is a touch too 'perfect', but her subordinate players are consistently well-rounded, and the settings usually more than a mere backdrop to the action. Furthermore, the mechanics of plot and puzzle are handled with an originality and competence that sometimes eluded Christie and Allingham. Marsh is at her very best in the stories that revolve around the theatre.

A Surfeit of Lampreys
[GK552] Fontana pbk **£2.95**
Clutch of Constables
[GK553] Fontana pbk **£2.50**
Colour Scheme
[GK554] Fontana pbk **£2.50**
Death at the Dolphin
[GK555] Fontana pbk **£2.95**
Died in the Wool
Although all her books are interesting, this benefits from a highly unusual setting, a New Zealand sheep station, which Alleyn visits in order to solve a year-old murder. The vastness of the landscape, with its mountains, valleys and sense of isolation, is

wonderfully and economically described, the local idiom expertly managed.
[GK556] Fontana pbk **£2.95**
Off with His Head
[GK557] Fontana pbk **£1.50**
Overture to Death
[GK558] Fontana pbk **£2.50**
Scales of Justice
[GK559] Fontana pbk **£1.95**
Swing, Brother, Swing
[GK560] Fontana pbk **£2.50**
The Final Curtain
[GK561] Fontana pbk **£2.95**
Tied up in Tinsel
[GK562] Fontana pbk **£2.50**
Vintage Murder
[GK563] Fontana pbk **£1.95**

MARSHALL, WILLIAM (Australian, 1944 -)
An underrated writer who brought both structural and stylistic originality to his Yellowthread Street series, which teeters between farce and horror in relating the antics of a Hong Kong police station and its multi-racial officers. Marshall has also started a similar series on Manila.

Far Away Man
[GK564] Futura pbk **£1.95**
Gelignite
[GK565] Futura pbk **£2.50**
Hatchet Man
[GK566] Futura pbk **£1.95**
Manila Bay
[GK567] Mysterious P pbk **£2.50**
Skullduggery
[GK568] Futura pbk **£2.50**
Whisper
The second in Marshall's frenetic series set in Manila.
[GK569] Mysterious P hbk **£10.95**
Yellowthread Street
[GK570] Futura pbk **£1.95**

MCBAIN, ED (US, 1926 -)
The 87th Precinct novels were the inspiration for the tremendously successful TV series 'Hill Street Blues', and there are no finer examples of the modern American procedural: Detective Carella and his colleagues have matured with time, and their fallibility prevents the series from becoming simply formulaic. McBain's Matthew Hope titles, about an East Coast lawyer, are also recommended.

Another Part of the City
[GK571] Pan pbk **£2.50**
Axe
[GK572] Pan pbk **£2.99**
Cop Hater
[GK573] Penguin pbk **£1.95**
Downtown `NEW`
A non-series novel, funny and fast-moving, about a Florida orange-grower up in Manhattan on business with a few hours to kill on Christmas Eve. Soon on the run from an assortment of crazies, and with a beautiful Chinese girl in tow, Barnes realizes he is a marked man. But why? An unusual departure for McBain - the caper novel with an edge.
[GK574] Heinemann hbk **£11.95**
Eight Black Horses
[GK575] Pan pbk **£2.99**
Ghosts
[GK576] Pan pbk **£2.99**
Give the Boys a Great Big Hand
[GK577] Penguin pbk **£2.50**
Ice
[GK578] Pan pbk **£3.50**
Jack and the Beanstalk
[GK579] Sphere pbk **£2.50**
Killer's Choice
[GK580] Penguin pbk **£2.50**
Killer's Payoff
[GK581] Penguin pbk **£1.95**

Killer's Wedge
[GK582] Penguin pbk **£1.95**
Let's Hear It for the Deaf Man
[GK583] Pan pbk **£1.95**
Lightning
[GK584] Pan pbk **£2.99**
Lullaby `NEW`
The latest (40th) 87th Precinct novel pits Carella and Meyer against two Chinese brothers and some murderous Jamaicans. Before New Year's Day is out, a child is murdered…
[GK585] H Hamilton hbk **£11.95**
Poison
[GK586] Pan pbk **£2.50**
Puss in Boots
[GK587] Sphere pbk **£2.99**
Sadie When She Died
[GK588] Pan pbk **£2.50**
So Long As You Both Shall Live
[GK589] Pan pbk **£1.95**
The Pusher
[GK590] Penguin pbk **£2.50**
Tricks
[GK591] Pan pbk **£2.95**

MCCABE, CAMERON (German, 1915 -)
Pseudonym of Ernest Borneman.
The Face on the Cutting-Room Floor
One-off oddity from the 1940s, recently 'rediscovered', containing structural and narrative pyrotechnics, with *three* alternative endings.
[GK592] Penguin pbk **£3.95**

MCGIVERN, WILLIAM P. (US, 1922 - 1982)
Undervalued American crimewriter, one of the first to tackle the subject of police corruption head-on (*Rogue Cop* deserves a reprint), and influential in his accurate depiction of homicide detection.
The Big Heat
[GK593] Simon & Sch pbk **£3.50**
Very Cold for May
[GK594] Penguin pbk **£3.95**

MCILVANNEY, WILLIAM (British, 1936 -)
Fans of Inspector Laidlaw wait patiently for his reappearance in a third story about Glasgow's underworld. The 'patter' is skilfully integrated into McIlvanney's sympathetic portrayal of a tough city undergoing change, and Laidlaw's own struggle for integrity in a depraved world is entirely believable.
Laidlaw
[GK595] Hodder pbk **£2.50**
The Papers of Tony Veitch
[GK596] Hodder pbk **£2.95**

MELVILLE, JAMES (British, 1931 -)
Pseudonym of Peter Roy Martin. Melville has built up a reputation of high regard with his series involving Japanese Detective Superintendent Otani. Gentler in tone than William Marshall's Hong Kong fables, Melville nevertheless provides humorous and instructive observations on Japanese customs and behaviour.
A Haiku for Hanae `NEW`
Another outing for Supt. Otani of the Hyogo prefectural police, who is reminded on holiday of a baffling 20 year old case involving a murdered American missionary, found with a small ceramic bushy-tailed fox in his hand. This is the police procedural at its most sophisticated.
[GK597] Headline hbk **£11.95**
Death of a Daimyo
[GK598] Dent pbk **£3.95**
Kimono for a Corpse
[GK599] Headline pbk **£2.50**
Ninth Netsuke
[GK600] Dent pbk **£3.95**
The Reluctant Ronin
[GK601] Headline pbk **£2.50**

FICTION

Ngaio Marsh, author of *Died in the Wool*
(Fontana pbk £2.95)

FICTION

MILLAR, MARGARET (Canadian, 1915 -)
Less well known in Britain, Millar is recognised in
the US as one of the five top crime fiction writers of
the post-war era, not least for the way in which she
has reflected the social attitudes of the times, and for
her ability to convey a consistent sense of unease.
Beast in View
Generally considered her finest work, ***Beast in View***
is both a baffling mystery and a clear-eyed glimpse of
madness. Superbly crafted.
[GK602] Penguin pbk **£2.50**
How Like an Angel
[GK603] Penguin pbk **£2.95**
Soft Talkers
[GK604] Penguin pbk **£2.99**
Spider Webs
[GK605] Penguin pbk **£2.99**
Stranger in My Grave
[GK606] Penguin pbk **£2.99**
Taste of Fears
[GK607] Penguin pbk **£2.50**

MITCHELL, GLADYS (British, 1901 - 1983)
One of the more eccentric creations in the annals of
'whodunnit' detective literature is Dame Beatrice
LeStrange Bradley, psychiatric advisor to the Home
Office. She features in over sixty of Mitchell's books
and can always be relied upon to provide wit,
mischievous humour and highly original methods of
solving a crime.
Lament for Leto
[GK608] Hogarth pbk **£3.50**
Laurels Are Poison
[GK609] Hogarth pbk **£3.95**
Rising of the Moon
[GK610] Hogarth pbk **£3.95**
Salt Marsh Murders
[GK611] Hogarth pbk **£3.95**
Speedy Death
[GK612] Hogarth pbk **£3.95**
St Peter's Finger
[GK613] Hogarth pbk **£3.50**
When Last I Died
[GK614] Hogarth pbk **£4.50**

NABB, MAGDALEN (British)
Resident in Florence, Nabb writes about the twilight
world of the city - the side the tourists don't see.
Often taking real events as her inspiration, she is
concerned with what turns ordinary people into
savage criminals.
Death in Autumn
[GK615] Fontana pbk **£1.95**

Death in Springtime
[GK616] Fontana pbk **£1.50**
Death of a Dutchman
[GK617] Fontana pbk **£2.95**
Death of an Englishman
[GK618] Fontana pbk **£2.50**
The Marshal and the Madwoman
[GK619] Fontana pbk **£2.95**
The Marshal and the Murderer
[GK620] Fontana pbk **£2.95**

PARETSKY, SARA (US)
Kansas-born writer, currently rated America's first
lady of crime. Vic Warshawski, her chic Chicago
private-eye, is not shy of becoming personally
involved in the cases she takes on and shows more
tenacity than most when the going gets rough. Well-
written dialogue and a thoroughly believable heroine.
Bitter Medicine
[GK621] Penguin pbk **£2.99**
Deadlock
[GK622] Penguin pbk **£2.99**
Indemnity Only
[GK623] Penguin pbk **£2.99**
Killing Orders
[GK624] Penguin pbk **£2.95**
Toxic Shock NEW
Warshawski arouses suspicions at a chemical plant
while investigating an old friend's paternity, and when
the body of an activist is discovered murdered on
polluted factory wasteland, she begins to unearth a
sickening trail of corruption. A highly topical and
complex story, grippingly told.
[GK625] Gollancz hbk **£11.95**

PARKER, ROBERT B. (US, 1932 -)
Increasingly popular writer in the hard-boiled
tradition, Parker's private-eye Spenser is almost
comic. However, none of his books can be described
as mere 'capers', dealing as they do with serious
subjects and realistic behaviour: the humour is
derived incidentally from 'real' situations and fuelled
by the wisecracks of the central character. In
recognition of his ability in this field, Parker has been
chosen for the task of 'completing' Raymond
Chandler's unfinished Marlowe novel, *The Poodle
Springs Story*.
Catskill Eagle
[GK626] Penguin pbk **£2.99**
Ceremony
[GK627] Penguin pbk **£2.99**
Crimson Joy NEW
The hooker, the waitress and the dancer, all murdered,
all black. Spencer goes out on a limb to link a man
who has falsely confessed to the killings with the
murderer's calling card - a blood red rose.
[GK628] Viking hbk **£11.95**
God Save the Child
[GK629] Penguin pbk **£2.99**
Godwulf Manuscript
[GK630] Penguin pbk **£2.99**
Judas Goat
[GK631] Penguin pbk **£2.50**
Looking for Rachel Wallace
[GK632] Penguin pbk **£2.99**
Promised Land
[GK633] Penguin pbk **£2.99**
Savage Place
[GK634] Penguin pbk **£2.99**
Taming a Sea-Horse
[GK635] Penguin pbk **£2.95**
Valediction
[GK636] Penguin pbk **£2.99**
Widening Gyre
[GK637] Penguin pbk **£2.99**

PETERS, ELLIS (British, 1913 -)
Pseudonym of Edith Pargeter, an historical novelist
who turned to crime writing with a successful series

of detective stories featuring CID Inspector George
Felse and his son Dominic, who travel extensively
(India, Czechoslovakia, Austria), giving the books
vivid settings full of unusual information. She is also
the creator of the 11th century monk, Brother Cadfael,
currently one of the most popular detectives in
English language fiction.
BROTHER CADFAEL
A Morbid Taste for Bones
[GK638] Futura pbk **£2.99**
A Rare Benedictine
Three vintage tales of intrigue and treachery which
chronicle the chain of events that led Brother Cadfael
into the Benedictine Order. Specially commissioned
colour illustrations by Clifford Harper punctuate the
text.
[GK639] Headline hbk **£12.95**
An Excellent Mystery
[GK640] Futura pbk **£2.50**
Dead Man's Ransom
[GK641] Futura pbk **£2.99**
Leper of St Giles
[GK642] Futura pbk **£2.99**
Monk's Hood
[GK643] Futura pbk **£2.50**
One Corpse Too Many
[GK644] Futura pbk **£2.99**
Pilgrim of Hate
[GK645] Futura pbk **£2.99**
Rose Rent
[GK646] Futura pbk **£2.99**
St Peter's Fair
[GK647] Futura pbk **£2.50**
The Confessions of Brother Haluin
[GK648] Futura pbk **£2.99**
The Devil's Novice
[GK649] Futura pbk **£2.99**
The Heretic's Apprentice NEW
Brother Cadfael is again called away from his
herbiary to assist his old friend the Sheriff, Hugh
Beringar, in a case which requires both a murder to be
solved and a charge of heresy to be rebutted. In this,
the sixteenth medieval mystery from Ellis Peters, the
philosophical issues are as intriguing as the solution
to the puzzle itself.
[GK650] Headline hbk **£10.95**
The Hermit of Eyton Forest
[GK651] Futura pbk **£2.99**
The Raven in the Foregate
[GK652] Futura pbk **£2.99**
The Sanctuary Sparrow
[GK653] Futura pbk **£2.99**
Virgin in the Ice
[GK654] Futura pbk **£2.99**
INSPECTOR FELSE
A Nice Derangement of Epitaphs
[GK655] Futura pbk **£2.99**
**Black Is the Colour of My True Love's
Heart**
[GK656] Futura pbk **£2.99**
City of Gold and Shadows
[GK657] Headline pbk **£2.99**
Death to the Landlords!
[GK658] Headline pbk **£2.99**
**Mourning Raga - An Indian
Whodunnit**
[GK659] Headline pbk **£2.50**
Piper on the Mountain
[GK660] Headline pbk **£2.99**

RADLEY, SHEILA (British)
Among the best of British newcomers, Radley and her
hero Inspector Quantrill delve into the murky private
lives of East Anglian folk: local colour abounds,
authenticity of dialogue improves with each book.
Radley must surely soon win an award from her
Crime Writers' Association colleagues.
Blood on the Happy Highway
[GK661] Penguin pbk **£2.50**

Chief Inspector's Daughter
[GK662] Penguin pbk **£2.99**
Death and the Maiden
[GK663] Penguin pbk **£2.99**
Fate Worse than Death
[GK664] Penguin pbk **£3.50**
Talent for Destruction
[GK665] Penguin pbk **£2.99**
This Way Out **NEW**
How a decent and honourable husband who hates his
mother-in-law and a cold-blooded psychopath
conspire to commit a double murder. When a staged
burglary goes disastrously wrong and Quantrill is
brought in to investigate a killing of unbelievable
savagery, this variation of *Strangers on a Train*
develops into Radley's most ambitious novel to date.
[GK666] Constable hbk **£10.95**
Who Saw Him Die?
[GK667] Penguin pbk **£2.99**

RAYMOND, DEREK (British)
Now resident in France, Raymond has produced three
of the nastiest studies in human perversity as one
could ever hope to find - or avoid. The unnamed
detective from the Unexplained Deaths division of the
Met, a rampant pessimist cold-shouldered by his
colleagues, encounters gruesome crimes committed
by pathological deviants. For strong stomachs only.
He Died with His Eyes Open
[GK668] Sphere pbk **£3.50**
How the Dead Live
[GK669] Sphere pbk **£3.99**
The Devil's Home on Leave
[GK670] Sphere pbk **£3.50**

RENDELL, RUTH (British, 1930 -)
Just now reaching the peak of her form (and finally
receiving the appropriate degree of support form her
publisher), Rendell is one of Britain's leading
practitioners of both the crime story, mostly involving
the provincial Chief Inspector Wexford, and the novel
of suspense. It is on these, dealing brilliantly and
disturbingly with decidedly odd characters and
unusual behaviour, that her reputation deserves to
rest. 'One of our most important novelists' (John
Mortimer).

Ruth Rendell, author of *The Bridesmaid* (Hutchinson
hbk £11.95) & *The Veiled One* (Arrow pbk £4.99)

A New Lease of Death
[GK671] Arrow pbk **£2.50**
Collected Short Stories
[GK672] Hutchinson hbk **£12.95**
Demon in My View
[GK673] Arrow pbk **£2.50**
Fallen Curtain & Other Stories
[GK674] Arrow pbk **£2.50**
Heartstones
[GK675] Arrow pbk **£2.50**
Judgment in Stone
[GK676] Arrow pbk **£2.50**
Live Flesh
[GK677] Arrow pbk **£2.75**
Make Death Love Me
[GK678] Arrow pbk **£2.50**
Master of the Moor
[GK679] Arrow pbk **£2.50**
Means of Evil & Other Stories
[GK680] Arrow pbk **£2.50**
One Across, Two Down
[GK681] Arrow pbk **£2.50**
Talking to Strange Men
[GK682] Arrow deluxe pbk **£5.95**
[GK683] Arrow pbk **£2.99**
The Bridesmaid **NEW**
A dark, brooding novel of suspense, appropriately
crowning 25 years as an author, and very possibly
Rendell's best so far. A young man's obsessive
fascination with a beautiful Renaissance statue known
as the Farnese Flora undergoes a surprising and
horrifying transformation when he meets a woman
whose face bears a remarkable resemblance to the
sculptured features of 'The Bridesmaid'. An
increasing sense of dread informs every page.
[GK684] Hutchinson hbk **£11.95**
The Face of Trespass
[GK685] Arrow pbk **£2.50**
The Fever Tree & Other Stories
[GK686] Arrow pbk **£2.50**
The Killing Doll
[GK687] Arrow pbk **£2.99**
The Lake of Darkness
[GK688] Arrow pbk **£2.50**
The New Girl Friend & Other Stories
[GK689] Arrow pbk **£2.50**
The Tree of Hands
[GK690] Arrow pbk **£2.99**
To Fear a Painted Devil
[GK691] Arrow pbk **£2.50**
Vanity Dies Hard
[GK692] Arrow pbk **£2.50**
INSPECTOR WEXFORD
A Guilty Thing Surprised
[GK693] Arrow pbk **£2.50**
A Sleeping Life
[GK694] Arrow pbk **£2.25**
An Unkindness of Ravens
[GK695] Arrow pbk **£2.50**
From Doon with Death
[GK696] Arrow pbk **£2.50**
Murder Being Once Done
[GK697] Arrow pbk **£2.50**
No More Dying Then
[GK698] Arrow pbk **£2.50**
Put on by Cunning
[GK699] Arrow pbk **£2.50**
Shake Hands for Ever
[GK700] Arrow pbk **£2.50**
Some Lie and Some Die
[GK701] Arrow pbk **£2.50**
The Best Man to Die
[GK702] Arrow pbk **£2.50**
The Speaker of Mandarin
[GK703] Arrow pbk **£2.50**
The Veiled One
Before Wexford can solve the mystery of a woman
garrotted in a Kingsmarkham car park, he narrowly
escapes death himself: a bomb underneath his

Ellis Peters, author of *The Heretic's Apprentice*
(Headline hbk £10.95) Photo: Roy Morgan

daughter's car explodes outside his house. Burden is
left to pursue the case alone, but he does not have the
deductive abilities of his boss.
[GK704] Arrow deluxe pbk **£4.99**
[GK705] Arrow pbk **£2.99**
Wexford: An Omnibus
From Doon With Death/A New Lease of Death/The
Best Man to Die.
[GK706] Mysterious P pbk **£5.99**
Wexford: The Second Omnibus
[GK707] Hutchinson hbk **£12.95**
Wolf to the Slaughter
[GK708] Arrow pbk **£2.50**

RINEHART, MARY ROBERTS (US, 1876 -
1958)
Wrote straight detective/adventure stories with
romantic undertones. *The Circular Staircase* extends
the theme of the country house with a guilty secret.
The Circular Staircase
[GK709] Dent pbk **£3.95**
The Wall
[GK710] Dent pbk **£4.95**

ROBINSON, ROBERT (British)
The television personality wrote this one crime novel
in 1956. Set in Oxford, it is predictably witty and
ingenious, and now a minor classic in the Oxbridge
detective story canon.
Landscape with Dead Dons
[GK711] Penguin pbk **£1.95**

ROHMER, SAX (1883 - 1959)
Fu Manchu is one of the more extravagant literary
arch-villans; these tales of the Yellow Peril now seem
unbelievably gung-ho, yet remain highly entertaining.
Mystery of Dr Fu Manchu
[GK712] Dent pbk **£2.95**

SAYERS, DOROTHY L. (British, 1893 - 1957)
Sayers is proof that good writing will always survive
the changes in moral and social values. Lord Peter
Wimsey, her dilettante detective, may appear
infuriatingly snobbish and chauvinistic to the modern
reader, but behind his Woosterish facade is a complex
man of strong principles, and Sayers' obvious
involvement with her character has ensured the books
a lasting popularity.
Busman's Honeymoon
[GK713] Hodder pbk **£3.50**

Clouds of Witness
[GK714] Hodder pbk **£2.95**
Documents in the Case
[GK715] Hodder pbk **£2.50**
Five Red Herrings
Wimsey arrives at an artist's colony in Galloway, South Scotland, to pinpoint Campbell's murderer. The classic whodunnit (there are six suspects), and Sayers' most ingenious plot.
[GK716] Hodder pbk **£2.95**
Gaudy Night
[GK717] Hodder pbk **£3.50**
Hangman's Holiday
[GK718] Hodder pbk **£2.50**
Have His Carcase
[GK719] Hodder pbk **£3.50**
In the Teeth of the Evidence
[GK720] Hodder pbk **£2.99**
Lord Peter Views the Body
[GK721] Hodder pbk **£2.95**
Murder Must Advertise
Along with *The Nine Tailors* this is Sayers' most meticulously researched novel. Wimsey joins an advertising agency in order to learn who killed Victor Dean, their star copywriter. In no other story does Wimsey encounter such really unpleasant characters, and the treatment of crimes such as blackmail and drug pushing is surprisingly forthright for the times.
[GK722] Hodder pbk **£2.95**
Striding Folly
[GK723] Hodder pbk **£1.95**
Strong Poison
[GK724] Hodder pbk **£2.50**
The Nine Tailors
[GK725] Hodder pbk **£2.99**
Unpleasantness at the Bellona Club
[GK726] Hodder pbk **£2.99**
Whose Body?
[GK727] Hodder pbk **£2.50**

SIMENON, GEORGES (Belgian, 1903 - 1985)
A colossus of the genre, even of the novel itself, and the creator of Maigret, the most famous fictional detective after Holmes, Simenon revolutionised the crime story in terms of the psychological depth of its characters and in making 'the implausible acceptable'. His best stories deal with events that have their origin far back in the past and his most memorable characters, both criminal and otherwise, are those who fight a losing battle with their own consciences. *Stain on the Snow*, *The Man Who Watched the Trains Go By* and *Maigret Mystified* are three of his very finest stories.
Act of Passion
[GK728] Penguin pbk **£3.95**
In Case of Emergency/Little Saint
[GK729] Penguin pbk **£3.95**
Iron Staircase & The Train
[GK730] Penguin pbk **£3.95**
Little Man from Archangel/Monsieur Monde Vanishes
[GK731] Penguin pbk **£3.95**
Maigret Mystified
[GK732] Penguin pbk **£3.99**
Maigret and the Ghost
Maigret and the Hotel Majestic/Three Beds in Manhattan/Maigret and the Ghost.
[GK733] Penguin pbk **£3.95**
Maigret's Pipe
[GK734] Penguin pbk **£3.95**
Maigret's Rival
[GK735] Penguin pbk **£3.95**
Rules of the Game   **NEW**
A model citizen in a small American town has his application to join the country club rejected, causing him to question the community's values and his own ambitions. Bitter and humiliated, he is determined to have his revenge.
[GK736] H Hamilton hbk **£10.95**

Simenon Omnibus
[GK737] H Hamilton hbk **£10.95**
Stain on the Snow
[GK738] Penguin pbk **£3.95**
The Man Who Watched the Trains Go/ Breton Sisters
[GK739] Penguin pbk **£3.95**

SIMPSON, DOROTHY (British, 1933 -)
Unfussy, methodical stories of detection featuring family-man Inspector Thanet (from Kent). Simpson's reputation grows apace among fans of the safe, English suspense story. She won the Silver Dagger Award in 1985.
Close Her Eyes
[GK740] Sphere pbk **£2.99**
Dead by Morning   **NEW**
Recently returned to Kent to claim a large inheritance after a twenty-five year absence, Leo Martindale is found dead in a ditch. Hit and run, or murder? Thanet, in his ninth case, confronts a plethora of suspects.
[GK741] M Joseph hbk **£11.95**
Dead on Arrival
[GK742] Sphere pbk **£2.99**
Element of Doubt
[GK743] Sphere pbk **£2.99**
Last Seen Alive
[GK744] Sphere pbk **£2.99**
Puppet for a Corpse
[GK745] Sphere pbk **£2.99**
Suspicious Death
[GK746] Sphere pbk **£2.99**

STARK, RICHARD
(US, 1933 -)
Pseudonym of *Donald Westlake* (qv). Stark invented the professional thief Parker, tough, mean and spare, in prose to match (and on film, for once, none of the flavour was lost in Lee Marvin's portrayal in *Point Blank*). Parker's motives are never questioned and one can only wonder how such a cold, ruthless character who kills wholesale, can have such a fatal attraction for the reader. There is nothing remotely like this series, nearly all of them now in print.
Black Ice Score
[GK747] Allison & B pbk **£2.95**
Green Eagle Score
[GK748] Allison & B pbk **£2.95**
Point Blank
[GK749] Allison & B pbk **£2.95**
Rare Coin Score
[GK750] Allison & B pbk **£3.99**
The Handle
[GK751] Allison & B pbk **£3.99**
The Jugger
[GK752] Allison & B pbk **£2.95**
The Man with the Getaway Face
[GK753] Allison & B pbk **£2.95**
The Mourner
[GK754] Allison & B pbk **£3.50**
The Outfit
[GK755] Allison & B pbk **£3.99**

STOUT, REX
(US, 1886 - 1975)
Creator of the gluttonous egg-head detective Nero Wolfe (*Even in the Best Families*), whose charm, wit and various eccentricities have endeared him to generations of readers. Considering Stout's prolific output, there is lamentably little to choose from at present.
Even in the Best Families
[GK756] Fontana pbk **£2.95**
Hand in the Glove
[GK757] Hogarth pbk **£3.95**
The Doorbell Rang
[GK758] Hogarth pbk **£2.99**

SYMONS, JULIAN (British, 1912 -)
Crime archivist *extraordinaire* who has contributed a great deal to the modern crime story and its subgenres, introducing a psychological depth in the 1950s (not previously attempted in this field) to stories such as *The Colour of Murder* and *The Narrowing Circle*. His Victorian trilogy and collections of short stories are models of their type, as are his more humorous efforts such as the Innes-like *Criminal Comedy of the Contented Couple*; the character of his sleuthing thespian, Sheridan Haynes, who specialises in the role of Sherlock Holmes, is a most amusing one.
Belting Inheritance
[GK759] Macmillan pbk **£3.99**
Criminal Comedy of the Contented Couple
[GK760] Penguin pbk **£2.99**
Detling Secret
New edition of *The Detling Murders*.
[GK761] Penguin pbk **£1.95**
End of Solomon Grundy
[GK762] Macmillan pbk **£3.95**
Julian Symons Omnibus
[GK763] Penguin pbk **£4.95**
The Colour of Murder
A turning point of sorts in the English crime story, being one of the first really successful attempts at dispensing with the rigid 'rules' of the genre. The plot, which centres around the arrest and trial of an underachiever for the murder of a librarian (once the object of his fantasy) is deliberately loose, and there are no cardboard characters to impinge upon the narrative, which is largely described by the victim himself.
[GK764] Macmillan pbk **£3.95**
The Kentish Manor Murders
[GK765] Macmillan pbk **£3.99**
The Narrowing Circle
[GK766] Penguin pbk **£3.95**
Three Pipe Problem
[GK767] Penguin pbk **£3.99**
Tigers of Subtopia
[GK768] Penguin pbk **£1.75**

TEY, JOSEPHINE (British, 1897 - 1952)
Pseudonym of Elizabeth Mackintosh. Detective novelist whose books are always in demand: *Brat Farrar* (recently televised), *The Franchise Affair* and *The Daughter of Time* are already minor classics, the latter featuring her regular hero, Inspector Alan Grant, another of those correct, unassuming men from the Yard. Despite almost belonging to another age now, the books are sufficiently 'universal' to ensure a continued readership.
Brat Farrar
[GK769] Penguin pbk **£2.95**
The Franchise Affair
[GK770] Penguin pbk **£2.95**
Man in the Queue
[GK771] Penguin pbk **£2.99**
Miss Pym Disposes
[GK772] Penguin pbk **£2.95**
Shilling for Candles
[GK773] Penguin pbk **£2.50**
Singing Sands
[GK774] Penguin pbk **£3.99**
The Daughter of Time
From his hospital bed, Grant re-examines the murder in 1480 by Richard III of his two nephews. Tey has indulged in genuine historical detective work to confound the accepted judgement of history and has ingeniously incorporated the process and results into a modern story of detection. The sheer uniqueness of this idea has ensured the book's lasting popularity.
[GK775] Penguin pbk **£3.99**
To Love and Be Wise
[GK776] Penguin pbk **£2.95**

THOMPSON, JIM (US, 1906 - 1976)
An American pulp-writer, without honour in any country except possibly France until very recently, whose genius and influence is now recognised by an ever growing band of critics and readers alike. The typical Thompson novel is a frightening descent into the psychopathic soul of a doomed character, shot through with emotion and inappropriate humour. There is something dangerous and out of control about Thompson's work and it is certainly not for the fainthearted.
After Dark My Sweet
[GK777] Creative Arts pbk **£2.95**
Recoil
[GK778] Creative Arts pbk **£2.95**
Swell Looking Babe
[GK779] Creative Arts pbk **£2.95**
The Alcoholics
[GK780] Creative Arts pbk **£2.95**
The Criminal
[GK781] Creative Arts pbk **£2.95**
Wild Town
[GK782] Creative Arts pbk **£2.95**

THOMSON, JUNE (British, 1930 -)
Whodunnit author of some subtlety, in the classic mould. The stories, which feature Detective Inspector Jack Finch, have been praised for their careful characterization and sure sense of place.
A Dying Fall
[GK783] Sphere pbk **£2.50**
Sound Evidence
[GK784] Sphere pbk **£2.50**
The Dark Stream
[GK785] Sphere pbk **£2.75**
The Spoils of Time **NEW**
Finch investigates a double murder at Houlett Hall, a decaying country house. With infinite patience he separates the clues from the red herrings, and finds a 'cat's cradle of avarice' throughout the Aston family.
[GK786] Constable hbk **£10.95**
To Make a Killing
[GK787] Sphere pbk **£2.50**

TUROW, SCOTT (US)
Presumed Innocent
For once the hype for a first novel was justified - but it will be a hard act to follow. The story of Rusty Sabich, chief prosecuting attorney in a large mid-western city, who is accused of a crime he has been instructed to solve. The authentic courtroom scene (based on the author's own experience as Chicago US Attorney's Office prosecutor) is the book's centrepiece. Absolutely riveting.
[GK788] Penguin pbk **£3.95**

UPFIELD, ARTHUR W.
(Australian, 1888 - 1964)
Australian writer whose half-caste police detective Napoleon Bonaparte, or 'Bony', is steeped in Aboriginal lore: the mysteries are genuinely tantalizing, the stories exciting and well-paced without the frenetic baggage of the big city thriller. A refreshing change.
Battling Prophet
[GK789] Angus & R pbk **£3.50**
Bony and the White Savage
[GK790] Angus & R pbk **£2.25**
Death of a Swagman
[GK791] Angus & R pbk **£1.95**
Man of Two Tribes
[GK792] Angus & R pbk **£3.50**
Mystery of Swordfish Reef
[GK793] Angus & R pbk **£3.50**
New Shoe
[GK794] Angus & R pbk **£2.25**
Venom House
[GK795] Angus & R pbk **£3.50**

Wings above the Diamantina
[GK796] Angus & R pbk **£2.25**

VACHSS, ANDREW
Blue Belle **NEW**
Bodley Head have imaginatively published the third of Vachss' stories about the New York outlaw detective Burke as a trade paperback. The subject matter is child abuse, and no punches are pulled: Vachss is himself a lawyer in private practice specializing in juvenile justice, and though the style may be supercharged, the depravity he describes is not fictional. In *Blue Belle*, a savage gang of predators is on the prowl, kidnapping and killing teenage prostitutes in a smooth and silent vehicle - the 'Ghost Van'.
[GK797] Bodley pbk **£6.99**
Flood
[GK798] Pan pbk **£2.50**
Strega
[GK799] Pan pbk **£2.99**

VALIN, JONATHAN
Fire Lake **NEW**
[GK800] Mysterious P hbk **£10.95**

VINE, BARBARA (British, 1930 -)
Pseudonym of Ruth Rendell.
A Dark Adapted Eye
[GK801] Penguin pbk **£2.95**
A Fatal Inversion
[GK802] Penguin pbk **£3.50**
The House of Stairs
Ruth Rendell seems to produce her most weird and sensual writing under the Vine pseudonym. The gothic setting, a huge mansion in North Kensington, is used to maximum effect, as it slowly fills up with bizarre characters who reveal their darker side. Nobody has evoked '60s London so imaginatively.
[GK803] Viking hbk **£11.95**
[GK804] Penguin pbk **£3.50**

WALLACE, EDGAR (British, 1875 - 1932)
Wallace wrote adventure stories, mysteries, horse racing thrillers and procedurals, all of which remain highly readable today.
Four Complete Novels
The Four Just Men/Eve's Island/Clue of the Twist Candle/The Man Who Knew.
[GK805] Robinson pbk **£3.50**
The Four Just Men
Dispensing their own individual brand of justice wherever they met crime, the eponymous Four Just Men, it could be argued, were the forerunners of today's judge-and-jury vigilante heroes from *Death Wish* and *The Equalizer*.
[GK806] Dent pbk **£2.95**
The Murder Book of J.G. Reeder
Subtitled 'The Mind of Mr Reeder' in the UK, this is the collection of outstanding short stories which raised Wallace above the level of a pulp-writer.
[GK807] Dover pbk **£3.50**

WAMBAUGH, JOSEPH (US, 1937 -)
If all policemen were like the protagonists of Wambaugh's comic but shocking procedurals, anarchy would surely reign - and yet the author is himself an ex-cop, and some of the books, such as *The Onion Field* and *Lines and Shadows* he describes as 'non-fiction novels'. The pressures of police work, and the expectations which the public (thanks to the media) have of it, are treated in a particularly distressing manner.
Blue Knight
[GK808] Sphere pbk **£2.95**
Choirboys
[GK809] Futura pbk **£2.50**
Delta Star
[GK810] Futura pbk **£2.95**

Georges Simenon, author of *Maigret and the Ghost* (Penguin pbk **£3.95**)

Glitter Dome
[GK811] Futura pbk **£2.50**
Lines and Shadows
[GK812] Futura pbk **£2.50**
New Centurions
[GK813] Sphere pbk **£2.95**
Secrets of Harry Bright
[GK814] Sphere pbk **£2.95**
The Blooding **NEW**
The true account of the Narborough murders in Leicester, the historic case in which genetic fingerprinting was used for the first time to convict a murderer.
[GK815] Bantam hbk **£12.95**
The Onion Field
[GK816] Futura pbk **£2.50**

WATSON, COLIN (British, 1920 - 1982)
The market town of Flaxborough owes something to the pre-war era of the Golden Age in spirit, but the situations are as comical as a saucy seaside postcard. Inspector Purbright catches the rustle of the lace curtains on his way down the street, and the Mayor and the butcher's wife meet secretly behind the bandstand: in such delightfully observed scenes, Colin Watson captures the essence of the English bourgeoisie.
Blue Murder
[GK817] Methuen pbk **£3.95**
Broomsticks over Flaxborough
[GK818] Methuen pbk **£3.95**
Bump in the Night
[GK819] Methuen pbk **£3.95**
Charity Ends at Home
[GK820] Methuen pbk **£3.50**
Coffin Scarcely Used
[GK821] Methuen pbk **£3.50**
Flaxborough Crab
[GK822] Methuen pbk **£3.50**
Hopjoy Was Here
[GK823] Methuen pbk **£3.95**
Lonely Heart 4122
[GK824] Methuen pbk **£3.50**
Naked Nuns
[GK825] Methuen pbk **£3.95**
One Man's Meat
[GK826] Methuen pbk **£4.50**
Plastic Sinners
[GK827] Methuen pbk **£3.50**
Whatever's Been Going on at Mumblesby?
[GK828] Methuen pbk **£3.95**

WENTWORTH, PATRICIA
(British, 1878 - 1961)

A cornerstone of the English 'Golden Age' of detective fiction, Wentworth wrote 40 straightforward and competent books featuring her professional detective Miss Maud Silver, very much in the Christie vein.

Benevant Treasure
[GK829] Hodder pbk **£2.50**
Case of William Smith
[GK830] Hodder pbk **£2.50**
Ladies Bane
[GK831] Hodder pbk **£2.50**
Pilgrim's Rest
[GK832] Hodder pbk **£2.50**
The Gazebo
[GK833] Hodder pbk **£2.50**
Traveller Returns
[GK834] Hodder pbk **£2.25**

WESTLAKE, DONALD E. (US, 1933 -)
The most versatile crime author alive, Westlake sees himself as specializing in 'bewilderment'. This is certainly true of the comic/caper novels he currently tends to favour (the Dortmunder stories, concerning the misadventures of a Jewish petty thief, are exciting and very funny - a rare achievement). His early work and the series written as *Richard Stark* (qv) are more hard-edged, but he is an adept in any field, including the blockbusting saga (*Kahawa*) and the playscript (*Transylvania Station*).

Good Behaviour
[GK835] Star pbk **£2.99**
Kahawa
[GK836] Star pbk **£3.99**
Transylvania Station
[GK837] D Macmillan pbk **£3.95**
Trust Me on This `NEW`
Westlake in comedic mood again, lifting the lid on a US tabloid newspaper office.
[GK838] Allison & B hbk **£11.95**
Wax Apple
[GK839] No Exit P pbk **£1.99**

WHITFIELD, RAOUL (US, 1908 - 1945)
Pulp-writer and backbone of *Black Mask* magazine, Whitfield's novels are what hard-boiled crime writing is all about.

Death in a Bowl
[GK840] Oldcastle P pbk **£3.99**
Green Ice
[GK841] Oldcastle P pbk **£3.99**
Virgin Kills
[GK842] Oldcastle P pbk **£3.99**

WILLEFORD, CHARLES (US, 1919 - 1988)
Virtually ignored throughout most of his writing career, Willeford suddenly stumbled upon fame with his recent novels about Hoke Moseley, the Miami Police Sergeant unglamorous enough to have false teeth. Now that Willeford is dead, the superb, underrated novels he wrote in the 1950s and 60s will surely be 'rediscovered' and given cult status. His study of the American psychopath, who appears in many different guises throughout the novels, is chillingly executed, reminiscent in some ways of Jim Thompson, another writer who had to die for his work to be rescued from obscurity. There are no more Mosely stories, but a wealth of very esoteric 'pulp' novels waiting to be reprinted by an enterprising editor.

Burnt Orange Heresy
[GK843] Creative Arts pbk **£2.95**
Cockfighter
[GK844] Creative Arts pbk **£2.95**
Kiss Your Ass Goodbye `NEW`
This is in fact a self-contained fragment from Willeford's longest novel *The Shark-Infested Custard*, an early 1970s work deemed 'too depressing' to publish. A pharmaceutical salesman is stalked by a jealous husband - or so it seems. The humour is as black as pitch, but it is also a story of high suspense.
[GK845] Gollancz hbk **£10.95**
Miami Blues
[GK846] Futura pbk **£2.50**
New Hope for the Dead
[GK847] Futura pbk **£2.50**
Pick-Up
[GK848] Creative Arts pbk **£2.95**
Sideswipe
[GK849] Gollancz hbk **£10.95**
The Way We Die Now `NEW`
The final Hoke Moseley book, bizarre and violent, in which Hoke heads for the Everglades where a pair of vicious red-neck slave-drivers are murdering Haitians wholesale.
[GK850] Gollancz hbk **£11.95**

WOOLRICH, CORNELL (US, 1903 - 1968)
A mysterious and pathetic figure in his lifetime, Woolrich, who also wrote as William Irish, was a colossus of suspense writing. Many of the long novels have the word 'black' in their titles, from which the French coined the phrase *roman noir* and *film noir*, conjuring up his bleak, night-time world of lonely city streets and losers driven by desperation to ruinous deeds.

Darkness at Dawn
[GK851] Xanadu hbk **£11.95**
Into the Night
Incomplete at the time of his death, this archetypal Woolrich story of hatred, passion and retribution has been patched together by *Lawrence Block* (qv) in a successfully seamless manner. One can quibble with his choice of ending, but for once this usually dubious practice (profit-inspired) has worked very well.
[GK852] Simon & Sch hbk **£10.95**
One Drop of Blood `NEW`
The first volume of *The Best Suspense Stories of Cornell Woolrich*, which includes many rare tales from the '30s and '40s. Selected and introduced by Maxim Jakubowski.
[GK853] Xanadu hbk **£12.99**
Rear Window & Other Stories
[GK854] Simon & Sch pbk **£4.50**
Waltz into Darkness
[GK855] Futura pbk **£1.95**

YORKE, MARGARET (British, 1924 -)
Pseudonym of Margaret Nicholson. Yorke has written some two dozen crime novels which divide roughly between the psychological study of *No Medals for the Major* and those featuring Patrick Grant, fellow and dean of St Mark's College, who is squarely in the tradition of the English 'don-detective'.

Crime in Question `NEW`
A boy's encounter with a criminal on work detail from the local prison turns a penchant for petty crime into a full-scale flight from justice, as a burglary ends in murder.
[GK856] Mysterious P hbk **£10.95**
Death on Account
[GK857] Mysterious P pbk **£2.50**
Devil's Work
[GK858] Mysterious P pbk **£2.25**
Evidence to Destroy
[GK859] Mysterious P pbk **£2.50**
Mortal Remains
[GK860] Mysterious P pbk **£2.99**
No Medals for the Major
[GK861] Mysterious P pbk **£2.25**
Safely to the Grave
[GK862] Mysterious P pbk **£2.25**
Silent Witness
[GK863] Mysterious P pbk **£2.25**
Smooth Face of Evil
[GK864] Mysterious P pbk **£1.95**

Margaret Yorke, author of *The Crime in Question* (Mysterious Press hbk **£10.95**)

Speak for the Dead
[GK865] Mysterious P pbk **£2.99**
The Hand of Death
[GK866] Mysterious P pbk **£2.99**
The Point of Murder
[GK867] Mysterious P pbk **£2.99**
The Small Hours of the Morning
[GK868] Mysterious P pbk **£2.25**

Eight Period Pieces
P.D. James

There are few bedtime books more comforting, reassuring and nostalgic than a familiar detective story and the fact that we can re-read our old favourites with pleasure, even when we know the who, how, where, when and why of the plot, is evidence that these classics offer more lasting satisfactions than the smelling-out of red-herrings and the final solving of the mystery. After a long and busy day I tend to eschew the new gritty realism in favour of gentler delights, and if the detectives tend to be more gentlemanly than is believable and their methods not always consistent with authorised police practice, that hardly worries me. Much detective fiction, after all, is fantasy, but fantasy which is well-written, ingenious and exciting can often tell us more about the age in which the books were written than more pretentious literature. So here are eight detective stories which for me have stood the test of time. None of their authors is still with us, but their books have endured. I make no claims that these are the eight best period pieces, but they

are novels which are worthy of that name and which I can still re-read with pleasure.

WILKIE COLLINS
The Moonstone

T.S. Eliot has described *The Moonstone* as the first, the longest and the best of English detective stories. It is arguably the first, certainly among the longest and most critics would, I think, unhesitatingly place it among the ten best detective stories ever written. Although there is a murder, the main mystery is the theft of the fabulous moonstone, a sacred diamond with a bloody history which was originally stolen from India. Many of the future developments of the detective story are embodied in this long and complicated Victorian novel. We have an innocent suspect trying to prove, despite all the evidence, that he did not commit the crime. There is an emphasis on physical clues and the importance of apparent trifles, and the fair play rule is scrupulously observed. Wilkie Collins is

accurate in his descriptions of contemporary medical, forensic and police procedure and in the rose-loving Sergeant Cuff he has created the prototype of the realistically-portrayed professional detective. But it is for the superb characterisation and the writing as well as for its influence on the genre that *The Moonstone* remains one of the most re-readable of detective stories.
(Dent, hbk £8.95/Oxford, pbk £1.95/Penguin, pbk £2.95)

CYRIL HARE
Tragedy at Law

Cyril Hare, who took his pseudonym from Cyril Mansions where he lived and Hare Court in the Temple where he practised, was a lawyer who became a judge and who brilliantly used his specialised legal knowledge both in plotting his detective novels and in creating his sympathetic lawyer-detective Francis Pettigrew, that typically English hero, the man with the first-class mind who has never fulfilled his early promise. In *Tragedy at Law* we are on wartime circuit with Mr Justice Barber and his retinue in the days before the establishment of the Crown Court when Assize judges processed the country in considerable pomp. But there are those who regard the harsh and disagreeable judge with less than due reverence and as one attempt on his life follows another we await with a familiar mixture of horror and excitement the moment when his enemy finally strikes. I first read this elegantly written novel in the war (it was published in 1942) and can remember rationing the chapters to make it last longer. If Cyril Hare had written no other books, *Tragedy at Law* would ensure his place in the canon of the British detective story.
(Faber, pbk £2.95)

MARGERY ALLINGHAM
The Tiger in the Smoke

Margery Allingham, who died in 1966, was a brilliant exponent of a classical English detective story whose later novels (her best) are cleverly plotted, closely observed and sophisticated studies of the English scene. Her Mr Albert Campion, a gentleman adventurer of aristocratic if unspecified lineage, is one of the enduring sleuths of detective fiction. But for me her real power lies in her creation of eccentrics who are larger-than-life but

always rooted in reality, in her use of the brilliantly described setting to evoke atmosphere and enhance plot, and in her moral authority. *The Tiger in the Smoke* is the story of a man-hunt in fog-shrouded London and with its contrasting characters of Jack Havoc, the murderer, and the gentle uncompromising Canon Avril, refutes the common assertion that the great absolutes of good and evil are necessarily outside the range of the detective novelist.
(Hogarth, pbk £3.95)

DOROTHY L. SAYERS
The Nine Tailors
It is a safe assumption that any *aficionado* of the classical detective story asked to name the six best writers in the genre would include the name of Dorothy L. Sayers. Yet paradoxically there is no other writer of the Golden Era who provokes such strong and often opposing responses from readers and critics. To her detractors she is outrageously snobbish, intellectually arrogant and, at times, dull. To her admirers, of whom I am one, she is a writer who did more than almost any other to make the detective story intellectually respectable and to change it from an ingenious sub-literary puzzle into a specialised branch of fiction. She was content to work within the conventions of the detective story: a central mystery, a closed circle of suspects, a superman amateur detective superior in talent and intelligence to the professional police, and a solution which the reader could arrive at by logical deduction from clues planted with deceptive cunning but essential fairness. Her novels, too, are very much of their age in the complexity and ingenuity of the methods of murder. She drew heavily on her own experiences in her books and in *The Nine Tailors* we are embroiled with Lord Peter in a mystery set in the Fens where Dorothy L. Sayers spent much of her girlhood. For me the strength and enduring pleasure of the book lies less in the ingenuity of the mystery than in the picture it gives of a long-vanished way of life.
(NEL, hbk £11.95)

EDMUND CRISPIN
The Moving Toyshop
Edmund Crispin is the pseudonym of Bruce Montgomery, mystery writer, critic and musician who, to the regret of his admirers, wrote only nine detective stories, his main job being that of composer. Crispin is unique in his successful blending of the carefully crafted plot with farcical humour, eccentricity and boisterous high spirits. The plot of *The Moving Toyshop*, set in Oxford, is indeed bizarre since we have here not only the disappearing body, that ploy beloved of mystery-mongers, but a whole disappearing toyshop. But if the plot is impossible the solution has its own logic and it would be ungrateful to strain after credibility when we are being borne forward on such a tide of youthful high spirits.
(Penguin, pbk £3.99)

AGATHA CHRISTIE
The Pale Horse
Agatha Christie is the undisputed Queen of Crime whose name is virtually synonymous with the cosy, middle-class, conventional British detective story. She was a prolific writer whose quality is uneven but at her best she is unsurpassed as a fabricator of mystery. Like a cunning conjuror she lays the cards face downwards on the table, shuffles them with her cunning hands and defies us to turn over the guilty face. *The Murder of Roger Ackroyd*, her best-known book, breaks all the accepted rules and succeeds brilliantly. But for me *The Pale Horse* is her most re-readable book for the brilliance of the central idea and for the inclusion of Mrs Ariadne Oliver, the delightful, if muddled, writer of detective stories who is at least partially based on the writer herself.
(Collins, hbk £8.95/Fontana, pbk £2.50)

NGAIO MARSH
The Final Curtain
If there is truth in the maxim that a good detective story is twenty-five percent mystery, twenty-five percent character and fifty percent what the writer knows best, then Ngaio Marsh's continued popularity is assured; few writers have made better use of their own interests and experience. She was knowledgeable about painting and even more knowledgeable about the theatre, and in *The Final Curtain* we find both enthusiasms combined in a carefully-crafted traditional detective story. Her gentlemanly sleuth, Chief Inspector Roderick Alleyn, is returning from overseas war service and, while awaiting their reunion, his wife Troy has been persuaded to visit Ancreton to paint the Grand Old Man of the theatre, Sir Henry Ancred, in his costume as Macbeth. The household includes a rich variety of the eccentrics, particularly theatrical eccentrics, in which Ngaio Marsh delighted and the plot, as always, is carefully worked-out although it is difficult to see why Alleyn, as a Scotland Yard detective, should have become involved in a suspected murder outside the Metropolitan Police district, particularly if his wife were a visitor to the household. But this is a quibble; there is no more civilised or urbane detective to soothe both suspects and reader alike.
(Collins, hbk £9.95/Fontana, pbk £2.50)

CHRISTIANNA BRAND
Green for Danger
Green for Danger, published in 1944 and Christianna Brand's best-known novel, is primarily an ingenious puzzle in the tradition of the Golden Age. What we have is a closed society, an army hospital at the time of the Blitz, a series of murders and six suspects, each of whom has a credible motive, means and opportunity to commit the crimes. But the book is something more than a highly ingenious and formalised dance of death. Miss Brand was herself a Red Cross nurse during the War and here we find again that mixture of mystery, excitement and personal knowledge which, by setting the detective story unambiguously in its time and place, so enhances credibility and interest. The murders are bizarre but the setting is realistic. This is what it must have been like to serve as a Red Cross nurse under bombardment in a wartime hospital. Christianna Brand is a versatile, highly individual and romantic author who writes with gusto and enthusiasm and whose obvious liking for her characters, even the villains, is infectious. Detective-Inspector Cockrill, her irascible Kentish detective with his disreputable old mackintosh and his hat pushed always to the back of his head, is in the best tradition of the English eccentric hero.
(Pandora, pbk £3.95)

Among the leading writers of detective fiction in Britain today, P.D. James has achieved both critical and popular success with her novels featuring Cordelia Gray and the poeticizing Inspector Dalgleish, who appears in *Devices and Desires*, to be published this Autumn by Faber.

Book Choice

The Crime Writers Association Awards

The most prestigious prize for Crime Writing, for which writers from any country are eligible. Two Gold Daggers are awarded each year, one for fiction and one for non-fiction (we have included only fiction here), and Silver Daggers are given to the runner-up. In 1985, for the first time, a Diamond Dagger was awarded 'for excellence'. Here are the winners over the last twenty years:

1969
Gold : *A Pride of Heroes* Peter Dickinson
Silver : *Another Way of Dying* Francis Clifford

1970
Gold : *Young Man I think You're Dying* Joan Fleming
Silver : *The Labyrinth Makers* Anthony Price

1971
Gold : *The Steam Pig* James McClure
Silver : *Shroud for a Nightingale* P D James

1972
Gold : *The Levanter* Eric Ambler
Silver : *The Rainbird Pattern* Victor Canning

1973
Gold : *The Defection of A J Lewinter* Robert Littell
Silver : *A Coffin for Pandora* Gwendoline Butler

1974
Gold : *Other Paths to Glory* Anthony Price
Silver : *The Grosvenor Square Goodbye* Francis Clifford

1975
Gold : *The Seven Per Cent Solution* Nicholas Meyer
Silver : *The Black Tower* P D James

1976
Gold : *A Demon in My View* Ruth Rendell
Silver : *Rogue Eagle* James McClure

1977
Gold : *The Honourable Schoolboy* John le Carré
Silver : *Laidlaw* William McIlvanney

1978
Gold : *The Chelsea Murders* Lionel Davidson
Silver : *Waxwork*

1979
Gold : *Whip Hand* Dick Francis
Silver : *Service of All Dead*

1980
Gold : *The Murder of the Maharajah* H R F Keating
Silver : *Monk's Hood* Ellis Peters

1981
Gold : *Gorky Park* Martin Cruz Smith
Silver : *The Dead of Jericho* Colin Dexter

1982
Gold : *The False Inspector Dew* Peter Lovesey
Silver : *Ritual Murder* S T Haymon

1983
Gold : *Accidental Crimes* John Hutton
Silver : *The Papers of Tony Veitch* William McIlvanney

1984
Gold : *The Twelfth Juror* B M Gill
Silver : *The Tree of Hands* Ruth Rendell

1985
Gold : *Monkey Puzzle* Paula Gosling
Silver : *Last Seen Alive* Dorothy Simpson
Diamond : Eric Ambler

1986
Gold : *Live Flesh* Ruth Rendell
Silver : *A Taste For Death* P D James
Diamond : P D James

1987
Gold : *A Fatal Inversion* Barbara Vine
Silver : *Presumed Innocent* Scott Turow

BESTSELLERS FROM COLLINS

Collins

Clive Barker
The Great and Secret Show
August £12.95

Maisie Mosco
Out of the Ashes
September £12.95

Tom Clancy
Clear and Present Danger
October £11.95

Bryan Forbes
Song at Twilight
November £11.95

John Jakes
California Gold
January £12.95

From Shore to Shore
The Final Years
The Diaries of
Earl Mountbatten of Burma
1953-79
September £18.00

Eric Newby
What the Traveller Saw
October £20.00

Collins Harvill

Raymond Carver
Elephant and Other Stories
September £4.95

Peter Matthiessen
On the River Styx
September £10.95

Martin Cruz Smith
Polar Star
October £12.95

Mikhail Bulgakov
The White Guard
November £6.95

Anna Akhmatova
Selected Poems
November £5.95

Fontana/Flamingo

Craig Thomas
All the Grey Cats
August £4.50

Anna Murdoch
Family Business
August £3.99

Ann Oakley
The Men's Room
September £3.95

Pete Dexter
Paris Trout
October £3.99

Tom Clancy
Cardinal of the Kremlin
November £3.95

Chet Flippo
McCartney: The Biography
October £4.50

Brian Aldiss

10 SF Novels

Here are not quite my Ten Favourite SF Novels. I have avoided some titles which are too famous (like *Dune*) in favour of some which should be better known. My list will contain few surprises for those who have read David Wingrove's and my history of SF, *Trillion Year Spree*.

GREG BEAR
Blood Music

Bear is one of the grand contemporary masters of SF, and hard SF at that, although with the technology goes a deep respect for human values. Here, in this astonishing novel of wonder, human values are defeated by the new biochip technics which get out of hand - with fatal but strangely elevating results. Other Bear novels also recommended.
(Gollancz, hbk £9.95/Arrow, pbk £2.95)

JAMES BLISH
Black Easter

All of Blish's novels are worth seeking out. This is a splendid affair, with a modern necromancer conjuring up the Devil. The infernal city of Dis rises in Death Valley, and Hell's minions take over Earth. Technology and the supernatural mingle, often to slyly funny

effect. And who will take over from God? There's a sequel, too: *The Day After Forever*.
(Arrow, pbk £1.50)

PHILIP K. DICK
Martian Time-Slip

The late Philip Dick is the ideal modern master of science fiction, slick, sophisticated, hag-ridden, witty, ashen, and Californian. Still too little appreciated, *Martian Time-Slip* has a brilliantly conceived plot and a fine setting, Mars as parcelled out among the United Nations. The story of drugs and psychosis is played out by human and unhuman characters. (Unfortunately this title is currently unavailable).

A Scanner Darkly

I could not resist having two Phil Dicks. This is a here-and-now novel about a deadly drug loose in California, and how one man, sent in to investigate the drug ring, falls victim to it. Black but often funny, and written in Dick's best fluent, unadorned style.
(Grafton, pbk £2.50)

HARRY HARRISON
Bill, The Galactic Hero

Really funny SF is hard to find. This delectable romp by one of SF's favourite authors has stood the test of time and laughter. Bill is a sort of Everyman of the future, bombarded by - and narrowly surviving - a series of events of galaxy-shaking seriousness, like War and Love and Surgery. Look up Harrison's *Stainless Steel Rat* series.
(Penguin, pbk £3.50)

DORIS LESSING
The Sirian Experiments

Doris Lessing is England's best and most versatile woman author. This novel is one of her continuing *Canopus in Argos: Archives* series - not the first of the series, but an easily approachable novel with a female narrator who begins by admiring the galactic empire to which she belongs, to meet later with disillusion. Very little hardware, very grand perspectives.
(Cape, hbk £9.95/Granada, pbk £2.95)

JOSEPH O'NEILL
Land Under England

As in many SF novels, a profound theme underlies a weird premise. A Roman legion manning Hadrian's Wall went underground and remains there still,

locked into a totalitarian regime. Enter the central character, looking for his father. A macabre psychological story in a gripping funereal setting. Should be better known.
(Unfortunately this title is unavailable)

MARY SHELLEY
Frankenstein, or The Modern Prometheus

Perhaps at last this striking and complex 1818 novel is becoming appreciated as more than just a horror novel. Frankenstein, bringing life to a DIY corpse, still stands as the figure of the socially irresponsible scientist, and his monster still stalks our imagination. There's a concealed autobiographical strain to the story. The Penguin edition has an excellent Introduction by Maurice Hindle.
(Penguin, pbk £3.50/Oxford, pbk £3.50)

OLAF STAPLEDON
Star Maker

Words cannot describe the grandeur of Stapledon's vision of a soul who quests outward from Earth to meet its Maker. The Creator of the Universe is a chilly being, itself restless, subject to evolutionary law. A chronicle, hardly a novel, of combined science and poetry, brilliant, durable, and irresistibly readable - but for the higher brow.
(Penguin, pbk £3.95)

H.G. WELLS
The Time Machine

This is the book which really started SF on its commercial career in the

Kurt Vonnegut, author of *Galapagos* (Cape hbk £9.95/ Grafton pbk £2.99)

Gabriel Garcia Marquez, author of *One Hundred Years of Solitude* (Cape hbk £11.95, Picador pbk £4.95)

magazines. Published in 'The New Review' first, and then in book form in 1895, Well's story contains powerful originality. Beneath the adventure into time lies a sombre meditation on evolution and society. Often imitated, never even rivalled. Literally marvellous. (Pan, pbk £2.99)

Ten Magical Novels

This is a listing of my Ten Favourite Magical Novels. There is no actual magic in any of them; they are books which are magical in themselves, and which improve on re-reading, the great test of any book. One or two of them verge upon science fiction although they are not always categorised as such; categories are not always helpful. Nor are suggestions always helpful, unless they remain mere suggestions. Fiction is a whole world. We are free to explore it, and should look for what best pleases us, rather than being cowed by critics. Individualism is the best policy.

KINGSLEY AMIS
The Green Man

Kinsley Amis's only excursion into the supernatural. 'The Green Man' is the name of a pub in Herefordshire - a pub haunted by a particularly unsavoury set of ghosts. And the landlord has a convincing drink problem. God appears, to great effect. A chilly and chilling novel, admirably rancid. (Penguin, pbk £2.99)

ALEJO CARPENTIER
The Lost Steps

A wonderful narrative by a Cuban writer of a quest into the jungles of South America for the origins of music and the self. And the necessity for civilisation. Not pretentious, superbly ironic, and written so luxuriously that a re-reading becomes necessary every other year. Magical realism à la Carl Jung. (Unfortunately this title is currently unavailable).

WILLIAM GODWIN
Caleb Williams

This is a dark tale of retribution, first published in 1794. Godwin is Mary Shelley's father, and we can see here one of the inspirations for her wonderful Frankenstein. The characters, following a bygone literary style, orate rather than converse, which adds grandeur to a story of injustice, pursuit, and death. (Oxford, pbk £3.99/Penguin, pbk £5.99)

WILLIAM GOLDING
The Inheritors

A fresh green world. But strange new creatures in it are making their presence felt. The Cro-magnons are coming. This beautiful prehistoric fantasy is told from the point of view of the doomed Neanderthals, as they try to escape their fate. An early and remarkable Golding novel. (Faber, pbk £2.95)

ANNA KAVAN
Ice

A strange surreal novel, the last to be published before its mysterious author died. In a world in which the ice and totalitarianism are closing in, pursuer and pursued change roles. The ice can be read as a metaphor for the heroin to which Kavan was habituated. She is now a cult author, but too little known. (P Owen, hbk £10.95)

GABRIEL GARCIA MARQUEZ
One Hundred Years of Solitude

This is perhaps the best-known of the books of the list. It is sometimes described as magical realism, and has had something of the same attraction for Europeans of our generation as the *Arabian Nights* did for earlier generations. Strange adventures, strange distortions in time, set in a mythic South America. (Cape, hbk £11.95/Pan, pbk £4.95)

SHERIDAN LE FANU
Uncle Silas

First published in 1864, *Uncle Silas* is Le Fanu's best novel, worthy to stand beside Wilkie Collins's better-known *Woman in White*. It's the story of a young vulnerable orphaned girl left in the care of her wicked uncle, who plans to dispose of her. Very sinister, a well-crafted piece of Victoriana. (Oxford, pbk £4.95)

ROBERT HOLDSTOCK
Mythago Wood

An intensely imaginative novel about a stretch of primitive English woodland in which mysterious forces draw archetypes from the brain. Jung comes slap up against the Celtic twilight. The personages in the woods are brutal and covincing. One reading is not enough. (A sequel, *Lavondyss*, is no disappointment.) (Gollancz, hbk £10.95/Grafton, pbk £2.50)

LAURENCE STERNE
Tristram Shandy

This triumph of the Absurd was first published from 1759-1769. I went without lunch to buy my first copy. Perhaps you either like it or you don't, but, once you enter thoroughly into its time-warrens, the story of Tristram's life, told by himself (he is born in Volume III), you are in an unforgettable witty world. Has been seen as a precursor to Proust's more famous novel. (Oxford, pbk £3.95/Penguin, pbk £3.99)

KURT VONNEGUT
Galapagos

Vonnegut denies he is a science fiction writer. But this outrageous novel, set one million years in the future, describes how humanity got rid of its troublesome Big Brain. Exemplary flashy story-telling, and alarmingly funny. The master's best novel. (Cape, hbk £9.95/Grafton, pbk £2.99)

For more than thirty years, Brian Aldiss has been one of Britain's most versatile writers - novelist, short story writer and critic. He has written an acclaimed history of Science Fiction, *Trillion Year Spree*, as well as a wide range of novels, including the *Helliconia* trilogy. A collection of his best Fantasy stories, *A Romance of the Equator*, will be published later this year, as a companion volume to *Man in His Time*, a collection of his SF stories.

SCIENCE FICTION

"Out of the earth of rest or range/Perpetual in perpetual change/The Unknown passing through the strange" (John Masefield). Science fiction is not so much a genre, more an attitude of mind. As hard to define as it is easy to recognise, it is an extraordinarily diverse area, and perhaps the quintessential 20th century form, emphasising as it does, the centrality of change and the human response to that change. Those who wish to learn more about science fiction should seek Brian Aldiss and David Wingrove's *Trillion Year Spree*, a magisterial history of science fiction from its beginnings in gothic fantasy. A wider, if shallower book, is James Gunn's *New Encyclopaedia of Science Fiction*, which includes everything from authors' biographies to science fiction films.

Anthologies & Studies

ALDISS, BRIAN W. (ED)
Galactic Empires
[GL1] Legend pbk **£3.99**
Penguin Science Fiction Omnibus
[GL2] Penguin pbk **£3.95**
Penguin World Omnibus of Science Fiction
[GL3] Penguin pbk **£3.50**

ALDISS, BRIAN W. & WINGROVE, DAVID (EDS)
Trillion Year Spree
[GL4] Gollancz pbk **£6.95**

ASIMOV, ISAAC (ED)
Before the Golden Age: Science Fiction Anthology of the 1930s
Vol 1
[GL5] Futura pbk **£2.50**
Vol 2
[GL6] Futura pbk **£2.50**
Vol 3
[GL7] Futura pbk **£2.50**

CLUTE, JOHN; PRINGLE, DAVID & OUNTSLEY, SIMON (EDS)
Interzone: The First Anthology
[GL8] Dent pbk **£3.95**
Interzone: The Second Anthology
[GL9] Hodder pbk **£2.95**

ELLISON, HARLAN (ED)
Dangerous Visions
1960s and early 1970s New Wave.
[GL10] Gollancz pbk **£6.95**

GARNETT, DAVID (ED)
Zenith   **NEW**
An anthology of the best SF writing in Britain today.
[GL11] Sphere pbk **£3.50**

GREEN, JEN & LE FANU, SARAH
Despatches from the Frontiers of the Female Mind
[GL12] Women's P pbk **£2.50**

GUNN, JAMES (ED)
The New Encyclopeadia of Science Fiction
A comprehensive guide to the history and particularities of the genre.
[GL13] Viking hbk **£17.95**

HOLDSTOCK, ROBERT & EVANS, CHRISTOPHER
Other Edens Vol 1
[GL14] Unwin pbk **£2.95**

LE FANU, SARAH
In the Chinks of the World Machine: Women and Science Fiction
[GL14A] Women's P pbk **£5.99**

MOORCOCK, MICHAEL (ED)
New Worlds
[GL15] Flamingo pbk **£3.50**

STERLING, BRUCE (ED)
Mirrorshades
The definitive cyberpunk anthology.
[GL16] Grafton pbk **£3.99**

Writers A - Z

ADAMS, DOUGLAS (British, 1952 -)
An ex-producer of radio and television, Adams belongs to that generation of Cambridge graduates heavily influenced by Monty Python.
Dirk Gently's Holistic Detective Agency
In this novel and its sequel, *The Long Dark Teatime*, Adams combines the influences of Monty Python and Raymond Chandler.
[GL17] Heinemann hbk **£10.95**
[GL18] Pan pbk **£2.99**
The Long Dark Tea Time of the Soul   **NEW**
[GL19] Heinemann hbk **£10.95**
[GL20] Pan pbk **£2.99**
HITCH HIKERS GUIDE SEQUENCE
1: The Hitch Hiker's Guide to the Galaxy
The sequence began as a radio series, and starts with the destruction of earth to make way for a hyperspace bypass.
[GL21] Pan pbk **£2.99**
2: The Restaurant at the End of the Universe
[GL22] Pan pbk **£2.99**
3: Life, the Universe & Everything
[GL23] Pan pbk **£2.99**
4: So Long, & Thanks for All the Fish
[GL24] Pan pbk **£2.99**

ALDISS, BRIAN W. (British, 1925 -)
A sophisticated Englishman, Aldiss has written many SF novels and has contributed much to SF criticism, notably in his *Trillion Year Spree*, which is probably the best history of SF. He writes thoughtful novels whose epic scale is well supported by his imaginative and literate style.
A Romance of the Equator   **NEW**
This collection of Aldiss's best Fantasy Stories shows his equal mastery in that genre.
[GL25] Gollancz hbk **£12.95**
Cracken at Critical
[GL26] NEL pbk **£2.99**
Cryptozoic
[GL27] Gollancz pbk **£2.95**
Earthworks
[GL28] Mandarin hbk **£2.95**
Galaxies Like Grains of Sand
[GL29] Gollancz pbk **£2.99**
Malacia Tapestry
[GL30] Grafton pbk **£3.50**
Man in his Time
Originally titled 'Best SF stories of Brian Aldiss', this is a companion volume to *A Romance of the Equator*.
[GL31] Gollancz pbk **£3.50**

HELLICONIA SERIES
1: Helliconia Spring
The trilogy presents the ebb and flow of civilization, both human colonist and native 'phagor', on a planet whose 'year' is 26 Earth centuries long.
[GL32] Grafton pbk **£3.99**
2: Helliconia Summer
[GL33] Grafton pbk **£3.50**
3: Helliconia Winter
[GL34] Grafton pbk **£2.95**

ANDERSON, POUL (1926 -)
Anderson's style is a mixture of hard scientific extrapolation (a reflection of his training as a physicist) and swashbuckling adventure, often based on Scandinavian myth: his creations of new worlds are skilful and highly believable.
A Circus of Hells
[GL35] Sphere pbk **£2.99**
Dancer from Atlantis
[GL36] Sphere pbk **£2.50**
Mirkheim
[GL37] Sphere pbk **£2.50**
Orion Shall Rise
[GL38] Sphere pbk **£3.50**
Twilight World
[GL39] Sphere pbk **£2.50**

ANTHONY, PIERS (US, 1934 -)
A prolific writer whose books range from space opera to scientific mythology. Anthony was one of the first to grasp the potential of the multivolume epic. See also *Fantasy*.
Out of Phaze   **NEW**
The first in a series involving parallel worlds.
[GL40] NEL pbk **£6.95**
BIOGRAPHY OF A SPACE TYRANT
1: Refugee
[GL41] Grafton pbk **£2.95**
2: Mercenary
[GL42] Grafton pbk **£2.95**
3: Politician
[GL43] Grafton pbk **£2.95**
4: Executive
[GL44] Grafton pbk **£2.95**
5: Statesman
[GL45] Grafton pbk **£2.95**

Douglas Adams, author of *The Long Dark Tea Time of the Soul* (Heinemann hbk £10.95, Pan pbk £2.99)

INCARNATIONS OF IMMORTALITY

1: On a Pale Horse
[GL46] Grafton pbk **£2.99**
2: Bearing an Hourglass
[GL47] Grafton pbk **£2.95**
3: With a Tangled Skein
[GL48] Grafton pbk **£3.50**
4: Wielding a Red Sword
[GL49] Grafton pbk **£2.95**
5: Being a Green Mother   `NEW`
[GL50] Grafton pbk **£3.50**

ASIMOV, ISAAC (US, 1920 -)
The amazingly prolific Asimov is author of more than 300 books covering most aspects of life on earth and off it. His SF is firmly grounded in the 'Golden Age', being idea- rather than character-based. In the 1980s he has returned to his earlier works and written sequels in an attempt to form a coherent future history. See also *Fantasy*.
Fantastic Voyage II: Destination Brain
[GL51] Grafton pbk **£3.50**
I, Robot
[GL52] Grafton pbk **£2.95**
Nemesis   `NEW`
Asimov's new SF novel, independent from any of his earlier series, is set on the mysterious dwarf-star Nemesis.
[GL53] Doubleday hbk **£12.95**
OPUS: The Best of Isaac Asimov   `NEW`
[GL54] Grafton pbk **£3.95**
Robot Dreams   `NEW`
[GL55] Gollancz pbk **£3.50**
The Complete Robot Stories
[GL56] Grafton pbk **£3.95**
The Rest of the Robots
[GL57] Grafton pbk **£2.50**
FOUNDATION SERIES
1: Foundation
The *Foundation* sequence describes the fall of a galactic empire, and the efforts of 'psychohistorian' Seldon and the Foundation he sets up to conserve human knowledge, and so shorten the millenia of barbarism before the rebirth of civilization.
[GL58] Grafton pbk **£2.50**
2: Foundation & Empire
[GL59] Grafton pbk **£2.99**
3: Second Foundation
[GL60] Grafton pbk **£2.95**
4: Foundation's Edge
[GL61] Grafton pbk **£3.50**
5: Foundation & Earth
[GL62] Grafton pbk **£3.50**
6: Prelude to Foundation   `NEW`
[GL63] Grafton hbk **£11.95**
[GL64] Grafton pbk **£3.99**
ROBOT SERIES
1: Caves of Steel
Asimov's own favourite, with an android helping to solve a murder.
[GL65] Grafton pbk **£2.50**
2: Naked Sun
[GL66] Grafton pbk **£2.99**
3: The Robots of Dawn
[GL67] Grafton pbk **£3.50**
4: Robots & Empire
[GL68] Grafton pbk **£2.95**

BALLARD, J.G. (British, 1930 -)
"I believe in madness, in the truth of the inexplicable, in the commonsense of stones, in the lunacy of flowers, in the disease stored up for the human race by the Apollo astronauts". Ballard is one of the most idiosyncratic writers of today. His world of wrecked aeroplanes, drained swimming pools, concrete and sand dunes is instantly recognisable (as it is in his autobiographical novel of wartime Shanghai, *Empire of the Sun*). His themes of disaster and the interplay between man and the environment are powerfully

evoked in a highly stylized way. See *20th Century British Fiction* for his other novels.
Concrete Island
[GL69] Grafton pbk **£2.50**
Crash
[GL70] Grafton pbk **£2.50**
Hello, America
[GL71] Grafton pbk **£2.50**
High Rise
[GL72] Grafton pbk **£2.50**
Low-Flying Aircraft
[GL73] Grafton pbk **£2.50**
Myths of the Near Future
[GL74] Grafton pbk **£2.50**
The Atrocity Exhibition
[GL75] Grafton pbk **£2.50**
The Crystal World
[GL76] Dent pbk **£2.95**
The Day of Forever
[GL77] Grafton pbk **£2.50**
The Disaster Area
[GL78] Grafton pbk **£2.50**
The Drought
[GL79] Grafton pbk **£2.50**
The Unlimited Dream Company
[GL80] Grafton pbk **£2.50**
The Venus Hunters
[GL81] Grafton pbk **£3.50**
The Voices of Time
[GL82] Dent pbk **£2.95**
Vermilion Sands
[GL83] Dent pbk **£2.95**

BANKS, IAIN M. (British)
This young British writer has written several SF influenced and absurdist novels. His only 'pure' SF is this authentic space opera. See also *20th Century British Fiction*.
Consider Phlebas
[GL84] Futura pbk **£4.99**

BAYLEY, B.J. (British, 1937 -)
Described by Michael Moorcock as 'the most original SF writer of his generation', Bayley's work cannot be too highly praised.
Rod of Light
[GL85] Methuen pbk **£2.50**
The Zen Gun
[GL86] Methuen pbk **£2.50**

Greg Bear, author of *Eternity* (Victor Gollancz hbk £14.95)

BEAR, GREG (US, 1951 -)
A rising star of the 1980s, Bear's powerful writing earned him the 1987 Nebula award.
1: Eon
Eon and its sequel *Eternity* cover everything from nuclear holocaust to alien contact and a mathematical exploration of trans-Einsteinian space. Complex themes are brilliantly handled.
[GL87] Legend pbk **£3.50**
2: Eternity   `NEW`
[GL88] Gollancz hbk **£14.95**
Beyond Heaven's River   `NEW`
[GL89] Gollancz pbk **£2.99**
Blood Music
[GL90] Legend pbk **£2.95**
Forge of God
[GL91] Legend pbk **£3.99**
Hegira
[GL92] Gollancz pbk **£2.95**
Infinity Concerto
[GL93] Legend pbk **£3.50**
Psychlone   `NEW`
[GL94] Gollancz pbk **£3.50**
Strength of Stones
[GL95] Gollancz pbk **£2.95**
Tangents   `NEW`
A first collection of stories, which strengthens Bear's growing reputation as a natural successor to Arthur C. Clarke.
[GL96] Gollancz hbk **£11.95**

BENFORD, GREGORY (US, 1941 -)
Another scientist turned SF writer, whose mixture of good writing and hard science have won him a large following.
Against Infinity
[GL97] NEL pbk **£1.95**
Great Sky River
[GL98] Gollancz pbk **£3.50**
In Alien Flesh
Short story collection.
[GL99] Gollancz pbk **£2.99**
Stars in Shroud
[GL100] Sphere pbk **£2.95**
Tides of Light   `NEW`
Sequel to *Great Sky River* in an emerging series chronicling life at the galaxy's centre many centuries in the future.
[GL101] Gollancz hbk **£12.95**

BESTER, ALFRED (US, 1913 - 1987)
One of the great mavericks of the field, Bester's baroque style and fast moving plots are tied to some of the most splendidly individual characters in SF. Gully Foyle, the anarchic hero of *Tiger, Tiger* (also known as *The Stars My Destination*) moves through the universe in his quest for revenge. Compared to the Jacobean tragedies, an inspiration to the New Wave and Cyberpunk movements, Bester's prose has to be read to be believed:*"The cold was the taste of lemons and the vacuum was a rake of talons on his skin. The sun and the stars were a shaking ague that racked his bones"*.
The Deceivers
[GL102] Pan pbk **£3.95**
The Demolished Man
[GL103] Penguin pbk **£3.95**
Tiger! Tiger!
[GL104] Penguin pbk **£3.95**

BISHOP, MICHAEL (US, 1945 -)
Mature and witty, Bishop is from the school of American writers inspired by Philip K. Dick. His current work would be an excellent introduction to state-of-the-art speculative fiction for devotees of the literary mainstream.
Ancient of Days
[GL105] Paladin pbk **£4.95**

Philip K Dick Is Dead Alas `NEW`
An alternative history where Nixon was
re-elected four times but not five, if Philip K. Dick
can help it. A well-written and affectionate literary
homage.
[GL106] Grafton pbk **£3.99**
Unicorn Mountain `NEW`
[GL107] Grafton pbk **£7.95**

BLISH, JAMES P. (US, 1921 -)
Much of Blish's work is scientifically plausible,
philosophically interesting and cracking good
adventure. He will be remembered for his creation of
the tramp cities wandering the universe in search of
work.
Black Easter & The Day After Forever
[GL108] Arrow pbk **£1.50**
Cities in Flight
[GL109] Arrow pbk **£3.95**

BOULLE, PIERRE (French)
Planet of the Apes
The novel is now known as the basis for a series of
rather poor SF films - those who read the original will
find it a witty moral fable.
[GL110] Penguin pbk **£1.95**

BOVA, BEN (US, 1932 -)
Bova writes 'hard' SF extrapolation of the near
future. He champions the cause of science against
bureaucracy and emotionalism.
1: Orion
[GL111] Methuen pbk **£3.50**
2: Vengeance of Orion
[GL112] Methuen pbk **£3.95**
Colony
[GL113] Mandarin pbk **£2.95**
Exiles Trilogy
[GL114] Methuen pbk **£2.95**
Kinsman `NEW`
A prequel to *Colony*, an epic about the near future of
space exploration.
[GL115] Mandarin pbk **£3.50**
Privateers
[GL116] Methuen pbk **£2.95**
Voyagers
[GL117] Methuen pbk **£2.95**
Voyagers II: The Alien Within
[GL118] Methuen pbk **£2.95**

BRADBURY, RAY (US, 1920 -)
Bradbury's often lyrical work emphasises his
nostalgia for his small town American boyhood. A
fabulist for the post-war era, his evocative writing,
often set on a post-Mariner Mars, is unscientific but
powerful.
Dandelion Wine
[GL119] Grafton pbk **£2.99**
Fahrenheit 451
A dystopia on fascism and book burning, this novel
stands outside the main body of Bradburys
work.However it does show his optimistic belief that
the humanist spirit will prevail.
[GL120] Grafton pbk **£2.50**
Something Wicked This Way Comes
[GL121] Grafton pbk **£2.50**
The Day It Rained For Ever
[GL122] Penguin pbk **£3.95**
The Golden Apples of the Sun
[GL123] Grafton pbk **£2.50**
The Illustrated Man
[GL124] Grafton pbk **£2.50**
The Machineries of Joy
[GL125] Grafton pbk **£2.95**
The Martian Chronicles
[GL126] Grafton pbk **£2.99**
The Novels of Ray Bradbury
[GL127] Grafton hbk **£11.95**
[GL128] Grafton hbk **£9.95**

Ben Bova, author of Orion (Methuen pbk **£3.50**)

The October Country
[GL129] Grafton pbk **£2.50**
The Stories of Ray Bradbury Vol 1
[GL130] Grafton pbk **£3.95**
The Stories of Ray Bradbury Vol 2
[GL131] Grafton pbk **£3.95**
The Toynbee Convector `NEW`
The first collection of short stories for more than a
decade: ranging from a time-traveller who rescues
the world by telling a lie, to the woman who
investigated strange noises in her attic and wishes she
hadn't.
[GL132] Grafton hbk **£11.95**

BRADFIELD, SCOTT
The Secret Life of Houses `NEW`
A novel that is ironic, funny and 'filled with the
tension between the mundane and the dreams that
flicker on the periphery of vision'.
[GL133] Unwin Hyman hbk **£11.95**
[GL134] Unwin Hyman pbk **£3.99**

BRADLEY, MARION ZIMMER (US, 1930 -)
Most of Bradley's work is in a long sequence
concerning a rediscovered colony world Darkover,
where the anti-technological telepathic feudal system
is in conflict with the Terran Empire. The sequence
was begun in 1962 and continues. Bradley's recent
work in re-examining myth, whether Arthurian or
classical, has proved very popular.
City of Sorcery
[GL135] Arrow pbk **£3.50**
Darkover Landfall
[GL136] Arrow pbk **£2.50**
Forbidden Tower
[GL137] Arrow pbk **£3.50**
Hawkmistress
[GL138] Arrow pbk **£2.99**
Sharra's Exile
[GL139] Arrow pbk **£3.50**
Shattered Chain
[GL140] Arrow pbk **£2.50**
Thendara House
[GL141] Arrow pbk **£3.50**

BRIN, DAVID (US, 1950 -)
A deceptively casual writer, Brin's works have
great depth and integrity. Old themes are
carefully re-worked into satisfying new tales. The
dolphin space crew of *Startide Rising* are a
delight.
A River of Time
[GL142] Transworld pbk **£2.50**
Startide Rising
[GL143] Transworld pbk **£3.50**
Sundiver
[GL144] Transworld pbk **£2.95**
The Practice Effect
[GL145] Transworld pbk **£1.95**
Uplift War
[GL146] Transworld pbk **£3.99**

BROSNAN, JOHN (Australian, 1947 -)
A writer and film-critic long resident in the UK,
Brosnan has now ventured into fiction with this series
describing a post genetic-war earth literally under the
rule of an airborne elite. Described by Terry Pratchett
as "genuine gosh-wow stuff...aerobics for the
imagination".
SKYLORDS SERIES
1: The Sky Lords
[GL147] Gollancz pbk **£3.50**
2: War of the Skylords `NEW`
[GL148] Gollancz hbk **£11.95**

BRUNNER, JOHN (British, 1934 -)
*"Poised between intransigent scepticism and
uncritical credulity, it (SF) is par excellence the
literature of the open mind"*. A most influential writer
whose masterpieces are in the British tradition of the
dystopia.
Interstellar Empire
[GL149] Arrow pbk **£2.50**
Shockwave Rider
Written in 1975, this novel is absolutely topical. It
includes the first description of a hacker letting loose
a computer virus.
[GL150] Mandarin pbk **£3.50**
Victims of the Nova
[GL151] Legend pbk **£3.99**

BURGESS, ANTHONY (British, 1917 -)
A world class mainstream writer, Burgess is also
well-known in SF for his dystopian novels, including
the famous *A Clockwork Orange*.
1985
[GL152] Arrow pbk **£1.95**
A Clockwork Orange
[GL153] Penguin pbk **£2.50**

BUTLER, OCTAVIA E. (US, 1947 -)
Drawing on Afro-American history, and exploring a
multi-racial future, Butler's sensitively drawn
characters deal with real issues of power,
responsibility and love.
Kindred
[GL154] Women's P pbk **£4.95**
XENOGENESIS
1: Dawn
[GL155] Gollancz pbk **£2.95**
2: Adulthood Rites `NEW`
[GL156] Gollancz pbk **£2.99**
3: Imago `NEW`
[GL157] Gollancz hbk **£11.95**

CARD, ORSON SCOTT
(US, 1951 -)
"If anything, I'm a Mormon writer dabbling in SF".
Card is a prize-winning author who provides a new
slant on SF. See also *Fantasy*.
Ender's Game
[GL158] Arrow pbk **£3.50**
Speaker for the Dead
[GL159] Arrow pbk **£2.95**

CHERRYH, C.J. (US, 1942 -)

Cherryh's coherent future history is spread over light-years and millenia. Her novels plot the conflicts that arise where change is forced. Believable alien societies, a true sense of politics, psychology and language make Cherryh one of the most important writers of the '80s. See also *Fantasy*.

Angel with the Sword
[GL160] Gollancz pbk **£2.95**

Cuckoo's Egg
[GL161] Methuen pbk **£2.95**

Cyteen NEW
The first book in a new series about a 24th Century planet.
[GL162] NEL pbk **£4.99**

Downbelow Station
[GL163] Methuen pbk **£3.50**

Faded Sun Trilogy
[GL164] Methuen pbk **£3.95**

Merchanter's Luck
[GL165] Methuen pbk **£3.50**

Visible Light (Stories)
[GL166] Methuen pbk **£2.95**

CHANUR SAGA

1: Pride of Chanur
[GL167] Methuen pbk **£2.99**

2: Chanur's Venture
[GL168] Methuen pbk **£2.95**

3: The Kif Strike Back
[GL169] Methuen pbk **£2.95**

4: Chanur's Homecoming NEW
The long awaited final volume in the Chanur series is a brilliant exploration of the difficulties of overcoming bias and misunderstanding imposed by race, gender,language and cultural heritage.
[GL170] Methuen pbk **£3.50**

Myth in Science Fiction and Fantasy

"Stories matter...what is history but another myth, with the poetry taken out" (C.J. Cherryh). Myth and science fiction/fantasy are closely intertwined. Whether in the conscious or unconscious use of archetypical plots and patterns à la Joseph Campbell; or in the retelling of specific myths, or their degenerate offspring fairytales, science fiction and fantasy have been enriched by myth. Prometheus stealing fire from the gods, and his later descendant Faust are science fiction's core myth - as scientists seek out knowledge and find, sometimes too late, its cost. Thus *Frankenstein* is subtitled 'A Modern Prometheus'. The central theme in fantasy is the quest or fantastic journey, something familiar to us all from Tolkien on.
The overt use of specific myths for plot and character is another strand: Zelasny's *Lord of Light* is based on Hindu mythology; Lewis successfully rewrites the temptation of Eve in *Perelandra*, while Arthurian legend is one of the bases for Delany's *Nova*. *Dune* drew on the legends of Arabia and Greece, and also helped form a tradition of 'new' mythology by its incorporation of 'internal' myths and stories in the telling. As Heinlein wrote: *"The World is Myth. We create it ourselves - and we change it ourselves"*

CLARKE, ARTHUR C. (British, 1917 -)

A prolific author for many years, his career has been marked by a dual enthusiasm for the excitement of scientific discovery and a mystical attachment to the idea of man as a child of the universe. These themes are most apparent in his best known work, on which the film 2001 was based.

2001: Odyssey 1
[GL171] Arrow pbk **£2.50**

2010 Odyssey II
[GL172] Grafton pbk **£2.99**

2061 Odyssey III
[GL173] Grafton pbk **£2.99**

A Fall of Moondust
[GL174] Gollancz pbk **£3.50**

Astounding Days NEW
A science fictional autobiography. One of the greats of SF looks back at the Golden Age.
[GL175] Gollancz hbk **£12.95**

Rama 2 NEW
A sequel to the astounding novel that won all the major SF awards.
[GL176] Gollancz hbk **£12.95**

Rendezvous With Rama
[GL177] Gollancz pbk **£2.95**

Songs of the Distant Earth
[GL178] Grafton pbk **£2.95**

Tales from Planet Earth NEW
A new collection of stories.
[GL179] Legend hbk **£11.95**
[GL180] Legend pbk **£5.95**

The City & the Stars
[GL181] Gollancz pbk **£2.95**

The Deep Range
[GL182] Gollancz pbk **£2.95**

The Fountains of Paradise
[GL183] Gollancz pbk **£2.99**

The Other Side of the Sky
[GL184] Gollancz pbk **£2.95**

CLARKE, ARTHUR C. & LEE, GENTRY

Cradle
[GL185] Gollancz hbk **£10.95**
[GL186] Futura pbk **£3.99**

CLARKE, JEREMY

Necrotrivia vs. Skull NEW
A brutally funny satire on the materialism of Western society: Raymond Chandler as cyberpunk.
[GL187] Fourth Estate pbk **£4.95**

CLEMENT, HAL (US, 1922 -)

One of the best of the 'Hard Science' writers, his extrapolation of a world where gravity varies from 3 to 700 times that of earth makes fascinating reading.

Mission of Gravity
[GL188] Gollancz pbk **£2.50**

CONEY, MICHAEL (British, 1932 -)

A picaresque writer of soft SF, concerned with the people of his worlds rather than the machines.

Cat Karina
[GL189] Futura pbk **£2.50**

Celestial Steam Locomotive
[GL190] Futura pbk **£2.95**

Fang the Gnome NEW
[GL191] Futura pbk **£3.99**

Gods of the Greataway
[GL192] Futura pbk **£2.50**

COWPER, R. (British, 1926 -)

(Pseudonym of John Middleton Murry Junior.) The *Bird of Time* trilogy, a sequence of post-holocaust novels, shows Cowper's splendid style and characterization as they plot a mystical story of a new religion.

BIRD OF TIME TRILOGY

1: The Road to Corlay
[GL193] Orbit pbk **£2.25**

2: A Dream of Kinship
[GL194] Orbit pbk **£2.50**

3: A Tapestry of Time
[GL195] Orbit pbk **£2.50**

CROWLEY, JOHN (British)

One of Britain's most respected speculative writers, his individual, esoteric work is consistently rewarding to readers. See also *Fantasy*.

Beasts
[GL196] Gollancz pbk **£3.95**

DELANY, SAMUEL R. (US, 1942 -)

Umberto Eco has written of Delany: *"I consider Delany not only one of the most important SF writers...but a fascinating writer in general who has invented a new style"*. The James Joyce of SF and the leading light of the American New Wave in the 1960s, his colourful experimental writing paints exciting visual pictures in the space opera tradition, yet transcends earlier writers in the genre through his sophisticated treatment of linguistic and sexual themes. A stirring combination of glamour and vertigo. See also *Fantasy*.

Babel-17
[GL197] Gollancz pbk **£3.95**

Nova
[GL198] Gollancz pbk **£3.50**

Stars in My Pocket Like Grains of Sand
[GL199] Grafton pbk **£2.95**

The Jewels of Aptor
[GL200] Gollancz pbk **£2.99**

DICK, PHILIP K. (US, 1928 -)

An exciting writer whose brilliant and playful stories and complex, believable characters have made him a cult figure. His themes of what it is that makes us human, and of schizophrenia as a social norm, often make for uncomfortable reading. The splendidly detailed backgrounds and minor figures enrich his novels. *The Man in the High Castle* is one of the finest Alternative Worlds novels. Dick has been introduced to a wider audience since his novel *Do Androids Dream of Electric Sheep* was filmed as *Bladerunner.*

A Scanner Darkly
[GL201] Grafton pbk **£2.50**

Clans of the Alphane Moon
[GL202] Grafton pbk **£2.50**

Cosmic Puppets
[GL203] Grafton pbk **£2.50**

Do Androids Dream of Electric Sheep?
[GL204] Grafton pbk **£2.95**

Flow My Tears, the Policeman Said
[GL205] Grafton hbk **£2.50**

Lies, Inc.
[GL206] Grafton pbk **£1.95**

Man in the High Castle
One of the finest alternate world novels. Set in a world where the Axis powers won WWII and divided the USA between them. In the buffer zone of the Rockies a writer, the man in the high castle, has written an alternate history suggesting that the Allies....
[GL207] Penguin pbk **£3.95**

Maze of Death
[GL208] Grafton pbk **£2.50**

Now Wait For Last Year
[GL209] Grafton pbk **£1.95**

Penultimate Truth
[GL210] Grafton pbk **£2.50**

Radio Free Albemuth
[GL211] Grafton pbk **£2.95**

Second Variety NEW
2nd volume of collected stories.
[GL212] Gollancz hbk **£12.95**

The Divine Invasion
[GL213] Grafton pbk **£2.99**

The Golden Man
[GL214] Magnum pbk **£2.50**

The Simulcra
[GL215] Methuen pbk **£2.95**

The Three Stigmata of Palmer Eldritch
[GL216] Grafton pbk **£2.50**

DICKSON, GORDON R. (US, 1923 -)

His belief in the manifest destiny of man to control the stars is made palatable by his skill as a writer and

his profound grasp of the unpleasant realities of warfare.

DORSAI SEQUENCE
1: Tactics of Mistake
[GL217] Sphere pbk £2.50
2: Soldier, Ask Not
[GL218] Sphere pbk £2.75
3: Dorsai
[GL219] Sphere pbk £2.50
4: The Spirit of Dorsai
[GL220] Sphere pbk £2.99
5: Lost Dorsai
[GL221] Sphere pbk £2.50
6: Chantry Guild   **NEW**
[GL222] Sphere pbk £3.99

EFFINGER, GEORGE A. US, 1947 -)
A writer of humorous, almost surrealistic prose.
The Bird of Time
[GL223] Hodder pbk £2.50
The Nick of Time
[GL224] Hodder pbk £2.50

ELGIN, SUZETTE HADEN (US, 1936 -)
Elgin's linguistic scholarship is to the fore in these fine novels based on a stark future where a few families act as interpreters to the alien universe. The invention of a new women's language shows the power of language as a force for change.
Judas Rose: Native Tongue II
[GL225] Women's P pbk £4.95
Native Tongue
[GL226] Women's P pbk £2.50

ELTON, BEN
Satirist Elton's first novel is a diatribe on the death of our planet.
Stark   **NEW**
[GL227] M Joseph hbk £12.95
[GL228] Sphere pbk £3.50

FARMER, PHILIP JOSE (US, 1918 -)
Best remembered for bringing sex (and hence maturity) into SF in the 1950s with stories like *The Lover's Flesh* and *Strange Relations*. The world has now caught up with Farmer, and critics no longer regard him as a shocker, but as a legitimate taboo breaker.
Dark is the Sun
[GL229] Grafton pbk £1.95
Dayworld
[GL230] Grafton hbk £9.95
Dayworld Rebel   **NEW**
[GL231] Grafton pbk £3.50
Strange Relations
[GL232] Grafton pbk £1.95
RIVERWORLD SAGA
1: To Your Scattered Bodies Go
Farmer has become a world bestselling author with his *Riverworld* series, in which the entire human race is resurrected on the banks of a seemingly endless river, and historic personalities as diverse as Tom Mix, Mark Twain, Jesus Christ and Hermann Goering explore this unexpected afterlife.
[GL233] Grafton pbk £2.50
2: The Fabulous Riverboat
[GL234] Grafton pbk £2.99
3: The Dark Design
[GL235] Grafton pbk £2.95
4: The Magic Labyrinth
[GL236] Grafton pbk £2.95
5: Riverworld & Other Stories
[GL237] Grafton pbk £2.95
6: Gods of Riverworld
[GL238] Grafton pbk £2.95
WORLD OF TIERS
1: Maker of Universes/Gates of Creation/Private Cosmos
[GL239] Sphere pbk £4.50

2: Behind the Walls of Terra/ Lavalite World
[GL240] Sphere pbk £3.99

FARREN, MICK (US, 1943 -)
Hero of 1970s counterculture, rock musician, rock journalist and SF writer, Farren's books are amusing and entertaining and possess colour in psychedelic profusion. Full of metaphoric rock and roll imagery, his work is finding a new popularity undiminished by the wane of flower power. Essential reading for fans of Moorcock or Iain Banks.
Corpse
[GL241] NEL pbk £2.50
Protectorate
[GL242] NEL pbk £2.95
The Song of Phaid, the Gambler
[GL243] NEL pbk £3.95

GENTLE, MARY (British, 1956 -)
Her novels are a splendid investigation of a world, Orthe, by her tough but sensitive diplomat hero, Christie. The alien Ortheans, their history, religion and culture are well realized, but not at the expense of the pace of the adventure.
Ancient Light
[GL244] Arrow pbk £3.99
Golden Witch Breed
[GL245] Arrow pbk £3.50

GEORGE, PETER (British, 1924 - 1966)
Dr. Strangelove, or How I Learned to Stop Worrying & Love the Bomb
Made into a classic film by Stanley Kubrick in 1963, this novel is a masterpiece of ironic despair.
[GL246] Oxford pbk £3.95

GIBSON, WILLIAM (US, 1948 -)
The foremost of the Cyberpunk writers, Gibson has brought SF into tune with contemporary pop culture and electronic hardware, drugs, multinational company espionage, high fashion and synthesised music: all these elements form the background to his 'cyberspace' trilogy. As its computer-based society is overrun with the technological savagery of its streetwise inhabitants, the computer jockeys risk their minds stealing data to sell to the highest bidder from the dimension of cyberspace.
Burning Chrome
[GL247] Grafton pbk £2.95
CYBERSPACE SEQUENCE
1: Neuromancer
[GL248] Grafton pbk £2.95
2: Count Zero
[GL249] Grafton pbk £2.95
3: Mona Lisa Overdrive   **NEW**
[GL250] Gollancz hbk £10.95
[GL251] Grafton pbk £3.50

GRIBBIN, JOHN & CHOWN, MARCUS
Double Planet
[GL252] Gollancz pbk £2.99

GUIN, URSULA LE (US, 1929 -)
Ursula le Guin was one of the most important writers of the 1970s. She has published less in the 1980s, and her masterworks are *The Left Hand of Darkness* (1969) and *The Dispossessed* (1974). An academic background and an interest in Taoist philosophy inform all her works. Her rich romantic novels show in beautifully lucid writing the character and moral growth once thought to be only found in mainstream literature. She tackles politics, sexuality, myth and alienation, death and loss of innocence. By any standard an important writer: *I write science fiction because that is what my publishers call my books. Left to myself I should call them novels.* See also *Fantasy*.

Always Coming Home
[GL253] Grafton pbk £5.95
Dancing on the Edge of the World   **NEW**
A collection of essays on many subjects including SF and Fantasy.
[GL254] Gollancz hbk £14.95
Orsinian Tales
[GL255] Grafton pbk £2.50
Planet of Exile & Rocannon's World
[GL256] Star pbk £1.95
The Compass Rose
[GL257] Grafton pbk £1.95
The Dispossessed
[GL258] Grafton pbk £2.95
The Lathe of Heaven
[GL259] Grafton pbk £2.50
The Left Hand of Darkness
[GL260] Futura pbk £2.99
Threshold
[GL261] Grafton pbk £1.95

Women and Science Fiction

"What women do is survive. We live by ones and twos in the chinks of your world machine" (Tiptree/ Sheldon). The Science Fiction historian Brian Aldiss has dated the beginning of science fiction proper from Mary Shelley's *Frankenstein*. Some of the greatest science fiction writers are women and yet the genre is popularly thought to be written by men for boys. Women writers used to have to be disguised, 'female men' Ursula Le Guin's first stories came out under the name U K Leguin, while C L Moore, Andre Norton, Leigh Bracket had androgenous names. There was widespread consternation in the science fiction community as late as 1976 when James Tiptree Junior turned out to be Alice Sheldon (author of the story *The Women Men Don't See*). The economic and political liberation of women in the 60s and 70s was paralleled by an increase in women writing science fiction, many more realistic women characters and many more women readers. There are now fewer examples of women being relegated to what Joanna Russ calls 'intergalactic suburbia' and superb examples of women writing at all points of the science fiction spectrum. See *In the Chinks of World Machine* by Sarah Le Fanu, and *Despatches from the Frontier of the Female Mind* by Sarah Le Fanu and Jan Green.

HALDEMAN, JOE (US, 1943 -)
A mixture of scientific training and experience in Vietnam are used to good effect in Haldeman's hard SF novels.
Infinite Dream
[GL262] Futura pbk £3.50
Study War No More
[GL263] Futura pbk £2.95
The Forever War
[GL264] Futura pbk £2.25
Tool of the Trade
[GL265] Futura pbk £3.50
Worlds
[GL266] Futura pbk £2.25
Worlds Apart
[GL267] Futura pbk £2.25

HALL, SANDI (US)
First novel by promising SF feminist. Set in the near future, it concerns a group of women whose local campaign brings them into tragic conflict with big business. The story links them with a witch-burning misogynistic past, a peaceful feminist future and the time of the Godmothers, past, present and future.
The Godmothers
[GL268] Women's P pbk £3.95

HARRISON, HARRY (1926 -)

Pseudonym of Henry Maxwell Dempsey. Harry Harrison's light touch in his spoof space operas and in the *Stainless Steel Rat* series, contrasts with some hard SF extrapolation in his other work. *Make Room, Make Room* is the novel of overpopulation. Always well written, sometimes lightweight in content: *"In the guise of entertainments, which SF must always be primarily, many moral, physical, social, philosophical questions can be examined, if not solved"*.

Bill the Galactic Hero
[GL270] Penguin pbk **£3.50**

Bill the Galactic hero on the Planet of Robot Slaves　NEW
Twenty years after the much acclaimed publication of *Bill the Galactic Hero*, comes a sequel, another riotous antiwar romp, which parodies the clichés of SF, from Edgar Rice Burroughs to cyberpunk.
[GL271] Gollancz hbk **£11.95**

Deathworld 1
[GL272] Sphere pbk **£2.50**

Deathworld 2
[GL273] Sphere pbk **£2.50**

Deathworld 3
[GL274] Sphere pbk **£2.50**

Invasion: Earth
[GL275] Sphere pbk **£1.95**

Make Room, Make Room
[GL276] Penguin pbk **£3.95**

One Step from Earth
[GL277] Arrow pbk **£1.75**

Plague from Space
[GL278] Sphere pbk **£2.50**

Planet of No Return
[GL279] Sphere pbk **£2.50**

Planet of the Damned
[GL280] Futura pbk **£2.50**

Star Smashers of the Galaxy Rangers
[GL281] Futura pbk **£2.50**

Starworld
[GL282] Grafton pbk **£2.50**

The Technicolour Time Machine
[GL283] Futura pbk **£2.99**

West of Eden
[GL284] Panther pbk **£2.95**

Winter in Eden
[GL285] Grafton pbk **£3.50**

Return to Eden　NEW
[GL269] Grafton pbk **£7.95**

THE STAINLESS STEEL RAT SERIES

1: The Stainless Steel Rat
Jim Digriz, the amoral anti-hero, is 'the stainless steel rat in the walls of the world' in this consistently entertaining series.
[GL286] Sphere pbk **£2.50**

2: The Stainless Steel Rat's Revenge
[GL287] Corgi pbk **£2.99**

3: The Stainless Steel Rat Saves the World
[GL288] Corgi pbk **£2.50**

4: The Stainless Steel Rat Wants You
[GL289] Sphere pbk **£2.50**

5: The Stainless Steel Rat For Your President
[GL290] Sphere pbk **£2.50**

6: Adventures of the Stainless Steel Rat
[GL291] Sphere pbk **£2.50**

7: The Stainless Steel Rat is Born
[GL292] Sphere pbk **£2.75**

8: The Stainless Steel Rat Gets Drafted
[GL293] Corgi pbk **£2.99**

HARRISON, M. JOHN (British, 1945 -)

A writer in the school of Moorcock. See also *Fantasy*.

The Centauri Device
[GL294] Unwin pbk **£2.95**

The Committed Men　NEW
A bleak polluted Britain brings forth a mutated humanity.
[GL295] Gollancz pbk **£2.99**

HEINLEIN, ROBERT A. (1907 - 1988)

One of the greats of SF and a most influential writer. He has written many books exploring his favourite themes of self-reliance, immortality and revolutions. His two-fisted heroes are typical of Golden Age SF, his heroines are brighter than usual, and his light touch is a relief. His style of wisecracking sentimentality owes much to the writings of Chandler and Hammett. The sentimentality becomes less diluted and harder to take in his more recent novels.

Friday
[GL296] Hodder pbk **£3.50**

I Will Fear No Evil
[GL297] Hodder pbk **£3.50**

Job: A Comedy of Justice
[GL298] Hodder pbk **£2.95**

Puppet-Masters
[GL299] Hodder pbk **£2.50**

Stranger in a Strange Land
A campus favourite in 60s America. We can expect a massive revival with the renewal of interest in '60s counterculture. An orphaned survivor of the human colony on Mars returns to Earth as the Messiah of a new cult.
[GL300] Hodder pbk **£3.50**

The Cat Who Walks Through Walls: A Comedy of Manners
[GL301] Hodder pbk **£2.95**

The Door into Summer
[GL302] Gollancz pbk **£3.50**

The Man Who Sold the Moon
[GL303] Hodder pbk **£2.50**

The Moon is a Harsh Mistress
[GL304] Hodder pbk **£2.95**

The Number of the Beast
[GL305] Hodder pbk **£3.95**

Time Enough For Love
[GL306] Hodder pbk **£3.50**

To Sail Beyond the Sunset
[GL307] Sphere pbk **£3.99**

Waldo & Magic Inc
[GL308] Hodder pbk **£1.95**

HERBERT, FRANK (US, 1920 - 1986)

Herbert has written several intelligent novels about the interplay of humanity and environment, but is best known however for the long sequence of Dune novels. Together with its immediate successors, it is powerful in the extreme - but the later novels are weakened by their more byzantine plots.

The White Plague
[GL309] Hodder pbk **£3.50**

DUNE SERIES

1: Dune
Dune itself (1963-4) takes the trappings of Space Opera (Galactic Empires, storm troopers, psi power, etc) and brings together these traditional elements in a novel of depth and intensity. Seldom can a planetary environment have been so well realised, seldom a galactic history so well documented. None of this concrete detail, however, means that the story is lost.
[GL310] Hodder pbk **£3.95**

2: Dune Messiah
[GL311] Hodder pbk **£2.50**

3: Children of Dune
[GL312] Hodder pbk **£2.95**

4: God Emperor of Dune
[GL313] Hodder pbk **£3.50**

5: Heretics of Dune
[GL314] Hodder pbk **£3.50**

6: Chapter House of Dune
[GL315] Hodder pbk **£3.50**

HOGAN, JAMES P. (US, 1941 -)

Reading like an early Heinlein - good plots, anti-liberal sentiment and all-American heroes.

Endgame Enigma
[GL316] Legend pbk **£3.50**

Inherit the Stars
[GL317] Grafton pbk **£2.99**

Proteus Operation
[GL318] Legend pbk **£3.50**

HOLDSTOCK, ROBERT (British, 1948 -)

Among the best-realized of anthropologically-based SF, Holdstock's work has a marvellous sense of the primordial and mystical. See also the *Fantasy* and *Dark Fantasy* sections, under the Robert Faulcon entry.

Eye Among the Blind
[GL319] Gollancz pbk **£2.50**

In the Valley of the Statues
[GL320] Gollancz pbk **£2.50**

Where the Winds Blow
[GL321] Gollancz pbk **£2.95**

HUXLEY, ALDOUS (British, 1894 - 1963)

The dystopia imagined in *Brave New World* (1932) and its sequel has been one of the most influential in SF, with its convincing exploration of the consequences of genetic engineering. Huxley portrays a society where babies are chemically adjusted to grow into the body type required, and where the drug Soma is used for social control. The book can be read as an antidote to the scientifically imagined utopias of H.G. Wells. Huxley explored other utopias/dystopias in *Island* and *Ape & Essence*.

Ape & Essence
[GL322] Panther pbk **£1.95**

Brave New World
[GL323] Grafton pbk **£2.75**

Brave New World Revisited
[GL324] Grafton pbk **£2.50**

Island
[GL325] Grafton pbk **£3.50**

JETER, K.W. (US, 1950 -)

Savage, intense and uncompromising, Kevin Jeter's work has all the attributes of good modern *New Wave* writing, and his novels are amongst the strangest in the SF canon. Metallic style makes him a master of cyberpunk, often dismissed by the uninformed as pornographic and violent. His thematic trilogy beginning with the outstandingly weird *Dr Adder* confronts its subject matter realistically, without flinching as it questions sexual mores and comments on the civilised brutality of modern technology. Thoughtful, ice-cold cyberpunk at its best.

Infernal Devices
[GL326] Grafton pbk **£2.95**

Morlock Nights　NEW
The original 'steam-punk' novel, a sequel to Wells's *Time Machine*.
[GL327] Grafton pbk **£2.99**

THE DR. ADDER THEMATIC TRILOGY

1: Dr. Adder
[GL328] Grafton pbk **£2.95**

2: The Glass Hammer
[GL329] Grafton pbk **£2.95**

3: Death Arms
[GL330] Grafton pbk **£2.99**

KELLOGG, MARJORIE & ROSSOW, WILLIAM

Andre Norton praised these works as 'fine delineations of alien civilizations'.

A Rumour of Angels
[GL331] NEL pbk **£2.95**

Reign of Fire
[GL332] Gollancz pbk **£3.99**

The Wave and the Flame
[GL333] Gollancz pbk **£3.50**

KEYES, DANIEL (US, 1927 -)
One of the most moving of SF stories: it is the diary of a man who starts with an IQ of 68 and has it artificially boosted to genius level - but only temporarily. It is an exploration of humanity, intelligence and our society.
Flowers for Algernon
[GL334] Gollancz pbk **£3.50**

KILWORTH, GARRY (British, 1941 -)
One of Britain's most evocative writers, whose inventive, stunning work has been too often ignored.
Cloudrock `NEW`
The darker possibilities of the family are presented in this conflation of Freud and geography. Very funny.
[GL335] Unwin hbk **£3.50**
Spiral Winds
Like *Witchwater Country*, a powerfully atmospheric mainstream novel.
[GL336] Grafton pbk **£2.99**
The Songbirds of Pain
[GL337] Unwin pbk **£2.95**
Theatre of Timesmiths
[GL338] Unwin pbk **£2.95**
Witchwater Country
[GL339] Grafton pbk **£2.99**

KRESS, NANCY (US)
"Nancy Kress has idea after idea...She knows ideas are nothing without people". (Gene Wolfe).
An Alien Light `NEW`
[GL340] Century pbk **£6.95**

LEM, STANISLAW (1921 -)
Lem, who is Polish, is probably the best known SF writer not writing in English. He writes in many styles, often comic, but shot through with a pessimism concerning the future of humanity. He is influenced by Jorge Luis Borges and Hermann Hesse and his virtuoso invention provides an interesting contrast to the generally more optimistic and less iconoclastic tradition of English language SF.
Fiasco
[GL341] Futura pbk **£4.99**
Hospital of the Transfiguration `NEW`
[GL342] Deutsch hbk **£11.95**
One Human Minute
[GL343] Deutsch pbk **£7.95**

LESSING, DORIS (British, 1919 -)
Doris Lessing's sequence of SF novels provides an interesting example of a writer distinguished in the literary mainstream who has recognised that the form of SF gives greater freedom in expression and plot.
CANOPUS IN ARGOS ARCHIVES
1: Shikasta
[GL344] Grafton pbk **£3.50**
2: Marriages Between Zones Three, Four & Five
[GL345] Grafton pbk **£2.95**
3: The Sirian Experiments
[GL346] Grafton pbk **£2.95**
4: Making of the Representative for Planet 8
[GL347] Grafton pbk **£2.50**
5: Sentimental Agents in the Volyen Empire
[GL348] Grafton pbk **£2.50**

LEWIS, C.S. (1898 - 1963)
Like most of Lewis's writing this trilogy is Christian apologetic, heavily disguised as SF, and containing some of the most glorious descriptions of other planets ever written.
1: Out of the Silent Planet
[GL349] Pan pbk **£2.99**
2: Perelandra
[GL350] Pan pbk **£2.99**

Doris Lessing, author of Shikasta (Grafton pbk £3.50)

3: That Hideous Strength
[GL351] Pan pbk **£3.99**

MANN, PHILLIP (British, 1942 -)
Thoughtful SF about the changes man and aliens cause each other.
1: The Eye of the Queen
[GL352] Grafton pbk **£2.95**
2: Master of PaxWax
[GL353] Grafton pbk **£3.50**
3: The Fall of the Families `NEW`
[GL354] Grafton pbk **£3.99**

MARTIN, G.R.R.
(US, 1948 -)
A stylish writer of 'traditional' space opera with well visualized settings and gloom undercut with humour. See also *Dark Fantasy*.
Tuf Voyaging
[GL355] Gollancz pbk **£3.50**

MARTIN, G.R.R. & TUTTLE, L.
Windhaven
[GL356] Gollancz pbk **£2.95**

MAY, JULIAN
(US, 1931 -)
A well-known '50s writer now returning to fashion. Celtic mythology forms the background for a splendid tale of Pliocene earth, alien invasion and psychically 'operant' human beings.
THE SAGA OF THE EXILES
1: The Many-Coloured Land
[GL357] Pan pbk **£3.99**
2: The Golden Torc
[GL358] Pan pbk **£3.99**
3: The Nonborn King
[GL359] Pan pbk **£3.99**
4: The Adversary
[GL360] Pan pbk **£3.99**
Prequel: Intervention
[GL361] Pan pbk **£3.99**

MITCHELL, L.
The Revolution of St. Jane `NEW`
A complex novel that explores with wit and insight the vagaries of religious ideology.
[GL362] Women's P pbk **£4.95**

MITCHISON, NAOMI (British, 1897 -)
Best known for her other works on Mass Observation, her journeys to Africa, and her historical and mythological novels, her only SF work is an early attempt to show that both sexes might leave the earth.
Memoirs of a Spacewoman
[GL363] Women's P pbk **£1.95**

MCCAFFREY, ANNE (US, 1926 -)
The soft SF of Anne McCaffrey is more concerned with character rather than with adventure. Her interests in music and psychology are well integrated into her work.
Killashandra
[GL364] Corgi pbk **£2.99**
Restoree
[GL365] Corgi pbk **£2.95**
The Crystal Singer
[GL366] Corgi pbk **£2.95**
The Ship Who Sang
[GL367] Corgi pbk **£1.95**
To Ride Pegasus
[GL368] Sphere pbk **£2.99**

MCINTYRE, VONDA N. (US, 1948 -)
She is chiefly known as an accomplished noveliser of SF films, but her own work deserves a wider audience. Tautly written and intricately plotted, her humanistic and vital stories are always compelling.
Dreamsnake
[GL369] Gollancz pbk **£3.50**
Voyage Home
[GL370] Pan pbk **£2.50**

MCKILLIP, P.
Fool's Run `NEW`
Fantasy writer McKillip moves into SF with this blend of romanticism and cyberpunk.
[GL371] Futura pbk **£2.50**

NIVEN, LARRY (US, 1938 -)
The majority of Niven's numerous books form a coherent future history of 'Known Space', covering a thousand years. The novels and short stories interlock but can all be read separately. Though known as one of the most scientifically orientated of SF writers, he also creates delightful characters and/or aliens. *'"All your languages seem to use one possessive for all purposes - My arm, My husband, My mother" she said, using the intrinsic 'my' for her arm, the 'my' of property for her husband and the 'my' of relationship for her mother'* (Larry Niven).
A Gift From Earth
[GL372] Futura pbk **£2.99**
A World Out of Time
[GL373] Futura pbk **£3.50**
A1: Ringworld
[GL374] Sphere pbk **£3.50**
A2: Ringworld Engineers
[GL375] Futura pbk **£3.50**
B1: The Integral Trees
[GL376] Futura pbk **£2.99**
B2: The Smoke Ring
[GL377] Futura pbk **£3.99**
Limits
[GL378] Futura pbk **£3.50**
Neutron Star
[GL379] Futura pbk **£2.50**
Protector
[GL380] Futura pbk **£2.50**
Tales of Known Space
[GL381] Futura pbk **£3.50**
The Flight of the Horse
[GL382] Futura pbk **£3.50**
The Long Arm of Gil Hamilton
[GL383] Futura pbk **£1.95**
The World of Ptavvs
[GL384] Futura pbk **£2.50**

NIVEN, LARRY & BARNES, STEVEN
Descent of Anansi
[GL385] Futura pbk £2.95
Dream Park
[GL386] Futura pbk £3.50

NIVEN, LARRY & POURNELLE, JERRY
Footfall
[GL387] Sphere pbk £3.99
Lucifer's Hammer
[GL388] Futura pbk £3.99
Oath of Fealty
[GL389] Futura pbk £2.50

NIVEN, LARRY; POURNELLE, JERRY & BARNES, STEVEN
The Legacy of Heorot
[GL390] Sphere pbk £3.50

NIVEN, LARRY & POURNELLE, JERRY
The Mote in God's Eye
[GL391] Futura pbk £3.99

PALMER, DAVID (US, 1941 -)
One of the best of the new SF authors of the '80s, Palmer is, however, not prolific.
Emergence
[GL392] Hodder pbk £2.95
Threshold
[GL393] Hodder pbk £2.95

POHL, FREDERIK (US, 1919 -)
In a writing career spanning more than 50 years Pohl has produced a large body of work which combines invention with wit, as shown admirably in the recent *Heechee Saga*.
Demon in the Skull
[GL394] Penguin pbk £3.99
Man Plus
[GL395] Gollancz pbk £3.50
The Coming of the Quantum Cats
One of the better alternate world novels.
[GL396] Gollancz pbk £2.99
The Merchants' War
[GL397] Futura pbk £2.50
The Years of the City
[GL398] NEL hbk £2.95
HEECHEE SAGA
1: Beyond the Blue Event Horizon
The neurotic hero of the saga gains in self-knowledge (with the help of his computer psychiatrist Von Shrink), as humanity makes use of the mysterious artefacts left by the alien Heechee.
[GL399] Futura hbk £2.50
2: Heechee Rendezvous
[GL400] Futura pbk £2.50
3: Gateway
[GL401] Futura pbk £2.50
4: Annals of the Heechee `NEW`
[GL402] Gollancz hbk £9.95

POURNELLE, JERRY (US, 1933 -)
Pournelle's most successful work has been in conjuction with Larry Niven. His solo novels concentrate on military virtue and hard science.
Future History
[GL403] Futura pbk £2.95
High Justice
[GL404] Futura pbk £2.95
King David's Spaceship
[GL405] Futura pbk £3.50

POWERS, TIM (US, 1952 -)
An up-and-coming author who writes hard-edged SF with echoes of Zelazny and Delany. A writer to watch, whether writing traditional time-travel and paradox novels such as *The Anubis Gates*, or his post-holocaust *Dinner at the Deviant's Palace*.

Dinner at the Deviant's Palace
[GL406] Grafton pbk £2.95
On Stranger Tides
[GL407] Gollancz pbk £6.95
The Anubis Gates
[GL408] Grafton hbk £2.95
The Drawing of the Dark
[GL409] Grafton pbk £3.50

PRATCHETT, TERRY (British)
Space opera for the humourist. See also *Fantasy*.
Dark Side of the Sun
[GL410] Corgi pbk £2.50
Strata
[GL411] Corgi pbk £2.50

PRIEST, CHRISTOPHER (British, 1943 -)
A writer much admired by the literary mainstream. His work is compelling and brilliant, and is pioneering the SF advance to true literary recognition. His writing is often detached yet enthralling as he is adept at pulling the rug of reality from beneath the reader's feet in his absorbing explorations of perception - what is real and what is unreal. He is also a master of more traditional forms, as his exciting tribute to H.G. Wells in *The Space Machine* shows.
A Dream of Wessex
[GL412] Abacus pbk £3.95
Inverted World
[GL413] Gollancz pbk £3.50
The Affirmation
[GL414] Gollancz pbk £2.99
The Glamour
[GL415] Sphere pbk £2.95
The Space Machine
[GL416] Gollancz pbk £3.50

QUICK, W.T. (US)
Sombre realism in the cyberpunk vein, set at the cutting edge of technology. First in a projected trilogy.
Dreams of Flesh and Sand `NEW`
[GL417] Futura pbk £3.50

REED, ROBERT
Winner of the first Writers of the Future Gold Award. In *The Hormone Jungle*, a genetically changed humanity, set 2,000 years in the future, is still motivated by lust and lucre.
The Hormone Jungle `NEW`
[GL418] Orbit pbk £6.99

ROBERTS, KEITH (British, 1935 -)
Considered along with Aldiss and Ballard to be one of the top British SF authors. Roberts transcends the genre. He is famous for his well-realised alternative history *Pavane* in which Elizabeth I is assassinated and Catholicism supresses science well into the 20th Century. Roberts has won admiration for his sympathetic treatment of memorable female characters and of the Celtic landscapes they often inhabit in past, present or future.
Kiteworld
[GL419] Penguin pbk £3.95
Pavane
[GL420] Penguin pbk £3.95

ROBINSON, KIM STANLEY (US, 1952 -)
With its weird collisions of consumerism and post-history, Robinson's work has the character of P.H. Dick's. He has been described by Gene Wolfe as "simply one of our best authors".
Icehenge
[GL421] Futura pbk £2.50
Planet on the Table
[GL422] Futura pbk £2.95
The Gold Coast `NEW`
[GL423] Orbit pbk £6.99
The Memory of Whiteness
[GL424] Futura pbk £2.95

The Wild Shore
[GL425] Futura pbk £2.50

RUCKER, RUDY (US, 1946 -)
Cyberpunk, Hegelian philosophy and mathematical speculation co-exist in these stylish books.
Softwave `NEW`
[GL426] NEL pbk £2.50
Wetwave `NEW`
[GL427] NEL pbk £2.50

RUSS, JOANNA (US, 1937 -)
She writes some of the most thoughtful and provocative SF and fantasy today. Her clever slanting of stereotypes shows how much more important is character than expectation. Her angry novel of the female condition *The Female Man* is a superbly sustained diatribe against injustice. No one just 'likes' Russ - you either hate her or love her. According to B. Searles: "SF has its Mozarts...Joanna Russ is one of them".
Extra(ordinary) People
[GL428] Women's P pbk £1.95
Hidden Side of the Moon `NEW`
A new short story collection.
[GL429] Women's P pbk £4.95
The Female Man
[GL430] Women's P pbk £1.95
The Two of Them
[GL431] Women's P pbk £2.25
We Who Are About To
[GL432] Women's P pbk £3.50

RUSSELL, ERIC FRANK (British, 1905 - 1978)
He is a writer with a fine sense of humour and a deep hatred of bureaucracy. He has also created some of the most believable aliens in the genre.
Best of E.F. Russell
[GL433] Futura pbk £2.95
Next of Kin
[GL434] Methuen pbk £2.99
Sentinels from Space
[GL435] Methuen pbk £2.95
Sinister Barrier
[GL436] Methuen pbk £2.50
Three to Conquer
[GL437] Methuen pbk £2.95
Wasp
[GL438] Methuen pbk £2.50

SABERHAGEN, FRED (US, 1930 -)
The *Beserker Saga*, a story of robots programmed to exterminate all life, is an intelligently written Space Opera, combined with speculations about the nature of consciousness; it will finally run to 8 volumes. See also *Fantasy*.
BESERKER SAGA
1: Brother Beserker
[GL439] Gollancz pbk £2.99
2: Brother Beserker
[GL440] Gollancz pbk £2.99
3: Beserker's Planet
[GL441] Gollancz pbk £2.99
4: The Ultimate Enemy `NEW`
[GL442] Gollancz pbk £3.50

SARGENT, PAMELA (US, 1948 -)
Believable characters and a skilful use of language enhance a feminist tale of civilized women in cities and the savage men outside.
Shore of Women
[GL443] Pan pbk £3.99

SAXTON, J. (British, 1935 -)
An acute eye for human foibles is enhanced by Saxton's mordant humour.
Queen of States
[GL444] Women's P pbk £1.95

Joanna Russ, author of *Hidden Side of the Moon* (Women's Press pbk £4.95)

Travails of Jane Saint
[GL445] Women's P pbk £2.50

SCHMITZ, JAMES (US, 1911 - 1981)
The Witches of Karres
First published in 1966 this funny novel stars fledgling witches aboard a spacecraft.
[GL446] Gollancz pbk £3.50

SCOTT, MELISSA
SILENCE LEIGH SERIES
1: Five Twelfths of Heaven
Scott's trilogy has combined gripping space adventure with elements of magic, physics and the mysterious alchemical arts.
[GL447] Gollancz pbk £3.50
2: Silence in Solitude
[GL448] Gollancz pbk £3.50
3: The Empress of Earth   **NEW**
[GL449] Gollancz pbk £3.50

SHAW, BOB (Irish, 1931 -)
Bob Shaw is one of the most literate writers of the hard science school. His scientific ideas are usually original and exciting, tempered with good characterisations. He is one of the genre's finest, most intelligent entertainers, his work described by Zelazny as possessing "memorable characters, intense action, engaging notions, exotic locales".
1: The Ragged Astronauts
[GL450] Orbit pbk £2.95
2: The Wooden Spaceships
[GL451] Orbit hbk £3.50
3: The Fugitive Worlds   **NEW**
The concluding volume of the trilogy finds Toller Maraquine 11, grandson of the protagonist of the first two works, facing a new threat to the twin worlds of Land and Overland.
[GL452] Gollancz hbk £11.95
A Wreath of Stars
[GL453] Gollancz pbk £3.50
Medusa's Children
[GL454] Gollancz pbk £2.50
Night Walk
[GL455] Gollanz pbk £2.50

The Peace Machine
[GL456] Grafton pbk £2.50
The Ship of Strangers
[GL457] Gollancz pbk £2.99
Who Goes There?
[GL458] Gollancz pbk £2.95

SHEA, R. & WILSON, R.A.
ILLUMINATUS!
1: The Eye in the Pyramid
The collaborative trilogy has been described as "a *reductio ad absurdum* of all mammalian politics".
[GL459] Sphere pbk £3.50
2: The Golden Apple
[GL460] Sphere pbk £3.50
3: Leviathan
[GL461] Sphere pbk £3.50

SHECKLEY, ROBERT (US, 1928 -)
"Suddenly SF was in, it was chic, it was flashy, it was meaningful, and it was a whole load of fun".
(Sheckley, 1976). A great satirist, Sheckley is SF's Voltaire. His characters are innocents placed in Candide-like situations, and their attempts to come to terms with them are both touching and highly amusing. A writer of admirable subtlety, he is often compared to Kurt Vonnegut, and is one of Douglas Adams's sources of inspiration.
Hunter/Victim
[GL462] Mandarin pbk £3.50
The Alchemical Marriage of Alistair Crompton
[GL463] Methuen pbk £2.25
The Status Civilization
[GL464] Methuen pbk £2.25
The Tenth Victim
[GL465] Methuen pbk £2.50
Victim Prime
[GL466] Methuen pbk £2.50

SHEPPARD, LUCIUS
Sheppard's work is closer to the magic realism of Marques and Fuentes than to the military fiction of Heinlein and Dickson to which it is often compared.
Green Eyes
[GL467] Grafton pbk £3.50
Life During Wartime
[GL468] Grafton pbk £4.99

SILVERBERG, ROBERT (US, 1935 -)
If ever a man was undeservedly haunted by his past it is Robert Silverberg. A 'pulp' writer of the 1950s he achieved new status in the 1960s with novels such as *Thorns* and *Nightwings*. His later work is influenced by Borges and warrants close reading.
1: At Winter's End
[GL469] Gollancz hbk £11.95
1: Lord Valentine's Castle
[GL470] Pan pbk £3.50
2: The Majipoor Chronicles
[GL471] Pan pbk £3.50
2: The Queen of Springtime   **NEW**
Sequel to *At Winter's End*, continuing the story, 40 years on, of Hresh and his people's attempts to rebuild civilization on the surface of the Earth. A concluding volume will be published in 1990.
[GL472] Gollancz hbk £12.95
3: Valentine Pontifex
[GL473] Pan pbk £3.99
Dying Inside
[GL474] Gollancz pbk £2.99
Star of Gypsies
[GL475] Futura pbk £3.99
The Masks of Time
[GL476] Gollancz pbk £2.95
Time of Changes
[GL477] Gollancz pbk £3.50

To the Land of the Living   **NEW**
Silverberg's new book is concerned with what would happen if there *were* an afterworld.
[GL478] Gollancz hbk £11.95
Tom O'Bedlam
[GL479] Futura pbk £2.95
Up The Line
[GL480] Gollancz pbk £2.95

SIMAK, CLIFFORD D. (US, 1904 -)
Like Bradbury, Simak is obsessed with his midwestern roots. Instead of leaving Wisconsin for the stars he brings them down to earth. A writer of considerable sentimental charm.
A Heritage of Stars
[GL481] Methuen pbk £2.50
All Flesh is Grass
[GL482] Methuen pbk £2.50
Brothers and Other Stories
[GL483] Methuen pbk £2.95
City
[GL484] Methuen pbk £2.95
Highway of Eternity
[GL485] Mandarin pbk £2.99
Where The Evil Dwells
[GL486] Methuen pbk £2.50

SLADEK, JOHN (US, 1937 -)
A satirist of considerable power and complexity, Sladek is also a very funny writer. He is at odds with the optimistic wing of SF that feels every problem has its solution. His new novel *Bugs* is a comic fantasy about an Englishman lost in high-tech America.
Bugs   **NEW**
[GL487] Macmillan hbk £11.95
The Reproductive System
[GL488] Gollancz pbk £2.95

SLONCZEWSKI, J.
A Door Into Ocean
Violence and non-violence meet in the ocean world of Shora.
[GL489] Women's P pbk £4.95

SMITH, CORDWAINER (US, 1913 - 1966)
Involved from his youth in Asian politics, and the author of the definitive text on psychological warfare, Smith's work is surprisingly lyrical.
Instrumentality of Mankind
[GL490] Gollancz pbk £3.50
Norstrilia
[GL491] Gollancz pbk £2.95
Quest of the Three Worlds
[GL492] Gollancz pbk £2.50
Rediscovery of Man
[GL493] Gollancz pbk £3.50

SPINRAD, N. (US)
Uncompromising and intelligent, Spinrad is one of America's best New Wave writers, and his work has the characteristic power and verve of today's Cyberpunk.
Bug Jack Barron
[GL494] Grafton pbk £3.50
Little Heroes   **NEW**
[GL495] Grafton pbk £4.99
The Men in the Jungle   **NEW**
[GL496] Grafton pbk £3.50

STAPLEDON, O. (British, 1886 - 1950)
An early British writer of much-acclaimed SF.
Last & First Men
A classic future history spanning 2,000 million years from the First Men (us) to the Eighteenth Men.
[GL497] Penguin pbk £4.50
Star Maker
Described by Brian Aldiss as "*a chronicle, hardly a*

novel, of combined science and poetry, brilliant, durable and irresistably readable".
[GL498] Penguin pbk **£3.95**

STERLING, BRUCE
Involution Ocean
[GL499] Legend pbk **£2.50**
Islands in the Net
[GL500] Century pbk **£5.95**

SWANWICK, MICHAEL (US, 1950 -)
Somewhere between the humanists and Cyberpunk, Swanwick's work has been very successful. His new novel, *In the Drift*, is an alternate world story in which the Three Mile Island reactor *did* melt down, with a consequent escape of radio-active material.
In the Drift　`NEW`
[GL501] Century hbk **£10.95**
Vacuum Flowers
[GL502] Legend hbk **£2.99**

TENN, WILLIAM
Of Men and Monsters
The only novel by a prolific short story writer, which tells of a world in which aliens have taken over the Earth, and humans exist like mice.
[GL503] Gollancz pbk **£3.50**

TEPPER, S. SHERI
Grass　`NEW`
Tepper's new novel is set on Grass, the only planet in the universe untouched by a deadly plague. The inhabitants of Earth send a clandestine mission to discover the secret of the planet's immunity...
[GL504] Bantam hbk **£12.95**
[GL505] Bantam pbk **£6.95**

THOMPSON, E.P.
First venture into SF by the radical social historian, which tells of an alien visitor to Earth and his attempts to come to terms with the noisy, graceless beasts he finds. A combination of scientific imagination, political ideas, and an almost Swiftian satire.
The Sykaos Papers
[GL506] Bloomsbury pbk **£6.99**

TILLEY, PATRICK (British, 1928 -)
Tilley's popularity stems from his convincing combination of believable characters and complex plots.
THE AMTRAK WARS
1: Cloud Warrior
[GL507] Sphere pbk **£3.50**
2: First Family
[GL508] Sphere pbk **£3.50**
3: The Iron Master
[GL509] Sphere pbk **£3.50**
4: Blood River　`NEW`
[GL510] Sphere pbk **£3.50**

TIPTREE, JAMES (1916 -)
Pseudonym of Alice Sheldon. Sophisticated and intelligent writing and well thought-out plots characterise Tiptree's writing.
Brightness Falls from the Air
[GL511] Sphere pbk **£3.50**
Starry Rift
[GL512] Sphere pbk **£2.99**

TURNER, GEORGE (Australian, 1916 -)
Turner is concerned with the ethics of survival in a post-holocaust world. A 21st century Melbourne is beset by the greenhouse effect, a collapsed world economy and brutal class division.
The Sea and Summer
[GL513] Grafton pbk **£3.99**

TURTLEDOVE, H.
A trilogy founded on the idea that Mohammed never founded Islam, but became a Christian saint: thus, Byzantium endures. For more of Turtledove's work, see *Fantasy*.
BYZANTIUM
1: Agent of Byzantium
[GL514] NEL pbk **£2.95**
2: Non Interference
[GL515] NEL pbk **£2.95**
3: A Different Flesh
[GL516] NEL pbk **£2.95**

TUTTLE, L. (US, 1952 -)
A Spaceship Built of Stone
Collection of stories which concerns the undermining of ordinary life by dream and nightmare, occasionally crossing the boundary into Fantasy and Horror.
[GL517] Women's P pbk **£4.50**

VANCE, JACK (US, 1920 -)
Vance is a superb creator of other worlds, and a master of baroque style and incisive humour.
Araminta Station　`NEW`
[GL518] NEL pbk **£3.50**
The Planet of Adventure Omnibus
[GL519] Grafton pbk **£3.95**
DEMON PRINCES
1: Starking
[GL520] Grafton pbk **£2.50**
2: The Killing Machine
[GL521] Grafton pbk **£2.50**
3: The Palace of Love
[GL522] Grafton pbk **£2.95**
4: The Face
[GL523] Grafton pbk **£2.95**
5: The Book of Dreams
[GL524] Grafton pbk **£2.99**

VARDEMAN, R. & MILAN, V.
Jade Demons Quartet
[GL525] NEL pbk **£4.95**
Weapons of Chaos
[GL526] Hodder pbk **£4.50**
THE WAR OF THE POWERS
1: War of the Powers
[GL527] Hodder pbk **£3.95**
2: Istu Awakened　`NEW`
[GL528] Hodder pbk **£3.95**

VERNE, JULES (French, 1828 - 1905)
One of the first to succeed as a commercial SF writer, Verne owed a great and acknowledged debt to Poe. His heroes, like Captain Nemo, stand aloof from society and the military conquest ethic of the Imperialist Age. Of his 64 novels, these are the only two SF works which remain in print.
Journey to the Centre of the Earth
[GL529] Penguin pbk **£2.50**
Twenty Thousand Leagues Under the Sea
[GL530] Penguin pbk **£2.50**

VINGE, JOAN D. (US, 1948 -)
"SF is a lot like anthropology...it lets you glimpse other possible lifestyles, other ways of looking at things, other ways of dealing with problems".
Sensitive writing and an adept sense of fairytale and myth make Joan Vinge very engaging. Her sweeping saga *The Snow Queen* has been her most successful work so far.
1: The Snow Queen
[GL531] Futura pbk **£3.99**
2: World's End
[GL532] Futura pbk **£2.50**

VONNEGUT, KURT (US, 1922 -)
Even though Vonnegut himself likes to deny that his novels and stories are SF, his themes and

developments are classic examples of the genre. A strong humanist and humorous writer, he is regarded by many as the most brilliant craftsman in the genre, unlike his recurring character, the pathetically unsuccessful SF writer Kilgore Trout.
Breakfast of Champions
[GL533] Panther pbk **£2.95**
Cat's Cradle
[GL534] Penguin pbk **£3.95**
Catspaw　`NEW`
[GL535] Gollancz hbk **£12.95**
Deadeye Dick
[GL536] Panther pbk **£2.50**
Galapagos
[GL537] Panther pbk **£2.99**
God Bless You Mr Rosewater
[GL538] Panther pbk **£2.50**
Happy Birthday Wanda June
[GL539] Panther pbk **£2.50**
Jailbird
[GL540] Panther pbk **£2.50**
Mother Night
[GL541] Panther pbk **£1.95**
Palm Sunday
[GL542] Panther pbk **£2.95**
Sirens of Titan
[GL543] Gollancz pbk **£3.50**
Slapstick, or Lonesome No More
[GL544] Grafton pbk **£3.99**
Slaughterhouse Five
Vonnegut's most famous novel was inspired by his experiences as a POW during the firestorm bombing of Dresden at the end of the Second World War.
[GL545] Panther pbk **£3.99**
Welcome to the Monkey House
[GL546] Panther pbk **£2.50**

WATSON, IAN (British, 1924 -)
An interest in linguistics and anthropology inform Watson's intelligent novels.
Evil Water
[GL547] Grafton pbk **£2.95**
Salvage Rites (Short Stories)　`NEW`
[GL548] Gollancz hbk **£11.95**
Slowbirds
[GL549] Grafton pbk **£2.50**
Whores of Babylon
[GL550] Grafton pbk **£3.95**
THE GOD MIND & YALEEN
1: The Book of the River
[GL551] Grafton pbk **£2.99**
2: The Book of the Stars
[GL552] Grafton pbk **£2.99**
3: The Book of Being
[GL553] Grafton pbk **£2.99**

Science Fiction & the Media

Science fiction and the electronic media have had a strong reciprocal relationship. Film has fed off the written word (*Forbidden Planet* as a version of *The Tempest*) and vice versa (the ever expanding list of *Star Trek* novels and novelisations). There have even been feedbacks into reality; what some science fiction (or more likely SciFi) fans, call the 'Mundane' with NASA's first space shuttle being named the 'Enterprise'. Radio programmes have become books (*Hitchhiker's Guide*); books have been turned into radio. In 1938 thousands of Americans took to the hills as Orson Welles broadcast his version of H G Wells' *War of the Worlds*. The fantastic success of *Star Wars* and *Close Encounters* led to a boom in the production of science fiction and fantasy books which fed back into the production of films from classic novels and stories - P K Dick's *Do Androids Dream* - filmed as *Bladerunner*.

WATERSTONE'S BOOKSELLERS · ORDER FORM

MAIL ORDER DIVISION · 4 MILSOM STREET BATH BA1 1DA · ☎ 0225 448595 · FAX: 0225 444732

ORDERED BY: Please write your permanent address
PLEASE PRINT

NAME

ADDRESS

POSTCODE/ZIPCODE

COUNTRY

SEND TO: if different from ordered by
PLEASE PRINT

NAME

ADDRESS

POSTCODE/ZIPCODE

COUNTRY

BOOK REF. NO.	AUTHOR	TITLE	PUBLISHER	EDITION	QTY	PRICE

METHOD OF PAYMENT

❶ **I enclose** (PLEASE TICK)

£ CHEQUE/MONEY ORDER ☐ CREDIT CARD (see below) ☐
OTHER ☐ (Please specify)_____

❷ **Credit Cards** (PLEASE TICK)

ACCESS/MASTERCHARGE ☐ VISA ☐ DINERS ☐ AMEX ☐

☐☐☐☐☐☐☐☐☐☐☐☐☐☐

EXPIRY DATE

TOTAL BOOKS _____

POSTAGE & PACKING:
please see overleaf for postal charges

IF OUTSIDE UK ☐ _____
AIR MAIL ☐ _____
SURFACE ☐ _____
(USA only) AIR SPEEDED ☐ _____

TOTAL AMOUNT ENCLOSED _____

DATE _____

SIGNATURE

For full details of how to pay please turn over

WATERSTONE'S BOOKSELLERS · ORDER FORM

MAIL ORDER DIVISION · 4 MILSOM STREET BATH BA1 1DA · ☎ 0225 448595 · FAX: 0225 444732

HOW TO ORDER

❶ BY MAIL

Please complete an order form. Please write clearly and quote the full reference number from the catalogue entry. Post and packing costs can be calculated from the table below and should be added to the total.

❷ BY TELEPHONE

Please telephone your order on 0225 448595, quoting the details of the books you require (24 hour telephone answering service).

❸ BY FAX

You can fax your orders to us on 0225 444732.

TO ORDER BOOKS NOT LISTED IN THE GUIDE

We will supply any British book in print. Complete the order form in the same way giving author, title, and publisher and return it to us.

SPECIAL NOTE

Books bought from a United Kingdom bookseller are free of Value Added Tax and any other sales tax.

HOW TO PAY

❶ BY STERLING CHEQUE

Please make cheques payable to *Waterstone & Co. Limited* We can only accept sterling cheques drawn on a British bank.

❷ BY CREDIT CARD

Please give us the full credit card number, expiry date, plus the registered billing address for the account if different to the despatch address. We accept Access/Mastercard, American Express, Diner's, and Visa. We will charge your Credit Card when we despatch the books to you.

AMERICAN CUSTOMERS PLEASE NOTE: *If you choose to pay by credit card then there is no need to work out the conversion from dollars to sterling as the credit card company will do this for you automatically charging you in dollars even though you have ordered books priced in sterling.*

❸ BY BOOK TOKEN

In addition to Waterstone's Book Vouchers, we will accept Book Tokens as payment or part-payment of an order.

❹ OTHER METHODS

We also accept: Travellers' Cheques, British Postal Orders, International Money Orders (in Sterling).

AVAILABILITY

We try to keep in stock as many of the titles listed in our catalogues as we can. Sometimes, however, we have to order books directly from the publishers which can take an additional two weeks. If any title has gone out of print or is reprinting we will advise you by post. Should the money enclosed with your order result in a surplus due to the unavailability of some of the books we will send you a credit voucher which you can use for your next order. Alternatively, should you require a cheque or credit card refund, please let us know.

PRICE

Although every care is taken in the preparation of our catalogues, we cannot guarantee the prices of all the titles listed since the publishers quite frequently increase them without warning. If the price increase is less than 20% we will send you the books anyway either charging your credit card the additional cost or asking for a further cheque to cover it. Should the price increase exceed 20% we will inform you immediately and ask you whether you still require the books.

GUARANTEE

If a book arrives in a faulty or damaged condition please let us know immediately so that we can replace it.

POSTAGE & PACKAGING RATES

To calculate the full cost of your order you can use the table below.

How to calculate your postage charge
❶ Add up the cost of your books
❷ Using the left hand column follow the table across until you coincide with the destination of your order and the method by which you want it sent. For example; the cost of sending **£18.95** of books by Air-Speeded Post to the US would be **£4.80**
❸ Add the postage amount to the cost of your books and you will arrive at the total cost of your order.

VALUE OF ORDER	UK	EUROPE		USA		REST OF WORLD	
Up to	:	Surface	Air	Air-Speeded	Airmail	Surface	Airmail
£10	2.10	2.70	6.00	3.00	6.35	2.70	6.70
£20	3.00	4.40	9.00	4.80	10.35	4.40	10.70
£30	3.50	5.20	12.00	6.60	14.35	5.20	14.70
£40	4.00	6.50	15.00	8.40	18.35	6.50	18.70
£50	4.50	7.80	18.00	10.20	22.35	7.80	22.70
Increment per £10 extra	£0.50	£1.30	£3.00	£1.80	£4.00	£1.80	£4.00

WATERSTONE'S BOOKSELLERS · ORDER FORM

MAIL ORDER DIVISION · 4 MILSOM STREET BATH BA1 1DA · ☎ 0225 448595 · FAX: 0225 444732

ORDERED BY: Please write your permanent address
PLEASE PRINT

NAME

ADDRESS

POSTCODE/ZIPCODE

COUNTRY

SEND TO: if different from ordered by
PLEASE PRINT

NAME

ADDRESS

POSTCODE/ZIPCODE

COUNTRY

BOOK REF. NO.	AUTHOR	TITLE	PUBLISHER	EDITION	QTY	PRICE

METHOD OF PAYMENT

❶ **I enclose** (PLEASE TICK)

£ CHEQUE/MONEY ORDER ☐ CREDIT CARD (see below) ☐
OTHER ☐ (Please specify)_____

❷ **Credit Cards** (PLEASE TICK)

ACCESS/MASTERCHARGE ☐ VISA ☐ DINERS ☐ AMEX ☐

EXPIRY DATE

TOTAL BOOKS _____

POSTAGE & PACKING:
please see overleaf for postal charges

IF OUTSIDE UK ☐ _____
AIR MAIL ☐ _____
SURFACE ☐ _____
(USA only) AIR SPEEDED ☐ _____

TOTAL AMOUNT ENCLOSED _____

DATE _____

SIGNATURE

For full details of how to pay please turn over

Registered as Waterstone & Co. Limited Registered in England No. 1766696 Registered Address 121/125 Charing Cross Road London WC2

WATERSTONE'S BOOKSELLERS · ORDER FORM

MAIL ORDER DIVISION · 4 MILSOM STREET BATH BA1 1DA · ☎ 0225 448595 · FAX: 0225 444732

HOW TO ORDER

❶ BY MAIL

Please complete an order form. Please write clearly and quote the full reference number from the catalogue entry. Post and packing costs can be calculated from the table below and should be added to the total.

❷ BY TELEPHONE

Please telephone your order on 0225 448595, quoting the details of the books you require (24 hour telephone answering service).

❸ BY FAX

You can fax your orders to us on 0225 444732.

TO ORDER BOOKS NOT LISTED IN THE GUIDE

We will supply any British book in print. Complete the order form in the same way giving author, title, and publisher and return it to us.

SPECIAL NOTE

Books bought from a United Kingdom bookseller are free of Value Added Tax and any other sales tax.

HOW TO PAY

❶ BY STERLING CHEQUE

Please make cheques payable to *Waterstone & Co. Limited* We can only accept sterling cheques drawn on a British bank.

❷ BY CREDIT CARD

Please give us the full credit card number, expiry date, plus the registered billing address for the account if different to the despatch address. We accept Access/Mastercard, American Express, Diner's, and Visa. We will charge your Credit Card when we despatch the books to you.

AMERICAN CUSTOMERS PLEASE NOTE:

If you choose to pay by credit card then there is no need to work out the conversion from dollars to sterling as the credit card company will do this for you automatically charging you in dollars even though you have ordered books priced in sterling.

❸ BY BOOK TOKEN

In addition to Waterstone's Book Vouchers, we will accept Book Tokens as payment or part-payment of an order.

❹ OTHER METHODS

We also accept: Travellers' Cheques, British Postal Orders, International Money Orders (in Sterling).

AVAILABILITY

We try to keep in stock as many of the titles listed in our catalogues as we can. Sometimes, however, we have to order books directly from the publishers which can take an additional two weeks. If any title has gone out of print or is reprinting we will advise you by post. Should the money enclosed with your order result in a surplus due to the unavailability of some of the books we will send you a credit voucher which you can use for your next order. Alternatively, should you require a cheque or credit card refund, please let us know.

PRICE

Although every care is taken in the preparation of our catalogues, we cannot guarantee the prices of all the titles listed since the publishers quite frequently increase them without warning. If the price increase is less than 20% we will send you the books anyway either charging your credit card the additional cost or asking for a further cheque to cover it. Should the price increase exceed 20% we will inform you immediately and ask you whether you still require the books.

GUARANTEE

If a book arrives in a faulty or damaged condition please let us know immediately so that we can replace it.

POSTAGE & PACKAGING RATES

To calculate the full cost of your order you can use the table below.

How to calculate your postage charge
❶ Add up the cost of your books
❷ Using the left hand column follow the table across until you

coincide with the destination of your order and the method by which you want it sent. For example; the cost of sending **£18.95** of books by Air-Speeded Post to the US would be **£4.80**
❸ Add the postage amount to the cost of your books and you will arrive at the total cost of your order.

VALUE OF ORDER	UK	EUROPE		USA		REST OF WORLD	
Up to	:	Surface	Air	Air-Speeded	Airmail	Surface	Airmail
£10	2.10	2.70	6.00	3.00	6.35	2.70	6.70
£20	3.00	4.40	9.00	4.80	10.35	4.40	10.70
£30	3.50	5.20	12.00	6.60	14.35	5.20	14.70
£40	4.00	6.50	15.00	8.40	18.35	6.50	18.70
£50	4.50	7.80	18.00	10.20	22.35	7.80	22.70
Increment per £10 extra	£0.50	£1.30	£3.00	£1.80	£4.00	£1.80	£4.00

WATERSTONE'S BOOKSELLERS · ORDER FORM

MAIL ORDER DIVISION · 4 MILSOM STREET BATH BA1 1DA · ☎ 0225 448595 · FAX: 0225 444732

ORDERED BY: Please write your permanent address
PLEASE PRINT

NAME

ADDRESS

POSTCODE/ZIPCODE

COUNTRY

SEND TO: if different from ordered by
PLEASE PRINT

NAME

ADDRESS

POSTCODE/ZIPCODE

COUNTRY

BOOK REF. NO.	AUTHOR	TITLE	PUBLISHER	EDITION	QTY	PRICE

METHOD OF PAYMENT

❶ **I enclose (PLEASE TICK)**

£ CHEQUE/MONEY ORDER ☐ CREDIT CARD (see below) ☐

OTHER ☐ (Please specify) _____

❷ **Credit Cards (PLEASE TICK)**

ACCESS/MASTERCHARGE ☐ VISA ☐ DINERS ☐ AMEX ☐

☐☐☐☐☐☐☐☐☐☐☐☐☐☐☐☐

EXPIRY DATE

TOTAL BOOKS _____

POSTAGE & PACKING:

please see overleaf for postal charges

IF OUTSIDE UK ☐ _____

AIR MAIL ☐ _____

SURFACE ☐ _____

(USA only) AIR SPEEDED ☐ _____

TOTAL AMOUNT ENCLOSED _____

DATE _____

SIGNATURE

For full details of how to pay please turn over

Registered as Waterstone & Co. Limited Registered in England No. 1766696 *Registered Address* 121/125 Charing Cross Road London WC2

WATERSTONE'S BOOKSELLERS · ORDER FORM

MAIL ORDER DIVISION · 4 MILSOM STREET BATH BA1 1DA · ☎ 0225 448595 · FAX: 0225 444732

HOW TO ORDER

❶ BY MAIL
Please complete an order form. Please write clearly and quote the full reference number from the catalogue entry. Post and packing costs can be calculated from the table below and should be added to the total.

❷ BY TELEPHONE
Please telephone your order on 0225 448595, quoting the details of the books you require (24 hour telephone answering service).

❸ BY FAX
You can fax your orders to us on 0225 444732.

TO ORDER BOOKS NOT LISTED IN THE GUIDE

We will supply any British book in print. Complete the order form in the same way giving author, title, and publisher and return it to us.

SPECIAL NOTE

Books bought from a United Kingdom bookseller are free of Value Added Tax and any other sales tax.

HOW TO PAY

❶ BY STERLING CHEQUE
Please make cheques payable to *Waterstone & Co. Limited* We can only accept sterling cheques drawn on a British bank.

❷ BY CREDIT CARD
Please give us the full credit card number, expiry date, plus the registered billing address for the account if different to the despatch address. We accept Access/Mastercard, American Express, Diner's, and Visa. We will charge your Credit Card when we despatch the books to you.

AMERICAN CUSTOMERS PLEASE NOTE:
If you choose to pay by credit card then there is no need to work out the conversion from dollars to sterling as the credit card company will do this for you automatically charging you in dollars even though you have ordered books priced in sterling.

❸ BY BOOK TOKEN
In addition to Waterstone's Book Vouchers, we will accept Book Tokens as payment or part-payment of an order.

❹ OTHER METHODS
We also accept: Travellers' Cheques, British Postal Orders, International Money Orders (in Sterling).

AVAILABILITY

We try to keep in stock as many of the titles listed in our catalogues as we can. Sometimes, however, we have to order books directly from the publishers which can take an additional two weeks. If any title has gone out of print or is reprinting we will advise you by post. Should the money enclosed with your order result in a surplus due to the unavailability of some of the books we will send you a credit voucher which you can use for your next order. Alternatively, should you require a cheque or credit card refund, please let us know.

PRICE

Although every care is taken in the preparation of our catalogues, we cannot guarantee the prices of all the titles listed since the publishers quite frequently increase them without warning. If the price increase is less than 20% we will send you the books anyway either charging your credit card the additional cost or asking for a further cheque to cover it. Should the price increase exceed 20% we will inform you immediately and ask you whether you still require the books.

GUARANTEE

If a book arrives in a faulty or damaged condition please let us know immediately so that we can replace it.

POSTAGE & PACKAGING RATES

To calculate the full cost of your order you can use the table below.

How to calculate your postage charge
❶ Add up the cost of your books
❷ Using the left hand column follow the table across until you

coincide with the destination of your order and the method by which you want it sent. For example; the cost of sending **£18.95** of books by Air-Speeded Post to the US would be **£4.80**
❸ Add the postage amount to the cost of your books and you will arrive at the total cost of your order.

VALUE OF ORDER	UK	EUROPE		USA		REST OF WORLD	
Up to	:	Surface	Air	Air-Speeded	Airmail	Surface	Airmail
£10	2.10	2.70	6.00	3.00	6.35	2.70	6.70
£20	3.00	4.40	9.00	4.80	10.35	4.40	10.70
£30	3.50	5.20	12.00	6.60	14.35	5.20	14.70
£40	4.00	6.50	15.00	8.40	18.35	6.50	18.70
£50	4.50	7.80	18.00	10.20	22.35	7.80	22.70
Increment per £10 extra	£0.50	£1.30	£3.00	£1.80	£4.00	£1.80	£4.00

WATERSTONE'S BOOKSELLERS · ORDER FORM

MAIL ORDER DIVISION · 4 MILSOM STREET BATH BA1 1DA · ☎ 0225 448595 · FAX: 0225 444732

ORDERED BY: Please write your permanent address
PLEASE PRINT

NAME

ADDRESS

POSTCODE/ZIPCODE

COUNTRY

SEND TO: if different from ordered by
PLEASE PRINT

NAME

ADDRESS

POSTCODE/ZIPCODE

COUNTRY

BOOK REF. NO.	AUTHOR	TITLE	PUBLISHER	EDITION	QTY	PRICE

METHOD OF PAYMENT

❶ **I enclose** (PLEASE TICK)

£ CHEQUE/MONEY ORDER ☐ CREDIT CARD (see below) ☐
OTHER ☐ (Please specify) _____

❷ **Credit Cards** (PLEASE TICK)

ACCESS/MASTERCHARGE ☐ VISA ☐ DINERS ☐ AMEX ☐

☐☐☐☐☐☐☐☐☐☐☐☐☐☐☐☐

EXPIRY DATE

TOTAL BOOKS _____

POSTAGE & PACKING:
please see overleaf for postal charges

IF OUTSIDE UK ☐ _____
AIR MAIL ☐ _____
SURFACE ☐ _____
(USA only) AIR SPEEDED ☐ _____

TOTAL AMOUNT ENCLOSED _____

DATE _____

SIGNATURE

For full details of how to pay please turn over

Registered as Waterstone & Co. Limited *Registered in England* No. 1766696 *Registered Address* 171/173 Charing Cross Road London WC2

WATERSTONE'S BOOKSELLERS · ORDER FORM

MAIL ORDER DIVISION · 4 MILSOM STREET BATH BA1 1DA · ☎ 0225 448595 · FAX: 0225 444732

HOW TO ORDER

❶ BY MAIL

Please complete an order form. Please write clearly and quote the full reference number from the catalogue entry. Post and packing costs can be calculated from the table below and should be added to the total.

❷ BY TELEPHONE

Please telephone your order on 0225 448595, quoting the details of the books you require (24 hour telephone answering service).

❸ BY FAX

You can fax your orders to us on 0225 444732.

TO ORDER BOOKS NOT LISTED IN THE GUIDE

We will supply any British book in print. Complete the order form in the same way giving author, title, and publisher and return it to us.

SPECIAL NOTE

Books bought from a United Kingdom bookseller are free of Value Added Tax and any other sales tax.

HOW TO PAY

❶ BY STERLING CHEQUE

Please make cheques payable to *Waterstone & Co. Limited* We can only accept sterling cheques drawn on a British bank.

❷ BY CREDIT CARD

Please give us the full credit card number, expiry date, plus the registered billing address for the account if different to the despatch address. We accept Access/Mastercard, American Express, Diner's, and Visa. We will charge your Credit Card when we despatch the books to you.

AMERICAN CUSTOMERS PLEASE NOTE:
If you choose to pay by credit card then there is no need to work out the conversion from dollars to sterling as the credit card company will do this for you automatically charging you in dollars even though you have ordered books priced in sterling.

❸ BY BOOK TOKEN

In addition to Waterstone's Book Vouchers, we will accept Book Tokens as payment or part-payment of an order.

❹ OTHER METHODS

We also accept: Travellers' Cheques, British Postal Orders, International Money Orders (in Sterling).

AVAILABILITY

We try to keep in stock as many of the titles listed in our catalogues as we can. Sometimes, however, we have to order books directly from the publishers which can take an additional two weeks. If any title has gone out of print or is reprinting we will advise you by post. Should the money enclosed with your order result in a surplus due to the unavailability of some of the books we will send you a credit voucher which you can use for your next order. Alternatively, should you require a cheque or credit card refund, please let us know.

PRICE

Although every care is taken in the preparation of our catalogues, we cannot guarantee the prices of all the titles listed since the publishers quite frequently increase them without warning. If the price increase is less than 20% we will send you the books anyway either charging your credit card the additional cost or asking for a further cheque to cover it. Should the price increase exceed 20% we will inform you immediately and ask you whether you still require the books.

GUARANTEE

If a book arrives in a faulty or damaged condition please let us know immediately so that we can replace it.

POSTAGE & PACKAGING RATES

To calculate the full cost of your order you can use the table below.

How to calculate your postage charge
❶ Add up the cost of your books
❷ Using the left hand column follow the table across until you coincide with the destination of your order and the method by which you want it sent. For example; the cost of sending **£18.95** of books by Air-Speeded Post to the US would be **£4.80**
❸ Add the postage amount to the cost of your books and you will arrive at the total cost of your order.

VALUE OF ORDER	UK	EUROPE		USA		REST OF WORLD	
Up to	:	Surface	Air	Air-Speeded	Airmail	Surface	Airmail
£10	2.10	2.70	6.00	3.00	6.35	2.70	6.70
£20	3.00	4.40	9.00	4.80	10.35	4.40	10.70
£30	3.50	5.20	12.00	6.60	14.35	5.20	14.70
£40	4.00	6.50	15.00	8.40	18.35	6.50	18.70
£50	4.50	7.80	18.00	10.20	22.35	7.80	22.70
Increment per £10 extra	£0.50	£1.30	£3.00	£1.80	£4.00	£1.80	£4.00

WATERSTONE'S BOOKSELLERS · ORDER FORM

MAIL ORDER DIVISION · 4 MILSOM STREET BATH BA1 1DA · ☎ 0225 448595 · FAX: 0225 444732

ORDERED BY: Please write your permanent address
PLEASE PRINT

NAME

ADDRESS

POSTCODE/ZIPCODE

COUNTRY

SEND TO: if different from ordered by
PLEASE PRINT

NAME

ADDRESS

POSTCODE/ZIPCODE

COUNTRY

BOOK REF. NO.	AUTHOR	TITLE	PUBLISHER	EDITION	QTY	PRICE

METHOD OF PAYMENT

❶   **I enclose** (PLEASE TICK)

£ CHEQUE/MONEY ORDER ☐ CREDIT CARD (see below) ☐

OTHER ☐ (Please specify) _____

❷   **Credit Cards** (PLEASE TICK)

ACCESS/MASTERCHARGE ☐ VISA ☐ DINERS ☐ AMEX ☐

☐☐☐☐☐☐☐☐☐☐☐☐☐

EXPIRY DATE

TOTAL BOOKS _____

POSTAGE & PACKING:
please see overleaf for postal charges

IF OUTSIDE UK ☐ _____

AIR MAIL ☐ _____

SURFACE ☐ _____

(USA only) AIR SPEEDED ☐ _____

TOTAL AMOUNT ENCLOSED _____

DATE _____

SIGNATURE

For full details of how to pay please turn over

Registered as Waterstone & Co. Limited *Registered in England* No. 1760090 *Registered Address* 121/125 Charing Cross Road London WC2

WATERSTONE'S BOOKSELLERS · ORDER FORM

MAIL ORDER DIVISION · 4 MILSOM STREET BATH BA1 1DA · ☎ 0225 448595 · FAX: 0225 444732

HOW TO ORDER

❶ BY MAIL

Please complete an order form. Please write clearly and quote the full reference number from the catalogue entry. Post and packing costs can be calculated from the table below and should be added to the total.

❷ BY TELEPHONE

Please telephone your order on 0225 448595, quoting the details of the books you require (24 hour telephone answering service).

❸ BY FAX

You can fax your orders to us on 0225 444732.

TO ORDER BOOKS NOT LISTED IN THE GUIDE

We will supply any British book in print. Complete the order form in the same way giving author, title, and publisher and return it to us.

SPECIAL NOTE

Books bought from a United Kingdom bookseller are free of Value Added Tax and any other sales tax.

HOW TO PAY

❶ BY STERLING CHEQUE

Please make cheques payable to *Waterstone & Co. Limited* We can only accept sterling cheques drawn on a British bank.

❷ BY CREDIT CARD

Please give us the full credit card number, expiry date, plus the registered billing address for the account if different to the despatch address. We accept Access/Mastercard, American Express, Diner's, and Visa. We will charge your Credit Card when we despatch the books to you.

AMERICAN CUSTOMERS PLEASE NOTE:
If you choose to pay by credit card then there is no need to work out the conversion from dollars to sterling as the credit card company will do this for you automatically charging you in dollars even though you have ordered books priced in sterling.

❸ BY BOOK TOKEN

In addition to Waterstone's Book Vouchers, we will accept Book Tokens as payment or part-payment of an order.

❹ OTHER METHODS

We also accept: Travellers' Cheques, British Postal Orders, International Money Orders (in Sterling).

AVAILABILITY

We try to keep in stock as many of the titles listed in our catalogues as we can. Sometimes, however, we have to order books directly from the publishers which can take an additional two weeks. If any title has gone out of print or is reprinting we will advise you by post. Should the money enclosed with your order result in a surplus due to the unavailability of some of the books we will send you a credit voucher which you can use for your next order. Alternatively, should you require a cheque or credit card refund, please let us know.

PRICE

Although every care is taken in the preparation of our catalogues, we cannot guarantee the prices of all the titles listed since the publishers quite frequently increase them without warning. If the price increase is less than 20% we will send you the books anyway either charging your credit card the additional cost or asking for a further cheque to cover it. Should the price increase exceed 20% we will inform you immediately and ask you whether you still require the books.

GUARANTEE

If a book arrives in a faulty or damaged condition please let us know immediately so that we can replace it.

POSTAGE & PACKAGING RATES

To calculate the full cost of your order you can use the table below.

How to calculate your postage charge
❶ Add up the cost of your books
❷ Using the left hand column follow the table across until you

coincide with the destination of your order and the method by which you want it sent. For example; the cost of sending **£18.95** of books by Air-Speeded Post to the US would be **£4.80**
❸ Add the postage amount to the cost of your books and you will arrive at the total cost of your order.

VALUE OF ORDER	UK	EUROPE		USA		REST OF WORLD	
Up to	:	Surface	Air	Air-Speeded	Airmail	Surface	Airmail
£10	2.10	2.70	6.00	3.00	6.35	2.70	6.70
£20	3.00	4.40	9.00	4.80	10.35	4.40	10.70
£30	3.50	5.20	12.00	6.60	14.35	5.20	14.70
£40	4.00	6.50	15.00	8.40	18.35	6.50	18.70
£50	4.50	7.80	18.00	10.20	22.35	7.80	22.70
Increment per £10 extra	£0.50	£1.30	£3.00	£1.80	£4.00	£1.80	£4.00

WATERSTONE'S BOOKSELLERS · ORDER FORM

MAIL ORDER DIVISION · 4 MILSOM STREET BATH BA1 1DA · ☎ 0225 448595 · FAX: 0225 444732

ORDERED BY: Please write your permanent address
PLEASE PRINT

NAME

ADDRESS

POSTCODE/ZIPCODE

COUNTRY

SEND TO: if different from ordered by
PLEASE PRINT

NAME

ADDRESS

POSTCODE/ZIPCODE

COUNTRY

BOOK REF. NO.	AUTHOR	TITLE	PUBLISHER	EDITION	QTY	PRICE

METHOD OF PAYMENT

❶ **I enclose** (PLEASE TICK)

£ CHEQUE/MONEY ORDER ☐ CREDIT CARD (see below) ☐
OTHER ☐ (Please specify)

❷ **Credit Cards** (PLEASE TICK)

ACCESS/MASTERCHARGE ☐ VISA ☐ DINERS ☐ AMEX ☐

EXPIRY DATE

TOTAL BOOKS

POSTAGE & PACKING:
please see overleaf for postal charges

IF OUTSIDE UK ☐
AIR MAIL ☐
SURFACE ☐
(USA only) AIR SPEEDED ☐

TOTAL AMOUNT ENCLOSED

DATE

SIGNATURE

For full details of how to pay please turn over

Registered as Waterstone & Co. Limited Registered in England No. 1766696 Registered Address 121/123 Charing Cross Road London WC2

WGTB

WATERSTONE'S BOOKSELLERS · ORDER FORM

MAIL ORDER DIVISION · 4 MILSOM STREET BATH BA1 1DA · ☎ 0225 448595 · FAX: 0225 444732

HOW TO ORDER

❶ BY MAIL
Please complete an order form. Please write clearly and quote the full reference number from the catalogue entry. Post and packing costs can be calculated from the table below and should be added to the total.

❷ BY TELEPHONE
Please telephone your order on 0225 448595, quoting the details of the books you require (24 hour telephone answering service).

❸ BY FAX
You can fax your orders to us on 0225 444732.

TO ORDER BOOKS NOT LISTED IN THE GUIDE

We will supply any British book in print. Complete the order form in the same way giving author, title, and publisher and return it to us.

SPECIAL NOTE

Books bought from a United Kingdom bookseller are free of Value Added Tax and any other sales tax.

HOW TO PAY

❶ BY STERLING CHEQUE
Please make cheques payable to *Waterstone & Co. Limited* We can only accept sterling cheques drawn on a British bank.

❷ BY CREDIT CARD
Please give us the full credit card number, expiry date, plus the registered billing address for the account if different to the despatch address. We accept Access/Mastercard, American Express, Diner's, and Visa. We will charge your Credit Card when we despatch the books to you.

AMERICAN CUSTOMERS PLEASE NOTE:
If you choose to pay by credit card then there is no need to work out the conversion from dollars to sterling as the credit card company will do this for you automatically charging you in dollars even though you have ordered books priced in sterling.

❸ BY BOOK TOKEN
In addition to Waterstone's Book Vouchers, we will accept Book Tokens as payment or part-payment of an order.

❹ OTHER METHODS
We also accept: Travellers' Cheques, British Postal Orders, International Money Orders (in Sterling).

AVAILABILITY

We try to keep in stock as many of the titles listed in our catalogues as we can. Sometimes, however, we have to order books directly from the publishers which can take an additional two weeks. If any title has gone out of print or is reprinting we will advise you by post. Should the money enclosed with your order result in a surplus due to the unavailability of some of the books we will send you a credit voucher which you can use for your next order. Alternatively, should you require a cheque or credit card refund, please let us know.

PRICE

Although every care is taken in the preparation of our catalogues, we cannot guarantee the prices of all the titles listed since the publishers quite frequently increase them without warning. If the price increase is less than 20% we will send you the books anyway either charging your credit card the additional cost or asking for a further cheque to cover it. Should the price increase exceed 20% we will inform you immediately and ask you whether you still require the books.

GUARANTEE

If a book arrives in a faulty or damaged condition please let us know immediately so that we can replace it.

POSTAGE & PACKAGING RATES

To calculate the full cost of your order you can use the table below.

How to calculate your postage charge
❶ Add up the cost of your books
❷ Using the left hand column follow the table across until you

coincide with the destination of your order and the method by which you want it sent. For example; the cost of sending **£18.95** of books by Air-Speeded Post to the US would be **£4.80**
❸ Add the postage amount to the cost of your books and you will arrive at the total cost of your order.

VALUE OF ORDER	UK	EUROPE		USA		REST OF WORLD	
Up to	:	Surface	Air	Air-Speeded	Airmail	Surface	Airmail
£10	2.10	2.70	6.00	3.00	6.35	2.70	6.70
£20	3.00	4.40	9.00	4.80	10.35	4.40	10.70
£30	3.50	5.20	12.00	6.60	14.35	5.20	14.70
£40	4.00	6.50	15.00	8.40	18.35	6.50	18.70
£50	4.50	7.80	18.00	10.20	22.35	7.80	22.70
Increment per £10 extra	£0.50	£1.30	£3.00	£1.80	£4.00	£1.80	£4.00

WATERSTONE'S BOOKSELLERS · ORDER FORM

MAIL ORDER DIVISION · 4 MILSOM STREET BATH BA1 1DA · ☎ 0225 448595 · FAX: 0225 444732

ORDERED BY: Please write your permanent address
PLEASE PRINT

NAME

ADDRESS

POSTCODE/ZIPCODE

COUNTRY

SEND TO: if different from ordered by
PLEASE PRINT

NAME

ADDRESS

POSTCODE/ZIPCODE

COUNTRY

BOOK REF. NO.	AUTHOR	TITLE	PUBLISHER	EDITION	QTY	PRICE

METHOD OF PAYMENT

❶ **I enclose (PLEASE TICK)**

£ CHEQUE/MONEY ORDER ☐ CREDIT CARD (see below) ☐
OTHER ☐ (Please specify) _____

❷ **Credit Cards (PLEASE TICK)**

ACCESS/MASTERCHARGE ☐ VISA ☐ DINERS ☐ AMEX ☐

☐☐☐☐☐☐☐☐☐☐☐☐☐☐☐☐

EXPIRY DATE

TOTAL BOOKS _____

POSTAGE & PACKING:
please see overleaf for postal charges

IF OUTSIDE UK ☐ _____
AIR MAIL ☐ _____
SURFACE ☐ _____
(USA only) AIR SPEEDED ☐ _____

TOTAL AMOUNT ENCLOSED _____

DATE _____

SIGNATURE

For full details of how to pay please turn over

Registered as Waterstone & Co. Limited Registered in England No. 1706696 Registered Address 121/125 Charing Cross Road London WC2

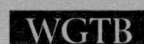
WGTB

WATERSTONE'S BOOKSELLERS · ORDER FORM

MAIL ORDER DIVISION · 4 MILSOM STREET BATH BA1 1DA · ☎ 0225 448595 · FAX: 0225 444732

HOW TO ORDER

❶ BY MAIL

Please complete an order form. Please write clearly and quote the full reference number from the catalogue entry. Post and packing costs can be calculated from the table below and should be added to the total.

❷ BY TELEPHONE

Please telephone your order on 0225 448595, quoting the details of the books you require (24 hour telephone answering service).

❸ BY FAX

You can fax your orders to us on 0225 444732.

TO ORDER BOOKS NOT LISTED IN THE GUIDE

We will supply any British book in print. Complete the order form in the same way giving author, title, and publisher and return it to us.

SPECIAL NOTE

Books bought from a United Kingdom bookseller are free of Value Added Tax and any other sales tax.

HOW TO PAY

❶ BY STERLING CHEQUE

Please make cheques payable to *Waterstone & Co. Limited* We can only accept sterling cheques drawn on a British bank.

❷ BY CREDIT CARD

Please give us the full credit card number, expiry date, plus the registered billing address for the account if different to the despatch address. We accept Access/Mastercard, American Express, Diner's, and Visa. We will charge your Credit Card when we despatch the books to you.

AMERICAN CUSTOMERS PLEASE NOTE:
If you choose to pay by credit card then there is no need to work out the conversion from dollars to sterling as the credit card company will do this for you automatically charging you in dollars even though you have ordered books priced in sterling.

❸ BY BOOK TOKEN

In addition to Waterstone's Book Vouchers, we will accept Book Tokens as payment or part-payment of an order.

❹ OTHER METHODS

We also accept: Travellers' Cheques, British Postal Orders, International Money Orders (in Sterling).

AVAILABILITY

We try to keep in stock as many of the titles listed in our catalogues as we can. Sometimes, however, we have to order books directly from the publishers which can take an additional two weeks. If any title has gone out of print or is reprinting we will advise you by post. Should the money enclosed with your order result in a surplus due to the unavailability of some of the books we will send you a credit voucher which you can use for your next order. Alternatively, should you require a cheque or credit card refund, please let us know.

PRICE

Although every care is taken in the preparation of our catalogues, we cannot guarantee the prices of all the titles listed since the publishers quite frequently increase them without warning. If the price increase is less than 20% we will send you the books anyway either charging your credit card the additional cost or asking for a further cheque to cover it. Should the price increase exceed 20% we will inform you immediately and ask you whether you still require the books.

GUARANTEE

If a book arrives in a faulty or damaged condition please let us know immediately so that we can replace it.

POSTAGE & PACKAGING RATES

To calculate the full cost of your order you can use the table below.

How to calculate your postage charge
❶ Add up the cost of your books
❷ Using the left hand column follow the table across until you coincide with the destination of your order and the method by which you want it sent. For example; the cost of sending £18.95 of books by Air-Speeded Post to the US would be **£4.80**
❸ Add the postage amount to the cost of your books and you will arrive at the total cost of your order.

VALUE OF ORDER	UK	EUROPE		USA		REST OF WORLD	
Up to	:	Surface	Air	Air-Speeded	Airmail	Surface	Airmail
£10	2.10	2.70	6.00	3.00	6.35	2.70	6.70
£20	3.00	4.40	9.00	4.80	10.35	4.40	10.70
£30	3.50	5.20	12.00	6.60	14.35	5.20	14.70
£40	4.00	6.50	15.00	8.40	18.35	6.50	18.70
£50	4.50	7.80	18.00	10.20	22.35	7.80	22.70
Increment per £10 extra	£0.50	£1.30	£3.00	£1.80	£4.00	£1.80	£4.00

WATERSTONE'S BOOKSELLERS · ORDER FORM

MAIL ORDER DIVISION · 4 MILSOM STREET BATH BA1 1DA · ☎ 0225 448595 · FAX: 0225 444732

ORDERED BY: Please write your permanent address
PLEASE PRINT

NAME

ADDRESS

POSTCODE/ZIPCODE

COUNTRY

SEND TO: if different from ordered by
PLEASE PRINT

NAME

ADDRESS

POSTCODE/ZIPCODE

COUNTRY

BOOK REF. NO.	AUTHOR	TITLE	PUBLISHER	EDITION	QTY	PRICE

METHOD OF PAYMENT

❶ I enclose (PLEASE TICK)

£ CHEQUE/MONEY ORDER ☐ CREDIT CARD (see below) ☐
OTHER ☐ (Please specify) _____

❷ Credit Cards (PLEASE TICK)

ACCESS/MASTERCHARGE ☐ VISA ☐ DINERS ☐ AMEX ☐

☐☐☐☐☐☐☐☐☐☐☐☐☐☐☐☐

EXPIRY DATE

TOTAL BOOKS _____

POSTAGE & PACKING:
please see overleaf for postal charges

IF OUTSIDE UK ☐ _____
AIR MAIL ☐ _____
SURFACE ☐ _____
(USA only) AIR SPEEDED ☐ _____

TOTAL AMOUNT ENCLOSED _____

DATE _____

SIGNATURE

For full details of how to pay please turn over

Registered as Waterstone & Co. Limited *Registered in England* No. 1700090 Registered Address 121/125 Charing Cross Road London WC2

WATERSTONE'S BOOKSELLERS · ORDER FORM

MAIL ORDER DIVISION · 4 MILSOM STREET BATH BA1 1DA · ☎ 0225 448595 · FAX: 0225 444732

HOW TO ORDER

❶ BY MAIL
Please complete an order form. Please write clearly and quote the full reference number from the catalogue entry. Post and packing costs can be calculated from the table below and should be added to the total.

❷ BY TELEPHONE
Please telephone your order on 0225 448595, quoting the details of the books you require (24 hour telephone answering service).

❸ BY FAX
You can fax your orders to us on 0225 444732.

TO ORDER BOOKS NOT LISTED IN THE GUIDE
We will supply any British book in print. Complete the order form in the same way giving author, title, and publisher and return it to us.

SPECIAL NOTE
Books bought from a United Kingdom bookseller are free of Value Added Tax and any other sales tax.

HOW TO PAY

❶ BY STERLING CHEQUE
Please make cheques payable to *Waterstone & Co. Limited* We can only accept sterling cheques drawn on a British bank.

❷ BY CREDIT CARD
Please give us the full credit card number, expiry date, plus the registered billing address for the account if different to the despatch address. We accept Access/Mastercard, American Express, Diner's, and Visa. We will charge your Credit Card when we despatch the books to you.

AMERICAN CUSTOMERS PLEASE NOTE:
If you choose to pay by credit card then there is no need to work out the conversion from dollars to sterling as the credit card company will do this for you automatically charging you in dollars even though you have ordered books priced in sterling.

❸ BY BOOK TOKEN
In addition to Waterstone's Book Vouchers, we will accept Book Tokens as payment or part-payment of an order.

❹ OTHER METHODS
We also accept: Travellers' Cheques, British Postal Orders, International Money Orders (in Sterling).

AVAILABILITY
We try to keep in stock as many of the titles listed in our catalogues as we can. Sometimes, however, we have to order books directly from the publishers which can take an additional two weeks. If any title has gone out of print or is reprinting we will advise you by post. Should the money enclosed with your order result in a surplus due to the unavailability of some of the books we will send you a credit voucher which you can use for your next order. Alternatively, should you require a cheque or credit card refund, please let us know.

PRICE
Although every care is taken in the preparation of our catalogues, we cannot guarantee the prices of all the titles listed since the publishers quite frequently increase them without warning. If the price increase is less than 20% we will send you the books anyway either charging your credit card the additional cost or asking for a further cheque to cover it. Should the price increase exceed 20% we will inform you immediately and ask you whether you still require the books.

GUARANTEE
If a book arrives in a faulty or damaged condition please let us know immediately so that we can replace it.

POSTAGE & PACKAGING RATES

To calculate the full cost of your order you can use the table below.

How to calculate your postage charge
❶ Add up the cost of your books
❷ Using the left hand column follow the table across until you coincide with the destination of your order and the method by which you want it sent. For example; the cost of sending £18.95 of books by Air-Speeded Post to the US would be £4.80
❸ Add the postage amount to the cost of your books and you will arrive at the total cost of your order.

VALUE OF ORDER	UK	EUROPE		USA		REST OF WORLD	
Up to	:	Surface	Air	Air-Speeded	Airmail	Surface	Airmail
£10	2.10	2.70	6.00	3.00	6.35	2.70	6.70
£20	3.00	4.40	9.00	4.80	10.35	4.40	10.70
£30	3.50	5.20	12.00	6.60	14.35	5.20	14.70
£40	4.00	6.50	15.00	8.40	18.35	6.50	18.70
£50	4.50	7.80	18.00	10.20	22.35	7.80	22.70
Increment per £10 extra	£0.50	£1.30	£3.00	£1.80	£4.00	£1.80	£4.00

WELLS, H.G. (British, 1886 - 1946)
Wells was the originator of many of SF's key concepts - the Time Machine, the Invading Alien, the Atom Bomb. His books are superbly written, often laden with 'messages' about the moral use of science, but ultimately optimistic and always compelling.
The First Men in the Moon
[GL554] Penguin pbk **£3.95**
The Invisible Man
[GL555] Pan pbk **£2.50**
The Time Machine
[GL556] Pan pbk **£2.50**
The War of the Worlds
[GL557] Pan pbk **£2.99**

WILLIAMS, WALTER JON (US, 1953 -)
A new American writer, likened to Roger Zelazny, whose *Cyberpunk* novel, *Hardwired*, is one of the best representatives of the sub-genre.
Ambassador of Progress
[GL558] Futura pbk **£3.50**
Knight Moves
[GL559] Futura pbk **£2.95**
NOVELS OF HUMAN DESTINY
1: Hardwired
[GL560] Futura pbk **£3.50**
2: Voice of the Whirlwind NEW
[GL561] Orbit hbk **£11.95**
[GL562] Orbit pbk **£6.99**

WILSON, COLIN (British, 1931 -)
Wilson is the author of many non-fiction works on the occult, psychology and crime. He has turned his hand to an exciting SF adventure reinforced by his own theories about mankind's future evolution.
THE SPIDERWORLD SAGA
1: The Tower
[GL563] Grafton pbk **£6.95**
2: The Delta
[GL564] Grafton pbk **£6.95**

WINGROVE, DAVID
Chung Kuo NEW
The first book of a 7-volume future history, epic in scope and powerfully dramatic.
[GL565] NEL hbk **£13.95**

WOLFE, GENE (US, 1931 -)
Wolfe is one of the finest prose-writers working in the genre. His semi-autobiographical novel, *Peace*, uses time travel as a metaphor for memory. See also *Fantasy*.
Peace
[GL566] NEL pbk **£2.99**
The Fifth Head of Cerberus
[GL567] Arrow pbk **£1.75**
The Island of Doctor Death & Other Stories
[GL568] Arrow pbk **£2.25**
There Are Doors NEW
[GL569] Gollancz hbk **£11.95**

WOMACK, JACK (US)
"Totally unexpected...syncs ultraviolent cyberpunk tropes with an achingly nostalgic alternate world/time travel riff" (William Gibson).
Ambient
[GL570] Unwin pbk **£2.95**
Terraplane NEW
[GL571] Unwin hbk **£10.95**

WRIGHT, HELEN
Wright is a talented newcomer whose work recalls that of C.J. Cherryh.
A Matter of Oaths NEW
[GL572] Methuen pbk **£2.50**

WYNDHAM, JOHN (British, 1903 - 1969)
Wyndham is known as the writer of the British

disaster novel *par excellence*. His matter of fact heroes cope with blindness, killer plants and alien invaders in unambiguous adventure stories of 'apocalypse tamed'.
Chocky
[GL573] Penguin pbk **£2.25**
Consider Her Ways & Others
[GL574] Penguin pbk **£2.50**
The Chrysalids
[GL575] Penguin pbk **£2.50**
The Day of the Triffids
[GL576] Penguin pbk **£2.95**
The Kraken Wakes
[GL577] Penguin pbk **£2.50**
The Midwich Cuckoos
[GL578] Penguin pbk **£2.50**
The Trouble with Lichen
[GL579] Penguin pbk **£2.50**
Web
[GL580] Penguin pbk **£1.95**

ZAMYATIN, Y. (USSR, 1884 - 1937)
We
Written in the 1920s, published in the West in the 1950s, and still unpublished in the USSR, *We* is a classic judgment on a utopia gone wrong, and was a major influence on Huxley's *Brave New World* and Orwell's *1984*.
[GL581] Penguin pbk **£3.50**

ZELAZNY, ROGER (US, 1937 -)
His dark, densely-plotted novels and stories, mythically resonant and poetically written, have deservedly won many of SF's most coveted awards.
Dream Master
[GL582] Methuen pbk **£1.95**
Isle of the Dead
[GL583] Mandarin pbk **£2.50**
Lord of Light
[GL584] Methuen pbk **£2.50**
The Doors of His Face, The Lamps of His Mind & Other Stories
[GL585] Methuen pbk **£2.50**
This Immortal
[GL586] Mandarin pbk **£1.95**

ZINDELL, DAVID
Zindell's work has been compared to Herbert's *Dune* for its imaginative sweep and technical virtuosity.
Neverness NEW
[GL587] Grafton hbk **£12.95**
[GL588] Grafton pbk **£7.95**

FANTASY FICTION

Anthologies

DATLOW, ELLEN & WINDLING, TERRI (EDS.)
Demons and Dreams: The Best Fantasy and Horror
[GL590] Century hbk **£11.95**
[GL591] Century pbk **£5.95**

JONES, STEPHEN (ED)
Fantasy Tales Vol 1
Fantasy Tales is Britain's best-selling paperback magazine of fantasy and terror; each of these issues contains new stories from major writers in the genre.
[GL592] Robinson pbk **£0.99**
Vol 2
[GL593] Robinson pbk **£0.99**
Vol 3 NEW
[GL594] Robinson pbk **£0.99**

Writers A - Z

ANTHONY, PIERS (US, 1934 -)
A prolific author with a wicked sense of humour and a predelection for bad puns. See also *Science Fiction*.
Castle Roogna
[GL595] Futura hbk **£3.50**
Centaur Aisle
[GL596] Futura pbk **£3.50**
Crewel Lye
[GL597] Futura pbk **£3.50**
Dragon on a Pedestal
[GL598] Futura pbk **£2.50**
Golem in the Gears
[GL599] Futura pbk **£2.95**
Ogre Ogre
[GL600] Futura pbk **£3.50**
Source of Magic
[GL601] Futura pbk **£2.95**
Spell for Chameleon
[GL602] Futura pbk **£2.95**
MAGIC OF XANTU TRILOGY
1: Vale of the Vole
[GL603] NEL pbk **£6.95**
2: Heavencent NEW
[GL604] NEL pbk **£10.95**
[GL605] NEL pbk **£6.95**

ASIMOV, ISAAC
Azazel NEW
Humourous fantasy from one of the masters of SF; this collection of stories follows the adventures of a two-centimetre tall fiery red imp, and his discoverer.
[GL606] Doubleday hbk **£10.95**

BEAR, G.
See also *Science Fiction*.
Serpent Mage
[GL607] Arrow pbk **£2.99**

BLAYLOCK, JAMES P. (US)
An original author, grounded in the classics of the genre, yet always ready to astonish.
Land of Dreams
[GL608] Grafton hbk **£2.99**
The Digging Leviathan
[GL609] Grafton pbk **£3.50**
The Disappearing Dwarf
[GL610] Grafton pbk **£3.50**
The Elfin Ship
[GL611] Grafton pbk **£3.99**
The Last Coin NEW
[GL612] Grafton hbk **£12.95**
[GL613] Grafton pbk **£7.95**

BRADLEY, MARION ZIMMER (US, 1930 -)
See also *Science Fiction*. As well as her SF-based *Darkover* series, Bradley has re-interpreted Arthurian and classical myth. She has also edited a series of anthologies on women and heroic fiction, the *Sword & Sorceress* titles.
Mist Over Avalon
[GL614] Sphere pbk **£3.99**
The Firebrand
[GL615] Sphere pbk **£3.99**
(EDITED)
Sword & Sorceress Vol 1
[GL616] Headline pbk **£2.95**
Vol 2
[GL617] Headline pbk **£2.95**
Vol 3
[GL618] Headline pbk **£2.95**

BROOKS, TERRY (US, 1944 -)
His years as an attorney gave Brooks a ready wit and strong sense of plot. His adventurous stories have

Isaac Asimov, author of *Azazel* (Doubleday hbk £10.95) and *Robot Dreams* (Victor Gollancz pbk £3.50)

FICTION

achieved great popularity.
MAGIC KINGDOM OF LANDOVER SERIES
1: Magic Kingdom For Sale/Sold
[GL619] Futura pbk **£3.50**
2: The Black Unicorn
[GL620] Futura hbk **£2.99**
3: Wizard at Large
[GL621] Futura pbk **£4.99**
SHANNARA SERIES
1: The Sword of Shannara
[GL622] Futura pbk **£3.95**
2: The Elfstones of Shannara
[GL623] Futura pbk **£3.99**
3: Wishsong of Shannara
[GL624] Futura pbk **£3.99**

CAMP, L. SPRAGUE DE & PRATT, FLETCHER
The Intrepid Enchanter
[GL625] Sphere pbk **£4.50**

CARD, O.S. (US)
A practising Mormon, Card's combination of adventure and morality is reminiscent of C.S. Lewis. His major theme is the rite of passage to a new maturity.
Hart's Hope
[GL626] Unwin pbk **£2.95**
Wyrms
[GL627] Arrow hbk **£3.50**
THE TALES OF ALVIN MAKER
1: Seventh Son
This series purports to be a 'spiritual biography' of Joseph Smith, founder of the Church of Latterday Saints. Four more volumes are promised. The 7th son of a 7th son comes of age in a United States where folk magic is real.
[GL628] Arrow pbk **£3.50**
2: Red Prophet NEW
[GL629] Arrow hbk **£11.95**
[GL630] Arrow pbk **£5.95**

CHERRYH, C.J. (US, 1942 -)
See also *Science Fiction*.
1: Chronicles of Morgaine
An omnibus edition of *Gate of Ivrel*, *Well of Shinan* & *Fires of Azeroth*.
[GL631] Mandarin hbk **£4.99**
2: Exile's Gate NEW
The white-haired and deadly Morgaine returns with a new adventure, in which she finds love and meets a friend of her father's.
[GL632] Mandarin hbk **£3.99**

Port Eternity NEW
A vivid and powerful fantasy which blends Arthurian legend with high-tech space adventure.
[GL633] Gollancz pbk **£2.99**
The Dreamstone
[GL634] Gollancz pbk **£2.50**
Tree of Sword & Jewels
[GL635] Gollancz pbk **£2.95**

CONSTANTINE, STORM
WRAETHTHU
1: The Enchanters of Flesh and Spirit
[GL636] Orbit pbk **£3.95**
2: The Bewitchments of Love and Hate
[GL637] Orbit pbk **£4.99**

COOPER, LOUISE (British)
"The person I like to read most is Louise Cooper, because she is so incredibly cinematic, and has a power of structural climax". (Tanith Lee).
INDIGO SERIES
1: Nemesis
[GL638] Unwin pbk **£3.50**
2: Mirage
[GL639] Unwin pbk **£2.95**
3: Infanta NEW
[GL640] Unwin pbk **£3.50**
TIME MASTER
1: The Initiate
[GL641] Unwin pbk **£2.95**
2: The Master
[GL642] Unwin pbk **£2.95**
3: The Outcast
[GL643] Unwin pbk **£2.95**

COOPER, SUSAN (British, 1935 -)
An unsentimental and skilful writer. Cooper's works, based on Anglo-Celtic mythology, are nominally for teenagers but can be read with pleasure at any age. *The Dark is Rising* is an anthology of 5 novels that deal with young people coming to maturity as well as the continuing struggle between Dark and Light.
The Dark is Rising (Sequence)
[GL644] Puffin pbk **£5.95**

CROWLEY, JOHN (US, 1942 -)
A difficult but rewarding writer, who seems to take as his motto Benedetto Croce's *"All history is fiction, just as all fiction is history"*.
Aegypt
A quest for hermetic philosophy in an alternate history. A difficult and ambiguous book; this is the first in a projected series exploring the secret history of our world.
[GL645] Gollancz pbk **£3.95**
Beasts
[GL646] Gollancz pbk **£3.95**
Little Big
[GL647] Methuen pbk **£3.95**

DEITZ, TOM
Fireshaper's Doom
[GL648] Futura pbk **£3.50**
Windmaster's Bane
[GL649] Futura pbk **£3.50**

DELANY, SAMUEL (US, 1942 -)
The episodic heroic fantasy of the *Neveryon* books attempts to stretch the limits of the genre; incorporating linguistics, anthropology and the holistic perception of economic and political organization as found in the French historian Braudel. Delany describes it as a 'dark comedy about the intricate relations of sex, narrative and power'.
NEVERYON SERIES
1: Tales of Neveryon
[GL650] Grafton pbk **£3.50**
2: Neveryona
[GL651] Grafton pbk **£3.99**

3: Flight from Neveryon NEW
[GL652] Grafton pbk **£3.99**
4: Return to Neveryon NEW
[GL653] Grafton pbk **£3.99**

DONALDSON, STEPHEN (US, 1947 -)
Often compared to Tolkien, Donaldson's work is massively realised with splendid baroque detail.
Daughter of Regals and Other Tales
[GL654] Fontana pbk **£3.95**
MORDANT'S NEED
1: Mirror of Her Dreams
In this diptych Donaldson is more reminiscent of a verbose Hambly than of Tolkien.
[GL655] Fontana pbk **£3.95**
2: A Man Rides Through
[GL656] Fontana pbk **£4.95**
THE FIRST CHRONICLES OF THOMAS COVENANT
1: Lord Foul's Bane
[GL657] Fontana pbk **£3.50**
2: The Illearth War
[GL658] Fontana pbk **£3.95**
3: The Power That Preserves
[GL659] Fontana pbk **£3.95**
THE SECOND CHRONICLES OF THOMAS COVENANT
1: The Wounded Land
[GL660] Fontana pbk **£3.95**
2: The One Tree
[GL661] Fontana pbk **£3.95**
3: White Gold Wielder
[GL662] Fontana pbk **£3.95**

EDDINGS, DAVID (US, 1931 -)
This massively popular fantasy series shows flawed and therefore human characters staggering under the weight of being both person and archetype. The plot and settings may be standard, the characters and their interaction are not.
ELENIUM SERIES
1: The Diamond Throne
[GL663] Grafton pbk **£6.99**
1: The Diamond Throne NEW
The first book in a new series unrelated to his others: *"A troll discovers a marvellous diamond..."*
[GL664] Grafton hbk **£11.95**
THE BELGARIAD SEQUENCE
1: Pawn of Prophecy
[GL665] Transworld hbk **£2.99**
2: Queen of Sorcery
[GL666] Transworld pbk **£2.99**
3: Magician's Gambit
[GL667] Transworld pbk **£2.99**
4: Castle of Wizardry
[GL668] Transworld pbk **£2.99**

C.J. Cherryh, author of *Port Eternity* (Victor Gollancz pbk £2.99)

5: Enchanters' End Game
[GL669] Corgi pbk **£3.50**
THE MALLOREON SEQUENCE
1: Guardians of the West
[GL670] Corgi pbk **£3.50**
2: King of the Murgos
[GL671] Corgi hbk **£3.95**
3: Demon Lord of Karanda `NEW`
[GL672] Bantam **£11.95**
[GL673] Bantam pbk **£6.95**
4: The Sorceress of Darshiva `NEW`
[GL674] Bantam hbk **£11.95**

EMSHWILLER, C. (US, 1921 -)
Largely a writer of SF short stories, this fantasy is a departure for Emshwiller. In it an ex-golden setter (yes, a dog) and the Womens' movement try to find out why women are turning into animals and vice versa.
Carmendog
[GL675] Women's P pbk **£4.95**

FEIST, RAYMOND
A splendidly detailed world and a sure hand with plot have justifiably made Feist very popular.
Faerie Tale `NEW`
[GL676] Grafton pbk **£6.95**
THE RIFTWAR SAGA
1: Silverthorn
[GL677] Grafton pbk **£3.50**
2: Magician
[GL678] Grafton pbk **£3.95**
3: Darkness at Sethanon
[GL679] Grafton pbk **£3.95**
4: Prince of the Blood `NEW`
[GL680] Grafton hbk **£12.95**
[GL681] Grafton pbk **£7.95**

FEIST, RAYMOND & WURTS, JANNY
Daughter of Empire
[GL682] Grafton pbk **£3.99**

GEMMELL, DAVID (British, 1948 -)
A background of Celtic mythology is used to great effect in these Sword and Sorcery novels.
Knights of Dark Renown `NEW`
[GL683] Century **£11.95**
[GL684] Century pbk **£5.95**
The Last Guardian `NEW`
[GL685] Legend hbk **£11.95**
[GL686] Legend pbk **£5.95**
DRENAI SERIES
1: Legend
[GL687] Arrow pbk **£3.99**
2: King Beyond the Gate
[GL688] Arrow pbk **£3.50**
3: Waylander
[GL689] Arrow pbk **£3.99**
SIPSTRASSI SERIES
1: Wolf in Shadow
[GL690] Arrow pbk **£3.50**
2: Ghost King
[GL691] Legend pbk **£3.50**
3: Last Sword of Power `NEW`
[GL692] Legend pbk **£3.50**

GORDON, STUART (British, 1947 -)
Contemporary characters, including a London social worker, must take sides in a battle of the Gods. Cathar France provides a fascinating backdrop.
THE WATCHERS
1: Archon
[GL693] Orbit pbk **£3.50**
2: Hidden World
[GL694] Orbit pbk **£2.99**
3: Azazel `NEW`
[GL695] Macdonald hbk **£11.95**

GREGORIAN, JOYCE BALLON
TREDANA TRILOGY
1: The Broken Citadel `NEW`
The first of a trilogy which opens with a young girl slipping into another world.
[GL696] Futura pbk **£4.99**

GUIN, URSULA LE (US, 1929 -)
See also *Science Fiction* for this powerful and influential writer. The *Earthsea* trilogy is a sensitive story of coming to terms with responsibility and death, set in a magical world of sea, swords and sorcery. *Malafrena* reads like a historical romance, but one set in an imaginary 'middle European' country where revolution is planned.
Always Coming Home
[GL697] Grafton pbk **£5.95**
Earthsea Trilogy
[GL698] Penguin hbk **£4.95**
Malafrena
[GL699] Grafton pbk **£1.95**

HAMBLY, BARBARA (US)
Likeable characters, a feel for politics and a masterly touch with menace make Hambly's novels a joy to read and re-read.
1: Ladies of Mandrigyn
[GL700] Unwin pbk **£2.95**
2: The Witches of Wenshar
[GL701] Unwin pbk **£2.95**
1: Silicon Mage
[GL702] Unwin pbk **£2.95**
2: Silent Tower `NEW`
[GL703] Unwin pbk **£2.95**
Dragonsbane
[GL704] Unwin pbk **£2.95**
DARWATH TRILOGY
1: Time of the Dark
[GL705] Unwin pbk **£2.95**
2: Walls of the Air
[GL706] Unwin pbk **£2.95**
3: Armies of Daylight
[GL707] Unwin pbk **£2.95**

HARRISON, M. JOHN
"The best fantasy is terra incognita. The reader is first lured into it, and then abandoned". Harrison's fiction is a weird mixture of narrative discontinuities and Sword & Sorcery - Borges crossed with Ballard and Burroughs.
Climbers `NEW`
A novel based on rock climbing, but really about an escape from the mundane.
[GL708] Gollancz hbk **£11.95**
Pastel City
[GL709] Unwin pbk **£2.95**
Storm of Wings `NEW`
[GL710] Unwin hbk **£2.95**
The Ice Monkey & Other Stories
[GL711] Unwin pbk **£2.95**
Viriconium
In Viriconium and *Viriconium Nights* in one volume.
[GL712] Unwin pbk **£3.95**

HOLDSTOCK, ROBERT (British, 1948 -)
A splendid writer whose prize-winning *Mythago Wood* and *Lavondyss*, its sequel, are inspired by Celtic mythology.
Earthwind
[GL713] Gollancz pbk **£2.95**
Lavondyss `NEW`
[GL714] Gollancz pbk **£6.95**
Mythago Wood
[GL715] Grafton pbk **£2.50**

KAY, GUY GAVRIEL
An impressive new writer, who deserves to be compared to Tolkien, and who, in the *Fionvar Tapestry*, has created a marvellous world: as he

himself has said - *"To be successful in fantasy, you have to take the measure of Tolkien - work with his strengths and away from his weaknesses"*.
FIONVAR TAPESTRY
1: Summer Tree
[GL716] Unicorn pbk **£2.95**
2: The Wandering Fire
[GL717] Unwin pbk **£2.95**
3: The Darkest Road
[GL718] Unwin pbk **£3.50**

KERR, KATHERINE
A standard Celtic myth based fantasy is redeemed by a splendid sense of place, superb dialogue and great narrative pace.
THE DEVERRY SERIES
1: Dawnspell
[GL719] Grafton pbk **£7.95**
2: Daggerspell
[GL720] Grafton pbk **£6.95**
3: Darkspell `NEW`
[GL721] Grafton pbk **£3.99**

KING, BERNARD
Skyfire
[GL722] Sphere pbk **£3.50**
The Destroying Angel
[GL723] Sphere pbk **£3.50**
Time-Fighters
[GL724] Sphere pbk **£3.50**

LAWHEAD, STEPHEN
An overtly Christian fantasy intended to fall into the tradition of Lewis, Williams and Macdonald, set against the background of Roman Britain and the legends of Arthur and Atlantis.
PENDRAGON CYCLE
1: Merlin
[GL725] Lion pbk **£3.50**
2: Taliesin
[GL726] Lion pbk **£3.50**
3: Arthur `NEW`
[GL727] Lion pbk **£3.50**

LEE, TANITH (British, 1947 -)
Lee specializes in the invention and interpretation of myth. Her hard-driving fiction can seem a strange combination of heroic fantasy and the wildest gothic romance.
East of Midnight
[GL728] Arrow pbk **£1.99**
Forests of the Night `NEW`
Lee's own selection of her short fiction.
[GL729] Unwin pbk **£12.95**
Night's Sorceries
[GL730] Arrow pbk **£2.99**
Women as Demons `NEW`
The male perception of women through time and space.
[GL731] Women's P pbk **£4.95**
DEMON LORD TRILOGY
1: Night's Master
[GL732] Arrow pbk **£2.50**
2: Death's Master
[GL733] Arrow pbk **£2.50**
3: Delusion's Master
[GL734] Arrow pbk **£2.50**

LEIBER, FRITZ (US, 1910 -)
Fafhrd and the Gray Mouser are the splendid heroes of Leiber's heroic fantasies. Complex and enjoyable, Leiber's work at once sets the pattern for, and makes fun of, the Sword & Sorcery genre. A seventh story is promised.
SWORDS SERIES
1: Swords & Devilry
[GL735] Grafton pbk **£2.50**
2: Swords Against Death
[GL736] Grafton pbk **£2.50**

Ursula le Guin, author of *Malafrena* (Grafton pbk £1.95) and *Dancing at the Edge of the World* (Victor Gollancz hbk £14.95) (Photo: Lisa Kroeber)

3: Swords in the Mist
[GL737] Grafton pbk **£2.50**
4: Swords Against Wizardry
[GL738] Grafton pbk **£2.50**
5: Swords of Lankhmar
[GL739] Grafton pbk **£2.50**
6: Swords & Ice Magic
[GL740] Grafton pbk **£2.50**

MACAVOY, R.A.
Sentimental without becoming 'twee', her fantasies have vividly-rendered imaginary settings and complex human characters.
BLACK DRAGON SERIES
1: Tea with the Black Dragon
[GL741] Transworld pbk **£1.95**
2: Twisting the Rope
[GL742] Transworld pbk **£2.50**

MCCAFFREY, ANNE
(US, 1926 -)
The *Dragon* books of McCaffrey, though provided with a SF rationale, work best if considered as fantasy. The relationship between men and dragons is well expressed.
DRAGONWORLD SERIES
1: Dragonflight
[GL743] Corgi pbk **£2.95**
2: Dragonquest
[GL744] Corgi pbk **£2.95**
3: Dragonsong
[GL745] Corgi pbk **£2.50**
4: Dragonsinger: Harper of Pern
[GL746] Corgi pbk **£2.50**
5: The White Dragon
[GL747] Corgi pbk **£3.99**
6: Dragondrums
[GL748] Corgi pbk **£2.50**
7: Moreta: Dragonlady of Pern
[GL749] Transworld pbk **£2.95**
8: Dragonsdawn NEW
[GL750] Bantam hbk **£10.95**
[GL751] Bantam pbk **£6.95**

MCDONALD, GEORGE (British, 1824 - 1905)
A strange combination of high Victorian Calvinism and anticipations of Jung and Kafka. See also *Childrens*.
Lilith
[GL752] Lion pbk **£2.50**
Phantastes
[GL753] Lion pbk **£2.50**

MCKILLIP, PATRICIA A.
The thoughtful fantasies of McKillip have strong characters, plots with a twist, and a refreshing humour.
RIDDLE MASTER TRILOGY
1: Riddle Master of Hed
[GL754] Futura pbk **£2.50**
2: Heir of Sea & Fire
[GL755] Futura pbk **£2.50**
3: Harpist in the Wind
[GL756] Futura pbk **£2.50**

MCKINLEY, ROBIN
Her high fantasy and retelling of fairy stories have authentic characters and are told in a muscular but subtle style.
Beauty
[GL757] Futura pbk **£2.50**
Door in the Hedge
[GL758] Futura pbk **£2.50**
CHRONICLES OF DAMAR
1: Blue Sword
[GL759] Futura pbk **£2.50**
2: Hero & the Crown
[GL760] Futura pbk **£2.50**

MCKINLEY, ROBIN (ED)
Imaginary Lands
[GL761] Futura pbk **£3.95**

MOORCOCK, MICHAEL (British, 1939 -)
The conflict of order and chaos is central to the many works of Moorcock. A mixture of Sword & Sorcery, time travel, space opera and literary pastiche, peopled by a cast of weird and wonderful players, Moorcock's novels are hard to describe but can be quite gripping. He also writes 'mainstream' fiction. A selection only of his work appears here.
Between the Wars - Colonel Pyat: Byzantium Endures
[GL762] Flamingo pbk **£3.95**
Gloriana
[GL763] Flamingo pbk **£4.95**
The Bull and the Spear
[GL764] Grafton pbk **£2.99**
The Chronicles of Castle Brass (Omnibus)
[GL765] Grafton pbk **£3.95**
The Chronicles of Corum
[GL766] Grafton pbk **£3.50**
The Dancers at the End of Time (Omnibus)
[GL767] Grafton pbk **£3.95**
The History of the Runestaff (Omnibus)
[GL768] Grafton pbk **£3.95**
The Laughter of Carthage
[GL769] Flamingo pbk **£4.50**
The Nomad of Time (Omnibus)
[GL770] Grafton pbk **£3.50**
The Swords of Corum (Omnibus)
[GL771] Grafton pbk **£3.95**
The Time Dweller
[GL772] Grafton pbk **£2.99**
Wizardry & Wild Romance
Moorcock's descriptive (and sometimes prescriptive) account of fantasy fiction from its beginnings.
[GL773] Gollancz pbk **£2.95**
CORNELIUS CHRONICLES
English Assassin & Condition of Muzak
[GL774] Fontana pbk **£4.95**

Final Programme & Cure for Cancer
[GL775] Fontana pbk **£4.95**
The Adventures of Una Persson and Catherine Cornelius in the 20th Century
[GL776] Grafton pbk **£2.50**
The Lives & Times of Jerry Cornelius
[GL777] Grafton pbk **£2.50**
ELRIC
1: Elric of Melnibone
[GL778] Grafton pbk **£2.99**
2: The Sailor on the Seas of Fate
[GL779] Grafton pbk **£2.50**
3: Weird of the White Wolf
[GL780] Grafton pbk **£2.50**
4: The Vanishing Tower
[GL781] Grafton pbk **£2.50**
5: The Bane of the Black Sword
[GL782] Grafton pbk **£1.95**
6: Stormbringer
[GL783] Grafton pbk **£2.50**
7: Elric at the End of Time
[GL784] Grafton pbk **£2.50**
8: The Fortress of the Pearl NEW
"Lost in the immensities of the Sighing Desert lies the city of Quarzhasaat..." There Elric finds a new quest, in the first new novel in the series in more than a decade.
[GL785] Gollancz hbk **£11.95**

MORWOOD, PETER
The *Alban Saga* forms a competent attack on the oldest of fantasy subjects: a boy growing up to become a world-saving hero.
ALBAN SAGA
1: Horse Lord
[GL786] Arrow pbk **£3.95**
2: Demon Lord
[GL787] Arrow pbk **£3.50**
3: Dragon Lord
[GL788] Arrow pbk **£2.95**
4: The Warlord's Domain NEW
[GL789] Arrow pbk **£5.95**

NORTON, ANDRE (US, 1912 -)
A prolific writer of SF and fantasy, Norton has often been classed as a children's writer. Her novels frequently have teenage heroes and heroines, but can be read with pleasure at any age. Much of the *Witch World* series has now been re-issued by Gollancz.
WITCH WORLD
1: Witch World
[GL790] Gollancz pbk **£2.50**
2: Web of the Witch World
[GL791] Gollancz pbk **£2.50**
3: Year of the Unicorn
[GL792] Gollancz pbk **£2.50**
4: Warlock of the Witchworld
[GL793] Gollancz pbk **£2.50**
5: Three Against Witch World
[GL794] Gollancz pbk **£2.50**
6: Sorceress of the Witch World
[GL795] Gollancz pbk **£2.95**
7: Spell of the Witch World
[GL796] Gollancz pbk **£2.95**
8: Trey of Swords
[GL797] Gollancz pbk **£2.99**
9: Ware Hawk NEW
[GL798] Gollancz pbk **£3.50**
Tales of the Witch World
A selection of short stories by many authors set in Norton's Witchworld.
[GL799] Pan pbk **£3.99**

PEAKE, MERVYN (British, 1911 - 1968)
The *Gormenghast* trilogy is one of the great neglected works of world literature, and not just of fantasy. Interestingly, those who find Tolkien slow, often take to Peake immediately.

GORMENGHAST
1: Titus Groan
[GL800] Methuen pbk **£1.95**
2: Gormenghast
[GL801] Methuen pbk **£2.95**
3: Titus Alone
[GL802] Methuen pbk **£2.95**

PRATCHETT, TERRY (British, 1948 -)
These satires on heroic fantasy are irresistible.
Pratchett's comic genius and charming characters are
displayed in fast-moving plots. The 'Discworld',
carried through space on the back of an enormous
turtle, is a masterful invention.
DISCWORLD
1: The Colour of Magic
[GL803] Corgi pbk **£2.99**
2: Light Fantastic
[GL804] Corgi pbk **£2.99**
3: Equal Rites
[GL805] Corgi pbk **£2.99**
4: Mort
[GL806] Corgi pbk **£2.99**
5: Sourcery
[GL807] Corgi pbk **£2.99**
6: Wyrd Sisters   `NEW`
[GL808] Gollancz hbk **£10.95**
[GL809] Corgi pbk **£2.99**
7: Pyramids   `NEW`
*"It isn't easy being a teenage Pharaoh...all you really
wanted was the chance to do something for young
people and the inner cities"*. A beguiling tale,
also introducing Ibid, a philosopher who thinks himself
the greatest authority on everything.
[GL810] Gollancz hbk **£11.95**
8: Guards! Guards!   `NEW`
*"Of all the cities in the world it could have
flown into, it flew into mine..."*.
[GL811] Gollancz hbk **£11.95**

ROHAN, M.S. (British, 1951 -)
The author lists Wagner and the Vikings among his
interests. Both may be found in this magnificent
trilogy of a world menaced by the encroaching ice.
The author also writes as *Michael Scott*
(see below).
WINTER OF WORLD
1: Anvil of Ice
[GL812] Futura pbk **£3.50**
2: The Forge in the Forest
[GL813] Orbit pbk **£3.50**
3: The Hammer of the Sun   `NEW`
[GL814] Orbit pbk **£3.99**

RUSS, JOANNA
The Adventures of Alyx
[GL815] Women's P pbk **£1.95**

SABERHAGEN, FRED (US, 1930 -)
A technologist and gamester, whose worlds combine
science and magic. See also *Science Fiction*.
Empire of the East
[GL816] Futura pbk **£2.95**
Sightblinders Story   `NEW`
[GL817] Futura pbk **£2.99**
Woundhealer's Story   `NEW`
[GL818] Futura pbk **£3.50**
SWORDS SERIES
1st Book of Swords
[GL819] Futura pbk **£3.50**
2nd Book of Swords
[GL820] Futura pbk **£3.50**
3rd Book of Swords
[GL821] Futura pbk **£2.50**

SCOTT, MICHAEL
TALES OF THE BARD
1: Magician's Law
[GL822] Sphere pbk **£3.50**

2: Demon's Law
[GL823] Sphere pbk **£3.99**
3: Death's Law   `NEW`
[GL824] Sphere pbk **£3.99**

SPEDDING
A fantasic re-evaluation of Alexander the Great's
conquests and their dissolution on his death. The
complex heroine Aleizon Ailix Ayndra is like no
other.
A WALK IN THE DARK TRILOGY
1: The Road and the Hills   `NEW`
[GL825] Unwin pbk **£3.95**
2: A Cloud over Water   `NEW`
[GL826] Unwin pbk **£3.95**
3: The Streets of the City   `NEW`
[GL827] Unwin pbk **£3.95**

TEPPER, S. SHERI
*"I don't know which I like more, the worlds she
creates or the way she writes about them"* (Stephen
Donaldson).
Blood Heritage
[GL828] Corgi pbk **£2.95**
Chronicles of Marvin Manyshaped
[GL829] Corgi pbk **£3.99**
Dervish Daughter
[GL830] Corgi pbk **£2.75**
Enigma Score
[GL831] Corgi pbk **£3.50**
Jinian Footseer
[GL832] Corgi pbk **£2.50**
The Awakeners
[GL833] Corgi pbk **£3.99**
The Bones
[GL834] Corgi pbk **£2.95**
The Gate to Women's Country
[GL835] Transworld pbk **£6.95**
The Revenants
[GL836] Corgi pbk **£2.95**

TOLKIEN, J.R.R. (British, 1892 - 1973)
*"Fantasy, the making or glimpsing of Other Worlds,
was the heart of the desire of Faerie. I desired
dragons with a profound desire"*. Tolkien is the doyen
and exemplar of fantasy fiction. It is unlikely that
without the massive success of *The Lord of the Rings*
there would have been such an interest in, and so
wide a production of, fantasy. Seldom can so detailed
a secondary world have been created, and never for so
esoteric a purpose: Tolkien created Middle Earth and
its inhabitants to provide a setting and speakers for
the Elvish languages he had devised.
Adventures of Tom Bombadil
[GL838] Unwin pbk **£5.95**
Farmer Giles of Ham
[GL839] Unwin pbk **£1.75**
Smith of Wootton Major/Leaf by Niggle
[GL840] Unwin pbk **£1.75**
The Hobbit (1937)
The deluxe edition is illustrated by Michael Hague.
[GL841] Unwin deluxe hbk **£20.00**
[GL842] Unwin hbk **£14.95**
[GL843] Unwin pbk **£2.50**

The Misty Mountains from *The Hobbit* (Unwin
Hyman hbk £14.95, pbk £2.50)

The Hobbit: The Annotated Edition `NEW`
Annotations by Douglas A. Anderson; many
illustrations by Tolkien and others. Appendix of
revisions, comprehensive gloss.
[GL844] Unwin hbk **£14.95**
Tree and Leaf
[GL845] Unwin pbk **£7.95**
LORD OF THE RINGS
Vol 1: The Fellowship of the Ring
[GL846] Unwin hbk **£10.95**
[GL847] Unwin pbk **£3.50**
Vol 2: The Two Towers
[GL848] Unwin hbk **£10.95**
[GL849] Unwin pbk **£3.50**
Vol 3: The Return of the King
[GL850] Unwin hbk **£10.95**
[GL851] Unwin pbk **£3.50**
Vols 1, 2 & 3
[GL852] Unwin pbk **£8.95**
The Silmarillion (1977)
Tolkien was working on *The Silmarillion* when he
died. Like the series of Chronicles of Middle Earth,
the published version was completed and put together
by his son Christopher.
[GL853] Unwin hbk **£11.95**
[GL854] Unwin pbk **£3.95**
THE CHRONICLES OF MIDDLE EARTH
1: The Book of Lost Tales: Vol 1
[GL855] Unwin pbk **£3.95**
2: The Book of Lost Tales: Vol 2
[GL837] Unwin pbk **£4.50**
3: Lays of Beleriand
[GL856] Unwin hbk **£18.95**
[GL857] Unwin pbk **£3.95**
4: The Shaping of Middle Earth
[GL858] Unwin pbk **£4.95**
5: Unfinished Tales
[GL859] Unwin hbk **£15.95**
[GL860] Unwin pbk **£4.95**
6: The Lost Road & Other Writings
[GL861] Unwin hbk **£17.95**
7: The Return of the Shadow
[GL862] Unwin **£17.95**
8: Treason in Isengard   `NEW`
[GL863] Unwin hbk **£17.95**

TOLSTOY, NICOLAI
The Coming of the King
The first book of a projected Merlin trilogy, which has
proved very popular.
[GL864] Bantam hbk **£12.95**
[GL865] Corgi pbk **£4.50**

VANCE, JACK (US, 1920 -)
Vance's dry wit is hidden by the glittering surface of
his baroque plots. The lush sensuality of the worlds he
conjures up is matched by a vivid and elegant prose
style.
Cugel's Saga
[GL866] Grafton pbk **£2.50**
Lyonesse
[GL867] Grafton pbk **£3.95**
Lyonesse 2: The Green Pearl
[GL868] Grafton pbk **£3.99**
Rhial to the Marvellous
[GL869] Grafton pb **£1.95**
The Dying Earth
[GL870] Grafton pbk **£1.95**
The Eyes of the Overworld
[GL871] Grafton pbk **£1.95**

WEIS, M. & HICKMAN, T. (US)
From the creators of *Dungeons & Dragons* come a
series of fast-moving Sword & Sorcery epics.
DARKSWORD
1: Forging of the Darksword
[GL872] Bantam pbk **£3.50**
2: Doom of the Dark Sword
[GL873] Bantam **£3.50**

3: Triumph of the Darksword **NEW**
[GL874] Bantam pbk £3.50
DRAGON LANCE CHRONICLES
1: Dragons of the Autumn Twilight
[GL875] Penguin hbk £3.50
2: Dragons of Winter Night
[GL876] Penguin pbk £3.50
3: Dragons of Spring Dawning
[GL877] Penguin pbk £3.50
Chronicles Omnibus
[GL878] Penguin pbk £7.99
DRAGON LANCE LEGENDS
1: Time of the Twins
[GL879] Penguin pbk £3.95
2: War of the Twins
[GL880] Penguin pbk £3.95
3: Test of the Twins
[GL881] Penguin pbk £3.50
DRAGON LANCE TALES
1: The Magic of Krynn
[GL882] Penguin pbk £3.50
2: Kender, Gully, Dwarves and Gnomes
[GL883] Penguin pbk £3.50
3: Love and War
[GL884] Penguin pbk £3.95

WHITE, T.H.
Author of highly imaginative Arthurian romances,
drawn from Malory's *Morte D'Arthur*.
The Book of Merlyn (1978)
Sequel to *The Once and Future King*.
[GL885] Fontana pbk £2.95
The Once and Future King (1958)
Comprising three volumes, re-telling the full story of
Arthur. The first of the trilogy, *The Sword in the
Stone*, gives a humorous, believable portrait of
growing up in a castle. In the later books, White
deepened and darkened his attitude, and re-wrote
parts of the first book with more threatening
overtones.
[GL886] Fontana pbk £4.95

WILLIAMS, CHARLES (British, 1886 - 1945)
With C.S. Lewis and Tolkien, Williams was a
member of the small Oxford group, the Inklings. His
fantasy thrillers share the Christian concerns and
allegorical methods of Lewis's work.
All Hallow's Eve
[GL887] Eardmans pbk £6.95
Descent into Hell
[GL888] Eardmans pbk £6.25
Greater Trumps
[GL889] Eardmans pbk £6.25
Place of the Lion
[GL890] Eardmans pbk £6.25
Shadows of Ecstasy
[GL891] Eardmans pbk £4.75
War in Heaven
[GL892] Eardmans pbk £6.25

WILSON, DAVID
The Coachman Rat **NEW**
A gripping novel that transforms a traditional
fairytale into a haunting image of the modern world.
[GL893] Robinson hbk £9.95
[GL894] Robinson pbk £5.95

WOLFE, GENE (US, 1931 -)
The sequence, *The Book of the New Sun*, is set on a
Vance-like dying world, and tells the story of
Severian who rises from apprentice torturer to ruler of
the planet. See also *Science Fiction*.
Soldier of the Mist **NEW**
[GL895] Orbit pbk £2.95
THE BOOK OF THE NEW SUN
1: The Shadow of the Torturer
[GL896] Arrow pbk £2.95
2: The Claw of the Conciliator
[GL897] Arrow pbk £2.95

3: The Sword of the Lictor
[GL898] Arrow pbk £2.50
4: The Citadel of the Autarch
[GL899] Arrow pbk £2.95
5: The Urth of the New Sun **NEW**
[GL900] Futura pbk £4.99

WURTS, JENNY
Sorcerer's legacy **NEW**
[GL901] Grafton pbk £3.50
Stormwarden
Wurts' first solo book is the beginning of a fantasy
saga sequence *The Cycle of Fire*. She has also
collaborated with Raymond Feist and others.
[GL902] Grafton pbk £7.95

ZELAZNY, ROGER (US, 1937 -)
Best known as a writer of SF, Zelazny's fantasy draws
on a base of mythology and folklore. His long
sequence on the land of *Amber*, and on the
troublesome family which rules it, has proved very
popular.
Dark Travelling
[GL903] Century pbk £6.95
This Immortal
[GL904] Methuen pbk £1.95
CHRONICLES OF AMBER
1: Nine Princes in Amber
[GL905] Sphere pbk £2.50
2: The Guns of Avalon
[GL906] Sphere pbk £2.50
3: Sign of the Unicorn
[GL907] Sphere pbk £2.50
4: The Hand of Oberon
[GL908] Sphere pbk £2.50
5: The Courts of Chaos
[GL909] Sphere pbk £2.50
6: Rhapsody of Amber
[GL910] Sphere pbk £2.50
7: Trumps of Doom
[GL911] Sphere pbk £2.99
8: Blood of Amber
[GL912] Sphere pbk £2.99
9: Sign of Chaos **NEW**
[GL913] Sphere pbk £2.99

DARK FANTASY & HORROR

Of all fictional forms, none are more maligned than
the most malignant - the weird, fearsome realms of
Dark Fantasy, ghost stories, horror novels and supernatural tales, both gothic and modern. The origins of
horror stem from the oral tradition of campfire warnings of 'things in the swamp, the dark...'; recognisable
strands reappear in later fields as diverse as the Bible
and *Beowulf*, before, with the emergence of the
gothic novels of Mrs Radcliffe and Monk Lewis, the
genteel English ghost story (M.R. James), the pulps
(Lovecraft, Block) and the modern novelists (King,
Herbert and Barker), the genre became established.
Some of the anthologies listed provide useful introductions to many writers and themes of the genre.

Anthologies

Great Tales of the Supernatural
[GL920] Dent pbk £1.35

**The Penguin Encyclopaedia of Horror &
the Supernatural**
[GL921] Viking hbk £14.95

Thirteen Famous Ghost Stories
[GL922] Dent pbk £1.50

ASHLEY, MIKE (ED)
**The Mammoth Book of Short Horror
Novels**
Wide-ranging collection including archaic and
modern works, from Blackwood to King and Shepard.
[GL923] Robinson pbk £4.95

BLEILER, E.F. (ED)
Five Victorian Ghost Novels
Including Vernon Lee, J.H. Ridder, Amelia Edwards,
Charles Beale, Wilhelm Meinhold, in a collection
revealing an interesting sub-genre.
[GL924] Dover pbk £4.90

COX, MICHAEL & GILBERT, R.A.
**The Oxford Book of English Ghost
Stories**
[GL925] Oxford hbk £13.95

CUDDON, J.A. (ED)
Penguin Book of Ghost Stories
[GL926] Penguin pbk £5.95
Penguin Book of Horror Stories
[GL927] Penguin pbk £5.99

ETCHISON, DENNIS (ED)
Cutting Edge
[GL928] Futura pbk £2.95

GORDON, GILES (ED)
Prevailing Spirits
A collection of Scottish ghostly tales by Robert Nye,
Antonia Fraser, George McKay Brown and others.
[GL929] Grafton pbk £2.50

GRANT, CHARLES L. (ED)
Shadows
Includes such modern masters as Bloch, King,
Campbell, Etchison & Tuttle.
[GL930] Headline pbk £2.50
Shadows 11
[GL931] Headline pbk £2.50

HAYDOCK, TIM (ED)
The Mammoth Book of Classic Chillers
[GL932] Robinson pbk £4.95

JONES, STEPHEN & NEWMAN, KIM (EDS)
Horror: 100 Best Books
Excellent reference book with entries by major
writers in the Dark Fantasy genre.
[GL933] Xanadu hbk £11.99

JONES, STEPHEN & SUTTON, DAVID (EDS)
Best Horror from Fantasy Tales
Stories taken from the cult magazine, including work
by Barker, Campbell, King and Grant.
[GL934] Robinson hbk £11.95

**KING, STEPHEN; SIMMONS, DAN & MARTIN,
GEORGE**
Dark Visions **NEW**
Three new stories from King and Simmons
respectively, and a 'werewolf' novella from Martin.
[GL935] Gollancz hbk £11.95

LAMB, HUGH (ED)
**Gaslit Nightmares: An Anthology of
Victorian Tales of Terror**
Wonderfully nostalgic collection by writers such as
Dickens & Jerome K. Jerome.
[GL936] Futura pbk £4.50

MARTIN, R.R. GEORGE (ED)
Night Visions
[GL937] Arrow pbk £2.95

James Herbert

Making a list of ten favourite books was almost as difficult as deciding upon eight gramophone records for that dreaded Desert Island. The only way to do it was to choose those that have meant something to me through the years, eliminate most of them, then cut the choice down to the final ten. The sheer pleasure of reading each one has been the test for including them on my list, but the genuine insight they've provided runs a close second.

H.G. WELLS
The History of Mr Polly
This 'simple' man's quest for love and fortune, but ultimately for contentment, was the first school book that I took seriously. Although I loved Wells' science fiction novels, this became, and still is, a firm favourite of all the great man's work.
(Pan, pbk £2.99)

RICHARD MATHESON
I Am Legend
The first non-Gothic horror story I'd ever read, an allegory really of how the isolated normal becomes the abnormal among a world of mutants. The main character finds himself living in a land of vampires whose sole purpose is to 'convert' him, to make him conform, to become one of them. Quite riveting, and one of Matheson's best.
(Robinson, pbk £2.95)

WILLIAM GOLDMAN
Colour of Light
An American writer who produced some of the most entertaining and moving novels of relationships and manners in the sixties and seventies, but known better now for his screenplays (*A Bridge Too Far*, *Butch Cassidy*, *The Princess Bride*). He's still the master of slick one-liners and sad humour, though.
(Granada, pbk £3.50)

KEN KESEY
One Flew Over the Cuckoo's Nest
A cult success twenty years ago, only the film version brought it mass appeal. It was then, and still is for me, a stunning tale of a misfit's rebellion against Establishment rule - in this case, the strictures of a mental institution. Comically, and tragically brilliant.
(Boyars, hbk £8.95/Picador, pbk £3.99)

LESLIE THOMAS
This Time Next Week
The author's account of his own boyhood in an orphanage. Although Leslie Thomas' novels have been hugely successful over the years, I still consider him to be one of our most underestimated writers. A little classic this one.
(Pan, pbk £2.99)

THOMAS HARRIS
The Silence of the Lambs
The most gripping thriller so far this year. Beautifully plotted, immense tension - a

Stephen King, author of *The Shining* (Hodder pbk £2.95) (Photo: James Leonard)

pleasure to read. One of those with which you regret turning over the last page.
(Heinemann, hbk £10.95)

BRAM STOKER
Dracula
Need I say more?
(Oxford, pbk £2.95/Penguin pbk £3.99)

ARTHUR C. CLARKE
Childhood's End
True science fiction can often be a bit too technically clever for its own good, but Arthur C. Clarke has the knack (unique, I think) of making the 'science' of his stories both understandable and awesome at the same time. The fate of mankind when the Earth has run its natural course makes wonderful fiction.
(Pan, pbk £2.99)

STEPHEN KING
The Shining
A deceptively simple plot of one man's degeneration into evil madness in an isolated and empty hotel, and the resulting terror into which his wife and son are plunged. The son has 'the shining' - he's psychic - and ultimately it's this gift that saves himself and his mother. Steve King's work never fails to impress.
(NEL, hbk £12.95, pbk £3.95)

COLIN WILSON
The Occult
My bible. An incredibly perceptive and well-informed study of all things paranormal and supernatural. Mind expansion is one of its many themes and, in fact, the book itself provides a trigger for that very thing.
(Panther, pbk £4.95)

James Herbert is Britain's favourite horror writer, and a pioneer of Dark Fantasy. Since the publication of his first novel, **The Rats,** his work has set new standards for writers in the genre, and has been successfully filmed.

MCKAULEY, KIRBY (ED)
Dark Forces
23 tales by both genre & mainstream authors.
[GL938] Futura pbk £3.50

RYAN, ALAN (ED)
The Penguin Book of Vampire Stories
The definitive anthology, spanning centuries of
Vampire literature, from Lord Byron to Tanith
Lee.
[GL939] Penguin pbk £5.95

WINTER, DOUGLAS (ED)
Prime Evil
Set to become the bestselling genre anthology ever,
all new original tales by modern masters as diverse as
David Morrel & M. John Harrison.
[GL940] Bantam hbk £10.95

Writers A - Z

AICKMAN, ROBERT
One of the most significant writers of modern Dark
Fantasy. Fascination with the immensity of the
unknown in comparison to human knowledge and
experience is the central theme of Aickman's
thoughtful work.
Cold Hand in Mine
[GL941] Robinson pbk £3.50
The Model
[GL942] Robinson pbk £2.95

ANDREWS, VIRGINIA
A writer of dark forces in a black world. The four
novels which comprise the story of the Dollanganger
family are based on a true story, and are a powerful
exposition of evil and revenge.
Dark Angel
[GL943] Fontana pbk £3.50
Fallen Hearts
[GL944] Flamingo pbk £3.50
Flowers in the Attic
[GL945] Fontana pbk £2.95
Garden of Shadows
[GL946] Collins hbk £10.95
Gates of Paradise   **NEW**
[GL947] Collins hbk £12.95
Heaven
[GL948] Fontana pbk £3.50
If There Be Thorns
[GL949] Fontana pbk £3.50
My Sweet Andrina
[GL950] Fontana pbk £3.50
Petals in the Wind
[GL951] Fontana pbk £3.50
Seeds of Yesterday
[GL952] Fontana pbk £3.50

BARKER, CLIVE
*"Every body is a book of blood; wherever we're
opened, we're red"*. Winner of the World Fantasy
Award, Barker is one of the most influential authors
writing in the genre today, his work unique for its
combination of uncompromising malevolence with
consummate literary skill. Unafraid of the repulsive
aspects of horror, his rich prose renders the excesses
as descriptions of considerable beauty.
Books of Blood: Vols 1 - 3
His first published works, critically acclaimed by
masters such as Stephen King and Ramsey
Campbell.
[GL953] Weidenfeld hbk £12.95
[GL954] Sphere pbk £4.99
Books of Blood: Vols 4 - 6
[GL955] Weidenfeld hbk £12.95
[GL956] Sphere pbk £4.99

Cabal: The Nightbreed
First of a new trilogy. The story of Cabal and his
people - the dead, yet alive, nightbreed. Barker's film
of the novel is to be released later this year.
[GL957] Fontana £2.95
The Damnation Game
Barker's first novel, the story of a gambler, his
unwilling bodyguard and their nemesis, Mamoulian, a
card sharper from...Hell?
[GL958] Sphere pbk £3.50
The Great and Secret Show   **NEW**
Set in the sultry landscape of California and
Hollywood, Barker's new novel tells of how two men
fight to possess 'The Art', the greatest power known
to mankind. The first part of a new trilogy.
[GL959] Collins hbk £12.95
Weaveworld
Barker's most successful novel yet. A true dark
fantasy, melding supernatural horror and the classic
'Sword & Sorcery' quest motif. An exciting, vibrant
and colourful tale of a world within a carpet, and of
the two mortals who struggle to possess the
Weaveworld - Cal, the hero, & Shadwell, the weird,
'businessman' villain.
[GL960] Collins pbk £3.95

BIERCE, AMBROSE
A great American writer in the Poe mould, who wrote
some marvellous tales set against the background of
the Civil War. His involvement in the War appalled
him, for he was a man of noble intent and cynical
idealism (as in his most famous work *The Devil's
Dictionary*). His dark fantasies are economically
written, original and disturbing. He came to an end as
mysterious as his work, vanishing into Mexico to join
Pancho Villa, never to be seen again...
Collected Writings
[GL961] Picador pbk £6.95
Ghost & Horror Stories
[GL962] Dover pbk £3.15
The Enlarged Devil's Dictionary
His famous collection of cynical definitions &
epigrams.
[GL963] Penguin pbk £5.95

BLACKWOOD, ALGERNON
Classic ghost stories by one of the masters. Those
who find M.R. James over-civilized and mannered are
more likely to enjoy Blackwood's darker style.
Best Ghost Stories
[GL964] Dover pbk £5.35

BLOCH, ROBERT
Veteran horror & SF author, with a delightfully
twisted imagination best illustrated by *Psycho*, based
on a true life murder case and later filmed by
Hitchcock.
Night of the Ripper
[GL965] Grafton pbk £2.50
Psycho
Bloch examines the deranged psyche of his anti-hero,
Norman Bates, an apparently normal middle-aged
motel owner who is actually a schizoid necromaniac.
[GL966] Corgi pbk £1.25

CAMPBELL, RAMSEY
Britain's greatest horror writer in terms of technique
and execution, who began writing *Cthulhu* style
stories in the '60s. Realistic, subtle and arcane, he is
adept at creating oppressive atmospheres from
seemingly normal situations (as in *Obsession*).
Ancient Images
The chilling story of an old horror film which can kill
its viewers.
[GL967] Century hbk £10.95
Cold Print (Stories)
[GL968] Grafton pbk £2.95
Dark Feasts (Stories)
[GL969] Robinson pbk £3.95

Obsession
[GL970] Grafton £8.95
The Doll Who Ate His Mother
[GL971] Arrow pbk £2.95
The Hungry Moon
Winner of the latest British Fantasy Award for Best
Novel.
[GL972] Arrow pbk £2.95
The Influence
[GL973] Arrow pbk £3.50

CARROLL, JONATHAN
Eccentric and humorous works of dark fantasy:
dogs talk in their sleep, dead author's characters
come to life. Many other quirky events take place in
Carroll's work: *Bones on the Moon* is his best
work.
Bones on the Moon
[GL974] Arrow pbk £2.50
Sleeping in Flame
[GL975] Century pbk £5.95
The Land of Laughs
[GL976] Arrow pbk £2.50

DERLETH, AUGUST
Creator of Arkham House Publishing, originally
dedicated to the works of H.P. Lovecraft. Derleth
augmented and extended Lovecraft's *Cthulhu* mythos
by incorporating HPL's own books into the pantheon
of malefic tomes.
The Mask of Cthulhu
[GL977] Grafton pbk £2.50
The Trail of Cthulthu
A 'fix-up' novel composed of novellas originally
published in various magazines.
[GL978] Grafton pbk £2.95

FARMER, JOSE PHILIP
Famous for his SF and Fantasy, Farmer's *Exorcism
Diptych* features Private Detective Herald
Childe clashing with a cadre of perverse
vampires and werewolves from an alternate universe.
THE EXORCISM DIPTYCH
Ritual One: The Image of the Beast
[GL979] Granada pbk £2.99
Ritual Two: Blown
[GL980] Grafton pbk £2.99

FAULCON, ROBERT
As *Robert Holdstock*, the best-selling author of
Mythago Wood, and winner of the World Fantasy
Award. Faulcon's *Nighthunter Sextet* (appearing in
three omnibus editions) is the least-known of his
work, and displays his knowledge of the occult and its
fantastic implications.
THE NIGHTHUNTER SEXTET
1: The Stalking/The Talisman
[GL981] Arrow pbk £3.50
2: The Ghost Dance/The Shrine
[GL982] Arrow pbk £3.50
3: The Hexing/The Labyrinth
[GL983] Arrow pbk £3.50

GALLAGHER, STEPHEN
Gallagher writes in a mainstream style catalysed
by elements of SF and Crime writing. His experience
in the field of radio scripts has given his work a
'matter of fact' approach that makes it convincing and
accessible to the general reader.
Down River
Another thriller-cum-chiller mutation, this is
Gallagher's best novel to date.
[GL984] Hodder hbk £10.95
Oktober
[GL985] Hodder pbk £2.99
Valley of Lights
A major film of this original crime/horror novel is to
be released this year.
[GL986] Hodder pbk £2.50

GRANT, CHARLES L.
One of the best modern American writers in the genre, Grant's work has a rare economy and self-restraint. Like Stephen King, his settings are familiar to the reader, without falling into the clichéd, while the weird elements of his work are elegant, colourful and highly convincing.

For Fear of the Night
[GL987] Futura pbk **£2.99**
Tales from the Nightside (Stories)
[GL988] Futura pbk **£2.95**
The Orchard
[GL989] Futura pbk **£2.99**
The Pet
[GL990] Futura pbk **£3.50**

GREGORY, STEPHEN
A young Welsh writer of considerable lyric gift, especially when describing the beautiful but terrifying landscapes of his native country. A winner of the Somerset Maugham award, his books of dark obsession would be relished by admirers of Iain Banks' *The Wasp Factory*.

The Cormorant
[GL991] Sceptre pbk **£2.95**
The Woodwitch
[GL992] Heinemann **£10.95**

HAMBLY, BARBARA
Restrained and elegant vampire novel by the bestselling fantasy authoress. See also *Fantasy*.

Immortal Blood
[GL993] Unwin pbk **£3.50**

HERBERT, JAMES
Britain's favourite horror writer, and a massive bestseller since his first novel *The Rats* exploded onto the scene in the 1970s. His novels, a number of which have been filmed, range from the gory realism of the early works (*Fluke*) and inventive fantasies (*Fluke*) and recently to subtle well-crafted ghost stories (*Haunted*). Along with his US counterpart, Stephen King, he has set a standard for other writers to aspire to.

Domain
[GL994] Hodder pbk **£3.50**
Fluke
[GL995] Hodder pbk **£2.50**
Haunted
[GL996] Hodder hbk **£10.95**
Lair
[GL997] Hodder pbk **£2.99**
Moon
[GL998] Hodder pbk **£3.50**
Sepulchre
[GL999] Hodder pbk **£3.50**
Shrine
[GL1000] Hodder pbk **£3.99**
The Dark
[GL1001] Hodder hbk **£11.95**
[GL1002] Hodder pbk **£3.50**
The Fog
[GL1003] Hodder pbk **£2.50**
The Jonah
[GL1004] Hodder pbk **£2.50**
The Magic Cottage
[GL1005] Hodder pbk **£3.50**
The Rats
[GL1006] Hodder hbk **£9.95**
[GL1007] Hodder pbk **£1.95**
The Spear
[GL1008] Hodder pbk **£2.99**
The Survivor
[GL1009] Hodder pbk **£2.99**

HIGGINS-CLARK, MARY
A writer of murderous horror tales played out against a background of glamorous locations, Higgins-Clark

is one of the most accomplished contemporary American writers of suspense tales.

A Cry in the Night
[GL1010] Fontana pbk **£2.95**
A Stranger is Watching
[GL1011] Fontana pbk **£2.50**
Stillwatch
[GL1012] Fontana pbk **£2.95**
The Cradle Will Fall
[GL1013] Fontana pbk **£2.95**
Where are the Children?
[GL1014] Fontana pbk **£2.50**
While My Pretty One Sleeps `NEW`
[GL1015] Century hbk **£11.95**

HJORTSBERG, WILLIAM
Falling Angel
Although marketed as a crime novel, and written in a gentle variant of the 'hardboiled' Private Eye style, this novel, filmed as *Angel Heart*, soon reveals itself to be more than a mere mystery, and chillingly incorporates aspects of voodoo and satanism.
[GL1016] Mysterious P pbk **£2.95**

HODGSON, WILLIAM HOPE
The House on the Borderland
Weird fiction at its most overwhelming: the reader is drowned in the cosmic sargasso of time and space.
[GL1017] Robinson pbk **£3.50**

HUTSON, SHAUN
Rebel, black comedian, and Rabelesian master of the Trash Art Horror Novel. Sometime road crew member for Heavy Metal rock bands, Hutson's work combines sleaze and satire in a way which enriches the genre, and makes him one of the more original voices of his generation.

Assassin
[GL1018] WH Allen hbk **£11.95**
Breeding Ground
[GL1019] Star pbk **£2.50**
Erebus
[GL1020] Star pbk **£2.95**
Relics
[GL1021] Star pbk **£2.95**
Shadows
[GL1022] Star pbk **£3.50**

JAMES, M.R.
The best ghost story writer that England has produced, James was a medievalist and biblical scholar. His writing is highly atmospheric, and exemplifies the appealing Victorian mannerist style of storytelling.

A Warning to the Curious (Ed. Rendell, Ruth)
[GL1023] Arrow pbk **£3.50**
Casting the Runes & Other Ghost Stories
[GL1024] Oxford pbk **£3.95**
Complete Ghost Stories
[GL1025] Penguin pbk **£3.95**
Ghost Stories
[GL1026] Arnold hbk **£16.95**

KING, STEPHEN
King's work excels in its ability to invest suburban America with visions of terror and destruction. His plots often derive from the 'world turned upside down' motif, and his writing shows an excellent and witty facility for observing the details of ordinary life. Manipulating characters so that the wildly improbable becomes allied with their own psycho-sexual complexes, his best work (such as *Carrie* or *The Shining*) shows genuine imaginative flair and an instinct for the truly startling that can transcend the strictures of his chosen genre.

Bachman Books
[GL1027] Hodder hbk **£14.95**

Carrie
[GL1028] Hodder pbk **£2.50**
Christine
[GL1029] Hodder pbk **£3.50**
Cujo
[GL1030] Futura pbk **£3.50**
Cycle of the Werewolf
[GL1031] Hodder pbk **£4.95**
Danse Macabre
[GL1032] Futura pbk **£3.50**
Different Seasons
[GL1033] Futura pbk **£3.95**
Firestarter XC
[GL1034] Futura pbk **£3.50**
It
[GL1035] Futura pbk **£5.99**
Misery
[GL1036] Hodder hbk **£11.95**
Night Shift
[GL1037] Hodder pbk **£3.50**
Pet Cemetary
[GL1038] Hodder pbk **£3.50**
Salem's Lot
[GL1039] Hodder pbk **£3.50**
Selected Works: The Shining/Salem's Lot/Carrie
[GL1040] Octopus hbk **£8.95**
Skeleton Crew
[GL1041] Futura pbk **£3.95**
The Dark Half `NEW`
King's new novel tells the story of a writer who tries to kill off the pseudonym under which he had been writing - only to find that he is unwilling to die...
[GL1042] Hodder hbk **£11.95**
The Dead Zone XC
[GL1043] Futura pbk **£3.50**
The Shining
[GL1044] Hodder pbk **£2.95**
The Stand
[GL1045] Hodder pbk **£3.95**

KOONTZ, DEAN R.
Prolific and entertaining American writer who has successfully evaded classification by producing novels with elements of SF, Fantasy, Thriller and Romantic Fiction. He is best known as a horror writer, recently becoming popular in the UK with the publication of *Watchers*, and now stands ready to rival Stephen King.

Darkness Comes
[GL1046] Star pbk **£3.50**
Lightning
[GL1047] Headline pbk **£3.99**
Midnight
[GL1048] Headline hbk **£12.95**
Night Chills
[GL1049] Star pbk **£3.50**
Strangers
[GL1050] Star pbk **£3.95**
The Vision
[GL1051] Star pbk **£2.99**
Twilight Eyes
[GL1052] Star pbk **£3.50**
Voice of the Night
[GL1053] Star pbk **£2.95**
Watchers
[GL1054] Headline pbk **£3.50**
Whispers
[GL1055] Star pbk **£3.50**

LAWS, STEPHEN
Inventive Geordie writer of three exciting novels set in an original but fitting contemporary location - the industrial heartland of Newcastle.

Ghost Train
[GL1056] Sphere pbk **£2.95**
Spectre
[GL1057] Sphere pbk **£3.50**

The Wyrm
[GL1058] Sphere pbk **£3.50**

LE FANU, J. SHERIDAN
The father of the modern ghost story, Le Fanu was a 19th century Irish writer whose entertaining fiction includes much sharp social criticism. His finest work is *Uncle Silas*, which appears at first to be simply a Victorian sensationalist novel, but goes beyond this to create a parable rich with Anglo-Irish symbols.

Best Ghost Stories
[GL1059] Dover pbk **£6.35**
Ghost Stories & Mysteries
[GL1060] Dover pbk **£5.55**
Uncle Silas (1864)
[GL1061] Dover pbk **£5.20**
Wylder's Hand
[GL1062] Dover pbk **£6.75**

LEROUX, GASTON
Phantom of the Opera
Unavailable for many years, this novel (which recently inspired the musical) is original, charming and melodramatic.
[GL1063] Star pbk **£2.99**

LEVIN, IRA
A Kiss Before Dying
[GL1064] Pan pbk **£2.95**
Rosemary's Baby
[GL1066] Pan pbk **£2.95**
The Boys From Brazil
[GL1067] Pan pbk **£2.95**
This Perfect Day
[GL1068] Pan pbk **£3.50**

LOVECRAFT, H.P.
After Poe (whose work will be found in the *American* fiction chapter) Lovecraft was the most significant Dark Fantasist ever, and like him a haunted New Englander. Lovecraft hated the scientifically advanced world he lived in, seeing mankind as a pathetic stumbler in a dark void. His prose is impassioned and purple, and achieves memorable cumulative effects. Little of his work appeared in his lifetime in book form, and became increasingly obscure until its re-appearance in the late 1970s.

Omnibus Vol 1: At the Mountains of Madness
Contains his few short novels, and the essential Mythos tale *Charles Dexter Ward*.
[GL1069] Grafton pbk **£3.50**
Omnibus Vol 2: Dagon & Other Macabre Tales
Contains all the major short stories.
[GL1070] Grafton pbk **£3.95**
Omnibus Vol 3: The Haunter of the Dark
Contains the bulk of the essential Cthulhu Mythos tales.
[GL1071] Grafton pbk **£3.50**

MARTIN, R.R. GEORGE
Fevre Dream
One of the great vampire novels, set on a Mississippi steamboat, with an unlikely bellicose hero.
[GL1072] Gollancz pbk **£3.50**
The Armageddon Rag
The definitive psychedelic rock horror novel, and a Gothic wonder for anyone who loved the Sixties.
[GL1073] Hodder pbk **£2.95**

MASTERTON, GRAHAM
International bestseller, author of mainstream, historical and SF disaster novels. Masterton relies more on ideas than exploitation, and his well-researched and plotted novels concern ordinary people adapting to the infernal aspects of the supernatural.

Charnel House
[GL1074] Sphere pbk **£2.99**
Death Trance
[GL1075] Sphere pbk **£2.99**
Mirror
[GL1076] Sphere pbk **£3.50**
Night Warriors
[GL1077] Sphere pbk **£3.50**
Plague
[GL1078] Star pbk **£2.99**
Revenge of the Manitou
[GL1079] Sphere pbk **£2.99**
Tengu
[GL1080] Sphere pbk **£3.50**
The Heirloom
[GL1081] Sphere pbk **£2.99**

NESBIT, E.
In the Dark
Best known as a classic children's author, this light collection of ghost stories has been recently re-issued.
[GL1082] Equation pbk **£3.50**

RICE, ANNE
Rice has written the most successful of the modern vampire novels, exploring the sensual elements of the genre. They tell the story of two men, Louis and Lestat, rendered immortal in their lust for blood; moments of gothic violence alternate with visions of loneliness and the unceasing search for the meaning of evil.

The Mummy   `NEW`
The story of Ramses the Damned, doomed to wander the earth - Rice once again memorably explores the interplay of the dead with their mortal brethren.
[GL1082A] Chatto hbk **£12.95**
THE VAMPIRE CHRONICLES
1: Interview with the Vampire
[GL1083] Futura pbk **£3.50**
2: Vampire Lestat
[GL1084] Futura pbk **£3.50**
3: Queen of the Damned   `NEW`
[GL1085] Macdonald hbk **£11.95**

SAUL, JOHN
Standard horror involving the metaphors of childhood, blindness and mental instability, with the traditional devices of reincarnation and retribution: all the tricks of the trade.

All Fall Down
[GL1086] Transworld pbk **£1.95**
Brainchild
[GL1087] Transworld pbk **£2.50**
Comes the Blind Fury
[GL1088] Hodder pbk **£2.95**
Cry for the Strangers
[GL1089] Hodder pbk **£2.95**
Punish the Sinners
[GL1090] Hodder pbk **£2.95**
Suffer the Children
[GL1091] Hodder pbk **£2.95**
The Unwanted
[GL1092] Bantam pbk **£2.95**
When the Wind Blows
[GL1093] Hodder pbk **£2.95**

SHEPPARD, LUCIUS
The Jaguar Hunter
Described as a 'magical realist' by critics, Sheppard's one story collection contains some of the most haunting supernatural tales ever written. See also *Science Fiction*.
[GL1094] Grafton pbk **£5.95**

SIMMONS, DAN
Song of Kali
An excellent world fantasy award-winning novel of spiritual and human evil set in the mystic East.
[GL1095] Headline pbk **£2.95**

STOKER, BRAM
In *Dracula* Stoker created the last of the great Gothic novels, with its virtuous heroes, succumbing maidens and hellish vampires; it has been interpreted as a metaphor for the syphilis which infected Victorian England (and Stoker himself), and as a reworking of the Flying Dutchman/Wandering Jew legends, and is a richly visual novel. The original first chapter 'Dracula's Guest', deleted by Stoker's editor, is available in the *Penguin Book of Vampire Stories*.

Dracula
[GL1096] Oxford pbk **£2.95**
[GL1097] Penguin pbk **£3.95**

STRAUB, PETER
One of America's finest horror writers, as yet unrecognised in the UK; his work is more literary than Stephen King, his collaborator on *The Talisman*, and relies on his writing skills rather than gaudy padding.

Full Circle
[GL1098] Corgi pbk **£2.99**
Ghost Story
[GL1099] Fontana pbk **£3.99**
If You Could See Me Now
[GL1100] Futura pbk **£2.95**
Koko
[GL1101] Penguin pbk **£3.95**
The Talisman
[GL1102] Penguin pbk **£3.95**

STRIEBER, WHITLEY
Before astounding the world with revelations of his contacts with extra-terrestrials in *Communion*, Strieber was best known as a writer of SF and Horror.

Black Magic
[GL1103] Grafton pbk **£2.99**
Catmagic
[GL1104] Grafton pbk **£3.50**
The Night Church
[GL1105] Grafton pbk **£2.99**

TUTTLE, LISA
Texan writer currently living in the UK, widely known for her writing on feminism. Her fiction encompasses SF, Fantasy and superb psychological horror, written with a feminist slant.

A Nest of Nightmares
[GL1106] Sphere pbk **£2.50**
Gabriel
[GL1107] Sphere pbk **£2.99**

WATSON, IAN
Inventive British SF author, recently turned to Dark Fantasy. His work is left-wing, socially aware and inspired by anti-nuclear, environmentalist polemics - politics merges with loathsome moments of staggering imagination.

Meat
[GL1108] Headline pbk **£2.99**
The Fire Worm
[GL1109] Gollancz hbk **£10.95**
The Power
[GL1110] Headline pbk **£2.50**

WRIGHT, T.M.
Two titles from one of America's most highly-regarded horror writers, both compared to and praised by Stephen King.

A Manhattan Ghost Story
[GL1111] Gollancz pbk **£3.50**
The Island
[GL1112] Gollancz pbk **£2.99**

FICTION

The WH Smith Annual Literary Award

An annual award of £10,000 for the book considered by the judges to have made the most outstanding contribution to literature during the previous twelve months. The book must be published in the UK and be written in English, but the author can come from anywhere in the Commonwealth. The judges make their decision independently, without submissions from publishers.

1959 Patrick White *Voss*
       (Eyre & Spottiswoode)
1960 Laurie Lee *Cider With Rosie*
       (Hogarth)
1961 Nadine Gordimer
       Friday's Footprint (Gollancz)
1962 J R Ackerley
       We Think the World of You
       (Bodley head)
1963 Gabriel Fielding
       The Birthday King (Hutchinson)
1964 E H Gombrich
       Meditations on a Hobby Horse
       (Phaidon)
1965 Leonard Woolf *Beginning Again*
       (Hogarth)
1966 R C Hutchinson
       A Child Possessed (Geoffrey Bles)
1967 Jean Rhys *Wide Sargasso Sea*
       (Deutsch)
1968 V S Naipaul
       The Mimic Men (Deutsch)
1969 Robert Gittings
       John Keats (Heinemann)
1970 John Fowles
       The French Lieutenant's Woman
       (Cape)
1971 Nan Fairbrother
       New Lives, New Landscapes
       (Architectural Press)
1972 Kathleen Raine
       The Lost Country
       (Hamish Hamilton/Dolmen Press)
1973 Brian Moore *Catholics* (Cape)
1974 Anthony Powell
       Temporary Kings (Heinemann)
1975 Jon Stallworthy
       Wilfred Owen: A Biography
       (Oxford/Chatto)
1976 Seamus Heaney *North* (Faber)
1977 Ronald Lewin *SLIM: The*
       Standardbearer (Leo Cooper)
1978 Patrick Leigh Fermor
       A Time of Gifts (J Murray)
1979 Mark Girouard
       Life in the English Country House
       (Yale UP)
1980 Thom Gunn
       Selected Poems 1950 - 1975 (Faber)
1981 Isabel Colegate
       The Shooting Party
       (Hamish Hamilton)
1982 George Clare
       Last Waltz in Vienna (Macmillan)
1983 A N Wilson *Wise Virgin* (Secker)
1984 Philip Larkin
       Required Writing (Miscellaneous
       Pieces 1955 - 1962) (Faber)
1985 David Hughes *The Pork Butcher*
       (Constable)
1986 Doris Lessing *The Good Terrorist*
       (Cape)
1987 Elizabeth Jennings
       Collected Poems 1953 - 1985
       (Carcanet)
1988 Robert Hughes *The Fatal Shore*
       (Collins Harvill)

Film:
History & Reference
Theory & Criticism
Monographs
World Film: By Area
Practical Film-Making
Video, Television, Radio

Photography:
History & Reference
Theory & Criticism
Catalogues & Collections
Monographs
Practical Photography

**Film &
Photography**

Jeremy Isaacs

All my life, my greatest pleasure has been in books. At school, at university, on National Service in the Army, I was never without a book, ready, whenever a gap in time appeared, to bury my nose in it. And there always seemed to be books around me. My parents' shelves, for which I am ever grateful to them, were loaded with fine reading. The Everyman Library tempted me early to the classics. Wielding the traditional torch under the bedclothes, I read late into the night, shedding tears on the pillow, I remember, for the plight of *Oliver Twist*.

In later life I have come to be something of a workaholic, and work has played havoc with reading, consuming hours of the day and night that would be much better spent with a book. So I read now at weekends, and on holidays. The heaviest bag in the car or on the plane is the one with the books in. Then, whether walking or lounging, I read a book a day.

I can never recapture the first pleasure of reading Dickens or Jane Austen, or Hemingway or George Eliot. But I can and do re-read them. Some of the best and biggest, Tolstoy and Dostoevsky, I save for rainy days yet to come. I cannot now long postpone re-reading another favourite, Anthony Powell. Proust is still ahead of me. I not only re-read fiction. Comforting myself before sleep, I read my favourite essayists not just once and again, but, like the young lady of Spain who was sick in the train, again and again and again; Hazlitt, Mencken, Liebling.

In crime fiction or thrillers, nothing is more exciting than to come across a new name guaranteed to please. I wish I could come across a dozen fresh Simenons. A book review by Anthony Quinton led me to the whole of P.M. Hubbard. His psychologically grim landscapes screw up the tension and his spare prose reminds me now that it is time I re-read another classically cool story-teller, Alfred Duggan.

Narrative history is another pleasure. Christopher Hibbert has taken me to Agincourt and Corunna. I forgot to re-read Garrett Mattingly's superb account of the Armada last year, dammit. C.L.R. James's death the other day recalls his *Black Jacobins*, and *Beyond the Boundary*, as good a book on cricket as ever was. I bless the fact that I read, enjoyed, admired and benefited from Robert Kee's history of Irish Nationalism *The Green Flag*, before the BBC asked me to work with him on a television version of it. The reviews strongly suggest I should ear-mark time this summer for Simon Schama's history of the French Revolution, *Citizens*.

Here's ten of the best, according to me. It could be a hundred:

ROBERT LOUIS STEVENSON
Kidnapped

From its marvellous first page to the famous last sentence, this is, I think, the best told story in English. The competition at the pipes is my favourite set piece. Through his adventures at sea and in the wild Highlands, David Balfour grows to manhood, and comes into his own. I read it every year.
(Oxford, pbk £3.50)

ELIZABETH DAVID
French Provincial Cooking

The recipes are appetising, but it is the introductory pages to each section that I read with special pleasure. They are beautifully written. I love the lovingly precise description of Madame Barattero's charcuterie at Lamastre. In *Mediterranean Food* the chapters are headed by quotations from others; Arnold Bennett's thirteen course meal for a few francs at Vars, and the drill for a nineteenth century gentleman's breakfast - we should say lunch - in Venice, ham and crab and liver and cheese and fruit, are especially mouthwatering.
(Penguin, pbk £8.99)

A.J. LIEBLING
The Sweet Science

All my Liebling is in anthologies and collections published in America. I cannot read often enough his accounts of Earl Long, out of the loony-bin, electioneering again in Louisiana. Or of eating in Paris, or drinking in Burgundy. His are the best sporting essays since Hazlitt's *The Fight*. *The Sweet Science*, on boxing, has just been re-issued here.
(Simon & Schuster, pbk £5.95)

KOBBE
(Edited by the Earl of Harewood)
Kobbé's Complete Opera Book

Who has done or is going to do what to whom; indispensable. And some plots, read late enough at night, send one ever so gently to sleep.
(Bodley Head, hbk £30.00)

GEORGE ELIOT
Middlemarch

I discovered this late, and still cannot quite grasp the full range of pleasures it affords. A masterpiece of narrative and character depiction.
(Chatto, hbk £9.95/Oxford, pbk £2.95/Penguin, pbk £2.95)

JANE AUSTEN
Persuasion

I discovered this early, and have spent years rearranging my preferences in Jane Austen's work. I like Anne Elliot and her sea captain so much I have to put this here. Time to turn again to *Emma* and to *Mansfield Park*? Oh! How I miss those cherished Hamish Hamilton Novel Library editions!
(Chatto, hbk £9.95/Oxford, pbk £1.95/Penguin, pbk £1.99)

PHILIP LARKIN
Collected Poems
(Ed. Anthony Thwaite)
The slim volumes - *High Windows*, *The Less Deceived* - gave much pleasure.

Jane Austen (Picture: National Portrait Gallery)

Useful though to have all this most readable of poets wrote in one full volume, scholarly presented.
(Faber, hbk £16.95)

MADAME LA TOUR DU PIN
Memoirs

Here's someone who survived the French Revolution and went to live in America. One of the most informative eye-witness accounts of history ever written, just because it is so sensibly matter-of-fact. This lady lived a full, troubled life, and put it all down plain on paper. It is still fresh today.
(Century, pbk £6.95)

GEORGE PSYCHOUNDAKIS
The Cretan Runner

(Trans. Patrick Leigh-Fermor)
The British in German-occupied Crete had heroic Cretan comrades. The shepherd George Pyschoundakis ran messages, up and down the mountain crags. They put him on a submarine for a break; he saw Jerusalem. The British officers assumed he was illiterate. After the war he handed Patrick Leigh-Fermor a close written manuscript, his story of the war. This is it, clear as a mountain stream. Since he wrote it, Psychoundakis has gone on to translate *The Odyssey* and *The Iliad* into Cretan rhyming couplets.
(John Murray, pbk £5.95)

ANTHONY POWELL
A Dance to the Music of Time

I have re-read all my other Powell favourites, *Afternoon Men*, *Venusberg*, *What's Become of Waring* - but have saved the twelve novels that constitute this wonderful narrative for a long-breathed space. Each elegant page pleases, bringing smiles, chuckles, laughter. And the hero's understated love affair, that starts and ends and is remembered, lasts in our minds too.
(12 volumes: Heinemann, hbks £9.95/Fontana, pbks £3.95)

In a distinguished and varied career in television and the Arts, Jeremy Isaacs has been associated with the BBC, Thames TV, the BFI, and Channel 4 (where he was Chief Executive, 1981 - 88). He is now General Director of the Royal Opera House, Covent Garden.

Anthony Powell (Photo: Heinemann)

Book Choice

FILM

Books can never match the thrill of the darkened cinema, but they can provide the magic of 'behind-the-scenes' detail, or a framework for a more critical appreciation of the medium. In a rapidly expanding field, with many titles having a remarkably short shelf-life, most of the books chosen for inclusion here are by specialist film writers or people working within the industry itself. Only a relatively small number can be included in each category, so new books have been favoured alongside recognised classics.

History & Reference

Particularly recommended are Christopher Lyon's *International Dictionary of Films and Filmakers*, and the range of new guides from Bloomsbury, which are attractively produced and all-encompassing.

Encyclopaedia of Musical Film NEW
1,600 entries covering actors, composers, lyricists, directors, choreographers and the most memorable songs and best-loved films.
[H1] Oxford pbk **£8.95**

Incredibly Strange Films NEW
A homage to crazed, low-budget features and cult films with interviews, biographies, filmographies and anecdotes.
[H2] Plexus pbk **£7.95**

ANDREW, GEOFF
The Film Handbook NEW
A guide to more than two hundred films, covering the work of every major director this century, by *Time Out* film critic Geoff Andrew. Each entry includes information on the director's other work.
[H3] Longman pbk **£10.95**

BERGAN, RONALD & KARNEY, ROBYN
Bloomsbury Foreign Film Guide NEW
Over 2,000 non-English language films are included with original titles, full credits, plot summaries, critical assessment and details of awards won. The best of its kind.
[H4] Bloomsbury pbk **£10.95**

BUSCOMBE, EDWARD (ED)
BFI Companion to the Western NEW
A Western-lover's guide complete with a short history of the genre, a cultural/historical dictionary (covering everything from Indian tribes to railroads and individual battles - both real and fictional), and a select guide to films. Beautifully produced, with colour illustrations, maps and comment from over 40 contributors.
[H5] Deutsch hbk **£19.95**

CAMERON-WILSON, J & SPEED, F. MAURICE
Film Review 1988 - 89
Surveys the year's film releases, including foreign language films, awards ceremonies, festivals, events in Hollywood and the most promising new faces. Also includes a listing of the year's new cinema books.
[H6] Columbus hbk **£15.95**
[H7] Columbus pbk **£9.95**

GARFIELD, B
Western Films: A Complete Guide NEW
Screenwriter, producer and author of *Death Wish* and *Wild Times*, Garfield has compiled a buff's guide which covers the silents, the talkies, crews, actors, directors and spaghettis.
[H9] Da Capo pbk **£12.95**

HALLIWELL, LESLIE
Halliwell's Film Guide
Sixth updated edition with over 1,000 new entries covering the whole history of cinema, plus updates on video availability.
[H11] Paladin pbk **£7.95**
Halliwell's Filmgoer's Companion
Ninth edition, now updated and revised for the first time since 1984. Includes two previous Halliwell titles, the *Movie Quiz* and the *Book of Quotes*, a hundred new illustrations, and new entries on actors such as Kevin Costner and Kathleen Turner.
[H12] Grafton hbk **£19.95**

KAEL, PAULINE
5001 Nights at the Movies
New Yorker film critic, Kael has possibly reviewed more films than any other critic of her generation. A witty guide, with informed and critical narratives and information on cast and crews.
[H14] Hamlyn pbk **£5.95**

KONIGSBERG, IRA
The Complete Film Dictionary NEW
What is an 'inky dink'? an infra-red travelling matt process? a pan shot?...This comprehensive source book on motion pictures as art, technology and industry answers all these and more. Over 3,500 illustrated mini-essays on technique, history, criticism and all aspects of film-making.
[H15] Bloomsbury pbk **£14.95**

LLOYD, ANNE & ROBINSON, DAVID
History of the Movies NEW
A film-buff's dream: seven decades of cinema history lovingly compiled with special features and photo-essays by experts and enthusiasts; from 'Space Invaders: Sci-fi in the Fifties' to 'The Brat Pack', silent movies to technicolour extravaganzas. Over 150 illustrations, including film-stills and posters.
[H16] MacDonald/Orbis pbk **£15.00**

LYON, CHRISTOPHER (ED)
Fast becoming the most comprehensive and useful reference work available. An introductory essay, written by a distinguished critic or historian, is provided for each person or film listed along with extensive biographical and cast/crew information.
International Dictionary of Films and Filmakers
Volume 1: Films
[H17] Macmillan pbk **£12.95**
Volume 2: Directors
[H18] Macmillan pbk **£12.95**
Volume 3: Actors and Actresses
[H19] Macmillan pbk **£12.95**

PEARY, DANNY
Close Ups: The Movie Star Book NEW
A classic, re-issued with a new introduction. The stars are seen as never before, through candid remarks from those in the know. Includes 1,000 photographs, filmographies and an index to 1,200 films.
[H22] Simon & Schuster pbk **£8.95**

ROBERTSON, PATRICK
The Guinness Book of Movie Facts
Revised third edition, for both the casual movie-goer and the film buff, including new chapters on locations and home videos.
[H23] Guinness pbk **£8.95**

SHIPMAN, DAVID
Movie Talk NEW
What did Bette Davis think of Ronald Reagan the actor? What does Steven Speilberg have to say about Harrison Ford? Over 5,000 of the most witty quotations from the world of movies.
[H24] Bloomsbury hbk **£14.95**

SILVER, ALAIN & WARD, ELIZABETH
Film Noir NEW
A excellent reference book with detailed entries on over 300 films with credits, storylines and a critique of each film.
[H25] Bloomsbury pbk **£14.95**

WELDON, M.
The Psychotronic Encyclopaedia of Film NEW
A guide to over 3,000 of the wildest movies ever made from *Attack of the Killer Tomatoes* to *I Dismember Mama*, with illustrations and information on cast, crew and characters. Uniquely eccentric reviews.
[H26] Plexus pbk **£9.95**

WYVER, JOHN
The Moving Image: An International History of Film, Television & Video NEW
One of the most all-encompassing histories of 'the moving image' available. This volume was originally produced as a guide and catalogue for the recently opened Museum of the Moving Image in London. Carefully researched with access to an impressive amount of primary source material.
[H29] Blackwell pbk **£15.00**

Theory & Criticism

Included in this section are collections of writing about film by those outside film-making itself (with a few exceptions, eg. directors like Sergei Eisenstein or Laura Mulvey, who are equally recognised for their contributions to film theory). The selection covers classic theory and critics, writings on genre and specialist studies. However, some of the most interesting 'theory' has been written by film-makers themselves: general 'reflections on the cinema' may be found in the *Monographs* section - particularly recommended are the new books by renowned directors Martin Scorsese and Wim Wenders.

ALBRECHT, DONALD
Designing Dreams: Modern Architecture in the Movies
Beautifully-illustrated study of how set-designers used the architectural language of modernism to enrich movie décor and create dreams of a better future for audiences during the bleak years of the Depression.
[H30] Thames & H pbk **£10.95**

ALTMAN, RICK
The American Film Musical
A re-issue of one of the best books on the musical and on 'genre' in general. Includes theory on genre analysis and essays on the musical, from folk, through fairytale to extravaganza.
[H31] BFI pbk **£9.95**

ARNHEIM, RUDOLF
Film as Art
Classic exploration of the psychological aspects of visual perception in film. Arnheim was one of the first film critics to defend the potential of film as an 'art'
[H34] Faber pbk **£3.95**

BARNOUW, ERIK
Documentary: A History of the Non-Fiction Film
The most comprehensive text on the subject available, richly researched and recently updated to accommodate the influence of new technological breakthroughs such as portable video and cable television.
[H35] Oxford pbk **£6.95**

BAZIN, ANDRE
The most influential 'realist' film critic, who founded and edited *Cahiers du Cinema*, a landmark in film history and the starting point of the careers of Truffaut, Godard, Chabrol and other French New Wave directors.
Cahiers du Cinema:
Vol 1: The 1950s (Ed. Hillier, Jim)
Neo-Realism, Hollywood, New Wave.
[H36] Routledge hbk **£25.00**
Vol 2: 1960 - 68 (Ed. Hillier, Jim)
New Wave, New Cinema, Re-Evaluating Cinema.
[H37] Routledge hbk **£25.00**
Vol 3: 1968 - 1972 (Ed. Browne, Nick)
Outlines the impact which the events of May 1968 had on French cultural theory and how this in turn had a dramatic effect on the direction of *Cahiers du Cinema*.
[H38] Routledge hbk **£25.00**

BRUNSDON, CHARLOTTE (ED)
Films for Women
Examines women in films, films made by women and above all films for women, and traces the changes that have occurred in the debate about women's cinema since the sixties.
[H40] BFI pbk **£6.95**

CAUGHIE, JOHN
Theories of Authorship: A Reader
An excellent series of essays which discuss the 'auteur' theory of cinema: who is an auteur, who is not and exactly what is meant by the term.
[H41] Routledge hbk **£8.50**

Robert Montgomery (as Philip Marlowe) in 'Lady in the Lake' from *Film Noir* (Bloomsbury pbk **£14.95**)

COLLICK, JOHN
Shakespeare, Cinema and Society `NEW`
Collick's study of the cultural, historical and economic development of Shakespearean cinema, takes in a diverse cross-section of films from all over the world, including early silent interpretations and the BBC/Time Life series.
[H43] Manchester UP pbk **£6.95**

DAVIS, ANTHONY
Filming Shakespeare's Plays: The Adaptations of Laurence Olivier, Orson Welles, Peter Brooke and Akira Kurosawa `NEW`
Davis discusses the dramatic problems which the 'staging' of Shakespearian plays posed for the four eminent film directors and examines how their films have influenced later theatrical stagings.
[H44] Cambridge hbk **£25.00**

DE LAURETIS, TERESA
Technologies of Gender: Essays on Theory, Film and Fiction
Builds a bridge between fashionable academic theory and frequently marginalised feminist theory. Recommended by Umberto Eco as an original approach to semiotics.
[H45] Indiana UP pbk **£9.95**

DELEUZE, GILLES
French philosopher, famous for his assaults on classical psychoanalysis, here turns his attention to film. His work is demanding reading but potentially the most influential philosophical analysis of cinematic language published so far.
Cinema Vol 1: The Movement-Image
[H46] Athlone P pbk **£11.95**
Cinema Vol 2: The Time-Image
[H47] Athlone P pbk **£11.95**

DOHERTY, THOMAS
Teenagers and Teenpics `NEW`
A serious study of the origins and development of teenage exploitation movies.
[H49] Unwin Hyman pbk **£8.95**

DONALD, JAMES (ED)
Fantasy and the Cinema `NEW`
A reader whose contributors submerge themselves in escapism, entertainment, pleasure and horror in the cinema.
[H51] BFI pbk **£9.95**

DYER, RICHARD
Heavenly Bodies: Studies in the Star System
An attempt to consider the 'film star' phenomenon from a wide range of critical and theoretical angles.
[H53] Macmillan pbk **£7.95**

EISENSTEIN, SERGEI
The Film Sense
The definitive edition of Eisenstein's writings in translation, in which he discusses film as a medium that should appeal to all the senses, not just the emotions and intellect. Includes a complete list of his work and a bibliography.
[H54] Faber pbk **£3.95**

FISCHER, LUCY
Shot/Countershot `NEW`
A survey of feminism and film, bringing together feminist analysis of mainstream film and examining attempts to establish a feminist film practice.
[H57] Macmillan pbk **£8.95**

FRENCH, PHILIP
Westerns
An accessible and lucid account of the Western and of

its essentially symbolic function in the growth of American cinema's sense of its own identity.
[H58] Secker pbk **£5.50**

GIDAL, PETER
Materialist Film
Polemical introduction to avant-garde and experimental film. Gidal refers to films by Andy Warhol, Godard, Liz Rhodes and many others.
[H59] Routledge pbk **£6.95**

GLADHILL, CHRISTINE
Home is Where the Heart is: Studies in Melodrama and the Women's Film
An exciting and thought-provoking collection of essays from two decades of film criticism. Includes contributions from Thomas Elsaesser, Laura Mulvey and E Ann Kaplan.
[H61] BFI pbk **£7.95**

GORMAN, CLAUDIA
Unheard Melodies: Narrative Film Music
A theoretical account of the various functions of the music that generally goes unremarked in the soundtrack of a narrative.
[H63] BFI pbk **£7.95**

GRIERSON, JOHN
One of the central figures in the British documentary movement, a film-maker and theorist in love with the potential of film to capture *"all the rhythmic energies that contribute to the blazing fact of the matter"*.
HARDY, FORSYTH (ED)
Grierson on Documentary
A selection of articles charting the intellectual energies of one of the central figures in the British documentary movement. Covers work from the 1930s as a film-maker to more recent work on mass communications.
[H65] Faber pbk **£2.50**

HEATH, STEPHEN
Heath's name is often linked with that of Colin McCabe. He has been instrumental in bringing to bear continental influences (Barthes, Derrida, Lacan) on contemporary British film theory.
Questions of Cinema
[H66] Macmillan pbk **£10.95**

HIRSCH, FOSTER
The Dark Side of the Screen: Film Noir
For all devotees of the wet streets at night, femmes fatale, murder, fate, cigarettes and bourbon. A generously illustrated and informative companion, one of the best in its field.
[H67] Da Capo pbk **£13.95**

KAEL, PAULINE
Film critic with *The New Yorker* for over 20 years, Kael's combination of caustic wit, erudition and expansive populist taste is often imitated but rarely matched. Her work has been of central importance in restoring a sense of experiment and moral imperative to the obsessively cash-conscious New Hollywood.
Deeper into the Movies
[H68] Boyars hbk **£9.95**
Kiss Kiss, Bang Bang
Film writings 1965-67.
[H69] Arrow pbk **£5.95**
Reeling
[H70] Boyars hbk **£9.95**
Taking It All In
[H71] Arrow pbk **£5.95**
The State of the Art
[H72] Arrow pbk **£5.95**
When the Lights go Down
[H73] Boyars pbk **£12.95**

KAPLAN, E. ANN
**Women and Film: Both Sides of
the Camera**
[H74] Methuen pbk **£8.95**
Women in Film Noir
A feminist analysis of the characteristic 'strong' and
dangerous woman portrayed in the thrillers and
melodramas of the 1940s and 1950s.
[H75] BFI pbk **£4.95**

KUHN, ANNETTE
**Cinema Censorship and
Sexuality 1909 - 1925**
An authoritative social history of censorship in the
early cinema.
[H76] Routledge pbk **£9.95**
**The Power or the Image: Essays on
Representation and Sexuality**
A collection of essays analysing a wide range of
films, to explore and develop an understanding of
how culturally dominant images of sexuality are
constructed and their impact socially, morally and
historically.
[H77] Routledge pbk **£7.95**

LOVELL, TERRY
**Pictures of Reality: Aesthetics,
Politics, Pleasure**
An interesting and polemical book which suggests,
taking its inspiration from Althusser, that Marxist
film theory need not mean realism.
[H79] BFI pbk **£3.95**

MAST, GERALD
**The Comic Mind: Comedy and the
Movies**
A second edition of a classic text on the subject by
one of America's leading film writers.
[H80] Chicago UP hbk **£22.50**

MAST, GERALD & COHEN, MARSHALL (EDS)
**Film Theory and Criticism:
Introductory Readings**
The best general anthology of film theory currently
available. Essential for students or anyone interested
in the development of 20th century aesthetics as a
whole.
[H81] Oxford pbk **£11.50**

MCCABE, COLIN
Former *enfant terrible* who lost his post at
Cambridge in the infamous 'structuralism
controversy' and went on to become head of
production at the BFI. His work is always
provocative, challenging accepted notions of
'culture' and the elitism it often implies.
**High Theory/Low Culture: Analysing
Popular TV and Film**
[H82] Manchester UP hbk **£8.95**

METZ, CHRISTIAN
Influenced by Bazin, Metz explores the ontology of
film images. He writes from a psycholgical point of
view, examining the role of perception in our
understanding of images.
**Film Language: A Semiotics of
the Cinema**
[H83] Oxford hbk **£19.50**
**Psychoanalysis and Cinema: The
Imaginary Signifier**
[H85] Macmillan pbk **£9.95**

MONACO, JAMES
How to Read a Film
An excellent place to start the study of film: lucid,
comprehensive and careful to define all technical
terms employed, this book is required reading for all
those baffled by film theory.
[H86] Oxford pbk **£9.95**

NEWMAN, KIM
Nightmare Movies `NEW`
A critical history of the horror movie from 1968 and
classical gothic to the post-modern horror of
Apocalypse Now and *Blood Simple*. Compiled by a
woman who fell in love with her first Dracula movie
at the age of 12.
[H88] Bloomsbury pbk **£12.95**

PALMER, JERRY
**The Logic of the Absurd: On Film &
TV Comedy**
Drawing on anthroplogy, psychoanalysis and
semiotics as theoretical aids this is a surprisingly
light-hearted analysis of what makes us laugh and
why.
[H90] BFI pbk **£7.95**

PEARY, DANNY
Cult Movies III `NEW`
A personal selection of sleazy and queasy cult films
with comment and information; includes *New York,
New York*, *One Eyed Jacks*, and *Faster Pussycat!
Kill! Kill!*.
[H91] Sidgwick pbk **£9.95**

POWELL, DILYS
The Golden Screen `NEW`
George Perry introduces this selection of reviews of
film classics and recent releases by Dilys Powell, to
celebrate her 50 years as a film columnist for the
Sunday Times.
[H92] Pavilion hbk **£14.95**

PRIBRAM, DEIDRE (ED)
**Female Spectators: Looking at
Film and Television** `NEW`
High-powered essays by contemporary feminist film-
makers and theorists on the complexity of the female
audience, and the nature of voyeurism. Includes
readings of individual films and TV programmes
from *Rear Window* to MTV Rock Videos.
[H93] Verso pbk **£8.95**

PUDOVKIN, V.I.
Film Technique and Film Acting
One of the major film-makers from the heroic era of
Soviet cinema. This book has long been one of the
fundamental text books on cinema.
[H94] Vision P hbk **£7.95**

ROTHMAN, WILLIAM
**The 'I' of Camera: Essays in Film
Criticism, History and Aesthetics** `NEW`
From the Cambridge *Studies in Film* series. This
study includes essays on Hitchcock, Griffith, Chaplin,
Renoir and Hawks, as well as discussion on the role
of the camera in theatrical melodrama, eroticism in
film, 'documentary' vs 'fiction' and the 'American-
ness' of American film.
[H96] Cambridge pbk **£9.95**

RUSSET, ROBERT & STARR, CECILE
**Experimental Animation: Origins
of a New Art** `NEW`
The best book available on the subject and an
indispensible source book. From the pioneers of
abstract animation in Europe to animators of new
technology, from Len Lye to Hans Richter. Lots of
illustrations, film stills, information on technique, a
glossary and list of distributors.
[H97] Da Capo pbk **£11.50**

SCHOEL, WILLIAM
**Stay Out of the Shower: The
Shocker Film Phenomenon** `NEW`
A passionate study of 'splatter movies', their making
and their fascination.
[H98] Robinson pbk **£6.95**

Clint Eastwood in 'The Outlaw Josey Wales' from
Philip French's *Westerns* (Secker pbk £5.50)

WALSH, MARTIN & GRIFFITHS, KEITH
**The Brechtian Aspect of
Radical Cinema**
A trenchant Brechtian crtique, distinguished by its
commitment to the ideal of a truly radical cinema and
by clear analysis of 'difficult' film-makers like
Medvedkin and Jean-Marie Straub.
[H100] BFI pbk **£4.95**

WILLIAMS, CHRISTOPHER (ED)
Realism and the Cinema: A Reader
This book gathers all the essential texts from a wide
range of sources, providing a stimulating cross-
cultural dialogue.
[H102] Routledge pbk **£7.95**

WOLLEN, PETER
**Readings and Writings: Semiotic
Counterstrategies**
A collection of essays, script ideas and reprinted
pieces by one of the most influential and accessible of
film theorists. Includes essays on Welles, Hitchcock
and Chaplin and an excellent piece on the
development of cinematic technology.
[H104] Verso pbk **£7.95**

Monographs

Monographs are usually published in recognition
of the more established or 'great' directors, and it is
they therefore who dominate this section. Wherever
possible, lesser-known film-makers (like
experimental animator Len Lye or Spike Lee)
have been included where books are available. There
are only a few technicians included here: their
experience of cinema is equally fascinating and is
often found in the technical books of practical film-
making, e.g *Film Magic* by David Hutchings, or
Film Lighting by Kris Malkiewicz. It must also
be noted that there are no women listed in this
section, due entirely to a lack of books! It is hoped
that the great numbers of feminist critics and
theorcticians included in the previous section goes

some way towards righting the balance. For further information on individual film-makers see also the *Biography* section.

ALLEN, WOODY

New Yorker Woody Allen is responsible for such soul-searching comedies as *Hannah and her Sisters* and *Annie Hall*; his style is eclectic and influenced by Fellini and Bergman in particular.
BRODE
Woody Allen
A critical overview of Allen's career.
[H105] Columbus pbk **£8.95**
HIRSCH, FOSTER
Love, Sex, Death and the Meaning of Life: Woody Allen's Comedy
[H106] McGraw Hill pbk **£9.95**
NAVACELLE, THIERRY DE
Woody Allen on Location
A privileged insight into the Director's working habits, since he rarely allows writers on set.
[H107] Sidgwick pbk **£7.95**

ALMENDROS, NESTOR
Man with a Camera
The internationally acclaimed cinematographer who shot many of Truffaut's films, as well as the unforgettable landscapes in *Days of Heaven*, here gives a cameraman's eye view of film-making.
[H108] Faber pbk **£9.95**

ANTONIONI, MICHELANGELO
Acclaimed Italian director of such modernist masterpieces as *Blow Up* and *The Passenger*, he is famous for his visual representation of existential situations.
That Bowling Alley on the Tiber: Tales of a Director
A notebook of essays by the director who claims his thoughts are always about film. Includes 33 ideas for films yet unmade, inspired by everything from T.S. Eliot to travels in the desert.
[H109] Oxford hbk **£9.50**
[H110] Oxford pbk **£6.95**

APPIGNANESI, RICHARD
Axis: Fassbinder, Mishima, Pasolini **NEW**
Extended essay on the careers and impact of three controversial and innovative post-war film-makers.
[H111] Plexus pbk **£6.95**

BERGMAN, INGMAR
Swedish theatre director and perhaps cinema's most profound psychologist, his films plumb the heights and depths of religious faith and sexual anxiety; his work includes *Persona* and *Fanny and Alexander*.
MOSLEY, PHILIP
Ingmar Bergman: The Cinema as Mistress
A critical history of his films - the development of his individual technique is related alongside biographical detail.
[H112] Boyars pbk **£4.95**

BERTOLUCCI, BERNARDO
KOLKER, ROBERT PHILLIP
Bernardo Bertolucci
Various critical perspectives on his life and work.
[H113] BFI pbk **£7.95**

BOORMAN, JOHN
British film-maker with a superb instinct for popular narrative. His films are often based on the idea of a quest or journey, often with magical or fantastical overtones.
Money into Light: The Emerald Forest Diary
Boorman's diary of the immense difficulties he

encountered from every side when making *The Emerald Forest*.
[H114] Faber pbk **£4.95**
CIMENT, MICHEL
John Boorman
A lavishly-illustrated and impeccably-researched monograph by the distinguished French critic.
[H115] Faber hbk **£14.95**

BRESSON, ROBERT
Originally a painter, Bresson's work is an investigation into the nature of cinematic narration. In films such as *Four Nights of a Dreamer*, Bresson uses mainly untrained actors and strips down image and sound to create emotional tension.
Notes on the Cinematographer
Reflections on the art of cinema.
[H116] Quartet pbk **£4.95**
HANLON, LINDLEY
Fragments: Bresson's Film Style
[H117] Associated UP hbk **£18.95**

BUNUEL, LUIS
Spanish filmmaker and one time collaborator with Dali, Buñuel was unrelenting in his assault on bourgeois values, exposing deceit and decadence in such films as *The Exterminating Angel* and *That Obscure Desire*.
EDWARDS, GWYNNE
The Discreet Art of Luis Buñuel: A Reading of his Films
One of the most all-encompassing works on Buñuel.
[H118] Boyars hbk **£16.00**

CAPRA, FRANK
Starting in the pre-talkies days Capra went on to become skilled in the manipulation of actors and narrative, particularly sensitive to the importance of the spoken word in sound film. Director of the award-winning comedy, *It Happened One Night*.
BASINGER, JEANINE
It's a Wonderful Life
A film book classic, which tells the story of Capra's life and times, and of the making of his masterpiece.
[H119] Pavilion pbk **£9.95**

CHAPLIN, CHARLIE
Universally known through his great comic icon, the 'Little Tramp', Chaplin also developed a cinema of great moral and technical complexity. Films such as *Modern Times* and *City Lights* show best his use of sound and long, exactly choreographed sequences.
CONWAY, M.; MCDONALD, G. & RICCI, M.
The Complete Films of Charlie Chaplin
Includes stills, credits, synopses and details of critical reception.
[H120] Citadel P pbk **£12.95**
MALAND, C.J.
Chaplin and American Culture: The Evolution of a Star Image
[H122] Princeton UP hbk **£20.95**
SMITH, JULIAN
Charlie Chaplin
A good (if brief) monograph, covering all aspects of Chaplin's career.
[H123] Columbus pbk **£5.95**

CIMINO, MICHAEL
Maker of popular epics, unmatched in scale and ambition by anyone since Griffith, Cimino is now best remembered for the huge financial disaster of *Heaven's Gate*, the film that destroyed a whole studio (United Artists) single-handed.
BACH, STEVEN
Final Cut: Dreams and Disaster in the Making of Heaven's Gate
One of the truly essential books on the mechanics of contemporary film making.
[H124] Faber pbk **£5.95**

Charlie Chaplin from Maureen Bessy's biography (Thames & Hudson hbk £20.00)

COCTEAU, JEAN
Poet, playwright and boxing manager, Cocteau created some of the most perfectly-realised examples of pure poetry ever committed to celluloid. His career spanned the 1920s-1950s.
Beauty and the Beast: Diary of a Film
[H125] Dover pbk **£4.45**

EISENSTEIN, SERGI
Russian director of *Battleship Potempkin* and *Ivan the Terrible*, Eisenstein was a tireless explorer of the possibilities of cinema, now, through his innovative use of montage, generally recognised as the first architect of film language.
AUMONT, JACQUES
Montage Eisenstein
The first major study of the film-maker that had access to the previously unknown material uncovered in the Soviet Union in the 1960s and early 70s. Particularly illuminating on Eisenstein's development as an aesthetician.
[H126] BFI pbk **£9.95**
LEYDA, JAY & VOYNOW, ZINA
Eisenstein At Work
A compilation of Eisenstein's own sketches, notes, letters and photos, as well as eye-witness accounts, building up an intimate record of the genesis of his film projects. Includes details of his lost epic *Que Viva Mexico*.
[H127] Methuen pbk **£9.95**

FASSBINDER, RAINER WERNER
Central figure in the New German Cinema. He developed an exciting blend of Hollywood narrative and politically motivated critique in such films as *Beware of a Holy Whore* and *Querelle*.
KATZ, ROBERT & BERLING, PETER
Love is Colder than Death
An illustrated portrait of the director who lived fast and died young, relating his life to his work.
[H128] Grafton pbk **£4.99**

FELLINI, FEDERICO
Fellini's place in film history is secure with such greats as *La Dolce Vita* and *8 1/2*. His worth is

controversial, combining an exuberant visual style with a series of mythic explorations of his own psychology and personal history.

BURKE, FRANK
Federico Fellini: Variety Lights to Dolce Vita
Absorbing and scholarly perspective on his career.
[H129] Columbus pbk **£5.95**

FAVA, CLAUDIO & VIGANO, ALDO
The Films of Federico Fellini
Includes a brief introduction by Fellini, biographical information, synopses and details of cast and crew.
[H130] Citadel P pbk **£12.95**

FORD, JOHN
The great poet of America's landscape and its pioneering spirit, Ford grew up with the American cinema, and in his own films chronicles the society of half a century. Only a third of his films were westerns, but he is best remembered for such epics as *The Searchers* and *Stagecoach*.

ANDERSON, LINDSAY
About John Ford
A passionate study by a British film-maker whose own films are also concerned with the relationship between an individual and his environment.
[H132] Plexus pbk **£8.95**

MACBRIDE, JOSEPH & WILLINGTON, M.
John Ford
A good general introduction to the man and his work.
[H133] Secker pbk **£6.95**

GANCE, ABEL
The first director to use widescreen and multi-screen projection, and creator of some of the most extravagant and impressive scenes ever filmed. With the recent recovery of *Napoleon*, he has been established as one of the greatest directors of all time.

KING, NORMAN
Abel Gance: Politics of Spectacle
[H135] BFI pbk **£7.95**

GODARD, JEAN LUC
One of the most influential directors of the last 30 years. Central to the French New Wave, his films bring together an enthusiasm for the Hollywood 'B' movie with a Brechtian aesthetic of alienation.

MCCABE, COLIN
Images, Sounds, Politics
Godard's work in the context of his radical politics.
[H136] Macmillan pbk **£8.50**

MILNE, TOM (ED)
Godard on Godard
Godard came to film through criticism, this collection of essays and interviews also double as an outrageous self-portrait.
[H137] Da Capo pbk **£10.95**

GRIFFITH, D.W.
Simultaneously described as a director of 'genius' and criticized for his 'vulgarity' and 'inanity', Griffith was one of the most prolific and influential of the early American directors and a founder member of United Artists. Amongst his 485 films are the silent epics, *The Birth of a Nation* and *Intolerance*.

BROWN, KARL
Adventures with D.W. Griffith
Described by Kevin Brownlow as 'the most exciting and the most perceptive volume of reminiscence ever published on the cinema'.
[H138] Faber pbk **£6.95**

GEDULD, HARRY (ED)
Focus on D.W. Griffiths
Places Griffith's work in the context of film history.
[H139] Prentice-Hall pbk **£1.60**

HADLEIGH, BOZE
Conversations with My Elders **NEW**
Six well-known personalities, including Rock Hudson

and photographer Cecil Beaton, discuss the cinema and the secret they all shared - their homosexuality.
[H140] GMP pbk **£4.95**

HAWKS, HOWARD
The greatest American director of genre films, responsible for *To Have and Have Not* and *Scarface*. His consistency and self-referential wit made him a darling of the *auteur* movement in 1960s criticism.

MAST, GERALD
Howard Hawks Storyteller
His life and work, written by an experienced film writer and teacher.
[H141] Oxford hbk **£17.50**

HERZOG, WERNER
German film-maker working in an eccentric tradition of visionary romanticism. Herzog's vision is intense and often profoundly disturbing, in such films as *The Enigma of Kaspar Hauser* and *Cobra Verde*.

CORRIGAN, T. (ED)
Films of Werner Herzog
[H142] Methuen pbk **£9.95**
The Films of Werner Herzog: Betwen Mirage and History
Juxtaposes Herzog's controversial career as a director with a critical analysis of his films.
[H143] Methuen pbk **£9.95**

HITCHCOCK, ALFRED
Hitchcock remains a by-word for suspense and psycho-sexual anxiety. His influence is everywhere but his instinct for entertainment with an edge is unequalled.

LEFF, LEONARD
Hitchcock and Selznick
The rich and strange collaboration of Alfred Hitchcock and David O. Selznick in Hollywood.
[H144] Weidenfeld pbk **£9.95**

MODLESKI, TANIA
The Women Who Knew Too Much: Hitchcock and Feminist Theory
A feminist reading of Hitchcock's films, with essays covering everything from 'Rape vs Manslaughter' to 'Women and the Labyrinth'.
[H145] Methuen pbk **£7.95**

RYALL, TOM
Alfred Hitchcock: British Cinema
A study of Hitchcock's formative years in Britain, when he directed 23 of his 53 films. Ryall examines these films in the context of the period.
[H146] C Helm hbk **£13.95**

TRUFFAUT, FRANCOIS (ED)
Hitchcock
The best insight into the work and mind of Hitchcock. In conversation with Truffaut he reveals details of the construction of famous sequences and information about his relationship to actors and film in general.
[H147] Grafton pbk **£8.95**

JARMAN, DEREK
A provocative and experimental contemporary British director, Jarman has been greatly influenced by Pasolini and his parallel career as a painter.
Dancing Ledge
Musings on the inter-relation of art and life, and in particular the relation his homosexuality bears to his films. The account of the development of films like *Sebastiane* and *The Tempest* are fascinating insights into the mechanics of independent film-making.
[H148] Quartet pbk **£7.95**
Derek Jarman's Caravaggio
Illustrated book of his avant-garde low-budget film.
[H149] Thames & H pbk **£10.00**
The Last of England
The political, sexual and aesthetic quandaries of contemporary Britain form a beautifully-written accompaniment to the film.
[H150] Constable hbk **£10.95**

LANG, FRITZ
An early German expressionist who developed his style and thematic preoccupations in Hollywood. Resulting films such as *The Big Heat* and *Human Desire* are lean and atmospheric tales.

JENKINS, STEPHEN (ED)
Fritz Lang
Good selection of critical essays covering all aspects of his career.
[H151] BFI hbk **£9.00**
[H152] BFI pbk **£4.95**

LASSALLY, WALTER
Itinerant Cameraman
Engaging account of life on location by the man who shot, amongst other things, *Lawrence of Arabia*.
[H153] J Murray hbk **£14.95**

LEAN, DAVID
British director of such movie greats as *Lawrence of Arabia*, *Doctor Zhivago* and *Bridge Over the River Kwai*, Lean is also a respected editor who has collaborated with, amongst others, Powell & Pressburger and Noel Coward.

SILVERMAN, STEPHEN, M.
David Lean **NEW**
Stunning pictorial record of a career spanning sixty years. Contains screen images as well as behind-the-scenes and private archive material.
[H154] Deutsch hbk **£25.00**

LEE, SPIKE
Contemporary American director, working on relatively low-budget independent films which bring black actors and a black perspective into the commercial cinema, with a quirky, 'Woody Allen' style of social comedy.
Spike Lee's Gotta Have It: Inside Guerilla Film-Making **NEW**
Lee's own journal and production notes documenting the birth of the idea and 'the actual pure hell' he went through to realise the film, *She's Gotta Have It*. As entertaining as the film itself and an informative glimpse at the mechanics of film-making. Includes a full length interview by Nelson George and the entire screenplay.
[H155] Simon & Sch pbk **£6.95**

Jack Birkett (as Caliban) in 'The Tempest' from Derek Jarman's *Dancing Ledge* (Quartet pbk **£7.95**)

LESTER, RICHARD

British director famed for his Beatles collaboration *A Hard Day's Night* and, more recently, for *Superman II & III*.
SINYARD, NEIL
The Films of Richard Lester
Critical analysis of his films, giving them a serious place in film history.
[H156] C Helm hbk **£22.50**

LOSEY, JOSEPH

American film-maker whose career in film and theatre spanned five decades; his collaborations with Harold Pinter included *The Servant* and *The Go-Between*.
CIMENT, MICHEL (ED)
Conversations with Losey
[H157] Methuen hbk **£30.00**
[H158] Methuen pbk **£14.95**

LYE, LEN

New Zealand-born pioneer of experimental film, kinetic sculptor and painter, Lye emigrated to London in the 1920s and worked with the GPO Film Unit before moving to New York. He invented 'direct film': scratching, stencilling or painting direct onto celluloid, thus *"making movies"*, as he put it *"without a camera"*.
CURNOW, WYSTAN & HORROCKS, R (EDS)
Figures of Motion: Selected Writings
Len Lye's own theories of film and the Art of motion, including 'Beginnings', his childhood memories of the New Zealand landscape and his formative experiences, as well as prose and poetry.
[H159] Oxford hbk **£18.50**

OZU, YASUJIRO

One of Japan's greatest directors, Ozu has been praised for his formal perfection but criticized for being a social conservative. His work is preoccupied with the patience and devotion of women in love.

Images of a 'stencil pattern' aircraft and a 'man signalling' from Len Lye's *Figures of Motion* (Editors: Curnow & Horrocks) (Oxford hbk £18.50)

BORDWELL, DAVID
Ozu and the Poetics of Cinema
Bordwell subjects Ozu's reputation to rigorous analysis with an in-depth look at his films and career as a director.
[H161] BFI pbk **£15.00**

POLANSKI, ROMAN

Polish-born director of great originality, his films confront problems of isolation, violence and evil. He directed *Rosemary's Baby* and *Chinatown*, films tinged with sadism and a fascination with pagan superstition.
WEXMAN, VIRGINIA WRIGHT (ED)
Roman Polanski
Polanski's sensational private life has dominated discussion of his films: this study focuses on his critical and commercial successes and the themes of his work.
[H162] Columbus pbk **£5.95**

POWELL, MICHAEL & PRESSBURGER, EMERIC

The pointed observations and humanity of Pressburger's scripts found their exact counterpoint in the almost mystical raptures of Powell's visual style. Experimental, challenging and popular, they number amongst Britain's greatest, renowned for films like *Colonel Blimp* and *Black Narcissus*.
CHRISTIE, IAN (ED)
Powell, Pressburger and Others
A study of the writer/director collaboration in the context of the times.
[H163] BFI pbk **£2.95**

ROSSELLINI, ROBERTO

Rossellini's name is inseperable from the post-war school of Italian neo-realism. His work is concerned with the unique experience of the individual within a social context, from Nazi Germany to the time of Louis XIV.
BRUNETTE, PETER
Roberto Rossellini
A study of the career of the great Italian film director. Published to commemorate the tenth anniversary of his death.
[H165] Oxford pbk **£8.95**

SCORSESE, MARTIN

Contemporary American film-maker whose assaults on the foundations of male sexuality and whose perennial themes of violence, guilt and redemption have never impaired his general popularity. Director of *Taxi Driver*, *Raging Bull* and *The Last Temptation of Christ*.
CHRISTIE, IAN & THOMPSON, D (EDS)
Scorsese on Scorsese `NEW`
Scorsese discusses his passionate and personal view of the cinema, highlighting the successes and failures of his own career. Illustrated with stills and sketches from his own archive.
[H166] Faber hbk **£14.95**

SEMBENE, OUSMANE

Africa's premier film-maker, a Marxist with a true Buñuelian feel for the absurd. Much of his work concerns the degradation of African culture after the achievement of independence.
PFAFF, FRANCOISE
The Cinema of Ousmane Sembene: A Pioneer of African Film
[H167] Greenwood P hbk **£26.95**

SPIELBERG, STEVEN

Spielberg's films are amongst the most successful of all time. A brilliant craftsman and storyteller, his work includes *Jaws*, *ET*, *The Color Purple* and the *Indiana Jones* trilogy.

MOTT, DONALD R. & SAUNDERS, CHERYL MCALLISTER
Steven Spielberg
Potted history of Spielberg's career, selection of critical essays and filmography.
[H168] Columbus pbk **£5.95**
SINYARD, NEIL
The Films of Steven Spielberg
[H169] Hamlyn pbk **£7.95**

STRAUB, JEAN-MARIE

Austere formalist whose films address the nature of cinematic signification and its political implications.
ROUD, RICHARD
Jean-Marie Straub
[H170] Secker pbk **£5.50**

TARKOVSKY, ANDREI

Russian film-maker, pre-occupied with cinema as a language of time and its ability to explore the 'spiritual'. His work, including *The Sacrifice* and *Solaris*, has opened a new chapter in film history.
Sculpting in Time: Reflections on the Cinema
A working through of his own understanding of the fundamental laws of cinema. Illustrated with stills and includes poetry by his father, Arseniy Tarkovsky.
[H171] Faber pbk **£14.99**
LE FANU, MARK
The Cinema of Andrei Tarkovsky
The first general study of Tarkovsky in English.
[H172] BFI hbk **£16.00**
[H173] BFI pbk **£7.95**
TUROVSKAYA, MAYA
Cinema as Poetry `NEW`
The first book about Tarkovsky by a leading Soviet critic to be translated into English. Forms a companion volume to Tarkovsky's own work *Sculpting in Time*.
[H174] Faber hbk **£14.99**

TRUFFAUT, FRANCOIS

A central figure of the French New Wave, as a theorist and a director, whose films are often exercises in style and genre. He believed in the formal potential of film to create a humane and meaningful response to the seeming chaos of reality.
Truffaut by Truffaut
Brings together Truffaut's insights on his own life and work and illustrates them with intriguing personal documents, many of them never before published. Includes 500 photogrpahs from all areas of his life.
[H175] Abrams hbk **£35.00**

VERTOV, DZIGA

Pioneer Soviet documentarist and leader of the revolutionary Kino-Pravda group, Vertov's films are composed of 'fragments of actuality' juxtaposed in provocative ways.
PETRIC, VLADA
The Man with the Movie Camera: Constructivism in Film
[H177] Cambridge hbk **£32.50**

VISCONTI, LUCHINO

A Marxist, Visconti's concern for the the process of historical change is usually counterpointed by a rich, almost baroque use of colour and camera movement. His subjects are often historical melodramas, as in *The Leopard*.
TONETTI, CLORETTA
Luchino Visconti
[H178] Columbus pbk **£5.95**

VON STERNBERG, JOSEF

Best remembered for his work with Marlene Dietrich in strange films such as *The Blue Angel*, memorable for their deadpan dialogue, black humour and elliptical melodramatic plots.

Fun in a Chinese Laundry
Von Sternberg's autobiography and reflections on life, love, Hollywood, Marlene Dietrich and the cinema.
[H179] Columbus pbk **£5.95**
BAXTER, PETER (ED)
Sternberg
Selection of essays covering all aspects of his career, including contributions from Arnheim and Kracauer, and 'The Von Sternberg Principle' by the director himself.
[H181] BFI pbk **£3.95**
ZUCKER, CAROL
The Idea of the Image: Josef von Sternberg's Dietrich Films
In-depth study of Von Sternberg's film language.
[H182] Assoc UP hbk **£18.00**

VON STROHEIM, ERICH
The archetypal 'Great Director' (later to parody himself in Wilder's *Sunset Boulevard*), his career was frustrated by an inability to adapt to the Hollywood machine. *Greed*, his greatest film, is a masterpiece of stylised realism.
KOZARSKI, RICHARD
The Man You Loved to Hate: Erich Von Stroheim and Hollywood
[H183] Oxford pbk **£9.95**

WAJDA, ANDRZEJ
Double Vision: My Life in Film   NEW
Wajda traces his own artistic development alongside historic events in Poland, from the Second World War, to the evolution of Solidarity.
[H184] Faber pbk **£5.95**

WATERS, JOHN
Underground cult film-maker, responsible for sleazy classics (usually assisted by the inimitable and dominating presence of Divine) such as *Desperate Living*, *Pink Flamingoes* and more recently, *Hairspray*.
Crackpot: The Obsessions of John Waters   NEW
A taste of Waters's outrageous excursions into journalism.
[H185] Fourth Estate pbk **£5.95**

WELLES, ORSON
A pioneering and passionate film-maker whose creative use of the long shot, deep focus, wide-angle lenses and baroque compositions is still making its influence felt today.
CARRINGER, ROBERT L.
The Making of Citizen Kane
A fabulous document containing the script, storyboard fragments, visuals and production details.
[H186] J Murray pbk **£8.95**
COWIE, PETER
The Cinema of Orson Welles
[H187] Da Capo pbk **£9.50**
WELLES, ORSON & MANKIEWICZ, HERMAN J.
The Citizen Kane Book
Background on the making of *Citizen Kane*, by the men themselves.
[H188] Methuen pbk **£7.50**

WENDERS, WIM
Emotion Pictures   NEW
Wenders explores the obsessions and experiences that fire his films, and as a European film-maker in Hollywood, he also contemplates the meaning of the 'American Dream' both for himself and for America. His films include *Paris, Texas* and *Wings of Desire*.
[H189] Faber hbk **£14.95**
WENDERS, WIM & SHEPARD, SAM
Paris, Texas
[H566] Ecco P pbk **£15.95**

World Film by Area

Britain & Ireland

BFI Film and Television Yearbook 1988 - 89   NEW
Invaluable reference work, packed with information on production companies, facilities and prime-movers in the British film and television industries.
[H190] BFI pbk **£10.95**

Directory of Irish and Irish-Related Films   NEW
A unique reference work on the Irish cinema, with contributions from film-makers, producers and cameramen throughout Ireland, Europe and the US.
[H191] Flicks Bks pbk **£17.00**

ALDGATE, ANTHONY & RICHARDS, JEFFREY
Britain Can Take it
A study of the extraordinary achievements of the British film industry's finest hour - in the service of the Ministry of Information during the Second World War - placing the films in a wider social and political context by drawing on official information, box office returns and scripts.
[H194] Blackwell hbk **£15.00**

AUTY, MARTIN & RODDICK, NICK
British Cinema Now
Powerful and informative short study of the contemporary scene; the hype, the triumphs and the abysmal failures are all dealt with in an authoritative manner.
[H196] BFI pbk **£6.95**

BARR, CHARLES (ED)
All Our Yesterdays: 90 Years of British Cinema
A marvellously refreshing read that gives the lie to the notion that 'British Cinema' is a contradiction in terms. A truly comprehensive overview.
[H197] BFI pbk **£12.95**

DOCHERTY, DAVID; MORRISON, DAVID & TRACY, MICHAEL
The Last Picture Show? Britain's Changing Film Audience
A meticulously researched survey that draws some surprising conclusions.
[H199] BFI pbk **£4.95**

HILL, JOHN
Sex, Class and Realism: British Cinema 1956 - 63
A brilliantly incisive history of the gritty social realist films that burst out of Britain in the late 1950s. Indispensable as a reference source and a major work of criticism in its own right.
[H201] BFI pbk **£7.95**

HUTCHINSON, TOM
The Goldcrest Story
An interesting account of the seemingly doomed British production company that delivered *Revolution* and *Absolute Beginners* to a largely indifferent public.
[H202] Ebury hbk **£12.95**

MCARTHUR, COLIN (ED)
Scotch Reels: Scotland in Cinema and Television
Polemical in tone and fascinating in content.
[H203] BFI pbk **£3.95**

RICHARDS, J. & SHERIDAN, D.
Mass Observation at the Movies
Movie-going was the great social habit of the 1930s and 40s, and Mass Observation (as part of a huge and on-going documentary project) charted the effect films had on the lives of ordinary people by recording first-hand their reactions to what they saw.
[H207] Routledge hbk **£37.50**

ROBERTSON, JAMES
The Hidden Cinema   NEW
An investigation into film censorship and how it operated in Britain from 1913-1972.
[H208] Routledge hbk **£30.00**

WALKER, ALEXANDER
Hollywood England: The British Film Industry in the 1960s
A general study by entertaining and highly influential film critic of the *Evening Standard*.
[H209] Harrap pbk **£7.95**
National Heroes: British Cinema in the '70s and '80s
Critical account of the changing face of the industry.
[H211] Harrap pbk **£6.95**

WARREN, PATRICIA
Elstree: The British Hollywood   NEW
An entertaining account of life under the bright lights and in the shadows of Elstree Studios, by actress and film-buff Warren, who writes with much first-hand knowledge.
[H212] Columbus pbk **£9.95**

United States & Hollywood

ADAIR, GILBERT
Hollywood's Vietnam: From 'The Green Berets' to 'Apocalypse Now'
Revised edition of a book examining the treatment of the war in over 60 films, and analysing the various approaches and ideological stances of film-makers.
[H213] Heinemann pbk **£7.95**

ALTMAN, RICK (ED)
Genre: The Musical
An excellent anthology of essays which looks at many different aspects of the American Musical: the development from stagebound set pieces to Gene Kelly's integrated musicals at MGM, Busby Berkeley's escapist fantasies and beyond.
[H214] Routledge pbk **£7.50**

ANGER, KENNETH
Hollywood Babylon
Representing a kind of landmark in grime, gossip and salacious misrepresentation, the two 'Holly Babies' are underground classics.
[H215] Arrow pbk **£4.99**
Hollywood Babylon II
[H216] Arrow pbk **£7.95**

BAILEY, MARGARET J.
Those Glorious Glamour Years   NEW
A celebration of classic Hollywood costume design from the 1930s. Over 700 illustrations featuring the work of Adrian, Orry-Kely and others, modelled by such stars as Vivien Leigh, Joan Crawford and Marlene Dietrich.
[H218] Columbus pbk **£14.95**

BLACK, D & KOPPS, C
Hollywood Goes to War
[H219] IB Tauris hbk **£14.95**

Marlon Brando from Kenneth Anger's *Hollywood Babylon II* (Arrow pbk £7.95)

BORDWELL, DAVID; STAIGER, JANET & THOMPSON, KRISTIN
The Classical Hollywood Cinema: Film Style and Mode of Production to 1960
An exhaustive and indispensable history. The combination of judicious analysis and factual weight is unlikely to be surpassed for many years to come.
[H221] Routledge pbk **£12.95**

BROOKS, LOUISE
Lulu in Hollywood
One of the world's most beautiful women tells of her early success in Hollywood, her most famous role in G.W. Pabst's *Pandora's Box* and her ultimate rejection by the sychophantic male-dominated studio system. A remarkable book by a uniquely well-informed and eloquent commentator.
[H222] Arrow pbk **£6.95**

CRIPPS, THOMAS
Slow Fade to Black: The Negro in American Film 1900 - 42
A fascinating and carefully documented history; particularly revealing on D.W. Griffith's *Birth of a Nation*.
[H223] Oxford hbk **£13.00**

EYLES, ALLAN
That Was Hollywood: The 1930s
First in a series of reference guides to Hollywood's film releases.
[H224] Batsford hbk **£14.95**
That Was Hollywood: The 1940s **NEW**
[H225] Batsford hbk **£14.95**

FAHEY, DAVID & RICH, LINDA
Masters of Starlight **NEW**
A tribute to the legion of stills photographers working in Hollywood between 1910-1970, whose single aim was to make mere men and women objects of fantasy, aspiration and longing. Compiled by Fahey and Rich, of the Hollywood Photographer's Archives.
[H226] Columbus pbk **£19.95**

FELL, JOHN C.
Before Hollywood: Turn of the Century American Film
Studies the first two decades of American Cinema.
[H227] Hudson Hills P hbk **£25.00**

HIRSCHHORN, CLIVE
The Hollywood Musical
If you want an illustrated book on musicals, this is the one to buy. Includes a foreword by Gene Kelly.
[H233] Octopus pbk **£9.95**

IZOD, JOHN
Hollywood and the Box Office 1895 - 1986
How the continual threat of financial collapse has moulded the methods and philosophies of the studios and corporations that control Hollywood.
[H235] Macmillan pbk **£9.95**

KOLKER, ROBERT PHILLIP
A Cinema of Loneliness: Penn, Kubrick, Altman, Scorcese, Coppola
Kolker places the films of these directors in an ideological perspective, and charts the relationship they have to one another with particular emphasis on the statements their films make about American society.
[H236] Oxford pbk **£12.50**

NORMAN, BARRY
Talking Pictures: The Story of Hollywood
Companion to a recent TV series, this book traces the development of Hollywood and the Hollywood Movie. Compiled by the television presenter and arbiter of British film taste.
[H240] BBC/Hodder hbk **£14.95**

OCTOPUS HISTORY OF THE HOLLYWOOD MOVIES
Excellent series of well-illustrated reference books which cover the films and stars of each of the major Hollywood studios.
The Disney Studio Story **NEW**
The story of 'the greatest dream factory in Hollywood' with full filmography and bibliography, it covers Disney landmarks from Mickey Mouse's début in 1928 to the modern box-office hits.
[H241] Octopus pbk **£16.95**
BERGEN, RONALD
The United Artists Story
[H242] Octopus hbk **£14.95**
EAMES, JOHN DOUGLAS
The MGM Story
[H243] Octopus pbk **£9.95**
The Paramount Story
[H244] Octopus hbk **£14.95**
HIRSCHHORN, CLIVE
The Universal Story
[H245] Octopus hbk **£9.95**
The Warner Bros Story
[H246] Octopus hbk **£11.95**

PETRIE, GRAHAM
Hollywood Destinies: European Directors in America 1922 - 1931
A study of the impact foreign talent had on Hollywood and how, in turn, Hollywood made its mark on these newcomers.
[H247] Routledge hbk **£25.00**

SINCLAIR, M.
Hollywood Lolita **NEW**
A provocative history of the alluring child-woman images portrayed in the movies, from sexy Victorians like Lilian Gish to the devil's daughters of the present day.
[H248] Plexus pbk **£6.95**

SMITH, T.G.
Industrial Light and Magic
ILM are responsible for the 'movie magic' in such films as *Star Wars* and *ET*. Smith, manager of ILM for 5 years, takes us behind the scenes for a complete analysis of the special effects process - from creature development to optical composing, looking at the technology involved and the evolution of the studio itself. A feast of photos, paintings and technical illustrations with a glossary of terms and screen credits for all ILM's productions. A luxurious book for anyone in love with movies.
[H249] Columbus hbk **£39.95**

STEVEN, PETER (ED)
Jump Cut: Hollywood Politics and Counter-Cinema
Articles from the influential alternative film magazine. It reveals a politicised, eclectic and subversive Hollywood that we very rarely hear about. A fascinating book.
[H250] BFI pbk **£9.95**

WILEY, MASON & BONA, DAMIEN
Inside Oscar: The Unofficial History of the Academy Awards
[H252] Columbus hbk **£12.95**

Europe

BERGSON, PHILLIP
World Cinema Vol 4: Holland
Good introduction to the subject combining interviews, bibliography and film stills with general information.
[H253] Flicks Bks hbk **£11.95**

BREN, FRANK
World Cinema Vol 1: Poland
Excellent short survey containing general information, interviews and good bibliographies.
[H254] Flicks Bks hbk **£11.95**

FRANCE
BLAKEWAY, CLAIRE
Jacques Prévert and Popular French Theatre and Cinema **NEW**
Examines the growth of the surrealist movement in the visual arts in France, and in particular Prévert's influence on film-makers Carné and Jean Renoir.
[H255] Assoc UP hbk **£17.50**
BUSS, ROBIN
The French through Their Films
A book which examines how far modern French culture has analysed and defined itself through the medium of film. Contains a reference guide to nearly 200 films.
[H256] Batsford hbk **£12.95**
MARTIN, JOHN W.
The Golden Age of French Cinema 1929 - 39
A succinct and accessible history in the excellent Columbus series. Ideal for the student.
[H257] Columbus hbk **£5.95**

GERMANY
FRANKLIN, JAMES
New German Cinema
Fassbinder, Herzog, Schlöndorff, et al, put in a clear historical and critical perspective.
[H258] Columbus pbk **£5.95**
RENTSCHLER, E. (ED)
German Film and Literature: Adaptions and Transformations
An interesting and varied series of articles which examine the influence of literary themes, techniques

and genres on both classic and contemporary German cinema.
[H259] Methuen pbk **£11.95**

ITALY

BUSS, ROBIN
The Italians through Their Films NEW
A short history of Italian cinema, relating the films to the mood of their times, both historically and socially. Contains a reference guide to over 100 films, including plots, credits and contemporary reviews.
[H261] Batsford pbk **£14.95**

GUILIANA, BRUNO & NADOTTIS, MARIA
Off Screen: Women and Film in Italy
An Italian perspective on women and film from two of the country's leading feminist film critics.
[H262] Routledge hbk **£25.00**
[H263] Routledge pbk **£8.95**

WITCOMBE, R.T.
The New Italian Cinema
Covers the most important film-makers of the generation following Rossellini, such as Bertolucci, Rosi, the Taviani Brothers and Visconti.
[H264] Secker pbk **£8.50**

MCILROY, BRIAN
World Cinema Vol 2: Sweden
Good short survey including interviews, bibliographies and many b/w stills.
[H265] Flicks Bks hbk **£11.95**

RUSSIA

MARSHALL, HERBERT
Masters of Soviet Cinema: Crippled Creative Biographies
Creative biographies of film-makers including Vselolod, Pudovkin, Dziga, Vertov, Alexander Dovzhenko and Sergei Eisenstein.
[H267] Routledge hbk **£25.00**

SCHNITZER, LUDA & MARCEL, JEAN & MARTIN
Cinema in Revolution: The Heroic Era of the Soviet Film
[H268] Da Capo pbk **£9.95**

TAYLOR, RICHARD & CHRISTIE, IAN
The Film Factory: Russian and Soviet Cinema in Documents 1896 - 1939
A treasure trove of background information to one of the great explosions of 20th century culture. A must for the student but marvellous just for browsing.
[H269] Routledge hbk **£35.00**

World

BARNARD, TIM
Argentine Cinema* NEW
Barnard is a Canadian film producer, particularly interested in political and censorship issues, as well as in the artistic development of cinema in Argentina. Contributions from leading commentators including Jorge Luis Borges.
[H270] Apollo P hbk **£9.95**

BARNOUW, ERIK
Indian Film
This book provides an excellent introduction to the world's largest film industry by a distinguished film historian.
[H271] Galaxy P pbk **£8.95**

BARRETT, GREGORY
Archetypes in Japanese Film NEW
A sociological study of the significance of the heroes and heroines in Japanese films and their influence on popular culture and religion.
[H272] Assoc UP hbk **£24.00**

BURCH, NOEL
To the Distant Observer: Form and Meaning in the Japanese Cinema
A comprehensive survey of Japanese directors such as Kurosawa, Ozu, Oshima and Mizoguchi, but also particularly illuminating on the Japanese studio system from which they emerged.
[H273] Scolar P pbk **£6.95**

CHANAN, MICHAEL
The Cuban Image
The first history of Cuban cinema to be written in English, this is a fascinating introduction to a film industry that has been at the centre of its country's cultural and political debates since the revolution.
[H274] BFI pbk **£8.95**

CLARKE, PAUL
Chinese Cinema: Culture and Politics since 1949
Traces the Chinese film industry's development from the foundation of the People's Republic in 1949 to the mid-1980s new wave, which boasts such films as the acclaimed *Yellow Earth*.
[H275] Cambridge hbk **£27.50**

DOWNING, J.D.H.
Film and Politics in the Third World
The only anthology of its kind in English with analysis of individual films, interviews with important directors such as Ousmene, Xie Jin and Jorge Sanjinés, studies of national industries and political and aesthetic manifestos.
[H276] Praeger hbk **£24.95**

MCFARLANE, BRIAN
Australian Cinema 1970 - 1985
The success of directors like Peter Weir, Bruce Beresford and Paul Cox bears witness to the current fertility of the Australian film industry. An excellent introduction to the subject.
[H277] Secker pbk **£9.95**

PFAFF, FRANCOISE (ED)
25 Black African Film-Makers
A critical study with exhaustive filmographies, biographies and bibliographies.
[H278] Greenwood P hbk **£40.95**

TOMASELLI, K
The Cinema of Apartheid: Race and Class in South African Film
Analysis of the historical development and the present state of South African cinema, describing the films themselves and linking them to the reality of life in the country.
[H281] Routledge pbk **£9.95**

Practical Film-making

A selection of some of the best manuals, from a huge and often highly specialised area. The books included are accessible but professional in approach, many of them from the Focal Press, one of the most respected publishers of practical books with titles for almost every aspect of film-making.

BERNSTEIN, STEVEN
The Technique of Film Production NEW
Essential reference work for practitioners and a good primer for students, this new handbook covers all the bases of professional film production, from film 'language' to basic photography, directing, camera work, post-production and finance.
[H282] Focal P hbk **£24.95**

BURDER, JOHN
The Technique of Editing 16mm Films
An updated edition answering all the basic questions concerning each step of the editing process, designed to assist newcomers to the professional cutting room.
[H283] Focal P hbk **£21.00**

DMYTRYK, EDWARD
Director of more than 50 films, including *The Caine Mutiny* and *Murder, My Sweet*. Dmytryk brings over 60 years of experience to all his books.
Cinema: Concept and Practice NEW
Here Dmytryk bridges the gap between abstract film theory and the practical realities of production.
[H284] Focal P pbk **£13.50**

HAPPE, BERNARD
Your Film and the Lab
An important guide for anyone wishing to extend their understanding of processing techniques and to communicate effectively with lab technicians.
[H290] Focal P pbk **£10.50**

HARCOURT; HOWLETT; DAVIES & MOSCOVIC
The Independent Producer
Excellent guidance for anyone who wants to break into film-making but does not know where to begin - here is everything you need to know.
[H291] Faber pbk **£7.50**

HUTCHINGS, DAVID
Film Magic
A useful and well-illustrated guide to the use and development of special effects in contemporary film, by a specialist who has spent years prowling around special effects houses.
[H292] Simon & Sch pbk **£9.95**

KERNER, MARVIN NEW
The Art of the Sound Effects Editor
A unique look at the workaday world and job responsibilities of the Hollywood sound editor by a veteran of both TV and film. The book relates, through personal anecdotes and procedures, the actual production of a soundtrack, including backgrounds, dialogue, special sound effects and dubbing.
[H293] Focal P hbk **£10.95**

Busby Berkley from Kenneth Anger's *Hollywood Babylon II* (Arrow pbk **£7.95**)

MILLER, WILLIAM
Screenwriting for Narrative Film and Television
The best guide currently available to the writing of effective dialogue. It also contains invaluable advice on narrative structure, characterisation and setting.
[H294] Columbus pbk **£7.95**

MILLERSON, GERALD
The Technique of Lighting for Television and Motion Pictures
An extremely useful professional but accessible guide to equipment and its practical use on set.
[H295] Focal P pbk **£22.95**

MUIR, ANN ROSS
A Women's Guide to Jobs in Film and Television
[H296] Pandora pbk **£6.95**

NISBETT, ALEC
The Technique of the Sound Studio
Complete coverage of sound and microphone characteristics, balance, volume control, fades, mixes, and more.
[H297] Focal P pbk **£19.95**

RABINGER, MICHAEL
Directing the Documentary
Rabinger explains all the processes that go into directing a technically-crafted picture from camera-angles to post-production methods. He also uncovers the pitfalls you may face during a project and outlines how to avoid them.
[H298] Focal P hbk **£21.95**
Directing: Film Techniques and Aesthetics **NEW**
The art, science and practice of directing. Includes hands-on exercises and production projects designed to identify individual strengths and weaknesses.
[H299] Focal P pbk **£19.95**

REISZ, KAREL & MILLAR, GAVIN
The Technique of Film Editing
Classic study of editing by two fine directors, looking in detail at the principles of continuity, selection of shots, timing and sound editing, as well as techniques for editing action sequences and documentaries.
[H301] Focal P pbk **£15.95**

SAMUELSON, DAVID
Motion Picture Camera Techniques
Exploration of the motion picture camera in action.
[H302] Focal P hbk **£1.50**

SWAIN, DWIGHT & SWAIN, JOYE
Film Scriptwriting: A Practical Manual
A clear step-by-step guide for the working writer or the beginner alike, from getting and developing ideas to writing of master scene or shooting script. Features annotated excerpts from some of today's most successful films and interviews with professionals.
[H304] Focal P pbk **£13.50**

WIESE, MICHAEL
Film and Video Marketing **NEW**
All the practical, realistic advice you need to promote and sell your independent feature film or original home video, from a skilled professional. He pinpoints common problems and offers solutions by drawing on numerous case-study examples.
[H305] Focal P hbk **£13.95**

WILKIE, BERNARD
Creating Special Effects for TV and Films
A professional guide to a fascinating and creative area of film practice.
[H306] Focal P hbk **£10.50**

Video

Video is a new but rapidly expanding medium; for many it is more accessible than film, both in terms of equipment and finance. These books have been chosen to assist the keen amateur, or to encourage the would-be professional. *The New Electronic Media* by Hoyt R. Hilsman is particularly illuminating as a guide to a wide range of video techniques and their applications.

Newnes Book of Creative Video
A guide designed to inspire the video user to explore the medium's creative potential
[H309] Heinneman hbk **£8.95**

ARMES, ROY
On Video
A serious attempt to rescue video from its position as cinema's poor relation.
H310] Methuen hbk **£20.00**
H310A] Methuen pbk **£6.95**

BROWNE, STEVEN E.
Videotape Editing **NEW**
A practical book guiding the reader through basic concepts of videotape use and editing into the specific procedures and techniques of the editing room. Browne has been a professional videotape editor for over 13 years.
[H311] Focal P pbk **£17.95**

HEDGECOE, JOHN
Hedgecoe on Video **NEW**
An accessible guide to successful home video, with technical information on the medium and its equipment, by one of the most prolific writers of film and photography guides.
[H312] Pyramid hbk **£16.95**

HILSMAN, HOYT R.
The New Electronic Media: Innovations in Video Technologies **NEW**
Keep pace with the dazzling world of electronic media with this comprehensive reference guide; it charts the blossoming of home video technologies from the simple television set to the complex integrated video systems that are set to dominate the future.
[H313] Focal P pbk **£13.50**

LEWELL, JOHN
Multivision: The Planning, Preparation and Projection of Audio-Visual Presentations
A thorough guide to the art of audio-visual presentation.
[H314] Focal P hbk **£22.50**

LEWIS, ROLAND
The Video Maker's Handbook
An easy to follow handy-sized guide to the essentials.
[H315] Pan pbk **£9.95**

MILLERSON, GERALD
Video Camera Techniques
The fundamentals of handling, principles of operation, and proper applications for the video camera.
[H316] Focal P hbk **£10.50**
Video Production Handbook
Explains the entire process of low-cost video-making. Readable and clearly written, ideal for students, industrial and public educators, cable TV producers and hobbyists.
[H317] Focal P pbk **£17.50**

Television

Television has a complex and significant place in our mass-media culture. This selection tries to represent many relevant areas of interest from the sociological to 'soap'. The emphasis is on critical or specialist studies, but much can be learnt about the mechanics of television production and reception from more technically oriented manuals (see in particular *Directing: The Television Commercial* and *Live TV*).

Cult TV **NEW**
Photo-history of TV classics like *Batman*, *Star Trek* and *Bewitched* compiled by a fanatic
[H318] Plexus pbk **£6.95**

Shakespeare on Television **NEW**
Anthology of essays, reviews and commentaries collectively assessing the impact of televising Shakespeare's plays.
[H319] New England UP pbk **£9.95**

Who's Who on Television
The fourth revised edition with 1,000 of the best known faces on TV, from Bonnie Langford to Jonathan Ross. Includes biographical information and a special section of 'unforgettables'.
[H320] ITV pbk **£7.95**

BAER, HELEN & DYER, GILLIAN
Boxed In: Women and Televison
[H322] Pandora pbk **£7.95**

BENNETT, TONY (ED)
Popular Television and Film
An Open University set text, this book is the ideal introduction to contemporary media studies.
[H323] BFI pbk **£6.95**

BLUM, RICHARD
Television Writing: From Concept to Contract
An excellent breakdown of different script types, which also outlines the entire pre-production process through practical examples and illustrations. Includes appendices with listings of funding agencies, programmers, agents and production companies.
[H324] Focal P pbk **£16.00**

BLUM, RICHARD & LINDHEIM, RICHARD
Primetime: Network Television Programming
Thorough look at the creators, sellers, and buyers of TV programmes, and the only full explanation of the individual responsibilities of all key creative, network and production positions established in the industry.
[H325] Focal P pbk **£19.95**

BUCKINGHAM, DAVID
Public Secrets: Eastenders and its Audience
A study which deals with the relationship between Britain's most popular 'soap' and its audience. The techniques of marketing employed by the BBC and the viewer's reponse to them, as well as the interpretations imposed by the media, reveal some significant ambiguities and contradictions in the role of popular television in contemporary society.
[H326] BFI pbk **£6.95**

DANIELS, THERESE & GERSON, JANE
The Colour Black **NEW**
What is the current relationship between Black people and popular television? This collection of original and previously published articles evaluates the nature of Black images on British television.
[H327] BFI pbk **£4.95**

DAVIES, MAIRE MESSENGER
Television is Good for Your Kids `NEW`
A challenge to the view that TV is damaging to
child development, by a psychologist and writer
specialising in the media (who is also a mother
of four).
[H328] Shipman pbk **£6.95**

DAY-LEWIS, SEAN (ED)
One Day in the Life of Television `NEW`
On 1 November 1988, people throughout the British
Isles were invited to record their experiences and
feelings as they watched TV. From the diaries of the
public and those in the industry itself, Day-Lewis has
selected the most interesting to make a fascinating
portrait of the British audience's attitudes to
television.
[H329] Grafton pbk **£9.95**

FISKE, JOHN
**Television Culture: Popular Pleasures
and Politics**
Examines the complex role TV plays on our multi-
media society, its significance as a public service and
as entertainment.
[H331] Methuen pbk **£7.95**

GRADUS, BEN
Directing: The Television Commercial
Both a guide to techniques of production and a
study of the philosophy of commercial directing.
Drawing on his own experience as well as that of
dozens of other professionals in the field, the
author offers insights into the ethical decisions that
directors face. An appendix includes sample
production budgets.
[H333] Focal P hbk **£22.50**

HACKMAN, SUE & WINK
Constructing Television `NEW`
An investigation into the processes by which
television programmes are created and interpreted.
[H334] Hodder pbk **£5.95**

HOBSON, DOROTHY
Channel 4: A History `NEW`
Account of the evolution of this controversial and
fairly new channel which has become a major force in
British broadcasting in the six years since its launch.
[H335] Secker hbk **£12.95**

John Grierson from Barnouw's *Documentary: A
History of the Non-Fiction Film* (Oxford University
Press pbk £6.95)

KINGSLEY, HILARY
**Soap Box: The Papermac Guide
to Soap Opera** `NEW`
Thousands of inside stories covering almost every
'soap' ever seen on British TV: how shows got
started, their crises, scandals and oddities. A light-
hearted look at the themes and traditions of 'soap'.
[H339] Macmillan pbk **£7.95**

MACDONALD, BARRIE
**Broadcasting in the United Kingdom:
A Guide to Information Sources**
First integrated guide to information sources on UK
broadcasting, its history, structure and organisation.
[H342] Mansell hbk **£35.00**

MALTIN, LEONARD
TV Movies & Video Guide 1989
Reliable companion to films made available for TV
broadcast or that have already appeared on video.
[H343] Penguin pbk **£4.99**

MAYBURY, RICHARD
A Beginner's Guide to Satellite TV
[H344] Penguin pbk **£3.95**

POSTMAN, NEIL
Amusing Ourselves to Death
A pointed analysis of the implications of mass-media
based culture. Essential (and unnerving) reading.
[H345] Methuen pbk **£4.99**

POTTER, JEREMY
Great Independent Television in `NEW`
Britain: Politics and Control 1968 - 80
The third volume of a series focusing on the central
issues facing the Broadcasting Authority and TV
companies as they establish themselves.
[H348] Macmillan hbk **£25.00**

SCHLESINGER, PHILIP
Putting 'Reality' Together: BBC News
Provocative analysis of the cultural assumptions
embedded in apparently 'objective' news broadcasts.
[H349] Methuen pbk **£9.95**

SILJ, ALLESANDRO
**East of Dallas: The European
Challenge to American Television** `NEW`
The success of US TV exports and their cultural
'threat' has resulted in European broadcasters fighting
back with home-grown 'soaps' designed to beat
Dallas in the ratings war.
[H351] BFI pbk **£7.95**

SILVERSTONE, ROGER
**Framing Science: The Making of a
BBC Documentary**
The record of the making of a *Horizon* programme
from initial research to final broadcast.
[H352] BFI pbk **£7.95**

VERNA, TONY
**Live TV: An Inside Look at Directing
and Producing**
Tony Verna was World Director for ABC during the
1984 Olympics in LA, and he was Executive Director
for the famous 'Live Aid' concert. This book takes an
honest look at how news, sports and special events are
presented to the public. Fascinating reading for
anyone interested in, or already working for TV.
[H355] Focal P hbk **£19.95**

WILLIAMS, RAYMOND
**Raymond Williams on Television:
Selected Writings**
A collection drawing on the TV column, turned out
every few weeks from 1968-1972, for *The Listener*.
Williams comments on world events, and through the

reviews we glimpse his everyday life and the ongoing
development of a personal sociology of culture.
[H356] Routledge pbk **£7.95**
**Television: Technology and
Cultural Form**
An updated edition of this seminal work by the great
historian and critic of contemporary culture.
[H357] Routledge pbk **£7.95**

YORKE, IVOR
Technique of Television News
Outlines the latest in production methods and includes
details on cable and satellite services, the techniques
behind electronic news gathering and electronic
picture editing. Basically a technical manual, the book
(based on Yorke's long experience with the BBC) is a
good insight into the mechanics of news-making too.
[H358] Focal P hbk **£22.95**

Radio

Although undermined by the bigger media network of
TV, radio has unique potential for access (both for
audience 'talk-back' and amateur 'pirate' stations) as
well as being important historically, with the format
of TV and other journalistic media still largely based
on radio broadcasting. This selection aims to give a
behind-the-scenes look at the industry, and technical
information for those interested in working within it.

**Listener Speaks: Radio Audience and
the Future of Radio**
[H359] HMSO pbk **£7.95**

Who's Who in Broadcasting
[H360] Carrick hbk **£15.00**

ASH, WILLIAM
The Way to Write Radio Drama
[H361] H Hamilton pbk **£6.95**

DARRINGTON, PHILIP
Guide to Broadcasting Stations
[H362] Heinemann pbk **£9.95**

DRAKAKIS, JOHN (ED)
British Radio Drama
[H363] Cambridge pbk **£11.95**

KEITH, MICHAEL & KRAUSE, JOSEPH
The Radio Station
Contemporary, candid and complete exploration of
what it's like to work in commercial radio. Updated
and expanded, this second edition uses the insights of
many top professionals and is lavishly illustrated.
[H364] Focal P hbk **£27.50**

MCLEISH, ROBERT
The Technique of Radio Production
Written for newcomers to radio, this new edition
details production methods, including the mixing
desk, scriptwriting, interviewing and compilation of
news, music and drama. The book also confronts the
use of broadcasting by and for society, highlighting
the ethical values of radio journalism and the
problems associated with commmercial advertising.
[H365] Focal P hbk **£24.95**

MONEY, STEVE
**Newnes Radio Amateur and Listener's
Pocket Book**
[H366] Heinemann hbk **£8.95**

TOOK, BARRY
**Laughter in the Air: An Informal History
of British Radio Comedy**
[H367] Robson pbk **£3.95**

PHOTOGRAPHY

Roget's Thesaurus lists 33 fields of photography, from aerophotography to x-rays. This section is limited to a small sampling of photographic works with an emphasis on 'art' and 'documentary' photographers, and a bias towards newer publications.

History & Reference

Photography is a relatively new medium and yet is everywhere amongst us, evolving faster than we are able to 'place' it in history. The books listed below are general histories, which attempt to present an over-view; often more detailed analyses of photographic history can be found in the introductions to catalogues and collections (see in particular *Photography Now*), or in monographs examining the evolution of a particular style or form.

FORD, COLIN (ED)
The Story of Popular Photography NEW
Compiled in recognition of the 150th anniversary of the birth of photography and based on photos from the Kodak museum. The book outlines the technical innovations that have created and contributed to the development of popular photography.
[H380] Century pbk **£10.95**

HICKS, ROGER
A History of the 35mm Still Camera
A technically-based and detailed survey of the development of the camera that was to revolutionise photographic practices.
[H382] Focal P hbk **£29.50**

JEFFEREY, IAN
Photography: A Concise History
Jefferey traces the development of photography by linking the work of major photographers, combining autobiographical detail with historical background.
[H383] Thames & H pbk **£5.95**

LANGFORD, MICHAEL
The Story of Photography
A succinct and accessible summary of the development of photographic processes, followed by a survey of subjects, styles and approaches to the medium.
[H384] Focal P pbk **£10.95**

LEMAGNY, J-CLAUDE & ROUILLE, A (EDS)
A History of Photography
An international team of photographic historians collaborate in this volume to create a thematic history of photography. Essays address aspects of the development of photography - including amateur, press and art photography, with reference to the social and historical context.
[H385] Cambridge hbk **£27.50**

NEWHALL, BEAUMONT
History of Photography
Hailed as a classic work on the subject, this history maps the aesthetic evolution of the 'art' of photography, relating this to technical innovation and establishing a canon of 'master' photographers.
[H387] Secker pbk **£12.95**

OLIVER, GEORGE
Photographs and Local History NEW
[H388] Batsford hbk **£14.95**

ROOSENS, LAURENT & SALA, LUC
A History of Photography: A Bibliography of Books NEW
Contains approximately 7,000 entries, arranged alphabetically by subject and cross-referenced.
[H389] Mansell hbk **£30.00**

ROSENBLUM
A World History of Photography NEW
A history of photography with an emphasis on the image as a universal language. Contains chapters on photography and documentation, art, photography and modernism, photography in the media, and the application of photography in science. Lavishly produced, this giant volume is generously illustrated using photographs from all over the world.
[H390] Abbeville hbk **£35.00**

SOBIESZEK, ROBERT
The Art of Persuasion NEW
The first in-depth history of advertising photography, tracing its evolution from 19th century posters, to its rapid development in the 20th century under the influence of social realism and avant-garde art.
[H391] Abrams hbk **£29.00**

WILLIAMS, VAL
Women Photographers: The Other Observers 1900 to the Present
An historical survey examining the marginalisation of women in the photographic arts. Produced in conjunction with an exhibition honouring and re-introducing the work of British women photographers - from the glamorous suffrage portraits of Christina Broom to the surrealist images of Madame Yevonde.
[H393] Virago pbk **£11.50**

Theory & Criticism

Photography theory is a new and inter-disciplinary field. This is a selection of those writers who are laying its foundations and widening the debate.

BARTHES, ROLAND
Camera Lucida: Reflections on Photography
Barthes's final text combines a selection of photographs with reflections on photography. The meditations gravitate around the themes of presence and absence, examining the relationship between photography and theatre, history and death. One of the most exciting theoretical attempts to place photography so far, this book is also accessible and entertaining.
[H394] Fontana pbk **£3.95**

BERGER, JOHN & MOHR, JEAN
Another Way of Telling NEW
Produced in conjunction with a television series screened this year. Writer and photographer collaborate to record the lives of mountain peasants and to explore 'photography' - a new means of expression more closely associated with memory than any other. A pioneering work which includes a 'photo-essay' of 150 images.
[H395] Granta pbk **£7.99**

BURGIN, VICTOR (ED)
Thinking Photography
A comprehensive and diverse anthology of articles by Umberto Eco, Walter Benjamin, John Tagg and others, essentially concerned with the 'production of meaning' in photographs. The best introduction to photography theory (as distinct from criticism) and its relation to contemporary cultural studies.
[H396] Macmillan pbk **£8.50**

FOSTER, ALASTAIR & MCGRATH, ROBERTA
Behold the Man: The Male Nude in Photography NEW
A unique mix of photographs and text, reflecting on the male nude in photography over the last 150 years: covering issues such as identity and image, gender in a patriachal society and the nude as form.
[H397] Stills Gallery pbk **£6.95**

JAY, BILL & MOORE, MARGARET (ED)
Shaw on Photography NEW
Essays by Bernard Shaw on the subject of photography. Originally published between 1901 and 1909, the book is illustrated by a generous selection of his own photographs.
[H398] Equation pbk **£12.95**

NEWHALL, BEAUMONT (ED)
Photography: Essays and Images
Described by the author as an 'autobiography of the art of photography' this collection includes the first news accounts of the Daguerreotype and essays by interested parties from Baudelaire to Minor White.
[H400] MOMA pbk **£9.95**

SCHARF, AARON
Art and Photography
Photography and its development related to the 'history of art' - in particular to 19th century art and debates about realism, impressionism and beyond.
[H401] Penguin **£9.95**

SONTAG, SUSAN
On Photography
Sontag trys to explain the mystery and authority of photographic images in our mass-media society and analyses the power of the camera - as a 'ray-gun', as 'tourism', and as an instrument of memory and desire.
[H402] Penguin pbk **£4.99**

TAGG, JOHN
The Burden of Representation
Drawing on semiotics and debates in cultural theory, Tagg questions the relationship of photographs to 'reality' and examines the political significance of new modes of representation, with emphasis on their use in the process of social regulation (passports, police work, hospitals, permits etc).
[H404] Macmillan pbk **£8.95**

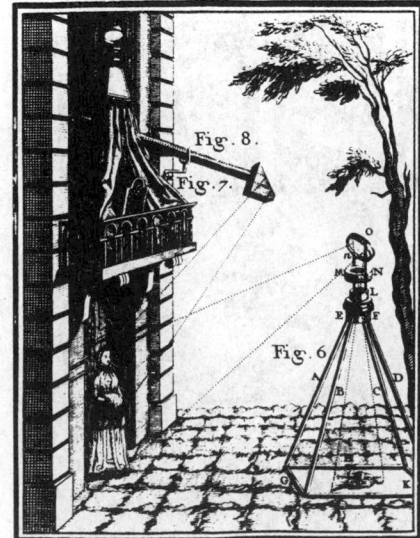

Illustration from *A History of Photography* edited by Jean-Claude Lemagny & Andre Rouille (Cambridge University Press hbk £27.50)

Catalogues & Collections

Photography books are often lavish and expensively produced: this section lists a broad selection of variously priced books, all of good quality. The most expensive titles have been included because they are particularly good or unusual collections with a very high standard of reproduction. For the more indulgent purchase, any work published by the New York Graphic Society, MOMA, or Abbeville is particularly recommended. New series worth looking out for are the Dirk Nishen collections of archival photographs (*River Thames*, *Streets of London* and *Island Women*), which comprise fascinating and beautiful photographs by known and unknown photographers; and the Thames & Hudson *Photofile* series (priced at £4.95), which offers well-researched representative selections of work by great photographers at an affordable price and was recently awarded the first annual prize for distinguished photographic books by the International Center of Photography, New York.

Art or Nature: 20th Century French Photography
Beautifully-produced catalogue for an exhibition based on the work of both native and foreign photographers, drawn to Paris for its atmosphere of innovation and experimentation. Robert Demachy, Brassai, Man Ray, Cartier-Bresson and many others are represented as contributors to the development of photography as an 'art'.
[H405] Trefoil hbk **£25.00**

Blitz: Exposure!
Accompanied an exhibition at the V & A Museum, wild and stylish work from *Blitz* - a glossy, state-of-the-art fashion magazine.
[H406] Ebury pbk **£8.95**

Eyewitness: World Press Photo 1989
Selection of press photographs from around the world, chosen for the annual international press photography competition run by the World Press Photo Foundation (an independent, non-commercial cultural organization). The cream of a journalistic art form that has grown more sophisticated with transmission technology.
[H408] Phaidon hbk **£14.95**

Mysterious Coincidences
An exhibition catalogue of work by a cross-section of contemporary British photographers particularly concerned with the manipulation of colour and the construction of an image.
[H409] Photographer's Gall pbk **£9.95**

ADES, DAWN
Photomontage
An exploration of photomontage in all its permutations, and its potential as an art both expressive and manipulative.
[H411] Thames & H pbk **£5.95**

BAILEY, D. & HARRISON, M. (EDS)
The Naked Eye
Beautifully bound and presented photographs of the nude, spanning a century of photography from Edgar Degas to Joel-Peter Witkin. Selected and introduced by David Bailey.
[H412] Barrie & J hbk **£16.95**

BUTLER, SUSAN (ED)
Shifting Focus: An International NEW
Exhibition of Women's Photography
With a long essay by the curator, Susan Butler, this catalogue is a survey of the range of themes and techniques adopted by women photographers in a creative decade.
[H413] Arnolfini pbk **£8.95**

CARMICHAEL, JANE
First World War Photographers NEW
Examines the work of official, press and amateur photographers with over 100 photographs reproduced from the archive of the Imperial War Museum. Carmichael focuses on the growing use of the photograph as a medium for the masses and as an historical document.
[H414] Routledge hbk **£20.00**

ENYEART, JAMES (ED)
Decade by Decade NEW
Principal movements and figures of American photography are traced from the late 19th century to 1985. Edited by the Director of the Center for Creative Photography, 100 of the Center's masterworks are reproduced in duotone and colour.
[H417] NY Graph Soc hbk **£25.00**
[H418] NY Graph Soc pbk **£14.95**

EVANS, D. & GOHL, S.
Photomontage: A Political Weapon
Material from the Heartfield Archive in East Berlin, and contemporary photomontage, including work by Peter Kennard, are presented in conjunction with essays covering the history of the medium and its relationship to caricature and politically inspired art.
[H419] G Fraser pbk **£9.95**

FISHER, ANDREA (ED)
Let Us Now Praise Famous Women
The work of eight women photographers employed by the Farm Security Administration project on a documentary assignment for the US government during 1935-44. Including Dorothea Lange, Ann Rosener and Pauline Ehrlich.
[H420] Pandora pbk **£9.95**

GRUNDBERG, A. & GAUSS, K.
Photography and Art: Interactions since 1946
An attractive volume of photographs highlighting the relationship between modern painting and photographs of the same period.
[H421] Abbeville hbk **£29.95**

HAWORTH-BOOTH, MARK
Photography Now NEW
A 'diagrammatic survey' of contemporary photography from all over the world, designed to illustrate a 'series of oppositions or varieties' in new approaches to the medium. Produced in conjunction with the V&A exhibition in recognition of the 150 year anniversary of photography, this catalogue also contains a miniature history of photography.
[H422] Dirk Nishen/V&A pbk **£14.95**

JEFFREY, IAN & ROGERS, BRETT (EDS)
Inscriptions and Inventions: British Photography in the 1980s
A useful *catalogue raisonné* featuring the work of ten contemporary British photographers, including Peter Fraser, Verdi Yahooda, Richard Wentworth, Martin Parr, Jem Southam, Ron O'Donnell and Boyd Webb.
[H423] Brit Council pbk **£7.00**

KISMARIC, SUSAN
California Photography:
Remaking Make-Believe NEW
Challenging selection of recent work by John Baldessari, Robert Heinecken, Larry Sultan, John Divola, Jo Ann Callis, Nancy Burton and Larry Johnson, all of whom live and work in California.
[H424] Thames & H pbk **£10.95**

KRAUSS, R; LIVINGSTONE, J & ADES, D
L'Amour Fou
A huge collection of photographs and essays highlighting the crucial role photography played in the surrealist movement. Includes artists bibliographies and biographies.
[H425] Abbeville hbk **£29.98**

MANCHESTER, WILLIAM
In Our Times: The World as
Seen by Magnum Photographers NEW
Over the past fifty years, Magnum, the universally acclaimed photo-journalists' co-operative, has produced some of the most arresting, terrible and beautiful images of our recent world history. A monumental volume drawing together the work of such photographers as Robert Capa, George Rodger and Cartier-Bresson.
[H426] Deutsch hbk **£40.00**

OWUSU & ROSS
Behind the Masquerade: The Story of Notting Hill Carnival
Photographs by David A. Bailey, Jacob Ross and Ian Watts illustrating the carnival from many perspectives - its meaning and significance, and its construction as a spectacle.
[H428] Arts Media pbk **£6.95**

REID, GEORGE (ED)
River Thames
Archive photographs of the Thames in the early 1920s and 1930s, when London was still the greatest port in the world.
[H429] Dirk Nishen pbk **£2.95**
Streets of London
Period photographs from the late 1920s and early 1930s by largely unknown photographers.
[H430] Dirk Nishen pbk **£2.95**

RICHTER, STEFAN
The Art of the Daguerrotype NEW
Contains some 80 examples from the first 20 years of photography. Chosen from Richter's private collection, most of them are published here for the first time and many are hand-tinted.
[H431] Viking pbk **£20.00**

ROTHSTEIN, ARTHUR
Documentary Photography
Rothstein explains the contributions of the photographers who forged and refined the documentary style. Quality reproductions represent the work of William Henry Jackson, Paul Strand, Walker Evans, Robert Capa, Weegee and many others. The book also briefly surveys the contemporary scene.
[H432] Focal P pbk **£19.95**

SEABORNE, MIKE (ED)
Shelters
Photographs of life underground during the London blitz, by Bill Brandt and other unrecorded photographers.
[H433] Dirk Nishen pbk **£2.95**

SHUDAKOV, GRIGORY
Pioneers of Soviet Photography
A comprehensive survey, carefully researched with an exciting selection of photographs.
[H434] Thames & H hbk **£24.00**

SMITH, JOSHUA
The Photography of Invention:
American Pictures of the 1980s NEW
An experimental collection of photographs that are made, not taken. Shows off the work of some of the decades' most interesting image-makers.
[H435] MIT hbk **£35.95**

STEICHEN, EDWARD
The Family of Man
Based on the original exhibition which contained 503 photographs by 273 photographers and became something of a milestone in the history of photography. Photographers attempted to capture all aspects of the 'human condition', documenting love, work, death, birth...as expressed all over the world.
[H437] Simon & Sch pbk **£9.95**

WITKIN, JOEL PETER
Masterpieces of Medical Photography
Selection of weird and wonderful medical photographs from the Burns archive, a personal choice from a photographer who is himself obsessed by the body and its potential for deformity.
[H438] Twelve Trees hbk **£35.00**

Monographs

ABBOTT, BERENICE
Considered one of the first documentary photographers, Abbott widened the concept of the 'portrait' to include a long term project based on New York City. She wrote: *"To make the portrait of a city is a life work and no one portrait suffices, because the city is always changing. Everything in the city is properly part of its story..."*.
New York in the Thirties
[H439] Dover pbk **£6.00**
O'NEAL, HANK
Berenice Abbott: Sixty Years of Photography
A representative and comprehensive collection of her work.
[H440] Thames & H hbk **£30.00**

ADAMS, ANSEL
Originally trained as a musician, Adams eventually turned to photography as an expressive medium. His work is mainly concerned with capturing the sublime in the American landscape. He studied the complexities of photo-mechanical reproduction to ensure that reproduction of his work came as close as possible to his original concept: consequently these volumes are works of art in themselves.
Examples: The Making of Forty Photographs
Adams unravels the process of creating some of his most famous photographs, giving a valuable insight into the photographer's working methods.
[H441] Little Brown hbk **£29.95**
Manzanaar   **NEW**
Collection of photos of Japanese men, women and children in an American prison camp during the Second World War. Includes an essay by Pulitzer Prize winner, John Hersey.
[H442] Secker hbk **£25.00**
Portfolios of Ansel Adams
[H443] NY Graph Soc pbk **£17.95**
Singular Images
[H444] NY Graph Soc hbk **£11.95**
Yosemite and the Range of Light
[H445] NY Graph Soc pbk **£19.95**
ALINDER & STILLMAN
Letters and Images 1916 - 1984   **NEW**
This compilation of letters provides a full record of his life and travels. A beautifully produced book with many photographs, including proof sheets and a page from the photographer's first photo album.
[H446] NY Graph Soc hbk **£25.00**

ATGET, EUGENE
Atget's ambition was *"to create a collection of all that which in Paris was artistic and picturesque"*. He died in 1927, virtually unknown, but was adopted by the

Parisian surrealists and cubists who eventually contributed to his recognition as an artist.
REYNAUD, FRANCOISE
Eugène Atget
One of the excellent (prize-winning) *Photofile* series.
[H449] Thames & H pbk **£4.95**
SZARKOWSKI, JOHN & HAMBOURG, MARIA MORRIS (EDS)
The Work of Eugene Atget
Vol 1: Old France
A fabulous collection of Atget's work, carefully collated from the thousands of photographs he produced in and around Paris. Originally Atget printed by daylight and toned with gold chloride: the silvery surface of his photographs has been captured, as far as is possible, in high-quality reproductions.
[H450] G Fraser hbk **£35.00**
Vol 2: Art of Old Paris
[H451] G Fraser hbk **£35.00**
Vol 3: Ancien Régime
[H452] G Fraser hbk **£35.00**
Vol 4: Modern Times
[H453] G Fraser hbk **£35.00**

AVEDON, RICHARD
Avedon's photographs of the South West of America are highly acclaimed: setting up his camera at a number of local fairs and other gatherings, he captures the personalities, and eccentricities, of many of his subjects in a uniquely memorable way.
In the American West
[H454] Thames & H hbk **£40.00**

BAILEY, DAVID
Bailey found fame in the sixties as a fashion photographer for *Vogue*, and for his work with Jean Shrimpton. His style was cool, minimal and modern and has evolved to include more personal work with his former wife Marie Helven in *Trouble and Strife* and recently, an interest in the English landscape.
Bailey NW1: Urban Landscapes
[H455] Dent hbk **£18.50**
Black and White Memories: 1948 - 1969
The most representative volume of his work up to the end of the 1960s, this includes fashion photographs, portraits, some personal pictures and street scenes.
[H456] Dent hbk **£25.00**
Nudes
[H457] Dent hbk **£16.50**
Trouble and Strife
[H458] Thames & H hbk **£15.00**

BARKER, CHRISTOPHER
Portraits of Poets
Notable English poets pictured in environments carefully chosen to reflect some aspect of their life or work. Each portrait is accompanied by biographical information and a poem.
[H459] Carcanet pbk **£9.95**

BARKSHIRE, PAUL
Other London   **NEW**
Portraits of hidden villages, country houses, little towns, and waterways of Greater London.
[H460] Lennard hbk **£14.95**

BEATON, CECIL
For many years photographer to the Royal Family, Beaton was in love with the romance and glamour of the aristocracy. Carefully constructed and re-touched, his fairytale portraits capture not just likenesses but a dream of England that was always to elude him.
MELLOR, DAVID (ED)
Cecil Beaton
[H462] Weidenfeld hbk **£18.95**
STRONG, ROY
The Royal Portraits   **NEW**
Selected from nearly 10,000 vintage prints preserved in Beaton's private archive. Includes work in

progress, with contact sheets and untouched proofs, together with snapshots of the photographer at work.
[H463] Thames & H pbk **£18.00**

BRANDT, BILL
Brandt began in the 1930s to photograph the English at home and by night. In the spirit of surrealism, his contrasting black and white images give a dream-like quality to his documentation. His later work is more concerned with the nude, form and distortion.
Literary Britain
A photographic 'literary tour' of Britain. Great figures from literary history are represented by a photograph capturing a birthplace or some landmark evocative of their style or work.
[H467] Hurtwood hbk **£19.95**
[H468] Hurtwood/V&A pbk **£8.95**
London in the Thirties
[H469] G Fraser hbk **£14.50**
[H470] G Fraser pbk **£8.95**
Nudes 1945 - 1980
[H471] G Fraser hbk **£19.50**
[H472] G Fraser pbk **£10.95**
Portraits
[H473] G Fraser hbk **£19.50**
MELLOR, DAVID
Bill Brandt: Behind the Camera - Photographs 1928 - 1983
[H474] Phaidon hbk **£14.95**

BRASSAI
Brassai studied art in Budapest, eventually moving to Paris. Here he produced many portraits of the artists he befriended, including photgraphs taken in Picasso's studios, and contributed images of graffiti for surrealist manifestos. Later work explores the strange and sometimes seedy nocturnal Paris, it was well received at the time and led to regular work for *Verve* and *Harper's Bazaar*.
Artists of My life
[H475] Thames & H hbk **£24.00**
Paris After Dark
[H476] Thames & H hbk **£35.00**
The Secret Paris of the Thirties
[H477] Thames & H pbk **£12.50**
GRENIER, ROGER
Brassai   **NEW**
One of the excellent (prize-winning) *Photofile* series.
[H478] Thames & H pbk **£4.95**

BURGIN, VICTOR
Between
A collection of image/text narratives drawn from cinema, advertising and all aspects of our 'multi-media' society, to explore the nature of the photograph and its presence in contemporary life.
[H479] ICA/Blackwell pbk **£17.50**

CAMERON, JULIA MARGARET
Friend of the Pre-Raphaelites and self-taught photographer, she ignored the 'rules' of focus and clarity to create portraits and allegorical costume pieces. Cameron aspired to 'ennoble Photography and to secure for it the character and uses of High Art'.
WEAVER, MIKE
Julia Margaret Cameron 1815 - 1879
[H480] Herbert P hbk **£12.50**

CAPA, ROBERT
The most famous of all war photographers, Capa's images have helped to define the emotional landscape of human conflict in the 20th century. Always an 'active' rather than a 'passive' observer, Capa was killed by a landmine whilst working in Vietnam in 1954.
LACOUTURE, JEAN
Robert Capa   **NEW**
One of the excellent (prize-winning) *Photofile* series.
[H481] Thames & H pbk **£4.95**

FILM & PHOTOGRAPHY

CARTIER-BRESSON, HENRI
Once a hunter in Africa, Cartier-Bresson later seized upon the potential of the portable 35mm camera and set out to 'capture the moment'. He travelled and photographed, worked in the cinema and was later hired by Capa as a photo-journalist. In his format and methods, Cartier-Bresson blurs the distinction between commercial and 'art' photography.
Cartier-Bresson in India
[H482] Thames & H hbk **£20.00**
Early Work
[H483] MOMA hbk **£22.00**
BRENSON, MICHAEL
Henri Cartier-Bresson   NEW
One of the excellent (prize-winning) *Photofile* series.
[H485] Thames & H pbk **£4.95**

DAVIES, JOHN
Green and Pleasant Land
Graceful black and white images of the everyday but extraordinary landscapes of Britain's post industrial cities, canals and disused collieries.
[H487] Cornerhouse pbk **£8.95**

EGGLESTON, WILLIAM
Important American photographer of the 'modernist' generation, noted for his innovative use of colour.
The Democratic Forest   NEW
This modern epic contains 150 colour photographs chosen from many thousands made during the 1980s by Eggleston. The sequence of images forms an almost autobiographical narrative starting in his home territory of Tennessee and the Mississippi Delta. It radiates out across America and a common international landscape as far as the Berlin Wall. Introduction by Eudora Welty.
[H488] Secker hbk **£15.00**

EVANS, WALKER
One of the first documentary photographers, Evans was employed by the Farm Security Administration to document the plight of tenant farmers and their environment, as part of a vast project to record American rural life during the depression. He later utilized sequences of images and combined text to explore 'the physiognomy of a nation'.
Photographs for the Farm Security Administration 1935 - 38
A thoroughly-documented catalogue of Evans's work for the FSA.
[H492] Da Capo pbk **£14.95**
Walker Evans at Work
[H493] Thames & H hbk **£12.50**
[H494] Thames & H pbk **£8.95**

FRANK, ROBERT
Frank arrived in New York in 1947 from Switzerland and travelled extensively in America documenting 'Americans'. His first book of photographs *The Americans*, and its view of the 'American Dream' is a landmark in post-war American culture.
The Lines of My Hand   NEW
Famous sequel to *The Americans*, now re-edited to include his latest work. It forms a photographic autobiography, documenting his travels, friends and family. Frank has also worked in the cinema and the book itself takes the shape of a 'road movie'.
[H496] Pantheon hbk **£30.00**

GIBSON, RALPH
As a photographer and a publisher, Gibson was one of the first to promote the 'book' as a legitimate and formal vehicle for the exhibition of photographs. His own work is dream-like in atmosphere but sharp and graphic in composition.
L'Anonyme
[H497] Aperture hbk **£25.00**
Tropism
[H498] Phaidon hbk **£29.50**

GODWIN, FAY
British landscape photographer working in the Romantic tradition of Ansel Adams.
The Secret Forest of Dean
[H499] Radcliffe P pbk **£7.95**
GODWIN, FAY & FOWLES, JOHN
Islands
[H500] Cape hbk **£7.95**
Land
[H501] Heinemann pbk **£12.95**

GOLDIN, NAN
Born in Washington DC in 1953, for more than a decade Goldin has obsessively photographed her life and that of her extended family from New York to London and Berlin. Her slide show of nearly 1,000 images combined with music was shown in NY nightclubs, and by 1985 was recognised as a major work of art by many institutions.
The Ballad of Sexual Dependency   NEW
The dominant theme of these photographs is the destructive nature of the relationships between man and women and the recurring need for love. The cumulative impact is one of harrowing intimacy. On its publication in the US in 1986, the *New York Times* described the book as a 'masterwork for the 1980s'.
[H502] Secker hbk **£12.95**

GROOVER, JAN
Jan Groover
Originally an exhibition catalogue to accompany a major retrospective, this offers a good selection of work, including colour work, early triptychs, still-lives and late Gelatin-silver prints.
[H503] MOMA pbk **£13.50**

HAAS, ERNST
Haas's photography was singularly intense and personal, ranging from still-lifes of flowers and abstract images of motion to photo-essays of cities and countries, most notably Japan.
Ernst Haas: A Colour Retrospective 1952 - 86
[H504] Thames & H hbk **£40.00**

HOCKNEY, DAVID
Contemporary British painter and collagist, now resident in California.
Cameraworks
Giant volume of Hockney's photo-montage and polaroid-collages. A kaleidoscope of palms, pools and friends - 176 illustrations of work produced between 1981-1983.
[H505] Thames & H hbk **£35.00**
Hockney on Photography
Hockney in conversation with Paul Joyce, reflects on paintings and photographs that have influenced him, looking back in particular to the beginnings of his interest in photography. Generously illustrated this book evolves into a personal history of art.
[H506] Cape hbk **£20.00**

KAR, IDA
Kar came to London in 1945, leaving behind her in Cairo a reputation as a stylish avant-garde photographer. In London she found a new bohemia and spent the next fifteen years portraying it. She photographed amongst others Marc Chagall, David Hockney, T.S. Eliot and Doris Lessing.
WILLIAMS, VAL
Ida Kar - Photographer: 1907 - 74   NEW
Kar's life and work in both biographical and aesthetic terms, making extensive use of correspondence and interviews from her recent past, and bringing together her most haunting and evocative photographs.
[H507] October pbk **£17.99**

KERTESZ, ANDRE
Kertész, born in Budapest and originally a stock-

market account clerk, became interested in photography which he eventually made a full-time profession after moving to Paris. He freelanced for many years and is considered by many to be one of the first truly 'modern' photographers.
NAEF, PHILIPS & TRAVIS
André Kertész of Paris and New York
[H509] Thames & H hbk **£35.00**
RILEY, HAROLD (ED)
André Kertész
[H510] Manchester Coll hbk **£30.00**
[H511] Manchester Coll pbk **£19.95**
SALLENAVE, DANIELLE
André Kertész   NEW
One of the excellent (prize-winning) *Photofile* series.
[H512] Thames & H pbk **£4.95**

KILLIP, CHRIS
In Flagrante
Photos of the North Eastern sea-coal gatherers, itinerants living in a nomadic camp, who derive their livelihood from collecting coal dumped in the sea by the coal industry. The book bears witness to a society in decline, ravaged by forces outside its control - a desolate and evocative body of photographs.
[H513] Secker hbk **£20.00**
[H514] Secker pbk **£9.95**

KLEIN, WILLIAM
Klein, a New Yorker, studied painting in Leger's studio and initially used photography for experiments in abstraction. His later work is especially concerned with the concept of the 'modern city', his photographs are influenced by an interest in graphics and the desire to subvert accepted techniques.
Close Up   NEW
Klein's latest collection is an exciting series of point blank wide-angle images of the anonymous and the famous, which attempts to redefine the relationship between photographer and subject. Klein's own text is both revealing and provocative.
[H515] Thames & H hbk **£24.00**

LARTIGUE, JACQUES-HENRI
Lartigue's photography is a celebration of the world immediately around him; his images are almost family snapshots, full of relations and friends at home or on holiday. What makes him a great a photographer is his unparalleled feel for motion: many of his best photographs explore the moving human figure, especially in relation to those objects we have developed to help us move: cars, bicycles, balloons and aeroplanes.
DAMADE, JACQUE
Jacques-Henri Lartigue
One of the excellent (prize-winning) *Photofile* series.
[H517] Thames & H pbk **£4.95**

LEWINSKI, J.
Portrait of the Artist
A detailed and personal survey of 25 years of British art. Artists' portraits include Howard Hodgkin, Henry Moore and Allen Jones, and are presented alongside information about their homes and studios.
[H518] Carcanet pbk **£12.95**

LINK, WINSTON O.
Steam, Steel and Stars: America's Last Steam Railroad
A massive project commissioned to document the power and beauty of the steam train. The photographs are taken at night using huge flash set-ups and split second timing: Link captures the thrust of the train speeding through the night as teenagers swim below or as it streaks past the screen of a drive-in movie.
[H519] Abrams hbk **£25.00**
MACDONALD, IAN

Smith's Dock
A collaboration between photographer MacDonald and artist Len Tabner, documenting the stages of construction of the last ship to be built at Smith's Dock Shipyard on Teeside. A tribute to a great industry and the end of an era.
[H520] Seaworks pbk **£7.50**

MAPPLETHORPE, ROBERT
Certain People
Powerful portraits from the last decade with subjects from New York 'high-life' and 'low-life'. Foreword by Susan Sontag.
[H521] Twelve Trees pbk **£45.00**
Robert Mapplethorpe
Spans his whole career, from art school portraits and early work with men in leather, to later portraits and still-lives. Includes essays by Richard Marshall and Ingrid Sischy.
[H522] Secker hbk **£25.00**
CONRAD, PETER (ED)
Portraits
[H523] NPG pbk **£12.95**
DIDION, JOAN (ED)
Some Women
Elegant and intimate portaits revealing **NEW** appreciation for the sculptural forms of the human body, as well as a personal engagement with women friends. Also includes lesser known portraits of children.
[H524] Little Brown hbk **£30.00**

MCBEAN, ANGUS
English surrealist photographer best known for his portraits of the glamourous and theatrical. McBean employed montage, multiple exposure and elaborate props, to create bizarre and entertaining images.
Vivien: A Love Affair in Camera **NEW**
Personal account of the friendship which grew up between the photographer and Vivien Leigh.
[H525] Phaidon pbk **£19.95**
WOODHOUSE, ADRIAN & MCBEAN, ANGUS
Angus McBean
[H526] Quartet hbk **£20.00**
[H527] Quartet pbk **£12.50**

MCCABE, EAMONN
Eamonn McCabe: Photographer
Selection of images, including recent landscape work, from the prize-winning sports photographer.
[H528] Heinemann hbk **£15.00**

MCCULLIN, DON
McCullin's first war assignment was in 1964 when he was sent to Cyprus by the *Sunday Times*, he has since built a considerable reputation for his brutally direct war reportage of fighting all over the world.
Open Skies **NEW**
McCullin turns his skills to a new battle, 'the terrible and senseless conflict ... between man and his environment'. The photographs capture the uneasy spirit of rural England, and include recent still-lives and a selection of war pictures.
[H529] Cape pbk **£9.95**
Perspectives
A large selection, including landscapes, haunting portraits, and pictures taken in Bradford and London.
[H530] Harrap hbk **£12.95**
HAWORTH-BOOTH, MARK
Donald McCullin
[H531] Collins pbk **£4.95**

MICHALS, DUANE
Innovative contemporary US photographer, influenced by everything from cubism to the cinema, the dreams of de Chirico to the life of Christ.
Album **NEW**
Giant portraits of Warhol, Gere, Novak and others.
[H532] Twelve Trees Press hbk **£30.00**

LIVINGSTONE, M. (ED)
Photographs/Sequences/Texts 1958-1984
Careful selection from a major retrospective exhibition, providing an overview of his career. Includes an interview with Michals, a bibliography and a list of exhibitions and works.
[H533] MOMA pbk **£5.95**

MILLER, LEE
Highly innovative US-born photographer, Miller has travelled extensively and worked as a fashion and war photographer (she was amongst the first to document the horrors of Nazi concentration camps after the war's end). Her formative years were spent living with Man Ray in Paris, and she invented, with him, the 'solarised' photograph: her own style was strongly influenced by surrealism.
LIVINGSTONE, JANE (ED)
Lee Miller: A Photographer Rediscovered **NEW**
The most extensive collection of her work so far published, reproductions in duotone.
[H534] Thames & H hbk **£30.00**
PENROSE, ANTHONY (ED)
Lives of Lee Miller
A celebration of all her lives - from surrealist Paris to fashionable New York and wartime London. Her son Anthony Penrose has compiled tantalysing, detailed glimpses into her life , and has rescued from relative obscurity a treasure trove of photographs which chart the struggle and successes of her innovative art.
[H535] Thames & H hbk **£14.95**

MOHOLY-NAGY
A leading theorist at the Bauhaus, a constructivist and suprematist artist and photographer. He experimented with the practices of photographic reproduction to create photograms, photoplastics and photomontage.
HAUS, ANDREAS
Moholy-Nagy
A good and well-illustrated overview of his work and the times in which he lived.
[H536] Thames & H hbk **£18.00**

MUNCH, EDVARD
EGGUM, ARNE
Munch and Photography **NEW**
Eggum relates Munch's painting to his early photographic experiments, revealing a much deeper and more complex dependence on photography than had been realised. Working with Strindberg, Munch began to understand and deploy the symbolic applications of photography. Lavishly illustrated with many unpublished images.
[H537] Yale hbk **£30.00**

NEWTON, HELMUT
HONNEF, KLAUS
Helmut Newton: Portraits
Newton's cool and kinky portraits document a contemporary elite of the rich and glamourous, film stars and art personalites.
[H540] Quartet hbk **£30.00**
LAGERFELD, KARL
Helmut Newton **NEW**
One of the excellent (prize-winning) *Photofile* series
[H541] Thames & H pbk **£4.95**

PAGE, TIM
A British photographer well respected for his hard-hitting reportage of the Vietnam war. He later immersed himself in the 'counter-culture' of 1960's West-Coast America, documenting its heroes as they rose and fell.
Ten Years After: Vietnam Today
[H542] Thames & H hbk **£15.95**
Tim Page's Nam
[H543] Thames & H pbk **£7.50**

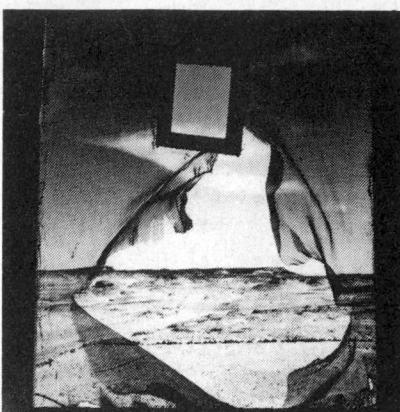
Illustration from *The Lives of Lee Miller*, edited by Anthony Penrose (Thames & H hbk £14.95)

PENN, IRVING
Penn worked for many years for *Vogue*. His work is diverse both in form and content - from intricate still-lives of New York street trash taken with a large format camera, to posed fashion-type portaits of tribesmen.
SZARKOWSKI, JOHN
Irving Penn
Beautifully produced retrospective covering all parts of Penn's career - originally intended as a catalogue for the recent V & A Museum exhibition.
[H544] MOMA hbk **£37.50**
[H545] MOMA pbk **£19.95**

RAY, MAN
A surrealist/dada artist who utilised every accident in the photographic process to explore new techniques, most famously the solarised print and the 'Rayograph' - a photograph made without a camera.
Bazaar Years **NEW**
Photographs made while working for *Harper's Bazaar*. A meeting of the disposable mass-media and the quintessential avante-garde - a truly surrealist event which transformed fashion photography.
[H546] Rizzoli pbk **£12.95**
Man Ray: Photographs
Over 300 of Man Ray's photographs including classic images, lesser known portraits and a large selection of erotic pictures.
[H547] Thames & H pbk **£17.95**
[H548] Dover pbk **£6.50**
FORESTA, MERRY A.
Man Ray **NEW**
One of the excellent (prize-winning) *Photofile* series
[H549] Thames & H hbk **£4.95**

REAS, PAUL
I Can Help
Suburbia, from the fluorescent bright supermarket to the interiors of an 'ideal home'; the 'dream' is contrasted with the ironies of human presence. Jewel-like reproduction and text by Stuart Cosgrove.
[H550] Cornerhouse Pubt pbk **£8.95**

ROBERTSON, GRACE
At 19 Robertson broke into the largely male domain of photojournalism, submitting her first pictures under a male pseudonym. Throughout the 1950s she worked for *Picture Post* and *Life* magazine, and ranged over subjects as diverse as a Battersea women's pub outing and the story of a woman giving birth (a story turned down by *Picture Post* for being 'too raw').
Grace Robertson: Photojournalist of the 50s **NEW**
Stunning collection of her photographs and accompanying text telling us what it was like to have

been one of the few women photographers active in the 'golden age of photojournalism', Robertson also gives us the low-down on working for *Life* magazine.
[H551] October pbk **£15.99**

ROBINSON, HENRY PEACH
A painter and etcher, Robinson took up photography in 1852 and produced 'art photographs', frequently using composite negatives. He wrote prolifically on the subject of applying the academic rules of composition to the construction of photographs.
HARKER, MARGARET
Henry Peach Robinson: Master of the Photographic Art 1830 - 1901
First ever collection of his work, containing over 100 plates, presented in the context of his life and theory.
[H552] Blackwell hbk **£37.50**
[H553] Blackwell pbk **£14.95**

SEIDNER, DAVID
MAURIES, PATRICK
David Seidner   **NEW**
Trained as a sculptor and best known for his fashion work, Seidner has gathered a considerable reputation over the last ten years and this book, his first retrospective collection, shows why. Sophisticated fashion shots jostle with early, John Cage-inspired portraits and the more recent experiments, which utilise mirrors and broken glass to startling effect
[H555] Thames & H hbk **£28.00**

SHERMAN, CINDY
Sherman's work, made up mainly of 'self-portrait' images is concerned with role-playing and identity. She has been influenced by television and cinema imagery, and more recently by mythology.
Cindy Sherman
A monograph reproducing a wide range of Sherman's work from the early fifties-style film stills to more contemporary work concerned with 'repulsion'.
[H556] Art Data pbk **£23.50**

SMITH, EDWIN
Post-war British photographer, famous for his calm, dream-like interiors and views of formal gardens.
Edwin Smith: Photographs 1935 - 1971
New edition introduced by Olive Cook, containing over 250 photographs, some previously unpublished.
[H557] Thames & H hbk **£25.00**
[H558] Thames & H pbk **£14.95**

SPENCE, JO
Putting Myself in the Picture
A political, personal and photographic autobiography that has evolved in part from Spence's involvement with photo-therapy as a framework for exploring the problem of identity.
[H559] Camden P pbk **£8.95**

SPENDER, HUMPHREY
Spender was one of the first British photographers to exploit the potential of the 35mm camera for documentary journalism. He is considered by many to be one of Britain's finest photographers.
Lensman
A collection of photographs taken between 1934-52.
[H560] Chatto pbk **£12.95**
Worktown People: Photographs from Northern England 1937 - 38
[H561] Falling Wall P pbk **£7.95**

TRESS, ARTHUR
New York gay photographer, whose work explores sexuality, masculinity and the possibility, through photographs, of engendering a 'ritualistic sense of delirium'
Machinations
Photographs of the male nude in all its glory, an exploration of man the machine, man the hero, man

the victim, man the shaper of his own destiny. Includes biographical information and a monograph by Mario Livingstone.
[H562] GMP hbk **£12.95**
Talisman
Retrospective of Tress's work from 1967-1980, produced in conjunction with a touring exhibition.
[H563] Thames & H pbk **£12.00**

WEEGEE
Weegee was one of the most extraordinary photographers of the century. His subject was invariably crime and he would follow and document its progress all over New York city using a police radio, developing the film in a mobile darkroom installed in the boot of his Chevrolet.
LAUDE, ANDRE
Weegee   **NEW**
One of the excellent (prize-winning) *Photofile* series.
[H564] Thames & H pbk **£4.95**

WENDERS, WIM
German film-maker, resident in America. His films include *Paris, Texas* and *Wings of Desire*.
Written in the West   **NEW**
Glorious colour photographs of the big skies and small towns of wild Western America, by the man who directed *Paris, Texas*. Text in German.
[H565] Deustch hbk **£25.00**

WESTON, EDWARD
One of the most important 'modernist' photographers, Weston was obsessed by beauty in form, from the curve of a thigh to the hollows in a capsicum.
NEWHALL, BEAUMONT & WESTON, EDWARD
Supreme Instants: The Photography of Edward Weston
Essays by Newhall and James Enyeart on Weston's life and work accompany a collection of exquisite reproductions, including early platinum toned works.
[H567] Thames & H hbk **£30.00**

ZOLA, EMILE
Zola: Photographer   **NEW**
Collection of over 200 photographs by one of the greatest French writers of the 19th century.
[H568] Collins pbk **£15.00**

Practical Photography

Dozens of practical guides are produced each year, often similar in content and approach. This is a selection of the best, covering all areas, with an emphasis on established books and authors. Ansel Adams's books are particularly recommended, as they relate the technical process to creative expression, steering the photographer towards a more complete control over the image; also recommended is anything from Focal Press, who have a large number of specialist texts, always meticulously researched and constantly updated by professionals in the field.

The Amateur Photographer's Guide to Perfect Pictures   **NEW**
How to take high quality photographs in any situation, by the editor of *Amateur Photography*. It also has fully illustrated features by six distinguished photographers including Lord Litchfield.
[H569] Hamlyn pbk **£7.95**

ADAMS, ANSEL
BASIC PHOTOGRAPHY
Highly recommended, these books combine a lifetime's technical experience with a passionate love

of photography as an 'art', making them challenging and instructive guides for photographers at any level. See Listings below for details of individual volumes.

BLACKLOW, LAURA
New Dimensions in Photo Imaging   **NEW**
Unique manual providing step-by-step illustrated instructions to ten processes, including photo imaging on paper, fabric and other 'non-silver' mediums. Includes a safety section and a special colour portfolio with contemporary examples by such artists as Robert Rauschenberg.
[H574] Focal P hbk **£0.00**

BLAKER, ALFRED A.
Photography: Art and Technique
A sharp overview of what it means to be a photographer. This new edition includes new sections on recent developments in automated and close-up flash, exposure techniques, new films and equipment systems. Special topics such as close-up, photomacrography, filters, view cameras and alternative printing methods are discussed in depth.
[H575] Focal P pbk **£25.00**

BUSCELLE, MICHAEL
Photographers' Question and Answer Book
A handy vinyl-coated handbook, providing three different levels of advice and ready solutions to common picture-taking problems.
[H576] Collins pbk **£8.95**

CALDER, JULIAN & GARRETT, JOHN
The Travelling Photographer's Handbook
How to do it, what you need - anywhere.
[H577] Pan pbk **£2.99**

CHAMBERLAIN, D.
Classic and Contemporary Nude Photography   **NEW**
An illustrated combination of art porfolio, 'how-to' photographic tips and studio technique.
[H578] Blandford P pbk **£16.95**

COLBECK, ANNIE & MARTIN, JUDY
Handtinting Photographs: History, Techniques and Materials   **NEW**
Traces the history of the art from Victorian prints to the hand-tinted pop videos of the eighties.
[H579] Macdonald Orbis hbk **£16.95**

DAFFURN, RAY & HICKS, ROGER
Pictures that Sell: A Guide to Successful Stock Photography
Tips on breaking into a difficult but rewarding area.
[H580] Collins hbk **£12.95**

DUNN, PHILIP
Press Photography
A comprehensive and well-illustrated guide by a professional in the business, to all aspects of the profession: tips on how to begin a career in news photography, the pros and cons of being a staff photographer and information on technical aspects of the job (cropping, captions, print quality etc).
[H581] Oxford hbk **£14.95**

HEDGECOE, JOHN
One of the most prolific writiers of technical manuals, Hedgecoe's books are always meticulously researched, both accessible and challenging, with equal attention paid to technique and to aesthetic effects.
Nude Photography
[H582] Ebury hbk **£15.00**
Practical Landscape Photography
[H583] Ebury hbk **£12.95**

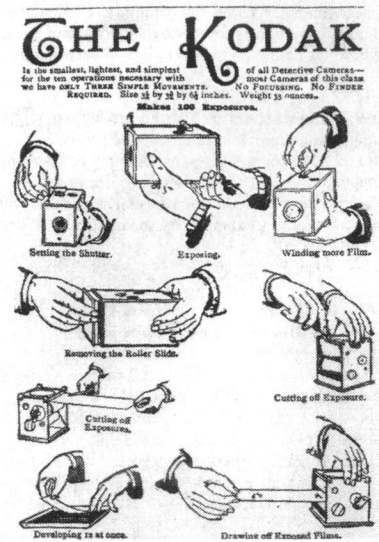

THE KODAK

Setting the Shutter. | Exposing. | Winding more Film.

Removing the Roller Slide.

Cutting off Exposure.

Cutting off Exposure.

Developing is at once. | Drawing off Exposed Films.

Illustration from *A History of Photography* edited by Jean-Claude Lemagny & Andre Rouille Cambridge University Press hbk £27.50)

Practical Portrait Photography
[H584] Ebury hbk **£12.95**
The Art of Colour Photography
[H585] Mitchell Beazley hbk **£9.25**

LANGFORD, MICHAEL J.
Widely considered to be the best introductory books available, Langford provides a complete guide to the principles of photographic practice and information about equipment and techniques. Experience teaching at the Royal College of Art means that his work is always up-to-the-minute and accessible at all levels.
35mm Handbook
[H586] Focal P hbk **£6.95**
Advanced Photography
[H587] Focal P pbk **£17.50**
Basic Photography
[H588] Focal P hbk **£24.50**
[H589] Focal P pbk **£14.95**

O'CONNOR, M. (ED)
Image Bank
Source book of ideas for the colour photographer.
[H592] Amphoto pbk **£17.50**

SHAW, JOHN
Nature Photographer's Complete Guide to Professional Field Techniques
Handy tips on how to 'capture' subjects in the wild.
[H593] Ampohoto pbk **£14.95**

TCHEREVKOFF
Tcherevkoff - The Image Maker: Developing Concepts for Special Effects **NEW**
Tcherevkoff is a pre-eminent name in special-effects photography in the US. His work is often seen on magazines and is used by the world's top companies.
[H594] Columbus pbk **£15.95**

WYLIE, GUS
The Complete Photographer **NEW**
A new encyclopaedia with the latest developments in photographic equipment and creative approaches to composition and lighting. Also includes sections on films, processing, subjects and approaches, and a 'gallery' of photographs (nearly 400 b/w and colour photos and diagrams).
[H595] Pyramid hbk **£17.95**

Cameras & Equipment

ADAMS, ANSEL
The Camera
BASIC PHOTOGRAPHY Vol 1
A classic text by landscape photographer Adams, this technical manual extends its focus to 'image management'; the careful choice of equipment to enable the photographer to create the image that he/she can 'see'.
[H596] NY Graph Soc hbk **£19.95**

RAY, SIDNEY
Camera Systems: A Technical Guide to Cameras and their Accessories
Useful for anyone wishing to broaden their knowledge of camera systems and their application.
[H599] Focal P hbk **£24.00**

ROBERTSON, GARY
Photographic Equipment: How to Choose and Buy it
One of the best available guides to help with important and often expensive purchases.
[H600] Focal P pbk **£17.50**

STOEBEL, LESLIE
View Camera Technique
Fifth edition of the book which continues to be the most comprehensive and practical source on equipment systems, movements, uses and applications. It examines 81 brand-name cameras and 77 different features.
[H601] Focal P hbk **£0.00**

Studio & Lighting

ANGELOLOU, CHRISTOPHER
Creative Photographic Lighting
A general guide to both natural and artificial lighting practices.
[H602] Collins pbk **£4.95**

ADAMS, ANSEL
Natural Light
BASIC PHOTOGRAPHY Vol 4
[H603] NY Graph Soc pbk **£5.95**
Artificial Light
BASIC PHOTOGRAPHY Vol 5
[H604] NY Graph Soc pbk **£5.95**

PERWEILER, GARY
Secrets of Studio Still Life Photography
Information on lighting, backdrops and overcoming common problems encountered when photographing difficult compositions.
[H605] Amphoto pbk **£14.95**

PINKARD, BRUCE
Creative Techniques in Studio Photography
[H606] Batsford hbk **£12.50**

SCHWARZ & STOPPE
Photographer's Guide to Using Light
This guide expands upon the photographic medium as the 'manipulation of light'. Giving information and ideas about achieving successful results in a wide variety of lighting 'set-ups'.
[H607] Amphoto pbk **£16.95**

Printing & Darkroom

ADAMS, ANSEL
The Negative
BASIC PHOTOGRAPHY Vol 2
Links the creative act of 'visualizing' a photograph with the choice of film, exposure and processing. Also includes a detailed discussion on the Zone System.
[H608] NY Graph Soc hbk **£19.95**
[H609] NY Graph Soc pbk **£5.95**
The Print
BASIC PHOTOGRAPHY Vol 3
The making of a fine print is the culmination of the creative process. Adams has spent many years studying processes to enable him to achieve exactly the effects he requires. Here he gives information on high-volume printing, very large print formats, processing for archival quality, as well as chemical formulae and test data.
[H610] NY Graph Soc hbk **£19.95**
[H611] NY Graph Soc pbk **£5.95**

CURRENT, IRA B.
Photographic Colour Printing: Theory and Technique
Well-illustrated, this book gives photographers a complete explanation of the elements of photographic colour printing and duplicating methods. Hands-on exercises provide practical demonstrations of important concepts and procedures.
[H612] Focal P hbk **£25.00**

CURTIN, DENNIS & DE MAIO, JOE
The Darkroom Handbook
Valuble and detailed technical reference.
[H613] Focal P pbk **£14.95**

NOCON, GENE
Photographic Printing
An accessible guide for both professional and amateur photographers, Nocon presents a method of printing based on his own experience as a professional photographic printer.
[H615] Planet hbk **£8.95**

STONE, JIM
Darkroom Dynamics: A Guide to Creative Darkroom Techniques
Creative darkroom techniques in a step-by-step format. Includes multiple printing, montage, toning, reticulation, infrared film, dye transfer, high contrast and much more.
[H616] Focal P hbk **£23.00**

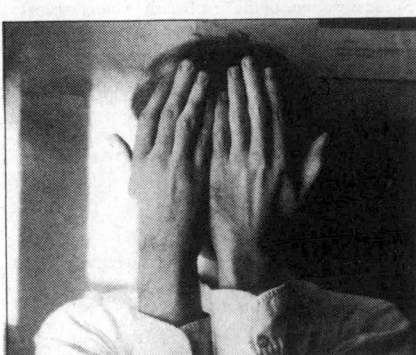

Andy Warhol from Duane Michals' *Photographs/ Sequences/Texts* (MOMA pbk £5.95)

General Cookery
Cookery by Country
Particular Foods
Drink

Food & Drink

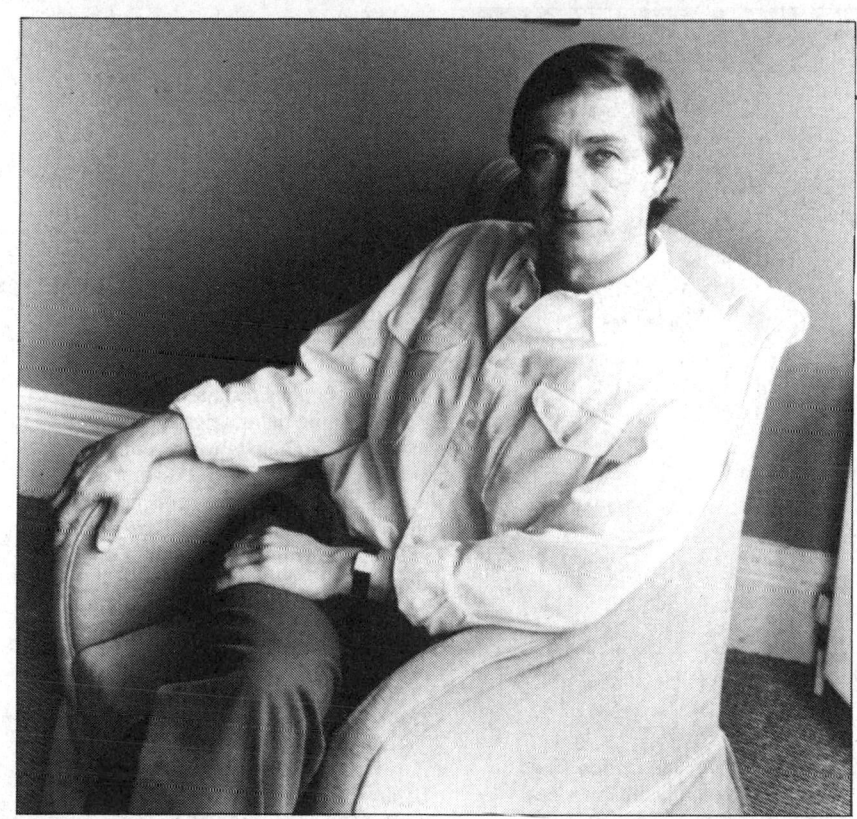

Cooking by the Book
Julian Barnes

Like many people who learned to cook after they learned to vote, I am incapable of preparing anything beyond breakfast without a prose text at my elbow telling me what to do. No reckless serendipity in the larder for me, no airy addition of a dozen crushed cardamom pods, no dazzling last-minute substitution of some Caribbean root vegetable which could equally be crafted into a truncheon. In my kitchen the cooking is done, quite literally, by the book. The shopping is militaristic, the weighing judicial, the chopping and dicing accurate to the last required millimetre. I scour the text of each recipe with fundamentalist rigour, scowling at any possible ambiguity. I demand precision, lucidity, plus a firm implication that someone of my culinary standard is capable of mastering the dish under discussion. I may not have become much of a cook as a result of all this, but I've

certainly become an expert on cookbooks.

At one time all you needed was Mrs Beeton; later, *The Joy of Cooking*; later still, two or three volumes of Elizabeth David. Nowadays, it seems, you have to display something between forty and eighty instruction manuals next to your stove before anyone will deign to dine with you. This means that I own far more cookbooks than I have dishes I know how to prepare. It also means that I know very clearly what I *don't* want from a cookbook.

I don't, for instance, want gastroporn colour illustrations whose sheeny charm mocks the sepia parody which emerges from the amateur's oven, or tricksy layout (like that ring-bound manual with each page sliced into three so that flicking through offered an infinite array of possible three-course dinner parties). I don't want books which make cocky predictions ('By now the sauce will have

reduced to a small amount of dense, dark liquid...' *Oh no it hasn't, so what do I do?*) or which expect impossible skills ('Clamping the tail of the fish between your knees, twist the flensing knife in a spiralling motion and the skin will slip smoothly off...'). Even theoretically

---

I don't want gastroporn colour illustrations whose sheeny charm mocks the sepia parody which emerges from the amateur's oven

---

helpful touches can be counterproductive: the confident listing of exact preparation times, for instance, ought to be useful, but in practice always flatters the efficiency of the writer rather than reflects the cack-handed reality of the domestic chef. Don't they realise you can't chop an onion - not properly, anyway, not as finely as they insist - in under about six minutes?

What I *do* want is books which guide and nanny me without being patronizing, which say, 'Don't be scared, go for it' (every time I make a soufflée I silently thank Fay Maschler for a piece of dulcet chivvying in the London *Standard*); books which tip you off about doing most of the preparation the day before, and suggest a range of substitutes in case the fishmonger is out of Goan hake or the greengrocer's lemon-grass is less than *à point*. I want books whose recipes concentrate on taste and scorn production values; books which tell me I don't have to skin, core and depip every tomato (when I do this there's nothing left at the end but a pool of juice on the chopping-board). Finally, I want books which can be made to lie flat on the work-surface without their pages falling out when you put them back on the shelf.

In China it's taken as a compliment at the end of a meal if the tablecloth around you is splattered with spilt food, soy sauce, bits of rice, and so on (at least, that's what the courteous Chinese guide once told me); and the same principle applies to cookbooks. The messier they are, the more you use and value them. By this token, my top kitchen guide is Jane Grigson's *Vegetable Book*, full of beetroot thumbprints and spinach

bookmarks. I relish her catholicity of cuisine, scholarly divagations, excellent prose and trenchant views (she refuses to be swayed by swede, and quite right too); beyond this she manages to convey the sturdy pleasure of cooking and eating. The dangers of food-writing are many (snobbery, effeteness, authoritarianism), and no writer could be further from them than Jane Grigson; open any of her books and you seem to get a warming whiff of

---

Open any of her books and you seem to get a warming whiff of some rich and bubbling stock

---

some rich and bubbling stock - which may be because you once dropped the book in the saucepan. Her *Fruit Book* (blackcurrant stains), *Fish Cookery* (cod-bone place-keepers) and *English Food* (dubious squidge-marks) are much in use; and how could anyone resist so unequivocal and encouraging a title as *Good Things*?

For some absurd reason Marcella Hazan isn't incredibly famous in Italy (perhaps because Italians all think they can cook anyway and don't need advice). This means it's even more important for us to bump up her royalties in this country. Her two *Classic Italian Cookbooks* constantly surprise me; first, because the food really comes out tasting as it does in Italy - more authentic than in most 'Italian' restaurants in this country; secondly, because her recipes seem literally fool-proof (I haven't been able to mess up a single one so far); thirdly, because she teaches you to cook pork - or what is sold as 'pork' by your local butcher - so that it tastes like meat rather than compacted cardboard.

I fought shy of Elizabeth David for many years, partly because of her reputation (I somehow felt she'd disapprove more if I spoiled one of her dishes) and partly because her recipes are comparatively short: this I took as a sign that only those with a decent amount of background know-how need bother. But this isn't, of course, the case: brevity of expression here indicates clarity of thought and instruction; so the new editions of *French Country Cooking*,

Delia Smith, author of *One is Fun!* (Hodder hbk £7.95, pbk £5.95)

Summer Cooking and *Italian Food* (illustrated - but with still-lives not gastroporn) are now being gravely baptised with sauce.

Fay Maschler's *Eating In* is full of inventive dishes and excellent for bluffers: your guests won't guess how comparatively easy some of its exotica are. Josceline Dimbleby is splendid for ambushing the jaded palate. Delia Smith is pompously looked down upon by Foodies, so whenever a paid-up Foodie crosses my threshold he or she gets a

---

For some absurd reason Marcella Hazan isn't incredibly famous in Italy

---

Delia recipe in the gob on principle. Also well-thumbed (if they'll forgive the expression) are Marguerite Costa and Claudia Roden; while Myrtle Allen's *The Ballymaloe Cookbook* and Susan Campbell's *English Cookery New and Old* are on constant stand-by. The only male cookery writer I turn to is Richard Olney, who is inclined to be bossy but whose *Simple French Cooking* (simple! hah!) is just right for when one fancies

being kicked around the kitchen like the humblest plate-scrubber. I cook my lamb according to Olney, beef according to Leith (it rhymes, for a start), chicken according to Grigson, and goose according to Shona Crawford Poole. This isn't showing off, merely an indication of neuroticism: once you find a recipe that works, you stick to it with furious loyalty.

Which leaves some forty or so dust-bearing volumes on my shelf, all bought in that spasm of enthusiasm which persuades you that your culinary style is infinitely expandable. These include: books by famous restaurant chefs (no point opening them unless you have a team of six to help you); several freezer cookbooks and food-processor manuals; a dozen guides to Chinese cuisine (I keep them in the rusting wok); three-volume anthologies which lack a cumulative index; books with too ambitious a catchment area - usually called *Great Dishes of the World* and found in the finest remainder shops, or too narrow a one - like *Fjord Food* or *The Vine-Twig Barbecue Guide*; books containing famous recipes from the past (just look how unhealthy they were in the past); books called things like *Pulses for Longevity*; Jacques Médicin's *Cuisine Niçoise*; plus an array of works picked up on holiday, in which category I am especially proud of *La Gastronomie Auvergnate*, every one of whose recipes contains at least one ingredient I can't even find in my dictionary, let alone in the shops. I'm sure I won't be able to prevent those just starting on the long road to cookbook folly from buying the sort of disasters listed above (people tried to stop me); all I can usefully do is suggest that you buy them in the summer. By late November you'll begin to realise what handy Christmas presents they could make for people you are not utterly fond of. But in the meantime, try not to autograph them with a sauce-coloured fingerprint.

Beyond his activities in the kitchen, Julian Barnes is one of the most considerable English novelists; his work includes *Metroland, Flaubert's Parrot, Staring at the Sun* and, published this summer, *A History of the World in 10 1/2 Chapters.* He also writes crime novels under the pseudonym Dan Kavanagh.

Feature

FOOD & DRINK

General Cookery

Everyone, whether they be a respected chef or merely a curious reader, has a different set of requirements for a cookbook. This section includes books that provide a general introduction to cooking, perhaps an explanation of the approach of a particular chef, or more wide-ranging reference works which aim to cover every aspect of the art of cooking.

Dining à La Carte
A collection of recipes by top chefs including Raymond Blanc and Anton Mosimann.
[I2] Octopus hbk **£14.95**

The Good Food Guide 1990 (Ed. Smith, D.)
One of the best known guides to Britain's restaurants, listing over 1,000 places that offer good food.
[I3] Hodder pbk **£11.95**

The Savoy Food and Drink Book
A richly illustrated history of one of the world's most distinguished hotels, the Savoy. Introduced by Kingsley Amis, there are recipes and anecdotes from Anton Edelmann, the Savoy's celebrated maître des cuisines, and cocktail recipes from the incomparable American Bar.
[I4] Pyramid hbk **£16.95**

ACKERMAN, ROY
Roy Ackerman's Recipe Collection
Recipe from top chefs collected by a leading restaurateur and food critic.
[I5] Penguin pbk **£6.95**
The Chef's Apprentice
Roy Ackerman plays apprentice to leading chefs.
[I6] Headline hbk **£12.95**

AGAR, ANNE
Lean Cuisine
[I7] Octopus hbk **£8.95**

ANDERSON, DIGBY
The Spectator Book of Imperative Cooking
[I8] Harrap hbk **£9.95**

ASHER, JANE
Easy Entertaining with Jane Asher
This book is full of good ideas for making the most of entertaining at home.
[I9] Conran Octopus hbk **£10.95**

AVILA, KAY
Based on the successful Channel Four television series with each chapter showing a different top-class chef who specialises in one particular course, enabling the reader to recreate the delicious dishes shown on the show.
Take Six More Cooks
[I10] Macdonald hbk **£8.95**
Take Twelve Cooks
[I11] Macdonald hbk **£8.95**

BAKER, JENNY
Student Cookbook
Newly revised edition of a useful work that shows how to make quick and simple food on a student budget.
[I12] Faber pbk **£2.95**

BEARD, JAMES A.
Beard on Entertaining
Recipes for breakfast, lunch, dinner and cocktail parties. Covers formal and informal entertaining with an interesting collection of recipes ranging from the effortlessly simple to the more complex.
[I13] Headline pbk **£7.95**

BEETON, MRS ISABELLA
Cookery & Household Management
The standard work by one of the earliest popular cookery writers, who completed this magnum opus before her death at the early age of 28. Despite its Victorian origin, many of the recipes and household hints are just as useful and entertaining today.
[I14] Ward Lock hbk **£19.95**
The Shorter Mrs Beeton
Based on the original work, this new revised edition contains over 400 recipes and is illustrated throughout in colour.
[I15] Ward Lock hbk **£14.95**

BERRIEDALE-JOHNSON, MICHELLE
British Museum Cookbook
An original cookbook including historical recipes from across the centuries illustrated with a wide range of contemporary engravings and woodcuts.
[I16] Brit Mus P hbk **£9.95**

BERRY, MARY
Buffets
[I17] Piatkus hbk **£9.95**
[I940] Sphere pbk **£2.95**
Cooking for Celebrations
[I18] Macdonald pbk **£2.95**
Creative Cook
[I19] Collins hbk **£14.95**

BLANCH, LESLEY
From Wilder Shores **NEW**
A work of nostalgia evoking dishes, places and people encountered while on the move through life — such as pushta kebabs of lamb marinated in yoghurt and vinegar shared with dusty Afghan horsemen, their eyes rimmed with kohl and their guns studded with turquoise.
[I20] J Murray hbk **£13.95**

BLUE, RABBI LIONEL
Kitchen Blues: Recipes for Body & Soul
Recipes for 'comfort food' for those whose body or soul is in need of comfort.
[I21] Gollancz pbk **£2.95**

BOXER, LADY ARABELLA
The Sunday Times Complete Cookbook
[I22] Weidenfeld hbk **£11.95**

CARRIER, ROBERT
Cooking with Robert Carrier
[I23] Hamlyn hbk **£10.95**
Great Dishes of the World
[I24] Sphere pbk **£3.25**

CAWLEY, RICHARD
The Artful Cook: Secrets of a Shoestring Gourmet
A personal interpretation of how to cook with imagination and eat with enthusiasm on a limited budget.
[I25] Macdonald Orbis hbk **£10.95**

CESERANI, VICTOR & KINTON, RONALD F.
Practical Cookery
This textbook is used by almost every catering college in Britain but don't be put off by that - it is a very good introduction to basic cooking techniques.
[I26] Arnold pbk **£7.95**

Illustration from *Summer Cooking* by Elizabeth David (Penguin pbk £7.95)

CHRISTIAN, GLYNN
Contemporary Home Cooking
[I27] Octopus hbk **£10.95**

CONRAN, CAROLINE
Good Home Cooking
[I28] Conran Octopus hbk **£8.95**

COSTA, MARGARET
The Four Seasons Cookery Book
Reccomended by Katie Stewart of *The Times* as a 'book for all who love and are interested in food'.
[I29] Macmillan pbk **£7.95**

COURTINE, ROBERT J. (ED)
Larousse Gastronomique: The World's Greatest Cookery Encyclopaedia
As the title unashamedly announces, this is the world's best culinary reference work. While concentrating on things French, its range of entries on both food and wine from round the world is staggering. The entries are accompanied by over 4,000 recipes and illustrated throughout in colour.
[I30] Hamlyn hbk **£25.00**

COX, NICOLA
Country Cooking from Farthinghoe
[I31] Gollancz hbk **£10.95**
Good Food from Farthinghoe
The author is a former *Sunday Times* Cook of Britain who now runs a successful cookery school. This book is filled with practical advice on entertaining and has a wide selection of recipes.
[I32] Gollancz pbk **£6.95**

CRAWFORD-POOLE, SHONA
The New 'Times' Cook Book
A further selection of recipes which tend to stress the unusual and up-market.
[I33] Collins hbk **£9.95**

DAVENPORT, PHILIPPA
The Country Living Country Cook
[I34] Ebury hbk **£10.95**

DAVID, ELIZABETH
More than any other single writer, Elizabeth David has awakened the British to the joys of food and

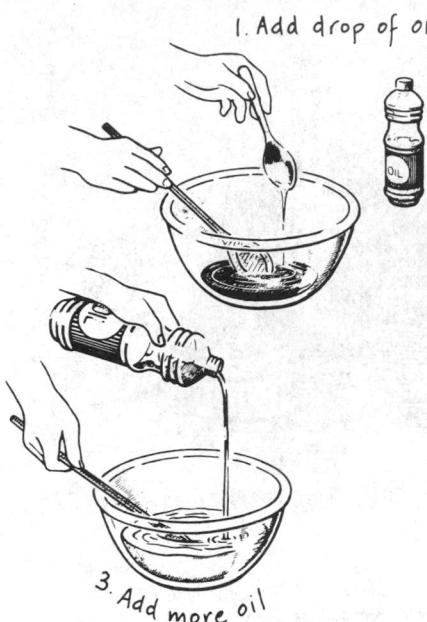

1. Add drop of oil

3. Add more oil

Illustration from *The Book of National Trust Recipes* by Sarah Eddington (National Trust hbk £6.95)

cooking. Her writing has that particular ability to evoke a vision of the perfection of the finished dish, as well as the pleasure of consuming it. For decades now she has inspired not only the cooks with her commonsense, and the clarity of her instructions, but also the discerning eater. Her other works, such as *French Country Cooking* and *Italian Food*, will be found under the appropriate sections later in the chapter.

An Omelette & A Glass of Wine
A collection of essays exploring her philosophy of cooking and dining, that display her culinary enthusiasm and acerbic wit.
[I35] D Kindersley hbk £10.95
[I36] Penguin pbk £6.95
Summer Cooking
Another classic - the perfect British summer day may be rare but when it arrives there is no excuse not to ensure that all elements combine to enhance it — including the food that is eaten.
[I37] D Kindersley hbk £12.95
[I38] Penguin pbk £7.95

DAVIES, LOUISE
Easy Cooking for One or Two
[I39] Penguin pbk £3.99
More Easy Cooking for One or Two
[I40] Penguin pbk £3.99

DIMBLEBY, JOSCELINE
A Taste of Dreams
[I41] Sphere pbk £1.95

DOWELL, PHILIP & BAILEY, ADRIAN
The Book of Ingredients
A re-issue of a standard reference work offering hints and methods with almost every ingredient known to cooks.
[I42] M Joseph pbk £12.95

DOWNING, BERYL
Quick Cook
Simple but tasty recipes that can be prepared in thirty minutes - or less.
[I43] Penguin pbk £3.95

DOWNES, MURIEL & PIERCY, HAROLD
Cordon Bleu & Constance Spry Entertaining
Two top names get together to give a comprehensive guide to traditional cordon bleu entertaining.
[I44] Octopus hbk £10.95

DRIVER, CHRISTOPHER & BERRIEDALE-JOHNSON, MICHELLE
Pepys at Table: 17th Century Recipes for the Modern Cook `NEW`
Recipes from the 17th century cookbooks contemporary with Samuel Pepys, adapted for the modern cook and accompanied by quotes from Pepys' diary and woodblock illustrations.
[I45] Unwin Hyman hbk £5.95

ELLE
The Elle Cookbook
A translation of a standard French work, whose elegant recipes are useful for all occasions.
[I48] M Joseph pbk £9.95

ELLIOT, ROSE
An innovative cook renowned for her writings on vegetarian cuisine. A fuller list of this author's books will be found in the section on Vegetarian cooking.
Simply Delicious
[I53] Fontana pbk £2.50
Your Very Good Health
[I54] Fontana pbk £3.95

ELLWOOD, CAROLINE & WADEY, ROSEMARY
The Hamlyn Cookery Course
[I55] Hamlyn hbk £9.95

FLOYD, KEITH
A Feast of Floyd `NEW`
From a family recipe for Old-fashioned Bread Pudding to methods of serving sushi, this is the most complete and wide ranging of Floyd's cookbooks, combining his indefatigable sense of fun with clear, reliable instructions and beautiful colour reproductions for many of the dishes described.
[I941] Collins hbk £14.95
Floyd in the Soup
An often hilarious autobiographical account of the rise and rise of this indefatigable restaurateur, author and television presenter - including an account of his

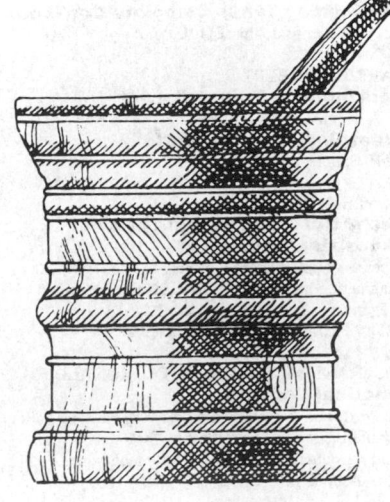

debut performance on the BBC involving roast guinea fowl uniquely stuffed with giblets still in their plastic bags.
[I56] Pan pbk £4.99
Floyd's Food
This was published before Floyd's first television series. It adheres to his principles of simple food cooked in season. Many of the recipes here can be cooked in one pot.
[I57] Absolute pbk £3.50

GOOD HOUSEKEEPING
The Good Housekeeping Series represents excellent value, with well-illustrated, simple recipes that produce flavoursome and stylish dishes.
All-Colour Cookbook
New to this excellent series, containing over 300 recipes.
[I58] Ebury hbk £8.95
Best Recipes
[I59] M Joseph pbk £8.95
Cookery Book
[I60] Ebury hbk £15.95
Cookery Encyclopaedia
[I61] Treasure hbk £11.95
Good Cookery
350 recipes whose emphasis is on healthy living.
[I62] Ebury hbk £14.95
New Basic Cookery
[I63] Ebury pbk £4.95
Step by Step Cook Book
One of the few cookery books to contain a colour illustration of every recipe together with detailed step-by-step instructions for each method.
[I64] Ebury hbk £14.95

GOODE, SHIRLEY
Recipes from the television series designed for the lone cook.
Goode for One
[I65] BBC pbk £1.95
The Shirley Goode Kitchen
[I66] BBC pbk £1.95

HAIGH, RACHEL & THE NEAL'S YARD BAKERY CO-OPERATIVE
Neal's Yard Bakery Wholefood Cook Book
Wholefood recipes from the famous Neal's Yard restaurant and bakery in London's Covent Garden.
[I67] D Kindersley hbk £12.95
[I67] D Kindersley pbk £7.95

HAMBRO, NATHALIE
Particular Delights
[I68] Macmillan pbk £6.95
Visual Delights
Stylish and well-presented seasonal recipes.
[I69] Conran Octopus hbk £9.95

HOLT, GERALDENE
Budget Gourmet
[I70] Penguin pbk £3.95

HORSELY, JANET
The Weekend Cook
[I71] Collins pbk £5.95

HOWARD, ELIZABETH JANE & MASCHLER, FAY
Howard & Maschler on Food
A variety of recipes giving innovative ideas for entertaining at home, from first courses to desserts.
[I73] Sphere pbk £3.99

HUME, ROSEMARY & DOWNES, MURIEL
Cordon Bleu Cookery
A straightforward and perennially useful introduction

to cooking, whose simplicity belies its sophisticated heritage.
[I174] Viking hbk **£14.95**
[I175] Penguin pbk **£4.95**

INNES, JOCASTA
Eatability
Imaginative food on a budget.
[I77] Macdonald hbk **£9.95**

ISITT, VERITY
Take a Buttock of Beefe
This is based on a 17th century cookbook, adapted for current use.
[I178] Headline pbk **£6.95**

JAINE, TOM
Cooking in the Country
[I179] Chatto hbk **£12.95**

JOHNSON, ALISON
Scarista Style: A Free Range & Humane Approach to Cooking & Eating
Scarista House is an award-winning restaurant on the Hebridean island of Harris. Alison Johnson has a commitment to free range food and most of these recipes can be used by vegetarians. The book is written with a wry sense of humour which makes for entertaining reading.
[I180] Gollancz hbk **£10.95**

JONES, JULIA & DEER, BARBARA
Cattern Cakes & Lace
Cooking for traditional festivals.
[I181] D Kindersley hbk **£12.95**

LAWRENCE, BERNADINE
The Benefit Book   NEW
A month's worth of nutritious recipes enabling a family of four to feed themselves three times a day on a high fibre, low fat diet - on a budget of £28 a week.
[I182] Thorsons pbk **£3.50**

LEITH, PRUE
Prue Leith's Dinner Parties
[I183] Macmillan pbk **£6.95**

LEITH, PRUE & TYRER, POLLY
Entertaining with Style
Unusual party ideas from an aphrodisiac dinner for two to a Creole party for 300.
[I184] Macdonald hbk **£14.95**

LEITH, PRUE & WALDEGRAVE, CAROLINE
The heads of a successful London cookery school impart their joint wisdom.
Leith's Cook Book
[I185] Fontana pbk **£5.95**
Leith's Cookery School
[I186] Macdonald hbk **£14.95**

LEVY, PAUL
Out to Lunch
A collection of entertaining anecdotes on the subject of the pleasures and perils of being Britain's best-known writer on food and drink. Including essays on obscure cuisines, how astronauts eat, what to eat with blue cheese and the real truth about eating dogs and monkeys in China.
[I187] Penguin pbk **£6.95**

LONG, ANN
Ann Long's Dinner Party Book
[I188] Hodder hbk **£12.95**

LOUSADA, PATRICIA
Easy to Entertain
[I189] Penguin pbk **£6.95**

MASCHLER, FAY
Eating In
Anton Mosimann regards Fay Maschler as 'one of Britain's best food writers'. This is a collection of recipes from her excellent column in the London *Evening Standard*.
[I90] Bloomsbury hbk **£9.95**
[I943] Bloomsbury pbk **£4.95**

Teach Your Child to Cook
A straightforward and helpful book addressed to both parent and child which demonstrates the various cooking techniques and skills needed both to stay alive and produce good food in the kitchen.
[I191] Bloomsbury pbk **£6.95**

MOINE, MARIE-PIERRE (ED)
The Best of Taste   NEW
A glittering collection of impressionistic essays and original menus by some of the world's best food writers and cooks, who were asked by *Taste* magazine about how they entertain their own family and friends.
[I192] Macdonald hbk **£16.95**

MOORE, HENRY (ED)
The Artist's Cookbook
Illustrated by artists from the Royal Academy
[I194] Macdonald hbk **£12.95**

MOSIMANN, ANTON
Cooking with Mosimann   NEW
A wide-ranging selection of innovative recipes emphasising healthily cooked foods using the minimum of fats and cream.
[I195] Macmillan hbk **£15.95**

MCCARTNEY, LINDA
Linda McCartney's Home Cooking   NEW
Over 300 recipes from McCartney's family kitchen.
[I196] Bloomsbury hbk **£13.99**

NILSON, BEE
Penguin Cookery Book
[I197] Penguin pbk **£3.95**

NORMAN, CECILIA
Cordon Vitesse
[I98] Thorsons pbk **£6.99**

PASTON-WILLIAMS, SARA
National Trust Book of Christmas & Festive Day Recipes
[I99] Penguin pbk **£3.50**

PATTEN, MARGUERITE
Every Day Cookbook in Colour
[I100] Hamlyn hbk **£4.95**

POOLE, SHONA CRAWFORD
The New Times Cook Book
[I103] Fontana pbk **£3.95**

RINZLER, CAROL ANN
Food Facts and What They Mean
A very informative book about the foods we eat and what is in them. Useful guide for the health-conscious, explaining and discussing all the major additives present in raw and processed foods.
[I105] Bloomsbury hbk **£13.95**
[I944] Bloomsbury pbk **£4.95**

ROGERS, JENNY (ED)
The Taste of Health
The book that accompanies the BBC series.
[I106] BBC hbk **£8.95**
[I107] BBC pbk **£5.50**

RONAY, EGON
Master Chefs of Europe
A beautifully designed collection of the work of 50 leading gourmets in Europe, brought together by the International Academy of Gastronomy. Each chef provides an exclusive menu as might be found in their restaurants, giving the reader opportunity to recreate these dishes at home.
[I108] Macdonald hbk **£16.95**
The Unforgettable Dishes of My Life   NEW
Egon Ronay, editor of the famous restaurant guides, presents his first cookery book, each recipe garnished with nostalgic gastronomic reminiscence.
[I109] Gollancz hbk **£17.95**

ROUND, JEREMY
The Independent Cook
From the *Independent*'s food correspondent, a calendar of produce and recipes showing when to buy and consume foods to get the most flavour and natural goodness, with recipes to enhance these things.
[I110] Barrie & J hbk **£12.95**

SCOTT, DAVID
The Fish, Vegetable, Cheese and Chicken Cookbook   NEW
From the writer who produced the not-quite-vegetarian cookbook the *Demiveg Cookbook*, a cookbook specialising in these culinary and nutritional favourites.
[I111] Bloomsbury pbk **£7.99**

SEKULES, VERONICA
Friends of the Earth Cookbook
[I112] Penguin pbk **£3.95**

SMITH, DELIA
It is now ten years since Delia Smith's cookery course was first broadcast on BBC television, but time has in no way diminished the appeal of her writing. Her *Complete Cookery Course* is arguably the finest single cookery book available — its instructions are clear, comprehensive and pretty nearly infallible. If you were allowed only one cookbook, it would have to be this.
Delia Smith's Complete Cookery Course
All three volumes collected in one easy volume.
[I114] BBC hbk **£12.95**
Delia Smith's Cookery Course: Part 1
[I115] BBC pbk **£5.25**
Delia Smith's Cookery Course: Part 2
[I116] BBC pbk **£4.25**
Delia Smith's Cookery Course: Part 3
[I117] BBC pbk **£4.25**
Frugal Food
A useful book for all those starting out on their own, with many simple but tasty recipes for those on a limited budget.
[I119] Hodder pbk **£2.50**
One is Fun!
[I120] Hodder hbk **£7.95**
[I121] Hodder pbk **£5.95**

SPRY, CONSTANCE & HUME, ROSEMARY
Constance Spry Cookery Book
First published in 1956 this elegantly composed book has established itself as a classic work of reference with comprehensive and wide-ranging recipes on all kinds of food.
[I122] Dent hbk **£17.50**

STEWART, KATIE
Katie Stewart's Cookbook
Recipes from the food columnist for *The Times*.
[I123] Gollancz hbk **£12.95**
[I123] Pan pbk **£3.95**

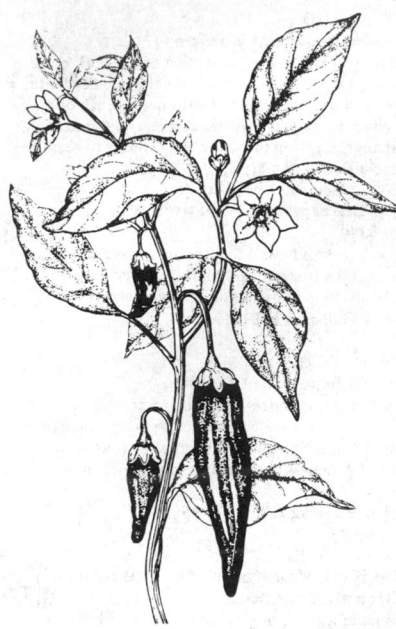

Illustration from *The Covent Garden Cookery Book* by Diana Troy (Sidgwick & Jackson pbk £6.95)

STEWART, MARTHA
Martha Stewart's Entertaining
[I124] Sidgwick hbk **£17.95**

TOVEY, JOHN
Eating Out with Tovey
[I125] BBC pbk **£6.95**
John Tovey's Country Weekends
Original country cooking and recipes for those in the country just for the weekend.
[I126] Ebury hbk **£14.95**

TROY, DIANA
The Covent Garden Cookery Book
[I126A] Sidgwick pbk **£6.95**

VERNON, TOM
Fat Man in the Kitchen
[I127] BBC hbk **£8.95**
[I128] BBC pbk **£4.95**

VOGUE
Food in 'Vogue' **NEW**
A collection of recipes and tips contributed to *Vogue* magazine since the 1920's when Michel Boulestin began his monthly column. Illustrated by a wide range of artists and with contributions from writers of the calibre of Elizabeth David and Robert Carrier, this book beautifully captures the period flavour of the various recipes.
[I129] Octopus hbk **£16.95**

WATERHOUSE, KEITH
The personal view of this aging social dissenter, casting a witty, world-weary eye on the political and social scene through that most pleasurable institution, lunch.
The Theory and Practice of Lunch
[I131] Grafton pbk **£2.99**

WATTS, MARY (ED)
The Complete Farmhouse Kitchen Cookbook
Recipes for traditional fare submitted by viewers of the popular Yorkshire television series.
[I132] Collins hbk **£9.95**

WOMAN'S REALM
Woman's Realm Cookbook
[I133] Octopus hbk **£12.95**

WRIGHT, JENI
The New Cordon Bleu Cookbook **NEW**
Concentrating on developing the reader's cooking skills and at the same time giving the cook confidence to tackle even the most complicated dishes, these recipes invite the cook to experiment with ingredients and techniques. It includes ideas to suit every occasion and stunning modern photographs that emphasise the stylish and appealing presentation for which the Cordon Bleu school is known.
[I134] Macdonald hbk **£12.95**

Cookery by Country

France

French cuisine still represents the pinnacle of culinary achievement, with an impressive depth of skill, knowledge, and excellence wedded to a tradition of innovation and experimentation. Look for the authoritative accounts of Simone Beck (et al) in classic cuisine, of Michel Guerard or the Troisgros brothers in nouvelle cuisine, or Elizabeth David for French provincial and country cooking.

A Little French Cookbook **NEW**
An introduction to the world's foremost cuisine in the Little Cookbooks series.
[I136] Appletree hbk **£3.50**

BECK, SIMONE; BERTHOLLE, LOUISETTE & CHILD, JULIA
These two thorough and authoritative volumes constitute the finest practical guide to French classical cuisine in English, with step-by-step instructions to all the recipes and excellent illustrations. Essential reading for anyone interested in the subject, whether a beginner or a proficient chef.
Mastering the Art of French Cooking: Vol 1
[I137] Penguin pbk **£9.95**
Vol 2
[I138] Penguin pbk **£12.99**

BENTLEY, JAMES
Life & Food in the Dordogne
James Bentley has lived, cooked and eaten for many years in the heart of Périgord and describes the life of the region and its cuisine, exploring a range of fascinating regional food including truffle, walnuts, cèpes, morilles, and girolles, fish, foie gras and goose.
[I139] Weidenfeld hbk **£10.95**
[I140] Weidenfeld pbk **£6.95**

BLANC, BEVERLY LE (ED)
Secrets of French Hors d'Oeuvres
[I141] Macdonald hbk **£3.95**
Secrets of French Sauces
Over 100 authentic sauce recipes.
[I142] Macdonald hbk **£3.95**

BLANC, GEORGES
Ma Cuisine des Saisons
One of the best works on nouvelle cuisine, with original recipes from the master chef and restaurateur Georges Blanc, reflecting his belief in seasonal cooking and the lighter, fresher style favoured by that school.
[I143] Macmillan hbk **£12.95**
[I945] Macmillan pbk **£8.95**

Natural Cuisine of Georges Blanc
Vegetarian, and wholefood recipes from one of the acknowledged masters of nouvelle cuisine.
[I144] Webb & B hbk **£19.95**

BLANC, RAYMOND
Recipes from Le Manoir aux Quat' Saisons
Raymond Blanc's Oxfordshire restaurant has been showered with awards since it opened in 1984, receiving 2 Michelin stars even before it opened. He is an inspired, self-taught cook now widely regarded as the best chef in Britain: here he shares some of his special recipes and explains his innovative methods with detailed instructions and advice on selecting ingredients, menus and wine.
[I145] Macdonald Orbis hbk **£17.50**

BOCUSE, PAUL
Bocuse à La Carte: Cooking for Family & Friends
[I146] Aurum hbk **£9.95**
The Cuisine of Paul Bocuse
An introduction to, and a revelation of, the methods and recipes of this famous Lyonnais chef.
[I147] Granada pbk **£9.95**

CHRISTIAN, GLYN
Edible France
A guide to the foods and specialities and the restaurants and markets of each region.
[I148] Ebury pbk **£7.95**

DAVID, ELIZABETH
French Country Cooking
A classic by any standards, introducing a cuisine through its recipes and its culture in typically evocative prose.
[I149] D Kindersley hbk **£12.95**
[I150] Penguin pbk **£6.95**
French Provincial Cooking
[I151] M Joseph hbk **£17.95**
[I152] Penguin pbk **£9.99**

DEIGHTON, LEN
The ABC of French Food **NEW**
A personal guide to French food by the bestselling thriller writer, based on conversations and jottings from Deighton's notebook compiled as he travelled through France, and accompanied by his own line drawings.
[I153] Century hbk **£14.95**

ESCOFFIER, GEORGES AUGUSTE
Born the son of a blacksmith in 1846, Escoffier rose rapidly to become the head chef at the Savoy in London, achieving there phenomenal fame and success. A culinary genius, he went on to open, with César Ritz, the Ritz in Paris and the Carlton in London.
Hors d'Oeuvres
The second Escoffier Kitchen Handbook.
[I154] Heinemann hbk **£5.95**
Stocks, Sauces and Garnishes
An Escoffier Kitchen Handbook, comprising an excerpt from the Complete Guide that deals just with stocks, sauces and garnishes
[I155] Heinemann hbk **£5.95**
The Complete Guide to the Art of Modern Cookery
[I156] Heinemann hbk **£25.00**

FLOYD, KEITH
Floyd on France
The latest book from the winner of the 1987 TV Glenfiddich award. A highly personal selection of around 300 of Keith Floyd's favourite classic French dishes, presented with irrepressible Floyd panache.
[I158] BBC pbk **£6.95**

FORBES, LESLIE
A Table in Provence
Leslie Forbes' second delightfully pretty and evocative culinary odyssey. Her first was *A Table in Tuscany*. Illustrated throughout by the author.
[I159] Webb & B hbk **£12.95**

GAULET, CHRISTIAN; CHAUSSEAUD, BERNARD; & HUS, EDMOND
Menus de Saison NEW
Combining exquisite food photography with practical cooking advice, this book offers a calendar of French cuisine, recipes, menus, and wine.
[I160] Equation hbk **£16.99**

GIRARDET, FREDY
Cuisine Spontanée
[I161] Macmillan pbk **£6.95**

GRIGSON, JANE
Charcuterie & French Pork Cookery
Grigson's first cookery book. It is entertaining, authentic and erudite, as are all her later books.
[I162] Penguin pbk **£9.99**

GUERARD, MICHEL
Cuisine Gourmande
[I163] Macmillan pbk **£8.99**
Cuisine Minceur
A collection of low cholesterol recipes in the nouvelle cuisine style.
[I164] Pan pbk **£0.95**

HOLT, GERALDENE
French Country Kitchen
This book won critical acclaim for combining wonderfully evocative recipes with very practical methods. She not only re-interprets some of the classic dishes of southern France but adds her own recipes inspired by the Midi and its local ingredients.
[I165] Penguin pbk **£6.95**
Recipes from a French Herb Garden NEW
Vivid, authentic recipes demonstrating the pervasive influence of wild herbs on the classical cuisine of France, magnificently illustrated with photographs that evocatively capture the atmosphere of the landscape, country markets and herb gardens of France.
[I166] Conran Octopus hbk **£14.95**

JOHNSTON, MIREILLE
The Cuisine of the Rose: Classical French Cuisine from Burgundy & Lyonnais
A comprehensive guide to the flavoursome cooking of the Rhône Valley.
[I167] Penguin pbk **£5.95**

KOFFMANN, PIERRE
Memories of Gascony NEW
Described as 'a chef's chef' and owner of La Tante Claire in London, Koffmann here gives an intimate account of the traditional regional cooking of his native Gascony.
[I168] Macdonald hbk **£17.50**

LADENIS, NICO
My Gastronomy NEW
The controversial Franco-Greek chef and owner of the internationally renowned London restaurants Chez Nico and Simply Nico combines here brilliantly innovative recipes with his own firm and outspoken views of food, customers and cooking.
[I169] Headline pbk **£5.99**

MARIE CLAIRE
French Cooking at its Best NEW
A stylishly presented new book offering an exciting

range of French recipes from traditional dishes to classic 'grande cuisine'.
[I170] Octopus hbk **£14.95**

MILLAU, CHRISTIAN
Dining in France
The co-editor of the most influential guide to good eating, Christian Millau visits the restaurants of France's greatest chefs.
[I171] Sidgwick hbk **£12.95**
[I172] Sidgwick pbk **£6.95**

MOSIMANN, ANTON
Cuisine Naturelle
A display of Mosimann's new style of health-conscious nouvelle cuisine.
[I173] Macmillan hbk **£18.95**
[I174] Macmillan pbk **£7.95**
Cuisine à La Carte
[I175] Macmillan pbk **£7.95**

OLNEY, RICHARD
An American who has spent much of his life in France, Olney here offers a collection of simple French recipes for English speakers.
Simple French Food
[I176] Hale hbk **£8.95**
[I177] Penguin pbk **£3.95**
Ten Vineyard Lunches
Explores the wine-producing regions of France to produce ten menus inspired by ten distinctive wines.
[I178] Ebury pbk **£8.95**

POMIANE, EDOUARD DE
Cooking in Ten Minutes
A French gastronôme who has adopted a surprisingly un-Gallic, scientific approach to the techniques of cooking.
[I180] Faber pbk **£3.95**
Cooking with Pomiane
[I181] Faber pbk **£1.25**

RANCE, PATRICK
The French Cheese Book NEW
The famous cheese expert dissects France region by region to examine in detail the great cheeses of the country, describing their appearance, texture, aroma, flavour, origins, and development.
[I183] Macmillan hbk **£16.95**

ROUX, MICHEL & ALBERT
Owners of the three Michelin star restaurant Le Gavroche, and the two starred Waterside Inn, the Roux brothers are at the pinnacle of English culinary achievement. Consummate television presenters, they have won the Glenfiddich Award for their beautifully illustrated and original cookery books.
French Country Cooking NEW
A region by region guide to the best local specialities and delicacies France can offer.
[I184] Sidgwick hbk **£16.95**
New Classic Cuisine
The distillation of their comprehensive range of recipes and menus.
[I185] Macdonald hbk **£14.50**
The Roux Brothers on Pâtisserie
Outstanding, authentic and imaginative French pâtisserie from the two brothers, who both served their apprenticeships as pâtissiers.
[I186] Macdonald hbk **£15.00**

SENDERENS, ALAIN
The Cuisine of Alain Senderens: La Cuisine Réussie
[I187] Macmillan pbk **£6.50**

SHARMAN, FAY & CHADWICK, BRIAN
The Taste of France
A dictionary of French food and wine designed to

enable the visitor to decipher any menu and discover the delights and variety of French food and wine.
[I188] Macmillan pbk **£5.95**

SHULMAN, MARTHA ROSE
Chez Martha Rose: The Pleasures of Parisian Eating NEW
Recipes with a distinctive Parisian flavour, spiced with entertaining anecdotes.
[I189] Macmillan hbk **£14.95**

TROISGROS, JEAN & PIERRE
Cuisine Nouvelle
Paul Levy described this stunning collection of innovative dishes as a 'collection every serious cook will want'.
[I190] Macmillan pbk **£6.95**

VERGE, ROGER
Cuisine of the Sun
[I191] Macmillan pbk **£8.95**
Entertaining in the French Style
[I192] Webb & B hbk **£30.00**

VERGNE, ELISA
Classic French Dishes for Microwave Cooking NEW
[I193] Macdonald hbk **£14.95**

WELLS, PATRICIA
The Food Lover's Guide to France
A practical and handy tourist guide to gastronomic France.
[I194] Methuen pbk **£6.95**

WILLAN, ANNE & L'ECOLE DE CUISINE LA VARENNE, PARIS
French Regional Cooking NEW
The founder of a celebrated cookery school in Paris presents the food of the 12 major regions of provincial France. Winner of the André Simon Book Award.
[I195] Century pbk **£6.99**

WOLFERT, PAULA
The Cooking of South-West France
This passionate and illuminating book describes the gastronomy of the region that stretches from Périgord to the Pyrenees, from Gascony across to Ganique, a cuisine both rustic and sophisticated.
[I196] D Kindersley hbk **£14.95**

Great Britain

The cooking of the British Isles has undergone something of a renaissance in recent years. Some writers such as Elisabeth Ayrton have looked at traditional and historical cooking, others have explored modern styles using traditional regional materials.

ALLEN, MYRTLE
The Ballymaloe Cookbook
[I197] Gill & Macmillan pbk **£6.95**

AYRTON, ELISABETH
English Provincial Cooking
[I198] M Beazley pbk **£4.95**
The Cookery of England
A fascinating and beautifully compiled history and recipe book of English cooking from the 15th century to the present day.
[I199] Penguin pbk **£8.99**

BOYD, LIZZIE
British Cookery NEW
A new edition of a classic account of the regional and

Illustration from *English Food* by Jane Grigson (Penguin pbk £7.99)

traditional cooking of the British Isles, giving backgound information about each recipe explained with clear and precise instructions.
[I200] Ch Helm hbk **£12.95**

BROWN, CATHERINE
Scottish Cookery
A new edition of this classic of Scots cuisine, illustrated with specially commissioned artworks by Fiona Brown.
[I201] Richard Drew hbk **£10.95**
[I946] Richard Drew pbk **£5.99**

DAVID, ELIZABETH
English Bread & Yeast Cookery
A comprehensive investigation of the processes, materials and techniques of yeast cookery and the bread-making of England.
[I202] Penguin pbk **£8.95**
Spices, Salt & Aromatics in the English Kitchen
[I203] Penguin pbk **£7.95**

DAVIES, GILLI
Lambs, Leeks and Laverbread `NEW`
A guide to the best of Welsh cookery, with an accent on the fresh, the healthy, and the naturally produced.
[I204] Grafton pbk **£4.99**

FITZGIBBON, THEODORA
A series of very regional recipes, accompanied by plenty of social history and anecdotes. Fully illustrated with old photographs.
A Taste of England
[I205] Pan pbk **£4.95**
A Taste of Ireland
[I206] Pan pbk **£4.95**
A Taste of the Lake District
[I209] Pan pbk **£3.95**
A Taste of the West Country
[I210] Pan pbk **£3.95**

GILLON, JACK
The Scottish Food Book `NEW`
A celebration of Scottish food with over sixty recipes using Scottish produce in modern dishes, illustrated with archive pictures and colour photographs.
[I211] Chambers hbk **£9.95**

GLASSE, HANNAH
The Art of Cookery Made Plain & Easy
A facsimile of one of the earliest of English Cookery books.
[I212] Prospect hbk **£22.50**

GRIGSON, JANE
English Food
The superb classic on the topic from Jane Grigson.
[I213] Penguin pbk **£7.99**
Good Things
[I214] Penguin pbk **£5.99**
The Observer Guide to British Cookery
A region by region look at the best of British food, with an appreciation of local ingredients and customs.
[I215] M Joseph hbk **£12.95**

HALL, ALLAN
Great Dishes from the British Gastronomic Academy
A collection of reminiscences and recipes from 50 famous food lovers including Len Deighton, Albert Roux, Prue Leith and Egon Ronay. The contributors' favourite dishes are complemented by wine chosen by Hugh Johnson and other experts.
[I217] Macdonald hbk **£12.95**

HARTLEY, DOROTHY
Food in England
Recipes, household hints, anecdotes, spells, history - a kitchen classic.
[I218] Futura pbk **£5.95**

HEGARTY, PATRICIA
An English Flavour: Food from Hope End Country House Hotel `NEW`
From Hope End, a country house formerly the home of Elizabeth Barret Browning, comes this elegant collection of recipes that use local produce, organic production and emphasise freshness and originality.
[I219] Equation hbk **£16.95**

LAVERTY, MAURA
Full & Plenty
Vol 1: Bread, Cakes & Pastry
An Irish household legend, with a wonderful and comprehensive account of Irish country kitchen from a writer now more famous for her evocative novels of Irish life and manners.
[I220] Anvil pbk **£3.95**
Vol 2: Fish & Meat
[I221] Anvil pbk **£4.95**

MACDONALD, CLAIRE
Celebrations `NEW`
Practical yet extravagant dishes for any celebration from this well known exponent of Scottish cooking.
[I222] Bantam hbk **£14.95**

MACLEAN, LADY VERONICA
Lady Maclean's Cookbook
A personal collection of recipes gathered together from several generations of Lady Maclean's family, her travels and friends.
[I223] Collins hbk **£9.95**

MENHINICK, GLADYS
Grampian Cookbook
[I225] Aberdeen UP pbk **£2.95**

ORTIZ, ELISABETH LAMBERT
A Taste of Excellence: Recipes from the Best of British Chefs `NEW`
A superb selection of new recipes, introduced by Anton Mosimann, from British chefs all over the country, including recipes from Raymond Blanc, David Adlard and Francis Coulson.
[I947] Collins hbk **£9.95**
[I226] Headline pbk **£4.99**

PASTON-WILLIAMS, SARA
Christmas Fayre `NEW`
Recipes and ideas for Christmas including festive menus, traditional customs, gifts and decorations.
[I227] David & Ch hbk **£9.95**

PATTULLO, DIONNE
Best of Scottish Cooking
[I228] Johnston & B pbk **£1.75**

RAY, ELIZABETH
The Best of Eliza Acton
The influential recipes of a pre-Beeton cook.
[I229] Penguin pbk **£6.95**

REEKIE, JENNIE
British Charcuterie `NEW`
Traditional British recipes for pork, including pies, puddings and sausages from each region of the country.
[I230] Ward Lock hbk **£12.95**

SMITH, MICHAEL
New English Cookery
[I231] BBC hbk **£8.75**
[I232] BBC pbk **£5.50**

SPURLING, HILARY
Elinor Fettiplace's Receipt Book
A recently discovered Elizabethan recipe book brought to life. A practical cookery book, social document and a unique glimpse into Elizabethan England.
[I233] Penguin pbk **£7.95**

WALDEN, HILARY
Harrods Book of Traditional English Cookery
[I235] Ebury hbk **£7.95**

WESTLAND, PAMELA
British Country Cheeses `NEW`
An illustrated guide to cheese-making past and present, covering in detail all the great regional cheeses of Britain, including a guide of where to find and buy them.
[I236] Ward Lock hbk **£12.95**

Greek & Middle Eastern

This section deals with all the myriad cuisines of the Eastern Mediterranean and North Africa, including Greek, Turkish, Lebanese, Moroccan and Arabic.

ANTHONY, D.
Lebanese Cookbook
[I238] Rigby hbk **£5.50**

CARRIER, ROBERT
A Taste of Morocco
An introductory guide to this North African cuisine by one of the foremost Western food writers.
[I239] Century hbk **£16.95**

HAROUTUNIAN, ARTO DE
Along with Claudia Roden, Haroutunian is regarded as the foremost authority on Middle Eastern cuisine.
Turkish Cookery
Highly recommended book from this prolific cookery writer who is best known for his Middle Eastern recipes.
[I241] Ebury hbk **£8.95**
[I242] Ebury pbk **£5.95**
Complete Arab Cookery
[I243] Grafton pbk **£2.50**
Middle Eastern Cookery
[I244] Pan pbk **£3.95**
North African Cookery
[I245] Century pbk **£7.95**
The Barbecue Cookbook
[I247] Pan pbk **£2.95**

Vegetarian Dishes from the Middle East
[I248] Century pbk **£5.95**
The Yoghurt Book
[I250] Penguin pbk **£3.50**

MAN, ROSAMUND
Complete Meze Table
A mouth-watering collection of the 'little dishes' of
Greece, Turkey, and the Middle East. In some ways
similar to hors d'oeuvres, a succession of meze can be
used to make up an entire meal.
[I251] M Joseph hbk **£8.95**
[I252] M Joseph pbk **£4.95**

PARADISSIS, CHRISSA
Best Book of Greek Cookery
An international bestselling classic, full of
unpretentious, authentic recipes.
[I254] Efstathiadis pbk **£5.00**

RODEN, CLAUDIA
An acknowledged expert in this field, Claudia Roden
has done much to popularize Middle Eastern cuisine,
offering simple and imaginative recipes which
concentrate on making the most of fresh ingredients
in season.
A New Book of Middle Eastern Food
[I255] Viking hbk **£13.95**
[I948] Penguin pbk **£8.99**
**Picnic: The Complete Guide to
Outdoor Food**
[I256] Hale hbk **£9.50**

SALAMAN, RENA
Greek Island Cookery
The essence of a varied cuisine is captured with
words, recipes and watercolours evoking the
atmosphere of the Greek Islands.
[I258] Ebury hbk **£9.95**

SANTA MARIA, JACK
Greek Vegetarian Cookery
[I253] Century pbk **£3.95**

STUBBS, JOYCE M.
Home Book of Greek Cookery
[I259] Faber pbk **£2.95**

WOLFERT, PAULA
Good Food from Morocco　　**NEW**
A classic work on the food of Morocco, originally
published under the title *Couscous*, recently revised
and updated to reflect modern tastes and the new
interest in Moroccan cuisine.
[I260] J Murray hbk **£15.95**

Indian

AITKEN, RHONA
The Memsahib's Cookbook　　**NEW**
A delightful guide to Anglo-Indian recipes of the Raj,
adapted for cooking today. Accompanied by the evoc-
ative observations of the author's grandfather Edward
Hamilton Aitken who was born in Bombay in 1851.
[I261] Piatkus hbk **£10.95**

DALAL, TARLA
New Indian Vegetarian Cookery
[I262] Ebury hbk **£6.95**

DAY, HARVEY
Complete Book of Curries
[I263] Heinemann pbk **£6.95**

DEVI, YAMUNA
The Art of Indian Vegetarian Cooking
Many Indians are vegetarian for religious or cultural

Illustration from *An Invitation to Italian Cooking* by
Antonio Carluccio (Pan hbk £8.95)

reasons, so Indian vegetarian cooking has been raised
to a very fine art.
[I264] Angus & R hbk **£19.95**

FERNANDEZ, RAFI
Indian Vegetarian Cooking
[I265] Fontana pbk **£3.95**

GOOD, NAOMI
Indian Cooking
[I266] Octopus pbk **£0.99**

GUPTA, SIPRA DAS
Home Book of Indian Cookery
[I267] Faber pbk **£3.25**

JAFFREY, MADHUR
A Taste of India
A personal guide to the sights, sounds, culture and
food of India, including 32 pages of colour
photographs.
[I268] Pan pbk **£6.95**
Eastern Vegetarian Cooking
[I269] Cape pbk **£7.95**
Invitation to Indian Cooking
[I270] Cape pbk **£7.95**
Madhur Jaffrey's Cookbook
A personal selection of over one hundred
favourite recipes, illustrated with colour
photographs.
[I949] Pavilion hbk **£14.95**
[I271] Pan pbk **£7.95**
Madhur Jaffrey's Indian Cookery
The book that accompanied the television series of the
same name.
[I272] BBC hbk **£8.25**
[I273] BBC pbk **£5.95**

MERCHANT, ISMAIL
**Ismail Merchant's Indian
Cuisine**
The famous and ebullient film producer shows that he
is also a talented and imaginative chef.
[I275] Futura pbk **£4.95**

SAHNI, JULIE
Classic Indian Cooking
[I276] D Kindersley pbk **£7.95**

SINGH, DHARAMJIT
Indian Cookery
[I277] Penguin pbk **£2.95**

TANEJA, MEERA
**Good Housekeeping Pakistani
Cookery**
[I278] Ebury pbk **£4.95**
New Indian Cookery
[I279] Fontana pbk **£2.95**

Italian

The essence of Italian cuisine is simple food prepared
from the best ingredients - perfect for the home cook.
Look for the classic works of Marcella Hazan, or
Claudia Roden's new book.

BLANC, BEVERLY LE (ED)
**Secrets of Italian Meat & Poultry
Dishes**
[I282] Macdonald hbk **£3.95**

BUGIALLI, GIULIANO
The Taste of Italy
A well presented book, with lots of lavish colour
photographs, that seeks to define Italian style and
culture through its cuisine.
[I284] Conran Octopus hbk **£12.95**
[I284] Conran Octopus pbk **£9.95**

BUONASSISI, VINCENZO
Classic Book of Pasta
Over 650 ways to prepare pasta. This is the
masterwork of one of Italy's most prestigious writers.
[I285] Futura pbk **£3.95**

CARLUCCIO, ANTONIO
An Invitation to Italian Cooking
The owner and chef of the popular Neal Street
restaurant in Covent Garden presents an attractively
illustrated book laced with personal anecdotes and
full of practical advice, showing a fresh approach to
classic Italian cooking.
[I286] Pavilion hbk **£14.95**
[I450] Pan hbk **£8.95**

DAVID, ELIZABETH
Italian Food
When this classic collection of authentic Italian
regional dishes first came out in 1954, it was a
revelation to British readers and inspired a whole
generation of cooks. The book also gives a fascinating
insight into the country, its history and people. The
revised and updated hardback edition is lavishly
illustrated with Italian paintings through the ages.
[I287] Barrie & J hbk **£14.95**
[I288] Penguin pbk **£7.99**

DE'MEDICI, LORENZA
Italy the Beautiful Cookbook　　**NEW**
A guide not only to Italian regional cuisine but also to
the Italian countryside and the Latin way of life,
presenting over 240 recipes of uncontrived full-
flavoured refinement.
[I289] Merehurst hbk **£19.95**

DEL CONTE, ANNA
Pasta Perfect
[I290] Conran Octopus pbk **£3.99**
The Gastronomy of Italy
A new encyclopaedia/dictionary with over 1,200
entries including nearly 200 recipes constituting a
history cookbook and invaluable reference work from
Apicus to Zabaglione.
[I291] Transworld hbk **£19.95**
Secrets from an Italian Kitchen　　**NEW**
A new collection from this popular Italian cookery
author, containing original and traditional recipes
based on ingredients essential to Italian cooking.
[I292] Bantam hbk **£14.95**

DEL NERO, CONTANCE & ROSARIO
Risotto　　　　**NEW**
An anthology of recipes, recollections amd
illustrations, focusing on this versatile North Italian
rice dish.
[I293] Harper & R hbk **£9.95**

DELLA CROCE, JULIA
Pasta Classica: The Art of Italian
Pasta Cooking　　**NEW**
An illustrated celebration of the Italian creative
staple - pasta - with recipes for cooks of all ability.
[I294] J Murray hbk **£16.95**

ELLIS, AUDREY
The Pasta Book
[I295] Piatkus hbk **£3.50**

FORBES, LESLIE
A Table in Tuscany
A delightful collection of Tuscan recipes interspersed
with observations, conversations and local gossip.
Stunningly illustrated throughout by the author's own
vibrantly coloured drawings, it was voted the
'prettiest cookery book of 1985' by *The Times*.
[I296] Webb & B hbk **£12.95**

GAVIN, PAOLA
Italian Vegetarian Cookery
[I297] Optima pbk **£4.95**

HARRIS, VALENTINA
Perfect Pasta
[I298] Barrie & J pbk **£2.99**

HAZAN, MARCELLA
Marcella's Kitchen
In her latest book the author introduces a more
personal note, explaining the origin and development
of her original recipes and digressing into personal
anecdote.
[I299] Macmillan hbk **£12.95**
[I284] Macmillan pbk **£6.95**
The Classic Italian Cookbook
This, her first book, won an André Simon memorial
prize and was acclaimed as the best general Italian
cookbook available in English.
[I300] Macmillan pbk **£7.95**
The Second Classic Italian
Cookbook
[I301] Macmillan pbk **£7.95**

NORDIO, JEANETTE NANCE
Taste of Venice
A collection of traditional Venetian recipes, with
some dating from the 13th century. The recipes are
placed against a backdrop of glorious colour
photographs of Venice.
[I302] Webb & B hbk **£12.95**

PICCINARDI, ANTONIO
Taste of Pasta
[I303] Webb & B pbk **£8.95**

RODEN, CLAUDIA
The Food of Italy　　**NEW**
Based on the award winning *Sunday Times* series, this
is an evocative region by region tour of Italian cuisine
and culinary practice, beautifully illustrated
throughout with both colour photographs, and
fascinating background information.
[I305] Chatto hbk **£16.00**

ROMER, ELIZABETH
Italian Pizza & Savoury Breads
All about pizza, schiacciata, foccaccia, calzone and
torte, with plenty of information on history, regional
variations and practical recipes.
[I306] M O'Mara hbk **£3.95**

The Tuscan Year
A wonderfully evocative personal cookbook,
illustrated with the author's own drawings.
[I307] Weidenfeld hbk **£9.95**
[I308] Weidenfeld pbk **£6.95**

ROSS, JANET & WATERFIELD, MICHAEL
Leaves from Our Tuscan Kitchen
A classic of Italian vegetable cooking first published
in 1899, then revised and updated by the original
author's great-great nephew.
[I309] Penguin pbk **£3.95**

SEED, DIANE
Top 100 Pasta Sauces
Authentic regional recipes accompanied by beautiful
illustrations.
[I310] Rosendale hbk **£8.95**

SHARMAN, FAY & CHADWICK, BRIAN
The Taste of Italy
A dictionary-cum-phrase book of Italian food and
wine. Invaluable for the non-Italian speaker in the
restaurant, market or food shop.
[I311] Macmillan pbk **£4.95**

SPENDER, LIZZIE
Pastability
[I312] Faber pbk **£3.95**

STREET, MYRA & MILLS, SONIA (EDS)
The Art of Italian Cooking
A record of many authentic regional recipes; it
includes a large number of dinner party menus, with
step-by-step photographs to accompany each recipe.
[I313] Hamlyn hbk **£15.00**

STREET, MYRA (ED)
La Cucina: The Complete Book of
Italian Cooking
This marvellous and comprehensive work is
translated from the Italian and edited by an Italian
cookery expert. There is a section on Italian wine by
Serena Sutcliffe.
[I314] Macdonald hbk **£17.50**

WRIGHT, JENI; IN ASSOCIATION WITH
'LA FORNAIA'
Pâtisserie of Italy
A mouth-watering collection of recipes for such
Italian delights as panettone, fruit tarts, ice-cream
cakes, little almond biscuits, polenta and ricotta cakes,
illustrated with beautiful colour photographs.
[I315] Macdonald hbk **£8.95**

Oriental

Oriental food has one of the most popular and
interesting culinary traditions in the world - especially
given the number and variations of its regions,
including Japanese, Chinese, Vietnamese, Thai,
Indonesian, and Korean. The growth in popularity of
these cuisines has been helped by the number of
restaurants in the West, and the easy availability of
special ingredients, as well as the work of cookery
writers such as Ken Hom and Kenneth Lo.

The Book of Sushi　　**NEW**
One of the definitive accounts of sushi preparation,
from simple sushi like norimaki through to more
spectacular varieties, covering the history and
nutritional value of this traditional Japanese dish.
[I316] Kodansha Int pbk **£9.95**

BHUMICHITR, VATCHARIN
The Taste of Thailand　　**NEW**
The definitive Thai cookery book, discussing Thai

culture, traditions and history in relation to the food
and recipes embraced in the text.
[I317] Pavilion hbk **£16.95**

BRENNAN, JENNIFER
Thai Cookery
[I318] Hale hbk **£8.50**
[I319] Futura pbk **£3.99**

CHASLIN, PIERRE; CANUNGMAI, PIYATEP &
INVERNIZZI, LUCA
Discover Thai Cooking
200 recipes set within the context of Thai culture,
illustrated with over 90 colour photographs and line
drawings.
[I322] Ward Lock hbk **£12.95**

DEKURA, HIDEO
The Fine Art of Japanese Cooking
Many superb colour photographs of finished dishes
and step-by-step photographs to help with technique.
Good value.
[I323] Bay Bks pbk **£3.95**

DOWNER, LESLEY
Japanese Vegetarian Cookery
[I324] Cape pbk **£7.95**

ELLWOOD, CAROLINE
Chinese Cooking
This is one of a series of almost pocket-sized recipe
books full of authentic well-tested recipes every one
illustrated by a colour photograph.
[I325] Octopus pbk **£0.99**

FERNANDEZ, RAFI
Malaysian Cookery
[I326] Penguin pbk **£3.95**

FULTON, MARGARET (ED)
Encyclopaedia of Asian & Oriental
Cookery
[I327] Octopus pbk **£5.95**

HOM, KEN
A young and energetic cook whose television series
has helped popularize Chinese cooking in the home.
Ken Hom's Chinese Cookery
[I328] BBC hbk **£8.95**
[I329] BBC pbk **£5.95**
Ken Hom's East Meets West Cuisine
A personal fusion of many different cuisines but
ending up in inimitable Hom style.
[I330] Macmillan hbk **£14.95**
[I951] Macmillan pbk **£6.95**
Ken Hom's Vegetable & Pasta Book
[I331] BBC pbk **£5.95**

HSIUNG DEH - TA
Home Book of Chinese Cookery
[I333] Faber pbk **£3.95**
Microwave Chinese Cooking
[I334] Macdonald hbk **£8.95**

LAMB, CORINNE
The Chinese Festive Board
A charming compilation of Chinese manners and
dining etiquette as accurate today as when it was first
published in 1935. Complemented by a selection of
Chinese proverbs and illustrated with line drawings
and photographs, chapters deal with wine, cooking
methods, ingredients and how to order a meal.
[I335] Oxford pbk **£4.95**

LEEMING, MARGARET & KOHSAKA,
MUTSUKO
Japanese Cookery
All the recipes have been tested in British kitchens
using ingredients readily available in this country. The

Illustration from *The Taste of Thailand* by Vatcharin Bhumichitr (Pavilion hbk £16.95)

emphasis is on the low-fat, healthy aspects of Japanese cuisine.
[I336] Century pbk **£4.95**

LO, KENNETH
The celebrated expert of Chinese cookery writing, renowned for his ability to present Chinese cuisine in English without compromising standards.
Chinese Cookery Course
[I337] Futura pbk **£1.50**
Chinese Food
An excellent introduction to the recipes and techniques of Chinese cooking.
[I338] Penguin pbk **£3.95**
Chinese Vegetable & Vegetarian Cookery
[I339] Faber pbk **£2.95**
Complete Encyclopaedia of Chinese Cooking
[I340] Treasure hbk **£11.95**
[I952] Hamlyn hbk **£4.95**
Cooking & Eating the Chinese Way
[I341] Mayflower pbk **£1.95**
Kenneth Lo's Healthy Chinese Cooking
[I342] Pan pbk **£2.95**
Kenneth Lo's New Chinese Cookery Course NEW
A course on traditional and modern Chinese food, including information on equipping a kitchen with the necessary utensils and preparing menus for a varying number of guests.
[I343] Macdonald pbk **£10.95**

Wok Cookbook
[I344] Mayflower pbk **£2.50**

MARTIN, PETER & JOAN
Japanese Cooking
[I346] Penguin pbk **£3.99**

ORTIZ, ELIZABETH LAMBERT
Japanese Cookery
[I347] Collins hbk **£9.95**
[I348] Fontana pbk **£3.95**

OWEN, SRI
Indonesian and Thai Cookery NEW
Informative introductions and clear reliable instructions help guide the reader and cook through the basics of these cuisines.
[I349] Piatkus pbk **£6.95**

PASSMORE, JACKI
Asia: The Beautiful Cookbook
This book describes the cuisine of each of the many regions of Asia in its cultural context, with lots of colour photographs of food and scenery.
[I350] Merehurst hbk **£19.95**
Wok Cookery Step-by-Step
[I351] Collins hbk **£9.95**

SANTA MARIA, JACK
Chinese Vegetarian Cookery
[I345] Century pbk **£5.95**

SCOTT, DAVID
A Taste of Thailand
(With Inwood, Kristiaan)
[I352] Century pbk **£6.95**
Far Eastern Vegetarian Cookery
[I353] Century pbk **£4.95**
Indonesian Cookery
(With Winata, Surya)
[I354] Rider pbk **£5.95**
Japanese Cook Book
[I355] Mayflower pbk **£1.95**

SOLOMAN, CHARMAINE
Mastering the Art of Chinese Cooking
[I356] Ebury hbk **£9.95**

SPAYDE, JON
Japanese Cookery NEW
Over 100 recipes from Japan's increasingly popular cuisine, including information on the culture, customs, and regions of Japan.
[I357] Ward Lock hbk **£9.95**

SPUNT, GEORGES
Step-by-Step Chinese Cookbook
An eminently practical and clear guide to how to create real Chinese food at home. Ideal for beginners.
[I358] Penguin pbk **£3.95**

TSUJI, SHIZUO
Japanese Cooking
[I359] Kodansha hbk **£15.95**

WOLF, REINHARDT & TERZANI, ANGELA
Japan: The Beauty of Food
An attractive book of photographs showing how Japanese foods are grown, prepared and served. The text reveals the secrets behind thousands of years of tradition.
[I361] Thames & H hbk **£30.00**

YAN-KIT SO
Yan-Kit So's Chinese Cookery
[I362] Walker hbk **£9.95**
[I953] Walker pbk **£4.99**
Yan-Kit's Classic Chinese Cookbook
[I363] D Kindersley pbk **£7.95**

European Cuisines

ANDREWS, COLMAN
Catalan Cuisine: Europe's Last Great Culinary Secret NEW
A celebrated new book exploring the little known cooking of the Catalan region of Spain and France, a cuisine heavily influenced by French, Moroccan and Roman cooking.
[I365] Headline hbk **£14.95**

BACON, JOSEPHINE
Pâtisserie of Vienna
An attractive book with many colour photographs and authentic recipes for such classic Viennese delicacies as sachertorte, strudel and gugelhopf.
[I366] Macdonald hbk **£8.95**

BEER, GRETEL
Austrian Cooking
[I367] Deutsch pbk **£4.95**

BOURNE, URSULA
Portuguese Cookery
[I368] Penguin pbk **£2.50**

BOXER, LADY ARABELLA
Mediterranean Food
[I369] Penguin pbk **£3.95**

CASAS, PENELOPE
Tapas: The Little Dishes of Spain
[I370] Pavilion hbk **£12.95**

CHAMBERLAIN, LESLEY
The Food & Cooking of Russia
[I371] Penguin pbk **£7.99**

CHATTO, JAMES & MARTIN, WENDY
A Kitchen in Corfu NEW
Away from the tourist beaches, old traditions of eating and living still flourish. This introduction to the cuisine of Corfu, influenced by Greek, Dalmatian and Italian cooking, describes the customs surrounding the growing and preparation of food.
[I372] Weidenfeld hbk **£7.95**

DAVID, ELIZABETH
A Book of Mediterranean Food
One of the classic accounts of food from the Mediterranean, gathered when the author lived in France, Italy, the Greek Islands and Egypt. The new hardback edition is completely redesigned and is accompanied by a large number of handsome illustrations.
[I373] D Kindersley hbk **£12.95**
[I374] Penguin pbk **£6.95**

DAVIDSON, ALAN
Mediterranean Seafood
[I375] Penguin pbk **£8.95**

GOLDSTEIN, DARRA
A Taste of Russia
Classic recipes set within the context of literature, history and social customs.
[I376] Sphere pbk **£3.95**

GRUNAUER, PETER & KISLER, ANDREAS
Viennese Cuisine: The New Approach NEW
Viennese cuisine is famed for its sumptuous richness. Here is a new approach demonstrating that it is possible to eat well and healthily without sacrificing variety and flavour.
[I377] J Murray hbk **£15.95**

HARDISTY, JYTTE
Scandinavian Cooking
[I378] Hamlyn hbk **£3.95**
[I379] Hamlyn pbk **£1.99**

HOWE, ROBIN
German Cooking
[I380] Mayflower pbk **£1.95**

KAYE, ANN & RANCE, HETTY
So This is Kosher? A New Approach to Jewish Cuisine
[I381] Ward Lock hbk **£9.95**

LANG, GEORGE
Cuisine of Hungary
Much more than a cookbook, this is an erudite and fascinating treatise on Hungarian cuisine and the culture and history surrounding its formation. Jane Grigson has said: 'Every country's cooking should have a book like this'
[I382] Penguin pbk **£8.95**

MIRODAN, VLADIMIR
The Balkan Cookbook
A Romanian actor/director and lifelong gourmet, Vladimir Mirodan provides a comprehensive look at the cuisine of the Balkans, based on a family collection of recipes and including advice on wines and spirits.
[I383] Lennard hbk **£10.95**

NELSON, KAY SHAW
Eastern European Cookbook
[I384] Dover pbk **£2.95**

READ, JAN
The Wine & Food of Spain
[I385] Weidenfeld hbk **£12.95**

REDWOOD, JEAN
Russian Food: All the Peoples, All the Republics NEW
Along with an introduction to Russian regional cuisines, this book offers a geographical profile of each region along with quotations from Russian writers, artists, and travellers.
[I386] Oldwicks hbk **£16.95**

RODEN, CLAUDIA
Mediterranean Cookery
Following her immensely successful television series this is one of the best books currently available on Mediterranean cookery.
[I387] BBC hbk **£12.95**

ROSE, EVELYN
Evelyn Rose Goes Microwave in the Jewish Kitchen NEW
Bestselling cookery writer Evelyn Rose turns her attention to the microwave oven, offering reassuring and practical advice on microwave cooking for Jewish cuisine.
[I388] Robson hbk **£12.95**
The New Jewish Cuisine
More than 400 recipes of one of the world's great cookery traditions are brought into the age of the food processor, the microwave oven and health-conscious eating.
[I389] Robson hbk **£12.95**
[I390] Macmillan pbk **£8.95**

SALAMAN, RENA
Mediterranean Vegetable Cookery
[I391] Collins hbk **£8.95**

TORRES, MARIMAR
The Spanish Table
[I392] Ebury hbk **£10.95**

VIEIRA, EDITE
The Taste of Portugal: Traditional Portuguese Cuisine
The authoritative book on one of Europe's forgotten cuisines now fast gaining popularity.
[I394] Hale hbk **£15.95**
[I395] Robinson pbk **£5.99**

Other Cuisines

Including the Cajun and Creole cooking of the Caribbean and the American South, along with Mexican and Tex-Mex, and the traditional cooking of America.

BAYLESS, RICK AND DEANN
Authentic Mexican NEW
The whole range of Mexican cuisine is covered by this husband and wife team of restaurateurs.
[I396] Headline hbk **£14.95**

BENGHIAT, NORMA
Traditional Jamaican Cookery
The definitive work on Jamaican cuisine. Placed in their social and historical context, the recipes range from the lavish eating of the Colonial days to imaginative and ingenious peasant and slave dishes.
[I397] Penguin pbk **£3.99**

BOOTH, GEORGE C.
Food & Drink of Mexico
[I398] Dover pbk **£3.15**

CLEMENTS, CAROLE
Traditional American Cooking NEW
Classic recipes from America with photographs illustrating the regions from which they come, emphasising the diversity of culinary experience encountered in this huge country.
[I400] Hamlyn hbk **£25.00**

FERGUSON, SHEILA
Soul Food: Classic Cuisine from the Deep South
Ferguson was lead singer with the legendary Philly sound pop group 'The Three Degrees' in the seventies, and has written a vivid account of this truly American cuisine of the Deep South.
[I401] Weidenfield hbk **£12.95**

FREDERICK, J. GEORGE & JOYCE, JEAN
Long Island Sea Food Cook Book
[I402] Dover pbk **£4.20**

GARDNIER, KENNETH
Creole Caribbean Cooking
A Dominican-born chef-restaurateur presents a range of recipes from his kitchen.
[I403] Grafton pbk **£3.95**
Creole Vegetarian Cookery
Caribbean and American recipes with an exotic French influence.
[I404] Grafton hbk **£5.99**

GRANT, ROSAMUND
Caribbean and African Cookery NEW
A passionate guide to the eclectic cuisine of the Caribbean, sprinkled generously with anecdotes and tributes to West Africa and Guyana.
[I405] Virago pbk **£6.50**

GRUVER, SUZANNE CARY
Cape Cod Cookbook
[I406] Dover pbk **£3.60**

MICKLER, ERNEST MATTHEW
White Trash Cooking
[I407] Ten Speed pbk **£9.95**

NICHOLS, LOURDES
Mexican Cookery
[I408] Fontana pbk **£3.95**

ORTIZ, ELIZABETH LAMBERT
Caribbean Cookery
A gastronomic tour of the whole Caribbean region, presenting recipes that can be made with ingredients which are readily available in British shops and markets.
[I409] Penguin pbk **£4.50**
Latin American Cooking
[I410] Hale hbk **£10.25**
[I411] Penguin pbk **£5.95**

ROMBAUER, IRMA & BECKER, MARION
The Joy of Cooking
[I412] Dent pbk **£8.95**

ROSSO, JULEE
Silver Palate Cookbook
A highly popular American book of old favourites.
[I413] Ebury pbk **£9.95**

TOKLAS, ALICE B.
Cookbook
[I414] Brilliance hbk **£11.95**
[I415] Brilliance pbk **£4.95**

WALKER, CLARE & CHRISTIANSEN, KERYN
Taste of American Cooking
[I416] Penguin pbk **£3.95**

WOLFE, L.
Cooking of the Caribbean Islands
[I417] Macmillan hbk **£9.95**
[I418] Macmillan spiral **£3.95**

Particular Foods

A selection of titles providing recipes for specific types of food (i.e. fish, poultry, game and cheese) as well as specialist guides to baking, confectionery, hors d'oeuvres, desserts, beverages, soups, preserves and the use of oils, herbs and spices. The Good Housekeeping and Time Life series make excellent basic reference libraries; for more detailed and inspirational guidance the Penguin Cookery Library is to be recommended (particulary the National Trust books edited by Sara Paston-Williams), as is the National Trust *Little Library* series published by Dorling Kindersley.

Baking, Bread & Cakes

Baking: Step-by-Step to Perfect Cakes: Pastries & Bread
[I720] Hamlyn hbk **£12.95**

ALBUREY, PAT
Harrods Book of Cakes & Desserts
[I721] Ebury hbk **£7.95**

ASHER, JANE
Jane Asher's Party Cakes
Ideas for very imaginative presentation and decoration from the multi-talented actress.
[I723] M Joseph pbk **£7.95**
Quick Party Cakes
[I724] Walker hbk **£8.95**
[I725] Walker pbk **£4.99**

BACON, JOSEPHINE
Pâtisserie of Vienna
[I726] Macdonald Orbis hbk **£8.95**

BERRY, MARY
Fast Cakes
[I727] Sphere pbk **£2.99**
Mary Berry's New Cake Book **NEW**
Cookery columnist Mary Berry's new collection of over 100 recipes for cakes and biscuits.
[I728] Piatkus hbk **£10.95**
More Fast Cakes
[I729] Piatkus hbk **£8.95**

CLARK, MAXINE; FARROW, JOANNE & MAN, KATHY
Children's Party Cakes
A full-colour book of 30 cakes including castles, hot air balloons, spaceships and monsters.
[I730] Macdonald Orbis hbk **£9.95**

COLLINS, VAL
Microwave Baking
[I731] David & Ch hbk **£7.95**

DAVESON, ELAINE
How to Design Beautiful Cakes **NEW**
The application of the principles of design to cake decorating.
[I732] Merehurst hbk **£5.95**

DAVID, ELIZABETH
English Bread & Yeast Cookery
There is surprisingly little published on bread-making other than technical works - but this is undoubtedly the classic on the subject: delightful to read as well as to use.
[I733] Penguin pbk **£8.95**

ELLIOT, ROSE
Rose Elliot's Book of Cakes
Simple and straightforward, from the expert on vegetarian cookery.
[I734] Fontana pbk **£1.25**

ELLISON, AUDREY
Bread Book
[I735] Apple hbk **£5.95**

GARFIELD, SANDY
Character Cakes and Cookies **NEW**
A creative introduction to children's character cakes, with instructions on how to assemble your own Mickey Mouse gâteau or Miss Piggy cooky.
[I736] Sidgwick hbk **£9.95**

GOOD HOUSEKEEPING
Complete Book of Cakes & Pastries
[I737] Ebury hbk **£8.95**
Successful Microwave Baking
[I738] Ebury hbk **£8.95**

GOODBODY, MARY & STACEY, JANE
Pretty Cakes **NEW**
An illustrated collection of more than 50 home cake decorating ideas.
[I739] Cassell hbk **£12.95**

HOLT, GERALDENE
Geraldene Holt's Cake Stall
[I741] Penguin pbk **£3.99**

LEBRECHT, ELBIE
Sugar-Free Cakes & Biscuits **NEW**
An innovative cookbook that demonstrates how to bake cakes and biscuits without sugar, using instead only naturally sweet flavours and high-fibre low-fat ingredients.
[I743] Faber pbk **£3.95**

LIDDELL, CAROLINE
The New Baking
Over 150 wholesome and delicious recipes for cakes, pastries, muffins, pies, biscuits and bread. A real treat.
[I744] Bloomsbury hbk **£14.95**

ODDIE, JANE
How to Decorate Cakes, Desserts & Savouries
[I748] Merehurst hbk **£4.95**

ORSINI, ELIZABETH
The Book of Pies
[I749] Pan pbk **£1.95**

PATTEN, MARGUERITE
Successful Baking
A comprehensive introduction with well-detailed accounts of the methods involved.
[I750] Collins hbk **£9.95**

ROBINSON, GREG & SCHOFIELD, MAX
The Icing on the Cake: Innovative Cakes for all Occasions
Illustrated with over 500 step-by-step photographs, this covers a wide range of techniques from simple cakes for the beginner to extravaganzas for the expert.
[I751] Bloomsbury hbk **£14.95**

ROUX, MICHEL & ALBERT
The Roux Brothers on Pâtisserie
Recipes and ideas for pastries and desserts from the master chefs of the celebrated Waterside Inn and Le Gavroche - each of which has three Michelin stars. The recipes included here are definitely in the advanced category.
[I752] Macdonald hbk **£15.00**

SMITH, DELIA
Book of Cakes
A good range of basic cakes with easy to follow instructions. From experience, these recipes are almost foolproof.
[I753] Hodder hbk **£8.95**
[I754] Hodder hbk **£4.95**

TEMBNER, CHRISTINE & WOLTER, ANNETTE
Best of Baking
[I755] Hamlyn hbk **£9.95**

TIME LIFE
The two *Time Life* series offer a very solid base for the inexperienced cook. The books are robustly made and traditional in their range of recipes, combining clear instructions with valuable colour illustrations of dishes and ingredients. The 27 volumes in *The Good Cook* series provide a complete cookery reference library for the home; the *Healthy Home Cooking* books (i.e. *Fresh Ways with…*) are more recent, offering imaginative recipes for those with an eye on their diet.
Biscuits
[I756] Time Life hbk **£13.95**
Bread
[I757] Time Life hbk **£13.95**
Cakes & Pastries
This is an excellent introduction to the making of cakes and pastries. There are clear illustrations and a wide variety of recipes.
[I758] Time Life hbk **£13.95**
Fresh Ways with Cakes
[I759] Time Life hbk **£13.95**
Fresh Ways with Pâtisserie **NEW**
[I760] Time Life hbk **£13.95**

WALLACE, EVELYN
Cake Decorating & Sugar Craft
[I761] Hamlyn hbk **£8.95**

Illustration from *English Bread and Yeast Cookery* by Elizabeth David (Penguin pbk £8.95)

WELSH, VIRGINIA & FRENCH, ALISON
Cake Magic: 50 Spectacular Cakes to Ice & Decorate
Fifty cakes illustrated in full colour.
[I762] Conran Octopus hbk **£8.95**
[I763] Conran Octopus pbk **£8.95**

WOMEN'S INSTITUTE
A companion series to the Good Housekeeping books, providing a wealth of useful recipes and straightforward advice on technique. The WI cake stalls are legendary.
Book of Biscuits
[I764] Ebury pbk **£1.95**
Book of Bread & Cakes
[I765] Ebury pbk **£1.95**
Book of Cakes
[I766] Ebury pbk **£1.95**
Book of Pastry
[I767] Ebury pbk **£1.95**

WRIGHT, JENI
Pâtisserie of Italy
[I768] Macdonald hbk **£8.95**

Chocolates & Confectionery

Chocolate Delights
[I768] Sphere pbk **£2.50**

HUNT, JANET
Wholefood Sweets Book
A guide to sweet things made of wholefoods and natural products.
[I424] Thorsons pbk **£3.95**

HUTTON, D.F & BODE, E.M.
Simple Sweetmaking
[I425] Faber pbk **£1.50**

NORMAN, JILL
Sweet Flavourings **NEW**
An interesting cookbook designed to give every cook ideas for developing the sweet flavours in food, using a range of ingredients from sharp to sweet: citrus fruits to almonds, honey, vanilla, and flower waters. A National Trust *Little Library* book.
[I427] D Kindersley hbk **£3.95**

NORWAK, MARY
The Wicked Chocolate Book NEW
Utterly hedonistic, a book for sybarites whose
consumption of chocolate inclines to the conspicuous.
[I428] Gollancz hbk **£12.95**

PINDER, POLLY
Polly Pinder's Chocolate Cookbook NEW
Packed with illustrations and photographs, this is a
recipe book just for chocolate lovers, showing new
and original ways with chocolate - such as a design
for a chocolate Christmas cracker.
[I429] Search hbk **£11.95**

POOLE, SHONA CRAWFORD
The Sweets Book: Home-Made Sweets,
Chocolates & Candies
[I421] Collins hbk **£7.95**
[I954] Fontana pbk **£3.95**

RUBINSTEIN, HELGE
The Chocolate Book
[I430] Penguin pbk **£4.99**

Coffee & Tea

A Little Book of Afternoon Teas
A celebration of the English institution of afternoon
tea, with recipes for both high society and country
teas.
[I433] Appletree hbk **£3.50**

National Trust Book of Afternoon Teas
[I434] David & Ch pbk **£5.95**

FOLEY, TRICIA
Having Tea
Looks at British tea-time traditions and offers over 50
recipes.
[I436] Sidgwick hbk **£9.95**

NORMAN, JILL
Teas and Tisanes NEW
A guide to teas, tisanes and herbal teas from China,
India, Sri Lanka and Kenya, as well as suggestions
for spiced teas, ices and desserts. A National Trust
Little Library book.
[I437] D Kindersley hbk **£3.95**

PATTEN, MARGUERITE
The Complete Book of Tea NEW
Tea-time themes from round the world, with over 100
varied recipes for food and tea-based drinks.
[I438] Piatkus hbk **£10.95**

RODEN, CLAUDIA
Coffee
[I439] Penguin pbk **£3.95**

ROLNICK, H.
Complete Book of Coffee
[I440] Melitta hbk **£6.95**

SIMPSON, HELEN
The London Ritz Book of Afternoon Tea
[I441] Ebury hbk **£5.95**

Desserts & Puddings

BINGHAM, JOAN & RICCIO, DOLORES
Sensational Desserts
[I443] Thorsons pbk **£5.99**

COOPER-ENGLISH, COLIN
National Trust Book of Sorbets,
Flummeries & Fools
[I444] David & Ch hbk **£5.95**

DIMBLEBY, JOSCELINE
Josceline Dimbleby's Book of Puddings,
Desserts & Savouries
[I446] Penguin pbk **£2.50**

HANDLY, LUCY
The Book of Cheesecakes
[I447] Hodder hbk **£6.95**

HURST, BERNICE
The Home-Made Ice-Cream Book
[I448] Apple P hbk **£6.95**

LAW, DIGBY
A Dessert Cookbook NEW
Hundreds of innovative ideas for desserts to suit every
occasion, from light and refreshing fruit compotes to
rich and extravagant gâteaux and mousses.
[I449] Hodder hbk **£9.95**

PASSMORE, JACKI
The Book of Ice-Creams & Sorbets
[I442] Hodder hbk **£5.95**

PASTON-WILLIAMS, SARA
National Trust Book of Traditional
Puddings
A pleasure to read as well as to cook from, tracing the
complex development of the British pudding with
easy, clearly-written recipes set in their proper
historical context.
[I450] Penguin pbk **£3.95**

POOLE, SHONA CRAWFORD
Iced Delights
Covers sorbets, classic ice-creams, soufflés, coupes
and bombes.
[I445] Octopus pbk **£3.99**

RUBINSTEIN, HELGE & BUSH
Ices Galore
[I451] Penguin pbk **£2.95**

TIME LIFE
Fresh Ways with Desserts
[I452] Time Life hbk **£13.95**

YOUNG, MARK & MURDOCH, LESLEY
HOWARD
Home-Made Ice Cream Naturally
[I453] Bay Bks pbk **£4.50**

Fish

BAKER, JENNY
Simply Fish
Featuring over 90 fish, this book describes each one
in detail and explains how to buy, prepare and cook
them.
[I955] Faber hbk **£13.95**
[I454] Faber pbk **£4.95**

CONIL, JEAN & FRANKLIN, FAY
French Fish Cuisine
[I455] Thorsons hbk **£10.95**

DAVIDSON, ALAN
Mediterranean Seafood
[I456] Penguin pbk **£8.95**
North Atlantic Seafood
[I457] Penguin pbk **£6.95**

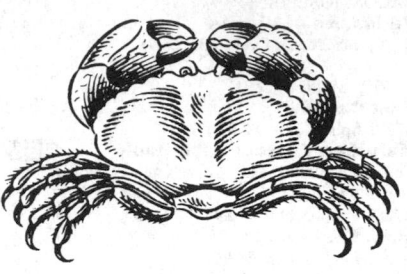

A crab from *The Fish Book* by Karin Perry (Chatto &
Windus hbk £14.95).

FLOYD, KEITH
Floyd on Fish
[I459] BBC pbk **£3.95**

GORDON-SMITH, CLAIRE
Fish Dishes
[I460] Octopus pbk **£1.25**

GRIGSON, JANE
Fish Cookery
[I461] Penguin pbk **£4.99**

HAYES, PATRICIA ANNE
The Trout Book NEW
A collection of over 100 recipes aimed at anglers and
all who love to eat trout, emphasizing the versatility
of the fish. Full details are given on filleting, storage
and preparation.
[I462] Crowood hbk **£8.95**

HICKS, SUSAN
The Fish Course
[I463] BBC pbk **£6.95**

KENWARD, JOHN & ROE, NICHOLAS
Swish Fish NEW
A collection of original and innovative recipes for flat
fish, describing buying, preparing and cooking them;
illustrated with detailed line drawings.
[I464] Hodder hbk **£12.95**

LASSALLE, G.
The Adventurous Fish Cook
[I465] Macmillan pbk **£7.95**

MACDONALD, CLAIRE
Delicious Fish
[I466] Grafton hbk **£10.95**

MCANDREW, IAN
A Feast of Fish
[I467] Macdonald hbk **£14.95**
[I467] Macdonald pbk **£9.95**

MOSIMANN, ANTON
Anton Mosimann's Fish Cuisine
A new collection of innovative recipes for fish and
seafood dishes.
[I468] Macmillan hbk **£16.95**

MOSIMANN, ANTON & HOFMANN, HOLGAR
Shellfish
[I469] Hamlyn hbk **£15.00**

PASTON-WILLIAMS, SARA
The National Trust Book of Fish
Cookery
[I470] National Trust hbk **£7.95**

PERRY, KARIN
The Fish Book: Buying and Cooking Fish in Britain NEW
This beautifully designed and yet immensely practical book gives the reader a region by region guide to the various fishes available in Britain, supplemented by delicious recipes for both the fish we know well and the more exotic varieties.
[I471] Chatto hbk **£14.95**

SPENCER, COLIN
Colin Spencer's Fish Cookbook
[I473] Pan pbk **£6.95**

STEIN, RICHARD
English Seafood Cookery
An inspired guide to the subject. Winner of the 1989 Glenfiddich Award
[I472] Penguin pbk **£7.95**

TIME LIFE
Fish and Shellfish
[I474] Time Life hbk **£13.95**
Fresh Ways with Fish and Shellfish
[I475] Time Life hbk **£13.95**

WILLIAMS, ANNE
F for Fish
[I476] Dent pbk **£6.95**

WILSON, ROBYN
Fish
[I477] Sphere **£3.50**

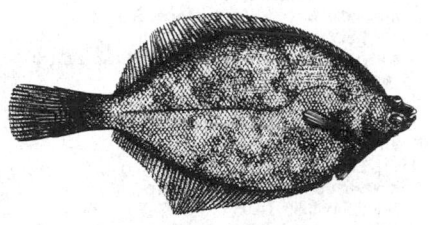

A dab from *The National Trust Book of Fish Cookery* by Sara Paston-Williams (The National Trust hbk £7.95)

Herbs & Spices

The Garlic Lover's Cookbook
Vol 1
[I478] Celest Arts pbk **£6.50**
Vol 2
[I479] Celest Arts pbk **£6.95**

DAVID, ELIZABETH
Spices, Salt & Aromatics in the English Kitchen
[I481] Penguin pbk **£7.95**

DUFF, GAIL
A Book of Herbs & Spices
[I482] Merehurst hbk **£7.95**

HALL, DOROTHY
The Book of Herbs
[I484] Pan pbk **£2.50**

HEMPHILL, ROSEMARY
Herbs & Spices
[I485] Penguin pbk **£2.95**

JUMP, MEG
Cooking with Chillies NEW
The best chilli recipes from all of the globe's culinary hot spots - a feast for lovers of hot spicy foods.
[I486] Bodley hbk **£12.95**

LAKE, MARK
The Pocket Book of Oils, Vinegars and Seasonings NEW
A guide to the ingredients for salad dressings.
[I487] M Beazley hbk **£5.95**

MAN, R. & WEIR, R.
The Compleat Mustard NEW
An authoritative guide to all aspects of mustard - cultivation, history, culinary, and medicinal uses.
[I488] Constable hbk **£10.95**

NORMAN, JILL
Salad Herbs NEW
Recipes for all the fresh herbs of summer, used in unusual salads, butters and sauces. A National Trust *Little Library* book.
[I489] D Kindersley hbk **£3.95**
Spices, Roots and Fruits NEW
A fascinating history of the spice trade augmenting a thorough examination of over 20 different spices and spice mixtures. A National Trust *Little Library* book.
[I490] D Kindersley hbk **£3.95**

RICHARDSON, ROSAMOND
Exotic Spices
[I491] Piatkus hbk **£5.95**
The Little Herb Book
[I492] Piatkus pbk **£2.50**
The Little Spice Book
[I493] Piatkus pbk **£2.50**

STOBART, TOM
Herbs, Spices & Flavourings
[I495] Penguin pbk **£4.95**

SUMMERS, NIGEL
Cooking with Herbs NEW
Over 120 recipes giving a new look at the many herbs used in cooking traditional and exotic dishes.
[I496] Crowood hbk **£3.95**

TREWBY, MARY
A Gourmet's Book of Herbs and Spices
[I497] Hodder hbk **£7.95**

Meat, Poultry & Game

365 Ways to Cook Chicken NEW
Enough recipes to cook chicken every day of the year and never serve up the same dish twice.
[I498] Harper & R binder **£9.95**

ARNOLD, MARY LOU
All Occasion Chicken Cookbook
[I499] Bay Books pbk **£2.95**

BLANC, BEVERLY LE
Secrets of Italian Meat & Poultry Dishes
[I500] Macdonald hbk **£3.95**

COX, NICOLA
Nicola Cox on Game Cookery NEW
A collection of recipes using game, ranging from ideas for elegant dinner parties to suggestions for homely and warming leftovers.
[I502] Gollancz hbk **£18.95**

FERGUSON, CLARE
Chicken Dishes
[I503] Octopus pbk **£1.25**

HIPPISLEY-COXE, ANTHONY & ARAMINTA
Book of Sausages
[I504] Gollancz hbk **£12.95**

HUMPHREYS, ANGELA
Game Cookery
[I505] David & Ch hbk **£10.95**

MCANDREW, IAN
Ian McAndrew on Poultry and Game NEW
This Michelin-starred chef offers 150 exciting and creative recipes using game and poultry, showing his special flair for unusual combinations of ingredients. Fully illustrated with colour photographs.
[I506] Macdonald Orbis hbk **£16.95**

SCOTT, PHILIPPA
Gourmet Game NEW
A fascinating cookery book devoted to traditional game cookery from around the world.
[I508] Barrie & J hbk **£12.95**

TIME LIFE
Beef & Veal
[I509] Time Life hbk **£13.95**
Fresh Ways with Beef & Veal
[I510] Time Life hbk **£13.95**
Fresh Ways with Lamb
[I511] Time Life hbk **£13.95**
Fresh Ways with Pork
[I512] Time Life hbk **£13.95**
Fresh Ways with Poultry
[I513] Time Life hbk **£13.95**
Lamb
[I514] Time Life hbk **£13.95**
Offal
[I515] Time Life hbk **£13.95**
Poultry
[I516] Time Life hbk **£13.95**

Preserves & Pickling

ERLANDSON, KEITH
Home-Smoking & Curing
[I519] Century pbk **£5.95**

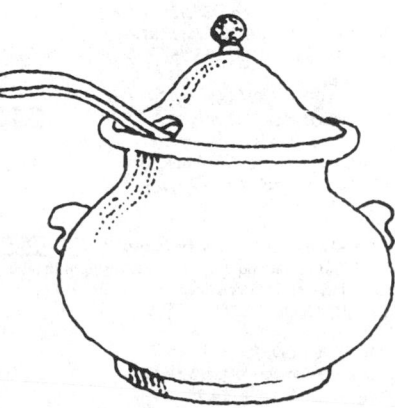

A basil pot from *A Book of Herbs and Spices* by Gail Duff (Merehurst hbk £7.95)

GOOD HOUSEKEEPING
Complete Book of Home Preserving
[I520] Ebury hbk **£9.95**

LAW, DIGBY
A Pickle & Chutney Cookbook
[I521] Hodder hbk **£9.95**

NORWAK, MARY
Book of Preserves
[I517] Hodder hbk **£6.95**

PASTON-WILLIAMS, SARA
**National Trust Book of the Country
Kitchen Store Cupboard**
[I523] David & Ch pbk **£5.95**

TIME LIFE
Preserving
[I524] Time Life hbk **£13.95**

Soups & Starters

BRIDGER, JUNE
Book of Hors d'Oeuvres
[I525] Hodder hbk **£5.95**

REDINGTON, CATHERINE
Perfect Picnics
[I527] Ward Lock hbk **£12.95**

BERRY, MARY
Buffets
[I528] Sphere pbk **£3.99**

BLANC, BEVERLY LE
Secrets of French Hors d'Oeuvres
[I535] Macdonald hbk **£3.95**

BOXER, ARABELLA
Starters with Style
An exquisite collection of recipes for first courses by
the food writer for English *Vogue*.
[I529] Octopus pbk **£3.99**

CARY, PAM
The Cheese Cookbook   NEW
A large range of recipes featuring the use of cheese in
soups, salads, party snacks and vegetarian foods.
[I530] Crowood hbk **£3.95**

CRACKNELL, H.L. & KAUFMANN, R.J. (EDS)
Hors d'Oeuvres
[I531] Kingswood hbk **£5.95**
Stocks, Sauces & Garnishes
[I532] Kingswood hbk **£5.95**

KAY, PAMELA & WARD, SUSIE
The Art of the Picnic   NEW
An anthology of historical and fictional picnic
recipes, ranging from the simple to the grand.
[I533] Cassell hbk **£12.95**

LAW, DIGBY
Light Meals with Digby Law   NEW
Over 300 original and exciting ideas for light lunches,
snacks and simple special occasion meals.
[I534] Hodder hbk **£9.95**

MARCANGELO, JO
Creative Cheese Cookery
[I536] Thorsons pbk **£4.95**

MENZIES, YVES
The Complete Book of Starters
[I537] Hale hbk **£12.95**

MILLS, SONIA
World Guide to Cheese
[I538] Apple hbk **£5.95**

PERTORCE, INGEBORG
Pâtés & Terrines
[I539] Hamlyn hbk **£15.00**

RODEN, CLAUDIA
**Picnic: The Complete Guide to Outdoor
Food**
[I540] Hale hbk **£9.50**

SMITH, MICHAEL
**Michael Smith's
Glyndebourne Picnic**   NEW
Hints and recipes about how to become more creative
in the composition of picnics.
[I542] Lennard hbk **£20.00**

TIME LIFE
Eggs & Cheese
[I544] Time Life hbk **£13.95**
Fresh Ways with Breakfasts & Brunch
[I545] Time Life hbk **£13.95**
Fresh Ways with Hors d'Oeuvres
[I546] Time Life hbk **£13.95**
Fresh Ways with Snacks & Canapés
[I547] Time Life hbk **£13.95**
Fresh Ways with Soups & Stews
[I548] Time Life hbk **£13.95**
Fresh Ways with Terrines and Pâtés
[I549] Time Life hbk **£13.95**
Hot Hors d'Oeuvres
[I550] Time Life hbk **£13.95**
Salads and Cold Hors d'Oeuvres
[I551] Time Life hbk **£13.95**
Sauces
[I552] Time Life hbk **£13.95**
Snacks & Canapés
[I553] Time Life hbk **£13.95**
Soups
[I554] Time Life hbk **£13.95**
Terrines, Pâtés & Galantines
[I555] Time Life hbk **£13.95**

VINEGRAAD, BERIT
Tempting Treats: Picnics
[I556] Macdonald Orbis hbk **£4.95**

WRIGHT, HANNAH
Soups
[I557] Hale pbk **£5.95**

Techniques

This section deals with the methods and techniques of
cooking, from the classical methods of French cuisine
as presented by Jaques Pepin, to the newer skills
needed for microwave ovens and barbecues.

ALLISON, SONIA
Book of Microwave Cookery
[I561] David & Ch hbk **£6.95**
Microwave for One
[I562] Partridge hbk **£9.95**

ALTHAUS, CATHERINE & FRENCH-HODGES,
PETER
Cook Now, Dine Later
[I563] Faber pbk **£3.95**

BENSON, KATE
Creative Steam Cuisine
[I564] Hamlyn hbk **£7.95**

BERRY, MARY
Mary Berry's New Freezer Cookbook
[I565] Piatkus hbk **£7.95**

BOWEN, CAROL
A-Z Microwave Cookery
[I566] Pan pbk **£3.99**
Barbecue Cookbook
[I567] Hamlyn hbk **£3.99**
**The Basic Basics Combination &
Microwave Cookbook**
[I568] Grub Street pbk **£4.95**
Combination Microwave Cookery
[I558] Pan pbk **£2.99**
Microwave Cookbook
[I559] Pan pbk **£2.99**

COLLINS, VAL
Beginner's Guide to Microwave Cookery
[I569] David & Ch hbk **£4.95**
Complete Microwave Cookbook
[I570] David & Ch hbk **£10.95**
Microwave Baking
[I571] David & Ch hbk **£7.95**
Microwave Cookery Cordon Bleu Style
[I572] David & Ch hbk **£6.95**
Microwave Fish Cookbook
[I573] David & Ch hbk **£6.95**
Microwave Wholefood Cookbook
[I575] David & Ch hbk **£6.95**

FLOYD, KEITH
Floyd on Fire
[I580] BBC pbk **£3.95**

GOOD HOUSEKEEPING
Complete Microwave Cook Book
[I581] Ebury pbk **£5.95**
Creative Food Processor Cookbook
[I576] Ebury pbk **£5.95**
Family Microwave Cookery Book
[I582] Ebury pbk **£6.95**
Freezer Handbook
[I583] Ebury pbk **£5.95**
Microwave Cookery Course
[I578] Ebury pbk **£6.95**
Microwave Cooking for One or Two
[I584] Ebury pbk **£6.95**
Microwave Encyclopaedia
[I585] Ebury hbk **£10.95**
Microwave Handbook
[I586] Ebury pbk **£5.95**
Slim & Healthy Microwave Cookery
[I587] Ebury pbk **£5.95**
Step-by-Step Food Processor Cookbook
[I588] Ebury pbk **£4.95**
Step-by-Step Microwave Cook Book
[I589] Ebury pbk **£5.95**
Successful Microwave Baking
[I590] Ebury pbk **£5.95**

GRIMSDALE, GORDON
Book of Sauces
[I591] Hodder hbk **£6.95**

HAROUTUNIAN, ARTO DER
The Barbecue Cookbook
[I593] Pan pbk **£2.95**

LEITH, PRUE
The Cook's Handbook
A good basic reference book for techniques, cooking
times, storing, freezing, equipment and ingredients.
[I594] Macmillan pbk **£8.95**

MCWILLIAM, JILL
The Practical Freezer Handbook
[I597] Octopus pbk **£1.75**

Illustration from *Creative Steam Cuisine* by Kate Benson (Hamlyn hbk £7.95)

NORMAN, CECILIA
The Book of Grilling & Barbeques NEW
A new title in the Creative Cookery series.
[I598] Hodder hbk **£6.95**

PEPIN, JACQUES
A pair of authoritative and well-illustrated guides to all the techniques of classical French cooking.
La Méthode: An Illustrated Guide to the Fundamental Skills of Cooking
[I599] Macmillan pbk **£11.95**
La Technique: An Illustrated Guide to the Fundamental Techniques of Cooking
[I600] Macmillan pbk **£13.95**

PIPER, BEVERLEY
Microwave Cooking for Health
[I601] Penguin pbk **£2.95**

RHODES, LORNA
The Steamer Cookbook NEW
An introduction to this health-conscious technique of cooking using steam, a traditional Oriental technique now adapted by modern Western cooking, and valued for the way it seals in the goodness of the ingredients.
[I602] Martin pbk **£3.95**

ROBERTS, SUE
Good Food from the Microwave
A guide to what tastes good when cooked in the microwave, concentrating particularly on fruit and vegetables.
[I603] D Kindersley hbk **£12.95**

RUBINSTEIN, HELGE & BUSH, SHEILA
Good Food from Your Freezer
[I604] Penguin pbk **£2.95**

SMITH, JANET
Vegetarian Microwave Cook Book
[I605] Ebury pbk **£6.95**

TIME LIFE
Fresh Ways with Picnics and Barbecues
[I607] Time Life hbk **£13.95**
Outdoor Cookery
[I608] Time Life hbk **£13.95**

VEALE, WENDY
Step by Step Garnishing NEW
A beautifully presented book exploring how to present your food with style and flair.
[I609] Apple hbk **£6.95**

WEALE, MARGARET
Beginning Microwave Cookery
[I610] Angell hbk **£7.95**
[I611] Angell pbk **£3.95**
Microwave Recipes for One or Two
[I612] Angell pbk **£3.95**
Slimmers' Microwave Cookbook
[I613] Angell hbk **£6.95**

Vegetables & Fruits

BAKER, JANICE
Salad: The Taste of Summer NEW
Recipes and ideas for the use of salad ingredients.
[I615] Bay pbk **£3.95**

BOXER, ARABELLA
Arabella Boxer's Garden Cookbook
[I616] Weidenfeld pbk **£5.95**

BRADFORD, PETER & MONTSE
Cooking with Sea Vegetables
Innovative and traditional ideas for seaweeds.
[I617] Thorsons pbk **£3.95**

BYRNE, PADDY & SCOTT, DAVID
Seasonal Salads
[I618] M Joseph pbk **£2.95**

CARY, PAM
The Fresh Fruit Cookbook
Explores new ways of using fruit with recipes, covering starters, soups, main courses, sauces and desserts.
[I619] Crowood hbk **£10.95**

CONIL, JEAN & FRANKLIN, FAY
Fabulous French Fruit Cuisine
[I620] Thorsons pbk **£6.99**

DOLOMORE, ANNE
The Essential Olive Oil Companion NEW
As well as giving over 100 traditional recipes, this book examines the history of this precious and medicinal oil, and how it is produced and cultivated.
[I621] Macmillan hbk **£10.95**

GOOD HOUSEKEEPING
Best of Vegetable Cooking
[I622] Ebury hbk **£7.95**

GRIGSON, JANE
All the books and recipes from this author are a safe bet: each one reveals an exemplary knowledge and flair.
Fruit Book
[I623] Penguin pbk **£4.95**
The Mushroom Feast
[I624] Penguin pbk **£7.50**
Vegetable Book
[I625] Penguin pbk **£4.95**

GRIGSON, JANE & KNOX, CHARLOTTE
Exotic Fruits & Vegetables
[I626] Cape hbk **£12.95**

HANDSLIP, CAROLE
Salad Book
[I627] Pan pbk **£2.95**

HAROUTUNIAN, ARTO DER
Classic Vegetable Cookery
A classic from the writer best known for his books on Middle Eastern cuisine.
[I628] Ebury pbk **£6.95**

JACKSON, JUDY
Microwave Vegetable Cooking NEW
Over 100 recipes describing how to cook vegetables in a microwave, while retaining colour and vitamins.
[I629] Macdonald hbk **£8.95**

LEVY, FAYE NEW
Fresh from France: Vegetable Creations
A teacher from the famous La Varenne cookery school in Paris explains the basic rules for cooking vegetables to retain maximum flavour and colour.
[I631] Grafton hbk **£12.95**

MABEY, RICHARD
Food for Free NEW
An updated, all-colour edition of the classic guide to Britain's wild foods, providing a useful identification guide for recognising edible fruits of the hedgerow, and recipes for preparing them for consumption.
[I632] Collins pbk **£7.95**

MARIA, JACK SANTA
The French Way with Vegetables NEW
Alphabetically-arranged cookery book offering recipes for vegetables from artichokes to watercress.
[I634] Century pbk **£3.95**

PHILLIPS ROGER
Wild Food
[I635] Pan pbk **£6.95**

RHODES, LORNA
The Book of Salads NEW
A new addition to the *Creative Cookery* series.
[I636] Hodder hbk **£6.95**

RIDGWAY, JUDY
The Vegetable Year Cookbook
[I638] Piatkus hbk **£9.95**

SALAMAN, RENA
Mediterranean Vegetable Cookery
[I639] Collins hbk **£8.95**

TIME LIFE
Fresh Ways with Salads
[I641] Time Life hbk **£13.95**
Fresh Ways with Vegetables
[I642] Time Life hbk **£13.95**
Fruits
[I643] Time Life hbk **£13.95**
Vegetables
[I644] Time Life **£13.95**

Vegetarian

Vegetarian food has become commonplace in recent years with the increasing rise in awareness of the value of healthy eating. Vegetarian cuisine now covers an enormous range of styles and degrees, ranging from those who merely want to eat less red meat, to the purer macrobiotic and vegan diets.

ALEXANDER, LYNNE
Staying Vegetarian
[I646] Fontana hbk **£3.95**

BAKER, JENNY
Vegetarian Student
[I647] Faber pbk **£2.95**

BATT, EVA
Vegan Cookery
[I648] Thorsons pbk £2.99

BLANC, GEORGES
Natural Cuisine
[I649] Webb & B hbk £19.95

BROWN, SARAH
Quick and Easy Vegetarian Cookery NEW
How to speed things up in the vegetarian kitchen.
[I650] BBC hbk £4.95
Sarah Brown's New Vegetarian Kitchen
[I651] BBC hbk £10.95
[I652] BBC pbk £6.95
Sarah Brown's Vegetarian Cookbook
[I653] D Kindersley hbk £12.95
[I654] Grafton pbk £3.95
Sarah Brown's Vegetarian Microwave Cookbook
[I655] D Kindersley hbk £9.95
Vegetarian Kitchen
An accompaniment to the immensely successful television series of the same name.
[I656] BBC pbk £5.25

CAMPION, KITTY
Vegetarian Encyclopaedia
[I657] Century hbk £10.95
[I658] Century pbk £4.95

CANTER, KAY & SWANN, DAPHNE
When the authors started their first restaurant in London their innovative approach became very popular, helping remove the 'cranky' image from vegetarian food. Approachable and delicious recipes throughout.
Cranks Recipe Book
[I659] Dent hbk £14.95
[I660] Grafton pbk £4.99
Entertaining with Cranks
[I661] Dent hbk £12.95
[I662] Grafton pbk £4.95

DUFF, GAIL
Vegetarian Cookbook
[I664] Pan pbk £4.99

ELLIOT, ROSE
One of the leading writers on vegetarian cooking, who offers particularly imaginative recipes for pulses.
Bean Book
[I665] Fontana pbk £3.95
Beanfeast
[I666] Fontana pbk £2.50
Book of Beans & Lentils
[I667] Fontana pbk £1.25
Book of Fruits
[I668] Fontana pbk £0.99
Book of Salads
[I669] Fontana pbk £0.99
Book of Savoury Flans & Pies
All vegetarian.
[I670] Fontana pbk £1.25
Book of Vegetables
[I671] Fontana pbk £0.99
Cheap & Easy
[I672] Fontana pbk £3.95
Gourmet Vegetarian Cooking
[I673] Fontana pbk £3.95
Not Just a Load of Old Lentils
[I674] Fontana pbk £3.95
Rose Elliot's Complete Vegetarian Cookbook
With over 1,000 recipes this is excellent value.
[I675] Collins hbk £9.95
Rose Elliot's Vegetarian Cookery
[I676] Collins hbk £14.95

Rose Elliot's Vegetarian Mother & Baby Book
[I677] Fontana pbk £3.95
Rose Elliott's New Vegetarian Cookbook
[I678] Octopus hbk £8.95
Simply Delicious
[I679] Fontana pbk £2.50
Vegetarian Dishes of the World
[I680] Fontana pbk £3.95
Your Very Good Health
[I681] Fontana pbk £3.95

FERGUSON, CLARE
Creative Vegetarian Cooking
Upmarket, international recipes with exotic and tempting dishes such as 'hot avocado and goat's cheese sandwiches'.
[I682] Ebury hbk £9.95

FLIESS, W. & J.
Modern Vegetarian Cooking
[I683] Penguin pbk £3.95

GARRET, GUY & NORMAN, KIT
Food for Thought Cookbook
A selection of recipes from the renowned Covent Garden restaurant.
[I684] Thorsons pbk £8.99

GIBBON, JILL
Wharf Street Vegetarian Café Cookbook
[I685] Thorsons pbk £4.99

GOOD HOUSEKEEPING
Vegetarian Gourmet
[I712] Ebury hbk £8.95
Vegetarian Microwave Cook Book
[I707] Ebury hbk £9.95
[I708] Ebury pbk £6.95

HAIGH, RACHEL
Neal's Yard Wholefood Cookbook
Recipes from the famous centre for healthy food in London's Covent Garden.
[I686] D Kindersley pbk £7.95

HIGHTON, N.B. & R.B.
The Home Book of Vegetarian Cookery
[I687] Faber pbk £4.95

KATZEN, MOLLIE
Katzen is the guiding light of the Moosewood Collective, a justifiably famous group who run a natural foods restaurant in upstate New York.
Moosewood Cookbook
[I688] Ten Speed pbk £7.95
New Recipes from the Moosewood Restaurants NEW
[I689] Ten Speed pbk £9.95
The Enchanted Broccoli Forest
[I690] Ten Speed pbk £9.95

LEEMING, ALISON
A Vegetarian Sampler
[I691] Thorsons pbk £6.99

LENEMAN, LEAH
The Single Vegan NEW
A vegan cookbook featuring simple, convenient and appetising meals for one, including hints and advice such as a weekly shopping list and 'staple' foods for the store cupboard.
[I692] Thorsons pbk £4.99

MANN, JENNY (ED)
Vegetarian Cuisine
[I695] Fontana pbk £2.50

MARSHALL, JANETTE
Fast Food for Vegetarians
[I695] Penguin pbk £3.99

MICHELL, KEITH
Practically Macrobiotic
[I696] Thorsons pbk £8.99

NORMAN, CECILIA
Cordon Vitesse
Entertaining for the vegetarian host in a hurry.
[I697] Thorsons pbk £5.99
Thorsons Vegetarian Microwave Cookbook
[I698] Thorsons pbk £3.50

SCOTT, DAVID
Far Eastern Vegetarian Cookery
[I699] Hutchinson hbk £4.95
The Demiveg Cookbook
A collection of recipes to suit the growing number of people who avoid red meat but eat fish and poultry.
[I701] Bloomsbury hbk £12.95
The Vegetarian Gourmet
[I703] Windward hbk £6.95

SHULMAN, MARTHA ROSE
Spicy Vegetarian Feasts
[I704] Thorsons pbk £5.99
The Vegetarian Feast
[I705] Thorsons pbk £5.99

SMITH, CHRISTINE
Good Children's Food
Vegetarian cookery for children.
[I706] Century pbk £5.95

SPENCER, COLIN
Cordon Vert
Dinner party menus for gourmet vegetarians.
[I709] Thorsons hbk £10.95
Green Cuisine
A selection of recipes submitted as entries for a competition organised by the *Guardian*.
[I710] Thorsons hbk £10.95
The Romantic Vegetarian
Menus for lovers, with month-by-month suggestions including table settings, music and flowers.
[I711] Thorsons hbk £9.95

THOMAS, ANNA
The Vegetarian Epicure
A popular classic, first published in 1973, and since reprinted 12 times. There is a wide variety of recipes with very good suggestions for dinner parties.
[I713] Penguin pbk £3.95

TIME LIFE
Fresh Ways with Pasta
[I714] Time Life hbk £13.95
Fresh Ways with Vegetarian Dishes
[I715] Time Life hbk £13.95 NEW
Grains, Pasta & Pulses
[I716] Time Life hbk £13.95

TRACY, LISA
The Gradual Vegetarian
[I717] Arrow pbk £3.95

TROY, DIANA
The Covent Garden Cookery Book
Diana Troy, adviser to the famous Neal's Yard Warehouse, presents delicious wholefood recipes from worldwide cooking traditions.
[I718] Sidgwick pbk £6.95

WAKEMAN, ALAN & BASKERVILLE, GORDON
The Vegan Cookbook
[I719] Faber pbk £4.95

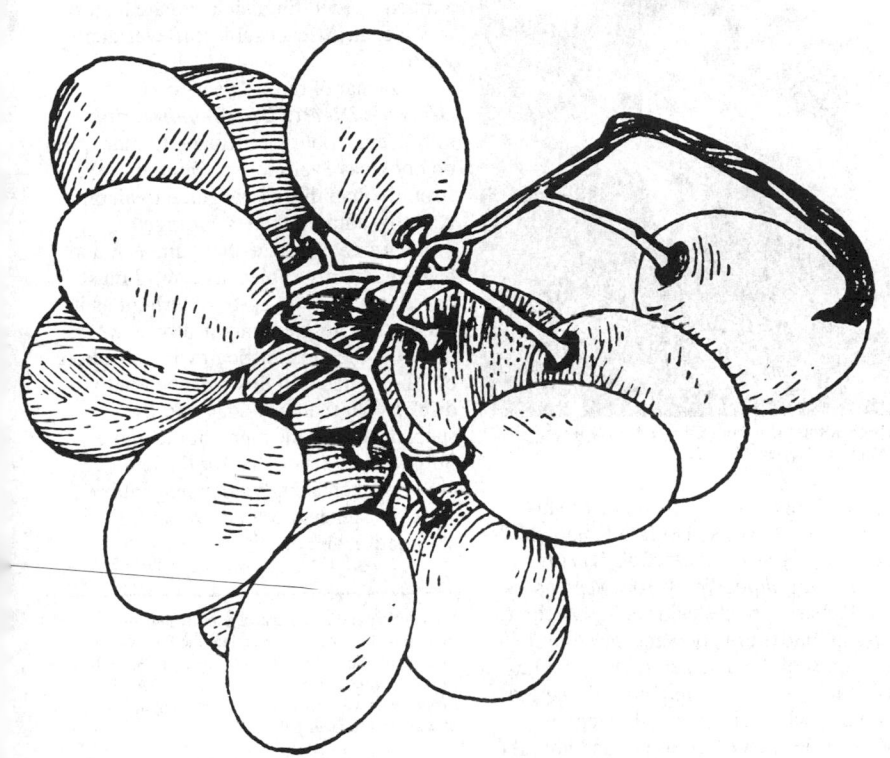

Illustration from *Jane Grigson's Fruit Book* (Penguin pbk £8.95)

'Wine is Fun!' and After
Jancis Robinson

I wonder how many readers, or even writers, of wine literature have noticed its subtle shifts in content and form over the last decade or so - and whether they appreciate the changing attitudes to wine these shifts reflect?

When I started writing about wine in 1976, Britons were beginning to marvel at their daring in managing six whole litres a head per year of this exotic beverage imported from what Jimmy Young was still able to refer to as 'le Continong', as though it were unthinkably distant and bizarre. To those of us who wrote about or sold wine then, six litres was about the amount we reckoned to drink or spit out every *week*. That national average therefore had to include a challengingly high proportion of non wine drinkers. We knew all too clearly that our *raison d'être* was at that stage a minority taste; in the mid-

seventies there were whole tracts of Britain in which the word wine was so charged with suspect elitist symbolism that, just like the words polo and Barbados, it had to be given audible quotation marks whenever it was mentioned.

We compared these attitudes with those prevailing in France and Italy, where wine was part of everyday life and per capita annual wine consumption was, incredibly, more than 100 litres (140 bottles - half a bottle a *day*...?)

Our task was clear. We had to boost our puny little British average, by going out and preaching the gospel of wine-drinking as an integral part of life. We had to rid wine of its image in this country as a drink weighed down not only by its association with outmoded concepts of privilege, but also by its complication as a subject. Our job was to dispel the

mystique surrounding wine. We had to persuade the British to set aside their innate horror of foreign languages and to teach them that they could enjoy wine without embarking on a series of night classes.

This resulted in the Wine is Fun!!! school of wine writing of which I must confess I was probably a founder

member. Even the title of the wine newsletter I started in 1977, *Drinker's Digest*, hinted at the breathless prose within. I see that top of the list of new books reviewed in the first issue was one called ***Plonk and Superplonk***, very much a book of its time. By 1980 when the Consumers' Association bought my stripling publication, things had sobered up sufficiently to warrant a name change, to *Which? Wine Monthly* (the question mark irritatingly but perhaps necessarily reminding the reader of the Association's most famous publication, giving the misleading impression that methods used to test washing machines could somehow be applied to wine assessment).

At the beginning of the eighties, Britain's per capita annual wine consumption was already more than eight litres. Package holidays had introduced millions of Britons to the notion of wine drinking with meals, even if they spun out their single bottle of Vino da Mesa marked with their hotel room number over so many dinners that they saw it at its worst. Supermarkets such as Sainsbury's and Waitrose were beginning to put real effort into finding interesting wine at prices that reflected their ability to buy in bulk. Women were quietly taking over as stockers of the notional family cellar, typically a brace of bottles on top of the fridge. Wine was beginning to infiltrate the British way of life.

Already in 1981 the arbiter-controllers of television had overcome their Reithian conviction that wine was too elitist to deserve a place on the screen. An

increasing proportion of publicans were prepared to allow this cuckoo into the beery nest. (Licensee's Liebfraumilch is yet to convince us connoisseurs of the pleasures of the pub, but it has presumably helped to recruit women to replace the pubs' traditional customers as they die off).

The masses had been fully exposed to wine drinking as a viable concept by the mid-eighties. Our per capita consumption of wine reached 12 litres, twice the mid-seventies level, in 1987, but even the most optimistic wine merchants are less bullish about the prospects for making millions of new converts in the nineties. Rather, they are relying on selling better and better quality wine to the present core of established wine drinkers as consumers become more health-conscious and more susceptible to anti-alcohol propaganda. Even the French Government's agricultural export arm, which has officially identified Britain as one of the few markets where any growth can be

Microscopic insights into a single aspect of wine, wine science or wine region seem to be what is required

expected, are predicting increases in quality rather than quantity here.

And our ideas about what, as well as how much, we ingest have changed too. Today's typical wine drinker differs from her counterpart of the mid-seventies not only in her gender but in that she feels strongly that drinks as well as food should be as 'natural' as possible (even if she doesn't understand too clearly what that means). She wants a wine guaranteed not to give her a headache, and guaranteed to be the wine specified on the label (even if she might be hard pushed to describe the characteristics of that wine). She is worried about all these wine frauds and wants some reliable direct line to the goodies in the wine world.

This, of course, has direct implications for wine writing. Wine writers are now expected to supply A-level information rather than kindergarten jollification. For the established troop of wine devotees, wine books must offer new

Hugh Johnson, author of *World Atlas of Wine* (Mitchell Beazley hbk £22.50)

interpretations of the texts rather than make new converts. Dorling Kindersley's intensely statistical *Sotheby's World Wine Encyclopaedia* by Tom Stevenson, and Robert Parker's painstakingly scored buying guides are good and successful examples of the new genre. Increasingly microscopic insights into a single aspect of wine, wine science or wine region seem to be what is required - and hold the jokes.

King of the jokes, and king of the blind tasters too, is Oz Clarke, whose output has subtly evolved over the years from entreating people to drink wine at all to treating them to a sort of end-of-term report on the world's winemakers. And even he, the only man I know who can enthuse for more than half an hour about a single wine, has been persuaded to take off his wine-soaked blinkers; Oz is currently writing a book about art and design for an American publisher. It will doubtless dazzle.

Hugh Johnson's way of encouraging the masses to drink wine was perhaps more elegant. Just as important an ingredient in the seminal *World Atlas of Wine* as the maps that gave us the illusion we somehow understood more about the liquid in our mouths by looking at the blob on the map whence it came, were his frustratingly short essays on the wines of each area. His enviably masterful prose could be distinguished from advertising copy chiefly by its glorious syntax and perfect punctuation, and had every reader reaching for the corkscrew within seconds. Now however, he has responded

to the changing wine market by diversifying into television and producing a much-needed English language history of wine, an A-level subject if ever there was one.

And what of me, 12 years on from *Drinker's Digest*? **The Demon Drink** may seem a poor progression to many, but no book has ever motivated me more strongly than this user's guide to alcohol. And this autumn there's **Vintage Timecharts**, evidence that I am as much beguiled by my subject as ever. I must have been crazy to agree to write it as it attempts to answer, graphically as well as verbally, the most difficult wine question of all - 'When will this wine be ready to drink? - but then nowadays, folks, specialisation's the name of the game. Sorry, I'll rephrase that for the late eighties: increasingly knowledgeable wine consumers deserve ever more stimulation and erudition.

Wine writer and broadcaster Jancis Robinson was the first journalist to be accepted into the fellowship of Masters of Wine. She has published widely on both food and wine, and her television series *The Wine Programme* was instrumental in opening up the world of wine to a broader public.

Jancis Robinson, author of *The Demon Drink* (Mitchell Beazley hbk £9.95)

DRINK

The last few years have seen a marked rise in wine consumption in Britain, and as the public's taste for wine has increased, so has its thirst for knowledge. There has always been a tradition of erudite and entertaining writing on wine in the English language; now the range of books has expanded to include works on every aspect of its distribution and appreciation. All the various regions of the world where wine is produced are now covered, with the recent appearance of authoritative guides to the fashionable New World wines of California and New Zealand. Perhaps the best known writers on wine in Britain today are Jancis Robinson and Hugh Johnson. Both have done much to explode myths, expand our fund of knowledge, and increase the public awareness of what wine is, what it does and how to enjoy it. Add to these names the distinguished work of foreign writers such as Hubrecht Duijker, and America's hugely influential wine guru Robert Parker, and the standard of writing becomes apparent.

Wine

Collins' Gem Guide to Wine
This tiny guide, with over 4,000 entries, lists each wine alphabetically, providing all the basic information you need to understand wine.
[I771] Collins pbk £1.95

Sunday Telegraph Good Wine Guide
[I772] Telegraph pbk £4.95

ARLOTT, JOHN
Arlott on Wine
Nearly 100 articles on the other great love of this famous cricketing enthusiast.
[I774] Collins hbk £12.95
[I774] Collins pbk £8.95

BROADBENT, MICHAEL
The Compleat Winetaster & Cellarman
[I775] M Beazley hbk £8.95
The Great Vintage Wine Book
Tastings of over 4,000 wines of vintages from 1945 by the erudite Master of Wines from Christie's.
[I776] M Beazley hbk £13.95

BURROUGHS, D. & BEZZANT, N.
New Wine Companion
Good introductory book on wine, the wine trade, spirits and other drinks.
[I777] Heinemann pbk £8.95
Wine Regions of the World
Indispensable guide to all aspects of wine from production to consumption. Required book for the Wine and Spirit Education Trust Higher Certificate.
[I778] Heinemann pbk £9.95

CLARKE, OZ
Oz Clarke's Wine Fact Finder & Taste Guide
[I779] M Beazley hbk £10.95
Webster's Wine Price Guide 1989
Comprehensive wine buyer's handbook, including prices and where they can be bought.
[I780] M Beazley hbk £9.95

EDWARDS, GRAHAM
The Language of Drink
A dictionary with over 42,000 entries covering all aspects of drink, both alcoholic and non-alcoholic:

vineyards, breweries, cocktails, coffees and teas, societies, recipes, milks and minerals.
[I781] Sutton hbk £9.95

FOREST, LOUIS
Wine Album
The first section of this book deals with buying, storing, serving and drinking wine, while the second section is an Art Deco inspired cellar book.
[I782] Gollancz hbk £7.95

HALLGARTEN, FRITZ
Wine Scandal
An investigative examination of the age-old and sadly continuing practice of adulterating wines.
[I783] Weidenfeld hbk £10.95

JOHNSON, HUGH
Perhaps the only man in England to make a fortune in the wine trade, Hugh Johnson has produced a range of enormously popular wine books. Always fair and encyclopaedic, he writes on all the major and minor wines of the old and new worlds with a degree of wit and a sensibly restrained rhetoric.
How to Enjoy Your Wine: Understanding, Storing, Serving
[I784] M Beazley hbk £5.95
Hugh Johnson's Pocket Wine Book 1988
The best of its field, small enough to fit in your pocket.
[I785] M Beazley hbk £4.95
Hugh Johnson's Wine Companion
[I786] M Beazley hbk £17.95
Hugh Johnson's Wine Pop-Up Book   **NEW**
An entertaining yet informative guide to the story of wine and wine production, told with the aid of some jokey and amusing paper engineering.
[I787] Hamlyn hbk £9.95
The Hugh Johnson Cellar Book
Designed to record all the information needed to keep a cellar of wine up to date.
[I788] M Beazley hbk £14.95
The World Atlas of Wine
Johnson's lavishly produced magnum opus now in its 3rd edition.
[I789] M Beazley hbk £25.00
Wine
A useful introduction from this acknowledged master of wine lore.
[I790] M Beazley hbk £9.95

JORDAN, BRIAN
**Jordan's Good Wine Guides
Vol 1: Supermarket Wines**
[I791] Witherby hbk £2.99
Vol 2: High Street Wines
[I792] Witherby hbk £2.99

JOSEPH, ROBERT (ED)
The Art of the Wine Label
The wine correspondent of the *Daily Telegraph* traces the history of the wine label from its 18th century beginnings to the modern designs of Miró, Picasso, Hockney and others.
[I793] Windward hbk £9.95

KING, ALICE
Winewise
A humorous and unpompous guide.
[I794] Methuen pbk £5.95

LAITHWAITE, TONY
Laithwaite's Great Wine Trek: A Journey through Every Wine Region of the World
[I795] Harrap pbk £7.95

LICHINE, ALEXIS
Encyclopaedia of Wines & Spirits
The 6th edition of one of the most authoritative works in this field, written by the erudite wine maker from Bordeaux.
[I796] Cassell hbk £35.00
[I797] Cassell pbk £14.95

LITTLEWOOD, J. (TRANS)
Milady Vine: The Autobiography of Philippe de Rothschild
[I798] Century pbk £4.95

MATTHEWS, PATRICK (ED)
Christie's Wine Companion
[I799] Webb & B hbk £14.95

NARDELLA, GINO & DOUGHERTY, KEITH
Wine & Wine Service
Invaluable wine waiter's handbook.
[I800] Batsford pbk £9.95

PARKER, ROBERT
Influential American wine critic, famous for his points system of grading wine.
The Wine Buyer's Guide: 1987-1988
Purchasing guide accompanied by the celebrated American wine critic's tasting comments and rating system.
[I801] D Kindersley hbk £10.95

PEYNAUD, EMILE
The Taste of Wine
First English language translation of the fascinating classic *Le Goût du Vin*, by the Director of the Bordeaux University Centre of Oenology.
[I802] Macdonald hbk £14.95
[I802] Macdonald pbk £9.95

RAINBIRD, GEORGE
An Illustrated Guide to Wine
[I803] Octopus hbk £6.95

RAY, CYRIL (ED)
The New Compleat Imbiber: A Literary Anthology
[I804] Collins hbk £9.95

ROBINSON, JANCIS
Presenter of *The Wine Programme*, and one of the most distinguished writers on wine and food in England today, Jancis Robinson has helped to open the world of wine up to a wider public. Her books are well and entertainingly written, as well as being authoritative.
Food and Wine Adventures
[I805] Headline hbk £7.95
Masterglass: A Practical Course in Tasting Wine
[I806] Pan pbk £4.50
On the Demon Drink
An invaluable and entertaining user's guide to alcohol.
[I807] Mandarin pbk £4.99
The Great Wine Book
[I808] Sidgwick pbk £9.95
Vines, Grapes & Wines
An illustrated gazetteer of over 1,000 grape varieties. It has been acclaimed as the most important book on wine since Hugh Johnson's *World Atlas of Wine* in 1970.
[I809] M Beazley hbk £16.95
Wine Book
[I811] Fontana pbk £2.95

ROOTES, NICHOLAS
The Drinker's Companion
[I812] Gollancz hbk £9.95

Oz Clarke, author of *Wine Fact Finder and Taste Guide* (Mitchell Beazley hbk £10.95) and *Webster's Wine Price Guide 1989* (Mitchell Beazley hbk £9.95)

SAMPSON, BETTY
The Art of Making Wine
[I813] Aurum pbk **£4.95**

SEARLE, RONALD
Something in the Cellar
Outrageous and hilarious cartoons on a vinous theme from a master humorist.
[I814] Souvenir hbk **£8.95**

SPURRIER, STEVEN
Académie du Vin Wine Cellar Book
[I816] Collins hbk **£9.95**

SPURRIER, STEVEN & DOVAZ, MICHEL
The Académie du Vin Wine Course
Wine appreciation and tasting course, as taught at the prestigious Paris Académie du Vin.
[I818] Century pbk **£7.95**

SPURRIER, STEVEN & WARD, JACK
How to Buy Fine Wines
An investor's guide to fine wines.
[I819] Phaidon hbk **£14.95**

STEVENSON, TOM
Sotheby's World Wine Encyclopaedia   **NEW**
A comprehensive and luxuriously produced guide to the wine producing countries of the world and the wines they create, featuring especially commissioned maps of the wine regions and districts combined with detailed information about individual wines - tasting notes, grapes used, recent vintages of note and how long the wine should be stored. A major new reference for the wine-lover.
[I820] D Kindersley hbk **£25.00**

SUTCLIFFE, SERENA
The Wine Drinker's Handbook
[I822] Pan pbk **£9.99**

VOSS, ROGER
The 1988 Which? Wine Guide
The independent findings of the Consumers' Association.
[I826] Hodder pbk **£9.95**
The Pocket Guide to Fortified & Dessert Wines   **NEW**
A diminutive guide full of useful information, including assessments of over 750 examples of fortified wines from both the old and new worlds.
[I827] M Beazley hbk **£5.95**

WAUGH, AUBERON
Waugh on Wine
Humorous vinous anecdotes from this versatile wine and food writer.
[I828] Fourth Estate hbk **£10.95**
[I956] Fontana pbk **£3.95**

YOUNG, ALAN
Making Sense of Wine Tasting
[I829] Lennard hbk **£9.95**

YOUNG, ROBIN
The Really Useful Wine Guide
[I830] Sidgwick hbk **£12.95**
[I831] Sidgwick pbk **£6.95**

Wines of France

BENSON, J. & MACKENZIE, A.
Sauternes: A Study of the Great Sweet Wines of Bordeaux
[I832] Sotheby hbk **£9.95**
The Wines of St Emilion & Pomerol
[I833] Sotheby hbk **£19.95**

BENSON, JEFFREY & MACKENZIE, ALASTAIR
Sauternes
A sumptuously produced revised edition of the classic book on the great sweet wines of Bordeaux, with tasting notes and many illustrations and maps.
[I834] Sotheby hbk **£18.00**

BERRY, CHARLES WALTER
In Search of Wines: A Tour of the Vineyards of France
Jancis Robinson introduces a 1930s classic.
[I835] Sidgwick hbk **£13.95**

BERRY, LIZ
The Wines of Alsace: A Buyer's Guide
Covering every variety of Alsace wine and eau-de-vie, offering buyers advice and an introduction to the history and profile of each wine.
[I836] Bodley hbk **£10.95**

BUSSELLE, MICHAEL
The Wine Lover's Guide to France
[I837] Pavilion pbk **£9.95**

DUIJKER, HUBRECHT
An outstanding wine writer and critic from the Netherlands.
The Good Wines of Bordeaux
[I841] M Beazley hbk **£14.95**
The Great Wine Châteaux of Bordeaux
[I840] M Beazley hbk **£14.95**
The Great Wines of Burgundy
[I8412] M Beazley hbk **£13.95**
The Traveller's Guide to the Wine Regions of France   **NEW**
A pocket guide to take with you on holiday.
[I843] M Beazley hbk **£5.95**

FAITH, NICHOLAS
The Story of Champagne
[I844] H Hamilton hbk **£17.95**

FORBES, PATRICK
Champagne: The Wine, the Land & the People
[I845] Gollancz hbk **£15.00**

GEORGE, ROSEMARY
The Wines of Chablis & the Yonne
[I846] Sotheby hbk **£15.95**

GINESTET, BERNARD
The Wines of France: Margaux
Foreword by Hugh Johnson
[I847] Aurum hbk **£12.95**
The Wines of France: St Julien
[I848] Aurum hbk **£12.95**

HANSON, ANTHONY
Burgundy
[I849] Faber pbk **£6.95**

JOHNSON, HUGH & DUIJKER, HUBRECHT
The Wine Atlas of France & Traveller's Guide to the Vineyards
In this very useful guide there are maps for touring the wine regions, pinpointing growers, wine makers and places of interest to the wine enthusiast.
[I851] M Beazley hbk **£16.95**

LEARMONTH, J. & MASTER, C.H.
The Wines of the Rhône
[I852] Faber hbk **£12.50**
[I853] Faber pbk **£6.95**

LICHINE, ALEXIS
Alexis Lichine's Guide to the Wines & Vineyards of France
Excellent and authoritative companion for the wines and regions of France.
[I854] Weidenfeld hbk **£12.95**
[I855] Macmillan pbk **£9.95**

MACQUITTY, JANE
Champagne & Sparkling Wines
A worldwide guide to over 1,000 sparkling wines from the wine correspondent of *The Times*.
[I857] M Beazley hbk **£4.95**

PARKER, ROBERT
Bordeaux: The Definitive Guide
[I858] D Kindersley hbk **£14.95**
The Wines of the Rhône Valley & Provence
Parker turns his attention to Southern France. A buyer's guide with tasting notes and evaluation of wines and vintages.
[I859] D Kindersley hbk **£14.95**

PEPPERCORN, DAVID
Bordeaux
[I860] Faber pbk **£6.95**
David Peppercorn's Pocket Guide to the Wines of Bordeaux
[I861] M Beazley hbk **£4.95**

REGIONAL GUIDES TO THE WINES OF FRANCE
The Red Wines of Bordeaux
[I862] Octopus hbk **£4.95**
The Red Wines of Burgundy
[I863] Octopus hbk **£4.95**
The White Wines of Bordeaux
[I864] Octopus hbk **£4.95**
The White Wines of Burgundy
[I865] Octopus hbk **£4.95**

SEELY, JAMES
The Loire Valley and Its Wines   **NEW**
The most comprehensive guide available to the fine wine growers of the region that includes the *appellations* of Sancerre, Pouilly-Fumé, Vouvray and Muscadet.
[I866] Lennard hbk **£16.95**

SEELY, JAMES & CHRISTIAN
Great Bordeaux Wines
Detailed study of 147 châteaux members of the Union des Grands Crus de Bordeaux.
[I867] Secker hbk **£30.00**

SPURRIER, STEPHEN
French Country Wines
[1868] Collins hbk **£5.95**
French Fine Wines
[1869] Collins hbk **£5.95**
The Académie du Vin Guide to French Wines
[1870] Collins hbk **£12.95**

SUTCLIFFE, SERENA
Serena Sutcliffe's Pocket Guide to the Wines of Burgundy
[1871] M Beazley hbk **£4.95**

VEDEL, ANDRE (ED)
The Macdonald Guide to French Wines 1988
The best guide to purchasing French wine. 11 major regions are listed together with 400 *appellations* and over 5,000 entries, each with tasting notes.
[1875] Macdonald hbk **£14.95**

VOSS, ROGER
Pocket Guide to French Regional Wines **NEW**
[1876] M Beazley hbk **£4.95**

Wines of Europe

ANDERSON, BURTON
The Pocket Guide to Italian Wines
[1877] M Beazley hbk **£4.95**

BARTY-KING, HUGH
A Taste of English Wine **NEW**
An examination of both the history and future of English wine, with a guide to where and how English wine is made, which of England's 300 or so vineyards are open to the public and where to taste and buy their produce.
[1878] Pelham hbk **£16.95**

DALLAS, PHILIP
Italian Wines
Newly revised and updated edition of this useful guide to the myriad varieties of Italian wine.
[1880] Faber pbk **£6.99**

DUIJKER, HUBRECHT
The Wines of Rioja
[1881] M Beazley hbk **£14.95**

FLOWER, R.
Chianti: The Land, the People & the Wine
[1882] Ch Helm hbk **£12.95**
[1957] Ch Helm pbk **£7.95**

SOCIÉTÉ CIVILE DU DOMAINE DE LA ROMANÉE-CONTI
PROPRIÉTAIRE A VOSNE-ROMANÉE (COTE-D'OR) FRANCE

ROMANÉE-CONTI
APPELLATION ROMANÉE-CONTI CONTROLÉE
5.443 *Bouteilles Récoltées*
N° 00000   LES ASSOCIÉS-GÉRANTS
ANNÉE 1985
Mise en bouteille au domaine
PRODUCT OF FRANCE   75 cl

A wine label from *The Red Wines of Burgundy* in the *Regional Guides to the Wines of France Series* (Octopus hbk £4.95)

GLEAVE, DAVID
The Wines of Italy
[1958] Hodder hbk **£8.95**

HAZAN, MARCELLA
Italian Wine
[1885] Penguin hbk **£4.99**

JEFFS, JULIAN
Sherry
[1886] Faber pbk **£3.95**

JOHNSON, HUGH
Hugh Johnson's Map of the English Vineyards **NEW**
Both a touring guide and an introduction to over 250 vineyards which are members of the English Vineyards Association.
[1887] EVA map **£3.50**
The Atlas of German Wines
A comprehensive guide, including touring and road maps with detailed information on leading growers and wine estates.
[1888] M Beazley hbk **£14.95**

METCALFE, CHARLES & MCWHIRTER, KATHRYN
The Wines of Spain and Portugal
[1889] Hodder hbk **£7.95**

RAY, CYRIL
New Book of Italian Wines
[1890] Sidgwick hbk **£10.00**

READ, JAN
The most widely read author in the field of Iberian wines. His books include information on the people and customs of the wine areas he describes, as well as comprehensive details of the wines and their production.
The Pocket Guide to Spanish Wines
[1892] M Beazley hbk **£5.95**
The Wine of Portugal
[1893] Faber pbk **£6.95**
The Wines of Spain
[1894] Faber pbk **£6.95**

ROBERTSON, GEORGE
Port
[1895] Faber pbk **£4.95**

SCHOONMAKER, FRANK
The Wines of Germany
[1897] Faber pbk **£4.95**

WARD, JACK
The Complete Book of Vine Growing in the British Isles
[1898] Faber pbk **£5.25**

Wines of the New World

COOPER, MICHAEL
The Wines & Vineyards of New Zealand
The definitive work on the fashionable cool-climate wines of New Zealand, with detailed discussion of the different regions, winemakers, and vintages of recent years. This is a revised and updated version of the first edition that won the UK Wine Magazine Book of the Year Award in 1986.
[1899] Hodder hbk **£17.95**

A wine label from *Alexis Lichine's Guide to the Wines and Vineyards of France* (Weidenfeld hbk £12.95, Macmillan pbk £9.95)

HALLIDAY, JAMES
Halliday's Australian Wine Guide 1988
[1901] Angus & R pbk **£10.95**
The Australian Wine Compendium
[1902] Angus & R hbk **£19.95**

MAYO, OLIVER
The Wines of Australia
[1903] Faber hbk **£12.95**
[1904] Faber pbk **£6.95**

MUSCATINE, D. AMERINE, M. & THOMPSON, R. (EDS)
California Wine
A very detailed study of all aspects of Californian wine - the definitive guide.
[1905] Sotheby hbk **£37.50**

READ, JAN
Chilean Wines
Valuable guide to the viticulture of Chile, the wines of which are fast gaining in international reputation and popularity. An introduction and tasting notes are provided by Hugh Johnson.
[1959] Sotheby hbk **£19.95**

Spirits & Cocktails

CRADDOCK, HARRY
The Savoy Cocktail Book
[1907] Hamlyn pbk **£3.95**

FAITH, NICHOLAS
Pocket Guide to Cognac & Other Brandies
[1908] M Beazley hbk **£4.95**

HALLGARTEN, PETER A.
Spirits & Liqueurs
[1909] Faber pbk **£4.99**

JACKSON, MICHAEL
Michael Jackson's Pocket Cocktail & Bar Book
[1910] M Beazley hbk **£3.95**

JUNGE, EWALD
Armagnac: The Spirit of Gascony **NEW**
A comprehensive survey of Armagnac, the earthy and more expressive cousin of cognac. Junge describes the history of the spirit and explores the secrets of this region of Gascony.
[1911] Bloomsbury hbk **£12.95**

MACELHONE, HARRY
Harry's ABC of Mixing Cocktails
[I913] Souvenir P hbk **£5.95**

RAY, CYRIL
Cognac
[I914] Harrap hbk **£9.95**
[I915] Harrap pbk **£5.95**

Whisky

COOPER, DEREK
A Taste of Scotch   **NEW**
A delightful anthology of wit and wisdom about
Scotch.
[I918] Deutsch hbk **£9.95**

ELDER, A.
The Whisky Map of Scotland
[I920] Bartholomew pbk **£1.95**

JACKSON, MICHAEL
The World Guide to Whisky
Tastings of hundreds of whiskies each accompanied
by colour reproductions of the labels.
[I921] D Kindersley hbk **£14.95**

MCDOWALL, R.J.S.
The Whiskies of Scotland
[I923] J Murray pbk **£6.95**

Beer & Brewing

The 1990 Good Pub Guide   **NEW**
A guide to over 1200 of the best pubs in Britain.
[I925] Hodder pbk **£9.95**

DAFT, ROLAND
Daft about Lager   **NEW**
A no-nonsense guide to all the lagers available in the
UK.
[I926] Sphere pbk **£3.50**

GLOVER, BRIAN
CAMRA New Beer Guide
The official guide to real beer and brewers.
[I924] David & Ch pbk **£3.95**

HURT, NICK & CHARLIE
**The Perfect Pub Primer: A Guide
to Britain's Best Boozers**   **NEW**
A guide to over 100 pubs which offer not only good
beer but pleasant décor, ambience, service and fellow
drinkers.
[I928] Sidgwick hbk **£5.95**

JACKSON, MICHAEL
**Michael Jackson's Pocket Beer
Book**
[I929] M Beazley hbk **£4.95**

The Glenfiddich Awards

The Glenfiddich Awards, made annually
since 1970, are for writers and
broadcasters who have contributed most
to the civilised appreciation of food and
drink. All written material, apart from
published books, is retyped before being
submitted to the panel to ensure
anonymity. Each category winner
receives a gold medallion, a case of
Glenfiddich malt whisky and a cheque for
£100. The overall winner also receives a
silver pot still trophy and a further cheque
for £750. Here are the respective winners
of the Food and Drink Book of the Year
categories from 1978:

1978   Elizabeth David
English Bread and Yeast Cookery
(Penguin)
1979   Jane Grigson
Jane Grigson's Vegetable Book
(Michael Joseph)
1980   Alan Davidson
North Atlantic Seafood
(Macmillan)
Cyril Ray
Ray On Wine (Dent)
1981   Anne Willan
*The Observer French Cookery
School* (Macdonald)
Derek Cooper
Wine with Food
(Marks & Spencer)
1982   Michael Smith
Cooking with Michael Smith
(Dent)
Burton Anderson *Vino*
(Hutchinson)
1983   Jane Grigson
Jane Grigson's Fruit Book
(M Joseph)
Jancis Robinson
The Great Wine Book
(Sidgwick & Jackson)
1984   Michel & Albert Roux
New Classic Cuisine (Macdonald)
Hugh Johnson:
Hugh Johnson's Wine Companion
(Mitchell Beazley)
1985   Yan-kit So
*Yan-kit So's Classic Chinese
Cookbook*   (D Kindersley)
Rosemary George
The Wines of Chablis (Sotheby)
1986   Lesley Downer & Minoru Yoneda
Step-by-Step Japanese Cooking
(Macdonald)
Kathryn McWhirter (Ed) *Which?
Wine Guide* (Hodder)
1987   Claudia Roden
Middle Eastern Cooking
(Walker Books)
Robert Parker
Bordeaux (Mitchell Beazley)
1988   Julie Sahni
*Classic Indian Vegetarian
Cooking* (D Kindersley)
Hubert Djuiker
The Wines of Rioja
(Mitchell Beazley)
1989   Richard Stein
English Seafood Cookery
(Penguin)
Charles Metcalfe & Kathryn
McWhirter
The Wines of Spain & Portugal
(Salamander Books)

Gardening

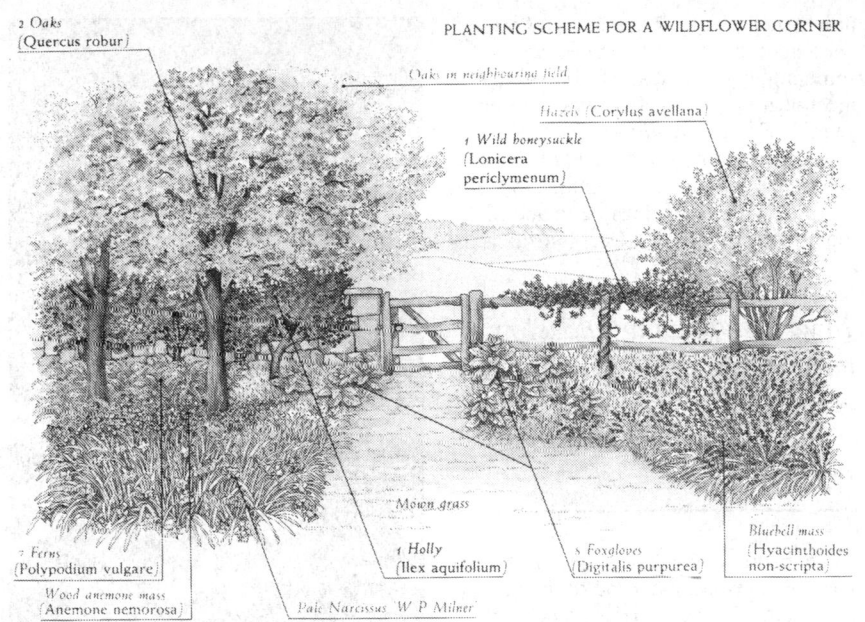

PLANTING SCHEME FOR A WILDFLOWER CORNER

2 Oaks
(Quercus robur)

Oaks in neighbouring field

Hazels (Corylus avellana)

1 Wild honeysuckle
(Lonicera
periclymenum)

Mown grass

7 Ferns
(Polypodium vulgare)

1 Holly
(Ilex aquifolium)

5 Foxgloves
(Digitalis purpurea)

Bluebell mass
(Hyacinthoides
non-scripta)

Wood anemone mass
(Anemone nemorosa)

Pale Narcissus W P Milner

A planting scheme for a Wildflower corner by John Brookes (Photo: Dorling Kindersley)

The Best of Garden Writing Today
Stefan Buczacki

Perhaps it is no more true of gardening than it is of other passionate leisure pursuits. But I find myself unavoidably saying that, as a breed, good gardeners don't generally make good writers. I am unsure why this should be and in a sense I suppose the acres of books in the gardening departments of bookshops would seem to belie my suggestion. But whilst there are indeed (and long have been) gardening books by the score, the presence of good writing between their covers is a very much rarer commodity. In the course of a season, around thirty or forty new titles find their way into my own library. Among them, perhaps half are by writers of whom I have never heard; and a proportion of these by gardeners of whom I have never heard. It is rather unusual for these new titles to throw up a gem, either a literary one or, I am afraid, a very useful one. But things pretty to behold are there in plenty, for the gardening book of today seems rather unfortunately to have become something of a vehicle to keep photographers in employment. But

Pegging out the strawberries from *The Conran Beginner's Guide to Gardening* by Stefan Buczacki (Conran Octopus hbk £12.95)

every season too, I am delighted to say, one of the old and trusted horticultural names produces a book to treasure; a volume that really can keep my attention

even on a warm summer evening with *lilium regale* beckoning across the terrace and a blend of charcoal embers, olive oil, garlic, thyme and the thought of a light Muscadet reminding me that a barbecue is ready. That surely must be the test of any gardening book.

Ask the man in the proverbial street or allotment to name a gardening name and the one that most immediately springs to

The gardening book of today seems rather unfortunately to have become something of a vehicle to keep photographers in employment

his lips will still be that of the late Percy Thrower. But Percy, fine man and great communicator, was not a born writer. His popular titles and compendia have stayed popular and stayed in print because he *was* Percy, not because they are great literature. But press the slightly more serious gardener and ask him to name a gardening author and I will lay short odds and my collection of primulas on their suggesting Christopher Lloyd. Lloyd's gardening reputation was built on a sound pedigree - that of his father Nathaniel Lloyd whose collaboration with Edwin Lutyens produced Great Dixter. But his reputation as an author is based on one of the modern gardening classics, *The Well Tempered Garden*, first published in 1970. And what a breath of fresh air it was and is, coming from Collins (although they have since lost him) in the middle of an era when Hamlyn and other publishing houses seemed to produce nothing more stimulating than X, Y or Z's 'ABC of Gardening'. Lloyd was and is so good because he is individual, happy to strike out and even on rather frequent occasion to become outrageous. You can't possibly always agree with him, but you seldom fail to admire his work.

If Christopher Lloyd has a failing, it is that, almost unavoidably it seems, he can slip into mere cataloguing. If John Brookes has a failing, it is because many people find him too square. To preach gardening design to the masses must have been a lonely and frustrating furrow to plough. But with *The Small Garden* John Brookes succeeded, his approach

having its only drawbacks in that squareness, that angularity that marks so many of his designs. It was with much relief therefore that I welcomed his *A Place in the Country* a few years later for this revealed that he does, after all, have a softer, country garden side to his character. More recently still, he has joined the Dorling Kindersley bandwagon to produce the rather lovely *The Indoor Garden Book* but this says much more about Dorling Kindersley's design department than it does about the author and the poor man has been reduced, like so many others today, to writing a book based on fitting caption words to page layouts. Come on John Brookes: back to what you do best.

Beth Chatto is a name that trips from the lips of the gardening cognoscenti as readily as *rhododendron yakushimanum*. Her Gold Medal winning exhibits of

---

His writing takes some adjusting to, and in its more florid moments is as colourful as the carpet bedding which he shuns

---

unusual plants have become an accepted and regular feature of Chelsea. Recently, she has won many friends with her *Gardening Notebook*, but still I feel has yet to communicate much of the secret behind her evident empathy with

ornamental plants. Nonetheless, I owe her a debt for having produced, with some highly talented artists, one of the most beguilingly lovely books of recent years in *Plant Portraits*.

Geoffrey Smith is a good gardener and a born and individual communicator. His writing takes some adjusting to and in its more florid moments is as colourful as the

---

To write a popular encyclo-paedia with a £30 price tag requires an enthusiastic authority and a compelling tale to tell

---

carpet bedding which he shuns. But at his best, he is inspirational and for me his most valuable and readable work is an early one, *Easy Plants for Difficult Places*, a treasure trove of useful advice from someone who has probably never grown anything in any other than very difficult places in his entire life.

Graham Stuart Thomas was for long Gardens Adviser to the National Trust. But for very much longer he will be adviser to rose growers everywhere. His trilogy - *Climbing Roses Old and New*, *Old Shrub Roses* and *Shrub Roses of Today* are as close to modern classics on specific plants as you will find. Their only rival among my greatly-used rose literature has come from one of England's finest rosarians, Peter Beales. To write a popular encyclopaedia with a £30 price tag requires an enthusiastic authority and a compelling tale to tell. Peter Beales offers both in *Classic Roses*. I am sure his sequel, *Twentieth Century Roses* is equally well crafted; I just can't be as enthusiastic about the subject matter.

It isn't easy to write an exciting book on vegetables. I am not sure that Joy Larkcom managed it with *Vegetables from Small Gardens*, but this handy little book has become a Bible for those with handy little gardens and, together with the late Denys de Saulles' *Home Grown*, should provide the vegetable enthusiast with all that they need. But neither is great literature: the challenge to produce fine words about fine edible plants remains untaken and there is nothing at all on fruit by modern authors to compare remotely with Taylor or Bunyard. That

Stefan Buczacki, author of *Ground Rules for Gardening* (Collins hbk £9.95) (Photo: BBC)

popular modern vogue for wildlife gardening also has yet to produce a worthy literature to compare with that of William Robinson; as indeed has water gardening to stand with Jekyll, so-called organic gardening to stand with anything, or, of course, rock gardening to compare with Reginald Farrer.

But I have left until last Dr David Hessayon, a man whose books must be on every gardener's bookshelf in the land. His is a one-man book production industry without parallel in the history of gardening. Perhaps his success and that of his *Expert* books is to be understood by the fact that he clearly has never set out to produce fine literature, nor indeed been the slave to the photographer's Union. He may not even be a great gardener (although I suspect that he is a very good one), but he knows what gardeners need to know; and he has a first-rate marketing outfit from which many more conventional publishers could learn a lesson.

Stefan Buczacki is the Gardening correspondent of *The Guardian*, and the author of *Ground Rules for Gardening* and *The Conran Beginner's Guide to Gardening*.

GARDENING

Reference & History

BRAY, LYS DE
The Art of Botanical Illustration **NEW**
A fascinating, highly-illustrated survey of botanical illustration from the earliest practitioners, covering the work of Redouté, Hill, Sowerby and many others.
[J0] C Helm hbk **£25.00**

CROWE, SYLVIA
Garden Design
Essential reading for all landscape architects and students. Describes different styles including Oasis, Sino-Japanese, Hispano-Arabic, and Italian.
[J1] Packard hbk **£20.00**

FELTWELL, JOHN
The Naturalist's Garden
From gardeners of antiquity (2000 BC - 1485 AD) through the Pleasure Garden to the Naturalist's garden of today. Achievements of naturalists from Pliny to William Robinson. Excellent and well-illustrated text. Worth looking at if you have never explored garden history.
[J2] Ebury P hbk **£12.95**

FISHER, JOHN
The Origins of Garden Plants
A substantial and well-illustrated history of the discovery and origins of nearly 1,000 of the flowers and shrubs found in our gardens today. The work of the early merchant adventurers, the great planthunters, the botanists and famous nurserymen is vividly brought to life. Excellent index and bibliography.
[J3] Constable hbk **£12.95**

GLEDHILL, D.
The Names of Plants **NEW**
A new edition of a very useful compilation of the Latin names of plants, with explanatory notes on their meanings.
[J4] Cambridge pbk **£8.95**

GOODE, PATRICK & LANCASTER, MICHAEL (EDS)
The Oxford Companion to Gardens
As with all the Oxford Companions this is an excellent and authoritative work.
[J5] Oxford hbk **£29.50**

JELLICOE, SIR GEOFFREY & SUSAN
Landscape of Man
The shaping of the environment from prehistory to the present day. A revised and expanded edition of this important work by the man who worked on Sutton Place, the largest landscaping project in this half of the century.
[J6] Thames & H pbk **£12.95**

JOYCE, DAVID
An Illustrated History of Garden Design
[J7] Hamlyn hbk **£17.95**

ROYAL HORTICULTURAL SOCIETY
Dictionary of Gardening
Edited by F.J. Chittenden in 4 volumes and supplement. This is a standard reference work for gardeners in the British Isles. It contains cultural and botanical details of garden plants and technical summaries of horticultural operations.
[J8] Oxford hbk **£195.00**
Supplement
Published in 1969, it contains revisions, amendments and updating of articles in the main volumes.
[J9] Oxford hbk **£45.00**

STEARN, W.T.
Botanical Latin
A standard comprehensive guidebook of descriptive terminology in both English and Latin for botanists and gardeners.
[J10] David & Ch hbk **£18.00**

THACKER, CHRISTOPHER
The History of Gardens
[J11] C Helm hbk **£13.95**

USHER, GEORGE
Dictionary of Botany
[J12] Constable hbk **£5.95**

Gardens Open in the UK

Gardens of England and Wales Open to the Public 1989
[J13] Seymour pbk **£1.50**

Historic Houses, Castles and Gardens Open to the Public 1989
Revised annually. Magazine format. Lists all important details.
[J14] BLP pbk **£4.50**

COTTON, SARAH (ED)
Guide to the Specialist Nurseries and Garden Suppliers of Britain and Ireland
An invaluable sourcebook on where to obtain more unusual or specialist items.
[J15] Garden Art P pbk **£8.95**

PHILIP, C. (ED)
The Plant Finder: Hardy Plant Society's Directory
Over 20,000 plants in general cultivation are brought together in one alphabetical list together with the relevant details of more than 300 nurseries which sell them. Includes addresses, opening times, prices etc.
[J16] Moorland pbk **£7.95**

RIX, ALISON & MARTYN
Gardens Open Today
A guide to gardens open to the public through the National Gardens Scheme. Published to celebrate the Diamond Jubilee of the scheme, through which 2,000 gardens in England and Wales are regularly open to the public. More than 600 of these gardens have been chosen for this guide, and in each case the owner or head gardener has written about his garden. 100 commissioned colour photos.
[J17] Mermaid pbk **£9.95**

British Gardening & Gardeners

The British tradition of gardening can be said to have had its real starting point in the Renaissance, when the dissemination of European culture, particularly that of France and Italy, gave rise to a recognisable Tudor style, incorporating highly intricate mazes, topiary

Illustration from *The Naturalist's Garden* by John Feltwell (Ebury Press hbk £12.95)

and the so-called 'knot-gardens'. By the 18th century, with the emergence of the country house as a distinct feature of British life and landscape, the influence and esteem in which the gardener/designer was held had grown tremendously. *William Kent* and *Capability Brown*, the pioneers of the landscape tradition, were the first in a long line of designers who have influenced the shape and history of British gardening. Also included here are several modern gardening writers who have in recent years helped and inspired the modern gardener: *Christopher Lloyd*, *Beth Chatto* and *Graham Stuart Thomas* are now universally regarded as required reading.

BEST, C. & BOISSET, C.
Leaves from the Garden
200 years of inspired garden writing by the best and most famous gardeners from Humphry Repton and William Cobbett to Margery Fish and John Brookes. The only anthology of its kind, illustrated with charming early b/w photos and some colour. An excellent reference work, source of new ideas for the practising gardener, and a good value gift for the armchair gardener.
[J18] J Murray hbk **£14.95**

BLOOM, ALAN
A contemporary nurseryman, and creator of the outstanding Bressingham gardens in Norfolk, which contain some 5,000 species. He himself is a specialist in hardy, herbaceous plants.
A Plantsman's Perspective: Experiences and Thoughts
[J19] Collins hbk **£9.95**

BOYD, ARABELLA LENNOX- & CLAY, PERRY
Traditional English Gardens
Explores the 'English Style' through 28 gardens in the care of the National Trust.
[J20] Weidenfeld hbk **£10.95**
[J21] Weidenfeld pbk **£6.95**

BROOKES, JOHN
The New Small Garden **NEW**
[J22] D Kindersley **£14.95**

BROWN, CAPABILITY (1715 - 1783)
English 18th century landscape gardener of genius whose nickname referred to his custom of assessing the 'capabilities' of a landscape. The surroundings of many great country houses, including Harewood and Blenheim bear witness to his skill. His unique style of landscape design was influenced by the 'picturesque' principle of creating gardens in the manner of pictures, offering views of perfect composition.

Landscape gardeners such as Brown constructed parks which looked like wild nature, but were in fact an ingenious man-made creation, with artificial lakes and slopes.

STROUD, DOROTHY
Capability Brown
Definitive work on Brown. Gives accounts of his commissions and achievements. Concludes with his principles and a list of works.
[J23] Faber pbk **£9.95**

TURNER, ROGER
Capability Brown and the 18th Century English Landscape
[J24] Weidenfeld hbk **£16.95**

BROWN, JANE
The English Garden in our Time: From Gertrude Jekyll to Geoffrey Jellicoe
The garden writer of the moment discusses famous garden designers including Jekyll, Jellicoe and Vita Sackville-West. Informative on formal and natural designs.
[J25] Antique Coll Club hbk **£19.50**

CHATTO, BETH
Garden Notebook
A charming and fascinating account of the author's gardening year.
[J26] Dent **£12.95**
Plant Portraits
A selection of 100 plants discussed by this highly experienced gardener and illustrated by leading botanical artists. Full of tips, and well presented.
[J27] Dent hbk **£12.95**
The Green Tapestry NEW
A quite magnificent book looking at Beth Chatto's own garden. 250 full colour illustrations.
[J28] Collins **£16.95**

COUNTRY LIFE
Gardens in Edwardian England
Recent reprint of a volume of gloriously nostalgic b/w photographs from the *Country Life* collections showing the great houses and gardens of the turn of this century in their heyday. Many of these gardens have since disappeared or changed radically, making this a fascinating reference record.
[J29] Antique Coll Club pbk **£25.00**

ELLACOMBE, CANON HENRY NICHOLSON (1822 - 1916)
A contemporary and friend of Gertrude Jekyll, who spent most of his life at Bitton vicarage in Gloucestershire.
In a Gloucestershire Garden
In this series of articles, Canon Ellacombe recounts how he chose, planted, pruned and shaped the flowers, trees and shrubs which drew visitors to his garden.
[J30] Century pbk **£4.95**

FISH, MARGERY (1893 - 1969)
Well known for her vitality, Margery Fish created her own garden at East Lambrook manor in Somerset, and brought back into fashion some of the old flowers used by Gertrude Jekyll.
A Flower for Every Day
[J31] Faber pbk **£3.95**
Carefree Gardening NEW
[J32] Faber pbk **£4.95**
Cottage Garden Flowers
[J33] Faber pbk **£4.95**
Gardening in the Shade
[J34] Faber pbk **£4.50**
Ground Cover Plants
[J35] Faber pbk **£4.95**
We Made a Garden
[J36] Faber pbk **£3.50**

CLARK, TIMOTHY
Margery Fish's Country Gardening NEW
[J37] David & Ch **£14.95**

GRAY, R. & FRANKEL, E.
Cambridge Gardens
Outlines the development of Cambridge's open spaces. Describes each of the established college gardens and the University Botanic Garden. Full of colour photographs.
[J38] Pevensey pbk **£5.95**
Oxford Gardens
Extensive description of the major college gardens and a survey of the Botanical Gardens - the oldest in Britain, dating back to the 17th century.
[J39] Pevensey pbk **£7.95**

HADFIELD, MILES
A History of British Gardening
The essential book in this field: informative and reliable on all subjects from the introduction of potatoes to the importance of Kew. Wonderful appendix by the Jellicoes on modern garden history, and a comprehensive bibliography.
[J40] J Murray pbk **£15.00**
[J41] Penguin pbk **£6.95**

HARVEY, JOHN
Medieval Gardens NEW
[J42] Batsford hbk **£12.95**
Restoring Period Gardens
Describes British gardens from the Middle Ages to George IV with guidance on the principles and practice.
[J43] Shire pbk **£3.95**

HAYDEN, PETER
Biddulph Grange, Staffordshire: A Victorian Garden Rediscovered NEW
Recently acquired by the National Trust, Biddulph Grange was one of the greatest gardens of Victorian times, now being restored after nearly a century of neglect.
[J44] G Philip hbk **£14.95**

HILL, THOMAS
Probably the author of the first published book on gardening, which appeared in 1563. It was a practical book for the Elizabethan era which apparently had a public prepared to buy such works.
The Gardener's Labyrinth
Blend of down-to-earth advice and superstition. Informal and enthusiastic, and giving an insight into life in the 16th and 17th centuries.
[J45] Oxford hbk **£14.95**
[J46] Oxford pbk **£7.95**

HOBHOUSE, PENELOPE
Gertrude Jekyll on Gardening
[J47] Collins hbk **£15.00**
[J48] Macmillan pbk **£6.95**
Private Gardens of England
33 of England's private living gardens selected for their diversity in style.
[J49] Weidenfeld pbk **£20.00**

HUNT, JOHN DIXON
William Kent: Landscape Garden Designer
A study of Kent's landscape garden designs. Assesses his contribution to the English landscape garden.
[J50] Zwemmer hbk **£29.95**

JACKSON-STOPS, GERVASE
The Country House Garden: A Grand Tour
Contemplates exceptional garden features of the great British country houses. Includes avenues, gates and

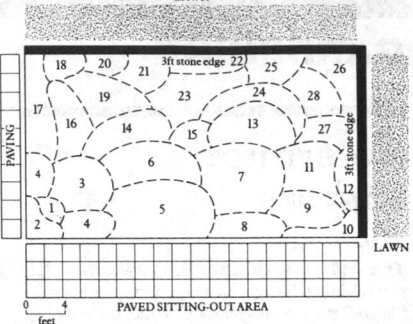

An open site with low permanent contents. Contents in the order they are described:

1. *Senecio elaeagnifolius buchananii*
2. *Festuca glauca*
3. *Acaena affinis*
4. *Ajuga reptans* 'Multicolor'
5. *Juniperus procumbens* 'Nana'
6. *Hebe* 'Mrs Winder'
7. *Euonymus fortunei* 'Silver Queen'
8. *Euphorbia myrsinites*
9. *Arum italicum* 'Pictum'
10. *Geranium renardii*
11. *Euphorbia amygdaloides* 'Rubra'
12. *Pulmonaria saccharata*
13. *Pinus mugo pumilio*
14. *Ballota pseudodictamnus*
15. *Genista lydia*
16. *Hebe* 'Edinensis'
17. *Calluna vulgaris* 'Golden Feather'
18. *Phormium tenax* 'Bronze Baby'
19. *Ruta graveolens* 'Jackman's Blue'
20. *Mentha rotundifolia* 'Variegata'
21. *Artemisia pontica*
22. *Helianthemum* 'Wisley Pink'
23. *Helictotrichon sempervirens*
24. *Hebe ochracea* (armstrongii)
25. *Hebe albicans*
26. *Anthemis cupaniana*
27. *Santolina pinnata neapolitana*
28. *Eryngium bourgati*

A planting plan from *Foliage Plants* by Christopher Lloyd (Viking hbk £12.95, Penguin pbk £7.95)

gatehouses, knots and parterres, cascades and fountains. Lively text and full colour photographs.
[J51] Weidenfeld hbk **£16.00**

JEKYLL, GERTRUDE (1843 - 1932)
As one of the most influential designers in this century, gardeners still look to her for ideas, advice and inspiration. She possessed a remarkable ability to visualise colour, form and texture to create, in particular, herbaceous borders of outstanding natural beauty. A significant part of her work was in collaboration with Lutyens - together they worked on at least 100 designs.
Children and Gardens
[J52] Antique Coll Club hbk **£12.95**
Colour Schemes for the Flower Garden
Practical and inspirational. Includes her planting plans in colour and an appendix of previously unpublished designs.
[J53] Windward hbk **£14.95**
[J54] Antique Coll Club hbk **£12.95**
Gardener's Essential Gertrude Jekyll
[J55] Breshich & F pbk **£3.95**
Gardener's Testament
[J56] Antique Coll Club hbk **£12.95**
Gardens for Small Country Houses
[J57] Antique Coll Club hbk **£17.50**
Home and Garden
[J58] Antique Coll Club hbk **£12.95**
Roses for English Gardens
[J59] Antique Coll Club hbk **£12.95**
[J60] Penguin pbk **£7.95**
The Making of a Garden: An Anthology
[J61] Antique Coll Club pbk **£12.95**
Wall, Water and Woodland Gardens
[J62] Antique Coll Club hbk **£12.95**
Wood and Garden
[J63] Antique Coll Club hbk **£12.95**

MASSINGHAM, BETTY
Miss Jekyll: Portrait of a Great Gardener
The popular biography. Of general interest to all

gardeners and plantsmen. Many quotations from Jekyll's own books and b/w illustrations.
[J64] David & Ch hbk **£12.50**
[J66] David & Ch pbk **£6.50**

TANKARD, JUDITH B. & VALKEEN-BURGH, M. VAN
Gertrude Jekyll: A Vision of
Garden and Wood   **NEW**
A beautiful collection of Jekyll's own photographs.
[J65] J Murray **£20.00**

KEEN, LADY MARY
The Glory of the English Garden   **NEW**
An example of the most sumptuous in gardening publishing, with an authoritative and interesting text.
[J67] Barrie & J hbk **£25.00**

LLEWELLYN, RODDY
Elegance and Eccentricity   **NEW**
Profusely illustrated, this book is both a history of, and a guide to, the styles and features of the country house garden.
[J68] Ward Lock hbk **£20.00**

LLOYD, CHRISTOPHER
Head gardener at Great Dixter, Northiam in East Sussex, and a prolific writer for *Country Life*, the *Guardian* and the *Observer*. Regarded by many as essential, as well as very entertaining, reading.
Foliage Plants
[J69] Viking hbk **£12.95**
[J70] Penguin pbk **£7.95**
The Adventurous Gardener
A survey of the preoccupations, reflections, prejudices and passions of this witty, wise and influential gardener.
[J71] Viking hbk **£12.95**
[J72] Penguin pbk **£5.95**
The Well-Chosen Garden
[J73] H Hamilton hbk **£12.50**
The Well-Tempered Garden
[J74] Viking hbk **£12.95**
[J75] Penguin pbk **£9.99**
The Year at Great Dixter
A very personal account of the events and pattern of life through a year at this famous Lutyens garden - the home of Lloyd himself. The pictures are, on the whole, decorative rather than informative.
[J76] Viking hbk **£15.95**

MILNE, AVILDE LEES- & VEREY, ROSEMARY
The Englishman's Garden
[J77] Viking hbk **£14.95**

PAGE, RUSSELL (1906 - 1985)
Education of a Gardener
Described by Anne Scott-James as 'a book for the connoisseur - not a how-to-do-it book but a thoughtful reminiscence of his gardening experience by one of the best garden designers of our time'.
[J78] Penguin pbk **£5.95**

PLUMPTRE, GEORGE
The Latest Country Gardens
A survey of the period since 1945: the emergence of British gardens from the stagnation and destruction of the war years and the picture of achievements since the 1950s. Includes a gazetteer of new gardens, many of which are open to the public.
[J79] Bodley pbk **£16.00**

RIDGE, ANTONIA
For Love of a Rose
The story of two families, the Meillands in Lyons and the Paolinos in Antibes, who shared a common devotion to roses. United through marriage and their work together, they around the world famous Peace Rose at the end of the Second World War.
[J80] Faber pbk **£2.95**

ROBINSON, WILLIAM (1838 - 1935)
Irish-born plantsman, editor, writer and curator of the Royal Botanic Society, Regent's Park. His travels abroad inspired his appreciation of the natural habitat, and in Britain heralded a movement of naturalistic planting of indigenous wild flowers.
Wild Garden
Published in 1870, Robinson's book has had a profound influence on gardening thought and theory and has never been more topical than today, when so many of our wayside and woodland flowers are being lost to urban development and insecticides. Robinson attacks the formal artificiality of high-Victorian gardens and passionately advocates the planting of wild and native flowers.
[J81] Century pbk **£5.95**

ROPER, LANNING (1912 - 1983)
American-born landscape gardener and garden correspondent to the *Sunday Times*. He was responsible for various National Trust gardens, at the same time as designing on a large scale for private clients - notably the Aga Khan.
BROWN, JANE
Lanning Roper and his Gardens
With access to Roper's private papers Brown has produced a thorough and sympathetic biography and critique of his work. Illustrations include many of Roper's own photographs and architect's plans etc.
[J82] Weidenfeld hbk **£20.00**
[J83] Weidenfeld pbk **£10.95**

SACKVILLE-WEST, V. (1892 - 1962)
English poet, novelist, close friend of Virginia Woolf, and a passionate gardener. With her husband Sir Harold Nicolson, she created Sissinghurst, now one of the National Trust's most widely visited gardens.
V. Sackville-West's Garden Book
A compilation of the best of her garden journalism originally published in the *Observer* between 1947 and 1961. Her informal style is engaging and accessible, revealing amazing insights including her conception of the White Garden.
[J84] M Joseph pbk **£7.95**
BROWN, JANE
Gardens of a Golden Afternoon: The Story of a Partnership
[J85] Penguin pbk **£8.95**
SACKVILLE -WEST, V. & FOX, ROBIN LANE
The Illustrated Garden Book
A new anthology of her gardening articles. Fox

A Dahlia from *The Best Plants for Your Garden* by Anne Scott-James (Conran Octopus hbk £14.95)

A Rosa Alba 'Celestial' from *The Illustrated Garden Book* by V. Sackville-West and Robin Lane Fox (Mermaid pbk £9.99)

supplies an excellent introduction and background to the articles which explains the influences on Vita's gardening principles. Outstanding photographs of Sissinghurst as it is today.
[J86] Mermaid pbk **£9.99**

SAVILLE, DIANA
Gardens for Small Country Houses
[J87] Macmillan pbk **£7.95**

SCOTT-JAMES, ANNE
A radio personality and a specialist in garden writing, whose individual approach endears her to garden lovers everywhere.
Down to Earth
[J88] M Joseph hbk **£9.95**
Sissinghurst: The Making of a Garden
From the Nicolsons' own notes, diaries and letters, the author records how this famous garden was made - how Harold designed it and Vita chose the plants. A fascinating story, well told.
[J89] M Joseph pbk **£8.95**
The Best Plants for Your Garden
A selection of 200 plants each of which is individually illustrated and described in a very personal way.
[J90] Octopus hbk **£14.95**
The Cottage Garden
[J91] Penguin pbk **£6.95**
The Language of the Garden: A Personal Anthology
[J92] Penguin pbk **£5.95**

STRONG, ROY
The Renaissance Garden in England
A good account of the evolution, design and meaning of palace gardens and great gardens. It explores the people and ideas that led to the creation of the great formal gardens of England under the Tudors and Stuarts, which were later destroyed en masse by the exponents of Landscape Style. The book includes surviving plans and diagrams of these lost gardens of England.
[J93] Thames & H pbk **£9.95**

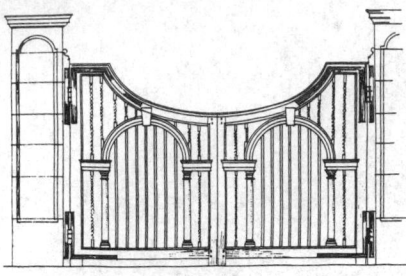

WOODEN GATES (NOW DISUSED)

Wooden gates from *Formal Gardens in England and Scotland* by Inigo Triggs (Antique Collectors Club hbk £25.00)

THOMAS, GRAHAM STUART
A prolific artist, writer and plantsman, whose speciality is roses, of which he has established a unique collection. He is also a consultant to the National Trust.
Art of Planting
Or, *The Planter's Handbook*.
[J94] Dent pbk **£13.50**
Climbing Roses, Old and New
[J95] Dent hbk **£12.95**
Complete Flower Paintings and Drawings of Graham Stuart Thomas
[J96] Thames & H hbk **£25.00**
Garden of Roses
[J97] Pavilion hbk **£16.95**
Gardens of the National Trust
[J98] Weidenfeld hbk **£14.95**
Old Shrub Roses
[J99] Dent hbk **£11.50**
Perennial Garden Plants
Or, *The Modern Florilegium*.
[J100] Dent hbk **£16.00**
Plants for Ground Cover
[J101] Dent hbk **£14.50**
Recreating the Period Garden
[J102] Collins hbk **£9.95**
Shrub Roses of Today
[J103] Dent hbk **£10.95**

TRIGGS, INIGO
Formal Gardens in England and Scotland
[J104] Antique Coll Club hbk **£25.00**

TURNER, TOM
English Garden Design: History and Styles since 1650
Describes eleven main styles: Enclosed, French, Dutch, Forest, Serpentine, Irregular, Transition, Italian, Mixed, Arts and Crafts and Abstract, developed by designers from Kent, Brown and Repton to Jekyll, Lutyens and Jellicoe. 300 illustrations.
[J104A] Antique Coll Club hbk **£19.95**

Foreign Styles of Gardening

AGNELLI, MARELLA
Gardens of the Italian Villas
[J105] Weidenfeld hbk **£35.00**

BROOKES, JOHN
Gardens of Paradise
The history and design of the great Islamic gardens. Extensively illustrated, the book includes maps of the garden locations and plans of layouts.
[J106] Weidenfeld hbk **£20.00**

DOHNA, V.
Private Gardens of Germany
Superb collection of photographs and descriptions of the finest German gardens.
[J107] Weidenfeld hbk **£30.00**

ITOH, TEIJI
The Gardens of Japan
Photographs of the finest gardens of Japan and text on the essence of Japanese gardening and its relation to houses and people.
[J108] Kodansha hbk **£72.00**

KESWICK, MAGGIE
The Chinese Garden
[J109] Academy Eds hbk **£24.95**
[J110] Academy Eds pbk **£14.95**

KUCK, LORAINE
The World of the Japanese Garden
[J111] Weatherhill hbk **£27.50**

MASSON, GEORGINA
Italian Gardens
[J112] Antique Coll Club hbk **£25.00**

SAWANO, TAKASHI (ED)
Art of Japanese Gardening   **NEW**
[J113] Hamlyn hbk **£9.95**

SCHINZ, MARINA & LITTLEFIELD, SUSAN
Visions of Paradise
280 superb evocative photographs of the Western World's best loved gardens. The text is good and chapters include 'The Herb Garden', 'The Designed Landscape' etc. Reasonable value for such a good-looking book.
[J114] Thames & H hbk **£25.00**

SEIKE, KIYOSHI; MASANOBU, KUDO & ENGEL, DAVID H.
A Japanese Touch for Your Garden
A concise introduction to the practical aspects of making a Japanese garden. Learn about Japanese lanterns, miniature pagodas, water basins, gates and walls. Detailed information on plants and trees, moss, bamboo etc. Packed with colour illustrations.
[J115] Kodansha hbk **£14.95**

VALDES, MARQUESA DE CASA
Spanish Gardens
An extensive study of Spanish gardens from Roman times to the present day.
[J116] Antique Coll Club hbk **£29.95**

WOODBRIDGE, K.
Princely Gardens
Traces the origins and development of the French formal style. Examples of great gardens are illustrated with contemporary engravings and modern b/w photographs.
[J117] Thames & H hbk **£32.00**

Theory & Practice of Design

Titles under this heading are concerned primarily with the conception, planning and construction of a garden, rather than with plantsmanship. There is some overlap, however, with the section covering *Practical Gardening*. For specific garden styles - eg. Container, Town and Water - see *Types of Gardens*.

ALEXANDER, R.
The English Gardening School
A complete course in garden planning and design useful for both the amateur and the professional. Based on courses held at the English Gardening School at the Chelsea Physic Garden, the book is abundantly illustrated with diagrams, line drawings, charts and colour photographs. Surely one of the best books of its type, as it gives equal weight to the practical/structural and the planting/colour aspects of design.
[J118] M Joseph pbk **£14.95**

BROOKES, JOHN
Place in the Country
[J119] Thames & H hbk **£12.50**
Room Outside: New Approach to Garden Design
This new approach to garden design sees the garden as a usable extension of the home, and here Brookes deals with the creation of a contemporary garden. Excellent advice on planting as well as on surfacing, walling, soil, etc. For the ordinary gardener who wants to make something worthwhile of his small plot. Very good clear illustrations.
[J120] Thames & H pbk **£4.95**
The Country Garden: How to Create the Natural Look in Your Garden
Principles of garden design sympathetic to the ways of nature by this leading garden designer and writer. Includes information on how to create a 'country style' in the town or country. Includes a plant list for different types of soil.
[J121] D Kindersley hbk **£16.95**
The Garden Book
[J122] D Kindersley hbk **£14.95**

BROOKS, JUDY
Garden Plans: New Designs for Small Gardens
[J123] G Philip hbk **£12.95**

FOX, ROBIN LANE
Variations on a Garden
Conveys a clear style of planting and design and picks out the plants and arrangements which mark out the changing seasons.
[J124] Lane Fox hbk **£10.95**

HOBHOUSE, PENELOPE
Garden Style
[J125] Windward hbk **£14.95**
The National Trust Book of Gardening
Explains how gardening is done on the National Trust properties. States the policies and theories underlying the work of the Trust in maintaining and recreating Britain's great gardens.
[J126] Pavilion pbk **£9.95**
The Smaller Garden
[J127] Collins hbk **£9.95**

KELLY, JOHN
The All-Seasons Gardens
How to plan a year-round framework of evergreens with garden features such as walls, hedges, pergolas

GARDENING

A Tudor knot from *Classic Garden Design* by Rosemary Verey (John Murray pbk £9.95)

and lawns, and then plant for colour. With good illustrations and charts giving in season and out-of-season features, it is aimed at the ambitious amateur.
[J128] Windward hbk **£9.95**

MANSFIELD, DEREK
Fitted Garden: Wall to Wall Garden Design
To help beginners understand that structure is as important as plants. Useful sections on pricing, engaging professional help, and on gardens for children and the disabled.
[J129] Ward Lock hbk **£9.95**

PAUL, ANTHONY & REES, YVONNE
The Garden Design Book
Examines the principles on which 15 of the best of today's garden designers work and explains how to make them work for you. Covers the basic framework - boundaries, paths and patios - and special features such as fountains, and garden furniture.
[J130] Collins hbk **£19.95**

THOMAS, GRAHAM STUART
Recreating the Period Garden
A practical book offering all the necessary information you will need to begin to reconstruct single features or whole gardens in a period suited to your house and surroundings. Plenty of diagrams and old photos.
[J131] Collins hbk **£9.95**

VEREY, ROSEMARY
Classic Garden Design NEW
Recreating features of gardens in the past.
[J132] J Murray pbk **£9.95**

WHITEN, FAITH & GEOFF
The Chelsea Flower Show
An affectionate tribute to the great institution which inspires thousands of people who visit it every year. Up-to-date design ideas. Includes many full-colour pictures taken at the 1987 Show.
[J133] Cassell hbk **£16.95**
[J134] Cassell pbk **£9.95**

Garden Ornament

RALSTON, MICHAEL
The Well-Furnished Garden
A new treasury and directory for all kinds of garden ornament - very useful.
[J135] M Beazley hbk **£12.95**

CARR, DAVID
Topiary and Plant Sculpture NEW
A beginner's step-by-step guide.
[J136] Crowood hbk **£10.95**

CLARKE, ETHNE & CLAY, PERRY
English Topiary Gardens
Not a practical book but included here for inspiration.
[J137] Weidenfeld hbk **£10.95**

CLEVELY, A.M.
Topiary: The Art of Clipped Trees and Ornamental Hedges
A history of topiary from the days of Ancient Rome. Also detailed instructions for creating different shapes plus methods of espaliering, pleaching, pollarding and other effects.
[J138] Collins hbk **£14.95**

JEKYLL, GERTRUDE
Garden Ornament
Invaluable reprint of one of Jekyll's last books which consists mainly of magnificent b/w photos (from the *Country Life* collection) showing examples of ornament and its proper use. Gates, steps, urns, orangeries, dovecotes, sundials, topiary, pergolas, ponds, and bridges arc all illustrated. A wonderful source of inspiration for gardening on a grander scale.
[J139] Antique Coll Club hbk **£25.00**

LACEY, GERALDINE
Creating Topiary
Highly illustrated practical book which combines history and practical advice on the art of topiary. Techniques for both formal and whimsical shapes explained.
[J140] Garden Art P hbk **£14.95**

PLUMPTRE, GEORGE
Garden Ornament NEW
A highly illustrated new survey of ornamental features throughout the history of the Western garden.
[J141] Thames & H hbk **£25.00**

STEVENS, DAVID
Pergolas, Arbours, Gazebos, Follies
Many finely photographed examples to inspire the enthusiastic amateur garden designer.
[J142] Ward Lock hbk **£12.95**

Practical Guides & Manuals

Titles under this heading are in most cases general, covering a wide selection of techniques, planting schemes etc in one volume. For the beginner there is a bewildering choice. Any authors whose work appears in the *British Gardening & Gardeners* section will always be excellent. There are also some series: any titles published by, or in association with, the Royal Horticultural Society (viz the *RHS Encyclopaedia of Practical Gardening*) is recommended. Excellent too are the *Wisley Handbooks*, which cover nearly every topic, and are written by experts in the field - at £2.95 they are splendid value. There is still little to compare with the *Expert* series by Dr. Hessayon, published by PBI - not expensive, and packed with information, they are excellent for quick reference. Another recommended series is the *Garden Bookshelf* from Windward, which concentrates on the planting schemes and designs of particular styles.

BALL, JEFF & CRESSON, CHARLES
The Sixty Minute Flower Garden
A garden full of flowers in just one hour a week.
[J143] WH Allen pbk **£10.95**

BISGROVE, RICHARD
The Flower Garden NEW
[J144] Windward hbk **£10.95**

BONAR, ANN
The Garden Plant Survival Manual
The quick, authoritative answer to every gardener's day-to-day questions about gardening, from soil types, light and water needs, through propagation, pruning, and planting, to the best treatment for pests and disease. Includes a plant-by-plant guide with specific information on the care of individual plants and varieties.
[J145] Ward Lock pbk **£7.95**

BOWN, DENNY
Alba NEW
Creating the entirely 'white' garden.
[J146] Unwin Hyman **£14.95**

BRAY, LYS DE
Borders: A Guide to Spring, Summer, and Autumn Colour
[J147] Ward Lock hbk **£14.95**
The Green Garden: The Art of Foliage Planting
Shows that labour-saving foliage plants can provide a wide range of colour and for a much longer season of interest too.
[J148] Ward Lock hbk **£8.95**

BRICKELL, CHRISTOPHER (ED)
RHS Encyclopaedia of Plants and Flowers NEW
A lavishly produced book, from the most reliable of organisations, the RHS. It will undoubtedly become a classic.
[J149] D Kindersley hbk **£25.00**

BROOKES, JOHN & BECKETT, KENNETH
The Gardener's Index of Plants and Flowers
A quick reference guide to the characteristics and cultivation of over 4,000 popular plants. Divided into categories, eg. shrubs, perennials, bulbs, water, plants, with charts giving information on height, flowering season, colour and soil preference. One of the best of its type.
[J150] D Kindersley hbk **£10.95**

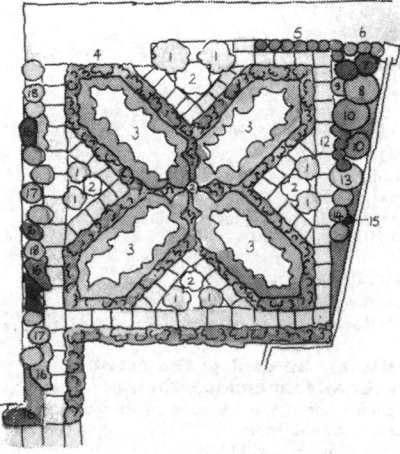

A plant scheme from *The Flower Garden* by Richard Bisgrove (Windward hbk £10.95)

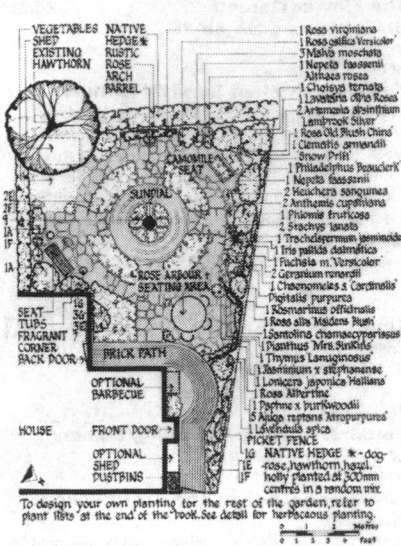

A garden plan from *Trouble-Free Gardening* by Susan Hampshire (Elm Tree Books hbk £13.95)

BUCHAN, URSULA
The Pleasures of Gardening
An intelligent look at what is involved in gardening for the beginner who wants more than glossy photographs.
[J151] Dent hbk **£12.95**

BUCZACKI, STEFAN
The Conran Beginner's Guide to Gardening
Looks at every aspect of gardening from scratch covering, planning, flowers, vegetables, fruit, even the buying of gardening tools.
[J152] Octopus hbk **£12.95**

CARR, DAVID
Getting the Best from Clay Gardens **NEW**
[J153] Ward Lock hbk **£8.95**

CHATTO, BETH
Damp Garden
Cannot be bettered as a source of advice and inspiration for those gardening on wet soil.
[J154] Dent pbk **£6.50**
Dry Garden
Invaluable for anyone who has struggled on dry soil - ideas on selecting plants for dry soils and in dry seasons and on improving conditions.
[J155] Dent pbk **£4.95**

COLBORN, NIGEL
Getting the Best from Exposed Gardens **NEW**
[J156] Ward Lock hbk **£8.95**
Leisurely Gardening: The Art of the Low-Maintenance Garden **NEW**
A guide to creating an attractive garden with the minimum of effort.
[J157] C Helm hbk **£12.95**

COMPTON, JAMES
Success with Unusual Plants
With photos by David Russell.
[J158] Collins hbk **£12.95**

EVANS, ALFRED
The Peat Garden
[J159] Cassell/Wisley pbk **£1.15**

EVISON, J.R.B.
Gardening on Lime and Chalk
[J160] Cassell/Wisley pbk **£2.95**

FERGUSON, NICOLA
Right Plant, Right Place
Unique in layout, this book will lead gardeners quickly and easily to the plants which will look best and grow best in their own particular garden. The plants are organised according to growing conditions, purpose and appearance.
[J161] Pan hbk **£8.95**

FOX, ROBIN LANE
Better Gardening
Entered in this sub-section because it could be missed elsewhere by the keen amateur. In format this does not appear to be a practical guide or manual, but it is a treasure-trove of useful hints - and the author's experience and good taste show through everywhere.
[J162] Penguin pbk **£5.95**

HAMPSHIRE, SUSAN
Trouble-Free Gardening **NEW**
Gardens which require little or no attention.
[J163] Elm Tree hbk **£13.95**

HAY, ROY & SYNGE, PATRICK M.
The Dictionary of Garden Plants in Colour with House and Greenhouse Plants
An enduring classic with lots of colour pictures and entirely reliable information laid out clearly.
[J164] M Joseph hbk **£19.95**
[J165] Mermaid pbk **£12.95**

HESSAYON, DR D.G.
The Armchair Book of the Garden
[J166] Century hbk **£9.95**
[J167] PBI pbk **£4.95**
The Garden Expert
[J168] PBI pbk **£2.95**
The Lawn Expert
[J169] PBI pbk **£2.95**

HOBHOUSE, PENELOPE
Borders **NEW**
[J170] Pavilion **£10.95**
Colour in Your Garden
Outlines the principles of colour and shows how to make garden pictures. More than 1,000 plants are grouped by colour and then by season. Beautifully produced and in full colour.
[J171] Collins hbk **£17.50**
The Country Gardener **NEW**
This will undoubtedly become another classic from Penelope Hobhouse.
[J172] Windward hbk **£14.95**

LACEY, STEPHEN
Startling Jungle: Colour and Scent in the Romantic Garden
Very readable and enthusiastic: it offers the gardener creative and practical advice on the use of colour and scent and the selection and artistic grouping of plants.
[J173] Viking hbk **£12.95**
[J174] Penguin pbk **£7.95**

LLOYD, CHRISTOPHER
The Adventurous Gardener
[J175] Penguin pbk **£5.95**
The Mixed Border
[J176] RHS/Cassell pbk **£2.95**

MCHOY, PETER
Getting the Best from Chalky Gardens **NEW**
[J177] Ward Lock hbk **£8.95**

PEARSON, ROBERT
The Winter Garden **NEW**
[J178] RHS/Cassell pbk **£2.95**

PHILLIPS, SUE, ET AL
The Book of Garden Styles **NEW**
[J179] Hamlyn hbk **£12.95**

PLEASE, PETER
Gardening for All **NEW**
Adapting garden styles to suit the elderly or disabled.
[J180] Batsford hbk **£7.95**

PYCRAFT, DAVID
Lawns
[J181] RHS pbk **£1.15**

READER'S DIGEST
Encyclopaedia of Garden Plants and Flowers
The A-Z illustrated guide to over 3,000 species of plants, trees, flowers and shrubs.
[J182] Hodder hbk **£18.95**
New Illustrated Guide to Gardening
An illustrated step-by-step guide to a host of gardening tasks and techniques. Exceptionally good value. Contributions from many experts under Roy Hay as the Consultant Editor. Laid out by subject in A-Z order, eg Cacti, Ferns, Lawns, Roses, Vegetables. Easy to follow diagrams, an A-Z guide to flowers and plants, and a helpful identification guide to plant disorders.
[J183] Hodder hbk **£14.95**
The Gardening Year
Not just a month-by-month guide but also a how-to-do-it book and a planner's aid as well. There is a section on plants and diseases of plants, and glossary of gardening terms.
[J184] Hodder hbk **£14.95**
Your Gardening Questions Answered
A valuable source of information for amateurs and professionals alike and a fascinating read. Compiled by a team of 18 experts including John Chambers (wild-flower seed expert) and Dr Stefan Buczacki (BBC Radio's 'Gardeners Question Time' adviser.)
[J185] Hodder hbk **£16.95**

RHS ENCYCLOPAEDIA OF PRACTICAL GARDENING
BRICKELL, CHRISTOPHER (ED)
Concise Encyclopaedia of Gardening Techniques
A condensed version in one volume of the 8-volume RHS Encyclopaedia of Practical Gardening listed individually below. 1,250 drawings.
[J186] M Beazley pbk **£7.95**
Fruit
[J187] M Beazley pbk **£5.95**
Garden Pests and Diseases
[J188] M Beazley pbk **£5.95**
Gardening Techniques
[J189] M Beazley pbk **£5.95**
Growing under Glass
[J190] M Beazley pbk **£5.95**
Lawns, Ground Cover, and Weed Control
[J191] M Beazley pbk **£5.95**
Propagation
[J192] M Beazley pbk **£5.95**
Pruning
[J193] M Beazley pbk **£5.95**
Vegetables
[J194] M Beazley pbk **£5.95**

RICE, GRAHAM
Plants for Problem Places
A dozen problem places are dealt with, and
suggestions made for plants which will thrive in
them.
[J195] C Helm hbk **£12.95**

ROSE, GRAHAM
The Low Maintenance Garden
[J196] Windward hbk **£10.95**
Traditional Garden Book   **NEW**
Beautifully produced and very inspiring.
[J197] D Kindersely hbk **£14.95**

RUSHFORTH
**The Hillier Book of Garden Planning
and Planting**
Describes how to plant your ideal garden with the
minimum of work and worry.
[J198] David & Ch hbk **£12.95**

SANECKI, KAY N.
Fragrant and Aromatic Plants
[J199] Cassell/Wisley pbk **£2.95**

SAVILLE, DIANA
Illustrated Garden Planter
Beginner's guide to plants and planting. No photos,
only drawings but easy to follow.
[J200] Penguin pbk **£5.95**

SCOTT-JAMES, ANNE
The Best Plants for Your Garden
A selection of plants which have a special value to the
author and earn their keep in gardens where space is
at a premium.
[J201] Octopus hbk **£14.95**

SHARMAN, FAY
Plants for Shade
[J202] Cassell pbk **£2.95**

SMITH, GEOFFREY
Easy Plants for Difficult Places
From a gardener who has battled with the Yorkshire
climate, sound advice on placing plants to give them
the best chance in life.
[J203] Hamlyn hbk **£8.95**

THOMAS, GRAHAM STUART
Art of Planting
Authoritative and extremely practical guide to the use
of plants in gardens, and to plant association. Good
illustrations and comprehensive plant lists.
[J204] Dent hbk **£13.50**

TOOGOOD, ALAN
Border Plants
A good introduction to border gardening with
chapters on planting shady borders, clay borders and
hot dry borders.
[J205] Ward Lock pbk **£3.95**
**Getting the Best from Lime-Free
Gardens**   **NEW**
[J206] Ward Lock hbk **£8.95**

VEREY, ROSEMARY
The Scented Garden
More a bedside than a practical book, this is
endearingly chatty and pretty.
[J207] M Joseph pbk **£9.95**

WILLIAMS, HUGH
The Hamlyn Guide to Plant Selection
Comprehensive colour charts, complemented by a
pictorial section detailing growing and propagation
techniques.
[J208] Hamlyn hbk **£12.95**

WILLIS, KEITH
Cultivating Rough Ground
[J209] Thorsons pbk **£2.95**

WRIGHT, MICHAEL (ED)
The Complete Book of Gardening
[J210] M Joseph pbk **£10.95**
**The Complete Handbook of Garden
Plants**
[J211] M Joseph pbk **£6.95**

Propagation

BROWN, GEORGE E.
**The Pruning of Trees, Shrubs and
Conifers**
A highly useful text for all gardeners.
[J212] Faber pbk **£5.95**

BROWSE, P.D.A. MCMILLAN
Plant Propagation
One of the RHS 'Practical Gardening' series.
Contains all that the serious gardener needs to know
to grow his own plants by all methods. Very good
drawings.
[J213] M Beazley pbk **£5.95**

CLARKE, GRAHAM
Practical Pruning
[J214] Ward Lock pbk **£3.95**

CLAYTON, J.
Pruning Ornamental Shrubs
[J215] RHS/Cassell pbk **£2.95**

COURTIER, JANE
Simple Plant Propagation
One of the recent 'Concorde Gardening' series from
Ward Lock aimed at beginners, very clearly laid out
and well-illustrated.
[J216] Ward Lock pbk **£2.95**

DOUGLAS, JAMES S.
A Beginner's Guide to Hydroponics
This first volume is an introduction to growing
vegetables, fruit and flowers without soil. The
technique involves providing the plants with balanced
amounts of food in the form of fertilising nutrients
and water. A useful book for keen gardeners who lack
space.
[J217] M Joseph pbk **£10.95**
Advanced Guide to Hydroponics
This second volume is for the very dedicated and the
scientifically minded only.
[J218] M Joseph pbk **£12.95**

GARNER, R.J.
The Grafter's Handbook
[J219] Cassell hbk **£10.95**

JOHNS, PATRICK
Ward Lock Book of Pruning   **NEW**
[J220] Ward Lock hbk **£14.95**

MOSSMAN, KEITH
The Pip Book
For those who would grow oranges, lemons, avocados
and more from the seeds which can be found in
everyday fruits.
[J221] Penguin pbk **£2.95**

**SCHUBERT, MARGOT & BLAICHER,
WOLFGANG**
The ABC of Hydroponics
[J222] Blandford pbk **£6.95**

SEDDON, GEORGE & BICKNELL, ANDREW
Plants Plus
All-embracing guide to successful plant propagation
for both indoor and outdoor plants.
[J223] Collins hbk **£10.95**
[J224] Collins pbk **£7.95**

THOMPSON, PETER
Creative Propagation   **NEW**
[J225] C Helm hbk **£15.95**

WRIGHT, ROBERT C.M. & TITCHMARSH, ALAN
Complete Book of Plant Propagation
[J226] Ward Lock pbk **£5.95**

Diseases & Pests

HARRIS, K. & BUCZACKI, STEFAN
**Pests, Diseases and Disorders of
Garden Plants**
[J227] Collins hbk **£9.95**

HAY, J.
Natural Pest and Disease Control
[J228] Century pbk **£5.95**

PHILLIPS, ROGER
Garden and Field Weeds
[J229] Elm Tree hbk **£7.95**
[J230] Elm Tree pbk **£3.95**

Types of Gardens

Container
Gardening

BAXENDALE, MARTIN
Window Boxes
[J232] Ward Lock hbk **£7.95**
[J233] Ward Lock pbk **£4.99**

BROWN, KATHLEEN & ROMAIN, EFFIE
Creative Container Gardening
Examples of designs to copy and inspiring pointers.
[J234] M Joseph pbk **£10.95**

DALEY, ALLEN & STELLA
**Making and Using Terrariums &
Planters**
A terrarium is an enclosed glass structure in which to
grow plants - this Victorian fashion seems to be in
vogue at the moment. Good diagrams and instructions
on how to cut the glass etc., plus suggestions for
suitable plants.
[J235] Blandford hbk **£12.95**
[J236] Blandford pbk **£7.95**

MCHOY, PETER
Bottle Gardening
[J237] Blandford pbk **£4.95**

SPOOZYNSKAU, JOY I.O.
The Indoor Vegetable Garden
[J238] David & Ch hbk **£4.95**

WHITE, RAY
Gardening in Ornamental Containers
[J239] Cassell/Wisley pbk **£2.95**

Indoor Gardening

ADAMS, DEENAGH GOOLD-
The Small Greenhouse
A Wisley Handbook with everything the beginner
needs to know about, from siting the greenhouse and
ventilating it, to the pests and diseases which attack
greenhouse plants.
[J240] Cassell/Wisley pbk **£2.95**

BECKETT, KENNETH
Growing Under Glass
[J241] M Beazley hbk **£5.95**

BONAR, ANN
House Plants
[J242] Cassell/Wisley pbk **£2.95**
The Conservatory Handbook
A comprehensive book which is accessible and
informative. Illustrated with good colour and b/w
photographs and some line drawings.
[J243] C Helm hbk **£14.95**

BRADBURN, ANTON
The Amdega Book of Conservatories
A guide to the extensive range of purpose-built and
do-it-yourself conservatories from one of Britain's
most respected firms.
[J244] David & Ch pbk **£12.95**

BROOKES, JOHN
The Indoor Garden Book
A new approach to the use of plants in decorating the
home, written by one of today's most influential
garden designers.
[J245] D Kindersley hbk **£14.95**
[J246] D Kindersley pbk **£9.95**

CHIUSOLI, ALESSANDRO & BOMANI, LUISA
**Macdonald Encyclopaedia of
Houseplants**
[J247] Macdonald pbk **£8.95**

CONDER, SUSAN
Terence Conran's Plants at Home
Of the large number of 'interior-decoration-with-
plants' titles which appeared recently, this is arguably
the least whimsical, and the most inspiring. Some
good ideas, and the photos are fun.
[J248] Octopus hbk **£9.95**

DAVIDSON, WILLIAM
Terraria & Bottle Gardens   NEW
[J249] Ward Lock pbk **£3.95**
The Houseplant Survival Manual
How to keep your houseplants healthy: what to do if
your rubber plant develops yellow leaves, or your
cyclamen begins to wilt. A plant-by-plant illustrated
guide, with detailed information on care, areas of risk,
treatment and cures.
[J250] Ward Lock pbk **£7.95**

DICKSON, ELIZABETH & SCHULENBURG,
FRITZ VON DER
The English Garden Room
25 gardeners describe their own garden rooms and
how they combine the arts of gardening and interior
design. Well illustrated with colour photographs.
Foreword by Sir Geoffrey Jellicoe.
[J251] Weidenfeld hbk **£16.00**
[J252] Weidenfeld pbk **£8.95**

HESSAYON, DR D.G.
Gold Plated Houseplant Expert
An expanded hardback edition of this gardening
classic.
[J253] Hutchinson hbk **£12.95**

House Plant Jotter   NEW
[J254] PBI pbk **£1.75**
The House Plant Expert
[J255] Pan pbk **£2.95**
The Indoor Plant Spotter
[J256] PBI pbk **£2.95**

MACSELF, A.J. & TURNER, ARTHUR
Handbook of Greenhouse Gardening
[J257] Collingridge hbk **£8.95**

MENAGE, RONALD HERBERT
Growing Indoor Plants
A good beginner's guide, and very practical.
[J258] Ward Lock hbk **£3.95**

READER'S DIGEST
Success with House Plants
Full of helpful information.
[J259] Reader's Digest hbk **£14.95**

SIMMONS, JOHN
**The Kew Gardens Book of Exotic
Indoor Plants**
A guide to growing the main groups of exotic indoor
plants in home conservatories, porches, on window
sills and in containers.
[J260] G Philip pbk **£15.95**

TRESIDDER, J. & CLIFF, S.
**Living Under Glass: Conservatories and
Sunrooms**
Traces the history of the conservatory and garden
room and looks at practicalities of building and
furnishing one today. Lavishly illustrated.
[J261] Thames & H hbk **£16.95**

WALLS, IAN
Complete Book of the Greenhouse
Fourth edition of this classic among gardening books.
One of the most complete and systematic
presentations of the subject.
[J262] Ward Lock hbk **£15.95**

WOODS, MAY & WARREN, ARETE SWARTZ
Glass Houses
A history of greenhouses, conservatories and
orangeries. Interwoven throughout is the account of
the people whose search for the perfect environment
for exotic plants brought about the marriage of
practicality and aesthetics which distinguishes these
buildings.
[J263] Aurum P hbk **£25.00**

Organic & Ecological Gardening

BUCZACKI, STEFAN
Ground Rules for Gardeners
A practical guide to garden ecology. Looks at the
basic principles and examines how they may be
utilised in the garden. Essentially a very practical
book.
[J264] Collins hbk **£12.95**

HAMILTON, GEOFF
Successful Organic Gardening
Complete guide to growing flowers, fruit, and
vegetables naturally. An important new book for
gardeners and all who care about their own health and
that of the environment. Includes colour photos and
drawings.
[J265] D Kindersley hbk **£14.95**

HILLS, L.D.
**Month By Month Guide to Organic
Gardening**
[J266] Thorsons pbk **£3.99**
Organic Gardening
As the longest lived of all the books in the recent
huge crop of books on organic gardening, this is
probably the best for the really serious gardener.
Practical information on different types of organic
fertiliser and growing instructions for specific crops,
with a special emphasis on long-forgotten fruit and
vegetables. Good advice on compost-making.
[J267] Penguin pbk **£3.95**

KENTON, BRANTON
Quantum Carrot
Describes how you can cultivate healthy plants for
food and decoration, naturally and in the smallest of
spaces.
[J268] Ebury P pbk **£5.95**

KITTO, DICK
Composting
Useful information on a subject fundamental for the
organic gardener.
[J269] Thorsons pbk **£5.99**
Planning the Organic Vegetable Garden
[J270] Thorsons pbk **£5.99**

O'BRIEN, K.D.
Veganic Gardening
[J271] Thorsons pbk **£6.99**

STICKLAND, SUE
Planning the Organic Flower Garden
[J272] Thorsons pbk **£5.99**
Planning the Organic Herb Garden
[J273] Thorsons pbk **£5.99**

Rock & Wall Gardens

FOERSTER, KARL
Rock Gardens Through the Year
A seasonal guide to plants and planting for the rock
garden.
[J274] Macdonald Orbis hbk **£12.95**

SCHACHT, WILHELM
Rock Garden
[J275] Alphabooks pbk **£7.95**

THOMAS, GRAHAM STUART
**The Rock Garden and its Plants:
From Grotto to Alpine House**   NEW
Published in association with the Royal Horticultural
Society. It is essentially a history of rock gardening,
but includes some practical and aesthetic advice for
those wishing to build a rock garden or enrich an
existing one.
[J276] Dent hbk **£18.00**

Small, Town & Enclosed Gardens

BOISSET, CAROLINE
The Town Garden   NEW
A good combination of history, practical advice and
inspirational ideas.
[J277] Windward hbk **£16.95**

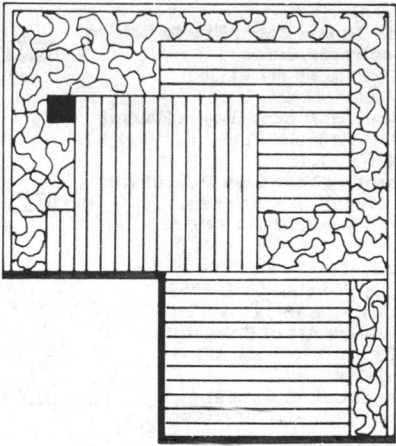

3 The paving pattern here creates a sense of movement.

A diagram showing paving designs from *The New Small Garden Book* by John Brookes (Dorling Kindersley hbk £14.95)

BROOKES, JOHN
The New Small Garden **NEW**
Another inspirational book from John Brookes, creating oases in a small courtyard or a town garden.
[J278] D Kindersley **£14.95**

COOMBS, G.K.
Plans for Small Gardens
[J279] Cassell/Wisley pbk **£2.95**
Plans for Small Gardens 2
[J280] Cassell/Wisley pbk **£2.95**

HOBHOUSE, PENELOPE
The Smaller Garden
[J281] Collins hbk **£9.95**

LLEWELLYN, RODDY
Beautiful Backyards
An 'ideas' book with a strong practical theme. Particularly good on perspective extension for tiny gardens, eg. 'Trompe l'oeil' painting.
[J282] Ward Lock pbk **£5.95**

PAGE, GILL
Town Gardens
[J283] Ward Lock hbk **£7.95**
[J284] Ward Lock pbk **£4.99**

PEARSON, ROBERT
Gardening in a Small Space
[J285] Cassell/Wisley pbk **£2.95**

STRONG, ROY
Creating Small Gardens
An inspiring and beautiful book, full of stunning ideas for garden layouts, with photos and plans to illustrate them, by the former director of the Victoria and Albert Museum.
[J286] Octopus hbk **£12.95**

TOOGOOD, ALAN
Planning and Making a Small Garden
Explains the potential in the pocket handkerchief size plot.
[J287] Ward Lock pbk **£3.95**

Water Gardens

ASLETT, KEN
Water Gardens
[J288] Cassell/Wisley pbk **£2.95**

LEDBETTER, GORDON T.
Patios and Ponds
[J289] Alphabooks pbk **£4.95**
Water Gardens **NEW**
A very practical guide to their design, construction, stocking and maintenance.
[J290] Alphabooks hbk **£9.95**

LLEWELLYN, RODDY
Water Gardens: The Connoisseur's Choice
Over 80 specially commissioned colour photographs illustrate the best examples of water gardens around the country, from Chatsworth and Bodnant to small private gardens that feature unusual items of interest. A visual feast, with a sprinkling of practical detail - basically a book from which to draw inspiration.
[J291] Ward Lock hbk **£16.95**

MOORES, ANDREW BOOTH-
Garden Pools, Waterfalls & Fountains
[J292] Ward Lock pbk **£3.95**

SIMMONS, JOHN
Pool and Waterside Gardening
One of the few Kew gardening guides. Considers the design elements of water gardening and gives practical information on construction and plant selection. Detailed descriptions of over 200 aquatic, marginal and moisture-loving plants. Well illustrated with diagrams and colour photos.
[J293] Hamlyn hbk **£7.95**

SWINDELLS, PHILIP & MASON, DAVID
The Complete Book of the Water Garden **NEW**
Written by two leading experts in the field, and lavishly illustrated with diagrams and photos, this is probably the most comprehensive book available.
[J294] Ward Lock hbk **£17.95**

An illustration from *The Butterfly Gardener* by Miriam Rothschild & Clive Farrell (Michael Joseph pbk £5.95)

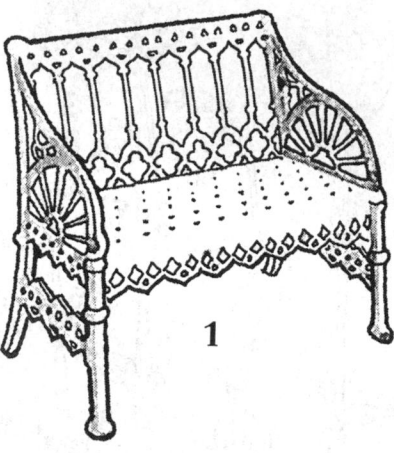

1

A reproduction Gothic garden seat from *Creating Small Gardens* by Roy Strong (Conran Octopus hbk £12.95)

Wild & Wildlife Gardens

BAINES, CHRIS
How to Make a Wildlife Garden
[J295] H Hamilton hbk **£10.95**
[J296] Elm Tree pbk **£7.95**

BRICKELL, CHRISTOPHER & SHARMAN, FAY
Vanishing Garden: A Conservation Guide to Garden Plants
[J297] J Murray hbk **£15.00**

CHINNERY, MICHAEL
The Living Garden
Practical guide to attracting and conserving garden wildlife. By a member of the BBC *Wildlife* panel, and bursting with intriguing information about the unseen life of the garden. Learn the benefits of attracting butterflies, bees, ladybirds, newts, dragonflies etc. A delightfully different gardening book.
[J298] D Kindersley hbk **£10.95**

GIBBONS, BOB & LIZ
Creating a Wildlife Garden **NEW**
[J299] Hamlyn hbk **£10.95**

GRAHAM, ROSE
Sunday Times Book of Woodland and Wildflower Gardening
Based on the best ideas from the *Sunday Times* competition to design a woodland garden for the Chelsea Flower Show.
[J300] David & Ch hbk **£12.95**

HOOPER, TED & TAYLOR, MIKE
The Beekeeper's Garden
How to encourage bees to your garden.
[J301] A & C Black hbk **£9.95**

ROBINSON, WILLIAM
The Wild Garden
[J302] Century pbk **£5.95**

ROTHSCHILD, MIRIAM & FARRELL, CLIVE
The Butterfly Gardener
The owners of even very small gardens can, by

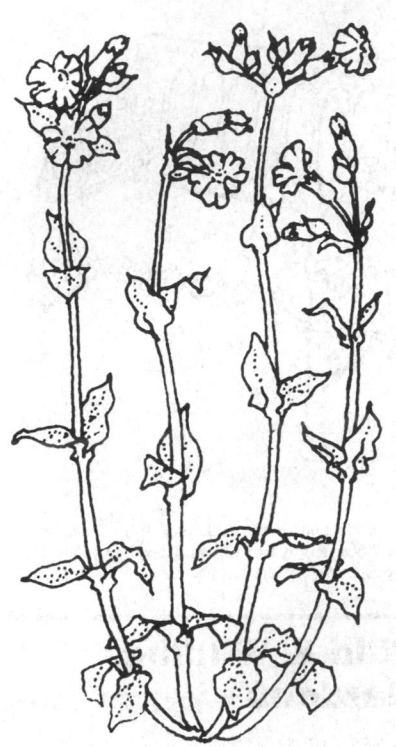

Red Campion from *The National Trust Book of Wild Flower Gardening* by John Stevens (Dorling Kindersley hbk **£14.95**)

introducing wild flowers, grasses etc, mimic the natural habitats of our native butterflies and so entice them to visit. Enthusiastic and knowledgeable.
[J303] M Joseph pbk **£5.95**

SMITH, GEOFFREY
The Joy of Wildlife Gardening NEW
An RSPB guide to preparing a garden to encourage wildlife.
[J304] C Helm hbk **£14.95**

STEVENS, JOHN
The National Trust Book of Wild Flower Gardening
The first book to satisfy the demand for straightforward, practical information on how to cultivate wild plants.
[J305] D Kindersley hbk **£14.95**

Plant Species A-Z

AFRICAN VIOLETS (SAINTPAULIA)
CLEMENTS, TONY
African Violets
A specialist nurseryman and Chelsea Medal winner writes on his subject and reveals all the secrets of how to keep these supposedly 'tricky' plants in beautiful condition.
[J306] David & Ch hbk **£9.95**
WALL, BILL
Saintpaulias & Related Plants NEW
[J307] RHS/Cassell pbk **£2.95**

ALPINES
ELLIOTT, JOE
Alpines the Easy Way
[J308] RHS/Cassell pbk **£2.95**
HEATH, R.E.
Collector's Alpines
Their cultivation in frames and alpine houses. Updated edition of this classic.
[J309] Collingridge hbk **£30.00**
INGWERSEN, W.
Manual of Alpine Plants
The famous collector and grower of alpines lists, genus by genus, a vast range of plants. Essential reference for the real enthusiast.
[J310] Hamlyn pbk **£9.95**
THOMAS, GRAHAM STUART
The Rock Garden and its Plants: From Grotto to Alpine House
The latest indispensable title from one of our greatest authors and plantsmen. Here he turns his attention to a complete study of rock plants.
[J311] Dent hbk **£18.00**

ANNUALS
GOULD, RALPH
Annuals and Biennials
[J312] RHS pbk **£0.95**
RICE, GRAHAM
Handbook of Annuals and Bedding Plants
Straightforward advice on basic soil preparation, care and cultivation is supplemented with ideas on displaying the plants to maximum effect in beds and borders, hanging-baskets, tubs and window-boxes.
[J313] C Helm pbk **£12.95**

AZALEAS
GALLE, FRED
Azaleas
[J314] Timber P hbk **£50.00**
IHEI ITO
A Brocade Pillow: The Azaleas of Old Japan
[J315] Weatherhill hbk **£17.50**

BEGONIAS
CATTERALL, ERIC
Growing Begonias
[J316] C Helm pbk **£6.95**
LANGDON, BRIAN
Begonias NEW
[J317] Cassell hbk **£12.95**

BONSAI
ADAMS, PETER
Art of Bonsai
[J318] Ward Lock hbk **£9.95**
[J319] Ward Lock pbk **£6.95**

BARTON, DAN
The Bonsai Book: The Definitive Illustrated Guide NEW
[J320] Ebury P hbk **£15.95**
BOLLMANN, W.E.
Karmuti: A New Way in Bonsai
[J321] Faber pbk **£2.95**
CHAN, PETER
Creating Your Own Bonsai with Everyday Garden Plants NEW
[J322] Ward Lock hbk **£9.95**
ROGER, ALAN
Bonsai
[J323] RHS/Cassell pbk **£2.95**
SAMSON, ISABELLE & REMY
Creative Art of Bonsai
[J324] Wark Lock pbk **£12.95**
SWINTON, ANN
Handbook of Bonsai NEW
[J325] Collingridge hbk **£8.95**
[J326] Collingridge pbk **£7.95**
YOSHIMURA, Y. & HALFORD, G.M.
The Japanese Art of Miniature Trees and Landscape
[J327] Tuttle pbk **£17.50**

BULBS
MATHEW, BRIAN
Flowering Bulbs for the Garden
An authoritative Kew gardening guide, superbly illustrated and with much information on special bulbs for the enthusiast.
[J328] Collingridge hbk **£7.95**
RIX, MARTYN
Growing Bulbs
[J329] C Helm pbk **£8.95**
RIX, MARTYN & PHILLIPS, ROGER
The Bulb Book
[J330] Pan pbk **£6.95**

CACTI
CULLMAN, WILLY ET AL
Encyclopaedia of Cacti
[J331] Alphabooks hbk **£30.00**
GRAHAM, VICTOR
Growing Succulent Plants Including Cacti
An indispensable aid to the successful cultivation of succulent plants.
[J332] David & Ch pbk **£12.95**
INNES, CLIVE
Cacti
[J333] RHS/Cassell pbk **£2.95**
Cacti and Other Succulent Plants
An excellent introduction giving practical advice on the care and cultivation of the most attractive and easy to grow varieties.
[J334] Ward Lock pbk **£3.95**

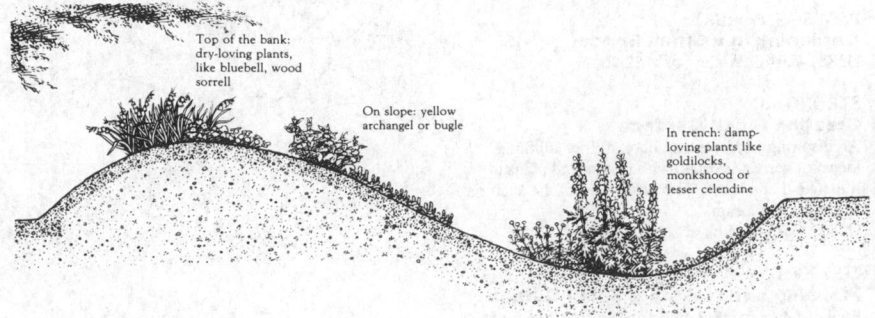

An artificial woodbank from *Creating a Wildlife Garden* by Bob & Liz Gibbons (Hamlyn hbk **£10.95**)

The Handbook of Cacti and Other Succulents
More than 300 full-colour pictures make this book one of the most comprehensively illustrated and informative guides available.
[J335] Ward Lock hbk **£12.95**
PILBEAM, JOHN
Cacti for the Connoisseur
A guide for growers and collectors. A new detailed edition by one of the great experts in the field. The focus is on the most rewarding and exciting species for the grower.
[J336] Batsford hbk **£29.95**
SIMMONS, JOHN (ED)
Kew Guide to Cacti NEW
[J337] Collingridge hbk **£8.95**

CAMELLIAS
BARTHOLOMEW, BRUCE & CHANG, HUNG TA
Camellias
Revised and augmented translation of Professor Chang's monograph published in Chinese in 1981.
[J338] Batsford hbk **£40.00**
KUNMING INSTITUTE OF BOTANY (ED)
Yunnan Camellias of China
Essentially a study of Yunnan Camellias in their natural environment, rather than of their cultivation in Britain. Nevertheless, this is a beautifully illustrated book.
[J339] Batsford hbk **£45.00**
MACOBOY, S.
Colour Dictionary of Camellias
New edition. A well researched and lively text with superb illustrations.
[J340] Lansdowne P hbk **£19.95**
TREHANE, DAVID
Camellias
[J341] RHS/Cassell pbk **£2.50**

CAMPANULAS
LEWIS, P. & LYNCH, M.
Campanulas NEW
[J342] C Helm hbk **£14.95**

CARNATIONS & PINKS
BIRD, R.
Carnations and Pinks
[J343] Collins pbk **£1.75**

CARNIVOROUS PLANTS
SLACK, ADRIAN
Carnivorous Plants
[J344] Alphabooks pbk **£12.50**
Insect-Eating Plants and How to Grow Them
[J345] Alphabooks pbk **£6.95**
TEMPLE, P.
Carnivorous Plants
[J346] RHS/Cassell pbk **£2.95**

CHRYSANTHEMUMS
BIRCUMSHAW, DEREK & DAMP, PHILIP
Chrysanthemums & Dahlias
[J347] RHS/Cassell pbk **£2.95**
RANDALL & WREN
Growing Chrysanthemums
[J348] C Helm pbk **£8.95**
SMITH, JAMES F.
Chrysanthemums
[J349] Batsford hbk **£20.00**
WOOLMAN, JACK
Chrysanthemums: A Plantsman's Guide NEW
[J350] Ward Lock hbk **£8.95**

CLEMATIS
FISK, JIM
Clematis
[J351] RHS/Cassell pbk **£2.50**

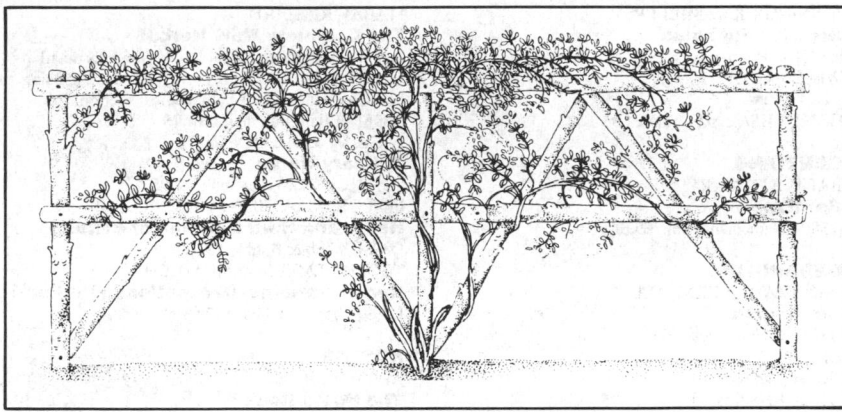

An illustration from *The National Trust Book of Wild Flower Gardening* by John Stevens (Dorling Kindersley hbk **£14.95**)

Clematis NEW
A superb book on every aspect of growing this plant.
[J352] Cassell hbk **£12.95**
LLOYD, CHRISTOPHER
Clematis NEW
Extensively revised edition by the garden author 'par excellence'.
[J353] Viking hbk **£14.95**

CLIMBING PLANTS
BECKETT, KENNETH
Climbing Plants
[J354] C Helm hbk **£8.95**
PRESTON, GEORGE
Climbing and Wall Plants
[J355] RHS/Cassell pbk **£2.95**
TAYLOR, JANE
Climbing Plants
A Kew gardening guide. Includes a lot of less well known climbers. Advice on how to train and prune the plants etc. Good colour plates.
[J356] Collingridge hbk **£7.95**

CROCUS
MATHEW, BRIAN
The Crocus
A complete recent revision of the genus. Descriptions of the species, habitats and flowering periods.
[J357] Batsford hbk **£35.00**

CYCLAMEN
NIGHTINGALE, GAY
Growing Cyclamen
[J358] C Helm pbk **£8.95**
WILSON, C. GREY-
The Genus Cyclamen
[J359] C Helm hbk **£14.95**

DAFFODILS
BARNES, D.
Daffodils
[J360] David & Ch hbk **£12.95**
SHEPHERD, F.W.
Daffodils
[J361] Cassell/Wisley pbk **£2.95**

DAHLIAS
BIRCUMSHAW, DEREK & DAMP, PHILIP
Chrysanthemums & Dahlias
[J362] RHS/Cassell pbk **£2.50**
DAMP, PHILIP
Dahlias NEW
[J363] Crowood hbk **£12.95**
Growing Dahlias
[J364] C Helm pbk **£6.95**

DAPHNE
BRICKELL, CHRISTOPHER & MATHEW, BRIAN
Daphne: The Genus in the Wild and in Cultivation
[J365] Alpine Garden pbk **£6.25**

DELPHINIUMS
EDWARDS, COLIN
Delphiniums NEW
A long-awaited study, covering every aspect of growing this delightful plant.
[J366] Crowood hbk **£12.95**

FERNS
GILBERT, ZOE
Ferns for the Garden & Home
A beautifully produced and very informative book. Excellent value.
[J367] New Holland pbk **£1.99**
GOUDEY, CHRISTOPHER
Maidenhair Ferns in Cultivation
[J368] C Helm hbk **£30.00**
KAYE, REGINALD
Ferns
[J369] RHS pbk **£0.95**

FOLIAGE PLANTS
BRAY, LYS DE
The Green Garden
The art of foliage planting. Shows that labour-saving foliage can provide a wide range of colour and for a much longer season of interest than most flowers.
[J370] Ward Lock hbk **£8.95**
BROWN, MICHAEL JEFFERSON-
Leaves NEW
[J371] David & Ch hbk **£10.95**
GORER, RICHARD
Hardy Foliage Plants
[J372] Collingridge hbk **£8.95**
LLOYD, CHRISTOPHER
Foliage Plants
[J373] Viking pbk **£12.95**
[J374] Penguin pbk **£7.95**

FUCHSIAS
BOULLEMIER, LEO
Fuchsias: A Plantsman's Guide NEW
[J375] Ward Lock hbk **£8.95**
EWART, RON
Fuchsia Lexicon
Revised edition, incorporating new information and photos of nearly 70 of today's most popular cultivars, with descriptions of some 2,000 species and varieties.
[J376] Blandford hbk **£14.95**
[J377] Blandford pbk **£11.95**

GARDENING

515

JENNINGS, K. & MILLER, V.
Growing Fuchsias
[J378] C Helm pbk **£8.95**
WELLS, GEORGE
Fuchsias
[J379] RHS/Cassell pbk **£2.95**

GENTIANS
BARTLETT, MARY
Gentians
[J380] Heinemann pbk **£9.50**

GERANIUMS
DELAMAIN & KENDALL
Geraniums
[J381] C Helm pbk **£5.95**
KEY, HAZEL
Pelargoniums
[J382] RHS/Cassell pbk **£2.95**
TAYLOR, JAN
Geraniums and Pelargoniums
A comprehensive guide to all aspects of cultivation, propagation and exhibition.
[J383] Crowood hbk **£12.95**
YEO, PETER
Hardy Geraniums
Complete guide to identification and cultivation. Also covers history, nomenclature and classification.
[J384] C Helm hbk **£25.00**

GLADIOLI
PARK, RON & ANDERTON, ERIC
Growing Gladioli   NEW
[J385] C Helm hbk **£13.95**

GRASSES
GROUNDS, ROGER
Ornamental Grasses   NEW
[J386] C Helm hbk **£17.95**
REINHARDT
Ornamental Grass Gardening
[J387] Macdonald hbk **£12.95**

GROUND COVER PLANTS
BROWNE, JANET
Ground Cover Plants
An invaluable guide devoted to those highly effective and attractive 'space fillers', giving useful advice on buying, planting, general maintenance and methods of propagation.
[J388] Ward Lock pbk **£3.95**
NAPIER, E. & SHARMAN, F.
Ground Cover Plants   NEW
[J389] RHS pbk **£2.95**

HEATHERS
KNIGHT, F.P.
Heaths and Heathers
[J390] RHS/Cassell pbk **£2.95**
PROUDLY & PROUDLY
Heathers in Colour
[J391] Blandford pbk **£5.95**

HERBS
BREMNESS, LESLEY
The Complete Book of Herbs
Arguably, the most attractive and informative book available.
[J392] D Kindersley hbk **£14.95**
COOPER, GUY & TAYLOR, GORDON
English Herb Gardens
A selection of England's finest herb gardens showing a wide diversity of design. Descriptions are complemented by a herb glossary.
[J393] Weidenfeld hbk **£10.95**
[J394] Weidenfeld pbk **£6.95**
LOWENFELD, C.
Herb Gardening
[J395] Faber pbk **£4.99**

MABEY, RICHARD
The Complete New Herbal
A practical guide to herbal living. Includes detailed instruction on cultivation, drying, storing and using herbs, as well as a self-help medical section.
[J396] H Hamilton hbk **£14.95**
PAGE, M. & STEARN, W.T.
Culinary Herbs
[J397] Cassell/Wisley pbk **£2.95**
PEPLOW, ELIZABETH & REGINALD
Herbs and Herb Gardens of Britain
[J398] Webb & B hbk **£9.95**
TOOLEY, EMELIE & MEAD, CHRIS
Herbs: Gardens, Decorations and Food
[J399] Sidgwick hbk **£17.95**

HOSTAS
ADEN, PAUL (ED)
The Hosta Book
[J400] C Helm hbk **£16.95**

HYDRANGEAS
BOOTH, H.M. HAWORTH-
The Hydrangeas
5th edition, incorporating new information and photographs of nearly 70 of today's most popular cultivars, with descriptions of some 2,000 species and varieties.
[J401] Constable hbk **£9.95**

IRISES
CASSIDY, G.E. & LINNEGAR, S.
Growing Irises
[J402] C Helm pbk **£8.95**
DYKES, W.R.
Genus Iris
A reprint that will appeal to all gardeners who love irises. Originally published in 1924.
[J403] Dover hbk **£29.75**
KOHLEIN
The Iris
[J404] C Helm **£25.00**

IVIES
KEY, HAZEL
Ivies
[J405] RHS pbk **£0.95**

LILIES
BROWN, M. JEFFERSON-
Lilies: A Plantsman's Guide   NEW
[J406] Ward Lock hbk **£8.95**

FOX, DEREK
Growing Lilies
[J407] C Helm pbk **£9.95**
Lilies
[J408] RHS/Cassell pbk **£2.95**
JEKYLL, GERTRUDE
Lilies for English Gardens
[J409] Antique Coll Club hbk **£12.95**
SYNGE, PATRICK M.
Lilies
A most important book on the Lilium species and its hybrids based on Elwes's monograph on the genus Lilium and its supplement, but with extra text to bring it up to date and new paintings by Margaret Stones.
[J410] Batsford hbk **£50.00**

MAGNOLIAS
BLAMEY, MARJORIE & TRESEDER, NEIL G.
Book of Magnolias
[J411] Collins hbk **£25.00**
GARDINER, JIM
Magnolias   NEW
[J412] Cassell pbk **£14.95**

MECANOPSIS
COBB, JAMES
Mecanopsis   NEW
[J413] C Helm hbk **£16.95**

ORCHIDS
BRISTOW, ALEX
Orchids
[J414] RHS/Cassell pbk **£2.95**
CRIBB, PHILLIP & BAILES, CHRISTOPHER
Hardy Orchids   NEW
[J415] C Helm hbk **£50.00**
HAWKES, ALEX D.
Encyclopaedia of Cultivated Orchids
An illustrated descriptive manual of the members of the Orchidaceae currently in cultivation.
[J416] Faber hbk **£50.00**
RITTERSHAUSEN, B. & W.
Orchids as Houseplants   NEW
[J417] Ward Lock hbk **£14.95**
RITTERSHAUSEN, W.
Illustrated Guide to Growing Your Own Orchids
[J418] Salamander pbk **£3.95**
STEWART, JOYCE
Orchids
A Kew Gardening Guide.
[J419] Collingridge hbk **£7.95**

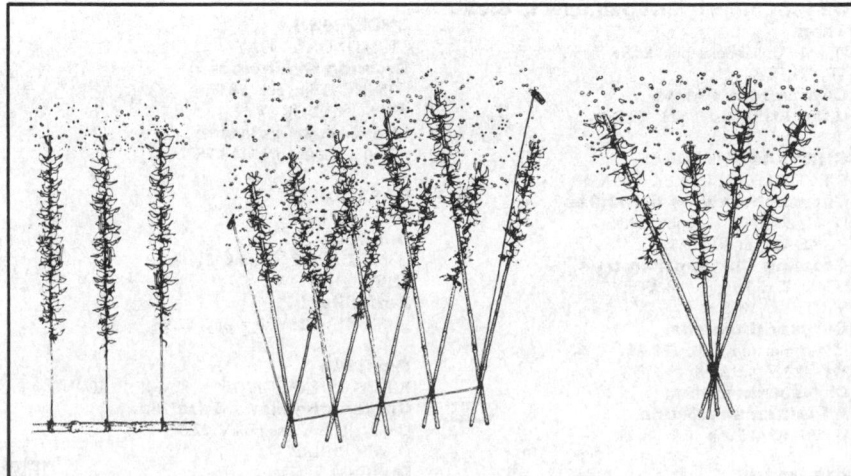

An illustration from *Successful Organic Gardening* by Geoff Hamilton (Dorling Kindersley hbk £14.95)

516

PERENNIALS

BECKETT, KENNETH
Growing Hardy Perennials
[J420] C Helm pbk **£6.95**

JELLITO, L. & SCHACT, W.
Manual of Cultivated Perennials **NEW**
In two volumes, the definitive work on the subject, for the professional and the serious amateur.
[J421] Batsford **£100.00**

SIMMONS, JOHN (ED)
Kew Guide to Tender Perennials **NEW**
[J422] Collingridge hbk **£8.95**

THOMAS, GRAHAM STUART
Perennial Garden Plants
Or, *The Modern Florilegium*.
[J423] Dent hbk **£16.00**

TOOGOOD, ALAN
Perennials
[J424] Macdonald Orbis pbk **£6.95**

PRIMULAS

DUTHIE, R.
Florists' Flowers and Societies
The National Auricula and Primula Society are one of the few old florists' societies still flourishing.
[J425] Shire pbk **£3.95**

HYATT, BRENDA
Auriculas **NEW**
[J426] Cassell hbk **£12.95**
Primroses & Auriculas **NEW**
[J427] RHS pbk **£2.95**

SWINDELLS, PHILLIP
Primulas: A Plantsman's Guide **NEW**
[J428] Ward Lock hbk **£8.95**

RHODODENDRONS

COX, KENNETH
Rhododendrons: A Plantsman's Guide **NEW**
[J429] Ward Lock hbk **£8.95**

COX, PETER A.
Rhododendrons
[J430] RHS/Cassell pbk **£2.95**

COX, PETER A. & KENNETH
Encyclopaedia of Rhododendron Hybrids
Alphabetically arranged descriptions of some 1,400 of the most important rhododendron hybrids. Based on 40 years of experience.
[J431] Batsford hbk **£25.00**

SALLEY, HOMER & GREER, HAROLD
Rhododendron Hybrids
A guide to the origins of over 4,000 named hybrids.
[J432] Batsford hbk **£45.00**

ROSES

AUSTIN, DAVID
Heritage of the Rose
With a foreword by Graham Stuart Thomas. Describes the place of the rose in history and art, and looks at both the theory and practice of rose growing.
[J433] Antique Coll Club hbk **£29.95**

BEALES, PETER
Classic Roses
First-class encyclopaedia of all old rose species, their cultivars and varieties. All aspects of history, cultivation and planting design with a comprehensive dictionary of over 1,000 old roses.
[J434] Collins hbk **£30.00**

Twentieth Century Roses
Individual descriptions of 650 of the most outstanding and most readily available modern roses plus details of their breeding, size, shape and flowering characters.
[J435] Collins hbk **£20.00**

COGGIATTI, STELVIO
Macdonald Encyclopedia of Roses
[J436] Macdonald pbk **£8.95**

EAGLE, DAWN & BARRY
Miniature Roses
A practical book written in straightforward, non-technical language on a very popular subject.
[J437] Collins hbk **£8.95**

FEARNLEY-WHITTINGSTALL, JANE
Rose Gardens: Thier History and Design
[J437A] Chatto hbk **£18.00**

GIBSON, MICHAEL
Growing Roses
[J438] C Helm pbk **£7.95**
Roses **NEW**
[J439] RHS pbk **£2.95**

GRIFFITHS, TREVOR
Book of Classic Old Roses
Over 600 varieties, accompanied by colour photos. Pretty and non-technical.
[J440] M Joseph pbk **£8.95**

HESSAYON, DR D.G.
The Rose Expert
[J441] PBI pbk **£2.95**
The Rose Jotter **NEW**
[J442] PBI pbk **£1.75**

MILLAR, GAULT S. & SYNGE, PATRICK M.
Dictionary of Roses in Colour
[J444] M Joseph pbk **£11.95**

PHILLIPS, ROGER & RIX, MARTYN
Roses
A colour-illustrated reference book, accompanied by descriptions of each rose's origin and parentage, appearance, characteristics and growing conditions.
[J445] Macmillan hbk **£16.95**
[J446] Pan pbk **£10.95**

SWAIN, BILL
Roses: Questions & Answers **NEW**
An invaluable reference book.
[J447] Cassell hbk **£12.95**

THOMAS, GRAHAM STUART
Climbing Roses Old and New
The guru of rose growing combines history with invaluable advice on choosing, planting and tending roses. This book and Thomas' next two books listed here are all good value.
[J448] Dent hbk **£12.95**
Old Shrub Roses
[J449] Dent hbk **£11.50**
Shrub Roses of Today
[J450] Dent hbk **£10.95**

WHITTINGSTALL, JANE FEARNLEY-
Rose Gardens: Their History and Design **NEW**
[J443] Chatto hbk **£18.00**

SAXIFRAGES

KOHLEIN, FRITZ
Saxifrages and Related Genera
Comprehensive coverage of this huge genus with descriptions of both species and hybrids, together with detailed information on all aspects of cultivation.
[J451] Batsford hbk **£25.00**

WEBB, DAVID & GORNAU, RICHARD
Saxifrages
[J452] C Helm hbk **£30.00**

SEDUMS

EVANS, R.L.
Handbook of Cultivated Sedums
A book for the enthusiast, using keys, descriptive text and colour plates to track down species.
[J453] Science Reviews hbk **£15.00**

SWEET PEAS

UNWIN, C.W.J.
Sweet Peas
Their history, development and culture. First published in 1926, this long-awaited revised edition covers every aspect of sweet pea cultivation including

A Victorian rose arch from *Rose Gardens: Their History & Design* by Jane Fearnley-Whittingstall (Chatto & Windus hbk **£18.00**)

the cordon method of culture and raising new varieties.
[J454] Silent Books hbk **£4.95**

WATERLILIES

ROBINSON, PETER
Waterlilies and Other Aquatic Plants **NEW**
A guide to more than 100 varieties, all illustrated in colour.
[J455] Collins hbk **£14.95**

SWINDELLS, PHILIP
Waterlilies
[J456] C Helm hbk **£8.95**

Fruit & Vegetables

BAKER, HARRY A. & WAITE, RAY
Grapes: Indoors and Out
[J457] Cassell/Wisley pbk **£2.95**

CLARKE, ETHNE
Art of the Kitchen Garden
Combines gardening history, growing suggestions, practical advice and recipes.
[J458] M Joseph hbk **£14.95**

CROUCH, DAVID & WARD, COLIN
The Allotment: Its Landscape and Culture
[J459] Faber hbk **£12.95**

DAVIES, JENNIFER
The Victorian Kitchen Garden
Based around the kitchen garden of Chiltern Foliat in Berkshire which was recently restored. It was the subject of a recent BBC series, which recorded the reconstruction of the garden in which the flowers, fruit and vegetables of the Victorian period were grown.
[J460] BBC hbk **£10.95**

GENDERS, ROY
Mushroom Growing for Everyone
[J461] Faber pbk **£3.95**

A bookplate by W.R. Lethaby from *The Edwardian Garden* by David Ottewill (currently unavailable)

HESSAYON, DR D.G.
The Vegetable Expert
[J462] PBI pbk **£2.95**
The Vegetable Jotter NEW
[J463] PBI pbk **£1.75**

HILLS, LAWRENCE D.
Grow Your Own Fruit and Vegetables
[J464] Faber pbk **£3.50**

LARKCOM, JOY
Vegetables from Small Gardens
[J465] Faber pbk **£3.95**

MAZE, PETER BLACKBURNE-
Simple Fruit Growing
A concise introduction to the art of fruit growing -
especially suitable for the beginner.
[J466] Ward Lock pbk **£3.95**
The Complete Guide to Fruit Growing
Looks at the many varieties that can be cultivated in
the average garden, and each stage in the cultivation
process.
[J467] Crowood hbk **£9.95**

PEARKES, GILLIAN
Vinegrowing in Britain
[J468] Dent hbk **£13.50**

READER'S DIGEST
Food from Your Garden
The complete how-to-grow-it, how-to-cook-it guide
to vegetables, herbs and fruit.
[J469] Reader's Digest hbk **£13.95**

ROACH, F.A.
Cultivated Fruits of Britain
[J470] Blackwell hbk **£25.00**
[J471] Blackwell pbk **£8.95**

ROYAL HORTICULTURAL SOCIETY
Fruit Garden Displayed
[J472] RHS pbk **£6.95**
Vegetable Garden Displayed
Timely reprints of these standard works, fully
updated. Practical books on producing food from the
garden with added colour. Reliable, and extremely
good value.
[J473] RHS pbk **£4.95**

SAULLES, DENYS DE
Home Grown
A comprehensive and attractively produced guide to
growing, storing, preserving your own fruit and
vegetables. Informative and well illustrated with
colour plates and line drawings.
[J474] Macmillan hbk **£14.95**

WALLS, IAN
Growing Tomatoes
[J475] David & Ch hbk **£14.95**
Simple Tomato Growing
[J476] Ward Lock pbk **£3.95**
Simple Vegetable Growing
How to avoid poor planning and unskilled cultivation.
[J477] Ward Lock pbk **£3.95**

WOODWARD, JACK
Pruning Hardy Fruits NEW
[J478] RHS/Cassell pbk **£2.95**

Trees & Shrubs

BEAN, W.J.
**Trees and Shrubs: Hardy in the British
Isles**
The standard work, in four volumes. A detailed
botanical and horticultural guide, genus by genus, to
hardy trees and shrubs. (Each volume available
individually at £50.)
[J479] J Murray 4 vols hbk **£200.00**
Trees and Shrubs: Supplement
A valuable update to the four previous volumes,
containing an index to them.
[J480] J Murray hbk **£35.00**

BIRD, RICHARD
Flowering Trees & Shrubs NEW
Beautifully illustrated.
[J481] Ward Lock hbk **£14.95**

COMPTON, JAMES
Success with Unusual Plants
An important book for 'tree connoisseurs'.
[J482] Collins hbk **£12.95**

DAVIS, BRIAN
Flowering Trees and Shrubs
[J483] Pelham hbk **£5.95**
Trees for Small Gardens
Over 250 popular varieties of trees arranged
alphabetically under a genus or species name, with
additional information about cultivation requirements
and varieties of similar appearance.
[J484] Pelham hbk **£5.95**

HESSAYON, DR D.G.
The Tree and Shrub Expert
[J485] PBI pbk **£2.95**

HILLIER, H.G.
Manual of Trees and Shrubs
This masterpiece is a must for the keen gardener and
garden visitor.
[J486] David & Ch hbk **£12.95**
**The Hillier Colour Dictionary of Trees
and Shrubs**
Gloriously illustrated and comprehensive.
[J487] David & Ch hbk **£10.95**

JOHNSON, HUGH
Encyclopaedia of Trees
A fully illustrated and completely revised guide to all
the major garden and forest trees of the temperate
world. It includes a 65 page A-Z index of tree species.
[J488] M Beazley hbk **£19.95**

KINAHAR, SONIA
Gardening with Trees NEW
[J489] C Helm hbk **£12.95**

KNIGHT, FRANK P.
Trees for Small Gardens
[J490] RHS pbk **£2.95**

LUNARDI, COSTANZA
**Macdonald Encyclopaedia of Shrubs
and Trees**
A guide which contains many useful practical hints.
[J491] Macdonald pbk **£6.95**

PAUL, ANTHONY & REES, YVONNE
Designing with Trees NEW
Growing trees for their greatest effect, in any
situation.
[J492] Windward hbk **£16.95**

PHILLIPS, ROGER & RIX, MARTYN
Shrubs NEW
A magnificent photographic reference book of over
1,200 species.
[J493] Pan pbk **£10.95**

RUSHFORTH, KEITH
Conifers
A major recent work offering a wealth of information
including propagation, planting, pests and diseases,
not only on all the commonly available species, but
also on rarer plants. Temperate conifers receive
detailed attention, and an overview of tropical
conifers is also given.
[J494] C Helm hbk **£19.95**
Shrubs for Small Gardens NEW
[J495] RHS pbk **£2.95**
**The Hillier Book of Tree Planting and
Management**
Expert advice on a difficult subject.
[J496] David & Ch hbk **£12.95**

SWAIN, BILL
Trees: Questions & Answers NEW
[J497] Cassell hbk **£14.95**

Pruning and tying in climbing roses on an arched
arbour from *The Gardener's Labyrinth* by Thomas
Hill (Oxford hbk £14.95, pbk £7.95)

Health & Fitness

Reference
Specific Ailments A - Z
Psychological Health and Self-Help
Women's Health
Diet & Nutrition
Fitness
Health & Beauty

HEALTH & FITNESS

Reference

Not intended as medical text books, the titles in this section present a selection for the layman, offering clear information and advice on general health matters and current medical practice.

Black's Medical Dictionary
[K1] A & C Black pbk **£15.00**

Medicines: The Complete Guide
[K2] Bloomsbury pbk **£6.95**

Oxford Companion to Medicine
In 2 volumes: the outstanding reference book of this section - covers absolutely everything.
[K3] Oxford hbk **£65.00**

Reader's Digest A-Z of the Human Body
Another excellent Reader's Digest reference book for the layman showing how the mind and body function in health and disease.
[K4] Hodder hbk **£13.95**

The British Medical Association Family Doctor Home Adviser
A general handbook to help with all sorts of medical problems, presented with the backing of the BMA.
[K5] D Kindersley hbk **£14.95**

The British Red Cross First Aid Manual
The first aid book compiled and used by the St John's Ambulance Brigade.
[K6] D Kindersley hbk **£9.95**
[K7] D Kindersley pbk **£4.95**

The Essential Guide to Prescription Drugs NEW
Provides information on the benefits and side-effects of over 200 prescription drugs. Easily understood by the layperson.
[K8] Harper & R pbk **£8.95**

BROWN, J.
Pears' Medical Encyclopaedia
[K9] Sphere pbk **£4.99**

COLEMAN, DR VERNON
The Health Scandal
The well-known author takes a critical look at the current state of the NHS.
[K10] Mandarin pbk **£4.99**

DAVIS, DR ALAN MARYON & ROGERS, JENNY
How to Save a Life
An indispensable family guide from the recent TV series. Simple clear explanations to help you cope in an emergency when every second counts.
[K11] BBC pbk **£4.95**

GRIFFITH, DR H. WINTER
The Complete Guide to Symptoms, Illness and Surgery
An experienced doctor answers the most frequent questions on illness from infancy to old age.
[K12] Equation pbk **£9.99**

HENRY, JOHN (ED)
The British Medical Association Guide to Medicine and Drugs
[K13] D Kindersley pbk **£15.00**

MARTLEW, GILLIAN & SILVER, SHELLEY
The Medicine Chest
[K14] Thorsons pbk **£4.99**

MUIR, DR J.A.
The PM System: Preventative Medicine for Total Health
[K15] Arrow hbk **£5.99**

ORME, PROFESSOR M. & GRAHAM-JONES, DR SUSANNA
Medicine: The Self-Help Guide
An easy-to-understand and thorough account of medicines and medical practice for the layman.
[K16] Viking hbk **£10.95**

SMITH, DR TONY
The Family Doctor Home Adviser NEW
Contains sensible, straightforward advice for the diagnosis and treatment of common ailments at home.
[K17] D Kindersley pbk **£9.95**

TREVELYAN, DOWSON & WEST
The Thorsons Guide to Medical Tests
[K18] Thorsons pbk **£5.99**

TURNER, DR ANTHONY
First Aid and Home Safety
[K19] Hamlyn hbk **£4.95**

Specific Ailments A-Z

This section contains titles on particular health problems, offering background information and practical advice on how to alleviate them. All are designed for the general reader. Among the major series are: the *Equation* 'The Family Doctor Guides', published in collaboration with the British Medical Association and written by leading practitioners and designed to cover all aspects of family health; *Optima's* 'Positive Health Series' of well-illustrated guides which give clear and up-to-date information on a wide range of ailments, and from *Sheldon*, the 'Overcoming Problems Series', clearly-written and well-produced books on various common complaints.

AIDS
Living with Aids
An excellent guide written by people with Aids, and produced by a group associated with the Terrence Higgins Trust.
[K20] Frontliners pbk **£9.95**
The Aids Handbook
[K21] Penguin pbk **£3.99**
CHAITOW, LEON & MARTIN, SIMON
Aids: The Holistic Approach to its Prevention and Treatment
Two well-known health authors tell the story of the striking success of holistic therapy witnessed in America and the implications this could have for other countries.
[K22] Thorsons pbk **£6.99**
SHILTS, RANDY
And the Band Played On: Politics, People and the Aids Epidemic
A provocative account of the first five years of the Aids epidemic in San Fransisco and a full discussion of the failures at the highest level of the medical, political and media establishments in reacting to it.
[K23] Penguin pbk **£8.95**
STARKIE, DR J. & DALE, R.
Understanding Aids
[K24] Hodder pbk **£6.95**

WATNEY, SIMON
Policing Desire: Aids, Pornography and the Media
A thorough and stimulating analysis of how Aids has been used, in some quarters, to oppress and stifle growth.
[K25] Comedia pbk **£6.95**
WATNEY, SIMON & CARTER, ERICA (EDS)
Taking Liberties: Aids and Cultural Politics NEW
A collection of provocative essays addressing the complex social and political issues raised by health education to prevent Aids. Particular focus on representation, and the role of the Gay community.
[K26] Serpent's Tail pbk **£8.95**

ALLERGIES
MCKENZIE, DR JOHN
Living with Allergies
[K27] Penguin pbk **£3.95**
MUMBY, DR KEITH
The Allergy Handbook
[K28] Thorsons pbk **£3.99**
STEEL, MARY
Understanding Allergies
[K29] Hodder pbk **£6.95**

ALZHEIMER'S DISEASE
FORSYTHE, ELIZABETH
Alzheimer's Disease: The Long Bereavement NEW
The author, who has herself cared for a husband with dementia, offers practical advice to relatives and friends, and covers the emotional and psychological aspects of caring.
[K30] Faber pbk **£3.99**

ANOREXIA & BULIMIA
ABRAHAM & LLEWELLYN-JONES
Eating Disorders: The Facts
[K31] Oxford pbk **£5.95**
FRENCH, BARBARA
Coping with Bulimia
[K32] Thorsons pbk **£4.99**
MELVILLE, JOY
ABC of Eating
[K33] Sheldon pbk **£2.95**
PALMER, R.L.
Anorexia Nervosa: A Guide for Sufferers and their Families
[K34] Penguin pbk **£2.95**

ARTHRITIS & RHEUMATISM
BRUSSEAU, PEGGY
Overcoming Rheumatism and Arthritis Naturally
One of the Women's Institute 'Help Yourself' guides. A useful book which examines the various orthodox and alternative treatments available.
[K35] Century pbk **£3.95**
CAMPBELL, G.W. & STONE, ROBERT B.
Doctor's Proven New Home Cure for Arthritis
Classic and recommended title.
[K36] Thorsons pbk **£2.50**
DIEPPE, PROF. PAUL
Arthritis
[K37] Equation pbk **£2.99**
HART, DR FRANK DUDLEY
Overcoming Arthritis
[K38] Dunitz/Futura pbk **£3.95**
HILLS, MARGARET
Curing Arthritis: The Drug Free Way
Popular value-for-money guide.
[K39] Sheldon pbk **£2.95**
SAYCE, VALERIE
Exercise Beats Arthritis
[K40] Thorsons pbk **£3.99**

VAN DEN BERGH, TONY
Answers to Arthritis
[K41] Optima/Futura pbk £4.95

ASTHMA & HAYFEVER
CARSON, PAUL
Coping Successfully with Your Child's Asthma
[K42] Sheldon pbk £2.95
KNIGHT, DR ALAN
Asthma and Hayfever
[K43] Optima pbk £3.95
REES, DR P.J.
Asthma
[K44] Equation pbk £2.99
TURNER, ROGER NEWMAN
The Hayfever Handbook
[K45] Thorsons pbk £2.99

BACK & OTHER PAIN
DE VRIES, JAN
Neck and Back Problems
[K46] Mainstream pbk £3.95
LEWITH & HORN
Drug-Free Pain Relief
[K47] Thorsons pbk £4.99
LIPTON, DR SAMPSON
Conquering Pain
[K48] Optima pbk £3.95
MOUNAYER, BONNIE & WYNN-WILLIAMS, SUSIE
The Back Shop Book: An A-Z of Family Back Care NEW
A well-illustrated guide containing comprehensive practical advice and exercises.
[K49] Optima pbk £8.99
TAGG, DAVID & LINDA
Back Pain
[K50] Crowood pbk £2.95
THE CONSUMERS' ASSOCIATION
Understanding Back Trouble
Useful information on symptoms, causes, treatment and exercises.
[K51] Hodder pbk £6.95

CANCER
DOBREE, DR CHARLES
Cancer: Your Questions Answered
[K52] Ebury pbk £4.95
HARRISON, S.
New Approaches to Cancer
[K53] Rider pbk £6.95
REYNOLDS, TRISH
Your Cancer Your Life
Written for cancer patients and those close to them, this book answers common questions and discusses the different forms of cancer and their treatment.
[K54] Optima pbk £6.95
THE CONSUMERS' ASSOCIATION
Understanding Cancer
[K55] Hodder pbk £6.95

CYSTIC FIBROSIS
BRAY, PERCY
Cystic Fibrosis
[K56] Souvenir pbk £6.95

DEAFNESS
FREELAND, ANDREW P.
Deafness
[K57] Oxford pbk £4.95

DIABETES
ANDERSON, DR JIM
Diabetes
[K58] Optima pbk £3.95
DAY, DR JOHN L.
Insulin-Dependent Diabetes
[K59] Thorsons pbk £9.99

Non-Insulin-Dependent Diabetes
[K60] Thorsons pbk £6.99
YOUNGSTON, DR R.M.
Learning to Live with Diabetes
[K61] Corgi pbk £3.50

DIGESTIVE & URINARY DISORDERS
GARTLEY, CHERYLE B.
Managing Incontinence
[K62] Souvenir pbk £6.95
JANOWITZ, HENRY D.
Your Gut Feelings
[K63] Oxford pbk £12.95
MILLARD, RICHARD T.
Overcoming Urinary Incontinence
[K64] Thorsons hbk £6.99
NICHOL, ROSEMARY
Coping Successfully with Your Irritable Bowel NEW
This common complaint is covered sympathetically and advice is offered on diet, and ways to cut down on stress factors which may cause this condition.
[K65] Sheldon pbk £2.95

DYSLEXIA
QUIN, VERA & MACAUSLAN, ALAN
Dyslexia
[K66] Penguin pbk £5.99

EPILEPSY
CHADWICK, DR D. & USISKIN, S.
Living with Epilepsy
[K67] Optima pbk £4.99
MCGOVERN, SHELAGH
Epilepsy Handbook
[K68] Sheldon pbk £3.95

EYESIGHT
AWDRY, PHILIP & NICHOLLS, C.S.
Cataract
[K69] Faber pbk £2.50
LEYDHECKER, WOLFGANG & CRICK, RONALD PITTS
All about Glaucoma
[K70] Faber pbk £2.25
YOUNGSTON, DR R.M.
Everything You Need to Know About Your Eyes
Covers common problems, diseases and treatments.
[K71] Sheldon pbk £2.95

HAEMOPHILIA
BERGER, MARIE
Understanding Haemophilia NEW
A thorough book, which undertakes to answer the kind of question which any parent might ask.
[K72] Ashgrove P pbk £4.95

HEART PROBLEMS & STROKES
FALK, BERNARD & BLACKWOOD, DR ROGER
Why Kill Yourself?
[K73] NEL pbk £2.99
MCCORMICK, ELIZABETH WILDE
Heart Attack Recovery Book
[K74] Unwin Hyman pbk £4.95
MULCAHY, RISTEARD
Beat Heart Disease
[K75] Optima pbk £3.95
SHILLINGFORD, J. P.
Coronary Heart Disease: The Facts
[K76] Oxford pbk £2.95
YOUNGSTON, DR R.M.
Stroke: A Self-Help Manual
[K77] David & Ch pbk £5.95

HIGH BLOOD PRESSURE
O'BRIEN & O'MALLEY
High Blood Pressure
[K78] Optima pbk £4.99

SHREEVE, DR CAROLINE
The High Blood Pressure Handbook NEW
Drug-free ways to relieve high blood pressure by means of improved diet and relaxation.
[K79] Thorsons pbk £3.99

MIGRAINE & HEADACHES
CRITCHLEY, DR EDMUND
The Pocket Guide to Migraines & Headaches
[K80] Arlington pbk £1.95
MANSFIELD, DR JOHN
The Migraine Revolution
[K81] Thorsons pbk £3.99
SACKS, OLIVER
Migraine: Understanding the Common Disorder
[K82] Pan pbk £3.95
WILKINSON, DR MARCIA
Migraine and Headaches
[K83] Dunitz/Futura pbk £3.95

MULTIPLE SCLEROSIS
DOWIE, POVEY & PRETT
Learning to Live with Multiple Sclerosis
A helpful book offering guidelines for sufferers on how to overcome their disabilities in everyday life. It includes a list of sources of help.
[K84] Sheldon pbk £2.95
FORSYTHE, ELIZABETH
Multiple Sclerosis: Exploring Sickness and Health
[K85] Faber pbk £4.95
GRAHAM, JUDY
Multiple Sclerosis
One of the best books on the subject.
[K86] Thorsons pbk £5.99

POST-VIRAL FATIGUE SYNDROME
FRANKLIN, MIKE & SULLIVAN, JANE
M.E.
A sensitive book on this only recently recognised, but much-discussed illness.
[K87] Century pbk £4.95
MACINTYRE, ANNE
M.E.: Post-Viral Fatigue Syndrome
[K88] Unwin Hyman pbk £4.95

SKIN PROBLEMS
MARKS, PROF RONALD
Acne
Part of the popular 'Positive Health' series.
[K89] Optima pbk £3.95
ORTON, CHRISTINE
Eczma
[K90] Thorsons pbk £2.50

THRUSH
CLAYTOW, CAROLINE
Coping with Thrush
[K91] Sheldon pbk £2.95

Psychological Health & Self Help

This section is designed to cover those problems which, though their outward symptoms may be physical, are more psychological in their origins. Thus Addictions are covered, along with Sexuality; Self-Help includes a section of Practical Psychology, with guides for anxiety, phobias and old age.

Addictions

ALCOHOLISM
DITZLER, JAMES & JOYCE
Coming Off Drink
[K93] Macmillan pbk **£5.95**
MCNEILL, KEITH
How to Say No to Alcohol
[K94] Sheldon pbk **£2.95**

DRUG ABUSE
COLEMAN, DR VERNON
Life without Tranquillisers
[K95] Piatkus pbk **£7.95**
GOSDEN, TONY BLAZE
Drug Abuse
[K96] David & Ch pbk **£5.95**
LEECH, KENNETH
What Everyone Should Know About Drugs
[K97] Sheldon pbk **£2.95**
WILLIS, JAMES
Drug Use and Abuse `NEW`
A thought provoking enquiry by a psychiatrist with wide experience in the field. Examines the need for intoxication, and gives new insights into how cultural aspects influence our attitude to drugs.
[K98] Faber pbk **£3.99**

SMOKING
CARR, ALAN
The Easy Way to Stop Smoking
[K99] Penguin pbk **£2.95**
TARGET, GEORGE
How to Stop Smoking
[K100] Sheldon pbk **£2.95**

Anxiety & Stress

FAELTEN, SHARON & DIAMOND, DAVID
The Complete Book of Stress Relief
[K101] Ebury P pbk **£8.95**

HANSON, PETER
The Joy of Stress
How to make stress work for you and help improve your life.
[K102] Pan pbk **£3.99**

LAKE, TONY
Overcoming Your Nerves
[K103] Sheldon pbk **£2.95**

LIVINGSTON-BOOTH, DR AUDREY
Less Stress, More Success
[K104] Severn H pbk **£11.95**

LOOKER, DR JENNY & GREGSON, DR OLGA
Stresswise `NEW`
A new illustrated guide to recognising the symptoms of stress and then tackling them.
[K105] Hodder pbk **£4.95**

MARSHALL, LYNN
Lynn Marshall's Instant Stress Cure
Well-known TV yoga expert shares her techniques for relaxation.
[K106] Century pbk **£6.95**

THE CONSUMERS' ASSOCIATION
Understanding Stress
[K107] Hodder pbk **£6.95**

WALLACE, JOE MACDONALD
Stress: A Practical Guide to Coping
[K108] Crowood pbk **£2.95**

Depression

HORWOOD, JANET
Comfort for Depression
[K109] Sheldon pbk **£2.95**

LAKE, TONY
Defeating Depression
[K110] Penguin pbk **£3.99**

PRIEST, ROBERT
Anxiety and Depression
[K111] Optima pbk **£5.99**

RUSH, DR JOHN
Beating Depression
[K112] Century pbk **£2.95**

WILKINSON, DR GREG
Depression `NEW`
A new title in the British Medical Association's Family Doctor Guide series.
[K113] Equation pbk **£2.99**

Practical Psychology

This section covers titles which offer a practical guide to Self-Help, and which promote a greater general confidence and sense of well-being.

BLAIR, PAT
Coping with Old Age
[K114] Optima pbk **£4.99**

DOUBTFIRE, DIANNE
Overcoming Shyness: A Woman's Guide
[K115] Sheldon pbk **£2.95**

FENSTERHEIM, HERBERT & BAER, JEAN
Don't Say Yes When You Want to Say No
[K116] Futura pbk **£2.50**
Making Life Right When it Feels All Wrong
[K117] Futura pbk **£2.99**

GREIST, JOHN
Anxiety and its Treatment
[K118] Cambridge pbk **£15.00**

HAMBLY, KENNETH
The Nervous Person's Companion
[K119] Sheldon pbk **£2.95**

HARRIS, THOMAS
I'm OK, You're OK
[K120] Pan pbk **£3.99**

HARRIS, THOMAS & DJORK, AMY
Staying OK
[K121] Pan pbk **£3.50**

HOBMAN, DAVID
Coming of Age `NEW`
A comprehensive and practical guide to health for those over the age of 55.
[K122] Hamlyn pbk **£7.95**

HUNT, DOUGLAS
No More Fears `NEW`
Argues that common phobias, such as the fear of flying or of confined spaces, can be alleviated by a

non-drug nutritional programme of vitamins, minerals and amino acids.
[K123] Thorsons pbk **£3.99**

JEFFERS, SUSAN
Feel the Fear and Do it Anyway
[K124] Century pbk **£3.95**

KNIGHT, LINDSEY
Talking to a Stranger: A Consumer's Guide
[K125] Fontana pbk **£2.95**

LEWIS, DAVID
Fight Your Phobia - and Win
[K126] Sheldon pbk **£3.95**

PEALE, NORMAN VINCENT
A Guide to Confident Living
[K127] Heinemann pbk **£2.95**

REISS, E. & HOROWITZ, K.
Stay Healthy in Later Life `NEW`
Healthy living for the over-fifties.
[K128] Grafton pbk **£2.99**

SIMON, DR SIDNEY
Getting Unstuck `NEW`
A personal programme for getting out of a rut, with continuing advice on what positive action can be taken to overcome self-defeating behaviour.
[K129] Thorsons pbk **£5.99**

STOPPARD, DR MIRIAM
The Prime of Your Life
The well-known TV personality offers some tips in this popular book.
[K130] Penguin pbk **£5.95**

VINES, ROBYN
Agoraphobia
[K131] Fontana pbk **£4.95**

VOSE, RUTH HURST
Agoraphobia
[K132] Faber pbk **£4.95**

WATTIS, DR. J.P.
Confusion in Old Age
[K133] Equation pbk **£2.99**

Sexuality

This section covers all aspects of sexuality, from general manuals on how to improve your sex life, to expert advice on specific problems. It also includes books on contraception.

BROMWICK & PARSONS
Contraception: The Facts
[K134] Oxford pbk **£8.95**

BROWN, PAUL & FAULDER, CAROLYN
Treat Yourself to Sex
[K135] Penguin pbk **£3.50**

COMFORT, ALEX
The Joy of Sex
The popular sex manual that everyone knows, along with its sequel.
[K137] M Beazley hbk **£10.95**
[K138] Quartet pbk **£3.95**
More Joy of Sex
[K136] Quartet pbk **£3.95**
The Pocket Joy of Sex
[K139] M Beazley pbk **£4.95**

Liz Hodgkinson, author of *Bodyshock* (Harrap Columbus pbk £5.95)

COOPER, WENDY & SMITH, TOM
Everything You Need to Know About the Pill
[K140] Sheldon pbk **£2.95**

DIAGRAM GROUP
Questions of Sex **NEW**
Sensitive advice on a range of sexual problems arranged in a question and answer format.
[K141] NEL pbk **£2.50**

GOLDENSON, R. & ANDERSON, K.
Everything You Ever Wanted to Know About Sex
[K142] Bloomsbury pbk **£3.95**
Sex A-Z
An attractively presented and informative dictionary of sex.
[K143] Bloomsbury hbk **£13.95**

GORDON, PETER & MITCHELL, LOUISE
Safer Sex: A New Look at Sexual Pleasure
[K144] Faber pbk **£3.95**

HART, JOHN
So You Think You're Attracted to the Same Sex?
Sensible advice on sexuality.
[K145] Penguin pbk **£1.95**

HODGKINSON, LIZ
Bodyshock
A sympathetic look at transexualism. Few books touch on the subject, so this one is particularly welcome.
[K146] Columbus pbk **£5.95**
Sex is Not Compulsory
[K147] Columbus pbk **£4.95**

JONES, LLEWLLYN
Herpes, AIDS and Other Sexually Transmitted Diseases
[K148] Faber pbk **£3.95**

MARTLEW, GILLIAN & SILVER, SHELLEY
The Pill Protection Plan
[K149] Thorsons pbk **£2.99**

MCCOY, WIBBELSMAN & HAYMAN (EDS)
The Teenage Body Book **NEW**
A practical guide for every teenager, which deals with both the physical and the emotional changes which adolescence brings.
[K150] Piatkus hbk **£12.95**
[K151] Piatkus pbk **£7.95**

PEARSALL, DR PAUL
Super Marital Sex
Argues that sex and intimacy are better within marriage. Includes practical advice.
[K152] Futura pbk **£3.99**

SANDFORD, CHRISTINE E.
Enjoy Sex in the Middle Years
[K153] Optima pbk **£3.95**

SNOWDEN, ROBERT
The IUD: A Woman's Guide
A complete guide to the pros and cons of this form of contraception.
[K154] Unwin Hyman pbk **£3.95**

Terminal Care

BOSTON, SARAH & TREZISE, RACHEL
Merely Mortal: Coping with Dying, Death and Bereavement
[K155] Methuen pbk **£3.95**

LAKE, TONY
Living with Grief
[K156] Sheldon pbk **£3.95**

LAMERTON, RICHARD
Care of the Dying
How to cope both practically and psychologically when caring for a terminally ill friend or relative.
[K157] Penguin pbk **£4.50**

PINCUS, LILY
Death and the Family: The Importance of Mourning
[K158] Faber pbk **£4.95**

WINN, DENISE
The Hospice Way
This book encourages the use of hospices for the terminally ill, which frequently provide the patient with a much more peaceful alternative than staying at home.
[K159] Optima pbk **£3.95**

YOUNGSTON, DR R.M.
Grief
[K160] David & Ch pbk **£5.95**

Women's Health

Covering health matters particular to women, this section includes self-help treatments for minor disorders, as well as guidance on how to look out for more serious problems, and how to cope with them when they arise.

AMMER, CHRISTINE
The A-Z of Women's Health
[K161] Grapevine pbk **£6.99**

BOSTON WOMEN'S HEALTH BOOK COLLECTIVE
Our Bodies Ourselves
The essential guide to all aspects of women's health: as it says on the cover, all women should really be issued with a copy free of charge.
[K162] Penguin pbk **£8.95**

CAMPBELL, MARIA CLAIRE
Snakes and Ladders: The Handbook of Women's Emotional Health
[K163] Century pbk **£5.95**

COLEMAN, DR VERNON
Women's Problems: An A-Z
[K164] Sheldon pbk **£2.95**

COOPER, WENDY
No Change
[K165] Arrow pbk **£2.99**

LLEWELLYN-JONES, DEREK
Everywoman: A Gynaecological Guide for Life **NEW**
A new edition of this sensitively written and comprehensive guide.
[K166] Faber pbk **£4.95**

STOPPARD, MIRIAM
Every Girl's Life Guide
[K167] D Kindersley hbk **£9.95**
[K167A] D Kindersley pbk **£4.95**
Everywoman's Life Guide
[K167B] Macdonald pbk **£9.95**
Everywoman's Medical Handbook
[K168] D Kindersley hbk **£14.95**
Health & Beauty Book
[K168A] D Kindersley hbk **£8.95**
[K168B] D Kindersley pbk **£5.95**

Miriam Stoppard, author of *Everywoman's Medical Handbook* (Dorling Kindersley hbk £14.95) and *Everywoman's Lifeb Guide* (Macdonald pbk £9.95)

Specific Ailments A-Z

ABORTION

KENYON, EDWIN
The Dilemma of Abortion
Helpful objective advice.
[K169] Faber pbk £6.50

WINN, DENISE
Experiences of Abortion
[K170] Optima pbk £4.99

AIDS

RICHARDSON, DIANE
Women and the Aids Crisis
[K171] Pandora pbk £3.95

RIEDER, INES & RUPPELT, PATRICIA (EDS)
Matter of Life and Death: Women Speak about Aids
Documents how women across the globe are fighting the Aids epidemic, and discusses the profound implications which it has for all of us.
[K172] Virago pbk £6.50

BREAST DISEASES

BAUM, MICHAEL
Breast Cancer: The Facts
A useful, comprehensive guide to diagnosis and treatment. Second edition.
[K173] Oxford pbk £4.95

CIRKET, CATH
Breast Health NEW
Contains helpful information on how the breasts function, and how disease is caused.
[K174] Thorsons pbk £5.99

ROBINSON, NANCY & SWASH, IAN
Masectomy: A Patient's Guide to Coping with Breast Surgery
[K175] Thorsons pbk £3.95

CANCER

FAULDER, CAROLYN
The Women's Cancer Book NEW
An extremely informative book covering every aspect of the detection, treatment and care of cancer. Honest and reassuring, it is relevant to women of all ages.
[K176] Virago pbk £5.95

CERVICAL CANCER

CHOMET, DR JANE & JULIAN
Cervical Cancer
[K177] Thorsons pbk £4.99

HARVEY, J.
Cervical Cancer and How to Stop Worrying about it
A useful guide to this important aspect of women's healthcare.
[K178] Faber pbk £3.95

SINGER, DR. ALBERT & SZAREWSKI, DR ANNE
The Cervical Smear Test: What Every Woman Should Know
[K179] Optima pbk £5.99

CYSTITIS

GILLESPIE, DR LARRIAN
You Don't Have to Live with Cystitis
[K180] Century pbk £4.95

KILMARTIN, ANGELA
Sexual Cystitis
[K181] Arrow pbk £3.99

SCHROTENBOER, KATHRYN
Cystitis
Sensitive alternative health remedies.
[K182] Optima pbk £4.99

ENDOMETRIOSIS

BREITKOPF, LYLE & BAKOULIS, MARION GORDON
Coping with Endometriosis
[K183] Thorsons pbk £4.99

HAWKRIDGE, CAROLINE
Understanding Endometriosis NEW
Clear advice on this, the second most common gynaecological complaint.
[K184] Optima pbk £5.99

HYSTERECTOMY

HAYMAN, SUZIE
Hysterectomy: What it is and How to Cope with it Successfully
Helpful and reassuring book discussing the physical and psychological effects.
[K185] Sheldon pbk £2.95

MENOPAUSE

BROMWICH, DR PETER
Menopause NEW
[K186] Equation pbk £2.99

COOPE, DR JEAN
The Menopause
[K187] Optima pbk £5.99

KAHN, ADA & HOLT, LINDA
Menopause: The Best Years of Your Life
[K188] Bloomsbury hbk £12.95

PERIODS & PMT

STEWART, MARION
Beat PMT Through Diet
Self-help for period pain and pre-menstrual tension.
[K189] Ebury pbk £3.95

WELLER, STELLA
Pain-free Periods
[K190] Thorsons pbk £2.50

SMOKING

JACOBSON, BOBBIE
Beating the Ladykillers: Women and Smoking
[K191] Gollancz pbk £4.95

VAGINISMUS

VALLINS, LINDA
Vaginismus
Involuntary spasms of vaginal muscles affect thousands of women. This book discusses the causes and methods of treatment.
[K192] Ashgrove P pbk £3.95

Pregnancy & Childcare

A very wide choice of literature is available on this subject. We include a selection, including the work of the acknowledged experts in the field - Hugh Jolly, Penelope Leach and Sheila Kitzinger.

ANDERSON, MARY
Infertility: A Guide for the Anxious Couple
[K193] Faber pbk £3.95
Pregnancy after Thirty
[K194] Faber pbk £2.95

BALASKAS, JANET
Active Birth
[K195] Unwin Hyman pbk £3.95

BALASKAS, JANET & ARTHUR
New Life
[K196] Sidgwick pbk £8.95

Sheila Kitzinger, author of *The Crying Baby* (Viking hbk £14.95)

BALASKAS, JANET & GORDON, YEHUDI
Encyclopaedia of Pregnancy and Birth
[K197] Macdonald pbk £9.95
Pregnancy, Birth and Infancy
Superb guide for parents covering conception, birth and the first year.
[K198] Orbis hbk £14.95

BLACK, JIM
The Working Mother's Survival Guide
[K199] Simon & Sch pbk £4.95

BOURNE, GORDON
Pregnancy
The highly acclaimed bestseller.
[K200] Pan pbk £5.99

BROOKS, MELISSA & ROGERS, DR MICHAEL
Caesarean Birth: A Practical Guide NEW
Clear and reassuring advice for mothers facing this kind of delivery.
[K201] Optima pbk £5.99

CARSON, DR PAUL
How to Cope with Your Child's Allergies
[K202] Sheldon pbk £2.95

COREA, GENA
The Mother Machine
Reproductive technologies from artificial insemination to artificial wombs.
[K203] Women's P pbk £6.95

DALTON, KATHARINE
Depression After Childbirth
[K204] Oxford pbk £4.95

DAVIS, ADELE
Let's Have Healthy Children
The well-known nutritionist Adele Davis adapts her theories on diet to the child's needs.
[K205] Unwin Hyman pbk £4.50

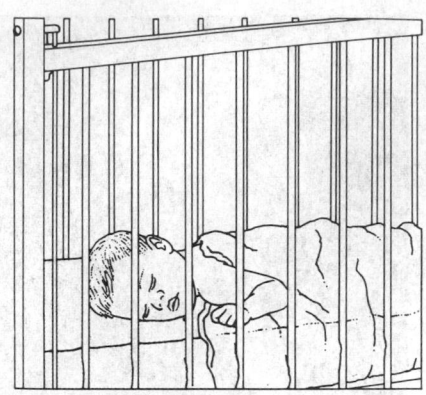

● Don't give him a pillow when he is sleeping. If you want to prop him when he is awake use a pillow under the mattress.

Illustration from *Baby and Child* by Penelope Leach (Penguin pbk £10.95)

EINON, DOROTHY
Parenthood: The Whole Story
A comprehensive guide for parents, which is informative without being didactic or condescending. Easy to use, it contains a refreshing approach to the subject.
[K206] Bloomsbury hbk **£12.95**
[K207] Bloomsbury pbk **£7.99**

EISENBERG, ARLENE
What to Eat When You're Expecting
[K208] Thorsons pbk **£5.99**

FERBER, RICHARD
Solve Your Child's Sleep Problems
[K209] D Kindersley pbk **£5.95**

JOLLY, HUGH
Hugh Jolly's Book of Child Care
An encyclopaedic volume by one of the most famous doctors in the field of child-care.
[K210] Unwin Hyman pbk **£8.95**
The First Five Years
[K211] Pagoda pbk **£4.95**

JONES, MAGGIE
Everything You Need to Know about Adoption
[K212] Sheldon pbk **£2.95**

KITZINGER, SHEILA
Kitzinger is a childbirth educator and social anthropologist who has been developing her own 'psycho-sexual approach' for over 30 years. She has studied attitudes to childbearing in many different cultures, from the US to Africa and the Caribbean.
Being Born
[K213] D Kindersley pbk **£5.95**
Experience of Breast Feeding
[K214] Penguin pbk **£3.99**
Experience of Childbirth
[K215] Penguin pbk **£3.99**
Giving Birth: How it Really Feels
Thirty first-hand descriptions.
[K216] Gollancz pbk **£4.95**
Pregnancy and Childbirth
[K217] M Joseph hbk **£10.95**
[K218] Penguin pbk **£5.95**
The Crying Baby NEW
Kitzinger's latest book, a practical and constructive approach to this common, but often distressing problem for all parents.
[K219] Viking hbk **£14.95**

KNIGHT, BERNARD
Sudden Death in Infancy: The 'Cot-Death' Syndrome
[K220] Faber pbk **£3.95**

KNOPFLER, ANNA
Diabetes in Pregnancy
[K221] Optima pbk **£5.99**

KOHNER, NANCY
Having a Baby
Based on the BBC television series.
[K222] BBC pbk **£5.95**

LEACH, PENELOPE
Penelope Leach is widely regarded as one of the great experts on caring for young children. Her particular concern has been to bridge the gap between professionals in the field and parents - between theories of childbirth and their practice.
Baby and Child
New edition.
[K223] Penguin pbk **£10.95**
Babyhood: Infant Development from Birth to Two Years
The next step on from *Baby and Child*. Second edition.
[K224] Penguin pbk **£6.99**
First Six Months
[K225] Fontana pbk **£4.95**

LEROY, MARGARET
Miscarriage
[K226] Optima pbk **£5.95**

ODENT, MICHEL
Birth Reborn
[K227] Fontana pbk **£5.95**
Entering the World
[K228] Penguin pbk **£6.95**

STANWAY, ANDREW & PENNY
The Baby and Child Book
[K229] Pan pbk **£5.95**

STANWAY, DR PENNY
The Mothercare Guide to Child Health
[K230] Conran Octopus pbk **£7.99**

STOPPARD, DR MIRIAM
The Baby & Child Medical Handbook
[K231] D Kindersley pbk **£6.95**
The Baby Care Book
All of Dr Stoppard's books are sensible, no-nonsense guides for parents.
[K232] D Kindersley pbk **£6.95**
The First Weeks of Life NEW
Another invaluable guide from the popular TV doctor.
[K233] D Kindersley pbk **£6.95**
The Pregnancy and Birth Book
[K234] D Kindersley pbk **£4.95**

WALKER, PETER & FIONA
Natural Parenting
A practical guide for fathers and mothers. Covering the period from conception to age three, it offers general health advice as well as play-orientated exercises and massage programmes.
[K235] Bloomsbury pbk **£6.95**

WARD, JANE
One Parent Plus: A Handbook for Single Parents NEW
Practical, but sensitive advice for the single parent.
[K236] Optima pbk **£5.99**

WELFORD, HEATHER
A-Z of Feeding in the First Year
[K237] Unwin Hyman pbk **£3.95**

WELLS, ROSEMARY
Helping Children Cope with Divorce
Offers advice and information on how to help NEW children overcome the pain of divorce.
[K238] Sheldon pbk **£2.95**

WHITBY, JENNY
The Pre-Natal Exercise Handbook NEW
A well-illustrated guide to all those important exercises which will best prepare the mother physically for the birth of her child.
[K239] Sidgwick pbk **£7.95**

WHITEFORD, BARBARA & POLDEN, MAGGIE
Postnatal Exercises
[K240] Century pbk **£5.95**

YNTEMA, SHARON
Vegetarian Children NEW
Advice on nutrition and education to help in the raising of a happy, healthy vegetarian family.
[K241] Thorsons pbk **£3.99**

Alternative Medicine

Alternative therapies have become increasingly popular as a safe, drug-free way of alleviating pain and maintaining good health. This is a selection of the best general guides, as well as books on individual methods and techniques.

Bloomsbury Good Health Guide: Common Problems and How to Solve Them
A self-help guide to improving your health naturally.
[K242] Bloomsbury pbk **£15.95**

CURTIS, SUSAN
Neal's Yard Natural Remedies
[K390] Routledge pbk **£5.95**

COLEMAN, DR VERNON
A-Z of Alternative Medicine
A comprehensive guide to the numerous therapies now available.
[K243] Corgi pbk **£3.95**

DRURY, NEVILL & SUSAN
The Illustrated Dictionary of Natural Health NEW
Extremely comprehensive, this encyclopaedic guide covers over 1500 different ailments, healing plants and therapies.
[K244] David & Ch pbk **£8.95**

FULDER, STEPHEN
Handbook of Complementary Medicine
[K245] Oxford hbk **£17.50**

MILLS, SIMON (ED)
Alternatives to Healing
[K246] Macmillan hbk **£14.95**

MURRAY, MICHAEL & PIZZORNO, JOSEPH
The Encyclopaedia of Natural Medicine NEW
Well-produced and comprehensive.
[K247] Optima hbk **£14.99**
[K248] Optima pbk **£12.99**

TRATTLER, RON
Better Health Through Natural Healing
[K249] Thorsons pbk **£4.99**

Specific Therapies A-Z

ACUPUNCTURE
The ancient Chinese method of stimulating the flow of energy through the body using needles.
FIREBRACE, PETER & HILL, SANDRA
Acupuncture
[K250] Hamlyn pbk **£4.95**
LEVER, DR R.
Acupuncture for Everyone
[K251] Penguin pbk **£3.95**
NIGHTINGALE, M.
Acupuncture
[K252] Optima pbk **£3.95**
WORSLEY, J.R.
Acupuncture: Is it Fit for You?
[K253] Element pbk **£5.95**

ALEXANDER TECHNIQUE
A comprehensive method of body awareness and postural integration, useful for relieving stress and maintaining general well-being.
GELB, MICHAEL
Body Learning: An Introduction to the Alexander Technique
[K254] Aurum pbk **£5.95**
HODGKINSON, LIZ
The Alexander Technique
[K255] Piatkus pbk **£8.95**

AROMATHERAPY
The ancient art of massaging pure essential oils into the body for their rejuvenating and therapeutic effects.
JACKSON, JUDITH
Aromatherapy
Aromatherapy is gaining credibility as a healing power: this is one of the most attractive books on the subject.
[K256] D Kindersley pbk **£5.95**
MARTIN, GILL
Aromatherapy
[K257] Optima pbk **£4.99**

HERBAL MEDICINE
The age-old tradition of using medicinal plants to treat disease safely continues to be popular today.
Macdonald Encyclopaedia of Medicinal Plants
Lists over 300 plants used to treat disease.
[K258] Macdonald pbk **£7.95**
BUCHMAN, DIAN DINCIN
Herbal Medicine
[K258A] Rider pbk **£6.95**

F

Deadly Nightshade - (Atropa belladonna)

Deadly Nightshade from Neal's Yard Natural Remedies by Susan Curtis (Routledge pbk £5.95)

CAMPION, KITTY
The Family Medical Herbal
[K259] D Kindersley pbk **£7.95**
HOFFMAN, DAVID
The Holistic Herbal
A revised edition of this excellent book. Recommended for all those wanting a more in-depth study of herbal medicine.
[K260] Element pbk **£8.95**
MCINTYRE, ANNE
Herbal Medicine
[K261] Optima pbk **£3.95**
MCINTYRE, MICHAEL
Herbal Medicine for Everyone
[K262] Penguin pbk **£3.95**

HOMOEOPATHY
A highly principled system of holistic medicine using minute doses of substances to stimulate the body's own healing powers. Safe, effective and without side-effects, it is suitable for babies, children and adults.
BRUNTON, DR NELSON
Homoeopathy
[K263] Optima pbk **£4.99**
GIBSON & GIBSON
Homoeopathy for Everyone
[K264] Penguin pbk **£3.95**
HOMOEOPATHIC DEVELOPMENT FOUNDATION
Homoeopathy: The Family Handbook
An easy-to-understand guide to the selection and use of homoeopathic medicines.
[K265] Unwin Hyman pbk **£3.95**
KOEHLER, GERHARD
The Handbook of Homoeopathy
A comprehensive guide for beginners, students and professionals.
[K266] Thorsons pbk **£6.99**
SMITH, DR TREVOR
Homoeopathic Medicine
One of the most popular authors on the subject.
[K267] Thorsons pbk **£4.99**
ULLMAN, DANA
Homoeopathy: Medicine for the 21st Century NEW
Presents clear explanations of the principles of homoeopathy, and some of the background of research into this new form of medicine.
[K268] Thorsons hbk **£8.99**

HYPNOTHERAPY
An increasingly popular but still little-known therapy.
LEVER, RUTH
Hypnotherapy for Everyone
[K269] Penguin pbk **£3.95**
SLEET, ROGER
Hypnotherapy: Is it For You?
[K270] Element pbk **£4.95**

MANIPULATIVE THERAPY
Included here are Osteopathy, Chiropractic, and Shiatsu. These therapies are useful in the treatment of physical injury and pain as well as for improving general well-being *Chiropractic* is the gentle manipulation of the spine to restore mobility and relieve pain; *Osteopathy* is a system of diagnosis and treatment based on the structural and mechanical problems of the musculo-skeletal system; *Shiatsu* is the Japanese art of applying pressure to various points on meridians around the body. It is used to stimulate the energy flow and increase vitality.
DOWNING, GEORGE
Massage Book
Massage books are in ever-increasing demand. This is one of the most attractive and most popular.
[K271] Penguin pbk **£4.95**
EYERMAN, KEN
Massage
[K272] Sidgwick pbk **£9.95**

HEINL, TINA
Baby Massage Book
An excellent book showing the therapeutic effects of touch on the very young.
[K273] Thorsons pbk **£5.25**
HUDSON, C. MAXWELL
The Book of Massage
A complete step-by-step guide to Eastern and Western techniques, beautifully illustrated.
[K274] Ebury pbk **£6.95**
INKELES, GORDON
Unwind: Simple Massage Techniques for Stress Control NEW
Massage for quick and easy stress relief.
[K275] Piatkus pbk **£6.95**
KAYE, ANNA & MATCHAN, DON C.
Reflexology
[K276] Thorsons pbk **£4.99**
KUNTZ, KEVIN & BARBARA
Hand and Foot Reflexology
One of a growing number of books about pressure-point therapy.
[K277] Thorsons pbk **£6.99**
MASTERS, PAUL
Osteopathy for Everyone
[K278] Penguin pbk **£4.95**
MOORE, SUSAN
A Guide to Chiropractic
[K279] Hamlyn pbk **£4.95**
NAMIKOSHI, TORU
The Shiatsu Way to Health
[K280] Kodansha pbk **£9.50**
OHASHI, WATARU
Do-It-Yourself Shiatsu
A straightforward guide taking the reader through the various techniques associated with learning Shiatsu.
[K281] Unwin Hyman pbk **£7.95**
SANDLER, S.
Osteopathy
[K282] Optima pbk **£3.95**

SPIRITUAL HEALING
HERZBERG, EILEEN
Spiritual Healing: A Patient's Guide
[K283] Thorsons pbk **£2.99**

Diet & Nutrition

This section covers general books on nutrition and diet, a selection of popular slimming diets, and books which give advice on special diets, allergy, additives and vitamins.

BRITISH NUTRITIONAL FOUNDATION
Food Fit to Eat NEW
[K284] Sphere pbk **£3.99**

CARPER, JANET
The Food Pharmacy
[K285] Simon & Sch hbk **£12.95**

CONSUMER'S ASSOCIATION
Healthy Eating: Fact and Fiction
[K286] Hodder pbk **£6.95**

DIAMOND, MARILYN & HARVEY
Fit for Life
Written by an American nutritionist husband and wife team, this is the US bestseller on diet and lifestyle. The emphasis is on a natural diet with high water content, including plenty of fruit and vegetables. A sensible diet to help you lose weight and feel fitter.
[K287] Bantam pbk **£3.50**
Living Health: Fit for Life II NEW
The sequel to the bestseller.
[K288] Bantam pbk **£3.99**

Rosemary Conley, author of *Complete Hip and Thigh Diet* (Arrow pbk £2.99)

GRANT, DORIS
Food Combining for Health: A New Look at the Hay System
Has to be the best-selling alternative health book to date - a very plausible look at the theories behind food combinations. Plenty of recipes included.
[K289] Thorsons pbk **£5.99**

LAPORTE, CAROLINE
High Energy Living
[K290] Century pbk **£3.95**

LEFANU, DR JAMES
Eat Your Heart Out
[K291] Macmillan pbk **£5.95**

LOBSTEIN, TIM
Fast Food Facts
[K292] Camden P pbk **£4.95**

LONDON FOOD COMMISSION
Food Adulteration and How to Beat it
Discusses the way in which the food industry manipulates the things we eat, giving the facts about preservatives, fertilisers and related subjects.
[K293] Unwin Hyman pbk **£4.95**

MAYES, ADRIENNE
The Dictionary of Nutritional Health
[K294] Thorsons pbk **£7.99**

MELVILLE, DR ARABELLA & JOHNSON, COLIN
Immunity Plus
Written by the same team who produced *The Complete Diet Book*, this is a wider exploration of diet and health.
[K295] Penguin pbk **£3.95**
The Complete Diet Book   NEW
A new edition.
[K296] Grafton pbk **£10.95**

MORSE, ELISABETH
The Family Guide to Food and Health
[K297] Barrie & J hbk **£12.95**
[K298] Barrie & J pbk **£8.95**

MCCONNELL, CAROL & MALCOLM
The Mediterranean Diet
[K299] Bodley pbk **£7.95**

POLUNIN, MIRIAM
The Right Way to Eat
Very readable approach to healthy eating from the editors of *Here's to Health.*
[K300] Dent pbk **£2.50**

SHREEVE, CAROLINE
Mood Food
A doctor qualified in both conventional and alternative medicine, Caroline Shreeve describes how what we eat can affect the way we feel and aggravate health problems such as depression and hyperactiviy. She offers suggestions on the right diet to improve our health.
[K301] Pan pbk **£3.50**

STANWAY, PENNY
Diet for Common Ailments   NEW
A comprehensive self-help guide, this book offers clear advice on how to treat and prevent common ailments by changes in our eating habits.
[K302] Sidgwick pbk **£5.99**

STEWART, ALAN & JACKSON, MARGARET
Second Bite of the Cherry
[K303] Optima pbk **£5.99**

YETIV, TAEK
Sense and Nonsense in Nutrition
[K304] Penguin pbk **£7.95**

YUDKIN, JOHN
Pure, White and Deadly
The classic book on the effect of sugar on our health, newly updated and now available in paperback.
[K305] Penguin pbk **£3.95**
The Penguin Encyclopaedia of Nutrition
[K306] Penguin pbk **£5.99**

Allergies & Additives

BROSTOFF, DR JONATHAN & GAMLIN, LINDA
The Complete Guide to Food Allergy and Intolerance
[K307] Bloomsbury pbk **£7.95**

FAELTEN, SHARON
The Allergy Self-Help Book
Shows how to identify and avoid specific foods or environmental factors which cause allergies.
[K308] Pan pbk **£4.99**

GREY, JULIET
**Food Intolerance:
Fact and Fiction**
[K309] Grafton pbk **£2.50**

HANSSEN, MAURICE
The New E for Additives
A completely revised edition of the bestselling guide to food additives. Hanssen is a renowned French expert in the field.
[K310] Thorsons pbk **£3.50**

HUNTER, JOHN
Allergy Diet: How to Overcome Food Intolerance
[K311] Optima pbk **£3.95**
Food Intolerance Diet Book
[K312] Optima pbk **£4.99**

Slimming Diets

The BBC Diet
[K313] BBC pbk **£2.95**

CONLEY, ROSEMARY
Complete Hip and Thigh Diet
The complete version of the phenomenal bestseller.
[K314] Arrow pbk **£2.99**

EYTON, AUDREY
Eyton's phenomenally successful F-plan diet sold two million copies worldwide. She is also the founder of *Slimming Magazine*, and of Rydale Hall Health Farm. She has a deep understanding of her subject, having worked with some of the world's leading nutritionists.
F-Plan
Bestselling diet book based on the simple and sensible idea of eating more fibre.
[K315] Penguin pbk **£2.50**
F-Plan Calorie Chart
[K316] Penguin pbk **£2.25**
F-Plus
[K317] Penguin pbk **£2.50**

GILBERT, SARA
Tomorrow I'll be Slim
[K318] Routledge pbk **£5.50**

HOWARD, ALAN NORMAN
The Cambridge Diet
[K319] Corgi pbk **£2.50**

KATAHN, MARTIN
The Rotation Diet
Very low calorie diet increasing from as little as 600 calories per day, in rotation over a 3-week period. The long-term aim is to speed up the metabolism.
[K320] Bantam pbk **£3.50**

KENTON, LESLIE
Kenton is a former broadcaster and Health & Beauty editor of *Harper's & Queen*, whose sparkling health and vitality are the best advertisement for her diet books. The diet she has devised consists of a high proportion of raw food, and has led to her being described as 'the most original guru of health and fitness'.
The Biogenic Diet
[K321] Century pbk **£3.99**

KOWALSKI, ROBERT
Cholesterol and Children   NEW
Argues that the build-up of cholesterol begins in childhood, and presents ways of modifying family eating habits to prevent this.
[K322] Thorsons hbk **£8.95**

MAZEL, JUDY
The Beverly Hills Diet
[K323] Arrow pbk **£2.95**

SPODNIK, JEAN PERRY & GIBBONS, BARBARA
The 35-Plus Diet for Women
[K324] Souvenir hbk **£9.95**

TARNOWER, HERMAN & BAKER, SAM SINCLAIR
The Complete Scarsdale Medical Diet
A sensible diet system based on sound, long-term nutritional advice. Recommended.
[K325] Transworld pbk **£2.99**

TEFF, MICHAEL
The Businessman's Diet Book
An eating plan for businessmen, based on easily available food and drink, which will help you lose

weight without hunger pangs. It includes advice on surviving business lunches and a pull-out questionnaire which can be returned to the author for a personal diet plan.
[K326] NEL pbk **£2.99**

WRIGHT, CELIA
The Wright Diet
[K327] Grafton pbk **£2.99**

WRIGHT, M. (ED)
The Salt Counter
[K328] Pan pbk **£1.50**

Special Diets

ALEXANDER, DALE
The New Arthritis & Commonsense
Revised and expanded edition of Alexander's classic book on arthritis and diet.
[K329] Cedar pbk **£3.95**

BRUSSEAU, PEGGY
Healthy Eating for Diabetics
[K330] Century pbk **£3.95**
The Healthy Heart Book   NEW
How to change your diet and lifestyle for a healthier heart.
[K331] Century pbk **£3.95**

BURKITT, DR D.
Don't Forget Fibre in Your Diet
Burkitt is the acknowledged expert on fibre.
[K332] Optima pbk **£3.95**

GREER, RITA
Healthier Special Diets
The most comprehensive, up-to-date book of its kind, covering nineteen basic diets, ranging from slimming to gluten-free, with 500 recipes written by an expert on diet, nutrition and allergy.
[K333] Dent pbk **£5.95**

HAUSMAN, PATRICIA
Foods That Fight Cancer
This book supports a now widely-held belief that cancer can be alleviated by a dramatic change in diet.
[K334] Ebury pbk **£3.95**

HILLS, MARGERET
The Curing Arthritis Cookbook
[K335] Sheldon pbk **£2.95**

HINE, JAQUI
Low Sugar Cooking
Delicious recipes, illustrated in colour.
[K336] Thorsons pbk **£5.99**

KOWALSKI, ROBERT
The Eight-Week Cholesterol Cure
After two major heart operations the author devised this book on how to reduce cholesterol in the diet without depriving oneself too much.
[K337] Thorsons pbk **£5.99**

KUSHI, MICHIO
The Cancer Prevention Diet
New edition of this macrobiotic approach to preventing and treating cancer.
[K338] Thorsons pbk **£6.99**

LEBRECHT, ELLIE
Living Without Sugar
[K339] Grafton pbk **£3.99**

MACGREGOR, GRAHAM
Salt Free Diet Book
[K340] Optima pbk **£3.95**

RAWCLIFFE, PETER & ROLF, RUTH
Gluten-Free Diet Book
[K341] Optima pbk **£3.95**

STANTON, ROSEMARY
Eating for Peak Performance
[K342] Unwin pbk **£5.95**

THOMAS, JANE
The Fat Counter
[K343] Pan pbk **£1.50**

Vitamins & Minerals

ERDMANN, DR ROBERT & JONES, MEIRION
Minerals
[K344] Century pbk **£4.95**

GRIFFITH, DR H. WINTER
The Vital Vitamin Fact-File
[K345] Thorsons pbk **£6.99**

MERVYN, LEONARD
Beat the Iron Crisis
Stresses the importance of iron and how to ensure sufficient intake.
[K346] Thorsons pbk **£1.99**
Thorson's Complete Guide to Vitamins and Minerals
Excellent value-for-money reference work giving the latest information in an accessible and clear form.
[K347] Thorsons pbk **£2.99**

MINDELL, EARL
A-Z of Vitamins and Minerals
The latest title from this leading American nutritionist.
[K348] Arlington pbk **£1.95**

SCOTT, DAVID
The Vitamin & Mineral Cookbook
[K349] Bloomsbury pbk **£4.99**

Fitness

Exercise

CHAITOW, LEON
The Beat Fatigue Workbook
[K351] Thorsons pbk **£6.99**

FONDA, JANE
Jane Fonda's Workout Book
The exercise book which led the way for the fitness craze of the late 1980s.
[K352] Penguin pbk **£7.99**

KENTON, LESLIE
Ultrahealth
[K353] Arrow pbk **£3.50**

KENTON, LESLIE & SUSANNAH
Time Alive
[K354] Conran Octopus hbk **£10.95**

LYCHOLAT, TONY
Shape Your Body, Shape Your Life
[K355] Thorsons pbk **£3.99**

MOREHOUSE, LAWRENCE E. & GROSS, LEONARD
Total Fitness in 30 Minutes a Week
[K356] Grafton pbk **£2.95**

PINCKNEY, CALLAN
Callanetics
The new exercise routine, which has taken the fitness world by storm.
[K357] Arrow pbk **£6.99**

RCAF
Famous exercises from the Royal Canadian Air Force.
Physical Fitness for Men
[K358] Penguin pbk **£2.95**
Physical Fitness for Women
[K359] Penguin pbk **£2.95**

RUSSELL, RONALD
Swimming for Life   NEW
The author presents the therapeutic value of regular swimming, especially in relation to many different ailments and disabilities.
[K360] Pelham pbk **£7.95**

SEARCH, GAY & DENISON, DAVID
Getting in Shape
Illustrated by cartoonist Gray Joliffe, this book contains a fitness programme specially formulated for those unused to exercise.
[K361] NEL pbk **£6.95**

TOBIAS, MAXINE & STEWART, MARY
Stretch and Relax
A fitness programme for all - supple or not - based on 20 minutes per day of stretching and relaxing. Recommended.
[K362] D Kindersley pbk **£7.95**

WINTERSON, JEANETTE
Fit for the Future
A guide for women who want to live well, by the contemporary fiction writer.
[K363] Pandora pbk **£3.95**

Relaxation, Tai Chi, Yoga

BENSON, HERBERT
The Relaxation Response
[K364] Fontana pbk **£2.95**

CROMPTON, PAUL
Chinese Soft Exercise
[K365] Unwin Hyman pbk **£12.95**

HEWITT, JAMES
The Complete Relaxation Book
[K366] Rider pbk **£4.95**

HORWITZ, TEM & KIMMELMAN, SUSAN
Tai Chi Chu'an: The Technique of Power
An accessible introduction to the Taoist idea of harmony of mind, body and environment through formalised exercises
[K367] Rider/Huchinson pbk **£7.95**

MITCHELL, LAURA
Simple Relaxation: The Physiological Method for Easing Tension (new edn.)
[K368] J Murray pbk **£4.95**

Leslie Kenton, author of *The Joy of Beauty* (Arrow pbk £5.95)

SIVANDA YOGA CENTRE
The Book of Yoga
Excellent introduction to yoga with accessible text and outstanding illustrations.
[K369] Ebury pbk **£6.95**

Health & Beauty

Vogue Beauty and Health Encyclopaedia
[K370] Octopus hbk **£12.95**

ANDERSON, MARIE
Model
[K371] Dragon's World pbk **£8.95**
BAIKIE, PAT
Natural Beauty
[K372] Orbis pbk **£5.95**

CLARK, FELICITY
Vogue Guide to Hair Care
[K373] Penguin pbk **£2.95**

DALY, BARBARA
New Looks from Barbara Daly
[K374] Orbis pbk **£5.95**

HARRIS, DR ANTHONY
The Safe Tan Book **NEW**
Tanning without tears by means of diet and proper sunscreens.
[K375] Sphere pbk **£2.99**

JACKSON, CAROLE
Colour Me Beautiful
A very popular guide to matching colours for beauty: once you have discovered your colour type, you can find out which colours will enhance your looks.
[K376] Piatkus pbk **£4.95**
Colour Me Beautiful Make-Up Book
[K377] Piatkus hbk **£10.95**

JACKSON, CAROLE & LULOW, KALIA
Colour for Men
[K378] Piatkus pbk **£5.95**

KENTON, LESLIE
The Joy of Beauty
Leslie Kenton is the most successful health and beauty writer today, perhaps because her glowing healthy looks defy contradiction. These are some of her secrets.
[K379] Arrow pbk **£5.95**

MEREDITH, BRONWEN
A Change for the Better: A Guide to Plastic Surgery
The latest ideas from this well-known beauty author on the dos and don'ts of cosmetic surgery.
[K380] Grafton pbk **£6.95**

PAINELL, CHRISSIE
Zest: Cosmopolitan's Health and Beauty Handbook
[K381] Ebury pbk **£7.95**

RICHARDS, AYO VAUGHAN
Black and Beautiful
[K382] Collins pbk **£5.95**

RODDICK, ANITA
The Body Shop Book
The well-known high street shop scores another hit.
[K383] Orbis pbk **£7.95**

SEDDON, CAROL
The Complete Man
The latest word on fashion, hairstyles and looks for today's man.
[K384] Ward Lock hbk **£12.95**

STOPPARD, MIRIAM
The Miriam Stoppard Health and Beauty Book
[K385] D Kindersley pbk **£5.95**

530

History

British History
European History
World History
Military History

HISTORY

BRITISH HISTORY

British history is arranged chronologically by period, and alphabetically by author within each period. The chapter begins with a general section covering survey histories, series which treat the whole of English history, and broad thematic studies. Within the chronological sections, books which deal with more than one period are placed with the earliest period covered. There is no demarcation between political and social history - a distinction that is often confusing - but the emphasis of the list is towards social history. Highly academic or specialist titles are not included.

General

Mastering British Economic and Social History
Concise and up-to-date introductory text from 1750 to the present century.
[L1] Macmillan pbk **£5.95**

ADKINS, LESLEY & ROY
The Handbook of British Archaeology
Standard textbook introduction to the subject.
[L2] Macmillan pbk **£7.95**

BECKETT, J.V.
The Aristocracy in England 1660 - 1914
[L3] Blackwell pbk **£10.50**

BLAKE, LORD ROBERT (ED)
The English World: History, Character and People
Highly illustrated, includes contributions from Hugh Trevor-Roper, Max Beloff, Asa Briggs and Kenneth Muir.
[L4] Thames & H hbk **£20.00**

BRIGGS, ASA
A Social History of England
Excellent survey of England over the centuries, well-illustrated and accessible.
[L5] Penguin pbk **£4.95**
[L6] Penguin pbk/illus **£8.99**

BRITISH HISTORICAL FACTS
British Historical Facts is an excellent reference series for students and professional historians.
COOK, CHRIS
English Historical Facts 1603 - 1688
[L7] Macmillan hbk **£33.00**
British Historical Facts 1688 - 1760
[L8] Macmillan hbk **£35.00**
British Historical Facts 1760 - 1830
[L9] Macmillan hbk **£35.00**
British Historical Facts 1830 - 1900
[L10] Macmillan Hbk **£35.00**
[L10A] Macmillan pbk **£9.95**

BRYANT, SIR ARTHUR
One of the most popular British historians of the century, but now somewhat unfashionable because of his unabashed imperialism and right-wing views.

A History of Britain and the British People
Vol 1: Set in a Silver Sea
Traditional, well-received narrative history of Britain.
[L11] Collins hbk **£15.00**
[L12] Grafton pbk **£3.95**
Vol 2: Freedom's Own Island
[L13] Collins hbk **£15.00**
[L14] Grafton pbk **£5.95**
Vol 3: The Search for Justice   NEW
Discovered after the author's death, the final volume had been substantially finished and has been completed using the author's notes. *The Search for Justice* covers the period from the Battle of Waterloo to the liberation of Europe in 1945.
[L15] Collins hbk **£15.00**

BURKE, JOHN
An Illustrated History of England
[L16] Collins hbk **£15.00**

CANNON, JOHN & GRIFFITHS, RALPH
The Oxford Illustrated History of the British Monarchy
[L16A] Oxford hbk **£19.95**

CANBY, COURTLAND
A Guide to the Archaeological Sites of the British Isles   NEW
The first of a seven-volume series on the archaeological sites of Europe.
[L17] Facts on File hbk **£13.95**

CHURCHILL, SIR WINSTON
Churchill's skills as an historian have largely been discredited for his lack of empirical discipline, however his sweeping, majestic history of England remains a great work for its lucidity and literary style.
A History of the English-Speaking Peoples
Vol 1: The Birth of Britain
[L18] Cassell hbk **£14.95**
[L19] Cassell pbk **£6.95**
Vol 2: The New World
[L20] Cassell hbk **£14.95**
[L21] Cassell pbk **£6.95**
Vol 3: The Age of Revolution
[L22] Cassell hbk **£14.95**
[L23] Cassell pbk **£6.95**
Vol 4: The Great Democracies
[L24] Cassell hbk **£14.95**
[L25] Cassell pbk **£6.95**

CLARK, PETER
The English Ale House: A Social History 1200 - 1830
[L26] Longman pbk **£12.50**

COOK, CHRIS
The Longman Handbook of Modern British History
A comprehensive reference book.
[L27] Longman hbk **£16.95**
[L29] Longman pbk **£8.95**

ENGLISH HISTORICAL DOCUMENTS
Vital primary sources for the professional historian.
Vol 1: c.500 - 1042
[L32] Methuen hbk **£65.00**
Vol 2: 1042 - 1189
[L33] Methuen hbk **£65.00**
Vol 3: 1189 - 1327
[L34] Eyre & S hbk **£65.00**
Vol 4: 1320 - 1485
[L35] Eyre & S hbk **£65.00**
Vol 5: 1485 - 1558
[L36] Eyre & S hbk **£65.00**
Vol 8: 1660 - 1714
[L37] Eyre & S hbk **£65.00**

Vol 9: American Colonial Documents to 1776
[L38] Eyre & S hbk **£65.00**
Vol 10: 1714 - 1783
[L39] Eyre & S hbk **£65.00**
Vol 11: 1783 - 1832
[L40] Eyre & S hbk **£65.00**
Vol 12 Part i: 1833 - 1874
[L41] Eyre & S hbk **£65.00**
Vol 12 Part ii: 1874 - 1914
[L42] Eyre & S hbk **£65.00**

HALLIDAY, F.E.
A Concise History of England
[L43] Thames & H pbk **£4.50**

HIBBERT, CHRISTOPHER
The English: A Social History 1066 - 1945
Comprehensive and compelling illustrated story of 900 years of English society.
[L44] Grafton hbk **£20.00**
[L45] Grafton pbk **£8.95**

HILL, CHRISTOPHER
Reformation to Industrial Revolution 1530 - 1780
Stimulating overview of three centuries from the historian well-known for his Marxist perspective.
[L46] Penguin pbk **£2.50**

HINDE, THOMAS
Courtiers: 900 Years of English Court Life
Public and private lives of over 100 characters in court history.
[L47] Gollancz pbk **£5.95**

HOBSBAWM, E.J.
Industry and Empire
Classic economic history of Britain since 1750 from a celebrated Marxist historian.
[L48] Weidenfeld hbk **£15.00**

HOSKINS, W.G.
Local History in England
An indispensable guide to the subject. 'The book contains an enormous amount of information - it would not be easy to discover anything really important that has been overlooked' (*TLS*)
[L49] Longman pbk **£7.95**
The Making of the English Landscape
[L50] Hodder Hbk **£17.95**

Gin Lane by Hogarth from *A Social History of England* by Asa Briggs (Penguin pbk **£8.99**) (Picture: Weidenfeld & Nicholson)

HUDSON, KENNETH & NICHOLLS, ANN
The Cambridge Guide to the Historic Places of Britain and Ireland `NEW`
A guide which treats everyday places, as well as the normal cultural sites.
[L51] Cambridge hbk **£15.00**

JOHNSON, PAUL
A History of the English People
[L52] Weidenfeld pbk **£6.95**

KEARNEY, HUGH
The British Isles `NEW`
Illustrated survey history of the British Isles, which treats of the four nations as one historical area, a history of dependence and interdependence.
[L53] Cambridge hbk **£15.00**

KENYON, JOHN (ED)
A Dictionary of British History
[L54] Secker hbk **£15.00**
[L55] Sphere pbk **£4.99**

LONGFORD, ELIZABETH
The Oxford Book of Royal Anecdotes `NEW`
Highly illustrated anthology of everything Royal and British, from Bodicca to Elizabeth II.
[L57] Oxford hbk **£15.00**

LONGFORD, LORD
A History of the House of Lords `NEW`
Anecdotal, popular history of the Upper House.
[L58] Collins hbk **£15.00**

MACAULAY, LORD THOMAS BABINGTON
History of England
[L59] Penguin pbk **£4.95**
The Illustrated History of England
This edition is published to coincide with the tercentenary of the Glorious Revolution.
[L60] Weidenfeld hbk **£14.95**

MAITLAND, F.W.
The Constitutional History of England
[L62] Cambridge pbk **£22.50**

MARWICK, ARTHUR (ED)
The Illustrated Dictionary of British History
[L63] Thames & H pbk **£6.95**

MCDOWELL, DAVID
Illustrated History of Britain `NEW`
Introduction to British history for younger readers.
[L64] Longman hbk **£9.95**

MORGAN, KENNETH O. (ED)
The Oxford Illustrated History of Britain
A recent and attractive general history. Ten authors supply lucid overviews of consecutive periods from the Roman occupation to the present day. The text which is excellently illustrated is the best introduction to British history for the general reader.
[L72] Oxford hbk **£19.50**
[L73] Oxford pbk **£9.95**

MORTON, A.L. & TATE, GEORGE
The British Labour Movement 1770 - 1920
A concise but complete popular history of the Labour Movement from its earliest beginnings.
[L65] Lawrence & W pbk **£5.95**

NEWBY, HOWARD
Country Life `NEW`
Social history of rural England from the Enclosure Movement to the present.
[L68] Sphere pbk **£4.99**

NORMAN, EDWARD
Roman Catholicism in England
From the Elizabethan Settlement to the Second Vatican Council.
[L69] Oxford pbk **£5.95**

NORWICH, JOHN JULIUS
Britain's Heritage
[L70] Grafton hbk **£14.95**
[L71] Grafton pbk **£6.95**

PORTER, ROY
Living with Sickness: The English Experience 1650 - 1850
Innovative and highly acclaimed social history.
[L74] Fourth Estate hbk **£25.00**

RIDLEY, JASPER
The History of England
Jasper Ridley offers a new insight upon the past, a marvel of compression and a model of lucidity. The author combines something of the enquiring mind of Toynbee with the prose of Bryant.
[L75] Routledge hbk **£10.50**

TAYLOR, A.J.P.
Essays in English History
One of Britain's most eminent historians writes on a wide range of topics, including genocide, Lloyd George, World War I and Cobbett.
[L76] Penguin pbk **£4.95**

THE OXFORD HISTORY OF ENGLAND
From the Roman invasion of Britain to the end of the Second World War, the scope, authoritative writing and well-balanced viewpoint makes it a truly great work, despite some of the volumes now being quite dated.
Vol 1a: Roman Britain
[L77] Oxford hbk **£25.00**
Vol 1b: The English Settlements
[L78] Oxford hbk **£17.50**
Vol 2: Anglo-Saxon England 550 - 1087
[L79] Oxford hbk **£25.00**
Vol 3: From Domesday Book to Magna Carta 1087 - 1216
[L80] Oxford hbk **£25.00**
Vol 4: The Thirteenth Century 1216 - 1307
[L81] Oxford hbk **£25.00**
Vol 5: The Fourteenth Century 1307 - 1399
[L82] Oxford hbk **£25.00**
Vol 6: The Fifteenth Century 1399 - 1485
[L83] Oxford hbk **£25.00**
Vol 7: The Early Tudors 1485 - 1558
[L84] Oxford hbk **£25.00**
Vol 8: The Reign of Elizabeth I 1558 - 1603
[L85] Oxford hbk **£25.00**
Vol 9: The Early Stuarts 1603 - 1660
[L86] Oxford hbk **£25.00**
Vol 10: The Later Stuarts 1660 - 1714
[L87] Oxford hbk **£25.00**
Vol 11: The Whig Supremacy 1714 - 1760
[L88] Oxford hbk **£25.00**
Vol 12: The Reign of George III 1760 - 1815
[L89] Oxford hbk **£25.00**
Vol 13: The Age of Reform 1815 - 1870
[L90] Oxford hbk **£25.00**
Vol 14: England 1870 - 1914
[L91] Oxford hbk **£25.00**
Vol 15: English History 1914 - 1945
[L92] Oxford hbk **£25.00**

A.J.P. Taylor, author of *Essays in English History* (Penguin pbk £4.95)

THOMPSON, E.P.
The Making of the English Working Class
The major work on the development of class structure and its role before, and during the Industrial Revolution.
[L93] Penguin pbk **£7.95**

TREVELYAN, G.M.
Originally a member of the Cambridge Apostles, Trevelyan served in the First World War and became Cambridge Regius Professor of Modern History in 1927. He is probably best remembered for his popular and nostalgic *English Social History*.
A Shortened History of England
[L94] Penguin pbk **£5.99**
Illustrated English Social History
Classic narrative of 600 years of social evolution from Chaucer's England to the turn of the 20th century.
[L95] Longman hbk **£22.50**
[L96] Penguin pbk **£5.99**
Illustrated History of England
Introduction by Asa Briggs
[L97] Longman hbk **£22.50**

WRIGLEY, E.A. & SCHOLFIELD, R.S.
The Population History of England 1541 - 1871
[L100] Cambridge pbk **£17.50**

British History by Period

A number of useful series are available, covering English history from its beginnings to the present day: the Pelican *History of England* and *Social History of Britain*, Paladin *Making of Britain* and *History of England* and Fontana series are suitable for the general reader, offering scholarly, but brief and readable accounts of each period. A longer, and more detailed series, intended for 'A' level and undergraduate students, but suitable for other readers, is the Arnold *New History of England*, published in ten volumes. Two other shorter series which focus on particular topics are the Macmillan *Problems in Focus* (priced at £8.95) and Longman *Seminar Studies* (priced at £3.45)

534

Pre-Roman & Roman Britain

ALLASON-JONES, LINDSAY
Women in Roman Britain `NEW`
Recent archaeological research forms the basis of this first survey of women in Roman Britain.
[L101] Brit Mus Pub pbk **£9.95**

BIRLEY, ANTHONY
People of Roman Britain
[L102] Batsford pbk **£10.95**

BURL, AUBREY
Prehistoric Stone Circles
[L103] Shire pbk **£2.95**
The Stonehenge People
The author vividly recreates the daily lives of megalithic people with special reference to Stonehenge as a social and ritual centre. He dismisses many of the far-fetched theories concerning Stonehenge while examining the importance of the stones.
[L104] Barrie & J pbk **£6.95**

CAESAR, JULIUS (102/100 - 44 BC.)
Conquests of Gaul
Includes an account of his campaigns in Britain, and offers a fascinating portrait of the military customs of the early Britons.
[L105] Penguin pbk **£3.95**

CHADWICK, NORA
Celts
Good general introduction and survey of the early Celts.
[L106] Penguin pbk **£4.99**

DOBSON & BREEZE
Hadrian's Wall
[L107] Penguin pbk **£6.95**

DYER, JAMES
Hill Forts of England and Wales
[L108] Shire pbk **£2.50**
Southern England: An Archaeological Guide
A guide to prehistoric and Roman remains.
[L109] Faber pbk **£4.95**

JOHNSON, S
Later Roman Britain
In the Paladin *Making of Britain* series
[L110] Grafton pbk **£4.95**

LAING, LLOYD
Celtic Britain
In the Paladin *Making of Britain* series..
[L110A] Grafton pbk **£5.95**

MANLEY, JOHN
Atlas of Prehistoric Britain `NEW`
A combination of narrative, artwork and photography, which gives a highly detailed picture of the period, and shows how prehistoric monuments contain evidence of everyday life.
[L111] Phaidon hbk **£22.50**

MARSDEN, PETER
Roman London
[L112] Thames & H pbk **£4.95**

MUIR, RICHARD
Shell Guide to Reading the Landscape
[L113] M Joseph hbk **£13.95**
[L114] M Joseph pbk **£4.95**

The Lost Villages of Britain
[L115] M Joseph pbk **£10.95**
The Stones of Britain
[L116] M Joseph hbk **£15.95**

POWELL, T.G.E.
The Celts
[L117] Thames & H pbk **£6.95**

RICHMOND, I.A.
Roman Britain
A study from the Roman invasion to the 5th century. In the Pelican *History of England* series.
[L118] Penguin pbk **£3.99**

SALWAY, PETER
Frontier People of Roman Britain
[L119] Cambridge hbk **£19.50**
Roman Britain
First volume of Oxford's prestigious series charts the history of Britain under Roman rule and is informed by archaeological discoveries of the last 50 years.
[L120] Oxford pbk **£8.95**

SCULLARD, H.H.
Roman Britain: Outpost of the Empire
[L121] Thames & H pbk **£5.95**

SELKIRK, ANDREW
The Riches of British Archaeology
[L122] Cambridge pbk **£12.95**

TACITUS (c. 55 - 117)
Agricola/Germania
Germania is an account of the Germanic tribes, including interesting descriptions of Roman Britain such as the customs of woad painting in the time of war.
[L123] Penguin pbk **£3.95**

TODD, MALCOLM
Roman Britain 55 BC - AD 400
[L124] Fontana pbk **£5.95**

WACHER, JOHN
Roman Britain
[L125] Dent pbk **£4.50**
The Coming of Rome
In the Paladin *Making of Britain* series.
[L126] Grafton pbk **£2.95**
Towns of Roman Britain
[L127] Batsford pbk **£14.95**

Anglo-Saxon Britain

AELFRIC
A monk of Winchester and the most prominent Anglo-Saxon prose writer, whose *Lives* provide narrative accounts of such saints as King Edmund who was murdered by the Vikings.
Lives of the Saints Vol 1
[L128] Oxford pbk **£9.50**
Lives of the Saints Vol 2
[L129] Oxford pbk **£9.50**

ALCOCK, LESLIE
Arthur's Britain
[L130] Penguin pbk **£4.95**

BEDE
The Venerable Bede was a scholar and historian and one of the leading writers of Anglo-Latin in Anglo-Saxon England. His history of Britain since 55 BC was based on a constant search for material in official documents, letters and other written records. He lived and died at Jarrow where he taught many of the monks.

Ecclesiastical History of the English People
Single narrative history of the conversion of the English to Christianity and the history of the English Church to the early 8th century. This version contains both the original Latin text and an English translation.
[L131] Oxford hbk **£50.00**
History of the English Church & People
[L132] Penguin pbk **£3.95**
MARSDEN, JOHN (ED)
The Illustrated Bede `NEW`
Lavishly illustrated edition, with facsimile reproductions of the original text.
[L133] Macmillan hbk **£16.95**

BLAIR, PETER HUNTER
An Introduction to Anglo-Saxon England
[L134] Cambridge pbk **£13.95**

FINBERG, H.P.R.
The Formation of England 550 - 1042
An accessible guide through the Dark Ages from the Anglo-Saxon invasions to the eve of the Norman conquest. In the Paladin *History of England* series.
[L135] Grafton pbk **£3.95**
The Norman Conquest
[L136] Grafton pbk **£3.95**

FISHER, J.V.D.
The Anglo Saxon Age 400 - 1042
[L137] Longman pbk **£9.50**

GEOFFREY OF MONMOUTH
History of the Kings of Britain
The *History of the Kings of Britain* covers a period of 1,900 years: it begins with Brutus, great grandson of Aeneas, and ends with Cadwallader (AD 689), dealing in particular with the Arthurian legends. The author, said to have been a Benedictine, claimed ancient Welsh documents as his sources, but there is considerable doubt to the validity of this claim and to the factual authority of the History.
[L138] Penguin pbk **£3.99**

JONES, MARTIN
England Before Domesday
[L139] Batsford hbk **£19.95**
[L140] Batsford pbk **£10.95**

LAING, LLOYD & JENNIFER
Two volumes in the Paladin *Making of Britain* series.
Anglo-Saxon England
[L141] Grafton hbk **£4.95**
The Origins of Britain
[L142] Grafton pbk **£5.95**

LOYN, H.R.
Anglo-Saxon England and the Norman Conquest
[L143] Longman hbk **£9.95**

MYRES, J.N.L.
The English Settlements `NEW`
Recently issued in paperback, this and Stenton's *Anglo-Saxon England* (both volumes from the Oxford History of England) are the best accounts of the period.
[L144] Oxford pbk **£6.95**

SAVAGE, ANNE (ED)
The Anglo-Saxon Chronicles
Translation of the Old English chronicles which form a remarkable record of one thousand years of English history from the time of Julius Caesar to the coronation of Henry II. Written mainly by monks, it provides a vivid and lively picture of the Anglo-Saxon world.
[L145] Macmillan pbk **£8.95**

STENTON, SIR FRANK
Anglo-Saxon England **NEW**
From the Oxford History of England.
[L146] Oxford pbk **£8.95**

WHITELOCK, DOROTHY
Beginnings of English Society
In the Pelican *History of England* series.
[L147] Penguin pbk **£3.95**

WILSON, D.
The Archaeology of Anglo-Saxon England
[L148] Cambridge pbk **£17.50**

WOOD, MICHAEL
In Search of the Dark Ages
Popular, concise and well-illustrated account from the successful BBC television series.
[L149] BBC pbk **£8.95**

Medieval Britain

ALLMAND, CHRISTOPHER
The Hundred Years War: England and France at War 1300 - 1450
[L150] Cambridge pbk **£20.00**
[L151] Cambridge pbk **£6.95**

ASTILL & GRANT (EDS)
The Countryside of Medieval England
Contributions from historians, archaeologists and environmentalists giving an integrated perspective on the 11th-15th centuries.
[L152] Blackwell hbk **£35.00**

BARLOW, FRANK
The English Church 1000 - 1066
A history of the Later Anglo-Saxon Church.
[L153] Longman pbk **£11.50**
The English Church 1066 - 1154
A history of the Anglo-Norman Church.
[L154] Longman hbk **£25.00**
The Feudal Kingdom of England 1042 - 1216
[L155] Longman pbk **£9.95**
Thomas à Becket
[L156] Weidenfeld pbk **£8.95**

BATES, DAVID
William the Conqueror
Major new account placing the Norman Conquest of England in the context of events in Western Europe, showing the problems of ruling a kingdom divided by sea and culture.
[L157] G Philip hbk **£14.95**

BEAN, J.M.W.
From Lord to Patron **NEW**
The author analyses the relationship between Lord and Man in late medieval England, the so-called 'bastard feudalism'.
[L157A] Manchester UP hbk **£29.95**

BENNETT, HENRY
Life on the English Manor: A Study of Peasant Conditions 1150 - 1400
[L158] Cambridge hbk **£12.95**

BERESFORD, MAURICE
The Lost Villages of England
[L159] Sutton pbk **£8.95**
The New Towns of the Middle Ages
Out of print for 20 years, the sequel to *The Lost Villages of England* describes town plantation in England, Wales and Gascony.
[L160] Sutton hbk **£19.50**

BOLTON, J.L.
Medieval English Economy 1150 - 1500
[L161] Dent pbk **£7.95**

BROOKE, CHRISTOPHER
The Saxon and Norman Kings
[L162] Fontana pbk **£3.95**

BROOKE, Z.N.
The English Church and the Papacy
A re-issue of a book, which, although written in 1931, remains the best study of the early English Church from the Conquest to the reign of John.
[L163] Cambridge pbk **£10.95**

BUTT, RONALD
A History of Parliament: The Middle Ages **NEW**
A narrative account of the birth of Parliament from the Magna Carta, through the Plantagenet councils, up to 1485.
[L164] Constable hbk **£30.00**

CHIBNALL, MARJORIE
Anglo-Norman England 1066 - 1166
[L165] Blackwell hbk **£32.50**
[L166] Blackwell pbk **£8.95**

CLANCHY, M.T.
England and its Rulers 1066 - 1272
[L167] Fontana pbk **£5.95**

COLLINS, MARIE
Caxton: The Description of Britain
[L167A] Sidgwick hbk **£14.95**

COOK, D.R.
Lancastrians and Yorkists: The War of the Roses
[L168] Longman pbk **£3.45**

DARBY, H.C.
Domesday England
[L169] Cambridge pbk **£15.00**

DAVIS, R.H.C.
King Stephen
[L170] Longman pbk **£6.95**

DREWETT & REDHEAD
The Trial of Richard III
A mock trial to discover whether or not he did kill the Princes in the Tower.
[L171] Sutton pbk **£5.95**

View of an inhabited medieval landscape from *Caxton: The Description of Britain* by Marie Collins (Sidgwick & Jackson hbk **£14.95**)

DYER, CHRISTOPHER
Standards of Living in the Late Middle Ages **NEW**
The author focuses on the varying fortunes of social groups in medieval English society from 1200 to 1520, an age dominated by war and disease.
[L171A] Cambridge pbk **£8.95**

ELTON, G.R.
England 1200 - 1640
[L172] Cambridge pbk **£5.95**

FLETCHER & STEVENSON (EDS)
Order and Disorder in Early Modern England
[L173] Cambridge pbk **£8.95**

GOUGH, RICHARD
History of Myddle
[L174] Penguin pbk **£4.95**

HALLAM, ELIZABETH
Chronicles of the Age of Chivalry
The Plantagenet dynasty from 1216-1377. Covers Henry III, the three Edwards, the era of the Black Prince and the Black Death.
[L175] Weidenfeld hbk **£16.95**
The Plantagenet Chronicles
[L176] Macmillan pbk **£10.95**

HALLAM, H.E.
Rural England 1066 - 1272
[L177] Fontana hbk **£3.50**

HAMMOND & SUTTON
Richard III: The Road to Bosworth Field
[L178] Constable hbk **£12.95**

HARRISS, G.L.
Henry V: The Practice of Kingship
[L179] Oxford pbk **£9.95**

HILTON & ASHTON (EDS)
The English Rising of 1381
[L180] Cambridge pbk **£9.50**

KEEN, M.H.
England in the Later Middle Ages: A Political History
This is one of the standard texts used by A-level history students. An excellent introduction and overview.
[L181] Methuen hbk **£20.00**
[L182] Methuen pbk **£10.95**

KERR, MARY & NIGEL
A Guide to Medieval Sites in Britain
[L183] Grafton pbk **£8.99**
A Guide to Norman Sites in Britain
[L184] Grafton pbk **£4.95**

LANDER, J.R.
Government and Community 1450 - 1509
In the Arnold *New History of England* series.
[L184A] Arnold pbk **£10.95**

MAITLAND, F.W.
Domesday Book and Beyond: Three Essays in the Early History of England
A reissue of the classic study (first published 1897) on the nature of English society at the time of the Domesday survey. Maitland describes what we now know of medieval England and discusses the methodology of the complex Domesday survey.
[L185] Cambridge hbk **£35.00**
[L186] Cambridge pbk **£12.95**

MYERS, A.R.
England in the Late Middle Ages
In the Pelican *History of England* series.
[L187] Penguin pbk **£4.50**

PASTON FAMILY
The Pastons: A Family in the Wars of the Roses
One of the best contemporary accounts of the turmoil of medieval England from the papers of a relatively undistinguished Norfolk family.
[L188] Penguin pbk **£3.95**

POSTAN, M.M.
Medieval Economy and Society: Economic History of Britain 1100 - 1500
[L189] Penguin pbk **£4.99**

PRESTWICH, MICHAEL
Edward I
[L190] Methuen hbk **£25.00**
Three Edwards: War and State in England 1272 - 1377
[L191] Methuen pbk **£8.95**

ROSS, CHARLES
Richard 111
[L192] Methuen pbk **£7.95**
The Wars of the Roses: A Concise History
One of the excellent illustrated history series from Thames & Hudson.
[L193] Thames & H pbk **£5.95**

ROWLEY, TREVOR
Two volumes in the Paladin *Making of Britain* series.
Norman Heritage
[L194] Grafton pbk **£3.95**
The High Middle Ages 1200 - 1500
[L194] Grafton pbk **£6.95**

SEWARD, DESMOND
Henry V as Warlord
[L195] Sidgwick hbk **£15.00**
The Hundred Years War: The English in France 1337 - 1453
[L196] Constable pbk **£6.95**

STENTON, LADY DORIS MARY
English Society in the Early Middle Ages
In the Pelican *History of England* series.
[L197] Penguin pbk **£4.50**

THOMPSON, M.W.
The Decline of the Castle
Examines the decline of the castle as both fortification and seigneurial residence, from the 15th century to the English Civil War.
[L198] Cambridge hbk **£15.00**

THOMSON, JOHN
The Transformation of Medieval England 1370 - 1529
[L199] Longman pbk **£10.95**

TUCK, ANTHONY
Crown and Nobility 1272 - 1461
[L200] Fontana pbk **£4.95**

WARREN, W.L.
King John
[L201] Methuen pbk **£7.50**

WILKINSON & CANTRELL
The Normans in Britain
[L202] Macmillan pbk **£4.25**

WILKINSON, B.
The Later Middle Ages in England 1216 - 1485
[L203] Longman pbk **£9.95**

WILLIAMSON, AUDREY
The Mystery of the Princes
An investigation into the supposed murder of 1483.
[L204] Sutton pbk **£5.95**

Tudor & Stuart Britain

ASHTON, ROBERT
Reformation and Revolution 1558 - 1660
[L205] Grafton pbk **£4.95**

COLEMAN, DONALD
The Economy of England 1450 - 1750
[L206] Oxford pbk **£5.95**

CROSS, CLAIRE
Church and People 1450 - 1660
[L207] Fontana pbk **£5.95**

DICKENS, A.G.
The English Reformation
Exhaustive account of one of the most complex periods in British history. Regarded as a 'masterly' work.
[L208] Fontana pbk **£5.95**

FRASER, ANTONIA
The Weaker Vessel: Woman's Lot in 17th Century England
A look at women in the 17th century, a time when their social standing was at its lowest, but also a time when the seeds of improvement were sown.
[L209] Methuen pbk **£4.50**

HOLDERNESS, B.A.
Pre-Industrial England
Standard text charting the development of the economy and society from the 16th century to 1750.
[L210] Dent pbk **£5.95**

HOULBROOKE, RALPH A.
The English Family 1450 - 1700
[L211] Longman pbk **£8.50**

LOADES, DAVID
Politics and the Nation 1450 - 1660: Obedience, Resistance and Public Order
[L212] Fontana pbk **£6.95**

LOCKYER, ROGER
Tudor & Stuart Britain
One of the standard texts used by students of A-Level history, Lockyer provides an excellent introduction to the whole period.
[L213] Longman pbk **£7.50**

REARDON, B.
Religious Thought in the Reformation
[L214] Longman hbk **£8.95**

REED, MICHAEL
The Age of Exuberance
In the Paladin *History of England* series.
[L214A] Grafton pbk **£6.95**

Lady Antonia Fraser, author of *The Weaker Vessel* (Methuen pbk **£4.50**)

ROPER, HUGH TREVOR
Catholics, Anglicans and Puritans: 17th Century Essays
Essays looking at the intellectual and religious movements behind the Puritan Revolution. Includes essays on Nicholas Hill the English Atomist; Laudism and political power; Archbishop Usher of Armagh; the Great Tew Circle, and Milton and politics.
[L215] Secker hbk **£17.50**
[L216] Fontana pbk **£5.95**

RUSSELL, CONRAD
Crisis of Parliaments: English History 1509 - 1660
[L217] Oxford pbk **£10.95**

SCARISBRICK, J.J.
The Reformation and the English People
How 'ordinary' women and men responded to the Reformation.
[L218] Blackwell hbk **£7.50**

SLACK, PAUL
Poverty and Policy in Tudor and Stuart England
[L219] Longman pbk **£7.50**

SMITH, A.G.R.
The Emergence of a Nation State 1529 - 1660
[L219A] Longman pbk **£10.95**

STARKEY, DAVID
The English Court: From the Wars of the Roses to the Civil War
An examination of the royal household, the internal workings of the Court and its personnel, showing the fundamentally personal nature of the monarchy, unthreatened and undivided by any revolution in government or extension of Parliamentary functions.
[L220] Longman hbk **£17.50**
[L221] Longman pbk **£8.50**

STONE, LAWRENCE
Family, Sex and Marriage in England 1500 - 1800
Compulsively readable study of the evolvement of family relationships from the impersonal extended family to the nuclear unit.
[L222] Penguin pbk **£7.95**

STONE, LAWRENCE & FAWTIER, JEANNE
An Open Elite? England 1540 - 1880
A radical reassessment of the landed classes 1540-1880 which tests the traditional view that for centuries English landed society had been open to new families made rich by business or public office.
[L223] Oxford hbk **£30.00**
[L223A] Oxford abridged pbk **£7.95**

The Tudors

BENNETT, MICHAEL J.
The Battle of Bosworth
A detailed and authoritative reconstruction of the battle which opened Henry VII's way to the English throne.
[L224] Sutton pbk **£7.95**

BINDOFF, S.T.
Tudor England
In the Pelican *History of England* series.
[L225] Penguin pbk **£3.99**

BYRNE, M. ST. CLARE (ED)
The Lisle Letters
Almost 2,000 edited letters which bring to life the intimate concerns of the Lisle household, set against a backdrop of Tudor politics and court intrigue.
[L226] Secker hbk **£14.95**
[L227] Penguin pbk **£5.99**

CHRIMES, S.B.
Henry VII
[L228] Methuen pbk **£12.95**

COLLINSON, PATRICK
Queen and Realm 1558 - 1603 NEW
In the Arnold *New History of England* series.
[L228A] Arnold pbk **£10.95**

DAVIS, C.S.L.
Peace, Print and Protestantism 1450 - 1558
Absorbing study of the impact of the printing press and its relationship with the growth of Protestantism from the Wars of the Roses to the dawn of Elizabethan England. In the Paladin *History of England* series.
[L229] Grafton pbk **£3.95**

ELTON, G.R.
England Under the Tudors
Perhaps the best introduction to Tudor history as a whole, and one which champions the role of Thomas Cromwell as a radical administrator, contrary to previous opinion, and as a statesman who established far-reaching administrative procedures.
[L230] Methuen hbk **£10.95**
Policy and Police: The Enforcement of the Reformation in the Age of Thomas Cromwell
How the break with Rome was enforced and accepted in England.
[L274] Cambridge pbk **£12.95**
Reform and Reformation: England 1509 - 1558
Looks at the Reformation in context of Tudor politics and social change showing the influence exerted by

Thomas Cromwell as Henry VIII's chief administrator. In the Arnold *New History of England* series.
[L231] Arnold pbk **£10.95**
The Parliament of England 1559 - 1581
The standard authority on 16th-century constitutional and political history investigates the role of Parliament in political matters, and challenges previously held views of Sir John Neale that the Commons acquired a major role as a consistent body of Puritan agitators in opposition to government and monarchy in the first half of Elizabeth's reign.
[L232] Cambridge hbk **£35.00**
The Tudor Constitution
[L233] Cambridge hbk **£42.50**
[L234] Cambridge pbk **£17.50**

ERICKSON, CAROLLY
The First Elizabeth
[L235] Macmillan pbk **£3.50**

FLETCHER, ANTHONY
Tudor Rebellions
Looks at the causes of rebellions in the period (Pilgrimage of Grace 1536, Western Rebellion 1547, Kett's Rebellion 1549, Wyatt's Rebellion 1553, and the Northern Rebellion 1569).
[L236] Longman pbk **£3.45**

FOX, ALISTAIR
Thomas More: History and Providence
[L237] Blackwell pbk **£8.95**

FRASER, ANTONIA
Mary Queen of Scots
Masterful lengthy biography from the author of *Cromwell: Our Chief of Men*.
[L238] Methuen pbk **£3.50**

GRAVES, MICHAEL A.R.
The Tudor Parliaments: Crown, Lords and Commons 1485 - 1603
[L239] Longman pbk **£6.95**

HAIGH, CHRISTOPHER (ED)
Reign of Elizabeth I
[L240] Macmillan pbk **£8.95**

HARRISON, S.M.
Henry VIII and the Dissolution of the Monasteries
[L241] Macmillan pbk **£3.25**

HOSKINS, W.G.
The Age of Plunder: The England of Henry VIII 1500 - 1547
[L242] Longman hbk **£8.95**

IVES, E.W.
Anne Boleyn
[L243] Blackwell pbk **£8.95**

LANDER, J.
Conflict and Stability in 15th Century England
[L244] Hutchinson pbk **£8.95**
Government and Community 1450 - 1509
On the control of nobility under Henry VII and Henry VIII through the use of attainder and coercion bonds, which increased the control of government over society and led to Henry VII's reputation as a rapacious monarch.
[L245] Arnold pbk **£9.95**

LOCKYER, ROGER
Henry VII
[L246] Longman pbk **£3.45**

MARIUS, RICHARD
Thomas More
An important new biography adding to our knowledge of More and the tempestuous age in which he lived: a picture of a saint, humanist, and politician whose inner conflicts resulted in his execution.
[L247] Dent hbk **£16.95**
[L248] Fontana pbk **£7.95**

MATTINGLY, GARRETT
The Defeat of the Spanish Armada
The best and most accesible account from the English perspective.
[L249] Cape hbk **£16.00**
[L250] Penguin pbk **£8.95**

MORRIS, CHRISTOPHER
The Tudors
[L251] Fontana pbk **£2.75**

PALLISER, D.M.
The Age of Elizabeth: England Under the Later Tudors
[L252] Longman hbk **£9.95**

PALMER, M.D.
Henry VIII
[L253] Longman pbk **£3.45**

RIDLEY, JASPER
Elizabeth I
[L254] Constable hbk **£15.00**
The Statesman and the Fanatic: Thomas Wolsey and Thomas More
[L255] Constable pbk **£6.95**
The Tudor Age
[L255A] Constable hbk **£25.00**

ROWSE, A.L.
Court and Country: Studies in Tudor Social History
Examines the relations between the Tudor court, the centre of government and the localities.
[L256] Harvester pbk **£22.50**
Eminent Elizabethans
[L257] Macmillan hbk **£35.00**

SALTER, RICHARD
Elizabeth I and Her Reign
Contains 122 documents from the period.
[L258] Macmillan pbk **£4.25**

SCARISBRICK, J.J.
Henry VIII
A landmark in historical biography this remains the most interesting study of a fascinating, complicated and sometimes grotesque monarch.
[L259] Methuen hbk **£17.50**
[L260] Methuen pbk **£9.95**

STRONG, ROY
Gloriana: The Portraits of Queen Elizabeth I
An important study of early propaganda and the development of Tudor iconography, which shows mythology as a vital historical force.
[L261] Thames & H hbk **£18.00**
The Cult of Elizabeth
[L262] Thames & H pbk **£8.95**

THOMAS, KEITH
Religion and the Decline of Magic
Outstanding, seminal study of the changing roles of religion, popular piety, magic and other manifestations of the supernatural in early modern Britain.
[L263] Weidenfeld hbk **£20.00**
[L264] Penguin pbk **£10.95**

THOMSON, GEORGE MALCOLM
Sir Francis Drake
Recently re-issued, Thomson's biography of Drake was first published in 1972.
Deutsch pbk **£7.95**

TITTLER, ROBERT
The Reign of Mary I
[L265] Longman pbk **£3.45**

WARNICKE, RETHA
The Rise and Fall of Anne Boleyn **NEW**
Yet another study of the most famous of Henry VIII's victims which returns to the original belief that her execution was the result of the King's concern about the future of the dynasty not the result of a factional conspiracy within the court.
[L266] Cambridge hbk **£15.00**

WILLIAMS, PENRY
The Tudor Regime
One of the most acclaimed surveys of the Tudor era in the last decade, which treats all the controversies with judicious balance and clarity, assessing the effects of Tudor policies on the quality of daily life.
[L267] Oxford pbk **£9.95**

WILLIAMSON, JAMES A.
The Tudor Age 1485 - 1603
[L268] Longman pbk **£9.95**

YOUINGS, JOYCE
16th Century England
In the Pelican *Social History of Britain* series.
[L269] Penguin pbk **£5.95**

The Stuarts & the Civil War

ASHTON, ROBERT
Reformation and Revolution 1558 - 1660
Charts the religious controversies and factional disputes that marked the period from the accession of Elizabeth I to the Restoration. In the Paladin *History of England* series.
[L270] Grafton pbk **£4.95**

CLARENDON, EDWARD HYDE LORD
Selections from The History of the Rebellion/The Life by Himself
An unsurpassed narrative of the period by the leading supporter of both Charles I and Charles II, which he wrote for posterity *"when the passion, rage, and fury of this time shall be forgotten"*.
[L271] Oxford pbk **£3.50**

COWARD, BARRY
The Stuart Age 1603 - 1714
[L272] Longman pbk **£10.95**

CUST & HUGHES
Conflict in Early Stuart England **NEW**
[L273] Longman pbk **£7.95**

FRASER, ANTONIA
Cromwell: Our Chief of Men
Excellent lengthy biography of this extraordinary man, an unwilling leader who emerged from comparative obscurity to become such a key figure in English history.
[L275] Weidenfeld hbk **£16.50**
[L276] Methuen pbk **£4.95**

GARDINER, SAMUEL
A great, scholarly work recently reissued with an introduction by Christopher Hill.
History of the Great Civil War
Vol 1: 1642 - 44
[L277] Windrush P pbk **£9.95**
Vol 2: 1644 - 45
[L278] Windrush P pbk **£9.95**
Vol 3: 1645 - 47
[L279] Windrush P pbk **£9.95**
Vol 4: 1647 - 49
[L280] Windrush P pbk **£9.95**

GREGG, PAULINE
Free-Born John
A biography of John Lilburne, the radical leader of the Levellers during the Civil War who sought extreme egalitarian social reform.
[L281] Dent pbk **£5.95**
King Charles I
[L282] Dent pbk **£5.95**

HILL, CHRISTOPHER
A Marxist historian, Hill is one of the leading authorities on 17th-century England. Steeped in every aspect of the period, from religious thought to the literature of Milton and his contemporaries, Hill writes from a wide context. His brilliance can be measured by the controversy he arouses.
God's Englishman
Hill's compelling biography of Oliver Cromwell, the man who exerted such an extraordinary influence over the course of English history.
[L283] Penguin pbk **£4.99**
Intellectual Origins of the English Revolution
[L284] Oxford pbk **£8.95**
Puritanism and Revolution
Absorbing interdisciplinary summary of ideas generated by the Puritan revolution.
[L285] Penguin pbk **£6.99**
Society and Puritanism in Pre-Revolutionary England
[L286] Penguin pbk **£6.95**
The World Turned Upside Down
A fascinating and seminal piece of work in the field of social history, which examines the responses of the population at large to the English Civil War. Presents a serious challenge to previous studies of the period.
[L287] Penguin pbk **£6.95**

HIRST, DEREK
Authority and Conflict 1603 - 1658
In the Arnold *New History of England* series.
[L67D] Arnold pbk **£10.95**

HUTTON, RONALD
The Royalist War Effort
[L288] Longman pbk **£8.50**

KENYON, J.P.
Stuart Constitution 1603 - 1688
First published in 1966, this updated edition comprises essential documents of the Stuart period with illuminating commentaries incorporating the latest research.
[L289] Cambridge pbk **£15.00**
Stuart England
In the Pelican *History of England* series.
[L290] Penguin pbk **£3.95**
The Civil Wars of England
[L291] Weidenfeld hbk **£16.95**
The Stuarts
[L292] Fontana pbk **£3.50**

LOCKYER, ROGER
Buckingham
The Life and Political Career of George Villiers, First Duke of Buckingham 1592-1628. The disasters experienced by the Stuart kings were in many cases precipitated by the extraordinary, irresponsible aristocrat George Buckingham who as favourite of James I and Charles I was central to the downfall of the Early Stuarts.
[L293] Longman pbk **£12.95**
The Early Stuarts **NEW**
Narrative history of England 1603-1642.
[L294] Longman pbk **£9.95**

MORRILL, J.S.
Reactions to the English Civil War 1642 - 1649
[L295] Macmillan pbk **£8.95**
Revolt of the Provinces
Conservatives and Radicals in the English Civil War 1630-1650. Morrill argues that the English Civil War was not only a conflict between Puritans and Popish Royalists, but was at a more fundamental level a conflict between the Court and the provinces.
[L296] Longman pbk **£6.95**

POCOCK, J.G.A.
The Ancient Constitution and the Feudal Law
English historical thought in the 17th century, with explanations of current ideas of constitutionalism and common law.
[L297] Cambridge pbk **£10.95**

The conspirators in the Gunpowder Plot, a detail from a contemporary German print, reproduced in *The Oxford Illustrated Encyclopaedia: World History Volume 1* (Oxford hbk **£19.50**)

ROWSE, A.L.
Reflections on the Puritan Revolution
[L298] Methuen hbk **£14.95**

RUSSELL, CONRAD
The Origins of the English Civil War
[L299] Macmillan pbk **£8.95**

SANDERSON, JOHN
But the People's Creatures NEW
The author's thesis is that common to the debates of
the period 1642-49 was the idea of the magistracy as
the creation of those over whom it was to preside.
[L299A] Manchester UP hbk **£29.95**

SOMMERVILLE, J.P.
**Politics and Ideology in England
1603 - 1640**
The critical political and constitutional developments
in the years running up to the Civil War had important
foundations in the conflicting ideologies of the divine
right of Kings and government by consent.
[L300] Longman pbk **£7.95**

STONE, LAWRENCE
**The Causes of the English Revolution
1529-1642**
A highly-rated book with scholarly analysis of the
arguments on this complex subject, incorporating the
latest research.
[L301] Ark pbk **£5.95**
**The Crisis of the Aristocracy
1558 - 1641**
Based on the private papers of aristocratic families,
Stone presents a new interpretation of the long-term
social changes leading up to the English Revolution.
[L302] Oxford hbk **£35.00**
[L303] Oxford pbk **£6.95**

TREVELYAN, G.M.
England Under the Stuarts
In its 21st Edition. Long regarded as a standard work
on the period.
[L304] Methuen pbk **£9.95**

WEDGWOOD, C.V.
One of the most accessible and entertaining historians
to write on this period.
Oliver Cromwell
[L305] Duckworth hbk **£6.95**
The King's Peace 1637 - 41
[L306] Collins hbk **£15.00**
The King's War 1641 - 47
[L307] Collins hbk **£15.00**
The Trial of Charles 1
[L308] Collins hbk **£15.00**
[L309] Penguin pbk **£2.95**

WILLEY, BASIL
The Seventeenth Century Background
Classic study of the century describing its intellectual
climate, and focusing on eminent thinkers of the day.
[L310] Ark pbk **£4.95**

WOOLRYCH, AUSTIN
Commonwealth to Protectorate
'...Will be essential reading for all students of the
period' (Christopher Hill).
[L311] Oxford pbk **£12.50**

The Restoration

CLARK, J.C.D.
The scourge of Marxist historians, Jonathan Clark has
been inaccurately dubbed 'Mrs Thatcher's Historian'
engaged in the task of revising British History. His
argument with the Marxist historians is based on the
claim that they (Hill, Hobsbawm, Thompson et al)
have searched for facts to suit their prejudiced
views. Clark argues that the British political
system has not devoloped according to Marxist
theories, but that democracy was the fortuitous
by-product of personal power struggles. Undoubtedly
a brilliant historian, it remains to be seen if the
body of his work will eventually compare with
that of his adversaries, Hill and Hobsbawm in
particular.
English Society 1688 - 1832
Ideology, Social Structure and Political Practice
during the Ancien Regime.
[L312] Cambridge hbk **£37.50**
[L313] Cambridge pbk **£12.95**
**Revolution and Rebellion: State and
Society in England in 17th and 18th
Centuries**
Refutes the Marxist interpretation of the 1640s as the
English Revolution, and attempts to show the non-
revolutionary nature of the 1688 Revolt, the American
Revolution, the Industrial revolution and the Great
Reform Bill controversy.
[L314] Cambridge hbk **£22.50**
[L315] Cambridge pbk **£7.95**

EARLE, PETER
**The Making of the English Middle
Class** NEW
In this heavily researched and detailed history the
author argues that the growth of the London middle
classes in the period 1660-1730 was the crucial
factor in the development of the modern British
economy.
[L316] Methuen hbk **£25.00**

GREGG, EDWARD
Queen Anne
[L317] Ark pbk **£5.50**

HALEY, KEN H.D.
Politics in the Reign of Charles II
[L318] Blackwell pbk **£3.50**

HOLMES, GEOFFREY
**Britain after the Glorious Revolution
1689 - 1714**
[L319] Macmillan pbk **£8.95**

HUTTON, RONALD
Charles II NEW
The first scholarly, full-length biography of Charles
II, which incorporates new source material; its
attention to his rule over Scotland and Ireland as well
as England gives a united history of the British Isles
in this period.
[L319A] Oxford hbk **£20.00**
The Restoration
[L320] Oxford pbk **£5.95**

JONES, J.R.
Britain and the World 1649 - 1815
[L321] Fontana pbk **£2.95**
Country and Court 1658 - 1714
In the Arnold *New History of England* series.
[L321A] Arnold pbk **£10.95**
The Restored Monarchy 1660 - 1688
[L322] Macmillan pbk **£6.95**

KENYON, J.P.
The Popish Plot
[L323] Penguin pbk **£4.50**

MILLER, JOHN
The Glorious Revolution
[L324] Longman pbk **£3.45**
**The Restoration and the Reign of
Charles II**
[L325] Longman pbk **£3.45**

SPECK, W.A.
Reluctant Revolutionaries NEW
A history of the 1688 revolution which argues that the
revolution saw a decisive move towards constitutional
monarchy, but that this was by no means inevitable.
[L327] Oxford hbk **£17.50**

WILSON, CHARLES
England's Apprenticeship 1603 - 1763
[L329] Longman hbk **£9.95**

ZEE, HENRI & BARBARA VAN DER
1688: Revolution in the Family
A good introduction to a difficult subject.
[L331] Penguin pbk **£5.95**

18th Century
Britain

ASHTON, T.S.
The Industrial Revolution 1780 - 1830
The classic account of the Industrial Revolution
which still remains influential. Informative and
accessible.
[L332] Oxford pbk **£4.50**

BENTLEY, MICHAEL
Politics without Democracy
[L333] Fontana pbk **£4.50**

BERG, MAXINE
**The Age of Manufacturers:
Industry, Innovation and Work in Britain
1700 - 1820**
[L334] Fontana pbk **£4.95**

BLACK, JEREMY
Britain in the Age of Walpole
[L335] Macmillan pbk **£8.95**

BROOKE, JOHN
King George III 1760 - 1820
[L336] Constable pbk **£7.95**

CANNON, JOHN
**Aristocratic Century: The Peerage of
18th Century England**
Discusses the volatile nature of Hanoverian society
and establishes that the English peerage was more
exclusive in nature than it had been considered in
Namier's day.
[L337] Cambridge hbk **£27.50**
[L338] Cambridge pbk **£9.95**

CHRISTIE, IAN R.
Wars and Revolution 1760 - 1815
In the Arnold *New History of England* series.
[L67G] Arnold pbk **£10.95**

CORFIELD, P.J.
**The Impact of English Towns
1700 - 1800**
A general survey of towns and their development over
the century.
[L339] Oxford pbk **£4.95**

DEAN, PHYLLIS
The First Industrial Revolution
A standard analysis of economic, industrial and
technological change brought about by industrial
development 1750 to 1850.
[L340] Cambridge pbk **£8.50**

DINWIDDY, J.R.
From Luddism to the First Reform Bill
[L341] Blackwell pbk **£3.50**

EHRMAN, JOHN
The Younger Pitt
Vol 1: The Years of Acclaim
[L342] Constable pbk **£9.95**
Vol 2: The Reluctant Transition
[L343] Constable pbk **£9.95**

EVANS, ERIC J.
**The Forging of the Modern State
1783 - 1870**
A text book on early industrial Britain.
[L344] Longman pbk **£10.95**

FLOUD, R. & MCCLOSKEY, D.N. (EDS)
**The Economic History of Great Britain
1700 - 1860**
Excellent study of the main developments in
technology and economic growth, explaining the
nature of the first industrial revolution.
[L346] Cambridge pbk **£13.50**

FULFORD, ROGER
Hanover to Windsor
[L347] Fontana pbk **£2.50**

HAMMOND, J.L. & BARBARA
The Village Labourer 1760 - 1832
A study of the government of England before the
Reform Bill.
[L349] Sutton pbk **£6.95**

HILTON, BOYD
Corn, Cash & Commerce
Economic policies of the Tory Government 1815-30.
[L350] Oxford pbk **£8.95**

HIMMELFARB, GERTRUDE
**The Idea of Poverty: England in the
Early Industrial Age**
Discerning and thoroughly researched study of the
developing attitudes of 18th and 19th century social
thinkers and political radicals.
[L351] Faber pbk **£12.95**

HORN, PAMELA
**Life and Labour in Rural England
1760 - 1850**
[L352] Macmillan pbk **£7.95**

JARRETT, DEREK
Britain 1688 - 1815
[L353] Longman pbk **£8.95**

LANGFORD, PAUL
**A Polite and Commercial People:
England 1727 - 83**   **NEW**
The first volume in the *New Oxford History of
England*.
[L56] Oxford hbk **£19.50**

MARLOW, JOYCE
The Life and Times of George I
[L354] Weidenfeld hbk **£10.95**

MARSHALL, DOROTHY
18th Century England 1714 - 1784
General overview of political events of the century,
incorporating social, religious and economic factors.
[L355] Longman pbk **£9.95**

MATHIAS, PETER
**First Industrial Nation: An Economic
History of Britain 1700 - 1914**
[L356] Methuen pbk **£12.95**

NAMIER, LEWIS
**The Structure of Politics at the
Accession of George III**
The major work of this Polish/British historian,

published in 1929, in which he reassessed historical
studies of 18th century political history by arguing
that the so-called struggle between the Whigs and the
Tories was not nearly so clean-cut as had been
assumed. One of the seminal works in British
historiography.
[L357] Macmillan pbk **£16.95**

PLUMB, J.H.
England in the 18th Century
In the Pelican *History of England* series.
[L358] Penguin pbk **£3.95**
The First Four Georges
[L359] Fontana pbk **£3.50**

PORTER, ROY
English Society in the 18th Century
In the Pelican *Social History of Britain*
series.
[L359A] Penguin pbk **£4.99**

PORTER, ROY & DOROTHY
**In Sickness and in Health: The British
Experience 1650 to 1800**
[L360] Fourth Estate hbk **£25.00**

REED, MICHAEL
The Georgian Triumph 1700 - 1830
In the Paladin *History of England* series.
[L361] Grafton pbk **£3.95**

RUDE, GEORGE
Wilkes and Liberty
Wilkes was the editor of an 18th century radical
newspaper and an early champion of democratic
rights and freedom of the press. A classic study of the
movement he led, and the challenge it posed to
autocratic government, by a pre-eminent
contemporary historian.
[L363] Lawrence & W pbk **£6.95**

SPECK, W.A.
Stability and Strife 1714 - 1760
In the Arnold *New History of England* series.
[L67F] Arnold pbk **£10.95**

STEVENSON, JOHN
**Popular Disturbances in England 1700 -
1870**
[L364] Longman pbk **£8.95**

WALVIN, JAMES
Slavery and British Society
[L365] Macmillan pbk **£8.95**

WHITE, T.H.
The Age of Scandal
An excursion through a minor period.
[L366] Oxford pbk **£4.95**

WILLEY, BASIL
**The Eighteenth Century
Background**
Celebrated exposition of the development of the
theme of nature in 18th century thought and literature
which culminates in a study of its use by the romantic
poet Wordsworth.
[L367] Ark pbk **£4.95**

19th Century
Britain

ADELMAN, PAUL
**Gladstone, Disraeli and Later Victorian
Politics**
[L368] Longman pbk **£3.45**

**Victorian Radicalism: The Middle Class
Experience 1830 - 1914**
A valuable political and social history, which is one of
the standard texts on this period.
[L369] Longman pbk **£6.95**

ASHTON, ROSEMARY
Little Germany
An excellent history of Victorian Britain focusing on
the German community, which included Marx, Engels
and others.
[L370] Oxford pbk **£6.95**

BENTLEY, MICHAEL
**Politics without Democracy
1815 - 1914**
Examination of 19th century political change from the
perspective of individuals in government.
[L371] Fontana pbk **£4.50**

BEST, GEOFFREY
Mid-Victorian Britain 1851 - 1875
[L372] Fontana pbk **£4.95**

BLAKE, LORD ROBERT
Disraeli
Still the definitive biography of Queen Victoria's
favourite Prime Minister.
[L374] Methuen pbk **£12.95**

BRIGGS, ASA
The Age of Improvement 1783 - 1867
A large, informative work widely used in schools but
also readily accessible to the general reader. It
concentrates on Victorian Britain, stressing the
underlying unity of the age, from which appeared a
new economic technology with its consequent social
problems.
[L375] Longman pbk **£10.95**
Victorian Cities
Explores the growth of six major cities during the
Victorian era.
[L376] Penguin pbk **£5.99**
Victorian People
Companion to *Victorian Cities*. An assessment of
'persons and themes' from the Great Exhibition to the
Second Reform Bill.
[L377] Penguin pbk **£4.95**

Queen Victoria by Franz Xaver Winterhalter, by kind
permission of Her Majesty the Queen

Victorian Things NEW
The long-awaited final volume of Briggs'
trilogy on Victorian life.
[L378] Batsford hbk **£19.95**

BROWN & DANIELS
The Chartists
A study of the working class movement which arose
as a consequence of the Reform Bill of 1832, which
had denied political rights to the working classes
through its property qualifications.
[L379] Macmillan pbk **£3.95**

BRYANT, SIR ARTHUR
The Great Duke
Bryant's sound, if somewhat traditional, biography of
the Duke of Wellington.
[L379A] Collins hbk **£12.95**

CECIL, DAVID
**Melbourne: Young Melbourne and
Lord Melbourne**
[L379B] Constable pbk **£8.95**

CHAMBERLAIN, MURIEL E.
**Pax Brittannica? British Foreign
Policy 1789 - 1914** NEW
[L380] Longman pbk **£6.95**

CHAMBERS, J.D.
The Workshop of the World
Authoritative summary of development 1820-1880.
[L381] Oxford pbk **£2.95**

CHECKLAND, S.G.
**The Rise of Industrial Society in
England 1815 - 1885**
Both this study and *The Great Victorian Boom* below
provide excellent surveys of the social, economic and
political conditions of 19th century England.
[L382] Longman pbk **£9.95**

CHURCH, R.A.
The Great Victorian Boom
Excellent studies in economic and social history.
[L383] Macmillan pbk **£4.50**

ELDRIDGE, C.C.
**British Imperialism in the 19th
Century**
[L385] Macmillan pbk **£8.95**

ENSOR, R.C.K.
England: 1870 - 1914
Comprehensive classic embracing a period of rapid
change from Gladstone to Asquith.
[L386] Oxford hbk **£25.00**
[L387] Oxford pbk **£10.95**

FEUCHTWANGER, E.J.
Democracy and Empire 1865 - 1914
In the Arnold *New History of England* series.
[L67I] Arnold pbk **£10.95**

GASH, NORMAN
One of the most acclaimed writers on the 19th
century, Gash's two-volume biography of Peel is
accepted as the definitive work.
Aristocracy and People 1815 - 1865
In the Arnold *New History of England* series.
[L67H] Arnold pbk **£10.95**
Lord Liverpool
[L387A] Weidenfeld hbk **£16.95**
**Mr Secretary Peel: The Life of Sir
Robert Peel to 1830**
[L388] Longman pbk **£12.50**
**Sir Robert Peel: The Life of Sir Robert
Peel after 1830**
[L389] Longman pbk **£12.50**

GAY, PETER
Acclaimed exposition on the sexual mores and
behaviour of the Victorians, based on
psychoanalytical studies.
**The Bourgeois Experience: Victoria
to Freud
Vol 1: Education of the Senses**
[L390] Oxford pbk **£8.95**
Vol 2: The Tender Passion
[L391] Oxford pbk **£8.95**

GOURVISH & O'DAY
Later Victorian Britain
[L392] Macmillan pbk **£8.95**

HALEVY, ELIE
Renowned classic first published in 1912 in 6
volumes. The first volumes are here reprinted, and
provide a detailed analysis of economic, political and
cultural issues of the years covered.
**A History of the English People in the
19th Century:
Vol 1: England in 1815**
[L348] Ark pbk **£7.95**
Vol 2: The Liberal Awakening
[L348A] Ark pbk **£4.95**
Vol 3: The Triumph of Reform 1830 - 41
[L393] Ark pbk **£5.95**

HARRISON, J.F.C.
Early Victorian Britain 1832 - 1851
[L394] Fontana pbk **£5.95**

HOBSBAWM & RUDE
Captain Swing
A major study of the agricultural riots which shook
rural England in the 1830s.
[L395] Penguin pbk **£5.95**

HORN, PAMELA
Labouring in the Victorian Countryside
[L396] Sutton pbk **£6.95**
**The Rise and Fall of the Victorian
Servant**
[L397] Sutton pbk **£5.95**

LONGFORD, ELIZABETH
Longford's two-volume study of one of the most
important figures of the early part of the century is
both informative and entertaining.
Wellington: Years of the Sword
[L398A] Grafton pbk **£3.95**
Wellington: Pillar of State
[L398B] Grafton pbk **£3.95**

MARLOW, JOYCE
The Tolpuddle Martyrs
[L399] Grafton pbk **£2.95**

MATTHEW, H.C.G.
Gladstone: 1809 - 1874
[L400] Oxford pbk **£5.95**

MAYHEW, HENRY
**London Labour and the London Poor:
Articles 1849 - 1850**
A selection from the classic social survey, by this
distinguished Victorian author and editor of *Punch*.
[L401] Penguin pbk **£6.95**

MIDWINTER, E.C.
Victorian Social Reform
[L402] Longman pbk **£3.45**

MINGAY, G.E.
**The Transformation of Britain
1830 - 1939**
In the Paladin *History of England* series.
[L403] Grafton pbk **£5.95**

MORRIS, JAMES
A trilogy which tells the tale of the rise and fall
of the British Empire in a lively, almost novelistic
manner, distinguished by the author's majestic
prose.
**Heaven's Command: An Imperial
Progress**
[L404] Penguin pbk **£6.99**
Pax Britannica
[L405] Penguin pbk **£5.95**
Farewell the Trumpets
[L406] Penguin pbk **£6.95**

PEARSALL, R.
**The Worms in the Bud: Aspects of
Victorian Sexuality**
[L407] Penguin pbk **£5.95**

PEARSON & WILLIAMS
**Political Thought and Public Policy in
the 19th Century**
[L408] Longman pbk **£7.50**

POCOCK, TOM
Nelson
[L408A] Cassell pbk **£9.95**

PREST, JOHN
Politics in the Age of Cobden
[L409] Macmillan hbk **£29.50**

READ, DONALD
**The Age of Urban Democracy
1868 - 1914**
[L410] Longman pbk **£10.95**
Peel and the Victorians
[L411] Blackwell hbk **£27.50**

RICHARDS & MACKENZIE
**The Railway Station: A Social
History**
A fascinating study of a romantic obsession.
[L412] Oxford pbk **£5.95**

ROBBINS, KEITH
**19th Century Britain: Integration
and Diversity** NEW
The author develops the thesis that the nineteenth
century saw the consolidation of England, Scotland
and Wales into one nation, yet cultural diversity was
maintained.
[L413] Oxford hbk **£12.95**
[L414] Oxford pbk **£5.95**
**The Eclipse of a Great Power: Modern
Britain 1870 - 1975**
[L456] Longman pbk **£10.95**

ROYLE, EDWARD
Chartism
[L415] Longman pbk **£3.45**

SEAMAN, L.C.B.
**Victorian England: Aspects of English
and Imperial History 1837 - 1901**
A standard survey of the period with emphasis on the
years after 1875.
[L416] Methuen pbk **£8.95**

SHANNON, RICHARD
Gladstone
[L417] H Hamilton hbk **£20.00**
[L418] Methuen pbk **£11.95**
**The Crisis of Imperialism
1865 - 1915**
Detailed study of the transformation of Imperial
Britain from the death of Palmerston to the beginning
of World War I. In the Paladin *History of England*
series.
[L420] Grafton pbk **£4.95**

HISTORY

SMITH, CECIL WOODHAM
Queen Victoria: Her Life and Times 1819 - 1861
[L421] H Hamilton pbk **£5.95**

THOMPSON & EPSTEIN
The Chartist Experience
Studies in working-class radicalism and culture 1830-1860.
[L422] Macmillan pbk **£9.95**

THOMSON, DAVID
England in the 19th Century
In the Pelican *History of England* series.
[L423] Penguin pbk **£3.99**

WALVIN, JAMES
Victorian Values
A timely study of what Victorian values actually were, as opposed to what they are now popularly believed to be have been.
[L425] Deutsch hbk **£9.95**

WIENER, MARTIN
English Culture and the Decline of the Industrial Spirit
An examination of British moves away from industrialism from the early 19th century onwards, which Wiener fascinatingly traces to the industrial decline of the late 1970s.
[L425A] Penguin pbk **£4.50**

WOOD, ANTHONY
19th Century Britain 1815 - 1914
[L426] Longman pbk **£7.25**

WRIGHT, D.G.
Democracy and Reform 1815 - 1885
[L427] Longman pbk **£3.45**

YOUNG, G.M.
Portrait of an Age
A fascinating interpretation of life and conditions in Victorian Britain.
[L428] Oxford pbk **£4.95**

20th Century Britain

ADDISON, PAUL
The Road to 1945: British Politics and the Second World War
[L429] Quartet pbk **£4.95**

ADELMAN, PAUL
The Decline of the Liberal Party 1910 - 31
With its companion volume, these are standard texts for students of Political History; in the *Seminar Studies in History* Series.
[L430] Longman pbk **£3.45**
The Rise of the Labour Party 1880 - 1945
[L431] Longman pbk **£3.45**

ANDERSON, G. (ED)
The White Blouse Revolution **NEW**
An examination of how the sexual composition of office work changed radically since 1870, from being a male preserve, to a state where the majority of office workers are women; in the process, it shows how historical events, such as World Wars, can radically change social structure.
[L431A] Manchester UP hbk **£27.50**

BARNETT, CORRELLI
The Audit of War: The Illusion and Reality of Britain as a Great Nation
A challenging and important work which places Britain's decline since the Second World War in a startling new perspective.
[L432] Macmillan pbk **£7.95**
The Collapse of British Power
[L433] Sutton pbk **£8.95**

BELOFF, MAX
Wars and Welfare 1914 - 1945
In the Arnold *New History of England* series.
[L67J] Arnold pbk **£10.95**

BLAKE, LORD ROBERT
The Decline of Power 1915 - 1964
In the Paladin *History of England* series.
[L434] Collins hbk **£18.00**
[L435] Grafton pbk **£4.95**

BROOK, STEPHEN
The Club **NEW**
A study of the Jewish communities of modern Britain.
[L436] Constable hbk **£15.95**

BULLOCK, ALAN
Ernest Bevin: Foreign Secretary
Definitive biography of the man who had as much responsibility as anyone in negotiating Britain's place in the post-war world order.
[L437] Oxford pbk **£12.50**

CALDER, ANGUS
The People's War: Britain 1939 - 45
Oral history of daily life in Britain during the war.
[L439] Grafton pbk **£3.95**

CHILDS, D.
Britain Since 1945: A Political History
[L440] Methuen pbk **£6.95**

COOK, CHRIS
Short History of the Liberal Party 1900 - 84
[L441] Macmillan pbk **£9.95**

COSTELLO, J.
Love, Sex and War
Loaded with statistics and anecdotes, with chapters on women in war, VD, and homosexuality.
[L442] Pan pbk **£3.95**

Neville Chamberlain returning from Munich in September 1938 taken from *Oxford Illustrated Encyclopaedia: World History Vol 2* (Oxford hbk £19.50)

FISHWICK, N.
Association Football and English Social Life 1910 - 50 **NEW**
In examining the impact of football on people's lives the author reveals aspects of contemporary working-class culture, and finds that, while football has improved the quality of everyday life, it has also illustrated the limitations of people's opportunities.
[L442A] Manchester UP hbk **£25.00**

HINTON, JAMES
Protests and Visions: Peace Politics in 20th Century Britain **NEW**
[L443] Hutchinson pbk **£8.95**

JAMES, ROBERT RHODES
The British Revolution/British Politics 1880 - 1939
[L444] Methuen pbk **£10.95**

JENKINS, ROY
Baldwin
[L444A] Collins pbk **£8.95**
Mr Balfour's Poodle: Peers versus People **NEW**
A reprint of Jenkins's classic study of the constitutional crises 1906-1911 which resulted in the House of Lords passing the Parliament Bill.
[L445] Collins pbk **£9.95**

KENNEDY, PAUL
The Realities Behind Diplomacy **NEW**
In explaining the decline of Britain's standing in the world, from its height in 1865, Kennedy focuses on the connection between industrial power and foreign policy. Newly re-issued.
[L446] Fontana pbk **£5.95**

KUSHNER & LUNN (EDS)
Traditions of Intolerance **NEW**
Essays on the history of British intolerance in the 20th century.
[L447] Manchester UP hbk **£29.95**

KUSHNER, TONY
The Persistence of Prejudice **NEW**
A study of anti-semitism in Britain during WWII.
[L448] Manchester UP pbk **£9.95**

MARWICK, ARTHUR
British Society since 1945
In the Pelican *Social History of Britain* series.
[L448A] Penguin pbk **£4.95**

MEDLICOTT, W.N.
Contemporary England 1914 - 1964
With an epilogue, covering 1964-74.
[L449] Longman pbk **£9.95**

MORGAN, KENNETH
Consensus and Disunity: The Lloyd George Coalition Government 1918 - 22
[L429A] Oxford pbk **£12.50**
Labour in Power
Notable study of the Attlee administration 1945-1951.
[L450] Oxford pbk **£6.95**
Labour People
Leaders and Lieutenants: Hardie to Kinnock
[L450A] Oxford hbk **£12.95**

NUTTGENS, P.
The Home Front **NEW**
Accompanying the television series, this examines the historical development of housing - from the corporatism of the Victorians, through the post-Great War council housing and post-1945 planning schemes, to the controversial high-rise developments of the 1960s.
[L451] BBC hbk **£10.95**

O'GORMAN, FRANK
British Conservatism: Conservative Thought from Burke to Thatcher
A concise account of the origins and development of Conservative ideology, showing just how much it has changed since the late 18th century.
[L452] Longman pbk **£6.95**

PANKHURST, SYLVIA
Suffragette Movement: An Intimate Account of Persons and Ideals
Primary source for the history of the movement from its origins in the late 19th century to the end of the Great War.
[L453] Virago pbk **£10.99**

PELLING, HENRY
History of British Trade Unionism
[L454] Penguin pbk **£5.99**
Short History of the Labour Party
The best account of the development of the Labour Party, which concentrates on the balance of power between the trade unions, the ideologues and the Parliamentary Party.
[L455] Macmillan pbk **£8.95**

SISSONS & FRENCH (EDS)
The Age of Austerity
Collection of essays by 15 different writers, providing a stimulating portrait of the immediate post-war period 1945-51.
[L457] Oxford pbk **£4.95**

SKED & COOK
Post-War Britain: A Political History
[L458] Penguin pbk **£6.99**

STEVENSON, JOHN
British Society 1914 - 1945
In the Pelican *Social History of Britain* series.
[L458A] Penguin pbk **£4.99**

SYMONS, JULIAN
The General Strike: A Historical Portrait
Lively and detailed portrait of this crucial 1926 episode in the development of modern Britain.
[L459] Hutchinson pbk **£5.95**

TAYLOR, A.J.P.
English History 1914 - 1945
Account of the closing years of the British Empire. During ten of these 31 years the English people were involved in world war; for 19 of these years they lived in the shadow of mass-unemployment. Taylor's study of the period remains the classic account.
[L460] Penguin pbk **£7.95**

TAYLOR, R. & YOUNG, N.
Campaigns for Peace   **NEW**
Essays on the development of British peace movements since the late 19th century.
[L460A] Manchester UP pbk **£9.95**

THOMAS, HUGH
The Suez Affair
[L461] Weidenfeld pbk **£5.95**

THOMSON, DAVID
England in the 20th Century 1914 - 1963
In the Pelican *History of England* series.
[L461A] Penguin pbk **£3.95**

WARK, WESLEY K.
The Ultimate Enemy: British Intelligence and Nazi Germany 1933 - 39
Throws new light on appeasement by examining the role played by British intelligence in shaping policy toward Nazi Germany in the 1930s.
[L462] Oxford pbk **£5.95**

Irish History

The vital nature of Irish historiography and a constantly growing corpus of historical research has led to a vast range of work published on Irish history in the past few decades. This recent revision is not only prolific but controversial, casting new light on present problems, and reflecting changing cultural beliefs and social values. The list, which is necessarily selective, is biased towards the most recent publications and general histories. Particularly worthy of note is Roy Foster's *Modern Ireland*, which makes excellent use of recent research to provide the most stimulating new history of Ireland.

A NEW HISTORY OF IRELAND
Planned and established by the late T.W. Moody, this series is the culmination of a renaissance in Irish historiography, and will surely become the definitive history of Ireland. It will eventually consist of 10 volumes, of which seven will be text and three will be reference, written by some seventy contributors. Those volumes that have already been published have dealt with all aspects of Irish history in their particular period and reflect the recent emphasis on social history.
Vol 2: Medieval Ireland 1169 - 1534
[L463] Oxford hbk **£75.00**
Vol 3: Early Modern Ireland 1534 - 1691
[L464] Oxford hbk **£55.00**
Vol 4: 18th Century Ireland 1691 - 1800
[L465] Oxford hbk **£65.00**
Vol 8: A Chronology of Irish History to 1976
[L466] Oxford hbk **£60.00**
Vol 9: Maps, Genealogies, Lists
[L467] Oxford hbk **£95.00**

BECKETT, J.C.
The Making of Modern Ireland 1603 - 1923
A scholarly and challenging history of modern Ireland.
[L468] Faber pbk **£6.95**

BENCE-JONES, MARK
Twilight of the Ascendancy
For fans of Molly Keane and the Irish RM, Mark Bence-Jones has written the real story of the decline of the Anglo-Irish aristocracy. Highly atmospheric and enjoyable.
[L469] Constable pbk **£6.95**

BERESFORD ELLIS, PETER
Hell or Connaught   **NEW**
History of the Cromwellian campaign in Ireland.
[L470] Blackstaff pbk **£5.95**
The Boyne Water   **NEW**
A popular history of the Battle of the Boyne which explains why the event has become such a potent symbol in Irish history.
[L471] Blackstaff pbk **£5.95**

BISHOP & O'MALLEY
The Provisional IRA
An excellent and detailed study on the present day IRA by two Irish journalists. For the background to the IRA and a history of its origins, see Tim Pat Coogan below.
[L472] Corgi pbk **£3.99**

BOYCE, D.G.
The Irish Question in British Politics
[L473] Macmillan pbk **£5.95**
The Revolution in Ireland 1879 - 1923
[L473A] Macmillan pbk **£8.95**

BROWN, TERENCE
Ireland: A Social and Cultural History 1922 - 1985
A highly readable account of recent Irish history that serves as an excellent introduction to contemporary Irish culture, and is essential background material to a study of 20th century Irish literature.
[L474] Fontana pbk **£5.95**

COOGAN, TIM PAT
The IRA
For the background to the IRA and a history of the old IRA Tim Pat Coogan's book, recently re-issued in paperback, is the standard text.
[L475] Fontana pbk **£4.95**

CULLEN, L.M.
The Economic History of Ireland since 1660
A new edition of the classic text on Irish economic history by the foremost authority on the subject.
[L476] Batsford pbk **£8.95**

FISK, ROBERT
In Time of War
A fascinating and lively account of Ireland during the war years by the highly respected English journalist. It cannot be too highly recommended.
[L477] Grafton pbk **£6.95**

FOSTER, ROY
Modern Ireland 1600 - 1972   **NEW**
A masterful, engrossing and erudite study of Irish history from the 17th century to the present day, providing a unique synthesis of recent Irish historical studies. The book, which is highly controversial, assumes a basic knowledge of Irish history.
[L478] Allen Lane hbk **£25.00**

FOSTER, R.F. (ED)
The Oxford Illustrated History of Ireland   **NEW**
The Oxford Illustrated Histories are the most readable and approachable books on their subjects. Written by a team of distinguished Irish historians, the text promises to be more than an introduction; combined with the 200 illustrations and full reference material, this may become the standard one-volume history of Ireland.
[L478A] Oxford hbk **£17.50**

HOPKINSON, MICHAEL
Green Against Green: The Irish Civil War
The cataclysmic event of recent Irish history and politics, the Civil War (1922-3) remains a highly contentious and rarely examined issue. Up to now the standard work has been Calton Younger's (see below) but this recent study uses previously unavailable sources to give a highly detailed account of the war.
[L479] Gill & Macmillan pbk **£12.95**

HOPPEN, THEODORE K.
Ireland since 1800: Conflict and Conformity   **NEW**
[L480] Longman pbk **£8.95**

KEE, ROBERT
A reissue in paperback of Kee's excellent introduction to Irish history. Admirably lucid and readable, *The Green Flag* is a narrative history which concentrates on the great events rather than themes of Irish history.

The Green Flag:
Vol 1: The Most Distressful Country
[L481] Penguin pbk **£4.99**
Vol 2: The Bold Fenian Men
[L482] Penguin pbk **£4.99**
Vol 3: Ourselves Alone
[L483] Penguin pbk **£4.99**

LEE, JOSEPH
Ireland 1912 - 1985   **NEW**
The first major examination of Irish performance in
the 20th century. The author places the main political
events within the broad cultural and economic
framework and discusses the importance of rhetoric
and reality in the Irish mind.
[L484] Cambridge hbk **£14.95**
**The Modernisation of Irish Society
1848 - 1918**
A reissue of a standard textbook on Irish life and
history from the Famine to the election of the first
Dail. The book was originally volume 10 in the
discontinued Gill History of Ireland.
[L485] Gill and Macmillan pbk **£7.95**

LYONS, F.S.L.
**Culture and Anarchy in Ireland
1890 - 1939**
A re-issue of Lyons's study of the four conflicting
cultures which have co-existed in Ireland - Gaelic,
English, Anglo-Irish and Ulster Protestant.
[L485A] Oxford pbk **£5.95**
Ireland since the Famine
A massive work that has become the text of modern
Irish history. Scholarly, incisive, and readable it is
without doubt the best 1-volume history of the period.
[L486] Fontana pbk **£7.95**

MACDONAGH, OLIVER
**States of Mind: A Study of Anglo-Irish
Conflict 1780 - 1980**
A fascinating study of the Anglo-Irish tradition,
particularly good on Irish historiography.
[L487] Unwin Hyman pbk **£9.50**
The Hereditary Bondsman
The most recent and authoritative study of Daniel
O'Connell, this is the first of two volumes, covering
his life from 1775 to 1829 and dealing with the period
up to Catholic Emancipation.
[L488] Weidenfeld hbk **£16.95**

MOODY & MARTIN
The Course of Irish History
Slightly dated but excellent survey of Irish history.
The best in one volume dealing with early Irish
history.
[L489] Mercier/RTE pbk **£12.95**

MURPHY, JOHN A.
Ireland in the 20th Century
A reissue of volume 11 in the discontinued Gill
History of Ireland, this title is the clearest
introduction to an extremely complex period,
covering Independence, the partition of the island and
the development of the new state.
[L490] Gill and Macmillan pbk **£7.95**

NEW GILL HISTORY OF IRELAND
This new series is intended to replace the old *Gill
History of Ireland*, with completely new titles and
authors. It will eventually consist of six volumes
providing a complete survey of Irish history from
early medieval times to the present. Like the old Gill
History the volumes in this series will undoubtedly
become standard texts for schools and
undergraduates.
RICHTER, MICHAEL
**Vol 1: Medieval Ireland: The
Enduring Tradition**   **NEW**
[L491] Gill and Macmillan pbk **£8.95**

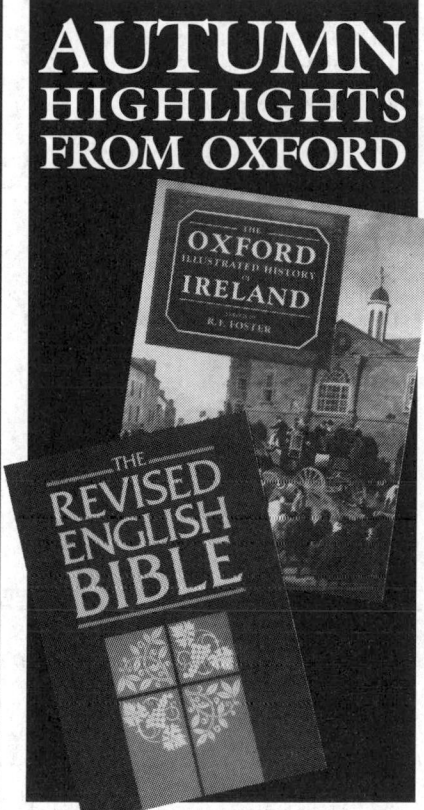

AUTUMN HIGHLIGHTS FROM OXFORD

The Oxford Illustrated History of Ireland
Edited by ROY FOSTER

A lavishly illustrated, authoritative account
that traces Irish history from prehistoric
communities, through centuries of
turbulent change and creativity, to the
present day.
0 19 822970 4 October £17.50

The Revised English Bible
A major new version of the Bible for the
1990s and beyond, written in clear,
contemporary English for use by all
denominations.
Bible only *0 19 101210 6 £8.95*
Bible with Apocrypha *0 19 101220 3 £9.95*
(Also available in handsome leather
presentation editions)
September
Jointly published with Cambridge University
Press

Wartime
Understanding and Behaviour in the Second World War
PAUL FUSSELL

Marking the 50th anniversary of the
outbreak of the Second World War, this
compelling book offers vivid recollections
of life on the home and battle fronts.
0 19 503797 9 September £15

I'm a Health Freak Too!
ANN MCPHERSON and
AIDAN MACFARLANE

Following the bestselling *Diary of a
Teenage Health Freak*, Susie Payne has
written the ultimate guide to teenage
RUDE health, covering many subjects
brother Pete would never have dreamed of!
0 19 282232 2 September £2.95
Oxford Paperbacks

The Selfish Gene
Second Edition
RICHARD DAWKINS

The revised and considerably expanded
edition of a science bestseller, the most
important book on evolution since Darwin.
0 19 286092 5 September £5.95
Oxford Paperbacks

A Dictionary of Superstitions
Edited by IONA OPIE and
MOIRA TATEM

Published in time for Halloween, this
intriguing guide to centuries of folk belief
delves into spells, cures, rituals, charms,
omens, and much more.
0 19 211597 9 October £17.50

The Oxford Reference Dictionary
Flexi Edition
A new flexi edition of this unique reference
book, with over 75,000 definitions, 6,000
encyclopaedic entries, and nearly 100 pages
of illustrations and maps.
0 19 861238 9 July £9.95

OXFORD UNIVERSITY PRESS
Publishers of the Second Edition of *The Oxford English Dictionary*

Digging for potatoes during the Irish Famine, taken from *Oxford Illustrated Encyclopaedia: World History : Volume 2* (Oxford hbk £19.50)

FITZPATRICK, BRENDAN
Vol 3: 17th Century Ireland: The Wars of Religion NEW
[L492] Gill and Macmillan pbk **£8.95**
JOHNSON, E.M.
Vol 4: 18th Century Ireland NEW
[L493] Gill and Macmillan pbk **£8.95**

O'KELLY, MICHAEL J.
Early Ireland NEW
Up-to-date introduction to Irish pre-history.
[L494] Cambridge pbk **£9.95**

SMITH, CECIL WOODHAM
The Great Hunger
Compulsive reading from the author of *The Reason Why*, a terrifying account of the Great Famine of 1846 - 1848.
[L495] H Hamilton pbk **£6.95**

STEWART, A.T.Q.
The Narrow Ground
An excellent 'Unionist' history of Ulster from 1609 to 1969. Essential reading for anyone trying to understand the Northern Ireland problem.
[L496] Pretari P pbk **£4.95**
The Ulster Crisis: Resistance to Home Rule 1912 - 1914
A study of the formation of Ulster unionist politics.
[L497] Faber pbk **£2.95**

YOUNGER, C.
Ireland's Civil War
[L498] Fontana pbk **£6.95**

Scottish History

CAMERON, DAVID KERR
The Ballad and the Plough
Celebrated folk history of Scottish farm life.
[L499] Gollancz pbk **£5.95**

EDINBURGH HISTORY OF SCOTLAND
DUNCAN, A.A.M.
Vol 1: Making of the Kingdom
[L503] Mercat P pbk **£12.95**
NICHOLSON, R.
Vol 2: The Later Middle Age
[L504] Mercat P pbk **£12.95**
DONALDSON, G.
Vol 3: James V to James VII
[L505] Mercat P pbk **£12.95**
FERGUSON, W.
Vol 4: 1689 to Present
[L506] Mercat P pbk **£12.95**

KYBETT, SUSAN MACLEAN
Bonnie Prince Charlie: A Biography of Charles Edward Stuart
[L507] Unwin Hyman hbk **£15.00**
[L507] Unwin Hyman pbk **£5.99**

LENMAN, BRUCE
Jacobite Risings in Britain 1689 - 1746
[L508] Methuen pbk **£8.50**
The Jacobite Cause
[L509] R Drew pbk **£4.95**

MACDONALD FRASER, GEORGE
The Steel Bonnets NEW
New edition of the classic account of the Border reivers, the great raiding families of the Marches in Elizabethan times, of whom it was said *"if Jesus Christ was amongst them they would deceave him"*.
[L510] Collins pbk **£6.95**

MACKIE, J.D.
A History of Scotland
Popular, short history of Scotland in one volume.
[L511] Penguin pbk **£4.99**

MACLEAN, FITZROY
A Concise History of Scotland
[L512] Thames & H pbk **£4.50**

MCLYNN, FRANK
Charles Edward Stuart
[L513] Routledge hbk **£24.95**
The Jacobites
[L514] Routledge pbk **£6.95**

PREBBLE, JOHN
Culloden
[L515] Penguin pbk **£4.99**
Glencoe
[L516] Penguin pbk **£4.99**
Mutiny: Highland Regiments in Revolt 1743 - 1804
[L516A] Penguin pbk **£6.99**
The Highland Clearances
[L517] Penguin pbk **£4.99**
The King's Jaunt
The visit of George IV to Scotland in 1822 was the first by a British monarch for nearly 200 years. Prebble looks behind Sir Walter Scott's elaborately staged festival to find the real importance of the King's jaunt.
[L518] Fontana pbk **£3.95**
The Lion in the North
[L519] Penguin pbk **£4.99**
[L519A] Penguin pbk/large format **£7.95**

SCOTT, RONALD MCNAIR
Robert the Bruce
Hero of the Scottish War of Independence who routed the English troops at the memorable Battle of Bannockburn (1314).
[L520] Canongate pbk **£5.95**

SMOUT, T.C.
A Century of the Scottish People 1830 - 1950
With its companion volume *A History of the Scottish People* this is the best narrative history of Scotland available, scholarly and accessible. The two volumes cover the period from the Reformation to the present.
[L521] Collins pbk **£6.95**
A History of the Scottish People
[L522] Fontana pbk **£6.95**

WITHERS, C.J.
Gaelic Scotland: The Transformation of a Culture Region NEW
An important history of the Highlands and Islands, focusing on the transformation of the region through the policy of anglicisation.
[L523] Routledge hbk **£47.50**

Welsh History

DAVIES, JOHN
Hanes Cymru NEW
One-volume survey history of Wales in Welsh.
[L524] Allen Lane hbk **£20.00**

JONES & HERBERT
In People and Protest 1815 - 1880
[L525] Welsh UP pbk **£7.95**
Wales Between the Wars
[L526] Welsh UP pbk **£7.95**

OWEN, HUW
Settlement and Society in Wales
[L528] Welsh UP hbk **£35.00**

OXFORD HISTORY OF WALES
DAVIES, R.R.
Vol 1: Conquest, Coexistence and Change: Wales 1063 - 1415
This volume covers the period when Wales struggled to retain its independence and identity in the face of the Anglo-Norman conquest and subsequent English rule.
[L529] Oxford hbk **£40.00**
WILLIAMS, GLANMOR
Vol 2: Recovery, Reorientation and Reformation: Wales c.1415 - 1642
Presents for the first time a comprehensive account of the two decisive centuries in Welsh history which followed the defeat of Owain Glyn Dwr.
[L530] Oxford hbk **£40.00**
JENKINS, GERAINT H.
Vol 3: The Foundations of Modern Wales: Wales 1642 - 1780
Explores the important but neglected period between the Civil War and the beginnings of the Industrial Revolution, showing the development of powerful social forces which took an impoverished downtrodden nation to the threshold of unprecedented social, economic and political change.
[L531] Oxford hbk **£40.00**
MORGAN, KENNETH O.
Vol 4: Rebirth of a Nation: Wales 1880 - 1980
[L532] Oxford hbk **£27.50**
[L533] Oxford pbk **£6.95**

WILLIAMS, G.A.
When Was Wales
[L534] Penguin pbk **£5.50**

Danton and Desmoulins on the steps of the scaffold. From *The Days of the French Revolution* by Christopher Hibbert. (Penguin pbk £12.99)

Reflections on a Revolution
Michael Foot

1789: A good year to start the study of modern times. So the text books would softly suggest, but there is a better reason for the pre-eminence accorded to this precise moment and the revolutionary decade which followed. History is a perpetual unfinished argument. Historians are not, as they sometimes choose to pretend, the careful collectors of facts, the recreators of the past. All the best of them are engaged in a furious ideological debate about the present and the future. And 1789 and the aftermath certainly offer something worth arguing about.

This point was blandly but potently put by one of the very greatest of twentieth century historians, Pieter Geyl. He was writing an essay on historical inevitability, and the claim slipped out almost casually: "History is often thought of as a study contentedly remote from the present, or as a hobby of scholars who have elected to fly from the world around them into the dead and gone past. The truth is rather that history is an active force in the struggles of every generation and that the historian by his interpretation of the past, consciously or half-consciously or even unconsciously, takes his part in them, for good or for evil. History, then, is a factor to be reckoned with in the present: some will maintain, the decisive one."

Pieter Geyl was a modest-mannered man, the model almost of his retiring scholar in the first part of that description. But we see that he makes the most immodest claim on behalf of his profession and its products - the *decisive* factor in shaping the present and the future.

Although he has written on many other themes, Pieter Geyl made his fame and name with a book called **Napoleon For and Against**, which he conceived while he was held as a hostage by the Germans at Buchenwald. It is indeed one of the most enthralling and instructive books on the subject ever written, although some French historians may at once protest that, on his own reckoning, the moment when he wrote his book, poisoned his mind against Napoleon. To permit any comparison whatever between Napoleon and Hitler, even by remote application, is insulting and intolerable.

Geyl must be acquitted at once of so wretched a charge: he knew what were the civilising influences at work in the French conquests which Napoleon carried across Europe, even if his countrymen, like most of ours, managed to keep the matter in proportion. Yet the portrait of the man himself which emerged from the clashing descriptions was certainly not a pleasant one: the balance came down much more *against* than *for*. But of

course that was not the theme of the book. What he showed, better than ever before, was how the fashion changed among the French historians; how throughout the century and beyond, the verdict on Napoleon had much more to do with the new political battles of the period, and how the new Napoleon could be invoked as an ally or an enemy.

Pieter Geyl applied the same technique to the Revolution itself, and his book on Napoleon contains several backward glances across the revolutionary period. Once upon a time, Jacobin or left-wing or Marxist historians would picture Napoleon as the child of the Revolution, 'Robespierre on horseback'. Napoleon himself at St Helena was eager to foster this myth, or variations of it, and the very fact that he had an interest in doing so helps to show what may have been his true, youthful temperament.

Many contemporary critics or would-be historians saw this Napoleon as the real man: Hazlitt in England, Heine in Germany, Stendhal in France. These three men of genius drew the same enduring inspiration from the events of 1789 and the years that followed. Nothing that happened later could blot out from their minds the scale of the revolutionary achievement, and indeed subsequent events seem to uphold the wisdom of their judgement. All the setbacks for the revolutionary cause which they saw around them and marked with such pain did not destroy their faith that the cause itself would revive and prosper in the end.

Just to clinch the Geyl thesis, we can eagerly note that it was a French historian who stepped forward to change the way in which the French, or at least great sections of the French people, judged their history and prepared for their future. Fortunately, Pieter Geyl has written on this theme, on Jules Michelet, 'the great national historian', who transformed the whole story in the 1840s and the 1850s in such a 'decisive' manner. To read Michelet is to renew the spirit of the revolutionary times, and in particular the earliest years of the greatest promise. He tells of the fall of the Bastille as no one had told it before or since. A few sentences can offer only a hint:

"The attack on the Bastille was by no means reasonable. It was an act of faith. Nobody proposed; but all believed, and all acted...Then let that grand day remain ever one of the eternal fêtes of the human

race, not only as having been the first of deliverance, but as having been superlatively the day of concord. What happened during that short night on which nobody slept, for every difference of opinion to disappear with the shades of darkness, and all to have the same thoughts in the morning? What took place at the Palais Royal and the Hotel de Ville is well known: but what would be far more important to know, is, what took place on the domestic hearth of the people."

The people played the leading role in Michelet's beloved Paris, and, as he described their achievement, the city assumed a mightier proportionate part in events than ever before - "when I reflect on what Paris has done for the liberties of our human race, I feel impelled to kiss the stones of its monuments and the pavements of its streets." How many travellers in Paris, how many readers of Michelet, have been swept along by his passionate reconstruction of the scene. Pieter Geyl warns against the peril, without avail.

The last name to figure on Geyl's Napoleonic list, George Lefebvre, is even more closely associated with the re-writing of the history of the Revolution itself. However, this example illustrates how the flaming torch of historical revision could be handed on from one master to another. Lefebvre died in 1959 at the age of 86. In the art of exposition he had made himself at least the equal of two of his famous predecessors at the Sorbonne, Alphonse Aulard and Albert Mathiez. However, he regarded himself rather as a direct pupil of Jean Jaurés, the Socialist leader and historian who was martyred by an assassin in 1914. Like Jaurés, Lefebvre was a rationalist humanitarian in the tradition of the Enlightenment who believed that his own age, in allegiance to that same tradition, called for a great adventure in democratic socialism - "I saw and heard Jaurés only two times, lost in the crowd, but if anyone cares to assign me a maître, I recognise only him." And, of course, both Lefebvre and Jaurés had been powerfully influenced in their view of history by Karl Marx, and had no wish to conceal the debt.

Thanks partly to Lefebvre's persisting influence, Marxist or near-Marxist interpretations became positively fashionable. The achievement was celebrated in the appropriate year, 1968, when an avowed fellow-Marxist on this side of the Channel, Gwyn Williams, surveyed the latest developments in French Revolutionary scholarship in his **Artisans and Sans-Culottes**. His new edition, published twenty years later, brought the survey up-to-date, and showed how substantial efforts had been made to fill some of the gaps. He noted how the words *Britain* or *British* were sometimes clumsily used to conceal the contribution which the Welsh, the Scots or the Irish made to that of their English comrades, and he noted even more forcibly the change in role accorded to women.

But let the last word be left to celebrate this most notable of all restorations. Meantime, we may note that the English-writing world, to use the term in its most expansive form, has naturally made efforts to keep pace with the French. No single method or theme may be attributed to these bicentennial productions. However, one tendency may be emphasised which is most directly seen in Simon Schama's **Citizens: A Chronicle of the French Revolution**. He has aimed more boldly and ambitiously than any other modern historian to embrace the story once more in a single narrative. He invites comparison with the very greatest who have known that this was the necessary supreme accomplishment; Thomas Carlyle, for example, or even Jules Michelet himself, although he, as we shall see in a moment, had an even larger purpose.

Many tens of thousands of readers, I trust, will pass their own judgement. May I, at least, with Gwyn Williams' safe hand to guide me, return to the women's question. "My 1968 text," he wrote, "could not fail to note the role of women in many of the journées in France and the quite spectacular *leadership* they exercised in the last revolts of Germinal and Prairial. Twenty years on, however, I cannot fail to note, in pain and shame, the barely concealed surprise which informs my writing at that point...It is certainly the advance of women's history which is beginning to transform our understanding of the popular movement in France."

It may now be recalled in wonder that the historian described by Pieter Geyl as 'the greatest writer of them all', had written almost in the same sense nearly 150 years before. Jules Michelet saw 'the spirit of the Revolution' as his teacher: "it knows; and the others do not know. It possesses the secret of all the preceding ages." The epic of the liberation of the French people, nay, the liberation of the

---

"When I reflect on what Paris has done for the liberties of our human race, I feel impelled to kiss the stones of its monuments and the pavements of its streets."

---

human mind itself - that was what *his* history of the Revolution was to be. And maybe because he saw its comprehensive character, Michelet, before any other historian, always searched for the role which the women - or their chosen champions - had played.

The house of Marquis de Condorcet had been the place in pre-Revolutionary times where the rights and claims of women were first elaborated. His salon in Paris became, with his wife's association, 'the hearth of the republic'. Some other famous women, notably Olympe de Gouges, joined with them in drafting a Declaration of the Rights of Women. She, the notorious Olympe - notorious for her seductions as well as her Declarations - established the rights of women, according to Michelet, "by one just and sublime saying: 'They have as good a right to mount the tribune as they have of ascending the scaffold'."

The English have usually liked to pretend that Jules Michelet wrote only for the French. His critics would have been wiser to note how he strove to make all causes, including the women's cause, part of the same liberation. We readers in these anniversary years may help to re-establish his reputation as an historian along with the restitution to its proper pedestal of the French Revolution itself.

Michael Foot was Leader of the Labour Party from 1980 to 1983, and has spent much of his life in Parliament, representing successively Plymouth, Ebbw Vale and Gwent. A journalist and critic, he has published widely, including the autobiography *Loyalists and Loners*, and most recently a study of Byron, *The Politics of Paradise*.

Feature

EUROPEAN HISTORY

European history is divided into chronological sections for books that treat more than one European country, followed by listings for individual countries. In the section below, general European titles, covering a range of periods, are listed, together with the major series. Where a title covers more than one period, it will be found in the first period to which it refers.

General

BARZINI, LUIGI
The Europeans
[1000] Penguin pbk **£4.99**

COOK, CHRIS
European Political Facts 1789 - 1848
[L1001] Macmillan hbk **£35.00**
European Political Facts 1848 - 1918
[L1002] Macmillan hbk **£35.00**
European Political Facts 1918 - 84
[L1003] Macmillan pbk **£10.95**
The Longman Handbook to Modern European History 1763 - 1985
A valuable reference book which lists the key events of the last two centuries. Included are short biographies of the major figures, a glossary of historical terms and bibliographies for the various topics.
[L1004] Longman hbk **£15.95**
[L1005] Longman pbk **£7.95**

EUSEBIUS
The History of the Church
A classic history covering the period from the foundation of the Church until the beginning of the 4th century.
[L1006] Penguin pbk **£4.95**

EVANS, E.P.
The Criminal Prosecution of and Capital Punishment of Animals
A fascinating study based on law reports of the prosecution of animals throughout European history, reflecting the changing religious and superstitious values of European society.
[L1007] Faber pbk **£4.95**

FISHER, H.A.L.
Not to be confused with the *Fontana History of Europe* (see below) this is a more general history which gives a useful overview. Unfortunately one or other of the volumes seem to be always unavailable.
A History of Europe Vol 1
[L1008] Fontana pbk **£3.95**
A History of Europe Vol 2
[L1009] Fontana pbk **£3.50**
A History of Europe Vol 3
[L1010] Fontana pbk **£3.95**
A History of Europe Vol 5 part ii
[L1011] Fontana pbk **£3.50**

FONTANA HISTORY OF EUROPE
A particularly accessible series, each volume is by a leading authority in the particular field and is a synthesis of many years research. Used primarily by 'A' Level students, the volumes are the best introductions to their subjects for the general reader.

HOLMES, GEORGE
Europe: Hierarchy and Revolt 1320 - 1450
[L1012] Fontana pbk **£2.95**
HALE, J.R.
Renaissance Europe 1480 - 1520
[L1013] Fontana pbk **£3.95**
ELTON, G.R.
Reformation Europe 1517 - 1559
[L1014] Fontana pbk **£4.95**
ELLIOTT, J.H.
Europe Divided 1559 - 1598
[L1015] Fontana pbk **£4.95**
PARKER, GEOFFREY
Europe in Crisis 1598 - 1648
[L1016] Fontana pbk **£2.95**
STOYE, JOHN
Europe Unfolding 1648 - 1688
[L1017] Fontana pbk **£2.75**
OLWEN, HUFTON
Europe: Privilege and Protest 1730 - 1789
[L1018] Fontana pbk **£3.95**
RUDE, GEORGE
Revolutionary Europe 1783 - 1815
[L1019] Fontana pbk **£3.95**
DROZ, J.
Europe Between Revolutions 1815 - 1848
[L1020] Fontana pbk **£3.95**
GRENVILLE, J.A.S.
Europe Reshaped 1848 - 1878
[L1021] Fontana pbk **£4.95**
STONE, NORMAN
Europe Transformed 1878 - 1919
[L1022] Fontana pbk **£3.95**
WISKEMANN, ELIZABETH
Europe of the Dictators 1919 - 1945
[L1023] Fontana pbk **£3.95**

GOODY, J.
The Development of Family and Marriage in Europe
[L1024] Cambridge pbk **£10.95**

KENNEDY, PAUL
Strategy and Diplomacy 1870 - 1945　**NEW**
A reissue of the author's essays on the background to 20th century conflicts. The essays come under three headings: Britain's world policy 1865-1945; Germany & England, the naval aspects and strategy in a global context.
[L1025] Fontana pbk **£4.95**

LEE, STEPHEN J.
Aspects of European History 1789 - 1980
[L1026] Methuen pbk **£6.95**

LOCKYER, ROGER
Habsburg and Bourbon Europe 1470 - 1720
This is the standard survey of this period in Europe: authoritative, lucid, accessible and stimulating, Lockyer offers an indispensable overview of the shifting balance of power in Europe across three centuries.
[L1027] Longman pbk **£8.95**

LONGMAN GENERAL HISTORY OF EUROPE
Longmans have an excellent reputation as history publishers and this series confirms their reputation - each volume is by a leading historian in the particular subject and the series is valued by undergraduates for its lucid presentation and consistent standard of scholarship. The series is constantly revised, with some revised editions recently published.

JONES, A.H.M.
Decline of the Ancient World
[L1028] Longman pbk **£9.95**
BROOKE, CHRISTOPHER
Europe in the Central Middle Ages 962 - 1154
[L1029] Longman pbk **£9.95**
MUNDY, J.
Europe in the High Middle Ages 1150 - 1309
[L1030] Longman pbk **£11.50**
HAY, DENYS
Europe in the 14th and 15th Centuries　**NEW**
Second, revised edition.
[L1031] Longman pbk **£10.95**
KOENIGSBERGER, H.G.
Europe in the 16th Century
Second, revised edition.
[L1032] Longman pbk **£9.95**
PENNINGTON, D.H.
Europe in the 17th Century　**NEW**
New, revised edition.
[L1033] Longman pbk **£9.95**
ANDERSON, M.S.
Europe in the 18th Century 1713 - 1783
[L1034] Longman pbk **£9.95**
FORD, F.L.
Europe 1780 - 1830　**NEW**
Second, revised edition.
[L1035] Longman pbk **£10.95**
HEARDER, H.
Europe in the 19th Century 1830 - 1880
[L1036] Longman pbk **£9.95**
ROBERTS, J.M.
Europe 1880 - 1945
New, revised edition.
[L1037] Longman pbk **£10.95**

MCEVEDY, COLIN
Atlas of Modern History to 1815
[L1038] Penguin pbk **£4.95**

MITTERAUER, M. & SIEDER, R.
European Family
Discusses how the forms and function of the basic social unit have changed through religious, political, and social upheaval.
[L1039] Blackwell pbk **£8.95**

NEW CAMBRIDGE MODERN HISTORY
This series includes essays by some of the front-rank scholars in the area, who for one reason or another decided not to develop their ideas in a form accessible to the non-specialist, and accordingly never earned the reputation of the Eltons and the A.J.P. Taylors. Particularly worthy of mention are Hans Baron and Cecilia M. Ady. Each volume is the work of several scholars, thus providing a more balanced picture than single author works.
Vol 1: The Renaissance 1493 - 1520
[L1040] Cambridge hbk **£50.00**
[L1041] Cambridge pbk **£25.00**
Vol 2: The Reformation 1520 - 1559
[L1042] Cambridge hbk **£55.00**
Vol 3: The Counter-Reformation and the Price Revolution 1559 - 1610
[L1043] Cambridge hbk **£50.00**
Vol 4: The Decline of Spain and the Thirty Years War 1609 - 1659
[L1044] Cambridge hbk **£65.00**
[L1045] Cambridge pbk **£27.50**
Vol 6: The Rise of Great Britain and Russia 1688 - 1725
[L1046] Cambridge hbk **£65.00**
[L1047] Cambridge pbk **£27.50**
Vol 7: The Old Regime 1713 - 1763
[L1048] Cambridge hbk **£60.00**

Vol 9: War and Peace in an Age of Upheaval 1793 - 1830
[L1049] Cambridge hbk £65.00
Vol 10: The Zenith of European Power 1830 - 1870
[L1050] Cambridge hbk £65.00
Vol 11: Material Progress and World-Wide Problems 1870 - 1898
[L1051] Cambridge pbk £27.50
Vol 12: The Shifting Balance of World Forces 1898 - 1945
[L1052] Cambridge hbk £65.00
Vol 13: Companion Volume
[L10453] Cambridge hbk £45.00
Vol 14: Atlas
[L1054] Cambridge hbk £65.00
[L1055] Cambridge pbk £30.00

The Classical World

The Classical World covers the history of Ancient Greece and Rome. The first section is composed of general ancient histories and reference works, the following sections dealing with Greece and Rome separately. The list combines classical contemporary accounts, good general histories and notable new titles.

CHADWICK, J.
The Decipherment of Linear B
The story of the phenomenal achievement of Michael Ventris in providing the key to unlock the secrets of the great Minoan Civilisation.
[L1056] Cambridge pbk £8.50
The Mycenean World
[L1057] Cambridge pbk £9.95

FERGUSON, JOHN
Utopias of the Classical World
[L1058] Thames & H pbk £14.00

FINLEY, M.I.
One of the most renowned academics in this field, whose lucid surveys combine accessibility with erudition.
Politics in the Ancient World
[L1060] Cambridge pbk £8.50
The Ancient Economy
[L1061] Hogarth pbk £5.95

GRANT, MICHAEL
Ancient History Atlas
A comprehensive atlas of the ancient world which breaks from the traditional emphasis upon political history. In 87 clear and informative maps, Michael Grant portrays the history of ancient times from the second millennium BC to the reign of Justinian I.
[L1062] Weidenfeld pbk £6.95
Greece and Rome: The Birth of Western Civilization
[L1063] Thames & H hbk £20.00

HAMMOND, N.G.L. & SCULLARD, H.H. (EDS)
The Oxford Classical Dictionary
Excellent reference work listing people, events and classical terminology.
[L1064] Oxford hbk £35.00

OXFORD HISTORY OF THE CLASSICAL WORLD
Eminently readable, with chapters by different historians to provide a balanced and authoritative history. Despite its length it is an ideal history for the general reader interested in the classical world, with valuable illustrations.

BOARDMAN, JOHN (ED)
Oxford History of the Classical World
[L1065] Oxford hbk £27.50
Vol 1: Greece and the Hellenistic World
[L1066] Oxford pbk £9.95
Vol 2: Rome
[L1067] Oxford pbk £9.95

RADICE, BETTY
Who's Who in the Ancient World
Useful reference work placing real and mythological people in context.
[L1068] Penguin pbk £5.95

THE CAMBRIDGE ANCIENT HISTORY
This series is the bible of Ancient History studies: by far the most scholarly and complete source available. It is currently being slowly rewritten to take account of the latest research and archaeological studies.
Vol 1 Part i: Prolegomena and Prehistory
[L1069] Cambridge hbk £50.00
[L1070] Cambridge pbk £22.50
Vol 1 Part ii: Early History of the Middle East
[L1071] Cambridge hbk £65.00
[L1072] Cambridge pbk £22.50
Vol 2 Part i: The Middle East & the Aegean Region c.1800 - 1380 BC
[L1073] Cambridge hbk £60.00
[L1074] Cambridge pbk £22.50
Vol 2 Part ii: The Middle East & the Aegean Region c.1380 - 1000 BC
[L1075] Cambridge hbk £65.00
[L1076] Cambridge pbk £22.50
Vols 1 & 2: Plates
[L1077] Cambridge hbk £30.00
Vol 3 Part i: Prehistory of the Balkans/The Middle East 10th to 8th Centuries BC
[L1078] Cambridge hbk £65.00
Vol 3 Part iii: Expansion of the Greek World, 8th to 6th Centuries BC
[L1079] Cambridge hbk £40.00
Vol 3: Plates
[L1080] Cambridge hbk £30.00
Vol 4: Persia, Greece and the Western Mediterranean 525 - 479 BC
[L1081] Cambridge hbk £60.00
Vol 5: Athens 470 - 401 BC
[L1082] Cambridge hbk £42.50
Vol 6: Macedon 401 - 301 BC
[L1083] Cambridge hbk £45.00

The acropolis at Athens from *Oxford Illustrated Encyclopaedia: World History Volume 1* (Oxford hbk £19.50)

Vols 5 & 6: Plates
[L1084] Cambridge hbk £32.50
Vol 7 Part i: The Hellenistic World
[L1085] Cambridge hbk £45.00
Vol 7 Part i: Plates
[L1086] Cambridge hbk £25.00
Vol 8: Rome and the Mediterranean 218 - 133 BC
[L1087] Cambridge hbk £60.00
Vol 9: The Roman Republic 133 - 44 BC
[L1088] Cambridge hbk £65.00
Vol 10: The Augustan Empire 44 BC - 70 AD
[L1089] Cambridge hbk £65.00
Vol 11: The Imperial Peace AD 70 - 192
[L1090] Cambridge hbk £65.00
Vol 12: The Imperial Crisis and Recovery AD 193 - 324
[L1091] Cambridge hbk £60.00

Ancient Greece

ADCOCK, F. & MOSLEY, D.J.
Diplomacy in Ancient Greece
[L1092] Thames & H hbk £14.00

ANDREWES, ANTONY
Greek Society
[L1093] Penguin pbk £5.95

ARRIAN (c.95 - 175)
Although Greek, Arrian enjoyed a successful career as an officer in the Roman army. He wrote a valuable account of Alexander the Great's career, narrating his campaigns.
Campaigns of Alexander
[L1094] Penguin pbk £4.99

BOWDER, DIANA (ED)
Who Was Who in the Greek World
[L1095] Phaidon hbk £18.00

BROWNING, ROBERT (ED)
The Greek World
Classical, Byzantine and Modern.
[L1096] Thames & H hbk £20.00

BURN, A.R.
Persia and the Greeks
[L1097] Duckworth hbk £9.95
The Pelican History of Greece
[L1098] Penguin pbk £5.95

CAMP, JOHN M.
Athenian Agora Excavations in the Heart of Classical Athens
[L1099] Thames & H hbk £16.00

CHADWICK, J.
The Mycenean World
[L1100] Cambridge pbk £9.95

DAVIS, J.K.
Democracy and Classical Greece
[L1101] Fontana pbk £3.50

DOVER, K.J.
The Greeks
[L1102] Oxford pbk £3.95
The Greeks and their Legacy
The second collection of Sir Kenneth Dover's papers. This volume deals with the transmission of Greek classical culture throughout history down to the present day.
[L1103] Blackwell hbk £37.50

HISTORY

EASTERLING & MUIR
Greek Religion and Society
[L1104] Cambridge pbk **£9.50**

ELLIS, J.T.
Philip II and Macedonian Imperialism
History of Macedonian expansion under the rule of
Alexander the Great's father Philip.
[L1105] Thames & H pbk **£7.95**

FINLEY, M.I.
Ancient Greeks
[L1106] Penguin pbk **£4.99**
**Economy and Society in Ancient
Greece**
[L1107] Chatto hbk **£15.00**
The World of Odysseus
[L1108] Penguin pbk **£2.95**

FITZHARDINGE, L.F.
The Spartans
[L1109] Thames & H pbk **£6.95**

FOX, ROBIN LANE
Alexander the Great
Highly enjoyable account of Alexander which was
published to great acclaim a few years ago.
[L1110] Penguin pbk **£6.99**

GRANT, MICHAEL
The Classical Greeks
[L1111] Weidenfeld hbk **£18.00**
The Rise of the Greeks
[L1112] Weidenfeld hbk **£17.95**

GREEN, PETER
A Concise History of Ancient Greece
[L1113] Thames & H pbk **£5.95**

JONES, A.H.M.
Athenian Democracy
[L1114] Blackwell pbk **£8.95**

KITTO, H.D.F.
The Greeks
[L1115] Penguin pbk **£3.95**

KUHRT, A. & SHERWIN-WHITE, S. (EDS)
Hellenism in the East   `NEW`
The first study to combine evidence from both Greek
and non-Greek languages to examine the role of
Hellenism in Persia, as power was transferred from
Achaemenid Persian to Macedonian Greek rule.
[L1116] Duckworth hbk **£28.00**

LEVI, PETER
Atlas of the Greek World
[L1117] Phaidon hbk **£18.50**

MEIGGS, RUSSELL
The Athenian Empire
[L1118] Oxford pbk **£17.50**

MURRAY, OSWYN
Early Greece
[L1119] Fontana pbk **£5.95**

PLUTARCH (c.46 - 120)
Plutarch wrote in a number of different fields but is
chiefly remembered as a biographer who used anec-
dote to illustrate the moral character of his subjects.
Age of Alexander
[L1120] Penguin pbk **£4.99**
Rise and Fall of Athens
[L1121] Penguin pbk **£4.99**

ROBINSON, C.E.
History of Greece (9th Edition)
[L1122] Methuen pbk **£8.95**

STOBART, J.C.
The Glory That Was Greece
[L1123] Sidgwick pbk **£10.95**

TAYLOR, LORD WILLIAM
The Myceneans
[L1124] Thames & H hbk **£12.95**

VEYNE, PAUL
Bread and Circuses   `NEW`
A study of ruler obligation and the practice of
political pluralism in the Greek city state.
[L1125] Allen Lane hbk **£20.00**

WALBANK, F.W.
The Hellenistic World
[L1126] Fontana pbk **£3.50**

WOOD, E.M.
Peasant-Citizen and Slave   `NEW`
A controversial study of Athenian society which
argues that the most distinctive feature of Athenian
democracy was the prominence given to labour,
despite slavery, which saw the emergence of peasant
as citizen.
[L1127] Verso pbk **£9.95**

WOOD, MICHAEL
In Search of the Trojan War
Based on the popular television series.
[L1128] BBC pbk **£8.95**

XENOPHON (c.430 - 352 BC)
Athenian historian who has been dubbed the world's
first journalist for his eye-witness reports of military
campaigns, and for his celebrated account of the
period in which he lived.
History of My Times
[L1129] Penguin pbk **£5.95**

Ancient Rome

ALFOLDY, GEZA
The Social History of Rome
[L1130] Routledge pbk **£9.95**
The Social History of Rome   `NEW`
Substantially revised edition of the classic study
of Ancient Rome - principally of the Empire,
but also covering the Republic - written to
provide a background for students of Roman
history.
[L1131] Routledge pbk **£9.95**

AMMIANUS (330 - ?)
Roman soldier and historian whose history acts as a
continuation of those of Tacitus's, covering the period
from the death of Domitian in AD 36 to the death of
Valens in 378.
Later Roman Empire
[L1132] Penguin pbk **£6.99**

BARROW, R.H.
The Romans
Barrow looks at the Roman personality through their
religion, writing and achievements. The concluding
chapters cover the period from Constantine to the 5th
century, providing a background to the medieval
period.
[L1133] Penguin pbk **£4.99**

BEARD, M. & CRAWFORD, N.
Rome in the Late Republic
[L1134] Duckworth pbk **£5.95**

BREEZE, D.J.
Roman Forts in Britain
[L1136] Shire pbk **£2.50**

CAESAR, JULIUS (102/100 - 44 BC)
Caesar's accounts of his military campaigns cannot be
taken as accurate records of what actually happened.
Their value lies in being primary sources for a study
of Caesar and in the details of the army and their
equipment.
Civil War
[L1137] Penguin pbk **£3.95**
Conquest of Gaul
[L1138] Penguin pbk **£3.99**

CARCOPINO, JEROME
Daily Life in Ancient Rome
[L1139] Penguin pbk **£5.99**

CHEVALLIER, RAYMOND
Roman Roads   `NEW`
The most complete study available, dealing with all
aspects from the planning and building of the roads,
their strategic and economic importance, to the
vehicles that used them.
[L1140] Batsford pbk **£14.95**

CHISHOLM, K. & FERGUSON, J.
Rome: The Augustan Age
A compilation of primary sources in translation
covering Roman politics, art, literature, social history
and philosophy.
[L1141] Oxford pbk **£14.50**

CICERO (c.106 - 43 BC)
Philosopher, lawyer, politican and rhetoricican, Cicero
was finally put to death by Mark Anthony during the
instability that followed Caesar's death. His influence
has been widespread, and his writings were among
the standard texts of medieval learning.
Selected Letters
[L1142] Penguin pbk **£4.99**
Selected Political Speeches
[L1143] Penguin pbk **£5.99**
Selected Works
[L1144] Penguin pbk **£3.99**

CORNELL & MATHEWS
Atlas of the Roman World
[L1145] Phaidon pbk **£18.50**

CRAWFORD, MICHAEL
The Roman Republic
[L1146] Fontana pbk **£3.50**

DUDLEY, DONALD
Roman Society
[L1147] Penguin pbk **£3.50**

FERGUSON, J.
The Religions of the Roman Empire
[L1148] Thames & H pbk **£5.95**

FERRILL, ARTHUR
The Fall of the Roman Empire
[L1149] Thames & H pbk **£7.95**

GIBBON, EDWARD
**The Decline and Fall of the Roman
Empire**
A highly regarded one-volume abridgement by D.M.
Low.
[L1150] Chatto hbk **£12.95**
[L1151] Penguin pbk **£5.99**

GRANT, MICHAEL
History of Rome
[L1152] Weidenfeld hbk **£15.00**
[L1153] Faber pbk **£7.95**

JONES, A.H.M.
Augustus
[L1154] Hogarth pbk **£4.95**

LIVY (c.59 BC - AD 17)

Livy wrote a history of Rome from its earliest beginnings up to his own lifetime. Not all his books have survived, but we still have his version of Rome's legendary foundation and his account of the Punic Wars.

The Early History of Rome
Covers books 1 - 5 of the original History
[L1155] Penguin pbk **£4.99**
Rome and Italy
Books 6 - 10
[L1156] Penguin pbk **£4.95**
Rome and the Mediterranean
Books 21 - 30
[L1157] Penguin pbk **£6.95**
War With Hannibal
Books 31 - 45
[L1158] Penguin pbk **£5.99**

MASSIE, ALAN
The Caesars
First paperback edition of the novelist's introduction to the personalities of the Caesars.
[L1159] Sphere pbk **£3.99**

OGILVIE, R.M.
Early Rome and the Etruscans
[L1160] Fontana pbk **£2.95**
The Romans and their Gods
[L1161] Hogarth pbk **£5.95**

PLINY (62 - c.114)
Roman letter writer. Pliny's correspondence was translated during the vogue for letters in the 17th and 18th centuries. He is remembered for his stately style and his description of the eruption of Vesuvius.
Letters of the Younger Pliny
[L1162] Penguin pbk **£4.95**

PLUTARCH (c.46 - 120)
Fall of the Roman Republic
[L1163] Penguin pbk **£4.99**
Makers of Rome
[L1164] Penguin pbk **£3.95**

POLYBIUS (c. 203 - 120 BC)
Historian of the Hellenistic period whose major theme, however, was the rise and universality of Rome.
The Rise of the Roman Empire
[L1165] Penguin pbk **£5.99**

ROBINSON, C.E.
History of Rome 753 BC - AD 410
[L1166] Methuen pbk **£9.95**

SALLUST (c.86 - 35 BC)
Sallust's writings survive only in fragments. He wrote the first important historical monographs on near contemporary events in a dramatic and vigorous style.
The Jugurthine War/Conspiracy of Cataline
[L1167] Penguin pbk **£4.95**

SALMON, E.T.
Making of Roman Italy
A history of the Italian Peninsula during the earliest years of Roman expansion.
[L1168] Thames & H hbk **£14.00**

SIMKINS, M.
Warriors of Rome NEW
Excellently illustrated by James Field, this traces the development of the Roman soldier, his armour, his daily life and methods of warfare. A good introduction for the general reader.
[L1170] Blandford hbk **£14.95**

STOBART, J.C.
The Grandeur That Was Rome
[L1171] Sidgwick pbk **£11.95**

STOCKTON, DAVID
The Gracchi
[L1172] Oxford pbk **£10.50**

SUETONIUS (70 - 140)
Roman biographer and secretary to Hadrian, remembered for his *Lives* of the first 12 Caesars.
The Twelve Caesars
[L1173] Penguin pbk **£4.50**

SYME, RONALD
The Augustan Aristocracy NEW
[L1174] Oxford pbk **£15.00**

TACITUS (c.55 - 117)
Acclaimed as Imperial Rome's greatest historian, Tacitus wrote about recent events so was probably reasonably accurate, though he was not above prejudice. He was a master of the damning aside for which his theme - despotic absolutism - gave him plenty of scope.
Agricola/Germania
[L1175] Penguin pbk **£3.50**
Annals of Imperial Rome
[L1176] Penguin pbk **£4.99**
Histories
[L1177] Penguin pbk **£4.50**

WELLS, COLIN
The Roman Empire
[L1179] Fontana pbk **£4.95**

The Middle Ages

Covers the period from the fall of Rome to the Renaissance.

ANGOLD, M.
The Byzantine Empire: A Political History
[L1180] Longman pbk **£9.95**

BARBER, MALCOLM
The Trial of the Templars
Interest in the Templars, their beliefs and mysteries remains high. This factual account of their fall exposes many strange aspects of their story.
[L1181] Cambridge pbk **£11.95**

BARBER, RICHARD
The Penguin Guide to Medieval Europe
[L1182] Penguin pbk **£8.99**

BARRACLOUGH, GEOFFREY
The Medieval Papacy
[L1183] Thames & H pbk **£4.95**

BOSWELL, JOHN
The Kindness of Strangers NEW
Subtitled 'The Abandonment of Children in Western Europe from Late Antiquity to the Renaissance', the author has taken as his starting point the medieval belief that men should not visit brothels lest they unwittingly commit incest.
[L1184] Allen Lane hbk **£20.00**

BRONDSTED
The Vikings
Another excellent Penguin introduction to this period.
[L1185] Penguin pbk **£5.99**

BULLOCK, ALAN
The Humanist Tradition in the West
From the Renaissance to present day this book shows how the rediscovery of the classical world changed men's thought.
[L1186] Thames & H hbk **£15.00**

BYRON, ROBERT
Byzantine Achievement
[L1187] Routledge hbk **£25.00**

CAMBRIDGE MEDIEVAL HISTORY
Vol 1: The Christian Roman Empire and the Foundation of the Teutonic Kingdoms
[L1188] Cambridge hbk **£75.00**
Vol 3: Germany and the Western Empire
[L1189] Cambridge hbk **£55.00**
Vol 4 Part i: The Byzantine Empire - Byzantium and Its Neighbours
[L1190] Cambridge hbk **£85.00**
Vol 4 Part ii: The Byzantine Empire - Government, Church and Civilisation
[L1191] Cambridge hbk **£55.00**
Vol 6: Victory of the Papacy
[L1192] Cambridge hbk **£85.00**

CHADWICK, HENRY
Early Church
[L1193] Penguin pbk **£4.99**

CONTAMINE, PHILIPPE
War in the Middle Ages
Incorporated with the study of medieval warfare is the wider issue of the role of War in medieval society.
[L1194] Blackwell pbk **£10.50**

DAVIS, RALPH H.C.
A History of Medieval Europe: From Constantine to St Louis
A clear and comprehensive account. Included are chapters on the medieval church and Papacy, the Carolingian, Frankish and Saxon Empires, and the Barbarian and Christian invasions.
[L1195] Longman pbk **£8.95**

DELANEY, FRANK
A Walk in the Dark Ages
Traces the imaginary wanderings of an Irish monk/scholar across the Europe of 7th century.
[L1196] Collins hbk **£15.00**

EINHARD & NOTKER THE STAMMERER
Two Lives of Charlemagne
The two chronicles are important sources for the history of the Carolingian Empire. Largely hagiographical, the truth can be found between the lines (particularly in the case of the subtler Einhard).
[L1197] Penguin pbk **£4.50**

FOOTE & WILSON
Viking Achievement
[L1198] Sidgwick pbk **£10.95**

FOSSIER, ROBERT (ED)
The Middle Ages 350 - 950 NEW
Translated from the French, volume 1 of the *Cambridge Illustrated History of the Middle Ages* covers the rise of Byzantium in the East and the Holy Roman Empire in the West.
[L1199] Cambridge hbk **£30.00**

FROISSART, JEAN (c.1337 - c.1410)
This contemporary of Chaucer is best known as the historian of the Hundred Years War. His account abounds in factual errors but brilliantly mirrors the spirit of the Age of Chivalry.
Chronicles
[L1200] Penguin pbk **£5.99**

GANSHOF, F.L.
Feudalism
A classic study of the organisation of late medieval society.
[L1201] Longman pbk **£6.95**

GIERKE, OTTO
Political Theories of the Middle Ages
One of the seminal texts in the historiography of political thought.
[L1202] Cambridge hbk **£27.50**

GOTTFRIED, R.
The Black Death
[L1203] Macmillan pbk **£5.95**

GREGORY OF TOURS (c. 538-594)
Ecclesiastic whose attempt to be objective was limited by his scorn for secular rulers, but whose History remains an essential source for the study of early medieval France.
History of the Franks
[L1204] Penguin pbk **£6.95**

HOLMES, GEORGE
Oxford Illustrated History of Medieval Europe
A lively, authoritative and highly illustrated history covering life in medieval Europe between the fall of the Roman Empire and the dawn of the Renaissance. It is the best one-volume history of the period.
[L1205] Oxford hbk **£17.50**

HUIZINGA, J.
The Waning of the Middle Ages
Huizinga's stimulating account of the end of the Middle Ages and the beginning of the new era has long been hailed as a classic overview, offering endless insights into two major ages of Western civilisation.
[L1206] Penguin pbk **£5.95**

JAMES, EDWARD
The Franks
A new volume in the excellent Peoples of Europe series. James charts the transformation of the Franks from barbarians to heirs of the Roman Empire.
[L1207] Blackwell hbk **£16.95**

JONES, GWYN
A History of the Vikings
Jones looks at the culture of the Scandinavian people and their movement overseas in the Viking Age of 780-1070.
[L1208] Oxford pbk **£6.95**

JONES, JOHN A.P.
The Crusades
[L1209] Macmillan pbk **£3.25**

KEEN, M.H.
Chivalry
A social ideal with a profound and pervasive influence on history of early modern Europe.
[L1210] Yale UP pbk **£8.95**

KIECKHEFER, RICHARD
Magic in the Middle Ages   NEW
An interdisciplinary approach combining history, religion and psychology. The author sees the practice of magic as a focal point for an understanding of life in the period.
[L1211] Cambridge pbk **£6.95**

KING, P.D.
Charlemagne
This looks at the early years of Charlemagne up to his period as Emperor. The aim of the 'Lancaster' pamphlets from Methuen, of which this is one, is to

provide 'A' level students with recent research which may be missing from course texts.
[L1212] Methuen pbk **£3.95**

KIRSHNER & WEMPLE
Women of the Medieval World
Essays examining the roles of women in religious, sexual and domestic affairs.
[L1213] Blackwell pbk **£9.95**

KOENIGSBERGER, H.G.
Medieval Europe 400 - 1500
Along with Roger Lockyer's *Habsburg and Bourbon Europe* Koenigsberger offers an indispensable introduction to an extended period.
[L1214] Longman pbk **£8.95**

LE GOFF, JACQUES
Medieval Civilisation   NEW
Translated from the French, a popular overview of the period.
[L1215] Blackwell hbk **£19.50**

MAYER, HANS EBERHARD
The Crusades
[L1216] Oxford pbk **£9.95**

MCEVEDY, COLIN
Atlas of Medieval History
[L1217] Penguin pbk **£4.95**

MCKITTERICK, ROSAMUND
The Carolingians and the Written Word   NEW
McKitterick examines the role of literacy in the Carolingian renaissance and the development of medieval universities.
[L1218] Cambridge hbk **£30.00**

NORWICH, JOHN JULIUS
Byzantium: The Early Centuries   NEW
The first in a three-volume history of Byzantium. This volume covers the period from the dedication of Constantinople by Constantine the Great in AD 330 to the coronation of Byzantium's first European rival, Charlemagne, in 800.
[L1219] Viking hbk **£17.95**

OSTROGORSKY, GEORGE
History of the Byzantine State
Now an undergraduate text, this is an indispensable guide to a difficult subject.
[L1220] Blackwell pbk **£14.95**

PIGGOTT, STUART
The Druids
[L1221] Thames & H pbk **£6.95**

POUNDS, N.J.G.
An Economic History of Medieval Europe
[L1222] Longman hbk **£12.50**

PREVITE-ORTON, C.W. (ED)
The Shorter Cambridge Medieval History
Vol 1: The Later Roman Empire to the 12th Century
[L1223] Cambridge hbk **£60.00**

ROPER, HUGH TREVOR
The Golden Age of Europe: From Elizabeth I to the Sun King
Lavishly illustrated cultural history.
[L1224] Thames & H Hbk **£22.50**
The Rise of Christian Europe
Excellent illustrated survey of the development of Christendom.
[L1225] Thames & H pbk **£4.95**

RUNCIMAN, SIR STEVEN
The most distinguished of Byzantine historians, whose writing is wonderfully lucid and accessible.
Medieval Manichee: A Study of the Christian Dualist Heresy
[L1226] Cambridge pbk **£11.95**
Mistra: Byzantine Capital of the Peloponnese
[L1227] Thames & H pbk **£12.50**
Sicilian Vespers: A History of the Mediterranean World in the Later 13th Century
[L1228] Cambridge pbk **£12.95**
The Great Church in Captivity
Study of the Patriarchate of Constantinople from the Eve of the Turkish Conquest to the Greek War of Independence.
[L1229] Cambridge pbk **£13.95**
The History of the Crusades (3 Vols)
Runciman describes the tale of the crusades as 'one of faith and folly, courage and greed, hope and disillusion'. The three volumes cover the capture of Jerusalem by Christian knights, the fall of the Holy City to Saladin and the decline of the crusading movement.
[L1230] Cambridge 3 vols hbk **£65.00**
Vol 1: The First Crusade
[L1231] Cambridge hbk **£27.50**
[L1232] Penguin pbk **£7.99**
Vol 2: The Kingdom of Jerusalem
[L1233] Cambridge hbk **£27.50**
[L1234] Penguin pbk **£8.95**
Vol 3: The Kingdom of Acre
[L1235] Cambridge hbk **£27.50**
[L1236] Penguin pbk **£7.95**

SOUTHERN, RICHARD W.
The Making of the Middle Ages
Dated but good, clear, short introduction to the period.
[L1237] Hutchinson pbk **£5.95**
Western Society and the Church in the Middle Ages
[L1238] Penguin pbk **£5.99**

TUCHMAN, BARBARA
A Distant Mirror: The Calamitous 14th Century
A magnificent sweeping history of the 14th century in Western Europe - the century of the Hundred Years War and the Black Death.
[L1239] Macmillan pbk **£7.99**

Martin Luther meets Charles V at Worms, in Germany, from *Oxford Illustrated Encyclopaedia: World History Volume 1* (Oxford hbk £19.50)

WALEY, DANIEL
Later Medieval Europe: From Saint Louis to Luther
[L1240] Longman pbk **£8.95**

WHITTING, PHILIP (ED)
Byzantium: An Introduction
[L1241] Blackwell pbk **£8.95**

WOLFF, PHILIPPE
Awakening of Europe
The history of ideas developing through the Middle Ages.
[L1242] Penguin pbk **£5.95**

Early Modern Europe

Renaissance, Reformation and the 'Ancien Régime'.

ANDERSON, M.S.
War and Society in 18th Century Europe
[L1243] Fontana pbk **£4.95**

BEHRENS, C.B.A.
Society, Government and the Enlightenment
The experiences of 18th century France and Prussia.
[L1244] Thames & H hbk **£16.00**

BOSSY, JOHN
Christianity in the West 1400 - 1700
A highly original and absorbing long essay which examines fundamental shifts in the Christian faith during a volatile period.
[L1246] Oxford pbk **£5.95**

BRAUDEL, FERNAND
Braudel is the most famous of the 'Annales' historians (named after the *Annales* Journal). Where most historians in trying to produce works of geographic and political macro-history face the problem of integrating their very diverse material into a credible unity, Braudel's very different approach - beginning with the bases of those forces, such as geography and climate, whose effects exhibit themselves over long periods and whose impact are profound - achieves the most satisfying integration.
Capitalism and Material Life 1400 - 1800
A new edition of the first volume of *Civilisation and Capitalism*.
[L1247] Collins hbk **£25.00**
Civilization and Capitalism
Painstaking and minute study of everyday life in Europe in the period 1400-1800.
Vol 1
[L1248] Collins hbk **£25.00**
[L1249] Fontana pbk **£15.00**
Vol 2
[L1250] Collins hbk **£25.00**
Vol 3
[L1251] Collins hbk **£25.00**
[L1252] Fontana pbk **£15.00**
**The Mediterranean and the Mediterranean World
Vol 1**
The product of 25 years research, the first volume describes the geography and environment of the Mediterranean, which shaped its history, and outlines the subsequent historical, economic and social trends.
[L1253] Fontana pbk **£7.95**

Vol 2
Braudel brings his massive study to a dramatic climax with the political and physical confrontation between the Spanish-Hapsburg and Ottoman-Turkish empires at the Battle of Lepanto.
[L1254] Fontana pbk **£7.95**

CAIRNS, T.
Renaissance and Reformation
[L1255] Cambridge pbk **£4.95**

CAMPORESI, PIERO
Bread of Dreams   `NEW`
An original approach to the history of people in medieval Europe: Camporesi develops the thesis that they lived in a state of almost permanent hallucination due to hunger or to bread adulterated with halluciogenic herbs.
[L1256] Blackwell hbk **£22.50**

CHADWICK, O.
The Reformation
Pelican History of the Church series. Deals with the formative work of Erasmus, Luther, Zwingli and Calvin, guiding the reader through the theological minefield of the Reformation.
[L1257] Penguin pbk **£5.99**

DAVIDSON, N.
The Counter Reformation
History of Catholic doctrine and the efforts of the Church to reform priesthood and administration.
[L1258] Blackwell pbk **£3.25**

DOYLE, WILLIAM
The Ancien Régime
A succinct guide to a much-used and misleading historical concept which explains how the term originated and developed down to our own times.
[L1259] Macmillan pbk **£4.50**

EIRE, CARLOS M.N.
War against the Idols
This study follows the development of iconoclasm, a crucial instrument of the Protestant Reformation, from Erasmus to Calvin.
[L1259A] Cambridge pbk **£9.95**

ELTON, G.R.
Reformation Europe 1517 - 1559
Examines the issues and preoccupations central to the age. Alongside Chadwick's *The Reformation* this remains the standard introduction which treats both the theological and political arguments.
[L1260] Fontana pbk **£4.95**

EVANS, R.J.W.
The Making of the Hapsburg Monarchy 1550 - 1700
[L1261] Oxford pbk **£14.95**

FOSSIER, ROBERT (ED)
The Cambridge Illustrated History of the Middle Ages 1250 - 1520
Excellent and authoritative survey with a wide range of illustrative material. Translated from the French.
[L1262] Cambridge hbk **£30.00**

HAMPSON, N.
The Enlightenment
A judicious introduction to the implications of this ubiquitous concept in terms of political, social, religious and intellectual history.
[L1263] Penguin pbk **£4.95**

HOUSTON, R.A.
Literacy in Early Modern Europe   `NEW`
Culture and education 1500 to 1800.
[L1264] Longman pbk **£7.95**

KAMEN, HENRY
European Society 1500 - 1700
[L1265] Hutchinson pbk **£7.95**

KOENIGSBERGER, H.G.
Early Modern Europe 1500 - 1789
[L1266] Longman pbk **£8.95**

LEE, STEPHEN J.
Aspects of European History 1494 - 1789
[L1267] Methuen pbk **£6.95**

MCKAY, DEREK
The Rise of the Great Powers 1648 - 1815
[L1268] Longman pbk **£8.95**

MULLETT, M.
Luther
[L1269] Methuen pbk **£3.50**

PARKER, T.H.L.
John Calvin
A full-scale life of Geneva's controversial reformation leader and influential theologian.
[L1271] Lion P pbk **£4.95**

RABB, THEODORE K.
The Struggle for Stability in Early Modern Europe
[L1272] Oxford pbk **£5.95**

ROPER, HUGH TREVOR
Renaissance Essays
[L1273] Fontana pbk **£5.95**

RUDE, GEORGE
Europe in the 18th Century
This highly acclaimed study of 18th century Europe covers all aspects of the period - social, intellectual, economic, political, diplomatic, military and colonial history. The material is organised thematically rather than chronologically, and treats of Europe as a whole.
[L1274] Weidenfeld pbk **£8.95**

SCARRE, G.
Witchcraft and Magic in 16th & 17th Century Europe
Belief in witchcraft was widespread - this book addresses many of the most significant questions.
[L1275] Macmillan pbk **£4.50**

SHENNAN, J.H.
Liberty and Order in Early Modern Europe
The Subject and the State 1650-1800.
[L1276] Longman pbk **£6.50**

WEDGWOOD, C.V.
The Thirty Years War
Very highly regarded work of historical literature. Wedgwood's command of the printed sources and of the enormous literature in German, Swedish, Dutch, French, Italian and Spanish is as impressive as her economy of style.
[L1277] Methuen pbk **£8.95**

WILLIAMS, E.N.
Ancien Régime in Europe
A good complement to the works of Anderson and Rudé, and a major work in its own right. Each state is taken in turn and analysed in terms of political, social and economic structures. A highly detailed work most advantageously used in conjunction with the comparatively lively work of Rudé.
[L1278] Penguin pbk **£6.99**

HISTORY

French society of the 'ancien régime', as depicted in a contemporary cartoon. Illustration from *Oxford Illustrated Encyclopaedia: World History Volume 1* (Oxford hbk £19.50)

Europe in the Age of Revolution & Empire

ANDERSON, M.S.
The Ascendancy of Europe 1815 - 1914
[L1279] Longman pbk **£9.95**

BEST, GEOFFREY
War and Society in Revolutionary Europe 1770 - 1870
[L1280] Fontana pbk **£3.50**

BRIDGE, ROY
The Great Powers & the European States System 1815 - 1914
[L1281] Longman pbk **£7.95**
The Great Powers and the European States System 1815 - 1914
[L1282] Longman pbk **£7.50**

CRANKSHAW, E.
The Fall of the House of Habsburg
Classic, lively account of the crucial events leading to the First World War.
[L1284] Macmillan pbk **£7.99**

HOBSBAWM, E.J.
One of the leading figures from the (broadly speaking) Marxist coterie of British historians, his books have been adopted by people of all political persuasions as the best introduction to 19th century Europe. His account of so great a subject achieves admirable clarity and brevity through highlighting key themes. By literary standards all his works are of a high order.
The Age of Revolution 1789 - 1848
[L1285] Sphere pbk **£4.99**
The Age of Capital 1848 - 75
[L1286] Weidenfeld hbk **£15.00**
[L1287] Sphere pbk **£4.95**
The Age of Empire 1874 - 1914
[L1288] Sphere pbk **£9.95**
Worlds of Labour
Ranges over many of the major themes in the history of working men and women in the late 18th and mid-19th centuries.
[L1289] Weidenfeld hbk **£15.95**

JOLL, JAMES
Europe since 1870: An International History
One of the major texts for 'A' level and undergraduate study. It provides a lucid account enabling one to distinguish the main trends generated by the mass movements of the period. The viewpoint of the book is provided by the idea of Europe as an historical entity.
[L1290] Penguin pbk **£6.99**

KIERNAN, VICTOR
European Empires from Conquest to Collapse 1815 - 1960
[L1291] Fontana pbk **£3.50**

LEE, STEPHEN J.
Aspects of European History 1789 - 1980
[L1292] Methuen pbk **£6.95**

MCEVEDY, COLIN
Atlas of Recent History since 1815
[L1293] Penguin pbk **£4.95**

OKEY, R.
Eastern Europe 1780 - 1985
[L1294] Hutchinson pbk **£9.95**

RUDE, GEORGE
Revolutionary Europe 1783 - 1815
[L1295] Fontana pbk **£4.95**

SKED, ALAN
The Decline and Fall of the Hapsburg Empire NEW
The author argues, on the basis of recent research, that the Hapsburg Empire's decline was not due to inherent weaknesses (as Taylor suggests) but as a direct consequence of Germany's losing the First World War.
[L1296] Longman pbk **£8.95**

TAYLOR, A.J.P.
Europe: Grandeur and Decline
A collection of essays that provides a range of controversial perspectives on largely post-1848 Europe. There are brilliant portraits of leading figures such as Metternich, Napoleon, and Bismarck.
[L1297] Penguin pbk **£4.99**
The Habsburg Monarchy
Taylor describes the last phase in the long history of the Habsburgs. Their empire stretching across Central and Eastern Europe led to insuperable problems, which were compounded by their attempts to provide a heterogeneous population with stable government.
[L1298] Penguin pbk **£5.95**
The Struggle for Mastery in Europe: 1848 - 1918
This work focuses on a period whose leading feature was the often precarious balance struck by the conflicting self-interests of nation-states and the desire to maintain a balance of power. Primarily a study of the political/diplomatic machinations of the major powers, the whole is set in an economic context.
[L1299] Oxford pbk **£7.95**

THOMSON, DAVID
Europe since Napoleon
Very popular school text, admired for its accessibility and range.
[L1300] Penguin pbk **£6.95**

TUCHMAN, BARBARA
Tuchman was an eminent American historian, who died recently. *The Proud Tower* is an evocative and sensitive portrait of the world before the war, in the period 1890 1914.

August 1914
[L1301] Constable hbk **£12.95**
[L1302] Macmillan pbk **£8.95**
The Proud Tower
[L1303] Macmillan pbk **£9.99**

VIDLER
The Church in the Age of Revolution: 1789 to Present Day
[L1304] Penguin pbk **£5.99**

WOOD, ANTHONY
Europe 1815 - 1960
Widely used at 'A' and first degree levels this far-ranging account appeals to those who distrust the tendency of the newer kind of historical writing which plays down the explanatory force of the motives of rulers and governments. This is political history first and foremost.
[L1305] Longman hbk **£13.95**
[L1306] Longman pbk **£9.50**

Europe in the 20th Century

ALEXANDER, M.S. & GRAHAM, H. (EDS)
The French and Spanish Popular Fronts NEW
A collection of essays providing a comparative study of the development of popular fronts in Europe, showing them to be genuine mass-movements rather than élite partnerships.
[L1306A] Cambridge hbk **£29.50**

DAWIDOWICZ, LUCY
The War against the Jews
[L1307] Penguin pbk **£6.95**

GILBERT, MARTIN
The Holocaust
It is very hard not to lapse into one form or another of bad taste or moral crusade when dealing with the horror of the final solution. Gilbert, while providing the most thorough single-volume account yet available, does not. This alone is enough to make his work the authority on the Holocaust.
[L1308] Fontana pbk **£6.95**

HOGAN, M.J.
The Marshall Plan
The most complete history of American aid in post-war Europe, which argues that the Marshall plan was an attempt by the US government to create an integrated, mixed single-market economy.
[L1308A] Cambridge pbk **£15.00**

HOGGART, R. & JOHNSON, P.
An Idea of Europe
An innovative assessment of the European ideal.
[L1309] Chatto hbk **£12.95**

HOWARTH, STEPHEN
August 1939: The Last Few Weeks of Peace in Europe NEW
[L1310] Hodder hbk **£12.95**

KITCHEN, MARTIN
Europe between the Wars
[L1311] Longman pbk **£8.50**

LEE, STEPHEN J.
Aspects of European History 1789 - 1980
[L1312] Methuen pbk **£6.95**

LENTIN, A.
Guilt at Versailles
[L1313] Methuen pbk **£7.95**

MILANES, VICTOR MALLIA **NEW**
The Origins of the Second World War
A selection of primary source material on the origins of the Second World War 1919-1939. Eight chapters document the post-World War I settlement and its gradual disintegration.
[L1314] Macmillan pbk **£3.95**

PALMER, ALAN
Dictionary of 20th Century History
[L1315] Penguin pbk **£5.95**
Dictionary of Modern History 1789 - 1945
[L1316] Penguin pbk **£4.99**

ROSS, GRAHAM
The Great Powers and the Decline of the European States System 1914 - 1945
[L1317] Longman pbk **£7.50**

SEAMAN, L.C.B.
From Vienna to Versailles
[L1318] Methuen pbk **£6.95**

TAYLOR, A.J.P.
The First World War 1914 - 1918
[L1320] Penguin pbk **£5.99**
The Origins of the Second World War
This work wreaked considerable havoc when it first appeared as it seemed to redistribute blame for the origins of WW2 in such a way as to make Hitler less of a devil and Chamberlain more of a gullible fool. It is flawed in places but remains a provocative and compelling read.
[L1321] Penguin pbk **£4.99**
From Sarajevo to Potsdam
[L1319] Thames & H pbk **£4.95**

WISKEMANN, ELIZABETH
Europe of the Dictators 1919 - 1945
A short work with an almost overwhelming amount of detail in a very small space. This book focuses on political changes of the period but also treats of social and economic developments.
[L1322] Fontana pbk **£3.95**

Europe by Country

The French Revolution

A comprehensive selection from the vast number of books published to mark the bicentenary are listed below, with an emphasis on new titles and important reprints, and a bias towards French historians. It aims to show the variety of approach, from broad narrative histories to studies of specific topics. Unfortunately the work of many of the most important historians remains untranslated, or has gone out of print.

BEST, GEOFFREY (ED)
The Permanent Revolution
Excellent collection of essays by eight prominent scholars on the effect of the French Revolution today, treating of such topics as Nationalism, human rights, counter-revolution and the conduct of war.
[L1323] Fontana pbk **£4.95**

Illustration from *The Oxford History of the French Revolution* by William Doyle (Oxford hbk £19.50)

BINDMAN, DAVID
The Shadow of the Guillotine **NEW**
Catalogue of the exhibition of British prints on the subject of the Revolution, including Blake's illuminations, Gillray's satirical drawings and Wedgwood medallions.
[L1324] Brit Mus P pbk **£14.95**

BURLEY, PETER
Witness to the Revolution **NEW**
The correspondence of British and American observers in Paris, such as Thomas Jefferson (then American Ambassador in Paris) and Arthur Young.
[L1325] Weidenfeld hbk **£16.95**

CAMBRIDGE HISTORY OF THE FRENCH REVOLUTION **NEW**
Cambridge made the imaginative decision not to commission yet another history of the revolution, but to translate these three recent studies by active French historians/researchers. Scholarly and challenging, the three volumes contain much recent material, and provide the most up-to-date synthesis of French research. Particularly notable is Vovelle's account of the early years of the Revolution.
VOVELLE, MICHEL
Vol 1: The Fall of the French Monarchy
[L1326] Cambridge pbk **£10.95**
BOULOISLAU, MARC
Vol 2: The Jacobin Republic 1792 - 94
[L1327] Cambridge pbk **£10.95**
WORONOFF, DENIS
Vol 3: The Thermidorean Régime and the Directory 1794 - 99
[L1328] Cambridge pbk **£9.95**

CARLYLE, THOMAS
A Carlyle Reader
[L1329] Cambridge pbk **£8.50**
The French Revolution
Carlyle's best-known historical work is one of outstanding narrative and descriptive power, with an impressive and memorable array of character portraits including Lafayette, Danton and Robespierre.
[L1330] Oxford pbk **£7.95**

CHAPMAN, PAULINE
The French Revolution as Seen by Madame Tussaud, Witness Extraordinaire **NEW**
A reconstruction of the Revolution in Paris, largely based on the diaries of Marie Grosholtz (later Madame Tussaud), whose fame began with her waxes of guillotined heads.
[L1331] Quiller hbk **£12.95**

CHRONICLE **NEW**
Chronicle of the French Revolution
Chronicle have attempted to follow up the enormous success of *Chronicle of the 20th Century* by treating the French Revolution in a similar way, resulting in an enormous, very highly-, and well- illustrated 'diary', written in the present tense to simulate newspaper accounts. Unfortunately it lacks historical perspective, and, strangely for its length, fails to create much of the flavour of the Revolution.
[L1332] Longman hbk **£29.95**

COBB, RICHARD
The People's Armies
Recently translated from the French, this is the major work of one of the most highly regarded historians of today. The People's Armies were revolutionary civilian groups created to obtain food and equipment from rural areas for the French army. The interaction of the largely urban and highly politicised *armées* with rural villagers is one of the most revealing aspects in the social history of the Revolution.
[L1333] Yale UP pbk **£9.95**

CRONIN, VINCENT
Louis and Antoinette **NEW**
Cronin argues that Louis and Antoinette have been the most consistently misrepresented Royal figures - they were not the frivolous pleasure-seekers of lore, but hard-working reformers. According to Robin Lane Fox, 'an impressive addition to the small list of biographies which are neither journalism nor Christmas Pudding'.
[L1334] Collins Harvill pbk **£7.95**

DOYLE, WILLIAM
The Oxford History of the French Revolution **NEW**
The author, one of the leading historians today, has written a compelling, highly-detailed, narrative history of the Revolution. The book's accessibility and scholarship, a hallmark of Oxford Histories, will surely make it the standard textbook for years to come.
[L1335] Oxford hbk **£19.50**

FREGOSI, PAUL
Dreams of Empire **NEW**
Subtitled 'Napoleon and the First World War, 1792-1815', this examines Napoleon's campaigns outside continental Europe, in Africa, Asia, the West Indies, South America, Ireland and Louisiana.
[L1336] Hutchinson hbk **£19.95**

FURET, FRANCOISE
Interpreting the French Revolution
[L1337] Cambridge pbk **£8.95**

GEYL, PIETER
Napoleon: For and Against
See Michael Foot's article on pages 547-548.
[L1338] Penguin pbk **£7.95**

GOUGH, HUGH
The Newspaper Press in the French Revolution **NEW**
1789 saw a free press in France for the first time. The press subsequently played a vital part in influencing political debate, not just among the Parisian clubs, but

throughout the provinces. This is the first major study in English on the subject, and the first to integrate the study of the provincial press into a study of the Parisian press.
[L1339] Routledge hbk **£29.00**

HAMPSON, NORMAN
Danton
A biography of one of the key figures of this period.
[L1340] Duckworth hbk **£15.00**
[L2340] Blackwell pbk **£6.95**

HAYCRAFT, JOHN **NEW**
In Search of the French Revolution
A mix of narrative history and travelogue, based on the author's journeys to key sites of the Revolution.
[L1340A] Secker hbk **£14.95**

HIBBERT, CHRISTOPHER **NEW**
The Days of the French Revolution
New abridged and illustrated edition of a popular history of the Revolution. A commendable introduction by the most prolific of historians.
[L1341] Penguin pbk **£12.99**

HUNT, LYNN
Politics, Culture and Class in the French Revolution
The best book on the iconography and mythology of the Revolution.
[L1342] Methuen pbk **£8.95**

JARRET, DEREK **NEW**
Three Faces of Revolution
The revolution as viewed from Paris, London and New York in 1789.
[L1343] G Philip hbk **£14.95**

JONES, COLIN
The Longman Companion to the French Revolution **NEW**
Encyclopaedic reference work. The wealth of information includes: lists of all the members of the numerous committees, parliaments and revolutionary groups; prices of food staples; a guide to taxes and levies; biographies of the main characters; glossary of revolutionary terms, and a chronology of the Revolution. It *is* indispensable.
[L1344] Longman hbk **£40.00**

JONES, P.M.
The Peasantry in the French Revolution
Excellent re-appraisal of Lefebvre's studies on 18th century French rural culture. Jones has found that recent research confirms Lefebvre's view that the peasantry occupied centre stage in the early years of the Revolution, but argues with his thesis that such peasant participation ran counter to its main capitalist trend.
[L1345] Cambridge pbk **£9.95**

KENNEDY, EMMET
A Cultural History of the French Revolution **NEW**
An acclaimed overview of the culture of the Revolution which examines painting, music, fiction, theatre, festivals, philosophy and science from the mid-18th century to the Napoleonic era. Illustrated.
[L1346] Yale UP hbk **£19.95**

LEFEBVRE, GEORGES
The Coming of the French Revolution
A reprint of the classic Marxist interpretation of the causes of 1789, notable for its lucid exposition and powerful, thrusting argument. The book was written to mark the 150th anniversary of the Revolution, but was soon suppressed by the Vichy government on account of its 'corruptingly' democratic tone.
[L1347] Princeton UP pbk **£8.95**

The French Revolution Vol 1
[L1348] Princeton UP pbk **£8.95**
The French Revolution Vol 2
[L1349] Princeton UP pbk **£8.95**

MICHELET, JULES
History of the French Revolution
An abridged version, edited by Gordon Wright, of Michelet's great history, originally in seven volumes, written between 1847-53. See Michael Foot's article at the head of this chapter.
[L1350] Chicago UP pbk **£11.95**

OUTRAM, DORINDA
The Body and the French Revolution **NEW**
Subtitled 'Sex, Class and Political Culture', this is one of the more original books to appear in the bicentennial year. The author argues that the dignity and authority of the human body was diminished by a Revolution that excluded females from public life because of their physical constitution, and promoted such practices as heroic suicide and death by guillotine; this diminution was crucial, she claims, in the subsequent development of bourgeois culture.
[L1351] Yale UP hbk **£17.50**

ROBERTS, J.M.
The French Revolution
Good, very short, introduction.
[L1352] Oxford pbk **£4.95**

RUDE, GEORGE
The Crowd in the French Revolution
A classic study of the composition of the revolutionary 'crowd' or 'mob'. Rudé's aim was to dissect scientifically the 'crowd' into its constituent social parts, avoiding the ideological prejudices that led Burke and Taine to see it as a bloodthirsty mob, or allowed republican historians like Michelet and Aulard to believe that it was the personificaion of all virtue.
[L1353] Oxford pbk **£5.95**

SCHAMA, SIMON
Citizens **NEW**
The most enjoyable new history of the Revolution. Schama has combined a new voice with an old historical tradition to achieve the near impossible - to make a scholarly history a bestseller. *Citizens* is in the great 19th century narrative/epic tradition, emphasising the role of the individual as the historical force, in a cultured and immensely broad text. Commenting on the book, Schama concludes *"the violence of the Revolution was not just an unfortunate moment, a means to a higher end, it was the heart of the Revolution itself: this is a disenchanted book - an epitaph for revolutionary romance"*.
[L1354] Viking hbk **£19.95**

SOBOUL, ALBERT
Understanding the French Revolution
Seventeen essays on areas of historical dispute by the pre-eminent, post-war historian of the Revolution. Heavily influenced by Lefebvre, Soboul denied he was a Marxist historian, but his work has a strong ideological structure. Thus the most interesting essays are on the historiography of the Revolution.
[L1355] Merlin pbk **£7.95**

THOMPSON, J.M.
Two good, concise introductions to the history of the revolution by an historian noted for his unideological approach and clear structure.
Leaders of the French Revolution
[L1356] Blackwell pbk **£8.95**
The French Revolution
[L1357] Blackwell pbk **£9.95**

VANSITTART, PETER
Voices of the Revolution **NEW**
Well-constructed anthology of contrasting accounts compiled in chronological order to recreate the chaos of the Revolution as it stumbled from one momentous event to another. Many of the accounts have not appeared in print before.
[L1358] Collins hbk **£10.95**

WILLIAMS, GWYN A.
Artisans and Sans-Culottes
Williams challenged the claim of those French historians who called themselves 'Marxist' and in doing so produced a controversial and original history of radical popular movements in Britain and France at the time of the Revolution. A very welcome reprint.
[L1359] Libris pbk **£7.95**

France

ANDERSON, R.D.
France 1870 - 1914
[L1360] Routledge pbk **£6.95**

BENEDICT, PHILIP (ED)
Cities and Social Change in Early Modern France **NEW**
Essays on the evolution of urban life 1500-1789.
[L1361] Unwin Hyman hbk **£30.00**

BIERMAN, JOHN **NEW**
Napoleon III and His Carnival Empire
A court history of the colourful and decadent Second Empire.
[L1362] J Murray hbk **£15.95**

BONNEY, RICHARD
Political Life in France under Richelieu and Mazarin 1624 - 61
The 17th century is frequently described as an age of crisis in the relations between governments and subjects. This book examines the growth of monarchical power during which ministerial competence and provincial administration were developed.
[L1363] Oxford hbk **£40.00**

BRAUDEL, FERNAND
The Identity of France
Braudel's approach is through the human situation in correlation to the geographical circumstances (affecting communications, fertility etc), and through this he explores the development of France as a nation, its limitations as a power and its place in relation to Europe and the world. This is the first volume of a massive history of France, sadly unfinished on the author's death.
[L1365] Collins hbk **£20.00**

BRIGGS, ROBIN
Early Modern France 1550 - 1715
A remarkable study that is of interest to both students of history as the general reader. This formative period of French history is handled in a vigorous manner providing one of the best accounts available of the French provinces in the age of Louis XIV.
[L1366] Oxford pbk **£5.95**

BURY, J.P.T.
France 1814 - 1940
[L1367] Methuen hbk **£7.95**

CAMBRIDGE HISTORY OF MODERN FRANCE
JARDIN, A. & TUDESQ, A-J.
Restoration and Reaction 1815 - 1848
[L1368] Cambridge hbk **£45.00**
[L1369] Cambridge pbk **£11.95**

AGULHON, M.
The Republican Experiment
1848 - 1852
[L1370] Cambridge hbk **£30.00**
[L1371] Cambridge pbk **£9.95**
PLESSIS, ALAIN
The Rise and Fall of the Second Empire
1852 - 1871
[L1372] Cambridge pbk **£8.95**
MAYEUR, J-M. & REBERIOUX, M.
The Third Republic from its Origins to
the Great War 1871 - 1914
[L1373] Cambridge hbk **£42.50**
[L1374] Cambridge pbk **£11.95**
BERNARD, P. & DUBRIEF, H.
The Decline of the Third Republic
1914 - 1938
[L1375] Cambridge hbk **£37.50**
[L1376] Cambridge pbk **£10.95**
AZEMA, JEAN-PIERRE
From Munich to the Liberation
1938 - 1944
[L1377] Cambridge hbk **£30.00**
[L1378] Cambridge pbk **£12.95**
RIOUX, JEAN-PIERRE
The Fourth Republic 1944 - 1958
[L1379] Cambridge hbk **£40.00**

CHAUSSINAND-NOGARET, GUY
The French Nobility in the Eighteenth
Century: From Feudalism to
Enlightenment
[L1398] Cambridge pbk **£9.95**

COBBAN, ALFRED
In schools and universities Cobban's three-volume
history has established itself as an indispensable
introduction to modern France. Its strength lies in the
lucid manner in which he presents the great turning
points in terms of forces, mass movements and
leading individuals, whose nature and motives his
narrative clearly delineates.
History of Modern France: 1715 - 1799
[L1380] Penguin pbk **£4.99**
History of Modern France: 1799 - 1871
[L1381] Penguin pbk **£4.50**
History of Modern France: 1871 - 1962
[L1382] Penguin pbk **£4.50**

COLLINGHAM, H.A.C.
The July Monarchy: A Political History
of France 1830 - 1848
[L1383] Longman pbk **£13.00**

CRONIN, VINCENT
Paris on the Eve   **NEW**
An evocative picture of daily life in Paris in the
decade leading up to the Great War.
[L1384] Collins pbk **£17.50**

GREENGRASS, MARK
France in the Age of Henri IV: The
Struggle for Stability
[L1385] Longman pbk **£7.50**

HALLAM, ELIZABETH M.
Capetian France 987 - 1328
[L1386] Longman pbk **£11.50**

HASLIP, JOAN
Marie Antoinette
[L1386A] Weidenfeld pbk **£8.95**

HORNE, ALISTAIR
The Fall of Paris: The Siege and the
Commune 1870 - 71
An excellent, harrowing account that established the
author's reputation.
[L1387] Penguin pbk **£7.50**

JACKSON, JULIAN
The Popular Front in France
The only full-length study in English of the left-wing
coalition which emerged in France in the 1930s,
leading to the election of the country's first Socialist
Premier, Léon Blum.
[L1388] Cambridge hbk **£30.00**

KNECHT, R.J.
Francis I
[L1389] Cambridge pbk **£11.95**

LARKIN, MAURICE
France since the Popular Front   **NEW**
A comprehensive history of contemporary France that
places special emphasis on France's role within the
EEC
[L1390] Cambridge hbk **£10.95**

MAGRAW, ROGER
France 1815 - 1914: The Bourgeois
Century
[L1391] Fontana pbk **£6.95**

MANSEL, PHILIP
The Court of France 1789-1830   **NEW**
Mansel argues that the Revolution, paradoxically,
strengthened the Monarchy and produced a more
élitist court.
[L1393] Cambridge hbk **£25.00**

MARX, KARL & ENGELS, F.
The Paris Commune
[L1394] Lawrence & W pbk **£2.95**

MCKITTERICK, ROSAMUND
The Frankish Kingdoms under the
Carolingians 751 - 987
The best account we have of the Carolingian Empire
in the West.
[L1395] Longman pbk **£12.50**

MCMANNERS, J.
Death and the Enlightenment
Subtitled 'Changing Attitudes to Death among
Christians and Unbelievers in 18th Century France', it
tells how 'death was at the centre of life as the
graveyard was at the centre of the village.' An
inspirational social history which, given the subject
matter, was a surprising bestseller.
[L1396] Oxford pbk **£7.95**

PRICE, ROGER
A Social History of 19th Century France
The author proposes that the Revolution had little
social impact, thus in 1815 France was predominantly
rural and unindustrialised. He argues that the
economic revolution occurred in the mid-19th
century.
[L1399] Hutchinson pbk **£9.95**

REARICK, CHARLES
Pleasures of the Belle Epoque   **NEW**
Social history of fin-de-siècle France, focusing on
'places of pleasure'.
[L1400] Yale UP pbk **£12.95**

RUDE, GEORGE
The Crowd in History
Study of Popular Disturbances in France & England
1730 - 1848.
[L1401] Lawrence & W hbk **£14.95**
[L1402] Lawrence & W pbk **£6.95**

TAPIE, V.L.
France in the Age of Louis XIII and
Richelieu
[L1403] Cambridge hbk **£30.00**
[L1404] Cambridge pbk **£13.95**

ZELDIN, THEODORE
The French
A new edition of Zeldin's lively, masterful study of
contemporary France.
[L1405] Collins pbk **£6.95**
France 1848 - 1945
Although this work provides a reliable and
stimulating account of the political and economic
forces that shaped France in this period, what is most
impressive is his treatment of the broader cultural and
social issues, and the manner in which this diversity
of themes is worked into a greater unity. The erudition
is staggering and exhibits as great a familiarity with
sociological and psychological themes as with the
purely historical. The hardback editions contain the
full text, which is subdivided in each of the paperback
volumes.
Vol 1: Ambition, Love and Politics
[L1406] Oxford hbk **£30.00**
Vol 1 Parts i & ii: Ambition and Love
[L1407] Oxford pbk **£6.95**
Vol 1 Part iii: Politics and Anger
[L1408] Oxford pbk **£6.95**
Vol 2: Intellect, Taste and Anxiety
[L1409] Oxford pbk **£30.00**
Vol 2 Part i: Intellect and Pride
[L1410] Oxford pbk **£5.95**
Vol 2 Part ii: Taste and Corruption
[L1411] Oxford pbk **£5.95**
Vol 2 Part iii: Anxiety and Hypocrisy
[L1412] Oxford pbk **£5.95**

ZWEIG, STEFAN
Marie Antoinette: Portrait of an
Average Woman
[L1412A] Cassell pbk **£7.95**

Germany

ARDAGH, J.
Germany and the Germans
An excellent account of contemporary Germany
comparable to Barzini's *The Italians* or Zeldin's *The
French*.
[L1414] Penguin pbk **£6.99**

BARK, DENNIS & GRESS, DAVID
A History of West Germany   **NEW**
Vol 1: From Shadow to Substance
Published to mark the fortieth anniversary of the
Federal Republic of Germany.
[L1415] Blackwell hbk **£50.00**
Vol 2: Democracy and Its Discontents
[L1416] Blackwell hbk **£50.00**

BARRACLOUGH, G.
The Origins of Modern Germany
[L1417] Blackwell pbk **£10.95**

BERGHAHN, V.
Germany and the Approach of War
in 1914
[L1418] Macmillan pbk **£8.95**
Modern Germany: Society, Economics
and Politics of the 20th Century
A comprehensive overview and interpretation of the
developments of 20th century Germany.
[L1419] Cambridge pbk **£10.95**

BESSEL, R. (ED)
Life in the Third Reich
[L1420] Oxford pbk **£4.95**

BRACHER
German Dictatorship
Origins, structure and effects of national socialism.
[L1421] Penguin pbk **£9.95**

BULLOCK, A.
Hitler: A Study in Tyranny
Regarded as a masterpiece of historical biography, Bullock provides an absorbing, dispassionate account.
[L1423] Penguin pbk **£7.99**

CARR, WILLIAM
A History of Germany 1815 - 1985
Essential reading for all students of modern Germany.
[L1424] Arnold pbk **£9.95**

CLARE, GEORGE
Berlin Days 1946 - 1947 **NEW**
George Clare, a Vienna-born Jew, found himself in Norfolk at the end of the War, but decided he had to go to Germany to discover the reasons why the great 19th century intellectual homeland had become the world's worst dictatorship. This is his account of his years spent in Berlin, which was then 'the most harrowing, yet most fascinating, place on earth'.
[L1425] Macmillan hbk **£12.95**

CRAIG, G.A.
Germany 1866 - 1945
[L1426] Oxford pbk **£8.95**
The Germans
Using a broad historical perspective the author probes the complex make-up of the German identity.
[L1427] Penguin pbk **£5.95**

CRANKSHAW, E.
Bismarck
Study of the Prussian general who became chief architect of modern Germany through his military genius.
[L1428] Macmillan pbk **£7.95**

DONALD, J. & SHAW, W.
Dictionary of the Third Reich
Includes succinct and detailed biographies of the major figures.
[L1429] Grafton pbk **£4.99**

DULMEN, RICHARD VAN
Theatre of Horror: Crime and Punishment in Early Modern Germany **NEW**
The author treats of punishment within the context of the medieval world when the idea of the rehabilitation of criminals did not exist. Punishment existed purely as a means of retribution and deterrence.
[L1430] Blackwell hbk **£22.50**

ENGLEMANN, B.
In Hitler's Germany
Gives fascinating insights into how everyday lives were affected by Hitler, and includes a number of individual portraits.
[L1431] Methuen hbk **£12.95**

FEST, JOACHIM
Hitler
[L1432] Weidenfeld hbk **£8.95**
The Face of the Third Reich
Examines the Nazi regime through individual studies of its leaders. Translated from the German by Alan Bullock.
[L1433] Penguin pbk **£7.95**

FRIEDHOFF, HERMAN
Requiem for the Resistance
Subtitled 'Civilian Struggle against Nazism in Holland and Germany', this is a gripping account by a member of the underground movement.
[L1434] Bloomsbury hbk **£14.95**

FUHRMANN, HORST
Germany in the High Middle Ages 1050 - 1200
A text-book covering the economic background and social transformation brought about by the emergence of new classes and and intellectual renewal set against the decline of the Empire.
[L1435] Cambridge pbk **£7.50**

GRUNBERGER, RICHARD
A Social History of the Third Reich
A massive documentary of facts compiled from letters, newspapers, chronicles and other contemporary sources.
[L1436] Penguin pbk **£8.95**

HAFFNER, SEBASTIAN
Germany's Self Destruction: The Reich from Bismarck to Hitler **NEW**
[L1437] Simon & Sch hbk **£14.95**

HIDEN, J.W.
Germany & Europe 1919 - 1939
[L1438] Longman pbk **£6.95**

HILDEBRAND, K.
The Third Reich
Examines the major problem areas in interpretations of this period by historians.
[L1440] Unwin Hyman pbk **£9.40**

HOFFMAN, P.
German Resistance to Hitler
Charts the growing recognition by some Germans in the 1930s of the malign nature of the Nazi regime and the degree of their resistance.
[L1441] Harvard UP pbk **£7.95**

HUBATSCH, W.
Frederick the Great: Absolutism & Administration
[L1442] Thames & H hbk **£12.50**
Studies in Medieval and Modern Germany
The author focuses on the main periods in German history from the Crusades to the Second World War.
[L1444] Macmillan pbk **£9.95**

JAMES, HAROLD
A German Identity **NEW**
In searching for the causes of Germany's post-war success Professor James argues that the politics of German nationality have always been a product of international trends and that economic success has always been the German ideal.
[L1445] Weidenfeld hbk **£16.95**

KOCH, H.W.
A Constitutional History of Germany: 19th & 20th Centuries
[L1446] Longman pbk **£9.95**
Aspects of the Third Reich
[L1447] Macmillan hbk **£12.95**
Prussia: A History
[L1448] Longman pbk **£9.95**

KOLB, EBERHARD
Weimar Republic
[L1449] Unwin Hyman pbk **£7.95**

LAFFAN, MICHAEL
The Burden of German History 1919 - 45 **NEW**
From a series of Goethe Institute lectures on the Weimar Republic and the rise of National Socialism.
[L1450] Methuen pbk **£7.95**

MANN, G.
History of Germany since 1789
A work that offers a complete overview of the German people in this period including discussions of intellectual and artistic development. The chief virtue of this sensitive narrative is the way in which it turns to good account the notion of paradox: this provides the key to rendering intelligible the course of a people's history which has at one time exhibited a temperament for intellectual development and at another a tolerance for dictatorship. Widely used in schools and universities.
[L1451] Penguin pbk **£7.95**

MARSHALL, BARBARA
The Origins of Post-War German Politics
Discusses the Allies' role in restructuring German political life and looks at the German political scene in terms of mutual interaction of personalities, belief and economics, and of indigenous and foreign influences.
[L1452] Routledge hbk **£25.00**

PASSANT, E.J.
A Short History of Germany 1815 - 1945
[L1453] Cambridge pbk **£9.95**

ROPER, HUGH TREVOR
Hitler's Table Talk: His Private Conversations 1941 - 44
[L1454] Oxford pbk **£6.95**
The Last Days of Hitler
Highly acclaimed study of the period leading up to Hitler's final defeat.
[L1455] Macmillan pbk **£6.95**

SAGARRA, E.
Introduction to 19th Century Germany
An excellent account with a bias towards social history of a century dominated by Nationalism and the unification of Germany.
[L1456] Longman pbk **£7.50**

SCRIBNER, R.W.
The German Reformation
[L1457] Macmillan pbk **£4.50**

SHIRER, WILLIAM L.
The Rise and Fall of the Third Reich
A massive book written by an American journalist in Germany shortly after the war. Despite his closeness to events Schirer has written an excellent, captivating narrative which focuses on events within Germany. His account of the final days of the Reich is unsurpassable.
[L1458] Pan pbk **£6.95**

STERN, F.
Gold and Iron
Focuses on the extraordinary relationship between Bleichroder and Bismarck, 'Junker and Jew', who together worked at building Germany into a great Empire.
[L1460] Penguin pbk **£8.95**

STYLES, A.
The Unification of Germany
[L1461] Arnold pbk **£3.50**

TAYLOR, A.J.P.
Bismarck: The Man and the Statesman
The standard biography of one of the most dominant figures in 19th century Europe.
[L1462] H Hamilton pbk **£5.95**
Course of German History
A Survey of the Development of German History since 1815.
[L1463] Methuen pbk **£6.25**

TURNER, HENRY ASHBY
The Two Germanies Since 1945
Turner sees East and West Germany as inextricably linked and that their reciprocal interaction has been the major element in their evolution.
[L1464] Yale UP hbk **£17.50**

VIERHAUS, RUDOLF
Germany in the Age of Absolutism NEW
A history covering the period from the Thirty Years War to the end of the Seven Years War, arranged thematically, dealing with cultural and economic developments as well as political life.
[L1464A] Cambridge pbk **£9.95**

Italy

The Italian World
Highly illustrated overview of Italian culture with essays by John Julius Norwich, Francis Haskell, J.R. Hale and others.
[L1466] Thames & H hbk **£20.00**

BARZINI, L.
The Italians
An unsurpassed account of contemporary Italian life which treats of the historical factors of Italian identity and of regional diversity.
[L1467] H Hamilton pbk **£7.95**

BEALES, D.
The Risorgimento and the Unification of Italy
[L1468] Longman pbk **£5.95**

BURCKHARDT, JACOB
Cultural historian whose work established the Renaissance as a distinct period. His history of civilisation (unfinished at his death) argued that culture, in its widest sense, was the sole creative factor, while the state and religion were both repressive forces.
The Civilisation of the Renaissance in Italy
This is the most influential work on the subject. It has been the basis for all subsequent enquiry, either as the authoritative study of the period or as an object for radical attack. A formally complete and unified picture of the age is produced by handling the material thematically through the study of a narrow range of characters and city-states.
[L1470] Phaidon pbk **£7.50**

BURKE, P.
The Italian Renaissance
A brilliant and original work. The main theme concerns the interplay between philosophical and religious ideas, political power, and economic affluence, which produced enormous artistic energy and unprecedented artistic output.
[L1471] Polity pbk **£8.50**

BURMAN, EDWARD
Italian Dynasties NEW
Highly illustrated, potted studies of the Colonna, Medici, Sforza and Visconti families.
[L1472] Thorsons hbk **£14.95**

GINZBURG, CARLO
The Cheese and the Worms: The Cosmos of a 16th Century Miller
[L1473] Routledge pbk **£8.95**

HAY, DENYS
The Italian Renaissance in its Historical Background
Remains the best single-volume introduction to the Italian Renaissance.
[L1474] Cambridge hbk **£22.50**
[L1475] Cambridge pbk **£8.50**

HEARDER & WALEY
A Short History of Italy
[L1476] Cambridge pbk **£8.95**

HIBBERT, CHRISTOPHER
Garibaldi and His Enemies
[L1478] Penguin pbk **£5.99**
Rise and Fall of the House of Medici
[L1479] Penguin pbk **£5.99**

HOLMES, GEORGE
Florence, Rome and the Origins of the Renaissance
[L1480] Oxford pbk **£10.95**

LONGMAN HISTORY OF ITALY
LARNER, JOHN
Italy in the Age of Dante & Petrarch 1216 - 1380
[L1481] Longman pbk **£9.95**
HAY, DENYS
Italy in the Age of the Renaissance NEW
[L1482] Longman pbk **£12.00**
COCHRANE, ERIC
Italy 1530 - 1630 NEW
[L1483] Longman pbk **£12.00**
CARPANETTO, D.
Italy in the Age of Reason 1685 - 1789
[L1484] Longman pbk **£10.50**
HEARDER, HARRY
Italy in the Age of the Risorgimento 1790 - 1870
[L1485] Longman pbk **£12.00**
CLARK, M.
Modern Italy 1871 - 1982
[L1486] Longman pbk **£13.50**

MACHIAVELLI, NICCOLO
The Prince
Machiavelli's most famous work. A treatise on statecraft in which he argues the need for political realism: that the prosperity of the state depends on finding a leader who is not afraid to resort to unethical means which will secure the higher interests of a harmonious state. *The Prince* needs to be viewed in the context of a proliferation of 'handbooks for princes' not just as a book of political machination which created the misleading term 'Machiavellian'.
[L1487] Penguin pbk **£2.99**

MACK SMITH, DENIS
Italy and its Monarchy NEW
The history of the four Savoyard Kings who ruled from 1861 until 1946. The author argues that the Italian monarchy was discredited as an institution of government because they accepted a burden of responsibility for events without the power to control them.
[L1488] Yale UP hbk **£16.95**
Mussolini
[L1488A] Grafton pbk **£4.95**

NORWICH, JOHN JULIUS
A History of Venice
A wide-ranging but nonetheless detailed treatment of the history of one of the most enigmatic cities of the Mediterranean. An accessible and stimulating work.
[L1489] Penguin pbk **£11.95**

ORIGO, IRIS
The Merchant of Prato
An evergreen and famous study of an Italian merchant who lived towards the end of the Middle Ages. He was not famous and achieved little of lasting effect but his Life illuminates all aspects of his time. Based on some 150,000 business and private letters discovered in 1810, it provides a picture of intricate and brilliant detail showing us in the example of one 14th century Tuscan merchant, Italian domestic life on the eve of the Renaissance.
[L1490] Penguin pbk **£6.99**

PHILLIPS, MARK (ED)
The Memoirs of Marco Parenti NEW
The diary of a Florentine silk merchant which gives a contemporary account of the uprising against the Medici in the 15th century.
[L1491] Heinemann hbk **£12.95**

PROCACCI, GIULIANO
History of the Italian People
[L1492] Penguin pbk **£5.99**

SASSOON, DONALD
Contemporary Italy
A socio-economic history of Italy since 1945.
[L1493] Longman pbk **£9.95**

SMITH, DENIS MACK
Cavour
[L1494] Methuen pbk **£8.95**
Mussolini
[L1495] Grafton pbk **£4.95**
The Making of Italy 1796 - 1866
Italy was beginning to change before the French Revolution came in 1789 which added new impetus in a new direction. The author establishes how Italian unification occurred, arguing that it was one of those complex movements which developed along lines that were sometimes far removed from the intentions of any participants.
[L1496] Macmillan hbk **£29.50**
[L1497] Macmillan pbk **£9.50**

TREVELYAN, G.M.
Garibaldi and the Thousand NEW
A re-issue of the second volume of Trevelyan's remarkable trilogy on the unification of Italy. Based on Garibaldi's memoirs (which had been given to Trevelyan as a present) the book remains an essential source on the subject.
[L1498] Cassell hbk **£8.95**

WALEY, DANIEL
The Italian City Republics
[L1499] Longman hbk **£15.95**
[L1500] Longman pbk **£6.95**

WISKEMANN, ELIZABETH
Fascism in Italy: Its Development and Influence
[L1501] Macmillan pbk **£8.95**

Russia and the Soviet Union

A Companion to Russian History
[L1502] Facts on File pbk **£7.95**

The Cambridge Encyclopaedia of Russia and the Soviet Union NEW
An excellent, well-illustrated overview of Russian/Soviet history and culture, showing the diversity of contemporary USSR.
[L1503] Cambridge hbk **£27.50**

ACTON, EDWARD
Russia: Present and Past
Despite the uninformative title, Acton's contribution to Longman's Present and Past series is an excellent one-volume beginner's history of modern Russia, illustrated with maps and photographs.
[L1504] Longman hbk **£8.95**

ALEXANDER, JOHN T.
Catherine the Great NEW
New, highly detailed and lengthy biography making use of the most recent research.
[L1505] Oxford hbk **£16.95**

CARR, E.H.
A radically inclined scholar whose famous work of historiography *What is History?* aroused wide controversy on its publication in 1961. Carr rejects the old liberal historians' notion that historical objectivity is possible, arguing that all historians are socially conditioned and determined, and cannot possibly view past events with detachment. Paradoxically his massive *History of the Soviet Union* is so skilfully researched and highly detailed it is a model of historical science.
A History of the Soviet Union 1917 - 1929
Massive, 14-volume history (details on request). The most interesting volumes for the general reader are available in paperback.
[L1506] Macmillan hbk **£295.00**
The Bolshevik Revolution Part 1
[L1507] Penguin pbk **£7.99**
The Bolshevik Revolution Part 2
[L1508] Penguin pbk **£7.95**
The Bolshevik Revolution Part 3
[L1509] Penguin pbk **£8.95**
The Russian Revolution from Lenin to Stalin 1917 - 1929
[L1510] Macmillan pbk **£6.99**
The Twenty Years' Crisis 1919 - 1939
[L1511] Macmillan pbk **£7.99**
The Twilight of Comintern 1930 - 35
Following the completion of his fourteen volume *History of the Soviet Union* which carried the record of the Revolution down to the end of 1929, Carr explored the relationship of Moscow with communist parties in the rest of the World.
[L1512] Macmillan pbk **£11.50**

Nikolai Bukharin, Marxist theoretician and economist, from *Oxford Illustrated Encyclopaedia. World History Volume 2* (Oxford hbk £19.50)

CLARK, RONALD
Lenin
The most recent biography, which received excellent reviews on publication.
[L1513] Faber hbk **£17.95**

COHEN, STEPHEN F.
Bukharin and the Bolshevik Revolution
Currently in the process of being posthumously rehabilitated by the Soviet Union's new leadership Bukharin was at one point the only major alternative to Stalin. The latter's subsequent revision of the history books consigned the talented Bukharin to obscurity: Cohen's biography, the first attempt to restore him, was published in 1971.
[L1514] Oxford pbk **£4.95**
Rethinking the Soviet Experience: Politics and History since 1917
[L1515] Oxford pbk **£5.95**

CONQUEST, ROBERT
Harvest of Sorrow
Between 1929 and 1932 the Soviet government struck a double blow at the peasantry of the USSR: dekulakisation, the dispossession and deportation of millions of peasant families; and collectivisation, the effective abolition of private property. Conquest's long-awaited, impassioned study tells the story of one of the most shameful episodes in modern history.
[L1516] Arrow pbk **£5.99**
Stalin and the Kirov Murder NEW
Conquest debates the case of Stalin's involvement in the murder of Sergei Kirov, the next-most powerful member of the Politburo at the time of his death in 1934, which allowed Stalin free rein to dominate the Soviet Union.
[L1517] Hutchinson hbk **£14.95**

CRANKSHAW, E.
The Shadow of the Winter Palace
This popular volume details the final years of the Romanov dynasty from the accession of Nicholas I to the abdication of his namesake Nicholas II. The narrative is stronger dealing with the disintegration of the old order than with analysing the roots of the new.
[L1518] Macmillan pbk **£8.95**

DEUTSCHER, ISAAC
Expelled from Poland in 1932 for his activities as leader of the anti-Stalinist faction in the Polish Communist Party, Deutscher has written one of the standard histories of the Soviet Union, and an acclaimed three-volume biography of Trotsky.
Russia 1917 - 1967
[L1519] Oxford pbk **£3.95**
Stalin: A Political Biography
This controversial political biography was first published in 1948. Substantially revised and updated in 1966, it remains an important portrait from a particular viewpoint.
[L1520] Penguin pbk **£6.99**
The Prophet Armed 1879 - 1921
[L1521] Oxford pbk **£6.95**
The Prophet Outcast 1929 - 1940
[L1522] Oxford pbk **£6.95**
The Prophet Unarmed 1921 - 1929
[L1523] Oxford pbk **£6.95**

FALKUS, M.E.
The Industrialisation of Russia 1700 - 1914
[L1524] Macmillan pbk **£4.50**

FITZPATRICK, SHEILA
The Russian Revolution 1917 - 1932
An excellent single-volume introduction to the Revolution and its aftermath.
[L1525] Oxford pbk **£4.95**

GITELMAN, ZVI
A Century of Ambivalence: The Jews of Russia and the Soviet Union NEW
Photographic album of the Russian Jews since 1881 with explanatory text.
[L1526] Viking hbk **£20.00**

GORBACHEV, MIKHAIL
Perestroika
The blueprint for a new Soviet Union which contains a frank, incisive account of the contemporary USSR.
[L1527] Fontana hbk **£3.95**

HALPERIN, CHARLES
Russia and the Golden Horde NEW
A much-needed reinterpretation of the impact of the Mongol conquest and rule of Russia from the 13th to the 15th centuries. Halperin analyses the influence of the Mongols on Medieval Russia's political history, culture and thought.
[L1528] Tauris pbk **£9.50**

HELLER, M. & NEKRICH, N.
Utopia in Power: A History of the USSR from 1917 to the Present
This first substantial new history of the Soviet Union to be published for many years, which despite its obvious scholarship has been criticised for giving way to anti-Soviet rhetoric.
[L1529] Hutchinson hbk **£25.00**
[L1530] Hutchinson pbk **£16.95**

HILL, CHRISTOPHER
Lenin and the Russian Revolution
Excellent study by the Marxist historian who specialises in 17th century English history, and in particular the English Civil War.
[L1531] Penguin pbk **£4.50**

HOPKIRK, PETER
Setting the East Ablaze
Lenin's dream of an Empire in Asia.
[L1532] Oxford pbk **£4.50**

HOSKING, GEOFFREY
A History of the Soviet Union
Professor Hosking's study provides us with a well-balanced overview of Soviet society in the last 70 years.
[L1533] Collins hbk **£12.95**
[L1534] Fontana pbk **£5.95**

HOUSE, FRANCIS
The Russian Phoenix
This short history of the Russian Christian experience before and after the Revolution was published to coincide with the celebration of the millennium of the Russian Orthodox Church.
[L1535] SPCK pbk **£7.95**

JONGE, ALEX DE
Stalin and the Shaping of the Soviet Union
[L1536] Fontana pbk **£5.95**

KAGARLITSKY, BORIS
The Thinking Reed NEW
Subtitled 'Intellectuals and the Soviet State from 1917 to the Present Day'. In his account of Soviet intellectual life since 1917 Boris Kagarlitsky, a young Soviet sociologist, addresses all aspects of the difficult relationship between the state and the intelligentsia, including the policy of Glasnost.
[L1537] Verso pbk **£9.95**

KOCHAN, LIONEL
Russia in Revolution
[L1538] Grafton pbk **£2.95**

The Jews in Soviet Russia since 1917
[L1539] Oxford pbk **£3.50**

KOCHAN, LIONEL & ABRAHAM
The Making of Modern Russia
A very accessible single-volume history of Russia and the Soviet Union.
[L1540] Penguin pbk **£6.99**

LIEVIN, DOMINIC
Russia's Rulers under the Old Regime **NEW**
A detailed examination of every member of the State Council under Tsar Nicholas II.
[L1541] Yale UP hbk **£27.50**

LONGMAN HISTORY OF RUSSIA
FENNELL, J.
The Crisis of Medieval Russia 1200 - 1304
[L1542] Longman pbk **£10.50**
CRUMMEY, ROBERT
The Formation of Muscovy 1304 - 1613
This second volume is a comprehensive account of the late medieval Russian monarchy and the emergence of Muscovy as the dominant state in North Eastern Russia.
[L1543] Longman pbk **£10.95**
DUKES, PAUL
The Making of Russian Absolutism 1613 - 1801
Covers the first two centuries of Romanov rule from the foundation of the dynasty to the accession of Alexander I. As with its companion volumes it is a very useful introductory narrative on a crucial period of change in the history of Russia.
[L1544] Longman pbk **£8.95**
ROGGER, HANS
Russia in the Age of Modernisation and Revolution 1881 - 1917
Professor Rogger's book concentrates on the relationship between the state and society in late 19th century Russia.
[L1545] Longman pbk **£10.95**
MCCAULEY, MARTIN
The Soviet Union since 1917
[L1546] Longman pbk **£10.95**

MASSIE, ROBERT K.
Nicholas and Alexandra
[L1548] Gollancz pbk **£6.95**
Peter the Great
One of the most outstanding historical biographies, Massie's *Peter the Great* deservedly won a Pulitzer Prize. It is not only an enormously detailed study of one of the most influential and charismatic figures in Russian history, but also a superb evocation of life in Petrine Russia.
[L1549] Sphere pbk **£5.95**

MCCAULEY & WALDRON
The Emergence of the Modern Russian State 1856 - 1881
[L1550] Macmillan hbk **£35.00**

MEDVEDEV, ROY
Let History Judge: The Origins and Consequences of Stalinism **NEW**
A revised and expanded edition of Medvedev's 1971 work: much new material has been incorporated, covering the Kirov assassination, the show trials, and the fate of Trotsky.
[L1552A] Oxford hbk **£25.00**

NOVE, ALEC
An Economic History of the USSR
[L1553] Penguin pbk **£5.95**

PIPES, RICHARD
Russia Under the Old Regime
This authoritative volume covers the period from the 9th century to the late 19th. Part One describes the evolution of the Russian state, the second part treats of the various social groups of the Empire, and the final part analyses the intelligentsia's challenge to the regime and the regime's response in creating a police state.
[L1554] Weidenfeld hbk **£15.00**
[L1555] Penguin pbk **£6.95**

REED, JOHN
Ten Days that Shook the World
John Reed, the American journalist and political activist, holds the distinction of being buried in Red Square in the Heroes Grave. His book has been revered in the Soviet Union, made into a film - *Reds* - in America, but has been disparaged by historians as the product of an overactive imagination. Nevertheless, it conveys the chaos and excitement of the revolution in Leningrad.
[L1556] Penguin pbk **£4.95**

SCHAPIRO, LEONARD
The Communist Party of the Soviet Union
[L1557] Routledge pbk **£12.95**
The Russian Revolution
[L1558] Penguin pbk **£3.95**

SETON-WATSON, HUGH
The Russian Empire 1801 - 1917
This volume in the Oxford History of Modern Europe surveys the development of the Russian Empire from the reign of Alexander I to the abdication of Nicholas II.
[L1559] Oxford hbk **£30.00**
[L1560] Oxford pbk **£14.95**

SHUKMAN, HAROLD (ED)
The Blackwell Encyclopaedia of the Russian Revolution
The encyclopaedia is written by 40 specialists and covers every aspect of the period from the development of the revolutionary movement to an analysis of revolutionary culture.
[L1561] Blackwell hbk **£37.50**

SOLZHENITSYN, ALEXANDER
The Gulag Archipelago
This monumental study of the Soviet prison camp system is now available in one abridged volume in paperback.
[L1563] Collins Harv pbk **£6.95**

SUMMERS, ANTHONY & MANGOLD, TOM
File on the Tsar
In July 1918 Tsar Nicholas II, his wife Alexandra and his five children, disappeared whilst in Communist hands, never to be seen again. Summers and Mangold investigate the theories that they may have survived, in a thrilling and chilling account of their 'last' days.
[L1564] Gollancz pbk **£4.95**

TROYAT, HENRI
A Russian-born Frenchman, Troyat is one of the most readable and prolific of contemporary biographers. He has been criticised for his unacademic approach but his *oeuvre*, including biographies not just of the Tsars but also of Tolstoy, Pushkin, Gogol and Chekov, is impressive.
Alexander of Russia
[L1565] Hodder hbk **£10.95**
Catherine the Great
[L1566] Ellis hbk **£9.50**
Ivan the Terrible
[L1567] Hodder hbk **£14.95**

Peter the Great
Peter the Great, fascinated equally by progress and absolute power, changed the face of Russia completely, turning it towards Europe with the development of St Petersburg as a modern political and cultural centre.
[L1568] H Hamilton hbk **£15.95**

WOOD, ALAN
The Origins of the Russian Revolution 1861 - 1917
[L1570] Methuen pbk **£3.50**

Spain

BALFOUR, SEBASTIAN **NEW**
Dictatorship, Workers and the City
A history of the Spanish labour movement from 1939 to 1988.
[L1571] Oxford hbk **£30.00**

BORKENAU, F.
The Spanish Cockpit
This book, together with Brenan's *Spanish Labyrinth* and Orwell's *Homage to Catalonia*, represents a vivid first-hand portrayal of the civil war. All three authors possess sensitivity towards the limitations of power and the fate of individuals to give reasonably balanced accounts whilst portraying the horrors of the war.
[L1572] Pluto pbk **£5.95**

BRENAN, GERALD
The Spanish Labyrinth
[L1573] Cambridge pbk **£12.95**

CARR, RAYMOND
Modern Spain: 1875 - 1980
The most concise and lucid history of modern Spain.
[L1574] Oxford pbk **£6.95**
Spain: 1808 - 1975
A lengthy and highly-detailed history which has become a standard undergraduate text.
[L1575] Oxford pbk **£14.95**

COLLINS, ROGER
Spain in the Eighth Century **NEW**
The first volume to appear in the new Blackwell History of Spain.
[L1576] Blackwell hbk **£29.50**

ELLIOTT, J.H.
Spain and its World 1500 - 1700 **NEW**
Essays from the pre-eminent historian of early modern Spain, under four headings: Spain and the Americas; the European world; the world of the Court, and the decline of Spain.
[L1577] Yale UP hbk **£20.00**
The Count Duke of Olivares
An exceptional biography of Philip IV's principal minister and Richelieu's arch-rival in European diplomacy. A monumental and readable work of scholarship. Newly published in paperback.
[L1578] Yale UP pbk **£12.95**
Imperial Spain
[L1579] Penguin pbk **£5.95**

HOOPER
The Spaniards
A lively portrayal of contemporary Spain which is particularly good on the Francoist legacy and the problems of regional diversity.
[L1580] Penguin pbk **£4.95**

INNES, HAMMOND
The Conquistadors
[L1581] Collins pbk **£9.95**

JACKSON, G.
A Concise History of the Spanish Civil War
[L1582] Thames & H pbk **£4.95**

KAMEN, HENRY
One of the foremost authorities on Spanish history, best known for his examination of the Spanish Inquisition.
Inquisition and Society in Spain
[L1583] Weidenfeld hbk **£16.95**
[L1584] Weidenfeld pbk **£9.95**
Spain 1469 - 1714: A Society in Conflict
[L1585] Longman pbk **£8.50**
Spain in the Later 17th Century 1665-1700
[L1586] Longman pbk **£13.00**

LYNCH, J.
Spain Under the Hapsburgs Vol 1
[L1587] Blackwell pbk **£9.95**
Spain Under the Hapsburgs Vol 2
[L1588] Blackwell pbk **£9.95**

ORWELL, GEORGE
Homage to Catalonia
[L1589] Secker hbk **£12.95**
[L1590] Penguin pbk **£2.95**

PARKER, GEOFFREY
Philip II
[L1591] Sphere pbk **£4.99**

PRESTON, PAUL
Revolution and War in Spain 1931 - 39
[L1593] Methuen pbk **£9.95**
The Triumph of Democracy in Spain
[L1594] Methuen pbk **£7.95**

STRADLING, R.A.
Philip IV and the Government of Spain
An attempt to rehabilitate the figure of Philip IV, establishing him as an independently minded politician who deserves to be remembered for more than being the King who had Olivares as his first minister.
[L1595] Oxford hbk **£35.00**

THOMAS, HUGH
The Spanish Civil War
A very long and very detailed account whose monumental breadth defies brief summary or comment, it is a leading authority, although not definitive. If it has a weakness it lies in the ungenerous judgement on the political good sense of the Spanish Anarchist Movement.
[L1596] Penguin pbk **£10.95**

Other European Countries

ALBANIA
POLLO, S. & PUTO, A.
A History of Albania
[L1597] Routledge hbk **£30.00**

AUSTRIA
BELLER, STEPHEN
Vienna and the Jews 1867 - 1938 `NEW`
[L1598] Cambridge hbk **£25.00**
PYNSENT, ROBERT (ED)
Decadence and Innovation `NEW`
Essays on the role of decadence in propagating culture in *fin-de-siècle* Austro-Hungary.
[L1599] Weidenfeld hbk **£25.00**

BULGARIA
CRAMPTON, R.J.
A Short History of Modern Bulgaria
[L1600] Cambridge pbk **£8.95**

GREECE
CLOGG, RICHARD
A Short History of Modern Greece
The best history available in English.
[L1601] Cambridge pbk **£8.95**
Balkan Society in the Age of Greek Independence
[L1602] Macmillan hbk **£35.00**
WOODHOUSE, C.M.
Modern Greece: A Short History
[L1604] Faber pbk **£4.95**

HUNGARY
HOENSCH, JORG K.
A History of Modern Hungary
[L1605] Longman pbk **£9.95**
KOPACSI, SANDOR
In the Name of the Working Class `NEW`
Kopacsi was the Budapest Chief of Police at the outbreak of the 1956 uprising but refused to carry out Russian orders and subsequently became a leader in the revolution. His angry account of the events is a unique historical record.
[L1606] Fontana pbk **£4.95**
LUKACS, JOHN
Budapest 1900 `NEW`
A cultural portrait of one of Europe's great cities at the height of its power and a study of its subsequent decline.
[L1607] Weidenfeld hbk **£16.95**

LOW COUNTRIES
BOXER, C.N.
The Dutch Seaborne Empire
[L1608] Penguin pbk **£5.95**
GEYL, PIETER
The Revolt of the Netherlands `NEW`
A reissue of the first volume of Geyl's classic history of the Dutch Speaking Peoples (which he never finished). The new Cassells history series is a very welcome collection of great histories which should never have been allowed to go out of print.
[L1609] Cassell pbk **£6.95**
HALEY, KEN
The British and the Dutch
Traces their relationship from the Middle Ages, through 1688 when the Dutch Prince William of Orange became King of England, to the present.
[L1610] G Philip hbk **£11.95**
KOSSMAN, E.H.
The Low Countries 1780 - 1940
[L1611] Oxford hbk **£30.00**
PARKER, GEOFFREY
The Dutch Revolt
As an expert on Spanish history Parker is well qualified to understand the broad context of the struggle between the Netherlands and Spain in this enthralling narrative of an event of European significance.
[L1612] Penguin pbk **£5.99**
ROWEN, HERBERT H.
The Princes of Orange
Relates the personal lives and characters of the Princes with the development of the unique institution of the Stadholderate and the broader political history of the republic.
[L1613] Cambridge hbk **£25.00**
SCHAMA, SIMON
The Embarrassment of Riches
This great, sweeping narrative history of Holland in the Golden Age established Schama as one of the great stylists amongst contemporary historians. Equal weight is given to cultural, social and political developments in a book which constantly focuses on

individuals like characters in a novel. The many illustrations are integral to the text.
[L1614] Collins hbk **£19.95**
[L1615] Fontana pbk **£12.95**

POLAND
ASCHERSON, NEAL
Struggles for Poland
[L1616] Pan pbk **£4.99**
DAVIES, NORMAN
God's Playground: A History of Poland Vol 1: The Origins to 1795
[L1617] Oxford pbk **£15.00**
Vol 2: 1795 to the Present
[L1618] Oxford pbk **£15.00**
The Heart of Europe: A Short History of Poland
[L1619] Oxford pbk **£7.95**
HALECKI, OSKAR
A History of Poland
[L1620] Routledge hbk **£9.95**
LESLIE, R.F.
The History of Poland since 1863 `NEW`
New edition of standard text.
[L1621] Cambridge pbk **£12.95**
TORANSKA, TERESA
'Oni' Stalin's Polish Puppets
[L1622] Collins Harv pbk **£9.95**
ZAMOYSKI, ADAM
The Polish Way
Subtitled 'A Thousand Year History of the Poles and Their Culture', this is the best one-volume introduction to Polish history and culture.
[L1624] J Murray pbk **£11.95**

PORTUGAL
RABY, D.L.
Fascism and Resistance in Portugal
Communists, Liberals and Military Dissidents in the Opposition to Salazar 1941-74.
[L1625] Manchester UP hbk **£35.00**

ROUMANIA
MACKENZIE, ANDREW
A Concise History of Roumania
[L1626] Hale hbk **£15.95**

SWEDEN
ROBERTS, MICHAEL
The Swedish Imperial Experience 1560 - 1718
[L1627] Cambridge pbk **£9.50**

TURKEY
COOKE, M.A. (ED)
A History of the Ottoman Empire to 1730
Composed of chapters selected from the *New Cambridge Modern History* and the *Cambridge History of Islam*.
[L1628] Cambridge pbk **£17.95**
SHAW, S.J.
History of the Ottoman Empire & Modern Turkey Vol 1
Empire of the Gazis: The Rise & Decline of the Ottoman Empire 1208 - 1808.
[L1629] Cambridge pbk **£15.00**
Vol 2: Reform, Revolution and Republic
The Rise of Modern Turkey 1808 - 1975.
[L1630] Cambridge pbk **£22.50**

YUGOSLAVIA
JELAVICH B.
History of the Balkans Vol 1: 18th & 19th Century
[L1632] Cambridge pbk **£17.50**
History of the Balkans Vol 2: 20th Century
[L1633] Cambridge pbk **£17.50**

WORLD HISTORY

As a subject for academic study, 'world history' is a recent phenomenon. The subject matter, whether a World War, the development of the superpowers, or global economic and environmental problems, undoubtedly exists, but the problems of working such a vast amount of material into a satisfactory whole has rarely been overcome. The question of choosing a reasonable vantage point (should 'world history' be Eurocentric?), establishing a framework (is a chronological method suitable?), and the limiting of subject matter (is a history of the super powers 'world history'?) have yet to be answered. The titles below address themselves to some of these questions. Also listed are some general 'social' histories, which do not fit into other categories, but cannot truly be termed 'world history'.

General

Chronicle of the Twentieth Century
A phenomenal bestseller, the Chronicle gives a month by month account in newspaper format of the events of the Twentieth Century. It is a remarkable publishing feat and fascinating to browse through, but lacks historical perspective.
[L2000] Longman hbk **£29.95**

BITTERLI, URS
Cultures in Conflict **NEW**
A study from both sides of the clash between European colonists and native civilizations.
[L2001] Polity hbk **£27.50**

COOK, DON
Forging the Alliance **NEW**
A history of NATO to celebrate its 40th anniversary, introduced by Lord Carrington.
[L2002] Secker hbk **£15.00**

DENNIS, DENISE
Black History for Beginners
In documentary comic form, the author tackles a much neglected subject.
[L2003] Pluto pbk **£5.95**

GRENVILLE, J.A.S.
A World History of the Twentieth Century:
Vol 1: Western Dominance
[L2004] Fontana pbk **£5.95**

HOBHOUSE, HENRY
Forces of Change **NEW**
Bestselling author of *Seeds of Change*, Hobhouse treats historical forces in an easily accessible manner.
[L2005] Sidgwick hbk **£17.95**

JOHNSON, PAUL
A History of the Modern World from 1917 to the 1980s
An eminently readable text, informed, however, by many of the author's prejudices.
[L2006] Weidenfeld pbk **£8.95**

KENNEDY, PAUL
The Rise and Fall of the Great Powers
'Economic Change and Military Conflict from 1500 to 2000'. A global view of economic and military history with a controversial futurology section. Although limiting himself to a study of the great powers, Kennedy's grasp of the themes of history and

understanding of diplomacy make this the most interesting and successful of 'world' histories.
[L2007] Unwin Hyman hbk **£18.95**
[L2008] Fontana pbk **£6.95**

LESBIAN HISTORY GROUP
Not a Passing Phase
Essays which shed new light on old events from a radical source.
[L2022] Women's P pbk **£5.95**

LITVINOFF, BARNET
The Burning Bush: Antisemitism and World History **NEW**
The author sees antisemitism as a crucial force in the evolution of nationhood.
[L2009] Fontana pbk **£5.95**

MACNEILL, WILLIAM
Plagues and People **NEW**
[L2010] Penguin pbk **£6.99**

OXFORD ILLUSTRATED ENCYCLOPAEDIA OF WORLD HISTORY
From Earliest Times to 1800
[L2011] Oxford hbk **£19.50**
From 1800 to the Present Day
[L2012] Oxford hbk **£19.50**

PENGUIN ATLAS OF WORLD HISTORY
Vol 1: From the Beginning to the Eve of the French Revolution
[L2013] Penguin pbk **£5.95**
Vol 2: From the French Revolution to the Present
[L2014] Penguin pbk **£5.50**

PENGUIN HISTORY OF THE WORLD ECONOMY
Vol 1: First World War 1914 - 1918
[L2015] Penguin pbk **£5.99**
Vol 2: From Versailles to Wall Street 1919 - 1929
[L2016] Penguin pbk **£5.99**
Vol 3: World in Depression 1929 - 1939
[L2017] Penguin pbk **£5.99**
Vol 4: War, Economy and Society 1939 - 1945
[L2018] Penguin pbk **£6.95**
Vol 5: Prosperity and Upheaval 1945 - 1980
[L2019] Penguin pbk **£7.95**

ROBERTS, J.M.
The Hutchinson History of the World
This lucid and wide-ranging account of world history has received considerable acclaim and remains consistently popular. A judicious overview of an impossibly large subject.
[L2020] Hutchinson hbk **£19.95**
The Pelican History of the World
[L2021] Penguin pbk **£7.99**

THOMAS, HUGH
Unfinished History of the World
[L2023] Pan pbk **£9.99**

TOYNBEE, ARNOLD
A Study of History
One volume abridgement, with the original illustrations as chosen by Toynbee.
[L2024] Thames & H pbk **£14.95**
A Study of History: Vols 1 - 6
An abridged version, in two volumes, of this classic study of the rise and fall of the great civilisations, which attempts to trace the recurring patterns of history. Adored and reviled in equal measure.
[L2025] Oxford pbk **£7.95**

Vols 7 - 10
[L2026] Oxford pbk **£6.95**

VADNEY, TOM
The World since 1945
[L2027] Penguin pbk **£5.99**

WEDGWOOD, C.V.
Spoils of Times
'A Short History of the World from Earliest Times to the 16th Century'.
[L2028] Collins hbk **£15.00**

WEE, HERMAN VAN DER
Collins Atlas of World History
[L2029] Collins hbk **£20.00**
The World: An Illustrated History
Excellent, illustrated guide to the complexities of the human story from the Ice Age to the Cold War.
[L2030] Times Bks pbk **£9.95**
Times Atlas of World History
The most authoritative historical atlas, it contains a vast amount of information, but reading the maps requires a considerable effort.
[L2031] Times Bks hbk **£27.50**
Times Concise Atlas of World History
[L2032] Times Bks pbk **£7.95**

WELLS, H.G.
An Illustrated Short History of the World
A new edition of this classic introduction to world history by the author of *The Time Machine* with an introduction and added material by Philip Ziegler.
[L2033] Webb & B hbk **£14.95**
Short History of the World
[L2034] Penguin pbk **£4.95**

Ancient Civilisations

The two sciences of history and archaeology are distinguished by their use of different sources and evidence, and development of different methodologies; but in the 'pre-history' of ancient civilizations these distinctions are blurred, and the two sciences merge to produce a picture of the ancient world. For this reason some archaeology titles have been listed below. The recent resurgence of interest in this area has led to considerable dispute over the chronology and nature of ancient civilisations, seriously questioning the value of earlier studies.

Macmillan Dictionary of Archaeology
A standard reference book, giving an A-Z listing of archaeological terms, sites and archaeologists.
[L2035] Macmillan hbk **£25.00**
[L2036] Macmillan pbk **£9.95**

ALDRED, CYRIL
The Egyptians
[L2037] Thames & H pbk **£6.95**

BAINES, JOHN & MALEK, JAROMIR
Atlas of Ancient Egypt
[L2038] Phaidon pbk **£18.50**

BARKER, PHILIP
Techniques of Archaeological Excavation
[L2039] Batsford pbk **£12.95**
Understanding Archaeological Excavation
[L2040] Batsford pbk **£10.95**

BICKERMAN, E.J.
Chronology of the Ancient World
[L2041] Thames & H pbk **£5.95**

BINDFORD, LEWIS
In Pursuit of the Past
A classic work by the leading American
archaeologist.
[L2042] Thames & H pbk **£9.95**

BRAY, WARRICK & TRUMP, DAVID H.
**The Penguin Dictionary of
Archaeology**
[L2043] Penguin pbk **£5.95**

CERAM
Gods, Graves and Scholars
The classic account of the age of archaeological
discovery in the 19th century.
[L2044] Penguin hbk **£5.95**

CHADWICK, JOHN
The Decipherment of Linear B
The story of the phenomenal achievement of Michael
Ventris in providing the key to unlock the secrets of
the great Minoan civilisation.
[L2045] Cambridge pbk **£8.50**

CLARK, GRAHAME & PIGGOTT, STUART
Prehistoric Societies
[L2046] Penguin hbk **£4.95**

CLARK, GRAHAME
World Prehistory in New Perspective
[L2047] Cambridge pbk **£15.00**

CLAYTON, PETER & PRICE, MARTIN (EDS)
**The Seven Wonders of the Ancient
World**
[L2048] Routledge hbk **£17.95**

COE, MICHAEL D.
Mexico
[L2049] Thames & H pbk **£6.95**
The Maya
[L2050] Thames & H pbk **£6.95**

COLES, BRYONY AND JOHN
People of the Wetlands **NEW**
The book tells the story of the excavations of
the world's wetlands, unique environments which
have preserved remnants of ancient civilisations.
Included is a guide to wetland sites and
museums.
[L2051] Thames & H hbk **£17.95**

COTTERELL, ARTHUR (ED)
**The Penguin Encyclopaedia of Ancient
Civilisations**
Well-illustrated and reliable introduction to the
subject, with contributions from thirty international
experts.
[L2052] Penguin pbk **£9.95**

CUNLIFFE, BARRY (ED)
**Origins: Roots of European
Civilisation**
Published to celebrate the 10th anniversary of
Radio 4's influential series, the book contains
ten articles by leading scholars on their current
research.
[L2053] BBC hbk **£16.95**

DANIEL, GLYN (ED)
The Pastmasters **NEW**
Biographies of eleven major archaeologists: Childe,
Piggot, Phillips, Hawkes, Lloyd, Braidwood, Willey,
Becker, De Laet, Clark and Mulvaney.
[L2054] Thames & H hbk **£18.00**

DAVID, ROSALIE
**The Pyramid Builders of Ancient
Egypt** **NEW**
A Modern Investigation of Pharaoh's Workforce. The
builders of the pyramids are revealed as simple people
with ordinary preoccupations, skilled craftsmen rather
than the popular image of slaves.
[L2055] Routledge pbk **£16.95**

DAVIES, NIGEL
Ancient Kingdoms of Mexico
[L2056] Penguin pbk **£4.95**

DELANEY, FRANK
The Celts
Popular, lively account, based on the BBC series,
which is aimed at the general reader not the
student.
[L2057] Grafton pbk **£5.99**

DIEHL, RICHARD A.
Tula
The Toltec capital of Ancient Mexico.
[L2058] Thames & H pbk **£18.00**

DYER, JAMES
Teaching Archaeology in Schools
[L2059] Shire pbk **£1.95**

EDWARDS, I.E.S.
Pyramids of Egypt
[L2060] Penguin pbk **£6.95**

EMERY, WALTER B.
Archaic Egypt
[L2061] Penguin pbk **£4.95**

FAGIN, BRIAN M.
**The Great Journey: The Peopling
of Ancient America** **NEW**
An account of the ancient trek from tropical Africa
across Asia and the Arctic to North America.
[L2062] Thames & H hbk **£14.95**

GARDINER, A.H.
Egypt of the Pharaohs
[L2063] Oxford pbk **£8.95**

GRAHAM-CAMPBELL, JAMES
The Viking World **NEW**
Well-illustrated introduction to the Vikings based on
recent archaeological research.
[L2064] Windward pbk **£9.95**

A gold coin of Philip II of Macedonia from *Oxford
Illustrated Encyclopedia of World History Volume 1*
(Oxford hbk £19.50)

GREENE, KEVIN
Archaeology: An Introduction
[L2065] Batsford pbk **£9.95**

GROVE, DAVID C.
**Chalcatzingo: Excavations on the
Olmec Frontier**
[L2068] Thames & H pbk **£18.00**

HARRISON, RICHARD J.
**The Beaker Folk: Copper Age
Archaeology in Western Europe**
[L2070] Thames & H hbk **£12.95**

HODDINOTT, R. F.
The Thracians
[L2071] Thames & H hbk **£12.95**

HUDSON, KENNETH
World Industrial Archaeology
[L2072] Cambridge pbk **£7.95**

JAMES, T.G.H.
Ancient Egypt **NEW**
Lavishly illustrated guide to Ancient Egypt by the
former Keeper of Antiquities at the British
Museum.
[L2073] Brit Mus P hbk **£14.95**

JORDAN, PAUL
Face of the Past
[L2074] Batsford pbk **£14.95**

KATZ, FRIEDRICH
Ancient American Civilisations
[L2075] Weidenfeld pbk **£5.50**

KEMP, DAVID
Living Underground **NEW**
The first comprehensive survey of troglodytes
and ancient cave dwellers throughout the
world.
[L2076] Herbet P hbk **£18.00**

LLOYD, SETON
Archaeology of Mesopotamia
From the Old Stone Age to the Conquest.
[L2077] Thames & H pbk **£7.95**
**Ancient Turkey: A Traveller's
Guide to Anatolia** **NEW**
An account, for the general reader, of Turkey's
early history which saw the spread of Hittites,
Phrygians, Persians, Greeks and Romans across
Anatolia. Seton Lloyd focuses on the many
archaeological sites to show the contributions of the
various cultures.
[L20771] Brit Mus P hbk **£16.95**

LLOYD, SETON & MULLER, H.W.
**Ancient Architecture of Egypt
and the Near East**
[L2078] Faber pbk **£14.95**

MACQUEEN, J.G. (ED)
The Hittites
With their contemporaries in Asia Minor.
[L2079] Thames & H pbk **£12.95**

MALLORY, J.R.
In Search of the Indo-Europeans **NEW**
Subtitled 'Language, Archaeology and Myth',
the book absorbs recent archaeological discoveries
to give a picture of the earliest European
culture.
[L2080] Thames & H hbk **£24.00**

MELLAART, JAMES
Earliest Civilizations of the Near East
[L2081] Thames & H pbk **£2.95**

MOCTEZUMA, EDUARDO MATOS
The Great Temple of the Aztecs
The story of the chance discovery in 1978 of the remains of Tenochtitlan.
[L2082] Thames & H pbk **£24.00**

MURNANE, W.
The Penguin Guide to Ancient Egypt
[L2083] Penguin pbk **£8.95**

MURRAY, MARGARET ALICE
The Splendour That Was Egypt
The evergreen classic on Ancient Egypt.
[L2084] Sidgwick pbk **£10.95**

O'KELLY, MICHAEL
Newgrange
Standard work on one of Ireland's most impressive sites.
[L2085] Thames & H hbk **£12.95**

OATES, JOHN
Babylon
[L2086] Thames & H hbk **£6.95**

PENNICK, NIGEL & DEVERAUX, PAUL
Lines on the Landscape `NEW`
The authors examine linear features of the past, using aerial photography to examine the debates about leys and pre-historic linear arrangements.
[L2087] Hale hbk **£15.95**

RENFREW, COLIN
Archaeology and Language
An important contribution to recent archaeological study, using language as evidence for the early history of Indo-European culture.
[L2088] Cape hbk **£16.00**

ROMER, JOHN
Ancient Lives
[L2089] Weidenfeld pbk **£16.00**
People of the Nile: New Light on the Civilization of Ancient Egypt `NEW`
New paperback edition of Romer's Egypt: a personal journey through the ancient civilization.
[L2090] M Joseph pbk **£10.95**

ROUX, GEORGES
Ancient Iraq
[L2091] Penguin pbk **£5.99**

SAGGS, H.W.F.
The Might That Was Assyria
[L2092] Sidgwick pbk **£10.95**

SANDARS, N.K.
The Sea Peoples
A study of the warriors of the ancient Mediterranean.
[L2093] Thames & H pbk **£6.95**

SCARRE, CHRIS (ED)
Past Worlds: Times Atlas of Archaeology
Superbly illustrated with maps, graphs and photos, giving an excellent, comprehensive overview.
[L2094] Times Bks hbk **£29.50**

SORRELL, MARK
Reconstructing the Past
[L2095] Batsford pbk **£12.95**

SPENCER, A.J.
Death in Ancient Egypt
[L2096] Penguin pbk **£4.95**

TRIGGER, BRUCE G.
A History of Archaeological Thought
The first book on the subject, it places the development of archaeological thought within a broad social and intellectual framework.
[L2097] Cambridge hbk **£40.00**

WENKE, R.J.
Patterns in Prehistory
Mankind's First Three Million Years.
[L2098] Oxford pbk **£12.95**

WHITTLE, ALASDAIR
Neolithic Europe: A Survey
[L2099] Cambridge pbk **£12.50**

WILLETS
Civilisation of Ancient Crete
[L2100] Batsford hbk **£20.00**

Africa

The majority of books on African history in an English bookshop concern themselves with South Africa or the study of colonisation, reflecting the limits of European interest. Recently, with post-colonialism, more attention has been paid to the history of the African peoples but most titles are academic studies at academic prices. Some of the more general titles have been included here, as well as some of the major works of African historians themselves.

BERNAL, MARTIN
Black Athena: Afro-Asiatic Roots of Classical Civilisation
Vol 1: The Fabrication of Ancient Greece
A revolutionary work of scholarship which suggests that the Afro-Asiatic roots of Classical civilisation have been systematically denied since the 18th century, chiefly for racist reasons.
[L2104] Free Assoc pbk **£15.00**

BERNSTEIN, HILDA
The World That Was Ours
The story of the Rivonia trial when Nelson Mandela and seven others were sentenced to life imprisonment.
[L2105] South African Writers pbk **£5.95**

BIRMINGHAM, DAVID
Central Africa to 1870
[L2106] Cambridge pbk **£9.50**

DAVENPORT, T.R.H.
South Africa: A Modern History
[L2109] Macmillan pbk **£18.95**

DAVIDSON, BASIL
Africa in Modern History
[L2110] Penguin pbk **£4.95**
The Story of Africa
[L2111] M Beazley pbk **£8.95**

DIOP, CHEIK ANTA
Pre-Colonial Black Africa
Duly available in English this is one of three major works by Diop that attempt to reconstruct African history and the black contribution to the foundation of Western civilisation. A milestone in African historiography.
[L2112] L Hill hbk **£6.95**

FAGE, J.D. (ED)
Cambridge History of Africa
The most comprehensive history of Africa, from the

earliest times to 1975, in eight volumes: further details on request.
[L2113] Cambridge hbk **£455.00**

HARGREAVES, JOHN D.
Decolonisation in Africa
[L2114] Longman pbk **£7.95**

HARRISON, DAVID
The White Tribe of Africa
[L2115] BBC pbk **£5.25**

HOLT, P.M. & DALY, M.W.
A History of the Sudan `NEW`
Completely revised new edition.
[L2116] Longman pbk **£6.95**

ILIFFE, JOHN
The Emergence of African Capitalism
[L2117] Macmillan pbk **£5.95**

JAFFE, HOSEA
A History of Africa `NEW`
A non-Eurocentric perspective by an African historian.
[L2118] Zed pbk **£6.95**

KAPUSCINSKI, RYSZARD
Another Day of Life
Eyewitness account of the birth of independent Angola. Kapuscinski has a unique ability to see the historical importance of contemporary events.
[L2119] Picador pbk **£3.50**
The Emperor: Downfall of an Autocrat
A portrait of the final days of Haile Selaisse, emperor of Ethiopia and founder of Rastafarianism.
[L2120] Picador pbk **£3.95**

KNOX-JOHNSTON, ROBIN
The Cape of Good Hope: A Maritime History `NEW`
The first of a proposed two-volume series on the great capes by the renowned sailor.
[L2121] Hodder hbk **£12.95**

KRAMER, GUDRUN
The Jews of Modern Egypt `NEW`
The author catalogues the dispersion of Egypt's once large Jewish community after the redefinition of Egyptian nationalism.
[L2122] IB Tauris hbk **£24.50**

LAPPING, BRIAN
Apartheid: A History
An excellent introduction by the television journalist.
[L2123] Grafton pbk **£3.95**

LEWIS, DAVID LEVERING
The Race to Fashoda
European Colonialism and Black Resistance in the Scramble for Africa.
[L2124] Bloomsbury hbk **£13.95**

MANNING, P.
Francophone Sub-Saharan Africa 1880 - 1985 `NEW`
Colonial and post-colonial history of Mauritania, Mali, Niger, Chad, Cameroon, Congo, Zaire, Senegal, Guinea, and the Ivory Coast.
[L2125] Cambridge pbk **£8.95**

MARSOT, A.L. AL SAYYID
A Short History of Modern Egypt
[L2126] Cambridge hbk **£7.95**

MAZRUI, ALI A.
The Africans: A Triple Heritage
[L2127] BBC pbk **£14.95**

MCEVEDY, COLIN
Atlas of African History
[L2128] Penguin pbk **£5.95**

MOOREHEAD, ALAN
The Blue Nile
[L2129] Penguin pbk **£8.95**
The White Nile
[L2130] Penguin pbk **£8.95**

MORRIS, DONALD R.
The Washing of the Spears `NEW`
A re-issue of the classic account of the Zulu wars and
the Zulu nation, with a new introduction by Chief
Buthelezi.
[L2131] Cape hbk **£19.50**

MURRAY, JOCELYN
Cultural Atlas of Africa
[L2101] Phaidon hbk **£18.50**

OLIVER, ROLAND & FAGE, J D
A Short History of Africa
[L2132] Penguin pbk **£4.99**

OLIVER, ROLAND & CROWDER, MICHAEL
**The Cambridge Encyclopaedia of
Africa** `NEW`
The best one-volume study of Africa.
[L2133] Cambridge hbk **£25.00**

PHIMISTER, IAN
**An Economic and Social History of
Zimbabwe 1890 - 1948**
[L2134] Longman hbk **£28.00**

PORCH, DOUGLAS
The Conquest of Morocco
[L2135] Macmillan pbk **£7.95**
The Conquest of Sahara
[L2136] Oxford pbk **£5.95**

ROTBERG, ROBERT
**The Founder: Cecil Rhodes and
the Pursuit of Power** `NEW`
An exhaustive biography of the colonial 'monarch',
ruthless businessman and founder of Rhodesia.
[L2137] Oxford hbk **£25.00**

SHILLINGTON, KEVIN
A History of Southern Africa
Primarily a social history which gives prominence to
the indigenous population.
[L2138] Longman pbk **£4.20**

SMITH, ROBIN BROOKE
The Scramble for Africa
[L2139] Macmillan pbk **£4.25**

SWEARINGER, W.D.
Moroccan Mirages `NEW`
The author argues that Morocco's future is
threatened by the economic policies adopted by
the French for the 'jewel' of their Empire, and
continued by the Moroccan government since
independence.
[L2140] IB Tauris pbk **£12.50**

ULLENDORFF, EDWARD
The Ethiopians
[L2141] Oxford pbk **£2.50**

WHEATCROFT, GEOFFREY
**The Randlords: The Men who Made
South Africa**
[L2142] Weidenfeld pbk **£6.95**

WILKS, IVOR
Asante in the 19th Century `NEW`
Asante was one of the most powerful kingdoms in
Africa in the 19th century: this study shows how an
African political order developed outside the colonial
experience.
[L2143] Cambridge pbk **£15.00**

North America

AMBROSE, STEPHEN E.
**Rise to Globalism: American Foreign
Policy since 1938**
The Cold War, Korea, the Cuba invasion and Vietnam
are some of the events discussed by the former
personal secretary to Eisenhower, Stephen
Ambrose.
[L2144] Penguin pbk **£4.95**

BADGER, A.J.
The New Deal
[L2145] Macmillan pbk **£6.95**

BELOFF, MAX
The Federalist
[L2146] Blackwell pbk **£9.95**

BIRMINGHAM, JOHN
**The Rest of US: The Rise of America's
Eastern European Jews**
[L2147] Futura pbk **£3.95**

BLACKBURN, ROBIN
**The Overthrow of Colonial Slavery
1776 - 1848**
Study on the impact of anti-slavery and revolution on
the systems of colonial slavery.
[L2148] Verso pbk **£12.95**

BLUM, WILLIAM
The CIA: A Forgotten History
From covert action in China in the 1950's to aid for
the Nicaraguan Contras. Blum talks of high office
deception but blames the ineffectiveness of the
media for the ease with which the CIA have acted
illegally.
[L2149] Zed pbk **£8.95**

BOORSTIN, DANIEL
**The Americans
Vol 1: The Colonial Experience**
[L2150] Sphere pbk **£6.99**
Vol 2: The National Experience
[L2151] Sphere pbk **£6.99**
Vol 3: The Democratic Experience
[L2152] Sphere pbk **£7.99**

BRANCH, TAYLOR
Parting the Waters `NEW`
The first volume of what promises to be the definitive
history of Martin Luther King and the civil rights
movement treats of the rise of the movement to its
high point in 1963. The second volume will cover the
Johnson years 1963-69.
[L2153] Macmillan hbk **£18.95**

BROGAN, HUGH
**Longman History of the United
States of America**
[L2154] Longman hbk **£24.95**
**Pelican History of the United
States of America**
The best one-volume history available, Brogan is
particularly astute on the run-up to America's
involvement in Vietnam.
[L2155] Arrow pbk **£7.50**

BROWN, DEE
**Bury My Heart at Wounded Knee:
Indian History of the American
West**
[L2156] Pan pbk **£5.99**

BUMSTED, J.M.
**Interpreting Canada's Past
Vol 1: Before Confederation**
[L2157] Oxford pbk **£10.95**
Vol 2: After Confederation
[L2158] Oxford pbk **£10.95**

CARROLL, PETER N. & NOBLE, DAVID W.
**The Free and the Unfree: A New History
of the United States**
A challenging interpretative history that hinges, as the
title suggests, on the changing relationship between
the holders of power, the possessors of wealth, and
the repressed sections of society.
[L2159] Penguin pbk **£4.95**

A poster published by the African National Congress from *Oxford Illustrated Encyclopaedia of World History
Volume 2* (Oxford hbk £19.50)

CHAFE, W.H.
The Unfinished Journey: America since World War II
Readings on post-war America. A selection of essays on major post-war issues, presenting opposing views and eyewitness accounts.
[L2160] Oxford pbk **£13.50**

CONNELL, EVAN S.
Son of the Morning Star: General Custer and the Battle of Little Big Horn
[L2161] Pan pbk **£4.50**

COOKE, ALISTAIR
Alistair Cooke's America
Alistair Cooke's celebrated and entertaining dispatches on all aspects of American life.
[L2162] BBC pbk **£7.75**

COUNTRYMAN, EDWARD
The American Revolution
Highly readable account summarising recent views, presenting central characters and re-examining key events. By introducing us to six 'types' from slave to landowner, the struggle for independence is vividly recreated at the level of ordinary experience.
[L2163] Penguin pbk **£4.95**

GARRATY, JOHN A.
A Short History of the American Nation Vol 1   `NEW`
Culled from articles in the *American Heritage* magazine, the first volume covers the period up to 1877, while the second continues the story to the present day.
[L2164] Harper & R pbk **£13.50**
Vol 2   `NEW`
[L2165] Harper & R pbk **£13.50**

GILBERT, MARTIN
American History Atlas
[L2166] Weidenfeld hbk **£10.95**
[L2167] Weidenfeld pbk **£5.95**

GORDON, ARTHUR A.
The American Jews
[L2168] Harvard UP pbk **£4.50**

HAWKE, DAVID FREEMAN
Everyday Life in Early America   `NEW`
A new three volume social history of America. The first volume covers the 18th century, the second deals with the period 1790-1840 and volume three with the post Civil War period up to 1870.
[L2169] Harper & R hbk **£11.50**
The Reshaping of Everyday Life in the US   `NEW`
[L2170] Harper & R hbk **£12.95**
The Expansion of Everyday Life in the US   `NEW`
See below: SUTHERLAND, DAVID

JOHNSON, THOMAS H. & WISH, HARVEY
Oxford Companion to American History
Like all the Oxford Companions this provides an excellent and authoritative guide to the main events and movements of the subject.
[L2171] Oxford hbk **£35.00**

JONES, MALDWIN A.
Limits of Liberty: American History 1607 - 1980
A major survey of the American past tracing the political, intellectual, economic and cultural development of a distinctive society while stressing continuity with the Old World.
[L2172] Oxford pbk **£10.95**

KIMBALL, J (ED)
Churchill & Roosevelt: The Complete Correspondence
'These three volumes read like a skilful and compelling history of World War II. They are a unique literary landmark.' *(New York Times)*
[L2192] Collins 3 vols hbk **£35.00**

MCNAUGHT, KENNETH
The Penguin History of Canada   `NEW`
New edition, revised throughout, with two new chapters and an excellent historiographical essay.
[L2174] Penguin pbk **£4.95**

MCPHERSON
Battle Cry of Freedom: Civil War Era   `NEW`
The first volume of the Oxford History of the United States to appear in England, it was received with almost unanimous acclaim as the best recent account of the Civil War.
[L2175] Oxford hbk **£19.50**

MIDDLEKAUFF, R.
The Glorious Cause: The American Revolution 1763 - 1789
'An impressive performance...a fine general account which will justly rank as a standard work.' *(English Historical Review)*.
[L2176] Oxford hbk **£25.00**
[L2177] Oxford pbk **£9.95**

MORISON, SAMUEL ELIOT
The Great Explorers
An abridgement of Morison's two-volume history of the European voyagers to America.
[L2178] Oxford pbk **£8.95**

MORISON, SAMUEL (ED)
A Concise History of the American Republic
Morison's full *Oxford History of the American People* is unfortunately out of print, but this is an equally useful overview of American History.
[L2179] Oxford hbk **£29.00**
[L2180] Oxford pbk **£13.95**
The Growth of the American Republic: Vol 1
A classic history of the United States from pre-Columbian times to the Carter Administration.
[L2181] Oxford hbk **£19.50**
Vol 2
[L2182] Oxford hbk **£22.50**

NEWMAN, PETER.C.
Company of Adventurers: Story of the Hudson's Bay Company
[L2183] Penguin hbk **£5.95**
Caesars of the Wilderness
[L2184] Penguin pbk **£5.99**

PAINE, THOMAS
Common Sense
Paine's advocacy of independence for the American colonies was crucially important at the time of the Revolution.
[L2185] Penguin pbk **£2.50**

PLUMB, J.H.
An American Experience   `NEW`
The second collection of essays on American history from the most prolific and widely read English historian.
[L2186] Harvester hbk **£30.00**

POLENBERG, RICHARD
One Nation Divisible: Class, Race and Ethnicity since 1938
[L2187] Penguin pbk **£5.95**

PRUCHA, FRANCIS PAUL
Indians in American Society: From the Revolutionary War to the Present
A more or less dispassionate history of American Indian policy.
[L2188] California UP pbk **£7.95**

RANELAGH, JOHN
The Agency: The Rise and Decline of the CIA
Winner of the National Intelligence Book Prize, *The Agency* is the most detailed account of CIA intentions and operations currently in print.
[L2189] Hodder pbk **£7.95**

RANSOM, ROGER L.
Conflict and Compromise   `NEW`
Subtitled 'The Political Economy of Slavery, Emancipation and the American Civil War', the book's central thesis is that slavery not only caused the Civil War but decided its outcome by crippling the Southern war effort.
[L2190] Cambridge pbk **£9.95**

REDIKER, MARCUS
Between the Devil and the Deep Blue Sea   `NEW`
Subtitled 'Merchant Seamen, Pirates, and the Anglo-American World, 1700-1750' the book highlights the wider historical issues of the rise of Capitalism and the genesis of free-wage labour.
[L2191] Cambridge pbk **£9.95**

ROOSEVELT, F.D. & CHURCHILL, WINSTON
Churchill & Roosevelt: The Complete Correspondence
'These three volumes read like a skilful and compelling history of World War II. They are a unique literary landmark.' *(New York Times)*.
[L2192] Collins hbk **£35.00**

SCHLESINGER, ARTHUR M.
Cycles of American History
Recent views on American history by the renowned essayist, which attempts to find an historical pattern.
[L2193] Deutsch hbk **£14.95**

SUTHERLAND, DAVID
The Expansion of Everyday Life in the US   `NEW`
[L2194] Harper & R hbk **£12.95**

TERKEL, STUDS
American Dreams: Lost and Found
[L2195] Grafton hbk **£3.95**
The Great Divide   `NEW`
Oral history American-style. Studs talks to the American people about what happened to the American dream.
[L2196] H Hamilton hbk **£15.95**

THOMPSON, VINCENT B.
The Making of the African Diaspora in the Americas 1441 - 1900
Chronicles the dispersal of African people through the New World.
[L2197] Longman pbk **£17.00**

WADE, WYN CRAIG
The Fiery Cross: The Ku Klux Klan in America
[L2198] Simon & Sch pbk **£7.95**

WALDMAN, CARL & BRAWN, MOLLY
Atlas of the North American Indians
[L2199] Facts on File pbk **£9.95**

WASHINGTON, BOOKER T.
Up From Slavery
[L2200] Penguin pbk **£3.99**

WHITE, J.
**Black Leadership in America
1895 - 1965**
[L2201] Longman pbk **£6.95**

WOODCOCK, GEORGE
A Social History of Canada   **NEW**
An excellent companion to Penguin's recent *History
of Canada*.
[L2202] Viking hbk **£14.95**

ZINN, HOWARD
**A People's History of the
United States**
[L2203] Longman hbk **£10.95**

Central & Southern America

ARCHETTI; CAMMACK & ROBERTS
Latin America
Drawing on the work of British, American and Latin
American social scientists, this book presents a broad
overview of social structure and change from the
conquest to the present day. The comprehensive
treatment of contemporary themes includes the
development of the state system, the military in
government, class formation and the role of
women.
[L2204] Macmillan hbk **£20.00**
[L2205] Macmillan pbk **£6.95**

BAZANT, JAN
**A Concise History of Mexico from
Hidalgo to Cardenas 1805 - 1940**
[L2206] Cambridge pbk **£9.95**

BECKLES, DR HILARY
A History of Barbados   **NEW**
A history of Barbados from the first human
settlement by the Amerindians about 650 A.D. to the
present day which has as its central theme the
struggle for social equality and material
improvement.
[L2207] Cambridge pbk **£8.95**

A warning from the Ku Klux Klan in the aftermath of
the South's defeat in the American Civil War.
Illustration from *Oxford Illustrated Encyclopedia of
World History Volume 2* (Oxford hbk £19.50)

BERNAL, IGNACIO
**A History of Mexican Archaeology: The
Vanished Civilizations of Middle
America**
[L2208] Thames & H pbk **£6.95**

BETHELL, LESLIE (ED)
**The Cambridge Encyclopaedia of Latin
America and the Caribbean**
[L2209] Cambridge hbk **£25.00**
**Brazil: Empire and 1st Republic
1822 - 1930**
A selection of chapters from the **Cambridge History
of Latin America** which presents the history of a
single region for students.
[L2209] Cambridge pbk **£8.95**

BOURNE, PETER
Castro
Biography of the revolutionary leader written by an
eminent American psychiatrist.
[L2210] Macmillan pbk **£7.95**

CAMBRIDGE HISTORY OF LATIN AMERICA
Edited by Leslie Bethell.
Vol 1: Colonial Latin America
[L2211] Cambridge hbk **£60.00**
Vol 2: Colonial Latin America
[L2212] Cambridge hbk **£75.00**
Vol 3: From Independence to 1870
[L2213] Cambridge hbk **£75.00**
Vol 4: 1870 - 1930
[L2214] Cambridge hbk **£60.00**
Vol 5: 1870 - 1930
[L2215] Cambridge hbk **£75.00**

CASTRO, FIDEL
Nothing Can Stop the Course of History
Transcript of a major interview by an American
journalist with the Cuban leader.
[L2216] Pathfinder P hbk **£5.75**

CORTES, HERNAN
Letters from Mexico
The thoughts and impressions of the Spanish
conquistador.
[L2217] Yale UP pbk **£15.95**

DIAZ, BERNAL
Conquest of New Spain
Diaz served under Hernan Cortes when, with his
small band of men, he conquered the entire Aztec
Empire. Fifty years after the event Diaz wrote this
classic account of their expedition.
[L2218] Penguin pbk **£5.50**

FAUNDEZ, JULIO
Marxism and Democracy in Chile   **NEW**
A history of what was South America's model
democracy - Chile from 1932 to the military coup that
ended Allende's government in 1973.
[L2219] Yale UP hbk **£18.50**

GALLEANO, EDUARDO
**Memory of Fire
Vol I: Genesis**
[L2220] Minerva pbk **£4.99**
Vol II: Faces and Masks
[L2221] Minerva pbk **£4.99**
Vol III: Century of Wind   **NEW**
The final volume of Galleano's extraordinary,
idiosyncratic, semi-fictional history of Latin America.
As much a work of literature as of history.
[L2222] Quartet hbk **£14.95**

GALLENKAMP, C.
**Maya: The Riddle and Rediscovery of a
Lost Civilisation**
[L2223] Penguin pbk **£4.95**

HEMMING, JOHN
**Red Gold: Conquest of the
Brazilian Indians**
[L2224] Macmillan hbk **£8.95**
The Conquest of the Incas
[L2225] Penguin pbk **£5.95**

INNES, HAMMOND
The Conquistadors
[L2226] Collins hbk **£9.95**

JAMES, C.L.R.
The Black Jacobins
A reprint of the classic study of the only successful
slave-revolt in history, which occurred in San
Domingo in 1791 under the leadership of a 45-year
old slave, Toussaint l'Ouverture. The history is a
powerful polemic against slavery and racism by the
greatest West Indian writer and thinker of our times.
[L2227] Allison & B pbk **£5.99**

JOHNSON, HOWARD
After the Crossing   **NEW**
The story of immigrants in the Caribbean and the
development of Creole society after slavery.
[L2228] Frank Cass hbk **£15.00**

KLEIN, HERBERT S.
Bolivia
A study of the evolution of a multi-ethnic society.
[L2229] Oxford pbk **£8.95**

LOCKHART, JAMES & SCHWARTZ, STUART B.
Early Latin America
[L2230] Cambridge pbk **£12.95**

MASON, J.A.
The Ancient Civilizations of Peru
Radiocarbon dating places an embryonic civilisation
in Peru in 7,566 BC: this book examines the
archaeological discoveries at Machu Pichu, Cuzco
and Titicaca.
[L2231] Penguin pbk **£5.99**

MEYER, MICHAEL C. & SHERMAN,
WILLIAM L.
The Course of Mexican History
Remains the major text in its field. In this revised
edition new chapters include recent developments
under the governments under Lopez Portillo and de la
Madrid.
[L2232] Oxford pbk **£16.50**

NAIPAUL, V.S.
The Loss of El Dorado: A History
[L2233] Penguin pbk **£4.95**

PENDLE, GEORGE
A History of Latin America
[L2234] Penguin pbk **£4.50**

POPPINO, ROLLIE E.
Brazil: The Land and the People
[L2235] Oxford pbk **£4.95**

REED, DAVID
**Insurgent Mexico: Ten Days that
Shook the World**
[L2236] Penguin pbk **£4.95**

SKIDMORE, THOMAS E. & SMITH, PETER H.
Modern Latin America   **NEW**
The second edition of the standard history of
Latin America: the antithesis of Galleano's work.
[L2237] Oxford pbk **£12.50**

THOMAS, HUGH
The Cuban Revolution
[L2238] Weidenfeld pbk **£12.95**

HISTORY

WARD, J.R.
Poverty and Progress in the Caribbean 1800 - 1960
This study surveys recent research and debate on the economic history of the Caribbean since 1800. The region is treated as a whole through the common themes of slavery and colonial rule, and particular emphasis is placed on the ways in which historical experience has contributed to current difficulties in achieving sustained economic growth.
[L2239] Macmillan pbk **£4.50**

WOODWARD, RALPH LEE
Central America: A Nation Divided
[L2240] Oxford pbk **£8.95**

WORCESTER, DONALD E. & SCHAEFFER, WENDELL G.
The Growth and Culture of Latin America
Vol 1: From Conquest to Independence
[L2241] Oxford pbk **£17.75**

China

There is a dearth of reasonably-priced histories of China and most of these are accounts of contemporary China which have been thrown out-of-date by recent events. This short list can be supplemented by the relevant sections in the *Fiction* and *Travel* chapters.

ADSHEAD, S.A.M.
China in World History
China's political, economic, cultural, social and technological relations with the non-Chinese world.
[L2242] Macmillan hbk **£35.00**

BLUNDEN, CAROLINE & ELVIN, MARK
Cultural Atlas of China
[L2243] Phaidon hbk **£18.50**

CHEO YING, ESTHER
Black Country to Red China NEW
An extraordinary personal insight to post-Civil War China by an English-educated Red Army soldier.
[L2244] Hutchinson pbk **£5.95**

CHING, FRANK
Ancestors
Through the 900 year history of his family, Ching, an American Journalist, provides a political and social history of China as it moves from ancient, isolated empire to communist regime.
[L2245] Harrap hbk **£12.95**

COTTERELL, ARTHUR
China: A Concise Cultural History NEW
Superb one-volume survey of Chinese history divided into three parts - the pre-imperial (down to 221BC), Imperial (221BC to 1912) and the post-Imperial periods.
[L2246] J Murray pbk **£10.95**

DE HARTOG, LEO
Genghis Khan: Conqueror of the World NEW
A new account of Genghis Khan and his Mongol hordes which focuses on the diplomatic and administrative skills behind their successes.
[L2247] IB Tauris hbk **£14.95**

FAIRBANK, JOHN KING
The Great Chinese Revolution 1800 - 1985
[L2256] Picador pbk **£4.95**

FLEMING, PETER
Bayonets to Lhasa
Now verging on the dated but very enjoyable as travel literature as well as history.
[L2248] Oxford hbk **£6.95**
The Siege of Peking
[L2249] Oxford pbk **£5.95**

GERNET, JACQUES
A History of Chinese Civilisation
[L2250] Cambridge pbk **£17.50**

GITTINGS, JOHN
China Changes Face: The Road from Revolution 1949 - 1989 NEW
Written before the recent student revolt and the subsequent massacre the *Guardian* correspondent's study of the emergence of the new China is the best book we have on the subject.
[L2251] Oxford hbk **£17.50**

HOOK, BRIAN (ED)
The Cambridge Encyclopaedia of China
[L2252] Cambridge pbk **£27.50**

HOOKER, MARY
Behind the Scenes in Peking
First published in 1910 this is a gripping eye-witness account of the siege of the Legation quarters during the Boxer Rebellion, by a young American girl caught up in the events.
[L2253] Oxford pbk **£4.95**

HOPKIRK, P.
Foreign Devils on the Silk Road
A fascinating account of the trading contacts between the cultures of Europe and China. Both were aware of the other's existence but the development of contact was slow and restricted.
[L2254] Oxford pbk **£5.95**
Trespassers on the Roof of the World: The Race for Lhasa
[L2255] Oxford pbk **£5.95**

MACKERRAS, COLIN P.
Modern China: A Chronology from 1842 to the Present
[L2257] Thames & H hbk **£22.50**

NAIPAUL, SHIVA
Beyond the Dragon's Mouth
[L2259] Sphere pbk **£4.99**

RODZINSKI, WITOLD
The People's Republic of China
Excellent overview of recent Chinese History and portrait of modern China.
[L2260] Collins hbk **£17.50**
[L2261] Fontana pbk **£5.95**

SALISBURY, HARRISON E.
The Long March: The Untold Story
[L2262] Pan pbk **£3.95**

SCHELL, ORVILLE
Discos and Democracy NEW
A study of the rapidly changing culture of modern China.
[L2263] Random House hbk **£14.95**

SPENCE, JONATHAN D.
The Gate of Heavenly Peace: The Chinese and their Revolution 1895 - 1980
[L2264] Faber hbk **£11.50**
[L2265] Penguin pbk **£7.50**

South Asia, India & South East Asia

ALI, TARIQ
The Nehrus and the Gandhis: An Indian Dynasty
[L2267] Pan pbk **£2.50**

ANDAYA, BARBARA, & WATSON, LEONARD Y.
A History of Malaysia
[L2268] Macmillan pbk **£7.95**

BASHAM, A.L.
The Wonder That Was India Vol 1
The two volumes trace the development of the Indian civilisation from earliest times to the eighteenth century. Comprehensive and well illustrated.
[L2270] Sidgwick pbk **£14.95**
RIZVI, S.A.A.
Vol 2
[L2271] Sidgwick hbk **£18.95**

BENCE-JONES, MARK
Clive of India
Authoritative biography of British India's founding father.
[L2272] Constable pbk **£7.95**
The Viceroys of India
[L2273] Constable pbk **£5.95**

BROWN, JUDITH M.
Modern India: The Origins of an Asian Democracy
Accessible introduction to the labyrinthine complexities of modern India.
[L2274] Oxford pbk **£10.95**

CHOUDHURY, GOLUM
Pakistan NEW
A new history of Pakistan since its inception as an independent state in 1947, concentrating on the recent transition from military to civil rule.
[L2275] Scorpion hbk **£15.00**

COLLINS, LARRY & LAPIERRE, DOMINIQUE
City of Joy
Account of contemporary Calcutta.
[L2276] Arrow pbk **£3.95**
Freedom at Midnight
Journalistic account of the countdown to Indian independence.
[L2277] Grafton pbk **£4.50**

GASCOIGNE, BAMBER
The Great Moghuls
[L2278] Cape pbk **£9.95**

HALL, D.G.E.
A History of South East Asia
The most comprehensive single-volume history of the region.
[L2279] Macmillan pbk **£12.95**

HIBBERT, CHRISTOPHER
The Great Mutiny: India, 1857
A grim account of a terrible conflict. Both sides displayed extraordinary heroism and horrible savagery.
[L2280] Penguin pbk **£6.95**

JEFFREY, ROBIN
Asia: The Winning of Independence
[L2281] Macmillan pbk **£8.95**

MACDONALD, MALCOLM
Angkor and the Khmers
Angkor was one of the world's great empires
influencing not only mainland South East Asia but far
beyond - yet little has published on the subject.
[L2282] Oxford pbk **£4.95**

MOORHOUSE, GEOFFREY
India Britannica
[L2283] Grafton pbk **£3.95**

NAIPAUL, V.S.
India: A Wounded Civilisation
A pessimistic account of Naipaul's return to India,
which is one of his best travel narratives.
[L2284] Penguin pbk **£2.95**

NEHRU, JAWAHARLAL
Glimpses of World History
[L2285] Oxford pbk **£4.95**
The Discovery of India
[L2286] Oxford pbk **£4.95**

PERKINS, ROGER
The Amritsar Legacy **NEW**
A history of the Sikhs since 1919.
[L2287] Picton hbk **£14.95**

ROBINSON, FRANCIS (ED) **NEW**
The Cambridge Encyclopaedia of India
The encyclopaedia also covers Pakistan, Bangladesh,
Sri Lanka, Nepal, Bhutan and the Maldives. The only
comprehensive study of South Asia in one volume,
the encyclopaedia is highly illustrated with maps and
photographs and deals with all aspects of life in the
region.
[L2288] Cambridge hbk **£30.00**

SANGATHANA, STREE
**We Were Making History: Women
in the Telengana Movement** **NEW**
[L2289] Zed Books hbk **£28.95**

SARKAR, A
Modern India 1885 - 1947
Primarily a history of the imperialist struggles based
on the most recent research.
[L2290] Macmillan pbk **£14.95**

SEAGRAVE, STERLING
The Marcos Dynasty **NEW**
The seedy, chilling story of how Ferdinand Marcos
came to power in the Philippines and of the
culpability of the US in maintaining his brutal regime.
[L2292] Macmillan hbk **£16.95**

SHAWCROSS, WILLIAM
Ten Years After: Vietnam Today
A record of the country's recovery from the effects of
war, with photographs by Tim Page.
[L2293] Thames & H hbk **£16.50**

SMITH, V.A.
The Oxford History of India
[L2294] Oxford pbk **£6.95**

SNELLGROVE, DAVID AND RICHARDSON,
HUGH.
A Cultural History of Tibet **NEW**
[L2295] Element pbk **£10.50**

SPEAR, T.G.P.
**The Oxford History of Modern India,
1740 - 1975**
[L2296] Oxford pbk **£5.50**

THAPAR, ROMILA
History of India Vol 1
[L2297] Penguin pbk **£3.90**

Agni, the god of fire, from *The Cambridge
Encyclopaedia of India* (Cambridge hbk **£30.00**)

SPEAR, T.G.P.
History of India Vol 2
[L2298] Penguin pbk **£3.95**

TINKER, HUGH
South Asia: A Short History **NEW**
New edition of an integrated history of South Asia,
which covers Pakistan, India, Bangladesh, Burma,
and Sri Lanka.
[L2299] Macmillan hbk **£29.00**

TURNBULL, C. MARY
A History of Singapore 1819 - 1975
[L2300] Oxford pbk **£8.50**

WILLIAMS, E. LEA
Southeast Asia: A History
[L2301] Oxford pbk **£12.50**

WYATT, DAVID K.
Thailand: A Short History
[L2302] Yale UP pbk **£14.95**

Japan

BARR, PATRICIA
The Deer Cry Pavilion
Travelogue history of the lives of Westerners in 19th
century Japan.
[L2303] Penguin pbk **£4.99**
The Coming of the Barbarians
[L2304] Penguin pbk **£4.99**

BEHR, EDWARD
Hirohito **NEW**
Marshals an abundance of evidence in support of the
view that Hirohito was a cunning waverer and
opportunist who skilfully concealed his own
complicity in war crimes.
[L2304A] Hamish Hamilton hbk **£14.95**

BERNSTEIN, GAIL LEE & FUKUI, HARUHIRO
(EDS)
Japan and the World
Focuses on Japan over the past century with special
emphasis on the contemporary period.
[L2305] Macmillan hbk **£35.00**

THE CAMBRIDGE HISTORY OF JAPAN
Another major multi-volume history from Cambridge
which is guaranteed to be the most scholarly and up-
to-date history of Japan in English. As usual the first
volumes published are not in consecutive order.
Vol 3 : Medieval Japan **NEW**
[L2312] Cambridge hbk **£55.00**
Vol 5: The Nineteenth Century **NEW**
[L2313] Cambridge hbk **£55.00**
Vol 6: The Twentieth Century
[L2314] Cambridge hbk **£60.00**

HARRIES, M AND S
Sheathing the Sword **NEW**
First of a four-volume history of Japan in paperback.
This volume treats of the immediate post WW II
period.
[L2306] Heinemann pbk **£6.95**

LEHMANN, J.P.
The Roots of Modern Japan
[L2307] Macmillan pbk **£9.95**

MONTGOMERY, MICHAEL
Imperialist Japan **NEW**
The author focuses on the cultural/psychological
background to Japanese imperialism: the effects of a
long period of isolation and the sense of inferiority
with the adoption of Chinese culture.
[L2308] Croom Helm hbk **£19.95**

MORRIS, IVAN
The World of the Shining Prince
A study of the cultural aesthetic world of the Heian
period in Japan.
[L2309] Penguin pbk **£5.95**

SCHALLER, MICHAEL
**The American Occupation of Japan:
The Origins of the Cold War in Asia**
[L2310] Oxford pbk **£7.95**

STORRY, RICHARD
A History of Modern Japan
[L2311] Penguin pbk **£3.99**

Emperor Hirohito from *Hirohito* by Edward Behr
(Hamish Hamilton hbk **£14.95**)

WATANABE, SOLCHI
The Peasant Soul of Japan NEW
[L2315] Macmillan hbk **£29.50**

The Middle East

The contemporary historiography of the Middle East
is almost totally dominated by the Arab-Israeli
conflict and Muslim fundamentalism. Most of the
histories adopt polemical stances, and are thus best
read in conjunction with an opposing view.

**Atlas of the Middle East and
North Africa**
A reference source book concentrating on the
economic and social development of the modern
nations.
[L2316] Cambridge pbk **£45.00**

BEHR, ARNOLD
Israel 1948
Photographs and recollections by Behr who arrived in
Israel soon after its creation as a state. From 1948 to
1951 he travelled extensively taking some 3,000
photographs.
[L2318] G Fraser hbk **£15.00**
[L2319] G Fraser pbk **£9.95**

CHOUEIRI, YOUSSEF
Arab History and the Nation State NEW
Detailed, academic study of Arab political culture.
[L2324] Routledge hbk **£30.00**

COLLINS, LARRY & LAPIERRE, DOMINIQUE
O Jerusalem!
[L2325] Grafton pbk **£4.99**

FEUERLICHT, ROBERTA
The Fate of the Jews NEW
A new, critical history of the Jews, concentrating on
the American diaspora, by a Jewish historian.
[L2326] Quartet pbk **£6.95**

FRYE, RICHARD
The Golden Age of Persia NEW
A study of the development of Persian civilisation
after the Arab conquest in the 7th century AD,
showing the continuity of Persian/Iranian culture.
[L2327] Weidenfeld pbk **£9.95**

GILBERT, MARTIN
**Exile and Return: The Emergence of
Jewish Statehood**
[L2328] Weidenfeld hbk **£8.95**
[L2329] Weidenfeld pbk **£5.95**
Jewish History Atlas
[L2330] Weidenfeld pbk **£10.95**

HAYES, J.R. (ED)
The Genius of Arab Civilisation
[L2331] KPI pbk **£15.00**

HILLEL, SHLOMO
Operation Babylon
Focuses on Israeli activity in Arab lands prior to the
establishment of the State of Israel.
[L2332] Fontana pbk **£4.95**

HOLDEN, DAVID & JOHNS, RICHARD
The House of Saud
[L2333] Pan pbk **£4.50**

HOLT, P M
CAMBRIDGE HISTORY OF ISLAM
**Vol 1a: The Central Islamic Lands from
Pre-Islamic Times to World War I**
[L2320] Cambridge pbk **£22.50**

**Vol 1b: The Central Islamic Lands since
1918**
[L2321] Cambridge pbk **£15.00**
**Vol 2a: The Indian Sub-Continent, South
East Asia**
[L2322] Cambridge pbk **£22.50**
Vol 2b: Islamic Society and Civilization
[L2323] Cambridge pbk **£22.50**

HOPWOOD, DEREK
Syria 1945 - 1986
Explains the policies and objectives of the nation set
in their historical background.
[L2334] Unwin Hyman pbk **£7.95**

JOHNSON, PAUL
History of the Jews
[L2335] Weidenfeld hbk **£16.95**
[L2336] Weidenfeld pbk **£8.95**

KEPEL, GILLES
The Prophet and the Pharoah
A look at Islamic fundamentalism in Egypt, the
country of its birth, which includes an analysis of the
Jihad group responsible for the murder of President
Sadat.
[L2337] Al Saqi Bks pbk **£5.95**

KIERNAN, THOMAS
The Arabs
[L2338] Sphere pbk **£3.50**

LAMBTON, ANN
Qujar Persia NEW
A history of 19th century Persia and the crucial
involvement of the West which led to the emergence
of modern Iran.
[L2340] IB Tauris hbk **£24.50**

LAPIDUS, IRA M.
A History of Islamic Societies
Surveys Muslim life throughout the world.
[L2341] Cambridge hbk **£35.00**

LAQUEUR & RUBIN (EDS)
The Israel-Arab Reader
[L2342] Penguin pbk **£6.95**

LEWIS, BERNARD (ED)
**The World of Islam: Faith, People,
Culture**
[L2317] Thames & H pbk **£20.00**

LYONS, MALCOLM & JACKSON, DAVID
**Saladin: The Politics of the
Holy War**
[L2343] Cambridge pbk **£11.95**

MANSFIELD, PETER
The Arabs
[L2344] Penguin pbk **£6.99**

MORRIS, BENNY
**The Birth of the Palestinian
Refugee Problem** NEW
[L2345] Cambridge pbk **£12.95**

MOTTAHEDEH, ROY
**The Mantle of the Prophet: Politics and
Religion in Iran**
[L2346] Penguin pbk **£6.95**

O'BRIEN, CONOR CRUISE
**The Siege: Saga of Zionism and
Israel**
History of Zionism from its 19th century origins to
the establishment of the state of Israel by one of that
country's most attentive observers.
[L2347] Grafton pbk **£8.95**

OVENDALE, RITCHIE
The Origins of the Arab-Israeli Wars
[L2348] Longman pbk **£7.95**

PALUMBO, MICHAEL
The Palestinian Catastrophe NEW
The author uses reports from international
observers of the 1948 war to argue that the expulsion
of the Palestinians was the inevitable result of
Zionism.
[L2349] Quartet pbk **£6.95**

PAPPE, ILAN
**Great Britain and the Arab/Israeli
Conflict 1948 - 51**
An analysis of Britain's policy towards Palestine in
the post-war Mandate using primary sources only
recently made available from British archives.
[L2350] Macmillan hbk **£35.00**

ROBINSON, FRANCIS
**Atlas of the Islamic World since
1500**
[L2353] Phaidon hbk **£18.50**

ROTH, STEPHEN (ED)
The Impact of the Six Day War NEW
Essays on the fundamental changes that occurred in
Israeli society after the war.
[L2354] Macmillan hbk **£33.00**

SACHER, HOWARD M.
A History of Israel Volume 2 NEW
The long-awaited sequel to Sacher's History of Israel
(now unavailable), this volume covers the period from
the Yom Kippur war to the present.
[L2355] Oxford pbk **£7.95**

SAID, EDWARD
Covering Islam
How the media and the experts determine how we see
the rest of the world - by a leading contemporary
literary critic and Palestinian intellectual.
[L2356] Routledge pbk **£7.95**

SAMUEL, RINNA
History of Israel NEW
[L2357] Weidenfeld hbk **£12.95**

One way of tying the Indian dhoti from *The
Cambridge Encyclopaedia of India* (Cambridge hbk
£30.00)

HISTORY

SHIBLAK, ABBAS
The Lure of Zion
An analysis of the controversy that still surrounds the mass exodus of Iraqi Jews to Israel in the early 1950s.
[L2358] Al Saqi Bks pbk **£4.95**

SHIPLER, DAVID K.
Arab and Jew: Wounded Spirits in a Promised Land
Pulitzer prize-winning study of contemporary Israel.
[L2359] Bloomsbury pbk **£6.95**

WATT, W.MONTGOMERY
The Majesty That Was Islam
[L2361] Sidgwick pbk **£10.95**

Australasia

Bicentenaries see the publication of an enormous number of histories, but as they pass, so the books go out of print. There are now no more titles available on Australian history than there were before the bicentenary (and still fewer histories of New Zealand available), but a few have endured. The best of these is Robert Hughes's monumental study of the transportation of convicts to Australia.

BASSETT, JAN (ED)
The Concise Oxford Dictionary of Australian History
[L2362] Oxford hbk **£8.95**

CARTER, PAUL
The Road to Botany Bay
[L2363] Faber pbk **£6.95**

CONNOLLY, BOB & ANDERSON, ROBIN
First Contact
Chronicles the 1930s discovery of an isolated civilisation in the highlands of New Guinea.
[L2364] Penguin hbk **£6.99**

HAWKE, ROBERT
Making of New Zealand
[L2365] Cambridge hbk **£42.50**
[L2366] Cambridge pbk **£17.50**

HUGHES, ROBERT
The Fatal Shore
International best seller on Australia's 'convict years'. A brilliantly researched study of the convicts' transportation to Australia and the establishment there of a new culture.
[L2367] Collins hbk **£15.00**
[L2368] Pan pbk **£5.99**

MACDONALD, ROBERT
Fire Down Below `NEW`
Part travelogue, part history of the Maoris.
[L2370] Bloomsbury hbk **£14.95**

MOOREHEAD, ALAN
Fatal Impact: The Invasion of the South Pacific 1767 - 1840
[L2371] Penguin pbk **£4.95**

OLIVER, W.H. & WILLIAMS, B.R.
Oxford History of New Zealand
[L2373] Oxford hbk **£12.50**

PILGER, JOHN
A Secret Country `NEW`
A history of Aboriginal Australia by the journalist and film-maker, John Pilger.
[L2374] Cape hbk **£12.95**

RICKARD, JOHN
Australia: A Cultural History `NEW`
From the Longman *Present and Past* series, the book focuses on the transmission of values, beliefs and customs through generations.
[L2375] Longman pbk **£8.95**

WALKER, MIKE
Australia: A History
Anecdotal account of Australia's history based on the BBC Radio 4 series.
[L2377] Macdonald pbk **£4.95**

WILSON, CHARLES
Australia 1788 - 1988: The Creation of a Nation
[L2378] Weidenfeld hbk **£16.95**

Historians & Writing History

When E.H. Carr's *What Is History?* was published in 1961, it aroused great controversy. To many historians, Carr's thesis of the impossibility of historical objectivity seemed to deny their raison d'etre. Ever since Ranke claimed 'to tell it as it was' in the early 19th century, historical research and methodology have been constantly refined, and the discipline of history has progressed to such an extent that it has come to resemble a science. Carr's thesis did not dismiss this progress, but argued that the role of the historian as interpreter of the past was a crucial part of the historical process. He is vindicated by the variety of approaches which have been adopted by modern historians: the structures of the Marxists; the recent revivial of epic narrative; Braudel's belief in Total History, and Bloch's advocacy of comparative history; 'history from below' as seen by Rudé in *The Crowd in History*; and psychological history as promoted by Peter Gay in *Freud for Historians*. There is no substitute for reading the histories written by the great historians, but below is a selective guide intended to highlight the variety of answers to the question 'What is History?'.

BARRACLOUGH, GEOFFREY
An Introduction to Contemporary History
[L2379] Penguin pbk **£4.99**

BLOCH, MARC
The Historian's Craft
[L2380] Manchester UP pbk **£8.95**

BRAUDEL, FERNAND
On History
Definitive statement of the aims of the influential French *Annales* school which concerns itself with the study of 'mentalities' rather than historical events.
[L2381] Weidenfeld pbk **£10.95**

BURROW, JOHN W.
A Liberal Descent: Victorian Historians and the English Past
[L2382] Cambridge hbk **£35.00**
[L2383] Cambridge pbk **£12.95**

BUTTERFIELD, HERBERT
George III and the Historians `NEW`
A re-issue of Butterfield's classic work which is largely a polemic on the writing and revision of English history.
[L2384] Cassell pbk **£6.95**

CANNADINE, DAVID
The Pleasure of the Past `NEW`
Thirty essays on the study and writing of history for the general reader.
[L2385] Collins hbk **£17.50**

CANNON, JOHN (ED)
The Blackwell Dictionary of Historians
This book fills an obvious gap and promises to be a standard reference work on the subject. There are entries on 500 historians with 50 essays on the historiography of various countries and events. The book is indexed and contains bibliographies of the historians' writings.
[L2386] Blackwell hbk **£39.50**

CARR, EDWARD H.
What is History?
Stimulating reflections on history by a radically-inclined scholar who rejects the old liberal notions that historical objectivity is possible. Carr argues that all historians are socially conditioned and determined, and cannot possibly view past events with pure detachment. His views aroused wide controversy among historians on their publication in 1961.
[L2387] Macmillan hbk **£33.00**
[L2388] Penguin pbk **£3.95**

CHARTIER, ROGER
Cultural History `NEW`
Chartier examines various approaches to the history of cultural forms, including the work of the *Annales* in France, of Foucault and Elias, and more recent contributions.
[L2389] Polity hbk **£25.00**

COLLEY, LINDA
Namier `NEW`
A brilliant historian, although now out of vogue, Namier deserves a critical biography for his contribution to historical methodology. This is the most recent title in Weidenfeld's excellent *Historians on Historians* series.
[L2390] Weidenfeld pbk **£5.95**

COLLINGWOOD, R.G.
The Idea of History
Reflections on differing concepts of history through the ages by the Oxford historian and philosopher.
[L2391] Oxford pbk **£6.95**

COOK, ALBERT
History Writing `NEW`
The author studies the literary dimension to the writing of history concentrating on the difficult marriage of historical truth to historical rhetoric.
[L2392] Cambridge hbk **£25.00**

COOK, CHRIS
Dictionary of Historical Terms
[L2393] Macmillan pbk **£8.95**

ELTON, G.R.
The Practice of History
Forthright pronouncements - many of them directed against E.H. Carr - by a leading conservative scourge of the 'new' history.
[L2394] Fontana pbk **£3.50**

EVANS, GEORGE EWART
Spoken History
[L2395] Faber pbk **£10.95**

FERRO, MARC
The Use and Abuse of History: or, How the Past is Taught
[L2396] Routledge hbk **£25.00**

FINLEY, M.I.
The Use and Abuse of History
[L2397] Hogarth pbk **£4.95**

FURET, FRANCOIS
In the Workshop of History
[L2398] Chicago UP hbk **£21.95**

GAY, PETER
Freud for Historians
'A writer of brilliant allusiveness and scintillating style - never better demonstrated than in this enormously enjoyable book' (John Keegan, *The Sunday Times*).
[L2399] Oxford pbk **£5.95**
Style in History NEW
Style and eloquence are the unsung skills of the historian. Peter Gay places them at the centre of the historian's art through studies of Burckhardt, Macauley, Ranke and Gibbon.
[L2400] Norton pbk **£5.95**

GELLNER, ERNEST
Plough, Sword and Book
His own philosophy of history, which sharply conflicts with the prevailing views that philosophical history in the tradition of Marx, Comte and Spencer has little to teach us.
[L2401] Collins hbk **£15.00**

GINZBURG, CARLO
Myths, Emblems, Clues NEW
An interdisciplinary approach to the past: the importance of symbols in history.
[L2402] Hutchinson hbk **£16.95**

HAMBURGER, JOSEPH
Macaulay and the Whig Tradition
Macaulay was the greatest of the 'Whig' historians. His unfinished history reflected his belief in England's manifest destiny .
[L2403] Chicago UP hbk **£13.95**

HAY, DENYS
Annalists and Historians
Useful study of ancient and medieval historiography.
[L2404] Methuen hbk **£9.95**

HIMMELFARB, GERTRUDE
The New History and the Old
Provocative analysis of current fashions in the writing of history by a noted American scholar who is an uncompromising champion of the 'traditional' approach.
[L2405] Harvard UP pbk **£7.25**

HOBSBAWM, ERIC & RANGER, TERENCE
The Invention of Tradition
[L2406] Cambridge pbk **£10.95**

HOSKINS, W.G.
Fieldwork in Local History
[L2407] Faber pbk **£4.95**

KENYON, JOHN
The History Men
Highly readable account of the development of professional history in England since the Renaissance, particularly strong on the great Victorian practitioners.
[L2408] Weidenfeld pbk **£7.95**

KRANTZ, FRIEDRICH
History from Below
Essays illustrating the methods of grassroots history by Christopher Hill, John Bromley, V.G. Kiernan and E.J. Hobsbawm.
[L2409] Blackwell pbk **£11.95**

KRIEGER, LEONARD
Ranke: The Meaning of History
Ranke's work developed from the intention 'simply to show how it really was'. He is the doyen of the empirical school of history, laying down a systematic method of collecting archive material.
[L2410] Chicago UP hbk **£24.75**

LOWENTHAL, DAVID
The Past is a Foreign Country
This book draws on the arts, the humanities, and the social sciences to show how man has come to terms with his past since the Renaissance.
[L2411] Cambridge pbk **£13.95**

MARWICK, ARTHUR
The Nature of History
Comprehensive introduction to the subject. Newly revised third edition.
[L2412] Macmillan pbk **£7.95**

OAKESHOTT, MICHAEL
On History NEW
Three essays on historiography, the rule of law and the Tower of Babel myth.
[L2413] Blackwell pbk **£7.95**

PHILLIPSON, NICHOLAS
Hume
Recognised now for his philosophical work, the *Treatise on Human Nature*, Hume's reputation in his lifetime was for his historical writing, in particular the eight volume *History of England*.
[L2414] Weidenfeld pbk **£5.95**

PORTER, ROY
Gibbon
[L2415] Weidenfeld pbk **£5.95**

PORTER, ROY & TEICH, MIKULAS (EDS)
Revolution in History
Essays by leading historians examining ideas of revolution within historical development. Major questions are raised about historiographical interpretation.
[L2416] Cambridge pbk **£10.95**

Barbara Tuchman, author of *Practising History* (Macmillan pbk **£8.95**) (Photo: Bruce Davidson)

ROWSE, A.L.
Froude the Historian: Victorian Man of Letters
Like Macaulay, Froude has been accused of lacking the true discipline of a scholar. His work is more noted now for its literary elegance.
[L2417] Sutton pbk **£7.95**

THOMPSON, PAUL
The Voice of the Past: Oral History
Revised edition
[L2418] Oxford pbk **£6.95**

TOSH, JOHN
The Pursuit of History
A textbook for students of history which gives a comprehensive outline to the various methods employed.
[L2419] Longman pbk **£7.50**

TUCHMAN, BARBARA
Practising History
A collection of essays by the well-known American historian, author of *The Proud Tower* and *The March of Folly*.
[L2420] Macmillan pbk **£8.95**

TULLOCH, HUGH
Acton
[L2421] Weidenfeld hbk **£5.95**
WEDGWOOD, C.V.
History and Hope
The collected essays of a 'popular' historian who has written extensively on 17th century England and Europe.
[L2422] Collins pbk **£17.50**

WRIGHT, ANTHONY
R.H. Tawney
Tawney is widely regarded as the patron saint of 20th Century British socialism, and this book acts as a guide to the interpretation of his works.
[L2423] Manchester UP pbk **£6.95**

Simon Schama, author of *Citizens* (Viking hbk **£20.00**)

MILITARY HISTORY

This year sees the 75th anniversary of the outbreak of World War I, and the 50th of World War II. Both occasions have prompted yet more books on these popular subjects - at the rate of more than a dozen a week in mid-1989. This applies particularly to Hitler's war - surely the pivotal event of the century - as is reflected in the space it occupies here. Much is bound to be ephemeral, but the work of, among others, Martin Gilbert and John Keegan, has been eagerly awaited. What follows is a selection of the recent highlights, alongside classics by Liddell Hart, Taylor, Terraine and others.

General

CHANDLER, DAVID
A Guide to the Battlefields of Europe　**NEW**
New edition of a standard guide, particularly useful for its coverage of sites in Eastern Europe.
[LA1] P Stephens hbk **£19.95**

CHANDLER, DAVID (ED)
The Dictionary of Battles
[LA2] Ebury hbk **£12.95**

CREVELD, MARTIN VAN
Command in War
[LA3] Harvard UP pbk **£8.75**
Supplying War
Eschews strategy in favour of the crucial but often neglected subject of logistics.
[LA4] Cambridge pbk **£12.95**

DIXON, NORMAN F.
On the Psychology of Military Incompetence
Provocative study by a British psychologist of the effect of 'bull' and other military rituals on decision-making in the field.
[LA5] Cape hbk **£10.95**
[LA6] Futura pbk **£6.95**

GLOVER, MICHAEL
A New Guide to the Battlefields of Northern France and the Low Countries
[LA10] M Joseph hbk **£14.95**

HASTINGS, MAX (ED)
The Oxford Book of Military Anecdotes
Absorbing collection in the now quite extensive series of Oxford anthologies.
[LA11] Oxford hbk **£12.50**
[LA12] Oxford pbk **£5.95**

HMSO
Exploring Museums
Provides descriptions of museums to visit in different regions: London, South-West England, North East England, North West England and the Isle of Man. State which one of the series you wish to buy when ordering.
[LA13A] HMSO pbk **£7.95**

HOLMES, RICHARD
The Firing Line
[LA13] Penguin pbk **£5.99**

HOWARD, MICHAEL
The Causes of Wars
[LA14] Unwin Hyman pbk **£4.95**

War and the Liberal Conscience
[LA15] Oxford pbk **£4.95**
War in European History
[LA16] Oxford pbk **£5.95**

KEEGAN, JOHN
The Face of Battle
This book attempts to reconstruct what exactly happened at Agincourt, Waterloo and the Somme. The result is as close as we are likely to come to an understanding of the individual's experience in conflict.
[LA17] Barrie & Jenkins hbk **£14.95**
[LA18] Penguin pbk **£5.99**
The Mask of Command
Here Keegan considers 'heroic' leadership as reflected in the careers of Alexander the Great, Wellington, Ulysses S. Grant and Hitler.
[LA19] Cape hbk **£12.95**
[LA19A] Penguin pbk **£5.99**
The Price of Admiralty　**NEW**
Keegan's most recent book, and perhaps his best to date (despite its title). A landlubber's view of naval warfare, as incisive as its military predecessor *The Face of Battle*.
[LA20] Hutchinson hbk **£14.95**

KEEGAN, JOHN & HOLMES, RICHARD
Soldiers
[LA22] Sphere pbk **£5.95**

KEEGAN, JOHN & WHEATCROFT, A.
Who's Who in Military History
[LA23] Hutchinson hbk **£9.95**
[LA24] Hutchinson pbk **£4.95**

MACDONALD, JOHN
Great Battlefields of the World
[LA25] M Joseph hbk **£16.95**

PARET, PETER (ED)
Makers of Modern Strategy: From Machiavelli to the Nuclear Age
[LA26] Oxford pbk **£15.00**

ROYLE, TREVOR
War Report　**NEW**
[LA28] Grafton pbk **£3.99**

SEYMOUR, WILLIAM
Battles in Britain 1066 - 1746
[LA29] Sidgwick pbk **£9.95**

General Montgomery from *Oxford Illustrated Encyclopaedia of World History:Volume 2* (Oxford hbk £19.50)

SUN-ZTU
The Art of War
This edition of the classic work on strategy written over 24 centuries ago is introduced by Tao Hanshang, Chinese general and veteran of the Long March.
[LA30] David & Ch hbk **£9.95**

TUCHMAN, BARBARA
The March of Folly: From Troy to Vietnam
[LA3001] Sphere pbk **£5.99**

WINTLE, JUSTIN
Dictionary of War Quotations　**NEW**
A vade-mecum of over 4,000 quotations illuminating the attractions, the pity and (even) the humour of war.
[LA31] Hodder hbk **£17.95**

YOUNG, PETER & ADAIR, JOHN
From Hastings to Culloden
[LA32] Roundwood pbk **£12.00**

Pre-19th Century Conflicts

ARMESTO, FELIPE FERNANDEZ
The Spanish Armada: The Experience of War in 1588
The campaign as seen from the Spanish viewpoint, which sets out to debunk the myth of a heaven-sent victory.
[LA34] Oxford pbk **£7.95**

CHANDLER, DAVID
Campaigns of Napoleon
Still the best single-volume survey of Napoleon's military career from the siege of Toulon in 1793 right through to his ultimate defeat at Waterloo.
[LA35] Weidenfeld hbk **£30.00**
Napoleon's Marshals
The Napoleonic marshalate was varied in temperament and approach, ranging from laconic professionals like Davout and Berthier to fire-eaters like Murat and Ney. Each is given a biographical chapter in this study, which spans 117 years of French history.
[LA36] Weidenfeld hbk **£25.00**

CONTAMINE, PHILIPPE
War in the Middle Ages
An indispensable study: 'quite simply the best book on medieval European warfare available in any language' (*History Today*).
[LA37] Blackwell pbk **£10.50**

DUFFY, CHRISTOPHER
Frederick the Great: A Military Life
[LA38] Routledge pbk **£9.95**

FERRILL, ARTHUR
The Fall of the Roman Empire: The Military Explanation
[LA40] Thames & H pbk **£7.95**
The Origins of War from the Stone Age to Alexander the Great
[LA41] Thames & H pbk **£5.95**

FOX, ROBIN LANE
Alexander the Great
[LA42] Penguin pbk **£6.99**

GATES, DAVID
The Spanish Ulcer: A History of the Peninsular War
Comprehensive study of the bitter seven year war which tied down 200,000 French troops. Besides

discussing Wellington's victories the author (unusually for a British historian) also gives due weight to the part played by the people of Spain in resisting the invader.
[LA43] Unwin Hyman hbk **£15.00**

GOODMAN, ANTHONY
The Wars of the Roses
[LA44] Routledge hbk **£25.00**

HACKETT, GENERAL SIR JOHN
Warfare in the Ancient World   NEW
Comprehensive survey of military systems from earliest recorded times to the Late Roman Empire. Given the added bonus of superb illustrations by Peter Connolly, this promises to be one of the best books on the subject.
[LA46] Sidgwick hbk **£16.95**

HIBBERT, CHRISTOPHER (ED)
The Recollections of Rifleman Harris
John Harris started out in life as a Dorset shepherd and ended as a Soho shoemaker. The days between were spent as an ordinary soldier, vividly recalled in this personal memoir of the Peninsular War.
[LA47] Century pbk **£3.95**

LONGMATE, NORMAN
Defending the Island
[LA48] Hutchinson hbk **£16.95**

MARTIN, COLIN & PARKER, GEOFFREY
The Spanish Armada
A book which combines a re-assessment of the campaign with new material gleaned from a study of surviving Armada wrecks. Probably the best of the recent crop of Armada books.
[LA49] H Hamilton hbk **£14.95**

MATTINGLY, GARRETT
The Defeat of the Spanish Armada
This work, originally published in 1959, is probably still the best introduction to the subject for the general reader.
[LA50] Cape hbk **£12.95**

NEWARK, TIM
Celtic Warriors
[LA51] Blandford pbk **£6.95**
Medieval Warlords
[LA52] Blandford hbk **£14.95**
The Barbarians
[LA53] Blandford pbk **£6.95**

PARKER, GEOFFREY
The Army of Flanders and the Spanish Road 1567 - 1659
The 'Spanish Road' was the vital military corridor between Savoy and Luxembourg through which Spain supplied her armies during the Dutch revolt.
[LA56] Cambridge pbk **£13.95**
The Military Revolution
An important re-assessment of the role of military power in the rise of the West between 1500-1800.
[LA57] Cambridge hbk **£15.00**

POPE, DUDLEY
The Devil Himself: The Mutiny of the 'Danae' in 1800
By the celebrated writer of naval adventure, creator of Ramage.
[LA58] Secker hbk **£10.95**

ROSS, CHARLES
The Wars of the Roses: A Concise History
Excellent illustrated history of the whole period.
[LA59] Thames & H pbk **£5.95**

RUSSELL, FREDERICK H.
The Just War in the Middle Ages
[LA60] Cambridge pbk **£10.95**

SEWARD, DESMOND
Henry V as Warlord
A book that will come as a surprise to those of us reared on the Shakespearean myth. In this revisionist study, Henry emerges as a cold-blooded professional, whose warlike policies crippled England's economy and reduced the country to civil war after his death.
[LA61] Sidgwick hbk **£15.00**
The Hundred Years' War
[LA62] Constable pbk **£6.95**

TURNBULL, STEPHEN
Battles of the Samurai
[LA63] Blandford hbk **£12.95**
Samurai Warlords   NEW
The latest in a well-researched series by the leading authority in this country on warfare in medieval Japan.
[LA64] Blandford hbk **£14.95**
Samurai Warriors
[LA65] Blandford hbk **£14.95**
The Samurai
[LA66] G Philip hbk **£14.95**

WAILLY, HENRI DE
Crécy 1346: Anatomy of a Battle
A blow-by-blow reconstruction of the Black Prince's great victory over France which began the Hundred Years' War.
[LA67] Blandford hbk **£14.95**

WATSON, G.R.
The Roman Soldier
[LA68] Thames & H pbk **£6.95**

YOUNG, PETER
Naseby 1645
Brigadier Young, who died recently, was the foremost authority on the military history of the English Civil War. This is the final part of his trilogy of battles, following earlier studies of Edgehill and Marston Moor.
[LA70] Century hbk **£14.95**

19th Century Conflicts

ASCOLI, DAVID
The Day of Battle: Mars-la-Tour 16th August 1870
Careful reconstruction of a battle which, though not in itself decisive, foreshadowed the French surrender at Sedan three weeks later.
[LA71] Harrap hbk **£17.95**

BATTY, PETER & PARISH, PETER
The Divided Union: The Story of the American Civil War 1861 - 65
[LA72] Penguin pbk **£9.99**

CONNELL, EVAN S.
Son of the Morning Star: General Custer & the Battle of the Little Bighorn
[LA73] Pan pbk **£4.50**

ELTING, JOHN R.
Swords Around the Throne   NEW
[LA74] Weidenfeld hbk **£18.95**

HORNE, ALISTAIR
The Fall of Paris: The Siege and the Commune 1870 - 71
[LA77] Penguin pbk **£7.50**

HOWARD, MICHAEL
The Franco-Prussian War: The German Invasion of France 1870 - 71
Highly-regarded study by a leading historian of the conflict which humbled Napoleon III's France and ushered in the Second Reich.
[LA78] Methuen pbk **£7.95**

LUNT, JAMES (ED)
From Sepoy to Subedar
First-hand account of the career of Sitar Ram, a soldier in the Bengal army during the 19th century.
[LA80] Macmillan pbk **£6.95**

MACRORY, PATRICK
Kabul Catastrophe
Published in 1966 as 'Signal Catastrophe' but retitled after the author found it in the Railways section of a well-known London bookshop. The story of the ill-fated British expedition into Afghanistan.
[LA81] Oxford pbk **£6.95**

MASON, PHILIP
A Matter of Honour: An Account of the Indian Army, its Officers and Men
Absorbing study of the British army in its second home.
[LA82] Macmillan pbk **£7.95**

PAKENHAM, THOMAS
The Boer War
[LA83] Futura pbk **£6 99**

REITZ, DENYS
Commando: A Boer Journal of the Boer War
[LA84] Faber pbk **£3.95**

RODGER, N.A.M.
The Wooden World
An absorbing account of the Georgian navy. This is not a technical study of ships and gunnery, nor a narrative history. Instead, it is a comprehensive survey of the men and their milieu: recruitment, diet, life on-board ship and so on. The picture which emerges is very different to that depicted in naval adventure fiction.
[LA85] Collins hbk **£17.50**
[LA86] Fontana pbk **£6.95**

SIFAKIS, STEWART
Who Was Who in the American Civil War
Over 2,500 concise biographies, arranged alphabetically, of the major participants on both sides in the war.
[LA87] Facts on File hbk **£25.00**

SYMONDS, CRAIG L.
Battlefield Atlas of the American Civil War
[LA89] Ian Allan hbk **£10.95**

WOODHAM-SMITH, CECIL
The Reason Why
Highly readable account of the Charge of the Light Brigade in 1854, which sheds light on the military system which made such a disaster possible.
[LA90] Penguin pbk **£3.95**

The First World War

BABINGTON, ANTHONY
For the Sake of Example: Capital Courts Martial 1914 - 1918
[LA91] Grafton pbk **£3.95**

BARNETT, CORRELLI
The Swordbearers: Studies in Supreme Command in the First World War
Outstanding study of the great commanders of World War I - Von Moltke, Jellicoe, Petain and Ludendorff.
[LA93] Hodder pbk **£9.95**

BOND, BRIAN (ED)
Staff Officer: The Diaries of Lord Moyne 1914 - 1918
[LA94] Leo Cooper hbk **£17.50**

BRUCE, ANTHONY
Great Battles of the First World War **NEW**
Over 800 entries in A-Z format, covering the personalities, battles, technology and political background of the war. Includes over 200 contemporary photographs.
[LA95] M Joseph hbk **£20.00**

GILBERT, MARTIN
First World War Atlas
[LA96] Weidenfeld hbk **£10.95**
[LA97] Weidenfeld pbk **£6.95**

HART, BASIL H. LIDDELL
History of the First World War
[LA98] Pan pbk **£5.95**

LIVESEY, ANTHONY
Great Battles of World War I **NEW**
The latest in the exceptionally well-produced *Great Battles* series. Three-dimensional computer maps and colour spreads recreate all the major encounters, including Tannenberg, Caporetto, the Marne and the Somme.
[LA99] M Joseph hbk **£19.95**

MACDONALD, LYN
1914 - 1918: Voices & Images of the Great War
Lyn Macdonald has made a name for herself as an

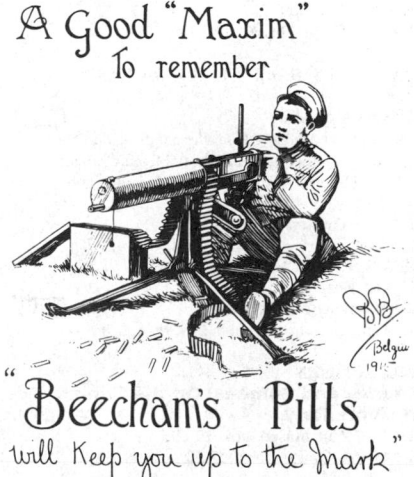

Illustration from *1914 - 1918: Voices & Images of the Great War* (Michael Joseph hbk £15.95)

oral historian of the Great War. Her work combines a sympathy for the experience of ordinary soldiers with a concern for the wider issues facing generals and politicians.
[LA100] M Joseph hbk **£15.95**

MOORE, WILLIAM
Gas Attack: Chemical Warfare 1914 - 1918 and Afterwards
A work which analyses the successive use of chlorine, phosgene, mustard gas and arsenicals during the war.
[LA101] Leo Cooper hbk **£14.95**

ROBBINS, KEITH
The First World War
[LA102] Oxford pbk **£5.95**

STONE, NORMAN
The Eastern Front 1914 - 1917
[LA103] Hodder pbk **£12.95**

TAYLOR, A.J.P.
The First World War 1914 - 1918
[LA104] Penguin pbk **£5.95**

VAUGHAN, EDWIN C.
Some Desperate Glory
Edwin Vaughan joined the Artist's Rifles OTC in 1914 and served throughout the war. His diary of life on the Western Front is a classic of its kind.
[LA105] Macmillan pbk **£4.95**

WILSON, TREVOR
The Myriad Faces of War: Britain and the Great War 1914 -1918
A truly exhaustive study of the British experience, covering not only military events but also the social and economic background. Wilson's monograph is a major contribution to First World War historiography.
[LA106] Blackwell/Polity pbk **£14.95**

Specific Campaigns & Battles

ASCOLI, DAVID
The Mons Star: The British Expeditionary Force 5th August - 22nd November 1914
[LA107] Harrap hbk **£10.95**

BENNETT, G.
Naval Battles of the First World War
[LA109] Pan pbk **£2.95**

BULLOCK, DAVID
Allenby's War
[LA110] Blandford hbk **£12.95**

COPPARD, GEORGE
With a Machine Gun to Cambrai
[LA111] Macmillan pbk **£3.95**

HOCKLEY, A.H. FARRAR
The Somme
[LA114] Pan pbk **£2.95**

HORNE, ALASTAIR
The Price of Glory: Verdun 1916
[LA1141] Penguin pbk **£6.95**

HOUGH, RICHARD
The Great War at Sea 1914 - 1918
[LA115] Oxford pbk **£5.95**

JAMES, ROBERT RHODES
Gallipoli **NEW**
[LA116] Macmillan pbk **£8.99**

LIDDLE, PETER H.
Men of Gallipoli
[LA117] David & Ch pbk **£4.95**
The Airman's War 1914 - 1918
[LA118] Blandford hbk **£17.50**

MACDONALD, LYN
1914
[LA119] Penguin pbk **£5.99**
The Roses of No Man's Land
'Lyn Macdonald has uncovered an extraordinarily rich mass of personal reminiscence written and oral…the well known horrors of the Western front are unexpectedly illuminated'. (*The Times*).
[LA120] Macmillan pbk **£6.95**
The Somme
[LA121] Macmillan pbk **£7.95**
They Called It Passchendaele
The story of the Third Battle of Ypres and of the men who fought in it.
[LA122] Macmillan pbk **£6.99**

MIDDLEBROOKE, MARTIN
First Day on the Somme: 1st July 1916
[LA123] Penguin pbk **£4.95**
The Kaiser's Battle
On 21 March 1918 the Germans launched their long-awaited 'Spring Offensive' designed to knock Britain out of the war. How nearly they came to achieving their goal is revealed in this compelling account.
[LA124] Penguin pbk **£5.95**

MOORE, WILLIAM
A Wood Called Bourlon
[LA125] Leo Cooper hbk **£12.95**

PITT, BARRIE
1918: The Last Act
[LA126] Macmillan pbk **£7.95**

TERRAINE, JOHN
The Road to Passchendaele
[LA127] Secker hbk **£7.95**
To Win a War: 1918, the Year of Victory
For years John Terraine has argued that the First World War generals are unfairly criticised. In this book he shows how the Allies campaigned with skill and determination to win the war in 1918.
[LA128] Macmillan pbk **£5.95**

VAT, DAN VAN DER
The Ship that Changed the World
The Escape of the Goeben to the Dardenelles in 1914.
[LA129] Hodder hbk **£12.95**
[LA129A] Grafton pbk **£3.50**

WARNER, PHILIP
The Battle of Passchendaele
New study of the battle which became a by-word for the horrific fighting conditions on the Western Front.
[LA130] Sidgwick pbk **£8.95**

The Second World War

The World at Arms **NEW**
Mammoth 50th anniversary treatment of 'the war that touched the lives of every man, woman and child'. Maps, diorama and rarely published photographs from both Allied and Axis archives.
[LA131] Hodder hbk **£16.95**

BARNETT, CORRELLI
The Desert Generals
The book which caused a storm of controversy when
it first appeared in 1960 because of its thesis that
Auchinleck, not Montgomery, was the architect of
victory at El Alamein.
[LA132] Pan pbk **£2.95**

BARNETT, CORRELLI (ED)
Hitler's Generals `NEW`
Corelli Barnett has assembled a distinguished group
of military historians to produce this collective
biography of twenty-six generals of the Third Reich.
[LA133] Weidenfeld hbk **£12.95**

BLUMENSON, MARTIN
Patton: The Man Behind the Legend
[LA135] Cape hbk **£14.95**

BOND, BRIAN
**British Military Policy between the Two
World Wars**
[LA136] Oxford hbk **£30.00**

BOULLE, PIERRE
The Bridge on the River Kwai
[LA137] Fontana pbk **£1.95**

BRICKHILL, PAUL
The Great Escape
[LA138] Arrow pbk **£1.75**

BRYANT, SIR ARTHUR
The Turn of the Tide 1939 - 1943
[LA139] Grafton pbk **£5.95**
Triumph in the West 1943 - 45
[LA140] Grafton pbk **£5.95**

CALDER, ANGUS
The People's War
[LA141] Grafton pbk **£3.95**

CALVOCORESSI, PETER; WINT, GUY &
PRITCHARD, JOHN
Total War `NEW`
Revised edition of a valuable study which first
appeared in 1972. The story is now updated and incl-
udes the Ultra revelations, which Calvocoressi was
not allowed to publish when the book first appeared.
[LA142] Viking hbk **£25.00**
[LA142A] Penguin pbk **£12.99**

CHURCHILL, WINSTON S.
History of the Second World War
Vol 1: The Gathering Storm
[LA143] Penguin pbk **£5.99**
Vol 2: The Finest Hour
[LA144] Penguin pbk **£5.99**
Vol 3: The Grand Alliance
[LA145] Penguin pbk **£5.99**
Vol 4: Hinge of Fate
[LA146] Penguin pbk **£5.99**
Vol 5: Closing the Ring
[LA147] Penguin pbk **£5.99**
Vol 6: Triumph and Tragedy
[LA148] Penguin pbk **£5.99**

COOPER, ARTEMIS
Cairo in the War 1939 - 45 `NEW`
Polo at the Geriza Club, drinks at Shepheard's,
Rommel at the gates…
[LA149] H Hamilton hbk **£16.95**

DAILY TELEGRAPH `NEW`
Chronicle of the Second World War
The war seen through the pages of *The Daily
Telegraph* 1939-45, with commentaries by Max
Hastings (the present editor) and others.
[LA150] Sidgwick hbk **£15.95**

DAVIES, TONY
**When the Moon Rises: An Escape
through Wartime Italy**
[LA151] Sphere pbk **£2.75**

DUNLOP, SIR EDWARD
**The War Diaries of Weary Dunlop: Java
and the Burma-Thailand Railway
1942 - 45**
[LA153] Lennard hbk **£16.95**

FRASER, DAVID
And We Shall Shock Them
Absorbing history of the very mixed fortunes of the
British army during 1939 - 45.
[LA154] Hodder pbk **£5.95**

FRIEDHOFF, HERMAN
Requiem for the Resistance
First-hand account of the Dutch struggle against
Nazism.
[LA155] Bloomsbury hbk **£14.95**

FUSSELL, PAUL
**Wartime: Understanding and Behaviour
in the Second World War** `NEW`
[LA1555] Oxford hbk **£15 00.**

GILBERT, MARTIN
The Second World War `NEW`
Martin Gilbert recently completed his multi-volume
biography of Winston Churchil to great acclaim. This
definitive study, published to coincide with the 50th
anniversary of the war's outbreak, is sure to be just as
warmly received.
[LA156] Weidenfeld hbk **£18.95**

HAMILTON, NIGEL
**Monty: The Life of Montgomery of
Alamein**
Hamilton has written the official biography of
Montgomery. In three volumes; it is a masterly work
which considers not only his undoubted military
talents, but also his political naivety and his
unendearing personality in retirement.
**Vol 1: The Making of a General,
1887 - 1942**
[LA157A1] Hodder pbk **£7.95**
**Vol 2: Master of the Battlefield,
1942 - 44**
[LA157A2] Hodder pbk **£9.95**
Vol 3: The Field Marshall, 1944 - 76
[LA157A3] Hodder pbk **£7.95**
Monty: The Man behind the Legend
[LA157] Sphere pbk **£3.99**

HART, BASIL H. LIDDELL
History of the Second World War
[LA158] Pan pbk **£7.99**

INGLIS, RUTH
The Children's War 1939 - 45
The experiences of wartime evacuees in their own
words collected by an author who was herself
evacuated (from China to the US) during the
war.
[LA159] Collins hbk **£12.95**

IRVING, DAVID
**Churchill's War Vol 1: The Struggle
for Power**
First volume (of two) in Irving's reassessment of the
British war effort. The book's more sensational
aspects, including accusations of cowardice and
drunkenness, do not obscure its virtues as a study of
its protagonist's ruthless devotion to the anti-Hitler
crusade.
[LA160] Veritas hbk **£16.95**
[LA160A] Arrow pbk **£7.99**

Hitler's War 1939 - 42
[LA161] Macmillan pbk **£7.95**
Hitler's War 1942 - 45
[LA162] Macmillan pbk **£7.95**
The War Path
[LA163] Macmillan pbk **£6.95**

KEEGAN, JOHN
The Second World War `NEW`
Keegan's latest book looks at the war in its
broad historical context, using a thematic
approach. There are sections on each of the key
events of the war, from the fall of France to the War
in the Pacific. Certain to be one of the highlights of
the year.
[LA1631] Hutchinson hbk **£18.95**

KENNEDY, LUDOVIC
War Papers `NEW`
Popular collection of historic front pages from
both the British and American press
1939-45.
[LA164] Fontana pbk **£10.95**

KESSLER, LEO
SS Peiper
[LA165] Grafton pbk **£2.95**

KNOX, MACGREGOR
Mussolini Unleashed
Politics and Strategy in Fascist Italy's Last War
1919-41.
[LA166] Cambridge pbk **£12.95**

LARRABEE, ERIC
**Commander in Chief:
Franklin Delano Roosevelt, his
Lieutenants and their War**
[LA167] Deutsch hbk **£15.95**

LUCAS, JAMES
Last Days of the Reich
[LA170] Grafton pbk **£3.95**
**Reich! World War II through German
Eyes**
[LA171] Grafton pbk **£3.95**

MACKNESS, ROBIN
Oradour: Massacre and Aftermath
The story of the destruction of a remote French
village by the SS in 1944 is well known. When the
author of this book returned to Oradour forty years
later, he discovered some disturbing inconsistencies in
the official version…
[LA172] Corgi pbk **£3.50**

MARSDEN-SMEDLEY, PHILIP & GLASS,
FIONA (EDS)
Articles of War `NEW`
Contemporary writing from the pages of *The
Spectator*, including contributions from Graham
Greene, Harold Nicholson, Rose Macaulay and
Diana Mosley.
[LA173] Grafton hbk **£14.95**

MESSENGER, CHARLES
**World War II:
Chronological Atlas** `NEW`
[LA175] Bloomsbury hbk **£19.95**

MILLER, JOHN
**Friends and Romans: On the Run in
Wartime Italy**
[LA176] Hutchinson hbk **£13.95**
[LA176A] Grafton pbk **£3.50**

MORLEY, JOHN DAVID
In the Labyrinth
[LA179] Sphere pbk **£3.99**

MORRIS, ERIC
Guerillas in Uniform `NEW`
Churchill's Private Armies in the Middle East and the
War against Japan, 1940-1945.
[LA180] Hutchinson hbk **£16.95**

MOSS, W. STANLEY
Ill Met by Moonlight
Boy's Own adventures in occupied Crete.
[LA181] Buchan & En pbk **£5.95**

PARKER, DR R.A.C.
Struggle for Survival: The History
of the Second World War `NEW`
[LA1811] Oxford hbk **£14.95**

PERRETT, BRYAN & HOGG, IAN
Encyclopaedia of the Second
World War `NEW`
Billed as 'the ultimate reference book on the subject',
this covers every conceivable aspect of the conflict,
by land, sea and air.
[LA182] Longman hbk **£19.99**

PITT, BARRIE
Churchill and his Generals
[LA183] David & Ch pbk **£4.95**
The Crucible of War
Vol 1: Wavell's Command
[LA184] Macmillan pbk **£6.95**
Vol 2: Auchinleck's Command
[LA185] Macmillan pbk **£7.95**
Vol 3: Montgomery and Alamein
[LA186] Macmillan pbk **£6.95**

PITT, BARRIE & FRANCES
Chronological Atlas of World
War II `NEW`
Over 350 maps in full colour throughout, supported
by essays on the major topics.
[LA187] Macmillan hbk **£30.00**

PSYCHOUNDAKIS, GEORGE
The Cretan Runner
[LA188] J Murray pbk **£5.95**

REID, P.R.
The Colditz Story: The Latter Days
of Colditz
[LA189] Hodder pbk **£4.99**

SMALL, KEN
The Forgotten Dead `NEW`
In 1944 the Allies staged a dress rehearsal for D-day
on the Devon coast - with disastrous results. The
author, a local hotelier, was the first to piece together
the tragic events that led to the deaths of nearly 1,000
US servicemen.
[LA192] Bloomsbury pbk **£3.99**

TAYLOR, A.J.P.
The Second World War: An Illustrated
History
[LA195] H Hamilton hbk **£14.95**
War Lords
Considers Mussolini, Hitler, Churchill, Stalin and
Roosevelt in Taylor's inimitable style.
[LA196] Penguin pbk **£3.99**

TAYLOR, ERIC
Women Who Went to War 1938 - 46
A study of operational roles of British women in the
war, whether as ferry pilots, Wrens, SOE agents or
VAD nurses staying behind with POWs in Burma.
This book does not draw a veil over prejudice - even
flying ace Amy Johnson could not become a bomber
pilot - nevertheless it shows the vital contribution of
women to the war effort.
[LA197] Hale hbk **£12.95**

TEC, NECHAMA
When Light Pierced the Darkness
[LA198] Oxford hbk **£17.50**
[LA198A] Oxford pbk **£6.95**

TOWNSEND, COLIN & EILEEN
War Wives
A tribute to the unsung heroines of the war: 'ordinary'
housewives of Britain and Germany, left to carry on
with their lives without their menfolk, in some cases
for over seven years.
[LA200] Grafton hbk **£13.95**

TREVOR-ROPER, HUGH
The Last Days of Hitler
The definitive account, originally published in 1947,
to confound rumours that the Führer had not died in
the Berlin bunker.
[LA191] Macmillan hbk **£6.95**
[LA191A] Pan pbk **£2.50**

WALLER, JANE & VAUGHAN-REES, MICHAEL
Women in Uniform
[LA201] Macmillan pbk **£9.95**

WICKS, BEN
No Time to Wave Goodbye
The true story of Britain's 3,500,000 evacuees - a
moving collection of personal memories, at once
humorous and tragic. With an introduction by one-
time evacuee Michael Caine.
[LA202] Bloomsbury pbk **£3.50**

WILMOTT, H.P.
The Great Crusade `NEW`
[LA203] M Joseph hbk **£17.95**

Specific Campaigns & Battles

ALLEN, LOUIS
Burma: The Longest War 1941 - 45
[LA204] Dent pbk **£8.95**

BELFIELD, EVERSLEY & ESSAME, H.
The Battle for Normandy
[LA205] Pan pbk **£2.95**

BROOKS, STEPHEN & ECKSTEIN, EVE
Operation Overlord: Embroidery,
History, Invasion `NEW`
A celebration of the 45th anniversary of the D-day
landings, and the events that led up to it.
[LA207] Ashford hbk **£12.95**

CLARK, ALAN
Barbarossa
Compelling study of the German invasion of Russia
1941-45, the greatest and most destructive land
campaign in history. Here Hitler staked everything -
and lost.
[LA208] Macmillan pbk **£3.95**

COSTELLO, JOHN
The Pacific War
[LA209] Pan pbk **£3.95**
Love, Sex and War
[LA2091] Pan pbk **£3.95**

D'ESTE, CARLO
Bitter Victory
The campaign for Sicily in 1943.
[LA210] Collins hbk **£17.50**
Decision in Normandy
[LA211] Pan pbk **£3.95**

John Keegan, author of *The Second World War*
(Hutchinson hbk £18.95)

DEIGHTON, LEN
Blitzkrieg: From the Rise of Hitler to
the Fall of Dunkirk
[LA212] Grafton pbk **£3.95**
Bomber
[LA213] Grafton pbk **£3.95**
Fighter: The True Story of the Battle of
Britain
[LA214] Grafton pbk **£3.50**

ELLIS, JOHN
Cassino: The Hollow Victory
[LA215] Sphere pbk **£4.95**

ERICKSON, JOHN
Stalin's War with Germany:
Vol 1: The Road to Stalingrad
[LA216] Grafton pbk **£6.95**
Vol 2: The Road to Berlin
[LA217] Grafton pbk **£8.95**

FLEMING, PETER
Operation Sea Lion
Classic account of German plans for the invasion of
Britain in 1940.
[LA218] Pan pbk **£3.50**

GRENFELL, RUSSELL
Main Fleet to Singapore
[LA219] Oxford pbk **£4.95**

HARRIS, JOHN
Dunkirk
[LA220] David & Ch pbk **£4.95**

HASTINGS, MAX
Bomber Command
[LA221] Pan pbk **£4.99**
Das Reich
Resistance and the March of the Second SS Panzer
Division through France, June 1944.
[LA222] Pan pbk **£3.99**
Overlord
[LA223] Pan pbk **£4.99**
Victory in Europe
[LA224] Weidenfeld hbk **£10.95**

HILLARY, RICHARD
The Last Enemy   **NEW**
[LA225] Pan pbk **£2.99**

HORNE, ALASTAIR
To Lose a Battle: France 1940
Complements Horne's earlier books on the siege of
Paris and Verdun.
[LA226] Penguin pbk **£6.95**

HOUGH, RICHARD
**The Longest Battle: The War at
Sea 1939 - 45**
[LA227] Weidenfeld hbk **£14.95**
[LA228] Pan pbk **£3.95**

HOYT, EDWIN P.
The Invasion before Normandy
[LA229] Hale pbk **£5.95**
U-Boat Wars
[LA230] R Hale hbk **£10.95**

IRVING, DAVID
The Destruction of Dresden
[LA231] Macmillan pbk **£5.95**

KEEGAN, JOHN
Six Armies in Normandy
[LA233] Penguin pbk **£4.95**

KENNEDY, LUDOVIC
'Pursuit': The Sinking of the Bismarck
[LA234] Fontana pbk **£1.75**

LEWIS, NORMAN
Naples '44
[LA235] Eland pbk **£4.95**

LUCAS, LADDIE
**Flying Colours: The Epic Story of
Douglas Bader**
[LA236] Grafton pbk **£1.95**
Out of the Blue
The role of luck in air warfare 1917-66.
[LA237] Grafton pbk **£3.95**

LUNT, JAMES
**A Hell of a Licking: The Retreat from
Burma 1941 - 42**
[LA238] Collins hbk **£15.00**

MCINTYRE, DONALD
The Battle of the Atlantic
[LA239] Pan pbk **£2.95**

MCKEE, ALASTAIR.
Caen: Anvil of Victory
[LA240] Macmillan pbk **£5.95**

MIDDLEBROOK, MARTIN
Lincolnshire poultry-farmer, turned military historian,
Middlebrook is also known for his excellent First
World War books (see above).
Convoy
[LA241] Penguin pbk **£4.99**
Peenemunde Raid: 17 - 18 August 1943
[LA242] Penguin pbk **£4.99**
The Battle of Hamburg
[LA243] Penguin pbk **£6.95**

MURRAY, WILLIAMSON
Luftwaffe
[LA244] Grafton pbk **£5.95**

ROSIGNOLI, GUIDO
Allied Forces in Italy 1943 - 45   **NEW**
Comprehensive account of the Italian campaign, with
details of Allied insignia, badges and uniforms.
[LA245] David & Ch hbk **£12.95**

RYAN, CORNELIUS
A Bridge Too Far
[LA246] Hodder pbk **£4.99**
The Last Battle
[LA247] Hodder pbk **£2.95**
The Longest Day
[LA248] Hodder pbk **£2.95**

SAINSBURY, KEITH
The Turning Point
[LA249] Oxford pbk **£6.95**

SALISBURY, H.E.
**The 900 Days: The Siege of
Leningrad**
[LA250] Macmillan pbk **£3.95**

SAWARD, DUDLEY
**'Bomber' Harris: The Authorised
Biography**
[LA252] Sphere pbk **£3.95**
**Victory Denied:
The Rise of Air Power and the Defeat
of Germany 1920 - 45**
[LA253] Buchan & En hbk **£12.95**

SEARLE, RONALD
To the Kwai and Back
[LA254] Collins hbk **£15.00**

SHULMAN, MILTON
Defeat in the West
[LA255] Pan pbk **£4.99**

SLIM, FIELD MARSHAL LORD
Defeat into Victory
[LA256] Macmillan pbk **£8.95**

TAYLOR, E.
**Operation Millennium:
The 1,000 Bomber Raid on Cologne
1942**
[LA258] Hale hbk **£12.95**

TERRAINE, JOHN
The Right of the Line
The story of the RAF during World War II.
[LA259] Hodder pbk **£7.95**

TISSIER, TONY LE
The Battle for Berlin 1945
[LA260] Cape hbk **£15.00**

TOWNSEND, PETER
**Duel in the Dark: A Fighter Pilot's Story
of the Blitz**
[LA261] Arrow pbk **£3.95**

TRUE STORIES OF WORLD WAR II
A collection of re-issued personal accounts of
combat in various campaigns and arenas of World
War II.
BRADDON, RUSSELL
Nancy Wake
[LA262] Pan pbk **£3.99**
The Naked Island
[LA263] Pan pbk **£3.99**
BRICKHILL, PAUL
The Dam Busters
[LA264] Pan pbk **£3.99**
MARSHALL, BRUCE
The White Rabbit
[LA265] Pan pbk **£3.99**
PHILIPS, C.E. LUCAS
The Cockleshell Heroes
[LA266] Pan pbk **£3.99**
URQUHART, MAJOR GEN R.E.
Arnhem
[LA267] Pan pbk **£3.99**

TUTE, WARREN
The Reluctant Enemies   **NEW**
The often tragic story of relations between Britain and
France 1940-42, when (officially at least) Britain was
at war with France.
[LA268] Collins hbk **£15.00**

WHITING, CHARLES
Bounce the Rhine
[LA271] Secker pbk **£2.95**
**Operation Northwind: The Second
Battle of the Bulge**
[LA272] Grafton pbk **£3.50**
**The Long March on Rome: The
Forgotten War**
[LA273] Century pbk **£9.95**

The Intelligence War

BENNETT, RALPH
**Ultra and Mediterranean Strategy
1941 - 45**   **NEW**
An important contribution to our knowledge of the
vital role played by Ultra in the Allied success in the
war.
[LA274] H Hamilton hbk **£17.95**

BROWN, ANTHONY CAVE
Bodyguard of Lies
[LA275] Star pbk **£6.95**

CABINET OFFICE
**British Intelligence in the Second World
War: Vol 1**
The 'Secret War' against the Axis powers has
attracted a great deal of attention in recent years.
This is the official version of Ultra, the raid on
Coventry and other shadowy episodes in the
conflict.
[LA276] HMSO hbk **£12.95**
Vol 2
[LA277] HMSO hbk **£15.95**
Vol 3 pt 1
[LA278] HMSO hbk **£17.95**
Vol 3 pt 2
[LA279] HMSO hbk **£29.95**

CHANT, CHRISTOPHER
**The Encyclopaedia of Codenames of
World War II**
[LA280] Routledge hbk **£30.00**

CRUICKSHANK, C.G.
SOE in the Far East
[LA282] Oxford pbk **£5.95**

DAVIDSON, BASIL
Special Operations Europe
[LA283] Gollancz hbk **£10.95**
[LA283A] Grafton pbk **£3.95**

DEACON, RICHARD
The Silent War
[LA284] Grafton pbk **£3.50**

FISHER, DAVID E.
**Radar: A Dance on the Edge of
Time**
[LA285] Hale hbk **£12.95**

FOOT, M.R.D.
**SOE: Special Operations Executive
1940 - 46**
[LA286] BBC hbk **£8.50**

JONES, R.V.
Most Secret War: British Scientific Intelligence 1939 - 45
The Battle of the Beams, the war against the German Radar, the 'V' weapons. How the British found out about them, by the man most deeply involved in the new world of electronic warfare.
[LA287] Hodder pbk **£5.95**
Reflections on Intelligence **NEW**
Fascinating follow-up to *Most Secret War*, ten years on. Here Professor Jones draws on his long experience to explore the business of intelligence, official secrecy, deception and related topics.
[LA288] Heinemann hbk **£17.50**

LOCKHART, R. BRUCE
Memoirs of a British Agent
[LA290] Macmillan pbk **£6.50**

RUBY, MARCEL
F Section SOE
First-hand account of clandestine activities in Occupied France.
[LA292] Leo Cooper hbk **£17.50**

STEVENSON, WILLIAM
A Man Called Intrepid
[LA293] Sphere pbk **£2.95**

WINTERBOTHAM, F.W.
Ultra Secret
[LA294] Futura pbk **£1.00**

Modern Conflicts

ADAMS, JAMES
Secret Armies
On Grenada in 1983 a US Ranger officer was reduced to using his credit card in a payphone to call Fort Bragg and ask them to ask Washington to call up the USS Guam and give him an air strike. This and other anecdotes are recounted in this absorbing study of modern Special forces, including Spetsnaz, Delta Force and the SAS.
[LA295] Pan pbk **£3.99**

BARKER, DENNIS
Ruling the Waves
[LA296] Viking hbk **£12.95**
[LA296A] Sphere pbk **£3.99**

BROGAN, PATRICK
World Conflicts **NEW**
This book tackles each of the fifty or more countries which are currently experiencing some form of conflict - be it terrorism, foreign intervention, or outright war - in the world today.
[LA297] Bloomsbury pbk **£7.99**

HACKETT, GENERAL SIR JOHN
Third World War: The Untold Story
[LA298] Sidgwick hbk **£9.95**

HOCKLEY, ANTHONY FARRAR
Opening Rounds
The former C-in-C Allied Forces Northern Europe assesses the chances of a Third World War using conventional rather than nuclear weapons.
[LA299] Deutsch hbk **£12.95**

KITSON, FRANK
Bunch of Five
General Kitson's account of his experiences in Kenya, Malaya, Oman and Cyprus 1952-67.
[LA301] Faber pbk **£5.95**
Directing Operations **NEW**
What is the point of governments spending phenomenal sums on defence if properly prepared and qualified commanders are not available to direct military operations? General Kitson's new book sets out to show what is required of generals in the nuclear age.
[LA302] Faber hbk **£12.99**
Warfare as a Whole
[LA303] Faber hbk **£10.99**

MOYNAHAN, BRIAN
The Claws of the Bear **NEW**
A study of the modern Soviet military machine by the European editor of the *Sunday Times*.
[LA304] Hutchinson hbk **£16.95**

SUVOROV, VIKTOR
Spetsnaz: The Story of the Soviet SAS
[LA305] Grafton pbk **£3.99**

Korea

CUMINGS, BRUCE & HALLIDAY, JON
Korea: The Unknown War
[LA306] Viking hbk **£14.95**

HASTINGS, MAX
The Korean War
[LA307] Pan pbk **£4.99**

HOCKLEY, ANTHONY FARRAR
The Edge of the Sword
The defence of Hill 235 on the Imjin River by British troops in 1951 was one of the more stirring episodes of the war. A first-hand account of the battle, and of the author's experiences as a prisoner of the Chinese.
[LA308] Buchan & En pbk **£5.95**

MERRILL, JOHN
Korea
[LA309] AUP hbk **£26.50**

RIDGWAY, MATTHEW B.
The Korean War
General Ridgway replaced MacArthur as United Nations Supreme Commander in April 1951.
[LA310] Da Capo pbk **£11.95**

Vietnam

BUTLER, DAVID
The Fall of Saigon
[LA311] Sphere pbk **£4.99**

CAPUTO, PHILIP
A Rumour of War
[LA312] Arrow pbk **£3.50**

DONOVAN, DAVID
Once a Warrior King
The experiences of a US infantry officer operating in the Mekong delta during the Vietnam conflict.
[LA313] Corgi pbk **£3.99**

Guernica by Pablo Picasso. Illustration from *Oxford Illustrated Encyclopaedia of World History Volume 2* (Oxford hbk **£19.50**).

HERR, MICHAEL
Dispatches
'We have all spent ten years trying to explain what happened to our heads and our lives in the decade we finally survived - but Michael Herr's *Dispatches* puts all the rest of us in the shade'.(Hunter S. Thompson).
[LA314] Picador pbk **£3.95**

MANGOLD, TOM & PENYCOT, JOHN
The Tunnels of Cu Chi: A Remarkable Story of War
[LA317] Pan pbk **£3.99**

SANTOLI, AL
To Bear Any Burden
An oral history of Vietnam based on the recollections of GIs, diplomats, POWs, wives, refugees and even former VC soldiers.
[LA319] Sphere pbk **£4.50**

SHEEHAN, NEIL
A Bright Shining Lie   **NEW**
Colonel John Paul Vann went out to Vietnam in 1962, where Neil Sheehan met him and followed his career with fascination. Vann epitomised the US presence: reckless, outspoken, tragic. 'Superb. If you ever read just one history of the Vietnam war, read and admire and celebrate this one'. (John le Carré).
[LA320] Cape hbk **£15.95**

The Falklands

ARTHUR, MAX
Above All Courage
First-hand accounts of the Falklands front line.
[LA321] Sphere pbk **£3.95**

BILTON, MICHAEL & KOMINSKY, PETER
Speaking Out: Untold Stories from the Falklands War   **NEW**
An oral history of the conflict, based on the acclaimed Yorkshire TV film screened in April 1987.
[LA322] Deutsch hbk **£14.95**

HASTINGS, MAX & JENKINS, SIMON
The Battle for the Falklands
[LA323] Pan pbk **£4.99**

LAWRENCE, ROBERT
When the Fighting is Over
The story behind the controversial TV film *Tumbledown*: the author's experiences on the islands and after his return to Britain with massive head injuries.
[LA324] Bloomsbury pbk **£3.95**

MCMANNERS, HUGH
Falklands Commando
[LA325] Grafton pbk **£2.95**

MIDDLEBROOK, MARTIN
Task Force: The Falklands War 1982
Originally published as 'Operation Corporate', this is the most balanced study of the war to date.
[LA326] Penguin pbk **£6.99**
The Fight for the 'Malvinas'   **NEW**
This is the Falklands story from the *Argentine* point of view, the result of Middlebrook's extensive interviews in Buenos Aires. A disturbing study of deception, muddle and patriotism.
[LA327] Viking hbk **£14.95**

RICE, DESMOND & GAVSHON, ARTHUR
The Sinking of the Belgrano
Includes a controversial examination of Mrs

Thatcher's role in the loss of lives sustained by the Argentinians when their ship was torpedoed by a British submarine.
[LA328] Hodder pbk **£8.95**

THOMPSON, JULIAN
No Picnic: 3 Commando Brigade in the South Atlantic
[LA329] Fontana pbk **£2.95**

Other Recent Conflicts

ARTHUR, MAX
Northern Ireland: Soldiers Talking
First-hand accounts.
[LA330A] Sidgwick hbk **£13.95**
[LA330A] Sidgwick pbk **£8.95**

HORNE, ALISTAIR
A Savage War of Peace
Re-issue of the definitive account of the bloody civil war in Algeria 1954 - 62.
[LA332] Macmillan pbk **£8.95**

ISBY, DAVID
War in a Distant Country   **NEW**
The first study of the Afghanistan conflict since the Russian withdrawal.
[LA333] Arms & Arm hbk **£14.95**

URBAN, MARK
War in Afghanistan
[LA334] Macmillan pbk **£9.95**

Exploring MUSEUMS

Museum visitors will discover in this new and unique series of eleven Museums' Association guides a superbly illustrated, discriminating and enthusiastic introduction to the best and most interesting museums in the British Isles. Each book lists museums alphabetically by place name and includes a brief description of their location, plus access details and descriptions of what's on view. Each book is about 130 pages, illus in colour & b/w. Price **7.95** *net.*

February 1990

The Home Counties   0 11 290471 8
Southern England and the Channel Islands
0 11 290468 8
Scotland   0 11 290474 2
Wales   0 11 290467 X

Out now

London
0 11 290465 3

South-West England
0 11 290469 6

North East England
0 11 290470 X

North West England and the Isle of Man
0 11 290473 4

May 1990

East Anglia   0 11 290472 6
The Midlands   0 11 290466 1
Ireland   0 11 290475 0

Published by HMSO for the Museums and Galleries Commission.

HMSO BOOKS

Humour

HUMOUR

Everyman's Book of Nonsense
[M1] Dent pbk **£1.95**

Faber Book of Parodies
[M2] Faber pbk **£5.95**

The Penguin Book of Modern Humour
Edited by Alan Coren, former editor of *Punch*.
[M3] Penguin pbk **£3.50**

'AUGUSTUS CARP'
Augustus Carp Esquire by Himself:
Being the Autobiography of a
Really Good Man
The assessment is his own: one of the more
unpleasant characters of fiction, a gross counterpoint
to Mr. Pooter, and almost as funny.
[M4] Penguin pbk **£2.50**

AYRES, PAM
Country housewife poet who rose to sudden and
unexpected fame in the 1970's, as a result of an
appearance on the original 'Opportunity Knocks'.
Ballad of Bill Spink's Bedstead
& Other Poems
[M5] Severn H pbk **£1.75**

BAIRNSFATHER, BRUCE
Best of 'Fragments from France'
The best First World War cartoonist, whose work
revealed some of the miseries of trench life: *"Well, if*
you knows of a better 'ole, go to it".
[M6] Milestone pbk **£4.95**

BATEMAN, H.M.
The Best of H.M. Bateman: Tatler
Cartoons 1922 - 26
Apoplexy rules in these wonderful drawings of the
extraordinary in the everyday.
[M7] Bodley pbk **£5.95**

BAXTER, GLEN
Has cornered the market in incongruous captions to
Angela Brazil-type drawings.
Atlas
[M8] Fontana pbk **£2.95**
Glen Baxter: His Life
A spoof autobiography in Baxter's predictable style
of incongruence.
[M9] Fontana pbk **£4.95**
Impending Gleam
[M10] Fontana pbk **£2.95**

BEACHCOMBER (J.B. MORTON)
Eccentric English humour from the long-running
Daily Express column. A delightful gallimaufry of
bizarre characters.
The Best of Beachcomber **NEW**
[M11] Heinemann pbk **£5.95**

BELL, STEVE
Cartoonery of a savagery of line and content
reminiscent of Rowlandson or Gillray. Occasionally
over-cloacal but consistently withering.
'If'...Only Again
[M12] Methuen pbk **£3.50**
Another Load of 'If'
[M13] Methuen pbk **£3.95**
'If'...Bounces Back
[M14] Methuen pbk **£3.95**
Maggie's Farm: The Last Roundup
[M15] Methuen pbk **£4.95**
The 'If' Chronicles
[M16] Methuen pbk **£3.95**

The Unrepeatable 'If'
[M17] Methuen pbk **£3.95**
The Vengenace of 'If' **NEW**
Bell's seventh collection evokes 'the last days
of President Reagan, the relentless continuation of
Margaret Thatcher and the amazing fashion for
religious intolerance which was the hallmark
of 1989'.
[M18] Methuen pbk **£4.50**

BELLOC, HILAIRE
Cautionary Tales for Children
A classic of wit and imagination.
[M19] Duckworth pbk **£3.95**
Cautionary Verses
[M20] Duckworth hbk **£12.95**

BENCHLEY, ROBERT
American humorous short story and article writer.
Benchley Lost & Found
[M21] Dover pbk **£3.35**
Benchley Roundup
[M22] Chicago UP pbk **£7.95**

BENNETT, ALAN, ET AL
The Complete 'Beyond the Fringe'
The original scripts of the epoch-making revue by the
Cambridge Footlights team of c. 1960.
[M23] Methuen pbk **£5.95**

BERNARD, JEFFREY
Low Life
A man who spends his days propping up bars in Soho
drinking vodka and tonic, chainsmoking Players and
following turf form; and regularly turns out lucid and
amusing essays. An inspiration to all journalists.
[M24] Duckworth hbk **£9.95**
[M25] Pan pbk **£3.95**

BETJEMAN, JOHN
A borderline case for inclusion in Humour, this is
quintessential English verse, gentle and ironic.
Collected Poems
[M26] J Murray hbk **£9.95**

BLUE, RABBI LIONEL
Famous for his Radio 4 'Thoughts for Today'.
Portrays life with a delightful self-deprecation.
Back Door to Heaven
[M27] Fount pbk **£1.95**
Blue Heaven
[M28] Hodder hbk **£6.95**
Blue Horizons **NEW**
A new collection of stories offering Blue's unique
blend of humour and wisdom.
[M29] Hodder hbk **£8.95**
Bolts from the Blue
[M30] Hodder pbk **£1.95**
Bright Blue
[M31] BBC pbk **£2.50**

BOND, SIMON
Odd Dogs: 101 Scenes of
Canine Life **NEW**
Bond turns to dogs for his new collection.
[M32] Methuen pbk **£3.99**
One Hundred and One Uses of a
Dead Cat
An essential book for all felinophobes.
[M33] Methuen pbk **£3.50**
One Hundred and One More Uses
of a Dead Cat
[M34] Methuen pbk **£3.50**
Success and How to Be One
[M35] Methuen pbk **£2.95**
Teddy
[M36] Methuen pbk **£2.95**
Uniformity
[M37] Methuen pbk **£4.95**

Unspeakable Acts
[M38] Methuen pbk **£2.50**
What Shall We Do with the Kids in
the Holidays?
[M39] Ashford pbk **£2.99**

BOXER, MARC
Late aristocratic cartoonist, who specialized in deft
caricature.
Marc Time
[M40] Hodder pbk **£2.95**
People Like Us
[M41] Hodder hbk **£4.95**
The Times We Live In
[M42] Cape pbk **£2.50**

BOYNTON, SANDRA
Chocolate: A Consuming Passion
The illustrations are a delight, and the approach to
chocolate is sensible and even profound.
[M43] Methuen pbk **£3.95**

BROWN, CRAIG
Illustrated Collection of
Parliamentary Sketches 1987-8 **NEW**
[M44] Times Bks hbk **£7.95**

BUCKLAND, ELFREDA
The World of Donald McGill
The man who made the saucy seaside postcard into an
art form and made the rude joke a respectable
message to send home. Inimitable, naive and even
touching.
[M45] Javelin pbk **£3.95**

CAMPBELL, PATRICK
The Campbell Companion
Droll Anglo-Irish humour.
[M46] Pavilion hbk **£4.95**

CARROLL, LEWIS
Children's classics into which grown-ups love to read
things.
Humorous Verse
[M47] Dover pbk **£5.85**
The Annotated Alice (Ed. Gardener, Martin)
[M48] Penguin pbk **£2.25**
The Annotated Snark
[M49] Penguin pbk **£1.50**

Rabbi Lionel Blue, author of *Blue Horizons* (Hodder
and Stoughton hbk **£8.95**)

CARROTT, JASPER
TV comedian commits his mock-bewilderment, mock-outrage to print.
Carrott Roots
[M50] Arrow pbk **£2.50**
Little Zit on the Side
[M51] Arrow pbk **£1.95**
Sweet & Sour Labrador
[M52] Arrow pbk **£1.95**

COOK, BERYL
Prominent naive artist, either refreshingly direct or repetitively vulgar, according to one's.point of view.
Beryl Cook's New York
[M53] Penguin pbk **£3.95**
One Man Show
[M54] Penguin pbk **£3.95**
The Works
[M55] Penguin pbk **£3.95**

COOPER, JILLY
The renowned writer of potboilers and romantic novels turns her hand to domestic comedies: unashamedly over-laden with snobbery.
British in Love
A witty anthology of English romantic verse.
[M56] Arlington hbk **£6.50**
Class
[M57] Corgi pbk **£2.50**
How to Survive Christmas
[M58] Methuen pbk **£2.95**
Love & Other Heartaches
[M59] Arlington hbk **£6.50**
Super Cooper
[M60] Corgi pbk **£1.25**
Turn Right at the Spotted Dog
More of her writings from the *Mail on Sunday*.
[M61] Methuen pbk **£2.95**
Work & Wedlock
[M62] Methuen pbk **£1.50**

COWARD, NOEL
Historically interesting dissector of upper-middle class English mores of the 1930s. An elegant songsmith.
Lyrics of Noel Coward
[M63] Methuen pbk **£4.95**
Noel Coward Songbook
[M64] Methuen hbk **£15.00**

Noel Coward, author of the *Noel Coward Songbook* (Methuen hbk £15.00) (Cartoon by Marc Boxer)

DANDY / BEANO
Fifty years of 'The Dandy' & 'The Beano'
These comics have kept generations of children (and adults) entertained. With such favourites as Korky the Cat, Desperate Dan and Dennis the Menace.
[M65] DC Thompson hbk **£4.95**

DAVIS, JIM
The adventures of the popular yellow comic strip cat...
Garfield Gallery: Vols 1 - 5
[M66] Hodder hbk **£4.95**
Garfield Treasury: Vol 1
[M67] Ravette hbk **£4.95**
Garfield Treasury: Vol 2
[M68] Ravette pbk **£2.95**
Garfield Treasury: Vol 3
[M69] Ravette pbk **£2.95**

DONALDSON, WILLIAM
Great Disasters of the Stage
[M70] A Barker pbk **£4.95**

DUNN, MARY
A series of very amusing spoof autobiographies.
Lady Addle Remembers
[M71] Transworld pbk **£2.50**
Lady Addle at Home
[M72] Corgi pbk **£2.95**
The Memoirs of Mipsie
[M73] Transworld pbk **£2.50**

EBDON, JOHN
Ebdon's England
A cultivated and dry sense of humour guides the visitor round the vagaries of England and the English.
[M74] Sphere pbk **£2.75**

EDMONDS, FRANCES
Cricket XXXX Cricket
A cricketer's wife who joined her husband in Australia to watch England retain the Ashes and wrote a book the cricket elite would rather she had not.
[M75] Pan pbk **£2.99**
Members Only   NEW
Edmonds turns her one-nation Tory sarcasm on our Parliamentary representatives.
[M76] Heinemann hbk **£10.95**

FANTONI, BARRY
Cartoons
His own selection of his cartoons from *The Times* and *The Listener*.
[M77] Star pbk **£2.50**

FROST, DAVID & DEAKIN, MICHAEL
Who Wants to be a Millionaire?
[M78] Deutsch hbk **£4.95**

FROST, DAVID & SHEA, MICHAEL
Mid-Atlantic Companion
[M79] Sphere pbk **£2.95**

FULTON, RIKKI
Scotch & Wry
Since the death of Chic Murray, Scotland's best comic. His annual scoff at the idiosyncrasies of the Scottish nation are the best thing about Hogmanay.
[M80] Gordon Wr hbk **£5.95**

GRAHAM, HARRY
When Granmama Fell off the Boat: The Best of Harry Graham
Very funny Edwardian blackly comic poetry.
[M81] Methuen pbk **£4.95**

Joyce Grenfell, whose autobiography *The Time of My Life* is published by Hodder & Stoughton (hbk £15.00)

GRAHAM, LAURIE
A Marriage Survival Guide   NEW
Very funny, sardonic guide to spotting, and coping with, a partner's peccadilloes.
[M82] Chatto hbk **£8.95**

GRENFELL, JOYCE
A good example of where the enunciation of the comedienne is required for full effect. Still delightful and popular: witness Maureen Lipman's successful stage show this year.
George - Don't Do That
[M83] Futura pbk **£2.99**
In Pleasant Places
[M84] Futura pbk **£3.50**
Stately as a Galleon
[M85] Futura pbk **£2.99**
Turn Back the Clock
[M86] Futura pbk **£3.50**

GROSSMITH, GEORGE & WEEDON
The Diary of a Nobody
The shortcomings of the aspiring and perspiring Victorian clerk Mr. Pooter. A never-bettered comedy of social embarrassment.
[M87] H Hamilton hbk **£12.95**
[M88] Penguin pbk **£1.50**

HANCOCK, TONY
Truly timeless comedy of the little man everywhere conspired against. Internally consistent, and brilliantly constructed by Galton and Simpson, the 1950s radio scripts pass the test in being just as funny on the page as on the air.
Best of Hancock
[M89] Robson hbk **£6.95**
[M90] Penguin pbk **£3.95**
Hancock
[M91] BBC pbk **£2.95**
The Illustrated Hancock: The Pictorial Biography
[M92] Macdonald hbk **£10.95**
[M93] Macdonald pbk **£6.95**
Tony Hancock 'Artiste': The Complete Tony Hancock Companion
(Ed. Wilmut, Roger)
[M94] Methuen pbk **£5.95**

HEATH-ROBINSON, W.
One of Britain's most influential and inventive humorists, who perfected a style of depicting carefully-detailed and preposterous machinery.
Best of Heath Robinson
[M95] Duckworth pbk **£4.95**
The Gentle Art of Advertising
[M96] Duckworth pbk **£4.95**

Great British Industries
[M97] Duckworth pbk **£4.95**
Heath Robinson at War
[M98] Duckworth pbk **£4.95**

HERBERT, A.P.
The classic cases of Albert Haddock, exposing the farce of the Law.
Common Law
[M100] Methuen pbk **£5.95**
More Uncommon Law
[M101] Methuen pbk **£5.50**

JAMES, CLIVE
Definitely the best of an ephemeral group, the television critics. His stint at the *Observer* (*Visions Before Midnight* 1972-76 & *The Crystal Bucket* 1976-79) reveals current practitioners as derivative and flabby. James understands TV's triviality, and yet makes you interested in programmes you did not even know were on. Consistently amusing.
The Crystal Bucket
[M102] Pan pbk **£3.95**
Glued to the Box
[M103] Pan pbk **£3.95**
Visions before Midnight
[M104] Pan pbk **£3.95**

JOAN COLLINS FAN CLUB
My Life With Fanny the Wonderdog NEW
A lavishly illustrated history of Julian Clary's partnership with Fanny the Wonderdog which, as *The Joan Collins Fan Club*, has proved one of the funniest club acts of recent years.
[M105] Macmillan pbk **£5.99**

JOHNSTON, BRIAN
World's Best Maggie Thatcher Jokes NEW
[M106] BBC pbk **£1.99**

KEILLOR, GARRISON
Perfectly observed small town life in Minnesota. All human life is here. One of the rare examples of comedy which justifies the adjective 'wry'.
Happy to be Here
[M107] Faber pbk **£3.95**
Lake Wobegon Days
[M108] Faber pbk **£3.95**
Leaving Home
[M109] Faber pbk **£3.99**

Garrison Keillor, author of *Leaving Home* (Faber hbk £9.95)

Clive James, author of *The Crystal Bucket* (Pan pbk £3.95)

KINGTON, MILES
Un Four-Pack de Franglais
A collection of Kington's four volumes of Anglo-French linguistic drollery.
[M110] Penguin pbk **£3.95**

LANCASTER, OSBERT
Lady Maudie was the central character of his Pocket Cartoon in the *Daily Express*. By being consistently snobbish, self-centred and simplistic, her comments showed up the folly of politics and politicians.
Cartoon History of Architecture
[M111] Murray pbk **£7.95**
Draynflete Revealed
[M112] Murray hbk **£6.95**
Sailing to Byzantium
[M113] Murray pbk **£5.95**
Saracen's Head, or the Reluctant Crusader
[M114] Murray hbk **£6.95**
Sign of the Times: Pocket Cartoons
[M115] Murray hbk **£10.95**
The Essential Osbert Lancaster
[M116] Barrie & J hbk **£15.95**
The Life & Times of Maudie Littlehampton
[M117] Murray hbk **£7.95**
With an Eye to the Future (Memoirs)
[M118] Century pbk **£4.95**

LEAR, EDWARD
Rather like Carroll, Lear's warped, incomplete personality produced unique comedy. The best of nonsense.
Book of Learned Nonsense
[M119] WH Allen hbk **£10.95**

LEHRER, TOM
Too Many Songs by Tom Lehrer
Harvard Maths professor, and celebrated satiric song writer of the 1950s, Lehrer's lyrics have kept their satiric force: the world he sees today is too desperate even for satire, he claims.
[M120] Methuen hbk **£9.95**
[M121] Methuen pbk **£5.95**

LEWIS-SMITH, VICTOR & SPARKES, PAUL
Loose Ends: The Book
Ned Sherrin's cult Saturday morning radio programme, where he surrounds himself with the bright, and not so bright, young things, now appears in print.
[M122] Ebury pbk **£6.95**

LOW, DAVID
A New Zealander, the greatest of political cartoonists.
The Years of Wrath: A Cartoon History 1932 - 45
[M123] Gollancz pbk **£5.95**

LYNN, JONATHAN & JAY, ANTHONY
Highly perspicacious Whitehall and Downing Street satire; despite rising from ministerial to prime-ministerial rank, politician Jim Hacker needs the advice of his foil, Sir Humphrey Appleby, as much as ever.
Complete Yes Minister
[M124] BBC hbk **£12.95**
Yes Prime Minister: Volume 1
[M125] BBC hbk **£9.95**
Yes Prime Minister: Volume 2
[M126] BBC hbk **£9.95**

MARSHALL, ARTHUR
Gentle humour of a fastidious campery, now sadly old-fashioned.
Giggling in the Shrubbery
[M127] Fontana pbk **£2.50**
Whimpering in the Rhododendrons
[M128] Fontana pbk **£1.95**

MARX, GROUCHO
Groucho & Me
[M129] Columbus pbk **£5.95**
Memoirs of a Mangy Lover
[M130] Futura pbk **£1.95**

MAYLE, PETER & JOLIFFE, GRAY
Have made a fortune personalizing that part of a man that dare not speak its name. The titles tell all.
Man's Best Friend
[M131] Pan pbk **£3.95**
Twinkle Winkle: Man's Best Friend and Your Star Signs
[M132] Pan pbk **£3.95**
Wicked Willie's Guide to Male Misbehaviour
[M133] Pan pbk **£3.95**
Wicked Willie's Low Down on Women
[M134] Pan pbk **£3.95**
Willie's Away
A collection of postcards to tear out and send.
[M135] Pan pbk **£2.99**

MCALLISTER, BRIAN
Look, No Feet
A collection of political cartoons of the last few years from the *Guardian*'s front page cartoonist.
[M136] Gollancz pbk **£2.95**

MCGONAGALL, WILLIAM
The world's worst poet, who wrote some of the best unintentionally humorous poetry ever.
Library Omnibus
A collection of all of McGonagall's important writings and poetry.
[M137] Duckworth hbk **£12.95**
Poetic Gems
[M138] Duckworth pbk **£2.95**

MIKES, GEORGE
Hungarian emigré whose work shows his fascination with his adopted culture.
How To Be A Brit: A Mikes Minibus
[M139] Penguin pbk **£2.95**

How To Be An Alien
Still one of the best humorous analyses of the peculiarities of the British.
[M140] Penguin pbk **£1.95**
How To Be Decadent
[M141] Penguin pbk **£1.75**
How To Be God
[M142] Deutsch hbk **£6.95**
How To Be Poor
[M143] Penguin pbk **£1.95**

MILLIGAN, SPIKE
Madcap English humorist, some of whose best work was done in the 1950's with the Goon Shows, with Harry Secombe, Michael Bentine and Peter Sellers.
A Dustbin of Milligan
[M144] Star pbk **£1.99**
Bedside Milligan
[M145] Star pbk **£1.99**
Mirror Running
[M146] Hutchinson pbk **£5.95**
Puckoon
[M147] Penguin pbk **£2.95**
Small Dreams of a Scorpion
[M148] Penguin pbk **£1.95**
The Loony: An Irish Fantasy
[M149] Penguin pbk **£2.99**
Transports of Delight
[M150] Penguin pbk **£2.95**
Further Transports of Delight
[M151] Penguin pbk **£2.95**
AUTOBIOGRAPHY
Adolf Hitler: My Part in His Downfall
[M152] Penguin pbk **£2.50**
Goodbye Soldier
[M153] Penguin pbk **£2.95**
Monty: His Part in My Victory
[M154] Penguin pbk **£2.50**
Mussolini: His Part in My Downfall
[M155] Penguin pbk **£2.99**
Rommel? Gunner Who?
[M156] Penguin pbk **£2.50**
Where Have All the Bullets Gone?
[M157] Penguin pbk **£2.95**
Milligan's War
A selection from the six volumes of Milligan's war memoirs.
[M158] M Joseph hbk **£12.95**
GOONS
Book of the Goons
[M159] Robson pbk **£5.50**
Goon Show Scripts
[M160] Sphere pbk **£2.50**
Lost Goon Show Scripts
[M161] Sphere pbk **£3.99**
More Goon Show Scripts
[M162] Sphere pbk **£2.50**

MITFORD, NANCY
Noblesse Oblige
Concepts of class, still widely understood thirty years on, produced this witty guide to what is 'U' (upper class), and 'non-U'.
[M163] Futura pbk **£1.95**

MONTY PYTHON
A comic team which emerged from the universities in the 1960s, notable for their anarchic and very English humour; still hugely popular and commonly reprised, although its members (Cleese, Palin, Idle, Gilliam et al) have gone their separate ways.
Brand New Monty Python Papperbok
[M164] Methuen pbk **£4.95**
Complete Works of Shakespeare & Monty Python: Volume 1
[M165] Methuen pbk **£9.99**
Monty Python Gift Boks
[M166] Methuen pbk **£6.95**

Monty Python and the Holy Grail
[M167] Methuen pbk **£4.99**
Monty Python's Big Red Book
[M168] Methuen pbk **£4.95**
Monty Python: The Meaning of Life
[M169] Methuen pbk **£5.50**
The Complete Monty Python's Flying Circus: Volume 1 **NEW**
[M170] Methuen hbk **£7.99**
The Complete Monty Python's Flying Circus: Volume 2 **NEW**
[M171] Methuen hbk **£7.99**

MUNRO, MICHAEL
The Patter
A humorous look at the current Glaswegian use of English.
[M172] Glasgow District Lib pbk **£3.50**
The Patter: Another Blast
[M173] Canongate pbk **£3.95**

NALLON, STEVE
I Margaret: The Unofficial Autobiography **NEW**
Spoof autobiography written by the man who provides her voice for *Spitting Image*.
[M174] Macmillan pbk **£6.95**

Cartoon from *The New Yorker Album of Drawings 1925-75* (Penguin pbk **£4.50**)

NASH, OGDEN
Candy is Dandy: The Best of Ogden Nash
America's most popular comic poet.
[M175] Methuen pbk **£5.95**

NEW YORKER
Collections from the leading literary magazine.
The New Yorker Album of Drawings 1925 - 75
[M176] Penguin pbk **£4.50**
The New Yorker Cartoon Album 1975 - 1985
[M177] Deutsch hbk **£14.95**
[M178] Penguin pbk **£6.95**

O'ROURKE, P.J.
Holidays in Hell **NEW**
Extremely sharp & youngish Republican journalist travels to troublespots in America's 'back yard', and unerringly unearths the seedy and (unconsciously) comic aspects. Well-written, funny, cool.
[M179] Picador pbk **£3.99**
Republican Party Reptile
The confessions, adventures, essays (and other) outrages of P.J. O'Rourke.
[M180] Picador pbk **£3.50**

OXFORD ANECDOTES
A series of marvellously entertaining collections of quotations and stories, ranging in tone from the humorous to the more serious.
Oxford Book of Legal Anecdotes
[M181] Oxford hbk **£12.95**
Oxford Book of Literary Anecdotes
[M182] Oxford pbk **£5.95**
Oxford Book of Military Anecdotes
[M183] Oxford hbk **£12.50**
[M184] Oxford pbk **£5.95**
Oxford Book of Political Anecdotes
[M185] Oxford hbk **£12.50**
[M186] Oxford pbk **£4.95**

PALIN, MICHAEL & JONES, TERRY
Very funny spoof 1930s Boys' Own adventures.
Ripping Yarns
[M187] Methuen pbk **£4.95**
More Ripping Yarns
[M188] Methuen pbk **£3.95**

PARKER, DOROTHY
Classic American 20th century wit: urbane and acerbic.
Best of Dorothy Parker
[M189] Duckworth hbk **£6.95**
Collected Works
[M190] Duckworth hbk **£9.80**
Penguin Dorothy Parker
[M191] Penguin pbk **£5.95**

PARKINSON, C. NORTHCOTE
Became a household name through his Law: *"work expands to fill the time allocated to it"*.
In-Laws & Outlaws
[M192] J Murray pbk **£1.50**
Parkinson's Law or the Pursuit of Progress
[M193] Penguin pbk **£2.95**
The Law & the Profits
[M194] J Murray pbk **£1.50**
The Law, or Still in Pursuit
[M195] Penguin pbk **£3.95**

PEATTIE & TAYLOR
Alex
Post Big Bang, and Great Crash, yuppie scoundrel cartoons from the *Independent*.
[M196] Heinemann pbk **£4.95**

HUMOUR

PERELMAN, S.J.
Sophisticated American humorist who collaborated
with Groucho Marx on scripts for the Marx Brothers
films.
Best of S.J. Perelman NEW
[M197] Methuen hbk **£7.50**
Eastward Ha!
[M198] Methuen pbk **£1.95**
Last Laugh
[M199] Methuen pbk **£4.95**
**Westward Ha!: Around the World
in 80 Clichés**
[M200] Da Capo pbk **£7.95**

POTTER, STEPHEN
The Complete Upmanship
Though predicated on a politer society than that
of the present day, this is a delightful guide-book to
gaining the upper hand at work and play, brazenly or
subtly. Full of classic dinner-party gambits: if
someone talks of a country of which you know
nothing, and other guests appear equally stumped,
lean back in your chair and murmur 'But not in the
south, of course'. Don't be put off by the vulgar
cover.
[M201] Grafton pbk **£6.95**

PRATCHETT, TERRY & JOLIFFE, GRAY
The Unadulterated Cat NEW
Britains's fastest-selling cartoonist and leading SF
novelist combine in a 'Campaign for Real Cats' -
those 'not adulterated by TV commercials'.
[M202] Gollancz pbk **£3.99**

PRIVATE EYE
Originally the house magazine of some clever
Oxbridge graduates, the Eye gained great
popularity in the 1960s through some campaigning
journalism. Many consider its best days to be
behind it, but newish editor Ian Hislop (28) is
determined to recapture pole position among
satirical magazines despite a recent libel action
placing its future in the balance.
FANTONI, BARRY (ED)
Colemanballs
The malapropisms and spoonerisms of media
commentators.
[M203] Deutsch pbk **£1.95**
Colemanballs 2
[M204] Deutsch pbk **£1.95**
Colemanballs 3
[M205] Deutsch pbk **£1.95**
Colemanballs 4 NEW
[M206] Deutsch pbk **£2.50**
HISLOP, IAN
Monty Stubble: Battle for Britain
[M207] Deutsch pbk **£2.95**
**Satiric Verses: The Best of
Private Eye 1987 - 89** NEW
[M208] Deutsch pbk **£3.50**
**Secret Diary of Lord Gnome
Aged 73 & 3/4**
[M209] Deutsch pbk **£3.95**
HISLOP, IAN & INGRAMS, RICHARD
**Umberto Estrobes: The Gnome
of the Rose**
[M210] Deutsch pbk **£3.50**
HUSBAND, TONY
Yobs and Other Cartoons NEW
[M211] Deutsch pbk **£2.50**
INGRAMS, RICHARD
**Cover-Up:
Private Eye Covers** NEW
[M212] Deutsch pbk **£4.50**
INGRAMS, RICHARD & WELLS, JOHN
For several years the funniest thing in the
'Eye' by far. Perfect caricature of the Prime
Ministerial consort as a gin-swilling,
golf-club reactionary.

Self-caricature form *Scarfe on Scarfe* (Hamish
Hamilton hbk £14.95)

**Bottoms Up! Further Letters of Denis
Thatcher**
[M213] Deutsch pbk **£2.50**
**Dear Bill: The Collected Letters of
Denis Thatcher**
[M214] Deutsch pbk **£2.50**
**Just the One: Further Letters of Denis
Thatcher**
[M215] Deutsch pbk **£2.50**
No 10 NEW
Celebrating the Boss's 10 years in office and the
world's being told 'We Are a Grandmother'. Denis's
dreams turn again to retirement.
[M216] Deutsch pbk **£2.95**
**The Best of Dear Bill:
The Collected Letters of Denis
Thatcher**
[M217] Deutsch hbk **£7.95**
[M218] Sphere pbk **£3.99**

PUNCH
The old comic warhorse has still to regain its feet, a
year after the departure of Alan Coren. These
collections are from happier days.
More Cartoons from Punch
[M219] Robson pbk **£2.95**
Pick of Punch NEW
A celebration to mark the approaching 150th birthday
of *Punch*.
[M220] Grafton hbk **£10.95**
Punch at the Theatre
[M221] Robson hbk **£6.50**
Travelling Light: Punch Goes Abroad
[M222] Grafton hbk **£9.95**
APPELBAUM & KELLY (EDS)
**Great Drawings & Illustrations from
Punch 1841 - 1901**
[M223] Dover pbk **£6.00**
BARNES, PETER
Dead Funny: Punch in the Afterlife
[M224] Grafton pbk **£2.95**
COREN, ALAN
Best of Alan Coren
[M225] Robson hbk **£7.50**
HEWISON, B. (ED)
Cartoons from Punch
[M226] Robson pbk **£2.95**

HUMOUR

589

POWELL, DILYS
Punch at the Cinema
[M227] Robson hbk **£7.50**

RASPE, R.E.
The Adventures of Baron Munchausen
Extravagant fantasy this year filmed by Terry Gilliam.
[M228] Methuen pbk **£6.95**

RIGG, DIANA
No Turn Unstoned
Diana Rigg collects together some of the worst,
and the most amusing, theatrical reviews
ever written.
[M229] Arrow pbk **£2.25**

ROOT, HENRY
A brilliant idea. One man wrote spurious, ludicrous
but literate and cogent letters to famous people. Very
few saw through his wheeze, and most replied (often
pompously or patronisingly) to his absurd questions.
The Collected Letters
[M230] Futura pbk **£5.95**

ROSEN, MICHAEL
**Rude Rhymes: Mother Goose
Goes Behind the Bike Shed**   NEW
A collection of children's rhymes which, for
once, *does* include the really rude ones.
[M231] Deutsch pbk **£2.95**

SAYLE, ALEXEI
Train to Hell
The erstwhile aggressive, foul-mouthed Liverpudlian
Marxist graduate of the School of Hard Knocks offers
a surreal discursive murder mystery.
[M232] Methuen pbk **£2.95**

SCARFE, GERALD
Savage, distorted caricatures drawn by a gentle,
thoughtful man.
**Line of Attack: Collected
Political Drawings**   NEW
[M233] H Hamilton hbk **£25.00**
**Scarfe on Scarfe: An Autobiography
in Pictures**
[M234] H Hamilton hbk **£14.95**
Seven Deadly Sins
[M235] H Hamilton hbk **£14.95**

SCHULZ, CHARLES
Snoopy and Charlie Brown come from 'Peanuts', the
world's most successful comic strip.
Good 'Ol' Snoopy
[M236] Hodder pbk **£1.50**
Here Comes Snoopy
[M237] Hodder pbk **£1.50**
It's Your Turn Snoopy
[M238] Hodder pbk **£1.95**

© 1958 by United Feature Syndicate, Inc.
Snoopy, from *Good Ol' Snoopy* (Hodder pbk £1.50)

Illustration from *The Compleet Molesworth* (Pavilion
pbk £6.95)

SEARLE, RONALD
A cartoonist of distinctive line, and with a gentle
affection for those he portrays. His early reputation
was built on the rowdy girls of St. Trinian's, filmed in
the 1950s with a cast including the inimitable
Alistair Sim.
Golden Oldies
[M239] Pavilion hbk **£8.95**
Illustrated Winespeak
What the recondite terms of the wine buff mean in
pictorial terms.
[M240] Souvenir hbk **£6.95**
Ronald Searle in Perspective
A collection of work from many sources.
[M241] Hodder hbk **£19.95**
Searle's Cats
[M242] Souvenir pbk **£6.95**
Something in the Cellar
More fun at the expense of the drinker.
[M243] Souvenir hbk **£9.95**
Take One Toad
[M244] Dobson hbk **£4.50**
The Addict
[M245] Dobson hbk **£1.95**
To the Kwai and Back
Autobiography of his time as a Far East Prisoner
of War.
[M246] Collins hbk **£15.00**

SEARLE, RONALD & WILLANS, GEOFFREY
The Compleet Molesworth
Forerunner of Adrian Mole, Molesworth is the
hopeless schoolboy whose shoe laces are forever
undone.
[M247] Pavilion hbk **£8.95**
[M248] Pavilion pbk **£6.95**

SELLAR, W.C. & YEATMAN, R.J.
1066 & All That
A comic classic: a guide to English history as gleaned
by inattentive pellet-hurling schoolchildren. In the
Civil War the Roundheads (right but repulsive)
defeated the Cavaliers (wrong but wromantic).
[M249] Methuen pbk **£2.95**
And Now All This
[M250] Methuen pbk **£2.50**

SILVER, BURTON & BENNET, JEREMY
**The Naughty Victorian
Handbook**   NEW
Subtitled 'The Rediscovered Art of Erotic Hand
Manipulation', this book offers, apparently uniquely,
'tactile participation by the reader'
[M251] Bloomsbury pbk **£7.95**

SIMMONDS, POSY
Chronicler of the pretensions and problems of what
happened when the radical students of 1968 grew up,
got married and had to work. Intricate drawings
which repay close study.
Mrs Weber's Diary
[M252] Cape hbk **£6.50**
Pick of Posy
[M253] Cape hbk **£6.50**
True Love
[M254] Fontana pbk **£2.95**
Very Posy
[M255] Fontana pbk **£3.95**

SMITH, PHIL
The Phil Smith Collection   NEW
Compilation of conversations from his Radio 4
programmes where he coaxes extraordinary, touching
reminiscences from Lancashire working people. Deft,
funny and original.
[M256] BBC pbk **£2.95**

SPECTATOR, THE
The Spectator Cartoon Book
Cartoons on an enormous range of subjects - from
politics to sex, marriage, art, religion, health, food,
pets and drink. Edited by William Deedes.
[M257] Deutsch hbk **£8.95**

STAVEACRE, TONY
**Slapstick! Illustrated Story of
Knockabout Comedy**
[M258] Angus & R pbk **£7.95**

STEPTOE & SON
The Best of Steptoe and Son   NEW
Classic scripts from the television series, written
by the partnership of Galton and Simpson, and
memorably starring Wilfrid Brambell and Harry
H. Corbett.
[M259] Pan hbk **£7.95**

THE DANDY/BEANO
**Fifty Years of 'The Dandy' & 'The
Beano'**
These comics have kept generations of children
(and adults) entertained. With such favourites as
Korky the Cat, Desperate Dan and Dennis the
Menace.
[M260] DC Thompson hbk **£4.95**

THELWELL, NORMAN
Prolific cartoonist who has specialized in animals and
their owners. Most well-known for his little girls on
enormous ponies, this is innocent, old-fashioned
work, where nubile women are likely to be called
Miss Hipkiss.
A Leg at Each Corner
[M261] Methuen pbk **£2.50**
Angels on Horseback
[M262] Methuen pbk **£2.50**
Belt Up!
Thelwell's Motoring Manual
[M263] Methuen pbk **£1.99**
Effluent Society
[M264] Methuen pbk **£2.50**
Play it as it Lies
Cartoons on Golf.
[M265] Methuen pbk **£2.50**
Pony Cavalcade
[M266] Methuen pbk **£3.95**
**Some Damned Fool's Signed the
Rubens Again**
The perils of opening a Stately Home to the
undeserving public.
[M267] Methuen pbk **£2.50**
The Compleat Tangler
Fishing is the subject.
[M268] Methuen pbk **£2.50**

HUMOUR

ICTION AND FANTASY · FOOD AND COOKERY · HEALTH AND FITNESS · HUMOUR · GAMES AND PUZZLES · CRIME

ND THRILLERS · PHILOSOPHY AND POLITICS · PSYCHOLOGY AND SCIENCE · TRAVEL WRITING AND GUIDE BOOKS

REVISION NOTES AND STUDY AIDS · RELIGION AND REFERENCE · ECONOMICS AND ENVIRONMENT · LANGUAGE

ND LINGUISTICS · TWENTIETH CENTURY CLASSICS · NEW AGE AND SHORT STORIES · AUTOBIOGRAPHY AND

IOGRAPHY · POLITICS AND CURRENT AFFAIRS · CONTEMPORARY FICTION · PENGUIN CLASSICS · GIFT BOOKS

ND GARDENING · ART AND AR   CIENCE FICTION AND FANTASY ·

OOD AND COOKERY · HEALTH   CRIME AND THRILLERS · PHI-

OSOPHY AND POLITICS · PSYC   IDE BOOKS · REVISION NOTES

ND STUDY AIDS · RELIGION A   LANGUAGE AND LINGUISTICS ·

WENTIETH CENTURY CLASSIC   HY AND BIOGRAPHY · POLITICS

PENGUIN
BOOKS

All your reading needs

ND CURRENT AFFAIRS · CONT   OOKS AND GARDENING · ART AND

RCHITECTURE · HISTORY · P   Y · FOOD AND COOKERY ·

EALTH AND FITNESS · HUMOU   · PHILOSOPHY AND POLITICS ·

YCHOLOGY AND SCIENCE · TRAVEL WRITING AND GUIDE BOOKS · REVISION NOTES AND STUDY AIDS · RELIGION

ND REFERENCE · ECONOMICS AND ENVIRONMENT · LANGUAGE AND LINGUISTICS · TWENTIETH CENTURY CLAS-

CS · NEW AGE AND SHORT STORIES · AUTOBIOGRAPHY AND BIOGRAPHY · POLITICS AND CURRENT AFFAIRS ·

ONTEMPORARY FICTION · PENGUIN CLASSICS · GIFT BOOKS AND GARDENING · ART AND ARCHITECTURE · HIS-

ORY · POETRY AND PLAYS · SCIENCE FICTION AND FANTASY · FOOD AND COOKERY · HEALTH AND FITNESS ·

UMOUR · GAMES AND PUZZLES · CRIME AND THRILLERS · PHILOSOPHY AND POLITICS · PSYCHOLOGY AND

CIENCE · TRAVEL WRITING AND GUIDE BOOKS · REVISION NOTES AND STUDY AIDS · RELIGION AND REFERENCE ·

CONOMICS AND ENVIRONMENT · LANGUAGE AND LINGUISTICS · TWENTIETH CENTURY CLASSICS · NEW AGE AND

ORT STORIES · AUTOBIOGRAPHY AND BIOGRAPHY · POLITICS AND CURRENT AFFAIRS · CONTEMPORARY FICTION

ENGUIN CLASSICS · GIFT BOOKS AND GARDENING · ART AND ARCHITECTURE · HISTORY · POETRY AND PLAYS ·

IENCE FICTION AND FANTASY · FOOD AND COOKERY · HEALTH AND FITNESS · HUMOUR · GAMES AND PUZZLES

RIME AND THRILLERS · PHILOSOPHY AND POLITICS · PSYCHOLOGY AND SCIENCE · TRAVEL WRITING AND

UIDE BOOKS · REVISION NOTES AND STUDY AIDS · RELIGION AND REFERENCE · ECONOMICS AND ENVIRONMENT

Cartoon by **Thelwell**, all of whose work is published by Methuen.

The Pony Panorama
Includes *Penelope*, *Thellwell's Gymkhana* and *Thelwell Goes West*.
[M269] Methuen pbk **£8.95**
Thelwell Country
Collected cartoons.
[M270] Methuen pbk **£1.99**
Thelwell's Brat Race
His children can be at times less than endearing.
[M271] Methuen pbk **£2.50**
Thelwell's Riding Academy
[M272] Magnum books pbk **£2.50**
This Desirable Plot
The problems of acquiring a house.
[M273] Methuen pbk **£2.50**
Three Sheets in the Wind
Thelwell goes sailing.
[M274] Methuen pbk **£2.50**
Top Dog: Thelwell's Complete Canine Companion
[M275] Methuen pbk **£2.50**
Up the Garden Path
[M276] Methuen pbk **£2.50**
Wrestling with a Pencil: The Life of a Freelance Artist
Autobiography.
[M277] Methuen hbk **£12.50**

THOMAS-ELLIS, ALICE
As with Jeffrey Bernard above, this is a collection of essays from *The Spectator*, but as befits a famous lady novelist, more gentle and domestic, and showing a different but no less effective brand of humour.
Home Life
[M278] Fontana pbk **£2.95**
More Home Life
[M279] Flamingo pbk **£3.95**
Home Life Three **NEW**
[M280] Duckworth hbk **£9.95**

THOMPSON, HUNTER S.
Life on the edge in America. Cult comedies of debauchery, drugs, despair and delirium.
Fear and Loathing in Las Vegas
[M281] Grafton pbk **£2.95**
The Great Shark Hunt
[M282] Pan pbk **£5.95**

THURBER, JAMES
The most affecting American humorist (whose humour grew from experiences which disturbed or embarrassed him), whether writing about his own fantasy life, or the plight of mild unworldly men trying to deal with bullies or domineering women.
Let Your Mind Alone
[M283] Methuen pbk **£3.95**
Middle Aged Man & the Flying Trapeze
[M284] Methuen pbk **£3.50**

The Thirteen Clocks & the Wonderful 'O'
[M285] Penguin pbk **£1.95**
Thurber Carnival
[M286] Penguin pbk **£5.95**
Thurber's Dogs
[M287] Dent pbk **£2.95**
Vintage Thurber: Vol 1
[M288] H Hamilton hbk **£9.95**
[M289] H Hamilton pbk **£4.99**
Vintage Thurber: Vol 2 **NEW**
[M290] H Hamilton hbk **£9.95**
[M291] H hamilton pbk **£4.99**

TIMPSON, JOHN
The former stalwart of the Radio 4 flagship looks on the funnier side of the long-running programme.
Early Morning Book
[M292] Fontana pbk **£3.95**
Lighter Side of 'Today'
[M293] Unwin Hyman pbk **£1.75**

TOWNSEND, SUE
Adrian Mole is *the* infamous media star, diarist and anxiety-ridden pseudo-intellectual teenager. Fatally spotty and gauche, he has proved fodder for spin-offs (and rip-offs).
Bits and Pieces from Adrian Mole **NEW**
A collection of Adrian Mole's further writings and broadcasts which take him to the age of 21 1/3; as well as celebrated pages from the diary of Margaret Hilda Roberts, the Grantham grocer's daughter, and pieces written under Townsend's own name.
[M294] Methuen pbk **£4.99**
The Adrian Mole Diaries Omnibus
[M295] Methuen hbk **£7.95**
The Diary of Adrian Mole Aged 13 & 3/4
[M296] Methuen pbk **£2.95**
The Growing Pains of Adrian Mole
[M297] Methuen pbk **£2.95**

TRUDEAU, GARY
Dry, syndicated cartoonist of North American politics.
Check Your Eyes at the Door
[M298] Sphere pbk **£2.95**
In Search of Reagan's Brain
[M299] Hodder pbk **£1.95**
That's Doctor Sinatra, You Little Bimbo
[M300] Sphere pbk **£2.95**
You Give Great Meeting, Sid
[M301] Hodder pbk **£1.95**

TWEEDIE, JILL
Ex-*Guardian* columnist offers gently ironic advice for the young woman of today.
It's Only Me
[M302] Robson hbk **£6.95**
Letters from a Fainthearted Feminist
[M303] Robson hbk **£5.95**
More from Martha **NEW**
[M304] Robson hbk **£5.95**

VIZ
Big Pink Stiff One
A collection of editions 18 to 25 of the publishing sensation of the last twelve months. A comic produced on a shoestring by Newcastle schoolfriends in their mid-twenties, it now sells ten times as many copies as *Private Eye*. It is a vicious parody of children's comics, the popular press, women's magazine letters pages, and anything else in sight. The humour is largely lavatorial, leavened with ultra-violence.
[M305] John Brown hbk **£5.95**

WATERHOUSE, KEITH
Top-notch journalist, now ensconced at the *Daily Mail*, Waterhouse has for years been offering a trenchant Northerner's view of goings-on. A gifted playwright and novelist to boot.
Collected Letters of a Nobody
[M306] M Joseph hbk **£9.95**
Office Life
[M307] Grafton pbk **£2.50**
Theory and Practice of Lunch
A set text for journalists.
[M308] M Joseph pbk **£5.95**
Waterhouse at Large
[M309] Grafton pbk **£3.95**

WAUGH, AUBERON
Waugh decided early in life to emulate his father Evelyn and adopted an extremely reactionary satirical stance, observing life with disdain from his Somerset squirarchical fastness. Aged beyond his years, now at fifty he seems rather to have caught himself up. His aim in his *Private Eye* and now *Sunday Telegraph* columns has been to provoke reaction in others. Life viewed amusingly through the bottom of a fine glass of claret.
Another Voice
[M310] Fontana pbk **£3.95**

WINOKUR, JON
The Portable Curmudgeon **NEW**
A collection of the utterances of Curmudgeons (a species defined as 'a cynic, debunker or awkward cuss') from Oscar Wilde to Evelyn Waugh, and Dorothy Parker to S.J. Perelman. Over 1,000 wicked quotations.
[M311] Gollancz pbk **£3.99**

WOOD, VICTORIA
Prize-winning comedienne, currently one of the funniest of either sex, who specializes in vulgarity and brilliantly-sustained comedies of embarrassment.
Barmy **NEW**
[M312] Methuen pbk **£3.95**
Lucky Bag: The Victoria Wood Songbook
[M313] Methuen pbk **£4.95**
Up to You Porky: The Victoria Wood Sketch Book
[M314] Methuen pbk **£2.95**

Victoria Wood, author of *Barmy* (Methuen pbk **£3.95**)

English Literature: General & by Period
American Literature
European & World Literature
Literary Theory
Language & Linguistics

Literature

LITERARY CRITICISM

Literary criticism is a huge field, ranging from illustrated biographies of famous authors to advanced philosophical accounts of the function of language. This chapter attempts to give a broad selection of books available from the important publishers (i.e. Oxford, Cambridge, Harvester, Routledge, Blackwell, Macmillan) providing for the needs of both the student and the general reader. It is roughly divided in two halves: the first section lists historical and thematic studies by region; the second is devoted to literary theory. The emphasis throughout is on new and recent books; studies of themes or histories are preferred over monographs and secondary texts. Literary biographies are listed separately in the *Biography* chapter.

English Literature

Reference

BENET, WILLIAM ROSE (ED)
The Reader's Encyclopaedia (3rd Ed)
More than 9,000 entries on World Literature from the earliest times to the present day. In addition to information on specific authors and works, the encyclopaedia also provides details of historical events, characters, myths, legends, relevant artistic movements, terminology and literary awards.
[N1] A & C Black hbk **£19.95**

BOLD, ALAN & GIDDINGS, ROBERT
Who Was Really Who in Fiction
A study of 600 real people on whom fictional characters were based.
[N3] Longman hbk **£12.95**

CUDDON, J.A.
Dictionary of Literary Terms
[N5] Penguin pbk **£7.99**

DRABBLE, MARGARET (ED)
Oxford Companion to English Literature
Fifth edition of the most detailed reference guide to literature in English from all periods. It covers authors, individual works, literary schools and movements.
[N6] Oxford hbk **£19.50**
[N7] Oxford leather **£35.00**
Concise Oxford Companion to English Literature
An abridged version of the *Oxford Companion* which includes updates and a number of new entries.
[N8] Oxford hbk **£12.95**

EAGLE, DOROTHY (ED)
Concise Oxford Dictionary of English Literature
An abridgement of Sir Paul Harvey's *Oxford Companion to English Literature*.
[N9] Oxford pbk **£5.95**

MCLEISH, KENNETH (ED)
Bloomsbury Good Reading Guide
Guide through world literature which is both an A - Z reference book for particulars and, by cross-referencing, a thematic guide for popular fiction and classic literature.
[N14] Bloomsbury pbk **£5.99**

MYERS, JACK & SIMMS, MICHAEL (EDS)
Longman Dictionary and Handbook of Poetry
Combining the features of a dictionary and an encyclopaedia this compendium gathers together definitions of poetry from the classical era through to the present.
[N15] Longman hbk **£23.00**

OUSBY, IAN (ED)
The Cambridge Guide to Literature in English
Biographical and critical articles on creative writers, critics, themes and genres. It is particularly impressive on non-British writing in English and on contemporary writers. Introduced by Maragaret Atwood.
[N16] Cambridge hbk **£17.95**

ROYLE, TREVOR (ED)
Macmillan Companion to Scottish Literature
[N17] Macmillan pbk **£9.95**

STEPHENS, MEIC (ED)
Oxford Companion to the Literature of Wales
[N18] Oxford hbk **£17.50**

WYNNE-DAVIES, MARION (ED)
Bloomsbury Guide to English Literature   NEW
An impressive new reference book which, in addition to 6,500 entries arranged A-Z, includes 12 essays on the historical and social context of English literature, contemporary critical approaches to literature, the history and development of the main genres, and medieval literature.
[N20] Bloomsbury hbk **£19.95**

History

A CRITICAL HISTORY OF ENGLISH LITERATURE
A new edition of his classic history of English literature.
DAICHES, DAVID
Vol 1: From the Beginnings to the 16th Century
[N22] Secker pbk **£9.95**
Vol 2: Shakespeare to Milton
[N24] Secker pbk **£8.95**
Vol 3: The Restoration to 1800
[N26] Secker pbk **£9.95**
Vol 4: The Romantics to the Present Day
[N28] Secker pbk **£9.95**

A HISTORY OF MODERN CRITICISM 1750 - 1950
'Professor Wellek's highly readable study is an excellent introduction to the history of modern criticism for both the general student and the specialist alike.' (*Times Literary Supplement*)
WELLEK, RENE
Vol 1: The Later 18th Century
[N29] Cambridge pbk **£12.95**
Vol 2: The Romantic Age
[N30] Cambridge pbk **£15.00**
Vol 3: The Later 19th Century
[N31] Cambridge pbk **£15.00**
Vol 4: The Age of Transitions
[N32] Cambridge pbk **£15.00**

Vol 5: English Criticism 1900 - 1950
[N33] Cape hbk **£20.00**
Vol 6: American Criticism 1900 - 1950
[N34] Cape hbk **£20.00**

BLAMIRES, HARRY
A Short History of English Literature
Second edition of this concise history of English literature from Chaucer to the 1980s. Blamires provides information on individual authors' lives, works and personalities as well as a general sense of each period and the development of literature as a whole.
[N36] Methuen pbk **£6.50**

CONRAD, PETER
Everyman History of English Literature
A brilliant study of the development of literature over a period of 1,200 years which stresses the relationships between individual writers and continuities of form and theme.
[N37] Dent pbk **£7.95**

DEANE, SEAMUS (ED)
Short History of Irish Literature
[N38] Hutchinson pbk **£6.95**

ENGLISH LITERATURE IN ITS CONTEXT
Subtitled 'Studies in the Idea of Nature in the Thought of the Period', both these classic studies appear on most reading lists for their respective periods.
WILLEY, BASIL
Vol 1: The 17th Century Background
[N39] Ark pbk **£3.95**
Vol 2: The 18th Century Background
[N40] Ark pbk **£3.95**

EVANS, SIR IFOR
Short History of English Literature
Updated by Bernard Bergonzi for the present edition (1974), Ifor Evans's book is still a very popular and respected study of literature from the earliest times to the 20th century.
[N41] Penguin pbk **£3.99**

FOWLER, ALASTAIR
A History of English Literature
Ambitious, stylish overview of writers, literary genres, forms and historical events from the Middle Ages to Post Modernism.
[N42] Blackwell hbk **£17.50**

MACMILLAN ANTHOLOGIES OF ENGLISH LITERATURE   NEW
A series of beautifully produced anthologies which contain a representative and wide-ranging selection of drama, poetry and prose arranged chronologically, supported by full notes and biographical details of authors included. The first real alternative to the Norton series and excellent value for money.
JEFFARES, A. NORMAN & ALEXANDER, MICHAEL (EDS)
Vol 1: The Middle Ages 700 - 1500
(Ed. Alexander, M. & Liddy, F.)
[N44] Macmillan hbk **£29.95**
[N45] Macmillan pbk **£8.95**
Vol 2: The Renaissance 1550 - 1660
(Ed. Campbell, G.)
[N46] Macmillan hbk **£29.95**
[N47] Macmillan pbk **£8.95**
Vol 3: The Restoration and 18th Century 1660 - 1798
(Ed. McGowan, I.)
[N48] Macmillan hbk **£29.95**
[N48A] Macmillan pbk **£8.95**

Volume 4: The 19th Century
1798 - 1900 (Ed. Martin, Brian)
[N51] Macmillan hbk **£29.95**
[N52] Macmillan pbk **£8.95**
Volume 5: The 20th Century
1900 - The Present (Ed. McEwan, Neil)
[N49] Macmillan hbk **£29.95**
[N50] Macmillan pbk **£8.95**

NEW PELICAN GUIDE TO ENGLISH LITERATURE
The standard literary history series for anyone who
wants to seek out the context which informs English
literature. Each volume includes a selection of essays
on the key figures of the period.
FORD, BORIS (ED)
Vol 1: Part 1 Medieval Literature
[N53] Penguin pbk **£4.99**
Vol 1: Part 2 The European Inheritance
[N54] Penguin pbk **£5.99**
Vol 2: The Age of Shakespeare
[N55] Penguin pbk **£4.99**
Vol 3: From Donne to Marvell
[N56] Penguin pbk **£4.95**
Vol 4: From Dryden to Johnson
[N57] Penguin pbk **£4.99**
Vol 5: From Blake to Byron
[N58] Penguin pbk **£4.99**
Vol 6: From Dickens to Hardy
[N59] Penguin pbk **£4.99**
Vol 7: From James to Eliot
[N60] Penguin pbk **£5.50**
Vol 8: The Present Day
[N61] Penguin pbk **£5.50**
Vol 9: American Literature
[N62] Penguin pbk **£6.99**

ROGERS, PAT (ED)
Oxford Illustrated History of English Literature
In this lavishly illustrated volume, the richness,
diversity and continuity of Britain's literary tradition
is explored by a group of prominent scholars.
[N63] Oxford hbk **£16.50**

SAMPSON, GEORGE (ED)
Concise Cambridge History of English Literature
[N65] Cambridge pbk **£17.50**

SPHERE HISTORY OF LITERATURE
Straightforward general accounts, uncluttered by
jargon, informed by English critical attitudes.
Vol 1: The Middle Ages (Ed. Bolton, N.F.)
[N67] Sphere pbk **£4.95**
Vol 2: English Poetry and Prose
1540 - 16 (Ed. Ricks, C.)
[N68] Sphere pbk **£4.95**
Vol 3: English Drama to 1710
(Ed. Ricks, C.)
[N69] Sphere pbk **£5.99**
Vol 4: Dryden to Johnson (Ed. Lonsdale, R.)
[N70] Sphere pbk **£5.99**
Vol 6: The Victorians (Ed. Pollard, A.)
[N71] Sphere pbk **£5.99**
Vol 8: American Literature to 1800
(Ed. Cunliffe, M.)
[N72] Sphere pbk **£4.95**
Vol 9: American Literature to 1900
(Ed. Cunliffe, M.)
[N73] Sphere pbk **£5.99**
Vol 10: The English Language
(Ed. Bolton, N.F.)
[N66] Sphere pbk **£5.99**

THE HISTORY OF SCOTTISH LITERATURE
The research of more than eighty scholars gives a
comprehensive modern view of Scottish literature that

spills over into the wider cultural context; the essays
cover many authors and themes and all three
languages of Scotland.
CRAIG, CAIRNS (ED)
Vol 1: Medieval and Renaissance
[N74] Aberdeen UP hbk **£18.50**
Vol 2: 1660-1800
[N75] Aberdeen UP hbk **£18.50**
Vol 3: 19th Century
[N76] Aberdeen UP hbk **£18.50**
Vol 4: 20th Century
[N77] Aberdeen UP hbk **£18.50**

THE NORTON ANTHOLOGY OF ENGLISH LITERATURE
These anthologies of poetry and prose provide so
much in the way of introductions, notes and
discussion of contemporary assumptions that they
serve as superb guides through the whole span of
English literature, from Anglo-Saxon poetry right up
to the modern novel.
ABRAMS, M.H. & OTHERS (EDS)
Volume 1
Covers the period from the Middle Ages to the
Restoration.
[N81] Norton pbk **£12.95**
Volume 2
Begins with a study of the Romantic poets and goes
on to cover the 19th and 20th centuries.
[N83] Norton pbk **£12.95**
Major Authors
[N79] Norton pbk **£14.50**

THE OXFORD ANTHOLOGY OF ENGLISH LITERATURE
Two-volume anthology (also available in six
individual volumes) edited by two of the most
distinguished contemporary literary critics. They
include useful notes, a glossary of theories and terms,
and excellent bibliographies.
KERMODE, FRANK & HOLLANDER, JOHN (EDS)
Vol 1 - 3
From medieval literature to the end of the 18th
century.
[N84] Oxford pbk **£16.50**
Vol 4 - 6
From the Romantic period through to modern British
literature.
[N85] Oxford pbk **£16.50**

WATSON, RODERICK
The Literature of Scotland
A broad survey of writing in English and Gaelic with
considerable space allotted to less-celebrated Scottish
authors and special emphasis on parallel
developments in music and the fine arts.
[N86] Macmillan pbk **£8.95**

Series

CRITICAL IDIOM SERIES
The volumes of this series deal with the key terms of
our critical vocabulary. The studies examine the
nature of each term, its historical development and its
meaning for the contemporary reader. The following
titles are currently available:
Romance, Rhetoric, Genre, Metre Rhyme and Free
Verse, The Sonnet, Romanticism, Realism, The
Absurd, Lyric, Allegory, Comedy, The Epic, Satire.
[N87] Methuen pbk **£3.95 -£4.50**

HARVESTER FEMINIST READINGS
A new series which investigates the links between
creative writing and feminist reading by surveying the
key works of English literature from a feminist

perspective. The following titles available:
Nathaniel Hawthorne, Alfred Lord Tennyson,
Renaissance Dramatists, Thomas Hardy, James
Joyce, D.H. Lawrence, Milton, Marvell, Geoffrey
Chaucer, T.S. Eliot, Shakespeare.
[N100] Harvester pbk **£7.95**

HARVESTER KEY WOMEN WRITERS
Useful series of feminist readings of major women
writers. These are readable and concise studies
offering both social and literary criticism. Titles
available:
George Eliot , Emily Dickinson, Charlotte Brontë,
H.D. The Career of that Struggle, Katherine
Mansfield, Iris Murdoch, Colette, Rebecca West,
Elizabeth Barrett Browning, Elizabeth Gaskell.
[N110] Harvester pbk **£7.95**

MACMILLAN CASEBOOKS
Excellent series of collected critical essays covering
all the major authors and works in English literature.
Recent highlights include the following thematic
titles:
The Gothic Novel, Issues in Contemporary Critical
Theory, Poetry Criticism: Developments since the
Symbolists, Studying Shakespeare: Critical
Approaches.
[N111] Macmillan pbk **£7.95**

MACMILLAN MODERN NOVELISTS
A series which charts the radical changes that have
taken place in the novel in the 20th century, featuring
those writers who have thematically, structurally, or
stylistically extended the genre. Titles available:
H.G. Wells, William Golding, Graham Greene, John
Updike, E.M. Forster, Doris Lessing, Gustave
Flaubert, Fyodor Dostoevsky, Albert Camus,
William Faulkner, Henry James, Evelyn Waugh,
Macolm Lowry, Marcel Proust, Six Women
Novelists.
[N117] Macmillan pbk **£6.95**

MACMILLAN WOMEN WRITERS
A series of critical introductions to women writers,
written by women. Invaluable as background reading
for 'A' level. Titles available:
Sylvia Plath, Christina Stead, Margaret Atwood,
Fanny Burney, Charlotte Brontë.
[N121] Macmillan pbk **£5.95**

METHUEN CONTEMPORARY WRITERS
Stimulating series of monographs that provide an
ideal introduction to the major names in
contemporary world literature. The following titles
are available:
J.G. Farrell, Muriel Spark, Saul Bellow, John
Fowles, Margaret Drabble, Alain Robbe-Grillet,
Kurt Vonnegut, Seamus Heaney, Philip Larkin,
Doris Lessing, Graham Greene, Iris Murdoch, John
Barth, Joe Orton, Harold Pinter, Ted Hughes.
[N134] Methuen pbk **£3.95 - £4.50**

HARVESTER NEW READINGS
Like Blackwell's *Rereading Literature* series, these
studies seek to apply the most appropriate critical and
theoretical principles to each individual author (rather
than applying a single traditional or contemporary
approach to the whole series). Titles available:
Chaucer, D.H. Lawrence, Dickens, Donne, George
Eliot, Keats, Pope, Shakespeare, Spenser, Swift, T.S.
Eliot, Wordsworth.
[N141] Harvester pbk **£7.95**

LONGMAN PREFACE SERIES
Straightforward introductions to each writer,
concentrating on individual works. They are most
useful as school/university study aids. The following

titles are available:

James Joyce, E.M.Forster, Jane Austen, Dickens, Shelley, Milton, George Eliot, Wordsworth, Henry James, Auden, Lawrence, Hopkins, Keats, Hardy, Donne, Orwell, The Brontës, T.S. Eliot, Pope.
[N166] Longman pbk **£7.95**

BLACKWELL REREADING LITERATURE SERIES

Challenging and intelligent use of modern critical practice as a way of elucidating the particular nature of individual writers. This series has commissioned some of the most stimulating young British critics; especially interesting are the studies of Chaucer (Knight), Milton (Belsey), Dickens (Connor), and Wordsworth (Hamilton).
Titles available:
John Milton, James Joyce, Virginia Woolf, Pope, Charles Dickens, Wordsworth, Samuel Beckett, Geoffrey Chaucer, Blake, Alfred Tennyson, W.H. Auden, Ben Jonson, Charlotte Brontë, Thomas Hardy, William Shakespeare.
[N178] Blackwell pbk **£4.95**

READER'S GUIDES

Detailed companions to an author's work, combining close readings of the texts with biographical, historical and cultural contexts. Hugh Kenner 's *Beckett*, and John Unterecker's *Yeats* are outstanding critical works in their own right. Titles available:
Charles Dickens, D.H. Lawrence, Samuel Beckett, Gerard Manley Hopkins, George Orwell, W.B. Yeats, T.S. Eliot, Geoffrey Chaucer, Graham Greene, The Metaphysical Poets, Robert Lowell.
[N179] Thames & H pbk **£6.95**

THE CRITICAL HERITAGE

Each volume traces the critical reception of a writer and his work from the earliest reviews to the present day. Invaluable for the student; fascinating for the general reader. Titles available: *Auden, Jane Austen (2 vols), Chekhov, Conrad, Dickens, Hawthorne, Hemingway, Hopkins, Henry James, Joyce, Lawrence, Malory, Somerset Maugham, Dos Passos, Orwell, Poe, Shakespeare (6 vols), Smollett, Sterne, Stevens, Tennyson, Walpole, Woolf, Dante, Proust, Plath, Congreve.*
[N187] Routledge hbk **£30.00 - £75.00**

TWENTIETH CENTURY VIEWS

Prestigious American series. Each volume is edited by a well-known critic and includes a range of modern critical essays based around authors rather than works. The complete list covers most of the major names in English literature; recent titles include: *Austen, Donne, Hardy, Wilde, Dickens, Forster, Greene, Dylan Thomas, Camus.*
[N1871] Prentice Hall pbk **£4.95**

WRITERS AT WORK.

PLIMPTON, GEORGE (ED)
Compelling series of interviews with modern writers from the *Paris Review.*
Series 1
Includes E.M. Forster, Faulkner, Capote and Moravia.
[N188] Penguin pbk **£5.95**
Series 2
Includes T.S. Eliot, Pasternak, Henry Miller, and Aldous Huxley.
[N189] Penguin pbk **£6.50**
Series 3
Includes Cocteau, Burroughs, Waugh and William Carlos Williams.
[N190] Penguin pbk **£5.95**
Series 4
Includes Auden, Borges, Kerouac and Updike.
[N191] Penguin pbk **£6.99**

Series 5
Includes Neruda, Vidal, Wodehouse and Isaac Bashevis Singer.
[N192] Penguin pbk **£5.95**
Series 6
Includes Marquez, Spender, Vonnegut and Rebecca West.
[N193] Penguin pbk **£6.99**

General Studies

ALLEN, WALTER
The English Novel
A stimulating appraisal of important novelists and their work from *Pilgrim's Progress* to *Sons and Lovers*.
[N194] Penguin pbk **£4.99**
The Short Story in English
[N195] Oxford pbk **£7.95**

BILLINGTON, SANDRA
Social History of the Fool
This fascinating book pursues the history of the Fool and his role in society and literature from 1220 to 1850.
[N197] Harvester pbk **£10.95**

BOULTON, MARJORIE
The Anatomy of Poetry
'Its analysis of poetic methods and processes is both lucid and acute.' (*Listener*)
[N198] Routledge pbk **£6.95**
The Anatomy of the Novel
A basic analysis of the formal elements of the novel.
[N199] Routledge pbk **£6.95**

BULL, JOHN A.
The Framework of Fiction: Socio-Cultural Approaches to the Novel
Evaluates the main theoretical attempts from Marx onwards to relate the novel to society and ideology, and also examines how factors such as publishing methods and audience composition have influenced its formal development.
[N200] Macmillan pbk **£7.95**

CHAMBERLAIN, MARY
Writing Lives
This collection brings together the older generation of Virago's writers with their younger successors who interview them. Features Maya Angelou, Molly Keane, Rosamund Lehmann, Grace Paley and Eudora Welty.
[N201] Virago pbk **£7.95**

FORD, FORD MADOX
The English Novel
A respected study, particularly illuminating on the development and legacy of the 19th century novel (with special reference to the work of Flaubert and Conrad). '*In perusing this book,*' Ford writes, '*the reader must be prepared to do a great deal of the work himself - within his own mind.*'
[N203] Carcanet pbk **£3.95**

HAFFENDEN, JOHN (ED)
Novelists in Interview
'Intelligent, scrupulous, detailed interviews with leading British novelists, with among others a slightly cagey William Golding, a somewhat dismayingly articulate Martin Amis and a remarkably revealing Anita Brookner.' (*Sunday Times*)
[N204] Methuen pbk **£8.95**

HOUGH, GRAHAM
Selected Essays
Hough's subjects include Coleridge, Austen,

Tennyson, Poe, Yeats, T.S. Eliot and John Crowe Ransom.
[N208] Cambridge pbk **£8.50**

KENYON, OLGA
Women Novelists Today
An ambitious and wide-ranging study which considers the development of a tradition in women's writing since the feminist 'revolution' of the 1960s.
[N209] Harvester pbk **£9.95**

KETTLE, ARNOLD
Introduction to the English Novel
A famous introduction to the novel from a Marxist perspective, recently updated.
Vol 1
[N210] Hutchinson pbk **£7.95**
Vol 2
[N211] Hutchinson pbk **£8.50**

KNIGHTS, L.C.
Selected Essays in Criticism
Covers authors as diverse as Marlowe, George Herbert, Clarendon, and Henry James.
[N212] Cambridge pbk **£12.95**

MILLER, KARL
Doubles: Studies in Literary History
The double - man's duality, the doppelänger, the second self - has preoccupied writers from antiquity to the present. Miller examines this phenomenon from the Wolf man in the Romantic era to modern examples in the work of Norman Mailer, Sylvia Plath and Martin Amis, ending with a note to John Lennon.
[N213] Oxford pbk **£6.95**

Medieval Literature

GENERAL STUDIES

ALEXANDER, MICHAEL
Old English Literature
Surveys Old English poetry and prose from its Germanic origins until its eclipse after the Norman Conquest, with generous verse extracts.
[N215] Macmillan pbk **£7.95**

Geoffrey Chaucer from an illustration in *The Reader's Digest Great Illustrated Dictionary* (hbk £19.95)

BENNETT, J.A.W
Middle English Literature
A comprehensive, authoritative and readable study of
English literature from *The Owl and the Nightingale*
to *Piers Plowman*.
[N216] Oxford hbk **£25.00**

BREWER, DEREK
English Gothic Literature
Brewer argues for a formal style in works such as
those of Chaucer, Langland's *Piers Plowman*,
Malory's *Morte D'Arthur* and the poems of the
Gawain Poet. This style is as characteristic as the
religious achievement of Gothic art and
architecture.
[N217] Macmillan pbk **£7.95**

BURROW, JOHN
**Medieval Writers and Their Work:
Literature and its Background
1100 - 1500**
An enjoyable and informative introduction to English
language, literature and society from the Norman
Conquest to the Middle Ages.
[N218] Oxford pbk **£4.95**

LEWIS, C.S.
Lewis's criticism of medieval literature is both
scholarly and romantic, drawing parallels throughout
with subsequent literary developments.
**Studies in Medieval and Renaissance
Literature**
[N220] Cambridge pbk **£10.95**
The Allegory of Love
[N221] Oxford pbk **£6.95**
**The Discarded Image:
An Introduction to Medieval and
Renaissance Literature**
[N222] Cambridge pbk **£8.95**

SPEARING, A.C.
The leading critic of medieval poetry.
Medieval Dream Poetry
[N223] Cambridge pbk **£11.95**
**Medieval to Renaissance in
English Poetry**
[N224] Cambridge pbk **£11.95**
Readings in Medieval Poetry **NEW**
A stimulating collection of linked essays covering the
medieval romances, Chaucer, Langland, Malory and
the Gawain Poet.
[N226] Cambridge pbk **£9.95**

SWANTON, MICHAEL
English Literature Before Chaucer
This stimulating introduction to the literature of
the pre-Chaucerian centuries (from *Beowulf* to *The
Owl and the Nightinglae*) abandons the division of
the Old and Middle English worlds, in order to
encourage more direct appreciation and critical
appraisal.
[N227] Longman pbk **£7.95**

VANCE, EUGENE
**Marvellous Signals: Poetics and Sign
Theory in the Middle Ages**
This is an important study of poetry in the
medieval era, showing the link between semiotics
and poetics. It elucidates the background of such
writers as St Augustine, Spenser, Chaucer and
Dante.
[N228] Nebraska UP pbk **£11.65**

WRENN, C.L.
A Study of Old English Literature
A classic which surveys literary writing in
England from Caedmon to the Norman
Conquest.
[N229] Harrap pbk **£10.35**

INDIVIDUAL WRITERS
CHAUCER, GEOFFREY
BREWER, DEREK
An Introduction to Chaucer
Arranged chronologically, with detailed critical
analyses of the poems woven skilfully into an account
of what is known about Chaucer's life and career.
[N230] Longman pbk **£7.95**
BURNLEY, DAVID
The Language of Chaucer
Reissued in the new Macmillan *Language of
Literature* series.
[N2301] Macmillan pbk **£6.95**
HOWARD, DONALD R.
Chaucer and the Medieval World
The most ambitious and convincing attempt yet at a
biography of Chaucer. Howard's scholarship is
exhaustive, building up a detailed picture of the
medieval context in which the poet wrote, and
offering some provocative theories about the coherent
structure of the apparently 'unfinished' *Canterbury
Tales*.
[N231] Weidenfeld hbk **£16.95**
KANE, GEORGE
Chaucer
An Oxford *Past Master* which offers a short
introduction to Chaucer, concentrating on the poetry
and available social and biographical details.
[N232] Oxford pbk **£3.95**
WETHERBEE, WINTHROP
Chaucer: The Canterbury Tales **NEW**
Places the *Canterbury Tales* in the context of the
crisis of English society in the 14th century.
Wetherbee also discusses the language of the poem
and the place of Chaucer in subsequent literary
tradition.
[N234] Cambridge pbk **£4.95**

THE GAWAIN POET
DAVENPORT, W.A.
The Art of the Gawain Poet
Classic account of the complex alliterative poetry of
the anonymous 14th century northern writer, probable
author of *Sir Gawain and the Green Knight*, *Pearl*,
Cleanness and *Patience*.
[N235] Athlone pbk **£8.95**

Renaissance &
17th Century
Literature

GENERAL STUDIES
BENNETT, JOAN
**Five Metaphysical Poets: Donne,
Herbert, Vaughan, Crashaw, Marvell**
A traditional literary critic who offers a very readable
introduction to the Metaphysical poets.
[N236] Cambridge pbk **£6.95**

DAVIES, STEVIE
**The Idea of Woman in Renaissance
Literature: The Feminine Reclaimed**
Explores the humanist and Platonist revival of ancient
classical learning in terms of its reclamation of the
feminine principle in the work of Spenser, Milton and
Shakespeare.
[N643] Harvester pbk **£9.95**

DONNO, ELIZABETH STOREY (ED)
The Renaissance Excluding Drama
Spenser, Shakespeare, Marlowe, Donne, and Milton
are included here, as well as fiction and prose writers.
[N238] Macmillan pbk **£6.95**

KING, BRUCE
17th Century English Literature
A comprehensive one-volume history, covering the
major movements, influences, genres and styles.
[N242] Macmillan pbk **£7.95**

PATRIDES, C.A. & WITTREICH, JOSEPH
**The Apocalypse in Renaissance
Thought and Literature**
A fascinating study of Renaissance thought through
its obsession with the image of the Apocalypse.
[N245] Manchester UP pbk **£12.95**

RIVERS, ISABEL
**Classical and Christian Ideas in English
Renaissance Poetry**
Highly illuminating guide to the context of ideas and
assumptions which inform English Renaissance
poetry, including extensive quotation from seminal
writers and thinkers.
[N246] Unwin Hyman pbk **£9.95**

ROSTON, MURRAY
16th Century English Literature
A stimulating account of the major literary
developments of the period, including the rise of the
English language, the use of new poetic forms, the
growth of the playhouse, and the emergence of the
middle class writer.
[N247] Macmillan pbk **£7.95**

TILLYARD, E.M.W.
The Elizabethan World Picture
Classic introduction to the context of Elizabethan
literature by the well-known Shakespearean critic.
[N248] Penguin pbk **£3.95**

TUVE, ROSEMUND
Elizabethan and Metaphysical Imagery
One of the earliest studies to be specifically
concerned with imagery in Elizabethan and 17th
century literature.
[N249] Chicago UP pbk **£7.25**

INDIVIDUAL WRITERS
DONNE, JOHN
CAREY, JOHN
John Donne: Life, Mind and Art
An acclaimed critical biography.
[N250] Faber pbk **£4.95**
DOCHERTY, THOMAS
John Donne, Undone
A rigorous and historical account of Donne in relation
to the specific culture of the late Renaissance, through
a broadly post-structuralist reading of his verse.
[N251] Methuen pbk **£8.95**

HERBERT, GEORGE
VENDLER, HELEN
The Poetry of George Herbert
A study by one of America's leading critics well-
known for her imaginative and sensitive close
readings of the text.
[N252] Harvard hbk **£15.50**

MARVELL, ANDREW
WILCHER, ROBERT
Andrew Marvell
A good general introduction to Marvell's writing, in
particular his lyric poems.
[N253] Cambridge pbk **£7.95**

MILTON, JOHN **NEW**
DANIELSON, DENNIS
The Cambidge Companion to Milton
Essays from 18 distinguished contributors which
provide a comprehensive and often provocative
introduction to Milton's life and work.
[N254] Cambridge pbk **£8.95**

EMPSON, WILLIAM
Milton's God
Milton according to Empson's study 'is struggling to make his God appear less wicked ... and does succeed in making him noticeably less wicked than the traditional Christian one.' Empson carefully traces what he feels to be Milton's 'large minded' account of the temptation and fall of Lucifer, Adam and Eve, and places a good deal of weight, finally, on the very remote possibility that Milton's God intends to abdicate.
[N255] Cambridge pbk **£10.95**

HILL, CHRISTOPHER
Milton and the English Revolution
Illuminating and justly famous study by the historian Christopher Hill, whose numerous works on the English Civil War give him special authority to write about the context of events and ideas within which Milton was writing.
[N256] Faber hbk **£17.50**

MARTZ, LOUIS L.
Milton: Poet of Exile
'The most important single study of Milton that has appeared in years ... For a long time to come it will be the book from which Milton's *oeuvre* is reviewed and from which Milton criticism seeks renewal.' (*Modern Language Quarterly*)
[N257] Yale UP pbk **£10.95**

RICKS, CHRISTOPHER
Milton's Grand Style
Milton's 'grand style', has been vigorously attacked in the 20th century (by T.S. Eliot among others) and this book is an attempt to refute Milton's detractors by showing the delicacy and subtlety which is to be found in the verse of *Paradise Lost*.
[N258] Oxford pbk **£6.50**

SIDNEY, SIR PHILIP
BUXTON, JOHN
Sir Philip Sidney and the English Renaissance (3rd Ed)
This book is a study of the patronage of literature by Sir Philip Sidney and his family from 1575 to 1630 and shows that the sudden flowering of the English spirit in the poetry of the time owed much to the intelligent direction and patient experiments of Sidney and his friends.
[N259] Macmillan pbk **£12.95**

18th Century Literature

GENERAL STUDIES

DAY, GEOFFREY
From Fiction to the Novel
Geoffrey Day argues that to regard the 18th century as the era which saw the birth of the novel is to read history backwards. He shows that it is more relevant to consider the 'novels' of the period as radical experiments in form which completely undermine the standard modern account of fiction's calm and ordered development.
[N261] Blackwell hbk **£25.00**

DE BOLLA, PETER
The Discourse of the Sublime: History, Aesthetics and the Subject NEW
An original study which combines discussion of contemporary historiography and literary theory with an examination of rare 18th century archive material, to link the birth of modern consumerism with the developing concept of the individual.
[N6431] Blackwell hbk **£27.50**

MULLAN, JOHN
Sentiment and Sociability: The Language of Feeling in the 18th Century
A discursive examination of the sentimental novel in the 18th century, looking beyond novels to understand sentimentalism as the expression of a culture's anxiety about the nature of social relations.
[N262] Oxford hbk **£25.00**

NOVAK, MAXIMILLIAN E.
18th Century English Literature
This study examines the major literary trends of the 18th century, paying special attention to the development of political satire, the rise of the novel and the comparative decline of both epic and tragedy. A bibliography and chronological table are provided.
[N263] Macmillan pbk **£5.95**

NUSSBAUM, FELICITY & BROWN, LAURA
The New 18th Century: Theory, Politics, English Literature
New theoretical approaches (feminist, Marxist, new historicist and psychoanalytic) that reinterpret and reinstate canonical works (Fielding, Goldsmith, Sterne) and explore areas and figures that are increasingly important to 18th century study.
[N264] Methuen pbk **£9.95**

ROGERS, PAT (ED)
Restoration and 18th Century Prose and Poetry 1660 - 1780
The introduction discusses the usual division of the period into three sections dominated by Dryden, Pope and Johnson, with consideration of the terms commonly associated with them: neo-classical, Augustan and pre-Romantic. Examines the work of more than 80 writers.
[N265] Macmillan pbk **£6.95**

SAMBROOK, JAMES
The 18th Century: The Context of English Literature 1700 - 1789
A useful survey of science, religion, philosophy, history and aesthetics in the period, questioning the labels literary historians have attached to the period traditionally known as the Augustan age or the 'Age of Reason'.
[N267] Longman pbk **£8.50**

SPENCER, JANE
The Rise of the Woman Novelist
By outlining a history of the novel composed of women writers rather than the canonical male writers, Spencer challenges the standard histories of the novel.
[N268] Blackwell pbk **£7.95**

SPENDER, DALE
Mothers of the Novel
Dale Spender argues that women more than men were responsible for the introduction and promotion of the novel as a literary form, and the role of writers such as Jane Austen has been exaggerated at the expense of earlier women writers of the 18th century.
[N269] Pandora pbk **£5.95**

TODD, JANET
Sensibility
Charts the growth and context of the intellectual and literary movement known as 'sensibility' or 'sentimentalism' in the mid-18th century.
[N270] Methuen pbk **£7.95**

WATT, IAN
Rise of the Novel: Studies in Defoe, Richardson and Fielding
Remains one of the seminal texts on both the novel

and the 18th century: describing the links between the rise of the novel and the development of a middle class social ideology.
[N271] Hogarth pbk **£4.95**

INDIVIDUAL WRITERS

FIELDING, HENRY
SMALLWOOD, ANGELA J.
Fielding and the Woman Question NEW
A subtle and insightful reading of Fielding's work against the context of the predicament of women in Britain in the early 18th century.
[N272] Harvester hbk **£35.00**

VAREY, SIMON
Henry Fielding
Concise, lucid introduction to all his novels, stressing Fielding's technique in combining opposites to satiric and comic effect.
[N273] Cambridge pbk **£7.50**

POPE, ALEXANDER
ROGERS, PAT
An Introduction to Pope
[N274] Methuen pbk **£8.95**

RICHARDSON, SAMUEL
EAGLETON, TERRY
The Rape of Clarissa: Writing, Sexuality and Class Struggle in Samuel Richardson
Brilliant but contrasexual analysis, developing and discussing feminist, Marxist and post-structuralist approaches to the text.
[N277] Blackwell pbk **£6.95**

HARRIS, JOCELYN
Samuel Richardson
[N278] Cambridge pbk **£7.50**

SMOLLETT, TOBIAS
BASKER, JAMES G.
Tobias Smollet: Critic and Journalist
Examines Smollet's role as critic and journalist at the centre of 18th century culture, providing useful background material to his major works.
[N279] Assoc UP hbk **£26.00**

STERNE, LAURENCE
BYRD, MAX
Tristram Shandy (1985)
Brief but authoritative general introduction both to the novel and the current state of criticism.
[N280] Unwin Hyman pbk **£8.95**

ISER, WOLFGANG
Tristram Shandy
Shows how Sterne exploits the philosophy of his day and its cognitive deficiencies, using digression, humour and play to convey the experience of subjectivity, and implicitly expose the classical concept of the self.
[N281] Cambridge pbk **£3.95**

LAMB, JONATHAN
Sterne's Fiction and the Double Principle NEW
An exciting new study which aims to sever Sterne from the Locke tradition, asking why the collection and arrangement of fragments had such an appeal for Sterne, and why his most original effects are derived from limitations and repetitions.
[N282] Cambridge hbk **£22.50**

MYER, VALERIE (ED)
Laurence Sterne: Riddles and Mysteries
Useful and perceptive collection of essays by major Shandean scholars, stressing the novel's humorous, erotic and satiric aspects.
[N283] Vision P pbk **£7.95**

19th Century Literature

GENERAL STUDIES

ABRAMS, M.H.
Natural Supernaturalism: Tradition and Revolution in Romantic Literature
Traces the workings of Romantic thought from St Augustine to modern writers such as Wallace Stevens and James Joyce, concentrating in particular on Wordsworth, the chief architect of English Romanticism.
[N285] Norton pbk **£7.95**
The Correspondent Breeze: Essays on English Romanticism
[N286] Norton pbk **£7.95**
The Mirror and the Lamp
A classic study of Romantic poetics which concentrates on the distinction between mirrors (Aristotelian art, which reflects and imitates) and lamps (Platonic art, which projects a self-created inner world), which is one of the major constituitive images underlying Romanticism.
[N287] Oxford pbk **£6.95**

BEER, PATRICIA
Reader, I Married Him
A pioneering study of the women characters in Jane Austen, Charlotte Brontë, Mrs Gaskell and George Eliot.
[N288] Macmillan pbk **£6.95**

BOWRA, C.M.
The Romantic Imagination
Classic series of essays on Blake, Coleridge, Wordsworth, Shelley, Keats, Byron, Edgar Allan Poe, Christina and Dante Gabriel Rossetti, and Swinburne.
[N289] Oxford pbk **£5.95**

BROMWICH, DAVID (ED)
Romantic Critical Essays
This selection of 21 essays comprises all the major works of public criticism from Wordsworth's Preface to the *Lyrical Ballads* through to Shelley's *A Defence of Poetry*, concentrating on popular critics rather than aesthetic theorists.
[N290] Cambridge pbk **£8.95**

BUTLER, MARILYN
Romantics, Rebels and Reactionaries
Subtitled 'English Literature and its Background 1760 - 1830', this study takes a fresh look at one of the most fertile periods in literary history, and questions the validity of grouping such diverse talents as Blake, Keats, Coleridge, Wordsworth, Byron, Scott and Austen under the label 'Romantic'.
[N291] Oxford pbk **£5.95**

CROSS, NIGEL
The Common Writer: Life in 19th Century Grub Street
The most detailed account yet of the social, cultural and economic factors that controlled literary activity in the last century.
[N292] Cambridge pbk **£11.95**

GAULL, MARILYN
English Romanticism
Provides a detailed background to Romantic literature with discussion of particular topics, including the Gothic influence and the various religious and classical themes which dominated creative imaginations during the period.
[N294] Norton pbk **£9.95**

HARDY, BARBARA
Forms of Feeling in Victorian Fiction
'Barbara Hardy's study is English academic criticism at its best: scrupulous, intelligent, rich in local illumination and subtle discrimination … I came away with my sense of these writers deepened and enlarged.' (*New Statesman*)
[N295] Methuen pbk **£8.95**
Narrators and Novelists: The Collected Essays of Barbara Hardy Vol 1
[N296] Harvester hbk **£35.00**

HAYTER, ALETHEA
Opium and the Romantic Imagination
A fascinating study of the effect of widespread opium use on the literature of the period. Includes discussion of well-known addicts such as Coleridge and De Quincey, and of other less obvious users like Charlotte Brontë.
[N297] Crucible pbk **£7.99**

KERMODE, FRANK
The Romantic Image
'In this extremely important book of speculative and scholarly criticism, Mr Kermode is setting out to redefine the notion of the Romantic tradition, especially in its relation to English poetry and criticism. He makes us realise the extraordinary strength of the Romantic movement.' (*Times Literary Supplement*)
[N298] Routledge pbk **£4.95**

KITSON, PETER
Romantic Criticism 1800 - 1825   `NEW`
Launch title in the new *Key Documents in Literary Criticism* series from Batsford. Includes an introduction to the period, a chronology of creative and critical writing, and annotated texts of major statements by Romantic writers and critics.
[N299] Batsford pbk **£6.95**

LOVELL, TERRY
Consuming Fiction
This is a study of the development of the English novel from commodity to literature in the 18th and 19th centuries. The author argues that as its literary stake rose, the form of the novel changed, and so did the part played by women in producing (writing) and consuming (reading).
[N300] Verso pbk **£7.95**

MUIR, KENNETH (ED)
The Romantic Period Excluding the Novel
A collection of essays by leading scholars with an introduction by Kenneth Muir.
[N301] Macmillan pbk **£8.95**

POLLARD, ARTHUR (ED)
The Victorian Period Excluding the Novel
Includes illuminating studies of over 70 writers.
[N302] Macmillan pbk **£8.95**

PRAZ, MARIO
The Romantic Agony
A classic study of Romantic background themes, ideas and literature, with an introduction by Frank Kermode.
[N303] Oxford pbk **£7.95**

SEDGEWICK, EVE KOKOFSKY
The Coherence of Gothic Conventions
Through readings of classic Gothic authors, as well as of De Quincey and the Brontës, the most characteristic thematic conventions of the Gothic are firmly linked to the genre's more psychologically subversive elements.
[N304] Methuen pbk **£8.95**

SHAW, W. DAVID
The Lucid Veil
Study of theory and practice of Victorian poetics in relation to changing axioms of knowledge and perception.
[N305] Athlone hbk **£25.00**

STONYK, MARGARET
19th Century English Literature
This volume provides a comprehensive chronological outline of the period, with biographical information on each writer and a discussion of the dominant literary genres.
[N307] Macmillan pbk **£7.95**

SUTHERLAND, JOHN
The Longman Companion to Victorian Fiction   `NEW`
Over 1,000 biographical entries and over 600 novels are synopsised in this, the fullest account of English fiction between 1837 and 1901.
[N308] Longman hbk **£25.00**

TURNER, PAUL
English Literature 1832 - 1890 Excluding the Novel   `NEW`
Discusses 19th century poetry, drama, history, biography and scientific writing in the light of the most recent scholarship.
[N817] Oxford hbk **£25.00**

WATSON, J.R.
English Poetry of the Romantic Period 1789 - 1830
Looks in detail at the shared preoccupations of the Romantic poets and their response to the events which were transfoming their world: the French Revolution, the Napoleonic Wars, and the Industrial Revolution.
[N310] Longman pbk **£8.50**

WHEELER, MICHAEL
English Fiction of the Victorian Period 1830 - 1890
A comprehensive overview and analysis of Victorian fiction. Contains a chronological table, as well as biographical and bibliographical information.
[N311] Longman pbk **£7.50**

WILLIAMS, RAYMOND
The English Novel from Dickens to Lawrence
Penetrating, subtle and influential study by one of the most prominent post-war Marxist critics.
[N312] Hogarth pbk **£5.95**

INDIVIDUAL WRITERS

AUSTEN, JANE
BURROWS, J.F.
Computation into Criticism
In most discussions of works of English fiction the commonest words - such as prepositions, pronouns, articles and the verb 'to be' - are generally overlooked. However, in this study, detailed statistics are used to show how much they can reveal about the way a novelist like Jane Austen draws her characters.
[N313] Oxford hbk **£25.00**
BUTLER, MARILYN
Jane Austen and the War of Ideas
'There can be no doubt of the immense value for the critical reader of this impressive exposition of conflicting views concerning the individual and society at the end of the 18th century.' (*Review of English Studies*)
[N314] Oxford pbk **£9.95**
HARDY, BARBARA
A Reading of Jane Austen
[N315] Athlone pbk **£8.95**

SOUTHAM, B.C. (ED)
Critical Essays on Jane Austen
Essays by John Bayley, Brigid Brophy, Denis
Donoghue, Tony Tanner, Angus Wilson and
others.
[N316] Routledge pbk **£6.95**
TANNER, TONY
Jane Austen
[N317] Methuen pbk **£7.95**

BRONTE, CHARLOTTE
GLEN, HEATHER
Charlotte Brontë: A Reappraisal
Combining techniques of close stylistic analysis with
detailed historical scholarship, this book offers a
challenging new reading of the novels.
[N319] Blackwell pbk **£7.95**

BRONTE, EMILY
SPARK, MURIEL & STANFORD, DEREK
Emily Brontë
This book is in two parts: firstly a biography by
Muriel Spark; and secondly a critical examination of
her work by Derek Stanford.
[N320] Arrow pbk **£3.95**

CARROLL, LEWIS
DELEUZE, GILLES
Logic of Sense   **NEW**
A very important study by a French philosopher and
psychoanalytic critic of the nature of meaning and
meaninglessness in Lewis Carroll.
[N321] Athlone hbk **£35.00**

COLERIDGE, SAMUEL TAYLOR
BEER, JOHN
Coleridge's Poetic Intelligence
'Dr John Beer is perhaps the best living Coleridge
scholar. This book, as might be expected, is a
valuable contribution to the unravelling of
Coleridge's thought and the reading that guided it.'
(*Times Literary Supplement*)
[N322] Macmillan pbk **£8.95**
HAMILTON, PAUL
Coleridge's Poetics
Illuminating account of Coleridge as a thinker
dealing particularly with his radical view of
language.
[N323] Blackwell pbk **£9.95**

DICKENS, CHARLES
BENTLEY NICOLAS; SLATER, MICHAEL &
BURGIS, NINA
The Dickens Index
An illuminating guide to all Dickens' novels, short
stories, pamphlets, plays, collections of journalism,
and travel books. Its unique formula of alphabetically
arranged entries, keyed to the individual works, plus
chapter rather than page references, makes it an ideal
companion.
[N324] Oxford hbk **£40.00**
CAREY, JOHN
**The Violent Effigy: A Study of Dickens'
Imagination**
An imaginative study. Carey concentrates on the
images and symbols of violence, death, disfigure-
ment, and nightmare which abound in Dickens'
world.
[N325] Faber pbk **£3.99**
SLATER, MICHAEL
Dickens and Women
[N326] Dent pbk **£5.95**

ELIOT, GEORGE
ASHTON, ROSEMARY
George Eliot
An Oxford *Past Master*. An informative study of
Eliot's ideas, influence, and influences.
[N328] Oxford pbk **£2.95**

HARDY, BARBARA
The Novels of George Eliot
[N329] Athlone pbk **£7.95**

HARDY, THOMAS
BAYLEY, JOHN
An Essay on Hardy
A highly recommended essay by one of the most
engaging and sympathetic of contemporary English
critics.
[N331] Cambridge pbk **£11.95**
PAULIN, TOM
**Thomas Hardy: The Poetry of
Perception**
An original account which combines a discussion of
the major literary and philosophical influences on
Hardy's work with a series of close readings of
individual poems.
[N335] Macmillan pbk **£9.95**
SUMNER, ROSEMARY
**Thomas Hardy: Psychological
Novelist**
'Rosemary Sumner's book constitutes not just an
invaluable first step in coming to terms with Hardy as
a psychological novelist but, no less immediately, a
freshly conceived, cogently argued and crisply written
study in its own right.'(Michael Millgate)
[N336] Macmillan pbk **£9.95**

KEATS, JOHN
LEVINSON, MARJORIE
Keats's Life of Allegory
A brilliantly iconoclastic reinterpretation of Keats's
work (in particular the five romances) by one of
America's most exciting critics, in which the excesses
of Keats's poetry, the overwritten sentiment that the
majority of modern critics have chosen to ignore or
explain away, are focused on.
[N337] Blackwell hbk **£29.50**
RICKS, CHRISTOPHER
Keats and Embarrassment
Enjoyable book on a poet who was 'probably more
widely and subtly gifted with powers of empathy than
any other English poet', by a prominent contemporary
English critic, noted for his sensitivity to the minutiae
of poetic nuance.
[N338] Oxford pbk **£5.95**

MORRIS, WILLIAM
THOMPSON, E.P.
**William Morris: Romantic to
Revolutionary**
This is a revised edition of E.P. Thompson's classic
intellectual biography of Morris. He seeks to show
how Morris's political and artistic ideas co-exist and
inform each other.
[N339] Merlin pbk **£7.95**

THACKERAY, WILLIAM
CAREY, JOHN
Prodigal Genius
[N341] Faber pbk **£3.25**
HARDY, BARBARA
**The Exposure of Luxury: Radical
Themes in Thackeray**
[N342] P Owen pbk **£7.50**
PETERS, CATHERINE
**Thackeray's Universe: Shifting Worlds
of Imagination and Reality**
A recent, well-received illustrated biographical study.
[N342A] Faber hbk **£12.95**

TROLLOPE, ANTHONY
GEROULD, WINFRED GREGORY & GEROULD,
JAMES THAYER
A Guide to Trollope
An A-Z of characters and places featured in
Trollope's novels and short stories.
[N343] Sutton pbk **£7.95**

HALPERIN, JOHN
Trollope and Politics
[N344] Macmillan pbk **£9.95**
WALL, STEPHEN
Trollope and Character
Modern criticism has tended to concentrate on
Trollope as a moralist and critic of society but
Stephen Wall's recent book follows the novelist's own
view that a writer should live with his characters in
the 'full reality of established intimacy' and
concentrates on Trollope as an exceptional creator of
fictional persons.
[N345] Faber hbk **£17.50**

WORDSWORTH, WILLIAM
AUSTEN, FRANCES
**The Language of Wordsworth
and Coleridge**   **NEW**
Launch title in the new Macmillan *Language of
Literature* series.
[N2302] Macmillan pbk **£6.95**
BEER, JOHN
Wordsworth and the Human Heart
'This is a remarkable and very important book.
Through his focus on the human heart, John Beer
shows us a Wordsworth who is more passionate, more
feeling, than many of us admitted him to be. He also
shows us a Wordsworth who has something important
to say to the modern world.' (J. Robert Bath)
[N346] Macmillan pbk **£8.95**
HARTMAN, GEOFFREY
The Unremarkable Wordsworth
Hartman's capacity to open up a dialogue between
contemporary theory and Wordsworth's verse informs
all these essays, written since his masterly
Wordsworth's Poetry was published in 1964.
[N348] Methuen pbk **£9.95**
Wordsworth's Poetry 1787 - 1814
One of the most acclaimed studies of Wordsworth, it
marked an epoch in the study of the poet, and of
Romantic poetry in general.
[N349] Yale UP pbk **£9.95**
WORDSWORTH, JONATHAN
**William Wordsworth: The Borders
of Vision**
An invigorating and illuminating account of
Wordsworth as a 'border poet' - that is a poet
preoccupied with transition between states of being
and levels of consciousness.
[N350] Oxford pbk **£15.00**

20th Century
Literature

GENERAL STUDIES

BLAMIRES, HARRY
**A Guide to 20th Century Literature
in English**
A compact and readable encyclopaedia of 500 writers
and their writing in English from all over the world,
excluding America.
[N351] Methuen pbk **£7.95**
Twentieth Century English Literature
(2nd Ed)
Puts writers in their historical and literary context,
fills out their cultural background in art and music
and defines wider movements of thought and fashion.
Both the chronological table and further reading lists
have been fully revised.
[N352] Macmillan pbk **£9.95**

BOLD, ALAN
Modern Scottish Literature
While the approach is critically objective throughout,
Bold, himself a poet, critic and a Scot, makes this a

lively and enjoyable companion as well as a shrewd and serious study.
[N353] Longman pbk **£8.95**

BRADBURY, M. & MCFARLANE (EDS)
Modernism
Excellent introduction to the broad context of Modernism, with a selection of essays on different writers, movements, periods and places.
[N354] Penguin pbk **£7.99**

CALDER, JOHN
The Defense of Literature   **NEW**
A collection of essays examining the significant international literature of our time including accounts of Proust, Joyce, Brecht, Kafka, Burroughs and the French *nouveau roman*.
[N356] Calder hbk **£12.95**

CAREY, JOHN
Original Copy: Selected Reviews and Journalism 1969 - 1986
"*A recurrent theme in the book is the contention that English writing in the 20th century has persistently catered for minorities and elites to the exclusion of a large potential readership of ordinary, intelligent people who have developed over the years, a thoroughly understandable dislike of 'culture' and 'the culture'.*" (From the introduction)
[N357] Faber hbk **£10.95**

CONNOLLY, CYRIL
100 Key Books of the Modern Movement
A selection from France, England and America, 1880 - 1950.
[N358] Allison & B pbk **£3.95**

CUNNINGHAM, VALENTINE
British Writers of the Thirties
This acclaimed, wide-ranging discussion of British writing in a momentous decade offers interpretations of central texts of the period, not in linguistic isolation but in the contexts - social, political, historical, ideological, personal - in which they were written.
[N359] Oxford hbk **£30.00**
[N359A] Oxford pbk **£9.95**

DAVIE, DONALD
A History of Poetry in Britain 1960 - 1985   **NEW**
A judicious and provocative critical survey. As well as placing the major poets - Larkin, Bunting, MacDiarmid, Heaney - in context, Davie also explores specific themes: the rise of poetic theory, the influence of Eliot and Hardy, and the role of translation.
[N360] Carcanet hbk **£18.95**

DIPPLE, ELIZABETH
The Unresolvable Plot: Reading Contemporary Fiction
An informative guide focusing on the work of Greene, Marquez, Borges, Nabokov, Calvino, Beckett, Eco, Spark, Russell Hoban, Murdoch, Bellow and Lessing.
[N361] Routledge pbk **£8.95**

DONOGHUE, DENIS
We Irish: Selected Essays
W.B. Yeats and James Joyce are the commanding figures in this first volume and each is considered as embodying one distinctive way of 'being Irish'. The other writers discussed include George Russell, Frank O'Connor. George Moore, Sean O'Faiolain, Austin Clarke, Samuel Beckett and Seamus Heaney.
[N362] Harvester hbk **£32.50**

ELLMANN, MAUD
The Poetics of Impersonality
Subtitled 'The Question of the Subject in T.S. Eliot and Ezra Pound'. 'Accomplished and ambitious: a virtuoso performance by a critic who is genuinely at home in the world of contemporary theory.' (Patrick Parrinder)
[N363] Harvester pbk **£10.95**

ELLMANN, RICHARD & FEIDELSON, C. (EDS)
The Modern Tradition: Backgrounds of Modern Literature
Invaluable source book, covering the key texts in philosophy, literature and criticism from the mid-19th century onwards.
[N364] Oxford hbk **£29.50**

FAULKENER, PETER
A Modernist Reader: Modernism in England, 1910 - 1930
This is a selection of key documents from the modernist period. It includes critical essays, letters and manifestoes from all the main writers and thinkers linked with Modernism, Futurism, Imagism and Vorticism in England (includes James, Lewis, Pound, Joyce, Eliot, Lawrence).
[N365] Batsford pbk **£6.99**

FISHER, MARK (ED)
Letters to an Editor   **NEW**
A collection of letters to Michael Schmidt, editorial director of Carcanet Press, one of the most innovative post-war publishers. The book contains correspondence from established writers, as well as many newcomers whom the press have helped to launch. Published to coincide with Carcanet's 20th anniversary.
[N365A] Carcanet hbk **£12.95**

HYNES, SAMUEL
The Auden Generation: Literature and Politics in England in the 1930s
A standard work on the background to the literature of the period.
[N369] Faber pbk **£3.95**

JOSIPOVICI, GABRIEL
The Lessons of Modernism (2nd Ed)
A stimulating meditation centred on three key questions: how does a person's life relate to their art? What is the place of modern art in the culture and educational system of today? What are the limits of human expression and of the expressivity of voice and body?
[N370] Macmillan pbk **£9.95**
The Modern English Novel
[N371] Open Bks pbk **£4.00**

KENNER, HUGH
The Mechanic Muse
This unusual investigation of the works of Eliot, Pound, Joyce, and Beckett, examines how the rapid developments in technology changed their way of viewing and depicting the modern world.
[N372] Oxford pbk **£5.95**
A Sinking Island   **NEW**
In this admirably iconoclastic book, Kenner proposes that England, which earlier in this century saw some of the greatest achievements of modernism, has steadily turned its back on these developments. This has left our culture foundering in a sea of mediocrity, provincialism and media-manipulation.
[N372A] Barrie & J hbk **£16.95**

LEVIN, HARRY
Refractions: Essays in Comparative Literature
Levin is a versatile critic of broadly humanist sympathies, who is particularly illuminating on the relationship between realism and myth in modern writers like Joyce, and on the development of the Naturalist school in 19th century French fiction.
[N373] Oxford pbk **£4.50**

MCHALE, BRIAN
Post-Modernist Fiction
Proposes a canon of post-modern fiction capacious enough to include North American metafiction, Latin American magic realism, the French *nouveau roman*, concrete prose and science fiction.
[N374] Methuen pbk **£8.95**

MORRISON, BLAKE
The Movement: English Poetry and Fiction of the 1950s
Important study of the anti-Romantic movement in the literature of the 1950s (which included Philip Larkin, Donald Davie, and Kingsley Amis) by a contemporary poet whose own work demonstrates its continuing influence.
[N375] Methuen pbk **£9.95**

NICHOLLS, PETER
Modernisms: A Literary Guide
Conceived as both an analytic introduction to a complex and fascinating body of theory and as an invitation to rethink our reading of seminal works of modern British, American and European literature.
[N376] Macmillan pbk **£6.95**

SILKIN, JON
Out of Battle:
The Poetry of the Great War
No other book ranges so widely or probes so deeply into the responses of the 'war poets' - Silkin discusses Brooke, Blunden, Edward Thomas, Ivor Gurney, Ford Madox Ford, Wilfred Owen, and David Jones, amongst others.
[N377] Routledge pbk **£4.95**

SISSON, C.H.
English Poetry 1900 - 1950:
An Assessment
A typically astringent account by the renowned poet and critic, which turns a cold douche of common sense on some of the more messianic pretensions of modernism.
[N378] Carcanet hbk **£12.95**

SMITH, STAN (ED)
Twentieth Century Poetry
Entries on over 200 poets in the English language.
[N380] Macmillan pbk **£8.95**

STEAD, C.K.
Pound, Yeats, Eliot and the Modernist Movement
Partly a history of modernism in English poetry during the first fifty years of this century and partly an exploration of what the term 'modernism' means, this book looks at the poetry of Hardy, Yeats, Pound, Eliot and Auden and assesses the extent to which the label 'modernist' is relevant to their work.
[N381] Macmillan pbk **£9.95**
The New Poetic
Classic introduction to modernism and a perennial favourite on all student reading lists.
[N382] Hutchinson pbk **£8.95**

SULTAN, STANLEY
Eliot, Joyce and Company
Explores the relationship of Eliot and Joyce to certain antecedents (Dante, Flaubert, Baudelaire, Dostoevsky) and contemporaries (Pound, Yeats), as well as to their readers, in order to illuminate essential similarities in their aims and methods.
[N383] Oxford hbk **£25.00**

TAYLOR, D.J.
Writers at the Crossroads `NEW`
A witty and intellectually assured polemic on the
terminal state of the English novel by a young and
controversial critic. Taylor attacks the complacent,
deferential literary establishment, the play-safe
middlebrow publishers and the feckless authors
themselves (Amis, Drabble, Murdoch) for allowing
our fiction to lag far behind the vast chaos of
contemporary life.
[N385] Bloomsbury pbk **£4.99**

THWAITE, ANTHONY
**Poetry Today: A Critical Guide to
British Poetry 1960 - 1984**
A comprehensive critical survey beginning with
Robert Graves and David Jones and going on to
consider the work of Hughes, Larkin, Heaney and
Porter, ending with an examination of younger poets,
including James Fenton and Craig Raine.
[N386] Longman pbk **£5.50**

WOODCOCK, GEORGE (ED)
Twentieth Century Fiction
Contains details of 300 major writers: the
introduction considers the novel from the beginning
of the century and gives a particularly useful
overview of recent writing from the Commonwealth.
[N388] Macmillan pbk **£12.95**

INDIVIDUAL WRITERS
BECKETT, SAMUEL
ALVAREZ, A.
Beckett
A Fontana *Modern Master*, which provides an
excellent brief introduction to Beckett's fiction and
drama, particularly strong on unravelling the complex
ideas which underpin them.
[N389] Fontana pbk **£2.95**
O'CONNOR, STEVEN
Samuel Beckett
A study in which post-structuralist analysis (with
particular reference to Deleuze and Derrida) provides
the key to understanding Beckett's use of repetition.
[N391] Blackwell hbk **£27.50**

DOUGLAS, KEITH
SCAMMELL, WILLIAM
Keith Douglas
Since his death in action in 1944, Douglas's
reputation has steadily grown. Scammell, himself a
poet, makes a convincing claim for Douglas as the
finest English poet to have emerged during World
War II, and as a major poet in his own right.
[N393] Faber pbk **£4.95**

ELIOT, T.S.
GARDNER, HELEN
The Art of T.S. Eliot
One of the earliest and most famous studies of Eliot's
work; it still provides a very solid introduction, being
particularly illuminating on the context of his later
religious verse.
[N394] Faber pbk **£2.95**
KENNER, HUGH
The Invisible Poet: T.S. Eliot
A highly original and popular study by a
distinguished contemporary American critic.
[N396] Methuen pbk **£8.95**
SPENDER, STEPHEN
Eliot
Interesting account of Eliot and his work by a poet of
the Auden Generation and a personal friend.
[N397] Fontana pbk **£3.95**

GOLDING, WILLLIAM
BOYD, STEPHEN J.
The Novels of William Golding
Acclaimed study which shows how Golding's

'poetry' is used to defamiliarise the everyday world,
so that a sense of wonder may be restored and that his
fiction may retain an ambiguous kernel.
[N398] Harvester hbk **£29.95**
CAREY, JOHN (ED)
**William Golding:
The Man and his Books**
A tribute on his 75th birthday which contains essays
by well-known writers, including Seamus Heaney,
Ted Hughes, John Fowles, Ian McEwan, and an
interview with John Carey.
[N399] Faber hbk **£12.50**

HEANEY, SEAMUS
CORCORAN, NEIL
Seamus Heaney: A Student's Guide
A detailed study by an acknowledged expert, covering
all Heaney's work up to the 1984 collection *Station
Island*. Provides a convincing account of the
influence of Yeats and Heaney's imaginative use of
the archetypal stories of Irish antiquity.
[N401] Faber pbk **£3.95**

HILL, GEOFFREY
ROBINSON, P.
Geoffrey Hill: Essays on His Work
A distinguished collection of essays which explore
the many complex themes in Hill's work.
[N402] Open UP pbk **£7.95**

HUGHES, TED
SAGAR, KEITH (ED)
The Art of Ted Hughes
Collection of essays which includes 30 previously
unpublished poems.
[N403] Cambridge pbk **£11.95**

JOYCE, JAMES
ATTRIDGE, DEREK & FERRER, DANIEL (EDS)
**Post-Structuralist Joyce: Essays from
the French**
The most significant criticism to have appeared in the
last 20 years, including essays by Derek Attridge,
Daniel Ferrars, Hélène Cixous, Stephen Heath,
Jacques Aubert, Jean Micheal Rabaté, André Topia
and Jacques Derrida.
[N404] Cambridge pbk **£8.50**
BLAMIRES, HARRY
**Bloomsday Book: A Guide through
Joyce's Ulysses** (2nd Edition)
An indispensible guide through Joyce's *Ulysses*,
which explains each episode and its relation to *The*

Geoffrey Hill (Photo: Fay Godwin Photo File)

Odyssey as well as other works. Blamires also gives
admirable guidance to the structure and thematic
development of the novel.
[N405] Routledge pbk **£7.95**
ELLMANN, RICHARD
Ulysses on the Liffey
Brilliant exposition of the themes and structure of
Joyce's masterpiece by his most distinguished modern
critic and biographer.
[N406] Faber pbk **£4.99**
MCCABE, COLIN
**James Joyce and the Revolution
of the Word**
'The most exciting and original book on Joyce to
have appeared for many years.' (*New Statesman*)
[N407] Macmillan pbk **£6.95**
James Joyce: New Perspectives
[N408] Harvester pbk **£9.95**
PARRINDER, PATRICK
James Joyce
[N409] Cambridge pbk **£7.95**

KIPLING, RUDYARD
KEMP, SANDRA
Kipling's Vision
A thorough re-reading of both published and
unpublished work, and an original examination of
Kipling's involvement with early theories of
psychology and the paranormal.
[N411] Blackwell hbk **£25.00**

LARKIN, PHILIP
SALWAK, DALE
Philip Larkin: The Man and His Work
Eighteen distinguished contributors, many of them
friends of Larkin, celebrate his talents as a poet and
reveal the man behind the writing.
[N414] Carcanet hbk **£27.50**

LAWRENCE, D.H.
HOUGH, GRAHAM
**The Dark Sun: A Critical Study of
D.H. Lawrence**
[N415] Duckworth pbk **£9.95**
KERMODE, FRANK
Lawrence
Excellent brief introduction by the celebrated critic.
One of the Fontana *Modern Masters* series.
[N416] Fontana pbk **£2.95**
LEAVIS, F.R.
D.H. Lawrence: Novelist
A famous and pioneering study by the well-known
Cambridge liberal critic of the 1930s and 1940s.
[N417] Penguin pbk **£4.95**
SAGAR, KEITH
The Art of D.H. Lawrence
[N418] Cambridge pbk **£12.50**

MURDOCH, IRIS
CONRADI, PETER J.
**Iris Murdoch: The Saint and the
Artist**
An important and sympathetic study which draws on
new material to argue that Murdcoh's early novels -
fine as they are - and her early theory have obscured
the achievement of the later work.
[N420] Macmillan hbk **£35.00**

ORWELL, GEORGE
WILLIAMS, RAYMOND
Orwell
In the Fontana *Modern Masters* series, a perceptive
introduction by the respected Marxist critic.
[N422] Fontana pbk **£2.95**
WOODCOCK, GEORGE
The Crystal Spirit
A reprinted study of Orwell with a new introduction
by the author.
[N423] Fourth Estate pbk **£5.95**

LITERATURE

WOOLF, VIRGINIA

BISHOP, EDWARD
Virginia Woolf
A useful overview of Virginia Woolf's life and career which discusses the letters and diaries, as well as the major novels, in order to trace the development of her experimental techniques.
[N428] Macmillan pbk **£4.95**

MARCUS, JANE (ED)
Virginia Woolf and Bloomsbury: A Centenary
Brings together 15 essays from Nöel Annan, Nigel Nicolson, Michael Holroyd, Louise Desalvo and Sandra Gilbert ranging from the biographical, to feminist and neo-Freudian readings.
[N429] Macmillan pbk **£10.95**

MARCUS, JANE (ED)
New Feminist Essays on Virginia Woolf
'These essays offer the student of Virginia Woolf a good deal of new, exciting material and some radically fresh perspectives on Woolf's development as an artist and theoretician.'(*Women's Studies*)
[N430] Macmillan pbk **£9.95**

YEATS, W.B.

DONOGHUE, DENIS
Yeats
A Fontana *Modern Master*: an excellent brief introduction by one of Yeats's most imaginative contemporary critics.
[N431] Fontana pbk **£1.95**

ELLMANN, RICHARD
The Identity of Yeats
Excellent study of Yeats's life and work by one of this century's most distinguished literary critics, best known for definitive biographies of Joyce and Wilde.
[N432] Faber pbk **£6.99**

JEFFARES, A. NORMAN
A New Commentary on the Poems of W.B. Yeats
A documented guide to Yeats's poems quoting where apposite from his other writings (both published and unpublished) and from critical work on his poems. Dates of composition and publication are included.
[N433] Macmillan hbk **£35.00**

American Literature

Reference

CONN, PETER
Literature in America `NEW`
A large and beautifully illustrated history of American literature from the early 17th century to the late 1980s, with helpful chronological tables and annotated guides to further reading.
[N441] Cambridge hbk **£25.00**

CUNLIFFE, MARCUS
Literature of the United States
A popular study of writers and themes in American literature from colonial times to the present day.
[N442] Penguin pbk **£6.99**

FRENCH, WARREN (ED)
Twentieth Century American Literature
Covers some 250 novelists, poets and playwrights.
[N443] Macmillan pbk **£9.95**

HART, JAMES D.
Oxford Companion to American Literature
A comprehensive source of information on all aspects of American literature from 1578 to 1982.
[N435] Oxford hbk **£39.50**

Concise Oxford Companion to American Literature
[N434] Oxford hbk **£19.50**
[N434A] Oxford pbk **£7.95**

HIGH, PETER B.
An Outline of American Literature
An informative survey of prose, poetry and drama from colonial times to the present day. Illustrated throughout with black and white photographs, the guide also provides a list of literary terms and a chronology of literary and historical events.
[N444] Longman pbk **£6.50**

LEARY, LEWIS (ED)
American Literature to 1900
Melville, Emerson, Whitman and James are among the 130 writers featured; there is also an introduction giving the historical background and specific topics.
[N447] Macmillan pbk **£6.95**

SALZMAN, JACK (ED)
Cambridge Handbook of American Literature
An A-Z of writers and writing including entries on principle magazines, literary movements and chronological tables of American history and literature.
[N436] Cambridge hbk **£19.50**

THE NORTON ANTHOLOGY OF AMERICAN LITERATURE (3rd Edition)
New edition of a classic reference work, introducing more women, Afro-American and Native-American writers.
BAYM, NINA & OTHERS (EDS)
Shorter Edition
[N448] Norton pbk **£14.95**
Volume 1
Covers the period between 1820 and 1865.
[N449] Norton pbk **£13.95**
Volume 2
Covers the period between 1865 and 1985.
[N450] Norton pbk **£13.95**

TOYE, WILLIAM (ED)
Oxford Companion to Canadian Literature
A companion to the English and French literature of Canada, including articles on the writing of the Indian, Inuit and Ukranian communities.
[N437] Oxford hbk **£35.00**

WALKER, MARSHALL
The Literature of the United States of America
Marshall Walker has updated his classic study of American literature, paying more detailed attention to modern writers, including pieces on Hart Crane, e.e. cummings, John Ashbery, William Burroughs, and John Irving.
[N451] Macmillan pbk **£8.95**

General Studies

ALLEN, WALTER
Tradition and Dream
A respected study of the Anglo-American novel from the 1920s onwards.
[N453] Hogarth pbk **£5.95**

ALTIERI, CHARLES
Painterly Abstraction in Modernist American Poetry
Analyses the idea of abstraction in the visual arts and the challenge it posed to literature. Altieri then applies the term 'abstract' to poetry and traces it through the work of Wordsworth and Baudelaire to the modernists: Pound, Eliot, Williams, Moore, Stein, Stevens.
[N454] Cambridge hbk **£45.00**

BRADBURY, MALCOLM
The Modern American Novel
'A compressed history of the subject I cannot see anyone bettering for a long time to come ... absolutely first-rate.' (*Irish Times*)
[N456] Oxford pbk **£5.95**

DAVIDSON, CATHY N.
Revolution and the Word: The Rise of the Novel in America
Offers a unique perspective on the origins of American fiction, showing how in the aftermath of the Revolution, the novel found a special place among the less privileged citizens of the new Republic.
[N457] Oxford hbk **£22.50**

FAAS, EKBERT
Towards a New American Poetics
Essays and interviews with diverse American writers: includes Charles Olson, Robert Duncan, Robert Creeley, Allen Ginsberg, etc.
[N458] B Sparrow pbk **£6.95**

FIELDER, LESLIE
Love and Death in the American Novel
A classic, contentious study of the great themes of American fiction, this is a highly readable account for both the popular reader and the student.
[N459] Penguin pbk **£6.99**

HANCOCK, GEOFF
Canadian Writers at Work
A collection of interviews, including Margaret Atwood, Mavis Gallant, Jack Hodgins, Robert Kroetsch, Bharati Mukherjee, Alice Munro, Jane Rule and Josef Skvorecky.
[N460] Oxford hbk **£12.50**

KELLER, LYNN
Re-Making it New: Contemporary American Poetry and the Modernist Tradition
Explores how early 20th century modernist poetry has influenced contemporary writers: John Ashbery is discussed in conjunction with Wallace Stevens, Elizabeth Bishop with Marianne Moore, and Robert Creeley with William Carlos Williams.
[N462] Cambridge hbk **£30.00**

KENNER, HUGH
A Homemade World: American Modernist Writers
An impassioned look at those artists who stayed in America - William Carlos Williams, Wallace Stevens, Marianne Moore, Fitzgerald and Faulkner - to hammer out a poetic 'as American as the Kitty Hawk plane, not really in the debt of the international example, austere and astringent.'
[N446] Boyars pbk **£4.50**

LAWRENCE, D.H.
Studies in Classic American Literature
Lawrence's critique of the destruction of the American dream of freedom and liberation as experienced in its classic works of fiction. It includes some of the most convincing close criticism of Hawthorne, Melville, Whitman and Poe.
[N452] Penguin pbk **£3.99**

MORSE, DAVID
American Romanticism
Offers a continuous analysis of the development of
19th century literature from its beginnings with
Brockden Brown and Cooper to the post-Civil War
achievement of Mark Twain and Henry James.
Vol 1
[N465] Macmillan hbk **£29.50**
Vol 2
[N464] Macmillan hbk **£29.50**

ROWE, JOYCE A.
**Equivocal Endings in Classic
American Novels**
Approaches four classic American novels from an
original perspective: the strangely equivocal nature of
the vision with which each of them ends. The novels
are Hawthorne's *The Scarlet Letter*, Mark Twain's
Adventures of Huckleberry Finn, Henry James's
The Ambassadors and Scott Fitzgerald's *The Great
Gatsby*.
[N466] Cambridge hbk **£20.00**

TANNER, TONY
Scenes of Nature, Signs of Man
Subtitled 'Essays in 19th & 20th Century American
Literature'. Examines how American romantic
writing differs from European, and how
contemporary writers like Pynchon, Barth and
DeLillo negotiate their complex relationships to their
homeland.
[N426] Cambridge pbk **£11.95**

WILSON, EDMUND
**Patriotic Gore: Studies in the Literature
of the American Civil War**
With a new introduction by Malcolm Bradbury.
[N467] Hogarth pbk **£8.95**

Individual Writers

DICKINSON, EMILY
ROBINSON, JOHN
Emily Dickinson: A Student's Guide
[N470] Faber pbk **£4.99**

FAULKNER, WILLIAM
BROOKS, CLEANTH
William Faulkner: First Encounters
One of the founders of American New Criticism,
Brook is also authoritative Faulkner critic, bringing
an Empsonian rigour and wit to bear on the manifold
difficulties of his subject's *oeuvre*.
[N471] Yale pbk **£9.50**
**William Faulkner:
The Yoknapatawpha Country**
[N472] Yale pbk **£17.95**
**William Faulkner: Toward the
Yoknapatawpha and Beyond**
[N473A] Yale hbk **£46.25**
[N473] Yale pbk **£14.95**

FROST, ROBERT
POIRIER, RICHARD
Robert Frost: The Work of Knowing
[N474] Oxford pbk **£6.95**

MELVILLE, HERMAN
OLSON, CHARLES
Call Me Ishmael
A poet's account of Melville's influences in *Moby
Dick*. Olson's book is stimulating and eccentric in
style, somewhat in the manner of Lawrence's
American criticism, or the essays of Olson's mentor
Edward Dahlberg.
[N476] City Lights pbk **£4.95**

NABOKOV, VLADIMIR
RAMPTON, DAVID
**Vladimir Nabokov:
A Critical Study of the Novels**
[N477] Cambridge pbk **£8.95**
WOOD, MICHAEL
Vladimir Nabokov
This study concentrates on key motifs like betrayal,
conspiracy, and accident in Nabokov's work and
provides a thorough analysis of his witty and
inventive attitude to language. It looks most closely at
Lolita, *Ada* and Nabokov's fictional treatment of
writers.
[N478] Routledge pbk **£3.75**

PLATH, SYLVIA
HOLBROOK, DAVID
Sylvia Plath: Poetry and Existence
Holbrook deploys psychoanalysis and
phenomenology in a pioneering work of literary,
personal and cultural interpretation.
[N479] Athlone pbk **£9.95**

POUND, EZRA
BROOKER, PETER
**A Student's Guide to the Selected
Poems of Ezra Pound**
[N480] Faber pbk **£4.99**
LINDBERG, KATHRYNE V.
**Reading Pound Reading:
Modernism After Nietzsche**
Through a careful analysis of Pound's often forgotten
literary and cultural criticism, this book reveals the
elements it shared with certain Nietzschean habits of
reading, uncovering surprising links with an unlikely
list of accomplices, which includes Emerson,
Whitman, William Carlos Williams and Charles
Olson.
[N481] Oxford hbk **£22.50**
PERLOFF, MARJORIE
**The Dance of the Intellect: Studies in
the Poetry of the Pound Tradition**
Essays on the poetry of Swinburne, Yeats, Wallace
Stevens, Joyce, William Carlos Williams and John
Cage, tracing many of the new directions in post-
modern poetry back to Pound.
[N482] Cambridge pbk **£10.95**

PYNCHON, THOMAS
SEED, DAVID
**The Fictional Labyrinths of
Thomas Pynchon**
A close and detailed reading of Pynchon's fiction
from his early short stories through to *Gravity's
Rainbow*.
[N485] Macmillan hbk **£29.50**

STEIN, GERTRUDE
NEUMANN, SHIRLEY & NADEL, IRA (EDS)
**Gertrude Stein and the Making
of Literature**
Eleven essays: some situate Gertrude Stein's work
in terms of modernist and post-modernist literary
theory and practice; several provide close readings of
works that have previously received scant critical
attention; others bring new manuscript evidence to
bear on our understanding of Stein's compositional
techniques.
[N487] Macmillan hbk **£29.50**

STEVENS, WALLACE
KERMODE, FRANK
Wallace Stevens **NEW**
A new edition of a fifties classic. It contains a fully
up-to-date bibliography and a new introduction, in
which Kermode reminds us, among other things, just
how insecure was Steven's reputation as a poet when
the essay was first published.
[N488] Faber pbk **£4.99**

VENDLER, HELEN
**On Extended Wings:
Wallace Stevens's Longer Poems**
Vendler's technique of imaginative close reading
makes her the ideal critic for the elusive genius of
Stevens; her studies of his work have been
instrumental in securing his reputation as a major
poet.
[N483] Harvard UP pbk **£6.95**
**Wallace Stevens:
Words Chosen Out of Desire**
[N484] Harvard UP pbk **£3.95**

THE AMERICAN NOVEL
Excellent series of new critical essays devoted to
single works of American fiction. A range of
approaches are used from traditional 'close reading'
to post-structuralist theory. Titles available:
The American, *Moby Dick*, *Huckleberry Finn*, *The
Scarlet Letter*, *Light in August*, *The Great Gatsby*,
Uncle Tom's Cabin, *The Sun Also Rises*, *Invisible
Man*, *The Red Badge of Courage*, *The Awakening*.
[N496] Cambridge pbk **£6.95**

European & World Literature

Reference & History

BONDANELLA, PETER & CONWAY, JULIA
**Macmillan Dictionary of Italian
Literature**
[N497] Macmillan hbk **£29.50**

DOVER, KENNETH
Ancient Greek Literature
An historical survey of Greek literature from c.700
BC to 550 AD produced by distinguished scholars
and experts.
[N550] Oxford pbk **£5.95**

GARLAND, HENRY & MARY (EDS)
Oxford Companion to German literature
(2nd Ed)
An excellent reference book covering all aspects of
German literature from the 8th century to the present
day with extended entries on authors whose
reputations have been confirmed in the last ten years.
[N498] Oxford hbk **£29.50**

GOODWIN, KEN
A History of Australian Literature
Shows how the recurrent themes of the quest to
recover the past, the idea of the alien, the need to
endure, and the imminence of violence, combine to
produce the unique qualities found in Australian
literature.
[N570] Macmillan pbk **£8.95**

HARVEY, SIR PAUL (ED)
**Oxford Companion to Classical
Literature**
A comprehensive encyclopaedia to all aspects of the
classical world.
[N551] Oxford hbk **£25.00**
[N549] Oxford pbk **£5.95**

HARVEY, P. & HESELTINE, J.E. (EDS)
Oxford Companion to French Literature
A comprehensive source of information on all aspects

LITERATURE

of French literature, from c.400 AD to just after 1945, containing a few updated entries on the works of important authors after 1945.
[N499] Oxford hbk **£27.50**

LEMPRIERE, JOHN
Lemprière's Classical Dictionary
For almost 200 years Lemprière's *Classical Dictionary of Proper Names in Ancient Authors* has been a faithful 'who's who' for the complex world of classical literature.
[N554] Routledge pbk **£12.95**

LEVI, PETER
Pelican History of Greek Literature
An excellent guide and a useful addition to the *Pelican Guide to English Literature* series, including interesting material on some of the lost plays.
[N555] Penguin pbk **£6.99**

REID, JOYCE M.H. (ED)
Concise Oxford Dictionary of French Literature
An abridged form of the *Oxford Companion to French Literature*. Entries from the *Companion* are condensed rather than omitted and all are fully cross-referenced.
[N500] Oxford hbk **£12.95**
[N501] Oxford pbk **£7.50**

SEYMOUR-SMITH, MARTIN
The Macmillan Guide to Modern World Literature
A robustly-argued, 1,400 page study of 20th century writing, divided into chapters on specific countries or groups of countries whose literature is related. Includes information on a range of countries whose literature has previously been neglected by both readers and critics, including Iceland, Armenia, Pakistan and many more.
[N563] Macmillan hbk **£40.00**
[N563A] Macmillan pbk **£14.95**

WARD, PHILIP
Oxford Companion to Spanish Literature
A comprehensive source of information on authors, texts, groups, movements, styles, critics and influences in Spanish literature from Roman times to the present day. Includes information on Spanish literature in all its linguistic forms, both from mainland Spain and from Central and Southern America.
[N502] Oxford hbk **£22.50**

WILDE, WILLIAM & HOOTON, JOY
Oxford Companion to Australian Literature
A comprehensive guide to Australian literature, attempting to place it in all the possible contexts of Australian culture from the first settlements in 1788 to the early 1980s.
[N564] Oxford hbk **£35.00**

General Studies

BAKER, CANDIDA
**Yackers:
Australian Writers Talk About Their Work**
Contains interviews with twelve writers, including Christina Stead, Peter Carey, Elizabeth Jolley, David Malouf, and Thea Astley.
[N565] Pan pbk **£3.95**

BROWN, DEMING
Soviet Russian Literature since Stalin
The most up-to-date general survey of post-war Russian literature, studying the work in its political, social and ideological contexts.
[N504] Cambridge pbk **£8.95**

BULLIVANT, KEITH (ED)
The Modern German Novel
Essays on Thomas Bernhard, Heinrich Böll, Max Frisch, Günter Grass, Peter Handke, Arno Schmidt, Botho Strauss, Martin Walser and Christa Wolf.
[N505] Berg hbk **£27.95**

CAESAR, M. & HAINSWORTH, P. (EDS)
Writers and Society in Contemporary Italy: A Collection of Essays
This volume is the first attempt to acquaint English readers with the wide range of literary and intellectual activity in Italy over the last 30 years.
[N506] Berg pbk **£7.95**

FAIRLIE, ALISON·
Imagination and Language
Essays on Constant, Baudelaire, Nerval, and Flaubert.
[N507] Cambridge pbk **£17.50**

FRANCO, JEAN
An Introduction to Spanish-American Literature
[N569] Cambridge hbk **£13.95**

HAMBURGER, MICHAEL
A Proliferation of Prophets
Essays on German Writers from Nietzsche to Brecht by the distinguished German translator and poet.
[N514] Carcanet pbk **£7.95**
After the Second Flood: Essays in Modern German Literature
[N515] Carcanet hbk **£16.95**

KING, JOHN (ED)
Modern Latin American Fiction: A Survey
Writers included are Isabel Allende, Borges, Gabriel García Marquez, Manuel Puig and Mario Vargas Llosa.
[N571] Faber pbk **£4.95**

LANDMARKS OF WORLD LITERATURE
This is a new series devoted to single literary texts. It concentrates on the relation to other texts and to the historical, cultural, and intellectual background. There is an impressive breadth of works chosen from world literature, from classical antiquity to the 20th century. Titles available:
Buddenbrooks, Anna Karenina, Old Goriot, The Tale of Genji, Faust: Part One, Rousseau: Confessions, The Odyssey, Tristram Shandy, The Divine Comedy, The Stranger, The Iliad, Bleak House, The Sorrows of Young Werther, The Waves, Nostromo, Adolphe, The Red and the Black, Swann's Way, Doctor Zhivago, Pound: The Cantos, Waiting for Godot, The Canterbury Tales.
[N537] Cambridge pbk **£3.95 - £4.50**

LUKACS, GEORG
Studies in European Realism
A sociological survey of the writings of Balzac, Stendhal, Tolstoy, Zola, Gorky, and others. It is a celebration of the humanist tradition in European literature.
[N516] Merlin pbk **£7.95**

NABOKOV, VLADIMIR
Lectures in Russian Literature
[N517] Picador pbk **£3.95**

NKOSI, LEWIS
Home and Exile & Other Selections
'An essential document for anyone interested in African, and especially South African, writing.'
(*Times Literary Supplement*)
[N572] Longman pbk **£11.75**

SHATTUCK, ROGER
The Innocent Eye
Examines the influence of French art and literature on contemporary culture.
[N520] Faber hbk **£15.00**

SPENDER, DALE
Writing a New World: Two Centuries of Australian Women Writers
This book relates how white women settlers in Australia wrote of their new lives in a strange land, through their letters home. Spender shows how this developed into the literature of today's Australian women writers such as Christina Stead and Thea Astley.
[N574] Pandora hbk **£16.95**

WALSH, WILLIAM (ED)
Commonwealth Literature
This volume includes some 120 writers and a useful introduction traces the origins of literature in English in Canada, Australia, New Zealand, India, Africa and the East Indies, as well as discussing specific national achievements in poetry, fiction and drama.
[N576] Macmillan pbk **£11.95**

Individual Writers

BAUDELAIRE, CHARLES
BENJAMIN, WALTER
Charles Baudelaire: A Lyric Poet in the Era of High Capitalism
A classic study by the German Marxist critic, something of a landmark in the development of materialist criticism.
[N522] Verso pbk **£7.95**

BORGES, JORGE LUIS
THOMAS, EDWARD (ED)
In Memory of Borges
Lectures by Greene, Borges, Henry Ferns, Mario Vargas Llosa, and Alicia Jurado.
[N578] Constable pbk **£6.95**

DANTE
TAMBLING, JEREMY
Dante and Difference
A new approach to the *Divine Comedy* drawing on medieval theories of reading and comparing them to current post-structuralist and hermeneutical analyses.
[N526] Cambridge hbk **£25.00**

DOSTOEVSKY, FEODOR
BAKHTIN, M.M.
Problems of Dostoevsky's Poetics
A complex study by a prominent literary theorist.
[N527] Manchester UP pbk **£11.50**
JONES, JOHN
Dostoevsky
A brilliant, if eccentric, study of narrative techniques and language in Dostoevsky's work by the author of acclaimed books on Wordsworth, Keats and Aristotle.
[N528] Oxford pbk **£5.95**
STEINER, GEORGE
Tolstoy or Dostoevsky: An Essay in Contrast
[N529] Faber pbk **£6.95**

FLAUBERT, GUSTAVE
SARTRE, JEAN-PAUL
**Family Idiot: Gustave Flaubert
1821 - 1857
Vol 1**
Sartre's critical masterpiece: massive, tendentious, unfinished. As revealing about its author as its subject, maybe more so.
[N530] Chicago UP hbk **£19.95**
Vol 2
[N531] Chicago UP hbk **£21.95**

GOETHE, J.W. VON
LUKACS, GEORG
Goethe in his Age
[N532] Merlin pbk **£6.95**

MALLARME, STEPHANE
BERSANI, LEO
The Death of Stephane Mallarmé
In this highly original and provocative study Bersani explores a paradox within Mallarmé's work - as a prime example of textual imperialism and yet as an extraordinary assault on literature's claims to importance.
[N521] Cambridge hbk **£12.95**

MANN, THOMAS
LUKACS, GEORG
Essays on Thomas Mann
[N538] Merlin pbk **£4.95**

MISHIMA, YUKIO
YOURCENAR, MARGUERITE
Yukio Mishima
[N583] A Ellis hbk **£8.95**

PROUST, MARCEL
BECKETT, SAMUEL
**Proust/Three Dialogues with
Georges Duthuit**
Beckett's early study of Proust also helps illuminate his own preoccupations.
[N539] Calder pbk **£3.95**
COCKING, J.M.
**Proust: Collected Essays on the
Writer and His Art**
[N540] Cambridge pbk **£12.95**
KILMARTIN, TERENCE
Guide to Proust
A comprehensive guide by the man who recently produced the standard Penguin translation of *A La Recherche duTemps Perdu*.
[N541] Chatto hbk **£10.95**
SHATTUCK, ROGER
Proust
Excellent brief introduction in the Fontana *Modern Masters* series.
[N542] Fontana pbk **£1.95**

PUSHKIN, ALEKSANDR
BAYLEY, JOHN
Pushkin: A Comparative Study
Bayley is one of the most skilful and illuminating of contemporary English critics to write on Russian literature; he is particularly good on Pushkin.
[N543] Cambridge hbk **£27.50**

SARTRE, JEAN-PAUL
GOLDTHORPE, RHIANNON
Sartre: Literature and Theory
'The nine essays collected in this well-printed volume contain some of the most scholarly and perceptive writing available on Sartre, either in English or in French.' (*Journal of European Studies*)
[N545] Cambridge pbk **£11.95**
MURDOCH, IRIS
Sartre: Romantic Rationalist
The philosophical strain which shows itself in all Iris

Murdoch's novels is fully employed in this study of Sartre's philosophy, looking at his ideas of consciousness, individuality and his theory of '*la litérature engagée*'.
[N546] Chatto hbk **£11.95**

SOLZHENITSYN, ALEXANDER
LUKACS, GEORG
Solzhenitsyn
Lukács sees Solzhenitsyn as the true heir to the socialist-realist writers of post-Revolutionary Russia, and as a major novelist on a world scale.
[N547] Merlin pbk **£6.00**

WOLF, CHRISTA
**The Fourth Dimension: Interviews with
Christa Wolf**
Wolf discusses the practice of creating her own fiction, and she asserts the importance of the authorial presence in her work and in the history of the novel.
[N548] Verso pbk **£7.95**

Literary Theory

There has been no greater site for debate in current literary study, or indeed any academic discpline, than that described by the term 'theory'. Broadly speaking, literary theory has in this century followed two main paths - the linguistic (whose main schools are formalism, semiotics and structuralism) and the historico-political (Marxism, feminism, new historicism). Other theorists have sought to undermine or complicate this binary opposition, as in the project of the most recent post-structuralism and deconstruction. Many of the writers most influential in literary theory will be found in other sections of the Guide: for example, Derrida, Lacan, and Lyotard in *Philosophy*; and Althusser, Habermas and Foucault in *Social Sciences*. As well as the individual works by the major theorists, this section contains many lucid and useful introductory works designed for tthe student and general reader, the best of which are by Jonathan Culler, Frank Lentricchia and Terry Eagleton.

ATTRIDGE, DEREK
**Peculiar Language: Literature as
Difference from the Renaissance to
James Joyce**
A lucid introduction to the uses of deconstruction, offering a vigorous set of essays that challenge the assumption that post-structuralist analysis ignores the social and political in literature.
[N586] Methuen pbk **£8.95**

ATTRIDGE, DEREK; BENNINGTON, GEOFF &
YOUNG, ROBERT (EDS)
**Post-Structuralism and the Question
of History**
A collection of essays anatomizing the central debate in literary theory today: the relationship between post-structuralism and historical (especially Marxist) literary theory. Contributors include Gashé, Derrida, Lyotard, Culler, Gayatri Chakravorty Spivak, and Maud Ellmann.
[N587] Cambridge pbk **£11.95**

AUERBACH, ERICH
Mimesis
A wide-ranging study of the classical concept of representation of reality in Western literature taking texts from Homer, Dante, Cervantes, Shakespeare and Proust.
[N588] Princeton UP pbk **£8.95**

BAKHTIN, M.M.
Influential Russian theorist whose work

problematizes the junction between Russian formalist theory and the dialogic flux of history.
Problem of Dostoevsky's Poetics
A classic work on Dostoevsky that also serves as a useful introduction to Bakhtin's literary theory.
[N589] Manchester UP pbk **£12.95**
CLARK, KATERINA & HOLQUIST, MICHAEL
Mikhail Bakhtin
Both a biography and a lucid introduction to the whole range of Bakhtin's literary and cultural theory.
[N590] Harvard UP pbk **£7.95**

BARRELL, JOHN
Poetry, Politics and Language
Bold new readings of canonical poetry, displaying how poetry analysis can absorb new approaches to literature focusing on issues of discourse, class and gender.
[N591] Manchester UP pbk **£6.95**

BARTHES, ROLAND
One of the most influential writers in literary theory, Barthes' work displays the transition from structuralism and semiotics to its problematization as post-structuralism, under the twin pressures of dcconstruction and historicism.
Criticism and Truth
Offers a definition of structuralist poetics.
[N592] Athlone hbk **£25.00**
Empire of Signs
A reading of the figure of Japan in Western thought.
[N593] Cape hbk **£10.95**
Michelet
Barthes' favourite book; it offers a series of interelated thematic summaries on the writings of one of France's greatest historians.
[N594] Blackwell pbk **£9.50**
Mythologies
Seminal text in the development of semiotics: a powerful yet subtle series of essays studyng the signs, gestures and messages through which Western society sustains, perpetuates and obscures itself.
[N595] Cape hbk **£9.95**
[N596] Grafton pbk **£3.99**
**Roland Barthes by Roland
Barthes**
A kind of autobiography both personal and theoretical, the book is an archaeology of Barthes' interests and obsessions.
[N597] Macmillan hbk **£29.50**
[N598] Macmillan pbk **£9.95**
Sade, Fourier, Loyola
[N599] Cape hbk **£9.95**
Sollers Writer
A reading of the controversial French writer Phillipe Sollers, raising the issues of the nature of narrative, the theory of language and the problems of traditional realism.
[N600] Athlone hbk **£25.00**
**The Grain of the Voice:
Interviews 1962 - 1980**
[N600A] Cape hbk **£25.00**
The Rustle of Language
A collection of essays espousing Barthes' poetic, in which he elegantly and subtly attempts to define the rustle of language, an elusive music of meaning.
[N601] Blackwell hbk **£29.50**
[N602] Blackwell pbk **£9.95**
The Semiotic Challenge
Fifteen essays, some analytic, some playful, from 1963 to 1973.
[N6021] Blackwell pbk **£9.95**
The Responsibility of Forms
Essays and reflections from 1961 to 1975, ranging from Art Deco via Greek Theatre and Pop Art to the songs of Schumann.
[N6011] Blackwell hbk **£27.50**

Writing Degree Zero and Elements of Semiology
Barthes' earliest writings, important in the development of structuralism.
[N603] Cape hbk **£8.95**

CULLER, JONATHAN
Barthes
Useful introduction; clear, but not overly simple.
[N604] Fontana pbk **£2.95**

SONTAG, SUSAN (ED)
The Roland Barthes Reader
[N605] Fontana pbk **£7.95**

BAYLEY, JOHN
Selected Essays
Essays which exemplify Bayley's dictum that the critic's function is to intensify enjoyment and enhance the value of the experience of reading.
[N606] Cambridge pbk **£9.95**

The Order of Battle at Trafalgar & Other Essays
Includes essays on Keats, Hardy and Larkin but concentrates on the great figures in the Russian tradition from Pushkin and Turgenev to Brodsky.
[N607] Collins hbk **£12.00**

BELSEY, CATHERINE
Critical Practice
Straightforward and articulate introduction to the new approaches to literary criticism.
[N609] Methuen hbk **£19.95**

The Subject of Tragedy
'This is a committed book which may go some way to converting the uncommitted ... Although she uses the specialized vocabulary of modern critical theory, she writes with a clarity and zest which can carry along even an uninitiated reader.' (*Times Higher Education Supplement*)
[N610] Methuen pbk **£8.95**

BENJAMIN, WALTER
German Marxist critic who studied literature and philosophy before collaborating with Brecht and Adorno. Benjamin moved to Paris to escape Nazi persecution and later committed suicide after failing to escape from Occupied France in 1940.
Illuminations
Essays which combine metaphysics and materialism, including his seminal piece: 'The Work of Art in the Age of Mechanical Reproduction'.
[N611] Fontana pbk **£3.95**

One Way Street & Other Writings
Essays introduced by Susan Sontag, including writings on language, character, and revolutionary violence; and essays on photography and surrealism.
[N613] New Left hbk **£29.95**

BENNETT, TONY
Formalism and Marxism
The best introductory guide to the work of the Russian Formalists and that of contemporary Marxist critics such as Macherey and Eagleton.
[N614] Methuen pbk **£6.95**

BERGONZI, BERNARD
The Myth of Modernism and 20th Century Literature
Collection of essays spanning fifteen years: a recurring theme is the effect of Modernism on major writers and literary opinion.
[N615] Harvester pbk **£11.95**

BLONSKY, MARSHALL (ED)
On Signs: A Semiotics Reader
Essays united only in their belief that the world and its human and cultural contents may be 'read' as texts and that the less explicit a society's codes and signals, the more revealing they become when subject to the

semiotician's scrutiny. Contributors include Barthes, Derrida, Foucault, Jakobson, Kristeva and Lacan.
[N616] Blackwell pbk **£10.95**

BLOOM, HAROLD
Bloom first emerged in the campaign started by Northrop Frye against the poetics of T.S. Eliot and the New Critics. He championed the Romantic line, which he insisted ran from Milton and Blake to Wallace Stevens and John Ashbery. His studies of individual writers were followed by his important tetralogy of books on poetic influence. Bloom's *Romanticism* sets him apart from the deconstructionist critics, as does his Judaism and the all-consuming influence of Freud.

A Map of Misreading
"The history of fruitful poetic influence ... is a history of anxiety and self-saving caricature, of distortion, of perverse, wilful revisionism without which modern poetry as such could not exist." (Bloom)
[N617] Oxford pbk **£6.95**

Poetry and Repression: Revisionism from Blake to Stevens
Reinterpretation of the full sweep of English and American Romantic poetry offering close readings of the major Romantic poets, alongside a review of the crucial ideas of Emerson, Nietzsche and Freud.
[N618] Yale UP pbk **£10.95**

The Anxiety of Influence
"True poetic history is the study of how poets as poets have suffered from other poets, just as any true biography is the story of how anyone suffered his own family - or his own displacement into lovers and friends." (Bloom)
[N619] Oxford pbk **£6.50**

The Breaking of the Vessels
Bloom argues for the *agon*, or struggle between poets, in a concise study of the Freudian mode of influence in literature. He examines criticism of the Bible, the Romantic tradition and Freud's own texts. The study intriguingly suggests the direction of Bloom's forthcoming magnum opus: his critical analysis of Freud.
[N620] Chicago UP pbk **£3.95**

The Ringers in the Tower: Studies in the Romantic Tradition
[N621] Chicago UP pbk **£3.75**

DE BOLLA, PETER
Harold Bloom: Towards Historical Rhetorics
A discursive appraisal of the nature of rhetoric in Bloom's writing, arguing for a historical conception of rhetoric.
[N622] Routledge pbk **£7.95**

BOOTH, WAYNE C.
Critical Understanding: The Powers and Limits of Pluralism
Expresses his belief that there is an important connection between understanding moral virtue and personal fulfillment.
[N624] Chicago UP pbk **£7.25**

The Company We Keep: An Ethics of Fiction
Booth argues that the relocation of ethics to the centre of our engagement with literature has affected the relationship between reader and writer.
[N625] California UP hbk **£18.95**

The Rhetoric of Fiction
A highly influential work of criticism which concentrates on how authors use consistent systems of rhetoric in order to achieve specific effects, which attempt to manipulate audience response in a determined way.
[N626] Penguin pbk **£8.95**

The Rhetoric of Irony
A systematic analysis of the rhetoric, or tropes, of irony and its effect on readers.
[N627] Chicago UP pbk **£10.25**

BOWIE, MALCOLM
Freud, Proust, Lacan: Theory as Fiction
Provocative reading of psychoanalytic texts with early 20th century fiction, using each to disrupt and disturb a simple understanding of the other.
[N628] Cambridge pbk **£10.95**

BUTLER, CHRISTOPHER
Interpretation, Deconstruction & Ideology
An introduction to some current issues in literary theory, outlining a pragmatic theory of interpretation based on structuralism, deconstruction and Marxist approaches.
[N631] Oxford pbk **£8.95**

CARROLL, DAVID
Paraesthetics: Foucault, Lyotard & Derrida
Probably the most insightful introduction to the work of these three writers, which by demonstrating the interpretation of post-structural theory with the 'new historicism' offers a defense of critical theory itself.
[N632] Methuen pbk **£9.95**

COHEN, RALPH (ED)
The Future of Literary Theory   **NEW**
The editor of *New Literary History* brings together an influential group of scholars and asks them to trace the future of theory.
[N633] Routledge pbk **£14.95**

COOMBES, HARRY
Literature and Criticism
A precise, clear and unpretentious introduction to the art of the literary critic taking the reader through the different aspects of rhythm, rhyme, imagery, poetic thought, feeling and diction.
[N634] Penguin pbk **£3.99**

CULLER, JONATHAN
Probably the best apologist for French theory writing in English, Culler's introductions have done much to explain and popularize structuralism and later developments.
Framing the Sign
Addresses the historical relationship between literary studies and the university, showing how criticism has become a university-based activity, designed to produce literary interpretations of canonical texts.
[N635] Blackwell pbk **£8.95**

On Deconstruction: Theory and Criticism after Structuralism
The best single introduction to deconstructive critical practice, describing with lucidity and acuteness the operation of the major writings of deconstructive (and feminist) theorists.
[N636] Routledge pbk **£8.95**

On Puns
Essays explaining ways in which puns reveal the fundamental workings of language.
[N637] Blackwell pbk **£8.95**

Structuralist Poetics: Structuralism, Linguistics and the Study of Literature
A major work studying the use of structuralism in literary criticism, showing both its strengths and weaknesses as a possible model for a poetics of the future.
[N638] Routledge pbk **£8.95**

The Pursuit of Signs
An investigation of the semiotics of literature, reader-response criticism and the implications of deconstruction.
[N639] Routledge pbk **£9.95**

DAICHES, DAVID
Critical Approaches to Literature
Poses and answers three questions: what is the nature and value of imaginative literature; how can we judge

the relative merits of individual literary works; and how is literature related to other human activities? [N641] Longman pbk **£9.95**

DE MAN, PAUL
Since his death in 1983 there has been a reassessment of Paul De Man and of deconstruction, the critical practice of which he was the most celebrated advocate in the US. De Man's collaborationist stance in World War II has been seen as indicative of the weakness of deconstruction, which denies the possibility of truth and justice. Certainly De Man's audacious synthesis of the ideas of Nietzsche with the methods of Derrida is ultimately anti-political, mesmerised by the beauty of ideas. However, it is De Man who carries the strongest influence on contemporary American criticism, and this is justified by the brilliance of analysis in his finest essays, collected in *Blindness and Insight*.

Allegories of Reading: Figural Language in Rousseau, Nietzsche, Rilke & Proust
[N644] Yale UP pbk **£11.95**

Blindness and Insight: Essays in the Rhetoric of Contemporary Criticism
Argues that critics owe their best insights to assumptions that these insights disprove.
[N645] Methuen pbk **£9.95**

The Rhetoric of Romanticism
'This collection holds special interest for its long chronological range. The praise that De Man granted Yeats applies equally to his own work: it constantly warns against the danger of unwarranted hopeful solutions.' (Jonathan Arac)
[N647] Columbia UP pbk **£9.50**

DOCHERTY, THOMAS
On Modern Authority: The Theory and Condition of Writing, 1500 to the Present Day
Original and insightful post-structuralist re-reading of literary and political history, exploring the condition of authority, writing and gender in modern culture.
[N648] Harvester pbk **£10.95**

EAGLETON, MARY (ED)
Feminist Literary Theory: A Reader
Drawing on the writing of around 50 French American and British writers, from Virginia Woolf to Joyce Carol Oates, this anthology makes available works previously only found in disparate academic journals.
[N649] Blackwell pbk **£8.95**

EAGLETON, TERRY
Leading English Marxist critic, who teaches at Oxford.

Against the Grain
Essays on Joseph Conrad, John Bayley, Wittgenstein, and Brecht, demonstrating his theory about the necessity of reading 'against the grain': that is to say, challenging the text's assumptions about its readers and reception.
[N650] Verso pbk **£7.95**

Criticism and Ideology
A wide-ranging analysis in which Eagleton asserts that the function of criticism is to question the immediate presence of the work, to deny naturalness in order to reveal the components of its making.
[N651] Verso pbk **£7.95**

The Function of Criticism
Useful introduction to the history of literary criticism, from the early 18th century to the present day.
[N652] Verso pbk **£6.95**

Literary Theory: An Introduction
One of the best introductions to literary theory, designed for an undergraduate audience. Recommended for its witty and lucid explication, and its remarkable condensation and synthesis.
[N653] Blackwell pbk **£6.95**

Marxism and Literary Criticism
[N654] Methuen pbk **£5.95**

The Ideology of the Aesthetic   **NEW**
Eagleton's major work to date, it aims to present nothing less than a history and critique of the concept of the aesthetic throughout modern Western thought, from Kant to Habermas.
[N655] Blackwell pbk **£9.95**

Walter Benjamin: Or Towards a Revolutionary Criticism
[N656] Verso pbk **£6.95**

ECO, UMBERTO
Semiotics and the Philosophy of Language
In this learned, stimulating and witty book Eco seeks to delineate the components of general semiotics: a formidable attempt at a unified theory.
[N659] Macmillan pbk **£9.95**

The Role of the Reader: Explorations in the Semiotics of Texts
Nine essays focusing on the role of the reader in textual interpretation, proposing a dialectic between 'open' and 'closed' texts; between a work of art that actively involves the reader in its production and one that holds a reader at bay and seeks to evoke a limited and predetermined response.
[N660] Hutchinson pbk **£9.95**

Travels in Hyperreality
An eclectic and entertaining series of essays in the semiotic manner, originally written for the popular press (first published as *Faith in Fakes*).
[N661] Picador pbk **£3.95**

ELIOT, T.S.
The critical theories of this famous poet are, despite his own hesitations, amongst the most influential in 20th century British scholarship, attacking as they do the conventions of traditional liberal literary appreciation.

For Lancelot Andrewes: Essays on Style and Order
[N662] Faber pbk **£3.95**

Notes towards the Definition of Culture
[N663] Faber pbk **£3.95**

On Poetry and Poets
[N664] Faber pbk **£3.95**

Selected Essays
Includes essays on Elizabethan and Restoration dramatists, 'The Function of Criticism', and 'Tradition and the Individual Talent', in which Eliot asserts, with reference to Western literary tradition, that the historical sense compels the writer to work consciously within that entire tradition.
[N665] Faber hbk **£14.95**

Selected Prose of T.S. Eliot
(Ed. Kermode, Frank)
[N666] Faber pbk **£5.95**

The Sacred Wood
Contains essays from the years 1917 to 1920 including 'The Perfect Critic' and essays on Blake, Dante, and Euripides.
[N667] Methuen pbk **£6.95**

The Use of Poetry and the Use of Criticism
[N668] Faber pbk **£4.99**

To Criticise the Critic
[N669] Faber pbk **£4.95**

NEWTON-DE-MOLINA, DAVID (ED)
The Literary Criticism of T.S. Eliot
Recent essays by F.W. Bateson, Denis Donoghue, Graham Hough, Samuel Hynes and others.
[N670] Athlone hbk **£30.00**

EMPSON, WILLIAM
English critic who played a key role in the development and popularization of New Criticism in Britain.

Argufying (Ed. Haffenden, John)
A posthumous collection of essays on literature and culture which exemplify the scope, wit, and passionate sanity of Empson's imagination.
[N671] Hogarth pbk **£15.00**

Faustus and the Censor
[N672] Blackwell hbk **£25.00**

Seven Types of Ambiguity
One of the most important modern critical works: in it Empson outlines a close (almost scientific) reading of the text, advocating the positive aspects of ambiguous words and phrases, with their multiple layers of meaning. 'Ambiguity' itself can mean an indecision as to what you mean, an intention to mean several things, a problem that one or other or both of two things has been meant, and the fact that a statement has several meanings.
[N673] Hogarth pbk **£5.95**

Some Versions of Pastoral
A purposefully difficult rendering of the pastoral mode which, according to fellow critic Robert Sale, expresses 'the collapse of the old pastoral relation of the swain-hero to the sheep-people and the consequence of that collapse in the period between the end of the 16th and the beginning of the 19th centuries'. Includes memorable readings of Shakespeare's Sonnet 94, *The Beggar's Opera*, and *Alice in Wonderland*.
[N674] Hogarth pbk **£5.95**

The Structure of Complex Words
Includes a series of exacting analyses of key words, including 'wit' in Pope's *Essay on Criticism*; 'all' in *Paradise Lost*; 'fool' in *King Lear* and 'sense' in *The Prelude*.
[N675] Hogarth pbk **£5.95**

NORRIS, CHRISTOPHER
William Empson and the Philosophy of Literary Criticism
The first full-length study of Empson's work, which among its other concerns accounts for the gulf that has emerged between Empson's viewpoint and the understanding of his work by others.
[N676] Athlone hbk **£32.50**

FELPERIN, HOWARD
Beyond Deconstruction: The Uses and Abuses of Literary Theory
An account of the swiftly developing discipline of contemporary literary theory, and its consequences for future literary study.
[N679] Oxford pbk **£9.95**

FISH, STANLEY
Doing What Comes Naturally   **NEW**
Essays on the rational basis of our literary, legal and psychoanalytic interpretation. Fish assesses the place of reason in a rhetorical world.
[N680] Oxford hbk **£35.00**

Is There a Text in this Class? The Authority of Interpretative Communities
One of the seminal texts in the reader-response school, which places the emphasis on the experience of the reader in constructing the meaning of the text.
[N681] Harvard UP pbk **£7.95**

FORSTER, E.M.
Aspects of the Novel
A friendly, popular and unsystematic attempt to establish a 'poetics of fiction'.
[N682] Penguin pbk **£3.99**

FRYE, NORTHROP
Practical Imagination: Poetry
[N683] Harper & R pbk **£7.75**

T.S. Eliot: An Introduction
[N684] Chicago UP pbk **£5.25**

The Anatomy of Criticism
Historical, ethical, archetypal and rhetorical criticism are paired with their analogues - modes, symbols, myths and genres.
[N685] Princeton pbk **£9.95**

The Critical Path: Essays on the Social Context of Literary Criticism
Poses three questions: what are the specific functions of poetry and criticism; in what sense can the past be said 'to know' anything; and what is the relationship between a society and its art?
[N686] Harvard UP pbk **£8.95**

GENETTE, GERARD
Narrative Discourse: An Essay in Method
'Probably the best articulation ... of the ways in which narrative disposes itself in time, mood and 'voice': but it is also full of insight into the chief source of its examples - *A la Recherche du Temps Perdu.'*
(*London Review of Books*)
[N689] Blackwell pbk **£10.50**

GILBERT, SANDRA & GUBAR, SUSAN
No Man's Land: The Place of the Woman Writer in the 20th Century
An innovative reading of modernist works, tracing the role of anxious male chauvinism and of the problems of gender in the development of modernism.
[N690] Yale UP hbk **£12.95**

Shakespeare's Sisters: Feminist Essays on Women Poets
Beginning with Jane Lead and Anne Bradstreet, the essays examine the work of H.D., Denise Levertov, Edna St. Vincent Millay, Christina Rossetti, Emily Dickinson and Adrienne Rich.
[N691] Indiana UP pbk **£12.95**

The Madwoman in the Attic
A massive work that uses the metaphor of madness to trace the genesis of writing by women in the 19th century. A skilful and commanding example of feminist literary theory, offering revisionist essays on Wollestonecraft, the Brontës, Mary Shelley, Elizabeth Barrett Browning, Emily Dickinson and Virginia Woolf.
[N692] Yale pbk **£16.95**

GIRARD, RENE
Influential but unclassifiable critic who is currently teaching at Stanford University in California. His work 'presents a self-sufficient and internally coherent system of thought; it is both a rationally articulated study and a prophetic vision of the hidden origins of culture and the nature of cultural process.'
(*Comparative Literature*)
Deceit, Desire and the Novel
A key work in both our understanding of the novel and the application of post-structuralism and psychoanalytic criticism to reading method, in all its social, economic, political and spiritual dimensions.
[N693] Athlone pbk **£15.95**

To Double Business Bound: Essays on Literature, Mimesis and Anthropology
Essays on Dante, Camus, Lévi-Strauss, Dostoevsky and others, which explore and develop Girard's central idea of mimesis and scapegoating.
[N694] Athlone hbk **£35.00**

Violence and the Sacred
'Abounds in fresh and stimulating interpretations of psychoanalysis, of anthropological theories, and dramatic situations in Greek Tragedies.' (Wallace Fowlie)
[N695] Athlone pbk **£15.95**

GUIRAUD, PIERRE
Semiology
A compressed survey of the general principles of semiotics.
[N697] Routledge pbk **£7.95**

HARLAND, RICHARD
Superstructuralism
A comprehensive, jargon-free and accessible guide to all the major figures of recent theoretical movements, including sections on Saussure, Lévi-Strauss, Lacan, Althusser, Barthes, Foucault, Derrida, Kristeva and Deleuze and Guattari.
[N701] Routledge pbk **£6.95**

HARTMAN, GEOFFREY
Easy Pieces
An eclectic and insightful collection of essays on diverse cultural topics including Hitchcock, Barthes, Borges and Malraux.
[N702] Columbia UP pbk **£9.60**

Criticism in the Wilderness: The Study of Literature Today
A critical study of the difference between literature and criticism, examining the rise of new theory in the American academy, and its effect on literature.
[N703] Yale UP pbk **£11.95**

HARVEY, DAVID
The Condition of Postmodernity: An Enquiry into the Origins of Cultural Change NEW
'Devastating. The most brilliant study of postmodernity to date. David Harvey cuts beneath the theoretical debates about postmodernist culture to reveal the social and economic basis of this apparently free-floating phenomenon.' (Terry Eagleton)
[N6431] Blackwell pbk **£9.95**

HAWKES, TERENCE
Structuralism and Semiotics
A lucid introduction, designed for the undergraduate student.
[N705] Methuen pbk **£4.95**

HEATH, STEPHEN
Representation and Sexual Difference
Looks at various approaches to the great sexual imponderable first articulated by Freud - 'What does a woman want?' - moving on to review the question of man/women and its analogue, conscious/unconscious in Hardy's *Jude the Obscure* and Stevenson's *Dr Jekyll and Mr Hyde*.
[N706] Blackwell pbk **£7.95**

The Sexual Fix
[N707] Macmillan pbk **£7.95**

HUME, KATHRYN
Fantasy and Mimesis: Response to Reality in Western
In an analysis that ranges from the Icelandic sagas to Science Fiction, and the Odyssey to the *nouveau roman*, Hume examines the ways in which fantasy and mimesis contribute to literary representations of reality.
[N708] Routledge pbk **£9.95**

HUTCHEON, LINDA
A Poetics of Postmodernism: History, Theory, Fiction
In this, her third study of formal self-consciousness in art, Hutcheon adds both a historical and an ideological dimension.
[N709] Routledge pbk **£9.95**

A Theory of Parody: Teachings of the 20th Century Artform
'This thoughtful engagement with the theory of parody picks its way meticulously through this conceptual minefield, to emerge with a convincing map of the terrain which admirably complements her previous account of the nature of artistic self-reflection.' (*Times Literary Supplement*)
[N710] Routledge pbk **£9.95**

JACOBUS, MARY
Reading Women: Readings in Feminist Criticism
One of the foremost contemporary feminist critics considers the relations between women, literary theory, and psychoanalysis; reflecting the current concerns in Anglo-American and French theory.
[N712] Routledge pbk **£8.95**

JAKOBSON, ROMAN
Leading figure in the Russian and Prague school of formalists, and later a key influence on Barthes, Lévi-Strauss and American structuralism and linguistics.
Language in Literature
The first presentation in English of Jakobson's major essays on the intertwining of language and literature in which he reveals himself as a great explorer of literary art, re-inventing the freshness of poets like Shakespeare and Pushkin.
[N713] Harvard UP hbk **£21.25**

JAMESON, FREDERIC
Foremost American Marxist literary and cultural theorist.
The Ideologies of Modelling: Vol 1
Collected essays on theory, mostly examining the tension between literary criticism and the need to explain the Marxist intellectual tradition.
[N714] Routledge pbk **£8.95**

The Ideologies of Modelling: Vol 2
[N715] Routledge pbk **£8.95**

The Political Unconscious: Narrative as a Socially Symbolic Act
Ambitious and rewarding attempt to politicize the deconstruction of textual gaps and inconsistencies, seen as the 'unconscious', produced by a collision of language, form and ideology.
[N716] Routledge pbk **£8.95**

JAUSS, HANS ROBERT
Toward an Aesthetic of Reception
The seminal text in reception theory. Contains an introduction by Paul De Man.
[N717] Harvester pbk **£8.95**

JOHNSON, BARBARA
A World of Difference
Extends and rethinks the theoretical perspectives on literature in *The Critical Difference* and contains subtle and probing analyses of texts by Molière, Wordsworth, Poe, Baudelaire, Mallarmé and De Man.
[N719] J Hopkins hbk **£17.40**

The Critical Difference
Johnson's analysis of deconstruction (she is the translator of Derrida's *Dissemination*) has made the discipline more relevant to literary studies, concentrating (unlike much of De Man and Derrida) on accessible literary texts, such as those of Melville and Poe.
[N720] J Hopkins hbk **£17.40**

JOSIPOVICI, GABRIEL
The World and the Book: A Study of Modern Fiction
Engagingly crafted study of modern fiction and its predecessors, subtly demonstrating the use of structuralist and formalist theory.
[N721] Macmillan pbk **£8.95**

Writing and the Body
An unusual, deeply personal, highly original and suggestive exploration of a central literary question through the work of Kafka, Shakespeare, Sterne and Dante.
[N722] Harvester hbk **£37.50**

KERMODE, FRANK
An Appetite for Poetry: Essays in Literary Interpretation NEW
Essays on Milton, Eliot, Wallace Stevens, William

Empson, biblical criticism and an extended polemical prologue which reaffirms Kermode's belief in the vital interdependence of literature, criticism and theory.
[N724] Collins hbk **£15.00**

Essays on Fiction 1971 - 1982
[N725] Routledge pbk **£7.50**

Forms of Attention
Three essays: the formation of the Botticelli canon, a *scherzo* on Hamlet, and lastly a piece that shows how disentangling opinion from knowledge is less important than preserving what we value against loss.
[N726] Chicago UP pbk **£4.75**

History and Value
[N727] Oxford hbk **£15.00**

The Genesis of Secrecy
An eloquent, provocative book which argues that the reader approaches the text as he does the world - with the understanding (ultimately disappointed) that he will find a semblance of order, meaning and authority.
[N728] Harvard UP pbk **£6.25**

The Sense of an Ending: Studies in the Theory of Fiction
A pioneering attempt to relate 'the theory of literary fictions to the theory of fictions in general' using fictions of apocalypse as a model.
[N729] Oxford pbk **£5.95**

KRISTEVA, JULIA
French theorist of language and science who is best known for her examinations of the relationship between language, the body, and the limits of personal identity (particularly female), which draw heavily upon Lacanian psychoanalysis and semiotics.

Desire in Language: A Semiotic Approach to Literature and Art
In this work Kristeva proposes and tests theories involving first the origin and development of the novel, and second what she has defined as a signifying practice in 'poetic language' and pictorial works. Includes essays on Beckett, Sollers, Giotto and Bellini.
[N730] Blackwell pbk **£9.95**

Language: The Unknown - An Initiation into Linguistics `NEW`
Kristeva's first book examines language as the material object of thought and focuses on the representative or semiotic processes of linguistic communication.
[N731] Harvester hbk **£20.00**

The Kristeva Reader (Ed. Moi, Toril)
The first comprehensive and accessible introduction to Kristeva's work in English. The essays are selected as representative of the three main areas of her work: semiotics, psychoanalysis and political theory.
[N732] Blackwell pbk **£9.95**

LEAVIS, F.R.
Leavis's influence on the way literature is taught at school and university can hardly be overestimated, though his 'Practical Criticism', liberal humanism and canonical tradition are now deeply unfashionable.

English Literature in Our Time and the University
[N733] Cambridge pbk **£6.95**

New Bearings in English Poetry
Influential study of Eliot, Pound and Hopkins which asserted them as *the* major poets for the following generation.
[N734] Penguin pbk **£5.95**

The Common Pursuit
[N735] Hogarth pbk **£5.95**

The Great Tradition
A study of George Eliot, Henry James, and Joseph Conrad; all of whom are distinguished by their 'vital capacity for experience' and in whose works 'certain human potentialities are nobly celebrated'.
[N736] Penguin pbk **£6.99**

SINGH, J.
Valuation in Criticism & Other Essays
Gathers together essays, reviews, articles, lectures and notes which have not appeared in volume form before: including pieces on T.S. Eliot, Lawrence, Empson, George Eliot, Henry James, Yeats, and his reflections on Marxism.
[N737] Cambridge pbk **£10.95**

LEAVIS, Q.D.
Collected Essays Vol 1: The Englishness of the English Novel
Essays on Jane Austen, Emily and Charlotte Brontë, and George Eliot.
[N738] Cambridge pbk **£13.50**

Vol 2: The American Novel and Reflections on the European Novel
[N739] Cambridge pbk **£12.95**

Vol 3: The Novel of Religious Controversy `NEW`
Focuses on the Anglo-Irish novel and women writers of the 19th century. 'Her *Collected Essays* easily surpass *The Great Tradition* for depth of perception, originality of thought, and plain, forceful masculine expression.' (*The Times*)
[N740] Cambridge hbk **£30.00**

LENTRICCHIA, FRANK
After the New Criticism (1980)
From this self-styled historian of the critical scene, an ambitious account of the rise of American deconstruction and its continental sources. A valuable critical introduction.
[N741] Methuen pbk **£9.95**

Ariel and the Police: Michel Foucault, William James, Wallace Stevens
Argues that the desire for power is comparable with the desire for freedom and articulation.
[N742] Harvester hbk **£29.95**

LERNER, LAURENCE
Reconstructing Literature
Essays by Wayne C. Booth, John Holloway, Gabriel Josipovici, Laurence Lerner, Roger Scruton, Anthony Thorlby, and Cedric Watts, covering texts as diverse as Sophocles, Proust and Kafka.
[N743] Blackwell pbk **£9.95**

The Frontiers of Literature
Examines discourses that share a border with literature, such as narrative history and religion, and goes on to explore the signficance of the material periphery of books themselves: titles, prefaces, authorship, rejected drafts.
[N744] Blackwell hbk **£27.50**

LEVINAS, EMMANUEL & HAND, SEAN (ED)
The Levinas Reader `NEW`
A major influence on the development of 20th century continental philosophy through works such as *Totality and Infinity* and *Otherwise than Being*, Levinas has provided inspiration for Derrida, Lyotard, Blanchot and Irigaray. This is the most representative selection of his writing to have appeared in English.
[N746] Blackwell pbk **£9.95**

LEVINSON, MARJORIE; BUTLER, MARILYN; MCGANN, JEROME & HAMILTON, PAUL
Rethinking Historicism: Critical Readings in Romantic History `NEW`
Four distinguished scholars of Romanticism address the problematic concept of 'History' within Romantic studies, interrogating the methods and assumptions of both 'new' and 'old' historicism to provide alternative ways of reading the literary past.
[N747] Blackwell hbk **£25.00**

LEWIS, C.S
An Experiment in Criticism
Shows Lewis's primary concerns of the notion of good reading, the surrender of the reader to the text, and the affinities this process shares with love and morality.
[N748] Cambridge pbk **£7.95**

Selected Literary Essays
Containing the essay 'The Anthropological Approach', in which Lewis proposes that criticism is a body of knowledge that 'enables the reader to enter more fully into the author's intentions.'
[N749] Cambridge pbk **£13.95**

LODGE, DAVID
Modes of Modern Writing: Metaphor, Metonymy & the Typology of Modern Literature
Incisive and exploratory essay on the polarity between metaphoric and metonymic techniques of expression, supported by detailed analysis of critical and literary texts.
[N751] Arnold pbk **£12.00**

The Language of Fiction
Argues against the belief that the language of poetry is somehow essentially different from the language of prose.
[N752] Routledge pbk **£7.95**

The Novelist at the Crossroads & Other Essays on Fiction and Criticism
The 'crossroads' which the modern novelist faces refers to his choice between conventional naturalism and the various escapes from realism which Robert Scholes calls 'fabulation'.
[N753] Routledge pbk **£3.95**

Working with Structuralism: Essays and Reviews on 19th & 20th Century Literature
A collection of reviews and essays that display the assimilation of structuralist method without becoming confusing or exclusively theoretical.
[N754] Routledge pbk **£5.95**

Write On: Occasional Essays 1965 - 1985
This selection of occasional essays provides a humane and witty anthology of writing on a wide range of topics - including Catholicism, Norman Mailer and literature in general. As Lodge puts it: 'you pays your money, and takes your Joyce'.
[N755] Penguin pbk **£3.95**

LUKACS, GEORG
Hungarian-born Marxist critic, theorist and Stalinist academic.
The Historical Novel
Lukács's major work, displaying almost all of his critical concepts in a Hegelian/Marxist defence of the European realist novel.
[N757] Penguin pbk **£5.95**

Theory of the Novel (1920)
Written in 1914, this pre-Marxist work is influenced by Hegel, and describes the novel as a bourgeois epic 'of alienation and pessimism'.
[N758] Merlin pbk **£4.95**

Writer and Critic
An eclectic collection of critical articles, most notably an important defense of the 'reflectionist' concept of art.
[N759] Merlin pbk **£5.95**

MACDONELL, DIANE
Theories of Discourse: An Introduction
Critical introduction to theories of discourse advanced by Foucault, Althusser, Pecheux, and Hirst, which propose that speech and writing encode the structures of power in society, and that because society is defined by struggle and conflict, our discourses reflect and create conflict.
[N760] Blackwell pbk **£7.95**

MACHEREY, PIERRE
French Marxist literary theorist.
The Theory of Literary Production (1970)
Innovative and influential application of the Marxist theory of Althusser to literary criticism, decisively breaking with 'neo-Hegelian' Marxist criticism.
[N761] Routledge pbk **£9.95**

MACHIN, RICHARD & NORRIS, CHRISTOPHER (EDS)
Post-Structuralist Readings of English Poetry
Exemplary essays in the post-structural method on texts ranging from Shakepeare to the modernists, from contributors including Catherine Belsey, Harold Bloom, Maud Ellmann, Geoffrey Hartman, J. Hillis Miller, and Gayatri Chakravorty Spivak.
[N762] Cambridge pbk **£10.95**

MARKS, ELAINE & COURTIVRON, ISABELLE DE (EDS)
New French Feminisms
An anthology presenting the different theoretical approaches of the new French feminists (Kristeva, Cixous, Irigaray, et al). An excellent starting point for the uninitiated.
[N763] Harvester pbk **£9.95**

MCGANN, JEROME J.
The Beauty of Inflections: Literary Investigations in Historical Method & Theory
Explores the problems of historical literary studies in post-structuralism, through essays mainly in Romantic literature, and attempts to develop a fully elaborated socio-historical criticism for literary works.
[N764] Oxford pbk **£12.95**

MILLER, J. HILLIS
Leading proponent of the american school of deconstruction at Yale.
Fiction and Repetition: Seven English Novels
Exemplary readings in deconstruction: analysing *Wuthering Heights*, *Henry Esmond*, *Tess of the D'Urbervilles*, *The Well-Beloved*, *Lord Jim*, *Mrs Dalloway* and *Between the Acts* for the resistance they themselves produce to their own totalizing forces.
[N765] Blackwell pbk **£9.95**
The Ethics of Reading
A clear and helpful introduction to the deconstruction debate and a skilful examination of the ethical questions usually thought unanswerable by deconstruction.
[N766] Columbia UP pbk **£9.50**

MILLER, KARL
Authors   **NEW**
A spirited defence of the author and authorial presence, ranging from *Hamlet* and Cervantes to Kingsley Amis, Milan Kundera and Primo Levi.
[N768] Oxford hbk **£15.00**

MOI, TORIL
French Feminist Thought
A useful anthology that includes contributions from well-known theorists such as Luce Irigaray and Julia Kristeva, and provides a cross-section of texts from the women's movement, recent feminist research and intellectual debate in France.
[N770] Blackwell pbk **£9.50**
Sexual/Textual Politics: Feminist Textual Theory
Combining detailed exposition with a coherent argument of its own, this book examines the strengths and limitations of Anglo-American and French feminist literary theory, in a balanced comparative analysis.
[N769] Routledge pbk **£6.95**

MONTEFIORE, JAN
Feminism and Poetry
Describes what is specific to women's poetry and shows how women poets deal with the masculine literary and critical tradition by which poetry is defined.
[N771] Pandora pbk **£4.95**

MORETTI, FRANCO
Signs Taken for Wonders
Moretti's 'wonders' are the most celebrated moments in modern literature. He examines them through different critical approaches to create a 'sociology of literary forms'.
[N773] Verso pbk **£9.95**

NORRIS, CHRISTOPHER
Deconstruction: Theory and Practice
[N775] Methuen pbk **£6.95**
The Contest of Faculties
Controversial and adventurous reading of deconstruction and literary theory in the context of contemporary analytic philosophy.
[N776] Methuen pbk **£8.95**

PARKER, PATRICIA
Literary Fat Ladies: Rhetoric, Gender and Property
Discussing a wide range of texts to discover patterns in written rhetoric that reveal more general questions of literary plotting, hierarchy, ideological framing and political consequence.
[N777] Methuen pbk **£10.95**

PARRINDER, PATRICK
Authors and Authority
Subtitled 'A Study of English Literary Criticism and its Relation to Culture, 1750 -1900', this is an interesting theoretical account of the history of literary criticism.
[N778] Routledge pbk **£7.50**
The Failure of Theory
Controversial collection of essays that argue that the theoretical revolution in literary studies is visibly failing, and furthermore has had a detrimental effect on contemporary creative writing.
[N779] Harvester pbk **£9.95**

POIRIER, RICHARD
A World Elsewhere: The Place of Style in American Fiction
Style for Poirier is used to encompass all aspects of the writer - 'sounds, identities and presences' - as expressed in the work of Emerson, Hawthorne and Twain, amongst others.
[N780] Oxford pbk **£4.95**
The Renewal of Literature: Emersonian Reflections
'A massive dose of brilliance ... a wonderfully invigorating and always challenging work' (Edward Said). Poirier turns to Emerson, Frost, Stevens and William James to find support for this powerful critique of modernism in creative and critical writing.
[N781] Faber hbk **£14.95**

POUND, EZRA
Seminal figure in British modernist poetry and criticism, whose articles and prescriptions (on Imagism and Vorticism in particular) were widely influential in the method and technique of many modernist poets.
ABC of Reading
Proposes that prose and poetry have important psychological and ethical functions to discharge but that it is in poetry that language is 'charged with meaning to the utmost possible degree.'
[N782] Faber pbk **£3.99**
Confucian Analects
[N783] P Owen hbk **£10.95**

Guide to Kulchur
[N784] P Owen hbk **£15.95**
Literary Essays of Ezra Pound
[N785] Faber pbk **£8.95**
Selected Prose 1909 - 1965
'Chosen from hundreds of articles and shorter pieces of journalism to which until now only scholars have had access.' (*Times Literary Supplement*)
[N786] Faber pbk **£3.95**
The Spirit of Romance
[N787] P Owen pbk **£9.95**

RICHARDS, I.A.
Practical Criticism
Examples of the method of practical criticism.
[N790] Routledge pbk **£9.95**
Principles of Literary Criticism
A key work in the theory of 'practical criticism', the empirical approach that still informs most literary studies in British education.
[N791] Routledge pbk **£7.95**
RICHARDS, I.A. & OGDEN, C.K.
The Meaning of Meaning
A classic work dealing directly with the central problem of meaning and providing a fundamental and lively critique of language itself.
[N793] Routledge pbk **£6.95**

RICOEUR, PAUL
French philosopher whose work synthesizes elements of phenomenology, hermeneutics, structuralism and psychoanalysis.
The Rule of Metaphor
An exhaustive account of the ways metaphors operate to generate meaning in language.
[N795] Routledge pbk **£9.95**

RIMMON-KENAN, SHLOMITH
Narrative Fiction: Contemporary Poetics
A synthesis of contemporary approaches to narrative fiction, including Anglo-American new criticism, Russian formalism, French structuralism, and the phenomenology of reading.
[N797] Methuen pbk **£6.95**

ROE, SUE (ED)
Women Reading Women's Writing
Offers illuminating answers to the question of how women readers approach the problems inherent in writing about men. Discusses the work of Virginia Woolf, the Brontës, Angela Carter and Sylvia Plath.
[N798] Harvester pbk **£8.95**

RORTY, RICHARD
Contingency, Irony and Despair   **NEW**
Continues Rorty's assault on foundationalist metaphysics, carrying it into the literary arena. Whereas the work of philosophers like Nietzsche, Freud and Wittgenstein enable socities to see themselves as mere historical contingencies, imaginative literature (Orwell and Nabokov are cited) can promote the solidarity a truly liberal culture needs.
[N799] Cambridge pbk **£8.95**

ROSE, JACQUELINE
Sexuality in the Field of Vision
An exploration of the encounter between feminism, psychoanalysis, semiotics, and film theory. Includes a memorable reading of *Hamlet*.
[N800] Verso pbk **£7.95**

RUTHVEN, KEN
Critical Assumptions
A clear and discursive guide to the pragmatic assumptions made in literary criticism.
[N801] Cambridge pbk **£9.95**
Feminist Literary Studies

A rigorous and oft-referred to account of the questions that ground a comparatively new discipline.
[N802] Cambridge pbk **£7.50**

SAID, EDWARD W.
Beginnings
An eloquently argued thesis on the concept of origin, authorship and beginning in writing, this is one of the best examples of American deconstructive practice.
[N803] Columbia UP pbk **£7.50**
The World, the Text and the Critic
An impressive series of essays, offering a discussion of the secular state of contemporary criticism in the West and brilliant investigations into Derrida, Foucault, Swift, Conrad and Lukács.
[N804] Faber pbk **£6.95**

SALUSINSKY, IMRE
Criticism in Society
Interviews with Jacques Derrida, Northrop Frye, Harold Bloom, Geoffrey Hartman, Frank Kermode, Edward Said, Frank Lentricchia, and J. Hillis Miller, wherein each is asked to discuss general modes of criticism as well as offering some close analysis of the same Wallace Stevens poem.
[N805] Routledge pbk **£6.95**

SCHOLES, ROBERT
Semiotics and Interpretation
Applies the full range of semiotic theory to a series of texts - poems, stories, films, a scene from a play, bumper stickers. 'Accessible yet challenging, this book will be the indispensable new introductory text for semiotics.' (*Choice*)
[N806] Yale UP pbk **£7.95**
Textual Power: Literary Theory and the Teaching of English
A discussion of the uses and abuses of theory in the teaching of literature, arguing that teaching is unavoidably a theoretical activity.
[N807] Yale UP pbk **£5.95**
The Elements of Poetry
[N808] Oxford pbk **£3.25**

SELDEN, RAMAN
A Reader's Guide to Contemporary Literary Theory
'This book is an admirable compression of a huge area of critical activity and discussion. Selden takes on nothing less than the whole of contemporary theory and is wonderfully lucid.' (Robert Con Davis)
[N809] Harvester pbk **£5.95**
Practising Theory and Reading Literature: An Introduction
'Remarkably concise but informative summaries of just about every major critical movement ... achieves minor miracles in the way of compressed argument and lucid explanation.' (Christopher Norris)
[N810] Harvester pbk **£6.95**
The Theory of Criticism from Plato to the Present: A Reader
[N811] Longman pbk **£10.95**

SHOWALTER, EILEEN
New Feminist Criticism: Essays on Women, Literature and Theory (Ed)
Essays which range from the Brontës to modern romance by the critics Rosalind Coward, Sandra Gilbert, Susan Gubar, Carolyn Heilbrun, Annette Kolodny.
[N812] Virago pbk **£7.50**
Speaking of Gender `NEW`
Innovative collection of essays that move beyond feminism to gender theory through deconstruction and reader-reponse criticism.
[N813] Routledge pbk **£8.95**

SKURA, MERDITH ANNE
The Literary Use of the Psychoanalytic Process
'A landmark in the theory and practice of psychoanalytic criticism indispensable to the critic interested in this subject.' (*Choice*)
[N814] Yale UP pbk **£11.50**

SONTAG, SUSAN
Popular American critic who has remained stimulating on all aspects of contemporary culture. Her early essays in *Against Interpretation* championed an emotional intuitive approach to art rather than an intellectual one, but more recent work has centred on her defence of the life of the mind against the excesses of the 'radical will' she herself helped define in the 1960s, which sought to alter consciousness for aesthetic reasons, as in the use of drugs.
Against Interpretation
[N814A] Deutsch pbk **£5.95**
AIDS and its Metaphors `NEW`
Sontag considers the metaphors with which AIDS is encumbered, such as 'plague'. She scrutinizes the appetite in our society for worst-case scenarios, what Saul Bellow calls 'apocalyptic thinking'.
[N814B] Viking hbk **£9.95**
Illness as Metaphor
[N814C] Penguin pbk **£3.50**
Susan Sontag Reader
[N814D] Penguin pbk **£7.99**
Under the Sign of Saturn
[N814E] Writers & R pbk **£4.95**

SPIVAK, GAYATRI CHAKRAVORTY
In Other Worlds
Important synthesis of Derridean deconstruction and feminist theory, applying that model to major debates in the study of literature, culture and theory.
[N815] Routledge pbk **£9.95**

STEINER, GEORGE
Versatile humanist critic and cultural sage.
After Babel: Aspects of Language and Translation
An examination of the difficulties of literary translation which proceeds to analyse the wider issue of language as a means of human adaption and survival.
[N816] Oxford pbk **£6.95**
Antigones
The Antigone myth as evidenced in Western literature, art and thought.
[N817] Oxford pbk **£5.95**
George Steiner: A Reader
[N818] Penguin pbk **£6.99**
Language and Silence: Essays and Notes 1958 - 1956
[N819] Faber pbk **£6.99**
On Difficulty and Other Essays
Asks in what ways the classical and human ideals and values which have animated Western literature and habits of thought have been eroded, and how our ability to read has been affected by the decline of privacy.
[N820] Oxford pbk **£4.95**
Real Prescences: Is there Anything in What We Say? `NEW`
Asserts that the 'death of God' pervades our culture, underwriting the modish arguments for emptiness and absence in current theories of meaning.
[N8173] Faber hbk **£14.99**
The Death of Tragedy
No 'neat abstract definition' of tragedy is here given; instead tragedy is seen to arise when a hero (Oedipus, Lear, Phèdre or Pentheus) is forced to suffer an extra-judicial punishment which far exceeds his or her apparent guilt.
[N821] Faber pbk **£4.25**

STRICKLAND, GEOFFREY
Structuralism or Criticism?: Thoughts on How We Read
A critical introduction to the structuralist debate in the academy, offering both an introduction to, and a critique of, the use of theory in literary criticism.
[N823] Cambridge pbk **£10.95**

THOMPSON, E.P.
The Poverty of Theory & Other Essays
A fusion of political ideas and literary influence, this is a polemic drawing on the English poetic tradition in the form of Blake, Wordsworth and William Morris.
[N826] Merlin pbk **£7.95**

TODOROV, TZETVAN
Bulgarian-French literary theorist and historian of ideas, Todorov is best known for his work on hermeneutics and his exacting structural analyses of literary prose.
French Literary Theory Today: A Reader
An anthology of studies representing the most significant contributions made in France in the last 15 years.
[N827] Cambridge pbk **£9.95**
Introduction to Poetics
[N828] Harvester pbk **£5.95**
Mikhail Bakhtin: The Dialogical Principle
Study of the Russian formalist whose work continues to influence contemporary post-structuralist and Marxist literary theory.
[N829] Manchester UP pbk **£13.95**
Symbolism and Interpretation
[N830] Routledge hbk **£17.95**

VEESER, HAROLD (ED)
The New Historicism `NEW`
New Historicism has helped replace a fact-finding model of historical study with a descriptive and narrative model. This collection of essays examines and explains the 'New' history.
[N832] Routledge pbk **£9.95**

VICKERS, BRIAN
In Defence of Rhetoric `NEW`
Sets out to intellectually reinstate rhetoric, providing a bold and detailed history of the discipline from classical times through to the critical theories of Roman Jakobson and Paul De Man.
[N833] Oxford hbk **£14.95**

WASHINGTON, PETER
Fraud Theory `NEW`
A spirited attack on the theoretical 'house style' which dominates literary studies (i.e. the combination of structuralism, semiotics, Marxism, and feminism). 'After reading this energetic and lucid attack on theory, I began to feel that dons in English should only get tenure if they stuck to teaching their subject, and should be sacked for writing theoretical books about it.' (John Bayley)
[N834] Fontana pbk **£3.95**

WELLEK, RENE & WARREN, AUSTIN
Theory of Literature
Attempts to outline a coherent theory of literature by both placing structuralism within a wider context, and returning again to stress that the work of literature is the central subject matter.
[N835] Penguin pbk **£6.99**

WHITE, ALLON & STALLYBRASS, PETER
Politics and Poetics of Transgression
Penetrating and discursive analysis of middle-class culture from the 17th - 19th centuries, interplaying Bakhtin and Freud to display the limits and trans-gresssions in psychic, literary, and class processes.
[N836] Methuen pbk **£7.50**

WHITMAN, JON
Allegory: The Dynamics of an Ancient and Medieval Technique
A discussion of allegory, both as a philosophical strategy for interpreting texts and as a literary method for composing them.
[N837] Oxford hbk **£30.00**

WILLIAMS, RAYMOND
One of the foremost English Marxist literary critics, whose work included analysis of film, television and popular culture as well as literature.
Communications
[N838] Penguin pbk **£2.50**
Culture and Society from Coleridge to Orwell
A reading of the term culture in 19th and 20th century literary texts, seen against the industrial revolution and the socio-political changes it wrought.
[N839] Hogarth pbk **£6.95**
Keywords
A very useful guide to the key words used in intellectual debate, tracing their change and development through history.
[N840] Fontana pbk **£4.95**
Marxism and Literature
A major work in British theory: both an introduction to, and innovative discussion of, the problem of 'literature' and the Marxist analysis of historical forces.
[N841] Oxford pbk **£5.95**
Politics and Letters
Interviews with *The New Left Review*.
[N842] Verso pbk **£6.95**
Second Generation
[N843] Hogarth pbk **£5.95**
The Country and the City
[N844] Hogarth pbk **£5.95**
The Politics of Modernism **NEW**
A posthumous collection of unpublished essays.
[N8172] Verso pbk **£8.95**
Writing in Society
[N845] Verso pbk **£8.95**
EAGLETON, TERRY (ED) **NEW**
Raymond Williams: A Critical Reader
Features essays by Stuart Hall, Edward Said, Lisa Jardine and others.
[N8171] Polity pbk **£7.95**

WRIGHT, ELIZABETH
Psychoanalytic Criticism: Theory in Practice
One of Britain's leading exponents of psychoanalytic theory in literature, moves through historical approaches of classical psychoanalysis to the contemporary debate centred around psychoanalysis, discourse and power.
[N846] Methuen pbk **£8.95**

YOUNG, ROBERT (ED)
Untying the Text: A Post-Structuralist Anthology
A useful introduction to the best post-structuralist theorists, including important essays by Barthes, Foucault, Barbara Johnson, Maud Ellmann and Paul De Man.
[N847] Routledge pbk **£8.95**

Language & Linguistics

BARBER, C.L.
The Story of Language
A brief but extremely clear account of the development of English.
[N848] Pan pbk **£2.95**

BURCHFIELD, ROBERT
The English Language
'It can be recommended without reservation to all who are sensitive to the subtlety, richness, and power of the language they speak.' (*British Book News*)
[N849] Oxford pbk **£3.95**
Unlocking the English Language **NEW**
An optimistic portrait of the English language by one of its most distinguished contemporary custodians. Burchfield argues that the rich and diverse linguistic system that we inherited some 1,500 years ago has remained *unweakened*, though substantially changed, by the social and political events of the intervening period.
[N850] Faber hbk **£12.95**

CHAPMAN, RAYMOND
Linguistics and Literature: An Introductory to Literary Stylistics
Argues that linguistic analysis can make a precise and stimulating contribution to literary criticism, rather than simply fulfil the role of 'a mere technology or service station'.
[N852] Arnold pbk **£5.95**

CULLER, JONATHAN
Saussure (2nd Ed)
Excellent monograph on the influential linguist by a leading contemporary literary theorist. A Fontana *Modern Master*.
[N853] Fontana pbk **£4.95**

FABB; ATTRIDGE; DURANT & MACCABE (EDS)
The Linguistics of Writing: Arguments Between Language and Literature
Contributors include Ann Banfield, Jonathan Culler, Jacques Derrida, Stanley Fish, John Hollander, Frederic Jameson, David Lodge and Raymond Williams.
[N854] Manchester UP pbk **£12.50**

FOWLER, ROGER
Linguistics and the Novel
[N856] Methuen pbk **£6.95**

GREENBAUM, SIDNEY
Good English and the Grammarian
It is quite possible to write grammatically and badly at the same time. Greenbaum examines the various senses of the word 'grammar' and argues that grammarians should present their work to a larger public, particularly on matters of language prescription.
[N857] Longman pbk **£7.95**

HORROCKS, GEOFFREY
Generative Grammar
A comprehensive history of, and practical guide to Chomskyan linguistic theory.
[N858] Longman pbk **£9.95**

JESPERSEN, OTTO
Growth and Structure of the English Language
Tenth edition of a seminal work, with an introduction by Randolph Quirk.
[N859] Blackwell pbk **£6.95**

LEECH, CHRISTOPHER
Semantics
[N860] Penguin pbk **£7.99**

LYONS, JOHN
Chomsky
Brief introduction to the work of the man who discovered 'deep structures'. A Fontana *Modern Master*.
[N862] Fontana hbk **£2.95**

MILROY, JAMES & LESLEY
Authority in Language
This exploration of the notions of 'correct' and 'incorrect' language looks at the problem from both the historical and the practical perspectives. It examines ideas on language held by writers from Swift to Orwell, tracing them through to present day views on correctness.
[N864] Routledge pbk **£9.95**

NASH, WALTER
English Usage
'In this essential student reference text Walter Nash deals thorough and entertainingly with the changing patterns of English usage and patterned choice in English style.' (*Language Monthly*)
[N865] Routledge pbk **£8.95**

ONIONS, C.T.
Modern English Syntax
[N866] Routledge pbk **£7.50**

PALMER, F.R.
Grammar
[N867] Penguin pbk **£4.99**
The English Verb
[N868] Longman pbk **£8.95**

QUIRK, RANDOLPH; GREENBAUM, SIDNEY; LEECH, GEOFFREY & SVARTVIK, JAN
A Grammar of Contemporary English
[N869] Longman hbk **£29.00**
A Comprehensive Grammar of the English Language
The largest, most authoritative grammar of the English language ever written, produced by the world's most distinguished grammarians after twenty years of collaborative work.
[N872] Longman hbk **£70.00**

QUIRK, RANDOLPH
Use of English
A classic text, ideal for students or anyone interested in exploring the complexities of modern English usage.
[N870] Longman pbk **£7.95**

QUIRK, RANDOLPH & GREENBAUM, SIDNEY
A University Grammar of English
[N871] Longman pbk **£11.50**

RICKS, CHRISTOPHER & MICHAELS, LEONARD (EDS) **NEW**
The State of the Language (1990 Edition)
Ten years on from their controversial first edition, Ricks and Michaels have assembled a new set of essays, stories and poems which reflect the state of English today: how it has changed, what it has lost, and where it might be going.
[N873] Faber hbk **£12.95**

ROBINS, R.H.
General Linguistics: An Introductory Survey
The third edition of a book written as an introduction to the contemporary state of the whole subject of linguistics, in a language understandable to all.
[N874] Longman pbk **£9.95**
A Short History of Linguistics
[N875] Longman pbk **£9.50**

WARDHAUGH, RONALD
Languages in Competition
In this lucid account of the spread and decline of the world's languages, particularly English and French, Professor Wardhaugh examines the historical and political importance of language as the expression of national identity and power.
[N877] Routledge pbk **£9.95**

Music

MUSIC

Reference

AMIS, JOHN & ROSE, MICHAEL
Words about Music: A Faber Anthology `NEW`
The ideal musical bedside book, containing a consistently varied collection of writing on all aspects of music and musicians.
[O1] Faber hbk **£14.95**

ARNOLD, DENIS (ED)
The New Oxford Companion to Music
A comprehensive encyclopaedia of music, with 6,000 articles on composers and their works (including opera, jazz and popular music), definitions of musical terms, the history of music, and of musical instruments. A standard reference work, and good value.
[O2] Oxford hbk **£60.00**

BARLOW, HAROLD & MORGENSTERN, SAM
A Dictionary of Musical Themes
A unique reference work which offers an immediate answer when a naggingly familiar but unidentifiable snatch of music is heard. All the themes listed are written out in musical notation, arranged alphabetically by composer, and then gathered into a notation index, arranged alphabetically after all themes have been transcribed into C.
[O3] Faber hbk **£17.50**

CUMMINGS, DAVID
New Everyman Dictionary of Music
Originally compiled by Eric Blom, and now in its 6th edition, this is one of the finest and most comprehensive one-volume reference works on music. Now thoroughly revised and containing over 1,500 new entries.
[O4] Dent hbk **£25.00**
[O5] Dent pbk **£8.95**

GANZL, KURT & LAMB, ANDREW
Ganzl's Book of the Musical Theatre
Ganzl is to light theatrical music what Kobbé is to opera, with summaries of the libretti and songs of nearly 300 of the best and most popular shows, from Gilbert and Sullivan to *La Cage aux Folles*.
[O6] Bodley hbk **£30.00**

GREENFIELD, LAYTON & MARCH
The New Penguin Guide to Compact Discs and Cassettes
An essential companion for the CD collector, this 1,366 page guide discusses the relative merits of all the important recordings of the classical repertoire. Its editors, three of *Gramophone*'s most experienced and respected critics, give consistently well-balanced and helpful advice, with a gratifying enthusiasm for the recordings of lesser-known composers.
[O7] Penguin pbk **£12.95**

GRIFFITHS, PAUL
The Thames & Hudson Encyclopaedia of 20th Century Music
A companion volume to the same author's *Modern Music: A Concise History from Debussy to Boulez*. Contains over a thousand entries on all aspects of the century's music, as well as a useful appendix listing the principal composers in chronological order.
[O8] Thames & H pbk **£5.95**

JACOBS, ARTHUR
The New Penguin Dictionary of Music
[O9] Penguin pbk **£5.95**

KENNEDY, MICHAEL (ED)
The Oxford Dictionary of Music
Without question the most comprehensive, detailed, reliable and best-value one-volume reference work on music now available.
[O10] Oxford hbk **£17.95**
The Concise Oxford Dictionary of Music
The third edition of this popular dictionary has been rewritten not only to take account of recent research in some areas, but to cover fully the development of music in the 20th century.
[O11] Oxford pbk **£5.95**

OSBORNE, CHARLES (ED)
Dictionary of Composers
[O12] Macmillan pbk **£7.95**

SADIE, STANLEY & HITCHCOCK, H. WILEY (EDS)
The New Grove Dictionary of American Music
In 4 volumes. The first comprehensive dictionary of American music, with articles commissioned from the major authorities, and a balanced coverage of concert and popular forms.
[O13] Macmillan hbk **£395.00**

SADIE, STANLEY & LATHAM, ALISON (EDS)
The Cambridge Music Guide
A relative newcomer amongst music reference books, which received critical praise on its appearance in 1985; well illustrated throughout.
[O14] Cambridge hbk **£22.50**

SADIE, STANLEY (ED)
The Grove Concise Dictionary of Music `NEW`
As might be expected, an excellent dictionary, based on the 1980 *New Grove Encyclopaedia*.
[O15] Macmillan hbk **£19.95**
The New Grove Dictionary of Music and Musicians
In 20 volumes. The *New Grove* is as much an encyclopaedia as a dictionary. It embraces the entire world of musical knowledge, with over 22,500 articles by 2,300 contributors from over 70 countries. An immense achievement.
[O16] Macmillan hbk **£1,100.00**
The New Grove Dictionary of Musical Instruments
In 3 volumes. This set provides a uniquely comprehensive, authoritative and up-to-date guide to the history, construction and performance of over 12,000 musical instruments from every culture; it encompasses Western and non-Western, ethnic, folk and classical, and ranges from the earliest to the most modern.
[O17] Macmillan hbk **£295.00**

SCHOLES, PERCY A. (ED)
The Oxford Companion to Music
Now in its tenth edition, this old faithful is still a reliable, user-friendly single-volume reference work.
[O18] Oxford hbk **£22.50**

History of Music

ABRAHAM, GERALD
100 Years of Music
The classic survey of music in the 19th century: it contains an excellent chapter on Wagner, and charts the gradual transformation of classical tonality into the new musical language of Schoenberg and the Second Viennese School.
[O19] Duckworth pbk **£9.95**
The Concise Oxford History of Music
A companion volume to the *Oxford Dictionary of Music*, and a scholarly and accessible general survey.
[O20] Oxford pbk **£12.95**

BRINDLE, REGINALD SMITH
The New Music
The second edition of this authoritative guide to modern music, subtitled 'The Avant-Garde since 1945', includes a new chapter reviewing the decade after the book's first appearance. The author threads his way through the maze of movements and technological developments with the sureness of one involved with the avant-garde as critic, composer and observer.
[O21] Oxford pbk **£9.50**

FOREMAN, LEWIS (ED)
From Parry to Britten: British Music 1900 - 1945 in Letters
A collection of letters by British composers, commenting on the musical scene of their times.
[O22] Batsford pbk **£12.95**

GRIFFITHS, PAUL
Modern Music: A Concise History from Debussy to Boulez
A straightforward and lucid history which gives appropriate weight to all the main musical movements of the century; punctuated with 128 well-selected illustrations.
[O23] Thames & H pbk **£5.95**

GROUT, DONALD J. & PALISCA, CLAUDE V.
A History of Western Music
The prescribed single-volume history of music on most reading lists: the fourth edition was planned by Donald Grout before his death, and completed by Professor Palisca of Yale University.
[O24] Dent hbk **£18.95**

HARMAN, ALEC & MELLERS, WILFRED
Man and his Music
Re-issue of this classic introduction to Western music. The paperback edition comes in 4 volumes.
[O25] Barrie & J hbk **£30.00**
Vol 1: Medieval and Early Renaissance Music
[O26] Barrie & J pbk **£8.95**
Vol 2: Late Renaissance and Baroque Music
[O27] Barrie & J pbk **£8.95**
Vol 3: The Sonata Principle
[O28] Barrie & J pbk **£8.95**
Vol 4: Romanticism and the Twentieth Century
[O29] Barrie & J pbk **£8.95**

MACHLIS, JOSEPH
Introduction to Contemporary Music
A thorough survey of the development of modern music and of current trends. The first chapter in particular is extremely helpful, and provides a genuine introduction to a difficult subject, making the rest of the book's material more accessible.
[O30] Dent hbk **£18.50**

MERTENS, WIM
American Minimal Music: Reich, Glass & Riley
One of the very few books that introduces the interested reader to the techniques and ideas behind minimalism, and to the leading composers in the field.
[O31] Kahn & A hbk **£6.50**

MITCHELL, DONALD
The Language of Modern Music
A lucid and perceptive text which examines the aesthetic and intellectual background to the fragmentation of form which has occurred in this century's music. It attempts to explain why artists have found it necessary to search for new means of expression.
[O32] Faber pbk **£3.95**

PRENTICE-HALL HISTORY OF MUSIC SERIES
One of the best surveys of musical history available at present; although the individual volumes are expensive, they are worth every penny.
SEAY, ALBERT
Music in the Medieval World
Beginning with the role of music in church ritual, the author examines the development of musical techniques, and the introduction of new sonorities that culminate in the work of the Notre Dame School; it also examines the work of Guillaume de Machaut, the first major individual figure to emerge.
[O33] Prentice-Hall pbk **£12.95**
BROWN, HOWARD MAYER
Music in the Renaissance
A comprehensive survey of the music of the 15th and 16th centuries, with an emphasis on the contribution of the major composers.
[O34] Prentice-Hall pbk **£12.95**
PALISCA, CLAUDE V.
Baroque Music
Examines the criteria and terminology of baroque music, and introduces the reader to the various composition techniques.
[O35] Prentice-Hall pbk **£12.95**
PAULY, REINHARD G.
Music in the Classic Period
Focusing on the lives and works of Haydn, Mozart and Beethoven, the author traces the evolution of musical style through the period and clarifies its main characteristics.
[O36] Prentice-Hall pbk **£27.80**
LONGYEAR, REY M.
Nineteenth-Century Romanticism in Music
With background information on Romanticism, musical styles and forms, on performance and practice, this survey ranges from Beethoven to 1905.
[O37] Prentice-Hall pbk **£28.90**
SALZMANN, ERIC
Twentieth-Century Music: An Introduction
Discusses the relationship, and differences, between contemporary musical ideas and those of the past.
[O38] Prentice-Hall pbk **£12.95**

ROSEN, CHARLES
These two works by the American scholar Charles Rosen are essential reading for anyone interested in the classical composers beyond a superficial level, and the reader who studies them in depth will be constantly repaid by the author's deep understanding of his subject.
Sonata Forms
[O39] Norton pbk **£7.95**
The Classical Style
[O40] Faber pbk **£8.95**

RUSHTON, JULIAN
Classical Music: A Concise History From Gluck to Beethoven
A tautly written history of the Classical style, broad in range, including philosophical and scientific discussions of the times and their influence on the prevailing artistic climate.
[O41] Thames & H hbk **£12.50**

SAMSON, JIM
Music in Transition
A book that charts the transition in musical style from the music of late Romantic masters such as Brahms, Wagner, Bruckner and Mahler to the early masterworks of the composers of the modern school; particularly good on Busoni and Scriabin.
[O42] Dent hbk **£13.50**

SCHONBERG, HAROLD C.
Lives of the Great Composers
38 essays which, taken as a whole, provide a highly readable account of the development of Western music from Bach to Webern. The author firmly distances himself from the school of thought which says that music is entirely self-contained and explicable without reference to the lives of composers: the result is a series of affectionate yet scholarly portraits.
[O43] Futura pbk **£6.95**

WHITTALL, ARNOLD
Romantic Music: A Concise History
A recently published survey of Romantic music, describing the emergence of a new form of musical expression, as seen in the work of Weber, Schumann, Donizetti, Berlioz and Chopin, and its development by Wagner and Verdi.
[O44] Thames & H hbk **£12.50**

WULSTAN, DAVID
Tudor Music
In this informative and analytical survey of the golden age of English music, Wulstan focuses on all the major kinds of Tudor music, both popular and private, and discusses them in their historical and technical context.
[O45] Dent hbk **£25.00**

Composers - Biographies & Studies

Series

DENT MASTER MUSICIANS
This immensely popular series was begun ninety years ago, and has developed since under the editorship of four scholars, Frederick J. Crowest, Eric Blom, Sir Jack Westrup and, since 1976, Stanley Sadie. Great care is taken over the selection of authors, and the result is that each volume is written by an acknowledged expert in the field. A fine balance is struck between biography and musical discussion, and the series is regularly revised, with volumes being replaced altogether if superseded by modern scholarship. In general, if you want to read only one book on a composer, the *Master Musicians* series gives the most reliable, readable introductions available. In the following list of titles available, the first price listed is for the hardback, the second for the paperback. Some volumes exist in only one format.
Bach Malcolm Boyd £11.50/4.95
Bartók Paul Griffiths £11.50/5.95
Beethoven Denis Matthews £13.50/4.95
Berlioz Hugh MacDonald £9.50/NA
Bizet Winton Dean NA/£3.50
Brahms Malcolm MacDonald £16.95/NA
Britten Michael Kennedy NA/£5.95
Bruckner Derek Watson £9.50/NA
Dufay David Fallows £11.50/5.95
Dvořák Alec Robertson £9.50/NA
Grieg John Horton £9.50/3.50
Handel Percy M. Young £9.50/NA
Haydn Rosemary Hughes £9.50/5.95
Liszt Derek Watson £16.95/NA
Mahler Michael Kennedy £9.50/5.95
Mendelssohn Philip Radcliffe £9.50/NA
Monteverdi Denis Arnold £9.50/NA
Mozart Eric Blom NA/£5.95
Mussorgsky M.D. Calvocoressi £9.50/NA
Ravel Roger Nichols £9.50/NA
Rossini Richard Osborne NA/£5.95
Schoenberg Malcolm MacDonald £9.50/5.95
Schubert John Reed £14.95/5.95
Schumann Joan Chissell £9.50/5.95
Sibelius Robert Layton NA/£4.95
Richard Strauss Michael Kennedy NA/£5.95
Stravinsky Francis Routh £9.50/NA
Tchaikovsky Edward Garden £9.50/4.95
Verdi Julian Budden £13.50/4.95
Vivaldi Michael Talbot £9.50/4.95
Wagner Barry Millington £13.50/4.95

NEW GROVE BIOGRAPHIES
A series of individual and collected biographies from Macmillan, which are greatly expanded versions of the articles in the *New Grove Dictionary*. They incorporate the latest scholarship, combining biographical details with comment on the major works, and an up-to-date bibliography and full list of works. The prices below are for the paperback editions.
Bach Family Wolff £7.95
Beethoven Wolff £7.95
Handel Dean £7.95
Haydn Larsen £7.95
Mozart Sadie £7.95
Schubert Brown £5.95
Wagner Dahlhaus & Deathridge £4.95
French Baroque Masters Anthony £8.95
High Renaissance Masters Noble & Reese £6.95
Early Romantic Masters 1 Temperley £7.95
Early Romantic Masters 2 Warrack £7.95
Italian Baroque Masters Arnold et al £6.95
Late Romantic Masters Cooke £7.95
Masters of Italian Opera Gossett £5.50
Modern Masters Lampert et al £4.95
North European Baroque Masters Rifkin £7.95
Russian Masters 1 Brown £8.95
Russian Masters 2 Abraham £8.95
Second Viennese School Griffiths £6.95
Twentieth Century American Masters £9.95
Twentieth Century French Masters Nectoux £8.95
Turn of the Century Masters Tyrell £7.95

BBC MUSIC GUIDES
A continuing series of short, inexpensive commentaries on a particular aspect of a composer's output. They are written by a particular authority on the topic or work under consideration (for example Robert Simpson on the Beethoven symphonies) and generally find a happy medium between an intelligent and helpful programme note and a serious analysis of the work being discussed. Excellent pre- or post-listening material. Available for the following works, at between £2.25 - £2.95 for each paperback volume:
Bach Cantatas/Organ Music
Bartók Chamber Music/Orchestral Music
Beethoven Concertos and Overtures/Piano Sonatas/String Quartets/Symphonies
Berlioz Orchestral Music
Brahms Chamber Music/Piano Music/Orchestral Music/Songs

Bruckner Symphonies
Couperin Works
Debussy Orchestral Music/Piano Music
Dvořák Symphonies and Concertos
Elgar Orchestral Music
Fall Works
Handel Concertos
Haydn String Quartets/Symphonies
Mahler Symphonies and Songs
Mendelssohn Chamber Music
Monteverdi Church Music/Madrigals
Mozart Chamber Music/Piano
Concertos/Serenades and Divertimenti/Wind and
String Concertos
Purcell Works
Rachmaninov Orchestral Music
Ravel Orchestral Music
Schoenberg Chamber Music
Schubert Chamber Music/Piano
Sonatas/Songs/Symphonies
Schumann Orchestral Music/Piano Music/Songs
Shostakovitch Symphonies
Tchaikovsky Ballet Music/Symphonies and
Concertos
The Trio Sonata
Vaughan Williams Syphonies
Vivaldi Works
Hugo Wolf Songs

Composers A-Z

BACH, JOHANN SEBASTIAN
ARNOLD, DENIS
Bach
[O46] Oxford pbk **£2.95**
DAVID, HANS T. & MENDEL, A. (EDS)
The Bach Reader
A book of recollections and memoirs of the great
composer from his own contemporaries and later
historians, with translations of the composer's letters,
and appreciations by his pupils. Many important
documents appear here.
[O47] Norton pbk **£9.95**
KIRKPATRICK, RALPH
**Interpreting Bach's 'Well-Tempered
Clavier'**
Subtitled 'A Performer's Discourse on Method', this
makes no attempt at analysis, but instead suggests a
way of thinking about the music that again and again
throws up helpful insights.
[O48] Yale UP pbk **£6.95**
WILLIAMS, PETER
An immense feat of scholarship, indispensable for
organists.
The Organ Music of J.S. Bach Vol 1
Contains BWV 525-598, 802-805 Preludes, Toccatas,
Fantasias, Fugues, Sonatas, Concertos and
Miscellaneous Pieces.
[O49] Cambridge pbk **£15.00**
The Organ Music of J.S. Bach Vol 2
BWV 599 - 771, works based on Chorales.
[O50] Cambridge pbk **£15.00**
**The Organ Music of J.S. Bach Vol 3: A
Background**
[O51] Cambridge pbk **£15.00**

BARTOK, BELA
LENDVAI, ERNO
Béla Bartók: An Analysis of His Music
A highly technical survey, the main thesis of the book
is that Bartók evolved for himself a method of
integrating all the elements of music, and that
everything he wrote after his thirties followed one
single, basic principle.
[O52] Kahn & A hbk **£6.50**

BAX, SIR ARNOLD
FOREMAN, LEWIS
Bax: A Composer and his Times
The neglected works of Arnold Bax are finally
enjoying a wider currency, thanks to the series of
recordings made by Bryden Thompson for Chandos.
This excellent work is the only study of the composer
currently available.
[O53] Scolar P hbk **£40.00**

BEETHOVEN, LUDWIG VAN
Selected Letters
Translated by J.S. Shedlock, with explanatory notes
by A.C. Kalischer. A selection of 457 letters written
through the composer's life which will provide a good
idea of his forceful prose style for those unwilling to
invest in the collected edition.
[O54] Dover pbk **£5.55**
The Letters of Beethoven
In 3 Volumes, edited by Emily Anderson. This is a
reprint of the standard edition of Beethoven's letters.
[O55] Macmillan hbk **£60.00**
ARNOLD, DENIS & FORTUNE, NIGEL
The Beethoven Companion
An invaluable collection covering every aspect of
Beethoven's life and work.
[O56] Faber pbk **£10.99**
COOPER, MARTIN
**Beethoven: The Last Decade 1817 -
1827**
One review called this the most outstanding
monograph in the English language on a musical
subject to have appeared since the War.
[O57] Oxford pbk **£10.95**
HOPKINS, ANTONY
The Nine Symphonies of Beethoven
An accessible yet scholarly survey by the popular
broadcaster.
[O58] Pan pbk **£3.95**
ROSTAL, MAX
The Sonatas for Violin and Piano
A detailed analysis of the ten sonatas which form the
backbone of the violinist's repertoire.
[O59] Toccata P pbk **£6.95**
WEGELER, FRANZ & RIES, FERDINAND
Remembering Beethoven
The publication of this book is an event of major
importance for Beethoven bibliography in English.
The impressions conveyed by two of the composer's
closest intimates are of a loved and treasured friend,
much misunderstood, who, despite occasional lapses,
reciprocated the affection in which he was held.
[O60] Deutsch hbk **£11.95**

BERG, ALBAN
CARNER, MOSCO
Alban Berg
Mosco Carner's book on Alban Berg is a sympathetic
study of perhaps the most accessible composer of the
Second Viennese School. The section on the
composer's work is particularly perceptive,
concentrating on its dramatic and musical aspects.
[O61] Duckworth pbk **£12.95**

BERLIOZ, HECTOR
Memoirs of Hector Berlioz
The most valuable memoirs written by any composer:
they chart the course of his mostly unhappy career
with good-natured humour and occasional outbursts
of rage.
[O62] Dover pbk **£7.45**
CAIRNS, DAVID
**Berlioz Vol 1: 1803 - 1832 The
Making of an Artist** **NEW**
The first volume of what is likely to be the definitive
biography of the composer. A work of immense
scholarship as well as great affection for the subject.
[O63] Deutsch hbk **£25.00**

BIRTWISTLE, HARRISON
HALL, MICHAEL
Harrison Birtwistle
The first monograph on the British composer
Harrison Birtwistle whose opera *The Mask of
Orpheus* received such critical acclaim when
produced by the ENO.
[O64] Robson pbk **£8.95**

BOULEZ, PIERRE
One of the most influential and controversial figures
in contemporary music. All these works offer
valuable insights into his personality and musical
views.
**Orientations: Collected Writings by
Pierre Boulez**
[O65] Faber hbk **£25.00**
**Pierre Boulez: Conversations with
Célestin Deliège**
[O66] Eulenburg pbk **£4.95**
GLOCK, WILLIAM (ED)
Pierre Boulez: A Symposium
[O67] Eulenburg pbk **£7.95**

BRAHMS, JOHANNES
GEIRINGER, KARL
Brahms: His Life and Work
A standard life of Brahms, first published in 1947.
[O68] Da Capo hbk **£25.00**
KEYS, IVOR
Johannes Brahms **NEW**
The first major new study of Brahms in English since
the 1940s; a chronological account of the composer's
life followed by a work-by-work analysis of his entire
oeuvre.
[O69] C Helm hbk **£16.95**

BRIAN, HAVERGAL
MACDONALD, MALCOLM (ED)
Havergal Brian on Music
Brian's journalistic output was as large (incredibly) as
his musical output, and this volume brings together
some of his writings on British composers. Essential
reading for those interested in neglected British
composers (not just Bax and Bantock, but also Scott
and Sorabji), and with excellent chapters on Elgar and
Delius.
[O70] Toccata P pbk **£9.50**

BRITTEN, BENJAMIN
PALMER, CHRISTOPHER
The Britten Companion
[O71] Faber pbk **£9.95**

Ludwig van Beethoven from *The Cambridge Music
Guide* edited by Stanley Sadie and Alison Latham
(Cambridge hbk **£22.50**)

WHITE, ERIC WALTER
Benjamin Britten: His Life and Operas
Although obviously concentrating on the operas, this is a good general introduction to Britten's music.
[O72] Faber pbk **£9.95**
WHITTALL, ARNOLD
The Music of Britten and Tippett
A technical survey that offers a unique double portrait of the two leading composers of their generation.
[O73] Cambridge hbk **£35.00**

BUSONI, FERRUCCIO
BEAUMONT, ANTONY
Busoni the Composer
That Busoni is at last being recognized as a major composer is at least partly the result of Antony Beaumont's masterly biography.
[O74] Faber hbk **£35.00**
DENT, EDWARD
Ferruccio Busoni
[O75] Eulenburg pbk **£8.95**

CAGE, JOHN
The fact that all these titles have exactly the same format and yet such different prices has a randomness that seems wholly appropriate to this writer. Much of his iconoclasm now seems eminently sensible; *For the Birds* is probably the best place to start.
Empty Words
[O76] Boyars pbk **£5.95**
For the Birds
[O77] Boyars pbk **£5.95**
Silence
[O78] Boyars pbk **£12.95**
X
[O79] Boyars pbk **£12.95**

CARTER, ELLIOTT
SCHIFF, DAVID
Music of Elliott Carter
Generally considered to be among the most important composers writing at the moment, this is the first full-length study of this American composer to appear in Britain.
[O80] Eulenburg pbk **£9.95**

CHARPENTIER, MARC-ANTOINE
HITCHCOCK, H. WILEY
Marc-Antoine Charpentier   NEW
A concise and fluent introduction to an important 17th century composer, who is only now emerging from a long period of neglect.
[O81] Oxford pbk **£7.95**

CHOPIN, FREDERIC
EIGELDINGER, JEAN-JACQUES
Chopin: Pianist and Teacher
First paperback English edition of an important collection of documents which reveal Chopin as teacher and interpreter of his own music.
[O82] Cambridge pbk **£12.95**

COPLAND, AARON
BUTTERWORTH, NEIL
The Music of Aaron Copland
A painstaking chronological survey of Copland's entire output, including a conversation with the composer on his piano music.
[O83] Toccata P pbk **£6.95**
COPLAND & PERLIS, VIVIAN
Copland: Vol 1 1900 - 1942
This first volume of autobiography covers the composer's childhood in Brooklyn, his period of study with Boulanger in Paris, his involvement with the Group Theatre in New York, and his time in Hollywood.
[O84] Faber hbk **£18.50**

COUPERIN, FRANCOIS
MELLERS, WILFRED
François Couperin and the French Classical Tradition
A wholly revised and rewritten editon of the standard work on this composer. It sheds much light on all aspects of cultural life in France at the time of Louis XIV.
[O85] Faber hbk **£27.50**

DAVIES, PETER MAXWELL
GRIFFITHS, PAUL
Peter Maxwell Davies
Written with the composer's full co-operation, this is a thorough-going introduction, complete with a list of works and discography, that will inspire the adventurous listener to seek out the music.
[O86] Robson pbk **£4.95**

DEBUSSY, CLAUDE
LESURE, FRANCOIS & NICHOLS, ROGER (EDS)
Letters
The long awaited publication in English of the letters of a great and popular French composer. Attractively written, they throw light on his personality and music. His correspondence with some 75 recipients spans the whole spectrum of the arts (literature, theatre and music) at a time of great artistic activity in France.
[O87] Faber hbk **£27.50**
NICHOLS, ROGER
Debussy
[O88] Oxford pbk **£5.95**

DELIUS, FREDERICK
PALMER, CHRISTOPHER
Delius: Portrait of a Cosmopolitan
[O89] Duckworth pbk **£9.95**
REDWOOD, CHRISTOPHER (ED)
A Delius Companion
Published originally as a 70th birthday tribute to Eric Fenby, this symposium is essential reading for admirers of Delius.
[O90] Calder pbk **£4.95**

DUNSTABLE, JOHN
BENT, MARGARET
Dunstable
A short critical survey which places emphasis on the music rather than biographical detail.
[O91] Oxford pbk **£6.95**

DVORAK, ANTONIN
CLAPHAM, JOHN
Dvorák
An authoritative biography of the popular Czech composer.
[O92] Calder pbk **£4.95**

ELGAR, SIR EDWARD
Elgar and His Publishers
In 2 volumes, edited by Jerrold Northrop Moore. This book collects all of Elgar's letters to his publishers with their replies. More importantly, the book includes for the first time correspondence with his friend A.J. Jaeger (inspiration for the *Nimrod* variation).
[O93] Oxford hbk **£55.00**
KENNEDY, MICHAEL
Portrait of Elgar
Michael Kennedy's sympathetic biography of Elgar was clearly a labour of love, as is evident from almost every page. Now in its third edition, and revised to take account of the additional material made available by Moore's *Life*, it will give much pleasure to anyone wanting to look past the popular, but misconceived, image of the composer as the archetypal, patriotic Edwardian gentleman.
[O94] Oxford pbk **£6.95**

MOORE, JERROLD NORTHROP
Edward Elgar: A Creative Life
The culmination of twenty years' research, this major new biography is without doubt the most complete and perceptive study of the composer to date.
[O95] Oxford pbk **£12.50**
The Windflower Letters   NEW
Another fruit of the tireless labours of Elgar's American biographer. 'Windflower' was the composer's pet name for Alice Stuart Wortley, daughter of the painter Millais: she is thought by some to have been the secret dedicatee of the Violin Concerto.
[O96] Oxford hbk **£25.00**
NOY, MICHAEL DE-LA
Elgar the Man
De-la-Noy takes a dispassionate look at Elgar's complex and at times unattractive personality. A book for all Elgarians.
[O97] H Hamilton pbk **£6.95**
REED, W.H.
Elgar As I Knew Him   NEW
First published in 1936, this important document is again available in an edition which contains all the sketches for the Third Symphony in facsimile. Reed was approached by Elgar in 1910 to help with the arrangement of the Violin Concerto, and subsequently became one of the composer's closest friends. His memoir provides one of the best insights into Elgar's personality that we have.
[O98] Oxford pbk **£5.95**

FAURE, GABRIEL
JONES, J. BARRIE (ED)
Gabriel Fauré: A Life in Letters   NEW
This clearly translated text is the nearest thing we have to an autobiography, and sheds much new light on a constantly underrated composer.
[O99] Batsford hbk **£19.95**
LONG, MARGUERITE
At the Piano with Fauré
An interesting little book about the French pianist and her friendship with the ageing composer Gabriel Fauré, and their work together on his piano compositions.
[O100] Kahn & A hbk **£6.95**
ORLEDGE, ROBERT
Gabriel Fauré
The only major work on this important French composer available in English at present. A very fine introduction to and survey of Fauré's work, with a detailed investigation into the elements that make up his style.
[O101] Eulenburg pbk **£11.50**

GERSHWIN, GEORGE
JABLONSKI, EDWARD
Gershwin
A recent, critically acclaimed biography written with sympathy and insight by a close friend of the composer's brother, Ira. Illustrated with 83 photographs.
[O102] Simon & Sch pbk **£9.95**

GILBERT, W.S. & SULLIVAN, ARTHUR
AYRE, LESLIE
The Gilbert & Sullivan Companion
An entertaining and informative reference book, self-recommending for G & S lovers.
[O103] Macmillan pbk **£7.95**
GILBERT, WILLIAM SCHWENK
The Savoy Operas
[O104] Macmillan pbk **£7.50**
JACOBS, ARTHUR
Arthur Sullivan: A Victorian Musician
Sullivan deserved a modern, thoroughly researched biography to himself; Jacobs has written a compassionate portrait, which nevertheless does not

Sir Edward Elgar from *Kings, Queens and Courtiers* by Kenneth Rose (Weidenfeld hbk £12.95, pbk £8.95)

attempt to ignore the less pleasant aspects of the composer's personality.
[O105] Oxford pbk **£5.95**

GLASS, PHILIP
Opera on the Beach
The most commercially successful of the so-called minimalist school here tells the story of his life and music.
[O106] Faber pbk **£6.99**

HANDEL, GEORGE FREDERICK
HOGWOOD, CHRISTOPHER
Handel
A scholarly and entertaining biography by one of the composer's best modern interpreters. Well illustrated, and with an excellent final chapter on Handel's treatment by posterity.
[O107] Thames & H pbk **£7.95**
KEATES, JONATHAN
Handel: The Man and his Music
An enthusiastic and readable life by a self-confessed layman, which is nonetheless particularly good on the music.
[O108] H Hamilton pbk **£6.95**

HAYDN, JOSEPH
KELLER, HANS
The Great Haydn Quartets
The late Hans Keller was one of the most revered and important writers on, and critics of music. This book, which appeared not long before his death, draws on his long experience of teaching and thinking about music that was particularly close to him.
[O109] Dent hbk **£16.95**
ROBBINS LANDON, H.C. & JONES, DAVID WYN
Haydn: His Life and Work **NEW**
[O110] Thames & H hbk **£24.00**
ROBBINS LANDON, H.C.
The Life of Haydn Vol 1: The Early Years
[O111] Thames & H hbk **£35.00**
Vol 2: At Esterhaza
[O112] Thames & H hbk **£35.00**
Vol 3: In England
[O113] Thames & H hbk **£35.00**
Vol 4: The Years of 'The Creation'
[O114] Thames & H hbk **£35.00**

Vol 5: The Late Years
[O115] Thames & H hbk **£35.00**

HINDEMITH, PAUL
SKELTON, GEOFFREY
Paul Hindemith: The Man Behind the Music
Hindemith's reputation suffered a serious decline in the 25 years following his death, but his truly original music is now once more beginning to enjoy a wider circulation. This penetrating biography is the only one in English, and at its low price should be snapped up before it goes out of print.
[O116] Gollancz hbk **£6.00**

HOLST, GUSTAV
HOLST, IMOGEN
Gustav Holst: A Biography
Written by the composer's daughter, this is the most authoritative book likely to be written on Holst. Published here for the first time in paperback.
[O117] Oxford pbk **£4.95**

IVES, CHARLES
Memos
A primary source-book containing most of the composer's previously unpublished writings.
[O118] Calder pbk **£5.50**
BURKHOLDER, J. PETER
Charles Ives
All writers on Ives need to be slightly evangelical in some respects, and Burkholder's enthusiastic exegesis is no exception. A book which will offer much to assist a greater understanding of this extraordinary composer.
[O119] Yale UP pbk **£6.95**

LASSUS, ORLANDUS
ROCHE, JEROME
Lassus
[O120] Oxford pbk **£6.95**

LIGETI, GYORGY
GRIFFITHS, PAUL
Gyorgy Ligeti
The only study of this major modern composer currently available, written by a leading authority on 20th century music.
[O121] Robson pbk **£8.95**

LISZT, FRANZ
SEARLE, HUMPHREY
The Music of Liszt
A composer's eye view of Liszt, first published in 1954, but still recognized today as a valuable survey.
[O122] Dover pbk **£5.20**
SITWELL, SIR SACHEVERELL
Liszt
A literary biography rather than a musical one. With a foreword by Louis Kentner.
[O123] Columbus pbk **£5.95**

MAHLER, GUSTAV
COOKE, DERYCK
Gustav Mahler: An Introduction to his Music
[O124] Faber pbk **£4.95**
LEBRECHT, NORMAN
Mahler Remembered
These eye-witness accounts by the composer's contemporaries and friends form a remarkable and deeply illuminating image of a towering personality.
[O125] Faber pbk **£6.95**
MARTNER, KNUD (ED)
Selected Letters of Gustav Mahler
[O126] Faber hbk **£15.00**

MITCHELL, DONALD
Life of Gustav Mahler Vol 1: The Early Years
[O127] Faber hbk **£35.00**
Vol 2: The Wunderhorn Years
[O128] Faber hbk **£30.00**
Vol 3: Songs and Symphonies of Life and Death
[O129] Faber hbk **£35.00**

MENDELSSOHN, FELIX **NEW**
Felix Mendelssohn: A Life in Letters
Mendelssohn's letters, written with charm and humour, provide an unsurpassed insight into 19th century musical affairs as well as an intimate and lively portrait of the composer himself.
[O130] Cassell hbk **£14.95**

MESSIAEN, OLIVIER
GRIFFITHS, PAUL
Olivier Messiaen and the Music of Time
Covering the whole of Messiaen's musical career up to and including his opera, *St François d'Assise*, this is the most comprehensive and stimulating treatment of the composer to date.
[O131] Faber hbk **£17.50**
JOHNSON, ROBERT SHERLAW
Messiaen
A full-length assessment of Messiaen's musical language.
[O132] Dent hbk **£16.00**

MOERAN, E.J.
SELF, GEOFFREY
The Music of E.J. Moeran
Pioneering study of this neglected Irish composer whose work is long overdue for revival.
[O133] Toccata P pbk **£7.95**

MONTEVERDI, CLAUDIO
ARNOLD, DENIS & FORTUNE, NIGEL
The New Monteverdi Companion
[O134] Faber pbk **£10.00**

MOZART, WOLFGANG AMADEUS
ANDERSON, EMILY (ED & TRANS)
Letters of Mozart and His Family
His letters make fascinating reading, available now in a new, thoroughly revised and annotated edition.
[O135] Macmillan hbk **£45.00**
BROPHY, BRIGID
Mozart the Dramatist
A new edition of a book which first appeared in 1964, by the well-known contemporary novelist and journalist.
[O136] Libris hbk **£17.50**
HILDESHEIMER, WOLFGANG
Mozart
Not the book to buy if you want a straightforward 'life and works' approach to Mozart (Blom's volume in the *Master Musicians* series can be highly recommended), but a fascinating psychological study nonetheless.
[O137] Dent pbk **£4.95**
HUTCHINGS, ARTHUR
A Companion to Mozart's Piano Concertos
An acknowledged classic of Mozart studies, now back in print.
[O138] Oxford pbk **£9.95**
LEVEY, MICHAEL
The Life and Death of Mozart
A recent biography of Mozart by the distinguished art historian.
[O139] Sphere pbk **£4.99**
OSBORNE, CHARLES
The Complete Operas of Mozart
Especially useful for those interested in Mozart's

lesser-known operas; all 20 are discussed in detail, as well as two unfinished works.
[O140] Gollancz pbk **£5.95**
ROBBINS LANDON, H.C.
1791: Mozart's Last Year
In this important work, Professor Robbins-Landon draws on his unrivalled knowledge of the sources and a substantial amount of new information to reconstruct the events of Mozart's last year. He is at pains to discover the true sequence of events, and dispose of the accumulated controversy and mythology.
[O141] Thames & H hbk **£12.95**
Mozart: The Golden Years 1781 - 1791
NEW
An important successor to the above work, this is equally entertaining and authoritative.
[O142] Thames & H hbk **£14.95**
ROBBINS LANDON, H.C. & MITCHELL, DONALD
The Mozart Companion
A series of articles by authorities on the composer covering all the major musical forms in which he wrote.
[O143] Faber pbk **£6.95**

NIELSEN, CARL
SIMPSON, ROBERT
Carl Nielsen: Symphonist
Robert Simpson is a leading authority on the music of the Danish composer Nielsen.
[O144] Kahn & A hbk **£7.95**

POULENC, FRANCIS
BERNAC, PIERRE
Francis Poulenc: The Man & His Songs
A completely authoritative book by the baritone who toured Europe over a period of 25 years with Poulenc at the piano, and for whom many of the songs were written.
[O145] Gollancz hbk **£11.95**

PROKOFIEV, SERGEI
ROBINSON, HARLOW
Sergei Prokofiev: A Biography
A completed biography and general discussion of Prokofiev's music.
[O146] Hale hbk **£22.95**
SAMUEL
Prokofiev
A serviceable biography, first published in 1960 and translated from the French. Well illustrated.
[O147] Boyars pbk **£3.95**

PUCCINI, GIACOMO
ASHBROOK, WILLIAM
Operas of Puccini
An excellent general introduction to the works of Puccini.
[O148] Oxford pbk **£9.95**
CARNER, MOSCO
Puccini: A Critical Biography
The definitive biography of the composer.
[O149] Duckworth pbk **£12.95**

RAVEL, MAURICE
NICHOLS, ROGER
Ravel Remembered
The common view of Ravel as cold and retiring is refuted in this intriguing collection of recollections by his friends and colleagues.
[O150] Faber pbk **£6.95**

RIMSKY-KORSAKOV, N.A.
My Musical Life
A uniquely valuable record of the growth of Russian national music and the daily lives and work of 'The Five', as well as an honest and clear description of the composer's own musical career.
[O151] Eulenburg hbk **£19.95**

SATIE, ERIK
WILKINS, NIGEL (ED & TRANS)
The Writings of Erik Satie
A collection of miscellaneous pieces on various topics, musical and otherwise, which fully display the wit that characterizes much of his music.
[O152] Eulenburg hbk **£12.95**

SCHOENBERG, ARNOLD
ROSEN, CHARLES
Schoenberg
Charles Rosen's short monograph on Schoenberg remains one of the best introductions to the work of this towering figure in 20th century music.
[O153] Boyars hbk **£6.95**
STUCKENSCHMIDT, H.H.
Arnold Schoenberg: His Life & Works
Stuckenschmidt is considered an authority on Schoenberg.
[O154] Calder hbk **£15.00**

SCHUBERT, FRANZ
WIGMORE, RICHARD (TRANS)
Schubert: The Complete Song Texts
A parallel text of Schubert's entire output of *lieder*, with clear prose translations.
[O155] Gollancz hbk **£19.95**

SCHUMANN, CLARA
REICH, NANCY B.
Clara Schumann: The Artist and the Woman
Illuminating biography, written with affection as well as scholarship, of an important but too often neglected figure in the Romantic movement in music. Newly published in paperback.
[O156] Oxford pbk **£6.95**

SCHUMANN, ROBERT
OSTWALD, PETER F.
Schumann: Music and Madness
An important recent biography. The author, who is Professor of Psychiatry at the University of California, draws a correlation between the composer's creativity and his recurring mental instability, and throws new light on the more general relationship between genius and madness.
[O157] Gollancz hbk **£15.00**
SAMS, ERIC
The Songs of Robert Schumann
A thoroughly researched full-length study of Schumann's 246 songs for voice and piano.
[O158] Eulenberg hbk **£12.95**
SCHUMANN, EUGENIE
Memoirs of Robert Schumann
[O159] Eulenburg pbk **£7.95**

SCRIABIN, ALEXANDER
MACDONALD, HUGH
Scriabin
[O160] Oxford pbk **£6.95**

SHOSTAKOVITCH, DMITRI
Testimony: The Memoirs of Dmitri Shostakovich
Written with Solomon Volkov. This is not an autobiography in the conventional sense. Shostakovich himself called it the 'testimony of an eyewitness'. Shostakovich survived, and composed through the worst excesses of the Stalinist purge: this book and much of his greatest music is a celebration and commemoration of those who didn't.
[O161] Faber pbk **£7.95**

SIBELIUS, JEAN
TAWASTJERNA, ERIK
Life of Sibelius Vol 2: 1904-1914
This second volume covers the crucial years of the Third and Fourth Symphonies. The author had access

to Sibelius's papers and diaries, which give a day-by-day account of his life at this period. Volume 1 is out of print.
[O162] Faber hbk **£17.50**

STOCKHAUSEN, KARLHEINZ
MACONIE, ROBIN
Stockhausen
[O163] Boyars pbk **£9.95**

STRAUSS, RICHARD
Correspondence of Richard Strauss & Hugo von Hofmannstahl
[O164] Cambridge pbk **£12.95**
DEL MAR, NORMAN
Richard Strauss Vol 2
A critical commentary on his life and work. The British conductor Norman Del Mar is an authority on the works of Strauss. His three-volume study is the standard work; volume 1 is currently out of print.
[O165] Faber pbk **£10.00**
Vol 3
[O166] Faber pbk **£10.00**

STRAVINSKY, IGOR
Autobiography
[O167] Boyars pbk **£4.50**
BOUCOURECHLIEV, ANDREI
Stravinsky
An outstanding critical biography of the great Russian composer by a distinguished musicologist that challenges many widely-held views on Stravinsky's music.
[O168] Gollancz pbk **£9.95**

SWEELINCK, JAN PIETERSZOON
NOSKE, FOITS
Sweelinck
A new study of this Dutch contemporary of Byrd. He is deservedly remembered as one of the most important composers of keyboard music before J.S. Bach.
[O169] Oxford pbk **£7.95**

SZYMANOWSKI, KAROL
SAMSON, JIM
The Music of Szymanowski
The first study in English of this neglected Polish composer.
[O170] Kahn & A hbk **£11.95**

TCHAIKOVSKY, PETER ILLYCH
BROWN, DAVID
Tchaikovsky Vol 1: The Early Years 1840-1874
Rapidly establishing itself as the definitive 'life and works', Brown's series of books has now reached the years following the crisis precipitated by Tchaikovsky's disastrous marriage, and the recovery and consolidation of his confidence as a composer.
[O171] Gollancz hbk **£17.50**
Vol 2: The Crisis Years 1874-1878
[O172] Gollancz hbk **£17.50**
Vol 3: The Years of Wandering 1878-1885
[O173] Gollancz hbk **£25.00**
KENDALL, ALAN
Tchaikovsky
A very important new book on the Russian composer which incorporates much information concerning the composer's demise, taken from an edition of his family's letters, banned in the Soviet Union and smuggled to the West in 1979.
[O174] Bodley hbk **£15.00**
WARRACK, JOHN
Tchaikovsky
A perceptive biography of the tormented composer which discusses the music in non-technical language.
[O175] H Hamilton pbk **£6.95**

TIPPETT, SIR MICHAEL
Moving into Aquarius
[O176] Grafton pbk **£3.50**
Music of the Angels
Containing nearly all the essays and broadcasts that
were not included in *Moving into Aquarius*, as well
as the sketchbooks for *A Child of Our Time*: essential
reading for anyone interested in appreciating our most
eminent living composer.
[O177] Eulenburg pbk **£7.95**
BOWEN, MEIRION
Michael Tippett
[O178] Robson pbk **£4.95**
KEMP, IAN
Tippett: The Composer and his Music
The authorized biography of the great British
composer.
[O179] Oxford pbk **£12.50**
MATTHEWS, DAVID
Michael Tippett: An Introductory Study
[O180] Faber pbk **£3.95**

VARESE, EDGARD
OUELLETTE, FERNAND
Edgard Varèse
[O181] Boyars pbk **£4.50**
VARESE, LOUISE
Varèse: A Looking-Glass Diary
A personal memoir of the pioneering French
composer by his second wife.
[O182] Eulenburg pbk **£6.95**

VAUGHAN WILLIAMS, RALPH
VAUGHAN WILLIAMS, URSULA
RVW
An intimate and clearly authoritative biography of the
composer by his widow, first published in 1964, and
re-issued in paperback with 16 pages of photographs,
in the Oxford Lives Series.
[O183] Oxford pbk **£6.95**

VERDI, GIUSEPPE
KIMBELL, DAVID R.B.
Verdi in the Age of Italian Romanticism
[O187] Cambridge pbk **£15.00**
OSBORNE, CHARLES
The Complete Operas of Verdi
The standard one-volume work on the subject. All the
operas (including the lesser-known ones) are
included, as well as the *Requiem* and other
miscellaneous works. Well-researched accounts of the
genesis, composition and performance of each are
coupled with percipient musical analyses.
[O188] Gollancz pbk **£4.95**

WAGNER, RICHARD
My Life
A wonderfully outrageous autobiography, by a man
obsessed with the vision of his own greatness and the
worthlessness of all those who refused to submit
themselves to serving his genius.
[O189] Cambridge pbk **£17.50**
BURBIDGE, PETER & SUTTON, RICHARD
The Wagner Companion
[O190] Faber pbk **£8.95**
COOKE, DERYCK
**I Saw the World End: A Study of
Wagner's 'Ring'**
The distinguished writer on music, Deryck Cooke,
was working on this book at the time of his death.
Had he been able to complete it, there is no doubt the
result would have been a very considerable work. As
it stands, it is a very interesting fragment.
[O191] Oxford pbk **£4.50**
MANN, THOMAS
Pro and Contra Wagner
By the Nobel Prize-winning novelist, who
acknowledged the influence of Wagner.
[O192] Faber pbk **£7.95**

NEWMAN, ERNEST
Wagner Nights
An essential book for all Wagnerians, first published
in 1949 but for some time out of print, until its 1988
reappearance in this paperback edition. It comprises a
series of lucidly written commentaries designed, as
the author says, 'to help the opera-goer see the
Wagnerian works as nearly as possible as Wagner
must have seen them.'
[O193] Bodley pbk **£9.95**
PORTER, ANDREW (TRANS)
The Ring of the Nibelung
German text with English translation, as used in the
highly acclaimed ENO production.
[O194] Faber pbk **£4.95**
SABOR, RUDOLPH
The Real Wagner **NEW**
A useful addition to the Wagner bibliography, 25
years in the writing, which takes full advantage of all
major documentary sources.
[O195] Cardinal pbk **£5.99**

WALTON, WILLIAM
KENNEDY, MICHAEL
Portrait of Walton **NEW**
An illuminating assessment of Walton's life and work
by one of the foremost authorities on English music.
[O196] Oxford hbk **£17.50**
WALTON, SUSANA
Behind the Façade
A long-awaited biography of William Walton by his
widow. It discusses his life and character and is rather
sketchy about the music (Walton would have
approved). Full of marvellous stories about their
acquaintances.
[O197] Oxford pbk **£4.95**

WEBER, CARL MARIA VON
WARRACK, JOHN
Carl Maria von Weber
[O198] Cambridge pbk **£15.00**

WEBERN, ANTON VON
MOLDENHAUER, HANS
Anton von Webern
The definitive work on the life and music of Webern.
[O199] Gollancz hbk **£25.00**
WILDGANS, FRIEDRICH
Anton von Webern
A useful introduction to the composer including brief
discussions of all the published works.
[O200] Calder hbk **£5.50**

WEILL, KURT
DREW, DAVID
Kurt Weill: A Handbook
This handbook is the result of many years' work, and
is the first of a number of projects that Drew is
undertaking to champion the music of Weill.
[O201] Faber hbk **£25.00**

WIDOR, CHARLES-MARIE
THOMSON, ANDREW
**The Life and Times of Charles-
Marie Widor 1844 - 1937** **NEW**
A comprehensive biography of a composer whose life
and music have hitherto remained in obscurity,
despite the fact that his Toccata is one of the most
popular pieces of music ever written.
[O202] Oxford pbk **£6.95**

XENAKIS, IANNIS
MATOSSIAN, NOURITZA
Xenakis
The fruit of ten years' study and close collaboration
with the composer, this is an authoritative biography
of one of the most controversial of living composers,
with a full discussion of the music.
[O203] Kahn & A hbk **£13.95**

Igor Stravinsky from *The Book of the Violin* by
Dominic Gill (Phaidon hbk **£20.00**)

Performer's Biographies

ASHKENAZY, VLADIMIR
PARROTT, JASPER
Beyond Frontiers
Written by Ashkenazy's long-time manager and
friend, ***Beyond Frontiers*** tells the story of the great
pianist's beginnings as a child prodigy under the
Soviet system, and his subsequent defection to the
West. One of the most intelligently written books
about a virtuoso.
[O204] H Hamilton pbk **£4.95**

BEECHAM, SIR THOMAS
ATKINS, HAROLD & NEWMAN, ARCHIE
Beecham Stories
Beecham on everything from Jazz to Hitler. Perfect
bedside reading.
[O205] Futura pbk **£2.50**

BERNSTEIN, LEONARD
GRADENWITZ, PETER
**Leonard Bernstein: The Infinite Variety
of a Musician**
A comprehensive and authoritative biography by a
close friend and observer of over forty years. It is a
colourful picture of his personality and achievements
that is further illustrated by colleagues, including
Menuhin, Dorati and Stern.
[O206] Berg hbk **£14.95**

BOULT, SIR ADRIAN
Boult on Music
A collection of the conductor's radio talks and essays
on composers (particularly Elgar), conductors
(Nikisch) and favourite pieces.
[O207] Toccata P pbk **£4.95**
KENNEDY, MICHAEL
Adrian Boult **NEW**
A sympathetic yet objective biography of one of our
greatest conductors. Boult, who died in 1983, aged
94, did more than most for English music,
paradoxically because his musicality was truly
cosmopolitan. His love for, and knowledge of, the
European classical tradition gave his championing of
Elgar, Vaughan Williams and others a greater weight.
[O208] Macmillan pbk **£8.99**

MUSIC

BRAIN, DENNIS
PETTITT, STEPHEN J.
Dennis Brain: A Biography
Brain's tragic death in a car crash at the age of 36 deprived the musical world of an exceptionally gifted instrumentalist who, in his modest way, altered the public's perception of the horn as a musical instrument. He fully deserved this clearly written biography, which in this paperback reissue, contains a full discography and list of works either written for him, or of which he gave the first performance.
[O209] Hale pbk **£7.95**

BRENDEL, ALFRED
Musical Thoughts and Afterthoughts
The acclaimed concert pianist Alfred Brendel writes thoughtfully on many musical subjects, most notably on the great Viennese masters, Haydn, Mozart, Beethoven and Schubert.
[O210] Robson pbk **£3.95**

CALLAS, MARIA
JELLINEK, GEORGE
Callas: Portrait of a Prima Donna
Written in 1960 at the height of her fame, this is a fascinating eye-witness account of the diva's career before its final tragic phase; illustrated with 64 black and white photographs.
[O212] Dover pbk **£6.35**
STASSINOPOULOS, ARIANNA
Maria Callas
Thoroughly researched and warmly sympathetic biography of the charismatic, but ultimately tragic, singer.
[O211] Arrow pbk **£4.95**

CARUSO, ENRICO
SCOTT, MICHAEL
The Great Caruso
A recent biography of 'the greatest tenor ever'.
[O213] H Hamilton hbk **£16.95**

CASALS, PABLO
Song of the Birds: Sayings, Stories & Impressions of Pablo Casals
[O214] Robson hbk **£7.95**

CHALIAPIN, FEODOR
GORKY, MAXIM
Chaliapin
An enthralling account of the life of the great Russian bass by the influential Russian writer. Gorky was a close friend of Chaliapin's, and this biography has the feel of reported anecdote.
[O215] Columbus pbk **£5.95**

DU PRE, JACQUELINE
Impressions   **NEW**
As the title suggests, not a biography, but a series of perspectives on the achievements and paradoxes of du Pré's life, from her friends and colleagues.
[O216] Grafton pbk **£7.95**
EASTON, CAROL
Jacqueline du Pré: A Biography
A biography frowned on by du Pré's family and widower, by a woman who spent more time than anyone with her during the last five years of her life.
[O217] Hodder hbk **£14.95**

FERRIER, KATHLEEN
LEONARD, MAURICE
Kathleen
A recent biography of one of the most popular British singers this century. Published to mark the 35th anniversary of her death in 1953, it includes many new letters, memoirs and photographs.
[O218] Hutchinson hbk **£14.95**

Jacqueline du Pré from a biography by Carol Easton (Hodder & Stoughton hbk £14.95)

FLAGSTAD, KIRSTEN
VOGT, HOWARD
Flagstad
[O219] Secker hbk **£20.00**

GOULD, GLENN
COTT, JONATHAN
Conversations with Glenn Gould
Conversations with the controversial pianist and writer Glenn Gould, covering the wide range of his interests (not only musical) but concentrating on his views and interpretation of Bach.
[O220] Hutchinson pbk **£4.95**
PAGE, TIM (ED)
The Glenn Gould Reader
A more or less complete collection of writings by the extraordinary Canadian pianist. Highly entertaining - his condemnation of middle-period Beethoven, or his appreciation of Petula Clark, have to be read to be believed.
[O221] Faber pbk **£12.95**

HOFFNUNG, GERARD
HOFFNUNG, ANNETTE
Gerard Hoffnung
A biography of the musical humorist, famous for his animated cartoons and his gentle, mocking vision of the world of music.
[O222] Gordon Fraser hbk **£17.50**

KLEMPERER, OTTO
Klemperer on Music
Subtitled 'Sayings from a Musician's Workbench', and illustrated throughout with sketches by different artists, this well-produced paperback will be of interest to all admirers of Otto Klemperer as conductor, composer and champion of modern music.
[O223] Toccata P pbk **£5.95**
HEYWORTH, PETER (ED)
Conversations with Klemperer
[O224] Faber pbk **£4.95**
Otto Klemperer: His Life and Times Vol 1: 1885 - 1933
[O225] Cambridge hbk **£22.50**

LEGGE, WALTER
SCHWARZKOPF, ELISABETH
On and Off the Record: A Memoir of Walter Legge
A fascinating compilation of anecdotes about, and writings by, the autocratic EMI producer who described himself as 'a midwife to music', and who brought into the world such classic performances as the Flagstad/Furtwängler *Tristan*, Klemperer's Beethoven, Beecham's *Magic Flute*, as well as the recorded legacies of Cantelli, Lipatti and Neveu.
[O226] Faber pbk **£5.95**

LLOYD WEBBER, JULIAN
Travels with My Cello
Entertaining volume of anecdotes.
[O227] Pavilion pbk **£4.95**

OGDON, JOHN
OGDON, BRENDA LUCAS & KERR, MICHAEL
Virtuoso
The painful story of Ogdon's breakdown and ultimate recovery is told with brutal frankness by his wife.
[O228] H Hamilton pbk **£6.95**

RATTLE, SIMON
KENYON, NICHOLAS
Simon Rattle: The Making of a Conductor
An account of the leading light among younger English musicians, following him through the course of a year; Rattle speaks of his relationship with the City of Birmingham Symphony Orchestra, and of his plans for the future.
[O229] Faber pbk **£7.99**

RUBINSTEIN, ARTUR
My Many Years
Memoirs of the great Polish concert pianist, who was also a bon viveur, raconteur, womanizer and card-player.
[O230] H Hamilton pbk **£7.95**

SUTHERLAND, JOAN
MAJOR, NORMA
Joan Sutherland
[O231] Futura pbk **£3.95**

TOSCANINI, ARTURO
HOROWITZ, JOSEPH
Understanding Toscanini
A passionately written study of one of the most celebrated and complex of all conductors.
[O232] Faber hbk **£20.00**
SACHS, HARVEY
Toscanini
[O232A] Weidenfeld hbk **£12.50**

Illustration from *Toscanini* by Harvey Sachs (Weidenfeld hbk £12.50)

VISHNEVSKYA, GALINA
Galina
Autobiography of the renowned Russian soprano and wife of cellist Mstislav Rostropovitch.
[O233] Hodder pbk **£3.95**

Opera

BARLOW, HAROLD & MORGENSTERN, SAM
Dictionary of Opera and Song Themes
[O234] Faber hbk **£17.50**

CLEMENT, CATHERINE
Opera, or the Undoing of Women **NEW**
Perhaps the first important text in feminist music criticism, this provocative book amply demonstrates that 19th century librettists helped to perpetuate a social order of which the subjection of women was a vital constituent.
[O235] Virago pbk **£7.50**

CONRAD, PETER
A Song of Love and Death
A history of opera and a discussion of archetypal roles in opera by an Oxford English don who is regarded as one of the brightest critics of contemporary culture.
[O236] Chatto pbk **£6.95**

DONALDSON, FRANCIS
The Royal Opera House
An account of Covent Garden in the 20th century.
[O237] Weidenfeld hbk **£16.95**

HAMILTON, DAVID (ED)
The Metropolitan Opera Encyclopaedia
Brief entries on opera composers, singers and conductors, with short essays by international stars.
[O238] Thames & H hbk **£20.00**

HEADINGTON, CHRISTOPHER
Opera: A History
A comprehensive yet concise history, giving coverage to lesser-known areas.
[O239] Bodley hbk **£16.00**

JACOBS, ARTHUR & SADIE, STANLEY
The Pan Book of Opera
For those who can't afford Kobbé, this is the ideal opera handbook, newly revised and now containing synopses of 83 operas.
[O240] Pan pbk **£5.99**

KOBBE
Kobbé's Complete Opera Book
Tenth edition, edited by the Earl of Harewood; completely redesigned and reset. The standard reference book on opera.
[O241] Bodley hbk **£30.00**

LAZARUS, JOHN
The Opera Handbook
A guide to the history of opera.
[O242] Longman hbk **£9.95**

MORDDEN, ETHAN
Opera Anecdotes
A vastly entertaining selection of stories, some famous, some less well-known, about composers, singers, impresarios and audiences.
[O243] Oxford pbk **£5.95**

PLEASANTS, HENRY
Opera in Crisis **NEW**
A collection of essays which analyses the current state of opera presenting a personal viewpoint. The crisis is twofold according to Pleasants: a dearth of original material combined with a tendency for directors and designers to reinterpret works, often in an outlandish way which is false to the intentions of the composer.
[O244] Thames & H hbk **£12.00**

ROSENTHAL, HAROLD & WARRACK, JOHN
Concise Oxford Dictionary of Opera
An invaluable source of information on all aspects of opera containing entries on individual operas, composers, librettists, singers, conductors, technical terms, and other subjects.
[O245] Oxford pbk **£7.95**

SADIE, STANLEY
New Grove: Opera
The latest New Grove handbook reprinted from the *New Grove Dictionary of Music and Musicians*.
[O246] Macmillan hbk **£32.50**

Series

CAMBRIDGE OPERA HANDBOOKS
The volumes in this excellent series are aimed at the opera-goer as well as the student. They contain a full description of the history of each work (both its writing and subsequent stage history), followed by a detailed synopsis and an analysis of the score. The writings of past commentators are taken into consideration, and each volume concludes with a bibliography and discography, together with guides to other sources where relevant. The following volumes are currently available, priced at £27.50 in hardback, £9.95 in paperback, unless otherwise stated.
Britten: **Death in Venice/Peter Grimes/ The Turn of the Screw**
Gluck: **Orfeo** £17.50/8.95
Janácek: **Kátá Kabanová** £25.00/9.95
Monteverdi: **Orfeo**
Mozart: **Die Entführung aus dem Serail/Le Nozze di Figaro/ Don Giovanni** £25.00/8.95
Puccini: **La Bohème/Tosca**
Strauss: **Der Rosenkavalier**
Stravinsky: **The Rake's Progress** £20.00/7.95
Verdi: **Falstaff** £22.50/8.95/**Othello**
Wagner: **Parsifal** £22.50/9.95

ENO OPERA GUIDES
Over the last few years the *English National Opera* has been publishing a series of guides, in association with *John Calder* and *The Royal Opera House*, to the works that form the basis of their repertoire. Each guide (usually produced on the occasion of a new production) is a lavishly illustrated programme book, consisting of a series of essays which describes the historical background to the making of the opera and the music. There is a complete libretto in the original language and a translation into English, as well as a full plot synopsis. All guides are priced at £4.00, unless otherwise stated.
Beethoven: **Fidelio**
Bizet : **Carmen**
Britten: **Peter Grimes/Gloriana**
Debussy: **Pelléas & Mélisande**
Janácek: **Jenufa/Kátá Kabanová**
Mozart: **The Marriage of Figaro/ Don Giovanni/The Magic Flute/ Cosi Fan Tutte**
Mussorgsky: **Boris Godunov**
Puccini: **La Bohème/Tosca/Manon/**
Madame Butterfly/Turandot (£5.00)
Rossini: **The Barber of Seville & Moses/ La Cenerentola**
Strauss: **Der Rosenkavalier/Salome & Electra//Arabella**
Tchaikovsky: **Eugene Onegin**
Tippett: **Operas of Michael Tippett**
Verdi: **Falstaff/Rigoletto/Il Trovatore/ The Force of Destiny/Aida/Simon Boccanegra/ La Traviata/Othello**
Wagner: **Tristan and Isolde/Tannhäuser/ The Flying Dutchman/Mastersingers of Nuremberg/Rheingold/ The Valkyrie/Parsifal/ Siegfried/ Twilight of the Gods**

Music Studies

BACH, C.P.E.
Essay on The True Art of Playing Keyboard Instruments
This is a classic manual on the art of playing keyboard instruments. Written by the second son of J.S. Bach, it appeared in the 1780s, and soon established itself as a major text and teaching aid.
[O247] Eulenburg pbk **£7.95**

BENT, IAN WITH DRABKIN, WILLIAM
Analysis
Probably the best general study of analysis available, this book is an expansion of Ian Bent's highly acclaimed article in the *New Grove Encyclopaedia*. Beginning with a chapter in which he examines the place of analysis in the study of music, it continues with an exhaustive survey of analytical history, and ends with a discussion of various of its types, including musical semiotics and set theory.
[O248] Macmillan pbk **£9.95**

BERNAC, PIERRE
Interpretation of French Song
Much acclaimed on its publication in 1970, this is still the standard work on the subject.
[O249] Gollancz hbk **£9.95**

BLADES, JAMES
Percussion Instruments and their History
[O250] Faber pbk **£15.00**

BLOCH, ERNST
Essays on the Philosophy of Music
An anthology of essays by the influential German philosopher on different aspects of musical experience. Sometimes very difficult to follow, but the reader who perseveres will find much to enhance his or her understanding of the place of music in human existence.
[O251] Cambridge pbk **£11.95**

BLUM, DAVID & THE GUARNERI QUARTET
Art of Quartet Playing
An unusual book, written in the form of conversations, which sheds much light on how an interpretation is reached.
[O252] Gollancz hbk **£15.95**

BRINDLE, REGINALD SMITH
Musical Composition
This book, for students of all levels of ability, first guides students through the basic elements before covering a variety of special subjects such as vocal and choral music, accompaniments and film and TV music.
[O253] Oxford pbk **£9.95**

BUSONI/DEBUSSY/IVES
Three Classics in the Aesthetic of Music
An important and inexpensive collection of articles and essays by three of the century's great maverick composers.
[O254] Dover pbk **£3.60**

CARDUS, NEVILLE
Cardus on Music: A Centenary Collection (Ed. Wright, Donald)
Cardus can lay claim to being one of the most important music critics in English; his work appeared in the *Manchester Guardian* for many years.
[O255] H Hamilton hbk **£14.95**

COOK, NICHOLAS
A Guide to Musical Analysis
The first book to examine thoroughly all the main techniques of musical analysis. The author compares the different methods, contrasting their strong and weak points, with the aid of 182 musical examples.
[O256] Dent hbk **£25.00**

COOKE, DERYCK
The Language of Music
Reissue of a controversial and influential study.
[O257] Oxford pbk **£9.95**

COPLAND, AARON
Music and Imagination
The original form of this book was a series of six lectures given at Harvard University in 1951-52. Their purpose, in Copland's own words, was to provide *"..a free improvisation on the general theme of the role imagination plays in the art of music"*.
[O258] Harvard UP pbk **£3.95**

DART, THURSTON
Interpretation of Music
Thurston Dart was one of the key figures responsible for the growth of interest in pre-classical and early music, using his great gifts as a keyboard player to perform the music on the instruments of the time. His scholarship was much respected for its penetrating insights.
[O259] Hutchinson pbk **£4.95**

DEL MAR, NORMAN
The British conductor's knowledge of the orchestra and of orchestral music is second to none; these three works are a testament to this, and are highly recommended.
Anatomy of the Orchestra
A commendably thorough and highly entertaining treatise on the instruments of the orchestra and their technique. A worthy successor to Cecil Forsyth's *Orchestration*.
[O260] Faber pbk **£9.95**
Companion to the Orchestra
This Companion has been expressly written for the student and the lay listener, and provides a good survey of the orchestra and its instruments for the music-lover at large.
[O261] Faber pbk **£9.95**
Orchestral Variations
A trail of hope through the labyrinth of misprints and editorial *faux pas* found in orchestral material.
[O262] Eulenburg pbk **£7.25**

DENYER, R.
Guitar Handbook
This is a very popular well-illustrated guide on Guitar playing, suitable for most types of learner, from beginner to more accomplished player.
[O263] Pan pbk **£10.95**

DONINGTON, ROBERT
The Interpretation of Early Music
A standard work on the basis of performance practice in Early Music.
[O264] Faber pbk **£14.95**

FISCHER-DIESKAU, DIETRICH
Fischer-Dieskau Book of Lieder
[O265] Gollancz hbk **£10.95**

FORSYTH, CECIL
Orchestration
It is a tribute to Forsyth's accuracy and user-friendliness that his manual, first published 75 years ago, is not only still in print, but is as valuable to the orchestral student as any more modern text.
[O266] Dover pbk **£7.95**

FRANKLIN, PETER
Idea of Music: Schoenberg and Others
Why has modern music evolved as it has? Starting from the premise that Austro-German music in the late 19th century was dominated by philosophical ideas, Franklin sets the writing of Schoenberg, Adorno and Thomas Mann alongside the music of the time, in a compelling argument for revising the standard historical account of the period.
[O267] Macmillan pbk **£9.95**

GILL, DOMINIC
The Book of the Piano
[O515] Phaidon hbk **£19.50**
The Book of the Violin
[O515A] Phaidon hbk **£20.00**

GREEN, BARRY & GALLWEY, W. TIMOTHY
The Inner Game of Music
Explains the psychology of music so that both performers and listeners can gain a deeper insight into the art.
[O268] Pan pbk **£3.99**

GRIFFITHS, PAUL
Guide to Electronic Music
[O269] Thames & H pbk **£3.95**

HOLST, IMOGEN
An ABC of Music
A short practical guide to the basic essentials of rudiments, harmony and form. With a foreword by Benjamin Britten.
[O270] Oxford pbk **£4.95**
Conducting a Choir
A guide for amateurs.
[O271] Oxford pbk **£6.95**

HOPKINS, ANTONY
Hopkins is a well-known writer, and presenter of programmes for the BBC and World Service. His writing is commendable for its clarity and perception, and he is able to bring more technical matters before the uninformed listener, in ways that can be easily understood.
Concertgoer's Companion
Vol 1
[O272] Dent hbk **£10.95**
Vol 2
[O273] Dent hbk **£15.00**
Talking about Music
[O274] Pan pbk **£3.95**
Understanding Music
[O275] Dent pbk **£4.95**

JACOB, GORDON
Orchestral Technique
A manual for students but of interest to the general reader. A standard book on the subject.
[O276] Oxford pbk **£7.95**

JACOBS, ARTHUR
The Pan Book of Orchestral Music
A useful volume for the layman, this concise guide begins with a brief introduction to orchestral forms and the evolution of the orchestra itself. The main part of the book consists of programme notes on the works of some 75 composers from Bach to Boulez.
[O277] Pan pbk **£5.99**

KAROLYI, OTTO
Introducing Music
Starts with the basics of music and moves on to score reading and harmony. One of the best short introductions to music theory.
[O278] Penguin pbk **£3.99**

KERMAN, JOSEPH
Musicology
An introduction to the subject of musicology. With the increasing interest in authentic performance and the rediscovery of the music of the past, this is an area that has seen much recent growth.
[O279] Fontana pbk **£3.95**

LEPPARD, RAYMOND
Authenticity in Music
An examination of the current trend towards authentic performance, and of the kind of knowledge that performers need to have, by the British conductor known for his re-introduction of Renaissance and Baroque music in authentic performance conditions.
[O280] Faber pbk **£4.95**

LOVELOCK, WILLIAM
The Rudiments of Music
A standard text which contains all the essential information needed for a thorough grounding in musical theory.
[O281] Unwin Hyman pbk **£3.95**

MUNROW, DAVID
Instruments of the Middle Ages & Renaissance
[O282] Oxford pbk **£9.95**

PHILLIPS, LOIS
Lieder Line by Line
In addition to straightforward prose translations of the best-known *lieder* of the great composers, this most valuable book for singers also contains a word by word translation printed directly below the original, as an aid to interpretation.
[O283] Duckworth pbk **£12.95**

PILKINGTON, MICHAEL
The first two volumes in a projected series which aims to offer a complete guide to the rich repertoire of English song over the last 500 years. Each song is briefly described in respect of tonality, range, metre, duration and difficulty.
Campion, Dowland and the Lutenist Songwriters **NEW**
[O284] Duckworth hbk **£14.95**
Gurney, Ireland, Quilter and Warlock **NEW**
[O285] Duckworth hbk **£14.95**

PISTON, WALTER
This American composer was Professor of Music at Harvard for more than 40 years. His three works, based on his teaching experiences, are highly regarded textbooks.
Counterpoint
[O286] Gollancz hbk **£7.95**
Harmony
[O287] Gollancz hbk **£10.95**
Orchestration
[O288] Gollancz pbk **£8.95**

PRENDERGAST, ROY M.
Film Music: A Neglected Art
One of only two books currently available that treats the subject of film music in any detail. Among the composers discussed are Bernard Herrmann, Elmer Bernstein, Miklos Rosza and Max Steiner.
[O289] Norton pbk **£6.35**

RASTALL, R.
Notation of Western Music
A study of the semiology of Western music.
[O290] Dent hbk **£17.50**

SACHS, CURT
History of Musical Instruments
A standard text on the subject.
[O291] Dent hbk **£15.00**

SADIE, STANLEY (ED)
Reprinted and expanded versions of articles from the *New Grove Dictionary of Music and Musicians*.
New Grove: Early Keyboard Instruments
[O292] Macmillan pbk **£9.95**
New Grove: The Organ
[O292] Macmillan pbk **£9.95**
New Grove: The Piano
[O293] Macmillan pbk **£9.95**
New Grove: The Violin Family
[O293] Macmillan pbk **£9.95**

SCHOENBERG, ARNOLD
Schoenberg's theoretical writings are fascinating, but should be approached with the utmost caution by those who want clear guidance.
Fundamentals of Musical Composition
An idiosyncratic approach to composition teaching.
[O294] Faber pbk **£6.95**
Preliminary Exercises in Counterpoint
[O295] Faber pbk **£5.95**
Structural Functions of Harmony
[O296] Faber pbk **£3.95**
Style and Idea: Selected Writings of Arnold Schoenberg
One of Schoenberg's most important collections of writings.
[O297] Faber pbk **£9.95**
Theory of Harmony (Harmonielehre)
An interesting view of the way harmony works. This volume informs the reader more of Schoenberg's own view of harmony rather than providing a working guide for students.
[O298] Faber pbk **£14.95**

SHAW, GEORGE BERNARD
A major collection of Shaw's music criticism, which includes many of his most perceptive, brilliant and witty critiques of concert life around the turn of the century.
Collected Music Criticism Vol 1
[O299] Bodley pbk **£12.95**
Vol 2
[O300] Bodley pbk **£12.95**
Vol 3
[O301] Bodley pbk **£12.95**

SPINK, IAN
English Song: Dowland to Purcell
A comprehensive survey of 17th century English song.
[O302] Batsford pbk **£8.95**

TOVEY, DONALD FRANCIS
Tovey's *Essays in Musical Analysis* have been the bedrock of British analysis since their publication just before the War, and they are still the means by which the layman is most likely to increase his enjoyment of the classical repertoire.

Chamber Music
[O303] Oxford pbk **£6.95**
Concertos and Choral Works
[O304] Oxford pbk **£6.95**
Symphonies and Other Orchestral Works
[O305] Oxford pbk **£6.95**

VAUGHAN WILLIAMS, RALPH
National Music and Other Essays
A collection of essays on subjects such as English music, Beethoven and his contemporaries; according to Michael Kennedy, editor of the second edition, it effectively comprises Vaughan Williams' musical autobiography.
[O306] Oxford pbk **£5.95**

Jazz

B Flat, Bebop, Scat
Anthology of short stories and poems capturing the feeling and swing of the music.
[O307] Quartet hbk **£10.95**

BALLIETT, WHITNEY
American Musicians: 56 Portraits in Jazz
The celebrated Jazz columnist of the *New Yorker* brings together all the personalities he has chronicled during a period of 25 years, including Fats Waller, Duke Ellington, Elven Jones and Ornette Coleman.
[O308] Oxford hbk **£17.50**
American Singers
[O309] Oxford hbk **£10.95**
Improvising: Sixteen Jazz Musicians and Their Art
[O310] Oxford hbk **£19.50**
Night Creature: Journal of Jazz 1975-80
[O311] Oxford hbk **£11.00**

BERENDT, JOACHIM
Jazz Book
A useful book for listeners looking for an introduction to the history of Jazz. Divided into 'The Styles of Jazz', 'The Musicians of Jazz', 'The Elements of Jazz' etc, it provides a source of useful information, yet remains highly readable.
[O312] Grafton pbk **£4.95**

BERNHARDT, CLYDE
I Remember: Eighty Years of Black Entertainment, Big Band & Blues
An interesting account of Jazz in the early years as told to Sheldon Harris.
[O313] Pennsylvania UP pbk **£12.95**

CARR; FAIRWEATHER & PRIESTLEY
Jazz: The Essential Companion
Three highly qualified and knowledgeable men have brought together their skills to produce the most comprehensive and usable dictionary of Jazz in its class. Covers musicians, terms etc from 'the original Dixieland Jazz band' to 'Loose Tubes'. Highly recommended.
[O314] Grafton pbk **£8.95**

CASE, BRITT & MURRAY
The Illustrated Encyclopaedia of Jazz
A large-format, recently updated reference work.
[O315] Salamander pbk **£9.95**

CHILTON, JOHN
Who's Who of Jazz
A strong book, especially for lovers of early Jazz.
[O316] Macmillan pbk **£7.95**

COLLIER, JAMES LINCOLN
Making of Jazz: A Comprehensive History
Possibly the best study of Jazz from its African roots to its present point of departure. A well-written and searching book containing a good discography/bibliography.
[O317] Macmillan pbk **£9.99**

CROWETT, BRUCE & PINFOLD, MIKE
The Jazz Singers
The authors set out the case for the often overlooked and underrated musicians who are so central to the popular appeal of the music as well as its development.
[O318] Javelin pbk **£5.95**

DANCE, STANLEY
World of Swing
Focusing on the era in which the big bands of Benny Goodman et al were predominant.
[O319] Da Capo pbk **£7.50**

DANKWORTH, AVRIL
Jazz: An Introduction to Its Musical Basis
[O320] Oxford pbk **£5.95**

ELLISON, MARY
Extensions of the Blues `NEW`
More than a book on Blues and its players, this is a study of the music's foundation and its deeper effects. As well as looking at the origins of the form with the arrival of African slaves in the deep South, it explores the relation of Blues to Jazz, Rock, and American poetry, fiction and drama. A work of great and general interest.
[O321] Calder hbk **£14.95**

FEATHER, LEONARD
From Satchmo to Miles
A study of trumpet in Jazz.
[O322] Da Capo pbk **£9.95**
Inside Jazz, Inside Be-Bop
[O323] Da Capo hbk **£20.95**
Laughter from the Hip: The Lighter Side of Jazz
[O324] Da Capo pbk **£5.75**

FEIGIN, LEO
Russian Jazz: A New Identity
Taking off from where *Red and Hot* finished, a history of the development of Russian Jazz since the 1970s, collecting opinions from a multinational array of critics, poets and musicians. Of equal interest to lovers of improvised music and to those concerned with music and politics.
[O325] Quartet hbk **£12.95**

GELLY, DAVE
The Giants of Jazz
A small introductory book with brief biographies of some major stars of the genres.
[O326] Aurum pbk **£5.95**

GIDDINS, GARY
Rhythm-A-Ning: Jazz Tradition & Innovation in the 80s
The 1980s have been an exciting time for Jazz, as reflected in this volume of selected criticism from the *Village Voice*.
[O327] Oxford pbk **£6.95**

GIOIA, TED
The Imperfect Art: Reflections on Jazz and Modern Culture `NEW`
A collection of seven essays which cover a wide range of viewpoints on Jazz: Gioia sets out the

case for Jazz as an art form, one which relies as much on error and correction as premeditation. Focusing on its artistic validity, this is a work suitable for a wider readership than that of the Jazz *aficionado*.
[O328] Oxford hbk **£15.00**

GITLER, IRA
Jazz Masters of the Forties
[O329] Da Capo pbk **£8.95**

GODBOLT, JIM
All This: And Many a Dog
'Memoirs of a loser and pessimist'. The title belies the hilarity of the anecdotes, as well as the accurate portraits and personal insight of a true Jazz devotee.
[O330] Quartet pbk **£5.95**
In the Moment: History of Jazz in Britain 1919 - 1950
A British perspective on Jazz, recounting the effect American musicians, the Musicians' Union ban, and British players have had on the music scene from the arrival of ODJB, to Ronnie Scott and Tubby Haynes in the late 1940s.
[O331] Grafton pbk **£4.95**
Jazz in Britain: 1950 - 1970   NEW
[O332] Quartet hbk **£14.95**

GOLDBERG, JOE
Jazz Masters of the Fifties
[O333] Da Capo pbk **£7.50**

HARRIS, STEVE
A Critical Guide to Jazz on Compact Disc
An illustrated discography covering most of the Jazz now widely available.
[O334] Salamander pbk **£8.95**

HARRISON, FOX & THACKER
The Essential Jazz Records Vol 1: Jazz to Swing
The definitive book on Jazz recordings, covering over 250 of the greatest.
[O335] Mansell pbk **£15.00**

HASSE, JOHN
Ragtime: Its History, Composers, Music
The first book to chronicle the genre in any detail, and in an accessible way.
[O336] Macmillan pbk **£15.00**

HORRICKS, RAYMOND
Tongue and Groove: Profiles in Jazz
A humorous look at Jazz and its musicians.
[O337] Costello hbk **£18.50**

JONES, MAX
Talking Jazz
Interviews with 39 artists from many fields of Jazz, both mainstream and off-beat, giving a varied perspective on its past and future.
[O338] Macmillan hbk **£14.95**

KERNFELD, BARRY (ED)   NEW
The New Grove Dictionary of Jazz
The ultimate reference tool for the Jazz enthusiast, with 4,500 entries over 1,300 pages. Little is left out, and in the true Grove dictionary fashion, the entries are informative and highly usable, with bibliographies, discographies and cross-references. Although expensive, it's highly recommended.
[O339] Macmillan 2 vols hbk **£225.00**

LARKIN, PHILIP
All What Jazz: A Record Diary, 1961 - 1971
A collection of essays which illuminate the poet's love for Jazz. Interesting and lyrical.
[O340] Faber pbk **£4.95**

LEES, GENE
The Singer & the Song
Social history seen through the mirror of past popular music: the author argues convincingly for the artistic merits of the popular song and singer.
[O341] Oxford hbk **£12.95**

LYONS, LEN
The Great Jazz Pianists   NEW
Covering 27 pianists in interview, with an interesting opening chapter surveying the tradition; artists such as Ahmad Jamal and Marion McPartland are included, along with giants like Oscar Peterson, Herbie Hancock and Cecil Taylor.
[O342] Da Capo pbk **£9.95**

LYTTELTON, HUMPHREY
Best of Jazz Vol 2: Enter the Giants
A good book by the well-known musician and writer, who both commands respect and gives it to the players he covers here.
[O343] Robson hbk **£6.95**

MACRAE, BARRY
The Jazz Handbook   NEW
A well-arranged reference work, set out chronologically by decade, and alphabetically within each period: some provocative entries.
[O344] Longman hbk **£10.95**

MCPARTLAND, MARION
All in Good Time
A collection of essays by a celebrated pianist and critic. The host of *Jazz Piano*, the long-running radio programme, she gives sympathetic and interesting accounts of some of the great players of Jazz.
[O345] Oxford hbk **£13.50**

OLIVER, PAUL
Blues Off the Record: 30 Years of Blues Commentary
[O346] Baton P hbk **£12.50**
Gospel, Blues and Jazz
[O347] Macmillan pbk **£6.95**

ROSE, AL
I Remember Jazz
A collection of reminiscences from one of the most prolific producers of Jazz albums.
[O348] Thorsons pbk **£6.99**

SCHULLER, GUNTHER
Early Jazz
This is *the* book about the roots of the music. Scholarly yet accessible, from the man who played on the Miles Davies album 'Birth of the Cool', and is a respected musicologist.
[O349] Oxford pbk **£6.95**

SHAPIRO, N. & HENTOF, NAT
Hear Me Talkin' to Ya
A kaleidoscopic history of Jazz from the players and singers whose history it has been.
[O350] Dover pbk **£6.95**

SHAW, ARNOLD
Black Popular Music in America
Covering in detail the development of Black music, including Jazz, into the era of popular music.
[O351] Macmillan hbk **£17.95**

SILVESTER, PETER
A Left Hand Like God: A Study of Boogie-Woogie   NEW
A thorough and interesting work on one of the least studied areas of Jazz. Silvester discusses the form's history and development, with an appendix analysing the music of some of the pianists associated with it.
[O352] Quartet hbk **£18.50**

STEWART, REX
Jazz Masters of the Thirties
[O353] Da Capo pbk **£7.50**

TIRRO, F.
Jazz: A History
Well researched and presented, this is an accessible history of Jazz.
[O354] Dent hbk **£17.50**

VIAN, BORIS
Round About Close to Midnight: The Selected Jazz Writings of Boris Vian
Vian's style echoes the fluid improvisation of the music: this contains his articles from *Jazz Hot* and *Combat*.
[O355] Quartet hbk **£14.95**

WAITE, BRIAN
Modern Jazz Piano   NEW
Essentially a theoretical and practical work, this is of interest to all players and other readers with a basic grounding in the rudiments of the music. Waite analyses the harmony and scales the modern Jazz pianist needs to know, in a succinct and well-illustrated fashion.
[O356] Spellmount hbk **£15.95**

WHITCOMB, IAN
Irving Berlin and Ragtime America
The author takes Irving Berlin as the product of an era, and proceeds to discuss the pulse and current of popular music, and its industry, in the first half of the century.
[O357] Century pbk **£7.95**

WILLIAMS, MARTIN T.
Art of Jazz
Essays on the development of Jazz as an art.
[O358] Da Capo pbk **£6.75**
Jazz Heritage
A companion volume to his prize-winning book *The Jazz Tradition*.
[O359] Oxford pbk **£6.95**
Jazz Masters in Transition: 1957 - 1969
Covering the birth of hard bop and modal playing, up to the first experiments in Jazz fusion.
[O360] Oxford hbk **£25.00**
The Jazz Tradition
An intelligent account from a respected critic. Second edition.
[O361] Oxford pbk **£4.95**

Biographies

ARMSTRONG, LOUIS
My Life in New Orleans
The autobiography of 'Satchmo' the leading trumpeter of the early Jazz Age.
[O362] Da Capo hbk **£9.95**
JONES, MAX & CHILTON, JOHN
'Louis': The Louis Armstrong Story 1900 - 1971
The definitive biography of Armstrong - worth reading even if Jazz is not a special interest.
[O363] Da Capo pbk **£8.50**

BAKER, JOSEPHINE
HANEY, LYNN
Naked at the Feast: The Biography of Josephine Baker
A life of the Black singer whose career began at the Folies Bergères, and who later starred in many films.
[O364] Robson hbk **£7.50**

BARKER, DANNY
A Life in Jazz
Another inside story of Jazz from a Big Band player, who played with Cab Calloway and others.
[O365] Macmillan pbk **£15.00**

BASIE, BILL 'COUNT'
Good Morning Blues
The autobiography of one of the great Big Band legends, legendary for his spare blues touch at the piano, and for his subtle scoring.
[O366] Grafton pbk **£6.95**

BECHET, SIDNEY
CHILTON, JOHN
Sidney Bechet: Wizard of Jazz
A deeply searching and well-written account of the life and times of Sidney Bechet, a pioneer improviser.
[O367] Macmillan hbk **£14.95**

BERLIN, IRVING
FREEDLAND, MICHAEL
A Salute to Irving Berlin
An interesting account of the hugely successful American song writer, famous for 'White Christmas' and many others.
[O368] Comet pbk **£5.95**

BOLDEN, BUDDY
MARQUIS, D.
In Search of Buddy Bolden
One of the first famous stars of Jazz: Michael Ondaatje presents a fictional version of his life in *Coming Through Slaughter*.
[O369] Da Capo pbk **£6.95**

CLAYTON, BUCK
ELLIOTT, NANCY MILLER (ED)
Buck Clayton's Jazz World
75 years of Jazz history recorded with charm and wit.
[O370] Macmillan hbk **£16.95**

COLE, NAT KING
HASKINS & BENSON
Nat King Cole
Renowned both as a jazz pianist in his trio, and as the song writer of such classics as 'When I Fall in Love'.
[O371] Robson hbk **£8.95**

COLTRANE, JOHN
PRIESTLEY, BRIAN
John Coltrane
Since Bill Cole's book has gone out of print, this is the only easily available account of the most influential tenor saxophone player Jazz has yet known. In the *Apollo* Jazz series, a useful pocket-sized introduction to many important figures.
[O372] Apollo pbk **£4.95**

DAVIS, MILES
CARR, IAN
Miles Davis: A Critical Biography
An important book on the figure who has deeply influenced Jazz trumpet playing since his debut with Charlie Parker, up to 'Amandla', his new album, at the age of 63. 'Critical' is not the right way to define Carr's approach - it sometimes borders on idolatry.
[O373] Grafton pbk **£3.95**
MCRAE, BARRY
Miles Davis
The other view of Davis's career - and a far less generous look at a performer who has always been controversial.
[O374] Apollo pbk **£4.95**

DOLPHY, ERIC
HORRICKS, RAYMOND
The Importance of Being Eric Dolphy
Horricks explains the life, music and influence of a deeply persuasive champion of progressive Jazz. Dolphy was known for his alto saxophone and bass clarinet playing, and his particular style of angular improvisation.
[O375] Costello pbk **£5.95**

DORSEY, TOMMY & JIMMY
SANFORD, H.
Tommy & Jimmy: The Dorsey Years
[O376] Da Capo pbk **£8.95**

ELLINGTON, DUKE
COLLIER, JAMES LINCOLN
Duke Ellington
The author of *Jazz: A Comprehensive History* has produced a book of fundamental importance on possibly the greatest composer/pianist to write for Big Band.
[O377] Pan pbk **£5.99**
GAMMOND, PETER
Duke Ellington: His Life and Music
[O378] Apollo pbk **£4.95**

FEATHER, LEONARD
Jazz Years: Earwitness to an Era
One of the better pieces of Jazz autobiography.
[O379] Quartet hbk **£12.95**

FITZGERALD, ELLA
COLIN, SID
Ella: The Life and Times of Ella Fitzgerald
Central to the tradition of Black Jazz singing and its popularization, Ella Fitzgerald is still one of the most powerful and popular performers today.
[O380] Elm Tree hbk **£9.95**

FOSTER, POPS
Pops Foster: Autobiography of a New Orleans Jazzman
[O381] California UP pbk **£4.95**

GARNER, ERROL
DORAN, J.M.
Errol Garner: The Most Happy Piano
Famous for 'Misty', and rich, lyrical piano playing, Errol Garner is undoubtedly a major figure in Jazz history.
[O382] Scarecrow hbk **£32.50**

GETZ, STAN
PALMER, RICHARD
Stan Getz
Probably most famous for his work with Antonio Carlos Jobim in the 1960s, which produced the Latin/samba classics Jazz Samba and Getz/Gilberto, Stan Getz has been a serious tenor player of the 'Cool School' from the West Coast - yet his early nickname was 'the Steamer'.
[O383] Apollo pbk **£4.95**

GILLESPIE, DIZZY
FRAZER, ALAN
Dizzy: To Be or Not to Bop
An excellent book on a great trumpeter, with a sense of the freshness of Be-Bop, and the glow of Latin American rhythms that Gillespie pioneered in fusion with Jazz.
[O384] Quartet pbk **£8.95**

GORDON, DEXTER
BRITT, STAN
Long Tall Dexter   NEW
An influential player for many years, Gordon started with Louis Armstrong, and was one of the pioneers of Be-Bop, working with 'Wardill Gray' on the West Coast scene. His stay in Europe and subsequent return to America in the 1970s put him in an ideal position to play Lester Young in the film *Round Midnight*.
Stan Britt follows Gordon's career, and analyses his recordings and tenor style.
[O385] Quartet hbk **£14.95**

GRAPPELLI, STEPHANE
SMITH, GEOFFREY
Stephane Grappelli: A Biography
A well-illustrated book telling the story of one of the great violinists of Jazz, who worked with Django Reinhardt in the 'Hot Club of Paris', and has earned the respect of classical greats such as Yehudi Menuhin and Nigel Kennedy.
[O386] Pavilion hbk **£12.95**

HERMAN, WOODY
VOCE, STEVE
Woody Herman
This biography traces the varied career of a great and respected player up to 1985.
[O387] Apollo pbk **£4.99**

HOLIDAY, BILLIE
Lady Sings the Blues
[O388] Penguin pbk **£3.95**
WHITE, JOHN
Billie Holiday: Life & Times
[O389] Omnibus P pbk **£6.95**

KERN, JEROME
FREEDLAND, MICHAEL
Jerome Kern: A Biography
[O390] Robson pbk **£3.95**

MILLER, GLENN
BUTCHER, GEOFFREY
Next to a Letter From Home
A wartime chronicle of the Miller band and its sound that produced Big Band classics 'Pennsylvania 65000' and 'In the Mood'.
[O391] Sphere pbk **£4.95**

MINGUS, CHARLIE
PRIESTLEY, BRIAN
Mingus: A Critical Biography
Similar to the Miles Davis counterpart, this biography records the often hard times of an outcast, half-caste bass player, dealing with the innovation which he brought about, and which produced 'Scenes in the City' and other major albums.
[O392] Grafton pbk **£3.95**

MULLIGAN, GERRY
HORRICKS, RAYMOND
Gerry Mulligan
Mulligan pioneered the 'pianoless' quartet and was probably the most influential baritone saxophone player on the West Coast, which produced the 'Cool School'.
[O393] Apollo pbk **£4.95**

PARKER, CHARLIE
RUSSELL, ROSS
'Bird Lives':
High Life and Hard Times of Charlie 'Yardbird' Parker
Probably the best book on the short but extremely important career of 'Bird'; recent interest has grown in the wake of Clint Eastwood's film on the inventor of Be-Bop, and thus of modern Jazz.
[O394] Quartet pbk **£4.95**

PETERSON, OSCAR
PALMER
Oscar Peterson
One of the slim but informative volumes from Spellmount, exploring the blues-based piano style of a well-loved pianist.
[O395] Spellmount pbk **£3.95**

PIAF, EDITH

BERTEAUT, SIMONE
Piaf
A biography by Piaf's sister.
[O396] Penguin pbk **£5.95**

CROSLAND, MARGARET
Piaf
[O397] Hodder pbk **£2.95**

SCOTT, RONNIE

FORDHAM, JOHN
Let's Join Hands and Contact the Living: Ronnie Scott and His Club
[O398] H Hamilton pbk **£6.95**

SINATRA, FRANK

HOWLETT, JOHN
Frank Sinatra
[O399] Plexus pbk **£5.95**

KELLEY, KITTY
His Way: The Unauthorized Biography of Frank Sinatra
[O400] Bantam pbk **£3.95**

SINATRA, NANCY
Frank Sinatra: My Father
[O401] Hodder pbk **£3.50**

SMITH, BESSIE

FEINSTEIN, ELAINE
Bessie Smith: Empress of the Blues
A long awaited tribute to a great singer.
[O402] Penguin pbk **£2.95**

WALLER, FATS

KIRKEBY
Ain't Misbehavin'
[O403] Da Capo pbk **£7.95**

Pop

CHAMBERS, IAIN
Urban Rhythms: Pop Music and Popular Culture
The first critical historical analysis of British pop music since 1956 which seriously explores the relationship of each new fashion, from Rock'n'Roll through to Reggae, Disco and Punk.
[O404] Macmillan pbk **£7.95**

CLARKE, DONALD (ED)
The Penguin Encyclopaedia of Popular Music NEW
Reviewers inevitably cited omissions and quarrelled with judgements: nevertheless this is a mammoth undertaking which has resulted in a more than respectable single-volume reference work.
[O405] Viking hbk **£25.00**

COHN, NIK
Ball the Wall
Seminal collection of essays by the man who pointed out that everything you need to know about pop music can be found in the chorus of *Tutti Frutti*.
[O406] Picador pbk **£4.99**

FRITH, SIMON
Art into Pop
Co-written with Howard Horne, this is an interesting examination and exploration of the links between pop music and art, especially in such areas as use of image to promote and define the pop artist.
[O407] Methuen pbk **£6.95**
Music for Pleasure
Something of a hotch-potch compared with *Sound Effects*, but still full of provocative opinions and a reasonable attempt to disprove Nik Cohn's remark

(quoted in the text) that *"...there isn't that much to say about rock'n'roll"*.
[O408] Polity P pbk **£7.95**
Sound Effects: Youth, Leisure and the Politics of Rock'n'Roll
Originally titled 'The Sociology of Rock', Frith's book is as earnest as it sounds, but is nonetheless one of the tiny handful of works that provides an intelligent analysis of the impact of popular music.
[O409] Constable pbk **£5.95**

GAMBACCINI, PAUL
Top 100 Albums
The Radio One DJ's personal choice of 100 classic albums. An attractively designed book and great fun to read.
[O410] M Joseph pbk **£8.95**

GARFIELD, SIMON
Expensive Habits: The Dark Side of the Music Industry
An excellent survey of the bitter lawsuits that characterize the greed and exploitation of the music business.
[O411] Faber pbk **£5.95**

GEORGE, NELSON
Where Did Our Love Go?
The classic account of the rise and fall of the Motown sound.
[O412] Omnibus P pbk **£6.95**

GILLETT, CHARLIE
Making Tracks: The Story of Atlantic Records
The fascinating biography of the only pioneer Indie R'n'B label that survived into the 1980s, based on interviews with its founders and senior executives.
[O413] Souvenir P pbk **£8.95**
The Sound of the City
The only book in the *New Oxford Dictionary of Music*'s pop music bibliography, this has long been regarded as the most intelligently written history of the music of the 1950s and 60s.
[O414] Souvenir P pbk **£8.95**

GREIG, CHARLOTTE
Will You Still Love Me Tomorrow? Girl Groups from the 50s On NEW
Starting with the doo-wop groups of the 1950s, and going on to the rap and hip-hop groups of the 80s, this is a fully illustrated survey of one of the most purely enjoyable currents in pop music, as well as a reflection of the changing aspirations of women in the music business over the years.
[O415] Virago pbk **£8.99**

HIRSHEY, GERRI
Nowhere to Run: The Story of Soul Music
The author's passion for her subject shows through on every page - essential reading for soul fans.
[O416] Pan pbk **£4.99**

HOSKYNS, BARNEY
Say It One More Time for the Broken Hearted
A perceptive exploration of the roots of soul in the American South by a leading journalist of the *New Musical Express*.
[O417] Fontana pbk **£4.95**

HOUNSOME, TERRY
New Rock Record
This is a massive pop music reference work, of special interest to serious record collectors.
[O418] Blandford pbk **£12.95**

MALONE, BILL C.
Country Music USA
Described by no less an authority than *The Nashville Tennessean* as 'the most accurate, complete and serious study of country music ever published'.
[O419] Thorsons pbk **£9.95**

MARCUS, GREIL
Lipstick Traces NEW
Subtitled 'A Secret History of the 20th Century', this is a remarkable combination of pop music and social history.
[O420] Secker hbk **£14.95**
Mystery Train
Certainly one of the few indispensable rock books - passionate, opinionated and dazzlingly well-written.
[O421] Omnibus P pbk **£7.95**

PIDGEON, JOHN
The Encyclopedia of Popular Song
[O422] Sidgwick hbk **£15.95**

RICE, TIM & JO; GAMBACCINI, PAUL
The latest editions of the most authoritative popular music reference books, containing thousands of entries listing hit singles and albums.
The Guinness Book of No 1 Hits
[O423] Guinness pbk **£7.95**
The Guinness Book of British Hit Singles
[O424] Guinness pbk **£7.95**
The Guinness Book of British Hit Albums
[O425] Guinness pbk **£7.95**

RIMMER, DAVE
Like Punk Never Happened NEW
An entertaining account of the horror story that was pop in the 80s.
[O426] Faber pbk **£4.95**

ROGAN, JOHNNY
Starmakers & Svengalis
Seventeen case studies of pop managers and the bands they managed, including Brian Epstein, Andrew Loog Oldham, Simon Napier-Bell and Malcolm MacLaren.
[O427] Futura pbk **£4.99**

ROLLING STONE MAGAZINE
What A Long Strange Trip It's Been: 20 Years of Rolling Stone
The respected American rock magazine provides a serious assessment of the popular music scene since the 60s. Now available at a bargain price.
[O428] Ebury pbk **£5.99**

SHAPIRO, HARRY
Waiting for the Man
The inescapable truth that drugs are, and have always been, an integral part of the music business is here intelligently and compassionately expounded.
[O429] Quartet hbk **£14.95**

STREET, JOHN
Rebel Rock: The Politics of Popular Music
A thoughtful book which, as well as discussing what happens when pop stars take up political stances, aims to show why rock and pop can be such an important influence in some people's lives.
[O430] Blackwell pbk **£6.95**

TOSCHES, NICK
Country
First published in 1977, but appearing in this country for the first time, Tosches's book explores the darker side of the music.
[O431] Secker pbk **£6.95**

TUCKER, KEN
Rock of Ages: The Rolling Stone History of Rock & Roll
An authoritative history of popular music. Written from an American standpoint, it covers a wide field.
[O432] Penguin pbk **£7.95**

Biographies

BAEZ, JOAN
And a Voice to Sing With
Compelling autobiography of the politically committed American singer.
[O433] Arrow pbk **£3.99**

BERRY, CHUCK
Chuck Berry: The Autobiography
As the first Black rock'n'roll star, Berry's personal account of the change in race relations in the music business makes his story of especial interest.
[O434] Faber pbk **£4.95**

BOWIE, DAVID
GILLMAN, PETER & LENI
Alias David Bowie
One of the most accomplished and enigmatic figures in the world of entertainment, Bowie's multi-faceted career is fully covered in this biography, which draws on new material.
[O435] Hodder pbk **£4.95**
MILES & CHARLESWORTH, CHRIS
The David Bowie Black Book
An illustrated biography, selected from the myriad of Bowie books as being particularly good on facts and well-presented.
[O436] Omnibus P pbk **£8.95**

BROWN, JAMES
BROWN, JAMES WITH TUCKER, BRUCE
James Brown: The Godfather of Soul
Not the most modest autobiography ever written, Brown's story is nonetheless compelling reading.
[O437] Fontana pbk **£3.95**

CLAPTON, ERIC
COLEMAN, RAY
Survivor: The Authorized Biography of Eric Clapton
A truthful biography of the archetypal 'rock-star', which neither hero-worships, nor overdramatizes.
[O438] Futura pbk **£3.95**

CROSBY, DAVID
Long Time Gone   `NEW`
A wonderful account of the sheer degradation that can be a rock star's life.
[O439] Heinemann hbk **£12.95**

DYLAN, BOB
Lyrics: 1962 - 1985
A major collection of Dylan's lyrics.
[O440] Grafton pbk **£6.95**
GRAY, MICHAEL & BAULDIE, JOHN
All Across the Telegraph: A Bob Dylan Handbook
A miscellaneous collection of Dylanalia from the pages of *The Telegraph*; probably one of the most useful of the great glut of books on Dylan.
[O441] Futura pbk **£4.99**
HEYLIN, CLINTON
Bob Dylan: Stolen Moments
The product of six years' research by a leading Dylan authority, this is a beautifully presented chronological list of events (as opposed to biography) which will be indispensable to Dylanophiles.
[O442] Wanted Man pbk **£12.95**

SHELTON, ROBERT
No Direction Home
A major biography and assessment of Bob Dylan.
[O443] Penguin pbk **£4.95**

ENO, BRIAN
TAMM, ERIC
Brian Eno: His Music and the Vertical Colour of Sound   `NEW`
A detailed and thoughtful critique of an immensely influential composer, producer and sometime performer.
[O444] Faber pbk **£7.50**

GABRIEL, PETER
BRIGHT, SPENCER
Peter Gabriel: The Authorised Biography
The dichotomy between Gabriel's flamboyant stage persona and his shy, thoughtful personality is one of the themes fully explored in this sympathetic biography.
[O445] Headline pbk **£4.99**

GAYE, MARVIN
RITZ, DAVID
Divided Soul: The Life of Marvin Gaye
[O446] Grafton pbk **£4.95**

HENDRIX, JIMI
MURRAY, CHARLES SHAAR
Crosstown Traffic: Jimi Hendrix and Post-War Pop   `NEW`
A penetrating survey of pop music using the career and subsequent influence of Hendrix as a starting point. Murray is one of the most widely respected rock journalists.
[O447] Faber pbk **£7.95**

JACKSON, MICHAEL
Moonwalk
Interestingly dedicated to Fred Astaire, the bestselling autobiography of 'a very special human being'.
[O448] Mandarin pbk **£3.99**

JOPLIN, JANIS
FRIEDMAND, M.
Buried Alive: The Story of Janis Joplin
[O449] Plexus pbk **£5.95**

LENNON, JOHN
COLEMAN, J.
John Lennon
[O450] Futura pbk **£4.99**

David Bowie from *Alias David Bowie* by Peter & Leni Gillman (Hodder & Stoughton pbk £4.95)

Bruce Springsteen, whose biographies *Born to Run* (Omnibus Press pbk £8.95) & *Glory Days* (Arrow pbk £6.95) are written by Dave Marsh

LITTLE RICHARD
WHITE, CHARLES
Little Richard
[O451] Pan pbk **£3.95**

MORRISON, JIM
HOPKINS, JERRY & SUGERMAN, DANNY
No One Here Gets Out Alive: The Biography of Jim Morrison
[O452] Plexus pbk **£6.95**

NEW ORDER
EDGE, BRIAN
New Order & Joy Division: Pleasures and Wayward Distractions
Updated edition of a good, illustrated biography.
[O453] Omnibus P pbk **£6.95**

POGUES
MCGOWAN, HEWITT & PIKE
Poguetry: The Illustrated Pogues Songbook   `NEW`
A record of the Pogues' 1988-9 tour of Europe and the USA, together with the lyrics of thirty of their songs, appropriately illustrated by John Hewitt.
[O454] Faber pbk **£8.99**

POP, IGGY
NILSEN, PER & SHERMAN, DOROTHY
The Wild One: The True Story of Iggy Pop
Described on its jacket as 'an essential Iggophile purchase', this is indeed full of facts, anecdotes and photos of the great man.
[O455] Omnibus P pbk **£6.95**

REES, CRAMPTON & LAZELL (EDS)
Guinness Book of Rock Stars
A reference book which chronologically documents the careers of all the major acts of the past thirty years.
[O456] Guinness pbk **£9.95**

SPRINGSTEEN, BRUCE
Born to Run was Marsh's first book which took the story up to 1978-9, and the preparations for *The River*. Its sequel, *Glory Days* covers Springsteen's career in the 80s, and is Marsh's eleventh book. Both are needed for a full survey, but *Born to Run* is

unquestionably the better book, especially in its assessment of Springsteen's lyrics.

MARSH, DAVE
Born to Run: The Bruce Springsteen Story
[O457] Omnibus P pbk **£8.95**
Glory Days
[O458] Arrow pbk **£6.99**

THE BEATLES
The Beatles Lyrics
[O459] Futura pbk **£3.50**
LEWISOHN, MARK
The Complete Beatles Recordings
The ultimate reference work on the group's recordings and albums.
[O460] Hamlyn hbk **£12.95**

THE SMITHS
MIDDLES, NICK
The Smiths
Updated after the band broke up in 1987, this attempts to analyse their appeal as well as providing a detailed history.
[O461] Omnibus P pbk **£6.95**

U2
DUNPHY, EAMON
Unforgettable Fire: The Story of U2
[O462] Penguin pbk **£3.99**

VELVET UNDERGROUND
BOCKRIS, VICTOR & MALANGA, G.
Uptight: The Velvet Underground Story
Easily the best book so far written on the band, it tells you all you need to know, and much you don't.
[O463] Omnibus P pbk **£6.95**

WILSON, MARY
My Life as a Supreme
A strangely touching autobiography that is really the story of how the author coped with Diana Ross's gradual domination of the group through her relationship with Berry Gordy.
[O464] Arrow pbk **£3.99**

ZAPPA, FRANK
The Real Frank Zappa Book   `NEW`
The autobiography of one of the few genuinely iconoclastic figures in contemporary music.
[O465] Picador hbk **£12.95**

BALLET

Biography

AUSTIN, RICHARD
Two distinguished biographies, of the legendary Russian ballerina Pavlova, and of one of the outstanding talents of our time, Makarova, who has distinguished herself in the fields of jazz and contemporary dance as well as in her classical performances.
Anna Pavlova
[O470] H Hamilton pbk **£4.95**
Natalia Makarova
[O471] Dance hbk **£6.95**

BUCKLE, RICHARD
Buckle has established himself as a leading dance writer with these three classic biographies of figures closely involved with Diaghilev's Ballets Russes; the collection of his own reviews offers a glimpse of some of the best, and worst, moments of British dance.
Buckle at the Ballet
[O472] Dance hbk **£8.95**
Diaghilev
[O473] H Hamilton pbk **£8.95**
George Balanchine: Ballet Master
[O474] H Hamilton hbk **£20.00**
Nijinsky
[O475] Penguin pbk **£4.99**

DUNCAN, ISADORA
My Life
[O476] Sphere pbk **£3.99**

FONTEYN, MARGOT
Autobiography   `NEW`
A revised edition of a classic autobiography, telling of Fonteyn's involvement with British ballet from the 1930s to the present day, with a new chapter which brings the story up to date.
[O477] H Hamilton pbk **£7.95**
Pavlova
A critical assessment of one of Ballet's legendary stars.
[O478] Weidenfeld pbk **£8.95**

KARSAVINA, TAMARA
Theatre Street
An autobiography, widely hailed as a masterpiece of dance writing, it is energetically written, anecdotal and amusing.
[O479] Dance hbk **£10.95**

Margot Fonteyn from her new revised *Autobiography* (Hamish Hamilton pbk £7.95)

KIRKLAND, GELSEY
Dancing on My Grave
The moving and powerful story of a famous American ballerina's nightmarish experiences in the world of dance.
[O480] Penguin pbk **£3.99**

MAKAROVA, NATALIA
Dance Autobiography
An elegantly produced volume from one of the most popular and versatile Russian ballerinas, which will interest all who value ballet.
[O481] A & C Black hbk **£9.95**

MEYER, ADOLF DE
L'Après-Midi d'Un Faune: Nijinsky 1912
A record of Nijinsky's first, notorious choreographic work. Includes many photographs of the legendary dancer and his cast.
[O482] Dance pbk **£9.95**

MILLE, AGNES DE
Dance to the Piper
Autobiography by one of the most innovative and influential choreographers, the daughter of Cecil B. de Mille.
[O483] Columbus pbk **£5.95**

PARKER, DEREK
Nijinsky: God of Dance
A recent biography, including interviews with surviving members of the Ballets Russes.
[O484] Equation hbk **£14.95**

STODELLE, ERNESTINE
Dance Story of Martha Graham: Deep Song
Along with Agnes de Mille, Martha Graham is one of the influential and innovative of 20th century American choreographers.
[O485] Macmillan hbk **£21.00**

WALKER, KATHERINE SORLEY
Ninette de Valois
British ballerina who toured with Diaghilev's Ballets Russes and later founded the Sadler's Wells Ballet School in 1931.
[O486] H Hamilton hbk **£20.00**

Theory & History

World Ballet & Dance 1989 - 1990   `NEW`
The first edition of a new dance year-book, providing detailed coverage of all major British classical and contemporary dance companies, and worldwide coverage of dance abroad.
[O487] Dance pbk **£10.95**

ADSHEAD, JANET (ED)
Dance Analysis: Theory and Practice
[O488] Dance pbk **£10.00**

ARNHEIM, DANIEL D.
Dance Injuries: Their Prevention and Care
An invaluable book for dancers, this is an expertly written text on the ailments which afflict them.
[O489] Dance pbk **£10.00**

AU, SUSAN
Ballet & Modern Dance
An excellent volume on ballet in its many forms: in the Thames & Hudson *World of Art* series.
[O490] Thames & H pbk **£5.95**

BAZAROVA & MEY
Alphabet of Classical Dance
Ballet theory drawn from classes taught by two great
Russian ballerinas.
[O491] Dance pbk **£7.95**

BROWN, JEAN MORRISON (ED)
The Vision of Modern Dance
A fascinating selection of writings by 21 of today's
finest American dancers.
[O492] Dance pbk **£6.00**

BROWN, ANN KIPLING & PARKER, MONICA
Dance Notation for Beginners
The Labomotation and the Beresh movement notation
are explained simply and succinctly.
[O493] Dance pbk **£6.95**

CLARKE, MARY & CRISP, CLEMENT
Ballerina
A survey of ballerinas past and present.
[O494] BBC hbk **£14.95**
London Contemporary Dance **NEW**
An illustrated study of the largest modern
dance company in Britain, and its development in its
permanent home, The Place.
[O495] Dance hbk **£15.95**

CRICKMAY, ANTHONY
A Portrait of the Royal Ballet
[O514] M O'Mara hbk **£12.95**

CUNNINGHAM, MERCE
The Dancer and the Dance
One of the most innovative contemporary American
choreographers here discusses his poetic of dance.
[O496] Boyars hbk **£18.00**

DUFORT, ANTHONY
Ballet Steps **NEW**
[O497] Heinemann hbk **£10.95**

EWING, WILLIAM A.
**The Fugitive Gesture: Masterpieces of
Dance Photography**
A book of magnificent photographs showing ballet
dancers in performance.
[O498] Thames & H hbk **£25.00**

FRASER, DONALD HAMILTON
Dancers **NEW**
An evocative collection of paintings and drawings of
dancers, on and off stage.
[O499] Phaidon hbk **£14.95**

FRASER, JOHN
Private View
[O499A] H Hamilton hbk **£20.00**

GRIGOROVITCH, YURI & VANSLOV, V.
The Bolshoi Ballet
A survey of the highly disciplined Moscow ballet
company, famed for the athleticism of its productions.
[O500] Paganiniana hbk **£25.00**

GUEST, IVOR
The Romantic Ballet in Paris
[O501] Dance hbk **£9.95**

HUMPHREY, DORIS
The Art of Making Dances
An excellent introduction to the art of choreography,
from an important figure in contemporary American
dance.
[O502] Dance pbk **£6.95**

Sir Kenneth Macmillan from, *A Portrait of The
Royal Ballet*. Photographs by Anthony Crickmay
(Michael O'Mara Books hbk £12.95)

KOEGLER, HORST
Concise Oxford Dictionary of Ballet
An authoritative and well-written book with over
5,000 entries on all aspects of ballet.
[O503] Oxford pbk **£7.95**

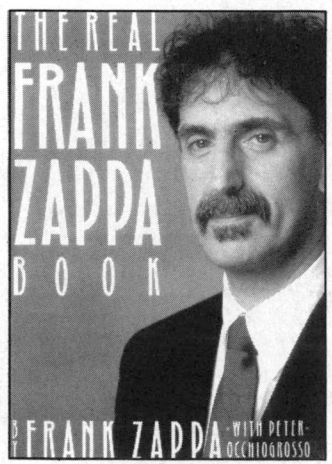

MUSIC

Susan Jaffe from *Private View* by John Fraser, photographs by Eve Arnold (H Hamilton hbk £20.00)

LAWSON, JOAN
The Principles of Classical Dance
[O504] A & C Black hbk **£10.95**

MAGRI, GENNARO
Theoretical and Practical Treatise on Dancing
A crucial, pre-Romantic treatise on dance, regarded in its day as the pre-eminent work on the subject.
[O505] Dance hbk **£20.00**

ORLOFF, ALEXANDER
The Russian Ballet on Tour **NEW**
A photographic insight into the lives and work of one of the great Russian companies.
[O506] Barrie & J hbk **£25.00**

ROBERTSON & HUTERA
The Dance Handbook
An excellent guide through 200 entries on influential works, dancers, choreographers and companies.
[O507] Longman pbk **£10.95**

SEARLE, HUMPHREY
Ballet Music: An Introduction
British composer Humphrey Searle (himself author of many a ballet score) writes a thorough survey and introduction to ballet music.
[O508] Dover pbk **£4.75**

SHOOK, KAREL
Elements of Classical Ballet Technique
Recommended reading for all ballet teachers.
[O509] Dance pbk **£2.95**

SIEGEL, MARCIA B.
Days on Earth: The Dance of Doris Humphreys
A study of one of the key figures of modern American dance, which provides a full account of her work.
[O510] Yale UP hbk **£27.00**

VAUGHAN, DAVID
Frederick Ashton and His Ballets
A valuable study of the choreographic work of one of the leading British dancers and choreographers of the century.
[O511] A & C Black hbk **£16.00**

WALKER, KATHERINE SORLEY & WOODCOCK, SARAH C.
The Royal Ballet: A Picture History
A magnificent collection of black and white photographs which capture the best moments in the history of the Royal Ballet.
[O512] Threshold pbk **£9.95**

WHITE, JOHN (ED)
20th Century Dance in Britain
A history of five companies - London Contemporary Dance Theatre, the Royal Ballet, Ballet Rambert, the London Festival and the Scottish Ballet.
[O513] Dance pbk **£6.95**

Natural History:
General & Reference
Field Guides
By Region
By Subject

Science:
General
By Subject

NATURAL HISTORY & SCIENCE

Natural history covers a very broad range of books from detailed texts on individual flora and fauna to lavishly illustrated picture books. As far as possible, we have tried to select the best and the newest titles for the general reader, though we have also included some practical books of specialist interest and some introductory texts which could lead to more detailed study. Science books are selected for their suitability for the general reader. Thus specialist science books, and academic texts, are not to be found in the following listing.

Natural History: General & Reference

Atlas of the Living World
A compelling survey of the ever-changing patterns of life on earth and the possible patterns of the future.
[P1] Weidenfeld hbk **£19.95**

COMPLETE UNWIN ANIMAL LIBRARY
A superb, attractively presented encyclopaedia set. The standard reference work on animals.
BANISTER, DR K. & CAMPBELL, DR A.
Encyclopaedia of Reptiles & Amphibia
[P3] Unwin Hyman hbk **£17.50**
Encyclopaedia of Insects
[P4] Unwin Hyman hbk **£17.50**
Encyclopaedia of Birds
[P5] Unwin Hyman hbk **£30.00**
Encyclopaedia of Mammals
Vol 1
[P6] Unwin Hyman hbk **£30.00**
Vol 2
[P7] Unwin Hyman hbk **£30.00**

Encyclopaedia of World Wildlife
Includes a foreword by David Attenborough.
[P8] Octopus hbk **£10.95**

ALLABY, M. (ED)
Oxford Dictionary of Natural History
Foreword by David Attenborough. This dictionary makes the increasingly specialised vocabulary of Natural History accessible to all.
[P9] Oxford hbk **£20.00**

ATTENBOROUGH, SIR DAVID
As a popular TV presenter, David Attenborough has done more than any other natural historian to bring the world of nature into the home. In *Life on Earth* and *The Living Planet* he led the viewer on a comprehensive tour, from the Tundra to the Coral Reef, from amoeba to the orang-utan and these diverse wonders are recaptured in his books. The superb photography is best presented in the Reader's Digest augmented editions, but Attenborough's text is accessible in any form. His most recent work - *The First Eden* - (again written for television) arose from his concern over man's contempt for the animals he once worshipped.
Discovering Life on Earth
[P10] Collins hbk **£6.95**
[P11] Collins pbk **£4.95**

Life on Earth
Based on the TV series, this book provides a history of nature through 3,500 million years.
[P12] Collins hbk **£12.95**
[P13] Fontana pbk **£6.95**
The Living Planet
[P15] Collins hbk **£12.95**
[P16] Fontana pbk **£9.95**
The Living Planet : Reader's Digest Augmented and Enlarged Edition
[P17] Collins hbk **£14.95**
The First Eden: The Mediterranean World and Man
A very popular, beautifully illustrated book. Examines the relationship between man and the natural habitat of the Mediterranean, an area first inhabited by human beings some two million years ago.
[P18] Collins hbk **£12.95**
[P19] Fontana pbk **£5.99**

BELLAMY, DAVID & QUALYLE, BRENDAN
Turning the Tide: Exploring the Options for Life on Earth
The book of the TV series, it assesses the environmental state of the world today and suggests a 'greenprint for the future'.
[P20] Collins hbk **£14.95**

BIRKHEAD, MIKE & TIM
The Survival Factor   **NEW**
The book to accompany a recent Anglia TV programme. Discusses the role of natural selection in the animal kingdom. Examines in depth adaptive strategies which some species have adopted in order to survive, such as the spadefoot toad's ability to absorb water through its permeable skin, and the cuckoo's breeding habits. Includes colour photos and line drawings.
[P21] Boxtree hbk **£14.95**

BRIGHT, MICHAEL
There are Giants in the Sea   **NEW**
Examines the evidence for the existence of unusual and mysterious sea monsters.
[P22] Robson hbk **£10.95**

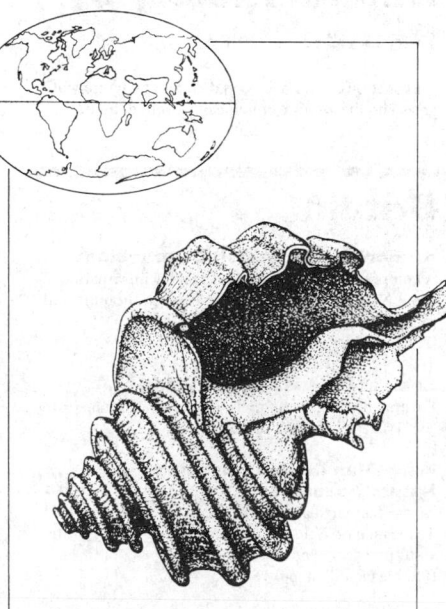

Illustration from *Life Pulse* by Niles Eldredge (Penguin pbk £4.99)

CHRISTIE, DAVID
Remarkable Animals: A Unique Encyclopaedia of Wildlife Wonders
A collection of the world's weirdest and most wonderful creatures, their habitats, breeding patterns and vital statistics.
[P27] Guinness hbk **£12.95**

COUSTEAU, JACQUES
The Silent World
The pioneering marine explorer describes the rich and exciting progress in underwater discoveries.
[P28] H Hamilton hbk **£11.95**

DALTON, STEPHEN
Secret Lives
A personal selection of over 100 photos from 25 years of the work of one of the world's greatest world wildlife photographers. Pictures of birds, mammals, insects, and plants are accompanied by commentaries, both from an aesthetic and a scientific angle.
[P29] Century hbk **£14.95**

DOWNER, JOHN
Supersense: Perception in the Animal World
Accompanying the major BBC TV series of 1988, this book documents the spectacularly innovative project which aimed to determine how animals and plants perceive and interpret the world around them.
[P30] BBC **£12.95**

HRH THE DUKE OF EDINBURGH
Down to Earth
A collection of writings, drawn from speeches, made as President of the World Wildlife Fund, on the exploitation of the natural environment by man.
[P31] Fontana pbk **£4.50**

GAMLIN, LINDA & VINES, GAIL (EDS)
The Evolution of Life
The ideal reference book for anyone interested in the living world. Full of colour illustrations on every page and many helpful detailed diagrams.
[P32] Collins hbk **£14.95**

JENKINS, SID
Animals Have More Sense
The chief Inspector in the RSPCA reveals the extent of human cruelty to animals, a subject which was brought to light in the successful BBC TV series 'Animal Squad'.
[P34] Fontana pbk **£2.95**

LINCOLN, R.J. & BOXSHALL, G.A.
Cambridge Illustrated Dictionary of Natural History
A concise dictionary of organisms and their ecology designed for reference and for use in the field, with over 700 illustrations.
[P36] Cambridge hbk **£17.50**

MABEY, R.; CLIFFORD, S. & KING, A.
Second Nature   **NEW**
Examines the inter-relationship between man and the natural world.
[P37] Cape hbk **£7.95**

MALLINSON, JEREMY
Travels in Search of Threatened Species   **NEW**
A world-wide search reveals the vast numbers of threatened and endangered species.
[P38] David & Ch hbk **£10.95**

MATTHEWS, RUPERT
The Atlas of Natural Wonders
A guide to the world's most spectacular phenomena.
[P39] Ebury P hbk **£16.95**

MUIR, RICHARD
The Countryside Encyclopaedia
An authoritative reference book.
[P40] Macmillan hbk **£14.95**

PACKHAM, CHRIS
Wild Habitats `NEW`
Photographer and TV personality presents a
completely fresh view of the habitats of Europe.
Combines evocative descriptive text with basic
biology and ecology, and contains a field guide
section with descriptions of all the major species an
explorer is likely to find.
Grasslands & Scrub
[P41] Collins pbk **£4.95**
Heathlands
[P42] Collins pbk **£4.95**
Rocky Shorelands
[P43] Collins pbk **£4.95**
Deciduous Woodlands
[P44] Collins pbk **£4.95**

SOPER, TONY
Discovering Animals
[P47] BBC pbk **£4.95**

TUDGE, COLIN (ED)
Encyclopaedia of the Environment
An excellent illustrated survey of the animal
kingdom, world ecology and ecosystems.
[P49] C Helm hbk **£19.95**

Field Guides

The number of Field Guides available on the
market is increasing all the time in a wide range of
quality, detail and price. Here is a brief survey of
the major series, which should enable you to
choose the ones most suitable to your needs. Most
cover the main areas of birds, wild animals and
plants.

COLLINS FIELD GUIDES
Classic guides, still unchallenged in their coverage of
such a wide range of topics. Despite their rather old
fashioned design, with colour plates and illustrations
packed onto the page, two decades of use have
created a degree of familiarity with their format. For
the serious naturalist.

COLLINS GEMS
Pocket-sized, cheap and ideal for the young, these
cover a wide range of topics from farm animals to
wild beasts. Expert but simple treatment of the most
familiar species.

**COLLINS NEW GENERATION FIELD
GUIDES**
A new series, with David Attenborough as its general
editor, which offers more than the traditional field
guide. Clearly set out, well illustrated and with the
relevant descriptive text, they contain additional
background information on modern classification and
an account of every stage in the life of their subject
(at the moment the series only covers birds, wild
flowers and mushrooms). Excellent individual guides
which, as a series, offer a sound general introduction
to the natural world.

COLLINS PHOTOGUIDES
Another recent Collins series. Though designed for
the beginner, they still cover a surprising range of
species. Their high quality colour photographs make
identification easy and their subject is not over
simplified or pulled out of context. Protected by a
flexi-cover they are durable and practical.

HAMISH HAMILTON PHOTOGUIDES
Another high quality series illustrated with full colour
photographs. A compact format with separate titles
devoted to different areas of plant identification.

KINGFISHER FIELD GUIDES
A very attractive series clearly illustrated and well set
out. The illustrations are of particularly high quality
and space has been given for additional points of
interest. The wild flower section of the Plant Life
Guide includes (along with the descriptive text) a
brief summary of each plant's traditional uses, both
medicinal and cosmetic. A strong, comprehensive
series.

MACMILLAN FIELD GUIDES `NEW`
A brand new series of field guides designed to
provide more accurate and descriptive identification
of the natural world. Includes books on Bird
Identification, British Wild flowers, Geological
Structures and North Atlantic Shorebirds.

LONGMAN GUIDES
Practical pocket sized guides whose low price reflects
the fact that they are aimed at the younger nature
enthusiast.

MITCHELL BEAZLEY POCKET GUIDES
Despite their size these guides are comprehensive and
packed with information. Well produced and with
high quality illustrations they are the best of the
pocket-sized series.

OCTOPUS COLOUR GUIDES
A cheaper alternative to other field guides. They do
cut corners, largely through the illustrations, but are
good value.

OBSERVER'S GUIDES
Like the *Collins Gems* these are aimed at the younger
market. Not all of the series is available but most of
the natural history titles are.

Natural History by Region

This section covers books on different geographical
areas and the wildlife which can be found there.

Britain

AA Book of the British Countryside
A comprehensive A-Z guide. Includes information
about National Parks as well as fishing, shooting and
footpath laws.
[P50] Hodder hbk **£16.95**

Book of the Irish Countryside
Illustrated with photographs, drawings and maps.
[P51] Blackstaff hbk **£14.95**

**Macmillan Guide to Britain's
Nature Reserves** `NEW`
Revised and updated, it includes a foreword by HRH
The Prince of Wales. A comprehensive survey of the
wildlife reserves of Britain.
[P52] Macmillan pbk **£19.95**

Reader's Digest Animals of Britain
Descriptions of over 150 species of mammals,
reptiles, amphibians and farm animals.
[P60] Hodder hbk **£8.95**

ARLOTT; FITTER & FITTER
Complete Guide to British Wildlife
[P61] Collins pbk **£5.95**

ASHBY, ERIC `NEW`
The Secret Life of The New Forest
This book reveals the secrets of one of Britain's oldest
and most beautiful forests. Photographer Eric Ashby
observes, with infinite patience, giant oaks, deer and
ponies, fox cubs and badgers, rare orchids and
butterflies.
[P62] Chatto hbk **£14.95**

BAINES, CHRIS
The Wild Side of Town
Based on the BBC television programme which
explored the unexpected wealth of wildlife in our
towns, cities and urban wasteland areas.
[P64] BBC pbk **£6.95**

BELLAMY, DAVID
Bellamy's Ireland: The Wild Boglands
[P67] Ch Helm pbk **£9.95**

BURTON, JOHN
**The National Trust Book of British Wild
Animals**
The history, life-styles and habitats of animals, birds
and fish species, described in depth and accompanied
by beautiful illustrations.
[P73] Deutsch pbk **£8.95**

CHINERY, MICHAEL
**Field Guide to the Wildlife of Britain
and Europe**
Good quality, well illustrated and informative -
recommended.
[P75] Kingfisher pbk **£6.95**
**The Natural History of Britain and
Europe**
[P76] Kingfisher hbk **£14.95**

COOPER, ANDREW
The Secret Nature of Britain `NEW`
An absorbing book which documents hours of patient
observation. His camera here records rare lizards, the
hatching of bird's eggs, and pheasants relased into the
wild during the shooting season.
[P78] BBC hbk **£12.95**

DUNN, MICHAEL
The Lake District
A guide to its geology, plant and animal life and
history.
[P80] David & Ch hbk **£12.95**

FITTER, R. & MANUAL, R..
**Field Guide to Freshwater Life in
Britain and North-West Europe**
[P81] Collins pbk **£7.95**

FITTER, RICHARD
London's Natural History
[P82] Collins hbk **£6.50**

FRANKS, ELAINE
The Undercliffe `NEW`
A sketchbook of the Axmouth-Lyme Regis Nature
Reserve. It reflects how the many different types of
wildlife interact in the unique environment of this
stretch of coastline.
[P83] Weidenfeld hbk **£14.95**

GOODERS, JOHN
The Outdoor Guide to Britain
Provides detailed information on over 150 different
national parks, nature reserves, zoos and safari
parks.
[P86] Webb & B hbk **£16.95**

HOSKINS, W.G.
The Making of the English Landscape
Classic book tracing the development of the appearance of the countryside as a result of the different uses that man has made of it. Newly revised and updated, the hardback edition points out some more recent advances in our knowledge of the past.
[P87] Hodder hbk **£17.95**
[P88] Penguin pbk **£5.95**

INGRAMS, RICHARD
The Ridgeway: Europe's Oldest Road
A well written, illustrated account of the ancient Ridgeway which runs for 40 miles along the escarpment of the Berkshire and Wiltshire Downs.
[P89] Phaidon hbk **£14.95**

MERCER, DERRICK & PUTTNAM, DAVID
Rural England: Our Countryside at the Crossroads
A celebration of the English countryside and a plea for its conservation from the Council for the Protection of Rural England.
[P93] Macdonald hbk **£14.95**

MILLS, STEPHEN
Nature in its Place: The Habitats of Ireland
From Dublin and Cape Clear to the Mountains of Mourne and the Wetlands, this illuminating book traces how species of birds, animals and plants have made their habitat in Ireland.
[P95] Bodley pbk **£8.95**

MUIR, RICHARD
The Countryside Encyclopaedia
An illustrated and authoritative companion to our countryside heritage.
[P96] Macmillan hbk **£14.95**
The Shell Guide to Reading the Landscape
A fascinating guide to understanding the many ways in which different facets of the English landscape have been created.
[P97] M Joseph hbk **£13.95**

PURSEGLOVE, JEREMY
Taming the Flood: A History and Natural History of Rivers and Wetlands NEW
A definitive study of the ecology of British wetlands, based on the recent Channel 4 series.
[P100] Oxford hbk **£16.95**

RACKHAM, OLIVER
History of the Countryside: The Full Fascinating Story of Britain's Landscape
[P101] Dent pbk **£8.95**
The Last Forest: The Story of Hatfield Forest NEW
A detailed examination of the complex interaction between man and nature in the last medieval forest in England.
[P102] Dent hbk **£15.95**

SOOTHILL, ERIC & THOMAS, MICHAEL J
Natural History of Britain's Coasts
A reference book and field guide for explorers of the British coastline, whether as birdwatchers, ramblers, photographers or holiday visitors.
[P105] Blandford pbk **£8.95**

SMYTH, BOB
Green Guide to Urban Wildlife NEW
Each entry describes urban wildlife sites and their locations, history, nature interest and management, who to contact and where to seek further information.
[P106] A & C Black hbk **£9.95**

TUBBS, COLIN
The New Forest
[P109] Collins pbk **£9.95**

World

LEOPOLD, ALDO
Sand County Almanac
A classic work from one of America's foremost conservationists, the almanac traces a year in the life of the Wisconsin countryside and includes pieces written over a forty year period on the philosophical issues involved in wildlife conservation.
[P112] Oxford hbk **£12.95**

AMMANN, KARL & KATHERINE
The Hunters and the Hunted NEW
A vivid, beatifully photographed record of East African wildlife and the constant cycle of life and death.
[P113] Bodley hbk **£22.50**

ANDREWS, MICHAEL
The Flight of the Condor
Based on the spectacularly photographed television series, following the path of the condor's flight through many different kinds of landscape in South America.
[P114] Collins pbk **£8.95**

BROWNLIE, BETTY & LOCKLRY, RONALD
The Secrets of Natural New Zealand
A guide to the rich variety of New Zealand's flora and fauna, well illustrated with pencil drawings and watercolour paintings.
[P116] Viking hbk **£30.00**

CHERNOV, YU I.
The Living Tundra
A wide-ranging account of wildlife in the Tundra offering an insight into the ways in which animals, plants and climate interact in an inhospitable environment.
[P118] Cambridge pbk **£12.95**

CHINERY, MICHAEL
Field Guide to the Wildlife of Britain and Europe
An attractive reference work, detailing over 1,500 species and including advice on identification.
[P119] Kingfisher pbk **£6.95**

COUSTEAU, JAQUES
Amazon Journey
Superb illustrations of this trip down the Amazon by the French deep sea diver.
[P120] Abrams hbk **£30.00**

GOODALL, JANE
Chimpanzees of the Gombe: Patterns of Behaviour
The most recent and comprehensive account of Jane Goodall's years in the Gombe. She has been criticised for crossing the barrier of mere observation and becoming too closely involved in the chimps' lives, but this work remains an authoritative and detailed account of their behaviour.
[P121] Harvard UP hbk **£21.95**

GREENPEACE
The Greenpeace Book of Antarctica
Archive photographs trace the history of the continent and its threatened wildlife.
[P122] Dorling Kindersley hbk **£14.95**
Insight Guide to Indian Wildlife
[P123] Harrap pbk **£9.95**

KANE, JOE
Running the Amazon NEW
Exciting account of the first men to travel the whole length of the Amazon.
[P124] Bodley hbk **£15.00**

KINGDON, JONATHAN
Island Africa NEW
Reveals how varieties of African plants and animals have been shaped throughout time. Illustrated by the author's own drawings.
[P125] Collins hbk **£25.00**

KNYSTAUTAS, ALGIRDAS
The Natural History of the USSR
[P126] Century hbk **£14.95**

LAWICK, HUGO VON
Two stunning books from one of the great wildlife photographers.
Among Predators and Prey
[P127] H Hamilton hbk **£25.00**
Savage Paradise
[P128] Collins hbk **£30.00**

LAWS, RICHARD
Antarctica: The Last Frontier NEW
A beautifully illustrated portrait, based on the acclaimed Anglia TV series.
[P129] Boxtree hbk **£14.95**

LOPEZ, BARRY
Arctic Dreams: Imagination and Desire in a Northern Landscape
[P130] Picador pbk **£4.95**

MATTHIESSEN, PETER
The Tree Where Man Was Born: African Experience
[P132] Picador pbk **£4.95**

MITCHEL, ANDREW
The Enchanted Canopy: Secrets from the Rainforest Roof
A thousand feet from the floor of the South American rainforest lies another world. By constructing a gantry in the tree tops, Mitchel and his colleagues have been able to make some remarkable studies.
[P133] Fontana pbk **£9.95**

MJOBEREG, ERIC
Forest Life and Adventures in the Malay Archipelago
A compendium of the flora and fauna of the islands of Borneo and Sumatra, including the largest flower of the world - Rafflesia tuan mudae.
[P134] Oxford pbk **£4.95**

MOYAL, ANN
A Bright and Savage Land: Scientists in Colonial Australia
The isolation of this continent has produced a unique natural history. This is a historical record of observations by explorers and natural historians, among them Cook and Darwin, superbly illustrated with early photographs and sketches.
[P135] Collins hbk **£17.50**

NATIONAL GEOGRAPHIC SOCIETY
As with all their magazines, these books contain breathtaking photographs.
The Natural History of America
[P136] Nat Geographic hbk **£17.50**
Wild Animals of North America
[P137] Nat Geographic hbk **£19.50**

PRATER, S.H. NEW
The Book of Indian Animals (3rd Edition)
[P138] Oxford hbk **£7.95**

ROSS, KAREN
Okavango: The Jewel of the Kalahari
Okavango is a little known wilderness area in Botswana where the Okavango river meets and disappears into the Kalahari. This fascinating book, based on the BBC series, describes its history, its unique environment and the challenges it faces in the future.
[P139] BBC hbk **£12.95**

SMITH, JO STEWART
In the Shadow of Fujisan
From a BBC television series, this is an exploration of Japanese wildlife and its vivid representation in their cultural life. Sadly their attitude towards conservation is still very ambivalent.
[P140] Viking hbk **£14.95**

By Subject

Fish & Molluscs

Observer's Book of Pond Life
Good quality handbook for the younger reader.
[P143] Penguin pbk **£3.95**

ADE, ROBIN
The Trout and Salmon Handbook   **NEW**
The definitive guide to salmon, trout and char throughout the world, with ample information on their lifecycles and their sporting characteristics.
[P144] C Helm hbk **£12.95**

BANISTER, DR. K. & CAMPBELL, DR. A.
Encyclopaedia of Underwater Life
[P145] Unwin Hyman hbk **£25.00**

BARRETT & YONGE
Collins Pocket Guide to the Sea Shore
[P146] Collins hbk **£7.95**

CHATFIELD, JUNE
Field Guide to the Snails of Britain and Europe
Photographic guide to terrestrial and freshwater snails with an additional section on slugs.
[P147] Hamlyn hbk **£8.95**

COUSTEAU, JACQUES
The Silent World
Reissue of Cousteau's account of his pioneering deep-sea diving explorations.
[P148] Elm Tree hbk **£11.95**

FITTER, R. & MANUEL, R.
Field Guide to Freshwater Life in Britain and North-West Europe
[P150] Collins hbk **£12.95**

MARSHALL, N.B.
Life of Fishes
[P151] Weidenfeld hbk **£12.50**

MUUS & DAHLSTROM
Field Guide to the Sea Fishes of Britain and North-West Europe
[P152] Collins pbk **£7.95**

PHILLIPS, ROGER
Freshwater Fish of Britain, Ireland & Europe
[P153] Pan pbk **£7.95**

PHILLIPS, ROGER & RIX, MARTYN
Sea Shells and Sea Weeds
[P155] H Hamilton pbk **£4.95**

PIRNICKA & CERNY
Illustrated Book of Fish
[P156] Octopus hbk **£7.95**

READER'S DIGEST
Part of their excellent 'Living Countryside' series.
Secrets of the Seashore
[P158] Hodder hbk **£9.95**
The World of Still Water
[P159] Hodder hbk **£9.95**

THOMPSON; BERNARD & COLDREY
The Pond
[P161] Collins hbk **£9.95**

WALLS, JERRY G.
Shell Collecting
[P162] TFH hbk **£3.95**
Conches, Tibias and Harps
[P163] TFH hbk **£19.95**

WHEELER, A.
World Encyclopaedia of Fish
[P166] Macdonald hbk **£19.95**

WYE, KENNETH   **NEW**
Pocket Guide to Shells of the World
Includes colour photographs of more than 8000 shells, captioned with both Latin and common names, as well as size and description, global location and natural habitat.
[P168] M Beazley hbk **£5.95**

Insects & Spiders

Observer's Book of Insects
[P170] Penguin pbk **£3.95**

AGUILLAR; DOMMANGET & PRECHAC
Field Guide to the Dragonflies and Damselflies of Britain, Europe and North Africa
[P171] Collins hbk **£14.95**

BELLMAN, HEIKO
Field Guide to the Grasshoppers and Crickets of Britain and Northern Europe
The only identification guide currently available to Northern Europe's seventy-eight species of grasshopper and cricket, with clear illustrations and a key to grasshopper songs.
[P172] Collins hbk **£10.95**

CARTER, DAVID
Butterflies and Moths in Britain and Europe
[P175] Pan pbk **£7.95**

CARTER, DAVID & HARGREAVES, BRIAN
Field Guide to the Caterpillars of Britain and Europe
[P176] Collins hbk **£9.95**

CHINERY, MICHAEL
Field Guide to Insects of Britain and Europe
[P177] Collins hbk **£6.95**

EVANS, JEREMY
The Complete Guide to Beekeeping
The foremost practical guide to the first three years of beekeeping. It tells you what you need to buy when starting, how to deal with the honey flows and

harvests in the second years, and how to deal with swarms in the third year.
[P543] Unwin Hyman hbk **£15.95**

HARDE & SEVERA
Field Guide in Colour to Beetles
[P179] Octopus hbk **£3.95**

HIGGINS, L.G. & RILEY, N.D.
Field Guide to the Butterflies of Britain and Europe
[P181] Collins hbk **£8.95**

MACE, HERBERT
Complete Handbook of Beekeeping
[P548] Ward Lock pbk **£6.95**

MAFHAM & MAFHAM
Spiders of the World
[P182] Blandford hbk **£14.95**

MORSE, HOOPER
Illustrated Encyclopaedia of Beekeeping
[P549] Blandford hbk **£19.95**

READER'S DIGEST
Butterflies and Other Insects of Britain
[P186] Hodder hbk **£8.95**
Field Guide to Butterflies of Britain
[P187] Hodder hbk **£8.95**

TRIBERTI; DACCORDI & ZANNETTI
Macdonald Encyclopaedia of Butterflies and Moths
A beautifully illustrated guide detailing over 300 species from the equator to the polar regions.
[P190] Macdonald hbk **£9.95**

WHALLEY, PAUL
Pocket Guide to Butterflies
Good quality practical handbooks.
[P191] M Beazley pbk **£3.95**

Mammals

Encyclopaedia of Mammals
A superb and attractively illustrated encyclopaedia.
Vol 1
[P192] Unwin Hyman hbk **£30.00**
Vol 2
[P193] Unwin Hyman hbk **£30.00**

CORBET, GORDON & OVENDEN, DENYS
Mammals of Britain and Europe
[P194] Collins hbk **£6.95**

HALTENORTH, T. & DILLER, H.
Field Guide to the Mammals of Africa including Madagascar
[P196] Collins hbk **£8.95**

MATTHEWS, L. HARRISON
Mammals in the British Isles
[P197] Collins hbk **£10.95**

INDIVIDUAL SPECIES

BRUEMMER, FRED
Seasons of the Seal   **NEW**
A celebration of the harp seal and a tribute to all those who have fought to save it from extinction.
[P201] Bloomsbury hbk **£16.95**

COUSTEAU, JACQUES
Whales
A tribute to the intelligence and grace of the largest of

the mammals by the legendary marine biologist. Cousteau himself describes this book as the 'product of anger and love'.
[P203] WH Allen hbk **£25.00**

DOAK, WADE **[NEW]**
Encounters with Whales & Dolphins
A valuable introduction to the understanding and preservation of these uniquely intelligent mammals.
[P204] Hodder hbk **£16.95**

DOBBS, HORACE
Tale of Two Dolphins **[NEW]**
An exciting account of Dobbs' attempts to define the powerful anti-depressant effects that dolphins have on human beings.
[P205] Cape pbk **£5.95**

DOMICO, TERRY
Bears of the World **[NEW]**
A definitive study which describes each species.
[P206] Facts on File hbk **£15.95**

FERRIS, CHRIS
Out of the Darkness
One of Britain's leading badger experts, Chris Ferris has been studying badgers in her local woods for over 20 years. Here she describes their lives and their persecution by poachers.
[P209] Unwin Hyman pbk **£4.95**

HAYES, HOWARD **[NEW]**
The Dark Romance of Dian Fossey
The extraordinary story of the American naturalist whose reclusive existence spent in detailed study of the mountain gorilla ended with her being brutally murdered in 1985. The subject of a recent feature film.
[P211] Chatto hbk **£12.95**

HEYMANN, DANIELLE
The Bear **[NEW]**
How does the world appear to an orphaned bearcub? This is the book of Jean-Jacques Annaud's extraordinary new film based on the struggles to survive and developing friendship of two bears.
[P212] Sidgwick hbk **£8.95**

MOSS, CYNTHIA **[NEW]**
Elephant Memories: Thirteen Years in the Life of an Elephant Family
Born Free-style fictionalised account of an elephant family, based on the factual knowledge Moss has culled from years of detailed research.
[P217] Fontana pbk **£4.99**

MOWATT, FARLEY
Woman in the Mists **[NEW]**
The authorized biography of naturalist Dian Fossey (see Hayes, Howard above).
[P218] Macdonald hbk **£12.95**

PENNY, MALCOLM
Rhinos: An Endangered Species
A moving account of the plight of one of the world's most threatened animals.
[P220] C Helm hbk **£14.95**

SAVAGE, CANDACE
Wolves **[NEW]**
A beautifully illustrated portrait of this highly intelligent, much-misunderstood animal.
[P221] Hale hbk **£15.95**

SCHWARTZ, JEFFREY
Red Ape: Orang-Utans & Human Origins
Interesting argument that our closest relative is not the chimpanzee, but the largely ignored orang-utan.
[P222] Elm Tree hbk **£14.95**

SCOTT, JONATHAN
The Leopard's Tale
[P223] H Hamilton hbk **£16.95**

STOCKER, LES
The Complete Hedgehog
Everything you need to know from the expert on hedgehogs.
[P225] Chatto pbk **£6.95**

STRUM, SHIRLEY
Almost Human: A Journey into the World of Baboons
The result of 14 years study, this book reveals some fascinating insights into their behaviour.
[P226] Elm Tree hbk **£14.95**

THAPAR, VALMIK
Tiger: Portrait of a Predator
[P227] Collins hbk **£15.00**

WAYRE, PHILIP
Operation Otter **[NEW]**
A moving account of a couples' attempts to re-stock the rivers of England with otters, which also provides a great deal of incidental information about the animals themselves.
[P228] Chatto pbk **£7.95**

WILLIAMS, HEATHCOTE
Whale Nation
A celebration of the world's largest mammal in poetry, prose and pictures.
[P229] Cape pbk **£8.95**
Sacred Elephant **[NEW]**
A moving and eloquent tribute to the wisdom and suffering of the beast John Donne called 'Nature's Great Masterpiece'.
[P230] Cape pbk **£9.95**

Reptiles & Amphibians

ARNOLD, BURTON & OVENDEN
Field Guide to the Reptiles and Amphibians of Britain and Europe
[P231] Collins hbk **£7.95**

HALLIDAY & ALDER
Encyclopaedia of Reptiles and Amphibians
[P233] Unwin Hyman hbk **£15.00**

ROSS, CHARLES A.
Crocodiles and Alligators **[NEW]**
Combines up-to-date scientific information with a survey of the place of these fearsome creatures in literature, art and folklore.
[P234] Merehurst hbk **£19.95**

STEEL, RODNEY
Crocodiles **[NEW]**
An attempt to rehabilitate the reputation of the crocodile by a naturalist who has spent years in detailed study of their behaviour. A comprehensive portrait of the nearest surviving relatives of the dinosaurs.
[P235] C Helm hbk **£14.95**

Birds

There is an immense range of books on birds, reflecting the abiding popularity of birdwatching as well as the grace and beauty of birds themselves. For specific species it is hard to better the publications of T. & A.D. Poyser, while the range of field guides published by Collins are the staple fare for the birdwatcher, beaten only by the New Generation Guides, also published by Collins, and edited by David Attenborough.

REFERENCE & GENERAL

Bird Identification **[NEW]**
Solves the problem by using the technique of comparing 'confusion species'.
[P236] Macmillan hbk **£14.95**

CAMPBELL, BRUCE & LACK, ELIZABETH
Dictionary of Birds
Standard work for the enthusiast covering modern ornithology and related subjects.
[P238] Poyser hbk **£45.00**

DIAMOND; SCHREBER; ATTENBOROUGH & PRESTT
Save the Birds
A magnificent volume, which not only introduces us to the rarer species, but also explains why all birds are being threatened and what we can do to help.
[P239] Cambridge hbk **£22.50**

SOPER, TONY
Discovering Birds
[P241] BBC pbk **£3.95**
A Passion for Birds
Published to commemorate the centenary of the RSPB, this book is a bird-lover's delight featuring the contributions of many well-known ornithologists.
[P242] David & Ch hbk **£10.95**

BRITISH & EUROPEAN BIRDS

AA Book of British Birds
Beautifully illustrated and well set-out, this comprehensive guide includes a practical section on building nest boxes, as well as highlighting the best areas for birdwatching in Britain.
[P243] Hodder hbk **£14.95**

Field Guide to the Birds of Europe
Excellent, well-illustrated and comprehensive guide for the enthusiast.
[P244] Kingfisher pbk **£6.95**

Reader's Digest Field Guide to the Birds of Britain
Delightful, comprehensive reference work.
[P245] Hodder hbk **£8.95**

ANDREWS, JOHN
Birds of Britain and Europe
A pocket identification guide in the Hamlyn Nature Guides series. Good value.
[P249] Hamlyn pbk **£2.99**

BERTEL; HAKAN & SVENSSON
Hamlyn Guide to the Birds of Britain and Europe **[NEW]**
A field guide accompanied by three cassettes featuring birdsong of more than 360 species.
[P250] Hamlyn hbk **£17.95**

BROWN, LESLIE
British Birds of Prey
[P251] Collins hbk **£10.50**

FULLER, R.J.
Bird Habitats in Britain
Comprehensive guide describing the main habitat types and their associated bird life through the seasons and the distribution of sites in Britain.
[P257] Poyser hbk **£17.00**

GOODERS, JOHN
The Complete Birdwatcher's Guide
A comprehensive ornithological reference work and practical field guide rolled into one. Also gives useful information on Britain's prime birdwatching locations.
[P258] Kingfisher hbk **£16.95**

HARRISON, COLIN
Field Guide to the Nest Eggs and Nestlings of British and European Birds
Recommended for the keen birdwatcher.
[P259] Collins pbk **£6.95**

HAYMAN, PETER & BURTON, PHILIP
Birdlife of Britain and Europe
Excellent reference book.
[P260] Mitchell Beazley hbk **£12.95**

HOLDEN, PETER & SHARROCK, J.T.R.
RSPB Book of British Birds
New edition of this identification guide covering the 272 most common species found in the British Isles.
[P262] Macmillan pbk **£6.95**

LAMBERS, TERENCE & GOODERS, JOHN
Collins British Birds
One of the best reference guides available - highly recommended.
[P264] Collins pbk **£8.95**

PERRINS, CHRISTOPHER
Collins New Generation Guide to Birds of Britain and Europe
Edited by David Attenborough. Ideal for the enthusiast.
[P265] Collins hbk **£10.95**
[P266] Collins pbk **£7.95**

PETERSON; MOUNTFORD & HOLLOM
Field Guide to the Birds of Britain and Europe
[P267] Collins hbk **£8.95**

SCOTT, BOB
Atlas of British Birdlife
A county-by-county guide to bird-watching sites, containing a checklist of every species regularly visiting or breeding in the British Isles, with distribution maps and migration routes.
[P269] Hamlyn hbk **£15.00**

SHARROCK, J.T.R.
Birds New to Britain and Ireland
'First-sighting' accounts of 83 species unrecorded in Britain and Ireland before 1946.
[P270] Poyser hbk **£14.00**

SVENSSON, LARS & DELIN, HAKAN
Photographic Guide to the Birds of Britain and Europe NEW
A definitive photographic guide that features more than 1,500 colour photographs, and explanatory line drawings for each species.
[P271] Hamlyn hbk **£14.95**

THOM, VALERIE M.
Birds in Scotland
Comprehensive guide for birdwatchers.
[P272] Poyser hbk **£24.00**

TUNNICLIFFE, C.F.
The painstaking detail of Tunnicliffe's paintings make them unique. The paperback editions of his work are successful because the reproductions have not been reduced or cut to fit a smaller format. The most aesthetically successful book is *Tunnicliffe's Birds*, much care being taken to reproduce the colour and texture of the originals.

Sketches of Birdlife
[P275] Gollancz hbk **£12.95**
Tunnicliffe's Birds
[P276] Gollancz hbk **£40.00**
Portrait of a Country Artist
[P278] Gollancz pbk **£6.95**

BIRDS OF THE WORLD

Collins Field Guides
New Guide to the Birds of New Zealand
[P280] Collins hbk **£9.95**
Field Guide to the Birds of Galapagos
[P281] Collins hbk **£8.95**
Field Guide to the Birds of SE Asia
[P282] Collins hbk **£9.95**
Field Guide to the Birds of Australia
[P283] Collins pbk **£9.95**
Field Guide to the Birds of Southern Africa
[P284] Collins hbk **£8.95**
Field Guide to the Birds of West Africa
[P285] Collins hbk **£9.95**
Field Guide to the Birds of East Africa
[P286] Collins hbk **£8.95**

CEMMICK, DAVID & VEITCH, DICK
Kakapo Country: The Story of the World's Most Unusual Bird
Fascinating book on a rare and endangered breed of parrot, which is completely defenceless against predators and leads a solitary nocturnal life in remote parts of New Zealand.
[P287] Hodder hbk **£17.95**

FERGUSON-LEES; BURTON; FRANKLIN & MEAD
Birds of Prey: An Identification Guide to the Raptors of the World NEW
The first guide of its kind to cover all 300 + species: detailed, well-illustrated and authoritative.
[P292] Helm hbk **£25.00**

MACKENZIE, JOHN P.S.
Waterfowl NEW
A beautifully produced guide to the world's waterfowl in the excellent Harrap Birds of the World series.
[P293] Harrap hbk **£12.95**

BIRD WATCHING

Where to Watch... Series
East Anglia
[P298] Helm pbk **£8.95**
Bedfordshire, Berkshire, Buckinghamshire, Hertfordshire and Oxfordshire
[P299] Helm pbk **£9.95**
Lancashire, Cumbria and Cheshire
[P300] Helm pbk **£8.95**
Where to Watch Birds in Britain and Europe
A revised edition describing 200 of the best birdwatching sites in Britain and Europe with information on the birds and maps to help site location.
[P301] Helm pbk **£9.95**
Somerset, Avon, Gloucestershire and Wiltshire
[P302] Helm pbk **£9.95**
The West Midlands
[P303] Helm pbk **£9.95**
Kent, Surrey and Sussex
[P304] Helm pbk **£9.95**
Where to Watch Birds in Wales
[P305] Helm pbk **£9.95**
Where to Watch Birds in Scotland NEW
[P306] Helm pbk **£9.95**

FISHER, JAMES & FLEGG, JIM
Watching Birds
Very good general introduction for beginners.
[P309] Poyser hbk **£6.00**

HAYMAN, PETER
Birdwatcher's Pocket Guide
Another in this excellent series of handy guides.
[P310] M Beazley pbk **£4.95**

MORRISON, PAUL
Bird Habitats of Great Britain and Ireland: A New Approach to Birdwatching NEW
Shows how to identify birds, not in isolation, but in their natural context, looking at all the habitats in the British Isles and the delicate balances that exist between birds and their environment.
[P311] M Joseph hbk **£16.95**

ODDIE, BILL
Birdwatching with Bill Oddie
A practical guide with advice on how to choose the best gear, where and how to look for birds and how to recognise what you're looking at.
[P312] Macmillan pbk **£4.99**

ORTON, DICK
The Hawkwatcher NEW
Affectinate account of a lifetime's birdwatching, which details a particular obsession with hawks.
[P313] Unwin Hyman hbk **£14.95**

SULLIVAN, SYLVIA
The RSPB Book of the Birdwatching Year NEW
Twelve famous birdwatchers write about a particular place or time of year special to them.
[P316] Thorsons hbk **£14.95**

SOPER, TONY
Birdwatching
[P317] BBC pbk **£8.95**
The Birdtable Book
[P318] David & Charles hbk **£9.95**

SOPER, TONY & LOVEGROVE, ROGER
Birds in Your Garden: A Month-by-Month Guide NEW
An illustrated identification guide with advice on how to attract birds into the garden.
[P319] Webb & B hbk **£12.95**

Plants & Trees

This section offers a selection of field guides and reference books on trees, plants, fungi and flowers. We have highlighted some of the best titles here, but for further guidance on the variety of Field Guides available and what they offer, turn to the beginning of this chapter. There is considerable overlap between this section and the *Gardening* chapter, which includes works on specific species of flowers.

LONGMAN NATURE GUIDES
Practical, pocket-sized guides for the younger enthusiast.
Berries of Britain and Europe
[P321] Longman pbk **£1.95**
Conifers of Britain and Europe
[P322] Longman pbk **£1.95**
Deciduous Trees of Britain and Europe
[P323] Longman pbk **£1.95**
Flowers of Field and Meadow
[P324] Longman pbk **£1.95**

Observer's Book of Trees
[P325] Penguin hbk **£3.95**

BLAMEY & GREY-WILSON
The Illustrated Flora of Britain and Northern Europe **NEW**
The first illustrated flora for the region representing the distilled life's work of Europe's premier botanical artist.
[P343] Hodder hbk **£24.95**

BLAMEY, MARJORIE & PHILIP
Marjorie Blamey's Portraits of Wild Flowers
Probably one of the best-known and best-loved natural history illustrators.
[P345] Collins hbk **£6.95**

BUCZACKI, STEFAN
Guide to Fungi of Britain & Europe
[P348] Collins pbk **£8.95**

CHINERY, MICHAEL
**Field Guide:
The Plant Life of Britain and Europe**
A well known natural historian, Chinery is the general editor of the Kingfisher Field Guide series. They cover a wide variety of plant life and are well-illustrated and informative.
[P350] Kingfisher pbk **£6.95**
The Wild Life of Britain and Europe
[P352] Kingfisher pbk **£7.95**

CLAPHAM, A.R. & TUTIN, D.G.
Flora of the British Isles
This standard British Flora was first published in 1952. This new edition revises descriptions of the species in order to provide an accurate identification of all British plants. Also includes commonly related garden plants and well established aliens.
[P353] Cambridge pbk **£25.00**

DAVIS, P.H. & CULLEN, J.
The Identification of Flowering Plant Families
A guide to the scientific basis of plant identification. This third edition of an established work, outlines changes which have occured over the last decade in taxonomic thinking and public attitudes to plants and wildlife.
[P356] Cambridge pbk **£6.95**

FITTER, ALASTAIR
New Generation Guide to Wild Flowers
Like the Kingfisher series, these are good quality, informative guides. In addition they offer an explanation of classification and describe each stage in the life of the wild flower.
[P357] Collins pbk **£7.95**

FITTER; FITTER & BLAMEY
The Wild Flowers of Britain and Northern Europe
[P359] Collins pbk **£6.95**
The Grasses, Sedges, Rushes and Ferns of Britain and Northern Europe
[P360] Collins pbk **£5.95**

GILMOUR, JOHN & WALTERS, MAX
Wild Flowers
An updated edition of this classic reference work.
[P361] Collins pbk **£6.50**

LANG, DAVID
A Guide to the Wild Orchids of Great Britain and Ireland
An updated edition of this essential reference work, including information on two new species of orchid.
[P373] Oxford pbk **£8.95**

MABBERLEY, D.J.
The Plant Book: A Portable Dictionary of the Higher Plants
For the more advanced botanist, a comprehensive dictionary of flowering plants with common names and uses, arranged according to Cronquist's system.
[P374] Cambridge pbk **£22.50**

MITCHELL, ALAN & WILKINSON, JOHN
The Trees of Britain & Northern Europe
New edition of this complete pocket guide to trees, with additional information on the finest specimens of tree and notable tree collections found in the British Isles.
[P377] Collins pbk **£6.95**

MOORE, PETER D.
Pocket Guide to Wild Flowers
A slim volume packed with information. The illustrations are remarkably detailed for its size.
[P378] Mitchell Beazley pbk **£3.95**

PERRING, FRANKLYN **NEW**
RSNC Guide to British Wild Flowers
Produced in collaboration with the Royal Society for Nature Conservation; features artwork for each species opposite its description, for easy reference.
[P379] Hamlyn pbk **£3.95**

PHILLIPS, ROGER & RIX, MARTIN
A practical, comprehensive series of photoguides.
Coastal Wild Flowers
[P381] H Hamilton pbk **£4.95**
Garden and Field Weeds
[P383] H Hamilton pbk **£4.95**
Mediterranean Wild Flowers
[P385] H Hamilton pbk **£4.95**
Native and Common Trees
[P386] H Hamilton pbk **£4.95**
Wild Flowers of Mountain and Moorland
[P388] H Hamilton pbk **£4.95**
Wild Flowers of the Roadside and Waste Places
[P390] H Hamilton pbk **£4.95**
Woodland Wild Flowers
[P392] H Hamilton pbk **£4.95**

POLUNIN, OLEG
Polunin has long been respected for his work in this area for the quality of his botanic photographs.
Collins Photoguide to the Wild Flowers of Britain and Northern Ireland
Ideal for the beginner as well as the professional botanist, this guide contains over 1,750 species arranged in colour order to aid identification. Line drawings and some excellent photography.
[P393] Collins pbk **£9.95**
Concise Flowers of Europe
[P395] Oxford pbk **£6.95**
Flowers of Greece and the Balkans
[P396] Oxford pbk **£12.95**
with SMYTHIES, B.E.
Flowers of South-West Europe: A Field Guide
A superb guide to the flowers of the Iberian Peninsula.
[P398] Oxford pbk **£9.95**
with STAINTON, ADAM
Flowers of the Himalayas
A definitive guide, now available in condensed form for amateur botanists and students.
[P399] Oxford hbk **£35.00**
Concise Flowers of the Himalayas
[P400] Oxford pbk **£19.50**

PURSEY, HELEN L.
Wild Flowers of Britain and Europe **NEW**
A guide to 220 of the commonest flowers.
[P401] Hamlyn pbk **£2.99**

RAVEN, JOHN & WALTERS, MAX
Mountain Flowers
First published around 20 years ago, this classic work has now been updated, but retains its original format.
[P402] Collins pbk **£6.50**

ROSE, FRANCIS
The Colour Identification Guide to the Grasses, Sedges, Rushes & Ferns of the British Isles & North-Western Europe
Describes over 420 species and illustrates more than 350 in colour, with a glossary of technical terms and plan structures.
[P406] Viking hbk **£30.00**

SUMMERHAYES, V.S.
Wild Orchids of Britain
New edition of a classic from a leading authority on orchids.
[P410] Collins hbk **£6.50**

TURNER, WILLIAM **NEW**
A New Herbal
This book has not been reprinted since 1551, and this facsimile edition includes Fuch's fine woodcuts. William Turner, the 'father of English botany', was the first person to provide detailed observations of the appearance and habitat of plants.
[P411] Carcanet hbk **£20.00**

WILKINS, MALCOLM
Plantwatching
Remarkable book on the inner workings of the plants: their form, function, behaviour and chemical engineering. Fully illustrated with diagrams and photos.
[P412] Macmillan hbk **£14.95**

WILLIAMS; WILLIAMS & ARLOTT
Field Guide to the Orchids of Britain and Europe
[P413] Collins hbk **£7.95**

WILSON & BLAMEY
Alpine Flowers of Britain and Europe
[P414] Collins pbk **£6.95**

Pets & Domesticated Animals

The variety of books available on pets is very extensive, dominated of course by cats and dogs. The main ranges, both of which are detailed and well illustrated, are published by Century and Michael Joseph. TFH, the American publishers also produce an extensive range on all varieties of pets with good illustrations and a clear text, using American vocabulary and references.

BROCK, JULIET CLUTTON
The Natural History of Domesticated Mammals
An illustrated history of animals that man has domesticated from early times to the present day.
[P415] Cambridge pbk **£9.95**

MORRIS, DESMOND
The Animals Roadshow
Based on the popular television series, this book looks at the long and fascinating relationship between man and animal, talks to animal-lovers throughout Britain and includes intriguing facts on some very unusual pets.
[P420] Cape pbk **£6.95**

STOCKER, LES
Something in a Cardboard Box
Stocker runs a wildlife hospital with his wife, in their back garden. This book gives an account of their ten years of wildlife rescue, full of tales of heartbreak and hilarity. The book features badgers, deer, stoats and hedgehogs, amongst others, as well as a wonderful story about a python.
[P422] Chatto pbk **£7.95**

BIRDS

ALDERTON, DAVID
Birdkeeper's Guide to Breeding Birds
Featuring over 50 species from finches to waterfowl, this illustrated guide contains all you need to know about how to breed birds, how to recognise pairs, hand rearing, colour breeding and establishing and exhibiting stud.
[P423] Salamander pbk **£4.95**

CHRISTIE, IRENE
Understanding Your Parrot
Covers all the important points that a beginner should know, including excellent sections on parrot maintenance and on the body language of parrots.
[P427] Witherby hbk **£10.95**

MOIZER, STAN & BARBARA
Budgerigars: A Complete Guide
An encyclopaedic guide to the breeding and care of all kinds of budgerigars.
[P433] Merehurst hbk **£12.95**

PORTER, VALERIE
Domestic and Ordinary Fowl　`NEW`
This book seeks to generate interest in domestic and ornamental fowl. It features chickens, turkeys, guineafowl, peafowl, pheasants and quail, amongst others. Each species is examined in detail, with photographs and analyses of behaviour.
[P435] Pelham hbk **£14.95**

CATS

People's fascination and love for cats is reflected in the wide range of the following titles. Among the practical guides to cat care there are also books which cover their many-faceted character.

Observer's Book of Cats
A guide for the younger reader.
[P436] Penguin hbk **£3.99**

GETTINGS, FRED
The Secret Lore of the Cat　`NEW`
[P437] Grafton hbk **£14.95**

Illustration from **Favourite Cats** by John P. O'Neill (Gollancz hbk £12.95)

MCHATTIE, GRACE
The Cat Lover's Dictionary　`NEW`
A comprehensive reference book with colour illustrations, which prvides information on well-known and lesser-known breeds.
[P438] Witherby hbk **£10.95**

MORRIS, DESMOND
Catlore
How many tail signals does a cat make? Why are they attracted to people who don't like them? Sequel to the tremendously successful *'Catwatching'*, this book answers some more intriguing questions on cat psychology and body language.
[P440] Cape hbk **£5.95**

O'NEILL, JOHN P.
Favourite Cats
[P441A] Gollancz hbk **£12.95**

POND & RALEIGH
Standard Guide to Cat Breeds
[P442] Macmillan hbk **£12.95**

SAYER, ANGELA
The Complete Book of the Cat
Essential tips on choosing a cat, with invaluable advice on caring for kittens and full grown cats. Includes a special section on pedigree cats.
[P445] Hamlyn pbk **£6.95**

STURGIS, MATTHEW
The English Cat at Home
A delightful collection of engaging cats and their engaged owners, seen together in their surroundings, whether a stately home, country garden, bachelor pad, farmhouse kitchen, Oxford college or Downing Street.
[P447] Chatto hbk **£16.95**

TAYLOR, ROGER
You and Your Cat
Probably the most comprehensive guide to cat care available at the moment. Written by the vet from the One by One series on television, it covers the different cat breeds, helps you choose the one best suited to you and gives information on feeding, grooming, health care and first aid. Clearly set out and well-illustrated.
[P449] Dorling Kindersley pbk **£6.95**

VINER
Cat Care Manual
This book traces a cat's life giving tips and advice on how to care for it as it gets older. The question-and-answer format covers general health and popular breeds with step-by-step photographs on grooming. Ideal for the slightly younger cat owner.
[P450] Stanley Paul hbk **£10.95**

DOGS

Encyclopaedia of Dog Breeds
[P452] TFH hbk **£12.50**

Observer's Book of Dogs
For the younger dog-owner.
[P453] Penguin hbk **£3.95**

DRABBLE, PHIL
One Man and His Dog
A new book published to coincide with the 100th programme in the popular TV series. Drabble was initially sceptical about whether the series would be successful or not, but believes that there are two main reasons: the stunningly beautiful country in which 'One Man and His Dog' is shot, and the interviews he conducts with local people during the programmes.
[P462] Pelham hbk **£12.95**

MORRIS, DESMOND
Dog Watching
Even the honest hound reveals secrets by its body language. Another examination of animal psychology from the author of **Manwatching** and *Catwatching*.
[P470] Cape hbk **£5.95**

PET FISH

Observer's Book of Tropical Fish
A guide for the younger reader.
[P476] Penguin pbk **£3.95**

ALLGAYER, R. & TETON, J.
Complete Book of Aquarium Plants
Plants are essential for the wellbeing of aquarium fish as well as being aesthetically pleasing. This guide provides detailed descriptions and colour photographs of over 150 freshwater aquarium plants, together with information on their environmental needs.
[P479] Ward Lock hbk **£16.95**

ANDREWS & CARRINGTON
The Manual of Fish Health
A complete guide to keeping fish in peak condition from providing a healthy environment to recognizing and treating a wide range of diseases. Publication August 1988.
[P480] Salamander hbk **£12.95**

AXELROD, HERBERT RICHARD
Complete Introduction to Community Aquariums
[P481] TFH hbk **£3.95**
Complete Introduction to Koi and Garden Pools
[P482] TFH hbk **£3.95**
Dr Axelrod's Atlas of Tropical Freshwater Aquarium Fishes
[P483] TFH hbk **£50.00**
How to Set Up a Tropical Aquarium
[P484] TFH hbk **£4.50**
Starting Your Tropical Aquarium
[P485] TFH hbk **£7.50**
Tropical Fish for Beginners
[P486] TFH hbk **£6.95**
with VORDEWINKLER, WILLIAM
Encyclopaedia of Tropical Fishes
[P488] TFH hbk **£13.50**
Goldfish and Koi in Your Home
[P489] TFH hbk **£10.95**
with BURGESS, WARREN
Marine Fish
[P490] TFH hbk **£3.95**
Salt Water Aquarium
[P491] TFH hbk **£11.95**
Axelrod, Herbert Richard, et al
Exotic Marine Fishes
[P492] TFH hbk **£16.95**

MCINNERNEY, DEREK & GERARD, GEOFFREY
All About Tropical Fish　`NEW`
A complete guide to the construction of a n aquarium, its maintenance and the breeding and care of tropical, freshwar and some marine fish. The standard book on the subject.
[P497] Harrap hbk **£14.95**

MILLS, DICK
Practical Encyclopaedia of the Marine Aquarium
Fully illustrated guide to the brilliant fish and invertebrates of the world's tropical and coral reefs as well as those creatures from temperate waters which can thrive in captivity.
[P498] Salamander hbk **£12.95**

SCIENCE

General

Cambridge Illustrated Thesaurus of Science and Technology
(Ed. Godman, A. & Denney, R.)
[PA1] Cambridge hbk **£6.50**

Chambers Science and Technology Dictionary (Ed. Walker, Peter)
Excellent and comprehensive coverage of scientific and technological terminology.
[PA2] Chambers pbk **£16.95**

Concise Science Dictionary (Ed. Isaacs)
[PA3] Oxford pbk **£5.95**

From Creation to Chaos `NEW`
Scientists speak out on facts and theories, ideas and discoveries in this anthology of prose writings.
[PA4] Blackwell hbk **£15.00**

ARTHUR, WALLACE
**Theories of Life:
Darwin, Mendel and Beyond**
Examines rival theories of life, including that of the 'creationists', from an evolutionist's standpoint.
[PA7] Penguin pbk **£3.95**

ASIMOV, ISAAC `NEW`
As Far as the Human Eye Could See
A collection of essays on scientific subjects, ranging from the centre of the earth to the far reaches of the universe.
[PA8] Grafton pbk **£3.50**
New Guide to Science
A masterly summary of current knowledge in all the physical and biological sciences: from sub-atomic particles to immense galaxies and from dinosaurs to bacteria.
[PA9] Penguin pbk **£8.99**
The Relativity of Wrong `NEW`
Asimov here discusses the composition of the Milky Way, the discovery of the stars and the 'Moon Effect' on human behaviour. Newly available in paperback.
[PA10] Oxford pbk **£5.95**
The Roving Mind
A collection of essays on the many facets of modern science and scientific thought.
[PA11] Prometheus pbk **£8.95**
The Subatomic Monsters: Essays on Science
Wide-ranging scientific essays written with wit and clarity on subjects such as 'thinking about thinking', 'the world of the red sun' and 'the properties of chaos'.
[PA12] Grafton pbk **£2.95**

BODANIS, DAVID
The Secret House
Reveals what really goes on in your home - from eggs breathing in the pantry to tins spluttering on kitchen shelves. Accompanied by 70 full-colour photographs, it is not for the squeamish.
[PA13] Sidgwick pbk **£7.95**

BURGESS J.; MARTEN, M. & TAYLOR, R.
Microcosmos
A visual exploration of objects which are too small to be seen, including atoms, genes, bedbugs, tastebuds and even silicon chips.
[PA17] Cambridge hbk **£15.00**

CAPRA, FRITJOF
The Turning Point: Science, Society and the Rising Culture
An essential guide for anyone interested in the place of science and metascience in our contemporary culture.
[PA21] Fontanta pbk **£4.95**
Uncommon Wisdom `NEW`
Conversations with remarkable people, all of whom helped to stimulate Capra's intellectual achievements.
[PA20] Fontana pbk **£4.95**

DAVIES, PAUL
God and the New Physics
Shows how far the recent explosive discoveries of the new physics are revolutionising our view of the world, and in particular throwing light on many questions formerly posed by religion.
[PA22] Penguin pbk **£4.99**

DYSON, FREEMAN
Origins of Life
A historical survey of theories and experiments on the origin of life plus a sketch of new ideas and experiments.
[PA23] Cambridge hbk **£8.50**

GARDNER, MARTIN
Whys & Wherefores `NEW`
More fun essays ranging from James Joyce and fantasy novels to physics and philosophy.
[PA24] Chicago UP hbk **£15.95**

GARDNER, MARTIN (ED)
Sacred Beetle and Other Great Essays in Science
A collection of essays by over thirty leading interpreters of science, on subjects ranging from Darwin to Einstein.
[PA25] Oxford pbk **£5.95**

GLEICK, JAMES
Chaos: Making a New New Science `NEW`
Nominated for a National Book award in the USA. It cuts across traditional scientific disciplines, tying together unrelated kinds of wildness and irregularity: from the turbulence of weather to the complicated rhythms of the human heart. Stimulating and exciting.
[PA26] Heinemann hbk **£12.95**
[PA27] Cardinal pbk **£5.99**

GONZALEZ-CRUSSI, F.
Notes of an Anatomist
Entertaining and witty essays on varied and often bizarre subjects including two-headed babies, Egyptian burial customs, penile nicknames and castration. References include Balzac, Gogol, Simone de Beauvoir and El Greco.
[PA28] Pan pbk **£2.95**
Three Forms of Sudden Death
Reflections on the grandeur and misery of the body. Essays include 'On Ageing' and 'The Female Breast'.
[PA29] Pan pbk **£3.50**

HALDANE, J.B.S.
On Being the Right Size and Other Essays
Essays on subjects such as the origin of life and the meaning of 'hot'.
[PA31] Oxford pbk **£5.95**

HARRE, ROMANO
Great Scientific Experiments
20 experiments that have changed our view of the world.
[PA32] Oxford pbk **£5.95**

HAWKING, STEPHEN
**A Brief History of Time:
From the Big Bang to Black Holes**
A very popular book by the leading Cambridge theoretical physicist and cosmologist, which leads the way forward for contemporary theories on the cosmos. It is written for the non-mathematical layman.
[PA75] Bantam hbk **£14.95**

KOESTLER, ARTHUR
The Sleepwalkers
Examines the whole history of cosmology, including the split between science and religion, the roles of great scientists and the significance of politics.
[PA78] Peregrine pbk **£7.95**

LORENZ, KONRAD
Lorenz is well-known for his controversial theories on human behaviour. He has attempted to prove that general laws govern behaviour and cites experiments with animals as examples where behavioural adaptations lead to stimulus responses.
Behind the Mirror
[PA78A] Methuen pbk **£4.50**
On Aggression
Argues that the act of aggression is inbred in some animals, including man. An emotive book which has aroused strong criticism.
[PA78B] Methuen pbk **£8.95**
Waning of Humaneness
Lorenz's most recent book, which argues that this century has witnessed a deterioration in 'human qualities'. Opposition to this book has been vociferous.
[PA78C] Unwin Hyman hbk **£11.95**

MEDAWAR, PETER
Advice to a Young Scientist
[PA34] Pan pbk **£2.95**
Limits of Science
[PA35] Oxford pbk **£4.95**
Memoirs of a Thinking Radish
An autobiography of a great scientist, including anecdotes on the Rockerfeller Institute, life in Oxford, Karl Popper and J.B.S. Haldane.
[PA36] Oxford pbk **£4.95**
Pluto's Republic
Incorporating *The Art of the Soluble* and *Induction and Intuition in Scientific Thought*. A reasoned and well-written view of science which incorporates both the good and the bad aspects.
[PA37] Oxford pbk **£5.95**

PEARCE, FRED
Turning up the Heat `NEW`
Our perilous future in the global greenhouse is discussed and alarming findings are revealed.
[PA190] Bodley H hbk **£12.95**

PERUTZ, MAX
Is Science Necessary? Essays on Science and Scientists `NEW`
Nobel prize-winning chemist provides an overview of science for the general reader.
[PA38] Barrie & J hbk **£14.95**

POPPER, KARL
The Logic of Scientific Discovery
A philosophical examination of science. One of the most important documents of the 20th century, in which the fields of modern science are brought together.
[PA39] Unwin Hyman pbk **£9.95**

ROSE, STEVEN & APPIGNANESI, LISA
Science and Beyond
Leading scientists assess the place of science today.
[PA41] Blackwell hbk **£25.00**

THOMAS, LEWIS
**The Youngest Science:
Notes of a Medicine Watcher**
An enthralling history of modern medicine.
[PA49] Oxford pbk **£4.95**

UVAROV & ISAACS, ALAN
The Penguin Dictionary of Science
A reliable and clear explanation of the basic
vocabulary of physics, chemistry, maths and
astronomy with a smattering of words used in
biochemistry, biophysics and molecular biology. New
edition.
[PA50] Viking hbk **£16.95**
[PA51] Penguin pbk **£5.50**

WOODCOCK, ALEXANDER & MONTE, D.
Catastrophe Theory
A revolutionary way of understanding how things
change.
[PA53] Penguin pbk **£3.95**

Astronomy

Cambridge Atlas of Astronomy
An outstanding book which clarifies the most
complex developments and scientific investigations
for the non-specialist. Extensive use of superb colour
illustrations.
[PA54] Cambridge hbk **£35.00**

ASIMOV, ISAAC
Exploring the Earth and the Cosmos
Covers everything from the expanding universe and
the theory of relativity to black holes and the building
of a time machine.
[PA57] Penguin pbk **£5.50**

BARROW, JOHN & TIPLER, FRANK
The Anthropic Cosmological Principle
Addresses the puzzle of the existence of the universe
and reintroduces the idea of 'grand design' - a notion
which has returned to fly in the face of accepted
scientific ideas.
[PA58] Oxford pbk **£9.95**

BOSLOUGH, JOHN
Beyond the Black Hole
An introduction to the life and work of Stephen
Hawking whose ideas have been crucial to our
understanding of the universe's deepest mysteries.
[PA60] Fontana pbk **£2.50**

BRIGGS, G.A. & TAYLOR, F.W.
Photographic Atlas of the Planets
The best collection of photographs of the planets over
the last two decades. Also included are global maps
of the planets and their satellites.
[PA61] Cambridge pbk **£8.95**

CADOGAN, PETER
From Quark to Quasar
A pictorial journey spanning some 42 orders of
magnitude to provide a unique insight into the scale
of our universe.
[PA62] Cambridge hbk **£13.95**

CLOSE, FRANK
**End: Cosmic Catastrophe and the
Fate of the Universe** NEW
Points to the possible natural disasters which
could bring about the end of the universe, including
huge asteroids, comets and rocks the size of New
York. Makes the frightening suggestion that the
universe may not be as stable as we had previously
thought.
[PA64] Simon & Sch hbk **£12.95**

CONSOLMAGNO, GUY & DAVIS, DANIEL
Turn Left at Orion NEW
How to find night sky objects in a small
telescope. Aimed at the beginner.
[PA65] Cambridge hbk **£12.50**

DAVIES, PAUL
**Other Worlds: Space, Superspace and
the Quantum Universe**
Reveals the unpredictability of the world in which we
live.
[PA67] Penguin pbk **£3.99**
The Cosmic Blueprint NEW
Challenges the contemporary view that we live in a
dying universe. Davies examines claims that there are
definite 'organising principles' in nature, and
proposes that the universe as a whole possesses a
tendency to develop towards progressively higher
levels of complex organisation.
[PA68] Unwin Hyman pbk **£5.95**

FERRIS, TIMOTHY
Coming of Age in the Milky Way NEW
The story of the struggle towards understanding
cosmic space and time.
[PA69] Bodley H hbk **£14.95**

GARDNER, MARTIN
Ambidextrous Universe
In an argument touching on poetry, music, art, and
even magic, Gardner shows how polarity and its
problems have contributed to our knowledge of the
origin of life, the fourth and fifth dimensions of anti-
matter and the difficulties of communication with
other galaxies.
[PA70] Penguin pbk **£4.95**

GRIBBIN, JOHN
In Search of the Big Bang
Explores the mysteries of cosmic creation.
[PA73] Corgi pbk **£5.95**
The Omega Point
The search for the missing mass and the ultimate fate
of the universe.
[PA74] Heinemann hbk **£12.95**

HENBEST, NIGEL & COUPER, HEATHER
The Restless Universe
Draws on the most recent astronomical discoveries to
present a comprehensive and fascinating picture of
our dramatic universe.
[PA76] G Philip hbk **£8.95**

HOYLE, FRED & WICKRAMASINGHE,
CHANDRA
**Cosmic Life-Force: The Power of Life
Across the Universe**
Proposes the controversial theory that the universe as
a whole is controlled by an intelligent life-force that
overcomes all other forces of nature. This theory not
only encompasses Earth, but stretches out to include

neighbouring planets and their satellites and beyond
them to other galaxies.
[PA77] Dent hbk **£12.95**

LILLER, WILLIAN & MAYER, BEN
The Cambridge Guide to Astronomy
A practical introduction which tells you how to get
outside and actually practice astronomy, even if you
own nothing more than a simple camera.
[PA79] Cambridge hbk **£15.00**

MALIN, STUART
**The Greenwich Guide to Stars,
Galaxies and Nebulae** NEW
Goes beyond our own solar system to four distant and
mysteriously beautiful galaxies.
[PA80] G Philip hbk **£5.95**

MOORE, PATRICK
1989 Yearbook of Astronomy NEW
[PA82] Sidgwick hbk **£9.95**
A-Z of Astronomy
Over 400 entries and dozens of photographs explain
astronomical subjects from Aberrations of Starlight
and Absolute Magnitude to Zero Gravity and the
zodiac.
[PA83] P Stephens pbk **£6.99**
Exploring the Night Sky with Binoculars
Moore carefully explains the rudiments of astronomy
and the selection of suitable binoculars. Also
discusses in more detail the array of beautiful
astronomical objects that await the binocular observer
including stars, clusters, nebulae and galaxies.
[PA84] Cambridge pbk **£6.95**
The Amateur Astronomer
A thorough introduction to astronomy, starting with a
fascinating account of the historical background,
followed by hints on choosing and maintaining
observation equipment.
[PA88] Cambridge hbk **£14.95**
The Sky at Night NEW
Charts astronomical developments from the beginning
of 1985 through to the autumn of 1988, and includes
the return of Halley's comet, the passing of Uranus by
the Voyager 2, and the explosion of a supernova in the
large Cloud of Magellan.
[PA89] Harrap hbk **£12.95**

MOORE, PATRICK & HUNT, GARRY
The Atlas of the Solar System
[PA90] M Beazley hbk **£19.95**

MOORE, PATRICK & JACKSON, F.
Life in the Universe
Ideas on the origins of life and the possibilities of life
on other planets.
[PA91] Routledge pbk **£9.95**

MULLER, RICHARD
Nemesis, The Death Star NEW
Propounds the theory that a 'killer star' is orbiting the
sun and causing comet storms to 'rain' on Earth every
26 million years. Viewed with scepticism by the
scientific world.
[PA92] Heinemann hbk **£10.95**

NICOLSON, IAIN & MOORE, PATRICK
The Universe
Over 200 original artwork subjects reconstruct the
theory and the drama of the Cosmos. Subjects
include: inside a black hole; the creation of the
planets, and the birth, life and death of stars.
[PA95] Collins hbk **£15.00**

PELTIER, LESLIE
A Guide to the Stars
Basic guide to the night sky including things that can
be seen with the naked eye.
[PA96] Cambridge pbk **£7.50**

Patrick Moore, co-author of *The Atlas of the Solar
System* (Mitchell Beazley hbk £19.95)

REES, MARTIN & GRIBBIN, JOHN
The Stuff of the Universe
A probing study of the special relationship between
mankind and the cosmos.
[PA98] Heinemann hbk **£12.95**

RIDPATH, IAN & TIRION, WILL
The Monthly Sky Guide `NEW`
Contains maps of the sky for each month of the year,
realistically depicting the stars visible to the naked
eye.
[PA100] Cambridge pbk **£5.25**

SAGAN, CARL
Cosmic Connection
[PA101] Macmillan pbk **£2.95**
Cosmos
[PA102] Futura pbk **£3.50**

Biology

**Cambridge Illustrated Thesaurus of
Biology** (Ed. Gutteridge, Anne)
[PA107] Cambridge hbk **£6.50**

Concise Dictionary of Biology
[PA108] Oxford hbk **£7.95**

BRITISH MUSEUM
**Human Biology: An Exhibition of
Ourselves**
A lively introduction to human biology, aided by
cartoons, photographs and colourful diagrams. It
invites readers to look more closely at themselves and
the way their bodies work.
[PA109] Cambridge pbk **£6.50**

BRONOWSKI, JACOB
**The Origins of Knowledge and
Imagination**
Explains how we receive and translate our experience
of the world to achieve knowledge. Examines the
mechanisms of our perception and the origin and
nature of language.
[PA110] Yale UP pbk **£7.95**

DESOWITZ, ROBERT
The Thorn in the Starfish
A clear explanation of how the immune system
works: a subject which, since the spread of AIDS, has
been the focus of greater attention.
[PA112] Nortons pbk **£14.95**

EDWARDS, ROBERT
Life Before Birth `NEW`
Reflections on the embryo debate by one of the
doctors responsible for the birth of the first test-tube
baby.
[PA113] Century hbk **£14.95**

GORMAN, JAMES
The Man with No Endomorphins `NEW`
A witty and intriguing account of the scientific
relevance to everyday life covering an enormous
range of subjects
[PA114] WH Allen hbk **£10.95**

MEDAWAR, PETER
The Uniqueness of the Individual
Essays written by Medawar as a rising young
biologist.
[PA116] Dover pbk **£4.75**

MEDAWAR, PETER & JEAN
Aristotle to Zoos
An authoritative and witty guide to central topics in

biology, for example, a definition of interferon, a
useful explanation of the immune system, and essays
on eugenics and ageing.
[PA117] Oxford pbk **£5.95**

SCOTT, ANDREW
Pirates of the Cell
A clear and lively introduction to viruses, including
what they are made of, and how they manage to
invade the vulnerable cells within our bodies. Also
examines the effectiveness of vaccinations and
describes successful attempts to turn viruses into
useful biological systems.
[PA121] Blackwell pbk **£7.95**

SMITH, JOHN MAYNARD
The Problems of Biology
Starting from a definition of life and the mechanics of
replication heredity, Maynard Smith covers a wide
range of topics, including the pattern of nature, animal
behaviour, the brain's function and finally the origin
of life.
[PA122] Oxford pbk **£4.95**

THOMAS, LEWIS
**The Wonderful Mistake:
Notes of a Biology Watcher**
Incorporates two of his most famous essays: 'The
Lives of a Cell' and 'The Medusa and the Snail'.
[PA123] Oxford pbk **£6.95**
The Youngest Science
Discusses the role of medicine in the autobiography
of a famous doctor.
[PA124] Oxford pbk **£4.95**

**WALMSLEY, JANE & MARGOLIS,
JONATHAN**
Hot House People
An analysis of whether we can create 'superpeople',
and an examination of the ethics.
[PA126] Pan pbk **£4.95**

YOUNG, J.Z.
An Introduction to the Study of Man
Shows that a biological framework is useful to help
man understand himself. Investigates such topics as
homeostasis and cybernetics, and heredity and
reproduction, and includes discussions of some of the
philosophical, sociological and environmental
problems raised by a biological study of man.
[PA127] Oxford pbk **£5.95**

Chemistry

**Cambridge Illustrated Thesaurus of
Chemistry** (Ed. Godman, Arthur & Denney)
[PA128] Cambridge hbk **£6.50**

CRONE, HUGH
Chemicals and Society
The use and misuse of chemicals in society from
Agent Orange to Bhopal, plus the effect of hairsprays
on the Ozone layer.
[PA129] Cambridge pbk **£9.95**

RICHARDS, W. GRAHAM
The Problems of Chemistry
For the non-specialist, an eye-opener into the
problems currently faced by chemists, and a
discussion of the likely direction of future
developments.
[PA130] Oxford pbk **£5.95**

SHARP, DAVID WILLIAM ARTHUR (ED)
Dictionary of Chemistry
[PA132] Penguin pbk **£5.95**

Genetics &
Evolution

BAKKER, ROBERT
Dinosaur Heresies
A revolutionary view of dinosaurs.
[PA134] Penguin pbk **£7.95**

BATESON, GREGORY
Mind and Nature: A Necessary Unity
Bateson compares genetic and cultural evolution,
seeing rigour and imagination as the two great
contraries of the mental process, and analogues to
genetic replication and mutation respectively.
[PA135] Fontana pbk **£3.50**

CHERFAS, JEREMY
**Man Made Life: Genetic Engineering
Primer**
Explains the techniques of genetic engineering in a
clear and simple way. Also reveals intriguing
possibilities for harnessing these methods for the
production of drugs, fuel, food and cures for diseases.
[PA138] Blackwell pbk **£9.95**

CHERFAS, JEREMY & GRIBBIN, JOHN
The Redundant Male
Argues that sex is an inefficient method of
reproduction in evolutionary terms, and thus
questions its continuous practice among many
species. A controversial book with far-reaching
implications.
[PA139] Paladin pbk **£2.95**

CRICK, FRANCIS
**What Mad Pursuit?:
A Personal View of Scientific
Discovery** `NEW`
A first-hand account of the discovery of the double-
helix.
[PA140] Weidenfeld hbk **£14.95**

DARWIN, CHARLES
In 1859, when *Origin of Species by Natural
Selection* was published, there was enormous
opposition, especially from the Church. Today
however Darwinism is widely accepted in the
scientific world, and has had a revolutionary impact
on the study of life on earth.
The Essential Darwin Ridley, Mark (Ed)
Selections of writings plus commentary by a leading
scientist of today, Kenneth Korey.
[PA142] Unwin Hyman pbk **£5.95**
Origin of Species (Ed. Burrow, J.W.)
[PA141] Penguin pbk **£4.50**
Voyage of the Beagle
[PA143] Penguin hbk **£5.99**
KEYNES, R.D. (ED)
Charles Darwin's Beagle Diary
Fresh transcript of the diary recording daily activities
and long journeys made in Patagonia and Chile, with
biological notes.
[PA144] Cambridge hbk **£35.00**

DAWKINS, RICHARD
Selfish Gene
Classic book which suggests that genes govern
behaviour in order to ensure their own survival: a new
face of the theory of evolution, soundly based in fact
and explained in plain, jargon-free language.
[PA145] Oxford pbk **£4.95**
The Blind Watchmaker
The winner of the Royal Society of Literature Award.
It is a brilliant and controversial update on evolution,
intelligible both to the scientist and layperson.
[PA146] Penguin pbk **£4.99**

ELDREGE, NILES
Life Pulse: Episodes from the Story of the Fossil Record
Discusses the crucial episodes in the history of the Earth and links these events to the theories of evolution and extinction.
[PA148] Penguin pbk **£4.99**

GOULD, STEPHEN JAY
An Urchin in the Storm
Contests the imperial claims and tidy theories of those who seek to narrow the world around us. With wit and vigour, Gould scourges the fallacies of evolutionary biology and determinism and celebrates the diversity of life, the mystery of human intelligence and the wisdom of Charles Darwin.
[PA149] Collins hbk **£10.95**
Ever Since Darwin
A fascinating collection of essays on subjects such as the impact and relevance of Darwinism, the question of size in nature and the bizarre sex life of a mushroom maggot.
[PA150] Penguin pbk **£4.99**
Hen's Teeth & Horse's Toes
Re-examines the theories on why all species, including our own, eventually die out.
[PA151] Penguin pbk **£5.95**
Mismeasure of Man
Exposes the 'fatal flaws' of intelligence testing.
[PA152] Penguin pbk **£4.95**
Panda's Thumb
A quirky and provocative exploration of the nature of evolution.
[PA153] Penguin pbk **£4.99**
Time's Arrow, Time's Cycle
Myth and methaphor in the discovery of geological time. Includes an examination of rival theories on man's conception of time.
[PA154] penguin pbk **£4.99**

GRIBBIN, JOHN
Genesis: The Origins of Man and the Universe
[PA156] Oxford pbk **£4.95**
In Search of the Double Helix
The entire story of evolution from Darwin to DNA, and beyond.
[PA158] Corgi pbk **£4.95**

HALL, STEPHEN
Invisible Frontiers
A book about the race to synthesise the human gene in the late 1970s - the race in which egos collided, rules were broken, scientific breakthroughs were achieved, and fortunes made.
[PA159] Sidgwick hbk **£14.95**

HARSANYI, ZSOLT & HUTTON, RICHARD
Genetic Prophecy: Beyond the Double Helix
Examines the use of genetic markers to predict man's susceptibility to various diseases, using techniques already used to diagnose diabetes and some forms of cancer. The arguments in this book will have fundamental effects on the future of medicine.
[PA160] Paladin pbk **£1.95**

LEWIN, ROGER
Bones of Contention: Controversies in the Search for Human Origins
Winner of the 1989 Science Book Prize, organised by Britain's Committee for Public Understanding of Science. Lewin bases his discoveries on interviews with many field-leaders and seeks to unravel the mysteries of man's origin.
[PA161] Penguin pbk **£5.99**

Human Evolution: An Illustrated Introduction
Helps the reader achieve a wider perspective on the study of human origins.
[PA162] Blackwell pbk **£7.50**

NOSSAL, G. & COPPEL, R.
Reshaping Life   `NEW`
An updated and expanded edition of the very popular introduction to genetic engineering.
[PA165] Cambridge pbk **£8.95**

ROSE, KAMIN & LEWONTIN
Not in our Genes: Biology, Ideology and Human Nature
A vigorous attack on the apparent recent rise in biological determinism, which the authors associate with right-wing politics.
[PA166] Penguin pbk **£5.99**

ROSE, STEVEN
Chemistry of Life
A book which helps us to unify our knowledge of the mechanisms of life.
[PA167] Penguin pbk **£5.95**

SHAPIRO, ROBERT
Origins
A sceptic's guide to the creation of life on earth. A vivid explanation which covers the many theories attempting to explain the origin of life on earth.
[PA169] Penguin pbk **£5.95**

SHELDRAKE, RUPERT
A New Science of Life: The Hypothesis of Formative Causation
Challenges orthodox science with a theory of causal connection across space and time. Why is it, for instance, that when rats have learned a new trick in one place, other rats elsewhere seem to be able to learn it more quickly?
[PA170] Grafton pbk **£4.95**
The Presence of the Past
A controversial attack on modern theories in the natural sciences which challenges our approach to the universe. Sheldrake expands and develops his theory that all natural systems have a collective memory, or 'morphic field'.
[PA171] Collins hbk **£12.95**

SMITH, JOHN MAYNARD
The Evolution of Sex
Considers the selective forces responsible for the origin and evolution of sexual reproduction.
[PA172] Cambridge pbk **£8.95**

WATSON, J.D.
Along with Francis Crick, Watson won the Nobel Prize for unravelling the mystery of the structure of DNA, the basis of all life on earth.
Double Helix
A personal account of one of the greatest scientific discoveries of the century.
[PA173] Penguin pbk **£3.95**

Mathematics

DEVLIN, KEITH
Mathematics: The New Golden Age
Famous media mathematician, Devlin makes difficult topics accessible and introduces us to the revolution in thought of the last quarter century.
[PA196] Penguin pbk **£7.99**

GARDNER, MARTIN
Mathematical Carnival
Maddening and entertaining puzzles - an amalgam of

infinity, fun and physics.
[PA199] Penguin pbk **£3.95**
Mathematical Circus
[PA200] Penguin pbk **£4.95**
Mathematical Magic Show
Treats include Mobius bands, coin and card trickery, finger arithmetics and the post-Ticktacktoe game of Tri-Hex.
[PA201] Penguin pbk **£4.99**
Mathematical Puzzles and Diversions
More treats including Diophantine brain-teasers and diabolic squares.
[PA202] Penguin pbk **£3.99**
More Mathematical Puzzles and Diversions
[PA203] Penguin pbk **£1.75**

HODGES, ANDREW
Alan Turing: The Enigma of Intelligence
An intimate and perceptive biography of the brilliant mathematician who cracked the German enigma code during the war. He was obsessed by the idea of machine intelligence and is in effect the father of the modern computer.
[PA204] Unwin hbk **£6.95**

MORONEY, M.J.
Facts from Figures
The basics of statistics for understanding their use in our everyday lives.
[PA207] Penguin pbk **£4.99**

ROWNTREE, DEREK
Statistics Without Tears
A primer for non-mathematicians who wish to become acquainted with the subject before getting involved with calculations.
[PA208] Penguin pbk **£3.99**

Physics

COHEN, I. BERNARD
Birth of a New Physics
The story of one of the greatest advances in human thought: the scientific revolution of the 17th century.
[PA218] Penguin pbk **£4.95**
The Newtonian Revolution
A provocative account of the beginnings of modern science.
[PA219] Cambridge pbk **£13.95**

DAVIES, PAUL
The New Physics
A complete and comprehensive account of the new and most exciting discoveries in modern physics. The text, illustrated in colour throughout, is accessible to any readers wanting to understand the latest developments in modern physics.
[PA223] Cambridge hbk **£30.00**

HAZEN, ROBERT
Superconductors: The Breakthrough
Retells the exciting story of the discovery of superconductors - materials that conduct electricity with virtually no resistance - which operate at workable temperatures. Secrecy, false formulae and stolen patent rights all feature in the high drama.
[PA230] Unwin Hyman hbk **£12.95**

MOORE, WALTER
Schrodinger: Life and Thought   `NEW`
A biography of the brilliant Austrian scientist, which draws on recollections of Schrodinger's friends, family and colleagues, as well as on contemporary records, letters and diaries.
[PA234] Cambridge hbk **£25.00**

Philosophy

Reference & Introductions
History of Philosophy
Ancient & Medieval Philosophers
Modern Philosophers
Topics of Philosophy
Continental Philosophy

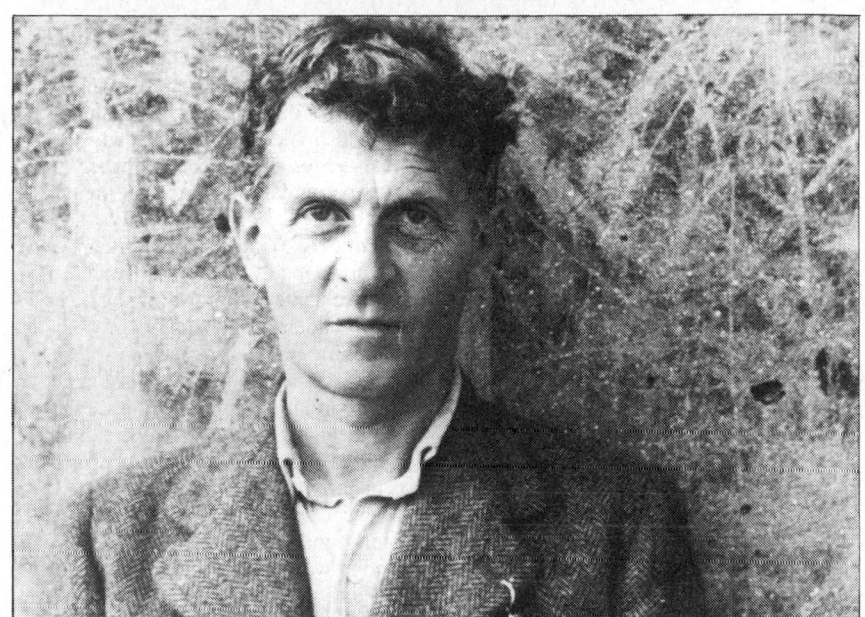

Biographical Investigations: Writing the Life of Ludwig Wittgenstein

Ray Monk

We live in an age preoccupied - perhaps to an unhealthy extent - with the celebration of anniversaries. As everybody who reads a newspaper, listens to the radio, or watches television must know, it is ten years since Margaret Thatcher first became Prime Minister, a hundred years since the births of Charlie Chaplin and Adolf Hitler, and two hundred years since the French Revolution.

It is also - though this has occasioned considerably less comment in the media - a hundred years since the birth of Ludwig Wittgenstein, acknowledged by many to be the greatest philosopher of the twentieth century. By an unplanned coincidence, a biography of Wittgenstein upon which I have been engaged for the last five years has been completed in this, his centenary year.

With a few notable exceptions (Bertrand Russell and Martin Heidegger come immediately to mind), the lives of philosophers rarely excite much interest or controversy. Wittgenstein is perhaps chief among those exceptions. Since his death in 1951, there has been a veritable flood of memoirs of him written by friends, students and even casual

acquaintances (F.R. Leavis, who met him on perhaps four or five occasions, has made his 'Memories of Wittgenstein' the subject of a seventeen-page article). Portraits of him have been drawn in print by Bertrand Russell, G.E. Moore, John Wisdom and Rudolf Carnap - to name only the most famous. Recollections of him have been published by the lady who taught him Russian, the man who delivered peat to his cottage in Ireland and the person who - though he did not know him very well - happened to take the last photographs of him. His correspondence, accounts of his lectures, notes of his conversations - these have all been published and found a surprisingly wide and enthusiastic readership. A novel drawing on these sources (*The World As I Found It* by Bruce Duffy) has received great critical acclaim and was, for a time, numbered among the ten best-selling books in the United States. Poems have been written about him, works of music and art inspired by him, and at least five television documentaries produced about him.

All this attests to the great interest Wittgenstein's life and personality has inspired *outside* the academic community.

Among professional philosophers his work continues to be interpreted and commented upon. A recent bibliography lists nearly six thousand books and articles written by academic philosophers on his work. Very few of these draw upon the biographical sources mentioned in the previous paragraph. Here it is not his private conversations and his personal preoccupations that are under discussion, but the themes of his (notoriously difficult) philosophical work. Most of this immense secondary literature is of little interest (or even intelligible) to anyone outside academia.

Introductions to Wittgenstein's philosophy typically begin with a biographical chapter, which runs through the salient facts of his life: that he was born in Vienna of an immensely wealthy family, that he studied under Bertrand Russell, went to live alone in a hut by a fjord in Norway where he worked out the theory of logic expounded in *Tractatus Logico-Philosophicus*, fought with the Austrians in the First World War, became a mystic under the influence of Tolstoy's *Gospel in Brief*, ended the *Tractatus* on a curiously mystical note, gave away his inherited wealth, gave up philosophy to teach in elementary schools, returned to Cambridge and to philosophy in 1929, and then developed a technique of philosophising that sought to dismantle many of the structures erected by his earlier work. It is made clear that his life was dominated by religious, spiritual and cultural attitudes he felt to be deeply at odds with the age in which he lived. These introductions then go on to provide a discussion of Wittgenstein's work as it has been assimilated into contemporary philosophy, a discussion that seems strangely at variance with the character described in the opening chapter.

I began my biography with the conviction that this gap had to be breached, that the connection between the themes of Wittgenstein's work and the concerns evident in his life and his personal remarks had to be made explicit. His close friend Maurice Drury - whose notes on conversations with Wittgenstein provide the most interesting and revealing source for Wittgenstein's religious thoughts - explained his decision to publish those notes by saying:

"The number of introductions to and commentaries on Wittgenstein's philosophy is steadily increasing. Yet to

one of his former pupils something that was central to his thinking is not being said ... It would be a tragedy if well-meaning commentators make it appear that his writings were now easily assimilable into the very intellectual milieu they were largely a warning against."

Drury's notes are indispensable for understanding this 'something', but on the question of *how* it is central to Wittgenstein's thinking, Drury himself is

---

"The philosopher is not a citizen of any community of ideas, that is what makes him a philosopher"

---

too reticent. Another close friend, Paul Englemann, has been more explicit - at least in relation to the *Tractatus*. His letters from Wittgenstein abound with religious and ethical reflections, and, in making them public, Englemann was at pains to stress their relevance to Wittgenstein's philosophical work, to make clear, as he put it, that in the *Tractatus*, 'logic and mysticism have sprung from the same root'. The famous last sentence of the book, "Whereof one cannot speak, thereof one must be silent", has a positive as well as a negative import; though it denies the expressibility of transcendental truths, it affirms their existence. The Vienna Circle of logical positivists (upon whom the book had an impact that was decisive for the development of philosophy in the twentieth century) saw things differently. 'We must be silent', said Otto Neurath, the most uncompromisingly positivist of them, 'but not *about* anything'. But, as Wittgenstein explained to a potential publisher (Ludwig von Ficker), it was just the things he had *not* said in the book, things he believed *could* not be said, that he regarded as most important.

Since the publication of Wittgenstein's letters to Englemann and von Ficker, an alternative tradition of commentary has grown up that, in contrast to the received Anglocentric view, stresses Wittgenstein's *Austrian* background. *Wittgenstein's Vienna* by Alan Janik and Stephen Toulmin - perhaps the best known and most influential work of this sort - seeks

to understand the *Tractatus* by placing Wittgenstein's work in the context of that of his Austrian contemporaries, a context that includes the psychology of Freud and Weininger, the music of Mahler and Schoenberg, the art of Klimt and Kokoschka, and the architecture of Otto Wagner and Adolf Loos.

Though necessary, this cultural re-orientation is not sufficient. The gap that separates Wittgenstein's work from that of most academic philosophers is not geographical but spiritual. There is no reason to think he would have felt any less isolated at Vienna University than he did at Cambridge, no reason to regard Viennese philosophers, such as Rudolf Carnap and Otto Neurath, as any closer to him than Bertrand Russell. "The philosopher is not a citizen of any community of ideas," Wittgenstein wrote, "that is what makes him a philosopher."

Wittgenstein felt isolated, not just from British culture, but from the whole of twentieth century civilisation. And it is this sense of complete isolation that gives his life its special poignancy and its peculiarly compelling fascination. Whether he lived among the wealthy and cultured in Vienna, the privileged and learned in Cambridge, the uneducated poor in rural Austria, or the fishermen on the west coast of Ireland, he lived as an *outsider*. Philosophically he was most prolific when he lived entirely alone in Norway.

In considering Wittgenstein's relation to what is often called the 'philosophical community' (a phrase all too often used as a euphemism for the Philosophy sub-faculty at Oxford), two aspects of twentieth century civilisation stand out as being particularly relevant: its dominance by science and its increasingly professional nature. Wittgenstein abhorred both. His detestation of popular works of science was based on his conviction that they served as propaganda for the idol-worship of science and scientists. He was, he told a lecture class, making propaganda for an opposing style of thinking: "I am honestly disgusted with the other...I'm saying: 'For God's sake don't do this'."

The idea that philosophy could seriously be pursued as a profession, a career, similarly disgusted him. He stayed away from academic conferences, refused to write articles for academic journals, and urged his students not to

become academic philosophers. Of his later work, *Philosophical Investigations*, he wrote: "May it soon - this is what I wish for it - be completely forgotten by the philosophical journalists, and so be preserved for a better sort of reader".

It is particularly unfortunate, then, that when one sees a chapter in a book about him entitled 'Wittgenstein's Influence', one knows in advance it will concern itself exclusively with the impact he has had on academic philosophy. In researching my book, I became increasingly aware that there is a large and important part of his influence that is not, indeed could not be, reflected in the large body of academic literature his work has inspired. Drury, for example, was influenced by Wittgenstein to seek a career in medicine. Another friend I talked to was persuaded by Wittgenstein to leave Cambridge to join Woolworth's (he now works as a gardener), another became a nurse, yet another worked as an accountant. All felt themselves to be deeply influenced by Wittgenstein. Some of them showed me large collections of letters from Wittgenstein which reveal the interest he showed in their lives and his determination to have an *ethical* influence upon them.

Wittgenstein had an extraordinarily compelling and charismatic personality, and it is indeed appropriate to talk of his 'disciples'. But the lines of apostolic succession reach far beyond the academy. In fact it was precisely about those of his students who became professional philosophers that he felt most ambivalent. "The only seed I am likely to sow," he said, "is a certain jargon."

When one studies Wittgenstein's work as it has been assimilated into contemporary philosophy, one misses what he himself regarded as its most fundamental aspect: the spirit which informs it. Similarly, if one reads nothing but his correspondence, his private conversations, memoirs of him and accounts of his life, one leaves out the very thing which provided the central point of that life: his philosophical work. What I have tried to do is describe the one in terms of the other; to, so to speak, put the life back into his philosophy.

Ray Monk's biography of Wittgenstein, due to be published by Cape at the end of 1989, will be the first full-length biography of the philosopher to appear in English.

PHILOSOPHY

Reference & Introductions

BULLOCK, A. & STALLYBRASS, O. (EDS)
Fontana Dictionary of Modern Thought
[Q1] Fontana pbk **£9.95**
Fontana Dictionary of Modern Thinkers
A wide-ranging guide to 20th century thought in general. Contains admirably succinct entries on most contemporary philosophers.
[Q2] Fontana pbk **£5.95**

CAVELL, STANLEY
Must We Mean What We Say?
Famous studies on various topics, from aesthetics to Wittgenstein.
[Q3] Cambridge pbk **£11.95**

COLLINSON, DIANE
Fifty Major Philosophers: A Reference Guide
Ranging from Plato to Wittgenstein, the thinkers treated here include Aristotle, medieval philosophers and modern philosophers from Descartes to the contemporary continental schools.
[Q4] Routledge hbk **£22.50**

EDWARDS, P. (ED)
The Encyclopaedia of Philosophy (4 vols)
This is the most substantial reference work available. Most of the articles, by leading contemporary philosophers, are an ideal introduction to the serious study of any part of philosophy.
[Q5] Macmillan hbk **£275.00**

EMMET, E.R.
Learning to Philosophise
[Q6] Penguin pbk **£3.95**

EWING, A.C.
Fundamental Questions of Philosophy
[Q7] Routledge pbk **£5.25**

FLEW, ANTONY (ED)
A Dictionary of Philosophy
Probably the best single-volume dictionary available. Written by a distinguished list of contributors, it provides succinct, clear definitions of the special terms used in philosophical discourse and has extended entries on the most important philosophers.
[Q8] Macmillan hbk **£25.00**
[Q9] Pan pbk **£4.99**

HOLLIS, MARTIN
Invitation to Philosophy
One of the best brief introductions to contemporary philosophy, couched in plain language and assuming little previous acqaintance with the subject.
[Q10] Blackwell pbk **£4.95**

HOSPERS, JOHN
An Introduction to Philosophical Analysis
[Q11] Routledge pbk **£8.50**

KORNER, S.
Fundamental Questions of Philosophy: One Philosopher's Answers
[Q12] Harvester pbk **£9.95**

LACEY, ALAN R.
A Dictionary of Philosophy
Contains entries on most of the topics and concepts central to analytical philosophy.
[Q13] Routledge pbk **£5.95**
Modern Philosophy
A very thorough introduction. It contains a topic by topic account followed by a short historical survey.
[Q14] Routledge pbk **£5.25**

MACINTYRE, ALASDAIR
Against the Self-Images of the Age
A collection of essays on a variety of topics that demonstrate the lucidity and originality that have made MacIntyre one of the most respected philosophers of our time.
[Q15] Duckworth pbk **£9.95**

MAGEE, BRYAN
Great Philosophers
Based on Magee's most recent television series, this adopts a historical approach to the subject. Each chapter has Magee talking to a contemporary philosopher about an important figure from the past: Bernard Williams on Descartes, John Passmore on Hume, John Searle on Wittgenstein, etc.
[Q16] Oxford pbk **£5.95**
Men of Ideas: Some Creators of Contemporary Philosophy
[Q17] Oxford pbk **£5.95**
Modern British Philosophy
Originating as a radio series, this presents a collection of dialogues on the state of British philosophy between Magee and prominent writers in the field such as Karl Popper and A.J. Ayer.
[Q18] Oxford pbk **£5.95**

MITCHELL, S. & ROSEN, M.
The Need for Interpretations: Contemporary Conceptions of the Philosopher's Task
[Q19] Athlone P pbk **£10.95**

NAGEL, THOMAS
What Does It All Mean?
Written in vivid, accessible prose, this provides an introduction to some of the central problems of philosophy: What really exists? Can we know anything? Is anything really right or wrong? Does life have any meaning? In short: What does it all mean?
[Q20] Oxford hbk **£8.95**

NEEDLEMAN, J.
The Heart of Philosophy
[Q21] Routledge pbk **£5.95**

NOZICK, ROBERT
Philosophical Explanations
Not an introductory book, but one which, unusually, deals with the entire range of philosophical problems and (even more unusually) offers convincing solutions to many of them.
[Q22] Oxford pbk **£11.50**

O'HEAR, A.
What Philosophy Is
[Q23] Penguin pbk **£5.95**

PINCHIN, CALVIN LEWIS
Issues in Philosophy
Written specifically for the new 'A' level courses in philosophy, this introduces some of the main problems in the subject through a critical examination of the works of major philosophers past and present.
[Q24] Macmillan pbk **£6.95**

RUSSELL, BERTRAND
Problems of Philosophy
First published in 1912, this is one of the classic

introductions to the subjects of philosophical analysis.
[Q25] Oxford pbk **£2.95**

WILSON, JOHN
What Philosophy Can Do
An attempt to counteract the impression that is often formed of the sterility of contemporary Anglo-Saxon philosophy by demonstrating the practical force that its analytical techniques can have when applied to political and ethical questions.
[Q26] Macmillan pbk **£8.95**

History of Philosophy

ALLEN, REGINALD E.
Greek Philosophy: Thales to Aristotle
A popular chronological introduction to the Presocratics, Plato and Aristotle.
[Q27] Macmillan pbk **£9.95**

AYER, A.J.
Philosophy in the Twentieth Century
Reliable survey in transparent prose of various movements in modern philosophy, intended as a continuation of Bertrand Russell's famous *History of Western Philosophy*.
[Q28] Unwin pbk **£4.95**

BERLIN, ISAIAH
Against the Current: Essays in the History of Ideas
[Q29] Oxford pbk **£4.95**
Russian Thinkers
[Q30] Penguin pbk **£4.95**
The Age of Enlightenment: The Eighteenth Century Philosophers
(Ed. Berlin, Isaiah)
[Q31] Oxford pbk **£3.95**
Vico and Herder: Two Studies in the History of Ideas
[Q32] Chatto pbk **£4.95**

COPLESTON, F.C.
Copleston is a prolific philosopher and historian of philosophy who has won particular acclaim for his studies of Schopenhauer and Nietzsche.
Philosophies and Cultures
Essays on the nature of the history of philosophy and on its relationship to philosophy itself.
[Q33] Oxford hbk **£8.50**
The History of Philosophy: Vol 1: Greece & Rome
[Q34] Search hbk **£12.50**
Vol 2: Augustine to Scotus
[Q35] Search hbk **£12.50**
Vol 3: Ockham to Suarez
[Q36] Search hbk **£12.50**
Vol 4: Descartes to Leibniz
[Q37] Search hbk **£12.50**
Vol 5: Hobbes to Hume
[Q38] Search hbk **£12.50**
Vol 6: Wolff to Kant
[Q39] Search hbk **£12.50**
Vol 7: Fichte to Nietzsche
[Q40] Search hbk **£12.50**
Vol 8: Bentham to Russell
[Q41] Search hbk **£12.50**
Vol 9: Maine de Biran to Sartre
[Q42] Search hbk **£12.50**

COTTINGHAM, JOHN
The Rationalists
A study of 17th century philosophy, focusing on the main figures - Descartes, Spinoza and Leibniz.
[Q43] Oxford pbk **£5.95**

GUTHRIE, W.K.C.
A History of Greek Philosophy
**Vol 1: The Early Pre-Socratics &
Pythagoreans**
The standard text on Ancient Greek Philosophy.
[Q44] Cambridge pbk **£15.00**
**Vol 2: The Pre-Socratic Tradition:
Parmenides to Democritus**
[Q45] Cambridge pbk **£15.00**
**Vol 3: The Fifth Century Enlightenment
Pt 1: The Sophists**
[Q46] Cambridge pbk **£9.50**
Pt 2: Socrates
[Q47] Cambridge pbk **£11.95**
Vol 4: Plato: The Man and his Dialogues
[Q48] Cambridge pbk **£15.00**
Vol 5: The Later Plato & The Academy
[Q49] Cambridge pbk **£15.00**

HAMLYN, DAVID WALTER
A History of Western Philosophy
The first new history to be written for several years.
[Q50] Penguin pbk **£4.95**

HONDERICH, T. (ED)
Philosophy Through its Past
Various contemporary British and American
philosophers on aspects of the work of famous
philosophers of the past. Demonstrates how the
history of philosophy can invigorate present
philosophical debates.
[Q51] Penguin pbk **£6.95**

KENNY, ANTHONY
**The Heritage of Wisdom: Essays on the
History of Philosophy**
[Q52] Blackwell hbk **£22.50**

KENNY, ANTHONY (ED)
Rationalism, Empiricism and Idealism
British Academy lectures on the History of
Philosophy.
[Q53] Oxford pbk **£9.95**

O'CONNER, D.J.
**A Critical History of Western
Philosophy**
[Q54] Macmillan pbk **£11.95**

PASSMORE, J.
Hundred Years of Philosophy
A very thorough history of late 19th century and 20th
century philosophy, concentrating particularly on the
areas of epistemology, logic, philosophy of language
and philosophy of science.
[Q55] Penguin pbk **£6.95**
Some Recent Philosophers
A continuation of the above including discussion of
Davidson and Kripke.
[Q56] Duckworth hbk **£12.50**

RIST, J.M.
Stoic Philosophy
[Q57] Cambridge pbk **£10.95**

RUSSELL, BERTRAND
A History of Western Philosophy
Still the most widely-read history of philosophy, this
is unique in the literature in providing, not only
summaries of the ideas of the major philosophers of
the past, but also essays on the social and economic
backgrounds to their thought.
[Q58] Unwin Hyman pbk **£7.95**

SCRUTON, ROGER
**A Short History of Modern Philosophy:
From Descartes to Wittgenstein**
[Q59] Routledge pbk **£3.95**

SORABJI, RICHARD
**Matter, Space and Motion: Theories in
Antiquity and their Sequel**
A companion to *Time, Creation & the Continuum*.
Sorabji explores the views of Aristotle and his
predecessors as they were adapted by Stoics,
Christians and Neoplatonists and filtered through to
modern times.
[Q60] Duckworth **£35.00**
Time, Creation & the Continuum
An enquiry into ancient Greek physics and
metaphysics and their influence on later thought.
[Q61] Duckworth pbk **£12.50**

WALLIS, R.T.
Neoplatonism
A conspectus of the whole neoplatonic movement
with particularly detailed studies of Plotinus and
Porphyry.
[Q62] Duckworth pbk **£9.95**

WEDBERG, ANDERS
**A History of Philosophy:
Vol 1: Antiquity and the Middle
Ages**
An analytical history that gives emphasis to the
intellectual problems and the theories of the great
philosophers, rather than to their personalities and
historical circumstances.
[Q63] Oxford pbk **£7.50**
Vol 2: The Modern Age to Romanticism
[Q64] Oxford pbk **£6.50**
Vol 3: From Bolzano to Wittgenstein
[Q65] Oxford pbk **£8.95**

WOODHOUSE, R.S.
The Empiricists
[Q66] Oxford pbk **£4.95**

Ancient & Medieval Philosophers

(Arranged in chronological order)

BARNES, JONATHAN (ED)
Early Greek Philosophy   **NEW**
An accessible introduction to the work of the
Presocratics that contains translations of the primary
sources together with commentary on particular texts
and a general introduction.
[Q67] Penguin pbk **£4.95**

KIRK, G.S.; RAVEN, J.E. & SCHOFIELD, M.
The Presocratic Philosophers
An indispensable source book for the study of the
Presocratics. It contains all the known fragments,
together with detailed commentary and an exhaustive
list of sources.
[Q68] Cambridge pbk **£15.00**

HERACLITUS (d.c. 480 BC)
The oracular pronouncements of Heraclitus -
preserved in *The Fragments* - were proverbial, even
in ancient times, for their obscurity. They espouse a
mystical view expressed in a series of now familiar
metaphors ('The sun is new each day', etc) for the
continuous flux of existence.
KAHN, CHARLES (ED)
The Art and Thought of Heraclitus
A new arrangement and translation of *The
Fragments* with literary and philosophical
commentary.
[Q69] Cambridge pbk **£12.50**

PARMENIDES (b.c. 510 BC)
More of Parmenides' work survives than that of any
other Presocratic. His metaphysical view of the
indivisibility of reality is preserved in his poem, the
'Way of Truth', and in Plato's account in the dialogue,
Parmenides.
**Parmenides' 'Way of Truth' and Plato's
'Parmenides'**
[Q70] Routledge pbk **£16.95**

SOCRATES (c. 469 - 399 BC)
Though he wrote nothing, Socrates must, primarily
through his influence on Plato, be counted the first
great philosopher of the Western tradition. In Plato's
early dialogues one can see something of the 'Socratic
method' of philosophical enquiry. Conficting portraits
of his personality are drawn in Xenophon's respectful
memoir (the *Memorabilia*) and Aristophanes'
irreverent caricature in *The Clouds* (see *Drama*).
SANTAS, GERASINIOS XENOPHON
Socrates
A detailed study of Socrates's philosophy as it
appears in Plato's early dialogues.
[Q71] Routledge pbk **£9.95**
STONE, I.F.
The Trial of Socrates
A historical re-examination of the circumstances
surrounding the life and trial of Socrates, written by a
renowned American journalist.
[Q72] Picador pbk **£5.95**

PLATO (c. 428 - 348)
Plato's influence is universal; it extends throughout
Western philosophy from his pupil, Aristotle, to the
present day. His dialogues are equally works of
literature and philosophy. They are customarily
grouped in three periods: early, middle and late. The
early dialogues are concerned primarily with
presenting the personality and the philosophic style of
his teacher, Socrates. In the middle period (which
reaches its peak with the *Republic*) Socrates appears
as a mouthpiece for Plato's own doctrines. In the later
dialogues, chief among which are *Theaetetus* and
Parmenides, these doctrines are subjected to a
rigorous and sophisticated analysis.
Early Socratic Dialogues
An invaluable collection which contains most of the
well known early dialogues.
[Q73] Penguin pbk **£5.95**
Gorgias
A dialogue from Plato's middle period which contains
a famous discussion between Socrates and Callicles, a
young Athenian who brashly maintains that might is
right.
[Q74] Penguin pbk **£2.95**
Laws
[Q75] Penguin pbk **£4.50**
Phaedrus and Letters 7 & 8
[Q76] Penguin pbk **£3.95**
Philebus
One of the best known of Plato's late dialogues, this
comprises an examination of how human beings
ought to live: What characterizes the 'good life'?
[Q77] Penguin pbk **£3.50**
Protagoras/Meno
The *Protagoras* presents a debate on whether virtue
can be taught. The *Meno* contains the first distinctly
Platonic doctrines, most notably the first expression
of the theory that knowledge is recollection.
[Q78] Penguin pbk **£2.50**
Theaetetus
[Q79] Penguin pbk **£4.95**
The Last Days of Socrates
A series of early dialogues - *Euthyphro*, *Apology*,
Crito and *Phaedo* - which together present Plato's
admiring picture of Socrates's conduct during his
trial.
[Q80] Penguin pbk **£2.95**

The Portable Plato

This contains the famous Benjamin Jowett translations of *Protagoras*, *Symposium*, *Phaedo* and *The Republic*.
[Q81] Penguin pbk **£5.95**

The Republic

Possibly the best known of all Platonic dialogues, this presents the fullest account of Plato's 'Theory of Forms' in the context of his prescriptions for a just state.
[Q82] Penguin pbk **£3.95**

The Symposium

A debate about love in which both Socrates and Aristophanes make memorable speeches, this is the most poetic of Plato's dialogues and a delight to read.
[Q83] Penguin pbk **£2.50**

Theaetetus

The dialogue in which Plato's concerns most closely correspond to those of contemporary philosophers, the *Theaetetus* investigates the nature of perception and knowledge.
[Q84] Oxford pbk **£12.50**

Timaeus and Critias

The cosmology of the *Timaeus*, being reconcilable with Christian doctrine concerning the Creation, was particularly influential during the Middle Ages and was, until the Renaissance revival of Plato, one of the few Platonic works that were widely known.
[Q85] Penguin pbk **£2.95**
ANNAS J.

An Introduction to Plato's Republic

[Q86] Oxford pbk **£7.95**
CROSS, R.C. & WOOZLEY, A.D.

Plato's Republic: A Philosophical Commentary

An outstandingly clear exposition of the central arguments of *The Republic*.
[Q87] Macmillan pbk **£7.95**
GOSLING, J.C.B.

Plato

[Q88] Routledge pbk **£7.95**
GRISWOLD, CHARLES (ED)

Platonic Writings/Platonic Readings

A collection of essays which focus on two main themes: the general problem of interpreting a Platonic dialogue and Plato's reasons for presenting his thought in that form.
[Q89] Routledge pbk **£9.95**
HARE, R.M.

Plato

Possibly the best short survey for the general reader.
[Q90] Oxford pbk **£2.95**
IRWIN, TERRENCE

Plato's Moral Theory: The Early and Middle Dialogues

[Q91] Oxford pbk **£10.95**
MELLING D.J.

Understanding Plato

[Q92] Oxford pbk **£4.95**
ROSEN, STANLEY

Plato's Sophist: The Drama of Original and Image

[Q93] Yale pbk **£10.95**

Plato's Symposium

[Q94] Yale pbk **£16.95**
STRAUSS, LEO

Studies in Platonic Political Philosophy

The best known, and most highly acclaimed study of Plato as a political theorist.
[Q95] Chicago pbk **£7.25**

ARISTOTLE (384 - 322 BC)

A pupil of Plato, Aristotle is, perhaps second only to his master, one of the most influential of all Western philosophers. Throughout the medieval period he was the supreme authority in all fields of intellectual endeavour. His science was superseded by the discoveries of Copernicus and Galileo, and his authority in logic - after a reign of over two thousand years - was finally challenged by the growth of Fregean mathematical logic in the twentieth century. Today, his continued importance as a philosopher rests chiefly on his *Metaphysics* and his *Ethics*.

A New Aristotle Reader

A comprehensive selection of texts, which includes all the passages most frequently discussed in the secondary literature.
[Q96] Oxford pbk **£12.50**

Aristotle on His Predecessors

[Q97] Open Court pbk **£4.95**

Athenian Constitution

The only fragment to survive of a survey carried out by Aristotle's students of the constitutions of the various Greek city states.
[Q98] Penguin pbk **£3.95**

Classical Literary Criticism

Contains translations, with Aristotle's *Poetics*, of Horace's *Ars Poetica* & Longinus' *On the Sublime*.
[Q99] Penguin pbk **£2.95**

De Anima (On the Soul)

[Q100] Penguin pbk **£3.95**

Ethics

[Q101] Penguin pbk **£3.99**

Eudemian Ethics: Books 1, 2 & 8

[Q102] Oxford pbk **£12.50**

Metaphysics Books M & N

[Q103] Oxford pbk **£12.50**

Nichomachean Ethics

[Q104] Oxford pbk **£2.95**

On Memory

A new translation by Richard Sorabji of *De Memoria* with extensive introductory material, summaries and commentary.
[Q105] Duckworth pbk **£5.95**

Poetics

[Q106] Oxford pbk **£12.50**

Politics

Politics contains Aristotle's criticisms of Plato's *Republic* and gives his own views on democracy, the state and the responsibilities of the citizen.
[Q107] Penguin pbk **£4.50**

Posterior Analytics

This contains Aristotle's theory of logic, and, as such, was for centuries considered one of his most important works.
[Q108] Oxford pbk **£12.50**

The Art of Poetry

[Q109] Oxford pbk **£3.95**
ACKRILL, J.L.

Aristotle the Philosopher

[Q110] Oxford pbk **£5.95**
BARNES, JONATHAN

Aristotle

A recommended introduction that manages to be clear and concise while avoiding superficiality.
[Q111] Oxford pbk **£2.95**
CHARLES, DAVID

Aristotle's Theory of Action

[Q112] Duckworth hbk **£12.95**
FORTENBAUGH, W.W.

Aristotle on Emotion

[Q113] Duckworth **£5.95**
GRAYEFF, FELIX

Aristotle and His School

On the basis of new investigations, Grayeff challenges the traditional view that Aristotle was the sole author of most of the treatises that go under his name.
[Q114] Duckworth **£8.95**
HARDIE, W.F.

Aristotle's Ethical Theory

[Q115] Oxford pbk **£17.50**
KENNY, ANTHONY

Aristotle's Theory of the Will

An account of Aristotle on free will which stresses the superiority of the *Eudemian* (over the *Nichomachean*) *Ethics*.
[Q116] Duckworth pbk **£9.95**

Aristotle (Picture: The British Museum)

LEAR, JONATHAN

Aristotle: The Desire to Understand

[Q117] Cambridge pbk **£8.95**
LLOYD, GEOFFREY E.R.

Aristotle: The Growth and Structure of his Thought

[Q118] Cambridge pbk **£9.95**
SORABJI, RICHARD

Necessity, Cause & Blame: Aristotle's Theory

[Q119] Duckworth pbk **£12.95**
URMSON, J.O.

Aristotle on Ethics

[Q120] Blackwell pbk **£6.95**

LUCRETIUS (99 - 55 BC)

On the Nature of the Universe

The best-known work of the Epicurean School of philosophy that flourished in the post-Aristotelian period. In six books it gives a complete exposition of the metaphysical materialism that characterizses Epicureanism.
[Q121] Penguin pbk **£2.95**

SENECA, LUCIUS ANNAEUS

(4 BC - 64 AD)

Letters from a Stoic

Seneca's letters - together with the *Meditations* of Marcus Aurelius - are the classic texts of Stoicism, the austere ethical creed that dominated Roman philosophy during the first and second centuries AD.
[Q122] Penguin pbk **£3.95**

MARCUS AURELIUS (121 - 180 AD)

Meditations

[Q123] Penguin pbk **£2.95**

PLOTINUS (205 - 270)

Plotinus is widely regarded as the founder of Neoplatonism, a mystical doctrine (influential during the Renaissance) based on the supposition of a hierarchy of increasingly perfect realities, culminating in 'The One'.

The Essential Plotinus

[Q124] Hackett pbk **£3.50**
RIST, J.M.

Plotinus: The Road to Reality

[Q125] Cambridge pbk **£10.95**

Boethius (Picture: The British Museum)

AUGUSTINE OF HIPPO, ST (354 - 430)
St Augustine is without doubt the most important Christian philosopher of the early medieval period. He was a North African convert to Christianity whose work exercised an enormous influence both on later medieval thought and on the theological doctrines of the Reformation.
City of God
A monumental work which succeeded in articulating and establishing a comprehensive vision of Christianity at a time when the Church was being undermined by rival pagan groups.
[Q126] Penguin pbk **£8.95**
Confessions
A classic of philosophy and introspective autobiography, which recounts Augustine's conversion to Christianity via Neoplatonism.
[Q127] Penguin pbk **£4.95**

BOETHIUS (c. 475 - 524)
Boethius was a Roman philosopher whose translations ensured the dissemination of many of Aristotle's works, most notably, his logic. His own *Consolation of Philosophy* was one of the most widely read philosophical works of the Middle Ages. Written while Boethius was in prison awaiting execution, it presents a poetic declaration of the insecurity of everything save virtue.
Consolation of Philosophy
[Q128] Penguin pbk **£3.95**

AQUINAS, ST THOMAS (1225 - 1274)
Aquinas is regarded as the most important scholastic theologian of the Middle Ages, and he remains to this day the standard authority in the Roman Catholic Church. His major philosophical achievement was to provide a systematic reconciliation of Greek (chiefly Aristotelian) philosophy with Christian dogma.
Aquinas on Politics & Ethics
[Q129] Norton pbk **£5.95**
The Philosophy of Thomas Aquinas: Introductory Readings
Aimed specifically at those who feel daunted by the sheer size of Aquinas's major works, this provides extracts from his work which illustrate the central themes of his philosophy.
[Q130] Routledge pbk **£9.95**
COPLESTON, F.C.
Aquinas
A sympathetic guide to the complexities of Aquinas's thought.
[Q131] Penguin pbk **£4.95**

KENNY, ANTHONY
Aquinas
A brief and exceptionally lucid introduction.
[Q132] Oxford pbk **£3.95**

Modern Philosophers

(Arranged in chronological order)

BACON, FRANCIS (1561 - 1626)
A major figure of the English Renaissance, Bacon is known as an essayist, historian, politician and propagandist for science. In his insistence on the value of observation in science, he could be regarded as the grandfather of British empiricism.
Essays
[Q134] Penguin pbk **£4.50**
The Advancement of Learning
[Q135] Dent pbk **£3.50**
QUINTON, ANTHONY
Francis Bacon
In keeping with the other books in the *Past Masters* series, this presents a general overview of Bacon's thought for those coming to him for the first time.
[Q136] Oxford pbk **£1.95**

HOBBES, THOMAS (1588 - 1671)
The importance of Hobbes's seminal work, the *Leviathan*, rests primarily on its attempt to establish the study of politics as a scientific enquiry analogous to astronomy or biology. It is of more general philosophical interest, however, because of its classic formulation of metaphysical materialism, the view that everything in the universe is corporeal.
Leviathan
[Q137] Penguin pbk **£4.95**
SORELL, TOM
Hobbes
A detailed and sympathetic study.
[Q138] Routledge hbk **£18.95**

DESCARTES, RENE (1596 - 1650)
More than any other philosopher, Descartes has determined the development of modern philosophy, and is often regarded as the first great modern philosopher. Rejecting all beliefs that were subject to doubt, he endeavoured to rebuild knowledge on the foundation provided by the apparent certainty of his most famous inference: *"I think, therefore I am"*.
Discourse on Method & Other Writings
Originally published as an introduction to a series of essays on scientific topics (including, most famously, the *Geometry*), this has since become Descartes's best known work.
[Q139] Penguin pbk **£2.95**

Francis Bacon (Picture: The British Museum)

Geometry
[Q140] Dover pbk **£4.80**
Meditations on First Philosophy
With selections from *Objections and Replies*.
[Q141] Cambridge pbk **£4.95**
Philosophical Writings of Descartes Vol 1
A completely new translation of Descartes's philosophical works. Intended to replace the translation of Haldane and Ross, it contains all the works included in the earlier edition, together with a number of additional texts, including some of Descartes's scientific writings.
[Q142] Cambridge pbk **£10.95**
Vol 2
[Q143] Cambridge pbk **£10.95**
Selected Philosophical Writings of Descartes `NEW`
Based on the new edition of Descartes's philosophical works listed above, this selection contains the most important and widely studied of those works, including the *Discourse on Method* and *Meditations*.
[Q144] Oxford pbk **£7.95**
COTTINGHAM, JOHN
Descartes
A detailed study (and partial defence) of Descartes's rationalism.
[Q145] Blackwell pbk **£8.50**
KATZ, J.J.
Cogitations
Reflections on Descartes's *cogito* in relation to contemporary philosophy of language.
[Q146] Oxford pbk **£9.95**
SORELL, TOM
Descartes
A brief introduction for the beginner.
[Q147] Oxford pbk **£2.95**
WILLIAMS, BERNARD
Descartes: The Project of Pure Enquiry
[Q148] Penguin pbk **£3.95**

PASCAL, BLAISE (1632 - 1677)
Regarded in his lifetime as one of the greatest mathematicians of his day, Pascal is now better known for the works of theology and apologetics he wrote towards the end of his life (listed below), after a religious revelation had convinced him that *"the heart has reasons of which reason is ignorant"*.
Pensées
[Q149] Penguin pbk **£4.99**
Provincial Letters
[Q150] Penguin pbk **£4.99**

SPINOZA, BENEDICT (1632 - 1677)
Of Spinoza's two great works of philosophy, the *Tractatus Theologico-Politicus* was published anonymously and the *Ethics* posthumously. Both challenged prevailing orthodoxies; the *Tractatus* by defending the principle of secular, constitutional government, and the *Ethics* by propounding a pantheism that was considered to be inimical to religious faith. Recognition of their greatness came later and has persisted to this day.
Ethics & On the Improvement of the Understanding & Correspondence
[Q151] Dover pbk **£5.55**
Tractatus Theologico-Politicus
[Q152] Dover pbk **£5.55**
BENNETT, JONATHAN
A Study of Spinoza's 'Ethics'
[Q153] Cambridge pbk **£11.95**
SCRUTON, ROGER
Spinoza
An accessibly-written, brief introduction to the whole of Spinoza's thought.
[Q154] Oxford pbk **£2.95**

LOCKE, JOHN (1632 - 1704)

Locke is possibly the most influential of all English philosophers. His two chief works, *An Essay Concerning Human Understanding* and *Two Treatises of Government*, have laid the foundations for the traditions of, respectively, British empiricism and liberal democracy.

A Locke Reader
Extracts from Locke's most important works, together with commentary and a general introduction.
[Q155] Cambridge pbk **£9.95**

An Essay Concerning Human Understanding (Ed. Nidditch, Peter H.)
This is the standard student edition of the *Essay*; scrupulously edited and abundantly supplied with explanatory material.
[Q156] Oxford pbk **£12.50**

Two Treatises of Government
(Ed. Laslett, Peter)
A newly revised version of Peter Laslett's definitive edition.
[Q157] Cambridge pbk **£4.95**

DUNN, J.
Locke
A short introduction aimed at the general reader.
[Q158] Oxford pbk **£2.95**

MACKIE, J.L.
Problems from Locke
One of the most widely-used secondary texts on Locke.
[Q159] Oxford pbk **£8.95**

LEIBNIZ, GOTTFRIED W. VON
(1646 - 1716)

Though he wrote on a wide variety of subjects, it is chiefly for his logic and metaphysics that Leibniz is studied today. His metaphysics - outlined in *New Essays on Human Understanding* and *Monadology* - centres on the notoriously obscure notion of 'windowless monads', supposed by Leibniz to be the irreducible substances of which the world is composed. This metaphysic is in turn based on the theories expounded in the writings on logic, a selection of which is offered in *Philosophical Writings*.

Discourse on Metaphysics & Monadology
[Q160] Open Court pbk **£5.25**

New Essays on Human Understanding
(Complete)
[Q161] Cambridge pbk **£17.50**

New Essays on Human Understanding
(Abridged)
[Q162] Cambridge pbk **£7.95**

Philosophical Writings
[Q163] Dent pbk **£3.50**

BROWN, STUART
Leibniz
A comprehensive introduction.
[Q164] Harvester pbk **£19.50**

ROSS, G. MACDONALD
Leibniz
A short, introductory overview.
[Q165] Oxford pbk **£2.95**

WOOLHOUSE, R.S. (ED)
Leibniz: Metaphysics and Philosophy of Science
A collection of recent essays by distinguished academic philosophers.
[Q166] Oxford pbk **£5.95**

BERKELEY, GEORGE (1685 - 1753)

One of the great British empiricists, Berkeley is most famous for putting forward an extreme form of subjective idealism according to which nothing exists except in the minds of men and God. It is a view he advances in *The Principles of Human Knowledge* and defends against criticism in the *Three Dialogues*.

Philosophical Works
A collection of Berkeley's early works, including, most notably, *An Essay towards a New Theory of Vision*.
[Q167] Dent pbk **£4.50**

The Principles of Human Knowledge & Three Dialogues between Hylas and Philonous
[Q168] Penguin pbk **£4.95**

DANCY, JONATHAN
Berkeley: An Introduction
A sympathetic interpretation of Berkeley's idealism that defends it at least to the extent of accepting that realism is mistaken.
[Q169] Blackwell pbk **£6.50**

URMSON, J.O.
Berkeley
A brief, introductory account.
[Q170] Oxford pbk **£1.95**

HUME, DAVID (1711 - 1776)

Hume's *Treatise of Human Nature* is recognised as one of the most penetrating works of philosophical analysis ever written. Its scepticism, abhorrent to common sense yet founded on apparently inescapable logic, set the agenda for philosophical debate for the next two hundred years. Its arguments are re-stated, sometimes in a more accessible form, in Hume's other great philosophical works, the two *Enquiries*.

A Treatise of Human Nature
[Q171] Penguin pbk **£4.95**
[Q172] Oxford pbk **£6.95**

Enquiries Concerning Human Understanding & the Principles of Morals
[Q173] Oxford pbk **£6.50**

Of Miracles
[Q174] Open Court pbk **£2.50**

AYER, A.J.
Hume
A sympathetic and exceptionally well-written introduction.
[Q175] Oxford pbk **£2.95**

STROUD, BARRY
Hume
Contains an extended - and influential - discussion of Hume's analysis of induction.
[Q176] Routledge pbk **£7.95**

KANT, IMMANUEL (1724 - 1804)

Stirred from his 'dogmatic slumber' by Hume's corrosive scepticism, Kant founded his philosophy on investigations into the scope of human knowledge. His huge philosophical achievement was to combine the insights of the two opposing traditions of rationalism and empiricism into a single theory, known as 'transcendental idealism', the statement of which forms the core of his classic, *Critique of Pure Reason*.

Critique of Judgement
Otherwise known as the 'Third Critique', this contains Kant's theory of aesthetics, and is still recognized as a central text in aesthetic theory.
[Q177] Oxford pbk **£8.95**

Critique of Pure Reason
This translation by Norman Kemp Smith has long been recognized as the definitive English text.
[Q178] Macmillan pbk **£9.95**

The Moral Law (Trans. Paton, H.J.)
Kant's *Groundwork of the Metaphysics of Morals*.
[Q179] Hutchinson pbk **£4.95**

CASSIRER, E.
Kant's Life and Thought
A detailed biography that contains much philosophical exposition.
[Q180] Yale UP pbk **£14.95**

KEMP, J.
The Philosophy of Kant
[Q181] Oxford pbk **£2.50**

KORNER, S.
Kant
[Q182] Penguin pbk **£4.95**

SCRUTON, ROGER
Kant
Perhaps the most accessible, brief introduction available.
[Q183] Oxford pbk **£2.95**

WALKER, R.C.S.
Kant
One of the few recent commentaries to take Kant's metaphysics seriously.
[Q184] Routledge pbk **£8.50**

Kant on Pure Reason
A collection of recent essays by contemporary philosophers, edited by Walker.
[Q185] Oxford pbk **£6.95**

BENTHAM, JEREMY (1748 - 1832)

One of the earliest exponents of the utilitarian view of moral judgements, Bentham was interested primarily in its applications to the problems of legal theory. In his major work, *Introduction to the Principles of Morals and Legislation* he puts forward and defends the view that the morality of actions can be judged quantitatively in terms of their consequences.

Introduction to the Principles of Morals and Legislation
[Q186] Methuen pbk **£8.95**

HARRISON, ROSS
Bentham
[Q187] Routledge pbk **£8.95**

HEGEL, GEORG W.F. (1770 - 1831)

Of all the great system builders in the history of philosophy, Hegel is perhaps the greatest - or at any rate, his system is the most comprehensive, embracing as it does history, politics, morality, art and religion. The metaphysical basis of the system is laid out in *The Phenomenology of Spirit*, while its political consequences are outlined in *The Philosophy of Right*, which, partly because of its influence on Karl Marx, is probably Hegel's best-known work. The *Introduction to the Lectures on the History of Philosophy* is often recommended as a way into the whole theory.

Hegel: The Essential Writings
[Q188] Harper & R pbk **£7.95**

Introduction to the Lectures on the History of Philosophy
[Q189] Oxford pbk **£8.95**

Immanuel Kant (Picture: The British Museum)

The Phenomenology of Spirit
[Q190] Oxford pbk **£12.95**
The Philosophy of Right
[Q191] Oxford pbk **£8.95**
INWOOD, M. (ED)
Hegel
A collection of essays by contemporary philosophers.
[Q192] Oxford pbk **£6.95**
PLANT, R.
Hegel: An Introduction
One of the most acclaimed recent introductions to
Hegel's thought.
[Q193] Blackwell pbk **£7.50**
SINGER, P.
Hegel
[Q194] Oxford pbk **£2.95**
TAYLOR, C.
Hegel
A major study. Influential in the recent revival of
Hegel.
[Q195] Cambridge pbk **£15.00**

SCHOPENHAUER, ARTHUR (1788 - 1860)
Though he has always been outside the mainstream of
philosophical activity - both in Britain and in his
native Germany - Schopenhauer remains a potent
force in our culture at large. Acknowledged as one of
the great literary stylists of philosophy, his work has
exerted a powerful influence on many artists and
creative writers, most notably Joseph Conrad and
Thomas Mann. Traces of his influence are also
evident in Wittgenstein's *Tractatus Logico-
Philosophicus*.
Essays and Aphorisms
[Q196] Penguin pbk **£2.95**
**On the Fourfold Root of the Principles
of Sufficient Reason**
[Q197] Open Court pbk **£7.75**
On the Freedom of the Will
[Q198] Blackwell pbk **£6.95**
World as Will and Representation Vol 1
[Q199] Dover pbk **£8.05**
World as Will and Representation Vol 2
[Q200] Dover pbk **£8.05**
COPLESTON, F.C.
**Arthur Schopenhauer: Philosopher of
Pessimism**
[Q201] Search hbk **£8.95**
HAMLYN, D.W.
Schopenhauer
A rigorously analytical introduction.
[Q202] Routledge pbk **£6.95**
MAGEE, BRYAN
The Philosophy of Schopenhauer
More than is usual in books of this type, Magee
provides a discussion of the impact Schopenhauer has
had on the Arts, and on our culture in general.
[Q203] Oxford pbk **£9.95**

MILL, JOHN STUART (1806 - 1873)
Though in the history of philosophy, Mill is equally
important as a logician, today it is as a moral
philosopher, as the author of *On Liberty* and
Utilitarianism that he is most frequently studied. *On
Liberty* remains the definitive statement of liberal
individualism, while in *Utilitarianism* Mill refines
Bentham's 'hedonic calculus' to produce a more
sophisticated version of utilitarian theory.
On Liberty
[Q204] Penguin pbk **£2.99**
Utilitarianism and Other Essays
[Q205] Penguin pbk **£4.95**

KIERKEGAARD, SOREN (1813 - 1855)
In his emphasis on the importance of personal
experience, Kierkegaard introduced a new,
'existentialist' note into philosophical thinking. His
work is, in part, a reaction against the prevailing
Hegelianism of his day, and many of his most famous

Friedrich W. Nietzsche (Picture: The British
Museum)

books, for example, *Concluding Unscientific
Postscript* are dominated by a fierce polemic against
Hegel. Much of his other work is concerned with a
psychological investigation into the aspects of human
consciousness - anxiety, fear, uncertainty - that impel
the 'leap of faith' into religious belief.
Concluding Unscientific Postscript
[Q206] Princeton UP pbk **£7.50**
Fear and Trembling
[Q207] Penguin pbk **£3.95**
The Concept of Anxiety
[Q208] Princeton UP pbk **£5.95**
The Sickness Unto Death
[Q209] Princeton UP pbk **£5.95**
GARDINER, PATRICK
Kierkegaard
[Q210] Oxford pbk **£3.95**

NIETZSCHE, FRIEDRICH W. (1844 - 1900)
Nietzsche's writings - masterpieces of both literature
and philosophical thought - contain no systematic
attempt to solve the traditional problems of
philosophy. Rejecting the comforts of both religious
faith and philosophical theory, his work has themes
rather than dogmas. Among those themes are: the
inadequacy of utilitarian ethics, the primacy of the
human will, and the need - after the 'death of God' -
to assume for ourselves the responsibility for our
moral choices.
A Nietzsche Reader
[Q211] Penguin pbk **£3.50**
Beyond Good and Evil
[Q212] Penguin pbk **£2.95**
**Daybreak: Thoughts on the Prejudices
of Morality**
[Q213] Cambridge pbk **£6.95**
Ecce Homo
[Q214] Penguin pbk **£3.95**
Human All Too Human
[Q215] Cambridge pbk **£8.95**
Joyful Wisdom
[Q216] F Ungar pbk **£9.95**
Selected Letters
[Q217] Soho pbk **£6.95**
**The Birth of Tragedy & On the
Genealogy of Morals**
[Q218] Anchor pbk **£4.50**
The Nietzsche/Wagner Correspondence
[Q219] Liveright pbk **£9.75**

**The Will to Power: In Science, Nature,
Society and Art**
[Q220] Vintage pbk **£6.95**
Thus Spake Zarathustra
[Q221] Penguin pbk **£3.99**
Twilight of the Idols & Anti-Christ
[Q222] Penguin pbk **£2.95**
Untimely Meditations
[Q223] Cambridge pbk **£7.50**
HEIDEGGER, MARTIN
Nietzsche Vol 1: The Will to Power
[Q224] Routledge pbk **£16.95**
**Vol 2: The Eternal Recurrence of the
Same**
[Q225] Harper & R pbk **£18.95**
**Vol 3: The Will to Power as Knowledge
and as Metaphysics**
[Q226] Harper & R hbk **£18.95**
HOLLINGDALE, R.J.
Nietzsche
A sympathetic introduction that concentrates on
Nietzsche as a moral philosopher.
[Q227] Routledge pbk **£3.95**
SCHACHT, R.
Nietzsche
[Q228] Routledge pbk **£10.95**
STERN, J.P.
Nietzsche
In this short, introductory study, Stern emphasizes the
role that Nietzsche's thought has played in the history
of Europe in the 20th century.
[Q229] Fontana pbk **£2.95**

FREGE, GOTTLOB (1848 - 1925)
Frege's definition of number in terms of classes in
The Foundations of Arithmetic, though neglected for
much of his life, is now recognized as a crucially
important landmark in the development of
mathematical logic. Even more influential are his
classic essays, 'Sense and Reference' and 'Concept
and Object' in *Philosophical Writings*. These have
had an enormous impact on the development of
philosophical logic and establish Frege as the
founding father of analytical philosophy.
Philosophical Writings
[Q230] Blackwell pbk **£7.50**
The Foundations of Arithmetic
[Q231] Blackwell pbk **£7.50**
DUMMETT, MICHAEL
Frege: Philosophy of Language
Not only the most influential reading of Frege, but
also in itself a major contribution to philosophical
literature.
[Q232] Duckworth pbk **£9.95**

SANTAYANA, GEORGE (1863 - 1952)
A student of William James at Harvard, Santayana
developed further the scepticism implicit in James's
pragmatism, arguing that human reason is but an
expression of an animal compulsion to believe.
Reason in Art
[Q233] Dover pbk **£3.85**
Reason in Common Sense
[Q234] Dover pbk **£4.25**
Reason in Religion
[Q235] Dover pbk **£5.00**
Reason in Science
[Q236] Dover pbk **£6.00**
Reason in Society
[Q237] Dover pbk **£4.50**
Scepticism & Animal Faith
[Q238] Dover pbk **£5.10**
The Sense of Beauty
[Q239] Dover pbk **£3.35**

RUSSELL, BERTRAND (1872 - 1970)
The importance of Russell's more technical work -
particularly *Principles of Mathematics* and the essays
collected in *Logic and Knowledge* - in shaping the

content and method of analytical philosophy makes him arguably the greatest philosopher of the 20th century. More certainly, his popular essays have made him the most respected and best-loved philosopher among the general public.

An Inquiry into Meaning and Truth
[Q240] Unwin Hyman pbk **£3.95**

Authority and the Individual
Delivered in 1949, this was the first of the BBC's series of Reith Lectures. In them Russell discusses the question: which is more important, freedom or order?
[Q241] Unwin Hyman pbk **£3.95**

Bertrand Russell's Best
[Q242] Unwin Hyman pbk **£3.95**

Education and the Social Order
[Q243] Unwin Hyman pbk **£3.95**

In Praise of Idleness
[Q244] Unwin Hyman pbk **£3.95**

Introduction to Mathematical Philosophy
[Q245] Unwin Hyman hbk **£20.00**

Logic and Knowledge
[Q246] Unwin Hyman pbk **£9.95**

Marriage and Morals
Russell's advocacy of 'free love' and open marriages outraged religious opinion in the United States, but contributed enormously to his reputation as a philosopher with something to say on issues of general interest.
[Q247] Unwin Hyman pbk **£3.95**

Mysticism and Logic and Other Essays
Includes 'A Free Man's Worship', one of Russell's most popular essays.
[Q248] Unwin Hyman hbk **£5.95**

On Education
The first - and most radical - of Russell's statements on educational theory.
[Q249] Unwin Hyman pbk **£3.95**

Our Knowledge of the External World
[Q250] Unwin Hyman hbk **£18.95**

Philosophical Essays
[Q251] Unwin Hyman hbk **£20.00**

Political Ideals
A strident statement of Russell's political creed. Delivered as a public lecture during the First World War, and banned by the British government, it remained unpublished in the UK until the 1960s.
[Q252] Unwin Hyman pbk **£3.95**

Power: A New Social Analysis
[Q253] Unwin Hyman pbk **£3.50**

Principles of Social Reconstruction
A book which began as a co-operative venture between Russell and D.H. Lawrence (united in their opposition to the First World War), but which ended (after acrimonious dispute between the two) as a personal statement of Russell's political philosophy.
[Q254] Unwin Hyman pbk **£3.95**

Religion and Science
[Q255] Oxford pbk **£6.95**

Roads to Freedom
Written in the aftermath of the First World War, this presents a brief exploration of the various kinds of socialism and anarchism.
[Q256] Unwin Hyman pbk **£3.95**

Sceptical Essays
[Q257] Unwin Hyman pbk **£2.50**

The ABC of Relativity
A masterly popularization of Einstein's theories.
[Q258] Unwin Hyman pbk **£3.95**

The Conquest of Happiness
[Q259] Unwin Hyman pbk **£3.95**

The Impact of Science on Society
[Q260] Unwin Hyman pbk **£3.95**

The Philosophy of Leibniz
[Q261] Unwin Hyman hbk **£12.50**

The Principles of Mathematics
[Q262] Unwin Hyman hbk **£25.00**

The Problems of Philosophy
[Q263] Oxford pbk **£2.95**

Unpopular Essays
[Q264] Unwin Hyman pbk **£3.95**

Why I Am Not a Christian
[Q265] Unwin Hyman pbk **£2.95**

AYER, A.J.

Russell
An introduction from the most distinguished contemporary Russellian philosopher.
[Q266] Chicago UP pbk **£7.95**

KILMINSTER, C.W.

Russell
[Q267] Harvester pbk **£10.95**

SAINSBURY, R.M.

Russell
One of the surprisingly few recent discussions of Russell's work from an analytical perspective.
[Q268] Routledge pbk **£8.50**

WITTGENSTEIN, LUDWIG (1889 - 1951)
Though the Wittgenstein corpus is now large and intensively studied, in his lifetime he published just one, short, philosophical work, *Tractatus Logico-Philosophicus*, a formidably distilled presentation of logical atomism that ends with a mystical affirmation of the importance of the ineffable. In his later work - chief among which is *Philosophical Investigations* - the earlier theory is dismantled and replaced with a unique linguistic method for dissolving philosophical confusion - a method based on the construction of imaginary 'language-games'. The difficulty and importance of his work has inspired an enormous secondary literature.

Culture and Value
A collection of aphorisms on literature, music, religion and morality.
[Q269] Blackwell hbk **£7.95**

Last Writings on the Philosophy of Psychology Vol 1
The last manuscript of the series from which *Philosophical Investigations Part II* was compiled.
[Q270] Blackwell pbk **£29.50**

On Certainty: Uber Gewissheit
Written shortly before his death, the remarks collected here centre on an attack on Moore's 'Defence of Common Sense' and constitute one of Wittgenstein's clearest and most accessible works.
[Q271] Blackwell pbk **£7.95**

Philosophical Grammar
Written from 1931-1934, this is of interest primarily for its second part, which contains some of Wittgenstein's very finest writings on mathematics.
[Q272] Blackwell pbk **£7.95**

Philosophical Investigations
The central text of Wittgenstein's later period.
[Q273] Blackwell pbk **£9.95**

Philosophical Remarks
Written shortly after Wittgenstein's return to Cambridge in 1929, this represents a 'transitional

Ludwig Wittgenstein (Photo: Oxford University Press)

stage' between his early and later work.
[Q274] Blackwell pbk **£7.95**

Remarks on Colour
Written during the last few months of his life, this contains Wittgenstein's critical engagement with Goethe's theory of colour.
[Q275] Blackwell pbk **£6.95**

Remarks on the Foundations of Mathematics
Though widely neglected, his later work on mathematics was considered by Wittgenstein himself to be the peak of his philosophical achievement.
[Q276] Blackwell pbk **£8.95**

Remarks on the Philosophy of Psychology Vol 1
The remarks collected in these two volumes contain preliminary studies for the work that now forms part II of *Philosophical Investigations*.
[Q277] Blackwell pbk **£12.50**

Remarks on the Philosophy of Psychology Vol 2
[Q278] Blackwell pbk **£12.50**

The Blue and Brown Books
Preliminary studies for the *Philosophical Investigations*, dictated between 1933 and 1935.
[Q279] Blackwell pbk **£8.95**

Tractatus Logico-Philosophicus
(Trans C.K. Ogden)
This edition contains the first translation, together with the original German text.
[Q280] Routledge pbk **£6.95**

Tractatus Logico-Philosophicus
(Trans Pears & McGuinness)
[Q281] Routledge pbk **£5.50**
A more recent translation, considered by many to be more rigorous.

Zettel
A collection of fragments mainly written in the years 1946-48.
[Q282] Blackwell pbk **£7.50**

BAKER, G.P. & HACKER, P.M.S.

An Analytical Commentary on Wittgenstein's Philosophical Investigations
The first volume of what is generally considered to be the definitive commentary.
[Q283] Blackwell pbk **£9.50**

Meaning and Understanding: Essays on the Philosophical Investigations
[Q284] Blackwell pbk **£9.50**

CAVELL, STANLEY

The Claim of Reason: Wittgenstein, Scepticism, Morality and Tragedy
[Q285] Oxford pbk **£9.95**

GRAYLING, A.C.

Wittgenstein
A brief, critical study.
[Q286] Oxford pbk **£3.95**

HACKER, P.M.S.

Insight and Illusion: Themes in the Philosophy of Wittgenstein
A new, extensively revised edition of one of the most widely-read expositions of Wittgenstein's thought.
[Q287] Oxford pbk **£9.95**

HALLER, RUDOLF

Questions on Wittgenstein
A series of essays on Wittgenstein's relationships to his Austrian predecessors and peers.
[Q288] Routledge pbk **£7.95**

KENNY, ANTHONY

The Legacy of Wittgenstein
A collection of essays by one of the most lucid and reliable of Wittgenstein's commentators. Includes 'Wittgenstein's Conception of Philosophy', one of the best discussions of the topic available.
[Q289] Blackwell pbk **£7.95**

Wittgenstein
Perhaps the best general introduction available.
[Q290] Penguin pbk **£4.95**

KRIPKE, SAUL A.
Wittgenstein on Rules and Private Language
[Q291] Blackwell pbk **£7.95**

MALCOLM, NORMAN
Ludwig Wittgenstein: A Memoir
Published here with von Wright's *Biographical Sketch*, this provides a vivid picture of the strength and fascination of Wittgenstein's personality.
[Q292] Oxford pbk **£4.95**

MCGINN, COLIN
Wittgenstein on Meaning: An Interpretation and Evaluation
[Q293] Blackwell pbk **£7.95**

MCGUINNESS, BRIAN
Wittgenstein: A Life. 1889-1921: Young Ludwig
The first volume of the long-awaited definitive biography.
[Q294] Duckworth hbk **£15.95**

MCGUINNESS, BRIAN (ED)
Ludwig Wittgenstein and the Vienna Circle
Notes of conversations between Wittgenstein, Moritz Schlick and Friedrich Waismann that took place in Vienna between 1929 and 1932 - a critical stage in Wittgenstein's development.
[Q295] Blackwell pbk **£6.95**

Wittgenstein and His Times
Five essays by distinguished philosophers that relate Wittgenstein's work to that of his contemporaries, such as Freud, Weininger and Spengler.
[Q296] Blackwell pbk **£6.95**

MONK, R.
Wittgenstein: A Biography **NEW**
The first full-length, complete biography of Wittgenstein.
[Q297] Cape pbk **£16.95**

PEARS, DAVID
The False Prison: A Study of the Development of Wittgenstein's Philosophy Vol 1
A major study that is intended to fill the gap between short introductions and specialized discussions.
[Q298] Oxford pbk **£6.95**

Vol 2 **NEW**
[Q299] Oxford pbk **£9.95**

Wittgenstein
[Q300] Fontana pbk **£3.50**

HEIDEGGER, MARTIN (1889 - 1976)
Although Heidegger's reputation has suffered from his involvement with the Nazis, he remains one of this century's most profound philosophers. The rejection of metaphysics and the analysis of existence that form the core of his major work, *Being and Time*, have had a decisive impact on the development of contemporary continental philosophy.

Being and Time
[Q301] Blackwell pbk **£12.50**

Discourse on Thinking
[Q302] Harper & R pbk **£5.50**

Early Greek Thinking: The Dawn of Western Philosophy
[Q303] Harper & R pbk **£8.75**

Introduction to Metaphysics
[Q304] Yale UP pbk **£9.95**

On Time and Being
[Q305] Harper & R pbk **£3.75**

Question Concerning Technology and Other Essays
[Q306] Harper & R pbk **£5.75**

What is a Thing?
[Q307] America UP pbk **£7.70**

STEINER, GEORGE
Heidegger
An invaluable introduction to many of the central themes of Heidegger's difficult writings.
[Q308] Fontana pbk **£4.95**

Martin Heidegger, author of *Nietzsche Vol 1: The Will to Power* (Routledge pbk £16.95)

POPPER, KARL (1902 -)
Karl Popper is possibly the most influential living philosopher. His great work in the philosophy of science, *The Logic of Scientific Discovery*, has dominated the field since its publication in 1935. Its great achievement was to establish a new, and more tenable, criterion for science. Much of his other work is concerned to deny the possibility of a scientific study of human society.

A Pocket Popper
[Q309] Fontana pbk **£4.95**

Conjectures and Refutations
[Q310] Routledge hbk **£20.00**

Objective Knowledge: An Evolutionary Approach
[Q311] Oxford pbk **£7.95**

The Logic of Scientific Discovery
[Q312] Hutchinson pbk **£9.95**

The Open Society and Its Enemies Vol 1: The Spell of Plato
[Q313] Routledge pbk **£8.95**

The Open Society and Its Enemies Vol 2: The High Tide of Prophecy
The volume of *The Open Society* concerned with Hegel and Marx.
[Q314] Routledge pbk **£8.95**

The Poverty of Historicism
[Q315] Ark pbk **£4.95**

The Self and its Brain
Co-written with the neurobiologist, Sir John Eccles, this presents an interactionist view of the mind and the brain that denies that they are identical.
[Q316] Routledge pbk **£10.95**

Unended Quest
An intellectual autobiography that describes the evolution of Popper's thought on both philosophy and politics.
[Q317] Fontana pbk **£3.95**

MAGEE, BRYAN
Popper
A brief introduction to Popper's work on both science and politics.
[Q318] Fontana pbk **£2.95**

O'HEAR, ANTHONY
Karl Popper
A detailed and rigorous study that concentrates on Popper as a philosopher of science.
[Q319] Routledge pbk **£7.50**

Topics of Philosophy

Aesthetics

ADORNO, THEODOR
Aesthetic Theory
An important social analysis from the most gifted and versatile philosopher of the influential Frankfurt School.
[Q321] Routledge pbk **£7.95**

In Search of Wagner
[Q322] Verso pbk **£6.95**

Philosophy of Modern Music
Adorno's seminal work, written in 1948, the core of which is provided by his famous discussion of Stravinsky.
[Q323] Sheed & W pbk **£6.95**

Prisms
Includes essays on Benjamin, Bach, Proust, Kafka, Schoenberg and Jazz.
[Q324] MIT pbk **£6.95**

BARNES, ANNETTE **NEW**
On Interpretation: A Critical Analysis
Argues that works of art do have determinate meanings, even though the interpretative task is essentially open-ended.
[Q325] Blackwell pbk **£8.95**

BEARDSLEY, MONROE C.
Aesthetics from Classical Greece to the Present: A Short History
A standard introduction to the subject.
[Q326] Alabama UP pbk **£8.54**

The Aesthetic Point of View: Selected Essays
[Q327] Cornell UP pbk **£17.00**

BLOCH, ERNST, ET AL
Aesthetics and Politics
Collected here are the key texts in the Marxist controversies over literature and art involving Ernst Bloch, Georg Lukács, Bertolt Brecht, Walter Benjamin and Theodor Adorno.
[Q328] Verso pbk **£7.95**

BOURDIEU, P.
Distinction: A Social Critique of the Judgement of Taste
An examination of the strategies of pretension in present-day France. Bourdieu describes how class distinctions are preserved by attitudes to art and beauty.
[Q329] Routledge pbk **£9.95**

BURGIN, VICTOR
The End of Art Theory: Criticism and Post-Modernity
Essays examining the interdependency of advertising, film, painting and photography constituting a call for a 'new art theory'.
[Q330] Macmillan pbk **£7.95**

BURKE, EDMUND
A Philosophical Enquiry into Our Ideas of the Sublime and the Beautiful
A seminal 18th century work on aesthetic experience.
[Q331] Blackwell pbk **£9.95**

CROCE, BENEDETTO
Guide to Aesthetics
An accessible introduction to the work of the greatest

idealist philosopher of aesthetics this century.
[Q332] America UP pbk £4.35

GOODMAN, NELSON & ELGIN, CATHERINE Z.
**Reconceptions: In Philosophy
and Other Arts & Sciences** NEW
An important new statement of Goodman's
'philosophy of understanding', which is here
explained, revised and shown to illuminate painting,
music, architecture and literary theory.
[Q333] Routledge hbk £25.00

GRIFFITHS, A. PHILLIPS (ED)
Philosophy and Literature
[Q334] Cambridge pbk £10.95

HOSPERS, JOHN
Introductory Readings in Aesthetics
[Q335] Macmillan pbk £14.95

HULME, T.E.
**Speculations: Essays on Humanism
and the Philosophy of Art**
A classic work of aesthetics, first published in 1918.
Its anti-Romantic tenor had a large influence on a
whole generation of poets and literary critics.
[Q336] Routledge pbk £6.95

LANGER, SUSANNE K.
**Feeling and Form: A Theory of Art
Developed from Philosophy in a New
Key**
[Q337] Routledge hbk £19.95
**Philosophy in a New Key: A Study In
the Symbolism of Reason, Rite and Art**
Susanne Langer's theory of art as an articulation of
human emotions has had an enormous influence on
the subsequent development of aesthetics.
[Q338] Harvard UP pbk £6.25

LEWIS, PETER
The Philosophy of Art
A new book which introduces in a clear and non-
technical way the complex question of the nature of
art and its place in human culture.
[Q339] Blackwell pbk £6.95

MAQUET, JACQUES
**The Aesthetic Experience: An
Anthropologist Looks at the Visual Arts**
[Q340] Yale UP pbk £13.50

MARCUSE, HERBERT
The Aesthetic Dimension
[Q341] Macmillan pbk £3.95

MOTHERSILL, MARY
**Beauty Restored: An Essay in
Aesthetic Theory**
[Q342] Oxford pbk £12.50

OLSEN, S.H.
**The Structure of Literary
Understanding**
[Q343] Cambridge pbk £9.95

OSBORNE, H. (ED)
Aesthetics
[Q344] Oxford pbk £3.95

READ, SIR HERBERT
The Meaning of Art
Read's most famous work of aesthetics; written in
1931, it is now regarded as a standard text in the
subject.
[Q345] Faber pbk £3.95
The Philosophy of Modern Art
[Q346] Faber pbk £3.95

ROSE, MARGARET
**Marx's Lost Aesthetics: Karl Marx and
the Visual Arts**
[Q347] Cambridge pbk £9.95

SAVILE, ANTHONY
**The Test of Time: An Essay in
Philosophical Aesthetics**
[Q348] Oxford pbk £10.95

SCHILLER, J.C.F.
On the Aesthetic Education of Man
[Q349] Oxford pbk £9.95

SCRUTON, ROGER
Aesthetic Understanding
Scruton is a lucid and engaging writer whose
reputation as the 'Philosopher of the New Right' does
little to suggest the sophistication of his work on
aesthetics.
[Q350] Routledge pbk £10.95
Aesthetics of Architecture
[Q351] Routledge pbk £10.95
Art and the Imagination
[Q352] Routledge pbk £10.95

SHEPPARD, A.
**Aesthetics: An Introduction to the
Philosophy of Art**
An up-to-date introduction to aesthetics for the
general reader with particular emphasis on
literature.
[Q353] Oxford pbk £4.95

SIMPSON, DAVID (ED)
**German Aesthetic and Literary
Criticism**
Essays on Kant, Fichte, Schelling, Schopenhauer and
Hegel.
[Q354] Cambridge pbk £9.95

SPRINKLER, MICHAEL
Imaginary Relations
An attempt to extend Althusser's Marxism to the
domain of aesthetics.
[Q355] Verso pbk £9.95

WOLFF, JANET
The Social Production of Art
[Q356] Macmillan pbk £6.95

WOLLHEIM, R.
Art and its Objects
A standard work that has had much to do with the
revival of the subject.
[Q357] Cambridge pbk £7.95

Epistemology

AYER, A.J.
Central Questions of Philosophy
Among contemporary philosophers, Ayer was almost
alone in seeing epistemology as the core of the
subject, but the books listed here present a lucid and
spirited defence of his position.
[Q358] Penguin pbk £3.50
Probability and Evidence
[Q359] Macmillan pbk £5.95
**The Foundations of Empirical
Knowledge**
First published in 1940, this is Ayer's best-known
work of epistemology.
[Q360] Penguin pbk £3.95
The Problem of Knowledge
[Q361] Penguin pbk £3.95

COHEN, J.L.
**The Dialogues of Reason: An Analysis
of Analytical Philosophy**
[Q362] Oxford pbk £10.95

DANCY, JONATHAN
**An Introduction to Contemporary
Epistemology**
[Q363] Blackwell pbk £8.95
Perceptual Knowledge (Ed. Dancy, Jonathan)
Contributors include: H.P. Grice, David Lewis, P.F.
Strawson and John MacDowell.
[Q364] Oxford pbk £6.95

GRAYLING, A.C.
The Refutation of Scepticism
A defence of transcendental arguments in the tradition
of Kant and Strawson.
[Q365] Duckworth pbk £8.95

GREGORY, R.L.
**Concepts and Mechanisms of
Perception**
A collection of more than fifty essays, representing
Gregory's work since 1950.
[Q366] Duckworth hbk £14.95

GRIFFITHS, A. PHILLIPS (ED)
Knowledge and Belief
[Q367] Oxford pbk £5.95

HAMLYN, D.W.
The Theory of Knowledge
[Q368] Macmillan pbk £7.95

LYCAN, WILLIAM G.
Judgement and Justification
A new and original analysis of the difference between
justified and unjustified belief.
[Q369] Cambridge pbk £8.95

MACDONALD, G.F. (ED)
Perception and Identity
Essays presented to A.J. Ayer, together with his
replies to them.
[Q370] Macmillan pbk £7.95

MELLOR, D.H.
**The Warrant of Induction:
An Inaugural Lecture** NEW
The text of the inaugural lecture delivered by
Professor Mellor on his appointment to the Chair of
Philosophy at Cambridge, in which he attempts to
solve Hume's notorious problem of legitimating
inductive inference.
[Q371] Cambridge pbk £2.50

MOSER, P.K. & VANDERNAT, ARNOLD (EDS)
**Human Knowledge: Classical and
Contemporary Approaches**
This collection of readings combines the foremost
classical sources with important contemporary
philosophers.
[Q372] Oxford pbk £6.95

MOSER, P.K. (ED)
A Priori Knowledge
This volume collects ten of the most important recent
essays on this subject. Among the philosophers
included are C.I. Lewis, A.J. Ayer, W.V. Quine, and
S.A. Kripke.
[Q373] Oxford pbk £6.95

RORTY, RICHARD
Philosophy and the Mirror of Nature
The most important contribution to the current debate
about the status of philosophy.
[Q374] Blackwell pbk £8.50

STRAWSON, P.F.
Scepticism and Naturalism: Some Varieties
[Q375] Routledge pbk **£5.95**

STROUD, BARRY
The Significance of Philosophical Scepticism
[Q376] Oxford pbk **£8.95**

UNGER, PETER
Ignorance: A Case for Scepticism
[Q377] Oxford pbk **£9.95**

Ethics

ANSCOMBE, G.E.M.
Collected Philosophical Papers Vol 3: Ethics, Religion & Politics
A stimulating collection of essays presenting an unfashionably traditional Catholic outlook.
[Q378] Blackwell pbk **£7.50**

AYER, A.J.
Freedom and Morality and Other Essays
[Q379] Oxford pbk **£8.95**

BERLIN, ISAIAH
Four Essays on Liberty
[Q380] Oxford pbk **£5.95**

BILLINGTON, R.
Living Philosophy: An Introduction to Applied Ethics
An accessible introduction to ethics which presupposes no knowledge of philosophy. Constructing his analyses around the problems which occur in everyday life, the author stresses the link between certain elements of Western and Eastern philosophy.
[Q381] Routledge pbk **£9.95**

BLUM, L.A.
Friendship, Altruism & Morality
[Q382] Routledge pbk **£8.75**

BOK, S.
Secrets: On the Ethics of Concealment and Revelation
[Q383] Oxford pbk **£5.95**

A.J. Ayer, author of *Freedom and Morality and Other Essays* (Oxford University Press pbk £8.95)

BRANDT, R.B.
A Theory of the Good and the Right
[Q384] Oxford pbk **£10.95**

CLARK, S.
The Moral Status of Animals
[Q385] Oxford pbk **£4.95**

COLLINSON, DIANE & CAMPBELL, ROBERT
Ending Lives
A textbook that provides summaries of the controversies surrounding issues of life and death, including a detailed examination of the issues raised by suicide and euthanasia.
[Q386] Blackwell pbk **£6.95**

DWORKIN, RONALD
A Matter of Principle
[Q387] Oxford pbk **£9.95**
Taking Rights Seriously
[Q388] Duckworth pbk **£12.95**

EVANS, DAVID (ED)
Moral Philosophy and Contemporary Problems
[Q389] Cambridge pbk **£9.95**

FINNIS, J., ET AL
Nuclear Deterrence, Morality & Realism
On the basis of a detailed analysis of the realities of nuclear deterrence, the authors conclude that the deterrent is unjustifiable and examine the question of conscience that this raises for everyone.
[Q390] Oxford pbk **£12.50**

FINNIS, J.
Fundamentals of Ethics
[Q391] Oxford pbk **£7.95**

FOOT, PHILIPPA
Theories of Ethics (Ed. Foot, Philippa)
[Q392] Oxford **£5.95**
Virtues and Vices
[Q393] Blackwell pbk **£7.95**

FREY, R.G.
Rights, Killing and Suffering: Moral Vegetarianism and Applied Ethics
[Q394] Blackwell pbk **£7.95**

GAUTHIER, D.
Morals by Agreement
[Q395] Oxford pbk **£11.95**

GLOVER, JONATHAN
Causing Death and Saving Lives
[Q396] Penguin pbk **£3.95**

GOWANS, C.W.
Moral Dilemmas
Essays on a central topic in ethical theory from Kant, Mill, Bradley and Ross to recent work by Foot, Hare, Nagel, van Fraasen and others.
[Q397] Oxford pbk **£8.95**

HAMPSHIRE, STUART
Innocence and Experience   **NEW**
Hampshire's new work is a lucid examination of the conflicts between individuals and societies, and an evaluation of the validity of any concepts of justice which arise from such considerations.
[Q398] A Lane hbk **£16.95**
Private and Public Morality
[Q399] Cambridge pbk **£5.25**

HANFLING, OSWALD
Life and Meaning: A Philosophical Reader (Ed. Hanfling, Oswald)
Classic texts on questions of value, life and death,

ranging from Ecclesiastes to Parfit and Nozick.
[Q400] Blackwell pbk **£6.95**
The Value of Life
In the context of discussions of medical and practical ethics, Hanfling addresses the central (but often overlooked) question: what is the value and meaning of human life?
[Q401] Blackwell pbk **£6.95**

HARE, R.M.
Freedom and Reason
[Q402] Oxford pbk **£7.95**
Moral Thinking: Its Levels, Methods and Point
Hare's most recent major work, in which he develops not only his account of moral language, but also a normative position on moral questions themselves.
[Q403] Oxford pbk **£7.95**
The Language of Morals
First published in 1952, this has become a standard text in ethical theory. Hare argues that moral judgements are not descriptive of any reality; they are, rather, *prescriptive*.
[Q404] Oxford pbk **£7.95**

HARMAN, GILBERT
The Nature of Morality: An Introduction to Ethics
[Q405] Oxford pbk **£6.95**

HARRIS, JOHN
The Value of Life: An Introduction to Medical Ethics
[Q406] Routledge pbk **£8.50**

HUDSON, W.D.
Modern Moral Philosophy
[Q407] Macmillan pbk **£8.50**

HURSTHOUSE, ROSALIND
Beginning Lives
A textbook that seeks to clarify the complex questions surrounding the morality of abortion and to contribute to their solution.
[Q408] Blackwell pbk **£7.95**

KAMENKA, EUGENE
Marxism and Ethics
[Q409] Macmillan pbk **£3.95**

LEE, SIMON
Law and Morals: Warnock, Gillick and Beyond
[Q410] Oxford **£3.95**

LUCAS, J.R.
On Justice
[Q411] Oxford pbk **£9.95**

MACINTYRE, ALASDAIR
A Short History of Ethics
A history of moral philosophy from the Homeric Age to the 20th century.
[Q412] Routledge pbk **£6.95**
After Virtue
A seminal work of modern ethics which concludes that *"we still, in spite of the efforts of three centuries of moral philosophy and one of sociology, lack any coherent rationally defensible statement of a liberal individualist point of view"*.
[Q413] Duckworth pbk **£12.95**
Whose Justice? Which Rationality?
The long-awaited sequel to *After Virtue*.   **NEW**
[Q414] Duckworth pbk **£12.95**

MACKIE, J.L.
Ethics: Inventing Right and Wrong
A standard introduction to the whole subject.
[Q415] Penguin pbk **£3.95**

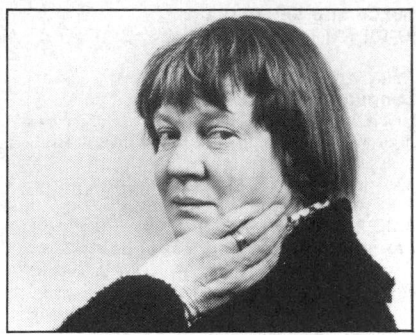

Iris Murdoch, author of *The Sovereignty of Good*
(Routledge pbk **£3.95**)

MAYO, BERNARD
The Philosophy of Right and Wrong
A clear general introduction to ethics for
undergraduates.
[Q416] Routledge pbk **£5.95**

MCNAUGHTON, DAVID A.
Moral Vision: An Introduction to Ethics
Concentrating on recent work in the subject, and in
particular the debate among contemporary
philosophers between moral realism and non-
cognitivism, McNaughton both clarifies the issues
involved and gives his own original point of view.
[Q417] Blackwell pbk **£7.95**

MIDGLEY, MARY
**Beast and Man: The Roots of Human
Nature**
Mary Midgley's work has breathed new life into
contemporary discussions of ethics.
[Q418] Routledge pbk **£7.95**
**Evolution as a Religion: Strange Hopes
and Stranger Fears**
[Q419] Routledge pbk **£5.95**
**Heart and Mind: The Varieties of Moral
Experience**
[Q420] Routledge pbk **£5.50**
Wickedness: A Philosophical Essay
[Q421] Routledge pbk **£4.95**

MOORE, G.E.
Ethics
[Q422] Oxford pbk **£2.95**
Principia Ethica
The classic text of 'ethical intuitionism'.
[Q423] Cambridge pbk **£8.95**

MURDOCH, IRIS
The Sovereignty of Good
Argues that the account of nature and value provided
by contemporary academic analytic philosophy is
inadequate.
[Q424] Routledge pbk **£3.95**

NAGEL, THOMAS
Mortal Questions
[Q425] Cambridge pbk **£7.50**

NORMAN, R.
The Moral Philosophers
An introduction to ethics, via a critical examination of
the theories of some of the major moral philosophers
of the past.
[Q426] Oxford pbk **£6.95**

PARFIT, DEREK
Reasons and Persons
One of the most important works of moral philosophy
in recent years.
[Q427] Oxford pbk **£8.95**

PASSMORE, JOHN
Man's Responsibility for Nature
[Q428] Duckworth pbk **£9.95**

PATON, W.
**Man and Mouse: Animals in Medical
Research**
A riposte to animal rights theorists.
[Q429] Oxford pbk **£2.95**

QUINTON, ANTHONY
Utilitarian Ethics
The second edition of the best short survey of
Utilitarianism, with a new preface outlining the work
on the subject written during the last decade.
[Q430] Duckworth pbk **£5.95**

RACHELS, JAMES
**The End of Life: Euthanasia and
Morality**
[Q431] Oxford pbk **£4.95**

RAPHAEL, D.D.
Moral Philosophy
[Q432] Oxford pbk **£4.95**

SANDEL, M.
Liberalism and the Limits of Justice
[Q433] Cambridge pbk **£7.95**

SCHEFFLER, S.
Consequentialism and Its Critics
(Ed. Scheffler, S.)
This volume presents papers discussing arguments on
both sides of the consequentialist debate. The
distinguished contributors include: John Rawls,
Bernard Williams, Thomas Nagel and Derek
Parfit.
[Q434] Oxford pbk **£7.95**
The Rejection of Consequentialism
[Q435] Oxford pbk **£7.95**

SCRUTON, ROGER
**Sexual Desire: A Philosophical
Investigation**
[Q436] Weidenfeld pbk **£8.95**

SEN, AMARTYA & WILLIAMS, BERNARD (EDS)
Utilitarianism and Beyond
[Q437] Cambridge pbk **£10.95**

SINGER, PETER
Applied Ethics (Ed. Singer, Peter)
[Q438] Oxford pbk **£6.95**
In Defence of Animals
(Ed. Singer, Peter)
[Q439] Blackwell pbk **£6.95**
Practical Ethics
[Q440] Cambridge pbk **£7.50**
**The Expanding Circle: Ethics and
Sociobiology**
[Q441] Oxford pbk **£4.95**

SINGER, PETER & WELLS, DEANE
**The Reproduction Revolution: New
Ways of Making Babies**
[Q442] Oxford pbk **£3.95**

SMART, J.J.C. & WILLIAMS, BERNARD
Utilitarianism: For and Against
[Q443] Cambridge pbk **£7.50**

SOREL, T.
Moral Theory and Capital Punishment
[Q444] Blackwell pbk **£6.95**

SUMNER, L.W.
The Moral Foundation of Rights
[Q445] Oxford pbk **£9.95**

TEN, C.L.
**Crime, Guilt and Punishment: A
Philosophical Introduction**
[Q446] Oxford pbk **£8.95**

TOOLEY, MICHAEL
Abortion and Infanticide
[Q447] Oxford pbk **£14.00**

WALDRON, JEREMY (ED)
Theories of Rights
[Q448] Oxford pbk **£5.95**

WARNOCK, G.J. (ED)
Contemporary Moral Philosophy
[Q449] Macmillan pbk **£3.95**

WARNOCK, MARY
**A Question of Life: The Warnock Report
on Human Fertilization and Embryology**
[Q450] Blackwell pbk **£5.95**
Ethics since 1900
[Q451] Oxford pbk **£4.50**

WHITE, A.R.
Rights
[Q452] Oxford pbk **£7.95**

WILLIAMS, BERNARD
Ethics and the Limits of Philosophy
[Q453] Fontana pbk **£3.95**
**Moral Luck: Philosophical Essays
1973 - 80**
[Q454] Cambridge pbk **£8.95**
Morality: An Introduction to Ethics
[Q455] Cambridge pbk **£5.50**
Obscenity and Film Censorship
[Q456] Cambridge pbk **£7.50**

WILSON, JOHN
A Preface to Morality
Wilson presents a Platonic view of morality that sees
it, not in terms of action and will, but as a matter of
mental health and the ability to love.
[Q457] Macmillan pbk **£7.95**

Logic

COPI, I.M.
Introduction to Logic
A standard textbook for several generations of logic
students. It covers both formal and informal
arguments, and both inductive and deductive logic.
[Q458] Macmillan pbk **£12.95**

FISHER, ALEC
The Logic of Real Arguments **NEW**
A book designed to help students (not only in
philosophy but in other subjects too) to evaluate the
arguments encountered in the course of their studies.
[Q459] Cambridge pbk **£6.95**

GRAYLING, TONY
Introduction to Philosophical Logic
[Q460] Harvester pbk **£9.95**

GUTTENPLAN, S.D.
Languages of Logic
[Q461] Blackwell pbk **£7.95**

HAACK, SUSAN
Philosophy of Logics
[Q462] Cambridge pbk **£9.95**

HODGES, W.
Logic: Introduction to Elementary Logic
[Q463] Penguin pbk **£4.95**

KNEALE, W. & KNEALE, M.
The Development of Logic
The definitive history of the subject.
[Q464] Oxford pbk **£15.00**

NEWTON-SMITH, H.H.
Logic
A complete introduction to logic for first-year
university students with no background in logic,
philosophy or mathematics.
[Q465] Routledge pbk **£6.95**

QUINE, W.V.
Elementary Logic
[Q466] Harvard UP pbk **£4.75**
From a Logical Point of View
A great logician and an influential philosopher in the
Russellian tradition, Quine is always a pleasure to
read. The volumes of essays listed here are classic
examples of the clarity of his thought and the sparse,
witty style of his writing.
[Q467] Harvard UP hbk **£9.95**
Methods of Logic
[Q468] Routledge pbk **£5.95**
Philosophy of Logic
[Q469] Harvard UP pbk **£5.50**
Ways of Paradox and Other Essays
[Q470] Harvard UP pbk **£7.95**

SMULLYAN, RAYMOND
**Forever Undecided:
A Puzzle Guide to Gödel**   **NEW**
An entertaining and accessible introduction to the
works of the great mathematician and logician
Kurt Gödel.
[Q471] Oxford pbk **£5.95**

STRAWSON, P. (ED)
Philosophical Logic
[Q472] Oxford pbk **£5.95**

TOULMIN, STEPHEN E.
The Uses of Argument
[Q473] Cambridge pbk **£9.50**

Metaphysics

ARMSTRONG, D.M.
What is a Law of Nature?
[Q474] Cambridge pbk **£8.50**

BARRETT, WILLIAM
**Death of the Soul: From Descartes to
the Computer**
The author examines the diminishing place of the
spirit in philosophical thought and demonstrates that
the pervasive influence of scientific materialism
seriously compromises our ability to form an
adequate idea of the conscious mind.
[Q475] Oxford pbk **£4.95**

BENADETTE, J.A.
**Metaphysics:
The Logical Approach**
[Q476] Oxford pbk **£7.95**

BERGSON, H.L.
**Creative Mind: An Introduction to
Metaphysics**
[Q477] Citidel P pbk **£7.50**

CARR, BRIAN
Metaphysics: An Introduction
A general introduction to the major problems of
descriptive metaphysics.
[Q478] Macmillan pbk **£7.95**

HAMLYN, D.W.
Metaphysics
[Q479] Cambridge pbk **£8.50**

KLEMKE, E.D. (ED)
The Meaning of Life
[Q480] Oxford pbk **£8.95**

KOLAKOWSKI, LESZEK
Metaphysical Horror   **NEW**
Studies on the search for the Absolute: *"The
search for the ultimate foundation is as much an
unremovable part of human culture as the denial of
the legitimacy of this search."*
[Q481] Blackwell hbk **£12.95**

KORNER, STEPHAN
**Metaphysics: Its Structure and
Function**
[Q482] Cambridge pbk **£9.95**

LEWIS, DAVID
On the Plurality of Worlds
An influential and much-discussed defence of 'modal
realism', the idea that ours is but one of a plurality of
possible worlds.
[Q483] Blackwell pbk **£8.95**

MACKIE, J.L.
**The Cement of the Universe:
A Study of Causation**
[Q484] Oxford pbk **£10.95**

QUINTON, ANTHONY
The Nature of Things
[Q485] Routledge pbk **£9.95**

SPRAGUE, E.
Metaphysical Thinking
[Q486] Oxford pbk **£5.95**

SPRIGGE, T.
Theories of Existence
[Q487] Penguin pbk **£3.50**

STEVENSON, L.
The Metaphysics of Experience
[Q488] Oxford pbk **£7.95**

STRAWSON, P.F.
Individuals
Strawson's most celebrated work; a defence of
'descriptive metaphysics' and the legitimacy of
transcendental arguments.
[Q489] Routledge pbk **£7.95**

SUPPES, PATRICK
Probabilistic Metaphysics
[Q490] Blackwell pbk **£8.95**

WIGGINS, DAVID
Sameness and Substance
[Q491] Blackwell pbk **£7.50**

Philosophy of
Language

AUSTIN, J.L.
How to Do Things with Words
The William James Lectures of 1955, which provide
Austin's fullest account of the notion for which he is
most famous: the idea of a 'speech act', an utterance
(such as 'I promise') that is itself the performance of
an action.
[Q492] Oxford pbk **£4.95**

Sense and Sensibilia
[Q493] Oxford pbk **£5.95**

AYER, A.J.
Language, Truth and Logic
First published in 1936, this remains one of the most
strident statements of the case for the logical positivist
analysis of meaning.
[Q494] Penguin pbk **£3.95**

BAKER, G.P. & HACKER, P.M.S.
Language Sense and Nonsense
A polemical analysis - from a Wittgensteinian point
of view - of contemporary work in linguistics and
philosophy of language, including that of Chomsky,
Davidson and Dummett.
[Q495] Blackwell pbk **£9.50**

BARTHES, ROLAND
Selected Writings
A useful selection which provides an excellent
introduction to the work of this widely influential
French semiologist.
[Q496] Fontana pbk **£4.95**

BENNETT, JONATHAN
Linguistic Behaviour
[Q497] Cambridge pbk **£8.50**

BLACKBURN, S.
Spreading the Word
An admirably lucid overview of modern philosophy
of language, written with the non-specialist in
mind.
[Q498] Oxford pbk **£6.95**

CHOMSKY, NOAM
Language and Mind
Chomsky's theory of 'transformational grammar' has
not only revolutionized the study of linguistics, but
has also had a great impact on the philosophy of
language, particularly in its appeal to the anti-
empiricist notion of an innate 'universal grammar'.
[Q499] Harcourt B pbk **£10.95**
**Language and Problems of
Knowledge**
[Q500] MIT pbk **£7.95**
Rules and Representations
[Q501] Blackwell pbk **£8.95**

CLARKE, D.S., JR
Principles of Semiotic
[Q502] Routledge pbk **£6.95**

CULLER, JONATHAN
Barthes
[Q503] Fontana pbk **£2.95**
Saussure
[Q504] Fontana pbk **£4.95**

DAVIDSON, DONALD
Inquiries into Truth and Interpretation
Contains all Davidson's best-known papers on the
philosophy of language, papers which have made his
one of the dominant voices in contemporary
philosophy.
[Q505] Oxford pbk **£8.95**

DEVITT, MICHAEL & STERELNY, KIM
**Language and Reality:
An Introduction to the Philosophy
of Language**
A comprehensive and up-to-date introduction that
provides surveys of the competing theories of truth
and meaning that have been advanced recently, and
explains their relevance to traditional problems in
epistemology, metaphysics and ethics.
[Q506] Blackwell pbk **£8.95**

DUMMETT, MICHAEL
Truth & Other Enigmas
A collection of Dummett's widely influential essays,
together with a long explanatory preface.
[Q507] Duckworth pbk **£19.95**

GELLNER, ERNEST
Words and Things
A spirited attack on analytical and linguistic
philosophy first published in 1959.
[Q508] Routledge pbk **£6.95**

HACKING, IAN
**Why Does Language Matter to
Philosophy?**
An excellent survey of the 'linguistic turn' taken by
philosophy in the twentieth century, including an
account of Wittgenstein's impact and discussions of
the work of contemporary philosophers such as
Feyerabend and Davidson.
[Q509] Cambridge pbk **£6.50**

HARRIS, ROY
The Language Makers
A critique of the views on language put forward by a
long line of philosophers, including Plato, St
Augustine, Locke, Saussure, Russell and
Wittgenstein.
[Q510] Duckworth pbk **£5.95**
The Language Myth
[Q511] Duckworth pbk **£7.95**

KATZ, JEROLD J. (ED)
The Philosophy of Linguistics
[Q512] Oxford pbk **£6.95**

KRIPKE, SAUL A.
Naming and Necessity
A work that more than any other has influenced the
content and style of contemporary debates on the
philosophy of language.
[Q513] Blackwell pbk **£6.95**

LYONS, JOHN
Chomsky
An excellent survey of Chomsky's thought including
an explanation of his widely influential work on the
'deep structure' of grammar.
[Q514] Fontana pbk **£2.95**

OGDEN, C.K. & RICHARDS, I.A.
The Meaning of Meaning
First published in the 1920s and now regarded as a
classic in its field, this presents a Russellian causal
analysis of meaning.
[Q515] Routledge pbk **£4.95**

PARKINSON, G.H.R. (ED)
The Theory of Meaning
[Q516] Oxford pbk **£2.95**

PLATTS, MARK (ED)
**Reference, Truth and Reality: Essays
on the Philosophy of Language**
[Q517] Routledge pbk **£8.95**

PUTNAM, HILARY
Meaning and the Moral Sciences
[Q518] Routledge pbk **£7.50**

SAUSSURE, FERDINAND DE
Course in General Linguistics
Saussure's most famous work. First published in
1915, it introduced the terminology (sign, signifier,
etc.) and the analysis of form that were later adopted
by semiologists such as Roland Barthes, and have
since become the hallmarks of the entire
'structuralist' tradition.
[Q519] Duckworth pbk **£9.95**

SEARLE, J.R.
**Expression and Meaning: Studies in the
Theory of Speech Acts**
A student of Austin's at Oxford, Searle has since
become the leading exponent of speech act theory.
[Q520] Cambridge pbk **£8.50**
**Speech Acts: An Essay in the
Philosophy of Language**
[Q521] Cambridge pbk **£5.95**
The Philosophy of Language
(Ed. Searle, J.R.)
[Q522] Oxford pbk **£5.95**

Philosophy of Mind

ANSCOMBE, G.E.M.
**Collected Philosophical Papers Vol 2:
Metaphysics and the Philosophy of
Mind**
[Q523] Blackwell pbk **£7.95**
Intention
Anscombe's most famous work; an analysis of
intentional states, profoundly influenced by
Wittgenstein.
[Q524] Blackwell pbk **£6.95**

ARMSTRONG, D.M. & MALCOLM, NORMAN
Consciousness and Causality
[Q525] Blackwell pbk **£7.95**

BORN, RAINER (ED)
**Artificial Intelligence: The Case
Against**
A collection of essays by distinguished analytical
philosophers, psychologists and computer scientists,
including Hilary Putnam, John Searle and Hubert
Dreyfus.
[Q526] Routledge pbk **£9.95**

DAVIDSON, DONALD
Essays on Actions and Events
A collection of all the essential articles on the
philosophy of mind written by this much discussed
contemporary American philosopher.
[Q527] Oxford pbk **£8.95**

DENNETT, DANIEL C.
Dennett is possibly the most interesting contemporary
philosopher of mind. He expresses his materialism in
a sophisticated and clear manner congenial to
professional and layman alike.
**Brainstorms: Philosophical Essays on
Mind and Psychology**
[Q528] Harvester pbk **£10.95**
Content and Consciousness
[Q529] Routledge pbk **£5.95**
**Elbow Room: The Varieties of Free Will
Worth Wanting**
[Q530] Oxford pbk **£9.95**

FLEW, ANTHONY
Body, Mind and Death
[Q531] Macmillan pbk **£3.95**

FODOR, JERRY
**Representations: Philosophical Essays
on the Foundations of Cognitive
Science**
[Q532] Harvester pbk **£10.95**

FRANKFURT, HARRY G.
**The Importance of What We
Care About**   **NEW**
A collection of thirteen essays on ethics and the
philosophy of mind by one of America's leading
philosophers.
[Q533] Cambridge pbk **£9.95**

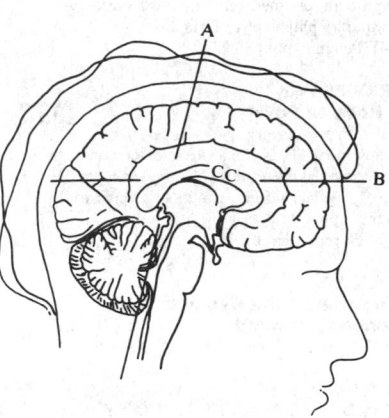

Cross-section of the brain from *The Oxford
Companion to the Mind* edited by R.L. Gregory
(Oxford University Press hbk £25.00)

GEACH, P.
Mental Acts
[Q534] Routledge pbk **£2.50**

GLOVER, J. (ED)
The Philosophy of Mind
[Q535] Oxford pbk **£5.95**

GREGORY, R.L. (ED)
Oxford Companion to the Mind
Contains over 900 entries covering a wide range of
subject matter including philosophy, psychology and
the physiology of the brain.
[Q536] Oxford hbk **£25.00**

HAMLYN, D.W.
The Psychology of Perception
A philosophical critique of Gestalt Theory and
derivative theories of perception.
[Q537] Routledge pbk **£4.75**

HUMPHREY, NICHOLAS
**Consciousness Regained: Chapters in
the Development of Mind**
[Q538] Cambridge pbk **£4.95**

KENNY, ANTHONY
Action, Emotion and Will
[Q539] Routledge pbk **£7.50**

MACINTYRE, ALASDAIR
**The Unconscious: A Conceptual
Analysis**
[Q540] Routledge pbk **£5.50**

MCGINN, COLIN
The Character of Mind
An engaging introduction to the philosophy of mind.
[Q541] Oxford pbk **£5.95**

PEARS, DAVID
Motivated Irrationality
[Q542] Oxford pbk **£9.95**

POLANYI, MICHAEL
**Personal Knowledge: Towards a Post-
Critical Philosophy**
[Q543] Routledge pbk **£9.50**

RYLE, GILBERT
The Concept of Mind
First published in 1949, the theory of 'logical

behaviourism' outlined here remains a presence in contemporary philosophy of mind.
[Q544] Penguin pbk **£5.95**

SCARRY, ELAINE
The Body in Pain `NEW`
Drawing on a wide variety of sources, including medical case histories and documents on torture compiled by Amnesty, Scarry explores the nature of physical suffering and its inexpressibility in language.
[Q545] Oxford pbk **£7.95**

SEARLE, J.R.
Intentionality: An Essay in the Philosophy of Mind
[Q546] Cambridge pbk **£8.95**

SHOEMAKER, SYDNEY & SWINBURNE, RICHARD
Personal Identity
[Q547] Blackwell pbk **£7.95**

SMITH, PETER & JONES, O.R.
The Philosophy of Mind: An Introduction
[Q548] Cambridge pbk **£6.95**

TAYLOR, G.
Pride, Shame and Guilt: Emotions of Self-Assessment
The author's discussion centres on the similarity of the beliefs involved in the experience of these emotions.
[Q549] Oxford pbk **£7.95**

TEICHMAN, JENNY
Philosophy and the Mind
[Q550] Blackwell pbk **£7.95**
The Mind and Soul: An Introduction to the Philosophy of Mind
[Q551] Routledge pbk **£5.25**

YOUNG, J.Z.
Philosophy and the Brain
Written for the general reader as well as for students, this book seeks to show the relevance of biological knowledge to philosophical problems, and, conversely, the importance of philosophical concepts to the study of biology.
[Q552] Oxford pbk **£4.95**

Philosophy of Science

BARROW, JOHN D. & TIPLER, FRANK J.
The Anthropic Cosmological Principle
With a general audience in mind, this book addresses a central problem for scientists and philosophers: the position and role of man in the universe.
[Q553] Oxford pbk **£9.95**

BHASKAR, ROY
Scientific Realism and Human Emancipation
[Q554] Verso pbk **£9.95**

DAVIES, PAUL
God and the New Physics
Shows how far the recent explosive discoveries of the new physics are revolutionizing our view of the world and in particular throwing new light on many of the questions formerly posed by religion.
[Q555] Penguin pbk **£4.95**

FEYERABEND, PAUL
Against Method
Feyerabend is an astute critic of orthodoxy and a fine polemical writer. *Against Method* - his most famous work - is an uncompromising statement of 'epistemological anarchism'. This new edition incorporates essays from its sequel, *Science in a Free Society*.
[Q556] Verso pbk **£7.95**
Farewell to Reason
A new series of essays, in which Feyerabend continues his assault on what he regards as the empty claims of reason, and defends his iconoclastic relativism.
[Q557] Verso pbk **£9.95**

HARRE, ROM
The Philosophies of Science
A good general introduction to the relationship between science and philosophy.
[Q558] Oxford pbk **£4.95**

HEMPEL, CARL G.
Aspects of Scientific Explanation
Outlines Hempel's enormously influential model of scientific theory in terms of a hierarchy of increasingly general laws.
[Q559] Macmillan pbk **£14.95**

HOLLIS, MARTIN & LUKES, STEVEN (EDS)
Rationality and Relativism
[Q560] Blackwell pbk **£7.95**

KUHN, THOMAS S.
The Copernican Revolution
[Q561] Harvard UP pbk **£7.95**
The Essential Tension: Selected Studies in Scientific Tradition and Change
[Q562] Chicago UP pbk **£11.25**
The Structure of Scientific Explanations
One of the most important works in modern philosophy of science, this introduces Kuhn's much discussed notion of a 'paradigm shift', the radical change in explanatory frameworks that follows a crisis in science.
[Q563] Chicago UP pbk **£6.25**

LAKATOS, IMRE
Proofs and Refutations: The Logic of Mathematical Discovery
[Q564] Cambridge pbk **£6.95**

MAXWELL, NICHOLAS
From Knowledge to Wisdom: A Revolution in the Aims and Methods of Science
[Q565] Blackwell pbk **£8.95**

NAGEL, ERNST
The Structure of Science
A weighty modern classic.
[Q566] Routledge pbk **£9.50**

NEWTON-SMITH, W.H.
The Rationality of Science
Includes a rationalist rejoinder to Feyerabend.
[Q567] Routledge pbk **£7.50**
The Structure of Time
[Q568] Routledge pbk **£8.50**

POINCARE, R.
Science and Hypothesis
A collection of stimulating reflections from a renowned mathematician. Written for a general audience.
[Q569] Dover pbk **£4.50**

REICHENBACH, HANS
Philosophy of Space and Time
[Q570] Dover pbk **£4.40**

RICHARDS, STEWART
Philosophy and Sociology of Science: An Introduction
[Q571] Blackwell pbk **£7.95**

RUSE, MICHAEL
Taking Darwin Seriously: A Naturalistic Approach to Philosophy
An argument for making the ideas of natural selection central to the issues in philosophy.
[Q572] Blackwell pbk **£7.50**

TRUSTED, JENNIFER
The Logic of Scientific Inference: An Introduction
[Q573] Macmillan pbk **£7.95**

Continental Philosophy

The term 'continental' to describe philosophers with a particular set of concerns (rather than simply originating from a certain area) has a comparatively short history. It has its origin in the neglect by Anglo-American philosophers of texts - such as Merleau-Ponty's *Phenomenology of Perception*, Sartre's *Being and Nothingness*, and Saussure's *Course in General Linguistics* - which have had a decisive influence on philosophy in France and Germany. We list here those key texts, together with more recent works inspired by them, which have come to constitute a tradition, or set of traditions (phenomenology, structuralism, critical theory and deconstructionism) that is still largely neglected by philosophers in the English-speaking world.

ADORNO, THEODOR
Minima Moralia: Reflections from a Damaged Life
Adorno's best-known work; a series of aphorisms on everyday existence in 'late capitalism'.
[Q574] Verso pbk **£7.95**
Negative Dialectics
The fullest statement of Adorno's general philosophical position, *Negative Dialectics* presents a determinedly unsystematic approach, a kind of anti-logic.
[Q575] Routledge hbk **£25.00**
The Jargon of Authenticity
[Q576] Routledge pbk **£5.95**
JAY, MARTIN
Adorno
[Q577] Fontana pbk **£2.50**

ADORNO, T. & HORKHEIMER, W.
Dialectic of Enlightenment
One of the key works of the Frankfurt School of Critical Theory.
[Q578] Verso pbk **£7.95**

BACHELARD, GASTON
On Poetic Imagination and Reverie
[Q579] Spring Pubs pbk **£10.95**
The New Scientific Spirit
An analysis of modern science that sees its essence in the advance of mathematical abstraction, and that draws from that implications for our understanding of the mind and the imagination.
[Q580] Beacon pbk **£7.95**
The Poetics of Space
[Q581] Beacon pbk **£6.95**

The Psychoanalysis of Fire
[Q582] Beacon pbk **£6.95**

BAUDRILLARD, JEAN
Selected Writings
Baudrillard is one of Europe's most fashionable and
controversial philosophers. This volume makes
available for the first time some of his most important
work, from his early writings on advertising and
commodity culture to his recent work on simulation
and desire.
[Q583] Polity pbk **£8.95**
KELLNER, DOUGLAS
Jean Baudrillard:
From Marxism to Post-Modernism
and Beyond
[Q584] Polity pbk **£8.50**

BLACKHAM, H.J.
Six Existentialist Thinkers
[Q585] Routledge pbk **£4.95**

BLEICHER, JOSEF
Contemporary Hermeneutics
[Q586] Routledge pbk **£9.50**
The Hermeneutic Imagination
[Q587] Routledge pbk **£8.95**

BUBNER, RUDIGER
Modern German Philosophy
On Husserl, Heidegger, Gadamer, Lukacs, Adorno
and Habermas.
[Q588] Cambridge pbk **£8.95**

DELEUZE, GILLES
Cinema 1: The Movement-Image
[Q589] Athlone pbk **£11.95**

DELEUZE, GILLES &
GUTTARI, FELIX
A Thousand Plateaux: Capitalism and
Schizophrenia
[Q590] Athlone pbk **£16.00**
Anti-Oedipus: Capitalism and
Schizophrenia
[Q591] Athlone pbk **£18.00**

DERRIDA, JACQUES
Largely because of his impact on contemporary
literary theory, Derrida has become the most widely
discussed continental philosopher. His most famous
work is *Writing and Difference* which makes the case
for Derrida's notorious claim that writing, rather than
speech, is the primordial form of language.
Margins of Philosophy
[Q592] Harvester pbk **£10.95**
Positions
[Q593] Athlone hbk **£20.00**
Spurs: Nietzsche's Styles
[Q594] Chicago UP pbk **£6.25**
The Postcard: From Socrates to Freud
and Beyond
[Q595] Chicago UP pbk **£15.25**
Writing and Difference
[Q596] Routledge pbk **£7.95**

DEWS, PETER
Logics of Disintegration
A study of Derrida, Lacan, Lyotard and Foucault that
sets their work in relation to the more explicitly
critical tradition of the Frankfurt School and
concludes that post-structuralism ultimately becomes
entangled in its own 'logic of disintegration'.
[Q597] Verso pbk **£7.95**

FOUCAULT, MICHEL
Archaeology of Knowledge
[Q598] Tavistock pbk **£6.95**

Jürgen Habermas, author of *Knowledge and
Human Interests* (Polity Press pbk £12.50) and *The
Philosophical Discourse of Modernity* (Polity Press
hbk £25.00)

Discipline and Punishment: Birth of the
Prison
[Q599] Penguin pbk **£6.95**
Madness and Civilization
Foucault's celebrated study of the social construction
of 'madness'.
[Q600] Tavistock pbk **£7.95**
The Birth of the Clinic
More than medical history it *"is about space, about
language and about death: it is about the act of
seeing the gaze"*.
[Q601] Tavistock pbk **£8.95**
The Foucault Reader
[Q602] Penguin pbk **£6.95**
A History of Sexuality
Vol 1: An Introduction
Now complete in three volumes, Foucault originally
planned a six-volume history of sexuality. This work
provides a radical reassessment of received ideas
about sex, society and human life.
[Q603] Penguin pbk **£4.95**
Vol 2: The Uses of Pleasure
[Q604] Penguin pbk **£7.95**
Vol 3: The Care of the Self
[Q605] A Lane hbk **£17.95**
HOY, DAVID (ED)
Foucault: A Critical Reader
Includes contributions by Richard Rorty, David
Couzens Hoy and Edward W. Said.
[Q606] Blackwell pbk **£8.95**

GADAMER, HANS-GEORG
Hegel's Dialectic: Five Hermeneutical
Studies
[Q607] Yale UP pbk **£7.95**
Philosophical Apprenticeships
[Q608] MIT pbk **£8.95**
The Relevance of the Beautiful and
Other Essays
[Q609] Cambridge pbk **£8.50**
Truth and Method
Gadamer's major work; an influential analysis of the
phenomenon of understanding within a general theory
of hermeneutics, the theory of interpretation.
[Q610] Sheed & W pbk **£15.50**

GEUSS, R.
The Idea of a Critical Theory:
Habermas and the Frankfurt School
[Q611] Routledge pbk **£5.95**

GROSSMAN, REINHARDT
Phenomenology and Existentialism: An
Introduction
[Q612] Routledge pbk **£7.95**

HABERMAS, JURGEN
Knowledge and Human Interests
Habermas's major work on the theory of knowledge,
which outlines his distinction between 'empirico-
analytical' and 'hermeneutic' enquiries and argues for
the development of a critical theory which would
combine the two.
[Q613] Polity pbk **£12.50**
The Philosophical Discourse of
Modernity
Habermas's most recent major work, in which he
traces the philosophical origins of contemporary
critiques of modernity and gives his own critical
assessment of the new scepticism.
[Q614] Polity hbk **£25.00**

KEARNEY, RICHARD
Modern Movements in European
Philosophy
Views continental European philosophy as a series of
responses to crises in modern culture and society. A
useful introduction with helpful bibliographies.
[Q615] Manchester UP pbk **£8.95**

LEVIN, DAVID MICHAEL
The Opening of Vision: Nihilism and the
Postmodern Situation
[Q616] Routledge pbk **£12.95**

LYOTARD, JEAN-FRANCOIS &
THEBAUD, J.
Just Gaming
An investigation of the problem of justice through the
use of Wittgenstein's theory of language games.
[Q617] Manchester UP pbk **£5.95**

LYOTARD, JEAN-FRANCOIS
The Differend
A wide-ranging discussion of aspects of
postmodernism: the 'linguistic turn' of modern
philosophy, the decline of metaphysics, and the
intellectual retreat of Marxism.
[Q618] Manchester UP pbk **£7.95**
The Postmodern Condition: A Report on
Knowledge
An influential investigation into the problem of
legitimizing knowledge when there is no
unified public sphere, only discordant language
games.
[Q619] Manchester UP pbk **£8.95**

MACQUARRIE, J.
Existentialism
[Q620] Penguin pbk **£3.50**

MERLEAU-PONTY, MAURICE
The Phenomenology of Perception
First published in 1945, this is Merleau-Ponty's major
work, and a key text in the continental tradition of
phenomenology. It presents an analysis of
consciousness that rejects both dualism and
materialism and puts in their stead an enigmatic
'philosophy of ambiguity'.
[Q621] Routledge pbk **£12.50**
SCHMIDT, JAMES
Maurice Merleau-Ponty: Between
Phenomenology and Structuralism
A re-examination of Merleau-Ponty's writings against
a background of recent developments in French social
theory.
[Q622] Macmillan pbk **£8.95**

MONTEFIORE, A. (ED)
Philosophy in France Today
A representative selection of contemporary articles
chief among which is Derrida's contribution specially
written for this collection.
[Q623] Cambridge pbk **£8.95**

RICOEUR, PAUL
Freud and Philosophy: An Essay on Interpretation
[Q624] Yale UP pbk **£15.95**
The Rule of Metaphor
[Q625] Routledge pbk **£8.95**

ROBERTS, JULIAN
German Philosophy: An Introduction
Takes Kant to be the main source of modern
metaphysics and includes chapters on most modern
German philosophers, including Hegel,
Schopenhauer, Nietzsche, Heidegger and Adorno.
[Q626] Blackwell pbk **£8.95**

SARTRE, JEAN-PAUL
Being and Nothingness
Sartre's chief philosophical work, first published in
1943. It presents a complex phenomenological
analysis of existence, the self, and the nature of the
imagination and the emotions.
[Q627] Routledge pbk **£11.95**
Critique of Dialectical Reason
Written in 1960, this presents a reappraisal of the
whole of Sartre's philosophical and political thought,
an attempt to synthesize existentialism with a
reconstructed Marxism.
[Q628] Verso pbk **£14.95**
Sketch for a Theory of the Emotions
[Q629] Routledge pbk **£6.95**
The Psychology of Imagination
[Q630] Routledge pbk **£6.95**
**War Diaries: Notebooks from a Phoney
War 1939 - 40**
A series of notes on philosophy, literature, politics,
history and autobiography that anticipate the themes
of Sartre's later work.
[Q631] Verso pbk **£6.95**
CAWS, PETER
Sartre
[Q632] Routledge pbk **£8.95**

SCHNADELBACH, H.
Philoscphy in Germany 1831 - 1933
[Q633] Cambridge pbk **£9.50**

SILVERMAN, H.J.
**Inscriptions: Between Phenomenology
and Structuralism**
An enquiry into the contemporary state of continental
philosophy. Silverman traces the path that leads from
Merleau-Ponty to Derrida.
[Q634] Routledge hbk **£22.95**

SILVERMAN, H.J. (ED)
Derrida and Deconstruction
[Q635] Routledge pbk **£9.95**
**Philosophy and Non-Philosophy since
Merleau-Ponty**
A series of essays by Anglo-American philosophers,
each devoted to one of the major continental figures.
Merleau-Ponty, Sartre, Heidegger, Deleuze, Foucault,
Lyotard, Habermas and Derrida are among those
discussed.
[Q636] Routledge pbk **£9.95**

SOLOMON, ROBERT C.
**Continental Philosophy since 1750:
The Rise and Fall of the Self**
[Q637] Oxford pbk **£4.95**

STURROCK, JOHN (ED)
**Structuralism and Since: From
Lévi-Strauss to Derrida**
[Q638] Oxford pbk **£4.95**

Poetry

Michael Schmidt (Photo: Stephen Raw)

Carcanet: The First 20 Years
Michael Schmidt

As an editor, I am just as happy restoring to the light living works by neglected writers as I am in delivering new writers to the world. Publishing at Carcanet is a matter of adventure *and* restitution, in equal parts. We publish a major fiction list, but here I would like to concentrate on poetry, which is where Carcanet started.

As a student in the 1960s I often found it hard to get my hands on books that *might* be important: there was virtually no Wyndham Lewis, H.D., or Ford (beyond the 'major novels'); no Yvor Winters, Blunden's poems, Cornford's writings, Charlotte Mew's poems and prose, Delmore Schwartz's work - the list was long. Inexpensive selections of important, if not major, poets from Gower and Charles of Orleans to Barnes and Arthur Symons were lacking, too. In many cases there was simply no edition in print.

As the feminists found, neglect is not always accidental. It can have to do with fashion, politics or 'dominant ideologies', and it can impoverish the present. Where I diverge from feminist editors is in my belief that gender contributes less to neglect than fashion and politics do. Most polemical editorial programmes - including the feminist - tend to generate their own orthodoxies: design and blurb-styles signal not only a book but a cause.

Carcanet was the fruit of student unrest - but not precisely of the kind that was rife in 1969 when the Press started at Pin Farm, South Hinksey, Oxford, near the 'causeway chill' of Arnold's poem. Our unrest had two aspects, one selfish, one selfless. We were young poets who couldn't get a London publisher: we had our geniuses to launch. But we were also children of our time, we wanted the widest possible readership to have access to what we considered to be the best English poetry of the past and present. How could we properly read the present if we could not read back from it? The historical sense of poetry readers grows shorter and less stable each year. There is a premium on the new, at the expense of the old. In the last twenty years the wheel has been invented by at least three groups of poets, each a 'new generation'. The less past we have, the faster the clock-hands turn and the sooner we are dust and ashes.

It is a triumph of sorts: poetry is newsworthy, a pretext for journalism. The shop-life of poetry books can be almost as short as that of fiction and annuals. The people we used to call 'readers' are now collectivised into a 'poetry market', centred largely on the educational establishment. Each publisher with a poetry list craves admittance to the syllabus, as in years gone by poets might crave admittance to Parnassus. Poetry has embraced the secular forces of supply and demand, accepting the determinants it so vigorously resisted earlier in this century.

Almost from the beginning in 1969, when Carcanet published seven

---

In the last twenty years the wheel has been invented by at least three groups of poets, each a 'new generation'

---

pamphlets of poems, I had a vision of the end, though perhaps I expected it would come sooner than it has. A firm like Carcanet is unlikely to outlive the chance intersection of lives and enthusiasms which nurture it. Constant financial over-exposure results from a non-programmatic commitment to books and writers who seem excellent and are published without primary regard to the market place. When Carcanet's last chapter is written, about twenty-three years hence I trust, it will be possible for an archaeologist to survey the entire list and piece together a pattern, as in a Roman mosaic. There will be gaps and some ugly figures there: false starts, false endings, those blemishes of error or failed assurance. But many lines will be clear: the insistence on Anglo-American modernism, for instance, resolutely pursued into a period increasingly hostile to it; the presence of a handful of major writers who have drawn into the Press some of the neglected writing which gives them context and makes their work *effective* today. I have in mind especially C.H. Sisson, Donald Davie, Octavio Paz, Michael Hamburger, Christopher Middleton and John Ashbery. I ought to add the names of Edgell Rickword and Idris Parry, two of the best essayists of the century.

Our 'new poets' - several of them now well established - will fit into the centre of the mosaic. Their introduction will be the durable contribution that Carcanet has made.

Carcanet has not followed a single line. The young editor who shaped the early lists, including a range of poetry in translation (much of it from Eastern Europe) passed through various phases of

enthusiasm and influence. Some of the original authors survive on the list; they too have changed. Editors fresh out of university respond to certain kinds of wit in a text - local wit, one might say, the fruit of study and cleverness. If, leaving the dreaming spires behind them, they are knocked sideways by an unexpected gale - in my case the poems of C.H. Sisson

> *Sisson's work had that effect on me. Later, Yvor Winters seemed a wonderful antidote to certain forms of levity and formal laxness*

and W.S. Graham, the criticism of Donald Davie and Christopher Middleton - they look rather different when they have righted themselves. Sisson writes of the way that Pound effected an adjustment of the way he actually *heard* poetry. Sisson's work had that effect on me. Later, Yvor Winters seemed a wonderful antidote to certain forms of levity and formal laxness. Later still John Ashbery suggested a world of utterance I had wilfully deafened myself to. All three,

very different in kind, took their bearings from what academics call Modernism but what I would prefer to call Pound, Eliot, Stevens, Ford, H.D., Lewis, Williams, those writers whom modern criticism has done so much to assimilate into an academy which they themselves might have despised.

Carcanet has enjoyed for twenty years an unusual freedom: to publish without the compulsion to make a profit. Supported first from private resources, then by the Arts Council and our proprietor and chairman Robert Gavron, we have something over 700 titles to our credit, about a third of them still in print. We have found that a book can sell 150 copies in the first year, 70 in the second, and 500 in the third: it is a matter, where possible, of keeping faith with a work long enough for that work to make its way if it can. We find it possible to break even on short print-runs (sometimes as few was 750 copies). We try to publish Selected and Collected Poems by our authors so that each subsequent collection has a past available to the interested reader, and the poet need not jump up and down forever on the same spot.

Carcanet, described as 'the Radio three of literary publishing' by a hostile critic, is something of an anachronism in its attitudes to stock-turn, market and 'product range'. Among the smaller independent presses, it has an impossibly vast programme of making available neglected and new writing, working with a staff of four and a half people. Each year it produces six issues of the magazine *PN Review* (how can any publisher exist without the catalyst of a magazine?) and roughly forty titles, along with thirty or forty reprints and new editions. We still believe in a diaspora of general readers hungry for the new but also for the contexts and antecedents of the new. Publishing is a dialogue with that usually silent partner...rather like Radio Three, which addresses us as if we were *really* there. And we are.

C.H. Sisson, author of *In the Trojan Ditch* (Carcanet hbk £8.95) (Photo: Carcanet Press)

Michael Schmidt founded Carcanet Press while at Oxford in 1969; an academic at the University of Manchester, he is himself a poet and critic, and has edited the anthology **Some Contemporary Poets of Britain and Ireland**.

Feature

POETRY

British & Irish Poetry

General Anthologies

Anglo-Welsh Poetry 1480 - 1980
(Ed. Garlick, R. & Mathias, R.)
The only anthology to concentrate wholly on English language writing by Welsh authors.
[R1] Poetry Wales P hbk **£12.95**
[R2] Poetry Wales P pbk **£5.95**

Everyman's Book of English Verse
(Ed. Wain, John)
[R3] Dent Hbk **£12.00**

Faber Book of Irish Verse
(Ed. Montague, John)
[R4] Faber pbk **£5.95**

Irish Verse
[R5] Penguin pbk **£3.95**

The Golden Treasury of the Best Songs and Lyrical Poems in the English Language (Ed. Palgrave, Francis Turner)
This remains the classic popular anthology of English verse, still going strong, with many additions and alterations by subsequent editors since its inception in 1861.
[R6] Oxford hbk **£9.95**
[R7] Oxford pbk **£3.95**

The New Oxford Book of English Verse 1250 - 1950 (Ed. Gardner, Helen)
[R8] Oxford hbk **£13.95**

The New Oxford Book of Irish Verse
(Ed. Kinsella, Thomas)
Kinsella features the Irish poetic tradition in its entirety - from pre-Christian writers to Heaney and Mahon.
[R9] Oxford hbk **£14.95**
[R10] Oxford pbk **£5.95**

The Oxford Book of English Verse 1250 - 1918 (Ed. Quiller-Couch, A.T.)
[R11] Oxford hbk **£14.95**

The Oxford Book of Scottish Verse NEW
(Ed. MacQueen, John & Scott, Tom)
Spanning seven centuries of Scottish verse, MacQueen and Scott have chosen to emphasize work written in Scots rather than English, and to devote considerable space to neglected poets of the 15th and 16th centuries.
[R12] Oxford pbk **£5.95**

The Oxford Book of Welsh Poetry
(Ed. Parry, Thomas)
[R13] Oxford pbk **£9.50**

The Penguin Book of English Verse
(Ed. Hayward, John)
Authoritative selection of English verse running from Wyatt to Dylan Thomas.
[R14] Penguin pbk **£3.99**

The Rattle Bag (Ed. Hughes, Ted & Heaney, Seamus)
In Heaney and Hughes' fine anthology, which is more conventional than it pretends to be, the emphasis is on poetry as a means of communication with mystery. Along with 'Anon' and snippets from Shakespeare, the most represented poets are Hardy, Lawrence, Hopkins and Yeats - there is little from the 18th century.
[R15] Faber pbk **£6.95**

Welsh Verse (Trans. Conran, Tony)
Welsh language poetry dates back to the 6th Century, making it one of Europe's oldest living languages. Tony Conran translates works from 13 centuries, from poets likE Gwyn Thomas and Aneirin to modern writers.
[R16] Poetry Wales P hbk **£10.95**
[R17] Poetry Wales P pbk **£4.95**

Anglo-Saxon & Medieval Verse

A Choice of Anglo-Saxon Verse
[R18] Faber pbk **£3.95**

A Choice of Scottish Verse 1470 - 1570
Contains selections from the major Makars of the period, such as Henryson, Dunbar, Gavin Douglas and David Lyndsay as well as anonymous work.
[R19] Faber pbk **£1.95**

An Anthology of Old English Poetry
[R20] Oxford pbk **£8.50**

Anglo-Saxon Poetry (Ed. Bradley)
[R22] Dent pbk **£4.95**

Earliest English Poems
[R23] Penguin pbk **£3.95**

English Verse 1300 - 1500
(Ed. Burrows, John)
[R24] Longman pbk **£9.50**

Medieval English Lyrics (Ed. Davies, R.T.)
[R25] Faber pbk **£5.95**

Middle English Lyrics (Ed. Luria, Maxwell & Hoffman, Richard)
[R26] Norton pbk **£6.95**

The Oxford Book of Late Medieval Verse and Prose (Ed. Gray, Douglas)
[R27] Oxford Hbk **£19.50**
[R28] Oxford pbk **£6.95**

BEOWULF POET
The most famous surviving Old English poem, *Beowulf*, was written in the West Saxon dialect in c.1000, although it was probably developed orally. It is an epic which records the heroic deeds of the eponymous warrior, set in southern Scandanavia. He eventually kills the monster Grendel (and Grendel's mother); fifty years later Beowulf and a dragon fatally wound each other. The poem is preoccupied with the strength of the hero, feasting and fighting, and its philosophical considerations to do with good and evil, life and death, have lead to many differing interpretations - Christian, mythic and allegorical.
Beowulf (Trans. Crossley-Holland, Kevin)
[R29] Oxford hbk **£5.95**
[R30] Oxford pbk **£2.50**
Beowulf (Trans. Michael, Alexander)
[R31] Penguin pbk **£2.50**

CHAUCER, GEOFFREY (1343/4 - 1400)
"Whan that Aprill with his shoures soote/The droghte of March hath perced to the roote…" Referred to by Dryden as 'the father of English poetry', Chaucer was the first poet to mould continental models into distinctly English forms. While most contemporary court poets were still writing in Latin or Anglo-Norman, Chaucer was enriching the English vocabulary - as Ezra Pound puts it, Chaucer's is 'the earliest English that one can read without a dictionary, but for which a glossary is needed'. His humour and realism, his philosophic wisdom and technical skills, are unchallenged, and he combines a brilliant talent for dialogue and vivid characterization with a humane and inclusive world view. The language's first great poet.
Love Visions
Includes *Book of the Duchess*, *House of Fame*, *Parlement of Foules* and *Legend of Good Women*, translated into modern English by B. Stone.
[R32] Penguin pbk **£4.50**
The Canterbury Tales (Trans. Coghill, Nevill)
In his most famous work, *The Canterbury Tales*, Chaucer brings in specifically English subject matter, observing the whole of society from courtly knight to bawdy miller. This unfinished work consists of tales told by specific characters, set in the framework of a pilgrimage from Southwalk to Canterbury.
[R33] Penguin pbk **£3.99**
The Canterbury Tales (Trans. Wright, David)
An acclaimed new translation.
[R34] Oxford hbk **£17.50**
[R35] Oxford pbk **£3.95**
The Riverside Chaucer (Ed. Benson, Larry)
In Middle English, this is the standard version of Chaucer for those who want to read him in his original language. Published in 1988, and based on the previous edition of F.N. Robinson, it includes a number of textual changes and clarifications, all of which combine to make it a definitive edition.
[R36] Oxford pbk **£9.95**
Troilus and Criseyde (Trans. Coghill, Nevill)
"Go lytel bok, go lytel my tragedie..." Chaucer's great five-part poem tells the story of the love of Troilus and Criseyde, set during the Trojan war: it is a masterpiece on a human and philosophical scale, here available in a very readable translation, with an excellent introduction.
[R37] Penguin pbk **£3.95**

GAWAIN POET
The identity of the author of *Gawain and the Green Knight*, *Pearl*, *Patience* and *Cleanness* is unknown. *Gawain*, his finest work, is a 2,500 line alliterative poem, written in a north-west midlands dialect very different from that of Chaucer. Set in the early days of Arthur's court, it follows the heroic adventures of one of his knights; gently comic and psychologically observant, the vigorous narrative is matched by passages of splendid sensuous beauty. It is the finest of the surviving Middle English romances.
Pearl (Ed. Gordon, E.V.)
Pearl is a great medieval allegory of personal and spiritual crisis, written within a strict but fluent verse pattern; this edition presents it in its Middle English language form. ♪
[R38] Oxford pbk **£7.50**
Pearl (Ed. Cawley, A.C.)
With *Cleaness*, *Patience*, *Gawain and the Green Knight*.
[R39] Dent pbk **£1.95**
Sir Gawain and the Green Knight
[R40] Manchester UP pbk **£5.95**
Sir Gawain and the Green Knight (Ed. Burrow, John A.)
[R41] Penguin pbk **£3.99**
Sir Gawain and the Green Knight (Ed. Tolkien, J.R.R. & Gordon, E.V.)
[R42] Oxford pbk **£5.50**

GOWER, JOHN (c.1330 - 1408)
"O gentile Engleterre, a toi j' escrits". The pre-eminence of his friend Chaucer has tended, unjustly, to make Gower a mere also-ran. Shakespeare, of course, thought highly enough of him to include him as the Chorus in *Pericles*, and Skelton thought Gower's 'matter was worth gold'. 'Matter' is crucial: in Gower's work it is his deep moral concerns - except for an odd leniency towards incest! - communicated in efficient, precise language which are important. In *Confessio Amantis* - a collection of tales set in the framework of a lover's confession to Venus's priest, his handling of the potentially tedious iambic tetrameter couplets is light and compelling.
Selected Poetry
[R43] Carcanet pbk **£3.95**

GWILYM, DAFYDD AP (Welsh, c.1320)
Little known outside his native Wales, Gwilym successfully combined the native Bardic traditions of Wales with Anglo-Norman forms, bringing a new vocabulary and metrical patterns into use.
Selected Poems
[R43A] Penguin pbk **£5.95**

HENRYSON, ROBERT (c.1424 - c.1506)
One of the Scottish Chaucerians, Henryson's best known work is *The Testament of Cresseid*, a moralizing sequel to Chaucer's *Troilus and Criseyde*: a story-teller and allegorist, Henryson was essentially a moralist who wrote poetry.
Poems & Fables (Ed. Wood, Harriet Harvey)
[R44] Mercat P pbk **£5.95**
Selected Poems (Ed. Barron, Ray)
[R45] Carcanet pbk **£3.95**

HOCCLEVE, THOMAS (1348 - 1430)
"O Engelond, stande upright on thy feet!" Among the few important English poets of the 15th century, Hoccleve's wildly uneven *oeuvre* has suffered heavily at the hands of the critics. Yet he has a strikingly personal tone: much autobiographical material is found in his best poems, which deal with his mental breakdown.
Selected Poems (Ed. O'Donoghue, Bernard)
[R46] Carcanet pbk **£3.95**

LANGLAND, WILLIAM (1360 - 87)
Little is known of his life, but his masterpiece and only extant work, *Piers Plowman*, survives in three versions. A religious allegory in alliterative verse, it centres on the dreamer-narrator's search for true Christianity, the resultant path to salvation consisting of introspection and a condemnation of the established church. In parts a poem of great beauty, it is also an attempt to assert human rights - the keynote of the poem is in the words *'There the poor dare plead'*.
Piers the Ploughman (Trans. Goodridge)
[R47] Dent pbk **£3.95**
[R48] Penguin pbk **£2.95**
Selections from the B-Text (Ed. Brock, S.)
[R49] Manchester UP pbk **£5.95**

Elizabethan & 17th Century Verse

Elizabethan Lyrics (Ed. Ault, Norman)
[R50] Faber pbk **£6.95**

Elizabethan Verse
[R51] Penguin pbk **£3.95**

Kissing the Rod: An Anthology of 17th Century Verse by Women
(Ed. Greer, Germaine)
[R52] Virago hbk **£27.50**

Metaphysical Lyrics
[R53] Oxford pbk **£4.95**

Metaphysical Poets (Ed. Gardner, Helen)
A classic, and still valuable anthology.
[R54] Penguin pbk **£3.50**

Silver Poets of the 16th Century
[R55] Dent pbk **£2.50**

The Oxford Book of 16th Century Verse
(Ed. Chambers, E.K.)
[R56] Oxford hbk **£21.50**

The Oxford Book of 17th Century Verse
(Ed. Grierson, H.J.C.)
[R57] Oxford hbk **£17.50**

CAMPION, THOMAS (1565 - 1620)
"When thou hast told these honours done to thee,/Then tell, O tell, how thou didst murder me". A doctor, musician and poet, Campion is best remembered for his 'ayres', poems sung by a solo voice with harmonized accompaniment. In his *Observations in the Art of English Poesy*, he argued in vain for the application of classical quantitative metre, although the system he proposes is useless. His poems are at once over-refined and incomparably skilful.
Ayres and Observations (Ed. Hart, Joan)
[R58] Carcanet pbk **£3.95**

CHAPMAN, GEORGE (c.1559 - 1634)
"Kneel then with me, fall worm-like on the ground,/And from th' infectious hill of this round,/From men's brass wits and golden foolery,/Weep, weep your souls, into felicity." Chapman's reputation comes second-hand - too often he is known as the collaborator with Fletcher or Massinger as a playwright, or from Keats' sonnet 'On First Looking into Chapman's Homer'. His version of Homer, scandalously out of print, is the finest translation. Carcanet's selection is a useful introduction to the poems.
Selected Poems
[R59] Carcanet pbk **£2.50**

COTTON, CHARLES (1630 - 87)
"From the bustle of the town,/And the knavish tribe of the gown,/From long bills where we are debtors,/From bum-bailiffs, and their setters,/From the tedious city lectures,/And thanksgiving for Protectors, Libera nos, etc..." Friend of Lovelace and Izaac Walton, whose *The Compleat Angler* he finished, Cotton is a neglected figure. Walton refers to his 'old-fashioned poetry, but choicely good'.
Selected Poems (Ed. Robinson, Ken)
[R60] Carcanet pbk **£3.95**

DONNE, JOHN (1572 - 1631)
Although his contemporary Ben Jonson thought that he deserved to be hanged 'for not keeping number', the energetic phrasing of Donne's metres has proved more congenial to our century. In the 1590s he produced his five satires and the best love poetry, which is frequently erotic, and turns on paradox and puns; it is a forceful riposte to the tired conventions of the Petrachan sonneteers. As T.S. Eliot wrote, 'a thought to Donne was an experience; it modified his sensibility.' The love poems are complimented by the more difficult divine ones; they are intellectually unresolved and to some less stylistically arresting. A Roman Catholic apostate, he took orders in the Anglican church in 1615, and as Dean of St Pauls he was a severe and brilliant sermon writer. The finest metaphysical poet.
Complete English Poems
(Ed. Smith, Albert James)
[R61] Penguin pbk **£6.99**

Complete English Poems
(Ed. Patrides, C.A.)
[R62] Dent pbk **£3.95**
John Donne's Poetry (Ed. Clemens, A.L.)
An excellent Norton Critical Edition for those who want notes on the poems.
[R63] Norton pbk **£5.95**
Poetical Works (Ed. Grierson, Sir Herbert)
[R64] Oxford pbk **£6.95**
Selected Prose
[R65] Penguin pbk **£4.99**
Selection of Poetry (Ed. Hayward, John)
[R66] Penguin pbk **£2.99**

DRAYTON, MICHAEL (1563 - 1631)
"Since there's no help, come let us kiss and part..." This is Drayton's most famous line, from his sonnet sequence *Idea*, and although he wrote in many other forms - eclogues, verse letters, the topographical poem on England *Poly-Olbion* - he is best remembered for his sonnets.
Selected Poems (Ed. Thomas, Vivien)
[R67] Carcanet pbk **£2.50**

GASCOIGNE, GEORGE (1530 - 1577)
"My worthy Lord, I pray you wonder not/To see your woodsman shoot so oft awry,/Nor that he stands amazed like a sot/And lets the harmless deer, unhurt, go by." Gascoigne is a transitional poet, a stepping stone between the first and second halves of the 16th century, between Wyatt and Spencer. He was also an innovator, writing the first English treatise on prosody, the first original blank verse poem, and the first prose comedy *The Adventures of Master F.J.*. Yvor Winters called Gascoigne's plain-spokenness 'almost an affectation of plainness, even of brusqueness' and believed him to be 'one of the masters of the short poem of the century'.
The Green Knight: Selected Poems and Prose (Ed. Pooley, Roger)
[R68] Carcanet hbk **£8.95**
[R69] Carcanet pbk **£4.95**

HERBERT, GEORGE (1593 - 1633)
"Of what an easy quick access,/My blessed Lord, art thou! how suddenly/May our requests thine ear invade!" Along with Donne, Herbert is the finest of the Anglican devotional poets. Despite the appeal to 17th century contemporaries, not least the Puritans, Herbert's work became unfashionable after his death because of its piety, and it took Coleridge to reassess it, perceiving the complex thought expressed with exemplary clarity and plainness. His work is characterized by simple, undecorated diction deployed in complex sentence structures: a master of form, his stanzas visually corroborate the meaning. Herbert saw his work as *"a picture of the many spiritual conflicts that have passed betwixt God and my soul, before I could subject myself to the will of Jesus my Master."*
English Poems (Ed. Patrides, C.A.)
[R70] Dent pbk **£2.50**
George Herbert and Henry Vaughan
(Oxford Authors)
[R71] Oxford hbk **£19.50**
[R72] Oxford pbk **£7.95**
Poems and Prose (Ed. Auden, W.H.)
[R73] Penguin pbk **£2.99**

HERRICK, ROBERT (1591 - 1673)
"When as in silks my Julia goes,/Then, then (methinks) how sweetly flows/The liquefaction of her clothes". Referred to by Swinburne as 'the greatest song-writer ever born to the English race', Herrick's work is characterized by its figurative language, delightful conceits and a concentration on the *sound* of the poems - even at the expense of meaning. A Cavalier poet, he owed poetic debts to Donne, Jonson and the classics.

Selected Poems (Ed. Jesson-Dibbley, David)
[R74] Carcanet pbk **£3.95**

HOWARD, HENRY, EARL OF SURREY
(1517 - 47)
"Set me where as the sun doth parch the green,/Or where his beams may not dissolve the ice…"
Beheaded for conspiring against the succession of Edward VI, Surrey was described by Thomas Wharton as 'the most elegant traveller, the most polite lover, the most learned nobleman, and the most accomplished gentleman of his age', and his life was idealized in Thomas Nashe's *The Unfortunate Traveller*. Often neglected during this century for the work of Wyatt, Surrey is a major innovative poet; he 'invented' blank verse, and domesticated the sonnet.
Selected Poems (Ed. Keene, Dennis)
[R75] Carcanet pbk **£3.95**

JONSON, BEN (1572 - 1637)
"Drink to me only, with thine eyes,/And I will pledge with mine;/Or leave a kiss but in the cup,/And I'll not ask for wine." Better known as a playwright, Jonson is also a considerable poet. When Swinburne talks of him as 'one of the singers who could not sing', he refers to Jonson's 'plainness'. His language is natural, and his poems contain little figurative excursion, but, based on classical models, they exhibit a masterly control of rhetoric, a perfect sense of balance and a subtle complexity of tone. If he could not sing, he could at least *speak* - if not a master of music, then he is a master of stress. If, as T.S. Eliot alleged, 'his poetry is of the surface', then it is a brilliantly articulated surface. Jonson's distinctive contributions are his 'country house' poems, his elegies and his epigrams - even his long poems tend towards the epigrammatic.
Ben Jonson and the Cavalier Poets (Ed. McLean, H.)
[R76] Norton pbk **£5.95**
Complete Poems
[R77] Penguin pbk **£7.95**
Selected Works (Oxford Authors)
[R78] Oxford hbk **£19.50**
[R79] Oxford pbk **£8.95**

LOVELACE, RICHARD (1618 - 57/8)
"Stone walls do not a prison make,/Nor iron bars a cage". A favourite at the court of Charles I, Lovelace wrote perhaps 30 perfectly accomplished poems, which merge metaphysical toughness with Jonsonian elegance; too often though, he preferred brilliance and surprise to clarity.
Selected Poems (Ed. Hammond, Gerald)
[R80] Carcanet pbk **£3.95**

MARLOWE, CHRISTOPHER (1564 - 93)
"Come live with me, and be my love,/And we will all the pleasures prove…" Better known as the author of plays such as *Tamburlaine* and *Doctor Faustus*, Marlowe's poetical output stands on its own strengths, and certainly its language is less strident than in the plays. His major work was *Hero and Leander*, a minature epic, about which Edgell Rickword commented: 'putting aside *Paradise Lost*, it would seem impossible to find a later rival to *Hero and Leander*'. It is the most classical of English love poems. As well as translations of Ovid and Lucan, Marlowe's *oeuvre* includes the famous lyric 'The Passionate Shepherd to His Love', which prompted replies from Ralegh and Donne.
Complete Poems and Plays
(Ed. Pendry & Maxwell)
[R81] Dent hbk **£8.95**
[R82] Dent pbk **£3.50**
Complete Poems and Translations
(Ed. Orgel, Stephen)
[R83] Penguin pbk **£4.95**

MARVELL, ANDREW (1621 - 78)
"My love is of a birth as rare/As 'tis for object strange and high:/It was begotten by despair/Upon impossibility". Known as MP for Hull, patriot, satirist and foe to tyranny, Marvell's lyric poetry was little known in his lifetime. A partial revival was started by Charles Lamb, continued in the 19th century by Tennyson, and only in the 20th century, with T.S. Eliot's influential essay, did his reputation reach its current height. Less brittle than Donne, his poems are oblique, witty and often enigmatic, with a microscopic visual correctness. His 'Horatian Ode upon Cromwell's Return from Ireland' is the finest political poem in the language.
Complete Poems (Ed. Donno, E.S.)
[R84] Penguin pbk **£5.95**
Complete Poetry (Ed. Lord)
[R85] Dent pbk **£2.95**
Selected Poems (Ed. Hutchings, Bill)
[R86] Carcanet pbk **£3.95**

MILTON, JOHN (1608 - 74)
"Of Man's first disobedience and the fruit/Of that forbidden tree whose mortal taste/Brought death into the world and all our woe,/With loss of Eden…" Given the widespread influence of Milton's blank verse, especially on 18th and 19th century poets, 20th century commentators - Leavis and Eliot, for example - have tended to stress only the harmful effects of Milton's latinate verse. Milton's strength - and sin - is his language, Leavis calling it 'cut off from speech'; whilst it has undeniable power and grandeur, it is easy to miss other qualities - it is delicate and subtle, witty and precise. Important works include *Comus*, the elegy 'Lycidas', and *Samson Agonistes*, but his masterpiece, and arguably the language's finest poem, is *Paradise Lost*, which deals with the fall from which Christ redeems man.
Complete Shorter Poems (Ed. Carey, John)
[R87] Longman pbk **£9.95**
Paradise Lost (Ed. Fowler, Alistair)
Many critics have disliked *Paradise Lost*: Dr. Johnson believed there was a 'want of human interest' in the poem, and Yvor Winters talked of the 'pompous redundancy of the verse', its dependence on 'literary stereotypes'. With its voluptuous blank verse, its biblical and classical allusions, and huge scope, Milton might appear a difficult poet; however, no literate person should be ignorant of his work, which is second only to Shakespeare. This edition is comprehensively edited and annotated, elucidating the poem's complexities.
[R88] Longman pbk **£9.95**

John Milton (Picture: National Portrait Gallery)

Poetical Works (Ed. Bush, Douglas)
[R89] Oxford pbk **£7.95**
Portable Milton
[R90] Penguin pbk **£5.95**
Prose Works
[R91] Dent hbk **£8.95**
Selected Poems of John Milton
(Ed. Lerner, Laurence)
[R92] Penguin pbk **£2.95**

RALEIGH, SIR WALTER (1552 - 1618)
"Of all which past, the sorrow only stays…" Scholar, soldier, poet, alchemist, introducer of the potato to Ireland and tobacco to England, court favourite, explorer and atheist, Raleigh was the paradigm of the 'renaissance man', but the prevailing tone of his work is of defeat and disappointment.
Selected Writings (Ed. Hammond, Gerald)
[R93] Carcanet hbk **£14.95**
[R94] Penguin pbk **£4.95**

SIDNEY, SIR PHILIP (1554 - 1618)
"Loving in truth, and fain in verse my love to show,/That the dear She might take some pleasure of my pain…" The first major English poet-critic, Sidney is a model of correctness, clarity and measure. Raleigh refers to him as the 'Scipio, Cicero and Petrach of our time'.
A Defence of Poetry
[R95] Oxford pbk **£2.25**
Selected Poems (Ed. Jones, Katherine Duncan)
[R96] Oxford pbk **£5.95**
Selected Writings (Ed. Dutton, R.)
[R97] Carcanet pbk **£3.95**
Sidney (Oxford Authors)   **NEW**
[R97A] Oxford hbk **£30.00**

SKELTON, JOHN (?1460 - 1529)
Although Pope dismissed him as 'beastly Skelton', and Wharton commented on his grotesque humour and lack of decorum, our century has been more generous: W.H. Auden and Robert Graves saw him as the transitional poet between the Middle Ages and the Renaissance. He is often seen as a difficult poet, and his 'skeltonics' - headlong, breath-less doggerel, featuring irregular lines, often with no apparent metre and aggresive, rattling rhymes - are unique. He referred to his own poems as 'trifles of honest mirth'.
Complete English Poems
(Ed. Scattergood, John)
[R98] Penguin pbk **£8.99**
Selected Poems (Ed. Hammond, Gerald)
[R99] Carcanet pbk **£3.95**

SPENSER, EDMUND (1552 - 99)
"Sweet Thames! run softly, till I end my song…" Referred to by Keats as the 'elfin poet', Spenser is a crucial influence on most major poets until the end of the 19th century - Milton, Blake, Wordsworth, Hardy and Byron all learned from him (his greatest detractor was Landor: 'Thee gentle Spenser fondly led/But me he mostly sent to bed'). As well as writing *The Shepheardes Calender*, his masterpiece is *The Faerie Queene*. Often called a poet's poet, he is now, sadly, often merely a scholar's poet. One of the essential writers in the English tradition.
Poetical Works (Ed. Smith & Selincourt)
[R100] Oxford pbk **£7.95**
The Faerie Queene (Ed. Hamilton, Albert C.)
Coleridge called *The Faerie Queene* 'an almost continued instance of beauty'. Written in the 'Spenserian stanza' (eight iambic pentameter lines and a linal hexameter, rhyming 'ababbcbcc'), it is deliberately archaic, allegorical, tending towards the figurative and ideal, yet also tender and lucid, if perhaps lacking in 'human interest'. It works by cumulative effect, and should be read in large chunks. This is an excellent annotated edition.
[R101] Longman pbk **£15.95**

The Faerie Queene (Ed. Roche & O'Donnell)
[R102] Penguin pbk **£12.95**

TRAHERNE, THOMAS (1637 - 74)
Initially thought to be the work of Henry Vaughan, Traherne's poetry has always lived in that shadow. Yet his exuberant, spontaneous verse, though written with visionary precision and rejecting the doctrine of original sin, rapturously celebrates creation and the boundless potential of man's mind and spirit, often foreshadowing Whitman!
Selected Writings (Ed. Davis, Dick)
[R103] Carcanet pbk **£3.95**

VAUGHAN, HENRY (Welsh, 1621 - 95)
*"I saw Eternity the other night/Like a great **Ring** of pure and endless light,/All calm, as it was bright..."* Clearly influenced by George Herbert, the work of Vaughan - who said of his mentor that 'holy life and verse gained many pious converts (of whom I am the least)' - is more rarified by comparison: his God is less present. His achievement was to bring the transcendent into the reach of the senses.
Complete Poems (Ed. Rudrum, Alan)
[R104] Penguin pbk **£6.95**
Selected Poems (Ed. Shaw, Robert B.)
[R105] Carcanet pbk **£3.95**

WYATT, SIR THOMAS (1503? - 42)
"They flee from me that sometime did me seek..." The introducer of new forms into English verse, including the Petrachan sonnet, Wyatt, at his best, is one of our finest lyric voices. His prosodic irregularity - a mixture of metrical and the older accentual verse - reveals an exciting rhythmic skill, contrasting with the 'smoothness' of his contemporary Surrey. His carnal, lusty sonnets are decidedly un-Petrachan; his language is colloquial and undecorated.
Complete Poems (Ed. Rebholz, R.A.)
[R106] Penguin pbk **£7.50**

Restoration & 18th Century Verse

18th Century Verse
[R107] Penguin pbk **£4.95**

Silver Poets of the 18th Century
[R108] Dent hbk **£8.95**

The New Oxford Book of 18th Century Verse (Ed. Lonsdale, Roger)
Lonsdale's 1984 anthology was a crucial attempt to re-adjust perceptions of the 18th century, away from received ideas of order; his range of poems is wide, and draws effectively on popular and vernacular work.
[R109] Oxford hbk **£19.50**
[R110] Oxford pbk **£6.95**

CHATTERTON, THOMAS (1752 - 70)
Referred to by Wordsworth as *"the marvellous boy,/The sleepless soul that perished in his pride"*, Chatterton's legend is better known than the work. After writing 'medieval' poems which he passed off as originals, attributing them to one Sir Thomas Rowley, he left his native Bristol for London, where after six months of struggling to survive, he committed suicide by taking arsenic. Admired by Keats, Shelley and Wordsworth, Chatterton's language is plain, its rhythms wonderfully resonant.
Selected Poems (Ed. Lindop, Grevel)
[R111] Carcanet pbk **£3.95**

COLLINS, WILLIAM (1721 - 59)
Although he only left 1,500 lines of verse after his short, troubled life, Collins is one of the most influential figures of the early 18th century. Dr Johnson commented on his wildness and extravagance, which produced obscurity as well as 'sublimity and splendour'. Later poets responded to his struggle against conventionality, his lyrical intensity, and his conception of poetry as sacred and visionary. His best known work is the 'Ode to Evening'.
Poems of Gray, Collins and Goldsmith (Ed. Lonsdale, Roger)
[R112] Longman pbk **£12.95**
Poetical Works (Thomas Gray and William Collins) (Ed. Johnstone, A.)
[R113] Oxford pbk **£7.50**

COWPER, WILLIAM (1731-1800)
"God moves in a mysterious way,/His wonders to perform..." Norman Nicholson talks of Cowper's verse having 'the merit of good conversation', and in *Table Talk*, Cowper presents himself with a similar modesty: *"I play with syllables, and sport in song"*. Yet many of his poems were written under the pressures of mental breakdown, and they mark a movement away fom the neo-classical themes of the 18th century towards Romanticism.
Selected Poems (Ed. Rhodes, Nick)
[R114] Carcanet pbk **£3.95**

CRABBE, GEORGE (1754 - 1832)
"Old Peter Grimes made fishing his employ,/His wife he cabin'd with him and his boy..." Crabbe wanted his readers to feel his writing - accounts of rural and provincial life, of individuals and communities, landscapes - was true; his contact with the physicality of things, and his eye for circumstantial detail led Byron to refer to him as 'though nature's sternest painter, yet the best'. Edward Fitzgerald believed that 'every thinking man will like him more as he grows older'.
Selected Poems (Ed. Poster, Jem)
[R115] Carcanet pbk **£4.95**

DRYDEN, JOHN (1631 - 1700)
A writer who redirected the current of English literature, Dryden is the successor of Marlowe and Jonson, and the father of the 18th century. His language is above all *efficient*, and if it lacks the intimacy and doubt of his predecessors, it is supremely suited to public, civic and social discourses rather than personal statement and evocation, as can be seen from the political satire *Absalom and Achitophel*. As T.S. Eliot put it, Dryden 'remains one of those who have set standards for English verse which it is desperate to ignore', and 'is one of the tests of a catholic appreciation of poetry.'
Dryden (Oxford Authors)
[R116] Oxford hbk **£22.50**
[R117] Oxford pbk **£8.95**
Poems and Prose (Ed. Douglas, Grant)
[R120] Penguin pbk **£3.50**

FINCH, ANNE - COUNTESS OF WINCHILSEA (1661 - 1720)
"How we are fallen! fallen by mistaken rules/And Education's, more than Nature's fools,/Debarred from all improvments of the mind,/And to be dull, expected and designed..." One of the earliest English women poets of importance, Finch was the friend of Pope, Swift and Purcell (who set one of her poems to music), and has been admired by Wordsworth and Arnold; although neglected in this century, she has been invoked by Virginia Woolf. Apparently happy in her marriage, she remained conservative in an age of liberal sentiment. Her poetry was influenced by 'the solitude and security of the country', and Wordsworth described it as 'chaste, tender, and vigorous'.

Selected Poems (Ed. Thompson, Denys)
[R121] Carcanet pbk **£3.95**

GAY, JOHN (1685 - 1732)
"Life is a jest; and all things show it,/I thought so once, but now I know it." Although better known for **The Beggar's Opera**, Gay was a master of the heroic couplet. His *Trivia* is one of the best poems about London, and owes its success to his ear for rhythms of speech and tones of voice. Despite a sybaritic lifestyle and a lack of ambition which ensured that he did not achieve all that he might have done, Gay remains an enjoyable figure, if a minor one in comparison to his fellow member of the Scriblerus club, Pope.
Selected Poetry (Ed. Walsh, Marcus)
[R122] Carcanet pbk **£3.95**

GOLDSMITH, OLIVER (1730 - 1774)
"Ill fares the land, to hastening ills a prey,/Where wealth accumulates and man decay..." Better known for his plays and the novel, **The Vicar of Wakefield**, Goldsmith's reputation as a poet rests on a handful of superb pieces. His finest poem is 'The Deserted Village': focusing on one imaginary place, Auburn, he elegizes the destruction of rural communities for the sake of commerce and exploitation, and vividly captures the charms of rural life.
Poems and Plays (Ed. Davis, Tom)
[R123] Dent hbk **£8.95**
Poems of Gray, Collins and Goldsmith (Ed. Lonsdale, Roger)
[R112] Longman pbk **£12.95**
Selected Writings (Ed. Lucas, John)
[R125] Carcanet pbk **£3.95**

GRAY, THOMAS (1716 - 71)
"The curfew tolls the knell of parting day,/The lowing herd winds sowly o' er the lea..." Among the most considerable of mid-18th century poets, Gray has the distinction of having written what is probably the best-known poem in the language - the 'Elegy'. His work is both solemn and light-hearted, and Donald Davie has commented that Gray 'was the last serious and greatly gifted poet to practice a rhetorical art'.
Poems of Gray, Collins and Goldsmith
[R112] Longman pbk **£12.95**
Poetical Works (Thomas Gray & William Collins) (Ed. Lonsdale, R.)
[R113] Oxford pbk **£7.50**
Selected Poems
[R128] Carcanet pbk **£3.95**

JOHNSON, SAMUEL (1709 - 84)
Samuel Johnson - poet, novelist, lexicographer, editor, biographer, critic, conversationalist - was the moral and critical centre of his age. His severe Augustanism, a sceptical Toryism and a belief in Reason, lead to a poetry characterized by critical discrimination and moral insight, generality and instruction. T.S. Eliot regarded 'The Vanity of Human Wishes' as the most accomplished satire in the language.
Poems
[R129] Oxford hbk **£32.50**
Samuel Johnson (Oxford Authors)
[R130] Oxford pbk **£7.95**

OLDHAM, JOHN (1653 - 1683)
Oldham is perhaps best known from Dryden's elegy: *"Farewel, too little and too lately known,/Whom I began to think and call my own;/For sure our souls were near ally'd; and thine/Cast in the same Poetick mould with mine"*. Ken Robinson's selection re-introduces a little-known poet to a wider public, and his introduction places Oldham in the context of the Restoration period.
Selected Poems
[R131] Bloodaxe pbk **£4.95**

Alexander Pope (Picture: National Portrait Gallery)

POPE, ALEXANDER (1688 - 1744)
In his use of Dryden's measure, the heroic couplet, Pope rediscovered many of the complexities of the poetic process which Dryden had refined away. If Dryden's couplets are self-contained, Pope's best contain a paradox or an irresolution which compels one to read on. Pope thinks in metaphors, shapes and forms - he does not decorate a rational line of thought with a metaphor. *The Rape of the Lock* is a masterpiece of mock-heroic writing, which pursues social foible to absurd lengths; despite his assurance and authority, *The Dunciad* is only a partial success, and the *Essay on Man* a failure as didactic and philosophical poetry. Urbane and civilized, he is, bar none, the poet of culture.
Poems of Alexander Pope
[R132] Penguin pbk **£2.95**
Collected Poems
[R133] Dent pbk **£2.95**
Poetical Works
[R134] Oxford pbk **£7.95**

SMART, CHRISTOPHER (1722 - 71)
Although his madness has clouded a genuine appreciation of the poems, Smart was a radical figure in the conventional 18th century; an enthusiast, a consummate verbal artist, and the possessor of a distinctive *poetic* imagination, Smart was no mere versifier. Northrop Frye refers to the magnificent *Song of David* as a 'musical tour de force', while Donald Davie suggests Smart is 'the greatest English poet between Pope and Wordsworth'.
Selected Poems
[R135] Carcanet pbk **£3.95**

SWIFT, JONATHAN (1667 - 1745)
"If on Parnassus' top you sit,/You rarely bite, are always bit:/Each poet of inferior size/On you shall rail and criticize…" The Dean of St Patrick's, Dublin, Swift's verse (as well as his prose - most notably *Gulliver's Travels*) is characterized by a sense of disgust - often of bodily functions - and an interest in the common people. The 'I' in his poetry speaks with an uncompromised acerbity few poets have mastered. Edgell Rickword felt that Swift's verse 'is the most intricate labyrinth of personality that any poet built around himself, not excepting Donne.'

Complete Poems
[R136] Penguin pbk **£12.95**
Selected Poems (Ed. Sisson, C.H.)
[R137] Carcanet pbk **£3.95**
Selected Works (Oxford Authors)
[R138] Oxford pbk **£7.95**

THOMSON, JAMES (Scottish, 1700-48)
"An elegant sufficiency, content,/Retirement, rural quiet, friendship, books." Perhaps Thomson's most famous lines - though few would be able to put his name to them - are 'Rule Brittania'. Nowadays largely neglected, he was greatly respected by Wordsworth and Dr Johnson, who thought that Thomson had 'a mind that at once comprehends the vast and attends the minute'. Sadly, his particular genius seems muted by his chosen form, a Miltonic blank verse: his finest work is *The Seasons*, where neo-Miltonic language blends with scientific and political reflection.
The Seasons & The Castle of Indolence
[R139] Oxford pbk **£6.95**

WILMOT, JOHN - EARL OF ROCHESTER (1648 - 80)
"Love a woman! You're an ass,/'Tis a most insipid passion/To choose for your happiness/The silliest part of God's creation." Restoration court wit and notorious libertine, Rochester 'blazed out his youth and health in lavish voluptuousness', as Dr Johnson put it, and he was caricatured as Dorimant in Etherege's *Man of Mode*. Yet he is a seriously neglected poet, and it is hard not to admire the scurrility of his satire, the frankness about sex, and the wit and complexity of his lyrics.
Complete Poems
[R140] Yale pbk **£11.95**
The Debt to Pleasure
[R141] Carcanet pbk **£3.95**

YOUNG, EDWARD (1683 - 1765)
"Be wise today; 'tis madness to defer." Young's most famous work is his monumental *Night Thoughts*, of which Dr Johnson thought that 'the power is in the whole; and in the whole there is a magnificence like that ascribed to Chinese plantation, the magnificence of vast extent and endless diversity'. It not only allied him to the contemporary 'graveyard' poets, but, in the combination of primitive orientalism with the poetry of 'the Sublime', anticipates the ruminative poetry of Wordsworth and the 'creative imagination' of the Romantic movement.
Selected Poems
[R142] Carcanet pbk **£3.25**

Romantic Verse

English Romantic Verse
[R144] Penguin pbk **£3.95**

BEDDOES, THOMAS LOVELL (1803 - 49)
"If thou wilt ease thine heart/Of love and all its smart…" A bizarre literary enigma, Beddoes was obsessed with the macabre, the supernatural and bodily decay. He was heavily influenced by the Jacobean dramatists - Lytton Strachey called him 'the last Elizabethan' - and yet is comparable to Baudelaire or Poe; each page seems to feature grotesque imagery leavened only by grisly humour. His major work is *Death's Jest-Book*, but he is best known today for his short lyrics.
Selected Poems
[R146] Carcanet pbk **£2.50**

BLAKE, WILLIAM (1751 - 1827)
"O Rose, thou art sick!" Apart from the Royal Academy of Art - his graphics are central to his work - Blake received little formal education, and this lead to a crucial imaginative independence; F.R. Leavis claimed Blake was 'individual, original, and isolated enough to be without influence.' The originality is best found in his short lyrics in *The Songs of Innocence and Experience*. His individuality, however, and what Leavis calls 'the absence of adequate social collaboration' contributed to the pretensions of the bloated Prophetic books where visionary symbolism mixes with inert and opaque poetry; they are too remote from the real world, too occupied with esoteric ideas. His best poems exist independently of his symbolic philosophy.
Complete Poems
[R147] Penguin pbk **£10.95**
Poems
[R148] Longman pbk **£12.95**
Selected Poetry
[R149] Penguin pbk **£3.99**
Songs of Innocence and Experience
This volume, and its companion, the Oxford *Marriage of Heaven and Hell*, present Blake's poems accompanied by their original colour plates.
[R150] Oxford pbk **£5.95**
The Marriage of Heaven and Hell
[R151] Oxford pbk **£4.95**
William Blake (Oxford Authors)
[R152] Oxford hbk **£25.00**
[R153] Oxford pbk **£8.95**

BURNS, ROBERT (Scottish, 1759 - 96)
The case against Burns has been made by Hugh MacDiarmid: he set a disastrous example with his demotic Scots poems, leading to successors adopting an outmoded style and subject matter, producing a cultural and linguistic stereotype. Burns has not been helped by his fierce - if, as Donald Davie has pointed out, posthumous - adoption by chauvinistic Scots, which has seen him relegated to a cultural cul-de-sac. Yet Burns has a versatility, thematic and tonal, that few English poets can match. Matthew Arnold helped strip away the sentimental gloss Burns had received, talking of his 'fiery, reckless energy', and commenting that 'his view is large, free, shrewd, benignant - truly poetic'.
A Choice of Burns' Poems and Songs
[R154] Faber pbk **£3.95**
Poems and Songs
[R156] Oxford pbk **£7.95**

BYRON, LORD GEORGE (1788 - 1827)
The legend - scandals, exile, the death at Missolonghi - is better known than the poetry; Bertrand Russell commented that 'as a myth his importance, especially on the continent, was enormous'. Perhaps the Byronic hero is his most imporant invention, the outcast wandering in exile contemplating the injustices done him in the past. Poetically, he is the heir of Pope: in his masterpiece, *Don Juan*, where light satire mixes with impassioned writing, he controls his digressive manner superbly, and the narrative voice, by turns urbane, cynical and virulent, is a wonderful creation.
Byron (Oxford Authors)
[R157] Oxford hbk **£22.50**
[R158] Oxford pbk **£9.95**
Don Juan
[R159] Penguin pbk **£10.95**
Poetical Works
[R160] Oxford pbk **£8.95**

CLARE, JOHN (1793 - 1864)
"I AM: yet what I am none cares or knows…" Too often today Clare is admired for his poems which reveal a personal vulnerability, which resulted in his incarceration in Northampton General Asylum. More distinctively his poetry is a place away from man, where nature is evoked with a strong verbal and

visual facility. Edward Thomas calls him 'a peasant writing poetry...[who] had to do what he could with the current forms of polite literature.'

John Clare (Oxford Authors)
[R161] Oxford pbk **£5.95**
Selected Poems
[R162] Dent pbk **£3.50**
Selected Poems and Prose
[R163] Oxford pbk **£5.95**
The Parish
[R164] Penguin pbk **£2.95**
The Rural Muse
[R165] Carcanet pbk **£5.95**
The Shepherd's Calendar
[R167] Oxford pbk **£3.50**

COLERIDGE, SAMUEL TAYLOR
(1772 - 1834)
Drug addict, political turncoat and mystic humbug, Coleridge is, with Wordsworth, one of the central progenitors of English Romanticism, and with Samuel Johnson, the greatest critical intelligence among English poets. His *On the Constitution of Church and State*, the great book of conservative political ideas, and *Biographia Literaria*, his theories of Imagination and Fancy, are central contributions to English thought. His major poems are 'Christabel', 'Kubla Khan' and 'The Rime of the Ancient Mariner'.

Biographia Literaria
[R168] Dent pbk **£3.50**
Poems
[R169] Dent pbk **£2.50**
Poems and Prose
[R170] Penguin pbk **£2.95**
Poetical Works
[R171] Oxford pbk **£8.95**
Samuel Taylor Coleridge (Oxford Authors)
Contains much of the poetry, the complete *Biographia Literaria*, substantial extracts from the prose, as well as many of his more informal writings.
[R172] Oxford hbk **£19.50**
[R173] Oxford pbk **£7.95**
Selected Poems of Samuel Taylor Coleridge
[R174] Penguin pbk **£2.50**
Selected Poetry   NEW
(Ed. Empson & Pirie)
Re-issue of Empson's controversial edition.
[R175] Carcanet pbk **£4.95**

KEATS, JOHN (1795 - 1821)
"'*Beauty is truth, truth beauty*' - that is all/Ye know on earth, and all ye need to know". Keats is one of the central Romantic poets; Tennyson considered him the greatest poet of his century, and Matthew Arnold captured the essence of his work when he said that 'Keats as a poet is abundantly and enchantingly sensuous; the question with some people will be, whether he is anything else.' One of the virtues of his work, though, is that he does not 'philosophize', and he referred to his 'yearning passion for the Beautiful'. Dying at only 26, the last five years of his life were remarkably creative - *Endymion*, 'The Eve of St Agnes', 'La Belle Dame Sans Merci', the magnificent letters, and in particular, the *Odes* came in this period. If Keats lacked the intellectual resources of Coleridge or Shelley, he came closest to solving the problems of form they all struggled with.

Complete Poems
[R176] Penguin pbk **£7.99**
Poems
[R177] Longman pbk **£12.95**
Poetical Works
[R178] Oxford pbk **£6.95**
Selected Poetry
[R179] Penguin pbk **£2.99**

LANDOR, WALTER SAVAGE (1775 - 1864)
"*I strove with none; for none was worth my strife;/Nature I loved, and next to Nature, Art...*" Caricatured by Dickens as Boythorn in *Bleak House*, Landor is best remembered for his short lyrics to Ianthe and Rose Aylmer. In the period of the Romantics, Landor was a radical, a neo-classical poet with a Greek imagination. As his greatest 20th century champion, Ezra Pound, put it, 'the effect of his severe classical studies never deserts him'; he adopts traditional forms, and he writes with a quiet sensuousness in what Pound called a language 'far removed from any speech ever used anywhere'.

Selected Poems and Prose
[R180] Carcanet hbk **£12.95**

SHELLEY, PERCY BYSSHE (1792 - 1822)
"*Walk upon the winds with lightness,/Till they fail, as I am falling,/Dizzy, lost, yet unbewailing.*" Shelley saw no distinction between poetry and politics, and his work revitalizes the radicalism of earlier Romantic writing. His extraordinary lyric powers and glamorized life story tend to obscure other sides of him - his intellectual courage and his hatred of injustice. His work is sometimes marred by rhetorical abstraction and excesses, intellectual arrogance and an intense self-pity, but he explodes such limitations in poems such as 'Ode to the West Wind', or in 'The Defence of Poetry'. A poet of volcanic hope for a better future.

Poetical Works
[R181] Oxford pbk **£7.95**
Selected Poems
[R182] Dent pbk **£2.75**
Selected Poems of Percy Bysshe Shelley
[R183] Penguin pbk **£3.50**
Shelley's Poetry & Prose
[R184] Norton pbk **£8.95**
Shelley's Prose: or The Trumpet of a Prophecy
The eagerly awaited re-issue of the complete prose works with a new preface by Harold Bloom.
[R186] Fourth Estate pbk **£10.95**

WORDSWORTH, WILLIAM (1770 - 1850)
Chief architect of the Romantic movement, Wordsworth published the revolutionary *Lyrical Ballads* with Coleridge in 1798, which included the first of the descriptive meditations, *Tintern Abbey*. He is celebrated as the poet who could divine the secret pressures of the landscape and capture the powers of memory, and himself described his poetry as 'emotion recollected in tranquility', he often started from the lost sights of childhood - the fading 'visionary gleam' of *Ode: Intimations of Immortality from Recollections of Childhood*. His long autobiographical poem *The Prelude* (in three versions) stands as one of the major works of English poetry.

A Choice of Wordsworth's Verse
[R187] Faber pbk **£3.95**
Lyrical Ballads 1798
[R188] Oxford pbk **£2.95**
Poems Vol 1
[R189] Penguin pbk **£10.00**
Poetical Works
[R190] Oxford hbk **£37.50**
[R191] Oxford pbk **£7.95**
Selected Poems of William Wordsworth
[R192] Penguin pbk **£1.95**
Selected Poetry and Prose   NEW
(Ed. Hobsbaum, Philip)
[R193] Routledge pbk **£5.95**
Selected Prose Writings
[R195] Penguin pbk **£6.95**
The Prelude
[R196] Penguin pbk **£7.99**
[R197] Oxford pbk **£5.95**

The Prelude 1799, 1805, 1850
(Ed. Abrams, Gill & Wordsworth)
Wordsworth's long autobiographical poem, presented here in the three major stages of its development and modification.
[R198] Norton pbk **£8.95**
William Wordsworth (Oxford Authors)
[R199] Oxford pbk **£7.95**

Victorian Verse

Everyman's Book of Victorian Verse
(Ed. Watson, J.R.)
The main lights of Watson's slightly sentimental anthology are Tennyson and Arnold.
[R200] Dent hbk **£12.00**
[R201] Dent pbk **£4.50**

The New Oxford Book of Victorian Verse
(Ed. Ricks, Christopher)
Ricks' brilliant anthology casts an ironic eye on the Victorian age, and its purpose is to reproach those who tried 'to write as the great had successfully done'. Ricks' main poets are Browning and Clough, there is a good selection from Barnes, forgotten poets are revived, while Cosmo Monkhouse proves a witty antidote to pomposity.
[R202] Oxford hbk **£16.95**

Victorian Verse
[R204] Penguin pbk **£6.99**

ARNOLD, MATTHEW (1822 - 88)
"*And we are here as on a darkling plain/Swept with confused alarms of struggle and flight,/Where ignorant armies clash by night.*" There is great variety in Arnold's poetic output - he wrote lyrics ('Dover Beach'), narratives ('Sohrab and Rustum'), poetic drama ('Empedocles on Etna'), and elegies ('The Scholar Gipsy'). Often derived from classical subjects, and troubled by contemporary Victorian issues such as Darwinism, they are informed by alienation, despair, stoicism and spiritual emptiness.

Culture & Anarchy (Prose)
[R205] Cambridge pbk **£7.95**
Matthew Arnold (Oxford Authors)
[R206] Oxford hbk **£19.50**
[R207] Oxford pbk **£8.95**
Selected Poems and Prose
[R208] Dent hbk **£8.95**
[R209] Dent pbk **£2.95**
Selected Poems of Matthew Arnold
[R210] Penguin pbk **£2.99**
Selected Prose
[R211] Penguin pbk **£6.99**
The Poems of Matthew Arnold
[R212] Longman pbk **£13.95**

BARNES, WILLIAM (1801 - 1886)
"*Within the woodlands, flow'ry gleaded,/By the woak tree's mossed moot...*" Obsessed with the necessity of rejecting foreign words and returning to the purity of Anglo-Saxon English, Barnes brought his beliefs into his poetry, which evokes the Dorset landscape and country customs, by writing in dialect. Often thought of as a quaint provincial versifier, Barnes' command of folk idiom is of more than philological interest, and he attracted a small circle of admirers, including Hardy and Hopkins, who thought that 'Barnes is the perfect artist - it is as if Dorset life and Dorset landscape had taken flesh and blood in the man.'

Selected Poems
[R213] Carcanet pbk **£3.95**

POETRY

BRONTE SISTERS

"Cold in the earth, and the deep snow piled above thee!/Far, far removed, cold in the dreary grave!". Better known as novelists, Emily, Anne and Charlotte Brontë were also poets. Charlotte was only competent, Anne developed a distinguished personal voice, but Emily emerges from Stevie Davies' selection as one of the great women poets of our tradition.
Selected Poems (Ed. Davies, Stevie)
[R214] Carcanet pbk **£3.95**
[R215] Blackwell pbk **£7.95**

BROWNING, ELIZABETH BARRETT
(1806 - 61)
"How do I love thee? Let me count the ways/I love thee to the depth and breadth and height/My soul can reach..." Although the romance overshadows the work - she eloped with Robert Browning to escape her despotic father - Barrett Browning is a considerable poet: erudite, politically radical, she was independent minded, foreshadowing feminism in many ways, and an important innovator.
Selected Poems
[R216] Chatto hbk **£12.95**
[R217] Carcanet pbk **£3.95**

BROWNING, ROBERT (1812 - 1889)
"...Art remains the one way possible/Of speaking truth, to mouths like mine at least". It is Browning's use of the dramatic monologue - a trying on of a succession of masks - which has made him such an important influence on Eliot, Pound, and other 20th century poets. His development of the 'persona' poem, his insistence on something like the speaking voice in his poems, and the lack of an articulate philosophy make him an interesting, if suggestively incomplete, writer. A prolific poet, his major works are *The Ring and the Book*, a massive account of a 17th century Roman murder, and 'Childe Roland to the Dark Tower Came'.
Poems
Vol 1
[R219] Penguin pbk **£12.95**
Vol 2
[R218] Penguin pbk **£12.99**
Poetical Works 1833 - 1864
[R220] Oxford pbk **£16.25**
Selected Poems of Robert Browning
[R221] Penguin pbk **£3.50**
The Ring and the Book
[R222] Penguin pbk **£10.00**

CARROLL, LEWIS (1832 - 98)
"Twas brillig, and the slithy toves/Did gyre and gimble in the wabe;/All mimsy were the borogoves,/And the mome raths outgrabe". Lewis Carroll was the *nom de plume* of Charles Lutwidge Dodgson, a mathematics don at Oxford. *Alice's Adventures in Wonderland* revolutionized children's literature, and the clever puzzles and word games of his nonsense verse - such as *The Hunting of the Snark* - are as fresh as ever.
Humorous Verse
[R223] Dover pbk **£5.85**
The Annotated Snark
[R224] Penguin pbk **£4.99**

CLOUGH, ARTHUR HUGH (1819 - 61)
"Say not the struggle nought availeth,/The labour and the wounds are vain..." Clough is a strangely neglected poet: his two long, hexameter narrative poems - *The Bothie of Tober-na-Vuolich*, which is about a student reading party in Scotland, and *Amours de Voyage*, about sensitive English travellers in Europe - are elegant, compressed alternatives to bloated Victorian novels.
Selected Poems
[R225] Carcanet pbk **£3.95**

The Poems
[R226] Oxford pbk **£9.95**

HOPKINS, GERARD MANLEY (1844 - 89)
As a Jesuit priest, Hopkins felt there was an incompatability between his vocation and his writing. He burned much of his early poetry, but was encouraged to write *The Wreck of the Deutschland*, which was dedicated to the memory of five Franciscan nuns drowned in the Thames. Although this was denied periodical publication, he continued to write, and his best poems include 'The Windhover' and 'Pied Beauty'. His poetry deals with his spiritual relations with God, expressed in an ecstatic response to nature. His pursuit of a language of inspiration meant that he broke with conventional diction, and he revived archaisms; he called this method 'sprung rhythm', an attempt to reconcile speech rhythms with the greatest possible poetic emphasis, scanning stresses, the number of which remain constant, rather than the syllables. Partly because he did not gain a wide readership until the publication of Bridges' edition of 1918, he is often seen as a precursor of modernism.
Gerard Manley Hopkins (Oxford Authors)
[R227] Oxford hbk **£17.50**
[R228] Oxford pbk **£8.95**
Poems and Prose
[R229] Penguin pbk **£3.95**
Poems of Gerard Manley Hopkins
[R230] Oxford pbk **£3.95**
Selected Prose
[R231] Oxford pbk **£3.95**

LEAR, EDWARD (1812 - 88)
Lear began to write nonsense verse for the children of the Earl of Derby while working at Knowsley Hall; later he started to illustrate them, and these two talents combined to produce many charming books. His numerous well-known poems include 'The Owl and the Pussycat', 'The Jumblies', and 'The Courtship of the Yongy-Bongy-Bo'. Many of his creations - 'The Dong with the Luminous Nose' and 'The Pobble Who Has No Toes' - are partial self-portraits, and reflect his lonely, melancholy life.
The Nonsense Verse of Edward Lear
[R232] Methuen pbk **£5.95**

MEREDITH, GEORGE (1828 - 1909)
"Then each applied to each that fatal knife,/Deep questioning, which probes to endless dole./Ah, what a dusty answer gets the soul/When hot for certainties in this our life!" Perhaps most noted for his novels *The Egoist* and *Diana of the Crossways*, Meredith's verse is currently emerging from a period of eclipse. Among his diverse *oeuvre* most notable is *Modern Love*, a sonnet sequence examining marriage. It is peculiar in its use of the 'Meredithian' sonnet form, which consists of 16 lines, a form currently popularized by Tony Harrison.
Selected Poems
[R233] Carcanet pbk **£4.95**

ROSSETTI, CHRISTINA (1830 - 94)
"When I am dead, my dearest,/Sing no sad songs for me..." Referred to by Ford Madox Ford as 'the most valuable poet that the Victorian age produced', Rossetti has left us poems - devotional, love lyrics, descriptive pieces - which are quiet and unemphatic, controlled yet passionate. Philip Larkin thought her poetry 'unequalled for its objective expression of happiness denied and a certain unfamiliar steely stoicism.'
A Choice of Christina Rossetti's Verse
[R234] Faber pbk **£2.95**

Goblin Market (Illus. Rackham, Arthur)
[R235] Harrap pbk **£2.95**
Selected Poems
[R236] Carcanet pbk **£3.95**

SWINBURNE, ALGERNON CHARLES
(1837 - 1909)
Swinburne is an extraordinary and paradoxical figure; side by side exist a passion for liberty and a desire for subjection - his prostration before hired flagellants is notorious. He had a naive political and poetical romanticism, which led to a vagueness of thought which he mistook for a profound sensibility. Yet he had an extraordinary prosodic skill, and developed an extreme approach to diction, rhythm and form, where the flow of words is everything.
Selected Poems
[R239] Carcanet pbk **£3.95**

TENNYSON, ALFRED LORD (1809 - 92)
T.S. Eliot considered Tennyson to be a great poet because of the 'abundance, variety, and complete competence' of his work. He (rightly) commended the variety of metrical accomplishment, and said that he had 'the finest ear of any English poet since Milton.' The weaknesses of his poetry were pointed out by Matthew Arnold who, uncharitably, castigated Tennyson for being 'deficient in intellectual power'. If his greatest fault is a narrowness of register, his strength lies in his sense of the power and sound of language. *In Memoriam* and *Maud* remain as two of the finest 19th century poems, and present memorable depictions of grief.
'In Memoriam', 'Maud' and Other Poems
[R240] Dent pbk **£2.50**
A Selected Edition (Ed. Ricks, Christopher)
Selected from Ricks' acclaimed classic three-volume complete edition.
[R241] Longman pbk **£14.95**
Idylls of the King
[R242] Penguin pbk **£7.95**
Poems and Plays
[R243] Oxford pbk **£8.95**
Selected Poems of Alfred Lord Tennyson
[R244] Penguin pbk **£2.95**

John Keats (Picture: National Portrait Gallery)

Elizabeth Jennings (Photo: B.J. Harris, Oxford)

Elizabeth Jennings

If I listed every book which has been valuable to me in one way or another during my life, I might well use up almost a quarter of these splendid pages. But, of course, there are certain ones which came either at a formative stage in my writing life and others which are important simply for the great pleasure they still give me.

In my childhood, which was a long one as I was an extremely late developer, I liked Louisa Alcott's *Little Women*, *Good Wives* and *Little Men* as well as Susan Coolidge's *What Katy Did* and *What Katy Did at School*. I had a sister two years older than myself, but I always longed for a brother, a little younger, a little older or, best of all, a twin. So, like many children, I invented one called Jack Baycock. Thus I always loved stories about families and, to this day, have never been greatly drawn to fairy stories or science fiction. At one time I must have known *Little Women* and *What Katy Did* almost by heart, yet I always read from the books day and night. Children are in general callous (perhaps it is the only way they can survive) and I relished the dramatic illnesses of Beth and of Katy. I disliked, however, any form of piety and always skipped the long 'holy' scene between Cousin Helen and Katy.

Later on I read E. Nesbit's books; it is true that they contain an element of fantasy but not too much for my juvenile taste. And, although I have never sailed in my life, I had a passion for the children in Arthur Ransome's book, especially *Winter Holiday* and *We Didn't Mean to Go to Sea*. All of these books fed my hunger for a large family. At the age of thirteen (I was still in all senses a child) I loved *Pride and Prejudice* which is so sparingly written and astringently romantic. I disliked *Twelfth Night* at school because I thought its treatment of love was 'soppy'. In my early teens I read *Tom Brown's Schooldays* and *Stalky and Co*. I still return to the latter with enormous pleasure; it is so wonderfully subversive - the boys always get the better of the masters.

Perhaps surprisingly I did not much care for poetry at this time. I did not think of Shakespeare as poetry and I wallowed in *Macbeth*. Poetry came as a revelation to me; that is no exaggeration. In a school anthology called *The Dragon Book of English Verse* we one day 'did' Chesterton's great battle poem *Lepanto*. I was overwhelmed by its vivid language and striking rhythms "Dim drums throbbing in the hills half-heard...", "The shadow of the Valois is yawning at the Mass" and so on. This poem was the beginning of my passion for poetry. It was at this time that I began writing fairly well-crafted but ludicrously over-ambitious ballads and odes.

I was very lucky to be at the Oxford High School; we had such splendid teachers. From Chesterton we passed on to the Romantics. I know so many of Keats's and Coleridge's poems by heart that I would only want to put as the first item on my Book List Keats's superb letters. They are so vivid, so *right* about the making of poems. These letters, too, display a charming character, a literary saint. And all these letters were written by a young man who died, after much suffering, in his mid-twenties. I am tempted to choose Coleridge's wise *Biographia Literaria* but must confine myself to one book from this period in English poetry.

I have had a passion for the theatre from an early age. I never deluded myself that I had any acting ability but I did act a little in childhood and at Oxford. I saw John Gielgud's *Macbeth* when I was a child in a school party and he

remains my favourite actor. At 85 he is still working hard and I am fortunate enough to correspond with him from time to time. I would want his book *Stage Directions* on my list because it shows, with total humility, what one man alone has done for the English stage, especially for Shakespeare. His last *Hamlet* in 1944 remains my favourite one. I have never seen it surpassed.

I am a Roman Catholic and love the mystical writing in *The Cloud of Unknowing* and in Julian of Norwich's work. However, I would choose an inspired book from a much earlier period than the Middle Ages for my list of indispensables. It is St Augustine's *Confessions* and it must be in Pusey's poetic and lucid translation. This book reminds me of Ostia Antica near Rome and, indeed, of all that Rome meant to me in the late fifties and early sixties. I fell in love with the city and will not return because I could not bear to have my peerless memories spoilt. So I would add to my list Phaidon's full *Guide to Rome and Latium* with its coloured photographs and maps. Looking at this book I can easily recreate the many months I spent there in the Spring and in September and October.

I now come to the hardest part of this essay. It is very nearly impossible for me to choose poets but, after much struggling and arguing with myself, I would want

John Gielgud, by Clive Francis from *Blessings in Disguise* by Alec Guinness (Hamish Hamilton hbk £12.95, Fontana pbk £3.95)

W.H. Auden (Photo: BBC Hulton Picture Library)

the *Collected Poems* of Auden, the *Collected Poems* of Yeats and Richard Ellmann's *New Oxford Book of American Verse*. I have not included any poets from past periods except *The Collected Poems of George Herbert*. He has won a close race with Hopkins, Eliot, Donne, Wordsworth, Matthew Arnold and Chaucer. Echoes of all these poets ring in my ears. Shakespeare, of course, is in my blood.

This piece sounds more and more like a *Desert Island Discs* choice. Well, that is what it is in so far as all the books I have chosen are indispensable to me. When it comes to novels, choosing becomes excessively difficult, with the exception of Jane Austen and some of George Eliot, I find that it is the 20th century novels which excite me most. I could not do without some Evelyn Waugh. He writes simple, impeccable prose and his humour and range of characters are equal to that of Dickens. Penguin's *Sword of Honour* trilogy would suit me very well. In a totally different and experimental way, Virginia Woolf's *The Waves* is, for me, compulsive reading. It is closer to an extended prose poem than any conventional novel. It is a work of nuance and suggestion, of rhythm and music, of image and character.

Books:

John Keats: *Letters* (Oxford, pbk £6.95)
John Gielgud: *Stage Directions* (Hodder & Stoughton, pbk £7.95)
The Confessions of St Augustine (unfortunately Pusey's translation is currently unavailable)
Guide to Rome and Latium (Phaidon, pbk £9.95)
W.H. Auden: *Collected Shorter Poems 1927-57* (Faber, pbk £4.95)
W.H. Auden: *Collected Longer Poems* (Faber, pbk £5.95)
W.B. Yeats: *Collected Poems* (Macmillan, pbk £7.99)
The New Oxford Book of American Verse (edited by Richard Ellmann, Oxford, hbk £25.00)
George Herbert: *Collected Poems* (Penguin, pbk £2.99)
Evelyn Waugh: *The Sword of Honour Trilogy* (Methuen, hbk £10.95/Penguin, pbk £5.95)
Virginia Woolf: *The Waves* (Hogarth, hbk £10.95/Panther, pbk £2.95)

Since the publication of her first collections of poetry in the 1950s, Elizabeth Jennings has established herself as one of the distinctive voices of post-war British poetry. Her *Collected Poems 1953-86* won the W.H.Smith award in 1986; her most recent collection is *Tributes*.

John Keats by C.A. Brown
(Picture: The National Portrait Gallery)

The Geoffrey Faber Memorial Prize

Founded in 1963 in memory of the founder of Faber & Faber Ltd, the prize of £500 is awarded annually and given, alternately, for the work of fiction or verse from the previous two years that judges deem to possess the most abundant literary merit. The three judges must be reviewers of poetry or fiction and are nominated by the editors or literary editors of the newspapers and magazines for which they write.

1964 Christopher Middleton *Torse 3*
       George Macbeth *The Broken Places*
1965 Frank Tuohy *The Ice Saints*
1966 Jon Silkin *Nature With Man*
1967 William McIlvanney *Remedy is None* (Eyre & Spottiswoode)
       John Noone *The Man with the Chocolate Egg* (Hamish Hamilton)
1968 Seamus Heaney *Death of a Naturalist* (Faber)
1969 Piers Paul Read *The Junkers* (The Alison Press)
1970 Geoffrey Hill *King Log* (Deutsch)
1971 J G Farrell *Troubles* (Cape)
1972 Tony Harrison *The Loiners* (London Magazine Editions)
1973 David Storey *Pasmore* (Longman)
1974 John Fuller *Cannibals and Missionaries* (Secker)
       Epistles to Several Persons (Secker)
1975 Richard Wright *The Middle of a Life*
1976 Douglas Dunn *Love or Nothing* (Faber)
1977 Carolyn Slaughter *The Story of the Weasel* (Hart-Davis, MacGibbon)
1978 David Harsent *Dreams of the Dead* (Oxford)
       Kit Wright *The Bear Looked Over the Mountain* (Salamander)
1979 Timothy Mo *The Monkey King* (Deutsch)
1980 George Szirtes *The Slant Door* (Secker)
       Hugo Williams *Love Life* (Deutsch)
1981 J M Coetzee *Waiting for the Barbarians* (Secker)
1982 Paul Muldoon *Why Brownlee Left* (Faber)
       Tom Paulin *The Strange Museum* (Faber)
1983 Graham Swift *Shuttlecock* (Penguin)
1984 James Fenton *In Memory of War* (Salamander)
1985 Julian Barnes *Flaubert's Parrot* (Cape)
1986 David Scott *A Quiet Gathering* (Bloodaxe)
1987 Guy Vanderhaeghe *Man Descending* (Bodley Head)
1988 Michael Hoffman *Acrimony* (Faber)
1989 David Profumo *Sea Music* (Secker)

20th Century Poetry

Anthologies

A Various Art (Ed. Crozier, Andrew & Longville, Tim)
Adventurous selection of experimental poets who have chosen to work outside the establishment of British poetry. Poets include Roy Fisher, J.H. Prynne and John Riley.
[R245] Carcanet hbk **£12.95**

British Poetry since 1945
(Ed. Lucie-Smith, Edward)
Wide-ranging anthology which was judiciously revised in 1985.
[R246] Penguin pbk **£5.99**

Eleven British Poets   **NEW**
(Ed. Schmidt, Michael)
As an alternative to Alvarez, this is a fine survey of post-war poetry, with a more open-minded approach to important, modernist British writers - it includes large selections of Sisson, Graham and Tomlinson.
[R247] Routledge pbk **£6.95**

English Poetry 1918 - 1960
[R248] Penguin pbk **£3.95**

First and Always (Ed. Sail, Lawrence)
Charming anthology of contemporary poetry with a difference - the proceeds go to the Great Ormond Street Children's Hospital. Poets include Seamus Heaney and C.H. Sisson.
[R249] Faber pbk **£4.95**

Georgian Poetry (Ed. Reeves, James)
Judicious re-examination of Georgian verse which tries to answer the question 'what were the positive merits of the poetry which was wholly superceded in critical esteem in the late 1920s?'. It includes work by Blunden, de la Mare, W.H. Davies, Edward Thomas and Robert Graves.
[R250] Penguin pbk **£3.50**

New Chatto Poets II (Ed. Motion, Andrew)
Motion's anthology introduces six poets who, although they have appeared in magazines, have yet to publish in book form - they are Susanne Ehrhardt, Paul May, Lucy Anne Watt, Robert Crawford, Sarah Maguire and Mark Ford. A guide to the future of Chatto's list!
[R251] Chatto pbk **£5.95**

New Poetry (Ed. Alvarez, Al)
Seminal but dated collection of post-war verse, whose polemical introduction stresses the pre-eminence of the American confessional poets over those of the Movement.
[R252] Penguin pbk **£4.99**

Noise and Smokey Breath (Ed. Whyte, Hamish)
An anthology of Glasgow poems 1900-1983, this superb collection is profusely illustrated with paintings and photographs.
[R253] Third Eye Centre pbk **£5.95**

Nua-Bhardachd Ghàidhlig/Modern Scottish Gaelic Poems
Excellent bilingual selection of the work of Sorley MacLean, George Campbell Hay, Derick Thomson, Iain Crichton Smith and others.
[R254] Canongate pbk **£4.95**

Poetry of the Thirties (Ed. Skelton, Robin)
Interesting introduction to the period, with the poems divided into thematic sections.
[R256] Penguin pbk **£4.99**

Poetry of the Forties (Ed. Skelton, Robin)
Skelton offers poems divided into thematic sections, with work from major figures of the time - Dylan Thomas and Roy Fuller - and more interestingly, from neglected poets such as Julian Orde Abercrombie and Nicholas Moore.
[R255] Penguin pbk **£4.95**

Some Contemporary Poets of Britain and Ireland (Ed. Schmidt, Michael)
Intriguing alternative to Motion and Morrison's Penguin book; whilst there is some overlap of poets - Harrison, Wainwright, Scupham, for example - Schmidt's book has a less parochial selection, including work from Frank Kuppner, Dick Davis, and John Ash.
[R257] Carcanet hbk **£9.95**

The Faber Book of 20th Century Verse
(Ed. Heath-Stubbs, John & Wright, David)
Rather than defining one tradition (as Roberts did in his Faber anthology), Heath-Stubbs and Wright's indecisive anthology attempts to display the whole history of English poetry from Hardy until 1975 (when it was last revised). Its alphabetical order makes for some odd bedfellows, as the book includes Lascelles Abercrombie as well as Ezra Pound, and unread figures such as Paul Potts and J.C. Squire.
[R258] Faber pbk **£4.95**

The Faber Book of Contemporary Irish Poetry (Ed. Muldoon, Paul)
[R259] Faber pbk **£10.95**
[R260] Faber pbk **£5.95**

The Faber Book of Modern Verse
(Ed. Roberts, Michael)
Classic anthology which defined the modern movement. Getting hold of the original edition is vital, as each of the revisions has been disastrous; the revisions have not been made in the spirit of the original. Peter Porter's (1982) is the least convincing; rather than a book with an idiosyncratic and stimulating point of view, it is merely a hodge-podge.
[R261] Faber hbk **£12.50**

The New British Poetry   **NEW**
(Ed. D'Aguiar, Fred & Allnutt, Gillian)
This unusual anthology features Black, Feminist and modern writing; new writers rub shoulders with more established names, to produce what Peter Ackroyd has called 'one of the most important developments in the publishing of poetry in recent years'.
[R262] Paladin pbk **£6.95**

The Oxford Book of 20th Century Verse
(Ed. Larkin, Philip)
Controversial anthology with a characteristic anti-modernist slant, featuring a host of obscure Georgians at the expense of 'harder' modernist poems.
[R263] Oxford hbk **£13.50**

The Oxford Book of Contemporary Verse (Ed. Enright, D.J.)
Enright offers a selection from what he refers to as 'the poetry of civility, passion and order', casting a net which takes in Commonwealth and American as well as British work. Chronologically it runs from Stevie Smith (born 1902) to Douglas Dunn (born 1942), taking in James K. Baxter, Derek Walcott and Elizabeth Bishop.
[R264] Oxford pbk **£5.95**

The Penguin Book of Contemporary British Poetry (Ed. Motion, Andrew & Morrison, Blake)
Heavily criticised but influential gathering of work from younger poets; it includes good work from Heaney, Harrison and Fenton, but puts too heavy an emphasis on the 'Martian' poets.
[R265] Penguin pbk **£3.95**

The Poetry Book Society Anthology 1988 - 89   **NEW**
(Ed. Constantine, David)
A selection of new poems from poets including Fleur Adcock, R.S. Thomas, E.J. Scovell and Robert Wells.
[R266] Hutchinson pbk **£6.95**

Poets

ABSE, DANNIE (Welsh, 1923 -)
A practicing doctor from Welsh-Jewish stock, Abse tries to write poems which *"appear translucent but are in fact deceptions"*. They reflect a wide range of experience - especially that of a doctor and a Jewish cultural outsider - yet remain within the English tradition of intimate address to the reader.
Ask the Bloody Horse
[R268] Hutchinson pbk **£4.95**
Collected Poems 1948 - 1976
[R269] Hutchinson pbk **£6.95**

ADCOCK, FLEUR (New Zealand, 1934 -)
Although born in New Zealand, Adcock has settled in Britain. Perhaps her best known poem is 'Against Coupling', which is a homage to masturbation. Her latest book, *The Virgin and The Nightingale*, is a splendid collection of translations from medieval Latin, including erotic pieces by Peter du Blois and from the *Carmina Burana*.
Hotspur
[R270] Bloodaxe pbk **£2.50**
Meeting the Comet
[R271] Bloodaxe pbk **£2.95**
Selected Poems
[R272] Oxford pbk **£4.95**
The Virgin and the Nightingale
[R273] Bloodaxe pbk **£5.95**

AMIS, KINGSLEY (1922 -)
Better known for his novels such as *Lucky Jim*, Amis has written poetry influenced by Graves, Auden, and his friend and fellow member of the Movement, Philip Larkin, though without achieving the latter's skill and eminence. Amis takes a plain man's stance, distrusting extremes and relying on common sense, and his bluffly deflating language is intentionally unmusical and unresonant.
Collected Poems 1944 - 79
[R274] Hutchinson pbk **£6.95**

ASH, JOHN (1948 -)
"There are still more hairs on my head/Than there are croissant outlets in Seattle./People tell me I'm looking good, but should I believe them/..Is anyone more trustworthy than a newspaper?" Now living in New York, Ash is one of the best of younger British poets: he works through styles learnt from John Ashbery and the French Symbolists, and his work is filmic and witty, original and immediate, in a mode which Ash refers to as 'urban pastoral'. Dana Gioia comments that 'the effect is rather like reading Nabokov versified by Supervielle.'
Disbelief
[R275] Carcanet pbk **£6.95**
The Branching Stairs
[R276] Carcanet pbk **£4.95**
The Goodbyes
[R277] Carcanet pbk **£3.25**

ASHBY, CLIFF (1919 -)

Ashby's work suffers from an extraordinary neglect. He writes of the intensely respectable petty-bourgeois world of the West Yorkshire in which he lives, in a manner which is honest, vivid and refreshing.

Plain Song: Collected Poems
[R278] Carcanet hbk **£9.95**

AUDEN, W.H. (1907 - 73)

As the great poet of the 1930s, Auden's reputation is strangely uneven. His early poems are social and vivid, with left-wing sympathies, and show influences of Old English metrical forms, a love of the northern English landscape and a reading of Freud. But perhaps the greatest works are of the late 1930s and early 40s, and poems such as 'In Praise of Limestone', 'September 1, 1939' and 'Lay your sleeping head...'. He is least admired for his later work, which is lucid, bookish and over-intellectual, and where his Christianity is evident. Literature replaced life as his subject matter; yet his technical control is impeccable and the later work remains as a repository of poetic forms.

Collected Longer Poems
[R279] Faber pbk **£5.95**

Collected Poems (Ed. Mcndelson, Edward)
This is the first paperback publication of the *Collected Poems*, which presents the (often revised) versions of the poems which Auden wished to preserve.
[R280] Faber hbk **£15.00**
[R281] Faber pbk **£9.95**

Collected Shorter Poems
[R282] Faber pbk **£3.95**

Norse Poems
[R283] Faber pbk **£4.95**

Selected Poems
[R284] Faber hbk **£9.95**
[R285] Faber pbk **£3.95**

The English Auden
A valuable collection of Auden's writings - poetry, reviews, sketches and prose - up to the time of his departure for America in 1939. It includes poems removed by Auden from later collections, including one of his greatest, 'September 1, 1939'.
[R286] Faber pbk **£7.95**

BARKER, GEORGE (1913 -)

The misunderstood surrealism and garbled rhetoric of Barker's early work marked him out for comparisons with Dylan Thomas, and this unfortunate association has dogged him throughout his career. His first masterpiece was the notorious *True Confession of George Barker*, but perhaps his best work has come in the 1970s and 80s, in his collections *Dialogues, Etc*, *Villa Stellar*, and *Anno Domini*. It is only sad that his marvellous *Collected Poems* is issued in such an unattractive format.

Anno Domini
[R287] Faber pbk **£4.00**

Collected Poems
[R288] Faber hbk **£27.50**

Villar Stellar
[R289] Faber pbk **£2.50**

BARKER, HOWARD (1946 -)

The celebrated playwright, author of *The Love of a Good Man*, has published three collections of verse. Barker contemplates the modern world with its cruelties, dilemmas and tyrannies.

Don't Exaggerate: Desire and Abuse
[R290] Calder pbk **£3.95**

Lullabies for the Impatient
[R291] Calder pbk **£3.95**

The Breath of the Crowd
[R292] Calder pbk **£2.95**

BECKETT, SAMUEL (Irish, 1906 -)

Better-known as a novelist and dramatist, Beckett has also written verse; like Joyce's poems they are minor work, in the Irish tradition of melodious, subjective gloom. Yet in them we see a certain concentration, and something missing from the other texts, a peering into the intimate hurts of his heart.

Collected Poems 1930 - 1978
[R293] Calder pbk **£4.95**

Collected Poems in English and French
[R294] Calder pbk **£4.95**

BEER, PATRICIA (1924 -)

The appearance of Patricia Beer's *Collected Poems* is a major event. It represents three decades of work, and contains work from her seven previous volumes, as well as a number of new poems. The scope of her poetry is wide, and her formal concerns remain strong. Quirky yet dependable, her work moves from an early concentration on metrical verse to an interest in free verse and syllabics. Robert Lowell thought her to be one of the best contemporary poets.

Collected Poems
[R295] Carcanet hbk **£16.95**

BELL, MARTIN (1918 - 78)

As a member of the Group, whose meetings he parodied in 'Mr Hobsbaum's Monday Evening Meeting', Bell wrote deliberately populist poetry, by turns belligerent and delicate. His most famous poem is 'Headmaster: Modern Style'.

Collected Poems
[R296] Bloodaxe hbk **£12.95**
[R297] Bloodaxe pbk **£5.95**

BERRY, JAMES (Jamaican, 1948 -)

Berry came to England in 1948, and has since steadily made his name as a critic and poet. In *Chain of Days* he considers Old and New Worlds: from Africa, slavery, colonization and life in Britain and America, he gathers and reassesses both a past and a present.

Chain of Days
[R298] Oxford pbk **£4.95**

BETJEMAN, JOHN (1906 - 84)

"Come, friendly bombs, and fall on Slough..."
Betjeman was the most popular poet of his day, and that popularity tends to stand in the way of a proper assessment, although he was admired by W.H. Auden and Philip Larkin. His work is technically conservative, and reliant on well-worn rhymes and regular rhythms, but comments drily on English middle-class life, its aspirations shot through with sadness.

Best of Betjeman
[R299] Penguin pbk **£3.95**

Church Poems
[R300] J Murray pbk **£7.95**

Collected Poems
[R301] J Murray hbk **£11.95**
[R302] J.Murray pbk **£6.95**

Ring of Bells
[R303] J Murray pbk **£4.95**

Summoned by Bells
[R304] J Murray hbk **£11.95**
[R305] J Murray pbk **£6.95**

Uncollected Poems
[R306] J Murray hbk **£5.95**

BLUNDEN, EDMUND (1896 - 74)

"I have been young, and now am not too old..."
Blunden's poetry is characterized by the quiet authority and fine craftsmanship associated with the Georgians, and his best poems 'Report on Experience' and 'Third Ypres' come out of his participation in World War I.

Selected Poems of Edmund Blunden
[R307] Carcanet pbk **£5.95**

BOLAND, EAVAN (1944 -)

A teacher and friend of Derek Mahon's, Boland was at one time a poet of short, clipped lines, but has also written in longer rhythmical units.

The Journey and Other Poems
[R308] Carcanet pbk **£4.95**

BRACKENBURY, ALISON (1953 -)

After two highly-praised collections, *Dreams of Power* and *Breaking Ground*, Brackenbury's third, *Christmas Roses*, is a collection of her vivid short lyric poems. In subject they include childhood, animals shadowed by people, South Africa, risk, love: nothing is quite as one anticipates in her work.

Christmas Roses
[R312] Carcanet pbk **£6.95**

BROOKE, RUPERT (1887 - 1915)

His good looks and early death - of blood-poisoning on the way to the Dardanelles - guaranteed Brooke's transformation into a symbol of romantic patriotism. His verse is characteristically Georgian, colloquial and nostalgic. His light verse anthology pieces include 'The Old Vicarage, Grantchester' and 'Heaven'. His most famous poem 'The Soldier' (*"If I should die, think only this of me..."*), with its classically sentimental attitude to the slaughter on the Western Front, was rapturously received on its first publication in 1915.

Collected Poems
[R316] Sidgwick hbk **£10.95**

The Collected Poems　　　　**NEW**
Not the *Complete* Brooke, but it has a new - if somewhat unenthusiastic - introduction by Gavin Ewart.
[R317] Sidgwick pbk **£9.95**

The Poetical Works of Rupert Brooke
[R318] Faber pbk **£3.95**

BROWNJOHN, ALAN (1931 -)

One of the most considerable political poets writing today, Brownjohn's topical verse often comprises monologues delivered in character: he has commented that much of his verse tends towards the 'condition of fiction'.

Collected Poems 1952 - 86
[R320] Hutchinson pbk **£5.95**

BUNTING, BASIL (1911 - 85)

Ignored by the British reading public until the publication of the outstanding *Briggflatts* in 1966, Bunting has started to receive a proper recognition as one of the finest English poets since the war. Although his sensibility is profoundly English, Northumbrian even, his technique is American, shows the influence of Pound and Zukofsky. His work is notable for its brilliant compression and musical forms; as Donald Davie has said, 'this is where English poetry has got to, it is what English poets must assimilate and go on from'.

Collected Poems
[R322] Oxford pbk **£7.95**

FORDE, VICTORIA

The Poetry of Basil Bunting　　　**NEW**
This first critical study of Bunting's work draws upon the work and letters of Bunting and his contemporaries as well as interviews with family and friends.
[R323] Bloodaxe hbk **£17.95**
[R324] Bloodaxe pbk **£8.95**

BURNSIDE, JOHN (1955 -)

In his first collection, *The Hoop*, Burnside takes his bearings from Celtic mythology, and the Gloucestershire landscape. With a disciplined eye and ear, he endorses a belief that landscape, by being described, is valued and preserved.

The Hoop　　　**NEW**
[R330] Carcanet pbk **£5.95**

CAMERON, NORMAN (Scottish, 1905 - 53)

Although Cameron has never lacked admirers among fellow poets - who include Roy Fuller, Geoffrey Grigson, and Robert Graves - his skilful, moving and quietly memorable poems have lacked a wider

readership because of their unavailability - they were last printed in 1959. The *Collected Poems*, which includes 13 previously uncollected poems and his translations of Heine, Nezval and Villon, should repair this state of neglect.

Collected Poems
[R331] Anvil pbk **£12.95**

CARSON, CIARON (Irish)
Steeped in traditional Irish culture, Ciaron Carson is able to encapsulate history, terrifyingly, in an anecdote, and he is a fine story-teller in verse. His poems about Belfast are savagely grim, reminiscent of R.S. Thomas or Robert Frost.

The Irish for No
[R332] Bloodaxe pbk **£4.95**

CAUDWELL, CHRISTOPHER (1901 - 1937)
The pseudonym of Christopher St John Sprigg, Caudwell drove an ambulance in the Spanish Civil War, where he was killed. The work in his *Collected Poems* lacks literary sophistication and often falls in-to stilted earnestness, but the plain language and sim-ple forms have an unsentimental realism and urgency.

Collected Poems
[R333] Carcanet pbk **£5.95**

CAUSLEY, CHARLES (1917 -)
Although Causley began writing verse as a response to his experience of World War II and the personal losses this entailed, a recurrent pre-occupation is the possibility of innocence and renewal, an impulse which discovers resonant analogies in the rich folk traditions of his native Cornwall. Frequently introspective, his writing still maintains a kind of stubborn bouyancy that is derived from an obsessive interest in early ballad forms.

Collected Poems
[R334] Macmillan pbk **£5.95**
Secret Destinations
[R335] Macmillan pbk **£7.95**

CHARLTON, GEORGE (1950 -)
Charlton's poems are about the heroisms of ordinary lives. Most are set in his native North East - in the pubs, on the street, down the allotments. Douglas Dunn calls him 'deft in rich phrasing'.

Nightshift Workers
[R336] Bloodaxe pbk **£4.95**

CLARKE, GILLIAN (Welsh, 1937 -)
Among the best loved of contemporary Welsh poets, Clarke writes about Wales, and adopts Welsh-language patterns of assonance and metrical forms with great skill. She finds the subjects of her poems in legends and their modern embodiments, and her themes include fertility, endurance and natural duty.

Letting in the Rumour
[R338] Carcanet pbk **£4.95**

CLEMO, JACK (1916 -)
As he is blind and deaf, Clemo's career has sometimes been seen (unhelpfully) as a triumph over adversity. Yet the muscularity of his verse, which features a tortured Christian existentialism and blasted Cornish landscapes, is unique. His *Selected Poems* shows the full range of his work, from the strident, Calvinist work of his early period, to the later, more humane poetry in which a late appreciation of modernism is apparent.

Selected Poems
[R339] Bloodaxe pbk **£6.95**

CONRAN, TONY
Blodeuwedd (Lament for Children)
An elegiac new collection including homages for Sorley Maclean and 'Elegy for the Welsh Dead' written about the Falklands War.
[R340] Poetry Wales P pbk **£3.95**

CONSTANTINE, DAVID (1944 -)
Influenced by Robert Graves, Constantine's poems are erudite, erotic and culturally wide-ranging; he brings a classical, European sensibility to bear on observed reality. Although he has a descriptive accuracy, at times the erudition is too heavy, the biblical and mytholgical references too conspicuous - in his later collection *Madder* we are faced by Orpheus, Yseut, Don Giovanni, Pan and Christ. His distinctive and assured handling of syntax, though, makes him one of the best poets on the Bloodaxe list.

Madder
[R341] Bloodaxe pbk **£4.95**

COPE, WENDY (1945 -)
Britain's best-selling poet, Wendy Cope is noted for her parodies and satires.

Making Cocoa for Kingsley Amis
[R342] Faber pbk **£3.95**

CORNFORD, JOHN (1915 - 1936)
An English communist who served with the Interna-tional Brigade in the Spanish Civil War, Cornford was killed at the Cordoba front. His early poetry is influ-enced by the work of his mother, Frances Cornford, and his later work keeps its clarity and direct simplic-ity despite a rebellion in favour of the modernism of Graves, Auden and Eliot. Some of the love poems in *Poems from Spain, 1936* are his best work.

Collected Writings
[R343] Carcanet pbk **£5.95**

CRONIN, ANTHONY (Irish, 1925 -)
Cronin's best poems, such as 'Elegy for the Night-bound', combine urban anguish with an impressive command of rhetorical verse forms. C.H. Sisson com-ments that 'about the verse of Cronin there is neither twilight nor romanticism, and it is as if the strenuum of the best Irish prose had entered the verse at last.'

Letter to an Englishman (1985)
[R344] Raven Arts pbk **£2.95**
New and Selected Poems (1982)
[R345] Carcanet pbk **£3.95**
Reductionist Poem (1980)
[R346] Raven Arts pbk **£1.95**
The End of the Modern World
[R347] Raven Arts pbk **£4.95**

CURTIS, TONY (Welsh, 1946 -)
One of Wales' most popular poets, Tony Curtis' new collection, *The Last Candles*, confirms his range. He celebrates love and family ties, without sentimentality, and brings a vast range of historical and contemporary perspectives into play.

Selected Poems 1970 - 1985
[R348] Poetry Wales P pbk **£3.95**
The Last Candles **NEW**
[R349] Seren Books pbk **£4.95**

D'AGUIAR, FRED
Mama Dot
Immensely popular collection of poems from a buoyant, witty West Indian poet.
[R350] Chatto pbk **£3.95**

DAVIE, DONALD (1922 -)
After 20 years in the States, Davie has returned to the England which, in imagination, he never left - Northern, non-conformist, conservative and slightly cantankerous. This is the voice that informs his new collecton, *To Scorch or Freeze*, an investigation in 46 poems of what it is to be God-fearing. In the ancient tradition of versified paraphrases of Scripture, and drawing on Golding, Watts, Smart and the Book of Common Prayer, Davie asks why it is so hard to approach the big themes without irony and self-effacement.

Collected Poems
[R351] Carcanet pbk **£6.95**

To Scorch or Freeze **NEW**
[R352] Carcanet pbk **£6.95**
Under Briggflatts **NEW**
Under Briggflatts is a history of the last 25 years of British poetry, with excursions into criticism, philosophy and translation, written by one of the most notable critics of our time. Davie considers a vast range of writers, from Austin Clarke, Basil Bunting and Keith Douglas, through to Tony Harrison, Geoffrey Hill and Seamus Heaney.
[R353] Carcanet hbk **£18.95**

DAVIES, W.H. (Welsh, 1871 - 1940)
Davies' experiences as a tramp are described in *The Autobiography of a Super-Tramp*. His poems - there are over 600 in all - are uneven, but the best have a spontaneous freshness inspired by an unambiguous love of nature.

Selected Poems
[R354] Oxford pbk **£3.95**

DAVIS, DICK (1945 -)
Devices and Desires: New and Selected Poems adds 23 new poems to a substantial selection from Davis' three previous books. A practitioner of the 'plain style', in the tradition of Jonson, Winters and Gunn, his poems possess clarity of diction and syntax, use traditonal metres, and are morally evaluative; yet they have a distinct personal voice.

New and Selected Poems
[R355] Anvil hbk **£9.95**
[R356] Anvil pbk **£4.95**

DAY-LEWIS, CECIL (Irish, 1904 - 1972)
Generally considered as a minor figure of the 'MacSpaunday' group, Day-Lewis' early work was marked by a tension between Marxist poitics and a tendency towards romanticism. 'Newsreel' and 'The Bombers' are his best political poems. Despite many establishment honours, including the Poet Laureateship in 1968, his reputation declined, as his post-war work bore the hallmarks of a dry formalism.

Lasting Joy
[R357] Unwin pbk **£1.95**

DOUGLAS, KEITH (1920 - 1944)
Although he is regarded as the finest English poet of the Second World War, Douglas is not specifically a war poet, and his poems have not dated. He enlisted when war was declared - serving in England and then North Africa, and his prose book *Alamein to Zem Zem* is an outstanding account of the experience; wounded in Palestine, he soon returned to active service, and was killed in France. With his model, Isaac Rosenberg, he shares a sense of the choicelessness of the situation. His most chilling poem, because of the chilling neutrality of the tone, is 'How to Kill': *"How easy it is to make a ghost"*, he writes, as if sniper's work has become child's play.

A Prose Miscellany
[R358] Carcanet hbk **£10.95**
The Complete Poems
[R359] Oxford pbk **£5.95**

DUFFY, MAUREEN (1933 -)
Playwright, novelist and poet, Duffy has made a significant contribution to women's literature by dealing frankly and tenderly with lesbian relationships. Her poetry is fresh, accessible and often eloquent.

Collected Poems
[R362] H Hamilton hbk **£10.95**
[R363] H Hamilton pbk **£5.95**

DUNMORE, HELEN
Helen Dunmore's new collection *The Raw Garden* examines the changes in landscape - felled trees, drained land - wrought through centuries of human intervention; she asks us to explore our sense of the

POETRY

'natural'. This book of closely linked poems celebrates a world of landscapes and human relationships familiar from her two earlier collections.

The Raw Garden **NEW**
[R364] Bloodaxe pbk **£4.95**

DUNN, DOUGLAS (Scottish, 1942 -)
One of the best-selling contemporary poets, Dunn's work is continually evolving. His fine first collection *Terry Street*, influenced by Philip Larkin, has detailed explorations of underprivileged lives. Later collections developed more fantastical and surrealistic strands, and his early career can be overviewed in his *Selected Poems 1964 - 83*. *Elegies* mourns the death of the poet's wife. His latest collection, *Northlight*, contains an elegy for Larkin.

Elegies
[R365] Faber pbk **£3.95**
Northlight
[R366] Faber hbk **£8.95**
[R366A] Faber pbk **£3.95**
Selected Poems 1964 - 83
[R367] Faber pbk **£4.95**

DURCAN, PAUL (Irish, 1944 -)
Durcan's poems are cinematic and whimsical, cramming together ideas, reported speech, moments of dislocation and non-sequiturs. *Berlin Wall Café* was a Book Society Choice.

Berlin Wall Café
[R368] Blackstaff pbk **£4.95**
Going Home to Russia (1987)
[R369] Blackstaff pbk **£4.95**
The Selected Paul Durcan (1982)
[R371] Blackstaff pbk **£4.95**

DURRELL, LAWRENCE (1912 -)
Better known as the author of *The Alexandria Quartet*, Durrell is also a poet; he has written that *"thought-clusters, constellations of ideas linked by private assocations, characterize poetic thinking as against the ratiocinative, noetical operations of the philosophers"*, and it is in terms of the ideogram, that most concentrated and direct representation of the associative thought, that he views as the highest poetic achievement. Durrell comments that he has 'produced five or six good poems', and there are odd flashes of brilliance in the flawed works.

Collected Poems
[R372] Faber hbk **£9.00**
[R373] Faber pbk **£5.95**

DUTTON, G.F. (Scottish, 1924 -)
Characteristically Dutton's poems are minimalist and imagistic evocations of landscape. Anne Stevenson has commented that 'he stands alone in a new rank of an old tradition. I think he is one of the most important poets of our time'.

Camp One
[R374] Macdonald pbk **£2.00**
Squaring the Waves
[R375] Bloodaxe pbk **£3.95**

ELIOT, T.S. (1888 - 1965)
Eliot's influence on the development of 20th century verse has been profound. As a precocious Harvard philosophy graduate he arrived at Oxford to study with the metaphysician F.H. Bradley and much of his early verse and criticism is written from under the shadow of Bradley's magisterial *Appearance and Reality*. This scientific precision, with its impersonal presentation of the '*significant*' emotion' was leavened by Eliot's admiration for the ironic wit displayed by symbolists like Laforgue and his burgeoning interest in oriental mysticism. This distinctly anti-Romantic cross-fertilisation came to fruition in 1922 with *The Waste Land*, a brilliant, if bitter, tessellation of poetic fragments, skilfully reworked by Ezra Pound (then Eliot's mentor) into the definitive work of High

Modernism. Eliot's slow and difficult progression into the Christian faith forms the subject matter for his subsequent verse. Critics have complained at its lack of humour and its political conservatism, and bemoaned the apparent adandonment of poetic wit. However, *Four Quartets* represents the most convincing modern attempt to write a long meditative poem in the Dantean tradition; and in its complex musings on the interconnections of history, faith, memory, despair and elemental reality it is perhaps best seen as the logical extension of Eliot's early (paradoxical) aim to write as an escape from both emotion and personality: *"But, of course, only those who have personality and emotions know what it means to want to escape from these things."*

Collected Poems 1909 - 1962
[R378] Faber pbk **£3.95**
Complete Poems and Plays
[R379] Faber pbk **£10.00**
Four Quartets
[R380] Faber pbk **£1.95**
Old Possum's Book of Practical Cats
[R381] Faber pbk **£2.50**
Selected Poems
[R382] Faber pbk **£2.95**
The Illustrated Old Possum (Colour Illus. Nicolas Bentley)
[R383] Faber pbk **£3.50**
The Waste Land
[R384] Faber pbk **£2.95**
The Waste Land: A Facsimile
A facsimile and transcript of original drafts, including the annotations of Ezra Pound, edited by Valerie Eliot.
[R385] Faber hbk **£17.50**
[R386] Faber pbk **£9.95**

ELLIOT, ALISTAIR (1932 -)
Bringing together the work from his 5 earlier collections, and adding many new poems, Alistair Elliot's *Collected Poems* shows him as a poet of unusual scope. A traveller who immerses himelf in the places he visits, his *On the Appian Way* sequence recounts a trip on foot along the route Horace took in 37 BC, along the length of the Appian way, from Rome to Brindisi. Erudite and witty, his work is immediately attractive for its formal control and inventiveness.

Collected Poems
[R387] Carcanet hbk **£18.95**

EMPSON, WILLIAM (1906 - 1984)
When his *Collected Poems* first appeared in 1955, Empson was already regarded as one of the century's central writers, principally because of his brilliant critical works, which include *Seven Types of Ambiguity*. Empson is a poet of wit, in the metaphysical sense of having 'the intellect at the tip of the senses'. Often learned and allusive, his verse uses analytical argument and imagery drawn from modern physics and mathematics, that employs, with virtuoso skill, linguistic, metrical and syntactical complexities.

Collected Poems
[R388] Hogarth pbk **£4.95**

ENRIGHT, D.J. (1920 -)
An academic, critic and poet, Enright has made a plea for *"the poetry of civility, passion and order"* in reaction against the 'confessional' subjectivity of Robert Lowell or John Berryman. His own work is distinguished by its supple tone, which is detached and ironic, although not neccessarily cold.

Collected Poems (1987)
[R389] Oxford hbk **£10.95**
[R390] Oxford pbk **£6.95**
Instant Chronicles: A Life
[R391] Oxford pbk **£4.50**

EVANS, CHRISTINE
Cometary Phases **NEW**
[R392] Seren Books pbk **£4.95**

POETRY

EWART, GAVIN (1916 -)
The prolific Ewart is notable for his light and comic verse, with a skill for parody, and a penchant for erotic verse (which led WH Smith to ban his book *Pleasures of the Flesh*!). Martin Booth has described his work as 'risqué, charming, witty, blunt, rude, serious, touching, flippant and skilful.'
All My Little Ones
[R393] Anvil pbk **£3.95**
Collected Ewart 1933 - 80
[R394] Hutchinson pbk **£6.95**
Penultimate Poems `NEW`
Ewart's latest collection features poems about the harshness of wars and religions, (with reference to Gibbon), the literary scene, glimpses of the ancient world, and the consolation of cats.
[R395] Hutchinson pbk **£5.95**

FAINLIGHT, RUTH (1931 -)
Fainlight writes for a wide audience, and there are similarities in her work with Ted Hughes (of *Crow*), and the poetry of her husband, Alan Sillitoe. John Heath-Stubbs comments that 'this very accomplished poet is also a most delicate and sensitive observer.'
New and Collected Poems
[R396] Hutchinson pbk **£5.95**
Selected Poems
[R397] Hutchinson pbk **£5.95**

FANTHORPE, U.A. (1929 -)
Collecting the best of her work from her three Peterloo books, U.A. Fanthorpe's Penguin *Selected Poems* quickly drew her a large readership. Although she is erudite, at home in a classical past, her poems are often set in the decaying NHS of the present, as her characters face up to death with stoicism. Accomplished, painful and honest.
A Watching Brief
[R398] Peterloo pbk **£4.50**
Selected Poems
[R399] Peterloo hbk **£7.50**
[R400] Penguin pbk **£2.95**

FEINSTEIN, ELAINE 1930 -)
Feinstein has cited Wallace Stevens as an early influence, and her poems are notable for their exploration of perception and imagery.
Badlands
[R401] Hutchinson pbk **£5.95**
The Border
[R402] Hutchinson pbk **£6.95**

FENTON, JAMES (1949 -)
Fenton's poetry is a testament to chance: poems such as 'A German Requiem' and 'Chosun' owe their existence to chance reporting assignments, and he explores the ideas of the 'found' poem in 'Exempla', where library catalogues or Victorian geology books seem to have beem rummaged through. Yet he owes to W.H. Auden the discursive forms he uses to explore history and politics, as the poems deal with the aftermaths of wars in Cambodia and Germany; his poems deal with real places and people, but often capture the absurd, surreal side of events.
Memory of War/Children in Exile Poems 1968 - 83
[R403] Salamander hbk **£7.95**
[R404] Penguin pbk **£3.50**
Parting Time Hall (with Fuller, John)
[R405] Salamander pbk **£7.50**

FISHER, ROY (1930 -)
Influenced by the American Black Mountain School, Fisher's modernist and experimental approach mixes with a deliberately provincial subject matter, seeking material in the industrial landscapes of the West Midlands, as shown in his long poem 'The City', which is about Birmingham. His poetry is intensely English despite its American forms.

John Fuller whose *Selected Poems 1954 - 1982* are published by Secker & Warburg (hbk £10.95) & Penguin (pbk £3.95)

A Furnace
[R407] Oxford pbk **£4.95**
Poems 1955 - 1987 `NEW`
[R408] Oxford pbk **£7.95**

FULLER, JOHN (1937 -)
Like his friend and collaborator James Fenton, Fuller is indebted to W.H. Auden, and his early work is effortlessly fluent and urbane. Turning away from modernism, Fuller has preferred to use traditional verse forms, and achieved technical triumphs in the rigorously organized Petrarchan sonnet sequence *The Labours of Hercules*, and in *The Illusionists*, a long narrative poem which borrows the stanza form from Pushkin's *Eugene Onegin*.
Parting Time Hall (with James Fenton)
[R409] Salamander pbk **£7.50**
Selected Poems 1954 - 1982
[R410] Secker pbk **£10.95**
[R411] Penguin pbk **£3.95**
The Grey Among the Green
[R412] Chatto pbk **£4.96**

FULLER, ROY (1912 -)
Fuller's work is characterised by left-wing sympathies and an interest in man as a social animal; later he became interested in outlining individual psychologies, in his most interesting collections of the late 50s and 60s. He is a delightful technician, but his interest in form, his detachment and his easy use of irony leave him open to criticisms of unadventurousness. His powers remain undimmed, however.
Available for Dreams `NEW`
Available for Dreams continues Fuller's late flowering, in which a lifetime's thought and feeling, and a delight in the infinitely variable sonnet form, establish the Fuller world of music and science, birds and history and suburbia.
[R413] Collins hbk **£11.00**
Consolations
[R414] Secker pbk **£4.95**
New and Collected Poems
[R415] Secker hbk **£14.95**

GALLAS, JOHN (New Zealand, 1950 -)
John Gallas' first collection, *Practical Anarchy*, includes high comedy, satire and travel poems featuring Leicester Football Club, Turkey, New Zealand, Bulgaria and Northamptonshire. The poems map out a sort of 'spiritual geography', and, taken together, show how absurd it is to make sense of the world, and how brave of Man it is to try - hence the 'practical anarchy' of the title.
Practical Anarchy
[R416] Carcanet pbk **£6.95**

GARFITT, ROGER
In his new collection, *Given Ground*, Garfitt looks at the underside of history, as lived not by those who make it, but those who are caught up in it; he captures, for example, the mixture of fear and boredom felt by soldiers waiting to go to Northern Ireland. The central long poem, 'Lower Lumb Mill' satirizes the English pastoral tradition.
Given Ground `NEW`
[R417] Carcanet pbk **£6.95**

GARIOCH, ROBERT (Scottish, 1909 - 1981)
Most of Garioch's work is written in a form of Scots, and he has been successful in building unobtrusively on this speech basis; he has a fine ear, and the archaism is constantly being corrected by a nice colloquial accuracy. Often his poems combine a gift for comic impersonation with satirical observations of civic follies, but in meditations such as 'The Wire' and 'The Muir', he reveals a sombre vision; perhaps his best work, though, is his series of translations from the 19th century Italian dialect sonnets of Giuseppi Belli which catch the tone and movement of the original in an equivalent idiom.
A Garioch Miscellany
[R418] Macdonald pbk **£7.95**
Complete Poetical Works
[R419] Macdonald pbk **£12.95**

GASCOYNE, DAVID (1916 -)
The influence of European Surrealism pervades Gascoyne's work. His reputation suffered in the 1950s because he lacked the formal precision characteristic of the 'Movement' poets; however, if his work is less tight than theirs, it gains in a correspondingly more powerful visionary element.
Collected Poems
[R420] Oxford hbk **£14.95**
[R421] Oxford pbk **£7.95**

GLOVER, JON (1943 -)
There are more than 40 poems in Glover's first book, *Our Photographs*, which forms part of his 'Islanders' sequence. It concerns a man who leaves his home on a Scottish island and emigrates to the United States in the 19th century; his sense of space and of himself changes, and his letters home disturb those who remain to face eviction. As in Eliot or Hill there is a coldness or impersonality here, and an impressive sweep of different speakers, tones and forms.
Our Photographs
[R422] Carcanet pbk **£4.95**

GRAHAM, W.S. (Scottish, 1918 - 1986)
There is a Scots timbre in Graham's poetic voice, which contributes to the ability to change tone, in a single line, from raucousness to tenderness. His early work, indebted to Dylan Thomas, is rich in verbal inventiveness. The later poems have plain diction and syntax animated by strong and expressive rhythms. His mature theme is language, and its value in fending off silence, and its limited capacity for communication.
[R423] Faber hbk **£8.50**
[R424] Faber pbk **£4.50**

GRAVES, ROBERT (1895 - 1985)
Graves is a major English poet of the century who rejected the modernist experiments of Yeats and Eliot, and his spare, colloquial voice has more in common

with the quiet irony of Thomas Hardy. Love between the sexes is his most characteristic theme - his lightness and humour disguise a mastery of tone subtle enough to explore personal relationships with sharp insight.

Collected Poems
[R425] Cassell hbk **£18.95**
Poems
[R426] Penguin pbk **£3.95**
Selected Poems
[R427] Penguin pbk **£4.50**

GRAY, ALISTAIR (Scottish, 1934 -)
More widely known as a novelist (*Lanark*, *The Fall of Kelvin Walker*), Gray has written verse as well; *Old Negatives* collects together four verse sequences written at different times since 1952. His themes are love, faith and language; they are 'negative' because they describe love mainly by its absences and reverses.

Old Negatives
[R428] Cape pbk **£5.95**

GRIGSON, GEOFFREY (1905 - 1985)
Grigson edited the influential modernist periodical *New Verse* (1933-39), and was an acerbic critic given to attacking inflated reputations - such as Edith Sitwell, and championing lesser known but excellent poets such as Clere Parsons and E.J. Scovell. His early poems consist of precise, imagistic observations of the world; his later work is less austere and more emotional.

Collected Poems 1963 - 80
[R429] Allison & B hbk **£9.95**
[R430] Allison & B pbk **£4.95**
Persephone's Flowers
[R431] Secker pbk **£6.95**

GROSS & KANTARIS
The Air Mines of Mistila   `NEW`
Kantaris and Gross bring alive a place with imaginary figures and strange atmospheric conditions, Mistila, in Columbia, which neither of them has visited.
[R432] Bloodaxe pbk **£4.95**

GUNN, THOM (1929 -)
The tight verse forms and anti-Romanticism of his first collection *Fighting Terms* marked Gunn out as a movement poet, though he lacked that group's reductive irony. *The Sense of Movement* was dominated by a Sartrean existentialism, and an intriguing tension between the contemporary subject matter and the traditional forms. His later work experiments with syllabics, and has a tenderness missing from the earlier work.

Moly
[R433] Faber pbk **£4.95**
Selected Poems
[R434] Faber pbk **£3.50**

GURNEY, IVOR (1890 - 1937)
After studying at the Royal College of Music - he is one of England's finest song-writers - Gurney served as a private on the Western front from 1915, and the war damaged an already unstable mental condition; committed in 1922, he remained in the City of London Mental Hospital, Kent, until his death. It has taken Gurney a long time to achieve the eminence he deserves. His hideous experiences in WWI produced work which, as Andrew Motion has commented, 'cherishes a time-honoured rural vision in language which reflects the strength of forces working for its destruction.'

Collected Poems of Ivor Gurney
[R435] Oxford hbk **£12.00**
[R436] Oxford pbk **£4.95**
Severn & Somme/War's Embers
[R437] Carcanet hbk **£8.95**

HAMBURGER, MICHAEL
(Anglo-German, 1924 -)
As is often the case with all-round talents, Hamburger's important achievement as a poet has been overshadowed by his work as a translator and critic. His early work is devoutly literary, hermetic and obscure, and marked by a chilly craftsmanship - he refers in his autobiography to a wilful misunderstanding of Eliot's theory of impersonality. Erudite and rooted in two literary traditions, Hamburger's later work is more lucid, aiming for intellectual clarity, a complexity of thought rather than complexity of expression.

Collected Poems
[R439] Carcanet hbk **£14.95**
Selected Poems
[R440] Carcanet pbk **£4.95**

HAMILTON, IAN (1938 -)
Editor of *The Review* and the glossier *The New Review*, and controversial biographer of Robert Lowell and J.D. Salinger, Hamilton's poetic *oeuvre* is small but influential. He has characterized his own work as 'dramatic lyrics' where *"the reader is offered only the intense, climactic moment of a drama - the prose part, the part which provided the background data, is left to the imagination."*

Fifty Poems
[R441] Faber pbk **£4.95**

HARDY, THOMAS (1840 - 1928)
Perhaps better known as a novelist, Donald Davie has called Hardy 'the most far-reaching influence, for good or ill...in British poetry of the last 50 years'. His themes were constant throughout his poetic *oeuvre* - nature's indifference or hostility, thwarted or lost love, death - and he uses the same strategy in many poems, working through a plot to an unexpected conclusion. He is the first essentially 20th century poet.

Hardy's Love Poems
[R442] Macmillan pbk **£3.95**
Selected Poems
[R443] Dent pbk **£2.95**
Selected Poems of Thomas Hardy
[R444] Penguin pbk **£3.95**
The Complete Poems
[R445] Macmillan pbk **£14.95**
[R446] Macmillan pbk **£9.99**
Thomas Hardy (Oxford Authors)
[R447] Oxford pbk **£5.95**

HARRISON, TONY (1937 -)
Harrison sets out to speak for those who haven't had 'a voice'; in the Meredithian sonnets of the *School of Eloquence* sequence, he is concerned with the relationship with his dead parents, and the way his education has separated him from his working-class roots. The poems feature emphatic rhyming, a bold awkwardness of technique, and a distinctive, spoken, demotic English. His use of many language registers, and the tensions when they are brought together in traditional verse forms are fascinating. His more recent work, such as *A Kumquat for John Keats*, is more free-wheeling.

A Kumquat for John Keats
[R448] Bloodaxe pbk **£1.00**
Dramatic Verse 1973 - 1985
[R449] Bloodaxe hbk **£20.00**
Selected Poems
[R450] Penguin pbk **£5.99**
Ten Sonnets from 'The School of Eloquence'
[R451] Anvil pbk **£1.95**
The Fire-Gap
[R452] Bloodaxe pbk **£1.95**
Theatre Works 1973 - 1985
[R453] Penguin pbk **£4.95**
V. (Vee)
[R455] Bloodaxe pbk **£4.50**

ASTLEY, NEIL (ED)
Essays on Tony Harrison
The first critical guide to Harrison's work, Astley's selection of essays covers his poetry, translations and theatre work.
[R456] Bloodaxe hbk **£16.95**
[R457] Bloodaxe pbk **£7.95**

HARSENT, DAVID (1942 -)
Harsent's *Selected Poems* brings together work from his four individual Oxford collections published so far. The minimalism of his early work has affinities with the poets associated with *The Review* - Ian Hamilton and Hugo Williams - but this has been replaced by longer narrative sequences. His work exhibits a concern for craftsmanship, and is influenced by Berryman and Snodgrass.

Selected Poems   `NEW`
[R458] Oxford pbk **£7.95**

HARWOOD, LEE (1939 -)
John Ashbery has commented that Harwood's poetry 'lies open to the reader, like a meadow...the "great" poetry that I like best has this self-effacing, translucent quality. Self-effacing not from modesty, but because it is going somewhere and has no time to consider itself.'

Crossing the Frozen River   `NEW`
[R459] Paladin pbk **£5.95**

HEANEY, SEAMUS (Irish, 1939 -)
Heaney's early work - in *Death of a Naturalist* - explores his background, in poetry characterized by a primitive trust in the force of onomatopoeia to bring over an image, gained from a partial reading of Hopkins. There is a gain in technical assurance and thematic ambition from book to book, as he ventures on an exploration of Ireland through emblems of its past; the Irish 'troubles' are an important theme in many of the poems which probe Irish history and pre-history. He remains one of the language's most popular living poets.

Death of a Naturalist
[R460] Faber pbk **£3.95**
Door into the Dark
[R461] Faber pbk **£2.95**
Field Work
[R462] Faber pbk **£3.99**
North
[R463] Faber pbk **£3.95**
Preoccupations: Selected Prose 1968 - 78
[R464] Faber pbk **£4.95**
Selected Poems
[R465] Faber pbk **£2.95**
Station Island
[R466] Faber pbk **£3.95**
Sweeney Astray
[R467] Faber hbk **£6.95**
[R468] Faber pbk **£3.95**
The Government of the Tongue (Essays)
Stimulating and beautifully written, Heaney's collection of essays and lectures deals with the question of poetic responsibility, and the paradoxical relationship between the power wielded by the tongue, and the restraints that are sometimes placed on it; the essays deal with Auden, Lowell, Plath, Larkin and Walcott, as well as East Europeans Herbert and Holub.
[R469] Faber pbk **£4.99**
The Haw Lantern
[R470] Faber hbk **£7.95**
[R471] Faber pbk **£3.95**
Wintering Out
[R472] Faber pbk **£2.95**

HEATH-STUBBS, JOHN (1918 -)
No poet of our time has practiced so many genres with such success as Heath-Stubbs, from epic to epigram, handling free verse and strict metres with

equal assurance. Many of the poems have mythological and historical subjects; yet he also writes about animals, birds and insects. His recent poems are composed 'in the head' for the speaking voice - the poet being blind. Four decades of work are brought together in his elegant *Collected Poems*. *"As for the purpose of poetry"*, he writes, *"I can only fall back on the familiar Horatian tag that it is 'to instruct by pleasing'"*.

Collected Poems 1943 - 1987
[R473] Carcanet hbk **£25.00**
Naming the Beasts
[R474] Carcanet pbk **£3.95**
The Immolation of Aleph
[R475] Carcanet pbk **£4.95**

HENRI, ADRIAN (1932 -)
Mixing techniques from jazz, pop music and painting, Henri produces fresh and immediate verbal collages. His work is populist: he has written that *"I would like my poems to be read by as many people as possible, since I can't see any point either personally or politically in writing for an élite minority."*

Collected Poems
[R476] Allison & B pbk **£6.95**

HILL, GEOFFREY (1932 -)
Hill's dense and allusive verse has been praised for its 'latinity' (George Steiner), its 'strength' (Harold Bloom) and attacked for its wilful obscurantism (Tom Paulin). Hill himself describes the writing of poetry as an 'exemplary activity', a phrase which captures exactly the blend of the ceremonial, the self-consciously patrician and the morally rigorous that so distinguishes his work. As influenced by Housman, Gurney and Rosenberg as he is by Eliot or Pound, Hill has an unflagging gift for evoking the complex moral and emotional imperatives of the past, and what survives of the past in the present (in the English landscape, for example). The range of his erudition is daunting, but he wears it lightly, mixing in a droll good humour (particularly in the essays and footnotes) which provides an attractive counterpart to the high seriousness of his best work.

Collected Poems
[R477] Deutsch hbk **£9.95**
[R478] Penguin pbk **£3.95**
For the Unfallen
[R479] Deutsch pbk **£3.95**
Mercian Hymns
[R480] Deutsch pbk **£3.95**
Mystery of the Charity of Charles Péguy
[R481] Deutsch pbk **£3.00**
Tenebrae
[R482] Deutsch pbk **£3.95**
The Lords of Limit: Essays on Literature & Ideas
[R483] Deutsch hbk **£12.95**

HILL, SELIMA
Selima Hill's latest collection, *The Accumulation of Small Acts of Kindness*, takes the form of the diaries of a patient, before, during and after a time in a psychiatric hospital.

My Darling Camel
[R484] Chatto pbk **£4.95**
Saying Hello at the Station
[R485] Chatto pbk **£4.95**
The Accumulation of Small Acts of Kindness   NEW
[R486] Chatto pbk **£4.95**

HOFMANN, MICHAEL (1957 -)
Hofmann's two collections mark him out as as an original, unusual talent. His poems are off-beat, anecdotal meditations on the detritus of contemporary urban society, lonely people or personal disappointment, told in a flat, laconic voice. 'The Nomad, My Father' and 'My Father's House' are

wrested out of the poet's itinerant childhood and the resulting resentment of his unfathomable father - the distinguished German novelist Gert Hofmann.

Acrimony
[R487] Faber pbk **£3.95**
Nights in the Iron Hotel
[R488] Faber pbk **£4.00**

HOLDEN, MOLLY (1927 - 1981)
Holden's poetry has, for the last twenty years, commanded a loyal following. She takes her bearings from the work of Hardy. Her later years were spent in a wheelchair as a result of multiple sclerosis; from that point on, her important journeys were creative rather than physical. Clive James has written that 'she seemed to have turned her enforced immobility into a new kind of travel, giving minutely concentrated observations a ravishingly beautiful utterance.'

New and Selected Poems
(Ed. Curtis, Simon)
[R489] Carcanet pbk **£6.95**

HOUSMAN, A.E. (1859 - 1936)
"Here dead lie we because we did not choose/To die and shame the land from which we sprung." The pastoral nostalgia in Housman's poetry is bittersweet and melodious. His most famous work is *A Shropshire Lad*, a collection of nature and love poems, which is notable for its (often homosexual) sense of frustration and futility. The poems are most effective when his pessimism is cast in a historical perspective.

A Shropshire Lad
[R496] Ashford hbk illus **£20.00**
[R497] Harrap pbk **£2.95**
Collected Poems and Selected Prose
[R498] Penguin pbk **£6.99**
The Collected Poems
[R499] Cape pbk **£3.95**

HUGHES, TED (1930 -)
Although immensely popular, Hughes's selection as Poet Laureate in 1985 was something of a surprise, as his poems are far from 'occasional'. By projecting cruel and predatory instincts onto creatures of his own invention, he produces a kind of anthropological allegory. Whilst his linguistic tap-roots are deep in the Shakespearean age, his work shows the influence of Hopkins and Lawrence, as well as a broad spectrum of international writing. Despite his rare energy and exciting formal experiments, his work sometimes suffers from a sameness of tone and thematic narrowness.

Crow
[R500] Faber pbk **£2.95**
Flowers and Insects
[R501] Faber hbk **£7.95**
Gaudete
[R502] Faber pbk **£3.95**
Lupercal
[R503] Faber pbk **£2.95**
Moortown
[R504] Faber hbk **£5.25**
[R505] Faber pbk **£2.25**
Moortown Diary   NEW
Moortown Diary is a new edition of Hughes' acclaimed Devon farming sequence, with an introduction sketching in the background from which these poems emerged. Seen in isolation from the other poems in the collection in which they first appeared, these journal poems appear as some of the most original he has written.
[R506] Faber hbk **£8.99**
[R507] Faber pbk **£4.99**
Season Songs
[R509] Faber pbk **£2.95**
Selected Poems
[R510] Faber hbk **£12.50**
[R511] Faber pbk **£4.95**

The Hawk in the Rain
[R512] Faber pbk **£2.95**
Wodwo
[R514] Faber pbk **£3.95**
Wolfwatching   NEW
Hughes's 14th collection has many poems in which nature is presented with his customary power - but he also breaks new ground with a series of intimate family poems.
[R515] Faber hbk **£8.99**
[R516] Faber pbk **£3.99**

IMLAH, MICK
Imlah's poetry ranges across an unusually large range of subjects, often building up quirky narratives from the basis of a historical fact; his publishers described *Birthmarks* as 'sharp, contemporary, witty and disturbing'.

Birthmarks
[R517] Chatto pbk **£4.95**

JAMES, CLIVE (Australian, 1939 -)
Other Passports collects James's early lyric poems as well as the parodies and lampoons for which he is known, including his mock epics.

Other Passports: Poems 1958 - 85
[R518] Picador pbk **£3.95**

JENKINS, ALAN
In the Hot-House
An acclaimed debut collection from the Poetry Editor of the *TLS*.
[R520] Chatto pbk **£4.95**

JENNINGS, ELIZABETH (1926 -)
Although she was initially perceived as a Movement poet, Jennings's Catholicism has given her work a sense of faith, rather than reductive irony, as its dominant mode. Her recent work has traditional formal qualities, yet she extends them with a freedom like Hardy's, writing exuberant 'psalms', sonnets and her impeccable *terza rima*. Her subject matter is wide; she writes of love, friendship, childhood, places, religion and works of art, where painting, her 'second favourite art', is well represented. Peter Levi writes that Jennings is 'one of the few living poets we could not do without.'

Collected Poems
[R521] Carcanet hbk **£14.95**
[R522] Carcanet pbk **£5.95**
Moments of Grace
[R523] Carcanet pbk **£4.95**
Selected Poems
[R524] Carcanet pbk **£2.95**
Tributes   NEW
The dominant note of Jennings's new collection, *Tributes*, is one of celebration, even when poems touch on darker themes, as she evokes painters, composers, philosophers and writers whom she values.
[R525] Carcanet pbk **£6.95**

JONES, DAVID (Anglo-Welsh, 1895 - 1974)
The central themes of Jones's intense and difficult poetry are war and the Incarnation - he was a convert to Catholicism. *In Parenthesis* - which T.S. Eliot called 'a work of genius' - is an epic work that mixes prose and verse on the subject of the Great War, in which the sufferings of Private John Ball are intertwined with factual history and Welsh legend. His other major work is *The Anathemata*, which Auden called 'very probably the finest long poem written in English this century.'

In Parenthesis
[R526] Faber pbk **£4.95**
The Anathemata
[R527] Faber pbk **£3.95**

JOYCE, JAMES (Irish, 1882 - 1941)
Obviously better known as the century's best novelist, Joyce produced two collections of verse. *Chamber Music* was his first book to reach the public, and earned him a place in the *Imagist Anthology*. These poems are elusive and formal, above all musical. Faber's edition of *Pomes Penyeach* contains Joyce's scabrous satires 'The Holy Office' and 'Gas from a Burner'.
Chamber Music
[R528] Cape pbk **£3.95**
Pomes Penyeach and Other Poems
[R529] Faber pbk **£2.50**

KAVANAGH, P.J. (1931 -)
Kavanagh's poems are formally traditional and preoccupied with the pains and joys of life, the hope given by love, and death - especially the death of his wife which informs his outstanding autobiography *The Perfect Stranger*. His work is consistently surprising, fresh and deeply melodious.
People & Places (Prose)
This is Kavanagh's selected 'personal letters to the world' collecting together some of his occasional writings.
[R530] Carcanet hbk **£12.95**
Presences: New & Selected Poems
[R531] Chatto pbk **£4.95**
The Perfect Stranger (Autobiography)
[R532] Fontana pbk **£3.50**

KAVANAGH, PATRICK (Irish, 1904 - 1967)
Resenting Yeats' romanticised view of the peasantry, Kavanagh's major poem, *The Great Hunger*, is a grimly compassionate account of the poverty of rural Irish life, in which the rhythmic variety is impressive. He is now recognised as the greatest Irish poet of the mid-century.
Collected Poems
[R533] MB O'Keefe pbk **£3.50**

KEYES, SIDNEY (1922 - 1943)
Enlisting in 1942 - after Oxford, where he appeared alongside John Heath-Stubbs and Keith Douglas in *Eight Oxford Poets* - Keyes was killed the following year in Tunisia. Too often clumsy symbolism deprives the writing of immediacy and pressure, but his most enduring poems - 'The Migrant' and 'The Kestrels' - are those in which landscapes and seascapes appear in their least symbolically forced settings.
The Collected Poems of Sidney Keyes
[R534] Routledge pbk **£4.95**

KINSELLA, THOMAS (Irish, 1928 -)
The characteristic themes of Kinsella's early work are the difficulty of love, nightmare and illness, which he explores with formal elegance. More recently, his work has attempted to create mythic structures which rise above the disorder of contemporary life.
Blood and Family NEW
[R535] Oxford pbk **£6.95**
Fifteen Dead
In *Fifteen Dead*, which features elegies for the poet's contemporaries, there is a direct confrontation with the social and political realities of Ireland.
[R536] Dolmen pbk **£3.50**
One Fond Embrace
[R537] Gallery P pbk **£6.00**
One and Other Poems
[R538] Dolmen pbk **£3.50**
Poems 1956 - 73
[R539] Dolmen pbk **£4.95**
The Tain
Kinsella has emerged as a fine translator from Gaelic. *The Tain* is a version of the *Tain Bo Cuailnge*, the great Cattle Raid of Cooley.
[R540] Oxford pbk **£6.95**

KIPLING, RUDYARD (1865 - 1936)
"If any question why we died/Tell them, because our fathers lied." Kipling mastered a wide range of poetic forms, such as the dramatic monologue (where the personae, however, are often caricatures) and the narrative ballad. Poems such as 'Danny Deever', 'Gunga Din' and 'Mandalay', with their popular cockney demotic, have the verve of a music-hall turn. His plainspeaking, epigrammatic verse remains a poetry from the turn of the century that is not weary.
A Choice of Kipling's Verse
[R541] Faber pbk **£2.50**
Early Verse by Rudyard Kipling
[R542] Oxford hbk **£22.50**
[R543] Oxford pbk **£5.95**
Moon of Other Days: Favourite Poems
(Ed. Kaye, M.M.)
[R544] Hodder hbk **£14.95**
Selected Verse
[R545] Penguin pbk **£2.95**

KUPPNER, FRANK (Scottish, 1951 -)
Kuppner's first volume of poems, *A Bad Day for the Sung Dynasty*, consisting of 511 ludic quatrains, was 'a response to the discovery of a vast set of Chinese paintings', and 'feeling certain that the whole story was not being told'; his technique is 'a straight lift from the Chinese poetry translators', he writes.
A Bad Day for the Sung Dynasty
[R546] Carcanet pbk **£4.95**
Ridiculous! Absurd! Disgusting! NEW
The title of Kuppner's new book comes from Rimbaud's response, on being asked to characterize his own poetry. The book contains three works - one verse, one prose, one a mixture of the two - in which his aim is to produce *"something worth speaking over the phone to someone rung up more or less at random"*.
[R547] Carcanet pbk **£6.95**
The Intelligent Observation of Naked Women
[R548] Carcanet pbk **£6.95**

LARKIN, PHILIP (1922 - 1985)
Larkin's *Collected Poems* gathers together, for the first time, his small, varied *oeuvre*, comprising the four collections, juvenilia and unpublished later poems. It presents a picture of the development from the Yeats-haunted *The North Ship* to the desolate pictures of urban Britain in his mature collections, where characters like Mr. Bleaney are characterized by the objects with which they surround themselves, and where there is a passive acceptance of the frustrations of life.
Collected Poems (Ed. Thwaite, Anthony)
[R549] Faber/Marvell hbk **£16.95**
High Windows
[R550] Faber pbk **£2.95**
Required Writing (Prose)
A collection of Larkin's prose and occasional essays, which reveals much about his own poetic beliefs.
[R551] Faber pbk **£6.95**
The Less Deceived
[R552] Marvell P pbk **£3.60**
The North Ship
[R553] Faber pbk **£2.95**
The Whitsun Weddings
[R554] Faber pbk **£2.95**
HARTLEY, JEAN
Philip Larkin, the Marvell Press, and Me NEW
Amidst what is now a Larkin industry, Jean Hartley's book is a valuable personal memoir of the man; it is also a history of that odd little press, and creates a fascinating picture of provincial life in the 50s and 60s.
[R555] Carcanet hbk **£12.95**

FABER POETRY

Ted Hughes
Poet Laureate

Wolfwatching
A new fourteenth collection
0 571 14166 8   Cased   £8.99
Sept
0 571 14167 6   FPB   £3.99
Sept

Moortown Diary
The acclaimed farming sequence in a new edition
0 571 14169 2   Cased   £8.99
Sept
0 571 14084 X   FPB   £4.99
Sept

Seamus Heaney
Professor of Poetry at Oxford

The Government of the Tongue
Writings on poets
0 571 14151 X   FPB   £4.99
June

faber and faber

Andrew Motion, author of *Natural Causes* (Chatto pbk £4.95)

LAWRENCE, D.H. (1885 - 1930)
Extraordinarily Lawrence's poetry was featured in the anthologies of the seemingly incompatible Imagist and Georgian Movements. Under Whitman's influence, Lawrence believed in the necessity of free verse, where we 'look for the insurgent naked throb of the instant moment'. The often tiresome attitudes which dominate his didactic poems and the pettiness of some of his satires are countered by the accuracy and vividness of description in the great animal poems.
Complete Poems
[R556] Penguin pbk **£7.95**
Selected Poems
[R557] Penguin pbk **£3.50**

LEE, LAURIE (1914 -)
Best known for *Cider with Rosie* and *As I Walked Out One Midsummer Morning*, Lee also published poetry which captured the same nostalgic love of the pre-industrial countryside.
Selected Poems
[R558] Penguin pbk **£2.50**

LEVI, PETER (1931 -)
A translator, archaeologist and sometime Shakespeare scholar, Levi's versatile and delicate poetry betrays the considerable influence of Wallace Stevens. John Heath-Stubbs commends his work for displaying "a true humanism which accepts the inevitability of death and decay, and does not appear to seek for any consolation in the idea of transcendence."
Collected Poems 1955 - 1975
[R560] Anvil pbk **£7.95**
Death is a Pulpit
[R561] Anvil pbk **£2.95**
Five Ages
[R562] Anvil pbk **£3.95**
Goodbye to the Art of Poetry NEW
This is the text of Levi's valedictory lecture as Oxford Professor of Poetry; it is unusual in that it is composed in couplets. Written in couplets, it ranges widely and associatively about poets ancient and modern, about language, and the roots of poetry in the common language.
[R563] Anvil pbk **£3.95**
Shadow and Bone NEW
Levi's new collection gathers together work written over the last 8 years. There are sequences about

railway posters and America, poems for scholars or fellow poets, and a long poem on the meaning of Christmas.
[R564] Anvil pbk **£5.95**
Shakespeare's Birthday
[R565] Anvil pbk **£2.95**
The Echoing Green
[R566] Anvil pbk **£1.95**
The Noise Made by Poems (Prose)
[R567] Anvil pbk **£4.95**

LEWIS, ALUN (Welsh, 1915 - 1944)
Lewis's best writing concerned the tedium of army life and the all-pervasive fear of death upon which it is founded. A gifted disciple of Edward Thomas, he dedicated his most famous poem, 'All Day it has Rained…', to him ("…*Edward Thomas brooded long/On death and beauty - till a bullet stopped his song*"). Tragically Lewis himself died soon after arriving in Burma during WWII.
A Miscellany of His Writings
[R568] Poetry Wales P pbk **£6.95**
Letters NEW
[R568A] Seren Books hbk **£12.95**
Selected Poems
[R569] Unwin Hyman pbk **£2.50**

LEWIS, WYNDHAM (1882 - 1957)
"*..to be busily balking/The tongue-tied Briton - that is my outlandish plot!*" Lewis's poetry is a neglected part of a neglected writer's *oeuvre*. His one collection, *One Way Song*, is verse satire; C.H. Sisson calls it the 'most subtle piece of argumentation put into English verse in the 20th century'.
Collected Poems & Plays
[R570] Carcanet pbk **£7.95**

LINDOP, GREVEL (1948 -)
Tourists is Lindop's first collection for 10 years, in which he mixes a graceful lyric mode with a slightly harrassed narrative strain. The book includes an impressive sequence which draws inspiration from the engravings of Thomas Bewick.
Tourists
[R571] Carcanet pbk **£6.95**

LOMAX, MARION
The Peepshow Girl NEW
[R574] Bloodaxe pbk **£4.95**

LONGLEY, MICHAEL (Irish, 1939 -)
One of Northern Ireland's most lauded poets, Longley's neat, formalist work continues to divide critics. James Fenton has written of the poems having 'matched a sense of history and the brutal present with a recurrent feeling for the lyrical moment and the fragility of experience.'
Poems 1963 - 83
[R575] Salamander hbk **£9.95**
[R576] Penguin pbk **£3.95**

MACBETH, GEORGE
According to Peter Porter, MacBeth is the most inventive poet of his generation, and certainly his darkly comic verse, preoccupied (to an unhealthy extent say some critics) with death, decay, violence, cruelty and lust, is highly distinctive. In recent years he has toned down this surrealistic extravagance but continued to experiment with form. The result is shown to best advantage in the moving collection *Anatomy of a Divorce*.
Anatomy of a Divorce
[R577] Hutchinson pbk **£5.95**
Poems of Love and Death
[R578] Secker pbk **£4.95**
The Cleaver Garden
[R579] Secker pbk **£6.95**
The Long Darkness
[R580] Secker pbk **£5.95**

MACCAIG, NORMAN (Scottish, 1910 -)
MacCaig's early work was marked by New Apocalyptic excesses, but his 1955 collection *Riding Lights* marked a new precision, what he calls 'the long haul to lucidity'. Much of his work centres on the theme of perception ("*I took my mind for a walk, or my mind took me for a walk*"), and it is notable for the use of 'strained metaphor to defamiliarize the familiar' which predates the Martian poets by several decades.
Collected Poems
[R581] Chatto pbk **£6.95**
Voice-Over
[R582] Chatto pbk **£5.95**

MACDIARMID, HUGH (Scottish, 1892 - 1978)
A communist and a Nationalist, MacDiarmid - the pen name of Christopher Grieve - revealed new potentialities for the use of Scots as a literary language. He was a voluminous and uneven writer, whose *oeuvre* ranges from the early Scots lyrics, through the intellectual epic *A Drunk Man Looks at the Thistle*, to the 'scientific' poems of the 30s and later. Full of looted words, half-digested geology and linguistics, and chunks lifted from other writers, his poems stand comparison with Eliot and Pound, and he is the finest Scottish poet since Burns.
A Drunk Man Looks at the Thistle
(Ed. Buthlay, Keith)
New annotated edition.
[R584] Scottish Acad P pbk **£4.95**
Complete Poems: Vol 1
[R585] Penguin pbk **£9.95**
Complete Poems: Vol 2
[R586] Penguin pbk **£9.95**

MACKINNON, LACHLAN
A witty, cerebral first collection by the well-known critic, who has recently published a biography of Elsa Triolet.
Monterey Cypress
'Mackinnon is essentially an autobiographical poet. The "I" in these poems is intriguing, never obtrusive. Erudite, Mackinnon is at all times accesible; his tone quiet, disarmingly laid-back, with its own slow rhythm.' (Carol Anne Duffy)
[R587] Chatto pbk **£4.95**

MACLEAN, SORLEY (Scottish, 1911 -)
MacLean is one of Britain's finest poets; he writes in Scots Gaelic, and has prepared his own translations for his *Collected Poems*, which is published in a parallel text format. His early work explores the conflict between public responsibility and private passions and needs, while the later work develops these themes in a specifically Gaelic setting.
Collected Poems NEW
Parallel Text, in Gaelic and English.
[R588] Carcanet hbk **£18.95**
Reothairt is Contraigh/Spring Tide & Neap Tide
Selected Poems 1932-72.
[R589] Canongate pbk **£3.95**

MACNEICE, LOUIS (Irish, 1907 - 1963)
Usually (but unhelpfully) linked with Auden and Spender under the 'MacSpaunday' grouping, MacNeice is a poet of urban rhythms, whose work is pervaded by a sense of loss. His most famous work is the long poem *Autumn Journal*; whilst capturing the political uncertainties of the 30s, it is always personal and subjective. He characterized the poet as "*able bodied, fond of talking, a reader of newspapers, capable of pity and laughter, appreciative of women, susceptible to physical impressions*".
Collected Poems
[R590] Faber pbk **£6.95**
Selected Poems (Ed. Auden, W.H.)
[R591] Faber pbk **£1.95**

Selected Poems (Ed. Longley, Michael)
[R592] Faber pbk **£4.95**

MAHON, DEREK (Irish, 1941 -)
Detached and unsentimental, Mahon's 'A Disused Shed in Co. Wexford' is his finest poem, a superb and moving metaphor for the persecuted peoples of history, which Andrew Waterman has described as 'a flight of the controlled yet haunted imagination'. His work is dominated by a sense of loss, isolation and exile, and, unlike some of his Ulster contemporaries (Heaney or Montague), Mahon has rarely confronted 'the troubles'.
Antarctica Poems
[R593] Gallery P pbk **£3.60**
High Time
[R594] Gallery P pbk **£4.50**
Hunt by Night
[R595] Oxford pbk **£4.95**
Kensington Notebook
[R596] Anvil pbk **£4.00**
Poems 1962 - 78
[R597] Oxford pbk **£5.95**
The Chimeras
[R598] Gallery P pbk **£2.70**

MARE, WALTER DE LA (1873 - 1956)
Walter de la Mare's poetry inhabits a special realm: *"the all-but-uttered, and yet out of reach"*. Mysterious travellers and dreamers cross the borders between fantasy and the waking world where a sense of wonder is coloured by a pervasive sense of loss and regret. Not always fashionable but consistently popular, de la Mare's cadenced, rhyming verse reveals a singularly inventive technician; the admiration of so inveterate an anti-Georgian as T.S. Eliot should give some indication of his measure and worth.
Behold, This Dreamer!
[R599] Faber pbk **£5.50**
Collected Rhymes and Verses
[R600] Faber pbk **£2.50**
Selected Poems
[R601] Faber pbk **£2.95**
The Collected Poems
[R602] Faber pbk **£9.95**

MASEFIELD, JOHN (1878 - 1967)
Although his poetry has been critically disparaged since he became Poet Laureate in 1930, Masefield is genuinely popular. His range is large: as well as being an exquisite lyricist and elegist, he is a narrative poet; his most famous works are sea poems such as 'Cargoes' and 'Sea-Fever', and 'Reynard the Fox', a perky narrative about a fox-hunt told by a man who hates hunting.
Selected Poems
[R603] Carcanet pbk **£9.95**

MCGOUGH, ROGER (1937 -)
An early success as one of the Liverpool Poets, McGough has established himself as one of the most powerful and distinctive voices of modern poetry. This new *Selected Poems* brings together over 20 years of work, from the early *The Mersey Sound* to his 1986 collection *Melting into the Foreground*. A founder member of the pop theatre groups 'Scaffold' and 'Grimms', he has also written several stage and television plays, and regularly gives poetry readings up and down the country.
Melting into the Foreground
[R608] Viking hbk **£6.95**
[R609] Penguin pbk **£4.95**
Selected Poems NEW
[R610] Cape hbk **£12.95**

MEW, CHARLOTTE (1869 - 1928)
Although admired by Masefield, de la Mare and Thomas Hardy, who called her 'the least pretentious but undoubtedly the best woman poet of our day',

Charlotte Mew is a strangely neglected figure. For her, if the poem is to be true, the content must violate the form, and she shares thematic concerns with her close friend Hardy - the ephemeral nature of passion, memory, the difficulties of love. She committed suicide by drinking disinfectant.
Collected Poems and Prose
[R612] Carcanet hbk **£12.50**
[R613] Virago pbk **£5.95**

MIDDLETON, CHRISTOPHER (1926 -)
Middleton's poetry is provocative, experimental and readable. The main thrust of his work is against a thematic, 'literary' poetry, and for a poetry of colour and conflict. Cast as avant-garde, modernist, or post-Surrealist, no category contains him; his poems explore the twilit zones between things and nothing, and areas of perception, reflection and imagination.
111 Poems
[R614] Carcanet pbk **£5.95**
A Reader: Selected Writings
Middleton's latest book is a generous compendium of work from his nine collections from between 1962 and 1986, as well as a section of recent work, accompanied by two essays.
[R615] Carcanet hbk **£18.95**
Two Horse Wagon Going By
[R616] Carcanet pbk **£5.95**

MITCHELL, ADRIAN (1932 -)
Star of the pop poetry scene of the late 1960s, Mitchell is committed to poetry as performance. Aiming to change the world, and gain a wide popular audience, his poems are simple and topical, although the subjects of his early work - Vietnam, the bomb and an anti-establishment stance - are becoming increasingly obscure. Anthony Thwaite summed up the pros and cons of his verses: 'They are clear, direct, funny, warm-hearted, and eloquent. They are also sometimes obvious, banal, whimsical, and too generally sure of a welcome...' - he preaches to the converted.
For Beauty Douglas: Collected Poems 1953 - 1979
[R619] Allison & B pbk **£6.95**
Love Songs of World War III NEW
[R620] Allison & B pbk **£5.99**
On the Beach at Cambridge
[R621] Allison & B pbk **£3.50**

MONTAGUE, JOHN (Irish, 1929 -)
Montague has written that *"all of us are uprooted, subject to the seismic waves of the late 20th century: we must warm and warn ourselves against a new ice age"*. He salvages from this personal and political breakdown some powerful, brief lyrics which achieve an exact, crystalline eloquence. His themes - symptomatic of the desolation which haunts him - are exile, the loss of gaelic and the dispossession of national identity.
A Slow Dance
[R624] Oxford pbk **£2.50**
Mount Eagle NEW
[R625] Bloodaxe hbk **£12.95**
[R626] Bloodaxe pbk **£5.95**
The Dead Kingdom
The underlying structure of this sequence is provided by the lore of place, or *Dinnseanchas*; this ancient form is recreated in linked narratives to mark Montague's poetic journey across Ireland from Cork - where he lives - to the locale of his early life in the Fermanagh-South Tyrone area, the scene of his mother's funeral.
[R627] Oxford pbk **£4.95**

MORGAN, EDWIN (Scottish, 1920 -)
Prolific and versatile, Morgan is an experimental, yet popular poet, whose various styles show the

influence of the American modernist tradition and the 'concrete poetry' movement, as well the local environment of Glasgow (in the tremendous *Glasgow Sonnets*). His work exhibits an exuberant linguistic playfulness and works with a wide variety of subjects - computers, science fiction, city life, and character sketches running from Ramases II to Marilyn Monroe.
Poems of Thirty Years
[R628] Carcanet hbk **£16.95**
Sonnets from Scotland
[R629] Mariscat p pbk **£3.75**
Themes on a Variation
[R630] Carcanet pbk **£6.95**

MORRISON, BLAKE (1950 -)
Morrison has been influenced by the quiet and ironic voice of the Movement, of which he has written an excellent critical study. The revised edition of *Dark Glasses* contains much new material.
Dark Glasses NEW
[R631] Chatto pbk **£5.95**
The Ballad of the Yorkshire Ripper
[R632] Chatto pbk **£4.95**

MOTION, ANDREW (1952 -)
In assessing Motion's work it is possible to see a move away from the tender lyrics about his mother's mute existence after a riding accident, towards an unobtrusive assurance with which he sets about rehabilitating the traditional narrative functions of verse. His use of 'secret narratives' (the title of his third collection) and historical personae - in *Independence*, for example - is a way of freeing personal feelings whilst distancing and impersonalizing them.
Dangerous Play: Poems 1974 - 84
[R633] Salamander hbk **£8.95**
[R634] Penguin pbk **£2.95**
Independence
[R635] Salamander pbk **£5.00**
Natural Causes
[R636] Chatto pbk **£4.95**
Secret Narratives
[R637] Salamander pbk **£3.00**
The Pleasure Steamers
[R638] Carcanet pbk **£4.95**

MUIR, EDWIN (Scottish, 1887 - 1959)
Unassertive, traditional, and out of the mainstream of contemporary verse, Muir's work made little impact in his lifetime. Although he was a clumsy technician, Eliot commented that 'under the pressure of emotional intensity, and possessed by his vision, he found, almost unconsciously, the right, the inevitable way of saying the things he wanted to say'.
Collected Poems
[R639] Faber pbk **£4.95**
Selected Poems
With a preface by T.S. Eliot.
[R640] Faber pbk **£1.95**
Selected Prose
[R641] J Murray hbk **£15.00**

MULDOON, PAUL (Irish, 1951 -)
Despite an over-easy reliance on slight anecdotes as the basis for his poems, Muldoon has developed into a poet notable for his enigmatic individuality - his work is witty, punning and posturing. One reviewer accurately characterised it as 'Hallucinatory Logic out of Surrealism by Martian Art'.
Meeting the British
[R642] Faber pbk **£3.95**
Quoof
[R643] Faber pbk **£3.95**
Selected Poems 1968 - 1983
[R644] Faber pbk **£3.95**

MURPHY, RICHARD (Irish, 1927 -)
Murphy has been described as the last of the Anglo-Irish poets and his vivid investigations of Irish history in 'The Battle of Aughrim' display an epic power and a classical purity of diction that links him immediately to Yeats, and beyond to alliterative Anglo-Saxon sea-poems and the rich assonances of traditional Gaelic verse. His latest collection *The Mirror Wall* represents a new departure, with verse freely inspired by the poems and frescoes on the walls of the fortress of Sigiriya in Sri Lanka, where he spent much of his early childhood.
New Selected Poems   **NEW**
[R645] Faber hbk £9.99
[R646] Faber pbk £4.99
The Mirror Wall   **NEW**
[R647] Bloodaxe hbk £12.95
[R648] Bloodaxe pbk £5.95

NICHOLS, GRACE (Guyana, 1950 -)
Grace Nichol's fat black woman is brash and self-celebrating, challenging a white world that still turns its back on black people. The poems have an engaging directness, wit and pathos, speaking of memory, love and of *"the power to be what I am: a woman, charting my own futures"*.
Lazy Thoughts of a Lazy Woman   **NEW**
[R649] Virago pbk £4.99
The Fat Black Woman's Poems
[R650] Virago pbk £3.50

NOLAN, CHRISTOPHER (Irish, 1965 -)
Nolan is perhaps best known for his best-selling autobiography *Under the Eye of the Clock*, which won the Whitbread Prize in 1987. Severely brain-damaged at birth, he learned to communicate by typing with a unicorn stick attached to his forehead. His poems - reminiscent in some ways of Dylan Thomas - feature heavy alliteration, and draw together disparate concepts with a powerful creative force.
Dam-Burst of Dreams
[R651] Weidenfeld pbk £3.95

O'BRIEN, SEAN
O'Brien's charactersistic territory is the urban pastoral; his poems are dramatic and aggressive, yet also witty. Douglas Dunn has written that 'his increasingly powerful and angry poetry confronts history head on...picking up a gauntlet that Thatcher's England has dropped at his feet'.
The Frighteners (1987)
[R652] Bloodaxe pbk £4.50

OWEN, WILFRED (1893 - 1918)
Widely regarded as the greatest World War I poet, Owen's impassioned eloquence is often forceful. The novelty in his work is its subject matter, and Owen's depiction of the horrors of the trenches is a nice corrective to the propaganda of Rupert Brooke; the internal contrast in Owen's work is heightened by his Keatsian sense of language.
Complete Poems (Ed. Stallworthy, J.H.)
[R653] Hogarth hbk £55.00
The Poems of Wilfred Owen
[R654] Hogarth pbk £2.95

PATTEN, BRIAN
A pop poet with a working-class background, Patten's poetry is perhaps the most lyrical and plaintive of the Liverpool poets. He has remarked: *"poetry is a private thing in itself...it's nothing to do with educating or saying anything."*
Grave Gossip
[R655] Unwin pbk £1.95
Notes to the Hurrying Man
[R656] Unwin pbk £2.95
Storm Damage   **NEW**
[R657] Unwin Hyman hbk £12.95
[R658] Unwin Hyman pbk £4.95

The Irrelevant Song
[R659] Unwin pbk £2.95

PAULIN, TOM (Irish, 1949 -)
Paulin's early work recorded, with a confining literalness, the claustrophobia of Ulster society in sparse verse - Andrew Waterman has talked of Paulin's insistence on 'bare floorboards, wet slates, grey sea'. His more recent poetry draws on an unexpected seam of imaginative openness, and he has developed - without relinquishing his political responsibility - into what he accused Joyce of being - *"a politicized aesthete"*.
Fivemiletown
[R660] Faber pbk £4.95
The Riot Act: A Version of Sophocles's Antigone
[R661] Faber pbk £3.95
The Strange Museum
[R662] Faber pbk £3.95

PITT-KETHLEY, FIONA (1954 -)
Pitt-Kethley's stock-in-trade is vulgar-cum-light verse which evokes the world of sordid swimming-pool changing rooms, dirty old men - indeed *any* 'crude, thoughtless, kinky men' - commenting acidly on the bizarre hypocrises of male sexuality.
Private Parts
[R666] Chatto pbk £4.95
Sky Ray Lolly
[R667] Chatto pbk £3.95

PORTER, PETER (1929 -)
Porter made his name with deft, incisive satires on the 'swinging sixties', and his work became associated with the protest poetry of 'The Group' in that period. Although primarily a social poet, his range has extended to lyrics, dramatic monlogues and elegies in a more meditative style, including a wide range of allusions through music and art.
A Porter Selected   **NEW**
A collection of nearly 100 poems chosen by Porter himself, representing 30 years of his work, from 11 original collections.
[R670] Oxford pbk £6.95
Collected Poems
[R668] Oxford hbk £15.00
[R669] Oxford pbk £4.95
Mars (Illustrated by Arthur Boyd)
[R671] Deutsch hbk £14.95
Possible Worlds   **NEW**
[R672 A] Oxford pbk £5.95
The Automatic Oracle
[R672] Oxford pbk £4.95

PRINCE, F.T.
Walks in Rome
Prince's latest book is a single poem in four sections; its occasion is a week's holiday in Rome which is juxtaposed with the author's recollections of pre- and post-war events.
[R673] Anvil hbk £7.95
[R674] Anvil pbk £4.95

RAINE, CRAIG (1944 -)
Raine's basic technique is to present startling metaphors, in order to re-awaken the reader's visual awareness. The title poem of his second collection *A Martian Sends a Postcard Home* - which gave the title 'Martians' to Raine and his like-minded practitioners - sets out to be an uncomprehending alien's report of events on earth, describing a watch as *'time is tied to the wrist/Or kept in a box, ticking with impatience'*.
A Martian Sends a Postcard Home
[R675] Oxford pbk £4.95
Rich
[R676] Faber pbk £3.50

The Electrification of the Soviet Union
[R677] Faber pbk £3.50
The Onion Memory
[R678] Oxford pbk £3.95

RAINE, KATHLEEN (1908 -)
Although Kathleen Raine was a contemporary of Auden, Day Lewis and Spender, she remained untouched by the influence of their socially committed poetry and her own work is dominated by (in her own words) 'a sense of the sacred'. The close observation of nature in her work often has a self-consciously mystical slant, very much in the Neo-Platonic tradition of her own favourite poets: Spenser, Milton, Shelley, Yeats and, above all, Blake.
Collected Poems 1935 - 80
[R679] Unwin Hyman hbk £17.50

RANDALL, DEBORAH
The Sin Eater   **NEW**
[R680] Bloodaxe pbk £4.95

RAWORTH, TOM
Tottering State: Selected Poems 1963 - 1987
[R681] Paladin pbk £5.95

READING, PETER (1946 -)
'He is an original - and in this case his originality lies in reconciling apparently incongruous areas of experience to make a genuine comedy of terrors.' (George Szirtes).
Essential Reading
[R682] Secker pbk £9.95
Final Demands
[R683] Secker pbk £5.00
Perduta Gente   **NEW**
The eponymous 'lost people' of Reading's new book are the dispossessed, the 'expendables, eyesores, winos, unworthies', those whose aspirations are 'gagged, disregarded, unsought'.
[R684] Secker pbk £5.00
Stet
[R685] Secker pbk £5.95

REDGROVE, PETER
A natural scientist by training, Redgrove affirms and celebrates both the power and the strangeness of nature. His poetry is pervaded by a sense of mystery, both religious and erotic, expressed in rich visual imagery. 'Of all living poets he is the one most likely to surprise us with a quality of pure inspiration' (Robert Nye, *The Times*).
Force and Other Poems
[R686] Routledge pbk £13.75
In the Hall of the Saurians
[R687] Secker pbk £5.00
Moon Disposes: Poems 1954 - 87
[R688] Secker pbk £10.00
Songs of My Skin: Selected Poems 1954 - 74
[R689] Routledge pbk £5.50
The First Earthquake
[R690] Secker pbk £5.00

REED, JEREMY (1951 -)
Award-winning young poet, whose intricate, linguistically inventive verse was thus praised by Seamus Heaney: *"It is full of rich and careful writing, dense with pleasure in words that pleasure the world and waken us to its lovely suprises."*
Engaging Form
[R691] Cape pbk £6.95
The Nineties   **NEW**
[R692] Cape pbk £7.95
Selected Poems
[R693] Penguin pbk £4.95

REID, ALISTAIR (1926 -)
Reid's poetry celebrates the surface of the earth with the devoted observation of unpossessive love - Robert Graves has noted his "verbal felicity and deep though controlled feeling". He has travelled widely and *Weathering* includes some of his translations of Spanish and Latin American poetry.
Weathering
[R694] Canongate pbk **£3.95**

REID, CHRISTOPHER (1949 -)
Reid's work is dominated by extravagant metaphors: as a Martian poet, he concentrates on unusual descriptions of day-to-day reality, using a technique built around a deliberate mis-recognition of signs. Comparisons with his Oxford tutor Craig Raine are inevitable, but Reid has a distinct - if less interesting - style; his third collection in particular, which purports to be the translated work of the eponymous if fictitious *Katerina Brac*, emphasizes his impersonality and rejection of autobiographical material.
Arcadia
[R695] Oxford pbk **£3.75**
Pea Soup
[R696] Oxford phk **£4.50**
Katerina Brac
[R696] Faber pbk **£3.95**

RICHARDS, I.A. (1893 - 1979)
Richards' application of Positivist philosophical analysis to poetry proved extremely influential, giving rise to the school of 'practical criticism', where texts were scrutinsed for ambiguity, irony and other linguistic (i.e. not simply emotional) complexities. Richards' own verse, while less distinguished than that of his pupil William Empson, is nevertheless interesting, being appropriately precise in its diction and engagingly ironic in tone.
New and Selected Poems
[R697] Carcanet pbk **£4.95**

RIDLER, ANNE (1912 -)
A devotional poet whose work has been compared to the Metaphysicals in its ability to place the facts of everyday experience at the service of a wide-ranging philosophical speculation.
New and Selected Poems
[R698] Faber pbk **£7.95**

ROMER, STEPHEN (1957 -)
Idols (1986)
Stephen Romer's eponymous idols are an odd mixture of high art and low life, Kierkegaard and Emma Bovary, philosophy and coffee. His poems possess a cool intellectual clarity but wide learning is only gently insinuated in a series of delicate meditations on history, urban life and the girl who left him.
[R699] Oxford pbk **£3.95**

ROSENBERG, ISAAC (1890 - 1918)
Neglected for many years after his death on the Somme in 1918, Rosenberg is now regarded as one of the most innovative poets of World War I. His verse was vividly realistic, written in response to the 'begloried sonnets' of Brooke, and his background - urban, working-class, Jewish - gives him a unique perspective on the horror of war. This standard edition of Rosenberg's poetry, which includes 32 (monochrome and colour) plates, commemorates the centenary of his birth.
The Collected Works of Isaac Rosenberg (Ed. Parsons, Ian) `NEW`
[R700] Chatto pbk **£12.95**

RUMENS, CAROL (1944 -)
A refreshingly direct poet whose sharply fin uned portraits of domestic life have been gradually replaced by darker and more complex poems dealing with exile, political persecution and the legacy of the Holocaust.
Direct Dialling
[R701] Chatto pbk **£3.95**
From Berlin to Heaven `NEW`
[R702] Chatto pbk **£5.95**
Making for the Open
[R703] Chatto pbk **£5.95**
Selected Poems
[R704] Chatto pbk **£5.95**
The Greening of Snow Beach `NEW`
Rumens' latest collection offers an unusual insight into her engagement with Russian culture; it includes several groups of poems, as well as translations of poets including Blok and Mandelstam.
[R705] Bloodaxe pbk **£5.95**

SASSOON, SIEGFRIED (1886 - 1967)
The bitter satire and irony of Sassoon's war poetry contrasts starkly with the life of cultured ease he enjoyed before first going to the trenches. Although his brutal experiences left him resentful and highly politicised, his poetry soon lost its sharpness, becoming increasingly reflective and devotional (he was received into the Catholic Church in 1957). Sassoon's only post-war masterpiece was a work of prose: the autobiographical *Memoirs of a Fox-Hunting Man* (1928).
Collected Poems
[R706] Faber pbk **£4.95**
Selected Poems
[R707] Faber pbk **£2.95**
The War Poems of Siegfried Sassoon
[R708] Faber hbk **£7.95**
[R709] Faber pbk **£2.95**

SCANNELL, VERNON (1922 -)
Anecdotal and colloquial, Scanell is an attractive poet who was originally characterized as part of the opposition to the Movement poets in the 1950s, although in retrospect his ironic way of dealing with urban situations and mundane daily life seems remarkably similar.
New & Collected Poems
[R713] Robson pbk **£3.95**
Selected Poems
[R714] Allison & B pbk **£2.50**
Soldiering On
[R715] Robson hbk **£6.95**

SCHMIDT, MICHAEL (Mexican, 1947 -)
"The mind is a garden as the garden is,/And hangs above a wilderness it comprehends." Perhaps because of his high profile as critic, anthologist, and most influentially, as managing director of Carcanet Press and editor of *PN Review*, Michael Schmidt's poetry has not received the attention it deserves. He has moved on from the slick impersonality of his early work, and reached a new maturity; anecdotal yet rhythmically exciting, *The Love of Strangers* consists of 20 extended evocations of important, yet often distant influences on him, ranging from Pasolini to Elizabeth Daryush, from Robert Frost to the matador Joselito Huerta.
The Love of Strangers `NEW`
[R716] Hutchinson pbk **£5.95**

SCOTT, DAVID
Playing for England `NEW`
'Scott belongs firmly to the long tradition of parson-poets that goes back at least as far as George Herbert...For all their reticence, there is a compassion in these poems and a sense of propriety' (Norman Nicholson *Church Times*.)
[R717] Bloodaxe pbk **£5.95**

SCOVELL, E.J. (1907 -)
Scovell's polished lyrics are quiet elegiac meditations on the English landscape and on the subtleties of everyday experience. She has written of her work: *"I should like the surface to be entirely clear, and the meaning to be entirely implicit; I should like the reader to understand what I say, so that along with it he may apprehend something I do not say, but which the subject of my poems expresses to me, and could to him."*
Collected Poems
[R718] Carcanet hbk **£16.95**

SCUPHAM, PETER (1933 -)
Scupham's technique is to submit his subjects - landscapes, heirlooms - to a detailed examination in formalist poems with strict rhyming schemes; as Neil Powell puts it, the poems 'invariably ritualize their subjects', but in a way that is oblique and without flashiness. Sometimes, however, his serious and accomplished poems appear constrained by such highly beautiful and articulated surfaces.
Out Late
[R719] Oxford pbk **£4.95**
Summer Palaces
[R720] Oxford pbk **£3.00**
The Air Show
[R721] Oxford pbk **£4.95**
Winter Quarters
[R722] Oxford pbk **£4.50**

SHAPCOTT, JO
Electroplating the Baby `NEW`
[R723] Bloodaxe pbk **£4.95**

SHERRARD, PHILIP
In the Sign of the Rainbow: Selected Poems 1940 - 1986
The first extensive selection of Sherrard's poetry.
[R724] Anvil pbk **£5.95**

SHUTTLE, PENELOPE (1947 -)
Penelope Shuttle writes about the mysteries of experience and the elusive areas of feminine life in a pure, controlled style which can seem almost incantatory. Well known as a novelist, she is married to fellow-poet Peter Redgrove.
Adventures with my Horse
[R725] Oxford pbk **£5.95**
The Child-Stealer
[R726] Oxford pbk **£4.95**
The Lion from Rio
[R727] Oxford pbk **£3.95**
The Orchard Upstairs
[R728] Oxford pbk **£3.95**

Vernon Scannell, author of *Soldiering On* (Robson Books hbk **£6.95**)

SILKIN, JON (1930 -)
Silkin's poetry may be read as an alternative to the more tame 'Movement' poets of his generation: emotive and strenuous, he writes for 'committed individuals', questioning man's inhumanity to man. In his most famous sequence, *Flower Poems*, Silkin exemplifies his own critical observation that poetry is born of the conflict between the twin urges of imagism and narrative.
Selected Poems
[R729] Routledge pbk **£7.95**

SIMMONS, JAMES (Irish, 1933 -)
Simmons's stock-in-trade is lively social satire - really doggerel - as he trawls marital problems and other tensions in his personal life. His belief in the richness of everyday life - expressed in *No Land Is Waste, Dr. Eliot* - is interspersed with moral speciousness and sentimentality: Simmons's 'man' is *"not hollow, he's a mate of mine"*, while T.S. Eliot is *"the pompous old swine"*.
Poems 1956 - 1986
[R730] Bloodaxe hbk **£12.95**
[R731] Bloodaxe pbk **£5.95**

SISSAY, LEMN
A recent collection from an acclaimed young Manchester poet, increasingly well-known for his lively performance poetry.
Tender Fingers in a Clenched Fist
[R732A] Bogle l'Ouverture pbk **£4.95**

SISSON, C.H. (English, 1914 -)
Sisson writes about decline, lust and death. His early work is a quest towards 'plain statement', and features a pervading pessimism and a tone *"chastening and acerbic to an unnatural degree"*. His belief in the unconsidered nature of poetic utterance has led to a 'softening' process, where dream states are reflected, meaning is unparaphrasable and syntax is ambiguous. He rejects whatever appears 'with the face of familiarity', and fluid rhythms are an outstanding feature of his work. He is one of the finest living UK poets.
Collected Poems
[R733] Carcanet hbk **£14.95**
God Bless Karl Marx!
[R734] Carcanet pbk **£4.95**
On the Look Out: A Partial Autobiography `NEW`
Carcanet have finally published Sisson's autobiography, which was written in the 60s. It concentrates on the first 50 years of his life and, often reversing chronology, moves from Whitehall to a Sergeant's mess in India, commuter Sevenoaks to Hitler's Berlin, pre-war Paris to working-class Bristol.
[R735] Carcanet hbk **£14.95**
Selected Poems
[R736] Carcanet pbk **£4.95**

SITWELL, EDITH (1887 - 1964)
An experimental poet active from the second decade of the century on, Edith Sitwell is remembered now for *Façade*, the collection of 'abstract poems' or 'patterns in sound', set to music by William Walton. In fact her later poetry, including that written after 1945, is more serious and interesting.
Collected Poems
[R737] Macmillan pbk **£2.95**

SMITH, IAIN CRICHTON (Scottish, 1928 -)
A bilingual poet in Gaelic and English, Crichton Smith has lived much of his life in the Outer Hebrides. He has commented: *"I have always believed in a poetry which contains fighting tensions and not in the poetry of statement"*.
A Life
[R738] Carcanet pbk **£4.95**
Selected Poems
[R739] Carcanet pbk **£2.95**

The Exiles
[R742] Carcanet pbk **£4.95**
The Village and Other Poems
Smith's *The Village* sequence of 50 poems evokes the world that shaped his imagination, celebrating and elegizing the everyday lives of the people of that world in a language of poise and control. The 37 *Other Poems* range widely in theme and subject, from television to apartheid.
[R743] Carcanet pbk **£6.95**

SMITH, KEN (1938 -)
For some time undervalued in Britain, Smith's work has undergone recent critical reassessment. *The Poet Reclining* collects much of his best work, including the longer poem, *Fox Running*, which memorably depicts his vision of the hostile environment of London.
A Book of Chinese Whispers (Prose)
[R744] Bloodaxe pbk **£4.95**
Burned Books
[R745] Bloodaxe pbk **£3.00**
Terra
[R746] Bloodaxe pbk **£4.95**
The Poet Reclining: Selected Poems 1962 - 80
[R747] Bloodaxe pbk **£8.95**
Wormwood
[R748] Bloodaxe pbk **£4.95**

SMITH, STEVIE (1902 - 1971)
Stevie Smith was a memorable performer of her own poetry: simple and colloquial, sometimes archaic, her tone moves freely between wit and pathos. She was also an acclaimed novelist.
A Selection (Ed. Lee, Hermione)
[R749] Faber pbk **£3.50**
Collected Poems
[R750] Penguin pbk **£6.95**
Selected Poems
[R751] Penguin pbk **£3.95**

SMITH, SYDNEY GOODSIR (New Zealand, 1915 - 1975)
Born to Scottish parents in Wellington, Smith consciously adopted the Middle Scots of the old Makars as his model, and wrote in a language that, despite its provenance in ancient texts, had a strangely fluent and spoken quality about it. His linguistic experimentation places him in the tradition of Hugh MacDiarmid.
Collected Poems
[R752] Calder hbk **£11.95**
[R753] Calder pbk **£6.95**

SPENDER, STEPHEN (1909 -)
Spender's work is associated with that of of the 1930s group of socially committed writers centred around Auden, although his flirtation with Communism was brief. His best work, much of it written early in his career, combines a bewildered and tentative despair with an idealistic desire for positive change.
Collected Poems
[R755] Faber hbk **£12.50**
[R756] Faber pbk **£5.95**

STALLWORTHY, JON (1935 -)
"My poems all/Are woven out of love's loose ends;/For myself and for my friends". Quiet and formally precise, Stallworthy's work has reacted against the public protest poetry of his generation, and insists on the equal value of private experience.
First Lines
[R757] Oxford pbk **£4.95**
The Anzac Sonata
[R758] Chatto pbk **£4.95**

SWEENEY, MATTHEW
Blue Shoes `NEW`
Sweeney takes as his subject the contrast of rural

Ireland and metropolitan England, the vitality of youth against the body's decay, the stability of the remembered moment in comparison with the flux of time.
[R759] Secker pbk **£5.00**

SYMONS, ARTHUR (1865 - 1945)
Given his acknowledged influence on the three major poets of the first half of the century - Yeats, Eliot and Pound, all of whom stress the importance of his introductory *The Symbolist Movement in Literature* to their own work - it is surprising that Symons languishes in obscurity. His poetry followed his 'desire to be modern' and, despite an occasional echo of Swinburne or Yeats, is original in dealing with urban themes, and for its colloquial tone. Eliot commented that he had learnt from Symons 'that one could write poetry in an English such as one would speak oneself. A colloquial idiom'.
Selected Writings
[R760] Carcanet pbk **£3.95**

SZIRTES, GEORGE (1948 -)
'One of the very best poets under 40. You might encapsulate his manner of writing by describing it as a contest between pictureable reality and the over-world of his imagination' (Peter Porter).
Metro
[R761] Oxford pbk **£4.95**
The Photographer in Winter
[R762] Secker pbk **£4.95**

THOMAS, D.M. (1935 -)
Thomas writes: *"My poetry does not move far from love and death. Early poems use science fiction themes as images of desire and separation. More recently, my most obsessive themes have been sexuality, family deaths and a search for lost roots."*
Selected Poems
[R763] Secker pbk **£7.95**

THOMAS, DYLAN (Welsh, 1914 - 1953)
Overpraised in his lifetime, Thomas's work has been much more critically received since his death. Elaborate, highly obscure and verbally energetic, his work was influenced by Hopkins, and (more marginally) by surrealism and psychoanalysis; he combines garbled rhetoric with archetypal imagery. Poems like 'And Death Shall Have No Dominion' and 'Do Not Go Gentle into that Good Night' remain popular, as does the radio play *Under Milk Wood*.
Collected Poems
[R764] Dent pbk **£1.95**
Collected Poems 1934 - 53 `NEW`
(Ed. Davies, Walford & Maud, Ralph)
This is the first detailed, scholarly edition of Thomas's poetry, with extensive annotation and a reliable text.
[R765] Dent hbk **£15.00**
Poems
[R766] Dent hbk **£10.50**
[R767] Dent pbk **£2.95**
The Notebook Poems, 1930 - 34 `NEW`
[R768] Dent hbk **£16.00**
Under Milk Wood (Radio Play)
[R769] Dent pbk **£1.75**

THOMAS, EDWARD (1878 - 1917)
"Rain, midnight rain, nothing but the wild rain/On this bleak hut, and solitude, and me/Remembering again that I shall die..." All of Edward Thomas's poetry was written in a short period preceding his death at Arras - and it was the impact of war, as well as the influence of Robert Frost, which prompted him to turn to verse after 22 years supporting himself as a reviewer and hack prose writer (this work is best read in the collection *A Language not to be Betrayed*). He stands as one of the handful of finest English poets of the century.

A Language not to be Betrayed
[R770] Carcanet pbk £5.95
Collected Poems
[R771] Faber pbk £3.95
Selected Poems (Ed. Thomas, R.S.)
[R772] Faber pbk £1.50
Selected Poems and Prose
[R773] Penguin pbk £3.99

THOMAS, R.S. (Welsh, 1913 -)
Thomas's early poetry is dominated by his
relations with his largely rural Welsh parishes and
parishoners. He has a remarkable instinct for the
vivid but unexpected metaphor - yet often poems are
merely contexts for points of vividness. His later
work - which, surprisingly, some critics have seen
as a falling-off - has a tendency towards prophecy
and allegory, and is less rooted in place, showing
a greater willingness to make formal experiments.
His fine, bare poetry has great depth.
Between Here and Now
[R774] Macmillan pbk £5.95
Experimenting with an Amen
[R775] Macmillan pbk £4.95
Selected Poems 1946 - 68
[R776] Bloodaxe pbk £4.95
Selected Prose
[R777] Poetry Wales P pbk £7.95
The Echoes Return Slowly (Memoirs)
[R778] Macmillan pbk £12.95
Welsh Airs
[R779] Poetry Wales P hbk £7.95
[R780] Poetry Wales P pbk £3.95

THORPE, ADAM (1956 -)
Mornings in the Baltic (1988)
A remarkable first collection displaying a
great range and vitality of form. Thorpe has a
richly ironic lyric voice which he adapts with
equal ease to narrative, elegy and dramatic
monologue.
[R781] Secker pbk £5.00

THWAITE, ANTHONY (1930 -)
Influenced by Larkin (whose **Collected Poems** he has
recently edited), Thwaite's work has an urbane and
accessible clarity. Technically elegant, it is shaped by
his sense of life's contradictions - his efforts to voice
conviction being undermined by a fear of futility. He
has held a number of editorial jobs - at the *New
Statesman* and *Encounter* - as well as working abroad
in Japan.
Letter from Tokyo (1987)
[R782] Hutchinson pbk £5.95
Poems 1953 - 1988   NEW
Re-issued in an updated form, this is Thwaite's own
selection of his work.
[R783] Hutchinson pbk £8.95
Victorian Voices
[R784] Oxford pbk £4.95

TOMLINSON, CHARLES (1927 -)
Indebted to American literature, Tomlinson's poetry
is in the tradition of Pound, Williams and Zukofsky.
In attempting to accord 'objects their own existence'
the poems are often imagistic, visual responses to
landscapes, experiences and events. Perhaps his finest
poems are the cinematic 'Swimming Chenango Lake'
and the political 'Prometheus'. He is among the finest
of living English poets.
Collected Poems
[R785] Oxford hbk £15.00
[R786] Oxford pbk £6.95
The Return
[R787] Oxford pbk £4.95

TRIPP, JOHN
Selected Poems   NEW
[R789] Seren Books pbk £4.95

WAIN, JOHN (1925 -)
Associated with the 'Movement' of the 1950s,
Wain's poetry is understated and technically
conservative, often dealing with 'ordinary life' in
urban settings.
Open Country
[R790] Hutchinson pbk £5.95
Poems 1949 - 79
[R791] Macmillan pbk £4.95

WAINWRIGHT, JEFFREY (1944 -)
Wainwright's scrupulous, terse language, his
historical sense and commitment to the larger world
of politics, marks him out from more frivolous
contemporaries. Although he writes fragile and tender
love lyrics, his most interesting works are his
historical poems, which are reminiscent of Geoffrey
Hill.
Selected Poems
[R792] Carcanet hbk £2.95

WATKINS, VERNON (Welsh, 1906 - 1967)
His romanticism has often placed Watkins as one of
the apocalyptic poets of the 1940s, but, although he
was a close friend of Dylan Thomas, his poetry is, as
Larkin commented, 'much more controlled than
theirs, reaching further back to the symbolist poets of
Europe'. He is often at his best in describing the
smallest particulars of nature.
Collected Poems
[R796] Golgonooza pbk £19.50

WELLS, ROBERT (1947 -)
Influenced by James Thomson, Gray, Cowper
and Collins, Wells's poetry is characterized by
controlled forms, archaic diction, and its use of
allegory, while the classical resonances of his verse
owe debts to Latin and Greek literature (he has
translated both Theocritus and Virgil's *Georgics*).
George Mackay Brown has commented of his work:
'the healing loneliness of hills and waters, and the
solitary figures who move among them - bathers,
woodcutters, hay-harvesters - are the setting and
characters of Wells's poems: all breathe a rare
wholesomeness'.
Selected Poems
[R797] Carcanet pbk £3.95
The Winter's Task
[R798] Carcanet pbk £2.95

WILLIAMS, HUGO (1942 -)
Williams was associated with the literary magazines
The Review and its successor *The New Review*, and he
produced slight, minimalist poems not dissimilar to
those of fellow contributors Colin Falck and David
Harsent. Devoid of rhetoric, his intense and resonant
work is anecdotal, yet riven with insight. As Peter
Levi has commented, 'someone who liked him might
own a Hockney, subscribe to the *London Magazine*,
and live in Hampstead.'
Selected Poems   NEW
Williams's new **Selected Poems** features the poet's
own choice of poems from his five previous
collections.
[R799] Oxford pbk £6.95
Writing Home
[R800] Oxford pbk £3.95

WRIGHT, DAVID (South African, 1920 -)
Born in Johannesburg, Wright became stone deaf at
the age of seven, and moved to England aged 14. His
work is evidence that much more than the ear enters
our perception of rhythm. After some apocalyptic
excesses in the 1940s, he developed a plainer style,
notable for what C.H. Sisson has called 'language
close to speech, but nourished by the surest and most
unpretentious of English traditions - the line from
Chaucer and his contemporaries to the world of Clare,
Clough and Hardy'.

Deafness (Autobiography)   NEW
Reissued with a substantial new introduction,
this is Wright's autobiography, which recalls his
childhood and education, as well as tracing the little-
known history of deafness.
[R801] Faber pbk £4.99
Selected Poems
[R802] Carcanet pbk £4.95

WRIGHT, KIT
Poems 1974 - 88
[R803] Hutchinson pbk £7.50

YEATS, WILLIAM BUTLER (1865 - 1939)
Nobel Prize for Literature 1923. Yeats's poetry
went through what Michael Hamburger has called 'an
extraordinary progression from melancholy
romantic reveries to prophetic or starkly realistic
encounters with the "Savage God". His early work
deals with traditional Irish themes - legend and the
Celtic revival - and with his unrequited love for Maud
Gonne, while the second half of his career is marked
by a turn towards sparer and more colloquial dramatic
speech, due partly to the influence of Ezra Pound.
Yeats referred to the 'quarrel with ourselves' out of
which poetry is made, and, despite some instances of
obscurity, the power of his late poems, written
towards the end of the 1930s, remains unmatched.
A Vision (Prose)
[R804] Macmillan pbk £11.95
Autobiographies (Prose)
[R805] Macmillan pbk £8.95
Collected Poems
[R806] Macmillan pbk £10.95
Selected Criticism & Prose
[R807] Pan pbk £3.50
Selected Poems
[R808] Pan pbk £3.95
The Secret Rose (Prose)
[R809] Macmillan pbk £6.95

YOUNG, ANDREW (Scottish, 1885 - 1971)
Young's career started quietly from 1910 with *Songs
of the Night*, and many volumes of quiet, reflective
verse followed. Although he built up a readership in
his lifetime, he is now little read, and remains a minor
Georgian.
Poetical Works
[R810] Secker hbk £12.95
[R811] Secker pbk £9.95

W.B. Yeats (Picture: National Portrait Gallery)

World Poetry in English

A New Book of South African Verse in English (Ed. Butler, Guy & Mann, Chris)
[R812] Oxford hbk **£10.00**

Hinterland: Afro-Caribbean & Black British Poetry (Ed. Markham, E.A.) **NEW**
Featuring 16 poets writing on both sides of the Atlantic, including Walcott and Brathwaite, Berry and D'Aguilar, Markham's anthology is characterized by local colour and tonal innovation, often thought to be lacking in the British 'mainstream'.
[R813] Bloodaxe pbk **£7.95**

Inside Black Australia: An Anthology of Aboriginal Poetry (Ed. Gilbert, Kevin) **NEW**
Gilbert introduces 40 aboriginal poets, and they write tough poems that resist the silence of genocide and the destruction of culture.
[R814] Penguin pbk **£4.95**

Modern African Poetry
Fresh and passionate gathering of 67 poets from 23 countries.
[R815] Penguin pbk **£4.95**

New Oxford Book of Canadian Verse in English (Ed. Atwood, Margaret)
[R816] Oxford hbk **£18.50**
[R817] Oxford pbk **£9.50**

New Zealand Verse
[R818] Penguin pbk **£5.95**

The Oxford Book of Australian Verse (Ed. Murray, Les)
[R819] Oxford pbk **£15.00**

The Oxford Book of Contemporary New Zealand Verse (Ed. Adcock, Fleur)
An excellent survey of the field, stretching from the older poets Allen Curnow and James K. Baxter to lesser-known names, such as Elizabeth Smither and Lauris Edmond.
[R820] Oxford pbk **£7.95**

The Penguin Book of Caribbean Verse in English (Ed. Burnett)
This unusual anthology mixes the oral tradition - performance and dub - with the more traditional literary one: Bob Marley and Peter Tosh rub shoulders with Derek Walcott and Edward Kamau Brathwaite.
[R821] Penguin pbk **£6.99**

The Penguin Book of South African Verse (Ed. Gray, Stephen)
Gray's anthology includes all the obvious figures such as David Wright, William Plomer, Roy Campbell and Breyten Breytenbach, but has some more surprising inclusions: Fernando Pessoa, de Camoens, Isaac Rosenberg and Rudyard Kipling.
[R822] Penguin pbk **£6.99**

Under Another Sky: The Commonwealth Poetry Prize Anthology (Ed. Niven, Alistair)
This book celebrates 25 years of the prize, which is dedicated to the proposition that a common language endows us with a common poetry - or poetries. It includes work by Chinua Achebe, Grace Nichols, Lauris Edmond and Vikram Seth.
[R823] Carcanet pbk **£6.95**

ATWOOD, MARGARET (Canada, 1939 -)
Poet and novelist, Atwood is one of Canada's most prominent writers. Her poetry is an exposure of the power politics of nationality and gender; it features a sharp and witty idiom, where the prosaic and the surreal interact.
True Stories
[R824] Cape pbk **£3.95**

BAXTER, JAMES K. (New Zealand, 1926 - 72)
Baxter is New Zealand's finest poet, and one of the language's finest poets of the century. Much of his career represented a crusade against his country's lack of spirituality; early bohemianism and Christian concern found a focus when he converted to Catholicism in 1958. The early verse featured lyrical renditions of a rural New Zealand world; later he moved towards narratives, and towards the end of his career evolved a fluid sonnet form in the superb *Jerusalem Sonnets*, which express his personal sense of religious conviction.
Collected Poems
[R825] Oxford hbk **£17.00**

BHATT, SUJATA (India, 1956 -)
Although she writes in English, Bhatt's mother tongue is Gujarati. Attached to both cultures, she cannot do without either. She writes of goats and lizards, real people and mythological figures, and of political strife and erotic love. *Brunizem*, the title of her first collection, refers to the dark brown prairie soil found in Asia, Europe and North America, the three very different worlds of her imagination.
Brunizem
[R826] Carcanet pbk **£5.95**

BRATHWAITE, EDWARD KAMAU (West Indian, 1930 -)
"The history of catastrophe requires such a literature to hold a mirror up to broken nature." Brathwaite articulates the complicated history of the Caribbean people in a poetry which combines literary English with Caribbean vernacular. Born in Barbados, he now teaches at the University of the West Indies in Kingston, Jamaica.
Mother Poem
[R313] Oxford pbk **£4.95**
Sun Poem
[R314] Oxford pbk **£4.95**
X-Self
This volume completes the trilogy begun by *Mother Poem* and *Sun Poem*, weaving together the strands of history and heredity that have contributed to his present self.
[R315] Oxford pbk **£6.95**

CURNOW, ALLEN (New Zealand, 1911 -)
All Curnow's poetry is concerned with the quest for cultural identity in his native New Zealand, and, believing that poets should not cut themselves off from ordinary people, he has been a champion of the demotic voice. *Continuum: New and Later Poems 1972-1988* brings together poems from his previous five volumes, and a number of important new poems. He is a gentle, compassionate and humorous voice.
Continuum: New and Later Poems 1972 - 1988 **NEW**
[R827] Auckland hbk **£16.95**
Look Back Harder: Critical Writings 1935 - 1984
[R828] Oxford pbk **£14.00**

EDMOND, LAURIS (New Zealand, 1924 -)
One of New Zealand's most distinguished poets, assured and prolific, Edmond did not publish a collection until 1975. Her work casts a subtle and compassionate light on the fragility of human relationships, and the impermanence of human existence; it is soft-spoken and mildly ironic.

Margaret Atwood, author of *True Stories* (Jonathan Cape pbk £3.95)

Seasons and Creatures
[R829] Bloodaxe pbk **£4.95**
Summer near the Arctic Circle
[R830] Oxford pbk **£5.95**

HOPE, A.D. (Australia, 1907 -)
"You cannot build bridges between the wandering islands;/The Mind has no neighbours..." Crassly condemned for obscurity, anti-Australianism and misogyny, Hope's work is characterized by sexual explicitness, a ferocious wit and an elegant formalism. It is fresh, powerful, European, and humanely erotic.
Selected Poems
[R831] Carcanet pbk **£3.95**

MANSFIELD, KATHERINE (New Zealand, 1888 - 1923)
Better known as a brilliant short-story writer, and for her marvellous diaries and letters, Katherine Mansfield also wrote poems. Vincent O'Sullivan has made a fresh selection from the uncollected work, and Mansfield appears from that selection as a technically innovative, highly accomplished poet.
The Poems of Katherine Mansfield **NEW**
[R832] Oxford hbk **£9.95**
[R833] Oxford pbk **£6.95**

MURRAY, LES A. (Australia, 1938 -)
Brought up on a dairy farm in New South Wales, Murray has written many poems which evoke the landscape, history and values implicit in that community, which he refers to as his 'spirit-country'. Others survey the oddities and idiocies of contemporary culture with a witty, sophisticated and sympathetic intelligence. He is at the front rank of poets now writing.
Selected Poems
[R834] Carcanet pbk **£3.95**
The Boys who Stole the Funeral **NEW**
In Murray's fast-paced novel in verse, which consists of 140 varied and resourceful sonnets, two boys steal the body of an old Digger, Clarrie Bunn, from an undertaker's, to return it to the country where he wished to be buried. Underlying the wry narrative, the theme of blood sacrifice contends with the more fragile theme of Christian reconciliation.
[R835] Carcanet pbk **£6.95**
The Daylight Moon
[R836] Carcanet pbk **£6.95**

SERVICE, ROBERT (Canada, 1874 - 1958)
Born in Glasgow, Service emigrated to Canada when he was 21. In 1904 he moved to the Yukon, where the Klondike gold rush had recently taken place, and this provided the impetus for his best-known verse. His melodramatic verse has little literary merit, but his ballads of Yukon life such as 'The Shooting of Dan McGrew' and 'The Cremation of Sam McGee' were immensely popular in their day.

Songs of the High North
[R837] Benn pbk **£3.25**
The Best of Robert Service
[R838] A & C Black pbk **£5.95**

SETH, VIKRAM (Indian, 1952 -)
Influenced by Thomas Hardy, Philip Larkin and
Timothy Steele, the poems in Seth's first collection,
The Humble Administrator's Garden, are quiet and
graceful, reflecting his encounters with his own and
alien cultures - England, the United States and China.
The Golden Gate is a novel in verse about yuppie
Californian life, and uses - with great verve and
panache - the Pushkin sonnet stanza inspired by
Charles Johnston's translation of *Eugene Onegin*.
The Golden Gate
[R839] Faber pbk **£3.95**
The Humble Administrator's Garden
[R840] Carcanet pbk **£5.95**

SOYINKA, WOLE (Nigerian, 1934 -)
Soyinka's poetry follows his better-known drama and
prose in both quality of language and subject matter:
the long title poem of *Idanre and Other Poems*
attempts to balance traditional African beliefs and
modern life, while *A Shuttle in the Crypt* describes
the period of his political imprisonment.
A Shuttle in the Crypt
[R841] Methuen pbk **£3.50**
Idanre and Other Poems
[R754] Methuen pbk **£3.95**

WALCOTT, DEREK (West Indian, 1930 -)
The publication of Walcott's *Collected Poems*
revealed him as one of the most talented and original
voices of the post-War era, whose language and tone
has developed consistently since the appearance of
major collections in the early 1960s. He has forged a
poetic language from literary English and local
vernacular, which accurately reflects the state of the
Caribbean today.
Collected Poems
[R793] Faber pbk **£20.00**
Midsummer
[R794] Faber pbk **£3.95**
The Arkansas Testament
[R795] Faber pbk **£4.95**

WALLACE-CRABBE, CHRIS
(Australia, 1934 -)
Often concerned with the shaping of beliefs, Wallace-
Crabbe's poetry moves beyond a personal lyric vision
to an objective consideration of political issues.
I'm Deadly Serious   NEW
[R842] Oxford pbk **£4.95**
The Amorous Cannibal
[R843] Oxford pbk **£4.50**

WEDDE, IAN (New Zealand)
Tendering: New Poems   NEW
This new collection pervaded by powerful images of
the sea, and voyages of exploration.
[R844] Auckland UP pbk **£10.95**

American Poetry

American Poetry (Ed. Hall, Donald)
[R845] Faber pbk **£2.25**

American Verse
[R846] Penguin pbk **£6.95**

American Verse of the 19th Century
[R847] Dent pbk **£1.75**

Contemporary American Poetry
[R848] Penguin pbk **£4.95**

**The Faber Book of Contemporary
American Verse** (Ed. Vendler, Helen)
[R849] Faber hbk **£14.95**

**The New Oxford Book of American
Verse** (Ed. Ellmann, Richard)
[R850] Oxford hbk **£25.00**

The Oxford Book of American Verse
(Ed. Matthiessen, F.O.)
[R851] Oxford hbk **£25.00**

ANGELOU, MAYA (1928 -)
The multi-talented Angelou has appeared in musicals,
written film scripts and, most notably, several
volumes of autobiography which examine the
challenges facing black American women. Her poetry
is enormously popular and highly readable.
And Still I Rise
[R852] Virago pbk **£3.95**
**Just Give Me a Cool Drink of Water
'Fore I Diiie**
[R853] Virago pbk **£3.95**
Now Sheba Sings the Song
[R854] Virago pbk **£6.95**

ASHBERY, JOHN (1927 -)
Associated with the New York poets such as Frank
O'Hara and James Schuyler, with whom he
collaborated on the novel *A Nest of Ninnies*, Ashbery
is an original - inscrutable, uncommitted and
unpolemical, his poems are self-referential and self-
enclosed. Influenced by Wallace Stevens and the
French surrealists, his poetry is by turns expansive
and elliptical, always evasive. At times his work is
spoiled by a wilful, contrived experimentalism, but
the best poems work as explorations of uncertainty.
A Wave (1984)
[R855] Carcanet pbk **£4.95**
April Galleons (1988)
This new volume combines the lyric directness of *A
Wave* with the baroque richness of language in his
earlier work.
[R856] Carcanet hbk **£8.95**
Selected Poems (1986)
[R857] Carcanet hbk **£16.95**
[R858] Paladin pbk **£4.95**
Self-Portrait in a Convex Mirror (1977)
[R859] Carcanet pbk **£4.95**
Shadow Train (1982)
[R860] Carcanet pbk **£5.95**

BERRYMAN, JOHN (1914 - 1972)
Berryman's life was turbulent, ending in suicide when
he jumped from a bridge in Minneapolis; his poetry is
personal and confessional, exploring religious doubts
and guilt. His early work has 'the aura of academic
contrivance about it', and his reputation rests on two
sequences: *Homage to Mistress Bradstreet*, a
celebration of the 17th century poet Anne Bradstreet,
and the *Dream Songs*, which Robert Lowell called
'one of the glories of the age'.
Selected Poems 1938 - 68
[R861] Faber pbk **£3.95**

BISHOP, ELIZABETH (1911 - 1979)
One of America's finest poets, Bishop's work is
notable for its brilliant observation of the world. Her
landscapes are not symbolic, but contain the *quidditas*
of place. Using classical forms, hers is a
representational art - one of statement and description,
where the visual world hints at the secrets of life,
objects are imbued with a dreamy unreality.
The Complete Poems
Bishop's *Complete Poems* gathers together all her
poetry, including fifty previously unpublished
poems, and her translations of Paz, Max Jacob, and
others.
[R862] Hogarth pbk **£9.99**

BLY, ROBERT (1926 -)
Reacting strongly against the hegemony of the
confessional poets, Bly ignores rhetoric and artifice,
and his poetry strives after 'naturalness'. Yet perhaps
because of this rejection of known, academic
measures, his verse, although possessing poise,
assurance and ease of movement, sometimes fails to
move us.
Jumping Out of Bed   NEW
Bly's latest book to appear in Britain, *Jumping Out
of Bed* is based on Taoist poems, and includes some
translations of the Chinese poet Wang Wei.
[R863] Forest pbk **£5.95**
The Love of Minute Particulars (1985)
[R864] Sceptre pbk **£4.95**

BUKOWSKI, CHARLES (1929 -)
The latest among Bukowski's 30 collections of poetry,
The Roominghouse Madrigals, reveals him as the
poet of the gritty backwaters of faceless cities and of
flophouse one-night stands. His work, indebted to the
Beats, is angry and irreverent, and he professes to
despise the poetry of the mainstream.
**Burning in Water Drowning in Flame:
Selected Poems 1955 - 73**
[R867] Black Sparrow pbk **£7.50**
Love Is a Dog from Hell
[R868] Black Sparrow pbk **£7.50**
**Play the Piano Drunk Like a Percussion
Instrument Until the Fingers Begin to
Bleed**
[R869] Black Sparrow pbk **£5.95**
The Days Run Wild Horses Over the Hill
[R870] Black Sparrow pbk **£6.50**
**The Roominghouse Madrigals: Early
Selected Poems 1946 - 1966**
[R871] Black Sparrow pbk **£10.95**
War All the Time
[R872] Black Sparrow pbk **£8.95**
**You Get so Alone at Times that it Just
Makes Sense**
[R873] Black Sparrow pbk **£11.95**

CARVER, RAYMOND (1939 - 1988)
Carver's keen eye and incisive verbal skill have made
him a highly acclaimed chronicler of contemporary
life. In his quietly beautiful poetry Carver fashions
landscapes of elusive mystery and danger.
A New Path to the Wall   NEW
Carver's new collection is beautifully organized, and
one in which the keynote is a delight in new ways to
enjoy the present, rather than regret for the past. His
widow, Tess Gallagher, contributes a memoir of his
last days.
[R874] Collins hbk **£11.00**
In a Marine Light: Selected Poems
[R875] Collins hbk **£11.50**
[R876] Picador pbk **£3.95**

CLAMPITT, AMY (1920 -)
Clampitt's work is characterized by a chastely
brilliant detail, a flowing syntax and a measured tone
which is able to accommodate the mundane and rise
to a sustained and controlled eloquence. James Fenton
has spoken of her 'beautiful gravity, scope and
movement'.
Archaic Figure
[R877] Faber pbk **£4.95**
What the Light Was Like
[R878] Faber pbk **£4.95**

CRANE, HART (1899 - 1932)
Crane's work is a very American poetry, rooted in
"that deep wonderment, our native clay". His major
work is *The Bridge*, which affirms all that Eliot
denies in *The Waste Land*. Crane commented that 'I
take Eliot as a point of departure toward an almost
complete reverse of direction' and, in his move
towards a 'more ecstatic goal', his psychological

models were Whitman and Melville. The poem remains a flawed masterpiece, where a mystical synthesis of America is presented, with Brooklyn Bridge standing as a symbol of hope; however, the poem's epic and romantic urges seem unresolved, and there is an obscurity of language and a forced optimism. This optimism was not borne out by his own life, and he commited suicide aged only 33.

Complete Poems
[R879] Bloodaxe pbk £6.95
The Bridge
[R880] Norton pbk £4.95
White Buildings: Poems
[R881] Norton pbk £3.20

CREELEY, ROBERT (1926 -)
After his early projectivist verse, with its presentation of reality as process, and his subsequent adoption of a manner of serial composition (freely associative 'scribbling'), Creeley has mellowed into a more meditative mode. He is considered by some as a major figure in post-war American poetry.

A Sense of Measure (Prose)
[R882] Boyars pbk £3.95
Collected Poems of Robert Creeley 1945 - 1975
[R883] Boyars pbk £9.95
Memory Gardens
[R884] Boyars pbk £5.95
Poems 1950 - 1965
[R885] Boyars pbk £4.50

CUMMINGS, E.E. (1894 - 1962)
There are two complementary urges in cummings' poetry; to celebrate the 'eternal us' now, and biting satire, often against what he called the 'busy monster, manunkind'. He is known for his experimental style: influenced by jazz and contemporary slang, he drops capital letters, plays wildly with typography, and formal devices (capital letters or punctuation in the middle of words, phrases split by parentheses) are used as a visual manifestation of a theme; he was original in making pronunciation 'mean' in itself. For all his experimentation, his work is sometimes sentimental and intellectually thin.

73 Poems
[R886] Faber pbk £3.95
Selected Poems 1923 - 1958
[R887] Faber pbk £3.95

DICKINSON, EMILY (1830 - 1886)
Now recognized as one of the most innovative poets of the 19th century, only seven of Emily Dickinson's 1,775 poems were published in her lifetime. Although she wrote on traditional subjects - love, nature, religion and mortality - her idiosyncratic handling of technique is startling. Often writing in stanzas of four lines, the technical irregularities - the frequent use of dashes, sporadic capitalization of nouns, convoluted phrasing, off-rhymes and broken metres - combine with her startling metaphors and aphoristic wit to produce extraordinary poetry.

A Choice of Emily Dickinson's Verse (Ed. Hughes, Ted)
[R888] Faber pbk £3.95
Selected Poems (Ed. Reeves, James)
[R889] Heinemann pbk £3.95
Complete Poems of Emily Dickinson
[R890] Faber pbk £7.95

DOOLITTLE, HILDA (H.D.) (1886 - 1961)
Only now, over a century after her birth and 28 years after her death, is H.D. being acknowledged as a major writer to be spoken of with Pound and Eliot. Her *Selected Poems* starts with her Imagistic poems, and includes the 'lost' poems of the 1930s, the prophetic *Trilogy* poems of the war years, and the visionary sequences *Helen in Egypt* and *Hermetic Definition*, perhaps her most distinctive writing.

Collected Poems 1912 - 1944
[R891] Carcanet hbk £18.95
Helen in Egypt
[R892] Carcanet pbk £6.95
Hermetic Definition
[R893] Carcanet pbk £4.95
Selected Poems `NEW`
[R894] Carcanet hbk £14.95
Trilogy
[R895] Carcanet pbk £6.95

EBERHARDT, RICHARD (1874 - 1963)
One might describe Eberhardt's early work as belonging to the 'dead sheep' school of poetry: *'I saw on a slant hill a putrid lamb,/Propped with daisies'*, or, *'In June, amid the golden fields,/I saw a groundhog lying dead'*. Much of his later work offers a (subtler) response to nature, from cancer cells to the Maine coastline. He has written that *"Poetry is a confrontation of the whole being with reality. It is a basic struggle of the soul, the mind and the body to comprehend life, to bring order to chaos, or to phenomena, and by will and insight to create communicable verbal forms for the pleasure of mankind."*

Collected Poems
[R896] Oxford hbk £25.00
Maine Poems `NEW`
[R897] Oxford pbk £9.95
Ways of Light: Poems 1972 - 80
[R898] Oxford pbk £5.95

FERLINGHETTI, LAWRENCE (1919 -)
Ferlinghetti was a central figure in the Beat movement, as founder of San Francisco's City Lights bookstore, and as the publisher of Ginsberg, Corso and Levertov. His own poetry is unacademic in form and satiric in tone, yet he has a strong interest in politics and cultural issues, often attacking American values.

Over All the Obscene Boundaries: European Poems & Translations
[R899] New Directions pbk £3.95

FROST, ROBERT (1874 - 1963)
Although posthumous biographical researches have shown him to be something of a vain careerist, the persona of the 'loveable New England sage' persists. Ruminative and aphoristic, his poems are often dramatic monologues, and he makes exemplary use of New England patterns of speech. Edward Thomas described his works as 'revolutionary, because they lack the exaggeration of rhetoric', whilst Randall Jarrell commented that Frost's poems 'express an attitude that at its most extreme, makes pessimism seem a hopeful evasion'. The later work is marked by a flatness of tone, which Frost described as 'a language absolutely unliterary'.

Robert Frost
[R900] Oxford pbk £4.95
[R901] Penguin pbk £2.95

GINSBERG, ALLEN (American, 1926 -)
The most famous of the Beat poets, Ginsberg is best-known for his poem *Howl*; with its driving colloquial beat and its drop-out romanticism, it represents the rhetorical voice of the popular American tradition. Ginsberg has spoken accurately of his 'Hebraic, Melvillian bardic breath', and it is clear that he is indebted to Whitman. He possesses a great flair for hyperbole and some lack of modesty, but the poems, and there are many, often lie dead on the page, needing the poet's performance.

Collected Poems
[R902] Viking hbk £17.95
[R903] Penguin pbk £10.95
Howl (Manuscript Version)
[R904] Viking hbk £16.95
White Shroud: Poems 1980 - 1985
[R905] Viking hbk £12.95

HECHT, ANTHONY (1926 -)
Hecht is a fastidious and neo-classical poet, though he is never bloodless. He sees all too clearly mankind's decline from some original standard of possibility, a 'Disorder at the heart of everything', against which he sets up his poetry as a 'searching discipline' which 'can keep/That eye still clear'. At his best he achieves *"a grace won by the way from all/Striving in what is difficult"*.

Millions of Strange Shadows
[R906] Oxford pbk £2.50

HUGHES, LANGSTON (1926 -)
The identification of Langston Hughes with the Black Civil Rights movement means that his work provides a clear reflection of Black achievements and aspirations of the period. If his literary models were Whitman, Vachel Lindsay and Carl Sandburg, a unique element was added by his ear for black rhythms, be they from jazz lyrics or revivalist meetings. He referred to his own work as *"like be-bop...marked by conflicting changes, sudden nuances, sharp and sudden interjections, broken rhythms..."*

Selected Poems
[R907] Pluto pbk £6.95

JEFFERS, ROBINSON (1887 - 1962)
Jeffers is best remembered for his long narratives which frequently return to the controversial themes of incest, parricide and bestial passion. His extreme pessimism has alienated many readers, as he expresses a profound contempt for almost everything connected with humanity - *"the animals Christ is rumoured to have died for"*.

Dear Judas
[R908] Norton pbk £5.95
Double Axe
[R909] Norton pbk £5.95
Selected Poems (Ed. Falck, Colin)
[R910] Carcanet pbk £6.95
The Women at Point Sur
[R911] Norton pbk £5.95

KORELITZ, JEAN HANFF (1961 -)
The Properties of Breath is Korelitz's first collection, and it is marked by an unforced yet musical speaking voice, an acute, telling eye for detail, and a readiness to listen to what remains unspoken. Amy Clampitt has commented that 'a strain of demotic intensity hints at the presence of Sylvia Plath', the feeling and the cadence are both the poet's own'.

The Properties of Breath `NEW`
[R912] Bloodaxe pbk £4.95

LEVERTOV, DENISE (1923 -)
An English woman living in America, Denise Levertov has long been known for her political poetry, and her new collection, *Breathing the Water*, contains some of her freshest and most powerful yet. She takes the reader back to more personal, spiritual concerns, and the poems are lit with a joyful awareness of the physical world.

Breathing the Water `NEW`
[R913] Bloodaxe pbk £5.95
Oblique Prayers (1986)
[R914] Bloodaxe pbk £4.95
Selected Poems
[R915] Bloodaxe pbk £6.95

LONGFELLOW, HENRY WADSWORTH (1807 - 1882)
One of the most popular writers of his time, Longfellow's work ranges from sentimental pieces such as 'The Village Blacksmith' to glorifications of the American past, as in 'Paul Revere's Ride'. His most famous work, *The Song of Hiawatha*, offers an escape into the fantastical world of adventure, and reflects a reading of European epics, plus an interest in creating a peculiarly American mythology.

POETRY

Poems
[R916] Dent pbk **£3.50**
Selected Poems
[R917] Penguin pbk **£5.95**

LOWELL, ROBERT (1917 - 1977)
Lowell's early work is marked by Catholic symbolism and formal conservatism, yet it is formally inventive, with the discordant rhythms and syntax focusing on the history of New England and his own family. His most famous collection, *Life Studies*, has a looser form, and is less rhetorical. Drawing heavily on intimate autobiographical material, it is one of the central works of the 'Confessional' school, and he is open about his darkest personal experiences, such as spells in mental hospitals and his marriages.
Collected Prose
[R918] Faber hbk **£17.50**
Day by Day
[R919] Faber hbk **£7.95**
For the Union Dead
[R920] Faber pbk **£3.50**
Imitations
[R921] Faber pbk **£3.50**
Life Studies
[R922] Faber pbk **£3.95**
Near the Ocean
[R923] Faber pbk **£3.50**
Robert Lowell's Poems: A Selection
(Ed. Raban, Jonathan)
[R924] Faber pbk **£3.95**
Selected Poems 1938 - 64
[R925] Faber pbk **£2.95**

MERRILL, JAMES (1926 -)
Regarded in America as a major poet, alongside Lowell, Ashbery and Bishop, Merrill is hardly known in Britain. He is legendary, or notorious, for his massive *The Changing of Light at Sandover* sequence, which includes *Mirabell: Books of Numbers*, where the poet communicates with the illustrious dead by means of a ouija board. Although his anthology appearances display him as a lightweight, formal lyricist, his more familiar ground - befitting a writer whose acknowledged master is Proust - is in extended poetic autobiography.
Mirabell: Books of Numbers
[R926] Oxford pbk **£3.25**

MOORE, MARIANNE (1887 - 1971)
Marianne Moore's poetry can be characterized as an examination of things with great clarity. She manipulates patterns of line endings, uses intricate rhymes, assonance and alliteration, and an exquisitely developed syntax, which are combined with peculiar ideas and facts. She usually writes in syllabics, in which, given the intricacy of the mathematically regular forms, she is able to develop her unique voice. Beyond the surface brilliance, there is a unique 'accessiblity to experience'.
Complete Poems
[R927] Faber pbk **£3.95**
The Complete Prose of Marianne Moore
[R928] Faber hbk **£35.00**

MOSS, STANLEY (American, 1925 -)
In Moss's third book, *The Intelligence of Clouds*, the thematic range is wide. There are tributes to Aristophanes and fellow-poet James Wright; an elegy for his mother; poems on Italian themes, butterflies, alphabets, China, centaurs, New York, rainbows, and a notable sequence set in Jerusalem. Yehudi Amichi refers to it as 'a book of great originality'.
The Intelligence of Clouds   **NEW**
[R929] Anvil pbk **£4.95**

NASH, OGDEN (1902 - 1971)
Nash is America's most popular comic poet. His outrageous rhymes and puns take a stand against all that is complicated and obscure: Nash speaks for the simple man who wishes he had missed out on growing up.
A Penny Saved is Impossible
[R930] Deutsch pbk **£7.95**
Candy is Dandy
[R931] Methuen pbk **£5.95**
I Wouldn't Have Missed It: Selected Poems
[R932] Deutsch pbk **£9.95**

O'HARA, FRANK (1926 - 1966)
Along with Kenneth Koch and John Ashbery, Frank O'Hara mounted an attack on the prevailing notions of taste in New York in the 50s (*"Not you, lean quarterlies and swarthy periodicals..."*) Interested in the painting of the Abstract Expressionists, such as Pollock and de Kooning, he likewise attacked received styles, and his work comes as close as possible to the technique of 'action painting'. His work is urban, conversational, and with a musical notion of prosody.
Lunch Poems (1964)
[R933] City Lights pbk **£3.50**

O'NEILL, EUGENE (American, 1888 - 1953)
Nobel Prize for Literature, 1936. Better-known as a playwright, O'Neill also wrote poetry. Some critics have complained that he is a clumsy stylist, whilst others have praised his ability to combine halting speech with lyrical phrasing into a controlled and vernacular poetry.
Poems 1912 - 1944
[R934] Cape pbk **£6.95**

OLSON, CHARLES (1910 - 1970)
As rector of Black Mountain College in North Carolina, Olson was the guiding light of the Black Mountain poets, who include Robert Creeley, Denise Levertov and Robert Duncan. They were influenced by Olson's provocative and polemical essay 'Projectivist Verse'. It called for a poetry of 'open forms' and 'composition by field', in which 'form is never more than an extension of contact', and the structure of a poem is determined by the breath of the poet and not by metrical feet. His major (indeed massive) work is *The Maximus Poems*.
Collected Poems
Contains all the poetry except for the *Maximus* series, and includes many short lyrics that have never previously appeared in print.
[R935] California UP hbk **£40.00**
The Maximus Poems (1987)
[R936] California UP hbk **£28.35**
[R937] California UP pbk **£6.90**

PIERCY, MARGE (1936 -)
Piercy's political activities have centred on her conviction that the women's movement is the surest way to fruitful social change. Margaret Atwood calls her poems 'rough, direct, hairy, political, tremendously energetic, visionary, vulnerable and real'.
My Mother's Body
[R938] Pandora pbk **£4.95**
Stone Paper Knife
[R939] Pandora pbk **£5.50**

PLATH, SYLVIA (1932 - 1963)
Shortly after the collapse of her marriage to the English poet Ted Hughes, Sylvia Plath committed suicide, leaving unpublished what has become her best-known collection of verse, *Ariel*. Although she has obvious affinities with the American 'confessional poets' of the 1950s, she possessed a firm, often sardonic detachment which enabled her to present the trauma of her final years in a sharply original way.
Ariel
[R940] Faber pbk **£3.95**

Ezra Pound, whose *Selected Poems 1908 - 1959* are published by Faber (pbk **£3.95**)(Photo: Associated Press)

Collected Poems (Ed. Hughes, Ted)
[R941] Faber hbk **£12.50**
[R942] Faber pbk **£5.95**
Selected Poems (Ed. Hughes, Ted)
[R943] Faber hbk **£6.95**
[R944] Faber pbk **£3.95**
The Bed Book
[R945] Faber pbk **£1.95**

POE, EDGAR ALLEN (1809 - 49)
Baudelaire (who translated many of his works), Swinburne, Wilde, Rossetti and Yeats were all admirers of Poe's poetry. Freudian critics, and Freud himself, have been intrigued by the macabre and pathological elements in his work, including hints of necrophilia in the poem 'Annabel Lee'. 'The Raven' remains his most popular poem.
Poems & Essays
[R946] Dent pbk **£2.50**
Portable Poe
[R947] Penguin pbk **£5.95**

POUND, EZRA (1885 - 1972)
Ezra Pound is the most controversial writer of the 20th century, and no other writer has excited such contradictory judgments. He was, as T.S. Eliot said, 'more responsible for the XXth Century revolution in poetry than any other individual'. After he moved away from the pared down style of Imagism, he found freedom through translation - from the Provçenal, early Italian, Old English and the Chinese of Li Po. His masterpiece is *The Cantos*: they remain difficult, because of their huge range of reference and assimilation of cultures, and combination of different linguistic registers, languages and parallel historical worlds, but must finally be counted among the century's finest poetic achievements.
Collected Shorter Poems
[R948] Faber pbk **£4.95**
Selected Cantos
[R949] Faber pbk **£3.95**
Selected Poems 1908 - 1959
[R950] Faber pbk **£3.95**
The Cantos of Ezra Pound
Sadly, Faber's new, enlarged *Cantos* is a disappointment, since Pound's corrections were never incorporated. It is only with the Italian publishing house Mondadori's bilingual *I Cantos* that the poem is actually even in the correct order.
[R951] Faber pbk **£12.50**

Translations
[R952] Faber pbk **£3.95**

RICH, ADRIENNE (1929 -)
Rich's poetry is marked by a consciousness of division, separation and dislocation. She sees her poetry as a procedure through which to heal divisions between the self and the world, attempting to re-integrate all the fragments into a more positive union.
The Fact of a Doorframe: Poems Selected and New 1950 - 1984
[R953] Norton hbk **£13.40**
[R954] Norton pbk **£7.05**

RIDING, LAURA (1901 -)
Laura Riding has commented that *"a poem is an uncovering of truth so fundamental and general that no other name besides poetry is adequate except truth"*; this definition reveals her commitment to lucidity, purity and truth in language - and when she lost this faith in 1938, she renounced poetry. Her poems are disciplined and precise, often rejecting the evasions of metaphor, their 'meaning' developing only through the process of the poem itself.
The Poems of Laura Riding
[R955] Carcanet hbk **£9.95**
[R956] Carcanet pbk **£5.95**

ROETHKE, THEODORE (1908 - 1963)
Roethke's early collection **The Lost Son** - his best book - contains many of his excellent 'greenhouse' poems: they feature a return to childhood landscapes and experiences (his father was the owner of a large floral business) in what he called a 'personal history and a history of race itself'. Roethke has written that *"in this kind of poem, the poet should not 'comment', or use many judgement words: instead he should render the experience, however condensed and elliptical that experience may be."*
Collected Poems
[R957] Faber pbk **£4.95**

SNODGRASS, W.D. (1926 -)
Snodgrass's first collection, **Heart's Needle**, appearing in 1959, the year after Robert Lowell's **Life Studies**, seemed to herald a new genre; both books are 'confessional', revealing intimate personal details. In the remarkable title sequence of that book, Snodgrass centres on the hurt caused by the separation from his daughter, via his divorce from his wife. Technically Snodgrass is notable for his use of traditional and complicated verse forms.
Heart's Needle
[R958] Marvell P pbk **£3.60**
Selected Poems 1957 - 1987 **NEW**
Snodgrass's **Selected Poems** features splendid works such as the dislocated 'Ten Days Leave' and 'Return to Frisco, 1946', which deals with Snodgrass's return from the war, as well as 'Heart's Needle' and excerpts from the controversial 'The Führer Bunker', consisting of imagined monologues from Hitler's bunker during the last month of the Reich.
[R959] Hutchinson pbk **£9.95**

SNYDER, GARY (1930 -)
Snyder's poetry synthesises the techniques of Imagism with the formal freedom of poets like Olson, to deal almost exclusively with the inter-relationship of nature and primitive religion. He has written that *"I hold the most archaic values...the fertility of the soul, the magic of animals, the power-vision in solitude...the common work of the tribe"*.
Axe Handles
[R961] North Point P pbk **£5.95**
Good Wild Sacred
[R962] Five Seasons P pbk **£3.00**
Left Out in the Rain: New Poems 1947 - 1985
[R964] North Point P pbk **£7.95**

STEVENS, WALLACE (1879 - 1955)
Along with Eliot and Pound, Stevens is one of the major American poets of the century. Behind the surface of dazzling rhetorical magnificence and rhythmic beauty in poems such as 'Le Monocle de Mon Oncle' and 'Sunday Morning', it is possible to find a structure of plain sense (it would be possible to write a prose paraphrase, not something one could do with **The Waste Land**). The other striking point of comparison with his great contemporaries is his metrical conservatism: he uses regular iambic pentameters, extraordinary in an age of revolutionary metrical experiment.
Collected Poems
[R965] Faber pbk **£5.95**
Selected Poems
[R966] Faber pbk **£3.95**
The Necessary Angel: Essays on Imagination & Reality
[R967] Faber pbk **£3.95**

STEVENSON, ANNE (1933 -)
Although she was born in England, and lives here now, Stevenson was brought up in the US. Her **Selected Poems 1956-1986** gathers together work from her 7 previous collections. As well as demonstrating the range of her work - passionate, wry and lyrical - it reprints in full **Correspondences**, an ambitious sequence which traces the history of a New England family over 150 years. The poems - all in the form of personal letters from members of that family, and the odd newspaper cutting - show how the Calvinist doctrine of Adam Chandler, the family's founder, dominates the lives of the succeeding generations.
Selected Poems 1956 - 1986
[R968] Oxford hbk **£10.95**
[R969] Oxford pbk **£6.95**
The Fiction-Makers
[R970] Oxford pbk **£3.95**

WALKER, ALICE (1944 -)
Better known for her novel **The Color Purple**, Walker writes brief, accessible poems which touch upon love, friendship, motherhood, racism and world pollution.
Goodnight Willy Lee, I'll See You in the Morning
[R971] Women's P pbk **£2.95**
Horses Make A Landscape Look More Beautiful
[R972] Women's P pbk **£2.95**
Once
[R973] Women's P pbk **£2.95**

WHITMAN, WALT (1819 - 1892)
Whitman's **Leaves of Grass** is one of America's great works. He described the 12 poems in the first edition as saturated *"with the vehemence of pride and audacity of freedom necessary to loosen the mind of still-to-be-form'd America from the folds, the superstitions, and all the long, tenacious and stifling anti-democratic authorities of Asiatic and European past."* New editions proliferated throughout his lifetime, as he added new work as he developed. The long exhalation of the lines, the rhetorical catalogues and repetitions achieve something like ritualistic rhythms, reminiscent of the Psalms. Recognized in England by Rossetti and Swinburne, Whitman's influence on world literature has been incalculable; Henry Miller, Allen Ginsberg and Hart Crane took him as a model, and subtler influences can be seen in work as different as Eliot and Lorca.
A Choice of Whitman's Verse
[R974] Faber pbk **£3.95**
Complete Poems
[R975] Penguin pbk **£7.95**
Leaves of Grass
[R976] Penguin pbk **£3.50**
Portable Walt Whitman
[R977] Penguin pbk **£5.95**

WILBUR, RICHARD (1921 -)
Wilbur chose the exacting craft of traditional forms because, as he puts it, *"the strength of the genie comes from his being confined in a bottle."* His first poems, 'written in answer to the inner and outer disorders of the Second World War', are marred by obtrusive word play, but the late work is more dramatic, with a plainer style and less precious language, although retaining the artifice and formal strictness. *"Poems"*, he believes, *"are conflicts with disorder, not messages from one person to another."*
New and Collected Poems **NEW**
[R978] Faber pbk **£9.99**

WILLIAMS, C.K.
C.K. Williams is a new poet to British readers, coming from the tradition of Jeffers and Whitman. His early work is extreme, as he progressively abandons syntax, form and punctuation, and his subjects are war, torture and the suffering of innocents. In later work he uses a long, flexible, unrhymed line to convey his vivid reports of contemporary malaise.
Flesh and Blood: Poems **NEW**
[R979] Bloodaxe pbk **£5.95**
Poems 1963 - 1983 **NEW**
[R980] Bloodaxe pbk **£7.95**

WILLIAMS, WILLIAM CARLOS (1883 - 1963)
Williams is one of America's most important poets; rejecting the allusive, European style of Eliot and Pound, he insisted upon an 'anti-poetic' American idiom. His poems illuminate the dictum in **Paterson**: *"no ideas, but in things."*
Collected Poems Vol 1: 1909 - 1939
[R981] Carcanet pbk **£18.95**
Vol 2: 1939 - 1963 **NEW**
The publication of the second volume of the **Collected Poems** completes the definitive edition of Williams' published poems, except for **Paterson**. This new volume includes a wealth of material previously unavailable in Britain, including Williams' translations, and the scholarly apparatus is as informative and discreet as possible.
[R982] Carcanet hbk **£25.00**

WINTERS, YVOR (1900 - 1968)
"The young are quick of speech./Grown middle aged, I teach/Corrosion and distrust,/Exacting what I must." Winter's **Collected Poems** allows us to follow his abrupt development. His early works reflect the Imagist experiments of Pound and Williams, while later collections are characterized by a rigorously disciplined form, containing rationally controlled reflections on experiences of moral significance.
Collected Poems
[R983] Carcanet hbk **£12.95**

European Poetry

Classical Greek

Greek Anthology
Selection of poignant and humorous Greek epigrams surveying the 700 years before and after Christ with subjects as varied as death and erotic love.
[R984] Penguin pbk **£4.95**

Three Archaic Poets: Archilochus, Sappho and Alcaeus (Trans. Burnett, A.)
[R985] Duckworth pbk **£12.95**

Three Classical Poets: Sappho, Catullus and Juvenal
[R986] Duckworth pbk **£9.95**

APPOLLONIUS OF RHODES
(Greek, 3rd Century BC)
Alexandrian epic poet who brought new narrative techniques to his rendition of the legendary voyage of Jason and the Argonauts.
The Voyage of the Argo
[R987] Penguin pbk **£2.95**

HESIOD & THEOGNIS (8th/6th Century BC)
Theogony/Works and Days/Elegies
Hesiod's major work **Works and Days** gives an account of a farmer's life which was to influence Virgil's **Georgics**. Theognis was an aristocrat of Megara who wrote his elegies at a time of violent civil strife between the aristocracy and the plebians.
[R988] Penguin pbk **£2.95**

HOMER (Greek, c.800 BC)
It is now considered unlikely that the same man wrote the two epics **The Iliad** and **The Odyssey**, which are traditionally ascribed to Homer; the figure of the blind bard lives on, however. The poems mark the beginning of Western European literature - as Ford Madox Ford says, 'to appreciate the beauties of Homer, all that is necessary is to read him.' Excellent translations of Homer have been made by Chapman, whose version was famously recommended by Keats and is now scandalously unavailable, and by Dryden and Pope; but in contemporary times, Robert Fitzgerald's attempt has been favourably received, as has Christoher Logue's **War Music**, an account of Books 16-19 of the **Iliad**, recently re-issued by Faber. Rieu's are the standard prose translations.
The Iliad (Trans. Rieu)
The Iliad describes the war raged by Achean princes against Troy, the object of which was to recover Helen, wife of Meneleus, whom Paris, son of the king of Troy, had carried off. It centres on the anger of Achilles at the slight put on him by Agamemnon, and his final return to the field, and slaying of Hector.
[R989] Penguin pbk **£2.95**
The Iliad (Trans. Fitzgerald, Robert)
[R990] Oxford pbk **£2.95**
The Odyssey (Trans. Rieu)
The Odyssey describes the adventures of Odysseus during his return from the Trojan War to his kingdom of Ithaca.
[R991] Penguin pbk **£3.50**
The Odyssey (Trans. Shewring, Walter)
[R992] Oxford pbk **£2.50**
The Odyssey (Trans. Lawrence, T.E.)
[R993] Sutton pbk **£5.95**
The Odyssey (Trans. Fitzgerald, Robert)
[R994] Collins Harv pbk **£6.95**
LOGUE, CHRISTOPHER
War Music　**NEW**
An account of Books 16-19 of Homer's **Iliad**
[R995] Faber pbk **£4.95**
POPE, ALEXANDER
Pope's Iliad: A Selection　**NEW**
(Ed. Rosslyn, Felicity)
[R996] Bristol Classics pbk **£11.95**

PINDAR (Greek, c.522 - 443 BC)
The majority of Pindar's surviving works are odes celebrating victories in the games at Olympia and elsewhere. His basic framework of strophe, anti-strophe and epode, now known as the Pindaric ode, has been much copied, yet his distinguished English translators - Dryden, Pope and Gray - employed much looser forms, and miss Pindar's architectural structures. His work is formal and serious, relying on bold imagery and gnomic utterance.
The Odes (Trans. Lattimore, Richmond)
[R999] Chicago UP pbk **£6.50**

SAPPHO (Greek, 7th Century BC)
Ford Madox Ford comments on the 'wonderful, frequently excruciating beauty' of Sappho's poetry, but adds that 'it is almost impossible to get over into another tongue the fullness of that beauty'. Ezra Pound thought that, in comparison with the Latin poet Catullus, she was 'just a little Swinburnian', though he considered her, along with Homer, as one of the two Greek poets worth reading, saying that 'I know of no better ode than the *poikilothron*'.
Poems and Fragments (Trans. Balmer, J.)
[R1000] Brilliance **£2.95**
Sappho: A New Translation
[R1001] California UP pbk **£5.95**

THEOCRITUS (Greek, c.308 - c.240 BC)
One of the most important Greek bucolic poets, Theocritus established the formal characteristics of the pastoral mode, which concerns the lives of shepherds. His subject matter, though, is huge, ranging from the sexual gossip of herdsmen to the praise of Hellenistic monarchs, from mythological scenes to the hectic life of contemporary Alexandria. European literature would be unimaginable without him - no Virgil's **Eclogues**, no Milton's **Lycidas** - yet until Robert Wells' superb translation of **The Idylls** appeared, there had been no convincing translation into English.
The Idylls
[R1002] Carcanet hbk **£9.95**
[R1003] Penguin pbk **£3.99**

Latin

Latin Literature: An Anthology
A collection of Latin poetry and prose, translated by English authors including Pope, Dryden and Graves.
[R1004] Penguin pbk **£5.95**

The Virgin and the Nightingale
(Trans. Adcock, Fleur)
Adcock's latest book is a splendid collection of translations from the medieval Latin, and includes erotic pieces by Peter du Blois and from the **Carmina Burana**.
[R1005] Bloodaxe pbk **£5.95**

CATULLUS (c.84 - c.54 BC)
One of the most versatile of Roman poets, Catullus wrote love poems, satires and elegies with equal success. His language is plain and direct, colloquial and pungent. He describes his love of Lesbia, alternately evoking disillusionment and ecstacy. His work is most easily available in the post-Poundian translations of Peter Whigham, who was praised by William Carlos Williams as 'the most delightful translator of Catullus'.
Poems (Trans. Whigham, Peter)
[R1006] Penguin pbk **£3.95**

HORACE (65 - 8 BC)
Horace's work is a celebration of a return to order after civil wars, and his **Odes** imitate the lyric poets of early Greece. Ironical and cultured, his work emphasizes the civilized values of wine, good company and a delight in nature. Horace's influence is crucial on many English poets, especially on the odes of Marvell and Dryden, and the satires of Wyatt and Jonson.
Complete Odes and Epodes
(Trans. Shepherd, W.G.)
[R1007] Penguin pbk **£4.99**
Satires (Horace and Persius)
[R1008] Penguin pbk **£4.99**

JUVENAL (c.55 - 104)
The last major poet of the ancient world, Juvenal wrote 16 satires fulminating against the vices of his age. Rhetorical and funny, he is perhaps the greatest of all satirists. His anger takes in virtually the whole of Roman society, from the pretentions of an outdated nobility to socially conspicuous homosexuals.
Sixteen Satires
[R1009] Penguin pbk **£4.50**

LUCRETIUS (c.99 - 55 BC)
Adopting the atomic theory of the universe of Epicurus, Lucretius seeks in his philosophical poem of six books and in hexameters, **De Rerum Natura**, to show that the world is inexplicable without recourse to divine intervention. Dryden talked of his 'plain sincerity', and Walter Savage Landor said *"there is about him a simple majesty, a calm and lofty scorn of everything pusillanimous and abject; and, consistently with this character, his poetry is masculine, plain, concentrated and energetic."*
On the Nature of Things
[R1010] Penguin pbk **£3.50**

MARTIAL (c.40 - c.104)
Roman epigrammatist whose 1,577 epigrams - satirical, witty, obscene - achieve a wonderful formal perfection. There have been many translators - his elegance and bile have impressed themselves on successive generations of English poets. Something of this tradition is reflected in the **Epigrams of Martial: Englished by Divers Hands**, which features translations by many contemporary poets, who include Alistair Elliot, Tony Harrison, J.V. Cunningham and Peter Porter.
Epigrams of Martial: Englished by Divers Hands (Ed. Sullivan & Whigham)
[R1011] California UP hbk **£15.00**
Letter to Juvenal and Other poems
(Trans. Whigham, Peter)
[R1013] Anvil pbk **£4.95**
The Epigrams (Trans. Michie, James)
[R1014] Penguin pbk **£4.95**
HARRISON, TONY
U.S. Martial
Tony Harrison's marvellous pamphlet features 18 satires in contemporary (un)dress, their targets the latter-day Romans of New York City; Martial's vernacular Latin is rendered into the fruity argot of the Big Apple.
[R1015] Bloodaxe pbk **£2.95**

OVID (PUBLIUS OVIDIUS NASO)
(43 BC - 18 AD)
Th great Roman writer of love elegies (**Amores**), as well as many other forms, Ovid was banished to the Black Sea in 8 AD for unknown indiscretions. An expert metrician in the **Metamorphoses**, where he retells the old myths, briefly, and with every possible rhetorical flourish, he proves to be a superb teller of stories. His **Amores** were brilliantly translated by Christopher Marlowe, and are available in his **Complete Poems and Translations**, from Penguin. The greatest version of the **Metamorphoses**, however, is unavailable; translated by Arthur Golding (1536-1605), Ezra Pound refers to it as 'the most beautiful book in the language'.
Erotic Poems
[R1016] Penguin pbk **£5.99**
Metamorphoses
[R1017] Penguin pbk **£3.99**
Metamorphoses (Trans. Melville, A.D.)
[R1018] Oxford pbk **£3.95**

PERSIUS (34 - 62)
Persius's powerful and uncompromising satires on Roman society in the time of Nero were greatly admired by such contemporaries as Lucan and Martial. Here they are translated by the distinguished American poet W.S. Merwin.
The Satires of Persius (Trans. Merwin, W.S.)
[R1019] Anvil pbk **£3.95**

TIBULLUS ALBIUS (c.48 - 19 BC)
The elegant poet, remembered for his quiet, melancholy elegies, and a gentle delight in country life.
Poems
[R1020] Penguin pbk **£3.95**

VIRGIL (70 - 19 BC)
The greatest of the Roman poets, Virgil successfully produced work which equalled their Greek models. His *Eclogues*, based on Theocritus, add new meaning to the pastoral's idealization of country life by alluding to contemporary matters, while the *Georgics* transformed the didacticism of Hesiod into a panegyric of Italy and the traditional ways of country life. His supreme achievement was the *Aeneid*, an epic in 12 books not fully completed at his death: his instructions to his executors to burn the work were fortunately ignored. Among the best of contemporary translations are Sisson's *Aeneid* and Robert Wells' *Georgics*.
The Aeneid (Trans. Fitzgerald, Robert)
Adding the presentation of a patriotic theme - that of the birth of Rome - to the genre of Homer, the *Aeneid* avoids panegyric, and in the personality of Aeneas rehearses a subtle dialogue between the private and public. Translated by Gavin Douglas, the Earl of Surrey and Dryden, his work has been a central touchstone in English literature; as Sisson remarks, 'everybody should know something of the *Aeneid*'.
[R1021] Collins Harv hbk **£12.50**
[R1021A] Penguin pbk **£5.95**
The Aeneid (Trans. Sisson, C.H.)
[R1022] Carcanet hbk **£16.95**
The Aeneid (Trans. Knight, F.W.J.)
[R1023] Penguin pbk **£3.99**
The Aeneid (Trans. Lewis, C. Day)
[R1025] Oxford pbk **£3.95**
The Eclogues (Trans. Lee, Guy)
[R1026] Penguin pbk **£3.50**
The Georgics (Trans. Robert, Wells)
[R1027] Carcanet hbk **£8.95**
The Georgics (Trans. Wilkinson, L.P.)
[R1028] Penguin pbk **£3.99**
DRYDEN, JOHN
Dryden's Aeneid
The enterprizing Bristol Classics Press have issued a generous selection from Dryden's *Aeneid*, and this is the only popular edition of this great translation.
[R1029] Bristol Classics hbk **£22.50**
[R1030] Bristol Classics pbk **£8.95**

Modern European Poetry

Anthology of French Poetry (Ed. Lawler, J.)
[R1031] Oxford pbk **£4.95**

German Poetry 1910 - 1975
(Ed. Hamburger, Michael)
Authoritative survey of this century's poets, translated by the excellent Hamburger. Poets include Rilke, Trakl, Brecht and Celan. A recommended introduction.
[R1032] Carcanet pbk **£6.95**

German Verse
[R1033] Penguin pbk **£5.99**

Ice Around Our Lips: Finnish and NEW
Swedish Poetry (Ed. McDuff, David)
McDuff's book contains substantial selections from the 10 most important figures, from the *fin de siècle* figure of Bertel Gripenberg to the Marxist Gosta Agren, by way of Edith Sondergran and Bo Carpelan.
[R1034] Bloodaxe pbk **£7.95**

Poets of Bulgaria (Ed. Meredith, William)
Introduced by Alan Brownjohn, this anthology contains the work of 24 contemporary poets, translated by American counterparts, including John Updike.
[R1035] Forest Books pbk **£6.95**

Post-War Russian Poetry (Ed. Weissbort, Daniel)
A comprehensive survey of the period; among the poets are Akhmadulina, Brodsky, Zabolotsky, Pasternak and Yevtushenko.
[R1036] Penguin pbk **£3.95**

Spanish Poetry
[R1037] Penguin pbk **£9.95**

The Burning Forest: Modern Polish NEW
Poetry (Ed. Czerniawski, Adam)
This anthology includes work from major poets such as Herbert, Rozewicz and Szymborska, wartime writer-heroes like Stroinski, and young dissidents such as Krynicki and Maj. A thoughtful historical sweep, the book includes a large selection of photographs and biographies.
[R1038] Bloodaxe pbk **£7.95**

The New Czech Poetry NEW
(Ed. Osers, Ewald)
This introduction to contemporary Czech poetry features 3 poets, all born in the 1940s. Jaroslav Cejka's work is gently humorous as the language of science is applied to emotions and human relationships, whilst Michal Cernik's evoke a strong sense of history, landscape and family. The work of Karel Kys, influenced by Rimbaud, is playful and sensuous.
[R1039] Bloodaxe pbk **£6.95**

The Oxford Book of French Verse
[R1040] Oxford hbk **£15.95**

The Poetry of Survival (Ed. Weissbort, Daniel)
A major anthology of post-war European poetry, especially from those countries under Soviet sway, many of whom are important influences on contemporary English writers. Celan, Milosz, Herbert, Popa and Amichai are among those featured.
[R1041] Anvil pbk **£6.95**

ANON
Lancelot of the Lake (Trans. Corley, Corin)
The first translation into English of the original short version of the old French prose poem, which tells of the adventures of Lancelot and his love affair with Guinevere at the court of King Arthur. A major work which influenced Dante.
[R1042] Oxford pbk **£5.95**
Nibelungenlied
German poem of the 13th century relating the saga which inspired Wagner's *Der Ring Des Nibelungen*.
[R1043] Penguin pbk **£3.95**
Poem of the Cid
[R1044] Penguin pbk **£4.50**
Song of Roland
C.H. Sisson's excellent translation of the medieval French poem, which deals with the legend of Roland, the most famous Paladin of Charlemagne.
[R1045] Carcanet hbk **£7.95**
[R1046] Penguin pbk **£2.95**
The Kalevala NEW
The Kalevala is a Finnish epic, on the scale of the *Iliad* or the *Odyssey*, which presents a rare portrait of an ancient people in peace and at war. It played a central role in the march towards Finnish independence, and inspired some of Sibelius' greatest works.
[R1047] Oxford pbk **£6.95**

AKHMATOVA, ANNA (Russian, 1889 - 1966)
Possibly Russia's greatest modern poet, Akhmatova's early love lyrics were attacked as anti-revolutionary, and by 1925 they were banned. Persecuted under Stalin, she became a 'non-person', and was unable to publish. The poems she wrote in this period - the cycle *Requiem*, and *Poem without a Hero* - are extraordinary: she was convinced of the need for poetry to speak harsh truths, only believing in its justification in a time of distress if the poet was prepared to bear witness. Her work is an enduring testimony to the sufferings of Russia after the Revolution.
Poems (Trans. Coffin, L.)
With an introduction by Joseph Brodsky.
[R1048] Norton pbk **£5.65**
Selected Poems (Trans. McKane, R.)
[R1049] Bloodaxe pbk **£7.95**
Selected Poems (Trans. Thomas, D.M.)
[R1050] Penguin pbk **£5.99**
Selected Poems NEW
[R1051] Collins Harv pbk **£5.95**
You Will Hear Thunder (Trans. Thomas, D.M.)
[R1052] Secker hbk **£10.95**

APOLLINAIRE, GUILLAUME
(French, 1880 - 1918)
Bohemian and patriot, iconoclast and pornographer, Apollinaire was a friend and supporter of the Cubists. His own experimental poetic forms employ both rhythms which dispense with punctuation and a style of typography derived from exercises on postcards sent from the front in World War I. Yet he is also, in France, the last of the poets whose lines people know by heart.
Selected Poems (Trans Oliver, Bernard)
[R1053] Anvil hbk **£10.95**
[R1054] Anvil pbk **£4.95**

ARIOSTO, LUDOVICO (Italian, 1474 - 1535)
The *Orlando Furioso* looks back to the tradition of Virgil and Homer to which Ariosto was represented by early admirers as the natural heir, just as surely as it looks forward to the christianized epic forms of Milton and Spenser, who consciously set himself to 'overgo' the poem. If it lacks the straight-forward moral sonorities that might have gratified Spenser, it offers instead a tortuously hedonistic celebration of the chivalric ideal, seamlessly combined with a highly piquant scepticism.
Orlando Furioso (Trans. Waldman, Guido)
[R1055] Oxford pbk **£5.95**
Orlando Furioso Vol 1
[R1056] Penguin pbk **£6.00**
Orlando Furioso Vol 2
[R1057] Penguin pbk **£8.95**

BAUDELAIRE, CHARLES
(French, 1821 - 1867)
Baudelaire is one of the central writers of the 19th century. *Les Fleurs du Mal*, his only collection of verse, was a lifetime's work, but one out of which all subsequent French poetry has come. It is an attempt to create beauty and order - notably in the discovery of hidden relations or *correspondences* - in a world largely perceived as ugly and oppressive. In musical language and evocative images, Baudelaire examines his sense of isolation and boredom, the power of love and the attractions of evil and vice.
Baudelaire
[R1058] Penguin pbk **£3.50**
Fleurs du Mal (Trans. Howard, Richard)
[R1059] Picador pbk **£5.95**
The Complete Verse (Trans. Scarfe, Francis)
[R1060] Anvil hbk **£12.95**
[R1061] Anvil pbk **£4.95**
The Poems in Prose
[R1062] Anvil hbk **£12.95**
[R1063] Anvil pbk **£5.95**

BLOK, ALEKSANDR (Russian, 1880 - 1921)
Blok's career might be seen as a prolonged duel between the instincts of a romantic idealist and the relentless social and political counter-claims of pre-revolutionary Russia. From the youthful aestheticism of the verses addressed to Sophia, Blok's poetry moves through cycles of faith and disillusion, mystical reverence and bleak irony, until in 'The Twelve' there comes a triumphant, mythopoeic resolution of the writer's internal conflicts.
Selected Poems
[R1064] Central hbk **£4.50**
The Twelve & The Scythians
[R1065] Journeyman pbk **£1.95**

BORCHERS, ELIZABETH (German)
As in the art of Paul Klee, whose painting gives her collection *Fish Magic* its title, there is a deceptively childlike surface which masks a tragic awareness of the human condition in the poetry of Borchers. Anneliese Wagner's translations, in this bilingual edition, are the first introduction to an English readership of this distinguished German poet. Echoes of fairy tales, folk song and nursery rhymes mingle with nightmarish moments in sharp, compelling poems.
Fish Magic NEW
[R1066] Anvil pbk **£5.95**

BRODSKY, JOSEPH (Russian, 1940 -)
Winner of the Nobel Prize for Literature in 1987, Brodsky is the first post-war Russian poet to successfully stand comparison with the pre-war generation of Akhmatova and Mandelstam, and like them, he was unacceptable to the regime. Arrested in 1963, he served five years in a labour camp near Archangel, and, after much harrassment, he chose exile in 1972. Now equally fluent in Russian and English, his poems stand as a testament to the anguish of permanent exile from one's native land and language. A poet of great facility and versatility, his fantastical realism has been replaced by a simplicity of language, creating a new kind of 'pure' utterance, which he calls 'silent speech'.
A Part of Speech (Trans. Walcott, Derek & Hecht, Anthony, et al)
[R1068] Oxford pbk **£4.95**
Less than One: Selected Essays
Brodsky writes of the role of poetry in resisting the destruction of the human spirit, as well as elucidating the political repercussions of his own verse, in this magisterial collection which includes autobiographical pieces and essays on other writers.
[R1069] Penguin pbk **£5.95**
To Urania
[R1070] Viking hbk **£14.95**
[R1071] Penguin pbk **£4.99**

CAMOES, LUIS DE (Portuguese, c.1524 - 1580)
Camoes, the 'national poet' of Portugal, wrote the first epic poem which, in scope and universality, spoke for the modern world. *The Lusiads* is a crucial poem of European conquest and its moral misgivings. Camoes himself possessed qualities of the epic hero: scholar, lover and soldier, he was blinded in the service of his king.
Selected Lyrics and Lusiads NEW
A notable new translation by the redoubtable Keith Bosley.
[R1072] Carcanet hbk **£14.95**
[R1073] Carcanet pbk **£6.95**
The Lusiads
[R1074] Penguin pbk **£3.95**

CARPELAN, BO (Finland, 1926 -)
Carpelan's brilliant novel *Axel* has been published recently by Carcanet: now Forest Books publish his poetry in English for the first time in volume form. This is a beautifully produced collection, illustrated by the Finnish artist Hannu Taina.

Rooms without Walls NEW
[R1075] Forest pbk **£7.95**

CAVAFY, C.P. (Greek, 1863 - 1933)
The best-known of modern Greek writers, Cavafy is one of the century's central poets. His ironical view of ancient Greek and Roman mythology and history, his stunning appreciation of his native Alexandria, are expressed in extremely laconic language. His work falls into two parts; the historical and the homosexual. Perhaps the best poems are the historical 'persona' poems that owe their subtlety and vividness to the freedom to escape from his 'empirical self', and which are set between 200 BC and 600 AD in the cities of Magna Graecia. His homosexual poems are more intimate, although with their obsessive concentration on the limbs of his lovers, perhaps less universal.
Collected Poems (Trans. Mavrogordato, J.)
[R1076] Hogarth pbk **£5.95**

CELAN, PAUL (German, 1920 - 1970)
Celan is among the most important German-language poets of the century; George Steiner refers to him as 'almost certainly the major European poet of the period after 1945'. His poems, written after and about the horrors of Auschwitz, often have a musical structure, an archetypal imagery and the absence of the word 'I', qualities which distance them from historical events. His work hinges on the question of what can be written in poetry, in a diction which vacillates between archaism and neologism, and silences become part of the poems.
Collected Prose
[R1077] Carcanet hbk **£8.95**
Poems (Trans. Hamburger, Michael)
This revised and enlarged edition of Hamburger's translations add 43 new versions to the previous edition.
[R1078] Anvil hbk **£15.95**

CORBIERE, TRISTAN (French, 1845 - 1875)
Although he cultivated a sense of disgust and a desperate elegance, presenting himself in his *Epitaphe* as a *poseur*, Corbière refused to escape from his fluid, multiple personality into a succession of personae. Instead his poems are the confessions of a man whose complaint is that he has no self. Corbière is modern because of his ironic tone and unusual diction - he adopts a colloquialism, which had its effect on Pound, who called him 'the most poignant poet since Villon', admiring his 'hard-bit lines'.
The Centenary Corbière
[R1079] Carcanet hbk **£6.95**

D'ANNUNZIO, GABRIELE
(Italian, 1863 - 1938)
D'Annunzio combined the role of European decadent with that of man of action; he lost an eye in World War I, and was a supporter of Mussolini. His poems - often descriptive and impressionistic - recall specific places and occasions, evoking the feelings, memories and myths they give rise to.
Halcyon (Trans. Nichols, J.G.)
This masterpiece was published in 1903; it consists of 88 lyrics drawn together with meticulous unity.
[R1080] Carcanet pbk **£6.95**

DANTE ALIGHIERI (Italian, 1265 - 1321)
T.S. Eliot commented that *"Dante and Shakespeare divide the world between them, there is no third."* Dante's masterpiece, *The Divine Comedy,* remains perhaps the most important poem in Western literature; it depicts the poet's journey through the spirals of the Inferno and across the levels of Purgatory, to the sublime heights of Paradise, a journey in which he is guided by his love for the ideal Beatrice.

La Vita Nuova
[R1081] Penguin pbk **£3.99**
Portable Dante
[R1082] Penguin pbk **£5.95**
The Divine Comedy (Trans. Sisson, C.H.)
[R1083] Carcanet hbk **£16.95**
The Divine Comedy
Vol 1: Inferno (Trans. Musa, Mark)
[R1084] Penguin pbk **£3.99**
Vol 2: Purgatory (Trans. Musa, Mark)
[R1085] Penguin pbk **£3.95**
Vol 3: Paradiso (Trans. Musa, Mark)
[R1086] Penguin pbk **£4.99**
Vol 1 (Trans. Sinclair, John D.)
Sinclair's translation appears in parallel text format with the original text.
[R1090] Oxford pbk **£6.95**
Vol 2 (Trans. Sinclair, John D.)
[R1091] Oxford pbk **£6.95**
Vol 3 (Trans. Sinclair, John D.)
[R1092] Oxford pbk **£6.95**

ELUARD, PAUL (French, 1895 - 1952)
A memorable lyric poet usually associated with the Surrealist movement, Eluard is remembered as a love poet of dream-like haunting images.
Selected Poems (Trans. Bowen, Gilbert)
[R1093] Calder pbk **£5.95**

EMIN, GEVORG
Land, Love, Century NEW
The poetry of Gevorg Emin in *Love, Land, Century*, is translated from the Armenian by Martin Robbins with Tatul Sonentz-Papazian; and Yevgeny Yevtushenko contributes a foreword.
[R1094] Forest Bks pbk **£7.95**

ENZENSBERGER, HANS MAGNUS
(German, 1929 -)
Influenced by Brecht's idea of poems as 'utensils', Enzensberger is a radical poet who is well aware of what is going on in the wider worlds of science, ecology and politics.
The Sinking of the Titanic
This sequence takes the eponymous historical event, and uses it as the central image in a work that examines large areas of contemporary culture; the great ship with its human freight becomes an emblem for the modern predicament. Translated by the author.
[R1095] Carcanet hbk **£5.95**

ESCHENBACH, WOLFRAM VON
(German, c.1200)
Bavarian Knight and epic poet, von Eschenbach's best-known work *Parzifal* concerns the legend of Sir Percevel's quest for the Holy Grail.
Parzival
[R1096] Penguin pbk **£4.50**
Willehalm
[R1097] Penguin pbk **£3.50**

ESENIN, SERGEI (Russian, 1895 - 1925)
The title of Esenin's *Confessions of a Hooligan* is particularly apt. His life was turbulent - he was from peasant stock, a hopeless drunkard, married to Isadora Duncan, and commited suicide by hanging at 30. His poetry is confessional, and his peasant background is reflected in the delightful simplicity of the pre-revolutionary lyrics. He celebrated the revolution ecstatically before disenchantment set in, and this is reflected in the brutality of his *Hooligan* poems. His later poems are taut lyrics, and anecdotal, conversational narratives.
Confessions of a Hooligan
[R1098] Carcanet hbk **£4.95**
Selected Poetry
[R1099] Central hbk **£4.95**

FONTAINE, JEAN DE LA
(French, 1621 - 1695)
The simplicity of the **Fables** is deceptive; La Font-aine mixes wit and affection, humour and elegance in a flexible style of alternate short and long lines, constantly changing rhyme schemes, and styles which alternate between the mythological and the colloquial.
Selected Fables
[R1100] Penguin pbk **£3.99**
Some Tales (Trans. Sisson, C.H.)
The popularity of the **Fables** has overshadowed the **Tales**, which are full of stock stories re-told in charm-ing verse, and which appear effortless and witty.
[R1101] Carcanet hbk **£4.50**

FRANCE, MARIE DE (French, c.1160 - 1190)
Marie de France wrote twelve famous Celtic stories in Anglo-Norman couplets. They became the best known examples of the 'Breton' lays, which were much imitated in Britain, for example in Chaucer's **Franklin's Tale**.
The Lais of Marie de France
[R1102] Penguin pbk **£4.50**

FRIED, ERICH (Austrian, 1921 - 1988)
A Viennese Jew by birth, Fried lived in London from 1938 until his death last year, although he continued to write in German. His lack of firm roots accounts for the title of his book **100 Poems without a Country**. A Marxist of the German school, his technique in the later work is similar to that of Brecht or Enzensberger, and his poems have a terse, ironic wit, that is incisive, laconic and humane.
100 Poems without a Country
[R1103] Calder pbk **£4.95**

GOETHE, JOHANN WOLFGANG VON
(German, 1749 - 1832)
As Germany's greatest writer, Goethe is best known for his play **Faust**, and his Romantic novel **Young Werther**. The poems in **The Roman Elegies** are marked by great linguistic and thematic range, a natural confidence and energy.
Poems and Epigrams (Trans. Hamburger, M.)
[R1104] Anvil pbk **£4.95**
Roman Elegies & The Diary
(Trans. Luke, David)
[R1105] Libris hbk **£22.50**
Selected Poems
[R1106] Calder pbk **£9.95**
Selected Verse
[R1107] Penguin pbk **£5.95**

GOZZANO, GUIDO (Italian, 1883 - 1916)
As Montale says, *"Gozzano made his début as no other poet has done since; that is, in a quite casual way, with his hands in his pockets."* He offered a new kind of poetry in Italian, one of grey semitones and harmonies, a poetry that was no longer heroic. Although he was influenced by d'Annunzio, Gozzano's work has stronger realistic elements. If it never *sings* as Pascoli's does, it has instead a fine narrative strain.
The Colloquies
[R1108] Carcanet pbk **£6.95**

HEINE, HEINRICH (German, 1797 - 1856)
Most famous as a lyric poet - many of his poems were set to music by 19th century German composers - Heine called himself 'the last Romantic'. His poetry is characterized by a combination of self-indulgent emotion and sharp self-criticism and deflating irony. As Matthew Arnold put it, Heine *"unites so much wit with so much pathos"*.
Deutschland: A Winter's Tale　`NEW`
(Trans. Reed, T.J.)
Angel Books have recently published an excellent translation of **Deutschland: Ein Wintermärchen**, a jaunty satirical account of Heine's return to his

homeland in 1843. His main satirical targets are Prussianism, censorship, the role of the church, and the fogs of German philosophy.
[R1109] Angel hbk **£8.95**
[R1110] Angel pbk **£4.95**
Selected Verse
[R1111] Penguin pbk **£3.95**
The Complete Poems (Trans. Draper, Hal)
[R1112] Oxford hbk **£14.95**

HERBERT, ZBIGNIEW (Polish, 1924 -)
Deeply embedded in the European cultural tradition, Herbert has been called 'a poet of historical irony' by Czeslaw Milosz. He achieves a precarious equilibrium by endowing the patterns of civilizations with meanings, in spite of all its horrors. Herbert uses history *"not for lessons in hope but to confront my experience with the experience of others"*. He writes 'persona' poems, not far removed from those of Cavafy, and his language is stripped down. His theory of art is based on a rejection of 'purity': *"poetry as a verbal art,"* he has written, *"bored me."*
Report from the Besieged City and Other Poems
[R1113] Oxford pbk **£5.95**
Selected Poems (Trans. Milosz, C.)
[R1114] Carcanet pbk **£4.95**

HOLUB, MIROSLAV (Czech, 1923 -)
Holub's poetry reflects the desire that people should *"read poems as naturally as they read the papers, or go to a football match. Not to consider it as anything more difficult, or effeminate, or praiseworthy."* Whilst it is lively and experimental, using free verse forms derived from Ferlinghetti, Corso and Enzensberger, it is based, as Al Alvarez has commented, 'on an unsentimental, probing, compassionate, witty sense of the modern world.' Holub treats his poetry as a hobby, and is by profession an eminent immunologist.
On the Contrary and Other Poems
(Trans. Osers, E.)
[R1115] Bloodaxe hbk **£8.95**
[R1116] Bloodaxe pbk **£4.95**
The Fly (Trans. Theiner; Osers & Milner)
[R1117] Bloodaxe pbk **£5.95**

HUGO, VICTOR (French, 1802 - 1885)
Although Hugo is well known for his novels such as **Les Miserables**, his poetry is undervalued in Britain, having been extravagantly praised in France by Baudelaire, Proust and Valéry. His poetry combines technical bravura with a startling Romantic energy, as he rages against injustice. Harry Guest's fine translations should help us to appreciate a poet whom the French adore.
The Distance, the Shadows: Selected Poems (Trans. Guest, Harry)
[R1118] Anvil pbk **£7.95**

HOLDERLIN, FRIEDRICH
(German, 1770 - 1843)
The authoritative translator of Hölderlin, Michael Hamburger, has written: 'Hölderlin's best work is literally incomparable. This uniqueness is difficult to explain or characterize. Historically speaking, Hölderlin achieved a fusion of native and foreign qualities, of emotional and spiritual dynamism with 'stillness of beauty', as he called it, of pathos with precision, of directness with grandeur, unmatched by any other German poet.' Although it would be difficult to challenge the excellence of Hamburger's translation, there is a new **Selected Poems** by David Constantine.
Selected Poems (Trans. Constantine, David)
[R1119] Bloodaxe pbk **£5.95**
Selected Verse (Trans. Hamburger, Michael)
[R1120] Anvil hbk **£12.95**
[R1121] Anvil pbk **£4.95**

Selected Verse of Hölderlin & Mörike
(Trans. Middleton, Christopher)
[R1122] Chicago UP hbk **£14.00**
[R1123] Chicago UP pbk **£2.95**

JACCOTTET, PHILIPPE (French, 1925 -)
Deeply involved with the visible world, like his countrymen Bonnefoy, Ponge and Guillevic, Jaccottet writes *"a poetry without images"* - which is in fact a poetry without metaphor, as he distinguishes between 'necessary' and 'ornamental' images. Poetry *"becomes the bare naming of things"*.
Selected Poems
[R1124] Viking hbk **£12.95**
[R1125] Penguin pbk **£5.99**

JANOVIC, VLADIMIR (Czech)
The House of the Tragic Poet　`NEW`
(Trans. Osers, Ewald)
In his epic poem, **The House of the Tragic Poet**, Janovic brings to life characters from a mosaic floor; a small theatrical company of six young men are about to enact a satyr play for the summer feast of Vulcania. But it is the year AD 79, only a few days before the eruption of Vesuvius. Not only about the last days of Pompeii, it is also about human relation-ships and man's ways of coping with life and death.
[R1126] Bloodaxe pbk **£6.95**

JIMENEZ, JUAN RAMON
(Spanish, 1881 - 1958)
Nobel Prize for Literature, 1956. A modern poet without being modernistic, Jimenez went through a process of purification similar to that of W.B. Yeats; the early symbolist poems were replaced by a naked diction. Although his work is rooted in the tradition of mystical, Christian writers such as Thomas à Kempis, he stressed the primacy of the imagination: *"The imagination is autonomous, and I am an imaginative autonomist."*
Light and Shadows: Selected Poems and Prose　`NEW`
[R1127] Forest Bks pbk **£5.95**

LAFORGUE, JULES (French, 1860 - 1887)
A sophisticated ironist, Laforgue's trademarks are self-mockery, colloquialism and verbal game-playing. His formal experiments are combined with an obsession with non-identity; he adopts the masks of buffoon and dreamer. T.S. Eliot's work is deeply indebted to Laforgue's work, not only in the appro-priation of lines and passages, tones and moods, but also for the rhapsodic structure of **The Waste Land**.
Poems of Jules Laforgue (Trans. Dale, Peter)
[R1128] Anvil hbk **£15.00**
[R1129] Anvil pbk **£9.95**

LERMONTOV, MIKHAIL
(Russian, 1814 - 1841)
Lermontov was an archetypal Romantic, absorbed in his own emotions; *"Moi"*, he once wrote, *"c'est la personne que je fréquente avec le plus de plaisir."* His work, which includes the novelistic narrative poems **The Novice**, **The Demon** and **The Treasurer's Wife of Tambov**, is heavily influenced by Byron, and is characterized by a revolt against accepted values and a craving for freedom, a sense of isolation, and an ingrained pessimism.
Major Poetry
[R1130] Croom H hbk **£45.00**
Selected Works
[R1131] Central hbk **£4.95**

LORCA, FEDERICO GARCIA
(Spanish, 1898 - 1936)
Lorca is the symbolic Spanish poet, largely because of the manner of his death, murdered by the Nationalists. He is not, though, a political poet, but a popular folk poet whose work, nevertheless, was as

sophisticated as more intellectual, cerebral writers. His poetry possesses the elusive quality of being able to delight the simple minded, and command the respect of the learned.

Deep Song & Other Prose
[R1132] Boyars hbk £7.95
[R1133] Boyars pbk £4.95
Poems (Trans. Rowe, A.)
[R1135] Aquila pbk £1.20
Poet in New York (Trans. Simon, Greg & White, Stephen)
Poet in New York is a genuinely modern poem. Faced with the brutality of life in the New World, Lorca is unable to impose a metaphorical order on this vision; the poem copes with this new subject matter by inconsistencies of style - plainness of diction alternates with rhetorical accumulations of metaphor.
[R1136] Viking hbk £12.95

MALLARME, STEPHANE
(French, 1842 - 1898)
The French Symbolist poet *par excellence*, Mallarmé was one of the founding fathers of modernism. For him the aesthetic experience was a matter of faith, and he elevated art to the status of a religion - he renounced the poetry of statement for poems whose finely-wrought suggestion and musical texture touch upon an undefined ideal perfection.
Selected Poems
[R1137] California UP pbk £4.40
Tomb for Anatole (Trans. Auster, Paul)
[R1138] North Point P pbk £9.95

MANDELSTAM, OSIP (Russian, 1891 - 1938?)
The harrowing story of Mandelstam's last years has been told in *Hope Against Hope*, the memoirs of his widow, Nadezda. After responding unsatisfactorily to the regime, he was effectively silenced from 1928, and was arrested after reciting his famous poem denouncing Stalin. He became a poet of 'the living word', his poems committed to flimsy notebooks and the memories of friends. The rest of his life was a liturgy of persecution, and he died (probably) in a labour camp. In even his bleakest work, where he assumes the mantle of the spokesman of the epoch, there is an intangible sense of elation.
Poems
[R1139] Angel hbk £10.95
[R1140] Angel pbk £5.95
Poems (Trans. Greene, J.)
[R1141] Elek pbk £5.95
Selected Poems
[R1142] Penguin pbk £3.95
The Noise of Time: The Prose of Osip Mandelstam
[R1143] Quartet pbk £5.95

MAYAKOVSKY, VLADIMIR
(Russian, 1893 - 1930)
Mayakovsky is a poet of springy and accessible vitality. He welcomed the Revolution and expected the Futurists to be the vanguard of the new state's art; Lenin, however, thought his work was 'incomprehensible rubbish'. Coarse, violent and declamatory political poems alternate with cycles of purely lyric verse.
Listen! Early Poems 1913 - 1918
[R1144] Redstone P boxed set £7.95
Poems (Ed. Marshall, Herbert)
[R1145] Dobson hbk £17.50
[R1146] Central hbk £2.50
Selected Works: Vol. 1 (Selected Verse)
[R1147] Central hbk £5.95
Selected Works: Vol. 2 (Longer Poems)
[R1148] Central hbk £5.95

MICHELANGELO BUONARROTI
(Italian, 1475 - 1564)
Michelangelo wrote over 300 poems, including Platonic sonnets to Tommaso de Cavalieri and

spiritual poems to Vittoria Colonna. Elizabeth Jennings's translation is highly recommended.
Sonnets (Trans. Jennings, Elizabeth)
[R1149] Carcanet pbk £6.95
The Complete Poems of Michelangelo
[R1150] P Owen hbk £11.95

MILOSZ, CZESLAW (Polish, 1911 -)
Nobel Prize for Literature, 1980. The landscape of his native Lithuania has always been at the core of Milosz's poetry. His poetic work presents a great variety of forms, ranging from mock odes and treatises in the spirit of the 18th century, to notebooks of dreams. He is a Symbolist in reverse, circumventing with his symbols the essential being of things, which seems to be his real concern. Joseph Brodsky calls Milosz 'one of the greatest poets of our time, perhaps the greatest'.
Bells in Winter: Selected Poems
(Trans. Milosz, with Vallee, L.)
[R1151] Carcanet pbk £4.95
Collected Poems 1931 - 1987 `NEW`
[R1152] Penguin pbk £7.99
New & Selected Poems
[R1153] Viking hbk £18.95
The Land of Ulro (Prose)
[R1154] Carcanet hbk £12.95
Visions from San Francisco Bay (Prose)
[R1155] Carcanet hbk £10.95

MONTALE, EUGENIO (Italian, 1896 - 1981)
Nobel Prize for Literature, 1975. The finest modern Italian poet, Montale is a formalist engaged in rekindling language to express the more elusive reaches of experience. His work is characterized by its sharp symbolism and richly suggestive language, and he is known in particular for his evocations of landscape, women and erotic feeling.
Poet in our Time (Trans. Hamilton, A.)
[R1157] Boyars pbk £3.95

PASOLINI, PIER PAOLO (Italian, 1922 - 1975)
Pasolini's early poetry, under the influence of Giovanni Pascoli, is written in the Friulan dialect, which he adopted as 'a sort of mystic act of love, a kind of *felibrisme*, like the Provçenal poets'. With his assimilation of Marxism through the writings of Gramsci, however, he moved away from the hermetic, towards a more objective and realistic style, reflecting his contact with the peasantry.
Selected Poems (Trans. MacAfee, N. & Martinengo, L.)
[R1159] Calder pbk £6.95

PASTERNAK, BORIS (Russian, 1890 - 1960)
Best known for the novel *Dr. Zhivago*, Pasternak's early poems seemed to Marina Tsvetayeva "*a downpour of light*", having a striking richness of words and images. Over the years he refined and simplified his work, trying to attain 'an unnoticeable style'. Among the finest poems are those he 'gave' to Dr. Zhivago in the last chapter of the novel.
Selected Poems (Trans. Stallworthy, J. & France, P.)
[R1160] Penguin pbk £3.95
The Voice of Prose
[R1161] Polygon pbk £8.95

PESSOA, FERNANDO
(Portuguese, 1888 - 1935)
Pessoa accepted the dividedness of human nature so completely that he wrote under four names, as himself, and under three heteronyms; the existence of the work of Alberto Caeiro, Ricardo Reis, Alvaro de Campos and Fernando Pessoa is a testament to their progenitor's propensity to disbelieve his own existence. All four poets have different characteristics, but all his work reveals a mind shaken by suffering.

Selected Poems
[R1163] Penguin pbk £5.99

PETRARCH (FRANCESCO PETRARCA)
(Italian, 1304 - 1374)
"*I find no peace and all my war is done./I fear and hope, I burn and freeze like ice./I fly above the wind, yet can I not arise.*" The Florentine contemporary of Dante and Boccaccio, who shared with them a passionate commitment to the ideals of classical antiquity, Petrarch remains the acknowledged father of Italian humanism. At his best, in the *Canzones*, which record his devotion to the unknown Laura, he pioneered the vocabulary of over 200 years of European love poetry. Sidney's wry weariness in speaking of 'poor Petrarch's long deceased woes' is a kind of ironic compliment; he was translated by Surrey and Wyatt, who provides the translation above.
Songs and Sonnets from Laura's Lifetime
[R1164] Anvil pbk £3.50

PILINSZKY, JANOS (Hungarian, 1921 - 81)
A compelling voice among the generation of European poets who bore first-hand witness to the horrors of the Second World War, the poetry of Pilinszky is marked by a spiritual and artistic distinction. `NEW`
The Desert of Love
(Trans. Hughes, Ted & Csokits, Janos)
The Desert of Love is a revised and enlarged version of the 1976 edition of his magnetic, intense and haunting poems. Ted Hughes provides an introduction which refers to Pilinszky's 'desolation of vision', which is only 'equalled by its radiance'.
[R1165] Anvil hbk £9.95
[R1166] Anvil pbk £4.95

PUSHKIN, ALEXANDER
(Russian, 1799 - 1837)
Generally regarded as Russia's greatest poet, the lack of adequate translations has impeded his recognition in Britain. This situation was changed by Charles Johnston's brilliant translation of *Eugene Onegin*, the story of Tatyana's artless love for the foppish Onegin.
Eugene Onegin
[R1167] Penguin pbk £3.99
On Literature
A valuable collection of Pushkin's prose writings.
[R1168] Athlone P hbk £45.00

RADNOTI, MIKLOS (Hungarian, 1909 - 1944)
Murdered by the fleeing Nazis towards the end of the War, Radnoti's last poems were later found on his person in the mass grave into which his body had been thrown. His late work, recorded in this volume, is powerful, moving and direct.
Forced March: Selected Poems
[R1169] Carcanet pbk £4.95

RATUSHINSKAYA, IRINA (Russian, 1954 -)
"*I know it won't be received/Or sent. The page will be/In shreds as soon as I have scribbled it.*" With these words, Ratushinskaya begins her *Pencil Letter*, which was written in prison, in 1982, as she waited to be tried for 'anti-Soviet agitation and propaganda'. In March 1983 she was sentenced to seven years hard labour. After an international campaign, she was released in October 1986, on the eve of the Reykjavik summit.
No, I'm Not Afraid (Trans. McDuff, David)
[R1170] Bloodaxe hbk £12.95
[R1171] Bloodaxe pbk £5.95
Pencil Letter
Many of the poems in *Pencil Letter* were written with burnt matchsticks on bars of soap, and then memorized, at the Barshevo labour camp.
[R1172] Bloodaxe hbk £10.95
[R1173] Bloodaxe pbk £4.95

Rainer Maria Rilke from *Lettre à Rodin, 1928* currently unavailable

RILKE, RAINER MARIA
(German, 1875 - 1926)
The subjective emotionalism of his early work, which featured a self-identification with the oppressed, developed into a period of pseudo-mystical lyricism; in his diverse experiments he used masks, vacillating between the personae of the aristocrat and the pariah. His finest works are the *Duino Elegies* and *Sonnets to Orpheus*.
Letters on Cézanne (Prose)
[R1174] Cape hbk **£9.95**
Selected Poetry (Trans. Mitchell, S.)
[R1175] Picador pbk **£4.99**
The Duino Elegies (Trans. Leishman, J.B. & Spender, S.)
[R1176] Chatto pbk **£3.95**
The Duino Elegies NEW
(Trans. Cohn, Stewart)
Stewart Cohn's new translations capture Rilke's fluidity and the blinding transparence of his diction, and they have classical qualities which set them apart from earlier, doggedly literal versions.
[R1177] Carcanet hbk **£15.00**
Unofficial Rilke (Trans. Hamburger, Michael)
[R1178] Anvil pbk **£3.95**

RIMBAUD, ARTHUR (French, 1854 - 1891)
By the age of 17 Rimbaud had written his most famous poem, 'Le Bateau Ivre'; between 1871 and 1873 he set out on a programme of 'disorientation of the senses', trying to turn himself into a seer, and this period saw him write the prose poems *Les Illuminations*. By the age of 20, his poetic career was over: after repudiating poetry, he wandered Europe and North Africa, gun-running and slave-trading. He is remarkable for his passion for extremity.
A Season in Hell and Selected Poems (Trans. Cameron, Norman) NEW
[R1179] Anvil hbk **£12.95**
[R1180] Anvil pbk **£5.95**
Complete Works
[R1181] Picador pbk **£5.95**
Complete Works: Selected Letters
(in French and English)
[R1182] Chicago UP pbk **£8.75**

RITSOS, YANNIS (Greek, 1909 -)
Exile and Return: Selected Poems 1969 - 1974 (Trans. Keeley, Edmund)
Exile and Return is translator Edmund Keeley's selection from Ritsos's poetry published during the dictatorship of the Greek colonels; a long-standing communist, he was gaoled after the 1967 coup. Although these poems are rarely overtly political, they vividly characterize the mood that dominated those years.
[R1183] Anvil pbk **£5.95**

SEFERIS, GEORGE (Greek, 1900 - 1970)
Seferis has long been regarded as the greatest Greek poet of the age, and second only to Cavafy among all modern Greek poets. His verse is notable for its Eliot-like impersonality. The poetry occupies a middle ground between the plots of myth and the circumstances of history.
Complete Poems of George Seferis (Trans. Keeley, E. & Sherrard, P.) NEW
This new edition of Sherrard and Keeley's now standard translation is designed for those readers to whom Greek is greek, and prefer a more compact book.
[R1185] Anvil hbk **£15.95**
[R1186] Anvil pbk **£5.95**

SEIFERT, JAROSLAV (Czech, 1901 - 1984)
Nobel Prize for Literature, 1984. This great lyric poet has long been a national figure in Czechoslovakia, but has begun to receive recognition in the West since winning the Nobel. In his introduction to the *Selected Poems*, George Gibian calls him a 'poet of the world of the senses, not of transcendence, angst, fear or trembling'.
Selected Poetry (Trans. Osers, E.)
[R1187] Deutsch pbk **£9.95**

SERENI, VITTORIO (Italian, 1913 - 1983)
Serini is widely regarded as the finest Italian poet of his generation after Montale. Although the background to the poems is specific in time and place, it is their developing metaphysical dimension which makes him a poet in whose work the fullest appreciation of life is to be found.
The Selected Poems of Vittorio Sereni
[R1188] Anvil pbk **£5.95**

STRASSBURG, GOTTFRIED VON
(German, c.1200)
Little is known of von Strassburg's life: his version of *Tristan* was the most important to survive from the Middle Ages.
Tristan
[R1189] Penguin pbk **£3.50**

SODERGRAN, EDITH (Finnish, 1892 - 1923)
Although she was influenced by German writing, and in particular Nietzsche, she wrote in Swedish, and her *Poems* of 1916 were the first 'modern' poems in that language. She is notable for her sense of simplicity and detail, and her response to nature. Through the *Complete Poems* - which includes extracts from her volatile letters - resignation changes to defiance.
Complete Poems (Trans. McDuff, David)
[R1190] Bloodaxe hbk **£9.95**
[R1191] Bloodaxe pbk **£5.50**

TRANSTROMER, TOMAS (Swedish, 1931 -)
Tranströmer's work is quizzical, serious and sombre. He has written that *"My poems are meeting places. Their intent is to make a sudden connection between aspects of reality that conventional languages and outlooks ordinarily keep apart"*.
Collected Poems (Trans. Fulton, Robin)
[R1192] Bloodaxe pbk **£6.95**

TROYES, CHRETIEN DE (French, c.1170)
Chrétien de Troyes was the greatest writer of courtly 'Romances'. His version of the tales of King Arthur influenced all subsequent versions.
Arthurian Romances
[R1193] Dent pbk **£3.95**
Perceval: The Story of the Grail
[R1194] DS Brewer pbk **£9.95**
Yvain
[R1195] Manchester UP pbk **£5.95**

TSVETAYEVA, MARINA
(Russian, 1892 - 1941)
Tsvetayeva's poetry is notable for the violence of her emotions and the ferocity of her expression. She saw poetry as an act of revelation: *"the target of all poetry is the heart"*, she wrote. Boris Pasternak spoke of her 'rich and compact and enveloping sequences of stanza after stanza in its vast periods of unbroken rhythm.'
A Captive Spirit (Prose)
[R1196] Virago pbk **£5.95**
Selected Poems (Trans. Feinstein, Elaine)
[R1197] Hutchinson pbk **£6.95**
Selected Poems (Trans. McDuff, David)
[R1198] Bloodaxe pbk **£6.95**

VALERY, PAUL (French, 1871 - 1945)
Inspired by the Symbolists, Valéry's language is distinguished by a remarkable purity of diction. T.S. Eliot commented that *"Valéry will remain for posterity the representative poet of the first half of the 20th Century - not Yeats, not Rilke, not anyone else."*
An Anthology (Trans. Lawler, James)
[R1199] Routledge pbk **£9.95**

VERLAINE, PAUL (French, 1844 - 1896)
Verlaine's life is notorious - apart from the almost vocational dissipation, he shot his lover Rimbaud in the wrist, and subsequently spent two years in jail. Technically, he broke every rule of prosody with his virtuoso experimentation; yet his poems are essentially simple, and close to music.
Femmes/Hombres
In his erotic collection *Femmes/Hombres*, Verlaine's best poems are made up of the happy minutes of people in bed, capturing a sense of continual sexual celebration, as both consequent sorrows and love are both passed over.
[R1200] Anvil pbk **£5.95**

VILLON, FRANCOIS
(French, 1431 - after 1463)
Villon's supple verse moves through a range of voices from gallows humour to haunting lyric flight. Ezra Pound called him *"the hardest, the most authentic, the most absolute poet of France. The underdog, the realist, also a scholar...An insuperable technician."*
Selected Poems (Trans. Dale, Peter)
[R1201] Penguin hbk **£4.99**
Selected Poems (Trans. Kinnell, G.)
[R1202] New England UP pbk **£7.30**

WEORES, SANDOR (Hungarian, 1913 -)
Weöres is considered the greatest living poet in his language, and is an important European poet. His bold use of associational imagery is coupled with a wide range of mythological and anthropological reference; he uses the primitive myths to remind us of our civilization.
Eternal Moment NEW
(Trans. Morgan, Edwin & Smith, William Jay etc)
Eternal Moment exhibits the diversity of Weöres's poetry, containing lyrics and satires, sonnets and prose poems, epigrams and concrete poems.
[R1203] Anvil hbk **£12.95**
[R1204] Anvil pbk **£6.95**

POETRY

YEVTUSHENKO, YEVGENY
(Russian, 1933 -)
Once seen as the young generation's literary spokesman, Yevtushenko's declamatory and colloquial poetry now seems over-reliant on an easy rhetoric. Influenced by Mayakovsky, his work is not innovative, but instead rather middlebrow. A natural revolutionary, he is a libertarian who is insistent that ends do not justify bad means.
Almost at the End
[R1205] Boyars hbk **£10.95**
Face Behind the Face
[R1207] Boyars pbk **£3.50**
Poetry
[R1208] Boyars pbk **£3.95**

ZAGAJEWSKI, ADAM (Polish, 1945 -)
Zagajewski's language is direct and simple, and his attitudes are uninhibited. He has clashed with the authorities in Poland, where his work has suffered temporary publication bans.
Tremor
[R1209] Collins pbk **£6.95**

World Poetry

170 Chinese Poems (Ed. Waley, Arthur)
[R1210] Constable pbk **£5.95**

Hebrew Verse
[R1211] Penguin pbk **£10.95**

Japanese Verse
[R1212] Penguin pbk **£5.95**

Modern Poetry of the Arab World
[R1213] Penguin pbk **£3.95**

Songs of the South: Anthology of Ancient Chinese Poetry
[R1214] Penguin pbk **£4.95**

Zen Poetry
[R1215] Penguin pbk **£3.99**

AKKO, YOSANO
Tangled Hair `NEW`
(Trans. Maloney, Dennis & Oshiro, Hide)
[R1216] Forest Bks pbk **£5.95**

AMICHAI, YEHUDA (Israel, 1924 -)
Born in Würzburg of German Jewish parents, Amichai emigrated to Jerusalem in 1936. He writes in his non-native language - Hebrew - and his clipped utterance is not unlike that of Paul Celan, though more accessible. Like Celan, he is sceptical of the stain on the silence which his words leave, and he confines himself to the short lyric; yet like Brecht, he does not let this scepticism get in the way of his clarity and 'low-brow' power to communicate.
Selected Poems (Trans. Bloch, C. & Mitchell, S.)
[R1217] Viking pbk **£12.95**
Selected Poems `NEW`
[R1218] Penguin pbk **£5.99**

BASHO, MATSUO (Japanese, 1644 - 1694)
Basho is remembered as a master of the 'haiku'. *The Narrow Road to the Deep North* is an episodic work in which Basho observes the mysteries of the natural world in a combination of haiku and prose reflection; *On Love and Barley* is a collection of 'haiku'.
On Love and Barley
[R1219] Penguin pbk **£2.99**
The Narrow Road to the Deep North
[R1220] Penguin pbk **£3.95**

DAO, BEI (Chinese, 1949 -)
British readers are perhaps familiar with Bei Dao's collection of short stories *Waves*. His poetry reflects - and criticizes - the conflicts of the cultural revolution. Experimental, subjective and apolitical, he remains uncompromising in his allegiance to the imaginative values that his poems advance. He is among China's foremost young poets.
The August Sleepwalker `NEW`
[R1221] Anvil hbk **£12.95**

GIBRAN, KAHLIL (Lebanese, 1883 - 1931)
Mystic, poet, philosopher and artist, Gibran invented the prose poem form in Arabic; he remains widely known for *The Prophet*.
The Prophet
[R1221A] Pan pbk **£3.99**
Treasury of Gibran
[R1222] Heinemann hbk **£10.95**

KHAYYAM, OMAR (Persian, c.12th century)
Omar Khayyam's rich quatrains evoke a cynical hedonism; he doubts the value of human endeavours, and celebrates instead the present moment.
The Rubaiyat of Omar Khayyam
(Trans. Fitzgerald, Edward)
Edward Fitzgerald's remarkable translation went unnoticed for many years, until it was discovered by Rossetti, remaindered on a bookstall. It is more than merely a translation, and is itself one of the most popular poems in the language.
[R1223] Collins hbk **£9.95**
The Rubaiyat of Omar Khayyam
(Trans. Avery & Heath-Stubbs)
[R1224] Penguin pbk **£2.99**
The Rubaiyat of Omar Khayyam
(Trans. Fitzgerald, Edward)
[R1225] Collins pbk **£4.95**

NERUDA, PABLO (Chilean, 1904 - 1973)
Nobel Prize for Literature, 1971. Chilean ambassador and communist, Neruda became, after a baroque beginning, a poet of the multitude, where communication is more important than finesse. He wanted a *"poetry like bread that can be shared by all, learned men and peasants alike"*. Michael Hamburger has commented acutely on Neruda's utilitarian view of poetry when he says that *"most 'ordinary people' turn to poetry not for bread, but for cream cakes, if they turn to it at all."*
Memoirs
[R1158] Penguin pbk **£4.99**
Selected Poems
[R1227] Penguin pbk **£5.99**
Twenty Love Poems and a Song of Despair
[R1228] Cape pbk **£3.95**

PAZ, OCTAVIO (Mexican, 1914 -)
Paz, the greatest living poet of Latin America, draws on both his native Mexican traditions and on the international avant-garde. He explores political themes - the suppression of native Mexican culture by colonial forces, and of colonial culture by modern nationalism, and the consequent severing of historical roots - and his civic poems explore the consequences of pollution and demographic growth. He is also a frank and visionary poet of the erotic.
Collected Poems `NEW`
The appearance of the *Collected Poems*, in its handsome bilingual edition, is an important event. The translations of Elizabeth Bishop, Charles Tomlinson and Denise Levertov are included.
[R1229] Carcanet hbk **£25.00**
Convergences (Prose)
[R1230] Bloomsbury hbk **£16.95**
On Poets and Others
[R1231] Carcanet hbk **£14.95**

Selected Poems (Ed. Tomlinson, Charles)
[R1232] Penguin pbk **£4.99**
The Labyrinth of Solitude
(Non-fiction, 1985)
This provides a compelling insight into Mexico and the meaning of its Revolution.
[R1233] Penguin pbk **£3.95**

TAGORE, RABINDRANATH
(Indian, 1861 - 1941)
Nobel Prize for Literature 1913. The lush note of Tagore's poetry has tended to make him a neglected poet, but he was admired by Yeats and Pound. Although he wrote in Bengali, he translated - rather banally - his own work into English.
Collected Poems & Plays
[R1234] Macmillan pbk **£14.95**
Selected Poems (Trans. Radice, William)
[R1235] Penguin pbk **£3.95**

VALLEJO, CESAR (Peruvian, 1892 - 1938)
Like Pablo Neruda, Vallejo broke with the tradition of 'pure' poetry under the pressure of his social and political conscience, though this commitment never turned him into a didactic poet. Although his diction is stark and direct, he never attained the degree of austerity that felt figurative or metaphorical language to be self-indulgent. His pity moves him to a revolt, not against society, but against God and life itself.
Selected Poetry (Trans. Higgins, J.)
[R1236] F Cairns pbk **£4.95**

Anthologies

100 Poems by 100 Poets (Ed. Pinter, Harold)
[R1237] Methuen pbk **£3.95**

A Personal Anthology of English Verse
(Ed. Amis, Kingsley)
[R1238] Hutchinson hbk **£12.95**

Common Ground (Ed. Laski, Marghanita)
Marghanita Laski's last book is an anthology which expresses her lifelong concern that the arts, especially poetry, should be accessible. This is a new selection of the best-loved and most durable poems in our tradition. It is a catholic 'refresher', and a radical old-fashioned anthology which is less guilded than Palgrave.
[R1239] Carcanet hbk **£9.95**

English Christian Verse
[R1240] Penguin pbk **£5.95**

English Love Poems
(Ed. Betjeman, J. & Taylor, G.)
[R1241] Faber pbk **£3.95**

English Pastoral Verse
[R1242] Penguin pbk **£4.50**

Favourite Love Poems `NEW`
(Ed. Osborne, Charles)
[R1243] Michael O'Mara hbk **£9.95**

Homosexual Verse
[R1244] Penguin pbk **£5.95**

Imagist Poetry
[R1245] Penguin pbk **£3.95**

Love Poetry
[R1246] Penguin pbk **£4.99**

Narrative Verse (Ed. Collins, V.H.)
[R1247] Oxford pbk **£3.95**

Other Men's Flowers (Ed. Wavell, A.P.)
[R1248] Cape hbk **£9.95**

Poetry with an Edge (Ed. Astley, Neil)
Publisher Neil Astley has chosen a selection of
international poets from his Bloodaxe list, to
celebrate its tenth anniversary, and includes work
from Tony Harrison, Ken Smith and Miroslav Holub.
[R1249] Bloodaxe pbk **£6.95**

**The Chatto Book of Nonsense
Verse** (Ed. Haughton, Hugh) **NEW**
[R1252] Chatto hbk **£12.95**

The Faber Book of Ballads
(Ed. Hodgart, M.)
[R1253] Faber pbk **£4.95**

**The Faber Book of English History in
Verse** (Ed. Baker, Kenneth)
Surprisingly fair-minded and balanced anthology
from the current Secretary of State for Education. It
traces the history of England from the time of
Bodicca to the coronation of Elizabeth II.
[R1254] Faber hbk **£12.95**
[R1255] Faber pbk **£6.99**

**The Faber Book of Epigrams and
Epitaphs** (Ed. Grigson, G.)
[R1256] Faber pbk **£3.95**

The Faber Book of Love Poems
(Ed. Grigson, G.)
[R1257] Faber hbk **£6.95**
[R1258] Faber pbk **£4.95**

The Faber Book of Political Verse
(Ed. Paulin, Tom)
[R1259] Faber pbk **£8.95**

The Faber Book of Popular Verse
(Ed. Grigson, G.)
[R1260] Faber pbk **£4.95**

The Faber Book of Religious Verse
(Ed. Gardner, Helen)
[R1261] Faber pbk **£4.95**

The Faber Book of Useful Verse
[R1262] Faber pbk **£4.95**

The Faber Popular Reciter
(Ed. Amis, Kingsley)
[R1263] Faber pbk **£3.95**

The Male Muse: A Gay Anthology
[R1264] Black Sparrow pbk **£3.95**

**The New Oxford Book of Christian
Verse** (Ed. Davie, Donald)
Typically forthright selection with a non-conformist
slant. Apart from bafflingly thin selections of Herbert,
Donne, Crashaw and Marvell, there is a rich selection
from the 18th century, of Watts, Wesley, and above
all, Cowper.
[R1265] Oxford hbk **£17.50**
[R1266] Oxford pbk **£4.95**

The Oxford Book of Ballads
(Ed. Kingsley, James)
Kingsley's selection covers the range of this popular
form - among the 150 ballads he includes are historical and biblical ballads, romances and seductions,
and over half are accompanied by their tune.
[R1267] Oxford pbk **£6.95**

**The Oxford Book of English Verse in
Translation** (Ed. Tomlinson, Charles)
[R1268] Oxford pbk **£4.95**

The Oxford Book of Narrative Verse
[R1269] Oxford hbk **£12.95**

The Oxford Book of Satirical Verse
(Ed. Grigson, G.)
[R1270] Oxford pbk **£5.95**

The Oxford Book of Short Poems
(Ed. Michie, J. & Kavanagh, P.J.)
One of Oxford's best anthologies. The editors have
selected poems shorter than sonnets, but longer than
epigrams. As well as those normally associated with
the short poem - Herrick, Dickinson, Jonson - there
are pieces from those we link with longer works -
Pope, Byron and Whitman. Most interesting, though,
are poems by virtually forgotten poets such as
Thomas Bastard, Mildmay Fane and Clement
Barksdale.
[R1271] Oxford pbk **£4.95**

The Oxford Book of Travel Verse
[R1272] Oxford hbk **£12.50**

Comic Verse

Century of Humorous Verse 1850 - 1950
(Ed. Green, Roger Lancelyn)
[R1275] Dent hbk **£8.95**

Choice of Comic and Curious Verse
[R1276] Penguin pbk **£5.95**

Everyman Book of Light Verse
(Ed. Robinson, Robert)
[R1277] Dent hbk **£13.50**

Everyman's Book of Nonsense Verse
[R1278] Dent hbk **£12.00**

Faber Book of Parodies (Ed. Brett, Simon)
[R1279] Faber pbk **£4.95**

Light Verse
[R1280] Penguin pbk **£6.95**

Oxford Book of Light Verse
(Ed. Auden, W.H.)
[R1281] Oxford pbk **£4.95**

The Faber Book of Comic Verse
(Ed. Roberts, Michael)
[R1282] Faber pbk **£4.95**

The Faber Book of Nonsense Verse
(Ed. Grigson, G.)
[R1283] Faber pbk **£4.95**

The New Oxford Book of Light Verse
(Ed. Amis, Kingsley)
[R1284] Oxford pbk **£4.95**

War Poetry

First World War Poetry (Ed. Silkin, Jon)
[R1285] Penguin pbk **£3.95**

Lost Voices of World War I (Ed. Cross, Tim)
An original international anthology of writers, poets
and playwrights, this collects the work of those
caught up in the Great War from all parts of the
world, including the better-known British and French
poets alongside Armenian and Hungarian writers; the
text appears in parallel language format.
[R1285A] Bloomsbury pbk **£14.95**

**Men Who March Away: Poems of the
First World War** (Ed. Parsons)
[R1286] Hogarth pbk **£2.95**

Poems of the Second World War
(Ed. Selwyn)
[R1287] Dent pbk **£4.95**

Spanish Civil War Poetry
(Ed. Cunningham, Valentine)
[R1288] Penguin pbk **£4.95**

The Oxford Book of War Poetry
(Ed. Stallworthy, J.H.)
Rather than focusing on the specifically British war
poetry of the 20th century, Stallworthy chooses from
all the world's poetry.
[R1273] Oxford hbk **£12.95**

The Terrible Rain: Poets 1939 - 1945
(Ed. Gardner, Brian)
[R1289] Methuen pbk **£3.95**

**Up the Line to Death: War Poets
1914 - 1918** (Ed. Gardner, Brian)
[R1290] Methuen pbk **£3.95**

GITTINGS, ROBERT
**The War Poets: The Lives and Writings
of the 1914 - 1918 War Poets**
The definitive illustrated guide to the lives, times and
poetry of the First World War poets by the well-
known contemporary poet and biographer.
[R1291] Bloomsbury hbk **£13.95**

Women's Poetry

**Bread and Roses: 19th and 20th
Century Women's Poetry**
(Ed. Scott, Diana)
[R1292] Virago pbk **£5.50**

**Early Ripening: American
Women's Poetry Now** **NEW**
(Ed. Piercy, Marge)
Anne Stevenson, Adrienne Rich, Denise Levertov and
Amy Clampitt are the better-known names in this
anthology which celebrates the diversity of women's
experiences in the United States.
[R1293] Pandora pbk **£5.95**

**Making for the Open: Post-Feminist
Poetry** (Ed. Rumens, Carol)
Rumens's wide ranging anthology - recently revised -
includes Eavan Boland, E.J. Scovell, Wendy Cope
and U.A. Fanthorpe.
[R1294] Chatto pbk **£5.95**

**Naming the Waves: Contemporary
Lesbian Poetry**
(Ed. McEwan, C.)
[R1295] Virago pbk **£5.95**

**The Bloodaxe Book of Contemporary
Women Poets** (Ed. Couzyn, J.)
[R1296] Bloodaxe pbk **£7.95**

**The Faber Book of 20th Century Women
Poets** (Ed. Adcock, Fleur)
[R1297] Faber pbk **£4.99**

**The World Split Open: Women Poets
1552 - 1950** (Ed. Bernikow)
[R1298] Women's P pbk **£4.95**

Women Poets
[R1299] Penguin pbk **£5.99**

General English Dictionaries
Specialized Dictionaries
Foreign Languages: Dictionaries & Courses
Encyclopaedias
Yearbooks
Practical Reference

Reference

REFERENCE & LANGUAGE

General English Dictionaries

Where once Dr Johnson toiled, computers now hum. The electronic revolution has meant the preparation of vast dictionary databases from which new or specialised editions can be prepared and updated with comparative ease. There is now, therefore, an even greater choice of dictionaries than ever, and to make a choice it is necessary to consider how the dictionary will be used: whether for learning English as a foreign language, for school or university work, for settling disputes or for doing crosswords or playing scrabble. There are dictionaries to suit each purpose and we reflect this in our selection, with prices ranging from £1.95 to £3,000.

CHAMBERS
Chambers English Dictionary
New Edition of the 20th Century Dictionary. Contains 15,000 new words and phrases with unparalleled coverage of scientific, technical and legal terms and the language of literature. It is a highly respected and widely used dictionary and is a serious rival to all the other English dictionaries. A favourite of crossword addicts.
[S0] Chambers hbk **£15.95**
[S1] Chambers hbk/thumb index **£17.95**
Chambers Minidictionary
[S2] Chambers pbk **£1.75**
Chambers Pocket Dictionary
[S3] Chambers pbk **£4.95**

COLLINS
Collins dictionaries are more user-friendly than their Oxford counterparts, expanding their definitions with encyclopaedic entries. Collins also score points by providing very clear guidance in regard to usage, spelling and etymology, and, aided by their huge COBUILD computer research project in Birmingham, their attention to the rapid changes in contemporary language.
Collins Cobuild English Language Dictionary
Based on the Collins Birmingham University Language Database this is invaluable for those learning English as a foreign language.
[S4] Collins hbk **£12.95**
[S5] Collins pbk **£7.95**
Collins Concise Dictionary Plus NEW
A breakthrough for paperback dictionaries: 1,600 pages combining Collins most up-to-date one-volume dictionary with over 15,000 geographical and biographical entries. Also contains an encyclopaedic supplement of essential information depicted in diagrams and charts. Easily the most useful (and inexpensive) reference book on the market.
[S6] Collins pbk **£8.95**
Collins Concise English Dictionary
[S7] Collins hbk **£9.50**
Collins Dictionary and Thesaurus
Dictionary and thesaurus in one volume, derived from Collins English Dictionary and New Collins Thesaurus. 71,000 dictionary references; 250,000 thesaurus synonyms; desk size. Material is conveniently arranged - thesaurus and dictionary entries on the same page. Excellent value.
[S8] Collins hbk **£11.95**

Collins English Dictionary
Arguably the best single-volume English dictionary. Recently completely re-edited, it has 170,000 references and 15,000 encyclopaedic entries. Covers both historical and modern usage.
[S9] Collins hbk **£14.95**
[S10] Collins hbk/thumb index **£16.95**
Collins Paperback English Dictionary
[S11] Collins pbk **£3.50**
Collins Pocket English Dictionary
[S12] Collins hbk **£4.95**
English Gem Dictionary
[S13] Collins flexi **£1.95**

FACTS ON FILE
MANSER, MARTIN
The Visual Dictionary
[S14] Facts On File hbk **£14.95**

HODDER
READER'S DIGEST
Reader's Digest Universal Dictionary
Based on the Reader's Digest Great Illustrated Dictionary. Selected for the *Daily Telegraph* crossword competition. Beautifully presented. Over 180,000 references. Excellent on slang, jargon and latest words.
[S15] Hodder hbk **£21.95**

JOHNSON, DR SAMUEL
The Dictionary of the English Language
(Abridged Edition)
Efforts to standardize the English language reached their fullest and most magnificent peak in this pioneering dictionary, first published in 1755 after nine years of work. It offers subjective evaluations of the worth of a word and personal definitions of what a word means, backed up by gloriously apt and eclectic quotations. Unfortunately a full version of Johnson's dictionary is currently unavailable but these abridged versions include a selection of the most interesting definitions.
[S16] Gollancz hbk **£10.95**
[S17] Macmillan pbk **£4.95**

LONGMAN
Longman Active Study Dictionary of English
A learning dictionary for intermediate English students clearly laid out with comprehensive notes on usage, grammar and pronunciation.
[S18] Longman pbk **£4.25**
Longman Dictionary of Contemporary English
[S19] Longman hbk **£9.50**
[S20] Longman pbk **£6.50**
Longman Dictionary of the English Language
The most comprehensive one-volume dictionary in existence. 250,000 definitions; easy pronunciation system.
[S21] Longman hbk **£17.95**
[S22] Longman hbk/thumb index **£22.50**
Longman Lexicon of Contemporary English
[S23] Longman hbk **£10.95**
[S24] Longman pbk **£7.95**
Longman Photo Dictionary
Colour photographs used to present words.
[S25] Longman pbk **£3.95**

OXFORD
Oxford continue to set the standard by which other dictionaries must measure themselves, although Collins are arguably the more innovative and contemporary. Oxford, however, corner the academic market, retaining the cachet of producing the world's largest dictionary and restricting themselves editorially to authoritative, accurate word-definition.

Concise Oxford Dictionary
Third in the hierarchy and an excellent and standard one-volume work.
[S26] Oxford hbk **£9.50**
[S27] Oxford hbk deluxe **£17.50**
[S28] Oxford hbk/thumb index **£10.95**
[S29] Oxford leather **£29.50**
Oxford Children's Dictionary
[S30] Oxford hbk **£6.95**
Oxford Dictionary of Current English
[S31] Oxford pbk **£2.50**
Oxford English Dictionary NEW
(2nd Edition)
The compilation of the OED has been one of the glories of English scholarship over the past century. It was radical in conception because whilst previous dictionaries had aimed to standardise the language, laying down rules for correct usage, the OED was conceived upon a more objective historical basis; that is, it does not select only those words in the language which it considers to be valuable and worthy of inclusion, but lists a comprehensive range of words without value judgements, concentrating on listing the facts (first recorded use, semantic changes, pronunciation etc.). The first fascicle was published in 1884 and the complete dictionary in 1928. Before the dictionary was partially completed it was obvious that a supplement would be required to cope with the additional material that was being supplied, as well as corrections, to say nothing of the changes in the language in the half century of the dictionary's compilation. Consequently, four supplementary volumes were published. The 20 volumes of the 2nd Edition integrate the original 12 volume edition with these 4 supplements, adding 5,000 new words and senses, in a redesigned and reset format.
[S32] Oxford hbk **£1,500.00**
[S33] Oxford leather **£2,750.00**
Oxford English Dictionary (1st Edition)
Three-volume complete text of the 1st edition, including the supplements volume; the text of the larger work has been photographically diminished, with 4 pages appearing on one. Supplied with magnifying reader. Given the enormous cost of the full set, the compact edition represents tremendous value.
[S34] Oxford hbk **£225.00**
Oxford English Dictionary
(1st Edition, Supplement)
Complete text of the four supplements to the 1st Edition reproduced micrographically in one volume.
[S35] Oxford hbk **£75.00**
Oxford Minidictionary
[S36] Oxford hbk **£1.75**
Oxford Paperback Dictionary (2nd Ed)
[S37] Oxford pbk **£3.75**
Oxford Reference Dictionary
[S38] Oxford flexi **£9.95**
Oxford-Duden Pictorial English Dictionary
[S39] Oxford pbk **£5.95**
Pocket English Dictionary
[S40] Oxford hbk **£4.95**
Shorter Oxford English Dictionary
A two-volume distillation of the first edition of the OED, without the quotations. Authoritative and easily used as a standard reference work.
[S41] Oxford hbk **£65.00**
[S42] Oxford hbk/thumb index **£75.00**
HORNBY, A.S.
Oxford Advanced Learner's Dictionary
[S43] Oxford flexi **£6.95**
[S44] Oxford hbk **£8.95**

PENGUIN
Penguin Pocket English Dictionary
[S45] Penguin pbk **£2.75**
The New Penguin English Dictionary
[S46] Penguin pbk **£4.95**

Anglophone Dictionaries

AMERICAN
Langenscheidt Universal Webster English
[S47] Hodder pbk **£1.75**
Longman Dictionary of American English
[S48] Longman hbk **£8.60**
[S49] Longman pbk **£6.00**
Oxford American Dictionary
[S50] Oxford hbk **£16.95**
Oxford Paperback American Dictionary
[S51] Oxford pbk **£4.95**
Webster's New World Dictionary NEW
A serious rival to the Ninth New Collegiate Dictionary, strong on Americanism.
[S52] Simon & Sch hbk **£14.50**
[S53] Simon & Sch hbk/thumb index **£15.50**
Webster's Ninth New Collegiate Dictionary
Webster's is undoubtedly the leading authority in American dictionaries. Indeed, over the years since the Ninth New Collegiate dictionary was first published, it has established itself as a household name. Offers what many other dictionaries lack - a guide to good usage.
[S54] Longman hbk **£19.95**
[S55] Longman hbk, deluxe **£27.00**
[S56] Longman hbk/thumb index **£24.00**

AUSTRALIAN
The Australian Concise Oxford Dictionary
[S57] Oxford hbk **£11.95**
The Australian Little Oxford Dictionary
[S58] Oxford pbk **£4.95**
The Australian National Dictionary NEW
A comprehensive record of Australia's distinctive variations on the English language - the fruit of ten years' work.
[S59] Oxford hbk **£50.00**
The Australian Oxford Minidictionary
[S60] Oxford pbk **£2.95**

SOUTH AFRICAN
A Dictionary of South African English
[S61] Oxford **£12.95**
The South African Pocket Oxford Dictionary
[S62] Oxford **£8.95**

Synonym Dictionaries & Thesauri

Bloomsbury Crossword Solver
Invaluable list of more than 3,000 unusual words.
[S63] Bloomsbury pbk **£6.99**

Chambers 20th Century Thesaurus
A thesaurus for day-to-day use by everyone who requires to extend and vary their vocabulary. 18,000 references with over 350,000 synonyms and antonyms. Unlike Roget, this thesaurus is arranged alphabetically like an ordinary dictionary, which makes it very convenient and easy to use. Its range of synonyms is less slangy and more literate than the Collins equivalent.
[S64] Chambers hbk **£8.95**

Collins Thesaurus
[S65] Collins hbk **£8.50**
[S66] Collins pbk **£2.95**
New Collins Thesaurus
[S67] Collins hbk **£8.95**
Gem Thesaurus
[S68] Collins hbk **£1.75**

Longman Synonym Dictionary
The most comprehensive British synonym dictionary in print with 17,000 headwords and over one million synonyms.
[S69] Longman hbk **£16.95**
Longman Top Pocket Thesaurus
[S70] Longman pbk **£1.95**

Modern Guide to Synonyms and Related Words
Unlike most other synonym dictionaries this handy paperback provides useful examples of the ways in which synonyms may be used. Antonyms are included as well.
[S71] Penguin pbk **£5.95**

Pan Dictionary of Synonyms & Antonyms
[S72] Pan pbk **£2.95**

Penguin Word Master Dictionary
Incorporates a thesaurus.
[S73] Penguin pbk **£4.95**

Roget's Thesaurus
This idiosyncratically designed synonym dictionary, originally compiled in 1805 by Romilly Roget, has become a classic and an indispensable companion for all writers, editors, speakers, translators and lovers of the English language. A new, revised edition appeared recently.
[S74] Longman hbk **£12.95**
[S75] Longman hbk, deluxe **£20.00**
[S76] Penguin pbk **£3.95**
[S77] Sphere pbk **£3.50**
Longman Pocket Roget's Thesaurus
[S78] Longman pbk **£4.95**
Roget's Thesaurus (Facsimile of the 1st Edition)
This luxury facsimile edition printed on acid-free paper and bound in real cloth provides a fascinating insight into Roget's achievement.
[S79] Bloomsbury hbk **£19.95**

The New Nuttall Dictionary of Synonyms & Antonyms
[S80] Viking hbk **£10.95**

COLMAN, JAMES
Collins Crossword Dictionary NEW
Contains all the usual listings of meanings plus information on the crossword context, helping the solver compete on more equal terms with the compiler.
[S81] Collins hbk **£13.95**
The Complete Guide to Cryptic Crosswords NEW
A comprehensive guide to the lateral thinking needed to understand cryptic clues, this guide gives an invaluable insight into the interpretation of clues and how to break down a clue into various components, for both the novice and the expert.
[S82] Collins pbk **£8.95**

ENRIGHT, D.J.
Fair of Speech: The Uses of Euphemism
Euphemisms in sex, death, the media, law, medicine and much more by a distinguished contemporary poet.
[S83] Oxford hbk **£9.95**
[S84] Oxford pbk **£4.95**

Usage & Grammar

Chambers Concise Usage Dictionary
Useful explanations of common difficulties in grammar, spelling and usage.
[S85] Chambers pbk **£4.50**
Chambers Pocket Guide to Phrasal Verbs
[S86] Chambers pbk **£2.50**
Chambers Spell Well
[S87] Chambers hbk **£2.95**

Gem Dictionary of English Usage
[S88] Collins pbk **£2.25**
Gem Dictionary of Spelling and Word Division
[S89] Collins pbk **£1.95**

Grammar and Vocabulary Practice
[S90] Collins pbk **£3.25**
Grammar for Everyday Use
[S91] Collins pbk **£4.95**

Longman Dictionary of Phrasal Verbs
[S92] Longman hbk **£10.95**

Oxford Spelling Dictionary
[S93] Oxford hbk **£9.95**
Oxford Minidictionary of Spelling
[S94] Oxford flexi **£1.95**

BODMER, FREDERICK
The Loom of Language
Interesting classic of linguistic study, *The Loom of Language* (also known as *A Guide to Foreign Languages for the Home Student*) will interest anyone who enjoys exploring the fascinating variety of language development.
[S95] Merlin hbk **£12.50**
[S96] Merlin pbk **£7.95**

BURCHFIELD, R.W.
The English Language
Following his momentous job of editing the Supplements to the *Oxford English Dictionary*, Dr Burchfield has produced a short and illuminating guide to the English language. It will be recommended reading for many years.
[S97] Oxford hbk **£10.95**
[S98] Oxford pbk **£3.95**
The Oxford Guide to the English Language
A well-designed and clearly laid out general reference guide for everyone who needs simple and direct guidance for the formation and use of English words. Examines spelling, pronunciation, meanings and grammar.
[S99] Oxford hbk **£16.95**
[S100] Oxford pbk **£3.95**

CAREY, G.V.
Mind the Stop
[S101] Penguin pbk **£2.25**

CLARK, JOHN O.E.
Word Perfect: A Dictionary of English Usage
[S102] Harrap flexi **£6.95**
[S103] Harrap hbk **£8.95**

CRYSTAL, DAVID
Cambridge Encyclopaedia of Language
The only one of its kind - an outstanding synthesis of language and its development. Comprehensive, richly illustrated, lively and accessible.
[S104] Cambridge hbk **£25.00**

DEAR, I.C.B.
Oxford English: A Guide to the Language
Excellent guide to correct written and spoken English and an accessible introduction to the English language in all its aspects.
[S105] Oxford hbk **£14.95**

FORSTER, KLAUS
Pronouncing Dictionary of English Place-Names
[S106] Routledge hbk **£14.95**

FOWLER, H.W.
Dictionary of Modern English Usage
A classic and standard reference tool.
[S107] Oxford hbk **£10.95**
[S108] Oxford pbk **£4.95**

FOWLER, H.W. & FOWLER, F.G.
The King's English (3rd Edition)
[S109] Oxford hbk **£9.50**
[S110] Oxford pbk **£4.95**

GOWERS, SIR ERNEST
Complete Plain Words
A classic attempt to reduce obfuscation in language.
[S111] Penguin pbk **£3.95**

GREENBAUM, SIDNEY & WHITCUT, JANET
Longman Guide to English Usage
[S112] Longman hbk **£12.50**

JONES & GIMSON
Everyman's English Pronouncing Dictionary
For many years a standard textbook for English pronunciation. In concentrating on difficult or unusual words it is a useful guide for the general reader, as well as those learning English.
[S113] Dent hbk **£6.95**

KATZNER, KENNETH
Languages of the World (Revised Edition)
[S114] Routledge pbk **£5.95**

LEECH, GEOFFREY
Semantics
Explores the ways in which the meanings of words change and develop.
[S115] Penguin pbk **£6.95**

MANSER, MARTIN H. (ED)
Bloomsbury Good Word Guide
How properly to use punctuation, spelling, grammar, and jargon. Accessible, authoritative and up-to-date.
[S116] Bloomsbury pbk **£5.99**

MCCRUM; CRAN & MCNEIL
The Story of English
Designed to accompany a highly successful television series, *The Story of English* is in itself an absorbing history of the English language with excellent chapters on the versions of English spoken in different parts of the world.
[S117] Faber pbk **£9.95**

O'CONNOR, J.D.
Phonetics
[S118] Penguin pbk **£5.95**

ONIONS, C.T.
A Modern English Syntax
[S119] Routledge pbk **£6.95**

PALMER, F.R.
Grammar
[S120] Penguin pbk **£2.95**

The English Verb
[S121] Longman pbk **£7.95**

PARTRIDGE, ERIC
Usage and Abusage: A Guide to Good English
The classic work from the Grand Old Man of English linguists.
[S122] H Hamilton hbk **£9.95**
[S123] Penguin pbk **£4.95**

QUIRK, SIR RANDOLPH
Grammar of Contemporary English
A shorter book than the *Comprehensive Grammar* and adequate for all but the dedicated specialist.
[S124] Longman hbk **£29.00**

QUIRK; GREENBAUM; LEECH & SVARTVIK
A Comprehensive Grammar of the English Language
The largest, most definitive grammar of the language ever written; produced after 20 years of collaborative work.
[S125] Longman hbk **£49.50**
[S126] Longman hbk, deluxe **£60.00**

RAMSARAN, SUSAN
An Introduction to the Pronunciation of English
[S127] Arnold pbk **£7.95**

READER'S DIGEST
Family Word Finder
Packed with synonyms, antonyms, sample sentences and spelling tips. A good family reference guide to English for all of us who have forgotten everything we ever learnt about grammar, syntax, synonyms, antonyms etc.
[S128] Hodder hbk **£12.95**
The Right Word at the Right Time
A recent addition to the aids to correct English from a house that has specialised in providing clear, accessible and authoritative guides for the general reader.
[S129] Hodder hbk **£13.95**

ROOM, ADRIAN
Dictionary of Changes in Meaning
[S130] Routledge hbk **£14.95**
Dictionary of Confusing Words & Meanings
[S131] Routledge pbk **£6.95**
Dictionary of Contrasting Pairs
Opposing concepts and words used in everyday life explained and clarified.
[S132] Routledge hbk **£14.95**
Room's Dictionary of Distinguishables
[S133] Routledge pbk **£7.95**

SWAN, MICHAEL
Practical English Usage
A handy reference book for correct usage of the English language.
[S134] Oxford pbk **£5.00**

THOMPSON
Practical English Grammar
[S135] Oxford pbk **£4.85**

URDANG, LAURENCE
Dictionary of Differences   **NEW**
Differences between difficult words in everyday use such as 'amoral/immoral', 'among/amongst/between'. Unique in that it reflects important historical events and the differences between prevailing attitudes of the time.
[S136] Bloomsbury pbk **£6.99**

WALDHORN, S. & ZEIGER, A.
English Made Simple
[S137] Heinemann pbk **£3.95**

WEINER, E.S.C.
Oxford Guide to English Usage
[S138] Oxford hbk **£8.95**
Oxford Miniguide to English Usage
[S139] Oxford pbk **£1.95**

WILEMAN, B. & WILEMAN, R.
Word Spell: A Spelling Dictionary
Gives in a good layout the correct spellings of commonly mis-spelt words. Contains useful hints to help readers improve their writing.
[S140] Harrap hbk **£8.95**

YULE, HENRY & BURNELL, A.C.
Hobson-Jobson
Indian English. Preface by Anthony Burgess.
[S141] Routledge hbk **£18.95**

Specialized Dictionaries

General

Bernstein's Reverse Dictionary
[S143] Routledge pbk **£6.95**

Brewer's Dictionary of Phrase & Fable
A riveting guide to the meaning and origins of many of the idioms and catchphrases, nicknames, clichés, classical and modern references which are often baffling. The place to look when you want to discover the correct word for an assemblage of nightingales (a watch), the symbolism of pub names or which of the muses was Terpsichore.
[S144] Cassell hbk **£14.95**

Dictionary of Jargon
[S145] Routledge hbk **£25.00**

Dictionary of Literary Terms
[S146] Penguin pbk **£7.50**

Longman Register of New Words
[S147] Longman **£10.95**
[S148] Longman pbk **£5.95**

DUNKLING, LESLIE
A Dictionary of Days
All Saints' Day, Twelfth Night, Mother's Day and many more not commonly found in dictionaries.
[S149] Routledge hbk **£14.95**

EHRLICH, EUGENE
Le Mot Juste: The Penguin Dictionary of Foreign Terms and Phrases
From Afrikaans to Zulu, more than 15,000 words are defined. Entertaining and educational, with the benefit of an excellent index.
[S150] Viking hbk **£15.95**

MACDONALD, JAMES
Dictionary of Obscenity, Taboo and Euphemisms
A fascinating study of why certain words are considered unsuitable in 'polite' conversation, and an indication of their origins.
[S151] Sphere pbk **£3.99**

MANSER, MARTIN
Dictionary of Eponyms
Listing the names of people after whom something is believed to be named, eg. Atlas, Biro, Cardigan, Wellingtons etc.
[S152] Sphere pbk **£4.99**

MILLER, STUART
The Concise Dictionary of Acronyms and Initialisms **NEW**
[S153] Facts on File **£18.95**

PARTRIDGE, ERIC
A Dictionary of Catch Phrases
[S154] Routledge hbk **£14.95**
[S155] Routledge pbk **£8.95**

PAXTON
Everyman's Dictionary of Abbreviations
[S156] Dent hbk **£10.95**

RHEINGOLD, HOWARD
They Have a Word for It
Foreign words and phrases for which there are no equivalents in English.
[S157] Severn House pbk **£5.95**

Etymology

Encyclopaedia of Word Origins
Fascinating and illuminating exploration of the roots of words we use everyday.
[S158] Routledge hbk **£25.00**

Oxford Dictionary of English Etymology
This is arguably the most complete and reliable etymological dictionary published in the English Language, drawing on the scholarship of the *Oxford English Dictionary*. Each word is accompanied by its pronunciation, present-day meaning, date of its first recorded use in English, its earliest form in written English and the chronology of the development of its sense(s). The total number of main entries is 24,000.
[S159] Oxford hbk **£27.50**
Concise Oxford Dictionary of English Etymology
[S160] Oxford hbk **£13.95**

ROOM, ADRIAN
A Dictionary of True Etymologies
[S161] Routledge hbk **£11.95**

Name Dictionaries

BBC Pronouncing Dictionary of British Names
[S162] BBC hbk **£7.95**

Gem Dictionary of First Names
[S163] Collins pbk **£1.95**

DUNKLING, LESLIE
Book of Names
[S164] Guinness pbk **£5.95**

GLENNON, JAMES
4,001 Babies' Names & Their Meanings
[S165] Hale hbk **£1.75**

HANKS, PATRICK & HODGES, FLAVIA
Oxford Minidictionary of First Names
[S166] Oxford flexi **£2.25**

JOHNSON, C. & SLEIGH, L.
Names for Boys & Girls
[S167] Pan pbk **£2.95**

PINE, L.G.
A Dictionary of Nicknames
[S168] Routledge hbk **£9.95**

REANEY, P.H.
A Dictionary of British Surnames
[S169] Routledge hbk **£22.50**
The Origin of English Place-Names
[S170] Routledge hbk **£13.95**
[S171] Routledge pbk **£4.95**
The Origin of English Surnames
[S172] Routledge hbk **£19.95**
[S173] Routledge pbk **£8.95**

ROOM, ADRIAN
Dictionary of Irish Place-Names
[S174] Appletree P pbk **£4.95**
Dictionary of Place-Names in the British Isles
A fascinating book by the acknowledged expert on British place-names. This is Room's most comprehensive work, with 4,000-plus entries uncovering a wealth of historical, linguistic and geographical information.
[S175] Bloomsbury hbk **£15.95**
[S176] Bloomsbury pbk **£7.99**
Dictionary of Trade Name Origins (2nd Edition)
[S177] Routledge hbk **£9.95**
Dictionary of World Place-Names Derived from British Names
[S178] Routledge hbk **£18.95**
Place-Name Changes Since 1900
[S179] Routledge hbk **£11.95**

WITHYCOMBE, ELIZABETH G.
Oxford Dictionary of English Christian Names
[S180] Oxford pbk **£4.95**

Quotations & Proverbs

Bloomsbury Dictionary of Quotations
Not as comprehensive as the *Oxford Dictionary of Quotations* but well-arranged and highly entertaining. A dictionary of quotations for the 1980s - contemporary, authoritative and thought-provoking.
[S181] Bloomsbury hbk **£14.95**

Bloomsbury Thematic Dictionary of Quotations
Entries are arranged by category or subject with a key word index. Cross-referencing and biographical listings are also included. Especially suited to public speakers, ideal for reference or browsing. Some 700 categories, ranging from money to sex, pollution, music and beyond.
[S182] Bloomsbury hbk **£14.95**

English Proverbs Explained
Limited number of entries but the meaning of every entry is clearly explained.
[S183] Pan pbk **£5.95**

Faber Book of Anecdotes
For those in need of wit, here is a treasure trove: from Aaron to Ziegfeld and everyone who was anyone. Some of the world's best stories are included.
[S184] Faber hbk **£17.50**

Gem Dictionary of Quotations
[S185] Collins pbk **£1.95**

International Thesaurus of Quotations
Unusual in being arranged by subject rather than author. Although it is thematically interesting, it draws rather heavily on a relatively small group of authors.
[S186] Penguin pbk **£7.95**

Oxford Dictionary of Proverbs
Largest number of proverbs in any single volume proverb dictionary.
[S187] Oxford hbk **£19.50**
Concise Oxford Dictionary of Proverbs
[S188] Oxford pbk **£4.95**

Oxford Dictionary of Quotations
The largest and most authoritative Quotation Dictionary, recently re-edited in a new edition.
[S189] Oxford hbk **£17.50**
[S190] Oxford leather **£29.50**
Concise Oxford Dictionary of Quotations
[S191] Oxford hbk **£10.95**
[S192] Oxford pbk **£4.95**

Oxford Minidictionary of Quotations
[S193] Oxford pbk **£1.95**

Routledge Dictionary of Quotations
Arranged by topic from Absence to Zed.
[S194] Routledge hbk **£12.95**

COHEN, J.M. & M.J.
Dictionary of Modern Quotations
[S195] Penguin pbk **£4.95**
Penguin Dictionary of Quotations
[S196] Penguin pbk **£4.95**

GROSS, JOHN (ED)
The Oxford Book of Aphorisms
[S199] Oxford pbk **£4.95**

O'KILL, BRIAN
Exit Lines: Last Words of the Famous and Infamous
[S200] Longman hbk **£10.95**

YAPP, PETER (ED)
Traveller's Dictionary of Quotation: Who Said What, about Where?
[S201] Routledge hbk **£30.00**
[S202] Routledge pbk **£11.95**

Rhyming Dictionaries

Poet's Manual and Rhyming Dictionary
The best rhyming dictionary currently available, with a superb guide to poetry metre and scansion in the first half for anyone who wants to learn how to write verse. It includes a wealth of slang and colloquial words, as well as many foreign expressions that have been accepted into the English language.
[S203] Thames & H pbk **£4.50**

Rhyming Dictionary
Whereas the Thames & Hudson rhyming dictionary (see above) is arranged by vowel sounds, this is arranged like an ordinary dictionary, A - Z. An unpretentious, useful book which includes a comprehensive range of rhymes.
[S204] Penguin hbk **£5.95**

ESPY, WILLARD R. (ED)
Words to Rhyme With
[S205] Macmillan hbk **£20.00**

WALKER, J.
Rhyming Dictionary of the English Language
[S206] Routledge hbk **£11.75**

Slang & Idiom

Chambers Idioms
A collection of idiomatic expressions giving their meanings in simple English. Includes sentences which show how idioms are used and information about their origins.
[S207] Chambers pbk **£4.50**

Dictionary of American Slang
[S208] Macmillan hbk **£16.95**

Longman Dictionary of English Idioms
[S209] Longman hbk **£10.95**

Word Wise: A Dictionary of English Idioms
A thorough examination into idioms and their correct usage for better English.
[S210] Harrap hbk **£8.95**
[S211] Harrap pbk **£6.95**

COWIE, A.P. & MACKIN, R.
Dictionary of Current Idiomatic English Vol 1: Verbs with Prepositions & Participles
[S212] Oxford hbk **£9.30**
[S213] Oxford pbk **£4.85**
Vol 2: Phrase, Clause & Sentence Idioms
[S214] Oxford hbk **£14.60**
[S215] Oxford pbk **£7.00**

GREEN, JONATHON
Concise Dictionary of English Slang
[S216] Hodder hbk **£8.95**
[S217] Hodder pbk **£4.95**
Dictionary of Contemporary Slang
[S218] Pan pbk **£3.95**
The Slang Thesaurus
[S219] H Hamilton hbk **£12.95**
[S220] Penguin pbk **£9.99**

LEWIN, ALBERT & ESTHER
The Thesaurus of Slang & Colloquialisms
[S221] Facts on File hbk **£25.00**

MAJOR, CLARENCE
Black Slang: A Dictionary of Afro-American Talk
[S222] Routledge pbk **£5.95**

PARTRIDGE, ERIC
A Dictionary of Clichés
[S223] Routledge pbk **£5.95**
A Dictionary of Slang & Unconventional English
The definitive slang dictionary.
[S224] Routledge hbk **£47.50**
Dictionary of Historical Slang
[S225] Penguin pbk **£7.95**
Smaller Slang Dictionary
[S226] Routledge pbk **£6.95**
The Routledge Dictionary of Historical Slang
[S227] Routledge hbk **£27.50**

Foreign Language Dictionaries & Courses

Arranged alphabetically by language. In this very competitive field, quality does roughly correlate to price; however, most dictionaries represent very good value for money, as do the language courses listed below.

Language Courses on Cassette

The modern obsession with self-study has produced a boom in this area of the market, with a bewildering variety of courses offered to the public. We hope that the descriptions provided will explain some of the important differences between the series.

HUGO 'IN THREE MONTHS'
Well established, highly regarded courses in all the major European languages: **Dutch**, **French**, **German**, **Italian**, **Russian**, **Spanish**, **Swedish** and **Japanese**. They consist of a book and four cassettes retailing at £28.75 and are suitable for the serious amateur.

PAN 'BREAKTHROUGH'
These are complete self-study courses developed for beginners who want a practical language course. They retail at £25.00 and consist of 3 cassettes and book. A *Further* series for the more advanced student is also available and costs £29.95. Available in **French**, **German**, **Italian**, **Spanish** and **Greek**.

BBC
The BBC has developed courses in modern European languages which are suitable for both self-study and evening classes, enjoying the advantage of the accompanying TV or radio series. They appear in the listings below under the appropriate languages.

The BBC also produce the *Get By In...* series, consisting of a short booklet, available either separately (at £2.95), or in a pack with 1 or 2 cassettes (at £7.95), specifically tailored to the practical needs of the traveller. Available for: **Arabic**, **Chinese**, **French**, **German**, **Greek**, **Italian**, **Japanese**, **Portuguese**, **Spanish** and **Turkish**.

BERLITZ 'FOR TRAVELLERS'
Excellent inexpensive phrase books and dictionaries in many languages.
Phrase Books available for: **Arabic, Chinese, Danish, Dutch, Finnish, French, German, Greek, Hebrew, Hungarian, Italian, Japanese, Korean, Latin American Spanish, Norwegian, Polish, Portuguese, Russian, Serbo-Croat, Spanish, Swahili, Swedish** and **Turkish**.
Pocket Dictionaries available for: **Danish, Dutch, Finnish, French, German, Italian, Norwegian, Portuguese**.
Both phrase books and dictionaries are priced at £2.25 each. There are accompanying tapes to many of the Phrasebooks: details on request.

HEINEMANN 'MADE SIMPLE'
Despite a limited selection (**French**, **German**, **Russian**, **Spanish** and **Italian**), both the books

and the cassettes are superb. Each book is accompanied by two cassette recordings, either of which may be purchased separately. The books retail at £5.95; the cassettes at £15.00.

HODDER 'TEACH YOURSELF'
Still the most popular of layman's guides and now extending to 37 languages, including some of the more unusual ones such as Esperanto, Hausa, Icelandic, Indonesian, Sanskrit, Swahili and Yoruba, where they are the only simple guides readily available. Prices range from £3.50 to £7.00. Cassette recordings are available only for the major languages. Further information on this series can be supplied on request.

MACMILLAN 'MASTERING'
A very good self-contained course for both individual and classroom study. Single cassettes are available to accompany the four titles: **French**, **German**, **Spanish** and **Italian**. For **French** and **Spanish**, a second, more advanced volume is available. The books are priced at £3.95 each; the cassettes at £7.95.

ROUTLEDGE 'COLLOQUIAL'
An extremely useful series, providing the reader with a simple and concise working knowledge of a foreign language. The books introduce the main grammatical points and provide a practical vocabulary to enable the beginner to speak the language as it is spoken by the people of the country of its origin. Prices range from £4.50 to £7.95; cassettes (available only in some languages) from £6.00 to £7.00. Courses are available in: **Arabic** (Gulf & Saudi Arabia; Egypt), **Chinese**, **Czech**, **Dutch**, **French**, **German**, **Greek**, **Hungarian**, **Italian**, **Japanese**, **Persian**, **Polish**, **Portuguese**, **Russian**, **Serbo-Croat**, **Spanish** and **Turkish**.

Major Languages A - Z

Arabic

Advanced Learner's Arabic-English Dictionary
[S229] Llewellyn pbk **£32.95**

Arabic for English Speaking Students
[S230] Llewellyn pbk **£12.50**

Course in Colloquial Arabic
[S231] Llewellyn hbk **£10.50**
Further Course in Colloquial Arabic
[S232] Llewellyn hbk **£12.50**

Dictionary of Modern Written Arabic
[S233] Harrap pbk **£11.95**

Oxford English-Arabic Dictionary of Current Usage
[S234] Oxford hbk **£27.50**
Concise Oxford English-Arabic Dictionary of Current Usage
[S235] Oxford hbk **£8.95**

Wortabet's Pocket Dictionary English-Arabic/Arabic-English
[S236] Llewellyn pbk **£8.50**

Chinese

Concise English-Chinese/Chinese-English Dictionary
An excellent pocket-size dictionary, probably the best Chinese dictionary. Massive number of entries despite its size.
[S237] Oxford pbk **£5.95**

BRUCE, R.
Teach Yourself Cantonese
[S238] Hodder pbk **£3.95**

FAZZIOLI, EDOARDO
Understanding Chinese Characters
The history and meaning of the most common Chinese characters elucidated.
[S239] Collins hbk **£11.95**

Dutch

Cassell's Standard Dutch Dictionary
This excellent Cassell's dictionary is at the top end of the range of Dutch dictionaries.
[S240] Cassell hbk **£24.00**

Dutch Phrase Book
[S241] Collins pbk **£1.50**

Oxford-Duden Pictorial Dutch & English Dictionary
[S242] Oxford hbk **£19.95**

Traveller's Dutch
[S243] Pan pbk **£1.50**

RENIER, F.G.
Dutch Dictionary: Dutch-English/English-Dutch
[S244] Routledge pbk **£6.95**

French

A - Z by publisher. There is a wide range of French dictionaries, as befits the language taught most frequently in English schools. The field is dominated by the excellent series from Collins and Harrap.

BBC LANGUAGE COURSES
1: A Vous La France
[S245] BBC 2 cassettes **£9.95**
[S246] BBC pbk **£6.95**
2: France Extra
[S247] BBC 3 cassettes **£14.95**
[S248] BBC pbk **£7.95**
3: Franc-Parler
[S249] BBC 2 cassettes **£9.95**
[S250] BBC pbk **£5.95**

COLLINS
The unquestioned leader in this field.
Collins-Robert French Dictionary: French-English/English-French
Arguably the best one-volume French dictionary available and certainly the most popular.
[S251] Collins hbk **£14.95**
[S252] Collins hbk/thumb index **£16.50**
Collins-Robert Concise French Dictionary
[S253] Collins hbk **£8.50**

Collins-Robert Paperback French Dictionary
[S254] Collins pbk **£3.50**
French Gem Dictionary
[S255] Collins pbk **£1.95**
French Gem Grammar
[S256] Collins pbk **£1.95**
French Gem Verb Tables
[S257] Collins pbk **£1.95**
French Pocket Dictionary
[S258] Collins hbk **£3.50**
French Traveller's Dictionary & Phrase Book
[S259] Collins pbk **£2.95**
Le Micro Robert-Dictionnaire du Français Primordial
[S260] Collins hbk **£10.50**
Le Petit Robert: Vol 1
[S261] Collins hbk **£35.00**
Le Petit Robert: Vol 2 Dictionnaire des Noms Propres
[S262] Collins hbk **£42.50**

EUROPEAN SCHOOLBOOKS
Lexis: Larousse de la Langue Française
Well-known French-French dictionary.
[S263] European Schoolbooks hbk **£23.95**

HARRAP
At the top of the range, Harrap's *Standard French/English Dictionary* in four volumes is unsurpassed in accuracy and authority, and is essential for serious students. In addition, Harrap have used their experience in this field to produce several other quality dictionaries.
Harrap's Concise French & English Dictionary (New Edition)
[S264] Harrap flexi **£6.95**
[S265] Harrap hbk **£8.95**
Harrap's French & English Business Dictionary
[S266] Harrap hbk **£24.95**
Harrap's French & English Science Dictionary
[S267] Harrap hbk **£17.50**
Harrap's French & English Slang Dictionary
[S268] Harrap pbk **£9.95**
Harrap's French Visual Dictionary
Invaluable for those who know what something looks like but not what it is called and vice-versa. Illustrations galore with entries in two colours to differentiate between French and English texts. Also indicates variations in usage of English and American English, as well as European and Canadian French.
[S269] Harrap hbk **£14.95**
Harrap's Mini French & English Dictionary
[S270] Harrap flexi **£1.95**
Harrap's Paperback French & English Dictionary
[S271] Harrap pbk **£2.95**
Harrap's Pocket French & English Dictionary
[S272] Harrap hbk **£3.50**
Harrap's Shorter French & English Dictionary
[S273] Harrap hbk **£13.95**
STANDARD FRENCH DICTIONARY
Vol 1: French-English: A - I
[S274] Harrap hbk **£25.00**
Vol 2: French-English: J - Z
[S275] Harrap hbk **£25.00**
Vol 3: English-French: A - K
[S276] Harrap hbk **£25.00**
Vol 4: English-French: L - Z
[S277] Harrap hbk **£25.00**

HODDER
French for Adults
[S278] Hodder pbk **£4.95**
Let's Talk French
[S279] Hodder pbk **£2.75**
Living French
[S280] Hodder pbk **£3.50**

OXFORD
Concise Oxford French Dictionary: French-English/English-French
(2nd Edition)
[S281] Oxford flexi **£7.50**
[S282] Oxford hbk **£11.95**
JANES, MICHAEL
Oxford French Minidictionary
[S283] Oxford flexi **£1.95**
Oxford Paperback French Dictionary
[S284] Oxford pbk **£3.95**
Oxford-Duden Pictorial French-English Dictionary
[S285] Oxford flexi **£8.95**
[S286] Oxford hbk **£19.50**

PAN
BESWICK, CHRIS
Companion French Grammar
[S287] Pan pbk **£2.50**

ROUTLEDGE
KETTRIDGE, J.O. (REVISED BY A.J. STRAHAN)
Handbook of Commercial French
Includes a section on the conventions of French business correspondence, and a selection of model letters and telexes on a whole range of subjects.
[S288] Routledge hbk **£18.95**
[S289] Routledge pbk **£6.95**

German

Arranged A - Z by publisher. BBC Publications offer excellent self-study courses, while the superb range from Collins and Hodder/Langenscheidt dominate the field as a whole.

BBC LANGUAGE COURSES
1: Deutsch Direkt
[S290] BBC 3 cassettes **£14.95**
[S291] BBC pbk **£6.95**
2: Deutsch Express
[S292] BBC 3 cassettes **£14.95**
[S293] BBC pbk **£7.95**
3: Ganz Spontan!
[S294] BBC 2 cassettes **£9.95**
[S295] BBC pbk **£8.95**

CAMBRIDGE
The Cambridge Eichborn German Dictionary
Ideal for the business and administrative fields.
[S296] Cambridge hbk **£22.50**

COLLINS
5,000 German Words
[S297] Collins pbk **£1.95**
Collins German Dictionary: German-English/English-German
Certainly one of the most highly rated single-volume German dictionaries. Competes with the equivalent Langenscheidt concise volume.
[S298] Collins hbk **£14.95**
[S399] Collins hbk/thumb index **£16.50**
Collins Concise German Dictionary
[S300] Collins hbk **£8.50**
Gem German Verb Tables
[S301] Collins pbk **£1.95**

German Gem Dictionary
[S302] Collins pbk £1.95
German Gem Grammar
[S303] Collins pbk £1.75
German Pocket Dictionary
[S304] Collins pbk £3.95
COLLINS-KLETT GERMAN DICTIONARY
Vol 1: German/English
[S305] Collins hbk £8.95
Vol 2: English/German
[S306] Collins hbk £8.95

HODDER
PAXTON, N.
German for Adults
[S307] Hodder pbk £4.95
German for Business
[S308] Hodder pbk £3.95
Let's Talk German
[S309] Hodder pbk £5.95
Living German
[S310] Hodder pbk £3.50

LANGENSCHEIDT
New Concise German-English/English-German
[S311] Hodder hbk £12.95
Pocket German-English/English-German
[S312] Hodder pbk £6.95
Shorter German-English/English-German
[S313] Hodder pbk £4.50
Standard German-English/English-German
[S314] Hodder hbk £7.95
Universal German-English/English-German
[S315] Hodder pbk £1.75
LANGENSCHEIDT MURET-SANDERS
ENCYCLOPAEDIC DICTIONARY
The most comprehensive German dictionary available, it has an excellent reputation, but at nearly £250.00 it is perhaps too large and expensive for the needs of most students. The condensed version, in two volumes, is more manageable.
Condensed English-German
[S316] Hodder hbk £42.50
Condensed German-English
[S317] Hodder hbk £42.50
English-German: A - M
[S318] Hodder hbk £59.50
English-German: N - Z
[S319] Hodder hbk £59.50
German-English: A - K
[S320] Hodder hbk £59.50
German-English: L - Z
[S321] Hodder hbk £59.50

OXFORD
Oxford-Duden Pictorial German-English Dictionary
[S322] Oxford flexi £8.95
[S323] Oxford hbk £19.50
Pocket Oxford German Dictionary: German-English/English-German
[S324] Oxford flexi £3.95

ROUTLEDGE
WICHMANN, K.
German Dictionary: German-English/English-German
[S325] Routledge hbk £4.95

Greek

Greek
[S326] Longman hbk £8.95

Greek Language & People
[S327] BBC 2 cassettes £9.95
[S328] BBC pbk £8.95

Greek Phrase Book
[S329] Collins pbk £1.50

Greek Pocket Dictionary
[S330] Collins pbk £3.95

Langenscheidt Pocket Greek (Classical)/English
[S331] Hodder hbk £4.95

LIDDELL, H.G. & SCOTT, R.A.
A Greek Lexicon (9th Edition)
The standard dictionary of classical Greek, well-established and revised.
[S332] Oxford hbk £65.00

PRING, J.T.
Oxford Dictionary of Modern Greek
[S333] Oxford flexi £6.95
[S334] Oxford hbk £10.95

Italian

Arranged A - Z by publisher. Again, BBC publications offer a wide range of courses both for beginners and advanced learners alike. Among the dictionaries, the four-volume Sansoni-Harrap is definitive, while Collins continue to dominate the single-volume market.

BBC LANGUAGE COURSES
1: Buongiorno Italia
[S335] BBC 3 cassettes £14.95
[S336] BBC pbk £6.95
2: L'Italia dal Vivo
[S337] BBC 3 cassettes £14.95
[S338] BBC pbk £7.95

CAMBRIDGE
Cambridge Italian Dictionary Vol 1: Italian-English
[S339] Cambridge hbk £55.00
Cambridge Italian Dictionary Vol 2: English-Italian
[S340] Cambridge hbk £55.00
Cambridge Concise Italian Dictionary
[S341] Cambridge hbk £22.50
Cambridge Signorelli Italian-English/English-Italian Dictionary
[S342] Cambridge hbk £27.50

COLLINS
Collins-Sansoni Italian Dictionary: English-Italian/Italian-English
[S343] Collins hbk £16.95
Collins Concise Italian Dictionary: Italian-English/English-Italian
[S344] Collins hbk £8.95
Italian Gem Dictionary
[S345] Collins pbk £1.95
Italian Pocket Dictionary
[S346] Collins pbk £3.95

HARRAP
Harrap's Pocket Italian & English Dictionary
[S347] Harrap hbk £6.50
SANSONI-HARRAP ENGLISH/ITALIAN DICTIONARY
English-Italian: A - L
[S348] Harrap hbk £35.00
English-Italian: M - Z
[S349] Harrap hbk £35.00

Italian-English: A - L
[S350] Harrap hbk £35.00
Italian-English: M - Z
[S351] Harrap hbk £35.00

HODDER
Italian for Adults
[S352] Hodder pbk £4.95
Let's Talk Italian
[S353] Hodder pbk £6.50
Living Italian
[S354] Hodder pbk £3.25

OXFORD
ANDREWS, JOYCE
English-Italian/Italian-English
[S355] Oxford hbk £24.85
Oxford Italian Minidictionary
[S356] Oxford flexi £1.95
Oxford Paperback Italian Dictionary
[S357] Oxford pbk £3.95

Japanese

Japanese Simplified Cassette Course
Part of Hugo's *In Three Months* series, the emphasis is on spoken Japanese but it takes an absolute beginner to a perfectly competent level. Good value.
[S358] Hugo cassette pack £34.50

Japanese for Beginners
[S359] Gakken hbk £18.90

Japanese for Busy People
An excellent beginner's language course.
[S360] Kodansha pbk £12.95

Japanese for Today
[S361] Gakken hbk £34.70

Oxford-Duden Pictorial English-Japanese Dictionary
[S362] Oxford hbk £19.50

THE MITSUBISHI CORPORATION
Japanese Business Language
[S363] Routledge hbk £9.95

Latin

Cassell's Standard Latin Dictionary
[S364] Cassell hbk £13.95
Cassell's Concise Latin Dictionary
[S365] Cassell hbk £5.95

Chambers Murray Latin-English Dictionary
[S366] Chambers pbk £9.95

Langenscheidt Shorter Latin-English/English-Latin
[S367] Hodder pbk £4.50

Langenscheidt Universal Latin-English/English-Latin
[S368] Hodder pbk £1.95

Latin Gem Dictionary
[S369] Collins pbk £1.95

HENDRICKS, R.A.
Latin Made Simple
[S370] Heinemann pbk £4.95

REFERENCE

LEWIS, C.T. & SHORT, C.
Latin Dictionary
[S371] Oxford hbk **£50.00**
Oxford Latin Dictionary
The most famous and distinguished Latin dictionary.
[S372] Oxford hbk **£135.00**

WOODHOUSE, S.C.
Routledge Latin-English/English-Latin Pocket Dictionary
[S373] Routledge pbk **£5.95**

Portuguese

Discovering Portuguese
[S374] BBC 2 cassettes **£9.95**
[S375] BBC pbk **£7.95**

Harrap's Portuguese-English Dictionary
[S376] Harrap hbk **£19.95**
Harrap's Pocket Portuguese-English/English-Portuguese Dictionary
[S377] Harrap hbk **£6.50**

Langenscheidt Pocket Portuguese-English/English-Portuguese
[S378] Hodder hbk **£8.95**
Langenscheidt Universal Portuguese-English/English-Portuguese
[S379] Hodder pbk **£1.95**

Portuguese Gem Dictionary
[S380] Collins pbk **£2.25**

Russian

Langenscheidt Pocket Russian-English/English-Russian
[S381] Hodder hbk **£7.95**

Oxford English-Russian Dictionary
[S382] Oxford hbk **£35.00**
Oxford Russian-English Dictionary
[S383] Oxford hbk **£35.00**
Pocket Oxford Russian Dictionary: Russian-English/English-Russian
[S384] Oxford flexi **£5.95**

Russian Gem Dictionary
[S385] Collins pbk **£2.25**

Russian Language & People
[S386] BBC 2 cassettes **£14.95**
[S387] BBC pbk **£7.95**

HARRISON, WILLIAM & FLEMING, SVETLANA LE
Russian Dictionary: Russian-English/English-Russian
[S388] Routledge pbk **£6.50**

VLASTO, A.P.A.
Russian Course
Self-contained Russian language course (one volume, no cassettes).
[S389] Penguin pbk **£4.50**

Scandinavian

Standard Danish Dictionary
Originally from the US publisher Holt Reinhart

Winston, this dictionary (as with the Standard Finnish and Swedish Dictionaries) is widely distributed by Cassells and fills a gap in the neglected area of Scandinavian languages.
[S390] Holt Reinhart hbk **£24.00**
Standard Finnish Dictionary
[S391] Holt Reinhart hbk **£18.95**
Standard Swedish Dictionary
[S392] Holt Reinhart hbk **£19.95**

Swedish in Three Months
[S393] Hugo pbk/4 cassettes **£29.95**

Traveller's Scandinavian
[S394] Pan pbk **£2.50**

HAUGEN, EINAR
Norwegian-English Dictionary
[S395] Oxford hbk **£35.00**

Spanish

Arranged A-Z by publisher. With no multi-volume Spanish dictionary currently available, the best single volume dictionaries are the *Collins Spanish Dictionary* and the *Harraps Vox Shorter Spanish-English Dictionary*.

BBC LANGUAGE COURSES
1: Digame
[S396] BBC 3 cassettes **£14.95**
[S397] BBC pbk **£6.95**
2: Por Aqui
[S398] BBC 3 cassettes **£14.95**
[S399] BBC pbk **£6.95**
A: España Viva
[S400] BBC 2 cassettes **£9.95**
[S401] BBC pbk **£6.95**
B: Paso Doble   **NEW**
[S402] BBC 2 cassettes **£9.95**
[S403] BBC pbk **£6.95**

COLLINS
Collins Spanish Dictionary: Spanish-English/English-Spanish
[S404] Collins hbk **£13.95**
[S405] Collins hbk/thumb index **£15.50**
Collins Concise Spanish Dictionary: Spanish-English/English-Spanish
[S406] Collins hbk **£8.50**
Spanish Gem Dictionary
[S407] Collins pbk **£1.95**
Spanish Gem Grammar & Verb Tables
[S408] Collins pbk **£1.95**
Spanish Pocket Dictionary
[S409] Collins pbk **£3.95**

HARRAP
Harrap's Concise Spanish/English Dictionary
[S410] Harrap hbk **£7.95**
Harrap's Mini Pocket Spanish/English Dictionary
[S411] Harrap flexi **£1.95**
Harrap's Pocket Spanish & English Dictionary
[S412] Harrap flexi **£3.95**
Vox Shorter Spanish-English Dictionary
[S413] Harrap hbk **£25.00**

OXFORD
Oxford-Duden Pictorial Spanish-English Dictionary
[S414] Oxford flexi **£8.95**
[S415] Oxford hbk **£19.50**

Other Languages

EGYPTIAN
WALLIS, E.A. BUDGE
Egyptian Language: Easy Lessons in Egyptian Hieroglyphics
[S416] Routledge hbk **£10.50**
[S417] Routledge pbk **£5.75**

GAELIC
Gaelic embodies both Scottish/Celtic and Irish/Celtic variants of the language, although the latter has been included only recently. As a result, many still refer to Gaelic as the Scottish variant, while Irish remains Irish. As regards learning the language, there is limited choice but what is available is of a high standard.
Etymological Dictionary of the Gaelic Language
[S418] Gairm Pub pbk **£6.90**
Everyday Gaelic
[S419] Gairm Pub hbk **£3.90**
Gaelic Dictionary
Based on a 'pronouncing Gaelic dictionary' by Neil Macalpine first published in 1831, this remains the most authoritative of current Gaelic dictionaries. Part of its strength lies with its emphasis on etymology and pronunciation, but no less important is the inclusion of many words found in contemporary speech.
[S420] Aberdeen UP pbk **£9.50**
Gaelic Self-Taught
[S421] Gairm Pub hbk **£3.90**
MacLennan's Gaelic Dictionary
Includes an English-Gaelic section. First published in 1925.
[S422] Acair & Aberdeen UP hbk **£17.50**
[S423] Acair & Aberdeen UP pbk **£9.50**
The New English-Gaelic Dictionary
[S424] Gairm Pub hbk **£7.50**
[S425] Gairm Pub pbk **£5.70**

HEBREW
Langenscheidt Pocket Hebrew (Old Testament)/English
[S426] Hodder hbk **£4.95**
Modern Hebrew
[S427] Oxford hbk **£11.50**

ICELANDIC
CLEASBY, RICHARD
An Icelandic-English Dictionary
[S428] Oxford hbk **£95.00**

IRISH
English/Irish Dictionary
[S429] Virtue & Co hbk **£9.00**
Irish/English Dictionary
[S430] Virtue & Co hbk **£9.00**
Pocket Irish Dictionary
[S431] Appletree P pbk **£1.95**
Teach Yourself Irish
[S432] Hodder pbk **£2.50**
O'SIADHAIL, MICHAEL
Learning Irish
[S433] Yale UP hbk **£19.95**

KOREAN
MARTIN, SAMUEL
Korean in a Hurry
A quick approach to spoken Korean.
[S434] Tuttle pbk **£4.25**

MALAY
Malay Gem Dictionary
[S435] Collins pbk **£1.95**

PERSIAN

STEINGASS, F.
A Comprehensive Persian-English Dictionary
[S436] Routledge hbk **£40.00**

POLISH

Langenscheidt Polish-English/English-Polish
[S437] Hodder flexi **£7.95**

SCOTS

Scots Dictionary
Includes words in use from 1650. Desk size. No serious rival for the price.
[S438] Chambers hbk **£9.95**
Scots Thesaurus
[S439] Aberdeen UP hbk **£17.50**
[S440] Aberdeen UP pbk **£9.95**
The Concise Scots Dictionary
[S441] Aberdeen UP hbk **£17.50**
[S442] Aberdeen UP pbk **£9.50**
GRAHAM, WILLIAM (ED)
The Scots Word Book
Contains a substantial English-Scots section, as well as sections on Scots grammar and idiom; it should be used with caution, and in conjunction with a dictionary.
[S443] Ramsey Head hbk **£7.50**
KAY, BILLY
Scots: The Mither Tongue
The history of the development of the language: its political and cultural traumas and its condition and potential for survival today, told with enthusiasm by one of its most kenspeckle promoters, who also made the accompanying television series.
[S444] Mainstream hbk **£9.95**
[S445] Grafton pbk **£2.95**
STEVENSON, JAMES & MACLEOD, ISEABAIL
Scoor-oot: A Dictionary of Scots Words & Phrases in Current Use   **NEW**
A short dictionary designed to reflect Scots as it is still spoken today, covering the most widely-used words and expressions.
[S446] Athlone hbk **£16.95**

SERBO-CROAT

Langenscheidt Serbo-Croatian Dictionary
[S447] Hodder pbk **£1.95**

SOUTH-EAST ASIAN

MACDONELL, A.A.A.
A Practical Sanskrit Dictionary
[S448] Oxford hbk **£22.50**
ZOGRAPH, G.A.
Languages of South Asia: A Guide
[S449] Routledge pbk **£13.75**

SWAHILI

MYACHINA, E.N.
Swahili Language
[S450] Routledge pbk **£10.75**

TAGALOG

ASPILLERA, PARALUMAN
Basic Tagalog for Beginners
Official language of the Philippines.
[S451] Tuttle hbk **£12.95**

THAI

ALLISON, GORDON
Easy Thai
Excellent introduction to the Thai language.
[S452] Tuttle pbk **£4.95**
ROBERTSON, RICHARD
Practical English-Thai Dictionary
Pocket size.
[S453] Tuttle pbk **£8.25**

TIBETAN

JASCHKE, H.A.
Tibetan-English Dictionary
With a English-Tibetan Vocabulary.
[S454] Routledge hbk **£32.00**

TURKISH

Langenscheidt Standard Turkish-English/English-Turkish
[S455] Hodder hbk **£9.95**
Langenscheidt Universal Turkish-English/English-Turkish
[S456] Hodder pbk **£1.95**
Oxford English-Turkish Dictionary
[S457] Oxford hbk **£27.50**
Oxford Turkish-English Dictionary
[S458] Oxford hbk **£27.50**
Concise Oxford Turkish Dictionary: Turkish-English/English-Turkish
[S459] Oxford hbk **£19.50**

WELSH

Collins-Spurrell Welsh Dictionary
[S460] Collins hbk **£3.95**

Multilingual

A Multi-Lingual Business Handbook
[S461] Pan pbk **£3.95**

European Menu Reader
How to read the menu in 14 European languages.
[S462] Berlitz pbk **£2.95**
European Phrase Book
14 European languages incorporated in this pocket size phrasebook.
[S463] Berlitz pbk **£2.95**

Languages of Asia and the Pacific: A Traveller's Phrase Book
Covering words and phrases in 25 languages. An excellent companion given the lack of alternatives.
[S464] Angus & R pbk **£7.95**

Motorist's Phrase Book: French/German/Spanish
[S465] Collins pbk **£2.50**

Traveller's Multi-Lingual Phrase Book in 8 European languages.
[S466] Pan pbk **£2.95**

Encyclopaedias

Collins Australian Encyclopaedia
[S467] Collins hbk **£30.00**

Encyclopaedia Britannica
(15th Edition, 1986)
Britannica is not only the most expensive encyclopaedia in the English language, it is also the best. We have listed only the standard binding in 32 volumes - more elaborate and expensive ones are available on request.
[S468] Ency Britannica Int hbk **£1,240.00**

Everyman's Encyclopaedia (6th edition)
12 volumes.
[S469] Dent hbk **£250.00**

Everyman's Fact Finder
[S470] Dent hbk **£10.95**

Prehistoric cave painting (Altamira, Spain) from *Junior Pears Encyclopaedia* (Pelham Books hbk £8.95)

Guinness Book of Answers
[S471] Guinness hbk **£9.95**
Guinness Book of Records
In the last few years this has become the bible for trivia hunters throughout the world and has spawned a small industry of its own. There is in all of us a fascination with and curiosity about things greater, faster, smaller than and generally different from ourselves. Published and updated annually.
[S472] Guinness hbk **£8.95**

Hamlyn Encyclopaedic World Dictionary
[S473] Hamlyn hbk **£14.95**

Hamlyn Illustrated Encyclopaedia of Knowledge
[S474] Hamlyn hbk **£19.95**

Hutchinson Factfinder
[S475] Hutchinson hbk **£10.95**

Hutchinson Pocket Encyclopaedia
[S476] Hutchinson hbk **£5.95**

Hutchinson Twentieth Century Encyclopaedia
A major revision for the 8th edition with 25 more entries.
[S477] Hutchinson hbk **£19.95**

Junior Pears Encyclopaedia
New and completely revised edition.
[S478] Pelham hbk **£8.95**

Macmillan Children's Encyclopaedia
[S479] Macmillan hbk **£16.95**

Macmillan Family Encyclopaedia
(21 Volumes)
Second probably only to the Britannica.
[S480] Macmillan hbk **£395.00**

New Junior Encyclopaedia in Colour
[S481] Hamlyn hbk **£7.95**

Pears Cyclopaedia (96th Edition)
Entries arranged according to subject. This remains the most authoritative reference book of its kind.
[S482] Pelham hbk **£10.95**

Penguin Columbia New Encyclopaedia
A brand new paperback encyclopaedia. It has a surprisingly wide range of references and is laid out in a clear and concise format.
[S483] Penguin pbk **£9.95**

BRIGGS, ASA (ED)
The Longman Encyclopaedia   **NEW**
A major new one-volume encyclopaedia which boasts an impressive editorial board (Prof Hermann Bondi,

Prof Stuart Hall, Prof Mary Warnock, A S Byatt) under the direction of Professor Briggs. Contains over 17,000 entries, 500 photographs, 250 drawings, dozens of useful quick reference tables, 150 maps and a full-colour atlas. Stern competition for Macmillan.
[S484] Longman hbk **£22.50**

ISAACS, DR ALAN (ED)
The Macmillan Encyclopaedia
The 1989 edition of this one-volume bestseller has undergone a major refit: 400 new articles; another 400 substantially revised; 4,000 updated and/or corrected. Plus the maps have been corrected and 10 new graphs added. All this and a new-look jacket too! 'The most comprehensive one-volume encyclopaedia' (The *Sunday Times*).
[S485] Macmillan hbk **£21.95**

JACKSON, PAUL
British Sources of Information
A guide and bibliography on 43 subjects from architecture to women.
[S486] Routledge hbk **£30.00**

Yearbooks

Crockford's Clerical Directory 1988/89
This is the authority on records of all the serving and retired clergy of the Church of England, the Church in Wales, and the Scottish Episcopal Church. The directory also provides an index of churches and other places of public worship in the Church of England, and the benefice to which each relates.
[S487] Church House Pub hbk **£27.50**

Debrett's Distinguished People of Today
[S488] Debrett's hbk **£55.00**

International Who's Who (52nd Edition)
[S489] Europa hbk **£75.00**

The Statesman's Yearbook 1989 - 90
A wealth of information on political, economic and social conditions of the world.
[S490] Macmillan hbk **£29.95**

Whitaker's Almanack 1989 (Shorter Edition)
[S491] J Whitaker hbk **£7.50**

Whitaker's Almanack 1989:
The Reference Book
An amazing variety of subjects in one renowned annual volume - all the facts at your fingertips at home or work.
[S492] J Whitaker hbk **£15.25**

Whitaker's Almanack 1989:
The Year Book
An invaluable guide to British and World affairs of the past year and essential dates and data for the year ahead.
[S493] J Whitaker hbk **£25.50**

Detail from the frontispiece of *Whitaker's Almanack 1989* (Whitaker hbk £15.25)

Who's Who 1990   **NEW**
A standard reference work: almost everything you need to know about people of influence, with short biographies of over 28,000 figures from all walks of life. The 1990 edition is available from January.
[S494] A & C Black hbk **£65.00**

Practical Reference

Adoption

So You're Adopted
[S495] Chambers pbk **£2.95**

BURNS
Stepmotherhood
[S496] Piatkus pbk **£3.95**

DAVENPORT, D.
One Parent Families
[S497] Sheldon pbk **£2.50**

JONES, MAGGIE
Everything You Needed to Know About Adoption
[S498] Sheldon pbk **£2.95**

RAPHAEL, KATE
Step-Parents Handbook
[S499] Sheldon pbk **£2.95**

Careers

Kogan Page produces an excellent series (entitled *Careers in...*) covering more than 30 vocations, priced at £3.95 each. More information on request.

CVs and Written Applications
Guide on constructing curricula vitae and filling in application forms.
[S500] Ward Lock pbk **£3.99**

Degree Course Offers 1988
[S501] Careers Consultants pbk **£9.95**

Great Answers to Tough Interview Questions
[S502] Kogan Page pbk **£3.95**

Higher Education in the UK 1988-89
[S503] Longman pbk **£9.95**

The Sunday Times Good University Guide
[S504] Collins pbk **£6.95**

Working Abroad
[S505] Kogan Page pbk **£6.95**

ATHA & DRUMMOND
The Good Schools Guide
[S506] Ebury P pbk **£8.95**

BOEHM, KLAUS
The Student Book 1989-90
What and Where to Study in the UK and How to Apply.
[S507] Macmillan pbk **£8.95**

INDEPENDENT SCHOOLS YEARBOOK 1989
Boys' Schools, Co-Educational Schools and Preparatory Schools
[S508] A & C Black pbk **£13.95**
Girls' Schools
[S509] A & C Black pbk **£9.50**

Consumer Law

Concise Dictionary of the Law
[S510] Oxford pbk **£4.95**

Handbook of Consumer Law
[S511] Hodder pbk **£5.95**

Taking Your Case to Court
[S512] Hodder pbk **£5.95**

Which: Way to Complain
[S513] Hodder pbk **£5.95**

ANDREWS, A.
How to Cope with Credit and Deal with Debt
[S514] Unwin Hyman pbk **£3.95**

BERLINS, M. (ED)
The Law and You
[S515] Hodder hbk **£14.95**

LANTIN, B.
How Not to Get Ripped Off
[S516] Unwin pbk **£3.95**

PRITCHARD, J.
Guide to the Law
[S517] Penguin pbk **£9.95**

WEDDERBURN, LORD
The Worker and the Law
[S518] Penguin pbk **£10.00**

WISEMAN, S.
How to Complain Effectively
[S519] Optima pbk **£3.95**

Divorce

Divorce: Legal Procedures
[S520] Hodder pbk **£5.95**

LELAND, J.
Breaking Up
[S521] Optima pbk **£3.95**

MITCHELL
Coping with Separation and Divorce
[S522] Chambers pbk **£2.95**

WILLIAMS, A.
Divorce and Separation
[S523] Sheldon pbk **£2.95**

Etiquette

Complete Book of Etiquette
[S524] Foulsham pbk **£1.95**

Debrett's Etiquette & Modern Manners
[S525] Pan pbk **£3.95**

Marriage Etiquette: 'Best Man'
[S526] Foulsham pbk £1.00

Speeches & Toasts
[S527] Foulsham pbk £2.50

Teach Yourself Public Speaking
[S528] Hodder pbk £2.95

The Best 'Best Man'
[S529] Foulsham pbk £1.20

**Titles & Forms of Address:
A Guide to the Correct Use**
[S530] A & C Black pbk £5.50

BRANDRETH, GYLES
Complete Public Speaker
From the humorist who has written a book on everything.
[S531] Sheldon pbk £2.50

DERRAUGH, WILLIAM
Wedding Etiquette
[S532] Foulsham pbk £2.25

JEFFERY, BARBARA
Wedding Speeches & Toasts
[S533] Foulsham pbk £1.50

KIRKPATRICK, A.L.
**Complete Public Speaker's
Manual**
[S534] Thorsons pbk £2.99

Home Ownership

Buying and Selling a Home
[S535] Telegraph Pubs pbk £3.95

**How to Sell Your House without
an Estate Agent**
[S536] Collins pbk £1.25

**Timesharing:
A Practical Guide**
[S537] David & Charles pbk £5.95

Which: Renting and Letting
[S538] Hodder pbk £6.95

**Which: The Legal Side of Buying
a House**
[S539] Hodder pbk £6.95

**Which: The Way to Buy, Sell and
Move House**
[S540] Hodder pbk £9.95

ARDEN, A.
Private Tenants' Handbook
[S541] Allison & B pbk £3.95

BOWERS, ARTHUR
Home Ownership A - Z
[S542] Collins pbk £1.75

LELAND, J.
Tenants' Rights
[S543] Optima pbk £3.95

VICKERS, L.
Buying a House or Flat
[S544] Penguin pbk £3.50

Retirement

KEMP
Handbook for Retirement
[S545] Macmillan hbk £12.95

WILLINGHAM, J.
Care for the Elderly
[S546] Optima pbk £3.95

Secretarial & Office

Chambers Office Oracle
Essential information on every aspect of modern office and business life - from public speaking to advertising services.
[S547] Chambers pbk £8.95

**Type Right: The Typist's
Spelling Checker**
How to spell all the most commonly used words in typing.
[S548] Chambers pbk £2.50

Webster's Secretarial Handbook
[S549] Longman hbk £21.00

ANSON, PENNY
Secretarial Duties
[S550] Chambers pbk £3.95

HUGHES, V. & HUGHES, C.
Secretary's Handbook
[S551] Hodder pbk £3.50

LEAFE, MARGARET
Practical Typing Skills: Student's Book
Office procedures and typing assignments to improve the student's grasp of the practicalities of office work.
[S552] Chambers pbk £4.95

SHAW, BARBARA
Word Processing
A comprehensive guide to all aspects of using a word processor.
[S553] Chambers pbk £3.95

STANANOUGHT, DEREK
Keyboarding
Information on how to acquire keyboard skills for typewriters, computers and word processors.
[S554] Chambers pbk £3.95

STANANOUGHT, JOYCE
**Typewriting Theory and Practice:
A Progressive Course**
The rules of typewriting theory with frequent exercises and practice.
[S555] Chambers pbk £4.95

Writing Guides

Hart's Rules for Compositors & Readers
The highest linguistic and lexicographic standards of editing and printing.
[S556] Oxford hbk £6.50

**Oxford Dictionary for Writers &
Editors**
[S557] Oxford hbk £8.95

The Complete Letter Writer
[S558] Ward Lock pbk £2.95

The New Business Letter Writer
[S559] Foulsham pbk £2.95

**Writers' and Artists' Yearbook
1990** NEW
Indispensable guide for writers, artists, publishers, composers etc. Contains articles and features on self-publishing, word-processing, paperback bestsellers, writing for television, opportunities for freelance artists, how to run a picture library and an updated 'who owns whom' in publishing. New material specially commissioned for this edition includes a detailed article on markets for poetry and an outline of the new Copyright, Designs and Patents Act.
[S560] A & C Black pbk £6.95

ASH, W.
The Way to Write Radio Drama
[S561] Elm Tree pbk £5.95

BALDWIN, MICHAEL
How to Write Short Stories
Deals with the basics of plot-making, location, character unity, dialogue, and tone of voice and goes on to discuss ways of achieving a personal style and theme.
[S562] Elm Tree pbk £5.95

BRAINE, JOHN
The author of *Room at the Top*.
Writing a Novel
[S563] Methuen pbk £5.50

BRANDE, DOROTHEA
Becoming a Writer
[S564] Macmillan pbk £4.95

BURTON, S.H.
Mastering Practical Writing
Looks at the written language of our daily lives, puts writing in a social context, and demonstrates that writing is an interpersonal skill which can be learnt and improved.
[S565] Macmillan pbk £3.25

BUTCHER, JUDITH
Copy Editing
A reference manual for those who prepare typescripts and illustrations for printing and publication.
[S566] Cambridge hbk £19.50
**Typescripts, Proofs and Indexes:
A Guide for Authors**
[S567] Cambridge pbk £3.75

CASTERTON, JULIA
**Creative Writing: A Practical
Guide**
This practical guide gives advice about style and form as well as useful hints about how to get published, and other ways of having work read or heard.
[S568] Macmillan pbk £3.95

FAIRFAX, JOHN & MOAT, JOHN
The Way to Write
A stimulating guide to the craft of writing, covering every aspect from the daunting moment of confrontation with the blank page.
[S569] Elm Tree pbk £6.95

FINCH, P.
How to Publish Your Poetry
[S570] Allison & B pbk £3.95
How to Publish Yourself
[S571] Allison & B pbk £3.95

GALLACHER, T.
The Way to Write for the Stage
[S572] Elm Tree pbk **£5.95**

HIGHSMITH, PATRICIA
Plotting and Writing Suspense Fiction
Advice from one of the most popular crime writers.
[S573] Poplar pbk **£4.95**

HINES, J.
The Way to Write Magazine Articles
[S574] Elm Tree pbk **£5.95**

HOFFMAN, A.
Research for Writers
[S575] A & C Black pbk **£6.95**

JUTE, ANDRE
Writing a Thriller
[S576] A & C Black pbk **£4.95**

KANE, THOMAS
Oxford Guide to Writing
A rhetoric and handbook for college students.
[S577] Oxford pbk **£15.00**

KANE, THOMAS & PETERS, LEONARD
**Writing Prose: Techniques and
Purposes**
A stimulating book based upon the theory that one
can learn to write by studying and imitating good
works. Examples of authors whose work is included
are V.S. Naipaul, Tom Wolfe, and Jonathan Raban.
[S578] Oxford pbk **£9.95**

KEATING, H.
Writing Crime Fiction
[S579] A & C Black pbk **£4.95**

KITCHEN, P.
The Way to Write Novels
[S580] Elm Tree pbk **£5.95**

LEGAT, MICHAEL
An Author's Guide to Publishing
[S581] Hale pbk **£4.95**
Writing for Pleasure and Profit
A practical guide to the craft of writing.
[S582] Hale pbk **£4.95**

PAICE, E.
The Way to Write for Television
[S583] Elm Tree pbk **£5.95**

PIRIE, DAVID B.
How to Write Critical Essays
'David Pirie provides detailed, well-organised, fully
discussed recommendations for writing critical
essays.' (*British Book News*)
[S584] Methuen pbk **£4.95**

ROGERS, GEOFFREY
Editing for Print
A useful handbook with good illustrations.
[S585] Macdonald hbk **£9.95**

SAUNDERS, JEAN
The Craft of Writing Romance
Practical advice from a succesful romantic novelist.
[S586] Allison & B pbk **£2.95**

SAVILLE, J.
The Business Letter Writer
[S587] Ward Lock pbk **£2.95**

TURNER, BARRY (ED)
The Writer's Handbook 1990
Lists all essential names and addresses of key
decision-makers and is updated every year. The 1990

edition contains fuller sections on Poetry Societies
and Picture Libraries.
[S588] Macmillan pbk **£7.95**

WATSON, GEORGE
Writing a Thesis
A witty and engaging discussion, aiming to stimulate
literary and historical research on the one hand, while
helping to lend it discipline on the other. Any students
faced with a thesis, dissertation or extended essay
should find it helpful and entertaining in equal
measure.
[S589] Longman pbk **£5.50**

WELLS, GORDON
Magazine Writers Handbook
A collection of names and addresses of non-specialist
magazines which accept unsolicited stories and
articles. Information is also given on fees, styles etc.
[S590] Allison & B pbk **£3.95**

REFERENCE

Religion

Reference
Philosophy of Religion
Christian Religion
Non-Christian Religions
Modern Spiritual Leaders
Mythology

RELIGION

Reference

Lion Handbooks
Excellent basic guides to religion, suitable for the general reader. Each volume is clearly written and well-illustrated. Four volumes presented in slip-case include *Handbook to the Bible*, *History of Christianity*, *The World's Religions*, *Handbook of Christian Belief*.
[T1] Lion 4 vols hbk **£49.80**

BISHOP, P. & DARTON, M. (EDS)
The Encyclopaedia of World Faiths
This authoritative text is accompanied throughout by maps, charts, photographs and diagrams.
[T2] Macdonald pbk **£19.95**

LING, TREVOR OSWALD
Buddha, Marx and God
A history of Eastern and Western religions.
[T3] Macmillan pbk **£4.95**
History of Religion East and West
[T4] Macmillan pbk **£9.95**

PEPPER, MARGARET (ED)
Dictionary of Religious Quotations
An entertaining and inspiring book, ranging from 'Abandonment' to 'Zeal' with quotations from all major world religions.
[T5] Deutsch hbk **£12.95**

SMART, NINIAN
Honorary Professor at Lancaster University and at the University of California at Santa Barbara, Ninian Smart is the foremost scholar in the field of comparative religions. His writings are clear and easily accessible to the general reader.
The World's Religions　　**NEW**
Smart's latest book is a glossy, informative examination of all religions. The faiths of every country and region are described, highlighting doctrine, sacred narrative/myth, ethics, experience, iconography, ritual and institutions. The first part considers the ways religions crystallised out of the ancient world, while the second follows the journey of conquest and discovery after the Renaissance, and considers how religions have been refashioned as the modern world develops.
[T6] Cambridge hbk **£25.00**

Philosophy of Religion

CAHN, STEVEN & SCHATZ, DAVID (EDS)
Contemporary Philosophy of Religion　　**NEW**
Scholarly review by distinguished philosophers of religion, both sympathetic to religion and highly critical. Considers conventional issues (eg. the problem of evil) and more neglected areas (the purpose of ritual, faith and rationality, and the conflicting claims of world religions).
[T7] Oxford pbk **£7.95**

DAVIES, BRIAN
Introduction to the Philosophy of Religion
A critical examination of the classic questions of evil and God, God's existence, life after death, and miracles. Davies examines the beliefs of past philosophers and modern thinkers, suggesting his own responses, but leaving the answers open for the reader.
[T8] Oxford pbk **£5.95**

DURKHEIM, EMILE
Born in France and brought up to be a rabbi, Durkheim instead became the founder of modern comparative sociology. He was a Positivist who believed that people are a product of their society and that their feelings and attitudes are conditioned by social forces. He argued that society is more than the sum of its parts, and that collective beliefs and behaviour cannot be explained in terms of individual psychology.
Elementary Forms of the Religious Life
Shows Durkheim's way of regarding beliefs and concepts not in terms of their ultimate truth or falsity, but as a product of specific social conditions.
[T9] Unwin Hyman pbk **£14.95**
On Religion
[T10] Routledge pbk **£5.95**

FLEW, ANTONY G.N.
Body, Mind and Death
[T11] Macmillan pbk **£3.95**

GRIFFITHS, BEDE
An important spiritual writer from a Christian middle-class background, who has adopted many aspects (in both thought and lifestyle) of Buddhism. He was a confidant of C.S. Lewis at Cambridge, and a member of the Benedictine community of Prinknash Abbey. He now lives as a Sannyasi, his ashram being a centre for prayer and meditation.
Marriage of East and West
[T12] Fount pbk **£2.50**

HICK, JOHN
An Interpretation of Religion　　**NEW**
Hick's latest book explores the notion that various religions are differing responses to the One Real. He addresses the principal topics as well as considering the basis for religious affirmation, and world interfaith dialogue. Taking account of the social and historical sciences he offers a religious interpretation with clarity, force and fresh insight.
[T13] Macmillan pbk **£12.95**
Arguments for the Existence of God
[T14] Macmillan hbk **£14.95**
Death and Eternal Life
[T15] Macmillan pbk **£9.95**
Evil and the God of Love
A modern theological classic considering the two reponses: Augustinian (looking to the past for a meaning), and Irenaean (looking to the future for a justifying completion). Focusing on the latter, Hick considers human nature as moving from that of human animal to child of God, and examines the dark mystery of the person-making process.
[T16] Macmillan pbk **£9.95**
Existence of God
A collection of essays and extracts.
[T17] Macmillan pbk **£4.95**

HICK, JOHN (ED)
The Myth of God Incarnate
A classic collection of essays and extracts examining the debate initiated by Bultmann of the concept of God made human.
[T18] SCM pbk **£6.95**

HUME, DAVID
Scottish empirical philosopher, historian and man of letters.
Dialogues Concerning Natural Religion
[T19] Hafner pbk **£6.95**

St Aidan from *A Calendar of Saints* by James Bentley (Macdonald Orbis hbk £12.95)

Of Miracles
[T20] Open Court pbk **£2.50**

JAMES, WILLIAM
American empirical philosopher and psychologist.
Varieties of Religious Experience
[T21] Penguin pbk **£4.95**

JUNG, C.G.
Swiss psychologist who began as a disciple of Freud but later severed this connection to found his own school of analytical psychology. He developed an idea of the psyche containing the personal unconscious, forgotten or repressed individual experiences, and the collective unconscious, being the residue of ideas and images shared by all human beings. This led him into a widely diverse series of studies including religion, folklore, mythology, astrology and mysticism.
Answer to Job: Researches into the Relation between Psychology and Religion
[T22] Routledge pbk **£5.50**

KENNY, ANTHONY JOHN PATRICK
Oxford philosopher noted for his work on Wittgenstein. For many years a Jesuit priest, until he left the order and became an academic. His work shows a sharp understanding of the philosophical tensions involved in religious faith.
The God of the Philosophers
[T23] Oxford pbk **£7.95**

KIERKEGAARD, SOREN
Danish philosopher and theologian perhaps best known for his religious views. Rejecting the false security of external justifications, he insisted that all belief in God could only be a 'leap of faith'. This is described as the necessary consequence of a preceding state of 'Angst'. His analyses of this state of spiritual crisis and radical uncertainty are remarkable for their psychological penetration.
Fear and Trembling
[T24] Penguin pbk **£3.99**
Gospel of Sufferings
[T25] J Clark pbk **£4.95**

KOLAKOWSKI, LESZEK
Religion
[T26] Fontana pbk **£2.50**

MOORE, GARETH, O.P.
Believing in God - A Philosophical Essay NEW
A sketch towards a philosophical understanding of Christianity - not the truth of a range of ideas, but what it means for Christians to believe the things they do.
[T27] T Clark hbk **£14.95**

PASCAL, BLAISE
Pensées
Pascal is famous for his 'wager' contained in his *Pensées*. If there is a God in whom we choose not to believe, then we run the risk of losing everything. But if we believe, then we stand to gain everything. If, having believed, there turns out to be no God, then we neither gain nor lose anything.
[T28] Penguin pbk **£4.99**

RUSSELL, BERTRAND
British philosopher noted for his atheism.
On God and Religion
[T29] Prometheus pbk **£10.45**
Religion and Science
[T30] Oxford pbk **£6.95**
Why I am not a Christian
[T31] Unwin Hyman pbk **£3.95**

SHARPE, ERIC J.
Comparative Religion
[T32] Duckworth pbk **£9.95**

SMART, NINIAN
Religious Experience of Mankind
[T33] Fontana pbk **£4.95**

SWINBURNE, RICHARD
Existence of God
[T34] Oxford pbk **£9.95**
Faith and Reason
[T35] Oxford pbk **£9.95**

WATTS, FRASER & WILLIAMS, MARK
The Psychology of Religious Knowing
Two clinical psychologists examine the psychological processes involved in arriving at religious knowledge, relating it to the ways people come to know other things, in particular, personal insights.
[T36] Cambridge hbk **£19.50**

WILBER, KEN
A Sociable God
A psychological view of religion. New Religious movements, the influx of Eastern mystery traditions to the West, and the sociology of religion, are explored by one of America's most interesting synthesists of religion and science.
[T37] Shambala pbk **£9.95**

Christian Religion

Liturgy, Missals & Prayer Books

Glenstal Bible Missal
[T105] Collins hbk **£16.95**

Oxford Bridesmaid's Prayer Book
[T106] Oxford hbk **£8.50**

Oxford Cycle of Prayer
[T107] Oxford hbk **£2.95**

Pica Prayer Book
[T108] Oxford hbk **£8.95**

The Alternative Service Book 1980 Oxford/Mowbray Pew Edition
[T109] Oxford hbk leather **£19.95**
[T110] Oxford hbk leatherex **£8.50**

The Alternative Service Book 1980
[T111] SPCK pbk **£7.95**

The Book of Common Prayer with Standard Hymns Ancient and Modern
[T112] Collins hbk **£6.95**
[T113] Collins pbk **£4.50**

Sunday Missal
[T114] Collins hbk **£7.95**
Weekday Missal
[T115] Collins hbk **£18.95**

BARCLAY, WILLIAM
Prayers for Help and Healing
[T116] Fount pbk **£1.75**
Prayers for Young People
[T117] Fount hbk **£1.95**

KOSSOFF, DAVID
You Have a Minute Lord? A Sort of Prayer Book
A popular book of prayers from the author best known for his version of the Bible stories for children.
[T118] Pan pbk **£3.99**

PATON, ALAN
Instrument of Thy Peace
[T119] Fontana hbk **£1.75**

RUNCIE, ROBERT & HUME, BASIL
Prayers for Peace
A selection of texts by the two eminent church leaders, one Anglican and one Catholic.
[T120] SPCK pbk **£2.50**

Bibles

Rather than list all the hundreds of editions of the Bible currently in print, here we have simply selected the standard versions offered by the main publishers. In each case there are many permutations: different qualities of binding, paper, boxes, slip cases; special editions for christenings, weddings and presentations; large print editions; pocket editions; illustrated editions; editions which contain the Apocrypha, concordances, maps and charts; red letter editions; editions for children and lectern Bibles for use in church. Further details are available on request.

AUTHORIZED VERSION
Despite the outdated language and the advances in biblical scholarship in intervening years, The King James Bible of 1611 remains the most widely accepted version of the Bible and a classic of the English language.
Brevier Reference Bible
The standard reference edition.
[T666] Collins pbk **£8.50**
[T667] Oxford leather **£25.00**
Cameo Reference Bible
The most popular of the many Cambridge editions of the Authorized Version.
[T668] Cambridge leather **£20.00**
Gem Pocket Bible
[T669] Collins pbk **£3.25**

St Petronela from *A Calendar of Saints* by James Bentley (Macdonald Orbis hbk **£12.95**)

GOOD NEWS BIBLE
Perhaps the most accessible of all translations, *The Bible in Today's English Version*, universally known as the *Good News Bible*, has, since its first appearance in 1971, successfully fulfilled the evangelical purposes for which it was created by the United Bible Societies.
Bible Society Edition
[T670] Bible Soc leather **£25.95**
[T672] Bible Soc hbk **£7.95**
[T673] Bible Soc pbk **£4.95**
Collins Edition
Contains 500 illustrations by Annette Valloton, a chart of Bible history, cross references, an introduction to each book and an index of important subjects.
[T674] Collins leather **£7.95**
[T675] Collins hbk **£6.50**
[T676] Collins pbk **£4.95**

JERUSALEM BIBLE
Originally a French translation produced in Jerusalem by Dominican scholars, the JB has been widely accepted within the international Catholic community.
[T677] Bible Soc leather **£35.00**
[T678] Bible Soc hbk **£8.95**
[T679] Bible Soc pbk **£6.50**

NEW ENGLISH BIBLE
An entirely new translation first published in 1970, this is an ecumenical and authoritative version approved by the major Christian bodies in Britain, and based on the most up-to-date biblical scholarship.
[T680] Oxford leather **£17.00**
[T681] Oxford hbk **£9.50**

NEW INTERNATIONAL VERSION
First published in 1978, the NIV is the fruit of the labours of over 100 scholars from many denominations and countries, and is widely regarded as an authoritative text within the evangelical community.
Popular Edition (Ed. D. Wiseman)
[T682] Hodder leather **£18.95**
[T683] Hodder hbk **£6.95**
[T684] Hodder pbk **£5.50**

REVISED ENGLISH BIBLE **NEW**

A major new version of the Bible for the 1990s and beyond, written in clear, contemporary English for use by all denominations.
[T687] Oxford/Cambridge hbk **£8.95**

With Apocrypha
[T688] Oxford/Cambridge hbk **£9.95**

REVISED STANDARD VERSION

The second major revision of the King James Bible (the first being the Revised Version of 1885), the RSV was first published in 1957 and is now used by churches and scholars throughout the English-speaking world.
[T685] Collins hbk **£7.95**
[T686] Oxford leather **£8.95**

Bible Commentaries

BARCLAY, WILLIAM
Scotish Biblical scholar, well known as a television and radio lecturer. His main achievement has been to rescue the New Testament from the abstruse erudition of scholars and to make it accessible, without compromising his own scholarly standards.

Daily Study Bible
Barclay's series of commentaries are available for the various books of the Bible at £2.75 each. The whole set is available in 18 volumes, with a slip case, as priced below.
[T121] St Andrew P 18 vols hbk **£47.00**

BARTH, KARL
The most important Protestant theologian of the century. A fuller listing of his work will be found in the *Theology* section.

Epistle to the Romans
An influential study that has acquired the status of a classic.
[T122] Oxford pbk **£8.95**

BRUCE, F.F.
The Acts of the Apostles
A detailed study of Acts based on the Greek text by Britain's leading conservative theologian.
[T123] IVP hbk **£16.95**

CAIRD, G.B.
Paul's Letters from Prison
[T124] Oxford pbk **£4.50**

CAMBRIDGE BIBLE COMMENTARY ON THE NEW ENGLISH BIBLE
A widely acclaimed series of over fifty paperbacks, designed to make the results of modern scholarship accessible to the general reader.
[T125] Cambridge pbk **£6.95 - £13.95**

LINDARS, BARNABAS
Gospel of John
The most renowned of the New Century Bible series.
[T126] Marshall pbk **£10.50**

NEW PELICAN TESTAMENT COMMENTARIES
Well-respected series of scholarly, but accessible, commentaries on the gospels by four leading contemporary scholars.
CAIRD, G.C.
St Luke
[T127] Penguin pbk **£4.95**
FENTON, JOHN C.
St Matthew
[T128] Penguin pbk **£5.95**

MARSH, JOHN
St John
[T129] Penguin pbk **£6.95**
NINEHAM, DENNIS ERIC
St Mark
[T130] Penguin pbk **£5.95**

REDHEAD, BRIAN & GUMLEY, FRANCES
Redhead is best known as the presenter of BBC Radio 4's *Today* programme; Frances Gumley is a Senior Producer in the BBC's Religious Department.
The Good Book **NEW**
A lively and easy-to-read guide through the Bible. The excellent introductory essay draws on worldwide learning and experience from Christian theologians, Rabbis and Islamic scholars. All books of the Old and New Testaments are considered in detail.
[T131] Duckworth pbk **£4.95**

RENDTORFF, ROLF
The Old Testament: An Introduction
[T132] SCM hbk **£12.50**

TYNDALE OLD AND NEW TESTAMENT COMMENTARIES
A popular series of inexpensive commentaries on individual books of the Bible. The authors are well-known evangelical and conservative writers and scholars. The books espouse a traditional outlook.
[T133] IVP pbk **£4.25 - £6.25**

Christian Reference

Lion Concise Bible Handbook
Concise version of the bestselling *The Lion Handbook of the Bible*. A very good book-by-book popular guide to the Old and New Testaments.
[T134] Lion pbk **£4.95**

Lion Handbook of Christianity: A World Faith
[T135] Lion hbk **£12.95**

Oxford Bible Reader's Dictionary and Concordance
[T136] Oxford hbk **£6.50**

Oxford Bible Reader's Pocket Concordance
[T137] Oxford hbk **£4.50**

ALEXANDER, PATRICIA J.
Lion Concise Bible Encyclopaedia
This guide is designed to elaborate on the historical, geographical and cultural setting of the people and events of the Bible. Arranged alphabetically in a concise format.
[T138] Lion hbk **£4.95**

ALTER, R. & KERMODE, FRANK (EDS)
The Literary Guide to the Bible
Two distinguished literary critics with Christian sympathies highlight the various literary qualities of the Bible. The book is designed to enhance general understanding of an area which has been neglected as a result of a prevailing academic approach to the work. Attractively presented, there are essays on every book of the Bible, as well as 7 general essays by well-respected scholars.
[T139] Collins hbk **£20.00**

AUNE, DAVID
The New Testament in its Literary Environment **NEW**
Good introduction to the major literary genres and forms found in the New Testament.
[T140] J Clarke hbk **£12.95**

BARRETT, DAVID B. (ED)
World Christian Encyclopaedia
A comparative survey of churches and religions in the modern world. This major reference book describes systematically the present extent, status and characteristics of the Christian religion throughout the world. Photographs, maps and tables throughout.
[T141] Oxford hbk **£110.00**

BENTLEY, JAMES
A Calendar of Saints
[T141A] Orbis hbk **£12.95**

CALVOCORESSI, PETER
Who's Who in the Bible
[T142] Penguin pbk **£4.99**

CROSS, F.L. & LIVINGSTONE, E.A. (EDS)
The Oxford Dictionary of the Christian Church
A comprehensive reference book on every aspect of Christianity, especially in its historical development. The Dictionary contains nearly 6,000 entries and over 4,500 bibliographies.
[T143] Oxford hbk **£37.50**

DRANE, J.
Introducing the New Testament
A popular introduction to the New Testament aimed to set the writings in a proper historical and social perspective. Main sections on Jesus, the Kingdom of God, and St Paul and his letters.
[T144] Lion pbk **£12.95**

Introducing the Old Testament
Same format as its companion volume above, this is divided into two main parts - one documents an account of the Old Testament, the other considers the faith of the Hebrew nation.
[T145] Lion pbk **£12.95**

FARMER, D.H. (ED)
The Oxford Dictionary of Saints
This dictionary gives concise accounts of about 1,100 saints who lived, died or were venerated in the British Isles, or who lived in the English-speaking world.
[T146] Oxford pbk **£5.95**

FERGUSON, SINCLAIR & WRIGHT, DAVID
New Dictionary of Theology
This extensive work contains the contributions of over 200 scholars. Subjects range widely from the more scholarly (the biblical basis of theology, black consciousness and African independent churches) to those of general interest (baptism in the Spirit, the sovereignty of God).
[T147] IVP hbk **£18.95**

GOODRICK, EDWARD W. & KOHLENBERGER, JOHN R.
New International Version Handy Concordance
Over 35,000 entries with special entries for over 200 Bible characters. Includes the listing of 44 familiar Authorised Version words cross-referenced to their NIV equivalents.
[T148] Hodder pbk **£4.95**

GROLLENBERG
Shorter Atlas of the Bible
[T149] Penguin pbk **£4.95**

HINNELLS, JOHN R. (ED)
Handbook of Living Religions
[T150] Penguin pbk **£6.99**
Penguin Dictionary of Religions
An excellent, comprehensive and authoritative guide, containing charts, maps and an invaluable bibliography.
[T151] Penguin pbk **£6.99**

Becket consecrated Archbishop of Canterbury, 3rd June 1162, from *Becket Leaves* by Janet Backhouse & Christopher de Hamel (British Library pbk £5.95)

KELLY (ED)
Oxford Dictionary of Popes
[T152] Oxford pbk **£5.95**

KOMONCHAK (ED)
New Dictionary of Theology
Compiled by English-speaking Roman Catholic theologians.
[T153] Gill & Macmillan hbk **£50.00**

LIVINGSTONE, E.A. (ED)
Concise Oxford Dictionary of the Christian Church
Attractively presented this dictionary ranges from Aaron to Zwingli with succinct, informative descriptions of key movements and people throughout the history of the church.
[T154] Oxford pbk **£5.95**

LODKYER, HERBERT (ED)
Illustrated Bible Dictionary
A recent one-volume Bible dictionary, with 500 colour illustrations and 5,500 up-to-date entries. Designed for the general reader.
[T155] Hodder pbk **£16.95**

MANSER, MARTIN H. (ED)
Concise Book of Bible Quotations
Contains nearly 300 themes arranged in alphabetical order, with a second listing in Biblical order. This two-part ordering is very useful in discovering the essential teachings of the Bible.
[T156] Lion pbk **£4.95**

METFORD, J.C.J.
Dictionary of Christian Lore and Legend
A lucid and concise guide through Christian themes which have inspired life and culture.
[T157] Thames & H pbk **£6.95**

METZGER, BRUCE M. & METZGER, I. (EDS)
Oxford Concise Concordance to RSV of Bible
[T158] Oxford pbk **£5.50**

PRITCHARD, J.B. (ED)
The Times Atlas of the Bible
Compiled by an international team of 50, including archaeologists, historians and theologians, this useful atlas contains 600 colour maps and illustrations. It gives a very visual appreciation of the setting of the Bible, yet also contains much scholarly text.
[T159] Times hbk **£25.00**

THE ILLUSTRATED BIBLE DICTIONARY
Probably the most comprehensive Bible dictionary available, containing an abundance of pictures, maps and diagrams, many in full colour. Consulting editors include F.F. Bruce and D. Guthrie.
Vol 1: Aaron to Golan
[T160] IVP hbk **£19.50**
Vol 2: Goliath to Papyri
[T161] IVP hbk **£19.50**
Vol 3: Parable to Zuzim
[T162] IVP hbk **£19.50**

Christian History

ALLEGRO, JOHN M.
The Dead Sea Scrolls: A Reappraisal
An assessment of the collection of papyrus texts found near the Dead Sea in 1947, which contained important new historical evidence about the time of Jesus, in particular about other communities of faith existing in the first century.
[T163] Penguin pbk **£4.50**

ARMSTRONG, KAREN
The First Christian: Saint Paul's Impact on Christianity
[T164] Pan pbk **£2.95**

BACKHOUSE, JANET & HAMEL, CHRISTOPHER DE
Becket Leaves
[T164A] British Library pbk **£5.95**

BACON, ERNEST W.
Pilgrim and Dreamer: John Bunyan, His Life and Work
Biography of the 17th century non-conformist priest, and author of *Pilgrim's Progress*.
[T165] Paternoster hbk **£4.99**

BEDE (673 - 735)
Probably the greatest historian of the Early Middle Ages. His history of Britain since 55 BC was based on a constant search for material in official documents, letters and other written records. He lived and died at Jarrow, where he taught many of the monks and composed bible commentaries, as well as his famous history of the English people, written in Anglo-Latin.
Age of Bede
Bede's *Life of St. Cuthbert*, Eddius Stephanus's *Life of Wilfrid*, and other works.
[T168] Penguin pbk **£5.99**
History of the English Church and People
[T169] Penguin pbk **£3.95**

BETHGE, EBERHARD
Dietrich Bonhoeffer
The moving story of the German pastor and theologian who was arrested on a charge of plotting to kill Hitler and executed by the Nazis in 1945.
[T170] Fount pbk **£6.95**
Dietrich Bonhoeffer: A Life in Pictures
[T171] SCM hbk **£12.95**

CARPENTER, HUMPHREY
Jesus
A dispassionate study of Jesus as a historical figure. Part of the *Modern Masters* series.
[T172] Oxford pbk **£2.95**

CHURTON, T.
The Gnostics
Based on a television series tracing the history and influence of Gnosticism - a philosophy seeking direct experience of God - from the time of Jesus to the present day.
[T173] Weidenfeld hbk **£10.95**

JOHNSON, PAUL
A History of Christianity
[T174] Weidenfeld hbk **£7.95**

MACCOBY, HYAM
Judaism in the First Century   **NEW**
Provides insight into many of the problems of New Testament interpretation by revealing the creative energy and vitality of the Jewish sects existing at the time of Jesus.
[T175] Sheldon pbk **£4.95**

MCDANNELL, COLLEEN & LANG, BERNHARD
Heaven: A History   **NEW**
Images of heaven from poetry, art, literature and popular culture are presented to describe and interpret the ways in which believers have understood the notion of everlasting life.
[T176] Yale UP hbk **£16.95**

PAGELS, ELAINE
The Gnostic Gospels
Examination and interpretation of a set of texts found at Nag Hammadi in Egypt in 1945 containing many important Gnostic texts. A central book for the study of this religious philosophy.
[T177] Penguin pbk **£3.95**

PELICAN HISTORY OF THE CHURCH
An excellent series of concise history books providing lucid and accessible overviews of each period. Owen

RELIGION

Chadwick's exposition of The Reformation is particularly acclaimed.

Vol 1: The Early Church
[T178] Penguin pbk **£4.99**
Vol 2: Western Society and the Church in the Middle Ages
[T179] Penguin pbk **£4.95**
Vol 3: The Reformation
[T180] Penguin pbk **£5.95**
Vol 4: The Church and the Age of Reason 1648 - 1789
[T181] Penguin pbk **£4.50**
Vol 5: The Church in an Age of Revolution: 1789 to the Present Day
[T182] Penguin pbk **£4.95**
Vol 6: Christian Missions
[T183] Penguin pbk **£5.95**

POLLOCK, JOHN
Wilberforce
Biography of the English politician and philanthropist famous for engineering the abolition of slavery.
[T184] Lion pbk **£4.95**

SCHWEITZER, ALBERT
Quest of the Historical Jesus
The most famous work of the German theologian and doctor.
[T185] SCM pbk **£8.50**

TAWNEY, R.H.
Religion and the Rise of Capitalism
An established and important work, extending in importance beyond the boundaries of theological discussion by assessing the fundamental impact of doctrine on social, economic and political issues. Taking the study from the Middle Ages to the early 18th century, Tawney concludes that the causes leading to the revolution of Capitalism were many, and that religion played an important (if less conspicuous) role, alongside the expansion of trade and rise of new classes to political power.
[T186] Penguin pbk **£4.95**

THEISSEN, GERD
The Shadow of the Gallilean
A fascinating, brilliantly constructed exploration of the life of Jesus. Firmly based within modern biblical scholarship, Theissen constructs a detective story of murder, mystery and intrigue, which opens up a deep understanding of the political nature of Jesus' ministry, and his role within the political structure of first century Palestine.
[T187] SCM pbk **£15.00**

WARD, BENEDICTA (ED)
Lives of the Desert Fathers
[T188] Mowbray pbk **£6.95**

WARE, KALLISTOS
The Orthodox Church
A clear guide to the history and traditions of the orthodox church, by a respected scholar and key figure in the orthodox church in Britain.
[T189] Penguin pbk **£4.99**

WILSON, EDMUND
Dead Sea Scrolls
Written by a non-specialist for non-specialists, Wilson's work provides a readable introduction to the significance of this important discovery.
[T190] Fontana pbk **£2.95**

WILSON, IAN
Jesus: The Evidence
Based on the TV series, Wilson presents the case in a straightforward, witty, and, at times sceptical manner.
[T191] Pan pbk **£3.50**

The Evidence of the Shroud
[T192] O'Mara pbk **£3.95**

Theology

ANSELM, ST (1033 - 1109)
Born of a noble family in Northern Italy who did not approve of his wish to enter the Church, Anselm joined the Abbey of Bec in Normandy where he became Prior in 1063. Appointed Archbishop of Canterbury in 1093, he wrote many philosophical and theological works emphasising the medieval theme of Faith seeking after Reason. A founder of scholasticism, he originated the famous ontological argument for the existence of God: God's existence is necessary because of God's perfection.
Basic Writings
Includes *Proslogium, Monologium, Gaunilon's In Behalf of the Fool* and *Cur deus Homo*.
[T193] Open Court pbk **£8.95**
Prayers and Meditations
This work sets a precedent in encouraging the layman as well as the monk in meditative prayer.
[T194] Penguin pbk **£4.95**
EVANS, GILLIAN ROSEMARY
Anselm `NEW`
[T195] Chapman pbk **£4.95**

AQUINAS, ST THOMAS (1225 - 1274)
The most important scholastic theologian of the Middle Ages, whose philosophical achievement was to reconcile Greek philosophy with Christianity. His assimilation of Aristotle's pagan philosophy into the Christian conception of the universe was influential in determining the tenor of later medieval philosophy. Aquinas, an Italian Dominican, still retains the status of a standard authority within the Roman Catholic church.
Summa Contra Gentiles Vol 1: God
[T196] Notre Dame UP pbk **£7.25**
Vol 2: Creation
[T197] Notre Dame UP pbk **£7.25**
Vol 3: Providence
[T198] Notre Dame UP pbk **£11.75**
Vol 4: Salvation
[T199] Notre Dame UP pbk **£7.25**
Summa Theologiae `NEW`
A new edition in 5 volumes. This vast, comprehensive work resolves all moral and political sciences into one great metaphysical system.
[T200] Sheed & W 5 vols pbk **£87.50**
Summa Theologiae: A Concise Translation `NEW`
A one-volume translation, edited by Timothy McDermott, of important parts of this masterwork. Presented in non-technical modern English, with modern chapter and paragraph format.
[T201] Methuen hbk **£20.00**
CLARK, MARY T. (ED)
Aquinas Reader `NEW`
[T202] Fordham UP hbk **£9.75**

AUGUSTINE, ST (354 - 430)
One of the greatest of the Church Fathers, and a supreme intellect of the Dark Ages. As Bishop of Hippo, he engaged in theological controversy with all the pagan groups undermining Christianity in the 4th century. He exercised considerable influence on Medieval thought, as well as on the theological doctrines of the Reformation, and contributed to many areas of philosophy, his conclusions being generally derived from Platonic premises.
Confessions
Although his mother was a devout Christian, Augustine rejected her faith as a young man. In 387 he was converted after hearing the sermons of St

Ambrose in Milan. This conversion is recounted in a moving passage in *The Confessions*, a classic of philosophy and one of the most celebrated spiritual biographies.
[T203] Penguin pbk **£4.99**
The City of God
This monumental work succeeded in articulating a comprehensive and monotheistic vision of God at a time when the Church was undermined by rival pagan groups. Its influence on subsequent Christian thought has been immense, in particular the emphasis on the power of God's grace.
[T204] Penguin pbk **£9.99**
CLARK, MARY T.
Selected Writings
In the *Classics of Western Spirituality* series.
[T205] SPCK pbk **£15.00**

BARR, JAMES
Fundamentalism
An important contribution to the debate on the nature of biblical criticism by this controversial writer. By examining the intellectual basis of biblical faith, he provides an excellent introduction to modern, critical methods of biblical scholarship.
[T206] SCM pbk **£12.50**

BARTH, KARL (1886 - 1968)
A Swiss theologian, Barth was the most prominent Protestant thinker of this century, whose work shows the influence of existential literature and thought. He was a serious critic of the Kaiser in the Great War, and later of the Nazis.
Church Dogmatics
14 volumes, at £17.95 each. Karl Barth's most famous work, systematizing his theological vision in an exhaustive catalogue of well-written theological exposition.
[T207] T Clark 14 vols hbk **£251.30**
Evangelical Theology
[T208] T Clark pbk **£7.95**
GREEN, CLIFFORD (ED)
Karl Barth, Theologian of Freedom - Selected Writings `NEW`
The essential Barth for students and the general reader. The selected writings are in 6 main areas: a critique of liberal theology; studies of Romans and Anselm; revelation and Biblical theology compared with natural theology; Christology, election and reconciliation; Christian ethics and public life; and socialism and the resistance to Nazism. With a clear introductory essay showing the connections between key texts, putting Barth into historical context, it charts the development of his thought and shows his significance within Christian theology.
[T209] Collins pbk **£4.95**

BONHOEFFER, DIETRICH (1906 - 1945)
Influential German theologian active in protests against the Nazis. He was arrested by the Gestapo on a charge of plotting to kill Hitler, and executed in 1945.
Letters and Papers from Prison
Written whilst a prisoner of the Nazis, Bonhoeffer's most celebrated writings celebrate the coming together of Christianity and secular humanism.
[T210] SCM pbk **£4.95**
GRUNCHY, JOHN DE
Dietrich Bonhoeffer
Part of the *Making of Modern Theology* series.
[T211] Collins pbk **£6.95**

BULTMANN, RUDOLPH (1884 - 1976)
One of the most influential 20th century German theologians. His existentialist interpretations of the New Testament reject historical reliability of the Gospels as an indicator of their truth and meaning. His knowledge and study of oral traditions show the

Gospels reflecting the theology of the early churches, rather than simply providing reports of facts about Jesus. He emphasises the need to demythologise Christianity to make it more relevant and accessible.

New Testament and Mythology and Other Basic Writings
[T212] SCM pbk **£7.95**

Theology of the New Testament: Vol 1
An excellent, thorough introduction to the New Testament and the range of criticism, as well as to Bultmann's theological perspective.
[T213] SCM hbk **£12.50**

Vol 2
[T214] SCM hbk **£9.50**

JOHNSON, ROGER (ED)
Rudolph Bultman
Part of the *Making of Modern Theology* series.
[T215] Collins pbk **£7.95**

CALVIN, JOHN (1509 - 1564)
A major figure of the Reformation whose faith was more extreme, severe and radical than that of Luther. His desire to set up a theocracy, a state governed by church leaders, came to short-lived fruition in Geneva.

Institutes of the Christian Religion
Calvin's major work is a defence of the Reformed-Faith. It proclaims the Bible as ultimate authority, and includes his famous views on Predestination.
[T216] Collins pbk **£17.95**

LANE, TONY & OSBORNE, HILARY (EDS)
Translated from Calvin's Latin original.
[T217] Hodder pbk **£2.95**

CHARDIN, PIERRE TEILHARD DE
(1881 - 1955)
French biologist, palaeontologist, Jesuit priest, mystic and cult figure who lived in China for many years. He applied his whole life, tremendous intellect and great spiritual faith to building a philosophy which would reconcile Christian theology with the scientific theory of evolution. His aim was to link the facts of religious experience with those of natural science.

A Hymn of the Universe
[T218] Fontana pbk **£2.50**

The Future of Man
[T219] Fontana pbk **£1.95**

The Phenomenon of Man
An original synthesis of Christianity and evolutionary ideas which has, since its posthumous publication in 1959, gained the status of a 20th century classic, and is regarded as Teilhard de Chardin's masterpiece.
[T220] Fount pbk **£2.95**

CUPITT, DON
A controversial Christian thinker, Cupitt is currently Dean of Emmanuel College, Cambridge. His television series *The Sea of Faith* looked at the reasons behind, and considered some answers to, the crisis of faith in modern times. He recognises the Church's success in redefining aspects of Christian teaching, but sees a failure to meet the challenge of demythologising doctrine. Cupitt makes an impassioned call for the renewal of a living faith, to be defined by the individual for him, or herself.

Christ and the Hiddenness of God
[T221] SCM **£6.50**

Nature of Man
[T222] Sheldon P pbk **£4.50**

Only Human
[T223] SCM pbk **£5.95**

Radicals and the Future of the Church `NEW`
Cupitt's latest book examines the doctrines of modern philosophy which influence radical Christians, and considers how they effect the notion of Christianity as One Church, One Faith, One Lord. Cupitt proposes strategies for survival by redesigning the church of

the future - one that is structurally democratic, credally minimalist and consistently libertarian.
[T224] SCM pbk **£6.95**

Taking Leave of God
When published in 1980, this book created a storm, and was the start of the controversy - could Cupitt remain a Christian and call for such a radical understanding of modern Christianity?
[T225] SCM pbk **£6.50**

The Leap of Reason
[T226] SCM pbk **£4.95**

The New Christian Ethics `NEW`
This recent book argues that all ethical positions are a matter of personal preference.
[T227] SCM pbk **£6.95**

COWDELL, SCOTT
Atheist Priest? Don Cupitt and Christianity `NEW`
An examination of how Cupitt has arrived at his controversial, non-realist interpretation of Christianity.
[T228] SCM pbk **£6.50**

ERASMUS, DESIDERIUS (c.1467 - 1536)
The greatest humanist and scholar of his age, this Dutch Augustinian monk was to revolutionise European literature with his writings and his many translations of the Bible.

In Praise of Folly
Sir Thomas More encouraged Erasmus in the writing of this, one of the most influential clerical satires ever written. It anticipated the Reformation in its attacks on the corruption and ideological barrenness of contemporary theologians, providing an ideal model of the 'new learning' then sweeping through Europe.
[T229] Penguin pbk **£3.99**

HEBBLETHWAITE, B.L.
The Problem of Theology
Is there such a subject? A standard introduction to the issues of 'rational talk about God', and the wider and looser senses in which the notion of 'theology' is used.
[T230] Cambridge pbk **£7.95**

KEMPIS, THOMAS A (1379 - 1471)
A German Augustinian monk who served his vocation as subprior and eventually Prior at the convent of Agnetenberg near Zwolle.

The Imitation of Christ
This, his best known mystical prose work, owes its wide appeal to the simplicity of its language and the piety and sincerity of its author. In it he traces the spiritual development of a Christian soul as it detaches itself from the world and moves towards a union with God.
[T231] A Clark hbk **£3.50**
[T232] Penguin pbk **£2.95**

KUNG, HANS (1928 -)
Widely influential Swiss theologian and controversial critic of the hierarchy of the Roman Catholic church. His licence to teach theology was revoked by the Doctrinal Congregation in Rome, following his questioning of the Pope's infallibility.

Christianity and the World Religions
[T233] Fount pbk **£5.95**

Does God Exist?
[T234] Fount pbk **£5.95**

Eternal Life?
[T235] Fount pbk **£5.95**

Infallible? An Inquiry
Kung's most controversial statement of the doubts about Catholic doctrine, which led to the withdrawal of his official licence to teach theology.
[T236] Fount pbk **£1.25**

On Being a Christian
[T237] Collins hbk **£15.00**
[T238] Fount pbk **£5.95**

Why I Am Still a Christian
[T239] T Clark pbk **£4.95**

KUNG, HANS & MOLTMANN, JURGEN (EDS)
Right to Dissent
[T240] T Clark pbk **£3.75**

LIBERATION THEOLOGY
Primarily a movement in Latin-American political and church life, Liberation Theology has spawned a whole school of theologies, many of them far more extreme than that espoused by Gutierrez in his classic book on the subject *A Theology of Liberation*. In its most radical form, Liberation Theology has caused controversy because of its mixture of Marxism and Christianity, as well as its acceptance of a level of violence necessary to ensure reform and change.

BOFF, LEONARD & CLODOVIS
Introducing Liberation Theology
In the series: *Liberation and Theology*. This volume addresses the fundamental issues tackled by Liberation Theology: oppression, the role of violence etc.
[T241] Burns & Oates pbk **£3.95**

GUTIERREZ, GUSTAVO
A Theology of Liberation
Gutierrez, a Peruvian theologian, is seen by many as the founder of Liberation Theology.
[T242] SCM pbk **£9.50**

Power of the Poor in History
[T243] SCM pbk **£7.95**

LOYOLA, ST IGNATIUS (1491 - 1556)
A soldier of considerable energy, Loyola was seriously wounded in the siege of Pamplona; during his convalescence he experienced a spiritual awakening and thereafter devoted himself to God. In 1534 he founded the Society of Jesus (the Jesuits), a spiritual army committed to zealous missionary work and austere self-abstinence.

Spiritual Exercises
A taxing set of rules for spiritual training, whose aim is to bring the soul closer to an understanding of God; the exercises are central to the training of Jesuit monks.
[T244] A Clark pbk **£3.75**

LUTHER, MARTIN (1483 - 1546)
German religious reformer, theologian and founder of the Protestant faith. In 1517 his outrage at the sale of Catholic indulgences led to the nailing of his ninety-five theses to the door of Wittenberg Cathedral, protesting against the authority of the Pope; with this symbolic act of dissent the Reformation began.

Bondage of the Will
[T245] J Clarke hbk **£8.50**

DILLENBERGER, JOHN (ED)
Selections from His Writings `NEW`
Thorough introduction to Luther's writing.
[T246] Anchor P pbk **£6.50**

NEWMAN, JOHN HENRY CARDINAL
(1801 - 1890)
Despite his mother's Calvinist influence on his early life, Newman's involvement with the High Church Tractarians and the Oxford Movement was the beginning of a spiritual journey which led to his conversion to Catholicism in 1845; he was made a cardinal in 1879 by Pope Leo XIII. A celebrated preacher and prose stylist, he used his great gifts for oratory and writing to expound the basis of his own belief.

Apologia Pro Vita Sua
Provoked by a controversy with Charles Kingsley, this spiritual biography contains a brilliant defence of Newman's conversion to Catholicism.
[T247] Sheed & W pbk **£6.50**

Dream of Gerontius
Newman's moving poem, memorably set to music by Elgar, depicts the journey of a soul to Heaven.
[T248] Mowbray pbk **£1.95**

RELIGION

Cardinal John Henry Newman
(Photo: BBC Hulton Picture Library)

Essay in Aid of a Grammer of Assent
An examination of the nature of belief, which places
importance on intuitive perception rather than the
results of logical reasoning.
[T249] Notre Dame UP pbk **£8.75**

SCHLEIERMACHER, FRIEDERICH
(1768 - 1834)
German theologian of the turn of the 19th century.
His writings form the basis for much modern
Protestant theology, emphasising the importance of
inner experience and the knowledge of God as
mediated through history.
Christian Faith
Written in 1821-22, and revised in 1830, this is
regarded as Schleiermacher's culminating
masterpiece.
[T250] T Clark hbk **£16.95**
CLEMENTS, KEITH (ED)
Friedrich Schleiermacher
Part of the *Making of Modern Theology* series.
[T251] Collins hbk **£7.95**

TILLICH, PAUL (1886 - 1965)
Existentialist theologian and philosopher who settled
in America after the rise of the Nazis in his native
Germany.
Love, Power and Justice
[T252] Oxford pbk **£6.50**
**Systematic Theology Vol 1: Reason and
Revelation, Being and God**
[T253] SCM pbk **£12.50**
The Courage to Be
Concise and clearly written introduction to Tillich's
main themes. Discusses the notion of 'ultimate
reality' - that which motivates individuals and forms
the goal of religious quests.
[T254] Fontana pbk **£1.95**
Vol 2: Existence and the Church
[T255] SCM hbk **£9.50**
**Vol 3: Life and the Spirit: Existence and
the Kingdom of God**
[T256] SCM hbk **£12.50**

TAYLOR, MARK KLINE (ED)
Paul Tillich
Part of the *Making of Modern Theology* series. A
survey of Tillich's work with commentaries on his
most important contributions to modern theological
writings.
[T257] Collins pbk **£7.95**

WARD, KEITH
Currently Professor of the History and Philosophy of
Religion at King's College, University of London.
The Rule of Love   NEW
A set of meditations on the text of the Sermon
on the Mount, which consider what the nature of true
happiness is, and look at ways of obeying God in
everyday life.
[T258] Daybreak pbk **£4.95**
**Turn of the Tide: Christianity in Britain
Today**
A survey of Christianity in present day society.
Initially produced as a series of radio talks, in which
he presented the evidence for the revitalisation of the
intellectual strength and vigour of Christianity.
[T259] BBC pbk **£3.50**

Devotional Literature

ANON
Cloud of Unknowing
A work of profound contemplation written by an
unknown Christian mystic of the 14th century.
[T260] SPCK pbk **£9.50**
[T261] Hodder pbk **£1.75**

ARMSTRONG, KAREN (ED)
**Tongues of Fire: An Anthology of
Religious and Poetic Experience**
[T262] Penguin pbk **£5.95**

ASSISI, ST FRANCIS OF (1181/2 - 1226)
Born the son of a prosperous merchant, Francis lived
an exuberant, extravagant youth until he became very
ill. This was the beginning of his conversion, later
completed on his return from a military venture
when he experienced a vision. He gave up his
inheritance and devoted himself to the sick and poor,
living as a hermit. He swiftly drew a following,
and by 1210 the Franciscan order had received
recognition from Pope Innocent III. He was canonised
in 1228.
Little Flowers of St. Francis
Includes the famous *All Creatures of our God and
King*. A simple, lyrical celebration of God's creation,
especially through the birds and animals of the natural
world.
[T263] Hodder pbk **£2.25**
Praying with St Francis
A book of the prayers, praises and meditations of St
Francis, through which the modern Christian may
share in his devotion to God.
[T264] SPCK pbk **£2.25**

AUGUSTINE, ST (354 - 430)
Praying with St Augustine
In a simple, accessible format this book contains
selected prayers, meditations and praises by Saint
Augustine.
[T265] SPCK pbk **£2.50**

BARCLAY, WILLIAM
The Lord is My Shepherd
This was William Barclay's last collections of
writings. Having spent his life interpreting and
lecturing on the New Testament, he was beginning to
turn his attention to the Old Testament shortly before
he died. This contains commentaries on a selection
from the Psalms.
[T266] Fount pbk **£1.50**

CASSIDY, SHEILA
Sharing the Darkness   NEW
A study of the spirituality of the carer by hospice
Doctor Cassidy.
[T267] DLT hbk **£4.95**

COLLIER, BETH
**Beyond Words: Prayer as a Way
of Life**
Born out of the harsh experience of a serious illness,
the author learnt the importance of contemplative
prayer. In this book she seeks to introduce others to a
similar way of life.
[T268] SPCK pbk **£2.25**

GRIFFITHS, BEDE
Return to the Centre
[T269] Fount pbk **£2.50**

HUDDLESTON, TREVOR
Ordained in 1937 after having travelled in India and
Africa. In 1943 the ministry took him to South Africa
where he became a vociferous champion for the rights
of black South Africans.
I Believe
A reflection, phrase by phrase, upon the words of the
Creed.
[T270] Fount pbk **£1.75**

JOHN OF THE CROSS, ST (1542 - 1591)
Spanish Carmelite friar who came into conflict with
the authorities for expressing sympathy with the
reformists. After being appointed to a convent in
Avila, he was arrested and imprisoned in Toledo,
during which time he composed his noblest mystical
writings, which are considered to be among the finest
in Spanish poetry.
Dark Night of the Soul
[T271] Burns & Oates pbk **£4.95**
[T272] Hodder pbk **£1.95**

JULIAN OF NORWICH, ST (c. 1342 - after 1416)
The mystic Julian of Norwich was a recluse in a cell
attached to the church of St. Julian at Norwich.
Revelations of Divine Love
Gives an account of the visions which appeared to her
whilst she was ill in 1373, together with her
meditations on these mystical experiences.
[T273] Penguin pbk **£3.95**

KROLL, UNA
Growing Older   NEW
A practical and inspiring approach to aging.
[T274] Collins pbk **£2.95**

LOYOLA, ST IGNATIUS
**Finding God in All Things: Praying with
St. Ignatius**
An interpretation of the ideas on prayer developed
and practised by St Ignatius Loyola.
[T275] Fount pbk **£2.95**

MADDOCKS, MORRIS BISHOP
A Healing House of Prayer   NEW
A selection of prayers structured for each day of the
month. The prayers guide the reader through rooms of
a house, taking the person through quiet
contemplation, healing presence, wisdom, praises,
stillness in the face of God, to preparation for
Christian living in the world.
[T276] Hodder pbk **£6.95**

MARSHALL, E. & HAMPLE, S.
Children's Letters to God
[T277] Fount pbk **£1.95**

RELIGION

RAMSEY, MICHAEL
Archbishop of Canterbury from 1961 - 1974, Ramsey died in 1988. The focus of his office was the quest for Christian unity - in 1966 he met with Pope Paul IV, the first such meeting since the Reformation. His ministry was one of contemplation and scholarship.
Be Still and Know
[T278] Fount pbk **£1.95**

ROLLE, RICHARD (c. 1300 - 1349)
One of the most important 14th century mystics, Rolle lived for many years at Hampole in Yorkshire.
English Writings NEW
In the *Classics of Western Spirituality* series.
[T279] SPCK pbk **£13.50**
The Fire of Love
Describes an intense personal relationship with Christ, likening it to a raging fire in the breast.
[T280] Penguin pbk **£3.99**

SEALY, HOPE (ED)
Prayer for the Day NEW
An anthology from contributors to the Radio 4 series over the past two years. Includes contributions from the Archbishop of Canterbury, Lady Longford and Wendy Craig.
[T281] BBC pbk **£3.50**

SMITH, DELIA
A Journey into God NEW
This popular writer shares her vision of the day-to-day reality of prayer.
[T282] Hodder hbk **£7.95**

SNOWDEN, RITA
Prayers in Large Print
A sharing of personal prayer, particularly aimed at those nearing the end of their lives.
[T283] Fount pbk **£2.50**

TERESA OF AVILA, ST (1515 - 1582)
Spanish Carmelite nun and author, famous for her mystical visions. She was also tirelessly practical, working hard to re-establish the simple strictures of the Carmelite order. By the time of her death she had founded 17 reformed convents throughout Spain.
Interior Castle or the Mansions
[T284] Hodder pbk **£2.50**
The Life of Saint Teresa of Avila by Herself
This autobiography includes a vivid account of her early life and tells of her transformation by profound religious experiences. It follows her progress towards the spiritual ecstasy of consummation or 'marriage' with God.
[T285] Penguin pbk **£4.95**
Way of Perfection
A spiritual guide for the nuns of her Order.
[T286] Sheed & W pbk **£5.50**

TERESA, MOTHER
Albanian-born missionary, now an Indian citizen. Her life has been dedicated to helping the underpriviledged in India and other countries. She was awarded the Nobel Peace Prize in 1979 and in 1980 the Bharat Ratna (Star of India).
Gift for God
[T287] Fount pbk **£1.50**
Love of Christ
[T288] Fount pbk **£1.95**

TOURVILLE, ABBE DE
One of the great spiritual figures of the 19th century. A French Catholic priest whose letters articulate the desire to know and to foster in oneself all the capabilities of the soul in order to make its potential and grace actual.
Letters of Direction
[T289] Mowbray pbk **£2.75**

'The Creation of the Stars' from a 12th century Hexameron of St Ambrose in *Painting in Europe 800-1200* by C.R. Dodwell (Penguin hbk £30.00)

Streams of Grace
A new selection from his letters, translated by Robin Waterfield.
[T290] Fount pbk **£2.50**

WILSON, WENDY (ED)
Pearls of Wisdom NEW
A collection of favourite quotations from famous people. Published to mark the 30th anniversary of Cruse, the charity which helps the bereaved.
[T291] DLT hbk **£4.95**

WIRT, SHERWOOD ELIOT
Spiritual Awakening
A collection of devotional writings from over a dozen spiritual leaders of the 18th century. Includes the writings of John Wesley, J. Newton and William Law.
[T292] Lion pbk **£3.95**

Modern Christianity

ARMSTRONG, KAREN
Armstrong entered an English teaching order of nuns in 1962, taking her vows in 1965. She was sent by the order to read English Literature and Language at Oxford University in 1967, with a view to her teaching in one of their schools. In 1969 she left the order.
The Gospel according to Women
With *The Testament of Woman: Christianity's Creation of the Sex War*.
[T293] Pan hbk **£3.50**
Through the Narrow Gate
The story of a young woman's decision to follow the life of Christ, the struggle, torment and the eventual failure of her faith.
[T294] Pan pbk **£3.50**

BARCLAY, OLIVER (ED)
Pacifism and War
Part of Inter-Varsity's *When Christians Disagree* series in which subjects of contention between Christians are debated by a number of contributors, each presenting her or his case.
[T295] IVP pbk **£6.95**

BARCLAY, WILLIAM
A Plain Man Looks at the Apostles' Creed
[T296] Fount pbk **£3.50**

A Plain Man Looks at the Beatitudes
[T297] Fount pbk **£1.95**
A Plain Man Looks at the Lord's Prayer
[T298] Fount pbk **£1.50**

BARTON, JOHN
People of the Book? NEW
The 1988 Bampton lectures present a positive and informed view of the authority of Scripture. There is a balance between critical awareness and sensitivity to the inspiring, enriching power of God.
[T299] Mowbray pbk **£9.95**

BAUCKHAM, RICHARD
The Bible in Politics - How to Read the Bible Politically NEW
This is not a summary of politics in the Bible, nor a programme for Christian political action, but rather a method of studying the Bible politically. The author describes how the notion of separating politics from religion is a modern notion, and he sees in the rediscovery of a political message a return to normality.
[T300] SPCK pbk **£6.95**

BEESON, TREVOR & PEARCE, JENNY
A Vision of Hope
Against the background of political instability, war and repression in eight representative countries of Latin America, this book tells of the positive response of the Christian churches.
[T301] Fount pbk **£2.95**

BERRY, R.J.
God and Evolution NEW
Recognising the difficulties many Christians encounter with the notion of evolution, Berry examines the biblical basis for God's control of the world, and seeks to reconcile this with the theory of evolution.
[T302] Hodder pbk **£6.95**

BOOM, CORRIE TEN
Jesus is Victor NEW
[T303] Kingsway pbk **£1.95**
The Hiding Place
The enthralling story of the writer's courageous and harrowing involvement in underground activities against the Nazis in Holland.
[T304] Hodder pbk **£2.95**

BORROWDALE, ANNE
A Woman's Work - Changing Christian Attitudes NEW
A challenging look at the Christian ideals of love and self-sacrifice, and the way in which this traditional ethic has done harm to women through the assumptions of the virtue of unceasing, unquestioning and often unrewarded service to others. Illustrated throughout with cartoons by Posy Simmonds.
[T305] SPCK pbk **£4.95**

BRIERLEY, PETER (ED)
UK Christian Handbook NEW
Revised and updated, this 1989 edition has over 4,000 entries with statistics and charts which give an insight into the changing fortunes of British churches since 1970.
[T306] MARC Europe hbk **£14.95**

BROWN, LAURENCE
The Psychology of Religion - An Introduction NEW
A clear and authoritative discussion of the nature of religious personality, conversion and development, religious experience and commitment.
[T307] SPCK pbk **£6.95**

BYRNE, LAVINIA

Sharing the Vision - Creative Encounters between Religious and Lay Life `NEW`

Explores the growing dialogue between religious and lay people. Set in various contexts, Byrne encourages the exploration and understanding of the past, the need to share present experiences, and hopes for a shared vision of the future.
[T308] SPCK pbk **£4.95**

COCKERELL, DAVID

Beginning Where We Are - A Theology of Pastoral Ministry `NEW`

Examines the need to respond to the economic and socio-cultural changes which have taken place since World War II. Cockerell presents a radical alternative to conventional approaches to ministry, proposing the starting point as listening to the insights and concerns of those ministered to.
[T309] SCM pbk **£8.50**

COLSON, CHARLES W.

Former aide of President Nixon who was implicated in the Watergate scandal and sent to prison, during which period he was converted to Christianity. Since his release, he has been active in setting up the worldwide network of Prison Fellowship - an organisation created to help and encourage prisoners whilst in prison, and on their release.

Born Again
The story of his conversion whilst in prison.
[T310] Hodder pbk **£2.95**

Kingdoms in Conflict
Reflects on the rightful place of the Christian within the political world, the conflicts between Church and State, and the temptations and responsibilities which befall those in power.
[T311] Hodder pbk **£3.50**

COOK, DAVID

The Moral Maze
In this clear and energetic book, David Cook outlines a method for considering ethical questions from a Christian perspective - this is then demonstrated with set examples (e.g. abortion). Cook does not impose an answer, but guides the reader as to the central issues which should be considered.
[T312] SPCK pbk **£5.95**

Thinking about Faith - A Beginner's Guide
A clear and lively introduction to the key themes in thinking about faith. Cook confronts the fear involved in applying philosophical ideas to religion and theology, and offers the reader reassurance and guidance.
[T313] IVP pbk **£5.95**

COSSTICK, VICKY (ED)

Aids: Meeting the Community Challenge
A good collection of essays which challenge and provoke the reader. The contributors, who include the Chief Rabbi and Cardinal Hume, do not present a unified voice, but display a range of religious thinking on responses to this health crisis.
[T314] St Paul pbk **£5.95**

DAVIES, PAUL

God and the New Physics
Shows how far the recent explosive discoveries of the new physics are revolutionising our view of the world, and in particular throwing new light on many of the questions formerly posed by religion.
[T315] Penguin pbk **£4.99**

DEVANANDA, ANGELO

Mother Teresa
[T316] Fount pbk **£3.50**

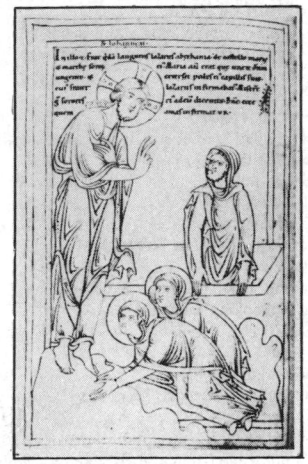

'The Raising of Lazarus' from a 12th century book of Necrologies, from *Painting in Europe 800-1200* by C.R. Dodwell (Penguin pbk £30.00)

FIELD, FRANK

The Politics of Paradise
A discussion of the Christian approach to politics by the Labour MP for Birkenhead. He suggests that politics is more to do with attitudes than a set of programmes.
[T317] Fount pbk **£3.50**

FOSKETT, JOHN & LYALL, DAVID

Helping the Helpers `NEW`
Describes models of supervision and discusses its problems and its value for pastoral education.
[T318] SPCK pbk **£5.95**

FYNN

Mister God, This is Anna
A very popular book, simply written, but one which confronts profound spiritual concerns.
[T319] Fount pbk **£2.50**

GERARD, GEOFFREY

Away from it All: A Guide to Retreat Houses `NEW`
This fourth edition contains a new section on retreat houses in Ireland, alongside updated material on over 150 guest houses, monasteries and retreats throughout the UK.
[T320] Lutterworth pbk **£3.95**

GRAHAM, BILLY

The charismatic American evangelist who has become the apologist for 'Born Again Christianity'. He is famous for his powerful and persuasive preaching at mass gatherings.

Angels: God's Secret Agents
[T321] Hodder pbk **£1.95**

Approaching Hoof-Beats
[T322] Hodder pbk **£1.95**

How to be Born Again
[T323] Hodder pbk **£2.25**

GREEN, MICHAEL

Previously rector of St. Aldate's, Oxford, where he built up one of the most energetic and enthusiastic evangelical congregations in England.

Baptism
[T324] Hodder pbk **£1.95**

The Day Death Died
Offers the evidence for and implications of the crux of the Christian faith - the death and resurrection of Jesus Christ.
[T325] IVP pbk **£1.50**

You Must Be Joking: Popular Excuses for Avoiding Jesus Christ
[T326] Hodder pbk **£1.95**

HUDDLESTON, TREVOR (1913 -)

Naught for Your Comfort
One of the first books to make the world aware of the suffering of black people in South Africa.
[T327] Fount pbk **£2.50**

HUME, BASIL CARDINAL

To Be a Pilgrim `NEW`
The Cardinal expounds his thoughts on the Christian pilgrimage to eternal happiness with God.
[T328] Tharpa pbk **£2.50**

IDLE, MAJORIE

Joy in the City `NEW`
The wife of a pastor describes her experiences of ministry in the East End of London, the lessons learned and encouragement gained there.
[T329] Kingsway pbk **£2.25**

JENKINS, DAVID E.

Controversial contemporary theologian and Bishop of Durham.

God, Miracle and the Church of England
Jenkins describes this book as 'being about the sort of God we believe in or should believe in, about what God does, what he wants and what he offers'. He sees the search for answers to these questions as forming the purpose of his own particular discipleship and local ministry. These pieces are elaborations of lectures and sermons given since his installation as Bishop of Durham.
[T330] SCM pbk **£4.95**

God, Politics and the Future
[T331] SCM pbk **£4.95**

KENNY, ANTHONY JOHN PATRICK

A Path from Rome: An Autobiography
Moving autobiography of Kenny's journey from priest to Oxford philosopher.
[T332] Oxford pbk **£4.95**

KING, MARTIN LUTHER (1929 - 1968)

American black civil rights leader and Baptist minister. He was awarded the Nobel Peace Prize in 1964. During the 1960s he lectured on, and discussed with religious and state leaders, the problems faced by blacks in their struggle for freedom. He was killed by a hired assassin in 1968 - the work of a conspiracy whose members have never been found.

Strength to Love
Coretta Scott King describes this book as 'the best explanation and exposition of Martin Luther King's philosophy of non-violence; his belief in a divine, loving presence that binds all of life'.
[T333] Fount pbk **£1.95**

Words of Martin Luther King
[T334] Fount pbk **£1.95**

KOSSOFF, DAVID

Award-winning actor and occasional writer and teller of his own stories. His television series *Stories from the Bible* made a great impact.

Bible Stories
Favourite episodes from the Bible vividly brought to life by Kossoff.
[T335] Fount pbk **£2.50**

Book of Witnesses
[T336] Fount pbk **£2.50**

KUSHNER, HAROLD S.

When All You've Ever Wanted isn't Enough
[T337] Pan pbk **£2.50**

When Bad Things Happen to Good People
A classic analysis, in comforting and accessible terms, of what theologians like to call 'theodicy'.
[T338] Pan pbk **£3.50**

LEES, SHIRLEY (ED)
The Role of Women
In the *When Christians Disagree* series: questions such as the women's role in the Church and home are here hotly debated.
[T339] IVP pbk **£6.25**

LEWIS, C.S. (1898 - 1963)
For many years an atheist, the celebrated Oxford scholar and don became a convert to Christianity in 1929. One of the finest and most popular Christian apologists of this century, he brought his discerning mind, wit and imagination to bear on a diverse range of subjects.
Christian Reflections
[T340] Fount pbk **£2.50**
Fern-Seed and Elephants
[T341] Fount pbk **£1.75**
First and Second Things
[T342] Fount pbk **£1.75**
God in the Dock
A collection of lectures, articles and sermons defending orthodox Christianity.
[T343] Fount pbk **£1.50**
Letters to Children
[T344] Fount pbk **£1.95**
Mere Christianity
[T345] Fount pbk **£2.50**
Miracles
'The central miracle asserted by Christians is the Incarnation. They say that God became Man. Every other miracle prepares the way for this or results from this' states Lewis, providing the key to the book.
[T346] Fount pbk **£2.50**
Of This and Other Worlds
[T347] Fount pbk **£2.50**
Prayer: Letters to Malcolm
Lewis's last book, this is an imaginative approach to the problems of prayer.
[T348] Fount hbk **£1.95**
Present Concerns
[T349] Fount pbk **£1.95**
Reflections on the Psalms
[T350] Fount pbk **£1.95**
Screwtape Letters
Recognised as a milestone in the history of popular theology and in the religious experience of many people; it is designed for those whose approach to their religion is beset by doubts and hesitations.
[T351] Fount pbk **£3.50**
Screwtape Proposes a Toast
[T352] Fount pbk **£2.50**
Surprised by Joy
An autobiographical volume charting Lewis's early life, culminating in his conversion to Christianity.
[T353] Fount pbk **£2.95**
The Abolition of Man
[T354] Fount pbk **£1.25**
The Business of Heaven
A delightful collection of readings, one for each day of the year, selected from the work of Lewis.
[T355] Fount pbk **£2.95**
The Four Loves
One of Lewis's finest books. The Four Loves are distinguished here as: Affection, Friendship, Eros and Charity. He discerns the dangers of the first three, which can become dangerous without Charity - the divine love which is the sum and goal of all.
[T356] Fount pbk **£1.95**
The Great Divorce
[T357] Fount pbk **£1.95**
The Pilgrim's Regress
[T358] Fount pbk **£2.50**

The Problem of Pain
Alongside the *Screwtape Letters*, this is one of Lewis's most important contributions to modern theological writing.
[T359] Fount pbk **£2.50**
Timeless at Heart
A recent compilation of essays, lectures and articles on aspects of faith.
[T360] Fount pbk **£2.50**

LINZEY, ANDREW
Christianity and the Rights of Animals
Deals with the status of animals in Christianity proposing a 'theology' of animals.
[T361] SPCK pbk **£5.95**

MAKOWER, FRANCES
Faith or Folly? Drugs, Ministry and Community   NEW
A moving and personal story of the work of a Roman Catholic nun (from a Jewish family) and her work in a Baptist community for people dependent on drugs. She displays the mutual enrichment of the meeting of faiths to work with a difficult contemporary problem.
[T362] DLT pbk **£4.95**

MCCARROLL, TOBIAS
Morning Glory Babies: Children   NEW
with Aids and the Celebration of Life
The response of a small Catholic community in the United States to the presence of AIDS in our world. Their response is practical - adopting and fostering babies with HIV & AIDS; political - as they start to appreciate the reasons for the state's neglect of these unfortunate infants; and spiritual - integrating the joy of these children's short lives into their understanding of God. Profoundly moving and inspiring.
[T363] Triangle pbk **£2.95**

MERTON, THOMAS
There has been recent renewed interest in the writings of Thomas Merton, now emerging as one of the most significant figures in modern American Catholicism. He had a wide-ranging, uncloistered intelligence, and a passion for Eastern religions and radical Western politics.
The Seven Storey Mountain
Merton's autobiography has been decribed as one of the few books about the life of the spirit which is flattering to contemporary intelligence, despite being written in thoroughly modern idiom. An important contribution to modern literature admired by Graham Greene, amongst others.
[T364] Sheldon pbk **£8.95**

MILLS, HAYLEY & MACLAINE, MARCUS (EDS)
My God: Letters from the Famous on God and the Life Hereafter   NEW
Over 100 people answer the questions 'Who or What is your idea of God?' and 'What do you think happens to you when you die?'. Contributors include the Archbishop of Canterbury, the Dalai Lama and cartoonist Mel Calman. Royalties go to Save the Children Fund.
[T365] Pelham hbk **£9.95**

MONTEFIORE, HUGH
Of Anglo-Jewish background, Montefiore was converted to Christianity at Rugby School. From 1978 until his retirement in 1987, he was Bishop of Birmingham and became well known for his outspoken views on political, moral and social issues.
Communicating the Gospel in a Scientific Age   NEW
[T366] St Andrew P pbk **£3.50**

MOSS, ROLAND
The Earth in our Hands
Professor Moss calls Christians to act in the face of the present ecological crisis.
[T367] IVP pbk **£2.25**

MUGGERIDGE, MALCOLM
For many years a journalist and broadcaster on current affairs, Muggeridge became more widely known for his commentaries on modern society, which took on philosophical and religious resonances. His growing commitment to Christianity culminated a few years ago in his conversion to Catholicism - an event which received widespread media coverage.
Conversion: A Spiritual Journey
[T368] Fount pbk **£2.95**
Jesus Rediscovered
[T369] Fount pbk **£2.50**
Jesus: The Man who Lives
[T370] Fount pbk **£2.50**
Something Beautiful for God
[T371] Fount pbk **£2.50**

O'DONOVAN, OLIVER
Peace and Certainty - A   NEW
Theological Essay on Deterrence
Instead of treating deterrence as an appendage to the current debates on the morality of nuclear weapons, Professor O'Donovan sees how the whole argument can turn on this issue. He considers deterrence as an alternative to war and analyses its morality from this perspective.
[T372] Oxford pbk **£4.95**

PAGELS, ELAINE
Adam, Eve and the Serpent   NEW
An important contribution to the study of sexual morality, social psychology and Christian doctrine.
[T373] Weidenfeld hbk **£14.95**

PARRATT, JOHN (ED)
A Reader in African Christian Theology
Contains 12 essays by leading African theologians on the major theological concerns in today's Africa.
[T374] SPCK pbk **£7.50**

PEBERDY, ALYSON (ED)
Women Priests?   NEW
Steps back from the debate to allow the main protagonists to present their arguments as to whether the ordination of women is consistent with orthodox faith. Includes contributions from John Austin Baker (Bishop of Salisbury), Alexina Murphy and Janet Martin Soskice.
[T375] Marshall P pbk **£3.99**

PIERIS, ALOYSIUS, S.J.
An Asian Theology of Liberation   NEW
Examines the complex issues presented by Third World poverty for modern Christian belief.
[T376] T Clark hbk **£7.95**

PRIESTLAND, GERALD
Priestland became Religious Affairs correspondent for the BBC in 1977, after a career as Foreign Correspondent in New Delhi and Beirut.
Gerald Priestland at Large
The third volume of the *Yours Faithfully* collection of radio talks.
[T377] Fount pbk **£1.95**
Priestland Right & Wrong
[T378] Fount pbk **£1.95**
Priestland's Progress
[T379] BBC pbk **£3.50**
Something Understood: An Autobiography
'He...managed to find God without losing his sense of humour' (Chaim Bermant, *Observer*).
[T380] Arrow pbk **£3.99**

The Case Against God
Gerald Priestland presses the case against God cross-examining a number of witnesses - A.J. Ayer, Shirley Williams, Iris Murdoch and Don Cupitt - for evidence against the possibility of a divine being.
[T381] Fount pbk **£2.75**
Yours Faithfully Vol 2
[T382] Fount pbk **£1.25**

REEVES, DONALD
Rector of St James Church, Piccadilly in London since 1980.
**Making Sense of Religion -
A Fresh Look at Christianity** NEW
Based on the series on BBC television, Donald Reeves examines many of the original and controversial ideas to make sense of religion. He considers new expressions for God (as mother and lover) and re-examines the roles of Jesus Christ and the church.
[T383] BBC pbk **£4.99**

SAMUEL, VINAY & SUGDEN, CHRISTOPHER
**Lambeth '88: A View from the
Two Thirds World** NEW
Describes the impact made upon, and by, bishops from developing countries attending the 1988 Lambeth conference.
[T384] SPCK pbk **£6.95**

SHEPPARD, DAVID & WORLOCK, DEREK
**Better Together: Christian Partnership
in a Hurt City**
Bishop Sheppard and Archbishop Worlock talk of their partnership in seeking to bring solace to the many social troubles of Liverpool.
[T385] Penguin pbk **£3.99**

STOTT, JOHN
Rector Emeritus of All Souls, Langham Place and President of the London Institute for Contemporary Christianity, Stott is regarded as one of the foremost spokespersons of the Evangelical community.
Basic Christianity
[T386] IVP pbk **£2.50**
The Cross of Christ
A detailed analysis of the significance of Christ's cross, meeting head-on difficulties encountered in the Atonement.
[T387] IVP pbk **£7.95**

SURIN, KENNETH
Theology and the Problem of Evil
An exciting journey into theodicy examining the theoretical and practical approaches to thinking on this issue. Through considering both 'process' and 'theoretical' approaches, Surin concludes that the only practical approach is one rooted in the reality of human suffering and grounded in the notion of God being justified through justifying sinners. He concludes with a call for a messianic and practical solidarity with all afflicted.
[T388] Blackwell pbk **£8.95**

TUTU, DESMOND
The first black Archbishop of Cape Town, recipient of the Nobel Peace Prize, and a passionate spokesperson for the blacks of South Africa.
Hope and Suffering
[T389] Fount pbk **£2.50**

WALLIS, JIM (ED)
The Rise of Christian Conscience
Explaining and outlining the new movement of conscience within today's Church, this contains pieces from many contributors, including Bishop Desmond Tutu.
[T390] Harper & R pbk **£7.95**

WALSH, JOHN
Growing Up Catholic NEW
A joyful romp through the Catholic religion with the experiences of famous and lapsed Catholics, including Wendy Perriam, Karen Armstrong, Edna O'Brien and Anthony Burgess.
[T391] Macmillan pbk **£5.99**

WARNER, MARINA
**Alone of All Her Sex: The Cult of the
Virgin Mary**
A fascinating and important book considering the history of adoration of Mary, and the effect of this on modern woman.
[T392] Picador pbk **£6.95**

WATSON, DAVID
One of the most important figures in the recent Evangelical movement in Britain, whose recent death from cancer was much mourned. He studied sciences at Cambridge, where he was converted, and went on to become a singularly powerful and charismatic preacher. His books are widely popular, setting out the fundamental concerns of Christianity in a clear and accessible manner.
Discipleship
A comprehensive study of what it is - and costs - to be a true disciple of Christ.
[T393] Hodder pbk **£2.95**
Fear No Evil
Written with the knowledge that he was suffering from cancer.
[T394] Hodder pbk **£1.95**
Live a New Life
[T395] IVP pbk **£1.50**
My God is Real
[T396] Falcon pbk **£1.50**

WEIL, SIMONE
A fascinating moralist and thinker, Weil was attracted to the twin edifices of Catholicism and Marxism, but never attached herself entirely to either. She has been recognised as an important Christian apologist, whose writings illuminate the great mysteries of Christianity. She considered communication to be an absolute moral imperative.
Gateway to God
[T397] Fontana pbk **£1.75**
Gravity and Grace
The quality of her analysis of Mediterranean religion and Platonic thought shows her intellectual rigour as well as her near-mystical identification with the oppressed. An object lesson in lucid philosophical enquiry.
[T398] Ark pbk **£3.95**
**Intimations of Christianity among the
Ancient Greeks**
[T399] Ark pbk **£4.95**
Lectures on Philosophy
[T400] Cambridge pbk **£7.50**
Simone Weil: An Anthology
[T401] Virago pbk **£7.99**
Waiting on God
In his introduction, Malcolm Muggeridge writes: *'the mounting tragedy of Western Man and the ever accelerating decomposition of his civilisation serve to underline the urgency of what she had to say.'*
[T402] Fontana pbk **£1.75**

WILES, MAURICE
God's Action in the World
The 1986 Bampton Lectures by Oxford Professor Maurice Wiles consider if, and how, and where God acts in the world.
[T403] SCM pbk **£5.95**

WILLIAMS, HARRY ABBOTT
One of the few contemporary Christian writers whose books have found acceptance and admiration with non-Christians and Christians alike.
Some Day I'll Find You
Harry Williams's spiritual autobiography. The many humorous aspects of the book belie its profound search for Good and for God.
[T404] Fount pbk **£3.50**

WILSON, A.N.
How Can We Know?
A frank and thoughtful book by the popular novelist which discusses how the author perceives the truths which underpin Christian doctrine and how he came to believe that the Christian religion was incontrovertibly true.
[T405] Penguin pbk **£3.50**

WURMBRAND, RICHARD
Pastor Wumbrand endured terrible privation during three years of solitary confinement in an underground prison in Bucharest. During these years he composed many sermons for an unseen congregation, now collected in the following books. His writings offer exceptionally eloquent and moving affirmations of faith.
100 Prison Meditations
[T406] M Pickering pbk **£1.95**
Alone with God
[T407] Hodder pbk **£2.25**
Reaching Towards the Heights
[T408] M Pickering pbk **£2.95**

Non Christian Religions

Buddhism

Buddhism is the Western name given to the teachings of Gautama, a teacher in India in the 5th century BC. It exists in two main forms: *Mahayana*, called the Northern School, since it embraces Tibet, Mongolia, China, Japan and Korea; and *Theravada*, practised in Sri Lanka, Burma and Cambodia. The latter school concentrates on the personal attainment of Nirvana (release from earthly limitations), whereas Mahayana Buddhists renounce this personal quietism in order to concentrate on helping humanity as a whole. Buddhism can be seen as a way of life, not a series of dogmas: its gentle, renunciatory character has given it an increasing apppeal to many dissatisfied with the materialism of Western societies, an interest somewhat ironically reflected in the profusion of recent books on the subject.

BROWN, KERRY & O'BRIEN, J. (EDS) NEW
Essential Teachings of Buddhism
Produced with the assistance of Buddhist priests in Thailand and Japan, this selection of fundamental texts aims to guide the outsider to the essence of Buddhism and aid practitioners in understanding their spiritual inheritance.
[T410] Rider pbk **£8.95**

CARRITHERS, MICHAEL
The Buddha
A brief survey of the life and teachings of the Buddha, locating them in their social and philosophical context. In the *Past Masters* series.
[T411] Oxford pbk **£2.95**

CAUSTON, RICHARD
Nichiren Shoshu Buddhism
Originating in Japan, Nichiren Shoshu is now established as one of the world's most important

contemporary schools; this highly accessible account of the teachings and practice of the movement elucidates a philosophy seeking to combine spiritual growth with practical action in the world.
[T412] Rider pbk **£4.95**

CONZE, EDWARD
A Short History of Buddhism
A chronological survey which traces the development of Buddhism through four major eras.
[T413] Unwin Hyman pbk **£4.95**
Buddhist Wisdom Books
Composed in India sometime between 100 BC and 600 AD, the Diamond and Heart Sutras are central to the Buddhism of Tibet and Japan. Conze provides an accessible translation of the two texts, accompanied by a previously unavailable commentary.
[T414] Unwin Hyman pbk **£5.95**

CONZE, EDWARD (ED)
Buddhist Scriptures
A selection of essential writings from the period AD 100-400, the Golden Age of Buddhist literature.
[T415] Penguin pbk **£3.99**

EASWARAN, EKNATH (TRANS)
The Dhammapada
A recent translation with an excellent general introduction and commentary by a scholar of Sanskrit and English literature, and teacher of meditation.
[T416] Arkana pbk **£4.99**

HUMPHREYS, CHRISTMAS
Humphreys enjoyed the distinction of being England's only Buddhist High Court Judge. He was one of the great advocates of Western Buddhism, and his writings show a clarity and humour that makes them ideal reading for Westerners interested in any aspect of historical or modern Buddhism.
A Popular Dictionary of Buddhism
Concise explanations of all the essential terms in Buddhism are provided here, along with biographical notes on its main figures.
[T417] Curzon pbk **£4.00**
Buddhism
Humphreys' now classic introduction to the history and thought of the many varieties of Buddhism.
[T418] Penguin pbk **£4.99**
Concentration and Meditation
With its basis in Buddhist ideas, but demanding no prior understanding of the subject, a book offering guidance in the development of the mind from simple methods to advanced meditation techniques.
[T419] Element pbk **£7.95**
Exploring Buddhism
The flowering of Buddhism has given rise to a vast range of concepts and enquiries; here some special topics are treated in detail in a series of individual essays.
[T420] Unwin Hyman pbk **£3.95**
The Buddhist Way of Life
[T421] Unwin Hyman pbk **£2.95**

MASCARO, J. (TRANS)
The Dhammapada
This collection of simple verses is believed to have been gathered from the Buddha's early disciples, and is hence the purest representation of his teaching; it has been called the 'Buddhist Sermon on the Mount', and offers a noble system of moral philosophy, the heart of Buddhist thought.
[T422] Penguin pbk **£1.95**

MCDONALD, KATHLEEN
How to Meditate
A practical guide, by a Western Buddhist nun and teacher, to the purpose and techniques of Buddhist meditations.
[T423] Wisdom pbk **£5.95**

Illustration from *Living Buddhism* by Andrew Powell and photographer Graham Harrison (British Museum Publications pbk £14.95)

MERRITT, JANE HAMILTON
A Meditator's Diary: A Western Woman's Unique Experiences in Thai Monasteries
A modern American journalist recounts the experience of her sojourn in a Thai Buddhist monastery, and her struggles to come to terms with an alien way of life.
[T424] Mandala pbk **£3.95**

POWELL, ANDREW
Living Buddhism   **NEW**
The author travelled throughout the Far East with photographer Graham Harrison to produce this record of contemporary Buddhism; a text detailing the pressures of modern society on Buddhist culture is accompanied by a wealth of colour photographs.
[T425] Brit Mus P hbk **£14.95**

SADDHATISSA, H.
The Life of the Buddha
This sensitive reconstruction of the Buddha's life story derives its narrative from careful study of early Sanskrit sources.
[T426] Unwin Hyman pbk **£2.75**

SANGHARAKSHITA
Sangarakshita (born Dennis Lingwood) studied Buddhism and Eastern philosophy in India and, as leader of the Friends of the Western Buddhist Order, is one of the most prominent of Western Buddhists. The following are a selection from his many writings.
A Survey of Buddhism
A comprehensive guide to Buddhist thought and practice, which seeks to demonstrate the essential unity of all Buddhist schools. One of the standard studies, first published in 1957.
[T427] Element pbk **£9.95**
Human Enlightenment
A brief introduction to the methods of Buddhist practice.
[T428] Windhorse pbk **£3.50**
The Three Jewels
The Three Jewels are the Buddha, the Dharma (his teaching) and the Sangha (his followers). An

introduction to Buddhism which emphasizes the three principles central to all forms of Budddhist thought.
[T429] Windhorse pbk **£5.95**

SNELLING, J.
The Buddhist Handbook
A comprehensive guide to the ideas, schools and practices of modern Buddhism.
[T430] Century pbk **£6.95**

SUBHUTI, DHARMACHIRI
Buddhism for Today
New edition of an introduction to contemporary Western Buddhism, providing a survey of various modern schools and an account of the Friends of the Western Buddhist Order, one of the foremost Western Buddhist organisations, in which the author has played an important role.
[T431] Windhorse pbk **£6.25**

SUZUKI, D.T. (TRANS)
Lankavatara Sutra: A Mahayana Text
Written in India (c. 350 AD). The central core of Mahayana teaching is contained here.
[T432] Routledge hbk **£16.95**

Tibetan Buddhism

Although introduced in 640, Tibetan Buddhism did not become established until the 11th century. Fused with the indigenous Bon religion, its practices include meditation, chanting and Tantric rituals. With the exile of the Dalai Lama (the Living God of Tibetan Buddhism) and the popular writings of authors like Trungpa, it has become one of the better known forms of Buddhism in the West; despite the rather sensational mythology which has always surrounded Tibet, it is at heart a very practical spiritual path.

BATCHELOR, STEPHEN (ED)
The Jewel in the Lotus
Unique in combining an approachable introduction to Tibetan Buddhism with selections from the teachings of the major traditions.
[T433] Wisdom pbk **£9.95**

CHOGYAM, NGAKPA
Journey into Vastness
With his informal approach, this English-born lama here offers to a wider audience Tibetan meditation techniques previously taught only in Himalayan monasteries.
[T434] Element pbk **£7.95**
Rainbow of Liberated Energy
A view of the colour and element symbolism of Tibetan Tantra, interwoven with anecdotes about the author's own experience of study in the Himalayas.
[T435] Element pbk **£6.95**

DAVID-NEEL, ALEXANDRA
Magic and Mystery in Tibet
The first European woman to reach Lhasa. This is a fascinating account of David-Neel's travels, weaving together the myths and legends of Tibetan Buddhism.
[T436] Unwin Hyman pbk **£4.95**

EVANS-WENTZ, YEELING
The Tibetan Book of the Dead
Published in 1937 this is an English version of a Tibetan 'Bardo'. It describes methods for a dying man to pass consciously through death and rebirth.
[T437] Oxford hbk **£12.95**
[T438] Oxford pbk **£5.95**

GYATSO, T.
The Buddhism of Tibet
An anthology of works by Gyatso, the fourteenth

Dalai Lama, written as an introduction for the Western reader; also included are two texts often used in the practice of meditation.
[T439] Unwin Hyman pbk **£9.95**

LAMA YESHE
An Introduction to Tantra
A clarification of the often misunderstood ideas of Tantra. The author shows that while our desires often bring dissatisfaction, if properly channelled they can be a useful tool to awaken our inner potential.
[T440] Wisdom pbk **£6.95**

LANDAW, JONATHAN & WEBER, ANDY
Images of Enlightenment **NEW**
With 24 full-colour illustrations taken from specially commissioned paintings, an introduction and guide to the iconography of Tibetan Buddhism through the examination of its most vital images.
[T441] Tharpa pbk **£7.95**

SPARHAM, G. (TRANS)
The Tibetan Dhammapada
The Tibetan version of the central Buddhist text, here presented in a newly revised translation.
[T442] Wisdom pbk **£7.95**

TRUNGPA, C.
Cutting Through Spiritual Materialism
Born and educated in Tibet, Trungpa was until his recent death a leading Buddhist teacher in America. Here he expounds the Buddhist approach to true spirituality.
[T443] Element pbk **£7.95**
The Myth of Freedom
An exploration of contrasting Buddhist and Western notions of freedom, demonstrating the path to true freedom through the Tibetan tradition.
[T444] Element pbk **£10.95**

Zen Buddhism

The school of Japanese Buddhism derived from the Chinese Ch'an, a mixture of Chinese and Buddhist philosophy. Zen is a very practical religion, relying more on intuitive experience (Satori) and the use of daily material to that end, rather than on texts. The use of Koans - paradoxes, eg. 'the sound of one hand clapping' - is designed to jolt the mind out of habitual physical and intellectual ruts. The variety of techniques used by Zen masters to awaken their students is reflected in the proliferation of titles, 'Zen and the Art of…'

BANCROFT, A.
Zen: Direct Pointing to Reality
A highly illustrated introduction to Zen Buddhism. In the *Art and the Imagination* series.
[T445] Thames & H pbk **£5.95**

BLACKSTONE, JUDITH & JOSIPOVIC, ZORAN
Zen for Beginners
One of an extremely popular series, fundamentally serious in intent but seeking to clarify their subjects through cartoons and a light, informal touch.
[T446] Unwin Hyman pbk **£3.95**

CLEARY, T. (TRANS)
Zen Dawn
The three 8th century texts gathered here contain the earliest known writings on Zen Buddhism, including treatises by Bodhidharma, the first Zen master.
[T447] Wisdom pbk **£6.95**

HAMMITZSCH, HORST
Zen in the Art of the Tea Ceremony
An exploration of *Chado*, the Tea Way; at their purest

level, the precise rituals of the tea ceremony function as one of the routes to Zen enlightenment.
[T448] Element hbk **£4.95**

HARDING, D.E.
On Having No Head: Zen and the Rediscovery of the Obvious
A vivid account of the nature of mystical experience: the author describes his own experience of sudden enlightenment, his 'headlessness' or loss of self, and explores his subsequent spiritual development.
[T449] Arkana pbk **£3.99**

HERRIGEL, E.
Zen in the Art of Archery
Like the Martial Arts, Kyudo, the practice of Archery, is regarded in Japan as a spiritual discipline, not merely a sport. Herrigel explores the philosophical basis of Kyudo along with an often amusing account of his training.
[T450] Arkana pbk **£3.99**

HOOVER, T.
Zen Culture
Japanese culture has been thoroughly permeated by Zen; Hoover traces its influence upon art and landscape and explains its place in everyday life via the tea ceremony, cuisine and poetry.
[T451] Arkana pbk **£5.99**

HUMPHREYS, CHRISTMAS
A Western Approach to Zen
For those with no easy access to Japanese teachers, or unable to undertake extensive study in Japan, a practical route to understanding and following the path of Zen.
[T452] Unwin Hyman pbk **£4.95**
Zen Buddhism
In his usual lucid style, Humphreys provides a general introduction to the history and concepts of Zen, attempting especially to define its practical aspects.
[T453] Unwin Hyman pbk **£4.95**

KAPLEAU, ROSHI PHILIP
The Three Pillars of Zen
Teaching, practice, enlightenment - these are the Three Pillars. This classic of modern Zen provides a sourcebook with extracts from the central Zen texts, notes on practice and letters to and from teachers and students.
[T454] Rider pbk **£7.95**

KRAFT, KENNETH (ED)
Zen: Tradition and Transition **NEW**
A collection of classic and contemporary essays and texts, ranging from accounts of personal experience to the history of modern American Zen.
[T455] Rider pbk **£5.95**

REPS, PAUL (ED)
Zen Flesh, Zen Bones
The renowned anthology of the teachings and stories of the Zen masters provides a striking introduction to the remarkble and witty methods of Zen enlightenment.
[T456] Penguin pbk **£3.95**

SANGHARAKSHITA, BHIKSU
The Essence of Zen
Five essays based on talks given by the author in 1965, which provide a brief yet lucid account of the heart of Zen philosophy.
[T457] Windhorse pbk **£2.50**

SUZUKI, D.T.
The Zen Doctrine of No Mind
An exposition of the teaching of the Zen master Hui-Neng, and its central place in Zen tradition.
[T458] Rider pbk **£4.95**

SUZUKI, DAISETZ TEITARO
The leading authority on Zen teaching for the West; the writings of Suzuki collectively provide an essential guide to the practice and philosophy of Zen.
A Manual of Zen Buddhism
An anthology of the most important Zen texts.
[T459] Century pbk **£4.95**
An Introduction to Zen Buddhism
[T460] Rider pbk **£4.95**
Awakening of Zen
[T461] Shambhala hbk **£3.50**
Living by Zen
An introduction which aims to provide a fresh approach to Zen enlightenment, clarifying its concepts through anecdotes drawn from the lives of Zen masters and their pupils.
[T462] Rider pbk **£5.95**

SUZUKI, SHUNRYU
Zen Mind, Beginner's Mind
This accessible series of talks emphasises the need for the Zen practitioner constantly to retain a state of openmindedness - the mind of the beginner; the author's ideas derive ultimately from the early Zen master Dogen, but he expresses the continuing relevance of Zen, in the West and East alike.
[T463] Weatherhill pbk **£4.95**

WATTS, ALAN W.
The Way of Zen
Alan Watts is one of the great 20th century populists of Eastern thought. Despite a somewhat turbulent life, his writings always show an intuitive grasp of the subject. One of the best Zen primers.
[T464] Penguin pbk **£4.50**

Chinese

The two main Chinese religions, apart from Buddhism, are Confucianism and Taoism. Both use the concept of the 'Tao' (the way or path). In Confucianism, the 'Way' is a set of guidelines governing behaviour, a code of manners as the traditional guide to life for the Chinese gentry. Taoism uses the 'Way' in a more mystical sense as 'the unity underlying the plurality of the universe: the unnamed and underlying principle behind all things'.

Confucianism

From the 5th century BC, the thoughts and attitudes offered by China's greatest sage provided the educational framework of the country for hundreds of years. Confucian teaching is dominated by secular concerns with the social relationships of people, and the workings of justice, loyalty and goodness. It was instrumental in moulding the moral fabric of Chinese society.

CHEN, LI FU
The Confucian Way: A New and Systematic Study of the Four Books
[T466] KPI pbk **£7.95**

CONFUCIUS
LAU, D.C. (TRANS)
The Analects
[T467] Penguin pbk **£4.99**
WALEY, ARTHUR (TRANS)
The Analects of Confucius
A new edition of the classic translation by one of this century's most renowned Oriental scholars, whose versions of Chinese and Japanese poetry did much to popularise Eastern literature earlier this century.
[T468] Unwin Hyman pbk **£6.95**

DAWSON, RAYMOND
Confucius
A concise attempt to provide the sayings attributed to Confucius in the **Analects** with a context in the development of Chinese civilisation.
[T469] Oxford pbk **£2.95**

HSU, L. SHIHLIEN
Confucianism: The Political Philosophy of Confucianism
An interpretation of the social and political ideas of Confucius, his forerunners and his early disciples.
[T470] Curzon P hbk **£5.50**

MENCIUS
Works
A collection of the philosophy of the first great follower of Confucius; his teachings are based on the innate moral goodness of man's nature.
[T471] Penguin pbk **£4.99**

SMITH, D. HOWARD
Confucius and Confucianism
Placing Confucius in his historical context, this useful introduction traces the development of his ideas and their revival in later Chinese dynasties.
[T472] Grafton pbk **£2.95**

Taoism

The principles of Yin and Yang, the two poles of negative and positive cosmic energy, lie at the root of Chinese thought. Taoism expresses the search for balance between these two poles, by which harmony may be found through the operation of *wu-wei*, 'not forcing'. These ideas, developed in China around the 5th century BC, have gained renewed attention in the 20th century through contemporary searches for a more balanced way of life.

BLOFELD, JOHN
Taoism: The Quest for Immortality
An introduction to Taoist philosphy and its practical applications; the place of Tao in modern Chinese life is also examined.
[T473] Unwin Hyman pbk **£4.95**

CHIH-HSU OU-I
The Buddhist I Ching
The only Buddhist interpretation of the Chinese classic.
[T474] Element pbk **£8.95**

CLEARY, THOMAS
Taoist I Ching
Consists of a full translation of the text of the *I Ching*, along with a commentary by the 18th century Taoist adept Liu I-Ming. The whole provides the only complete Taoist interpretation of this fundamental text.
[T475] Element pbk **£10.95**

The Inner Teachings of Taoism
A version of an 11th century Chinese classic which presents the spiritual theories of the Complete Reality School of Taoism.
[T476] Element pbk **£7.95**

I CHING
Of the five books of Confucianism, the *I Ching* or *Book of Changes* has gained an existence almost independent of the religion from which it came. As a text it reflects the Tao in Chinese thought - the ebb and flow of energy, *Yin* and *Yang* represented in the combination of complete and broken lines within its 64 hexagrams; used as a means of divination, it shows a gentler character than that of the Western mantic arts.

Illustration from *Masters of Enchantment: The Lives and Legends of 84 Mahasiddhas* by Keith Dowman (Routledge pbk £15.95)

BLOFELD, JOHN (ED)
I Ching Book of Changes
A translation designed for practical use in divination, briefer than the Wilhelm edition, by a leading modern Western scholar of Chinese thought.
[T477] Unwin Hyman pbk **£4.95**

WILHELM, R. (TRANS)
I Ching Book of Changes
Introduced by Carl Jung, this is the classic scholarly translation, providing detailed exposition of the development of the text and its imagery.
[T478] Arkana hbk **£17.95**
[T479] Arkana pbk **£7.99**

LAO TZU
Translatable as 'The Classical Book of Meaning and Life', the *Tao Te Ching*, the teaching of the semi-mythical contemporary of Confucius, is the essential text of Taoism. A work of morality as well as mysticism, it instructs how man may, through right action in government, attain balance between his simultaneous lives in the material world and the world of the spirit.

ENGLISH, JANE (TRANS)
Tao Te Ching
In large format, this most attractive edition accompanies its text with calligraphy, and with paintings and photographs capturing the essence of the Taoist Way.
[T480] Wildwood H pbk **£8.95**

LAU, D.C. (TRANS)
Tao Te Ching
A modern translation emphasising the moral and practical content of the work.
[T481] Penguin pbk **£2.99**

WILHELM, R. (TRANS)
Tao Te Ching
The best-known and most often-quoted version, a classic in its own right.
[T482] Arkana pbk **£4.99**

RAWSON, PHILIP & LEGEZA, LASZLO
Tao: The Chinese Philosophy of Time and Change
In the *Art and Imagination* series.
[T483] Thames & H pbk **£5.95**

WATTS, ALAN
Tao: The Watercourse Way
Wattss' final book, completed after his death by his collaborator Al Chung-Liang Huang; illustrated with examples of Chinese calligraphy, the text displays as

ever the author's ability to clarify complex philosophical ideas for the general reader.
[T484] Penguin pbk **£4.99**

WILHELM, R. (TRANS)
The Secret of the Golden Flower: A Chinese Book of Life
Wilhelm's version of a central Taoist text on Chinese yoga is accompanied by the 18th century *Hui Ming Cheng* ('The Book of Consciousness and Life'), a meditation manual combining Taoist and Buddhist practices; a commentary by Jung is also included.
[T485] Arkana pbk **£4.99**

WILLIS, BEN
The Tao of Art: The Inner Meaning of Chinese Art and Philosophy
Explores the application of the principles of Yin and Yang by Chinese artists, and relates this philosophy to the universal artistic impulse in its attempt to create harmony.
[T486] Rider pbk **£7.95**

Hinduism

The oldest Indian religion, Hinduism has no formal creed but is the result of five thousand years of continuous cultural development. In this time it has assimilated many of the beliefs and traditions of Buddhism, Christianity and Sikhism. Hinduism is intimately connected with the Indian caste system, and one of its central beliefs is that through devotion, good works and 'right action' one is reincarnated at a higher level of life, eventually escaping the cycle of death and rebirth. The essential texts of Hinduism, the **Mahabharata** and **Ramayana**, describe a complete path of spiritual development through the actions of the pantheon of Hindu gods; they were composed between the 5th and 2nd centuries BC.

BHAGAVAD-GITA
EASWARAN, EKNATH
The Bhagavad-Gita
A new translation with detailed commentary by this leading contemporary Indian scholar.
[T487] Arkana pbk **£4.99**

MASCARO, J. (TRANS)
The Bhagavad-Gita
The **Bhagavad-Gita** (lit: 'Song of the Lord') is the most popular book of Hindu scripture and for many Hindus represents the essence of their religion. One episode from the epic **Mahabharata**, it is a dialogue between the hero Arjuna and the Lord Krishna concerning the ways to salvation.
[T488] Penguin pbk **£2.50**

SHREE PUROHIT SWAMI (TRANS)
The Geeta
Not a literal translation, but one whose poetry offers for the Western reader a flavour of the true meaning of this essential text for the Hindu.
[T489] Faber pbk **£2.95**

BROWN, K. (ED)
Essential Teachings of Hinduism
A series of brief extracts, one for each day of the year, from the Hindu sacred texts; the accompanying commentaries seek to draw out the spiritual import of the readings for those with no background in Hindu tradition.
[T490] Rider pbk **£8.95**

DOWMAN, KEITH
Masters of Enchantment: The Lives & Legends of 84 Mahasiddhas
[T490A] Routledge pbk **£15.95**

MAHABHARATA
The Ramayana and Mahabharata
The classic translation, somewhat abridged but retaining all the essential matter of the original; reprinted continuously since its first publication in 1910.
[T491] Dent pbk **£2.50**

NARAYAN, R.K. (ED)
The Mahabharata
The major episodes from the greatest of Indian epics are here selected and put into modern English prose; Narayan's version benefits from the novelist's narrative skill.
[T492] Heinemann hbk **£9.95**

MAHESH, YOGI MAHARISHI
On the Bhagavad Gita
The Maharishi gained some considerable prominence as a spiritual teacher in the 1960s; here he offers a detailed re-evaluation of the first six books of the *Gita* for modern times. This edition provides the text in both English and Sanskrit.
[T493] Penguin pbk **£6.99**

MASCARO, J. (TRANS)
The Upanishads
Dating from the period 800 - 300 BC the *Upanishads* are the most philosophical of Hindu scriptures, but many of the verses are also literary masterpieces.
[T494] Penguin pbk **£2.99**

O'FLAHERTY, WENDY DONIGER (ED)
Hindu Myths
This selection from the *Rig Veda*, *Mahabharata* and other sources, collecting together tales of the principal Hindu gods, captures superbly the Indian delight in storytelling.
[T495] Penguin hbk **£4.50**
Hinduism: Textual Sources for the Study of Religion
One of a series offering extended selections from the important texts, including many previously unavailable in English.
[T496] Manchester UP pbk **£8.95**
The Rig Veda
Composed between 1500 and 1000 BC these hymns in praise of various gods constitute the most ancient and sacred scriptures of Hinduism.
[T497] Penguin pbk **£4.95**

Illustration from *Masters of Enchantment: The Lives and Legends of 84 Mahasiddhas* by Keith Dowman (Routledge pbk £15.95)

PATANJALI
The Aphorisms of Yoga
Regarded by Hindus as less important only than the *Bhagavad Gita* and *Upanishads*, this short collection of sayings contains the essentials of Hindu religious practice. Most probably written down in the 9th century AD, their origin is much older. This edition features an introduction by W.B. Yeats.
[T498] Faber hbk **£3.95**

RADHAKRISHNAN
The Hindu View of Life
Recent reprint of an attempt to find a way through the intricacies of Hindu belief as expressed in its multiplicity of stories and myths, to the underlying philosophy which has shaped Indian life.
[T499] Unwin Hyman hbk **£2.50**

RICHARDS, GLYN (ED)
A Sourcebook of Modern Hinduism
Indian religious thinkers in the last two centuries have attempted to re-evaluate many of the attitudes of traditional Hinduism; this anthology offers a selection of their most significant writings.
[T500] Curzon P hbk **£8.50**

SEN, K.M.
Hinduism
A concise, largely historical survey which manages, despite its brevity, to trace a clear line through the many complex strands of Hinduism.
[T501] Penguin hbk **£3.95**

STUTLEY, MARGARET
Dictionary of Hinduism: Its Mythology, Folklore & Development 1500 BC - 1500 AD
Another excellent reference guide from Routledge, enabling the reader with little prior knowledge of Hinduism to get a clear idea of its distinguishing features.
[T502] Routledge pbk **£12.95**
Hinduism: The Eternal Law
Exploring the essentials of Hindu belief by concentration on a series of topics, this introductory volume devotes chapters to the sacred literature, the gods and their cults, Hindu temples, and practices of worship, amongst many others.
[T503] Crucible pbk **£5.99**

YOGANANDA, PARAHAMSA
The Autobiography of a Yogi
In its purest form yoga is the Hindu science of meditation. This extraordinary book, reprinted many times since its first publication, recounts the experiences of a 20th century yogi, his encounters with modern Hindu saints during prolonged travels and studies. Stories of meetings with other spiritual explorers, such as Gandhi and Tagore, are combined with an exposition of the principles by which self-mastery may be attained.
[T504] Rider pbk **£5.95**

Sikhism

Founded in the 15th century by Guru Nanak, Sikhism reflects Hindu and Islamic influences, although its adherents no longer regard themselves as Hindus. While accepting the ideas of reincarnation and karma, the Indian caste system is rejected. Sikh practices include meditation, devotional singing and the guidance of a Guru (teacher).

COLE, OWEN
The Guru in Sikhism
[T505] DLT pbk **£3.95**

COLE, OWEN & SAMBHI
The Sikhs: Religious Beliefs and Practices
An examination of the political and social forces which have shaped the identity of Sikhism as a distinct religion.
[T506] Routledge pbk **£9.50**

MCLEOD, W.H.
Sikhism: Textual Sources for the Study of Religion
Designed primarily for the student of religion, this series also makes available for the practitioner many previously inaccessible but important texts.
[T507] Manchester UP pbk **£6.95**
Who is a Sikh? `NEW`
A new investigation of Sikh identity: McLeod traces the development of opinion on this question, attempting to find an answer relevant to the place of the Sikh in contemporary society.
[T508] Oxford hbk **£19.50**

Islam

The most widespread of the world's religions after Christianity, Islam retains a remarkable consistency in its teachings. Islam means 'submission', the unification of religion, government and daily life by the word of God as expressed through his prophet Muhammad. There exist two major sects, the majority Sunni following the principle that doctrinal authority rests on consensus between religious authorities; the Shi'ite minority, centred in Iran, Iraq and Pakistan, regard the Twelve Imams and their present day successors the Ayatollahs as the infallible guardians of spiritual truth. As a path to enlightenment, Islam has so far lacked the attraction of the more mystical religions from further East, except perhaps in its Sufi manifestation; as a powerful force, it has clearly shown itself worth reckoning with; as a religion, it deserves deeper understanding.

AHMED, AKBAR S.
Discovering Islam `NEW`
A sociological study of Muslim culture which attempts to counter the Western image of Islam as an aggressive, fanatical creed; an analysis of modern Islamic societies in the light of their history.
[T509] Routledge pbk **£9.95**

AL-MUZAFFAR, M.R.
The Faith of Shi'a Islam
Exploration of the beliefs of the Shi'ite sect which derives its law from its spiritual leaders, the Imams.
[T510] KPI pbk **£4.95**

BURMAN, E.
The Assassins: Holy Killers of Islam
A re-evaluation of this secret sect, placing them in context as members of the Isma'ili branch of Shi'a Islam.
[T511] Crucible pbk **£6.99**

COOK, M.
Muhammad
A concise introduction to the life and teaching of the Prophet. In the Oxford *Past Masters* series.
[T512] Oxford pbk **£1.95**

GIBB, H.A.R.
Islam
A brief but clear introduction to the essentials of Islam.
[T513] Oxford pbk **£4.95**

GLASSE, CYRIL
Concise Encyclopaedia of Islam NEW
A major reference work on the beliefs,
practices, history and culture of the Islamic world.
Written by an acclaimed scholar, its 1,200 entries
cover comprehensively all the major subjects.
[T514] Stacey Int hbk **£35.00**

GUILLAUME, A.
Islam
A more extensive history of the development and
spread of Islam, now well-established as one of the
standard introductions to the subject.
[T515] Penguin pbk **£3.99**

HIRO, DILIP
Islamic Fundamentalism
An objective account of the forces active in modern
Islam, focusing on the contrast between the Sunni
state of Saudi Arabia and Shi'ite Iran, and tracing
their contrasting views of an ideal Muslim society
back to rival schools of thought in the earliest days of
Islam.
[T516] Grafton pbk **£4.95**

KORAN
The 114 *Suras* or chapters of the *Koran* are a record
of the revelations of Allah to the prophet Muhammad
between the years 610 and 632, and provide the basis
for all the rules and practices of the Muslim way of
life. Their subject-matter is wide, ranging from re-
interpretations of Bible stories to visions of heaven
and hell, and guidance for the conduct of
Muhammad's early followers. Their theme, however,
is constant: that of the oneness of Allah, and his
rewards and punishments to believers and
disbelievers.
Arberry, A.J. (TRANS)
The Koran
A verse translation which seeks to approximate
closely to the poetic forms of the original.
[T517] Oxford pbk **£2.95**
Dawood, N.J. (TRANS)
The Koran
This excellent prose translation was, when published
in 1959, the first produced in contemporary Englsih.
[T518] Penguin pbk **£3.99**
ALI, A. YUSUF (TRANS)
**The Holy Qu'ran: Text, Translation and
Commentary**
This orthodox Muslim edition of the Koran, in Arabic
and English, was first published in 1934, and has
been recently revised.
[T519] PM Llewellyn hbk **£13.95**

LEWIS, BERNARD (ED)
**The World of Islam: Faith, People,
Culture**
A highly illustrated historical survey of the Islamic
world.
[T520] Thames & H hbk **£20.00**

LINGS, M.
**Muhammad: His Life Based on the
Earliest Sources**
Drawing on Arabic source-material from the 8th
and 9th centuries, Lings, a sensitive modern
interpreter of Middle Eastern culture, provides a vivid
narrative life.
[T521] Unwin Hyman hbk **£19.95**
[T522] Unwin Hyman pbk **£7.95**

NASR, SEYYED HOSSEIN (ED) NEW
Islamic Spirituality 1: Foundations
With contributions from many of the leading Islamic
scholars, this new volume in the *World Spirituality*
series provides a detailed account of the roots of
Muslim spiritual thought.
[T523] SCMP pbk **£19.50**

ROBINSON, F.
An Atlas of the Islamic World
A colourful and attractively presented historical atlas
concentrating on the diffusion of Islam since 1500;
one of the excellent series of Phaidon Historical
Atlases, with many maps and a full text.
[T524] Phaidon hbk **£18.50**

RUTHVEN, M.
Islam in the World
A Western journalist's analysis of contemporary
Islamic political movements, tracing their roots in a
sympathetic study of long-established beliefs and
practices.
[T525] Penguin pbk **£5.95**

SCHUON, FRITHJOF
Understanding Islam
Swiss-born, a poet and painter as well a largely self-
educated Arabic scholar, Schuon here offers an
exploration of Islam 'from within', seeking to explain
not what Muslims believe but how and why their
beliefs are shaped.
[T526] Unwin Hyman pbk **£4.95**

TABATABA'I, A.
A Shi'ite Anthology
The Shi'ite conception of the *Hadith*, the corpus of
sacred tradition, includes not only the words of
Muhammad but the sayings of the Imams. These are
here presented for the first time in English.
[T527] KPI hbk **£15.00**
[T528] KPI pbk **£7.95**

Sufism

The mystical branch of the Muslim tradition, Sufism
is a movement originally ascetic in nature. It was
much influenced by Gnostic and Neo-Platonic
philosophies and, having considerable common
ground with other mystical movements, is more
accessible to the Western world than orthodox Islam.
Sufi thought has also provided the stimulus for many
of the great poets of Islam.

ATTAR, FARID AL-DIN
Muslim Saints and Mystics
A collection of biographies of Sufi masters by this
great Persian 13th century poet.
[T529] Arkana pbk **£7.99**
The Conference of Birds (Trans. Darbandi,
Afkham & Davis, Dick)
The *Mantiq al-Tayr* ('Conference of the Birds') is the
most important work of the Persian poet and mystic
Attar. It is a complex allegorical rendering of the Sufi
quest, describing how all the birds of the earth
(representing human souls) begin a search for the
Simurgh, a mythical bird (representing the Supreme
Divinity). All but thirty perish in the process: the
survivors eventually realise that they themselves are
the Simurgh (in Persian *si murgh* means 'thirty
birds').
[T530] Penguin pbk **£4.95**

BAKHTAR, L.
Sufi: Expression of the Mystic Quest
A colourfully illustrated, mainly pictorial exploration
of Sufism and its influence on the creative arts in the
Middle East. In the *Art and Imagination* series.
[T531] Thames & H pbk **£5.95**

FEILD, R.
A contemporary Sufi master whose books describe
his spiritual quest across the world with great
philosophical insight.
Steps to Freedom
[T532] Element pbk **£6.95**

The Invisible Way
[T533] Element hbk **£6.95**
The Last Barrier
[T534] Element pbk **£6.95**

HAERI, SHAYKH FADHLALLA
The Elements of Sufism NEW
One of a new series, seeking to answer the
basic questions about the history and development of
Sufism and providing an account of its relationship to
other forms of mystical and religious thought.
[T535] Element pbk **£4.95**

LINGS, MARTIN
What is Sufism?
A lucid introduction to this branch of the Muslim
faith; a concise volume but one which nevertheless
successfully illuminates some of the more obscure
areas of its subject.
[T536] Unwin Hyman pbk **£2.95**

RUMI, JALALUD-DIN
Teachings of Rumi: The Mathnawi
The greatest of the Sufi mystics, whose rapturous
poems inspired the religious cult of the Whirling
Dervishes; the six books of the *Mathnawi* constitute
the principal work of this 13th century Persian poet.
[T537] Octagon hbk **£8.00**

SHAH, IDRIES
**Exploits of the Incomparable Mulla
Nasrudin/Subtleties of the Inimitable
Mulla Nasrudin**
An irrepressible prankster, the character of Mulla
Nasrudin embodies the startling and witty Sufi
attitude to life.
[T538] Octagon hbk **£4.00**
**Learning How to Learn: Psychology and
Spirituality in the Sufi Way**
Stories, discourses and conversations answering some
of the many questions on the Sufi way posed to Shah
by readers from all walks of life.
[T539] Penguin pbk **£4.99**
**Pleasantries of the Incredible Mulla
Nasrudin**
[T540] Octagon hbk **£6.95**
**Special Illumination: The Sufi Use of
Humour**
The use of humour to overturn conventional thought-
patterns is a distinctly Sufi approach to philosophy.
[T541] Octagon hbk **£4.00**
The Way of the Sufi
An anthology of writings, tales and ideas by and
about the great Sufi thinkers.
[T542] Penguin pbk **£3.50**
Thinkers of the East
A collection of stories, parables and aphorisms which,
like the parables of Zen, attempt to reveal truth by
giving a humorous jolt to habitual ways of seeing and
thinking.
[T543] Penguin pbk **£3.99**

TWEEDIE, IRINA
Daughter of Fire
In 1959, at the age of 52, Tweedie undertook a trip to
India; this diary of her five years in study with the
Sufi master she unexpectedly met there, tells the
extraordinary story of the first Western woman to
undergo training in this rigorous but wonderfully
rewarding spiritual discipline.
[T544] Blue Dolphin pbk **£15.95**

Judaism

The most ancient of the Western religions. The core
of Jewish belief lies in the *Torah*, the first five books
of the *Pentateuch*, of the Biblical Old Testament. The

contents of the *Torah*, where God's will and law are revealed to man, are the basis of all later teaching; these later texts include the rest of the Old Testament, and the *Talmud*, the body of law and practice codified in the 5th century. There is some debate about what precisely constitutes Judaism as a religion, the relationship between man and God being defined by a set of laws and observances rather than by an exact set of beliefs; the importance of history in maintaining Jewish identity is a theme reflected in the selection which follows.

BUBER, MARTIN
The most significant Jewish thinker of the 20th century, Buber was deeply interested in the possibilities for religious revival presented by the ideas of Hasidism, and was also a central figure in the Zionist movement, although always concerned for the rights of the Arab community. He denied he was a theologian or philosopher, preferring to be regarded as a spiritual guide.
On Judaism
These twelve lectures range across all aspects of the Jewish faith.
[T545] Schocken pbk **£6.50**
On Zion: The History of an Idea
Four talks delivered in 1944; poignantly just four years before the establishment of the state of Israel.
[T546] T Clark pbk **£5.95**

COHN-SHERBOK, D.
The Jewish Heritage
A comprehensive new history of Jewish religion and tradition.
[T547] Blackwell hbk **£25.00**
[T548] Blackwell pbk **£7.95**

EPSTEIN, ISIDORE
Judaism
An excellent brief survey of Judaism in the Penguin *Religion* series.
[T549] Penguin pbk **£4.99**

JOHNSON, PAUL
A History of the Jews
A comprehensive and accessible general history emphasising the Jewish contribution to world culture. Best-known as a journalist, Johnson is also a significant popular historian.
[T550] Weidenfeld hbk **£16.95**
[T551] Weidenfeld pbk **£8.95**

LANGE, NICHOLAS R.M. DE
An Atlas of the Jewish World
An historical atlas of the spread of Jewish influence, also providing a visual explanation of Jewish culture through its artefa`cts, and a fascinating pictorial record of modern Jewish communities.
[T552] Phaidon hbk **£18.50**
Judaism
A clear, concise introduction by the lecturer in Rabbinics at Cambridge University; he concentrates on defining the nature of Jewish belief, rather than providing an historical overview.
[T553] Oxford pbk **£4.95**

NEUSNER, J. (ED)
The Mishnah
A scholarly new translation of the collection of oral law which forms the basis of the Talmud.
[T554] Yale UP hbk **£45.00**

NIGOSIAN, SOLOMAN ALEXANDER
Judaism: The Way of Holiness
A sensitive and lucid new study of the growth of the Jewish spirit relating it to the central concept of Holiness.
[T555] Aquarian pbk **£6.99**

RAPHAEL, CHAIM
A Feast of History
The flight of the Israelites is commemorated at the feast of Passover; the Seder, a traditional family meal held on Passover Eve, is accompanied by the reading of the festival text, the Haggadah. Raphael's splendidly illustrated history of Passover also includes a version of the Haggadah.
[T556] Weidenfeld hbk **£10.95**

RAYNOR, JOHN D. & GOLDBERG, D.J.
The Jewish People: Their History and Their Religion
Jewish culture is analysed by two progressive Rabbis.
[T557] Viking hbk **£15.95**

RUNES, DAGOBERT D. (ED)
Dictionary of Judaism
[T558] Citadel pbk **£5.95**

WOUK, HERMAN
This is My God
A personal account, by the American novelist and practising Jew, of his religion and the history of his people, explaining its meaning for his own life and that of modern Jewry.
[T559] Fount pbk **£2.50**

Theology

The Authorised Daily Prayer Book in English and Hebrew
In parallel text, the standard service book of the United Hebrew Congregations.
[T560] Eyre & S pbk **£3.50**

ANDRIESSE, R.C. MUSAPH
From Torah to Kabbalah
A basic introduction to the writings of Judaism.
[T561] SCM pbk **£3.95**

BLUE, L. & MAJONET, RABBI J.
The Blue Guide to the Here & Hereafter
A treasury of Jewish spiritual thought, ranging in scope from Biblical quotations and Yiddish proverbs to lyrics by Gershwin and Oscar Hammerstein.
[T562] Collins pbk **£3.50**

BUBER, MARTIN
I and Thou
Buber's most influential book, a classic statement of the relationship between man and God.
[T563] T & T Clark pbk **£4.95**
Tales of the Hasidim Vol 1
Collections of vivid anecdotes illuminating the beliefs of the 18th century movement which marked the last flowering of Jewish mysticism; the parables by which the Hasidic Rabbis taught contain a rich and passionate faith.
[T564] Schocken hbk **£6.95**
Tales of the Hasidim Vol 2
[T565] Schocken pbk **£7.50**

GREEN, ARTHUR (ED)
Jewish Spirituality 1: From the Bible through the Middle Ages NEW
A new collection of essays tracing the development of Jewish religious philosophy from ancient Israel to Kabbalah. A volume in the *World Spirituality* series.
[T566] SCMP pbk **£17.50**

KENTON, WARREN
Kabbalah: Tradition of Hidden Knowledge
A visual history of Kabbalah and its symbolism in Jewish tradition. In the *Art and Imagination* series.
[T567] Thames & H pbk **£5.95**

KOLATCH, ALFRED J.
The Jewish Book of Why
An exploration, in question and answer format, of many of the fundamental problems of Jewish life and practice, offering guidance on the relevance of Jewish law in today's world.
[T568] Kuperard hbk **£10.95**
The Second Jewish Book of Why
In a similar way to the first volume, Rabbi Kolatch expands on the approach of Jewish scholars to the ethical problems of contemporary life; topics such as abortion and organ transplant are among the many considered.
[T569] Kuperard hbk **£11.95**

KOPCIOWSKI, ELIAS
Praying with the Jewish Tradition
An anthology of prayers from wide-ranging sources, including the Bible, the Talmud and traditional liturgies. Introduced by Rabbi Lionel Blue.
[T570] Triangle pbk **£2.50**

MATT, D.C. (ED)
The Zohar: Book of Enlightenment
The major text of Jewish mysticism, written as a commentary on the Pentateuch in the 13th Century by Moses de Leon.
[T571] SPCK pbk **£11.50**

RAPHAEL, CHAIM (ED)
A Jewish Book of Common Prayer
Relates the Jewish to the Anglican prayer book using the example of the Jewish service for Sabbath Eve.
[T572] Weidenfeld hbk **£10.95**

UNTERMAN, ALAN
The Jews: Their Religious Beliefs and Practices
Another in this useful series investigating the social context shaping the practices of religious communities.
[T573] Routledge pbk **£9.50**

VERMES, P.
Buber
A concise account of the life and thought of this profound and controversial philosopher.
[T574] P Halban pbk **£5.95**

Modern Spiritual Leaders

Bhagwan Shree Rajneesh

An amalgam of teachings from almost every major spiritual tradition, flavoured with modern psychological theories and bound together by his personal magnetism, has won Rajneesh many followers since the 1970s. This controversial figure's movement has been rent by disputes, but many remain loyal to his remarkable brand of instruction. The books listed here are a tiny selection from his total output, but they give some idea of his extraordinary eclecticism.

MILNE, HUGH
Bhagwan: The God that Failed
An occasionally sour but nonetheless interesting account from inside Rajneesh's movement, by his disillusioned bodyguard.
[T576] Sphere pbk **£3.50**

RAJNEESH, BHAGWAN SHREE
Gold Nuggets
Extracts from a series of talks given in 1986, when Rajneesh was on the run from the US, and capturing in adversity the essence of his spiritual approach.
[T577] Rebel PH hbk **£6.50**
I Teach Religiousness, Not Religion
Rajneesh's answers to followers on the relationship between organised religion and genuine belief.
[T578] Rebel PH pbk **£3.50**
Meditation: The First and Last Freedom
A practical guide to meditation in the contemporary world.
[T579] Rebel PH hbk **£9.50**
Roots and Wings: Talks on Zen
[T580] Arkana hbk **£8.99**
Tao: The Three Treasures
[T581] Wildwood H pbk **£4.95**
The Supreme Doctrine: Discourses on the Kenopanishad
Given in lectures in the Himalayas, here are Rajneesh's responses to one of the central texts of Indian religion.
[T582] Arkana pbk **£9.99**

THOMPSON, JUDITH
The Way of the Heart: The Rajneesh Movement
An even-handed assessment of Rajneesh and his critics; the author is an academic but writes with the general reader in mind.
[T583] Aquarian pbk **£5.99**

Gurdjieff

The son of a Greek carpenter, this Russian occult teacher was born in the Caucasus around 1874, and died in Paris in 1949. *"I have very good leather to sell to those who want to make shoes out of it"*, Gurdjieff once wrote. Aware of the erosion of traditional forms of religious teaching, he sought out elements of esoteric knowledge which were in danger of being lost. At the heart of his teaching is the recognition that man is not a fully conscious being - he is asleep but has the possibility of awakening, and can use the stuff of his daily life, as in Zen Buddhism, for this purpose. His system of ideas draws on many Eastern traditions, but is presented in a practical form adapted to the needs of 20th century man.

BENNETT, J.G.
Gurdjieff: Making a New World
The most prominent Western disseminator of Gurdjieff's ideas expounds his teacher's philosophy, and attempts to clarify the complex development of his thought.
[T584] Turnstone P pbk **£3.95**

GURDJIEFF, G.I.
All and Everything Books 1 - 3
In this challenging book Gurdjieff sets out with compassion and humour to *"corrode without mercy all the rubbish accumulated during the ages of human mentation."* The core of his teaching is presented here in a form which touches more than the usual intellectual processes.
[T585] Arkana hbk **£25.00**
All and Everything: Beelzebub's Tales to his Grandson Book 1
[T586] Arkana pbk **£5.99**
Book 2
[T587] Arkana pbk **£5.99**
Book 3
[T588] Arkana pbk **£5.99**
Life Is Real Only Then, When 'I Am'
The third and final series of Gurdjieff's writings.
[T589] Arkana pbk **£11.95**

Meetings with Remarkable Men
Gurdjieff's often allegorical evocation of his early life. Dissatisfied with the religious and scientific knowledge of his time, he recounts his travels through Central Asia and Egypt, his encounters with religious masters and the exploits of his fellow seekers in an attempt to find a new order of reality.
[T590] Arkana pbk **£5.99**
Views from the Real World
Early talks as recollected by his pupils.
[T591] Arkana pbk **£5.99**

OUSPENSKY, P.D.
A contemporary of Gurdjieff and the most influential of his followers with regard to the spread of his ideas in the West. He worked with Gurdjieff from 1915 to 1918, having been drawn to him by the preoccupations of his work with the problems of man's existence.
A Further Record: Extracts from Meetings
A verbatim record of talks with students which attempt to help them reach a deeper understanding of Ouspensky's philosophical method.
[T592] Arkana pbk **£7.99**
A New Model of the Universe
Largely written before his period of study with Gurdjieff, a volume exploring the place of his esoteric thought, occult ideas and modern scientific theory in man's future spiritual development.
[T593] Arkana pbk **£7.99**
In Search of the Miraculous: Fragments of an Unknown Teaching
The most detailed account of Gurdjieff's system and his early groups in Russia, this book also shows the development in Ouspensky's ideas which led to his eventual break with Gurdjieff.
[T594] Arkana pbk **£6.99**
The Fourth Way: Teachings of G.I. Gurdjieff
A series of questions and answers showing the dynamic effect of Gurdjieff's system within a group.
[T595] Arkana pbk **£7.99**

WILSON, COLIN
G.I. Gurdjieff: The War Against Sleep
A well-written and highly stimulating introduction to Gurdjieff's ideas.
[T596] Aquarian P pbk **£4.99**

Krishnamurti

Born in Madras in 1891, Krishnamurti was educated within the Theosophical movement. He was proclaimed as the Messiah by his teacher Annie Besant and other Theosophists, but rejected his role in 1929, declaring that man could find truth only by freeing himself from all conditioning. His wisdom and clarity of thought, expounded in talks and conversations throughout the world, have nevertheless gained him a huge and dedicated following. The great subtlety of his philosophy has attracted people from all fields, such as Bernard Shaw and Nehru; it has also led to revealing interviews with Mrs Gandhi, Iris Murdoch and Bernard Levin, amongst others. His talks, dialogues and writings have been published in a succession of volumes: what follows is a small selection.

JAYAKAR, PUPUL
Krishnamurti: A Biography
Drawing extensively on conversations with Krishnamurti and on her own diaries, the author of this recent biography reveals many little-known episodes from her friend's early life, his childhood celebrity, and the growth of his own spirituality.
[T597] Harper & R pbk **£9.95**

KRISHNAMURTI, J.
Commentaries on Living 1st Series
These were among the first of Krishnamurti's own writings to be published.
[T598] Gollancz pbk **£5.95**
Commentaries on Living 2nd Series
[T599] Gollancz pbk **£5.95**
Krishnamurti's Journal
A rare glimpse into Krishnamurti's mind through his own writings.
[T600] Gollancz hbk **£4.95**
Krishnamurti's Notebook
A daily record kept by Krishnamurti over seven months in 1961 and 1962; the remarkable intensity of his thoughts reflects not only the natural world, but his perceptions and mystical states of consciousness.
[T601] Gollancz pbk **£5.95**
Life Ahead
[T602] Gollancz pbk **£5.95**
The Awakening of Intelligence
A comprehensive record of Krishnamurti's teaching in conversation with religious and scientific thinkers.
[T603] Gollancz pbk **£6.95**
The Beginnings of Learning
[T604] Penguin pbk **£4.95**
The First and Last Freedom
Krishnamurti's first published book.
[T605] Gollancz hbk **£8.95**
The Future is Now: Krishnamurti's Last Talks in India
[T606] Gollancz hbk **£8.95**
The Impossible Question
[T607] Penguin pbk **£4.50**
The Penguin Krishnamurti Reader
Selections from *The First and Last Freedom*, *Life Ahead* and *This Matter of Culture*.
[T608] Penguin pbk **£4.95**
The Second Penguin Krishnamurti Reader
Selections from *The Urgency of Change* and *The Only Revolution*.
[T609] Penguin pbk **£4.95**
KRISHNAMURTI, J. & BOHM, DAVID
The Ending of Time
A stimulating collaboration with one of our most enlightened modern scientists, examining the limitations of rational Western traditions, and the neccessity to move beyond them.
[T610] Gollancz pbk **£5.95**

Mythology

The need for man to explain his place in the universe combines with the impulse to hear and tell a story, to create the great mythologies of the world. It's study is relatively recent, dating from the late 18th century, and owes much to knowledge gleaned from the parallel studies of anthropology, geography and history. The modern perception of the purpose of myth offers two main approaches: firstly as a means of explanation for the mysteries of creation, the interweaving cycles of nature and time, justification for political and social actions, and as a background to the growth of religious and ritual practices; secondly, the more psychological view of myth as an expression of human and social need, an embodiment (in Jungian terms) of a shared, collective unconscious representing a particular culture's perception of the universe and its place within it. The selection below seeks to highlight some of the systems which have a continuing resonance in modern culture.

CAMPBELL, JOSEPH
Unquestionably the premier mythographer of modern times. His studies range over the whole field of world

mythology, seeking constantly to emphasize the persistence of the impulse behind myth in contemporary cultures. Jung's theories on the collective unconscious are a strong influence on his work - one of the main tasks being to trace the common themes underlying myths of all cultures and periods.

An Open Life NEW
These selections from a series of American radio interviews with Michael Toms explore more informally Campbell's lifelong involvement with the study of myth.
[T611] Grafton pbk **£6.95**

Myths to Live By
Discussions of the place of myth in primitive societies, and the relevance of our own myths in contemporary life.
[T612] Grafton pbk **£2.95**

The Hero with a Thousand Faces
A pursuit of the significance of the hero figure across the world of myth.
[T613] Grafton pbk **£6.95**

The Masks of God
Remarkably erudite but also accessible, this monumental four-volume study covers the entire history of myth from its earliest flowerings to the creative impulse in modern societies.

Vol 1: Primitive Mythology
[T614] Penguin hbk **£6.99**

Vol 2: Oriental Mythology
[T615] Penguin pbk **£7.50**

Vol 3: Occidental Mythology
[T616] Penguin pbk **£6.95**

Vol 4: Creative Mythology
[T617] Penguin pbk **£6.95**

CHETWYND, TOM
A Dictionary of Sacred Myth
This reference work explores mythical symbols in relation to dreams and the creative imagination.
[T618] Unwin Hyman pbk **£4.95**

COTTERELL, A.
A Dictionary of World Mythology
A brief survey of the world's major mythological systems, arranged A-Z within a series of topics.
[T619] Oxford pbk **£4.95**

FRAZER, SIR J.G.
The Golden Bough
Frazer's extraordinary achievement began with an attempt to explain the violent practices of the priesthood of Diana at Aricia; his studies expanded into an exposition of the history of myth which still stands as a landmark of anthropological and mythological study. The abridged edition contains all Frazer's essential material.
[T620] Macmillan 13 vols hbk **£250.00**
[T621] Macmillan hbk (abridged) **£29.50**
[T622] Macmillan pbk (abridged) **£7.95**

GRAVES, ROBERT
The White Goddess: A Historical Grammar of Poetic Myth
Graves's search to rediscover the creative impulse behind poetry takes the exploration of medieval Welsh tales as its basis, but expands into a 'historical grammar of poetic myth', tracing the poetic urge through the myths of many cultures.
[T623] Faber pbk **£5.95**

GRIMAL, PIERRE (ED)
Larousse World Mythology NEW
Translated from French, this well-established and comprehensive work is now available in a new hardback edition. The text, accompanied by many illustrations, both retells the major myths of societies throughout the world, and seeks to assess their historical and cultural meaning.
[T624] Hamlyn hbk **£15.00**

MACLAGAN, DAVID
Creation Myths
Descriptions of the origins of the world as seen by various cultures with illustrations of their visual expression. In the *Art and Imagination* series.
[T625] Thames & H pbk **£5.95**

WALKER, BARBARA G.
A Woman's Encyclopaedia of Myths and Secrets
A wide-ranging and fascinatingly eclectic encyclopaedia of mythology, religion and folklore which seeks to reinstate women to the centre of the world's belief-systems.
[T626] Harper & R pbk **£14.95**

Celtic Mythology

Celtic mythology comprises Irish, Welsh, British and French legends. It retains elements of the common Indo-European mother-goddess cults, although these are largely subsumed within the tales of later patriarchal societies. The immediate sources of the myths are medieval, but reflect a far older tradition of storytelling; the mythological element has to some extent been degraded, but can be traced back to far earlier forms of the stories. The Arthurian cycle, one of the most powerful in world mythology, illustrates this process: around the semi-historical figure of Celtic Britain's last defender gather attributes of the archetypal hero, traditions of Germanic kings and the Grail motif - although added by medieval authors, these are often echoes of much older and even pre-Christian traditions.

BARBER (ED)
The Arthurian Legends: An Illustrated Anthology
A volume of selections from the most important versions of the stories of Arthur, accompanied by the interpretations of visual artists through the centuries.
[T627] Boydell pbk **£6.95**

GANTZ, JEFFREY (TRANS)
Early Irish Myths and Sagas
An anthology of the tales central to the Irish tradition; written down in around the 8th century AD, they represent the oral tradition of the Iron Age Celts.
[T628] Penguin pbk **£3.99**

Mabinogion
A superb modern translation of the Welsh tales which are among the most beautiful of Celtic myths.
[T629] Penguin pbk **£3.99**

GIMBUTAS, MARIJA
Goddesses and Gods of Old Europe
This important study of the goddess-cult of Stone Age Europe shows how recent archaeological discoveries establish the independence of Indo-European beliefs from the Middle Eastern societies from which they were once supposed to spring. Such evidence provides important new insights into the origins of Celtic myth.
[T630] Thames & H pbk **£8.95**

GREGORY, LADY AUGUSTA
One of the major figures of the Irish Revival movement of the late 19th century, and prominent in the literary world, Lady Gregory collected and translated many volumes of myth and folklore in her efforts to recover the roots of Irish literature. Her versions stand as some of the finest and most enchanting.
Cuchulain of Muirthemne
[T631] C Smythe pbk **£3.50**
Gods and Fighting Men
[T632] C Smythe pbk **£4.25**

MARKALE, JEAN
Women of the Celts
Celtic civilisation, standing halfway between a matriarchal and a patriarchal culture, gave a prominent place to women, as is reflected in its myths. This study explores images of women in Celtic mythology, their presence as a powerful force, and relates this to the contemporary representation of women.
[T633] Thorsons pbk **£10.95**

MATTHEWS, JOHN
The Grail: Quest for Eternal Life
Highly illustrated account of the Grail Myth as a Spiritual Quest. In the *Art and Imagination* series.
[T634] Thames & H pbk **£5.95**

ROLLESTON, T.W.
Myths and Legends of the Celtic Race
First published over fifty years ago, this excellent study has recently been made available again.
[T635] Constable pbk **£5.95**

RUTHERFORD, WARD
Celtic Mythology
An introductory survey of Celtic society and culture, tracing its influence on literature and customs to the present day.
[T636] Aquarian P pbk **£5.99**

SHARKEY, JOHN
Celtic Mysteries
The religion of the Celts is here explored with reference to the myths and the practices of Druidism, accompanied as ever by a fascinating range of illustrations. In the *Art and Imagination* series.
[T637] Thames & H pbk **£5.95**

Egyptian Mythology

Egyptian mythology was largely transmitted by oral tradition, and although many artefacts and temples inform us about the early gods, there is little source material for the legends themselves, apart from Plutarch's rendering of the myth of Osiris. The main deities are Ra - the Sun King, Horus (often represented with a hawk's head, as many gods emerged from earlier animal worship), Set and Isis. Prevalent themes are: creation, the unity of the two geographical lands of Upper and Lower Egypt, and the usual establishment of order upon chaos. The Pharaoh was seen as a temporal manifestation of divine attributes.

BUDGE, SIR E.A. WALLIS
A pioneering scholar of Egyptology whose writings, although published around the turn of the century, still stand as the definitive works on the subject of ancient Egyptian religion.
Book of the Dead
Translation of papyri describing the rituals which ensure the safe passage of the soul to the immortal world; the original hieroglyphics are reproduced with an interlinear rendering.
[T638] Arkana pbk **£8.99**
Egyptian Magic
[T639] Arkana pbk **£5.99**
Osiris and the Egyptian Resurrection Vol 1
The myth of Osiris stands as the archetype for myths of death and renewal; Budge traces the evidence for the Egyptian version of this myth, its analogues in related cultures and later accounts by Plutarch and others.
[T640] Dover pbk **£11.95**
Vol 2
[T641] Dover pbk **£7.95**

RELIGION

The Gods of the Egyptians Vol 1
[T642] Dover pbk **£17.00**
Vol 2
[T643] Dover pbk **£18.00**

DAVID, A. ROSALIE
The Ancient Egyptians: Religious Beliefs and Practices
A highly detailed study, concentrating on the shaping of belief by social and political requirements.
[T644] Routledge pbk **£8.50**

FAULKNER, R.O. (TRANS)
The Book of the Dead **NEW**
Illustrated with specially-commissioned photographs taken from the collection of Egyptian funeral papyri in the British Museum, a new translation of the body of texts collectively known as *The Book of the Dead*.
[T645] Brit Mus P pbk **£9.95**

HART, GEORGE
A Dictionary of Egyptian Gods and Goddesses
Recent archaeological discoveries have increased our knowledge of the Egyptian gods; this reference work utilises such learning to expand the brief but essential background information provided.
[T646] Routledge pbk **£5.95**

LAMY, L.
Egyptian Mysteries
A visual exploration of the esoteric knowledge of Ancient Egypt and its resonance in later cultures, including the occult groups to which the vague origins of Egyptian belief greatly appealed. In the *Art and Imagination* series.
[T647] Thames & H pbk **£5.95**

LURKER, M.
Gods and Symbols of Ancient Egypt
A dictionary illustrated with many photographs, placing the images and symbols of Egyptian religion in their social context.
[T648] Thames & H pbk **£5.95**

Greek & Roman Mythology

These are among the best known legends in mythology, forming a vital element of Western culture through the traditional emphasis on the importance of classical learning. While there are obvious correspondences (Zeus - Jupiter, Hera - Juno, Artemis - Diana etc), the different characteristics of the two cultures are represented in their myths. Greek mythology developed from circa 2,000 BC to the birth of the Christian era, and absorbed many cultures and religions in this time. There is a wit and exuberance in many of the legends, plays and poems, that became muted in their Roman versions, the latter being a more ordered society, bent on the imposition of a rigid code of life upon a barbarian world.

BULFINCH, THOMAS
The Myths of Greece and Rome
Introduced by Joseph Campbell. A highly recommended edition of the long-established classic version of the myths, here accompanied by their pictorial representations in Western art.
[T649] Penguin pbk **£7.95**

GRAVES, ROBERT
The Greek Myths
The poet Robert Graves's excellent retelling of Greek myth, with detailed commentaries on its sources, has deservedly become a standard work for the general

reader. This abridged and illustrated edition omits the commentary, concentrating on the tales themselves.
[T650] Penguin pbk **£9.99**
The Greek Myths
Vol 1
[T651] Penguin pbk **£4.99**
Vol 2
[T652] Penguin pbk **£4.99**

KERENYI, C.
Kerenyi, a colleague of Jung and a classical scholar, set out to write a book on Greek mythology 'for adults'. These volumes provide one of the prime psychological interpretations of the cycles of Greek myth and legend.
Gods of the Greeks
[T653] Thames & H pbk **£4.95**
Heroes of the Greeks
[T654] Thames & H pbk **£4.95**

KIRK, GEOFFREY
Nature of Greek Myths
An examination of the various theories about Greek mythology, analysing the general nature of myth, and the place of myths in ancient Greek society.
[T655] Penguin pbk **£5.99**

RADICE, BETTY
Who's Who in the Ancient World
An illustrated dictionary of the major figures in Classical mythology, literature and history, giving their origins, and particularly concerned to record their significant appearance in Western art and literature.
[T656] Penguin pbk **£5.95**

ROSE, H.J.
Handbook of Greek Mythology
Designed primarily for the student of Classical literature, a guide to to the development of the Greek myths through the great authors, and their transmission to the Roman world.
[T657] Methuen pbk **£9.95**

Middle Eastern Mythology

The myths of the ancient Near East are survivors from some of the world's oldest civilised societies. Dating from 2,000 BC and before, many have been rediscovered only recently, retrieved by archaeological activity in the last hundred years. They are important not only in themselves, but in their provision of a cultural background to the societies which produced the religions of Judaism and Christianity.

DRIVER, G.R.
Canaanite Myths and Legends
[T658] T Clark hbk **£15.95**

HOOKE, S.H.
Middle Eastern Mythology
Based on the recent work of archaeologists, a study which places the myths of the Bible in the context of those of the Mesopotamians, Egyptians and other Near Eastern cultures.
[T659] Penguin pbk **£3.95**

LEVY, R. (TRANS)
The Epic of the Kings: Shah-Nama
Written down in the 10th century, the national epic poem of Persia collects the myths, legends and folktales of the country into a single cycle, from creation to the coming of Islam. This selection seeks

to capture the literary essence of the original for the general reader.
[T660] Arkana pbk **£9.99**

SANDARS, NANCY (TRANS)
The Epic of Gilgamesh
The most famous masterpiece of Babylonian literature, telling of the exploits of the tyrannical semi-divine King of Uruk. Dating from the third millenium BC, it was first discovered and translated only in the last century.
[T661] Penguin pbk **£2.99**

Teutonic Mythology

Our knowledge of the Teutonic (Norse) mythology comes, like Celtic legend, from late, mainly Christian sources. Apart from brief mentions in the writings of Caesar and Tacitus, the main source is the *Edda* of Sturluson, a 12th century Icelandic historian. Again the myths revolve around a large pantheon of deities headed by the triad of Woden/Odin, ruler and lawgiver, Thor the god of thunder and work, and Tyr the war god. The cult of Woden was very much a religion until the Germans were converted to Christianity. The stories are rich in creation myths, tales of epic struggles and complex strata of minor spirits, giants and demons.

CROSSLEY-HOLLAND, KEVIN
The Norse Myths
A vivid retelling of the great Scandinavian myths by this gifted poet and translator; basing his versions on the original sources, he draws the sometimes confusing and conflicting accounts these provide into a coherent whole.
[T662] Penguin pbk **£7.95**

DAVIDSON, H.R.E.
Gods and Myths of Northern Europe
Very much the classic in its field, this study of the Northern myths analyses their place in Germanic and Scandinavian society between the first millenium BC and 1,000 AD, and examines why these ancient beliefs eventually gave way to Christianity.
[T663] Penguin pbk **£3.95**

STURLUSON, SNORRI
The Edda: Tales from Norse Mythology
Written mainly as a literary handbook for Icelandic poets, the *Prose Edda*, as Sturluson's work is known, is also our primary source for information on the Norse myths.
[T664] Dent pbk **£4.95**

TITCHENELL, E.B. (ED)
The Masks of Odin
Translations of lays from the Norse *Poetic* or *Elder Edda*, a 10th century verse collection constituting a cycle of tales of the Norse gods; the accompanying commentary explores the continuing relevance of the ideas expressed in these myths.
[T665] Theosophical UP pbk **£6.95**

RELIGION

Current Affairs
Politics
Economics
Sociology & Anthropology
Psychology
Women's Studies

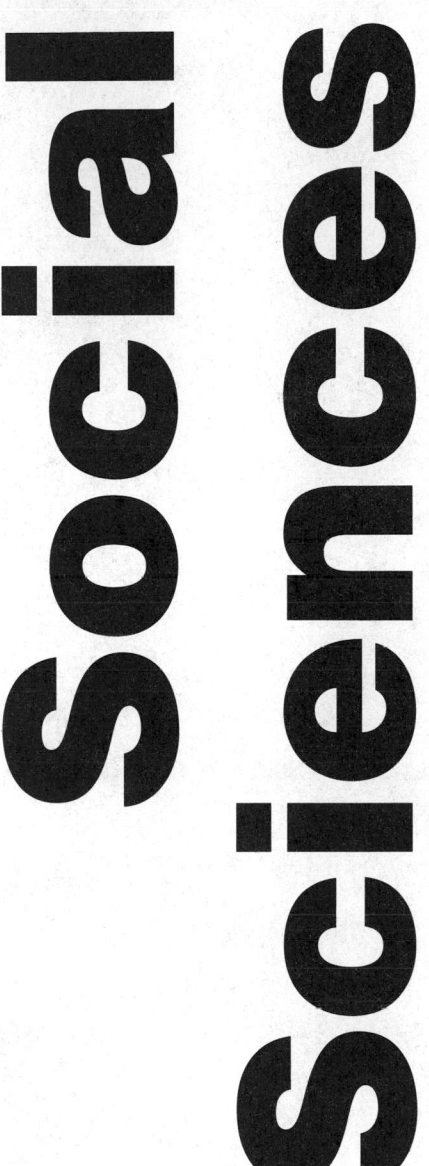

Social Sciences

SOCIAL SCIENCES

CURRENT AFFAIRS

General

New State of the World Atlas
A novel, inventive and illuminating reference work which shows, through a series of well-designed maps and diagrams the state of the world from various perspectives: military, agricultural, demographic, women's rights, etc.
[UA1] Pan pbk **£6.95**

The Statesman's Year Book 1988 - 89
A wealth of information on political, economic and social conditions of the world.
[UA2] Macmillan hbk **£26.95**

ARNOLD, GUY
The Third World Handbook
A survey of the Third World, including chronologies of conflict and independence, analysis of regional political groupings and consideration of the distinctive social, political and economic problems faced by third world countries in common.
[UA3] Cassell pbk **£12.95**

ASCHERSON, NEAL
Games with Shadows
A study of topics which illuminate our times, from the *Observer* columnist.
[UA4] Radius pbk **£6.95**

BARNABY, FRED (ED)
The Gaia Peace Atlas
The study of the prospects for peace and survival into the next millennium.
[UA41] Pan pbk **£10.95**

BULL, HEDLEY
The Anarchical Society: A Study of Order in World Politics
A study of questions including: what is order in world politics? How is order maintained in the contemporary states system? And what alternative paths to world order are desirable and feasible?
[UA5] Macmillan pbk **£9.95**

BUZAN, BARRY
An Introduction to Strategic Studies
Subtitled 'Military Technology and International Relations'. Buzan pays special attention in this textbook to the impact of the revolution in military technology on modern relations between states, the dynamics of the nuclear arms race, the theory of deterrence and the emergence of the means of violence as a problem in itself.
[UA6] Macmillan pbk **£12.99**
People, States and Fear
The national security problem in international relations. A sustained discussion of the issue of 'national security' - generally held to be both a permanent source of instability in the international system and an irreducible concern of every nation-state.
[UA7] Wheatsheaf pbk **£10.95**

CALVOCORESSI, PETER
World Politics since 1945
[UA8] Longman pbk **£11.95**

CARR, E.H.
The Twenty Years' Crisis, 1919 - 1939
Still a classic introduction to International Relations, Carr's study was the first major presentation of the 'realist' approach.
[UA9] Macmillan pbk **£7.99**

CHOMSKY, NOAM
The Chomsky Reader
Brings together the many different strands of his thought.
[UA10] Serpent's Tail pbk **£9.95**
The Culture of Terrorism
[UA11] Pluto pbk **£8.95**

CROW, BEN & THORPE, MARY (ED)
Survival and Change in the Third World
An Open University textbook covering a wide range of issues in development studies including: theories of development, colonial and post-colonial economies, the influence of the world economy on Third World development etc.
[UA12] Polity P pbk **£8.95**

FANON, FRANTZ
The Wretched of the Earth
The classic statement of imperialism by a leading Third World radical.
[UA13] Penguin pbk **£3.50**

GEORGE, SUSAN
A Fate Worse than Debt
[UA14] Penguin pbk **£4.99**

HALLIDAY, FRED
Cold War, Third World:
An Essay on Soviet-American Relations in the 1980s
A comparison of the roles played over the last decade by the superpowers in the Third World.
[UA16] Radius hbk **£16.95**
The Making of the Second Cold War
Halliday's analysis of the causes and significance of the sharpening of East-West hostilities in the late 1970s and early 1980s remains unrivalled.
[UA17] Verso pbk **£8.95**

HARRIS, NIGEL
End of the Third World
A survey of the social and economic dynamism of the Newly Industrialising Countries.
[UA18] Penguin pbk **£4.99**

HARRISON, PAUL
Inside the Third World
An analysis of poverty.
[UA19] Penguin pbk **£5.99**
The Third World Tomorrow
A report from the battlefront.
[UA20] Penguin pbk **£3.95**

JOHNSON, PAUL (ED)
The Oxford Book of Political Anecdotes
[UA22] Oxford pbk **£4.95**

KIDRON, M. & SMITH, D.
The War Atlas: Armed Conflict
A remarkable and sobering series of maps analysing the international scope and forms of modern militarism.
[UA23] Pan pbk **£2.99**

LAQUEUR, WALTER
The Age of Terrorism
A global survey of terrorist groups and their motives.
[UA24] Weidenfeld hbk **£17.95**

LINEAR, M.
Zapping the Third World: The Disaster of Development
[UA25] Pluto pbk **£5.50**

MIDDLETON, HAYDN (ED)
Atlas of Modern World History
The changing patterns of British and global political realities in our century colourfully brought to life in a fascinating series of maps.
[UA21] Oxford pbk **£7.95**

O'BRIEN, CONOR CRUISE
Passion and Cunning and Other Essays
Looks at the part played by politics and religion in world affairs.
[UA26] Weidenfeld hbk **£18.00**

ROBINS, L.
Introducing Political Science: Themes and Concepts in Studying Politics
An invaluable and very readable introductory guide to the content and methods of the many subject-areas which make up the contemporary discipline of Political Science. Includes chapters on political theory, comparative politics, urban politics, modern political economy, political sociology, public administration, international relations, political geography, development studies and political methodology.
[UA27] Longman pbk **£6.50**

SAMPSON, ANTHONY
Writer and journalist, one of the best known Current Affairs authors whose accounts of contemporary issues are always well-researched and stimulating.
Black and Gold
Apartheid, tycoons and revolutionaries.
[UA28] Hodder pbk **£3.95**
Drum: The Venture into New Africa
[UA29] Hodder pbk **£6.95**
Sovereign State
The secret history of International Telephone and Telegraph.
[UA30] Hodder pbk **£2.95**
The Arms Bazaar
The companies, dealers and bribes from Vickers to Lockheed.
[UA31] Hodder pbk **£4.50**
The Changing Anatomy of Britain
An updated edition of his classic report.
[UA32] Hodder pbk **£5.99**
The Empires of the Sky
An exposé of the major airlines.
[UA33] Hodder pbk **£2.50**
The Money Lenders
The story behind the 'World Bank Crisis'.
[UA34] Hodder pbk **£4.50**
The Seven Sisters
The oil corporations.
[UA35] Hodder pbk **£4.50**

SCHELL, JONATHAN
The Abolition
Schell advances his own solution to the nuclear threat.
[UA36] Picador pbk **£2.95**
The Fate of the Earth
Perhaps the most powerful evocation of the threat of nuclear war to humanity and to the planet.
[UA37] Picador pbk **£2.50**

SEGAL, GERALD
Guide to the World Today
An updated edition of this guide to world affairs which combines analysis, key facts and political background to give a full perspective on important international issues.
[UA38] Simon & Sch pbk **£5.95**

SMITH, M.; LITTLE, R. & SHACKLETON, M. (EDS)
Perspectives on World Politics
This Open University set text leads the reader through a well-chosen series of extracts, several of them from articles not otherwise easily obtainable, which cover the range of major issues in the discipline.
[UA39] Croom H pbk **£8.95**

TAYLOR, T. (ED)
Approaches and Theory in International Relations
A comprehensive and readable survey for students of the main schools within the discipline of International Relations.
[UA40] Longman pbk **£11.50**

VADNEY, THOMAS E.
The World Since 1945
An accessible history of world politics up to 1986 in one volume.
[UA42] Penguin pbk **£5.99**

International Politics

Arranged by area of the world.

Africa

BRITTAIN, VICTORIA
Hidden Lives, Hidden Deaths: South Africa's Crippling of a Continent
An overview, with eye-witness accounts of the situation in South Africa.
[UA44] Faber hbk **£12.95**

CHAZAN, NAOMI ET AL
Politics and Society in Contemporary Africa
An impressively comprehensive study of African politics, covering many aspects including political culture and the post-colonial state, political economy, regional relations of African states, under-development, ethnicity etc.
[UA45] Macmillan pbk **£9.95**

COMMONWEALTH EMINENT PERSONS' GROUP
Mission to South Africa
[UA46] Penguin pbk **£2.95**

DAVENPORT, THOMAS
South Africa: A Modern History
[UA48] Macmillan pbk **£18.95**

HALLIDAY, F. & MOLYNEUX, M.
The Ethiopian Revolution
An analysis of the Ethiopian case which seeks also to draw more general conclusions about Third World revolutions.
[UA50] Verso pbk **£6.95**

HARRISON, PAUL
The Greening of Africa: Breakthrough in the Battle for Land and Food
Commissioned by the Institute for Environment and Development, this persuasive and informative argument shows that an African Green Revolution is possible.
[UA51] Grafton pbk **£4.95**

HUBBARD, MICHAEL ET AL
Preventing Famine
Rethinking policies for avoiding such famines as those which have occurred in Ethiopia and the Sudan.
[UA47] Routledge pbk **£10.95**

ILIFFE, JOHN
The African Poor
[UA52] Cambridge pbk **£9.95**

JANSSON, K. ET AL
The Ethiopian Famine
A new edition, by the man who ran the UN relief operation in Ethiopia.
[UA53] Zed pbk **£6.95**

KAPUSCINSKI, RYSZARD
The Emperor
A portrait of the last days of Haile Selassie.
[UA54] Picador pbk **£2.95**

LAPPING, BRIAN
Apartheid: A History
A factual account covering every stage of the development of apartheid from the very first Cape settlements.
[UA55] Grafton pbk **£3.95**

LEACH, GRAHAM
South Africa
The BBC correspondent investigates apartheid and the nature of Afrikaner nationalism, as well as critically examining Botha's reforms.
[UA57] Methuen pbk **£2.95**
The Afrikaners
Surveys the dilemmas of white South African politics and the bitter division forming within the community.
[UA56] Macmillan **£15.95**

MANDELA, WINNIE
Part of My Soul
A defiant and moving autobiography by someone at the very centre of the black South African struggle.
[UA58] Penguin pbk **£3.99**

MARABLE, MANNING
African and Caribbean Politics: From Kwame Nkruma to Maurice Bishop
Marable focuses on the issue of the proliferation of authoritarian regimes and explores the political legacy of the experience of slavery and imperialism.
[UA59] Verso pbk **£8.95**

MAZRUI, ALI A.
The Africans
Challenges many of our received, Western notions about Africa, most interestingly in relation to the genesis of ancient civilisations.
[UA60] BBC hbk **£14.95**

SAVE THE CHILDREN FUND
Prospects for Africa's Children
[UA61] Hodder pbk **£5.95**

STRASBURG, TONI & BERNSTEIN, KEITH
Frontline Southern Africa
Based on a Channel 4 film, this is an account of the staggering effects of South Africa's policies on the frontline states.
[UA62] C Helm pbk **£12.95**

STONEMAN, COLIN
Zimbabwe: Politics, Economics and Society
[UA63] Pinter pbk **£9.95**

Britain

BAGEHOT, WALTER
English Constitution
[UA64] Fontana pbk **£3.95**

BENN, TONY
Parliament and People: Agenda for a Free Society
Interviews with *New Left Review*.
[UA65] Verso pbk **£3.25**

BROWN, MICHAEL & MAY, JOHN
The Greenpeace Story
Traces the rise of Greenpeace.
[UA66] D Kindersley pbk **£7.95**

BRUCE-GARDYNE, JOCK
Ministers and Mandarins: Inside the Whitehall Village
The author has served as a Minister of State in Mrs Thatcher's Government, and so presents an insider's view.
[UA67] Sidgwick hbk **£10.95**

BYRD, PETER (ED)
British Foreign Policy under Thatcher
Does the Thatcher revolution extend into the realm of foreign policy, or do the old continuities persist?
[UA68] P Allan pbk **£8.95**

CAMPBELL, BEATRIX ET AL
New Times
A collection of recent essays form *Marxism Today*, mapping the Left's re-assessment of the socialist future.
[UA73] Lawrence & W pbk **£7.95**

CANNON, GEOFFREY
The Politics of Food
Claims that the decisions of a closed circle of people in Whitehall and Westminster have resulted in the British diet being the most unhealthy in the Western world.
[UA69] Century pbk **£6.95**

CHESSHYRE, ROBERT
Return of a Native Reporter
An account of journalist Chesshyre's journeys around, and impressions of, Britain, after his return from a period of work in America: it becomes a memorable, and critical document of the social changes of the 1980s visible to one whose view is partly that of an 'outsider'.
[UA70] Penguin pbk **£4.95**

COLEMAN, TERRY
Movers and Shakers
A collection of the *Guardian* columnist's interviews and profiles, which gives a valuable insight into the mood of the times.
[UA70A] Deutsch hbk **£12.95**

FOOT, PAUL
Who Framed Colin Wallace?   **NEW**
Foot tells a story of official deception and secret-keeping, and of the campaign to discredit former military intelligence officer Colin Wallace, which resulted in his imprisonment for murder.
[UA70A] Macmillan hbk **£12.95**

GAMBLE, ANDREW
Britain in Decline
Second edition of this outstanding introduction to contemporary British politics.
[UA71] Macmillan pbk **£8.95**

The Free Economy and the Strong State
Probably the best and most accessible serious study of Thatcherism.
[UA72] Macmillan pbk **£7.95**

HARRIS, ROBERT
Gotcha! The Media, the Government and the Falklands Crisis
[UA74] Faber pbk **£3.95**

HENNESSY, PETER
Cabinet
A clear and comprehensive account of the workings of the Cabinet, including case studies of the Cabinet system in some key decision-making episodes of recent British politics.
[UA75] Blackwell pbk **£8.95**
Whitehall
Analyses the workings of the Civil Service.
[UA76] Secker hbk **£20.00**

HITCHENS, CHRISTOPHER
Prepared for the Worst **NEW**
A new collection of Hitchens' essays from the *Spectator*, *New Statesman* and American periodicals.
[UA77] Chatto hbk **£15.95**

HOBSBAWM, ERIC
Politics for a Rational Left **NEW**
A collection of articles on British politics by the noted Marxist historian - arguing the need for a broad coalition with the centre as the only means of defeating Thatcherism.
[UA78] Verso pbk **£7.95**

HOWE, S. (ED)
Lines of Dissent: Writing from the 'New Statesman', 1913 - 1988
[UA79] Verso hbk **£14.95**

JACK, IAN
Before the Oil Ran Out
[UA80] Flamingo pbk **£3.95**

JENKINS, PETER
Mrs Thatcher's Revolution: The Ending of the Socialist Era
[UA81] Pan pbk **£4.99**

JESSOP, B. ET AL
Thatcherism: A Tale of Two Nations
The only comprehensive review for students of the debates on the nature of Thatcherism.
[UA82] Polity P pbk **£7.95**

JOHNSTON, RONALD (ED)
National Dividing? The Electoral Map of Great Britain 1979 - 1987
An analysis of the widening North-South gap as reflected in successive General Elections.
[UA83] Longman pbk **£9.95**

JONES, B. & KAVANAGH, D.
British Politics Today
An accessible and comprehensive introduction to the subject for 'A' Level students.
[UA84] Mancheser UP pbk **£4.25**

JONES, B. (ED)
Political Issues in Britain Today
Clear, informative introductions to thinking about a whole range of political issues in contemporary Britain, including Secrecy in Government, Electoral Reform, Unemployment, Racism, Defence Issues, Northern Ireland, Nuclear Energy etc. A companion volume to the popular *British Politics Today*.
[UA85] Manchester UP pbk **£5.95**

KAVANAGH, DENNIS
Thatcherism and British Politics
[UA86] Oxford pbk **£5.95**

KLEIN, R.
The Politics of the National Health Service
An account of the development of the NHS from its inauguration in 1948, focusing on recurrent policy dilemmas and how successive governments have sought to meet them.
[UA87] Longman pbk **£6.95**

LEVIN, BERNARD
Levin's journalism and essays, collected in these volumes, establish him as one of the most individual and intelligent voices in Britain of the last two decades.
All Things Considered
[UA87A] Cape hbk **£12.95**
Conducted Tour
[UA87B] Hodder pbk **£4.95**
Enthusiasms
[UA87C] Hodder pbk **£3.95**
The Way We Live Now
[UA87D] Hodder pbk **£3.95**

LEYS, COLIN
Politics in Britain: From Labourism to Thatcherism
Revised edition of this admirably clear and stimulating introduction to modern British politics.
[UA88] Verso pbk **£6.95**

MARQUAND, DAVID
The Unprincipled Society
An analysis of Britain's condition.
[UA89] Fontana pbk **£4.95**

MERCER, DERRIK; MANGHAM, GEOFF & WILLIAMS, KEVIN
Fog of War
An analysis of the relationship between the media, armed forces and the government in the wake of the Falklands War.
[UA90] Heinemann hbk **£15.95**

MILIBAND, RALPH
Capitalist Democracy in Britain
[UA91] Oxford pbk **£5.95**

NAIRN, TOM
The Enchanted Glass
Tom Nairn's perceptive, witty and radical study of Royalty and the English. Probably the only serious intellectual treatment of the subject available.
[UA92] Radius pbk **£8.95**

NORTON, PHILIP
The British Polity
[UA93] Longman pbk **£10.50**
The Commons in Perspective
A comprehensive textbook on the institutions and working of parliament.
[UA94] Blackwell pbk **£8.50**

PINCHER, CHAPMAN
The 'Spycatcher' Affair: A Web of Deception
[UA94A] Hodder pbk **£2.95**

PONTING, CLIVE
Breach of Promise: Labour in Power, 1964 - 1970 **NEW**
Clive Ponting's history and reassessment of Harold Wilson's government.
[UA97] H Hamilton hbk **£15.95**

Clive Ponting, author of *Breach of Promise* (Hamish Hamilton hbk £15.95)

Whitehall: Tragedy and Farce
An exposé of Whitehall from the controversial former civil servant who 'leaked' information to Parliament on the Belgrano Affair.
[UA98] Sphere pbk **£4.95**

PORRITT, JONATHON & WINNER, DAVID
Coming of the Greens
[UA98A] Fontana pbk **£4.99**
Going Green
Demonstrates how far Green ideas have penetrated every aspect of our culture from movies to health food stores, and religion to big business.
[UA99] Fontana pbk **£3.50**

ROSE, RICHARD
Politics in England: Persistence and Change
[UA100] Faber hbk **£9.95**

RYLE, MICHAEL & RICHARDS, PETER
The Commons Under Scrutiny
This is the latest edition of the popular *The Commons Today*, revised and updated to include the impact of the 1987 General Election.
[UA101] Routledge pbk **£8.95**

SCHWARZ, WALTER
The New Dissenters
Moral responses to Thatcherism by leading Churchmen, activists and politicians.
[UA102] Bedford Sq pbk **£3.95**

SKED, ALAN & COOK, CHRIS
Post-War Britain: A Political History
A government-by-government account.
[UA103] Penguin pbk **£6.99**

THOMPSON, E.P.
Writing by Candlelight
A stimulating collection of Thompson's essays of the 1970s, including a large section on civil liberties in Britain.
[UA104] Merlin P pbk **£5.95**
Zero Option
A volume of Thompson's essays on European Nuclear Disarmament, including 'Notes on Exterminism: The Last Stage of Civilisation', which sparked a major debate on the nature of the nuclear arms race.
[UA105] Merlin P pbk **£4.95**

Margaret Thatcher (Photo: Sdrja Djukanovic)

TURNBULL, MALCOLM
The 'Spycatcher' Trial
An account of the Spycatcher trial from Peter Wright's defence lawyer, who gives a full account of the issues and personalities concerned.
[UA105A] Mandarin pbk **£3.99**

WEST, NIGEL
A Matter of Trust: MI5 1945 - 72
[UA105B] Hodder pbk **£2.95**
MI5: British Secret Intelligence Operations 1909 - 45
[UA105C] Grafton pbk **£3.95**
MI6: British Secret Service Operations 1909 - 45
[UA105D] Grafton pbk **£3.95**
The Friends
[UA105E] Weidenfeld hbk **£12.95**

WILLIAMS, RAYMOND
Resources of Hope: Culture, Democracy, Socialism   **NEW**
A new collection of Williams' essays, and a fitting tribute to one of the great post-war writers and intellects.
[UA106] Verso pbk **£9.95**

ZUCKERMAN, SOLLY
Nuclear Illusion and Reality
[UA107] Collins pbk **£4.95**

Europe

ARDAGH, JOHN
France Today
[UA199] Penguin pbk **£6.99**
Germany and the Germans
[UA200] Penguin pbk **£5.99**

ASCHESON, NEAL
Struggles for Poland
[UA201] Pan pbk **£4.99**

BARZINI, LUIGI
The Europeans
A series of witty and often revealing articles, one for each of the major Western European nationalities, attempting to portray their respective characters.
[UA202] Penguin pbk **£4.99**

BASSETT, RICHARD
Waldheim and Austria
[UA203] Penguin pbk **£4.99**

CAMILLER, P. (ED)
The Left in Western Europe
[UA204] Verso pbk **£8.95**

CONRADT, D.
The German Polity
1986 edition of this standard introductory text on West German politics.
[UA205] Longman hbk **£14.65**

DAWISHA, KAREN
Eastern Europe, Gorbachev and Reform
[UA206] Cambridge pbk **£7.95**

GUNN, S.
Europe's Radical Right
A critical overview of the New Right in Britain and Europe.
[UA207] Pluto pbk **£5.95**

HARMAN, C.
Class Struggles in Eastern Europe, 1945 - 83
[UA208] Bookmarks pbk **£7.95**

HEBBLETHWAITE, PETER
In the Vatican
The biographer of John XXIII on the inner workings of the Vatican.
[UA209] Oxford pbk **£4.95**

HOOPER, JOHN
The Spaniards
A portrait of the new Spain.
[UA210] Penguin pbk **£4.99**

HULSBERG, W.
The German Greens
The first in-depth study in English of the emergence, political character and prospects of one of the great radical successes in the politics of the 1980s.
[UA211] Verso pbk **£9.95**

JOHNSTONE, DIANA
The Politics of Euromissiles: Europe's Role in America's World
A compelling survey of the politics of the INF deployment and an account of the political forces which mobilised against it across Western Europe.
[UA212] Verso pbk **£5.95**

KALDOR, M. ET AL (EDS)
The New Detente: Rethinking East-West Relations
Writers from both sides of the continent and a wide political spectrum debate the future of Europe.
[UA213] Verso pbk **£9.95**

LOVENDUSKI, J. & WOODALL, J.
Politics and Society in Eastern Europe
[UA214] Macmillan pbk **£9.95**

MILOSZ, CZESLAW
The Captive Mind
A controversial analysis of society by the Nobel Prize-winning Polish poet which highlights the gullibility of the modern imagination in its willingness to accept totalitarianism on the basis of a promised future.
[UA215] Penguin pbk **£3.95**

PALMER, JOHN
Europe without America? The Crisis in Atlantic Relations
A thoughtful and compellingly argued assessment of the rising political and economic conflicts of interest within the Atlantic alliance.
[UA216] Oxford pbk **£5.95**
Trading Places
[UA217] Radius pbk **£6.95**

SMITH, GORDON
Politics in Western Europe
The fifth edition of this textbook introduction to the comparative study of European politics.
[UA218] Gower pbk **£8.50**

TORANSKA, TERESA
Oni: Poland's Stalinists Cross Examined
'Oni' is Polish for 'They' and refers to the shadowy leaders of the Soviet block between 1944 and 1956, recent interviews with whom form the basis of this enightening study.
[UA219] Collins pbk **£9.95**

URWIN, DEREK
Western Europe since 1945
Fourth edition of this standard political history of postwar Western Europe.
[UA221] Longman pbk **£8.50**

WRIGHT, VINCENT
The Government and Politics of France
1989 edition of this leading textbook on French government.
[UA222] Unwin Hyman pbk **£9.95**

India & Asia

ALI, TARIQ
The Nehrus and the Gandhis: An Indian Dynasty
A fine historical record, with an introduction by Salman Rushdie.
[UA108] Picador pbk **£2.50**

ANWAR, RAJA
The Tragedy of Afghanistan: A First-Hand Account
[UA109] Verso hbk **£17.95**

BENEWICK, R. & WINGROVE, P. (EDS)
Reforming the Revolution: China in Transition
A collection of essays assessing the progress of the momentous changes under way across Chinese social, political and economic life.
[UA110] Macmillan pbk **£7.95**

GITTINGS, JOHN
China Changes Face: The Road from Revolution, 1949 - 1989
Published to coincide with the 40th anniversary of the revolution, this is the most comprehensive non-specialist account of modern Chinese politics in English. By the Chinese correspondent of *The Guardian*.
[UA111] Oxford hbk **£17.50**

RODZINSKI, WITOLD
The People's Republic of China
Reflections on Chinese political history since 1949.
[UA112] Collins hbk **£17.50**
[UA112A] Fontana pbk **£5.95**

SEAGROVE, STERLING
The Marcos Dynasty   **NEW**
[UA113] Macmillan hbk **£16.95**

SHAWCROSS, WILLIAM
Sideshow
A welcome reprint of Shawcross's brilliant account of
the Cambodian conflict.
[UA114] Hogarth pbk **£6.95**
The Quality of Mercy
This follow-up study from William Shawcross on
Cambodia looks at world response to the state of
that country after the Vietnamese invasion, as the
full horror of the Khmer Rouge régime became
apparent.
[UA115] Fontana pbk **£3.95**

TULLY, MARK & JACOB, SATISH
**Amritsar: Mrs Gandhi's Last
Battle**
[UA116] Pan pbk **£3.95**

TULLY, MARK & MASANI, ZAREER
**From Raj to Rajiv: 40 Years of
Indian Independence**
The book to accompany the Radio 4 series.
[UA117] BBC hbk **£10.95**

WORONOFF, JON
Politics the Japanese Way
[UA118] Macmillan pbk **£13.95**

Middle East

BAKHASH, SHAUL
**The Reign of the Ayatollahs:
Iran and the Islamic Revolution**
One of the best general introductions on the
Revolution and its aftermath.
[UA119] Counterpoint pbk **£4.95**

CHOMSKY, NOAM
**Fateful Triangle: Israel, the US and
the Palestinians**
[UA120] Pluto P pbk **£8.95**

HARKABI, Y.
Israel's Fateful Decisions
[UA121] IB Tauris hbk **£14.95**

HEIKAL, MOHAMED
**Autumn of Fury: The Assassination
of Sadat**
Detailed account by one of the most acute
commentators on the Middle East.
[UA122] Corgi pbk **£3.95**
**The Return of the Ayatollah: The
Iranian Revolution from Mossadeq
to Khomeini**
[UA123] Deutsch pbk **£6.95**

HIRO, DILIP
Inside the Middle East
[UA124] Routledge pbk **£8.95**
Islamic Fundamentalism
[UA125] Grafton pbk **£4.95**
**The Longest Story of the Iran-Iraq
Conflict**
[UA126] Grafton hbk **£14.95**

HIRST, DAVID
**The Gun and the Olive Branch:
The Roots of Violence in the Middle
East**
[UA127] Faber hbk **£12.50**

LIPMAN, BEATA
Embattled Ground
An examination of the responses of women to the
conflict in Israel.
[UA128] Pandora pbk **£4.95**

MANSFIELD, PETER
The Arabs
An excellent introduction to the political and
historical developments of the Arabs from nomads to
oil-sheikhs.
[UA129] Penguin pbk **£6.99**

SAID, EDWARD
After the Last Sky
[UA131] Faber pbk **£6.95**
Covering Islam
A fascinating critical study of the portrayal of Islam
in the Western media.
[UA132] Routledge pbk **£7.95**

SHOUKRI, GHALI
**Egypt - Portrait of a President:
Sadat's Road to Jerusalem**
[UA133] Zed Bks pbk **£7.95**

SICK, GARY
**All Fall Down: America's Fateful
Encounter with Iran**
[UA134] IB Tauris hbk **£16.50**

TAHERI, AMIR
Holy Terror
[UA135] Sphere pbk **£3.95**

WRIGHT, M.
Iran: The Khomeini Revolution
A study of the domestic and international impact of
the Islamic revolution.
[UA136] Longman pbk **£6.95**

North America

AMBROSE, STEPHEN A.
Rise to Globalism
The latest edition of this classic study of
American foreign policy between 1938 to the
1980s.
[UA137] Penguin pbk **£5.99**

BENSON, P. & HILL, D.
Religion on Capitol Hill
A study of the influence of religious factors in
Congress
[UA138] Oxford pbk **£7.50**

BILL, JAMES A.
The Eagle and the Lion
The complex relationship between the USA and
Iran.
[UA139] Yale UP hbk **£16.95**

BLOOM, ALLAN
**The Closing of the American
Mind**
A savage, conservative critique of the American
educational system with an enthusiastic introduction
by Saul Bellow.
[UA140] Penguin pbk **£8.99**

COCKBURN, ALEXANDER
Corruptions of Empire
A collection of Cockburn's polemical journalism.
[UA141] Verso pbk **£7.95**

DAVIS, M.
**Prisoners of the American
Dream**
A series of essays in which Davis explores why
'the world's most industrially advanced nation
never spawned a mass party of the working
class.'
[UA143] Verso pbk **£7.95**

GRIFFITH, ERNEST S.
The American System of Government
A standard text, now in its sixth edition, outlining the
workings of US government institutions.
[UA144] Methuen pbk **£7.95**

KELLERMAN, BARBARA
The Political Presidency
The practice of leadership from Kennedy through
Reagan.
[UA145] Oxford pbk **£9.95**

KENNEDY, P.
**The Rise and Fall of the Great
Powers**
Now in paperback, this is the history book whose
predictions about the future of American world power
sent it to the top of the US bestseller lists in the
aftermath of the Crash of 1987.
[UA146] Fontana pbk **£6.95**

LEES, J. ET AL
American Politics Today
A clear introductory textbook on the institutions of
American government.
[UA147] Manchester UP pbk **£4.95**

MARABLE, MANNING
Black American Politics
New and revised edition of Marable's work, charting
the subject from the Washington Marches to Jesse
Jackson.
[UA148] Verso pbk **£9.95**

MAYER, JANE & MCMANUS, DOYLE
**Landslide: The Unmaking of President
Reagan**
[UA149] Fontana pbk **£5.99**

MCCONNELL, MALCOLM
Challenger: A Major Malfunction
[UA150] Unwin pbk **£3.95**

MCKAY, DAVID H.
American Politics and Society
[UA151] Blackwell pbk **£7.95**

MOLL, HERMAN & LEAPMAN, MICHAEL
**Broker of Death: An Insider's Story
of the Iran Arms Deal**
[UA152] Macmillan hbk **£12.95**

NICHOLAS, H.G.
The Nature of American Politics
[UA153] Oxford pbk **£6.95**

PEEL, G.
Revival and Reaction
A study of the political right in the United States
which seeks to explain the historical context of the
1980s ascendancy.
[UA154] Oxford pbk **£9.95**

SMITH, HEDRICK
**The Power Game: How Washington
Works**
[UA155] Fontana pbk **£5.95**

STOCKMAN, DAVID A.
The Triumph of Politics
A study of the recent crisis in American government
and its consequences for the rest of the world.
[UA156] Coronet pbk **£3.95**

TAHERI, AMIR
A Nest of Spies
Charts the relationship of the US and Iran up to recent
developments in the Gulf.
[UA157] Hutchinson hbk **£15.95**

WILLS, GARRY
Reagan's America: Innocents At Home
[UA158] Heinemann pbk **£6.95**

WOODWARD, BOB
**Veil: Secret Wars of the C.I.A.
1981 - 1987**
A revealing account of the CIA's institutionalised disregard for the law in the pursuit of a dimly perceived ideological policy.
[UA159] Headline pbk **£4.99**

Southern & Central America

Nunca Mas
A Report by Argentina's National Commission on Disappeared People: moving testimony to the victims of the Argentine military régime.
[UA160] Faber pbk **£7.95**

ANGEL, ADRIANNA & MACINTOSH, FIONA
Tiger's Milk
Women in Nicaragua describe their oppression, their suffering and their hope for change.
[UA161] Virago pbk **£9.99**

AZICRI, MAX
Cuba: Politics, Economics and Society
[UA162] Pinter hbk **£9.95**

CHOMSKY, NOAM
Turning the Tide
Written with Chomsky's characteristic combination of erudition and biting sarcasm, this volume examines the US intervention in Central America in historical perspective.
[UA163] Pluto pbk **£6.50**

CLOSE, DAVID
Nicaragua: Politics, Economics and Society
[UA164] Pinter pbk **£9.95**

COCKBURN, LESLIE
Out of Control
The story of the secret war in Nicaragua, the illegal arms pipeline and the Contras.
[UA142] Bloomsbury hbk **£13.95**

MARSHALL, PETER
Cuba Libre!: Breaking the Chains?
Looks at the successes and failures of Cuba, and examines the possible contenders who may succeed Castro.
[UA165] Unwin Hyman pbk **£6.95**

PEARCE, JENNY
Under the Eagle
US interventions in Central America and the Caribbean.
[UA166] Lat Am Bureau pbk **£5.95**

RUSHDIE, SALMAN
The Jaguar Smile: A Nicaraguan Journey
The story, plus personal commentary, of a journey to Central America at the invitation of the Sandinista government.
[UA167] Pan pbk **£3.95**

SIMPSON, JOHN & BENNETT, JANA
The Disappeared
The story of the victims of Argentina's secret war of oppression.
[UA168] Robson hbk **£12.95**

TRAGER, OLIVER
Latin America
Focuses on the effects of internal strife and external interference in this region.
[UA169] Facts on File hbk **£18.50**

WEBER, HENRI
Nicaragua: The Sandinista Revolution
[UA170] Verso pbk **£5.95**

Soviet Union

BLOOMFIELD, J. (ED)
Perestroika, State and Civil Society
A new collection, including essays by Martin Walker, Archie Brown and Mick Lampert, examining the momentous significance of the changes currently under way in the Soviet Union.
[UA171] Lawrence & W pbk **£8.95**

BOOKBINDER, ALAN ET AL
Comrades: Portraits of Soviet Life
[UA172] BBC hbk **£11.95**

COHEN, STEPHEN F.
Rethinking the Soviet Experience: Politics & History since 1917
[UA173] Oxford hbk **£5.95**

DAWISHA, KAREN
Gorbachev and Reform: The Great Challenge
[UA174] Cambridge pbk **£7.95**

DIBB, P.
Soviet Union: The Incomplete Superpower
[UA175] Macmillan hbk **£11.95**

EDMONDS, ROBIN
Soviet Foreign Policy: The Brezhnev Years
Covers the years 1956-1982.
[UA176] Oxford pbk **£5.95**

FRANKLAND, MARK
The Sixth Continent: Russia and Mikhail Gorbachev
The background to the new revolution in Russia.
[UA177] H Hamilton hbk **£12.95**

GILBERT, MARTIN
Jews of Hope
The plight of Soviet Jewry.
[UA178] Penguin pbk **£3.95**

GORBACHEV, MIKHAIL
Perestroika: Our Hopes for Our Country and Our World
Gorbachev's thoughts on reform and restructuring in the USSR. Includes ideas for an open foreign policy, the emancipation of women and a policy on racial and religious differences.
[UA179] Fontana pbk **£3.95**

HAYNES, V. & BOJCUN, M.
The Chernobyl Disaster
[UA180] Hogarth pbk **£5.95**

KARGALITSKY, B.
The Thinking Reed: Intellectuals and the Soviet State: 1917 to the Present
[UA181] Verso pbk **£9.95**

LANE, D.
Soviet Economy and Society
[UA182] Blackwell hbk **£10.95**

State and Politics in the USSR
[UA183] Blackwell hbk **£9.95**

LEWIN, MOSHE
The Gorbachev Phenomenon: An Historical Interpretation
Recounts the great changes in Soviet society which preceded the emergence of Gorbachev. Now available in paperback.
[UA184] Century pbk **£5.95**

MANDEL, E.
Beyond Perestroika
[UA185] Verso hbk **£10.95**

MCAULEY, MARTIN
The Soviet Union Under Gorbachev
A collection of essays which together constitute one of the best and most level-headed of the many recent attempts to analyse the rapidly changing face of the Soviet Union.
[UA187] Macmillan hbk **£9.95**

MEDVEDEV, ZHORES
Gorbachev
[UA188] Blackwell pbk **£7.95**

NAHAYLO, B. & SWOBODA, V.
National Tension in the USSR: The History of the Unfulfilled National Contract
Surveys those non-Russian parts of the Soviet Union now campaigning for cultural identity and political independence.
[UA189] H Hamilton hbk **£14.95**

NOVE, ALEC
Stalinism and After
[UA190] Unwin hbk **£25.00**

RESHETAR, JOHN
The Soviet Polity: Government and Politics in the USSR
[UA191] Harper & R hbk **£17.50**

ROXBURGH, ANGUS
Pravda: Inside the Soviet News Machine
[UA192] Gollancz hbk **£16.95**

Salman Rushdie, author of *The Jaguar Smile* (Pan pbk **£3.95**) (Photo: Viking)

SAKWA, RICHARD
Soviet Politics: An Introduction
This major new textbook combines a history of the development of the Soviet state since 1917 with a review of the contemporary political scene, and assesses the rise of Gorbachev.
[UA193] Routledge hbk **£12.95**

SCHAPIRO, LEONARD & REDDAWAY, PETER
Russian Studies
[UA194] Collins hbk **£15.00**

SMITH, GORDON
Soviet Politics
A major new textbook containing substantial historical background information and an examination of the first year of the Gorbachev regime.
[UA195] Macmillan pbk **£9.95**

WALKER, MARTIN
Russia
A collection of pieces from the Moscow Diary of the *Guardian* correspondent, chronicling the emergence of *glasnost*.
[UA196] Abacus pbk **£3.99**
The Waking Giant: The Soviet Union Under Gorbachev
A vivid portrayal of the new Russia of *glasnost* and détente.
[UA197] Sphere pbk **£4.99**

WHITE, STEPHEN & PRAVDA, ALEX
Ideology and Soviet Politics
Provides a detailed picture of the development of official ideology up to Gorbachev's 1986 Party Programme.
[UA198] Macmillan pbk **£12.95**

POLITICS

General

BOTTOMORE, TOM (ED)
Dictionary of Marxist Thought
The most impressive, detailed and wide-ranging reference work of its kind on Marxism.
[UB1] Blackwell hbk **£11.95**

ROBERTSON, DAVID (ED)
Penguin Dictionary of Politics
A useful and up-to-date aid.
[UB2] Penguin pbk **£4.99**

SCRUTON, ROGER
A Dictionary of Political Thought
A handy reference guide for the general reader which rarely reveals the conservative bias of its editor.
[UB3] Pan pbk **£5.99**

WILLIAMS, RAYMOND
Keywords: A Vocabulary of Culture and Society
Originally conceived as a glossary for Raymond Williams' *Culture and Society*, this volume is a unique record of the shifting meanings and associations of the most ideologically charged words of the vocabulary of politics and political thought.
[UB4] Fontana pbk **£4.95**

Histories of Political Thought

ARNHART, R.
Political Questions: Political Philosophy from Plato to Rawls
[UB5] Macmillan pbk **£12.95**

BERKI, R.N.
History of Political Thought
A compact study of the Western tradition organised around the major historical shifts in the conception of the relation between the individual and society.
[UB6] Dent pbk **£3.95**

FORSYTH, M. & KEENS-SOPER, M.
A Guide to the Political Classics: Plato to Rousseau
Introductory essays for students.
[UB7] Oxford pbk **£8.95**

LIVELY, J. & REEVE, A. (EDS)
Modern Political Theory from Hobbes to Marx: Key Debates
An accessible anthology of classic interpretations of the major figures in the tradition of Political Theory - with sections on Hobbes, Locke, Burke, Rousseau, Bentham, Mill and Marx.
[UB8] Routledge pbk **£9.95**

MUSCHAMP, DAVID (ED)
Political Thinkers
Fifteen introductory essays covering the history of political thought from Plato to the present. Includes a useful glossary and chronological table.
[UB9] Macmillan pbk **£8.95**

SABINE, G.H. & THORSON, T.L.
A History of Political Theory
The first of the many editions and revisions of this work was published in 1937, and it remains a standard work of reference.
[UB10] Holt RW hbk **£11.50**

THOMSON, DAVID
Political Ideas
A study of the most significant ideas of eminent European political thinkers over the last 500 years.
[UB11] Penguin pbk **£4.50**

Political Thinkers

In chronological order.

MACHIAVELLI, NICCOLO (1469 - 1527)
Machiavelli's advice on the exercise of state power cannot fully be understood outside the context of 'the present ruin of Italy' which it was his misfortune to witness. But his prescriptions for effective government, whatever moral criticism they have provoked, prefigure many of the central themes of modern 'realist' understandings of state behaviour such as: the state's monopoly of armed force; the separation of public from private morality; and the careful blend of consent and coercion required to sustain the legitimacy of a régime.
Portable Machiavelli
Edited and translated by Bondanella and Musa, this volume includes the complete *Prince*, an abridged version of the *Discourses*, selections from the *Art of War* and the *History of Florence* together with letters and much else besides. There is also a biographical and explanatory introduction.
[UB13] Penguin pbk **£5.95**

The Prince (Trans. Bull, George)
The classic justification of treachery and deceit for the establishment and maintenance of authority which gives the term 'Machiavellian' its meaning.
[UB14] Penguin pbk **£2.99**
The Prince (Ed. & trans. Adams, R.M.)
[UB15] Norton pbk **£4.95**
The Prince (Ed. Skinner, Quentin)
A new translation by Russell Price, introduced by Quentin Skinner.
[UB16] Cambridge pbk **£4.95**
SKINNER, Q.
Machiavelli
In the Oxford *Past Master* series.
[UB17] Oxford pbk **£2.95**

HOBBES, THOMAS (1588 - 1679)
Hobbes's political thought is distinctive both in the constitution which he advocated - absolutist rule - and in the materialist methodology which he used. The former derives from his pessimistic assumptions about human nature, strongly reinforced by his experience of the Civil War. The latter marked an attempt to found a 'science of politics' grounded in the principles of enquiry pioneered by Galileo and Harvey.
Leviathan
[UB18] Penguin pbk **£4.99**
[UB19] Dent pbk **£2.95**
OAKESHOTT, MICHAEL
Hobbes on Civil Association
[UB21] Blackwell pbk **£7.50**
TUCK
Hobbes
In the Oxford *Past Master* series.
[UB23] Oxford pbk **£3.95**

LOCKE, JOHN (1632 - 1704)
One of the undisputed fathers of modern Liberalism, Locke's works span its central themes: constitutional government, natural rights, private property - and toleration.
Second Treatise of Government
[UB24] H Davidson pbk **£3.75**
Two Treatises of Government
(Ed. Laslett, Peter)
Laslett's introduction places the *Treatises* in their historical and political context, and assesses Locke's attitude to the Glorious Revolution of 1688.
[UB25] Dent pbk **£2.95**
CRANSTON, M.
John Locke: A Biography
[UB26] Oxford pbk **£5.95**
DUNN, JOHN
Locke
[UB27] Oxford pbk **£3.50**
Political Thought of John Locke
[UB28] Cambridge pbk **£11.95**
JENKINS & JOHN
Understanding Locke
[UB29] Edinburgh UP pbk **£8.50**
PARRY, GERAINT
John Locke
[UB30] Unwin Hyman pbk **£8.95**
YOLTON, JOHN W.
A Locke Reader
[UB31] Cambridge pbk **£9.95**
John Locke: An Introduction
[UB32] Blackwell pbk **£8.95**

ROUSSEAU, JEAN-JACQUES (1712 - 1778)
Rousseau's ideas have influenced many currents of political thought - radical democratic, socialist, anarchist, populist-nationalist. This extraordinary fertility can be traced partly to the ambiguity which cloaks his central innovation: the *volonté générale*, an attempt to reconcile the antagonism between state sovereignty and the natural rights of citizens by redefining sovereignty in terms of the General Will.

Confessions (Trans Cohen, J.M.)
[UB33] Penguin pbk **£5.99**
Discourse on the Origins of Inequality
(Trans. Cranston, M.)
[UB34] Penguin pbk **£2.99**
Political Writings (Ed. Ritter & Bondanella)
[UB35] Norton pbk **£5.95**
The Indispensable Rousseau
(Ed. Mason, John Hope)
[UB36] Quartet pbk **£5.95**
The Social Contract
[UB37] Penguin pbk **£2.99**
GILDEN
Rousseau's Social Contract:
The Design of the Argument
[UB38] Chicago UP pbk **£6.25**
MILLER, JAMES
Rousseau: Dreamer of Democracy
[UB39] Yale UP pbk **£9.95**
SHKLAR, JUDITH
Men and Citizens: Study of Rousseau's
Social Thought
[UB40] Cambridge hbk **£10.95**

BURKE, EDMUND (1729 - 1797)
The father of conservatism in British political
thought, Burke expounded both a conception of
political change and a model of representative
democracy. The former involved an organic notion of
the political order in which conscious revolutionary
projects were held to disrupt the evolutionary capacity
of the state to accommodate new social forces. The
latter stressed the right and duty of elected
representatives, once elected, to act according to their
best judgement rather than the immediate desires of
their electors.
Reflections on the Revolution in
France: Selected Works
(Ed. O'Brien, Conor Cruise)
[UB41] Penguin pbk **£4.99**
HAMPSHER-MONK, IAIN (ED)
The Political Philosophy of
Edmund Burke
A new edition of this student reader, with an
introduction setting out the political and intellectual
background to Burke's writings.
[UB42] Longman pbk **£6.95**
MACPHERSON, C.B.
Burke
In the Oxford *Past Master* series.
[UB43] Oxford pbk **£1.95**

PAINE, THOMAS (1737 - 1809)
A key figure, not as a philosopher but as a
communicator of radical ideas. An ardent supporter of
the French and American revolutions, Paine wrote
pamphlets and treatises advocating political liberty
and the emancipation of slaves and women. His
writings (in colloquial, plain-speaking prose) became
one of the key influences on the Radical movement
after his death.
A Thomas Paine Reader
(Ed. Foot & Kramnick)
[UB45] Penguin pbk **£5.99**
Age of Reason
[UB46] Citadel pbk **£4.95**
Common Sense
Published in 1776, **Common Sense** is a plea for
American independence. There were 25 editions in its
first year alone.
[UB47] Penguin pbk **£2.99**
Rights of Man
A vigorous attack on the monarchy, the system of
hereditary wealth and Burke's critique of the
revolution in France, for which he was elected to the
National Assembly in France, and outlawed in
Britain.
[UB48] Citadel pbk **£3.95**
[UB49] Penguin pbk **£3.50**

AYER, A.J.
Thomas Paine
[UB50] Faber pbk **£4.99**
PHILIP, M.
Paine
In the Oxford *Past Master* series.
[UB51] Oxford pbk **£3.95**

MILL, JOHN STUART (1806 - 1873)
Mill is best known for his development and
refinement (in **Utilitarianism**, 1863) of Bentham's
'Utilitarian' views, which had advocated that the
greatest happiness of the greatest number should be
the first principle of social organisation. Perhaps of
greater importance, however, was his attempt to
reconcile the freedom of the individual with the need
to maintain social order. His prescription of a minimal
coercive state apparatus to guarantee fundamental
rights is a classic of liberal individualist thought.
On Bentham and Coleridge
[UB52] Cambridge pbk **£7.95**
On Liberty
[UB53] Penguin pbk **£2.99**
On Liberty (Ed. Spitz, David)
[UB54] Norton pbk **£4.95**
With 'Representative Government' and 'Subjection of
Women'.
[UB55] Oxford pbk **£5.95**
On Politics and Society
[UB56] Fontana pbk **£4.95**
Utilitarianism
Together with **On Liberty** and **Considerations on**
Representative Government.
[UB57] Dent pbk **£4.50**
Utilitarianism and Other Essays
[UB58] Penguin pbk **£4.99**
GRAY, JOHN
Mill on Liberty: A Defence
[UB60] Routledge hbk **£20.00**
HALLIDAY
John Stuart Mill
[UB61] Allen & Unwin pbk **£5.95**
MCCLOSKEY
John Stuart Mill: A Critical Study
[UB62] Papermac pbk **£3.95**
RYAN, ALAN
The Philosophy of John Stuart Mill
[UB63] Macmillan pbk **£9.95**
THOMAS, W.
Mill
In the Oxford *Past Master* series.
[UB64] Oxford pbk **£3.95**

MARX, KARL (1818 - 1883)
Many of the volumes listed below are in the Pelican
Marx library: prepared in association with the *New
Left Review*, they are probably the most accessible
edition of Marx's major works available in English.
Each volume is edited and introduced by
distinguished writers in the field of Marxist studies,
who situate the texts both within Marx's *oeuvre* and
within the political context of the time. Each volume
includes a comprehensive chronology of the
publications of works by Marx and Engels.
Early Writings
This volume includes a number of pieces crucial to
any understanding of Marx's work. The introduction
to the **Contribution to the Critique of Hegel's**
Philosophy of Right (1843-4) contains Marx's first
identification of the proletariat as the universal class
whose interests are identified with revolution. The
Appendix reproduces both the famous **Theses on**
Feuerbach (1845) and the **Preface to A Contribution**
to the Critique of Political Economy - the latter is
often held to comprise the most succinct statement of
the premises of historical materialism. Finally, the full
text is included of the **1844 Manuscripts** (also known
as the **Economic and Philosophical Manuscripts**),
seen by many as an early humanist phase of Marx's

thought. Whether Marx broke decisively from this
humanist paradigm in his mature writings has been a
point of furious debate within Marxist scholarship and
politics. Also included are the **Critique of Hegel's**
Doctrine of the State (1843) and **On the Jewish**
Question (1843).
[UB69] Penguin pbk **£6.95**
Capital Vol 1
With an extensive introduction by Ernest Mandel.
[UB65] Penguin pbk **£9.95**
Capital Vol 2
[UB66] Penguin pbk **£9.95**
Capital Vol 3
[UB67] Penguin pbk **£9.95**
Communist Manifesto
Issued on the eve of the 1848 revolutionary
upheavals, the **Communist Manifesto** contains some
of the most powerful, though simplified, formulations
of Marx's and Engels' analysis of the rise and
anticipated collapse of capitalism.
[UB68] Penguin pbk **£2.50**
Grundrisse: Foundations of the
Critique of Political Economy
A rough draft of **Capital**, often used as an
abridgement of the central arguments.
[UB70] Penguin pbk **£7.95**
Karl Marx: A Reader (Ed. Elster, Jon)
[UB71] Cambridge pbk **£7.95**
Political Writings Vol 1:
The Revolutions of 1848
Includes the full test of the **Communist Manifesto**,
and the series of articles from the *Neue Rheinische
Zeitung* in which Marx interpreted the significance of
the 1848 uprising in Vienna, Berlin and Prague.
Edited and introduced by David Fernbach.
[UB72] Penguin pbk **£6.99**
Political Writings Vol 2: Surveys
from Exile
Includes **The Eighteenth Brumaire of Louis**
Bonaparte (a crucial source of Marxian views on the
state), **The Class Struggles in France**, and articles on
Britain, India, China and the American Civil War.
Edited and introduced by David Fernbach.
[UB73] Penguin pbk **£6.99**
Political Writings Vol 3: The First
International and After
Includes speeches and documents relating to Marx's
involvement in the First International, letters on
Germany, Ireland and the Franco-Prussian War, **The
Civil War in France** and the famous **Critique of the
Gotha Programme** - where Marx came nearest to
speculation on the political organisation of a future
communist society. Edited and introduced by David
Fernbach.
[UB74] Penguin pbk **£6.99**
Portable Karl Marx (Ed. Kamenka, E.)
Edited, introduced and partly translated by Eugene
Kamenka, this includes a wide selection of Marx's
most important writings, a lengthy biographical and
expository introduction, and extensive chronology of
Marx's life and publications, a collection of
biographical documentation and a useful glossary of
key terms.
[UB75] Penguin pbk **£5.99**
Selected Writings (Ed. McLellan, D.)
Probably the best one-volume selection of extracts
from Marx's writings - by the author of leading
introductory commentaries on many aspects of
Marx's thought.
[UB76] Oxford pbk **£9.95**
ALTHUSSER, LOUIS
For Marx
'In 1845, Marx broke radically with every theory that
based history and politics on an essence of man...This
rupture with every... humanism is no secondary detail;
it is Marx's scientific discovery.' (**For Marx**).
Althusser's declared goal of reconstructing the
scientific claims of dialectical materialism fuelled a
heated debate in the Western left which lasted well

over a decade. The essays in this volume introduce the concepts at the heart of the Althusserian controversy: the 'problematics' of the younger and older Marx, the 'epistemological break' and the claim for a Marxian theoretical anti-humanism.
[UB77] Verso pbk **£8.95**
AVINERI, S.
The Social and Political Thought of Karl Marx
Avineri relates Marx's thought firmly to its Hegelian context, and argues strongly against the notion that Marx broke decisively from the humanist concerns of the *1844 Manuscripts*.
[UB78] Cambridge pbk **£8.95**
BREWER, ANTHONY
Guide to Marx's 'Capital'
Designed to be read side by side with Marx's text, this volume provides a chapter by chapter guide, explaining key terms and clarifying the central argument.
[UB79] Cambridge pbk **£8.95**
CARVER, T.
Marx's Social Theory
An introduction to Marx's theory of social formations and historical change, focusing on the classic formulation in the *1859 Preface*.
[UB80] Oxford pbk **£4.50**
COHEN, G.A.
Karl Marx's Theory of History: A Defence
A rigorous and systematic defence of historical materialism from an analytical Marxist perspective.
[UB81] Oxford pbk **£8.95**
ELSTER, JON
Introduction to Marx
[UB82] Cambridge pbk **£6.95**
GERAS, NORMAN
Marx and Human Nature: Refutation of a Legend
Implicitly a polemic against the Althusserian denial of a consistent Marxian concept of human nature, Geras's stimulating argument is built around a close analysis of the sixth of the famous *Theses on Feuerbach*.
[UB83] Verso pbk **£5.95**
MCLELLAN, DAVID
Karl Marx: His Life and Thought
McLellan's still growing oeuvre on Marx comprises an outstanding resource of readable introductions, lucid explication and wide reference. Each volume

Karl Marx (Picture: British Museum)

also includes an invaluable bibliography for further reading. This volume contains a full-length biography.
[UB84] Macmillan pbk **£8.95**
Marx
In the Fontana *Modern Masters* series.
[UB85] Fontana pbk **£3.95**
Marx before Marxism
Covers the development of Marx's thought up to and including the *1844 Manuscripts*.
[UB86] Macmillan pbk **£3.95**
Marxism after Marx
Traces the broad development of Marxist thought and politics over three continents up to the present, by focusing on the major schools and revolutionary ideologies. Can be read either as a sustained intellectual narrative or as a work of reference.
[UB87] Macmillan pbk **£7.95**
Marxism and Religion
[UB88] Macmillan pbk **£9.95**
The Thought of Karl Marx
First published in 1971, this volume has long been a standard introductory textbook on Marx.
[UB89] Macmillan pbk **£5.95**
The Young Hegelians and Karl Marx
A detailed and admirably clear account of the philosophical school which was the intellectual context of Marx's early thinking. The only readily accessible work on this for students.
[UB90] Macmillan pbk **£3.95**
MILIBAND, R.
Marxism and Politics
A lucid description of what is essential to Marxist politics, which is also (among much else) a close exegesis of Marx's writings on class power and the state.
[UB91] Oxford pbk **£5.95**
SINGER, PETER
Marx
In the Oxford *Past Master* series.
[UB92] Oxford pbk **£3.50**
SOWELL, T.
Marxism
An excellent brief introduction to the economic and historical dimensions of Marx's thought.
[UB93] Unwin Hyman pbk **£4.95**
THOMAS, P.
Karl Marx and the Anarchists
[UB94] Routledge pbk **£9.95**
WOLFF, ROBERT PAUL
Understanding Marx
[UB95] Blackwell hbk **£29.95**

ENGELS, FREDERICH (1820 - 1895)
It was Engels who coined the phrases 'historical materialism', 'materialist interpretation of history' and 'false consciousness'. *Anti-Duhring* constitutes the first systematic exposition of the Marxist position. His writings form the basis for the dialectical materialist ideology informing the Soviet state. But the crude positivism with which he has been associated in the West as a result of this is now being recognised as a misrepresentation.
Anti-Duhring
[UB96] Lawrence & W pbk **£3.95**
Origin of the Family, Private Property and the State
[UB97] Penguin pbk **£3.95**
The Condition of the Working Class in England (Kiernan, V.)
Industrial Manchester in the early 1840s. Highlights the material and human waste of capitalism, and boldly states the need for collective control of the means of production.
[UB98] Penguin pbk **£4.50**
CARVER, T.
Engels
In the Oxford *Past Master* series.
[UB99] Oxford pbk **£1.95**

MCLELLAN, DAVID
Engels
In the Fontana *Modern Masters* series.
[UB100] Fontana pbk **£6.99**

LENIN, VLADIMIR ILYICH (1870 - 1924)
The central figure in the development of Marxism in the 20th century. Within his contribution to Marxist political thought, three themes stand out in particular: his development of the idea of the vanguard party and its relationship to the proletariat (*What is to be Done?*, 1920); his analysis of the growing contradictions within world capitalism leading to world war and imminent revolution (*Imperialism: The Highest Stage of Capitalism*, 1916); and his polemic on the need for a violent overthrow of the state and the establishment of the 'Dictatorship of the Proletariat' (*State and Revolution*, 1917).
Essential Works (Ed. Christian, Henry)
[UB101] Dover pbk **£5.90**
What is to be Done? (Ed. Service, R.)
Includes an extensive biographical and explanatory introduction by Robert Service.
[UB102] Penguin pbk **£3.95**
HARDING, NEIL
Lenin's Political Thought
This is the best single study of Lenin's political thought available.
[UB103] Macmillan pbk **£17.50**
LANE, DAVID
Leninism: A Sociological Interpretation
[UB104] Cambridge pbk **£3.00**
LUKACS, G.
Lenin: A Study of the Unity of His Thought
A brief philosophical interpretation.
[UB105] Verso pbk **£5.95**
TUCKER, ROBERT C. (ED)
Lenin Anthology
[UB107] Norton pbk **£8.50**

TROTSKY, LEON (1879 - 1940)
Russian Marxist and revolutionary, leader of the October Uprising and the revolution that followed. Banished in 1929 and assassinated in Mexico in 1940, probably on the orders of Stalin. Famous for his *Theory of Permanent Revolution*.
Permanent Revolution (and 'Results and Prospects') (Ed. Pearce, B.)
[UB108] Pathfinder pbk **£5.75**
The Revolution Betrayed
(Trans. Eastman, M.)
[UB109] Pathfinder pbk **£5.75**
DEUTSCHER, I.
The Prophet Armed: Leon Trotsky 1879 - 1921
[UB110] Oxford pbk **£6.95**
The Prophet Unarmed: Leon Trotsky 1921 - 1929
[UB111] Oxford pbk **£6.95**
The Prophet Outcast: Leon Trotsky 1929 - 1940
[UB112] Oxford pbk **£6.95**
HALLAS, DUNCAN
Trotsky's Marxism
[UB113] Pluto P pbk **£2.50**
KNEI-PAZ, BARACH
Social and Political Thought of Leon Trotsky
[UB114] Oxford hbk **£12.50**

GRAMSCI, ANTONIO
Gramsci's writings have been seen as a basis of the major non-Leninist alternative tradition of Marxist politics. Whereas Lenin saw the state unequivocally as the repressive apparatus of the ruling class, requiring violent overthrow, Gramsci redefined it to include its consensual, or hegemonic aspects. The struggle for socialist transformation may therefore be

Antonio Gramsci (Picture: The Communist Party Library)

advanced not by a 'frontal attack' on the state, but by 'trench warfare' in which the state's legitimacy is undermined by the construction of an alternative, socialist, hegemony.

A Gramsci Reader (Ed. Forgacs, D.)
An accessible introductory selection for anyone beginning to read Gramsci.
[UB115] Lawrence & W pbk **£8.95**

Prison Notebooks
Covering a vast array of material, most of Gramsci's central ideas are to be found in the notebooks.
[UB116] Lawrence & W pbk **£6.95**

Selections from Cultural Writings
[UB117] Lawrence & W pbk **£6.95**

Selections from Political Writings 1910 - 1920
[UB118] Lawrence & W pbk **£4.95**

Selections from Political Writings 1921 - 1926
[UB119] Lawrence & W pbk **£6.95**

BOGGS, CARL
Gramsci's Marxism
[UB120] Pluto P pbk **£4.95**

FEMIA, JOSEPH V.
Gramsci's Political Thought
Hegemony, consciousness and the revolutionary process.
[UB121] Oxford pbk **£9.95**

JOLL, JAMES
Gramsci
A readable introduction to an increasingly influential thinker.
[UB122] Fontana pbk **£1.95**

SASSON, ANNE SHOWSTACK
Approaches to Gramsci (Ed)
[UB123] Writers & R pbk **£5.95**

Gramsci's Politics
Centred on Gramsci's theory of the state, this study forms an ideal introduction to his work.
[UB124] Hutchinson pbk **£7.95**

SIMON
Gramsci's Political Thought: An Introduction
[UB125] Lawrence & W pbk **£4.95**

SPRIANO
Antonio Gramsci and the Party: The Prison Years
[UB126] Lawrence & W pbk **£4.95**

HAYEK, FRIEDRICH AUGUST (1899 -)
One of the most distinguished and controversial thinkers of modern times. No friend of the Left in politics, Hayek is often viewed as the guru of the New Right. A proponent of liberalism in a classical sense, and an advocate of free market economies, he views capitalism as the protector of individual liberties. While his **Road to Serfdom** (1945) warned of the totalitarian consequences of the application of egalitarian and collectivist principle, his **Constitution of Liberty** (1961) seeks constitutional foundations for the liberal capitalist state. Elsewhere in his writings, he ranges freely through philosophy and intellectual history.

The Constitution of Liberty
Seeks constitutional foundations for the capitalist state.
[UB127] Routledge pbk **£9.95**

The Road to Serfdom
His most accessible work. A critique of economic planning, resting on the notion that totalitarianism is the inevitable unintended consequence of egalitarian and collectivist principles.
[UB128] Routledge pbk **£5.50**

BUTLER, EAMONN
Hayek: A Study of His Life and Work
[UB129] MT Smith pbk **£5.95**

GRAY, JOHN
Hayek on Liberty
The definitive account of his work.
[UB130] Blackwell pbk **£9.95**

Ideologies

Marxism

ANDERSON, P.
Arguments within English Marxism
An extended analysis of, and debate with, the work of E.P. Thompson.
[UB131] Verso pbk **£7.95**

Considerations on Western Marxism
A compelling brief account of the intellectual history of Western Marxism, focusing on the contributions of Lukacs, Korsch, Gramsci, Adorno, Marcuse, Benjamin, Sartre, Althusser, Della Volpe and Colletti.
[UB132] Verso pbk **£5.95**

In the Tracks of Historical Materialism
In this short book, Anderson extends his account of the development of Western Marxism beyond the mid-70s, where **Considerations** broke off. He goes on to provide a powerful critique of the major structuralist and post-structuralist philosophical challenges to historical materialism, concentrating on Foucault, Derrida, Lacan and Habermas.
[UB133] Verso pbk **£5.95**

ARONSON, RONALD
Dialectics of Disaster
Powerfully argues that the disasters of the 20th century, past and impending, challenge the rationalist assumptions of historical materialist analysis.
[UB134] Verso pbk **£7.95**

BAHRO, R.
From Red to Green
These interviews with *New Left Review* articulate the thinking behind Bahro's remarkable political odyssey, from loyal oppositionist in East Germany, to activist in the West German peace movement, to spokesman of the fundamentalist wing of the German Greens.
[UB135] Verso pbk **£7.95**

The Alternative in Eastern Europe
[UB136] Verso pbk **£9.95**

BENTLEY, JAMES
Between Marx and Christ
A history of the dialogue between Marxism and Christianity which underpins modern 'Liberation Theology'.
[UB137] Verso pbk **£5.95**

BUHLE, PAUL
Marxism in the USA
A balanced historical account of the strengths and weaknesses which have characterised the history of American Marxism.
[UB138] Verso pbk **£8.95**

COHEN, STEPHEN
Bukharin and the Bolshevik Revolution: A Political Biography
To many, Bukharin represents the lost alternative to Stalinism in the historical development of the Bolshevik revolution. Much more than a biography of one man, Cohen's narrative presents an outstanding reconstruction of the thought and experience of the early Bolshevik intelligentsia.
[UB139] Oxford pbk **£4.95**

COLLINS, HUGH
Marxism and Law
[UB140] Oxford pbk **£4.95**

FROLICH, P.
Rosa Luxemburg
[UB141] Pluto P pbk **£6.50**

GERAS, NORMAN
The Legacy of Rosa Luxemburg
The clearest and most comprehensive account available of Luxemburg's thought.
[UB143] Verso pbk **£7.95**

HELD, DAVID
Introduction to Critical Theory: From Horkheimer to Habermas
A clearly-written introductory survey of the Frankfurt School.
[UB144] Hutchinson pbk **£10.95**

JESSOP, BOB
The Capitalist State
[UB145] Blackwell pbk **£8.95**

KOLAKOWSKI, LESZEK
Main Currents of Marxism: Its Rise, Growth and Dissolution
Vol 1: The Founders
[UB146] Oxford pbk **£7.95**
Vol 2: The Golden Age
[UB147] Oxford pbk **£7.95**
Vol 3: Breakdown
[UB148] Oxford pbk **£7.95**

KUBALKOVA, V. & CRUIKSHANK, A.
Marxism and International Relations
[UB149] Oxford pbk **£6.95**

LARRAIN, JORGE
Marxism and Ideology
[UB150] Macmillan pbk **£9.50**

LICHTHEIM, GEORGE
A Short History of Socialism
[UB151] Fontana pbk **£2.95**
Marxism
[UB152] Routledge pbk **£9.95**

LUKES, STEVEN (ED)
Marxism and Morality
[UB153] Oxford pbk **£4.95**

MCLELLAN, DAVID
Marxism: Essential Writings
A collection of the major statements of classical and contemporary Marxism, with introductions and bibliographies.
[UB156] Oxford pbk **£9.95**
The Essential Left
[UB157] Unwin Hyman pbk **£4.95**

MERQUIOR, J.G.
Western Marxism
[UB158] Paladin pbk **£3.95**

MILIBAND, RALPH
Class Power and State Power
[UB159] Verso pbk **£6.95**

ROEMER, JOHN (ED)
Analytical Marxism
[UB161] Cambridge pbk **£8.95**

THOMPSON, E.P.
An outstanding British historian, essayist and pamphleteer, and a leading figure in the first New Left, Thompson's position has shifted considerably from the Marxism of earlier years.
Poverty of Theory and Other Essays
Includes the passionate attack on Althusser, and *An Open Letter to Leszek Kolakowski*, the fullest statement Thompson has made of his own position.
[UB162] Merlin pbk **£7.95**

TIMPANARO, SEBASTIANO
On Materialism
[UB163] Verso pbk **£8.95**

WILLIAMS, RAYMOND
Politics and Letters
[UB164] Verso pbk **£10.95**

WOOD, ELLEN MEIKSENS
The Retreat from Class
[UB165] Verso pbk **£8.95**

Liberalism

ARBLASTER, ANTHONY
The Rise and Decline of Western Liberalism
[UB166] Blackwell pbk **£9.95**

Friedrich August Hayek, author of *The Constitution of Liberty* (Routledge pbk **£9.95**)

BERLIN, ISAIAH
Against the Current: Essays in the History of Ideas
[UB167] Oxford pbk **£4.95**
Four Essays on Liberty
A classic philosophical work.
[UB168] Oxford pbk **£5.95**

BLAKE, LORD ROBERT
The Conservative Party from Peel to Thatcher
[UB169] Fontana pbk **£5.95**

BOBBIO, N.
The Future of Democracy
Argues for a radical extension of liberal representative democracy beyond political institutions and into the workplace and the sphere of public provision.
[UB170] Polity P pbk **£7.95**

BOSANQUET, N.
After the New Right
[UB171] Heinemann pbk **£8.95**

CRANSTON, MAURICE
Philosophers and Pamphleteers: Political Theorists of the Englightenment
Highly readable biographical and expository chapters on Montesquieu, Voltaire, Rousseau, Diderot, Holbach and Condorcet.
[UB172] Oxford pbk **£4.95**

DAHL, R.
Dilemmas of Pluralist Democracy
Explores the place of independent organisations and interest groups within the democratic state.
[UB173] Yale UP pbk **£9.95**

ECCLESHALL, R.
British Liberalism: Liberal Thought from the 1640s to the 1980s
An invaluable documentary history and reader in liberalism, which includes a useful introduction defining the broad historical and theoretical characteristics of liberalism.
[UB174] Longman pbk **£6.50**

ELLIS, ADRIAN & KUMAR, KRISHAN
Dilemmas of Liberal Thought
[UB175] Tavistock pbk **£13.95**

FREEDEN, MICHAEL
The New Liberalism
[UB176] Oxford pbk **£10.25**

GRAY, JOHN
Liberalism
[UB177] Open UP pbk **£5.50**

GREEN, DAVID G.
The New Right: The Counter Revolution in Political, Economic & Social Thought
A useful introduction to the diverse themes and strands in 'New Right' thought. Comprehensive and up-to-date, it includes a survey of the impact of the new liberalism on the Thatcher and Reagan governments, and the gap between new liberal thought and practical politics.
[UB178] Wheatsheaf pbk **£9.95**

GREEN, T.H.
Lectures on the Principles of Political Obligation and Other Writings
(Ed. Harris & Murrow)
[UB179] Cambridge pbk **£10.95**

HALL, JOHN A.
Liberalism: Politics, Ideology and the Market
[UB180] Paladin pbk **£3.95**

HOWARD, MICHAEL
War and the Liberal Conscience
In a stimulating series of polemical lectures, Howard traces the history of the liberal anti-war tradition whose ideas remain central to the modern peace movement.
[UB181] Oxford pbk **£3.95**

LEVITAS, R. (ED)
The Ideology of the New Right
A critical analysis of the major ideological aspects of the neo-conservative revival.
[UB182] Polity P pbk **£7.95**

LUKES, S.
Individualism
[UB183] Blackwell pbk **£8.95**

MACPHERSON, C.B.
Democratic Theory
[UB184] Oxford pbk **£8.95**
Life and Times of Liberal Democracy
An excellent tightly-reasoned analysis of liberal democracy.
[UB185] Oxford pbk **£4.95**
The Political Theory of Possessive Individualism
[UB186] Oxford pbk **£5.95**
The Rise and Fall of Economic Justice and Other Essays
[UB187] Oxford pbk **£5.95**

MAGEE, BRYAN
Popper
[UB188] Fontana pbk **£2.95**

MANNING, DAVID JOHN
Liberalism
[UB189] Dent pbk **£3.95**

NOZICK, ROBERT
Anarchy, State and Utopia
[UB190] Blackwell pbk **£9.95**

RAWLS, JOHN
Theory of Justice
[UB191] Oxford pbk **£7.95**

REISS, HANS (ED)
Kant's Political Writings
(Trans. Nisbet, H.B.)
[UB192] Cambridge pbk **£10.95**

SANDEL, MICHAEL J. (ED)
Liberalism and its Critics
[UB193] Blackwell pbk **£8.50**
Liberalism and the Limits of Justice
A discussion of philosophical dilemmas of modern liberalism focusing on a critique of Rawls's theory of justice.
[UB194] Cambridge pbk **£7.95**

SHAPIRO, IAN
The Evolution of Rights in Liberal Theory
A spirited exploration of the difficulties facing attempts to ground modern notions of rights and justice by recourse to the liberal philosophical tradition.
[UB195] Cambridge hbk **£10.95**

WEIL, S.
Oppression and Liberty
[UB196] Routledge pbk **£5.95**

Conservatism

The Portable Conservative Reader
[UB197] Penguin pbk **£6.99**

ALLISON, L.
Right Principles
[UB198] Blackwell pbk **£9.95**

NISBET, R.
Conservatism
[UB199] Open UP pbk **£5.50**

O'SULLIVAN, NOEL
Conservatism
A fascinating account of the French, German and British traditions together with an assessment of Conservative ideology in the 20th century.
[UB200] Dent pbk **£3.95**

OAKSHOTT, M.
On History
[UB201] Blackwell pbk **£7.95**

SCRUTON, ROGER
The Meaning of Conservatism
[UB203] Macmillan pbk **£7.95**
Untimely Tracts
[UB204] Macmillan hbk **£18.95**

Anarchism

BAKUNIN, M.
God and the State (Ed. Avrich, Paul)
[UB205] Dover pbk **£3.00**

GODWIN, WILLIAM
Anarchist Writings (Ed. Marshall, Peter)
[UB207] Freedom P pbk **£4.00**
Enquiry Concerning Political Justice
(Ed. Kramnick, Isaac)
[UB208] Penguin pbk **£6.99**

JOLL, J.
The Anarchists
[UB209] Routledge pbk **£8.95**

MILLER, DAVID
Anarchism
A popular student text.
[UB210] Dent pbk **£4.95**

TAYLOR, M.
Community, Anarchy and Liberty
[UB211] Cambridge pbk **£8.50**

WOODCOCK, GEORGE (ED)
The Anarchist Reader
[UB212] Fontana pbk **£4.95**

General Political Thought

ANDERSON, B.
Imagined Communities
A discussion of the phenomenon of nationalism.
[UB213] Verso pbk **£6.95**

ARBLASTER, A.
Democracy
[UB214] Open UP pbk **£5.50**

ARENDT, HANNAH (1906 - 1975)
Arendt's best known and most controversial work is *The Origins of Totalitarianism*, which sought the roots of totalitarianism in the historical replacement of classes by the masses,
and the emergence of a mass society. Her equation of Stalinism with Nazism was a key influence on 'the totalitarian school' which dominated American political science during the era of the Cold War.
Eichmann in Jerusalem
[UB215] Penguin pbk **£5.99**
On Revolution
Argues that the 'lost treasure' of the revolutionary tradition is the engagement in free political action.
[UB216] Penguin pbk **£5.99**
The Origins of Totalitarianism
[UB217] Deutsch pbk **£6.95**

BAKER, J.
Arguing for Equality
[UB218] Verso pbk **£6.95**

BARRY, N.
Introduction to Modern Political Thought
A comprehensive introduction organised around analyses of key issues in the discipline, including the State, Law, Justice, Authority and Power etc.
[UB219] Macmillan pbk **£7.95**

BAUMAN, Z.
Freedom
[UB220] Open UP pbk **£5.50**

BERKI, R.N.
Security and Society
[UB221] Dent pbk **£7.95**
Socialism
[UB222] Dent pbk **£5.95**

BERRY, C.J.
Human Nature
An analysis of the history and use of this concept in political argument.
[UB223] Macmillan pbk **£6.95**

BREUILLY
Nationalism and the State
[UB225] Manchester UP pbk **£7.95**

BROWN, ALAN
Modern Political Philosophy
This introductory volume includes full chapters on the thought of Rawls and Nozick.
[UB226] Penguin pbk **£4.50**

CLAUSEWITZ, KARL VON
On War
A classic of strategic theory and an influential study of the relationship between war and politics.
[UB227] Penguin pbk **£4.99**

CONNOLLY, WILLIAM (ED)
Legitimacy and the State
Excerpts and essays by major writers from Marx to Foucault.
[UB228] Blackwell pbk **£7.95**
Terms of Political Discourse
[UB229] M Robertson pbk **£7.95**

CRICK, BERNARD
In Defence of Politics
A central and classic work - tough-minded and thoughtful - by the distinguished biographer of George Orwell.
[UB230] Penguin pbk **£4.50**

CRICK, BERNARD & CRICK, THOMAS
What is Politics?
[UB231] Arnold pbk **£3.50**

DUNLEAVY, P. & O'LEARY, B.
Theories of the State: The Politics of Liberal Democracy
A popular textbook which reviews the major contending approaches to the role of the state. Perspectives outlined include: Pluralist, New Right, Elite Theory, Marxist, Neo-Pluralist.
[UB232] Macmillan pbk **£9.95**

DUNN, JOHN
Modern Revolutions
An introduction to the analysis of a political phenomenon which includes an examination of over eight different 20th century revolutions.
[UB233] Cambridge pbk **£9.50**
Politics of Socialism
[UB234] Cambridge pbk **£6.95**
Rethinking Modern Political Theory
Essays which explore the historical sources of the weaknesses in modern political theory.
[UB235] Cambridge pbk **£9.95**
Western Political Theory in the Face of the Future
Attempts to dissipate some of the central political superstitions of our day.
[UB236] Cambridge pbk **£7.50**

ECCLESHALL, R. ET AL
Political Ideologies: An Introduction
[UB237] Hutchinson pbk **£7.50**

EVANS, P.; RUESCHEMEYER, D. & SKOCPOL, T. (EDS)
Bringing the State Back In
[UB238] Cambridge pbk **£12.50**

FINE, BOB
Democracy and the Rule of Law
[UB239] Pluto P pbk **£7.95**

FINLEY, MOSES I.
Democracy Ancient and Modern
The author is a leading historian of the Ancient world.
[UB240] Hogarth pbk **£5.95**

FRANKEL, B.
The Post Industrial Utopians
A survey of the major theorists of post-industrial society.
[UB241] Polity P pbk **£8.95**

GAMBLE, A.
An Introduction to Modern Social and Political Thought
[UB242] Macmillan pbk **£7.95**

GELLNER, ERNEST
Nations and Nationalism
A stimulating theory of nationalism which argues that it is rooted in the functional needs of modernisation.
[UB243] Blackwell pbk **£7.95**

GIBBONS, M. (ED)
Interpreting Politics
[UB244] Blackwell pbk **£8.95**

GODWIN, B. & TAYLOR, K.
Politics of Utopia: A Study in Theory and Practice
[UB245] Hutchinson pbk **£8.50**

HELD, DAVID
Models of Democracy
An excellent and wide-ranging survey of the historical development and the present state of

SOCIAL SCIENCES

democratic theory. Discusses major thinkers including Plato, Hobbes, Mill, Marx, Weber, and Hayek.
[UB246] Polity P pbk **£7.95**
Political Theory and the Modern State
A review of the major debates in political science on the nature of the state.
[UB247] Polity P pbk **£8.95**

HELD, DAVID & POLITT, C.
New Forms of Democracy
[UB248] Sage pbk **£7.95**

HELD, DAVID ET AL
States and Societies
This Open University reader provides the student with a series of extracts from major political thinkers on the state (from Machiavelli to Hayek), followed by six sections of modern contributions covering almost every aspect of state behaviour.
[UB249] M Robertson pbk **£7.95**

HOWARD, MICHAEL
Clausewitz
In the Oxford *Past Master* series.
[UB250] Oxford pbk **£2.95**

JORDAN, B.
The State: Authority and Autonomy
[UB251] Blackwell pbk **£9.95**

KEDOURIE, ELIE
Nationalism
[UB252] Hutchinson pbk **£8.95**

KITCHEN, MARTIN
Fascism
A lucid introduction to the ongoing theoretical debates on the nature of fascism.
[UB253] Macmillan pbk **£6.95**

KUPER, ADAM (ED)
Political Science and Political Theory
[UB254] Routledge pbk **£6.50**

LARRAIN, JORGE
Concept of Ideology
A study of the concept of ideology from 18th century French thought, through Marx and Durkheim up to the present.
[UB256] Hutchinson pbk **£8.95**

LESSNOFF, M.
Social Contract
[UB257] Macmillan pbk **£7.95**

LINDLEY, R.
Autonomy
[UB258] Macmillan pbk **£7.95**

LIVELY, JACK
Democracy
[UB259] Blackwell pbk **£8.95**

LUKES, STEVEN (ED)
Power
A lucid and accessible introduction to the nature of power. Includes pieces by Bertrand Russell, Max Weber, Hannah Arendt, J.K. Galbraith and Raymond Aron.
[UB260] Blackwell pbk **£7.95**

MANUEL, FRANK & MANUEL, FRITZIE
Utopian Thought in the Western World
[UB261] Blackwell pbk **£14.95**

MORRIS, WILLIAM (1834 - 1896)
Artist, designer, poet, and socialist, Morris was a man of many talents who exerted a profound influence on his contemporaries, particularly as the founder of the

(anti-industrial) Arts and Crafts movement. *News from Nowhere* has been described as 'a socialist fantasy cast in a dream setting'.
News from Nowhere/Selected Writings & Designs
[UB262] Lawrence & W pbk **£4.95**
Political Writings of William Morris
[UB263] Lawrence & W pbk **£3.95**

QUINTON, ANTHONY
Political Philosophy
An excellent introduction for general reader and student alike.
[UB264] Oxford pbk **£5.95**

RENWICK, ALAN & SWINBURN, IAN
Basic Political Concepts
An introductory 'A' level textbook.
[UB265] Century pbk **£5.25**

RYAN, ALAN
Property and Political Theory
[UB266] Blackwell pbk **£8.95**

SCHUMPETER, JOSEPH
Capitalism, Socialism and Democracy
A famous classic of 20th century social science and modern thought. With great verve and brilliance the various elements of Marx's social theory are expounded - praise is mingled with severe criticism. Seen as a profound sociological analysis particularly for its development of a new and distinctive concept of democracy.
[UB267] Unwin Hyman pbk **£4.95**

SMITH, A.D.
Theories of Nationalism
[UB269] Duckworth pbk **£9.80**

TALMON, J.L.
Origins of Totalitarian Democracy
[UB270] Penguin pbk **£5.95**

VINCENT, ANDREW
Theories of the State
[UB271] Blackwell pbk **£9.95**

WRIGHT, ANTHONY
Socialism: Theories and Practices
[UB272] Oxford pbk **£4.95**

ECONOMICS

Economic Theory

BACKHOUSE, ROGER
A History of Modern Economic Analysis
A comprehensive treatment with the balance given over to modern economic analysis. Backhouse's judicious coverage and accessible style make this an ideal text.
[UC1] Blackwell pbk **£14.95**

BARBER, WILLIAM J.
History of Economic Thought
This is an elementary and readable introduction to the development of economics. By focusing on the major economists in each period, Barber provides a succinct account of classical, Marxist, neo-classical and Keynesian thought.
[UC3] Penguin pbk **£3.95**

BROWN, MICHAEL BARRATT
Models in Political Economy
An original introduction to the diversity of modern economic thought, which examines the basic models of the economy that underlie the diverse schools of analysis.
[UC5] Penguin pbk **£5.95**

CALDWELL, B.J.
Beyond Positivism: Economic Methodology in the 20th Century
A survey of the methodological debates which beset contemporary economic theory.
[UC6] Unwin Hyman pbk **£10.95**

CATEPHORES, GEORGE
An Introduction to Marxist Economics
[UC7] Macmillan pbk **£9.95**

CODDINGTON, A.
Keynesian Economics: The Search for First Principles
Cogently analyses and dissects the main varieties of Keynesian economics.
[UC8] Unwin Hyman pbk **£7.50**

DEANE, PHYLLIS
The Evolution of Economic Ideas
A history of economics which focuses on the discontinuities in the subject that result from the successive policy choices it has faced.
[UC9] Cambridge pbk **£10.95**

DEANE, PHYLLIS & KUPER, JESSICA (EDS)
A Lexicon of Economics
A dictionary of sorts: the entries are fewer but more detailed.
[UC10] Routledge pbk **£9.95**

DOBB, MAURICE
Theories of Value and Distribution since Adam Smith
A noted Marxist account of the break between the classical economics of Smith, Ricardo and Marx and the later neo-classical school.
[UC11] Cambridge pbk **£12.95**

DONALDSON, PETER
Donaldson has presented numerous television programmes on economics, and his books are addressed directly to the general reader. Well-written, clear and enjoyable, they are ideal starting-points.
10 x Economics
[UC12] Penguin pbk **£2.99**
Economics of the Real World
[UC13] Penguin pbk **£4.99**
Question of Economics
[UC14] Penguin pbk **£5.99**
Worlds Apart
[UC15] Penguin pbk **£3.95**

DOW, SHEILA C.
Macroeconomic Thought: A Methodological Approach
A widely-praised study of the methodological foundations of the diverse schools in modern economics.
[UC16] Blackwell pbk **£12.95**

EICHNER, ALFRED S.
Eichner is one of the leading American post-Keynesian economists, in a tradition that attempts to bring Keynes together with the American institutionalists and radical economics.
A Guide to Post-Keynesian Economics
[UC17] Macmillan pbk **£7.95**
Towards a New Economics: Essays in Post-Keynesian and Institutionalist Theory
[UC18] Macmillan pbk **£9.95**

Milton Friedman (Photo: Popperfoto)

Why Economics is Not Yet a Science
[UC19] Macmillan pbk **£9.95**

ELTIS, WALTER
Classical Theory of Economic Growth
A readable and non-technical study of the way economists have examined the sources of economic growth.
[UC20] Macmillan pbk **£9.95**

FINE, BEN
Marx's Capital
A simple introduction to the arguments of *Capital*.
[UC21] Macmillan pbk **£5.95**
Theories of the Capitalist Economy
A Marxist review of the main economic theories of the workings of capitalism.
[UC22] E Arnold pbk **£8.95**

FRIEDMAN, MILTON
Capitalism and Freedom
A collection of Friedman's non-technical papers which in general argue for reduced state intervention and market solutions to economic and social problems.
[UC23] Chicago UP pbk **£6.25**

GALBRAITH, J.K.
A noted populariser of liberal and Keynesian economics.
Almost Everyone's Guide to Economics
[UC25] Penguin pbk **£3.99**
The Affluent Society
[UC27] Penguin pbk **£5.99**
The Great Crash 1929
[UC28] Penguin pbk **£4.99**

GODLEY, W. & CRIPPS, F.
Macroeconomics
Although written as a textbook, this path-breaking account by two leading Cambridge economists is suitable for anyone not put off by simple mathematics.
[UC29] Fontana pbk **£3.95**

GOWLAND, D.
Controlling the Money Supply
Probably the most detailed review of the theory, and especially the practice, behind attempts to control monetary policy.
[UC30] Cr Helm pbk **£7.95**

Money, Inflation and Unemployment
An excellent undergraduate textbook on all aspects of monetary economics.
[UC31] Wheatsheaf pbk **£10.95**

GREEN, PETER & SUTCLIFFE, BOB
The Profit System
A non-technical and comprehensive Marxist guide to the institutions and workings of contemporary capitalism.
[UC32] Penguin pbk **£5.95**

HAHN, FRANK
Equilibrium and Macroeconomics
A collection of the author's non-technical papers on problems of general equilibrium theory and monetary economics.
[UC33] Blackwell pbk **£14.95**
Money and Inflation
Three lectures on the economics of monetarism and rational expectations.
[UC34] Blackwell pbk **£6.95**
Money, Growth and Stability
[UC35] Blackwell pbk **£14.95**

HICKS, SIR JOHN
The Crisis in Keynesian Economics
An early attempt to diagnose the problems in, and propose reformulations of, Keynesian economics by one of the century's leading (maverick) Keynesian economists.
[UC36] Blackwell pbk **£5.95**
The Economics of John Hicks
[UC37] Blackwell pbk **£12.95**

HOLLANDER, S.
Classical Economics
A study of the classical economists by a leading historian of economic ideas.
[UC39] Blackwell pbk **£15.00**

HOWARD, MICHAEL
Modern Theories of Income Distribution
[UC40] Macmillan pbk **£7.95**

HUNT, E.K. & SHERMAN, H.J.
Economics: An Introduction to Traditional and Radical Views
A widely-used radical textbook.
[UC42] Harper & R pbk **£11.95**

KALDOR, NICHOLAS
Further Essays on Applied Economics
[UC43] Duckworth pbk **£9.95**
Further Essays on Economic Theory
[UC44] Duckworth pbk **£9.95**
The Scourge of Monetarism
[UC45] Oxford pbk **£4.95**
THIRLWALL, A.P.
Nicholas Kaldor
The first full-length, comprehensive study of Kaldor's contribution to modern economics.
[UC46] Wheatsheaf pbk **£16.95**

KEYNES, JOHN MAYNARD
The General Theory of Employment Interest and Money
Probably the most important work of economics written this century, Keynes' *General Theory* and the theory of effective demand developed within it constitute a major critique of, and alternative to, orthodox theory.
[UC47] Macmillan pbk **£9.95**
MOGGRIDGE, D.
Keynes
One of the best short accounts of Keynes's work available, written by a leading economic historian.
[UC48] Macmillan pbk **£1.95**

LAIDLER, D.
Monetarist Perspectives
An elementary textbook review of the different doctrines which comprise 'monetarism'.
[UC49] P Allan pbk **£29.50**

MAINWARING, L.
Value and Distribution in Capitalist Economies
Subtitled 'An introduction to Sraffian Economics', this is a pioneering non-mathematical treatment of Sraffian theory.
[UC50] Cambridge pbk **£10.95**

MALTHUS, THOMAS ROBERT
An Essay on the Principles of Population
[UC51] Penguin pbk **£4.99**

O'CONNOR, JAMES
The Meaning of Crisis: A Theoretical Introduction
A non-technical but difficult review of Marxist and radical theories of capitalist crisis.
[UC52] Blackwell pbk **£8.50**

PURDY, DAVID
Social Power and the Labour Market
[UC53] Macmillan pbk **£9.95**

ROWTHORN, R.E.
Capitalism, Conflict and Inflation: Essays in Political Economy
A collection of essays by one of Britain's leading Marxist economists.
[UC54] Lawrence & W pbk **£6.95**

SAMUELSON, PAUL A.
Economics: An Introductory Analysis
The most popular and widely-sold economics textbook ever written.
[UC55] McGraw Hill pbk **£12.50**

SAWYER, M.C.
The Economics of Michal Kalecki
A detailed study of the work of this influential radical Polish economist, which covers Kalecki's work on capitalism and socialism, as well as the problems of development.
[UC56] Macmillan pbk **£10.50**

John Maynard Keynes (Photo: BBC Hulton Picture Library)

SOCIAL SCIENCES

SHAND, A.
The Capitalist Alternative: Introduction to Neo-Austrian Economics
One of the few textbook accounts of this often-neglected stream of economic theory.
[UC57] Wheatsheaf pbk **£10.95**

SHAW, G.K.
Rational Expectations: An Elementary Exposition
A balanced and illuminating introduction to the new economics of rational expectations.
[UC58] Wheatsheaf pbk **£6.95**

SMITH, ADAM
The Wealth of Nations
[UC59] Penguin pbk **£4.99**

THUROW, SCOTT
Zero-Sum Solution: The Route to Economic Growth
A noted liberal American economist offers solutions to the problems of low growth and inflation.
[UC60] Penguin pbk **£3.95**

International Economics

AGNEW, J.
The United States in the World Economy: A Regional Geography
A major survey of the emergence of the US economy to global dominance and its subsequent decline, with a concluding focus on the problems faced by America's world leadership.
[UC61] Cambridge pbk **£9.95**

ALDCROFT, DEREK
A leading economic historian whose work is notable for its readability and its non-technical nature.
From Versailles to Wall Street 1919 - 1980
[UC62] Penguin pbk **£5.99**
The European Economy 1914 - 1980
[UC63] Cr Helm pbk **£8.95**

ARTIS, M. & OSTREY, S.
International Economic Policy Coordination
A discussion of the problems of macroeconomic policy management among the leading Western economies.
[UC64] Routledge pbk **£7.95**

ASHWORTH, W.
A Short History of the International Economy since 1850
A standard and widely used textbook survey.
[UC65] Longman pbk **£7.95**

BALLANCE, R.H.
International Industry and Business
Structural change, industrial policy and industry strategies.
[UC66] Unwin Hyman pbk **£14.95**

BAUER, P.T.
Reality and Rhetoric: Studies in the Economies of Development
A noted exponent of free-market solutions argues for their relevance in the context of the Third World.
[UC67] Weidenfeld pbk **£5.95**

BEENSTOCK, M.
The World Economy in Transition
An influential neoclassical account of the structural changes in the world economy which have produced recession in the West and high growth in the leading Asian economies.
[UC68] Unwin Hyman pbk **£10.95**

BRETT, E.A.
The World Economy since the War: The Politics of Uneven Development
An important radical textbook which looks at international production, trade and monetary relations.
[UC69] Macmillan pbk **£78.95**

CAVES, R.E.
Multinational Enterprise and Economic Analysis
A survey of the orthodox economic literature on the multinationals.
[UC70] Cambridge pbk **£10.95**

EDWARDS, CHRIS
The Fragmented World: Competing Perspectives on Trade, Money and Crisis
A major undergraduate textbook of international economics.
[UC72] Methuen pbk **£9.95**

EL'AGRAA, A.M. (ED)
The Economics of the European Community
One of the best accounts of the institutions, policy making and economic activities of the EC available.
[UC73] P Allan pbk **£14.95**

FOREMAN-PECK, J.
A History of the World Economy: International Economic Relations since 1850
[UC74] Wheatsheaf pbk **£11.95**

FREY, B.S.
International Political Economics
A liberal account of the problems of policy making in the international economy.
[UC76] Blackwell pbk **£12.95**

GEORGE, SUSAN
A Fate Worse than Debt
A radical treatment of the Third World debt crisis, which sees its persistence in terms of Western political resistance to autonomous economic development in the poor countries.
[UC77] Penguin pbk **£4.99**

GILL, S. & LAW, D.
The Global Political Economy: Perspectives, Problems and Policies
[UC78] Wheatsheaf pbk **£12.95**

HARRIS, NIGEL
A Marxist economist noted for his writing on the Third World, Harris writes clearly and provides many illuminating examples.
The End of the Third World
Subtitled 'Newly Industrializing Countries and the Decline of an Ideology'.
[UC82] Penguin pbk **£4.99**

HOOD, N. & YOUNG, S.
The Economics of Multinational Enterprise
[UC83] Longman pbk **£12.50**

HOOGVELT, A. & PUXTY, A.
Multinational Enterprise: An Encyclopaedic Dictionary of Concepts and Terms
[UC84] Macmillan pbk **£8.95**

JENKINS, RHYS
Transnational Corporations and Uneven Development
The internationalisation of capital and the Third World.
[UC85] Methuen pbk **£8.95**

KIDRON, M. & SEGAL, R.
The Book of Business, Money and Power
[UC86] Pan pbk **£3.99**

KINDLEBERGER, CHARLES
The World in Depression: 1929 - 1939
One of the leading American economic historians of the postwar period, Kindleberger's account of the depression pioneered the argument that the absence of world leadership was a fundamental cause of inter-war instability.
[UC87] Penguin pbk **£5.99**

LEVER, HAROLD & HUHNE, CHRISTOPHER
Debt and Danger
A popular account of the international debt crisis by two leading economic commentators.
[UC88] Penguin pbk **£3.95**

LIPIETZ, A
Mirages and Miracles: The Crisis of Global Fordism
A readable example of the influential Marxist theory that the current period is witnessing a fundamental change in the forms of production and consumption.
[UC89] Verso pbk **£8.95**

MADDISON, ANGUS
Phases of Capitalist Development
A path-breaking attempt to examine the historical evidence, in order to isolate and explain the different phases of economic growth from the late 18th century to the present.
[UC90] Oxford pbk **£8.95**

MANDEL, ERNEST
Late Capitalism
Perhaps the major Marxist work of economics written since the War, Mandel provides a history and analysis of capitalism without rival.
[UC91] Verso pbk **£12.95**

MILWARD, ALAN
War, Economy and Society: 1939 - 1945
[UC92] Penguin pbk **£6.95**

MOORE, L.
Growth and Structure of International Trade since the Second World War
[UC93] Wheatsheaf pbk **£12.95**

ODELL, PETER R.
Oil and World Power
A popular outline of the world oil industry written by a leading energy economist.
[UC94] Penguin pbk **£5.99**

PARBONI, R.
The Dollar and its Rivals
A Marxist account of the trade and monetary rivalries between Europe and America which beset the 1970s.
[UC95] Verso pbk **£6.95**

PIORE, M.J. & SABEL, C.F.
The Second Industrial Divide: Possibilities for Prosperity
A very influential statement of the case for developing small-scale, high-technology production in the place of traditional mass production industries.
[UC96] Basic Bks pbk **£8.95**

SEITZ, J.L.
The Politics of Developments
Provides a general review of the problems associated with population growth, food production, energy and environmental issues, and technological development in the Third World.
[UC97] Blackwell pbk **£8.95**

SPERO, J.E.
The Politics of International Economic Relations
One of the standard liberal textbooks.
[UC98] Unwin Hyman pbk **£10.95**

STRANGE, S.
Casino Capitalism
An account of the financial instability which besets the world economy.
[UC99] Blackwell pbk **£9.95**
States and Markets: An Introduction to International Political Economy
A textbook which attempts to span the gap between international economics and international relations.
[UC100] Pinter pbk **£8.95**

SWANN, DENNIS
The Economics of the Common Market
[UC101] Penguin pbk **£6.99**

TOYE, J.
Dilemmas of Development
Reflections on the counter-revolution in development theory and policy.
[UC102] Blackwell pbk **£9.95**

VAN DER WEE, HERMAN
Prosperity and Upheaval: The World Economy 1945 - 1980
A comprehensive study of the causes of postwar growth, the main economic trends and the changes wrought in the international economy.
[UC103] Penguin pbk **£7.95**

WORLD COMMISSION ON ENVIRONMENT & DEVELOPMENT
Our Common Future
The report of the United Nations Bruntland Commission on the ecological implications of current patterns of global development - chilling reading.
[UC104] Oxford pbk **£5.95**

The British Economy

AARONVITCH, S. & SMITH, R.
The Political Economy of British Capitalism: A Marxist Analysis
The best textbook account of the British economy from a radical perspective.
[UC105] McGraw Hill pbk **£13.95**

ALDCROFT, DEREK
Full Employment: The Elusive Goal
A comparison with the unemployment problem in the 1930s. Aldcroft pays particular attention to the regional problem, the difficulties of declining industries, and the current sources of growth.
[UC106] Wheatsheaf pbk **£10.95**
The British Economy
Vol 1: The Years of Turmoil, 1920 - 1951
[UC107] Wheatsheaf hbk **£32.50**
Vol 2: The Growth Failure, 1950 - 1973
[UC108] Wheatsheaf pbk **£9.95**

BARR, N.A.
The Economics of the Welfare State
A comprehensive review of the economics of, and debates around, reform of the welfare state.
[UC109] Weidenfeld pbk **£12.95**

BLACK, J.
The Economics of Modern Britain: An Introduction to Macroeconomics
[UC110] Blackwell pbk **£9.95**

CAIRNCROSS, A.
The Years of Recovery: British Economic Policy 1945 - 51
A magisterial survey of the problems of post-war economic reconstruction. Cairncross was himself an adviser to the post-war Labour government and was thus a participant in the events he chronicles here.
[UC111] Methuen pbk **£14.95**

COATES, D. & HILLARD, J. (EDS)
The Economic Decline of Modern Britain: The Debate Between Left and Right
A collection of articles from across the political spectrum on the causes of Britain's present economic difficulties. Many of the pieces collected here are not easy to find elsewhere, making this an extremely useful compendium.
[UC112] Wheatsheaf pbk **£10.95**
The Economic Revival of Modern Britain: The Debate Between Left and Right
[UC113] E Elgar pbk **£9.95**

CRAFTS, N.F.R.
British Economic Growth during the Industrial Revolution
A major re-interpretation of the economic evidence on the origins and character of the industrial revolution in Britain. Crafts' book made a significant contribution to the historical debate on industrialisation and has major implications for the understanding of 20th century economic performance.
[UC114] Oxford pbk **£9.95**

CROSS, R.
Economic Theory and Policy in the UK
An outline and assessment of the controversies.
[UC115] M Robertson pbk **£10.95**

CUTLER, T. ET AL
Keynes, Beveridge and Beyond
The authors argue that the Keynesian techniques for full employment and the Beveridge-inspired system of social welfare were flawed from the start. The pattern of post-war economic growth has further undermined their effectiveness and so, the authors suggest, a radical overhaul of economic and social policy will be required in the 1990s.
[UC116] Routledge pbk **£8.95**

DORNBUSCH, R. & LAYARD, R. (EDS)
The Performance of the British Economy
A review of the degree to which the 'Thatcher experiment' has remedied the sources of slow growth in the British economy. The general verdict is that, despite many necessary changes, the deep-seated causes of relative decline have not been adequately addressed.
[UC117] Oxford pbk **£9.95**

ELBAUM, B. & LAZONICK, W. (EDS)
The Decline of the British Economy: An Institutional Perspective
An important collection of revisionist essays in economic history.
[UC118] Oxford pbk **£9.95**

FINE, B. & HARRIS, L.
The Peculiarities of the British Economy
A Marxist account of the current predicament of the British economy, providing interesting reviews of the fortunes of specific industries such as coal, nuclear power, armaments, cars, and electronics.
[UC119] Lawrence & W pbk **£8.95**

FLOUD, R. & MCCLOSKEY, D. (EDS)
The Economic History of Britain since 1700
Vol 1 1700 - 1860
The first volume of what has rapidly become the standard textbook on the economic history of Britain. The authors bring the techniques of modern economic analysis to bear on the central question of the industrial revolution. An indispensable work for students and specialists alike.
[UC120] Cambridge pbk **£13.50**
Vol 2 1860 - 1970
[UC121] Cambridge pbk **£17.50**

GARDNER, N.
Decade of Discontent: The Changing British Economy since 1973
[UC122] Blackwell pbk **£9.95**

GREENAWAY, D. & SHAW, G.K.
Macroeconomics and the British Economy: Theory and Policy in the UK
[UC123] Blackwell pbk **£12.95**

HARE, PAUL
Planning the British Economy
Hare argues that government intervention at the central and regional level is necessary to improve the level and quality of investment in the British economy. He also provides a survey of the theoretical economic arguments for and against economic planning and a review of the evidence on planning in practice.
[UC124] Macmillan pbk **£810.95**

HUTTON, WILL
The Revolution that Never Was: An Assessment of Keynesian Economics
The former *Newsnight* correspondent argues that Britain's economic problems derive in part from the fact that Keynesianism was never properly applied.
[UC125] Longman pbk **£7.50**

JAY, D.
Sterling: A Plea for Moderation
[UC126] Oxford pbk **£4.95**

KAY, J. ET AL (ED)
Privatisation and Regulation: The UK Experience
The most detailed and careful review of the economic implications of the privatisation and liberalising programmes of the Thatcher governments.
[UC127] Oxford pbk **£9.95**

KEEGAN, W.
Britain without Oil: What Lies Ahead
Keegan argues that Conservative management of the UK economy has wasted the opportunity provided by North Sea oil to increase Britain's growth and develop her international competitiveness. He suggests that a major economic crisis looms as the oil runs out.
[UC128] Penguin pbk **£2.95**

LAYARD, R.
How to Beat Unemployment
Layard provides a full account of the causes of unemployment, the competing theories that have been advanced to explain it and the policy debate over how to reduce it.
[UC129] Oxford pbk **£4.95**

Margaret Thatcher, from *Margaret Thatcher: The First Ten Years* (Sidgwick & Jackson hbk £12.95)

LEE, C.H.
The British Economy since 1700: A Macroeconomic Perspective
[UC130] Cambridge pbk **£9.95**

MAYNARD, G.
The Economy under Mrs Thatcher
An up-beat assessment of the 'Thatcher experiment'. Maynard provides a clear and accessible account of the range of government policies and argues that on balance they had a clearly favourable impact.
[UC131] Blackwell pbk **£7.95**

POLLARD, S.
The Development of the British Economy, 1914-1980
One of the standard histories of the British economy in the 20th century, now in its third edtion.
[UC132] E Arnold pbk **£10.95**
The Wasting of the British Economy: British Economic Policy, 1945 to the Present
A powerfully argued critique of the anti-industrial bias of UK economic policy by one of the leading contemporary economic historians.
[UC133] Cr Helm pbk **£8.95**

PRATTEN, C.
Applied Macroeconomics
[UC134] Oxford pbk **£9.95**

ROWTHORN, R.E. & WELLS, J.R.
Deindustrialisation and Foreign Trade
A major new addition to the voluminous literature on deindustrialisation. Rowthorn and Wells break genuinely new ground in two ways: they set the UK experience in a broad comparative and historical perspective, and they argue that the pattern of industrial development cannot be understood outside the context of the changing position of the whole economy in the international division of labour.
[UC136] Cambridge pbk **£15.00**

SMITH, D.
The Rise and Fall of Monetarism
A popular account of the development and perambulation of monetarist policy in the UK.
[UC137] Penguin pbk **£3.95**

STEWART, M.
After Keynes
A revised edition of the author's classic, this edition has now been up-dated to include a discussion of the monetarist reaction against Keynesianism.
[UC138] Penguin pbk **£4.50**

TOMLINSON, J.
British Macroeconomic Policy since 1940
One of the clearest accounts of British post-war macroeconomic policy available.
[UC140] Cr Helm hbk **£25.00**
Monetarism: Is There an Alternative?
A detailed review of the theoretical and policy alternatives to monetarism that have been offered by the opposition parties and critical economists in recent years.
[UC141] Blackwell pbk **£9.95**

Socialist Economies

AGANBEGYAN, ABEL
The Challenge: Economics of Perestroika
The author is the Chief Economic Adviser to Mikhail Gorbachev and a member of the Presidium of the Soviet Academy of Sciences. In this book he provides an extensive review of the kind of economic reforms that Gorbachev is seeking to introduce.
[UC142] Hutchinson pbk **£8.95**

BERGSON, A. & LEVIN, H. (EDS)
The Soviet Economy: Towards the Year 2000
An important collection of articles on the performance and future prospects of the Soviet economy.
[UC143] Unwin Hyman pbk **£15.95**

BIDELEUX, R.
Communism and Development
Bideleux provides a combination of a commentary on arguments about socialist economic development and a review of the empirical evidence of the success or otherwise of the latter. A forceful critique of the Stalinist model of forced industrialisation and compulsory collectivisation.
[UC144] Methuen pbk **£9.95**

ELLMAN, M.
Socialist Planning
A new edition of one of the standard treatments of socialist economies and economics. Ellman has included a new discussion of de-collectivisation in China, the *perestroika* in the USSR, and the Polish economic crisis.
[UC145] Cambridge pbk **£12.95**

GOLDMAN, MARSHALL, I.
Gorbachev's Challenge: Economic Reform in the Age of High Technology
A leading American specialist on the Soviet economy considers the obstacles facing the Gorbachev reforms.
[UC146] Norton pbk **£5.95**

GOMULKA, S.
Growth, Innovation and Reform in Eastern Europe
One of the most important contibutions to the examination of the growth process in East European economies written in recent years.
[UC147] Blackwell pbk **£9.95**

KORNAI, J.
Growth, Shortage and Efficiency
A path-breaking attempt to develop an economic model of the planned economies. Kornai regards these as characterised by chronic shortages as a result of the priority accorded to investment in their plans.
[UC148] Blackwell pbk **£8.50**

LANE, D. (ED)
Labour and Employment in the USSR
[UC149] Wheatsheaf pbk **£8.95**

NOLAN, P. & PAINE, S. (ED)
Rethinking Socialist Economics: A New Agenda for Britain
An attempt to take the lessons of planning and think through the implications for a market socialism in Britain.
[UC150] Polity P pbk **£3.45**

NOVE, ALEC
An Economic History of the USSR
Probably the best single-volume history available.
[UC151] Penguin pbk **£5.95**
Political Economy and Soviet Socialism
[UC152] Unwin Hyman pbk **£9.95**
Socialism, Economics and Development
[UC153] Unwin Hyman pbk **£10.95**
The Economics of Feasible Socialism
A powerful attack on the utopian elements in socialist economic thinking and an economic agenda for market socialism.
[UC154] Unwin Hyman pbk **£9.50**
The Soviet Economic System (3rd edn.)
This book is both an exhaustive review of the Soviet economy and Nove's own reflections on the questions of structural problems, economic change and the reform agenda.
[UC155] Unwin Hyman pbk **£10.95**

RISKIN, C.
China's Political Economy: The Quest for Development since 1949
A comprehensive study of the development and workings of the Chinese economy.
[UC156] Oxford pbk **£12.95**

SOCIOLOGY & ANTHROPOLOGY

Sociology & Social Theory

ABERCROMBIE, N. & WARDE A. ET AL
Contemporary British Society
A major new sociology textbook for 'A' level and undergraduate students, it covers all the main themes and is copiously illustrated with empirical material on British society.
[UD1] Polity P pbk **£7.95**

ABERCROMBIE, N.; HILL, S. & TURNER, B.S.
Dictionary of Sociology
[UD2] Penguin pbk **£4.99**

ARIES, P. & BEJIN, A.
Western Sexuality: Practice and Precepts in Past and Present Times
A wide-ranging collection of essays covering the diverse forms of 'normal' and 'abnormal' sexual practices in Western society from the middle ages to the 20th century.
[UD3] Blackwell pbk **£8.95**

ASHFORD, DOUGLAS E.
The Emergence of the Welfare States
An impressive, comparative polity or state-centred account of the emergence of welfare states in the US, Britain, France, Germany and Sweden.
[UD4] Blackwell pbk **£9.95**

BALL, STEPHEN
Education
[UD5] Longman pbk **£3.75**

BANTON, M.
Racial Consciousness
An examination of theories of racism and racial consciousness written by a leading specialist.
[UD6] Longman pbk **£5.95**
Racial Theories
[UD7] Cambridge pbk **£6.95**

BAUDRILLARD, J.
Jean Baudrillard: Selected Writings
A useful collection of the writings of the radical French post-structuralist theorist of symbolic forms.
[UD8] Polity P pbk **£8.95**

BERGER, PETER L.
Invitation to Sociology
A classic introduction.
[UD9] Penguin pbk **£4.50**

BILTON, T. ET AL
Introductory Sociology
In its revised third edition, with a complete new chapter, this book is probably the best 'A' level or first year undergraduate text. It covers the main areas of sociological inquiry while critically employing the main theoretical traditions.
[UD10] Macmillan pbk **£9.95**

BROCKOCK, ROBERT
Freud
A simple introduction for sociology students.
[UD11] Routledge pbk **£4.95**

BORONSKI, TOMAS
Knowledge
An 'A' level survey of the debates surrounding the sociology of knowledge.
[UD12] Longman pbk **£3.75**

BOTTOMORE, TOM
Classes in Modern Sociology
[UD13] Unwin Hyman pbk **£5.50**
Sociology and Socialism
A collection of Bottomore's vivid and readable essays on the close but problematic relationship between sociology and socialism.
[UD15] Wheatsheaf pbk **£10.95**

BOURDIEU, PIERRE
Outline of a Theory of Practice
One of the outstanding contributions to theory in anthropology and the social sciences more generally, Bourdieu attempts a general theory of the relations between social structure and human practice.
[UD17] Cambridge pbk **£9.95**

CALLINICOS, A.
Making History
A Marxist contribution to the debate in contemporary social theory on the relation of structure to agency.
[UD18] Polity P hbk **£27.50**

CASHMORE, E. ELLIS & TROYNA, B.
Introduction to Race Relations
[UD19] Routledge pbk **£7.95**

COHEN, S. & SCULL, A.
Social Control and the State: Comparative and Historical Essays
[UD20] Blackwell pbk **£9.50**

COHEN, STANLEY
Folk Devils and Moral Panics: The Creation of the Mods and Rockers
One of the classic texts of the radical sociology of deviance, Cohen argues that society's moral panics create the folk devils of popular concern, rather than reflect genuine upsurges of crime or disorder.
[UD21] Blackwell pbk **£9.95**

COLLINS, R.
Weberian Sociological Theory `NEW`
[UD22] Cambridge pbk **£11.95**

CONNELL, R.
Gender and Power
A review of the recent sociology of gender, the study of the personal and the social relations of identity, sexuality and power between the sexes.
[UD23] Polity P pbk **£8.50**

CORRIGAN, P. & SAYER, D.
The Great Arch: English State Formation as Cultural Revolution `NEW`
A Marxist social history of the British state from AD 1000 to the 19th century which draws widely on the work of historians and the other classical social theorists, Weber and Durkheim.
[UD24] Blackwell pbk **£9.95**

CRAIB, IAN
Modern Social Theory
An undergraduate textbook on social theory, from Parsons to Habermas, which focuses on the post-war development of the discipline.
[UD25] Wheatsheaf pbk **£9.95**

CROMPTON, R. & MANN, M.
Gender and Stratification
A collection of articles which attempt to examine the social relationships between class and gender.
[UD26] Polity P pbk **£8.95**

DAVIS, H. & SCASE, R.
Western Capitalism and State Socialism
A rare comparative treatment of the sociology of capitalism and socialism written for an undergraduate audience.
[UD27] Blackwell pbk **£8.95**

DOBASH, R.P.; DOBASH, R.E. & GUTTERIDGE, S.
The Imprisonment of Women
A forcefully-argued book which argues both that women receive punishment of greater severity as a result of patriarchal attitudes and that the law functions so as to reinforce women's subordination.
[UD28] Blackwell pbk **£7.95**

DURKHEIM, EMILE
A Positivist to the core, Durkheim was the driving force behind the theory of a 'collective conscience'. He is widely held to be the founder of modern comparative sociology.
Division of Labour in Society
[UD29] Macmillan pbk **£9.95**
Suicide: A Study in Sociology
One of the classic texts of sociology, Durkheim's study has served as a model of sociological research for subsequent generations.
[UD30] Routledge pbk **£9.95**
The Division of Labour in Society
Durkheim's first work, in which he argued for the classification of societies into mechanical and organic types, showing how modern society was increasingly of the latter type.
[UD31] Macmillan pbk **£9.95**
The Rules of Sociological Method
[UD32] Macmillan pbk **£7.95**
FENTON, STEVEN
Durkheim and Modern Sociology
[UD33] Cambridge pbk **£9.50**
GIDDENS, ANTHONY
One of the leading social theorists writing today, Giddens' work spans a range from abstract social theory through to more substantive studies and critical interpretative studies.
Durkheim
An excellent short but critical account of Durkheim's social theory and sociology.
[UD34] Fontana pbk **£4.95**
THOMPSON, K.
Emile Durkheim
A short interesting introduction to the full range of the classical French sociolgist's work.
[UD36] Routledge pbk **£3.95**

ELSTER, JON (ED)
Rational Choice
An important collection of articles on the new sociology of rational choice and game theory which is increasingly influential.
[UD37] Blackwell pbk **£9.95**

FARMER, MARY
The Family
An introductory text on the sociology of the family, designed primarily for 'A' level courses.
[UD38] Longman pbk **£7.95**

FEHER, F.; HELLER, A. & MARKUS, G.
Dictatorship Over Needs: An Analysis of Soviet Societies
Probably the most innovative radical analysis of state socialist societies to have appeared in the post-war period, this provides a comprehensive analysis of the political and economic relations within these societies.
[UD39] Blackwell pbk **£8.50**

SOCIAL SCIENCES

GEORGE, V. & MANNING, N.
Socialism, Social Welfare and the Soviet Union
One of the few systematic studies of the topic by two of the leading welfare sociologists.
[UD53] Routledge pbk **£10.95**

GIDDENS, ANTHONY
One of the leading social theorists writing today, Giddens' work ranges from abstract social theory through to more substantive studies and critical interpretative studies.
Capitalism and the Modern Social Theory
One of the best treatments of the sociology of Marx, Weber and Durkheim available for an undergraduate audience.
[UD54] Cambridge pbk **£8.95**
Social Theory and Modern Sociology
[UD55] Polity P pbk **£8.95**
Sociology NEW
A major new textbook with a specific focus on the international spread of social phenomena paying attention to conventionally overlooked topics - such as militarism and communications.
[UD56] Polity P pbk **£9.95**
The Constitution of Society
A comprehensive statement of Giddens' overall standpoint in social theory.
[UD57] Polity P pbk **£8.95**
The Nation-State and Violence
An advanced treatment of the administrative and military power of the modern nation-state.
[UD58] Polity P pbk **£8.95**

GIDDENS, ANTHONY & TURNER, J.
Social Theory Today
A series of essays by some of the leading figures in contemporary sociology review of the main schools of social theory.
[UD59] Polity P pbk **£9.95**

GILL, COLIN
Work, Unemployment and the New Technology
A very readable, critical introduction to the social issues surrounding the impact of new technology on the nature and organisation of work.
[UD60] Polity P pbk **£7.95**

GOFFMAN, ERVING
Famed for his study of the behaviour of inmates in 'total' institutions, Goffman's work on the management of the 'self' in social encounters is currently being positively re-evaluated.
Asylums
[UD61] Penguin pbk **£5.95**
The Presentation of Self in Everyday Life
[UD62] Penguin pbk **£4.99**

GOLDING, PETER
The Mass Media
An 'A' level textbook review of the sociology of television and the newspaper industry.
[UD63] Longman pbk **£6.50**

GOLDTHORPE, JOHN
An Introduction to Sociology
[UD64] Cambridge pbk **£8.95**

GOLDTHORPE; LLEWELYN & PAYNE
Social Mobility and Class Structure in Modern Britain
An exhaustive survey on social mobility during the 20th century.
[UD65] Oxford pbk **£9.95**

HABERMAS, JURGEN
Perhaps best-known for his work on the theory of knowledge, Habermas has also challenged the theoretical foundations and framework of critical social theory.
Communication and the Evolution of Society
[UD66] Polity P pbk **£8.95**
Knowledge and Human Interests
[UD67] Polity P pbk **£12.50**
Legitimation Crisis
[UD68] Polity P pbk **£9.50**
BERNSTEIN, R.
Habermas and Modernity NEW
A very valuable collection of critical essays on the recent work of Habermas, organised primarily around his recent defence of the philosophical and social claims of modernism.
[UD69] Polity P pbk **£8.95**
OUTHWAITE, W.
Habermas
An up-to-date guide to the work of Habermas which sets it in the context of critical theory and modern German society.
[UD70] Polity P pbk **£7.95**
PUSEY, M.
Jurgen Habermas
A simple introduction to the often complex work of Habermas.
[UD71] Routledge pbk **£4.95**

HALSEY, A.H.
Halsey's major work has centred on the British education system. He has brought to light the disproportionate achievements of the service class within the system, and has stressed the importance of education as a tool for social reform.
British Social Trends since 1900
[UD72] Macmillan pbk **£14.95**
Change in British Society
A broad-scale overview of the social changes that have transformed Britain over the last century.
[UD73] Oxford pbk **£4.95**

HALSEY; HEATH & RIDGE
Origins and Destinations
A study of the educational experience of Englishmen and Welshmen from World War I to the 1970s, offering an answer to the question of whether there is a class bias in education.
[UD74] Oxford pbk **£9.95**

HARALAMBOS, M.
Sociology: Themes and Perspectives
A noted 'A' level textbook which systematically reviews the main subject areas from the functionalist, Marxist and interactionist perspectives - popular among students.
[UD76] Unwin Hyman pbk **£11.25**

HARGREAVES, JOHN
Sport, Power and Culture
An important social and historical study of the connections between the popular sports and the wider structures of power in society.
[UD77] Polity P pbk **£8.95**

HAWTHORN, G.
Enlightenment and Despair
Approaches the development of social theory from a philosophical standpoint, seeing its origins in the project of the Enlightenment.
[UD80] Cambridge pbk **£8.95**

HEATH, ANTHONY ET AL
How Britain Votes
An analysis of the sociological factors which influence political behaviour.
[UD81] Pergamon pbk **£9.95**

HERITAGE, J.
Garfinkel and Ethnomethodology
A comprehensive study of ethnomethodology in general and the work of Garfinkel in particular, Heritage's study is probably the best account available.
[UD82] Polity P hbk **£27.50**

HILL, M.
Understanding Social Policy
A textbook account of the types of social policy in modern Britain, with a special focus on recent changes. In its third edition.
[UD83] Blackwell pbk **£8.50**

HILL, M. & BRAMLEY, G.
Analysing Social Policy
Directed towards an undergraduate audience, this is one of the best comparative reviews of theoretical approaches in the field of social policy analysis.
[UD84] Blackwell pbk **£8.95**

HODGE, R. & KRESS, G.
Social Semiotics
A major new textbook, designed for courses on communications and cultural studies, which treats the social study of the generation and dissemination of meaning in a systematic way.
[UD85] Polity P pbk **£8.95**

HOLDAWAY, SIMON
Inside the British Police
A study of the working of the British police based upon a considerable period of participant observation.
[UD86] Blackwell pbk **£8.95**

HORNE, JOHN
Work and Unemployment
An introductory survey to the sociological aspects of work and unemployment in modern society.
[UD87] Longman pbk **£3.75**

ILLICH, IVAN
Radical 'pop' sociologist and cultural critic noted for his critique of the role of the professions in society.
Deschooling Society
[UD88] Penguin pbk **£3.99**
The Limits to Medicine
[UD89] Boyars pbk **£5.95**

JACOBS, BRIAN
Racism in Britain
The social, political and economic influence of racism.
[UD91] C Helm pbk **£6.95**

JORDAN, BILL
Rethinking Welfare
A radical attempt to re-orient the debate on welfare away from state versus free-market provision towards a more general concern with the values which welfare policy seeks to secure.
[UD92] Blackwell pbk **£8.95**

JOSEPH, MARTIN
Sociology for Everyone
A basic 'O' level textbook in sociology.
[UD93] Polity P pbk **£6.95**

KINSEY, R.; LEA, J. & YOUNG, J.
Losing the Fight Against Crime
A controversial argument which urges the Left to take the issue of crime seriously in order to recapture the ground ceded to the Right.
[UD94] Blackwell **£8.95**

LASH, S. & URRY, J.
The End of Organised Capitalism
An ambitious comparative study of the rise and crisis

of organised capitalism and its replacement by a new form, disorganised capitalism.
[UD95] Polity P pbk **£9.95**

LAVER, M.
Social Choice and Public Policy
A respected undergraduate textbook in comparative social policy analysis.
[UD96] Blackwell pbk **£9.50**

LEE, D. & NEWBY, H.
The Problems of Sociology
A first-class introduction to the main classical traditions in social theory written for an undergraduate audience.
[UD97] Century pbk **£8.95**

LUKES, S.
Power
A valuable collection of essays which attempt to define and elaborate on this central but complex concept in social and politial theory.
[UD99] Blackwell pbk **£8.50**

MANN, MICHAEL (ED)
Macmillan Student Encyclopaedia of Sociology
A very useful reference book which contains entries on major sociologists, central concepts and brief accounts of theoretical perspectives.
[UD100] Macmillan pbk **£9.95**

MANNHEIM, KARL
Basing his writings on studies of German society during the first half of the 20th century, Mannheim has made important contributions to political sociology, the sociology of education and the study of social structure in modern society.
Ideology and Utopia
A classic in the sociological study of ideologies and 'world views' by the German-born theorist of the mass society.
[UD101] Routledge pbk **£8.95**

MARSH, C.
Exploring Data
A new, comprehensive textbook for undergraduates in the role of quantitative data in sociological research.
[UD102] Polity P pbk **£9.95**

MAYES, PAT
Gender
An introductory account of this relatively recent development in mainstream sociology.
[UD104] Longman pbk **£3.75**

MILES, ROBERT
Capitalism and Unfree Labour: Anomaly or Necessity?
[UD106] Routledge pbk **£10.95**
Racism
An introduction to the fierce debates around this contested concept in the social sciences.
[UD107] Routledge pbk **£7.95**
Racism and Migrant Labour
A radical account which seeks to locate the persistence of racist ideology in the political and economic postition of migrant labour in contemporary capitalism.
[UD108] Routledge pbk **£8.95**

MORISON, MURRAY
Methods in Sociology
An introductory treatment of both quantitative and qualitative methods of research in the social sciences.
[UD109] Longman pbk **£3.75**

OFFE, K.
Disorganised Capitalism
A valuable collection of Offe's most recent essays, subtitled 'Contemporary Transformations of Work and Politics', concerned with the crisis of social democratic politics and the emergence of the new social movements.
[UD110] Polity P pbk **£8.95**

PAHL, R.E.
Divisions of Labour
One of the most important contributions to the study of work in Britain of the last decade. Includes a fascinating case study of the Isle of Sheppey in Kent.
[UD111] Blackwell pbk **£10.95**

PARSONS, TALCOTT
Parsons attempted the impossible: to design an all-encompassing interdisciplinary general theory of social action. His scheme for social relations has inspired many later sociologists to address the relationships between individuals and society.
HAMILTON, P.
Readings from Talcott Parsons
[UD112] Routledge pbk **£6.95**
Talcott Parsons
A simple but comprehensive account of the work of the dominant figure of post-war North American sociology.
[UD113] Routledge pbk **£4.25**

POTTER, D. (ED)
Society and the Social Sciences
This Open University reader provides a useful collection of articles on British society.
[UD114] Routledge pbk **£9.95**

SCOTT, J.
The British Ruling Class
A comprehensive historical and sociological study written by a leading authority on the subject.
[UD115] Polity P pbk **£8.95**

SKINNER, Q. (ED)
The Return of Grand Theory in the Human Sciences
[UD117] Cambridge pbk **£6.95**

SKOCPOL, T. (ED)
Vision and Method in Historical Sociology
A collection of essays on the work of some of the major contributors to historical and comparative sociology.
[UD118] Cambridge pbk **£10.95**

SMITH, ANTHONY D.
The Ethnic Origins of Nations
A major contribution to the study of nationalism which concentrates on the ethnic communities constituted prior to the emergence of modern nation-states.
[UD119] Blackwell pbk **£10.95**

STONE, JOHN
Racial Conflict in Contemporary Society
An introduction to the sociology of race which pays particular attention to the importance of the connections between racial conflict, institutions and social change.
[UD120] Fontana pbk **£3.50**

SWINGEWOOD, ALAN
A Short History of Sociological Thought
A comprehensive history of the discipline from the Enlightenment, through the classical phase of

Durkheim, Marx, Weber and other, to the modern schools of functionalism, structuralism and interactionism.
[UD121] Macmillan pbk **£8.95**

TAYLOR, STEVE
Suicide
[UD122] Longman pbk **£3.75**

TERKEL, STUDS
Working
An oral history of the working lives of American citizens.
[UD123] Penguin pbk **£7.95**

THOMPSON, IAN
Religion
[UD124] Longman pbk **£3.75**

THOMPSON, J.
Studies in the Theory of Ideology
A number of critical studies which assess the state of theoretical work on the problem of ideology.
[UD125] Polity P pbk **£7.95**

THOMPSON, K.
Beliefs and Ideology
[UD126] Routledge pbk **£4.25**

TODD, EMMANUEL
The Explanation of Ideology: Family Structures and Social Systems
Todd's important contribution to social history and social theory advances the argument that different forms of belief system reflect the underlying family forms of a society.
[UD127] Blackwell pbk **£9.50**

TURNER, B.S.
Equality
The first systematic study of the subject since Tawney's classic work.
[UD128] Routledge pbk **£4.95**
The Body and Society
A major study of the social shaping of the forms and practices of the human body which considers the discourses of medicine, the law, religion and sexuality.
[UD129] Blackwell pbk **£9.95**

WALBY, S.
Patriarchy at Work
A radical study of the relations between patriarchy and capitalism in British employment from 1800-1984.
[UD130] Polity P pbk **£7.95**

WEBER, MAX
For many, *the* sociologist's sociologist. Weber's combination of historical erudition and sociological insight gives his work a coherence and power rarely matched.
Selection in Translation
(Ed. Runciman, W.G.)
[UD131] Cambridge pbk **£10.95**
The Agrarian Structure of Ancient Civilisations
[UD132] Verso pbk **£12.95**
The Protestant Ethic and the Spirit of Capitalism
Weber's celebrated discussion of the connections between Calvinism and the emergence of capitalism, together with his theory of rationalization.
[UD133] Unwin Hyman pbk **£5.95**
KASLER, DIRK
Max Weber: An Introduction to his Life and Work
A major new textbook on the great German sociologist, unique in its breadth and its attention to

Max Weber from the 1922 biography by his wife
(Picture: British Museum)

recent scholarship and debates. A comprehensive and
accessible account of Weber's work.
[UD134] Polity P pbk **£8.95**
PARKIN, FRANK
Weber
A somewhat idiosyncratic introduction to Weber by a
leading contemporary Weberian sociologist.
[UD135] Routledge pbk **£5.95**

WILLIAMS, RAYMOND
Culture
An examination of culture from the literary critic well
known for his Marxist perspective.
[UD136] Fontana pbk **£3.95**

WORSLEY, PETER
Modern Sociology
A collection of readings providing a background to
the main strands of sociological thought and styles of
sociological writing.
[UD137] Penguin pbk **£7.95**
The New Introducing Sociology
A classic and admirable, if somewhat dry,
textbook.
[UD138] Penguin pbk **£5.99**

YOUNG, MICHAEL & WILLMOTT, PETER
Family and Kinship in East London
A path-breaking study of the social consequence
of slum clearance in Bethnal Green, paying
particular attention to the changing family
forms which resulted as extended families were
separated.
[UD139] Penguin pbk **£5.95**

Anthropology

BARLEY, NIGEL
A Plague of Caterpillars
More anecdotes and insights into the Dowayo
lifestyle, including an account of the ancient
circumcision ceremony and a plague of black hairy
caterpillars.
[UD141] Penguin pbk **£2.99**

**Innocent Anthropologist: Notes from
a Mud Hut**
A witty and unconventional introduction to the life of
a social anthropologist. Inspiring reading.
[UD142] Penguin pbk **£4.99**

BEATTIE, JOHN H.M.
Other Cultures
A good introduction to the study of anthropology.
[UD143] Routledge pbk **£8.95**

BLOCH, MAURICE
**Marxism and Anthropology: The History
of a Relationship**
A penetrating study of both the use that Marx and
Engels made of anthropological evidence and the
contributions of Marxists to the development of
anthropology.
[UD144] Oxford pbk **£5.95**
**Marxist Analyses and Social
Anthropology**
[UD145] Routledge pbk **£7.95**

BRODY, HUGH
Living Arctic
The way of life - and the threats to it - in the Canadian
Arctic.
[UD146] Faber pbk **£4.95**

DOUGLAS, MARY
British sociologist renowned for her studies of
religion and symbolism.
Purity and Danger
An anthropological study of the social construction of
concepts of pollution and taboo.
[UD147] Routledge pbk **£4.95**

ENNEW, JUDITH
**Economic Anthropology:
An Introduction**
A textbook introduction to the comparative
anthropligical study of the economic institutions of
production, distribution, exchange and consumption.
[UD148] Polity P pbk **£8.50**

EVANS-PRITCHARD, E.E.
'E-P' is famous for his studies of the Azande and the
war-like Nuer of southern Sudan. He denied the
existence of universal laws of human social behaviour
and thus argued that anthropology could never be
'scientific'.
Nuer Religion
[UD149] Oxford pbk **£8.95**
Social Anthropology
A welcome reprint for this classic text of British
empirical social anthropology.
[UD150] Routledge pbk **£8.95**
Theories of Primitive Religion
[UD151] Oxford pbk **£6.95**
**Witchcraft, Oracles and Magic
among the Azande**
Evans-Pritchard's classic study of African belief
systems and their functional role in society.
[UD152] Oxford pbk **£7.95**
DOUGLAS, MARY
Evans-Pritchard
[UD153] Fontana pbk **£1.95**

FOX, ROBIN
**Kinship and Marriage: An
Anthropological Perspective**
[UD154] Penguin pbk **£3.95**

FRAZER, JAMES GEORGE
A key player in the move to gain recognition for
anthropology as an academic discipline in its own
right. He succeeded in holding the first British
university professorship bearing the title 'Social
Anthropology'.

The Golden Bough
A classic text which did more to popularize
anthropology than to advance its theoretical basis,
Frazer's study of myths, magic and religion was
immensely popular when published in 1890.
[UD155] Macmillan 13 vols hbk **£250.00**
[UD156] Macmillan hbk (abridged) **£29.50**
[UD157] Macmillan pbk (abridged) **£7.95**

GELLNER, ERNEST
Muslim Society
A comprehensive social and anthropological study of
Muslim sociey.
[UD158] Cambridge pbk **£10.95**

GODELIER, M.
**The Mental and the Material:
Thought, Economy and Society**
A major contribution to anthropological and social
theory by a leading French Marxist: Godelier draws
on his extensive fieldwork to produce a theory of the
relations between thought and practice in social life.
[UD159] Verso pbk **£8.95**

GOODY, JACK
Cooking, Cuisine and Class
[UD160] Cambridge pbk **£8.95**
Production and Reproduction
A comparative study of the sphere of domestic labour
and the organisation of domestic life.
[UD161] Cambridge pbk **£8.50**
The Domestication of the Savage Mind
A brilliant study of the impact on society of the
transition from oral to literate cultures.
[UD162] Cambridge pbk **£8.95**
**The Logic of Writing and the
Organisation of Society**
A detailed overview, both theoretical and empirical,
of this important subject.
[UD163] Cambridge pbk **£7.95**

HIRST, P. & WOOLLEY, P.
Social Relations and Human Attributes
A comprehensive review of psychological and
sociological theories of the development of human
capacities.
[UD164] Routledge pbk **£8.95**

KIRK, G.S.
**Myth: Its Meaning and Functions in
Ancient and Other Cultures**
A penetrating discussion by one of the authorities on
Greek mythology.
[UD165] Cambridge pbk **£11.95**

KUPER, ADAM
**Anthropology and Anthropologists:
The British School**
A critical study of the British anthropological
tradition from the mid-19th century through to the
present day.
[UD166] Routledge pbk **£7.95**

LARNER, CHRISTINA
Witchcraft and Religion
A study of the politics of popular religious belief.
[UD167] Blackwell pbk **£8.95**

LEACH, EDMUND
Culture and Communication
An introduction to the use of structuralist analysis in
social anthropology in order to elaborate the logic by
which symbols are connected into systems of
meaning.
[UD168] Cambridge pbk **£7.50**
Rethinking Anthropology
A powerful, if maverick, critique of mainstream
British anthropology.
[UD169] Athlone pbk **£10.95**

LEACH, EDMUND (ED)
The Structural Study of Myth and Totemism
[UD170] Routledge pbk **£9.95**

LEVI-STRAUSS, CLAUDE
Probably the most celebrated anthropologist since the war, Lévi-Strauss is noted for his structuralist approach to the study of kinship and myth.
Myth and Meaning
A short statement of Lévi-Strauss's main ideas on the subjects.
[UD171] Routledge pbk **£5.95**
Structural Anthropology Vol 1
[UD172] Penguin pbk **£7.95**
Structural Anthropology Vol 2
[UD173] Penguin pbk **£7.95**
The Elementary Structures of Kinship
Lévi-Strauss's pioneering structuralist study of kinship relations in primitive societies.
[UD174] Beacon pbk **£10.50**
The Raw and the Cooked
Demonstrates how myths can be reduced to a comprehensible psychological pattern.
[UD175] Penguin pbk **£5.95**
The Savage Mind
Lévi-Strauss's magisterial study of the nature of 'primitive' thought, where he develops his influential contrast between 'cold' and 'hot' cultures.
[UD176] Weidenfeld pbk **£6.50**
Tristes Tropiques
A lament for primitive cultures under threat from the West, Lévi-Strauss's autobiography is a fascinating introduction to his thought.
[UD177] Penguin pbk **£6.95**
LEACH, EDMUND
Lévi-Strauss
[UD178] Fontana pbk **£2.95**
PACE, D.
Claude Lévi-Strauss
A detailed but readily accessible study of the complex work of the French master.
[UD179] Routledge pbk **£5.95**

LEWIS, I.M.
Social Anthropology in Perspective
[UD180] Cambridge pbk **£9.95**

Claude Lévi-Strauss, author of *Myth and Meaning* (Routledge pbk £5.95) (Photo:Jerry Bauer)

MALINOWSKI, BRANISLAW
A pioneer of participant-observation, Malinowski believed that culture was a means of satisfying physiological needs, and thus he provided the foundations for the tradition of functionalism in anthropology.
The Argonauts of the Western Pacific
Widely and rightly seen as one of the literary classics of anthropological writing, Malinowski's study of the Trobriand Islanders in New Guinea seeks to elucidate the way in which institutions function in order to channel instinctual behaviour.
[UD181] Routledge pbk **£16.95**
The Sexual Life of Savages in North Western Melanesia
[UD182] Routledge pbk **£15.95**

MEAD, MARGARET
Margaret Mead was a household name in the States in the Sixties. Her work addresses the age-old question of whether human behaviour is biologically or culturally determined.
Male and Female
[UD183] Greenwood P hbk **£27.95**
The Coming of Age in Samoa
Mead's pioneering contribution to cultural anthropology argued that sex roles and gender identities were culturally variable - the book has recently been the subject of a heated controversy.
[UD184] Penguin pbk **£3.50**
FREEMAN, DEREK
Margaret Mead and Samoa: The Making and Unmaking of an Anthropological Myth
A detailed new look at Mead's seminal work and the evidence on which it was based, concludes that Mead was seriously misled by her own subjects and preconceptions.
[UD185] Penguin pbk **£5.95**

MEILLASSOUX, C.
Maidens, Meal and Money
A study of the relationship between capitalist development and the transformations of the position of women and domestic labour, by a leading French anthropologist.
[UD186] Cambridge pbk **£8.50**

MOORE, HENRIETTA L.
Feminism and Anthropology
A pioneering review of the way in which women have been studied within anthropology, as well as the light which conceptions of gender can cast on anthropological research.
[UD187] Polity P pbk **£8.95**

ORTNER, S. & WHITEHEAD, H. (ED)
Sexual Meanings: The Cultural Construction of Gender and Sexuality
[UD188] Cambridge pbk **£12.50**

PARKIN, DAVID (ED)
The Anthropology of Evil
14 anthropologists consider the nature of evil, reviewing general religious concepts and revealing obscure cultural ones.
[UD189] Blackwell pbk **£10.95**

PEACOCK, JAMES L.
Consciousness and Change
Symbolic anthropology in an evolutionary perspective.
[UD190] Blackwell pbk **£8.50**

POST, LAURENS VAN DER
Popular anthropologist whose work has reached a wide audience and has helped to publicise the cause of the outcast survivors of Stone Age Africa.

Laurens van der Post, author of *The Lost World of the Kalahari* (Penguin pbk £3.50)

A Walk with a White Bushman
A mixture of philosophy, biography and wisdom. Includes conversations with Jean-Marc Pottiez.
[UD191] Penguin pbk **£4.99**
The Heart of the Hunter
[UD192] Penguin pbk **£4.95**
The Lost World of the Kalahari
A fascinating account of a problematic expedition, and rediscovery of the Bushman, his cave art, spontaneous music-making and uncanny hunting skills.
[UD193] Penguin pbk **£3.50**

RADCLIFFE-BROWN, A.R.
Radcliffe-Brown was the leader of the 'structural-functionalists' and upheld the need for a cultural and social understanding of institutions and customs, as opposed to a reductionist and biological interpretation.
The Sociology of Radcliffe-Brown
(Ed. Kuper, Adam)
This valuable collection brings together many of Radcliffe-Brown's most important contributions to anthropology, demonstrating his distinctive brand of structural-functionalism.
[UD194] Routledge pbk **£8.50**
KUPER, ADAM
Social Anthropology of Radcliffe-Brown
A full-length study of the work of one of the leading exponents of functionalism in social anthropology.
[UD195] Routledge pbk **£8.95**

SAHLINS, M.
Stone-Age Economics
A classic study which argues that the stone age was the original 'affluent' society, in the sense that it lacked a dynamic compelling ever greater production of a material surplus.
[UD196] Routledge pbk **£8.95**

SANDAY, PEGGY REEVES
Female Power and Male Dominance
An anthropological study into the origins of women's subordination in society.
[UD197] Cambridge pbk **£11.95**

Nigel Barley, author of *A Plague of Caterpillars*
(Penguin pbk **£2.99**)

SCHNEEBAUM, TOBIAS
Where the Spirit Dwells
An encounter with the Asmat, a jungle-dwelling
people in New Guinea who have barely been touched
by modern civilisation.
[UD198] Weidenfeld hbk **£14.95**

SEYMOUR-SMITH, CHARLOTTE
**The Macmillan Dictionary of
Anthropology**
An invaluable reference work.
[UD199] Macmillan pbk **£9.95**

SMITH, R.J.
Japanese Society
A fascinating review of the anthropological evidence
relating to the connection between tradition, the sense
of self and the form of social order in Japan.
[UD200] Cambridge pbk **£8.50**

SPERBER, DAN
On Anthropological Knowledge
[UD201] Cambridge pbk **£7.50**
Rethinking Symbolism
[UD202] Cambridge pbk **£9.50**

STREET, BRIAN V.
Literacy in Theory and Practice
Based on the author's fieldwork in Iran, Street
argues that the study of literacy must be integrated
into an account of its social and political
context.
[UD203] Cambridge pbk **£9.50**

TURNBULL, COLIN
The Forest People
A portrayal of life among the Ba'Mbuti pygmies who
live in the inhospitable Ituri Forest of north-eastern
Zaire.
[UD204] Grafton pbk **£3.50**
The Mountain People
Turnbull's horrifying study of the Ik, a tribe in
Uganda where the old and the young are treated with
a brutality that is scarcely credible.
[UD205] Grafton pbk **£2.50**

PSYCHOLOGY

Reference & Introductory

ADCOCK, C.J.
Fundamentals of Psychology
Basic introduction to the scope of psychological
study.
[UE1] Penguin pbk **£4.95**

COHEN, DAVID (ED)
Psychologists on Psychology
[UE2] Ark pbk **£5.95**

GREGORY, R.L. (ED)
Oxford Companion to the Mind
A fascinating and wide-ranging reference work
covering all aspects of mental processes, with some
intriguing diversions into related fields. Many leading
figures have contributed specialist essays.
[UE3] Oxford hbk **£25.00**

GROSS, D.
**Psychology, the Science of Mind
& Behaviour**
A concise, balanced introduction for 'A' level,
undergraduate and general readers, covering social,
cognitive, and child psychology as well as mental
illness and therapies.
[UE4] E Arnold pbk **£1.95**

HAYES, N.
A First Course in Psychology
GCSE syllabus material clearly explained.
[UE5] Nelson pbk **£6.25**

LLOYD, PETER & MAYES, ANDREW
**Introduction to Psychology:
An Integrated Approach**
Introductory text which treats the subject
thematically, seeking to clarify the links between
diverse psychological schools.
[UE6] Fontana pbk **£7.95**

MILLER, GEORGE
Psychology: The Science of Mental Life
Classic introduction to the history and development of
the science of psychology.
[UE7] Penguin pbk **£4.95**

REBER, A.
Penguin Dictionary of Psychology
[UE8] Penguin pbk **£7.99**

SEARLE, J.
Minds, Brains, Science
Very readable account of the philosophy of
psychology.
[UE9] Penguin pbk **£3.99**

SUTHERLAND, STUART (ED)
Macmillan Dictionary of Psychology
[UE10] Macmillan hbk **£29.95**

Analysis & Therapy

BERNE, E.
**Layman's Guide to Psychiatry
and Psychoanalysis**
[UE11] Penguin pbk **£4.95**

**Transactional Analysis in
Psychotherapy**
A classic handbook of principles of 'Transactional
Analysis'.
[UE12] Souvenir P pbk **£5.95**

BETTELHEIM, BRUNO (1903 -)
An American psychologist who specialises in the
treatment of children with emotional disturbances.
Particularly well known for his work with autistic
children, he also studied human behaviour in extreme
situations, and used examples drawn from his own
experiences in a Nazi concentration camp.
Surviving the Holocaust
[UE13] Fontana pbk **£3.50**
The Informed Heart
[UE14] Penguin pbk **£6.99**
**The Uses of Enchantment: Meaning and
Importance of Fairy Tales**
[UE15] Penguin pbk **£7.95**

BLOCH, SIDNEY
What is Psychotherapy ?
[UE16] Oxford pbk **£5.95**

DINNAGE, ROSEMARY
**One to One: Experiences of
Psychotherapy**
Presents 20 case studies of the benefits and
drawbacks of such treatments, from the patient's
viewpoint.
[UE17] Penguin pbk **£4.50**

FARRELL, B.
The Standing of Psychoanalysis
Balanced review of doctrines and therapies.
[UE18] Oxford pbk **£4.95**

FOUCAULT, MICHEL (1926 - 1984)
French philosopher, psychologist, historian and
anthropologist best known for his *Histoire de la Folie*
(published in English as *Madness and Civilization*).
Central themes include social deviance, and society's
persecution of the mentally ill.
**Discipline and Punishment: Birth of
the Prison**
One of Foucault's most accessible and entertaining
works, this is a study of the development of modern
forms of surveillance and discipline centred around
the emergence of the modern prison system.
[UE19] Penguin pbk **£6.95**
Foucault Reader (Ed. Rabinow, P.)
A concise introduction to the work of the seminal
French post-structuralist thinker.
[UE20] Penguin pbk **£7.99**
History of Sexuality
Vol 1: An Introduction
[UE21] Penguin pbk **£4.99**
Vol 2: Use of Pleasure
[UE22] Penguin pbk **£7.95**
Vol 3: The Care of the Self
[UE23] A Lane hbk **£17.95**
Madness and Civilization
[UE24] Tavistock pbk **£8.95**
**Power/Knowledge: Selected Interviews
and Other Writings 1972 - 77**
[UE25] Harvester hbk **£10.95**
DELEUZE, GILLES
Foucault
Examines Foucault's principal themes - knowledge,
power and the nature of subjectivity. Both a critique
and an interpretation.
[UE26] Athlone P hbk **£29.50**
MERQUIOR, J.G.
Foucault
[UE27] Collins hbk **£17.50**
SMART, B.
Foucault
A fine review of Foucault's work which does justice

to the depth and breadth of his work for a new
audience, without superficiality.
[UE28] Routledge pbk **£5.95**

FREUD, SIGMUND (1856 - 1939)
The father of modern psychoanalysis. Although
some aspects of his work have been superseded,
his influence on our whole culture remains huge.
The standard translations of his work are those by
James Strachey, originally commissioned by
Leonard and Virginia Woolf for the Hogarth
Press.
Complete Introductory Lectures on Psychoanalysis (Ed. Stratchey, James)
[UE29] Unwin Hyman hbk **£25.00**
Essentials of Psychoanalysis
[UE30] Penguin pbk **£6.95**
Leonardo da Vinci
Freudian biography written by the master, this brief
study attempts to show the connections between the
artist's work and his childhood.
[UE31] Routledge pbk **£3.50**
PENGUIN FREUD LIBRARY
Vol 1: Introductory Lectures on Psychoanalysis
[UE38] Penguin pbk **£7.95**
Vol 2: New Introductory Lectures on Psychoanalysis
These clearly written lectures provide perhaps the
best introduction to Freudian theory for the general
reader.
[UE39] Penguin pbk **£5.95**
Vol 3: Studies on Hysteria
Written in collaboration with Josef Breuer, this is
Freud's first major work and the earliest statement of
his theory of suppression.
[UE40] Penguin pbk **£7.95**
Vol 4: Interpretation of Dreams
Justifiably Freud's most famous work. It is a
remarkable mixture of bold theorising and
imaginative insight.
[UE41] Penguin pbk **£8.95**
Vol 5: Psychopathology of Everyday Life
[UE42] Penguin pbk **£6.95**
Vol 6: Jokes and their Relation to the Unconscious
[UE43] Penguin pbk **£5.99**
Vol 7: On Sexuality
Includes Freud's seminal essays of 1903, the original
formulation of the celebrated (and much denigrated)
concept of the 'Oedipus Complex'.
[UE44] Penguin pbk **£6.95**
Vol 8: Case Histories 1: 'Dora' and Little Hans
'Dora' is one of Freud's best known cases. She was
an 18-year-old hysteric treated by Freud in 1900. The
case demonstrates Freud's use of dream
interpretation.
[UE45] Penguin pbk **£6.99**
Vol 9: Case Histories 2
Contains the last four of Freud's six major case
histories: Fat Man, Schreber, Wolf Man and Female
Homosexuality.
Vol 10: On Psychopathology
[UE32] Penguin pbk **£6.95**
Vol 11: On Metapsychology: The Theory of Psychoanalysis
[UE33] Penguin pbk **£7.95**
Vol 12: Civilisation, Society and Religion
Includes the illuminating 'Civilization and its
Discontents' bringing Freudian theory to bear on the
origins and consequences of social repression.
[UE34] Penguin pbk **£6.99**
Vol 13: Origins of Religion
[UE35] Penguin pbk **£7.99**
Vol 14: Art and Literature
[UE36] Penguin pbk **£7.95**

Vol 15: Historical and Expository Works on Psychoanalysis
[UE37] Penguin pbk **£7.95**
Totem and Taboo
Criticised for its flawed anthropology, this work
remains one of the great classics of psychological
literature.
[UE47] Routledge pbk **£4.50**
BADCOCK, CHRISTOPHER
The Essential Freud
An introduction to the topics and concepts that
characterise Freud's contribution to the contemporary
view of the world.
[UE48] Blackwell pbk **£7.95**
BROWN, J.A.C.
Freud and the Post-Freudians
[UE49] Penguin pbk **£4.95**
CLARK, R.W.
Freud: The Man and the Cause
[UE50] Grafton pbk **£4.95**
EYSENCK, HANS
Decline and Fall of the Freudian Empire
A critical account of Freud's legacy from one of the
world's most famous behaviourist psychologists.
[UE51] Penguin pbk **£4.50**
ISBITER, J.N.
Freud: An Introduction to his Life and Work
A new and controversial reading of psychoanalysis.
[UE52] Blackwell pbk **£7.95**
MALCOLM, JANET
In the Freud Archives
An absorbing journalistic account of the bitter rivalry
to gain access to Freud's unpublished papers.
[UE53] Fontana pbk **£3.50**
STAFFORD-CLARK, D.
What Freud Really Said
[UE54] Penguin pbk **£3.95**

FROMM, ERICH (1900 - 1980)
Fromm offers a humanistic blend of Freud and Marx
and his intelligible style has made him one of the
most popular and widely-read psychologists. He
combines acute insight into psychological motivation
with a deep concern for social issues.
Anatomy of Human Destructiveness
[UE55] Penguin pbk **£6.95**
Beyond the Chains of Illusion: My Encounter with Marx and Freud
[UE56] Sphere pbk **£3.95**
Man for Himself: An Enquiry into the Psychology of Ethics
[UE57] Routledge pbk **£4.95**
The Fear of Freedom
[UE58] Routledge pbk **£5.95**
The Sane Society
[UE59] Routledge pbk **£8.50**
To Have or To Be?
[UE60] Sphere pbk **£3.95**

HARRIS, THOMAS
I'm OK - You're OK
The most solid textbook on 'Transactional
Analysis'.
[UE61] Pan pbk **£3.99**

HOWARD, ALICE & WALDEN
Exploring the Road Less Travelled
A practical follow-up to 'The Road Less Travelled'
by M.S. Peck.
[UE62] Hutchinson pbk **£4.95**

JANOV, ARTHUR
Primal Therapy: The Cure for Neurosis
By an author famous for his theory of 'primal
therapy'.
[UE63] Sphere pbk **£3.95**

JUNG, CARL GUSTAV (1875 - 1961)
Jung worked with Freud until 1912 when he severed
his connection with the psychoanalytic movement and
founded his own school of analytical psychology. He
developed the idea of the psyche (whole personality)
containing the personal unconscious and the
collective unconscious.
Analytical Psychology
[UE64] Ark pbk **£4.95**
Aspects of the Feminine
A welcome collection of articles and extracts from
Jung's writings on marriage, Eros, the mother, the
maiden, and the 'anima/animus' concept.
[UE65] Routledge pbk **£5.50**
Dreams
Dreams interpreted in the context of mysticism,
religion, culture and symbolism.
[UE66] Routledge pbk **£5.50**
Four Archetypes: Mother, Rebirth, Spirit, Trickster
[UE67] Routledge pbk **£4.50**
Man and His Symbols
Written for the general reader, this provides a
refreshingly straightforward account of Jung's ideas.
[UE68] Pan pbk **£5.99**
Memories, Dreams, Reflections
An extraordinary autobiographical account of the
development of Jung's ideas.
[UE69] Collins pbk **£4.95**
Modern Man in Search of a Soul
[UE70] Routledge pbk **£4.95**
Psychological Reflections
A new anthology of writings including Jung's more
aphoristic remarks, drawn from a wide variety of
sources and arranged by theme.
[UE71] Routledge pbk **£5.50**
Psychology and the Occult
Includes Jung's 1902 MD dissertation, a psychiatric
study of a medium and the public lecture: 'On the
Spiritualist Phenomena'.
[UE72] Routledge pbk **£5.50**
Selected Writings
Perhaps the best one-volume collection of Jung's
work, judiciously selected by Anthony Storr. Nothing
essential has been left out.
[UE73] Fontana pbk **£4.95**
Seminars: Vol 1: Dream Analysis
The first of Jung's English seminars, given in
1928.
[UE74] Routledge hbk **£32.00**
The Psychology of Transference
A much-celebrated work providing practical
applications of Jung's ideas to familiar psychological
situations.
[UE75] Routledge pbk **£5.50**
HILLMAN, J.
Facing the Gods: From Jung to Freud
A comparative study of both views of the
unconscious.
[UE76] Spring pbk **£8.50**
JACOBI, JOLANDE
The Psychology of C.G. Jung
[UE77] Routledge pbk **£8.50**
SERRANO, MIGUEL
C.G. Jung and Hermann Hesse: A Record of Two Friendships
[UE78] Routledge pbk **£6.50**
STEIN, MURRAY (ED)
Jungian Analysis
A collection of essays by American analysts
providing a basic handbook of Jungian psychology.
[UE79] Shambhala pbk **£12.95**
STORR, ANTHONY
The Art of Psychotherapy
Storr is perhaps the most important contemporary
Jungian psychotherapist. Here he provides an outline
of theory and practice, cutting through Jung's
mysticism.
[UE80] Heinemann hbk **£12.50**

Carl Gustav Jung (Photo: Mary Evans Picture Library)

WILSON, COLIN
C.G. Jung: Lord of the Underworld
A clear and readable introduction to Jung and his ideas.
[UE81] Aquarian pbk **£5.99**
WOODWARD, M.
The Owl was a Baker's Daughter
Jungian perspective on obesity, anorexia and feminine repression.
[UE82] Airlift pbk **£5.95**

KLEIN, MELANIE (1882 - 1960)
An Austrian child psychoanalyst and follower of Freud. By analysing the unconscious at different levels she discovered new ways to treat character abnormalities. She led the field in applying these techniques to children. She is also known for her work on the psychology of ethics, group relations and aesthetics.
Envy, Gratitude and Other Works, 1946 - 1963
Introduces her theory of primal envy.
[UE83] Virago pbk **£9.95**
Love, Guilt and Repartition and Other Works, 1921 - 1945
Concerned with infant anxieties and the effects on child development.
[UE84] Virago pbk **£9.95**
Selected Melanie Klein
(Ed. Mitchell, Juliet)
A useful collection including essays in which Klein extends Freud's claim that young infants have death instincts.
[UE85] Penguin pbk **£5.95**
The Psychoanalysis of Children
[UE86] Virago pbk **£9.95**
GROSSKURTH, PHYLLIS
Melanie Klein
A recent and full biography
[UE87] Hodder hbk **£19.95**
SPILLINS, E. BOTT
Melanie Klein Today: Developments in Theory and Practice
Vol 1: Mainly Theory
[UE88] Routledge pbk **£14.95**
Vol 2: Mainly Practice
[UE89] Routledge pbk **£14.95**

KNIGHT, LINDSAY
Talking to a Stranger: A Consumer's Guide to Therapy
[UE90] Fontana pbk **£2.95**

LACAN, JACQUES (1901 - 1981)
French structuralist and psychoanalyst who emphasised the role of linguistic models in analysis.
Ecrits: A Selection
[UE91] Tavistock pbk **£9.95**
Feminine Sexuality
[UE92] Macmillan pbk **£9.95**
Four Fundamental Concepts of Psychoanalysis
[UE93] Penguin pbk **£5.95**
BENVENUTO, B. & KENNEDY R.
The Works of Jacques Lacan
Accessible introduction to a modern master.
[UE94] Free Assoc pbk **£8.95**

LAING, R.D. (1927 -)
British existentialist psychiatrist, who made his name in the 1960s with his radical view of schizophrenia as a disease with its roots in family politics.
Divided Self
The classic iconoclastic study of schizophrenia, challenging the assumptions of traditional medical psychiatry.
[UE95] Penguin pbk **£3.50**
Facts of Life
[UE96] Penguin pbk **£2.50**
Politics of Experience and Bird of Paradise
Explores more fully the conflicts between the individual's right to self-realisation and the demands of social conventions.
[UE97] Penguin pbk **£3.95**
Self and Others
[UE98] Penguin pbk **£3.95**
Voice of Experience
[UE99] Penguin pbk **£3.95**

MILNER, MARIAN
The Hands of the Living God
An account of psychoanalytic treatment including a case study in schizophrenia which lasted over 20 years.
[UE100] Virago pbk **£8.95**

PECK, M.S.
The Road Less Travelled
A very popular title by a practising psychiatrist on ways of facing difficulties and of reaching a higher level of understanding.
[UE101] Century pbk **£4.95**

REICH, WILHELM (1897 - 1957)
Best known for his work on sexual energy, 'Orgonomy', which led to his vilification by the scientific establishment. His theories on the flow of energy in the body, and on the relationship between the body and the emotions, have increased in popularity in recent years with the developments in holistic medicine.
Passion of Youth: An Autobiography
Reich's account of his own sexuality, and his encounters with Freud. **NEW**
[UE102] Pan hbk **£10.95**
BOADELLA, D.
In the Wake of Reich
[UE103] Coventure pbk **£5.50**
Wilhelm Reich: The Evolution of his Work
[UE104] Ark pbk **£6.95**
RYCROFT, CHARLES
Reich
One of the excellent *Modern Masters* series. A good introduction to Reich's ideas.
[UE105] Fontana pbk **£1.95**

STORR, ANTHONY (1920 -)
Perhaps the most important contemporary Jungian psychotherapist, Storr is well-known for his frequent broadcasts on radio and televison.

Dynamics of Creation
[UE106] Penguin pbk **£4.95**
Human Aggression
[UE107] Penguin pbk **£3.95**
The Art of Psychotherapy
[UE108] Secker hbk **£12.50**

SZASZ, THOMAS
Myth of Mental Illness
From a radical libertarian point of view, Szasz argues that the whole idea of mental illness is a socially damaging misconception. An important and stimulating polemic.
[UE109] Grafton pbk **£2.95**

General Psychology

ARGYLE, MICHAEL
Bodily Communication
The science of non-verbal communication explained.
[UE110] Methuen pbk **£10.95**
Psychology of Interpersonal Behaviour
A detailed analysis of social behaviour.
[UE111] Penguin pbk **£4.95**
The Psychology of Work
[UE112] Penguin pbk **£6.99**

BLAKEMORE, COLIN
The Mind Machine
A lavish book covering topics from the recent BBC television series.
[UE113] BBC hbk **£14.95**

BLAKEMORE, COLIN & GREENFIELD, SUSAN
Mindwaves
Well-known psychologists from many diverse areas apply the latest experimental findings to classic philosophical debates.
[UE114] Blackwell hbk **£22.50**

BODEN, M.
Computer Models of the Mind
Advances in Artificial Intelligence - what psychology and computer science have to offer each other: an excellent study.
[UE115] Cambridge pbk **£10.95**

BORBLEY, A.
Secrets of Sleep: New Light on Sleep, Dreams and Sleep Disorder
The science of sleep, dreaming and brain wave study.
[UE116] Penguin pbk **£4.95**

BROWN, GEORGE & HARRIS, TIRRIL
Social Origins of Depression
Case studies of female psychiatric disorder.
[UE117] Tavistock pbk **£10.95**

COOK, M. & MCHENRY, R.
Sexual Attraction
Everything you always wanted to know...
[UE118] Pergamon pbk **£6.00**

EISER, J. RICHARD
Social Psychology
[UE119] Cambridge pbk **£12.50**

GARNHAM, A.
Artificial Intelligence: An Introdution
Overview of this exciting and fast-growing field.
[UE120] Routledge pbk **£8.95**

GRAY, JEFFREY
The Psychology of Fear and Stress
Top contemporary behaviourist applies experimental findings to human and animal psychology.
[UE121] Cambridge pbk **£15.00**

GREGORY, R.L.
Eye and Brain: The Psychology of Seeing
An illustrated introduction to the psychology of perception.
[UE122] Weidenfeld pbk **£6.95**

JAMES, WILLIAM
The Principles of Psychology
Classic watershed work by a pioneering American figure in the field.
[UE123] Harvard UP Pbk **£15.25**

ORNSTEIN, R. & SOBEL, DAVID
The Healing Brain
Comprehensive overview of the brain, cognition, psycho-somatic and placebo effects.
[UE124] Macmillan hbk **£14.95**

PAVLOV, IVAN PETROVITCH
Russian experimental psychologist whose investigations into stimulus-response in dogs have provided the basis for modern behavioural science.
Conditioned Reflexes
Includes results of experiments on cerebral damage, conditioned reflexes, dogs, and sleep.
[UE125] Dover pbk **£7.45**
Lectures on Conditioned Reflexes
[UE126] Friedmann pbk **£4.95**
GRAY, JEFFREY
Pavlov
A brief and lucid introduction to Pavlov's work.
[UE127] Fontana pbk **£1.25**

SKINNER, B.F.
Leading American behaviourist whose work since the 1950s has been concerned with the development of techniques of social control, particularly the 'treatment' of criminal behaviour.
Beyond Freedom and Dignity
The most accessible introduction to Skinner's theories.
[UE128] Penguin pbk **£5.95**
Science and Human Behaviour
[UE129] Free P pbk **£9.50**

SMITH, ANTHONY
The Mind
A guided tour of the human brain.
[UE130] Penguin pbk **£4.95**

STERNBERG, ROBERT
The Psychologist's Companion
Invaluable guide to scientific writing style.
[UE131] Cambridge pbk **£7.50**

YOUNG, J.Z.
Philosophy and the Brain
Considers the nature of the mind from the levels of cell-biology and the anatomy of the brain to the nature of perception and will.
[UE132] Oxford pbk **£5.95**

Popular & Practical

See also the 'Psychological Health & Self-Help' section, in the *Health and Fitness* chapter.

BADDELEY, ALAN
Your Memory
A layman's guide to memory by a leading expert.
[UE133] Penguin pbk **£7.99**

BERNE, ERIC
Berne was an important early figure of 'Transactional Analysis'.

Games People Play
Not for fun, but to control their world, and the others in it.
[UE134] Penguin pbk **£2.30**
Sex in Human Loving
[UE135] Penguin pbk **£3.95**

BONO, EDWARD DE
The master of 'lateral thinking', his books are full of practical 'thought' experiments, and his ideas are easily absorbed.
De Bono's Thinking Course
[UE136] BBC pbk **£3.95**
Five-Day Course in Thinking
[UE137] Penguin pbk **£3.95**
Future Positive
[UE138] Penguin pbk **£3.99**
Lateral Thinking
Explains the difference between lateral and vertical thinking and the ways in which the former can short-circuit the latter. The secret is to look at problems any way but head-on.
[UE139] Penguin pbk **£3.95**
Letters to Thinkers: Further Thoughts on Lateral Thinking
A collection of 30 'letters' which summarise his 'thinking about thinking'.
[UE140] Penguin pbk **£4.99**
Mechanism of Mind
[UE141] Penguin pbk **£4.50**
Po: Beyond Yes and No
[UE142] Penguin pbk **£3.99**
Practical Thinking
Four ways to be right; five ways to be wrong; five ways to understand.
[UE143] Penguin pbk **£3.95**
Six Thinking Hats
[UE144] Penguin pbk **£4.50**
Teaching Thinking
[UE145] Penguin pbk **£4.95**
Use of Lateral Thinking
[UE146] Penguin pbk **£3.50**
Wordpower
Gain a new perspective on the meaning of words, and how to use them.
[UE147] Penguin pbk **£4.50**

BROMLEY, D.
Human Ageing
An introduction to gerontology.
[UE148] Penguin pbk **£6.95**

BROOK, STEPHEN
The Oxford Book of Dreams
An anthology of famous dreamers' recollections.
[UE149] Oxford pbk **£5.95**

BUZAN, TONY
Use Your Head
[UE150] BBC pbk **£3.95**

CHETWYND, T. (ED)
A Dictionary of Symbols
Jungian Archetypes in handy alphabetical format for the bedside table.
[UE151] Paladin pbk **£3.95**

DOMINIAN, JACK
Depression
Simple introduction to a condition that leads one in ten people to seek help during their lives.
[UE152] Fontana pbk **£1.95**

DYER, W.W.
Your Erroneous Zones
[UE153] Sphere pbk **£3.50**

EYSENCK, HANS
This clinical psychologist is best-known for developing scales and tests to quantify personality.
Check Your Own I.Q.
[UE154] Penguin pbk **£2.99**
Crime and Personality
[UE155] Grafton pbk **£1.25**
Know Your Own Personality
[UE156] Penguin pbk **£2.99**

FAST, JULIUS
American guru of the power dressers.
Body Language
[UE157] Pan pbk **£3.99**

FRIDAY, NANCY
Jealousy
[UE158] Fontana pbk **£3.95**
Men in Love
[UE159] Arrow pbk **£4.50**
My Mother My Self
[UE160] Fontana pbk **£4.50**

HAMPSON, SARAH E.
The Construction of Personality
Introduces current theory and research in the psychology of personality, from the perspective of constructivism.
[UE161] Routledge pbk **£8.95**

HINTON, J.
Dying
Psychiatrist's sympathetic study of patients with terminal illness.
[UE162] Penguin pbk **£4.99**

HOOPER, A.
The Body Electric: Sex Therapy for Women
[UE163] Unwin Hyman pbk **£2.50**

KIRSTA, ALIX
Victims: Surviving the Aftermath of Violent Crime
[UE164] Century **£5.95**

KUBLER-ROSS, ELISABETH
To Live Until We Say Goodbye
[UE165] Prentice-Hall pbk **£6.95**

LAKE, TONY
Living with Grief
[UE166] Sheldon P pbk **£3.95**
Loneliness
Why it happens and how to overcome it.
[UE167] Sheldon P pbk **£2.50**

LESSING, DORIS
Prisons We Choose to Live Inside
Why human beings continue to make the same mistakes.
[UE168] Cape hbk **£7.95**

LOWEN, ALEXANDER
Language of the Body
[UE169] Macmillan pbk **£3.95**
Love and Orgasm: Revolutionary Guide to Sexual Fulfilment
[UE170] Macmillan pbk **£3.95**

MASTERS, WILLIAM & JOHNSON, VIRGINIA
On Sex and Human Loving
[UE171] Papermac pbk **£9.95**

ORNSTEIN, ROBERT
Multimind
Compendium of psychological phenomena.
[UE172] Macmillan hbk **£10.95**

PARKES, COLIN
Bereavement
Studies of grief in adult life.
[UE173] Penguin pbk **£5.99**

PEASE, ALLAN
Body Language
How to read others' intentions and feelings by their gestures.
[UE174] Sheldon P pbk **£4.95**

PLANT, M.
Drugs in Perspective
Review of drug abuse in contemporary society with suggested therapies.
[UE175] Hodder pbk **£6.25**

POSTON, C.
Reclaiming Our Lives: Adult Survivors of Incest
Interviews with, and self-help for, victims of incest.
[UE176] Little Brown pbk **£10.95**

ROGERS, CARL
Client Centred Therapy
[UE177] Constable pbk **£6.95**

ROWE, DOROTHY
A leading clinical psychologist in the UK today.
Beyond Fear
An examination of fear, particularly the fear of self-destruction.
[UE178] Fontana pbk **£4.95**
Chosing Not Losing
The strange world of suffering inhabited by the depressive.
[UE179] Fontana pbk **£4.95**
Depression: Experience of Depression
The 'MIND Book of the Year' in 1983.
[UE180] Routledge pbk **£4.50**

SACKS, OLIVER
A specialist in disorders of the brain. Sacks writes in an accessible and entertaining style.
A Leg to Stand On
Sacks's most recent work which combines scientific analysis with profound philosophical meditation.
[UE181] Duckworth hbk **£12.95**
[UE182] Picador pbk **£3.95**
Awakenings
A fascinating account of the 1920s sleeping sickness epidemic, and the 'miracle drug' that cured its victims.
[UE183] Picador pbk **£4.95**
Migraine
[UE184] Pan pbk **£3.95**
The Man who Mistook his Wife for a Hat
Extraordinary neurological cases including a patient who leans like the Tower of Pisa, a woman who has lost all sense of her own body and a distinguished musician who fails to recognise everyday objects.
[UE185] Duckworth hbk **£12.95**
[UE186] Picador pbk **£3.99**

SARNOFF, DOROTHY & MOORE, GAYLEN
Never be Nervous Again
How to overcome nervousness and awkwardness when communicating in public.
[UE187] Century pbk **£4.95**

SCHREIBER, FLORA RHETA
Sybil
A popular and very moving story of the successful treatment of a woman whose personality was split into no less than sixteen different characters.
[UE188] Penguin pbk **£3.99**

SHEPARD, MARTIN
Do-It-Yourself Psychotherapy
A self-help alternative to formal psychotherapy.
[UE189] Macdonald Orbis pbk **£4.95**

SKYNNER, ROBIN & CLEESE, JOHN
Families and How to Survive Them
Family therapy explored in an accessible way.
[UE190] Methuen pbk **£4.99**

VINES, R.
Agoraphobia: The Fear of Panic
An investigation of the phobia, with advice on how phobias generally may be successfully treated by simple therapy.
[UE191] Fontana pbk **£3.95**

WARNOCK, MARY
Memory
A lucid examination which aims to discover why we set such value on our ability to recall the past. The book discusses famous poets, novelists and diarists.
[UE192] Faber pbk **£5.99**

WEEKES, C.
Self Help for Your Nerves
[UE193] Angus & R hbk **£5.95**

WEEKS, J.
Sexuality and its Discontents
[UE194] Routledge pbk **£9.95**

WILSON, COLIN
The Misfits: A Study of Sexual Outsiders
Well-documented historical profiles of eccentric sexuality.
[UE195] Grafton pbk **£4.50**

Child Psychology

AXLINE, VIRGINIA
Dibs: In Search of Self
Moving account of the journey of one child from his resistance to learning to a full realisation of his potential, written in a manner that is readable and engaging.
[UE196] Penguin pbk **£3.99**

BETTELHEIM, BRUNO
A Good Enough Parent
Drawing from a wealth of experience and a vast amount of information, Bettelheim reveals that there are no hard and fast rules for parenthood.
[UE197] Pan pbk **£6.99**

BOWER, T.
The Perceptual World of the Child
[UE198] Fontana pbk **£2.95**

BREMNER, GAVIN
Infancy
An introduction to the perceptual, cognitive and social development of infants.
[UE199] Blackwell pbk **£7.50**

DONALDSON, MARGARET
Children's Minds
[UE200] Fontana pbk **£3.95**

ERIKSON, ERIK
Childhood and Society
One of the most widely quoted and discussed works of developmental psychology.
[UE201] Grafton pbk **£3.95**

Toys and Reasons
Erikson's famous study of the 'ritualization of experience'.
[UE202] Boyars pbk **£3.95**

GARVEY, C.
Children's Talk
[UE203] Fontana pbk **£2.95**
Play
[UE204] Fontana pbk **£2.95**

HOLT, JOHN
How Children Fail
[UE205] Penguin pbk **£4.95**
How Children Learn
[UE206] Penguin pbk **£4.95**

MONTESSORI, MARIA
An Italian educationalist whose teaching methods are still practiced in special schools and as part of the curriculum in traditionally-run schools. Open classrooms, readiness programmes and team teaching can be traced back to the Montessori Method.
Secret of Childhood
[UE207] Longman pbk **£3.95**

PAPERT, SEYMOUR
Mindstorms: Children, Computers and Powerful Ideas
An important and readable study of the use of computers in education.
[UE208] Harvester pbk **£7.95**

PIAGET, JEAN
Piaget is best-known for his theories of how children learn to think.
Moral Judgement of the Child
[UE209] Penguin pbk **£6.90**
Origin of Intelligence in the Child
[UE210] Penguin pbk **£5.95**
The Child's Conception of Movement and Speed
[UE211] Routledge hbk **£9.75**
The Psychology of Intelligence
[UE212] Routledge hbk **£19.95**
ATKINSON, CHRISTINE
Making Sense of Piaget: The Philosophical Roots
An attempt to explain the metaphysical foundations of Piaget's work.
[UE213] Routledge hbk **£19.95**
BODEN, MARGARET
Piaget
[UE214] Fontana pbk **£4.95**
RICHMOND, P.G.
An Introduction to Piaget
[UE215] Routledge pbk **£5.95**

SCHAFFER, R.
Mothering
[UE216] Fontana pbk **£3.50**

STANWAY, ANDREW
Preparing for Life
A parent's guide to the psychological and emotional life of children from conception to puberty.
[UE217] Viking hbk **£12.95**

TREADWELL, P.
A Parent's Guide to the Problems of Adolescence
[UE218] Penguin pbk **£5.99**

VILLIERS, P. & J. DE
Early Language
How children learn to speak and the causes of autism.
[UE219] Fontana pbk **£2.50**

WINNICOTT, DONALD
Home is Where We Start From
A collection of papers written for laymen which provides perhaps the best introduction to the work of one of Britain's most perceptive and gifted analysts.
[UE220] Penguin pbk **£4.95**
Human Nature
An overview of his thinking.
[UE221] Free Assoc pbk **£8.95**
Playing and Reality
[UE222] Penguin pbk **£4.95**
The Child, the Family and the Outside World
[UE223] Penguin pbk **£4.50**

WOOD, DAVID
How Children Think and Learn
Interpreting studies of children's powers of attention concentration and and memory.
[UE224] Blackwell pbk **£7.95**

WOMEN'S STUDIES

Listed together here are critical and historical works on Women's Studies, the writings of major figures within the movement, and a range of more practical titles covering aspects of psychology and health.

ALEGRIA, CLARIBEL
They Won't Take Me Alive
Salvadorean women in the struggle for national liberation.
[UF1] Women's P pbk **£3.95**

ALIC, MARGARET
Hypatia's Heritage
A history of women in science from antiquity to the late 19th century.
[UF2] Women's P pbk **£4.95**

ALLEN, SHEILA & WOLKOWITZ, CAROL
Homeworking: Myths and Realities
A stimulating insight into the issue of waged work in the home. Lays the groundwork for a thorough critique.
[UF3] Macmillan pbk **£8.50**

ARCANA, JUDITH
Every Mother's Son: The Role of Mothers in the Making of Men
Asks if it is possible to raise boys in a non-sexist way.
[UF4] Women's P pbk **£4.95**
Our Mothers' Daughters
[UF5] Women's P pbk **£5.95**

ATIYA, NYRA
Khul-Khaal: Five Egyptian Women Tell Their Stories
Considers a country where boys are more precious than girls, and where the rituals include female circumcision.
[UF6] Virago pbk **£8.99**

ATTALLAH, NAIM
Women
An account of Attallah's interviews with 289 women from a wide variety of backgrounds and countries including novelists, businesswomen and aristocrats. They give their views of fundamental issues from sexuality and motherhood to feminism and the nature of relationships. This book is a forum in which women express their dilemmas and fears.
[UF7] Quartet pbk **£5.95**

BANKS, OLIVE
Becoming a Feminist: The Socal Origins of 'First Wave' Feminism
[UF8] Harvester **£27.50**
Faces of Feminism
The most complete history to date of women's movements across the centuries.
[UF9] M Robertson pbk **£9.95**
The Biographical Dictionary of British Feminists
[UF10] Harvester hbk **£60.00**

BARRETT, MICHELE
Women's Oppression Today
An incisive discussion of the uncertain common future of Marxism and feminism.
[UF11] Verso pbk **£8.95**

BARRETT, MICHELE & MCINTOSH, MARY
The Anti-Social Family
An illuminating critique on the seemingly indestructible institution of marriage.
[UF12] Verso pbk **£4.95**

BEAUVOIR, SIMONE DE (1908 - 1986)
Two of the most important elements of 20th century thought - existentialism and feminism - meet in the work of Simone de Beauvoir. Novelist, and chronicler of the cultural ferment of modern France, de Beauvoir's magnum opus is *The Second Sex*, a huge and controversial work tracing the oppression of women through the ages using the evidence of myth and psychology as well as history. Her work has exerted an incalculable influence on all subsequent feminist writing.
The Second Sex
A landmark in the history of feminism. It explores the misrepresentation of women throughout the ages from biological, historical, psychoanalytic and mythological view-points. Scholarly, witty and lucid.
[UF13] Picador pbk **£7.95**
APPIGNANESI, LISA
Simone de Beauvoir
Illuminates the conflicts caused by Simone de Beauvoir's lifelong devotion to Sartre, and examines the contradictions in her feminism.
[UF14] Penguin pbk **£3.95**
EVANS, MARY
Simone de Beauvoir: A Feminist Mandarin
Assesses the contribution of Simone de Beauvoir's work to Western feminism.
[UF15] Tavistock pbk **£6.95**

BEDDOE, DEIRDRE
Discovering Women's History
[UF16] Pandora pbk **£4.95**

BEECHEY, VERONICA
Unequal Work
A series of seminal essays on women's work, the labour process, patriarchy and unemployment.
[UF17] Verso pbk **£7.95**

BEECHEY, VERONICA & WHITLEGG, ELIZABETH (ED)
Women in Britain Today
A book mainly used by sociology students, it is also of interest to the general reader.
[UF18] Open UP pbk **£7.95**

BENHABIB, SEYLA & CORNELL, DRUCILLA
Feminism as Critique
Essays on the politics of gender in advanced capitalist societies, drawing upon the latest theoretical developments in innovative and challenging ways.
[UF19] Polity P pbk **£8.50**

Simone de Beauvoir, author of *The Second Sex* (Picador pbk £7.95)

BERNHEIMER, CHARLES & KAHANE, CLAIRE (EDS)
In Dora's Case: Freud, Hysteria & Feminism
Essays offering an analysis of Freud and the feminine. Contributions by notable thinkers, including Jane Gallop, Jacques Lacan and Erik Erikson. Questions the emphasis of the Oedipal father over the pre-Oedipal mother, and Freud's reluctance to admit his own counter-transference. Ground-breaking and controversial.
[UF20] Virago pbk **£7.99**

BETTERTON, ROSEMARY (ED)
Looking On: Images of Femininity in the Visual Arts and Media
[UF21] Pandora pbk **£7.95**

BIRKE, LYNDA
Women Feminism and Biology: The Feminist Challenge
An important step towards the development of a feminine science. Argues that an individual's biology is continually and dynamically interacting with the environment. Controversial and provocative.
[UF22] Harvester pbk **£9.95**

BLACK, CLEMENTINA
Married Women's Work
The report of an enquiry undertaken by the Women's Industrial Council.
[UF23] Virago pbk **£6.50**

BOSTON WOMEN'S HEALTH COLLECTIVE
Our Bodies Ourselves
[UF25] Penguin pbk **£8.95**

BOSTON, SARAH
Woman Workers and the Trade Unions
A history of women workers' organisations and struggles from the mid-19th century to the present day.
[UF26] Lawrence & W pbk **£8.95**

Women's Studies

Lynne Segal

Hidden from History was the title the pioneering contemporary feminist historian Sheila Rowbotham gave to her book summing up the lives and legacies of half of humanity back in 1973, when the women's liberation movement in Britain was at its most passionate and confident. Women's Studies in this country emerged from that movement to uncover and explore the neglected, complex patterns of women's participation in the making of history, and to inspire and to promote their self-conscious engagement in the rethinking of every field of academic endeavour to include the experiences and perspectives of women.

Like any youthful discipline, asserting while still discovering its identity and credentials, Women's Studies has always generated passionate controversy within and around itself. In the beginning, within feminist debate, as more and more Women's Studies courses were offered first of all in adult education (in the early 1970s) and then increasingly in schools, polytechnics and universities (from the late 1970s) some feminists stood firm against what they saw as the divorce of theory from practice. The feminist scholarship in the academy was often criticised for being too detached from the feminist activism of the movement. The first two texts written specifically for Women's Studies were the essays collected in *Feminism and Materialism* edited by Annette Kuhn and AnnMarie Wolpe in 1977, and *Women Take Issue* edited by the Women's Studies Group Centre for Contemporary Cultural Studies in 1978. They begin by addressing 'the problem of "theoreticism"' and 'disagreements over what our practice should be', respectively. Today, with the fragmentation of the women's movement into more distinctive feminisms and the decline of radical politics more generally, the question of the link between theory and practice is no longer a centre or, some Women's Studies scholars would suggest, even a relevant question.

Controversy from within feminist thinking now focuses on the distinctiveness of the theoretical framework and methodology of Women's Studies, and on the type of contribution it makes to specific disciplines through attention to women's experience and to men's dominance over women as a basic axis of power in all social relations (or do women's perspectives challenge the whole foundation of 'male-defined' academic disciplines?) Dale Spender, probably the most prolific author and organiser in the area of Women's Studies, rejects the former position in *Men's Studies Modified* (1981) contrasting the theoretical and methodological basis of women's studies with 'men's knowledge'. Women's Studies, she argues, needs to reclaim the separate and distinct knowledge of women throughout history. With her usual passionate eloquence and irony the US poet Adrienne Rich (1981) endorses this position: 'The question now facing Women's Studies ... is the extent to which she has, in the past decade, matured into the dutiful daughter of the white, patriarchal university - a daughter who threw tantrums and played the tomboy when she was younger but who has now learned to wear a dress and speak almost as nicely as Daddy wants her to.' It is shared also by many other well known US feminist writers, like Catherine MacKinnon (1982) or Andrea Dworkin (1976).

In contrast, other feminists would stress that what is distinctive about Women's Studies is not so much exploring the separate experience and knowledge of women (never separate from the conceptual frameworks women share with men), nor rejecting existing criteria for intellectual objectivity (critical assessment of competing theories), but cutting across and transforming all existing academic discourses through an examination of the power relations of gender as a basic category of analysis. This involves shifting the basis of existing analyses, like the recent impressive historical study by Leonore Davidoff and Catherine Hall: *Family Fortunes: Men and Women of the English Middle Class 1780-1850* (1987). This has meant beginning the laborious work of 'deconstructing' all existing conceptual frameworks to expose and move on from their traditional androcentric viewpoint. These issues of feminist theory and methodology, of how the addition of women's experience changes the epistemological basis of knowledge, are addressed in Dorothy Smith's (forthcoming) *Everyday World as Problematic*. Others, especially those like Bell Hooks in *Ain't I a Woman: Black Women and Feminism* (1982), mindful of the important recent contributions of black feminist theory and culture, or Anne Phillips addressing the problematic interaction of gender and class, in *Divided Loyalties* (1987), would question whether 'women' have a common experience, whether gender identity overrides other identities of race, class, religion, or ethnicity.

The field of Women's Studies, it should be clear, is exceptionally diverse. Writers agree on little other than the importance of creating a space for the broadest possible cross-disciplinary perspectives to focus upon the task of bringing women's complex experiences into view. This interest in women's experience has generated a vast flowering of both creative and critical writing by women. In literary criticism, for example, Elaine Showalter's *A Literature of their Own: British Women Novelists from Bronte to Lessing* (1977) is already a classic of this genre. Gayle Greene and Coppelia Kahn's *Making the Difference: Feminist Literary Criticism* (1985) is a more recent example. The parallel emphasis on gender relations as an axis of power has expanded to include the growing production of men's writing on the social construction and functioning of masculinity. Men, once merely the unprobed norm of humanity, with women and 'femininity' marginalised or studied as a 'social problem', are now the object rather than the unexamined subject of academic exploration - the new 'social problem' of our time.

Although the oldest and most prestigious British universities have been slow to acknowledge the academic legitimacy of Women's Studies, the impact of feminist ideas and research in the academy has been rapid and profound. Few disciplines in the humanities or social sciences today can appear credibly up to date without recognition of the feminist impact. This in turn has been nurtured and fostered by the space provided by Women's Studies.

Feature

BRENNAN, TERESA (ED)
Between Feminism and Psychoanalysis `NEW`
Contributors from Britain, France and the United States renegotiate the alternatives posed for feminism by psychoanalytic theory.
[UF27] Routledge pbk **£8.95**

BROD, HARRY (ED)
The Making of Masculinity: The New Men's Studies
[UF28] Unwin Hyman hbk **£30.00**

BROWNMILLER, SUSAN
Against Our Will: Men, Women and Rape
A startling account which reveals that rape, due to socialisation, has become a 'natural' condition of life.
[UF29] Penguin pbk **£5.99**

BRUMBERG, JOAN JACOBS
Fasting Girls: The Emergence of Anorexia Nervosa as a Modern Disease
Explains why anorexia is so prevalent today and shows that this malady is by no means peculiar to the 20th century.
[UF24] Harvard UP hbk **£19.95**

BURCHELL, HELEN & MILLMAN, VAL (ED)
Changing Perspectives on Gender
Looks at national initiatives which provide opportunities for work on gender equality.
[UF30] Open UP pbk **£8.95**

BUTLER, SANDRA & WINTRAM, CLARE
Feminist Groupwork `NEW`
A survey of the process by which women can work in groups to analyse their social and psychological worlds.
[UF31] Sage pbk **£7.95**

CALDECOTT, LEONIE & LELAND, STEPHANIE (EDS)
Reclaim the Earth: Women Speak Out for Life on Earth
[UF32] Women's P pbk **£4.95**

CAMERON, DEBORAH
Feminism and Linguistic Theory
A critical survey of recent work on sexism and language.
[UF33] Macmillan pbk **£8.95**

CAMERON, DEBORAH & FRAZER, ELIZABETH
The Lust to Kill
One of the first feminist analyses of sexual murder and its relation to the question of gender. Essential reading for those who wish to understand why women are the victims of such crimes and not the perpetrators.
[UF34] Polity P pbk **£7.95**

CAMPBELL, BEATRICE
The Iron Ladies: Why Do Women Vote Tory?
Prominent Tory women are interviewed by this Marxist feminist and asked about their politics.
[UF35] Virago pbk **£5.50**
Unofficial Secrets: Child Abuse
A critical look at the Cleveland affair from one of Britain's leading feminist journalists.
[UF36] Virago pbk **£4.99**
Wigan Pier Revisited
Unemployment in Britain in the 1980s, from a woman's perspective.
[UF37] Virago pbk **£4.95**

Angela Carter, author of *Nothing Sacred* (Virago pbk £4.99)

CARTER, ANGELA (1940 -)
Polemical and frequently hilarious, Angela Carter's essays bear as unconventional a relationship to doctrinaire feminism or literary criticism as her fiction does to the popular novel. Her analysis of de Sade's sexual politics is a tremendous achievement - a truly imaginative work of criticism which is funny, wise and disturbing by turns.
Nothing Sacred: Selected Writings
[UF38] Virago pbk **£4.99**
The Sadeian Woman: An Exercise in Cultural History
A bold and stylish assault on the clichés surrounding woman's sexuality.
[UF39] Virago pbk **£4.99**

CARTER, APRIL
The Politics of Women's Rights
Looks at the current status of women in Britain.
[UF40] Longman pbk **£5.95**

CARTER, ERICA & WATNEY, SIMON (EDS)
Taking Liberties: AIDS and Cultural Politics `NEW`
[UF41] Serpent's Tail pbk **£8.95**

CARTLEDGE, SUE & RYAN, JOANNA (EDS)
Sex and Love: New Thoughts on Old Contradictions
[UF42] Women's P pbk **£5.95**

CHAMBERLAIN, MARY
Growing Up in Lambeth `NEW`
[UF42A] Virago pbk **£6.99**

CHAPMAN, ROWENA & RUTHERFORD, JONATHAN (ED)
Male Order: Unwrapping Masculinity
Essays on the changing meaning of masculinity.
[UF43] Lawrence & W pbk **£7.95**

CHERNIN, KIM
The Hungry Self: Women, Eating and Identity
Explores women's problematic relationship with food.
[UF44] Virago pbk **£4.95**

CHODOROW, NANCY
Feminism and Psychoanalytic Theory `NEW`
A re-examination of a troubled relationship from the author of the classic *The Reproduction of Mothering* (1978).
[UF45] Polity P hbk **£25.00**

CLEMENT, CATHERINE (1939 -)
One of the leading French feminists and a practising analyst.
The Weary Sons of Freud
Addressing the question of the social function of psychoanalysis, this traces the history of the psychoanalytic movement from Freud to Lacan and their followers today, and calls into question the development of psychoanalysis. Alongside her attack on this elitist, self-perpetuating institution, Clement includes her own personal account of analysis at the end of each chapter.
[UF46] Verso pbk **£6.95**
Opera, or the Undoing of Women `NEW`
A new study of the ways in which the subject matter and form of opera enshrined a social order of which the repression of women was an integral part.
[UF46A] Virago pbk **£7.50**

COCKBURN, CYNTHIA
Brothers
The gendering of skill in the printers' unions.
[UF47] Pluto P pbk **£6.25**
The Machinery of Dominance
Essays on the gendering of technical knowledge.
[UF48] Pluto P pbk **£6.95**

CONNELL, ROBERT WILLIAM
Gender and Power: Society, the Person and Sexual Politics
Uncovers the power structures inherent in a phallocentric society. A lucid and rigorous debate.
[UF49] Blackwell pbk **£8.50**

COOTE, ANNA & CAMPBELL, BEATRICE
Sweet Freedom: The Struggle for Women's Liberation
[UF50] Blackwell pbk **£7.95**

COYLE, ANGELA
Redundant Women
[UF51] Women's P pbk **£3.95**

COYLE, ANGELA & SKINNER, JANE (EDS)
Women and Work: Positive Action for Change `NEW`
[UF52] Macmillan pbk **£7.95**

DALLEY, GILLIAN
Ideologies of Caring: Rethinking Community and Collectivism
As the burden of caring for the elderly and disabled falls mainly upon women, many feminists have tried to address this question. Dalley offers new practical solutions.
[UF53] Macmillan pbk **£7.95**

DALY, MARY (1928 -)
An American feminist and theological writer, Daly holds a radical feminist perspective towards patriarchal society. She led the way with 'spiritual feminism', a metaphysical alternative to patriarchal religions.
Beyond God the Father: Towards a Philosophy of Women's Liberation
[UF54] Women's P pbk **£4.95**
Gyn/Ecology
A radical work which portrays men as parasites on women and encourages women to withdraw from a man-centred world to create a new society.
[UF55] Women's P pbk **£6.95**

SOCIAL SCIENCES

Pure Lust: Elemental Feminist Philosophy
Reveals women's 'lust' for change.
[UF56] Women's P pbk **£5.95**
Wickedary
'Webster's first new intergalactic wickedary of the English language'.
[UF57] Womens P pbk **£8.95**
Women and Poverty NEW
[UF57A] Attic P pbk **£3.95**

DAVIDOFF, LEONORE & HALL, CATHERINE
Family Fortunes
Gender relations in the English middle classes, 1780-1850.
[UF58] Unwin Hyman pbk **£10.95**

DAVIDSON, CAROLINE
A Woman's Work is Never Done
An illustrated and informative account of labour in the home through the ages.
[UF59] Chatto pbk **£9.95**

DAVIES, K. ET AL
Out of Focus: Writings on Women and the Media
Madonna, Margaret Thatcher and Hilda Ogden are among those discussed in terms of media stereotypes of women.
[UF60] Women's P pbk **£5.95**

DAVIS, ANGELA
Women, Race and Class
Deals with the history of black women under slavery, and working women in industrial societies, showing the connections between racism, sexism and class oppression.
[UF61] Women's P pbk **£5.95**

DELACOSTE, FREDERIQUE & ALEXANDER, PRISCILLA
Sex Work
Writings by women in the sex industry.
[UF62] Virago pbk **£5.50**

DEX, SHIRLEY
The Sexual Division of Work: Conceptual Revolutions in the Social Sciences
[UF63] Harvester pbk **£9.95**

DICKSON, ANNE
A Woman in Your Own Right
Now a standard work of assertiveness training for women.
[UF64] Quartet pbk **£3.95**
The Mirror Within: A New Look at Sexuality
[UF65] Quartet pbk **£3.95**

DOWLING, COLETTE
Perfect Women NEW
[UF65A] Collins hbk **£15.00**
The Cinderella Complex: Women's Hidden Fear of Independence
Shows that the conflict between wanting to be independent and the the need to be taken care of can, when experienced together, defeat themselves.
[UF66] Fontana pbk **£3.50**

DWORKIN, ANDREA (1946 -)
An American writer, novelist, poet and political activist who is a powerful voice in the women's movement today. She is best known for her writings on male dominance, particularly as expressed through sex, violence against women, and pornography.
Intercourse
'The most shocking book any feminist has yet written', according to Germaine Greer. Dworkin

rethinks each implication of the sexual act and challenges morals and attitudes.
[UF67] Arrow pbk **£3.50**
Letters from a War Zone
Includes speeches, interviews and essays.
[UF68] Secker pbk **£5.95**
Pornography: Men Possessing Women
[UF69] Women's P pbk **£5.95**
Right-Wing Women: The Politics of Domesticated Females
[UF70] Women's P pbk **£5.95**

ECKER, GISELA (ED)
Feminist Aesthetics
Collected essays on writing, architecture and painting.
[UF71] Women's P pbk **£4.95**

EICHENBAUM, LUISE & ORBACH, SUSIE
Bittersweet
Subtitled 'Facing up to Feelings of Love, Envy and Competition in Women's Friendships', this is a recent study that has its roots in the authors' own relationship.
[UF72] Arrow pbk **£2.99**
Understanding Women
Major new theory of women's psychology. It challenges Freudian orthodoxy and biological determinism.
[UF73] Penguin pbk **£4.99**
What do Women Want?
[UF74] Fontana pbk **£3.50**

EISENSTEIN, HESTER
Contemporary Feminist Thought
[UF75] Unwin Hyman pbk **£3.95**

EISENSTEIN, SARAH
Give us Bread but Give us Roses
Working women's consciousness in the US between 1890 and World War I.
[UF76] Routledge pbk **£9.95**

ERNST, SHEILA & GOODISON, LUCY
In Our Own Hands: A Book of Self-Help Therapy
[UF77] Women's P pbk **£5.95**
Living with the Sphinx: Papers from the Women's Therapy Centre
[UF78] Women's P pbk **£5.95**

FADERMAN, LILLIAN
Surpassing the Love of Men
Romantic friendship and love between women from the Renaissance to the present.
[UF79] Women's P pbk **£6.95**

FEMINIST REVIEW
Sexuality: A Reader
Challenging and lively essays on themes central to feminist thought, including pornography, sexual violence, and the twin concepts of 'masculinity' and 'feminity'.
[UF80] Virago pbk **£7.99**
Waged Work: A Reader
13 essays including contributions by Veronica Beechey, Sheila Allen and Carol Wolkowitz.
[UF81] Virago pbk **£7.99**

FERGERSON, ANN
Blood at the Root NEW
An interesting new approach to current political debates about the future of feminism.
[UF82] Pandora pbk **£7.95**

FORSTER, MARGARET
Significant Sisters: The Grassroots of Active Feminism 1839 - 1939
Traces the lives and careers of eight women each of

whom pioneered vital changes in the spheres of law, education, the professions, morals and politics.
[UF83] Penguin pbk **£4.95**

FRIEDAN, BETTY (1921 -)
American pupil of the great Gestalt psychologist, Kurt Kaffka, she worked as a clinical psychologist and in applied social reseach. Founder of the National Organisation for Women in 1966, she was President for the first five years, and is prominent in many other women's organisations.
Feminine Mystique
A powerful and illuminating analysis of the position of women in Western society. When published in 1963 it met with an enormous response, and led to Friedan being called 'the mother of the New Feminist Movement'.
[UF84] Penguin pbk **£4.99**
Second Stage
An outspoken and incisive book which proposes a plan of action for today.
[UF85] Sphere pbk **£2.95**

GALLOP, JANE
Feminism and Psychoanalysis: The Daughter's Seduction
A classic work discussing the intersection between Lacanian psychoanalysis and feminist theory.
[UF86] Macmillan pbk **£9.95**

GAMMAN, LORRAINE & MARSHMENT, MARGARET
The Female Gaze
A provocative collection of essays showing how women's views affect and interact with popular culture from Madonna to Thatcher.
[UF87] Women's P pbk **£6.95**

GHADIALLY, REHANA (ED) NEW
Women in Indian Society: A Reader
[UF88] Sage pbk **£13.00**

GILBERT, HARRIET & ROCHE, CHRISTINE
Women's History of Sex
An amusing yet erudite exploration of Western woman's sexuality, throughout the ages. Ranging from the chastity-belt to the pill, it presents the full history of women's experiences of sex.
[UF89] Routledge pbk **£5.95**

GORDON, LINDA
Heroes of Their Own Lives NEW
A rich and detailed history of family violence in Boston from the standpoint of its victims.
[UF90] Virago pbk **£11.99**

GOSTELOW, MARY
Complete Woman's Reference Book
[UF92] Penguin pbk **£6.95**

Mary Daly, author of *Pure Lust: Elemental Feminist Philosophy* (Women's Press pbk £5.95)

Germaine Greer, author of *Daddy, We Hardly Knew You* (Hamish Hamilton hbk £13.95)

GREER, GERMAINE (1939 -)
Australian feminist critic. Well known as a *Sunday Times* columnist, a writer for *Punch* and as a freelance journalist, the British media have presented her as a leader of the Women's Liberation Movement. However, she prefers to be seen for her individual views, many of which have been considered controversial, and even offensive by some feminists.
Daddy, We Hardly Knew You   NEW
Greer's most recent book is a quest to uncover the reality behind her father's life.
[UF93] H Hamilton hbk **£13.95**
Mad Woman's Underclothes
Essays (1968 - 85)
[UF94] Picador pbk **£4.99**
Sex and Destiny: Politics of Human Fertility
Although it is criticized for contradicting her earlier ideas of the importance of sexual freedom, Greer has said that changes in her ideas have been developments rather than changes in direction, many of them coming out of her experience of life in other cultures. This book was researched in India.
[UF95] Pan pbk **£2.95**
The Female Eunuch
A great and far-reaching inspiration to the women's movement which brought Greer fame. It uncovers the many aspects of women's subordination and calls on women to fight individually for independence.
[UF96] Paladin pbk **£3.99**

GRIFFIN, SUSAN
Made from this Earth
A collection of essays dealing with the difficulties of being a woman and an artist in our divided society.
[UF97] Women's P pbk **£4.95**
Pornography and Silence
[UF98] Women's P pbk **£5.95**
Woman and Nature: The Roaring Inside Her
[UF99] Women's P pbk **£4.95**

HAMILTON, CICELY
Marriage as a Trade
A classic polemic against marriage, written during the suffragette struggle.
[UF100] Women's P pbk **£2.95**

HARDING, SANDRA (ED)
Feminism and Methodology
An excellent introduction to the methodological and epistemological issues faced by academics in all subjects concerned with feminism.
[UF101] Open UP pbk **£7.95**

HARDYMENT, C.
From Mangle to Microwave
An absorbing history of the mechanisation of housework which questions the meaning of labour-sharing devices. Also a fascinating social history from the 19th century kitchen-maid's point of view.
[UF102] Polity P hbk **£15.00**

HEWLETT, SYLVIA ANN
A Lesser Life: The Myth of Woman's Liberation
Controversial assertion that women are now worse off than their mothers, having lost the protection of traditional marriage.
[UF103] Sphere pbk **£4.99**

HIJAB, NADIA
Womanpower
The lively but little-reported debate on women's position in the modern Arab world.
[UF104] Cambridge pbk **£8.95**

HITE, SHERE
Women and Love: A Cultural Revolution in Progress
The controversial new 'Hite Report' is a survey of women's experience of love. The author, Shere Hite, spent seven years collecting opinions and views from a cross-section of American women, and her report contains some very interesting insights: in particular, a large proportion of married women claimed to feel extremely isolated and lonely even within their marriages.
[UF105] Penguin pbk **£5.99**

HOOKS, BELL
Ain't I a Woman: Black Women and Feminism
A classic of Black feminism.
[UF106] Pluto pbk **£5.95**
Talking Back: Thinking Feminism, Thinking Black   NEW
[UF106A] South End P pbk **£7.50**

IRIGARAY, LUCE (1939 -)
A practising psychoanalyst, well-known for her disagreement with Jacques Lacan. Her studies have concentrated on femininity and language and she argues that women's language, as well as their unique sexuality, is repressed in a patriarchal society.
Speculum of the Other Woman
Exposes the phallocentric nature of Western philosophy in which the feminine is relegated to the realm of the unthinkable. Also attacks psychoanalytic theory for its blind acceptance of the forms suggested by structuralism, and for its view of woman as a castrated man.
[UF107] Cornell UP pbk **£16.80**
This Sex Which is Not One
Continues the themes in *Speculum*, but this is a more accessible text. It envisages a world in which the feminine can function alongside the masculine, and is essential reading for anyone interested in French feminism.
[UF108] Cornell UP pbk **£12.85**

JORDAN, JUNE
Moving towards Home: Political Essays   NEW
[UF108A] Virago pbk **£5.99**

JOUVE, NICOLE WARD
The Street Cleaner
A sophisticated, in-depth study of Peter Sutcliffe, the 'Yorkshire Ripper'.
[UF109] Boyars pbk **£6.95**

KELLY, LIZ
Surviving Sexual Violence
[UF110] Polity P pbk **£8.50**

KENNEDY, ELLEN & MENDUS, SUSAN
Women in Western Political Philsophy
[UF111] Harvester pbk **£9.95**

KENNER, CHARMIAN
No Time for Women: Exploring Women's Health in the 1930s and Today
[UF112] Pandora pbk **£5.50**

KENYON, EDWIN
The Dilemma of Abortion
Discusses moral, religious, medical, legal, psychological and political issues of abortion. A critical look at the Warnock Report and comments on the Gillick case.
[UF113] Faber pbk **£6.50**

KIMMEL, MICHAEL S. (ED)
Changing Men
A wide-ranging collection from the emerging field of 'men's studies'.
[UF114] Sage pbk **£14.50**

KITZINGER, S.
Woman's Experience of Sex
Places sex in the context of life, and writes about women's feelings concerning their bodies and many different dimensions of sexual experience.
[UF115] Penguin pbk **£7.99**

KOONZ, CLAUDIA
Mothers in the Fatherland
A highly acclaimed study of women and the family in Nazi Germany.
[UF116] Methuen pbk **£8.50**

Shere Hite, author of *Women and Love: A Cultural Revolution in Progress* (Penguin pbk £5.99)

KRAMARAE, CHERIS & TREICHLER, PAUL
A Feminist Dictionary
[UF117] Pandora pbk **£6.95**

KRZOWSKI, SUE & LAND, PAT (EDS)
In Our Experience
Accounts of a series of workshops at the Women's
Therapy Centre.
[UF118] Women's P pbk **£6.95**

KUZWAYO, ELLEN
Call Me Woman
A remarkable autobiography written to represent
the struggles of all Black women in South
Africa.
[UF119] Women's P pbk **£5.95**

LAWRENCE, MARILYN (ED)
**Fed Up & Hungry: Women, Oppression
and Food**
Stimulating and positive collection of essays by
women who have direct experience, personal or
professional, of anorexia, bulimia and compulsive
eating.
[UF120] Women's P pbk **£5.95**
The Anorexic Experience
[UF121] Women's P pbk **£4.95**

LENNON, MARY; MCADAM, MARIE &
O'BRIEN, JOANNE
Across the Water
Looks at Irish women's lives in Britain.
[UF122] Virago pbk **£7.99**

LERNER, GERDA
The Creation of Patriarchy
A radical reassessment of gender role and its historic
basis in Western civilisation.
[UF123] Oxford pbk **£6.95**

LEWIS, CHARLIE & O'BRIEN, MARGARET
Reasessing Fatherhood
New observations on fatherhood in the modern
family.
[UF124] Sage pbk **£9.95**

LIDDINGTON, JILL
The Long Road to Greenham   **NEW**
A major new study of feminism and anti-militarism in
Britain since 1820.
[UF124A] Virago pbk **£9.99**

LLOYD, GENEVIEVE
The Man of Reason
Male and female in Western philosophy.
[UF125] Methuen pbk **£6.95**

LUCEY, HELEN & WALKERDINE, VALERIE
Democracy in the Kitchen
Regulating Mothers and Socialising Daughters.
[UF125A] Virago pbk **£8.99**

MACDONALD, JANET
**How to be a Successful
Businesswoman**
[UF126] Methuen pbk **£4.95**

MACDONALD, SHARON; HOLDEN, PAT &
ARDENER, SHIRLEY (EDS)
**Images of Women in Peace
and War**
A penetrating analysis which subverts the
conventional reading of woman's role in peacetime
and war.
[UF127] Macmillan pbk **£8.95**

MALLON, BRENDA
Women Dreaming
[UF128] Pandora pbk **£3.95**

MARKS, ELAINE & COURTIVRON,
ISABELLE DE
New French Feminisms
A superlative introduction to French feminist thought.
Includes essays from de Beauvoir, Cixous, Irigaray
and Kristeva. Also provides an extensive history and
analysis of the French movement.
[UF129] Harvester pbk **£9.95**

MCCAFFERTY, NEIL
**Peggy Deery: A Derry Family
at War**   **NEW**
[UF129A] Virago pbk **£4.99**

MCEWEN, CHRISTINA & O'SULLIVAN, SUE
**Out the Other Side: Contemporary
Lesbian Writings**
[UF130] Virago pbk **£5.95**

MENDUS, SUSAN & RENDALL, JANE (ED)
Sexuality and Subordination
Interdisciplinary essays on the construction of gender
in 19th century Britain and France.
[UF132] Routledge pbk **£8.95**

MILES, ROSALIND
The Women's History of the World
Challenges orthodox perceptions of history and the
part men and women have played in it.
[UF133] M Joseph hbk **£12.95**

MILKMAN, R. (ED)
**Women, Work and Protest: A Century of
US Women's Labour History**
[UF134] Routledge hbk **£10.95**

MILL, JOHN STUART
The Subjection of Women
English philosopher (associated with 'Utilitarianism')
and radical reformer; whose *The Subjection of
Women* uses reason and common sense to challenge
sexual discrimination.
[UF135] Prometheus pbk **£2.95**

MILLER, JEAN BAKER
**Towards a New Psychology of
Women**
Argues that qualities which women possess in
abundance, including co-operation, ability to nurture
and tenderness, have been consistently devalued by
both men and women.
[UF136] Penguin pbk **£4.99**

MILLETT, KATE (1934 -)
American feminist who was actively involved in the
civil rights movement during the 1960s and was one
of the early committee members of the National
Organisation for Women.
Sexual Politics
A seminal work in the women's liberation movements
in the US and UK. It vigorously attacks patriarchy
using feminist arguments on the subjects of religion,
psychoanalysis and literature, and demands radical
changes in sexual attitudes.
[UF137] Virago pbk **£6.99**

MITCHELL, JULIET (1940 -)
Born in New Zealand, Mitchell now works in London
as a psychoanalyst. She is one of Britain's foremost
feminist thinkers and has written essays on the
political theory of women's oppression. She presents
a more just understanding of women in socialist
theory than had previously been granted.
Psychoanalysis and Feminism
A radical reassessment of Freudian psychoanalysis in
an attempt to develop an understanding of the
psychology of femininity and the oppression of
women.
[UF138] Penguin pbk **£6.99**

Women: The Longest Revolution
[UF139] Virago pbk **£6.99**

MITCHELL, JULIET & OAKLEY, ANN (EDS)
Rights and Wrongs of Women
[UF140] Penguin pbk **£6.99**
What is Feminism?
Stimulating essays covering health, motherhood, child
abuse, social welfare and the law.
[UF141] Blackwell pbk **£8.50**

MITTER, SWASTI
Common Fate, Common Bond
The position of women in the global economy, and
their attempts to better it.
[UF142] Pluto P pbk **£5.95**

MOORE, HENRIETTA
Feminism and Anthropology
[UF143] Polity P pbk **£8.95**

NAIRNE, KATHY & SMITH, GERRILYN
Dealing with Depression
A practical book offering help in identifying the
causes of depression, seeking appropriate help, and
taking steps towards change.
[UF144] Women's P pbk **£3.95**

NEUSTATTER, ANGELA
The Feminist Years   **NEW**
Achievements and changes in the women's movement
since the 1960s.
[UF145] Harrap hbk **£12.95**

NGCOBO, LAURETTA
Let it Be Told
Essays by Black women writers in Britain.
[UF146] Virago pbk **£4.99**

NISSIM, RINA
Natural Healing in Gynaecology
[UF147] Pandora pbk **£4.95**

NORWOOD, ROBIN
Women Who Love Too Much
An alternative to the addictive patterns of
relationships to which so many women are drawn.
[UF148] Arrow pbk **£3.50**

Kate Millet, author of *Sexual Politics* (Virago pbk
£6.99)

Letters from Women who Love too Much
A closer look at relationship addiction and recovery.
[UF148A] Arrow pbk **£3.50**

OAKLEY, ANN (1944 -)
A key English feminist sociologist. She has published a number of books on the family, the position of women, and on health-care. She is currently the Deputy Director at the Thomas Coram Unit, University of London.
Housewife
[UF149] Penguin pbk **£4.95**
Sex, Gender and Society
Examines the real differences between the sexes. Draws on the evidence of biology, anthropology, sociology, and studies in animal behaviour.
[UF150] MT Smith pbk **£4.95**
Sociology of Housework
[UF150A] Blackwell pbk **£8.95**
Subject Women
A very general study.
[UF151] Fontana pbk **£3.95**
Taking It Like a Woman
An autobiography in which she describes the events which made her a feminist, wife, mother, academic and writer.
[UF152] Fontana pbk **£2.95**
Telling the Truth about Jerusalem
A collection of essays and poems on issues central to the lives of today's women, including motherhood and women's health.
[UF153] Blackwell pbk **£8.95**
The Captured Womb
The history of the medical care of pregnant women.
[UF154] Blackwell pbk **£8.50**

OLSON, ANN & SEAGER, JONI
Women in the World: An International Atlas
[UF155] Pan pbk **£3.99**

ORBACH, SUSIE
Fat is a Feminist Issue
A pioneering work in the feminist psychology of health.
[UF156] Arrow pbk **£2.99**
Hunger Strike
[UF157] Faber pbk **£2.95**

OWEN, ALEX
The Darkened Room `NEW`
Women, Power and Spiritualism in Late Victorian England.
[UF157A] Virago pbk **£11.99**

PADEL, UNA & STEVENSON, PRUE
Insiders: Women's Experience of Prison
[UF158] Virago pbk **£5.50**

PANKHURST, SYLVIA
The Suffragette Movement
[UF159] Virago pbk **£10.50**

PATEMAN, CAROLE
The Sexual Contract
A radical critique of the suppressed assumptions about sexual reference to the marriage contract.
[UF160] Polity P pbk **£8.95**

PETCHESKY, ROSALIND
Abortion and Women's Choice
A highly acclaimed examination of the issues involved in the abortion debate.
[UF161] Verso pbk **£8.95**

PHILLIPS, ANGELA; LEAN, NICKY & JACOBS, BARBARA
Your Body, Your Baby, Your Life
[UF162] Pandora pbk **£4.95**

PHILLIPS, ANNE
Divided Loyalties: Dilemmas of Sex and Class
[UF163] Virago pbk **£5.99**

PHILLIPS, ANNE (ED)
Feminism and Equality `NEW`
[UF164] Blackwell pbk **£8.95**

PIPES, MARY
Understanding Abortion
[UF165] Women's P pbk **£3.95**

PRINGLE, ROSEMARY
Secretaries Talk: Sexuality, Power and Work `NEW`
How women as secretaries negotiate power structures in the workplace.
[UF166] Verso pbk **£8.95**

RAMAZANOGLU, CAROLINE
Feminism and the Contradictions of Oppression
A comprehensive survey of feminist theory and strategy, this book looks at the ways in which class, race, subculture and sexuality divide women and explores ways out of the impasse.
[UF167] Routledge pbk **£9.95**
RANDALL, VICKY
Women and Politics
A comprehensive analysis of women's involvement in politics throughout the world.
[UF168] Macmillan pbk **£8.95**

RICH, ADRIENNE (1929 -)
An award-winning American poet who is very concerned with social problems and controversies, and has written two of the most influential works of contemporary radical feminism. (See also *Poetry*).
Of Woman Born: Motherhood as Experience and Institution
[UF169] Virago pbk **£6.50**
On Lies, Secrets and Silence
Includes essays on 'The Common World of Women', education, motherhood and neglected women writers.
[UF170] Virago pbk **£6.50**

RICHARDS, JANET RADCLIFFE
The Sceptical Feminist
A rigorously philosophical approach to the problems of liberation.
[UF171] Penguin pbk **£4.99**

RILEY, DENISE
Am I That Name? `NEW`
An exploration of the history of the idea of 'womanhood' from the 17th century to the present day.
[UF172] Macmillan pbk **£8.95**

ROBERTS, HELEN
The Patient Patients: Women and Their Doctors
[UF173] Pandora pbk **£3.95**

ROGERS, BARBARA
52%: Getting Women's Power into Politics
[UF174] Women's P pbk **£4.50**

ROOT, JANE
Pictures of Women: Sexuality
Written in association with 'Pictures of Women Co-operative'.
[UF175] Pandora pbk **£5.50**

ROUCHE, JANIE LA & RYAN, REGINA
Strategies for Women at Work
[UF176] Unwin Hyman pbk **£4.95**

ROWBOTHAM, SHEILA (1943 -)
An English socialist-feminist historian. Her pamphlet 'Women's Liberation and the New Politics' (1970) laid down the fundamental approaches and demands of the emerging women's movement in Britain.
Dreams and Dilemmas: Collected Writings
A wide-ranging and stimulating selection of essays, poems and polemic from the late 1960s to the early 1980s.
[UF177] Virago pbk **£7.99**
The Past is Before Us `NEW`
A major new history of the ideas of the women's movement over the last two decades.
[UF178] Pandora hbk **£15.00**
Women's Consciousness, Man's World
An analysis of women's position in a capitalist society. Looks at the psychological position of women in modern society and describes the growth of the new feminist consciousness.
[UF179] Penguin pbk **£3.99**

RUSSELL, DORA (1894 - 1986)
English feminist who moved in radical socialist circles. She was a founder member of the National Council of Civil Liberties and participated in the campaign for Nuclear Disarmament. In 1958 she inspired the Women's Caravan of Peace in protest against the atrocities of the Cold War. She was married to Bertrand Russell for 14 years.
The Dora Russell Reader: 57 Years of Writing and Journalism
[UF180] Pandora pbk **£4.50**
The Tamarisk Tree Vol 1: My Quest for Liberty and Love
A fascinating work which, in describing Dora Russell's life, chronicles the development of British feminism and the progressive movement in education from the 1920s to the present day.
[UF181] Virago pbk **£6.50**
Vol 2: My School and the Years of War
[UF182] Virago pbk **£4.50**
Vol 3
[UF183] Virago pbk **£6.99**

SADOFF, MELISSA
Woman as Chameleon
Offers advice on work, marriage and motherhood.
[UF184] NEL pbk **£2.50**

SAYERS, JANET
Sexual Contradictions: Psychology, Psychoanalysis and Feminism
[UF185] Tavistock pbk **£8.95**

SCARR, SANDRA & DUNN, JUDY
Mother Care/Other Care
Childcare dilemma for women and children.
[UF186] Penguin pbk **£3.95**

SCOTT, HILDA
Working Your Way to the Bottom: The Feminisation of Poverty
[UF187] Pandora pbk **£5.25**

SEGAL, LYNNE
Is the Future Female?
A controversial critical overview of the current state of feminist politics and theory from a leading socialist-feminist.
[UF188] Virago pbk **£6.50**

SHAPIRO, ROSE
Contraception: A Practical and Political Guide
The most acclaimed study available on contraception from the woman's point of view.
[UF189] Virago pbk **£5.99**

SHARPE, SUE
Falling for Love: Teenage Mothers Talk
[UF191] Virago pbk **£3.99**
Just Like a Girl
[UF192] Penguin pbk **£5.99**

SHOWALTER, ELAINE
The Female Malady
Women, madness and English culture, 1830-1980. Immensely readable, detailed historical and literary study of women's relationship with psychiatry and definitions of mental illness.
[UF193] Virago pbk **£7.50**

SHUTTLE, PENELOPE & REDGROVE, PETER
The Wise Wound: Menstruation and Everywoman
A very interesting study of the attitudes towards menstruation throughout the ages by these two acclaimed poets who are also husband and wife. Includes an excellent chapter on witch-hunts.
[UF194] Grafton pbk **£3.95**

SILMAN, JANET (ED)
Enough is Enough
Aboriginal women speak out.
[UF195] Women's P pbk **£7.50**

SKINNER, JANE & FRITCHIE, RENNIE
Working Choices: A Life-Planning Guide for Women Today
Advises women on choices and opportunities.
[UF196] Dent pbk **£4.50**

SOMJEE, GEETA
Narrowing the Gender Gap
Examines a variety of efforts to help women overcome the constraints imposed on them by a network of social relationships.
[UF198] Macmillan pbk **£9.95**

SOUHAMI, DIANA
Woman's Place
The changing picture of women in Britain.
[UF199] Penguin pbk **£6.95**

SPENDER, DALE (1943 -)
A major contemporary Australian feminist theorist devoted to the promotion of women's history. She argues that the control of knowledge, previously a male domain, must be woman's goal in order to achieve liberation.
Feminist Theorists: Three Centuries of Women's Intellectual Traditions
[UF200] Women's P pbk **£6.95**
For the Record: The Making and Meaning of Feminist Knowledge
A personal assessment of the writers who have shaped the liberation movement from Betty Friedan to Adrienne Rich.
[UF201] Women's P pbk **£4.95**
Invisible Women: The Schooling Scandal `NEW`
Re-issue of a classic study of sexism in education.
[UF201A] Women's P pbk **£4.95**
Mothers of the Novel
100 good women novelists before Jane Austen.
[UF201B] Pandora pbk **£4.95**
Time and Tide Wait for No Man
[UF202] Pandora pbk **£6.50**

SPENDER, DALE & SARAH, ELIZABETH (EDS)
Learning to Lose: Sexism and Education
[UF203] Women's P pbk **£5.95**

STANWORTH, MICHELLE (ED)
Reproductive Technologies: Gender, Motherhood and Medicine
The economic, political and legal implications of the new technologies of human reproduction.
[UF204] Polity P pbk **£7.95**

STIMPSON, CATHERINE R.
Where the Meanings Are
A collection of the best and most influential essays by the founding editor of the feminist journal *Signs*.
[UF205] Routledge hbk **£27.50**

TAYLOR, BARBARA
Eve and the New Jerusalem
Socialism and feminism in the 19th century.
[UF206] Virago pbk **£8.99**

THOMSON, MARTINA
On Art and Therapy `NEW`
[UF206A] Virago pbk **£6.99**

TICKNER, LISA
The Spectacle of Women
A detailed account of the iconography of women's suffrage.
[UF206A] Chatto pbk **£15.00**

TILLY, LOUISE A. & SCOTT, JOAN W.
Women, Work and Family
A classic of recent women's history, this book is still the only comprehensive account of the history of women's work in England and France.
[UF208] Methuen pbk **£8.95**

TUTTLE, LISA
Encyclopaedia of Feminism
[UF209] Arrow pbk **£6.95**
Heroines
Interviews with famous women including Shirley Williams, Germaine Greer and Mary Quant who talk about the women they most admire and whose example has inspired them.
[UF210] Harrap hbk **£10.95**

TWEEDIE, JILL
Letters from a Fainthearted Feminist/More from Martha: Further Letters
Two collections of the wry and witty letters which first appeared in *The Guardian:* Tweedie is well-known for her humorous contribution to the women's movement.
[UF212] Picador pbk **£3.95**

WALBY, SYLVIA
Patriarchy at Work
An examination of the complex relationship between patriarchy and capitalism, which shows it to be founded on tension and conflict.
[UF213] Polity P pbk **£7.95**

WARNER, MARINA (1946 -)
A freelance writer and novelist. She is an art critic for the *New Statesman*, *The Guardian* and *The Sunday Times*.
Alone of All Her Sex: The Myths and Cult of the Virgin Mary
[UF215] Picador pbk **£6.95**
Joan of Arc: The Image of Female Heroism
[UF215A] Penguin pbk **£5.95**

Monuments and Maidens: The Allegory of the Female Form
An erudite and invigorating analysis of the female figures that bombard us on coins, stamps, television and public buildings.
[UF216] Picador pbk **£5.95**

WEEDON, CHRIS
Feminist Practice and Post-Structuralist Theory
A very useful book for those intimidated by the highly theoretical nature of its subject. A clear and concise exposition on the inter-relations of these two disciplines.
[UF217] Blackwell pbk **£7.95**

WEIDEGER, PAULA
Female Cycles
[UF218] Women's P pbk **£3.95**

WHYTE, JUDITH (ED)
Girl-Friendly Schooling
An examination into why schools fail girls and how traditional roles are reinforced. The implications of a 'girl-friendly' curriculum are also discussed.
[UF219] Methuen pbk **£6.95**

WILKINSON, SUE (ED)
Feminist Social Psychology
A collection of essays exploring the realm of social psychology and its relationship with feminism.
[UF220] Open UP pbk **£8.95**

WILSON, ELIZABETH (1936 -)
One of Britain's leading socialist-feminists. Her work ranges from autobiography and fiction through fashion and cultural theory to sociology and politics.
Adorned in Dreams: Fashion and Modernity
A feminist history of fashion, at once critical and celebratory.
[UF221] Virago pbk **£7.99**
Hallucinations: Life in the Post-Modern City
Stories, vignettes and essays on contemporary urban culture.
[UF222] Radius pbk **£6.95**
Hidden Agendas: Theory, Politics and Experience in the Women's Movement
[UF222A] Tavistock pbk **£8.95**
Only Halfway to Paradise
The changing position of women in Britain, 1945 - 1968.
[UF223] Tavistock pbk **£6.50**
Woman and the Welfare State
[UF224] Tavistock pbk **£8.50**

Marina Warner, author of *Alone of All Her Sex: The Myths and Cult of the Virgin Mary* (Picador pbk £6.95)

WILTSHER, ANNE
**Most Dangerous Women: Feminist
Peace Campaigners of the Great War**
[UF225] Pandora pbk £5.95

WISE, SUE & STANLEY, LIZ
**Georgie Porgie: Harrassment in
Everyday Life**
[UF226] Pandora pbk £5.95

WOLLSTONECRAFT, MARY (1759 - 1797)
A radical English feminist who shocked her
contemporaries with arguments for equal
opportunities. Wife of William Godwin and mother of
Mary Shelley, Mary Wollstonecraft's most celebrated
work was her *Vindication of the Rights of Woman* in
which she set out her belief that the so-called follies
of women were a consequence of the 'tyranny of
man', and made a plea for improvement in women's
education.
Vindication of the Rights of Woman
[UF227] Penguin pbk £4.50

WOODMAN, MARION
The Owl was a Baker's Daughter
Obesity, Anorexia Nervosa and the repressed
feminine.
[UF228] Airlift pbk £5.95

WOOLF, VIRGINIA (1882 - 1941)
Doing justice to the protean influence of Virginia
Woolf's essays and criticism on women writers in this
century is far from easy. Suffice it to say that *A Room
of One's Own* is unmatched in feminist literature for
its analysis of what the writer actually needs to be
physically able to write, and why women find these
basic criteria - privacy, space, time - so difficult to
achieve. Moreover, her critical writings, as well as
being extremely astute and stimulating as criticism
per se, were among the first fully to articulate the idea
of a female aesthetic, which drew on the peculiarities
of women's experience and ceased to be content with
simply imitating the styles, themes and concerns of
men. Although she did not like to call herself a
feminist, her writing has inspired debate on women
and writing, and the role of women in a culture
defined by men.
A Room of One's Own & Three Guineas
Argues for the necessity of economic independence
for women.
[UF229] Chatto hbk £12.95
[UF230] Grafton pbk £2.99
Books and Portraits
[UF230A] Grafton pbk £2.95
Death of the Moth
[UF231] Hogarth pbk £7.95
Essays Vol 1
The first volumes in a projected six-volume collection
of Woolf's essays, from the earliest, unsigned reviews
for the *TLS* to her important later longer pieces.
[UF231A] Hogarth hbk £25.00
Essays Vol 2
[UF231B] Hogarth hbk £25.00
Essays Vol 3
[UF231C] Hogarth hbk £25.00
Moments of Being
[UF232] Hogarth hbk £12.95
[UF233] Grafton pbk £2.50
The Common Reader: 1
[UF234] Hogarth pbk £5.95
The Common Reader: 2
[UF235] Hogarth pbk £5.95
Three Guineas
[UF236] Hogarth pbk £5.95
Women and Writing
[UF237] Women's P pbk £4.95
A Writer's Diary
[UF238] Hogarth hbk £12.95
[UF239] Grafton pbk £2.95

Sport

General
Major Sports A - Z
Other Sports
Games: Chess & Bridge

SPORT

From the large number of sports titles published every year, a small selection appears here. Although literature and sport may be seen as uneasy bedfellows, there are a number of good titles and series available. Of the practical books, (ie those which offer instruction and guidance to the amateur or professional sportsman), the series listed below from *A & C Black*, *Crowood* and *Collins* offer excellent, clear and well-illustrated instruction at a variety of levels. Annual reference/statistical works come out for many sports, including the classic *Wisden* and the *Rothman's* and *Playfair* yearbooks. Other more 'literary' writing can be found for most sports, as Vernon Scannell's *Sporting Literature: An Anthology* shows, but cricket, fishing, and mountaineering offer outstanding non-practical titles, whether in the form of autobiographies, essays or lasting works of journalism. The *Sportspages* imprint from Simon & Schuster has recently produced a number of excellent new and reprinted titles, and specialist publishers such as *Witherby* offer uniformly high-quality titles.

General

Official Rules of Sports and Games
The rules of every sport played in Britain recently updated to include British American Football.
[V1] Heinemann hbk **£12.95**

BBC SPORTS REPORT TEAM
Sports Report
The best from forty years of the Radio 2 programme, with a free cassette of contemporary recordings.
[V2] Macdonald hbk **£12.95**

BLUE, ADRIANNE
Faster, Higher, Further: Women In the Olympics
[V3] Virago pbk **£7.95**

CONSIDINE, T.
The Language of Sport
A-Z dictionary of sporting terms.
[V4] Angus & R hbk **£7.95**

EMERY, DAVID & GREENBERG, STAN
World Sporting Records
[V5] Bodley hbk **£12.95**
[V6] Bodley pbk **£6.95**

FOX, SALLY
The Sporting Woman NEW
Illustrated with images from all over the world, from ancient times to the 1920s, this demonstrates the (often unexpected) involvement of women in sport: from 17th century Frenchwomen playing serious billiards to Victorian Englishwomen playing cricket.
[V7] NY Graph Soc hbk **£8.99**

GALLICO, PAUL
Farewell to Sport
First published in 1938, a reprinted classic. Gallico covered the best of American sport from the early 1920s to the Berlin Olympics of 1936.
[V8] Sportspages pbk **£5.95**

GREENBERG, S.
Guinness Olympic Records 776 BC to 1988
Contains a mass of information and statistics.
[V9] Guinness pbk **£8.95**

HART-DAVIS, DUFF
Hitler's Olympics
A look at the 1936 Berlin Olympics which Hitler attempted to use to prove Aryan supremacy.
[V10] Hodder pbk **£3.50**

MASON, TONY
Sport in Britain: A Historical Handbook
A cultural history examining the effects of politics, the media, drugs and hooliganism.
[V11] Faber pbk **£3.95**

MASON, TONY (ED)
Sport in Britain: A Social History NEW
A unique compendium of analysis and information relating to 150 years of British sport: ten historians write essays on the major sports, with illustrations, including, in some cases rare, period photographs.
[V12] Cambridge hbk **£19.50**

MATTHEWS, P.
Guinness Encyclopaedia of Sports: Records and Results
[V13] Guinness pbk **£9.95**

MORRISON, D.
The Dictionary of Sporting Champions
[V14] World pbk **£3.95**

SCANNELL, VERNON (ED)
Sporting Literature: An Anthology
Scannell's criteria for selecting these pieces was that they should show a thorough knowledge of the sports concerned, as well as being well-written: Shakespeare, Yeats, Johnson, Burns and Evelyn Waugh appear among a host of others.
[V15] Oxford hbk **£12.50**

SYER, JOHN
Team Spirit: The Elusive Experience NEW
A stimulating examination of the intangible factors that make the successful performance of a team so much more than the sum of its individual members.
[V16] Sportspages pbk **£6.95**

WILSON, NEIL
Sport Tycoons: The Men and the Money
The *Independent*'s columnist lifts the veil on the enormous amounts of money in very few hands in the background of sport, capitalism's lucrative pastime.
[V17] Piatkus hbk **£12.95**

WOOTTON, STEVE
Nutrition for Sport
An excellent study of the science of nutrition in sport; also useful as a practical book.
[V18] Sportspages pbk **£5.95**

Major Sports A-Z

Series

KNOW THE GAME
An excellent and comprehensive series of small-format introductions to common sports and pastimes; simple to use and regularly revised, they are intended as introductions for the beginner to intermediate level, and are suitable for introducing children to a sport. They are priced at £1.99.
American Football, Archery, Backgammon, Basketball, Billiards & Snooker, Bowls, Camping, Card Games , (also More Card Games), Chess,
Coarse Fishing, Contract Bridge, Cricket, Croquet, Darts, Diving, Fencing, Float Fishing, Fly Casting, Golf, Gymnastics, Hang Gliding, Ice Skating, Indoor Cricket, Indoor Hockey, Judo, Karate, Keeping Fit, Life Saving, Mah Jong, Netball, Patience Games, Pistol Shooting, Pool, Powerlifting, Riding, Rifle Shooting, Rounders, Rowing, Rugby Union, Sailing, Short Tennis, Shotgun Shooting, Skiing, Soccer, Sports Injuries, Squash, SubAqua, Swimming, Table Tennis, Tennis, Track and Field Athletics, Trout & Salmon Fishing, Volleyball, Weight Lifting, Wind Surfing, Weight Training, Wind Surfing, Women's Hockey, Yoga.

SKILLS OF THE GAME
More detailed and advanced than the above, this series from Crowood is well-illustrated and written by experts. Most paperback editions cost £4.95.
American Football, Badminton, Basketball, Crown Green Bowls, Canoeing, Cricket, Endurance Running, Fitness for Sport, Golf, Hockey, Judo, Karate, Rhythmic Gymnastics, Rugby League, Rugby Union, Soccer, Skiing, Sprinting & Hurdling, Squash, Swimming, Table Tennis, Tennis, Triathlon, Volleyball, Water Skiing, Windsurfing, Women's Lacrosse.

COLLINS 'IMPROVE YOUR.....'
Intended for the more advanced level, and priced at £12.95 for hardback editions. Available for:
Bowls, Golf, Skiing, Snooker, Squash, Windsurfing

Cricket

Excellent cricket writing abounds, whether practical, autobiographical or 'occasional', from writers such as Cardus, Arlott, Swanton and C.L.R. James to Brian Johnston, David Frith and the inimitable *Wisden*. Useful anthologies such as the *Faber Book of Cricket*, and Alan Ross's *Cricketer's Companion* collect many such sources together, while the *Pavilion Library* has reprinted a number of classic older works from writers such as Blunden and 'Crusoe' Robertson-Glasgow.

ARLOTT, JOHN
One of Britain's best-known voices, the former radio commentator is a sympathetic and perceptive writer.
On Cricket
[V20] Fontana pbk **£3.50** NEW
The Essential John Arlott
The best of 40 years of classic cricket writing: from famous matches to heroic failures, and memories of many of the great names.
[V21] Collins hbk **£14.95**
Two Summers at the Tests
[V22] Pavilion pbk **£5.95**

ARNOLD, PETER & WYNNE-THOMAS, PETER
The Illustrated History of the Test Match
Detailed history of the first Test match in 1877 to 1987. Profusely illustrated.
[V23] Sidgwick hbk **£14.95**

BERRY, SCYLD
'Observer' on Cricket
An anthology of the best cricket writing from the *Observer* newspaper.
[V24] Unwin Hyman hbk **£12.95**

BIRLEY, DEREK
The Willow Hand: NEW
Some Cricket Myths Explored
Affectionate, radical, look at the history of cricket.
[V25] Sportspages pbk **£5.95**

BLOFELD, HENRY
Reminiscences from one of the best cricket writers and radio commentators.
My Dear Old Thing `NEW`
[V26] S Paul hbk **£10.95**
One Test After Another: Life in International Cricket
[V27] S Paul hbk **£8.95**

BLUNDEN, EDMUND
Cricket Country:
The Game & the Dream
A wonderful look at all aspects of the summer game from the great poet.
[V28] Pavilion pbk **£4.95**

BORDER, ALLAN
A Peep at the Poms
[V29] Barker hbk **£9.95**

BREARLEY, MIKE
Phoenix from the Ashes: The Story of the England-Australia Series 1981
[V30] Unwin Hyman pbk **£1.95**
The Art of Captaincy
A fascinating study of the psychology of captaincy. Brearley captained Middlesex and England and was one of the most successful post-war leaders of sporting men.
[V31] Hodder pbk **£5.95**

CARDUS, NEVILLE
Cardus's *Autobiography* recounts the humble Mancunian upbringing of the greatest-ever cricketing writer, who brought the game vividly to life for his *Manchester Guardian* readership.
Autobiography
[V32] H Hamilton pbk **£6.95**

DAVIES, MICHAEL & DAVIES, SIMON
The Faber Book of Cricket
Excellent anthology of cricket writing.
[V33] Faber pbk **£3.95**

EAGAR, PATRICK
Botham
Photographs capture the power and charisma of England's 1980s hero better than words.
[V34] Kingswood hbk **£9.95**

EDMONDS, FRANCES
Another Bloody Tour
Wife of former England spinner Phil Edmonds covers the West Indies tour of 1985/86 in her acerbic style.
[V35] Fontana pbk **£2.50**
Cricket XXXX Cricket
[V36] Pan pbk **£2.99**

ENGEL, MATTHEW (ED.)
Guardian Book of Cricket
The best of cricket writing from The *Guardian*, from a range of writers including Cardus.
[V37] Penguin pbk **£6.95**

FINGLETON, JACK
Ashes Crown the Year
The story of the England-Australia series in 1953.
[V38] Pavilion pbk **£5.95**
Brightly Fades the Don
Bradman's climactic Test series in England in 1948.
[V39] Pavilion pbk **£5.95**

FRINDALL, BILL (ED)
England's Test Cricketers 1876 - 1988 `NEW`
[V40] Collins hbk **£20.00**
Playfair Cricket Annual 1989 `NEW`
[V41] QAP pbk **£1.75**

FRITH, DAVID
England versus Australia: Pictorial History of the Test Match
[V44] Collins hbk **£17.95**
England versus Australia: Test Match Records 1877-1985
[V45] Collins hbk **£9.95**

FRY, C.B.
A Life Worth Living
[V46] Pavilion pbk **£5.95**

GOWER,DAVID & HODGSON,DEREK
A Right Ambition
England's re-appointed captain. The most gifted English batsman of his generation.
[V47] Collins hbk **£8.95**

HUTTON, LEN
Fifty Years in Cricket
Immortalised by his 364 at the Oval versus Australia in 1938, then the highest score in a Test innings, made when he was 22 years old.
[V48] Star pbk **£3.25**

JAMES, C.L.R.
C.L.R. James looks at his native West Indies. Not just a tribute to cricket, James surveys many aspects of West Indian life.
Beyond a Boundary
[V49] S Paul pbk **£5.95**
Cricket
[V50] Allison & B hbk **£14.95**

JOHNSTON, BRIAN
The BBC radio commentator and celebrated personality looks back over his life and involvement with the sport.
Guide to Cricket
[V51] WH Allen hbk **£10.95**
It's Been a Lot of Fun
[V52] Star pbk **£1.95**
It's a Funny Game
[V53] Star pbk **£1.95**
Rain Stops Play
[V54] Unwin Hyman pbk **£1.75**

KEATING, FRANK
Gents & Players
[V55] Robson pbk **£4.95**

KHAN, IMRAN
All Round View
The 1980s saw four great all-rounders at the peak of their form: Hadlee, Botham, Kapil Dev and Imran. Pakistan's aristocratic captain writes extremely well about cricket and cricketers, and especially about the vicissitudes of the game in his native country.
[V56] Pan pbk **£3.99**

LAKER, JIM
Cricket Contrasts
[V57] S Paul pbk **£7.95**

LEWIS, TONY
Double Century: The Story of the MCC and the Spread of Cricket
[V58] Hodder hbk **£14.95**

MANLEY, MICHAEL
The History of West Indian Cricket
A well-written, comprehensive history by Jamaica's Prime Minister.
[V59] Deutsch hbk **£17.95**

MARTIN-JENKINS, CHRISTOPHER
Grand-Slam: England in Australia 1986-7
[V60] Simon & Sch pbk **£7.95**

MARTIN-JENKINS, CHRISTOPHER & RUSSELL, JACK
Sketchbook of a Season `NEW`
A combined record of this summer's season from the editor of The *Cricketer*, with visual sketches from England and Gloucestershire wicket-keeper Jack Russell.
[V61] Lennard hbk **£12.95**

MASON, RONALD
Jack Hobbs
[V62] Pavilion pbk **£6.95**

MELFORD,M & WIMBUSH,W (EDS)
Daily Telegraph Cricket Year Book 1989
[V63] Telegraph pbk **£7.95**

MELFORD, MICHAEL (ED)
Botham Rekindles the Ashes
Story of the unforgettable 1981 ashes series as seen through the match reports of The *Daily Telegraph*.
[V64] Daily Tel pbk **£1.95**

MIDWINTER, ERIC
W.G. Grace: His Life & Times
[V65] Unwin Hyman hbk **£10.95**

MOORHOUSE, GEOFFREY
Lord's
A biography of the home of cricket.
[V66] Hodder hbk **£9.95**
The Best Loved Game
[V67] Pavilion pbk **£5.95**

MOSEY, DON
Boycott
Either the Greatest Living Yorkshireman, or a boring, selfish batsman. Rely on Mosey to incline to the former view.
[V68] Penguin pbk **£2.95**

PLUMPTRE, GEORGE
Cricket Cartoon and Caricatures `NEW`
A wide range of illustrations of the game of cricket, providing a fascinating chronicle on the styles and humour of cricket artists over the years.
[V69] Collins hbk **£16.95**

RICHARDS, VIV
Viv Richards' Cricket Masterclass
Training manual for the advanced player by the greatest batsman of contemporary cricket.
[V70] Macdonald hbk **£12.95**

ROBERTSON-GLASGOW, R.C.
Crusoe on Cricket: Collected Writings
[V71] Pavilion hbk **£9.95**
[V72] Pavilion pbk **£4.95**

ROSS, ALAN
Three tour books which contain some of the best Cricket writing.
Cape Summer & The Australians in England
[V73] Constable hbk **£10.95**
Ranji: Prince of Cricketers
[V74] Pavilion pbk **£5.95**
Through the Caribbean
[V75] Pavilion pbk **£5.95**

ROSS, ALAN (ED)
Cricketers' Companion
[V76] Methuen hbk **£12.50**
[V77] Penguin pbk **£5.95**

SOBERS, GARFIELD
Twenty Years at the Top
The career of the greatest-ever all-rounder.
[V78] Macmillan hbk **£12.95**

SPORT

Illustration from *Double Century: Cricket in The Times* edited by **Marcus Williams** (Pavilion hbk £14.95)

SPROAT, IAIN (ED)
Cricketer's Who's Who 1989
[V79] Collins hbk **£12.95**

SWANTON, E.W.
As I Said at the Time: A Lifetime of Cricket
The *Daily Telegraph*'s doyen cricket writer looks back.
[V80] Unwin Hyman pbk **£6.95**

SWANTON, E.W. (ED)
Barclays World of Cricket
[V81] Collins hbk **£25.00**

WARNER, SIR PELHAM
Lord's 1787 - 1945
[V82] Pavilion pbk **£5.95**

WILLIAMS, MARCUS (ED)
Double Century: Cricket in The Times Volume 1: 1785-1935
[V821] Pavilion hbk £14.95

WISDEN ANTHOLOGIES
Past collections of the internationally famous annual reference book that is also a totem of a way of life.
Wisden Anthology 1864 - 1900
[V83] Macdonald hbk **£29.50**
Wisden Anthology 1900 - 1940
[V84] Macdonald hbk **£29.50**
Wisden Anthology 1940 - 1963
[V85] Macdonald hbk **£29.50**
Wisden Anthology 1963 - 1982
[V86] Macdonald hbk **£29.50**

FRINDALL, BILL (ED)
Wisden Book of Test Cricket
[V42] Macdonald hbk **£29.50**
Wisden Book of Test Records
[V43] Wisden hbk **£29.50**

WRIGHT, GRAEME (ED)
Wisden Cricketer's Almanack 1989
[V97] Wisden hbk **£16.95**
[V88] Wisden pbk **£14.95**

Field Sports

BACKHOUSE ET AL (ED)
Complete Book of Shooting
[V89] Octopus hbk **£13.95**

BLACKWOOD, CAROLINE
In the Pink
An unbiased view of huntsmen and 'antis'. Contains disturbing testimony from the widow of a former huntmaster of the abuse he suffered when he saw the error of his ways and repented shortly before his death, describing bloody and usually denied rituals.
[V90] Bloomsbury hbk **£11.95**

BLOW, SIMON
Fields Elysian: Portrait of a Hunting Society
An elegant book recording the heyday of hunting as a social activity and capturing the enthusiasm of its devotees.
[V91] Dent hbk **£14.50**

CARR, RAYMOND
English Fox Hunting: A History
An excellent social history of the hunting classes in Britain.
[V92] Weidenfeld pbk **£5.95**

CLAYTON, MICHAEL
The Chase
[V93] S Paul hbk **£14.95**

EGGAR, ROBIN
Shooting in Eight Days **NEW**
A new series, following the progress of a novice through a week spent with some of the sport's experts.
[V94] Osprey pbk **£7.95**

MARTIN, B.
Tales of the Old Gamekeepers **NEW**
[V95] David & Ch hbk **£10.95**

MOORE, JOHN
Sport and the English Countryside
An anthology of John Moore's angling, shooting and conservation writing compiled by his sister.
[V96] Sportsman's P hbk **£12.95**

MURSELL, NORMAN
Come Dawn, Come Dusk: Fifty Years a Gamekeeper
[V97] Unwin Hyman pbk **£3.50**
Green & Pleasant Land: A Countryman Remembers
[V98] Unwin Hyman pbk **£2.95**
Running a Successful Shoot
[V99] Blandford hbk **£10.95**
The Forgotten Skills: Country Crafts Remembered
[V100] Unwin Hyman pbk **£11.95**

PARRY-JONES, JEMIMA
Falconry and Conservation
How to approach falconry and captive breeding in a practical and ethical way.
[V101] David & Ch hbk **£8.95**

STANBURY, PERCY & CARLISLE, G.L.
Clay Pigeon Marksmanship
[V102] Century hbk **£9.95**

UPTON, PHIL
A.J. Smith's Guide to Sporting Shooting
Phil Upton is currently the World Sporting Shooting Champion.
[V103] Argus pbk **£7.95**

Fishing

Hamlyn Encyclopaedia of Angling
A good introduction to all aspects of fishing; well illustrated.
[V104] Hamlyn hbk **£9.95**

ALDRICH, B.
Ever Rolling Stream **NEW**
Environment and fishing at Earl Mountbatten's estate at Romsey, Hampshire through which rolls the River Test.
[V105] Blandford pbk **£4.95**

ALEXANDER, STUART
Fly Fishing in Eight Days **NEW**
[V106] Osprey pbk **£7.95**

ARDLEY, C.H.
A Handbook of Fly-Tying
[V107] Witherby hbk **£9.75**

ASHLEY-COOPER, J.
One of the most eloquent and memorable English fishing writers.
A Line on Salmon
[V108] Witherby hbk **£10.95**
A Ring of Wessex Waters
[V109] Witherby hbk **£9.95**
A Salmon Fisher's Odyssey
Recollections of a life spent fishing Salmon rivers in Scotland, England and Ireland.
[V110] Witherby hbk **£16.50**
The Great Salmon Rivers of Scotland
The authoritative guide to the world famous Scottish salmon rivers - the Dee, Spey, Tay and Tweed.
[V111] Witherby hbk **£16.50**

ASHURST, KEVIN & GRAHAM, COLIN
Encyclopaedia of Pole Fishing
[V112] M Joseph hbk **£9.95**
Pocket Guide to Bait & Lures
[V113] Collins pbk **£4.95**
Pocket Guide to Saltwater Fishing
[V114] Collins pbk **£4.95**

BULLER, FRED
Domesday Book of Mammoth Pike
Fred Buller has tracked down and documented 230 mammoth pike.
[V115] Century pbk **£9.95**
Pike and the Pike Angler
Dick Walker called this 'the best book about a single species of fish ever written'. Completely Revised.
[V116] Century hbk **£12.95**

CLARKE, BRIAN
The Pursuit of Stillwater Trout
[V117] A & C Black hbk **£9.95**

DARLING, JOHN
Sea Angler's Guide to Britain & Ireland
[V118] Lutterworth pbk **£5.95**

FALKUS, HUGH
Salmon Fishing: A Practical Guide
The best book on salmon fishing by the acknowledged expert on the subject.
[V119] Witherby hbk **£20.00**
Sea Trout Fishing
[V120] Witherby hbk **£16.00**

FALKUS, HUGH & BULLER, F.
Freshwater Fishing
Recently revised, this is the most comprehensive angling compendium.
[V121] S Paul hbk **£30.00**

GODDARD, J.
Waterside Guide
A comprehensive pocket guide, for anglers, to the insect life of rivers and lakes.
[V122] Unwin hyman pbk **£6.95**

HEAD, LEN
River Fishing
[V123] Crowood hbk **£8.95**

HOLBROOK, CYRIL
Fishing from My Angle
Anecdotes from a lifetime angler and journalist.
[V124] David & Ch hbk **£8.95**

HOLDEN, JOHN
Long Distance Casting: Complete Guide to Tackle & Technique
[V125] Crowood hbk **£9.95**

INGLAS-HALL, J.
Fishing a Highland Stream
A classic written thirty years ago and recently re-issued: John Inglas-Hall has written the biography of a river.
[V126] Viking hbk **£9.95**

PRICHARD, MICHAEL & SHEPLEY, MICHAEL
Guide to Coarse Fishing
[V127] Guinness hbk **£10.95**

PRICHARD, MICHAEL (ED)
Collins EncyclopAedia of Fishing in Britain & Ireland
[V128] Collins hbk **£12.95**

PROFUMO, JOHN & ROBINSON, ALAN
In Praise of Trout   NEW
An illustrated essay on the joys of fishing, (with an introduction by Ted Hughes), as well as a study of the trout, which mixes childhood memory with literary history, biology with speculation.
[V129] Viking hbk **£20.00**

RANSOME, ARTHUR
Rod & Line
Better known as a children's novelist, Ransome loved fishing and wrote well about it.
[V130] Oxford pbk **£2.95**

SHARMAN, GEORGE
Carp & the Carp Angler
[V131] Century pbk **£7.95**

WALTON, IZAAK
The classic work on angling: the Derbyshire fisherman still reads beautifully, three centuries on.
The Compleat Angler
[V132] Penguin pbk **£2.50**
[V133] Oxford pbk **£3.50**

Football

Football Association Guide to the Laws of the Game
[V134] Heinemann pbk **£1.95**

Playfair Football Annual 1988 - 89
[V135] Macdonald pbk **£1.95**

Referee's Chart & Player's Guide to the Laws of Association Football
[V136] Pan pbk **£1.50**

Rothman's Football Yearbook 1988 - 89
Football's 'Wisden'; contains every possible statistic.
[V137] Macdonald pbk **£10.95**

BUTLER, BRYON
The Football League 1888 - 1988: The Official Illustrated History
[V138] Macdonald hbk **£14.95**

DAVIES, HUNTER
Glory Game: A Year in the Life of Tottenham Hotspur
The best-written club 'biography'.
[V139] Mainstream pbk **£5.95**

DUNPHY, EAMON
Only a Game? The Diary of a Professional Footballer
A mediocre player who turned out to be an excellent writer and who has now made journalism his career. The most illuminating book you will find on the domestic game.
[V140] Viking hbk **£8.95**

FRANCIS, TONY
Clough: A Biography
Brian, of course, the controversial professional Yorkshireman, socialist and manager. Written before the fists started flying.
[V141] S Paul hbk **£9.95**

GLANVILLE, BRIAN (ED)
The History of the World Cup
[V142] Faber pbk **£5.95**
The Joy of Football
A discerning collection of writings on the game edited by one of Britain's foremost sports journalists.
[V143] Hodder hbk **£12.95**

HODDLE, GLEN & HARRIS, HARRY
Spurred to Success: The Autobiography of Glenn Hoddle
Born again ball wizard.
[V144] Macdonald hbk **£9.95**

INGLIS, SIMON
The Football Grounds of Great Britain
A club-by-club guide to the increasingly threatened football grounds of England and Scotland.
[V145] Willow flexi **£10.95**

KELLY, STEPHEN
You'll Never Walk Alone: Official Illustrated History of Liverpool Football Club
Valuable (though pre-Hillsborough) survey of the achievements thus far.
[V146] Macdonald hbk **£12.95**

MILLER, DAVID
England's Last Glory
1966 And All That.
[V147] Pavilion hbk **£9.95**

MOYNIHAN, JACK
The Soccer Syndrome
A celebration of the first twenty years of post-war British football. Introduction by Brian Glanville.
[V148] Simon & Sch pbk **£5.95**

NICHOLAS, CHARLIE
Autobiography
Story of the Aberdeen and Scotland ex-prodigy.
[V149] S Paul hbk **£8.95**

ROBSON, BOBBY
World Cup Diary
'We wuz robbed' cried the nation. Robson has roughly the same idea, but is an incisive observer. Lucky there won't be a European Championship Diary.
[V150] Collins hbk **£8.95**

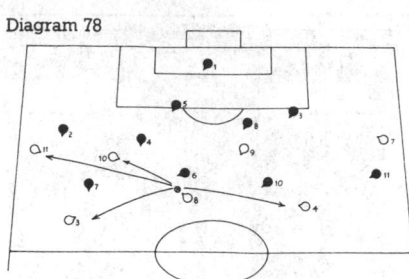
Diagram 78

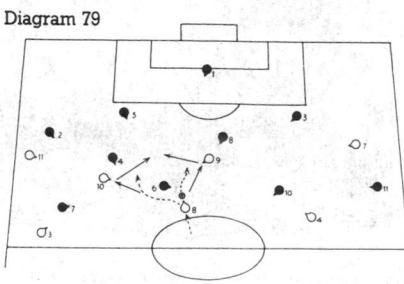
Diagram 79

Diagram (showing negative and positive passing opportunities) from *Soccer Strategies* by **Allen Wade** (Heinemann pbk £7.95)

ROBSON, BRYAN
Soccer Skills
Top tips from the fragile forward.
[V151] Hamlyn pbk **£5.95**

THOMAS, B. & HUGHES, B.
Gary Lineker
Biography of Barcelona and England centre forward.
[V152] Collins pbk **£8.95**

TYRRELL & MEEK
Manchester Utd Official History   NEW
The carnage of Munich, the beating of Benfica to win the European Cup ten years later, Edwards, Best and all the rest.
[V153] Hamlyn **£12.95**

WADE
Football Association Guide to Training and Coaching
[V154] Heinemann hbk **£6.95**

WADE, ALLEN
Soccer Strategies
[V154A] Heinemann pbk **£7.95**

Golf

Benson & Hedges Golfer's Handbook
The 84th edition of this comprehensive guide to golf in Britain and Ireland with full details of the European Tour.
[V155] Macmillan pbk **£10.95**

Following the Fairways 1990   NEW
3rd edition of a high-quality guide to the 1,770 courses of Britain and Ireland, with details of places to stay and visit, for the non-golfer.
[V156] Kensington West pbk **£13.95**

Historic Golf Courses of the British Isles
Introduction by Peter Alliss and Barry Took.
[V157] Duckworth hbk **£14.95**

The Holiday Golf Guide 1990 `NEW`
A new guide for golfers to Britain and Europe, with details on courses and other aspects of Golf, and more general information on the countries concerned.
[V158] Kensington West pbk **£10.95**

Who's Who in Golf
[V159] Hamlyn pbk **£4.95**

ALLISS, PETER
Play Better Golf with Peter Alliss `NEW`
[V160] BBC hbk **£10.95**
[V161] BBC pbk **£5.95**

ALLISS, PETER & FERRIER, BOB
The Best of Golf `NEW`
Illustrated panorama of the game's history, covering players, courses, changes in technique and equipment.
[V162] Partridge P hbk **£17.50**

ALLISS, PETER & HOBBS, MICHAEL
The Open: The British Championship Since the War
[V163] Collins hbk **£9.95**

BOOTH, ALLAN & HOBBS, MICHAEL
The Illustrated Dictionary of Golf
[V164] Sackville hbk **£14.95**

CANNON, DAVID
Severiano Ballesteros: A Celebration
[V165] Kingswood hbk **£12.95**

DOBEREINER, PETER
Down the 19th Fairway: A Golfing Anthology
[V166] Deutsch hbk **£8.95**
Golf Rules Explained
[V167] David & Ch hbk **£6.95**
Preferred Lies About Golf
[V168] S Paul hbk **£8.95**

FALDO, NICK
Golf: The Winning Formula
Tips from the affable 1989 US Masters champion.
[V169] S Paul hbk **£14.95**

GREEN, R.
Golf: An Illustrated History of the Game
[V170] Collins hbk **£14.95**

GREEN, ROBERT & MORGAN, BRIAN
72 Classic Holes of Golf `NEW`
A survey of the world's most beautiful golf courses, stunningly illustrated and elaborately descriptive.
[V171] Collins hbk **£16.95**

HOBBS, MICHAEL `NEW`
The Ryder Cup: An Illustrated History
[V172] Queen Anne P hbk **£14.95**

HOGAN, BEN
Modern Fundamentals of Golf
[V173] Heinemann pbk **£6.95**
Power Golf
One of the finest golf instruction books, a touchstone of the sport first published over 40 years ago.
[V174] Sportspages pbk **£5.95**

JACKLIN, TONY & DOBEREINER, PETER
Jacklin's Golf Secrets
Britain's Ryder Cup captain and the best of modern golf journalists combine to bring you their expertise.
[V175] S Paul hbk **£10.95**

JACOBS, JOHN & AULTMAN, DICK
Golf Doctor: Diagnosis, Explanation and Correction of Golfing Faults
[V176] S Paul hbk **£11.90**

LONGHURST, HENRY
Only on Sundays `NEW`
A collection of Longhurst's pieces from the *Sunday Times*; he is one of the essential writers on the sport, and a readable and entertaining essayist.
[V177] Sportspages pbk **£5.95**

LUCAS, LADDIE
John Jacob's Impact on Golf
[V178] S Paul hbk **£12.95**

LYLE, SANDY
The Championship Courses of Scotland
A re-issue of Lyle's guide to the courses of the game's birthplace, which leads on to an analysis of tactics.
[V179] Lennard hbk **£20.00**

NICKLAUS, JACK
Twenty 'majors' to his name, the Golden Bear is the most charismatic of post-war golfers.
Full Swing
[V180] Collins hbk **£12.95**
[V181] Collins pbk **£7.95**
Golf My Way
[V182] Heinemann hbk **£12.95**
My 55 Ways to Lower Your Golf Score
[V183] Hodder pbk **£8.95**
Play Better Golf Vol 1
[V184] Hodder pbk **£1.95**
Play Better Golf Vol 2
[V185] Hodder pbk **£1.95**
Play Better Golf Vol 3
[V186] Hodder pbk **£1.95**

PALMER, ARNOLD
The Complete Book of Putting
[V187] S Paul hbk **£12.95**

PLIMPTON, GEORGE
The Bogey Man: An 18-Handicap Account of the Pro-Golf Tour
Plimpton's account of a month spent on the professional golf circuit: golfing legends, adventures, superstition, stroke-saving theory and other lore.
[V188] Sportspages pbk **£5.95**

PRICE, CHARLES
Bobby Jones and the Masters
The story of the man and the Augusta 'major' he inaugurated and nurtured.
[V189] Century hbk **£20.00**

SAUNDERS, VIVIEN
Golf For Women `NEW`
[V190] A & C Black **£8.95**

SNEAD, SAM
How to Beat the Golf Hustler
Probably the only book in print on 'on-course' betting. A sardonic view by one of the greats.
[V191] S Paul hbk **£7.95**

STEEL, DONALD
Golf Facts & Feats
[V192] Guinness hbk **£12.95**

STIRK, DAVID
Carry Your Bag, Sir? `NEW`
An anecdotal and illustrated history of golf, seen from the rarely explored angle of the caddy.
[V193] Witherby hbk **£9.95**

THOMSON, PETER
The World Atlas of Golf
[V194] M Beazley hbk **£12.95**

WATSON, TOM & HANNIGAN, FRANK
New Rules of Golf 1988 - 1991
[V195] Hodder hbk **£8.95**

WATSON, TOM & SEITZ, NICK
Getting Up & Down: How to Save Strokes from 40 Yards
[V196] Hodder hbk **£9.95**

Horse-Racing & Equestrianism

Playfair Racing Annual 1989
[V197] Macdonald pbk **£2.95**

The Benson & Hedges Racing Year 1989
An encyclopaedia and almanac of horse racing in Britain and Ireland.
[V198] Pelham hbk **£15.95**

Travelling the Turf 1990 `NEW`
5th edition of a general guide to racing, centred around the 59 courses of Britain, with maps, details of accommodation, and of the racing calendar.
[V199] Kensington West pbk **£13.95**

BARNES, SIMON
Horsesweat and Tears `NEW`
Fascinating account of a year in the life of a racing stables.
[V200] Heinemann hbk **£12.95**

BERNARD, JEFFREY
Talking Horses
Amusing observations on his favourite sport and lifestyle by the *Spectator* columnist.
[V201] Fourth Estate hbk **£10.95**

BRADDOCK, PETER
Braddock's Complete Guide to Horse Racing Selection & Betting
[V202] Longman hbk **£12.95**

BRITISH HORSE SOCIETY
Manual of Stable Management
Book 1: The Horse
[V203] Harrap pbk **£4.95**
Book 2: Care of the Horse
[V204] Harrap pbk **£4.95**

CHAMPION, BOB
Champion's Story
Heartening story of Bob Champion who recovered from cancer to win the Grand National on Aldaniti.
[V205] Fontana pbk **£1.75**

GORDON-WATSON, MARY
The Handbook of Riding
[V206] M Joseph hbk **£12.95**

GREEN, LUCINDA
Regal Realm: A World Champion's Story
[V207] Methuen pbk **£4.95**

HILL, CHRISTOPHER
Horse Power: Politics of the Turf
General history of horse racing from 1950 onwards.
[V208] Manchester UP hbk **£21.50**

MAGEE, SEAN
The Channel Four Book of Racing `NEW`
An illustrated handbook, with introduction by Brough Scott, covering horses, courses, owners, trainers and jockeys, form and betting.
[V209] Sidgwick hbk **£15.00**

MORTIMER, ROGER & NELIGAN, TIM
The Epsom Derby
[V210] M Joseph hbk **£15.00**

O'NEIL, JONJO
Jonjo
An extremely popular jockey turned trainer who has
fought his way back from cancer.
[V211] Century hbk **£8.95**

OLIVER, KEN (ED)
**Ruff's Guide to the Turf & 'Sporting
Life' Annual 1989**
The most detailed and comprehensive reference
annual in racing.
[V212] Macdonald hbk **£50.00**

RANDALL & MORRIS (EDS)
Horse Racing: The Records
[V213] Guinness pbk **£7.95**

ROBERTS, PETER
The Basic Skills of Horse Riding
[V214] JA Allen pbk **£4.95**

SCUDAMORE, PETER　　　　**NEW**
Peter Scudamore on Steeplechasing
The first 200 winner National Hunt jockey for 35
years writes of the sport he was brought up in.
[V215] Partridge hbk **£13.95**

SERTH, G.W.
**Horse Owner's Guide to Common
Ailments**
[V216] M Joseph pbk **£3.95**

STEINKRAUS, WILLIAM & STONERIDGE,
MARJORIE
The Horse in Sport
[V217] Macdonald hbk **£14.95**

WILSON, JULIAN
Julian Wilson's 100 Great Horses
A tribute to 200 years of racing history from the BBC
racing commentator.
[V218] Macdonald hbk **£14.95**

XENOPHON
The Art of Horsemanship
Fourth century BC Athenian treatise, never bettered.
[V219] JA Allen pbk **£3.25**

Mountaineering

BELL, J.H.B.
Bell's Scottish Climbs
[V220] Gollancz pbk **£5.95**

BIRKETT, BILL
Classic Rock Climbs of Great Britain
A comprehensive guide to the best climbs in Britain.
[V221] Oxford hbk **£14.95**
Modern Rock and Ice Climbing
For the professional who wants to keep in touch with
the latest equipment and techniques.
[V222] A & C Black hbk **£12.50**

BONINGTON, CHRIS
Britain's best-known mountaineer tells of his
excitement and love of the sport in this three-volume
autobiography.
I Chose to Climb
[V223] Gollancz pbk **£4.95**
The Everest Years
[V224] Hodder pbk **£2.95**
The Next Horizon
[V225] Gollancz pbk **£4.95**
Mountaineer　　　　**NEW**
The illustrated autobiography of one of the world's
great climbers, covering his 30 years of climbing.
[V226] Diadem hbk **£16.95**

COLLISTER, ROB
Lightweight Expeditions　　**NEW**
A guide to lightweight climbing, written by
an expert with over 20 years experience.
[V227] Crowood hbk **£12.95**

CRAIG, D.
Native Stones: A Book about Climbing
One of the most popular sports books in recent years.
The poet David Craig sees rock climbing as a
metaphor for life.
[V228] Secker hbk **£10.95**
[V229] Fontana pbk **£3.50**

FAWCETT, GILL
The Alternative Guide to Rockclimbing
Much-needed information on pubs, cafe's and where
to sleep.
[V230] Unwin Hyman pbk **£6.95**

HOUSTON, CHARLES S.
**Going Higher: The Story of Man &
Altitude**
[V231] Cordee hbk **£9.95**

JONES, DAVID　　　　**NEW**
The Crag Guide to England and Wales
Listing every crag in England and Wales, with
location, maps and details of height and difficulty.
[V232] Crowood pbk **£9.95**

JUDSON, DAVID
Caving Practice & Equipment
[V233] David & Ch hbk **£14.95**

MCNEILL, CAROL
Orienteering　　　　**NEW**
[V234] Crowood hbk **£9.95**

MESSNER, REINHOLD
**The Crystal Ascent: Everest -
The First Solo Ascent**　　**NEW**
Messner writes of his 1980 solo ascent of Everest
without oxygen. More than simply an account of the
climb, it tells of his deep reaction to the environment,
and to the ultimate challenge of mountaineering.
[V235] Crowood hbk **£12.95**

MITCHELL, DICK
Mountaineering First Aid
[V236] Cordee hbk **£4.95**

PERRIN, JIM
Don Whillans
A biography of one of Britain's finest mountaineers.
[V237] Hodder hbk **£14.95**

SMITH, W.P. HASKETT
Climbing in the British Isles
[V238] Cordee hbk **£12.00**

TASKER, JOE
Savage Arena
Chris Bonington praises this as the 'greatest book on
mountaineering' he has read.
[V239] Methuen pbk **£4.95**

TULLIS, JULIE
Clouds from Both Sides
The story of the last tragic climb of Julie Tullis,
Britain's greatest female mountaineer.
[V240] Grafton pbk **£3.95**

WHYMPER, EDWARD
Victorian climber with a Ruskinesque prose style.
Scrambles Amongst the Alps 1860 - 69
[V241] Century pbk **£5.95**
The Ascent of the Matterhorn
[V242] Sutton pbk **£6.95**

Sailing

**Macmillan & Silk Cut Nautical
Almanac 1990**　　　　**NEW**
A new edition of the most popular of the sailing
almanacs.
[V243] Macmillan hbk **£15.95**

**Macmillan & Silk Cut Yachtsman's
Handbook**
[V244] Macmillan hbk **£19.95**

BOND, BOB
The Handbook of Sailing
[V245] Pelham pbk **£9.95**

CHICHESTER, SIR FRANCIS
The Lonely Sea and the Sky
Classic account of life on the sea, and of Chichester's
experience of the vast unknown forces of the natural
world.
[V246] Pan pbk **£3.50**

COLES, K. ADLARD
Close-Hauled
[V247] Conway Maritime pbk **£4.95**
Heavy Weather Sailing
[V248] Collins hbk **£18.95**
The Shell Pilot to the English Channel
Harbours on the South Coast of England: Ramsgate to
the Scillies.
[V249] Faber hbk **£17.50**

COOTE, J.
The Shell Pilot to the English Channel
Harbours in Northern France and the Channel Islands:
Dunkerque to Brest.
[V250] Faber hbk **£12.95**

COWES, BEKEN OF
A Century of Tall Ships
Impressively well-produced colour and older black
and white photographs of sailing ships by a long
established firm of Cowes photographers.
[V251] Harrap hbk **£25.00**

CUNLIFFE, T.
Inshore Navigation
[V252] Fernhurst hbk **£7.95**

DEAR & KEMP (EDS)
**The Pocket Oxford Guide to
Sailing Terms**
Recently published, this is the most up-to-date
sailing dictionary.
[V253] Oxford hbk **£12.95**
[V254] Oxford pbk **£6.95**

HAYES, J.
Sails
Illustrated guide on every possible aspect of sails.
[V255] Fernhurst pbk **£5.95**

HOLLANDER & MERTES
**The Yachtsman's Emergency
Handbook**
[V256] Angus & R hbk **£9.95**

HOWARD-WILLIAMS, JEREMY
Sails
[V257] Adlard Coles hbk **£24.95**

JARMAN, COLIN
Buying or Selling a Boat
[V258] Adlard Coles pbk **£6.95**
Cruising: Coastwise & Beyond
[V259] A & C Black hbk **£10.95**

Sailing & Boating: The Complete Equipment Guide
[V260] David & Ch hbk **£10.95**

KNOX-JOHNSTON, ROBIN
Seamanship
[V261] Hodder hbk **£12.95**

LUBBOCK, BASIL
China Clippers
Introduction by Eric Newby.
[V262] Century pbk **£4.95**

PERA, M.
Yacht Racing Rules 1989 - 1992   **NEW**
[V263] A & C Black pbk **£9.95**

POWELL, C.
Radio Position Fixing for Yachtsmen
[V264] Adlard Coles pbk **£5.95**

RABAN, JONATHAN
Coasting
Marvellously written journal of a trip around the British Isles.
[V265] Picador pbk **£3.99**

RANSOME, ARTHUR
Racundra's First Cruise
Introduced by C. Northcote Parkinson. In 1921 Ransome commissioned the boat in which he was to sail the Baltic.
[V266] Century pbk **£4.95**

ROLT, L.T.C.
Narrow Boat
Classic account of Rolt's early years on board his narrow boat 'Cressy' in the 1930s.
[V267] Methuen pbk **£5.95**

ROUSMANIERE, J.
Fastnet Force 10
A necessary reminder of the dangers of racing - the disastrous 1979 Fastnet Race.
[V268] A & C Black pbk **£6.95**

SLEIGHT, STEVE
Modern Boatbuilding
[V269] A & C Black hbk **£11.95**

SLOCUM, JOSHUA
Sailing Alone Around the World
[V270] Century pbk **£5.95**

Other Sports A-Z

AMERICAN FOOTBALL
ELSTRAN, BILL & NELSON, DAVID
American Football for the Viewer
[V271] S Paul pbk **£7.95**
American Football: How to Watch & Play
[V272] S Paul hbk **£7.95**
HORNE, NICKY
The Complete American Football Book
[V273] Robson hbk **£6.95**
The Viewer's Guide to American Football
[V274] Robson hbk **£4.95**
NAMATH, JOE & OATES, BOB J.
American Football: A Complete Guide to Playing the Game
[V275] Pan pbk **£6.95**
NELSON, COLIN
American Football
[V2751] Ward Lock pbk **£3.99**

RATCLIFFE & PHILIPS (EDS)
American Football Official Rulebook
[V276] Columbus pbk **£3.95**
ROWE, PETER
American Football Records, Facts and Champions   **NEW**
[V277] Guinness pbk **£8.95**

ARCHERY
The Archer's Digest
[V278] Cassell pbk **£10.95**
KEMBER-SMITH, JOHN
Archery Today
[V279] David & Ch hbk **£12.50**
PATERSON, W.F.
Encyclopaedia of Archery
[V280] Hale hbk **£12.95**

ATHLETICS
Hamlyn Encyclopaedia of Athletics
[V281] Hamlyn hbk **£4.99**
BAKER, WILLIAM J.
Jesse Owens: An American Life
[V282] Macmillan hbk **£12.95**
COE, PETER & SEBASTIAN
Running for Fitness
Includes the Runner's Log, a record which the Coes have found invaluable for long term training schedules.
[V283] Pavilion hbk **£9.95**
GLOVER & SHEPHERD
Runner's Handbook
[V284] Penguin pbk **£3.95**
GLOVER, BOB
Competitive Runner's Handbook
[V285] Penguin pbk **£4.95**
HEMERY, DAVID
Athletics in Action
[V286] S Paul pbk **£5.95**
SLOAN, LIZ & KRAMER, ANN
Running: The Women's Handbook
[V287] Pandora pbk **£3.95**
TEMPLE, CLIFF
Running from A to Z
Includes biographies of the major runners.
[V288] S Paul hbk **£10.95**
WARD, TONY (ED)
The AAA Guide to Better Athletics
Published with the Amateur Athletic Association. This guide includes a foreword by Britain's Steve Cram.
[V289] Pan pbk **£5.95**
WATT, WILSON & HORWILL
The Complete Middle Distance Runner
[V290] Century pbk **£4.95**

BADMINTON
BADDELEY, STEVE
Badminton in Action
Detailed training manual.
[V291] S Paul pbk **£5.95**
DAVIS, PAT
Badminton   **NEW**
[V292] David & Ch hbk **£7.95**

BALLOONING
CAMERON, DON
Ballooning Handbook
[V293] M Joseph hbk **£12.95**

BASEBALL
BOSWELL, THOMAS
Why Time Begins on Opening Day
[V294] Sportspages pbk **£5.95**
GARBER, ANGUS G.
Baseball Legends
[V295] Sportspages hbk **£10.95**

Blocking

Illustration from *American Football* by **Colin Nelson** (Ward Lock pbk £3.99)

SHATZKIN, MIKE
Baseball Explained
[V296] Pelham pbk **£7.95**
THOMAS, ANDREW
Guide to Baseball
[V297] Macdonald pbk **£2.95**

BOWLS
BRYANT, DAVID
Bryant on Bowls
[V298] Pelham pbk **£10.95**
ENGLISH BOWLING ASSOCIATION
Bowls: Know the Game
[V299] A & C Black pbk **£1.75**
NEWBY, DAVID
Daily Telegraph Bowls Yearbook 1989
[V300] Pan pbk **£7.95**
PILLEY (ED)
The Story of Bowls from Drake to Bryant
[V301] S Paul hbk **£14.95**
WEEKES, BARRY
Bowls (Crown and Flat Green)
Part of the *Play the Game* Series.
[V302] Ward Lock pbk **£3.99**

BOXING
Hamlyn Encyclopaedia of Boxing
[V303] Hamlyn **£9.95**
ANDRE & FLEISCHER
A Pictorial History of Boxing
A popular comprehensive history with good photographs.
[V304] Hamlyn pbk **£8.95**
GOLESWORTHY, MAURICE
Encyclopaedia of Boxing (8th Edition)
[V305] Hale hbk **£10.95**
HELLER, PETER
Mike Tyson   **NEW**
[V306] Robson **£10.95**
LIEBLING, A.J.
The Sweet Science
Liebling is one of the great American essayists; this volume on boxing is his only writing easily available in England.
[V307] Simon & Sch pbk **£5.95**
MCGHEE, FRANK
Boxing's Hall of Fame   **NEW**
A testimony to the giants of English boxing; highly-illustrated, it looks at the lives and careers of some 50 of England's all-time greats.
[V308] Bloomsbury pbk **£7.99**

MEAD, CHRIS
Champion Joe Louis: A Biography
[V309] Robson hbk **£9.50**
OATES, JOYCE CAROL
On Boxing
This popular American novelist. views the seedy New York boxing scene as metaphor, spectacle and history.
[V310] Pan pbk **£3.99**
TOPEROFF, SAM
Sugar Ray Leonard and Other Noble Warriors
[V311] Sportspages pbk **£6.95**

CROQUET
GILL, ANTON
Complete Guide to Croquet
[V312] Heinemann hbk **£14.95**
MCCULLOUGH, JOHN & MULLINER, STEVEN
The World of Croquet
Extensive book on this surprisingly vindictive sport.
[V313] Crowood hbk **£14.95**
SOLMON, J.
Croquet NEW
[V314] A & C Black **£7.95**

CYCLING
BALLANTINE, RICHARD
Richard's New Bicycle Book NEW
[V315] Oxford Illus hbk **£14.95**
LIGGETT, PHIL
Tour de France 1989
[V316] Harrap pbk **£9.95**
MERCKZ, EDDY
The Great Races
[V317] Cordee hbk **£16.95**
ROCHE, STEPHEN
My Road to Victory
Picture book of a victorious year which ended with him singing 'Irish Eyes Are Smiling' on French TV.
[V318] S Paul hbk **£10.95**
The Agony and the Ecstasy
A more serious study of how to win the world's greatest cycle race.
[V319] S Paul hbk **£12.95**
SLOANE, E.A.
The All New Complete Book of Cycling
The best technical book on cycling. Highly detailed and well illustrated.
[V320] Simon & Sch hbk **£9.95**
WATSON & GRAY
Penguin Book of the Bicycle
The A-Z of all you need to know about the bicycle.
[V321] Penguin pbk **£3.95**

HRH the Prince of Wales from *A Concise Guide to Polo* by **J N P Watson** (Sportsman's P hbk **£8.95**)

FENCING
PITMAN, BRIAN
Fencing NEW
[V322] Crowood hbk **£12.95**

HOCKEY
CADMAN, JOHN
Hockey Rules Illustrated
[V323] M Joseph hbk **£5.75**
Hockey: The Rules of the Game
[V324] Crowood hbk **£8.95**
TAYLOR, IAN & VEAR, DAVID
Taylor on Hockey
Tips from England's gold medal-winning goalkeeper.
[V325] Macdonald hbk **£9.95**

MARTIAL ARTS
Martial Arts of the Orient
[V326] Hamlyn pbk **£8.95**
Self Defence for Women
[V327] Hamlyn hbk **£6.95**
ANDREWS, C.
The KUGB Guide to Better Karate
A basic guide, officially sanctioned by the sport's ruling body in Britain.
[V328] Pan pbk **£4.99**
BRIGGS, KAREN
Judo Champion
Three times world champion tells her career story.
[V329] Crowood hbk **£9.95**
CAFFARY, BRIAN
The Judo Handbook NEW
[V330] Ward Lock hbk **£10.95**
CROMPTON, PAUL
Karate Training Methods
[V331] PH Crompton pbk **£4.95**
The Complete Martial Arts NEW
Covering all the major martial arts (such as Karate, Judo, Kick Boxing, Kendo and Tai Chi) this describes the physical and mental qualities necessary for each, and explains the history and tradition behind them.
[V332] Partridge P hbk **£15.95**
DONOVAN, TICKY
Traditional Karate
Ticky Donovan is the world's most successful karate coach and in 1986 led Britain to a fourth successive world championship.
[V333] Pelham hbk **£14.95**
Winning Karate
[V334] Pelham hbk **£10.95**
ENOEDA, K.
Karate Defence & Attack
[V335] PH Crompton hbk **£3.95**
FINN, M.
Martial Arts: A Complete Illustrated History
The development of the martial arts from their origins in Ancient Japan and India to their current worldwide popularity.
[V336] S Paul hbk **£16.95**
GOLDMAN, JOHN
Judo: The Complete Course
[V337] Guinness pbk **£7.95**
PAYNE, P.
Martial Arts: The Spiritual Dimension
[V338] Thames & H pbk **£4.95**
SHORTT, J & HASHIMOTO, KATSUHARA
Beginning Jujitsu
[V339] PH Crompton pbk **£5.95**
VALERA, DOMINIQUE
Competition Karate
[V340] PH Crompton pbk **£2.95**

MOTOR RACING
BOTSFORD, KEITH
The Champions of Formula 1
A detailed history of motoring racing champions from the 1950s to the present day.
[V341] S Paul hbk **£12.95**

HAMILTON, MAURICE
RAC Rally 1932 - 1988 NEW
The latest edition gives the up-to-date story of one of the toughest motoring events of the world.
[V342] Partridge P pbk **£8.95**
HILTON, CHRISTOPHER
Nigel Mansell
[V343] William Kimber hbk **£8.95**
LANG, MIKE
Grand Prix: 1977 - 1980
The third of three volumes which cover the recent history of the sport.
[V344] Haynes hbk **£14.95**
MANSELL, NIGEL
In the Driving Seat NEW
The perennial world championship hopeful and part time Isle of Man policeman offers his view from behind the wheel.
[V345] S Paul hbk **£14.95**
MORRISON, I.
Motor Racing: Records, Facts & Champions
[V346] Guinness pbk **£8.95**
MOSS, STIRLING & NYE, DOUG
Stirling Moss
[V347] P Stephens hbk **£14.95**

POLO
WATSON, J.N.P.
A Concise Guide to Polo
By the polo correspondent of *The Times*.
[V348] Sportsman's P hbk **£8.95**

RHYTHMIC GYMNASTICS
BOTT, JENNY
Rhythmic Gymnastics NEW
[V349] Crowood hbk **£9.95**

ROWING
BURNELL, R.
Henley Royal Regatta NEW
[V350] Heinemann hbk **£16.95**
TOPOLSKI, DANIEL & CLARK, GEORGE
Henley - The Regatta NEW
A photographic study capturing the history of the world's greatest rowing event in its anniversary year. Topolski, coach of the Oxford Boat Race team for 15 years, provides the commentary.
[V351] Murray pbk **£10.95**

RUGBY LEAGUE
Rothman's Rugby League Yearbook 1988 - 89
[V352] Macdonald pbk **£10.95**
LARDER, PHIL
Rugby League Coaching Manual NEW
[V353] Heinemann pbk **£9.95**

RUGBY UNION
Rothman's Rugby Union Yearbook 1988 - 89
[V354] Macdonald pbk **£10.95**
EDWARDS, GARETH
100 Great Rugby Players
[V355] Macdonald hbk **£14.95**
GODWIN, TERRY
Rugby Facts & Feats
[V356] Guinness hbk **£8.95**
The Complete Who's Who of International Rugby
[V357] Blandford hbk **£19.95**
PARRY-JONES, DAVID
Out of the Ruck: A Selection of Rugby Writing
[V358] Pelham hbk **£12.95**
STARMER-SMITH, NIGEL & ROBERTSON, IAN
BBC Rugby Special
The book of BBC2's rejuvenated Sunday magazine.
[V359] BBC hbk **£7.95**

SPORT

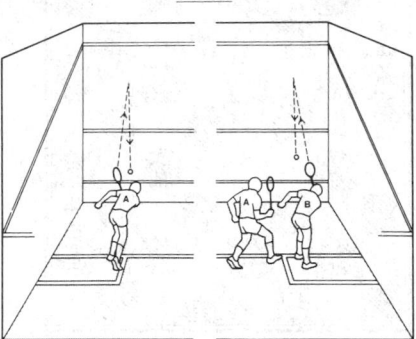

SQUASH

Illustration from *Squash* by **David Hawkey** (Ward Lock pbk £3.99)

SKIING
EPP, MARTIN
Ski Powder
Basic introduction to skiing by a famous Swiss ski guide.
[V360] Fernhurst **£5.95**
HELLER, MARK
Skiing School
[V361] Macdonald pbk **£7.95**
LANG, SERGE
21 Years of World Cup Ski Racing
[V362] Grafton hbk **£12.95**

SNOOKER
Benson & Hedges Snooker Year 1989
[V363] Pelham pbk **£5.99**
Rothman's Snooker Yearbook 1988-89
Rankings, career guides, major results plus coverage of billiards and amateur snooker. A most comprehensive guide.
[V364] Macdonald pbk **£9.95**
BURN, GORDON
Pocket Money: Inside the World of Snooker
A marvellous insight into the world of snooker that goes behind the popular TV image. Brutal and hard-hitting.
[V365] Pan pbk **£3.99**
CALLAN, FRANK & DEE, JOHN
Frank Callan's Snooker Clinic **NEW**
Assistance in improving your game from one of the sport's top professional coaches.
[V366] Partridge P pbk **£10.95**
DAVIS, STEVE
Successful Snooker
The six-times world champion offers insights into his relentless pursuit of consistency.
[V367] Letts pbk **£2.95**
EVERTON, CLIVE
Guinness Book of Snooker
[V368] Guinness pbk **£6.95**
Improve Your Snooker
[V369] Collins hbk **£12.95**
KARNEHM, JACK
Understanding Billiards & Snooker
This title has now been adopted by the Billiards and Snooker Association. Mr Karnehm is the most knowledgeable and enthusiastic of coaches and commentators.
[V370] Pelham pbk **£8.95**
TRELFORD, DONALD
Snookered
The *Observer*'s editor tries to come to terms with his obsessive interest in the game.
[V371] Faber pbk **£4.95**

SQUASH
SRA/WSRA Guide to Better Squash
Lessons from top coaches such as Bob Lincoln, Jane Poynder, Claire Chapman and Paul Wright.
[V372] Pan pbk **£4.99**
COLLOWN, ALAN
Squash: The Ambitious Player's Guide
[V373] Faber pbk **£3.95**
HAWKEY, DAVID
Squash
[V3731] Ward Lock pbk **£3.99**
KHAN, JAHANGIR
Winning Squash
[V374] S Paul pbk **£6.95**
POYNDER, J.
Pocket Guide to Squash Tactics
[V375] Unwin Hyman hbk **£5.95**
SWIFT, T.
Squash Rackets
[V376] A & C Black hbk **£5.95**
TAYLOR, J.
Squash
[V377] Pelham pbk **£8.95**

SWIMMING & DIVING
Sport Diving: British Sub Aqua Club Diving Manual
A comprehensive, well-illustrated guide to all aspects of sport diving.
[V378] S Paul pbk **£12.95**
AMATEUR SWIMMING ASSOCIATION
The Teaching of Swimming
[V379] A & C Black pbk **£4.00**
ASSOCIATION OF SWIMMING THERAPY
Swimming for the Disabled
[V380] A & C Black pbk **£5.50**
DEAKIN, JOAN
Scuba Diving
[V381] David & Charles hbk **£6.95**
WILKIE, DAVID & JUBA, KELVIN
The Handbook of Swimming
[V382] Pelham hbk **£12.95**

TENNIS
APPLEWHAITE, CHARLES & POYNDER, JANE
The L.T.A. Guide to Better Tennis
[V383] Pan pbk **£4.95**
BECKER, BORIS
Boris Becker's Tennis
Training programme from the extraordinarily powerful young German who has won Wimbledon twice.
[V384] Springfield hbk **£8.95**
DOUGLAS, PAUL
The Handbook of Tennis
[V385] Pelham hbk **£9.95**
EVANS, RICHARD
McEnroe: A Rage for Perfection
[V386] Hodder pbk **£2.50**
Open Tennis: The First 20 Years
The world of professional tennis: the players, the politics and the passions.
[V387] Bloomsbury hbk **£12.95**
FORBES, GORDON
A Handful of Summers
[V388] Sportspages pbk **£5.95**
MASKELL, DAN
A Life in Tennis
Autobiography of former player and famous BBC commentator. 'Oh I say, that's a peach of a life story. He's done it, he really has done it!'.
[V389] Collins hbk **£14.95**

WATER-SKIING
WEST, JOHN
Water-Skiing **NEW**
[V390] Crowood hbk **£9.95**

GAMES

Chess

The recent increase in the popularity of chess has been reflected in the range of titles published, a small selection of which appears here. Batsford are the major publisher, and their classification system, by three levels of difficulty (A: Basic Level; B: Middle Level; C: Advanced Level), has been followed here, where applicable. Pergamon offers another excellent range, with an emphasis on more advanced works.

The Official Laws of Chess, 1989 Edition **NEW**
From the Fédération Internationale des Echecs, this new edition includes the latest amendments to the laws of the game.
[V400] Batsford pbk **£6.95**

ADDISON, STEPHEN
The Book of Extraordinary Chess Problems **NEW**
Aimed at players of all levels, this is a collection of unorthodox or 'alternative' problems, which offer a fascinating exercise in chess lateral thinking.
[V401] Crowood hbk **£8.95**

AVERBAKH, Y.
Chess Endings: Essential Knowledge (B)
[V402] Pergamon pbk **£8.50**

BENJAMIN & SCHILLER
Unorthodox Openings (B)
Intended for the club player searching for new openings.
[V403] Batsford pbk **£6.95**

CAPABLANCA, JOSE RAOUL
My Chess Career
[V404] Dover pbk **£3.85**

Martina Navratilova from *Eammon McCabe: Photographer* (Heinemann hbk £15.00)

**World Championship
Matches 1921 & 1927**
[V405] Dover pbk **£3.00**

CHERNEV, IRVING
Logical Chess: Move By Move (A)
Excellent lay out for the beginner.
[V406] Faber pbk **£3.95**
**The Most Instructive Game of Chess
Ever Played** (A)
[V407] Faber pbk **£4.95**

CHERNEV, IRVING & REINFELD, FRED
Winning Chess (B)
Aimed at the average player.
[V408] Faber pbk **£3.95**

FINE, REUBEN
**The Ideas Behind the
Chess Openings**   **NEW**
An useful introductory guide for novices.
[V409] Batsford pbk **£7.95**

FISCHER, BOBBY
My 60 Memorable Games
With introductions to the games by Larry Evans.
[V410] Faber pbk **£4.95**

GELLER, EFIM
The Application of Chess Theory (C)
[V411] Pergamon pbk **£11.95**

GOLOMBEK, HARRY
Beginning Chess (A)
A classic beginner's guide.
[V412] Penguin pbk **£2.50**
**Capablanca's 100 Best Games of
Chess** (B)
[V413] Batsford hbk **£8.95**
The Game of Chess (A)
[V414] Penguin pbk **£3.95**

GUFELD, EDWARD
**The Sicilian for the Tournament
Player**   **NEW**
[V415] Batsford pbk **£8.95**

HARDING, TIM & BARDEN, LEONARD
Openings for the Club Player (B)
[V416] Batsford pbk **£7.95**

HOOPER, DAVID
Pocket Guide to Endgames (A)
[V417] Batsford pbk **£5.95**

Illustration by John Tenniel from **Lewis Carroll**'s
Through the Looking Glass (Macmillian hbk £4.95)

KARPOV, ANATOLY
Learn from Your Defeats (A)
[V418] Batsford pbk **£5.95**
Miniatures from the World Champions
[V419] Batsford pbk **£6.95**

KASPAROV & KEENE
Batsford Chess Openings 2 (A)   **NEW**
A rewriting of the openings reference manual,
including new variations.
[V420] Batsford hbk **£14.95**

KASPAROV, GARY
A Child of Change: The Autobiography
Early autobiography of current and youngest World
Champion in history.
[V421] Hutchinson hbk **£12.95**
Kasparov Teaches Chess (A)
[V422] Batsford pbk **£5.95**
My Games (A)
[V423] Batsford pbk **£9.95**
The Test of Time
[V424] Pergamon pbk **£8.25**

KAZIC, KEENE & LIM
The Official Laws of Chess (A)
[V425] Batsford pbk **£4.95**

KEENE & LEVY
**Opening Repertoire for the
Attacking Player** (B)
[V426] Batsford pbk **£7.95**

KEENE, RAYMOND
**The Evolution of Chess
Opening Theory** (B)
The author traces the development of opening
theory from the old rigid views to the present, more
creative, styles.
[V427] Pergamon pbk **£7.25**

KEENE, RAYMOND & GOODMAN, DAVID
**Kasparov v Karpov
Centenary Match** (A)
[V428] Batsford pbk **£6.95**

KOPEC & CHANDLER
**Master Class: A Course in
21 Lessons** (B)
Well established course for the competent player to
reach higher standards.
[V429] Pergamon hbk **£13.95**
[V430] Pergamon pbk **£7.95**

LASKER, EDWARD
Chess: Complete Self Tutor (A)
A very useful guide for testing your own ability
[V431] Batsford pbk **£7.95**

MCLEOD, W & MONGREDIEN, R
Chess for Beginners
[4311] Collins hbk **£5.95**

MORAN, PABLO
**World Chess Championship: Steinitz
to Alekhine** (B)
[V432] Batsford pbk **£12.95**

NIMZOWITSCH, ARON
Chess Praxis (A)
[V433] Batsford hbk **£14.95**
My System (B)
[V434] Batsford pbk **£8.95**

NUNN, JOHN
Tactical Chess Endings (B)
[V435] Batsford pbk **£8.95**
The Complex Pirc
[V436] Batsford pbk **£9.95**

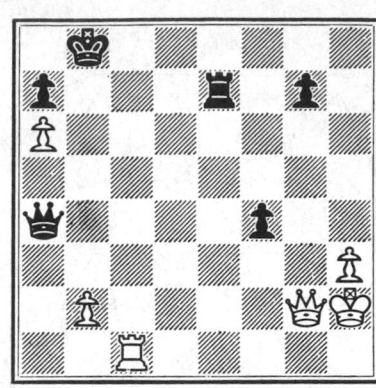

Illustration from *Chess for Young Beginners* by
William Mcleod and **Ronald Mongredien** (Collins
hbk **£5.95**)

POLUGAEVSKY, L.
Grandmaster Performance (C)
[V437] Pergamon pbk **£7.95**
Grandmaster Preparation (C)
[V438] Pergamon pbk **£7.95**
The Art of Defence in Chess (B)
[V439] Pergamon pbk **£9.95**

SAPI & SCHNEIDER
**The Sicilian Dragon:
Yugoslav 9 Bc4** (A)   **NEW**
[V440] Batsford pbk **£9.95**

SHAMKOVICH & SCHILLER
Kasparov's Opening Repertoire   **NEW**
[V441] Batsford pbk **£7.95**

SPANIER, DAVID
Total Chess (A)
[V442] Sphere pbk **£3.95**

SPEELMAN, JON
Endgame Preparation (C)
[V443] Batsford pbk **£8.95**

SUETIN, A.S.
Modern Chess Opening Theory (B)
[V444] Pergamon pbk **£5.95**

TAL, MIKHAIL
Selected Chess Games (A)
[V445] Dover pbk **£3.15**

TALBUT, SHAUN
Positional Chess   **NEW**
[V446] Batsford pbk **£7.95**

WADE & O'CONNELL
Games of Robert J. Fischer (B)
[V447] Batsford pbk **£14.95**

WADE, ROBERT; WHITELY, ANDREW &
KEENE, RAYMOND
**World Chess Championship: Botvinnik
to Kasparov** (B)
[V448] Batsford hbk **£12.95**

WHYLD, KEN
Chess: The Records (A)
[V449] Guinness pbk **£7.95**

WINTER, E.G. (ED)
World Chess Champions (B)
[V450] Pergamon pbk **£6.00**

TION AND FANTASY · FOOD AND COOKERY · HEALTH AND FITNESS · HUMOUR · GAMES AND PUZZLES · CRIME

D THRILLERS · PHILOSOPHY AND POLITICS · PSYCHOLOGY AND SCIENCE · TRAVEL WRITING AND GUIDE BOOKS

REVISION NOTES AND STUDY AIDS · RELIGION AND REFERENCE · ECONOMICS AND ENVIRONMENT · LANGUAGE

D LINGUISTICS · TWENTIETH CENTURY CLASSICS · NEW AGE AND SHORT STORIES · AUTOBIOGRAPHY AND

OGRAPHY · POLITICS AND CURRENT AFFAIRS · CONTEMPORARY FICTION · PENGUIN CLASSICS · GIFT BOOKS

D GARDENING · ART AND ARCIENCE FICTION AND FANTASY ·

OD AND COOKERY · HEALTCRIME AND THRILLERS · PHI-

SOPHY AND POLITICS · PSYCIDE BOOKS · REVISION NOTES

D STUDY AIDS · RELIGION ALANGUAGE AND LINGUISTICS ·

ENTIETH CENTURY CLASSICHY AND BIOGRAPHY · POLITICS

D CURRENT AFFAIRS · CONTOKS AND GARDENING · ART AND

CHITECTURE · HISTORY · Y · FOOD AND COOKERY ·

ALTH AND FITNESS · HUMOU· PHILOSOPHY AND POLITICS ·

PENGUIN
BOOKS

All your reading needs

YCHOLOGY AND SCIENCE · TRAVEL WRITING AND GUIDE BOOKS · REVISION NOTES AND STUDY AIDS · RELIGION

D REFERENCE · ECONOMICS AND ENVIRONMENT · LANGUAGE AND LINGUISTICS · TWENTIETH CENTURY CLAS-

S · NEW AGE AND SHORT STORIES · AUTOBIOGRAPHY AND BIOGRAPHY · POLITICS AND CURRENT AFFAIRS ·

NTEMPORARY FICTION · PENGUIN CLASSICS · GIFT BOOKS AND GARDENING · ART AND ARCHITECTURE · HIS-

RY · POETRY AND PLAYS · SCIENCE FICTION AND FANTASY · FOOD AND COOKERY · HEALTH AND FITNESS ·

MOUR · GAMES AND PUZZLES · CRIME AND THRILLERS · PHILOSOPHY AND POLITICS · PSYCHOLOGY AND

ENCE · TRAVEL WRITING AND GUIDE BOOKS · REVISION NOTES AND STUDY AIDS · RELIGION AND REFERENCE ·

ONOMICS AND ENVIRONMENT · LANGUAGE AND LINGUISTICS · TWENTIETH CENTURY CLASSICS · NEW AGE AND

RT STORIES · AUTOBIOGRAPHY AND BIOGRAPHY · POLITICS AND CURRENT AFFAIRS · CONTEMPORARY FICTION

ENGUIN CLASSICS · GIFT BOOKS AND GARDENING · ART AND ARCHITECTURE · HISTORY · POETRY AND PLAYS ·

ENCE FICTION AND FANTASY · FOOD AND COOKERY · HEALTH AND FITNESS · HUMOUR · GAMES AND PUZZLES

RIME AND THRILLERS · PHILOSOPHY AND POLITICS · PSYCHOLOGY AND SCIENCE · TRAVEL WRITING AND

DE BOOKS · REVISION NOTES AND STUDY AIDS · RELIGION AND REFERENCE · ECONOMICS AND ENVIRONMENT

Bridge

A small selection from the wide selection of Bridge literature appears here, with titles by British players such as JHugh Kelsey and Terence Reese prominent. The dominant publisher is Gollancz who offer the three valuable series listed below.

TEST YOUR GAME

An excellent series of handbooks, using examples and quizzes to improve the reader's skill in particular areas of the game. Priced at £3.50.
Finessing, Trump Control, Card-Reading, Communications, Defensive Play, Pairs Play, Percentages, Timing, Elimination Play, Safety Play

BRIDGE FLIPPERS

Ingenious and accessible basic tools of reference, suitable for use at the table. Priced at £1.95.
Basic Acol, Acol, Duplicate, Five-Card Major, Rubber Bridge Laws

TASK-MASTERS

A new series, with short summaries of Acol bidding, and exercises for consolidating lessons and testing knowledge. Written by expert teachers, they are priced at £1.25.
Introduction to Acol Bidding, Overcalling in Acol, Strategic Acol Bidding, Play Your Cards Right

CULBERTSON, JOSEPHINE
Contract Bridge Made Easy: The New Point Count Way
Simple and clear manual on bridge play.
[V451] Faber pbk **£2.50**

EWEN, ROBERT
Opening Leads   NEW
[V452] Hale pbk **£6.95**

FLINT, JEREMY & GILLICK, JOHN
The First Bridge Book
[V453] Pan pbk **£3.95**

KELSEY, HUGH
Advanced Play at Bridge
Series of problem hands to bring the reader to a high level of play.
[V454] Faber pbk **£3.95**
Challenge Match
Problems and solutions that will improve any reader's game.
[V455] Faber pbk **£3.95**
Killing Defence at Bridge
Classic book on defence.
[V456] Faber pbk **£3.95**
Match-Point Bridge
Many examples bring the anatomy of duplicate to life.
[V457] Faber pbk **£3.50**
Start Bridge the Easy Way
[V458] Gollancz pbk **£4.95**
Winning Card Play   NEW
[V459] Gollancz pbk **£5.95**

KELSEY, HUGH & GLAUERT, MICHAEL
Bridge Odds for Practical Beginners
[V460] Gollancz pbk **£5.95**

KELSEY, HUGH & MATHESON, JOHN
Improve Your Opening Leads
[V461] Gollancz pbk **£4.95**

KLINGER, RON
100 Winning Bridge Tips for the Improving Player
[V462] Gollancz pbk **£4.95**

KLINGER, RON
Guide to Better Acol Bridge   NEW
[V463] Gollancz pbk **£7.95**
World Championship Pairs Bridge
[V464] Gollancz hbk **£8.95**

MARKUS, RIXI
Aces & Places: The International Bridge Circuit
[V465] Unwin Hyman pbk **£2.50**
Book of Bridge
[V466] Collins hbk **£9.95**

MOLLO, VICTOR & GARDENER, NICO
Card Play Technique or The Art of Being Lucky
[V467] Faber pbk **£4.50**

NOVRUP, SVEND & KELSEY, HUGH
First Steps in Card Play   NEW
An acclaimed teaching text from a Danish expert.
[V468] Gollancz pbk **£3.95**

REESE, TERENCE
Bridge
[V469] Penguin pbk **£3.50**
Bridge for Ambitious Players
[V470] Gollancz pbk **£5.95**
Learn Bridge with Reese
Usefully set out including quizzes to test knowledge.
[V471] Faber pbk **£3.95**
Reese On Play
A classic; first published 40 years ago for the advanced player.
[V472] Hale pbk **£4.95**

REESE, TERENCE & BIRD, DAVID
Bridge: Tricks of the Trade   NEW
A guide to some of the particular areas where amateur players often make mistakes.
[V473] Gollancz hbk **£8.95**
Miracles of Card Play   NEW
The first in a sequence of humorous bridge stories.
[V474] Gollancz pbk **£5.95**
Unholy Tricks: More Miraculous Card Play
Stories of the bridge playing monks of St. Titus.
[V475] Gollancz pbk **£5.95**

REESE, TERENCE & MARKUS, RIXI
Better Bridge for Club Players   NEW
[V476] Gollancz pbk **£5.95**

REESE, TERENCE & POTTAGE, JULIAN
Positive Defence
A collection of difficult hands to improve defence technique.
[V477] Gollancz pbk **£4.95**

REESE, TERENCE & TREZEL, ROGER
Elimination Play in Bridge
[V478] Gollancz pbk **£2.95**
Master the Odds in Bridge
Enables one to correctly assess the odds in a situation.
[V479] Gollancz pbk **£2.95**
The Art of Defence in Bridge
[V480] Gollancz pbk **£3.50**
The Mistakes You Make at Bridge   NEW
[V481] Gollancz pbk **£5.95**

REESE, TERENCE (ED)
Bridge Tips by World Masters
[V482] Hale pbk **£4.95**

SHARIF, OMAR
Omar Sharif's Life in Bridge
The suave actor of *Dr Zhivago* is also a serious, cerebral player of both bridge and chess.
[V483] Faber pbk **£3.95**

SHEINWOLD, ALFRED
First Book of Bridge
Amusing and instructive primer.
[V484] Faber pbk **£3.50**

STUBBINGS, DEREK & MELBOURNE, HOWARD
Bridge for Beginners
[V485] Crowood pbk **£6.95**
Bridge for Improvers
[V486] Crowood pbk **£6.95**

Other Games

Hoyle's Modern Encyclopaedia of Card Games
The card-player's bible and the most authoritative rule book for all the basic games and popular variants.
[V487] Hale pbk **£5.95**

Hoyle's Rules of Games
Hoyle's is the accepted source for settling disputes on all games (not sports).
[V488] Signet hbk **£12.95**

Waddington's Illustrated Encyclopaedia of Games
[V489] Pan pbk **£4.95**

ARNOLD, PETER
The Book of Card Games   NEW
[V490] Ch Helm pbk **£6.95**

GOLDSMITH
Easy Guide to Backgammon
[V491] Harrap pbk **£1.95**

HARGRAVE, C.P.
A History of Playing Cards & Bibliography of Cards & Gamery
A reprint of a 1930s classic.
[V492] Dover hbk **£8.95**

HENRY & PHILLIPS
Creative Poker
A guide to avoiding the obvious plays.
[V493] Pan pbk **£3.95**

MOREHEAD, ALBERT H. & MOTT-SMITH, GEOFFREY
The Complete Book of Patience
Numerous variations of card games for one.
[V494] Faber pbk **£3.95**

Illustration by Tenniel from **Lewis Carroll**'s *Alice's Adventures in Wonderland* (Macmillan hbk **£4.95**)

Travel

Major Travel Writers
General Literary Travel

Atlases
Practical Travel Advice
Travel Guides Series

Britain: By Region
Western Europe
Eastern Europe
Africa
North America
Caribbean & Latin America
South America
Asia
Australasia & Oceania

Reflections of a Dinosaur

Dervla Murphy

The travel writing boom, while making us all Fat (or at least not-so-lean) Cats, has provoked a raging epidemic of navel-contemplation. In my youngish days, a quarter of a century ago, travellers went on their journeys, wrote their books and were taken for granted. Now, all of a sudden, we're *interesting*. Other people write books about us, and compile anthologies of our too frequently mortal prose, and base television and wireless programmes on our rarely profound thoughts and elusive 'motives'. Regularly we are tempted to indulge in ludicrous orgies of introspection - and generally we follow Oscar Wilde's advice. Having one's ego massaged is quite pleasurable, though the media masseuse may be over-earnest and under-comprehending.

Recently a solemn young man with an incipient pot-belly and prematurely wrinkled brow began his interview by asking me, "how do you define *travel*?"

I don't delude myself that the general public yearns to know how *I* define *travel*. But when offered the opportunity, most people leap on their hobby-horses. At once I did just that and rode away into the moon-rise, leaving the young man far behind - so far behind that an unhappy note subsequently apologised for his editor having thrown that interview into the waste paper basket.

Only then did I realise that those who share my concept of 'travel' are almost extinct. And this melancholy awareness of belonging to an endangered species was initially strengthened by Jan Morris's remarking in the second edition of this *Guide* that "books of a geographical description or day-by-day narrative...have mostly been superseded now - universal tourism and the techniques of television mean that nearly all of us know the look of the world and the sensations of travel". But then I noticed a certain semantic confusion here, uncharacteristic of Jan Morris. Can 'universal tourism' really be said to provide 'the sensations of travel'? Can 'the techniques of television' really enable us to 'know the look of the world'?

Tourists and travellers are, indisputably, polar opposites: the former essentially passive, the latter essentially active. Travellers (according to my archaic definition) seek 'undeveloped' regions and relish close contact with the locals - if any. They accept as inevitable smelly and/or noisy sleeping quarters, unpredictable paths, punishing climates, beetles expiring in their soup. In contrast, the tourist's first priority is considerable 'development' and they tend to regard the locals as relentless predators - which in Third World countries they usually are, so swiftly does mass tourism corrode human relationships. Moreover, the average tourist feels indignant and cheated if exposed to the most trivial inconvenience: a defective shower, a capricious electricity supply, dubiously laundered sheets. Flying regularly to distant places, there to sprawl on sand or visit those 'sights' accessible to motor vehicles, may give millions the illusion of 'widened horizons'. But it most certainly does not provide them with 'the sensations of travel'.

As for television, by showing spectacularly beautiful pictures of unfamiliar places, it of course enables us to 'know the look of the world' - though not the *feel* of the world. Nor can it ever bring us close to unfamiliar *peoples*. The arrival of a camera crew in a remote area (approached if possible by helicopter) notoriously changes the chemistry of the inhabitants' behaviour - as the arrival of a solo traveller, on foot or horseback, does not.

In 1889, Isabella Bird Bishop, while riding from Baghdad to Teheran, was weather-bound in the Allah-forsaken little town of Khannikin near the Persian border. There she discreetly observed a day in the life of a peasant family and precisely recorded, as was her wont, every nuance of those people's normal behaviour - a feat beyond the capacity of any television team. After all, even the most sophisticated Western victims of 'The Camera' are forced to become other than - and usually *less* than - themselves for the duration of their performance. So perhaps there remains some justification for us dinosaurs continuing to do our own small-brained thing: riding around New Guinea, cycling up the Nile or walking through Cameroon while quietly recording our observations of village life en route.

Meanwhile, more evolved creatures are all the time pursuing their diverse and often complex quests to the considerable enrichment of English literature: up the Orinoco, down the Mississippi, across the USA in a motor car - or happily recalling pre-war Europe, unhappily digging for ancestral roots in India, probing Russia and China, suffering in and with Calcutta, exposing the manic brutality of Christian missionaries in Latin America.

Jan Morris's suggestion that "Travel writing...can be very nearly as fictional as a novel" is disturbing for dinosaurs, who tend to be pedestrian in both senses and to side with Lady Mary Wortley Montagu: *"Perhaps it would be more entertaining to add a few surprising customs of my own invention, but nothing seems to me so agreeable as truth..."* Maybe some more specific labelling is needed, to help readers to distinguish between 'traditional' factual travel writers and authors who treat travel imaginatively, as "a mystic anagram of life itself" (Jan Morris again).

Playing with labels is risky but fun. It seems that by now two categories of modern writers inspired by *places* have emerged: Thinkers and Doers. (I am ignoring semi-literate descriptions of stunt-journeys, undertaken primarily for profit and/or notoriety and often

televised). Nowadays the Thinkers are not true *travellers*, in the Isabella Bird, Alexandra David-NeEel, Freya Stark tradition. But they can write more memorably about a weekend in Bath, or a flying visit to Sydney, than the Doers can about months of slogging through Far-Flungery. Many of their books contain the preservative spices of literary excellence and are likely to be enjoyed by our great-grandchildren, presuming the general public is still literate a century hence. Usually their mastery of language and intellectual vigour so exhilarate the reader that he or she doesn't give a damn if the books in question *are* "very nearly as fictional as a novel."

However, such subtle 'evocations of place' differ fundamentally, not only in execution but in *purpose*, from the Doers' descriptions of encounters with places and peoples. Your average Doer, chiefly notable for physical vigour and information-gathering, blends more or less entertaining accounts of personal adventures with reliable records of obscure corners and may spend half a day checking one fact. The results are rarely as satisfying, for the reader, as Thinkers' distillations - impressionistic, idiosyncratic, reflective - of their spiritual and emotional reactions to new surroundings. But can such author-dominated volumes fairly claim to be *travel* books?

This Thinkers/Doers distinction leaves lots of space for stimulating, or friendship-ending, arguments about who qualifies for which label. Obviously some authors can claim both and one could go on inventing labels for numerous sub-categories. Publishers and booksellers would, of course, consider such labelling very bad for business. They have to pretend, briefly, that *all* new books are of outstanding merit and would hate potential buyers to be warned that Petunia Bloggs-Wittering is a mere Doer. Yet the dinosaurs now urgently need to defend their territory against Jan Morris's thesis that "when it comes to the definition of travel writing, anything goes". Traditional travel writers, who try to be honest reporters, cannot accept that *in volumes labelled travel books*, the artistic imagination may be let off its leash.

TRAVEL

Major Travel Writers

BECKFORD, WILLIAM (1759 - 1844)
Grand Tour of William Beckford (1834)
Alternatively entitled *Italy, with Sketches of Spain and Portugal* but also *Dreams, Waking Thoughts and Incidents*, Beckford describes the places and cultures through which he travelled with genuine insight, tempered with an ironical eye.
[W1] Penguin pbk **£3.95**

BELLOC, HILAIRE (1870 - 1953)
Born in France, Belloc was educated in England and Scotland, and became a British citizen in 1902. From 1906 to 1910 he was MP for Salford, but quit politics to take up writing. His travel writing forms a small part of his output, which consisted mainly of verse, historical biographies and children's stories.
Cruise of the Nona (1925)
[W2] Century pbk **£4.95**
The Path to Rome (1902)
[W3] Penguin pbk **£3.95**

BIRD, ISABELLA (1831 - 1904)
The Victorian traveller Isabella Bird led a remarkable life of travel, despite chronic illness. At 26, she went to America on doctor's orders, only to return to Edinburgh four years later. A decade after that saw her arrival in Australia, via Hawaii, followed by her now famous trip through North America's Western Cordillera; her finest books cover these early travels. Later in life, she visited Japan and other parts of South-East Asia, seeing eventually the Himalayan plateaus, China, Korea and Mesopotamia.
A Lady's Life in the Rocky Mountains
[W4] Virago pbk **£5.50**
Journeys in Persia and Kurdistan
[W5] Virago pbk **£7.95**
Journeys in Persia and Kurdistan II
Introduction by Shusha Guppy.
[W6] Virago pbk **£7.50**
Korea and Her Neighbours
[W7] KPI pbk **£9.95**
Six Months in Hawaii
[W8] KPI pbk **£7.95**
**The Golden Chersonese &
The Way Thither**
[W9] Oxford pbk **£6.95**
The Yangtse Valley and Beyond
[W10] Virago pbk **£6.50**
Unbeaten Tracks in Japan
[W11] Virago pbk **£5.50**

BORROW, GEORGE (1803 - 1881)
With little formal education, yet speaking some 12 languages, Borrow moved from his home in Norfolk to London, where he attempted to establish himself as a writer. His language proficiencies led to an introduction to the British and Foreign Bible Society, for which he was commissioned to translate various Bibles. His travel writing stems from this association.
The Bible in Spain (1843)
[W12] Century pbk **£6.95**
Wild Wales (1857)
[W13] Whittet Bks pbk **£7.95**

BURTON, RICHARD (SIR) (1821 - 1890)
Orientalist, traveller and diplomat, Burton by the end of his life had mastered some 25 languages, the result of a childhood spent touring the continent. His proficiency in Arabic and knowledge of Arabia led to his most famous literary work, a translation of *The Arabian Nights*. His equally famous pilgrimage to Mecca, during which he was disguised as an Indian Pathan, made him very popular.
**A Personal Narrative of a Visit
to Al-Madinah** (Vols 1 & 2)
[W14] Dover hbk **£14.90**
First Footsteps in East Africa (2 vols)
[W15] Dover pbk **£8.95**

BYRON, ROBERT (1905 - 1941)
Before his premature death at sea during World War II, Byron had travelled extensively in Greece, India, Tibet, Afghanistan, Russia, China and Egypt. His travel writings are enlightened, sparkling evocations of both the ancient world and more recent epochs.
First Russia, Then Tibet
[W15A] Penguin pbk **£4.50**
The Byzantine Achievement (1929)
[W16] Routledge hbk **£25.00**
The Road to Oxiana (1937)
[W17] Picador pbk **£3.95**
The Station: Athos - Treasures and Men
[W18] Century pbk **£4.95**

CHATWIN, BRUCE (1940 - 1989)
Chatwin's writing consistently merged forms in refreshing, original ways. His travel writing bears similarities to later novels such as *The Songlines*: invented characters are set in non-fictional settings and circumstances, moving within the interstices between reality and fantasy, parable and paradox. *In Patagonia* describes his travels through the Southern tip of South America, and is one of the masterpieces of post-war travel writing.
In Patagonia
[W19] Cape hbk **£9.95**
[W20] Picador pbk **£3.99**

COBBETT, WILLIAM (1763 - 1835)
Primarily a radical reformer, though always a 'loyalist and a patriot', Cobbett wrote several million words on the need and ways of political change. Immensely popular during his lifetime, his outspoken criticism of the government of the day resulted in court appearances for libel , and periods in prison.
Rural Rides
[W21] Penguin pbk **£4.99**
**William Cobbett's Illustrated
Rural Rides**
Cobbett's best-known work records fact-finding tours, made on horseback, through the South of England.
[W22] Webb & B hbk **£14.95**

CURZON, GEORGE NATHANIEL
(1859 - 1925)
Inside Persia
[W23] Sigdwick hbk **£13.95**
Tales of Travel
Curzon travelled to the Levant both following graduation from University and later in life, recording entertaining accounts of the many joys and the pitfalls.
[W24] Century pbk **£5.95**

DOUGHTY, CHARLES MONTAGU
(1843 - 1926)
Passages from Arabia Deserta
Selections from the original *Travels in Arabia Deserta*.
[W25] Penguin pbk **£2.95**
Travels in Arabia Deserta Vols 1 & 2
(1888, revised 1921)
With an introduction by T.E. Lawrence. The eccentric and at times evocative product of a year wandering in Northern Arabia (Egypt east of the Nile and Sinai).
[W26] Bloomsbury hbk **£16.95**

DOUGLAS, NORMAN (Scotland, 1868 - 1952)
Born into the Scottish gentry, Douglas as a young man was a diplomat to the Tsarist court before leaving the profession to wander freely around Europe, principally within sight of the Mediterranean. His writing is often satirical and iconoclastic, but demonstrates great insight, offering one man's hedonistic yet credible accounts of early 20th century European life.
Fountains in the Sand
[W27] Secker hbk **£8.95**
[W28] Oxford pbk **£3.95**
Old Calabria
[W29] Century pbk **£5.95**
Siren Land
[W30] Penguin pbk **£3.95**

DUMAS, ALEXANDRE (France, 1802 - 1870)
Most famous for his witty, politicized historical novels, which were among the first of the 'researched' variety, Dumas' travel writing stands as enthusiastic appreciations of the places he visited.
Adventures in the Caucasus
[W31] P Owen hbk **£10.95**
From Paris to Cadiz
[W32] P Owen hbk **£10.95**
Tangier to Tunis
[W33] P Owen hbk **£10.95**
Travels in Switzerland
[W34] P Owen hbk **£10.95**

DURRELL, LAWRENCE (1912 -)
Born in India, Durrell returned to England in the late 1920s, and lived in Paris for part of the 1930s. He has spent most of his later life around the Eastern Mediterranean, and has written incisive, sensuous evocations of many places in the area.
Bitter Lemons (1957)
[W35] Faber pbk **£2.95**
Greek Islands
[W36] Faber pbk **£9.95**
Prospero's Cell (1945)
[W37] Faber pbk **£2.95**
Reflections on a Marine Venus
[W38] Faber pbk **£3.50**
**Spirit of Place: Letters and
Essays on Travel**
[W39] Faber pbk **£5.95**

FERMOR, PATRICK LEIGH (1915 -)
Fermor walked through pre-war Europe, from the Low Countries to Istanbul. His description of the continent during this period is recorded in his three volume travelogue, consisting of the first three titles listed here. He lives in the Mani, an area of Greece, which is the subject of one of his finest works.
A Time of Gifts
[W40] Penguin pbk **£4.99**
A Time to Keep Silence
[W41] Penguin pbk **£3.95**
Between the Woods and the Water
[W42] Penguin pbk **£4.99**
**Mani: Travels in the Southern
Peloponnese**
[W43] Penguin pbk **£4.95**
Roumeli: Travels in Northern Greece
[W44] Penguin pbk **£3.95**
Traveller's Tree
[W45] Penguin pbk **£4.95**

FLEMING, PETER (1907 - 1971)
A regular contributor to *The Spectator* and *The Times*, Fleming is principally known for his travel writing. They are frequently debonair and amusing accounts of high, but safe, adventure. His most memorable work is *News from Tartary* (1936), an account of his overland journey from Peking to Kashmir.
Bayonets to Lhasa
[W46] Oxford pbk **£6.95**

Brazilian Adventure (1933)
[W47] Penguin pbk **£4.95**
News from Tartary (1936)
[W48] Futura pbk **£2.95**
One's Company: A Journey to China
[W49] Penguin pbk **£4.95**

FORSTER, E.M. (1879 - 1970)
Forster's accounts of his travels to Egypt and India mix the highly factual with the impressionistic. They are all based directly upon trips made in the first half of his life.
Alexandria: A History and a Guide (1922)
[W50] M Haag pbk **£7.95**
Hill of Devi and Other Indian Writings (1953)
[W51] Penguin pbk **£3.99**
Pharos and Pharillon (1923)
[W52] M Haag pbk **£4.95**

GOETHE, JOHANN WOLFGANG VON
(Germany, 1749 - 1832)
Goethe made two important visits to Italy towards the end of his life which, significantly, helped to change his views on art, moving him closer to the classicists whom he had largely ignored during his youth.
Italian Journey is an account of this journey and, to a lesser extent, of the transformation of his ideas.
Italian Journey (1817)
[W53] Penguin pbk **£5.95**

GREENE, GRAHAM (1904 -)
Greene's travel writing varies little in tone from his fiction, though its concerns are often more overtly political.
Journey without Maps (1936)
An up-country journey in Liberia made in the mid-1930s, which becomes a metaphor, through psychoanalysis, for Greene's private journey into himself.
[W54] Penguin pbk **£3.95**
The Lawless Roads (1939)
Sponsored by the Roman Catholic Church, Greene went to Mexico to investigate allegations of religious persecution.
[W55] Bodley/Heinemann hbk **£12.95**
[W56] Penguin pbk **£3.50**

HAKLUYT, RICHARD (1552 - 1616)
Voyages 1589 - 1599
Hakluyt was for a time geographical adviser to the East India Company, and an original member of the Virginia Company, the full inception and history of which is the subject of this book.
[W57] Century pbk **£5.95**
Voyages and Discoveries of the English Nation (1589)
A record of the many explorers who flew the English flag.
[W58] Penguin pbk **£5.99**
Voyages to the Virginia Colonies
[W59] Century pbk **£5.95**

HEYERDAHL, THOR (1914 -)
Anthropologist and author, Heyerdahl has actively pursued data to underpin his theories about the movements of early man across continents and seas. He is most famous for his arduous sea journeys in theoretical replicas of pre-historic boats, undertaken to demonstrate the plausibility of his ideas.
Aku-Aku: The Secrets of Easter Island (1957)
[W60] Unwin pbk **£4.95**
Fatu-Hiva: Back to Nature (1974)
[W61] Unwin hbk **£15.00**
Maldive Mystery (1986)
[W62] Unwin pbk **£4.95**

The Kon-Tiki Expedition (1948)
A trip to prove that North American Indians had once sailed the Pacific.
[W63] Unwin pbk **£3.95**
The Ra Expeditions (1970)
[W64] Unwin hbk **£12.95**
The Tigris Expedition: In Search of Our Beginnings (1986)
[W65] Unwin pbk **£3.95**

HILLABY, JOHN (1917 -)
Hillaby's accounts of walks through Britain, Europe and the Far East are lively and accessible and have made him immensely popular.
Journey Home
[W66] Grafton pbk **£2.95**
Journey through Britain
[W67] Grafton pbk **£2.95**
Journey through Europe
[W68] Grafton pbk **£2.95**
Journey through Love
[W69] Constable hbk **£4.95**
Journey to the Jade Sea
[W70] Grafton pbk **£3.50**

JAMES, HENRY (1843 - 1916)
The subtlety of the Jamesian examination, prominent in his fiction, can equally be found in his travel writings, which are part cultural commentary, part visual and sensual reconnaissance.
A Little Tour in France (1884)
[W71] Penguin pbk **£4.50**
English Hours (New edition)
A collection of James's slighter pieces, occasional essays written over a period of 25 years on different parts of the country. The England depicted was as much a figment of the imagination when he wrote it, as it appears today.
[W72] Barrie & J hbk **£14.95**
[W73] Oxford pbk **£2.95**
Italian Hours
[W74] Century pbk **£5.95**
The American Scene (1907)
Returning to America after an absence of twenty five years, James was filled with horror at the evolving continent which he found: the book which resulted is one of his very finest, and shows his descriptive powers engaged to the full.
[W75] Granville pbk **£5.95**

JOHNSON, SAMUEL & BOSWELL, JAMES
Separate accounts of a journey they made together to the Hebrides, the first by Johnson (1775) and the second by Boswell (1785).
Journey to the Western Islands of Scotland & Journal of a Tour to the Hebrides
[W76] Oxford pbk **£6.95**
[W77] Penguin pbk **£4.99**

KEAY, JOHN
Keay's travel writing re-creates history, looking both at life in times very much in the past, and at the adventures of explorers and travellers who followed in the 19th century.
Eccentric Travellers
[W78] BBC pbk **£3.95**
Explorers Extraordinary
[W79] J Murray hbk **£10.95**
Highland Drover
[W80] J Murray hbk **£10.95**
India Discovered
[W81] Collins pbk **£8.95**
Into India
[W82] J Murray pbk **£6.95**
The Gilgit Game
[W83] Century pbk **£5.95**

Patrick Leigh Fermor, author of *Mani: Travels in the Southern Peloponnese* (Penguin pbk **£4.95**)

When Men and Mountains Meet
This story of the quest for access to Central Asia and inland China through the formidable barrier of the Western Himalayas involves some characters as exceptional as the terrain through which they journey.
[W84] Century pbk **£5.95**

KINGLAKE, A.E. (1809 - 1891)
Eothen: or, Traces of Travel Brought Home from the East (1844)
A famous account of his trip to the Eastern Mediterranean and the Holy Land, written in the form of a personal missive to an intimate friend, and thereby avoiding the old style of researched reconstructions. The result is a lively, personal record of Kinglake's own responses to what he encountered.
[W85] Century pbk **£4.95**

LAWRENCE, D.H. (1885 - 1930)
Lawrence's dislike of many elements of English life, as well as the state of his health, led him to travel abroad: most important were the periods spent in Italy and New Mexico, landscapes in which he felt more closely in touch with the primal, non-mental powers which feature so much in his later writings.
D.H. Lawrence and Italy
[W86] Penguin pbk **£4.95**
Etruscan Places
[W87] Olive P pbk **£6.95**
Mornings in Mexico
[W88] Penguin pbk **£3.50**
Twilight in Italy
[W89] Heinemann hbk **£9.95**

LEWIS, NORMAN (1913 -)
Since the publication of his first book in 1938, Lewis's body of travel writing has consisted of wide-ranging and often personal accounts based not only on travels, but also on the other events in his life, such as his experience during World War II, which he has tied into his later pieces.
A Dragon Apparent: Travels in Laos, Cambodia and Vietnam
[W90] Eland pbk **£5.95**
Golden Earth: Travels in Burma
[W91] Eland pbk **£4.95**
Naples '44
[W92] Eland pbk **£4.95**
The Missionaries
Lewis believes this is his most important work. In it he takes us among the Indians of Central and Latin America, and exposes the catastrophic effect which Western missionaries have wrought on their cultures.
[W93] Secker hbk **£10.95**

TRAVEL

To Run Across the Sea NEW
[W94] Cape hbk **£12.95**
Voices of the Old Sea
[W95] Penguin pbk **£3.99**

MACAULAY, ROSE (1881 - 1958)
Popular satirical novelist of the 1920s and 30s, whose travel writing painted a dry, witty picture of the places under examination.
Fabled Shore: From Pyrénées to Portugal (1949)
[W96] Oxford pbk **£4.95**
Pleasure of Ruins (1953)
[W97] Thames & H hbk **£14.00**
They Went to Portugal (1946)
[W98] Penguin pbk **£3.95**

MACLEAN, FITZROY (1911 -)
Maclean's books stress the cultural heritage and diversity of given societies, and above all, the importance of, and manner in which, political and religious history play a central part in any nation's modern life.
Holy Russia: An Historical Companion to European Russia
A comprehensive survey of the whole of European Russia, from the founding of the Kievan Rus in the 10th century through the Tsars and the Revolution to the era of Khruschev and his successors in the Kremlin.
[W99] Century pbk **£5.95**
Isles of the Sea
[W100] Collins hbk **£9.95**
Person from England and Other Travellers to Turkestan
[W101] Century pbk **£4.95**
To Caucusus: The End of the Earth
[W102] Cape hbk **£12.50**

MANDEVILLE, SIR JOHN (14th century)
Travels (c.1357)
Supposedly by the pen of one Sir John Mandeville, the author of this account, originally in Middle English, has not been confirmed. It recounts for pilgrims a journey through the Holy Land, and draws on a number of sources: geography, natural history, as well as romance and fantasia. It was an important influence on writers from Chaucer through to the Elizabethans.
[W103] Penguin pbk **£4.50**

MATTHIESSEN, PETER (1927 -)
Matthiessen's writing is principally concerned with the social anthropology of a wide range of peoples. He records with great detail the lifestyles of primitive tribes and their relationships with the natural world they inhabit.
Cloud Forest
[W104] Collins hbk **£5.95**
Indian Country
[W105] Fontana pbk **£3.95**
Nine-Headed Dragon River: Zen Journals
[W106] Collins hbk **£11.50**
The Snow Leopard
[W107] Collins Harr pbk **£6.95**
The Tree Where Man Was Born
[W108] Pan pbk **£3.95**

MOOREHEAD, ALAN (1931 -)
Moorehead has written several revisionist travel pieces on already well-covered territory. His two books on the Nile follow in the footsteps of earlier explorers, and place them in a new, late 20th century perspective.
Cooper's Creek
[W109] Penguin pbk **£4.95**
Darwin and the 'Beagle'
[W110] H Hamilton hbk **£8.95**

The Blue Nile
[W111] Penguin pbk **£8.95**
The White Nile
[W112] Penguin pbk **£8.99**

MOORHOUSE, GEOFFREY (1931 -)
Moorhouse is one of a select band of modern adventurers who search for extreme experiences, such as a solo traverse of the Sahara - described in *A Fearful Void* - or living firsthand, albeit temporarily, many of Calcutta's lifestyles.
Calcutta (1971)
[W113] Penguin pbk **£4.95**
Imperial City: The Rise and Rise of New York (1988)
[W114] Hodder pbk **£4.99**
Rail Across India
Co-written with Brian Hollingsworth.
[W115] Methuen hbk **£29.95**
The Fearful Void (1974)
[W116] Penguin pbk **£4.50**
To the Frontier (1974)
[W117] Hodder pbk **£4.95**

MORRIS, JAN (1926 -)
A smooth and compelling prose stylist, Morris's skill lies in her ability to discover and develop the imaginative essences of the societies and cultures among whom she finds herself, and to convey their 'true' nature as she interprets it. Her fist two books, on *Venice* and *Oxford*, established her as a writer of the highest class.
Among the Cities (1985)
[W118] Penguin pbk **£4.95**
Destinations
[W119] Oxford pbk **£4.95**
Journeys (1984)
[W120] Oxford pbk **£4.95**
Manhattan '45 (1987)
[W121] Penguin pbk **£4.99**
Matter of Wales: Epic Views of a Small Country (1984)
[W122] Penguin pbk **£5.95**
Oxford (1965)
[W123] Oxford pbk **£4.95**
Scotland: Place of Visions (1986)
[W124] Aurum hbk **£14.95**
Spain (1964)
Originally entitled 'The Presence of Spain', the hardback edition is illustrated with watercolours and lithographs by Joan Mirò.
[W125] Barrie & J hbk **£6.95**
[W126] Penguin pbk **£3.99**
Venice (1960)
[W127] Faber pbk **£3.95**
Wales: The First Place (1982)
[W128] Aurum pbk **£8.95**

MORTON, H.V. (1892 - 1979)
Morton's work, mainly published in the 30s, remains interesting for its attention to detail and the sympathy and sensitivity of its approach to its subject matter, although other aspects of it now appear rather dated.
A Traveller in Italy
[W129] Methuen pbk **£8.95**
A Traveller in Rome
[W130] Methuen pbk **£7.95**
A Traveller in Southern Italy
[W131] Methuen pbk **£7.50**
In Search of Ireland
[W132] Methuen pbk **£5.95**
In Search of London
[W133] Methuen pbk **£7.95**
In Search of Scotland
[W134] Methuen pbk **£5.95**
In Search of Wales
[W135] Methuen pbk **£5.95**
In the Steps of the Master
[W136] Methuen pbk **£5.95**

Magic of Ireland
[W137] Methuen pbk **£6.95**

MURPHY, DERVLA (Ireland, 1931 -)
In 1963 Murphy rode from France to India on a bicycle: as a solitary woman, she drew much attention and her study of people's reactions forms a large part of the journey through Europe, Iran, Afghanistan, Pakistan and India, which she recorded in *Full Tilt*. Her other works show equal evidence of her empirical curiosity, as well as a human compulsion to understand the underlying motivation of the peoples whose lives she witnesses.
A Place Apart (1978)
An examination of life in Northern Ireland.
[W138] Penguin pbk **£4.50**
Eight Feet in the Andes: Travels on a Donkey from Ecuador to Cuzco (1983)
[W139] J Murray hbk **£11.95**
Full Tilt: Ireland to India with a Bicycle (1965)
[W140] Arrow pbk **£2.99**
In Cameroon with Egbert (1989) NEW
Murphy travels in Cameroon on a four-legged creature.
[W141] J Murray hbk **£13.95**
Muddling through in Madagascar (1985)
In 1983 Murphy and her 14 year old daughter undertook an extensive journey through the lush, unique landscape of the Malagasi Republic.
[W142] Century pbk **£5.95**
On a Shoestring to Coorg: Experience of Southern India (1976)
[W143] Century pbk **£4.95**
Tales from Two Cities (1987)
Something of a departure for Murphy, she 'tours' two of Britain's inner cities.
[W144] Penguin pbk **£4.99**
The Waiting Land: A Spell in Nepal (1967)
It is 1965: Murphy braves bureaucracy, danger and squalour to help the Tibetans who are seeking refuge in Nepal.
[W145] Century pbk **£4.95**
Wheels within Wheels: Autobiography (1979)
[W146] Penguin pbk **£3.95**
Where the Indus is Young: Winter in Baltistan (1977)
The account of her five-month walk through 'little Tibet' to near the source of the Indus.
[W147] Century pbk **£3.95**

NAIPAUL, SHIVA (Trinidad, 1945 - 1985)
Born in the Caribbean, Naipaul moved to England in 1964, from where he wrote about the themes of displacement, alienation and racial discord. His record of his travels through Kenya and Tanzania, *North of South*, is a classic of its kind.
An Unfinished Journey
[W148] Abacus pbk **£4.99**
Black and White
[W149] Abacus pbk **£2.95**
North of South: An African Journey
[W150] Penguin pbk **£4.99**

NAIPAUL, V.S. (Trinidad, 1932 -)
The wide-ranging, melancholic evocation of human nature, prominent in Naipaul's fiction, is also to be found in his many slow, incisive travel books. The intense sympathy of his outlook is not without a certain hard-edged critical side, although this ususally appears in the shape of a metaphor or allusion. His records of his journeys around India (*An Area of Darkness* and *A Wounded Civilization*) are particularly acclaimed.
A Turn in the South (1989) NEW
Naipaul in the southern states of America, observing

V.S. Naipaul, author of *A Turn in the South* (Viking hbk £14.95)

lucidly the current social structure and the lives of several compelling individuals.
[W151] Viking hbk **£14.95**
Among the Believers: An Islamic Journey (1981)
[W152] Penguin pbk **£4.99**
An Area of Darkness: An Experience of India (1964)
[W153] Penguin pbk **£2.95**
Finding the Centre (1984)
[W154] Penguin pbk **£3.99**
India: A Wounded Civilization (1977)
[W155] Penguin pbk **£2.95**
Loss of El Dorado (1969)
[W156] Penguin pbk **£4.95**
The Middle Passage: The Caribbean Revisted (1962)
[W157] Penguin pbk **£3.99**
The Overcrowded Barracoon, and Other Articles (1972)
[W158] Penguin pbk **£4.95**

NEWBY, ERIC (1911 -)
Eric Newby's early travel writing reflects the high adventure which characterized his life in those supremely exciting times. His later works, which rose out of 'premeditated adventure', are enjoyably light-hearted, humorous and entertaining. The subjects of his work are many and varied ranging from an exploration of distant Nuristan, to an hilarious account of crossing Russia by train (*The Big Red Train Ride*); *Love and War in the Apennines* tells of three eventful months spent in war-time Italy, during which Newby evaded capture by the Germans, and met his wife-to-be, Wanda.
A Book of Travellers' Tales (1985)
[W159] Picador pbk **£5.95**
A Short Walk in the Hindu Kush (1958)
[W160] Picador pbk **£3.99**
Love and War in the Apennines (1971)
[W161] Picador pbk **£3.95**
On the Shores of the Mediterranean (1984)
[W162] Picador pbk **£4.95**
Slowly Down the Ganges (1966)
[W163] Picador pbk **£4.50**
The Big Red Train Ride (1978)
[W164] Penguin pbk **£4.50**
The Last Grain Race (1956)
[W165] Grafton pbk **£3.95**

What the Traveller Saw (1989) NEW
A collection of Newby's own black and white photographs taken during some 50 years of travel.
[W166] Collins hbk **£17.50**

PARK, MUNGO (Scotland, 1771 - 1806)
Park was a Scottish physician who went to Africa, then the greatest of unknowns, and ended up exploring what is now called the Niger region. His fame came upon his return to Britain, when he wrote about what he encountered.
Travels into the Interior of Africa
[W167] Eland pbk **£5.95**

POLO, MARCO (1254 - 1324)
Polo travelled with his Papal diplomat father and uncle to the court of Kublai Khan: the trio were to remain in Asia for more than a quarter-century. Polo's account, written toward the end of his life, is viewed as one of the first travel books immediately recognisable as such in modern terms.
Travels of Marco Polo
An epic journey, in three stages: from a thriving Venice to the court of the troublesome Kublai Khan; followed by 17 years within the Khan's orbit; and concluded with a six year return journey by sea to Italy.
[W168] Penguin pbk **£3.99**

POST, LAURENS VAN DER
(South Africa, 1906 -)
An erudite anthropologist, as well as traveller and adventurer, van der Post's work is informed both by an impassioned belief in the supremacy of nature and by many of the writings of Carl Jung.
Heart of the Hunter
[W169] Chatto hbk **£12.95**
[W170] Penguin pbk **£3.95**
Hunter and the Whale
[W171] Penguin pbk **£4.50**
Journey into Russia
[W172] Chatto hbk **£12.95**
[W173] Penguin pbk **£4.95**
Lost World of the Kalahari
An account of his expedition and rediscovery of the Bushman.
[W174] Hogarth hbk **£20.00**
[W175] Penguin pbk **£4.99**
Venture into the Interior
[W176] Chatto hbk **£12.95**
[W177] Penguin pbk **£4.50**
Walk with a White Bushman
A combination of philosophy and biography; includes conversations with Jean-Marc Pottiez.
[W178] Chatto hbk **£14.95**
[W179] Penguin pbk **£4.99**

SEVERIN, TIM (1940 -)
Echoing Heyerdahl, Severin reconstructs epic voyages in precise replicas of ancient sea-going vessels. His predecessors, however, are often more likely to be mythologized, if not entirely fictitious, heroes: his service to them is in establishing realistically the possibility that they once existed.
The Crusader NEW
Retracing the steps of the crusaders, starting in Belgium.
[W180] Century hbk **£11.95**
The Brendan Voyage (1977)
From the west coast of Ireland to North America.
[W181] Arrow pbk **£3.95**
The Jason Voyage: The Quest for the Golden Fleece (1984)
Iolkos to Colchis.
[W182] Arrow pbk **£3.50**
The Sinbad Voyage (1981)
From Oman to China.
[W183] Arrow pbk **£2.75**

The Ulysses Voyage (1985)
From Troy to Ithaca.
[W184] Arrow pbk **£3.50**
Tracking Marco Polo (1961)
A motorcycle team follows the route supposedly taken by Marco Polo.
[W185] Arrow pbk **£2.75**

SMOLLET, TOBIAS (Scotland, 1721 - 1771)
When young, Smollett travelled with the Army, as a surgeon's mate, and saw much of Europe. He was to return later in life, now established as one of the foremost Scottish novelists, and wrote with the cantankerousness of an aging gentleman.
Travels through France & Italy (1766)
In stark contrast with Sterne's similarly conceived work, Smollett's account of his meanderings in Europe is characterized by several prejudicial attitudes and outright disgust. However, the subliminal enthusiasm and eccentricity in his writing makes the book entertaining and it was extremely popular upon publication.
[W186] Oxford pbk **£4.95**

STARK, FREYA (1893 -)
Stark travelled to the Near East as a young graduate, and was to visit the region several more times. A natural traveller, she often ignored her own well-being and put little above a humane, humble approach to lives of others. The many villages and officials she encountered opened themselves up to her, subsequently allowing her to write engaging, 'accurate' portraits.
A Peak in Darien: Essays
[W187] J Murray hbk **£9.95**
A Winter in Arabia (1940)
A record of day-to-day life in Hadramaut in 1937 while Freya Stark was excavating the ancient city of Hureidha.
[W188] J Murray hbk **£15.00**
[W189] Century pbk **£5.95**
Alexander's Path: From Caria to Cilicia
A vivid description of the southern coastline and mountains of Turkey, tracing the route of Alexander the Great.
[W190] J Murray hbk **£15.00**
[W191] Century pbk **£6.95**
East is West (1945)
Concentrates on the author's war years in Arabia, Egypt, Syria, Iraq and Persia.
[W193] J Murray hbk **£10.95**
[W194] Century pbk **£4.95**
Ionia: A Quest (1954)
Stark's scholarly yet lively commentary on, and interpretation of, the historical, cultural and environmental background of the classical sites in Turkey.
[W195] Century pbk **£5.95**
Perseus in the Wind (1948)
The title was inspired by the memory of a summer she spent in the mountains of Elburz in Iran.
[W196] Century pbk **£4.95**
Riding to the Tigris
[W197] J Murray hbk **£12.50**
Rome on the Euphrates: The Story of a Frontier
[W198] J Murray hbk **£15.00**
Southern Gates of Arabia (1936)
[W199] J Murray hbk **£15.00**
[W200] Century pbk **£6.95**
Autobiography: Traveller's Prelude: 1893 - 1927 (1950)
The story of Freya Stark's cosmopolitan upbringing which shaped her disposition as a travel writer.
[W201] Century pbk **£4.95**
Beyond Euphrates: 1928 - 1933 (1951)
The sequel to *Traveller's Prelude,* this is Freya Stark's description of her independent journeys to the East.
[W202] Century pbk **£5.95**

Coast of Incense: 1933 - 1939 (1953)
[W203] J Murray hbk **£15.00**
Dust in the Lion's Paw:
1939 - 1946 (1961)
Covers the period of World War II when Stark
worked for the Foreign Office in the Middle East.
[W204] J Murray hbk **£15.00**
Valleys of the Assassins
[W205] J Murray hbk **£15.00**
[W206] Century pbk **£6.95**
Zodiac Arch
[W207] J Murray hbk **£9.95**

STERNE, LAURENCE (1713 - 1768)
A Sentimental Journey through
France & Italy (1768)
The Author's impressions of France and Italy,
drawn from several months spent in the two countries
during 1765.
[W208] Oxford pbk **£1.95**
[W209] Penguin pbk **£2.25**

STEVENSON, ROBERT LOUIS (1850 - 94)
Afflicted by ill-health, Stevenson was able to
travel much of the world because he was not fit to
follow his father into engineering. Several accounts
of his travels preceded his major fiction, though
the family journey to the South Seas, where he
hoped to recover his health, was at the very end of
his life. The plainness of travel narrative suited his
temperament, as can be seen most clearly in the
description of his steerage passage to America,
and subsequent crossing of the continent by train,
in *The Amateur Emigrant*.
In the South Seas: The Marquesas,
Paumotus and Gilbert Islands (1896)
[W210] KPI pbk **£7.95**
The Amateur Emigrant (1895)
[W211] Hogarth pbk **£5.95**
Travels with a Donkey in
the Cevennes (1879)
Robert Louis Stevenson's much-loved classic,
which describes a twelve day tour of that
mountainous region.
[W212] Century pbk **£4.95**

THEROUX, PAUL (US, 1941 -)
Stylish and often humorous, Theroux's travel writing
draws on many sources and evinces substantial
curiosity about atmosphere and place. Each of his
journeys is epic: across continents by train (in *The
Great Railway Bazaar*), or following the coastline of
Great Britain (*The Kingdom by the Sea*). He is
skilled at uncovering his own prejudices to locate a
'truer' impression.
Riding the Iron Rooster (1988)
Through China on a train.
[W213] Penguin pbk **£3.99**
Sunrise with Seamonsters: Travels and
Discoveries 1964 - 1984 (1985)
[W214] Penguin pbk **£4.95**
The Great Railway Bazaar:
By Train through Asia (1975)
[W215] Penguin pbk **£3.95**
The Kingdom by the Sea (1983)
[W216] Penguin pbk **£3.95**
The Old Patagonian Express:
By Train through the Americas (1979)
[W217] Penguin pbk **£4.50**

THESIGER, WILFRED (1910 -)
Thesiger's first journeys to the Near East were under
the auspices of the British Government, later with the
Army, and eventually on his own. His books record
the immersion he sought when travelling among the
Arab tribes, many of them nomadic, just before and
then after World War II.
Arabian Sands (1959)
[W218] Penguin pbk **£4.99**

Desert Marsh and Mountain:
World of a Nomad (1979)
[W219] Collins hbk **£20.00**
The Life of My Choice (1987)
A volume of autobiography.
[W220] Fontana pbk **£5.95**
The Marsh Arabs (1964)
[W221] Penguin pbk **£4.95**
Visions of a Nomad (1987)
A photographic record of Thesiger's life and
extensive travels.
[W222] Collins hbk **£20.00**

THUBRON, COLIN (1939 -)
Thubron has travelled extensively in Asia, the Near
East and in Europe. His prose is poetically informed,
and he demonstrates a cultural sensitivity which
allows him, more so than many others, to get 'under
the skin' of a place.
Among the Russians (1983)
[W223] Heinemann hbk **£10.95**
[W224] Penguin pbk **£3.99**
Behind the Wall: Journey through
China (1987)
[W225] Heinemann hbk **£10.95**
[W226] Penguin pbk **£4.99**
Jerusalem (1969)
[W227] Century pbk **£5.95**
Journey into Cyprus (1975)
[W228] Penguin pbk **£4.50**
Mirror to Damascus (1967)
An enthralling and fascinating history of Damascus
from the Amorites of the Bible to the revolution
of 1966.
[W229] Century pbk **£4.95**
The Hills of Adonis (1968)
[W230] Penguin pbk **£4.50**

TWAIN, MARK (US, 1835 - 1910)
Twain's travel writing is limited effectively to
three titles which come from the first half of his life,
when he was at his humorous and financial peak. In
later life, he was plagued by depression and
frequent insolvency.
A Tramp Abroad (1880)
[W231] Century pbk **£5.95**
Innocents Abroad (The New Pilgrim's
Progress) (1869)
A light-hearted reconstruction of his voyage through
the Mediterranean.
[W232] Century pbk **£5.95**
Roughing It (1872)
A travelogue of Twain's adventures in the
Western United States related with unfailing
humour, if not total veracity. A treasure-trove of
tall stories.
[W233] Penguin pbk **£4.95**

WAUGH, EVELYN (1903 - 1966)
Waugh's journeys abroad as foreign
correspondent began in the 1930s, after the success
of his early novels. The locations and characters
which he encounters allow his satirical gifts
free reign.
A Tourist in Africa (1960)
[W234] Methuen hbk **£9.50**
Labels: A Mediterranean Journal (1930)
[W235] Penguin pbk **£3.99**
Ninety-Two Days: A Journey in Guiana
and Brazil, 1932 (1934)
[W236] Penguin pbk **£3.99**
Remote People (1931)
[W237] Duckworth hbk **£12.95**
[W238] Penguin pbk **£3.95**
Waugh in Abyssinia (1936)
Concerned with the Italian occupation of Abyssinia in
the 1930s.
[W239] Methuen hbk **£9.50**
[W240] Penguin pbk **£3.99**

YOUNG, GAVIN (1928 -)
Young combines a sense of old-fashioned
adventure transplanted to modern times with an
elegant, cultivated prose style, in narratives which
make compelling reading. His most acclaimed works
are *Slow Boats to China* and its sequel *Slow
Boats Home*.
Return to the Marshes: Life with the
Marsh Arabs of Iraq (1977)
[W241] Penguin pbk **£3.99**
Slow Boats Home (1985)
[W242] Penguin pbk **£4.99**
Slow Boats to China (1981)
[W243] Penguin pbk **£4.95**
Worlds Apart (1987)
[W244] Hutchinson pbk **£4.95**

General Literary Travel

Granta 26: Travel (1989)
Includes pieces from Kapuscinski, Thubron and
Lewis amongst others.
[W250] Penguin pbk **£4.99**

The Best of the 'Sunday Times'
Travel Book
A selection from the two volumes so far published.
[W250A] David & Ch pbk **£4.95**

Views from Abroad: The 'Spectator'
Book of Travel Writing
[W251] Grafton pbk **£5.99**

AITKEN, MARIA
A Girdle Round the Earth
A brief, lively account of many of the famous and
lesser-known women travellers.
[W252] Constable hbk **£12.95**

Illustration from *Return to the Marshes: Life with
the Marsh Arabs of Iraq* by Gavin Young
(Penguin pbk £3.99)

BARZINI, LUIGI
Peking to Paris: Across Two Continents in an Itala
An account of the benefits of having answered a 1907 newspaper challenge which asked for a companion to travel from Peking to Paris by motorcar.
[W253] Penguin pbk **£5.95**

BATES, E.S.
Touring in 1600: A Study in the Development of Travel as a Means of Education
A scholarly and readable examination of the concept of the 'Grand Tour' as a complement to domestic education.
[W254] Century pbk **£6.95**

BRASSEY, LADY
A Voyage in the Sunbeam: Our Home on the Ocean for Eleven Months
A travelogue of a long and hazardous sea journey around the world in 1876-77.
[W255] Century pbk **£4.95**

CHICHESTER, FRANCIS
The Lonely Sea and the Sky
A classic picture of life at sea and Chichester's own relationship with the vast unknown forces of the natural world.
[W256] Pan pbk **£3.50**
The Romantic Challenge
An illustrated account of Chichester's dramatic Atlantic crossing in Gypsy Moth V in 1970.
[W257] Grafton hbk **£6.95**

CLARKE, THURSTON
Equator: A Journey Around the World   NEW
The author spent six months circumnavigating the earth via the equator and here recounts his story, punctuated by heat, dust and adventure.
[W258] Century hbk **£14.95**

DAVIES, MIRANDA (ED)
Half the Earth: Women's Experiences of Travel Worldwide
[W259] Pandora pbk **£4.95**

FENTON, JAMES
All the Wrong Places   NEW
One such situation was when the author found himself playing Bach on Ferdinand Marcos's grand piano while an angry mob broke the windows of the palace. Fenton also writes on experiences in Korea and Vietnam.
[W260] Viking hbk **£12.95**

FRATER, ALEXANDER
Beyond the Blue Horizon: On the Tracks of Imperial Airways
A history of the airline in its early, less regulated days.
[W261] Penguin pbk **£4.99**

FUSSELL, PAUL
Abroad: British Literary Travelling Between the Wars
A study of the genre, covering Robert Byron, Evelyn Waugh, Peter Fleming and others.
[W262] Oxford pbk **£3.95**

GELLHORN, MARTHA
The View from the Ground   NEW
Twenty nine of Gellhorn's articles, starting from the 1930s. The majority focus upon Eastern Europe, the island of Haiti, and the Middle East, in particular Israel.
[W263] Granta hbk **£11.95**

HIGGINS, AIDAN
Ronda Gorge and Other Precipices   NEW
Higgins recounts his long journey through Africa and Europe to Berlin, across to southern Spain and eventually on to his birthplace in County Kildare.
[W264] Secker hbk **£10.95**

HOUGH, CHRISTOPHER
A Pedaller to Peking
An account of his journey from Blackheath to Peking by bicycle.
[W265] Headline pbk **£2.99**

NORWICH, JOHN JULIUS
A Taste for Travel: An Anthology
[W266] Macmillan pbk **£7.95**

REID, ALASTAIR
Whereabouts: Notes on Being a Foreigner
[W267] Canongate hbk **£9.95**

ROBINSON, JANE
Wayward Women: A Guide to Women Travellers   NEW
A look at the lives, and journeys, of over three hundred female travellers; from 381 AD up to the present day.
[W268] Oxford hbk **£17.50**

RUSSELL, MARY
The Blessings of a Good Thick Skirt: Women Travellers and their World (1986)
Thematic history of many accomplished adventurers.
[W269] Collins pbk **£7.95**

SCOTT, ALASTAIR
Scot Free: A Journey from the Arctic to New Mexico
[W270] J Murray hbk **£10.95**
A Scot Goes South: A Journey from Mexico to Ayers Rock
The sequel to *Scot Free*.
[W271] J Murray hbk **£12.95**
A Scot Returns: A Journey from Bali to Skye   NEW
The last volume of the trilogy: Scott describes the final leg of his 194,000-mile journey to all corners of the earth.
[W272] J Murray hbk **£13.95**

SIMON, TED
Jupiter's Travel (1979)
Around the world on a motorcyle.
[W273] Penguin pbk **£4.50**
Riding Home (1984)
From the south of France to California: a cultural re-awakening.
[W274] Penguin pbk **£3.99**

SMEETON, MILES & BERYL
The Misty Islands   NEW
The Smeetons' account of their sailing trip across half the planet: starting in Japan, they crossed the Pacific 'diagonally' from north to south and, via Cape Horn and the unpredictable Atlantic, dropped anchor in the Hebrides.
[W275] Grafton hbk **£6.95**

SPITTELER, MIRANDA
Fours Corners World Bike Ride   NEW
To raise money for Intermediate Technology four teams of cyclists canvassed sponsorship and then set out from Harare, Hong Kong, La Paz and Sydney respectively to head for London, where they converged a year later.
[W276] Oxford hbk **£12.95**

STOYE, JOHN
English Travellers Abroad, 1604 - 1667
Retracing the steps of 17th century British travellers in France, Italy, Spain and the Netherlands.
[W277] Yale UP pbk **£12.95**

TAMBS, ERLING
The Cruise of the 'Teddy'   NEW
Without even a sextant, never mind a barometer or money, the author sailed for three years in, apparently, many directions. It is not entirely clear how he can now recount where he has been, though he clearly had a good time.
[W278] Grafton pbk **£6.95**

TURNBULL, COLIN M.
Forest People
[W279] Grafton pbk **£3.50**
Mountain People
[W280] Grafton pbk **£2.50**

VOSS, J.C.
Venturesome Voyages (1913)   NEW
The author's story of sailing around the world, in a small(ish) canoe, in search of the dubious treasure of the Cocos Island.
[W281] Grafton hbk **£6.95**

WATERHOUSE, KEITH
The Theory and Practice of Travel
Waterhouse's humorous, anecdotal tour of many diverse places.
[W282] Hodder pbk **£7.95**

WINCHESTER, SIMON
Outposts
The outposts are the relics of the British Empire which are still there to explore; Winchester focuses upon their historical and cultural resonances.
[W283] Hodder pbk **£4.95**

Atlases

Britain

3 Mile Road Atlas of Britain
3 miles = 1 inch. Contains new mapping from the AA's Automaps database.
[W284] AA hbk **£16.95**

Bartholomew's Road Atlas of Britain
3 miles = 1 inch.
[W285] Bartholomew pbk **£4.95**

Collins Road Atlas, Britain
1 mile = 1 inch; with 58 town plans.
[W286] Collins pbk **£4.95**

Collins Superscale Atlas Britain   NEW
2.25 miles = 1 inch.
[W287] Collins hbk **£12.95**

Comprehensive Motorists' Atlas of Britain   NEW
4 miles = 1 inch. Created from the newly-applied digital database, offering high quality, clear maps supplemented by tourist information.
[W288] Bartholomew hbk **£10.95**

Ordnance Survey Road Atlas of Great Britain
Utilizes a unique grid referencing system, for the rapid location of towns.
[W289] Hamlyn pbk **£10.95**

RAC Motoring Atlas of Britain 1989 NEW
4 miles = 1 inch. Apart from the usual national mapping coverage, there are town plans, approach maps to major urban centres, and a full index.
[W290] G Philip pbk **£4.95**

RAC Road Atlas of Southern England NEW
1.5 miles = 1 inch. Part of the urban 'navigator' series, which uses a very generous scale.
[W291] G Philip hbk **£8.95**

Road Atlas, Great Britain
[W292] AA hbk **£15.95**

Street Maps of British Towns
More town plans than any book of similar intention.
[W293] Yellow Pages hbk **£16.50**

Europe

AA Atlas Ireland
[W294] AA pbk **£2.99**

Big Road Atlas of Europe
1:1 000 000 (Central Western Europe); 1:1 250 000 (South Eastern Europe); 1:1.500 000 (Scandinavia).
[W295] AA pbk **£5.95**

Collins Road Atlas, Europe
1:4 000 000 (majority) 1:1 000 000 (certain urban areas).
[W296] Collins pbk **£6.95**

Collins Road Atlas, France
1:25 000; the UK edition of the French Hachette Maxi route atlas.
[W297] Collins pbk **£6.95**

Collins Road Atlas, Italy
1:25 000. With cartography produced by Agostini; includes 33 town plans and approach routes.
[W298] Collins pbk **£6.95**

Michelin Motoring Atlas France
1:200 000.
[W299] Hamlyn pbk **£7.95**

Michelin Motoring Atlas of Europe
Varying scales. Includes route-planning maps, 70 town plans, a map showing climatic variations, and advice on driving the roads of Europe.
[W300] Hamlyn pbk **£7.95**

RAC Road Atlas of Europe
[W301] G Philip pbk **£6.95**

Road Atlas Europe
[W302] Hamlyn hbk **£12.95**

North America

Atlas of North America
Produced by the American National Geographic Society; its quality and breadth are similar to that of the *Times Atlas of the World*.
[W303] National Geog hbk **£40.00**
[W304] National Geog pbk **£30.00**

Big Road Atlas USA, Canada, Mexico
[W305] AA pbk **£5.95**

Collins Road Atlas, USA
[W306] Collins pbk **£6.95**

North American Road Atlas
Inexpensive, American-produced, clearly laid-out.
[W307] Prentice-Hall pbk **£3.95**

US-Canada-Mexico Road Atlas and Vacation Guide
[W308] Rand McNally hbk **£12.95**
[W309] Rand McNally pbk **£9.95**

World

Collins Compact Atlas of the World
[W310] Collins hbk **£4.95**

Concise Atlas of the World
[W311] Collins hbk **£9.95**

Encyclopaedic Atlas of the World
[W312] Apple P hbk **£9.95**

Mini World Atlas
[W313] Bartholomew pbk **£2.75**

Peters Atlas of the World NEW
The Peters Atlas uses an entirely new projection of the Earth, reproducing proportionally the seven continents (thereby avoiding a European bias); some consider it to be revolutionary. The information on world topography and vegetation employs the latest satellite photography.
[W314] Longman hbk **£29.95**

Philip's Great World Atlas
[W315] G Philip hbk **£29.95**

Philip's International Atlas
[W316] G Philip hbk **£15.95**

Philip's Small World Atlas
[W317] G Philip pbk **£3.95**

Philip's World Atlas
[W318] G Philip hbk **£7.95**

Times Atlas of the World
The 'atlas's atlas': covers the world in great detail, and in coverage amounts to a compilation of all the world's national atlases.
[W319] Times Books hbk **£60.00**

Times Concise Atlas of the World
[W320] Times Books hbk **£27.50**

Practical Travel Advice

'Business Traveller' Guide to the Business Cities of the World
[W321] Simon & Sch pbk **£9.95**

Thomas Cook International Top 50 Ski Resorts NEW
Covers Italy, Switzerland, France, Austria, and countries outside Europe including Japan, the United States, Canada, South America, Australia and New Zealand.
[W322] Webb & B hbk **£15.95**

Traveller's Handbook
All the information needed to help the independent-minded traveller plan a trip to (almost) anywhere in the world.
[W323] Wexus pbk **£9.95**

CHESTER, CAROLE
Going Alone: The Women's Guide to Travel Know-how
Written by a woman for women. Especially helpful for solo travellers, it includes an abundance of practical information.
[W324] Ch Helm pbk **£4.95**

DODWELL, CHRISTINA
Explorer's Handbook
A source of advice for the independent traveller driven by above-average curiosity.
[W325] Hodder pbk **£6.95**

HANNA, NICK
BMW Tropical Beach Handbook NEW
First ever guide of its kind.
[W326] Fourth Estate pbk **£12.95**

HICKS, ROGER & SCHULTZ, FRANCES
Out-of-Season Holiday Guide
A detailed guide to the benefits of beating the mad August rush - how to choose and organise an out-of-season holiday.
[W327] Ch Helm pbk **£5.95**

LEES, DAN & MOLLY
Travel in Retirement
Information and advice on places and facilities especially suited to the needs of people over the age of 50.
[W328] Simon & Sch pbk **£4.95**

LIGHTMAN, SIDNEY
Jewish Travel Guide
Annually revised guide to all that is Jewish on the travel routes of the world.
[W329] Jewish Chron pbk **£5.95**

WOOD, KATIE & MCDONALD, GEORGE
Round the World Air Guide
A guide to the myriad possibilities (both good and bad) to be encountered when travelling the world by air.
[W330] Fontana pbk **£9.95**

WRIGHT, CAROL
Global Guide to Health Holidays
Provides up-to-date information on the types of resorts and their various facilities.
[W331] Ch Helm pbk **£5.95**

TRAVELLER'S HEALTH

Tropical Traveller: An Essential Guide to Travel in Hot Climates
Advice on preventative measures, medical treatment and a common sense approach to alien climates and conditions.
[W332] Pan pbk **£3.95**

DAWOOD, RICHARD (ED)
Traveller's Health
[W333] Oxford pbk **£5.95**

TURNER, ANTHONY C.
Traveller's Health Guide
[W334] Lascelles pbk **£4.95**

TRAVELLING WITH CHILDREN

GROSSMAN, SUSAN
Have Kids, Will Travel
[W335] Ch Helm pbk **£4.95**

HASLAM, DR DAVID
Travelling with Children
[W336] Futura pbk **£3.50**

Travel Guide Series

Owing to the fact that the majority of travel guides appear within a range of series many of the titles in the following sections do not have an individual description. Instead, where applicable, the series to which they belong has been indicated, with brief descriptions of the salient and distinguishing qualities of each one given below.

A TRAVELLER'S HISTORY (Windrush Press)

As the series name suggests, these are travellers' introductions which emphasize the historical. They examine the history of a given place and, with a view to experiencing it first-hand, clearly stipulate what still actually remains to be seen.

AA HACHETTE (AA)

For the most part, these consist of listings of hotels and restaurants, which are rated within a star system. However, there are listings of points of interest, with concise local histories, as well as an index (all the more useful given the thoroughness of the main body). The emphasis on facts, in particular on what prices to expect, accentuates their practicality.

ART GUIDE PUBLICATIONS (Art Guide Publications/A & C Black)

Comprehensive companions to the art domains in many of the major art capitals. Though they address artists, principally, they are useful for anyone seeking access to practical information on art production and exhibitions, as well as the factors which would make a given place unique.

BAEDEKER (AA, trans. from German)

Baedeker rests comfortably near the top of the concise practical guide category. Produced with a very good binding, they tend to carry information of a nature that does not rapidly go out of date. Colour photography, bird's-eye drawings, and a very reliable accommodations and restaurants listings guarantee their utility. Each one comes with a helpful city map.

BLUE GUIDES (A & C Black)

Famous for their background essays, in particular local history, they offer discriminating, practical listings of what is available, though not accommodation or restaurants. The maps are detailed, and the organization, with careful arrangement into sub-sections, makes them easy to use.

CADOGAN GUIDES (Cadogan Books)

Compiled by writers who benefit from an in-depth understanding of the locations concerned, chapters tend not to be organized on a purely geographical basis but, instead, often examine places according to 'what must be told first'. There are short, to-the-point surveys of the culture and history, and then, by means of 'headlined' paragraphs, more geographically-based listings of a considered and practical nature. There are also suggested itineraries and excursions, examining the various locations in terms of art and architecture rather than simply 'sights'.

COLLINS ILLUSTRATED GUIDES (Collins)

Moderately detailed and fully-illustrated guides which endeavour to visually represent their subjects. There is also written information on selected hotels and restaurants, basic practical information on prominent points of interest, suggested excursions and general overview maps, balanced by brief outlines of history.

COMPANION GUIDES (Collins)

Purposeful cultural guides which can just as easily be read independently, as in the context of the country to be visited. The tone, rather than the content, is scholarly, yet they remain completely accessible, written in clear, intelligent prose. They tend to be organised into areas or excursions (though not specifically into routes), and benefit from topical essays on local history, accompanied by area maps and floor plans of prominent architectural sites.

FAMILY WELCOME GUIDES (Futura)

Organized in a gazetteer format, these are specifically for people in small groups. They list reassuring information such as the proprietors of bed-and-breakfasts, general price ranges, as well as facilities suited to families. There are also general area plans (though not for the motorist), a brief outline of what is available to the visitor, and details of activities: each entry includes a brief set of directions.

FODOR'S (Fodor, US)

Comprehensive American guides whose strength is found in their simple method of organization, particularly in the use of sub-sections and paragraph 'headlines'. The use of acronyms and/or abbreviations side-steps the possibility of confusing symbols. The town plans and practical information on accommodation, restaurants and touring are clear and easy to use.

FROMMER'S DOLLAR-A-DAY (Simon & Schuster)

Guides concerned with reasonable economies while still acknowledging the need to fully 'experience' a place. Each guide provides basic information on accommodation and restaurants and the most prominent points of interest. Their usefulness for short visits is increased by the addition of a few diagrammatic maps.

FROMMER'S DOLLARWISE (Simon & Schuster)

Concise guides covering tourist activities and the daily requirements of individuals or families on holiday. Mainly they list prominent sights and, through a system of symbols, offers suggestions on accommodation and restaurants.

GAULT MILLAU 'BEST' SERIES (Penguin, Simon & Schuster)

Irreverent guides which swept through the small world of the French gastronomic review like a storm, setting new standards. They are lucid, firm and ultimately fair.

HILDEBRAND'S GUIDES (Harrap)

A series of concise general guides for the tourist, supplemented by colour photographs. They are organized on a strict geographical basis and are especially good for short visits by the uninitiated traveller. The practical information is condensed to offer the reader essential information, quickly and efficiently.

INDEPENDENT TRAVELLER'S GUIDES (Collins)

Accessible straightforward guides which list main points of interest and which offer solid practical information, aided by simple, general maps. The supplementary information consists of such things as a summary of local events and a list of titles for further reading.

INDEPENDENT TRAVELLER'S GUIDES (Moorland)

This series is oriented toward 'activities', that is, things one can do. There is an abundance of colour photographs, brief surveys of the history of a given place, as well as some practical information on accommodation and restaurants. The guides are organized in an easy-to-use gazetteer format. An inserted map is included.

INSIGHT GUIDES (APA Productions)

Historical and cultural guides which contain no specifically practical information and, as the series' name suggests, are for superficial background reading. They are complemented by an abundance of well-produced colour photographs, usually of the people, life and the landscape.

LASCELLES (Roger Lascelles)

Lascelles produce a very wide range of guides which covers literally the whole world. They also distribute an extensive selection published by others, from both within Britain and abroad. In general, they address travellers, as opposed to tourists, and offer great detail, along with sober practical advice both for the novice and the more experienced traveller.

LET'S GO (Pan)

For the kind of tourist they address, which seems to be the back-packing, casual American university student on holiday, these guides are probably without equal. Even if you do not fall into this category, they remain a perfectly adequate choice. Through the use of chatty, idiomatic yet concise journalistic language, they offer solid coverage of the various points of interest to be found in the place concerned and intelligently anticipate problems that can easily be avoided.

MICHAEL'S GUIDE SERIES (Lascelles)

Detailed, yet concise guides with a rational, no-nonsense approach, reflecting the independence of mind with which they have been produced.

MICHELIN GREEN TOURIST GUIDES (Michelin Tyre Co plc)

Each is an exhaustive listing of places to see, compiled for the inquisitive tourist - and they are strikingly thorough. Imaginatively illustrated, often with bird's-eye line-diagrams of towns and cities, they are especially good for opening times and details of museum collections. Contains no information on accommodation and restaurants. Some editions - particularly those covering the rural areas of France - are only available in French versions.

MICHELIN RED GUIDES (Michelin Tyre Co plc)

Despite the omnipresence of symbols, these guides are without equal as an exhaustive listing on accommodation, restaurants and some basic demographic information. They include trouble-shooting facts such as local trade fairs and other major events which may (or may not) oblige the visitor to postpone. Distances between destinations and major road routes, as well as exceptional maps, complement the gazetteer.

MONEYWISE GUIDES (BUNAC Travel Services)

Published by the British Universities North America Club. Well-rounded overviews of the North American destination concerned. Concise listings of the main points of interest, as well as suggested activities (supplemented by helpful maps) ensure that readers are offered a clear picture of what to expect.

OFF THE BEATEN TRACK (Moorland)

Strong on suggested excursions and on important places to visit (with an explanation of why they are 'important'), these guides are as useful for independent travellers as they are for those on a driving holiday. The 'further information' sections, which contain background material, help the reader form an overall picture.

ON A SHOESTRING
(Lonely Planet, Australia)

General guides for the independent traveller or tourist with advice on how to watch one's budget in the area concerned. The practical information is thorough, recommending accommodation and restaurants, and identifies the better excursions and local points of interest. The guides are comprehensive and good on background information, and are a slightly leaner version of their cousin the *Travel Survival Kit*.

ORDNANCE SURVEY GUIDES
(AA, Ordnance Survey)

In some ways these are the 'definitive' guides to a given place or region, although their coverage is intentionally middle-of-the-road. Reliability and accuracy are their forte.

ROUGH GUIDES (Harrap)

An extremely accessible series of guides with information in a narrative format, intended as British, or European, competition to the previously ubiquitous American *Let's Go* series. Available for a rapidly increasing number of places, they include practical information on accommodation, restaurants, opening times, and regular overview maps, with good detail on the cultural interest of each area or location. The familiar, yet logical tone of the prose reinforces their reputation for being both conscientious and thorough.

SELF-GUIDED SERIES
(Langenscheidt, trans. from German)

These guides are organized into excursions or routes through the country concerned and include colour photographs. They look at what pleasurable places and things can be found (as opposed to what can be done) and carry brief sections on history, cuisine, art and architecture. They contain no practical information on accommodation or restaurants.

TRAVEL SURVIVAL KITS
(Lonely Planet, Australia)

Well-conceived general guides for the independent traveller or tourist; the series offers especially good coverage of the Far East. The practical information is thorough and the position of money important but not central. They recommend accommodation and restaurants and identify the better local excursions and points of interest. Of particular value is the manner in which they build up the subject from first impressions through to fairly extensive detail.

WALKING THROUGH FRANCE
(Robertson McCarta)

A number of extremely detailed small-scale maps, which benefit from the use of full-colour, form the core of these guides, translated into English from the French. Charts giving distances to, from, and between given locations accompany the prescribed walks, which are illustrated with route diagrams showing the topography. Other useful information relating to the surrounding physical features is included along with advice on what is necessary for a particular day's outing.

WHERE WOULD YOU BE WITHOUT OUR TRAVEL GUIDES AND MOTORING MAPS? OUR RED GUIDES DESCRIBE MORE HOTELS AND RESTAURANTS THAN ANY OTHERS. OUR GREEN GUIDES MARK PLACES-OF-INTEREST WITH ONE, TWO, OR THREE STARS. OUR MAPS ARE UP-DATED EVERY YEAR. AND THEY'RE ALL CROSS-REFERENCED, SO YOU CAN MOVE EASILY FROM ONE TO ANOTHER. **MAKE SURE IT'S A MICHELIN. YOU'LL BE ALL OVER THE PLACE WITHOUT US.**

WHERE TO STAY
WHAT TO SEE
WHERE TO GO

MICHELIN MAPS AND GUIDES

TRAVEL

Britain

BRITISH SERIES

BARTHOLOMEW WALKING SERIES
(Bartholomew)

A series devoted to providing the sort of information that any rambler or walker would necessarily need on a walking holiday in the wilds. They are comprehensive, common sensical and reliable.

CAMRA "Best Pubs" Series

The *Campaign for Real Ale* was founded in the 1970s with the self-appointed remit to improve beer, full-stop. They have met with some success and, a few years ago, began to identify the pubs, nationwide, which offered jolly good beer, the real stuff. The resultant series is credible and fair-minded.

DISCOVERING SCOTLAND (John Donald)

Devoted to regional Scotland, these are touring guides which examine in some detail the many points of interest, with a particular emphasis on the architecture and landscape. They more or less assume one is on a motoring holiday and include a selection of black and white photographs. There is no practical information on opening times, accommodation or restaurants.

SHELL GUIDES (David & Charles, Faber, M Joseph, Macmillan)

A-Z gazetteer of towns: especially concerned with famous figures, local history (early, medieval and modern, where applicable) and each town's main points of interest as it emerges from that history. The colour photographs are of a high quality and, unlike in most guides, form an integral part of their appeal and use.

GENERAL GUIDES

AA 250 Tours of Britain
A wide range of day, weekend and holiday drives, clearly described and mapped.
[W371] Drive hbk **£16.95**

AA Discovering Britain
A beautifully photographed guide to the often ignored scenic treasures not always on the main tourist routes.
[W372] Drive hbk **£14.95**

AA Touring England
An illustrated guide consisting of route maps, town-plans and interesting topographical information.
[W373] AA hbk **£24.95**

AA Treasures of Britain
The treasures referred to are part of the architecture and art of Britain. Many photographs and historical information.
[W374] Drive hbk **£16.95**

AA Where to Go in Britain
[W375] AA hbk **£12.95**

AA Where to Go in the Countryside
Descriptions of 500 places in the countryside such as national parks, country parks and nature reserves.
[W376] AA hbk **£14.95**

Britain by Bicycle
Advice on the most scenic, not to mention safest, cycle routes.
[W377] Weidenfeld pbk **£4.95**

CTC Book of Cycle-touring
Published in conjunction with the Cyclists' Touring Club.
[W378] Grafton pbk **£3.95**

Collins Guide to Great Britain
[W379] Fontana pbk **£10.95**

Country Lover's Holiday Guide   NEW
Introduced by David Bellamy. Each county is introduced by a local historian, and includes many line-drawings, maps showing places of interest and information on opening times.
[W380] Butterfly Pubs hbk **£14.95**

Countryside Directory   NEW
A handbook for days out in the British countryside.
[W381] Sphere pbk **£3.99**

Exploring Rural England and Wales
Exploring Rural Europe series.
[W382] Ch Helm pbk **£5.95**

Family Welcome Guide: Britain
Family Welcome series.
[W383] Futura pbk **£7.50**

Fodor's Great Britain
[W384] Random Cen pbk **£9.95**

Fontana Guide to Great Britain
[W385] Collins hbk **£15.00**

Great Cycle Tours of Britain   NEW
Includes information on routes, access, accommodation, tourist information offices, cycle shops and suggested maps.
[W386] Ward L hbk **£14.95**

Guide to National Trust Properties
An illustrated gazetteer of the 800 or so houses owned by the National Trust.
[W387] AA pbk **£7.95**

Holiday Which? Guide to Weekend Breaks
Ideas for short breaks in all parts of Britain, and for making the most of your time away.
[W388] Hodder pbk **£9.95**

Les Routiers Guide to Britain   NEW
[W389] Macdonald pbk **£6.95**

Let's Go Britain and Ireland
[W390] Pan pbk **£9.95**

Markets and Fairs of Britain
A guide to British markets and fairs, including those for livestock.
[W391] Collins pbk **£6.95**

National Trust Book of the English Country Town
An illustrated history charting the development of the 'typical' town.
[W392] Grafton pbk **£4.95**

Off the Motorway
[W393] Cadogan pbk **£3.95**

Outdoor Guide to Britain   NEW
National parks, nature reserves, zoos and safari parks.
[W394] Webb & B hbk **£16.95**

See Britain by Train   NEW
50 scenic routes on Britain's contracting rail network; engineering features, landmarks, and intriguing places to stop off.
[W395] AA pbk **£8.95**

Traveller's Key to Sacred England
[W396] Harrap pbk **£9.95**

BLUE GUIDE SERIES
England (Newly revised)
[W397] A & C Black hbk **£13.95**
Exploring British Cities
[W398] A & C Black pbk **£9.95**
Green Guide to Urban Wildlife   NEW
[W399] A & C Black pbk **£11.95**

ELLSWORTH-JONES, WILL & WALKER, CHRISTINE (EDS.)
Sunday Times Weekend Breaks   NEW
[W400] Hodder pbk **£9.95**

GIBBONS, GARY & BEESLEY, EARL
Treasure Houses of England   NEW
[W401] Viking hbk **£30.00**

SHELL GUIDE SERIES
New Shell Guide to England
[W402] M Joseph hbk **£15.00**
Shell Book of English Villages
[W403] Peerage Books hbk **£9.95**
Shell Book of Exploring Britain
[W404] A & C Black hbk **£12.95**
Shell Book of Rural Britain
[W405] David & Ch hbk **£8.95**
Shell Book of Undiscovered Britain and Ireland
[W406] David & Ch pbk **£10.95**
Shell Guide to Reading the Landscape
Describes what can be gained from visiting the many and varied archaeological remains in rural parts of Britain.
[W407] M Joseph hbk **£13.95**

SOMERVILLE-LARGE, PETER
Skying   NEW
A journey around and above Britain in a microlight aircraft.
[W408] H Hamilton hbk **£13.95**

WALKING GUIDES

Holiday Which? Good Walks Guide
200 walks with a map to represent each one.
[W409] Hodder pbk **£8.95**

Long Distance Paths of England and Wales
[W410] David & Ch hbk **£10.95**

Shell Book of British Walks
Over one hundred routes arranged thematically: mountain walks, railway walks, and more, of varying length.
[W411] David & Ch hbk **£14.95**

WAINWRIGHT, ALFRED
Fell Walking with Wainwright: 18 of the Author's Favourite Walks
An illustrated guided tour through some of the many walks the author has developed in his lifetime.
[W412] M Joseph hbk **£12.95**

COASTS AND WATERWAYS

DURHAM, DICK
On and Offshore   NEW
With a backdrop of the Thames and Britain's south eastern coast, the author offers a blend of historical information, an account of his rather short journey, and of his personal experiences.
[W413] Ashford P hbk **£12.95**

ORDNANCE SURVEY GUIDE TO THE WATERWAYS
Indispensable guides for boat-owners, walkers and lovers of inland waterways. Useful pocket size.
Vol 1: South
[W414] Nicholson pbk **£6.95**
Vol 2: Central
[W415] Nicholson pbk **£6.95**
Vol 3: North
[W416] Nicholson pbk **£6.95**

PURVES, LIBBY
One Summer's Grace NEW
An illustrated personal travelogue of a journey around the coastline of Britain.
[W417] Grafton hbk **£12.95**

SALE, RICHARD
Walking Britain's Coast NEW
[W418] Unwin hbk **£17.95**

SOMERVILLE, CHRISTOPHER
Britain Beside the Sea NEW
An illustrated look at selected seaside towns.
[W419] Grafton hbk **£14.95**
Coastal Walks in England and Wales
[W420] Grafton pbk **£6.95**
Fifty Best River Walks
[W422] Webb & B hbk **£14.95**

SOMERVILLE, CHRISTOPHER & BETHELL, J
English Harbours and Coastal Villages NEW
A combination of text and photographs (by Bethell) introduces the reader to a selection of the historic ports and harbours of Britain.
[W421] Weidenfeld hbk **£11.95**

LITERARY & HISTORICAL GUIDES

A Guide to the Ancient Sites in Britain
[W423] Grafton pbk **£4.95**

Cambridge Guide to the Historic Places of Britain and Ireland
On offer is not only the more stately of stately homes, but also public houses, steam railways and the wonderful Blackpool Tower.
[W424] Cambridge hbk **£14.95**

Cambridge Guide to the Museums of Britain and Ireland
An exhaustive listing of the British and Irish collections. New edition.
[W425] Cambridge pbk **£8.95**

Historic Houses, Castles and Gardens in Great Britain and Ireland
Full visiting details of almost every prominent place of interest that is normally open to the public.
[W426] British Leisure pbk **£4.50**

Secret Britain
A guide to what is not always on the tourist route.
[W427] AA hbk **£16.95**

Shell Book of British Buildings
Illustrated companion to older British architecture, with brief social and political histories.
[W428] David & Ch hbk **£12.50**

BAINBRIDGE, BERYL (1934 -)
English Journey
The retracing of J.B. Priestley's 1938 tour which reveals, for the most part, that change does not come easily. It was made into a television series.
[W429] Fontana pbk **£2.50**

Forever England: North and South
[W430] Duckworth hbk **£9.95**

BARLEY, NIGEL
Native Land NEW
An anthropologist's look at many aspects of contemporary English life.
[W431] Viking hbk **£11.95**

BETJEMAN, JOHN (ED)
Guide to Selected English Parish Churches (Revised, in one volume)
[W432] Collins hbk **£9.95**

BURTON, ANTHONY
Britain Revisited: One Man's Journey in the Steps of the Travellers
[W433] Oxford hbk **£10.95**

DAICHES, DAVID & FLOWERS, RAYMOND
Literary Landscapes of the British Isles
A narrative atlas which endeavours to trace the footsteps of some well known literary figures and to re-situate a selection of stories in their real life settings.
[W434] Penguin pbk **£5.95**

EAGLE, DOROTHY
Oxford Literary Guide to the British Isles
A reference guide to the literary side of a selection of towns, villages and regions throughout the British Isles.
[W435] Oxford pbk **£5.95**

GOODMAN, ANTHONY
A Traveller's Guide to Early Medieval Britain
A selection of recommended visits to places of interest in Britain which have their origins in medieval times.
[W436] Routledge hbk **£12.95**

NEW, ANTHONY
Guide to the Abbeys of England and Wales
A pocket guide to the history and local lore which shrouds each abbey.
[W437] Constable hbk **£7.95**
Guide to the Cathedrals of Britain
[W438] Constable hbk **£6.95**

OTTAWAY, PATRICK & CYPRIEN, MICHAEL
Traveller's Guide to Roman Britain
A guide to the visible remains of the period during which Britain was under the authority of the Roman Empire.
[W439] Routledge hbk **£9.95**

PRIESTLEY, J.B. (1894 - 1984)
English Journey
During the latter part of the Depression Priestley travelled around Britain by train, sympathetically examining the British people and, indirectly, the state of the nation.
[W440] Penguin pbk **£4.95**

RABAN, JONATHAN (1942 -)
Coasting
Based on a sailing trip made around the coastline of Britain.
[W441] Picador pbk **£3.99**

THEROUX, PAUL (1941 -)
Kingdom by the Sea
The author looks humorously and wittily, at Britain, his adopted home, in the course of a journey made by train, bus and on foot around its coastline.
[W442] Penguin pbk **£3.95**

'TIRESIAS'
Notes from Overground
[W443] Grafton pbk **£3.50**

RESTAURANTS & ACCOMMODATION

AA Camping and Caravanning in Britain
[W444] Hodder pbk **£5.95**

Beer, Bed and Breakfast
CAMRA's guide to pubs with accommodation.
[W445] Robson pbk **£5.95**

Best of British Country House Hotels and Restaurants NEW
[W446] Fontana pbk **£5.95**

Country House Hotels of Britain and Ireland NEW
Featuring over two hundred country house hotels: the range is exhaustive, from the grandest to the more intimate, and the focus is upon character, quality of service and tranquility.
[W447] Ch Helm hbk **£9.95**

Country Inns and Backroads of Britain and Ireland NEW
[W448] Harper & R pbk **£7.50**

Good Food Guide
A newly revised edition of this comprehensive and enduringly useful guide to the restaurants of Great Britain.
[W449] Hodder pbk **£10.95**

Good Hotel Guide (Updated)
[W450] Hodder pbk **£11.95**

Great Britain and Ireland
Michelin Red guide.
[W451] Michelin hbk **£7.95**

Staying Off the Beaten Track
[W452] Arrow pbk **£7.00**

ACKERMAN, ROY
Ackerman Guide to the Best Restaurants and Hotels in the British Isles NEW
Second edition of Roy Ackerman's detailed description of what he considers to be the five hundred most satisfying places to eat and sleep in Britain.
[W453] Alfresco LP hbk **£9.95**

BROWN, SARAH
Sarah Brown's Best of Vegetarian Britain
An extensive guide to many of the better places around Britain in which to eat vegetarian and vegan food.
[W454] Thorsons pbk **£4.99**

HANSON, NEIL
Classic Country Pubs NEW
Written by a leading light in the Campaign for Real Ale. Hanson has travelled the length and breadth of Britain to seek out public houses deemed to be worthy of a visit, both for the beer served and for their atmosphere.
[W455] M Joseph hbk **£9.99**

RONAY, EGON
Cellnet Guide to Hotels, Restaurants and Inns
[W456] AA pbk **£9.95**

England By Region

Southern England

Including Bedfordshire, Berkshire, Buckinghamshire, Hampshire, Hertfordshire, Kent, Oxfordshire, Surrey and Sussex.

Explore the New Forest
[W457] HMSO pbk £4.95

Guide to the South Downs Way
[W458] Constable hbk £6.95

Guide to the Thames Path
[W459] Constable hbk £8.95

Guide to the Wealdway
[W460] Constable hbk £6.95

Hertfordshire: A Shell Guide
[W461] Faber pbk £4.95

Kent `NEW`
Hale County Leisure series.
[W462] Hale pbk £5.95

Kent and Sussex
Companion Guide series.
[W463] Collins hbk £10.95

Oxford and Cambridge
Blue Guide series.
[W464] A & C Black pbk £6.95

South Downs Way
[W465] HMSO pbk £4.95

Surrey `NEW`
Hale Country Leisure series.
[W466] Hale pbk £5.95

BARTHOLEMEW WALKING SERIES
Walk the New Forest
[W467] Bartholomew pbk £3.95
Walk the North Downs
[W468] Bartholomew pbk £3.95
Walk the South Downs
[W469] Bartholomew pbk £3.95
Walk the Thames and Chilterns
[W470] Bartholomew pbk £3.95

GLENDINNING, VICTORIA
Victoria Glendinning's Hertfordshire `NEW`
An intimate look at the county of her birth.
[W471] Weidenfeld hbk £14.95

MORRIS, JAN (ED)
Oxford Book of Oxford (1978)
An illustrated collection of writings on a city of many faces.
[W472] Oxford pbk £5.95

OORTHUYS, CAS
Oxford in Focus
[W473] Faber pbk £2.95

ORDNANCE SURVEY
Guide to the River Thames and River Way
[W474] Nicholson pbk £6.95
Historic County Guide to Hampshire and the Isle of Wight
[W475] G Philip hbk £9.95

Historic County Guide to Kent
[W476] G Philip hbk £9.95
Historic County Guide to Surrey
[W477] G Philip hbk £9.95

ORDNANCE SURVEY SERIES
Historic County Guide to Oxfordshire and Berkshire
[W478] G Philip hbk £9.95

WATKINS, BRUCE
Buckinghamshire
[W479] Faber pbk £4.95

WRIGHT, CHRISTOPHER JOHN
Guide to the Pilgrim's Way and North Downs Way
[W480] Constable hbk £7.95

South-West England

Including Avon, Cornwall, Devon, Dorset, Gloucestershire, Hereford & Worcester, Somerset and Wiltshire.

AA Touring the West Country
[W481] AA pbk £7.95

Best Pubs in Devon and Cornwall `NEW`
CAMRA Best Pubs series.
[W482] CAMRA pbk £4.95

Cotswolds `NEW`
[W483] Ordnance Survey pbk £6.95

Dartmoor and Exmoor
Great Walks in Britain series.
[W484] Ward Lock hbk £14.95

Dorset Coast Path
Guide to walking the 73-mile coastal path; with maps.
[W485] Penguin pbk £1.95

Exmoor National Park
A Countryside Commission Guide.
[W486] Webb & B pbk £5.95

Somerset
Cadogan Guide series.
[W487] Cadogan pbk £3.50

The Ridgeway `NEW`
[W488] Ordnance Survey pbk £6.95

BARTHOLEMEW WALKING SERIES
Walk Dartmoor: 35 Easy Walks
[W489] Bartholomew pbk £3.95
Walk Dorset and Hardy's Wessex `NEW`
[W490] Bartholomew pbk £3.95
Walk Exmoor `NEW`
[W491] Bartholomew pbk £3.95
Walk the Cornish Coastal Path `NEW`
[W492] Bartholomew pbk £3.95
Walk the Cotswolds `NEW`
[W493] Bartholomew pbk £3.95

BETJEMAN, JOHN (1906 - 1984)
Betjeman's Cornwall
[W494] J Murray pbk £5.95

COAST PATHS
Cornwall Coast Path
[W495] HMSO pbk £3.95
Dorset Coast Path
[W496] HMSO pbk £3.95

Somerset and North Devon Coast Path
[W497] HMSO pbk £3.95
South Devon Coast Path
[W498] HMSO pbk £3.95
South West Coast Path: Poole/ Exmouth Section `NEW`
[W499] Ordnance Survey pbk £6.95

GANT, ROLAND
A Guide to the South Devon & Dorset Coast Paths
A pocket guide to 500 miles of South West peninsula footpath.
[W500] Constable hbk £5.95

HILL, SUSAN (1942 -)
Spirit of the Cotswolds
Eloquent text by novelist Susan Hill with photographs of this part of England.
[W501] M Joseph hbk £14.95

LEA, HERMANN
The Hardy Guide Vol 1
Significantly, this guide was approved by the author himself.
[W502] Penguin pbk £4.95
The Hardy Guide Vol 2
[W503] Penguin pbk £4.95

MAURIER, DAPHNE DU (1907 - 1989)
Vanishing Cornwall
[W504] Penguin pbk £2.95

MOONEY, BEL
Bel Mooney's Somerset `NEW`
The author of *Fourth of July* portrays the county of her birth.
[W505] Weidenfeld hbk £14.95

PETTIT, PAUL
Devon, Cornwall and the Isles of Scilly: A Shell Guide
[W506] M Joseph pbk £4.99

RICHARDS, MARK
Cotswolds Way
[W507] Penguin pbk £4.50

ROBERTSON, CHARLES
Bath: An Architectural Guide
With an introduction by Jan Morris.
[W508] Faber hbk £11.50

SALE, RICHARD
Guide to the Cotswold Way
[W509] Constable hbk £7.95

SITWELL, EDITH (1887 - 1964)
Bath
Sitwell's evocation and re-creation of Bath society starts with the arrival of Beau Nash and his fashionable set in the early 18th century, which followed the visit by Queen Anne in 1702.
[W510] Century pbk £5.95

WEIR, JOHN
Dartmoor National Park
[W511] Webb & B pbk £5.95

East Anglia

Including Cambridgeshire, Essex, Norfolk and Suffolk.

AA Touring Central England and East Anglia
[W512] AA pbk £7.95

TRAVEL

East Anglia
OS/AA Leisure Guide Series
[W513] OS/AA pbk **£8.95** NEW

Explore the Broads
[W514] Bartholomew pbk **£3.50**

Guide to the Norfolk Way
A guide to one of Britain's newest long-distance footpaths, officially known as Peddlers Way or the Norfolk Coast Path.
[W515] Constable hbk **£6.95**

Norfolk Villages
[W516] Hale hbk **£7.95**

Oxford and Cambridge
Blue Guide series.
[W517] A & C Black pbk **£6.95**

Peddlers Way and Norfolk Coast Path
[W518] HMSO pbk **£4.95**

Visitor's Guide to East Anglia
[W519] Moorland pbk **£4.95**

JENNINGS, PAUL
East Anglia
[W520] G Fraser hbk **£9.95**

JESTY, CHRIS
East Anglian Town Trails NEW
34 town walks are covered, each supplemented by sketches by the author and extensive maps.
[W521] Hale pbk **£4.95**

RENDELL, RUTH (1930 -)
Suffolk NEW
The crime novelist's personal relationship with the landscape and history of the county.
[W522] Muller hbk **£14.95**

SCARFE, NORMAN
Cambridgeshire: A Shell Guide
[W523] Alastair P pbk **£6.95**

Midlands

Including Derbyshire, Leicestershire, Lincolnshire, Northamptonshire, Nottinghamshire, Shropshire, Staffordshire, Warwickshire and the West Midlands.

Pennine Way
[W524] HMSO pbk **£3.95**

DUERDEN, FRANK
Best Walks in the Peak District
[W525] Constable hbk **£8.95**

HILL, SUSAN (1942 -)
Shakespeare Country
[W526] M Joseph hbk **£12.95**

POUCHER, W.A.
Peak and Pennines
[W527] Constable hbk **£6.95**

SILLITOE, ALAN (1928 -)
Nottinghamshire
The author's evocation of his native county.
[W528] Grafton hbk **£14.95**

SKIPP, VICTOR
Centre of England
Covers Warwickshire, Worcestershire, Staffordshire, East Shropshire and North Gloucestershire.
[W529] Methuen pbk **£5.50**

THOROLD, HENRY
Nottinghamshire: A Shell Guide
[W530] Faber pbk **£6.95**

WRIGHT, CHRISTOPHER JOHN
Guide to the Pennine Way
[W531] Constable hbk **£7.95**

North-West England

Including Cheshire, Cumbria, Lancashire, Greater Manchester and Merseyside.

Best Pubs in Lakeland NEW
CAMRA Best Pubs Series.
[W532] CAMRA pbk **£3.95**

Holiday Which? Guide to the Lake District NEW
[W533] Hodder pbk **£7.95**

Lake District NEW
Companion Guide series.
[W534] Collins hbk **£10.95**

BARTHOLEMEW WALKING SERIES
Walk the Lakes: Forty Easy Walks
[W535] Bartholomew pbk **£3.50**
More Walks in the Lakes
[W536] Bartholomew pbk **£3.95**

BIRKETT, BILL & WHITE, JOHN
A Guide to Rock Climbing in Northern England NEW
The authors consider all the graded climbs in Yorkshire, Lancashire, Northumberland and in the Peak District.
[W537] Constable hbk **£7.95**

HARRIES, RICHARD
Cycling in the Lake District
[W538] Moorland pbk **£4.95**

POUCHER, W.A.
Lakeland Peaks
A pocket guidebook to some of the best routes in the Lakeland mountains.
[W539] Constable hbk **£7.95**

WAINWRIGHT, ALFRED
Coast to Coast Walk: St Bees Head to Robin Hood Bay
Wainwright describes the coast to coast walk from St Bees Head in Cumbria, across the Lake District and the Pennines into Swaledale, the North Yorkshire Moors and on to Robin Hood's Bay.
[W540] Westmorland pbk **£6.00**
Lakeland Mountain Passes NEW
Yet another in a long and illustrious series of Wainwright 'tours', complemented by photographs by Derry Brabbs.
[W541] M Joseph hbk **£14.95**
Pictorial Guide to Lakeland Fells
Vol 1: Eastern Fells
[W542] Westmorland hbk **£5.50**
Vol 2: Far Eastern Fells
[W543] Westmorland hbk **£5.50**
Vol 3: Central Fells
[W544] Westmorland hbk **£5.50**
Vol 4: Southern Fells
[W545] Westmorland hbk **£5.50**
Vol 5: Northern Fells
[W546] Westmorland hbk **£5.50**
Vol 6: North Western Fells
[W547] Westmorland hbk **£5.50**
Vol 7: Western Fells
[W548] Westmorland hbk **£5.50**

Wainwright on the Pennine Way
[W549] M Joseph pbk **£9.95**

WHITEMAN, ROBIN
The English Lakes NEW
An examination of the local history, geography and literary connections of several of the English lakes.
[W550] Weidenfeld hbk **£11.95**

WORDSWORTH, WILLIAM (1770 - 1850)
Wordsworth's Guide to the Lakes (1810)
Wordsworth's own vision of Cumbria, with which he was most familiar. It was originally entitled *A Description of the Scenery of the Lakes in the North of England*.
[W551] Webb & B hbk **£14.95**
[W552] Oxford pbk **£2.50**

North-East England

Including Cleveland, Durham, Humberside, Northumberland, Tyne & Wear and all counties of Yorkshire.

Cleveland Way
[W553] HMSO pbk **£3.95**

Cleveland Way NEW
National Trail Guides Series.
[W554] Ordnance Survey pbk **£6.95**

North York Moors
AA/Ordnance Survey Guide series.
[W555] AA pbk **£7.95**

Northumbria
Companion Guide series.
[W556] Collins pbk **£7.95**

Pennine Way North Section NEW
[W557] Ordnance Survey pbk **£6.95**

Yorkshire Dales NEW
[W558] Ordnance Survey pbk **£6.95**

Yorkshire and Humberside
Cadogan Guide series.
[W559] Cadogan pbk **£2.95**

BARTHOLEMEW WALKING SERIES
Walk the North Yorks Moors
[W560] Bartholomew pbk **£3.95**

COLLARD, GEORGE
Exploring Northumbria
Five routes which allow the visitor to explore the county and see something of its folklore, history, landscape and coastline.
[W561] Sutton hbk **£14.95**

COLLINS, MARTIN
North Yorks Moors: Walks in the National Park
[W562] Cicerone pbk **£4.95**

GUNN, PETER
Yorkshire Dales
A detailed history and guide to an enduringly beautiful and popular area of the country and its inhabitants.
[W563] Century pbk **£3.95**

SPENCER, BRIAN
New Shell Guide to North-East England
[W564] M Joseph pbk **£9.95**

WAINWRIGHT, ALFRED
Pennine Way Companion:
A Pictorial Guide
[W565] Westmorland hbk **£6.00**

WRIGHT, GEOFFREY
Yorkshire Dales National Park
[W566] David & Ch hbk **£12.95**

London

A-Z Information:
London's Handy Atlas-Guide
[W567] Geographers pbk **£2.95**

AA London Guide
[W568] AA pbk **£7.95**

Best of London
Gault Millau 'Best' series.
[W569] Penguin pbk **£9.95**

Children's London
For adults with children, this guide helpfully lists a
range of activities for the young. It includes
information on museums, galleries, parks, theatres,
cinemas, places to eat and (perhaps most
importantly!) where to park.
[W570] Nicholson pbk **£3.50**

Fodor's London
[W571] Random Cen pbk **£5.95**

Guide to Ethnic London
A guide covering the Chinese, Asian, Polish,
Italian, Jewish, Irish, Cypriot and Afro-Caribbean
communities.
[W572] M Haag pbk **£5.95**

Inside Soho
[W573] Nicholson pbk **£3.50**

London
Cultural Guide series.
[W574] Phaidon hbk **£9.95**

London Art and Artists Guide
(5th edition)
Art Guide Publications series.
[W575] A & C Black pbk **£6.95**

London Docklands Guide and
Street Atlas
[W576] Nicholson pbk **£5.95**

London Scene
An up-to-date guide to London specifically for gay
men.
[W577] GMP pbk **£5.00**

BANKS, F.R.
New Penguin Guide to London
Banks' comprehensive volume still stands as
perhaps the most detailed guide to London
in existence.
[W578] Penguin pbk **£3.99**

CLARKE, JENNIFER & PARKIN, JOANNA
'In Our Grandmothers' Footsteps':
The Virago Guide to London
[W579] Virago pbk **£5.95**

DANEFF, TIFFANY
London Walks　　　　　　　　**NEW**
Forty walks in Greater London.
[W580] M Joseph hbk **£15.95**

HAWKINS, ROY
Green London: A Handbook
[W581] Sidgwick pbk **£6.95**

HOLT, ELIZABETH & PERHAM, MOLLY
Kids' London
[W582] Pan pbk **£2.95**

NICHOLSON, LOUISE
London: Louise Nicholson's
Definitive Guide
A thoroughly researched guide which has integrated
the practical and the thematic. The old
neighbourhoods are identified, 'up-lifted' from
the pounding they have received from modern
life, and toured for the reader. The prose is
tight and the opinions offered by the author show
great insight.
[W583] Bodley hbk **£9.95**

PEPLOW, MARY & SHIPLEY, DEBORAH
Good Excursion Guide　　　**NEW**
[W584] Nicholson pbk **£3.95**

PEPLOW, MARY & SHIPLEY, DEBRA
London for Free
[W585] Grafton pbk **£2.95**

PICK, CHRISTOPHER
Children's Guide to London
Cadogan Guide series.
[W586] Cadogan pbk **£3.95**

ROSSITER, STUART (ED)
Blue Guide London
Blue Guide series.
[W587] A & C Black pbk **£9.95**

WHITAKER, JOANNA
London on Sunday
[W588] Grafton pbk **£2.50**

ZEFF, LINDA
Jewish London
[W589] Piatkus pbk **£4.95**

RESTAURANTS &
ACCOMMODATION

Best Pubs in London　　　　**NEW**
CAMRA Best Pub series.
[W590] CAMRA pbk **£4.95**

Greater London
Michelin pocket hotel and restaurant listing.
[W591] Michelin pbk **£2.10**

London Restaurant Guide
[W592] Nicholson pbk **£3.50**

BROWN, SARAH
Sarah Brown's
Vegetarian London
[W593] Thorsons pbk **£3.50**

LITERARY & HISTORICAL

BETJEMAN, JOHN
Betjeman's London
Edited by Pennie Denton. The former Poet Laureate's
distinctive prose and verse presented alongside his
own paintings and drawings.
[W594] J Murray pbk **£9.95**

BLATCH, MERVYN
A Guide to London's Churches
[W595] Constable hbk **£6.95**

HIBBERT, CHRISTOPHER
London: The Biography of a City
A concise, stimulating history of London with
inspired illustrations throughout.
[W596] Penguin pbk **£8.95**

HILLABY, JOHN
John Hillaby's London
[W597] Grafton pbk **£4.99**

PRITCHETT, V.S.
London Perceived (1962)
A sentimental tour of the metropolis by a
lifelong resident.
[W598] Hogarth pbk **£5.95**

SHAKESPEARE, NICHOLAS
Londoners
[W599] Sidgwick pbk **£8.95**

TRISTAN, FLORA
London Journals (1840-42)
An early socialist and feminist, Tristan came to
London from France to inspect life in the city,
especially how the poor lived.
[W600] Virago pbk **£7.50**

WEINREB, BEN & HIBBERT, CHRISTOPHER
London Encyclopaedia
An itemized history of the city, exhaustively
researched.
[W601] Macmillan pbk **£14.95**

WILLIAMS, GEORGE B.
Guide to Literary London
Aimed at those who have come to London in the
present to try to discover the stuff of the city's
literary past.
[W602] Batsford pbk **£9.95**

Scotland

Fodor's Scotland
[W606] Random Cen pbk **£10.50**

Scotland
Green tourist guide.
[W607] Michelin pbk **£5.25**

Scotland
Blue Guide series.
[W608] A & C Black pbk **£10.95**

BAXTER, COLIN
Scotland: The Light of the Land
[W609] David & Ch pbk **£7.95**

HAMILTON, RONALD
Holiday History of Scotland
An inevitably simplified history of Scotland,
which nonetheless adds depth and meaning to the
various sights that can be visited by the interested
holiday-maker.
[W610] Hogarth pbk **£3.95**

LINDSAY, MAURICE
Castles of Scotland
[W611] Constable hbk **£12.95**

MACKENZIE, R.F.
In Search of Scotland　　　　**NEW**
Mackenzie reflects upon his lifelong love for
Scotland, and examines its countryside, towns,
industrial heritage, ancient roads and winding
railways.
[W612] Collins hbk **£16.95**

MCNEISH, CAMERSON & SMITH, ROGER
Classic Walks in Scotland
[W613] Oxford hbk **£14.95**

MIERS, RICHENDA
Scotland
Cadogan Guide series.
[W614] Cadogan pbk **£7.95**

MUIR, EDWIN (1887 - 1959)
Scottish Journey
[W615] Fontana pbk **£3.50**

NAISMITH, ROBERT
**Buildings of the Scottish
Countryside**
[W616] Gollancz pbk **£7.95**

NEW, ANTHONY
Guide to the Abbeys of Scotland
[W617] Constable pbk **£9.95**

SANDISON, BRUCE
Hillwalker's Guide to Scotland `NEW`
Eighty walks of various lengths and degrees
of difficulty: from gentle, six mile hikes in the
lowlands to not-so-gentle sixteen mile scrambles
across mountains.
[W618] Unwin pbk **£8.95**

SLAVIN, KEN & SLAVIN, JULIE
Around Scotland
Cadogan Guide series.
[W619] Cadogan pbk **£5.95**

WEIR, TOM
Tom Weir's Scotland
[W620] Penguin pbk **£2.95**

Cities

ABERDEEN

BAXTER, COLIN
Aberdeen
[W621] R Drew pbk **£2.95**

EDINBURGH

Edinburgh Castle
[W622] HMSO pbk **£1.00**
BAXTER, COLIN
Edinburgh
[W623] R Drew pbk **£2.95**
DAICHES, DAVID
**Edinburgh: A Traveller's
Companion**
A guide by the Scottish literary critic.
[W624] Constable pbk **£6.95**
KERSTING, ANTHONY F. &
LINDSAY, MAURICE
Buildings of Edinburgh
[W625] Batsford pbk **£9.95**

GLASGOW

BAIN, ALISON
Glasgow Arts Guide `NEW`
Art Guide Publications series.
[W626] A & C Black hbk **£6.95**
BAXTER, COLIN
Glasgow
[W627] R Drew pbk **£2.95**
LINDSAY, MAURICE
Glasgow `NEW`
A look at increasingly chic Glasgow - European City
of Culture in 1990 - and how it has changed over the
past decade.
[W628] Hale pbk **£5.95**

PEPLOW, MARY & SHIPLEY, DEBRA
Glasgow for Free
[W629] Grafton pbk **£2.50**

Highlands &
Islands

**Northern Scotland and the Islands:
A Shell Guide**
[W630] M Joseph pbk **£9.95**

AITKEN, ROBERT
West Highland Way
[W631] HMSO pbk **£5.95**

BAILEY, PATRICK
Orkney
[W632] David & Ch hbk **£10.95**

BARTHOLMEW WALKING SERIES
[W665] Bartholomew pbk **£3.95**
**Walk Loch Lomond and
the Trossachs**
Including Stirling and the Ochils.
[W633] Bartholomew pbk **£3.95**
**Walk Loch Ness and the
River Spey**
Including Inverness and the Black Isle.
[W634] Bartholomew pbk **£3.95**
Walk Oban, Mull and Lochaber
[W635] Bartholomew pbk **£3.95**
**Walk Royal Deeside and North
East Scotland** `NEW`
Including Angus.
[W636] Bartholomew pbk **£3.95**
Walk South West Scotland
Including Arran and the Clyde.
[W637] Bartholomew pbk **£3.95**

BAXTER, COLIN
Cairngorm and Speyside
[W638] R Drew pbk **£2.95**
Mull and Iona
General guide, with colour illustrations.
[W639] R Drew pbk **£2.95**
Skye
[W640] R Drew pbk **£2.95**
West Highlands
[W641] R Drew pbk **£2.95**

BOWMAN, J.E.
**In the Highlands and Islands:
A 19th Century Tour**
[W642] Sutton pbk **£6.95**

BRAY, ELIZABETH
**Discovery of the Hebrides: Voyagers to
the Western Isles 1745 - 1881**
A scholarly treatment of the subject of British
internal expansionism during the second phase of
the Empire.
[W643] Collins hbk **£14.95**

BROWN, GEORGE MACKAY (1921 -)
A resident of Orkney for most of his life, Mackay
Brown is famous for his volumes of prose and poetry
focusing on the islands.
Portrait of Orkney (1981)
An intimate and poetic portrait of the author's
lifelong home.
[W644] J Murray pbk **£6.95**

CARMICHAEL, ALASDAIR
Kintyre
[W645] David & Ch hbk **£9.95**

HEDDERWICK, MHARI
An Eye on the Hebrides `NEW`
The author of the Katie Morag stories
provides an account of her six-month journey through
the Hebridean archipelago off the windy, and
sometimes wild, West coast.
[W646] Canongate hbk **£12.95**

HOWETT, KEVIN
**A Guide to Rock Climbing
in Scotland** `NEW`
An annotated listing of 450 graded climbs from Arran
to the Outer Hebrides.
[W647] Constable hbk **£8.95**

KERR, JOHN
**Highland Highways: Old Roads
in Atholl** `NEW`
Not surprisingly, successive generations have found it
difficult to build roads through the Grampians. Kerr
retells the history.
[W648] J Donald pbk **£2.50**

LAMONT-BROWN, RAYMOND
Discovering Fife
[W649] J Donald pbk **£7.50**

MACINNES, HAMISH (1930 -)
MacInnes was deputy leader of the British Everest
Expedition in 1975, was instrumental in the
development of mountain Search & Rescue, and has
invented several climbing implements, including a
special ice axe. He has also written some fiction set in
the mountains.
Highland Walks:
**Vol 1: Ben Lui to the Falls
of Glomach**
[W650] Hodder pbk **£6.95**
Vol 2: Sky to Cape Wrath
[W651] Hodder pbk **£6.95**
Vol 3: Arran to Ben Lui
[W652] Hodder pbk **£5.95**
**Vol 4: Cairngorms to
Royal Deeside**
[W653] Hodder pbk **£6.95**
Scottish Winter Climbs (1980)
[W654] Constable hbk **£6.50**

MURRAY, W.H.
West Highlands of Scotland
Companion Guide series.
[W655] Collins hbk **£7.95**

POUCHER, W.A.
Magic of Skye
[W656] Constable hbk **£7.95**
Scottish Peaks
A pictorial guide to walking in the highlands.
[W657] Constable hbk **£8.95**

SELBY, BETTINA
**Fragile Islands: A Journey
through the Outer Hebrides** `NEW`
A detailed and considered look at the whole of these
windswept islands. With illustrations.
[W658] R Drew hbk **£14.95**

STORER, RALPH
100 Best Routes on Scottish Mountains
[W659] David & Ch hbk **£14.95**
**Skye: Walking, Scrambling
and Exploring** `NEW`
An examination of the hidden landscape of the isle
of Skye.
[W660] David & Ch hbk **£12.95**

THOMPSON, FRANCIS
Harris and Lewis: Outer Hebrides
[W661] David & Ch hbk **£12.95**

St Kilda and other Hebridean Outliers
[W662] David & Ch hbk **£12.95**
Uists and Barra
[W663] David & Ch hbk **£7.95**

WAITE, CHARLIE
Scottish Islands NEW
The less accessible of the Scottish islands are given some long overdue attention by the author. The text is accompanied by over eighty full colour photographs.
[W664] Constable hbk **£15.95**

WEIR, TOM
Scottish Lochs
A guide to the banks of the lochs.
[W666] Constable hbk **£6.95**

WILLIAMS, DAVID
A Guide to the Southern Upland Way NEW
A detailed look at the route from Portpatrick on the south western coast of Scotland to Cockburnspath on the east.
[W667] Constable hbk **£7.95**

Lowlands

Lowlands and Borders of Scotland: A Shell Guide NEW
[W668] M Joseph pbk **£9.95**

BALDWIN, JOHN
Lothian and the Borders
[W669] HMSO pbk **£6.95**

BARTHOLEMEW WALKING SERIES
Walk Lothian, the Borders and Fife
[W670] Bartholomew pbk **£3.95**

SHEPHERD, IAN
Grampian
[W671] HMSO pbk **£6.95**

STELL, GEOFFREY
Dumfries and Galloway
[W672] HMSO pbk **£6.95**

STEVENSON, JACK
Clyde Estuary and Central Region
[W673] HMSO pbk **£6.95**

Wales

Brecon Beacons and Mid Wales NEW
AA/Ordnance Survey Leisure Guide series.
[W675] AA/OS pbk **£8.95**

Snowdonia and North Wales NEW
AA/OS Leisure Guide Series
[W676] AA/Ordnance Survey pbk **£8.95**

BARBER, CHRIS
Mysterious Wales
A treatment of some of the legends and mysteries of ancient Wales and their relevance to contemporary life.
[W678] Grafton pbk **£5.95**
More Mysterious Wales
[W677] Grafton pbk **£5.95**

CONDRY, WILLIAM
Snowdonia
[W679] David & Ch hbk **£12.95**

MILES, DILLWYN
Pembrokeshire Coast National Park
[W680] David & Ch hbk **£12.95**

REES, VYVYAN
South-West Wales
[W681] Faber pbk **£2.95**

THOMAS, EDWARD (1878 - 1917)
Thomas's small output as a poet was complemented by some compelling travel narratives which combined simple observation with a passive, contemplative quest for the spirit of his country. Born in London of Welsh parents, he was killed during World War I while fighting with the Artists' Rifles.
South Country (1909)
[W682] Dent pbk **£2.95**
Wales
[W683] Oxford pbk **£3.95**

THOMAS, ROGER
Brecon Beacons National Park
Produced by the Countryside Commission.
[W684] Webb & B pbk **£5.95**

WILLIAMS, HERBERT
Pembrokeshire Coast National Parks
Produced by the Countryside Commission.
[W685] Webb & B pbk **£5.95**

RESTAURANTS & ACCOMMODATION

Wales: Bed and Breakfast 1989
[W686] Welsh TB pbk **£2.50**

Wales: Hotels and Guest Houses
[W687] Welsh TB pbk **£2.75**

Wales: Self-Catering
[W688] Welsh TB pbk **£2.50**

Where to Eat in Wales
[W689] Kingsclere Pubs pbk **£2.95**

WALKING & CLIMBING

Best Walks in North Wales
[W690] Constable hbk **£7.95**

Brecon Beacons National Park
[W691] Penguin pbk **£2.50**

Offa's Dyke NEW
[W692] Ordnance Survey pbk **£6.95**

Pembrokeshire Coast Path
[W693] HMSO pbk **£3.95**

BARTHOLOMEW WALKING SERIES
Walk Snowdonia and North Wales
[W694] Bartholomew pbk **£3.95**
Walk South Wales and the Wye Valley NEW
[W695] Bartholomew pbk **£3.95**

SALE, RICHARD
A Cambrian Way: A Personal Guide to an Unofficial Route
A guide to the 260 footpaths that traverse Wales from Cardiff to Conway.
[W696] Constable hbk **£6.95**

STYLES, SHOWELL
Snowdonia National Park
Produced by the Countryside Commission.
[W697] Webb & B pbk **£5.95**

WILLIAMS, PAUL
A Guide to Rock Climbing in Snowdonia NEW
A guide to 500 challenging climbs around Snowdon, including the little-known route from Central Wales and the Lleyn Peninsula.
[W698] Constable hbk **£8.95**

WRIGHT, CHRISTOPHER JOHN
A Guide to Offa's Dyke Path
Footpath guide to the ancient mound built by King Offa to separate England and Wales.
[W699] Constable hbk **£7.95**
A Guide to the Pembrokeshire Coast Path
[W700] Constable hbk **£7.95**

Northern Ireland

Northern Ireland: Where to Eat
[W603] NITB pbk **£1.25**

Northern Ireland: Where to Stay
[W604] NITB pbk **£1.25**

Visitor's Guide to Northern Ireland
[W605] Moorland pbk **£6.95**

Channel Islands

Channel Islands
[W610] AA pbk **£7.95**

Channel Islands NEW
Blue Guide series.
[W611] A & C Black pbk **£6.95**

New Shell Guide to the Channel Islands
[W612] M Joseph pbk **£4.99**

Illustration from *Saddletramp* by Jeremy James (Pelham hbk £12.95).

Western Europe

GENERAL GUIDES

Alternative Holiday Guide to Exploring Nature in Western Europe
[W613] Ashford pbk **£8.95**

Alternative Holiday Guide to Golfing in Europe `NEW`
[W614] Ashford P pbk **£8.95**

Baedeker's Mediterranean Islands
[W615] AA pbk **£9.95**

Camping and Caravanning in Europe
A guide to Europe's camping sights.
[W616] AA hbk **£6.95**

Cycling in Europe
[W617] Pan pbk **£5.99**

Euroguide
A comprehensive tri-lingual guide to Europe, with maps.
[W618] Hallwag pbk **£15.95**

Europe by Eurail
[W619] Lascelles pbk **£7.95**

Europe by Train: The Complete Guide to Inter-Railing
[W620] Fontana pbk **£5.95**

Fodor's Europe
[W621] Random Cen pbk **£10.95**

Fodor's Selected Hotels of Europe
[W622] Random Cen pbk **£8.95**

Guesthouses, Farmhouses and Inns in Europe
[W623] AA hbk **£4.95**

Let's Go Europe
[W624] Pan pbk **£9.95**

Michelin Red Guide to the Main Cities, Europe
[W625] Michelin pbk **£8.25**

RAC Camping and Caravanning Guide to Europe
The RAC has inspected and approved some 2,300 sites across Europe for the camping and caravanning enthusiast.
[W626] RAC pbk **£5.75**

Traveller's Guide to Europe
A manual which contains information about hotels, restaurants, garages and general motoring all over Europe.
[W627] AA hbk **£6.95**

BENTLEY, JAMES
Weekend Cities
[W628] G Philip pbk **£6.95**

SPENCER, BRIAN
Walking in the Alps
A guide for ramblers, suggesting 90 routes of varying difficulty, from easy woodland strolls to high-level hikes.
[W629] Moorland pbk **£5.95**

LITERARY & HISTORICAL

APPLE, R.W.
Apple's Europe
A guide, by the former London-based correspondent of *The New York Times*, to the continent's art, architecture, music, and natural beauty.
[W630] Macmillan pbk **£7.95**

FARSON, NEGLEY
Sailing Across Europe
The 1926 account of an American's fulfilled dream of sailing across Europe in a 26-foot yawl (a small sailboat of the cutter class) via the Rhine and the Danube to the Black Sea.
[W631] Century pbk **£4.95**

GOODWIN, RICHARD
Leontyne `NEW`
The record of a journey by tug from London to Vienna.
[W632] Collins hbk **£16.00**

HARTY, RUSSELL (1934 - 1988)
Mr Harty's Grand Tour: A Journey from England to Naples
Russell Harty's life-long love affair with Europe culminated in this twentieth-century reconstruction of the *Grand Tour*, one that often tickled his wry, dry sense of humour.
[W633] Century hbk **£12.95**
[W634] Grafton pbk **£3.50**

HIBBERT, CHRISTOPHER (1924 -)
The Grand Tour (1969)
The historian's personal account of his tour of Europe.
[W635] Thames-Methuen hbk **£14.95**

JAMES, JEREMY
Saddletramp `NEW`
On horseback from Turkey to Wales, in eleven months.
[W636] Pelham hbk **£12.95**

JONES, TRISTAN
The Improbable Voyage of the Yacht 'Outward Leg'
[W637] Grafton pbk **£3.95**

MORRITT, J.B.S.
A Grand Tour: Letters (1794 - 96)
The collected letters of John Morritt, Esq. of Rokeby Hall, Yorkshire, which eloquently describe the progress of his late eighteenth-century tour through Austria, Hungary and Greece, to his ultimate destination the great city of Constantinople.
[W639] Century pbk **£4.95**

WILSON, EDMUND (US, 1895 - 1972)
The literary critic took great pains to be informed of international opinion, as well as international moods, realizing intrinsically that the United States' experience of the world, during his life-time, was markedly dissimilar to that of other nations.
Europe Without Baedeker
(1947, revised 1966)
A collection of travel sketches from an extremely sober tour of the continent in the wake of the 1945 peace.
[W640] Hogarth pbk **£5.95**

WILSON, MARY & WILSON, ANNE
A European Journal: Two Sisters Abroad in 1847
[W641] Bloomsbury hbk **£14.95**

By Country A - Z

Austria

Austria
Green tourist guide.
[W642] Michelin pbk **£5.50**

Austria
Cultural Guide series.
[W643] Phaidon hbk **£11.50**

Austria
Blue Guide series.
[W644] A & C Black hbk **£10.95**

Baedeker's Austria
[W645] AA pbk **£9.95**

Baedeker's Vienna
[W646] AA pbk **£5.95**

Fodor's Austria
[W647] Random Cen pbk **£8.95**

BASSETT, RICHARD
The Austrians: Tales from the Vienna Woods
A candid picture of contemporary Austrian life.
[W648] Faber hbk **£12.95**

BEER, GRETEL
Exploring Rural Austria `NEW`
Exploring Rural Europe series.
[W649] Chr Helm pbk **£5.95**

Belgium, Luxembourg, the Netherlands

Amsterdam `NEW`
[W650] AA pbk **£3.95**

Amsterdam Art Guide
Art Guide Publications series.
[W663] A & C Black pbk **£5.95**

Belgique-Luxembourg
Green tourist guide (French text only).
[W651] Michelin pbk **£5.50**

Belgium & Luxembourg
Blue Guide series.
[W652] A & C Black hbk **£11.95**

Benelux
Michelin Red Guide series.
[W653] Michelin hbk **£8.25**

Flandres, Artois et Picardie
Green tourist guide (French text only).
[W654] Michelin pbk **£5.25**

Fodor's Amsterdam
[W655] Random Cen pbk **£4.95**

Fodor's Belgium & Luxembourg
[W656] Random Cen pbk **£8.95**

Holland
Cultural Guide series.
[W657] Phaidon hbk **£9.95**

Holland
Blue Guide series.
[W658] A & C Black hbk **£10.95**

Hollande
Green tourist guide (French text only).
[W659] Michelin pbk **£5.50**

Rough Guide to Amsterdam
[W660] Harrap pbk **£4.95**

Rough Guide to the Low Countries NEW
[W661] Harrap pbk **£5.95**

HOPKINS, ADAM
**Holland: Its History, Paintings
and People** (1988)
Brings into focus the achievements of 'one of the
most surprising of all European nations'.
[W662] Faber pbk **£6.95**

Cyprus

Including both Greek Cyprus and Turkish Cyprus.

Cyprus
Blue Guide series.
[W664] A & C Black pbk **£7.95**

PARKER, DEREK & PARKER, JULIA
Cyprus
Cape Traveller's Guide series.
[W665] Cape pbk **£7.95**

WATKINS, P.
See Cyprus: A Complete Guide
[W666] Sidgwick hbk **£3.25**

France

GENERAL GUIDES

Exploring Rural France
Exploring Rural Europe series.
[W667] Chr Helm pbk **£5.95**

Fodor's France
[W668] Random Cen pbk **£9.95**

**Fontana/Hachette Guide
to France**
Translated from the French.
[W669] Fontana pbk **£9.95**

France
Blue Guide series.
[W670] A & C Black pbk **£14.95**

France
Michelin Red Guide series.
[W671] Michelin hbk **£9.50**

Let's Go France
[W672] Pan pbk **£9.95**

EPERON, ARTHUR
Le Weekend
A guide to *fins-de-semaine* in France.
[W673] Pan pbk **£4.99**

MADRON, SUSI
Cycling in France
Selection of relaxing routes through l'Hexagone.
[W674] G Philip hbk **£6.95**

RICCARDI-CUBITT, MONIQUE
Just Off the Autoroute
[W675] Cadogan pbk **£3.95**

LITERARY & HISTORICAL

ARDAGH, JOHN
**Writers' France: A Regional
Panorama** NEW
A tour of the French regions, keeping in mind how
they have been portrayed in literature.
[W676] H Hamilton hbk **£18.00**

BROWN, MICHAEL
South to Gascony NEW
[W677] H Hamilton hbk **£14.95**

CARRINGTON, DOROTHY
Granite Island: A Portrait of Corsica
A long-time resident of Corsica, Carrington writes of
the people, in some ways 'backwards', but also
enlightened, living lives overshadowed by history.
[W678] Penguin pbk **£4.95**

FISHER, M.F.K.
Two Towns in Provence
A deep affection for France, and for Aix-en-Provence
and Marseilles in particular, provides the impetus
behind this book.
[W679] Hogarth pbk **£5.95**

HAMILTON, RONALD
Holiday History of France
[W680] Hogarth pbk **£5.95**

HANBURY-TENISON, ROBIN
**White Horses over France: From the
Camargue to Cornwall**
[W681] Grafton hbk **£9.95**

MAYLE, PETER
A Year in Provence NEW
A month by month account of living in one of the
more enchanting regions of France.
[W682] H Hamilton hbk **£12.95**

MILLAR, GEORGE
**Isabel and the Sea: A Voyage through
the Canals of France to the
Mediterranean**
[W683] Century pbk **£4.95**

RAMBALI, PAUL
**French Blues: A Journey in
Modern France** NEW
The author investigates France's current atmosphere
of soul-searching.
[W684] Heinemann hbk **£11.95**

STOCK, DENNIS
Provence Memories NEW
An eminent photographer records the light, colour and
scenery originally captured by the Impressionists.
[W685] Little, Brown hbk **£25.00**

TROLLOPE, FRANCES (1780 - 1863)
Paris and the Parisians (1835)
[W686] Sutton pbk **£3.95**

WHITE, FREDA
Three Rivers of France (1952)
Re-issued with new photographs by Michael Busselle.
[W687] Pavilion hbk **£16.95**

NORTHERN FRANCE

**Coastal Walks: Normandy
and Brittany** NEW
McCarta Walking Guides to France series.
[W688] McCarta pbk **£9.95**

Normandy
Companion Guide series.
[W689] Collins pbk **£9.95**

Normandy and the Seine NEW
McCarta Walking Guides to France series.
[W690] McCarta pbk **£9.95**

Walking through Brittany NEW
McCarta Walking Guides to France series.
[W691] McCarta pbk **£9.95**

Walks in the Auvergne NEW
McCarta Walking Guides to France series.
[W692] McCarta pbk **£9.95**

BENTLEY, JAMES
Normandy NEW
Bentley offers a Normandy for the independent
traveller, and examines its history, landscape, religion
and cuisine. He also develops a few routes for the
exploration of its local history.
[W693] Aurum hbk **£14.95**

ELYS, MARY & NORMAN, JILL
Travels in Alsace and Lorraine
[W6931] Merehurst pbk **£6.95**

Illustration from *Travels in Alsace and Lorraine* by
Mary Elys and Jill Norman (Merehurst pbk £6.95)

FENN, PATRICIA (ED)
Normandy: French Entree Guide
[W6931] Quiller pbk **£3.95**

MICHELIN GREEN GUIDES
Titles marked § are only available with text in French.
Alsace et Lorraine §
[W694] Michelin pbk **£5.50**
Brittany
[W695] Michelin pbk **£5.50**
Champagne, Ardennes
[W696] Michelin pbk **£5.50**
Normandie-Cotentin §
[W697] Michelin pbk **£5.50**
Normandie-Seine §
[W698] Michelin pbk **£5.50**
Poitou-Vendée-Charentes §
[W699] Michelin pbk **£5.50**

NEILLANDS, ROBIN
Walking through France: From the Channel to the Camargue
[W700] Collins hbk **£10.95**

SNAILHAM, RICHARD
Normandy and Brittany
[W701] Weidenfeld hbk **£8.95**

PARIS

Country Round Paris
Companion Guide series.
[W702] Collins pbk **£9.95**

Environs de Paris
Green tourist guide (French text only)
[W703] Michelin pbk **£5.25**

Fodor's Paris
[W704] Random Cen pbk **£5.95**

Paris
Green tourist guide.
[W705] Michelin pbk **£5.25**

Paris
Michelin pocket hotel and restaurant guide.
[W708] Michelin pbk **£2.10**

Paris & Versailles (7th edition)
Blue Guide series.
[W706] A & C Black pbk **£9.95**

Paris NEW
[W707] AA pbk **£3.95**

Paris Art Guide
Art Guide Publications series.
[W709] A & C Black pbk **£5.95**

Paris and the Ile de France
Cultural Guide series.
[W710] Phaidon hbk **£7.95**

DELTHIL, FRANCOISE & BERNARD
Good Value Guide to Paris (Paris Pas Cher)
[W711] Aurum pbk **£6.95**

FITCH, NOEL RIDLEY
Hemingway in Paris NEW
20 walks in parts of Paris familiar to the novelist.
[W712] Equation pbk **£7.99**

GLYN, ANTHONY
Paris
Companion Guide series.
[W713] Collins pbk **£7.95**

LEITCH, MICHAEL
Slow Walks in Paris NEW
Twenty-two gentle walks for the ambler (or more appropriately the *flâneur*).
[W714] Hodder pbk **£7.95**

TURNER, CHRISTOPHER
Paris Step by Step NEW
A pocket guide to the cultural, historical and gastronomic of Paris, supplemented by 154 illustrations and 19 maps.
[W715] Pan pbk **£5.95**

SOUTHERN FRANCE

Corsica
Blue Guide series.
[W727] A & C Black pbk **£8.95**

Fodor's Loire Valley
[W728] Random Cen pbk **£5.95**

French Riviera NEW
[W729] AA pbk **£3.95**

Provence
Cultural Guide series.
[W730] Phaidon hbk **£11.50**

The Pyrénées
[W731] Harrap pbk **£9.95**

Walking the Pyrénées NEW
McCarta Walking Guides to France series.
[W732] McCarta pbk **£9.95**

BENTLEY, JAMES
A Guide to the Dordogne
[W733] Viking hbk **£10.95**
[W734] Penguin pbk **£6.95**
Languedoc
[W735] G Philip hbk **£14.95**

EPERON, ARTHUR & BARBARA
The Dordogne and Lot NEW
[W736] Chr Helm pbk **£9.95**

LOWE, JOHN
Corsica: A Traveller's Companion NEW
A narrative guide to the history, people and landscape of the island.
[W737] J Murray pbk **£8.95**

LYALL, ARCHIBALD
South of France
Companion Guide series.
[W738] Collins pbk **£8.95**

MANDELL, BARBARA
South of France
Cadogan Guide series.
[W739] Cadogan pbk **£7.95**

MICHELIN GREEN GUIDES
Titles marked § are only available with the text in French.
Auvergne §
[W740] Michelin pbk **£5.50**
Berry-Limousin §
[W741] Michelin pbk **£5.50**
Bourgogne §
[W742] Michelin pbk **£5.25**
Châteaux of the Loire
[W743] Michelin pbk **£5.50**
Corse §
[W744] Michelin pbk **£5.50**
Côte d'Azur §
[W745] Michelin pbk **£5.50**

Illustration of Mont St-Michel from *Normandy: French Entree Guide* edited by Patricia Fenn (Quiller pbk £3.95)

Dordogne
[W746] Michelin pbk **£5.50**
French Riviera
[W747] Michelin pbk **£5.25**
Gorges du Tarn §
[W748] Michelin pbk **£5.50**
Jura §
[W749] Michelin pbk **£5.50**
Provence
[W750] Michelin pbk **£5.50**
Pyrénées-Aquitaine §
[W751] Michelin pbk **£5.50**
Pyrénées-Roussillon §
[W752] Michelin pbk **£5.50**
Périgord-Quercy §
[W753] Michelin pbk **£5.50**
Rhone Valley
[W754] Michelin pbk **£5.25**

NEILLANDS, ROBIN
The Road to Compostela
A travelogue offering an overview of the famous pilgrim route from France across the Pyrénées.
[W755] Moorland hbk **£8.95**

STURROCK, JOHN
French Pyrénées
[W756] Faber pbk **£4.95**

SWINGLEHURST, EDMUND
The Midi
[W757] Weidenfeld hbk **£8.95**

WADE, RICHARD
Loire
Companion Guide series.
[W758] Collins pbk **£7.95**

RESTAURANTS & ACCOMMODATION

Best of France NEW
Gault Millau 'Best' series.
[W717] Simon & Sch pbk **£11.95**

Camp and Caravan Site Guide: France, Mediterranean Coast
[W718] Lascelles pbk **£2.95**

Camping and Caravanning in France
Michelin Red series.
[W719] Michelin pbk **£5.50**

French Food in France   `NEW`
Interprets and explains much of French gastronomic terminology, particularly that which is used in shops. There are also features on food, which help set the scene with useful background information.
[W720] AA pbk **£2.95**

EPERON, ARTHUR
Eperon's French Wine Tour
A traveller's guide to tasting and buying wine in France.
[W721] Pan pbk **£6.95**

EPERON, ARTHUR & EPERON, BARBARA
Self-Catering in France
[W722] Chr Helm pbk **£3.95**

HYMAN, PHILIP
Webster's Wine Tour: France
[W723] Prentice-Hall hbk **£9.95**

MILLON, MARC & MILLON, KIM
Wine Roads of France: A Complete Companion Guide
Practical information on the wine regions and their individual vineyards.
[W724] Equation hbk **£14.95**

PRICE, PAMELA VANDYKE
France for the Gourmet Traveller
A guide for enjoying the best of French cuisine.
[W725] Harrap pbk **£7.95**

WELLS, PATRICIA
Food Lovers' Guide to France
A selective guide to restaurants, shops and markets.
[W726] Methuen pbk **£9.95**

Germany
GENERAL GUIDES

BAEDEKER'S GUIDES
Baedeker's Berlin
[W759] AA pbk **£5.95**
Baedeker's Cologne
[W760] AA pbk **£5.95**
Baedeker's Frankfurt
[W761] AA pbk **£5.95**
Baedeker's Germany
[W762] AA pbk **£9.95**
Baedeker's Hamburg
[W763] AA pbk **£5.95**
Baedeker's Munich
[W764] AA pbk **£5.95**
Baedeker's Rhine
[W765] AA pbk **£5.95**
Baedeker's Stuttgart
[W766] AA pbk **£5.95**

Berlin Arts Guide
[W767] A & C Black pbk **£5.95**

Deutschland
Michelin Red Guide series.
[W768] Michelin hbk **£11.50**

Fodor's Germany
[W769] Random Cen pbk **£9.95**

Germany
Cultural Guide series.
[W770] Phaidon hbk **£11.50**

Rough Guide to Germany   `NEW`
[W771] Harrap pbk **£6.95**

BENTLEY, JAMES
Germany
Blue Guide series.
[W772] A & C Black pbk **£10.95**

PHILLIPS, JOHN
Coping with Germany   `NEW`
[W773] Blackwell pbk **£5.95**

LITERARY & HISTORICAL

LEVIN, BERNARD
To the End of the Rhine
An entirely subjective examination of the region's art, architecture, music, politics and people.
[W774] Hodder pbk **£4.50**

WALKER, IAN
Zoo Station: Adventures in East and West Berlin
A study of the 'two' Berlins: their culture, history and the lives of their inhabitants.
[W775] Sphere pbk **£3.99**

Greece
GENERAL GUIDES

Baedeker's Greece
[W776] AA pbk **£9.95**

Fodor's Greece
[W777] Random Cen pbk **£8.95**

Greece
Green tourist guide.
[W778] Michelin pbk **£5.50**

Greece
Cultural guides series.
[W779] Phaidon hbk **£11.50**

Greece
Blue Guide series.
[W780] A & C Black pbk **£12.95**

Let's Go Greece
[W781] Pan pbk **£9.95**

Rough Guide to Greece
[W782] Harrap pbk **£6.95**

LITERARY & HISTORICAL

ANDREWS, KEVIN
The Flight of Ikaros: Travels in Greece During a Civil War
[W798] Penguin pbk **£3.95**

GREENHALGH, PETER & ELIOPOULOS, EDWARD
Deep into Mani: A Journey to the Southern Tip of Greece
Part-guide and part-travelogue this was written by two *savants* and concentrates on the physical attributes of Mani.
[W799] Faber pbk **£3.95**

HOGARTH, PAUL & DURRELL, LAWRENCE
The Mediterranean Shore
Water-colours of 'Lawrence Durrell Country'.
[W800] Pavilion hbk **£20.00**

LEAR, EDWARD (1812 - 88)
Lear's travel pieces, all of which were edited by Lady Strachey, are considered to be valued 'for their discerning pictures of his times'. He was the subject of Tennyson's poem 'E.L. on his Travels'.
Journal of a Landscape Painter in Greece and Albania (1851)
A witty acccount of the nonsense poet's travels in the Balkans in 1848.
[W801] Century pbk **£5.95**

MILLER, HENRY (US, 1891 - 1980)
Colossus of Maroussi (1941)
Writing about his days in Greece, Miller devoted more space to people than place.
[W802] Penguin pbk **£4.50**

POWELL, DILYS
The Villa Ariadne
The author recalls the feats of her many famous friends during the war and just after in a story of high adventure.
[W803] M Haag pbk **£5.95**

SENIOR, MICHAEL
Greece and Its Myths
A traveller's companion to Greek mythology.
[W804] Gollancz hbk **£9.95**

STONEMAN, RICHARD
Literary Companion to Travel in Greece
[W805] Penguin pbk **£5.99**

GREEK ISLANDS

Crete
Blue Guide series.
[W783] A & C Black pbk **£7.95**

Crete   `NEW`
[W784] AA pbk **£3.95**

Greek Islands   `NEW`
[W785] AA pbk **£3.95**

North West Cyclades
[W786] Lascelles pbk **£4.95**

Rough Guide to Crete
[W787] Harrap pbk **£4.95**

BOWMAN, JOHN
Crete
[W788] Cape pbk **£7.95**

FACAROS, DANA
Greek Islands
Cadogan Guide series.
[W789] Cadogan pbk **£7.95**

FAWSETT, JOHN
North Aegean Islands
[W790] Lascelles pbk **£3.95**
Saronic Gulf Islands and Kythera
Covers Aegina, Hydra, Poros, and Salamis amongst many others.
[W791] Lascelles pbk **£4.95**

FREELY, JOHN
The Cyclades
[W792] Cape pbk **£7.95**

WALKER, VICTOR
Independent Traveller's Guide to the Greek Islands   `NEW`
Independent Traveller Guide series.
[W793] Collins hbk **£5.95**

GREEK MAINLAND

Athens and Attica
Cultural Guide series.
[W794] Phaidon pbk **£7.95**

Baedeker's Athens
[W795] AA pbk **£5.95**

Chalkidiki, Greece
A guide to over 500km of sandy beaches, which rim the North Aegean.
[W796] Moorland pbk **£7.95**

JONGH, BRIAN DE
Mainland Greece
Companion Guide series.
[W797] Collins hbk **£12.00**

Ireland

Not all guides include coverage of Northern Ireland.

GENERAL GUIDES

Fodor's Ireland
[W806] Random Cen pbk **£8.95**

Ireland
Companion Guide series.
[W807] Collins pbk **£8.95**

Ireland
Blue Guide series.
[W808] A & C Black pbk **£9.95**

Rough Guide to Ireland   NEW
[W809] Harrap pbk **£5.95**

Shell Guide to the Shannon   NEW
[W810] Gill & Macmillan hbk **£12.95**

Eric Newby, author of *Round Ireland in Low Gear*
(Picador pbk £4.99)

DAY, CATHARINA
Ireland
Cadogan Guide series.
[W811] Cadogan pbk **£8.95**

FULLINGTON, DON
Connoisseurs' Guide to Ireland   NEW
Ireland's countryside, county by county. Practical suggestions accompany this detailed and illustrated look at some of the picturesque sights and luxury hotels.
[W812] Aurum hbk **£8.95**

KILLANIN, LORD & DUIGNAN, MICHAEL
Shell Guide to Ireland (3rd edition)
[W813] Macmillan hbk **£16.95**

RYLE, MARTIN
By Bicycle in Ireland
The author has cycled each of the 22 routes described and offers a fresh and personal response to the country.
[W814] Impact Bks pbk **£4.95**

LITERARY & HISTORICAL

BOLL, HEINRICH (1917 - 1985)
Irish Journal (1967)
Written as the result of a long stay in the country; Böll was extremely 'sympathetic' towards Ireland, and even translated Behan and Synge partly for this reason.
[W815] Secker hbk **£8.95**

LYNAM, JOSS
The Irish Peak
[W816] Constable pbk **£7.95**

NEWBY, ERIC (1911 -)
Round Ireland in Low Gear
[W817] Picador pbk **£4.99**

PAKENHAM, THOMAS & VALERIE
Dublin: A Traveller's Companion
Letters, memoirs and commentaries describing the city.
[W818] Constable pbk **£7.95**

ROBINSON, TOM
Stones of Aran: Pilgrimage   NEW
A journey to Árainn, one of the three Aran Islands, and also one of the oldest (geologically) and stoniest landscapes in the world. Robinson looks at his subject in an invigorating variety of forms, both literary and philosophical.
[W819] Viking hbk **£12.95**

SOMERVILLE-LARGE, PETER
Cappaghlass (1985)
A contemplation of the changing ways in the west of Ireland.
[W820] Fontana pbk **£3.95**
From Bantry Bay to Leitrim: Journey in Search of O'Sullivan Beare (1974)
Somerville-Large retraces the route of O'Sullivan Beare, the Celtic chieftain who in 1602 marched his army north 300 miles to fight the invading English forces.
[W821] Arrow pbk **£3.95**
Grand Irish Tour
[W822] Penguin pbk **£4.95**

SYNGE, JOHN M. (1871 - 1909)
Originally a musician, Synge met Yeats in Paris and was encouraged by the poet to concentrate on his growing interest in Irish literature and language, a side of himself developed only in the second half of his life.

The Aran Islands (1907)
Drawn from the notebooks kept during his visit, *The Aran Islands* demonstrates Synge's expanding control 'over the music of speech'.
[W823] Blackstaff hbk **£9.95**

WYLIE, DONOVAN
32 Counties   NEW
The result of an itinerant tour of Ireland by a young man, not yet 20, who felt compelled to seek out its true nature and spirit. With photographs.
[W824] Secker hbk **£20.00**

Italy

Including Sicily, Sardinia and Malta.

GENERAL GUIDES

Baedeker's Italy
[W825] AA pbk **£9.95**

Fodor's Italy
[W826] Random Cen pbk **£9.95**

Italy
Cadogan Guide series.
[W827] Cadogan pbk **£10.95**

Italy
Green tourist guide.
[W828] Michelin pbk **£5.50**

Italy
Michelin Red guide series.
[W829] Michelin hbk **£10.50**

Italy
Cultural Guide series.
[W830] Phaidon hbk **£10.50**

Rough Guide to Italy   NEW
[W831] Harrap pbk **£9.95**

The Best of Italy   NEW
Gault Millau 'Best' series.
[W832] Simon & S pbk **£11.95**

GILL, CHRIS (ED)
Charming Small Hotels of Italy, Sicily and Sardinia
300 *pensions* and bed & breakfast stops.
[W833] Macmillan pbk **£3.95**

HOFMANN, PAUL
The Best of Italy   NEW
An illustrated companion guide to the *Cento Citta*, the hundred cities and towns that comprise the 'real' Italy, as the Italians know it. Most are provincial centres of great charm and beauty.
[W834] Equation pbk **£8.95**

SEED, DIANE
Eating Out in Italy   NEW
The English food writer, resident in Italy, takes the reader to some of her favourite restaurants.
[W835] Rosendale P hbk **£11.95**

LITERARY & HISTORICAL

EDWARDS, AMELIA B.
Untrodden Peaks and Unfrequented Valleys (1873)
A reminiscence of a summer ramble in the Dolomites.
[W836] Virago pbk **£7.50**

Illustration of the Chimaera Bronze, Florence from the *Cadogan Guide to Italy* edited by Dana Facaros and Michael Pauls (Cadogan pbk £10.95)

FARRER, REGINALD
The Dolomites: King Laurin's Garden
[W837] Cadogan pbk **£5.95**

HIBBERT, CHRISTOPHER
Rome: Biography of a City (1985)
Three millenia of history, from the Etruscan kings to Mussolini.
[W838] Viking hbk **£15.95**
[W839] Penguin pbk **£3.95**

LEES-MILNE, JAMES
Roman Mornings (1956)
Lees-Milne's personal impression of Rome.
[W840] Collins pbk **£8.95**
Venetian Evenings (1988)
The author's portrait of the Venice he has known for some sixty years, brought together in eleven elegant essays.
[W841] Collins hbk **£12.95**

MAXWELL, GAVIN
The Ten Pains of Death
[W842] Sutton pbk **£5.95**

MCCARTHY, MARY (1912 -)
Stones of Florence (1959)/**Venice Observed** (1956)
Two books which Mary McCarthy wrote in the late 1950s when, in her view, tourists were adversely affecting both of these cities. Now published in one volume.
[W843] Penguin pbk **£4.95**

PITT-KETHLEY, FIONA
Journeys to the Underworld
Pitt-Kethley travelled to Southern Italy and Sicily, her method of gauging the atmosphere of a place being contact with its menfolk.
[W844] Chatto hbk **£10.00**

RHODES, ANTHONY
A Sabine Journey: To Rome in Holy Year
In 1950 Anthony Rhodes travelled through the Sabine foothills of central Italy to Rome. Introduction by Peter Quennell.
[W845] Century pbk **£5.95**

ROSS, ALAN
Bandit on the Billiard Table: A Journey through Sardinia (1954, New edition)
Ross's account of a summer criss-crossing the alluring and, until recently, rarely-visited island.
[W846] Collins pbk **£6.95**

TEMPLETON, EDITH
Surprise of Cremona (1954)
One woman's adventures in six northern Italian towns: Cremona, Parma, Mantua, Ravenna, Urbino and Arezzo.
[W847] Methuen pbk **£4.95**

VIDAL, GORE (US, 1925 -)
Vidal in Venice (1987)
[W848] Weidenfeld pbk **£8.95**

NORTHERN ITALY

BAEDEKER'S GUIDES
Baedeker's Rome
[W851] AA pbk **£5.95**
Baedeker's Tuscany
[W852] AA pbk **£5.95**
Baedeker's Venice
[W853] AA pbk **£5.95**

Florence and Tuscany
[W854] Lascelles pbk **£5.95**

Florence: A Traveller's Companion
[W855] Constable pbk **£7.95**

Fodor's Florence and Venice
[W856] Random Cen pbk **£7.95**

Rome
Green tourist guide.
[W857] Michelin pbk **£5.50**

Rough Guide to Venice **NEW**
[W858] Harrap pbk **£5.95**

BENTLEY, JAMES
Umbria **NEW**
Bentley offers an Umbria for the independent traveller, and examines its history, landscape, religion and cuisine. He also develops some routes for exploring local history.
[W859] Aurum hbk **£14.95**

BLUE GUIDE SERIES
Florence
[W860] A & C Black pbk **£7.95**
Northern Italy
[W861] A & C Black pbk **£12.95**
Rome and Environs (4th edition)
[W862] A & C Black pbk **£11.95**
Venice (4th edition)
[W863] A & C Black pbk **£7.95**

COMPANION GUIDE SERIES
Florence
[W864] Collins pbk **£10.95**
Rome
[W865] Collins pbk **£9.95**
Venice
[W866] Collins pbk **£8.95**

CULTURAL GUIDE SERIES
Florence and Tuscany
[W867] Phaidon hbk **£7.50**
Rome and Latium
[W868] Phaidon hbk **£9.95**
Venice and the Veneto
[W869] Phaidon hbk **£9.95**

GOLDSMITH, JAMES & ANNE
The Dolomites of Italy: A Travel Guide **NEW**
An illustrated guide to summer and winter activities in the hills, as well as an overview of the region's history, geology, flora, fauna, and cuisine.
[W870] A & C Black hbk **£12.95**

JEPSON, TIM
Umbria: The Green Heart of Italy **NEW**
A guide to one of the most well known of Italy's north central provinces.
[W871] Equation pbk **£8.95**

KENT, JOHN
John Kent's Florence and Siena **NEW**
An illustrated companion to the cuisine, history and architecture of two beautiful Northern Italian cities.
[W872] Viking hbk **£9.95**

SCOTT, RUPERT
Florence Explored
[W873] Bodley pbk **£8.95**

STACE, CHRISTOPHER
Florence: City of the Lily **NEW**
An illustrated look at the history, culture and lifestyle of the Tuscan city.
[W874] Dent hbk **£14.95**

SOUTHERN ITALY & MALTA

Discover Malta
[W849] Heritage Ho pbk **£4.95**

Naples: A Traveller's Companion
[W875] Constable hbk **£9.95**

Rough Guide to Sicily **NEW**
[W876] Harrap pbk **£4.95**

Sicily
Blue Guide series.
[W877] A & C Black pbk **£9.95**

Southern Italy
Blue Guide series.
[W878] A & C Black pbk **£8.95**

KININMONTH, CHRISTOPHER
Malta & Gozo
[W850] Cape pbk **£7.95**
Sicily
[W879] Cape pbk **£7.95**

THOMSON, IAN
Independent Traveller's Guide Southern Italy **NEW**
A new title in the Collins Independent Traveller's Guide series.
[W880] Collins pbk **£5.95**

Portugal

Including the Canary Islands.

CANARY ISLANDS

Gran Canaria and the Eastern Canary Islands
[W882] Lascelles pbk **£4.95**

Tenerife and the Western Canary Islands
[W883] Lascelles pbk **£4.95**

SPOWART, NORAH B.
Tenerife and Other Canary Islands
[W884] Lascelles pbk **£4.50**

MAINLAND

Fodor's Lisbon
[W885] Random Cen pbk **£5.95**

Fodor's Portugal
[W886] Random Cen pbk **£8.95**

Portugal
Green tourist guide.
[W887] Michelin pbk **£5.50**

Portugal　　　　　　　　　　**NEW**
Cadogan Guide series.
[W888] Cadogan hbk **£7.95**

Portugal　　　　　　　　　　**NEW**
Blue Guide series.
[W889] A & C Black pbk **£8.95**

BALLARD, S. & BALLARD, J.
Pousadas of Portugal
A guide to the unique system of high-quality state-owned accommodation, including castles, palaces and houses of architectural and historical interest.
[W890] Moorland pbk **£7.95**

Scandinavia

Including Finland and Iceland.

BAEDEKER'S GUIDES
Baedeker's Copenhagen
[W891] AA pbk **£5.95**
Baedeker's Denmark
[W892] AA pbk **£9.95**
Baedeker's Scandinavia
[W893] AA pbk **£9.95**

Drive Around Denmark: A Handy Guide for the Motorist
[W894] Trafton hbk **£5.95**

Drive Around Sweden: A Handy Guide for the Motorist
[W895] Trafton hbk **£4.95**

Fodor's Stockholm, Copenhagen, Oslo, Helsinki and Reykjavik
[W896] Random Cen pbk **£5.95**

Fodor's Sweden
[W897] Random Cen pbk **£5.95**

Rough Guide to Scandinavia
[W898] Harrap pbk **£6.95**

AUDEN, W.H. & MACNEICE, LOUIS
Letters from Iceland (1937)
A collaboration which preceded Auden's emigration to the US (with Isherwood) in 1939 and represents a continued exploration of *un*-English environments.
[W899] Faber pbk **£3.95**

EDWARD, TED
Fight the Wild Island: A Solo Walk Across Iceland
The story of a walk across a fierce environment.
[W900] J Murray hbk **£11.95**

JONES, DAVID HAY
Night Times and Light Times: A Journey through Lapland　　**NEW**
Lapp (Sami) culture is strong despite encroachment from the south and the proliferation of hydro-electric projects during the last three decades.
[W901] H Hamilton hbk **£14.95**

Spain

Including the Balearic Islands.

GENERAL GUIDES

Baedeker's Madrid
[W943] AA pbk **£5.95**

Baedeker's Spain
[W944] AA pbk **£9.95**

Espana and Portugal
Michelin Red Guide series.
[W945] Michelin hbk **£8.25**

Fodor's Madrid
[W946] Random Cen pbk **£5.95**

Fodor's Spain
[W947] Random Cen pbk **£9.95**

Guide to Catalonia
[W948] Lascelles pbk **£8.95**

Let's Go Spain, Portugal and Morocco
[W949] Pan pbk **£9.95**

Madrid Art Guide　　　　　　**NEW**
Art Guide Publications series.
[W950] A & C Black hbk **£6.95**

Rough Guide to Spain
[W951] Harrap pbk **£6.95**

Spain
Green tourist guide.
[W952] Michelin pbk **£5.25**

Spain
Cultural Guide series.
[W953] Phaidon hbk **£11.50**

BOYD, ALASTAIR
Madrid and Central Spain
Companion Guide series.
[W954] Collins pbk **£9.95**

FACAROS, DANA & PAULS, MICHAEL
Spain
Cadogan Guide series.
[W955] Cadogan pbk **£9.95**

MCGIRK, JAN
Exploring Rural Spain
Exploring Rural Europe series.
[W956] Chr Helm pbk **£5.95**

TOMKIES, MIKE
In Spain's Secret Wilderness　　**NEW**
A discovery of the exotic wildlife in the sparsely-populated hinterland of the Iberian peninsula.
[W957] Cape hbk **£12.95**

LITERARY & HISTORICAL

BOYD, ALASTAIR
Essence of Catalonia
[W958] Deutsch pbk **£8.96**

BRENAN, GERALD
Face of Spain (1950)
A bird's-eye view of Spanish society under General Franco, c. 1949.
[W959] Penguin pbk **£4.50**

South from Granada (1957)
Brenan's detailed and personal homage to Andalucia and the village of Yegen, which he first visited in 1919.
[W960] Cambridge pbk **£9.95**

HEMINGWAY, ERNEST (1899 - 1961)
Death in the Afternoon (1932)
Hemingway's famously philosophical and in many ways timeless study of bullfighting.
[W961] Grafton pbk **£3.50**
The Dangerous Summer (1960)
[W962] Grafton pbk **£2.95**

LEE, LAURIE (1914 -)
As I Walked Out One Midsummer Morning (1969)
Laurie Lee here recounts his youthful adventures walking to London from his home in the peaceful Gloucestershire countryside and, later, in Spain in the months immediately preceding the Civil War.
[W963] Deutsch hbk **£9.95**
[W964] Penguin pbk **£2.50**

PRITCHETT, V.S. (1900 -)
The Spanish Temper (1954)
A book which has been acclaimed as one of the better introductions to an understanding of Spain in the post-war years. It was written during the first years of any real stability under the regime of General Franco.
[W965] Hogarth pbk **£5.95**

SEYMOUR-DAVIES, HUGH
Bottle-Brush Tree: A Village in Andalusia
After buying a house in a small Spanish village, Hugh Seymour-Davies attempts to settle into the closely-knit local community.
[W966] Constable hbk **£12.95**

TOIBON, COLM
Barcelona　　　　　　　　　**NEW**
Colm Toibon provides the reader with a cultural treatment of the fascinating city of Barcelona placing particular emphasis on the central role of its architecture.
[W967] Harrap hbk **£12.95**

WALKER, TED
In Spain
Poet Ted Walker's account of his long love affair with all aspects of Spain and most especially with its landscape, its people, its varied culture and its food.
[W9671] Corgi pbk **£4.99**

Switzerland

GENERAL GUIDES

Baedeker's Switzerland
[W968] AA pbk **£9.95**

Fodor's Switzerland
[W969] Random Cen pbk **£8.95**

Switzerland
Green tourist guide.
[W970] Michelin pbk **£5.25**

Switzerland
Cultural Guide series.
[W971] Phaidon hbk **£11.50**

TRAVEL

Turkey

Covers both Asian and European Turkey.

GENERAL GUIDES

Baedeker's Istanbul
[W972] AA pbk **£5.95**

Baedeker's Turkish Coast
[W973] AA pbk **£5.95**

Istanbul (2nd edition)
Blue Guide series.
[W974] A & C Black pbk **£9.95**

**Istanbul: A Traveller's
Companion**
[W975] Constable pbk **£8.95**

Turkey
Cultural Guide series.
[W976] Phaidon hbk **£12.95**

Turkey
[W977] Cadogan pbk **£7.95**

Turkey
Companion Guide series.
[W978] Collins pbk **£9.95**

Turkey: A Travel Survival Kit
[W979] Lonely Planet pbk **£7.95**

BOYD, H. SUMNER & FREELY, JOHN
Strolling through Istanbul
[W980] Routledge pbk **£7.95**

COLE, SIMON
Coping with Turkey   NEW
[W981] Blackwell pbk **£5.95**

MCDONAGH, BERNARD
Turkey   NEW
Blue Guide series.
[W982] A & C Black hbk **£11.95**

MULLER, MARTIN
Turkey: The Traveller's Guide NEW
This guide principally covers the Western regions
of Turkey.
[W983] Springfield Bks hbk **£8.95**

LITERARY & HISTORICAL

BEAN, GEORGE E.
Bean's four valuable guides to the regions of Turkey,
and their cultural and historical treasures, have
recently been re-issued.
Aegean Turkey
Includes Pergamum, Heracleia, Sardis, Ephesus,
Priene, Miletus and Didyma.
[W984] J Murray pbk **£9.95**
Lycian Turkey
Includes Myra, and the church of St Nicholas (*Santa
Claus*), Xanthus and Arycanda.
[W985] J Murray hbk **£15.95**
Turkey Beyond the Maeander
Includes Labraynda, Stratoniceia, Bargylia and
Halicarnassus.
[W986] J Murray hbk **£15.95**
Turkey's Southern Shore
Includes the stalactite caves and Red Tower of
Alanya, as well as Pergaean Artemis and the search
for her temple.
[W987] J Murray pbk **£8.95**

CUDDON, J.A.
The Owl's Watchsong
[W988] Century pbk **£4.95**

DODWELL, CHRISTINA
A Traveller on Horseback
[W989] Hodder pbk **£3.99**

FREELY, JOHN
Western Shores of Turkey
[W990] J Murray hbk **£13.95**

GLAZEBROOK, PHILIP
**Journey to Kars: A Modern Traveller in
the Ottoman Lands** (1984)
A journey among the relics of the Ottoman Empire.
[W991] Penguin pbk **£4.50**

HOLMES, PETER
Turkey: A Timeless Bridge
A sensitive photographic examination, with text by a
Briton long associated with Turkey.
[W992] Stork P hbk **£30.00**

SEWELL, BRIAN
**South from Ephesus: Travellers in
Aegean Turkey**
[W993] Century hbk **£12.95**

TAYLOR, JANE
Imperial Istanbul: Iznik, Bursa, Edirne
[W994] Weidenfeld pbk **£9.95**

Eastern Europe

GENERAL GUIDES

Eastern Europe on a Shoestring NEW
[W901A] Lonely Planet pbk **£9.95**

Fodor's Eastern Europe
[W913] Random Cen pbk **£10.50**

**Rough Guide to Eastern Europe:
Hungary, Romania and Bulgaria**
[W904] Harrap pbk **£6.95**

By Country A - Z

Albania

DURHAM, EDITH
High Albania (1909)
Durham travelled to the Balkans on doctor's orders.
Her anecdotal travelogue with digressions into the
history, religion and politics of Albania is unique.
[W995] Virago pbk **£6.99**

WARD, PHILIP
Albania - A Travel Guide
[W996] Oleander pbk **£6.95**

Bulgaria

Bulgaria   NEW
[W903] AA pbk **£3.95**

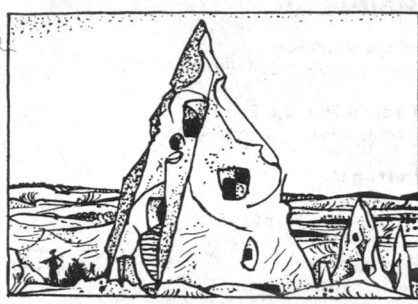

'The Rock Monastries of Cappodocia' from *Time to
Keep Silence* by Patrick Leigh Fermor (Penguin
pbk **£3.95**)

MIHAILOV, D. & SMOLENOV, P.
Bulgaria: A Guide
Translated from the Bulgarian.
[W906] Collets pbk **£4.95**

Czechoslovakia

Baedeker's Prague
[W909] AA pbk **£5.95**

Czechoslovakia Guidebook
Translated from the Czech.
[W910] Collets pbk **£4.95**

ARNOLD, GUY
Down the Danube   NEW
An account of his 1,750 mile journey down the
historic river to its Black Sea delta, reflecting upon its
cultural history and architecture.
[W914] Blandford P hbk **£14.95**

BAILEY, ANTHONY
**Along the Edge of the Forest: An Iron
Curtain Journey**
[W915] Faber pbk **£4.95**

FLEGL, M.
Prague Guidebook
Translated from the Czech.
[W911] Collets pbk **£8.95**

HAYMAN, SIMON
Guide to Czechoslovakia
[W912] Bradt pbk **£6.95**

MAGRIS, CLAUDIO
The Danube   NEW
A literary, historical and philosophical journey down
the Danube: the author contemplates everything from
Freud to Wittgenstein.
[W638] Collins hbk **£12.95**

Hungary

Baedeker's Budapest
[W902] AA pbk **£5.95**

Rough Guide to Hungary   NEW
[W905] Harrap pbk **£4.95**

HARDING, GEORGINA
**In Another Europe: A Journey
Across Hungary and Romania**   NEW
A bicycle trip across Hungary and Romania, which

concludes with the sharp realisation that Hungary is one of those countries changing with *glasnost* and that Romania is not.
[W918] Hodder hbk **£11.95**

PALLAI, K.
Your Guide to Budapest
Translated from the Hungarian.
[W907] Collets pbk **£7.50**

WELLNER, I.
Complete Guide to Budapest
Translated from the Hungarian.
[W908] Collets pbk **£8.50**

Poland

HILLS, DENIS
Return to Poland
[W923] Bodley hbk **£12.95**

SHARMAN, TIM
Poland
[W924] Columbus pbk **£9.95**

Soviet Union

GENERAL GUIDES

Baedeker's Moscow
[W925] AA pbk **£5.95**

Moscow and Leningrad
Blue Guide series.
[W933] A & C Black pbk **£10.95**

Fodor's Soviet Union
[W926] Random Cen pbk **£9.50**

BARTENEV, I. & BATAZHKOV, V.
Leningrad: An Illustrated Guide
Translated from the Russian.
[W927] Central Bks hbk **£6.95**

DAGLISH, ROBERT
Coping with Russia: A Beginner's Guide to the USSR
[W929] Blackwell pbk **£4.95**

LEVITSKY, H.
Kiev: A Short Guide
Translated from the Russian.
[W930] Central Bks hbk **£3.95**

LOUIS, V. & LOUIS, J.
Trans-Siberian Railway Guide
Translated from the Russian.
[W931] Collets pbk **£7.95**

LUDVIKOVA, L. & SKOKAN, L.
Soviet Union: Handbook and Guide
Translated from the Russian.
[W932] Collets pbk **£3.50**

MILOVSKY, A.V.
Ancient Russian Cities: A Guide
A thorough guide to what remains of pre-Revolutionary Russia as it is visible today, in particular to the many extant architectural and cultural treasures. Translated into English from the Russian.
[W934] Central Bks hbk **£5.95**

MUSHTUKOV, VICTOR & TIKHONOV, LEV
Museums of Leningrad
Translated from the Russian.
[W935] Central Bks hbk **£3.95**

POKIDOV, YURI
Brest, Minsk, Smolensk, Moscow
Translated from the Russian.
[W937] Central Bks hbk **£3.95**

STRAUSS, ROBERT
Trans-Siberian Rail Guide
[W940] Bradt pbk **£4.95**

THOMAS, BRYN
Trans-Siberian Handbook
[W941] Lascelles pbk **£8.95**

WALKER, MARTIN
Independent Traveller's Guide to the Soviet Union **NEW**
A new title in the Collins Independent Traveller Guide series.
[W942] Collins pbk **£5.95**

LITERARY & HISTORICAL

BURNABY, FRED
A Ride to Khiva: Travels and Adventures in Central Asia (1877)
With an introduction by Eric Newby.
In 1875 cavalry officer Fred Burnaby reads a newspaper article which prompts him to beg his superiors for leave from the army and dash to Khiva in mid-winter. The tale he tells is one of romantic high adventure, with a 'cast' that includes cossacks, sleigh-drivers and Tartar horsemen amongst others.
[W916] Century pbk **£4.95**

BYCHKOV, Y. & DESYATNIKOV, V.
Around the Golden Ring of Russia **NEW**
The authors provide a detailed examination of many of the fascinating churches which survived the Bolshevik Revolution and remain intact. The book has been translated from the original Russian text.
[W928] Collets hbk **£11.95**

CHEKHOV, ANTON (1860 - 1904)
The Island: A Journey to Sakhalin
Written at the turn of the century, *The Island* describes his gruelling trans-Siberian journey to the unwelcoming island off the eastern shores, directly north of Japan.
[W917] Century pbk **£5.95**

LEE, ANDREA
Russian Journal (1982)
A black American writer, Lee accompanied her husband on a United States Government exchange programme to Russia in 1978, and witnessed what is now very much a bygone era.
[W919] Faber pbk **£2.95**

MARSDEN, KATE
By Sledge and Horseback to the Outcast Siberian Lepers
With a recommendation by the Empress of Russia, Kate Marsden set out in 1890 for Yakutsk, in remotest Siberia, to work in a leper colony. Introduction by Eric Newby.
[W920] Century pbk **£4.95**

PENNINGTON, MICHAEL
Rossiya: A Journey through Siberia
[W936] Oleander pbk **£4.95**

POLONSKY, MARC & TAYLOR, RUSSELL
**USSR: From an Original Idea
by Karl Marx**
[W938] Faber pbk **£3.95**

POND, ELIZABETH
**Russia Perceived: A Trans-Siberian
Journey** (1981)
[W921] Century pbk **£6.95**

RANSOME, ARTHUR (1884 - 1967)
Ransome's trips to Russia and Asia between 1913 and
the 1920s had an impact on his later writing.
Racundra's First Cruise (1923)
Baltic sailing. Introduced by C. Northcote Parkinson.
[W922] Century pbk **£4.95**

SEMLER, HELEN
Discovering Moscow NEW
Culture, architecture and artistic potential as affected
by *glasnost*.
[W939] Equation pbk **£8.95**

Yugoslavia

Baedeker's Yugoslavia
[W997] AA pbk **£9.95**

Fodor's Yugoslavia
[W998] Random Cen pbk **£8.95**

Rough Guide to Yugoslavia
[W999] Harrap pbk **£4.95**

Yugoslavia NEW
Blue Guide series.
[W1000] A & C Black hbk **£12.95**

CUDDON, J.A.
Yugoslavia
Companion Guide series.
[W1001] Collins hbk **£9.95**

WOOD, KATIE & MCDONALD, GEORGE
Holiday Yugoslavia
[W1002] Fontana pbk **£4.95**

Illustration from *The Mediterranean Shore* by **Paul
Hogarth**; **Lawrence Durrell** (Pavilion hbk £20.00)

Africa

General

**Africa Overland: A Route and
Planning Guide**
[W1003] Lascelles hbk **£14.95**

Africa on a Shoestring
[W1004] Lonely Planet pbk **£9.95**

GELLHORN, MARTHA
The Weather in Africa (1978)
[W1005] Eland pbk **£3.95**
Travels with Myself and Another (1978)
[W1020] Eland pbk **£4.95**

HAMILTON, GENESTRA
**A Stone's Throw: Travels from Africa
in Six Decades**
[W1006] Century pbk **£7.95**

HAMPTON, CHARLES & HAMPTON, JANIE
A Family Outing in Africa
[W1007] Macmillan hbk **£12.95**

MARNHAM, PATRICK
**Fantastic Invasion: Dispatches
from Contemporary Africa**
Marnham explores the chaos of post-colonial Africa
in this book.
[W1008] Penguin pbk **£3.95**

WOODHEAD, LESLIE
**A Boxful of Spirits: Adventures
of a Film-maker in Africa**
[W1009] Heinemann pbk **£5.95**

By Region

East & Central
Africa

Covering the following countries: Burundi, Central
African Republic, Comoros, Congo, Djibouti,
Ethiopia, Kenya, Rwanda, Seychelles, Somalia,
Tanzania, Uganda and Zaire.

GENERAL GUIDES

East Africa: A Travel Survival Kit
[W1010] Lonely Planet pbk **£6.95**

East Africa: with Zambia and Malawi
[W1011] Lascelles pbk **£4.95**

Kenya
[W1012] Lascelles pbk **£5.95**

**Kenya and Northern Tanzania:
A Traveller's Guide**
[W1013] Lascelles pbk **£5.95**

HOBSON, CHRISTINE
Egypt Past and Present NEW
Past and Present series.
[W1014] Batsford hbk **£12.95**

READER, JOHN
Mount Kenya NEW
The gives an illustrated account of the uniquely
rich and varied landscape, ecology and wildlife of
Mount Kenya.
[W1015] Elm Tree Bks hbk **£25.00**

LITERARY & HISTORICAL

AMIN, MOHAMED
Journey through Kenya
[W1016] Bodley hbk **£18.00**
Kenya: The Magic Land
[W1017] Bodley hbk **£22.50**

AMIN, MOHAMED, ET AL
Railway Across the Equator
[W1018] Bodley hbk **£22.50**

BLIXEN, KAREN
Out of Africa (1937)
An autobiographical account of Blixen's (the writer
Isak Dinesen) life in Africa, married to her Danish
aristocrat cousin.
[W1019] Penguin pbk **£3.50**

HONE, JOSEPH
**Children of the Country: Coast to
Coast Across Africa**
[W1021] H Hamilton hbk **£12.95**

HUDSON, PETER
**A Leaf in the Wind: Travels in the
Heart of Africa**
An account of the author's journeys, alone and
often on foot, through some of the remotest regions
of Africa. He writes of the characters he met, such
as in simple fishing communities, and assesses
the way in which Africa is influenced by
Western culture.
[W1022] Fontana pbk **£3.99**

HUXLEY, ELSPETH
Mottled Lizard (1962)
[W1023] Penguin pbk **£4.50**
Out in the Midday Sun: My Kenya (1985)
[W1024] Penguin pbk **£4.50**
The Flame Trees of Thika (1959)
[W1025] Penguin pbk **£4.50**

HYLAND, PAUL
**The Black Heart: A Voyage
into Central Africa**
A journey through Zaire inspired and based on the
travels in the Congo by the author's great uncle in
the 1890s.
[W1026] Gollancz hbk **£12.95**

WARD, CLIVE; BOY, GORDON & ALLAN, IAIN
Snowcaps on the Equator
The fabled mountains of Kenya, Tanzania, Uganda
and Zaire.
[W1027] Bodley hbk **£22.50**

WINTERNITZ, HELEN
**East Along the Equator: A Congo
Journey** (1987)
A passionate account of a journey down the Congo
River and through the rainforest of eastern Zaire.
[W1028] Hodder pbk **£4.99**

YEOMAN, GUY
**Africa's Mountains of the Moon:
A Journey to the Ultimate
Sources of the Nile** NEW
The product of an artist's expedition into the heart of
central Africa; with botanical paintings.
[W1029] Elmtree Bks hbk **£20.00**

Northern Africa

Covering the following countries: Algeria, Chad, Egypt, Libya, Mauritania, Morocco, Sudan and Tunisia.

GENERAL GUIDES

Africa: The Nile Route
Overland from Cairo to Nairobi.
[W1030] Lascelles pbk **£4.95**

Discover Tunisia
[W1031] Lascelles pbk **£4.95**

Egypt
Blue Guide series.
[W1032] A & C Black pbk **£12.95**

Egypt
[W1033] Lascelles pbk **£8.95**

**Egypt and the Sudan: A Travel
Survival Kit**
[W1034] Lonely Planet pbk **£6.95**

Egypt: A MEED Practical Guide
From the *Middle East Economic Digest* .
[W1035] MEED pbk **£9.95**

Fodor's Egypt
[W1036] Random Cen pbk **£8.50**

Maroc
Green tourist guide. French text only.
[W1037] Michelin pbk **£5.50**

Morocco
[W1038] Lascelles pbk **£3.95**

Traveller's Guide to Egypt
[W1039] Cape pbk **£6.95**

Tunisia   NEW
[W1040] AA pbk **£3.95**

GLEN, SIMON & GLEN, JAN
Sahara Handbook
[W1041] Lascelles hbk **£18.95**

HAAG, MICHAEL VON
**Guide to Cairo, the Pyramids
and Saqqara**
[W1042] M Haag pbk **£5.95**
Guide to Egypt
[W1043] M Haag pbk **£9.95**

LITERARY & HISTORICAL

ASHER, MICHAEL
A Desert Dies (1986)
A despairing report on how the change in the Sahara is forcing thousands of nomads into the cities.
[W1044] Penguin pbk **£4.95**
**In Search of the Forty Days Road:
Adventures with the Nomads
of the Desert**
The road in question is an ancient trade route through the Sudan, now largely unmarked.
[W1045] Penguin pbk **£4.95**

EDWARD, TED
**Beyond the Last Oasis: A Solo Walk in
the Western Sahara** (1985)
A 19-day, 350-mile desert walk: the longest ever.
[W1046] Oxford pbk **£3.95**

FLAUBERT, GUSTAVE (1821 - 1880)
**Flaubert in Egypt: A Sensibility
on Tour**
A rare trip abroad: Flaubert seldom ventured beyond France, a fact which informs the disposition of his account.
[W1047] M Haag pbk **£5.95**

GOLDING, WILLIAM (1911 -)
Egyptian Journal
[W1048] Faber pbk **£4.99**

HOAGLAND, EDWARD
**African Calliope: Journey to
the Sudan**
A dense travelogue through modern Sudan, including a personal assessment of the politics of aid and the famine.
[W1049] Penguin pbk **£3.95**

KENNEDY, DOUGLAS
Beyond the Pyramids (1988)
A chronicle of travels through Egypt.
[W1050] Unwin pbk **£4.95**

LEWIS, WYNDHAM (1882 - 1957)
Journeys into Barbary (1932)
Writings and drawings of Morocco, c.1931-32.
[W1051] Penguin pbk **£4.50**

MAXWELL, GAVIN
**Lords of the Atlas: The Rise and Fall of
the House of Glaoua, 1893 - 1956**
A useful if somewhat circumspect introduction to Morocco, through the history of a prominent family.
[W1052] Century pbk **£5.95**

MAYNE, PETER
A Year in Marrakesh
[W1053] Eland pbk **£4.95**

MOORHOUSE, GEOFFREY & NOMACHI,
KAZUYOSHI
The Nile   NEW
A photographic and social exploration of the river's entire length.
[W1054] Barrie & J hbk **£19.95**

PIRAJNO, DUKE OF
**A Cure for Serpents: An Italian
Doctor in North Africa**
Rare insight into the Italian method of colonization; the Duke recounts his medical experiences in what many believe was the most humane colonial administration of the modern period.
[W1055] Eland pbk **£4.95**

PYE-SMITH, CHARLES
The Other Nile (1986)
Pye-Smith first travelled to Africa in 1975, and this record of his return trip, in 1984, illustrates with great lucidity the complex nature of change.
[W1056] Penguin pbk **£4.50**

SELBY, BETTINA
**Riding the Desert Trail: By Bicycle Up
the Nile**
[W1057] Sphere pbk **£3.99**

TRENCH, RICHARD
Forbidden Sands: Search in the Sahara
[W1058] J Murray hbk **£10.95**

WHARTON, EDITH (1862 - 1937)
In Morocco
In 1917 the American novelist visited Morocco where she purposefully began to collect material for a subsequent guide book.
[W1059] Century pbk **£5.95**

Southern Africa

Covering the following countries: Angola, Botswana, Lesotho, Madagascar, Malawi, Mauritius, Mozambique, Namibia, Swaziland, Zambia and Zimbabwe.

GENERAL GUIDES

Discovering Southern Africa
[W1060] Lascelles hbk **£21.95**

Discovery Guide to Zimbabwe
[W1061] M Haag pbk **£9.95**

South-West Africa/Namibia
[W1062] Lascelles pbk **£7.50**

LITERARY & HISTORICAL

BECKER, PETER
**The Pathfinders: A Saga of Exploration
in Southern Africa**
[W1063] Penguin pbk **£3.95**

POWELL, S.W.
Adventures of a Wanderer
An enthralling and sometimes cathartic tale of Africa before 1914, carousing and socializing, including slight brushes with the politics.
[W1064] Century pbk **£5.95**

SAITOTI, TEPILIT OLE
**The Worlds of a Maasai Warrior:
An Autobiography** (1986)
The early life of a Serengeti plainsman, latterly educated in Europe and America.
[W1065] Deutsch hbk **£12.95**

Western Africa

Covering the following countries: Benin, Burkina Fasso, Cameroon, Cape Verde, Equatorial Guinea, Gabon, Gambia, Ghana, Guinea, Guinea-Bissau, Ivory Coast, Liberia, Mali, Niger, Nigeria, Sao Tomé and Principe, Senegal, Sierra Leone and Togo.

GENERAL GUIDES

Discover the Gambia
[W1066] Lascelles pbk **£4.95**

Gambia   NEW
Insight Guide series.
[W1067] Harrap pbk **£10.95**

**Guide to West Africa: The Niger
and Gambia Rivers**
[W1068] M Haag pbk **£8.95**

West Africa: A Travel Survival Kit
[W1068] Lonely Planet pbk **£7.95**

LITERARY & HISTORICAL

ALEXANDER, CAROLINE
**One Dry Season: In the
Footsteps of Mary Kingsley**   NEW
Retracing the route of Kingsley's late 19th century journey to Gabon and part of West Africa.
[W1069] Bloomsbury hbk **£12.95**

DODWELL, CHRISTINA
Travels with Pegasus NEW
A microlight journey across West Africa.
[W1070] Hodder hbk **£12.95**

GIDE, ANDRE (1869 - 1951)
Travels in the Congo (1927)
The novelist's African travels, 'off the beaten track, to
see what one does not see ordinarily', while working
for the Colonial Ministry.
[W1071] Penguin pbk **£3.95**

KINGSLEY, MARY
Travels in West Africa (1897)
At the time of its publication *Travels in West Africa*
was an original and informative treatise on the
primitive religions of West Africa.
[W1072] Virago pbk **£7.99**

North America

Canada

GENERAL GUIDES

Canada
Green tourist guide.
[W1073] Michelin pbk **£5.25**

**Canada Scenic Rail Guide:
Central and Atlantic Canada**
[W1074] Lonely Planet pbk **£7.95**

**Canada Scenic Rail Guide:
Western Canada**
[W1075] Lonely Planet pbk **£7.95**

Canada: A Travel Survival Kit
[W1076] Lonely Planet pbk **£7.95**

**Collins Illustrated Guide
to Canada** NEW
[W1077] Collins pbk **£8.95**

FODOR'S GUIDES
Fodor's Canada
[W1078] Random Cen pbk **£9.95**
Fodor's Canada's Maritime Provinces
[W1079] Random Cen pbk **£6.95**
Fodor's Montreal
[W1080] Random Cen pbk **£5.95**
Fodor's Quebec
[W1081] Random Cen pbk **£7.95**
Fodor's Toronto
[W1082] Random Cen pbk **£6.95**

LITERARY & HISTORICAL

ABLEY, MARK
**Beyond Forget: Rediscovering
the Prairies**
The author gives a spiritual re-assessment of the
western flatlands: Manitoba, Saskatchewan, Alberta.
[W1083] Chatto hbk **£12.95**

BROOK, STEPHEN
Maple Leaf Rag: Travels Across Canada
Arriving with somewhat standard preconceptions,
Brook learns *'to admire the quirky but genuine
receptivity of the country's liberal-minded citizens'*.
[W1084] Picador pbk **£4.99**

MOODIE, SUSANNA
**Roughing It in the Bush: or Forest Life
in Canada** (1852)
Moodie emigrated at twenty-nine from England to
Canada, and recorded with great frankness the
difficult adjustment to her new life in the Canadian
wilderness.
[W1085] Virago pbk **£7.50**

MOWAT, FARLEY
People of the Deer NEW
The author takes up the cause of the virtually
forgotten and silenced Inuit tribe generally
known as the Ihalmiut, situated in the far north of
the continent.
[W1086] Souvenir pbk **£5.95**

PRYDE, DUNCAN
Nunaga: Ten Years of Eskimo Life (1971)
Pryde left Glasgow at 18 to try his hand at fur-trading.
He became entranced by Inuit life, and immersed
himself in their existence.
[W1087] Eland pbk **£4.95**

United States

GENERAL GUIDES

Dollarwise Guide to the USA NEW
Frommer Guide series.
[W1162] Simon & Sch pbk **£10.95**

Let's Go USA
[W1163] Pan pbk **£9.95**

Major Cities
[W1164] Simon & S pbk **£9.95**

Moneywise Guide to North America
From BUNAC.
[W1165] BUNAC pbk **£7.95**

National Parks (USA)
A large, illustrated guide to the wild places of the US.
[W1166] Rand McNally hbk **£19.95**
[W1167] Rand McNally pbk **£10.95**

**Travellers Survival Kit:
USA and Canada**
[W1168] Lascelles pbk **£6.95**

TRUDGILL, PETER
**Coping with America: A Beginner's
Guide to the USA**
A guide for those planning a long stay in America.
[W1169] Blackwell pbk **£5.95**

LITERARY & HISTORICAL

AMIS, MARTIN
The Moronic Inferno (1987)
A collection of Amis's essays on literary, social,
cultural and political aspects of the United States.
[W1131] Penguin pbk **£3.99**

BLOW, ROBERT (ED)
**Abroad in America: Literary
Discoverers of the New World
for the Past 500 Years** NEW
A chronological anthology of visitors' impressions of
America, including Sarah Bernhardt's response to the
adulation of others and George Harrison's opinion of
New York jelly babies.
[W1132] Lennard hbk **£14.95**

BROOK, STEPHEN
**Honky Tonk Gelato, Travels Through
Texas** (1985)
Observing in action the spirit of Texans, inspired by
their extravagant wealth and fierce independence,
both of which are more often portrayed in clichés.
[W1133] Picador pbk **£3.95**
New York Days, New York Nights
The author reels amidst the 'astonishing diversity' of
New York City.
[W1134] Picador pbk **£3.95**

BRYSON, BILL
The Lost Continent NEW
An American expatriate returns home after ten years
in England and encounters the subtle complexity of
first impressions renewed. His experiences are related
with incredulity, humour and admiration.
[W1135] Secker hbk **£12.95**

FAWCETT, EDMUND & THOMAS, TONY
America and the Americans
[W1136] Fontana pbk **£3.95**

FISHLOCK, TREVOR
The State of America (1986)
A personal, informed general treatise on American
life, and the social dimensions of the 'American
psyche'.
[W1137] Faber pbk **£4.95**

FITZGERALD, FRANCES
**Cities on a Hill: A Journey through
Contemporary American Cultures** (1986)
A collection of four essays on disparate
communities - San Francisco's 'Castro' and a
Florida retirement estate included - characterized by
entirely different collective attitudes, and on how
they are all the product of the same, very
'American', aspirations.
[W1138] Picador pbk **£4.50**

FRANCIS, NICK & BUTCHER, BILL
Mississippi Madness NEW
Two men attempt to canoe North America's
longest river.
[W1139] Oxford hbk **£12.95**

HANFF, HELENE
Apple of My Eye
Two New Yorkers try to gain an insight into
the outsider's view of their city and accordingly
metamorphose into tourists, with somewhat
intriguing results.
[W1140] Deutsch hbk **£9.95**

HEAT-MOON, WILLIAM LEAST
**Blue Highways:
A Journey into America**
On American road atlases the minor roads are
coloured blue: hence, Heat-Moon's journey on the
back roads, witnessing daily life and meeting
'ordinary folk'.
[W1141] Picador pbk **£4.95**

IRVING, WASHINGTON
**Astoria: Or Anecdotes of an Enterprise
Beyond the Rocky Mountains** (1836)
The tale of John Jacob Astor's fur-trading enterprise
in the untamed, unexplored west.
[W1142] KPI pbk **£8.95**

KENNEDY, DOUGLAS
**In God's Country: Travels
in the Bible Belt, USA**
An entertaining exploration of the reasons behind the
religious revival which has moved across the U.S.
over the past ten years.
[W1143] Unwin hbk **£12.95**

TRAVEL

Illustration from the Rhode Island section of *Fodor's 89: New England* (Fodor pbk £10.95)

KERRIDGE, ROY
In the Deep South `NEW`
An idiosyncratic coach ride through America, most of it in a less than comfortable Greyhound.
[W1144] M Joseph hbk **£14.95**

LEVIN, BERNARD
A Walk Up Fifth Avenue `NEW`
Levin indulges in the the physical opulence and cultural variety of New York.
[W1145] Cape hbk **£12.95**

LOPEZ, BARRY
Crossing Open Ground
14 essays on the author's own vision of man in his North American landscape.
[W1146] Macmillan hbk **£12.95**

NARAYAN, R.K. (1906 -)
My Dateless Diary: An American Journey (1964)
Narayan left India for the first time to travel to America at the age of 50. *My Dateless Diary* is a record of his observations.
[W1147] Penguin pbk **£3.99**

NICHOLSON, NIGEL & NICHOLSON, ADAM
Two Roads to Dodge City
[W1148] Weidenfeld hbk **£12.95**

NORDHOFF, CHARLES
Nordhoff's West Coast: California, Oregon and Hawaii (1874-75)
A historical alternative to many of the guides in the larger series.
[W1149] KPI pbk **£8.95**

RABAN, JONATHAN
Old Glory (1981)
A ride down the Mississippi in a 16-foot skiff, inspired by the author's childhood reading of *Huckleberry Finn*.
[W1150] Picador pbk **£4.95**

RAYNER, RICHARD
Los Angeles without a Map
A hilarious account of Englishman Rayner's experiences in America, where he met an insane off-duty playboy bunny called Barbara and a 150-foot green dinosaur.
[W1151] Grafton pbk **£3.99**

REES, DAVID
A Better Class of Blond: A Californian Diary
[W1152] Olive P pbk **£4.50**

RIEFF, DAVID
Going to Miami: Exiles, Tourists and Refugees in the New America
A personal view of the volatile American city, penetrating the conundrum of Nicaraguan Contras, Hondurans, Haitians and Vietnamese.
[W1153] Bloomsbury pbk **£4.95**

RUTHVEN, MALISE
The Divine Supermarket: Travels in Search of the Soul of America `NEW`
An examination of the diversity of American religions, keeping in mind its secular history and stipulation that church and state be separated.
[W1154] Chatto hbk **£14.95**

THOMPSON, HUNTER S.
Fear and Loathing in Las Vegas
Anxiety, drugs, weird quests and odd journeys colour the fantastical and nebulously comical world of an anarchic trip through the US. Which is Thompson more: the product or the producer of his fading cult?
[W1155] Grafton pbk **£3.99**

TROLLOPE, ANTHONY (1815 - 1882)
North America Vol 1 (1862)
Written while Trollope was working for the Post Office, a period which saw him travel to the West Indies, Australia, New Zealand and South Africa.
[W1156] Sutton pbk **£3.50**
North America Vol 2 (1862)
[W1157] Sutton pbk **£3.50**

TROLLOPE, FRANCES (1780 - 1863)
The Domestic Manners of the Americans (1832)
Trollope's American journey was born out of a scheme to raise the family's fortunes by emigrating to America to establish a fancy goods emporium in Cincinnati. The plan failed, and her impressions of America were far from favourable - nor were American reactions to her book.
[W1158] Century pbk **£4.95**

TURNER, FLORENCE
At the Chelsea
[W1159] H Hamilton hbk **£12.95**

WHITE, EDMUND
States of Desire: Travels in Gay America
A tour of the US to see what sort of lives the various gay communities are leading, 10 years after the grass-roots beginning of the Gay Liberation Movement.
[W1160] Picador pbk **£3.95**

YEVTUSHENKO, Y & NORTON, B
Divided Twins `NEW`
A celebration of Alaska and Siberia in words and photographs; the theme - two enormous and in many ways similar tracts of forest and snow.
[W1161] Viking hbk **£25.00**

FODOR'S U.S.A.

On their home territory, Fodor's Guides offer clearly laid-out and comprehensive information on all areas of the United States. Please specify with your order which titles are required.

Alaska (£7.95), **Atlantic City and the New Jersey Shore** (£6.95), **Boston** (£7.95), **California** (£9.95), **Cape Cod** (£7.95), **Carolinas and the Georgia Coast** (£7.95), **Chesapeake** (£6.95), **Chicago** (£6.95), **Colorado** (£7.95), **Far West** (£9.95), **Florida** (£8.95), **Hawaii** (£7.95), **Houston and Galveston** (£5.95), **Las Vegas** (£5.95), **Los Angeles** (£7.95), **New England** (£10.95), **New Mexico** (£7.95), **New Orleans** (£5.95),

New York City (£4.95), **New York State** (£8.95), **Pacific North Coast** (£8.95), **Philadelphia** (£7.95), **Rockies** (£7.95), **San Diego** (£6.95), **San Francisco** (£5.95), **Ski Resorts of North America** (£9.95), **South** (£9.95), **Texas** (£8.95), **USA** (£10.95), **Virginia** (£6.95), **Washington DC** (£5.95).
[W1102] Random Cen pbk **£5.95 - 10.95**

USA - MID-WEST

Best of Chicago
Gault Millau 'Best' Series.
[W1170] Simon & Sch pbk **£11.95**

Great Lakes Area
[W1171] Simon & Sch pbk **£9.95**

Northwest and Great Plains States
[W1172] Simon & Sch pbk **£9.95**

USA - NORTH EAST & NEW YORK

Baedeker's New York
[W1173] David & Ch hbk **£17.50**

Best of New England `NEW`
Gault Millau 'Best' series.
[W1174] Simon & S pbk **£11.95**

Best of New York
Gault Millau 'Best' series.
[W1175] Penguin pbk **£9.95**

Best of Washington DC
Gault Millau 'Best' series.
[W1176] Prentice-Hall pbk **£12.95**

New England
Green tourist guide.
[W1177] Michelin pbk **£5.50**

New York
Blue Guide series.
[W1186] A & C Black hbk **£14.95**

New York
Companion Guide series.
[W1178] Collins pbk **£7.95**

New York Art Guide
Art Guide Publications series.
[W1179] A & C Black pbk **£5.95**

New York City
Green tourist guide.
[W1180] Michelin pbk **£5.25**

North-Eastern States
[W1181] Simon & Sch pbk **£9.95**

Pauper's New York
[W1182] Pan pbk **£3.50**

Rough Guide to New York
[W1184] Harrap pbk **£4.95**

FISHER, BUBBLES
New York for Kids: Candy Apple?
Frommer Guides series.
[W1185] Prentice-Hall pbk **£9.95**

USA - SOUTH

Florida `NEW`
[W1187] AA pbk **£3.95**

Florida and Georgia
[W1188] Cadogan pbk **£3.95**

Middle Atlantic States
[W1189] Simon & Sch pbk **£9.95**

New Orleans NEW
[W1190] AA pbk **£3.95**

Old South
Cadogan Guide series.
[W1191] Cadogan pbk **£3.95**

Southeastern States
[W1192] Simon & Sch pbk **£9.95**

USA - WEST

Alaska: A Travel Survival Kit
[W1193] Lonely Planet pbk **£5.95**

Baedeker's San Francisco
[W1194] AA pbk **£4.95**
Best of San Francisco
Gault Millau 'Best' series.
[W1195] Prentice-Hall pbk **£12.95**

California and The West
[W1196] Simon & S pbk **£9.95**

Let's Go California and Hawaii
[W1197] Pan pbk **£9.95**

Let's Go Pacific Northwest, Alaska and Western Canada
[W1198] Pan pbk **£9.95**

Pacific Crest Trail Vol 1: California
[W1199] Wilderness P pbk **£14.95**

Pacific Crest Trail Vol 2: Oregon and Washington
[W1200] Wilderness P pbk **£12.95**

Rough Guide to California NEW
[W1201] Harrap pbk **£5.95**

San Francisco
[W1202] Prentice-Hall pbk **£4.95**

San Francisco on a Shoestring
[W1203] Lonely Planet pbk **£4.50**

Southwest and South Central Area
[W1204] Simon & Sch pbk **£9.95**

RIEGERT, RAY
Hidden Hawaii
[W1205] Moorland pbk **£7.95**

Mexico

GENERAL GUIDES

Baja California: A Travel Survival Kit
[W1088] Lonely Planet pbk **£5.95**

Fodor's Mexico
[W1089] Random Cen pbk **£10.95**

Let's Go Mexico
[W1090] Pan pbk **£9.95**

Mexico: A Travel Survival Kit
[W1091] Lonely Planet pbk **£11.95**

Rough Guide to Mexico
[W1092] Harrap pbk **£5.95**

EADIE, PETER MCGREGOR
Mexico Past and Present NEW
[W1093] Batsford hbk **£12.95**

FRANZ, CARL
People's Guide to Backpacking, Boating and Camping in Mexico
[W1094] J Muir Pubs hbk **£10.95**
People's Guide to Mexico
[W1095] J Muir Pubs hbk **£11.95**

LITERARY & HISTORICAL

FLANDRAU, CHARLES
Viva Mexico! A Traveller's Account of Life in Mexico
Mexico's beguiling land and people are admirably incapsulated by this entertaining writer.
[W1096] Eland pbk **£4.95**

LINCOLN, JOHN
One Man's Mexico (1966)
Among the more perceptive books on post-war Mexico, Lincoln's account is both a tribute and guide to its culture and former grandeur.
[W1097] Century pbk **£4.95**

MACKINTOSH, GRAHAM
Into a Desert Place (1988)
A 3000-mile walk around the coast of Baja, California, with all his supplies on his back, cacti everywhere…
[W1098] Unwin hbk **£14.95**

WRIGHT, RONALD
Time Among the Maya NEW
An investigation of the rise and fall of the Mayan civilization, starting in the first millenium A.D. The author also examines the 5 million people who today speak Mayan dialects and live 'with a Mayan identity'.
[W1099] Bodley hbk **£14.95**

Caribbean & Central America

Including the following Central American countries and Caribbean islands: Antigua (and Barbuda), Bahamas, Barbados, Belize, Costa Rica, Cuba, Dominican Republic, Dominica, El Salvador, Grenada, Guatemala, Haiti, Honduras, Jamaica, Nicaragua, Panama, Puerto Rico, Saint Kitts-Nevis, Saint Lucia, Saint Vincent and Trinidad & Tobago.

GENERAL GUIDES

Adventure Guide to Puerto Rico NEW
[W1206] Moorland pbk **£9.95**

Adventure Guide to the Virgin Islands NEW
[W1207] Moorland pbk **£8.95**

Baedeker's Caribbean
[W1208] AA pbk **£9.95**

Caribbean
Cadogan Guide series.
[W1209] Cadogan pbk **£8.95**

Caribbean Islands Handbook NEW
Very comprehensive guide which covers all of the English, French, Dutch and Spanish-speaking islands, and Bermuda, further out in the Atlantic.
[W1210] Trade & Trav hbk **£9.95**

Caribbean and the Bahamas NEW
[W1211] Harrap pbk **£9.95**

Cuba
Hildebrand Guide series.
[W1212] Harrap pbk **£3.95**

Fodor's Bahamas
[W1213] Random Cen pbk **£6.95**

Fodor's Bermuda
[W1214] Random Cen pbk **£6.95**

Fodor's Caribbean
[W1215] Random Cen pbk **£10.95**

Jamaica
Hildebrand Guide series.
[W1216] Harrap pbk **£3.95**
[W1217] Moon Pubs pbk **£6.95**

Puerto Rico
A guide to the U.S. protectorate, situated due west of the Dominican Republic.
[W1218] Harrap pbk **£9.95**

LITERARY & HISTORICAL

The Caribbean NEW
A thorough and well-researched political and cultural overview that should interest the traveller in search of solid background reading, and the teacher or student.
[W1219] Hansib Publ hbk **£7.95**

CREWE, QUENTIN
Touch the Happy Isles: Journey through the Caribbean
Crewe, who is confined to a wheel-chair, explores the whole chain of islands from Trinidad in the south to Jamaica, revealing the differences between their history, art and people.
[W1220] Headline pbk **£3.99**

DEREN, MAYA (1917 - 1961)
Divine Horsemen: The Living Gods of Haiti (1953)
A now classic account of the islands' deities, practitioners and rituals of *voodoo*.
[W1221] McPherson & Co pbk **£9.50**

GEBLER, CARLO
Driving through Cuba (1987)
Gebler's attempt to see for himself the realities of an island trying hard to live up its own ideological arguments.
[W1222] H Hamilton hbk **£13.95**

HUXLEY, ALDOUS
Beyond the Mexique Bay (1934)
Huxley's inimitable story which begins with his flight from a cruise liner in Jamaica in order to travel through the Central American mainland, Guatemala and Mexico.
[W1223] Grafton pbk **£1.95**

JOHNSON, AMRYL
Sequins for a Ragged Hem
Born in Trinidad, Johnson went to live in England when she was 11. Returning as an adult, she recounts her second impressions.
[W1224] Virago pbk **£5.50**

KINCAID, JAMAICA
A Small Place (1988)
Kincaid bears witness, with elegance and power, to
the 'true spirit' of the Caribbean.
[W1225] Virago pbk **£3.50**
At the Bottom of the River (1984)
Eccentric, visionary pieces about her life and her
island, Antigua.
[W1226] Picador pbk **£1.95**

LONGMORE, ZENGA
Tap Taps to Trinidad `NEW`
The author visits the West Indies for a look at what
could have been her homeland.
[W1227] Hodder hbk **£12.95**

MARNHAM, PATRICK
**So Far from God: Journey to
Central America**
An award-winning account of the troubles in Central
America, including an exposé of its religion,
terrorism and frequent barbarism.
[W1228] Penguin pbk **£4.99**

MASLOW, JONATHAN
Birds of Life, Birds of Death
An impression of the politics and violence of
Central America.
[W1229] Penguin pbk **£3.95**

RUSHDIE, SALMAN
**The Jaguar Smile: A Nicaraguan
Journey**
A personal commentary on a visit to Central
America, initiated by an invitation from the
Sandinista government.
[W1230] Picador pbk **£3.99**

STEPHENS, JOHN L.
**Incidents of Travel in Central America,
Chiapas and Yucatan**
An account of a 3000-mile trip through the region.
[W1231] Century pbk **£5.95**

TROLLOPE, ANTHONY (1815 - 1882)
West Indies and the Spanish Main (1859)
Through the Caribbean during the period in which the
novelist worked for the Post Office.
[W1232] Sutton pbk **£3.95**

WILENTZ, AMY
The Rainy Season `NEW`
Wilentz captures Haiti at the dawn of a new era, with
the fall of Duvalier, and the ensuing feelings of a
nation awaiting change.
[W1233] Cape hbk **£12.95**

Illustration from the Nicaragua section of *Fodor's
89: Central America* (Fodor pbk £7.95)

South America

Including the Galapagos Islands.

GENERAL GUIDES

Fodor's South America
[W1236] Random Cen pbk **£7.95**

Rough Guide to Brazil `NEW`
[W1238] Harrap pbk **£6.95**

Rough Guide to Peru
[W1239] Harrap pbk **£6.95**

South America on a Shoestring
The guide also covers Mexico and most of
Central America.
[W1240] Lonely Planet pbk **£7.95**

South American Handbook
Revised annually, the *South American
Handbook* is the most comprehensive and well-
researched traveller's guide, on any subject, available
in the English language. Accordingly it is worth
every penny.
[W1241] Trade & Trav hbk **£18.95**

Visitor's Guide to Peru `NEW`
[W1242] Moorland pbk **£8.95**

LONELY PLANET
**Chile and Easter Island: A Travel
Survival Kit**
[W1234] Lonely Planet pbk **£5.95**
Peru: A Travel Survival Kit
[W1237] Lonely Planet pbk **£7.95**
**Ecuador and the Galapagos Islands:
A Travel Survival Kit**
[W1235] Lonely Planet pbk **£4.95**

SHICHOR, MICHAEL & AMIR
These titles comprise three volumes of the Michael's
Guide series.
**Argentina, Chile, Paraguay
and Uruguay**
[W1243] Lascelles pbk **£5.95**
Bolivia and Peru
[W1244] Lascelles pbk **£5.95**
**Ecuador, Colombia and
Venezuela**
[W1245] Lascelles pbk **£5.95**

LITERARY & HISTORICAL

BRIDGES, LUCAS
Uttermost Part of the Earth
Born in Tierra del Fuego in 1874, Bridges looks back
upon his youth in the region, providing a mixture of
anthropology and natural history.
[W1246] Century pbk **£6.95**

BURNS, JIMMY
**Beyond the Silver River: South
American Encounters**
A collection of travel pieces indulging in the sensual
side of the continent.
[W1247] Bloomsbury pbk **£4.99**

CAUFIELD, CATHERINE
In the Rainforest
Every year an area of tropical rainforest the size of
Britain is lost to development. This is a moving and
often angry piece on this destruction and loss, and on
the world's improving attitude.
[W1248] Picador pbk **£3.99**

CREWE, QUENTIN
**In the Realms of Gold: Travels
through South America** `NEW`
An ironic, yet ultimately sympathetic guided tour
through this diverse, difficult and undeniably
beautiful contintent.
[W1249] M Joseph hbk **£14.95**

DANIELS, ANTHONY
**Coups and Cocaine: Two Journeys
in South America**
In search of the spirit of place and people Daniels
paints a contemporary portrait of the character of
South American life.
[W1250] Century pbk **£5.95**

FAWCETT, P.H.
Exploration Fawcett
Few adventure stories equal the terrifying experiences
endured by Colonel Fawcett in his search for a lost
city in Amazonia. Similarly, his later disappearance in
1925 remains a mystery.
[W1251] Century pbk **£5.95**

GRAHAM, R.B. CUNNINGHAME
**A Vanished Arcadia: Being Some
Account of the Jesuits in
Paraguay** (1901)
[W1252] Century pbk **£5.95**

HICKMAN, JOHN
**Enchanted Islands: The Galapagos
Discovered**
[W1253] Nelson hbk **£10.95**

HUDSON, W.H.
Idle Days in Patagonia (1893)
In straightforward, clear prose, Hudson recounts his
youth in Argentina, where he was born to English
parents resident in the trade colony.
[W1254] Dent pbk **£2.95**

KANE, JOE
Running the Amazon `NEW`
An exhilarating account of the author's 4,100 mile
boat trip down the Amazon and his reactions to its
wide variety of terrain, people and climate.
[W1255] Bodley hbk **£15.00**

NICHOLL, CHARLES
The Fruit Palace
Briefed to research an exposé on the Columbian
cocaine trade, what the author eventually produced
resembles an adventure thriller only real life
could orchestrate.
[W1256] Pan pbk **£2.95**

O'HANLAN, REDMOND
**In Trouble Again: A Journey Between
the Orinoco and the Amazon**
An amusing scramble into unknown territory
by the wonderfully eccentric perpetrator of
high adventure.
[W1257] H Hamilton hbk **£14.95**

SCHNEEBAUM, TOBIAS
Keep the River on Your Right (1969)
Forgoing all contact with civilization, Schneebaum
lived as a brother among the Akaramas, a primitive
tribe in Peru.
[W1258] GMP pbk **£4.50**

SHOUMATOFF, ALEX
The Rivers Amazon
An eight-month odyssey through Amazonia,
during which the author followed the river and
many of its tributaries to the headwaters high in
the Peruvian Andes.
[W1259] Century pbk **£5.95**

SIMPSON, JOE
Touching the Void (1988)
Climbing the west face of the *Siula Grande*, in the
Peruvian Andes, Simpson falls, disappears and is left
for dead only to struggle for his life with quite
frightening determination.
[W1260] Pan pbk **£3.99**

STARKELL, DON
Paddle to the Amazon
Starkell and his 'ordinary' family set out to canoe to
the Amazon from Central America, a journey which
covers some 12,000 miles.
[W1261] Futura pbk **£5.99**

SWALE, ROSIE
Back to Cape Horn (1986)
A journey on horseback down the length of Chile,
which took 14 months and covered 3,000 miles.
[W1262] Fontana pbk **£3.95**

TSCHIFFELY, A.F.
Southern Cross to Pole Star (1932)
The chronicle, in a loose diary format, of a man and
his horse travelling from Patagonia to Washington
D.C. in the late 1920s.
[W1263] Century pbk **£5.95**

URE, JOHN
Trepassers on the Amazon
[W1264] Constable hbk **£10.95**

WATERTON, CHARLES
Wanderings in South America
Waterton proclaimed he was happier living with
Indians and monkeys in the forests of Guiana than
with his other life as a Yorkshire gentleman.
[W1265] Century pbk **£5.95**

WRIGHT, RONALD
**Cut Stones and Crossroads: Journey
in the Two Worlds of Peru** (1984)
The author traces the history of the Incas, principally
through the close study of extant architecture; in so
doing he uncovers for himself the stark contrasts of
modern South America.
[W1266] Penguin pbk **£4.50**

Asia

Middle East &
Arabia

Covering the following countries: Afghanistan,
Bahrain, Dubai, Iran, Iraq, Israel, Jordan, Kuwait,
Lebanon, Maldives, Oman, Pakistan, Qatar, Saudi
Arabia, South Yemen, Syria, United Arab Emirates
and Yemen.

GENERAL GUIDES

Baedeker's Israel
[W1267] AA pbk **£9.95**

Baedeker's Jerusalem
[W1268] AA pbk **£5.95**

Bazak Guide to Israel 1989 - 90 `NEW`
A comprehensive guide supplemented by a five-
colour tourist map and colour photographs.
[W1269] Harper & R pbk **£9.95**

Carta's Israel Road and Touring Guide
Lists 78 touring itineraries, complete with road maps.
[W1270] Moorland pbk **£7.95**

Essentially Israel `NEW`
A guide to for first-time visitors.
[W1271] Cr Helm pbk **£5.95**

Fodor's Israel
[W1272] Random Cen pbk **£8.95**

Fodor's Jordan and the Holy Land
[W1273] Random Cen pbk **£8.95**

**International Herald Tribune Guide to
Business Travel and Entertainment:
Asia**
[W1274] A & C Black pbk **£7.95**

Israel
[W1275] Lascelles pbk **£4.95**

Let's Go Israel and Egypt
[W1276] Pan pbk **£9.95**

Maldives
[W1277] Lascelles pbk **£5.50**

MEED PRACTICAL GUIDES
Extremely detailed practical guides researched by the
Middle East Economic Digest.
Bahrain
[W1319] MEED pbk **£9.95**
Jordan
[W1313] MEED pbk **£9.95**
Kuwait
[W1314] MEED pbk **£9.95**
Oman
[W1315] MEED pbk **£9.95**
Qatar
[W1316] MEED pbk **£9.95**
Saudi Arabia
[W1317] MEED pbk **£9.95**
United Arab Emirates
[W1318] KPI pbk **£10.95**

New Guide to Bahrain
[W1278] Immel Pubs pbk **£9.95**

Pakistan Handbook `NEW`
Up-to-date, with close to 90 maps and full
trekking information.
[W1279] J Murray pbk **£14.95**

Rough Guide to Israel `NEW`
[W1280] Harrap pbk **£5.95**

**Travel with Children: A Survival Kit for
Travel in Asia**
Looks at the perennial problems of travel, including
health, food and maintaining a child's interest.
[W1281] Lascelles pbk **£3.50**

LONELY PLANET
Israel: A Travel Survival Kit
[W1283] Lonely Planet pbk **£7.95**
Jordan and Syria: A Travel Survival Kit
[W1284] Lonely Planet pbk **£5.95**
Pakistan: A Travel Survival Kit
[W1285] Lonely Planet pbk **£5.95**
West Asia on a Shoestring
[W1282] Lonely Planet pbk **£5.95**
Yemen: A Travel Survival Kit
[W1286] Lonely Planet pbk **£5.95**

WAGER, ELIAHU
Illustrated Guide to Jerusalem `NEW`
(Revised edition)
[W1287] Kuperard hbk **£9.95**

LITERARY & HISTORICAL

AMIN, MOHAMED
Journey through Pakistan
[W1288] Bodley hbk **£22.50**

BELL, GERTRUDE (1868 - 1926)
The Desert and the Sown (1907)
A description of Syrian life under the Ottomans, and
in particular its landscape, written during the first of
two archaeological expeditions to the Near East.
[W1289] Virago pbk **£6.99**

BELLOW, SAUL (1915-)
**To Jerusalem and Back:
A Personal Account**
A humane and patiently uplifting record of the
author's impressions made while touring the
ethnically diverse city.
[W1290] Penguin pbk **£3.95**

BIBBY, GEOFFREY
**Looking for Dilmun: The Search for
a Lost Civilization** (1970)
Bibby endeavoured to decipher the clues indicating
that there was a lost city on the island of Bahrain, an
project which consumed some 15 years.
[W1291] Penguin pbk **£4.99**

BLUNT, LADY ANNE
**A Pilgrimage to Nejd: The Cradle
of the Arab Race**
Introduction by Dervla Murphy. Lady Blunt, who
spoke Arabic, crossed 1,000 miles of the central
Arabian desert with her husband c.1878.
[W1292] Century pbk **£6.95**

BROWNE, EDWARD GRANVILLE
A Year amongst the Persians (1891)
Browne, a distinguished Islamicist, spent a year in
Iran (1887-88), and his subsequent book stands as an
early introduction to the perennial issues which face
that nation.
[W1293] Century pbk **£6.95**

BURUMA, IAN
**God's Dust: A Modern
Asian Journey** `NEW`
[W1294] Cape hbk **£12.95**

CURZON, ROBERT
Visits to Monasteries in the Levant
Robert Curzon's account of his wanderings in the
1830s through Egypt, Abyssinia, the Holy Land and
Albania in search of medieval manuscripts.
[W1295] Century pbk **£6.95**

DANZIGER, NICK
**Danziger's Travels: Beyond Forbidden
Frontiers** (1987)
An Asian experience: through Iran, Afghanistan,
Pakistan, Xinjiang, Tibet and Bhutan.
[W1296] Grafton pbk **£5.95**

DOUBLEDAY, VERONICA
Three Women of Herat
[W1297] Cape hbk **£12.95**

HODSON, PEREGRINE
**Under a Sickle Moon: A Journey
through Afghanistan**
A combination of personal impressions, war reportage
and contemporary history.
[W1298] Hodder pbk **£3.99**

LAWRENCE, T.E. (1888 - 1935)
Crusader Castles
Lawrence's illustrated survey of the many crusader
fortresses built near or on the shores of the

Mediterranean; many have since crumbled, a sad fact which has made his work virtually unique.
[W1299] M Haag pbk **£15.00**

LEVI, PETER
Light Garden of the Angel King: Journeys in Afghanistan (1972)
A search for historical and social clues behind the great migrations of people in Central Asia, a consistent theme through the ages.
[W1300] Penguin pbk **£4.99**

MAXWELL, GAVIN
Reed Shaken by the Wind (1957)
An exploration of the unfamiliar marshlands of western Iraq.
[W1301] Penguin pbk **£3.95**

MONFREID, HENRY DE
Hashish
[W1302] Penguin pbk **£3.95**

NERVAL, GERARD DE
Journey to the Orient
[W1303] P Owen hbk **£10.95**

OZ, AMOS
In the Land of Israel (1983)
A sabra (native-born Israeli), Oz assesses his countrymen's deepest fears, hopes and prejudices.
[W1304] Flamingo pbk **£3.99**

PHILBY, HARRY ST. JOHN
The Empty Quarter
Philby, among the more prominent British desert explorers, was to realise an earlier dream by crossing the *Rub' al Khali* (the 'Empty Quarter'), a most inhospitable tract of desert in the southern reaches of the Arab lands.
[W1305] Century pbk **£6.95**

RABAN, JONATHAN
Arabia through the Looking Glass
[W1306] Picador pbk **£4.95**

SACKVILLE-WEST, VITA
Twelve Days
An account of the author's journey across the Bakhtiari Mountains in the south west of Persia.
[W1307] M Haag pbk **£4.95**

SADLEIR, GEORGE FORSTER
Diary of a Journey Across Arabia (1819)
[W1308] Oleander hbk **£13.50**

SCHOFIELD, VICTORIA
Every Rock, Every Hill: A Plain Tale of the North-West Frontier & Afghanistan
A considered documentary on Afghan life and landscape antedating the Soviet occupation.
[W1309] Century pbk **£5.95**

SCHWARTZ, BRIAN
Travels through the Third World
[W1310] Sidgwick hbk **£12.95**

SELBY, BETTINA
Riding to Jerusalem: Journey through Turkey and the Middle East
[W1311] R Drew pbk **£6.95**

TRENCH, RICHARD
Arabian Travellers: The European Discovery of Arabia (1986)
A thematic examination of how successive Euro-centric travellers to the Near East have contributed to the creation of a romanticized notion of the Arab.
[W1312] Macmillan Pbk **£9.95**

East Asia

Covering the following countries and colonies: China, Hong Kong, Japan, Macau, Mongolia, North Korea, South Korea, Taiwan and Tibet.

GENERAL GUIDES

All Asia Guide (Pakistan to Japan)
Produced by the *Far Eastern Economic Review*, this has excellent, if brief, entries on all countries in the region. Written partly with the business traveller in mind, it nevertheless offers extensive cultural commentary.
[W1325] Lascelles pbk **£9.95**

Discovering Macau
[W1329] Lascelles pbk **£3.75**

Guide to Rajasthan, with Delhi and Agra
[W1331] M Haag pbk **£5.95**

Introducing Kyoto   `NEW`
A tour of one of Japan's oldest and historically significant cities.
[W1332] Kodansha hbk **£8.95**

North East Asia on a Shoestring
[W1333] Lascelles pbk **£4.95**

Rough Guide to China
[W1334] Harrap pbk **£6.95**

Shanghai: City Guide
[W1335] Lascelles pbk **£3.95**

Tibet   `NEW`
[W1336] Harrap hbk **£11.95**

Tibet Guide
Foreword by the Dalai Lama.
[W1337] Wisdom pbk **£13.95**

BAEDEKER'S GUIDES
Baedeker's Hong Kong
[W1326] AA pbk **£5.95**
Baedeker's Japan
[W1327] AA pbk **£9.95**
Baedeker's Tokyo
[W1328] AA pbk **£5.95**

FODOR'S ASIA
Beijing, Guangzhou and Shanghai
[W1320] Random Cen pbk **£5.95**
Fodor's Hong Kong and Macau
[W1330] Random Cen pbk **£7.95**
Japan
[W1322] Random Cen pbk **£9.95**
Korea
[W1323] Random Cen pbk **£8.95**
Tokyo and Vicinity
[W1324] Random Cen pbk **£5.95**

LONELY PLANET
China: A Travel Survival Kit
[W1338] Lonely Planet pbk **£11.95**
Hong Kong, Macau and Canton: A Travel Survival Kit
[W1339] Lonely Planet pbk **£6.95**
Japan: A Travel Survival Kit
[W1340] Lonely Planet pbk **£8.95**
Korea: A Travel Survival Kit
[W1341] Lonely Planet pbk **£5.95**
Taiwan: A Travel Survival Kit
[W1342] Lonely Planet pbk **£5.95**

Tibet: A Travel Survival Kit
[W1343] Lonely Planet pbk **£4.95**

LOWE, JOHN
Into China
[W1344] J Murray pbk **£8.95**
Into Japan
An introduction which addresses both the tourist and the prospective business traveller, looking at day-to-day life.
[W1345] J Murray pbk **£7.95**

RANDLE, JOHN & WATANABE, MARIKO
Coping with Japan
[W1346] Blackwell pbk **£5.95**

WALTERS, GARY
Day Walks Near Tokyo   `NEW`
26 popular walks in and around Tokyo, most within easy reach of the centre.
[W1347] Kodansha pbk **£7.95**

LITERARY & HISTORICAL

ALLEN, CHARLES
A Mountain in Tibet
The search for Mount Kailis and the sources of the great rivers of Asia.
[W1348] Futura pbk **£3.95**

BISHOP, PETER
Myth of Shangri-La   `NEW`
Tibet, travel writing and the western creation of a sacred landscape.
[W1349] Athlone hbk **£35.00**

BOOTH, ALAN
The Roads to Sata: A 2000 Mile Walk through Japan (1985)
Booth traverses three of Japan's four main islands, taking in the atmosphere and disposition of the people, as well as their lush countryside.
[W1350] Penguin pbk **£4.50**

BROOK, ELAINE
Land of the Snow Lion: An Adventure in Tibet
[W1351] Cape pbk **£6.95**

DALRYMPLE-HAMILTON, WILLIAM
The Road to Xanadu   `NEW`
An epic journey across Asia in search of the lost palaces of Kublai Khan.
[W1352] Collins hbk **£14.95**

DODWELL, CHRISTINA
A Traveller in China
[W1353] Hodder pbk **£3.95**

FORTUNE, ROBERT
A Journey through the Tea Countries of China and India
[W1354] Mildmay pbk **£6.95**
Three Years' Wandering in the Northern Provinces of China
[W1355] Mildmay pbk **£6.95**

GUIBAUT, ANDRE
Tibetan Venture
Expedition to study the lifestyles of remote tribesmen in Eastern Tibet, which cost one explorer his life.
[W1356] Oxford pbk **£4.95**

HARRER, HEINRICH
Return to Tibet (1983)
A return to see how the Chinese have tampered with the Tibetans' sense of national identity.
[W1357] Penguin pbk **£3.95**

TRAVEL

Seven Years in Tibet
Harrer's story of escaping from the British during
World War II, fleeing to Tibet, which was then
closed to the outside world, eventually to become the
Chief Engineer.
[W1358] Grafton pbk **£4.95**

HINTON, WILLIAM
Shenfan
It is 1971: Hinton returns to the Chinese village
where he had lived during the critical post-
revolutionary years to observe the changes.
[W1359] Picador pbk **£4.95**

HOPKIRK, PETER
Foreign Devils on the Silk Road (1980)
Searching for the lost cities and treasures of the trade
route through Chinese central Asia, which were lost
to the encroaching sands a millenium ago when the
Chinese lost control of the region.
[W1360] Oxford pbk **£5.95**

INOUYE, JUKICHI
Home Life in Tokyo
[W1361] KPI pbk **£9.95**

IYER, PICO
**Video Night in Kathmandu: And Other
Reports from the Not-so-far East**
The discovery that *Rambo* was on show from Tibet to
Bali, and other meetings of East and West.
[W1362] Transworld pbk **£4.99**

KAZANTZAKIS, NIKOS (Crete, 1883 - 1957)
**Japan/China: A Journal of Two
Voyages to the East**
[W1363] Creative Arts pbk **£8.50**

KELLOGG, DAVID
Big Nose, Tang Min and Little Liu NEW
Kellogg taught in China for more than four years
and in this book assesses his insight into Chinese
culture as it races, with interruptions, into
the 1990s.
[W1364] H Shipman hbk **£12.00**

KENNEDY, RICK
Home, Sweet Tokyo NEW
An American light-heartedly assesses his reactions to
the Eastern way of life.
[W1365] Kodansha pbk **£3.95**

LINDESAY, WILLIAM
**Along the Great Wall: From the
Desert to the Sea** NEW
Lindesay, a 31 year old geologist, ran the length
of the Great Wall, 2,470 miles of parched desert and
snow-covered mountains.
[W1366] Hodder hbk **£12.95**

LLOYD, SARAH
Chinese Characters
Through China on bike, bus, train and boat.
[W1367] Fontana pbk **£3.95**

LOTI, PIERRE
Japan: Madam Chrysanthemum (1920)
The first Western romance set in Japan, written
at the start of the European infatuation with all
things Eastern.
[W1368] KPI pbk **£7.95**

MAILLART, ELLA
Forbidden Journey
In 1935 Maillart set out in the footsteps of Marco
Polo from Peking to Kashmir, a journey that had
been deemed impossible for any Westerner
to complete.
[W1369] Century pbk **£5.95**

NEWSHAM, BRAD
All the Right Places NEW
Backpacking, hiking and biking through China, Japan
and, latterly, Russia.
[W1370] Hodder hbk **£12.95**

RITCHIE, DONALD
The Inland Sea
An elegant and at times poignant tribute to the people
who live within the little sea bounded by three of
Japan's four major islands.
[W1371] Century pbk **£4.95**

SETH, VIKRAM
**From Heaven Lake: Travels through
Sinkiang and Tibet** (1982)
In 1981 Indian-born Seth hitch-hiked through North-
West China, Tibet and Nepal: and his account relives
the adventure, which was as hazardous as his retelling
of it is humorous.
[W1372] Sphere pbk **£3.99**

STATLER, OLIVER
Japanese Inn
In Statler's almost magical creation is a seat in the
Minaguchi-ya, an ancient inn at the centre of his
odyssey through 400 years of history.
[W1373] Picador pbk **£3.95**

WELCH, DENTON
Maiden Voyage (1943)
A young writer's impression of 1930s China.
[W1374] Penguin pbk **£3.95**

WINCHESTER, SIMON
**Korea: A Walk through the Land
of Miracles** (1988)
An open-eyed, politically acute examination of
modern, highly-industrialised Korea, once known as
the 'Hermit Kingdom'.
[W1375] Grafton hbk **£12.95**

WOOD, HEATHER
Third-Class Ticket (1980)
The quite unusual story of how a Bengali land owner
left money to her villagers so that they may see 'all of
India'. It begins in 1969.
[W1376] Penguin pbk **£4.95**

India & South-East Asia

Covering the following countries: Bangladesh,
Bhutan, Burma, India, Cambodia, Laos, Nepal, Sri
Lanka, Thailand and Vietnam.

GENERAL GUIDES

Bangladesh: A Traveller's Guide
[W1377] Lascelles pbk **£4.95**

Collins Illustrated Guide to Burma
[W1378] Collins pbk **£8.95**

Collins Illustrated Guide to Delhi NEW
[W1379] Collins pbk **£8.95**

Fodor's India, Nepal and Sri Lanka
[W1380] Random Cen pbk **£9.95**

Fodor's South-East Asia
[W1381] Random Cen pbk **£9.95**

India: The Traveller's Companion
[W1382] Lascelles pbk **£4.95**

Kathmandu and the Everest Track
[W1383] Lascelles pbk **£4.95**

**Kathmandu and the Kingdom
of Nepal**
[W1384] Lascelles pbk **£5.95**

South East Asia on a Shoestring
[W1385] Lonely Planet pbk **£6.95**

Sri Lanka
[W1386] Lascelles pbk **£4.95**

Time Off in India and Nepal
A guide for the serious traveller which emphasizes
lifestyle and participation.
[W1387] Horizon pbk **£10.95**

Times Guide to Thailand
[W1388] Bartholomew pbk **£7.95**

**Trekking North of Pokhara Jomson,
the Thak Kola Canyon & the
Annapurna Sanctuary**
[W1389] Lascelles pbk **£3.95**

Trekking Peaks of Nepal NEW
Comprehensive guide to walking the peaks of Nepal,
with advice on local conditions and regulations.
[W1390] Crowood hbk **£14.95**

LONELY PLANET
**Bali and Lombok:
A Travel Survival Kit**
[W1391] Lonely Planet pbk **£6.95**
Bangladesh: A Travel Survival Kit
[W1392] Lonely Planet pbk **£4.95**
Burma: A Travel Survival Kit
[W1393] Lonely Planet pbk **£5.95**
India: A Travel Survival Kit
[W1394] Lonely Planet pbk **£11.95**
Kashmir, Ladakh and Zanskar
[W1395] Lonely Planet pbk **£4.95**
Sri Lanka: A Travel Survival Kit
[W1396] Lonely Planet pbk **£5.95**
Thailand: A Travel Survival Kit
[W1397] Lonely Planet pbk **£5.95**
Trekking in the Indian Himalaya
[W1398] Lonely Planet pbk **£4.95**
Trekking in the Nepal Himalaya
[W1399] Lonely Planet pbk **£4.95**

LITERARY & HISTORICAL

ACKERLEY, J.R.
Hindoo Holiday: An Indian Journal (1932)
The Maharajah of Chokrapur wanted a companion, a
tutor for his son, a private secretary; naturally he sent
away to England for one, advertising in a newspaper.
Ackerley answered the call.
[W1400] Penguin pbk **£4.50**

BAKER, SOPHIE
Caste: At Home in Hindu India NEW
An examination of contemporary Indian society.
[W1401] Cape hbk **£13.95**

CAMERON, JAMES
The Indian Summer (1974)
Cameron gives a clear, journalistic treatment of
events in India just before the 1971 war with Pakistan.
[W1402] Penguin pbk **£3.99**

EAMES, ANDREW
**Crossing the Shadow Line: Travels in
South-East Asia** (1986)
A trip after university (where the author had been
deeply interested in the writings of Joseph Conrad) to

the entirely different political and human realities of
South-East Asia.
[W1403] Hodder pbk **£4.95**

FISHLOCK, TREVOR
India File: Inside the Subcontinent
[W1404] J Murray pbk **£8.95**

GRASS, GUNTER
Show Your Tongue `NEW`
Grass presents an idiosyncratic exploration, in
prose, verse and with watercolours, of the human
tragedy of the poor he observed in several
Indian cities.
[W1405] Secker hbk **£20.00**

JONES, JOHN R.
Vietnam Now `NEW`
A look at Vietnam fifteen years after the final
withdrawal of American troops. The book is written
by an American who observed the country for
six months.
[W1406] Aston Pubs hbk **£16.95**

JONES, TRISTAN
Somewhere East of Suez
In July 1985 Tristan Jones, a disabled sailor, set out
from Istanbul on a journey to Phuket, partly to act as
an inspiration to handicapped young people.
[W1407] Bodley hbk **£12.95**

KAUL, H.K. (ED.)
Traveller's India: An Anthology
[W1408] Oxford hbk **£9.75**

LAPIERRE, DOMINIQUE
The City of Joy
Despite the dirt, rats and over-population, the author
discovers evidence of heroism, love and happiness in
the streets and slums of Calcutta.
[W1409] Arrow pbk **£3.95**

LINES, MAUREEN
**Beyond the North West Frontier:
Travels in the Hindu Kush and
Karakorams**
[W1410] Oxford hbk **£12.95**

MAUGHAM, W. SOMERSET (1874 - 1965)
On a Chinese Screen (1922)
A book derived from Maugham's two visits to
China in 1919 and 1921; the result mainly consists
of portraits of the various Europeans then in
residence there.
[W1411] Oxford pbk **£3.95**

MICHELL, GEORGE
**Penguin Guide to the Monuments
of India
Vol 1: Buddhist, Jain, Hindu** `NEW`
[W1412] Viking hbk **£30.00**
Vol 2: Islamic, Rajput, European `NEW`
[W1413] Viking hbk **£30.00**

SELBY, BETTINA
**Riding the Mountains Down:
A Journey by Bicycle to Kathmandu**
[W1414] Unwin pbk **£3.95**

SHEARER, ALISTAIR
Thailand: The Lotus Kingdom `NEW`
A cultural primer for the traveller.
[W1415] J Murray pbk **£9.95**

STEPHENS, JOY
Window onto Annapurna
Life in a remote mountain village situated 150 miles
west of Kathmandu.
[W1416] Gollancz hbk **£14.95**

THOMSON, ALEX & ROSSITER, NICK
**Ram Ram India: Notes from a
Ride in the Subcontinent**
An illustrated account of a bicycle journey from
Kashmir down to the southern tip of India.
[W1417] Grafton pbk **£4.99**

TURNER, J.A.
**Kwang Tung or Five Years
in South China** (1894)
An English Wesleyan minister, teacher and
missionary in China from 1886-91, Turner was one of
1,296 Protestant missionaries then working there.
[W1418] Oxford pbk **£4.95**

WARD, PHILIP
Bangkok: Portrait of a City
Philip Ward has painted his picture both for the
researcher and the general reader.
[W1419] Oleander pbk **£4.50**

WEBB, SIDNEY & WEBB, BEATRICE
Indian Diary
A diary kept by the two British socialists during
travels in India 1911-12 .
[W1420] Oxford hbk **£12.95**

East Indies

Including : Bali, Brunei, Indonesia, Malaysia, Papua
New Guinea, Philippines and Singapore.

GENERAL GUIDES

Baedeker's Singapore
[W1421] AA pbk **£5.95**

Bali
Cadogan Guide series.
[W1422] Cadogan pbk **£6.95**

Fodor's Singapore
[W1423] Random Cen pbk **£5.95**

Indonesia
[W1424] Lascelles pbk **£6.95**

Indonesia Handbook
[W1425] Moon Pubs pbk **£14.95**

Malaysia: A Guide to the Peninsula
[W1426] Lascelles pbk **£4.95**

LONELY PLANET
Indonesia: A Travel Survival Kit
[W1427] Lonely Planet pbk **£9.95**
**Malaysia, Singapore and Brunei:
A Travel Survival Kit**
[W1428] Lonely Planet pbk **£6.95**
Philippines: A Travel Survival Kit
[W1429] Lonely Planet pbk **£5.95**

LITERARY & HISTORICAL

ALLEN, BENEDICT
Hunting the Gugu `NEW`
On the islands of South East Asia, Allen sets off in
search of the legendary 'Lost Ape-Men of Sumatra'.
[W1430] Macmillan hbk **£12.95**

COLLIS, MAURICE
Raffles
The story of Thomas Stanford Raffles (1781-1835)
Singapore's 'founder'. Introduced by Jan Morris.
[W1431] Century pbk **£5.95**

HANSEN, ERIC
Stranger in the Forest
Despite his fears to the contrary Hansen survived his
travels through Borneo.
[W1432] Century pbk **£4.95**

HOSE, CHARLES
The Field-book of a Jungle Wallah (1929)
A description of shore, river and forest life
in Sarawack.
[W1433] Oxford pbk **£4.95**

KINLOCH, CHARLES WALTER
**Rambles in Java and the Straits
Settlements**
There are ghastly experiences recorded in these
memoirs of the 'Bengal Civilian'.
[W1434] Oxford pbk **£5.95**

MONBIOT, GEORGE
**Poison Arrows: An Investigative
Journey through Indonesia** `NEW`
A dangerous crossing of the mountainous swamps of
Indonesia, a place the author referred to as 'the most
remote tropical environment in the world'.
[W1435] M Joseph hbk **£14.95**

O'HANLON, REDMOND
Into the Heart of Borneo
An account of a journey made in 1983 to the
mountains of Batu Tiban with poet James Fenton.
O'Hanlon is one of the most engaging explorers of
today, whose work reveals him as a madcap eccentric;
on being invited to accompany O'Hanlon on his next
journey - along the Orinoco River, recorded in *In
Trouble Again* - Fenton replied that he would refuse
to go as far as High Wycombe with him, let alone to
South America.
[W1436] Penguin pbk **£4.99**

SUTTON, ANNABEL
The Islands in Between `NEW`
Two young women travel in the remote islands of
Indonesia, a journey the author describes with
humorous anecdotes and profiles of people they met.
[W1437] Impact Books pbk **£5.95**

W. Somerset Maugham, author of *On a Chinese
Screen* (Oxford pbk **£3.95**)

Australasia & Oceania

Covering Australia, New Zealand, Fiji, Kiribati, Nauru, Solomon Islands, Tonga, Tuvalu, Vanuatu and Western Samoa.

GENERAL GUIDES

Australia
Cadogan Guide series.
[W1438] Cadogan pbk **£9.95**

Australia `NEW`
[W1439] Tourist Pubs pbk **£7.95**

Australian Arts Guide
Art Guide Publications series.
[W1441] A & C Black hbk **£9.95**

Bush Walking in Australia
[W1442] Lonely Planet pbk **£5.95**

Dollarwise Guide to Australia `NEW`
Frommer Guide series.
[W1443] Simon & S pbk **£10.95**

Dollarwise Guide to the South Pacific
Frommer Guide series.
[W1444] Simon & S pbk **£9.95**

Fodor's Australia, New Zealand and the South Pacific
[W1445] Random Cen pbk **£10.95**

Fodor's South Pacific
[W1446] Random Cen pbk **£7.95**

Fodor's Sydney
[W1447] Random Cen pbk **£5.95**

Poster from *Riding the Skies: Classic Posters from the Golden Age of Flying* (Bloomsbury hbk £16.95)

Illustrated Guide to Australia `NEW`
[W1440] Collins pbk **£8.95**

New Zealand `NEW`
[W1448] Tourist Pubs pbk **£7.95**

South Pacific Handbook
A detailed guide to a large region with few people, now receiving more and more visitors each year.
[W1449] Moon Pubs hbk **£12.95**

Sydney and New South Wales `NEW`
[W1450] AA pbk **£3.95**

Tramping in New Zealand
[W1451] Lonely Planet pbk **£3.95**

LONELY PLANET
Australia: A Travel Survival Kit
[W1452] Lonely Planet pbk **£9.95**
Fiji: A Travel Survival Kit
[W1453] Lonely Planet pbk **£4.95**
Micronesia: A Travel Survival Kit
[W1454] Lonely Planet pbk **£5.95**
New Zealand: A Travel Survival Kit
[W1455] Lonely Planet pbk **£5.95**
Papua New Guinea: A Travel Survival Kit
[W1456] Lonely Planet pbk **£5.95**
Rarotonga and the Cook Islands: A Travel Survival Kit
[W1457] Lonely Planet pbk **£4.95**
Tahiti & French Polynesia: A Travel Survival Kit
[W1458] Lonely Planet pbk **£4.95**

LITERARY & HISTORICAL

ALLEN, BENEDICT
Into the Crocodile's Nest: A Journey inside New Guinea (1987)
To the heart of New Guinea to make contact with its hidden peoples and to learn the secrets of their harmonious communion with their land.
[W1459] Grafton pbk **£5.99**

CHRISTMAS, LINDA
The Ribbon and the Ragged Square: An Australian Journey
[W1460] Penguin pbk **£4.95**

DODWELL, CHRISTINA
In Papua New Guinea
Papua New Guinea is one of the less explored parts of the world; reason enough for Dodwell to go there.
[W1461] Picador pbk **£3.95**

FINKELSTEIN, DAVE & LONDON, JACK
Greater Nowhere: A Journey through the Australian Bush `NEW`
Two journalists, armed only with insect repellent and an 'esky' full of beer, set out to cross the outback in a Toyota truck.
[W1462] Ebury hbk **£14.95**

GRIMBLE, ARTHUR
A Pattern of Islands
As an officer in the colonial service on the Gilbert and Ellice Islands, Arthur Grimble spent 14 years documenting the daily life and rituals of the sorcerers, fisherman, fighters and poets he encountered.
[W1463] Penguin pbk **£4.99**

HALL, RODNEY
Journey through Australia (1988)
The Australian novelist's guided tour of his continent, enriched by years of earlier travel.
[W1464] J Murray hbk **£12.95**

Drawing from *Greater Nowhere: A Journey Through the Australian Bush* by **D. Finkelstein and J London** (Ebury P hbk £12.95)

HULME, KERI & MORRISON, ROBIN
Homeplaces `NEW`
An intimate, illustrated examination of Okarito, Moeraki and Stewart Island in New Zealand.
[W1465] Hodder hbk **£17.95**

JACOBSON, HOWARD
In the Land of Oz (1987)
Inspired by a 19th century explorer who ventured to Australia to familiarize its inhabitants with the British temperament, Jacobson went and here tells his humorous story with characteristic flair.
[W1466] Penguin pbk **£4.99**

LOTI, PIERRE
Tahiti: The Marriage of Loti (1880)
The tale of an amorous dalliance in Polynesia, c.1872.
[W1467] KPI pbk **£6.95**

SCHNEEBAUM, TOBIAS
Where the Spirits Dwell: Four Years in New Guinea
[W1468] Weidenfeld hbk **£14.95**

SHAND, MARK & MCCULLIN, DONALD
Skulduggery
[W1469] Cape hbk **£10.95**

Polar Regions

LOPEZ, BARRY
Arctic Dreams: Imagination and Desire in a Northern Landscape
A poetically evocative and romantic eulogy to the beauty of the extreme north.
[W1470] Picador pbk **£4.95**

LOWTHER, HUGH
A Victorian Earl in the Arctic `NEW`
Travels and collections of the fifth Earl of Lonsdale, who a century ago travelled the Great White North.
[W1471] Brit Mus P hbk **£19.95**

MEAR, ROGER & SWAN, ROBERT
In the Footsteps of Scott
[W1472] Cape hbk **£14.95**

PARFIT, MICHAEL
South Light: Journey to Antarctica
The thrill of being the first to explore uncharted territory is conveyed along with many other feelings.
[W1473] Bloomsbury pbk **£4.95**

PYNE, STEPHEN J.
The Ice
[W1474] Arlington hbk **£12.95**

SCOTT, ROBERT F.
Scott's Last Expedition
Scott's diary of his fatal 1911-12 expedition: a story of bravery in the face of a deteriorating situation.
[W1475] Methuen pbk **£6.95**

Colin Thubron

I always expect too much from a book. I don't simply want to be entertained; I want the heavens to open. And these few works - although a random choice - have mostly been stimulating for their unexpectedness or depth of insight. They include, I now realise, a preponderance of travel-books and foreign studies; but these are works which extend the medium in some way, whether intellectually (Lannoy, Chatwin, Stark), or through some depth of personal experience (Ratushinskaya, Heng, Thesiger). The only work in this brief list not set abroad (*The Perfectibility of Man*) is about a cultural or inner journey, an unattainable destination.

WILFRED THESIGER
The Life of My Choice
A rich, barbarian autobiography from the great traveller-explorer, who achieved his deepest sense of self in wandering among a people not his own. Beneath this account of the African childhood which shaped him, of his years in the Political Service in Sudan, and his wartime experiences in Afghanistan and North Africa, there runs an extraordinary subtext of boyish dreams sublimated into romantic action, and of values fiercely self-learnt and unfashionable.
(Collins, hbk £17.50/Fontana, pbk £5.95)

BRUCE CHATWIN
The Songlines
Bruce Chatwin's books defy category and this one - his masterpiece - is no exception. On one level it is an account of a journey in search of the Aboriginal songlines in Australia - an invisible web of tracks created by the Dreamtime ancestors. (Each track is still coupled with a song, whose knowledge entitles a native to travel it). But on a broader level the book is a celebration of the nomadism in man's primal nature, and an anthropological investigation into the origins of evil. A unique blend of intellectual passion and cool, stylistic precision.
(Cape, hbk £10.95/Picador, pbk £3.99)

RICHARD LANNOY
The Speaking Tree
Quite simply the most original and stimulating book about India that I have read. *The Speaking Tree* investigates early aesthetics (wonderful on the cave sanctuaries), relationships within the family, the caste system, and an enormous range of sacred and secular values and attitudes. It is one of those books whose insights, even where a reader disagrees with them, are more rich and thought-provoking than those of any more orthodox study.
(Oxford, pbk £7.50)

Bruce Chatwin, author of *The Songlines* (Cape hbk £10.95, Picador pbk £3.99) (Photo: Jerry Bauer)

PHILIP SHORT
The Dragon and the Bear:
Inside China and Russia Today
An imaginative, accessible report on the parallel courses traced by China and the Soviet Union, written by a BBC correspondent who worked in both countries. It describes not only how the two giants have eerily complemented one another's progress, but - more importantly - the profound differences which underlie their twin Communist veneers. The book predates *perestroika*, but is no less relevant for that.
(Unfortunately, currently unavailable)

IRINA RATUSHINSKAYA
Grey is the Colour of Hope
The Soviet poetess's four-year incarceration in a corrective prison camp is made bearable by a mixture of defiant sarcasm and an almost girlish vitality. The book is fascinating not only as a chronicle of physical survival but as a study in collective morale (the KGB made the fatal mistake of confining all the female prisoners of conscience together). Against an official world of confused values sanctioning cruelty in the name of patriotism, these few women pitted moral absolutes which the behaviour of their tormentors only confirmed.
(Hodder, hbk £12.95/pbk, £4.99)

LIANG HENG & JUDITH SHAPIRO
Return to China: A Survivor of the Cultural Revolution Reports on China Today
In many ways this is the most telling book to have emerged from China's 1966-76 Cultural Revolution - the account of a native Chinese's return to the land where his youth was laid waste as a Red Guard and an internal exile. It describes a country sickened with politics and still secretly scarred. Above all it asks: 'After the long nightmare, how many were looking seriously at themselves, beginning with the basic question of their behaviour towards other human beings?' The answer is an important and disturbing one.
(Chatto, hbk £12.95)

WILLIAM GOLDING
Close Quarters
The master triumphs again in this sequel to his *Rites of Passage*. Told in the unpromising but uncannily convincing

voice of a 19th century gentleman en route to a colonial posting in the Antipodes, it is a wonderful evocation of a creaking man-of-war which is slowly breaking up, and whose claustrophobia fills the book with its smells and noises. (Faber, hbk £10.95/pbk, £3.95)

PATRICK SUSKIND
Perfume: The Story of a Murderer

This compulsive and original novel introduces a grotesque literary being - an eighteenth-century dwarf who has 'the finest nose in Paris', but a vacuum instead of a soul. He is a genius of scent, and aspires to create a perfume which will satisfy his power-lust by rendering him instantly loveable. Filled with baroque details of *parfumerie*, the story becomes at last a vivid refutation that the unloving can become whole by being loved. (Hamish Hamilton hbk £10.95/Penguin pbk £4.50)

JOHN PASSMORE
The Perfectibility of Man

A rich, scholarly history of man's dream that he is perfectible, and of the different forms which the dream has taken. From the ancient Greek philosophies and Augustinian concept of grace, the author plunges into the Renaissance vision of man's completing himself in society, and onward through the modern dystopias and the fallacy that one particular class may create an earthly paradise. Man's desire for perfection, he suggests, is forever incompatible with the desire to be free. (Duckworth, hbk £24.00/pbk, £9.95)

Freya Stark, author of *Ionia: A Quest* (Century pbk £4.95)

FREYA STARK
Ionia: A Quest

One of the least known and most singular works of this doyenne of adventurers, *Ionia* is a traveller's study of the classical Greek cities of Turkey. Eschewing modern scholarship, it returns simply to the ancient historians and philosophers, and to the ruins themselves, depicting them with a delicacy of style which makes words live again. This is at once a magnificently dated and timeless work, grandly moralising and deeply personal. (Century, pbk £4.95)

A travel writer and novelist, Colin Thubron's early work included his studies of the Middle East *Mirror to Damascus* and *Jerusalem.* In the 1980s he has published two outstanding travel narratives, *Among the Russians* and *Behind the Wall*, telling of his journeys around the Soviet Union and China, and his contact with the people of both countries. His fourth novel, *Falling*, is due to be published by Heinemann in September 1989.

Irina Ratushinskaya, author of *Grey is the Colour of Hope* (Hodder & Stoughton hbk £12.95)

The Somerset Maugham Awards

The Somerset Maugham Awards, founded in 1947 by Maugham himself, are given on the strength of the promise of a published literary work. Authors must be British, under thirty-five years of age and ordinarily resident in the UK or Northern Ireland. The awards are given annually and total about £12,000. Their purpose is to enable the winners to travel and thereby widen the range and influence of contemporary English letters. One of Maugham's own stipulations was that the judges should not 'play for safety' in their selections, and 'literary work' makes for some interesting possibilities. Poetry, fiction, criticism, biography, history, philosophy, and belles-lettres have all featured amongst the winners; only dramatic works are excluded.

1947 A L Barker *Innocents* (Hogarth Press)

1948 P H Newby *Journey into the Interior* (Cape)

1949 Hamish Henderson *Elegies for the Dead in Cyrenaica* (J Lehmann)

1950 Nigel Kneale *Tomato Cain & Other Stories* (Collins)

1951 Roland Camberton *Scamp* (J Lehmann)

1952 Francis King *The Dividing Stream* (Longman)

1953 Emyr Humphreys *Hear and Forgive* (Gollancz)

1954 Doris Lessing *Five Short Novels* (M Joseph)

1955 Kingsley Amis *Lucky Jim* (Gollancz)

1956 Elizabeth Jennings *A Way of Looking* (Deutsch)

1957 George Lamming *In the Castle of My Skin* (M Joseph)

1958 John Wain *Preliminary Essays* (Macmillan)

1959 Thom Gunn *A Sense of Movement* (Faber)

1960 Ted Hughes *The Hawk in the Rain* (Faber)

1961 V S Naipaul *Miguel Street* (Deutsch)

1962 Hugh Thomas *The Spanish Civil War* (Eyre & Spottiswoode)

1963 David Storey *Flight into Camden* (Longman)

1964 Dan Jacobson *Time of Arrival* (Weidenfeld)
John le Carré *The Spy Who Came in From the Cold* (Gollancz)

1965 Peter Everett *Negatives* (Cape)

1966 Michael Frayn *The Tin Men* (Collins)

1967 B S Johnson *Trawl* (Secker)
Andrew Sinclair *The Better Half* (Cape)

1968 Paul Bailey *At the Jerusalem* (Cape)
Seamus Heaney *Death of a Naturalist* (Faber)

1969 Angela Carter *Several Perceptions* (Heinemann)

1970 Jane Gaskell *A Sweet Sweet Summer* (Hodder)
Piers Paul Read *Monk Dawson* (Secker)

1971 Susan Hill *I'm the King of the Castle* (Hamish Hamilton)
Richard Barber *The Knight and Chivalry* (Longman)
Michael Hastings *Tussy is Me* (Weidenfeld)

1972 Douglas Dunn *Terry Street* (Faber)
Gillian Tindall *Fly Away Home* (Hodder)

1973 Peter Prince *Play Things* (Gollancz)
Paul Strathern *A Season in Abbyssinia* (Macmillan)
Jonathan Street *Prudence Dictates* (Hart-Davis)

1974 Martin Amis *The Rachel Papers* (Cape)

1976 Dominic Cooper *The Dead of Winter* (Chatto)
Ian McEwan *First Love, Last Rites* (Cape)

1977 Richard Holmes *Shelley: The Pursuit* (Quartet)

1978 Tom Paulin *A State of Justice* (Faber)
Nigel Williams *My Life Closed Twice* (Secker)

1979 Helen Hodgman *Jack & Jill* (Duckworth)

Sara Maitland *Daughter of Jerusalem* (Blond & Briggs)

1980 Max Hastings *Bomber Command* (Michael Joseph)
Christopher Reid *Arcadia* (Oxford)
Humphrey Carpenter *The Inklings* (Allen & Unwin)

1981 Julian Barnes *Metroland* (Cape)
Clive Sinclair *Hearts of Gold* (Allison & Busby)
A N Wilson *The Healing Art* (Secker)

1982 William Boyd *A Good Man in Africa* (Hamish Hamilton)
Adam Mars-Jones *Lantern Lecture* (Faber)

1983 Lisa St Aubin de Teran *Keepers of the House* (Cape)

1984 Peter Ackroyd *The Last Testament of Oscar Wilde* (Hamish Hamilton)
Timothy Garton Ash *The Polish Revolution: Solidarity* (Cape)
Sean O'Brien *The Indoor Park* (Bloodaxe)

1985 Blake Morrison *Dark Glasses* (Chatto)
Jeremy Reed *By the Fisheries* (Cape)
Jane Rogers *Her Living Image* (Faber)

1986 Patricia Ferguson *Family Myths and Legends* (Deutsch)
Adam Nicholson *Frontiers* (Weidenfeld)
Tim Parks *Tongues of Flame* (Heinemann)

1987 Stephen Gregory *The Cormorant* (Heinemann)
Janni Howker *Isaac Campion* (McRae)
Andrew Motion *The Lamberts* (Chatto)

1988 Jimmy Burns *The Land that Lost Its Heroes* (Bloomsbury)
Carol Ann Duffy *Selling Manhattan* (Anvil)
Matthew Kneale *Whore Banquets* (Gollancz)

1989 Rupert Christiansen *Romantic Affinities* (Bodley Head)
Alan Hollinghurst *The Swimming Pool Library* (Chatto)
Deirdre Madden *The Birds of the Innocent Wood* (Faber)

Thomas Cook
Travel Book
Awards

Travel has provided the stimulus for some of the world's finest literature, from Homer and Herodotus to Dickens and Durrell. We therefore thought it appropriate to encourage the art of writing about travel by offering an award and by helping to promote the books entered for the award.
Sir John Cuckney, Chairman of Thomas Cook

The sudden popularity of travel writing has caused a publishing boom over the last few years, and the Thomas Cook awards, launched in 1980, have quickly become established as prestigious literary prizes. Two awards are given annually - one for the Best Narrative Travel Book (£2,000) and the other for the Best Guide Book (£1,000). In 1988 a new award was instituted for illustrated travel books. Winners over the last five years have been as follows:

1980
Travel: *Tracks* Robyn Davidson (Cape)
Guide: *The 1980 South American Handbook* John Brooks (Ed) (Trade & Travel)

1981
Travel: *Old Glory* Jonathan Raban (Collins)
Guide: *China Companion* Evelyne Garside (Deutsch)

1982
Travel: *The Sindbad Voyage* Tim Severin (Hutchinson)
Guide: *India* G Crowther, P A Raj & T Wheeler (Lonely Planet)

1983
Travel: *From Heaven Lake* Vikram Seth (Chatto)
Guide: *Companion Guide to New York* Michael Leapman (Collins)

1984
Travel: *To the Frontier* Geoffrey Moorhouse (Hodder)
Guide: *Cruising French Waterways* Hugh McKnight (Stanford)

1985
Travel: *So Far from God* Patrick Marnham (Cape)
Guide: *Shell Guide to Nottinghamshire* Henry Thorold (Faber)

1986/7
Travel: *Between the Woods and the Water* Patrick Leigh Fermor (J Murray)
Guide: *Fontana/Hachette Guide to France 1986* (Collins)

1988
Travel: *Behind the Wall* Colin Thubron (Heinemann)
Guide: *The Tibet Guide* Stephen Batchelor (Wisdom)
Illustrated Travel: *Languedoc* James Bentley & Charlie Waite (George Philip)

1989
Travel: *Riding the Iron Rooster* Paul Theroux (Hamish Hamilton)
Guide: *Landscapes of Madeira* John & Pat Underwood (Sunflower)
Illustrated Travel: *Landscapes of Madeira* Dr Richard B Fisher (Hodder)

G

INDEX OF ADVERTISERS